The Oxford Companion to

Wine

The Oxford Companion to

Wine

THIRD EDITION

Edited by Jancis Robinson

Assistant editor: Julia Harding

OXFORD

UNIVERSITY PRESS

OXFORD
UNIVERSITY PRESS

Great Clarendon Street, Oxford ox2 6dp

Oxford University Press is a department of the University of Oxford.
It furthers the University's objective of excellence in research, scholarship,
and education by publishing worldwide in

Oxford New York

Auckland Cape Town Dar es Salaam Hong Kong Karachi
Kuala Lumpur Madrid Melbourne Mexico City Nairobi
New Delhi Shanghai Taipei Toronto

With offices in

Argentina Austria Brazil Chile Czech Republic France Greece
Guatemala Hungary Italy Japan Poland Portugal Singapore
South Korea Switzerland Thailand Turkey Ukraine Vietnam

Oxford is a registered trade mark of Oxford University Press
in the UK and in certain other countries

Published in the United States
by Oxford University Press Inc., New York

Database right Oxford University Press (maker)

First published 1994
Second edition 1999
Third edition 2006

British Library Cataloguing in Publication Data

Data available

Library of Congress Cataloging in Publication Data

Data available

ISBN 978-0-19-860990-2

10 9 8

Typeset by Alliance Interactive Technology, Pondicherry, India
Corrected by Cepha Imaging Pvt Ltd
Printed and bound in Malaysia by Vivar Printing Sdn .Bhd.

Contents

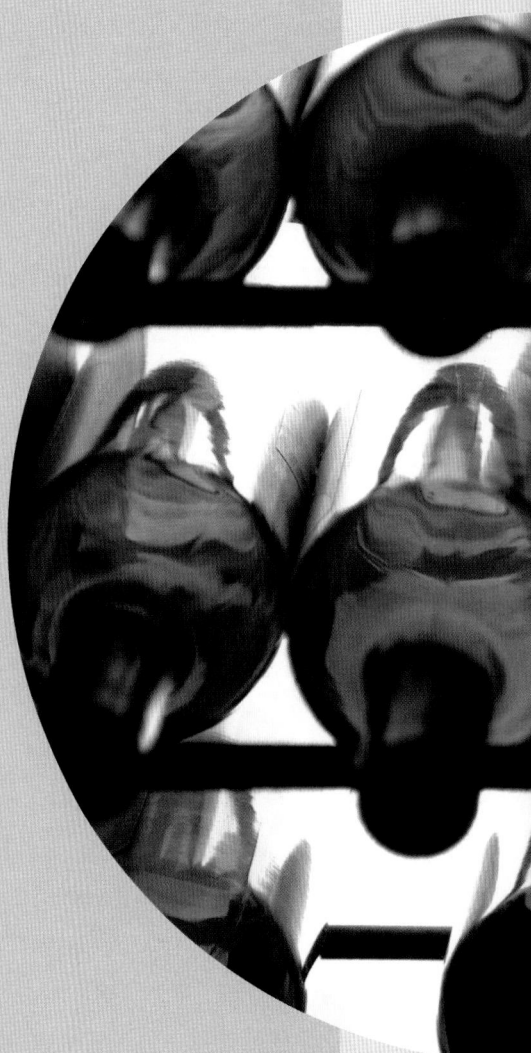

Preface

This book aims to be the definitive single-volume wine reference. It is not a directory of producers or individual wines; many excellent guides provide this sort of information, which can date particularly rapidly. *The Oxford Companion to Wine* seems to have found its niche worldwide as a comprehensive work, with attitude, aimed at curious, intelligent wine drinkers and wine students who want to understand more of the background to the delicious liquid they find in their glasses and bottles. Uniquely, this book provides extremely detailed and easily accessed information not just on the geography of wine but on its history, the science behind vine-growing and wine-making, the main grape varieties and wine personalities, and all the accoutrements of wine storage, serving, tasting, and consumption.

The information is presented in almost 4,000 alphabetically arranged articles of very varying lengths, each written by the editor, the assistant editor, or a recognized expert on that particular subject. Our 167 esteemed contributors (including 73 new to this edition) range from internationally renowned academics to some of the most famous wine writers and wine specialists in the world.

The first edition of this book, published in 1994, had 3,000 entries. The second (1999) edition had 3,650, but this third edition with its 3,900 entries is an even more concentrated wine resource: in order to make way for the extraordinary amount of new information required, we have had to omit all previous entries on brandy and other forms of distilled wine. There are thus more than 300 substantive new entries in this third edition.

The List of New Entries for this edition (pages xix–xx) is itself revealing. Politics, philosophy, and economics make their presence felt, but so too do globalization (plus Constellation, Diageo, and Foster's), price points, France's *crise viticole*, along with a host of new wine regions (notably in Australia and South Africa, but also whole new countries), new grape varieties, scores of new applications of science to vine-growing and wine-making, and, less benignly, vine pests and diseases that emerged only relatively recently.

These are the new entries, but of the old ones roughly three-quarters have been changed in some way, and a good 40 per cent of the total, about

1,600 entries in all, have been revised quite radically. The world of wine and our understanding of it—not least the revelations concerning grapevine relationships afforded by DNA typing—are changing so rapidly that updating is an obvious imperative.

In order to keep the book from becoming even heavier and more unwieldy, Oxford University Press insisted that we limit the increase in the number of pages to a mere 2 per cent, thereby imposing the tightest of editing disciplines on us. Thus readers will, we hope, find a minimum of extraneous detail and unnecessary repetition—just the information, all the information, and nothing but the information here, laced with the editorial opinion which is such a crucial ingredient of all Oxford Companions across a range of equally worthy subjects.

As editor of all three editions of *The Oxford Companion to Wine*, I would stress that my task has been considerably less onerous this time thanks to the diligence of Julia Harding MW, the book's first assistant editor, who brought a wealth of experience as a professional book editor 'fresh' from passing the Master of Wine exams at the first attempt, the top student of her year. She has been primarily responsible for the huge improvement in the viticulture and oenology sections of this book, injecting considerable effort to bring the articles up to date, taking account of the very latest research with the help of scores of generous scientists around the globe and making each entry as internationally relevant as possible. (We are aware of the dangers of Anglocentricity, and even Euro-centricity.) She has also co-ordinated the entire editorial process and somehow managed to copy-edit the manuscript with extraordinary rigour.

The team at OUP has as usual been exceptionally efficient and a pleasure to work with—notably the editorial team Judith Wilson and Pam Coote, production manager Emma McLeod, designer Nick Clarke, and picture researcher Carrie Hickman.

I am also blessed by an extremely tolerant family who have learnt to live with a work they sometimes call my fourth child.

JANCIS ROBINSON

London, 2006

Contributors

Viticulture Editor:
Dr Richard E. Smart

Oenology Editors:
Professor A. Dinsmoor Webb
Dr Patrick J. Williams

Contributors are listed in alphabetical order, first by surname, then by first name. MW stands for Master of Wine. Unsigned entries are written by the Editor or Assistant Editor.

H.H.A. Hamish Aird is a classicist and was Sub-Warden of Radley College, Oxfordshire in England.

J.A. Professor Jean Aitchison is Rupert Murdoch Professor of Language and Communication at the University of Oxford. She gave the Reith Lectures in 1996.

M.A. Mail Amanov is Director of the Azerbaijan Institute of Viniculture and Winemaking.

K.A. Kym Anderson is Lead Economist (Trade Policy) at the World Bank's Development Research Group in Washington DC. Since 1998 he has led a programme of wine economics research at the Centre for International Economic Studies at the University of Adelaide, where his projects include a global economic model for predicting the development of various national wine markets.

T.A. Tony Aspler, Canada's most widely read wine writer, wine columnist, and educator.

S.A. Susy Atkins is a wine writer who is based in Britain but travels widely.

H.G.B. Bill Baker, wine merchant whose distinctive wine list has long been decorated with unusual vinous quotations.

H.K.B. Helena Baker, a native of Prague who spent most of her working life in England

and France, is a wine and food writer now based in the Czech Republic. She publishes her own *Pocket Guide to the Wines and Winemakers of the Czech Republic*.

N.J.B. Nicolas Belfrage MW is a wine merchant and wine writer specializing in Italian wines.

E.J.R.B. Elizabeth Berry MW, wine merchant and author whose books include *The Wines of Alsace*.

H.B. Helen Bettinson, television producer, researcher for Hugh Johnson's *Story of Wine*.

D.B. David Bird MW is a Chartered Chemist and a Member of the Institute of Quality Assurance. He audits wineries throughout Europe and lectures on wine-making techniques. His publications include *Understanding Wine Technology*.

L.F.B. Dr Linda Bisson is a microbiologist trained in genetics and currently specializing in yeast biology. She is a Professor of Enology and holds the Maynard A. Amerine Endowed Chair at the University of California at Davis.

J.A.B. The late Dr Jeremy Black was Director of the British School of Archaeology in Iraq and later a Fellow of Wolfson College, Oxford, and University Lecturer in Akkadian. He wrote several studies on Sumerian and Babylonian literature and ancient philology.

B.B. Beverley Blanning MW is an independent UK-based wine writer who travels and tastes widely. She passed the Master of Wine exams at her first attempt in 2001, specializing for her dissertation in the subject of wine and health.

W.B. William Bolter, Bordeaux-based wine merchant, author, and wine-maker who worked for Alexis Lichine from 1958 to 1964.

L.Br. Dr Linda Bramble, wine writer and broadcaster based for several years at Brock

University's Cool Climate Oenology and Viticulture Institute in Ontario, Canada.

R.G.V.B. DR ROB BRAMLEY is a Principal Research Scientist with CSIRO in Adelaide, South Australia. Since 1998, he has been at the forefront of the development of Precision Viticulture, and leads several major research projects on vineyard variability.

J.M.B. MICHAEL BROADBENT MW, founder of Christie's Wine Department and author (see entry).

R.B. DR ROGER BROCK is a Lecturer in Classics at the University of Leeds and specialist in Greek history and historiography.

S.B. STEPHEN BROOK, journalist and author whose works include *Bordeaux: The Left Bank* and *The Wines of California*.

L.B. LARRY BROOKS studied plant pathology at the University of California at Davis and made wine for 20 years at Acacia winery in the Napa Valley.

R.M.B. ROSE MURRAY BROWN MW trained as a wine and wine antiques specialist with auctioneers Sotheby's and is now a freelance wine writer.

N.B. NICK BULLEID MW is a freelance wine-making consultant in Australia and a Visiting Professor at Charles Sturt University. He is also a wine writer and judge, and tries to coax Pinot Noir to ripeness in his 2-hectare vineyard in the chilly Southern Tablelands of New South Wales.

R.N.H.B. ROBIN BUTLER, antique dealer with a particular interest in wine, co-wrote *The Book of Wine Antiques* in 1986.

R.F.C. BOB CAMPBELL MW, New Zealand's best-known wine writer and founder of an exceptional wine school in Auckland.

T.R.C. TOM CARSON graduated from Roseworthy Agricultural College in 1991 and is now Chief Winemaker at Yering Station in the Yarra Valley in Victoria, Australia.

B.C.C. BRUCE CASS is a San Francisco-based wine writer and editor of the *Oxford Companion to the Wines of North America*.

S.J.C. DR STEVE CHARTERS MW lectures in wine marketing and wine studies at Edith Cowan University, Perth, Australia, with research interests in the consumer's engagement with wine. He is also an occasional wine writer.

V.C. Dr VÉRONIQUE CHEYNIER, Director of Research at the Institut National de la Recherche Agronomique (INRA), has been managing the internationally acclaimed research on wine polyphenols at INRA-Montpellier for 20 years. Dr Cheynier is on the editorial boards of the *AJGWR*, *AJEV*, and *JSFA*.

N.C. NODARI CHKHARTISHVILI is Director of the Georgian Research Institute of Horticulture and Viticulture.

T.C. DR TYLER COLMAN is a Visiting Scholar at Northwestern University, IL. He writes at www.drvino.com about how politics and economics affect the wines we drink.

B.G.C. DR BRYAN COOMBE, author, recently retired lecturer, and researcher specializing in grapevine physiology at Waite Agricultural Research Institute, Adelaide. The American Society of Enology and Viticulture awarded him Best Paper of the Year for viticulture in 1987 and oenology in 1991.

G.L.C. DR GLEN CREASY is a Senior Lecturer in Viticulture at Lincoln University's Centre for Viticulture and Oenology. His research specializes in cool climate viticulture and grape and wine phenolics.

B.C. PROFESSOR BARRY CUNLIFFE has been Professor of European Archaeology at the Institute of Archaeology, University of Oxford, since 1972.

L.D. LINDA DOMAS, Australian-based international consultant winemaker, was the first to make commercially successful bottled wines for export from Tunisia to Europe.

J. & M.D. PROFESSOR JAMES DOUGLAS was Visiting Professor of Political Science in various American universities while PROFESSOR MARY DOUGLAS is Emeritus Professor of Social Anthropology at the University of London.

P.R.D. DR PETER DRY, Associate Professor, School of Agriculture, Food and Wine, University of Adelaide.

A.J.D. ANNE DUGGAN is Professor of Medieval History at King's College, University of London.

A.D. ABI DUHR studied oenology at Geisenheim and Bordeaux. He lives and works in Luxembourg, where he is winemaker for his family's wine company and is in charge of Introduction to Oenology courses at the Lycée Technique Alexis Heck.

M.J.E. MARGARET EMERY was the librarian at Roseworthy Agricultural College from 1975 until 1995 and holds a Graduate Diploma in Wine.

N.F. NICHOLAS FAITH is a financial journalist whose numerous specialities include wine and brandy. He has written two important books on cognac and other brandies.

L.F. LUCY FAULKNER works in the wine trade and is based in Britain.

C.C.F. CHRISTOPHER FIELDEN is a British wine merchant and collector of wine books.

M.F. MICHAEL FRIDJHON is South Africa's leading wine writer, former adviser to the South African Minister of Agriculture, winery consultant, and liquor industry specialist.

M.Fr. MONTY FRIENDSHIP is a wine writer based in Zimbabwe.

D.F. DOUG FROST MW is a Kansas City author who is one of only three people in the world to be both a Master Sommelier and Master of Wine. He specializes in wines from America's less famous wine-producing states.

S.G. SAMUEL GASPARYAN, Director of the Armenian branch of the International Academy of Wine Growing and Winemaking.

D.G. DENIS GASTIN, once Senior Trade Commissioner in the Australian Embassy in Tokyo and now an Australian wine exporter and writer specializing in Japan and South East Asia.

B.G. BENNY GÉNSBØL, Danish wine writer and photographer, co-author with Jens Michael Gundersen of the book *Vinavl i Danmark* (Winegrowing in Denmark).

R.G. ROSEMARY GEORGE MW, wine writer, one of the first women to become a Master of Wine, whose books include the award-winning *Chablis*.

C.G. DR CAROLINE GILBY MW is a freelance lecturer and writer specializing in Eastern Europe. She has a PhD in plant sciences but left science to buy wine for a major UK retail chain before becoming an independent wine consultant.

D.J.G. DAVID GILL MW, wine merchant with considerable experience of importing wines from, among other countries, Bulgaria, Hungary, Malta, and Morocco.

J.G. DR JOHN GLADSTONES, author of *Viticulture and Environment*, is former Senior Lecturer in the University of Western Australia Department of Agriculture.

S.J.G. SAM GLAETZER worked as an environmental engineer and winemaker at Beringer Blass Wine Estates in South Australia before becoming their Senior

Commercial Winemaker. He grew up in a wine-making family and has a degree in Civil and Environmental Engineering and a graduate diploma in Oenology.

D.C.G. DAVID GLEAVE MW is Managing Director of Liberty Wines, a London-based wine importer and distributor. He has been extensively involved with Italian wines for over 20 years, spending three months of every year in Italy. He has written widely on the subject, including the 1989 book *The Wines of Italy*.

H.G. HOWARD G. GOLDBERG writes for *The New York Times* and lives in New York City.

J.A.G. JAMIE GOODE has a PhD in plant biology and for many years worked as a scientific editor. He publishes www.wineanorak.com and is currently wine writer for Britain's *Sunday Express*. His first book, *Wine Science*, was published in 2005.

R.Go. ROBERT GORJAK was raised in a wine-growing family in Ljutomer-Ormož. Today he is based in Ljubljana, Slovenia, and is active as a wine writer and wine educator.

R.d.G. RONALD DE GROOT owns and edits the leading Dutch wine magazine *Perswijn*. He is also active as a freelance contributor and consultant and a member of one of Europe's leading tasting panels, the Grand Jury Européen.

L.S.H. LISA SHARA HALL is a columnist and author who writes about wine from Portland, Oregon, specializing in the wines of the Pacific Northwest.

J.H. JAMES HALLIDAY, Australia's most prolific and most respected wine writer, an ex-lawyer who also found time to establish Coldstream Hills winery in the Yarra Valley.

J.M.H. The late JAKE HANCOCK was Professor of Geology at Imperial College, University of London, and a member of the editorial board of the *Journal of Wine Research*.

R.H. ROSEMARY HANSON, journalist and author of a book on the recipes and traditions of the French wine harvest.

J.Ha. JULIA HARDING MW, assistant editor of *The Oxford Companion to Wine*, studied modern languages at Cambridge before becoming a freelance book editor. She took the Wine and Spirit Education Trust intermediate and advanced certificates and diploma in the late 1990s before going on to work in the Wine Buying department at British wine retailer Waitrose in 2001. Julia qualified as a Master of

Wine in 2004, winning the Robert Mondavi award for best theory papers and the Tim Derouet Memorial Prize for excellence in all parts of the exam and dissertation. Now Jancis Robinson's full-time assistant, she was responsible for all entries on oenology and viticulture in this third edition of *The Oxford Companion to Wine*, and co-ordinated and copy-edited the new and revised text.

S.H. SAM HARROP MW comes from New Zealand and studied at both Auckland and Lincoln Universities before starting a career in wine-making. He has made wine for 13 years in many countries. After seven years as a winemaker for the UK retailer Marks & Spencer, he now runs his own wine-making consultancy in London and is also a shareholder in Domaine Matassa in Roussillon.

J.H.H. DR JUDITH HARVEY became a medical practitioner after a distinguished career as a research scientist.

P.H. DR PAUL HENSCHKE is Principal Research Microbiologist and co-leader of Biosciences at the Australian Wine Research Institute in Adelaide, South Australia.

H.-P.H. HANS-PETER HOEHNEN qualified at Geisenheim and worked in Australia, New Zealand, and his native Germany until 1997, when he moved to Thailand for three years. He now specializes as a consultant in tropical viticulture and wine-making throughout South East Asia.

L.H.-S. DR LEOFRANC HOLFORD-STREVENS is a classical scholar and author of *Aulus Gellius* who works for Oxford University Press.

R.Ho. ROMAN HORVATH is Managing Director of Freie Weingärtner Wachau, one of Austria's largest wine producers. He is also a wine educator and lectures at the Austrian Wine Academy.

I.J. IAN JAMIESON was, before retirement, a wine merchant-turned-wine writer who passed the Master of Wine examinations in 1970 and was best known for his articles and books on German wine.

H.J. HUGH JOHNSON is the world's most successful wine author and was introduced to specialist wine writing by the late André Simon (see entries on both).

R.J. RUSSELL JOHNSTONE is Technical Manager for Viticulture and Winemaking for the Orlando Wyndham Group.

G.V.J. DR GREGORY V. JONES is an Associate Professor at Southern Oregon University,

specializing in the study of how climate variability and change affect natural ecosystems and agriculture. He conducts applied research for the grape and wine industry in Oregon and has written widely on wine economics, grapevine phenology, climatological assessments of viticulture, and climate change.

T.J. DR TONY JORDAN started his career as research scientist and lecturer in oenology. He established the Yarra Valley winery and vineyard at Green Point for Moët Hennessy and is now CEO of the Moët Hennessy Wine Estates Group of Australian and New Zealand wineries.

R.H.N.J. RUPERT JOY is a Paris-based wine writer and consultant with a particular interest in Moroccan wine, on which he wrote his thesis at ESC Dijon.

E.K. EVA KALUZYNSKA, freelance journalist for long based in Brussels, with a special interest in wine, and a consultant to the European Commission.

M.R.K. MICHAEL KARAM is a Lebanese journalist and wine writer. He is a contributor to the *Wine Report* and the author of *Wines of Lebanon*.

F.K. FEDOR KAZAR is the Deputy Director of the National Institute of Wine Growing and Winemaking of Moldova.

P.K. DR PHILIP KENNEDY completed a doctorate in classical Arabic poetry at the Oriental Institute of Oxford University and is now based at the Department of Middle Eastern Studies, New York University.

J.D.K. JOHN KESBY, social anthropologist with a particular interest in metaphysical systems and myths, who teaches at the University of Kent.

S.K. SHALVA KHETSURIANI, President of Khetsuriani Winery in Georgia, won the 2004 Geoffrey Roberts Award and travelled extensively in France's wine regions as a result.

M.K. MEL KNOX is based in California where he has sold wine since 1972, taught wine appreciation classes at the University of California since 1974, and sold French barrels since 1980.

C.K. CHANDRA KURT, wine writer, author and consultant based in Zurich, has published several wine books and writes about wine for a variety of Swiss publications. www.chandrakurt.com

D.L. DAVID LAKE MW is the winemaker at the Columbia Winery in Woodinville, WA, where he has made more than 25 vintages. He studied viticulture and oenology at the University of California at Davis in the 1970s and was the first Master of Wine to make wine in North America. Both *Wine Spectator* and *Decanter* have described him as the 'Dean of Washington Winemakers'.

M.P.L. MARTIN LAM is the owner, chef, and celebrated wine buyer of Ransome's Dock restaurant in London.

M.L.-G. MILES LAMBERT-GOCS researches the wine history and traditions of eastern Europe, from Slovakia south through Greece.

R.S.L. RICHARD LANDER is an author and consultant advising companies on Internet, media, and business strategy.

G.J.L. GARETH LAWRENCE is Course Director of the Wine & Spirit Education Trust School in London and has a particular interest in the wines of central and south eastern Europe.

T.H.L. PROFESSOR TERRY LEE was Director of the Australian Wine Research Institute in Adelaide, then worked for Gallo in California.

H.L. HARRIET LEMBECK, noted wine educator and writer based in New York and a Charter Director of the Society of Wine Educators.

P.L. PETER LESKE was chief winemaker at Nepenthe in the Adelaide Hills. He now works as a technical consultant.

D.V.L. DENNIS LINDLEY was until his retirement Professor of Statistics and Head of the Department of Statistics at University College, London, having previously occupied similar positions at Cambridge University and the University College of Wales.

S.P.D.L. SIMON LOFTUS, English wine merchant and award-winning author.

Z.L. ZELMA LONG, second woman to enrol in the Department of Enology at the University of California at Davis, President of Simi Winery for much of the 1990s.

W.L. WINK LORCH, wine educator, writer, and editor, divides her time between England and Haute Savoie, France. A founder of the Association of Wine Educators, she has contributed to the *Williams-Sonoma Wine Guide*, the *Global Encyclopaedia of Wines*, and *Cordon Bleu Wine Essentials*.

A.L. PROFESSOR ALEXANDR LYANNOY is the Deputy Director of the Ukrainian National Centre of Science at the V.E. Tairov Institute of Wine Growing and Winemaking.

N.McG. NICO McGOUGH is a British-born Dutch wine merchant who is also editor of *De Wijnkrant*.

M.McN. MAGGIE McNIE MW, international wine consultant and once head of the Greek Wine Bureau in London.

N.M. NICO MANESSIS, Geneva-based journalist and author specializing in the wines of his native Greece. His books *The Greek Wine Guide* and *The Illustrated Greek Wine Book* introduced the new wines of this historic wine producing country to an international audience.

J.E.M. JANE MASTERS MW (née Kay) originally trained as an oenologist at the Institut d'Oenologie in Bordeaux. Having run the wine and drinks business at UK retailer Marks & Spencer, she now has her own consultancy business.

R.J.M. RICHARD MAYSON, the leading writer about Portuguese wines in the English language.

J.M. JOSIMAR MELO is food and wine journalist for the major Brazilian daily newspaper *Folha de São Paulo*. He is also owner of the gastronomic website *Basilico* (www.basilico.com.br). Among his books are *Guia Josimar Melo* (an annual gourmet guide to São Paulo) and *A Cerveja* (about beer).

A.S.M. ADAM SEBAG MONTEFIORE went to live in Israel after 13 years in the English wine trade. Working for Israel's two famous wineries, Carmel and Golan Heights, he acts as ambassador for Israeli wines worldwide, writing for a wide range of publications. He formed Handcrafted Wines of Israel, a consortium of Israel's finest boutique wineries.

J.T.C.M. JASPER MORRIS MW, joint founding editor of the *Journal of Wine Research*, wine merchant and author specializing in Burgundy.

F.M. FIONA MORRISON MW is a journalist based in Belgium with over 20 years' experience in the international wine business. She is married to Jacques Thienpont, Belgian wine merchant and owner of Le Pin, and they make and taste wine together.

L.M. LUCIE T. MORTON is an independent viticulturist in the US. She writes, lectures and consults on ampelography, rootstocks, and vineyard development, and is a founding member of the International Council on Grapevine Diseases. She translated *A Practical Ampelography* from Galet's original, and wrote *Winegrowing in Eastern America*.

E.S.M. EDEL SCHAUB MOSS is sommelière at the Presidente Intercontinental in Mexico, which has the largest cellar in Latin America.

A.H.M. ANGELA MUIR MW is a British-based roving wine-making consultant with a particular interest in central and eastern Europe.

R.M.M. REBECCA MURPHY is a wine writer based in Portland, OR, and founder and producer of the *Dallas Morning News* Wine Competition, one of the largest in the United States.

L.N. LOUISE NICHOLSON is a writer, lecturer, and adviser specializing in India which she has visited more than 50 times.

P.A.N. DR PHILIP NORRIE is a medical practitioner and wine producer in New South Wales, Australia, with a particular interest in wine history.

J.J.P. JEREMY PATERSON, Senior Lecturer in Ancient History at the University of Newcastle-upon-Tyne, is a specialist in Roman economic and social history with a particular interest in the Roman wine trade on which he has published.

E.P.-R. the late EDMUND PENNING-ROWSELL was one of the world's most respected wine writers, author of *The Wines of Bordeaux* (see entry).

T.P. PROFESSOR THOMAS PINNEY, Professor of English at Pomona College in Claremont, California, and author of the two-volume *History of Wine in America*.

J.P. JOHN PLATTER became a South African wine farmer and wine writer after a career as a foreign correspondent for United Press International. *John Platter's Guide to South African Wines* has become the country's best-selling wine book.

J.V.P. DR JOHN POSSINGHAM has degrees from the universities of Adelaide and Oxford and was foundation Chief of CSIRO's Division of Horticulture in Australia.

I.S.P. ISAK (SAKKIE) PRETORIUS is Managing Director of the Australian Wine Research Institute in Adelaide. He is also Professor Extraordinary in Oenology at the University of Stellenbosch, and Affiliate Professor in Oenology at the University of Adelaide. The main focus of his research is the genetic improvement of wine yeast strains.

P.V.P. PAMELA VANDYKE PRICE, prolific English author, and one of the first women wine writers.

A.H.P. ALEXANDER PURCELL is Professor of Entomology at the University of California at Berkeley. His research has focused on Pierce's disease and other bacterial diseases of plants spread by insect vectors.

M.R. MAGOMED RADZHABOV is the Dean of the Faculty of Fruit and Vegetable Growing at Moscow K.A.Timiryazev Agricultural Academy.

J.M.R. DR JANE RENFREW (Lady Renfrew of Kaimsthorn) is a prehistorian and palaeoethnobotanist and is an affiliated lecturer in the Department of Archaeology, University of Cambridge.

P.R.-G. PROFESSOR PASCAL RIBÉREAU-GAYON was head of the Faculty of Oenology at the University of Bordeaux and is recognized as one of the most renowned French authorities on making and tasting wine. His father, Jean Ribéreau-Gayon, was also Director of Bordeaux's Institute of Oenology and a descendant of Professor Ulysse Gayon, who worked with Louis Pasteur.

J.R. JANCIS ROBINSON MW, editor of *The Oxford Companion to Wine*, is one of the world's leading authorities on wine, voted the Wine Writers' Writer by her peers in *The Observer*. The first person outside the wine trade to have passed the notoriously tough Master of Wine exams, she is now the wine columnist for the *Financial Times* and writes a regular column for publications in ten countries on five continents. She is known to millions as a television presenter on wine and food, and wrote and presented the award-winning series *Jancis Robinson's Wine Course*. Voted the first ever International Wine Communicator of the Year in 1996, she has won a string of awards, and currently spends the majority of her time feeding her website www.jancisrobinson.com, which has subscribers from over 70 countries.

G.R. & G.M. DR GÁBOR ROHÁLY is a physician, a founding member of the Hungarian Wine Academy, and a wine writer who is widely credited with developing Hungary's wine vocabulary. DR GABRIELLA MÉSZÁROS trained as a lawyer and now writes regularly on wine in Hungary.

A.H.L.R. ANTHONY ROSE, British lawyer-turned-wine writer for *The Independent* newspaper who has written regularly on auctions and investment in wine for a wide range of publications.

B.T.A.R. BJØRN TORE AASTORP RUUD, Norwegian chef turned wine writer, has benefited from wine and spirit training in Norway, England and Mexico, where he is currently President of the Sociedad Mexicana de Vinos & Licores de Guadalajara.

V.R. VIACHESLAV RYBINSTEV was appointed Deputy Director of Research at the Magaratch (q.v.) wine research institute in Yalta in 1986 and has studied viticulture in Ukraine, Russia, Moldova, Kazakhstan, Uzbekistan, Georgia, Armenia, Azerbaijan, Turkmenistan, Germany, and the south of France.

D.S. DAVID SCHILDKNECHT is a philosopher by training but is now an Ohio-based wine importer–distributor who writes with increasing frequency about German, Austrian, and Hungarian wine. His annual reports from Germany have appeared in Stephen Tanzer's *International Wine Cellar* since 1986, more recently in Robert M. Parker's *The Wine Advocate*.

J.S. JOHN SCHREINER is a Vancouver-based writer who has been commenting on the wines of British Columbia since 1975. He has written nine books about Canadian wine.

H.S. PROFESSOR HANS SCHULTZ is Head of the Department of Viticulture at the Research Institute of Geisenheim in Germany and Professor of Viticulture at the University of Applied Sciences, Wiesbaden-Geisenheim. He has also worked and studied at Charles Sturt University in Australia, at ENSA/INRA Montpellier, and at the University of California at Davis. Professor Schultz grew up in the Mosel valley, where his parents have a small vineyard and winery.

M.W.E.S. MICHAEL SCHUSTER, writer who runs his own wine school in London and has translated the work of Professor Émile Peynaud.

T.S. TOM SCOTT, Honorary Professor in the Institute of Reformation Studies at the University of St Andrews, specializing in the economic and social history of Germany, 1300–1600, and part-time wine merchant.

M.A.S. DR MARK SEFTON is a Principal Research Chemist at the Australian Wine Research Institute, where he leads the Institute's research programmes on the chemistry of volatile grape and wine aroma and flavour compounds. He has also been extensively involved in industry 'troubleshooting' programmes, mostly involving wine taint problems.

V. DE LA S. VICTOR DE LA SERNA, Madrid-based journalist for *El Mundo*, wine writer, and wine producer.

S.S. STEPHEN SKELTON MW was a vineyard owner and winemaker in England between 1976 and 2001. He still works as a consultant to a number of vineyards in the United Kingdom. He also lectures on wine and has written two books on vineyards in the UK. He is currently running a retail and fine wine business in Putney, London.

R.E.S. DR RICHARD SMART, Viticulture Editor of the first two editions of this book and a substantial contributor to all three editions. World-famous viticultural scientist and author, now a consultant known particularly for his studies and applications of canopy management, with Tamar Ridge Wines of Tasmania as a major client.

B.C.S. DR BARRY C. SMITH is a Senior Lecturer in Philosophy at Birkbeck College, University of London. He is editor of *A Question of Taste: Philosophy and Wine* and co-editor of *Knowing Our Own Minds*. He has held visiting positions at the University of Cambridge, the University of California at Berkeley, and the École Normale Supérieure in Paris.

P.S. PIERRE SPAHNI comes from a family of wine brokers, was educated at the universities of Lausanne, California (Davis), and Newcastle upon Tyne, holds doctorate degrees in Business Administration and Agriculture, has written three books on the economics of wine, and provides independent wine-related research and consultancy services to institutions and companies (www.span-e.com).

P.K.C.S. PATRICIA STEFANOWICZ MW is a wine consultant and educator as well as a qualified architect and structural engineer. She is based in the UK and divides her working life between wine and construction project management.

T.M.S. TYSON STELZER, wine writer and scientist, is the world's most prolific writer on the topic of screw caps. His books include *Taming the Screw: A Manual for Winemaking with Screw Caps*.

K.B.S. KERRY BRADY STEWART was born in Missouri but has lived in the Rheingau since 1981. She has worked for the German Wine Information Service but now has her own public relations agency and writes books on wine, food, and travel.

K.S. KEITH SUTTON is Honorary Research Fellow in Geography at the University of Manchester and spent 20 years researching Algeria's socio-economic development.

M.T. MICHAEL TABONE is a wine lecturer and writer. He is the main wine correspondent for the *Sunday Times of Malta* and a consultant for a number of importers, restaurants and hotels. In 2001 he set up Scuola di Vino, Malta's first wine school.

P.T. PATRICIO TAPIA studied oenology at Bordeaux and journalism at Santiago University. He writes internationally about South American and Spanish wines and is editor and co-owner of the publishing company Planetavino (www.planetavino.com).

G.T. GEOFF TAYLOR BSc (Hons) CChem CSci MRSC has worked in the wine trade since 1976 and is the founder of Corkwise, the UK's leading wine analysis and technical consultancy laboratory.

D.E.T. DIANE E. TEITELBAUM is a wine consultant, wine educator, and freelance wine writer.

D.T. DANIEL THOMASES, American wine writer based in Florence who worked closely with Luigi Veronelli for many years.

J.T. JOELLE THOMSON is the wine writer for New Zealand's largest daily newspaper, *The New Zealand Herald*, and author of the best-selling annual *Joelle Thomson's Under $20 Wine Guide*. Her other books include *Celebrating New Zealand Wine* (2004).

R.T. DR ROY THORNTON has a PhD in Applied Microbiology from Strathclyde University, Scotland. He developed new strains of wine yeasts at Massey University, New Zealand, and has written extensively on wine microbiology. He was a Senior Research Microbiologist at E & J Gallo Winery for five years before joining CSU Fresno, CA.

S.T. STEVE TYERMAN is the Wine Industry Professor of Viticulture and Head of Wine and Horticulture at Adelaide University. He was President of the Australian Society of Plant Scientists (2004–05) and is a member of the Australian Society of Viticulture and Oenology. In 2003, he was elected as a fellow of the Australian Academy of Science.

P.T.H.U. TIM UNWIN is Professor of Geography at Royal Holloway, University of London. He is author of *Wine and the Vine* and was one of the founding editors of the *Journal of Wine Research*. His research now focuses on issues of poverty and inequality (see http://www.ict4d.org.uk), but he also retains a strong interest in wine and viticulture, and is currently the Institute of Masters of Wine's external examiner.

T.V. TIM VANDERGRIFT is Technical Services Manager for Winexpert Ltd. He writes about wine, teaches wine appreciation and wine-making, and is a consultant winemaker at several vineyards in British Columbia.

C.V.L. CORNELIS (KEES) VAN LEEUWEN is Professor of Viticulture and Head of the laboratory of vine ecophysiology at Bordeaux Agricultural University (ENITA). He is also the viticulturist at Cheval Blanc in Saint-Émilion, and has written extensively on various aspects of terroir and soil and wine quality.

K.V. KENNETH VEROSUB is Distinguished Professor in the Department of Geology of the University of California at Davis. In 1997, he was named Professor of the Year in California by the Carnegie Foundation for the Advancement of Teaching. He is a fellow of the Geological Society of America and the Royal Astronomical Society.

J.V. DR JOSÉ VOUILLAMOZ, Swiss botanist and plant molecular biologist who became a grape geneticist, until recently researcher at the University of California at Davis and Istituto Agrario di San Michele all'Adige, Italy. He specializes in the study of the origin and parentage of grape varieties through DNA typing.

M.W. MONTY WALDIN is a wine writer based in the UK. His first book, *The Organic Wine Guide*, was written after practical work experience in conventional and organic vineyards and wineries around the world had persuaded him that organics made sense. An internship on a biodynamic vineyard in Mendocino County, CA, in 1999 convinced him of the merits of biodynamics, and led him to write *Biodynamic Wines*. His other books include *Wines of South America* and *Bordeaux Wine Country*.

E.W. DR ELIZABETH WATERS is the Principal Research Biochemist with the Australian Wine Research Institute and an Associate Editor for the *Journal of Agricultural and Food Chemistry*. Her principal areas of research are protein, polysaccharide, flavour, and tannin chemistry.

B.M.W. The late DR BERNARD WATNEY was initially a physician but his many interests included wine, wine labels, and corkscrews. He co-wrote *Corkscrews for Collectors*, which has since been translated into French and German.

A.D.W. The late A. DINSMOOR WEBB, Oenology Editor of the first edition of this book, retired in 1982 as Professor Emeritus from the University of California at Davis and then continued to write and to act as consultant oenologist worldwide.

A.G.W. ANDREW WILLIAMS established the first British specialist organic wine importer before becoming a wine writer.

P.J.W. DR PATRICK WILLIAMS, Oenology Editor of the second edition of this book, was until his recent retirement the Deputy Director of, and a researcher for 24 years in, the Australian Wine Research Institute. The American Society of Enology and Viticulture awarded him best oenology paper of the year in 1991 and 1993, and the Accademia Italiana della Vite e del Vino recognized his work with the inaugural Corrado Cantarelli award for oenology and viticulture in 1995.

H.M.W. DR HANNEKE WILSON is the author of *Wine and Words in Classical Antiquity and the Middle Ages*; she is also a wine merchant specializing in Italy.

N.G.W. NIGEL WILSON, Fellow and Tutor in Classics (Emeritus) at Lincoln College, Oxford, where he continues to look after the college cellar. His main work as a classical scholar is as an expert in Greek palaeography and the history of the classical tradition.

T.K.W. TONY WOLF is Professor of Viticulture and has served as viticulturist with Virginia Tech since 1986. His education includes an MS from the Pennsylvania State University and a PhD from Cornell, both in viticulture research. Dr Wolf has written more than 50 scientific journal, trade, and extension publications.

V.Z. VANGJEL ZIGORI, Chairman of the Wine Department in the Food Research Institute of Tirana in Albania, professor, oenologist, and wine writer.

B.W.Z. BRUCE ZOECKLEIN is Professor and Enology Specialist and head of the Enology-Grape Chemistry Group at Virginia Tech. Before that he worked in the California wine industry and at the Viticulture and Enology Research Center, Fresno State. He has a BS in Microbiology, an MS in Horticulture and a PhD in Food Science. Dr Zoecklein has co-authored several books on wine chemistry and analysis. His research interests include secondary grape metabolites.

Acknowledgements

This book, like the two previous editions, owes most to a host of people around the world who have been extraordinarily generous with their time and knowledge, perhaps because wine is a subject which naturally inspires generosity and enthusiasm.

New sources of European expertise such as Véronique Cheynier and Kees van Leeuwen have added some of the latest European advances to the comprehensive base provided by the indefatigable Dr Richard Smart, Viticulture Editor of the first two editions, and Dr Patrick Williams and the late Professor A. Dinsmoor Webb, Oenology Editors of the second and first editions respectively. Both Dr Smart and Dr Williams are to be thanked for pointing out and contributing to essential updates for this third edition.

Assistant editor Julia Harding MW has drawn upon her impressive network of scientists and practitioners to make the entries on vine growing and wine-making as international as possible. The Australian Wine Research Institute was the single academic body contributed the greatest and most varied input but the list of advisers is long and multinational

The Organisation Internationale de la Vigne et du Vin (OIV) supplied the data on international production and consumption of wine, notably that presented in Appendix 2. Specifically Australian wine production data are used with permission from the Australian Bureau of Statistics (www.abs.gov.au). Global grape variety statistics were kindly provided by Pat Fegan of the Chicago School of Wine.

Historical entries have been reviewed by their authors to ensure that necessary updates have been made, and we are grateful that our many renowned academics, especially Dr Jane Renfrew, have taken such trouble to incorporate new discoveries in the relevant entries.

Some regional specialists were far more helpful than they need have been, updating their valuable contributions of seven and 12 years ago. James Halliday and Bob Campbell MW again gave us the benefit of their unparalleled knowledge of their native Australia and New Zealand respectively when they surely had far more lucrative calls on their time. Victor de la Serna and Richard Mayson manfully updated all of Spain and Portugal respectively. David Gleave MW, arguably the busiest man in the

British wine trade, somehow found the time to bring Daniel Thomases' extensive coverage of Italian wine up to date. His German counterpart, almost exactly, was American wine merchant David Schildknecht.

In North America, Howard Goldberg was particularly generous with his time and editorial eye, while Tim James was assiduous in his suggestions for improvements to the South African entries, thoroughly updated by Michael Fridjhon. Caroline Gilby MW has dramatically improved coverage of Bulgaria and Romania, while Patricio Tapia has done the same for Chile and Argentina. But perhaps the greatest hero of this third edition is Denis Gastin, who managed to convey his incredibly diverse knowledge of the emerging wine producers of Asia despite the intervention of back surgery.

Those who made notable contributions to the third edition, other than those recorded in the list of Contributors include:

Philip Bailey	Anupama Kumar
Rae Blair	Jean-Pierre Laurent
Achim Blau	Visooth Lohitnavy
Eveline Bartowsky	Karien Lourens
Piero Attilio Bianco	Pedro Marchevsky
Jorge Boehm	Christine Ontivero
The Budapest Bortársaság	Patrice Pellerin
Michel Bourqui	Alan Pollnitz
Jean-Michel Boursiquot	Paul Pontallier
Aurélie Chobert	Philip Quick
Monika Christmann	Christine Riou
Peter Clingeleffer	Dany Rolland
Adam Dakin	Michel Roux Jr
Denis Dubourdieu	Valerie Saxton
Ann Dumont	Steffen Schindler
Guy Duren	Ernie Sullivan
Neil Edkins	Charles and Philippa Sydney
Patrick Fegan	Paul Symington
Akos Forczek	Istvan Szepsy
Richard Gibson	Leon Terry
Jeanne M. Griffith	Rainer Töpfer
Michael Havens	Vertumne of Bordeaux
James Herrick	Kim Wachtveitl
Ailsa Hocking	Paul M. Whitehouse
Ben Howkins	David Wollan
Yakup Icgoren	Douglas Wregg
Tim James	Martin Yule
Michael Jarzebowski	George Zhao

Those who made a particular effort to help with the second edition include:

Fethi Askri
Julian Barnes
Alexis Bespaloff
Joán Bluske
Edmundo Bordeu
Michael Broadbent MW
Myriam Broggi
Stephen Browett
Dr Nicolas Catena
Sam Chafe
Sham Chougule
George Clowes
Christine Coletta
Jane Cranston
Simon Farr
Martin Fowke
Peter Gamble
Anna Garde
Richard Gawel
Howard Goldberg
Jerry Gough
Tim Hanni MW
Anthony Hanson MW
Ewald Junge
Eva Keresztury
Daniel Lehmann
Anne Le Meur

Nancy Light
Nico Manessis
José Milmo
Kym Milne MW
Adriano Miolo
Abigail Morris
Geoff Morris
Fiona Morrison MW
Hazel Murphy
John Parker
Sue Pike
Erica Platter
David Pollock
Paul Pontallier
Philippo Pszczolkowski
Zdenek Reimann
Lon J. Rombough
Julie and Richard Sellwood
Viktor Siegl
Jean-Louis Simon
Godfrey Spence
Andrew Stewart MW
Charles Sullivan
Zoran Tošovič
Peter Vinding-Diers
William Warre MW

The editor owes a great debt to these and many more both directly and indirectly and would like to apologise most sincerely to those who may have been overlooked.

List of new entries

Below is an alphabetical list of all the terms given their own new entry in this third edition of *The Oxford Companion to Wine.*

acetic acid bacteria
Acolon
Adelaide Plains
Adelaide Zone
agriturismo
Alcobaça
Alpine Valleys
anthesis
Arinarnoa
Arnsburger
Arribes (del Duero)
Asian lady beetle
atypical ageing
Australian Wine Research
    Institute
Azores
Babo
Baronnies, Coteaux du
barrel renewal
Beechworth
Beira Interior
Big Rivers Zone
biscoitos
black dead arm
black foot
Boisset
Bordeaux blend
Boutenac
Brachet
Breede River Valley
Brock
buffering capacity
California sprawl
Camarate
Cape
Cape Agulhas
Cape blend
carbonation
Castel
Catalunya
cation exchange capacity
Cayuga White
Central Ranges Zone
Cerceal Branca
Cercial
Charitois, Coteaux

Charles Sturt University
Charneco
Chaume
Chaves
Chelois
Chelva
Chenanson
Chenin Noir
Cienna
Classic
Clear Lake
Coastal
Coastal Region
co-fermentation
cold soak
Complexa
Constellation
co-pigmentation
Cornalin du Valais
Cornell University
Coruche
Corvinone
Cotarello
Couchois, Bourgogne Côtes du
crise viticole
Crljenak Kaštelanski
crown cap
Currency Creek
DAC
DAP
De Chaunac
délestage
Denmark
Diageo
diatomaceous earth
direct shipping
DMDC
Dominio de Valdepusa
drinking
Duché d'Uzès
Eastern Plains Zone
economics and wine
Egiodola
electrodialysis
Erstes Gewächs
estate wine
Évora
Far North Zone
Federspiel
feinherb
finca
Fladgate Partnership

flash détente
flavonols
flavour scalping
flight
Foster's
Foundation Plant Services
Fresno
Friulano
Frontenac
Gamaret
Garanoir
Garnacha Blanca
Gelber Muskateller
gemischter Satz
geographical information system
glassy winged sharpshooter
globalization
global positioning system
gluconobacter
glutathion
Gorbachev, Mikhail
Gracioso
Greater Perth Zone
Grés de Montpellier
Groenekloof
Grolleau Gris
Grosses Gewächs
Gundagai
Hastings River
Haut
Heathcote
Henty
Henriques, Justino
heritage varieties
Icewine
icon wine
IFOAM
Imperial Tokay
International Grape Genome
    Project
isoamyl acetate
isobutyl-methoxypyrazine
IVDP
Jacob's Creek
Kangaroo Island
Kékmedoc
Kövérszőlő
Lacrima Nera
Lafões
Lago
Lagos
Landot

List of new entries

xx

Maps of the wine regions

Note to the reader

Entries are arranged in letter-by-letter alphabetical order up to the first punctuation in the headword, except that names beginning with Mc are ordered as if they were spelt Mac, and St and Ste (French) are arranged as if they were spelt Saint and Sainte. Château and châteaux appear in full as headwords, but are abbreviated to ch and chx elsewhere. Entries appear under the name of the château, and not under C.

Typographical consistency is a particular issue in a book of this nature and length. In the interests of clarity, the non-specific part of the names of geographical features or political divisions not capitalized (e.g. Gavilan mountains, Napa valley, river Mosel, Washington state) except when they refer to a controlled wine appellation (e.g. Barossa Valley, Napa Valley, Santa Cruz Mountains) although in some cases they may be one and the same.

Cross-references are denoted by red small capitals and indicate the entry to which attention is being directed. Cross-references appear only where reference is likely to amplify or increase understanding of the entry being read. They are not given in all instances where the name of an entry appears in the text.

All wine-producing countries have an entry. The more significant ones also have individual entries for regions within them. German wines, since they carry the name of their region of origin on the bottle label, are discussed within regional entries. Individual people, wine producers, and properties which have played or are playing an important part in the history of wine have an entry, as do all significant appellations from France, Spain, and Portugal. Italy is extensively covered by a mixture of individual denominations and regional entries.

Measurements are given in metric accompanied by the United States equivalent. (See below for abbreviations.)

The format of this third edition is very similar to the second, including at the back of the book a Complete List of Entries by Subject to highlight more clearly just what the book holds, and to suggest another way of navigating your way through it. A revealing List of New Entries is included in the introductory matter; all new entries are of course included in the thematic listings too. To make way for extensive updating of old entries and more than 300 new entries, we have considerably increased the overall length of the book and have regretfully had to omit the entries on spirits and to abbreviate those on wine-related antiques.

The appendices include a complete list of wine appellations (not often found in printed form) together with details of those grape varieties specified by them (an even rarer listing), as well as listings of total vineyard area by country, total wine production, and per capita wine consumption. All have been thoroughly updated.

Abbreviations

ch, chx	château, châteaux
ft	feet
gal	US gallon
g/l	grams per litre
ha	hectare
hl	hectolitre
in	inches
l	litre
m	metre

abboccato, Italian for medium sweet (less sweet than AMABILE) or, literally, 'palatable' from *bocca* or 'mouth'. See also SWEETNESS.

ABC, acronym for the weary sentiment 'Anything But Chardonnay (or Cabernet)' which encouraged interest in grapes other than the (two most famous) INTERNATIONAL VARIETIES on the part of both producers and consumers. Rhône varieties have been the chief but by no means only beneficiaries.

abocado, Spanish for medium sweet. According to European Union labelling regulations, *semiseco* is the official Spanish term.

Abona, small denominated Spanish wine region covering the semi-desert south of Tenerife in the vinously revitalized CANARY ISLANDS. Inland, at Vilaflor, it boasts Europe's highest vineyard, reaching 1,600 m/5,200 ft above sea level. It produces an increasing number of ORGANIC wines and whites of little distinction from the LISTÁN Blanco grape.   V. de la S.

Abouriou, early-ripening minor south western dark-berried vine variety that was still grown on 420 ha/1037 acres of France in 2000. It is still theoretically allowed into Côtes du MARMANDAIS and is also found in some red VINS DE PAYS of the south west. Its wine is relatively high in tannin and low in acidity. French AMPELOGRAPHER Paul Truel identified the vine once grown in California as Early Burgundy as Abouriou.

Abruzzo, mountainous region in central Italy with a significant coastline on the Adriatic sea to the south of Marche and an important producer of wine (see map under ITALY). Abruzzo is fifth among Italy's regions in terms of production, with a total output of just under 4 million hl/105 million gal in 2004.

Despite the presence of one of Italy's better red grape varieties MONTEPULCIANO d'Abruzzo, despite the warm climate, and despite favourable vineyard sites where the hills descend towards the Adriatic and enjoy the benefits of summer heat and solar radiation from the sea, most of the region's production is undistinguished—even if close to a sixth of the region's production is DOC. The DOCs themselves are not particularly well conceived, with excessively generous production limits—100 hl/ha (5.7 ton/acre) for Montepulciano d'Abruzzo and over 120 hl/ha for Trebbiano d'Abruzzo—and little attempt to define suitable subzones for the varieties. In addition, the regional authorities virtually compelled growers in the 1970s to use the TENDONE system of training when replanting their vineyards (by withholding subsidies otherwise), which promoted quantity wildly in excess of quality.

In spite of this rickety legislative framework, some good wine is produced in Abruzzo. Fine, often keenly priced Montepulciano has long been produced in such townships as Brec-

ciarola, Città Sant'Angelo, Controguerra, Loreto Aprutino, Tocco da Casauria, Torano Nuovo, and Vasto. The Montepulciano grape was once openly (now clandestinely) prized as a blending wine in the north of Italy, particularly in Toscana, Veneto, and Piemonte. Montepulciano d'Abruzzo is generally produced in two styles: a young, quaffing style, robustly fruity and best drunk in its first two years; and a more serious, almost Syrah-like style, where the wildness of the fruit is often tempered by a bit of oak. Regardless of style, the wine frequently has a detectable animal quality to it, which can range from the attractively 'sweaty saddle' to the intolerably gamey. This REDUCTIVE character, probably caused by the high level of PHENOLICS in the variety's skins, could easily be tamed with a bit of care in the winery, but such care is sadly lacking in many wineries in the region.

An attempt to redeem the image of Montepulciano has been made with the introduction in 2003 of DOCG for Montepulciano d'Abruzzo Colline Teramane, for Montepulciano grown in the hills in the area around Teramo in the northern part of Abruzzo.

Trebbiano d'Abruzzo, mentioned as a wine of high quality by Cervantes in his *Novelas ejemplares*, is more complex. The best wines are not made from Trebbiano at all but rather from the BOMBINO of Puglia, while the great, dreary majority is made from high-yielding TREBBIANO TOSCANO. Better Trebbiano d'Abruzzo is a pleasurable, if not memorable, wine, but in the hands of Edoardo Valentini, who combines low YIELDS with a severe selection in the cellar, and ferments and ages his wine entirely in wood, it is one of Italy's most distinctive dry white wines.   D.T. & D.C.G.

Bastianich, J., and Lynch, D., *Vino Italiano: The Regional Wines of Italy* (New York, 2002).

Belfrage, N., *From Brunello to Zibibbo: The Wines of Southern Italy* (London, 2001).

abscisic acid, or **ABA**, HORMONE that occurs naturally in vines and regulates growth and physiology. Its synthesis is encouraged by physiological stresses including short days and WATER STRESS. In the vine, abscisic acid is involved in LEAF FALL, stunted shoots, bud dormancy, opening of STOMATA, and the biosynthesis of PHENOLICS during grape ripening. The irrigation technique PARTIAL ROOTZONE DRYING regulates vine growth, fruit composition, and likely wine quality by manipulating ABA levels.   R.E.S.

Champagnol, F., *Éléments de physiologie de la vigne et de viticulture générale* (Saint-Gely-du-Fesc, 1984).

Mullins, M. G., Bouquet, A., and Williams, L., *Biology of the Vine* (Cambridge, 1992).

Abu Nuwas (d. AD 814), half Arab/half Persian, was court poet and close friend of the Abbasid Caliph al-Amīn (reigned AD 809–813). He was one of the greatest ARAB POETS of classical Arabic/Islamic culture and, despite his eloquence in all the poetic genres, is remembered principally in the Arabic tradition for his wine poems (the *Khamriyyāt*). P.K.

Kennedy, P., *Abu Nuwas: A Genius of Poetry* (Oxford, 2005).

Abymes, named CRU just south of CHAMBÉRY whose name may be added to the eastern French appellation Vin de SAVOIE. The wines are typically light, dry whites made from the local JACQUÈRE grape, although there is some experimentation with Chardonnay.

AC, sometimes **AOC,** common abbreviation for APPELLATION CONTRÔLÉE, the French quality wine category.

academe, originally a Greek word for a site of scholastic endeavour, and today a term embracing all that is achieved there. It impinges considerably on the world of wine.

Wine-making was already a sophisticated practical art by the beginning of the 19th century, and Europe's first formal viticultural training school was established in SACHSEN in what is now eastern Germany in 1811–12. In the second half of the century, however, the seminal work of Louis PASTEUR heralded its transition to an applied science worthy of academic study. Vine-growing and wine-making were soon recognized as academic disciplines and in 1880, coincidentally, both the University of California (now established at DAVIS) and the Institut d'Oenologie at the University of BORDEAUX began teaching and researching VITICULTURE and OENOLOGY. The devastation caused in the mid to late 19th century by FUNGAL DISEASES and the PHYLLOXERA pest may help to explain the coincidence.

During the 20th and early 21st centuries, academic institutions throughout the world have worked in tandem with their local wine industries both to teach the scientific principles of vine-growing and wine-making (increasingly regarded as the single discipline of wine-growing) and to research refinements and solutions. Other academic institutions of importance to wine include ADELAIDE, AUSTRALIAN WINE RESEARCH INSTITUTE, BROCK, CHANGINS, CHARLES STURT UNIVERSITY, CONEGLIANO, CORNELL, DIJON, FRESNO, GEILWEILERHOF, GEISENHEIM, KLOSTERNEUBURG, LINCOLN, MAGARACH, MONTPELLIER, SAN MICHELE ALL'ADIGE, STELLENBOSCH, VIRGINIA TECH, and WÄDENSWIL. Some of these are government funded, although grants for specific research projects are increasingly sought from industry.

In traditional wine regions, wine-growing was taught by apprenticeship and apprentices were taught to respect TRADITION above SCIENCE. Formal academic training has long been the norm in the New World, on the other hand. By the late 20th century, however, it was customary for even a seventh generation Old World wine producer to have received some sort of formal academic training, certainly in his or her own region and very possibly abroad. This not only reflected a fundamental change of attitude towards the science of wine production on the part of Old World producers, but also played a crucial role in the widespread improvement in wine quality during the 1980s and 1990s. Academe, with its annual crop of graduates, could be said to have spawned FLYING WINEMAKERS. Wine courses today need not be focused on production or tasting, however, with such tertiary qualifications as the wine MBAs available in Bordeaux, Trieste, and Cirencester and that offered by the OIV.

Acadie, sometimes known as L'Acadie, winter-hardy grape variety speciality of Nova Scotia and Quebec in CANADA. Named after the French term for Nova Scotia, it is a crossing of SEIBEL 13053 and SEYVE-VILLARD 14–287 made in 1953 at Vineland Research, Ontario (now part of Guelph University). It ripens early and is particularly suitable for regions with very short growing seasons.

acetaldehyde, the most common member of the group of chemical compounds known as ALDEHYDES, a natural constituent of nearly all plant material, including grapes. Acetaldehyde is the next to last substance involved in the FERMENTATION pathway (and is therefore a minor constituent of all fermented products). Post-fermentation traces of acetaldehyde remain in all wines.

In pure liquid form, acetaldehyde has a particularly penetrating and unpleasant aroma. At the low concentrations normally present in wines, and mixed with wine's many other odorants, it is not unpleasant but above a certain level can make the wine smell 'flat' and vapid. At slightly higher concentrations, it contributes to the distinctive and characteristic smell of FINO sherry and other FLOR wines. Acetaldehyde binds with SULFUR DIOXIDE. It also adds to ANTHOCYANIN pigments, CATECHINS, and PROANTHOCYANIDINS (condensed TANNINS) and it is thus involved in the formation of PIGMENTED TANNINS and other derived pigments in wines.

Because it is the first compound formed when OXYGEN reacts with the ETHANOL in wine, winemakers are careful to minimize delicate white wines' exposure to air. (This is not so critical with heavier red wines, possibly because acetaldehyde reacts with tannins and anthocyanins.) Special care must be taken while BOTTLING white wines as this is when the introduction of oxygen can most easily damage the delicate aromas. When a bottle of white wine is only partially emptied, the freshness of its aroma is rapidly lost and replaced by a vapid OXIDIZED smell that is due to, among other reactions, the conversion of ethanol to acetaldehyde. The formation of perceptible acetaldehyde, accompanied by a browning of colour, is a typical sign of OXIDATION.

A.D.W., P.J.W., & V.C.

acetic acid, a simple two-carbon fatty acid and one of the more common organic chemicals encountered in foods, it is also the most common of the VOLATILE ACIDS, and the main flavour constituent responsible for the sour taste of VINEGAR. **Acetification** of a wine begins when it is exposed to OXYGEN, which allows ACETOBACTER bacteria to transform the wine's ALCOHOL into acetic acid. Such a wine may be described as **acetic**. Acetic acid is also directly produced during primary FERMENTATION and most wines have detectable acetic acid levels which are the result of normal YEAST activity. It is the main contributor to the measure of VOLATILE ACIDITY in wine. The perception threshold is generally around 600 mg/l.

A.D.W., P.J.W., & T.J.

acetic acid bacteria, a family of genera which includes ACETOBACTER and GLUCONOBACTER.

acetobacter, genus within the family of ACETIC ACID BACTERIA (AAB) capable of spoiling wine by converting it ultimately into VINEGAR. They are found on all grapes but especially rot-affected grapes. Acetobacter can survive only in OXYGEN and are also one of the very few groups of bacteria which can live in the high-acid (low pH) environment of wine (although see also LACTIC ACID BACTERIA).

Ideal conditions for the growth of acetobacter are temperatures between 30° and 40 °C (86° and 104 °F), relatively high pH values of between 3.5 and 4.0, low alcohol concentrations, absence of SULFUR DIOXIDE, and generous supplies of oxygen. For these reasons, safe wine-making favours low storage temperatures, good levels of ACIDITY and alcohol, use of appropriate levels of sulfur dioxide as a disinfectant and, to minimize oxygen contact, barrels, vats, and tanks kept full at all times, that is with minimum ULLAGE. If the latter cannot be avoided, the stored wine is blanketed with CARBON DIOXIDE, NITROGEN, or an INERT GAS MIXTURE. A.D.W. & P.J.W.

acid, when used as an adjectival tasting term rather than a chemical noun (see ACIDS), is usually pejorative and means that the wine has too much ACIDITY.

acid adjustment, euphemism for DEACIDIFICATION or more usually ACIDIFICATION.

acidification is the wine-making process of increasing the ACIDITY in a grape must or wine. This is a common practice in warm wine regions (as common as ENRICHMENT, or CHAPTALIZATION, in cool wine regions), and is often the only course open to a winemaker wanting to make a balanced wine from grapes which have been allowed a growing season long enough to develop flavour by reaching full physiological RIPENESS. This is because in warm conditions a large amount of the grape's natural malic acid is degraded during the ripening process. A good level of ACIDS (and therefore low PH) not only increases the apparent freshness and fruitiness of many wines, it also protects the wine against attack from BACTERIA, enhances the effectiveness of SULFUR DIOXIDE, and can improve COLOUR (as explained under acidity).

Acidification is usually sanctioned by local wine regulations within carefully delineated limits in order to prevent stretching of wine by adding sugar and water along with the permitted acid. In temperate zones such as Bordeaux and Burgundy, acidification is allowed, but with the understandable proviso that no wine may be both acidified and enriched.

The timing of the acid addition varies, but adding acid usually lowers pH so that an addition before or during FERMENTATION results in better microbiological control of subsequent processes and favours the formation of desirable aromas. Fine tuning of acid levels may take place at the final BLENDING stage but acid added at this stage can be too obvious.

Regulations vary from country to country but the most common permitted additives for acidification are, in descending order, TARTARIC ACID, CITRIC ACID, and MALIC ACID. Tartaric is the acid of choice for adding to grape juice before fermentation because, unlike both citric and malic acid, which can be attacked by LACTIC ACID BACTERIA, tartaric acid is rarely degraded. Tartaric acid has the disadvantages, however, that it is the most expensive of the three and that significant amounts of the acid may be precipitated as TARTRATES and lost from the wine. Malic acid is used infrequently because of its microbiological instability and its cost. Citric acid, while also being susceptible to microbiological attack, has the merit of being the least expensive and is used widely for inexpensive wines. It is often chosen for late acid additions because, unlike tartaric acid, it does not affect cold STABILIZATION. However, the use of citric acid for acidification is not permitted in wines made or sold in the EU. In many instances and where regulations permit (in the United States for example), a blend of acids is often used.

One of the problems with acidification is that it is difficult to calculate how much acid to add to reach a desired final pH, in part because each wine or must has its own BUFFERING CAPACITY.

See also DEACIDIFICATION, a less common wine-making measure used in cool climates.

A.D.W. & J.A.G.

acidity is a general term for the fresh, tart, or sour taste produced by the natural organic ACIDS present in a liquid. Wines, together with most other refreshing or appetizing drinks, owe their attractive qualities to a proper balance between this acidic character and the sweet and bitter sensations of other components. All refreshing drinks contain some acidity, which is typically sensed on the human palate by a prickling sensation on the sides of the tongue (see TASTING).

The acidity of the original grape juice has an important influence on wine quality because of its direct influence on COLOUR (see below), its effect on the growth of YEASTS and BACTERIA (harmful and beneficial), and its inherent effects on flavour qualities. It also plays a part in wine AGEING.

Grape juice acidity is highest just at the beginning of RIPENING, at which stage grapes have half as much concentration of acidity as lemons. See also VERJUS.

Acidity is one of the most important components in both grape juice and wine, and is also easily quantifiable. What is measured, although in different ways in different countries, is usually the TOTAL ACIDITY, which is the sum of the FIXED ACIDS and the VOLATILE ACIDS. To a scientist, acidity is the extent to which a solution is acid, caused by protons (hydrogen ions or H+), which may be present in either free or bound forms. Another way of measuring acidity is to measure the concentration of hydrogen ions (H+) free in solution, using the logarithmic PH scale. Generally the higher the total acidity of a wine, the lower is its pH.

Acidity helps to preserve the colour of red wines because the pH affects the ionization of ANTHOCYANINS, which in turn affects their colour. The lower the pH, the redder (less blue) the colour is and the greater the colour stability. As pH values rise (in less acid wines), pigments become increasingly blue and the colour becomes less stable with pigments eventually assuming muddy grey forms. Red wines from warmer regions and made without ACIDIFICATION can have colours that are less red (and often with a brownish tinge) than those from colder regions which produce wines with higher acidity. Higher pH values also cause the PHENOLICS of white wines to darken and eventually to polymerize as brown deposits.

Excessive acidity—resulting either from excessive concentrations of natural plant acids in less-than-ripe grapes or, more rarely, from over-enthusiastic acidification in the winery—makes wines sharp, tart, and sometimes unpleasant to drink. Too little acidity, on the other hand—the consequence of picking too late, or such heat during ripening that the natural plant acids are largely decomposed—results in wines that are flat, uninteresting, and described typically by wine tasters as 'flabby'.

See TOTAL ACIDITY for more details.

A.D.W., B.G.C., & P.J.W.

acids, members of a group of chemical compounds which are responsible for the sharp or sour taste of all drinks and foods, including wine. The most important acids contained in grapes are TARTARIC ACID and, in slightly lower concentrations, MALIC ACID. Malic acid occurs in many different plants and fruits, but vines are among the very few plants with large concentrations of tartaric acid in their fruit. The principal acid component in most plants is CITRIC ACID but VINIFERA vines are also unusual among plants in accumulating only very small amounts of citric acid.

Grapes contain a large number of acids other than their major constituents, tartaric and malic acids. Present in low concentrations are several of the fatty acids, of which the most common is ACETIC ACID, arising from the metabolic processes of fruit RIPENING.

Some other acids involved in the growth of vines accumulate in the berry in very small amounts and some of these persist into the wine. Other acids found in wines, while possibly present in traces in grapes, are formed mainly during FERMENTATION. Among those present in the largest concentrations are LACTIC ACID, SUCCINIC ACID, and CARBONIC ACID.

Various acids are also occasionally added during wine-making. (See ASCORBIC ACID, SORBIC ACID, and sulfurous acid, which is SULFUR DIOXIDE.)

Acids are important in wine not just because, in moderation, they make it taste refreshing, but also because they prevent the growth of harmful BACTERIA and can keep it microbiologically stable. Most bacteria, and all of those of greatest danger to man, are incapable of living in distinctly acid solutions such as wines. Two groups of bacteria are major exceptions to this rule, however, the ACETOBACTER and the various LACTIC ACID BACTERIA.

A wine's concentration of acids is called its ACIDITY, which can be measured in various ways. Acidity is closely, if inversely, related to PH.

A.D.W. & P.J.W.

acidulation, wine-making process more commonly known as ACIDIFICATION.

Acolon, GERMAN CROSSING of LEMBERGER and DORNFELDER.

adega, Portuguese word for cellar or winery.

Adelaide, usual abbreviation in the wine world for the **University of Adelaide**, in South Australia, with which ROSEWORTHY Agricultural College was merged in 1991 to form the Department of Horticulture, Viticulture, and Oenology, now a Discipline within the School of Agriculture and Wine, Australia's principal and influential centre of wine education and research (see ACADEME and AUSTRALIAN INFLUENCE).

Most of the teaching in oenology, viticulture, and wine business studies takes place in the South Australian capital city of Adelaide at the Waite Campus, 7 kilometres from the city centre, but the sensory classes are now held in the National Wine Centre in the heart of Adelaide. At the Waite Campus, students undertake their wine-making in the multi-million dollar Hickinbotham Roseworthy Wine Science Laboratory owned by the University of Adelaide. They also have access to the Commonwealth Scientific and Industrial Research

Organization (CSIRO) Division of Horticulture and the AUSTRALIAN WINE RESEARCH INSTITUTE (AWRI), both organizations having established a considerable international reputation for research in viticulture and oenology respectively.

T.H.L. & S.T.

Adelaide Hills, fashionable, relatively high (450–550 m/1,480–1,800 ft), cool wine region in SOUTH AUSTRALIA and one of Australia's best for growing fine Sauvignon Blanc, part of the MOUNT LOFTY RANGES ZONE with CLARE VALLEY. Lenswood and Piccadilly Valley are officially recognized subregions. Also notable for sparkling wine made from Pinot Noir and Chardonnay. In the north of the region, lower-altitude west-facing slopes produce fuller bodied wines from Shiraz. To complicate the picture, Shiraz (sometimes married with Viognier) also flourishes in the cooler parts to produce northern Rhône valley lookalikes.

Adelaide Plains, a flat, warm to hot region immediately north of Adelaide with one notable winery, Primo Estate (which sources much of its fruit from outside the region).

Adelaide Zone, Australian super zone encompassing the MOUNT LOFTY RANGES ZONE, FLEURIEU ZONE, and BAROSSA ZONE, plus the gaps in between. Thus, for example, Penfolds Magill Estate is a notable resident. Infrequently used as a Geographic Indication on wine labels.

adulteration and fraud have dogged the wine trade throughout its history. The variability and value of wine have traditionally made it a target for unscrupulous operators, as catalogued in the LITERATURE OF WINE. The long human chain stretching from grower to consumer affords many opportunities for illegal practices. It is important to remember, however, that at various times the law has viewed the same practices differently, sometimes condoning, sometimes condemning them. What we know as adulteration, our ancestors may have classed as a legitimate part of the wine-making process. See also MANIPULATION.

The simplest and most obvious form of adulterating wine is to add WATER. This is not necessarily fraudulent. In Ancient GREECE, for example, no civilized man would dream of drinking undiluted wine, and even today wine made from extremely ripe grapes may achieve better BALANCE if slightly diluted. The practice becomes illegal when done surreptitiously to cheat the consumer or defraud the taxman.

Another means of stretching wine is to 'cut', or blend, it with spirits or other (usually poorer-quality) wines. BORDEAUX merchants in the 18th century cut fine clarets with rough, stronger wine imported from Spain, the Rhône, or the Midi to increase profits, but also because it was genuinely believed that the resulting fuller bodied concoction was more to the English taste. JULLIEN describes this common practice as *travail à l'anglaise*. Similarly, merchants in 18th-century OPORTO began to adulterate port with brandy. The systematization of this process by the Portuguese government eventually led to an accepted method of 'adulteration', entirely lawful, to produce PORT as we know it today.

Other ways of altering the nature of a wine were perfectly legal. In the past, wines turned sour after a year or two and techniques used to cure or disguise 'sick' wines were commonplace. Classical and medieval recipes suggested adding various substances ranging from milk (perhaps a precursor of FINING with CASEIN) and mustard to ashes, nettles, and LEAD. Although home doctoring was routine, when these techniques were employed by merchants or taverners deliberately to mislead the customer, the practice was as illegal as it was ubiquitous. In the first century AD, PLINY the Elder bemoaned the fact that 'not even our nobility ever enjoys wines that are genuine'.

One particular method of altering the nature of wine remains controversial; the addition of sugar before or during fermentation to increase the eventual ALCOHOLIC STRENGTH, known as CHAPTALIZATION after the French minister CHAPTAL, who gave it respectability at the beginning of the 19th century. Producers in wine regions warm enough to need no such assistance tend to be scornful of the practice (although they may well indulge in ACIDIFICATION to increase the ACIDITY of their wines).

It is assumed today that, unless explicitly stated otherwise, wine is the product of naturally fermented grape juice. However, the practice of fabricating wine, as opposed to simply doctoring it, has a long and chequered history, often most prolific and ingenious at times when true grape wine has been difficult to obtain. In 1709 Joseph Addison wrote in the *Tatler* of the 'fraternity of chymical operators . . . who squeeze Bordeaux out of a sloe and draw Champagne from an apple', apparently a profession of long standing.

Wines were also fabricated from raisins, in the 1880s and 1890s during the scourge of PHYLLOXERA. In response, a thriving industry manufacturing wine from imported raisins sprang up on the Mediterranean coast. During American PROHIBITION in the 1920s, various methods were contrived to circumvent the law by producing wines at home from raisins, dried grape 'bricks', and tinned GRAPE CONCENTRATE (using techniques common to HOME WINE-MAKING today).

One of the most common forms of fraud does not involve any doctoring or fabricating of the wine, but merely the LABEL. Once a region made a name for its wines, others tried to steal it. In Roman times, ordinary wines were passed off as valuable FALERNIAN. From the 19th century, vine-growers have fought for the legal apparatus to protect their names (see APPELLATION CONTRÔLÉE) and today producers of some of the most expensive wines go to great lengths to design labels which cannot be counterfeited (see INVESTMENT).

The adulteration or fraudulent sale of wine can be dangerous. The consumer may even be put medically at risk, by the use of lead in ancient times and by METHANOL contamination in the 20th century.

Consumers, growers, and merchants are not alone in trying to prevent adulteration and fraud. Local authorities and (from the last century) governments have fought it. Regulations and legislation have been passed for many reasons: to protect the consumer; to preserve the good name of the local wine; or to facilitate TAXATION.

In medieval London it was illegal for taverners to keep French or Spanish wines in the same cellar as those from Germany to prevent mixing or substitution. A vintner found selling corrupt wine was forced to drink it, then banned from the trade. German punishments of the time were more severe, ranging from beatings and branding to hanging.

The legal apparatus existing to combat fraud and adulteration today is the culmination of many battles waged by both consumers and trade. In 1820 Frederick Accum published his *Treatise* stating that wine was the commodity most at risk. Thirteen years later Cyrus Redding reported no improvement and it was not until 1860 that the first British Food and Drug Act was passed.

As for wine-producing countries, the economic distress caused by phylloxera was the main stimulus to legislation. The French government produced a legal definition of wine in 1889, the Germans framed the first GERMAN WINE LAW in 1892 (superseded by the more thorough 1909 version), and the Italians in 1904. The French appellation contrôlée system, defining wines by geography rather than simply composition, did not become nationally viable until the 1930s.

Although once rife, adulteration and fraud have been considerably rarer in the wine trade since the adoption of CONTROLLED APPELLATION systems and methods by which to enforce them such as France's Service de la Répression des Fraudes. There have been examples of CONTAMINANTS in wine, both deliberate and accidental, but passing off has become increasingly difficult and, just possibly, less rewarding as wine consumers become ever more sophisticated and more concerned with inherent wine quality than the hierarchy of famous names. Consumers may with justification feel that the wine trade has attracted more than its fair share of charlatans because fraud in any field in which expertise is difficult to acquire and viewed with suspicion (such as wine and fine art) attracts more media attention than most other types of commercial fraud.

For details of modern fine wines encountered in fake form, see INVESTMENT.

H.B. & J.R.

Accum, F., *Treatise on Adulteration of Food and Culinary Poisons* (London, 1820).

Barr, A., *Wine Snobbery: An Insider's Guide to the Booze Business* (London, 1988).

Johnson, H., *The Story of Wine* (London and New York, 1989).

Jullien, A., *Topographie de tous les vignobles connus* (Paris, 1816).

Loubère, L. A., *The Red and the White: A History of Wine in France and Italy in the Nineteenth Century* (Albany, NY, 1978).

Redding, C., *The History and Description of Modern Wines* (London, 1833).

Aegean islands, islands in the Aegean Sea between modern GREECE and TURKEY. From 1050 BC onwards most of these islands were populated by Greeks. Some of the best Greek wine came from these islands, with CHIAN wine, from the island of Chios, ranked highly in both Ancient Greece and Ancient ROME. Wines from Lesbos, Thasos, and Cos also featured strongly. Chian wine was still highly valued in the Middle Ages and traded in quantity by the GENOANS, for example. H.H.A.

aeration, the deliberate and controlled exposure of a substance to air, and particularly to its reactive component OXYGEN.

The aeration of wine during WINE-MAKING must be carefully controlled, since excessive exposure to oxygen can result in OXIDATION and the possible formation of excess ACETIC ACID. At the beginning of FERMENTATION some aeration is necessary since YEAST needs oxygen for growth. The cellar operation of TOPPING UP can expose the wine to an amount of oxygen that contributes to the BARREL MATURATION process. The amount of aeration involved in the cellar techniques of RACKING wine from one container (usually a BARREL) to another, DÉLESTAGE, and PUMPING OVER can also be positively beneficial to a wine's development. Specifically, aeration can often cure wines suffering from REDUCTION and can usually remove malodorous and volatile HYDROGEN SULFIDE, MERCAPTANS, and some other SULFIDE from young wines.

Often for the same reasons, some aeration before SERVING by pouring the contents of a bottle from a great height or from one container into another can also benefit some wines after BOTTLE AGEING, as can simply swirling the wine in the glass. See also DECANTING and BREATHING.

aerial imagery. See REMOTE SENSING.

Afghanistan, Middle Eastern country in which about 50,000 ha/123,500 acres of vines are officially cultivated for TABLE GRAPES and DRYING GRAPES. At one time wine may have been made here and shipped along the old Silk Road to India.

Africa. See ALGERIA, EGYPT, ETHIOPIA, KENYA, MADAGASCAR, MOROCCO, NAMIBIA, TANZANIA, TUNISIA, SOUTH AFRICA, and ZIMBABWE.

age in a wine is not necessarily a virtue. See AGEING. See also VINE AGE.

ageing of wine, an important aspect of wine connoisseurship, and one which distinguishes wine from almost every other drink (see BACTERIA).

History

When a fine wine is allowed to age, spectacular changes can occur which increase both its complexity and monetary value. Ageing is dependent on several factors: the wine must be intrinsically capable of it; it must be correctly stored (in a cool place and out of contact with air); and some form of capital INVESTMENT is usually necessary.

Although the BIBLE suggests that Luke understood that old wine was finer than new wine, the Romans (see Ancient ROME and, specifically, HORACE) were the first connoisseurs systematically to appreciate fine wines which had been allowed to age, although there is some evidence of wine ageing in Ancient GREECE. Certain wines (DRIED GRAPE WINES, for example) were suitable for ageing because of their high sugar content and were stored in sealed earthenware jars or AMPHORAE. The best, FALERNIAN and SURRENTINE wines, required 15 to 20 years before they were considered at their best and were sometimes kept for decades.

The Greek physician GALEN (b. AD 130) noted that an 'aged' wine need not necessarily be old, but might simply have the characteristics of age. In other words it was possible, indeed very common, to age wines prematurely by means of heating or smoking them (see Ancient ROME). At one time the smoky taste of 'aged' wines became a vogue in itself, though Galen warned that they were not as wholesome as naturally old wines.

After the collapse of the Roman Empire, the appreciation of aged wines disappeared for a millennium. The thin, low-alcohol wines of northern Europe were good for only a few months, after which they turned sour and were sold cheap. The only wines that could be enjoyed a little longer were the sweeter and more alcoholic wines of the Mediterranean such as MALMSEY and SACK.

By the 16th century, exceptions to this rule could be found in the huge casks of top-quality wine made from RIESLING wine kept beneath German palaces (see GERMAN HISTORY). These wines were preserved through a combination of sweetness and ACIDITY in the must, the coldness of the cellar, and the cellarmaster's habit of constantly TOPPING UP the cask to avoid OXIDATION.

The real breakthrough came with the introduction in the 17th century of CORKS and glass BOTTLES. The ageing of wine in bottle was pioneered in England by connoisseurs of fine CLARET and port. English wine drinkers rediscovered pleasures largely unknown since Roman times.

Other methods of preserving wine were developed or rediscovered: the addition of spirits to a partially fermented wine to produce fortified wines (see FORTIFICATION); the systematic topping up of a SOLERA system to produce wines like sherry; and the heating of MADEIRA.

Demand for mature wines transformed the wine trade. Aside from a few wealthy owners, most vine-growers could not afford to keep stocks of past vintages. Only MERCHANTS could do that, and their economic power and hold over the producers increased during the 18th and 19th centuries. This was most demonstrably the case in BORDEAUX, BEAUNE, and OPORTO, where merchants amassed huge stocks, vast fortunes, and powerful reputations. H.B.

Johnson, H., *The Story of Wine* (London, 1989).

Younger, W., *Gods, Men and Wine* (London, 1966).

Which wines to age

The ageing of wine is an important element in getting the most from it but, contrary to popular opinion, only a small subgroup of wines benefit from extended BOTTLE AGEING. The great bulk of wine sold today, red as well as white and pink, is designed to be drunk within a year, or at most two, of BOTTLING.

Wines which generally do not improve with time spent in bottle, and which are usually best consumed as soon as possible after bottling (although after a few weeks in bottle has eliminated any BOTTLE SICKNESS) include the following—although the following is only the most approximate generalization: wines packaged in any containers other than bottles—BOXES, for example; wines with synthetic CLOSURES; wines designated TABLE WINES in the EUROPEAN UNION, JUG WINES in the US, and their everyday, commercial equivalents elsewhere; almost all branded wines, with the possible exception of some red bordeaux; most FIGHTING VARIETALS, with the possible exception of the best made from Cabernet Sauvignon grapes; many German QBA wines; almost all French VINS DE PAYS, Spanish VINO DE LA TIERRA, and the cheapest Italian IGT; almost all wine coloured pink; all wines released within less than six months of the vintage such as those labelled NOUVEAU and the like; FINO and MANZANILLA and similar light, dry sherries; basic ruby and tawny PORT; most wines labelled MOSCATO and all ASTI.

Even among finer wines, different wines mature at different rates, according to individual VINTAGE characteristics, their exact provenance, and how they were made. Such factors as BARREL FERMENTATION for whites and BARREL MATURATION for wines of any colour play a part in the likely life cycle of the wine. In general, the lower a wine's PH, the longer it is capable of evolving. Among reds, generally speaking the higher the level of FLAVOUR COMPOUNDS and PHENOLICS, particularly TANNINS, the longer it is capable of being aged. Wines made from the Cabernet Sauvignon and Nebbiolo grapes, for example, and many of those made from Syrah/Shiraz, should be aged longer than those based on Merlot or Pinot Noir—and certainly much longer than the average wine made from Gamay or Grenache. Among white wines, partly because of their higher acidity and FLAVOUR PRECURSORS, the finest Riesling and Loire Chenin Blanc evolve more slowly than wines based on Chardonnay.

In general terms, better-quality wines made from the following grape varieties should benefit from some bottle age, with a *very* approximate number of years in bottle in brackets:

Red wines
Aglianico of Taurasi (4–15)
Baga of Bairrada (4–8)
Cabernet Sauvignon (4–20)
Melnik of Bulgaria (3–7)
Merlot (2–12)
Nebbiolo (4–20)
Pinot Noir (2–8)
Raboso of Piave (4–8)
Sangiovese (2–8)
Saperavi (3–10)
Syrah/Shiraz (4–16)
Tannat of Madiran (4–12)
Tempranillo (2–10)
Xinomavro of Greece (4–10)
Zinfandel (2–6)

White wines
Chardonnay (1–6)
Chenin Blanc of the Loire (4–30)
Furmint of Hungary (3–25)
Petit Manseng of Jurançon (3–10)
Pinot Gris (1–6)
Riesling (2–30)
Semillon (dry wines) (2–7)
and all botrytized wines (5–25)

ICEWINE and all but the finest EISWEIN matures quite rapidly. Most fortified wines and their like, such as VINS DOUX NATURELS and VINS DE LIQUEUR, are bottled when their producers think they are ready to drink. Exceptions to this are the extremely rare bottle-aged sherries, vintage PORT (which is expressly designed for many years' bottle ageing), single quinta ports, and crusted port.

Producers of SPARKLING WINES usually claim that their wines are ready to drink on release, but this may not be true when demand exceeds supply. Even if yeast AUTOLYSIS ceases when the wine is disgorged, better-quality young sparkling wines with their high levels of acidity can often improve considerably with an additional year or so in bottle.

Factors affecting ageing
STORING WINE in particular conditions can affect the rate at which wine ages; the lower the TEMPERATURE, the slower the maturation. Conversely, ageing can be hastened by stripping a young wine of its solids (by very heavy FILTRATION or FINING, for example), and by storing wine in warmer conditions. Thus, a wine stored in a centrally heated Manhattan apartment will mature very much faster than one

stored in an unheated warehouse in Scandinavia. In general, the more slowly a wine matures, the greater the complexity of the flavour compounds that go to make up its BOUQUET (see below).

It is also popularly believed that in general, the smaller the BOTTLE SIZE, the faster its contents mature, presumably because of the greater proportion of OXYGEN in the bottle, both as a consequence of the bottling process and any possible oxygen ingress via the cork seal during ageing. This is part of the reason LARGE FORMATS carry a premium.

Wines under SCREW CAP tend to age very differently from the same wine under CORK, although it is too early for long-term scientific studies of this phenomenon.

For more details, see STORING WINE.

How wine ages
The descriptions below concern only those wines designed specifically to be aged. The great majority of wines in commercial circulation are ready to drink when sold.

Red wines To the untutored taster, older red wines seem to be softer and gentler than harsh, inky young ones. Those who notice such things will also observe a change in colour, typically from deep purple to light brick red. There should also be more SEDIMENT in an old wine than a young one. All these phenomena are related, and are related in particular to the behaviour of phenolics, the compounds of the grape, particularly the skins, including the blue/red ANTHOCYANINS which together with the astringent but colourless flavonoids form the PIGMENTED TANNINS (tannin-anthocyanin complexes) that are responsible for a red wine's COLOUR and TEXTURE.

Most phenolics are leeched out of the grape skins and seeds during RED WINE-MAKING. They react with each other, especially under the influence of the small amounts of oxygen dissolved in the wine during such processes as RACKING, topping up, and, later, bottling, to generate various derivatives including pigmented tannins. There is some evidence that these reactions start during the primary FERMENTATION process, and by about 18 months later the anthocyanins have mostly been converted to derived pigments responsible for the colour of older red wines. A fine red wine ready for bottling, therefore, may contain colourless tannins, a low concentration of anthocyanins, as well as pigmented tannins, and more complex COLLOIDS such as tannin-POLYSACCHARIDES, and tannin-PROTEINS. Reactions and aggregation continue in bottle. When the resulting polymers and particles reach a certain size, they precipitate as dark reddish-brown sediment, leaving wine that is progressively less astringent, some of the red/blue pigments and tannins having been precipitated. Thus, to a certain extent, holding a bottle of wine up to the light to determine how

much sediment it has precipitated can give some indication of its maturity (although the amount of sediment deposited is a function not just of time, but of storage conditions and the initial composition of the wine, phenolic and protein content for example).

At the same time as these visible changes occur, the impact of the wine on the nose and palate also evolves. A wide range of FLAVOUR PRECURSORS that were attached to glucose detach themselves (through a natural, and time-dependent, process of HYDROLYSIS) and contribute their individual flavour characteristics to the older wine.

Other flavour compounds responsible for the initial primary AROMAS of the grape and those of fermentation (sometimes called secondary aroma, or secondary bouquet) are also interacting, with each other and with other phenolics, so that gradually the smell of the wine is said to be transformed into a bouquet, of tertiary aromas, a very much more subtle array and arrangement of flavours which can be sensed by the nose (see TASTING).

ALDEHYDES are oxidized. ESTERS are formed from combinations of the increasingly complex array of wine ACIDS with ALCOHOLS. Continued esterification in bottle produces another range of possible aromas, all the more unpredictable since the esters are formed at very different rates. Esterification also makes the wine taste less acid (until the point at which other perceptible wine constituents have diminished to such an extent that the wine's acidity, which remains almost constant throughout bottle age, once more dominates its impact on the palate).

The rate at which all these things happen is influenced by a host of factors: storage conditions (particularly temperature), the state of the cork or other stopper, the ULLAGE when the wine was bottled, its pH level, and SULFUR DIOXIDE concentration, both of which can inhibit or slow the all-important influence of oxygen.

OENOLOGISTS understand this much about the maturation of age-worthy red wine, but are unable to predict with any degree of certainty when such a wine is likely to reach that complex stage called full MATURITY, when it has dispensed with its uncomfortably harsh tannins and acquired maximum complexity of flavour without starting to decay. Part of the joy of wine has long been said to be the monitoring of the progress of a case of wine, bottle by bottle, but this is strictly a rich person's sport.

White wines If our understanding of red wine maturation is incomplete, even less is known about the ageing process in white wines. Nevertheless, recent research has shown the importance of certain grape GLYCOSIDES (and the hydrolysis of these constituents) during white wine ageing, to the development of varietal aroma in the wine. White wines begin life in bottle with a much lower tally of phenolics, although those they have strongly influence colour and apparent astringency. White wines become browner with age, presumably because of the slow oxidation of their phenolic content. They may also throw a sediment, although very, very much less than a red wine of similar quality.

Ageing potential is clearly not directly related to a white wine's obvious concentration of phenolics since fine Rieslings, which are relatively low in phenolics, can in general age much longer than comparable Chardonnays, which contain more phenolics.

Experienced tasters, however, often note that wines affected by NOBLE ROT have a much greater ability to last than their non-botrytized counterparts. Experience also seems to suggest that white wines which undergo barrel fermentation also seem capable of lasting longer than those fermented in inert containers and then transferred to barrel for barrel maturation.

Most white wines which can mature over several decades rather than years are notably high in acidity, and few of them undergo MALOLACTIC FERMENTATION. Many of those venerable wines which demonstrate exceptional ageing ability today may well have been bottled with higher levels of sulfur dioxide than are acceptable to the modern consumer. See also ATYPICAL AGEING.

Stages of ageing

Maturing fine wines go through a number of perceptibly different stages. Very young wines are usually delicious, full of fruit and vivacity, but slightly simple. At some (unpredictable) time after bottling, anything between a few months and a few years, fine wines can seem to close up, to become surly, to lose their aroma without having gained a bouquet. Their dimensions can be sensed but little else (see TASTING). A variable number of years afterwards, they begin to smell like wine again and to have considerably more palate LENGTH. After this they enter into their most satisfying stage at which the bouquet seems fully developed and astringency has receded making the mouthfeel attractive, so that the wine is delightful in terms of flavour, texture, length, and all-important BALANCE. If, however, wine is aged for too long (and no one, alas, can predict when this will be), it enters a stage of decrepitude during which the acidity starts to predominate (see above). This unpredictable journey may help to explain apparently contradictory judgements of the same wine, from WINE WRITERS, wine professionals, and wine consumers alike.

Artificial ageing

This wine-making technique has been practised with varying degrees of enthusiasm according to the demands of the market. Current FASHION dictates that wine should be as 'natural' as possible (and, increasingly, that it should be youthful rather than mature), and so very few table wines are ever subjected to artificial ageing (even if many modern WINE-MAKING techniques such as MICRO-OXYGENATION are in fact designed to hasten some natural processes). Wine can be artificially aged by exposing it to oxygen or extremes of temperature, by shaking it to encourage effects of dissolved oxygen, or by exposing it to radiation or ultra-sonic or magnetic waves. The making of MADEIRA and some other RANCIO wines deliberately incorporates exposure to high temperatures, while storing wine in some modern domestic conditions can expose wine to high temperatures rather less deliberately.

See ANTHOCYANINS, ESTER, PH, PHENOLICS, TANNINS; also MATURITY and STORING WINE.

J.R., P.J.W., & V.C.

Ribéreau-Gayon, P., Glories, Y., Maujean, A., Dubourdieu, D., *Traité d'Œnologie 2: Chimie du vin: Stabilisation et traitements* (Paris, 1998), translated by Aquitrad Traduction as *Handbook of Enology 2: The Chemistry of Wine Stabilization and Treatments* (Chichester, 2000).

Robinson, J., *Vintage Timecharts* (London, 1989).

Aghiorghitiko, also known as **Agiorgitiko** and St George, red grape variety native to Neméa in the Peloponnese in GREECE, whose wines may be made from no other variety. It blends well with other varieties (notably with Cabernet Sauvignon grown many miles north in Metsovo to make the popular table wine Katoi) and can also produce good-quality rosé. The wine produced by Aghiorghitiko is fruity but can lack acidity. Grapes grown on the higher vineyards of Neméa can yield long-lived reds, however, and the grape is Greece's second most planted red, after XINOMAVRO.

Aglianico, a dark-skinned top-quality southern Italian grape variety for long thought to be of Greek origin (the name itself is a corruption of the word Ellenico, the Italian word for Hellenic). It retained the name Ellenico or Ellenica until the end of the 15th century, when it took its current name of Aglianico. First planted around the Greek colony of Cumae, close to present day Avellino (home of TAURASI), it is today cultivated in the mountainous centre of Italy's south, in particular in the provinces of Avellino and Benevento in CAMPANIA, and in the provinces of Potenza and Matera in BASILICATA. Scattered traces of this early-budding vine variety can also be found in CALABRIA, in PUGLIA, MOLISE, and on the island of Procida near Naples. A total of about 7,500 ha/18,500 acres was recorded in Italy in 2000. The vine can ripen so late even this far south that grapes may be picked in November. Attempts to pick it earlier, or to increase yields, invariably lead to a failure to tame its rather ferocious tannins. The grape's best wines are deep in colour with full chocolate and plum aromas, fine-grained tannins, and marked acidity on the palate. Aglianico seems to prefer soils of volcanic origin and achieves its finest results in the two DOCS of TAURASI in Campania and AGLIANICO DEL VULTURE in Basilicata. From the late 1990s, it and its wines have attracted sufficient international attention to inspire the export of various varietal bottlings. The DNA PROFILING work of Professor Attilio Scienza of Milan University in the early 2000s could find no relationship with any known Greek variety. D.C.G. & J.R.

Aglianico del Vulture is BASILICATA's only DOC wine but is also one of the most important wines of Italy's south, showing the potential, in its finest bottles, to offer worthy competition to a fine Sangiovese of Toscana or Nebbiolo of Piemonte. The DOC zone consists of close to 400 ha/1,000 acres, all on soil of volcanic origin from Mount Vulture in the north western part of the zone and benefiting from cool nights at an altitude of 450 to 600 m (1,970 ft).

The best producers have enjoyed great success in recent years, as higher prices have ensured that they can lower yields and pick later (and riper). Indeed, Aglianico is quite often one of the last grapes in Italy to be harvested, in late October or early November. The low-trained vines give great intensity of fruit, but the key to making drinkable Aglianico is to ripen the grapes, and this can only be done by reducing yields and picking late. New French oak barrels have largely replaced old chestnut casks in such superior cellars as those of Paternoster, Basilisco, and d'Angelo. D.T. & D.C.G.

Agliano, synonym for ALEATICO.

agricultural treatises are the source of much of our evidence for wine in Ancient GREECE and Ancient ROME. HESIOD was the first Greek to write on agriculture, in the 8th century BC. CATO, VARRO, COLUMELLA, PLINY, and VIRGIL were all important Roman writers.

agriturismo, important late 20th century phenomenon in rural Italy whereby unused or under-used farm buildings, a significant proportion of them on wine farms, are converted, typically with state aid, for TOURIST accommodation, thereby exposing many thousands of visitors each year to the practicalities of wine production. A similar **agroturismo** initiative has begun in Spain.

agrochemicals, the materials used in agriculture to control pests and diseases. They include FUNGICIDES, HERBICIDES, insecticides, bird repellents, plant GROWTH REGULATORS, rodenticides, and soil fumigants. A broader definition might also include FERTILIZERS.

Viticulture requires fewer agrochemicals than many other field crops, partly because such a high proportion of vines are grown in warm, dry summer environments in which

FUNGAL DISEASES are relatively rare, and also because vines require fewer fertilizers than most other crops (see VINE NUTRITION). Vines grown in humid, warm summers may require as many as ten SPRAYINGS, however. Vine-growers, like other farmers, are in general becoming less reliant on agrochemicals as a result of increased environmental awareness, and as alternative approaches become available. Some diseases, notably BOTRYTIS BUNCH ROT, develop tolerance to the repeated use of chemicals, and so their continued use is now discouraged. Alternative approaches may take the form of INTEGRATED PEST MANAGEMENT (IPM) programmes, which aim to apply chemicals more rationally, or the adoption of some form of ORGANIC or BIODYNAMIC VITICULTURE.

The use of agrochemicals in viticulture is strictly regulated by governments. The process of registering a new agrochemical with a government is lengthy and exacting, specifying, for example, withholding periods that must elapse between the last application and when the crop is harvested to allow residues of the agrochemical to diminish to suitably low concentrations.

In the case of wine, the effect the agrochemical may have on FERMENTATION is also assessed. For example, the fungicide folpet, which is used in some countries to protect vines against DOWNY MILDEW, may delay, or even prevent, fermentation.

Because an official maximum residue limit (MRL) may not exist for an agrochemical in all countries, world trade may be adversely affected. For example, the fungicide procymidone, which has been used in parts of Europe, is not registered in the US for use on any crop. When the American authorities detected residues of procymidone in some European wines in early 1990, they banned the importation of any European wine containing residues of procymidone in excess of 20 ρg/kg. This had a serious effect on many sectors of the European wine trade.

The *Codex Alimentarius* ('food code' in Latin) was established by the Food and Agricultural Organization (FAO) and the World Health Organization (WHO) to upgrade and simplify international food regulations and to avoid such incidents. *Codex* MRLs have been set for some agrochemicals in a range of crops, and several countries accept *Codex* MRLs in the absence of their own. The US does not recognize *Codex* MRLs, however.

Although an agrochemical may be present in formulations bearing different proprietary names, it usually has a single common name that is recommended by standards organizations. For example, the fungicide Rovral® (from manufacturers Rhône Poulenc) contains the agrochemical iprodione that is also used in the manufacture of several other fungicides.

See also RESIDUES. R.J.

Cabras, P., Meloni, M., and Pirisi, F. M., 'Pesticide fate from vine to wine', in G. W. Ware (ed.), *Reviews of Environmental Contamination and Toxicology*, 99 (New York, 1987).

Hassall, K. A., *The biochemistry and uses of pesticides: structure metabolism, mode of action and uses in crop protection* (2nd edn, Weinheim, NY, 1990).

Lemperle, E., 'Fungicide residues in musts and wine', in R. E. Smart, R. J. Thornton, S. B. Rodriguez, and J. E. Young (eds.), *Proceedings of the Second International Symposium for Cool Climate Viticulture and Oenology: 11–15 January 1988, Auckland, New Zealand* (Auckland, 1988).

Ahr, tiny German wine region of 530 ha/1,300 acres specializing in red wine and named after the river which flows east from the hills of the Eifel to join the Rhine near Remagen (see map under GERMANY). The most westerly vineyards are in dramatic, rocky, wooded scenery near Altenahr, where the steep slopes on either side of the river reach up to 300 m/980 ft above sea level, and sometimes narrow to the dimensions of a gorge. Many are covered in slate as well as basalt and greywacke clay of volcanic origin, well suited to SPÄTBURGUNDER (PINOT NOIR). The region lies between 50 and 51 degrees of LATITUDE, so that a good MESOCLIMATE is needed to ripen the grapes. Most of the best sites face south east to south west (see TOPOGRAPHY). The dark soil (see SOIL COLOUR), the reflected heat from the curious rock formations, and the protection from north winds that blow above the valley help to ensure the necessary summer warmth. Spätburgunder has been gaining ground steadily and was planted on 61 per cent of the area under vine by 2003, while PORTUGIESER, RIESLING, and MÜLLER-THURGAU vine varieties are on the decline. Many producers still offer soft, late-picked, medium sweet Spätburgunder with dominant RESIDUAL SUGAR.

Leading estates, however, produce fully fermented, dry, OAK aged, tannic Spätburgunder of good colour from low-yielding vineyards. More and more of the region's Spätburgunder wines are of this style (45 per cent were bottled dry by the mid 2000s) and they sell with ease at high prices to Germany's many red wine lovers. Almost 75 per cent of the region's grape harvest is processed by five CO-OPERATIVE cellars, and the state of Rheinland-Pfalz owns the largest estate, 14.5 ha/36 acres based on the 13th-century Kloster Marienthal. I.J. & D.S.

Aïdani, floral-scented variety grown on SANTORINI and other Greek islands for blending into mainly dry wines.

air drainage, important topographical and hence climatological consideration in VINEYARD SITE SELECTION. Cold air flows, or 'drains', downhill and so a continuous slope or HILLSIDE is much less prone to FROST and WINTER FREEZE than a hollow. In regions at risk from these phenomena, zones which accumulate cold air should be avoided as vineyard sites. R.E.S.

air dried. See BARREL MAKING.

Airén, Spain's most planted vine variety, and one that is planted at such a low VINE DENSITY that its vineyards cover more area than any other white wine variety in the world, 305,000 ha/753,350 acres in 2004, despite vigorous VINE PULL SCHEMES in La MANCHA where, as in VALDEPEÑAS, it is by far the most planted variety. The resultant wine is the major ingredient in the important Spanish brandy business. In central Spain it has traditionally been blended with dark-skinned Cencibel (TEMPRANILLO) grapes, which are steadily replacing Airén, to produce light red wines. It is increasingly vinified as an inexpensive white wine, however, nowadays using TEMPERATURE CONTROL to yield crisp, slightly neutral dry white wines for early consumption. In several ways, therefore, Airén is the Spanish equivalent of France's UGNI BLANC. Airén vines are trained into low BUSHES and have remarkable resistance to the DROUGHTS which plague central Spanish viticulture. The variety is also grown around MADRID and in ANDALUCÍA, where it is known as Lairén.

Aix-en-Provence, Coteaux d'. Mainly dry rosé and some red wines are made, often in spectacularly situated vineyards among the lavender and *garrigue* of PROVENCE. The extensive area entitled to this appellation stretches from the frontier with Les BAUX DE PROVENCE subappellation created in 1995 in the west as far as the Coteaux VAROIS. Within the area, a total of about 3,500 ha/8,645 acres of vineyards produce serviceable if generally unsophisticated reds and pale pink wines for early, often local, consumption. CO-OPERATIVES are relatively important here, but a number of individual estates such as Chx Calissanne and Revelette and CHAPOUTIER's Domaine de Béates are trying to establish a distinctive style from Grenache with Cinsaut, Mourvèdre, the local Counoise, Syrah, Carignan, and Cabernet Sauvignon grapes. Neither of the last two may make up more than 30 per cent of a blend. A little white is made from a wide range of southern, and SOUTH WEST FRANCE, grape varieties.

ORGANIC VITICULTURE has established a significant hold in this arid, Mediterranean climate.

Ajaccio. See CORSICA.

Alarije, white grape grown in the EXTREMADURA region of Spain.

Alba, town which provides a focus for the famous wines of the LANGHE hills in Piemonte in north west Italy. Regarded as the region's red wine, and white truffle, capital. See also ROERO and NEBBIOLO D'ALBA.

Albalonga is a 1951 Rieslaner Silvaner vine crossing grown to a very limited extent in Germany, notably Rheinhessen. It inherits from Rieslaner both a firm core of acidity and good rot resistance while dehydrating to MUST WEIGHTS above SPÄTLESE. The wine can smell more like a red, with black fruits and floral aromas, and Wittmann in Westhoven has high prices and complex old bottles to testify to the potential of this exotic variety.   D.S.

Albana, Italian vine made famous by the over-promoted ALBANA DI ROMAGNA. Now widely planted in the EMILIA-ROMAGNA region, its chief claim to fame is being mentioned in the 13th century by medieval agricultural writer PETRUS DI CRESCENTIIS. The thick-skinned **Albana Gentile di Bertinoro**, the most common clone, results in relatively deep-coloured white wines. Although Greco and Greco di Ancona are two of its synonyms, it is unrelated to GRECO di Tufo. A total of about 4,500 ha/11,000 acres of Italy were planted with Albana and its various subvarieties in 1990.

Albana di Romagna, dry white wine made in ROMAGNA in Central Italy from the ALBANA grape which was, amid much incredulity, awarded DOCG status in 1986. Albana di Romagna is Romagna's third most important VARIETAL wine, some way behind SANGIOVESE DI ROMAGNA and TREBBIANO DI ROMAGNA in terms of quantity produced. Albana, which needs good water supplies for ripening, has shown little aptitude either for heavy CLAY soils or for zones with little precipitation. Its high susceptibility to GREY ROT has further limited its cultivation to areas with a certain circulation of air to dry the bunches after heavy rainfall. Although the DOCG zone includes the Apennine strip of the provinces of Bologna, Forlì, and Ravenna, the best Albana comes almost entirely from the red clay soils of the hills between Faenza and the river Ronco to the east of Forlì, together with the CALCAREOUS subzone of Bertinoro, whose Albano enjoyed a significant renown in the past, and the words of Roman Empress Galla Placidia, that the wine should be drunk in gold goblets (*berti in oro*), are allegedly the origin of the township's name. The DOCG rules permit YIELDS of 100 hl/ha (5.7 tons/acre), hardly compatible with the supposed purpose of the DOCG.

Albana di Romagna comes in four different styles: *secco* (dry), *amabile* (medium dry), *dolce* (sweet), and PASSITO. Dry Albana is a rather neutral, characterless wine. Medium dry Albana normally seems neither fish nor fowl. Given the grape's inherent neutrality, its future seems to lie in the dessert version, achieved either with raisined grapes or, in more recent experiments, with NOBLE ROT and small BARREL MATURATION. These can be wines of surprisingly good quality, although they represent a minuscule portion of the total annual production of just under 28,000hl/739,200 gal from the 1,600 ha/4,000 acres of DOCG vineyards.   D.T. & D.C.G.

Albani, Colli, white wines from the hills south east of Rome. For more information, see CASTELLI ROMANI.

Albania, small European country on the Adriatic Sea with KOSOVO and MONTENEGRO to the north and GREECE to the south. It was under hard-line communist control for much of the 20th century but has been since 1996 in a state of some anarchy. Albania claims one of Europe's longest histories of viticulture. French historian Henri Enjalbert considered Albania, the Ionian islands of GREECE, and southern Dalmatia in what is now BOSNIA AND HERZEGOVINA may well have been the last European refuge of the vine after the Ice Age. Certainly there are written accounts of viticulture in Illyria, as it was known in classical times, as early as the 8th century BC. Early Latin writers also cited Illyria as source of a high-yielding vine that was introduced to Italy. By the 17th century, wine production diminished considerably under the influence of ISLAM.

Between the establishment of the first Albanian government in 1912 and 1944 viticulture increased rapidly, although PHYLLOXERA caused such devastation after its discovery in 1933 that by the end of the Second World War there were only 2,737 ha/6,760 acres of vines in Albania. During the 50 years of communist rule that followed, total vineyard area increased to 20,000 ha/49,400 acres, of which 14,000 ha/34,500 acres were devoted exclusively to wine, including imported international vine varieties such as 'Riesling', which is probably WELSCHRIESLING, and 'Tokay', which may be FURMINT.

In 1957, 24 wineries were established in all regions producing dry wines and a grape distillate called *raki rrushi* for local consumption and sweet wines, grape juice, and brandy for export. During the 1990s there was a programme of land privatization and attempts to establish a free market economy but the result, in the short term at least, has been a dramatic reduction in total vineyard area, from nearly 20,000 ha in 1990 to about 7,000 ha in 2002. Precise estimates are difficult because the typical vine-holding is tiny, in private hands, and poorly maintained. Since the decline of state vine nurseries, there is such a shortage of suitable plant material that new plantings are often ungrafted and uncertified imports from neighbouring MACEDONIA. Such wineries as remain suffer from antiquated equipment and the country's lack of oenological (though not viticultural) training.

Albania is divided into four wine regions. The coastal plain rises to 300 m/990 ft and encompasses the towns of Tirana, Durrësi, Shkodra, Lezha, Lushnja, Fier, Vlora, and Delvina. The hilly region varies between 300 and 600 m/1,980 ft altitude and includes Elbasan, Krujë, Gramsh, Berat, Prmet, Librazhd, and Mirdita. The submountainous region lies between 600 and 800 m and surrounds the towns of Pogradec, Korça, Leskovic, and Peshkopi. Some vines are also grown in the mountains as high as 1,000 m/3,300 ft.

The main indigenous vine varieties for winemaking are Shesh (both red, *zi*, and white *bardhë*), Kalmet (known as KADARKA in Hungary and thought to have originated in Albania), Vlosh, red and white Serinë grown in the south east of Albania, and Debine for red wines. Shesh i bardhë and Shesh i zi are the two most important vines, accounting for about 30 per cent of the crop, and take their name from the hill village of Shesh 15 km from the capital Tirana. At low yields the former has an attractive floral aroma while the latter is capable of producing wines worthy of ageing. Vlosh, a speciality of the village of Narta, makes full-bodied, quite astringent wines that may have some RANCIO character.

An experimental station designed to research local grape varieties and upgrade Albanian wine production was founded in 1990.
             V.Z. & J.R.

Enjalbert, H., *Histoire de la vigne et du vin* (Paris, 1975).
Frashri, K., *The History of Albania* (Tiranë, 1964).
Sotiri, P., Gjermani, T., and Nini, T., *Vitikultura* (Tiranë, 1973).
Vertumne et Associés, *Analysis of the Albanian Wine Industry* (Bordeaux, 2001).
Zigori, V., *Buletini Shkencave Natyrore*, 1966–70.

Albarello, rare but interesting white grape grown to a limited extent in the Ribera del Ulla wine region near La Coruña in north west Spain.

Albariño, Spanish name of the distinctive, aromatic, high-quality vine grown in Galicia (and as Alvarinho in the north of Portugal's Vinho Verde region). The grapes' thick skins help them withstand the particularly damp climate, and can result in white wines notably high in alcohol, acidity, and flavour. Albariño was one of the first Spanish white grape varieties produced as a varietal and encountered on labels. Most common in Spain in the RÍAS BAIXAS zone, it has become so popular (and expensive) that it accounts for about 90 per cent of all plantings. Sometimes oak-matured, and increasingly aged for several years in stainless steel tanks before release, it can age better than most light-skinned Spanish grapes however it is made. Occasionally blended with Loureiro, Treixadura, Caiño. Spanish plantings had grown to about 5,000 ha/12,350 acres by 2004. It is also grown in California, Oregon, and Australia.

albariza, a local, Andalusian term for the white, chalky-looking soil typical of parts of the JEREZ region in southern Spain. Grapes grown on this soil type produce some of the finest FINO and MANZANILLA sherries. The soil has a high LIMESTONE content, about 40 per cent, the remainder being CLAY and SAND. It appears dazzling white in summer, and has the characteristic of drying without caking, slowly releasing moisture to the vines during the growing season. This soil type is also present in the PENEDÈS region of north east Spain, where some of the best Spanish sparkling wine is produced (see CAVA). M.J.E.

Albarola, neutral white grape quite widely planted in the Cinqueterre zone of LIGURIA in north west Italy.

alberello, Italian term to describe free-standing BUSH VINES trained according to the GOBELET system.

Albillo, name of several different pale-skinned grape varieties grown in various parts of Spain, most notably RIBEIRO, CASTILLA Y LEÓN, and around MADRID. Its wines are typically neutral in flavour although they can be quite high in GLYCEROL, with obvious differences between the smaller-berried Albillo of Ribera del Duero and the larger-berried one grown round Madrid and in La Mancha.

V. de la S.

A light-skinned grape called **Albilla** is widely grown in Peru.

Alcañón, light, characterful, increasingly rare grape variety that is native to SOMONTANO in north east Spain.

Alcobaça, IPR centred on monastic town of the same name in western Portugal. See ESTREMADURA.

alcohol, the common name for ETHANOL. The term alcohol, which can be applied to any of the ALCOHOLS, derives from the Arabic *al-kuhl*, meaning 'the fine powder used to stain eyelids' (today's kohl), and thus by extension any kind of fine impalpable powder that represents the concentration, or quintessence, of the raw material involved. It was then more widely applied to fluids that represented the essence, or spirit, of something, and thus to any product of distillation.

alcohol reduction in wine can be achieved by a range of physico-chemical methods permitted in some countries but not in others. These include the use of a low-temperature DISTILLATION technique such as SPINNING CONE COLUMN, REVERSE OSMOSIS, ELECTRODIALYSIS, EVAPORATIVE PERSTRACTION, ULTRAFILTRATION, and NANOFILTRATION, as well as the more 'traditional' method of HUMIDIFICATION. The continuing debate over increasing ALCOHOLIC STRENGTH and extended HANG TIME has promoted the rapid development of such technologies as well as further research into the influences on alcohol levels of YEAST selection (some such as EC1118 are more efficient at producing alcohol than others) and FERMENTATION temperature.

Wollan, D., 'Controlling excess alcohol in wine', *Australia and New Zealand Wine Industry Journal*, 20/5 (Sept/Oct 2005), 48–50.

alcoholic, usually pejorative tasting term for a wine which tastes 'hot' and seems to contain excess ethyl alcohol, or ETHANOL.

alcoholic strength, an important measurement of any wine, is its concentration of the intoxicant ethyl alcohol, or ETHANOL. It can be measured in several different ways, the most common being the DEGREE first defined in France by Gay-Lussac in 1884. This was the number of litres of pure ethanol in 100 litres of wine, both measured at 15 °C/59 °F. Later a more precise definition, using 20 °C/68 °F as the reference temperature and some other minor refinements, was adopted in France and by most international organizations. The degree of alcohol is equivalent to its percentage by volume and is sometimes referred to as 'abv', alcohol by volume. In most countries it is mandatory to specify the alcoholic strength of all wines on the label, although it may be written either % or occasionally ° (see also DEGREE).

The alcoholic strength of wine that has not had alcohol added by FORTIFICATION is usually between nine and 16 per cent, with the great majority of wines being between 12.5 and 14.5 per cent alcohol—considerably higher than as recently as the 1980s thanks to CLIMATE CHANGE, current FASHION, a desire for riper PHENOLICS, and the resulting tendency to later picking after extended HANG TIME. A significant proportion of high-quality wine made today in warmer climates is deliberately subjected to some form of ALCOHOL REDUCTION to make it more palatable or to satisfy some legal requirement.

In Europe, fermented grape juice should usually reach at least 8.5 per cent alcohol before it legally constitutes wine, although exceptions are made for better-quality wines that have traditionally been low in alcohol such as German QMP wines and Italian MOSCATO. The technical European legal maximum alcoholic strength for wines that have had no alcohol added is 15 per cent, but derogations are frequently made at this upper limit too, not least for Italy's strongest wines such as AMARONE. In theory at least, all wines over 15 per cent imported into Europe should be labelled Special Late Harvested. In the United States, grape-based 'table wine' must legally be between seven and 14 per cent, while those between 14 and 24 per cent technically qualify as 'DESSERT WINES'.

Since alcohol is the product by FERMENTATION of grape sugar, itself the product of PHOTOSYNTHESIS driven by sunlight, the alcoholic strength of a wine is, very generally, proportional to the proximity of its provenance to the equator, although many other factors play a part. High vineyard ALTITUDE, poor WEATHER in a particular year, high YIELD, and any RESIDUAL SUGAR, are just some of the factors which may decrease alcoholic strength. Severe PRUNING in the vineyard, and cellar techniques such as ENRICHMENT, CONCENTRATION, and

fortification allow winemakers to manipulate alcoholic strength upwards. Some OLOROSO sherries, for example, can reach alcoholic strengths approaching 24 per cent after EVAPORATION. (See also DRIED GRAPE WINES.)

alcohols, those organic chemicals, the simplest members of which consist of carbon, hydrogen, and oxygen atoms arranged so that there is an -OH group present. Many different alcohols are used in commerce and industry but the most common is ethyl alcohol, or ETHANOL, the alcohol that is the important, and intoxicating, ingredient in wines and spirits. The presence of ethanol in foods and beverages, commonly referred to simply as 'alcohol', is the product of yeast FERMENTATION of natural sugars.

Other alcohols with more than two carbon atoms of ethanol are also the product of fermentation and these are sometimes called higher alcohols, or FUSEL OILS. The higher alcohols separated from ethanol by DISTILLATION are normally used as solvents in industrial processes. The major constituent of higher alcohols or fusel oils is the five-carbon isoamyl alcohol. A.D.W. & P.J.W.

aldehydes, a class of chemical compounds midway between the ALCOHOLS and the organic acids in their state of OXIDATION. They are formed during any phase of processing in which an alcoholic beverage is exposed to air. ACETALDEHYDE is the aldehyde of most interest to wine producers. Many aldehydes have quite potent odours, even if they are usually present in only trace concentrations in wines and spirits. As such, aldehydes contribute harmoniously to the overall character.

Those aldehydes containing more than the two carbon atoms of acetaldehyde are in general much more palatable. Vanillin, for example, is a complex aromatic aldehyde present in the vanilla bean and in many other plants, including some grapes where it is present as a GLYCOSIDE and is a FLAVOUR PRECURSOR. Vanillin also occurs as a component of the lignin structure of OAK wood. If new oak casks are used for wine maturation, some of this vanillin is extracted from the wood into the wine, where it adds complexity to the flavour. (See also OAK FLAVOUR.)

See also HERBACEOUS for the part played by **leaf aldehydes.** A.D.W. & P.J.W.

Aleatico, Italian red grape variety with a strong MUSCAT aroma. PETRUS DE CRESCENTIIS referred, as early as the 14th century, to the 'Livatica' vine which today is sometimes called Leatico or Agliano. DNA PROFILING at SAN MICHELE ALL'ADIGE strongly supports a parent–offspring relationship with the classic MUSCAT BLANC À PETITS GRAINS, hence the Muscat flavour. Aleatico certainly has the potential to produce fine, if somewhat esoteric, fragrant wine. Two DOCS enshrine the word Aleatico in the wine lexicon of LAZIO and PUGLIA, but the variety is becoming increasingly rare, although successful attempts such as Avignonesi's to revive the wine in the Tuscan MAREMMA are under way. Sweet red Aleatico is one of the few wines to be exported from the island of ELBA, and the variety is grown on the island of Corsica, although it is not authorized for any APPELLATION CONTRÔLÉE wine. Aleatico is also surprisingly popular in the central Asian republics, notably KAZAKHSTAN and UZBEKISTAN.   J.R. & J.V.

Alella, town near Barcelona in CATALUÑA (see map under SPAIN) which gives its name to a small Spanish denominated wine zone making mainly white wines in increasingly urbanized countryside. To compensate for the loss of agricultural land, this tiny DO was extended northwards in 1989 but by the mid 2000s there were still only 500 ha/1,250 acres of vineyard, a fraction of the area planted in 1956 when Alella was first awarded DO status. The zone used to be known for its old-fashioned, cask-aged, medium sweet white wines. The chief grape variety is the Pansá Blanca, the local name for XAREL-LO, which is now grown along with some CHENIN BLANC and CHARDONNAY to make both CAVA sparkling wines and dry, still white wine. The reputation of Alella was salvaged by Parxet/Marqués de Alella, which pioneered these new styles of wine. The local co-operative and a newer private producer, Roura, joined the drive to better quality in the late 1990s.   R.J.M. & V. de la S.

Alenquer, small, promising DOC in western Portugal. See ESTREMADURA.

Alentejo, DOC and VINHO REGIONAL (known as Vinho Regional Alentejano) in southern PORTUGAL corresponding with a province of the same name. In complete contrast to the north, this is a sparsely populated region where cereal farms and cork plantations (*latifúndios*) stretch as far as the eye can see. These large farms offer considerable ecomomies of scale compared with the smallholdings (*minifúndios*) of northern Portugal.

For centuries, the Alentejo's main link with wine was CORK. Over half the world's supply of cork is grown in Portugal and almost all of it is stripped from the cork oaks that fleck the vast Alentejo wheat fields. Southern Portugal bore the brunt of the military-led revolution that rocked the Lisbon establishment in 1974 and 1975 and, at the beginning of the 1980s, the economy of the Alentejo was in complete disarray, but over the next decade or so five vineyard enclaves emerged from the confusion. The towns of PORTALEGRE, BORBA, REDONDO, REGUENGOS de Monsaraz, GRANJA-AMARELEJA, and VIDIGUEIRA each had CO-OPERATIVE wineries built with government support in the pre-revolutionary 1960s and early 1970s. Until the early 1990s they produced wines for the

undemanding local market but, with financial assistance from the EUROPEAN UNION, they have begun to tap the Alentejo's wine-making potential and export their wines. Likewise single estates, all of which were returned to their former owners, are emerging with new wines. Vineyards now cover over 20,000 hectares of land.

The climate in much of the Alentejo is not naturally conducive to the production of fine wine, but modern technology can compensate for natural deficiencies. IRRIGATION supplements an annual rainfall total which rarely reaches 600 mm/23 in. Temperatures in the summer months frequently exceed 35 or even 40 °C (104 °F), so for white grapes which ripen as early as mid-August, sophisticated TEMPERATURE CONTROL is essential. The production of red wine, principally from ARAGÓNEZ, TRINCADEIRA, Moreto, and CASTELÃO grapes, exceeds white, although some growers see potential in white varieties such as ROUPEIRO and Antão Vaz. A number of producers are now making promising wines from SYRAH. Seven IPR regions were designated in the Alentejo around the six co-operatives listed above, together with EVORA, and MOURA. All of these are now sub-regions within the Alentejo DOC and feature as such on wine labels.   R.J.M.

Alexander Valley. California wine region and AVA in northern Sonoma county east of Healdsburg and south of Cloverdale. See SONOMA.

Alezio, DOC for robust red wine made mainly from NEGROAMARO grapes in south east Italy. For more details, see PUGLIA.

Alfrocheiro, one of the most promising, if not particularly widely planted, red grapes in the DÃO region of PORTUGAL. Alfrocheiro can also be found in the vineyards of ALENTEJO, RIBATEJO, and BAIRRADA. It is very susceptible to OIDIUM and GREY ROT and is not therefore as popular with growers as with winemakers. However, it yields reasonably well, ripens early, and produces deep-coloured wines with good alcohol and acid balance. It is often referred to as **Alfrocheiro Preto** ('black Alfrocheiro'). In the Douro it may sometimes be called Tinta Bastardinha.   R.J.M.

Algarve, the southernmost province of Portugal, now better known for TOURISM than for wine (see map under PORTUGAL). There is, however, evidence of a long wine-making tradition in the Algarve, principally fortified wines. Four DOCs have been designated, centred on local co-operatives at Lagos, Portimão, Lagoa, and Tavira. The entire province has also been designated as a VINHO REGIONAL. The climate and soils of the Algarve are generally thought to be better for citrus fruit and CORK trees than vines but private investment in a number of small wineries is proving that the Algarve has wine potential. The popular British singer Sir Cliff

Richard has helped put the Algarve on the wine map by planting a vineyard and building a winery near the resort of Albufeira.   R.J.M.

Algeria has known world renown in its turbulent recent history as a wine producer but has more recently been grappling with the economic and cultural problems posed by having almost as great an area under vine as Germany or South Africa, for example, but in an ISLAMIC environment. A colonial legacy became a problem of economic dependency. New initiatives, including a 10,000 ha/24,700 acre replanting programme, were begun in 1994.

History

In the late 1950s, France depended heavily on Algerian wine to provide its everyday blended red (and some smarter wines) with strength, colour, and concentration—all of them attributes entirely lacking in the ARAMON then grown so prolifically in the LANGUEDOC. Together with neighbouring MOROCCO and TUNISIA, Algeria accounted for two-thirds of international wine trade in the 1950s.

Although vine-growing was practised in pre-colonial Algeria, and indeed flourished in classical times, it was the French PHYLLOXERA crisis of the 1870s that was to convert the agriculture of this North African colony to vineyards (although there had been a certain influx of wine-growers from Baden in the mid 19th century—see GERMAN HISTORY). In the late 19th century, Algeria was so successfully developed as the prime alternative source for France's voracious wine drinkers that Algeria's total viticultural area grew from 16,688 ha/41,240 acres in 1872 to 110,042 ha/271,910 acres in 1890, largely thanks to settlers whose own European vineyards had been devastated by phylloxera, which eventually reached Algeria.

Vineyards reached their maximum extent of 400,000 ha/988,400 acres in 1938, when Algeria produced more than 21 million hl/550 million gal of wine. By then viticulture had shaped Algerian colonial society and by the year of independence, 1962, a dozen crus were accorded the honour of official VDQS recognition by the French. To the European vineyard owners, the so-called *pieds noirs*, or 'black feet', it gave economic and political power; for non-Europeans it provided valuable employment, but also dependence as the wine trade more than anything else integrated the colony with metropolitan France.

By the start of Algeria's war of independence in the mid 1950s, viticulture was still the leading sector of the colonial economy, accounting for half of Algeria's exports by value. In regions such as the Mitidja plain inland of Algiers and in parts of Oranais, around Aïn Temouchent for example, viticulture had acquired monocultural status.

At Algerian independence in 1962 nearly a million French settlers left as well as a sizeable army of occupation. Algeria's domestic wine

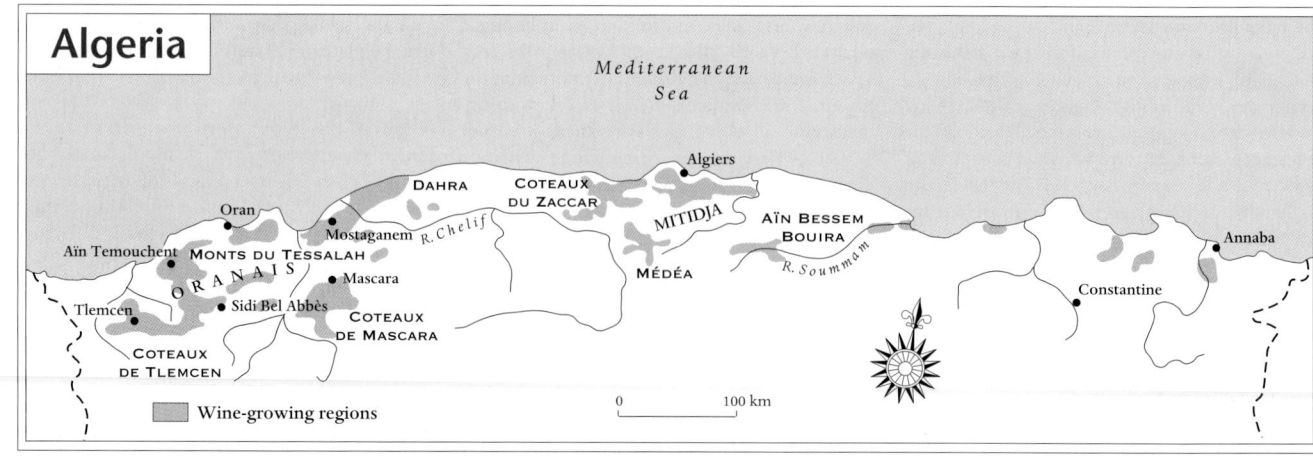

Algeria

market promptly collapsed and the inappropriateness of an Islamic country's heavy economic reliance on wine production became an immediate problem. The mass exodus of European technical skills adversely affected both quality and productivity. Most vineyards passed into a form of collective agriculture as total vineyard and, especially, total wine production began to decline. This posed economic problems as by the mid 1960s wine was still Algeria's second export commodity, after the country's burgeoning oil industry, and viticulture still provided half the man-days worked in the modern, commercialized sector of agriculture.

The modern wine industry

Marketing problems soon emerged after independence. France immediately reduced its imports of Algerian wine from 14.6 million hl/385 million gal in 1962 (about a fifth of France's own total production) to only 6.8 million hl/179 million gal in 1963. The USSR's agreement to buy 5 million hl/132 million gal a year between 1969 and 1975 eased these marketing difficulties somewhat but the agreed (barter) price represented less than half the prevailing world market rate. Negotiations with the EUROPEAN UNION resulted in reduced quantities of Algerian wine allowed into Europe.

These problems prompted various schemes in the late 1960s for the reconversion and reconstitution of Algeria's uneconomically ageing vineyards. The essential problem was, however, that few replacement crops such as cereals could match viticulture's employment opportunities. Only in the 1970s when the area under vine was steadily reduced was a real effort made to face up to the economic realities of the lack of markets. Urban and industrial expansion in the Mitidja plain behind Algiers also helped swallow up vineyards.

By 1990 only 102,000 ha/251,950 acres of vines remained, about one-quarter of the maximum extent in the 1930s, and by the early 21st century total vineyard area had declined further to about 65,000 ha/160,000 acres. A growing proportion of these vineyards now provide TABLE GRAPES rather than wine, about 60 per cent in 2002. Wine production levels have therefore fallen even more drastically than vineyard area, from between 1.8 and 2.8 million hl/47.5 and 74 million gal in the 1978–81 period to fewer than 400,000 hl in the late 1990s, although OIV estimates that this total is rising once more. Abandoned vineyards and wineries, lower yields, and lower prices have combined to make the relict Algerian wine industry a shadow of its former self.

Geography

In regional terms, by the mid 1990s western Algeria accounted for over 65 per cent of the area under vines, notably the districts of Aïn Temouchent, Mascara, Mostaganem, Sidi Bel Abbès, and Tlemcen. Seven regions have been designated quality zones by the country's Office National de Commercialisation des Produits Viti-vinicoles (ONCV). From west to east they are (see map) the Coteaux de Tlemcen, the Monts du Tessalah, the Coteaux de Mascara, the Dahra hills region, the Coteaux du Zaccar, inland from Algiers the Médéa region, and the Aïn Bessem Bouira region.

These viticultural regions all lie within the littoral Mediterranean climate zone of Algeria with its mild winters and hot, dry, and sunny summers. To the south and east of Algiers annual rainfall exceeds 600 mm/23 in while further west, around Tlemcen and Mascara, it usually exceeds 400 mm/15 in. Climatically this is similar to much of southern and eastern Spain.

These recognized quality zones produce mostly relatively concentrated red wines from old vines of those varieties planted, typically, in the 1950s. In 1962 at the time of independence, Algeria had 140,000 ha/345,900 acres of Carignan, 75,000 ha of Alicante Bouschet, 60,000 ha of Cinsaut, and 10,000 ha of Grenache planted, all producing fiery stuff that almost certainly contributed substantially to a high proportion of the wine then sold as burgundy as well as to everyday table wine. If Algerian wine has a fault today, it may be a lack of acidity or an overdose of alcohol but in no other country could the term VIEILLES VIGNES be so widely and literally applied with 80 per cent of vines estimated at more than 40 years old until a replanting programme got underway in the late 1990s.

Most wine is still vinified on a semi-industrial scale in the country's 70-plus wineries that demands fast fermentations and early bottling. The country saw practically zero investment in technology in the second half of the 20th century, although its mechanization and hot country technology at one time provided inspiration for many. The AUTOVINIFICATION tanks of the DOURO, for example, were developed in Algeria, where they were known as the Ducellier system.

The centralized ONCV, which exercises a near monopoly on both the production and sale of wine, embarked on a plan to establish the wine industry as necessary for the country's economy and by 1999 had achieved sufficient official recognition to be able to buy 40 farms and 26,000 ha in the west, close to the Moroccan border. There have also been plans for a joint venture with a British importer to harness all this potential and make wines specifically for export. Some Cabernet Sauvignon, Merlot, Syrah, Mourvèdre, and, perhaps inevitably, Chardonnay are being planted, although among light-skinned grapes Ugni Blanc and Clairette predominate. The introduction of TEMPERATURE CONTROL and keeping different vine varieties separate are two of the most pressing problems in Algeria's slowly recovering wineries. Finding a market is the next step.

Algeria is also a substantial producer of CORKS, which are mainly processed in Portugal and Spain.   K.S. & J.R.

Galet, P., *Dictionnaire encyclopédique des cépages* (Paris, 2000).

Isnard, H., 'Vigne et décolonisation en Algérie', in A. Huetz de Lemps (ed.), *Géographie historique des vignobles: actes du colloque de Bordeaux: octobre 1977* (Paris, 1978), vol. i.

Platter, J. & E., *Africa Uncorked* (London, 2002).

Sutton, K., 'Algeria's vineyards: an Islamic dilemma and a problem of decolonisation', *Journal of Wine Research* (1990), 101–20.

Alicante, city on Spain's Mediterranean coast long associated with strong, rustic wines which now gives its name to a denominated wine zone of 14,250 ha/35,200 acres. This DO in the LEVANTE extends from the city towards YECLA on the foothills of Spain's central plateau (see map under SPAIN) and allows eight different styles of wine including DOBLE PASTA, fortified wines, and a SOLERA-aged wine called FONDILLÓN, a speciality of the region made from very sweet, deliberately overripened grapes. A coastal sub-zone, the Marina Alta, produces mostly white MUSCAT-based wines. The climate becomes progressively hotter and the landscape more arid away from the coast and YIELDS rarely exceed 20 hl/ha (1.1 ton/acre). The principal grape variety, the red MONASTRELL, frequently ripens to produce wines with 16 to 18 per cent natural alcohol. Other red varieties well suited to the MEDITERRANEAN climate include GARNACHA and BOBAL. Ninety per cent of the region's wine is produced in poorly equipped CO-OPERATIVES but the Bocopa co-op at Petrer and such private firms as Gutiérrez de la Vega, Bernabé Navarro, Salvador Poveda, and Enrique Mendoza have made noticeable strides in quality.

Alicante is also a synonym for Garnacha Tintorera, or ALICANTE BOUSCHET, in Spain and is even sometimes used as a synonym for GRENACHE.   R.J.M. & V. de la S.

Alicante Bouschet, often known simply as **Alicante,** the most widely planted of France's red-fleshed TEINTURIER grape varieties. Although it declined in importance towards the end of the 20th century, it was still France's twelfth most planted black grape variety at the beginning of the 21st, with 8,800 ha/21,750 acres, mainly in the Languedoc-Roussillon (especially in the Hérault and Gard *départements*) but also in Provence and some plantings as far north as cognac country.

It was bred between 1865 and 1885 by Henri BOUSCHET from his father's crossing of Petit Bouschet with the popular Grenache, then often known as Alicante, and was an immediate success. Thanks to its deep red flesh, the wine it produced was about 15 times as red as that of the productive and rapidly spreading ARAMON. With distinctive purple patches on its leaves, it is also relatively high yielding and on fertile soils can easily produce more than 200 hl/ha (12 ton/acre) of wine with 12 per cent alcohol, if little character.

Alicante Bouschet also played a major role in late 19th- and early 20th-century viticulture as parent of a host of other Teinturiers, the products almost exclusively of crossings with non-VINIFERA varieties. In the second half of the 20th century it has profited from its status as the sole Teinturier to be a *Vitis vinifera*, and therefore officially sanctioned by the French authorities.

Outside France it is perhaps most widely cultivated in Spain, where it is also known as Garnacha Tintorera on a total of more than 16,000 ha/39,000 acres in 1990. It is particularly common in ALMANSA. The variety is also grown increasingly, often alongside its stablemate GRAND NOIR DE LA CALMETTE, in the arid climate of the ALENTEJO in southern Portugal, where VARIETAL versions are not uncommon.

Alicante is also grown in Corsica, Toscana, Calabria in southern Italy, former Yugoslavia, Israel, and North Africa; and there were still 1,300 acres/740 ha of it in California in 2002, mainly in the hot Central Valley.

Galet, P., *Dictionnaire encyclopédique des Cépages* (Paris, 2000).

Alicante Ganzin, very deeply coloured, red-fleshed vine which is the antecedent of TEINTURIER varieties such as ROYALTY and RUBIRED.

Aligoté, Burgundy's 'other' white grape variety, may be very much Chardonnay's underdog but in a fine year, when ripeness can compensate for its characteristic ACIDITY, Aligoté is not short of champions. It has been shown by DNA PROFILING to be a member of the greater PINOT family and was recorded in Burgundy at the end of the 18th century.

The vine is vigorous and its yield varies enormously according to the vineyard site. If grown on Burgundy's best slopes on the poorest soils in warmer years, Aligoté could produce fine dry whites with more nerve than most Chardonnays, but it would not be nearly as profitable.

In the Côte d'Or it is far less important than the two obviously nobler grape varieties Chardonnay and Pinot Noir, but there were still nearly 700 ha/1,700 acres at the beginning of the 21st century, and almost as much in southern Burgundy. It is now largely relegated to the highest and lowest vineyards, where it produces light, early-maturing wines allowed only the Bourgogne Aligoté appellation and drunk either with simple meals, by penny-pinchers, or, traditionally, mixed with blackcurrant liqueur as a KIR. Only the village of Bouzeron in the CÔTE CHALONNAISE, where some of the finest examples are produced, has its own appellation for Aligoté, Bouzeron, in which the maximum yield is only 45 hl/ha (2.5 ton/acre) as opposed to the 60 hl/ha allowed for Bourgogne Aligoté.

Plantings have also increased slightly in Chablis country, where it makes everyday dry white wine.

Aligoté is extraordinarily popular in eastern Europe. Bulgaria, for example, still grew a thousand or so hectares in the mid 2000s, and presumably prized it for its high natural acidity. In ROMANIA, nearly 6,000 ha/14,800 acres of the vine were in cultivation in 2005, particularly in Moldovia and Dobrogea, while it is grown on many thousands of hectares in the ex-Soviet republics according to some estimates, particularly in UKRAINE, MOLDOVA, GEORGIA, AZERBAIJAN, and KAZAKHSTAN.

allergies to wines of various sorts are by no means unknown. The most common **allergens,** chemicals capable of causing an allergic reaction in humans, are proteinaceous compounds. Among possible allergens in wines are traces of the natural PROTEINS not precipitated and removed with the dead yeast cells after FERMENTATION, and traces of proteins from a FINING agent used to clarify and stabilize the wine. The biogenic amines HISTAMINE and tyramine, thought to be produced by LACTIC ACID BACTERIA during MALOLACTIC FERMENTATION and present at higher levels in red wines, have been implicated in triggering headaches. There is still no agreement on whether histamine plays a role in wine-induced asthma.

The most common wine allergies are a sensitivity to either white wine or red wine. Since red wine contains a much wider range of constituents than white wine, having been fermented with the grape SKINS and other grape solids, an allergic reaction to all red wines and no whites seems more easily comprehensible than vice versa. SULFUR DIOXIDE, used at higher concentrations in making white wines than red, has been suggested as a cause of so-called white wine allergies, and a small proportion of the population, notably asthmatics, is particularly sensitive to SULFITES. (Though sensitivity to sulfites in red wine has also been reported.) However, most dried fruits are preserved with much higher levels of sulfites than most wines.

Some people, particularly members of some ethnic groups, experience some form of allergic reaction such as face flushing and high pulse rate to even quite moderate amounts of ETHANOL in any form.

This field is under-researched, perhaps because wine researchers are almost by definition unlikely to be allergic to wine themselves. See also HEALTH and LABELLING INFORMATION.

Vally, H., and Thompson, P. J., 'Allergic and asthmatic reactions to alcoholic drinks', *Addiction Biology*, 8 (2003), 3–11.

Allier is the name of a *département* in central France best known in the world of wine for its OAK, although it is also home to the wines of ST-POURÇAIN.

alluvium, type of sediment which can be described as **alluvial,** giving rise to soils which are often fine grained and typically fertile consisting of mud, SILT, SAND, and sometimes GRAVEL or stones deposited by flowing water on flood plains, in river beds, in deltas, and in estuaries. Alluvial soils are variable in texture, DRAINAGE, and age, and often such changes can be seen over a few metres. Where these soils are stony and sandy, they are highly valued for viticulture, as in the MÉDOC region of France and Marlborough in NEW ZEALAND. See entries prefixed SOIL.   R.E.S.

almacenista. From the Spanish word *almacén* meaning 'store', an almacenista is the term for a SHERRY stockholder who sells wine to shippers. It has been used as a marketing term by the sherry firm of Lustau, who buy in and bottle wines from almacenistas.

Almansa, small denominated wine zone in the eastern corner of CASTILE-LA MANCHA in central Spain (see map under SPAIN). The Almansa DO borders the LEVANTE regions JUMILLA and YECLA, which produce similarly strong, sturdy red wines, traditionally used for blending but increasingly sold in bottle, principally from MONASTRELL and GARNACHA TINTORERA grapes. The climate is extreme. Temperatures rise to 40 °C (104 °F) in summer but can dip below 0 °C (32 °F) in winter. Since the late 1980s, Bodegas Piqueras and the Tintoralba co-operative have been making consistently good wine using Cencibel (TEMPRANILLO) to lighten the load of Almansa's traditionally overripe grapes in addition to Garnacha Tintorera.

R.J.M. & V. de la S.

Almeirim, former IPR in central, southern Portugal dominated by a huge co-operative winery. Now a subregion of RIBATEJO.

Almuñeco, synonym for LISTÁN NEGRO.

Aloxe-Corton, a small village of charm at the northern end of the Côte de Beaune in Burgundy. First references to vineyards in Aloxe date back to 696, while in 775 CHARLEMAGNE ceded vines to the Abbey of St-Andoche at Saulieu. Aloxe is dominated by the hill of Corton, planted on three sides with vineyards including the GRANDS CRUS Corton (almost all red) and Corton-Charlemagne (white).

Corton is the sole grand cru appellation for red wine in the CÔTE DE BEAUNE and covers several vineyards which may be described simply as Corton or as Corton hyphenated with their names. While all Corton tends to be a dense, closed wine when young, Bressandes is noted for its comparative suppleness and charm; Renardes for its rustic, gamey character; Perrières for extra finesse; and Clos du Roi for the optimum balance between weight and elegance. It is often regarded as superior to Corton itself. Other Corton vineyards are Le Charlemagne, Les Pougets, and Les Languettes, all of which more often produce white Corton-Charlemagne, and Les Chaumes, Les Grèves, Les Fiètres, Les Meix, Clos de la Vigne au Saint, and part of Les Paulands and Les Maréchaudes. Further Corton vineyards extend into LADOIX-Serrigny. Although Corton is planted almost entirely with Pinot Noir vines, a tiny amount of white Corton is made, including the HOSPICES DE BEAUNE cuvée Paul Chanson from Chardonnay.

The great white wines, however, are those made within the **Corton-Charlemagne** appellation, which stretches in a narrow band around the top of the hill from Ladoix-Serrigny, through Aloxe-Corton to PERNAND-VERGELESSES, where it descends down the western edge of the hillside. The MESOCLIMATE governing Corton-Charlemagne is fractionally cooler than that of Corton and the soils are different. Whereas red Corton is mainly produced on reddish chalky clay which is rich in marl, the soil at the top of the hill and on the western edge is lighter and whiter, its stoniness believed locally to impart a gunflint edge to the wines of Corton-Charlemagne.

There remains some Pinot Blanc in the otherwise Chardonnay-dominated Corton-Charlemagne vineyards, which formerly were widely planted with Pinot Beurot (see PINOT GRIS) and Aligoté.

A great Corton may seem ungainly in its sturdiness when young but should have the power to develop into a rich wine with complex, gamey flavours at eight to ten years old. Cortons should, with POMMARD, be the most intense and longest-lived wines of the Côte de Beaune. Corton-Charlemagne also needs time to develop its exceptional character of breed, backbone, and racy power. Needing a minimum of five years, a good example will be better for a full decade in bottle.

Although more than half the vineyard area is given over to the grands crus, Aloxe-Corton also has its share of PREMIER CRU and village vineyards producing mainly red wines which can be supple and well coloured but mostly do not justify their significant premium over the wines of SAVIGNY-LÈS-BEAUNE. Apart from Les Guérets and Les Vercots, which are adjacent to Les Fichots in the commune of Pernand-Vergelesses, the premiers crus of Aloxe-Corton form a band just below the swathe of grand cru vineyards, extending into Ladoix-Serrigny.

See CÔTE D'OR and map under BURGUNDY.

J.T.C.M.

Chapuis, C., *Aloxe Corton* (Dijon, 1988), in French.

Alpine Valleys in NORTH EAST VICTORIA ZONE in Australia encompasses inter alia the Ovens, Buffalo, Kiewa, and Buckland valleys, and an important producer of a range of mainstream and ultra-eclectic varieties (Arneis, Saperavi, etc.).

Alsace, historically much-disputed region now on the eastern border of France, producing a unique style of largely VARIETAL wine, about 90 per cent of which is white. For much of its existence it has been the western German region Elsass. Because of its location it has been the subject of many a territorial dispute between France and Germany. Now separated from Germany by the river RHINE, and from France by the Vosges mountains, the language and culture of Alsace owe much to both origins, but are at the same time unique. Many families speak Alsacien, a dialect peculiar to the region, quite different from either French or German.

Of all the regions of France, this is the one in which it is still easiest to find villages outwardly much as they were in the Middle Ages, with traditional half-timbered houses and extant fortifications. The hilltops of the lower Vosges are dotted with ruined castles and fortresses, witnesses to past invasions.

Up to 2,000 growers bottle and sell their own wines, although over 80 per cent of the total volume is produced by just 175 companies. Even the large companies are usually family owned, however. One of the unique aspects of Alsace is that even the smallest growers regularly produce at least six to eight different wines each year, whilst the larger producers may extend to a range of 20 to 30 different bottlings.

All Alsace wines are, by law, bottled in the region of production in tall bottles called *flutes* (which some think may hinder sales because they are hardly the height of FASHION).

History

For details of the earlier history of the region, see GERMAN HISTORY. Annexed by France in the 17th century, Alsace was reclaimed, with part of Lorraine, by the new German empire in 1871. The vineyards were used to produce cheap blending wines. After the twin crises of oidium (POWDERY MILDEW) and PHYLLOXERA, HYBRIDS to give large, trouble-free crops were planted on the flat, easily accessible land on the plains. The finer, steeper, HILLSIDE sites, formerly revered, were largely abandoned.

Following the First World War, when Alsace returned to French rule, up to a third of these better sites were replanted with the noble VINIFERA varieties. A setback occurred with the Second World War, when export was impossible, and the area was once again overrun by Germany. Replanting of the better sites gathered momentum in the 1960s and 1970s, when Alsace once again started to build up export markets.

Geography and climate

Alsace lies between LATITUDES 47.5 degrees and 49 degrees north of the equator, giving a long, cool growing season. It is important for the vineyards to make the most of the sun's rays, and so most of the best vineyards are on south, south west, or south east facing slopes, sheltered from the wind by the Vosges. Average annual RAINFALL is one of the lowest in France, due to the influence of the Vosges mountains: 500 mm/19 in in Colmar, varying considerably according to site. Most vineyards are at an ALTITUDE of between 175 m and 420 m (2,017 ft), above which level much of the mountainside is covered with pine forests. Autumn humidity allows for the production of late-picked VENDANGE TARDIVE wines in good vintages.

The narrow vineyard strip runs from north to south, along the lower contours of the Vosges mountains, and spans the two French *départements* of Haut-Rhin and Bas-Rhin. The majority of large producers are based in the more southerly Haut-Rhin *département*, which is generally associated with better quality, especially for Gewürztraminer (often spelt Gewurztraminer in Alsace) and Pinot Gris, producing fatter, more powerful wines towards the south of the region. In the Bas-Rhin, individual vineyard sites become even more important to ensure full RIPENESS.

There are at least 20 major soil formations within the Alsace wine region, covering several eras. Higher, steeper slopes of the Vosges have thin topsoil, with subsoils of weathered gneiss, GRANITE, sandstone, SCHIST, and VOLCANIC sediments. The gentler lower slopes, derived from the Rhine delta bed, have deeper topsoils, over subsoils of CLAY, MARL, LIMESTONE, and sandstone. One of the most important subsoils is the pink *grès de Vosges*, Vosges sandstone, which was used extensively in the construction of churches and cathedrals, and which is much in evidence in Strasbourg. The plains at the foot of the Vosges are of ALLUVIAL soils, eroded from the Vosges, and are rich and fertile, generally more suited to the production of crops other than vines.

Winters can be very cold, spring is generally mild, and the summer is warm and sometimes very dry, with heavy hail and thunderstorms possible in summer and autumn. In some vintages summer DROUGHT can be a problem, and younger vines planted in the drier, sandy soils can suffer, whereas vineyards on the water-retentive clay soils have an advantage.

As a general rule, the heavier clay and marl soils give a wine with broader flavours, more body and weight, whilst a lighter limestone or sandy soil gives more elegance and finesse. Flint, schist, shale, and slate soils tend to give wines with a characteristic oily, minerally aroma reminiscent of petrol and sometimes described as 'gunflint', especially those made from the Riesling grape.

Viticulture

The varied styles of training in use depend partly on the steepness of the vineyard. Either single GUYOT, with up to 15 buds left on the cane, or double guyot, with up to eight buds on each cane, may be found, with a VINE DENSITY of between 4,400 and 4,800 vines per ha (1,940 per acre). There are also some CORDON-trained vines, with SPUR PRUNING, generally on older vines. The permitted yield is set at 100 hl/ha (6 ton/acre), higher than for any other APPELLATION CONTRÔLÉE—with the customary Plafond Limité de Classement (see PLC) of an extra 20 per cent, provided that wines are submitted for sampling, and show a certain TYPICALITY. Each year the permitted yield can be altered upwards or downwards by decree.

Quality-conscious producers will prune for a yield markedly lower than this, generally of between 40 and 50 hl/ha.

Vines are generally trained at a height of between 60 and 90 cm (35 in) above ground,

depending on the site. Vines on the plain are generally trained high to avoid FROSTS, whilst sloping vineyards can be trained closer to the ground, benefiting to the maximum from the available SUNLIGHT.

The steepest vineyard slopes may be TERRACED, as for example the GRAND CRU sites of Rangen and Kastelberg, or vines may be planted in rows either following the contours of the slope, or vertically from top to bottom, depending on the risk of SOIL EROSION. COVER CROPS may be planted to prevent erosion and to give more of a grip to tractors on moderate slopes.

Although MECHANICAL HARVESTING is used on the plains, many vineyards are too steep for machines, and many grapes are still hand picked. The vintage is always protracted, with varieties ripening at different times. Generally, harvesting starts in mid September, and often continues well into November.

A few growers have experimented with late-picked, BOTRYTIZED wines, not merely for the four permitted varietals (see Vendange Tardive below), but also with such diverse varieties as Auxerrois and Sylvaner, which can make outstanding wines. One or two growers produce a small quantity of VIN DE PAILLE, from healthy, ripe grapes picked in October, and dried on straw over the winter months. There have also been experiments with EISWEIN, from healthy grapes picked in December, and even in early January.

Vine varieties

At the beginning of the 20th century, the many varieties planted in Alsace were divided into 'noble' and others. The number has been rationalized over the years, and now the region produces eight major varietal wines: RIESLING, GEWÜRZTRAMINER, PINOT GRIS, PINOT NOIR, PINOT BLANC, MUSCAT, CHASSELAS, and SYLVANER. Chasselas is generally used for blending, and only a handful of producers still bottle it as a varietal. AUXERROIS is also planted, and is usually blended with Pinot Blanc, although it increasingly features on a label. There is also an increasing interest in planting the ubiquitous CHARDONNAY, forbidden by law, but tolerated when labelled as Pinot Blanc, or used in the sparkling wine CRÉMANT d'Alsace.

Most growers, wherever in the region they are based, plant all of the above varieties. As some varieties fetch higher prices, and some are much more fussy about vineyard site, each grower must make an economic as well as a practical decision when deciding what to plant where. Pinot Blanc and Auxerrois, both growing in popularity, are amongst the first to ripen, and are viticulturally easy to please. The later ripening Riesling and Sylvaner need to be planted on a sheltered site, and are amongst the most fussy. Muscat and Gewürztraminer are the most unreliable producers; unsettled weather at FLOWERING time can decimate the crop, so the site should be sheltered.

Riesling is the most widely planted variety, accounting for over 20 per cent of the area under vine. Plantations are steadily increasing, mainly in place of Sylvaner, which has been losing ground, and now accounts for only about 12 per cent of the area planted, with higher proportions in the Bas-Rhin than the Haut-Rhin. Pinot Blanc and the more common Auxerrois have also been on the increase, accounting for another 20 per cent between them. Gewürztraminer is grown on almost as much land but usually represents a smaller percentage of the production, which can fluctuate alarmingly. Its average yield is the smallest of all the varieties. The largest plantations of Gewürztraminer are in the Haut-Rhin. Pinot Gris is increasingly popular and now accounts for almost 12 per cent of the total area under vine. Pinot Noir has also increased its share as the only red varietal of Alsace (though Pinot Gris and Gewürztraminer are definitely pink skinned varieties). It represents nearly 9 per cent of the total vineyard area. The remaining vineyard area is planted with MUSCAT D'ALSACE, MUSCAT OTTONEL, Chasselas, Chardonnay, and small amounts of old plantings, of varieties no longer permitted but not yet replaced.

Wine-making

As in Germany, winemakers measure the sugar content of the grapes, or MUST WEIGHT, in degrees OECHSLE. Most Alsace wines are CHAPTALIZED, with the notable exception of VENDANGE TARDIVE wines, which must rely totally on natural sugars present in the grape. Indigenous YEASTS are generally sufficient, and few winemakers add yeast cultures, except in an abnormally wet vintage. ACIDIFICATION is not practised.

The number of different varieties, all to be vinified separately, can present a logistical problem. Small operations with one PRESS (increasingly a bladder press, which gives cleaner juice) will organize picking to allow each variety sufficient time in the press before the next variety is picked.

Most winemakers deliberately prevent MALOLACTIC FERMENTATION in white wines by keeping them cool and lightly sulfured, preferring to keep the fresh grape aromas—although some CUVÉES manage to complete malolactic fermentation, often by accident. Although initially making such wines softer, more vinous, and less floral, it does not seem to have altered the quality or keeping ability of the wines, so an increasing number of reputable cellars are allowing malolactic fermentation to take place. Pinot Noir needs to go through malolactic to soften and STABILIZE the wine, and is therefore often kept in an isolated part of the cellar to prevent cross-contamination from LACTIC ACID BACTERIA.

Because over 90 per cent of the wine is white, and because winemakers are emphasizing the primary grape flavours, most wine is vinified and stored in inert containers, and new wood is seldom used. Traditional cellars have large oval wood *cuves*, many over 100 years of age, literally built into the cellar. Traditionally the same cask will be used each year for the same varietal. The build-up of TARTRATES forms a glass-like lining to the cask, and there is no likelihood of oak flavours masking the wine's character. If a cask has to be replaced, the new cask will be well washed out to remove as much as possible of the OAK FLAVOUR, and will be used for Edelzwicker until all oak flavours have disappeared. A few growers are experimenting with BARREL MATURATION, most widely for Pinot Noir, but also occasionally with Pinot Blanc, Pinot Gris, Auxerrois, and even Sylvaner. Whilst this is considered acceptable for red and experimental wines, many growers and wine critics find it inappropriate for classic whites, one grower's BARRIQUE-aged Grand Cru Pinot Gris having been regularly rejected by tasting panels of his peers, and admitted under the Grand Cru label in the late 1990s only after years of vociferous persistence.

The cellars are generally quite cold by the time FERMENTATION is taking place, so many cellars have no cooling system.

Growers have found that the BOUQUET and AGEING potential can be enhanced by fermenting Riesling, Sylvaner, and Muscat at between 14 and 16 °C (61 °F), whilst Gewürztraminer will take a warmer temperature, of up to 21 °C (70 °F).

Alsace wines are in principle fermented dry; supposedly the only wines with significant RESIDUAL SUGAR are Vendange Tardive. A significant proportion of winemakers, however, leave 3 to 4 g/l or more residual sugar in their wines to give a softer flavour and it can be difficult to tell from the label just how sweet a given wine will taste.

Most wines are bottled within a year of the vintage, to retain freshness.

Some specific wines

Alsace was awarded AC status in 1962, with the one appellation Alsace, or Vin d'Alsace. The appellation Crémant d'Alsace was added in 1976, and Grand Cru in 1983. In addition, laws for Vendange Tardive wines were drawn up in 1983. For the still wines, the appellation Alsace can stand on its own, but is usually accompanied by one of the following names.

Riesling Considered by growers to be the most noble variety, Alsace Riesling is almost invariably bone dry. Young Riesling can display floral aromas, although it is sometimes fairly neutral. With age it takes on complex, gunflint, mineral aromas, with crisp steely acidity and very pure fruit flavours. It is one of the most difficult varieties for beginners, but one of the most rewarding wines for connoisseurs.

Gewürztraminer Usually dry to off-dry, but its low ACIDITY, combined with high alcohol and GLYCEROL, give an impression of sweetness.

Gewürztraminer has a distinctive spicy aroma and flavour, with hints of lychees and grapefruit. The naturally high sugar levels of Gewürztraminer make it ideal for late harvest sweet wines, and this is the most frequent varietal found as Vendange Tardive. Poorly made examples can be blowsy, flat, and overalcoholic. Gewürztraminer from the southern end of Alsace, around Eguisheim southwards, tends to have quite a different character, and is generally more aromatic as well as richer in weight.

Pinot Gris Traditionally known as Tokay-Pinot Gris or Tokay d'Alsace, Pinot Gris is the only accepted name according to a 1993 agreement between Hungary and the EU. Pinot Gris was for long underrated in Alsace. It combines some of the spicy flavours of Gewürztraminer with the firm backbone of acidity found in Riesling, giving a wine which ages particularly well. Young Pinot Gris is reminiscent of peaches and apricot, with a hint of smoke, developing biscuity, buttery flavours with age. It is very successful in a Vendange Tardive style.

Muscat Two varieties of Muscat are found in the Alsace region: MUSCAT BLANC À PETITS GRAINS, known as Muscat d'Alsace, and Muscat Ottonel. Most wines are a blend of the two. Alsace Muscat is always dry, and has a fresh grapey aroma and flavour. The taste should be reminiscent of biting into a fresh grape, with young, crisp fruitiness. Muscat is low in alcohol, and quite low in acidity. Because of its sensitivity to poor weather at flowering, Muscat only produces well in favourable vintages.

Sylvaner Sylvaner suffers from bad press in Alsace. It is difficult to grow, needs a good site, yet fetches comparatively little money. Good Sylvaner has a slightly bitter, slightly perfumed aroma and flavour, with very firm acidity. It has moderate alcohol, and is at its best when it is young and fresh. Sylvaner is at its best in hot vintages.

Pinot Blanc Also labelled Clevner or Klevner, Pinot Blanc is the workhorse of Alsace. As well as forming the base wine for Crémant d'Alsace, Pinot Blanc can produce very good, clean, dry white that is not particularly aromatic but has good acidity, with moderate alcohol.

Pinot Noir The only red varietal of Alsace struggles to achieve a particularly deep colour in this northerly climate. Many a Rouge d'Alsace has a light strawberry pink colour, whilst some Rosé d'Alsace can be deeper. Alsace Pinot Noir was always light, fresh quaffing wine, with raspberry fruit flavours, but increasingly it has suffered an identity crisis, with many growers experimenting with OAK AGEING. Good oak matured wines are increasingly the result of warmer vintages.

Edelzwicker Literally, this is German for 'noble mixture'. A blend of more than one variety can be labelled as Edelzwicker or, more occasionally, as Gentil. It can also be given a general name, such as 'Fruits de Mer'. Usually Edelzwicker is one of the cheapest wines in the range.

Auxerrois This variety is rarely mentioned on the label, although it may form the total or the majority of some wines labelled as Pinot Blanc, Klevner, or Clevner. A wine from pure Auxerrois is spicy, soft, and quite broad, with low acidity and good alcohol. It is occasionally vinified in oak, quite successfully.

Chasselas This variety's name is also seldom seen on the label. It is usually used for Edelzwicker, although the few growers who bottle Chasselas as a varietal can produce a very pretty, quite lightweight wine, dry with soft grapey fruit, low acidity, and light alcohol.

Klevener de Heiligenstein The village of Heiligenstein in the Bas-Rhin has always been known for its 'Klevener', a local name for SAVAGNIN Rosé of the Jura, a variety long forgotten in the rest of Alsace, produced within five neighbouring communes of Heiligenstein. Klevener has a lightly spicy, sometimes slightly buttery flavour. It is dry, less scented than Gewürztraminer, with less alcohol and a little more acidity. In good vintages it can age well. See KLEVENER DE HEILIGENSTEIN.

Crémant d'Alsace An increasing amount of sparkling wine is produced in Alsace, mostly from a base of Pinot Blanc, although some particularly good (white) Crémants are produced from Pinot Noir. See CRÉMANT for more details.

Vendange Tardive Late-picked wines have always been produced in small quantities in outstanding vintages. They were formerly sold as 'Spätlese', 'Auslese', and 'Beerenauslese', and the growers were free to decide which category they would choose. It was only in 1983, however, that legislation was passed to give a legal definition to Alsace's late-picked, sweet wines. To be labelled as Vendange Tardive, a term to which Alsace producers now claim exclusive rights in France, a wine must come from a single vintage, from one of the four permitted varieties Riesling, Muscat, Gewürztraminer, or Pinot Gris. The wine must not be ENRICHED in any way, and the minimum sugar concentration at harvest must be 220 g/l (95 °Oechsle) for Riesling or Muscat, and 243 g/l (105 °Oechsle) for Gewürztraminer or Pinot Gris. Picking must take place after a certain date, determined annually by the authorities, who must be informed beforehand of the grower's intention to pick a Vendange Tardive wine, and will inspect the vineyard at the time of picking to check the sugar concentration and quantity produced. The wine must also undergo an analysis and tasting after bottling, before the label is granted. Vendange Tardive wines do not have to be BOTRYTIS affected. The most commonly found varietal for Vendange

Tardive wines is Gewürztraminer, which can easily attain very high sugar levels. Muscat is the rarest of all, and is only possible in occasional vintages. Vendange Tardive wine is not necessarily sweet, and may vary from bone dry to medium sweet, and labels signify what style of wine to expect only very rarely. Although few producers made Vendange Tardive wines prior to 1983, the style has become very popular and quality varies widely.

Sélection de Grains Nobles SGN is a further refinement of Vendange Tardive, where the grapes have reached even higher sugar levels. Wines labelled as Sélection de Grains Nobles, however, nearly always contain a proportion of grapes affected by botrytis, or NOBLE ROT. The same four varieties are permitted, with minimum sugar levels of 256 g/l (110 °Oechsle) Oechsle) for Riesling and Muscat, and 279 g/l (120 °Oechsle) for Gewürztraminer and Pinot Gris. The same legislation as for Vendange Tardive governs production (see above). Sélection de Grains Nobles wine is sweet, although there is a variation in richness and quality, depending on the grape and the grower.

Alsace Grand Cru The Alsace Grand Cru appellation, created in 1983, signifies a wine from a single named vineyard site, a single vintage, from one of four permitted varieties, Riesling, Muscat, Gewürztraminer, or Pinot Gris (although under pressure from Deiss, a blend of varieties has been sanctioned for Altenberg de Bergheim). Maximum permitted yields are lower than for the basic appellation Alsace, and have been lowered from 70 to 60 hl/ha (plus a PLC of 10 per cent). Wines must undergo technical analysis and tasting for typicality. Minimum sugar levels are higher than for basic Alsace.

The appellation is the subject of much controversy. Out of 94 sites originally considered, 25 were initially chosen in 1983, and by the mid 1990s there were more than 50 provisional Grand Cru vineyard sites in Alsace, and some of the boundaries were still under discussion. This caused much confusion as it was possible to find a wine labelled for example Riesling Grand Cru Kaefferkopf and one labelled simply Riesling Kaefferkopf. Some of the nominated sites are of only moderate quality. Some named vineyards cover an unreasonably large area, often extending over a number of hillsides, including a number of soils and aspects, some greatly superior to others.

Whilst single-vineyard wines are an excellent way forward for quality wine production, much depends on the attitude of the grower, as well as on the quality of the vineyard site. The best sites and growers have undoubtedly benefited from the Grand Cru appellation, but many growers and co-operatives are producing wines of average quality, cashing in on the Grand Cru name. Some of the top négociants have Grand Cru vineyard sites, but prefer to use the names by which they have historically sold such wines: Trimbach's famous Clos Ste-Hune Riesling comes from the Grand Cru Rosacker, while Beyer's Riesling Cuvée Particulière is from the Grand Cru Pfersigberg. Some Grand Cru sites are only outstanding when planted with one or two of the four permitted varieties. On Kastelberg, for example, only Riesling is permitted.

In the following list, an approximate size has been indicated for those Grand Cru sites not yet fully delimited.

Altenberg de Bergbieten, Bergbieten, Bas-Rhin, 29.06 ha/71.8 acres
Altenberg de Bergheim, Bergheim, Haut-Rhin, 35.06 ha
Altenberg de Wolxheim, Wolxheim, Haut-Rhin, approx. 31.20 ha
Brand, Turckheim, Haut-Rhin, 57.95 ha
Bruderthal, Molsheim, Bas-Rhin, approx. 18.40 ha
Eichberg, Eguisheim, Haut-Rhin, 57.62 ha
Engelberg, Dahlenheim/Scharrachbergheim, Bas-Rhin, approx. 14.80 ha
Florimont, Ingersheim/Katzental, Haut-Rhin, approx. 21.00 ha
Frankstein, Dambach-la-Ville, Bas-Rhin, approx. 56.20 ha
Froehn, Zellenberg, Haut-Rhin, approx. 14.60 ha
Furstentum, Kientzheim/Sigolsheim, Haut-Rhin, 30.50 ha
Geisberg, Ribeauvillé, Haut-Rhin, 8.53 ha
Gloeckelberg (or Kloeckelberg), Rodern/St-Hippolyte, Haut-Rhin, 23.40 ha
Goldert, Gueberschwihr, Haut-Rhin, 45.35 ha
Hatschbourg, Hattstatt/Voegtlinshoffen, Haut-Rhin, 47.36 ha
Hengst, Wintzenheim, Haut-Rhin, 75.78 ha
Kaefferkopf, Ammerschwir, Haut-Rhin, 71 ha
Kanzlerberg, Bergheim, Haut-Rhin, 3.23 ha
Kastelberg, Andlau, Bas-Rhin, 5.82 ha
Kessler, Guebwiller, Haut-Rhin, 28.53 ha
Kirchberg de Barr, Barr, Bas-Rhin, 40.63 ha
Kirchberg de Ribeauvillé, Haut-Rhin, 11.40 ha
Kitterlé, Guebwiller, Haut-Rhin, 25.79 ha
Mambourg, Sigolsheim, Haut-Rhin, approx. 61.85 ha
Mandelberg, Mittelwihr/Beblenheim, Haut-Rhin, approx. 22.00 ha
Marckrain, Bennwihr/Sigolsheim, Haut-Rhin, approx. 58.35 ha
Moenchberg, Andlau/Eichhoffen, Bas-Rhin, 11.83 ha
Muenchberg, Nothalten, Bas-Rhin, 17.70 ha
Ollwiller, Wuenheim, Haut-Rhin, 35.86 ha
Osterberg, Ribeauvillé, Haut-Rhin, approx. 24.60 ha
Pfersigberg, Eguisheim/Wettolsheim, Haut-Rhin, approx. 74.55 ha
Pfingstberg, Orschwihr, Haut-Rhin, approx. 28.15 ha
Praelatenberg, Kintzheim, Bas-Rhin, approx. 18.70 ha
Rangen, Thann/Vieux-Thann, Haut-Rhin, 18.81 ha
Rosacker, Hunawihr, Haut-Rhin, 26.18 ha
Saering, Guebwiller, Haut-Rhin, 26.75 ha
Schlossberg, Kientzheim, Haut-Rhin, 80.28 ha
Schoenenbourg, Riquewihr/Zellenberg, Haut-Rhin, approx. 53.40 ha
Sommerberg, Niedermorschwihr/Katzenthal, Haut-Rhin, 28.36 ha
Sonnenglanz, Beblenheim, Haut-Rhin, 32.80 ha
Spiegel, Bergholtz/Guebwiller, Haut-Rhin, 18.26 ha
Sporen, Riquewihr, Haut-Rhin, approx. 23.70 ha
Steinert, Pfaffenheim/Westhalten, Haut-Rhin, 38.90 ha
Steingrubler, Wettolsheim, Haut-Rhin, 22.95 ha
Steinklotz, Marlenheim, Bas-Rhin, 40.60 ha
Vorbourg, Rouffach/Westhalten, Haut-Rhin, 72.55 ha
Wiebelsberg, Andlau, Bas-Rhin, 12.52 ha
Wineck-Schlossberg, Katzenthal/Ammerschwihr, Haut-Rhin, 27.40 ha
Winzenberg, Blienschwiller, Bas-Rhin, 19.20 ha
Zinnkoepflé, Westhalten/Soultzmatt, Haut-Rhin, 68.40 ha
Zotzenberg, Mittelbergheim, Bas-Rhin, 36.45 ha

See also MARC and CRÉMANT. E.J.R.B.

Stevenson, T., *The Wines of Alsace* (London, 1993).

Alternaria. Vine disease. See BUNCH ROTS.

alternative viticulture, forms of viticultural practice such as ORGANIC and BIODYNAMIC, which usually aim to minimize environmental degradation. See also SUSTAINABLE VITICULTURE.

Altesse, SAVOIE's finest white grape variety, once known as Roussette. Wines made from Altesse are called ROUSSETTE DE SAVOIE. The vine's origins are rich in mystery and intrigue.

The variety is a shy, late producer but it resists rot well and the wine produced is relatively exotically perfumed, has good acidity, and is well worth ageing. There were just 300 ha/740 acres in France in 2000.

altitude, the height above sea level of a vineyard, can have important effects on its climate and therefore on its viticultural potential. Other things being equal, temperature falls by about 0.6 °C (1.1 °F) per 100 m (330 ft) greater altitude. See also ELEVATION.

The lower temperatures at higher altitudes retard both vine BUDBREAK and, in particular, RIPENING. Small differences in elevation can have surprisingly big effects on wine quality and, indeed, on the ability of individual grape varieties to ripen at all. Becker refers to a major Rhine valley study illustrating this. Lower temperatures can be further compounded by the generally greater rainfall and cloudiness at higher altitudes.

Such effects are most marked in cool viticultural climates, where the rates of vine and berry development are directly limited by temperature. Similar altitude differences have much less effect in warmer climates (although they are sufficiently significant to explain, for example, why grapes may not always ripen fully in parts of TOSCANA). Gladstones' study quantifies these relationships.

With the increased market emphasis on TABLE WINES since the 1960s, ever higher vineyard sites have been sought, especially in the world's warmer wine regions (see CLIMATE AND WINE QUALITY and TEMPERATURE). Examples include the Adelaide Hills in SOUTH AUSTRALIA, the Central Ranges of NEW SOUTH WALES,

Tupungato and other high altitude plantings in ARGENTINA, the foothills of the Andes in CHILE, as well as the newer HILLSIDE VINEYARDS of California, Sicily, and Greece. Some of these vineyards have been planted not just in search of cooler temperatures, but to escape the deeper, more fertile soils of the valley floors and achieve vine BALANCE in shallower, hillside soils.

Whether diminishing concentrations of atmospheric CARBON DIOXIDE with altitude are a significant disadvantage for these plantings remains to be seen. On the other hand, current and future general rises in atmospheric carbon dioxide concentration may well largely override any such differences. See also CLIMATE CHANGE. Elevated vineyards also experience more ULTRAVIOLET RADIATION, which is likely to increase quality because of stimulation of PHENOLIC synthesis.

Most of the world's highest established vineyards are in Latin America but they are being challenged by new plantings in the Himalayas. Three of the world's highest commercial vineyards are Swiss-born Donald Hess's plantings in the northern province of Salta, Argentina. Colomé, near Molinos, is at 2,200–2,300 m (7,218–7,546 ft); El Arenal, Payogasta, is at 2,400–2,500 m (7,874–8,200 ft); and the 2-hectare El Arenal, Rio Blanco, is at 3,015 m (9,892 ft). BOLIVIA has vines up to 2,850m. In the Himalayas in Asia, a small vineyard has been reported at 2,750 m/9,000 ft in NEPAL, and BHUTAN is reputed to have a small vineyard planted at 2,300 m/7,500 ft. The highest European vineyards are probably those of ABONA in the Canary Islands, which are at altitudes up to 1,600 m/5,280 ft, although there are vines up to 1,100 m/3,630 ft and 1,300 m/4,260 ft in SWITZERLAND and AOSTA respectively.

J.G., R.E.S., & J.R.

Becker, H., 'Site climate effects on development, fruit maturation and harvest quality', in R. E. Smart *et al.* (eds.), *Proceedings of the Second International Symposium for Cool Climate Viticulture and Oenology: 11–15 January 1988, Auckland, New Zealand* (Auckland, 1988), 11–15.

Gladstones, J., *Viticulture and Environment* (Adelaide, 1992).

Alto Adige, the northern, predominantly German-speaking part of the TRENTINO-ALTO ADIGE region, bordering on the Austrian Tyrol. It was ceded to Italy only after the First World War and most of its inhabitants call it the Südtirol. (Throughout this article, German names appear in brackets after Italian names.) The region owes its Italian name to the river Adige (Etsch), which flows through it on its way to the Adriatic.

Viticulture follows the mountainous local TOPOGRAPHY, vine-growing being a feasible proposition only in the valleys of the Adige and Isarco (Eisach) rivers which meet at Bolzano (Bozen) to form a Y-shaped growing zone. The vine competes with apple trees for space in the warmer positions on the valley floors, and

it has been only recently that apples have been less remunerative, leading to an increase in vine plantings. The best vineyard sites, high up the hills, sometimes at 600–800 m, have been replanted only in recent years, and early results are very promising. This may be because these more forward-thinking producers have abandoned the PERGOLA system of vine training in favour of GUYOT, which has resulted in lower yields and more intense fruit.

Despite its septentrional position, Alto Adige enjoys a warm summer climate in the valleys and in the hills just off the valley floors, and the towns of Bolzano and Merano (Meran) are frequently among Italy's hottest in July and August. Virtually the entire production of wine qualifies as DOC; only 60 of the region's total 5,000 ha/12,350 acres of vineyards grow VINO DA TAVOLA grapes. The annual production of about 350,000 hl/9.2 million gal has increased from 320,000 hl in 1993, so this is one of the few regions in Italy where wine production has not declined. Viticulture is dominated by CO-OPERATIVES, which control about two-thirds of the total output, but many of these co-ops, in particular those of Colterenzio and San Michele Appiano, are run with high professional and managerial standards and produce excellent wine.

SCHIAVA (Vernatsch) was historically the dominant grape in Alto Adige, accounting for close to 60 per cent of the total wine produced. Today, it is rivalled by Chardonnay and Pinot Grigio, as the light to medium bodied red wines produced by Schiava have fallen from FASHION, and their traditional markets (Switzerland and Austria) seek fuller bodied reds. Schiava is the base of the 770 ha Caldaro (Kalterer), 14 ha Colli di Bolzano (Bozner Leiten), 175 ha Meranese (Meraner), and 286 ha SANTA MADDALENA (Sankt Magdalener) DOCs, and remains the most important varietal DOC within the overall Alto Adige appellation. In 2004, it accounted for 40,000 hl of the total of 240,000 hl produced as Alto Adige, followed by 32,000 hl of Pinot Grigio, 31,777 hl of Chardonnay, and 29,482 hl of Pinot Bianco. The second most important red variety was LAGREIN, with a total production of 24,000 hl, followed by Pinot Nero with 17,274 hl. The DOC structure of Alto Adige closely resembles that of the TRENTINO: a variety of geographically specific DOC zones together with a general DOC which embraces the entire zone, whose wines are further identified by VARIETAL, 18 in all. There are two other specific and delimited DOC zones in addition to these Schiava-dominated zones: Valle Isarco (Eisacktaler), where production is dominated by SILVANER and MÜLLER-THURGAU in addition to small amounts of GEWÜRZTRAMINER (itself supposedly a native of this region, named after the town of Tramin there); and Terlano (Terlaner), a white DOC based on PINOT BIANCO, and with limited but high-quality production of SAUVIGNON BLANC.

Lagrein is often championed by producers as it is planted only in Alto Adige. It produces deep coloured red wines that are frequently earthy and tannic, and has none of the charm of the region's best Pinot Nero. Lagrein is often blended with Schiava to deepen the colour and supply extra tannins and structure, giving a characteristic bitter finish which has, at times and not entirely accurately, been identified as a result of TERROIR. Lagrein was similarly used to boost the colour of Pinot Noir in the past, but a few producers—Gottardi, Haas, and Hofstätter in particular—are now producing varietally correct and decent examples of this grape, proving that Alto Adige is probably the Italian region best suited to the production of this most exasperating of varieties.

The simple white wines this region was producing in the late 1970s gave way to a richer and fuller style in the whites and a more polished character in the reds. BARRIQUES are increasingly used to add body. A substantial part of the improvement in the overall quality level has been the result of better matching of varieties to subzones, a matching which in many cases merely confirms the historic tradition of certain terroirs for certain grapes: Magré (Margreid) and Cortaccia (Kurtatsch) in the south west and Settequerce (Siebeneich) to the west of Bolzano for Cabernet and Merlot; Mazzon and Montagna (Montan) in the valley's south east, and Cornaiano (Girlan) to the south west of Bolzano for Pinot Noir (unlike in BURGUNDY, Pinot Noir prefers a south western ASPECT in this hotter region); Terlano (Terlan) for Sauvignon; Appiano (Eppan) and Monte (Berg) for Pinot Bianco; Ora (Auer) and the sandy and gravelly soils adjacent to Bolzano for Lagrein; Termeno (Tramin), Caldaro (Kaltern), and Cortaccia in addition to Santa Maddalena for Schiava; Cortaccia, Magré, and Salorno for Pinot Grigio.

In addition, some of the region's better producers, inspired by the blended whites of FRIULI, are successfully blending the likes of Pinot Bianco, Chardonnay, and Sauvignon with a bit of Riesling or Traminer.

See also SANTA MADDALENA, and compare with TRENTINO.

D.T. & D.C.G.

Alva, occasional name for SÍRIA in the Alentejo region of Portugal.

Alvarelhão, dark-berried vine planted all over northern Portugal, especially in the Douro valley but also in Trás-os-Montes and Dão. In GALICIA it is also known as BRANCELLÃO.

Alvarinho, the Portuguese name of a distinctive white grape variety grown around the town of Monção in the extreme north west of Portugal's VINHO VERDE country (and, as ALBARIÑO, in neighbouring GALICIA). The grapes' thick skins help them withstand the particularly damp climate, and can result in wines relatively high in alcohol (12 to 13 per cent), acidity, and flavour. Alvarinho was one of the first Portuguese varieties to appear on the labels of VARIETAL wines and is therefore one of the best known. Portuguese plantings totalled about 1,700 ha/4,200 acres in the mid 2000s.

amabile, Italian for sweet (sweeter than ABBOCCATO) or, literally, 'lovable'. See also SWEETNESS.

Amador, California county. See SIERRA FOOTHILLS.

Amarone. The most famous of Italy's dry DRIED GRAPE WINES has recently been revitalized with total volume produced increasing from 46,500 hl/1.23 million gal in 1990 to 148,000 hl in 2003. Historically Amarone was produced from some of the same grape varieties and in the same production zone as VALPOLICELLA, with the same distinction between the classical zone, where Amarone Classico is produced, and an enlarged zone where simple Amarone is produced. Amarone applied for DOCG status in February 2005 (granted in 2009) to ensure that it is made solely from CORVINA and CORVINONE, which together can comprise between 40 and 80 per cent of the blend, together with 5–30 per cent of the lesser RONDINELLA.

The wine is made from selected superior whole bunches which are dried or raisined in special drying lodges or chambers. Traditionally grapes were spread out on mats or wickerwork shelving, or strung up from the ceiling or rafters. Today, however, most producers pick the grapes directly into slatted packing cases, stack these cases on a pallet and then transport them to a drying room controlled for temperature and humidity. This new approach, which ensures minimal handling of the grapes, minimizing the risk of damage and consequent development of rot or mould, has resulted in cleaner, more balanced wines.

The length of the drying period varies from producer to producer but there has been a tendency to shorten the raisining period in recent years, as the new drying rooms have proved more efficient not only in drying the grapes but also in preventing the development of any BOTRYTIS, something that is now eschewed by all quality-conscious producers. The aim in the production of Amarone is to realise in the finished wine the intensity of colour, flavour, and tannin in the dried grapes. As all of these components reside in the skins, anything like botrytis that degrades the skins diminishes the intensity and purity of the wine. The drying process achieves more than desiccation; it also results in a metabolization of the acids in the grape and a polymerization of tannins in the skins, something that explains the richness yet balance of good Amarone. The use of drying rooms has also enabled producers to re-

duce the levels of alcohol to around 15 per cent while sacrificing none of the power and intensity that characterize good Amarone.

After the drying process is finished, the grapes are crushed and fermented dry. Since the grapes lose about 50 per cent of their liquid during the drying process, the must is quite rich, so fermentation is slow to start. A STUCK FERMENTATION can all too easily result if insufficient care is taken in the cellar, which explains why so many Amarone display regrettably high levels of VOLATILE ACIDITY.

Traditionally, the wines would have been aged in large BOTTI, usually made from Slovenian oak. Today, most of the best producers age at least part of their Amarone in BARRIQUES to encourage the development of supple tannins.

Much more important for quality than the drying process is the provenance of the grapes. This has been recognized in the proposed DOCG laws, where growers from the plains will only ever be permitted to devote 30 per cent of their total production to Amarone, while those on the hills where Amarone has always been produced (whether in the Classico zone or in the Valpantena) can transform up to 70 per cent of their production into Amarone. This is perhaps a recognition of the fact that too much wine is been made into Amarone. In 1990, Amarone comprised only eight per cent of total Valpolicella production, while in 2003 this figure had risen to 25 per cent. The problem, however, remains one of quality, for there is too much poorly made Amarone for sale, and not enough of the clean, balanced style. Good producers include Allegrini, Bussola, Ca' La Bionda, Quintarelli, and the more idiosyncratic Dal Forno.   D.T. & D.C.G.

amateur wine-making. See HOME WINE-MAKING.

amelioration, which strictly means improvement, is a euphemism for chemical intervention in wine-making with the express purpose of compensating for nature's deficiencies. Thus in cooler wine regions the term is commonly used interchangeably with ENRICHMENT or CHAPTALIZATION. Amelioration is sometimes used more widely to include both ACIDIFICATION and DEACIDIFICATION, and sometimes for any chemical adjustment to the constituents naturally present in grape juice or wine. Ameliorating operations condoned by each region's authorities tend to be those required, and vice versa, but limits are set. See also MANIPULATION.

American hybrids, group of vine HYBRIDS developed in the eastern United States, mainly in the early and mid 19th century and in some cases earlier. The term encompasses both hybrids between different native AMERICAN VINE SPECIES of the vine genus VITIS such as the *labrusca–riparia* CLINTON or, more commonly, an American species crossed with a

variety of the European vine species VINIFERA, such as Black Spanish, HERBEMONT, DELAWARE, and Othello. The hybrids' most common parents are the American species *V. labrusca* and *V. aestivalis*, along with *V. vinifera*.

These varieties are used to some extent for wine production and for TABLE GRAPES, but most are used commercially for unfermented GRAPE JUICE and jelly. The fruit is typically highly flavoured, and palates accustomed to the taste of *vinifera* varieties find the FOXY character of many American vines strong and objectionable.

See UNITED STATES, history, for more background. Following the devastation wreaked by the pest PHYLLOXERA in Europe at the end of the 19th century, the French began experimental hybridizing of *vinifera* with American species, producing the so-called FRENCH HYBRIDS or 'direct producers'.   T.P. & R.E.S.

Morton, L. T., *Winegrowing in Eastern America* (Ithaca, 1985).

American vines, loose term for both AMERICAN VINE SPECIES and also AMERICAN HYBRIDS.

American vine species, those members of the grapevine genus VITIS which originate in North America, including Mexico, and the Caribbean. About half the vine species of the world are native to America, but they are poorly suited to WINE-MAKING. When, however, all efforts to grow the imported European vine species *Vitis* VINIFERA in North America failed through disease or climatic extreme (see UNITED STATES, history), wine was made in North America of necessity from these species, detailed below.

After the discovery of AMERICAN HYBRIDS and the successful cultivation of *V. vinifera* vines in CALIFORNIA, native vines were no longer used for wine, with three notable exceptions: the *V. labrusca* CONCORD grape; some varieties of *V. rotundifolia*, notably the SCUPPERNONG; and last but not least *V. aestivalis* NORTON, which is currently enjoying a revival in Virginia and Missouri. The Concord has evolved a style of sweet, sometimes KOSHER, wine which is distinctively American (see NEW YORK), and the Scuppernong is also used for a sweet, musky wine popular in the southern United States where it is grown. Norton on the other hand produces a red wine which tastes like *vinifera* and is tolerant of the disease and environmental stresses of the eastern United States.

The most important role for the American species has been to provide the genetic basis for ROOTSTOCKS on to which European *vinifera* vines may be grafted (see MUNSON). This became a necessity in most of the world's wine regions at the end of the 19th century to counter the predations of the PHYLLOXERA louse, native to America and to which most American vine species had therefore developed resistance. The species *V. berlandieri*, *V. riparia*, and

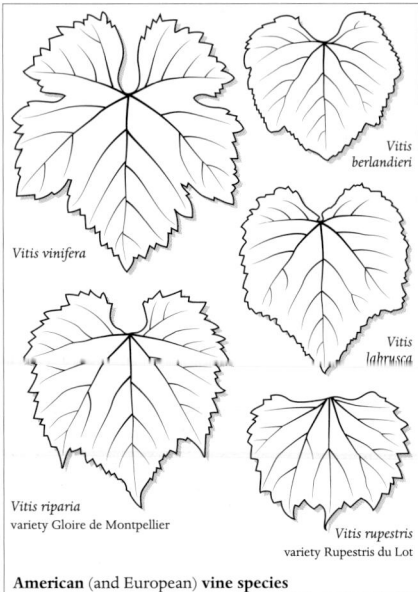

Vitis vinifera

Vitis berlandieri

Vitis labrusca

Vitis riparia
variety Gloire de Montpellier

Vitis rupestris
variety Rupestris du Lot

American (and European) **vine species**

V. rupestris are particularly important in this regard, and the great majority of the world's vineyards now grow on roots derived from them.

These are some of the more important American vine species (although others are listed under VITIS):

Vitis labrusca Vine species found in the north eastern United States producing strongly flavoured, dark berries whose almost rank aroma is sometimes described as FOXY. The berries fall easily when ripe and are called 'slip-skin', in that a berry squeezed between fingers will eject the flesh as a complete ball (non slip-skin varieties, which are the norm, are squashed when squeezed in this way). Most of the fruit of this species is black, and the leaves are large, thick, and covered on the lower surface with dense white or brown hairs. *Vitis labrusca* is a common parent in American hybrids.

Vitis aestivalis Vine species grown in the south eastern United States which, like *Vitis labrusca*, is a common parent in American hybrids. The fruit, however, is juicier and sweeter, and the grape skins are always black. This species shows good resistance to DOWNY MILDEW and POWDERY MILDEW and is therefore a common parent in VINE BREEDING programmes. Norton is the only variety with a reputation for wine quality. Early Spanish settlers of north eastern MEXICO made wine from WILD VINES of this species as early as 1597.

Vitis riparia This vigorous, tall-growing vine species is usually found along streams (its Latin name means 'river bank') and is widely distributed from Canada in the north to the Gulf of Mexico in the south. The grape has a black skin and its juice is acid without strong flavours. A common parent of many commercially important rootstocks, which are often early and of low to moderate vigour.

Vitis rupestris Unusual vine species in being a small shrub found typically on gravelly banks of streams or in watercourses in Texas. The leaves are small and kidney shaped and roots tend to grow vertically downwards rather than spread horizontally. A common parent of many commercially important rootstocks because of its phylloxera resistance.

Vitis berlandieri Vine species found on the limestone soils of Texas and Mexico. The grape is black and its juice is high in sugar and acid without strong flavours. This species is known for being difficult to root from cuttings, but because of its high phylloxera and lime resistance it is a common parent of many commercially important rootstocks.

Other American species include *V. cinerea*, *vulpina* (*cordifolia*), *candicans*, *longii*, *champini*, *monicola*, and *V. caribaea*. See VITIS. R.E.S.

Antcliff, A. J., 'Taxonomy: the grapevine as a member of the plant kingdom', in B.G. Coombe and P. R. Dry (eds.), *Viticulture*, i: *Resources in Australia* (Adelaide, 1988).

Galet, P., and Morton, L. T., *A Practical Ampelography* (Ithaca, NY, and London, 1979).

Morton, L. T., *Winegrowing in Eastern America* (Ithaca, 1985).

American Viticultural Area. See AVA.

Amerine, Maynard (1911–98), preeminent American OENOLOGIST, teacher, and writer, was trained as a plant physiologist at Berkeley in California before joining the revived Department of Viticulture and Enology at DAVIS in 1935. There he participated in some of the most important branches of its work, including the assessment of VINE VARIETIES for the different regions of California and the re-education of the wine industry to restore and advance the technical knowledge lost during PROHIBITION.

With A. J. WINKLER, Amerine developed the system of classifying wine regions by measuring heat summation. The list of his publications extends to nearly 400 items making substantial contributions to the literature of such subjects as wine JUDGING methods, wine and must ANALYSIS, COLOUR in wines, the AGEING of wine, the control of FERMENTATION, and the LITERATURE OF WINE.

Amerine served as chairman of his department from 1957 until 1962 and retired from the University in 1974, although he remained active as a writer and a recognized general expert on wine throughout his retirement. T.P. & B.C.C.

Amigne, Swiss white grape variety and a speciality of Vetroz in Valais, site of 20 ha/50 acres of the world's grand total of 25 ha/62.5 acres. Unpredictably, DNA PROFILING at DAVIS supported a parent–offspring relationship with PETIT MESLIER, the almost extinct variety of Champagne. In consequence, Amigne probably descends from GOUAIS BLANC and SAVAGNIN. The wine produced is either a powerful dry white with distinctive linden aromas or a sweet (see FLÉTRI) wine with flavours of citrus fruits and bitter almonds. J.V.

amino acids, the basic building blocks of PROTEINS, chemicals essential to all living systems. There are 20 amino acids involved in constructing thousands of proteins of living materials. When these proteins act as catalysts for specific biochemical reactions, they are called ENZYMES.

In ripe grapes, NITROGEN-containing compounds constitute about 1 g/l of juice, of which amino acids make up about half. The most common are proline, arginine, and glutamic acid (see UMAMI). During grape RIPENING, the concentrations of amino acids increase, arginine and proline especially; proline increases more than arginine if the fruit is exposed to light. High concentrations of arginine, resulting from soils with a high nitrogen content, present the danger of production of the carcinogen urethane (ethyl CARBAMATE) in wine.

YEASTS are able to make all the amino acids they require, but they will also use intact amino acids from the medium in which they find themselves if they are available. Thus FUSEL OILS are formed in wine as by-products of the nitrogen metabolism of the yeast cells living in grape juice. After fermentation has finished, yeast proteins break down, secreting smaller peptide units and amino acids into the wine if it is left in the presence of the LEES or dead yeast cells.

Bottle-fermented SPARKLING WINES owe some of their special flavour to the presence of substances associated with yeast breakdown, peptides, and amino acids (see AUTOLYSIS). A.D.W. & B.G.C.

Rantz, J. A. (ed.), 'Nitrogen in Grapes and Wine', Proceedings of the International Symposium, Seattle, June 1991, *American Society of Enology and Viticulture* (Davis, Calif., 1991).

amontillado, Spanish word which originally described sherry in the style of MONTILLA. Today it has two related meanings in the sherry-making process. The basic FINO wines become amontillado (Spanish for 'like Montilla') when the FLOR yeast dies and the wine is exposed to oxygen. This happens automatically if a fino type of sherry is fortified to 16 per cent since the flor yeast cannot work in such an alcoholic environment. The wine turns amber and tastes richer and nuttier. A true Amontillado-style sherry is therefore an aged Fino. Cheaper Amontillados, the most common Amontillado encountered commercially, are created artificially by blending and are usually sweetened. They tend to be quintessentially medium. For more details, see SHERRY.

Amorghiano, name for MANDELARIA on the island of Rhodes.

ampelography, the science of description and identification of the vine species VITIS and

Galet's **ampelographic** codes for some basic vine leaf shapes and the ruler and protractor used to measure them.

Galet protractor   Galet ruler

Austrian ampelographer Hermann Goethe proposed measuring the angle between leaf veins as an identifying character in 1876, and this concept was developed by the French ampelographer Louis Ravaz when in 1902 he published his, presumably much-needed, book *Les Vignes américaines*. Several large regional ampelographies were published near the turn of the century, including Pulliat (1888) and also Viala and Vermorel (1901–10) in France; Goethe (1878) in Austria; Rovasenda (1881) and Molon (1906) in Italy; and Hedrick (1908) and MUNSON (1909) in the US.

The most famous modern ampelographer, Dr Pierre GALET of MONTPELLIER, began his studies in 1944 by inspecting rootstock plantings, and this led to the publication of a distinguishing key in 1946. These studies were extended to include wine and table grape varieties and in 1952 his *Précis d'ampélographie pratique* was published, followed by, among other works, *Cépages et vignobles de France*. Galet's comprehensive quantitative description of leaf shape, attained by measuring the lengths and angles of the veins, the ratio of length to width, and the depth of sinuses, is highly objective. Other characteristics have been considered for identification, including the timing of phenological or development stages such as BUDBREAK, fruit maturation, or even LEAF FALL. Such features are known to be controlled by the environment, however, and can be used only in a relative sense for vine varieties in a single region.

The disadvantages of the technique are that, while some characteristics are quite stable, others, such as leaf shape, can vary markedly even on one vine. Major differences can be caused by environmental factors, but also and to a lesser degree by variation between different CLONES, plant age, and the influence of pests and vine DISEASES. There are, however, five characters which are quite stable: sex of the flower; grape skin colour; pulp colour; the taste of berries; and the presence of seeds.

Experience has shown that ampelography is a field of systematic botany requiring very specialized skills and interpretative ability, as well as an extraordinary memory. Very few people can walk into any vineyard and unequivocally identify varieties. Some modern acknowledged experts apart from Pierre Galet have included his colleague Paul Truel and successors Jean-Michel Boursiquot and Thierry Lacombe of Montpellier, and the late Alan Antcliff of Australia.

A complex ampelographic procedure was proposed by the Office International de la Vigne et du Vin (OIV) in 1951, based on 65 morphological characters. The International Board of Plant Genetic Resources (IBPGR) and l'Union International pour la Protection des Obtentions Végétales (UPOV) have also produced lists of descriptors and all three international systems have been harmonized by the introduction of numeric codes. Ampelographic

its cultivated VINE VARIETIES. A volume of vine descriptions is also called an ampelography, the word coming from the Greek *ampelos* for vine, and *graphe* for writing. Some system of distinguishing between grapevine varieties is clearly necessary since the early French **ampelographers** Viala and Vermorel (see below) were able to list about 24,000 names of varieties and their synonyms in their seven-volume *Ampélographie* published between 1901 and 1910. Some system of vine identification is particularly necessary in the modern era of VARIETAL wines (see below for examples of mistaken identification, especially in the NEW WORLD).

There has long been an awareness of differences between vine varieties, and PLINY the Elder could already produce vine descriptions and state that synonyms were creating confusion in Ancient ROME. While regional ampelographies emphasizing the aptitudes of various

cultivated varieties already existed in medieval Europe, it was not until the second half of the 19th century that a need for more systematic study developed. When serious vine diseases and pests were introduced to Europe from America (POWDERY MILDEW in 1845, PHYLLOXERA in 1863, DOWNY MILDEW in 1878, and BLACK ROT in 1885), it became essential to identify those species and varieties which showed most resistance to these hazards. Such species were soon used for VINE BREEDING and as ROOTSTOCKS.

Early ampelographic works emphasized fruit characters, and did not provide a key for classification, so that it was impossible to determine the name of a variety in a systematic fashion. Further, the distinguishing features of the vine varieties themselves were not emphasized. The vegetative parts of the vine were not used for identification since they were thought too variable and not stable. The studies have recently been facilitated by application of computers and electronic data storage and retrieval, but final identification still relies heavily on the judgement of ampelographers.

Attempts were therefore made to develop objective, laboratory-based tests for vine identification, including isozyme analysis and gel electrophoresis of enzyme banding patterns but DNA PROFILING has proved by far the most successful and effective.

Unfortunately, misnomers are common, especially in the New World, in government collections as well as in commercial nurseries and thus vineyards. Some of the early introductions of vine cuttings to these regions were made before European vine-growers had correctly identified their own varieties. Sometimes name tags on bundles of vine cuttings, all of which look remarkably similar, were simply misplaced or transposed. In other cases, confusion was caused by different synonyms in different European regions. James BUSBY's celebrated vine collection introduced to colonial Australia in 1832, for example, probably contained CINSAUT cuttings under seven different regional synonyms, and CHENIN BLANC under three. Paul Truel studied a large collection of French varieties at Domaine de Vassal on the Mediterranean coast (see INRA) in the 1960s and 1970s and found that as many as six distinct varieties grown in different parts of France were a single variety under different names, and there is even more variation in nomenclature between countries. The Graciano of Spain, for example, is the same as France's Morrastel, while the Ottavianello of Italy is the same as Cinsaut of France, but more complex examples abound.

Because its nursery has been able to provide virus-free, high-health vines, the FOUNDATION PLANT SERVICES at the University of California at DAVIS has been an important source of varieties for many establishing New World countries. Naming mistakes in this collection were legion, and caused inconvenience for both the California wine industry and importers of plant material from Davis. Some examples of such errors cited in California by French ampelographers Galet and Boursiquot, in Australia by Truel, and in New Zealand by Zuur include Abouriou (incorrectly called Early Burgundy), Petit Verdot (Gros Manseng), one clone of Pinot Noir (Gamay Beaujolais), Négrette (Pinot St George), Valdiguié (Napa Gamay), Melon (Pinot Blanc), Muscadelle (Sauvignon Vert), Tempranillo (Valdepeñas), a clone of Sauvignon Blanc (Savagnin Musqué), Trousseau Gris (Grey Riesling), and Touriga (Alvarelhão).

Generally rootstocks are more difficult to differentiate as they do not often fruit, so it is not surprising that problems have also occurred with their naming. In the 1990s, California growers were forced to replace the rootstock AXR1 as it succumbed to phylloxera.

This replanting effort was thwarted by finding that the rootstock thought to be SO4 was in fact 5C Teleki, and Riparia Gloire was mixed with Couderc 1616.   R.E.S.

Galet, P., *Cépages et vignobles de France* (2nd edn, Montpellier, 1990).

— *Dictionnaire encyclopédique des cépages* (Paris, 2000).

—and Morton, L. T., *A Practical Ampelography* (Ithaca, NY, and London, 1979).

Huglin, P., *Biologie et écologie de la vigne* (Paris, 1986).

amphora, Latin word from the Greek for a vessel with two handles. Although the term may refer sometimes to fine wares, it is normally used to describe the large pottery containers which were used for the bulk transport of many goods and liquids, including wine, in the Mediterranean world throughout classical antiquity (see Ancient EGYPT, for example). Despite the considerable variety of shape in amphorae, they mainly shared the characteristics of the two handles, a mouth narrow enough to be stoppered, and a bottom which tapered to a point (only a few, notably those of southern France, had flat bottoms). When full, many amphorae were a considerable weight; so the spike on the bottom served as a third handle, an essential point of purchase, when lifting and pouring. To carry wine the inner surface of the porous amphora was sealed with a coating of pine resin (see RESINATED WINES). To stop the mouth, either CORK or a lid of fired clay was pushed down the neck and then secured with a sealing of mortar. Modern study of amphorae began after the Second World War, when the use of the aqualung led to the discovery of many wrecks carrying cargoes of amphorae (see CELTS, for example). Later research has concentrated on the identification of kiln sites, where the vessels were produced. As a result, a much clearer picture of the pattern of trade in goods, such as wine, has emerged. The term amphora also became an expression of capacity, a cubic Roman foot, about 26 1/7 gal, although the actual vessels did not by any means conform to this. Indeed, it is likely that goods, such as wine, were frequently sold wholesale by weight and there were formulae for converting the weight of different goods into capacity.

                    J.J.P.

Peacock, D. P. S., and Williams, D. F., *Amphorae and the Roman Economy* (London, 1986).

Ampurdán-Costa Brava, Castilian name for the denominated Catalan wine zone EMPORDÀ-COSTA BRAVA.

Amtliche Prüfungsnummer. See AP NUMBER.

amurensis, an Asian vine species of the VITIS genus which takes its name from the Amur valley of northern China. The exceptionally cold climate in which it originates makes it useful to vine breeders seeking to introduce genes for cold hardiness. Professor Helmut

BECKER in particular developed HYBRIDS which shared some RIESLING characteristics, using *V. amurensis*.

amyl alcohols. See FUSEL OILS.

analysis of grapes, must, and wine is a regular and important part of the WINE-MAKING process.

Grapes and must

Traditional analysis of grapes and must is chiefly concerned with just three components: sugar, acid, and PH. For TABLE WINE, for instance, the grapes should ideally contain SUGARS capable of producing wines with an ALCOHOLIC STRENGTH between about 10 and 13 per cent by volume, which means that the grapes should have between 18 and 22 per cent of fermentable sugar by weight (see MUST WEIGHT for the various ways in which this can be measured).

The ACIDITY of the grapes or must should also ideally be such that the TOTAL ACIDITY is in the general range of 7 to 10 g/l expressed as tartaric acid. Some acid is always lost during wine-making, primarily as the alcohol content of the wine increases and the solubility of wine acids decreases. Acidity may be further reduced by MALOLACTIC FERMENTATION and cold STABILIZATION. It is therefore necessary to start with more acid in the grapes than is eventually wanted in the wine. However, it should be noted that the production of SUCCINIC ACID during fermentation may occasionally lead to a very slight increase in total acidity.

The chemistry of AGEING is strongly influenced by pH, and, although there is a relationship between pH and total acidity, it is important to measure pH separately. Two samples with the same acidity can have different pH readings because of the BUFFERING EFFECT of ions such as POTASSIUM.

Sugars are most simply measured by determining the DENSITY of a sample of clarified grape juice. Measurement of the juice's index of refraction (see REFRACTOMETER) can also provide a close estimate of its sugar content. In establishments with particularly well-equipped laboratories, modern chromatography can provide an extremely accurate sugar measurement. Sugar measurement is of primary concern in cool wine regions, as an indication of timing of HARVEST, the POTENTIAL ALCOHOL, and any need for ENRICHMENT.

In warm wine regions, the accumulation of sugars poses a different problem; in hot, dry weather, sugar synthesis (see PHOTOSYNTHESIS) and acid loss occur so rapidly that picking decisions have to be taken fast, and frequent field analysis may be necessary, normally involving a hand refractometer for sugar.

On arrival at the winery, harvested grapes may also be tested with a probe linked to an autoanalyser. This will typically analyse for sugar content and pH.   B.G.C.

amphora

22

Wine

Analysis of wine involves the measurement of various characteristics which relate to wine quality, stability, and legal requirements, ideally in a well-equipped laboratory. In most specialist wine laboratories, wine analysis also includes a critical tasting to ensure that the wine conforms to type and quality.

Common measurements include those of alcoholic strength, total acidity, VOLATILE ACIDITY, pH, density, RESIDUAL SUGAR, and SULFUR DIOXIDE. Laboratories in larger wineries may also be equipped to test for mineral elements such as IRON, COPPER, SODIUM, and potassium. All these parameters either play an important part in assessing quality and stability or are limited by law.

Not all wineries determine all these constituents, and many of the smaller ones have no laboratory at all and have to rely on samples sent to professional analysts.

More unusual determinations, such as quantifying pesticide RESIDUES, CHLOROANISOLES, or selected oak wood compounds that may be present in wines, and the detection of fraudulent CONTAMINANTS are only usually undertaken by specialist commercial laboratories.

Stability prediction tests for TARTRATES, PROTEIN, COLOUR sedimentation, and microbiology are also crucial analyses to ensure a commercially sound and stable product.

Modern analytical methods have become so sensitive that some trace components can be measured at concentrations of one part per trillion, levels unimaginable even as recently as the early 1980s. The wine analyst's increasingly difficult role is to assess which of the many hundreds of chemicals in finished wine at these very low concentrations are of constructive interest.

See also NUCLEAR MAGNETIC RESONANCE; and SOIL TESTING for the analysis of soils.

A.D.W. & G.T.

Coulter, A. D., Godden, P. W., and Pretorius, I. S., 'Succinic acid: how is it formed, what is its effect on titratable acidity, and what factors influence its concentration in wine?', *Australian and New Zealand Wine Industry Journal*, 19/6 (Nov/Dec 2004), 16–25.

Anbaugebiet, wine region in GERMANY, of which there are 13. The A in QBA stands for Anbaugebiet and these regions are fundamental to Germany's wine labelling and to GERMAN WINE LAW.

Ancellotta, Italian red wine grape valued for its deep colour as a blending ingredient, up to 15 per cent, in LAMBRUSCO. It is also widely used throughout central and northern Italy to add colour to wines deemed too pallid for today's market. Impressive VARIETAL versions are not unknown. According to the Italian vineyard census of 1990, Emilia-Romagna had 4,700 ha/11,750 acres planted, more than any subvariety of Lambrusco.

Ancenis, Coteaux d', small VDQS zone in the Loire around the historic town of Ancenis between Nantes and Angers. It is used for a limited number of VARIETAL wines, and the name of the variety must be stated on the label: Pineau de la Loire or Chenin Blanc; Malvoisie or Pinot Beurot (Pinot Gris); Gamay; or Cabernet. In fact the great majority of wine produced here is light red or pink made from Gamay, and some Cabernet, but a little serious medium sweet white wine is also produced. See also LOIRE, including map.

ancient vine varieties. THEOPHRASTUS (*c.*370–*c.*287 BC) remarked that there were as many kinds of grapes as there were kinds of soil (*Historia plantarum* 2. 5. 7; also *De causis plantarum* 4. 11. 6). He does not elaborate, but his remark shows how difficult it is to discuss VINE VARIETIES in the classical world. Are varieties that classical authors describe as different really different varieties, or are they examples of the same variety behaving differently in different conditions? Soil is only one factor; climate and wine-making methods are others. We cannot resort to tasting samples or nursery specimens; all we possess are CLASSICAL TEXTS written by authors who were not modern, scientifically trained AMPELOGRAPHERS.

The Greeks did not write systematic treatises on wine so we must turn to the Latin writers on agriculture and natural history, particularly VIRGIL, PLINY, and COLUMELLA. Virgil's treatment, in *Georgics* 2. 98–108, is the briefest and least systematic of the three, and he does not distinguish different wines, such as Lesbos, from different grape varieties, such as Aminean and Bumastus (the latter primarily a TABLE GRAPE). There are so many varieties, he concludes, that no one knows the number.

Only Democritus knew how many grape varieties existed, Pliny says (14. 20), but his account does not survive. Pliny himself announces that he will give us only the most important vine varieties. Pride of place among the Italian grapes goes to the Aminean, which has five subvarieties, then to the Nomentan, and third comes the Apian, which has two subvarieties and is the preferred grape of Etruria. All other vine varieties, Pliny asserts confidently, are imports from GREECE. Of these, the Graecula, from Chios or Thasos, is as good as the Aminean. Eugenia is good but only when planted in the Colli ALBANI. Elsewhere it does not produce good wine. The same goes for Rhaetic, which grows well in a cool climate, and the Allobrogian, which apparently ripens well in frost. These three grape varieties produce red wines which go lighter with age. The remaining varieties Pliny mentions are ones that he judges to be without distinction as wine grapes.

Columella agrees with Pliny for the most part but there are differences (3. 2. 7–31). He regards the Aminean as the best grape and puts the Nomentan second. He also recommends the Eugenian and Allobrogian wines, with the same reservation as Pliny, and the Apian. Then he mentions other varieties which are noted for their productivity rather than their flavour. He does not think highly of the Rhaetic, and he does not rank the Graecula with the Aminean. Vines were still being imported: Columella mentions three grapes which have only lately come to his notice so that he cannot give an opinion on their wines and also another grape which he says is a recent Greek import named Dracontion. Columella's aim is not to give a long and comprehensive list, for that would be impossible (he quotes Virgil's words, *Georgics* 2. 104–6). One should not quibble about names, he concludes, and, knowing that a variety can change out of all recognition if it is planted somewhere new, one should not approve a new grape until it has been tried and tested.

Columella's remarks indicate that farmers were prepared to experiment with new varieties, some of them imported from Greece. Some varieties were probably brought over with the Greek colonists from the 8th century BC onwards, others were growing in Italy long before they arrived. A Greek name is not a guarantee of Greek origin: some Greek names may be names given to Italian grapes which the Greeks of Sicily and southern Italy used when they started producing wine in their colonies. If so, these names reflect no more than the fact that the Greeks exploited the potential of these grapes commercially before the natives did.

H.M.W.

André, J., 'Contribution au vocabulaire de la viticulture: les noms de cépages', *Revue des études latines*, 30 (1952), 126–56.

McGovern, P. E., Fleming, S. J., and Kat, S. H. (eds.), *The Origins and Ancient History of Wine* (New York, 1995).

——*Ancient Wine* (Princeton and Oxford, 2003).

Tchernia, A., *Le Vin de l'Italie romaine* (Paris, 1986).

Ancient World. See Ancient ARMENIA, ASIA MINOR, CANAAN, CHINA, EGYPT, GREECE, INDIA, IRAN, MESOPOTAMIA, PHOENICIA, ROME, SUMER.

Andalucía, or **Andalusia**, the southernmost of Spain's autonomous regions, encompassing eight provinces and the DO regions of JEREZ, MÁLAGA, MONTILLA-MORILES, SIERRAS DE MÁLAGA, and CONDADO DE HUELVA (see map under SPAIN). Andalucía is the hottest part of Spain and has traditionally been associated with strong, alcoholic wines which have been exported from the Atlantic port of Cádiz since the PHOENICIANS first established their trading links around 1100 BC (see SPAIN, history). Wine continued to be produced during seven centuries of Moorish domination when Andalucía became one of the most prosperous parts of southern Europe. Since the 16th century, however, when cities such as Seville, Granada, and Córdoba were stepping-stones to the new colonies in SOUTH AMERICA, Andalucía has become one of the most impoverished regions of Spain.

The wines of Andalucía bear a strong resemblance to each other, and particularly to SHERRY, which has fashioned the region's wine industry since the city of Jerez was won back from the Moors in 1264. Most are FORTIFIED, although grapes from the arid plateau around Córdoba and Jaén are often so rich in natural sugar that they do not require the addition of spirit to reach an ALCOHOLIC STRENGTH of between 14 and 18 per cent. Until laws were tightened up following the foundation of the Jerez Consejo Regulador in 1934, wines from other parts of Andalucía would frequently find their way into sherry blends. Prince Alfonso de Hohenlohe's groundbreaking venture up in the Ronda hills, with an estate devoted to producing red and rosé table wines that first won acclaim in the late 1990s, opened up new perspectives for Andalusian wine which have been most convincingly confirmed in Granada province, where fine wine estates have sprouted on the slopes of Sierra Nevada.

R.J.M. & V. de la S.

Anderson Valley, cool California wine region and AVA on the western slope of the coastal mountain range 80 miles north of San Francisco. See MENDOCINO.

animals can cause serious damage in the vineyard, most obviously but not exclusively by eating grapes and foliage. Any reductions in foliage can prejudice fruit RIPENING and wine quality, and encourage sunburn.

Most animals may be kept out by fencing, but fences have to be sunk into the soil for smaller, burrowing animals, and high and cantilevered for animals as large and mobile as kangaroos. Deer, kangaroos, rabbits, rodents, and wild boar are some of the most common vineyard animal pests, but baboons can pose a threat in South Africa, as bears can in Canada, while rattlesnakes have been observed in an Arizona vineyard. Some vine-growers in New Zealand, on the other hand, deliberately use a combination of electric fencing and sheep to achieve judicious LEAF REMOVAL.

See also BIRDS. M.J.E. & R.E.S.

Flaherty, D. L., *et al.* (eds.), *Grape Pest Management* (2nd edn, Oakland, 1992).

Anjou, important, revitalized, and varied wine region in the western Loire centred on the town of Angers, whose influence once extended all over north west France. Anjou was the birthplace of Henri II, and its wines were some of France's most highly regarded in the Middle Ages (see LOIRE, history). It was the DUTCH WINE TRADE, however, that developed the sweet white wine production of the region in the 16th and 17th centuries, and it would be some centuries before the citizens of Paris rather than Rotterdam had the pick of each Angevin vintage. White grapes predominated

until the 19th century, when the Anjou vignoble reached its peak and PHYLLOXERA arrived. Since then a wide variety of less noble grape varieties have been planted, including a number of HYBRIDS, and the ENCÉPAGEMENT of this region is beginning to show some stability, with the total vineyard having shrunk by a half from its peak. White wine represents hardly 15 per cent of Anjou's total wine production with sweet Coteaux du Layon very much the cream of the crop, rosé may be its commercial mainstay, but reds are increasingly fine and important.

The region is relatively mild, being influenced by the Atlantic and protected by the woods of the Vendée to the south west (rather as the MÉDOC is protected by the Landes). Rainfall is particularly low here, for the land between here and the ocean is unremittingly flat, with annual totals of just 500 mm/19 in.

The GROLLEAU vine, and the sickly **Rosé d'Anjou** it all too often produced, are in retreat, although better vineyard management and an increase in the proportion of wine vinified by the négociants has resulted in an improvement in average quality. Much more refined, and incredibly long-lasting, is rosé **Cabernet d'Anjou**, which must be made from Cabernet Sauvignon or, much more likely, Cabernet Franc grapes. It can be quite sweet but usually has very high acidity which can preserve it for decades and makes it an interesting partner for a wide range of savoury dishes.

Cabernet Franc represents about one vine in three in Anjou and is increasingly favoured by growers there, encouraged by the creation in 1987 of the serious red wine appellation **Anjou-Villages**. The best area for such reds immediately south of Angers in the Coteaux de l'Aubance was given its own appellation **Anjou-Villages Brissac** in 1998. Lighter reds are produced as **Anjou Gamay**, from the Gamay grape of Beaujolais, and **Anjou Rouge** is the catch-all appellation for lighter, often quite crisp, red wines, although some excessively tannic wines result when growers draw off too much juice—and fruit—to make rosés.

Of dry white wines, **Anjou Blanc** is the most common, and is most successful when produced on the SCHIST and carboniferous rock close to the river. The wine must contain at least 80 per cent Chenin Blanc, but increasing proportions of Chardonnay, and Sauvignon, are included in the blend. Tiny amounts of sweet white **Anjou-Coteaux de la Loire**, made exclusively from Chenin Blanc, are also made. A significant and exciting development since the late 1990s has been the emergence of a new, high-quality style of dry Chenin Blanc in the Anjou, often using prime Layon sites to produce healthy, golden Chenin that is picked by hand in successive passages through the vineyard at full maturity before being fermented and then aged in 400 l double-barriques with a partial malolactic fermentation.

Superior producers of Anjou appellations include Domaine de Bablut, Philippe Delesvaux, Ch de Fesles, Domaine des Forges, Domaine de Haute Perche, Jo Pithon, Ogereau, Ch Pierre Bise, and Richou. Within the Anjou region are certain areas which have produced white wines of such quality that they have earned their own appellations: Coteaux de l'AUBANCE; BONNEZEAUX; Coteaux du LAYON; QUARTS DE CHAUME for sweet wines and SAVENNIÈRES for dry wines.

See also LOIRE, including map.

annual growth cycle of the vine. See VINE GROWTH CYCLE.

año, Spanish word for year. Some wines, particularly RIOJA, were once sold without a VINTAGE year but with the number of years' AGEING prior to bottling indicated on the label. **Ano** is the Portuguese word.

Ansonica, alternative name for Sicilia's white INZOLIA grape used particularly in the Tuscan Maremma, where it can produce wines of real character. It was planted on a total of nearly 9,500 ha/23,475 acres of Italian vineyard in the early 2000s, although total plantings were declining.

Antão Vaz, white grape increasingly favoured by winemakers in the ALENTEJO, southern PORTUGAL, where it is now producing sound VARIETAL wines.

anther, the pollen-bearing part of the STAMEN of a flower such as that of the vine. Each of the five anthers of the grape has sacs in which a large number of pollen mother cells develop into pollen grains, about two to three weeks before FLOWERING. The small, dry grains of POLLEN are released, possibly before the CALYPTRA or flower caps have fallen (see POLLINATION). In deliberate VINE BREEDING stamens and caps are removed early, before caps would normally fall, to prevent self-pollination and permit deliberate cross-pollination. B.G.C.

anthesis, another word for FLOWERING.

anthocyanins, members of a complex group of natural phenolic GLYCOSIDES (see also PHENOLICS) responsible for the colour of black and red grapes. They are also responsible for the colour of red wines, both as wine components and as precursors of PIGMENTED TANNINS and other derived pigments which are formed after the anthocyanins have reacted with other wine components. Anthocyanins are common in the plant world and are responsible for the red to blue colours of leaves, fruits, and flowers. The word comes from *anthos*, Greek for 'flower', together with the Greek-derived 'cyan' blue.

The particular anthocyanins found in grapes are limited in number, with mixtures of pigment molecules varying from species to species and from grape variety to grape variety. Indeed, chemical determination of the particular mixture of pigments present in an unidentified grape berry can aid vine identification. Pure *vinifera* varieties have anthocyanin pigments with only one molecule of glucose, while many of the AMERICAN VINES used in breeding ROOTSTOCKS and AMERICAN HYBRIDS also have anthocyanins with two molecules of glucose (a fact which greatly aided detection of non-*vinifera* wine in France in the mid 20th century; see University of BORDEAUX).

Anthocyanins have another important characteristic. They are capable of changing form slightly, depending upon the PH, or degree of ACIDITY, of the medium in which they are dissolved, the different forms being red, blue, and colourless. In general, the more acid the grape juice or wine, the greater the degree of ionization of the anthocyanins, and the brighter red the colour; as the acidity decreases, the proportion of colourless and blue forms increases. At wine pH values, grape anthocyanins should be mostly in colourless forms unless some pigment stabilizing mechanisms take place. (See also CO-PIGMENTATION and PIGMENTED TANNINS.)

The anthocyanin pigments are formed in the grapevine by a sequence of metabolic steps and are first visible when the berry begins to expand. The onset of this stage in the vine's metabolism is called VERAISON and is characterized by rapid growth and accumulation of sugar in the berry together with the first flush of colour in the berries.

The concentration of the pigments in the grape skin increases as the level of sugar increases in the grapes during ripening. The increase is intensified if sunlight falls on the berries, that is, if the berries are in an open CANOPY MICROCLIMATE. During veraison the anthocyanin pigments are formed and sequestered in the berry skins' outer cell layers in all but a few dark-berried grape varieties which have a portion of the pigment present in the pulp of the berry as well as in the skin (see TEINTURIERS).

One important operation during the FERMENTATION of most red wines, therefore, is to transfer the anthocyanin pigments from the skin cells to the wine. Colour transfer is achieved by keeping the skins adequately mixed with the fermenting wine (see MACERATION).

One might reasonably expect that the pigments in the new wine would be identical to those found in the grape skin. This may be the case for a few hours, but once the anthocyanins are mixed with the ACIDS of the wine and other phenolics as well as the many products of fermentation, they begin a series of reactions leading to more complicated molecules (see PIGMENTED TANNINS), in turn leading to a great diversity of derived pigments and colourless molecules. Derived pigments are classically assimilated to pigmented tannins arising from the addition of tannins to anthocyanins. However, they also include rather small molecules formed by the reaction of anthocyanins with other wine constituents such as ACETALDEHYDE or PYRUVIC ACID. Within a few years, only traces of the relatively simple monomeric anthocyanins remain. With wine ageing, polymers containing anthocyanin molecules may become larger and form aggregates so that some of them exceed their solubility in the wine and are precipitated as SEDIMENT. See AGEING.   A.D.W., B.G.C., & V.C.

Favretto, D., and Flamini, R., 'Application of electrospray ionization mass spectrometry to the study of grape anthocyanins', *American Journal of Enology and Viticulture*, 51/1 (2000), 55–64.

Somers, T. C., and Verette, E., 'Phenolic composition of natural wine types', in H. F. Linskens and J. F. Jackson (eds.), *Wine Analysis* (Modern methods of plant analysis, NS 6) (Berlin, 1988), 219–72.

anthracnose, one of the FUNGAL DISEASES of European origin which affects vines. It is also known as bird's eye rot or black spot. The disease is spread worldwide but is a particular problem in humid regions, as in the eastern UNITED STATES. Before the introduction of DOWNY MILDEW and POWDERY MILDEW, it was the most serious grape fungal disease in Europe, but since BORDEAUX MIXTURE was introduced in 1885 it has been controllable. The disease is caused by the fungus *Elsinoe ampelina*. Small black lesions are produced on the leaves and this area can die and drop out so that the leaves look as though peppered with gunshot. Small dark-coloured spots are also produced on young shoots, flower cluster stems, and berries. Anthracnose can reduce both the yield and quality of the fruit. The disease can be controlled by fungicides applied early in the growing season.   R.E.S.

Antinori, the most important wine producer in TOSCANA, and probably in the whole of ITALY. The modern wine firm was founded by brothers Lodovico and Piero Antinori in 1895, although the Antinori family can trace their history in the wine trade back to 1385, when Giovanni di Pietro Antinori enrolled in the Vintners Guild of Florence; like the vast majority of the Florentine nobility, the Antinori were, for centuries, producers of wine on their substantial country properties.

The work of the 19th-century brothers was continued by Piero's son Niccolò, who extended the house's commercial network both in Italy and into foreign markets and purchased the Castello della Sala estate near ORVIETO in Umbria. The house made a certain reputation for its white wines, sold under the Villa Antinori label, and for its Chianti, made in a soft and fruity style, by focusing its purchases of wine on various areas of the province of Florence, a style in contrast to the more austere wines of RICASOLI, the dominant Chianti house of the period. A vineyard was also planted with the Bordeaux grape variety CABERNET SAUVIGNON and cultivated during the 1930s. Although the family fortunes flourished, Antinori was only a medium-sized operation in 1966 when Piero Antinori, the son of Niccolò Antinori, took over.

By the early 1990s, he had increased the annual production 15-fold, giving the house a commanding position in Toscana, a position based both on the excellent quality of all the firm's wines at various price levels and, above all, on the innovative work of Antinori and house OENOLOGIST Giacomo Tachis in creating a new category of outstanding wines at the top of the range: Tignanello, the prototype SUPERTUSCAN, Solaia, which, together with SASSICAIA (initially marketed by the Antinori and whose development was assisted by Tachis), showed the potential for outstanding Cabernet in Toscana; Cervaro, a white wine produced at the Castello della Sala based on CHARDONNAY grapes and, then unusual for Italy, BARREL FERMENTED. While firmly anchored in central Italy, where vineyard holdings now approach 1,800 ha/4,450 acres, Antinori is, at the same time, becoming more international in its overall perspective, with JOINT VENTURES under way in Hungary, Malta, Chile, and Washington state and ownership of Atlas Peak in the Napa Valley. Piero's three daughters—Albiera, Allegra, and Alessia—are taking an increasingly prominent role in the company.

Piero's brother Lodovico Antinori independently created the internationally famous Supertuscans Ornellaia and the all-Merlot Masseto at his own estate near BOLGHERI (now owned by the Antinoris' great rivals the FRESCOBALDI). With their sister Ilaria, the brothers are now developing their own Campo di Sasso project at Bibona just north of Bolgheri. Lodovico, long a fan of Sauvignon Blanc, independently produces one in Marlborough, New Zealand, with Mount Nelson Estates.

D.T. & D.C.G.

Aosta, or the **Valle d'Aosta** (**Vallée d'Aoste** to the region's many French speakers), is Italy's smallest region (see map under ITALY). The long, narrow valley formed by the river Dora Baltea as it courses through the mountains of Italy's extreme north west is Italy's connecting link to France and Switzerland and to the north of Europe beyond.

This rugged alpine terrain is more suited to the grazing of animals than to the cultivation of the vine, and the vineyards—for the most part on HILLSIDES on either side of the Dora Baltea before the land rises to impossible ALTITUDES—are frequently terraced into dizzyingly steep slopes. No more than 30,000 hl/790,000 gal of wine is produced in an average year, of which only about 6,000 hl/157,800 gal qualifies as DOC. Most of it is sold privately either to the thriving tourist trade or to the intense flow of motorists which passes through the region. The two most important varieties are Torrette and Blanc de Morgex, which between them account for one third of the region's DOC production.

At the crossroads between northern and southern Europe, the Valle d'Aosta has found itself with an extremely rich diversity of vine varieties. Native regional and other Italian varieties include NEBBIOLO, DOLCETTO, Petit Rouge, Fumin, Vien de Nus, Prëmetta, Moscato di Chambave, and Prié or Blanc de Morgex. French varieties include PINOT NOIR, GAMAY, SYRAH, GRENACHE, PINOT GRIS or Malvoisie, PINOT BLANC, and CHARDONNAY. There is also the PETITE ARVINE of Switzerland and the MÜLLER-THURGAU of Germany.

The most interesting wines being made in the early 1990s were the Nebbiolo-based Donnas or Donnaz, produced close to CAREMA across the border in Piemonte and more interesting than the neighbouring Nebbiolo-based Arnad-Monjovet; the family of fruity reds with Petit Rouge as their base which encompass Enfer d'Arvier, Torrette, and Chambave Rosso; the Nus Rouge, made from Vien de Nus and Petit Rouge (spicier and more herbaceous than the Petit Rouge-based reds); the Moscato of Chambave, particularly in the PASSITO or dessert version; Gamay, fruity and soft but with some bitterness on the aftertaste which is not present in BEAUJOLAIS; Müller-Thurgau; the floral Blanc de Morgex et La Salle, produced in some of the highest vineyards in Europe, up to 1,200 m/3,9374 ft, made from ungrafted vines of the variety Prié (PHYLLOXERA does not survive at such high altitudes) trained in a low PERGOLA. Local producers are showing an interest in the Fumin, the grape which supplies structure and intensity in many of the Petit Rouge-based blends, and interesting experiments with small BARREL MATURATION of VARIETAL Fumin wines have begun.   D.T. & D.C.G.

aoûtement, French term for CANE RIPENING derived from *août*, French for August, the month in which it generally takes place in the northern hemisphere. The closest English term is periderm (shoot bark) formation. Careful observation shows that the first vineyards to start *aoûtement* and where it proceeds rapidly, are those which produce the finest wine. This is because early and rapid *aoûtement* indicates a modicum of WATER STRESS, as well as generous plant levels of CARBOHYDRATES, both of which contribute to rapid fruit RIPENING. *Aoûtement* has therefore been incorporated into vineyard SCORING systems used to predict wine quality.   R.E.S.

aperitifs, drinks served before a meal to 'open' (from the Latin *aperire*) the digestive system and stimulate the appetite, of which VERMOUTH and similar drinks are archetypal. Wines commonly served as aperitifs are dry, white, and not too alcoholic: CHAMPAGNE or any brut SPARKLING WINE; FINO and MANZANILLA sherry; MOSEL wines up to SPÄTLESE

level of sweetness; less rich ALSACE whites; MUSCADET, CHABLIS, and virtually any light, dry, still white wine without too much oak or alcohol. Customs vary nationally, however, and the French have customarily served spirits, FORTIFIED WINES, VINS DOUX NATURELS, VINS DE LIQUEUR, and strong, sweet wines such as SAUTERNES before meals. A common all-purpose aperitif, apparently acceptable to French and non-French alike, is the KIR, or *vin blanc cassis*, as well as a blend of white wine and sparkling water sometimes known as a spritzer. The port trade serves white port as an aperitif, sherry producers a dry oloroso or fino, too many amateurs a full-bodied Chardonnay.

aphids, small insects of the *Aphidiodae* family that feed by sucking the juices from plants. Several species of aphids attack grapes, but apart from PHYLLOXERA, they seldom cause serious damage in vineyards.   M.J.E.

AP number, or **Amtliche Prüfungsnummer**, adorns the label of every bottle of German quality wine, whether QBA or QMP. This 10-to 12-digit number is an outward sign that the wine has passed GERMANY's much-vaunted official testing procedure, which involves submitting samples of the wine to ANALYSIS and a BLIND TASTING test in which the wine is checked for FAULTS by a changing panel of fellow winemakers and other tasters. The test is hardly the most stringent procedure; the pass rate is well above 90 per cent. The first digit signifies which of the country's testing stations awarded the AP number (1 for Koblenz, 2 for Bernkastel, 3 for Trier—all three in the MOSEL-SAAR-RUWER—4 for Alzey in RHEINHESSEN, 5 for Neustadt in the PFALZ, 6 and 7 for Bad Kreuznach in the NAHE, where wines from SAALE-UNSTRUT and SACHSEN were also tested in the mid 1990s). The next code signifies the location of the vineyard. The penultimate pair of digits is the bottler's own code, which supplies a unique identification of the particular lot. If a vintner has bottled two or more wines of otherwise identical labelling (same site, Prädikat, and degree of dryness) this number is often used to distinguish them. The final two digits signify the year in which the wine was tested.

apoplexy. Vine disease. See ESCA.

appellation. See CONTROLLED APPELLATION.

appellation contrôlée, short for **appellation d'origine contrôlée,** is France's prototype CONTROLLED APPELLATION, her much-imitated system of designating and controlling her all-important geographically based names, not just of wines, but also of spirits such as cognac, armagnac, and calvados, as well as of many foods. This inherently protectionist system is administered by the INAO, a powerful Paris-based body which controls an

increasing proportion of French wine production, an average of 53 per cent of it in the early 2000s.

History

France's role as a wine producer had been gravely affected by the viticultural devastation caused by POWDERY MILDEW, DOWNY MILDEW, and PHYLLOXERA in the second half of the 19th century (see FRANCE, history). Fine wines were available in much-reduced quantity, but the LANGUEDOC and ALGERIA had become vast factories for the production of very ordinary wine at very low prices. Laws passed in the first two decades of the 20th century were aimed at bringing an end to the ADULTERATION AND FRAUD that was by then widespread. These were based simply on the principle of geographical DELIMITATION, and specified particular areas within which certain wines had to be produced. Bordeaux, Banyuls, and Clairette de Die were among the first; disagreement about exactly which districts should be allowed to produce France's most famous sparkling wine led to riots (see CHAMPAGNE, history).

It rapidly became clear, however, that France's famous wines depended on more than geography. The wrong grape varieties and careless wine-making would not result in a suitable expression of these carefully delimited TERROIRS. By 1923, Baron le Roy, the most influential and well-connected producer of CHÂTEAUNEUF-DU-PAPE, was implementing in his part of the southern Rhône a much more detailed set of rules including not just geographical delimitation but a specification of permitted VINE VARIETIES, PRUNING, and vine-TRAINING methods, and minimum ALCOHOLIC STRENGTH.

The French appellation contrôlée system evolved into a national reality in the 1930s when economic depression, widespread cultivation of HYBRIDS, and a serious wine SURPLUS increased the incentive for wine merchants to indulge in nefarious blending. The producers of genuine Pommard, for example, had a very real interest in limiting the use of their name to themselves. In 1935 the INAO was created with the express mission of drawing up and enforcing specifications for individual AOCs, or ACs, which broadly followed the Châteauneuf prototype, and in principle banned hybrids from AC wine. The great majority of the appellation regulations for France's most famous wines and spirits are therefore dated 1936 or 1937, although they have been continuously revised since. The VDQS category for wines deemed just below AC status was created in 1949 and is also administered by the INAO.

The French system of categorizing wine, including its main plank appellation contrôlée, has been taken as a model for EUROPEAN UNION wine legislation, and AC is France's equivalent of what the European authorities consider a QUALITY WINE. The legal powers of the INAO, both within France and in its dealings with the EU and beyond, were strengthened substantially in 1990, when it took the conscious decision to try to build the future of French wine on the concept of geographical appellations (eschewing even the mention of vine varieties on the main label) and adopted the specific aim of preserving agricultural activity in certain zones. But in 2004, when France's wine exports were clearly in significant decline and domestic sales stagnant, this policy was dramatically modified to make French wine labels easier to understand and the wines themselves more competitive in the global market. The aim was to raise the average quality of AC wines and introduce some new regional VIN DE PAYS categories. The INAO continues to wage war on all misused GENERIC wine and spirit names but the supremacy of the AC system is no longer unchallenged orthodoxy.

The regulations' scope

The INAO's detailed texts of its nearly 500 wine appellation regulations are already voluminous and constantly revised, covering the following aspects for each appellation and VDQS.

Production area All those communes allowed to produce the wine in question are listed, but within each of these communes only certain plots of land are deemed worthy, details of which are lodged with each commune's all-important *mairie* or administrative centre. Vines grown elsewhere within the commune are normally entitled only to be sold as a less specific appellation, a VIN DE PAYS or VIN DE TABLE.

Vine varieties The permitted grapes are specified in great detail, along with permitted maximum and minimum proportions. Many appellation regulations include long lists of half-forgotten but once-significant local varieties. White grape varieties are permitted to a certain extent in a number of red wine appellations.

Ripeness and alcoholic strength Specific MUST WEIGHTS are generally cited for freshly picked grapes before any CHAPTALIZATION, generally given in g/l of sugar. A maximum ALCOHOLIC STRENGTH after any chaptalization, if allowed, is also usually specified.

Yields Control of YIELDS is a fundamental tenet of the appellation contrôlée system, however sceptical some New World viticulturists are of the concept. The maximum yields cited in the regulations were almost routinely increased, however, by about 20 per cent throughout the 1970s and 1980s (see PLC). In 1993, the INAO announced its intention to curb yields (as the EU has done) but this has not been adopted with much noticeable enthusiasm.

This section usually includes information on a minimum VINE AGE allowed for appellation contrôlée production.

Viticulture This usually specifies a minimum VINE DENSITY, the approved PRUNING regime down to the number of buds, and the permitted vine-TRAINING SYSTEM. In some southern appellations the (limited) extent to which IRRIGATION is allowed may be outlined.

Wine-making and distillation This long section may well specify such aspects as compulsory DESTEMMING, method of ROSÉ WINE-MAKING (usually by SAIGNÉE), although there is generous use of the vague phrase *usages locaux*. Precise DISTILLATION techniques are usually specified for spirits.

Pros and cons

France's appellation contrôlée designation is in general a more reliable guide to the country's best wines than, for example, the QBA category of 'quality wines' in Germany, the liberally applied DOC designation in Italy and Portugal, and its DO counterpart in Spain (all of the last three modelled on the AC system). The French system is by no means perfect, however, and it remains to be seen whether the measures announced in 2004 to reserve appellation status to truly superior wines can possibly be effective. Policing remains a problem, and the Service de la Répression des Fraudes is probably understaffed. Contraventions of the regulations, particularly over-chaptalization, or chaptalization and ACIDIFICATION of the same wine, are difficult to detect (although a complex bureaucracy controls over-production). Misdemeanours are only very rarely publicized, and then usually only as a result of local politics.

A more serious disadvantage of the appellation contrôlée system is the extent to which it stifles experimentation. In dramatic contrast to the New World, vine-growers may plant only certain vine varieties. Those wishing to experiment have often been restricted to selling the wine not merely as a vin de pays, but as an anonymous, undated vin de table—or even forced to uproot the supposedly offending vines.

The appellation contrôlée regulations were drawn up not with a clean slate and a pencil devoted to the best possible options, but to legitimize the best current practices.

It is also fanciful to suggest that every wine produced within an appellation inevitably uniquely betrays its geographical provenance. Few blind tasters would unhesitatingly identify a Côtes du MARMANDAIS, for example. And then there are the catch-all appellations such as BORDEAUX AC, ALSACE, and CHAMPAGNE, whose quality variation is simply frustrating.
www.inao.gouv.fr

Apremont, named CRU just south of CHAMBÉRY (famous for its VERMOUTH) whose name may be added to the eastern French appellation Vin de SAVOIE. The wines are typically light, dry whites made from the local JACQUÈRE grape, although some Chardonnay is also grown.

Apulia, Anglicized form of the Italian region PUGLIA.

Aquileia, or **Aquileia del Friuli,** one of the more variable and less exported DOCs of the FRIULI region in north east Italy. The principal town is named after the Roman city which predated it.

Arab poets. The classical period of Arab civilization spawned a rich corpus of BACCHIC poetry which had its roots in pre-Islamic Arabia (AD 530 until the emergence of ISLAM). Wine was celebrated as one of a number of standard topics in the composite odes of pre-Islamic poetry. In its treatment, wine was underpinned by the rigid ethical code (*Muruwwa*, approximately *virtus*) that predicated the desert *Weltanschauung*, and thus gave voice to exaggerated notions of generosity. It was in this period, when wine was often compared to the saliva of women (to represent a kiss), that the seeds of the erotic register of later Arabic wine poetry were sown. Interestingly one such simile is even contained in the ode composed by Hassān Ibn Thābit, the Prophet's bard, to celebrate the conquest of Mecca shortly before Muhammad's death in AD 632. Traditional Muslim commentary, basing itself on the Islamic injunction against the consumption of wine, suggests that the simile is interpolated. But this argument is not entirely convincing; for Islam, while criticizing aspects of the culture of poetry, seems to have had little effect in censoring the poetic repertoire.

The essential model provided by this bedouin canon, which constituted the cornerstone of Arabian cultural and tribal identity, was absorbed virtually in its entirety into the nascent Islamic/Arab community; for this reason wine survived as a theme. Soon its treatment came to stand independently from the composite ode and, whilst the descriptive elements of Bacchic verse were based around a core of inherited imagery, a new defiant and anti-religious attitude was introduced that is reflected in a verse by the poet from al-Tā'if, Abū Mihjan al-Thaqafī: 'If I die bury me by the vine, so that its roots may satiate the thirst of my bones.' This solipsistic dirge, that shows the poet to have acquired notions of life after death, ignores the new imposing religious eschatology of the nascent Islamic community.

Islam did, of course, have a profound effect on the poets of Bacchism; for after a time, usually with the onset of old age, they would repent of their erring in pious Islamic terms. To replace them there was always a new generation of libertines, who were commonly men of high standing, such as governors and even, during the Umayyad period, caliphs. Al-Walīd ibn Yazīd, one of the last Umayyad caliphs

(d. AD 744), was a notorious hedonist (although perhaps maligned by later Abbasid propaganda) whose attitude in some Bacchic fragments is aggressively atheistic: 'Give wine [to drink] . . . for I know there is no Hell-fire!' In this period Bacchism became an urban phenomenon, notably amongst the libertines of Kufa (modern Iraq), and was eventually to gain a high profile in the Abbasid court circle of Baghdad, particularly during the reign of al-Amīn (reigned AD 809–13). This son of Hārūn al-Rashīd is famous in literary history as patron and boon companion of the great ABU NUWAS (d. AD 814).

In his wine poetry, Abu Nuwas synthesized a variety of impulses to produce sometimes complex poems which articulated all the issues relevant to the social dialectic of wine culture in an Islamic society: he expanded both the fantastical and mimetic descriptive repertoire of the *khamriyya*; he fused the Bacchic and erotic registers of poetry to create well-wrought seduction poems that gave voice to a sceptical world-view; he structured his poems in such a way as to support the simple rhetoric in defence of wine; finally, with literary sleights of hand, he reconciled the hedonistic ethic with Islamic dogma. It has rightly been said about the finest of these poems that they parallel the impulses and complexity of some English Metaphysical poetry.

From the descriptions of Abu Nuwas and other poets we gain a detailed picture of Bacchic culture: we are familiarized with the wine itself (its provenance, preparation, colour, bouquet, taste, and age—although here a mythological dimension enters into the poet's expression); its effects (physical, psychic, and spiritual); the personages (the boon companion, the pourer, the singing girl, the taverner (Jewish, Christian, or Persian), and the servant girl); the decorum of drinking (generosity, aristocracy, the quest for freedom, the Satanic pact, and, ultimately, belief in divine mercy); the venues of drinking (the caliphal palace, the tavern, the monastery, gardens, and the vine itself); finally we learn about the variety of vessels (for drinking: glass, silver and gold cups or goblets, ewers; for storage: jars, tanks or casks, and leather bottles).

After Abu Nuwas, poets who treated wine (throughout the Islamic lands, including al-Andalus in southern Spain) had little new to say; they simply reworked the imagery he had established, whilst discarding the careful structure of his finest poems. It was only amongst Sufi mystics that a new, important dimension was added to Bacchic poetry. Foremost amongst these was Ibn al-Fārid (d. 1235). For these ascetics DRUNKENNESS represented divine intoxication; they simply borrowed the imagery of Bacchic culture to articulate the otherwise ineffable states of mystical experience. Although Abu Nuwas himself was a ribald, Sufi sensitivity is perhaps foreshadowed in some of his most ethereal descriptions of wine:

[Last night I could not sleep] so give me to drink of the maiden wine who has donned the grey locks of old age whilst still in the womb;
A wine which [when poured] is replenished with youth . . .
One preserved for a day when its [seal] is pierced, though it is the confidant of Time itself;
It has been aged, such that if it were possessed of an eloquent tongue,
It would sit proudly amongst people and tell a tale of an ancient time . . .   P.K.
'Khamriyya', *The Encyclopaedia of Islam* (new edn.), vol. iv (Leiden, 1978), 998–1009.

Aragnan, old red and white grape varieties associated particularly with PALETTE in Provence. GALET reckons they are OEILLADE.

Aragón, known as **Aragon** in English. Once a powerful kingdom whose sphere of influence stretched from the LEVANTE in the west as far as NAPLES and SICILIA in the east, Aragón is now one of Spain's 17 autonomous regions. In the north east of the country, it spans the broad valley of the river Ebro which is flanked by mountains on either side (see map under SPAIN). The north is dominated by the Pyrenees, which feed water on to the arid Ebro plain. To the south and east the climate becomes progressively extreme as the land rises towards the central Spanish plateau.

The wines of Aragón have traditionally been strapping potions with natural alcohol reaching levels as high as 17 or 18 per cent. Red wines, made predominantly from the GARNACHA grape, were mostly sold in bulk for blending. However, four DO regions designated between 1980 and 1990 are helping to raise the profile of Aragón wines. SOMONTANO in the lush Pyrenean foothills east of the city of Huesca certainly has the most potential, but south of the Ebro wines from the DOs of CAMPO DE BORJA, CARIÑENA, and CALATAYUD are starting to benefit from investment in modern wine-making technology, which has revolutionized the style of modern-day garnacha. Throughout much of Aragón, large CO-OPERATIVES continue to dominate production, buying in grapes from smallholders.   R.J.M. & V. de la S.

Aragónez, once spelt **Aragónêz,** traditionally the principal Portuguese name for the Spanish red grape variety TEMPRANILLO in the ALENTEJO region, where it may be known as Tinta Aragóneza. It makes concentrated, deep-coloured reds, rather like those which go under the name Tinta Roriz in the Douro or, occasionally, Arinto Tinto in Dão and Tinta de Santiago in Setúbal.

Aramon is now, happily, a remnant of French viticultural history, a vine variety that burgeoned throughout the LANGUEDOC in the second half of the 19th century (the many who made their fortunes from wine around Béziers then were known as the **Aramonie**) and was displaced as France's most popular only in the 1960s by CARIGNAN. For decades, particularly

after the development of railway links with the populous north of France, Aramon vines were encouraged to spew forth light, everyday wine-for-the-workers that was with good reason called *petit rouge*.

Aramon's great attribute, apart from its prodigious productivity of up to 400 hl/ha (22.8 tons/acre), was its resistance to POWDERY MILDEW, the scourge of what were France's established wine regions in the mid 19th century. The variety was taken up with great enthusiasm and rapidly spread over terrain previously considered too flat and fertile for viticulture. GALET notes that its effects were particularly noticeable in the Hérault, where, between 1849 and 1869, the land under vine more than doubled, to 214,000 ha/528,800 acres.

Unless planted on poor soils and pruned extremely severely, Aramon produces some of the lightest red wine that could be considered red, often with a blue-black tinge and notably low in alcohol, extract, and character. To render the *rouge* sufficiently *rouge* for the French consumer, Aramon had invariably to be bolstered by such red-fleshed grapes as one of the TEINTURIERS, most often ALICANTE BOUSCHET. This gave Aramon a grave disadvantage compared with the deep, alcoholic reds of North Africa, and its popularity began to decline in the mid 20th century, a trend exacerbated by its toll from the 1956 and 1963 frosts. Aramon suffers from the twin disadvantages of budding early and ripening late and is therefore limited to hotter wine regions.

Not surprisingly, this variety has not been in great demand elsewhere (although it has been known in Algeria and Argentina and its origins are thought by some to be Spanish). The total French area planted with Aramon shrank from 34,700 ha/85,700 acres in 1988 to 9,100 ha in 2000 (almost exclusively in the Midi, particularly the Hérault). Some coarse VARIETAL examples have been marketed.

Aramon Gris and **Aramon Blanc**, lighter-berried mutations, can still be found, particularly in the Hérault.

Galet, P., *Dictionnaire encyclopédique des cépages* (Paris, 2000).

Arbin, CRU on the warm valley floor south east of the vermouth town CHAMBÉRY whose name can be added to the eastern French appellation Vin de SAVOIE. Arbin is particularly well known for the power and concentration of its red wine from the local MONDEUSE grape.

Arbois, the most important appellation in the JURA region in eastern France and named after the region's main wine town. The scientist Louis PASTEUR was brought up in the town, and conducted observations here when invited to turn his attention to wine health. More recently, Arbois has been famous as the location of the Jura's best-known wine producer, Henri Maire, whose energetic eponymous founder did much for the revival of the Jura wine region after the Second World War and died in 2003. The NÉGOCIANT grows, buys, blends, and sometimes bubbles by the TRANSFER METHOD about a third of the entire Jura wine production.

Arbois may be any colour, with some wines named *corail* or *rubis*, intermediate hues between pink and red which result from applying normal RED WINE-MAKING techniques to the light-coloured POULSARD grape or sometimes Pinot Noir, TROUSSEAU, or a blend. The northern part of the Arbois appellation is known for its well-structured Trousseau wines. In all, about half of all Arbois wine is red, making it the most important Jura appellation for red wine production. White wines are often VARIETAL Chardonnay made in unoxidized, Burgundian style. There are also blends in which some of the local SAVAGNIN, or Naturé, is included and these can taste distinctly nutty as the Savagnin will have been destined for VIN JAUNE. Small amounts of so called 'floral' Savagnin are now made without a trace of oxidation however. Top-quality producers include André et Mireille Tissot, Jacques Puffeney, Frédéric Lornet, Daniel Dugois, Rolet Père et Fils, and Jacques Tissot. A significant proportion of wine is made bubbly by the champagne traditional method of SPARKLING WINE-MAKING and sold as CRÉMANT du Jura.

Wines made from grapes grown within the commune of Pupillin, where Poulsard, often called Ploussard here, is a speciality, have the right to the appellation **Arbois Pupillin**.

See also VIN JAUNE and VIN DE PAILLE, both of which rarities are made within this appellation. W.L.

Arbois is also the name of a white grape variety of which about 300 ha/750 acres were still grown in the upper Loire in 2004 to produce such wines as VALENÇAY and CHEVERNY. Arbois is also a permitted ingredient in white wines labelled TOURAINE (and, in theory, Vouvray). The variety is declining in importance but was still the third most important variety of any colour in the Loir-et-Cher *département* in 1988. Often called Menu Pineau or Petit Pineau, it is a vigorous vine whose wines are softer than those of the Chenin Blanc that is more common in the middle Loire valley.

arbour, an overhead trellis structure used for VINE TRAINING, particularly in southern Italy. See TENDONE.

archaeology has been of great importance in tracing the ORIGINS OF VITICULTURE and plays a part in the ancient history of most wine regions. For a discussion of the techniques available and some of the more significant finds, see PALAEOETHNOBOTANY. For some more specific aspects, see also AMPHORAE and the CELTS.

Ardèche, region of France on the right bank of the Rhône between the main concentrations of vineyards which constitute the northern and southern Rhône valley in south east France. Its steadily improving wines are sold as VIN DE PAYS des Coteaux de l'Ardèche, from the southern VIVARAIS area, or Vin de Pays des Collines Rhodaniennes from the much larger surrounding region. VARIETAL Chardonnay and to a lesser extent Viognier have been particularly successful here. Louis LATOUR of Burgundy was a pioneer, notably with Grand Ardèche Chardonnay, and the Vignerons Ardechois is a co-operative with high standards.

Argaman, ISRAELI crossing of CARIGNAN and the Portuguese SOUSÃO which produces relatively ordinary wine.

Argentina, the most important wine-producing country in South America, and, since the late 1990s one of the most dynamic wine producers in the world. With a forecast output of 15.5 million hl/409 million gal in 2004, Argentina is the world's fifth biggest wine producer.

Of the 210,530 ha/520,229 acres of vineyard in 2003, 40 per cent was planted with dark-skinned varieties, 31 per cent (down from 50 per cent in 1996) with Argentina's famous pink-skinned varieties the CRIOLLAS and CEREZA, 22 per cent with light-skinned varieties, and just 7 per cent with 'others'. Considerable investments in new vineyard areas and improved wine-making technology continue to be made and the Argentine desire to export is now one of the most manifest in the world of wine.

History

Unlike North America where explorers and early settlers found VITIS *labrusca* growing in abundance, South America depended on the Spanish colonizers for imported European VINIFERA vines. The vine probably arrived in Argentina by four different routes. The first was directly from Spain in 1541 when vines are thought to have been cultivated, without great success, on the Atlantic coast around the river Plate. A year later, seeds of dried grapes were germinated as a result of an expedition from Peru to the current wine regions immediately east of the Andes. Another expedition from Peru in 1550 also imported vines to Argentina, while the fourth and most important vine importation came from Chile in 1556, just two years after the vine was introduced to Chile's Central Valley. (See SOUTH AMERICA, history, for more details.)

One of the most important grape varieties systematically cultivated for wine in South America was almost certainly the forerunner of Argentina's CRIOLLA CHICA, California's MISSION, and Chile's PAÍS, which were to be the backbone of South American wine production for the next 300 years.

Although Argentina was settled from both the east and the west, it was in the foothills of the Andes that the Jesuit MISSIONARIES found the best conditions for vine-growing. The first recorded vineyard was planted at Santiago del Estero in 1557. The city of Mendoza was founded in 1561 and vineyards in the province of San Juan to the north were established on a commercial scale between 1569 and 1589.

By the skilful use of dams and IRRIGATION channels, the early settlers were able to produce sufficient wine to meet the needs of a growing population and they also learned how to produce wine that could stand up to long wagon train journeys to the centres of population to the east.

In the 1820s, following the freeing of Argentina from Spanish colonial rule by General San Martín, there was a massive influx of European immigrants. In 1885 the RAILWAY between Buenos Aires and Mendoza was completed, lending still greater importance to the vineyards in the foothills of the Andes, and by 1900 a second wave of immigrants, many from wine-producing areas of Italy, Spain, and France, brought with them many new vine varieties and their own regional vine-growing and wine-making skills. The old colonial methods were quickly dispensed with, except the historic and essential irrigation system, and the foundations for Argentina's mammoth domestic wine industry were laid.

In the 1920s, Argentina was the eighth richest nation in the world, but the subsequent economic depression led to a steep decline in foreign investments and a disastrous drop in the export price of its primary products. While the landowning classes continued to prosper, or salted away their capital overseas, there was growing unrest among the largely disenfranchised, poorly paid urban masses. When General Juan Domingo Perón came to power in 1943 he appealed directly to the workers with promises of rapid industrialization, better working conditions, and organized, state-controlled unions. For a while Argentina's fortunes revived, but in the mid 1950s Perón and his ambitious and charismatic wife Eva were deposed by the military. From then on a succession of opportunist military governments led the country into spiralling decline. Throughout the 1960s and 1970s, Argentina had become so enmeshed in stifling bureaucracy that this was to lead to widespread corruption and ultimately to social and political unrest. Argentina grew increasingly isolated, by the early 1980s hyper-inflation was running at nearly 1,000 per cent a year and the wine industry was suffering from chronic lack of investment. Most producers were content to supply cheap, rustic VINO DE MESA to a domestic market that boasted the third highest per capita consumption of wine in the world. In the late 1960s and early 1970s, at a time when the UK was drinking approximately 3 l per capita per year and the Americans even less, the Argentines, despite all their troubles, were quaffing 90 l of wine per head. By 1996 that

Argentina

Wine-growing regions

0   250   500 km

PARAGUAY

JUJUY

SALTA

FORMOSA

● Cafayete

CATAMARCA   TUCUMÁN   SANTIAGO DEL ESTERO

BRAZIL

LA RIOJA   SANTA FE

SAN JUAN

CÓRDOBA

URUGUAY

Mt. Aconcagua

● Mendoza

MENDOZA   SAN LUIS

Buenos Aires ●

Pacific Ocean

LA PAMPA

Colorado

NEUQUÉN

RÍO NEGRO

Atlantic Ocean

CHILE

Andes Mountains

Paraná

Mendoza

Andes Mountains

LAVALLE

Mendoza ●   SAN MARTÍN

LUJÁN DE CUYO   MAIPÚ   JUNIN

TUPUNGATO   SANTA ROSA

RIVADAVIA

● Tunuyan

SAN CARLOS

San Rafael ●

SAN RAFAEL

0   100 km

figure had dropped dramatically to 41 l per capita (and by 2004 was down to 30 l).

Faced with this dramatic drop in home consumption, added to the pressing need to earn foreign currency, the more enlightened producers decided to go upmarket and in the late 1980s, for the first time, gave serious consideration to the possibilities of exporting, helped by political and economic stability not experienced for decades. Under President Menem, business confidence in Argentina's future was revitalized at home and

abroad and encouraged investment in a wine industry where time had stood still (see also CHILE).

It is a measure of changing attitudes that during the 1970s Argentina regularly produced well over 20 million hl/528 million gal of wine but by the early 2000s production had dropped to around 12.5 million hl. This was largely brought about by a reduction of a third during the 1980s in the total area planted with vines, especially red wine grape varieties. Despite the historic association of alcoholic, red wines

with good red Argentine beef, there was a noticeable swing to white wine drinking as the emerging middle class began to develop a life-style and taste of their own. In the 1960s, about 50,000 ha/123,500 acres were planted to Argentina's most distinctive red variety MALBEC, but uneconomically low prices for Malbec grapes in the 1970s and 1980s encouraged a reduction of this area to less than 10,000 ha in 1990, just as—as has so often been the case—the potential of the variety became apparent. Thanks to a dramatic VINE

PULL SCHEME, Argentina's total vineyard fell from 314,000 ha/775,580 acres in the early 1980s to 205,000 ha/506,350 acres in 1993 before a new wave of quality-orientated plantings which accounted for almost 50 per cent of all vines by the early 21st century.

Climate

Argentina's wine regions are widely dispersed, but are almost entirely confined to the western strip of the country bordering the foothills of the Andes. The vineyard area extends from the tropic of Capricorn in the north to the 40th parallel in the south. Apart from the southern, largely fruit-growing areas of the Río Negro and Neuquén, the climate is semi-desert with annual rainfall rarely more than 250 mm/10 in. The seasons are well defined, allowing the vines to rest.

Summer temperatures vary from 10 °C/50 °F at night to as much as 40 °C/104 °F during the day. Summers are hot in the regions of San Juan (except for the Calingasta valley), La Rioja, Catamarca, and the east of Mendoza (Santa Rosa, Rivadavia, San Martín, and Lavalle). In the Calchaquíes valley (Cafayate), upper Mendoza (Luján de Cuyo), Uco valley (Tupungato), and Río Negro, summers are TEMPERATE to warm, making them Regions II and III in the Winkler system of CLIMATE CLASSIFICATION. In winter, temperatures can drop below 0 °C/32 °F, although frost is rare, except where vines are grown at altitude.

The air is dry and particularly unpolluted, unlike the smog that is sometimes trapped over the Chilean vineyards closest to the capital, Santiago, just a short flight away over the Andes. Vine FLOWERING may occasionally be adversely affected by a hot, dry, hurricane-force storm called the *zonda*, which blows down from the north west in early summer. Grapes almost invariably reach full maturity and the lack of humidity reduces the risk of FUNGAL DISEASES, obviating the need for frequent and costly SPRAYING.

What little rain there is falls mainly in the summer months, often as potentially dangerous HAIL, although the 1998 vintage was plagued by unusually heavy and prolonged rain, and subsequent ROT, due to EL NIÑO. Heavy winter snow in the high Andes is important as this ensures plentiful supplies of water for the irrigation system on which the vines depend. If you buy older vineyard land in Argentina (parcels that were planted at the time the irrigation canals were dug), the purchase includes a government-regulated water allocation. Owners of newer vineyards generally have to rely on wells.

Regions
See map.

Mendoza In the far west of the country, only a (substantial) mountain range from Santiago in Chile, this is by far the biggest and most important wine-growing province in Argentina, accounting for about 70 per cent of all Argentina's wine production, although the area planted declined from a peak of 255,000 ha/629,850 acres in 1980 to about 146,081 ha/360,972 acres in 2003. The Andes dominate the western skyline, with mount Aconcagua, at over 7,000 m/23,000 ft, the highest mountain in the Americas, rising above the rest. Average vineyard altitudes are about 600 to 1,100 m (1,970–3,610 ft) above sea level. The climate is CONTINENTAL, with the four seasons clearly defined but without any extremes of temperature. Rainfall occurs mostly in the summer months, which encourages growth, but it seldom exceeds 300 mm/12 in a year with 200 mm/8 in being the average. Early summer HAIL, *La Piedra*, is the main risk to the vines and frost is rare.

The topsoil in Mendoza is of a loose, sandy, ALLUVIAL type with clay substructures. Water is in ample supply from four mountain rivers flowing from glaciers in the high Andes and 17,000 deep boreholes equal the flow of two additional rivers. The long rows of protective trees that line the vineyards and make summer temperatures of 36 °C/97 °F bearable are testimony to the effective and well-orchestrated system of reservoirs, canals, and IRRIGATION channels.

The most important wine-producing areas in and around Mendoza are:

Maipú department: Cruz de Piedra, Barrancas, Russell, Coquimbito, Lunlunta, and Maipú districts.

Luján department: Carrodilla, Chacras de Coria, Mayor Drummond, Luján, Vistalba, Las Compuertas, Pedriel, Agrelo, Ugarteche, Carrizal, Tres Esquinas, Anchoris.

San Martín to the east and San Rafael to the south of the region are also major centres of production, although less important than formerly following the swing to classic varieties.

Luján de Cuyo (which created Argentina's first CONTROLLED APPELLATION in 1993) is in the upper Mendoza valley at altitudes between 800 and 1,100 m (2,640 and 3,630 ft). Average rainfall is about 190 mm/7.2 in a year and the mean annual temperature is 15 °C/37.5 °F. The Malbec vine does particularly well here.

Pink-skinned grapes, notably CRIOLLA GRANDE and CEREZA, account for about a quarter of all Mendoza plantings and are used for inexpensive wine and grape concentrate. Red wine grapes account for more than half, with the Malbec predominating with a total of around 16,000 ha/40,000 acres, but Italian varieties and Tempranillo are also important. Cabernet Sauvignon is catching up with about 10,700 ha/26,440 acres by 2003. White wine varieties such as Chardonnay are increasingly common, especially in high altitude vineyards, such as those of Tupungato in the Uco valley south west of the city of Mendoza, which can be as high as 1,200 m/3,960 ft and are regarded as some of Argentina's most valuable vineyards.

San Juan This is Argentina's second biggest wine-producing region and had more than 47,000 ha/116,000 acres of vineyards in 2003. The capital of the province, San Juan, is 150 km/90 miles north of Mendoza. The climate is much hotter than that of Mendoza, with summer temperatures of 42 °C/107 °F not uncommon and with rainfall averaging only 150 mm/6 in per annum.

For long the home of high-yielding pink varieties, especially Cereza, whose high sugar content made them ideal for wine blending, concentrating, or for selling as fresh TABLE GRAPES or RAISINS, San Juan was being developed as a producer of quality wine in the late 1990s. A rapid reduction in the volume of wine produced has already taken place and is likely to continue, especially for red-skinned grapes such as BONARDA and SYRAH. It should be noted, however, that San Juan produces perfectly acceptable sherry-style wines and also provides the base for most of Argentina's BRANDY and VERMOUTHS. The best areas are in the Ullun, Zonda, and Tulum valleys.

La Rioja Historically the oldest of the wine-producing provinces, and home of the Torrontés Riojano, La Rioja had only 8,000 ha/20,000 acres of vineyard in 2003. By world standards the area is unimportant, although aromatic white wines from the TORRONTÉS grape can be good, and wines made from the Moscatel de Alexandria (MUSCAT OF ALEXANDRIA) have a following in Argentina itself. The lack of water for irrigation purposes makes wine-making a marginal activity.

Salta, Jujuy, and Catamarca These three far northern provinces cover 500,000 square km/193,000 square miles. Although of the three Catamarca has the biggest area under vine (2,300 ha/5,800 acres), it is in the province of Salta (1,900 ha/4,700 acres) that the best wine is produced (and some of the world's highest vineyards are situated; see ALTITUDE). Here the Torrontés Riojano is very much at home and around Cafayate in the Calchaquíes valley produces an outstandingly aromatic, full-bodied, dryish white wine. Promising TANNAT is also made here. The vineyards lie between 24 degrees and 26 degrees latitude, and can be 1,500 m/4,900 ft or more above sea level. The climate and soil are not dissimilar to Mendoza but the MESOCLIMATE there ensures a combination of good sugar levels at harvest (from 21 to 25 °BRIX) and above average TOTAL ACIDITY, thereby ensuring a wine of depth and balance. Of the other grape varieties grown in Salta, CABERNET SAUVIGNON is the most successful, producing a young wine with good fruit and concentration even without oak ageing.

Río Negro and Neuquén This southern area of Patagonia is much cooler than the higher-yielding areas to the north and, although there were some 3,800 ha/9,300 acres under vine in

2003, it may not yet have reached its full potential. Historically the Río Negro has been the fruit-growing centre of Argentina, producing particularly apples, but the cooler climate and chalky soil combined with a long, warm ripening season under clear skies make it ideal for the production of good-quality white wine (notably Torrontés Riojano and Semillon) and for sparkling wine base material. In the first five years of this century, new wineries—notably Bodegas del Fin del Mundo and Noemia—were established closer to the Andes in the Alto Valle del Río Negro producing perfumed and elegant Malbec, while in El Bolsón even further south, 1,600 km/990 miles from Mendoza, the renowned Bodega Weinert planted Pinot Noir, Chardonnay, and other early-ripening vines in the southernmost vineyard of the Americas.

Vine varieties

Red Paradoxically the predominant red wine grape variety in Argentina is one that has yet to achieve greatness in its original birthplace in the south west of France. The Malbec, often spelt Malbeck, of Bordeaux, BOURG, BLAYE, and CAHORS seems to have discovered its true home in upper Mendoza. There it produces a deep-coloured, robust, and fruity red wine with enough alcohol, weight, and structure to benefit from OAK ageing. Cabernet Sauvignon is as popular with Argentine wine-growers as any others, but there is no doubt that the Malbec produces by far the best and most balanced red wine and, with careful nurturing and strict temperature control during fermentation, has become Argentina's vinous trademark. Total plantings were over 20,000 ha/50,000 acres in 2003.

The second most planted red wine variety in Argentina, with 16,600 ha, is the increasingly fashionable variety called BONARDA, whose exact identity is still the subject of some debate among ampelographers. This variety, along with many other Italian varieties (most notably SANGIOVESE and BARBERA but also FREISA, NEBBIOLO, RABOSO, DOLCETTO, and LAMBRUSCO), was presumably brought to the country by the substantial numbers of Italian immigrants.

Plantings of Cabernet Sauvignon increased enormously, from under 2,500 ha/6,200 acres in 1990 to 15,440 ha/38,150 acres by 2003. Other red wine varieties apart from Merlot, often blended with Cabernet, include Pinot Noir, which has yet to find a suitable home in Argentina, and Syrah, which clearly has, in the hot San Juan valley, north of Mendoza. Total plantings of Syrah shot up from under 700 ha/1,730 acres in 1990 to more than 10,000 ha by 2003, making it Argentina's fourth most planted European variety after Malbec, Bonarda, and Cabernet Sauvignon.

Also significant is the Spanish variety TEMPRANILLO, often used to make light, fruity wines by CARBONIC MACERATION although

O. Fournier make a very serious example from 80 year-old vines in the Uco valley.

White Pedro Giménez (not identical to Spain's PEDRO XIMÉNEZ) is Argentina's most planted light-skinned grape variety, with 14,700 ha/36,300 acres grown particularly in Mendoza and the province of San Juan, where it yields alcoholic, full-bodied wine suitable for blending. It is also used for making GRAPE CONCENTRATE, which Argentina exports in vast quantities, particularly to JAPAN.

The second most planted light-skinned variety in 2003 was TORRONTÉS Riojano with 7,900 ha/19,100 acres, followed by Moscatel de Alejandria, or Muscat of Alexandria, with 5,400 ha/13,350 acres, then Chardonnay with 4,600 ha/11,400 acres, and Torrontés Sanjuanino with 3,100 ha/7,700 acres. The country's most interesting, and certainly the most distinctive, white wine grape variety is Torrontés in its various forms, which can produce a (relatively) light wine with a strong, floral, MUSCAT aroma. Use of the right strains of yeast and careful temperature control during fermentation can result in a Torrontés wine of great universal appeal. Originally it was planted almost exclusively in the northern province of Salta, particularly in the Calchaquies valley and around Cafayate. It can now be found in the province of Mendoza, where it is often used for blending.

Chardonnay is the wine that everyone wants to produce and the Argentines are no exception, particularly with their eye on the US and British markets. Of the classic white grape varieties, Chardonnay has proved to be perfectly and copiously at home in Argentina, even though fewer than 1,000 ha/2,470 acres were producing wine in 1990. Argentina has its own Chardonnay clone developed at DAVIS in California, the so-called Mendoza clone (see MILLERANDAGE), which is widely used in Australia and elsewhere. The variety has been particularly successfully grown at higher altitudes such as the Tupungato area at 1,200 m/3,940 ft.

True SAUVIGNON BLANC tends to be flabby in Argentina, and relatively rare with just 1,000 ha/2,500 acres planted. SAUVIGNONASSE is even rarer and less glorious. Other varieties include Pinot Gris, Viognier, Riesling, and Semillon.

Pinks The grapes of this, Argentina's most distinctive, category of vine varieties, which accounts for about 30 per cent of all vines planted, can hardly be described as either white skinned or dark skinned since at full ripeness their skins are distinctly pink. The CRIOLLA GRANDE, CRIOLLA CHICA, and CEREZA are some of Argentina's oldest varieties. Both Criolla and Cereza are extremely productive varieties of which one bunch on a well-irrigated vineyard can weigh as much as 4 kg/9 lbs. These pink-skinned varieties are typically planted in the hotter, flatter, most heavily irrigated vineyards. Moscatel Rosada is another

important pink-skinned variety, of which there were a total of 10,000 ha/25,000 acres in 2003. The wine produced from these varieties is usually very deeply coloured white, occasionally pink, often quite sweet, and sold at the bottom end of the market, either in bulk or in litre bottles or cardboard cartons, as everyday wine within Argentina, or blended with basic Malbec to produce a light red.

Alcalde, A. J., *Cultivares Viticolas Argentinas* (Mendoza, 1989).

Viticulture

Until the mid 1990s, more emphasis was placed on wine-making techniques and the equipment required for processing the huge yields of the Criolla Grande vine than on experimentation and innovation in the vineyards.

Warm, dry summers, clear skies, and ample supplies of water for irrigation can lead to very high yields, and certainly did in the 1970s when domestic consumption was at its peak. The drop in home sales in the 1980s and the growing realization among Argentine producers that they must export to survive has resulted in closer study of the art of the possible in existing vineyards and a search for new areas more suitable for the production of better-quality wine.

Almost all vines in Argentina are ungrafted, planted on their own roots. The root louse PHYLLOXERA has made only limited predations in Argentina, perhaps because the biotype present in the country is a relatively mild one, perhaps because there is a relatively high proportion of SAND in vineyard soils. The average vine life cycle in Argentina has been 50 years so that ROOTSTOCKS with particular resistances and attributes are likely to be introduced relatively slowly, if at all.

Before the construction of a new vineyard or the replanting of an old one can begin, the ground is cleared by bulldozer to leave slight slopes to facilitate the flow of the all-important water, which is stored nearby in strategically placed reservoirs and distributed by an intricate network of canals and ditches. Argentina's water distribution system is still one of the best in the world, despite having its origins in the 16th century. In more recent times, the channels of water that flow from the permanently snow-capped peaks of the high Andes have been augmented by the drilling of deep boreholes. These take water from between 60 and 200 m (650 ft) below the surface and can produce as much as 250,000 l/66,000 gal per hour. The landscape is unique, the cultivated areas resembling green oases in the scorched desert surroundings (as in the irrigated vineyards of AUSTRALIA but with the Andes as a backdrop).

Three methods of irrigation are used. Historically the most common was flood irrigation, whereby measured amounts of water are channelled into flat vineyards. Furrow irrigation involves the channelling of water along the furrows in which the vines are planted. By the late 1990s, more expensive but sensitive DRIP IRRIGATION techniques were widely used.

Soil structure varies from region to region but a loose greyish sandy texture predominates with substrates of GRAVEL, LIMESTONE, and CLAY. The Instituto Nacional de Vitivinicultura (INV), the Government's controlling body, and the National Institute of Agriculture Technology (INTA) were originally guided by Davis in California in selecting the right clones for the soil, but many vineyard owners subsequently looked to Australia for advice.

Although the immigrants who arrived in the early 20th century brought with them the vertical *espaldera* TRAINING SYSTEM of low training of vines along three wires, the need for greater volume led most vineyard owners to adopt the *parral cuyano* trellis system in the 1950s and 1960s (see TENDONE). As in Chile, however, the classic method is increasingly favoured once again, in order to facilitate both CANOPY MANAGEMENT and drip irrigation, although Cereza and Criolla Grande vines are still likely to be *parral* trained.

From BUDBREAK to HARVEST takes an average of five months and the long ripening season normally ensures grapes of full maturity. The INV declares the date of the harvest, which usually begins in mid February and, depending on the variety and the region, can extend until April. Many of the large new vineyards are several hours' drive from the wineries. Itinerant, low-paid grape pickers are still plentiful, despite recent dramatic rises in the cost of living, so the MECHANICAL HARVESTERS which would enable picking in the cool of the night and maximize wine quality are still far from common.

Much more rigorous control of yields, the gradual introduction of mechanical harvesting, and the building of wine-making facilities in the vineyard have been the main viticultural developments of the early 21st century.

Wine-making

The overwhelming demands of the domestic market in the late 1960s and early 1970s meant that wine-making techniques were geared to processing the vast yields of Criolla Grande, Criolla Chica, and Cereza grapes. The big producers concentrated their efforts and resources into perfecting a simple, somewhat brutal, but highly efficient system for receiving, destemming, crushing, macerating, and fermenting up to 2.5 million kg/2,500 tons of grapes a day. Even in the 1990s it was not unusual at the peak of the harvest to see lines of grape-laden trucks waiting patiently in the winery approaches to be weighed before tipping their loads into the giant crushers, often leading to dangerously oxidized fruit. Red wines were picked at 21 to 23 °Brix, crushed, fermented in concrete fermentation vessels, RACKED off the skins, at 10 °Brix, fermented to dryness off the skins, and then, in the more traditional bodegas, left for up to four years in large old wooden tanks before BOTTLING according to market demand.

Changes are well under way, however. The export-led drive for improved quality has forced even the biggest producers of cheap wine into a reappraisal of their wine-making techniques in order to supply international demand for sound VARIETAL wines.

Wine trade organization

The majority of Argentina's vineyards are in the hands of specialist grape-growers, of which many are relatively large commercial concerns. Wine producers exert increasing control on the grapes they buy in, however, and almost all of them own at least some vineyards.

The single greatest factor in making Argentina's wine suitable for export has arguably been the widespread use of foreign CONSULTANTS and in some cases FLYING WINE-MAKERS.

The great majority of Argentina's wineries, like the country's vineyards, are in Mendoza province, often on the outskirts of the city of Mendoza itself. The largest companies have traditionally had sales offices in the distant capital Buenos Aires, but the largest producer by far, Grupo Peñaflor, now masterminds its export campaign from Mendoza. Its main winery is at Coquimbito just outside Mendoza.

Valentin Bianchi, situated in San Rafael in the south of Mendoza province, is another producer to have exported successfully, particularly to the US, as have Finca Flichman (now owned by SOGRAPE of Portugal) and Pascual Toso and substantial vineyard owners Bodegas Lopez. Other successful exporters include Weinert, La Agricola, Santa Ana, Michel Torino, Norton, Luigi Bosca, Alta Vista, Terrazas de Los Andes, Salentein, and Balbi. Bodegas Esmeralda, Bodega La Rural, and Bodegas Escorihuela are part of the wine empire built up by Dr Nicolas Catena, who set a new standard for Argentina with a wide array of ambitious projects including a JOINT VENTURE with Ch LAFITE-ROTHSCHILD. Regional specialists with some degree of success outside Argentina include Etchart of Salta, for whom Michel ROLLAND has acted as consultant, and Canale in the Río Negro.

Bodega Norton of Luján de Cuyo was acquired by Austrian interests in 1989. In the 1990s, Argentina attracted a substantial wave of foreign investors, notably from Bordeaux, and Santa Rita, Concha y Toro, San Pedro, and then Montes from Chile, attracted by Argentina's lower land costs. Italian vermouth producers Martini & Rossi have long had Argentine investments, as have MOËT Hennessy, whose wholly owned subsidiary Chandon has been the biggest producer of sparkling 'Champaña' in Argentina for three decades. Other foreign investors include the champagne houses of Mumm, Deutz, and Piper-Heidsieck.   J.R. & P.T.

Anuario Internacional 2004 (Buenos Aires, annually).
Fielden, C., *The Wines of Argentina, Chile and Latin America* (London, 2003).
Goldin, C., *The Secrets of Argentine Malbec* (Buenos Aires, 2004).
Rolland, M., and Chrabolowsky, E., *Wines of Argentina* (Mendoza, 2003).
Spectator, A., *Vineyards, Bodegas & Wines of South America* (Buenos Aires, 2004).
Waldin, M., *Wines of South America* (London, 2003).

argols, another word for TARTRATES.

Arinarnoa, 1956 INRA crossing of Merlot and Petit Verdot of which 149 ha/368 acres grew in France in 2000. It can produce strong, dark red.

Galet, P., *Dictionnaire encyclopédique des cépages* (Paris, 2000).

Arinto, Portuguese white grape variety most commonly encountered in BUCELAS in which it must constitute at least 75 per cent of the blend. It is also grown in many other parts of Portugal, notably the RIBATEJO and TERRAS DO SADO. Arinto is respected for its high acidity and can yield wines which gain interest and, sometimes, a citrus quality with age. As an ingredient in VINHO VERDE it is known as Pedernã. Total plantings were 5,600 ha/13,800 acres in 2004.

Arinto do Dão is a different, less distinguished variety.

Arinto Tinto, Portuguese synonym for Aragónez, or TEMPRANILLO.

Aristophanes, Greek writer of comedies at the end of the 5th century BC. In his plays he extols the hard-working peasant farmer in the fields around Athens. One of his characters is a vine-dresser, or early vineyard worker (Trygaios in *The Peace*), and the goddess of peace is called wine-loving and 'giver of grapes'. Aristophanes criticizes the young for idling and drinking too much. Women also come in for criticism as topers in several of his plays.
                                                    H.H.A.

arm, viticultural term for that part of the vine's woody framework from which the CANES and SPURS arise. The location of arms depends on the vine-TRAINING system used. They may be borne along CORDONS, positioned at intervals so that the buds, after PRUNING, are placed to space the bearing shoots desirably. Alternatively, the arms may be positioned on a short HEAD at the top of the trunk as happens with some CANE PRUNING systems.
                                                    B.G.C.

armazém, Portuguese word literally meaning 'warehouse' or 'store'. In the towns of Vila Nova de Gaia (see OPORTO) and Funchal (see MADEIRA), *armazém* are the long, low LODGES where PORT and madeira are left to age.

Armenia, relatively small, mountainous, ex Soviet republic in the south Transcaucasus. One of the oldest viticultural regions, its altitude compensates for its LATITUDE, which is five to seven degrees more southerly than the famous vineyards of France. In 2002, Armenia had just 13,000 ha/32,100 acres of vineyard and produced 72,000 hl/1.9 million gal of wine (much of it strong, sweet, and often white), 6,200 hl of sparkling wine, and 47,000 hl of brandy.

History

The Transcaucasian region, including Armenia, is one of the world's oldest centres of viticulture. Ancient Armenia was much bigger than modern Armenia and in classical times included much of eastern TURKEY, AZERBAIJAN, and GEORGIA in the area between the Black Sea and the Caspian Sea. The vine was an indigenous plant in the valleys of Armenia, where the climate was particularly suitable for it. The wild vine *Vitis vinifera silvestris* (ancestor of the cultivated VINIFERA vine species) was established there over a million years ago. Carbonized or petrified grape pips have been found at several neolithic sites in the Caucasus, especially on the western (Black Sea) side. See PALAEOETHNOBOTANY and ORIGINS OF VITICULTURE.

Archaeological evidence has also revealed irrigation canals, wine cellars with processing facilities, and large clay jugs (*karas*). Raisins and grape seeds reminiscent of the varieties Voskeat, Makhali, and Garandmak cultivated today in the Ararat plain south west of Erevan were unearthed during excavations of the Teishebaini fortress from the 10th century BC. Wine cups and SULFUR sticks used in the 7th century BC were also found in the fortress.

Argishti I (785-753 BC), the king of Urartu (an ancient state which is regarded by modern Armenians as a predecessor of their homeland), made his capital Tushpa into a pleasant garden city planted with vineyards. An inscription of his descendant Rusa II (680-639 BC), who built Teishebaini (modern Karmir Blur), states: 'By command of the god Haldi I have planted these vineyards.' At Teishebaini wine cellars were excavated, with rows of *pithoi* (large ceramic wine jars) buried up to the neck and stamped with the year of production and the quality of the wine. Herodotus (*Histories* I. 194, see Ancient GREECE) described the river trade on the Tigris carried on by merchants operating from Armenia all the way downstream by the Assyrians. Transported on circular leather-covered rafts (like the modern *gufas* which could until recently still be seen on the river) was wine (*oinos* and therefore made from grapes; see WINE, etymology) in what he described as palm-wood casks.

But the Ancient Armenians fermented more than grapes. XENOPHON (*Anabasis* 4. 5. 26) describes how during his epic journey through the Near East he found in Armenia villages, 'also wheat, barley and beans; and barley-wine in *kraters* [see CRATER]. The actual grains of barley floated level with the brim, and reeds of various lengths but without nodes were in the bowls. When you were thirsty, you had to put one of these in your mouth and suck. It was a very strong wine, unless you mixed it with water. Once you got used to it, it was a very pleasant drink.'

Old manuscripts confirm Armenia's high level of viticultural development, yet this art often suffered periods of decline due to war and Arab, Turkish, and Persian invasions (see ISLAM).   J.A.B.

By the end of the 19th century, Armenia's viticulture was on a small scale. In 1913 vineyards covered 9,200 ha/22,700 acres and after the First World War this was reduced to 5,100 ha. In that period the average area of a peasant farm was just 1 ha. In the 1920s, private wineries were nationalized and amalgamated into the large Ararat wine trust, which later established a network of wine-processing plants in RUSSIA and in UKRAINE.

In 1940, the vineyard area reached 16,300 ha/40,261 acres. In the post-war period grape culture was developed mainly on land that had not been cultivated before, and specialized state farms were established based on collective farms. In 1990, Armenia had 29,000 ha/71,630 acres of vineyards.

Modern viticulture

Bounded by the Small Caucasus in the north and east and by the narrow Ararat plain in the south west, Armenia grows vines commercially at an altitude of 400 to 1,700 m (1,300–5,580 ft), altitude determining climate, which is dry and CONTINENTAL to dry subtropical, the annual rainfall being less than 500 mm/19 in. Summers are so dry that 85 per cent of vineyards need IRRIGATION. Winters are sufficiently severe for 85 per cent of vineyards to need WINTER PROTECTION, and there is a risk of FROST at both the beginning and end of the growing season. Only about 10 per cent of vines are GRAFTED, and roughly three vines in four are grown on a four-wire VERTICAL TRELLIS.

Armenia has five viticultural zones: the Ararat valley (65 per cent of vineyards and most of the wineries), the foothills of the Ararat valley (13 per cent), the north east zone (10 per cent), Vaiots Dzor region (10 per cent of vines), and Zangezur region (2 per cent). More than 400 different vine varieties are grown in Armenia, many of them for TABLE GRAPES, but notable wine varieties include Voskeat, Areni, Mskhali, Kakhet, RKATSITELI, Kangun, Akhtanak, Megrabuyr, and Karmrajut.

Since the late 1990s, demand for Armenian wine has risen considerably, particularly in Russia, with the most sought-after wine being made from the Areni vines in the Vaiots Dzor region.   V.R. & S.G.

armillaria root rot, worldwide FUNGAL DISEASE which lives in woody plant materials in the soil and attacks a wide range of plants including vines. It is sometimes called the mushroom, oak, or shoestring root rot. It is typically a problem on land where vines have replaced trees, and is frequently seen in new California vineyards where oak trees grew previously. Infected vines tend to occur in groups and slowly decline or sometimes die suddenly. The causal fungus, *Armillaria mellea*, produces white fungal mats with a distinct mushroom-like smell under the bark of the vine's lower trunk and roots. The land can be fumigated to ward off this fungus, for which there are no tolerant ROOTSTOCKS.   R.E.S.

Arnaldus de Villanova, sometimes called **Arnaud de Villeneuve**, was a Catalan who died in 1311. He taught medicine at MONTPELLIER, the most important medical school, with Salerno, in medieval Europe. He had an eventful life, attending the sickbeds of popes and kings and engaging in theological controversy. He was an influential physician, and his writings were still reprinted in the 16th century.

Arnaldus is not interested in wine for its own sake: his concern is with the medical proprieties of wine. One of his books, the *Liber de vinis* ('Book on Wines'), deals exclusively with wine as MEDICINE, but references to wine appear throughout his works. The *Liber de vinis* is short: in the 16th-century editions of the complete works it occupies no more than ten folio pages. To a modern reader it is bound to appear a strange mixture: GALEN and the Arab philosopher Avicenna; alchemy and astrology; some first-hand observation. Arnaldus' medicine draws heavily on the voluminous writings of Galen (129–99 BC), physician to the Emperor Marcus Aurelius, but Galen was a far better scientist. Galen wrote in Greek, but knowledge of Greek was rare in the medieval west: some of his works were, however, translated into Arabic and thence into Latin. Through Moorish Spain, Arabic influence on European influence was strong: hence Arnaldus' references to Avicenna and other Arabic authors.

Arnaldus praises wine as a remedy against melancholy and says that it is good for the liver, the urinary tract, and the veins, because it purifies the blood. He recommends it to the old, especially in winter, because it warms the kidneys as well as the entire body, it reduces the swelling of haemorrhoids, it is beneficial to digestion, gives one a healthy complexion, comforts the mind, and, best of all, slows down the greying of one's hair. Most of his remedies, however, do not involve the drinking of neat or watered wine. He uses wines FLAVOURED with rosemary or borage, recipes which go back to classical antiquity and which were supposed to cure a wide variety of ills; he exploits the antiseptic quality of wine for making poultices and, since the water was not usually reliable, to dissolve other medical substances.

One would not have been safe in Arnaldus' hands. An aside about making wine is spot on, however: the wooden casks in which wine was kept should be clean and free of odours, the grapes should mature properly, and any unripe grapes must be discarded.

He is popularly credited with introducing the first still to France, probably from Salerno, and George (1990) notes that he was granted a patent for his discovery of MUTAGE (which spawned wines such as those now known as VINS DOUX NATURELS) in 1299 from the powerful king of Majorca. H.M.W.

George, R., *French Country Wines* (London, 1990).

Lucia, S. P., *A History of Wine as Therapy* (New York, 1963).

Sigerist, H. E., *The Earliest Printed Book on Wine* (New York, 1943).

Thorndike, L., *A History of Magic and Experiential Science*, 7 vols. (New York and London, 1923-57), ii. 841-61.

Arneis, white grape variety and dry, scented VARIETAL wine of PIEMONTE in north west Italy. Originally from ROERO, it was traditionally used to soften the red Nebbiolo grape. Perhaps because of this, it is also sometimes called BAROLO Bianco, or white Barolo, by some of its more fervent admirers. Although the wine has a certain history in Piemonte, it seemed on the verge of disappearing in the early 1970s when only two houses, Vietti and Bruno Giacosa, were bottling Arneis. In the 1980s, however, thanks to growing demand for white wine in Piemonte, particularly from houses more renowned for their Barolo and BARBARESCO, there was an explosion of interest in Arneis, and plantings now total almost 600 ha/1,500 acres. The wine is DOC in the LANGHE and ROERO DOC zones and production in 2004 was 38,000 hl/1 million gal. It is a low-yielding variety that ripens in the second half of September and gives wines with subtle if interesting perfumes. Modern winemaking has, in the best cases, dealt with the variety's inherently low acidity. The best examples tend to be unoaked and drunk young. It is not planted anywhere else in Italy, but is planted to a very limited extent in California and Australia. The best producers in Piemonte are Malvira, Deltetto, Cascina Chicco, and Bruno Giacosa. D.C.G.

Arnsburger, white wine variety developed at GEISENHEIM for sparkling wine and exported to the island of MADEIRA due to an EU-funded project (with a German consultant). Planted on the north side of the island, the productive, disease-resistant variety is used to make rather tart, unfortified, dry white wine with limited local appeal. R.J.M.

aroma, imprecise tasting term for a relatively simple smell such as that of a grape, fermenting MUST, or young wine. Originally from the Greek word meaning 'spice', it has evolved so that in generally current English it means 'pleasant smell' (as opposed to odours, which may be distinctly nasty). Wine-tasting professionals tend to use the word aroma to distinguish the smells associated with young wines from the more complex aromatic compounds which result from extended BOTTLE AGE, generally referred to as BOUQUET. In Australia, the word aroma is often used to refer specifically to VARIETAL characteristics rather than those associated with wine-making. Those who distinguish between aroma and bouquet differ as to the point in a wine's life cycle which divides the use of the two terms. For tasters schooled at the University of BORDEAUX, bouquet includes fermentation smells, for example, as well as all those associated with oak ageing and bottle ageing. Others, particularly Burgundians, may refer to grape aromas as primary aromas, fermentation and oak ageing aromas as secondary aromas, and bottle ageing aromas as either tertiary aromas or bouquet. See also FLAVOUR, AROMA WHEEL, FLAVOUR COMPOUNDS, and ESTER. A.D.W.

aroma compounds. See FLAVOUR COMPOUNDS.

aromatized wines. See FLAVOURED WINES.

aroma wheel, graphical representation (see over) of TASTING TERMS used for AROMA, devised at the University of California at DAVIS by Ann C. Noble and others in the early 1980s. Her research into sensory evaluation of wine had indicated that there was no general agreement either on terminology or on its application. The aroma wheel was developed to provide a standardized lexicon which can be used widely to describe wine aroma in non-judgemental terms, grouping specific terms which can be defined to provide a basis for communication. In its attempt at clarification and categorization it is used by professionals and provides a good basis on which tasting terms for aroma can be taught to novices, even if with experience, most individuals tend to develop their own terms, which may be just as precise and descriptive. The aroma wheel does not include terms which describe the physical dimensions of a wine (such as 'full bodied' or 'tart').

The extensive use of the wine aroma wheel has led to the development of an analogous mouthfeel wheel to describe the TEXTURE and MOUTHFEEL sensations of red wines.

Noble, A. C., Arnold, R. A., Buechsenstein, J., Leach, E. J., Schmidy, J. O., and Stern, P. M., 'Modification of a standardized system of wine aroma terminology', *American Journal of Enology and Viticulture*, 38/2 (1987).

Arrábida, former IPR in southern Portugal named after the Serra da Arrábida and now part of the Palmela DOC. See TERRAS DO SADO.

arrachage, French term for RIPPING OUT vines. The *prime d'arrachage*, payment for participating in the European VINE PULL SCHEME, made its mark on the southern French landscape from the late 1980s.

Arribes (del Duero), promising VCIG Spanish wine region in CASTILE-LEÓN that it not unlike the DOURO valley over the Portuguese border with similar geology and precipitous slopes.

arrope, a syrup used for sweetening wine in Spain, especially SHERRY, made by boiling down and thus concentrating unfermented grape juice. See GRAPE CONCENTRATE.

Arroyo Grande. California wine region and AVA. See SAN LUIS OBISPO.

Arroyo Seco. California wine region and AVA. See MONTEREY.

Arruda, DOC in western Portugal with a large co-operative. See ESTREMADURA for more details.

Arrufiac, also known as **Arrufiat** and RUFFIAC, is a light-skinned grape variety enjoying a modest renaissance in Gascony in SOUTH WEST FRANCE. An ingredient in PACHERENC DU VIC-BILH and Côtes de ST-MONT, it was rescued from obscurity in the 1980s by André Dubosc of the Plaimont CO-OPERATIVE. It is typically blended with the MANSENGS and PETIT COURBU.

artists' labels, wine LABELS illustrated by works of art, often a different one for each vintage. Baron Philippe de ROTHSCHILD commissioned the Cubist Jean Carlu to design a mould-breaking label for the 1924 vintage of Ch MOUTON-ROTHSCHILD, the first to be CHÂTEAU BOTTLED. He instituted this as an annual custom from the 1945 vintage, with the result that COLLECTORS may seek particular missing labels, thereby adding value to Mouton Rothschild even in lesser or earlier maturing vintages (of which most bottles tend to have been opened). Since then, vintages of Mouton have enjoyed particular réclame in countries such as Japan, Denmark, Holland, and Spain associated with the artist responsible for that year's label. Wine producers all over the world have since emulated this phenomenon, notably Leeuwin Estate of WESTERN AUSTRALIA, although none to such clever effect.

(Exhibition catalogue) *Mouton Rothschild—Paintings for the Labels* (Bordeaux, 1995).

ascorbic acid, vitamin C, one of the first VITAMINS to be discovered, and a wine-making additive used chiefly as an antioxidant. As well as being essential to mankind's diet, it is involved in plant metabolic processes. The green grape contains significant levels of vitamin C but much is lost during fruit ripening

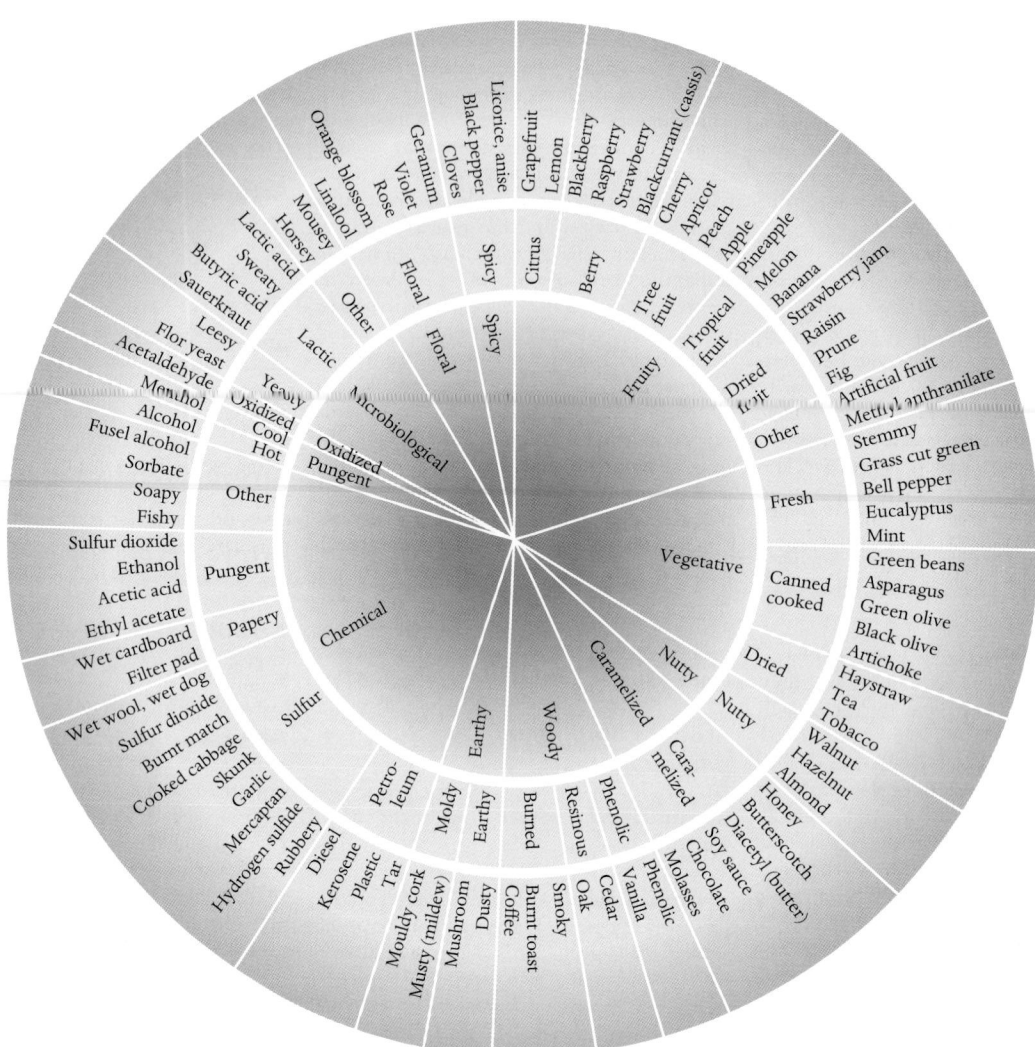

The **aroma wheel** was devised at the University of California at Davis by Professor Ann C. Noble in an attempt to instil some rigour into wine descriptions.

and later wine-making operations. In a wine context, ascorbic acid is of chief importance not to the wine drinker but to the winemaker as a permitted additive, within limits, for its ability to prevent OXIDATION by reacting directly with OXYGEN. The EU limit in a finished wine is 150 mg/l. It is added chiefly to light white wines, along with SULFUR DIOXIDE; because these two antioxidants act by different mechanisms, ascorbic acid is not a substitute for sulfur dioxide. Ascorbic acid is considered by many winemakers to be most effective when added at BOTTLING. Nevertheless, there is ongoing controversy about the overall antioxidative efficacy of ascorbic acid and this uncertainty is exacerbated by imprecise knowledge of both its mechanism of action with oxidants in wine and its interaction with sulfur dioxide. Accordingly, since 2000 there has been a renewed research effort to better understand the quite complex chemistry of ascorbic acid, sulfur dioxide, oxygen, and other agents of oxidation in wine. Erythorbic or iso-ascorbic acid

is often used, especially in Australia, as a less expensive alternative to ascorbic acid.

A.D.W., T.J., & P.J.W.

aseptic bottling. See STERILE BOTTLING.

Asia. Until the 1990s it was assumed—quite wrongly as it turned out—that this most populous of continents would never play an important role in the world of wine. There was something in the physical make-up of most Asians, it was thought by those in the continent which produces the lion's share of all wine, that made them prefer either non-alcoholic or grain-based drinks. This assumption was rapidly disproved in the mid to late 1990s when the world's AUCTION prices were inflated at an unprecedented rate thanks largely to sudden interest from buyers in Hong Kong, Singapore, and Taiwan. Thanks to a (short-lived) boom in the so-called tiger economies, and the much-vaunted HEALTH benefits claimed for red wine, wine-drinking changed from bizarre foreign

practice to status symbol in a remarkably short time in countries as varied as Thailand, Taiwan, India, Korea, and—the country with the greatest potential as both consumer and producer—China. Wine-drinking further infiltrated Japan meanwhile, while several other Asian countries have embarked on their own domestic wine industries since the early 1990s. Cambodia saw its first wine harvest in 2004: local grapes plus Shiraz picked and vinified by a local grower who previously specialised in TABLE GRAPES. For details of individual countries, see BHUTAN, CHINA, KOREA, INDIA, INDONESIA, JAPAN, MYANMAR, NEPAL, SRI LANKA, TAIWAN, and VIETNAM. See also the ex-Soviet Central Asian republics of TAJIKISTAN, KAZAKHSTAN, KYRGYZSTAN, TAJIKISTAN, TURKMENISTAN, and UZBEKISTAN. Countries such as AFGHANISTAN, IRAQ, IRAN, JORDAN, PAKISTAN, SYRIA, and Yemen devote most of their vineyards to the production of DRYING GRAPES but ISRAEL and LEBANON both have flourishing wine industries.

Asian lady beetle is an insect pest new to North American viticulture, first observed to cause problems in the 2001 vintage in the north east of the country. Normally considered a good sign in a vineyard, these insects feed on sugar from damaged grapes in the late ripening period, and are harvested with the fruit. Disturbed during the crushing process, they release a yellow-orange body fluid which taints the wine with a musty, nutty aroma and an astringent peanut-chocolate character on the palate. One adult beetle per 1.7 kg of grapes is enough to cause taint.

The insect was introduced to the US to control soya bean aphid, and this has been effective. However, at soya bean harvest it can move into adjacent vineyards searching for food. The Asian lady beetle (ladybird or ladybug in some countries) is now distributed all along the American eastern seaboard, into central states, and also in Washington and Oregon. At the time of writing, no solution to the problem has been found, and it has led to the disposal of a million litres of Ontario wine to date.

It has now also been reported in Italy, Germany, Holland, Belgium, and the UK.   R.E.S

Asia Minor, much of modern TURKEY, the land lying between the Black Sea and the Mediterranean.

In Ancient Asia Minor, grapes were harvested in September and October. In business documents of the Old Assyrian trading colonies in Asia Minor (dating to approximately the 19th century BC), this season of the year was called *qitip karānim,* or 'grape picking'. The location of the ancient vine-growing areas is uncertain, although they may well have been, as today, along the four great river valleys north of Adana, in the vicinities of Niğde, Nevşehir, Kayseri, Yozgat, and Sungurlu in central Turkey, towns which lie in a line between the east coast of the Black Sea and the east coast of the Mediterranean.

Among the Hittites, the Anatolian civilization in western Turkey in the second millennium BC, a grape harvesting festival took place every year. Viticulture was certainly important during the Hittite Old Kingdom (*c.*18th–15th centuries BC). The king's merit in the eyes of the storm god (who was regarded as the owner of the land) was reflected in the produce of the vineyards and in grain and livestock production. Wine was under the control of royal officials who distributed 'good wine' to certain pensioners (who complained when the quality was not satisfactory). Certain officials during the Old Kingdom bore a title which can be translated as 'wine chief', originally supervisor of the vineyards but later an exalted military rank comparable with general or field marshal.

In Hittite laws (also of the Old Kingdom), the price of grapes was regulated, together with the prices of barley and emmer (a species of wheat). One law makes provisions for damage caused to vines: the offender has to take the damaged vine himself and let the plaintiff take grapes from one of his own good vines at harvest time.

Another law prescribes penalties for the theft of a vine: six shekels for a free man, three if the offender was a slave. Previously the fine was lower, but the offender had been obliged to undergo corporal punishment in addition. Six shekels was also the fine for a free man who damaged another's vine by fire.

Viticultural images were used in ritual magic. In an archaic ritual performed during the foundation of a new palace, for example: 'They lay out a vine tendril and say, "Just as the vine puts down roots and sends up tendrils, so may the king and queen put down roots and send up tendrils!" '

Similarly in so-called 'vanishing god' texts we read: 'O Telepinu [a god of agriculture], hold goodness in your mind and heart, just as the grape holds wine in its heart!'   J.A.B.

Hoffner, H. A., Jr, *Alimenta Hethaeorum: Food Production in Hittite Asia Minor,* American Oriental Series 55 (New Haven, Conn., 1974).

aspect, the direction in which a slope faces, an important characteristic of vineyard sites, especially in cool climates. For more details, see TOPOGRAPHY.

aspergillus. Vine disease; see BUNCH ROTS.

aspersion, French for sprinkling and therefore a measure to reduce FROST damage to vines; see SPRINKLERS.

Aspiran, very old dark-skinned grape variety of the LANGUEDOC which once represented about a quarter of all vines planted in the Hérault *département,* but was not replanted on any great scale after PHYLLOXERA because it is not particularly productive. The odd hectare that remains yields limited quantities of light but perfumed red wine and it is a permitted grape variety in MINERVOIS.

Asprinio, light grape speciality of CAMPANIA in southern Italy, where it often makes slightly sparkling wines. DNA PROFILING at SAN MICHELE ALL'ADIGE showed that Asprinio and Greco di Tufo (see GRECO BIANCO), each used to produce distinct varietal wines, are in reality identical.   J.V.

Asprokondoura, Greek name for BOURBOULENC.

Assario Branco, Portuguese white grape encountered particularly in the Dão region which may be PALOMINO.

assemblage, French word for the important operation in the production of fine wines of deciding which lots will be assembled to make up the final blend. It plays a crucial role in SPARKLING WINE-MAKING when some CUVÉES may be assembled from several hundred different components. Here the complementary nature of each component is of great importance, as is, for all NON-VINTAGE sparkling wines, adherence to a house style.

Assemblage is of almost ritual significance in BORDEAUX, where many CHÂTEAUX make their so-called GRAND VIN carrying the château name by selecting and BLENDING only the best lots. The rejected lots may either be blended together to make a SECOND WINE (and occasionally even a third wine) or be sold off in bulk to a NÉGOCIANT carrying only the local APPELLATION (Margaux or St-Julien, for example).

This selection process typically takes place between the third and sixth month after the HARVEST (much later in SAUTERNES) and involves the MAÎTRE DE CHAI (winemaker), any OENOLOGIST regularly working for the property, and the proprietor, who must bear the considerable financial sacrifice of exclusions from the *grand vin,* which may sell for three or more times the price of the associated second wine. It is at this stage that the decision is usually taken over whether to incorporate any PRESS WINE.

The normal procedure is to taste samples from each *cuve* or FERMENTATION VESSEL and then simply decide whether it is of sufficiently high quality for the *grand vin.* It has usually been assumed that any blend of wines from the same property is likely to be harmonious. In most other Old World wine regions, especially BURGUNDY, holdings are too small to allow this selectivity, although Chave of HERMITAGE in the Rhône, for example, is notable for keeping lots from different parcels of vineyard separate until a final assembly just before bottling.

In the New World, such a process is likely to involve the assembly of blends of various different quality levels and character. In this case there may be extensive experiments with small samples of each lot—known as bench blending—before final blends are decided upon. Here the winemaker is concerned not just with each lot's inherent quality but also with its affinity with other components in the blend.

Assyrtico, or **Assyrtiko,** top-quality white grape variety grown increasingly widely in GREECE. Its origins lie on the island of SANTORINI but its ability to retain acidity in a hot climate has encouraged successful experimentation with it elsewhere, notably on the north eastern mainland around Halkidiki. Its severe mineral profile has made it a successful blending partner for MALAGOUSIA, Sauvignon Blanc, and Sémillon. Its wines can age relatively well.

Asti, town and province in PIEMONTE in north west Italy whose name appears in those of fruity local VARIETAL wines made from the likes of BARBERA, DOLCETTO, FREISA, GRIGNOLINO, MALVASIA, and MOSCATO D'ASTI. Moscato d'Asti is the superior version of the well-known sparkling wine that was until recently known as **Asti Spumante**, both of them being produced in a much wider area than the province of Asti.

In 1993, along with Moscato d'Asti, Asti Spumante was elevated to DOCG status and renamed **Asti**, largely in an effort to distinguish it from the host of FRIZZANTE or sparkling wines produced in Italy from a host of grape varieties of very varying quality.

The light, sweet SPUMANTE of Asti is, like the superior Moscato d'Asti, produced from the MOSCATO Bianco grape in the provinces of Asti, Cuneo, and Alessandria. The total area cultivated, which was 92,000 ha/227,000 acres worked by 80,000 vine-growers in the early 1960s, had declined 30 years later to 40,000 ha/98,800 acres worked by 37,000 growers. This contraction has not been mirrored by a dramatic fall in the amount of wine produced, however, since most of the land that has gone out of production was in marginal sites, while the remaining vineyard surface is more energetically exploited.

As a blended wine produced in extremely large quantities (nearly 650,000 hl/17 million gal per year, by far the largest single Italian DOC, more than half as much again as SOAVE, Italy's second most important DOC), Asti is dominated by the large commercial houses of Piemonte, most if not all clustered around the town of Canelli, where production of Asti Spumante began in the 1850s. The 18 largest houses control approximately 80 per cent of the total production, which has now surpassed 80 million bottles per year according to official figures, the great majority of them exported. The combination of large-volume production and small-scale viticulture has necessarily made Asti a blended wine from many sources, a fact which has tended to mask the significant quality differences from zone to zone and the different characteristics of the Moscato Bianco grape in a variety of TERROIRS. Thus far the NÉGOCIANT houses, unlike their counterparts in CHAMPAGNE, have shown no interest in any demarcation of subzones or of separate bottlings of wine of distinctive or superior provenances.

Asti differs significantly from its cousin, Moscato d'Asti: its ALCOHOLIC STRENGTH is higher (between 7 and 9.5 per cent against the maximum 5.5 per cent of Moscato d'Asti), as is its FIZZINESS (3.5–4 atmospheres of pressure in the bottle against a maximum of 1.7 atmospheres in Moscato d'Asti). The best and ripest grapes are used for Moscato d'Asti. As a more alcoholic wine with a smaller quantity of RESIDUAL SUGAR, Asti should, in theory, taste drier than Moscato d'Asti; in practice, the sweetness is even more marked due to the less pronounced aromas and flavours that are the inevitable result of less ripe grapes from zones that have been planted more to supply the needs of the négociant houses than for

any verifiable aptitude for producing fine Moscato.

One encouraging sign, however, is the recent decision on the part of important small estates, in many cases prestigious producers of Moscato d'Asti, to produce an Asti from their own grapes.   D.T. & D.C.G.

astringency is a complex of sensations resulting from the shrinking, drawing, or puckering of the tissues of the mouth. Earlier, astringency had been considered as one of the primary TASTE sensations, like sweetness, sourness, and particularly BITTERNESS, with which it has often been confused. It is now recognized as a tactile response not dependent on the taste receptors, however. The word is derived from the Latin *ad stringere*, meaning to bind, which presaged the finding that astringent materials could bind to, and precipitate, PROTEINS. The most important astringent materials are TANNINS, and it is these components of a wine that are responsible for the puckery, tactile sensation that is most noticeable in young red wines (but can be sensed in some white wines too, particularly those from hard-pressed grapes). However, an appropriate degree of astringency contributes very positively to the palatability of a red wine, and astringency is central to the TEXTURE and MOUTHFEEL of a wine. Some of the terms used by tasters to describe the astringency of a wine—hard, soft, green, resinous, leathery, gripping, aggressive, supple, for example—are the same as those used to describe the tannins of the wine. Although it is known that the astringent sensation is modified by acidity and sweetness, the influence of various wine components, including the PHENOLICS and particularly tannins and PIGMENTED TANNINS, on the astringent sensation has been an area of active research in contemporary OENOLOGY.   P.J.W.

Vidal, S., Francis, L., Noble, A., Kwiatkowski, M., Cheynier, V., and Waters, E., 'Taste and mouth-feel properties of different types of tannin-like polyphenolic compounds and anthocyanins in wine', *Analytica Chemica Acta*, 513 (2004), 57–65.

ATF, previously known as BATF. See TTB.

Athenaeus (flourished *c*.AD 200) was born in Naucratis, a Greek city in the Nile Delta in Egypt, and wrote in Greek. Nothing is known about his life, and his surviving work, the *Deipnosophistae*, meaning 'The masters of the art of dining', can be dated only from internal evidence. It describes at length how 23 men dine together in Ancient ROME and records their conversations; their two most frequent topics are HOMER and wine. Two of the participants are the physician GALEN and the lawyer Ulpian of Tyre; the others are not based on real persons. The work consists of 15 books, but the first two and part of the third survive only in excerpts.

Although wine is the second most frequent topic of the diners' conversation, Athenaeus

shows little interest in CONNOISSEURSHIP and none at all in VITICULTURE. Rather than engaging in systematic discussion, Athenaeus assembles curious facts, makes lists, and proposes (often incorrect) etymologies: his enumeration of types of CONTAINERS for wine in Book II exemplifies all these tendencies. Most of the wines which he mentions do not belong to his own day, e.g. Coan, Chian, Mendaean, and Thasian. The famous passage attributed to Galen on the wines of Italy (26c–27d) promises to be a discussion of Italian wines in Galen's day, the second half of the second century, but it has none of the rigour and acumen of the great medical writer; in fact, it is almost certainly not by Galen at all. The passage is a series of bald statements, telling us mainly whether a wine is sweet or dry and whether or not it was strong; it does not offer any comparison with wines of earlier periods or different regions. It gives some optimum drinking dates: Alban is best at 15 years old; FALERNIAN needs a minimum of 10 years' ageing, is best after 15 to 20 and, if any older, gives headaches. Falernian can be sweet or dry: we know from other writings (mainly Galen's own) that dry wines were popular in the second century AD, whereas in PLINY's day good wines appear to have been sweet. Athenaeus himself gives us no such historical perspective, however: he is not a historian but a contented collector of snippets.

H.M.W.

Brock, R., and Wilson, H., 'Wine in Athenaeus', in D. Braund and J. Wilkins (eds.), *Athenaeus and his World* (Exeter, 2000).

Athiri, widely grown white Greek vine variety whose lemony produce is often used for blending, notably with the nobler ASSYRTICO.

atypical ageing (ATA) or **untypical ageing** (UTA), known as *untypischer Alterungsnote* in Germany, where it was first documented in the late 1980s, is the term used to identify a phenomenon found predominantly in cool climate white wines. Affected wines lose their varietal character very early, develop atypical aromas and flavours described as naphthalene (moth balls), wet towel, or old furniture varnish, and are characterized by an increase in bitterness. Research so far suggests that this is linked to insufficient assimilable NITROGEN in the vine. The most likely cause is vine stress, particularly in dry vineyards and in dry years. This may explain why the phenomenon has so far been identified in regions such as northern Gemany, the Pacific Northwest, and the eastern US, but not in Australia.

B.W.Z & J.Ha.

Siebert, T., Herderich, M., Francis, L., Pollnitz, A., 'No evidence of "atypical ageing taint" in Australian white wine', *Australia and New Zealand Wine Industry Journal*, 18/5 (2003), 55–6, 58.

Zoecklein, B.W., 'Atypical ageing', Enology Notes, 77 (2003), www.fst.vt.edu/extension/enology/enologynotes.html

Aubance, Coteaux de l', small but sometimes excellent sweet white wine appellation in ANJOU on the left bank of the river Loire just south of the town of Angers and immediately north of Coteaux du Layon. It takes its name from the Aubance, a tributary of the Loire. Total production is rather more than that of SAVENNIÈRES across the river to the west, but the best results come from Chenin planted on outcrops of heat-retaining SLATE. The standard of wine-making is high, and a high proportion of the racy, sweet white Chenin Blanc wines made here is snapped up locally or in Paris. Red and dry white Anjou make up the bulk of production in this zone, but in exceptional years Coteaux de l'Aubance can be just as noble, if not always as long-lived, as the Loire's more famous sweet whites, and must owe their sweetness to a succession of TRIES through the vineyard, picking only the ripest grapes, a discipline, unusually, overseen by the INAO. According to the vintage, the wines may be BOTRYTIZED, as in 1997, and may carry the term Sélection de Grains Nobles on the label, or the grapes may be partly raisined on the vine. The wines must have a RESIDUAL SUGAR level of at least 17 g/l; any lower and they must be declassified to Anjou Blanc. Red wines produced in this zone are sold as Anjou-Villages Brissac. Domaines Daviau, de Montgilet, and Richou are star performers. See also LOIRE, including map.

Aubin Blanc, almost extinct white grape once grown in France's MOSELLE. DNA PROFILING at DAVIS confirmed that it is distinct from **Aubin Vert**, an even rarer local pale-skinned variety, and suggested that Aubin Blanc, like the PINOT family, is the possible progeny of GOUAIS BLANC and SAVAGNIN.

Aubun, rather ordinary black-berried vine variety of the southern Rhône. After a strange increase in popularity noted by the French agricultural census of 1979, it is in decline but was still almost among France's top 20 red wine vines in 2000 with a total of 1,400 ha/ 3,500 acres planted. It produces wine not unlike a softer version of CARIGNAN, and formed part of James BUSBY's original vine collection taken to Australia, where isolated plantings can still be found. Officially approved as an ingredient in many appellations of the southern Rhône, eastern Languedoc, and Provence (including CHÂTEAUNEUF-DU-PAPE), it yields well and buds late, offering good resistance to spring frosts. It is found in the southern Rhône, Gard, and the Aude, but is being systematically pulled up as a vine with no useful future for quality wine production.

auctions of wine are the sale of wine by lots by an auctioneer acting as agent for the seller or, in certain instances, as the seller in his or her own right.

History

Auctions have long been an integral part of the wine TRADE. Wine was sold by auction in Ancient ROME and, in the Middle Ages, before it became commonplace for buyers to visit wine regions, wine shipped in barrel to its final destination (see CONTAINERS) was frequently sold by auction as well as by private contract. In Britain, wine auctions were common at trading ports such as Leith in Edinburgh, Scotland, where the auction room in The Vaults testifies to a once lively auction trade in casks of fine bordeaux. In Germany, the practice of selling wine by auction under the names of village and vintage became well established in the 18th century. The Nassauer'sche Domäne in the Rheingau was among the first to initiate the movement towards establishing conditions of sale by auction in the 1830s.

As wine trading became increasingly competitive with improved transportation and more sophisticated communications, the need for producers to sell their wine by auction diminished. Whereas historically wine auctions were used as a means of selling young or relatively young wine in barrel, today's commercial auction trade relies on bottled wines at all stages of maturity. Once wine was packaged in BOTTLES stoppered with CORKS from the end of the 17th century, it became capable of BOTTLE AGEING and full maturation. With, literally, a new lease of life for fine wine, exceeding decades and, in rare instances, even a century or more, fine wine transcended its previous status as a short-term commodity.

Once wine became capable of being traded across generations, it naturally attracted admirers, collectors, and investors (see INVESTMENT). It became something that, at its finest, could be regarded with the same admiration as a work of art or any other classic auction room collectable. Wine captured in bottle led to a market in older wines whose reputation, based on VINTAGE and name, created a comprehensible and measurable scale of values.

Sales of wine were generally held as part of house sales until wine departments were established in the world's two leading auction houses. Christie's established its wine department in 1966, when Michael BROADBENT was recruited from the Bristol wine merchant HARVEYS to build up the department to meet the demands of an increasingly specialized and sophisticated international market. The first auction of the new era was held on 11 October 1966 and the first season achieved sales amounting to £220,634. Not to be outdone, Sotheby's entered the fray in 1970, holding the first auction of its newly formed wine department on 16 September 1970 in Glasgow.

While Christie's and Sotheby's dominated the wine auction scene for many decades, new auction systems and entrants have challenged the status quo. In the late 1970s, The Chicago Wine Company introduced and popularized the 'silent bid' wine auction system in the US.

Archaic laws in New York state prevented the spread of wine auctions in one of the world's most lucrative markets until the late 1980s. Christie's and Sotheby's initially teamed up with local wine merchants until deregulation in the late 1990s. The French auction market was also deregulated in the late 1990s.

Inefficiencies in the auction wine market during the 1980s also led to increased competition from specialist wine BROKERS such as Farr Vintners and others in the UK. The dot.com boom in the late 1990s spawned electronic wine auction houses. US-based WineBid.com, founded in 1996, established a worldwide network, but intense competition and organizational issues resulted in the closure of its UK, Australian, and European offices. The electronic auction format has been adopted by several wine auction companies, while electronic wine exchange businesses such as Uvine and Liv-ex have brought further competition to the secondary wine market.

Some notable annual auctions

Nevertheless, traditional auctions survive, most notably that of the HOSPICES DE BEAUNE. This former medieval hospice in Burgundy derives a substantial proportion of income for the modern hospital associated with it from the sale of wines produced from vineyards given as bequests over the centuries. Every third Sunday in November, the Hospices holds an annual charity auction accompanied by a long weekend of gargantuan feasting and decadent celebration. At the traditional candle auction, lots named after the Hospices' benefactors, each comprising a number of new 228-l/60-gal barrels, are sold. The auction is unique in that it is a public stage for the NÉGOCIANTS of Beaune to demonstrate their magnanimity, but whether it still also acts as a barometer of the market price for the new vintage in BURGUNDY is a moot point. The success of the Hospices de Beaune auction in combining the sale of wines with the glare of publicity has been the role model for a number of latter-day imitators from LIMOUX to California.

In the heart of Germany's Rheingau, at the Cistercian abbey KLOSTER EBERBACH, the CHARTA group of Riesling producers, which merged with the VDP in 1999, founded Die Glorreichen Tage in 1987, a three-day extravaganza whose focus is the traditional annual auction of German wines. South Africa's Nederburg enhanced its reputation for producing quality wines by establishing the Nederburg auction in 1975, at which lots of its top bottlings and those of other producers are offered for sale. The Nederburg sale in turn spawned the annual auction of the Cape Winemakers' Guild, a group of largely independent cellarmasters that started selling small lots of top wines at auction in 1985.

In the United States, distillers Heublein established the first New World wine auction in

Chicago in 1969. Since then a combination of strict licensing laws and tax advantages to buyers led to a boom in charity wine auctions in the United States, led by the now famous annual Napa Valley Wine Auction (which raised $52m between 1981 and 2005) and, latterly, the Naples Winter Wine Festival in Florida . The prices paid at these charity events are often so inflated by goodwill and/or welcome exhibitionism, however, that they cannot be compared as reliable indicators of the market with the United States' rapidly proliferating commercial auctions.

The professionals

Christie's is the oldest established wine auctioneer. Wine was a prominent feature in James Christie's first sale on 5 December 1766, which, along with household furniture, jewellery, and firearms, included the sale of 'a large quantity of Madeira and high Flavour'd Claret, late the Property of Noble Personage (Deceas'd)'. Three years later, on 7 and 8 September 1769, James Christie held his first sale entirely devoted to wine, a collection of 'Old Hock, Rich Burgundy, Calcavella [Portugal's CARCAVELOS], Malaga and TENT, the property of Captain Fletcher from the West Indies'.

Today's commercial auction scene is dominated by regular sales conducted by a number of professional auction houses, initially London-based. However, wine auctions elsewhere, particularly in the United States, started to present an increasingly serious challenge to London's hegemony in the late 1990s as American cellars started to become an increasingly lucrative source of supply. In the early 1990s, wine auctions were at long last permitted in New York, but only in association with an established retailer. As a result, Sotheby's established a presence in association with Sherry-Lehmann, holding its first sale in New York on 8 October 1994 while Christie's teamed up with Zachy's. The total value of wine sales in the US overtook the UK total in the mid 1990s.

By 2004, the five major companies holding significant live wine auctions in the US were Sotheby's with Aulden Cellars; NYWines-Christie's; Morrell; Acker Merrall & Condit, which holds its own separate on-line auctions; and Zachys, the last becoming one of the most successful thanks in part to the fact that sales are held in the great New York restaurant Daniel, where wining and dining during sales, already common in charity auctions, was introduced. Another American house, Hart Davis Hart, held its debut auction in 2005, thus returning glamorous bricks-and-mortar auctions to Chicago, although it also conducts on-line auctions.

In 2004, Christie's was the world's leading auctioneer with sales totalling $36,367,940 (£18,872,828) followed by Zachys with sales of $26,070,858, then Sotheby's, with sales of $20,750,330 (£11,415,892), then Acker Merrall &

Condit, whose sales totalled $17,079,942. Commercial auctions are also held to a certain extent in other countries, notably France, Belgium, Holland, Switzerland, Italy, and Australia, with occasional sales in Japan.

The introduction of the silent-bid wine auction in the 1980s, followed by the deployment of internet auction technology in the late 1990s has changed the auction format irrevocably. The vibrant cut and thrust of the live auction room is gradually dwindling as internet trading becomes part of our daily lives. While the auction process remains the same, the traditional expert wine auctioneer is increasingly becoming a market analyst and valuer, the electronic bidding system taking care of the sale process. Leading online auctioneers include WineBid.com and Brentwood.com, both California based; iDealwine in Paris; Langton's in Australia; Liv-ex, a trade-to-trade business in the UK; and, also in the UK, Uvine.com, which has moved increasingly from exchange to online auctions.

Trade structure

Broadly speaking, wine auction customers are split between private individuals, who constitute the majority of sellers and buyers, and the wine trade. Private buyers may have any number of different reasons for buying wine. They may be consumers, COLLECTORS, and/or investors (see INVESTMENT). Trade buyers also buy for investment, to fill gaps in a restaurant or merchant's wine list, or as brokers for trade or private clients. Reasons for selling wine vary equally, the traditional three d's of death, debt, and divorce having turned into four, as doctors' orders also become a factor. Private customers may want or need to sell in order to realize the value of their cellar, or part of it, or to finance further purchases, or as executors selling on behalf of an estate. The wine trade may sell to dispose of surplus or bankrupt stock.

Wines traded

Red bordeaux, or claret, remains the staple of the wine auction rooms, accounting for more than 60 per cent of saleroom throughput. It is long lived, enjoys widespread appeal, and it is in relatively plentiful supply. And the relative value of a particular red bordeaux is more readily identifiable than that of any other wine style, the 1855 CLASSIFICATION providing some sort of easily comprehensible framework for evaluating the red bordeaux châteaux most widely traded in the saleroom.

The FIRST GROWTHS—Chx LAFITE, LATOUR, MARGAUX, MOUTON-ROTHSCHILD in the Médoc, HAUT-BRION in what was Graves, AUSONE and CHEVAL BLANC in St-Emilion and the unofficial first growths Ch PÉTRUS and Le PIN of Pomerol—are undisputed members of today's élite. Owing to the classification's rigid composition, a second leading group of properties has emerged, commonly referred to as SUPER

SECONDS. Qualification for this group requires not only the strictest commitment to quality, but a record of consistently high prices, at least since the 1960s, which reflects that policy. More recently, a third group of so-called MICROCHÂTEAUX has emerged, inspired by the success of Le Pin.

Pre-PHYLLOXERA clarets are among the most highly prized items in any sale catalogue. Unique GRANDS FORMATS (large bottles) of old vintages, particularly of first growths, are much sought-after by collectors (see BOTTLE SIZE), although perhaps to a lesser degree than in the late 1980s. Specific VINTAGES play an important part, too, with the price of wines from consecutive years often fluctuating by a factor of three according to the reputation of the vintage. The most highly prized pre-war vintages of the 20th century are 1900, 1920, 1926, 1928, and 1929. In the immediate post-war period, the most sought-after trio are 1945, 1947, and 1949. In the latter half of the 20th century, 1953, 1959, 1961, 1982, 1990, and 2000 rank as the outstanding vintages with 1985, 1986, 1989, 1995, 1996, and 2003 running them close.

A recent saleroom phenomenon is the way prices for relatively recent vintages have started to outstrip the prices of older vintages. Although the state of the global economy plays a part, much of this has to do with the taste, and ratings, of the influential American critic, Robert M. PARKER, who writes mainly about young wines. Thus, for instance, prices of the top châteaux from the acclaimed 2000 vintage were already approaching the level of top 1982 prices by the mid 2000s. There are a number of additional reasons for this, among them the global trend towards drinking wines younger and a genuine shortage of great vintages tilting the balance of supply and demand even further towards demand.

Red bordeaux apart, burgundy is an increasingly significant player in the saleroom with Domaine de la ROMANÉE-CONTI, Roumier, Leflaive, Ramonet, Coche Dury, Ponsot, Rousseau, Jayer, Niellon, and Dugat among the most sought-after wines. In American auctions, California also accounts for a significant percentage of sales. Vintage port is a saleroom regular, albeit on a much smaller scale, with TAYLOR, FONSECA, GRAHAM, WARRE, DOW, CROFT, COCKBURN, and Quinta do NOVAL, the unofficial first growths, as it were, of a group of some 40 or more port houses. In recent years, the FASHION for the finest wines of the Rhône (Hermitage, Côte Rôtie and Châteauneuf-du-Pape) has seen a certain increase in popularity and prices, largely as a result of American demand. Italy and Spain are moving into the frame too as fine and rare wines from these countries begin to appear more frequently in the saleroom. On 9 July 1998, Christie's devoted a sale almost entirely to fine Italian wines. Among Italy's blue chips, GAJA's single-vineyard Barbaresco Sori San Lorenzo and Costa Russi and Barolo Sperss represent solid collectibles along with SUPERTUSCANS Sassicaia, Solaia, Tignanello, and Ornellaia. Older vintages of VEGA SICILIA, Marqués de Murrieta, Marqués de Riscal, CVNE, and Viña Tondonia from Lopez de Heredia are increasingly seen at auction. Wines from Germany, Alsace, Loire, MADEIRA, and TOKAJI make an occasional appearance.

The wines of the New World, California and Australia in particular, are beginning to make more of an impact too as their track record for ageing becomes more widely accepted and new wines appear on the secondary market. Demand for California wines is particularly strong in the US, less so elsewhere, with the 1994, 1997, and 2001 vintages being in particular demand. While such older rarities as the 1941 Inglenook Winery Cabernet can fetch very high prices, the focus today is on such CALIFORNIA CULT names as Bryant Family, Harlan Estate, and Screaming Eagle. It was a wine from Australia, PENFOLDS Grange, that was arguably the first New World wine to be recognized internationally as a collectable equivalent to a Bordeaux FIRST GROWTH. Grange is already a saleroom classic, while Henschke's Hill of Grace is also regarded as an important single-vineyard Shiraz. Langton's Classification of Australian Wine, first published in 1991, recognizes the track record of Australian wine at auction, reflecting an increasingly diverse market largely underpinned by BAROSSA VALLEY Shiraz, and COONAWARRA and MARGARET RIVER Cabernet Sauvignon. Australian cult names Chris Ringland (Three Rivers), Noon, Clarendon Hills, Wild Duck Creek, and Torbreck have further spiced up the auction market.

Record prices
Red bordeaux is the consistent pace-setter for wine auction PRICES, with almost all the red wine records being held by these wines. The record price for a single bottle of wine at auction was achieved at Christie's on 5 December 1985, when the late Malcolm Forbes, the American publishing magnate, paid £105,000 for a bottle of 1787 Ch Lafitte (sic). This bottle, said by its owner Hardy Rodenstock to have been found in a bricked-up cellar in Paris, and wheel-engraved with the markings '1787 Lafitte Th.J', was believed to have been a bottle of 1787 Ch Lafite belonging to Thomas JEFFERSON, the third president of the United States.

Although the circumstances surrounding the cache have never been disclosed, this has not prevented two more of the so-called Jefferson bottles from achieving world records. A half-bottle of 1784 Ch Margaux was sold for 180,000 French francs (about £18,000 at the prevailing exchange rate) to the American publisher Marvin Shanken at Bordeaux's wine fair Vinexpo in 1987, and in 1986 a world record was set for a bottle of white wine when a 1784 Ch d'YQUEM was sold at Christie's to Iyad Shiblaq, a Jordanian collector, for £36,000.

Other 20th-century records include £71,500 for a jeroboam (six bottles in one) of 1945 Ch Mouton Rothschild; $112,000 for a case of 1945 Ch Mouton Rothschild sold in New York on 13 April 1996; and, for a case of white wine, £15,400 for 1921 Ch d'Yquem. In May 1997, Sotheby's broke the record for an individual sale when a sizeable portion of a collection of wine amassed by the composer Andrew Lloyd Webber was sold for just under £3.7 million. The record was short-lived. Christie's Grand Cru sale held later that year on 18 and 19 September brought in more than £7 million from the sale of wine collected by a Norwegian businessman. In November 1999, Sotheby's offered 'The Greatest Private Wine Cellar in the World' in New York, a total of 3,235 lots going under the hammer for a world record total of $14,414,805.

How to buy and sell at auction
The public forum of the auction room and the intrinsically competitive aspect of bidding for lots often creates an atmosphere of tension and excitement in the saleroom in which it is easy for inexperienced participants to get carried away. The electronic format—which attempts to replicate the live auction environment—differs in that all lots are sold at exactly the same moment. The excitement of an auction sale occurs in the last 30 minutes before the auction closes. All the information required about a particular auction is contained in the auction catalogue which contains details of the lots, estimated prices, conditions of sale, and other general information on such matters as FILL LEVELS, bottlings, delivery charges, premiums, and other additions to the hammer price such as value added tax and excise duties payable where applicable. The internet auction format has taken catalogues one step further, providing potential buyers with instant information regarding vintage conditions, regional information, and tasting notes.

The wines to be sold are contained in numbered lots. Apart from a number and an estimated price band from lowest to highest, the description of each lot identifies the wine by name, bottle size, and vintage where applicable. The more reputable the auction house, the more it takes steps to guarantee the provenance of the wine to protect both the buyer and its own reputation. Given the importance of the condition of the wine, especially older wines, and since wines are not generally available for inspection, the catalogue specifies exact fill, or ULLAGE levels ('mid shoulder' or 'bottom neck', for example, levels illustrated in the catalogue), the condition of the LABEL, whether the wine comes in its own wooden CASE (sometimes abbreviated to 'owc.'), and will generally mention if a cellar is of exceptional pedigree or in previously undisturbed condition.

Auction house policy may vary on inspection and the condition of the wine to be sold.

Sotheby's do not open original wooden cases, while Christie's do unless the wines are young. Pre-sale tastings are not the lavish affairs they once were, but limited pre-sale tastings still take place occasionally. Lots which are of special interest may be supplemented by the auctioneer's tasting notes. Bidding may be by hand or, more often today, by waving a numbered paddle to attract the auctioneer's attention. Bidding is, unless otherwise stated, per dozen bottles. In the US, the auction room may be set up like a restaurant, with round tables and chairs, and lunch provided for all registered bidders.

Advance commission bids form a substantial proportion of bids received. Both Christie's and Sotheby's estimate that they may receive anything from 2,500 to 10,000 commission bids per sale. Whereas on average nearly two-thirds of lots used to go under the hammer in the saleroom itself, that proportion has dropped to only about a third in the intensely international fine wine market of the late 1990s. Commission, or absentee, bids are treated in exactly the same way as bids in the room. The successful bidders obtain their lot at one increment above the underbidder. In the event of two commission bids of the same amount, it is the one received first that takes precedence.

See COOPERAGE for details of French OAK auctions, and INFORMATION TECHNOLOGY for the auctioneer-free possibilities of wine auctions in the future. A.H.L.R.

Aurore, otherwise known as Seibel 5279, a FRENCH HYBRID once widely planted in the United States and still found in colder states. Adaptable and productive, it ripens early but it prone to ROT and its floral-scented wines are of no great distinction.

Ausbruch, famous wine style of AUSTRIA, a speciality of the town of RUST on the Neusiedlersee in Burgenland. Ausbruch is a close etymological relative of Aszú, a term commonly used in TOKAJI, where Hungary's most famous sweet wine is made. Tokaji and Ausbruch were probably developed at very much the same time, in the early 17th century. Ausbruch was traditionally made by adding a small proportion of non-botrytized grapes to the juice of, mainly FURMINT, grapes concentrated by NOBLE ROT, whose incidence is encouraged by the proximity of the shallow lake and the warm climate of the Pannonian plain. Austrian wine law requires Ausbruch to be made entirely from overripe, naturally shrivelled, or BOTRYTIZED grapes which reach a MUST WEIGHT of 27 °KMW (139 °OECHSLE). However, producers in Rust limit themselves to 30 °KMW. A mix of varieties is used, such as Welschriesling, Chardonay, Pinot Blanc, Traminer. Furmint, subject to a current revival in Austria, is so far only rarely grown.

Ausbruch may be fermented and aged in barrel or stainless steel.

Auslese, one of the riper Prädikats in the QMP quality wine category defined by the GERMAN WINE LAW. Auslese means literally 'selected harvest' and, from the 1994 vintage, the grapes should theoretically have been picked at least a week after a preliminary picking of less ripe grapes. In practice, an Auslese may well have been picked early in the harvest; the best BOTRYTIS for the best vinous results oftens occurs earlier on. Specific minimum MUST WEIGHTS are laid down for each combination of vine variety and region and range from 83 to 100 °Oechsle. At their finest, these are sweet, often BOTRYTIZED wines which can be sold at lower prices than the even riper and considerably rarer BEERENAUSLESE and TROCKENBEERENAUSLESE Prädikats. Auslese is usually associated with SWEET WINES. However, high-alcohol dry wines are on the increase in Germany. Such wines are often designated as Auslese trocken, but some vintners prefer to use the designation Spätlese even if the must weight on which their dry wine is based far exceeded the minimum for Auslese. Auslesen made from most of the new GERMAN CROSSINGS—with the notable exceptions of Rieslaner and Scheurebe—should be treated with suspicion as they rarely have the ACIDITY to balance the sweetness, but Riesling Auslesen can be some of Germany's finest and most characteristic wines. They can last for decades.

See also AUSTRIA.

Ausone, Château, minuscule but exceptionally fine estate on the edge of the town of ST-ÉMILION. It was named in 1781 after the Roman poet Ausonius who certainly had a vineyard in the Gironde, but probably one facing the river GARONNE than one in St-Émilion. Recorded in the 1868 Cocks et Féret's *Bordeaux et ses vins* (see LITERATURE OF WINE) as belonging to M. Cantenats, it then passed to a nephew, M. Lafargue, and then to his nephew, Edouard Dubois-Challon, who raised the reputation of the château to the leading position in St-Émilion up to the 1920s, when it was challenged by Ch CHEVAL-BLANC, the only other château to be ranked 'A' in the official CLASSIFICATION of St-Émilion in 1955. From 1939 to the mid 1970s, Ausone was not, with a few exceptional vintages, producing wines of the longevity of their 19th-century predecessors, although there was a marked improvement after the arrival of a new RÉGISSEUR, Pascal Delbeck, in 1976. Until the late 1990s, 50 per cent was owned by Mme Dubois-Challon, widow of Edouard, and 50 per cent by Alain Vauthier, who married Edouard's daughter Cécile, an unsatisfactory arrangement which ended with Vauthier taking control of, and completely renovating, the extraordinary cellars in limestone caves originally excavated to provide

stone for building the town. The wine itself has also been dramatically modernized, and the vineyard recuperated.

The estate consists of a mere 7 ha/18 acres—50 per cent MERLOT vines and 50 per cent CABERNET FRANC—on the steep slopes of the Côtes (see ST-ÉMILION) that run along the right bank of the DORDOGNE just below the town. Production of Ausone averages 2,000 cases. E.P.-R. & J.R.

Australia had become the world's sixth biggest wine producer by 2005, producing 14.7 million hl/388 million gal of wine in 2004 (an increase of 73 per cent on the amount produced five years previously). After a flurry of vineyard expansion, total vineyard area was almost 160,000 ha/395,000 acres by 2003. Australia makes every one of the major wine styles from aromatic, dry white table wine through to wines fashioned in the image of vintage port. Some of its wines—the unwooded Semillons of the Hunter Valley, the fortified Muscats and Tokays of north east Victoria—have no direct equivalent elsewhere, but overall the wines manage to be at once distinctively Australian yet fit easily into the world scene.

Nearly 2,000 wineries are spread through every state. Most of the wineries are small; 94 per cent of the annual CRUSH comes from one of the five largest companies, FOSTER'S (Lindemans, Rosemount, Penfolds), CONSTELLATION (Hardys, Banrock Station), PERNOD RICARD (Orlando, Jacob's Creek, Wyndham Estates), McGuigan Simeon, and Casella, owners of the hugely successful YELLOW TAIL brand.

As in California, over 1,800 of those small wineries have come into existence since 1970, offering weekend or retirement occupations for people from all walks of life, notably doctors and lawyers. In typical Australian style, however, the owners have frequently appointed themselves as hands-on viticulturists and winemakers. Nevertheless, perhaps due to the trickle-down effect of the renowned AUSTRALIAN WINE RESEARCH INSTITUTE at Adelaide and the university wine schools (see ADELAIDE), standards are extremely high.

The Australian wine SHOW system has also played a major role in promoting technical excellence and in shaping style. The lessons of the show ring have been reinforced by the well-known penchant Australians have for travel. Indeed, Australia spawned the so-called FLYING WINEMAKERS, a group of oenological guns for hire who follow the vintage around the world. On a less formal basis, many Australian winemakers have made a point of travelling and working overseas, principally in Europe. See AUSTRALIAN INFLUENCE.

Add this experience to the technological base, take in the effect of the sunny Australian climate, and allow for the surge in plantings of such popular grape varieties as Chardonnay and Cabernet Sauvignon, and it is not hard to see why Australian exports have increased

out of all recognition since 1983–4. In that year they were 8.9 million litres, worth $9.6 million. Australia simply did not rate a mention in the list of world wine exporters. By 2003–4, its exports were 575 million litres worth $2.55 billion dollars, placing it behind only France, Italy, and Spain in value of wine exports. It is not too fanciful to suggest that the wines have an openness, a confident, user-friendly style which reflects the national character (and climate). Australian winemakers have opted to preserve as much as possible of the flavour of the grape, yet to do so with a delicacy of touch, producing intensely fruity white wines and soft, mouth-filling red wines which appeal to the heart as much as to the mind. In so doing they have (willingly) sacrificed structural complexity at the altar of simple fruit flavour.

Between 1975 and 1985 sales of dry white wine quadrupled, while those of red wine were static, declining to a low point in 1979, but then recovering slowly. Since 1985 red wine sales have more than doubled, while those of white wine have marginally declined. What is more, the increase in sales of red wine has been mainly in 750 ml bottles, sales of which have risen by over 300 per cent and show no signs of stopping. FORTIFIED wines have declined (over a longer period) from 70 to 8 per cent. In turn, 50 per cent of all Australian wine sold locally is packaged in the ubiquitous wine 'cask' (see BOXES), usually in a 4.5-l (1.2-gal) configuration. It should come as no surprise to find that Australia has the highest annual per capita wine consumption in the English-speaking world, peaking at 21.6 l in 1986 before declining to a low of 17.6 l in 1991. It has since risen to 20.4 l, reflecting off-setting trends in 750 ml quality wine consumption (rising) and cask-quality consumption (falling).

History

'On 24th January two bunches of grapes were cut in the Governor's garden from cuttings of vines brought three years before from the Cape of Good Hope.' The year was 1791, the chronicler Watkin Tench, and the site of the garden is now occupied by the Hotel Inter-Continental in Sydney's Macquarie Street.

Between 1820 and 1840 commercial viticulture was progressively established in New South Wales, Tasmania, Western Australia, Victoria, and finally South Australia. It was based upon comprehensive collections of *Vitis vinifera* vines imported from Europe: there are no native vines in Australia, and neither CROSSINGS nor HYBRIDS have ever taken root. Italian immigrants (in the Riverlands), Silesians (in the Barossa and Clare valleys), Dalmatians (in the Swan valley of WESTERN AUSTRALIA), and Swiss (Yarra valley and Geelong in Victoria) all played key roles in the establishment of viticulture.

By 1870, South Australia, Victoria, and New South Wales all had substantial industries: that year they produced 8.7 million l/2.3 million

Australia

Wine-growing regions

UPPER HUNTER

MUDGEE

HUNTER VALLEY

NEW SOUTH WALES

ORANGE

SOUTH AUSTRALIA

CLARE VALLEY

COWRA

Sydney

RIVERINA

EDEN VALLEY RIVERLAND

MILDURA

SUNRAYSIA

Murrumbidgee

HILLTOPS

CANBERRA DISTRICT

BAROSSA VALLEY

Adelaide

ADELAIDE HILLS

McLAREN VALE

LANGHORNE CREEK

SWAN HILL

Murray

Canberra

GUNDAGAI

RUTHERGLEN TUMBARUMBA

PADTHAWAY

MOUNT BENSON

WRATTONBULLY

AVOCA

Bendigo

GLENROWAN

GOULBURN VALLEY

VICTORIA

Pacific Ocean

COONAWARRA

GRAMPIANS

Ballarat HEATHCOTE

YARRA VALLEY

HENTY

GEELONG

Melbourne

MORNINGTON PENINSULA

Tasman Sea

NORTHERN TERRITORY

WESTERN AUSTRALIA

QUEENSLAND

SOUTH AUSTRALIA

GRANITE BELT

SWAN VALLEY

NEW SOUTH WALES

GREAT SOUTHERN MARGARET RIVER

VICTORIA

GEOGRAPHE

TASMANIA

PIPERS BROOK

TAMAR RIVER Launceston

TASMANIA

COAL RIVER Hobart

0   200 km

gal of wine. Twenty years later Victoria alone was making twice that amount, more than the other two states combined. But PHYLLOXERA (discovered near Geelong in 1877), changing land use, a swing from dry wine production to fortified wine, the establishment of irrigated vineyards along the Murray river, and the removal of state trade barriers after Federation in 1901 saw South Australia comprehensively usurp Victoria's dominant position.

By 1930, South Australia was producing over 75 per cent of Australia's wine and the Barossa valley had become the centre of production, processing not only its own grapes but much of those grown in the RIVERLANDS, then and now the engine-room of Australian bulk wine production in the same way as California's CENTRAL VALLEY. As the geographic base moved from the cooler parts of Victoria to the warmer regions of South Australia, and specifically as the Murray and then Murrumbidgee Riverlands came into production, so the type of wine being produced changed.

Between 1927 and 1939 inclusive, Australia exported more wine to the United Kingdom than did France, mainly because of the Imperial Preference system which created trading advantages within the British Commonwealth. Most of this wine was fortified, the remainder being massively alcoholic and ferruginous red wine from north east Victoria, the Barossa valley, and the Southern vales, marketed (*inter alia*) under the Emu wine brand.

The industry of today started to take shape in the mid 1950s. Cold fermentation of white wine in STAINLESS STEEL was pioneered (see RE-FRIGERATION); the big wine companies moved into Coonawarra and (a decade later) nearby Padthaway; and the decline in fortified wine production and consumption contrasted with spectacular growth in the consumption of red table wine (up to 1970) and thereafter white table wine. The 1970s witnessed the arrival of the wine cask, of Cabernet Sauvignon and Chardonnay, the phenomenon of the boutique winery, and the re-establishment of viticulture across the cool corner of south eastern Australia, running east from Coonawarra and Padthaway right through Victoria.

Since the export boom started in the mid 1980s, the Australian industry has literally reinvented itself. Back in 1956, multi-purpose (eating, drying or wine-making) and non-premium varieties (Doradillo, Trebbiano, and such like) accounted for 85 per cent of the crush, premium grapes for 15 per cent. In 1986, the shares were 60 per cent and 40 per cent respectively; in 1994, 30 per cent and 70 per cent; and by 2004, 10 and 90 per cent. There may be a change within the mix of premium varieties, but the percentage of multi-purpose grapes is unlikely to fall much further (if at all) because of the safety valve they represent.

Looked at another way, in 1994, the 'big three' varieties Chardonnay, Shiraz, and Cabernet Sauvignon provided 27 per cent of production; in 2004 they provided just under 60 per cent. The extent and speed of this vineyard reconstruction, achieved without subsidy or direct government support (although tax breaks were offered for vineyard investment for a time), is a prime reason why Australia has such a competitive edge over Old World producers.

The last two decades of the 20th century saw more of the same: it is obvious, then, that the fine wines of today bear no resemblance to all but a tiny handful of those of 50 years ago. The next 50 years will bring further refinement, a continuation of the trend towards quality, and a decrease in the use of chemicals in all aspects of grape-growing and, to a lesser degree, wine-making. It is certain that the industry will continue to grow, but only the bravest prophet would suggest a further degree of change equivalent to that of the second half of the 20th century.

Climate

With a land mass similar to that of the United States of America, winter snowfields larger than those of Switzerland, and with viticulture in every state, one-line descriptions of the Australian climate are hazardous. For all that, there are two basic weather patterns, one affecting Western Australia, South Australia, Victoria, and Tasmania (the southern states), the other governing Queensland and New South Wales.

The southern states experience a winter–spring rainfall pattern, with a dry summer and early autumn. Ridges of high pressure sweep across the southern half of the continent from Perth to Melbourne during the vines' growing season, uninterrupted by mountain ranges; daytime temperatures typically range between 25 °C/77 °F and 35 °C/95 °F.

There is a less profound maritime influence than in California; the sea temperature is warmer, and the diurnal temperature ranges are less (see TEMPERATURE VARIABILITY). The resultant even accumulation of heat in the premium wine regions is seen by Australian researchers to be a major factor in promoting wine quality (and, more controversially, style).

Using the California heat degree system developed by WINKLER, the climate varies between region I and mid region III, with a preponderance in region II. Because of the lack of summer rainfall, IRRIGATION is considered as important for quality as for quantity. In the much hotter and drier Riverland of South Australia, Victoria, and New South Wales, it becomes as essential as it is in California's San Joaquin valley, and is unashamedly used to boost production.

The other, more northerly, weather system derives from the tropics. It provides a more even rainfall pattern, higher temperatures, and higher humidity. This system defines the subtropical climate for much of the rapidly increasing Queensland wine industry, and the coastal regions of New South Wales. The Hunter valley is prone to receive rather too much of its annual rainfall during HARVEST, only to suffer the subsequent dual burden of winter and spring drought. Its redeeming feature is the humidity and afternoon cloud cover which reduces stress on the vines and reduces the impact of its region IV heat load (see CLIMATE CLASSIFICATION for details).

Geography

Vine-growing in Australia is concentrated in the south eastern corner of this vast country. For more detail, see under the state or territory names which are, in declining order of importance as grape growers, SOUTH AUSTRALIA, NEW SOUTH WALES, VICTORIA, WESTERN AUSTRALIA, TASMANIA, QUEENSLAND, and CANBERRA. Considerable quantities of grapes and wine are trucked over state boundaries, however, for blending and bottling. EUROPEAN UNION laws demand that VARIETAL wines, labelled with a grape variety, be labelled with an officially recognized region. The **South Eastern Australia Zone** was created for this purpose and is a vast area encompassing all three of the most important wine states, including the important irrigated regions RIVERLAND and RIVERINA. This somewhat vague description is one of the most common on Australian lower-priced wine labels in export markets.

Viticulture

Equal pay for women, introduced in the latter part of the 1960s, had some unforeseen consequences. One was a major stimulus to the development of mechanized viticulture, initially MECHANICAL HARVESTING, which is responsible for about 80 per cent of the nation's crop, but in due course extending to pruning and, in the latter part of the 1980s, to all aspects of canopy management during the growing season. MECHANICAL PRUNING machines, which trim the canopy, lift and clip the foliage wires, pluck leaves in the fruiting zone, while simultaneously spraying herbicides were already common by the early 1990s. They have, however, fallen out of favour in some regions, and particularly in Coonawarra.

International cost comparisons carried out in the early 1990s for the Penfold Wine Group established what common sense suggested: Australia is able to grow and harvest grapes more economically than California or France (although not necessarily more economically than Chile, Argentina, or South Africa). This big-company, broad-acre approach to viticulture was carried to its logical conclusion with the development of so-called MINIMAL PRUNING in the late 1970s. This involves no winter pruning at all; the vine is allowed to grow unchecked save for light trimming and skirting during the summer months, demonstrating a hitherto unsuspected capacity for self-regulation.

At the other end of the spectrum, Australasian viticulturists and researchers have been at the forefront in developing advanced TRELLIS SYSTEMS and CANOPY MANAGEMENT systems. While these glory under such science fiction names as RT2T and TK2T, they can be seen as doing no more than recognizing what the French have practised for centuries: namely, that SUNLIGHT interception on buds and grape bunches is essential, as is a proper balance between CANOPY and crop level, or YIELD.

As in California, Oregon, and elsewhere, new vineyards in premium areas, particularly those in cooler regions, are being established with VINE DENSITIES two or three times greater than traditionally used, and with specifically adapted trellis systems. The aim is better-quality grapes at yields which may in fact be greater than those of traditional plantings.

The other major development is the move towards what is loosely called SUSTAINABLE VITICULTURE, with phrases such as INTEGRATED PEST MANAGEMENT coming into general (viticultural) usage. The Australian climate may prove less amenable than that of California (rather more growing season rainfall, higher humidity, and the scourge of DOWNY MILDEW), but there is an ineluctable move away from fungicides, pesticides, and herbicides towards more 'natural' grape growing (see ORGANIC VITICULTURE).

While the Australian climate is less suited to sustainable viticulture than might appear at first sight, the overall health of the vineyards appears to be good. PHYLLOXERA has never entered the states of South Australia, Western Australia, Tasmania, nor most of New South Wales (including the Hunter valley), and is not present in the bulk wine-producing Riverland. Small parts of Victoria remain affected, but very strict quarantine legislation, actively enforced and respected by viticulturists, prevented any spread from infested areas during the second half of the 20th century, with only one small exception.

Grafting, not as protection against phylloxera but for the entirely different purpose of changing vine variety, is practised (see TOP GRAFTING), and is playing a role in the shift towards premium grape varieties. However, the greater impetus comes from replanting and new plantings rather than from top grafting.

Wine-making

The typical medium-sized modern Australian winery is comprehensively equipped, especially in comparison with its counterpart in Europe. It has a laboratory capable of carrying out most basic ANALYSIS; a powerful REFRIGERATION system for cooling fermentation in insulated stainless steel fermenters, probably computer-controlled; and a must chiller to cool white grapes immediately after they have been crushed (unless they were machine harvested at night). The CRUSHER, PRESS, and FILTRATION equipment are usually of French, German, or Italian design and fabrication; and it is highly probable that there will be several large ROTOFERMENTERS supplementing the normal array of FERMENTATION VESSELS, including the Australian-designed Potter fermenters (see below).

The winery will routinely work 24 hours a day through the six to eight weeks of harvest using two shifts. The chief winemaker can work up to 18 hours a day. Scrupulous attention is paid to HYGIENE with OZONE (for barrels), caustic soda, and citric acid solutions having replaced chlorine-based products.

Up to this point there is nothing particularly unusual in an international context, unless it be the extent of the refrigeration capacity and the rotofermenter capacity. It is the way Australian winemakers use the equipment, and the underlying technology, which differentiates them (and their wines) from winemakers (and wines) in most other parts of the world.

The basic aims—the maximum preservation of varietal fruit flavour, and an essentially soft and supple structure for both wood-matured white and wood-matured red wines—are achieved in a number of ways.

Primary FERMENTATION and the secondary MALOLACTIC FERMENTATION are initiated speedily by the use of cultured YEASTS, although ambient yeasts are used increasingly. White wine fermentations are carried out at relatively low temperatures (typically 12–14 °C/53–7 °C), usually with clear juice which has been cold-settled (see SETTLING), or filtered and protected against prefermentation oxidation (see PROTECTIVE WINE-MAKING). The more complex, so-called 'dirty French' BARREL FERMENTATION of cloudy juice, LEES CONTACT, malolactic fermentation, and so forth is used for most of the best Chardonnay varietals and a handful of Sauvignon Blancs and Semillon/Sauvignon blends. The majority of aromatic (Riesling, Gewurztraminer) and unwooded whites are made without malolactic fermentation, and are bottled within six to nine months after the harvest.

Because grapes grown in the warmer regions reach chemical RIPENESS and PHYSIOLOGICAL RIPENESS with relatively low levels of acidity, TARTARIC ACID is routinely added during the primary fermentation. In cooler areas, makers of white wines in particular endeavour to harvest the grapes with sufficient natural acidity to preclude acid additions. Nonetheless, Australian winemakers believe that if the ACIDIFICATION takes place at this stage, rather than later (and specifically rather than at BOTTLING), it cannot be distinguished from natural ACIDITY. CHAPTALIZATION, by contrast, is prohibited, even in the coolest regions, although certain forms of ENRICHMENT are permitted.

Red wines other than Pinot Noir are fermented at intermediate temperatures (22–8 °C) in a wide variety of fermentation vessels. The once-popular Potter fermenter (with a central vertical sieve cylinder for draining and pumping over) has been superseded by newer designs with single slope floors and sieves which hug either wall or floor, often with provision for wooden header boards which hold the CAP of grape skins submerged. The handling of PINOT NOIR grapes is more complex: in this case, open-top fermenters are common, and an increasing number of wineries have the luxury of pneumatic devices for PUNCHING DOWN.

Extended MACERATION after fermentation is less commonly practised than in Europe or the United States, and is bypassed altogether with classic wines such as Penfolds Grange, which, like a significant proportion of fine Australian red wines, is pressed and put into barrel while still actively fermenting. The Australian belief is that post-fermentation maceration initially extracts more TANNINS, which entails extending the maceration to soften (by POLYMERIZATION) those tannins, and that this process dulls the fruit aroma and flavour, polymerization being an OXIDATIVE process (see OXIDATION). In the never-ending quest for complexity, it is common to put half the wine in new oak while still fermenting, the remaining half in old oak after extended post-fermentation maceration.

French OAK is preferred for top-quality white wines, for Pinot Noir, and much of the Cabernet Sauvignon produced. American oak is widely used for SHIRAZ, Cabernet–Shiraz blends, and for some Cabernet Sauvignon. Overall, the trend is towards the use of French oak, perhaps in tandem with American oak. Better barrel-making of American oak is lessening the contrast with French oak, and giving less overt oak flavours. For lesser-quality wines, the use of OAK CHIPS (in conjunction with older barrels) is widespread.

After a false start due to an over-enthusiastic rate of use, 'micro-ox' has become standard procedure for lower-priced, big-volume red wines intended for immediate consumption. For the reasons given in MICRO-OXYGENATION, it may also be part of the production of premium wines in the larger, more sophisticated wineries.

Although in certain vintages many winemakers wish it were otherwise, must CONCENTRATION equipment is not generally available. REVERSE OSMOSIS, as opposed to vacuum evaporation, is the preferred method, and some consultancy businesses bring the equipment on-site and carry out the procedure. The high cost limits its use.

Two issues have come to a head since 2000, seemingly unrelated, but both involving the use of SULFUR DIOXIDE. Up to that time, winemakers were following a politically correct path of reducing the total SO_2 in their wines, and adding it in small, incremental doses. Laudable though it may be from a perceived health point of view, the practice has been a root cause in the disconcertingly widespread appearance of BRETTANOMYCES, a problem which was rare as recently as the 1990s. The solution advocated by the AUSTRALIAN WINE RESEARCH INSTITUTE is to add sulfur dioxide in a dose of not less than 50 ppm if *Brett* is detected. A back-up of sterile FILTRATION may be necessary in extreme circumstances. In typical fashion, winemakers have reacted swiftly, and the incidence of *Brett* is in rapid retreat.

The other even more serious problem has been the increased incidence of RANDOM OXIDATION, particularly evident in cork-finished white wines, but also affecting red wines. Its tell-tale manifestation is the premature colour development of a varying but substantial number of white wines in a given case or bin. The percentage affected will grow with time, but once it first occurs, the percentage will be higher than that of CORK TAINT. Research into its causes has been underway for some time, but in the interim those who wish to continue to use corks are being advised to increase significantly the level of free SO_2 at bottling.

The twin problems of cork taint and random oxidation have led to the mass migration of winemakers from cork to SCREW CAP, starting with the Clare Valley Riesling makers, but now extending through all styles of white wines to some of the most prestigious and expensive red wines in the country. It is estimated that 50 per cent of premium to super premium wine bottled in 2005 was sealed with a screw cap.

Vine varieties

The following are the country's most widely planted varieties, red wine varieties first, in descending order of volume of wine produced.

Shiraz (442,102 tonnes in 2004) For long Australia's premier red wine grape in terms of area planted, Shiraz is also now securely planted on the throne. In 2004 it represented 41 per cent of the red wine crush and nearly 24 per cent of the all-grape total. It is grown in virtually every wine region, responding generously to the varying imperatives of TERROIR and climate. The variety is identical to the SYRAH of France and has a long Australian history. During the period in which Cabernet Sauvignon came into vogue, the familiarity of Shiraz led to its being treated with a thoroughly undeserved degree of contempt. However, the old DRY-LAND (non-irrigated) plantings of the Barossa Valley (producing voluptuously rich, potent wines) and the traditional Hunter Valley wines (which become silky with age) initiated a surge of popularity in both domestic and export markets.

If Chardonnay was the ship which launched Australia's export armada, it is Shiraz which took command in the late 1990s, and continues to lead the fleet. It has led to the proliferation of Shiraz plantings in Old and New Worlds alike, as competitors have sought to match the Australian offering. But Australia has four advantages, three of which cannot be lessened. The first is the bank of old vines from 80 to 150 years old in New South Wales, Victoria, and South Australia, all ungrafted and (usually) dry-grown. The second is the equally long experience vignerons have had in growing and making the wine. The third is an international icon, Grange, which only the northern Rhône can match. Fourth is the Joseph's Coat of styles from the huge range of terroir and climate, and the emergence of new regions as promising as Heathcote. Here 500-million-year-old Cambrian greenstone, an igneous rock, has weathered into a vivid red soil which, together with the climatic conditions, seems capable of becoming the greatest area for Shiraz in Australia.

Another new horizon for Shiraz is the looming ability to differentiate clones (of this or any other variety). There appear to be a number of different clones, but we do not know whether Busby's cuttings taken from the Hermitage hillside in 1832 were (as Busby's daily diary suggests) 'of three varieties of vines' (ie clones), or fewer, or more. Other importations may have added to clonal diversity, but there is also the belief that some apparently different clones may not be different at all, the difference in growth habit simply representing local terroir, climate, and several generations of viticultural techniques.

Finally, there has been a rapid and highly successful proliferation of Shiraz–Viognier blends from cooler climate regions.

Cabernet Sauvignon looks likely to challenge the supremacy of Shiraz as its production soared from 24,900 tonnes in 1989 to 317,472 tonnes in 2004. It barely existed in 1966 (100 ha/250 acres, 621 tonnes officially recorded) and, having reached 20,500 tonnes in 1979, lay largely becalmed until the end of the 1980s. Its quality epicentre is COONAWARRA, whence a disproportionate number of Australia's best Cabernet Sauvignons come. There is no question it performs best in moderately cool regions with a climate similar to that of Bordeaux. Its thick skins and relatively loosely formed bunches provide a natural defence against DOWNY MILDEW and BOTRYTIS, which threaten so many regions during the growing season. Thus MARGARET RIVER, GREAT SOUTHERN, WRATTONBULLY, CLARE VALLEY, and parts of central and southern VICTORIA produced most of the best Cabernets outside Coonawarra. That said, it is widely and successfully planted throughout Australia, except for the Riverland. While occasionally outstanding vintages such as 2002 manage to stand conventional wisdom on its head, the outlook is for the removal (or grafting) of Cabernet Sauvignon in the RIVERINA and RIVERLAND regions.

Merlot The rate of growth of Merlot has outpaced all others since 1990 even though Australia took an unusually long time to follow California's lead with the variety. In 1990, there were 509 ha/1,257 acres planted (almost 40 per cent of which was not yet bearing) whereas in 2004, 125,179 tonnes were picked.

As in California, there seems to be confusion over issues of flavour, structure, and style, well covered in the general discussion of the variety in this book. To the extent that there is consensus in Australia, it lies with structure and style: the wine should be medium-bodied, supple, and with soft, ripe tannins. As for flavour and style, some producers favour savoury, olive tones while others seek sweet, red berry fruit, just as some accept lashings of new oak and others do not. The marketplace (both domestic and export) apparently regards these issues as irrelevant, and happily soaks up the wine in all of its manifestations.

Pinot Noir While Pinot Noir (of which 42,427 tonnes were picked in 2004) has not increased at the same death-defying rate as Merlot, its growth has surprised many. Calculating how much is used in sparkling wine production is not easy, but it is the major part. That said, when grown in the right regions, it can produce table wine of genuine, at times exhilarating, distinction. The most consistent regions are Geelong, Gippsland, Mornington Peninsula, Yarra Valley (all around Melbourne), and Tasmania. The Macedon Ranges and Adelaide Hills have one or two excellent makers, the remainder are inconsistent. Australia's very strict and cumbersome QUARANTINE provisions have delayed the introduction of the newest Dijon clones of the now-retired Professor Raymond Bernard, giving New Zealand a distinct competitive advantage, and forcing Australia into a thoroughly unusual role of playing catch-up.

Ruby Cabernet (35,835 tonnes in 2004). This strictly non-premium workhorse CROSSING, used mainly for colour, is in retreat in the face of surplus Shiraz and Cabernet Sauvignon in Riverland and Riverina, where most Ruby Cabernet is planted. Most is used as a blend component in casks (see BOXES) and low-priced, generic, bottled wine.

Grenache (25,935 tonnes in 2004). Until the mid 1960s, 90 per cent of Australia's red wine was fashioned from the three Rhône varieties: Shiraz, Grenache, and Mourvèdre. Then Cabernet Sauvignon and its Bordeaux handmaidens started to make inroads, followed in due course—though initially less convincingly—by Pinot Noir. Shiraz became less fashionable, Grenache and Mourvèdre even less so. Just when it seemed these varieties would cease to be at all significant, the worldwide interest in the Rhône varieties and wine styles reversed the trend. Century-old, dry-farmed, BUSH-pruned Grenache in McLaren Vale (especially) and the Barossa Valley is now in great demand for table wine (previously most went into fortified wines). But, as ever, that portion of the crop produced from high-yielding, irrigated Riverland vineyards will make bland, lollyish wines. While total production has remained static, plantings have

increased since 1996, which masks the removal of Riverland plantings and new plantings in regions such as McLaren Vale and the Barossa Valley.

Petit Verdot first hit the statistical radar in 1999, when 110 ha/272 acres were bearing (and well over twice that were still to come into bearing). In the face of overall red wine surplus (however short-lived that may be), the meteoric rate of new plantings slowed, but has not stopped, and 22,044 tonnes were picked in 2004. It has been planted in many places, in the cooler regions as a blend component with Cabernet Sauvignon, as in the MÉDOC, but its greatest success has come in the Riverland and Riverina. The warm climate guarantees its ripeness, and its strong colour, robust flavour, and substantial tannins result in wines with ample character, even when yields are high. Here it is typically presented as a single varietal wine, and enjoying much success.

Mourvèdre (often called Mataro) is used in precisely the same fashion as Grenache, and has enjoyed the same recovery, plantings increasing from 583 ha/1,440 acres in 1996. A total of 13,583 tonnes were picked in 2004.

Other red varieties of importance: **Sangiovese** leads the Italian band, with **Barbera** and **Nebbiolo** well behind, and unlikely to close the gap. Enthusiasts have planted Sangiovese here, there, and everywhere, some with more success than others. A clear pattern is yet to emerge, but there is much more promise than there is for Nebbiolo. **Cabernet Franc** is becalmed; whether it is simply an issue of poor clones is not certain, but the wines generally lack focus except perhaps for some minor examples in Margaret River and Great Southern. **Malbec** has its moment of glory in the Clare Valley, where it has long formed a synergistic blend with Cabernet Sauvignon. **Durif** is gaining ground for precisely the same reasons as Petit Verdot, providing wines with abundant colour and flavour from high yields in warm regions. Lesser varieties such as **Tannat, Saperavi,** and **Lagrein** are now also in commercial production.

Muscat Gordo Blanco Australia's MUSCAT OF ALEXANDRIA (56,325 tonnes in 2004) provides a more positively flavoured wine than does SULTANA, but production will not increase and hence its relative importance will steadily decline (part is used for DRYING and part for grape juice).

Chardonnay (328,969 tonnes in 2004). In Australia as elsewhere in the world, Chardonnay is seen as the grape of today and of tomorrow. In the first few years of this century, there were predictions of a glut which were not fulfilled, and by 2003 (and 2004) demand comfortably exceeded supply. In a climate of uncertainty about the desirability of new plantings, Chardonnay stands apart, with positive sentiment certain to see increased tonnages in the years ahead, albeit at a less frantic pace. It is grown in every wine region, bending as much to the wills of the viticulturists and winemakers as to the influence of climate and terroir. The style varies from simple to complex, quality from mediocre to excellent, factors increasingly recognized by a widening range of prices. Fluctuations in supply and demand have seen blends with Semillon, Colombard, Chenin Blanc, and so forth come and go; only Western Australia has persisted with an enduring market for Houghton HWB (previously White Burgundy) and Margaret River Classic.

Semillon (rarely written Sémillon in the New World; 103,171 tonnes in 2004) is in one sense Australia's traditional counterpart to Shiraz. Yet it is a conundrum. On the one hand, it has failed to make any substantial headway in export markets, arguably because it is not an internationally recognized single varietal: consumers buy white bordeaux, not Semillon/Sauvignon Blanc. In the domestic market, mature Hunter Valley Semillon (anywhere between five and 20-plus years old) has an ardent following in Sydney, but not elsewhere. Yet despite this, its production continues to rise strongly: once a clear second to Riesling, it is now twice as important (in volume terms, at least). The answer is to be found in the Riverland and Riverina where it produces large crops of grapes which provide a superior wine to Trebbiano or Muscat Gordo Blanco. At the other end of the scale, the best Semillons are 100 per cent varietal, including unoaked versions from the Hunter with an alcohol level of 10.5 to 11 per cent, and those fermented in French oak, with or without a percentage of Sauvignon Blanc, from the Adelaide Hills and Margaret River at more conventional alcohol levels. The Semillon from the latter region, in particular, bears little or no resemblance to Hunter Valley Semillon, being much higher in alcohol (13.5° to 14°), richer, and more flavoursome in its youth.

Colombard (72,117 tonnes in 2004). The ability of this variety to retain ACIDITY has the same attractions in the warmer regions of Australia as in California, although its plantings are on nowhere near the same scale as those in California. The continual rise in importance of this variety is linked to that of Semillon, although it does not have any pretensions to the quality Semillon has at the top end. Rather, it has a prodigious yield (routinely over 130 hl/ha) while retaining high levels of natural acidity, making it an ideal component in blended white wines sold in casks. Its strongholds are the Riverland and Riverina.

Sauvignon Blanc The large increase in Sauvignon Blanc plantings and production (2,334 tonnes in 1995 to 43,107 tonnes in 2004) will come as a surprise to those who dislike the wine, mentally relegating it to second rank. It will be no less surprising to viticultural economists who look at the price/quality competition from New Zealand and, in particular, Marlborough. One explanation is that Marlborough's success has engendered greater interest in and demand for the wine in both domestic and international markets. It also seems that the various interpretations of style (from cold-fermented in stainless steel and early bottled through to complex barrel-fermented wines with a splash of Semillon) all find their mark. The number of producers of Sauvignon Blanc grows week by week, the apparently insatiable market demand pointing to increased plantings in the years ahead.

Riesling (36,585 tonnes in 2004) will surely never regain the pre-eminent position it lost to Chardonnay in 1992 (and other white varieties since that time) but there is tangible proof that the long-heralded Riesling renaissance is at hand, even if the statistics need careful interpretation. In terms of tonnes crushed, the high point came in 1985, with 46,481, the low point in 2000 with 26,800. But during this time Riesling was being removed from regions to which it was not suited (notably the Riverland and Riverina). New plantings in appropriate regions were taking place, but there was a time lag as they came into bearing. Thus the overall yield per hectare had fallen to 8.4 tonnes by 2004, down from 11.6 tonnes in 1991. The near-monopoly of the Clare and Eden Valleys for top-quality Riesling has been challenged by the Great Southern and, on a smaller scale, by Tasmania, but there will be no seismic shift in the foreseeable future.

Verdelho (25,967 tonnes in 2004). Mid 19th-century writings were consistent in their view that this was Australia's most valuable white variety, the counterpart, as it were, of Shiraz. It was first imported in 1825 from Madeira by the Australian Agriculture Company, and on several other occasions thereafter. Quite why Australia should have embarked on an enthusiastic but solo (with the exception of Portugal) programme of making table wine with it is a mystery. More mysterious still is why, having dwindled away to a few hectares in the Hunter Valley and South Australia, and a slightly less precarious toe-hold in the Swan Valley, it should have careered from a total production of 1,366 tonnes in 1990 to almost 26,000 tonnes in 2004. In this writer's view it is a tradesman-like variety, liking warmth, yielding well but not prodigiously, and producing a wine which epitomizes its working-class background.

Chenin Blanc (14,383 tonnes in 2004) has much in common with Verdelho, except that Chenin Blanc does make superb, long-lived wines in the Loire Valley, and once carpeted the Cape vineyards under the Steen nom-de-plume. In Australia, like South Africa, it yields very big crops, and is a compliant blend mate for other varieties.

Other white varieties: **Marsanne** has been grown at Tahbilk in the Goulburn valley for well over 100 years, having been taken there from Yeringberg in the Yarra valley (in turn having come from Switzerland). Until relatively recently, Tahbilk's was the largest single-vineyard planting in the world, but the Rhône's sudden popularity in the US and elsewhere has seen it lose that title. Much smaller plantings of **Roussanne** are mainly used to blend with Marsanne. **Viognier** is exciting a great deal of interest, and in percentage terms plantings are increasing at a greater rate (albeit from a low base) than those of any other variety. While most goes to make white wine, an increasing number of winemakers treasure it for the magic it works when co-fermented with Shiraz (see CO-FERMENTATION). **Gewurztraminer** has been around for a long time; blended with Riesling and made off-dry, it rightly inhabits Asian restaurant wine lists. Delicate—perhaps too delicate—dry, unblended versions are made in Tasmania and the cooler parts of Victoria. **Arneis**, **Cortese**, **Garganega**, **Gouais Blanc**, **Ondenc**, **Petit Manseng**, **Picolit**, **Schonburger**, and **Vermentino** are but some of the more obscure white wine varieties also in commercial production.

Labelling laws

A common geographical designation found on lower-priced wines is the barely helpful SOUTH EASTERN AUSTRALIA, which takes in part of Queensland, all of New South Wales, all of Victoria, and that part of South Australia in which it is possible to grow grapes. In practice, it often signifies a wine made from fruit grown in areas as unglamorous as RIVERLAND and/or RIVERINA.

Australia has had the major components of an APPELLATION system since 1963, initially through the framework of state legislation, but since 1987 effectively embodied in federal law, and since 1990 actively enforced by the official Wine and Brandy Corporation through the Label Integrity Programme (LIP). LIP annually carries out both general and specific audits, variously covering regions, varieties, and individual wineries, utilizing detailed production records which wineries must keep.

This is designed to ensure that where a variety or a region is specified, at least 85 per cent of the wine is of that variety and/or from that region; that 85 per cent is of the stated vintage; and, if more than one variety or region are specified, that they are listed in descending order. Thus Cabernet-Shiraz means the wine has more Cabernet Sauvignon grapes than Shiraz; Shiraz-Cabernet the reverse.

The missing link—a legislative definition of the boundaries of each region spurred on by the wine agreement signed between the EU and Australia in 1994—was completed in the late 1990s with the passing of regulations under the Federal Wine and Brandy Corporation Act. This has provided the framework for the methodical mapping of Australia into **zones**, **regions**, and **subregions**, all glorying under the ultimately bureaucratic and infinitely ugly term **Geographic Indications** (GI or GIs).

By 1996, each state had divided itself into **zones**: New South Wales has eight, Victoria six, South Australia eight, and Western Australia five. There was—and is—no requirement of geographic or climatic particularity, no rules for the drawing of the zone boundaries. Simple pragmatism ruled, although South Australia managed to complicate matters by introducing a **super zone**, and Western Australia came up with a series of utterly confusing and seemingly meaningless zone names. Compared with that which followed, it was a relatively simple and speedy process.

The legislation requires that a **region** is a single tract of land that is discrete and homogeneous in its grape growing attributes to a degree that is measurable; that it usually produces at least 500 tonnes of grapes a year; that it includes at least five differently owned vineyards each of at least 5 hectares; and that it may reasonably be regarded as a region.

A **subregion** must also be a single tract of land, comprising at least five independently owned wine grape vineyards of at least 5 hectares each, and must usually produce 500 tonnes of wine grapes in a year. However, a subregion is required to be substantially discrete within the region and have substantial homogeneity in grape growing attributes over the area.

The process of registration took far longer than expected. This was less to do with the requirements of the legislation and more to do with a mixture of in-fighting over names, apathy, and—in the case of Coonawarra—fierce arguments over boundary lines. Half a decade of argument and litigation plus several million dollars of legal fees has finally resolved the Coonawarra boundary lines. The ever-increasing spread of vineyards means new regions (and subregions) will continue to be created, but, it is hoped, without the acrimony of the early years.

By 2005, 56 regions had been finally determined, some work had been carried out on a further five regions, while yet more had still to take any steps towards registration under the legislation.

The once widespread but now largely discredited use of GENERIC names such as claret, burgundy, champagne, port, and sherry is being progressively phased out under the terms of 1994 EU wine agreement. Such names were never permitted on export labels (so that, for example, the famous Penfolds Grange Hermitage was renamed Grange for European customers), and have all but disappeared from wine labels within Australia. A phase-out date of 1 January 2008 has been agreed for the use of the names Sherry and Port, along with Fino, Amontillado, and Amoroso. The umbrella terms will become Australian Fortified White

Wine and Australian Fortified Red Wine respectively. The subcategories for White Fortified will be Dry, Medium Dry, and Mature Medium Dry respectively; for Red Fortified they will be Tawny and Vintage. Australian STICKIES Muscat and Tokay will also fall under the Red Fortified banner, and open up the pre-existing (but voluntary) categories of Classic, Grand, and Rare for both Tawny and Vintage.

Wine trade organization

The structure of the industry, measured by the size of the individual companies or groups, underwent profound changes in the first few years of the 21st century, with more to come. The largest was the assimilation of Hardys by CONSTELLATION of the US to form the world's largest wine group. The most publicized was the acquisition by Southcorp of Rosemount, and the financial haemorrhage which ensued. What seemed to be the most successful at the time was the 2000 acquisition of Beringer in California (by brewers FOSTER'S, who went on to swallow Southcorp/Rosemount) to form Beringer Blass, and the disappearance of the Mildara name. The 2002 merger of Simeon Wines and Brian McGuigan Wines, and the acquisition by that group of Miranda Wines the following year, lifted McGuigan into the top four, with a CRUSH twice that of Beringer Blass. Evans & Tate transformed itself from a small to medium winery based in the Margaret River to Australia's eighth-largest wine group by acquiring Cranswick Estate. Arguably, the greatest success story was that of Riverina-based Casella Wines, nowhere in the top 20 companies in 2000, and by 2004 sixth-largest thanks to its six million case sales of [yellow tail] (*sic*) (see YELLOW TAIL) into the United States and elsewhere. In the final result, the top ten producers crush 94 per cent of the total annual grape intake.

The sale of wine within Australia is relatively simple, and notably free of the restraints which apply in the UNITED STATES, unless it be the all-up tax on retail wine sales of over 40 per cent. Movement between the states is unhindered, and wine producers can sell to whomever they wish (distributors, retailers, or the public), wherever they wish. One of the particular freedoms of Australia is the BYO restaurant, 'BYO' standing for Bring Your Own. In Victoria, 'Licensed and BYO' restaurants which generously encourage patrons to bring their own wine are common. This ethic spreads across all restaurants in Australia. Most will permit patrons to bring their own wine upon payment of a CORKAGE fee, if the request is made in appropriate fashion. J.H.

Australia Wine Companion (Sydney, annually).
Halliday, J., numerous works including *The Wine Atlas of Australia and New Zealand* (2nd edn, Sydney, 1998).
www.awbc.com.au

Australian influence on wine production, marketing, and even distribution since the 1990s is difficult to overestimate. When the chips are finally counted, Australia will be credited with having had an enormous influence on the wine world of the late 20th century. Its VITICULTURISTS (notably the viticulture editor of this book) pioneered sophisticated CANOPY MANAGEMENT techniques and all sorts of tricks such as niceties of irrigation (see PARTIAL ROOTZONE DRYING) and hi-tech SOIL MAPPING. Australia's winemakers now travel the world—especially the northern hemisphere where the HARVEST conveniently takes place during the southern hemisphere lull—quietly infiltrating all manner of wineries with Australian technology, obsession with HYGIENE, and record WATER usage (see FLYING WINEMAKERS). One of their distinguishing marks is their commitment to long hours, ignoring weekends and evenings, at the critical periods during and immediately after harvest. Graduates of oenology and viticulture courses at Australian universities such as ROSEWORTHY, ADELAIDE, and CHARLES STURT UNIVERSITY are now dispersed around the world, and the AUSTRALIAN WINE RESEARCH INSTITUTE (AWRI) is increasingly recognized as one of the most important, and practical, forces in ACADEME. It is significant that the world's largest and canniest wine company, GALLO of California, deliberately recruited an Australian to lead its wine research department into the new millennium. Australia overtook France to be most important exporter of wine to the UK, one of the world's most significant markets, at the beginning of the century, and went on to perform the same trick in the US. Such has been Australia's success at developing and selling BRANDS to suit the modern international marketplace that it has increasingly been seen as a model even by such experienced wine exporters as the French. Alliances between Australian companies and global players in the drinks trade have been a notable feature of the GLOBALIZATION of the wine trade.

Australian Wine Research Institute

(**AWRI**) is a wine research organization owned and led by the Australian wine industry and based south east of Adelaide. Formed in 1955, its council includes members elected by Australian winemakers and vine-growers who pay the Wine Grapes and Grape Research levy. Research is designed to increase fundamental understanding while remaining responsive to the applied needs of producers and consumers.

Principal research areas are fourfold: wine composition, quality and sensory characteristics; industry development and support; transferring research outcomes to practice via a commercial Analytical Service; and coordinating oenological activities, including the collection, collation, and dissemination of oenology and viticultural research for the benefit of the Australian wine industry.

Strategic and applied research covers the chemical, microbiological, molecular, and sensory aspects of winemaking. For example, the identification, measurement, and enhanced control of non-volatile phenolic compounds responsible for colour and MOUTHFEEL in wine, the management of wine and oxygen in the making, maturing, and storing wine; developing tools to understand market preferences and shifts.

Industry development and support includes a problem-solving service, a consultancy service, advice on quality management and viticultural practices, and a self-help diagnostic service on the AWRI website on wine FAULTS and laboratory establishment. The Institute conducts seminars and workshops around the country and publishes more than 800 papers and articles every year. The AWRI supervises post-graduate students and provides lectures to undergraduates at ADELAIDE.

www.awri.com.au

Austria, qualitatively important wine-producing country in central Europe with an annual production of about 2.5 million hl/ 66 million gal, about a quarter as much as GERMANY to the north, with which it shares some grape varieties, wine styles, and labelling customs. The wines themselves are more varied and full bodied than the German norm, however. The majority of wines are white, dry, and VARIETAL, but the production of fine red wine continues to increase and Austria has a long tradition of botrytized SWEET WINE-MAKING. ADULTERATION on the part of certain merchants, resulting in a major wine scandal in 1985 (see History), led to major reforms in wine law and a determination to emphasize quality at the expense of quantity; average Austrian YIELDS from the country's 48,500 ha/ 119,800 acres of vines are about 50 hl/ha (3 tons/acre), half those in Germany. Austria is also famous for the quality of its wine GLASSES, the result of post-communist migration from BOHEMIA.

History
The CELTS are believed to have grown vines for wine in what is now Austria five centuries before the Christian era, and viticulture continued under Roman domination in what were then the Roman provinces of Noricum and Pannonia in the south east of modern Austria.

The Pannonian plain was repeatedly raided by waves of barbarians (almost defined by their lack of respect for viticulture), but by the era of CHARLEMAGNE, vines flourished once more, in many of what are still today regarded as the most important sites, under the influence of MONKS AND MONASTERIES, most concentrated around Krems on the Danube west of Vienna. Monasteries, often founded by Cistercians from BURGUNDY, and whose viticultural associations date from the Middle Ages, include Göttweig, Zwettl, Güssing, Heiligenkreuz, Klosterneuburg, and Melk. At this time

(as in Germany), the total area under vine was about ten times what it is today, and Austrian wines were widely exported. So great was this surplus production that a series of protectionist measures was undertaken in the 14th, 15th, and 16th centuries (when selling 'foreign' non-indigenous wines was prohibited from Lower Austria).

Once Hungary was also part of the Habsburg empire, Hungary's most famous wine TOKAJI somewhat overshadowed the reputation of other sweet wines produced within the Austro-Hungarian empire, even AUSBRUCH wines from Rust in the Neusiedlersee-Hügelland district of Burgenland (see below).

The Napoleonic wars did not leave Austrian vineyards unscathed, but the 19th century saw, as elsewhere, enthusiastic botanical experimentation, with perceptible effects on the development of Austria's vine varieties. Austria established its first viticultural and oenological school and research centre at KLOSTERNEUBURG in 1860.

The most damaging episode in 20th-century history was the discovery in 1985 that a small but highly publicized proportion of Austrian wine had been adulterated by diethylene glycol, a harmless but illegal additive designed to add apparent BODY and to make sweet wines taste sweeter. In the year after the scandal, Austria's wine exports were less than a fifth those of the year before. Hundreds of vine-growers found their produce unwanted outside Austria as a result of misdeeds on the part of some larger wine producers and blenders. Swingeing reforms were enacted and Austrian wine laws are currently some of the most exacting.

Climate
Austria's climate is decidedly CONTINENTAL, with much harsher winters but hotter, drier summers than those of France, for example. Average winter temperatures in the wine regions are only just above freezing point. Average summer temperatures, however, range from 18.5 °C/65 °F in Retz almost on the northern, Czech border in the Weinviertel to 19.3 °C/ 67 °F in Klöch in Styria (Steiermark) on the southern, Slovenian border.

Annual rainfall varies considerably more, with an average of 430 mm (16 in) in Retz but 854 (33 in) in Klöch. The Weinviertel (and indeed southern Moravia; see CZECH REPUBLIC) is one of the driest wine regions in Europe, while rain in the much wetter Styrian climate tends to fall mainly in summer. The most marked climate is in the Wachau region, source of Austria's most prized dry Rieslings and Grüner Veltliners, where the average annual rainfall in nearby Krems is 539 mm/21 in.

Burgenland enjoys the sunniest climate, with almost 2,000 hours of sunshine in an average year, while Gumpoldskirchen just south of Vienna has an average of only 1,805 hours. Local mesoclimates can vary enor-

mously however thanks to such factors as proximity to the river Danube, warm winds from the Pannonian plain in Burgenland, or cold air streams from the north.

Viticulture
Austria's fame viticulturally is as birthplace of the LENZ MOSER 'high culture' system whereby vines are trained far from the ground. This used to be by far the most common system of vine training in Austria, although modern vineyards are more likely to be planned with a higher VINE DENSITY and a lower TRAINING SYSTEM.

About 32,000 growers own vineyards in Austria. As in Germany, the great majority of vineyards are tended by part-time vine-growers and barely 2,500 growers own more than 5 hectares of vines. Many growers deliver their grapes to producers of sparkling wine producers or to the CO-OPERATIVES, which produce about 15 per cent of all Austrian wine.

Major climatological hazards are late spring FROSTS throughout Austria; HAIL in Styria, and in some years also in Vienna and Lower Austria; winter frosts in some sites with very little wind, although the Lenz Moser system offers some protection. On the terraces of the Wachau, IRRIGATION is necessary most years because of very thin soils and less than 500 mm average annual rainfall. Harvest dates vary from the end of August in Burgenland to the end of November for Wachau white wines. Late harvest wines may be picked even later. Machine harvesting is rare except for grapes for sparkling wines in the north east of Lower Austria.

Viticultural research is centred on KLOSTERNEUBURG, where some of Austria's most successful CROSSINGS such as ZWEIGELT were developed.

Wine-making
Dry wines with both EXTRACT and pronounced ACIDITY are fashionable with connoisseurs even more markedly in Austria than in Germany so that the most sought-after wines are those labelled TROCKEN (dry). All but the great sweet wines of Burgenland are fermented to almost complete dryness, with a RESIDUAL SUGAR level of not more than 4 g/l (or not more than 9 g/l provided that the TOTAL ACIDITY is not more than 2 g below the residual sugar content). In hot vintages such as 2000 and 2003, the residual sugar levels are sometimes closer to 6–8 g/l, though the wines are still technically dry.

Most wineries are well equipped and use stainless steel or large old wooden vats for fermentation and ageing. Bottling usually takes place in the spring following the vintage.

Many Austrian winemakers have travelled, however, and practices common in the fine wine regions of the world are increasingly employed by the more innovative producers. Red wine producers in Burgenland and Lower

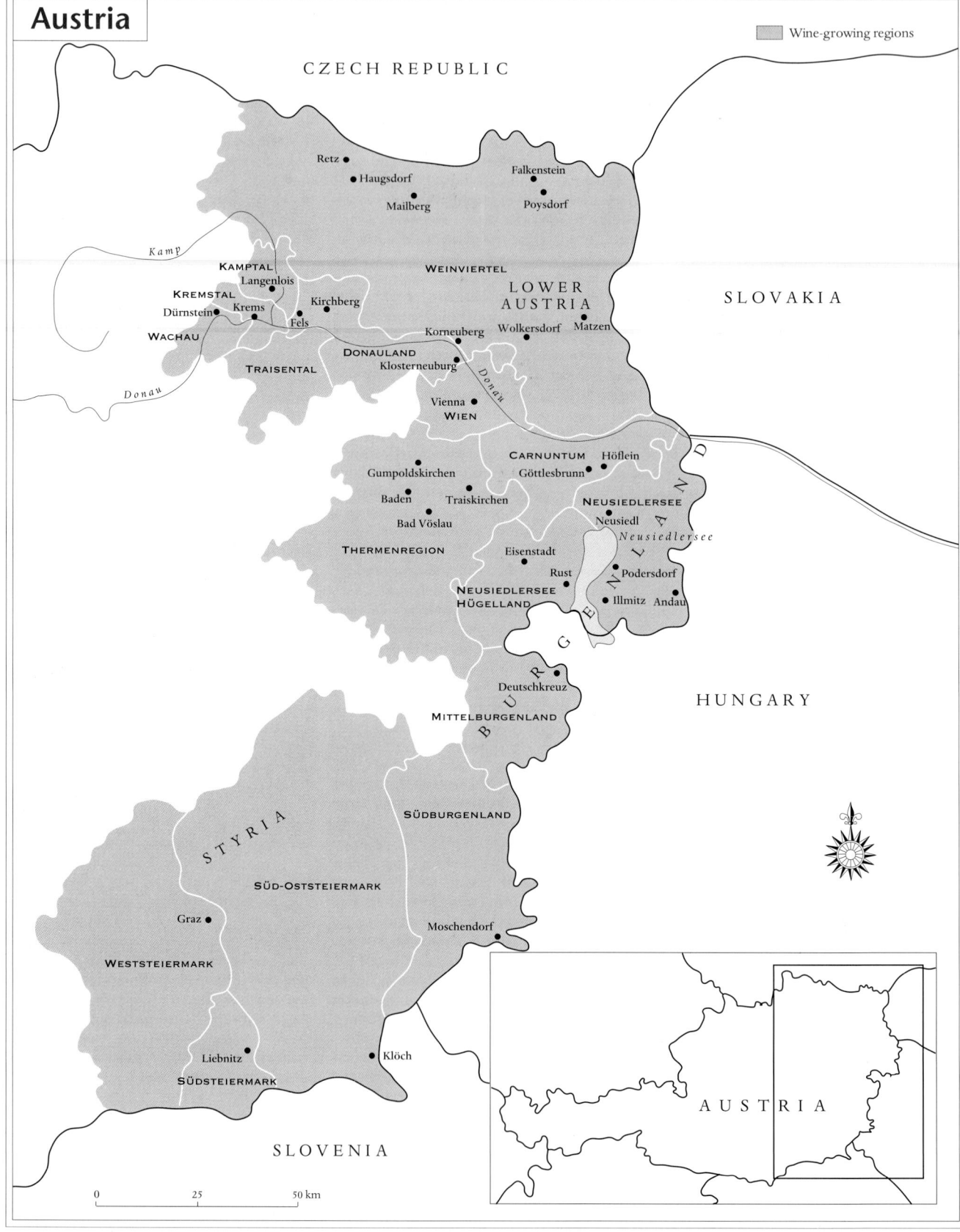

Austria

CZECH REPUBLIC

Wine-growing regions

Retz ●
● Haugsdorf
Mailberg ●

Falkenstein ●
Poysdorf ●

Kamp

KAMPTAL
Langenlois

KREMSTAL
Krems ●
Dürnstein ● ● Kirchberg
● Fels

WACHAU

Donau

TRAISENTAL

WEINVIERTEL

LOWER AUSTRIA

SLOVAKIA

DONAULAND
Klosterneuburg

Korneuburg ●
● Wolkersdorf
Matzen ●

Donau

Vienna ●
WIEN

CARNUNTUM Höflein ●
Göttlesbrunn ●

Gumpoldskirchen ●
Baden ● ● Traiskirchen
Bad Vöslau ●

NEUSIEDLERSEE
Neusiedl ●

Neusiedlersee

THERMENREGION

Eisenstadt ●
Rust ● ● Podersdorf
Illmitz ● ● Andau

NEUSIEDLERSEE HÜGELLAND

B U R G E N L A N D

Deutschkreuz ●

HUNGARY

MITTELBURGENLAND

SÜDBURGENLAND

S T Y R I A

SÜD-OSTSTEIERMARK

Graz ●

WESTSTEIERMARK

Moschendorf ●

Liebnitz ●
● Klöch

SÜDSTEIERMARK

SLOVENIA

0   25   50 km

AUSTRIA

Austria routinely use BARREL MATURATION and, for some fuller bodied white wines, BARREL FERMENTATION. Chemical ACIDIFICATION is usually strictly forbidden in Austria, although was exceptionally permitted in 2003, while DEACIDIFICATION is occasionally practised in lesser years. CHAPTALIZATION is allowed for Qualitätswein (see Wine labelling below) but not for wines of Kabinett quality or above, nor for STEINFEDER, FEDERSPIEL, and SMARAGD in Wachau. Modern winemaking techniques such as must CONCENTRATION and OAK CHIPS have been introduced to Austria, but only under the strict supervision of the wine control board.

Austrian wine research and teaching is centred on Klosterneuburg in Donauland. Austrian specialities include HEURIGER wine, G'spritzer (Heuriger wine mixed with an equal quantity of sparkling soda water), Schilcher (see Weststeiermark below), and STURM.

Despite the fashion for dry wines, MUST WEIGHT measurement is the key to wine labelling (see below) and wine quality in Austria, as it is in Germany. The Austrians have their own system of measuring must weight, expressed as degrees on the Klosterneuburg scale. One degree 'KMW' is equivalent to 1 per cent by weight of sugar in the must, or approximately 5 °OECHSLE.

Vine varieties

Austria's varietal mix reflects the country's geographical position between Germany on the one hand and Hungary and Slovenia on the other. Austria's most planted variety is the national speciality GRÜNER VELTLINER, which is planted in 36 per cent of Austria's total vineyard area. It is particularly important in Lower Austria, Vienna, and, to a lesser extent for simple wines, Burgenland. Second most important variety WELSCHRIESLING can produce sweet wines of great quality in Burgenland, and many perfectly respectable dry wines too, notably in Styria and some parts of Lower Austria. MÜLLER-THURGAU is declining in importance but was still the country's fourth most planted vine variety in the mid 2000s, even if rarely producing wines of real excitement. The indigenous red wine grape ZWEIGELT is now the country's second most planted variety of either colour and is found in all districts. The central European red grape varieties Blauer PORTUGIESER and BLAUFRÄNKISCH are also widely grown, with the former predominating in the basic reds of Lower Austria and the latter making increasingly high-quality wines in Burgenland. Weissburgunder (PINOT BLANC) is another widely planted white wine variety. CHARDONNAY has established itself as more than a fashionable novelty in most districts, and has been grown and known as Morillon (an old CHABLIS synonym) in Styria for more than a century. The specifically Austrian NEUBURGER was a speciality of Neusiedlersee, Thermenregion, and the Wachau, where RIES-

LING reigns, as it does in Kamptal, Kremstal, and Vienna. MUSCAT OTTONEL is Austria's most commonly planted Muscat variety (although the superior (Gelber) Muskateller, planted in Styria, enjoys more respect). GEWÜRZTRAMINER is widely planted, but its spiritual home is in Klöch in Styria. PINOT GRIS (known, as in Germany, both as Grauer Burgunder and Ruländer) is grown mainly in Styria, as is Sauvignon Blanc. ZIERFANDLER (or Spätrot) and ROTGIPFLER are the curious white wine grape specialities of Gumpoldskirchen in Thermenregion, while Blauer WILDBACHER is a light red grape grown almost exclusively in western Styria. CABERNET SAUVIGNON arrived only in the late 1980s and is concentrated in Burgenland, but Blauer Burgunder (PINOT NOIR) is another indigenous red variety with great potential in Lower Austria and Burgenland. ST-LAURENT is a useful variant of it particularly well adapted to conditions in Lower Austria and Burgenland. Other less common vine varieties include FRÜHROTER VELTLINER and ROTER VELTLINER, BOUVIER, GOLDBURGER, SYLVANER, Sämling 88 (see SCHEUREBE), and FURMINT. New varieties planted to a very limited extent include Syrah, Rössler and Rathay, the last two being new CROSSINGS from Klosterneuburg.

Wine regions

Almost all of Austria's vineyards are, like most of the country's agriculture, in the east of the country, far from the mountains that draw skiers from all over the world and constitute the majority of the country. Austrian wine law recogizes the four regions Weinland Österreich (the provinces of Lower Austria and Burgenland), Steierland (the province of Styria), Wien (Vienna), and Bergland Österreich (those few vineyards in western Austria). Weinland produces more than 90 per cent of all wines. Then there are 19 wine areas and five DAC regions. The first, WEINVIERTEL, was created in 2003.

More than six in every ten bottles produced come from Niederösterreich, or Lower Austria, on the fertile Danube plain in the north eastern corner of the country. Lower Austria includes, in declining order of the amount of wine produced, the areas of Weinviertel, Kamptal, Donauland, Thermenregion, Kremstal, the highly respected Wachau, Carnuntum, and Traisental.

Burgenland, on the Hungarian border in the far east, makes slightly less than a third of all Austrian wine, and a far higher proportion of Austria's best reds and sweet whites. Neusiedlersee on the eastern shores of the eponymous lake (or See) is by far the most important area, followed by Neusiedlersee-Hügelland on the western shores. Some fine Blaufränkisch is also produced in Mittelburgenland, Austria's red wine corner, and Südburgenland, in the middle and south of the region respectively.

Styria is a mountainous viticultural district with its own identity, producing mainly fresh white varietals. It is officially divided into south, south east, and west (Süd-, Süd-Ost-, and West- respectively) districts, which combine to produce less than 7 per cent of an average Austrian vintage.

The city of Vienna, or Wien, is given its own status as a wine region and area, climatically a particularly favoured enclave within Lower Austria.

Weinviertel Austria's largest wine area, the so-called 'wine quarter', with about 16,000 ha/39,500 acres of vineyards, is one of Austria's more dynamic. Weinviertel was the first to introduce the new DAC concept, which values origin over grape variety. DAC WEINVIERTEL is typically a fruity, spicy, dry Grüner Veltliner with at least 12 per cent alcohol. All other varieties from Weinviertel are labelled Lower Austria. Much of the land is flat, fertile, and very dry. The Müller-Thurgau and Welschriesling vines common here also help to bolster the volume produced. Some fine Weissburgunder (PINOT BLANC) and Riesling are made here as well. Wine growing centres in the western part of Weinviertel are Retz, Röschitz, and Seefeld-Kadolz, with some reputable producers such as Zull, Setzer, and Graf Hardegg. In the east of Weinviertel, Falkenstein, Poysdorf, Wolkersdorf, and especially around Korneuburg just north of Vienna are known for great Grüner Veltliner from producers such as Pfaffl and Taubenschuss. Matzen and Mannersdorf in the east benefit from warm autumns thanks to their proximity to the Pannonian plain; this, together with humidity from the March river, can result in botrytized wines in some years. Mailberg, almost due north of Vienna, and Haugsdorf have earned themselves a reputation for their confident red Blauer Portugieser and Zweigelt, notably from the Malteser estate managed by LENZ MOSER. Much of the base wine for Austria's sparkling wine, or SEKT, is produced in the north east part along the Brünner Strasse, the road north from Vienna to Brno in Moravia, especially around Poysdorf. These are sold to Sekt producers such as Schlumberger or Kattus.

Kamptal This 3,900-ha/9,600-acre district, named after the river Kamp, is centred on the important wine town Langenlois. Some of Austria's most concentrated Grüner Veltliner comes from this district, where LOESS is a common geological feature. Many fine Rieslings are also made here, notably on vineyards based on primary rock formation similar to some of the best in the famous and adjoining Wachau district. The most famous Riesling site is probably the Zöbinger Heiligenstein. The district is also associated with a number of Austria's most innovative winemakers (Angerer, Bründlmayer, Hirsch, Jurtschitsch, Loimer, Retzl, and Schloss Gobelsburg for example). Kamptal DAC was created in 2008.

Donauland This 2,900-ha/6,700-acre district stretches east along the Danube from just east of Krems to KLOSTERNEUBURG, which is both a centre of ACADEME, as Austria's leading viticultural and horticultural school, and the country's largest private vineyard owner Stift Klosterneuburg. The soils of Wagram, a long ridge overlooking the Danubian plain, are rich in loess and favour Grüner Veltliner. Other better-known villages in this western part are Kirchberg and Fels. Specialities of Wagram are EISWEIN and the white wine variety ROTER VELTLINER. The area around Klosterneuburg is dominated by CALCAREOUS soils and some fine Pinot Blanc is produced. More dynamic winemakers include Leth and Ott.

Thermenregion This 2,500-ha/6,100-acre district is centred on the once world-famous village of Gumpoldskirchen on the Südbahn, the southbound rail line from Vienna which gave its name to the region in the pre-1985 era. This is the warmest part of Lower Austria and can boast the longest uninterrupted tradition of vine-growing since Cistercians planted vineyards here in the 12th century. It is also one of the most distinctive wine regions in the world, dependent for its best wines on two specially adapted grape varieties found nowhere else (and here only in very limited quantity), ZIERFANDLER (or Spätrot) and ROTGIPFLER. Wines made from Spätrot-Rotgipfler grown in Gumpoldskirchen and ripened to AUSLESE level are rich, spicy, and potentially long-lived whites in quite a different style from the lean raciness evinced by the famous Rieslings of the Wachau, or even the BOTRYTIZED sweet wines of Burgenland. Neuburger is also planted here as well as Blauer Portugieser and Zweigelt for red wines. Other wine villages in the regions include Traiskirchen, Baden, Tattendorf, Sooss, and Bad Vöslau. Thermenregion is also well-known for its HEURIGEN, wine taverns operated by such reputable producers as Auer, Biegler, Fischer, and Reinisch.

Kremstal This 2,200-ha/5,400-acre district is centred on the beautiful twin towns of Krems and Stein, where huge quantities of wine were made under monastic auspices in the Middle Ages. Clay and limestone in the area east of Krems seem to imbue the finest Veltliners with a density all of their own. The headquarters of Lenz Moser is in Rohrendorf. The primary rock soils of the nearby Wachau are also found on the slopes of the north west Kremstal. Leading producers include Nigl, Malat, Sepp Moser, Undhof-Salomon, and the restructured Weingut der Stadt Krems. The co-operative Winzer Krems is one of Austria's largest producers. Kremstal DAC was created in 2007.

Wachau Austria's westernmost wine district is, with about 1,400 ha/3,500 acres of vines, one of Lower Austria's smallest. It is also the one of which many Austrian connoisseurs are most proud, however, on account of the elegance and refinement of its dry Rieslings and Grüner Veltliners, made from terraces sculpted from the steep banks of the river Danube as it flows through some of this beautiful country's most beautiful scenery. Primary rock formations, with occasional layers of loess, yield fine white wines with high levels of both EXTRACT and ACIDITY—Austria's (more consistent) answer to German RHEINGAU perhaps. As in the Rheingau, most of the vineyards are on the steeper northern bank of the broad river, and presumably benefit from some reflected sunlight. The climate is very particular here where a narrow spur of the eastern Pannonian zone meets cooler, moister, oxygen-enriched air from the northern forests. The effect is permanent air circulation, and the Danube stores heat and acts as an effective temperature regulator. More than any other Austrian wine region, the Wachau is marked by wide variations between day and night temperatures, which helps to preserve aroma and acidity (see TEMPERATURE VARIABILITY). Vineyards in the heartland of this region, which styles itself Vinea Wachau Nobilis Districtus, range hardly more than 20 km/12 miles as the crow flies from Schwallenbach in the west, downstream through Spitz, Weissenkirchen, Dürnstein (where the admirable and important co-operative Freie Weingärtner Wachau is based), and Loiben to Mautern. Some of these grapes are vinified by producers in the town of Krems just over the border in Kremstal, but respected family estates such as Alzinger, F. X. Pichler, Prager, Knoll, Jamek, and Hirtzberger which did much to create the Vinea Wachau association and affirm the district's commitment to quality in 1983 are all based in the medieval wine villages of the Wachau itself. The association has established three quality levels of its own for its distinctively racy dry white wines.

STEINFEDER is the lightest; FEDERSPIEL made from rather riper grapes. The most concentrated, and alcoholic, are those which qualify as SMARAGD. In very ripe years, sweet wines may also be made, and some producers are beginning to make BOTRYTIZED wines.

Carnuntum The 900-ha/2,200-acre district stretches east along the north bank of the Danube from the eastern outskirts of Vienna towards the Slovakian border. Its classical name comes from the eponymous Roman fortress town but the viticultural centre today are the tiny villages of Göttlesbrunn and Höflein. The region benefits from a MESOCLIMATE influenced by the Neusiedlersee and river Danube nearby. Carnuntum combines the freshness of Weinviertel and the weight of Burgenland. Red grape varieties are increasingly planted, with fruity Zweigelt predominating. Leading producers include Glatzer, Grassl, Markowitsch, and Pittnauer.

Traisental Lower Austria's smallest wine district of less than 700 ha/1,730 acres was born in 1995 after the somewhat varied Kamptal-Donauland region was split into four new entities. The vineyards are situated on both sides of the river Traisen, north of Lower Austria's capital St Pölten. On the right bank, clay and limestone soils predominate, generally resulting in softer, broader whites than on the left bank, where soils rich in lime produce racy wines comparable with those of the famous Wachau. Neumayer is the leading producer. Traisental DAC was created in 2006.

Neusiedlersee The shallow lake of Neusiedlersee, surrounded by sandy marshes, is the natural focus for Austria's Burgenland, and the district named after it consists of about 8,300 ha/20,500 acres of vines on the warm Pannonian plain between the lake and the Hungarian border, the Seewinkel, and the strip of land north of the lake. On gentle, south-facing slopes around villages such as Jois, Neusiedl, Weiden, Gols, and Mönchhof some of Austria's best red wines are produced. The PANNOBILE association includes such innovative wineries as Ah, Heinrich, and Nittnaus from Gols. Other notable producers include Pöckl, Schloss Halbturn, and Stieglmar. The so-called Haideboden and Seewinkel between the lake and the Hungarian border have mainly sandy, rich soils and produce outstanding red wines and some very fine, full-bodied white wines of all levels of sweetness, from dry and fiery to late harvest TROCKENBEERENAUSLESE, made more regularly than anywhere else in the world. The lake and its surrounding marshes encourage the formation of NOBLE ROT so that very sweet wines are a speciality of the lakeshore vineyards and, in the best vintages, have a balance and structure that can rival the world's finest sweet wines. Strohwein (straw wine) and EISWEIN are local sweet wine specialities. Some of Austria's more ambitious red wines come, in small quantities, from Neusiedlersee. ZWEIGELT is the most common red wine vine variety but Blaufränkisch and St-Laurent are also grown. In the Seewinkel, Apetlon, Neusiedl, Podersdorf, Frauenkirchen, Halbturn, Illmitz, and Andau are some of the more important wine villages. Some of the more dynamic producers include Kracher (world famous for his botrytized wines), Umathum, Velich, organic grower Michlits, and hypercreative Willi Opitz.

Neusiedlersee-Hügelland This is the name given to the wine region on the western shore of the lake, where soils are sometimes higher in loam, especially around Eisenstadt and Mattersburg. The gentle slopes of the Leithagebirge (the easternmost foothills of the Alps) are highly calcareous. The range of wines produced, from full-bodied dry and very sweet whites to increasingly 'international' reds, is very similar to that of the Neusiedlersee region on the opposite shore, with the addition of the famous sweet white AUSBRUCH wines from the town of Rust almost directly on the lake. Rust has a special mesoclimate supported by gentle slopes surrounding and protecting the vineyards and the warmth and humidity of lake Neusiedl that consistently favour botrytis. Specialists in this historic wine style include Feiler-Artinger, Schandl, Heidi Schröck, Triebaumer, and Wenzel. There are many family wine holdings here dedicated to both quality and innovation. Wine estates such as Kollwentz, Prieler, Schuster, and both Triebaumers produce wines as varied as a Sauvignon Blanc, Chardonnay, Welschriesling Eiswein, Cabernet Sauvignon, and, most proudly, an oakaged Blaufränkisch and Zweigelt. Total vineyard area is about 3,900 ha/9,600 acres.

Mittelburgenland The central Burgenland district, immediately south of the Neusiedlersee-Hügelland, harbours about 1,850 ha/4,500 acres of vineyard on mainly loamy flat land extending to the Hungarian border, sheltered by hills. With its warm climate, it has long been associated with red grapes, which constitute an unusually high proportion of those grown, about 80 per cent with Blaufränkisch by far the dominant variety. Mittelburgenland has its own association, the Verband Blaufränkischland, dedicated to extracting maximum quality from this lively eastern European red grape variety. Mittelburgenland DAC was created in 2005. Other varieties are Zweigelt and to a lesser extent Cabernet Sauvignon and Merlot. Besides the two successful co-operatives (Vereinte Winzer Horitschon and Winzerkeller Neckenmarkt), which vinify the majority of grapes from Mittelburgenland, estates such as Gesellmann, Heinrich, Igler, Kerschbaum, Wellanschitz, and Weninger are well known. Deutschkreutz, Neckenmarkt, and Horitschon are the important wine towns.

Südburgenland Southern Burgenland sprawls along the Hungarian border between Styria and Mittelburgenland but the total vineyard area is less than 450 ha/1,100 acres and producers have remained largely unaffected by fashions in wine-making and consumer taste. Best-known wines are Blaufränkisch made in the Eisenberg area, where, as German speakers will deduce, the soils are high in iron, and dry Welschrieslings from around Rechnitz. Uhudler is a curious speciality of the far south, well removed from the bureaucrats of the EU, made from a wide range of AMERICAN HYBRIDS which have been grown around the villages of Moschendorf and Heiligenbrunn (famous for its Kellergassen, clusters of thatched presshouses) since the 19th century, when they were presumably imported to offer resistance to the PHYLLOXERA louse. Krutzler, Wachter-Wiesler, and young Uwe Schiefer are probably the best producers of the region, specializing in Blaufränkisch.

Südsteiermark The wines of Styria, representing hardly 7 per cent of Austria's total production, became particularly fashionable during the 1990s, because of their dry and fragrant style. A majority of Styria's production is consumed at local HEURIGEN. The smallest of the Styrian areas, southern Styria around Leibnitz and some of it within sight of Slovenia, is the most important in terms of wine production, but even its 1,750 ha/4,330 acres of vines are widely scattered, grown vertically up steep, south-facing slopes in particularly sheltered spots, at altitudes of between 250 and 650 m (2,100 ft). The region has long cultivated two of the most popular INTERNATIONAL VARIETIES Sauvignon Blanc and Chardonnay (here usually called Morillon). Both varities are popular as crisp and fresh wines, but in good years barrel fermented versions are also produced. Welschriesling, Pinot Blanc (called Klevner here), and Gelber Muskateller (MUSCAT BLANC À PETITS GRAINS) are also grown and all of these varieties can produce distinctively crisp yet full and aromatic white wines. Many of the best producers belong to the Steirische Klassik association. JUNKER is an early bottled fresh, light blend, an Austrian answer to Beaujolais NOUVEAU. Alois Gross, Domäne Müller, Erich and Walter Polz, Sattlerhof, Tement, Tscheppe, and Wohlmuth are some of the best-known producers.

Süd-Oststeiermark South east Styria is a vast area in which there are about 1,100 ha/2,700 acres of widely dispersed vineyards, notably on the volcanic soils of Klöch, where Traminer is a speciality. Welschriesling, Pinot Blanc, Ruländer, Chardonnay, Sauvignon Blanc, and some Zweigelt are also cultivated in this relatively warm area. Neumeister and Winkler-Hermaden are notable producers.

Weststeiermark Western Styria, where there are about 430 ha/1,060 acres of vines, has its own extremely local speciality, Schilcher rosé made from lightly pressed Blauer Wildbacher grapes, known only here and, to a much more limited extent, in VENETO. The district produces little else, and exports little other than its fame beyond its own boundaries.

Vienna Vienna boasts of being the only capital city with a serious wine industry within its boundaries (although PARIS could at one time have made the same claim). Strict laws protect the city's 680 ha of vines, which were even more extensive in the Middle Ages, thanks to the influence of CHARLEMAGNE. Both monastic and aristocratic wine producers served the local populace with wine from specially built cellars, the precursors of Austria's unique HEURIGER tradition. Attractively youthful, relatively simple wines, typically made from Grüner Veltliner, are served to locals and tourists alike in these wine taverns in outlying suburbs such as Grinzing, Nussdorf, Neustift, and Sievering on the right bank of the Danube, and Stammersdorf, Strebersdorf, and Jedlersdorf on the left bank. Vienna also produces wines of real quality and ageing potential, however, notably those made from Grüner Veltliner and Riesling grown on vineyards on the slopes of the Nussberg and the Kahlenberg at Döbling, and those of Bisamberg on the left bank. Red grapes are increasingly important. Traditional customs are maintained in many less ambitious vineyards still cultivated with a mixture of grape varieties which are vinified together and called GEMISCHTER SATZ. Edelmoser, Franz Mayer, and Wieninger are three of Vienna's best producers.

Wine labelling

Wine laws drawn up since 1985 are some of the strictest in the world. They share much of the nomenclature of the GERMAN WINE LAW but standards in general and minimum MUST WEIGHTS in particular are higher (although warmer summers mean that it is easier to achieve higher Oechsle levels in most Austrian wine districts than in Germany). Qualitätswein is a genuinely exclusive category, for example, and Kabinett is regarded as a subcategory of Qualitätswein rather than a fully fledged Prädikatswein, as only Spätlese, Auslese, Strohwein, Eiswein, Beerenauslese, Ausbruch, and Trockenbeerenauslese are in Austria. All Austrian wines should have a red and white striped 'Banderole' around the neck or on top of the cork, which must be purchased by the producer to ensure that official quotas are not breached and to provide some sort of tracking system.

Wines are also labelled according to sugar content, the permitted limits having been increased in 1994. See SWEETNESS for the official European Union classification of trocken, halbtrocken, etc. A trocken wine must have a residual sugar level of no more than 9 g/l, a halbtrocken wine 9 to 12 g/l, a medium sweet, halbsüss or lieblich wine 12 to 45 g/l, and a sweet or süss wine more than 45 g/l. (The term extra trocken may be used for a wine with less than 4 g/l, the former standard for trocken.) Wines carrying the name of a grape variety or a vintage date must be composed of at least 85 per cent of that grape variety and 85 per cent of wine from that vintage respectively.

Tafelwein The bottom rung, for which grapes must achieve a must weight of 10.6 °KMW (51 °Oechsle). No Tafelwein other than BERGWEIN, wine produced on steeper slopes, may be sold in regular bottles. Traditionally these simple wines are bottled in two-litre bottles either by small, part-time growers or by négociants for supermarkets. Only a small percentage of Austria's total production is bottled as Tafelwein, which may state as its origin only Österreich. No grape variety or vintage may be cited.

Landwein One step up from Tafelwein, LANDWEIN must be made from certain specified grape varieties, must reach 14 °KMW (68 °Oechsle). Only about 5 per cent of all Austrian wine qualifies as Landwein, which may state as its origin only a wine region such as Weinland, Bergland, Steirerland, or Wien. Landwein has the same maximum yields per hectare as Qualitätswein (9,000 kg).

Qualitätswein This is the name both of a category which includes the subcategory Kabinett (below) and of a subcategory itself which represents the majority of Austrian wine. To qualify as Qualitätswein, the wine must come from a single area specified on the label and must demonstrate the characteristics of the recognized grape variety from which it is made. The must weight must reach 15 °KMW (73 °Oechsle) and, after chaptalization within certain limits, the wine must have 9 per cent alcohol. As in Germany, wines are tasted, analysed, and awarded a code that is the Austrian equivalent of Germany's AP NUMBER. The maximum yield per hectare may not exceed 9,000 kg or 6,750 litres.

Kabinett Regarded as merely a Qualitätswein in Austria, Kabinett wines, like Prädikatswein below, may nevertheless not be chaptalized. Oechsle levels must reach 84° (17 °KMW) and residual sugar cannot exceed 9 g/l (see SWEETNESS). This category is rarely used.

Prädikatswein All Prädikatswein (Spätlese, Auslese, Strohwein, Eiswein, Beerenauslese, Ausbruch, Trockenbeerenauslese) must be from one wine area, must be vintage dated, and must have its must weight officially certified. As in Germany, no Prädikatswein may be chaptalized. No Austrian Prädikatswein may be sweetened by added SÜSSRESERVE; all alcohol and residual sugar must be the result of natural grape sugars. Minimum alcohol is 5 per cent.

Spätlese A Spätlese must be made from fully ripe grapes picked at a minimum must weight of 19 °KMW (94 °Oechsle).

Auslese Must weight must be at least 21 °KMW (105 °Oechsle) and any unripe or unhealthy grapes must be excluded.

Strohwein 'Straw wine' made from overripe grapes with a must weight of at least 25 °KMW (127 °Oechsle) which are dried on straw or reeds until they reach the necessary must weight by dehydration (see DRIED GRAPE WINES).

Eiswein 'Ice wine' should be made from grapes with a must weight of 25 °KMW (127 °Oechsle), picked and pressed while still frozen at about −7 °C or even below. (see ICE WINE).

Beerenauslese Sweet wine made from grapes that are affected by noble rot with a must weight of at least 25 °KMW (127 °Oechsle).

Ausbruch A speciality of Rust in Neusiedlersee-Hügelland, made from grapes with a must weight of at least 27 °KMW (139 °Oechsle) that are naturally shrivelled, overripe, and affected by noble rot. See also AUSBRUCH.

Trockenbeerenauslese Very sweet wine made from grapes with a must weight of at least 30 °KMW (156 °Oechsle) that are naturally shrivelled, overripe and affected by noble rot.

R.Ho.

Blom, P., *The Wines of Austria* (London, 2000).

MacDonogh, G., *New Wines from the Old World* (Vienna, 1997).

Moser, P., *The Ultimate Austrian Wine Guide* (Klosterneuburg, 2004).

www.winesfromaustria.com

autolysis, the destruction of cells by their own ENZYMES. In a wine-making context, the term most commonly applies to the action of dead YEAST cells, or lees, after a second fermentation has taken place during SPARKLING WINE-MAKING. Its effects are greatest if wine is left in contact with the lees of a second fermentation in bottle for at least five years, and minimal if LEES CONTACT lasts for less than 18 months. Autolysis is unwelcome in most wines but in sparkling wines it is highly desirable: MOUTH-FEEL is improved through the release of POLY-SACCHARIDES; OXIDATION is inhibited through the release of reducing enzymes; and the production of certain MANNOPROTEINS reduces tartrate precipitation and improves protein stability. In addition, there is an increase in amino acids, which are the precursors of those flavour characteristics typically associated with CHAMPAGNE such as acacia, biscuity or bready notes, and other complex aromas from BOTTLE AGEING.

Charpentier, C., and Feuillat, M., 'Yeast autolysis', in G. H. Fleet (ed.), *Wine Microbiology and Biotechnology* (Switzerland, 1993).

autovinification, method of vinification designed to extract maximum COLOUR from red grapes and used primarily in the production of red port. Autovinification, a process involving automatic PUMPING OVER, was developed in ALGERIA in the 1960s, where it was known as the Ducellier system. Faced with a shortage of LABOUR in the 1960s, port producers were forced to abandon the traditional practice of treading grapes by foot in LAGARES. Many isolated QUINTAS had no electricity and so shippers built central wineries. The power supply was erratic and too weak for sophisticated pumps or presses so the shippers installed autovinification tanks in order to extract sufficient colour and TANNINS in the short FERMENTATION period prior to FORTIFICATION. Autovinification is a self-perpetuating process induced by the build-up of pressure; no external power source is needed.

Grapes which have been crushed and partially destemmed are pumped into specially constructed autovinification vats (see diagram) which are filled to within about 75 cm (29 in) of the top. The vat is closed and the autovinification unit (*a*) is screwed into place.

As the fermentation begins, CARBON DIOXIDE is given off and pressure builds up inside the vat. This drives the fermenting must up an escape valve (*b*) which spills out into an open reservoir (1) on top of the vat. Eventually the pressure will also force the water out of a second valve (*c*) into a smaller, separate reservoir (2). When the water has been expelled, the carbon dioxide that has built up in the vat escapes with explosive force through valve (*c*). The fermenting must in reservoir (1) falls back into the vat down the central autovinification unit (*a*), spraying the floating CAP of grape skins, so extracting colour and tannin. At the same moment, the water in reservoir (2) returns to valve (*c*), again sealing in the carbon dioxide, and the process repeats itself. The cycle continues until the winemaker judges that sufficient grape sugar has been fermented to alcohol, and sufficient COLOUR has been extracted, at which time the wine is run off and fortified just as described in PORT, wine-making.

At the start of fermentation, when a small amount of carbon dioxide is given off, the autovinification cycle is slow. But when the fermentation is in full swing, the pressure build-up is such that the cycle takes only 10–15 minutes to complete.

Originally autovinification vats were built from cement and lined with resin-painted concrete. However, significant modifications have accompanied improvements in both wine-making technology and the power supply to the DOURO valley, where port is produced. Modern autovinification tanks are made from STAINLESS STEEL and are equipped with REFRIGERATION units to prevent the must from overheating. Some shippers have resorted to traditional pumping over, or *remontage*, although this generally provides insufficient EXTRACTION for better-quality port. Other shippers have successfully combined pumping over with autovinification, thereby giving the winemaker greater control over port fermentation than ever before.

R.J.M.

Auvergne, Côtes d', VDQS which is administratively considered part of the greater LOIRE region, and basin, but these Massif Central vineyards, around Clermont-Ferrand, are in fact closer to the vineyards of the northern RHÔNE than they are to the river Loire itself. From fewer than 300 ha/750 acres of mainly Gamay and some Chardonnay vines, light reds and some pinks and whites are made in quantity, with considerable skill from some of the many small enterprises here. Gamay has long been grown here and this was one of the most important wine regions of France in the 19th century, before which Pinot Noir was grown in preference to Gamay. The names of the communes Boudes, Chanturgue, Château Gay-Corent (often rosé), and Madargue may be appended to Côtes d'Auvergne on wine labels. Most wines are consumed locally; none is expensive.

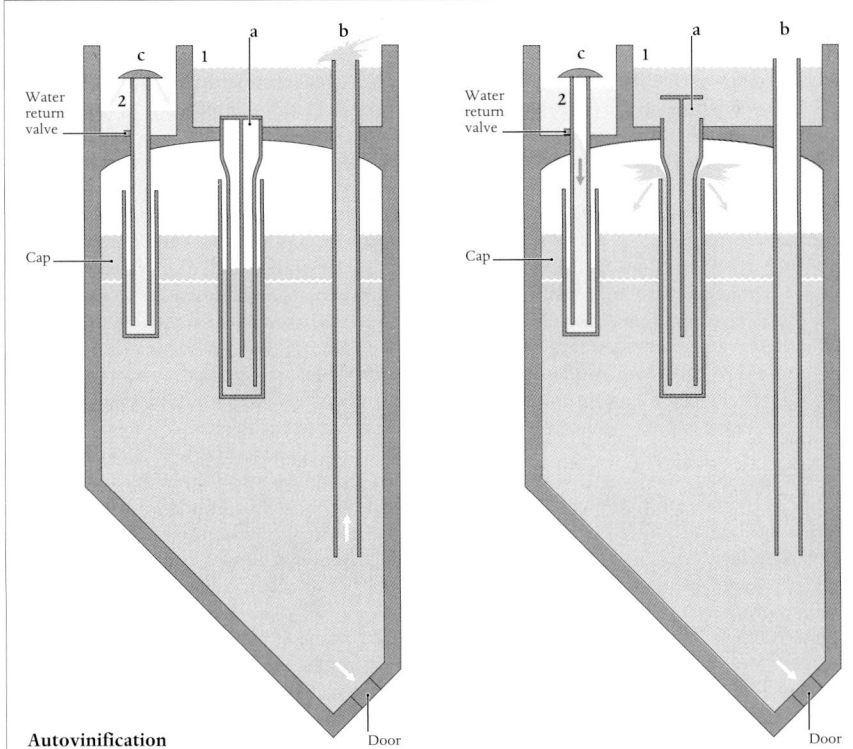

Autovinification

Water return valve

c 1 a b

2

Cap

Door

Auvernat, synonym for various Pinots and other grape varieties used in the Loire. Auvernat Noir is PINOT NOIR; Auvernat Gris is usually MEUNIER, sometimes PINOT GRIS; and Auvernat Blanc is CHARDONNAY.

Auxerre, once an important city in the Yonne *département* of north east France. Today CHABLIS is the Yonne's most famous and substantial wine appellation, but in the time of CHARLEMAGNE, the region centred on Auxerre 20 km/12 miles west had many more vineyards, being a larger centre of population and being conveniently situated on a river which leads directly into the Seine and thence to the PARIS basin. It is perhaps not surprising, given its historic importance, that so many vine varieties have the name or synonym AUXERROIS, meaning 'of Auxerre'.

Within the region, IRANCY has had its own appellation for Pinot Noir since 1999 and ST-BRIS for its Sauvignon Blanc. There are also regional appellations for light reds made from Pinot Noir with the local Cesar and Tressot and whites from Chardonnay sold as BOURGOGNE with one of these suffices: Chitry, Côtes d'Auxerre, Coulanges-la-Vineuse, Épineuil, and, for whites only, Vézelay.

Auxerrois is both the name used for the black-berried MALBEC in CAHORS, where it is the dominant vine variety, and the name of a relatively important white-berried variety in Alsace. And as if that were not confusing

enough, **Auxerrois Gris** is a synonym for PINOT GRIS in Alsace, while Chardonnay, before it became so famous, was once known as Auxerrois Blanc in the Moselle—as distinct from **Auxerrois Blanc de Laquenexy**, which is the variety today called Auxerrois in north east France (including Alsace) and LUXEMBOURG.

In 1999, DNA PROFILING at DAVIS showed that this Auxerrois is a progeny of Pinot and Gouais Blanc (see PINOT). There are still minuscule plantings of Auxerrois in the Loire but today it is most important in Alsace, the French Moselle (including Côtes de TOUL) and LUXEMBOURG, where it is most valued, particularly for its low acidity. If yields are suppressed, which they rarely are, the variety can produce excitingly rich wines in both Moselle regions that are worth ageing until they achieve a bouquet with a honeyed note like that of mature Chablis, the wine which today could be described as 'from Auxerre' or, in French, Auxerrois.

Auxerrois is Alsace's *éminence grise*, whose increasing total of 1,900 ha/4,800 acres (in France's 2000 census) covered considerably more Alsace vineyard than any one of the other three PINOTS planted there. Relatively rarely seen on a label, it produces slightly flabby, broad wines which are blended into many a wine labelled PINOT BLANC. Auxerrois can add substance if not subtlety to over-produced or under-ripened Pinot Blanc. Many Alsace wine enthusiasts have never heard of Auxerrois, which was the third most common

white wine grape in 2000 in the region's heartland, the Haut-Rhin—well over twice as much as plantings of the Pinot Blanc so much more familiar on wine labels. An Alsace wine labelled 'Pinot Blanc' could contain nothing but Auxerrois, which is also a major ingredient in EDELZWICKER.

Germany's plantings of Auxerrois reached 126 ha/310 acres in 2003, almost none of them, interestingly, in the Upper Mosel regions closest to Luxembourg but rather in Baden across the Rhine from Alsace. It has also recently been planted in the vineyards of some first class vintners in the Middle Nahe and adjacent Rheinhessen.

The variety achieved international fame in the 1980s when it was discovered that the first Chardonnay cuttings officially promulgated in SOUTH AFRICA were in fact nothing more glamorous than Auxerrois.

Galet, P., *Dictionnaire encyclopédique des cépages* (Paris, 2000).

Auxey-Duresses, a village in Burgundy producing medium-priced red and white wines not dissimilar to neighbouring VOLNAY and MEURSAULT respectively, although more austere in style. The vineyards, which include those of the hamlets of Petit Auxey and Melin, are located on either side of a valley subject to cooler winds than the main Côte de BEAUNE. PINOT NOIR vineyards, including such PREMIERS CRUS as Les Duresses and Le Climat de Val, are grown on the south east slope of the Montagne du Bourdon. White wines, made from CHARDONNAY, account for just above a quarter of the production, covering the slopes adjacent to Meursault. Some vines, atypically for Burgundy, are trained high.

In the past, wines from Auxey-Duresses were likely to have been sold under the names of grander neighbours. Many are now labelled as Côte de Beaune-Villages, although the village appellation is becoming more popular.

See CÔTE D'OR and map under BURGUNDY.

J.T.C.M.

auxins, one of a number of groups of natural HORMONES present in vines which regulate growth. They are produced in vine parts which are actively growing, such as shoot and root tips. Auxins favour cell growth over cell division, but are also involved in inhibiting the growth of LATERAL SHOOTS. Many chemicals have been synthesized which are chemically related and have a similar biological function. For example, the compounds 2,4-D and 2,4,5-T are auxin-like and form the basis of some HERBICIDES, which are used widely in cereal production. Vines, like tomatoes and cotton, are very sensitive to 2,4-D vapours such as can drift over vineyards when neighbouring farmers use aerial spraying, even from many miles away. Most vine-growing regions have now enacted laws to protect vineyards from the effects of such spraying.

R.E.S.

AVA, the acronym for **American Viticultural Area** and the UNITED STATES' relatively rudimentary answer to France's APPELLATION CONTRÔLÉE system of permitted geographical designations. The US federal government began developing this system in the early 1980s through its Bureau of Alcohol, Tobacco, and Firearms (BATF; see TTB). Under existing regulations, AVAs are theoretically defined by geographic and climatic boundaries, rather than pre-existing political ones, although this is not invariably true and there is some overlap of boundaries. The system requires no limitations on varieties planted, YIELDS, or other specifics familiar to those who know France's AC or Italy's DOC laws. The only requirement for their use is that 85 per cent of the grapes in a wine labelled with an AVA come from that region; if the wine is a VARIETAL, the legal minimum of 75 per cent of the named variety must come from the named AVA. (Unlike the AC, or DOC system, however, neither the expression 'AVA' nor 'American Viticultural Area' appears on wine labels.)

Between 1983 and 1991, BATF approved more than 100 AVAs in the country at large, more than 60 of those in California, but applications slowed to a trickle in the 1990s as producers were discouraged by the bureaucracy involved without any obvious commercial gain. Geography plays a much less important role for American wine consumers than for their European counterparts. San Francisco Bay is an example of a relatively new AVA devised primarily for commercial rather than geographical reasons.

The TTB website has a complete list of AVAs: http://www.ttb.gov/appellation/

Avery, Ronald (1899–1976), came from an old Cornish family which partly moved to Bristol, then an important port in the west of England, towards the end of the 18th century. The family wine merchants Avery & Co dates its origin from 1793 (three crucial years before the birth year of arch rivals HARVEYS of Bristol).

Born in the celebrated BORDEAUX vintage of 1899, he remained faithful to CLARET as his favourite red wine throughout his life. His time at Cambridge was cut short by the death of an uncle, who with his father ran the firm. To gain experience in the trade at a time when nearly all wine was imported in cask and bottled in Britain, he worked in cellars in London, Bordeaux, and Oporto before taking over the running of Averys in 1923.

In those days, wine merchants mostly bought from British agents or their principals, and only visited the wine regions for social purposes. But Avery had a keen, enquiring, even suspicious mind, became an excellent taster, and paid frequent visits abroad, particularly to Bordeaux. There he selected the casks he preferred, and when they arrived in Bristol docks was not averse to topping them up with another wine altogether. By the late 1930s

Averys produced an exceptionally extensive list with a large range of German wines and 100 clarets extending back 20 years, including unusually good stocks of 1923 burgundy and 1929 bordeaux whose quality he was astute enough to discern. At one time the list included seven vintages, back to the famous 1921, of Ch CHEVAL BLANC, a wine then little known in Britain but of which he was very fond. After the Second World War, he and Harry WAUGH, a friend and rival then working for Harveys, were the first to import Ch PÉTRUS into a distinctly unimpressed Britain. At this time he also became specially interested in burgundy in order to secure authentic wines, much subject then to blending from sources in southern France and ALGERIA.

The British wine trade was then an occupation for gentlemen, and Ronald Avery was an eccentric example. Habitually unpunctual, he seldom arrived at his office before 1 p.m., but then stayed late, writing heavily annotated letters of recommendation that turned many customers into friends. At this period most amateurs of fine wine in Britain had an account with Averys.

An excellent navigator, Ronald Avery frequently crossed the English Channel to France in his large motor yacht, which he had to sell to reduce the borrowings entailed by his enthusiastic investment in the Bordeaux vintages of the late 1940s and 1950s. He died in 1976, after which time the firm was run by his son John, although it lost its independence in 1987.

E.P.-R. & J.R.

Averys Bicentennial Wine List (Bristol, 1993).

Avesso, meaning 'contrary', a fitting description for this white grape planted in the VINHO VERDE region of northern PORTUGAL where, unlike the other principal grape varieties in the region, it ripens sufficiently to produce wines of 12–13 per cent alcohol. Mostly planted close to the lower reaches of the river DOURO, it is now being produced as a VARIETAL wine.

R.J.M.

AWRI. See AUSTRALIAN WINE RESEARCH INSTITUTE.

AXA, vast insurance group based in France whose wine division **AXA-Millésimes** is very small in the context of the company and very big in the context of fine wine in general and Bordeaux in particular. Claude Bébéar, the company's president and founder, was led to buy the small St-Émilion property Ch Franc-Mayne in 1984 as an indirect result of his friendship with Jean-Michel Cazes of PAUILLAC. Seeing the investment potential of good Bordeaux properties, he founded AXA-Millésimes in 1987 and it was managed by Cazes alongside his own wine holdings including Ch Lynch Bages until 2000 when Cazes retired and Christian Seely took over. Initial acquisitions included Clos de l'Arlot in NUITS-ST-

GEORGES, the CRU BOURGEOIS Ch Pibran and, also in Pauillac, the second growth Ch Pichon Baron, a fairy-tale chateau which has since been lavishly refurbished, re-equipped, and renamed Ch Pichon-Longueville. In 1989 another landmark building Ch Cantenac-Brown of MARGAUX was acquired, along with POMEROL's Ch Petit Village, sold by the Prats family of Cos in ST-ESTÈPHE. Three years later SAUTERNES first growth Ch Suduiraut and the Disznókő vineyard in TOKAJI were added, a sweet triumvirate being completed by the acquisition and subsequent restoration of the QUINTA DO NOVAL port business in 1993. AXA is by no means the only French insurance company to have invested in wine-related real estate but its distinguishing feature is how it uses wine as a unifying cultural aspect within the corporate ethic. Ch Petit Village was almost sold to the owner of Ch Pavie in St-Emilion in 2001 and Ch Cantenac Brown was put on the market in 2005, reportedly to allow diversification into Spain.

AXR1, variety of rootstock widely used in northern California until, in the late 1980s, it became fatally obvious that it was not resistant to PHYLLOXERA. For more information, see ROOTSTOCK.

Ayze, named, isolated CRU just outside Bonneville east of Geneva whose name may be added to the eastern French appellation Vin de SAVOIE. GRINGET is the principal grape variety used for the light white still and sparkling wines.

Azal Branco, Portuguese white grape variety which brings acidity to VINHO VERDE and is planted on a total of about 5,100 ha/ 12,600 acres, most of them in the MINHO, making it the second most planted white variety there after LOUREIRO. **Azal Tinto** is the dark-skinned version which is used for tart red Vinho Verde.

azeotrope, from the Greek 'to boil unchanged', a mixture of liquid chemicals which has a boiling point either higher or lower than any one of its components. The principal volatile components of wine tend to form azeotropes of two, three, or more components. Water, ETHANOL, volatile organic ACIDS, ALDEHYDES, ESTERS, acetals, and ketones, many of them powerfully aromatic, are among the azeotrope components in wines. The multiplicity of volatile compounds present in wine and our lack of detailed knowledge of all of the azeotropes possible makes it difficult to predict the composition of distillates (which depend on the varied boiling points of components).

Just as the formation of azeotropic mixtures in a liquid governs the boiling point and composition of the vapour during DISTILLATION, so it governs the composition of the vapours above a liquid in a glass at room temperature. When we smell a wine, our noses are recording the impression created by the azeotropic mixture rather than that of any single component.   A.D.W.

Azerbaijan, eastern state of the former Soviet Union situated between ARMENIA and the Caspian Sea producing only a fraction of the wine it produced before the fall of communism. Divided into the mountain system of the large and small Caucasus and the Kura and Araka lowlands, it includes the Republics of Nakhichevan and Nagorno Karabakh.

History

Grape-growing is the oldest branch of Azerbaijan's economy. Archaeology has revealed seeds of cultured grapes, stones for crushing grape berries, and stone fermentation and storage vessels dating back to the second millennium BC in the settlements of Kültan, Galabaglar, and Galajig (Nakhichevan).

HERODOTUS, describing a campaign of the SCYTHIAN chief Madyas in ASIA MINOR in the 7th century BC, mentioned that viticulture and wine-making were already developed in that region. The Greek geographer Strabo, in the 1st century BC, reported on grape culture in 'Albania', the old name of part of Azerbaijan.

The Arabian historians and geographers Abulfedy, Masudi, Khaukal, and El Mugaddasi recorded that vineyards existed near the towns of Gianji and Bardy during Arab domination. Viticulture of that region declined in the periods of war and revived in the time of peace. Viticulture was on a commercial scale after 1814, and developed especially fast at the end of the 19th century when two railways were built which provided access to the enormous wine market of RUSSIA.

By the beginning of the 20th century, small viticultural farms were established in the Kirovabad-Kazakh region as well as much larger enterprises in specialized zones of commercial grape and wine production. In 1940, the total vineyard area was 33,000 ha/ 81,500 acres, but the Second World War reduced this total to 21,000 ha/51,900 acres by 1947. Revival came in 1954, when expansion in grape cultivation began once more and gross yields also increased.

Climate and geography

The climate and the soils of mountainous regions are determined to a considerable extent by latitude, altitude, relief, and exposition of slopes. The climate of Azerbaijan varies between moderately warm with dry winters, to cold with abundant rainfall.

The average annual temperature is 10.5 to 15.5 °C (51–60 °F). The active temperature summation is between 3,000 and 4,600 °C in its varied wine regions. Annual rainfall in the low and premountainous parts of the country, where grapes are grown, is 250 and 600 mm (23 in) respectively.

Modern viticulture is concentrated in the Kirovabad-Kazakh and Shirvan regions, in the Republics of Nagorno-Karabakh and Nakhichevan, and in microregions of several other zones.

Viticulture

Only about 10 per cent of the vineyards, mainly in Nakhichevan, need the WINTER PROTECTION that is so necessary in Russian vineyards. About half of all vineyards need IRRIGATION and only about 20 per cent of them are grafted on to PHYLLOXERA-resistant ROOTSTOCKS. Irrigated vineyards are mainly in the Khanlar, Agdam, Mardakert, Tauz, Kazakh, Fizuli, and Shamkhor regions as well as in several zones of Nakhichevan.

Vine varieties

The country has 17 vine varieties officially recognized for wine production—and 16 table grape varieties are planted, accounting for 15 per cent of the total vineyard area. The most common varieties are RKATSITELI and PINOT NOIR.

New vineyards are planted to PINOT BLANC, ALIGOTÉ, Podarok Magaracha, Pervenets Magaracha (both developed at the Institute MAGARACH), Doina, Viorica, Ranni Magaracha, and Kishmish Moldavski.

Industry organization

In 1990, Azerbaijan's reported 181,000 ha/ 447,000 acres of vineyard yielded 1,196,000 tonnes of grapes and just 661,000 hl/17.5 million gal of wine, 18.2 million bottles of Soviet sparkling wine and 114,000 hl/3 million gal of brandy. By 2002, according to OIV statistics, total vineyard had shrivelled to just 10,000 ha/24,700 acres and total wine production to 73,000 hl. Commerce in this oil-rich republic can best be described as entrepreneurial.

In the mid 1990s, the leading wine enterprises of the country, which produce more than 90 different brands of wine and brandy, were the two Baku wineries, the Baku sparkling wines enterprise, and the Khanlar winery.
                                              V.R. & M.A.

azienda, Italian for a business. An **azienda agricola** is a farm, the equivalent of a French DOMAINE, and the phrase should appear on a wine label only if the grapes were grown and the wine produced on that estate; an **azienda vinicola**, on the other hand, may buy in grapes from elsewhere.

Azores, archipelago in the Atlantic and an autonomous region of PORTUGAL with three IPR regions. See BISCOITOS, PICO, and GRACIOSA.

BA, common abbreviation, used particularly by English-speakers, for the sweet-wine designation BEERENAUSLESE, the second sweetest Prädikat in GERMAN WINE LAW.

Băbească Neagră, Romania's second most planted red wine vine variety, after Merlot, whose name, meaning 'grandmother's grape', compares directly with FETEASCĂ or 'young girl's grape'. There were about 6,300 ha/15,560 acres of this variety planted in 2005, most of them producing light, fruity reds, considerably less 'serious' than Fetească Neagră.

Babo, alternative name for KMW, the Austrian unit of MUST WEIGHT. See KLOSTERNEUBURG.

Bacchus, common name in Ancient ROME for the classical god of wine whom the Greeks called Bacchos but, more usually, DIONYSUS. There was no official Roman festival of Bacchus: the Roman Senate suppressed the **Bacchanalia** in 186 BC because it saw them not only as a danger to the state, but also as a bacchanal in the modern sense, a scene of drunkenness and sexual licence. **Bacchic** poetry is verse with a vinous theme, a speciality of the ARAB POETS. Because the Romans concentrated on the vinous aspect of this much more complex god, and possibly because the word Bacchus is considerably easier to say and spell than Dionysus, the Roman name is much more commonly used in modern times, and is regarded as a word rich in wine connotations. The United States has its Society of Bacchus for committed wine enthusiasts, and the word is used emotively around the world to conjure up various conjunctions of wine and pleasure.

Dalby, A., *Bacchus. A Biography* (Los Angeles, 2003).

Bacchus is also the name of one of the most important GERMAN CROSSINGS. It was bred from a Silvaner × Riesling crossing and the lacklustre MÜLLER-THURGAU and in good years can provide growers in Germany with musts notching up the all-important numbers on the OECHSLE scale as well as powerful flavours and character, and is therefore useful for blending with Müller-Thurgau. Unlike the more aristocratic and more popular crossing KERNER, however, the wine produced lacks acidity and is not even useful for blending with high-acid musts in poor years since it too needs to be fully ripe before it can express its own exuberant flavours.

Bacchus's great allure for growers, however, is that it can be planted on sites on which Riesling is an unreliable ripener and will ripen as early and as productively as Müller-Thurgau. Total plantings in Germany reached a peak of around 3,500 ha/8,650 acres in 1990, about a third more than a decade previously, and more than half of this total was in Rheinhessen, where its substance is valued as an ingredient in QBA blends. This total had fallen to 2,500 ha/6,200 acres by 2003, making it the seventh most widely planted white variety, edging out SCHEUREBE. Franken produces some respectable varietal wines from its increasing area of 700 ha/1700 acres.

In the UK, Bacchus is the fourth most widely planted variety and can produce creditable wines vaguely reminiscent of Sauvignon Blanc. With the UK's generally lower yields and higher natural acid levels, it does not suffer from the flabbiness of warmer climate examples.

Bachet, ancient, dark-berried vine variety associated with the Aube in the south of the CHAMPAGNE region. It is a natural offspring of Pinot and Gouais Blanc (see PINOT).

Baco, François, was, like BOUSCHET, a nurseryman who saw his name live on in the names of some of the most successful of the vine varieties he bred. Baco's specialities were FRENCH HYBRIDS and his most successful was **Baco Blanc**, sometimes called **Baco 22A**, which was hybridized in 1898 and was, for much of the 20th century until the late 1970s, the prime ingredient in armagnac—a role now occupied by UGNI BLANC but previously occupied by FOLLE BLANCHE, although the French vineyard census of 2000 still noted 2,100 ha/ 5,200 acres of the variety, mainly in armagnac country. Baco Blanc, a crossing of Folle Blanche with the sturdy NOAH, was Baco's solution to Folle Blanche's reluctance to be grafted after the predations of PHYLLOXERA. Baco Blanc, once planted quite widely in western France, is now being fast pulled up, however, as the French authorities seek to purge hybrids from their vineyards. New Zealand grew Baco Blanc in some quantity at one time but here too evidence of a hybrid past is being rapidly eradicated.

Baco Noir, or **Baco 1,** resulted from crossing Folle Blanche with a variety of *Vitis riparia* in 1894 and was at one time cultivated in such disparate French wine regions as Burgundy, Anjou, and the Landes. It has also been widely planted in the eastern United States (see NEW YORK and CANADA), where its relatively fruity wines are not marked by the FOXY flavours associated with *Vitis* LABRUSCA and are sometimes harnessed to make NOUVEAU reds.

bacteria, very small micro-organisms which have serious implications in both viticulture and wine-making. Although not common pathogens of the grapevine, BACTERIAL DISEASES are potentially destructive and so very important.

In wine-making just two groups of bacteria are important, ACETOBACTER and LACTIC ACID BACTERIA. Since grape juice and wine are both high in ACIDITY, the great majority of bacteria, with the exception of these two groups, are incapable of living in them and, if introduced, do not survive. (Drinks such as cider, perry, orange juice, and beer are all much less acid than wine, are thereby subject to many forms of BACTERIAL SPOILAGE to which wine is immune, and therefore lack wine's AGEING potential.) No known human pathogenic bacteria can survive in wine, however, which is one of the reasons why it has been such a safe drink (safer than water at some times and in some places) through the ages.

Acetobacter (which do not harm humans) can turn wine, or any other dilute solution containing ETHANOL, into VINEGAR.

Acetobacter require OXYGEN for growth and survival and they die in the absence of oxygen (which is why care is taken to exclude oxygen from certain stages of wine-making and all stages of wine preservation—see LEFTOVER WINE).

Lactic acid bacteria produce LACTIC ACID and grow best in environments where there is a very small amount of oxygen. They are important as the agents of MALOLACTIC FERMENTATION in wines, by which excess MALIC ACID is decomposed.　　　　A.D.W., R.E.S., & P.J.W.

Kunkee, R., 'Bacteria in wine', in *Technology of Wine Making* (Westport, Conn., 1979).

bacterial blight,
vine BACTERIAL DISEASE caused by the bacterium *Xanthomonas ampelina*, so serious that it has led some Greek and French growers to abandon stricken vineyards. This disease shows its presence by retarding and killing young shoots. It is spread by rain and also by pruning tools. It can be controlled by removing and destroying infected plants and by disinfecting pruning tools between vines, as well as by copper sprays.　　　R.E.S.

bacterial diseases,
group of grapevine diseases caused by BACTERIA, small organisms which do not commonly attack vines but which can be deadly and are difficult to control. Of the bacterial diseases, PIERCE'S DISEASE is the most important and QUARANTINE authorities around the world are anxious to stop it spreading from America. In parts of North and Central America (southern California, Florida, and eastern Texas, for instance), viticulture can be rendered commercially impossible by the natural presence of this disease. Other economically important bacterial diseases are BACTERIAL BLIGHT and CROWN GALL.　　　R.E.S.

Flaherty, D. L., *et al.* (eds.), *Grape Pest Management* (Berkeley, Calif., 1981).

Pearson, R. C., and Goheen, A. C., *Compendium of Grape Diseases* (St Paul, Minn., 1988).

bacterial spoilage,
range of wine maladies or FAULTS including gas, haze, cloud, and off-flavours generated by the activity of BACTERIA in wine. These bacteria are either ACETOBACTER or LACTIC ACID BACTERIA. Acetobacter's tendency to transform wine into vinegar can be checked by keeping air away from wine, on the part of both winemaker and wine drinker (see LEFTOVER WINE). Lactic acid bacteria are more varied in their effects, which

include a wide range of unpleasant-smelling compounds, depending on the type of bacterium. These are relatively rarely seen today since great care is taken by winemakers (see STABILIZATION and HYGIENE) to guard against spoilage by lactic acid bacteria in the winery and to minimize the risk of a wine's being bottled with any spoilage bacteria (see FILTRATION, PASTEURIZATION, STERILE BOTTLING). If lactic acid bacteria do attack a wine in bottle, the results are usually detrimental to the taste and clarity of the wine, and gas is usually given off.　　A.D.W.

Baden,
GERMANY's longest wine region, stretching over 400 km/250 miles from the border with FRANKEN in the north to Lake Constance (the Bodensee) and German-speaking SWITZERLAND in the south (see map under GERMANY). The general and local climate, the varying soils, and the height above sea level have a marked effect on the wines of Baden's nine districts, or BEREICHE, which have a combined vineyard area of 15,900 ha/39,300 acres. Baden is Germany's stronghold of the PINOT family of vine varieties, with fashionable SPÄTBURGUNDER and GRAUBURGUNDER particular specialities.

This region's suitability for ripening a wide range of red grapes, in tandem with German consumer FASHION, has resulted in a surging red tide here, in 2003 surpassing 40 per cent of total acreage.

Baden is the southernmost region of Germany, with some of its vineyards at lower LATITUDES than those in ALSACE across the river RHINE in France. As a result, Baden wines are typically higher in ALCOHOLIC STRENGTH than most other German wines. This natural tendency is recognized by EUROPEAN UNION law, which has placed Baden in its administrative Zone B alongside the northern wine regions of France, while the rest of Germany is in Zone A. The annual RAINFALL rises to 1,200 mm/47 in in the Bereich Ortenau on the slopes of the Black Forest. It tends to rain briefly but powerfully, with water pouring out of the sky and then rushing through the storm channels that lead across the plain to the river Rhine. EROSION would have been a serious problem without the substantial vineyard modernization since the Second World War. Of those vineyards in the state of Baden-Württemberg where modernization (FLURBEREINIGUNG) has been possible, three-quarters have been reconstructed.

The Bereich **Tauberfranken** covers 714 ha/ 1,764 acres that intermittently follow the river Tauber until the confluence with the Main at Wertheim. Here, spring FROSTS are a great danger so that the vines (primarily MÜLLER-THURGAU and Spätburgunder) are grown mainly on slopes above the cool valley floor (see HILLSIDE VINEYARDS). The wine is similar to that of FRANKEN and for historical reasons the QUALITÄTSWEIN is sold in its neighbour's flagon-shaped BOCKSBEUTEL.

East across the Odenwald, the vineyards of the Bereiche **Badische Bergstrasse** (394 ha/974 acres) and **Kraichgau** (1,327 ha/ 3,249 acres) run north and south of Heidelberg. The first district is simply a continuation of the HESSISCHE BERGSTRASSE. In this southern stretch of the Bergstrasse, RIESLING is less widely grown and Müller-Thurgau is the leading vine. The northern Baden wines have good acidity, with Riesling on the granite soil showing charm and delicacy. Most of the harvest is handled by co-operative cellars.

There are two Bereiche in Baden whose wines are especially well known among wine lovers in Germany. In **Kaiserstuhl** and in the **Ortenau** the names of some communities are as familiar in the German wine world as the better-known villages of the MOSEL-SAAR-RUWER. This may be because almost the entire grape harvest of some villages is vinified by one good co-operative cellar.

South of Baden-Baden there are a few villages which, like those in Tauberfranken, sell their wines in the Bocksbeutel. Riesling predominates and certainly cheaper versions can be found further south in the Bereich Ortenau, away from the inflationary effect of Baden-Baden. The steep vineyards of Neuweier and Varnhalt are impressive and lie on the spurs of the Black Forest which run west, towards the Rhine. At nearby Bühl, Sasbachwalden, Kappelrodeck, and Waldulm, good Spätburgunder is produced at prices which reflect its quality.

Durbach near Offenburg is one of the best and most versatile Ortenau wine villages. Spätburgunder dominates, and the Riesling (known locally as Klingelberger) has that vital ingredient in Germany of good ACIDITY. Durbach also claims more Traminer, or Clevner as it is called in the Ortenau, than any other village in the country.

Low YIELDS contribute to the quality of better Baden wine today. Village co-operatives encourage the production of a crop far smaller than the maximum legal amount, through the way in which they pay their members. Nevertheless, yields from the white wine varieties are often greater in Baden than they are in Alsace, and the wines are usually not so concentrated as a result. Less sugar is added to them to increase the alcohol content (see ENRICHMENT) and many Baden wines are lighter in style. With the red wines the situation is different and the better Baden Spätburgunder is impressive, a dark-coloured wine with a wealth of flavour.

Between Offenburg and Freiburg, the capital of the Baden wine trade, the Bereich **Breisgau** rolls across the rural foothills of the Black Forest with much of the wine made by the vast central co-operative cellars in Kaiserstuhl, the Badischer Winzerkeller. Its members include 90 local CO-OPERATIVES and one wine estate incorporating a total vineyard area of 16,000 ha/39,500 acres. Co-operatives are responsible for some 85 per cent of Baden's wine production.

The wines of the Bereich **Tuniberg** are lighter than those of Kaiserstuhl and virtually all are produced by the Badischer Winzerkeller. South of Freiburg, the pleasant landscape of the Bereich **Markgräflerland** is known for its easy-to-drink wine from Gutedel (CHASSELAS), and near Lake Constance (Bodensee) the wines of the Bereich **Bodensee** have more acidity and elegance. I.J., K.B.S., & D.S.

Baga, red grape found throughout central PORTUGAL but mostly in the BAIRRADA region, where, unusually for Portugal, it accounts for as much as 90 per cent of black varieties. It is a vigorous variety, resistant to POWDERY MILDEW but ripens late and has a tendency to rot in the damp Atlantic climate of Portugal's western seaboard, threatened by early autumn rains. This small, thick-skinned variety (*baga* means 'berry') produces dark, fairly acidic, tannic wines that can be undrinkably astringent if the grapes are under-ripe when picked, a characteristic accentuated by fermentation on the stalks, which is still quite common. Well-made wines from a ripe year are full of fruit and capable of long ageing however. A large amount of Baga ends up as rosé: Sogrape, producers of MATEUS rosé have a large winery in the Bairrada region. Plantings totalled an estimated 10,200 ha/25,000 acres in 2004. R.J.M.

Baghdad, the capital of modern IRAQ, was founded by the first Abbasid caliph, al-Mansur, in AD 762. Early in its history the city became the focus of a Bacchic culture (see ARAB POETS), celebrated most eloquently by the poet ABU NUWAS. Although wine was imbibed in the Caliphal court and some outlying districts of the city (al-Karkh, for example), most wine was consumed where it was produced, in the small monasteries and towns that lay outside the city in various parts of Iraq. Their names are preserved in poetry and other sources ('Āna, Hīt, Qutrubbul in the vicinity of the city, for example, and Tīzanabādh further south near Kufa). P.K.

bag-in-box. See BOXES.

Bairrada, evolving DOC wine region in northern PORTUGAL (see map under PORTUGAL). The coastal belt south of OPORTO has been producing wine since Portugal gained independence from the Moors in the 10th century. By the early 1700s, Bairrada's dark, tannic red wines were widely drunk in Britain, masquerading as or blended with PORT from the DOURO valley to the north. Then in 1756, as part of his measures to protect the authenticity of port (see DELIMITATION), the Marquis of Pombal, Portugal's powerful prime minister, ordered that Bairrada's vineyards should be uprooted.

It has taken Bairrada more than two centuries to recover. The district was excluded from the list of wine regions demarcated by the

Portuguese government in 1908. After constant pressure from growers, Bairrada was awarded REGIÃO DEMARCADA status in 1979 and, like Portugal's other RDs, it is now designated a Denominação de Origem Controlada (DOC).

Like much of northern Portugal, Bairrada is an area of agricultural smallholdings. Cereals, beans, and vines thrive in between clumps of eucalyptus on the heavy but fertile clay soils. Most growers send their grapes to one of six CO-OPERATIVES but more than 20 merchants also have cellars in the region where wines from Bairrada and neighbouring DÃO are bought in for AGEING and BLENDING. Since the 1980s, a number of larger individual estates have started to produce their own wines, although one of the leading producers in the region Luis Pato now prefers to bottle his wines under the Vinho Regional BEIRAS designation.

Bairrada is unusual in Portugal in that it is almost a one-grape region. Over 70 per cent of the wines are red, made principally from the BAGA vine. In good years, Bairrada is capable of producing some of Portugal's leading reds which have the capacity to age in bottle for two decades or more. Over recent years wine styles have been changing and firms such as Aliança and SOGRAPE (who produce Mateus Rosé in Bairrada) are gradually adapting their vinification methods to make their wines softer and more approachable. Some other grape varieties such as TOURIGA NACIONAL, CABERNET SAUVIGNON, and MERLOT are also being planted to add roundness to Baga—although the last two have been bottled as Vinho Regional Beiras. White grapes, mostly Maria Gomes (or FERNÃO PIRES) and BICAL, are grown to produce TRADITIONAL METHOD sparkling wines, although these are not entitled to the Bairrada denomination.

On the edge of the region, the Palace Hotel at Buçaco blends its own red and white wines from grapes bought from growers in Dão and Bairrada. Older vintages are widely regarded as some of the best table wines in Portugal but are available only to guests dining at the hotel or one of its few associated establishments, apart from those few bottles which occasionally crop up at AUCTION. R.J.M.

Mayson, R., *The Wines and Vineyards of Portugal* (London, 2003).

Baiyu, Chinese name for RKATSITELI.

balance is essential for quality in both vine and wine.

Vines

Vine balance is a viticultural concept little appreciated by wine consumers, yet one which is essential for producing grapes for premium wine-making. A vine is in balance when the LEAF TO FRUIT RATIO is in the correct range. The amount of early season shoot growth should also be in balance with the

vine's reserves of CARBOHYDRATES. Vine balance concerns VIGOUR and it can be managed by the VITICULTURIST, with BALANCED PRUNING and WATER STRESS the principal tools. One of the best measures of vine balance is the ratio of fruit yield to pruning weight, now often called the Ravaz index, following its promotion by the French researcher of that name.

Balanced wine comes from balanced vines (a fact acknowledged even by such authors as Halliday and Johnson, who were previously critical of high YIELDS in any circumstances). A balanced vine has shoots of moderate vigour with no SHOOT TIP growth during fruit RIPENING. Leaves are of moderate size and number so excess SHADE is avoided, with both leaves and fruit well exposed to sunlight. Unbalanced vineyards are either too vigorous—in which case poor ripening results from shading and competition between the ripening grapes and shoot tips for carbohydrates—or not vigorous enough—in which case there is insufficient leaf

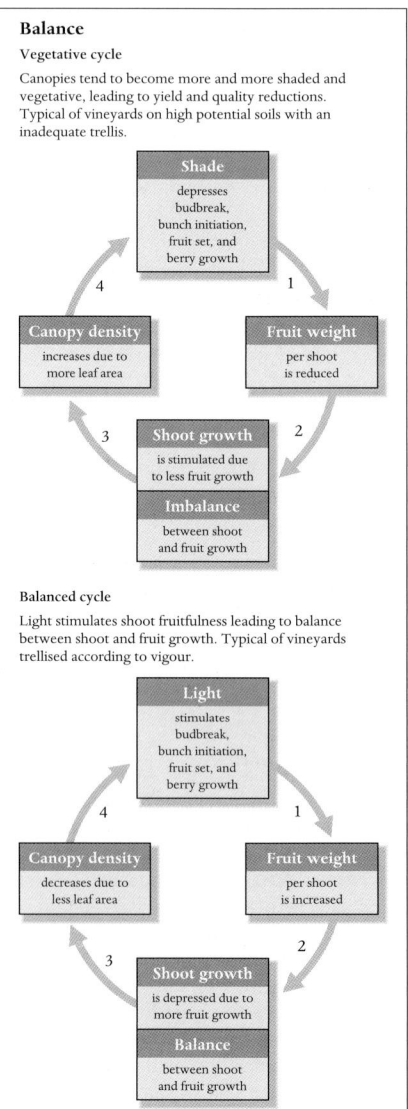

Balance

Vegetative cycle

Canopies tend to become more and more shaded and vegetative, leading to yield and quality reductions. Typical of vineyards on high potential soils with an inadequate trellis.

Shade
depresses budbreak, bunch initiation, fruit set, and berry growth

Fruit weight
per shoot is reduced

Shoot growth
is stimulated due to less fruit growth

Imbalance
between shoot and fruit growth

Canopy density
increases due to more leaf area

Balanced cycle

Light stimulates shoot fruitfulness leading to balance between shoot and fruit growth. Typical of vineyards trellised according to vigour.

Light
stimulates budbreak, bunch initiation, fruit set, and berry growth

Fruit weight
per shoot is increased

Shoot growth
is depressed due to more fruit growth

Balance
between shoot and fruit growth

Canopy density
decreases due to less leaf area

area for proper ripening. Monitoring shoot tip growth is seen as an important management tool for vine balance. R.E.S.

Wines

Wine tasters say that a wine has balance, or is well **balanced**, if its ALCOHOLIC STRENGTH, ACIDITY, RESIDUAL SUGAR, TANNINS, and FRUIT, complement each other so that no single one of them is obtrusive on the PALATE. (Young wines are expected to exhibit more marked tannins than mature ones however.) This extremely important wine characteristic is quite unrelated to FLAVOUR.

balanced pruning. The number of buds to be left on the vine at winter PRUNING should be judged relative to the vine's capacity early in the growing season to support the growth of shoots. In turn, a balanced pruned vine will have sufficient shoot growth to ripen the fruit it carries. The amount of late season growth is related to shoot growth early in the season. The amount of reserve, or stored, CARBOHYDRATES in the vine roots, trunk, and arms will determine how many developing shoots can be sustained. Of course, it is impossible to calculate the amount of stored reserves for each vine (which would involve excavation and chemical analysis), so pruning weights are used as an indication. The underlying principle is that the more the amount of shoot growth in summer, the higher will be the pruning weight and also the stored carbohydrate reserves.

Pruning weights are simply measured by weighing the cane prunings removed at winter pruning and using this figure to judge the appropriate bud numbers to leave at winter pruning. For example, one formula is to keep around 30 buds for each kg/2 lb of pruning weight. Experienced vine pruners can achieve a similar effect by looking at each vine, judging how it grew last growing season, and adjusting this year's number of buds accordingly.

If too few buds are left on the vine at winter pruning relative to the stored carbohydrates, then shoots in spring will grow quickly and have leaves which are too large and stems which are too thick. The vine will have a high LEAF TO FRUIT RATIO, which may result in poor fruit set (see COULURE). In any event, the leaf to fruit imbalance normally leads to a shaded CANOPY MICROCLIMATE and attendant problems of loss of YIELD and quality. Such a situation is common for vines planted close together on fertile soil.

On the other hand, if too many buds are left at pruning relative to stored carbohydrates, then the resulting large number of shoots will develop only slowly in spring. The leaves will be small and the stems spindly. The danger here is that the leaf area will be too low for the weight of grapes, which will ripen slowly and wine quality will suffer. This condition is often described as OVERCROPPING.

See also PRUNING. R.E.S.

Smart, R. E., and Robinson, M., *Sunlight into Wine: A Handbook for Winegrape Canopy Management* (Adelaide, 1991).

Tassie, E., and Freeman, B. M., 'Pruning', in B. G. Coombe and P. R. Dry (eds.), *Viticulture*, ii: *Practices* (Adelaide, 1992).

Winkler, A. J., *et al.*, *General Viticulture* (2nd edn, Berkeley, Calif., 1974).

Bali. See INDONESIA.

Balling, scale of measuring total dissolved compounds in grape juice, and therefore its approximate concentration of grape sugars. It is very similar to the BRIX scale used in the United States. For more details, see MUST WEIGHT.

Balsamina, or **Balsemina**, old Argentine name for SYRAH.

Banat Riesling or **Banat Rizling**, white grape variety grown in ROMANIA and just across the border with VOJVODINA. Its produce tends to be somewhat heavy, a sort of LAŠKI RIZLING (which the locals believe it to be) without the lift. Creata is a synonym.

Bandol, the most serious wine of PROVENCE, typically a deep-flavoured, lush red blend dominated by the MOURVÈDRE grape. Like CHÂTEAUNEUF-DU-PAPE, Bandol produces quintessentially Mediterranean red wines which are easy to appreciate in youth despite their longevity.

The appellation is named after the port from which they were once shipped all over the world. Bandol is now a Mediterranean resort town with little to offer the wine tourist, and the vineyards are on south-facing terraces well inland called locally *restanques*. As in the smaller appellation of CASSIS just along the coast, the vines are protected from the cold north winds, but have to fight property developers for their right to continued existence. A total of about 1,400 ha were cultivated in the early 2000s.

This particularly well-favoured southern corner is one of the few parts of France in which Mourvèdre, the characteristic grape of Bandol, can be relied upon to ripen. Other dark-berried varieties grown include Grenache and Cinsaut, much used for the local herby rosés which account for about one bottle of Bandol in three, together with strictly limited additions of Syrah and Carignan. A small quantity of white Bandol is made from Bourboulenc, Clairette, and Ugni Blanc with a maximum of 40 per cent Sauvignon Blanc, but little of it escapes the region's fish restaurants.

Wine-making techniques are traditional but evolving. All reds must have at least 18 months in cask. Mechanical harvesting is banned. Domaine Tempier is one of the few domaines to have a well-established market outside France but the likes of Domaines de la Bégude and de la Tour du Bon, and Chx La Rouvière,

Pibarnon, Pradeaux, and Vannières have all made fine wines.

Lynch, K., *Adventures along the Wine Route* (New York, 1988).

Banyuls and **Banyuls Grand Cru** are the appellations for France's finest and certainly most complex VINS DOUX NATURELS, made from vertiginous terraced vineyards above the Mediterranean at the southern limit of ROUSSILLON, and indeed mainland France. The dry but powerful red wine produced in the same vineyards is entitled to the appellation COLLIOURE, Banyuls-sur-Mer and Collioure being two of the four dramatic seaside communes included in these two appellations.

Banyuls differs from RIVESALTES, Roussillon's catch-all vin doux naturel, not only in terms of quality but also in style. There is not a hint of Muscat in Banyuls. Grenache Noir must dominate the blend, constituting at least 50 per cent of a Banyuls and 75 per cent of a Banyuls Grand Cru (which latter appellation is ignored by individual producers of the calibre of Dr Parcé of Domaine du Mas Blanc, who could be said to have re-energized the appellation in the mid 20th century). The grapes yield poorly and are often part shrivelled before being picked in early October. Alcohol is added while the must is still on the skins so that a wide range of flavour compounds are absorbed into the young wine, which, after perhaps five weeks' further MACERATION, is then subjected to one of a wide range of ÉLEVAGE techniques. A Banyuls Grand Cru must be matured in wood for at least 30 months. Others may be kept for as long as the producer desires and can afford, in glass BONBONNES or in barrels of all sizes, either carefully topped up in cool, damp conditions or deliberately evaporating, sometimes outdoors to achieve RANCIO flavours, or even in a local version of a SOLERA system.

Some Banyuls is made to preserve the heady aromas of macerated red fruits; others to display the characteristics of a particularly successful and long-past year (sometimes labelled RIMAGE); while other Banyuls demonstrate the extraordinary levels of concentration that can be achieved by Grenache, heat, and time. Such wines are some of the few that go well with chocolate, although many a French chef has created savoury dishes, often with a hint of sweetness, to be served expressly with a particular Banyuls. This is the only French wine region able to offer 20- and 30-year-old wines as a serious proportion of its total production. See also MAURY.

George, R., *The Wines of the South of France* (London, 2001).

Barbaresco, powerful red wine based on the NEBBIOLO grape grown around the village of Barbaresco in the PIEMONTE region in north west Italy. For long considered very much the junior of BAROLO in terms of its size and the power and prestige of its wines, Barbaresco emerged from Barolo's shadow in the 1960s to win recognition of its own striking qualities of elegance and aromatic intensity.

The wine is, in fact, a younger one than Barolo: it was not until the mid 1890s that Domizio Cavazza, professor at the Oenological School of ALBA and director of the Barbaresco CO-OPERATIVE, succeeded in fermenting all of the sugars and producing a completely dry wine, replicating the work of Louis Oudart in Barolo 50 years earlier. Barbaresco did not enjoy Barolo's connection with the House of Savoy and the nobility of the royal court in Turin, and suffered relative commercial obscurity until the efforts of Giovanni GAJA and Bruno Giacosa in the 1960s demonstrated the full potential of the wine.

The production zone of Barbaresco is to the north east and east of the city of Alba and is considerably smaller than that of Barolo but, as in Barolo, the area under vine has increased dramatically in recent years, from 484 ha/ 1,200 acres in the early 1990s to 680 ha/ 1,680 acres in 2004. The wine is produced in the townships of Barbaresco, Treiso (formerly part of Barbaresco), Neive, and a fragment of Alba, although 95 per cent of the cultivated vineyards lie in the first three. Neive calls itself 'the township of four wines' (the others being MOSCATO, BARBERA, DOLCETTO), and Nebbiolo only consolidated its position there after the Second World War. Even today Neive has fewer than 100 ha of Nebbiolo, less than that of Barbera or Dolcetto, and half the area planted with Moscato.

The soil of the Barbaresco zone is fundamentally a calcareous marl of the Tortonian epoch and the wines, in their relative softness and fruitiness and their perfumed aromas, bear a certain resemblance to Barolo produced on similar soils around the villages of La Morra and Barolo, although it is rare to find a Barbaresco with the body and concentration of a fine Cannubi or Brunate. A few positions in Neive, however—notably Santo Stefano and Bricco di Neive—give wines which are, in local parlance, *baroleggiano*, or resemble a Barolo.

Nebbiolo ripens earlier in Barbaresco than in Barolo, probably due to the vineyards' proximity to the river Tanaro, while the wines tend to be a bit lighter as the region is further east than Barolo, so marginally more susceptible to the maritime influence that makes the reds of Asti lighter than those from Alba. This lighter style of wine is reflected in the minimum ageing requirements, two years in total, a year of which must be in oak. This is a year less than for Barolo.

Wine-making techniques, which had previously favoured extremely prolonged MACERATION and CASK AGEING, evolved in the 1970s and 1980s, much as in Barolo, towards considerably shorter periods in cask in an effort to respond to modern tastes for rounder, fruitier

wines. If Barbaresco is generally a lighter-bodied wine than Barolo (although these are wines which must have a minimum ALCOHOLIC STRENGTH of 12.5 per cent and easily reach 13.5 per cent), it is not lacking in the TANNINS and ACIDITY that mark the Nebbiolo grape; young Barbaresco is by no means an inevitably pleasurable glass of wine. It does mature more rapidly than Barolo, however, and rarely ages as well. Barbaresco is normally at its best between five and ten years of age, with the exception of the above-mentioned vineyards in Neive. The general level of wine-making skills is today every bit as good as in Barolo, although this was not historically the case. The work done by the Produttori del Barbaresco, one of Italy's finest CO-OPERATIVES, and by individual producers such as Angelo Gaja and Bruno Giacosa, has helped to establish Barbaresco as a top-quality wine, and a number of smaller producers have benefited as a result.

Single-vineyard bottlings are a relatively recent phenomenon, in Barbaresco as in the rest of Italy. The first efforts date from 1967, and there is a less firmly established written record of CRU designation here than in Barolo. Lorenzo Fantini's monograph on Piedmontese viticulture of the late 19th century indicates very few 'choice positions' in Barbaresco (and none whatsoever in Neive). The first attempts to list and rate the finest positions date from the 1960s (Luigi VERONELLI) and the 1970s (Renato Ratti).

NÉGOCIANTS' willingness to pay higher prices for grapes from certain vineyards, however, does establish the existence of a certain consensus existing in the zone, a tradition which gave an undeniable prestige to Asili, Montefico, Montestefano, and Rabajà in Barbaresco; Albesani and Gallina in Neive; and Pajorè in Treiso. A certain number of the most famous vineyards—San Lorenzo, Tildin, and Martinenga in Barbaresco, Santo Stefano in Neive—are, in effect, 'man-made' crus which have gained their current prestige from the dedicated work and exacting standards of producers such as GAJA, Giacosa, and Alberto di Gresy, and have no precise historical tradition behind them.

Ultra-short FERMENTATIONS and BARRIQUE ageing of the wines were introduced to Barbaresco in the mid 1980s, although the former phenomenon has found fewer converts than in Barolo; the softer quality of Nebbiolo in Barbaresco—conserved by a shorter, one-year minimum ageing period in wood—makes radical innovations in wine-making techniques less of a necessity. The use of new OAK spread rapidly, however, due to the powerful influence of Angelo Gaja, headquartered in Barbaresco itself, and its spicy and aromatic qualities seem to blend well with the character of the wine.

D.T. & D.C.G.

barbarians, uncivilized ancient European people who were introduced to wine, and

therefore considered civilized, by CLASSICAL civilizations. See CELTS.

Barbarossa, red grape variety planted, and occasionally made into VARIETAL wine, in Emilia-Romagna and Corsica. The vine called Barbarossa in LIGURIA is not necessarily related. In PROVENCE it is known as **Barbaroux** and is a permitted, if little planted, grape variety in Côtes de Provence occasionally used for TABLE GRAPES.

Barbera, productive and versatile red grape variety which was Italy's third most planted dark-berried vine, after Sangiovese and Montepulciano, in 2000, when there were 28,300 ha/70,000 acres planted, a dramatic decrease since the nearly 50,000 ha in the 1990s, much of it used to produce tart, cheap wine. It has travelled widely, most notably to the Americas.

The MONFERRATO in Piemonte is frequently cited as the variety's birthplace, although the AMPELOGRAPHER Pierre Viala cites OLTREPÒ PAVESE in Lombardia as its original home. In any case, the archives of the cathedral chapters of Casale Monferrato conserve contracts leasing vineyard land between 1246 and 1277 provided that 'de bonis vitibus barbexinis' were planted.

Barbera ripens relatively late, as much as two weeks after the other 'lesser' black grape variety of Piemonte DOLCETTO, although traditionally still in advance of the stately NEBBIOLO. Its chief characteristic is its high level of natural acidity even when fully ripe, which has helped its popularity in hot climates. This high acidity has also led many ambitious producers to delay picking, and in some cases producers in the Langhe now pick Barbera after Nebbiolo. Such a widely planted variety (see below) has understandably developed various strains in its various spheres of Italian influence, Piemonte, Oltrepò Pavese, EMILIA-ROMAGNA, and the Mezzogiorno.

A white-berried **Barbera Bianca** is also known.

Piemonte

Barbera was once known as 'the people's wine' of Piemonte for its versatility and its abundant production. Its decline can be dated to the METHANOL scandal of 1984, when over 30 people died due to drinking cheap Barbera that had been adulterated with this deadly spirit. Perhaps because it was so widely planted, Barbera comes in a bewildering range of styles, from the young, cheap, and spritzy to powerful, intense, highly priced wines that need extended cellaring, reflecting the extreme heterogeneousness of the soils and MESOCLIMATES of the zones where it is planted.

Certain characteristics are constant none the less: a deep ruby colour (the wine was frequently used in the past to 'correct' the colour of Nebbiolo grapes grown in BAROLO and BARBARESCO); a full body with notably low levels of TANNINS; pronounced ACIDITY which is aggravated by over-production, Barbera being a variety of exemplary VIGOUR and productivity. The use of southern Italian blending wine to compensate for the thinness and sharpness of overcropped Barbera, a common practice in the past, seems to be coming to an end as YIELDS drop. The DOC regulations, which regrettably permit generous yields (70 hl/ha in Alba, 63 hl/ha in Asti), relatively low ALCOHOLIC STRENGTH (12 per cent in Alba and Asti, 11.5 in the Monferrato), and high minimum acidity in relation to the alcohol and body of the wines, do little to restrain yields or exalt quality.

ALBA, ASTI, and the Monferrato give their names to the three DOC zones of Piemonte, although the zones tend to sprawl across rather vast extensions of territory: there are 171 townships in the Asti DOC and 215 townships in the Monferrato DOC (with the two zones overlapping to a certain extent). Given the enormous acreage devoted to Barbera, it is no surprise that little mapping of the most suitable subzones has occurred, but, at the level of folk knowledge, the hills immediately to the north and south of Alba and Monforte d'Alba in the Alba DOC and, in the province of Asti, the area from Nizza Monferrato north west towards Vinchio, Castelnuovo Calcea, Agliano, Belveglio, and Rocchetta Tanaro are considered classic zones for Barbera. Much remains to be done, obviously, in matching variety and TERROIR. This was partly redressed in 2001 when Nizza was recognized as a specific subzone within the Barbera d'Asti DOC, with stricter regulations. Historically, Nizza, because it is one of the warmest parts of the Asti zone, has produced the ripest and best Barbera. In Asti, Barbera is given the best vineyard sites, whereas in Alba these sites go to Nebbiolo.

A small number of Barberas underwent a significant metamorphosis during the 1980s and 1990s as producers, in a parallel development to the Sangiovese-based SUPERTUSCANS, undertook BARREL MATURATION. The prototype was Giacomo Bologna's Bricco dell'Uccellone (although Émile PEYNAUD, while consulting for the ASTI house of Gancia in the early 1970s, had also suggested using BARRIQUES for Barbera, much to local bewilderment). There can be no question that new oak substantially modifies the character of Barbera, adding a real spiciness to its rather neutral aromas and a certain quantity of ligneous tannins which firm up its structure and soften the impact of its acidity. In addition, the extra oxygenation of the wine has helped to curb the variety's natural tendency to produce very reductive wines that stink of HYDROGEN SULFIDE. It should be remembered, however, that these avant-garde Barberas, being invariably the product of low yields and careful vinification, already have more body and flavour than traditional Barbera, even of a better sort, and that small barrels are unlikely

to become a panacea for this grape. This was illustrated by the fact that the great optimism in Barbera's future during the mid 1990s has proved to have been misplaced. The consumer has not shared this confidence, whether the wine is a mid-priced modern version or a higher priced 'turbo-charged' example.

D.T. & D.C.G.

Elsewhere in Italy

Barbera dominates much of Lombardia, in particular the vineyards of Oltrepò Pavese, where it makes VARIETAL wines of varying quality and degrees of fizziness, some fine and lively, as well as being blended with the softer local Croatina or BONARDA grape. It is a minor, and decreasing, ingredient in Terre di FRANCIACORTA and is found, as elsewhere in Italy, in oceans of basic VINO DA TAVOLA.

Barbera is also much planted immediately south east of Piemonte in the Colli Piacentini, the hills above Piacenza, of EMILIA-ROMAGNA. Here too it is often blended with Bonarda, particularly in the Val Tidone for the DOC red Gutturnio. It is also planted in the Bologna and Parma hills, the Colli Bolognesi and Colli di Parma, where it may also produce a VARIETAL wine which rarely has the concentration of Piemonte's best and is regularly fizzy. Most of central Italy's Barbera plays a minor role in blends with more locally indigenous varieties, not always adding useful acidity, although that is its real purpose in the deep south.

A Barbera Sarda is grown in Sardegna while in Sicily some argue that the local Perricone, or Pignatello, is also Barbera.   D.T.

Outside Italy

Only just outside Italy, Barbera is also grown over the border with SLOVENIA, chiefly in the Primorski coastal zone. Elsewhere in Europe it is barely known, but Italian immigrants took Barbera with them to both North and, particularly, South America. It is planted in Argentina where there are almost 1,000 ha, mainly in Mendoza and San Juan provinces. The variety is planted to a much more limited extent in the rest of South America. In California, however, there are well over 8,000 acres/3,200 ha, by no means all in the hot CENTRAL VALLEY, thanks to the fashion for all things Italian and epicurean. Among grape varieties hopefully brought to California from Piemonte, Barbera has consistently outperformed the nobler Nebbiolo. It is also planted in Australia, notably in Victoria, and in the warm zones of Paarl and Malmesbury in South Africa, where its naturally high acidity produces musts that do not need ACIDIFICATION.

Bardolino, cheerful and uncomplicated light red wine from the south eastern shores of lake Garda in the VENETO region of north east Italy. It is produced from CORVINA, Rondinella, and Molinara grapes. As in the

other two important Veneto DOCS SOAVE and VALPOLICELLA, the original production zone is that known as CLASSICO (Bardolino, Garda, Lazise, Affa, Costermano, and Cavaion). This has been extended to a considerably larger zone whose wines are simply called Bardolino. Exact TERROIR seems to have rather less effect on the quality of this relatively simple wine than it does on Soave and Valpolicella, and good Bardolino is regularly produced outside the Classico zone, notably in Sommacampagna. This is largely because the Bardolino zone, whether Classico or not, lies on a flat plain beside lake Garda. On the southern part of the zone, the soil is fertile, so yields are very high.

Total production in Bardolino is 182,000 hl/ 4,823,000 million gal each year, with 45 per cent coming from the Bardolino Classico heartland. Although the DOC blend, in terms of both the indicated grapes and the percentages to be employed, differs little from Valpolicella, Bardolino producers tend to use less Corvina (the variety which gives body and structure) and more of the somewhat neutral Rondinella than their neighbours in Valpolicella. Officially decreed yields of 13 tons per hectare are often superseded, which accounts for the lightness of many wines.

The rosé version of the wine is called Bardolino Chiaretto. Bardolino Superiore, a slightly headier wine with an extra 1 per cent of alcohol, must be aged a year before being released. Bardolino NOVELLO, an attempt to ape Beaujolais NOUVEAU, was born in the late 1980s, but the competition of similar *novello* wines from every grape and corner of Italy considerably lessened the marketing impact of the move.   D.T. & D.C.G.

Barolo, the most powerful and dramatic expression of the NEBBIOLO grape, takes its name from the village of the same name 15 km/ 9 miles to the south of the town of Alba in the region of PIEMONTE in north west Italy.

In the mid 19th century, the local viticultural output was transformed from a sweet to a dry wine, assuming the character it has maintained to this day. Up to this point the elevated sugar content of the late-maturing Nebbiolo grape, the cold cellars of Piemonte in November and December, and the unavailability of prepared YEASTS had combined to make a certain quantity of RESIDUAL SUGAR in the wines all but inevitable. The metamorphosis of the wines in the cellars of Giulietta Falletti, Marquise of Barolo, was effected by the French OENOLOGIST Louis Oudart, called to the zone by Camillo Cavour, the architect of Italian unity and mayor of Grinzano Cavour in the Barolo zone.

The wine, (one of several) widely termed 'the wine of kings, the king of wines' by its more avid admirers, enjoyed a privileged position from the very beginning, not merely among the nobility of Turin but also with the ruling House of Savoy (see PIEMONTE). Carlo Alberto di Savoia, who greatly appreciated the wines of Giulietta Falletti, purchased and developed the properties of the castles of Verduno and Roddi, both in the modern Barolo zone, while Emanuele, count of Mirafiori, Vittorio Emanuele II's son by the royal mistress Rosa Vercellana, developed the vineyards around the hunting lodge of Fontanafredda in Serralunga d'Alba. This association with what was then Italy's reigning dynasty has given Barolo an aura and a mystique which it has retained to this day.

The core of Barolo has always been the townships of Barolo, La Morra, Castiglione Falletto, Serralunga d'Alba, and the northern half of Monforte d'Alba, supplemented by outlying areas in a variety of other townships which have changed over the course of time. The Agricultural Commission of Alba added Grinzano, part of Verduno, and a section of Novello in 1909, confirming the previous DELIMITATION work of the Ministry of Agriculture in 1896. This became the official definition of the zone in 1934, not without protests from Barolo and Castiglione Falletto, which considered themselves the true standard-bearers of authentic Barolo. Parts of Diano d'Alba, Roddi, and Cherasco were added in the DOC decree of 1966, an error at least on paper, although growers in the zone have generally been careful to plant Nebbiolo only where it can ripen properly, and the villages of Roddi and Cherasco have respectively a mere 10.77 and 1.26 ha (26.4 and 3.1 acres) planted to Nebbiolo for Barolo.

The five core townships mentioned above contain 87 per cent of the total Barolo area. This sensible demarcation of the zone, disciplined YIELDS (56 hl/ha (3.2 tons/acre) maximum), and reasonable requirements for CASK AGEING (originally three years, subsequently lowered to two years) make this DOC (promoted to DOCG in 1980) one of Italy's most intelligent. These sensible restraints have also curbed the multiplicity of superior wines labelled IGT characteristic of other areas of Italy (see SUPERTUSCAN, for example).

Although Barolo is always a rich, concentrated, and heady wine, with pronounced TANNINS and ACIDITY, significant stylistic differences among the various wines of the zone do exist and tend to reflect the two major soil types which are conveniently separated by the Alba–Barolo road which runs along the valley floor, separating La Morra and Barolo to the west from Castiglione Falletto, Monforte d'Alba, and Serralunga d'Alba to the east. The first soil type, calcareous marls of the Tortonian epoch which are relatively compact, fresher, and more fertile, characterize the vineyards of the townships of La Morra and Barolo and produce softer, fruitier, aromatic wines which age relatively rapidly for a Barolo. The second soil type, from the Helvetian epoch, with a higher proportion of compressed

sandstone, is less compact, poorer, and less fertile, with the result that the townships of Monforte d'Alba and Serralunga d'Alba yield more intense, structured wines that mature more slowly. The vineyards of Castiglione Falletto are on a spur that divides these two valleys, and produces wines that have some of the elegant and more forward character of the wines from Barolo combined with the structure and backbone of those from Serralunga.

All fine Barolo, however, shares certain common traits: colour that is never deep (for Nebbiolo, like Pinot Noir, never produces opaque wines), ruby tending to garnet or brick with age; complex and expansive aromas of plums, dried roses, tar, liquorice, and—according to a few fortunate connoisseurs—the local white truffles. Full flavours are backed by substantial tannins, a dense texture, and real alcoholic warmth. (Barolo from Helvetian soils easily surpasses 14 per cent, and an ALCOHOLIC STRENGTH of over 15 per cent is by no means rare in superior vintages.) Excessive EXTRACTION and/or cask ageing can easily lead to overly tannic and bitter wines, and obtaining the proper richness while maintaining a certain drinkability is the fundamental, and not easy, task of the individual producer, a balancing act which is not rendered easier by the late-ripening character of the Nebbiolo grape.

Two developments have marked contemporary, post-DOC Barolo: the move towards estate bottling and single-vineyard bottling (principally by small producers), and an attempt to find a fruitier, less austere style of Barolo more in tune with modern palates. The marketing of the wine was dominated by NÉGOCIANT houses until 1960, unsurprisingly in a production zone where the average property is little more than 1 ha (1,107 growers divided 1,164 ha/2,875 acres in 1990). Estate bottling represented both an attempt by peasant proprietors to reap greater economic benefits from the production cycle and a desire to put their name, as well as that of their holdings, before the public eye. Négociant houses, dealing in large quantities, necessarily blended the wines of different provenances into a house Barolo (just like their counterparts in BURGUNDY). When skilfully done, this did—and still does—accomplish the creation of balanced and harmonious wines which exemplify the general characteristics of Barolo. It is none the less true that certain privileged positions have long enjoyed a greater prestige and given more distinctive wines in both the written tradition (from Lorenzo Fantini in the late 19th century to modern writers such as Luigi VERONELLI and Renato Ratti) and in the oral tradition of the zone, opinions made concretely significant by the higher prices paid by négociants for the grapes and wines of certain vineyards. While there is no absolute unanimity, most short lists of the finest CRUS include Rocche and Cerequio in La Morra; Cannubi, Sarmazza, and Brunate in Barolo

(this latter vineyard shared, *à la bourguignonne*, with La Morra); Rocche, Villero, and Monprivato in Castiglione Falletto; Bussia, Ginestra, and Santo Stefano di Perno in Monforte d'Alba; Lazzarito and Vigna Rionda in Serralunga d'Alba.

The multiplicity of single-vineyard bottlings in the 1980s, in the absence of an official CLASSIFICATION, has had the paradoxical result of focusing attention on and reinforcing confidence in the brand names of single producers. It should be remembered that estate bottling and single-vineyard bottling are parallel and not interlocking phenomena: small producers, in many cases, have continued to offer a generic Barolo in addition to those from a selected vineyard, and virtually all of the négociant houses could offer a selection of Barolo crus alongside their blended Barolo by the late 1980s.

Like many of the world's powerful and age-worthy red wines, Barolo has had to come to terms in the 1970s and 1980s with market demands for fruitier, less tannic wines that can more easily be drunk while young—not an easy transition for a zone where FERMENTATION and MACERATION have regularly lasted as long as two months. The leaders of the movement towards a softer style of Barolo were Renato Ratti, Paolo Cordero di Montezemolo, and the house of Ceretto. Their methods consisted of shorter fermentations (generally 10–14 days) and an abbreviated ageing period in wood followed by extended BOTTLE AGEING prior to commercial release.

The proponents of this new approach were termed 'modernists', while those who retained faith in the old methods were called 'traditionalists'. This rather facile distinction fascinated the wine world in the 1970s and 1980s, but in retrospect it can be seen as nothing more than the continuing evolution and modernization of wine-making in this small zone. There was no doubt that traditional Barolo, a product of long maceration on the skins, from relatively high-yielding grapes in which the tannins had yet to polymerize fully, needed extended ageing in cask in order to soften the hard tannins the wine displayed in youth. In truth, this softening of the tannins was brought about by oxidation, something that also oxidized the fruit. This resulted in wines that were garnet or brick in colour, with oxidation and the hard tannins still evident on the palate. Quite often, Barbera was added to the wine prior to bottling in order to add a youthful tinge to the tired old colour, and a liveliness to the withered fruit.

As the world of wine opened up in the 1960s, and as some of the producers in Barolo travelled further than Turin or Rome, they came to realize that their wines were badly in need of modernizing if they were not to become historical relics. There was a move to TEMPERATURE CONTROL during fermentation, a reduction in the length of MACERATION, a move to PUMPING OVER rather than submerged CAP in the belief that softer tannins were extracted and a shorter time in barrel were steps in this direction. Instead of a protracted length of time in large old oak, some producers started to introduce small oak BARRIQUES to the cellars in the late 1970s, in the belief that the sweeter oak tannins would help to moderate the aggressive grape tannins of the Nebbiolo. During the 1980s and 1990s, as prices climbed, producers were able to reduce yields, something that led not only to earlier picking (today, the harvest usually takes place in the first half of October, while historically the grapes were picked in late October) but also to riper tannins in the grape skins. This, as much as anything, has helped to temper Barolo's tannins. It was facilitated by the move to ROTOFERMENTERS in the late 1990s, a move which has resulted in a further abbreviation of the maceration time to between five and seven days.

Today, talk of 'modern' and 'traditional' styles is little more than a journalistic conceit. Wines from La Morra and Barolo, naturally more forward, are usually better suited to shorter ageing than those from Serralunga, where the greater intensity usually leads to a longer period of barrel ageing prior to bottling. Many producers have developed the historic trend for adding Barbera to Nebbiolo and today add Merlot, Syrah, or Cabernet in order not only to augment the colour but also to add impact and ripe berry notes to the more delicate character of Nebbiolo. Indeed, a proposal in the mid 1990s to reduce the minimum Nebbiolo content from 100 to 90 per cent was defeated, but only after intense debate in the region. Style wars still exist but, as elsewhere in the world of wine, they are often between those who want to produce impressive wines and those who want to make them more drinkable.

An unparalleled series of exceptional vintages in the late 1990s and early 2000s (in ascending order of quality, 1996, 2001, 1999, 2000, 1998, and 1997) saw the trend for price increases accelerate. This in turn led to an increase in plantings. In 2004, there were 1,714 ha/4,285 acres under vine, an increase of 47 per cent since 1990. This has seen Nebbiolo planted in sites that were traditionally reserved for such lesser varieties as DOLCETTO and BARBERA. It is unlikely that Nebbiolo will be able to ripen properly in these sites, so there is a grim pessimism among some producers that quality, just when it should be improving in order to justify the higher prices, will in fact decrease as these new plantings come to be used in the production of Barolo.

Price increases abetted by an increase in supply also led to a downturn in sales; annual production rose from 7 to 10.25 million bottles between the mid 1990s and mid 2000s, when many producers were struggling to sell their increasing backlog of vintages. As a result, prices stabilized, and a series of more affordable wines appeared on the market. Previous downturns in the region, the last of which was in the 1980s, led producers to improvements in the vineyard and the cellar. The same will undoubtedly happen this time.

See also BARBARESCO. **Barolo Bianco** is an occasional name for the ARNEIS grape.

D.T. & D.C.G.

Garner, M., and Merritt, P., *Barolo: Tar and Roses* (London, 1990).

Baronnies, Coteaux du. Vin de Pays in the Drôme *département* on the left bank of the Rhône whose producers are campaigning for elevation to VDQS status for its reds based mainly on Bordeaux grape varieties.

Baroque, sometimes spelt **Barroque**, is the intensely local grape variety of which white TURSAN must be made. Although it is now grown almost exclusively in the Landes *département*, it was at one time known throughout SOUTH WEST FRANCE and was valued by growers in the early 20th century for its resistance to POWDERY MILDEW. The total area planted with Baroque was quite literally decimated in the 1970s and 1980s by Landais disaffection with viticulture, but recent investment in the Tursan appellation by chef Michel Guérard of Eugénie-les-Bains has saved this characterful variety from extinction.

The wine produced, sold as Baron de Bachen, displays the unusual combination of high alcohol and fine aroma, something akin to ripe pears.

Barossa Valley, the heart of the Australian wine industry, the most famous wine region in AUSTRALIA, and the one in which most wine is produced, even if a high proportion of it is shipped in from vineyards outside the valley itself. There is an increasing trend towards planting off the valley floor and on higher ground on the hillsides. On the other side of the coin, the incalculable value of the viticultural bank of Shiraz, Grenache, and Mourvèdre vineyards, up to 150 years old, dry-grown, and ungrafted makes this a heritage area which can be neither duplicated nor replaced. According to Australia's official wine geography, the **Barossa Zone** includes the Barossa Valley and Eden Valley wine regions. For more detail, see SOUTH AUSTRALIA.

barrel, cylindrical container traditionally made from WOOD and historically used for the storage and transportation of a wide range of goods. Today, barrels are used almost exclusively in the production of fine wines and spirits, and are almost invariably made of wood (although TORRES and others have unsuccessfully experimented with various combinations of STAINLESS STEEL and wood in an effort to cut costs). The bulge, or bilge, of barrels means that they can be rolled and spun easily, and that, when they are kept horizontal, any sediment naturally collects in one place, from which the wine can easily be separated by RACKING.

Barrels come in many sizes (see BARREL TYPES) and qualities (see BARREL MAKING). The word barrel is conventionally used for a wooden container small enough to be moved, while VATS are larger, permanent containers, sometimes with an open top. COOPERAGE is the collective noun for all wooden containers, whether barrels or vats (as well as the term for the cooper's business or premises), and the word CASK is used for wooden containers of all sizes.

BARREL MATURATION is the term used in this book for ageing a wine in a barrel, while CASK AGEING has been used as a general term for keeping a wine in a larger wooden container. BARREL FERMENTATION is the technique of fermenting wine in barrel.

A barrel is made up of STAVES shaped into a bulging cylinder, with hoops round it, a flat circular head at either end, and at least one hole for a BUNG. See BARREL MAKING for details.

History

Although HERODOTUS refers to palm-wood casks being used to carry Armenian wine to Babylon in Mesopotamia, it is generally accepted that it was the Iron Age communities of northern Europe, notably the CELTS, who developed the wooden barrel for the large-scale transport of goods. Its origins cannot now be recovered but Julius Caesar encountered barrels during his campaigns in France in the 50s BC. In the second half of the 1st century AD, PLINY described transport barrels in GAUL in a way that suggests they would have been unfamiliar to his Roman audience. The Latin term *cupa*, which later came to mean barrel, at this time normally referred to wood storage tanks, the remains of one of which have been found at POMPEII, near Naples. Barrels or barrel staves have been preserved in waterlogged conditions on sites in Britain (at Silchester), and along the RHINE and the Danube. The wood used was frequently silver fir.

Famous monuments such as that from Neumagen on the German river MOSEL testify to the use of barrels for the transport of goods. When the Roman army served in northern Europe, it used barrels regularly; they are frequently illustrated in scenes from the columns of Trajan and Marcus Aurelius which commemorated the campaigns of these emperors in the 2nd century AD. From the middle of the 3rd century references in literature and art to the use of barrels in Italy and, to a lesser extent, elsewhere in the Mediterranean are much more frequent. It is possible that the more widespread use of the barrel explains the disappearance of various types of AMPHORAE in this period. It also means that from this period on it is much more difficult to trace trade routes, since wood is much less likely to survive on archaeological sites. Barrels were certainly used for the transport of wine, but also for other liquids and goods such as salt.

See also BARREL MAINTENANCE, BARREL RENEWAL, GRAIN, OAK, TOAST, OAK FLAVOUR, WOOD INFLUENCE, WOOD TYPES. J.J.P.

barrel fermentation, wine-making technique of fermenting grape juice or must in small BARRELS rather than in a larger FERMENTATION VESSEL. The technique is used principally for white wines because of the difficulty of extracting through a barrel's small BUNG-hole the mass of skins and seeds which necessarily remains after red wine fermentation. In Burgundy, California, and especially Australia, however, some winemakers deliberately put pressed red wines which still retain some unfermented sugars into barrel, thus allowing completion of red wine FERMENTATION in barrel in an attempt to make softer, more approachable wines.

Encouraged by the success of this technique, a few winemakers are taking this further and fermenting small quantities of red grapes entirely in barrels, either by removing the barrel head for an open top fermentation, or by using a specially designed barrel in which the bung hole in the side of the barrel has been replaced by a porthole in the head, sometimes with a paddle inside to help break up the CAP. Proponents claim that putting the must into barrel immediately after crushing results in softer tannins, increased stability, and better colour concentration.

Barrel fermentation seems particularly well adapted to wine made from CHARDONNAY grapes and some of the finest SWEET WINES. Its advantages are that it offers the possibility of extracting a controlled amount of OAK FLAVOUR into the wine and, since barrels have a large surface to volume ratio, artificial mechanized TEMPERATURE CONTROL may not be needed. It also provides a natural prelude to BARREL MATURATION and LEES STIRRING since the lees and the wine are already in the same container.

White wine which is fermented and stored in oak with its yeast solids, or LEES, has a softened, less obvious, and more integrated oak flavour than wine that has been fermented in a larger container before being matured in barrels. This may be because the YEAST acts on the highly aromatic oak flavour molecules to transform them biochemically into much less aromatic substances. (The secondary fermentation aromas, however, such as result from ESTERS, fatty acids, and higher alcohols, are substantially unaffected by barrel fermentation.) FINING also removes some oak compounds. Fermentation in barrel also gives large increases in POLYSACCHARIDES, or complex SUGARS, which add richness and apparent LENGTH of flavour on the palate. The amount

of yeast mass in the barrel and the frequency of stirring have a direct and considerable effect on the quantity of polysaccharides formed. The yeast also make and release ENZYMES that could reduce the stability of aromatic compounds in the wine.

White wines matured for a few months on their lees in barrel usually have a much lighter colour than those put into barrel after fermentation to mature. Certain COLLOIDS are liberated during fermentation and LEES CONTACT; this stabilizes some of the PHENOLICS extracted from the oak, causing pigment to be precipitated.

Stirring up the lees in the barrel also affects oak flavour. If the lees are stirred, they act as an even more effective buffer between the wine and the wood, limiting the extent to which wood TANNINS, and colouring matter, are extracted into the wine. Wines subjected to lees stirring therefore tend to be much paler and less tannic than those whose lees are not stirred. Stirring also minimizes the effects of stratification in the barrel and is a more efficient way to bring wine components in contact with the lees, and thereby increase extraction of materials from them.

Fermentation in barrel can also have secondary flavour effects due to temperature, lot size, and precise level of TOAST. The often higher temperature of fermentation in barrel rather than vat causes a loss of floral flavours and a reduction of the most obvious white wine fermentation AROMAS reminiscent of tropical fruit. There are fewer fatty acid esters and fatty acids which are described as perfumed or soapy, and more higher alcohols, which makes the wine taste fuller bodied. And because each fermentation even of identical juice has a slightly different flavour outcome, the larger number of small volume lots that are common in barrel fermentation create more complexity. A 10,000-l/2,642-gal lot would create one fermentation flavour if it were fermented in one tank, for example, but the same lot volume fermented in 70 barrels would produce a much more complex array of flavours.

The disadvantages of barrel fermentation are the relatively small size of the barrel and the time and effort required to clean, fill, and empty it, although the extra degree of complexity gained by the wine is usually worth any extra production costs. The cost of new barrels themselves is such, however, that the technique is restricted to higher-priced wines. With so many fermentations in a non-sterile material, it is always possible that some barrels may be infected with BACTERIA or undesirable yeasts, so extra vigilance is required to eliminate any defective wines.

Fermentation produces a protective blanket of CARBON DIOXIDE on the surface of the wine in the barrel. As fermentation slows and stops, the CO_2 will be displaced by air, allowing uptake of some oxygen from the HEAD SPACE into

the wine. The larger ratio of head space to wine volume in barrels will allow more oxygen to enter the wine than would occur if the same volume were in a large tank. However, it is important to keep barrels full to limit the amount of oxygen exposure so that the wine does not become OXIDIZED or affected by BACTERIAL SPOILAGE. See TOPPING UP.

When barrels are expensive and wine is not, winemakers and winery owners seek ways of economizing on barrel purchases. For alternatives to barrels, see INNER STAVES and OAK CHIPS.

A.D.W., L.F.B., & J.Ha.

Dubourdieu, D., 'Vinification des vins blancs secs en barriques', in *Le Bois et la qualité des vins et eaux-de-vie* (Bordeaux, 1992).

barrel inserts, imprecise and expanding term for pieces of wood, usually OAK, added to a barrel too old to impart much OAK FLAVOUR. For more detail, see BARREL RENEWAL, INNER STAVES, and OAK CHIPS.

barrel maintenance. BARRELS are an important investment for a winery, in terms of both their cost and their precious contents. The contents of a barrel may well have a wholesale value of thousands of dollars, while new barrels cost several, possibly six, hundred dollars (up to nine hundred for high-quality French oak). The preparation of new barrels and the maintenance of used ones is therefore an important activity for winemakers, and can play a part in determining WOOD INFLUENCE.

Preparation for use

Barrels are treated prior to use both to check for leaks and to ensure that the barrel offers the right flavours to the wine. In Burgundy, where the barrels are filled with either white grape MUST in the case of white wines or just-pressed wine in the case of reds, treatment is minimal. Usually the barrel is merely rinsed or filled with cold water to check for leaks and so that the grain can expand properly, thus reducing the amount of wine absorbed by the oak (which could be up to 30 l/8 gal per barrel). In Bordeaux, barrels are traditionally filled with 15 to 20 l/4 to 5 gal of hot water. The barrel is spun and shaken so that, in theory, some of the rough TANNINS are washed out as the steam created during the spinning process exposes any leaks. (If a small leak is found, it can usually be plugged with a small piece of wood. A leak near the head may indicate that some adjustment is necessary. Occasionally a STAVE may have to be replaced.) In practice, it is the toasting (see below) that has more influence on the tannins than the hot water.

New World wine regions used to be less systematic in their barrel preparation. In the late 1970s, it was still common to use soda ash, supposedly to remove unpleasant tannins, although it is now clear that soda ash prematurely ages the barrel and at the same time removes the barrel's TOAST and makes the wine taste more tannic. Most winemakers are wary of filling a barrel with lukewarm water as BACTERIA grow easily under such conditions. Nearly all winemakers will at least rinse the barrel prior to use and in parts of Europe ammonia is often used; although this is a harsh cleanser, it can provide nutrients for FERMENTATION. Ammonia may also be used deliberately to prepare barrels for a light vintage, supposedly to remove some of the wood tannins. At some point prior to first use, the exterior of the barrel is often coated with linseed oil or a commercial product such as Mildecide to combat MOULDS, although this is done principally for aesthetic reasons and linseed is used mainly on larger vats. It is becoming more common to use OZONE as a sanitizing agent in barrels because it is effective at killing both yeasts and bacteria. However, it can be dangerous if not used properly and requires appropriate safety measures in the winery. Several companies have developed high-pressure barrel washers that can be used in combination with hot water or steam to sanitize barrels with little impact on wood quality.

Identification

At many larger wineries a card is attached to the head of the barrel to enable the winemaker to follow the life of each individual barrel. In larger New World wineries, it is not uncommon to see the sort of bar code used by supermarkets, along with computerized tracking (see INFORMATION TECHNOLOGY). In smaller wineries, a few letters may suffice. In Burgundy, for example, the chalked letters 'CM/R' might serve to denote 'Chassagne Montrachet, Ruchottes'. And in very small cellars, the single individual in charge may know every barrel so intimately that formal markings are unnecessary. Some wineries are now experimenting with Radio Frequency Identification (RFID) systems.

Temperature and humidity

Storage conditions of full barrels are important (and see below for unused barrels). If the cellar is too cold, the wine will not develop. If it is too warm, off-flavours and harmful bacteria may develop, and the wine may age too rapidly. If the cellars are too dry, too much wine can evaporate and the barrels themselves can dry out. The ideal temperature is usually around 10 to 18 °C/50 to 66 °F, with a HUMIDITY over 75 per cent. Below 75 per cent, water evaporates, but above that figure alcohol evaporates. In warm regions, winemakers like to keep the humidity high, but not so high that it becomes impossible to control the growth of moulds.

The winemaker must consider the dew point, that combination of temperature and humidity at which evaporation occurs. Storing empty barrels (and full ones too) at temperatures higher than 65 °F invites problems, and storing barrels over 70 °F for more than three weeks runs the risk of BACTERIAL BLIGHT and the formation of VOLATILE ACIDS. Constancy of temperature is not as important as it is in a cellar for full bottles, and a winter drop in temperature assists precipitation and therefore CLARIFICATION. See also TOPPING UP.

Bungs

See BUNG.

Storage

The question of storage of all these barrels has both aesthetic and practical ramifications. In most wineries there are visitors to impress, although they tend to find efficient modern reality less impressive than cobwebbed tradition. Some much-visited wineries fill their barrels in full view of the tourists before trucking them down the road to a clinical modern barrel warehouse, carefully regulated for both temperature and humidity. In Bordeaux particularly, it is traditional to anoint the band around the middle of the barrel with wine, giving it a neat pink stripe—indeed in some of today's most immaculate barrel cellars this is the only visible sign that a liquid called wine is involved at all.

Touristic considerations aside, most wineries usually employ one of the following techniques: (1) Barrels are placed on metal pallets and fork-lifted into place. This looks industrial but is actually easiest on the cellar staff. Barrels can be stored either rolled to the side or with the bung straight up. (2) Barrels are piled one, two, or even three high in neat rows. (3) Barrels are stacked in huge pyramids. These may look good but the barrels are hard to work as disassembling the stack is a daunting task. Sometimes, as a result of this, the barrels are not properly cleaned. (4) A single row of barrels is rolled on to fixed barrel racks, which also look good but are often inefficient in terms of labour costs and use of space. (5) Barrels rest on rollers, supported by a steel framework, making access easier and reducing the need to move the barrels.

Topping up

When the barrels are full, winemakers like to keep them full to prevent excessive oxygenation. Most wineries 'top up' the barrels frequently to compensate for evaporation. The rate of wine evaporation is directly proportional to the temperature, which should be about 50 to 55 °F: not so cold as to hinder development but not so warm as to encourage bacterial growth. For more detail, see TOPPING UP.

Unused barrels and used empty barrels

Storage of empty barrels is always problematic, particularly because of the possible growth of harmful ACETOBACTER, and barrels may well be sheathed in plastic before being shipped long distances to minimize spoilage. Traditionally empty barrels were rinsed, dried, treated with SULFUR DIOXIDE, then bunged up. Recent experiments suggest that sulfuring an inverted barrel but not bunging up results in a much lower level of VOLATILE ACIDS since bunging up creates a humid environment, ideal for the growth of bacteria. Barrels so treated must be stored under the same conditions of low temperature and high, but not too high, humidity as full barrels. OZONE is now also used to treat barrels (see above, preparations for use).

Most winemakers prefer to avoid the cost and risks associated with the long-term storage of empty barrels by ordering very precise quantities and filling them as soon as possible.

M.K., L.B., & J.Ha.

Schahinger, G., and Rankine, B., *Cooperage for Winemakers* (Adelaide, 1992).

Taransaud, J., *Le Livre de la tonnellerie* (Paris, 1976).

barrel making involves far more than mere mechanics and the ability to fashion a watertight container out of nothing but bent wood. As outlined in detail in WOOD INFLUENCE, every stage of barrel manufacture has an impact on wine matured in that barrel. First, the tree is cut down, usually during the autumn or winter when the sap is down. COOPERS usually buy long sections of trunk, from trees that are ideally over 100 years old, and then the process that turns logs into stave wood begins.

Cutting: sawing versus splitting

Logs of appropriate lengths are cut and then split into four lengthwise. The bark and sap wood are cut off so that STAVES may be cut from transversal (rather than tangential) sections of wood.

Because American OAK is so much less porous than European, staves of American oak can simply be sawn from each quarter, to maximize the yield of each log. This is traditional quarter sawing. The mill worker tosses a quartered bolt on to a conveyor belt. A band saw parallel to the conveyor belt lops off a stave, which is sent on its way, while the rest of the log comes back on the conveyor belt to be sawn again.

European oak could well leak if thus sawn, however, and staves have to be cut, or split, much more carefully, minimizing the risk of leakage by following the oak GRAIN. Traditionally therefore European oak was split by hand so that the axe blade could follow the grain. Nowadays mechanically operated axes are guided through the wood sections and the resulting staves trimmed, still following the grain.

Some coopers do saw European wood and may paint the end of the staves, the chime, to block end-grain leaks. Since twice as many staves are produced by sawing as by hand-splitting, the waste involved in traditional European COOPERAGE practices is considerable.

French oak is so relatively expensive (the wood cost in a barrel was approaching 350 Euros in 2005) that sawn French barrels seem an economically alluring proposition. Experiments so far, however, suggest that experienced tasters systematically prefer wines from French barrels made from traditionally hand-split staves—perhaps because sawing oak exposes more grains, and therefore more raw TANNINS, to the wine. Proponents of sawing maintain that the wood is worked so much during manufacture it does not matter how the wood is cut, so long as the wood is sawed following the grain.

In France, wood split by hand from logs for use as staves is known as *merrain* and the men who do this work are known as *merrandiers*. Traditionally this work was done near the forest, but nowadays many cooperages have their own stave-splitting facilities.

Drying: air versus kiln

After the wood has been split or sawn, it must be dried. The drying process can be achieved either naturally in the open air or artificially using kilns. French oak has traditionally been air dried one year for every 10 mm/0.4 in width so that it takes between 18 and 36 months to 'season' wood by drying it, in stacks of potential staves, in the open, preferably on a site far from any industrial activity or any other source of pollution. This ties up so much capital that many cooperages have been forced to substitute artificial drying techniques which generally take no more than 12 months.

Many quality-conscious winemakers will pay a premium for wood dried in the open air, however, and an increasing number of them actually select and buy their own wood in advance of seasoning. Natural drying tends to reduce and modify the structure of the stable extractable compounds of the wood while heightening its aromatic potential. It has for long been thought that, as wood is seasoned outdoors and turns grey, darkening the ground beneath it, harsh tannins are being leached out of the wood. Wine matured in air-dried wood certainly tends to taste less aggressively tannic than the same wine matured in kiln-dried wood. Australian research by Sefton and others, however, indicates that tannin levels in wood do not in fact change during seasoning, but that their sensory effect does, with French oak tannins becoming much less noticeable with seasoning and American oak tannins more so.

Studies by Nicolas Vivas of the University of BORDEAUX indicate that moulds and enzymes formed on and in the wood during air drying play crucial roles in the flavour of oak and any wine matured in it. Moulds formed on the surface of the wood liberate exocellular ENZYMES, principally heterosidases. They permit the transformation of certain bitter components into molecules which taste more neutral. At the same time, glucose and POLYSACCHARIDES are liberated from the structural elements of the wood.

Other studies by Vivas show that natural air drying lowers the level of dry EXTRACT, total phenols, and ellagitannins and raises the level of lactones, vanillins, and eugenols (see OAK FLAVOUR). He cautions that if oak is dried under warm and dry conditions such as those found in much of Australia and California, the results will be similar to those produced in artificial dryers.

Some cooperages maintain that it is not the duration of the air-drying process that is important but the wood's exposure to rain and the temperature at which the wood is dried. Their wood may therefore be watered to simulate rain, but there has been little scientific analysis of results.

Assembling

Once the staves are dry enough, they can be assembled into barrels. Barrel making is made possible by the fact that wood can be bent when it has been heated. If the staves are shaped properly, the result will be a barrel. All edges will meet properly and the barrel will hold liquid without any agent other than the hoops which hold the staves together.

First, the staves are sized and trimmed into oblong lengths that might be called a double taper. Traditionally this work, known as 'dressing' the staves, was done by hand. The stave was 'listed', that is given the double taper shape, with a cooper's axe, known as a *doloire* in French. Then, the inside of the stave was 'scalloped' with a two-handled hollowing knife to allow for easier bending. Finally the staves were joined on a jointer, known as a *colombe* in French. Here the staves were given their final shape—rounded at the bilge (the middle) and narrowed at the heads (the ends). Nowadays most of this work is done with machines, even in France, at great savings of time and energy.

Finally, the cooper fits the staves into a frame so that each barrel will have the same circumference. An especially strong and wide stave is chosen for the stave into which the BUNG-hole will eventually be drilled (see below). Then he or she arranges these staves around an iron 'raising up' hoop, the result looking like a skirt or a teepee splayed out from the hoop at the top. This job calls for great manual dexterity, although in many American cooperages machines can do much of this work.

Shaping and toasting

Research has shown that the heating process is one of the most important in barrel manufacture, modifying the wood's physical and chemical composition and profoundly influencing any wine stored in the barrel. Heating allows the cooper to shape the barrel. Toasting degrades the wood structure and thereby produces aromatic compounds.

Various sources of heat can be used to shape the barrel: natural gas, steam and boiling water, or the fire of wood chips. Some cooperages combine techniques and shape the barrel with the aid of boiling water or steam, then finish the barrel with a fire toasting.

Coopers knocking down the hoops and bending the barrels over fire make an exciting spectacle for a high degree of co-ordination is required. The would-be barrel is rolled over a cylindrical, vented metal firepot, known as a *chaufferette*, in which small oak chips are burned. The coopers walk round the barrel knocking down the temporary iron hoops. They pound the hammer on a hoop driver—a short block of wood with a flat metal end—while slapping a wet rag on the wood to keep it from getting too toasted too quickly. After the top of the barrel has been shaped, the coopers wrap cables around the base of the barrel and use a capstan to cinch up the base.

Coopers often categorize the toasting and bending of staves in three stages: the warm-up (*chauffage*); the shaping (*cintrage*); and the toasting afterwards (*bousinage*). It is the last stage which determines the level of TOAST inside the barrel.

Natural gas, boiling water, and steam will heat the wood effectively and allow the cooper to bend the staves without the creation of blisters on the inside of the staves. Many winemakers prefer this technique as the barrel is easier to clean. Other winemakers prefer barrels shaped over a fire of wood chips, as the toast on the inside of the barrel provides an interesting 'toasty' flavour to the wine. These winemakers feel that any extra effort in BARREL MAINTENANCE is justified by the special flavour provided by this technique. The amount of time the barrel sits on the fire and the heat of the fire both have a dramatic impact on the appearance of the barrel's interior and on resultant wine flavour. Nowadays winemakers can order barrels 'toasted' to their specifications. Some cooperages use an electric ambient heater or a wood fire to toast the heads too, although these are usually left untoasted.

The heads

After the body of the barrel has been formed, then the heads, or barrel-ends, must be made and fitted. Five or six head staves are fitted together with wooden dowels or stainless steel gudgeons (headless nails). Then the head is cut to size, usually round but sometimes slightly oval in shape. Near each end of the body of the barrel, a groove, called the croze, is cut into the inside of the barrel. The head is cut at the edges so that it will fit into the croze. Some cooperages are now using a tongue and groove system.

Formerly all of this work was done by hand, but now virtually all of it is done on machines which have replaced an array of traditional cooper's tools with names (adze, chiv, etc.) to delight the dedicated Scrabble player. Finally the head is fitted into the barrel. To do this the hoops are loosened and the head is inserted into the croze.

Finishing

Before the barrel can be sold or shipped, its outside must be planed so that splinters will not dog cellar work. The barrel is tested for leaks, usually with steam or hot water injected through a small hole drilled in the bung stave. If the barrel passes the test, the small hole is drilled to bung-hole size and cauterized. The temporary iron hoops are removed and the final ones, usually made of metal and sometimes of chestnut, are fitted.

Developments

In the late 1980s, many American cooperages realized that the wine barrel market called for an entirely different barrel. They began to experiment with air drying staves and the results have been a significant improvement on the old-fashioned Bourbon/wine barrel. Whereas American oak barrels were sold without geographical origins, now winemakers can buy barrels made with staves from different states, forests, or regions. Several cooperages dry staves for up to three years.

The fact that expensive barrels lose their value so quickly has initiated various schemes for BARREL RENEWAL. See also BARREL INSERTS, INNER STAVES, and OAK CHIPS for other ways of imbuing wine with OAK FLAVOUR without having to buy new barrels.

See also BARREL TYPES, OAK, and WOOD INFLUENCE. M.K.

Chatonnet, P., 'Origin and processing of oak used in cooperage' and 'Aromatic compounds yielded by oak into wine', in *Le Bois et la qualité des vins et eaux-de-vie* (Bordeaux, 1992).

Schahinger, G., and Rankine, B., *Cooperage for Winemakers* (Adelaide, 1992).

Sefton, M. A., et al., 'Influence of seasoning on the sensory characteristics and composition of oak extracts', in *International Oak Symposium* (San Francisco, 1993).

Taransaud, J., *Le Livre de la tonnellerie* (Paris, 1976).

Vivas, N., *Manuel de tonnellerie à l'usage des utilisateurs de futaille* (2nd edn, Bordeaux, 2002).

barrel maturation is the wine-making operation of storing a fermented wine in wooden BARRELS to create ideal conditions for the components of the wine to evolve and so that the wood imparts some OAK FLAVOUR. This is an increasingly common practice for superior-quality still wines of all colours and styles, providing them, as it does, with the ideal preparation for BOTTLE AGEING.

The most obvious advantage of barrel maturation is that it encourages CLARIFICATION and STABILIZATION of the wine in the most natural, if not necessarily the fastest, way. It also helps to deepen and stabilize the COLOUR, to soften the TANNINS, and to increase the complexity of the flavour compounds.

Although some oak flavour is extracted directly into the wine, one of the more obvious secondary flavour effects of maturing a wine in barrel results from the slow oxygenation of the wine. When barrels are filled, stoppered, and rolled, they receive a small but significant amount of OXYGEN. Leaving barrels upright and topping up the evaporated wine weekly can triple the amount of oxygen the wine receives. This uptake of oxygen, however slow or fast, tends to reduce fresh, grapey primary AROMAS and also causes small tannin molecules to agglomerate, which changes the colour towards gold in whites and softens the astringency in both reds and whites. In red wines, oxygen aids in the formation of PIGMENTED TANNINS with colours that are more permanent than those of monomeric ANTHOCYANINS. For more details, see AGEING. MICROOXYGENATION in barrel or tank is seen by an increasing number of winemakers (and accountants) as an attractive alternative to prolonged barrel ageing.

WOOD INFLUENCE outlines the factors that govern the process of barrel maturation: size, age, and wood type of the barrel, techniques used in BARREL MAKING, storage conditions, characteristics of the vintage, wine-making techniques, and time. See also TOAST for details of how this plays a part in providing a buffer between the alcohol and the wood's PHENOLICS.

The better properties in BORDEAUX provide the paradigm for the barrel maturation of wines based on CABERNET SAUVIGNON and MERLOT grapes. Here top-quality wines are put into barrels with a light to medium toast immediately after (occasionally before, see below) MALOLACTIC FERMENTATION and left to mature for up to two years. RACKING every three or four months helps clarification, softens the oak flavour, and inevitably involves some oxygenation. Oxygenation is positively encouraged during the first six months by leaving the barrels with the BUNG up. Thereafter they are rotated so that oxygenation is reduced. FINING takes place at the beginning of the second year, further encouraging stabilization. The timing of BOTTLING is the final crucial human input of barrel maturation.

In the early 1980s, it was common for New World winemakers to practise these same techniques on wines made from the PINOT NOIR grape, but, because they lack the tannic structure of wines made from Cabernet Sauvignon or Merlot, such wines tasted bitter and excessively tannic. Heavier toast on the inside of the barrel can also act as a buffer between wood and wine. By racking Pinot Noir into barrel immediately after alcoholic fermentation and allowing malolactic fermentation to take place in barrel, much better integration of wood and wine has been achieved, together with greater complexity of flavour.

As a result of this success, some California winemakers began to apply this Pinot Noir

technique to varieties such as Cabernet Sauvignon, ZINFANDEL, and the RHÔNE varieties. Whereas in Bordeaux red wine has traditionally been racked into barrel only after malolactic fermentation, a significant proportion of New World Cabernet, Syrah, Zinfandel, and Merlot is now racked straight into barrel after primary alcoholic fermentation with the result that wine and wood oak flavours are better integrated. Even in Bordeaux, particularly on smaller properties where the necessary barrel-by-barrel surveillance is easier, there is a FASHION for encouraging malolactic fermentation in barrel in an attempt to make wines that are more flattering to taste young—particularly useful when selling EN PRIMEUR.

All over the world, many top-quality white wines are subjected to BARREL FERMENTATION prior to barrel maturation, another practice which tends to result in much better integration of wood and wine than putting white wine into barrel only after fermentation.

An alternative to barrel maturation for wines of all hues is CASK AGEING, whereby wine is stored in large, old wooden containers which impart no wood oak flavour but exert some of the favourable aspects of wood influence, provided they are kept clean. Other alternatives, and possible supplements, to barrel maturation are ageing in inert CONTAINERS; BOTTLE AGEING; and bottling almost immediately after fermentation as in NOUVEAU wines. See also INNER STAVES.

See BARREL MAINTENANCE for more details of some of the important practical aspects of barrel maturation. M.K. & L.B.

Naudin, R., *L'Élevage des vins de Bourgogne en fûts neufs* (Beaune, 1989).

Pontallier, P., 'Pratiques actuelles de l'élevage en barriques des grands vins rouges', in *Le Bois et la qualité des vins et eaux-de-vie* (Bordeaux, 1992).

Sefton, M. A., 'How does oak barrel maturation contribute to wine flavor?', *Australian and NZ Industry Journal* (Feb 1991).

Singleton, V. L., 'Some aspects of the wooden container as a factor in wine maturation', in *Chemistry of Winemaking*, American Chemical Society (Washington, DC, 1974).

barrel renewal is a way of saving money on expensive barrels that depreciate very quickly. One method, which is quite popular in the New World, involves shaving the interior of the barrel. A cooper removes the barrel head and shaves off all the pigmented wood from inside the barrel with a plane or grouter. In some cases, the barrel is allowed to dry out a bit, and then the cooper retoasts the inside in order to maintain the all-important buffer between the wine and the wood and seal the wood. The barrel is then reassembled. Barrels that are shaved but not toasted yield extremely astringent tannins. However, the toasting process is difficult because the wood is not entirely dry since it has been permeated by alcohol. Retoasting seems most effective on relatively young (two- to three-year-old) barrels. Wine aged in shaved and retoasted older barrels rarely has the subtlety of wine matured in new barrels. A further disadvantage is that this process makes the staves more fragile.

Another method involves inserting pieces of wood, usually OAK of various sizes and designs, into the barrel. With larger pieces of wood, the barrel head has to be removed. A food-grade device reminiscent of the tray in an automatic dishwasher is inserted. This holds small oak planks which may be renewed every other year or so. Alternatively such planks are linked together and attached inside the barrel. Sooner or later, however, the barrel falls apart from the repeated torture, and getting the right amount of new oak is difficult. Nevertheless, this technique can result in much better wines than those matured in shaved barrels. Smaller sections of oak, linked together or in some sort of sleeve, may be inserted through the bung hole, sometimes attached by a hook to the underside of the bung. See also INNER STAVES and OAK CHIPS.

barrel types vary considerably and this list includes some terms used for COOPERAGE, or wooden containers, that are, strictly speaking, larger than BARRELS.

Before concrete, STAINLESS STEEL, and other inert materials replaced WOOD as the most common material for wine FERMENTATION VESSELS and storage CONTAINERS in the 1960s, each wine region had its own legion of barrel types. Even today such terms as *feuillette*, TONNEAU, and FUDER may be used to measure volumes of wine long after the actual containers themselves have been abandoned. As recently as 1976, Jean Taransaud was able to list four pages of different barrel types used in various French wine regions (see below).

France
Barrel types, as most things French, are intensely regionalized. In many cases their capacity has changed over the years.

Bordeaux The **barrique bordelaise**, designated 225 l/59 gal for more than a century, is probably the most famous barrel of all and is now used widely outside the region. It is about 95 cm/37 in high and the staves are only about 20 mm/0.8 in thick (although the export version may be a cm or two lower and have rather thicker staves). The traditional BARRIQUE, sometimes called the 'château' model, has a wooden crossbar at each head and both a top and a racking BUNG.

The TONNEAU, at 900 l equivalent to four barriques, or 100 cases of wine, is still much used as a measurement by the Bordeaux trade, but this large cask no longer exists.

Burgundy Here the standard barrel is the 228-l **pièce**, which is relatively low (88 cm) and squat, supposedly for practicality given the narrow doorways and small scale of many Burgundian cellars, and to provide a deeper bilge for the LEES which accumulate in this region where RACKING is generally less frequent than in Bordeaux, for example. The staves are usually notably thicker than those of barriques, about 27 mm. Traditionally these barrels had chestnut hoops or iron hoops painted black, although some domaines have followed the American taste for more workmanlike galvanized hoops which need no repainting.

The traditional barrel in CHABLIS was the **feuillette**, at 132 l about half the size of the *pièce*. This is still the unit in which prices are commonly given, even though the barrel itself is increasingly rare.

Some domaines on the CÔTE D'OR may still have their own size of *feuillette*, holding 114 l, or even a **quartaut** holding 57 l, used primarily for TOPPING UP.

Cognac The standard cognac barrel now holds 350 l, although in 1900 it held only about 275 l, and only 200 l before the French Revolution. Cognac coopers make a wide range of different barrels for other wine regions.

Champagne A 205-l barrel is traditional here but those few houses which persist with BARREL FERMENTATION may also buy in Burgundy barrels.

Elsewhere in France A wide range of different barrel types is used in the Loire and the Rhône, from small new oak barrels to large wooden vats such as the 600-l **demi-muid** used in Châteauneuf-du-Pape. In Alsace, large ovals, or **foudres** of varying capacities, are most common.

Germany
Although Germany has formed its own group of daring iconoclasts, the Barrique Forum, most of the cooperage used until very recently has been large, old, and typically on the Mosel a **Fuder** holding 1,000 l or on the Rhine a **Stück** of 1,200 l. A **Halbfuder** and **Halbstück** are half these sizes respectively.

Spain
Spain's most characteristic barrel is the BUTT used for SHERRY. The American oak barrels used in RIOJA, and elsewhere, are 225-l **barricas bordelesas** modelled on Bordeaux BARRIQUES. Spanish cooperage can vary considerably in size and shape, however, and new wood was until recently not generally prized.

Portugal
The PIPE is Portugal's most famous wine measure. Portuguese cooperage, which can vary considerably in size and shape, may be made from French, American, or even Portuguese oak.

Italy
The large **botti**, or old wooden casks, traditionally used in Italy are typically made from Slavonian oak and have varying capacities. The barrique is increasingly common, however, sometimes called a **carato**, while the small barrels traditionally used for VIN SANTO are **caratelli** holding between 50 and 225 l. Large wooden casks standing vertical rather than being laid horizontal may be called **tini**. See BARRIQUE for a discussion of the use of this French barrel type in Italy today.

Hungary
Gönci holding 136 l are traditional in the production of TOKAJI and are named after the village in which they were usually made.

United States
Before the US became the world's best customer for exported French oak barrels (see COOPERAGE), American winemakers bought 50-gal/190-l American oak barrels produced for the whiskey business. A decline in bourbon sales in the 1980s led to American cooperages tailoring an increasing proportion of their output to wineries' needs, however, although variations on the *barrique* and *pièce* imported from France are the most desired, and most common, barrels used by American winemakers. 265-l barrels—Burgundy sized heads and Bordeaux length staves—have become popular for both aesthetic and practical reasons.

Australia and New Zealand
Barriques of 225 l have become the most commonly used barrel, and if imported from France, are imported whole. **Hogsheads** of 300 l and **puncheons** holding 450 or 500 l may also be found in New World wineries. While the latter are too large to manœuvre with ease and do not impart OAK FLAVOUR as fast as many winemakers desire, they may prove more suitable than *barriques*, for example, for some lighter wines.   M.K. & J.R.

Taransaud, J., *Le Livre de la tonnellerie* (Paris, 1976).

barrica, Spanish term for a barrel or BARRIQUE. A *barrica bordelesa* is the specific term for a Bordeaux *barrique*, the most common BARREL TYPE used in Spain.

barrique, the most famous of the BARREL TYPES, Bordeaux's relatively tall 225-l/59-gal wooden cask with thinner STAVES than the Burgundian *pièce* and most other barrels.

In the Middle Ages, the commercially acute Bordelais virtually trade-marked their distinctive *barrique bordelaise*, carefully designating its dimensions and prohibiting its use outside the region. By the end of the 18th century, it had replaced the unwieldy TONNEAU four times the size for transportation as well as storage, and in 1866 it was officially decreed that it must hold 225 l, rather than between 215 and 230 l as previously. Even as recently as this, it was common for some of the most highly regarded wines of Bordeaux to be shipped in *barrique* for bottling, if not by the NÉGOCIANTS of Bordeaux, then by wine merchants outside France, particularly in Britain.

Today the word *barrique* is often used, particularly outside France, for all manner of wooden BARRELS. In Germany and Italy, for example, the word is closely and emotively associated with iconoclasts who employ BARREL MATURATION in small, new OAK rather than traditional CASK AGEING in large, old, wooden casks. Germany has its Barrique Forum of innovators, and some Italian traditionalists are careful to use the Italian word *carati* for small wooden barrels in place of the French term employed by many internationalists.

J.R.

A note on Italy

Barrique, the Bordeaux name for the small oak barrels used for ageing the wines of the better châteaux, has been almost unanimously adopted in Italy to indicate these containers, to the exclusion of *pièce*, *fût*, or the other names which the French use. It is also improperly used in Italy not just for the 225-l size of Bordelais barrel, but for virtually any small format of oak cask, including **demi-muids**, **muids**, and other sizes. Small barrel ageing of wines began on a small scale in TOSCANA in the late 1960s and early 1970s. The two pioneering wines, TIGNANELLO and SASSICAIA, were of such outstanding quality and effected such a radical improvement on previous Italian versions of SANGIOVESE and CABERNET grapes that the advantages of *barrique* ageing became immediately evident to more open-minded Italian producers. Their use in Italy was none the less slow to increase in the 1970s and their suitability to Italian varieties was by no means universally accepted; a vocal school of native critics was not slow to denounce their use with indigenous varieties as a betrayal of the authentic character of the wines.

The 1980s saw a widespread and rapid expansion of *barrique* ageing, a key event being a 1981 tour of California by the influential Italian wine writer Luigi VERONELLI, accompanied by important producers Maurizio Zanella of FRANCIACORTA, Giacomo Bologna of PIEMONTE, and Mario Schiopetto of FRIULI, all amongst the most influential figures in Italian viticulture. Their conversion to the cause can only be compared to that of St Paul on the road to Damascus, and, upon their return, their vocal advocacy of the advantages of new oak and small formats had an immeasurable effect. Bologna was the pioneer in demonstrating how well the humble BARBERA could marry with new oak, and similar demonstrations, if with less uniform success, were first carried out for NEBBIOLO by Angelo Gaja, Aldo Conterno, and Elio Altare. By the end of the 1980s, the use of *barriques* had been extended to a large number of Italy's most important varieties, red and white: GARGANEGA, CORVINA, CORTESE, VERNACCIA, AGLIANICO, GAGLIOPPO, NERO D'AVOLA, and NEGROAMARO. The resulting wines have not always been a subtle blending of oak and varietal character, but an overall assessment of these wines as heavy handed or overly oaky would be inaccurate and unfair; however, much still needs to be learned about a correct employment of new oak with Italian grapes. The new popularity of *barriques* has also led to major changes in the style and personality of Italian versions of INTERNATIONAL VARIETIES. Once almost exclusively made in a fresh and fruity style, many have taken on a fuller and more powerful character as producers came to realize that *barriques* and light, refreshing wines were incompatible.

D.T.

Barsac, important sweet white wine appellation in BORDEAUX on the left bank of the river GARONNE just over the climatologically important cool river Ciron from the even bigger and more famous Sauternes appellation. All wines produced within Barsac are also entitled to use the appellation Sauternes (although the reverse is not the case). In the 2004 vintage, for example, 539 ha/1,330 acres of vineyard were declared as producing wine for the Barsac appellation, as opposed to 1,735 ha/4,290 acres for the Sauternes appellation. It is traditionally said that the wines of Barsac are slightly lighter than those of Sauternes, perhaps because the soils are more marked by SAND and LIMESTONE, and because the land is flatter, but much depends on individual properties and wine-making policies too. For more detail of viticultural and wine-making practices, see SAUTERNES. Some of the finest current achievers within the Barsac appellation are Chx Climens, Coutet, and Doisy-Daëne. See also the Barsac properties included in the Sauternes CLASSIFICATION.

Bartons, prominent family in BORDEAUX, originally from Lancashire in the north of England, which joined the Tudor Protestant Ascendancy in Ireland. Unlike most others who joined the BORDEAUX TRADE from abroad, the Bartons maintained their nationality, religion, and family connections with their country of origin. Thomas Barton arrived in Bordeaux in 1725, played a leading part in shipping fine CLARET back to Britain, and died in 1780 a very rich man. His son William (1723–99), with whom he bitterly quarrelled, formed his own company and was prominent in the trade on his own account. His son Hugh (1766–1854) married Anna, daughter of another prosperous merchant, Nathaniel Johnston. The association with Daniel Guestier of a Breton Huguenot family began in 1795 and Barton & Guestier, still an important NÉGOCIANT, was formed in 1802.

Highly successful, Hugh Barton bought Ch Langoa in ST-JULIEN in 1821, and acquired in 1826 part of the Léoville vineyard that was to become Ch Léoville-Barton, an even more prominent St-Julien. He died in England, having been succeeded by his son Nathaniel (1799–1867). Barton & Guestier continued to play a leading role in the Bordeaux trade, but PHYLLOXERA, the consequent shortage of authentic bordeaux, and the slump in English demand prior to the First World War led to unprecedented problems. Nathaniel's son Bertram Francis (1830–1904) worked first in the London office but came in 1873 to live in Bordeaux, rather than at Langoa. It was his third successor Ronald Barton (1902–86) who made Langoa his home. Business was difficult between the World Wars, and on the fall of France in 1940 Ronald had hurriedly to leave Langoa, which was soon occupied by the Germans. They did not pillage the cellars as Daniel Guestier told them that the estate belonged to a neutral Irishman who, however, volunteered for the British army. Although the quality and reputation of SECOND GROWTH Ch Léoville-Barton and third growth Ch Langoa-Barton steadily improved, the profitability of Barton & Guestier gradually declined, and in 1954 the American firm of Seagram took half the shares of Barton & Guestier and later acquired complete control.

Ronald Barton's nephew Anthony (1930–) joined Barton & Guestier in 1951, and subsequently left to form his own merchant business. In 1986 he moved into Langoa and took over complete control of the two classed growths, whose wines are both made at Langoa and have become models of sensibly priced, classic claret made for the long term.

E.P.-R.

Barton, A., and Petit-Castelli, C., *La Saga des Bartons* (Bordeaux, 1991).

Ray, C., *Fide et fortitudine: The Story of a Vineyard: Langoa-Léoville Barton 1821–1971* (Oxford, 1971).

basal buds, or **base buds**, the group of barely visible buds at the bottom of a shoot or cane. Normally they do not burst unless vines are severely pruned, and they are typically of low FRUITFULNESS.

R.E.S.

Basilicata, mountainous, virtually landlocked area of southern Italy, is the country's third least populated region, with approximately 600,000 inhabitants. Its name has become synonymous with the extreme poverty in, and abandonment of, much of Italy's deep south. Little commercial or industrial activity exists, and the countryside has been drained by emigration since the end of the Second World War. Little exists in the way of viticulture either, with the region's total wine production amounting to 500,000 hl/13.2 million gal, of which less than 2 per cent is of DOC status. The Basilicata has only one DOC wine, AGLIANICO del Vulture, although the Aglianico grape also gives interesting, if not superior, results in other areas of the region such as near Matera and in the Colli

Lucani in the east of the region. The most significant viticultural zone is undoubtedly that of the Vulture, an extinct volcano 56 km/35 miles to the north of Potenza, where, in addition to Aglianico, limited quantities of MALVASIA (dry, sweet, or sparkling) and MOSCATO (usually both sweet and lightly sparkling) are also produced.   D.T.

Bastianich, J., and Lynch, D., *Vino Italiano: The Regional Wines of Italy* (New York, 2002).

Belfrage, N., *From Brunello to Zibibbo: The Wines of Southern Italy* (London, 2001).

Basque country produces wines in Spain and France on either side of the western Pyrenees.

Spain

The Basque country (País Vasco in Castilian, Euskadi in Basque) is the most ferociously independent of all Spain's 17 autonomous regions. This densely populated, heavily industrialized strip of country facing the bay of Biscay is not normally associated with wine, even though the important RIOJA region stretches north of the river Ebro into the Basque province of Alava where the Rioja Alavesa subregion is located—home to such important estates as Marqués de Riscal, Contino, Artadi, Martínez Bujanda, Remelluri, and Remírez de Ganuza. The three wholly Basque DOS are the tiny region of **Getariako Txakoli** on the coast 25 km/15 miles west of San Sebastián, the smaller **Bizkaiko Txakoli** around Bilbao, and the newest one, **Arabako Txakoli**.

France
See BÉARN and IROULÉGUY.

Bastardo, serviceable but unexciting Portuguese dark-skinned grape variety still grown in the JURA, DÃO, and BAIRRADA regions, and to an extremely limited extent on the island of MADEIRA. Varieties called Bastardo abound, specifically associated with the Crimean Institute MAGARACH, but Galet insists it is identical to TROUSSEAU. Bastardo is also used as a synonym for the Spanish variety MERENZAO.

Galet, P., *Dictionnaire encyclopédique des cépages* (Paris, 2000).

Bâtard-Montrachet, great white GRAND CRU in Burgundy's CÔTE D'OR. For more details, see MONTRACHET.

bâtonnage, French term for the winemaking operation of LEES STIRRING.

Baumé, scale of measuring total dissolved compounds in grape juice, and therefore its approximate concentration of grape sugars (see MUST WEIGHT). It is used in much of Europe, including France, and Australia and, like other scales used elsewhere (see BRIX and OECHSLE), it can be measured with either

a REFRACTOMETER or a HYDROMETER. The Baumé scale is particularly useful in winemaking since the number of degrees Baumé indicates the POTENTIAL ALCOHOL in percentage by volume. (Grape juice of 12 °Baumé, for example, would produce a wine of about 12 per cent alcohol if fermented out to dryness.) The rate of fall in Baumé is one method used to follow the course of an alcoholic FERMENTATION, but it should be noted that its product, ETHANOL, has a low DENSITY and progressively depresses hydrometer readings.   B.G.C.

Baux de Provence, Les. A spectacular and famous small hilltop settlement in the far west of PROVENCE dominated by Michelin-starred restaurants and their customers' cars gives its name to a local APPELLATION CONTRÔLÉE created in 1995 and substantially amended ten years later. In the far north west, Les Baux is slightly warmer and wetter than much of Coteaux d'AIX-EN-PROVENCE from which it was ceded and the rules are stricter—possibly too strict. Red wines are made, from Grenache, Syrah, and Mourvèdre grapes, which must together make up at least 60 per cent of the blend, together with Cinsaut, Counoise, Carignan, and Cabernet Sauvignon (which last must represent no more than 20 per cent of the total, thus excluding the area's best estate, Domaine de Trévallon, from the appellation). Cinsaut takes the place of Mourvèdre in the rosés, which make up about a fifth of the appellation. Until the new AC regulations, white wines had to be sold as Coteaux d'Aix-en-Provence but now they have their own specifications which allow the inclusion of Marsanne and Roussanne, in addition to the usual white wine grapes of Provence. Even more significant however is that the appellation has become the first in France to demand that all wines are produced BIODYNAMICALLY. Domaine des Terres Blanches was one of France's earliest converts to ORGANIC VITICULTURE and now it and the equally reliable if smaller Domaine Hauvette are just two of the many producers able to abandon AGROCHEMICALS, partly because the Mistral keeps the vines healthy.

bearer, viticultural term used when pruning for what is effectively the fruiting unit of the vine, the selected long or shortened canes bearing the buds that will produce the next season's shoots and crop. See also PRUNING.

Béarn, rarely exported wine made in SOUTH WEST FRANCE either in the MADIRAN or JURANÇON zones, or in a third zone around Salies-de-Béarn and Bellocq dedicated exclusively to the production of **Béarn-Bellocq**. Characterful reds (often very similar to Madiran) and some firm rosés are made with up to 60 per cent Tannat grapes blended with Cabernet Franc, Cabernet Sauvignon, Fer,

Manseng Noir, while the very rare, tangy white wines may be made from such classic south west white grape varieties as Manseng, Petit Courbu, Lauzet, Camaralet (as in Jurançon), which together with Raffiat de Moncade (as well as Sauvignon), are conserved in the letter of the appellation law if not in the reality of the vineyard. Fewer than 300 ha/750 acres of vineyards are dedicated to the wines of Béarn (most of which are quite concentrated enough to go with a steak and Béarn's famous sauce), and the great majority of the wine is made by the CO-OPERATIVE at Bellocq.

Beaujolais, quantitatively extremely important wine region in east central France producing a unique style of fruity wine which is often relatively, nay unfashionably, light but is increasingly being made in a more concentrated, 'Burgundian' style. For administrative purposes, Beaujolais is often included as part of greater BURGUNDY, but in terms of climate, topography, soil types, and even distribution of grape varieties, it is quite different. In some years, Beaujolais has produced more than the whole of the rest of greater Burgundy to the north put together, well over a million hl of wine, almost all of which is produced from a single red grape variety, GAMAY Noir à Jus Blanc, and most of it by a single, distinctive wine-making method. Early-drinking Beaujolais at its best provides the yardstick for all the world's attempts to put red refreshment into a bottle, being a wine that is essentially flirtatious, with a juicy aroma which, combined with its promise of appetizing acidity, is sufficient to release the gastric juices before even a mouthful of the wine has been drunk. In this sense, Beaujolais is the very antithesis of the intense, BARREL MATURED reds currently considered the height of FASHION, and the region became too dependent on selling embryonic PRIMEUR wine. Producers paid the price of much-reduced demand for their wine in the late 1990s and early 2000s when they had to resort to compulsory DISTILLATION. In the French market place, Beaujolais had become almost a commodity, with attendant pressures on prices, so that generic blended Beaujolais was too often a thin, inky liquid that was in all senses lacklustre—or an ultra-commercial blend all too dependent on CHAPTALIZATION. There have been distinct stirrings of a revival from the 2003 vintage, which resulted in much denser wines than usual. As Harry WAUGH discovered so many years ago, a DOMAINE BOTTLED wine may well be the most direct route to quality (although see also Georges DUBŒUF, whose importance is that of a major NÉGOCIANT, but whose philosophy was based on an attempt to be true to TERROIR).

To the Burgundian, Beaujolais wines are *les vins du Rhône*, not because they are from the RHÔNE valley, but because the vineyards of the Beaujolais hills fall within the Rhône *département* that surrounds the city of Lyons.

Both lavender and vines thrive on shallow soils and in dry climates such as those here near Curnier in the southern Drôme *département* in the outer fringes of the increasingly popular **Rhône** valley in a vin de pays zone known as Coteaux des Baronnies.

History

The region is on the ancient Roman trade route up the Rhône and Saône valleys. It is hardly surprising, therefore, that there are records of Roman vineyards in the region, notably on Mont Brouilly (Brulliacus), just the sort of HILLSIDE VINEYARD site favoured by the Romans, and Morgon. Benedictine MONKS developed vineyards here as early as the 7th century and for much of the medieval period Beaujolais, in wine terms at least, was simply the southern neighbour of the great duchy of Burgundy.

Beaujolais is named after Beaujeu, the town in its western hills founded in the 10th century, and was ruled by the Dukes of Beaujeu before being ceded to the Bourbonnais for a time. The region achieved real viticultural identity when Philip the Bold issued his famous edict against the growing of Gamay in Burgundy proper. He was right in that Gamay performs so much better on the granite hillsides of Beaujolais than on the limestone escarpment of the CÔTE D'OR.

The Gamay wines of Beaujolais continued to flow down the Saône to Lyons so that Beaujolais became known as the city's third river, after the Rhône and Saône. When communications with Paris by canal and then RAILWAY were developed, demand for Beaujolais the wine increased yet further, and the region expanded to include much less suitable land in the south, the Bas Beaujolais. Beaujolais is a relatively recent wine of note. REDDING in the early 19th century does not mention the word and cites, of today's well-known names, only St-Amour, Moulin-à-Vent, and Chénas, noting that they sold for relatively low prices, and that they should be drunk young.

Geography and climate

The total vineyard area of the Beaujolais region is well over 20,000 ha/49,420 acres and includes nearly 100 communes with MÂCONNAIS on its northern boundary (indeed some vineyards may be classified as either Beaujolais Blanc or ST-VÉRAN). The climate is TEMPERATE and semi-CONTINENTAL; snow may fall in the foothills of the Massif Central to the immediate west by the time Beaujolais Nouveau is launched, but summers are sufficiently hot for the local houses to have the shutters and gentle, tiled roofs of the south of France.

In the northern, narrower part of the region, the TOPOGRAPHY is very varied, the landscape made up of gentle, rolling hills, based on GRANITE and SCHIST with some limestone, while the flatter, southern, more recently developed sector south of Villefranche has much richer soils, often with some clay, making much lighter wines, typically for earlier consumption, on the plains which stretch down towards Lyons. The result of the more favourable MESOCLIMATES on the granite hillsides is that ripening is always more advanced in the north

so that, apparently paradoxically, picking begins with the better-quality wines.

The appellations

About half of all Beaujolais is sold under the basic appellation Beaujolais, which comes from the Bas Beaujolais and the flatter land to the immediate west of the main north–south autoroute around Belleville. A small amount may be sold as Beaujolais Supérieur, for which the minimum POTENTIAL ALCOHOL of the grapes when picked must be 10.5 rather than 10 per cent.

The second most important Beaujolais appellation is Beaujolais-Villages, which accounts for about a quarter of total production. Beaujolais-Villages must come from the hillier, northern part of the Beaujolais region, its vineyards pushing up into the foothills of the Massif Central. If a Beaujolais-Villages is the produce of just one village or commune, it can append the name of that commune. In the finest sectors of this superior, northern part are the so-called Beaujolais crus, ten named communes or CRUS whose wines are considered so distinctive, and so good, that they have earned their own appellations. Some of these have the most evocative names in the wine lexicon, but their existence as separate entities can be confusing for newcomers to wine since there is rarely mention of the word Beaujolais on their labels. For more details of individual cru, see, approximately from north to south, ST-AMOUR, JULIÉNAS, CHÉNAS, MOULIN-À-VENT, FLEURIE, CHIROUBLES, MORGON, REGNIÉ, BROUILLY, and Côte de Brouilly.

A small amount of Beaujolais Blanc and Beaujolais-Villages Blanc is made each year, mainly from Chardonnay grapes. White grapes do best on patches of limestone and are planted mainly on these outcrops in the north of the region so that they are effectively southern neighbours of MÂCON Blanc and taste exactly like it. Growers are supposed to devote no more than 10 per cent of their vineyard to white grape varieties. Even smaller amounts of refreshing Beaujolais Rosé are made.

Basic maximum permitted YIELDS are 55 hl/ha (3.1 tons/acre) for Beaujolais AC, Beaujolais Supérieur, and white wines, 50 hl/ha for Beaujolais-Villages, with a curiously modest reduction to 48 hl/ha for the Beaujolais cru. The additional 20 per cent (PLC) has in practice been used to the maximum.

Another extremely important sort of Beaujolais is that sold as NOUVEAU, which may carry the appellation Beaujolais, Beaujolais Supérieur, or Beaujolais-Villages. When demand for Beaujolais Nouveau reached its peak, in 1992, nearly half of all Beaujolais AC was sold in this youthful state, for immediate consumption and, from the point of view of the producer, as an immediate generator of cash flow.

Viticulture

The GOBELET vine-training method is traditional in Beaujolais but in fact single GUYOT is much more likely in the southern Bas Beaujolais, with up to 12 buds. For Beaujolais-Villages as well as the crus, PRUNING methods must be much more restrained, either en gobelet or éventail (see TRAINING SYSTEMS). VINE DENSITY here is one of the highest in the world, between 9,000 and 13,000 vines per ha usually. All picking, typically in late September, has to be manual because whole bunches are needed for Beaujolais's winemaking technique.

Vine varieties

Gamay Noir à Jus Blanc (so called to distinguish it from the relatively widely planted red-fleshed Gamay TEINTURIERS) accounts for about 98 per cent of the Beaujolais vineyard, which makes Beaujolais the most *monocépagiste* (single variety) region of any size in France. Virtually all the rest is Chardonnay, although Aligoté is also allowed until 2024 (so long as it was planted before 2004) just as the tiny amount of Pinot Noir planted may be allowed in Beaujolais until 2015. According to the detail of the official regulations, up to 15 per cent of white varieties may be included in most Beaujolais appellations.

Considerable research into CLONAL SELECTION has taken place since 1960 so that the modern grower can choose from six approved clones, the best quality coming from small, thick-skinned berries.

ROOTSTOCKS used are SO 4, 3309, or, the Beaujolais speciality for granitic soils, Vialla.

Wine-making

Beaujolais is distinguished not just by the Gamay grape, but by its characteristic winemaking method, CARBONIC MACERATION or, more likely, SEMI-CARBONIC MACERATION. Only in Beaujolais is this technique used so widely, and, thanks to the commercial success of Nouveau, with such speed.

Another controversial issue in Beaujolais is chaptalization. In recent years the trend was to pick grapes at the legal minimum ripeness of 10 per cent potential alcohol (10.5 per cent for Beaujolais-Villages and crus), and then add sugar to bring the actual alcoholic strength dangerously close to the 13 (13.5) per cent maximum permitted final alcohol content.

Whole bunches arrive at the cellars and are emptied into cement or stainless steel FERMENTATION VESSELS generally of between 40 and 300 hl/1,056 and 7,920 gal capacity. The bottom 10 to 30 per cent of grapes are crushed by the weight above them and ferment in the normal way. This proportion increases with time. CARBON DIOXIDE is given off by this fermentation, and leaves the upper grapes bathed in the gas so that they undergo intracellular fermentation and produce the

---

Bunches of Pinot Noir grapes are generally of relatively modest size. The photogenic red colour between the leaf veins of this vine in Vosne-Romanée in Burgundy's Côte d'Or is a classic symptom of **magnesium** deficiency.

sort of aromas reminiscent of pear drops and bananas so closely associated with Beaujolais.

This combination of two different sorts of fermentation, together with MACERATION of the lower grapes and must, continues for perhaps as little as four days for Beaujolais Nouveau and ten days for cru wines destined for the long term. The pomace is then pressed and, unlike other regions, the PRESS WINE is automatically included in the final blend. MALOLACTIC FERMENTATION is then de rigueur, especially since the effect of carbonic fermentation is to increase MALIC ACID. After some form of STABILIZATION, the wine is bottled either at under two months, in the case of Nouveaux, or perhaps not until the second Christmas after the vintage for the most concentrated, long-lived crus. Bottling often takes place in the cellars of the négociants who soak up 90 per cent of the region's entire production (every BEAUNE merchant has to have its Beaujolais), or possibly at one of the village CO-OPERATIVES, which produce about a third of all the region's wine, or in a grower's cellar, using a mobile BOTTLING line.

An increasing proportion of Beaujolais, however, particularly in the crus, is made like 'proper' red burgundy at a much more leisurely pace, given some CASK AGEING, and possibly even bottled by hand from individual barrels. North Beaujolais is a region where TRADITION and the best of peasant culture have survived, looking down, perhaps with wry amusement, at the frenetic production of Nouveau in the Bas Beaujolais.

Serving Beaujolais

Beaujolais was traditionally served in a special 46-cl/1 pint bottle known as a *pot*. European standardization may not approve of this but the essential point is that most Beaujolais is designed to be *drunk* rather than discussed or collected. This is the archetypal lubrication wine, and can be particularly *gouleyant*, or gulpable, if served cellar cool. Most Beaujolais has been drunk within a year of harvest, most Beaujolais-Villages within two, most crus within three, although traditionally vinified wines, particularly Morgon, Moulin-à-Vent, Chénas, and Juliénas, can improve in bottle for up to ten years from a good vintage. The tendency with time, however, is for a serious old Beaujolais cru to taste increasingly like a red burgundy. Particularly well-respected producers of Beaujolais, most of them associated with one or two particular crus, include Chx des Jacques and Thivin, and Domaines Jean-Marc Burgaud, Jean-Claude Lapalu, des Terres Dorées, and du Vissoux.

See also the individual Beaujolais cru appellations BROUILLY, CHÉNAS, CHIROUBLES, FLEURIE, JULIÉNAS, MOULIN-À-VENT, MORGON, RÉGNIÉ, ST-AMOUR, as well as NOUVEAU.

Hanson, A., *Burgundy* (2nd edn, London, 1994).

Beaumes-de-Venise is a pretty village in Vaucluse that produced such characterful southern red Côtes-du-Rhône-Villages that it was awarded its own AC for them in 2005. The village has some excellent high altitude terroirs and such skilled winemakers as Domaines de la Ferme Saint-Martin and Saint-Amant. White and pink wines retain the Côtes du Rhône appellation. For decades, however, it was most famous for its unusually fragrant, sweet, pale gold VIN DOUX NATUREL. Muscat de Beaumes-de-Venise was particularly popular in northern Europe in the 1970s and early 1980s and could at that time be said to have been more widely appreciated than the great sweet whites of Bordeaux and Germany.

Like the Muscats of the Languedoc (see FRONTIGNAN, LUNEL, MIREVAL, and, particularly, ST-JEAN-DE-MINERVOIS), this southern Rhône Muscat is made exclusively from the best Muscat variety, MUSCAT BLANC À PETITS GRAINS, and occasionally its darker-berried mutation. (This appellation represents the Rhône's only dalliance with Muscat except for the vineyards that produce CLAIRETTE DE DIE to the north which have so successfully been invaded by the same variety.) Fermentation is arrested by the addition of alcohol to produce a wine of just over 15 per cent but Beaumes-de-Venise is usually more delicate and refreshing than the Languedoc Muscats, partly because its minimum RESIDUAL SUGAR level is 110 g/l, as opposed to 125 g/l. Some of the vineyards, such as that of Domaine de Durban, are particularly high and yield especially concentrated, aromatic wine. Most of the northern Rhône NÉGOCIANTS such as CHAPOUTIER, JABOULET, Vidal-Fleury, and Delas sell their own bottling of this popular appellation, which, apart from the extremely rare and expensive VIN DE PAILLE, is the Rhône's only sweet, still white (although see RASTEAU).

Beaune, vinous capital of BURGUNDY giving its name to the Côte de Beaune section of the CÔTE D'OR vineyards. Beaune was founded as a Roman camp by Julius Caesar, became the seat of the dukes of Burgundy until the 13th century, and, although losing political supremacy to Dijon thereafter, has always been the centre of the Burgundian wine industry. In the 18th century, the first merchant houses such as Champy (1720) and Bouchard (1731) were established and Beaune remains home to such leading NÉGOCIANTS as Louis JADOT, Joseph DROUHIN, Louis LATOUR, and BOUCHARD Père et Fils.

Beaune wines are mostly red, made from Pinot Noir grapes, although plantings of Chardonnay increased in the 1990s. There is more SAND in the soil here than in most Côte d'Or villages so the red wines tend to be no more than medium bodied, best drunk between five and ten years old. While neither as powerful as POMMARD nor as elegant as VOLNAY, Beaune

wines are more supple than Corton (see ALOXE-CORTON) and can be a charming introduction to good burgundy.

Before the enforcement of APPELLATION CONTRÔLÉE regulations, many local wines were sold as Beaune as a readily marketable label of convenience. Now the town has a good rather than great reputation for its wines, perhaps because there are few outstanding DOMAINES in an appellation dominated by merchants. However, Beaune is blessed with an unusually high proportion, nearly three-quarters, of PREMIER CRU vineyards. Indeed those of village status are the exception, being limited to small parcels of land clinging to unsuitable upper slopes and some low-lying vineyards with richer soils. Otherwise the vineyards of Beaune form a broad swathe of premiers crus from the border with SAVIGNY-LÈS-BEAUNE to Pommard.

The finest vineyards are regarded as those situated almost directly between the town and the hill of Les Mondes Rondes: Les Grèves, Les Bressandes, Les Teurons, Les Avaux, and Les Champs Pimont. Beaune-Grèves includes Bouchard's noted Vigne de l'Enfant Jésus vineyard, while Beaune-Boucherottes includes Louis Jadot's Clos des Ursules.

Other noted premier cru vineyards are Les Marconnets and Clos du Roi near the border with Savigny, and Clos des Mouches abutting Pommard. Although the red wines from this vineyard are not always memorable, Joseph Drouhin makes a rich, complex, and age-worthy white Clos des Mouches which is highly sought after.

Leading producers include Louis Jadot, Bouchard Père et Fils (from the 1996 vintage), and Albert Morot, although see also those of CHOREY-LÈS-BEAUNE.

In 1443 Nicolas Rolin founded the Hôtel Dieu, Beaune's principal tourist attraction. For more details, especially of the famous annual auction, see HOSPICES DE BEAUNE.

See also CÔTE D'OR, and map under BURGUNDY. J.T.C.M.

Beaune, Côte de. The Côte de Beaune is the southern half of the escarpment of the CÔTE D'OR, named after the important town and wine centre of Beaune. The greatest white wines of Burgundy and some very fine reds are grown on this stretch. The principal appellations, from north to south, are Corton and Corton-Charlemagne (see ALOXE-CORTON), BEAUNE, POMMARD, VOLNAY, MEURSAULT, PULIGNY-MONTRACHET, and CHASSAGNE-MONTRACHET. See also the separate entry under MONTRACHET.

Red wines from the lesser villages of the Côte may be sold under their own names or as **Côte de Beaune-Villages**. This appellation is available for the wines of AUXEY-DURESSES, Chassagne-Montrachet, CHOREY-LÈS-BEAUNE, LADOIX-SERRIGNY, Meursault, MONTHÉLIE, PERNAND-VERGELESSES, Puligny-Montrachet,

ST-AUBIN, ST-ROMAIN, SANTENAY, and SAVIGNY-LÈS-BEAUNE. See also MARANGES.

Whereas wines labelled Beaune come from the appellation adjoining the town, there is a small group of vineyards on the hill above whose wines are sold under the confusing appellation Côte de Beaune. Of these the best known are Clos des Monsnières and Les Topes Bizot. Both red and white wines are produced.

See also côte de NUITS and map under BURGUNDY.　　　　　　　　　　　　　J.T.C.M.

Beaunoir dark-berried vine variety special to the Aube district of CHAMPAGNE.

Beaunois, rarely used Burgundian synonym for CHARDONNAY.

Becker, Helmut (1927–89), academic and exceptionally cosmopolitan VITICULTURIST who was chief of the GEISENHEIM Grape Breeding Institute in Germany from 1964 until his death. Although he travelled, lectured, and learned extensively, he was essentially of this small town in the Rheingau region, having been born and educated there before studying biology at the nearby University of Mainz. He continued his academic career with a Ph.D. thesis on the biology of the PHYLLOXERA pest and then worked as a research scientist at the Neustadt viticultural station, where he was introduced to the field of VINE BREEDING, which was to dominate his work.

At Geisenheim from 1964, he continued the work of his predecessor Professor Heinrich Birk in CLONAL SELECTION and SCION breeding, but emphasized the need for deliberate cross-breeding for resistance to DOWNY MILDEW and POWDERY MILDEW. To achieve this end he used not only resistant genes from AMERICAN VINES, as many other vine breeders had, but also those from Asian species of VITIS, in particular V. amurensis. Under his leadership, the wine-making facilities of the institute were extended and became a model for small-scale wine-making in breeding stations around the world. The products of these micro-vinifications were filed like library books in the research institute's deep, cool cellar, in bottles closed with the CROWN CAPS of which Becker was a great proponent. Here Professor Becker would regale visitors with tastings of fine, Riesling-like wine made from NEW VARIETIES which were effectively HYBRIDS because of their non-VINIFERA genes, and therefore officially outlawed. (Some have since been officially embraced; see DISEASE-RESISTANT VARIETIES.)

He also intensified breeding of ROOTSTOCKS, aiming for complete phylloxera resistance rather than tolerance. This work yielded Börner, the first registered NEMATODE- and phylloxera-resistant rootstock (released after his death).

Apart from his research work, Helmut Becker was also a passionate teacher. He always saw viticulture from a global point of view and collaborated with numerous scientists around the world, participating in and organizing conferences as a platform for scientific discussion. Thanks to his willingness to travel, his often iconoclastic views, and lively delivery in several languages (including some colourful English learned while a 17-year-old prisoner of war), he was arguably the most internationally famous viticultural authority in the 1970s and 1980s. He made a particular contribution to the New Zealand wine industry, emphasizing viticulture's role in achieving wine quality, and encouraging the importation of important clones and varieties.　　　　　　　　　　　　　　R.E.S.

Beechworth, fashionable region in the foothills of the Victorian Alps with several iconic producers, notably Giaconda, in the NORTH EAST VICTORIA ZONE.

beer. This alcoholic drink made, like wine, by FERMENTATION, but of cereals rather than grapes, has impinged on wine mainly as a commercial competitor, the rivalry having ancient roots. Both beverages were enjoyed in the civilizations of MESOPOTAMIA, Ancient IRAN, and Ancient EGYPT, where brewing was associated with bread-making. Although beer was occasionally used for religious purposes, it was generally the drink of the common people, whereas the aristocracy and priesthood drank wine.

See also COFFEE HOUSES for details of other drinks which were historically in commercial competition with wine. See SPARKLING WINES for one area in which the technical concerns of the beer industry parallel those of some winemakers.　　　　　　　　　　　H.B.

Forbes, R. J., 'Food and drink', in C. Singer (ed.), *A History of Technology*, ii (Oxford, 1956).

Lutz, H. F., *Viticulture and Brewing in the Ancient Orient* (Leipzig and New York, 1922).

Beerenauslese, sometimes known as BA, one of the three ripest Prädikats in the QMP quality wine category defined by the GERMAN WINE LAW. Traditionally hardly any Beerenauslese wine was produced anywhere in Germany in many VINTAGES, but the combined effect of warm weather and particularly selective harvesting has meant that since 1988, ambitious estate-bottlers with good vineyards at their disposal have harvested Beerenauslese more years than not. This rich, usually deep golden wine should be made from individually selected overripe clusters or even individual grapes (**Beeren** means 'berries' in German), usually affected by NOBLE ROT. Specific minimum MUST WEIGHTS are laid down for each combination of vine variety and region and vary from 110 to 128 °OECHSLE. These rarities command extremely high prices but taste like honey-soaked raisins, essences of the relevant grape variety. Riesling in general produces the most refined and long-lasting examples, although many GERMAN CROSSINGS can reach the necessary ripeness.

See also AUSTRIA.

beetles, insects of the *Coleoptera* order, several of which attack grapevines as well as other horticultural crops and pastures. While particular species of beetles are often specific to a country or even region, beetles are a pest to grapevines worldwide. Black beetles (*Heteronychus arator*) attack young vines in spring, and can cause ring barking. They are native to South Africa, and are also known as African black beetles, but cause damage in other countries such as Australia. Apple curculio beetle (*Otiorhyncus cribricollis*), thought to be a native of Europe, and vegetable weevil (*Listorderes costirostris*) also attack young vines in late spring and early summer, causing damage by eating vine leaves and/or young shoots. Beetles of importance in France are *Altica ampelophaga* and *Adoxus vitis*, which eat leaves, and *Otiorhyncus sulcatus*, which eats young shoots and buds. *Rhynchites betuleti* is called *cigarier* in French because it damages PETIOLES so the leaves roll up like cigars. Control of beetles, if necessary, is by application of the appropriate insecticide. See also BORERS.

　　　　　　　　　　　　M.J.E. & R.E.S.

Flaherty, D. L., *et al.* (eds.), *Grape Pest Management* (2ⁿᵈ edn, Oakland, Calif., 1992).

Galet, P., *Précis de viticulture* (5ᵗʰ edn, Montpellier, 1988).

Beira Interior, large, diverse but sparsely planted DOC in central Portugal made up from the merger of three former IPRs which are now subregions. Castelo Rodrigo and Pinhel share many of the same characteristics with shallow GRANITE-based soils and a harsh CONTINENTAL climate. To the south, Cova de Beira encompasses softer country on the leeward side of Portugal's highest mountain range, the Serra da Estrela. This is prime fruit growing country and has a TERROIR well suited to viticulture but in the mid 2000s there were few producers other than the local co-operatives.　　　　　　　　　　R.J.M.

Beiras, VINHO REGIONAL covering most of central Portugal, embracing the DOCs of DÃO and BAIRRADA and including declassified wine from these areas. This diverse region stretching from the Spanish border to the coast includes Portugal's highest mountain range, the Serra da Estrela, as well as the fertile coastal littoral. The region has three internal subdivisions: Terras de Sicó, Beira Litoral, and Beira Alta. A wide range of grape varieties are permitted including Cabernet Sauvignon, Merlot, Chardonnay, and Sauvignon Blanc.　　　R.J.M.

Belgium, north European country which has traditionally been one of Bordeaux's best customers but is also evincing an increasing interest in NEW WORLD wines. It also produces a minuscule amount of wine of its own: about 1,400 hl/37,000 gal in 2004 and 2,000 hl predicted by 2010, despite its LATITUDE.

About 90 per cent of wines are white and 15 vine varieties are authorized, of which Müller-Thurgau, Chardonnay, and Pinot Noir are probably most successful although GERMAN CROSSINGS such as Kerner, Optima, and Dornfelder are common as well as Auxerrois and Pinot Gris. Local vine specialities such as Leopold III, Maréchal Joffre, and Loonse Vroege are not authorized for CONTROLLED APPELLATION wines.

Most vineyards are hardly more than 1 ha, produce wine merely for local sale, sometimes simply for HOME WINE-MAKING, and were, typically, planted in the 1960s and 1970s. Belgian wine is gradually gaining recognition at home and a few producers manage to export. The wine industry of LUXEMBOURG to the south east is much bigger, more successful, and older, having been established in Roman times. Belgian viticulture has a long, if not continuous, history, however. In the era of CHARLEMAGNE, vines were grown extensively in southern Belgium to provide wine for MONKS and were not abandoned until the 15th century, when a combination of CLIMATE CHANGE, military ravages, and the increasing influence of BURGUNDY prejudiced the continuation of Belgian viticulture.

Belgian wine is made with varying degrees of competence but is, typically, light, dry, white similar to that made just over the border in the southern NETHERLANDS.

There are five GEOGRAPHICAL DELIMITATIONS in Belgium. The first was Hageland, created in 1997 in the Flemish Brabant region around Leuven. Its 30 ha were farmed by nine officially recognized producers in 2005. The second appellation was Haspengouw, created in 2000 in eastern Limburg near the Dutch border covering 25 ha with six producers. Côtes de Sambres et Meuse in the south of the country near Liège between these two rivers was created in 2004, the first appellation in the French-speaking part of the country with almost 60 growers in Walloon sharing 20 ha of vines. The two newest appellations are Heuvelland and Viaamse Mousserende Kwaliteitswijn. For growers eschewing the confines of a controlled appellation, there are now two Belgian vins de pays—one for Flanders and one for Walloon. Appellations are overseen by the Belgian Federation of Wine and Spirits.

Courses in viticulture were recently introduced at Ghent and Leuven universities by a chemist from the Belgian beer industry.   F.M.

Beli, eastern European term for white or light, as in the colour of grapeskins. Beli Pinot is PINOT BLANC, for instance.

Belina, strictly **Belina Drobna,** historic middle European for GOUAIS BLANC, although

there can be confusion with other varieties prefixed BELI. It is still important in older vineyards of north east Slovenia and parts of Serbia, and Croatia, where it is also known as Stajerska Belina.

Bellet, historic, distinctive but minute appellation in the far south east of PROVENCE based on about 60 ha/150 acres of vines in the hills above Nice. It takes determination to find a bottle outside the Côte d'Azur, and even greater determination to find the vineyards themselves perched about 300 m/980 ft above the Mediterranean up the Var valley in the city's hinterland. Almost equal quantities of all three colours are produced. The scented, full-bodied whites made from the local Rolle grapes with some Chardonnay and occasionally Bourboulenc are the appellation's most distinctive wines, and reflect well the MESO-CLIMATE of these hillside vineyards, which is slightly cooler than in much of the rest of Provence. Rosés may be made from Braquet (the BRACHETTO of Piemonte across the Italian border) while the intriguing Folle Noire (Fuella) is traditional for red wines, although it is often supplemented by Grenache and Cinsaut. Chx de Crémat and de Bellet are the principal producers.

George, R., *The Wines of the South of France* (London, 2001).

Bellone, very juicy ancient white grape grown near Rome. About 3,000 ha/7,400 acres survived into the 1990s.

bench blending. See ASSEMBLAGE.

bench grafting, the viticultural operation of GRAFTING vines indoors rather than in the field. This procedure has allowed viticulturists around the world successfully to combat the ravages of PHYLLOXERA by economically grafting to resistant ROOTSTOCK. It permits mechanization and factory-style operations leading to mass production. The procedure is widely used in Europe, especially Italy and southern France, where it is an important industry. Dormant cuttings are saved for bench grafting, stored in the cold; after soaking in fungicide solution, rootstock cuttings are disbudded and SCION cuttings are cut into one-node pieces. Cuts of matching shape are made at the bottom of the scion and at the top of the rootstock, using cuttings of similar diameter. With a GRAFTING MACHINE, variously shaped cuts are used, such as 'omega' or 'sawtooth'. After matching together, the newly grafted cuttings are packed with a moistened, coarse-grained medium in boxes and stacked in humid, warm rooms (28–9 °C/82–4 °F) until the union has CALLUSED (in about two weeks). Once they have hardened, grafts are waxed to reduce water loss, then planted out, usually in a field NURSERY. Such was the demand for grafted plants in the 1990s that in many countries nurserymen have sold young grafted

plants in the summer of grafting for immediate planting in the field. Such young plants are called 'green grafts' (see GREEN GRAFTING) and are about half the price of a dormant, grafted vine which the nurseryman would sell the following winter. Green graft vines are now commonly available in many countries, and although they are younger than dormant vines, with fewer reserves, they can grow almost as well as dormant vines. However, good care is essential following transplanting, especially with regard to water supply.   B.G.C. & R.E.S.

Bendigo, historic (see GOLD RUSHES), temperate Australian region notable for full-bodied but smooth red wines. Lack of water for IRRIGATION (a potential problem with dry summers and periodic drought) limits expansion in an otherwise excellent region.

bentonite, a montmorillonite clay found principally in the state of Wyoming in the western United States, and in many other areas of the world. Like most clays, bentonite is a hydrated compound of aluminium and silicon oxides, but it differs in ways that are useful to winemakers. When mixed with water, it swells and assumes a form that has significant powers of adsorption.

Bentonite, so called because it was first discovered in the Fort Benton rock series, is widely used in the NEW WORLD to ensure PROTEIN stability, particularly to remove heat-unstable proteins from white wines.

Bentonite fining is also used in making everyday white wines for the CLARIFICATION of MUST before or, for more commercial wines, during FERMENTATION to remove solids that would otherwise make the wine look darker, taste coarser, and possibly form clouds in bottle. It is not used at this stage for top-quality white grape must whose constituents should have a beneficial effect on flavour. Bentonite is frequently used for fining after fermentation, however, to hasten the settling of LEES and thereby reduce the time between rackings. Bentonite is not generally used for red wines because their higher concentration of TANNINS can remove proteins naturally (but see BOTTLE DEPOSIT).

Even the most unsophisticated wine drinker prefers a clear white to a hazy one, however strange the idea of a Wyoming clay treatment may seem. An unwanted outcome of fining with bentonite is an inevitable loss of flavour resulting from adsorption of flavour molecules on the surface of the fining agent.   A.D.W.

Béquignol, rare Bordeaux red wine grape occasionally found in the nether reaches of SOUTH WEST FRANCE such as in the wines of LAVILLEDIEU. The wines are soft, light in body but deep in colour.

Bereich, German for a district, bigger than a GROSSLAGE but smaller than a region or

ANBAUGEBIET. The boundaries of these wine-making units in GERMANY are often drawn more for political than geographical reasons. A wine labelled Bereich Something (Bernkastel, for example) is unlikely to be very exciting.

Bergerac, extensive and renascent wine appellation in SOUTH WEST FRANCE producing red, dry white, and sweet white wines in the image of BORDEAUX to the immediate west of the region, often at more appealing prices. The greater Bergerac region, named after the principal town at its centre on the river DORDOGNE, is the principal appellation of the Dordogne *département*, and can boast more beautiful and varied countryside than that of its vinously more glamorous neighbour. Lacking distinctions other than touristic (and gastronomic; Périgord is the home of the truffle), it has long been difficult for the wines of Bergerac to escape from the shadow of Bordeaux's more serious wine reputation, but thanks to much more sophisticated use of OAK, pioneering producers such as Luc de Conti of Ch les Tour des Gendres and Gérard Cuisset of Ch les Miaudoux as well as a handful of sweet winemakers, and a new dynamism in wine production, some truly fine wine is being made.

The climate here is somewhere between MARITIME and CONTINENTAL, but overripeness is a rare characteristic of Bergerac grapes and wines. Soils vary from alluvial silt to clay and, on the higher terraces, limestone. Within the region are smaller districts, generally on higher sites with more obvious potential, which have their own appellations for specific wine types. MONBAZILLAC on the left bank of the river is potentially the greatest of these, and is making more and more good-quality BOTRYTIZED wine. MONTRAVEL on the right bank makes lightish dry and sweet white wines in the west of the region. Both these appellations were created in the late 1930s just after the creation of the Bergerac appellation. PÉCHARMANT won its own red wine appellation in 1946, as did the almost extinct sweet wine appellation of ROSETTE, while the SAUSSIGNAC sweet white wine appellation was created in 1982. Partly because these names, with the exception of Monbazillac, are hardly the most famous in the wine world, many producers choose to sell their wines simply as Bergerac.

The vine was grown in the region in Roman times but the wines were most obviously exported and appreciated in the Middle Ages, when viticulture thrived under the influence of MONKS AND MONASTERIES. The history of BORDEAUX outlines why the English were so fond of them, and why, as wines of the HAUT PAYS, they were discriminated against by the Bordeaux merchants. After the HUNDRED YEARS WAR, the DUTCH WINE TRADE dominated exports of Bergerac, developing the production of SWEET WINES here, as elsewhere, from the 16th century and, especially, after Protestant refugees left Périgord for northern Europe after the Revocation of the Edict of Nantes in 1685.

Bergerac was slow to recover from PHYLLOXERA and today's total of 8,000 ha/20,000 acres is just a fraction of the area planted with vines in the early 1870s—and much less than the 12,000 ha of total vineyard in the 1990s. Vines grown are the classic Bordeaux varieties: Cabernets and Merlot for red wines, and Sauvignon, Sémillon, and Muscadelle for whites. Sémillon is still the most planted light-skinned variety, Merlot the most popular grape for the red wines, which constitute the majority of production.

The most common form of Bergerac is as a still red wine generally very similar to red BORDEAUX AC. An increasing proportion of red wine is sold as longer-lasting, more usually barrel-aged **Côtes de Bergerac**, however, for which yields are generally lower (a maximum of 50 hl/ha or 3 tons/acre) and ALCOHOLIC STRENGTH higher (although rarely more than 12.5 per cent).

Some **Bergerac Rosé** is made, generally of Cabernet, but the second most common form of Bergerac is the dry white **Bergerac Sec**, increasingly well made thanks to the application of some of the techniques employed for better dry white bordeaux. About a quarter of all white wine is sweet, made mainly from Sémillon, and sold as **Côtes de Bergerac Moelleux**.

Bergeron, local name for ROUSSANNE in the Savoie appellation of Chignin.

Bergwein, term in AUSTRIA for wine made on slopes steeper than 26 per cent, most common in the Wachau and Styria.

Berlou. See ST-CHINIAN.

berry, botanical term for a class of fleshy fruit lacking a stony layer, so that all of the fruit wall is fleshy or pulpy. The grape berry, popularly known as the grape, is a prime example. It consists of two carpels, denoted by its two locules (internal spaces) in each of which are borne two ovules which may develop into SEEDS, giving in most cases a maximum of four seeds per berry. For more details, see GRAPE.
B.G.C.

berry rots. See BUNCH ROTS.

berry size is considered by many to be a factor in wine quality. It is often said that smaller berries contribute to better wine quality, especially for red wines, since the ANTHOCYANINS, PHENOLICS, and FLAVOUR COMPOUNDS are mostly contained in the skins. Smaller berries' higher surface-to-volume ratio results in a higher concentration of these skin compounds in the juice and hence in the wine. However, there are few scientific studies that confirm this.

Good-quality wine grape varieties typically have small berries, at least compared with both lower-quality varieties and TABLE GRAPES. The average weight of a premium wine grape at full ripeness is 1 to 2 g, whereas others weigh 3 to 10 g/0.35 oz. These values doubtless represent the selection of VINE VARIETIES for their end use, which has continued for centuries. This fact in itself would seem to support the idea that small berries are a prerequisite for premium wine production.

It is not the case, however, that any vineyard management practice which leads to smaller berries will necessarily improve wine quality. Certainly, WATER STRESS causes small berries, although some of the effects on wine quality may be the result of water stress on VINE PHYSIOLOGY rather than the direct result of small berries. The other simple means of reducing berry size is PRUNING to many buds in winter, but this is contrary to the principles of BALANCED PRUNING. Such pruning is likely to reduce wine quality since the vine may struggle to ripen grapes with insufficient leaf area for efficient PHOTOSYNTHESIS.

Recent controlled studies in California (with Cabernet Sauvignon) and Australia (with Shiraz) have shown that smaller berries do not necessarily make better wine. These studies concluded that it is the vineyard factors which make berries small, water stress in particular, which contribute directly to wine quality, not the small berries in themselves.
R.E.S.

Roby, G., Harbertson, J. F., Adams, D. A., and Mathews, M. A., 'Berry size and vine water deficits as factors in winegrape composition: Anthocyanins and tannins', *Australian Journal of Grape and Wine Research*, 10 (2004), 100–7.

Walker, R., Blackmore, H. B., Clingeleffer, P. R., Kerridge, G. H., Ruhl, E. R., and Nicholas, P. R., 'Shiraz berry size in relation to seed number and implications for juice and wine composition', *Australian Journal of Grape and Wine Research*, 11 (2005), 2–8.

Bhutan, Himalayan micro-kingdom with a single wine grape vineyard established in the early 1990s with the technical assistance of Australian wine company Taltarni. The vineyard is at 2,300 m/7,500 ft at Paro, near the capital Thimphu. About 7,000 vines were planted, including experimental plantings of Pinot Blanc, Pinot Noir, Riesling, Chardonnay, Cabernet Franc, Merlot, Gamay, Mondeuse, and Altesse.
D.G.

Biancame, ancient vine commonly planted along the east coast of northern Italy under several aliases, including **Bianchello**. About 3,000 ha/7,400 acres survived into the 1990s.

bianco means 'white' in Italian and the names of many Italian white wines therefore are Bianco d'/da/di/del Place-name. For more details, see under the place-name.

Note, however, that Bianco is also the name of a small town in CALABRIA and that GRECO di Bianco can be an exceptional sweet white wine.

Bianco d'Alessano, Italian light grape variety of PUGLIA.

Biancolella, Italian light grape variety of CAMPANIA often blended with more characterful grapes.

Bible. The vine, including its chief product, wine, is mentioned more often in the Bible than any other plant. The Book of Genesis presents the invention of viticulture as a step in the development of civilization. 'And Noah began to be an husbandman, and he planted a vineyard. And he drank of the wine and was drunken' (Gen. 9. 20–1). The original Hebrew text and its translations state clearly that Noah was the first to make wine, just as Abel was the first shepherd, Cain the first city builder, Jabel the first dweller in tents and keeper of cattle, Jubal the first musician, and Tubal-cain the first smith (Gen. 4. 2–22). By becoming the first winemaker, Noah fulfils his father's prophecy: 'this same shall comfort us concerning our work and toil of our hands, because of the ground which the Lord hath cursed' (Gen. 5. 29). VITICULTURE is divinely ordained: the art of WINE-MAKING will soften the rigours of human existence in a fallen world.

But wine is intoxicating if taken in excess: the invention of wine is also the occasion of the first DRUNKENNESS. Noah 'was uncovered within his tent'. Yet Genesis does not condemn Noah for his drunkenness and indecent exposure: it is Ham, the son who draws attention to his father's nakedness instead of respectfully covering it as Japheth and Shem do, who gets the blame. The impropriety is Ham's, not Noah's, and Noah curses Ham's offspring.

Even if Genesis was not troubled by drunkenness, the early Christian commentators were. The Church Fathers found all manner of excuses for Noah's behaviour: that Noah did not know the possible effects of wine, for example; that he drank to blot out his sorrow at the death and devastation wrought by the Flood; or that he was not drunk in a literal sense. Allegorically, Noah's drunkenness signifies divine ecstasy, the joy experienced by the Christian at the EUCHARIST, when wine is drunk. This interpretation is first offered by St Cyprian (d. 258), and, once it had been adopted by St Ambrose in the 4th century, it became the standard gloss on this text. Going yet further, because events in the Old Testament are read as foreshadowing parts of the life of Christ, Noah prefigures Christ. The wine that Noah drinks is the cup that God the Father would not allow to pass from Christ in the Garden of Gethsemane (Matt. 26. 39; cf. Mark 14. 35, Luke 22. 41–2), as St Augustine stated in Book 16 of *The City of God* (written in 429). In the eyes of Augustine

and those of medieval commentators after him, because Noah's drunkenness points forward to Christ's Passion, it is to be praised. Similarly, the speaker of Isaiah 63. 3, who has 'trodden the wine press alone', is interpreted as Christ, the man of sorrows (Isa. 53. 3).

In the Middle Ages, Christ in his Passion is often depicted as a man treading grapes or even—but not in English art—crushed in a wine press. These numerous mentions of grapes, wine, and the vintage in the Old Testament are allegorized as representing Christ's Passion: the bunch of grapes from the Promised Land (Num. 13. 24), for example; the vineyard in Isaiah 5. 1–7; and the wine in the Song of Songs.

Nowadays this method of biblical interpretation, known technically as typology, is used much less often: we may still hear Moses mentioned occasionally as a type of Christ but not Noah: modern biblical scholars restrict themselves to pointing out that in a primitive society lack of respect for one's elders is a far more serious offence than drunkenness.

The Bible is not suitable reading for teetotallers. As the Psalmist says, 'wine maketh glad the heart of man' (Ps. 104. 15). Although we may not realize it, Psalm 23, 'The Lord is my Shepherd', sings the praises of wine. In the line which is familiar to most English speakers as 'My cup runneth over', the cup contains wine, and the original version, followed by the various Latin translations, speaks approvingly of its intoxicating properties. To be deprived of wine is a terrible thing. Whenever the Prophets threaten doom and destruction, they say that the Lord will withhold the benefits of the vintage from the Israelites, as in Micah 6. 15, Amos 4. 9, Isaiah 17. 6, and Joel 1. 10. In the New Testament, Timothy is advised to give up drinking water and instead to 'use a little wine for thy stomach's sake and thine often infirmities' (1 Tim. 5. 23, now no longer thought to be by St Paul).

A rare disapproving reference would seem to be Acts 2. 13, when sceptical observers dismiss the Pentecostal miracle of speaking in tongues as drunkenness: the apostles 'are full of new wine', but the disapproval is aimed at the unseemly babble, not at wine; in any case, Pentecost is not the time of the vintage so the insult is perhaps not to be taken literally. 'New wine' evokes images of joyful abandon and drunken revelry, as in Joel 1. 5, where the Israelites, Joel prophesies, will labour in vain: 'Awake, ye drunkards, and weep, and howl, all ye drinkers of wine, because of the new wine, for it is cut off from your mouth.' But as a sign of God's mercy 'the mountains shall drop down new wine' (Joel 3. 18).

Old wine is never mentioned in the Old Testament, but it is in the New. Where the Synoptic Gospels explain that new wine should not be put into old 'bottles', wineskins in fact, as a matter of HYGIENE (Luke 5. 37–9, Matt. 9. 16–17, Mark 2. 21–2), only Luke adds,

'No man also, having drunk old wine, straightway desireth new; for he saith, The old is better.' The old wine would not of course have been stored and aged in a wineskin but in a sealed non-permeable container such as an AMPHORA. In the hot climate of the Holy Land, old wine would have been better than new, especially if it was a heavy tannic red. Compare Greek and Latin authors, who always prefer old wine to new (see AGEING, Ancient GREECE, and CLASSICAL TEXTS).

On one occasion, Christ himself expresses a desire to drink new wine. At the Last Supper, as the Synoptic Gospels tell us (Matt. 26. 29, Mark 14. 25, Luke 22. 18), he will not drink the wine until he drinks it new in the kingdom of his Father (Luke omits 'new'). These passages describe how the Eucharist was instituted. The new wine which Christ will drink when God's everlasting kingdom has come carried with it all the associations of the joy of the vintage. And Christ was aware of the importance of wine. His first miracle was to turn water into wine at the marriage feast in Cana, when the wine had run out. The governor of the feast, who does not know where the wine has come from, says to the bridegroom, 'Every man at the beginning doth set forth good wine and, when men have well drunk, then that which is worse; but thou hast kept the good wine until now' (John 2. 10). One would dearly like to know what this wine was like. But how delightful that Christ should be portrayed as a man of taste and discernment and that this should be the first tangible proof of his glory and the miracle that convinced the disciples. 'This beginning of miracles did Jesus in Cana, of Galilee, and manifested forth his glory; and his disciples believed in him' (John 2. 11). H.M.W.

Daube, D., *Wine in the Bible*, St Paul's Lecture (London, 1974).

Zapletal, V., *Der Wein in dem Bible* (Freiburg im Breisgau, 1920).

Bical, Portuguese white grape variety grown mainly in BAIRRADA, and DÃO, where it is called Borrado das Moscas, or fly droppings. The wines have good acidity and can be persuaded to display some aroma in some still VARIETAL versions, although in Bairrada the grapes are often used in blends for sparkling wines. Some capacity for AGEING has been demonstrated, Bical developing an almost RIESLING-like bouquet after a decade in bottle.

Bienvenues-Bâtard-Montrachet, a great white GRAND CRU in Burgundy's CÔTE D'OR. For more details, see MONTRACHET.

Bierzo, or **El Bierzo,** increasingly fashionable small DO region in north west Spain (see map under SPAIN) which administratively forms part of CASTILLA Y LEÓN. However, the river Sil, which bisects it, is a tributary of the Miño (Minho in Portugal) and the wines have more in common with those of GALICIA than those of the DOURO 140 km/88 miles to the south. Sheltered from the climatic excesses of the Atlantic and the central plateau, Bierzo shows promise as a wine region. The MENCÍA grape is capable of producing balanced, fruity red wines in well-drained soils on the SLATE and GRANITE of this part of Spain.

In the late 1990s, a group of small, mostly young growers reproduced in Bierzo the same 'miracle' which had happened in Priorat one decade earlier—they resurrected a moribund wine region. One of the protagonists, Álvaro Palacios, was indeed one of the Priorat pioneers as well. With his nephew Ricardo Pérez Palacios, he reclaimed small, old vineyards on slate slopes and produced wines with no resemblance to the light quaffable reds traditionally produced from fertile valley vineyards. In addition to Herederos de J. Palacios, the top new names by 2005 were Paixar, Pittacum, Dominio de Tares, Estefanía (Tilenus Pagos de Posada), and Castro Ventosa (Valtuille).

V. de la S.

Biferno, effectively the only DOC in the Italian MOLISE region.

Big Rivers Zone in NEW SOUTH WALES comprising the Murray Darling, Perricoota, Riverina, and Swan Hill regions.

bin, traditional term for a collection of wine bottles, normally stacked horizontally on top of each other, or the process of so storing, or **binning**, them. Thus these bins needed BIN LABELS, and a **bin end** has come to signify a small quantity of wine bottles left over from a larger lot.

bin labels were necessitated by the practice of BINNING unlabelled bottles.

The most common form of bin label was made of pottery and was approximately the shape of a coat hanger some 3–5 in/7–13 cm wide. At the apex there was an additional lug, pierced so that it formed a suspension ring. As many were nailed to the cellar masonry, they were often broken or cracked during removal.

Early English bin labels (dating to the mid 18th century) are delftware (tin-glazed earthenware) with blue or deep magenta calligraphy (upper case) on a white to pale blue ground. Almost all later ones have black lettering on white pottery, although coloured lettering is very occasionally seen. European labels came in a variety of forms and often with polychrome decoration; the language of the writing usually provides an obvious clue to the country of origin.

By the 19th century, labels developed rounded shoulders, the earlier ones being angled. Many had a portion of the face left unglazed where more precise details of the bin contents might be written. Home-made labels were sometimes fashioned from wood or slate and would likewise have written information.

In very large cellars and in commercial ones where the bin contents changed frequently, it was established practice to use circular bin labels with numbers that would cross-refer to the cellar records. Many of these, and the coat hanger variety, are marked with the manufacturer's name (Wedgwood, Copeland, etc.) or the vendor's name (e.g. Farrow & Jackson), almost invariably impressed during manufacture. Bin labels are not much collected in the world of wine antiques but the most sought after are delftware examples, those with spelling mistakes, and rarities of name, colour, or form.

R.N.H.B.

Binissalem. Wines from Spain's first offshore DO on the Mediterranean island of MAJORCA are mostly destined for the Balearic holiday resorts. Binissalem's dominant grape, the Manto Negro, is certainly capable of making well-balanced reds, although they can lack structure and character. The most common white variety is the Moll, also called Prensal Blanc, which produces bland, neutral wines.

V. de la S.

biodynamic viticulture is, depending on your perspective, an enhanced or extreme form of ORGANIC VITICULTURE. This controversial regime has produced some impressive results but without the reassurance of conclusive scientific explanation. It is based on theories expounded in the 1920s by the Austrian philosopher Rudolf Steiner (1861–1925) for agriculture in general. Biodynamics sees each vineyard as a living organism which can be maintained in a self-sustaining way (see SUSTAINABLE VITICULTURE). The Earth is also seen as a living organism with diurnal and seasonal rhythms dependent on, and receptive to, cosmic cycles. Agricultural work is timed to coincide with these rhythms and biodynamic spray and COMPOST preparations are used, at specified times, on the land or directly on the crops, to heighten their potentially beneficial effects. Although BORDEAUX MIXTURE and SULFUR are permitted to help control POWDERY MILDEW and DOWNY MILDEW respectively, conventional AGROCHEMICALS and FERTILIZERS are forbidden.

The two main biodynamic field sprays are horn manure and horn silica. Only a few grams of each are required per hectare. They are prepared by burying either cow manure or ground quartz (silica) in a cow horn for six months over winter or summer respectively. It is believed that horn helps to catalyze processes such as humus formation in the soil (horn manure), and the vitalizing of plant growth (horn silica). Horn manure is sprayed on the soil in the afternoon, as the sun descends, to stimulate microbial life in the soil, helping maintain soil structure and humus levels (see ORGANIC MATTER), and encouraging deeper vine roots. Horn silica is sprayed over the vines in the morning as the sun rises to regulate plant metabolism which favours

stronger, more upright vine growth, to ripen the wood, to improve fruit quality (sugar and dry matter content), and to discourage moisture- and shade-loving fungi. One further field spray, the silica-rich common horsetail, is used to encourage fungal spores to remain in the soil rather than affecting the vine.

Organic FERTILIZER in the form of compost is used to nourish the soil but biodynamic compost differs from other composts in that it is first activated by a series of starters or preparations, added in tiny quantities. Where yarrow, chamomile, stinging nettle, oak bark, dandelion, and valerian are not available, substitutes may be used. For example, *Casuarina stricta* is often substituted for common horsetail (*Equisetum arvense*) in Australia. Compost material should be generated on the vineyard, not bought in, and biodynamic growers are encouraged to keep their own livestock, with horses useful as a replacement for the tractor.

Like the horn manure and horn silica field sprays described above, most of the compost preparations are prepared (fermented) in animal organs which act as sheaths for, but not as ingredients in, the preparation. The animal organs are chosen for the supposed properties they possess as a result of their former function within the animal organism.

Biodynamic compost is said to make the soil especially receptive to the cosmic—earthly, solar, planetary, stellar, and especially lunar—rhythms by which biodynamic growers are supposed to time their vineyard work. For example, when the moon is descending a 'winter mood' is evoked, and activity below ground (the roots) is favoured where the sap is said to concentrate. This is seen as the best time to plant new vines, or to prune. When the moon is ascending, a 'summer mood' is evoked and the sap is rising high in the plant: this is the time to take cuttings for grafting, but pruning should be avoided.

Biodynamic growers see plants as having four components: root, leaf/shoot, flower, and fruit, and these are linked to the four elements of earth, water, air, and fire (solar heat). Each plant component is said to be favoured during particular points during the moon's cycle when the moon is positioned in front of one of the 12 signs of the zodiac. Thus, for example, spraying horn manure on the soil for root growth is said to be most effective if the moon is in front of an earth/root sign such as Taurus, Virgo, or Capricorn. These windows occur every nine days or so but for two or three days only, so only the smallest vineyards, or those with abundant labour, can time all their agricultural work according to the biodynamic calendar. Biodynamists claim that on conventional vineyards where neither biodynamic compost nor the field spray preparations are used, the effect of these earthy and cosmic rhythms will not be felt as the soil and the vines will not have been sensitized to them.

Cellar work is also said to benefit from the biodynamic calendar, with, it is claimed, bottling best under Leo if the wine is designed to age (the fruit 'force' will be most concentrated in the wine at this point, so bottling then will capture or seal it).

Where VINE PESTS need to be controlled in biodynamic farming, a number of the pests are collected, burnt, and their ashes scattered on the affected area to discourage future infestations.

All biodynamic preparations are 'dynamized' before application. In the case of the horn sprays, this involves stirring the horn manure or silica in water, first one way and then the other. When the direction of stirring is changed the water supposedly undergoes chaos, and this is when the influence of cosmic and earthly rhythms is said to be imprinted onto what is being stirred.

Biodynamics is seen by non-believers as an unscientific and disturbingly irrational cult. It remained little known in the wine world until increasing numbers of top-quality producers in France adopted it, including Nicolas Joly of Clos de la Coulée de Serrant in SAVENNIÈRES from the mid 1980s; Domaine Huet of Vouvray, Domaine Leflaive of PULIGNY-MONTRACHET, and Domaine LEROY in Vosne-Romanée from the late 1980s; CHAPOUTIER in Hermitage, Kreydenweiss, Ostertag, and Deiss in ALSACE in the early 1990s; and Comtes Lafon in MEURSAULT in the early 2000s. Other biodynamic domains include Nikolaihof in Austria's Wachau, Pingus in Spain's Ribera del Duero, and Viñedos Organicos Emiliana (VOE) in Chile.

Many of these producers were encouraged by former French government soil microbiologist Claude Bourguignon, who makes no claim to understanding how biodynamics works. His research showed that levels of microbial life in vineyard topsoils were significantly greater on organic and biodynamic plots than on those of conventionally farmed ones. In addition, Bourguignon found significant increases of microbial life on biodynamic vine roots at depths of several metres compared with conventionally and even organically farmed vines, and that the roots were thickest, longest and most able to penetrate the soil, and to assimilate trace elements, when grown biodynamically. He also found that levels of copper in the topsoils (from BORDEAUX MIXTURE) were reduced under biodynamics.

Biodynamic viticulture alone will not a great wine make: good viticultural and wine-making practices such as CANOPY MANAGEMENT and cellar HYGIENE are also essential. Aware of scepticism in some quarters, and often quizzical themselves, many biodynamic growers are reticent about their biodynamic practices, and may often adapt them for their particular situation.

Biodynamics gained a foothold in California in the early 1990s via the Fetzer family who, having sold the family winery to Brown Forman in 1992, wanted to 'get back to their roots' as grape growers. The word Biodynamic is trademarked worldwide by the Demeter Association of America and should strictly be spelt with a capital B. Demeter International acts as an umbrella body for many national certification bodies which adhere to internationally agreed production standards. In many countries, Demeter standards are additional to government-recognized organic standards.

Currently less than 1 per cent of the world's vineyards are farmed biodynamically. France has the greatest number of hectares and the world's biggest single biodynamic vineyard (150 ha at Domaine Cazes in Roussillon).

See also ORGANIC VITICULTURE, SUSTAINABLE VITICULTURE.   M.W.

Joly, N., *Wine from Sky to Earth* (New Orleans, 1998).
Proctor, P., and Cole, G., *Grasp The Nettle* (New Zealand, 1997).
Steiner, R., *Agriculture,* trans. by C. Greeger and M. Gardner (USA, 1993).
Waldin, M., *Biodynamic Wines* (London, 2004).

biological viticulture, a loose term since all viticulture involves biology, but for more details of the general philosophy implied, see ORGANIC VITICULTURE. In France, many ORGANIC WINES are sold as *vins biologiques*.

Biondi-Santi, family popularly credited with establishing the repute of BRUNELLO DI MONTALCINO in Toscana, central Italy. The wines were fabled for their longevity, but since the late 1970s, they have lived as much on their reputation as on current performance. As a result, the wines from their Il Greppo estate have failed to keep apace of the improvements made by other producers in the zone.
                                                            D.C.G.

biotechnology. See GENETIC MODIFICATION for some examples of viticultural biotechnology.

birds can be a more serious modern vine pest than PHYLLOXERA in some areas because they are so difficult to control, particularly during grape RIPENING when they feed on grapes. Birds have been feeding on grapes as they have evolved for about 60 million years, and in so doing have spread grape seeds in their excreta. This is one reason why grapes are thought to have developed small, black, sugary fruits which attract birds. (Subsequent selection of MUTATIONS has given us light-skinned grapes.)

For small vineyards in isolated regions, and particularly for early-ripening vine varieties, birds may destroy an entire crop. Unfortunately, the birds begin their destruction as soon as the grapes begin to ripen, so early harvest is not a solution. As well as the potential crop loss, bird pecks provide entry points for all sorts of BUNCH ROTS. Control measures are expensive and bird damage can make some vineyards uneconomic. Birds are often the greatest problem facing vineyards in new viticultural regions, especially if the vineyards are isolated (as in ENGLAND and Long Island in NEW YORK, for example).

The species of birds which attack grapes vary from region to region. The ubiquitous starling is one of the most widespread problem species but blackbirds, partridges, robins, sparrows, thrushes, and finches are also common. Starlings, for example, can eat 60 to 80 g/2.8 oz of grapes a day. The planting of a vineyard and the consequent provision of an extra food source can actually lead to a population increase of birds. Many growers notice that bird damage depends on the availability of alternative food sources. In the MARGARET RIVER region of Western Australia, for example, silvereye birds do more damage to vineyards when nectar from local eucalyptus trees and saltbush berries are limited. Where vineyards are extensive, and the varieties ripen together, then damage to individual vineyards is minor.

Many bird protection devices are based on scaring birds by sight or sound. In time, birds become accustomed to new objects or noises in a vineyard so that, for example, the traditional immobile scarecrow can rapidly lose effectiveness. Other scaring devices include a wide range of auditory contraptions, guns, gas-powered cannon, tape across the vineyards, cats, etc.

Netting of vineyards is becoming increasingly common. The nets are made of woven string or perforated plastic, can often be re-used, and tractor-mounted rollers assist installation and removal. Since the nets provide for virtually 100 per cent effective control yet do not harm birds, they are acceptable to growers and environmentalists alike.

Some local bird populations are affected by eating insects or grapes which contain pesticides used in vineyards, which bird lovers view as an argument against the use of AGROCHEMICALS.   R.E.S.

Buchanan, G. A., and Amos, T. G., 'Grape pests', in B. G. Coombe and P. R. Dry (eds.), *Viticulture,* ii: *Practices* (Adelaide, 1992).

bird's eye rot. Vine disease. See ANTHRACNOSE.

Biscoitos, IPR on the Azorean island of Terceira making small quantities of fortified wine from the VERDELHO grape. Biscoitos is so called because volcanic stones in the soil resemble biscuits.

bitterness, tasting attribute to which the flat part of the back of the tongue is generally most sensitive. It is not as common in wine as SWEETNESS and ACIDITY, and is often confused with the quite different tactile sensation of caused by ASTRINGENCY, which chiefly affects the insides of the cheeks. Some Italian red wines are relatively bitter, as are some less successful examples of particularly aromatic grape varieties such as Gewürztraminer, typically because of an excess of PHENOLICS. Poorly seasoned OAK can also make a wine taste bitter. Many flavoured VERMOUTHS, notably Punt e Mes, are deliberately very bitter. Sweetness can help to mask bitterness.

bitter rot, a FUNGAL DISEASE of ripe grapes that is active in warm, humid conditions. It is found only on damaged and almost senescent tissues, but the bitter fruit flavour can be detected in the finished wine. The cause is the fungus *Greeneria uvicola* and the disease is widespread in the eastern United States, Asia, Australia, and South Africa but not in France or Germany. The disease is easily controlled by most fungicides.   R.E.S.

black dead arm, fungal disease of grape wood caused by several species of *Botyrosphaeria*. It was first described by Hungarian scientists and later found to be widespread in other countries, where it has been confused with ESCA and EUTYPA DIEBACK. Deadly cankers form in trunks and arms, and spur positions die back. The same fungus is now known to cause dead patches in graft unions, on cluster stems, and also to rot and wither berries. (Formerly called Diplodia bunch rot.)   L.M.

Lehoczky, J., 'Black dead arm disease of grapevine caused by *Botyrosphaeria stevensii* infection', *Acta Phytopathologica Academiae Scientiarum Hungariacae*, 9 (1974), 319–27.
Larignon, P., Fulchic, R., Ceré, L., and Dubos, B., 'Observation of black dead arm in French vineyards', *Phytopathologica Mediterranea*, 40 (2001), S336–42.

black foot, fungal disease caused by *Cylindrocarpon* species which can lead to young vine decline and death. Symptoms include poor growth, chlorotic leaves, and brownish-black discoloration of rootstock trunks, roots, and graft unions. The fungus has been found on nursery material in high percentages from 25 to nearly 50 per cent, showing that control measures should begin here. The disease usually occurs where soil conditions are excessively wet, so careful irrigation and good drainage can reduce the risk of young plantings suffering from black foot.   L.M.

Rego, C., Nascimento, T., and Oliveira, H., 'Characterisation of *Cylindrocarpon destructans* isolates from grapevines in Portugal', *Phytopathologia Mediterranea* 40 (2001), S343–50.

black goo, name coined in 1995 by American viticulturist Lucie Morton to describe the symptoms of black spots and tarry ooze in xylem vessels produced by *Phaeomoniella chlamydospora*, a fungus that causes decline in young vines; it has now been identified as PETRI DISEASE. The same symptoms and fungus are found in older vines suffering from young ESCA, proper esca, and black measles disease.   L.M.

black knot. Vine disease. See CROWN GALL.

black measles. Vine disease. See ESCA.

Black Muscat, synonym for MUSCAT HAMBURG.

black rot, FUNGAL DISEASE which is one of the most economically important diseases of vines in the north eastern United States, Canada, and parts of Europe and South America. The disease is native to North America and was probably introduced to other countries by contaminated cuttings. It was introduced to France, for example, on PHYLLOXERA-tolerant rootstocks in 1885. The disease is caused by the fungus *Guignardia bidwelli*, which attacks young shoots, leaves, and berries. The disease spreads only in mild, wet weather. Crop losses can be high, up to 80 per cent. Control of the disease is based on fungicides sprayed from spring up to fruit ripening. As might be expected from the origin of the disease, some native American species are tolerant.   R.E.S.

black spot. Vine disease. See ANTHRACNOSE.

Blackwood Valley, relatively new, inland wine region on the same latitude as Margaret River in the South West Australia Zone of WESTERN AUSTRALIA.

black xylem decline, a more formal name for the condition BLACK GOO. Unhealthy young vineyards have been studied in South Africa for about 50 years, and more recently have been a cause for concern in California, where rapid expansion took place in the 1980s. Similar problems have been noted in Europe, Australia, and New Zealand.

The reason is not clear, but the majority of evidence implicates wood-rotting fungi, perhaps associated with infected planting material. The fungus *Phaeoacremonium* has been isolated from unhealthy vines; when combined with other fungi *Phellinus* and/or *Stereum* species, it appears to cause ESCA. There is some evidence that black xylem decline may be overcome by treating planting material with hot water, which is also useful against NEMATODES, PIERCE'S DISEASE, and PHYTOPLASMA disease.   R.E.S.

Blagny, small village in Burgundy's CÔTE D'OR. For more details, see both MEURSAULT and PULIGNY-MONTRACHET.

blanc, blanche, masculine and feminine French adjectives meaning 'white' and therefore a common suffix for light-berried grape variety names.

blanc de blancs, French for 'white of whites', may justifiably be used to describe white wines made from pale-skinned grapes, as the great majority of them are. The term has real significance, however, only when used for white SPARKLING WINES, in the production of which dark-skinned grapes often predominate. A blanc de blancs CHAMPAGNE, for example, is, unusually, made exclusively from CHARDONNAY grapes.

Blanc de Morgex, alpine white wine made from Prié, the only indigenous white grape speciality of the Valle d'AOSTA.

blanc de noirs, French for 'white of blacks', describes a white wine made from dark-skinned grapes by pressing them very gently and running the pale juice off the skins as early as possible. Many such still wines have a slightly pink tinge (see WHITE ZINFANDEL and DÔLE Blanche, for example). The term has a specific meaning in the Champagne region, where it is used to describe a CHAMPAGNE made exclusively from PINOT NOIR and MEUNIER grapes. It is a speciality of the Aube in Champagne. See also VIN GRIS and BLUSH.

Blanc Fumé is a French synonym for SAUVIGNON BLANC, notably in Pouilly-sur-Loire, centre of the POUILLY-FUMÉ, or **Blanc Fumé de Pouilly**, appellation, many of whose aromatic dry whites do indeed have a smoky, if not exactly smoked, perfume. Thanks to one imaginative American, FUMÉ BLANC is today a much more widely known term (see MONDAVI).

blanco, Spanish term for white as in *vino blanco*, or white wine.

Blandy, a name that is synonymous with MADEIRA, both the island and the wine. The Blandy family has extensive interests on Madeira and were formerly the owners of the famous Reid's Hotel. John Blandy of Dorset came to live on the island in 1811, having been introduced to the island and its wines while serving in the navy. His son Charles was astute enough to buy up considerable stocks of mature wine during the outbreak of POWDERY MILDEW in 1852, which contributed to the success of the madeira wine firm Blandy Brothers & Co. in the second half of the 19th century. In 1874, Charles's daughter married a Cossart, of the other important madeira wine firm COSSART GORDON. The tourist showpiece of the madeira wine industry, the old São Francisco lodge in Funchal, was once the Blandy family home and offices.

The difficult years of the early 20th century saw the formation of the Madeira Wine Association, which Blandy's joined in the 1920s, eventually acquiring a controlling interest. The group is now known as the Madeira Wine Company, includes all the British madeira firms (Cossart Gordon, Leacock, Rutherford & Miles), and is one of the largest producers on the island. The SYMINGTON family, a major force in the port wine trade, acquired a controlling interest in the Madeira Wine Company in 1988 and run it in partnership with the Blandys, who have other business interests on the island.

Cossart, N., *Madeira: The Island Vineyard* (London, 1984).

blanketing, wine-making term for protecting grapes, juice, or wine, particularly from OXYGEN, by applying a gas, usually INERT GAS or sometimes CARBON DIOXIDE.

Blanquette, occasionally used as a synonym for a wide range of white wine grapes in SOUTH WEST FRANCE including Bourboulenc, Clairette, Mauzac, and Ondenc. It has also been used for Clairette in Australia.

Blanquette de Limoux. See LIMOUX.

Blau or **Blauer** is the adjective meaning 'blue' in German, often used for darker-berried vine varieties. Blauer Burgunder and Blauburgunder are PINOT NOIR, for example, while Weisser Burgunder and Weissburgunder are PINOT BLANC.

Blauburger, Austrian red wine grape variety and, like the much more common ZWEIGELT, a crossing made in the 1920s by Dr Zweigelt at KLOSTERNEUBURG, in this case of Portugieser and Blaufränkisch. There are about 800 ha/2,000 acres of it, the majority planted in Lower Austria, where it produces relatively undistinguished light reds although its deep colour makes it a useful ingredient in blends.

Blauburgunder, sometimes **Blauer Burgunder,** common name for PINOT NOIR in Austria and Switzerland. In Germany, SPÄT-BURGUNDER (occasionally **Blauer Spätburgunder**) is more common.

Blaufränkisch is the Austrian name for the middle European black grape variety the Germans call LEMBERGER. From pre-medieval times it was common to divide grape varieties into the (superior) 'fränkisch', whose origins lay with the Franks, and the rest. It is today one of Austria's most widely planted dark-berried varieties producing wines of real character, if notably high acidity, when carefully grown. Its good colour, tannin, and raciness encourage the most ambitious Austrian producers to lavish new oak on it and treat it like SYRAH. Outsiders, however, can find its build reminiscent of, say, the MONDEUSE of Savoie or one of the denser crus of BEAUJOLAIS and for many years it was thought to be the Beaujolais grape GAMAY. Bulgarians still call it Gamé, while Hungarians translate its Austrian name more directly as KÉKFRANKOS, and occasionally call it Nagyburgundi. It is known in Romania as Burgund Mare. DNA PROFILING in Austria suggested a parent–offspring relationship with GOUAIS BLANC, known in Austria as Heunisch.

Its Austrian home is Burgenland, where most of its nearly 3,000 ha/7,400 acres are situated. It is grown particularly on the warm shores of the Neusiedlersee, in Mittelburgenland, and at Eisenberg in South Burgenland. As Kékfrankos it also grows on the Hungarian side of the lake, in Sopron, whose porty version has the distinction of having been singled out for mention by Napoleon. Today it is seen both at home and abroad as one of Austria's best local varieties. Blaufränkisch gives wines with firm acidity, good weight, deep colour, useful tannin and spicy character. It is often given BARREL MATURATION and has great ageing potential.

The variety called Frankovka in the CZECH REPUBLIC and VOJVODINA is one and the same and here can produce lively, fruity, vigorous wines for early consumption. In FRIULI in the far north eastern corner of Italy, the variety is called Franconia and can yield wines with zip and fruit.

The vine buds early and ripens late and can therefore thrive only in a relatively warm climate. It can suffer spring frost damage but is very vigorous and is not particularly disease prone. Yields are therefore quite high, around 75 hl/ha (4.3 tons/acre).

Blaye, fortified town on the north bank of the Gironde estuary just opposite Margaux in the BORDEAUX region which has been exporting wine much longer than the famous MÉDOC across the water. Today it lends its name to several of the so-called BORDEAUX CÔTES appellations, although at the beginning of the 20th century it produced mainly white wine for distillation into cognac to the immediate north. Today by far the most important wine produced here is robust red **Premières Côtes de Blaye**, made on just over 4,500 ha/11,100 acres of vineyard, mainly from Merlot grapes supplemented by Cabernet Sauvignon and some Malbec. Such wines vary in quality but the region is rich in conscientious PETITS CHÂTEAUX such as Chx Bel-Air La Royère, Haut Bertinerie, Gigault, Les Grands Maréchaux, Haut-Grelot, Les Jonqueyres, Mondésir-Gazin, and Montgillet, which can provide good value for early drinking. Soils vary considerably (much more than in neighbouring Côtes de BOURG). White wine may be called **Blaye** or **Côtes de Blaye**, the latter limited to a higher minimum ALCOHOLIC STRENGTH and lower maximum YIELD. Although plantings of SAUVIGNON BLANC are increasing, the much more neutral UGNI BLANC predominates here and, curiously, is supposed to make up 90 per cent of any white Blaye. Some is also distilled into FINE de Bordeaux.

bleeding. Vines are said to bleed when they lose fluid in spring from pruning cuts. This event can take place over several days, and is generally seen following the first few days of warm spring weather. Individual vines can

lose up to 5 l/1.3 gal of water. The liquid which drips from the pruning cuts is mostly water, with low concentrations of MINERALS, SUGARS, organic acids, and HORMONES. This is the first visible sign of the start of the new VINE GROWTH CYCLE, and corresponds to renewed activity of the root system. Osmotic forces create root pressure, which forces water up through the plant.   R.E.S.

The term is also used occasionally in wine-making; see SAIGNÉE.

Galet, P., *Précis de viticulture* (5th edn, Montpellier, 1988).

blend, any product of BLENDING but specifically a wine deliberately made from more than one grape variety rather than a single VARIETAL (which may contain only a small proportion of other varieties).

blending different batches of wine, or *coupage* as it is known in French, is a practice more distrusted than understood. Almost all of the world's finest wines are made by blending the contents of different vats and different barrels (see ASSEMBLAGE); CHAMPAGNE and SHERRY are examples of wines which are quintessentially blends. It is often the case, as has been proved by the most rigorous of experiments, that a wine blend is superior to any one of its component parts.

Blending earned its dubious reputation before the mid 20th century when wine laws were either non-existent or under-enforced, and 'stretching' a superior wine by blending it with inferior wines was commonplace (see ADULTERATION). Blending of different lots of the same wine as it is commonly practised today to ensure that quality is maximal and consistent was not possible before the days of large blending vats; before then wine was bottled from individual casks or vats, which is one explanation of the much higher degree of BOTTLE VARIATION in older vintages.

Modern blending, important in the production of both fine and everyday wines, may combine wines with different but complementary characteristics: heavily oak-influenced lots aged in new barrels may be muted by blending with less oaky lots of the same wine; wines that have undergone MALOLACTIC FERMENTATION may be blended with crisper ones that have not. In the case of ordinary table wines, blending is an important ingredient in smoothing out the difference between one VINTAGE and its successor. Such practices are by no means unknown in the realm of fine wine production, whether legally sanctioned or not. The wine regulations in many regions permit the addition of a certain proportion of another vintage to a vintage-dated wine, as they frequently do a certain proportion, generally less than 15 per cent, of wine from a region or even grape variety other than that specified on the label.

In today's competitive and quality-conscious wine market, motivation for blending is more often improvement than deception.

Perhaps the most enthusiastic blenders are the AUSTRALIANS, who regularly blend the produce of two or more different wine regions, possibly many hundreds of miles apart. There are philosophical differences between them and the European authorities, but a compromise solution to allow the importation of such wines into the EU was reached in the mid 1990s.

For details of **fractional blending**, see SOLERA. For an alternative approach, in which grape varieties are mixed before fermentation, see CO-FERMENTATION.

blind tasting, form of wine TASTING in which the taster attempts to evaluate and/or identify wines without knowing their identity. Only by blind tasting can a true assessment of a wine's style and quality be made, so subjective is the wine-tasting process. Many professional tastings, those designed to make significant judgements about quality and possibly value, are therefore conducted blind. A comparative tasting, for example, comprises a group of wines of the same approximate age and provenance served blind together in order to evaluate them without prejudicial knowledge of their identity.

Blind tasting with the sole purpose of identification is a particularly masochistic but potentially rewarding exercise, conducted sometimes round the dining table, sometimes in the examination room (as part of a MASTER OF WINE exam, for example). The blind taster generally attempts to identify VINE VARIETY, geographical provenance, and VINTAGE. The first of these should be the easiest but, while wines from different varieties are generally considered to be distinctive, trained tasters have been found unable correctly to identify varieties in University of California blind-tasting tests. The percentage of correct identification was high for characteristic varieties such as Muscat at 59 per cent; the success rate with Cabernet Sauvignon was 39 per cent, while some minor varieties could not be identified at all.

In some cases, a wine's geographical provenance can be easier to detect than specific grape variety or blend of varieties. Red bordeaux and white Alsace, for example, tend to express place before grape.

In identifying vintage and general maturity, a wine's COLOUR can be particularly helpful, although, given the extent of vintage variation, a vintage several years from the actual one may well be a better guess than the vintage either side of it. Blind tasting does not usually involve blindfolding the taster (although if this is done, many tasters can even be confused as to whether a wine is red or white). Common practice is to disguise labels or even whole bottles by swathing them in foil, paper, or fabric and identifying them simply by number.

The OPTIONS GAME was devised by Len EVANS as a way of combining the arcane process of blind tasting with general entertainment. Beginners often make the best blind tasters; experience can confuse.

bloom on a grape's skin (*pruine* in French) is the whitish covering consisting of waxes and cutin which protects the berry against water loss and helps stop the penetration of spores.

blue fining, largely outmoded though still widely used wine-making process whereby excess copper and iron are removed from wine by FINING with potassium ferrocyanide. The process works because soluble copper and iron form insoluble compounds with the ferrocyanide ion. A century ago, before STAINLESS STEEL was widely available, winery equipment was often made of iron, copper, or bronze, an alloy of copper and tin. They would be attacked by the ACIDS in wine. Wines containing more than 10 mg/l of iron or 0.25 mg/l of copper could easily form a haze, so blue fining was needed to remove the excess copper and iron dissolved from the equipment after prolonged contact with the metals.

The process was developed by the German chemist Möslinger at the end of the 19th century and is still legally used, under strict controls, in many countries. In contemporary wine-making, iron may be introduced from metal grape bins and from BENTONITE fining; vineyard sprays such as BORDEAUX MIXTURE are still a common source of copper. Because of fears that hydrogen cyanide could be formed from potassium ferrocyanide, the use of blue fining is a major regulatory issue for wine treatments internationally and is illegal in many countries. A.D.W. & P.J.W.

Blue Nun, the most successful German wine BRAND, and for most of the 20th century a LIEBFRAUMILCH owned by H. SICHEL Söhne of Mainz. It was launched with the 1921 vintage in 1923 as a more accessible product than the host of German bottles adorned with Gothic script and long, complicated names. A label was developed for the easy, medium dry style of young white wine sold in inns throughout Germany which initially showed several nuns in brown habits against a bright blue sky. The label, and subsequently the brand, became known as Blue Nun, featuring a single, alluring nun in a blue habit. Long before MATEUS Rosé, Blue Nun became a substantial commercial success as a result of heavy investment in advertising which preyed on the fears of what was then an unsophisticated wine drinking public. Blue Nun was advertised as the wine you could drink 'right through the meal', thereby solving the awkward problem of FOOD AND WINE MATCHING. It began to grow rapidly, mainly in Britain and America, in the 1950s when German wines enjoyed greater prestige than they do today and Blue Nun commanded about the same price as a SECOND GROWTH red bordeaux. At its zenith, in 1984/5, annual sales in the US alone were 1.25 million cases, with a further 750,000 cases sold elsewhere. Quality was reliably high, despite the quantities needed to satisfy world sales, and blending at the Mainz headquarters was conscientiously undertaken (at this stage by Rainer Lingenfelder among others, who went on to establish a reputation for himself as one of the best estate producers in Germany's PFALZ region). A static wine market, economic recession, and increasing sophistication on the part of wine consumers saw worldwide sales fall to well under a million cases in the 1990s. H. Sichel Söhne and the Blue Nun brand were bought by F. W. Langguth Erben in 1995. Since the brand's re-launch, the quality of the wine has substantially improved from a Liebfraumilch to a cool-fermented, drier QBA from RHEINHESSEN, and the packaging has been modernized. Increased sales volumes prompted the launch of brand extensions from 2001, including a Vin de Pays d'Oc Merlot, a Riesling from the Pfalz, a Spanish rosé, and a sparkling Riesling Secco from Italy. Global sales are now once again in excess of 1 million cases.

blush wine is a very pale pink popular American speciality made, rather like France's VIN GRIS, by using black-skinned grapes as if to make white wine. A marketing triumph emanating from California in the late 1980s (the name was originally coined by Mill Creek winery but the style was promulgated by Bob Trinchero of Sutter Home), it differs from ROSÉ mainly in ethos rather than substance, having become fashionable just when and where rosé was losing its market appeal (although a blush wine is likely to be perceptibly paler than a rosé). WHITE ZINFANDEL was initially the dominant type in this class, but it spawned many other pinks-from-reds such as VARIETALS labelled White Grenache, Cabernet Blanc, Merlot Blanc, Blanc de Pinot Noir, as well as GENERICS called Blanc de Noirs. Most are sweet, vaguely aromatic, and faintly fizzy. Blush wines' share of all wine consumed in the US fell from 22 per cent in 1997 to 15 per cent in 2003. See also SAIGNÉE. J.R. & B.C.C.

Boal, often Anglicized to Bual, is the name applied to several Portuguese white grape varieties much planted in the 19th century. Most famously, Bual came to represent a style of MADEIRA, richer than SERCIAL and VERDELHO, yet not as sweet as that called MALMSEY. Most of the Boal growing to a limited extent on Madeira today—though not nearly as limited as the island's other three 'noble' varieties—is **Boal Cachudo**. Portugal's Instituto da Vinha e do Vinho (IVV) lists four other subvarieties of Boal: **Boal Barreiro**, **Boal Branco**, **Boal**

Espinho, and **Boal Ratinho.** DNA PROFILING in Portugal confirmed that Boal Cachudo (or Boal da Madeira) is identical to MALVASIA Fina from the Douro, and that Boal Ratinho is the progeny of Boal Cachudo and CRATO Branco. Boal Branco is grown in the Algarve. Boal is known as Gual on the CANARY ISLANDS.

Bobal, important Spanish dark-skinned grape variety which produces deep-coloured red wines and even GRAPE CONCENTRATE in VALENCIA, ALICANTE, UTIEL-REQUENA, and to an extent in JUMILLA, YECLA, and BULLAS in south east Spain, mainly but not exclusively for BULK WINE production. It is widely planted, on a total of nearly 89,000 ha/220,000 acres in 2004, and its reputation has been growing as producers such as Mustiguillo have managed to fashion velvety reds from high altitude vineyards in Utiel-Requena. It retains its acidity better than MONASTRELL, which tends to be grown in slightly warmer, more southerly parts of Spain, and is notably lower in alcohol. It is allowed in four DO areas: Utiel-Requena, Valencia, MANCHUELA, and RIBERA DEL JÚCAR.

Bobal Blanco, also known as Tortosí, is still grown to a limited extent in Valencia.

Boca, rare but historically important red wine DOC in the Novara hills in the subalpine north of the PIEMONTE region of north west Italy. GHEMME, SIZZANO, and FARA, also in Novara, are similar, as are GATTINARA, LESSONA, and BRAMATERRA in the Vercelli hills across the river Sesia. For more details, see SPANNA.

Bocksbeutel, special bottle in the shape of a flattened flask used in the German wine region of FRANKEN and four communes in the northern Ortenau area of BADEN. The name probably derived from the Low German *Bockesbeutel*, a pouch to carry prayer-books and the like, rather than from any ostensible resemblance to a goat's scrotum (the literal translation). T.S.

BOD, biological oxygen demand. See WINERY WASTE.

bodega, Spanish term for a wine CELLAR, a WINERY, or a tavern or grocery store selling wine.

body, tasting term for the perceived 'weight'—the sensation of fullness, resulting from DENSITY or VISCOSITY—of a wine on the palate. Wines at either end of the scale are described as **full bodied** and **light bodied**.

Next to water, ALCOHOL is the major constituent of wines. It has a much higher viscosity than water and is the major component responsible for the sensation of fullness, or body, as a wine is rinsed around the mouth. ALCOHOLIC STRENGTH is therefore clearly an important factor: the more potent a wine the more full bodied it is usually said to be.

The dissolved solids in a wine, its EXTRACT, can also contribute significantly to body, although sweet wines are not necessarily full bodied (ASTI, for example, being sweet but very light bodied, thanks to its low alcohol content).

Contrary to popular conception, GLYCEROL makes only a very minor contribution to density, viscosity, and therefore to body (although it does have a slight effect on apparent sweetness).

Body is not related to wine quality, BALANCE being more important in a wine than whether it is full or light bodied. One of the less desirable effects of the increase in comparative TASTING, however, is that full-bodied wines make a more obvious impression and therefore tend to be glorified.

Amerine, M. A., and Roessler, E. B., *Wines: Their Sensory Evaluation* (2nd edn, New York, 1982).

Bohemia, western part of the CZECH REPUBLIC that is better known for the production of beer and GLASSES than wine. There are some small vineyard areas around the towns of Mělník and Roudnice, and the Lobkowicz estates in particular have made some good-quality red wine. A substantial business making sparkling wines generally from imported base wine is based in the region.

Boisset, Burgundy's largest wine producer and exporter and France's third biggest wine and spirit company, was formed as recently as 1961 by Jean-Claude Boisset when he was just 18 but is now one of the most diversified in France. The early business was successful enough to acquire rival NÉGOCIANTS Charles Vienot and Thomas-Bassot in 1982. The company was floated on the stock market in 1985 and took over Pierre Ponnelle, Morin Père et Fils, Jaffelin, and Bouchard Aîné during the next six years. In 1994 the company then diversified into sparkling wine production via such acquisitions as Varichon et Clerc and Charles de Fère while consolidating its Côte de Beaune holdings by buying Ropiteau, followed in the late 1990s by the Cellier de Samsons and Mommessin in Beaujolais, J. Moreau in Chablis, Domaine Bernard (now Louis Bernard) in the Rhône, and the fruit liqueur business L'Héritier-Guyot. Further acquisitions in Beaujolais and the Languedoc, including Caroline de Beaulieu, followed.

In 1998, Boisset formed its first overseas JOINT VENTURE to build Clos Jordan Pinot Noir winery with VINCOR of Canada. Others followed in 2003 with Pisano in Uruguay to form Progreso and Corpora in Chile to form Veranda. That same year the Boisset family regained full ownership of the company, now styled négociant-éleveur with a commitment to organic viticulture in its flagship 37-ha vineyard holding Domaine de la Vougeraie. The company then strengthened its positiong in the US by acquiring De Loach Vineyards,

Seven Peaks, as well as Marie Brizard US. They have offices in California and have a distribution joint venture in the UK.

Bolgheri, small town in the Tuscan MAREMMA which gives its name to a DOC for relatively ordinary white and rosé wines (including one from ANTINORI holdings here), but provides a geographical reference point for at least two of the most famous SUPERTUSCANS, SASSICAIA and Ornellaia, made by cousins and members of the extended Antinori family. Red wines from Bolgheri—principally from Cabernet and Merlot although Sangiovese is also permitted—were granted DOC status in 1994, with Sassicaia given its own DOC as a subzone of Bolgheri. Both Bolgheri and the neighbouring township of Castagneto Carducci have become magnets for investors from outside the zone, including Angelo GAJA of Piemonte, as the wines have attained wide international recognition and popularity. The proximity to the sea gives a more temperate climate than that found in the central Tuscan hills, resulting in grapes that ripen earlier, often before the autumn rains arrive. Such consistency has greatly increased the appeal of the area. D.T. & D.C.G.

Bolivia in SOUTH AMERICA has a long history of vine-growing but its modern wine industry is very small. Viticulture was brought to the high valleys of Bolivia from neighbouring PERU in the 16th century by Augustine MISSIONARIES. Between 1550 and 1570 they had reached the districts of Pilaya, Paspalla, and Cinti and had spread as far south as Tarija by 1600.

PHYLLOXERA and NEMATODES severely hampered Bolivian viticulture in much of the 20th century. Resistant ROOTSTOCKS and good-quality VINIFERA cuttings were imported in the 1980s in an effort to restore vineyard health and the proportion of grafted vines is increasing.

The climate here is both CONTINENTAL and TROPICAL, modified by ALTITUDE, so that the vines in the high Andean valleys are planted at 2,000 to 2,500 m/8,200 ft above sea level and La Concepción, the country's most important and highest altitude winery and one of four large wine enterprises in Tarija in the south near the Argentine border, grows vines between 1,600 and 2,800 m. It also buys CRIOLLA grapes from vines trained up trees at altitudes up to 2,850 m in Toropalca in the south of the country. Bolivia produces only about 20,000 hl/528,000 gal of wine a year according to OIV figures, most of it grown in Tarija. It would be classified as Region III or IV according to the WINKLER system, and annual RAINFALL averages 300 to 500 mm/19 in. A little wine is also produced in the south eastern zone of Camargo and the Cañón de Cinti denomination where conditions are similar to Tarija except that it is even hotter with an average temperature of 23 °C rather than 18.2

(66.5 °F). Rain can be concentrated in the early months of the year, encouraging FUNGAL DISEASES. The traditional system of training vines up the indigenous pepper tree (*Schinus molle*) helped retard the development of such diseases, but ESPALIER vine-training systems, with a VINE DENSITY of 3,000 to 3,500 vines per ha, are more common. IRRIGATION is widely practised.

MUSCAT OF ALEXANDRIA represents about 80 per cent of all light-coloured VINIFERA grape varieties planted, and is widely used for distillation into the aromatic local brandy singani, which can be a fine counterpart to the PISCO of Peru and Chile. Table wines are also produced from Muscat although plantings of a wide range of other varieties associated throughout the world with good-quality red and white wine are increasing. Some creditable Cabernet–Merlot blends are produced, notably from Aranjuez and as part of La Concepción's Cepas de Altura range, as well as examples of varietal Torrontés, Riesling, and Chenin Blanc.

The wine produced for domestic consumption by foot treading and vinification in clay jars is called *patero*.

Bollinger, independent Champagne house producing a range of top-quality wines based on Pinot Noir grapes. Bollinger was formed from the de Villermont family's holdings in the village of Aÿ near Rheims, where the company is still based. In 1829, Jacques Joseph Placide Bollinger, youngest son of a noblewoman and a legal officer in Württemberg, formed a partnership with Amiral Comte Athanase Louis Emmanuel de Villermont and Paul-Joseph Renaudin to form the house of Champagne Renaudin, Bollinger & Cie. In 1837, Jacques Bollinger married de Villermont's daughter Louise Charlotte and became a French citizen. In 1865, the house started to ship low DOSAGE champagne to Britain, which was unusual for a period in which most champagne reaching the country was sweet. Champagne Bollinger received the Royal Warrant as Official Purveyor of Champagne to Queen Victoria in 1884.

Control of the house eventually passed to Jacques's grandson (also named Jacques), who died young, leaving his widow Elizabeth Law 'Lily' Bollinger (1899–1977) in charge. Lily oversaw the family vineyards on foot and bicycle for four decades, enduring the 1944 German bombardment of Aÿ while sleeping in the Bollinger cellars. After the Second World War, she acquired the Beauregard vineyard at Mutigny as well as vineyards in Grauves, Bisseuil, and Champvoisy, bringing Bollinger's land holdings to 144 ha/356 acres, about 70 per cent of production needs. By the time of her death in 1977, Lily had seen sales double to 1 million bottles a year. She believed that nothing should change the traditional Bollinger style, which is achieved with a backbone of Pinot Noir from the Aÿ vineyards, a

certain proportion of BARREL FERMENTATION (unusual for sparkling wine), and TIRAGE in bottles stoppered, unusually, with corks rather than crown caps, often for a decade or more. Bollinger RD ('recently disgorged', with marked AUTOLYSIS as a result of being aged for a minimum of eight years) is the vintage dated Grande Année with extra age. Rarest of all the Bollinger range of champagnes is the Vieilles Vignes Françaises, a BLANC DE NOIRS produced exclusively from ungrafted Pinot Noir vines that grow in a vineyard behind Bollinger's headquarters which was never affected by PHYLLOXERA.

Bollinger also owns a majority stake in the SAUMUR house Langlois Chateau, as well as a much more recent minority stake in Delamain of Cognac. In 1985, Bollinger daringly took a 40 per cent share of Petaluma in SOUTH AUSTRALIA and now have a joint venture Tapanappa in Wrattonbully, South Australia. In 2005, the company bought the neighbouring house of Ayala. While other Champagne houses became defensive, Bollinger rose admirably to the challenge posed by critics of champagne in the early 1990s by issuing the Bollinger Charter of Ethics and Quality, in which it volunteered conditions for the production of its wines which protected both wine quality and the Bollinger name. Chief architect of the Bollinger Charter was the outspoken Christian Bizot, president of the house and nephew of Lily Bollinger. On his retirement he was succeeded by his nephew Ghislain de Montgolfier. His son Etienne also works for the company.

See also CHAMPAGNE.   S.A. & J.R.
Ray, C., *Bollinger: Tradition of a Champagne Family* (3ʳᵈ edn, London, 1988).

Bolognesi, Colli, small DOC zone in the hills of Bologna in north central Italy. See EMILIA-ROMAGNA for more details.

Bolzano, or **Bozen** in German, the main town of ALTO ADIGE in northern Italy. Local light red wines may carry the name **Colli di Bolzano** or **Bozner Leiten**.

Bombino Bianco, important white grape variety, especially in northern PUGLIA in southern Italy and also in EMILIA-ROMAGNA, LAZIO, MARCHE, and ABRUZZO where it has been confused with TREBBIANO d'Abruzzo.

The vine may have originated in Spain. It ripens late and yields extremely high quantities of relatively neutral wine, much of which has been shipped north, particularly to the energetic blenders of Germany. Many an ordinary SEKT or EU blend of TABLE WINE is made up substantially of Bombino Bianco, perhaps scented with a particularly aromatic German variety such as MORIO-MUSKAT. Some of its synonyms, Pagedebit ('it pays the debts') and Straccia Cambiale ('tear up the invoices') in particular, allude to its profitability to the

vine-grower. There is also a much less common dark-berried **Bombino Nero** in Puglia.

Bonarda, Italian red grape variety, or more accurately the name of three distinct varieties: (1) the Bonarda of the OLTREPÒ PAVESE and COLLI PIACENTINI (also planted in southern PUGLIA), which is, in fact, not Bonarda at all but rather the CROATINA grape; (2) the Bonarda Novarese, used to soften SPANNA in its range of DOC reds in the Novara and Vercelli hills, which again is not Bonarda, but UVA RARA, a variety more widely employed in the Oltrepò Pavese; and (3) the so-called Bonarda Piemontese, an aromatic variety which has been virtually abandoned because of its small bunches and low productivity, although it covered 30 per cent of the region's vineyard before the advent of PHYLLOXERA. Scattered patches remain on the left bank of the Tanaro, particularly in the township of Govone. In the mid 1990s, desultory attempts were being made to revive this last variety, in the belief that it will add aromatic interest when blended with the BARBERA grape. The only DOC wines in production which bear the name Bonarda are from the Oltrepò Pavese and are made from Croatina.   D.T.

Bonarda is also the name of the second most widely grown red wine grape variety in ARGENTINA, where total plantings had grown to 16,607 ha/39,702 acres planted by 2002. This means that Argentina has far more 'Bonarda' planted than Italy, although some authorities believe Argentine Bonarda is in fact CHARBONO, presumably the Italian, not the Savoie, version. More work is needed to establish its identity conclusively.

Alcalde, A. J., *Cultivares Viticolas Argentinas* (Mendoza, 1989).

bonbonne, a large glass jar or carboy, typically holding 25 l/6.6 gal, used as a neutral container to store wine, VIN DOUX NATUREL, or brandy, often after a period of wood ageing.

bonded warehouse or **bonded winery**, one in which no DUTY has been paid on the goods inside it. Prices for wines and, especially, spirits held **in bond** (IB) are therefore considerably lower than those quoted duty paid, or duty paid and delivered (DPD). It is sensible for any foreigner buying wine to store for possible shipment outside that country to buy it **in bond**.

Bondola, traditional *vinifera* grape of SWITZERLAND's Ticino, where it may be an ingredient in the local blend called Nostrano. Largely replaced by Merlot.

Bonnes Mares, great red GRAND CRU in Burgundy's CÔTE D'OR. For more details, see CHAMBOLLE-MUSIGNY and MOREY-ST-DENIS.

Bonnezeaux, particularly well-favoured enclave for sweet white wine production within the Coteaux du LAYON appellation in the Anjou district of the Loire. In this respect Bonnezeaux resembles QUARTS DE CHAUME to the north west but, perhaps because of its greater extent (about 110 ha/270 acres) spread across three *buttes* (small hills) and much more exposed situation, it has not enjoyed such fame. A Bonnezeaux from a producer as reliable as Ch de Fesles can be a deep green-gold nectar at 10 to 20 years old. The wines are made exclusively from Chenin Blanc grapes grown on steep slopes near Thouarcé. These grapes should ideally be attacked by NOBLE ROT, or at the very least have been picked only after several TRIES through the vineyard. POTENTIAL ALCOHOL should be at least 13.5 per cent, half a per cent more than Quarts de Chaume, but quality-conscious growers usually aim for at least 18 per cent, and yields are usually very low. See also LOIRE, including map.

books on wine. See the LITERATURE OF WINE and WINE WRITING. For references to wine in some more obviously literary works, see ENGLISH LITERATURE, WINE IN.

Borba, subregion of ALENTEJO in southern Portugal. It is also the name of a productive Spanish white grape grown in EXTREMADURA.

Bordeaux, important French port on the GARONNE river leading to the GIRONDE estuary on the west coast. Bordeaux gives its name to a wine region which includes the vineyards of the Gironde *département* and, as such, the wine region which produces more top-quality wine than any other, from a total vineyard area that had grown from about 114,000 ha in the mid 1990s to 124,000 ha/306,000 acres by 2004, divided among 18,000 increasingly impoverished producers as the gap in demand for the best wines and for the rest widened. Bordeaux has a higher proportion of large estates than any other French wine region, and produces more of the world's most expensive and sought-after wines than anywhere else. The most famous examples represent less than 5 per cent of the region's total production, however, and Bordeaux's most pressing problem in the early 21st century was how to sell the rest to a world increasingly accustomed to stronger, more concentrated reds. The best red bordeaux, known by the British as CLARET, are characterized by their subtlety and ability to evolve after years, sometimes decades, of BOTTLE AGEING. The worst can be thin and evanescent. The producers inbetween suffer because there are simply too many of them to make much impact. Throughout 2005, there was talk of declassifying much BORDEAUX AC to VIN DE PAYS de l'Aquitaine or de l'Atlantique.

The proportion of bordeaux that is white, both sweet and dry, has fallen from about a quarter in the 1990s to just over 10 per cent in the early 21st century. Small quantities of rosé, light red CLAIRET, and sparkling CRÉMANT

are also made. The total quantity of wine produced each year varies considerably according to VINTAGE but can be enough to fill more than 900 million bottles, which represents more than a quarter of France's total APPELLATION CONTRÔLÉE wine production. See BORDEAUX AC for bordeaux wine at its most basic, BORDEAUX TRADE for an account of the workings of the wine trade in Bordeaux, and University of BORDEAUX for details of its important Institut d'Oenologie.

History to medieval times
The Latin poet Ausonius (*c*.AD 310–393/4) is not only the first author to mention that wine was grown in his native Bordeaux, he was also the region's first known wine-grower. In his poem 'De herediolo' ('On his small inheritance'), dated 379, he tells us that he grows 100 *iugera* (a *iugerum* is approximately two-thirds of an acre or 0.25 ha) of vines. His estate was probably at Bazas, near the river Garonne (although some have suggested St-Émilion). In two of his other poems, 'Mosella' ('On the Moselle'), and 'Ordo urbium nobilium' ('The list of distinguished cities'), he describes the banks of the Garonne overgrown with vines. Ch AUSONE is named after him.

Although Ausonius' descriptions indicate that viticulture was well established in Bordeaux in his lifetime, no definite earlier evidence exists. Given that the Allobroges tribe were growing wine around Vienne in the RHÔNE valley in the 1st century AD, the Bituriges may have been doing the same in Bordeaux, but Strabo, author of the *Geography* (completed in 7 BC), merely says that Bordeaux ('Burdigala' in Latin and in Strabo's Greek) was a place of commerce, and PLINY, writing *c*.AD 77, does not tell us clearly that the Bituriges grew wine (although he does refer to a Biturica vine, which may have been associated with either the Bituriges tribe of Bordeaux or the other to the west of Bourges), so the likelihood is that viticulture spread to Bordeaux after it had come to the Rhône.

We know little about Bordeaux in the centuries following the fall of the Roman empire. The area was overrun by the Visigoths in the 5th century and when Clovis had defeated the Visigoths in 507 it became part of the Frankish kingdom. CHARLEMAGNE is said to have displayed a temporary interest in FRONSAC. With the economic expansion in Europe which started in the 11th century, demand for wine grew. Initially, the new port of LA ROCHELLE, on the Atlantic coast north of Bordeaux, brought wealth to the region in the 12th century; consequently, Bordeaux increased both its trade and its production. By 1200 wine was grown in BLAYE, BOURG, the lower DORDOGNE and the Garonne valley, and in the GRAVES. The Graves was the largest producer, with Ch Pape-Clément as its oldest named vineyard. In 1305 Archbishop Bertrand de Goth, who was to become Pope Clement V,

presented it to the see of Bordeaux. Throughout the Bordeaux region more red wine was grown than white, but SAUTERNES and CÉRONS probably had white wine, although these white wines cannot have been like the botrytis-affected wines of today, for the deliberate commercial use of NOBLE ROT in Sauternes and Cérons dates from after the Middle Ages. Until the late 17th century the MÉDOC was too marshy to produce much wine and was known mainly for its corn: there were just a few vineyards in what is now called the Bas-Médoc, north of ST-ESTÈPHE. ST-ÉMILION was already a wine-growing district, however. Some of the wine of Bordeaux was neither white nor red but a mixture of white and red grapes fermented together called 'clairet' in Old French, which is the origin of the modern English word CLARET.

Bordeaux's pre-eminence began as a result of the English connection. In 1152, Eleanor of Aquitaine married Henry Plantagenet, who in 1154 became king of England (and duke of Normandy) as well as acquiring Eleanor's territories, GASCONY and most of western France. In order to win the favour of the citizens of Bordeaux, King John (1199–1216) granted them numerous privileges. The most important of these was exemption from the Grand Coutume, the export tax imposed on ships sailing from Bordeaux. Also, Gascon merchants were given favoured treatment in London. All this made Gascon wine cheaper for the English than any other imported wine. In the 14th century, most French wine consumed in England was from Gascony, and a quarter of Bordeaux's wine exports went to England. Against these protective measures La Rochelle could not compete, despite its superior position right on the coast, while Bordeaux was 60 miles/100 km up river. And when La Rochelle fell to the French in 1224, it ceased to be a commercial threat to Bordeaux.

Not all the wines sold by the Gascon merchants were from the immediate Bordeaux area. In the HAUT PAYS (Gaillac, Quercy, Nérac, and Bergerac) the climate was more reliable and these wines were stronger than those of Bordeaux. The Haut Pays wines were more expensive because they were taxed in Bordeaux; and those from the parts of the Haut Pays which had fallen to the French were not allowed into Bordeaux until St Martin's Day, 11 November, or even until Christmas, so that Bordeaux wines dominated the wines available for the fleet which arrived each autumn to deliver the year's new wine to England, Scotland, Ireland, the Low Countries, and the Hanseatic ports. The wine of GAILLAC was especially prized in England.

In 1453, at the end of the HUNDRED YEARS WAR, Gascony reverted to French rule; yet its trade with England soon picked up again, even though it never regained its 14th-century volume. Bordeaux had been a major port before it became a wine-producing area to feed its wine

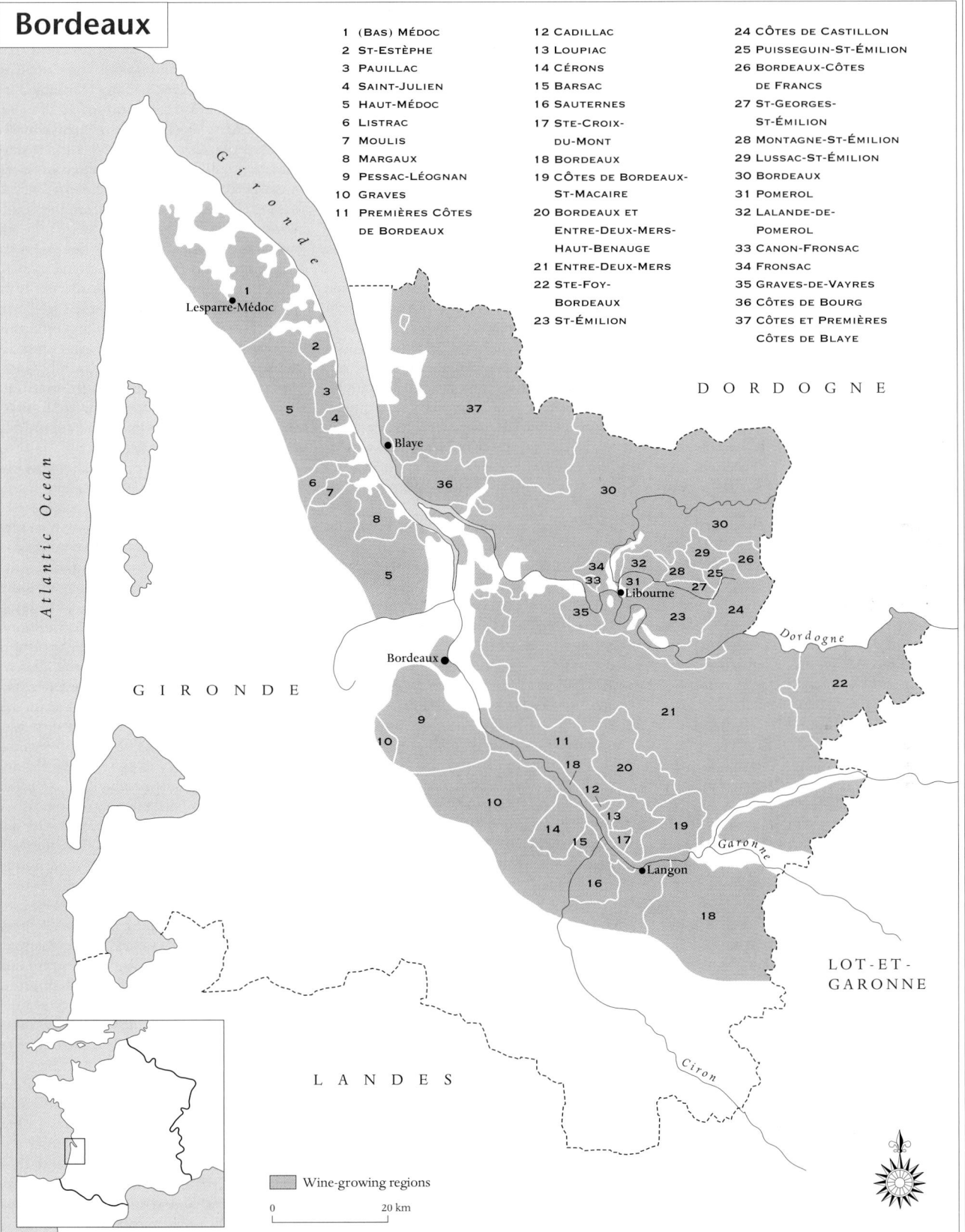

Bordeaux

1 (BAS) MÉDOC
2 ST-ESTÈPHE
3 PAUILLAC
4 SAINT-JULIEN
5 HAUT-MÉDOC
6 LISTRAC
7 MOULIS
8 MARGAUX
9 PESSAC-LÉOGNAN
10 GRAVES
11 PREMIÈRES CÔTES
   DE BORDEAUX

12 CADILLAC
13 LOUPIAC
14 CÉRONS
15 BARSAC
16 SAUTERNES
17 STE-CROIX-
   DU-MONT
18 BORDEAUX
19 CÔTES DE BORDEAUX-
   ST-MACAIRE
20 BORDEAUX ET
   ENTRE-DEUX-MERS-
   HAUT-BENAUGE
21 ENTRE-DEUX-MERS
22 STE-FOY-
   BORDEAUX
23 ST-ÉMILION

24 CÔTES DE CASTILLON
25 PUISSEGUIN-ST-ÉMILION
26 BORDEAUX-CÔTES
   DE FRANCS
27 ST-GEORGES-
   ST-ÉMILION
28 MONTAGNE-ST-ÉMILION
29 LUSSAC-ST-ÉMILION
30 BORDEAUX
31 POMEROL
32 LALANDE-DE-
   POMEROL
33 CANON-FRONSAC
34 FRONSAC
35 GRAVES-DE-VAYRES
36 CÔTES DE BOURG
37 CÔTES ET PREMIÈRES
   CÔTES DE BLAYE

DORDOGNE

Atlantic Ocean

Girondе

Lesparre-Médoc

Blaye

GIRONDE

Bordeaux

Libourne

Dordogne

Bordeaux

87

LANDES

Langon

Garonne

Ciron

LOT-ET-
GARONNE

Wine-growing regions

0   20 km

trade. Its winemakers were not patient monks, as they had often been in Burgundy, but opportunistic laymen, whose aim was to cash in on the huge demand for Bordeaux's chief export product, and so they switched from grain to wine. The thin wines of Bordeaux, which before the advent of glass BOTTLES and CORKS did not last from one vintage to the next, cannot have been anything like modern bordeaux.

H.M.W.

James, M. K., *Studies in the Medieval Wine Trade* (Oxford, 1971).

Penning-Rowsell, E., *The Wines of Bordeaux* (6th edn, London, 1989).

Simon, A. L., *The History of the Wine Trade in England*, 3 vols. (London, 1906–9).

Modern history

Trade with Britain continued after the English were expelled, but the DUTCH WINE TRADE gradually became dominant, not so much in wines for their own consumption but in inexpensive white wines for the rest of northern Europe and the Hanseatic states. The Bordeaux merchants had to fight hard to maintain their position in northern Europe, for the Dutch also bought from the Mediterranean countries.

It was the Dutch who drained the marshy MÉDOC in the mid 17th century, thereby creating the basis for the fine wines that made Bordeaux's reputation throughout the world. Before this the best wines were to be found in the well-drained GRAVES near the city, notably Ch HAUT-BRION. Today's leading Médocain estates—Chx LAFITE, LATOUR, and MARGAUX—were probably planted in the last third of the 17th century, and reached England, to be offered at auction in the COFFEE HOUSES of London, only after consignments had been captured at sea in the Anglo-French wars at the beginning of the 18th century.

The simultaneous trade war between Britain and France led to ever-increasing duties on French wines and the Anglo-Portuguese Methuen Treaty of 1703. In return for a Portuguese promise to admit British woollen goods in perpetuity, the British government agreed that duty on French wines should never be less than 50 per cent higher than on the wines of Portugal (and, in fact, Spain). Officially, British wine imports from Bordeaux declined sharply but smuggling must have been rife, to judge from the prevalence of bordeaux in the household sales conducted by Christie's (see AUCTIONS) after their foundation in 1766. Conditions in both Bordeaux and Britain were ripe for the development of trade in fine CLARET: in the Gironde there was a new affluent bourgeoisie, members of the legal Bordeaux Parlement, with the means to plant and maintain expensive vineyards, while in Britain bordeaux's almost exclusive market was created by a wealthy, landowning aristocracy and, soon, the new industrial middle class.

The necessary link was a Bordeaux merchant class, sufficiently well established to be able to buy, cellar, and export these 'new French clarets'. These merchants came largely from Britain, and Germany, which had long been prominent in the inexpensive red bordeaux trade. BARTON & Guestier originally started in 1725; William, later Nathaniel, Johnston began in 1734; and BROKERS Tastet & Lawton in 1740. These are some of the longer survivors of many more. The German firms of standing appear to have arrived later: CRUSE from Danish Schleswig-Holstein, later incorporated into Germany, arrived in 1819; Eschenauer in 1821; and Kressmann in 1858. A substantial French merchant, with its roots in the RHÔNE valley, was Calvet, which opened a Bordeaux office in 1870. It is also significant that the trade's 'bible' was the creation, in 1850, of an English teacher, Charles Cocks (see COCKS ET FÉRET).

Until well into the second half of the 20th century, most of these firms had their premises in the suburb of Les Chartrons, named after a medieval Carthusian monastery. The Quai des Chartrons, facing the river Garonne, and its side streets, was the headquarters of the so-called *aristocratie du bouchon* (aristocracy of the cork).

In 1852, Bordeaux was struck by oidium, or POWDERY MILDEW, the first of a series of vine plagues which were to devastate many other wine regions too. First noted in the sweet wine areas near the Garonne, it spread through the Graves and then into the Médoc. Between 1854 and 1856, all the properties which were rated CLASSED GROWTHS in the 1855 CLASSIFICATION produced a total of only 3,400 TONNEAUX of wine, not much more than half the crop in a prolific year. By 1858 this fungal disease was conquered by spraying with SULFUR, a practice which continues to this day (see below).

Trade with Britain increased as a result of the Anglo-French Treaty of 1860, for in the following year Gladstone, then Chancellor of the Exchequer, reduced duty on French wines to 2d. (less than 1p) a bottle. This was a particularly prosperous time for Bordeaux, which had also developed substantial markets in South America and Russia, and a small one in North America.

However, the severe onset of PHYLLOXERA in the late 1870s, followed by DOWNY MILDEW in the following decade, proved a serious setback to the trade in everyday GENERIC red and white bordeaux. For the first time ever an import BOND was established in Bordeaux, largely supplied with blending wine from the new vineyards of ALGERIA. On the other hand, excessive FERTILIZATION by important châteaux proprietors to compensate for losses by disease led to large crops of inferior quality and to a fall in reputation and price. In 1910, nevertheless, two out of every three bottles of French wine imported into Britain came from the Gironde. They totalled 110,000 hl/2.9 million gal, approximately the same as for BELGIUM, although Germany imported almost twice as much. In 1911, the Gironde *département* was delimited, leading eventually to the establishment of Bordeaux's APPELLATION CONTRÔLÉE system in 1936.

A serious slump followed soon after the First World War, with many châteaux changing hands, and this continued in the 1930s. After the First World War, the Russian market had disappeared, the South American one was much reduced, and the US market was closed by PROHIBITION between 1919 and 1933, when it hardly had time to recover before the Second World War.

At this time the market for fine wines was largely confined to the Médoc and the châteaux in the Graves near to Bordeaux. It was not until after the Second World War—during which Bordeaux, and many large châteaux, were occupied by the German army—that any ST-ÉMILION property other than Ch CHEVAL BLANC was widely known outside France, and the same was true of POMEROL, even Ch PÉTRUS, although there was a good market for inexpensive St-Émilions in Belgium.

It was not until the end of the 1950s that those châteaux with an international reputation made sufficient profits to begin serious replanting and the installation of modern equipment, notably FERMENTATION VESSELS made of STAINLESS STEEL, although this was an option which many châteaux, including Lafite, Margaux, and MOUTON-ROTHSCHILD, did not take. From the mid 1960s, the United States market became increasingly important, particularly for the classed growths. This was particularly marked with the successful 1970 vintage when large American purchases were made as futures, EN PRIMEUR, followed some years later in Britain. Previously, if a vintage was considered likely to be very fine, the BORDEAUX TRADE would sometimes buy SUR SOUCHE, but otherwise a vintage would not be marketed until shortly before or after BOTTLING, either by the château or by the Bordeaux merchants. In 1972, CHÂTEAU BOTTLING became compulsory for the classed growths, and was generally applied to the more important properties in the Graves, St-Émilion, and Pomerol. The leading red and white Graves had first been classified in 1953, and the St-Émilions in 1955 (see CLASSIFICATIONS). The Pomerols remain unclassified.

These en primeur campaigns reflected the changed financial situation in Bordeaux (although the generic wines, accounting for up to half the annual crop, continued, and continue, to be sold chiefly within 12 months of the harvest). No longer could most châteaux afford to hold several vintages in stock; nor could the Bordeaux merchants or their customers in France or abroad. For the most part in the 1970s and 1980s, consumers had to bear the financial responsibility of AGEING young red bordeaux, and some leading sweet wines.

The 'energy crisis' of 1973, in which Middle East oil producers greatly raised their prices, caused havoc in Bordeaux, where recent vintages had been sold en primeur at excessively high prices. This had applied at all quality levels, and one result was that in order to meet contracts for generic red bordeaux the distinguished house of CRUSE had bought wine from outside the region, involving altered appellation contrôlée documents. A sharp fall in prices occurred, as well as subsequent mass disposals of stock by both merchants and leading châteaux. Some of the traditional firms were saved from bankruptcy only by foreign ownership, and the old world of the Chartronnais disappeared for ever. Later, classed growth châteaux passed into the financial control of such outsiders as insurance companies (see AXA for example) and multinational corporations.

The succession of fine vintages in the 1980s improved the situation of many châteaux, but competition was so keen on the Bordeaux market that the merchants were unable as in the past to build up the financial reserves to tide them over poor years. So when Bordeaux was hit by the heavily FROST-damaged 1991 vintage and the record, diluted 1992, the en primeur trade virtually ceased internationally, and considerable financial problems arose—although the chiefly domestic trade in generic and humble appellation wines continued much as usual.

From the 18th century until 1939, the Bordeaux trade normally called the price tune, and with the exception of the *belle époque* from 1858 to 1878 the château owners had to fall into line. For the 30 years from 1961, the leading proprietors then held the whip hand in allocating their new wines to more than 100 Bordeaux merchants. In the early 1990s, when Bordeaux had no great vintages to sell, power was transferred to the consumer. The number of potential purchasers of fine bordeaux grew substantially, however, in the mid 1990s when the exciting 1995 and 1996 vintages were available, in the United States and for the first time in ASIA. This, coupled with widespread economic boom, helped create an unprecedented price spiral in Bordeaux, but this has been flattened somewhat in a market swollen by huge volumes of wine and by the strength of the euro in the early 21st century.

E.P.-R. & J.R.

Brook, S., *Bordeaux—People, Power and Politics* (London, 2001).

Faith, N., *The Winemasters* (3rd edn, London, 2005).

Penning-Rowsell, E., *The Wines of Bordeaux* (6th edn, London, 1989).

Geography

The wine districts of Bordeaux hug the Gironde estuary and the rivers DORDOGNE and GARONNE which flow into it (see map on p. 87). The largest and most important appellation is BORDEAUX AC, but there are more than 50 appellations in all, although many of them are rarely seen outside the region. The notably flat Bordeaux vineyards are rarely at altitudes of more than a few metres above sea level.

Conventionally, in terms of the all-important fine red wines at least, the whole region is split into 'left bank' and 'right bank', or MÉDOC and GRAVES on the west side of the Gironde, and ST-ÉMILION and POMEROL on the east side, leaving the vast ENTRE-DEUX-MERS ('between two seas') district in the middle. Within the Haut-Médoc, the superior land closer to Bordeaux, are the world-famous communes MARGAUX, ST-JULIEN, PAUILLAC, and ST-ESTÈPHE, together with the slightly less illustrious and, significantly, more inland appellations of LISTRAC and MOULIS. Most of the finest wines of the Graves, on the other hand, have come from an enclave awarded its own appellation in 1987, PESSAC-LÉOGNAN. Pomerol and St-Émilion have their 'satellite' appellations: LALANDE-DE-POMEROL; and Montagne-St-Émilion, Lussac-St-Émilion, St-Georges-St-Émilion, and Puisseguin-St-Émilion (for details of which see ST-ÉMILION). And just west of Pomerol are the increasingly respected appellations of FRONSAC and Canon-Fronsac.

Although a certain amount of white wine is made between the two rivers, most of Bordeaux's best white wines are made south of the river Garonne: dry wines from Graves and Pessac-Léognan, and sweet white wines which include some of the finest in the world from SAUTERNES and BARSAC. (See Climate below for a more detailed explanation.)

Also important quantitatively, however, are the so-called BORDEAUX CÔTES: the PREMIÈRES CÔTES DE BORDEAUX along the right bank of the Garonne; the GRAVES DE VAYRES enclave near Libourne on the left bank of the Dordogne; Côtes de BOURG across the wide Gironde estuary from Margaux; BLAYE, Côtes de Blaye, and Premières Côtes de Blaye in Côtes de Bourg's green, hilly hinterland; and the appellations which lie between Bordeaux and Bergerac to the east: Côtes de CASTILLON, Bordeaux Côtes de FRANCS, and STE-FOY-Bordeaux (not technically part of the Bordeaux Côtes).

The most famous vineyards are on particularly well-drained soils, notably gravels in the Médoc and Graves, and more calcareous terrain in parts of St-Émilion and Ste-Croix-du-Mont. For more details of local soils and conditions, see under these appellation names.

Duijker, H., and Broadbent, M., *The Bordeaux Atlas* (London, 1997).

Climate

The mild climate of Bordeaux is tailor-made to produce mild wines, wines that are marked more by subtlety than power. (It is the vine varieties, described below, which endow the wines with longevity.) Unlike the much more CONTINENTAL climate of inland France, or the more arid Mediterranean influence in the south of the country, the vineyards of Bordeaux are moderated and heavily influenced by their proximity to the Atlantic, here warmed by the Gulf Stream, and this gentle oceanic regulation of the climate extends well inland, thanks to the wide Gironde estuary. Most years the maritime climate protects the vines from WINTER FREEZE (although February 1956 was so cold that many vines were killed) and spring FROST (although April 1991 was so cold that much of that year's growth was frozen to extinction and the crop much reduced).

Spring is generally mild and damp, providing ample supplies of water for the growing season. Bordeaux's climate is hardly marginal, in that most grapes are usually ripened, but the region's weather is sufficiently unpredictable that the period of the FLOWERING in June is critical, with unsettled weather, especially cold rain and strong winds, seriously prejudicing the quantity of the forthcoming crop. COULURE and MILLERANDAGE are perennial threats, especially to the Merlot crop, although average rainfall in June is markedly lower than in any other month.

Summers are usually hot, with occasional storms but rarely prolonged rainfall. The forests of the Landes to the south help to moderate temperatures (and to protect the wine districts from strong winds off the Atlantic), which reach an average maximum of 26 °C/79 °F in August, the hottest month. July is usually the driest and sunniest month. Annual average sunshine is well over 2,000 hours. Occasionally, as in 1989 and 1990, some periods in August can be so hot and dry that the vines suffer WATER STRESS and the ripening process may stop altogether, and the exceptional summer of 2003 induced unparalleled HEAT STRESS in many vineyards, some of which had to be picked as early as late August. But generally Bordeaux's grapes ripen steadily, swollen by occasional rainfall, until a harvest between mid September and mid October. Rainfall can vary considerably from vintage to vintage and within the Bordeaux region itself, with the Médoc being wetter overall, with an average annual rainfall of 950 mm/37 in, than more inland districts.

Excessive rain is the chief hazard at harvest, especially in a year during which full ripeness has yet to be achieved. In the sweet wine areas, on the other hand, humidity is sought in autumn, particularly morning mists which evaporate during the day to encourage the spread of NOBLE ROT. It is no coincidence that Bordeaux's sweet white wine districts are clustered together on either side of the Garonne, about 20 miles upstream of the city, where the river Ciron flows into the Garonne. The waters of the Ciron, shaded for most of its length by the forests of the Landes, are invariably cooler than those of the Garonne and encourage the autumn morning mists which promote the BOTRYTIS fungus. In years when these are followed by warm, dry afternoons, the benevolent form of botrytis, noble rot, forms and great sweet white wine may be made. In damp years the malevolent form, GREY ROT, simply rots the fruit.

Vine varieties

Bordeaux's most famous, and best travelled, grape variety is that on which the Médoc and Graves depend for their red wines, CABERNET SAUVIGNON. Bordeaux's most planted variety by far, however, is MERLOT, which by the end of the 1980s occupied 40 per cent of all vineyard land. It predominates not just in the famous right bank appellations of St-Émilion and Pomerol but more importantly in the Entre-Deux-Mers and throughout the Bordeaux Côtes, in whose damper, cooler soils Cabernet Sauvignon can be difficult to ripen. CABERNET FRANC, also important on the right bank, where it is often called Bouchet, is the third most planted grape variety. PETIT VERDOT is the only other red grape variety of any importance, playing a minor, but in ripe vintages useful, role in the Médoc. Cot, Pressac, or MALBEC is an ingredient in some right bank wines on the other hand, and, perhaps thanks to some Argentine wines, is increasingly mentioned by producers, as is CARMENÈRE, a red grape variety of historical importance in Bordeaux (mentioned for reasons associated with Chile).

In the early 1970s, Bordeaux's single most planted grape variety of either colour was SÉMILLON but it is now much less important except for sweet wine production. SAUVIGNON BLANC is Sémillon's traditional minor blending partner in sweet white bordeaux but is used increasingly for dry white wines, often unblended. The only other white grape variety fully sanctioned by the appellation laws is the Bordeaux and Bergerac speciality MUSCADELLE, but small quantities of UGNI BLANC, COLOMBARD, and Merlot Blanc are also planted and used in white BORDEAUX AC.

In stark contrast to France's other famous fine wine, BURGUNDY, red bordeaux is quintessentially a wine made from a blend of different vine varieties. This is only partly because Merlot and Cabernet are complementary, the flesh of the former filling in the frame of the latter. It is also an insurance policy on the part of growers in an unpredictable climate. Merlot grapes bud, flower, and ripen earlier than Cabernet Sauvignon, and are much more susceptible to COULURE, which can seriously affect quantity. Cabernet Sauvignon, on the other hand, ripens so late that a cool, cloudy late summer can seriously affect its quality. Having several grape varieties mitigates the climatological disasters which struck Merlot in 1984 and 1991, for example, and Cabernet Sauvignon in 1992. Although the ENCÉPAGEMENT, the exact proportions of different vine varieties, varies from château to château, a typical Médoc recipe is 70 per cent Cabernet Sauvignon, 15 per cent Cabernet Franc, 15 per cent Merlot, while a typical St-Émilion recipe might be 60 per cent Merlot, 30 per cent Cabernet Franc, and 10 per cent Cabernet Sauvignon.

Among dry white wines, the recipe is less predictable, although some all-Sauvignon wines are produced. The classic recipe for sweet white wines is 80 per cent Sémillon to 20 per cent Sauvignon Blanc. Bordeaux produces some of the world's finest dry Sémillon-dominated wines, notably at Chx Haut-Brion and La Mission Haut-Brion.

Viticulture

With their neat, low rows of densely planted, GUYOT-trained, low-vigour vines, Bordeaux's vineyards are some of the world's most recognizable. Vine TRIMMING is a perennial activity, and VINE DENSITY in less glorious vineyards averages between 5,000 and 6,000 vines per ha, although it is often as high as 10,000 vines per ha/4,000 per acre in the Médoc.

FUNGAL DISEASES thrive in Bordeaux's damp climate, and frequent SPRAYING is a fact of life here. (This may explain the relative rarity of ORGANIC VITICULTURE in Bordeaux.) The incidence of EUTYPA DIEBACK became a serious preoccupation in the 1980s. BOTRYTIS BUNCH ROT is one of the most common hazards, although in sweet wine districts it is encouraged in its benevolent form as NOBLE ROT.

Fertilizers (including manure from specially reared herds at some top properties) and pesticides have played their part in increasing YIELDS. CROP THINNING and selective LEAF PLUCKING during the growing season has been widely employed since the late 1980s.

The flat, well-drained vineyards would submit easily to MECHANIZATION, although few have rows sufficiently widely spaced to permit MECHANICAL HARVESTING.

Traditionally the Bordeaux harvest would begin 100 days after the flowering, but the 1990s saw a tendency to leave the grapes on the vine to achieve full PHYSIOLOGICAL RIPENESS, or even overripeness (surmaturité in French), not just high SUGARS but fully ripe PHENOLICS. It has not been uncommon therefore to start picking 110 days or more after the flowering. Identifying the date of optimum maturity of each parcel of grapes, and managing to pick them as quickly as possible on and after that date, has become one of the chief preoccupations in Bordeaux.

The harvest generally starts in September, although in 1997 and 2003 a small proportion of the Sauvignon Blanc crop was picked, amidst a fanfare of misplaced publicity, much earlier. Ripening may be so slow in summers as cool as, for example, 2004 and 1984, that some red grapes are kept on the vine until well into October in the hope of boosting sugar levels in the grapes. Grapes for dry white wines and Merlot are in general picked before Cabernet Sauvignon and, especially, grapes for sweet white wines, which may not be picked until late October or even November in SAUTERNES.

Bordeaux must be the only region able to command prices high enough to justify hiring HELICOPTERS in an attempt to agitate cold air during spring FROSTS, or dry grapes during a wet vintage, as Chx MOUTON-ROTHSCHILD and PÉTRUS have been known to do. In the difficult vintages of the early 1990s, a high proportion of properties invested in SORTING tables in an attempt to maximize wine quality.

Wine-making

Wine-making techniques in Bordeaux's top estates are regarded as the paradigm by producers of Cabernet and Merlot wines, and fine sweet white wines, throughout the world. Under the guidance of the University of BORDEAUX, these techniques underwent considerable modernization in the 1970s and are continually being refined. Émile PEYNAUD in particular led the way towards much more approachable, more concentrated red wines, a trend intensified under the influence of consultant Michel ROLLAND. And the way in which dry white bordeaux is made was revolutionized in the 1980s, notably by Denis DUBOURDIEU.

Red wines Classic vinification of red bordeaux involves time and, because of the size of most top estates, considerable space in which to house the wine as it slowly makes itself (see RED WINE-MAKING). The process begins in the vat hall or *cuvier*, then moves to a first-year CHAI in which a year's production is stored in barrel, continues in the second-year *chai*, and may well necessitate an area for bottle storage.

Grapes are almost invariably DESTEMMED before crushing, and fermented in large FERMENTATION VESSELS, known as CUVES in Bordeaux, which may be made of cement, stainless steel, or even wood, for between five and ten or more days. Some form of TEMPERATURE CONTROL was installed at most properties in the 1970s or early 1980s, but is needed for only the hotter vintages; indeed it is increasingly common practice to heat the *cuves* at the beginning of FERMENTATION. Fermentation TEMPERATURES are generally slightly higher in Bordeaux than in the NEW WORLD, with 30 °C/86 °F being a common maximum during fermentation. The concentration of PHENOLICS in ripe Bordeaux Cabernet Sauvignon grapes is such that the precise techniques of EXTRACTION are an extremely important aspect of vinification. Much modern research is concentrated on the relative merits of various PUMPING OVER regimes, usually several times a day. The post-fermentation MACERATION is therefore seen as crucial by most winemakers, who allow the newly made wine at least a week 'on the skins'.

Some degree of CHAPTALIZATION is commonplace, and generally well judged, in Bordeaux, although CONCENTRATION techniques, including both osmosis and reverse osmosis, have been increasingly practised alternatives since the early 1990s. Ambient YEASTS are the norm and vines have been such an important crop in Bordeaux for so long that the indigenous yeast population is reliable and well adapted.

After fermentation and maceration, the FREE-RUN WINE is racked off the solids into another large vessel, either by PUMPING or, in the most meticulously or fortuitously designed properties, by gravity (see WINERY DESIGN). If the free-run wine is drained into a lower tank, the volume of harsher PRESS WINE can be reduced from more than 15 per cent to about 10 per cent, and the wine tastes softer and riper.

After, and increasingly before, MALOLACTIC FERMENTATION, the wine is racked into BARRELS made of French OAK, often LIMOUSIN with the typical Bordeaux barrel being called a BARRIQUE. The luxury of new barrels was introduced only in the 1980s, and the proportion of new barrels used even at top estates tends to be lower than in the most lavish New World wineries: rarely more than 60 per cent, and even lower in less ripe vintages. During the first year, the wine is racked off its LEES into a fresh barrel every three months or so, as well as being clarified by egg-white FINING. The wine is traditionally moved to a separate second-year *chai*, where it remains until the wine is blended immediately prior to BOTTLING, usually in early summer. The wine then undergoes the all-important period of BOTTLE AGEING, although this is likely, depending on the state of the market, to take place in the cellars of the BORDEAUX TRADE, the wine merchant, and, most typically, the consumer.

The ASSEMBLAGE is a crucial operation of selection, generally undertaken in the first few months after fermentation, during which it is decided which lots of wine will be blended together to form the principal *grand vin* for that year, which lots will form the SECOND WINE, and which may be sold off at an even lower level, either in bulk or in bottle. In less successful years, less than half of the wine produced on an estate might be selected for the *grand vin*. The actual blending may take place at any time up to bottling, according to the producer's preference.

The procedure above is that followed by the CLASSED GROWTHS and those who aspire to that quality level. Most wine which qualifies merely as BORDEAUX AC is more likely to be fairly ruthlessly filtered than fined, and is not given any BARREL MATURATION, but is bottled after a few months in tank. Some PETITS CHÂTEAUX may treat their wines to a stint in barrique, but such barrels are likely to be hand-me-downs from properties whose wines sell at a higher price.

For Bordeaux's exclusively red wine appellations, see MÉDOC, HAUT-MÉDOC, ST-ESTÈPHE, PAUILLAC, ST-JULIEN, MARGAUX, LISTRAC, MOULIS, ST-ÉMILION, POMEROL, FRONSAC, and CASTILLON.

Dry whites WHITE WINE-MAKING is relatively unremarkable in Bordeaux, except that the region was one of the last in France to cling to high doses of SULFUR in finished dry wines (perhaps because of its long history of turning its white grapes into sweet wines, which do need more sulfur), and in the upper echelons of white Graves and Pessac-Léognan BARREL MATURATION has one of the longest histories in the world. Bordeaux is also the home of cryomaceration, whereby additional flavour may be imbued by prefermentation SKIN CONTACT at low temperatures, known here as *macération pelliculaire*.

For Bordeaux's principal dry white wine appellations, see PESSAC-LÉOGNAN, GRAVES, ENTRE-DEUX-MERS, BLAYE, and GRAVES DE VAYRES.

Sweet whites Bordeaux's sweet white wine appellations are, in very approximate descending order of quality, SAUTERNES, BARSAC, STE-CROIX-DU-MONT, LOUPIAC, CÉRONS, CADILLAC, PREMIÈRES CÔTES DE BORDEAUX, GRAVES Supérieures, STE-FOY-Bordeaux, and Bordeaux ST-MACAIRE and Bordeaux Supérieur (for which see BORDEAUX AC).

Basic sweet white bordeaux, often described as *moelleux*, is a simple, sugary wine for which demand is falling. It is typically made by stopping the alcoholic FERMENTATION once it has reached the level of sweetness required. (See RESIDUAL SUGAR.) This is generally achieved by a combition of techniques: chilling, SULFUR DIOXIDE addition, and sterile FILTRATION. Winemakers in Sauternes and Barsac, however, and their more ambitious counterparts elsewhere, aim to make very rich BOTRYTIZED wines from grapes at the full limit of ripeness, which may be described as LIQUOREUX. This involves a considerably more painstaking wine-making regime, even more dependent than any other on events in the vineyard, which is described in SAUTERNES. The wine's selling PRICE, which in the 20th century was depressed by the whims of FASHION, may also play a part in determining whether its maker is able or prepared to take the risks involved in trying to maximize ripeness of the grapes. Since the late 1980s, some producers have also introduced the supplementary and controversial technique CRYOEXTRACTION in order to concentrate sugars by freezing.

CONCENTRATION of all sorts is becoming more common for all types of bordeaux. MICRO-OXYGENATION became increasingly popular in the 21st century, being especially useful for preparing early samples for the all-important annual PRIMEURS tastings which determine the reputation of each vintage.

Coates, C., *Grands Vins* (London, 1995).

Duijker, H., and Broadbent, M., *The Bordeaux Atlas* (London, 1997).

Parker, R., *Bordeaux* (4th edn, New York, 2003).

Bordeaux AC. The most important sort of wine produced in Bordeaux, quantitatively if not qualitatively, is that which qualifies for the simple appellation Bordeaux. Approximately 40 per cent of all red APPELLATION CONTRÔLÉE wine produced in the region, and almost 60 per cent of all white, is straightforward Bordeaux AC (although in 2005 there were proposals that a significant proportion of this wine should be reclassified VIN DE PAYS, possibly de l'Aquitaine or de l'Atlantique, so difficult had it become to sell Bordeaux AC). This wine is typically produced outside the more specific commune or regional appellations, although a great deal of red Bordeaux AC comes from the ENTRE-DEUX-MERS region, whose eponymous appellation applies only to white wine. (A counterpoint to this is the fact that the appellations of the Médoc apply only to red wines, so that even the Médoc's smartest white wines, such as Pavillon Blanc du Ch MARGAUX, are not allowed any appellation grander than Bordeaux AC. Similarly, dry white wines made from grapes usually grown for SAUTERNES qualify only for Bordeaux AC.) The other area with the greatest concentration of vineyard dedicated to the production of Bordeaux and Bordeaux Supérieur is that north of Libourne, where Merlot grapes predominate. In total, about 44,000 ha/109,000 acres of Bordeaux vineyard is dedicated to the production of red Bordeaux AC, less than 7,000 ha to white Bordeaux AC, and about 10,000 ha to the red Bordeaux Supérieur appellation.

The great majority of Bordeaux AC produced is made, often by CO-OPERATIVES, to be sold for blending anonymously into humble GENERIC wines, of very varying quality, but there are also individual properties, so called PETITS CHÂTEAUX, which lie outside any grander appellation but which express their own TERROIR and practise CHÂTEAU BOTTLING. About two-thirds of all Bordeaux AC produced is red, and the white, invariably dry, may be called **Bordeaux Sec**. Most AC Bordeaux is relatively low in alcohol, the minimum ALCOHOLIC STRENGTH after FERMENTATION being 10 per cent (although most wines are between 11 and 12.5).

More specific appellations which incorporate the word Bordeaux include **Bordeaux Rosé**, **Bordeaux Supérieur** (and its successor **Bordeaux Premier Cru**), whose minimum permitted alcoholic strength is half a per cent higher than Bordeaux AC and which is mainly red, but is occasionally sweet and white; **Bordeaux Clairet**, which is a light red recalling the precursors of CLARET; the bottle-fermented sparkling wine CRÉMANT de Bordeaux (which has replaced **Bordeaux Mousseux**); and a very minor dry white oddity, **Bordeaux Haut-Benauge**, just across the Garonne from Langon.

Most of these wines are designed to be drunk within a year of bottling if white, rosé, or clairet and within two or three years if red. The better examples are unmistakably lighter versions of Bordeaux's grander wines, while the worst can taste like homeless TABLE WINE. Few producers can afford to age these wines in OAK, and even fewer of the wines have the concentration to benefit from it, especially since expensive viticultural techniques such as CROP THINNING are hard to justify at this level, although exceptions are becoming more numerous. Most of the Bordeaux BRANDS are Bordeaux AC, most notably MOUTON CADET, which started off life with the much grander and more specific appellation of PAUILLAC.

The Bordeaux authorities call the above appellations the 'Bordeaux regional appellations' (all of which may much more simply be labelled Bordeaux), and include with them the Entre-Deux-Mers, STE-FOY-Bordeaux, and Côtes de Bordeaux-ST-MACAIRE appellation, which applies to the everyday sweet white wines made in a small district immediately south west of Haut-Benauge.

Other appellations which incorporate or have at one time incorporated the word Bordeaux are Bordeaux Côtes de CASTILLON, Bordeaux Côtes de FRANCS, and PREMIÈRES CÔTES DE BORDEAUX, all of which belong to the subgroup of Bordeaux appellations known as the BORDEAUX CÔTES.

Bordeaux blend, a red wine made up of some or all of CABERNET SAUVIGNON, CABERNET FRANC, MERLOT, PETIT VERDOT, and possibly MALBEC and CARMENÈRE. See also MERITAGE.

Bordeaux Côtes, local name in BORDEAUX for appellations on the, often historic, outer fringes of the region: BLAYE, Côtes de Blaye, Premières Côtes de Blaye; Côtes de BOURG; PREMIÈRES CÔTES DE BORDEAUX; Côtes de CASTILLON; Bordeaux Côtes de FRANCS; and GRAVES DE VAYRES. These wines tend to have considerably more personality than regular BORDEAUX AC, the result perhaps of local pride, and can provide some of Bordeaux's best wine value.

Bordeaux mixture, *bouillie bordelaise* in French, once much-used mixture of lime, copper sulfate, and water first recorded in 1885 by Alexis Millardet, Professor of Botany at Bordeaux University, as an effective control of DOWNY MILDEW. Use of the mixture was a historic event since it was to become the most important chemical for the control of both FUNGAL DISEASES and BACTERIAL DISEASES for 50 years. It has subsequently been replaced by other fungicides, many of them containing copper. It is still used today by very traditional growers in some regions and it is one of the few preparations permitted in ORGANIC VITICULTURE and BIODYNAMIC VITICULTURE.

There is some debate as to how the treatment was discovered. It was common for Bordeaux vignerons to spray the outside vineyard rows with the blue-staining copper sulfate to deter thieves. No doubt it was noticed that this practice halted the devastation caused by downy mildew which had begun in 1883. Continued use of Bordeaux mixture can lead to accumulation of COPPER in the soil, which can reach toxic levels especially in acidic soils. Some vineyards affected by copper toxicity in

the Bordeaux area are much reduced in vigour, but the problem can be overcome by adding LIME to the soil. Also, copper sprayed within 14 days of harvest can produce browning, turbidity, and SULFIDE characters in the wine and can result in incomplete FERMENTATIONS.

R.E.S.

Figiel, R., 'Bouillie bordelaise: the other gift from Bordeaux vineyards', *Practical Winery and Vineyard*, 11/3 (1990), 27–9.

Bordeaux trade. The sheer quantity of wine produced in Bordeaux, the fact that so much requires AGEING, and the historical importance of Bordeaux as a port (see BORDEAUX, history), mean that its wine trade is more stratified than most—even if wine is no longer the city's economically most important commodity.

Bordeaux wines have always been produced by one category of people and sold by another. The wine producers of the region range from world-famous estates with 200 ha/500 acres under vine, to owners of 2.5 ha or less, whose wines nowadays may also be world-famous (see MICROCHÂTEAUX) or whose grapes are delivered to one of the region's wine CO-OPERATIVES, or vinified in conditions of precarious HYGIENE for personal consumption.

The wine merchants, or NÉGOCIANTS, sometimes called *négociants-éleveurs* for their role in wine ÉLEVAGE, traditionally brought most of the wines they bought into their CHAIS in or around Bordeaux (notably its Quai des Chartrons) to be matured and shipped out to export customers, particularly in Britain and Scandinavia, either in barrels, or after bottling. They were joined in the early 20th century by merchants in LIBOURNE, who concentrated on markets in northern France and northern Europe (see POMEROL).

So great was the quantity of wine to be traded that numbers of middlemen were needed between producers and the merchants, of whom professional brokers, or *courtiers*, such as Tastet & Lawton have become an essential part of Bordeaux's vinous commercial structure. What the merchant supplied in addition to the mere buying and selling of wine was technical ability (his cellarmaster and team were likely to be considerably better technicians than the producers'), and financing for the grower.

This way of doing business changed considerably after 1945, when even some of the FIRST GROWTHS were still made available to the merchants in bulk, and most of the CLASSED GROWTHS have since 1959 been sold to the merchants on the condition that they are CHÂTEAU BOTTLED.

Since 1945, improvements in wine-making at all levels and, since the 1980s, PRICE increases and inflation levels which have made it impossible for even the biggest merchants to finance large quantities of wine, have tended to transform the role of the merchant from principal

to broker. Some of the merchants have been more aggressive than most in adapting winemaking techniques at the bottom end of the market, particularly for BORDEAUX AC, to international changes in taste. The mid 2000s saw a particular focus on the development of BRANDS in an effort to find a home for the increasing quantity of red wine produced in the region.

For examples of specific Bordeaux merchants, see BARTON, CRUSE, SICHEL, and MOUEIX.

W.B.

Brook, S., *Bordeaux—People, Power and Politics* (London, 2001).
Faith, N., *The Winemasters* (3rd edn, London, 2005).
Loftus, S., *Anatomy of the Wine Trade* (London, 1985).
Penning-Rowsell, E., *The Wines of Bordeaux* (6th edn, London, 1989).

Bordeaux, University of, university complex within sight of Ch HAUT-BRION on the outskirts of the city, whose Faculté (formerly Institut) d'Oenologie is a centre of oenological ACADEME of world renown. (Viticultural research is conducted under the auspices of INRA and the Ecole National des Travaux Agricoles, known as ENITA.)

The institute was founded in 1880 (the same year as the research institute that was to become the University of California at DAVIS) as a mere *station agronomique*, when Ulysse Gayon, the sole Professor of Chemistry at the associated University of Bordeaux, became its director.

Gayon had studied and worked with Louis PASTEUR, the founder of scientific OENOLOGY. He considered the *station*'s function was to promulgate sound methods of making and maturing wine. In addition to his contributions to the ANALYSIS of wines, he worked with Alexis Millardet on the development of the copper-based vine treatment designed to combat FUNGAL DISEASES which was to be known as BORDEAUX MIXTURE.

During the 40 years Gayon directed the *station*, its tradition of identifying the practical applications which could be made from research results was established, as was the importance of transmitting information to winemakers in unscientific language.

From 1927 the most significant research on wine and related subjects in the world was carried out at the University of Bordeaux through a collaboration between Jean Ribéreau-Gayon, the grandson of Ulysse Gayon, and Émile PEYNAUD, who did not officially join the University until 1949. From 1949, when Jean Ribéreau-Gayon became director of the *station*, the results of basic and extensive research became apparent to winemaker and consumer alike. Chromatography provided legally convincing evidence of the use of HYBRIDS in any wine sample, and encouraged their replacement by 'noble' VINIFERA vine varieties in the vineyards of Bordeaux, and thereby a great improvement in the quality of the region's basic BORDEAUX AC wines. At the same time, the understanding of the process of MALOLACTIC FERMENTATION gave wine producers the knowledge they needed to control a fundamental step in wine-making and gave them much greater control over the style and quality of the wines they made. Research into the influence of TERROIR on wine style and quality has been conducted at Bordeaux since the early 1960s.

The importance of the education of OENOLOGISTS was officially recognized in 1956 with the creation of an École Supérieure d'Oenologie empowered to award a winemaker's diploma. This became the Institut d'Oenologie in 1963, which was transformed into the Faculté d'Oenologie in 1995. During this period, oenology achieved full recognition as a new science and in 1971 the institute formally became part of the university, its work and educational titles enjoying full academic status.

The work of the institute has continued since 1976 under the direction of Pascal Ribéreau-Gayon, the son of the previous director. Since 1905 there has been close collaboration between the research carried out by the institute and a laboratory founded in that year by the French Ministry of Agriculture. The primary business of this laboratory is to check that French wine laws are respected by ensuring, for example, that all alcohol is grape based, that no fruits other than grapes have been used, that wines have not been subjected to both ACIDIFICATION and ENRICHMENT, and that a wine has not been stretched by dilution.

The Faculté is currently engaged in research on subjects which vary from explorations of the nature and effects of different YEASTS to investigations into the characteristics of different TANNINS. The most significant result of research in the 1980s was arguably the dramatic improvement in aroma and subtlety of dry white bordeaux, in which field DUBOURDIEU deserves much credit.

In addition to training oenologists who make wine throughout the world and belong to what is outside France referred to as the 'Bordeaux school' of wine-making, the Faculté supervises doctorates on vinous subjects and is the only French organization to enjoy this privilege. A prominent feature of the professional training at the Faculté is the importance attached to tasting wines and analysing their characteristics. Since 1949 the Faculté has also given series of tastings and lectures for growers and cellar workers without scientific training.

The Faculté is housed in its own buildings on the grounds of Bordeaux University. Viticultural research and lecturing is conducted under the auspices of INRA and ENITA at Bordeaux. However, MONTPELLIER has long been regarded as France's centre of viticultural academe. W.B. & C.V.L.

Bordo, occasional north-east Italian name for CABERNET FRANC.

bore, wine. For some reason, wine bores exist in public consciousness and, it has to be said, in reality in a more vividly pestilential way than art bores, music bores, or even sport bores. Perhaps this is because for most people wine is associated with sensual pleasure rather than analysis and verbal communication and so their wine-related boredom threshold is low. So far, wine bores are usually men, although women wine bores may be an eventual consequence of female financial emancipation. One woman's wine bore can be another person's wine expert, however.

borers, usually beetles or their larvae, which bore into the woody parts of plants, sometimes killing them. The branch and twig borer, *Melalgus confertus*, occurs throughout California and parts of Oregon and damages grape canes. Control is usually by cultural methods, by keeping vines healthy, pruning off all dying and dead parts and infested wood in winter. Beetle larvae causing problems to vineyards can be quite regionally specific. The fig longicorn (*Dihammus vastator*) beetle larvae causes vine damage only in the Hunter Valley region of Australia, for example. M.J.E.

boron, a MINERAL element required in minute quantities for healthy vine growth, and thus a so-called trace element. Boron deficiencies in vines are commonly found where SOIL ACIDITY and RAINFALL are high. Boron is required for the movement of SUGARS and the synthesis of AUXINS in the plant. A major effect of boron deficiency is poor FRUIT SET caused by the effect on POLLEN tube growth affecting germination, which can result in substantial reductions in YIELD. Bunches on boron-deficient vines often have many small berries. A quality gain from having more and smaller berries (see BERRY SIZE) is possible but this effect, while tantalizing, has not been proven.

Boron toxicity is also possible, sometimes due to over-application of fertilizer. Excess boron can also come from IRRIGATION water. See also FERTILIZERS. R.E.S.

Borraçal, synonym for Galicia's CAIÑO Tinto in Portugal's Vinho Verde region.

Borrado das Moscas, the DÃO region's name for the Portuguese variety BICAL.

Bosco, ordinary white grape of LIGURIA.

Bosnia and Herzegovina, central part of what was YUGOSLAVIA before civil war erupted. The vineyards are in Herzegovina, sometimes spelt Hertzegovina or Hercegovina, in the south. So much of the territory in the centre of the former Yugoslavia is wild, dry, pastoral upland that these vineyards cover only about 4,000 ha/1,000 acres of territory down towards the coast around Mostar, inland, and to the north of Dubrovnik, according to OIV figures for 2002, which recorded a total wine production of 75,000 hl.

The region has its own grape types: the white ZILAVKA, famed for its generous alcohol levels combined with unusually refreshing ACIDITY; and the much less impressive red Blatina. Zilavka has begun to be planted in neighbouring territories. A.H.M.

botanical classification, a system of classifying plants—including vines, yeasts, and the organisms responsible for FUNGAL DISEASES of the vine—which shows their relationship one to the other, and which also allows them to be uniquely described and identified. The basic unit of classification is the species; related species are sometimes grouped into genera (plural of genus); related genera into families; and related families into orders. In turn, species can be divided into subspecies.

Individual members of a single species are called varieties, or occasionally cultivars, and VINE VARIETIES can be further divided into three PROLES, according to their geographical origins. Different CLONES of individual varieties have also been selected. To summarize:

Order	Variety
Family	Prole
Genus	Clone
Species	

Classifications are created by botanists. Most commercially important grapevine varieties used for wine production, for example, are members of the genus VITIS, created in 1700 by Tournefort, and the species VINIFERA, first studied by Linnaeus in 1735. The full botanical binomial of the most common wine-producing vine species is therefore *Vitis vinifera L.*, often abbreviated to *V vinifera* or just *vinifera* (the person who describes the species often being listed, usually as initials, after the scientific name). Another convention is the use of Latin, often confected, and italics.

Grapevines belong to the order Rhamnales, and the family Vitaceae. There are two other families in the order Rhamnales: the Rhamnaceae family, which includes the jujube and the plant thought to be the lotus of ancient Greece; and the Leeaceae family, which consists mostly of shrubs.

The family Vitaceae contains the GRAPEVINE. The genus *Vitis* is one of 14 (some authorities say 12) genera, and *vinifera* is one of about 700 species in the family. This plant family is found in both tropical and temperate regions. Most of the plants are climbers and have tendrils opposite leaves on the shoots, the grapevine being representative. Galet lists 13 genera other than *Vitis* in this family (excluding two extinct species); the largest genus is *Cissus* with about 350 species, from succulent species such as cacti to the lianas of tropical jungles. *Ampelopsis* and *Parthenocissus* are two more genera closely related to each other and are observably similar to grapevines. Ornamental plants related to the grapevine include the Virginia creeper in the US and Europe, the kangaroo vine in Australia, and Japanese ivy and Crimson Glory in Japan.

The order **Rhamnales**

Vitaceae	Leeaceae
Rhamnaceae	

The family **Vitaceae** (according to Galet)

Vitis	*Rhoicissus*
Cissus	*Ampelopsis*
Cayratia	*Parthenocissus*
Clematicissus	*Acareosperma*
Tetrastigma	*Pterocissus*
Ampelocissus	*Landukia*
Pterisanthes	*Cyphostemma*

There are also the fossil genera *Cissites* and *Paleovitis*.

The *Vitis* genus has traditionally been divided into two distinct sections called *Euvitis* (now *Vitis*) and MUSCADINIA. (It should be noted, however, that some botanists consider *Muscadinia* as a separate genus to *Vitis*.) Galet's convention of the 14 extant genera listed above is used here. The two sections may be differentiated not only on the basis of appearance but also by chromosome number. *Muscadinia* has 40 chromosomes while *Vitis* has only 38. (This is a frustration to VINE BREEDERS, who would welcome ready access to the many pest and disease resistance genes of *Muscadinia*.)

The genus *Vitis*

There are many species of *Vitis*, most of which are native to North America (see AMERICAN VINE SPECIES), and some to Asia. The common wine grape species *Vitis vinifera* is native to Europe and west Asia. It shows great diversity as a result of selection and cultivation by man, and three basic groups of varieties, or proles, reflect differences between origin and end use. In the late 1990s the German Plant Variety Rights Office devised a new subspecies, *Vitis vinifera sativa*, for the new DISEASE-RESISTANT VARIETIES. See VITIS and VINIFERA for more details.

The full botanical pedigree of a bottle of wine made from Cabernet Sauvignon grapes might therefore be: order Rhamnales, family Vitaceae, genus *Vitis*, section *Vitis*, species *vinifera*, proles *Occidentalis*, variety Cabernet Sauvignon, clone INRA BX 5197.   R.E.S.

Antcliff, A. J., 'Taxonomy: the grapevine as a member of the plant kingdom', in B. G. Coombe and P. R. Dry (eds.), *Viticulture*, i: *Resources* (Adelaide, 1988).

Galet, P., *Précis de viticulture* (5th edn, Montpellier, 1988).

Mullins, M. G., Bouquet, A., and Williams, L., *Biology of the Grapevine* (Cambridge, 1992).

botryticine. See NOBLE ROT.

botrytis, without the capital B it botanically deserves, is commonly used as an abbreviation for BOTRYTIS BUNCH ROT, for the fungus that causes it *Botrytis cinerea* Pers, for its benevolent form NOBLE ROT, and occasionally for its malevolent form GREY ROT. Grapes affected by noble rot and the wines produced from them are often called BOTRYTIZED, or **botrytis affected.**

Elad, Y., Williamson, B., Tudzynski, P., and Delen, N. (eds.), *Botrytis: Biology, Pathology and Control* (Dordrecht, 2004).

botrytis bunch rot, vine disease which, of all FUNGAL DISEASES, has the greatest potential effect on wine quality. The disease can have a disastrous effect on both yield and quality when the fungus affects almost ripe, or damaged grapes, typically in humid weather. This malevolent form is known as GREY ROT, the most common of the BUNCH ROTS. On the other hand, if it affects ripe, healthy, whole, light-skinned grapes, and the weather conditions are favourable, botrytis develops in a benevolent form called NOBLE ROT, which is responsible for some of the world's finest sweet wines. (If it affects red grapes, it always damages PIGMENTS, resulting in wines with a greyish tinge and, often, off-odours associated with rot.)

The causal fungus for both forms of botrytis bunch rot is *Botryotinia fuckeliana* of which only a certain form (the so-called conidial form), termed *Botrytis cinerea*, is found in vineyards. The disease is widespread as it attacks not only vines but many cultivated and wild plants, and also survives as a saprophyte on dying and dead plant tissue.

Botrytis rot is a particular problem for vineyards in damp climates. In particular, rainfall near harvest causes severe infections, and thus can be a major climatic factor affecting the YIELD and quality of a particular vintage (as regularly happens in both BURGUNDY and BORDEAUX, for example). Botrytis spores germinate either on wet surfaces or where the ambient humidity is at least 90 per cent. Optimal infection temperatures are 15 to 20 °C/59–68 °F.

Although the botrytis fungus most commonly affects bunches of ripe grapes, it can also affect other parts of the vine such as emerging shoots in spring and young bunches which fall off with obvious effects on yield. The more common problem, however, is when flower parts are infected and remain trapped in the developing bunches. Infections of the fungus can spread in the bunch as it approaches maturity, especially after VERAISON when the grape berries are infected directly through the intact berry skin, or through wounds. The fungi can penetrate even healthy berries, gaining access through minute breathing pores called STOMATA, but more commonly the entry is through the broken skin. Such injuries may be caused by bird pecks, insect damage (in New Zealand, THRIPS have been found to carry botrytis spores), mechanical abrasion, or by tightly compressed berries which burst when the vine takes up water after rainfall.

The mould spreads progressively through the whole bunch, especially when berries are in close contact, as with vine varieties with compact bunches. If the weather turns dry, infected berries tend to dry out, and major changes to the fruit's chemistry can result in grapes suitable for classic botrytized wines influenced by noble rot. In continuing wet weather, however, the fungus rapidly spreads as grey rot, and the grape crop can literally rot before the owner's eyes. This explains the urgency of harvest when weather conditions are inclement. Early warning systems based on temperature or relative humidity have been developed to predict epidemics. Wines in such years are typically lower in alcohol as the fruit is harvested earlier. Research in Champagne has shown that botrytis can have a negative effect on the foaming properties of champagne.

Botrytis is a problem in other areas of viticulture. It is a common rot developing in stored TABLE GRAPES and also causes problems during GRAFTING operations in nurseries.

Vine varieties, and indeed various CLONES of vine varieties, differ in their susceptibility to botrytis depending on how tightly packed the berries are in the bunch, on the thickness of the skin, and to some extent also on the stage of ripeness. Varieties with compact bunches of high sugar content are the most susceptible. Sémillon, Sauvignon Blanc, Muscadelle, Carignan, Pinot Noir, and Merlot are particularly susceptible to botrytis bunch rot, with Chardonnay moderately susceptible and Cabernet Sauvignon quite tolerant. Interestingly, some varieties are made more resistant by producing PHYTOALEXINS which inhibit the fungus. Some varieties also have higher concentrations of preformed antifungal compounds.

Modern control measures take two forms. The first, the 'natural' approach, is to avoid excessive leafiness around the fruit, which means that bunches are better exposed to sun and wind which dry the fruit after rain or dew. Bunch thinning can also help. The removal of fallen leaves and prunings reduces the risk of overwintering spores and infection in spring due to rain splash. CANOPY MANAGEMENT practices such as leaf removal and improved trellis are most useful. Chemical control is the second route and still the most common method of control. The number of spray applications required depends on the climate. In wet regions, more than half a dozen sprayings may be needed, beginning at FLOWERING and ending before harvest. The last sprayings cannot be applied too close to harvest as yeast activity during fermentation may be inhibited, quite apart from any potentially harmful chemical RESIDUES.

While a relatively wide range of chemicals is now used for botrytis control, the fungus seems to be waging a war against the chemist. New chemicals seem to be used only for a few years before they become less effective, as the fungus develops resistance. Growers are now being forced to rely less on chemicals and to use more natural means of control. Newly bred varieties commonly have greater disease tolerance, and researchers are also attempting to control botrytis with two types of antagonistic fungus, *Trichoderma harzianum* and *Trichoderma atroviride*. This biological approach has led to the development of new products such as BOTRY-Zen® from New Zealand, which is claimed to be an effective control for botrytis. However, biological controls are variable in their efficacy.

See GREY ROT and NOBLE ROT for more details of the two different forms of botrytis. For details of how nobly rotten grapes are transformed into wine, and of the resulting wines, see BOTRYTIZED WINES.   R.E.S.

Galet, P., *Précis de viticulture* (5th edn, Montpellier, 1988).

Pearson, R. C., and Goheen, A. C., *Compendium of Grape Diseases* (St Paul, Minn., 1988).

Winkler, A. J., *et al.*, *General Viticulture* (Berkeley, Calif., 1974).

botrytized, or **botrytis-affected, wines** are those made from white grapes affected by the benevolent form of BOTRYTIS BUNCH ROT, known in English as NOBLE ROT. Distinctively scented in youth, and with considerably more EXTRACT than most wines, they are the most complex and longest lived of all the sweet, white table wines. The noble rot smell is often described as honeyed, but it can also have an (attractive) overtone of boiled cabbage.

History

There is no firm evidence that botrytized wines were recognized in antiquity, although Olney points out that a particularly fine Ancient Greek wine produced on Chios (see CHIAN) in the 5th century BC is described as *saprian* by ATHENAEUS, and that the literal translation of this may be 'rotten, putrid'. Noble rot is much more likely to occur in more humid climates than the MEDITERRANEAN CLIMATE of the Aegean islands, however, and the extremely unpleasant appearance of grapes infected by noble rot, and the difficulty with which they ferment, must have deterred many early winemakers.

Three important centres of botrytized wine production have their own accounts of the discovery that this particular sort of mouldy grape could be transformed into exceptional wine.

That of the TOKAJ region of north east Hungary is the oldest, dating from at least 1650 when the priest-cum-winemaker on a particular estate there delayed the HARVEST because of the threat of attack by the Turks. This allowed the development of noble rot and the grapes were duly vinified separately, as one would expect, and the resulting wine much admired. For diplomatic purposes it was introduced to the French court in the early 18th century,

long before French vine-growers had recognized the existence of the noble fungus.

In Germany, the principle of picking selected bunches of grapes (AUSLESE) was understood in the 18th century, but that of the widespread picking of grapes affected by NOBLE ROT dates, in the Rheingau region which became most famous for botrytized wines, from about 1820. In spite of popular beliefs to the contrary, precisely when and where vine-growers first realized the value of noble rot is not certain, although the discovery in Germany is thought to have been in the particularly suitable climate of the Rheingau. SCHLOSS JOHANNISBERG has certainly promulgated its own claim that in 1775 the traditional harvest messenger, as usual licensed to deliver permission to pick from the owner, the distant prince-abbot of Fulda, was delayed, thereby supposedly allowing a noble rot infection to proceed, and resulting in Germany's first botrytized SPÄTLESE.

The sweet wines of Bordeaux and the Loire were much treasured in the Middle Ages, particularly by the DUTCH, but without any specific mention of a special fungus, or acknowledgement of any special attribute. The principal French legend concerning the 'discovery' of noble rot—and legend it is widely believed to be—dates from as recently as 1847, at Ch d'YQUEM (although the quality, style, and youthfulness of earlier vintages of Yquem, such as the 1811, suggest that noble rot must have played an important part in wine production there before that date).

The risks and costs involved in making naturally botrytized wine make it necessarily expensive. It has therefore been an economical proposition only when sweet wines are highly valued. Germany's botrytized wines have always been regarded as precious rarities for which a ready market can be found within Germany. France's output of botrytized wines is potentially much greater, but when sweet wines were out of FASHION in the 1960s and 1970s, enthusiasm for producing them inevitably waned, only to be rekindled in the 1980s.

Geography and climate

Many conditions have to be met before botrytized wines can be produced. Not only is a MESOCLIMATE which favours misty mornings and warm afternoons in autumn needed, but producers must have the knowledge and the will to sacrifice quantity for nothing more certain than possible quality. Botrytized wines are very much a product of psyche as well as nature.

The district with the potential to produce the greatest quantity of top-quality botrytized wine is SAUTERNES (although it all depends, as everywhere, on the precise WEATHER of the year). The confluence of the rivers Ciron and GARONNE provide an ideal mesoclimate for the satisfactory development of noble rot. Nearby

sweet white wine districts CÉRONS, LOUPIAC, CADILLAC, and STE-CROIX-DU-MONT may also produce small quantities of botrytized wines, although the price fetched by these appellations rarely justifies the additional production costs.

Botrytized wine is also made by the most meticulous producers in MONBAZILLAC and SAUSSIGNAC. With viticultural commitment and skilful vinification, these districts can make botrytized wines to rival all but the very best Sauternes made similarly from Sémillon, Sauvignon, and particularly Muscadelle grapes. One or two fine examples of this style have also emerged from Gaillac.

On the river Loire, appellations such as Coteaux de l'AUBANCE, Coteaux du LAYON, QUARTS DE CHAUME, BONNEZEAUX, MONTLOUIS, and VOUVRAY can produce botrytized wines in good years, and they are given even greater ageing potential for being made from the acidic Chenin Blanc grape.

Botrytized wines may also be made from such varied grapes as Mâconnais Chardonnays and Alsace Rieslings in exceptional years.

Germany is the other famous source of botrytized wines, usually labelled BEERENAUSLESE or TROCKENBEERENAUSLESE, although the quantities made vary enormously according to vintage. Riesling is the classic grape, although some of the GERMAN CROSSINGS can be persuaded to rot nobly in an exceptionally suitable year. Noble rot infections are much more reliable in the Burgenland district of AUSTRIA, where, thanks to the influence of the Neusiedlersee, considerable quantities of botrytized Beerenauslesen and Trockenbeerenauslesen are made most years. Over the border in Hungary, Tokaj is still closely associated with botrytized wine-making, as are various parts of ROMANIA, notably COTNARI.

Botrytized wine-making is an embryonic art in Italy, Spain, and most of Portugal, where producers and consumers tend to favour either DRIED GRAPE WINES or FORTIFIED wines.

In the New World, botrytized wines are made with increasing frequency. Nederburg Edelkeur was a South African prototype which enjoyed international acclaim in the 1970s. Griffith in NEW SOUTH WALES's Riverina was producing Australian botrytized Pedro Ximénez as early as the late 1950s, and is now a centre for the production of relatively early maturing botrytized whites, particularly Semillon. In Australia, New Zealand, South Africa, and in California particularly, a host of botrytized Rieslings has emerged.

California has also seen attempts to simulate noble rot, by growing spores of the botrytis fungus in a laboratory and spraying them on picked, healthy, ripe grapes before subjecting them to alternately humid and warm conditions for a couple of weeks. The first of these wines was made in the late 1950s by Myron Nightingale in the Livermore valley. The result was called Premiere Semillon and has been followed by a series of similar wines made at Beringer in the Napa valley.

As awareness of noble rot and botrytized wines grows, the number of winemakers anxious to experiment also increases, even if the market is not always rapturous, and they are usually at the mercy of the weather. Even ENGLAND has succeeded in producing botrytized wine.

Vine varieties

Any white grape variety may be infected benevolently by the botrytis fungus; red varieties simply lose their colour. Certain varieties seem particularly sensitive to the fungus and well adapted to the production of botrytized wines, however: Sémillon, Sauvignon Blanc, Chenin Blanc, Riesling, Gewürztraminer, and Furmint are traditional.

Viticulture

The chief viticultural aspect of making botrytized wines is the number of passages or TRIES through the vineyard which may have to be made in order to pick grapes only at the optimum point of botrytis infection, because noble rot is so crucial to quality. See SAUTERNES for a description of the likely routine there. In a year as difficult as 1974 at Ch d'YQUEM (admittedly the most conscientious Sauternes estate), 11 *tries* were made over a ten-week period. In 1990, on the other hand, noble rot spread rapidly and uniformly and the grapes were picked by early October. Hand picking of these varied but usually disgusting-looking grapes is essential, and the cost of LABOUR is one important element in the price of botrytized wines.

In wet vintages, some producers use modern freeze concentration techniques, called CRYOEXTRACTION in French.

Wine-making

If picking botrytized grapes is painstaking, obtaining their juice and persuading it to ferment is at least as difficult because of its composition (see NOBLE ROT). PRESSING is a physically difficult operation, and, contrary to the usual practice, later pressings yield juice superior to the first pressing because it is richer in sugar and the chemical compounds produced by the botrytis fungus. The most dehydrated grapes in the press may not in any case yield juice until they have been pressed twice or three times.

A variety of wine-making methods are used, including the classic method described in SAUTERNES. Fermentation is necessarily extremely slow. The juice seems almost designed to inhibit YEASTS, being so high in sugar and antibiotics such as botryticine. Botrytized musts tend to lack nutrients such as thiamine and ammonia, which is another reason for stuck fermentations. Fermentation may be allowed to stop itself, or SULFUR DIOXIDE addition may be used. Care must be taken that

these wines, which often have a RESIDUAL SUGAR level equivalent to about 6 per cent alcoholic strength, do not suffer a SECOND FERMENTATION, and bottling, whether after two winters in new BARRIQUES as in the top Sauternes properties, or the following spring as in the Loire and many German cellars, has to be undertaken with care. Higher levels of SULFUR DIOXIDE are needed during vinification and at bottling because the enzyme LACCASE produced by botrytis increases the risk of oxidation and is tolerant of high levels of SO_2. In addition, the chemical composition of botrytized wines means they have significant power to bind SO_2. This is why EUROPEAN UNION regulations permit a higher level of total SO_2 for these wines than for all others. The development of *Botrytis cinerea* also results in the production of two POLYSACCHARIDES. One has antifungal properties and inhibits fermentation. The other, a β-glucan, can make FILTRATION much more difficult, especially if crushing, pumping, and pressing are carried out harshly.

Some wines, notably those made from aromatic varieties such as Muscat, are marked by a loss of varietal aroma. This is mainly because botrytis metabolizes the MONOTERPENES such as linalool and geraniol that are responsible for the distinctive aromas of such varieties.

Botrytized wines are capable of extremely long BOTTLE AGEING, for many decades in some cases.

Brook, S., *Liquid Gold: Dessert Wines of the World* (London, 1987).

Olney, R., *Yquem* (Paris, 1985, and London, 1986).

Ribéreau-Gayon, P., Dubourdieu, D., Donèche, B., and Lonvaud, D., *Traité d'Œnologie* 1: *Microbiologie du vin: Vinifications* (Paris, 1998), translated by J. M. Branco, as *Handbook of Enology* 1: *The Microbiology of Wine and Vinifications* (Chichester, 2000).

botte, Italian word for a large wooden cask, presumably from the same root as BUTT. The plural is **botti.**

bottle ageing, the process of deliberately maturing a wine after BOTTLING, whether for a few weeks as a conscious effort on the part of the bottler to allow the wine to recover from BOTTLE SICKNESS or, in the case of very fine wines, for many years in order to allow the wine to mature. Fine wines are usually vinified expressly so that they will benefit from ageing in bottle, with generous amounts of ACIDS, PHENOLICS, and FLAVOUR PRECURSORS extracted from the grape. These can often make them unattractive when consumed young, but provide them with all the necessary ingredients for bottle ageing. In some cases the high sugar, acid, and flavour compound levels, as in great Rieslings which may not contain much alcohol, can also benefit greatly from bottle ageing. However, some winemakers have adapted their wine-making techniques so that their wines have the capacity to age but are

nevertheless approachable much earlier. See, for example, MICRO-OXYGENATION.

The exact identification of the compounds produced during bottle ageing and responsible for the complex BOUQUET of a mature wine is yet to be completely resolved, although pioneering work has been conducted by chemists in ADELAIDE into the natural process of HYDROLYSIS on flavour precursors and in the role of these in bottle ageing. See AGEING for more detail. A.D.W. & P.J.W.

bottle deposit in red wines is a lacquerlike pigmented deposit adhering to the inner bottle surface and is different from SEDIMENT. This deposition, which may begin in the first few months after bottling, may cover only a small area of the bottle shoulder or may eventually cover the entire glass surface with which the wine is in contact. Wine quality is not affected by bottle deposit and experience has shown that premium reds (particularly those made from RHÔNE varieties) tend to exhibit this deposit more than lower-quality wines. The deposit is an insoluble complex polymer of PIGMENTED TANNINS and PROTEIN. P.J.W.

bottle fermented, description of some SPARKLING WINES made either by the traditional method, or by the transfer method. See SPARKLING WINE-MAKING for full details.

bottles, by far the most common CONTAINERS for finished wine. Being made of glass, bottles are inconveniently fragile and relatively heavy, but, importantly for long-term AGEING, they are inert. A standard bottle contains 75 cl/25 fl oz although see also BOTTLE SIZES.

History

Today it may be taken for granted that wine bottles of different colours and shapes will hold a precise capacity. Nor is it questioned that a paper LABEL will be firmly fixed to the bottle to give a plethora of information, much of it required by law. These are recent developments.

In classical antiquity wine was stored and transported in large, long jars called AMPHORAE. They varied considerably in size but it would certainly be difficult to pour a drinking quantity from such an awkward and big vessel, without using some sort of intermediate container. The Romans invented the technique of blowing glass bottles and some of these may well have been used to serve wine.

Pottery and stoneware jugs were used for centuries in Europe for serving wine, but glass took over as technology to make glass in commercial quantities spread in the 17th century, and by the end of it glass bottles were plentiful, although reserved for the upper classes.

Shape Early bottles have more or less globular bodies with long conical necks. The form

The local flora in Colchagua underline the Chilean wine industry's heavy reliance on **irrigation**. These Cabernet Sauvignon grapes are destined for Viña Bisquertt, Lihueimo.

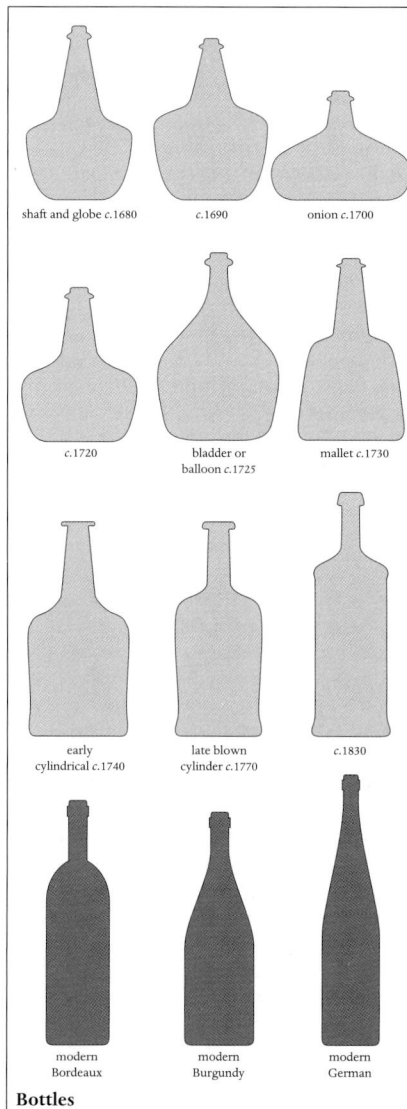

shaft and globe c.1680   c.1690   onion c.1700

c.1720   bladder or balloon c.1725   mallet c.1730

early cylindrical c.1740   late blown cylinder c.1770   c.1830

modern Bordeaux   modern Burgundy   modern German

Bottles

developed (see illustration), becoming lower and wider in Britain, while on mainland Europe the flask-shape with an oval cross-section was popular. From c. 1690 to 1720, the outline of a bottle resembled that of an onion—a wide compressed globular body with a short neck. Larger bottles were made too, whose shape resembled an inflated balloon or bladder. It is thought that all these forms were stored in beds of sand. By the 1720s the 'onion' became taller and the sides flatter—a form known by collectors as a 'mallet'. Naturally occurring impurities in the constituent ingredients gave glass an olive green hue which varied from pale to almost black and was beneficial to the bottled wine as it excluded light. Most bottles had an applied ring of glass just below the neck which gave an anchorage to the string used to hold in a variety of stoppers. These bottles were of substantial weight and thickness too.

Wine drinkers made an important discovery in the 1730s. While it was known that some

vintages of wine were better than others even in prehistory, their keeping and consequent maturing qualities were not realized until the introduction of BINNING, the storing of wine in bottles laid on their sides. The effectiveness of CORK as a CLOSURE was thereby enhanced because it was kept wet and expanded by the wine. All this was achieved by the abandoning of onion-, bladder-, and mallet-shaped bottles in favour of cylindrical ones which stack easily. Early cylindrical bottles have short wide bodies with tall necks, but as the century progressed the modern shape evolved. In 1821, Ricketts of Bristol patented a machine for moulding bottles of uniform size and shape, early examples of which are impressed 'patent' on the shoulder of the bottle and the legend 'H Ricketts & Co. Glassworks Bristol' on the base. Thus the modern wine bottle had evolved, all later shapes and colours being decided as a question of aesthetics rather than technical limitation.

Identification From 1636, at about the time of the first appearance of glass bottles in post-Roman Britain, it was illegal to sell wine by the bottle. This consumer protection measure was on account of vintners' willingness to take advantage of the varying capacity of blown bottles. From that time and for the next 230 years, wine was sold by the measure and then bottled. Customers who bought regularly had their own bottles and had them marked in order to distinguish them from any others that might be at the vintner's premises waiting to be filled. The usual marking was the attachment at the end of the production process of a disc seal of the same glass as the bottle, upon which was impressed the owner's initials, name, or heraldic device, often accompanied by the date. Innkeepers and taverners had appropriately marked, or 'sealed', bottles too. It may be noted here that these seals did not indicate the contents.

Sealed bottles are avidly collected today, the most prized being 17th-century ones, particularly those with dates incorporated in the seal. Named examples are preferred to ones with initials, and earlier ones to later.

Bottles with paper labels indicating the contents, first hand written and later printed, emerged during the opening years of the 19th century, but in Britain the law prohibiting wine from being sold by the bottle was not relaxed until 1860. Bottles with paper labels printed with pre-1860 vintages are probably relabelled or were intended for non-British markets.

Other materials Bottles in media other than glass are known, particularly in the 17th century, when glass was an expensive and scarce commodity. Leather bottles, jugs, and other vessels are sometimes associated with ale and beer but many will have been used in the service of wine. A large group of serving bottles is known, made in London, of white tin-glazed

earthenware (termed delftware). They are onion shaped with handles and vary from about half to 1½-bottle capacity. Their most charming feature is the calligraphy, usually opposite the handle, for 'CLARET', 'Whit Wine' (*sic*), 'SACK', or, more rarely, 'PORT' or other wine. They are frequently dated (from c.1630 to 1660) and the legend is often embellished with a curlicue.

Size The size and shape of early bottles was, to an extent, a hit and miss affair. Perhaps the 'standard' size was the natural result of a lungful of air, but bottles were made in a variety of sizes from early times. The onion or bladder shape can sometimes be found in extremely large sizes holding up to 30 bottles. The general term for a large early bottle is a carboy but the word magnum was also used somewhat impressively for a bottle of about double normal capacity. For a long while a bottle was more or less 1¼ UK pints (70 cl or 25 fl oz) and a magnum was a quart (1.12 l or 40 fl oz). Until the 1970s, when EUROPEAN UNION and other legislation enforced standardization, bottles varied from about 65 to 85 cl, CHAMPAGNE and BURGUNDY tending to be larger than those for BORDEAUX, while SHERRY bottles were often smaller.   R.N.H.B.

Morgan, R., *Sealed Bottles: Their History & Evolution (1630–1930)* (Burton-on-Trent, n.d.).
Ruggles-Brise, S., *Sealed Bottles* (London, 1949).

Modern bottles

Choice of LABEL and FOIL are not the only ways in which a wine producer can make a visual statement to a potential customer. Wine bottles are now made in an almost bewildering array of shapes, weights, colours of glass, and design, quite apart from their capacity (see BOTTLE SIZES).

In some regions one specific bottle has been adopted by all but the most anarchic producers, and indeed adoption of a special local, regional, or appellational bottle became particularly fashionable in the 1980s. Examples of special bottles are the heavy, embossed CHÂTEAUNEUF-DU-PAPE bottle (which comes in several rival versions); the BOCKSBEUTEL of FRANKEN; the CHÂTEAU GRILLET bottle peculiar to a single property; and the long-necked green bottle particular to MUSCADET, although it can sometimes seem that every French appellation has developed its own exclusive bottle.

In general, Italians, with their firm belief in the importance of design, offer the most dazzling range of wine bottles. Some of the particularly artful shapes used for grappa have been adopted by wine producers in Austria and further afield, especially for halves of sweet wine. Weight and darkness of glass seem to be highly valued by the Italians in particular, although it is a general rule throughout the wine world that the heavier a bottle, the greater the aspirations of the producer of the wine for

Electronically controlled **gyropalettes** such as these at Domaine Chandon in California's Napa valley have become the norm for sparkling wine-making and in Champagne as a much more effective alternative to shaking the sediment into individual bottlenecks by hand as shown on p. 288.

its longevity, or at least its price. Bottling wine in the lightest, cheapest glass is one way of paring production costs to a minimum.

The problem with some special bottle shapes, however, is that they may well be difficult to store, both on the shelf (many a special bottle is simply too tall for the average supermarket display) and, particularly, in a wine rack designed for standard bottles.

Bottle shapes Special designs apart, there are certain standard bottle shapes associated most commonly with certain regions or, increasingly, the styles of wine associated with those regions. Ambitiously made Chardonnays the world over, for example, tend to be put into burgundy bottles. Since the geographical provenance of most wines should be clear from the label, understanding bottle shapes is most useful for the clues they provide as to the intended style of the wine inside them. Some RIOJA producers, for example, put their Garnacha-dominated, richer blends into burgundy bottles, while their Tempranillo wines designed for longer ageing are put into bordeaux bottles. The red bordeaux bottle itself, incidentally, has been the subject of much research and revision to increase the durability of the wine stored inside it (see also Bottle colour below).

Many German wine producers in particular have employed bottle shapes as their most eloquent marketing tool in distancing drier, non-aromatic styles of wine from traditional German wines sold in the elongated bottle shape which has come to be associated with aromatic wines. The precise elongation of that shape evolved considerably in the 1970s and 1980s. Mass-market retailers objected to the inconvenient height of the traditional German bottle and so it was reduced by many, only to be increased again by some of the most quality-conscious German producers as a defiant statement of their reverence for tradition.

Most champagne and sparkling wines are sold in much the same shape of bottle, moulded to be thick and strong enough to withstand the pressure of up to six atmospheres inside each bottle. Considerable energy and money is expended, however, on designing special bottles for PRESTIGE CUVÉES, Moët & Chandon's Dom PÉRIGNON bottle having set a formidable standard. The precise shape of the lip of a champagne bottle indicates whether the second fermentation took place under a crown cap, or under a cork as it does in some very rare cases.

Bottles vary in the extent to which they have a punt, or inverse indentation, in their base. Most champagne and sparkling wine bottles have a particularly deep indentation because of the need to stack inverted bottles one on top of the other during the traditional method of SPARKLING WINE-MAKING. Punts are less obviously useful for still wines—although they can make 75-cl capacity bottles look bigger and more impressive—and deep punts can provide useful purchase for the thumb when SERVING wine from a bottle.

The exact shape and design of the neck and lip of the bottle is determined by what is used to stopper it. Most CLOSURES other than cork need some sort of modification and the widespread adoption of SCREW CAPS has entailed considerable redesign of bottles. The 1990s saw a marked but mercifully brief FASHION for bottles with a flange but no CAPSULE around the top, which damaged many a CORK-SCREW.

Bottle colour Wine keeps best in dark glass—as the Champenois, the most energetic researchers into the effects of bottle choice on wine, have found (ROEDERER Cristal, which has traditionally been sold in clear glass, is always swathed in an orange wrap designed to filter out ultraviolet light). On the other hand, dark glass prevents the consumer from being impressed by the colour of a wine. For this reason, most ROSÉS, not designed for BOTTLE AGEING in any case, are sold in clear glass. It is less clear why SAUTERNES and other sweet white bordeaux is sold in clear glass; TRADITION is the explanation. Most wine bottles are, for reasons of both tradition and the orientation of glass furnaces, some shade of green, from pale blueish green to a colour that to all intents and purposes is black. For traditional reasons again, brown glass is used for some Italian wines, for fortified wines, and was the traditional way of telling a HOCK or Rhine wine from a MOSELLE in green glass. German producers are increasingly using blue-green glass, however, a nod to Victorian times when blue glass was often used. One of the most distinctive glass colours for wine bottles is the yellow-green used for white burgundy, called *feuille morte* in France and therefore 'dead leaf' in much of the New World. As CHARDONNAY became the most fashionable wine in the world in the 1980s, so the dead leaf burgundy bottle became the most sought-after wine bottle, with especial frustration by producers in New World regions far from France until supply lines were established. Wines are occasionally marketed in bright blue and bright red bottles.

More clues from the bottle

Most wine bottles are moulded with the mark of their manufacturers, sometimes with their capacity, and all wine sold within Europe from the 1990s should have a LOT MARKING, a small code stamped on the label, foil, or bottle, so that each bottle can be traced back to its precise BOTTLING and dispatch.

bottle sickness, also known less politely as **bottle stink**, unpleasant and increasingly rare smell apparent in a wine immediately on opening which dissipates after a few minutes.

Off-odour compounds such as MERCAPTANS and SULFUR DIOXIDE may occasionally be formed by moulds embedded in poor CORKS, or by a small amount of wine which has escaped through the cork or capsule and is then acetified or otherwise subjected to BACTERIAL SPOILAGE. This is the principal reason why some people advocate allowing a bottle of wine to BREATHE before serving (and one of the reasons why it is wise to wipe the top of an opened bottle clean). DECANTING can achieve the same end.

A similar phenomenon should perhaps more properly be called 'bottling sickness' as it is usually an unpleasant smell that results directly from the BOTTLING process. Other than under perfect conditions, bottling may be a rough business involving so much aeration and agitation that a certain amount of potentially harmful OXYGEN is frequently dissolved in the wine. To counter possible OXIDATION, many bottlers add sulfur dioxide at this stage. If the wine is tasted in the first few weeks after bottling, the smell of sulfur dioxide may be obtrusive and it is wise to wait until the sulfur dioxide has reacted with the oxygen and the wine once more tastes as it did prior to bottling.

bottle sizes are standardized in most countries. A bottle containing 75 cl (25 fl oz) is now accepted almost universally as the standard wine (but not spirits, which is more usually 70 cl) bottle, with the magnum being 1.5 l, exactly twice the capacity. The standard bottle is about the same size as the first bottles (see BOTTLES, history), whose size may have been determined by the size of container conveniently blown by a (glassblower's) lungful of air. The bottle has in its time been variously described as a suitable ration of wine for one person at a sitting, one person per day, and two people at a sitting (see CONSUMPTION).

Half-bottles usually contain 37.5 cl and are believed to hasten wine AGEING, partly because they contain more OXYGEN per centilitre of wine since the bottle neck and ULLAGE are the same as for a full bottle. Most wine bottlers have viewed halves and other bottles smaller than the standard bottle as an unwelcome inconvenience, and BOTTLING technology has been focused on standard bottles, but there continues to be strong demand for half-bottles, particularly in restaurants. There have been various attempts to launch a 50-cl bottle, particularly common for SWEET WINES, and some champagne producers have had notable recent success with single-serve quarter-bottles.

The bottle capacities permitted within Europe for still wines are 10 cl, 25 cl, 37.5 cl, 50 cl, 75 cl, and 1, 1.5, 2, 3, 4, 5, 6, 8, 9, and 10 litres (and wine may be served in 18.7-cl bottles aboard trains, planes, and the like). Sparkling wine bottles come in 12.5-, 20-, 37.5- and 75-cl and 1.5-, 3-, 4.5-, 6- and 9-litre capacities. The

Capacity (l)	Bordeaux	Champagne/Burgundy
1.5 (2 bottles)	magnum	magnum
2.25 (3 bottles)	Marie-Jeanne	not found
3 (4 bottles)	double magnum	Jéroboam
4.5 (6 bottles)	Jéroboam*	Rehoboam
6 (8 bottles)	Impériale	Methuselah
9 (12 bottles)	not found	Salmanazar
12 (16 bottles)	not found	Balthazar
15 (20 bottles)	not found	Nebuchadnezzar

*5 litres since 1978

larger-sized bottles, some of them no longer in production, have different names in different regions.

A 24-bottle sized Melchior and a 34-bottle sized Sovereign are also known, in theory. Bordeaux COLLECTORS particularly treasure larger bottles (often known as 'large formats' or *grands formats*) up to Impériale size, as they favour slow but subtle wine AGEING. Giant champagne bottles, on the other hand, tend to favour publicity rather than wine quality (sizes larger than a magnum tend to be filled with wine made in smaller bottles).

bottle variation is one of the more tantalizing aspects of wine appreciation. It is only to be expected with a product as sensitive to STORAGE conditions as wine that bottles of the same wine will differ—perhaps because one has been exposed to higher temperatures or greater humidity. There can easily be a perceptible difference in quality and character between bottles from the very same CASE. SUBJECTIVISM may play a part, as well as a difference in FILL LEVELS, but it is also possible that the individual wines were different before they went into bottle, or were bottled under different conditions. It was not until the 1970s, for example, that it became commonplace for Bordeaux châteaux to ensure that a uniform blend was made before bottling; some of the world's more artisanal producers still bottle by hand from cask to cask. Similarly, wines bottled on two different occasions may find themselves packed in the same case (although modern LOT NUMBER marking provides more clues in this respect). CORKS can also contribute to bottle variation with individual bottles exhibiting odours from TRICHLOROANISOLE originating from the cork, and the ability of the cork seal to allow varying degrees of oxygen into bottles.

bottling, vital wine-making operation for all wines other than those packaged in containers other than bottles (see BOXES and CANS) and those few served straight from a cask or tank as BULK WINE.

Bottling techniques vary greatly according to the size, resources, technical ability, and modernity of the winery, although since the 1960s it has been customary almost everywhere to blend all casks or vats of a given lot of wine together before bottling, and to bottle it all at once. (Prior to this there could be

considerable BOTTLE VARIATION between different bottlings of even FIRST GROWTHS. And see CHAPOUTIER for a report of this practice extending well into the 1990s.)

Until recently, the high-speed, efficient bottling lines used for everyday wine subjected the wine to considerable AERATION and agitation so that wines would not taste as they should for some weeks after bottling, when the dissolved OXYGEN had fully reacted with the wine components, including added SULFUR DIOXIDE (as explained in BOTTLE SICKNESS). And wines containing RESIDUAL SUGAR may well have been subjected to PASTEURIZATION and 'hot bottled' to ensure microbiological stability. An increasing proportion of even inexpensive wine is bottled more carefully today, however, borrowing technology from the brewing industry.

Producers of high-quality wine with the means to invest in a bottling line (by no means all of them) use much more complicated and expensive equipment which subjects the wine to minimal aeration and agitation. NITROGEN or CARBON DIOXIDE is used to eliminate exposure to oxygen, and bottles are filled slowly so that there is no splashing or foaming. High-quality, low-alcohol, slightly sweet young wines may well be treated to STERILE BOTTLING.

Some small-scale wineries still follow the ancient tradition of bottling wine from casks or even individual barrels in the cellar. Many other small wineries, especially in France where *mis en bouteille au domaine* has considerable cachet, depend upon the services of outside mobile bottling lines, bottling equipment mounted in a truck or lorry which can be brought to the winery for a day or more.

The specific steps involved in bottling are the preparation of the wine itself (BLENDING, ANALYSIS, and possibly final FILTRATION) together with the preparation of the bottling line (sterilization and the preparation of the filler, corker or capper, labeller, capsuler, and casing machines, as appropriate). High-quality wines suitable for BOTTLE AGEING may not be labelled as soon as they are bottled, because they are stored for some time before being released and the labels may deteriorate in cellar conditions.

Bottling may take place either at any time from a few weeks after HARVEST (as with NOUVEAU wines) or when the wine is many years old (as in some of the most traditional Iberian BODEGAS). On smaller wine estates, bottling normally takes place at an otherwise quiet time for cellar staff such as in the spring or early summer.

Place of bottling may be many thousands of miles from where the grapes were originally grown, and even from where the wine was made, since BULK TRANSPORT is so very much cheaper than transporting wine in bottle. A 20-foot container will hold approximately 11,500 9-litre cases of bottled wine but a

disposable tank that fits into the same container will hold 24,000 litres of wine. The cost of bottling and bottles being so relatively high in California, Chile, and Australia, for example, some wines destined for sale in the US and Europe are bottled close to the market. In 2003, 10 per cent of wine imported into the UK was in bulk. Owing to low glass pricing in Europe, many New World wine producers are increasingly exporting their lower priced branded wines in bulk rather than in bottle. In eastern Europe and the FORMER SOVIET UNION in particular, bottling has traditionally taken place much closer to centres of population than to the vineyard. Producers of hand-crafted, top-quality wines, however, usually prefer to conduct the bottling operation themselves since they have greater control over the process and are able to reduce to a minimum the amount of treatment the wine needs prior to shipping. However, for high-volume wines with a limited shelf life in bottle of around nine months, there is the advantage that the wine is likely to reach the retailers' shelves much sooner after bottling than wine bottled at source. See BOTTLING INFORMATION for the significance of various bottling claims on the label.

As with any mechanical process, many things can go wrong during the bottling operation. The bottled wine itself can develop problems which were not previously apparent. Most result from incomplete STABILIZATION, but other contaminants may also intervene, such as those associated with CORKS.

See also BOTTLES. A.D.W., J.R., & J.Ha.

bottling information. Most wine labels should divulge where the wine was bottled. Wines bottled in the same place as they were vinified are described under CHÂTEAU BOTTLED, DOMAINE BOTTLED, ESTATE BOTTLED, ERZEUGERABFÜLLUNG, or GUTSABFÜLLUNG.

Common phrases for 'bottled' are *mis en bouteille* in French, *imbottigliato* in Italian, *embotellado* in Spanish, and *engarrafado* in Portuguese.

Many of the wines bottled by an enterprise other than the one which made the wine are labelled relatively obliquely. Within the EUROPEAN UNION, a bottler's address may not be specified on the label of a basic TABLE WINE if it incorporates the name of a QUALITY WINE; the bottler's postal code is usually employed instead. This is one of those well-intentioned rules designed to minimize the possibility of passing off, but it does make labels less informative to those not conversant with, for example, French *département* numbers or the two letters used for each Italian province.

Bouchalès is a dark-berried vine variety still grown to a limited extent in Bordeaux and in the Lot-et-Garonne *département*. It is not particularly easy to graft or grow and total French plantings fell from over 4,000 ha/9,900 acres in 1968 to less than 200 ha/500 acres by the 21st century.

Bouchard, Père et Fils, one of Beaune's large merchant houses (quite distinct from Bouchard Aîné), and the most important vineyard owner on Burgundy's Côte de BEAUNE. Based since 1731 in the 15th-century Ch de Beaune, a landmark in this medieval wine town, the house was established by Michel Bouchard, a Dauphiné textile merchant, and taken over in 1995 by Joseph Henriot of the eponymous champagne house who once ran VEUVE CLICQUOT. By that stage the beleaguered ninth generation of Bouchards had vineyard land acquired over the centuries that totalled more than 90 ha/230 acres. Bouchard have holdings in 25 different Beaune vineyards, including their exclusivities Beaune-Grèves, Vigne de l'Enfant Jésus, and Beaune, Clos de la Mousse. They are also particularly proud of their 1.1-ha/2.7-acre holding in Le MONTRACHET, their particularly significant share of Chevalier-Montrachet in their holding of 2.33 ha. In all, 71 of their 92 ha are in GRANDS CRUS or PREMIERS CRUS. In 1998, the Chablis firm William Fèvre was acquired and has been taken from strength to strength.

Wines from their own vineyards are undoubtedly Bouchard's best. For the much larger NÉGOCIANT business, the firm buys in considerable quantities of grapes (including all of those grown in the Clos-St-Marc premier cru in Nuits-St-Georges), must (notably in Chablis), and young wines for ÉLEVAGE in the medieval cellars on several levels below the Ch de Beaune. Under Henriot, even relatively inexpensive red wines have become noticeably deeper and more concentrated.

Bouchet, name for CABERNET FRANC commonly used in St-Émilion and elsewhere on the right bank of the GIRONDE.

bouchon is French for CORK and **bouchonné** describes a faulty, CORKED wine.

Bouchy, the local name for the CABERNET FRANC grape when grown in MADIRAN.

bouillie bordelaise, see BORDEAUX MIXTURE.

bouquet, oft-ridiculed tasting term for the smell of a wine, particularly that of a mature or maturing wine. Although its original French meaning was 'small wood' (from the same root as the Italian *bosco* and the English *bosky*), bouquet is a French word for a bunch of flowers which has been used to describe the perfume of a wine since the first half of the 19th century. It is used loosely by many wine tasters to describe any pleasant wine smell or smells but, just as a bouquet (rather than a bunch) of flowers suggests a composition of several varied elements, many wine professionals distinguish between the simple AROMA of the grape

and the bouquet of the more complex compounds which evolve as a result of FERMENTATION, ÉLEVAGE, and BOTTLE AGEING. There is little consistency in usage, however, and many authorities differ about which point in a wine's life cycle represents the point at which a wine's smell stops being an aroma and becomes a bouquet. See also AGEING, ESTER, FLAVOUR COMPOUNDS, and FLAVOUR PRECURSORS.

Bourboulenc is an ancient white grape variety that may well have originated in Greece, as the now rarely seen Asprokondoura, and has been grown throughout southern France for centuries. Ripening late but keeping its acidity well, it is allowed into a wide variety of Provençal and southern Rhône appellations (including Châteauneuf-du-Pape) but is rarely encountered as a dominant variety other than in the distinctively marine whites of La CLAPE and an increasing number of other Languedoc whites. France's total area planted with Bourboulenc halved in the 1970s and then doubled again, to its current level of about 800 ha/2,000 acres, in the 1980s thanks in part to a re-evaluation in the Languedoc, where it is also, confusingly, known as Malvoisie. Its tight bunches of large grapes can make it prone to rot in more difficult years but Bourboulenc, together with Maccabéo, should constitute more than 50 per cent of the blend for any white MINERVOIS, and the two, with Grenache Blanc, should dominate CORBIÈRES Blanc. Wine produced can be fine, with a hint of smoke.

Bourg, small town in the BORDEAUX region on the right bank of the river DORDOGNE, just up river of its confluence with the Garonne, which is surrounded by the **Côtes de Bourg** appellation, also known as **Bourg** and **Bourgeais**. In most years, more Côtes de Bourg red is produced than any other BORDEAUX CÔTES appellation, from about 3,850 ha/9,500 acres of vines. Grape varieties and organization are very similar to the larger BLAYE area to the immediate north, but the clay-limestone soils tend to be less varied in Bourg, and those vineyards on the edge of the Gironde estuary are particularly well protected from FROST damage, thanks to the maritime influence. Almost all wine produced is red, based on MERLOT grapes, and designed to last slightly longer than Premières Côtes de Blaye, to be consumed at four to six or even more years old. The average quality of Bourg's PETITS CHÂTEAUX (some of them not that small) has been improving. A little dry white wine is also made, chiefly from the eminently distillable UGNI BLANC and COLOMBARD grapes which still predominate here, even though it is decades since the region's wines were sent north to produce cognac. The star of the appellation is Ch Roc des Combes, produced by the owner of St-Émilion's Ch Tertre-Roteboeuf on a particularly well-favoured site

on the Gironde itself, but top cuvées of Chx Fougas, Tayac, and Terrefort-Bellegrave are also notable. This is an appellation worth watching. For more details, see BORDEAUX.

bourgeon is French for BUD, and **bourgeonnage** is the viticultural practice of thinning surplus developing buds before FLOWERING, a form of early CROP THINNING.

Bourgogne, the French name for both the region of BURGUNDY (La Bourgogne) and burgundy, the wines thereof (*le bourgogne*), which are red, white, and very occasionally rosé. In particular, Bourgogne refers to the most basic, generic category of APPELLATIONS in Burgundy.

For white wines the generic appellations are BOURGOGNE ALIGOTÉ, **Bourgogne Blanc** (made from Chardonnay grapes, although Pinot Blanc and Pinot Gris are tolerated), and **Bourgogne Grand Ordinaire**, which may contain Chardonnay, Aligoté, Melon de Bourgogne, and (in the Yonne, the Chablis *département*) Sacy.

For red wines the generic appellations are BOURGOGNE PASSETOUTGRAINS, **Bourgogne Grand Ordinaire**, and **Bourgogne Rouge**. The last is usually pure Pinot Noir, although it may technically include the César and Tressot once grown in the Yonne (Chablis country), and may be made from Gamay grapes if grown in one of the BEAUJOLAIS crus. Bourgogne Passetoutgrains is a blend of Gamay and Pinot Noir, requiring a minimum of one-third of the latter. Bourgogne Grand Ordinaire may include Pinot, Gamay, César, and Tressot.

A small amount of pink wine is sold as **Bourgogne Rosé**, or **Bourgogne Clairet**. In practice this may be the result of a SAIGNÉE of a red wine from a major vineyard in order to concentrate it—although by law this is not possible, since to declassify part of the crop into Bourgogne Rosé would necessitate declassifying the remainder into Bourgogne Rouge.

Bourgogne of whatever colour may be followed by a geographical suffix, either denoting a region (Hautes Côtes de Nuits, Hautes Côtes de Beaune, Côte Chalonnaise, Côtes d'AUXERRE, Côtes du COUCHOIS); a village (Chitry, Coulanges-la-Vineuse, Épineuil, Vézelay); or in certain cases a vineyard (Côte St-Jacques at Joigny, and La Chapelle Notre Dame, Le Chapitre, and Montrecul in the Côte d'Or).

Thus it is evident that the scope of 'Bourgogne', be it white, red, or pink, encompasses wide variations in provenance, quality, and style of wine, which may not be clear from the label. A Bourgogne Rouge or Bourgogne Blanc made by a grower in one of the major villages of the Côte d'Or (such as MEURSAULT for whites and VOLNAY or CHAMBOLLE-MUSIGNY for reds) is likely to be reliably fashioned in the image of classic CÔTE D'OR burgundy, however, and may well represent excellent value, being generally ready to drink sooner. There is every chance that the wine will be made from vines only just outside the village appellation yet will be sold at half the price.

CRÉMANT de Bourgogne is the generic appellation for sparkling Burgundy, either white or rosé, while the now rare red version is classified as **Bourgogne Mousseux**.

See also BOURGOGNE ALIGOTÉ and BOURGOGNE PASSETOUTGRAINS.   J.T.C.M.

Bourgogne Aligoté, a generic appellation of around 1,400 ha/3,460 acres in Burgundy for white wines made from the ALIGOTÉ grape. These wines vary between refreshingly crisp and disagreeably tart, although the latter characteristic suits their role as the basis for *vin blanc cassis*, or KIR. Aligoté is primarily for early consumption although wines from the best locations such as Chitry in the Yonne, Pernand-Vergelesses in the Côte de Beaune, and BOUZERON (which has its own appellation for Aligoté) can age well.   J.T.C.M.

Bourgogne Passetoutgrains, red thirst-quencher from Burgundy made from Pinot Noir (minimum one-third) and Gamay grapes. Often deep in colour and rather savagely animal when young, Passetoutgrains with age can attain greater refinement as the Pinot Noir flavours start to dominate. The best examples come from vineyards in the CÔTE D'OR lying in the plain beyond the main RN74 road which divides the finer vineyards from the generic. Almost two-thirds as much of this appellation is made each year as Bourgogne Rouge but relatively little leaves the region.   J.T.C.M.

Bourgogne, Université de. See DIJON.

Bourgueil, potentially captivating red wines made on the north bank of the Loire in the west of the TOURAINE district. The climate here is particularly gentle and rainfall is low, as in much of ANJOU to the immediate west. Of the 1,300 ha/3,200 acres of vineyard well over half are on the south-facing slopes which lead west from St-Patrice almost on the river to St-Nicolas (see below), where fewer than a third of the vineyard is on the slopes

The CABERNET FRANC grape is mainly responsible for these medium-bodied wines, which are typically marked by a more powerful aroma (reminding some of raspberries, others of pencil shavings) and slightly more noticeable tannins than the wines of CHINON to the south. As in Chinon, since 2000, Cabernet Sauvignon may represent up to 25 per cent of the blend. Bourgueil can be aged for five or many more years in really successful, fully ripe VINTAGES such as 1995, 1996, 1997, 2001, 2002, and 2003, while **St-Nicolas-de-Bourgueil**, produced on about 900 ha of lighter soils in the west of the region, is generally a lighter, earlier

maturing wine. These fragrant wines are extremely popular in Paris and northern France but have yet to be discovered by most non-French wine lovers.

A little dry rosé Bourgueil is also made, but the appellation does not, unlike Chinon, encompass white wines. Reliable producers include Yannick Amirault, Breton, Domaine de la Butte, and Druet. See LOIRE, including map.

Friedrich, J., *A Wine and Food Guide to the Loire* (New York, 1996 and London, 1977).

Bouschet is, like Müller, Scheu, and Seibel, a vine-breeder's surname that lives on in the name of his creations, although in this case there were two Bouschets, a 19th-century father and son whose work, perhaps unfortunately, made the spread of ARAMON possible. In 1824 Louis Bouschet de Bernard combined the productivity of Aramon with the colour expected of a red wine by crossing Aramon with TEINTURIER du Cher and modestly calling the result Petit Bouschet. This expedient crossing was popular in France throughout the second half of the 19th century and is still to be found in parts of North Africa and, according to GALET, Portugal. Louis's son Henri carried on where his father left off, producing most durably ALICANTE BOUSCHET and GRAND NOIR DE LA CALMETTE as well as a Carignan Bouschet.

Boutenac, relatively new subappellation of CORBIÈRES.

Bouvier, minor white grape variety bred as a TABLE GRAPE and now grown mainly in the Burgenland region of AUSTRIA, where it is particularly used for STURM, as well as for early-bottled wines. It is also grown in the Mátra Foothills of HUNGARY.

Bouzeron, village in the Côte CHALONNAISE famous for its BOURGOGNE ALIGOTÉ, which has had its own appellation, Bourgogne Aligoté de Bouzeron, since 1979, promoted to the simple appellation Bouzeron in 1997.

Bovale, dark-skinned grapes in SARDEGNA distinguished as **Bovale Sardo** and the more common **Bovale Grande**. Both are used mainly for blending. GALET refutes the suggestion that either is related to the BOBAL of Spain.

Galet, P., *Dictionnaire encyclopédique des cépages* (Paris, 2000).

boxes, wine. In the 1970s, an entirely new way of packaging wine was developed, expressly to provide a significant volume of wine in a package that is not as breakable or heavy as a bottle, and is better able to preserve any wine left in the container. It comprises a collapsible laminated bag inside a strong cardboard carton, and wine is drawn out of a tap specially designed to minimize the ingress of potentially harmful OXYGEN. The difficulty of making the wine container completely airtight

restricts the potential shelf life of **bag-in-box** wines. There are two main types of bag: in the silver-coloured ones, the oxygen barrier is provided by a thin layer of aluminium between layers of polyster; the clear bags are made from ethylene vinyl alcohol. The main disadvantage of the former is 'flex cracking' which tends to occur during transportation and weakens the oxygen barrier. The oxygen barrier in the clear bag becomes less effective as relative humidity increases.

The package, commonly holding four litres of wine, is particularly popular in Australia and New Zealand, where it is known flatteringly as the 'cask' or, more prosaically, 'bladder pack'. Wine boxes have also enjoyed success in northern Europe in the 3-l size. Boxes are generally filled with less expensive wines designed for early drinking and are bought either in bulk for parties or by those who want to enjoy a simple wine one glass at a time over several weeks. The wine inside a bag is best consumed within 4–6 weeks of opening, and has usually deteriorated quite markedly 9–12 months after filling, which is why some wine boxes are dated. (See LEFTOVER WINE for details of devices for preserving wine in partially empty bottles.) By the mid 2000s, almost a quarter of all wine sold in the US was packed in a box.

Brachet, sometimes called **Braquet**, historic light red grape variety of PROVENCE which is still a valued ingredient in the red and pink wines of BELLET near Nice. Yields are low and the vine is relatively delicate but the wine is truly distinctive. This variety is not related to the much more aromatic Italian BRACHETTO.

Brachetto, distinctively aromatic light red grape variety found principally round Asti, Roero, and Alessandria, where it is particularly successful, in the PIEMONTE region of Italy. It produces wines, notably **Brachetto d'Acqui** promoted to DOCG status in 1996, that are fizzy, relatively alcoholic, and have both the colour and flavour of strawberries—the light red equivalent of Moscato d'Asti. Occasional dry versions of Brachetto became even rarer from the late 1990s.

Bragato, Romeo, Dalmatian-born graduate of Italian viticulture studies and employee of the Victorian government in Australia who was invited in 1895 to investigate the prospects for viticulture and wine-making in New Zealand. His report was very favourable, and became an important document encouraging the development of the industry. Bragato found many regions 'pre-eminently suited' to viticulture, including important modern regions such as Hawkes Bay and Wairarapa. Following his visits, local growers' associations were formed, and a surge in plantings resulted.

Bragato identified PHYLLOXERA in New Zealand in 1895, and suggested the use of resistant

ROOTSTOCKS, but his advice was initially ignored. Offered the position of government viticulturist in 1902, he immediately began importing and distributing these rootstocks (which were to be used again to fight phylloxera outbreaks of the 1980s). He established a research station at Te Kauwhata with experimental vineyards and a training winery, and also published a handbook *Viticulture in New Zealand*. Bragato and the fledgling wine industry were, however, not supported by his masters in the Department of Agriculture. In 1908 he lost control of the Te Kauwhata Research Station and in 1909 migrated to Canada in disgust.   R.E.S.

Bramaterra, a lighter variation on the NEBBIOLO theme of LESSONA in the PIEMONTE region of north west Italy. Like the other wines of Novara/Vercelli, it is a blend of Nebbiolo, Croatina, and Vespolina. See SPANNA, the local name for Nebbiolo, for more details. See also the nearby BOCA, GATTINARA, GHEMME, SIZZANO, and FARA in Novara.

Brancellao, Galician vine once widely grown in north west Spain, particularly in RÍAS BAIXAS and known in Portugal's Vinho Verde region as **Brancelho** for its pale but sometimes aromatic wine. This is the ALVARELHÃO of the Douro.

branco, Portuguese word meaning 'white'. *Vinho branco* is therefore white wine.

brands, interpreted strictly as individual products marketed on the basis of their name and image rather than on their inherent qualities, have a much less dominant position in the market for wine than for drinks such as beer or cola, for instance, but thanks to GLOBALIZATION they are growing in importance. The leading industry resource IMPACT Databank calculated that the global market share of the top 25 wine brands in the world, while having grown significantly since the mid 1990s, was still less than 8 per cent in 2004. It is perhaps significant that IMPACT is based in the UNITED STATES, where distribution is tightly controlled and brands account for more than half of all wine sales. Most sectors of the wine market are relatively fragmented (although the FORTIFIED WINE business is not and has been built on brands), so that brand promotion is difficult to make cost effective, and can leave **branded wines** looking poor value. By far the most common promotion in the mid 2000s was based on PRICE and close relationships with the decreasing number of multiple retailers.

Wine brands offer a familiar lifeline to new wine consumers baffled by a multiplicity of unfamiliar, often foreign, proper names. But as wine drinkers become more sophisticated, they learn to decode what initially seems the arcane language of wine names, usually by identifying the major VARIETALS and some of the more important place-names. Thus, brands

are most sought after in embryonic and fast-growing markets, such as northern Europe and the rest of the English-speaking world between the 1950s and the 1980s, and in Africa, South America, and some Asian countries today.

It may be difficult to market branded wines in a competitive market, but it can be even more difficult to maintain consistency of a product as variable as wine. Supplies are strictly limited to an annual batch production process. Wine cannot be manufactured to suit demand, and different vintages impose their own characteristics on the product regardless of consumer taste. A high proportion of all wine drinkers were introduced to wine through brands, and it is to the credit of those brand owners most dedicated to maintaining quality standards whenever the introduction was a happy one.

Notably successful international individual wine brands are relatively few, and they have perforce to be based on wine of which there is no shortage of supply. BLUE NUN, LANCERS, MATEUS ROSÉ, and MOUTON CADET are all examples of brands which in the 20th century achieved annual sales measured in millions of cases.

There are those who argue that the grape variety CHARDONNAY, for example, has become a brand in its own right, so strong is consumer recognition of the name. Others claim that in certain markets, buyers' own brands have become so important, and so cleverly marketed, that, for example, some retailers' names have established themselves as brands.

Many of the world's bigger wine companies are attempting to market themselves to the consumer as a brand: GALLO, Sutter Home, Beringer, HARDYS, LINDEMANS, and YELLOW TAIL come immediately to mind. The definition of a wine brand is certainly a loose one. In some respects, the New French CLARETS, named for the estate which produced them, were the first wine brands. Today, the French wine industry blames some of its difficulty in selling everything it produces on its failure to build brands, in conspicuous contrast to the bigger companies in Australian and the US. And any definition which incorporates the notion of relatively elastic supply and some studied promotion would allow that the most successful wine brands of all are the so-called *grande marque* (which translates directly as 'big brand') CHAMPAGNES.

Brazil, Brasil in Portuguese, vast country and third most important wine producer in SOUTH AMERICA after Argentina and Chile with 68,000 ha/168,000 acres of vineyards in 2003 of which only a little over 5,000 ha were VINIFERA. Of the 3.48 million hl/92 million galls of wine produced in 2004, 43 per cent was still red, 34 per cent was still white, and a significant 22 per cent was sparkling. Only about 11 per cent of all wine made in Brazil is *vinho fino*, made from *vinifera* grapes. TABLE

GRAPES are the main products of Brazilian vineyards.

The vine was introduced in São Paulo state by the Portuguese as early as 1532. Spanish vines were introduced by the Jesuits in Rio Grande do Sul in 1626, but viticulture was abandoned after the destruction of Jesuit missions in the south of the country. In the 18th century, settlers from the Azores tried for a third time to establish *vinifera* vine cuttings brought from Madeira and the Azores, but encountered severe problems in the hot, humid climate. The first vines to be successfully cultivated in Brazil were the American vine ISABELLA (more often called Isabelle in Brazil) that was first planted on the south coast of Rio Grande in 1840, but it was not until the arrival of Italian immigrants in the high Serra Gaúcha region in the north east of Rio Grande do Sul that viticulture was definitively established in Brazil, and even then, in the late 1870s, it was mainly the AMERICAN VINES Isabella, CONCORD, CATAWBA, NORTON, Clinton, Delaware, Martha, and York Madeira that were cultivated, subsequently supplemented by Italian varieties such as Barbera, Bonarda, Moscato, and Trebbiano, and by Tannat as in Uruguay to the south.

Only in the early 20th century was any sort of national wine market established, with the development of communications between the centres of population such as Rio de Janeiro and the wine regions in the far south. The first CO-OPERATIVES were established in the late 1920s.

Wines with serious claims to quality were not developed until the 1970s, when several important multinational corporations, including MOËT & CHANDON, Seagram, Bacardi, Heublein, DOMECQ, and Martini & Rossi, established wine companies in Brazil and invested in modern wine-making equipment such as automatic TEMPERATURE CONTROL, STAINLESS STEEL, and imported BARRIQUES. Vine varieties such as Chardonnay, Welschriesling (Riesling Italico), Sémillon, Gewürztraminer, Cabernet Franc, Merlot, and Cabernet Sauvignon were also imported, and a programme of viticultural improvements embarked upon.

Modern Brazilian viticulture is concentrated in the extreme south of the country in the state of Rio Grande do Sul, principally in the high, hilly Serra Gaúcha region, north and inland of the state capital Porto Alegre, and also in the much smaller, newer Campanha, sometimes called Fronteira, wine region on the border with URUGUAY and Argentina.

Serra Gaúcha incorporates about 38,000 ha/93,700 acres of vines, all grafted, at an average ALTITUDE of 700 m/2,300 ft, which is difficult to mechanize, and shared between so many small farmers that the average vineyard holding is just 2.5 ha. The relatively acid soils are shallow, not particularly fertile, and have a high proportion of water-retaining clay. Average RAINFALL here is very high for a wine region, about 1,800 mm/70 in, of which at least 700 mm falls during the growing season of September to February. The resulting effect on grape RIPENING means that ENRICHMENT of some sort, usually CHAPTALIZATION, is almost always necessary. FUNGAL DISEASES are a constant threat in this humid climate, and more than 80 per cent of all vines are American vines or hybrids, still chiefly the usefully thick-skinned Isabella, grown to produce GRAPE JUICE, TABLE GRAPES, and wine, particularly sparkling wine, of the most basic quality.

The most common vine-TRAINING SYSTEMS are TENDONE to minimize the ROT that is a perennial problem and ESPALIER to encourage ripening of red wine varieties. For the *vinifera* varieties, efforts are being made to reduce YIELDS, however, in attempts to maximize wine quality.

The grapes are often picked before full ripeness is reached and the white wines of Serra Gaúcha are usually high in MALIC ACID. Different wineries have different policies on the desirability of MALOLACTIC FERMENTATION for white wines. Red wines are, inevitably in this climate, relatively light (yields can easily be 14 tonnes per ha) and acid, although there has been some experimentation with new OAK.

Within Serra Gaúcha, Garibaldi, where Moët-Hennessy do Brasil is based, is the centre for sparkling wine production, many of these wines being made in the image of SPUMANTE, for Italian influence is strong in the region. Farroupilha can produce good-quality grapes for red wine (and substantial quantities for local VERMOUTH), while Flores da Cunha is the source of much everyday wine. *Vinifera* production is centred on Bento Gonçalves, a sort of tourist centre for the wine industry.

Newer wine regions are notably less humid and produce deeper-coloured wines. By 2005 more than 1,300 ha/3,200 acres of vines, all *vinifera* varieties, had been planted in Campanha on the border with Uruguay, chiefly in the communes of Santana do Livramento and Pinheiro Machado. This is much flatter country, used substantially for pasture and cereal crops, with sandy soils and good DRAINAGE. Most vines are trained using some sort of espalier system, and the average annual rainfall is about 850 mm, considerably less than Serra Gaúcha but still high enough to prejudice ripening. Michel ROLLAND of Pomerol consults for Miolo here.

Another, even more distinctive new wine region is in the São Francisco Valley in the arid north of the country just nine degrees of LATITUDE south of the equator on the border between the states of Bahia and Pernambuco. TROPICAL VITICULTURE involving more than one harvest a year from PERGOLA training systems dependent on water from the local river is the rule here for the 500 ha of *vinifera* vines among a total vineyard area of 8,000 ha/ 19,800 acres in 2005. Some interesting, modern reds are emerging.

Despite these signs of viticultural life, local wine has yet to penetrate Brazilian culture very deeply, and average consumption is still extremely low, well below 2 l per head per year, except in the predominantly European communities of the south, although interest in Brazilian wine both domestically and on export markets is growing and the country has played host to the odd FLYING WINEMAKER.

J.R. & J.M.

Fielden, C., *The Wines of Argentina, Chile and Latin America* (London, 2003).

Waldin, M., *Wines of South America* (London, 2003).

breathing, an operation, believed beneficial by some consumers, involving pulling the cork and letting the open bottle stand for a few hours before it is poured. In fact, in such circumstances the wine can take only the most minimal of 'breaths', and any change is bound to be imperceptible (except possibly in the case of BOTTLE SICKNESS). The surface area of wine exposed to the air is so small that the effects of any AERATION are negligible. See DECANTING for details of effective aeration.

Breede River Valley, important wine region in SOUTH AFRICA.

breeding. See VINE BREEDING.

Breganze, DOC zone for a range of red and white often VARIETAL wines in the VENETO region of north east Italy. Although some of the vineyards are in the foothills of the alps to the north of the city of Vicenza, a large percentage of them are in the gravel soils of the plain. Some rather anonymous wines based on TOCAI, PINOT BLANC, VESPAIOLA, CABERNET, MERLOT, and PINOT NOIR are made, none of which is widely known outside the zone itself. Such international fame as the zone has is due to the efforts of a single producer, Fausto Maculan, who has travelled widely in France and California, planted CABERNET SAUVIGNON, CHARDONNAY, and SAUVIGNON BLANC, invested heavily in small oak barrels, and experimented with densely planted vineyards on French models, as well as producing important dessert wines from grapes with NOBLE ROT (the rare Acininobili, and the Torcolato mentioned under DRIED GRAPE WINES). Despite the excellence of his sweet wines, he has remained an isolated figure in Breganze.   D.T.

Breton, name used in the middle Loire for the CABERNET FRANC grape. The reference is not to Brittany but to Abbot Breton, who is reputed to have disseminated the vine in the 17th century.

Brettanomyces, sometimes called **Brett**, one of the YEAST genera found occasionally on grapes and in wines. *Brettanomyces* in its perfect or sporulating form is known as DEKKERA. While it is usually considered a spoilage yeast since it can produce off-flavours in wines, there is some evidence to indicate that at low levels some of the flavours produced by *Brettanomyces* can improve red wine complexity. (In some beers, for example Belgium's spontaneously fermented lambic and gueuze beers, *Brettanomyces* and its effects are essential.)

The first isolation of *Brettanomyces* in a bottled wine was in the 1950s by Schanderl and Draczynski of GEISENHEIM (Licker *et al.*). Olsen reports nine different species of *Brettanomyces*; the two most commonly found in wine are *B. intermidius*, and *B. lambicus*. These two species can grow in both red and white wine, although they are more often associated with red.

Brettanomyces is both an anaerobic and an aerobic organism. It is a resourceful microbe that can utilize a number of substrates at low levels and under restrictive conditions. The range and quantity of by-products produced by *Brettanomyces* depend on various factors, including levels of substrates, available precursors, and the size of the *Brettanomyces* population in the wine. The most important substrate is RESIDUAL SUGAR.

There are four key by-products of *Brettanomyces* growth which can affect the flavour and aroma of a wine: esterases, volatile fatty acids, tetrahydropyridines, and, arguably, the most important, volatile phenols. Two critical volatile phenol compounds have been isolated from *Brettanomyces* activity: 4-ethylphenol (4-EP) and 4-ethylguaiacol (4-EG). 4-EP is often described as introducing an 'animal' and 'sweaty saddle' flavour to wine. Its presence is an almost certain indicator of a *Brettanomyces* infection, and this is what most diagnostic laboratories test for to verify the presence of *Brettanomyces*. 4-EG in wine has a more appealing smoky, spicy, clove-like aroma.

Brettanomyces can create significant levels of volatile phenols in a short period of time and is difficult to manage in the cellar. However, the tools for monitoring *Brettanomyces* have never been more advanced, and winemakers can use analytical techniques such as gas chromatography/mass spectrometry to monitor high-risk wines.

Brettanomyces is sensitive to SULFUR DIOXIDE (SO_2) and can be controlled by maintaining 0.5 mg/l molecular SO_2. Hygiene is an important factor in controlling the growth of *Brettanomyces* in the cellar. Areas that provide suitable niches for *Brettanomyces* are must lines, dirty crush equipment, barrels, or any tank or transfer line that is not cleaned effectively. There have also been suggestions that the fruit fly can carry *Brettanomyces*. Once it is embedded in COOPERAGE, it can be difficult to eliminate from the cellar and barrels may need to be discarded to significantly reduce the populations. As with other microbes, the cleaner the winery, the more control one has over *Brettanomyces*. There are currently only two methods that virtually eliminate *Brettanomyces* at bottling: sterile FILTRATION and dimethyl dicarbonate (see DMDC). S.H.

Chatonnet, P., Dubourdieu, D., and Boidron, J. N., 'The influence of Brettanomyces/Dekkera sp. yeasts and lactic acid bacteria on the ethylphenol content of red wines', *American Journal of Enology and Viticulture*, 46/4 (1995), 463–8.

Heresztyn, T., 'Formation of substituted tetrahydropyridines by species of *Brettanomyces* and *Lactobacillus* isolated from mousey wines', *American Journal of Enology and Viticulture*, 37 (1986), 127–32.

Jefford, A., 'One brew's poison, another's nectar', *Financial Times* (Arts & Weekend supplement, 6 August 2005).

Licker, J. L., Acree, T. E., and Henick-Kling, T., 'What is "Brett" (Brettanomyces) flavour? A preliminary investigation', in A. L. Waterhouse and S. E. Ebeler (eds.), *Chemistry of Wine Flavour* (Washington, 1999), 96–115.

Olsen, E., '*Brettanomyces*: occurrence, flavour effects and control', 23rd annual New York Wine Industry Workshop hosted by N.Y.S.A.E.S., Cornell University (Geneva, NY, 1994).

Pollnitz, P. A, Pardon, K. H., and Sefton, M. A., 'Quantitative analysis of 4-ethylphenol and 4-ethylguaiacol in red wine', *Journal of Chromatography A*, 874/1 (2000), 101–9.

Silva, P., Cardoso, H., and Gerós, H., 'Studies on the wine spoilage capacity of *Brettanomyces/Dekkera* spp.', *American Journal of Enology and Viticulture*, 55/1 (2004), 65–72.

Brézème, curious small area just south of Valence in the northern RHÔNE which claims the right to prefix its name to the Côtes du Rhône appellation and produces sturdy, rather rustic reds from Syrah grapes.

bricco, or *bric* in the dialect of the north west Italian region of PIEMONTE, indicates the highest part of an elevation in the landscape or, in particular, a vineyard with a steep gradient at the top of a hill. The term was first used on a wine label by Luciano de Giacomi in 1969 for his Bricco del Drago, a blend of DOLCETTO and NEBBIOLO grapes from Alba, and has been extensively used for the other wines of Piemonte ever since. D.T.

Brindisi, Adriatic port and DOC for robust red wine made mainly from NEGROAMARO grapes in south east Italy. For more details see PUGLIA.

Britain, or **Great Britain**, has long been one of the most important international markets for wine. It regularly imports more wine than any country other than Germany and has shown unusually healthy growth in wine CONSUMPTION over the last 30 years. Its long wine-MERCHANT tradition has made it one of the most discerning, yet open-minded, wine-consuming nations. Domestic vine-growing in England and Wales is on too small a scale to affect consumers who expect to find the wines of the world on the shelves of their specialist merchants and, increasingly, supermarkets. A certain amount of wine is also made from imported grape concentrate (see BRITISH WINE). Historically, Britain's commercial influence helped shape the very existence of such wines as claret, madeira, marsala, port, and sherry (see BRITISH INFLUENCE).

See also ENGLAND (especially for history and modern viticulture), SCOTLAND, and WALES.

British influence on the wine trade. For centuries, wine consumption in Britain has had significant ramifications in many of the world's most important wine regions. A cool, wet climate has limited the production of wine in ENGLAND, so that British wine drinkers have had no choice but to look overseas for their supplies. Since they owe no permanent allegiance to any one wine region or wine-producing country, they have traditionally had a broad range from which to choose, although that choice has been dictated by convenience, FASHION, ECONOMICS, and POLITICS as often as by taste.

British influence on the wine trade resulted from more complex circumstances than a simple lack of native wines, however. (Otherwise, British influence on the wine trade would be no greater than, for example, Swedish or Danish—although see DUTCH WINE TRADE.) Britain enjoyed a unique combination of factors: relative prosperity and political power, a worldwide commercial empire supported by a strong navy, and a steadily increasing middle class. These circumstances not only helped to foster an interest in imported wines, but also provided the economic clout to acquire them. And at certain times in history, in specific wine regions, the British market was so influential that wine styles evolved, or completely new wines were invented, to satisfy its demands.

The first region fully to devote itself to British needs was SOUTH WEST FRANCE, when it belonged to the English crown. Indeed it could be argued that for 300 years, from 1152, Britain did have her own vines. During this period BORDEAUX was transformed into the most important wine centre in France. Vineyards were planted or extended around the city and far up the rivers Garonne and Dordogne to quench the English thirst. The loss of Bordeaux to the French in 1453 saw a decline in exports to England but this part of France was by now well established as a commercial wine region.

During the Middle Ages, wine was relatively cheap and plentiful in Britain. Wines from Germany, Portugal, Spain, Italy, Greece, the Mediterranean islands, and the Holy Land could all be found in London taverns, as well as those from France. It was not until the 16th century, however, that British merchants found, in southern Spain, a wine region to compensate for the loss of Bordeaux. Known collectively as SACK, the wines of Andalucía became immensely fashionable in Tudor times despite wars with Spain. Thousands of BUTTS of wine were sent back to England by British merchants settled in Sanlúcar and MÁLAGA. British taste and investment laid the foundations of what was to become the SHERRY industry.

The 17th century brought many problems for wine. The introduction of exotic new beverages such as coffee, chocolate, and teas (see COFFEE HOUSES), as well as the growing popularity of 'hopped' BEER, threatened the wine trade. The situation was not eased by the fact that the cost of wine had steadily grown to such a point that only the middle and upper classes could afford it. Crippling customs duties exacerbated the crisis. If the wine trade was to survive in Britain, some drastic changes were needed.

Medieval CLAIRET and Tudor sack had been staple beverages enjoyed by many Englishmen. British influence at the end of the 17th century was felt by a different sort of wine producer and encouraged the development of sophisticated superior-quality wines which only a limited clientele could afford. This select English market had particular influence in two areas of France: Bordeaux and CHAMPAGNE.

After the Restoration of Charles II in 1660, all things French were extremely fashionable in London. At this time individual producers in both Champagne and Bordeaux were making efforts to improve the quality of their wines. Champagne was promoted in London by French exiles (although it was English aristocrats who developed the taste for sparkling wine when French connoisseurs decried it as an aberration). Meanwhile a wealthy land-owner from Bordeaux, Arnaud de Pontac, succeeded in creating a stir when he opened a restaurant in London, Pontack's Head in Abchurch Street, to sell the wines of his Graves estate of HAUT-BRION.

The English aristocracy were delighted by these new styles of French wines, CLARET, and paid through the nose for them. Thus London became the chief market for fine wine and in turn influenced the quality of the wines themselves, for in the wine trade it is export that makes reputations, raises standards, and, above all, provides the driving force for investment. New vineyards were planted in Champagne and in the MÉDOC to exploit these refined English palates and purses.

The next great instance of a British-inspired wine was PORT. The exorbitant cost of champagne and good-quality claret, combined with the supply difficulties that resulted from WAR with France, caused British merchants to look elsewhere. Political rapprochement with Portugal signalled the possibility of a new, and cheap, source of wine. The British moved into OPORTO, prospected the DOURO valley for wine and vine-growing potential, and started a boom. Huge quantities of port were sent to Britain from the early 1700s, and as the century progressed the nature of the wine evolved to suit. Originally a rough red table wine, it was soon discovered to be improved by the addition of brandy, which made it even more palatable to the English, and considerably more stable for the sea voyage required. A whole new industry was created and the steep sides of the Douro valley terraced and planted to victual the English shires.

Similarly, Sicilia's MARSALA wine industry was developed by the British when, in the early years of the 19th century, Napoleon set up his Continental System hoping that, by depriving his enemies of French wine (among other things), he could cause British morale to collapse.

In 1860, William Gladstone stated that an Englishman's taste in wine 'is not an immutable, but a mutable thing'. He meant that British palates were capable of adapting to whatever was most available or pleasing at any particular period. A host of factors influenced taste and in turn demand influenced supply. Of all wine-drinking societies, Britain showed these developments most strikingly. Top-quality claret, sparkling champagne, and distinguished vintage port are today sought after all over the world. But ties of tradition and affection remain strong with the British market, a reminder of the fundamental part it played in the evolution of these and many other wines, and the wine trade in general.

Since the early 1980s, Great Britain has been targeted by many of the world's wine producers as one of the few substantial wine markets in which per capita wine consumption is growing. Only Germany imports more wine than Great Britain, but a substantial proportion of this is basic wine for processing into brandy, or TAFELWEIN or SEKT, much of which is re-exported.

The presence of the principal AUCTION houses and the resultant BROKERS made London the focus of the fine wine market, just as it is a production centre for the LITERATURE OF WINE and for wine EDUCATION.   H.B. & J.R.

Francis, A. D., *The Wine Trade* (London, 1972).
Johnson, H., *The Story of Wine* (London and New York, 1989).
Simon, A. L., *The History of the Wine Trade in England* (London, 1906-9).

British wine, a curious alcoholic drink made in the image of WINE from GRAPE CONCENTRATE imported into Great Britain. It is known as MADE WINE, and a decidedly manufactured product it is. Concentrated grape must, the consistency of thin honey, is imported in bulk throughout the year from wherever happens to be able to supply the best value (Spain was a notable source in the early 21st century). The must is eventually reconstituted by adding water and is fermented using selected YEAST strains, under the most rigorous technical controls, according to the wine style required. Until the 1980s, almost all British wine produced was FORTIFIED, and made to resemble sherry or port, or flavoured with ginger or other spices or fruits. Since the

early 1980s, British wines of normal TABLE WINE strength have also been made, much to the dismay of the producers of English wine (see ENGLAND), with whose products made from freshly picked grapes there is considerable confusion.

The British wine producers, few and relatively industrial, claim as initial historical precedent a Francis Chamberleyne, who was granted a charter by Charles I in 1635 to make wine from imported raisins. Wine continued to be made from imported raisins, but the real catalyst for the establishment of an economically viable British wine trade came when a technique for the CONCENTRATION of GRAPE JUICE was perfected by Emmanuel Roche of Toulouse, south west France, who promptly shared it with two Greek brothers Mitzotakis, members of his wife's family, to help them sell a surplus stock of Greek grapes and grape juice in London in 1900. Their Crown Grape Wine Company (on the site of a previous VINEGAR plant) eventually became Vine Products, whose premises outside the capital in Kingston-upon-Thames were described in the 1960s, in a reference to its production of sherry-style wines, as 'the biggest BODEGA in Europe'. This highly profitable concern was eventually taken over by Allied Breweries and, by the 1970s, was being run, somewhat incongruously, in tandem with HARVEYS of Bristol, the principal producers of real SHERRY.

Abbott, J. H. C., *British Wines* (London, 1975).

Brix, scale of measuring total dissolved compounds in grape juice, and therefore its approximate concentration of grape sugars. It is used in the United States and, like other scales used elsewhere (see BAUMÉ and OECHSLE), it can be measured with either a REFRACTOMETER or HYDROMETER. Degrees Brix indicate the percentage of solutes (of which about 90 per cent are sugars in ripe grapes) by weight in the liquid, at a temperature specified for the instrument used. One degree Brix corresponds approximately to 10 g/l sugar.

The **Balling** scale is similar although the specified temperature may differ.   B.G.C.

Broadbent, J. Michael (1927-), wine taster, writer, and auctioneer known particularly for his experience of fine, old wines. Broadbent trained initially as an architect in London but was not as enthused by its more prosaic aspects as by the fine wines to which a family friend had introduced him. He joined the late Tommy Layton as a wine trade trainee in 1952. Three years later he joined HARVEYS of Bristol, then in its heyday, where he worked for Harry WAUGH and eventually became UK sales director. In 1966, partly as a result of his own personal enterprise in corresponding with the chairman, Broadbent was taken on by Christie's to revive their wine AUCTION business. From then until 1992 he ran Christie's wine

department and in that capacity traded in and tasted a greater number of fine and rare wines than anyone else in the world.

Naturally didactic, he has been lecturing on wine since the late 1950s and it is as a conductor of wine tastings that he is distinguished. He sees it as his duty to ensure that tasting conditions are correct, and has no inhibitions about airing his elegant wine vocabulary in public. His passion is not for wine consumption, or for the relaxed sociability associated with it, but for the rigorous analysis of each measured mouthful of wine (he sees his wristwatch as an important TASTING accessory, monitoring how a wine evolves in the glass). In his architect's handwriting, he has recorded his disciplined impressions of every wine tasted, nearly 90,000 of them in more than 140 notebooks.

It is these notebooks, retyped by his equally hard-working wife Daphne, which form the basis for Broadbent's *Great Vintage Wine Book* and the more discursive *Vintage Wine*, unique records of wine-tasting history which stretch back to wines of the early 18th century. Unlike PARKER, his most obvious rival, Broadbent eschews scoring wines with NUMBERS between 50 and 100, but does award up to five stars to each wine.

As a result of his prominence as a literate and articulate wine taster, he is invited to attend and often conduct tastings of particularly grand or historic wines, many of these events arranged specifically around his frenetic international schedule.

Broadbent's life has been marked by competition, particularly with Sotheby's, and ambition. While at Christie's he not only wrote his own classic on the subject of *Wine Tasting*, first published in 1968 and much republished since, but instituted and directed Christie's Wine Publications, which issued many invaluable books—including the *Christie's Wine Review* anthologies—during the 1970s and 1980s. He has also written a monthly column of tasting notes for the British magazine *Decanter* since its inception.

Incurably active and apparently indefatigable, he became a MASTER OF WINE in 1960, a freeman of the City of London in 1964, chairman of the Institute of Masters of Wine in 1970, international president of the INTERNATIONAL WINE & FOOD SOCIETY in 1986, master of the City of London's Distillers' Company in 1990, council chairman of the Wine & Spirit Trades Benevolent Society in 1991, and even stood for sheriff of the City of London in 1993. He was made a Chevalier de l'Ordre du Mérite National in 1979. His son Bartholomew could be said to have helped establish the United States as the prime market for vintage PORT in the 1990s.

Parnell, C., 'Michael Broadbent: man of great taste', *Decanter* (Mar 1992).
Suckling, J., 'The world's most experienced taster', *The Wine Spectator* (15 Nov 1991).

Brock, leading university in CANADA for wine-related ACADEME. It is home to the Cool Climate Oenology and Viticulture Institute (CCOVI) established in 1996. Graduates make wine all over the world with particularly large contingents in California and Ontario. CCOVI is also the home of North America's only undergraduate degree programme in the study of COOL CLIMATE grape growing and wine-making. Student exchange programmes include partnerships with Okanagan University College in British Columbia, the Nova Scotia Agricultural College, LINCOLN University in New Zealand, the University of Udine in Italy, and DIJON. In viticulture, studies include the effects on wine quality of different vine training systems, vine spacing, irrigation, and shoot thinning; Niagara TERROIR using GPS, control of disease (particularly POWDERY MILDEW) and pests (particularly ASIAN LADY BEETLE), the elucidation of odour-active compounds in Canadian ICEWINES, and the effects of CANOPY MANAGEMENT and oenological treatments on red wine composition and taste. Studies in wine-making have focused, non exclusively, on the production of Icewine. L.Br.

brokers, important members of any trade, and increasingly important in the wine trade. Known charmingly as *courtiers* in French, brokers can play a vital role as middlemen between vine-growers and merchants, or NÉGOCIANTS, collecting and exhibiting hundreds of samples, or *échantillons*, taking a small percentage of any eventual sale. Another class of brokers, further along the distribution chain, guide those who sell wine through the maze of those who produce it, some of them nursing 'stables' of producers rather in the manner of a literary agent representing a rollcall of authors. And then, just one or two links away from those who actually pull the cork, there are the fine wine brokers, those who sell from a list of glamorous properties and vintages which may, but often do not, belong to them.

This last group, most of whom are based in Britain clustered round the two major AUCTION houses like bees round a honeypot, represents one of the very few sectors of the wine trade that has been highly profitable. Several London firms did extremely well in the 1990s as the number of wine COLLECTORS and INVESTORS around the world increased exponentially and ASIA woke up to the delights of fine wine; Farr Vintners regularly sell more wine than Sotheby's and Christie's combined. The sort of wine of interest to this new breed of wine merchant typically sits in an unbroken CASE in a BONDED WAREHOUSE in Britain while being traded so profitably around the world. The profitability of this business was so obviously attractive to traditional MERCHANTS more used to trading and delivering individual bottles and cases of much less valuable wine that in the early and mid 1990s many of them set up

their own broking divisions. Much of these brokers' trade is between their own established customers.

Brouilly, largest of the Beaujolais crus, produces some of the most robust, most textured of these red wines. About 1,300 ha/3,200 acres of vineyards flank the volcanic Mont Brouilly. **Côte de Brouilly** is an entirely separate appellation including just 310 ha/770 acres of land higher up the hillside. The wine produced tends to be more concentrated and longer lived than that of Brouilly. Ch de Thivin is a landmark producer. For more details, see BEAUJOLAIS.

Brulhois, Côtes du, red wine VDQS in SOUTH WEST FRANCE. About 190 ha/470 acres of Bordeaux vine varieties plus the Gascon TANNAT with a little FER are still grown in the rolling farmland down river of Moissac on both sides of the river Garonne. From medieval times the Brulhois wines of the HAUT PAYS were blended with those of Bordeaux down river but the ravages of PHYLLOXERA in the late 19th century were followed by widespread planting of HYBRIDS. The district's wines made from recently replanted VINIFERA vines were given VIN DE PAYS status initially before an elevation to VDQS in 1985. The wines are usually well coloured and the best can offer a good meeting-point between Gascon and Bordelais influences. Most are made by one of the two CO-OPERATIVES and consumed locally.

Brunello, conventionally the name for a strain of SANGIOVESE particularly well adapted to the vineyards of Montalcino in TOSCANA in central Italy producing most notably, therefore, BRUNELLO DI MONTALCINO. Today, it is accepted that Brunello is a local name for the Sangiovese grape, and that six to eight different clones of Sangiovese are planted in Montalcino.

Brunello di Montalcino, youngest of Italy's prestigious red wines, having been invented as a wine in its own right by Ferruccio BIONDI-SANTI, the first to bottle it and give it a distinctive name, in 1888. Conventional descriptions of the birth of the wine stress Biondi-Santi's successful isolation of a superior CLONE of SANGIOVESE, the Sangiovese Grosso or BRUNELLO, but enthusiastic descriptions of the wines of Montalcino by Cosimo Ridolfi (1831), and the fact that a wine of Clemente Santi, described as a 'select red wine (brunello)', had been a prize-winning entry in the agricultural fair of Montepulciano in 1865, indicate that genetically superior material was available in the zone at an earlier date. (And some records show the wines of Montalcino referred to as Brunello as early as the 14th century; see TOSCANA, history.)

Climate is perhaps a more significant factor than specific clones in creating the characteristics of the wine: the town of Montalcino,

112 km/70 miles south of Florence, enjoys a warmer, drier climate than the various zones of CHIANTI. Indeed, it is the most arid of all Tuscan DOCG zones, with an annual rainfall of about 700 mm/28 in (compared with over 900 in central Chianti Classico). In addition, a cool maritime breeze from the south west ensures both excellent ventilation and cool evenings and nights. Sangiovese reaches its maximum ripeness here, giving fuller, richer wines than anywhere else in Toscana, whose ALCOHOLIC STRENGTH is frequently over 14 per cent and whose levels of dry EXTRACT approach 30 g/l.

Popular myth has it that Brunello di Montalcino is the only important Tuscan red wine whose Sangiovese has never been blended with other varieties but this is not true. Prior to 1968 when DOC regulations, written largely by Biondi-Santi, were introduced, it was common for the few producers to augment their Sangiovese with other varieties in the zone. Biondi-Santi was an exception, so his monovarietal view prevailed. Following the earlier tradition, some producers currently add Merlot and Cabernet Sauvignon to their wines in order to give them an appeal they have been unable to achieve in either the vineyard or the cellar.

The oenological practices of first Ferruccio Biondi-Santi and then his son Tancredi Biondi-Santi—prolonged FERMENTATION and five to six years' CASK AGEING for the superior RISERVA—established a model of Brunello as a full, intense, and long-lasting wine. Only four vintages—1888, 1891, 1925, 1945—were declared in the first 57 years of production, contributing an aura of rarity to the wine that translated into high prices and, in Italy at least, incomparable prestige. The Biondi-Santi were the only commercial producers until after the Second World War and a government report of 1932 named Brunello as an exclusive product of the family and estimated its total annual production at just 200 hl/5,280 gal.

Even in 1960, there were only 11 bottlers, rising to 25 in 1970, 53 in 1980, 87 in 1990, and 175 in 2005. The total area planted was a mere 63.5 ha/157 acres in 1960, but it had jumped to 626 ha in 1980, 1,250 ha in 1993, and was almost 2,000 ha in 2004. Substantial amounts of outside capital have gone in to restoring vineyards and wine-making facilities and many small peasant proprietors also began to bottle their own Brunello in the 1980s and 1990s. Although the better wines have been widely in demand at high prices, quality levels have undeniably been irregular. The dubious condition of many of the casks and the lengthy obligatory ageing periods regardless of the characteristics of the vintage were sometimes deleterious.

The DOC regulations of 1960 established a minimum period of cask ageing of 42 months, confirmed in 1980 by the DOCG rules. The minimum cask ageing period was lowered to 36 months in 1990 and then to two years in 1998. Total ageing before release, however, remains 48 months, four months of which must be in bottle prior to release. Barrique ageing has become standard in Montalcino, as in other parts of Toscana. Some producers balance the oak with the wine better than others.

Stylistically, the zone can be split in two. On the GALESTRO soils in the northern part of the zone, the vineyards tend to be at a higher altitude than those in the south, whereas around Sant'Angelo in Colle the soil has more clay and the average temperature is higher. As a result, the harvest in the southern part of the zone is usually a week earlier than in the northern part, and the wines are fuller and more forward than the more aromatic wines from the north. As a result, some of the zone's producers have vineyards in both the north and south to give them the balance they seek.

Among Montalcino's better producers are Altesino, Argiano, Banfi, Case Basse, Costanti, Eredi Fuligni, Fossacolle, Lisini, Pieve di Santa Restituta (Gaja), and Poggio Antico.

The financial burden imposed by the lengthy ageing period has led to a corresponding increase in the production of Rosso di Montalcino, a red DOC wine that can be marketed after one year, with over 1.6 million bottles produced in 1995. (Brunello di Montalcino production totalled 3.5 million bottles in the same period, only 40 per cent of the theoretical potential of the zone.) The availability of a second DOC into which lesser wines can be declassified has, despite the quibbles expressed above, had a positive impact on the quality of Brunello, in addition to its obvious advantages for the cash flow of producers.

See also VINO NOBILE DI MONTEPULCIANO.

D.T. & D.C.G.

Brun Fourca, ancient Provençal vine associated with but hardly grown in PALETTE.

brush, the flesh remaining attached to the top of the berry stalk, or stem, after a grape is pulled off the bunch, as occurs during MECHANICAL HARVESTING or DESTEMMING, for example. The brush's size varies between vine varieties, from a barely discernible bit of flesh to a 'tongue' up to 5 mm/0.2 in long. The brush is caused by strong adhesion between the berry and stem, causing tearing of the skin, combined with particular characteristics of the zone of the flesh at the base of the berry. The cells of the brush are rich in TANNINS. The French term is *pinceau*.

The word brush is also used in the US for the total cane growth evident after leaf fall.

B.G.C.

brut, French word meaning 'crude' or 'raw', adapted by the CHAMPAGNE industry for wines made without (much) added sweetening or DOSAGE. It has come to be used widely for any SPARKLING WINE to indicate one that tastes

bone dry. Technically a brut champagne should contain fewer than 15 g/l RESIDUAL SUGAR, a maximum level which, in less naturally acidic still wines, would seem medium dry (see SWEETNESS). A wine labelled **extra brut** should contain less than 6 g/l residual sugar and may incorporate no dosage at all. Particularly dry wines may also be labelled **brut natur(e)**. These have less than 3 g/l residual sugar and are made without dosage. The word **bruto** may be used in Portugal.

Bual, Anglicized form of BOAL.

Buçaco, range of forested hills between DÃO and BAIRRADA in central Portugal where the Palace Hotel bottles some of the country's most sought-after wines. For more details, see BAIRRADA.

Bucelas, historic white wine, formerly spelt **Bucellas**, now a DOC, enjoying a revival of interest in its native Portugal. At one time it was fortified and it is thought to be Shakespeare's Charneco, mentioned in *2 Henry VI* and named after one of the local villages. The Duke of Wellington popularized the wine in Britain following the Peninsular Wars and for a time Bucelas was widely sold and appreciated in Victorian Britain as Portuguese Hock. (This undoubtedly helped to perpetuate the story that the ARINTO grape, the main variety in Bucelas, was related to Germany's RIESLING, a theory that does not stand up to AMPELOGRAPHIC scrutiny. Both Arinto and its aptly named partner ESGANA CÃO, meaning 'dog strangler', share the ability to make acidic, dry white wine in a sub-Mediterranean climate.) After such an illustrious past, this tiny white wine denomination just north of Lisbon, Portugal's capital city (see map under PORTUGAL), had almost disappeared by the early 1980s, the production of Bucelas having been concentrated in the hands of a single firm who let standards slip. A number of new enterprises helped to revive an old tradition. One producer has gone further and is now making TRADITIONAL METHOD sparkling wine and late harvest Bucelas.

R.J.M.

bud, *bourgeon* in French, is the name given to a small part of the vine shoot which rests between the leaf stalk or PETIOLE and the shoot stem. In the summer it is covered by green scales, which turn brown in winter. The bud contains three miniature, compressed (primordial) shoots. Normally the best developed of these shoots (from the 'primary' bud) bursts at BUDBREAK. Grapevine buds are classified as compound and fruitful; their development is complex.

B.G.C. & R.E.S.

Budai Zöld, Transylvanian white grape grown in Hungary around Lake Balaton making deep-coloured, full-bodied wine for local consumption.

budbreak, or **budburst**, a stage of annual vine development during which small shoots emerge from vine BUDS in the spring. This process begins the new growing season and signals the end of DORMANCY, their period of winter sleep. The first sign that budbreak is imminent is BLEEDING, when the vines begin to drip water from pruning cuts. The buds left at winter pruning begin to swell in the few weeks prior to budbreak, and budbreak itself is marked by the first signs of green in the vineyard, as the first young leaves unfold and push through the bud scales.

Budbreak takes place in early spring in cool climates, when the average air temperature is about 10 °C/50 °F. For many northern hemisphere regions, budbreak occurs in March, and for the southern hemisphere in September. Budbreak is more uniform when winters are cold but not subject to WINTER FREEZE. In warm to hot regions, budbreak is earlier, and in cooler regions it is delayed. In fact in TROPICAL VITICULTURE the vines never achieve proper dormancy, and budbreak can take place at any time of the year.

Not all varieties show budbreak at the same temperature. For example, French studies indicate that for the early TABLE GRAPE Pearl of Csaba budbreak occurs at 5.6 °C, MERLOT at 9.4 °C, and UGNI BLANC at 11.0 °C. Late pruning in winter delays budbreak, and this can be used to reduce the risk of winter FROST.

In temperate regions with warm winters, a few warm days, even in midwinter, can be enough to induce bud swelling, which can lead to budbreak if the warmth persists. One of the very few places around the world to show this problem is the MARGARET RIVER region in Western Australia. Because of the nearby moderating effects of the Indian ocean, the midwinter (July) mean temperature is a warm 13 °C. CHARDONNAY vines are particularly prone to this premature budbreak, with only a few buds breaking on the vine in midwinter, and the rest somewhat erratically later in spring.

For vines which are properly pruned (see BALANCED PRUNING) most of the buds left at winter pruning will burst, and budbreak is near 100 per cent. Budbreak is, however, normally lower for buds in the middle of long CANES. (When vines are left unpruned, as in MINIMAL PRUNING, it is the buds near the ends of canes which burst preferentially, as do higher buds. This adaptive physiology helped vines to climb trees and seek sunlight in their evolutionary forest habitat.) The two buds on either side of the cane just below the pruning cut typically burst. This is because of the flow of HORMONES in the plant and is the reason for pruning to two bud spurs.

For the vine-grower, budbreak represents the beginning of about eight months' work before HARVEST, during which the vine must be protected from pests, VINE DISEASES, and trained as necessary. The biggest problem for many vineyards at this time of the year is spring FROST, to which the young shoot growth is particularly sensitive. R.E.S.

Huglin, P., *Biologie et écologie de la vigne* (Paris, 1986).

Winkler, A. J., *et al.*, *General Viticulture* (2nd edn, Berkeley, Calif., 1974).

budding, the viticultural operation of GRAFTING where only a single bud is inserted. The term is also used in the context of BUDBREAK.

budwood, name given to vine CUTTINGS when they are destined for GRAFTING. Depending on the cutting length and bud spacing, four to 12 buds may be taken from each cutting. The budwood is typically put into cold storage to await grafting in the spring.

buffering capacity, the measure of resistance to change in PH by the addition of either acids or bases.

Bugey, Vins du, collective name for the wines of the Ain *département* in the southern Jura mountains just west of SAVOIE in eastern France. In 2005, vineyards totalled 500 ha/1,250 acres and elevation from VDQS to AC status was believed imminent. Bugey was once part of Burgundy and under the medieval influence of MONKS AND MONASTERIES the area was an important wine producer. Today, almost all of its varied wines are consumed locally. About half of all wines are white, but there are rosés as well as light reds, fully sparkling wines of all colours, notably the sweet pink **Vin du Bugey Cerdon**, varietal wines as in ROUSSETTE du Bugey, and wines to which the name of a CRU may be suffixed. The vines are widely dispersed and, among reds, may be the POULSARD of Jura, the MONDEUSE of Savoie, the Gamay of Beaujolais, or the Pinot Noir of Burgundy. White grapes grown are Burgundy's Chardonnay and Aligoté; Savoie's ALTESSE (Roussette), JACQUÈRE, and MOLETTE, and even a Mondeuse Blanche. Wines sold as VARIETALS are made exclusively from that variety. Most of these wines are drunk locally, notably with the local cuisine of Bresse. A particular speciality among this disparate collection of grape varieties, wine styles, and TERROIRS is the MÉTHODE ANCESTRALE, an unusually delicate, medium sweet sparkling wine. More of this wine is made than any other in Bugey, with about 170 ha planted in the cru Cerdon. A small amount of MÉTHODE TRADITIONNELLE Cerdon is also made. These were the wines with which the notable gastronome Anthelme Brillat-Savarin grew up. W.L.

George, R., *French Country Wines* (London, 1990).

Bukettraube, white grape variety used mainly in South Africa for sweet and occasionally BOTRYTIZED dessert wines, with a slightly grapey aroma. The precise parentage of this German import is unclear, but BULGARIA has a variety known as **Buket**, and there is an Alsace variety, originating in Würzburg, known as **Bouquettraube**. Less than 300 ha/740 acres remain in South Africa and are planted mainly in cooler coastal areas. J.P. & M.F.

Bulgaria, eastern European wine producer whose western export success in the 1980s was built on inexpensive VARIETAL wines, especially Cabernet Sauvignon. Viniculture has been practised in this part of the world for more than three millennia, even if it was interrupted by Ottoman domination for nearly 500 years from 1393 to 1878 (see ISLAM). The Turks retained substantial vineyards for TABLE GRAPE production, however, so that vine-growing has been consistently one of Bulgaria's principal agricultural activities.

Geography and climate

Bulgaria is a small country just 450 km/280 miles from the western border to the Black sea and 300 km/200 miles from Romania to the north and Greece and Turkey to the south. With the exception of the Balkan mountain range, which runs east to west, vines are planted all over the country, although the modern wine industry has been based on rolling fertile flatlands. On the Transdanubian and upper Thracian plains, for example, the vineyards lie mainly between 100 and 300 m in altitude, although some south western vineyards are as high as 1,000 m/3,280 ft.

Summers tend to be hot, with temperatures up to 40 °C/104 °F, while the temperature can fall to −25 °C in winter. Although the Black sea has a moderating effect on the eastern side of the country, the climate tends to be dramatically CONTINENTAL.

The most common climatological hazards are FUNGAL DISEASES caused by humidity. In non-drought years rainfall and high temperatures combine to promote rot and both sorts of mildew. Disease control varies considerably between larger commercial wineries, which either own vineyards or are prepared to fund AGROCHEMICALS for their growers, and small growers who cannot afford SPRAYING. Irrigation and CHAPTALIZATION are not generally necessary.

History

Despite its long vinous heritage, underlined by archaeological evidence of neolithic wine production, Bulgaria's present wine industry is less than a century old and has undergone many changes, most notably the effects of the rise, and fall, of communism and of Comecon economics and politics.

At the beginning of the 20th century, most Bulgarian wineries were CO-OPERATIVES with many smallholders pooling their resources. Private estates existed but tended to be somewhat inward looking. Then in the 1930s the growth in exports of both wine and table grapes, at this stage a much more important export than wine, made the country a significant supplier to central Europe. After the war, the new communist government, established in 1947, also nationalized wine production and quickly set about rationalizing the vineyards. In 1949, the state wine and spirits monopoly Vinprom was set up to control all the commercial-scale production and trade. Holdings of barely half a hectare gave way to much larger new co-operative enterprises. These were further developed in the 1960s when agro-industrial complexes were set up to grow a wide variety of crops on a very large commercial basis.

Even so, in the 1960s new grape varieties were introduced. Native varieties MAVRUD, MELNIK, PAMID, and Gamza gave way to Cabernet Sauvignon and Merlot. Among white varieties, RKATSITELI and WELSCHRIESLING yielded to proper Riesling, Chardonnay, and Sauvignon Blanc. It was this decision, allied to Vinprom's control of production and, to a certain extent, marketing, that set the scene for Bulgarian wine in the 1980s.

The vines were planted in vast vineyards, with high training and wide spacing to allow mechanization as well as hand picking. A standard CORDON, or occasionally double GUYOT, system of vine training replaced the straggly bush systems previously used for the likes of Mavrud.

At the same time, wineries were also set up by Vinprom, independently of vine-growing, to take advantage of the new, better-quality grape produce. Initially the emphasis was on red wine production, so no great influx of new equipment was needed, although Soviet demand for sparkling and sweet wines was so great that investment in stainless steel tanks, proper FILTRATION systems, and cement vats was initially financed by the Comecon Bank of the Eastern Bloc, the principal export market for Bulgarian wine. Subsequently, new technology was subsidized by cheap loans from the Bulgarian government and repaid from the income of the rapidly increasing exports to the west.

Western expertise came with the men from Pepsico, the giant American cola manufacturers. Eager to trade their soft drink concentrate for a saleable product, they provided links with California's wine faculty at DAVIS, with Professor Maynard AMERINE, and with other western establishments and wineries. Much of the original theory of modern wine production in Bulgaria is therefore Californian in origin. Some wineries such as Suhindol and Khan Krum initially, followed by Russe, Sliven, Preslav, and Burgas benefited greatly from this. Others, for reasons of management culture, were unwilling or unable to modernize.

Recent developments

Between the mid 1960s and mid 1980s, the Bulgarian wine industry was making significant progress, in terms of both quality and

Bulgaria

○ Wine cellar

ROMANIA

Vidin
Magura

Danube

RUSSE

STORK NEST

DANUBIAN PLAIN

BLACK SEA REGION

KHAN KRUM
NOVI PAZAR
SCHUMEN
Targovishte
VARNA

SUHINDOL

PRESLAV

Balkan Mountains

SERBIA

Sofia

BLUERIDGE SLAVYANTZI

SUB-BALKAN REGION
SLIVEN

POMORIE

Korten

IAMBOL
BOURGAS

Black Sea

Stara Zagora ORIACHOVITSA

Plovdiv

THRACIAN LOWLANDS
REGION

Perushtitza ASSENOVGRAD

STRUMA
VALLEY
REGION

Haskovo
Sakar

Stambolovo

Pirin Mountains

DAMIANITZA Melnik
Petrich Harsovo

TURKEY

GREECE

0   50 km

exports of inexpensive but competently made varietals to the west, especially to Britain, to which at one stage Bulgaria was the fourth biggest supplier of red wine overall. GORBA-CHEV's arrival as Soviet premier, however, had dire consequences for Bulgarian wine. His campaign to curb alcohol consumption in the USSR involved uprooting huge tracts of Bulgarian vineyard, some but not all of inferior quality. Grape prices were then fixed every year, irrespective of quality, which encouraged the co-operatives to turn their attention away from vines to other crops. Dead, dying, or diseased vines were not replaced. Many vineyards were simply abandoned, and few were treated to any systematic training or pruning systems.

In 1985, Bulgaria produced 4.5 million hl of wine, but in 1990, probably the best vintage in 45 years, the total crop was just 1.8 million hl/40 million gal, and this at a time when exports to the west were at record levels.

In 1990, the wine sector was suddenly liberalized and Vinprom disbanded in 1991 as part of the free market reforms introduced in the wake of the fall of communism in 1989, when Bulgaria's dictator Zhivkov was finally deposed. Throughout the early 1990s,

the Bulgarian wine industry was in disarray. Small-scale land restitution to those who could prove they owned it before 1947 was maladroitly handled. Rampant inflation took its toll on the domestic market and the export market was in the throes of substantial re-organization in response to the realities of the new free market economy. In the late 1990s, in a country where factories and collective farms seemed more often derelict than operational, the wine industry did at least move slowly forward with the process of privatization—although it took until 1999 for the largest state-owned wineries to be privatized, in most cases by management buy-outs. Foreign investment in the initial privatization process was virtually non-existent, unlike neighbouring HUNGARY, for example.

In the 2000s, many wineries have found themselves in trading difficulties, due to falling sales, reliance on bank loans, and lack of investment. A further round of secondary privatization and takeovers is taking place, with investment largely from foreign sources or, if Bulgarian, from outside the wine industry. See details of prominent specific wineries below.

With more obviously positive results, a number of smaller boutique wineries emerged

in the early 21st century making premium wines and investing in vineyards. Ch de Val in Gradetz valley near Vidin is owned by US-based robotics manufacturer Val Markov; Santa Sarah is a GARAGISTE operation owned by Bulgarian Ivo Genowski, a wine importer based in Germany; Ivan Todorov has invested money made from construction into his Todoroff winery also near Plovdiv and is developing vineyards; and the Bessa Valley project at Pazardijk near Plovdiv, owned by Stephan von Neipperg of Ch Canon La Gaffelière in St-Emilion with German partner Karl Hauptmann, has produced wine under the Enira label from the 2003 vintage. Maxxima is an ambitious NÉGOCIANT operation owned by two Bulgarian winemakers who since 2000 have sought out superior parcels of grapes all over the country.

Vineyards

The landscape of the Bulgarian wine industry has changed dramatically since the fall of the Iron Curtain and even more so since the completion of privatization. Vineyards were seriously neglected once it was clear that land would be returned to former ownership, but the process of identifying pre-1947 owners and resolving family disputes took until the late 1990s. Unfortunately this process has resulted in tiny, fragmented land holdings (under 0.5 ha on average), often owned by people with no experience in viticulture and who too often work abroad or in Bulgaria's cities. Many plots have been abandoned entirely.

Ministry of Agriculture statistics for 2004 show a vineyard area of 129,580 ha/320,000 acres, including around 34,000 ha of unmaintained or abandoned vineyards, and nearly 6,000 ha of table grapes. Approximately 53,000 ha are planted to red varieties. Registration of growers by the National Vine & Wine Chamber is proceeding—15,000 individual growers had registered by May 2005.

Another problem for Bulgaria is the age of its vine stock. Data for 2000 show 110,000 ha as over 20 years old, and 50,000 of those over 30 years old. New plantings have been severely limited by the difficulty of identifying owners and parcellation. Wineries frequently have teams dedicated solely to negotiating land purchases—each of which may require contracts with several hundred growers.

Because wineries have been so underfunded, EU funds have been made available for new plantings through the SAPARD (Special Accession Program for Agricultural and Rural Development) programme, which refunds 51 per cent of an investment. Most of the major commercial wineries have planted or are planning to plant vineyards to give better control over fruit quality and price, but in the mid 2000s only Stork Nest Estates claimed to be virtually self-sufficient.

Since Bulgaria's export peak in 1995-6, wine quality has suffered through inconsistency and poor fruit quality. Lack of vertical integration between growers and wineries, along with conflicting interests (growers want to pick early to ensure revenue and avoid theft) has meant substantial volumes being picked too early, while green and unripe. In addition, by 2004 Bulgaria had twice the crushing capacity it needed and competition for grapes forced prices up.

Harvest volumes in 2004 were estimated at 350,000 to 400,000 tonnes, although only around 200,000 tonnes were used by commercial wineries, giving 1.4 million hl/37 million gal of wine, meaning home production is still dominant. Average yields nationwide are estimated at only 4 tonnes/ha, although newer plantings can easily produce 7–8 tonnes/ha.

Markets

A developing professional middle class in Bulgarian cities is expected to increase the domestic market for bottled wine but it is prohibitively expensive for most country dwellers. Bulgaria also has a strong spirits culture, especially for the local *rakia*, of which almost 90 million bottles are consumed each year compared with around 28 million bottles of wine.

Exports accounted for 64 per cent of wine production by volume in 2004, showing an 11 per cent rise since 2001. Major markets are Russia, Poland, UK, and Germany, with sales to the former Soviet Union growing and sales to the west falling.

Winemaking

Foreign investment and SAPARD funds have been used to fund winery renovations and the installation of stainless steel, including ROTARY FERMENTERS, across Bulgaria, although Soviet-style concrete tanks are still widely used and may be lined with wax. Oak use is widespread, although until well into the 21st century barrels tended to be old and less than hygienic. OAK CHIPS are commonly used and improvements in COOPERAGE have meant that Bulgarian oak can be acceptable if seasoned properly. Some of the first foreign winemakers to work in Bulgaria were Australian Trevor Tucker at Stork Nest Estates, Frenchman Marc Dworkin at Bessa Valley, and Swedish winemaker Lars Torstenson at Assenovgrad.

Grape varieties

Red varieties account for about 63 per cent of plantings with whites dominating only the eastern Black Sea region. There are significant areas of such popular INTERNATIONAL VARIETIES as Cabernet Sauvignon (13,000 ha) and Merlot (14,000 ha). Other important varieties include the local PAMID (28,200 ha), which is claimed to be one of Bulgaria's oldest local varieties, but its light body, low acidity and low extract means at best it produces light table wines for early consumption. Gamza, the KADARKA of Hungary, is widely planted in the north of the country where it has a tendency to overproduce but can make interestingly spicy wines if the growing season is long enough. More interesting to many palates are the indigenous red grape varieties MAVRUD, grown mainly around Plovdiv and now the most popular varietal wine on the home market, where it is preferred in a tannic and extensively oak aged style. MELNIK is grown exclusively in the south west around the towns of Melnik, Sandinski, and Harsovo. It is very late ripening and can require extensive ageing. RUBIN is regarded by some as the variety with most potential to become Bulgaria's signature grape and is currently very much in demand. Some interestingly rich-fruited versions are now being made, notably by Damianitza and Santa Sarah. Bulgarian researchers have been enthusiastic developers of crosses, and another that shows some promise is Ruen, a Cabernet × Melnik cross registered for the south west. A number of lower quality varieties developed primarily for disease resistance are locally important such as dark-skinned Storgozia (a crossing of the local Buket with Villard Blanc) and Shevka. There is also some of the Georgian variety SAPERAVI imported from the Soviet Union.

Bulgaria grows a curious mix of white grape varieties, showing evidence of SERBIAN influence in its everyday DIMIAT (9,500 ha) and Georgian influence in its plantings of RKATSITELI (11,700 ha). Central European influence is evident in its WELSCHRIESLING, MUSCAT OTTONEL (3,600 ha, known as 'Misket Ottonel') and a local pink-skinned variety called MISKET Cherven, or Red Misket (4,700 ha), which produces distinctly grapey white wines, is mainly grown in the Rose Valley Sub-Balkan region, and is particularly noted for its frost resistance. Chardonnay (2,344 ha) is the fifth most planted white variety followed by Ugni Blanc (2,300 ha), while Riesling, Sauvignon, Aligoté, and Gewürztraminer are also grown.

The regions and quality designations

Although vines are grown all over Bulgaria, the country has generally been divided into five distinct wine regions: Danubian Plain, Rose Valley or Sub-Balkan region, Thracian Lowlands region, Black Sea region, and South West or Struma Valley region. The only part of Bulgaria which has no real wine production is the area round the capital Sofia. However, in the mid 2000s, the EU accepted just two wine regions for Bulgaria, which will be the Danubian Plain (the northern half of the country) and the Thracian Lowlands (the southern half). These will also be the two 'table wine with geographical indication' categories (or regional wines, equivalent to Vin de Pays). In addition are two quality wine categories: Quality wines with declared geographical origin (DGO) and Quality wines with guaranteed and controlled appellation of origin (the term Controliran may be used for this). There are 47 denominated regions for these quality wines.

In the mid 2000s, it was common for wineries to source grapes from all over Bulgaria and, because in many cases grapes are vinified outside the region where the grapes were grown, some of Bulgaria's top boutique wines do not qualify as quality wines. The winery, and its level of equipment, expertise, and commitment, plus any vineyards it owns or controls, remains the most important quality determinant for Bulgarian wine.

Danubian Plain and Black Sea region This area runs from Vidin in the north west across to Russe, then to the Black sea, and south to the Balkan foothills. The region's wineries, of which some are very important, take their grapes from the rolling Transdanubian plain, the Danube to the north providing water and moderation of summer temperatures. Key wineries include:

Russe or Rousse: a large-scale, well-equipped winery at Bulgaria's fourth city on the Danube and the Romanian border, under Russian ownership since 2003. Crushed 10,000 tonnes in 2004 and owned nearly 500 ha/1,235 acres in 2005.

Suhindol: possibly Bulgaria's best-known winery in the early 1990s when it was a major exporter to western markets, specializing in red wines, particularly Gamza, Cabernet, and Merlot. Another production site at Pavlikeni. Crushed 7,000 tonnes in 2004 and owned 2,000 ha in 2005.

Stork Nest Estates: the former Svishtov winery right on the Danube, now foreign-owned with an Australian winemaker. Owned 428 ha and almost self-sufficient in mid 2005.

Magura Winery: sources from approx 250 ha in the north west. Historically known for sparkling wines, including Bulgaria's only bottle-fermented examples, but otherwise mainly reds.

Festa Holdings: owns both Black Sea Gold at Pomorie and Vincom Bourgas (or Burgas) wineries near the coast making mainly whites.

Vinex Slavyantzi: based in the Sub-Balkan region, with five production sites and crushing around 15,000 tonnes, including substantial volumes for vermouth sold in Poland.

Targovischte: inland winery producing mainly whites for the domestic market.

Vinex Preslav, Khan Krum: both wineries owned by Strandzha Wine Cellar in Rosenovo. Known for white wines. Khan Krum reported to have crushed 2500 tonnes in 2004, Vinex Preslav crushed around 5,000 tonnes.

Thracian Lowlands, Struma Valley, and Sub-Balkan region Vast area on the flat upper Thracian plain from the Pirin mountains to the Black sea, producing cereals, rice, and a wide range of crops other than grapes. Main wineries include:

Vini Sliven: on the south eastern foothills of the Balkans, once Bulgaria's biggest producer but crush had fallen to under 20,000 tonnes by 2004; making spirits too. Same owner as 340-ha/840-acre Villa Liubimec project near Liubimetz.

Blueridge: impressive Australian-designed winery outside Sliven. Part of Domaine Boyar group, which also includes wineries at Schumen and Korten and a small premium vineyard at Elenovo. Joint venture with Italian textile manufacturer Miroglio for vineyard plantings. The group crushed 8,000 tonnes in 2004.

Belvedere Group: owns Domaine Menada (Stara Zagora), Sakar, Oriachovitza, and a 225-ha new Domaine Katerina vineyard project in the border zone. Also in partnership with Brestovitza co-operative near Plovdiv for Mavrud and Rubin. Estimated crush 15,000 tonnes.

Bessa Valley: winery and more than 100 ha of red wine vines planted on abandoned land in the village of Ognianovo near Plovdiv, Bulgaria's second city.

Vinzavod Assenovgrad: near Plovdiv, best known for reds, with robust Mavrud an Assenovgrad speciality. Swedish micro-winery with Lars Torstenson of Domaine Rabiega based here.

Peshtera Group: leading Bulgarian spirits group bought Vinis Iambol in 2004, adding to wineries at Saedinaenie and Vinprom-Pleven.

Owns 350 ha of vines and is aiming to increase to 1,300 ha. Estimated crush of 30,000 tonnes per annum.

Damianitza: based in the warm south west of the country by the Greek border and most notable for the picturesque town of MELNIK. Owned by publisher Philip Harmandjiev, Damianitza winery is the third biggest in Bulgaria in turnover due to its premium wines. One of the first wineries to launch a top end ICON WINE Redark. Also specializes in Bulgarian crosses and has trialled Italian varieties and Tempranillo.   C.G.

www.bulgarianwines.org/ (website of National Vines and Wine Chamber)
Bulgarian supplement, *Harpers* (July, 2005).
Peskett, S., 'Arrested development', *Harpers* (Oct 2004).

bulk method, alternative name for the Charmat or tank method of SPARKLING WINE-MAKING.

bulk storage of wine is important in the production and BLENDING of everyday commercial wines. Large storage tanks are usually made of stainless steel and may hold as much as 800,000 l/176,000 gal. OXIDATION is always a risk and, if the tank is not completely filled with wine, the head space must be filled with an INERT GAS. The lower its storage temperature, the better such a wine will keep. Many commercial blends are bottled throughout the year from such tanks, which are kept at relatively low temperatures. If consumers were to become more demanding of individuality in their wines, these large storage containers would become rarer and the wineries of the future might have only small and medium-sized storage containers.   A.D.W.

bulk transport of wine is the movement of large quantities of wine within a single winery or from one place to another, typically from where it was held in BULK STORAGE to the BOTTLING location, which may not even be in the same hemisphere.

Wine is most commonly transported in bulk from one installation to another by road tanker and/or ocean-going tank ships, although rail and barge are not unknown as means of transporting wine over long distances (while pipelines are occasionally used over short distances).

Whenever wine is moved, it is important to guard against OXIDATION. Danger points include the seals on pumps. Wine being delivered to a receiving tank should be filled from the bottom to prevent excessive aeration of the wine. If the tank must be filled from the top, then the tank should be filled with an INERT GAS such as nitrogen or carbon dioxide to displace any OXYGEN.   A.D.W.

bulk wine, or wine *en vrac*, as the French call it, is wine that is ready to drink, but has not been put into smaller CONTAINERS such as

BOTTLES. This may be because it is about to be packaged, or because it will be sold to another producer. Most of the wine that is sold in bulk is marketed at less than 10 US dollars per bottle, and is not meant for long term ageing. BULK TRANSPORT is by far the cheapest way of moving wine and it is common for wine to move in bulk between producer and blender or bottler, possibly between continents and hemispheres.

In Europe, Germany has emerged as the major importer of bulk wine from the New World, buying mainly red wine from Chile, Argentina, California, Australia, and South Africa. Most of this is sold through importers/bottlers in Germany and then bottled for various discount chains. China has emerged as a significant buyer of bulk wine, sourced wherever it is cheapest. The UK remains a significant market for bulk wine, both for brands and for private labels, a continuation of the country's wine BOTTLING tradition.

When SURPLUS PRODUCTION became an increasingly geographically widespread phenomenon in the early 21st century, the bulk wine market became an important feature of international wine trade, helped considerably by online trading.

Brokers of bulk wine follow the bulk markets daily and provide information to their client base. The internet has been a significant tool in managing and communicating up-to-date market information but few companies formed in the internet boom days, in the hope of replacing more traditional BROKERS, have survived because ebuyers need more information than price and location.

Bulk wine may even be sold in measured quantities drawn off from some form of BULK STORAGE. In southern Europe it is still commonplace to take a container, perhaps a BONBONNE or large plastic container, to be filled with bulk wine, which is charged by the litre.

Bullas, growing wine-producing zone in Spain's LEVANTE, now a DO. It shares many features with neighbouring JUMILLA and YECLA, including the predominance of the MONASTRELL grape.

Bull's Blood, historic and robust style of red wine made in HUNGARY, known as Bikavér in Hungarian. The town of EGER was most famously associated with it, producing a wine named Egri Bikavér within Hungary. As the export BRAND Bull's Blood, it enjoyed notable success in the 1970s, then produced exclusively by the state-owned Egervin winery, which shrouded the product in possibly convenient mystery. According to regulations drawn up in 2005, the wine must theoretically contain all theses varieties—KÉKFRANKOS, PORTUGIESER, KADARKA (traditionally the mainstay of the blend), BLAUBURGER, KÉKMEDOC, ZWEIGELT, CABERNET FRANC, CABERNET SAUVIGNON, MERLOT, and PINOT NOIR—none of them representing more than 50 per cent of the blend. The wines were the product of longer MACERATION than was perhaps common at the time, and the blend was certainly given some age before bottling. Today, Bikavér, based on Kadarka, is also made in Szekszárd, where the term was first used, at the end of the 19th century.

bunch, or cluster, the viticultural term for that part of the grapevine to which berries are attached. *Grappe* is the French term. Before the berries SET, each berry position is occupied by a flower; a bunch is an INFLORESCENCE of the vine after berries have set. In the grapevine the inflorescence grows at the node on the side of the stem opposite to a leaf, an unusual position within the plant kingdom. It is closely related to a TENDRIL, both deriving from the same embryonic organ, the anlage. Depending on the time of development, anlagen produce bunches, tendrils, or SECOND CROP.

Like a tendril, a grape bunch has two arms, called outer and inner. The inner arm develops the bulk of the bunch, while the outer arm may vary in form from a large, well-set 'wing' (as in UGNI BLANC) to a small tendril arm without berries, or it may even abort. Berries on wings sometimes ripen differently from those on the main crop.

Bunches vary hugely in size depending on that year's FRUIT SET and VINE VARIETY, from a few grams to many kilograms. They also vary in shape and tightness depending on the lengthening and flexibility of the BUNCHSTEM and branches and, of course, on setting and BERRY SIZE. B.G.C.

bunch rots, or **berry rots**, occur in vines all over the world and can be caused by many species of fungi including YEASTS and BACTERIA. Yield losses can be as high as 80 per cent and wine made from rotten fruit often smells and tastes tainted, typically mouldy, with a perceptible loss of fruit flavour. Vineyards badly infected with bunch rots themselves have a distinctive and unpleasant smell. Wet weather at HARVEST causes the worst cases of bunch rot, especially if grape skins are broken. The best known of the bunch rots is BOTRYTIS BUNCH ROT.

Some fungi, such as *Botrytis*, *Alternaria*, and *Cladosporium*, can infect healthy berries and these are called 'primary invaders'. 'Secondary invaders' such as *Aspergillus*, *Rhizopus*, and *Penicillium* gain access to berries split by rain, bird or insect attack, or diseases such as DOWNY MILDEW and POWDERY MILDEW, ESCA, or HAIL disease. So-called SOUR ROT is due to a mix of fungi, yeasts, acetic acid bacteria, and fruit fly larvae. Control measures can include SPRAYING, bunch thinning, increasing fruit exposure to wind and sun (see CANOPY MANAGEMENT), and avoiding other pests and diseases which can break berry skins. (See also FUNGAL DISEASES.) R.E.S.

Emmett, R. W., Harris, A. R., Taylor, R. H., and McGechan, J. K., 'Grape diseases and vineyard protection', in B. G. Coombe and P. R. Dry (eds.), *Viticulture*, ii: *Practices* (Adelaide, 1992).

Pearson, R. C., and Goheen, A. C., *Compendium of Grape Diseases* (St Paul, Minn., 1988).

bunchstem, the stem of a grapevine inflorescence, or bunch of grapes, known by botanists as the peduncle and in French as a *rafle*. The form of the bunchstem, especially the position and length of lateral branches, determines the shape of the BUNCH and is one of many characters used to identify vine varieties in the science of AMPELOGRAPHY. Winemakers often refer to bunchstems as stems or stalks (see DESTALKING, for instance). B.G.C.

bunchstem necrosis, or **BSN**, physiological condition which causes grape bunchstems to shrivel and die during RIPENING. This condition is also known as water berry in California, shanking in New Zealand, *Stiellähme* in Germany, and *dessèchement de la rafle* in French. Affected berries do not ripen properly and shrivel on the bunch, although it is rare for all berries to be affected. CABERNET SAUVIGNON vines are particularly prone to this disorder. Affected berries have lower SUGARS, ANTHOCYANINS, and fatty acids, but higher ACIDITY. The cause is unknown, but factors associated with the condition are vigorous shoot growth, the weather at FLOWERING, and levels of MAGNESIUM, CALCIUM, and ammonium in the plant tissue. Yield can be severely reduced, especially with MECHANICAL HARVESTING, as affected berries fall off. Wines can taste bitter and are poorly coloured. There is no widely accepted control, although magnesium sprays at VERAISON have sometimes reduced the problem. A similar disorder affects inflorescences at flowering and has been termed **early bunchstem necrosis**, or 'inflorescence necrosis'. R.E.S.

bung. A bung, made of glass, plastic, rubber, earthenware, silicone, or wood, is a barrel's stopper, analogous to the cork of a bottle. It is inserted in a **bung-hole**. If a barrel is stored so that the bung is at its highest point, this position is called **bung up** and the bung may be left so that gas can escape from the bung-hole. Some bungs even incorporate a device that encourages this. If a barrel is stored with the bung at either two or ten o'clock, the position is called **bung over**.

Since OXYGEN tends to enter a barrel around the bung-hole, silicone bungs are sometimes used to keep a particularly tight fit. These silicone bungs also have the advantage of being gentler on the **bung stave**, the stave in which the bung-hole is drilled, which is weakened and sometimes cracked by the constant hammering needed on wooden bungs.

Depending on the amount of evaporation (see BARREL MAINTENANCE and WOOD INFLUENCE), and the spare time available to the winery staff, TOPPING UP is done anywhere from twice a week to once every six weeks. In Bordeaux the bung is left at the top of the barrel so as to maximize AERATION of the young wine for the first six months, after which the barrel is rolled to one side so that the bung is in the so-called bung-over position. Thus the bung and bung-hole region are kept moist and aeration is reduced. Many New World wineries have adopted this practice, even for varieties as relatively fragile as Pinot Noir, as it is much less labour intensive than constant topping up.

Traditionally in Bordeaux and Burgundy barrels are filled through the top bung but racked via a RACKING bung on the head of the barrel. M.K.

Burgenland, umbrella wine area in AUSTRIA of 14,560 ha/36,000 acres, that comprises Neusiedlersee, Neusiedlersee-Hügelland, Mittelburgenland, and Südburgenland in the far east of the country on the Hungarian border. It is most famous for sweet white wines and for red wines made of local Blaufränksich, Zweigelt, and St-Laurent grapes.

Burger, white grape variety that was once very important in CALIFORNIA, where it was the state's most planted VINIFERA variety, having been promoted by one pioneer as greatly superior to the MISSION grape. The ampelographer GALET has identified it as the almost extinct southern French variety Monbadon that was cultivated to a limited extent in the Languedoc until the 1980s. It produces sizeable quantities of neutral wine. In the mid 2000s, it was planted on just 1,500 acres/600 ha, mainly in the hot SAN JOAQUIN VALLEY, many of them planted in the early 1980s.

Burgunder, common suffix in German, meaning literally 'of BURGUNDY', for such grape variety members of the PINOT family as Spätburgunder, Blauer Spätburgunder, Blauburgunder, or Blauer Burgunder (PINOT NOIR); Weissburgunder or Weisser Burgunder (PINOT BLANC); and Grauburgunder (drier styles of PINOT GRIS).

Burgund Mare means 'big Burgundian' in ROMANIA and is the local name for BLAUFRÄNKISCH.

Burgundy, known as BOURGOGNE in French, province of eastern France famous for its great red and white wines produced mostly from PINOT NOIR and CHARDONNAY grapes respectively. The province includes the viticultural regions of the Côte de Nuits and Côte de Beaune in the *département* of the CÔTE D'OR, the Côte CHALONNAISE and MÂCONNAIS in the Saône-et-Loire *département*, and CHABLIS and the wines of AUXERRE in the Yonne *département*. In 2003, the total area of Burgundy vineyard was 28,530 ha/ 70,470 acres.

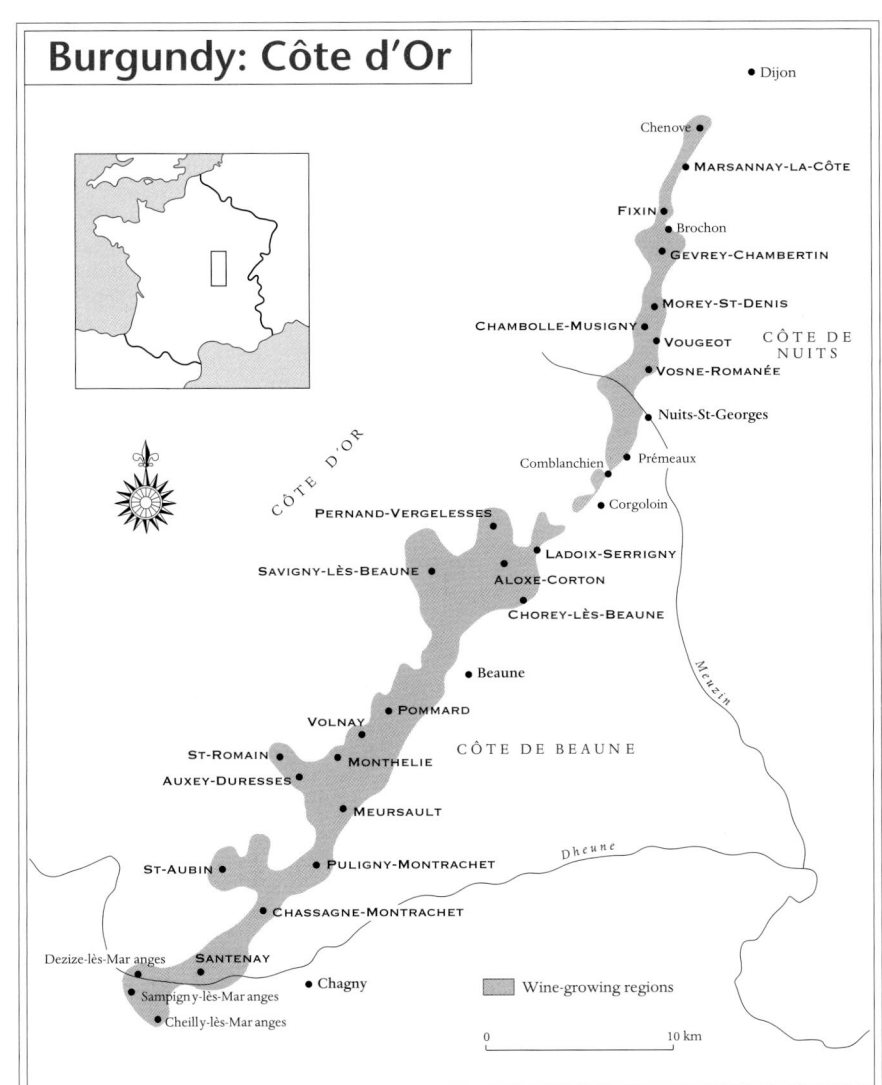

Burgundy: Côte d'Or

- Dijon
- Chenove
- MARSANNAY-LA-CÔTE
- FIXIN
- Brochon
- GEVREY-CHAMBERTIN
- MOREY-ST-DENIS
- CHAMBOLLE-MUSIGNY
- VOUGEOT
- VOSNE-ROMANÉE

CÔTE DE NUITS

- Nuits-St-Georges
- Comblanchien
- Prémeaux
- Corgoloin

CÔTE D'OR

- PERNAND-VERGELESSES
- LADOIX-SERRIGNY
- SAVIGNY-LÈS-BEAUNE
- ALOXE-CORTON
- CHOREY-LÈS-BEAUNE
- Beaune
- VOLNAY
- POMMARD

CÔTE DE BEAUNE

- ST-ROMAIN
- MONTHELIE
- AUXEY-DURESSES
- MEURSAULT
- ST-AUBIN
- PULIGNY-MONTRACHET
- CHASSAGNE-MONTRACHET
- Dezize-lès-Maranges
- SANTENAY
- Chagny
- Sampigny-lès-Maranges
- Cheilly-lès-Maranges

Meuzin

Dheune

Wine-growing regions

0 — 10 km

Ancient history

When the Romans (see Ancient ROME) conquered Gaul in 51 BC, they probably found the CELTS inhabiting what is now Burgundy already growing wine, although definite archaeological evidence for this goes back no further than the 2nd century AD. A tombstone in the village church of Corgoloin depicts what appears to be a Celtic god with a vine in his right hand; other gravestones have carvings of grapes. Also, archaeologists have found no Italian AMPHORAE of the mid 2nd century or later in Burgundy, which may indicate that from then on the region was producing enough wine of its own. From at least the 3rd century onwards, however, wine was transported from Italy in wooden BARRELS instead

BEAUJOLAIS in the Rhône département with 21,890 ha of vineyard, while sometimes being considered part of greater Burgundy, is a distinct region viticulturally, if not administratively, and is treated separately.

of amphorae, and wood is far more perishable than pottery.

The earliest literary evidence dates from AD 312. In a panegyric addressed to the Emperor Constantine the Great on the occasion of his visit to Autun (Augustodeunum), the citizens plead poverty. Part of the grim picture their orator paints is abandoned vineyards, the roots of the old vines so thickly intertwined that it would be impossible for a farmer to dig ditches. However old the vines were—and a mere human lifetime's worth of neglect would account for their tangled state—commercial viticulture had clearly been well established by the early 4th century.

As the Roman empire disintegrated, Burgundy came once more under barbarian rule, by the Franks, the Alamans, and the Vandals. The Burgundians, Scandinavians by origin, founded a kingdom in the RHÔNE valley, later including Lyons and Dijon, in 456; they were defeated by the Franks under Clovis's sons in 534. The first recorded words in praise of

Burgundian wine date from the Merovingian period. Gregory of Tours, who finished his History of the Franks in 591, says that the hills to the west of Dijon produce a noble wine that is like FALERNIAN—the highest praise possible from a Dark Age latinist. That wine, and the clear water flowing from the springs around the city, are sufficient reasons why in his opinion Dijon should become an episcopal see. In 587 King Guntramn, grandson of Clovis and son of Clotaire, gave a vineyard to the Abbey of St Benignus at Dijon, and in 630 the duke of Lower Burgundy donated vineyards at Gevrey, Vosne, and Beaune to the Abbey of Bèze, near Gevrey. The beginnings of monastic viticulture in Burgundy were in these Merovingian times.

Monastic influence

Nobles, peasants, and monks cultivated the vine under CHARLEMAGNE, when political stability brought prosperity. Medieval Burgundy owes its reputation as a producer of excellent wines largely to the MONKS AND MONASTERIES. The monks had several advantages over lay growers: they had cellars and store rooms in which to mature their wine; and, most importantly, they kept records and had the time and the degree of organization necessary to engage in systematic improvement. The first group of monks to acquire vineyards in Burgundy on a large scale were the Benedictines of Cluny. The foundation in 910 of the Abbey at Cluny in Mâconnais was the beginning of the Benedictine reform movement. Between 927 and 1157 Cluny became a vast organization with hundreds of dependent priories, not only in France but also in England, Germany, Spain, and Italy. Through benefactions from pious laymen, Cluny came to own all the vineyards around Gevrey by 1273, and in 1232 the duchess of Burgundy granted the Abbey of St-Vivant the vineyards now known as Romanée-Conti, La Romanée, La Tâche, Richebourg and Romanée-St-Vivant (see also DOMAINE DE LA ROMANÉE-CONTI). It also owned Pommard and vineyards at Auxey and Santenay.

The other group of monks to have a lasting effect on Burgundian viticulture were the Cistercians, an order founded in 1098 which took its name from the site of its first monastery, Cîteaux, east of modern Nuits-St-Georges. Although austerity and asceticism were the aims of the order, in contrast to the luxury and ostentation of the Benedictines, the Cistercians, often through donations, became rich and important landowners.

The Cistercians' first vineyard was given to them by the duke of Burgundy in 1098, not long after their foundation. Soon they were buying vineyards as well: in 1118 the Cistercians of Pontigny on the river Serein purchased, after much haggling, vineyards from the Benedictine monks of St-Martin at Tours from which they produced a white wine, the first CHABLIS. In 1110 the monks of Cîteaux were given land at Vougeot and went on to acquire more land there: it took them until 1336 to acquire enough to form one large vineyard, which they surrounded with a wall, the CLOS DE VOUGEOT. They bought or were given more vineyards all over the CÔTE D'OR and trained their lay brothers to work them: Beaune, Chambolle, Fixin, Pommard, and many more.

Aided by their skilled workforce, the monks had the time, the experience, and the learning necessary to experiment, record, and compare. By observing how different plots of vines produced different wines, the Cistercians discovered the importance of TERROIR and began to acknowledge different CRUS.

In the 12th and 13th centuries, white wine was preferred to red. In an age of murky drinking water, carefully made white wine was valued for its clarity. The wines that were most highly reputed, however, were not those of Burgundy but those of the Île-de-France centred on PARIS, which could easily be transported by RIVERS. Burgundy, on the other hand, was cut off, and its wines, which could only be transported north with much expense and difficulty along bumpy roads, were as yet little known. In medieval French texts, 'vin de Bourgogne' was from Auxerre, whose wines could easily reach Paris along the river Yonne: transport by boat was cheaper, easier, and less harmful to the wine than being carried by horse-drawn cart along bumpy roads. Until the 15th century what we call burgundy was known as 'Beaune'.

Upon his election in 1305 Clement V moved the papal court to Avignon. During this 'Babylonian captivity', which lasted until 1377, the court of the Avignonese popes was famous for its extravagance as well as its corruption, and demand for the wines of Burgundy to the north surged. The wines of 'Beaune' came generally to be regarded as second to none. Urban V (1362–70) went to Rome for three years in 1367 but, exasperated by the political infighting there, he returned to Avignon. In a letter, Petrarch made a vain attempt to persuade him to go back to Rome but had to admit that the best burgundy was not to be had south of the alps. The Babylonian captivity ended with Urban's successor Gregory XI, but the wines of Burgundy retained their high reputation.

The dukes of Burgundy

From a byword for largesse in Avignon, Burgundian wine became a status symbol with the Valois dukes, four generations of which governed Burgundy from 1363 to 1477. The first duke, Philip the Bold (1363–1404), son of King John of France, took a keen interest in the wine of the region, its most important export. In 1395, he issued a decree declaring the GAMAY grape variety to be harmful to human beings and its planting contrary to Burgundian practice. The first mention of the PINOT NOIR grape, named Noirien, dates only from the 1370s, but in all probability the grape had

been in use longer. Modern Gamay has a far higher yield than Pinot Noir, and documentary evidence suggests that the same was true in the 14th century. In the same decree, Philip inveighs against the use of organic FERTILIZERS, presumably because it also increased YIELDS. Philip was trying to maintain quality, while many growers thought that manure and Gamay would make for easy profits. Although Philip the Bold wanted every single Gamay plant uprooted by the next Easter, we find his grandson Philip the Good (1429–67) still thundering against the inferior vine, which he says is a threat to both the wines and the dukes of Burgundy. Fearing for his immortal soul, Philip the Good's rapacious Chancellor Nicolas Rolin built the famous HOSPICES DE BEAUNE in 1443.

But what were these famous wines really like? The white wines of Burgundy were probably made from the grape that also produced the highly reputed white wines of north eastern France, the Fromenteau, which had pale red berries and white juice, and could well be the ancestor of our PINOT GRIS. (The CHARDONNAY of modern white burgundy did not appear in the region until after the Middle Ages.) Also, in the Middle Ages wines were drunk in the year following the vintage, so properly matured burgundy would then have been unknown.   H.M.W.

Derlow, R. K., 'The "disloyal grape": the agrarian crisis of late fourteenth century Burgundy', *Agricultural History*, 56 (1982), 426–38.

Dion, R., *Histoire de la vigne et du vin en France* (Paris, 1959).

Modern burgundy

The duchy of Burgundy was once so proud of having the finest wines and finest court in Christendom that it developed into a state, and very nearly a kingdom in its own right. The defeat and death of the over-ambitious Charles the Rash, however, led to its being reincorporated into the kingdom of France. As the monarchy became stronger, the power of the Church declined slowly, so that during the 17th century many of the famous vineyards donated to the Church during the Middle Ages were sold to the increasingly important bourgeoisie in Dijon.

Although transport difficulties (see RIVERS) still hindered burgundy's fame abroad, the famous giant Pierre Brosse managed to interest Louis XIV in his Mâcon and the Sun King's physician, Fagon, prescribed old burgundy instead of champagne as the most suitable wine for his monarch's health. Roads began to improve in the 18th century and the tolls and tribulations inherent in road travel diminished, encouraging the start of commercial traffic in Burgundy. The first NÉGOCIANT (merchant) houses were founded in the 1720s and 1730s, including Champy (1720) and BOUCHARD PÈRE ET FILS (1731), names which have survived to this day.

The earliest major work on the wines of Burgundy, Claude Arnoux's *Dissertation on the Situation of Burgundy . . .* was published in 1728. It demonstrates the fame of the red wines of the Côte de Nuits and the special reputation of the Œil-de-Perdrix (partridge-eye) pink wines of Volnay, while the existence of white wine in the Côte de Beaune earns only a brief mention.

Most vineyards remained in the hands of Church or nobility until the French Revolution. From 1791, the vineyards were sold off, often split between several owners. Since then they have further fragmented as a result of the law of equal inheritance among children laid down in the Napoleonic Code. This process has caused much of the difficulty in understanding burgundy: the consumer must familiarize himself not only with a plethora of village and vineyard names but also with the relative merits of possibly dozens of producers of each one.

Burgundy prospered in the early 19th century, although wine PRICES were low even for the fine vineyards. In addition, there was widespread planting of the inferior GAMAY grape to provide wine that was plentiful and cheap, albeit mediocre. Transport conditions continued to improve with the opening of a canal system in Burgundy, and the Paris–Dijon railway in 1851.

Easy prosperity was first checked, however, by the spread of POWDERY MILDEW in the 1850s and then destroyed by the arrival of the PHYLLOXERA louse in the 1870s. This calamity was finally admitted in the Côte d'Or in 1878 when an infested vineyard in Meursault was surrounded by soldiers. The Burgundians did not find it easy to come to terms with the problem: there were riots in Bouze-lès-Beaune between factions in favour of treating vineyards and those against; a posse of growers in Chenôve actually attacked a team sent in to spray the vines; American ROOTSTOCKS, the eventual saviours of French vineyards, were banned from the region between 1874 and 1887. Eventually, however, common sense prevailed and by the 1890s post-phylloxera wines were again on the market. Only the best vineyards were worth replanting after the predations of phylloxera, a valuable side benefit of the disaster.

The Burgundians were well aware of the considerable variation in quality of the wines produced by different plots of land, or *climats*, as they are known in Burgundy. In 1855, Dr Lavalle published his influential *History and Statistics of the Côte d'Or*, which included an informal CLASSIFICATION of the best vineyards. This was formalized in 1861 by the Beaune Committee of Agriculture, which, with Lavalle's assistance, devised three classes. Most of the first class were in due course enfranchised as GRANDS CRUS when the APPELLATION CONTRÔLÉE system was introduced in the 1930s.

Most burgundy was sold through the flourishing NÉGOCIANT houses until the years of hardship after the First World War. The economic depression of the 1920s and early 1930s threatened to ruin many small growers. One solution was the CO-OPERATIVE, particularly useful in Mâconnais, where prices were lower. Another was for proprietors to bottle their own produce, a move which met with opposition from the merchants when growers such as the Marquis d'Angerville, Henri Gouges, and Armand Rousseau pioneered the concept of DOMAINE BOTTLING in the 1930s. Whereas in 1962 wines produced and bottled by growers accounted for only 15 per cent of production, by 1990 nearly half of all Côte d'Or wines were domaine bottled.

Geography and climate

The vineyards of Burgundy are based on LIMESTONE originating in the Jurassic period. This takes the form of undulating CHALK hills in Chablis; a long narrow escarpment running south and a touch west from Dijon to Chagny, the CÔTE D'OR; more isolated limestone outcrops in the Côte Chalonnaise and Mâconnais; with the vineyards of POUILLY-FUISSÉ beneath the imposing crags of Solutré and Vergisson in the extreme south.

The climate in Burgundy is broadly CONTINENTAL. In contrast to BORDEAUX, Burgundy is noticeably colder in the winter months, similar in temperature in the spring, but a little cooler during the summer. Although usually dry in winter, Burgundy tends to suffer from particularly heavy rainfall in May and June and again in October, which may or may not fall after the HARVEST. Spring FROST can be a problem (especially in CHABLIS), while HAIL causes local damage almost every year.

Overall, there is a shorter and more variable summer than in Bordeaux (which is why only early-ripening grape varieties can be grown there). And whereas the hardy CHARDONNAY vine can thrive under these conditions, producing what are widely considered the finest full-bodied dry white wines in the world, the temperamental PINOT NOIR vine is less regularly successful. For more details of Burgundy's special aptitude for top-quality wine production, see CLIMATE AND WINE QUALITY.

Burgundy is at the limit of successful RIPENING, the red wines of Auxerrois rarely achieving much depth or body. The great red wines of Burgundy are produced on the escarpment of the Côte d'Or, especially in the Côte de Nuits sector. Even here several vintages in a decade may lack sufficient sun to ripen properly.

Among the white wines of Burgundy, the wines of Chablis, reflecting their northern origin, are green tinted in colour and comparatively austere to taste. The most revered white wines are those of the Côte de Beaune, there being practically none in the Côte de Nuits, while the whites of the Côte Chalonnaise are lighter and attractive to drink young. Further south, the white wines of Mâconnais enjoy enough sun to make fat and ripe wines, although many of them lack finesse. J.T.C.M.

Viticulture

For details, see CÔTE D'OR; CHALONNAISE; and MÂCONNAIS.

Wine-making

For details, see CÔTE D'OR; CHALONNAISE; and MÂCONNAIS.

Vine varieties

Burgundy has one of the world's least varied ranges of vine varieties. Almost all of the region's best red and white wines are made from Pinot Noir and Chardonnay respectively. On the Côte d'Or, more than seven in every ten vines planted were Pinot Noir in the late 1980s, while Chardonnay plantings were increasing so that even at the most recent vineyard census of 1988 they represented nearly two in every ten vines. Gamay and ALIGOTÉ, the 'lesser' red and white wine vines respectively, were in hasty retreat, although BOURGOGNE ALIGOTÉ has its followers.

In the Côte Chalonnaise and Mâconnais, Chardonnay plantings increased notably during the 1970s and 1980s when the variety overtook Gamay as most important, and became an important source of wine labelled Bourgogne Blanc. In 1988, the Saône-et-Loire *département*, which includes these two southern Burgundy wine districts, had 4,500 ha/11,100 acres of Chardonnay (three times more than the Côte d'Or). Gamay plantings were just over 3,000 ha while those of Pinot Noir were 2,800 ha. There were also about 500 ha of Aligoté, approximately the same area as the Côte d'Or.

Organization of Burgundian vineyards

The vineyards of Burgundy, especially those of the Côte d'Or, are the most minutely parcelled in the world. This is mainly because the land has been continuously managed and owned by individual smallholders—there was no influx of outside capital with which to establish great estates as in BORDEAUX. But the combination of the Napoleonic Code, with its insistence on equal inheritance for every family member, and the fact that the land has proved so valuable, has meant that small family holdings have been divided and subdivided over generations. One vineyard, or *climat*, as it is known in this, the cradle of TERROIR, may therefore be owned by scores of different individual owners, each of them cultivating sometimes just a row or two of vines (see CLOS DE VOUGEOT, for example).

Organization of trade

Unlike the BORDEAUX TRADE with its large volume of single appellations, and many stratifications of those who sell it, the Burgundian wine trade is polarized between growers and NÉGOCIANTS, or merchants. Because the laws of equal inheritance have been strictly applied in a region of such valuable vineyards, individual growers may for example produce just one barrel, enough to fill just 25 cases, of a particular appellation. The market for burgundy was built by the merchants, who would buy grapes and wine from many different growers before blending and selling the results. Behind a merchant's Aloxe-Corton label, for example, may well be the produce of many different plots and cellars. Although in some cases these blends may be better than any individual ingredient, and in most cases today the merchants have better equipment and wine-making skills than the average Burgundian vine-grower, such blends have met increasing consumer resistance. Wine merchants such as Frank SCHOONMAKER and Alexis LICHINE introduced particularly the American public to the notion of DOMAINE BOTTLED burgundy in the 1950s and 1960s, creating a demand which resulted in a widespread improvement in the quality and authenticity of the merchants' produce. The merchants increasingly own their own vineyards, and are able to label the wines they produce 'mise en bouteille au domaine'. (Because few growers can afford their own BOTTLING equipment, mobile bottling units are much used in Burgundy.) Since the early 1990s, the distinctions between growers and merchants have become increasingly blurred, with many widely admired growers also producing another range of wines made from grapes they did not grow themselves. For more details, see NÉGOCIANTS.

See also HOSPICES DE BEAUNE and see BOURGOGNE for details of Burgundy's generic appellations. For the names of individual appellations, see BEAUNE; NUITS; CHALONNAISE; and MÂCON.

CHABLIS and BEAUJOLAIS are treated separately.

Coates, C., Côte d'Or (London, 1997).
Hanson, A. D., Burgundy (2nd edn, London, 1995).
Norman, R. H., The Great Domaines of Burgundy (2nd edn, London, 1996).
Pitiot, S., and Servant, J.-C., Les Vins de Bourgogne (11th edn of P. Poupon's original, Paris, 1992).

Busby, James (1801–71), the so-called father of Australian viticulture, although more recently the term prophet has been considered more appropriate. James Busby was born in Edinburgh and became interested in agriculture in Ireland, where his father managed estates. Before leaving Scotland for Australia, Busby became convinced of the future of the colony in viticulture, and so spent several months studying viticulture and wine-making in France. This allowed him to write his first book, *Treatise on the Culture of the Vine*, on the five-month voyage on the *Triton*. At 24, therefore, Busby was already an author of a viticultural textbook, although at the time it was considered too scientific and lacking in simple directions. A land grant of 800 ha/1,980 acres was made to Busby on the Hunter river in NEW SOUTH WALES in 1824, and the property was named Kirkton. Busby was initially employed to teach viticulture at the Male Orphan School near Liverpool, and to manage its 5,000-ha estate. Unfortunately the school was soon closed down, and in between several other posts Busby published in 1830 his second and much more successful book *A Manual of Plain Directions for Planting and Cultivating Vineyards and for Making Wine in New South Wales*. Busby, like others of his time, extolled the virtues of wine drinking compared with the then common excesses with spirits in the colony. His book contains the much quoted 'The man who could sit under the shade of his own vine, with his wife and children about him, and the ripe clusters hanging within their reach, in such a climate as this, and not feel the highest enjoyment, is incapable of happiness and does not know what the word means.'

Busby's greatest contribution to Australian viticulture was yet to be made. In 1831 he returned to England, and spent four months touring the Continent, primarily to make a collection of vine cuttings for Australia. His collection included cuttings for about 680 VINE VARIETIES (not necessarily all different) from the botanical gardens of MONTPELLIER, Luxembourg in Paris, and Kew in London, as well as from other parts of France and Spain. This collection was shipped to Sydney along with seeds of various vegetables, and by January 1833 was reported to be growing in the Sydney Botanic Gardens. In 1833 Busby published another book about his tour to Spain and France, and listed the varieties in his collection.

Busby's life entered a new dimension in 1833 with his appointment as the first British Resident at the Bay of Islands in New Zealand. The nearby town of Russell was a trading port for visiting whalers, and described as 'the hell hole of the Pacific'. Busby had neither the magisterial powers nor the constabulary to impose any order but, through his and others' efforts, New Zealand became a British possession in February 1840 with the signing of the Treaty of Waitangi by some fifty Maori chiefs. Busby had little time for viticulture in New Zealand, although he did establish a vineyard at Waitangi which was destroyed in 1845 during clashes with the Maoris. He is credited with being the first person to make wine in New Zealand.

Unfortunately, the Sydney vine collection was not tended as well as it should have been. Some of the vines were distributed to Kirkton in the Hunter, and some to the Adelaide Botanic Gardens in South Australia. Many of Busby's imports were to become the basis of the Australian wine industry which subsequently developed; indeed some CLONES of vine varieties such as Chardonnay and Shiraz that are important in the 1990s can be traced to Busby's imports. In later life Busby was aggrieved to discover that much of the credit for his vine introductions was erroneously given to William Macarthur, another pioneer of the Australian wine industry. Busby died in England in 1871. His great contribution to the Australian wine industry was his vine importations, his writings, and his enthusiasm for the notion that Australia should develop as John Bull's (England's) vineyard of the Antipodes.

R.E.S.

Evans, L., Australian Complete Book of Wine (Sydney, 1977).
Halliday, J., and Jarratt, R., The Wines & History of the Hunter Valley (Sydney, 1979).

bush vines, an alternative term to describe GOBELET-trained vines or HEAD TRAINING. The comparison with a bush is apt: the vines are trained to a short trunk, normally free standing (without a trellis system), and are pruned to a few spurs commonly arranged in a ring

on short arms from the trunk. The term bush vines is used in Australia and South Africa, and there was a FASHION for using it on labels in the late 1990s, although many of these old, and typically low-vigour, vineyards have been replaced by vines with a TRELLIS SYSTEM.

R.E.S.

butt, BARREL TYPE associated particularly with SHERRY production in the Jerez region. It is usually made from American oak and has a capacity of between 600 and 650 l/172 gal. A *bota chica* or shipping butt holds 500 l and is sometimes used as a unit of measurement. New butts are an inconvenience in the sherry-making process and have to be seasoned by being used for the FERMENTATION of lower-quality wines.

butterflies, regarded as pests in some vineyards. See MOTHS.

Buzet, archetypically Gascon red wine appellation in SOUTH WEST FRANCE up the Garonne river from BORDEAUX energetically producing notably bordeaux-like wines. The recent history of the appellation, created in 1973, is inextricably intertwined with the dynamism of the local CO-OPERATIVE, Les Vignerons de Buzet, which makes all but a tiny proportion of Buzet. Notably ambitious, the co-operative laid the foundation stones of a barrel-ageing cellar in 1958, for which their own COOPER today makes more than 500 BARRIQUES a year from specially chosen and seasoned French OAK. Thus, the average Buzet is given much more sophisticated ÉLEVAGE than the average BORDEAUX AC, without an enormous price differential.

The region, which extends along the left bank of the Garonne between Agen and Marmande, has known viticulture since Roman times but vine-growing was developed under monastic influence in the Middle Ages. The fortunes of the district's wines suffered during the HUNDRED YEARS WAR, when the district supported the English crown. The district was further hampered by the restrictions imposed by the Bordelais on all HAUT PAYS, or 'high country', wines, when the wines of the village of Nérac were particularly well known. PHYLLOXERA seriously affected viticulture in the late 19th century, and a ruling in the early 20th century that Bordeaux wines had to come from within the GIRONDE *département* was a further blow to a district which had habitually supplied BLENDING wines to the Bordeaux merchants.

Total vineyard area has shrunk to less than 1,400 ha from a late 1990s peak of more than 1,800 ha/4,450 acres. The gravels and clays of these inland hills are planted with classic red Bordeaux vine varieties Cabernet Sauvignon, Cabernet Franc, and, especially, Merlot. The co-operative has invested heavily in the most modern wine-making equipment, and its policy is to make strict selections according to TERROIR and quality each VINTAGE so that, although all Buzet should receive at least a year's BARREL MATURATION, the finest wines are blended to produce their top bottling Cuvée Napoléon. The co-operative also vinifies the produce of a number of individual parcels of land and bottles a plethora of them separately as CHÂTEAU wines. Ch de Gueyze and Baron d'Ardeuil are perhaps the two best known bottlings.

Byblos, ancient town in the LEBANON 40 km/25 miles north of modern Beirut. It had the reputation of being the oldest town in the world and was a PHOENICIAN centre of trading. Its wines were famous in classical times.

BYO stands for 'Bring Your Own' (Wine) and is a type of restaurant most common in Australia and New Zealand, where the term was coined. The term is associated with maximum wine-drinking pleasure at minimum cost to the restaurant-goer (in tandem with reduced profit to the restaurateur). New Zealanders claim that the BYO name and concept was born in 1976 when the New Zealand authorities, still notably cautious about the distribution of alcoholic drinks, devised the Bring Your Own licence for restaurants at which diners would be allowed to take their own wine. Australians in the state of Victoria, also famously restrictive in its legislative attitude to alcoholic drinks, maintain that Melbourne had BYO establishments in the 1960s. Wherever its origins, this arrangement has become common for a wide range of restaurants in Australia, New Zealand, and elsewhere, the wine often being bought in a nearby retail establishment. CORKAGE is sometimes but not always charged.

Cabardès, LANGUEDOC appellation (since 1999) of 550 ha/ 1,375 acres to the north of Carcassonne which produces red and some rosé wines that testify to its location on the cusp of Atlantic and Mediterranean influences. The grape varieties planted also represent a Bordeaux/Languedoc cocktail of Cabernet Sauvignon, Cabernet Franc, Merlot, Cot (Malbec), and some Fer Servadou (of MARCILLAC fame), spiced and fleshed out with the more meridional Syrah, Grenache, Cinsaut (mainly for rosé), and a limited, and declining, proportion of Carignan. The Bordelais varieties tend to prosper on the western, wetter, deeper soils, while wines produced from the hotter, shallower soils of the eastern Cabardès are more likely to have a high proportion of Mediterranean varieties. Winds almost constantly buffet the small hills punctuated by pines and *garrigue*, and minimize the local wine producers' dependence on AGROCHEMICALS. In contrast to the somewhat similar Côtes de la MALEPÈRE to the south of Carcassonne, production here is mainly in the hands of a small but committed band of individuals constrained by low financial returns. Wine-making equipment and methods are not always the most sophisticated, but the wines boast an originality and potential for longevity that is unusual for this part of France (which officials tend to classify as SOUTH WEST FRANCE rather than the LANGUEDOC to which its immediate eastern neighbour the Minervois belongs). Ch Pennautier has been the dominant producer while Domaine de Cabrol is making waves.

Cabernet is loosely used as an abbreviation for either or both of the black grape varieties CABERNET FRANC and CABERNET SAUVIGNON. In north east Italy in particular there has been a certain lack of precision about the precise identity of the Cabernet grown and allowed into the many Cabernet DOCs, although Cabernet Franc has tended to predominate. Elsewhere, Cabernet is more likely to be an abbreviation for Cabernet Sauvignon.

Cabernet Franc, fine French black grape variety, much blended with and overshadowed by the more widely planted CABERNET SAUVIGNON. Only in Anjou-Saumur and Touraine in the Loire valley, on the right bank of the Gironde in Bordeaux, and in parts of north east Italy is it quantitatively more important than Cabernet Sauvignon, but Cabernet Franc is still sufficiently widely grown to be one of the world's 20 most planted cultivars for wine.

In the vineyard it can be distinguished from Cabernet Sauvignon by its less dramatically indented leaves but the two share so many characteristics that they had for long been thought to be related. In 1997, thanks to DNA TYPING, it was established that Cabernet Franc was, with the Bordeaux white vine variety SAUVIGNON BLANC, a parent of the noble Cabernet Sauvignon (see CABERNET SAUVIGNON for more details).

By the end of the 18th century, Cabernet Franc was already documented as producing high-quality wine in the Libournais vineyards of St-Émilion, Pomerol, and Fronsac, where it is often called Bouchet today. Long before this, however, according to Odart, it had already been selected by Cardinal Richelieu, as a well-respected vine of south west France, to be planted at the Abbaye de St-Nicolas-de-Bourgueil in the Loire by an abbot called Breton, whose name persists as the Loire synonym for Cabernet Franc to this day.

Cabernet Franc is particularly well suited to cool, inland climates such as the middle Loire and the Libournais. It buds and matures more than a week earlier than Cabernet Sauvignon, which makes it more susceptible to COULURE, but it is easier to ripen fully and is much less susceptible to poor weather during harvest. In the Médoc and Graves districts of Bordeaux, where Cabernet Franc constitutes about 10 per cent of a typical vineyard (less than it once was because Merlot was so fashionable at the end of the 20th century) and is always blended with other varieties, it is regarded as a form of insurance against the weather's predations on Cabernet Sauvignon and Merlot grapes. Most Libournais bet on Cabernet Franc in preference to the later, and therefore more difficult to ripen, Cabernet Sauvignon to provide a framework for Merlot, Bordeaux's most planted variety.

In Bordeaux, plantings of Cabernet Franc and Cabernet Sauvignon were almost equal, at about 10,000 ha/25,000 acres, in the late 1960s but Cabernet Sauvignon was so often chosen in preference to Cabernet Franc by those replacing unprofitable white wine vineyards that 20 years later Cabernet Sauvignon covered almost twice Cabernet Franc's total area, a proportion that remains today, even though Cabernet Franc's total area in the Gironde has risen to 14,300 ha.

As a wine, Cabernet Franc tends to be rather lighter in colour and tannins, and therefore earlier maturing, than Cabernet Sauvignon although CHEVAL BLANC, the world's grandest Cabernet Franc-dominated wine, proves that majestic durability is also possible. Cabernet Franc is, typically, light to medium bodied with more immediate fruit than Cabernet Sauvignon and marked fragrance, including sometimes some of the herbaceous aromas evident in unripe Cabernet Sauvignon.

Cabernet Franc is still planted all over south west France, although, in appellations such as Bergerac and Madiran (where Cabernet Franc is known as Bouchy), Cabernet Sauvignon has been gaining ground.

Cabernet Franc was France's sixth most planted black grape variety by the most recent, 2000, census, almost half of its 36,000 ha total in the south west and half in the greater Loire valley. Steadily increasing appreciation (largely within France) of relatively light, early-maturing reds such as Saumur-Champigny, Bourgueil, Chinon, and Anjou-Villages fuelled demand for Cabernet Franc in the Loire at the expense of Rosé d'Anjou and Chenin Blanc whites.

Cabernet Franc is also well established in Italy, particularly in the north east (see FRIULI in particular), where it has typically been encouraged to yield such a quantity that over-herbaceous aromas scent wines that can be decidedly short on fruit. Tuscan and central Italian producers of Cabernet, many with decidedly lesser experience with Cabernet, are now showing a new interest in Cabernet Franc as a supplement to their Cabernet Sauvignon, in an effort to add more varietal aroma and complexity to their wines. The 2000 Italian vineyard survey found just over 7,000 ha of Cabernet Franc in Italy (slightly more than in 1990 but Cabernet Sauvignon had more than tripled). It is occasionally called Cabernet Frank or even Bordo, but more usually labelled simply Cabernet once in the bottle. An increasing proportion of 'Cabernet Franc' in north east Italy is being identified as Carmenère. While north eastern Italian vine-growers have tended to be as insouciant about the distinction between the two Cabernets as their counterparts over the border in SLOVENIA and further east, the Tuscans are beginning to view Cabernet Franc as a variety of real interest in BOLGHERI and the rest of the Maremma, where this late-ripening variety produces wines of great balance and elegance. Cabernet Franc has a presence in Hungary, KOSOVO and, it is thought, KAZAKHSTAN. It is also relatively significant in CHINA.

Elsewhere, with a few notable exceptions, Cabernet Franc has generally been grown for the express purpose of blending with Cabernet Sauvignon, following the Bordeaux recipe whether or not the climate suggests that such insurance would be wise. Cabernet Franc plantings have slowly increased in New World wine regions as winemakers embrace the sophistication of BORDEAUX BLENDS as opposed to single VARIETALS. In Australia, for example, Cabernet Franc plays a very minor part. The few hundred ha planted had by the mid 2000s barely added lustre to the variety's reputation. NEW ZEALAND also shows promise (although Cabernet Sauvignon grown in this relatively cool climate can often taste like Cabernet Franc) and plantings were expected to total 210 ha by 2006. South Africa had less than 1,000 ha planted in the mid 2000s, compared with over 13,000 ha of Cabernet Sauvignon, although it had its champions.

Although there was some early confusion between Cabernet Franc and Merlot, Californians have been rearing Cabernet Franc since the late 1960s, and with some zeal since the 1980s. This was originally a ploy to add complexity to Cabernet Sauvignons accused by some of simplicity. Some increasingly respected varietal Cabernet Francs and Bordeaux blends dominated by the variety are bottled in California today but the majority of the state's crop is used in MERITAGE-like blends. Total acreage had reached almost 3,400 acres/1,375 ha by 2004, most of it in Napa and Sonoma counties. Its relative scarcity make the grapes some of California's most expensive and it has been increasingly fashionable.

In the cooler northern and eastern wine regions of North America (especially the Niagara peninsula of CANADA, where ICEWINE has been made from it, Pennsylvania, VIRGINIA, and Long island in NEW YORK state), Cabernet Franc has emerged as the red VINIFERA variety of choice, ripening much more reliably than Cabernet Sauvignon and providing much more EXTRACT than do most HYBRIDS.

The variety has also been responsible for some well-balanced, fruity wines in the Pacific north western state of WASHINGTON, where the winter-hardy Cabernet Franc is more resistant to WINTER FREEZE than Merlot but is losing ground to the more fashionable Syrah.

The vine is increasingly planted in South America. ARGENTINA now grows Cabernet Franc to a limited extent with 300 ha/741 acres planted in 2003, most of it in Mendoza, while Chile had a substantial 925 ha/2,285 acres.

When the pendulum swings back from super-concentrated, high-alcohol reds, Cabernet Franc may be expected to benefit.

Bowers, J. E., and Meredith, C. P., 'The parentage of a classic wine grape, Cabernet Sauvignon', *Nature Genetics*, 16/1 (1997), 84–7.

Enjalbert, H., *Les Grands Vins de Saint-Émilion, Pomerol et Fronsac* (Paris, 1983).

Galet, P., *Dictionnaire encyclopédique des cépages* (Paris, 2000).

Odart, A.-P., *Ampélographie universelle* (Paris, 1845).

Cabernet Frank, occasional north east Italian name for CABERNET FRANC.

Cabernet Sauvignon, the world's most renowned, but relatively recent, red wine grape, rivalled only by Merlot as the world's most-planted dark-skinned grape variety. From its power base in Bordeaux, where it is almost invariably blended with other grapes, it has been taken up in other French wine regions and in much of the Old and New Worlds, where it has been blended with traditional native varieties and often used to produce pure VARIETAL wine.

Perhaps the most extraordinary aspect of Cabernet Sauvignon is its ability to produce a wine that is so recognizably Cabernet, even if remarkably few wine regions, considering its ubiquity, have so far proved reliable sources of seriously top-quality expressions of this potentially top-quality grape: MÉDOC, PESSAC-LÉOGNAN, NAPA, SONOMA, SANTA CRUZ MOUNTAINS, BOLGHERI, COONAWARRA, MARGARET RIVER, and part of PENEDÈS spring most readily to mind. What makes Cabernet Sauvignon remarkable to taste is not primarily its exact fruit flavour—although that is often likened to blackcurrants, its aroma sometimes to green bell peppers—but its structure and its ability to provide the perfect vehicle for individual vintage characteristics, wine-making and ÉLEVAGE techniques, and, especially, local physical attributes, or TERROIR. Unlike CHARDONNAY, which is as widely disseminated, late-ripening Cabernet Sauvignon must be grown in relatively warm climates, and can in some years fail to reach full RIPENESS even somewhere as mild as the Médoc.

It is Cabernet Sauvignon's remarkable concentration of PHENOLICS that really sets it apart from most other widely grown vine varieties. It is therefore capable of producing deeply coloured wines worthy of long MACERATION and long-term AGEING. Over the centuries, it has demonstrated a special but by no means exclusive affinity for densely textured French OAK. The particular appeal of Cabernet Sauvignon lies much less in primary fruit aromas (with which other varieties such as Gamay and Pinot Noir are more obviously associated) than in the much more subtle flavour compounds that evolve over years of BOTTLE AGEING from complex interaction between compounds derived from fruit, fermentation, alcohol, and oak. It is also true, however, that so distinctive is Cabernet Sauvignon's imprint on the palate memory that part of the reason why it is so widely planted is that even when irrigated to greedily high yields and hastily vinified without even a glimpse of wood, it can produce a wine with some recognizable relationship to the great Bordeaux growths of the Médoc and Graves on which its reputation has been built.

Cabernet Sauvignon's origins for long remained shrouded in mystery. There was speculation that, because one of its early synonyms, well established by the 17th century, was Bidure, it was the direct descendant of the vine called Biturica by PLINY. Bidure and Vidure were alternatively thought to be corruptions of *vigne dure*, a reference to the hardness of the vine's wood (which today makes it such a suitable candidate for MECHANICAL HARVESTING, and gives it good resistance to WINTER FREEZE).

The mystery of Cabernet Sauvignon's origins was solved in 1997, thanks to DNA PROFILING. Bowers and Meredith of the University of California at DAVIS showed beyond all reasonable doubt that Cabernet Sauvignon's parents are none other than CABERNET FRANC and the Bordeaux white wine grape SAUVIGNON BLANC, a crossing that is thought to have happened spontaneously in one of the many vineyards planted with a mixture of different vines in the old days. This neatly explains why Cabernet Sauvignon can smell like either or both of its parents, and why Cabernet Franc is mentioned in the literature long before Cabernet Sauvignon, and was already well established in Bordeaux by the end of the 18th century.

There are no early references to Cabernet Sauvignon in the LITERATURE OF WINE and the variety did not start to make any significant impact on the vineyards of Bordeaux until the end of the 18th century, when the great estates were built up and wine with real longevity emerged (see BORDEAUX, history). Baron Hector de Brane, once owner of Ch Mouton, together with his neighbour Armand d'Armailhacq, is credited with its promulgation, if not introduction, in the MÉDOC.

The distinguishing marks of the Cabernet Sauvignon berry are its small size, its high ratio of pip to pulp (one to 12, according to Peynaud, as opposed to one to 25 for Sémillon), and the thickness of its skins, so distinctively blue, as opposed to red or even purple, on the vine. The pips are a major factor in Cabernet Sauvignon's high TANNIN level while the thickness of its skins accounts for the depth of colour that is the tell-tale sign of a Cabernet Sauvignon in so many BLIND TASTINGS—as well as the variety's relatively good resistance to ROT.

The vine is susceptible however to POWDERY MILDEW, which can be treated quite easily, and the wood diseases EUTYPA and EXCORIOSE, which cannot. It is extremely vigorous and should ideally be grafted on to a weak ROOTSTOCK to keep its VIGOUR in check. It both buds and ripens late, one to two weeks after Merlot and Cabernet Franc, the two varieties with which it is typically blended in Bordeaux. Cabernet Sauvignon ripens slowly, which has the advantage that picking dates are less crucial than with other varieties (such as Syrah, for example); but this has the disadvantage that Cabernet Sauvignon simply cannot be relied upon to ripen in the coolest wine regions, especially when its energy can so easily be diverted into producing dangerously shady leaves, such as in Tasmania or New Zealand, unless CANOPY MANAGEMENT is employed. Cabernet Sauvignon that fails to reach full ripeness can taste eerily like Cabernet Franc (just as unripe Sémillon, coincidentally, resembles Sauvignon Blanc).

Even in the temperate climate of Bordeaux, the flowering of the vine can be dogged by cold weather and the ripening by rain, so that Bordeaux's vine-growers have traditionally hedged their bets by planting a mix of early and late local varieties, typically in the Médoc and Graves districts 75 per cent of Cabernet Sauvignon plus a mixture of Merlot, Cabernet Franc, and sometimes a little Petit Verdot. (See CABERNET FRANC for reasons why the Cabernet in St-Émilion and Pomerol is much less likely to be Cabernet Sauvignon.)

A practice that had its origins in judicious fruit farming has proved itself in the blending vat. The plump, fruity, earlier maturing Merlot is a natural blending partner for the more rigorous Cabernet Sauvignon, while Petit Verdot can add extra spice (if only in the sunniest years) and Cabernet Franc can perfume the blend to a

certain extent. Except in warmer wine regions, wines made solely from Cabernet Sauvignon can lack charm and stuffing; the framework is sensational but tannin and colour alone make poor nourishment. As demonstrated by the increasing popularity of Merlot and Cabernet Franc and even Petit Verdot cuttings, some producers in newer wine regions follow the Bordeaux example of blending their Cabernet Sauvignon with other varieties, although the Médoc recipe is by no means the only one. In Toscana it is sometimes blended with Sangiovese. In Australia and in Provence it is blended with SYRAH (SHIRAZ), with very different results.

Cabernet Sauvignon, with its sophisticated whiff of French glamour, was extraordinarily popular in the New World in the last two decades of the 20th century but in its homeland of Bordeaux, there was a concurrent tendency (now revised) to plant Merlot. The result has been that, while Cabernet Sauvignon was in the 1990s by quite a margin the most planted top-quality vine variety in the world, it was recently overtaken by Merlot. It could fairly be said that one of the first signs of 'modernization' of a wine region has been its importation of and experimentation with Cabernet Sauvignon cuttings. Only those regions, such as England, Germany, and Luxembourg, disbarred for reasons of climate, have been unable to join this particular club.

French plantings of Cabernet Sauvignon increased enormously in the 1980s and 1990s so that by 2000 there were 53,400 ha/132,000 acres, of which almost 60 per cent were in the Bordeaux *département* the Gironde (although within the Gironde the agriculturally more dependable Merlot has been consistently and considerably more popular). The vine's stronghold is the left bank of the river Gironde, most notably the famously well-drained gravels of the Médoc and Graves CRUS classés, whose selling price can well justify the efficacious luxury of ageing their wine in small, often new, oak barrels. Chx Latour and Mouton-Rothschild, two of the most famous wine farms in the world and both of them FIRST GROWTHS in Pauillac, are renowned for their high proportion of Cabernet Sauvignon: still approximately three vines in every four despite recent dramatic increases in Merlot plantings on both estates. Their wines, although differing in character, are known for their solidity and longevity.

The vine is also planted over much of SOUTH WEST FRANCE, often as an optional ingredient in its red, and occasionally rosé, wines. Only in BERGERAC and BUZET does it play a substantial part. In more internationally styled wines, however, it may add structure to the Négrette of GAILLAC and FRONTON, and the Tannat of BÉARN, IROULÉGUY, and MADIRAN. It is also increasingly used to add substance to the red Côtes de ST-MONT.

Plantings in the Languedoc-Roussillon

increased substantially in the 1980s to a total of more than 12,000 ha by 1997, but Cabernet Sauvignon has not been nearly as successful in this dry climate as Syrah, so by 2000 there were just 13,000 ha of Cabernet Sauvignon in the region to Syrah's 30,000 ha. Cabernet Sauvignon, which frequently demands IRRIGATION in the Languedoc-Roussillon, has made wines which have tended towards herbaceousness and suffered lack of substance.

The most obviously successful southern French Cabernet Sauvignons are those used as ingredients in low-yield blends with Syrah and other Rhône varieties, such as Mas de Daumas Gassac in the Hérault or, further east in Provence, Domaine de Trévallon and Ch Vignelaure.

Provence and the southern Rhône are no more impervious to the winds of FASHION than they are to the famous local mistral and according to the 2000 census there was as much Cabernet Sauvignon as Syrah in the Bouches-du-Rhône *département* in the southern Rhône valley, and a further 1,700 ha in the Var, Provence.

Cabernet Sauvignon's only other French territory is the Loire, where Cabernet Franc is generally more popular because easier to ripen but Cabernet Sauvignon is slowly gaining ground.

Outside France

According to the most accurate estimates available, there were approximately 30,000 ha/75,000 acres of Cabernet Sauvignon in the Soviet Union before it was broken up, with some of the most impressive bottle-aged examples coming from MOLDOVA. The variety is presumably still widely planted, although in the many wine regions susceptible to WINTER FREEZE, the cold-hardy hybrid CABERNET SEVERNY is popular. Cabernet Sauvignon is also grown in GEORGIA, AZERBAIJAN, KAZAKHSTAN, TAJIKISTAN, and KYRGYZSTAN. Of even greater significance to its global total plantings, it has also been the single most popular variety in CHINA's recent wave of plantings, which has seen the country's total vineyard area rise from 118,000 ha/291,600 acres in 1997 to an estimated 450,000 ha in 2004.

Another country with an extremely important area planted with the world's noblest black grape variety is Chile, whose grand total of ungrafted Cabernet Sauvignon grew from about 16,000 ha/39,500 acres to almost 40,000 ha between 1997 and 2003, making it the country's most important vine variety. Here the fruit is exceptionally healthy and the wine, if made carefully in one of the more modern wineries, almost rudely exuberant. See CHILE for more on Chilean Cabernet Sauvignon.

Not surprisingly, Cabernet Sauvignon also flourishes in the rest of South America's vineyards: in ARGENTINA, where in terms of quantity it is dwarfed by Malbec; in BRAZIL, URUGUAY, MEXICO, PERU, and BOLIVIA.

Cabernet Sauvignon, even less surprisingly, has been the bedrock of CALIFORNIA CULT wines. Such has been the quality of some of these wines that northern California could fairly be said to have proved itself Cabernet Sauvignon's second home, and indeed by 2004 the state grew about as much in total as Bordeaux, with a total which had more than doubled from 1996 to about 75,000 acres/ 30,000 ha, making it California's most important variety by far apart from Chardonnay. In the better, and often extremely carefully tended, sites of northern California, Cabernet Sauvignon can ripen quite well enough to need no grower's insurance or winemaker's additional complexity in terms of other grape varieties and 100 per cent Cabernet Sauvignon can be a hugely successful recipe. For more detail on the golden state's Cabernet achievements, see CALIFORNIA.

Cabernet Sauvignon is also one of WASHINGTON state's two major black grape varieties, even if it fell firmly into second place during the 1990s' mania for Merlot. The state's total plantings of Cabernet Sauvignon were just over 7,000 acres/2,830 ha in 2005. Cabernet Sauvignon's vigour and late ripening make it unattractive to growers in damp, cool Oregon but it has been most successful in other American states including Arizona and TEXAS. Even the wine industry in CANADA, with its natural climatic disadvantages, persists with the variety.

If Californians decided early on that the Napa Valley was their Cabernet Sauvignon hotspot, Australians did the same about Coonawarra. They, however, have for decades employed a much less reverential policy towards blending their Cabernet. Cabernet–Shiraz blends (a recipe recommended in Provence as long ago as 1865 by Dr GUYOT) have been popular items in the Australian market place since the 1960s. The richness and softness of Australian Shiraz is such that it fills in the gaps left by Cabernet Sauvignon even more effectively than can the French Syrah recommended by Dr Guyot. Cabernet Sauvignon was Australia's second most planted vine variety with more than 29,000 ha/71,600 acres by 2004. As plantings of Merlot have soared since 1996, joined more recently by Petit Verdot, Cabernet-dominant BORDEAUX BLENDS have become increasingly common in Australia and now outnumber Cabernet–Shiraz blends. See AUSTRALIA for more detail on Australian Cabernet Sauvignon.

Cabernet Sauvignon long played a quantitatively important part in the NEW ZEALAND wine industry and it was the country's fourth most planted vine variety in the 1990s but its 700-plus ha in the mid 2000s, which need careful CANOPY MANAGEMENT to ripen fully, had been outdone fivefold by Pinot Noir, now firmly the country's signature red.

Cabernet Sauvignon was equally revered in SOUTH AFRICA in the late 20th century and, with

13,500 ha/33,400 acres in 2004, it was the most planted red wine variety by far. In recent years, however, Bordeaux blends (often highly priced) have come to enjoy greater status in South Africa than wines made solely from Cabernet Sauvignon—and Syrah could be said to be more fashionable than Cabernet in any form.

Cabernet Sauvignon has been an increasingly popular choice for internationally minded wine producers in Spain, where it was planted by the Marqués de Riscal at his Rioja estate in the mid 19th century, and could also be found in the vineyards of VEGA SICILIA. It was otherwise virtually unknown on the Iberian peninsula until the 1960s, when it was imported into Penedès by both Miguel TORRES, Jr, and Jean León. It broadened its base in Spain, particularly Cataluña, in the late 20th century—not just for wines dominated by it but for blending, notably with Tempranillo. By 2004 there were 10,000 ha/ 24,700 acres of Cabernet Sauvignon in Spain, making it the sixth most planted red wine vine. In Portugal, it is much rarer but can be found, often blended with indigenous grape varieties, in a handful of lush red wines made in the Lisbon area.

Italy, where Cabernet Sauvignon was introduced, via Piemonte, in the 1820s, now has a very substantial area of Cabernet Sauvignon, about 8,000 ha/19,800 acres in 2000—quite an increase on 1990's total of 2,400 ha and now more than is recorded for Cabernet Franc. Remarkably few of the denominations which begin with the word Cabernet specify which should be used and in what proportions. Cabernet Sauvignon continues to spread southwards through Italy, even as far as the islands, and features in many of Italy's more cosmopolitan producers' most cherished wines. Cabernet Sauvignon has played a considerable role in the emergence of SUPER-TUSCANS, and can be found as a seasoning in an increasing proportion of CHIANTI. It is officially sanctioned, and individually specified, in such DOCs as CARMIGNANO in Toscana; Colli BOLOGNESI in Emilia-Romagna; in TRENTINO; in LISON-PRAMAGGIORE in Veneto; and in Friuli COLLI ORIENTALI, COLLIO, GRAVE DEL FRIULI, ISONZO, and Latisana. Cabernet Sauvignon is a major ingredient in such Tuscan wines as Solaia, Sassicaia, Venegazzù, and Castello di Rampolla's Sammarco, and is increasingly common (occasionally blended with BARBERA grapes) in the NEBBIOLO territory of Piemonte in such bottlings as Darmagi from GAJA and Alberto Bertelli's I Fossaretti.

East of Italy there are many thousands of hectares of Cabernet Sauvignon, which plays an important part in the wine industries of BULGARIA (13,000 ha/32,100 acres) in particular, ROMANIA (2,700 ha/6,700 acres—much less than of Merlot), and what was YUGOSLAVIA. Even when expected to produce relatively high yields, eastern European Cabernet Sauvignon is unmistakably Cabernet, and the best Roma-

nian and Bulgarian wines have real depth of flavour as well as colour, although quality of Bulgarian Cabernet fell dramatically after the fall of communism and the painstaking restitution of land, often to those who could not tend it. There are smaller amounts of Cabernet Sauvignon grown in HUNGARY, AUSTRIA, and GREECE, where it was first planted, in modern times at least, at the Carras domaine.

Perhaps the most tenacious Cabernet Sauvignon grower has been Serge Hochar of Ch Musar in the LEBANON, where in the last 20 years it has become, along with Cinsaut, the country's most planted wine grape accounting for almost 50 per cent of the total. There are other, rather less war-torn, pockets of Cabernet Sauvignon vines all over the eastern Mediterranean in TURKEY, ISRAEL, and CYPRUS, as well as increasing quantities in Morocco. In ASIA, there have also been experiments with the vine, notably in CHINA and JAPAN, where its strong links with the famous châteaux of Bordeaux are particularly prized.

Wherever there are any vine-growers with any grounding in the wines of the world, and late-ripening grapes are economically viable, they are almost certain to try Cabernet Sauvignon—unless they inhabit one of Bordeaux's great rival regions Burgundy and the Rhône.

Bowers, J. E., and Meredith, C. P., 'The parentage of a classic wine grape, Cabernet Sauvignon', *Nature Genetics*, 16/1 (1997), 84–7.

Eyres, H., *Cabernet Sauvignon* (London, 1991).

Galet, P., *Dictionnaire encyclopédique des cépages* (Paris, 2000).

Lake, M., *Cabernet* (Sydney, 1977).

Peynaud, E., *Connaissance et travail du vin* (Paris, 1981).

Cabernet Severny, red wine grape variety specially bred for cold climates at the All-Russia Potapenko Institute in the Rostov region of RUSSIA. It was created by pollination of a HYBRID of Galan × VITIS *amurensis* with a pollen mixture of other hybrid forms involving both the European vine species Vitis VINIFERA and the famously cold-hardy Mongolian vine species *Vitis amurensis*.

Cabinet, historical term, whose origins are disputed, for superior German wines. Wines made in Germany prior to the GERMAN WINE LAW of 1971 were labelled Cabinet if thought to be better than average and, by tradition, worthy of space in the producer's own Cabinet or cellar. Thus, an Auslese Kabinett would have denoted a selectively harvested wine the grower deemed particularly successful or precious. See GERMAN HISTORY.

Cabrières, village and named TERROIR within the Coteaux du LANGUEDOC in southern France, just east of FAUGÈRES and within the CLAIRETTE DU LANGUEDOC zone. The CO-OPERATIVE dominates production, which has historically favoured rosé, which must contain at least 45 per cent CINSAUT grapes.

Cadarcă, Romanian name for Hungary's KADARKA.

Cadillac, small sweet and medium sweet white appellation of less than 300 ha/740 acres just north of LOUPIAC in the BORDEAUX region, once particularly popular with the Dutch, named after the walled town built by the English in the 12th century. Until 1973 it was part of the surrounding PREMIÈRES CÔTES DE BORDEAUX appellation but its special combination of chalk and gravel theoretically justifies a distinction which is still too rarely found in the wines. Low selling prices make high-quality production methods such as those practised in SAUTERNES difficult to justify, and few producers are brave enough to try to make BOTRYTIZED WINES. The area's reds qualify as Premières Côtes de Bordeaux.

Caecuban wine was ranked by the connoisseurs of Ancient ROME among the finest wines of Italy for the last century BC and the first half of the 1st century AD. Caecuban wine was produced on a small vineyard in the low-lying marshy region, south of Terracina, on the west coast of central Italy, between the sea and the Lago di Fondi. The vines were trained up poplars. Caecuban was a white wine, which following standard Roman practice was aged for a number of years, during which it deepened to a 'flame' colour. It was described as 'sinewy' and 'packing a punch' by the medical writer Galen. The vineyard was largely destroyed in the middle of the 1st century AD by the ambitious, though abortive, scheme of the Emperor Nero to dig a canal to link the bay of Naples with the Tiber. Caecuban never recovered and the name became simply a generic term for wine with the characteristic colour of the true wine. Small quantities of undistinguished red wine called Cécubo are produced in the district today. J.J.P.

Cagnina, synonym for REFOSCO in Italy's Romagna region.

Cahors, increasingly significant wine region in the Quercy district in SOUTH WEST FRANCE, producing exclusively red wine, uniquely dependent on the MALBEC or Cot grape. In the 1980s and 1990s, it has benefited from considerable inward investment. The wine producers of Cahors long suffered from the protectionist measures against such HAUT PAYS wines inflicted on Cahors by the merchants of Bordeaux. The RIVER Lot provided an ideal trade route from the town of Cahors to the markets of northern Europe via the GARONNE and Bordeaux, and Cahors was making wines noted for their colour and BODY from at least the early Middle Ages. There are records of Cahors being sold in London in the early 13th century, but the HUNDRED YEARS WAR disrupted patterns of trade.

Cahors is influenced by the Mediterranean as well as by the Atlantic, and, although winters are rather colder than in Bordeaux, the wines tend to be more concentrated. They were appreciated as suitable blending material with the lighter wines of Bordeaux, and in the early 19th century were famed as the 'black wines of Cahors'. (Such was Cahors's international renown in the 19th century that imitation 'Cahors' was made by at least one of the Russian model wineries in the CRIMEA.) A method of making the wines even blacker had been adopted whereby a portion of the grape juice was boiled to concentrate its colour and fermentable sugars. The produce of this technique was designed specifically for blending rather than drinking. At this time there were almost 40,000 ha/100,000 acres of vineyards in the greater Cahors region, but PHYLLOXERA was to more than decimate this total, and resulted in considerable replanting with HYBRIDS. The arrival of the RAILWAYS also gave the populous north ready access to the cheap and plentiful wines of the LANGUEDOC. Cahors fell into decline.

The establishment of the Caves d'Olt COOPERATIVE at Parnac in 1947 marked the modest beginning of a new era during which the proportion of noble grape varieties and the incidence of good wine-making equipment and technology has steadily increased so that by the late 1990s more than 4,000 ha of vines were producing Cahors, awarded full APPELLATION CONTRÔLÉE status in 1971. Within south west France only BERGERAC makes more wine. Vines for Cahors may be planted either on the notably thin topsoil of the arid, limestone plateau, the *causses*, or on the sand and gravel terraces between the plateau and the river, the *coteaux*. The suitability of each is much debated (according to the location of the debater's own vines), although most agree that the *causses* tend to produce wine for long ageing, a more traditional style of Cahors, while the wine made on the *coteaux* can be drunk much younger.

The notorious WINTER FREEZE of 1956 had a marked effect on the Cahors *vignoble* and provided a clean slate at an appropriate moment in the appellation's evolution. By far the largest number of growers planted an overwhelming majority of Malbec, called here for obscure reasons Auxerrois, a traditional Cahors variety which is nowhere else associated with particularly long-living wines. The appellation rules stipulate at least 70 per cent Auxerrois, supplemented by the tannic TANNAT and/or the supple MERLOT. A strictly local variety known as Jurançon Noir has been virtually phased out, and most vines are now trained to a single GUYOT system (which is appropriate since this 19th-century scientist was particularly critical of the traditional GOBELET method for Auxerrois). Again, debate rages over the most suitable mix of grape varieties (although, like vineyard location, this is hardly a variable in practice, more a matter of long-term fact). Cahors is exceptional among the important south west French appellations in that neither Cabernet vine is allowed.

In the winery, MACERATION times are a genuine variable and can have a considerable effect on wine style, as of course does BARREL MATURATION, still a relatively rare phenomenon in the early 1990s. This has been changing, however, since Cahors has attracted more than its fair share of well-heeled outsiders. By the mid 2000s, the most prominent Cahors producers such as Ch du Cèdre, Ch Lagrezette, and Domaine Cosse Maisonneuve were making special cuvées so concentrated and velvety that they were difficult to distinguish from Argentina's most winning examples of the same grape—apart from their much higher prices. The great majority of wine produced is much lighter however and can often betray a certain rustic or animal character.

The local VIN DE PAYS, a speciality of the cooperative, is Vin de Pays des Coteaux de Quercy.

Caiño Tinto, strongly perfumed, delicate red wine vine grown on about 600 ha of Galicia in 2004 and found in tart reds in RÍAS BAIXAS and RIBEIRO. Known as BORRAÇAL in Portugal's Vinho Verde region. A light-berried **Caiño Blanco** is also found, particularly in Rías Baixas.

Cairanne, probably the best of the Côtes du Rhône villages, led by Domaines l'Oratoire St-Martin and Richaud. See RHÔNE.

Calabrese, meaning 'of Calabria', is a common synonym for the NERO D'AVOLA Sicilian red grape variety.

Calabria, the rugged toe of the boot of Italy, is closer to SICILIA than to Rome in every way. (In antiquity, Calabria was the name of the heel of Italy, part of modern PUGLIA.) It has lagged behind the rest of Italy in its agricultural and industrial development with a per capita income barely half the national average. It is not surprising, therefore, that its wines have made little impact and have little significance in national and international markets.

Only 5 per cent of the total surface area of the region's agricultural land is planted with vines, most of them close to the northern, Tyrrhenian coast or the southern, Ionian coast. The 35,000 ha/86,500 acres currently dedicated to vineyards—two-thirds of which are officially classified as HILLSIDE sites, with another 15 per cent promisingly mountainous but difficult to work—produce an average of just under 1 million hl/26.4 million gal of wine a year. The average size of the properties, whether in DOC zones or not, is hardly more than half a hectare, most of them yielding a particularly low annual income. The total DOC production of the region is only 3 per cent of the region's annual wine crop and almost 90 per cent of the wine produced is red.

The most important DOC by far is Cirò (on the sole of Italy's boot), where a certain viticultural tradition exists and where Tancredi BIONDI-SANTI of MONTALCINO operated as a consultant during the decades immediately following the Second World War. Even Cirò produces only a quarter of its potential, however, with barely 850 ha of the 2,700 ha of DOC Cirò vineyards planted actually employed in the production of a warm, alcoholic, DOC wine. Librandi is the best and most important producer in Cirò.

So uncommitted is Calabria to the business of making wine officially regarded as of superior quality that certain DOC wines have virtually disappeared from the market: Melissa Bianco, Donnici, Savuto (19 producers, and only 2,000 hl/53,000 gal produced in the official production declarations in the late 1990s), Sant'Anna Isola Capo Rizzuto—while Pollino made a token appearance with a paltry 7 hl. In a certain sense, therefore, the DOC system has ceased to function in Calabria.

GAGLIOPPO, the principal red grape of the region, is the base of Cirò, Savuto, and Pollino and seems to have real potential; interesting experiments with small oak BARREL MATURATION have begun in the zone in an effort to give the wine a more international character. It may be blended with red and white GRECO, TREBBIANO, and NERELLO grapes to produce Calabria's hefty reds and rosés. The white Greco grape, partially dried, produces a strong, coppery dessert wine of real interest and personality in its DOC zone around the town of Bianco almost at the tip of the boot, making the confusingly named Greco di Bianco Calabria's most distinguished wine. Cabernet Sauvignon and Cabernet Franc, Chardonnay, and Sauvignon Blanc are being experimented with in a desultory fashion, although real conviction and truly convincing results, with the exception of Librandi's Gravello, are rare. This is all too predictable in a region where, in the early 1990s, only three firms among the 65,000 registered grape-growers managed to export their wines.   D.T. & D.C.G.

Bastianich, J., and Lynch, D., *Vino Italiano: The Regional Wines of Italy* (New York, 2002).

Belfrage, N., *From Brunello to Zibibbo: The Wines of Southern Italy* (London, 2001).

Caladoc, dark-skinned grape variety created by French AMPELOGRAPHER Paul Truel under INRA auspices by crossing Grenache and Côt (Malbec) to produce a Grenache-like crossing less prone to COULURE. It has been planted in the southern Rhône but is not allowed into any APPELLATION CONTRÔLÉE wine, although it may be used to add TANNIN and aroma to red VINS DE PAYS. France grew a total of more than 1,400 ha/3,400 acres by 2000. It is also grown in the ESTREMADURA region of Portugal.

Calagraño, historic and nearly extinct Rioja grape which was shown in the early 2000s to be identical to CAYETANA Blanca.

Calatayud, dynamic denominated wine zone in ARAGÓN in north east Spain, in arid country on either side of the river Jalón, a tributary of the Ebro (see map under SPAIN). As in much of central Spain, YIELDS rarely rise above 20 hl/ha (1 ton/acre). The DO regulations limit growers to indigenous grape varieties, which are mostly sold to one of nine local CO-OPERATIVES. The GARNACHA grape, which accounts for around two-thirds of Calatayud's production, makes heady, potent red wine, although TEMPRANILLO is now also planted. Investment in new technology, particularly STAINLESS STEEL and REFRIGERATION, is increasing the proportion of Garnacha-based rosés and crisp white wines made from VIURA. The Maluenda and San Alejandro co-operatives have taken the lead in producing well-priced wines of an international standard.
                    R.J.M. & V. de la S.

calcaire, French word for LIMESTONE, a rock largely made up of CALCIUM carbonate, which may in English be described as **calcareous**. Many such soils have a reputation for high-quality wine. The term is used to describe, for example, the vineyard soils of CHAMPAGNE and some of the better parts of the CÔTE D'OR in France. Soils described as *argilo-calcaire* are a mixture of clay and limestone. See entries prefixed SOIL.   M.J.E.

calcium is a major nutrient required for vine growth. It enhances cell wall structure and contributes to grape skin defence against microbial attack. Calcium is immobile in the plant. It is taken up by roots during the period of rapid growth up to VERAISON, after which point there is little increase in calcium concentration in the plant.

In the soil, calcium is known as an element and it is rarely lacking in vineyards. Calcium-bearing soils come in many forms: MARL, calcite, CHALK, LIMESTONE, marble, and dolomite. These are predominantly calcium carbonate ($CaCO_3$), made up of the remains of marine creatures deposited over many millions of years. Presence of calcium in soils increases friability and DRAINAGE, especially where such calcareous soils underlie clay. See SOIL TEXTURE and SOIL AND WINE QUALITY. In regions where irrigation is not permitted, such as Burgundy and Champagne, calcium in the soils accounts for some of their suitability for premium viticulture.

Calcium in clays exists as cation Ca^{2+} and contributes to higher soil CATION EXCHANGE CAPACITY. The availability of elements as plant nutrients is broadly correlated with soil PH. Calcium in soils is usually accompanied by a pH of 6–7, at which point many plant nutrients and trace elements are at their most available (see SOIL ACIDITY, SOIL ALKALINITY). The presence of calcium in soils often correlates with optimum pH for grapes. Liming soils is mostly undertaken with the primary aim of increasing nutrient availability. Above pH 7, many elements become unavailable, and soils extremely high in calcium are not ideal for viticulture. See also CHLOROSIS.

Caldaro, or **Kaltern** in German, township in ALTO ADIGE, northern Italy. It gives its name to **Lago di Caldaro** or **Kalterersee**, a large DOC zone for lightish red wines which extends into neighbouring TRENTINO.

California, highly successful 'wine state' of the UNITED STATES and the largest source of American wine by far, producing 90 per cent of all US-grown wine, some years more than 550 million gal/20.8 million hl in total, and three out of every four bottles sold in the US, making the state effectively the world's fourth biggest producer of wine. California was also for years the only source of VINIFERA wine in the US. California wine, like most things Californian, has arrived at its current position by a series of bold investments, natural disasters, scientific achievements, external pressures, and political calamities. That the US is not a nation of wine drinkers has tended to exaggerate the cycle of giant strides and general retreats, and even relatively recent events can fast become history (see below).

History

Franciscan MISSIONARIES planted the first *vinifera* vines in California around 1770 (the native *Vitis californica* and *Vitis girdiana* are unfit for wine). For the next eighty years the Franciscans' MISSION grape remained the basis of California wine-growing, which passed from the missions to small growers as the mission lands were secularized under the newly independent Mexican government beginning in 1821. A French cooper, Louis Vignes, was an important pioneer when he planted *vinifera* vines at the sleepy little pueblo along the banks of Los Angeles river at the beginning of the decade. After the US annexation of Alta California in 1847, and the discovery of gold in 1848, wine-growing spread throughout the state. California's fame as a new wine region spread even as far as North Caucasus (see RUSSIA).

Following the GOLD RUSH of 1849, both population and vineyards expanded rapidly in the districts around San Francisco bay as frenzied commercialism gripped the region. Since almost all of the immigrants were male, there was enormous demand for domestic services such as laundries and restaurants as well as for less prosaic services and commodities, alcohol prominent among them. SONOMA valley had been a centre of wine-making activity since the 1820s thanks to spirited competition between Mariano Vallejo, the Mexicans' military commandant for Alta California, and Agoston HARASZTHY. By 1891, Sonoma had 22,683 acres/9,180 ha under vine to the NAPA valley's 18,000 acres. Driven in no small

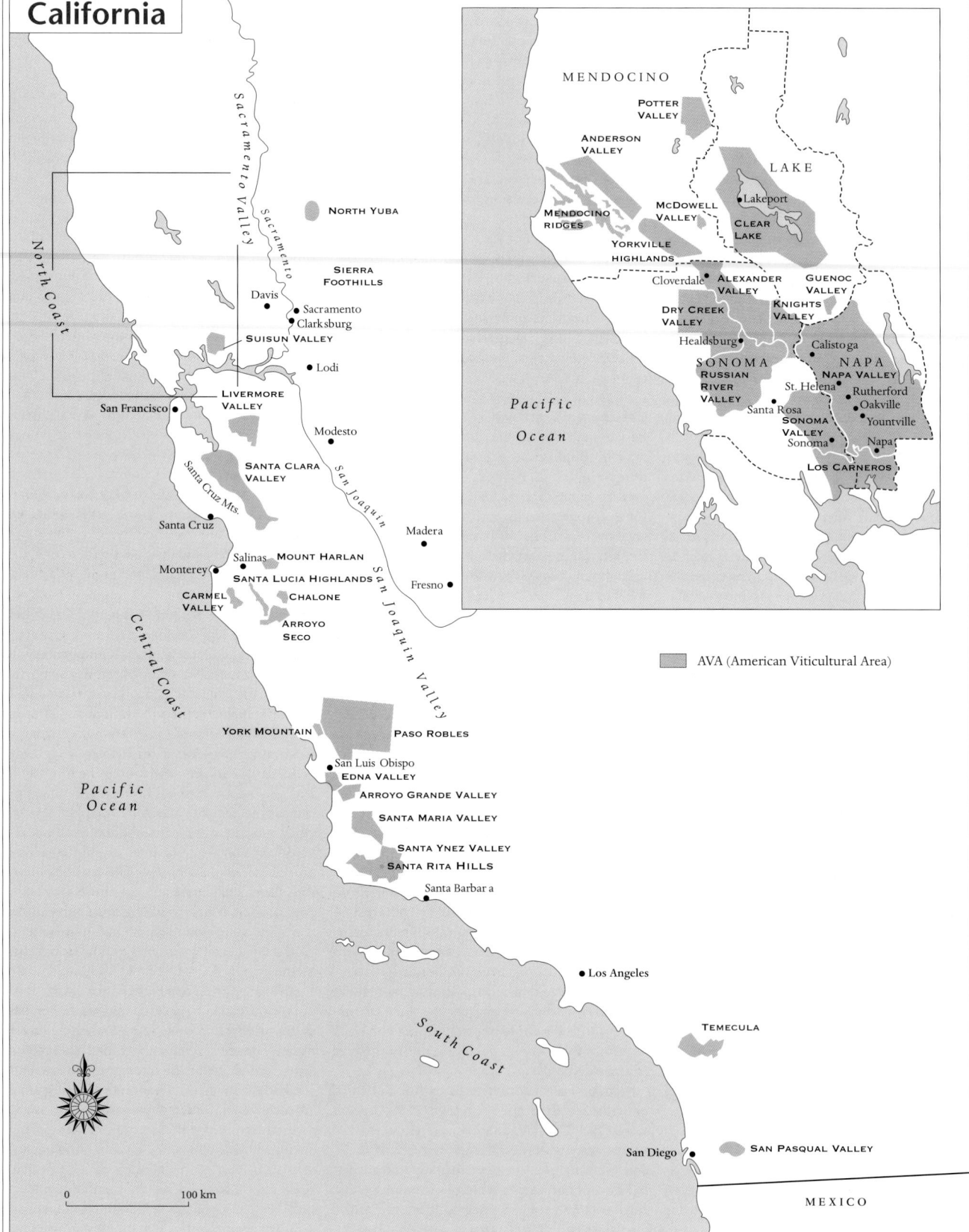

California

MENDOCINO

POTTER VALLEY

ANDERSON VALLEY

MENDOCINO RIDGES

McDOWELL VALLEY

YORKVILLE HIGHLANDS

LAKE

• Lakeport

CLEAR LAKE

Cloverdale •

ALEXANDER VALLEY

GUENOC VALLEY

KNIGHTS VALLEY

DRY CREEK VALLEY

Healdsburg •

• Calistoga

SONOMA

RUSSIAN RIVER VALLEY

St. Helena •

NAPA

NAPA VALLEY

Santa Rosa •

• Rutherford

Oakville •

Santa •

SONOMA VALLEY

• Yountville

Sonoma •

• Napa

LOS CARNEROS

Pacific Ocean

Sacramento Valley

Sacramento

North Coast

NORTH YUBA

SIERRA FOOTHILLS

Davis •

Sacramento •

Clarksburg •

SUISUN VALLEY

• Lodi

LIVERMORE VALLEY

San Francisco •

Modesto •

San Joaquin

Santa Cruz Mts.

SANTA CLARA VALLEY

Santa Cruz •

Madera •

Salinas •

MOUNT HARLAN

Monterey •

SANTA LUCIA HIGHLANDS

Fresno •

CARMEL VALLEY

CHALONE

ARROYO SECO

San Joaquin Valley

Central Coast

YORK MOUNTAIN

PASO ROBLES

San Luis Obispo •

EDNA VALLEY

ARROYO GRANDE VALLEY

SANTA MARIA VALLEY

Pacific Ocean

SANTA YNEZ VALLEY

SANTA RITA HILLS

Santa Barbara •

• Los Angeles

South Coast

TEMECULA

San Diego •

SAN PASQUAL VALLEY

MEXICO

0   100 km

AVA (American Viticultural Area)

measure by the devastation of Europe's vineyards by PHYLLOXERA, the 1870s and 1880s saw an extraordinary burst of investment in vineyards and wineries, benefiting not just these NORTH COAST counties, but also LIVERMORE VALLEY and SANTA CLARA VALLEY.

By the end of the century, nearly every region currently producing wine in California had been tried, and production was over 30 million gal/1.1 million hl, largely from the northern part of the state, especially Sonoma, Napa, and Santa Clara counties. The great central SAN JOAQUIN VALLEY began to develop for the large-scale production of inexpensive wines from the 1870s, especially in Fresno and Madera counties. The state had officially encouraged wine-growing from the earliest years, recognizing it as one of California's most distinctive contributions to the US economy. A board of State Viticultural Commissioners did useful work from 1880 to 1895, and the wine research and education of the University of California (first at Berkeley and subsequently in the warmer, more suitable location of DAVIS) began in 1880 and continues to the present.

California had neither viticultural traditions nor an entrenched peasantry in its early era, so aggressive research and education by E. W. Hilgard and Frederic T. Bioletti at the University produced immediate results. No later than 1881, scholars and growers alike saw clearly that the coastal counties were for finer table wines, the San Joaquin for everyday table wines and, perhaps, dessert wines of quality. Already California grew more than 300 *vinifera* varieties with CHASSELAS, ZINFANDEL, BURGER, and of course Mission, predominating, even if most of the nearly 800 wineries producing at California's 19th-century peak (about the same number as a century later) sold their wines anonymously in bulk to a handful of blender/bottlers who offered broad ranges of wine types to the trade.

Over-planting, however, and attempts by a couple of powerful merchants to corner the wine market, caused the price of grapes and wine to crash in the 1890s. Prices dropped below production costs. This and the first signs of phylloxera in California were the twin blows which caused the first major setback for this burgeoning industry, devastating the state's wine production. PROHIBITION, legally in force between 1920 and 1933, destroyed its market. It was many decades before some areas recovered their pre-Prohibition status as wine regions, unlike Napa and Sonoma to the north and the Central Valley which endured this second setback relatively robustly.

Immediately after the Repeal of Prohibition, the market demanded mostly sweet wines. Relatively few, small producers attempted to make superior table wines from superior varieties, with little recognition. By the end of the Second World War, wineries that bottled their own production were the norm. By then over-

all numbers had dwindled to about 120 producing wineries. A trade far more familiar with whiskey than wine encouraged the survivors to produce 'full lines', echoing, not the old blender/bottlers, but importers who were now bringing in broad arrays of wines from Europe sold under GENERIC names. In the three-tiered system of distributors (national or regional), district wholesalers, and local retailers, it may have been the retailers who were most to blame for wanting to keep their domestic orders as simple as their import invoices, reinforced by the general ignorance of the American drinking public. California thus produced wines sold under such generic names as Burgundy and Chablis.

After a period of struggle that lingered beyond the Great Depression and the Second World War, a second grand burst of investment was evident between 1970 and 1985, most obviously in Napa but also in Sonoma. (It was to be a new strain of phylloxera coupled with a new wave of prohibitionist sentiments that in the late 1980s helped cool this second burst too.) Growing populations around San Francisco pushed the new wave of vineyard planting south into MONTEREY, SAN LUIS OBISPO, and SANTA BARBARA counties. Then in the late 1990s a third wave of expansion, in no small part fuelled by the overnight entrepreneurial successes of the internet and multimedia bubble centred in northern California, pushed experimental planting up into the SIERRA FOOTHILLS as land in the Central Coast, Napa, and Sonoma became increasingly expensive.

In the 1970s and early 1980s, America became interested in wine. New wineries proliferated, production rose, better varieties were extensively planted, higher standards aimed at, and market demand swiftly answered. While California had fewer than 100 acres of Cabernet Sauvignon and practically no Chardonnay immediately after Prohibition in 1933, and only 600 and under 100 acres of these two major vine varieties by 1960, California's total plantings of Cabernet and Chardonnay had reached 30,000 acres/12,000 ha and 50,000 acres/20,000 ha by 1991. A decade later, those totals were 75,000 acres/30,000 ha and 100,000 acres/40,000 ha (more Chardonnay than is grown in the whole of France) and the names Cabernet and Chardonnay had become respectively almost synonymous with red wine and white wine for many Americans.

By the turn of the century, the state had nearly 800,000 acres of vines of grape-bearing age. Only 500,000 acres of these produced specifically wine grapes, however, with a significant proportion of grapes being varieties such as THOMPSON SEEDLESS. California is one of the world's most important producers of RAISINS.

As both consumers and trade matured in the 1970s, there was a proliferation of California wineries specializing in just two or three

wines, most of them labelled as VARIETAL wines closely tied to their region of origin, a distinct step up from the generic wines that had dominated the state's production since Prohibition. By 2005 the number of wine companies in the state had shot past the late 1980s record of 800 to nearly 1,700, almost all of them this time selling their production under their own labels. Prior to 1991, wines selling for less than $3 a bottle made up three-quarters of all California table wine shipments. By 2004 such wine accounted for just 13 per cent of California's total table wine shipments of 522 million gallons/20 million hl. In 2004, California table wines costing more than US$7 a bottle accounted for 32 per cent of the volume shipped and 64 per cent of winery revenues.

The market for wine in the United States continued to grow in the 2000s and there is no reason to believe that California will not continue to supply two-thirds of all domestic requirements. Meanwhile US wine exports, which were negligible after the Second World War, have grown steadily since the mid 1980s, and California supplies 95 per cent of that volume. In 1986, the US exported only 7.3 million gallons/0.275 million hl with a value to the wineries of US$35 million. In 2004, those figures had risen to 119 million gallons/4.5 million hl with a value to the wineries of US$794 million. The UK was the biggest importer, followed in order by Canada, Japan, the Netherlands, Germany, and France.

California's matching of vine variety to region remains so relatively immature that people continue to be more important than place. In the 19th century, immigrant Germans and Frenchmen showed the way for a larger population of Anglo-Americans. A later wave of Italian immigrants kept things going during and after Prohibition. And in the second half of the 20th century, the wine industry has been populated by an eclectic gathering of engineers, painters, physicians, pilots, retired industrialists, reformed hippies, and other second careerists who somehow found a calling in wine, and who have driven themselves with the same energy that made them successes in other fields, sometimes in spite of location rather than because of it.

Vine varieties (see below) are not necessarily planted because they are known to be the best adapted to that region—although there is a new awareness of the importance of matching site and variety (see Geography below and AVA). In Napa valley, the devastation wrought by phylloxera in the early 1990s made this an urgent practicality rather than a theoretical aim.

T.P. & B.C.C.

Adams, L., *The Wines of America* (4th edn, New York, 1990).

Carosso, V., *The California Wine Industry: A Study of the Formative Years* (Berkeley, Calif., 1951).

Muscatine, D., Amerine, M. A., and Thompson, B. (eds.), *The University of California/Sotheby's Book of California Wine* (Berkeley, Calif., 1984).

Pinney, T., *A History of Wine in America—From the Beginnings to Prohibition* (Berkeley, Calif., 1989).
——*A History of Wine in America—From Prohibition to the Present* (Berkeley, Calif., 2005).
Sullivan, C., *A Companion to California Wine* (Berkeley, Calif., 1998).

Climate

Those unfamiliar with California assign it a two-season MEDITERRANEAN CLIMATE. This is but a partial truth. Offshore ocean currents cause an intermittent fog-bank along California's coast, creating long stretches with insufficient sunshine to ripen most grapes. These fogs do not penetrate far inland, because of the 1,000-m/3,300-ft high coastal range, leaving the San Joaquin valley too warm and sunny—too Mediterranean if you will—to grow fine table wines. However, in the sharply convoluted in-between of the Coast ranges, jumbled terrain and variable fog produce more and less perfect growing season echoes of Castellina-in-CHIANTI, ST-ESTÈPHE, BEAUNE, and even Hattenheim in the RHEINGAU. There is no linear pattern. Napa, 20 miles north across the bay from San Francisco, is one of the warmer, drier regions on the coast. Westerly parts of Santa Barbara county, 300 miles/500 km to the south, are cooler and foggier than any part of Napa, while much of Mendocino, nearly 80 miles north of Napa, has hotter summers. Openings to the Pacific ocean in the Coast ranges indicate the cool spots, while mountain barriers locate the warmer ones.

The rainy season follows a more orderly pattern. Total annual RAINFALL north of San Francisco is between 24 and 45 in (615–1,150 mm), while from San Francisco southwards totals range from 20 in to the low teens. DROUGHT occurs regularly but since the phase of the cycle is 10–20 years, the last severe drought striking between 1987 to 1992, it can take new entrants on California's agricultural scene by surprise. Winters in California's grape-growing regions are mild to outright balmy. Damaging WINTER FREEZES are virtually unheard of.

Spring FROSTS vex growers more than any other fact of climate. Although late cold snaps occur infrequently, growers in the North Coast (north of San Francisco) are geared to mitigate the effects with SMUDGE POTS, overhead SPRINKLERS, and WIND MACHINES, huge fans that keep cold air moving in the vineyards. Spring rains sometimes interfere with flowering and fruit set, but never in disastrous proportion.

Geography

California's wine regions extend over more than 600 miles/960 km of the state's 900-mile length from north to south. They also extend 135 miles west to east from the Pacific coast up into the Sierra Nevada mountains. It is therefore difficult to typify soil types in California's vineyards because so much of the state's landforms have been emplaced on the North American tectonic plate, and then crumpled together by the action of the Pacific tectonic plate's sliding beneath it. Most vineyards have intrusions of several different soil types. Hence identification, and separate vinification, of different blocks within vineyards (see PRECISION VITICULTURE) became an increasingly valuable tool in the early 21st century for California's most quality-conscious winemakers. Nevertheless, it is still rare for wines from separately vinified vineyard blocks to appear as such in the market place. Most are blended (for complexity) at the winery into a range of styles and price levels more easily understood by consumers.

The US federal government began holding hearings in 1983 to approve AVA (American Viticultural Area) names for use on labels. That process is on-going, but it has been widely criticized for outcomes which often seem more politically expedient than educational or terribly useful to consumers. Before 1983, California's geographical appellations, by and large, were its counties. Those county names, still much used in practice on wine labels, have been, in very approximate descending order of popularity, NAPA, SONOMA, SANTA BARBARA, MONTEREY, SAN LUIS OBISPO, MENDOCINO, AMADOR, EL DORADO, and LAKE.

AVAs are rudimentary, imposing no restrictions on varieties planted or vineyard practices. By 2005, California had more than 87 (out of a national total of 145), many such complete unknowns that county names remain more effective at communicating vineyard location.

Individual AVAs are detailed in this book under the name of the county or larger geographical unit in which they fall, except for CARNEROS, LIVERMORE VALLEY, SANTA CLARA VALLEY, SANTA CRUZ MOUNTAINS, and TEMECULA.

Halliday, J., *Wine Atlas of California* (Sydney, 1993).
Kramer, M., *Making Sense of California Wine* (New York, 1992).
See www.wineinstitute.org/ava/index.html for more information on AVAs.

Viticulture

In the years following Repeal of Prohibition, California viticultural practices were relatively uniform: head-trained, SPUR PRUNED vines spaced about 8 ft apart on rows about 10 ft/3 m apart. Dry farming was the rule in the North Coast, while flood IRRIGATION was the universal practice in the San Joaquin Valley.

During the 1960s, vine TRAINING began to move on to wires, with cane PRUNING for lighter bearing vine varieties and CORDON for heavier yielders. Overhead sprinkler systems for irrigation became more common, especially in the emerging Central Coast. AXR1 became the ROOTSTOCK of choice because of its vigour and near universal adaptability, and heavy, dense canopies were the norm. Vine spacing remained at or near 8 × 10, or between 400 and 600 vines per acre (1,000 to 1,500 vines per ha).

Towards the mid 1980s, all of the old rules went by the way, impelled partly by a new mutation of phylloxera, the so-called biotype B, partly by a recurrence of PIERCE'S DISEASE, and, more significantly, by closer observation of the variables caused by California's turbulent geology. It was not uncommon in the early 1990s to see single properties on the North Coast with three or four different vine spacings, ranging between 800 and 2,000 vines per acre, and as many different systems of CANOPY MANAGEMENT. The aim was to take advantage of variations in soil structures and exposures as well as vine varieties. Since AXR1's resistance to phylloxera had proved disastrously low, rootstock selection was becoming a new art. The 1990s saw a major replanting programme, particularly in Napa and Sonoma, as a direct result of phylloxera and vine disease. The traditional alternative to AXR1 was Rupestris St George but around 30 different rootstocks were being trialled in the mid to late 1990s.

As the focus of winemakers' attention moved from flavour to TEXTURE in the 1990s, grapes have tended to be picked at ever higher BRIX. Since 2000 it has become common to see Cabernet Sauvignon destined for higher priced bottles left on the vine until 27 °Brix is achieved and pH levels rise above 3.7. This technique is unpopular with growers since dessication of the berries results in reduced tonnage, and less income. The technique also frequently requires an addition of WATER to the fermenting must to reduce alcohol levels to below 16 per cent. California wine legislation allows such 'watering back'. The result sought by these winemakers is mouth-filling EXTRACT but soft, luxurious texture from 'mature' tannins (see PHYSIOLOGICAL RIPENESS). These winemakers eschew herbal, green bean aromas in Cabernet in favour of berry and black stone-fruits' flavours.

MECHANICAL HARVESTING is widely employed in California but mainly in the CENTRAL VALLEY and the larger properties on the Salinas in MONTEREY. There is no shortage of Mexican LABOUR (cf. AUSTRALIA, for example), and the higher priced wines of Napa and Sonoma are almost always picked by hand. The Mexican labour force in California is well recompensed by international standards, very highly motivated, and remarkably adept. It is one of California's most important advantages over other wine producers worldwide.

ORGANIC VITICULTURE has grown from a cottage industry in the mid 1980s to a full-blown movement. The phrase 'sustainability' rolls easily off the tongue of most of the state's professional grape growers today, although interestingly it is not a topic widely promoted to consumers. Far fewer wines go to market with a label claiming 'Certified Organic Grapes' than would be expected from the number of vineyards growing grapes without AGROCHEMICALS. Many growers choose not to seek organic certification merely because they see no financial advantage in the market place and wish to leave their options open. BIODYNAMIC VITICULTURE has a few prominent adherents in California, where sceptics still vastly outnumber true believers.

Wine-making

Without tradition as either guide or limitation, most California winemakers have consistently looked to achieve the kind of reproducible results their university training exalts. Understanding a process and then controlling it are, thus, the first two goals of the state's typical OENOLOGIST. Of all the steps in wine-making, FERMENTATION has received the most vigorous attention.

Temperature-controlled fermentation began in California in the 1940s. With the advent of STAINLESS STEEL tanks and more integral cooling systems in the 1960s, there came 'designed' fermentation curves for each major grape variety. Ultra-hygienic, infinitely controllable stainless steel tanks and sterile FILTRATION allowed MALOLACTIC FERMENTATIONS to be brought under control at the same time. Today it is not at all unusual to have malolactic fermentation induced in one low PH batch of Chardonnay, deliberately inhibited in another (higher pH) batch, and then to blend these components for additional complexity in the resulting wine.

Throughout the modern era, ACIDIFICATION has been the norm across the state, but it is becoming slightly less commonplace as grapes are increasingly sourced from the more marginal climates of the coastal regions, where grapes often have higher natural ACIDITY than their counterparts in Bordeaux or Burgundy. DEACIDIFICATION is rarely practised or necessary. CHAPTALIZATION is not permitted, nor ever needed when wines and GRAPE CONCENTRATE from warm inland areas are consistently available for blending.

OAK barrels from French forests came into play as ageing vessels at the beginning of the 1960s; within a decade, BARREL FERMENTATION of white wines was the height of fashion. Chardonnay was and remains foremost among the varieties so fermented, but no white grape variety is immune. COOPERAGE activity in California surged in the 1990s after studies suggested that treatment and technique were more important than whether the oak was French or American. OAK CHIPS and INNER STAVES are commonly available in California but they are not yet widely employed. Nor is MICRO-OXYGENATION widespread.

With rare exceptions, red wines continue to be fermented in TANK, almost always in stainless steel, frequently in open topped vessels which allow mechanical PUNCHING DOWN. After years of separating MUST from CAP just as the fermentation approached dryness, the vogue of the 1980s was extended MACERATION for as long as 25 days after the end of fermentation. Today a broad panoply of maceration techniques is employed in a quest called 'TANNIN management'. As outlined above, the goal is soft MOUTHFEEL achieved through a high degree of EXTRACT and ripe tannins.

YEASTS, the very engine of fermentation, are also much studied and carefully monitored. For years pure strains of specially cultured yeast ruled in California. Towards the end of the 1980s, however, winemakers began to use various combinations of these strains, and were increasingly prepared to experiment with natural or ambient yeast and so-called wild yeasts. The stated goal is greater aromatic complexity. California's naturally arid summer climate lends itself well to minimal use of FUNGICIDES. The cultivation of an ambient yeast population is therefore much easier than it would be in regions subject to frequent spraying. By the turn of the century even large commercial wineries were fermenting as much as a quarter of their production with naturally occurring ambient yeasts.

Organic wine-making has been defined by the US government for labelling purposes since 2001. However, unlike European regulations, the US does not allow any addition of SULFITES which would raise the free sulfur dioxide level over 10 parts per million. The production of wines labelled 'organic' in California is therefore limited to a small, and somewhat eccentric, segment of the industry.

Wine types

The most important California wine type is the VARIETAL, the principal sorts of which are outlined below (see Vine varieties).

The production of inexpensive wines, largely from the Central or San Joaquin valleys, is in the hands of relatively few very large wineries. Most of the state's wineries concentrate on more expensive wines, many of limited production and available only in a few markets. Throughout the 1980s, production of red table wines, to which the state is well adapted, declined precipitously in response to the vagaries of the market. Only 14 per cent of the table wines shipped from California in 1989 were red, the rest being white (53 per cent), rosé (16 per cent), and so-called BLUSH wines (17 per cent). In 1991, this trend abruptly reversed itself thanks to the FRENCH PARADOX phenomenon. By 2004, 41 per cent of all California table wines were red with 40 per cent white and a still-considerable 19 per cent blush or rosé.

American wine diction tends to be based more on tax rates than wine characteristics. Table wine is anything with an ALCOHOLIC STRENGTH of up to 13.9 per cent. Even the finest late harvest imitations of TBAs (see TROCKENBEERENAUSLESE), the ones with 40 per cent residual sugar, are table wines to the taxman. Quality, or lack of it, is not implied by nomenclature as it is in Europe. Dessert wine, meanwhile, is anything with more than 16 per cent of alcohol, even the driest of SHERRY types. Sparkling wine, sensibly, is the stuff with bubbles.

That mastered, California offers few other terms not found elsewhere, or else mutated too little to require explanation, although see also FIGHTING VARIETAL, GENERIC, JUG WINE, and MERITAGE. In addition, there are the proprietary blends, which were originally only tarted-up generics. A Rhine would become Rhine Castle, a Chablis would become Golden Chablis, or somesuch. Some of those continue to exist. However, the advent of fighting varietals in the late 1980s called the supremacy of varietals into question and spawned a new breed of high-priced proprietaries based on blends of classic grape varieties that were traditional in Europe. Meritages, for example, imitate BORDEAUX and there are also equivalent counterparts to RHÔNE blends.

There is also a long and complex history of producing sparkling wine in California, which has had few inhibitions about calling it champagne. HARASZTHY began attempts to make sparkling wines of quality in the 1870s, using the traditional method (see SPARKLING WINE-MAKING). F. Korbel & Bros. came right behind, with rather more success.

In the years since 1970, European- and especially French-owned firms have come to dominate production of California traditional method wines made by traditional techniques using traditional grape varieties. Domaine Chandon was the forerunner. Piper-Sonoma, Mumm-Napa Valley, Roederer Estate, Maison Deutz, Domaine Carneros (Taittinger), and Scharffenberger (Pommery) followed from France, Gloria Ferrer (Freixenet) and Codorníu Napa from Spain. There remains a strong domestic element led by Schramsberg, Iron Horse, and, more recently, Jordan. During the 1990s, competition among foreign producers of sparkling wine in California produced a situation of immense benefit to consumers: quality rose dramatically while prices were ever more deeply discounted. In 1997, Deutz and Piper-Heidsieck sold their California properties and went back home to Champagne.

These are the sources of complexity in sparkling wines. Producers of inexpensive mass-market bubblies make less complicated wines yet complicate the story. American law permits wines made from a wide range of non-traditional grape varieties, made sparkling either by the Charmat CUVE CLOSE process or the Carstens TRANSFER process (which has almost been abandoned since the adoption of GYROPALETTES for RIDDLING), to be called Champagne so long as that word is accompanied by a clear appellation of origin (almost always 'California') and indication of the method used. Such wines are the sparkling equivalents of generic table wines. The 2005 EU–US wine agreement permitted continued use of the term champagne for already established brands of such wines.

Vine varieties

California's mix of vine varieties is one of the world's most fluid, thanks to its high proportion of professional grape farmers selling their produce to wineries in free market conditions, thanks to innate American flexibility, and thanks to the technique of FIELD GRAFTING.

The most planted varieties, in declining order, are Chardonnay, whose total area reached 100,000 acres/40,000 ha in 2003, Cabernet Sauvignon, which passed the 75,000 acre mark in 2003, Merlot (whose total plantings increased spectacularly from 11,000 to 52,000 acres between 1992 and 2003), Zinfandel (50,000 acres), French Colombard (29,800 acres), Pinot Noir (24,000 acres), Syrah (16,000 acres), Sauvignon Blanc (15,000 acres), and Chenin Blanc (11,400 acres). Of these, Chardonnay, Cabernet Sauvignon, Merlot, and Zinfandel dominate labels, while French Colombard and Chenin Blanc are more often non-trumpeted ingredients in less expensive blends, the great majority of them either white or blush. Italian influence is again likely to increase in California's vineyards, most particularly with Sangiovese, Barbera, and Pinot Grigio (sic). Other varieties enjoying modish popularity are Cabernet Franc and Rhône-related varieties such as Grenache, Petite Sirah, and Viognier.

Apart from Zinfandel, varieties that constitute a California speciality, many of them specifically bred in and for the state, are CARNELIAN, CHARBONO, EMERALD RIESLING, FLORA, GREEN HUNGARIAN, PETITE SIRAH, RUBIRED, RUBY CABERNET, and SYMPHONY.

AMPELOGRAPHY, the science of vine identification by human observation, has never been a popular sport with Californians. Nineteenth-century Californians were altogether casual about the identities of the vines they imported and grew. Modern researchers at Davis are using more sophisticated techniques of vine identification such as DNA PROFILING to try to sort out the ancestry of the varieties known in California as Petite Sirah, Valdepeñas (probably TEMPRANILLO), Pinot Blanc (MELON, the Muscadet grape, whose California existence is outlined below), Sauvignon Vert (MUSCADELLE), and Gray Riesling (TROUSSEAU Gris). Gamay presents a particularly confused picture in California. The variety traditionally known in California as Gamay Beaujolais is a clone of PINOT NOIR, with upright growth and an intense but simple aroma, while that called Napa Gamay is the obscure VALDIGUIÉ from south west France. In 1997, US labelling regulations were changed to allow the names Gamay and Gamay Beaujolais exclusively for the GAMAY Noir à Jus Blanc grown in France's Beaujolais region. Muscat Blanc should mean MUSCAT BLANC À PETITS GRAINS, although before a BATF (see TTB) ruling in the early 1990s it was also known as Muscat Frontignan and Muscat Canelli. Orange Muscat is a darker-berried mutation. Malvasia Bianca is a minor variety but has produced some impressive bottles of sweet and off-dry table wine.

The following are the most important varieties found on California wine labels, listed alphabetically. For details of other California vine varieties, see under the variety name.

Cabernet Sauvignon Of all the transplants of European varieties to California, it is Cabernet Sauvignon that seems most at home, particularly in the Napa Valley. Cabernet had surfaced as a leading success in Napa by the 1880s according to producers and critics of the time. Its primacy there has been recognized by authorities ever since, although not always by the consuming public. Other parts of the state have been trying to catch Napa since the 1880s, and most convincingly since the 1970s. The result was a state total of 75,000 acres/30,000 ha in 2003, of which Napa's share, despite vigorous increases in Cabernet acreage, is less than a quarter.

The best ones offer rich textures and an entrancing tennis match of opposing flavours, berries on one side, herbs on the other. Whether by natural gift or historic dominance, Napa produces a majority of the memorably distinctive, age-worthy examples from California. Some show off particular subzones such as the Rutherford-Oakville west side (of which two of the first to establish their credentials were Beaulieu Vineyard's Georges de Latour bottling and Heitz Cellars' Martha's Vineyard), Howell Mountain, or the Stags Leap District (from which a Stag's Leap Wine Cellars offering famously 'beat' some of the great names of France at a much-reported tasting in Paris in 1976). A long list of others come from less-defined regions or are blended from vineyards in differing parts of the valley.

Sonoma does not lag far behind with its finest examples, but they are fewer and more scattered in provenance. Its superior districts appear to be Alexander Valley and Sonoma Valley. The other coastal wine-growing northern county Mendocino shows a kinship in growing conditions, with similar wines. The Central Coast is generally cooler, and not as widely known today for Cabernet, although notable success at everyday price levels has been achieved by some of the larger wineries in the warmer districts inland of the coastal mountains such as Paso Robles and the southernmost sections of the Salinas valley. The inland side of the Santa Cruz Mountains was historically a magnificent district for California Cabernet and several smaller vineyards (Ridge's Montebello would be a premier example) persist today. Meanwhile new plantings in the Sierra Foothills are beginning to show distinct promise for broadening the range of California Cab style with their lighter body, high-toned fruit, and the more aggressive tannins found at increased elevation.

Chardonnay The great white grape variety of Burgundy came late to California but, once arrived, it swiftly came to play vanilla to Cabernet Sauvignon's chocolate. It has become so ubiquitous that many consumers use the name almost synonymously with white wine. However, grown in appropriate vineyards and made with care, it can be glorious and is still the premier white varietal wine of the state.

Wente Bros resolutely grew and made Chardonnay in LIVERMORE VALLEY during the 1940s. They were almost alone until 1952, when Napa's Stony Hill winery brought new attention to the varietal wine. With its celebrated 1957, Hanzell added the effects of new oak barrels to those of the vineyard, inspiring first dozens then scores to clamber on to that bandwagon. After a 1973 from Ch Montelena came first against some respectable white burgundies in a famous blind tasting in Paris in 1976, a whole new gold rush was on. Best estimates are that, by the early 21st century, California wineries were producing more than 1,500 different Chardonnays in each vintage.

During the 1970s, the majority of California Chardonnays were fermented in stainless steel, racked off their lees and presented untroubled by oak. As such, and given the warmer climate (Napa Valley is 37 rather than Burgundy's 47 degrees north of the equator), California did much to introduce the notion of FRUIT DRIVEN Chardonnays to the world. This approach was the technique advocated by UC DAVIS and was followed by most trained winemakers. Some more independent individuals began to experiment with what were then considered the much riskier techniques of BARREL FERMENTATION and LEES CONTACT.

Today, as in Burgundy, indeed because of Burgundy, California Chardonnay is often made as much or more in the cellar as in the vineyard. Barrel fermentation and OAK ageing, MALOLACTIC FERMENTATION, and all the other tricks in the winemaker's bag go into a wide range of styles from outright butterscotchy to straightforwardly fruity, with every stage in between. Most are dry, but a considerable number offer a softening dollop of sweetness (such as KENDALL-JACKSON's, whose supposed 'recipe' was the subject of a famous 1992 court case). Partly thanks to more powerful YEASTS, Chardonnays with more than 14 per cent alcohol are now common.

The grape variety has proven remarkably adaptable, growing well throughout the coastal counties, and not badly in the SIERRA FOOTHILLS. Chardonnay is most widely planted in Napa, Monterey, Santa Barbara, and Sonoma counties, in almost equal measure.

Gewürztraminer The California history of this distinctive ALSACE variety, most often spelt without the umlaut here, is relatively short. It did not come into its own as a varietal wine until the 1950s, and it remains limited in acreage. The variety takes on a particular flavour in California: floral, almost sweet pea, in most of Napa and the warmer parts of Sonoma; very close to lychee in the cooler climates of the Russian River district, the western portion of Santa Ynez Valley in Santa Barbara, Edna Valley in San Luis Obispo, the northern half of Salinas valley in Monterey, and, above all, Mendocino county's Anderson Valley. A substantial majority of California larger producers opt for off-dry styles, but a solid core make the wine fairly dry with only 6 to 8 g/l of RESIDUAL SUGAR. By and large, the dry wines are the ones to age in order to bring Gewürztraminer's perfumes to their most concentrated.

Merlot The historical record suggests that Merlot succeeded rarely and excelled never on its own in California in the years before Prohibition, although as a blending component with Cabernet it did win some important international prizes in the foothill districts of Santa Clara county. When those practitioners disappeared, Merlot disappeared too. It was not apparently grown in the state between 1919 and 1969, when, at last, a few curious growers (notably Louis Martini and Gundlach-Bundschu) began experimenting with it as a possible blending grape to soften the tannins in Cabernet Sauvignon once more. In the mid 1990s, Merlot suddenly took off, becoming the faddish red varietal of choice, a less tannic alternative to Cabernet Sauvignon, particularly when offered in restaurants by the glass. Between 1995 and 2003, Merlot acreage doubled from 26,000 to 52,000. There is much debate as to where in California is best suited to Merlot. Perception of the variety and its specific characteristics has in part been hampered by its mass-market success, which has yielded the bland sort of wines that may have caused it to disappear in the first place. However, more skilful growers and more determined winery owners have pushed several recent examples to heights heretofore not achieved, often with a stiffening soupçon of Cabernet Sauvignon. Of all the districts in which it has been tried to date, the most promising appear to be Napa's Stags Leap District, the Russian River Valley, and the Santa Ynez Valley. Many fine examples still go into blends with Cabernet Sauvignon, usually in the amount of 10 to 15 per cent, or into MERITAGE-like blends in larger proportions.

Pinot Gris/Grigio The faddishness of the American market place has winemakers constantly on the look-out for a new trend (see ABC). By 1998, Pinot Gris had begun to be discussed as a potential candidate, and in 2004 Pinot Gris (often labelled Pinot Grigio) inched passed Sauvignon Blanc to become the second most widely sold white wine in America. No single style has emerged as dominant but California's generally warm climate and its experimentally inclined winemakers tend more

toward Alsace richness than toward the crisper style found in Italy.

Pinot Noir The secrets of Pinot Noir in California turned out to be two: marine-induced fog in the vineyards (or, increasingly, planting at elevations too high to be much influenced by fog) and less time in wood in the cellars than it was given in the early 1980s. Pinot Noir perplexed California winemakers for decades by producing truly outstanding wine once in a great while, but dull stuff most of the time. André TCHELISTCHEFF symbolizes the struggle, never having equalled by his own judgement the splendid pair he made for Beaulieu Vineyard in 1946 and 1947. The harder people tried to make something grand, the more often they fell short. In the 1970s, the search for more suitable vineyards began to move ever closer to tidal shores. By the end of the 1980s, three districts had emerged, if not triumphant then at least much closer to triumph. Unified only by their proximity to a saltwater shore, they are Carneros, the Russian River Valley of Sonoma, and Santa Barbara county, especially its Santa Maria Valley and Santa Rita Hills. On a slightly later curve, more and more wineries were trimming the time they left their Pinot Noirs in French oak barrels from two years or more to one year or less. With rare exceptions, long wood ageing diminishes California-grown Pinot Noirs to extinction. They emerge browning, raisiny, and dried out. The shorter span confers complexity of bouquet, yet leaves the wines richer in texture and readier to age well in bottle. Pinot Noir enthusiasts tend to have their own favourites but Au Bon Climat, Gary Farrell (purchased by ALLIED DOMECQ in 2004), Rochioli, and Williams Selyem were some of the most consistently successful producers during the 1990s. Since then districts such as Anderson Valley, the new Fort Ross AVA in northern Sonoma, and the Santa Lucia Highlands on Salinas valley's western bench have created a considerable stir. Producers and growers such as Gary Pisoni, Siduri, Flowers, and Merry Edwards represent the new vanguard.

Riesling In the 1960s, Riesling was, with Cabernet Sauvignon, Chardonnay, and Pinot Noir, one of the Big Four in California. Beginning in the 1970s, its reputation began to decline, as an explosion in differing sweetness levels lacked a coherent set of semantic explanations. There may be a connection. During the 1980s, both sales and acreage tumbled, and scores of wineries abandoned Germany's noblest grape, leaving it in the hands of a few stubborn supporters. By the mid 2000s, barely 20 wineries produced a varietally labelled Riesling.

California Riesling cannot be mistaken for its German counterparts, being riper in flavour and weightier with higher alcohol. Its finest homes, albeit vestigial, in California include Mendocino's Anderson Valley, the higher reaches of El Dorado county, Mon-

terey's Arroyo Seco district, and Santa Barbara county. Although a winemakers' fascination with BOTRYTIS-affected sweet wines may have helped cause its downfall as a drier wine, examples of the former have been memorable from the likes of Freemark Abbey, Ch St Jean, and Joseph Phelps; examples of the latter from Greenwood Ridge, Madroña, and Claiborne-Churchill.

Sangiovese The classic Tuscan variety has received vigorous attention in California since the end of the 1980s, partly as a result of the ABC phenomenon and partly because of the success of Italianate restaurants throughout the US. Artistic success initially lagged well behind marketing interest, with many initial offerings appearing distinctly thin and often strawberry flavoured. Since the end of the 1990s, however, improvement in varietally labelled offerings has been noteworthy, perhaps due to VINE AGE—and a handful of blends (usually with Cabernet, Merlot, or Syrah) have on occasion been remarkable.

Sauvignon Blanc Dr Maynard A. AMERINE, long a voice of conscience for California winemakers in post at the University of California at Davis, used to call Sauvignon Blanc California's greatest white grape. He would also confess that the variety's forceful flavours probably needed tempering to appeal to the American public. There, in a nutshell, is its career, whether under its own name or under the California-coined synonym FUMÉ BLANC. It makes outstanding wines that many find too specific to enjoy, especially against the milder charms of Chardonnay. Some age their Sauvignons in new oak, disguising it as a sort of poor man's Chardonnay. Some blend in proportions of Semillon to temper the flavour and fill out a characteristically light body. Some do both.

In 2003, it was grown on 14,500 acres, which meant it was by far the most widely planted premium variety after Chardonnay. Memorable Sauvignon Blanc examples have come from Livermore Valley, Sonoma Valley, Napa Valley, and Santa Barbara. Scores of producers compete well; nearly every region in the state produces at least agreeably balanced wines from the variety. Generally speaking, straightforwardly styled Central Coast Sauvignon Blancs (Santa Ynez Valley, Monterey) smack sharply of the herbaceous or grassy flavours for which Sauvignon is so widely noted. Their North Coast counterparts are more subtly herbaceous from the cooler zones (Russian River Valley, lower Napa Valley), almost melony from warmer areas (upper Napa Valley, upper Alexander Valley). Temecula gives a curiously floral twist to the flavours, and Amador county in the Sierra Foothills yields a slightly brackish quality.

In recent years, an ever-increasing number of growers have been allowing grapes to become botrytis affected for sweet wines styled after SAUTERNES. Early results have charmed in youth, but tended to fade quickly.

Syrah California's RHÔNE RANGERS have generated growing interest in this French variety. Fleshy, clean, and plum-scented, perhaps more reminiscent of Australian Shiraz than the more microbiologically laden examples of the Rhône Valley. In fact California's surge in Syrah interest can trace its inception to a 1973 importation of cuttings from Australia. California Syrahs have achieved remarkable success in only a few years with acreage growing from 2,200 in 1995 to 16,000 in 2003. The Sierra Foothills, the warmer canyons of eastern Santa Barbara county, the Hopland area of Mendocino, and Sonoma's Dry Creek Valley have particularly distinguished themselves.

Viognier The 1980s' explosion of interest in red Rhône varieties was echoed in the 1990s with their white counterparts. Although a handful of California producers have dabbled with Marsanne and Roussanne, the majority of entrants have cast their lot with Viognier. Indeed while its cradle, the CONDRIEU appellation in France, boasted about 200 acres of the variety in 1995, California planted at least 600 acres in the 1990s alone, and boasted more than 2,000 acres by 2003. Pioneers included Ritchie Creek, La Jota, and Calera but the first major commitment was made by John Alban, who planted 30 acres in San Luis Obispo's Edna Valley district in 1989. Quality and style have been about as variable as the prices, with many expensive offerings being mediocre at best, prejudicing the variety's prospects although there have been some successes.

Zinfandel Conclusively shown in 2003 by Dr Carole Meredith of DAVIS to have originated on an island off the Dalmatian coast of CROATIA (see ZINFANDEL), California's signature grape languished to the point of extinction in its native home. It is a thin-skinned variety with compact, often large, clusters which are prone to rot in wet conditions. But from the time it arrived in the 1850s, Zin flourished in the dry California climate. Virtually a California exclusive for more than a century, the variety for long suffered from an image problem. Lacking a famous European forebear, it had to be taken on its own terms. Few critics had the independence of mind to do so, and so until the mid 1990s it was consigned to the category of a low-priced, honest, Italian-American working man's wine. All that has since changed. Mediocre Zinfandels now fetch US$20 per bottle and well-made examples from 80-year-old vines (one of California's great viticultural treasures) routinely command $35 to $60 a bottle. The variety even has its own four-day ZAP (Zinfandel Advocates and Producers) Festival, which draws 15,000 revellers from all over the world to San Francisco each January.

Although sometimes deliberately vinified to minimize this characteristic, Zinfandel can easily be chewier than a Cabernet. Beyond its robust textures, Zinfandel at the height of its powers tastes of the strain of raspberry Americans call boysenberry. Although it often has the structure and balance to age well, time does not replace its glorious flavours of berry with anything as pleasing. Flavours from oak barrels can also be difficult to work into harmony with the taste of berries. Many California producers opt for the sweet coconut flavours of American oak barrels to achieve this harmony. All the foregoing means that Zinfandel must come from a superior vineyard or be ordinary. Much inconclusive, artistic debate turns on vine age, and on trellising versus the traditional BUSH VINES.

The variety finds its most congenial home on dry-farmed hillsides originally identified in parts of California at the turn of the last century by immigrant Italians. A centrepiece of this cultural community is Sonoma's Dry Creek Valley, the Russian River district, Mendocino county, Sonoma Valley and, though the fact is little recognized, Napa Valley. San Luis Obispo county's Paso Robles has a long, strong history with Zinfandel, as does Amador county in the Sierra Foothills and Lodi and the Delta region of the Central Valley. All of these tend to make headier, riper wines than Sonoma, and heady, port-style wines made from late harvested old Zinfandel vines enjoyed a brief vogue in the early 1970s. See also WHITE ZINFANDEL.   B.C.C.

See also CARNEROS, CENTRAL COAST, CENTRAL VALLEY, LAKE COUNTY, LIVERMORE VALLEY, MENDOCINO, MONTEREY, NAPA, SAN LUIS OBISPO, SANTA BARBARA, SANTA CLARA VALLEY, SANTA CRUZ MOUNTAINS, SIERRA FOOTHILLS, SONOMA, and TEMECULA.

Cass, B. (ed.), *Oxford Companion to the Wines of North America* (Oxford and New York, 2000).

Darlington, D., *Angel's Visits: An Inquiry into the Mystery of Zinfandel* (New York, 1991).

Halliday, J., *Wine Atlas of California* (Sydney, 1993).

Kramer, M., *Matt Kramer's New California Wine: Making Sense of Napa Valley, Sonoma, Central Coast, and Beyond* (New York, 2004).

Muscatine, D., Amerine, M. A., and Thompson, B. (eds.), *The University of California/Sotheby's Book of California Wine* (Berkeley, Calif., 1984).

Sullivan, C., *A Companion to California Wine* (Berkeley, Calif., 1998).

Swinchatt, J., *Winemakers' Dance* (Berkeley, 2004).

California cult wines, a phrase coined in the 1990s to encompass wines made in the state of California, typically but not exclusively Napa Valley Cabernets, for which COLLECTORS, and possibly a few INVESTORS, would pay PRICES higher than those of Bordeaux's FIRST GROWTHS. They include such names as Araujo, Bryant Family, Colgin, Dalla Valle Maya, Grace Family, Harlan Estate, Moraga, Screaming Eagle, and Vineyard 29. What many of these names have in common is that they are made in extremely limited quantity, by talented winemaker CONSULTANTS (often female) currently favoured by FASHION.

California sprawl, term commonly used to describe the CANOPY of a vine trained on the simple TRELLIS SYSTEM adopted in many of the vineyards replanted in California in the mid 1980s in the wake of PHYLLOXERA damage. It generally refers to a trellis with a single fruiting wire plus one foliage wire above this, though there are some variations. This results in a sprawling vine without rigorous SHOOT POSITIONING. Although this inexpensive form of training can lead to a shaded canopy with poor bud fruitfulness and increased vegetative growth, this is more often a consequence of poor SITE SELECTION and inappropriate VINE DENSITY or ROOTSTOCK. Under such circumstances, any simple training system would be inadequate. See also CANOPY MANAGEMENT.

Calitor, almost extinct traditional Provençal vine allowed but rarely used in wines of the southern Rhône. Its wines tend to be light, but in hillside sites they can add character. This may be the Garriag of Cataluña.

Callet, Mallorcan grape often planted as a FIELD BLEND with Fogoneu Mallorqué or Fogoneu Francés, although Spanish statistics of 2004 recorded a total 176 ha/435 acres planted. All three tend to produce small quantities of deep-coloured wines with relatively little alcohol. Used mainly for rosés, but some Callet has shown it can make a lively young red.

callus, the white, formless tissue that grows from CAMBIUM tissue at cut and wounded surfaces of the grapevine on stems and roots. It is critical for vine GRAFTING since it signifies that the conditions for cell division are favourable and that the underlying graft or bud has united. High humidity, oxygen supply, and warm temperatures are the major requirements for rapid callus development. In the field, these conditions may be achieved by waxing or by wrapping the tissues tightly with plastic grafting tape. After BENCH GRAFTING, the cuttings are packed with moist material and held in a warm, humid room. (See also TISSUE CULTURE and illustration under GRAFTING.)   B.G.C.

Hartmann, H. T., and Kester, D. E., *Plant Propagation: Principles and Practices* (3rd edn, Englewood Cliffs, NJ, 1975).

Caluso, town in northern PIEMONTE most famous for its sweet white ERBALUCE.

calyptra, or flower cap, of the vine flower consists of the five petals joined together in the form of an inverted cup. The cap separates as a unit and falls from the grape flower at FLOWERING and exposes the STAMENS, which produce pollen, and the STIGMA, which receives pollen. The rate of capfall is slowed by cold and rain; the duration of capfall can stretch from a normal seven to ten days to as long as 15 to 20 days. FRUIT SET is impaired if the caps are retained and so this very small part of the grapevine can affect YIELD, especially for varieties such as MERLOT.   B.G.C.

Câmara de Lobos, or **Cama de Lobos**, occasionally found on bottles of ancient MADEIRA, is a wine district west of the capital Funchal on the south coast of the island associated with noble vine varieties and fine wine.

Camaralet, obscure vine allowed but hardly grown in BÉARN and JURANÇON in south west France that can make strongly flavoured white wine.

Camarate, Portuguese red wine grape also known as Mortágua in Arruda, and occasionally as Castelão Nacional (unrelated to CASTELÃO).

cambium, a zone of dividing cells in plants such as the grapevine; the inner cells develop into XYLEM and later differentiate into wood, while the outer cells develop into PHLOEM and, later, bark. The matching of cambial zones is important to the success of BUDDING and GRAFTING.

Another secondary cambium is the cork cambium, which cuts off non-living suberized cells yielding bark, as during vine CANE RIPENING. Of course the cork most readily associated with wine is the CORK derived from the secondary cambium of QUERCUS *suber* and used as CLOSURES.   B.G.C.

Campania, region of south west Italy of which Naples is the capital. In the ancient world, Campania was the home of some of the most renowned wines of Italy, if not of the whole Mediterranean basin: SURRENTINE, Calenian, MASSIC, and, most famous of all, FALERNIAN. Modern reality is considerably more modest: only 1,100 ha/2,700 acres of the region's total 48,000 ha/118,600 acres of vineyards are in DOC zones, and the regional production of DOC wines, which has risen to 80,000 hl/2.1 million gal, is still just over 3.5 per cent of the region's total production of 2.2 million hl, one of the lowest proportions of any of Italy's 20 regions.

Campania's natural beauty can be deceptive: the bay of Naples, Capri, and the Amalfi coast do not reflect the grinding poverty of the depopulated interior, which has also been severely damaged in recent earthquakes, and the desperate *plebs* of its regional capital of Naples, Italy's third largest city, offer little in terms of an interesting market. The possibility of good-quality viticulture none the less exists: abundant sunshine and HILLSIDE sites for vineyards, volcanic soil quite suitable for vinegrowing, and, most important of all, local vine varieties of real interest. AGLIANICO produces

red wine of unquestionable character in the TAURASI DOC near Avellino, and non-DOC Aglianico wines of some potential can also be found in the province of Avellino (in the townships of Sabato, Bonito, Fontanarosa, Grottaminarda, Montefredane, Santa Lucia di Serino, Solofra, and Tufo) and in the province of Benevento, where the IGT Aglianico del Sannio is produced.

The Solopaca DOC in the province of Benevento, with almost 500 ha/12,300 acres, produces an interesting, if rustic, red wine with occasional notes of tobacco, from a blend of 45 to 60 per cent SANGIOVESE grapes, Aglianico (10 to 20 per cent), PIEDIROSSO (20 to 25 per cent), and other red varieties. Attempts to revive the glory of Falernian are under way, with the recent Falerno del Massico DOC on the slopes of Monte Massico near Mondragone stipulating a blend of Aglianico (60 to 80 per cent), Piedirosso (20 to 40 per cent), plus PRIMITIVO or BARBERA (up to a maximum of 20 per cent). White and all-Primitivo versions are also made. The wines are still too young to be judged, although it seems safe to say that they will not match the 100-year-old Falernian served by Trimalchio in Petronius' *Satyricon*.

While Aglianico is the region's finest red wine variety, it is rivalled for interest by such white grapes as FIANO and GRECO.

Fiano d'Avellino, which takes its name from the variety the Romans called *Vitis apiana*, vine beloved of bees, is said to be redolent of pears and hazelnuts and bottles frequently carry the classical diction 'apianum'. Greco di Tufo, made from a clone of the GRECO BIANCO vine grown around the village of Tufo, is said to recall peaches and almonds. Both of these descriptions correspond to the epoch in which the wines underwent some ageing in wood. Now made in a fresher style, with fermentation at lower temperatures in order to capture the flavours accumulated in the grapes during the long growing season (the grapes are not picked until early October), the best wines have an aromatic dimension that few other native Italian varieties can match.

While the once-renowned viticulture of the island of Capri has virtually disappeared before the Gadarene onrush of modern tourism, ISCHIA has managed to maintain 64 ha of DOC vineyards, producing small quantities of white and minuscule quantities of red wine.

D.T. & D.C.G.

Bastianich, J., and Lynch, D., *Vino Italiano: The Regional Wines of Italy* (New York, 2002).
Belfrage, N., *From Brunello to Zibibbo: The Wines of Southern Italy* (London, 2001).

Campo de Borja, promising Spanish wine zone in the undulating plains around the town of Borja (after which the Borgia family was named) in the ARAGÓN region in the north east (see map under SPAIN), producing fairly alcoholic red wines. This is one of the most arid parts of the country and the

7,400 ha/18,290 acres of low-yielding vineyards, planted predominantly with GARNACHA vines, produce intensely sweet, dark grapes which are made into heady red wines. Tempranillo and Cabernet Sauvignon are now accepted varieties. The Borsao Borja co-operative has revolutionized the region with its young, intensely fruity reds that have won a large following on export markets and shown the way to the future for the DO. The best wines, notably the result of an Australo-American JOINT VENTURE, can command prices that would not even have been dreamt of in the late 1990s.

V. de la S. & J.R.

Canaan was the coastal region comprising a tiny part of modern TURKEY, the coast of modern SYRIA, LEBANON, and ISRAEL, from Gaza in the south to Hamath in the north, c.1000 BC. The pharaohs of Ancient EGYPT were struggling to maintain their control of this area during the 14th century BC, as we can read in the Amarna letters, an extensive correspondence between the pharaohs and the local puppet rulers and officials of Canaan. 'See that much food and wine—everything in great quantities—is made available for the archers of the king,' writes one Egyptian monarch.

Records on cuneiform tablets from the kingdom centres on the city of Ugarit (c.1200 BC; modern Ras Rhamra near Latakia about 160 km/100 miles north of the vineyards of modern Lebanon) indicate extensive viticulture. A standard formulation in describing properties for real estate transactions at this date mentions 'a house, together with its [watch-]tower, its olive grove and its vineyard'. However, life was as difficult in this area then as it was in the 1980s, since a complaint addressed by the prefect of Ugarit to a local great king, who was acting as mediator, stated that the people of Siyannu, a neighbouring city, 'have cut down our vines'. The people of Ugarit were obliged to swear not to cut down the vines of Siyannu, and moreover to swear (somewhat ingenuously) that they knew nothing of the identity of the perpetrators of such acts in the past. A similar dispute was adjudicated on the same occasion, this time concerning an allegation that wine from Ugarit had been stolen and sold unofficially to dealers at Beirut, down the coast.   J.A.B.

Canada has a thriving wine industry concentrated in four provinces, Ontario, British Columbia, and to a lesser extent Quebec and Nova Scotia. Given the exigencies of the Canadian climate, grapes are invariably grown near large bodies of water that moderate the effects of Canada's severe winters and decrease the risk of damaging WINTER FREEZE and spring FROSTS (see LAKE EFFECT). Until the late 1970s, the majority of Canadian vines were the winter-hardy North American LABRUSCA varieties such as CONCORD and Niagara. Next to follow were early-ripening, winter-resistant

FRENCH HYBRIDS such as VIDAL BLANC, SEYVAL BLANC, BACO NOIR, and MARCÉHAL FOCH, often called simply Foch in Canada. Since the late 1980s, however, growers have put greater emphasis on VINIFERA vine varieties, whose wines enjoy increasing success both at home and abroad. Riesling and Chardonnay are particularly important in Ontario, while Pinot Blanc and Merlot are specialities of British Columbia. In warm pockets, in both growing regions, Viognier, Syrah, and Petite Sirah can be found and some success has been established with Cabernets and Pinot Noir in warmer years.

Perhaps the most notable accomplishment has been the consistently high quality of sweet wines produced in Canada, especially ICEWINE and late harvest Riesling, Vidal, Ehrenfelser, and Optima. Canada is the world's largest producer of Icewine, which is not surprising since sustained temperatures of −8 °C can be relied upon each winter. The APPELLATION system (VQA) of Ontario, for instance, sets the minimum sugar levels for Icewine at 35 °BRIX, substantially higher than those for Germany's EISWEIN.

History

The Canadian wine industry dates from the early 19th century (although see also VÍNLAND). In 1811, a retired German corporal, Johann Schiller, domesticated the *labrusca* vines he found growing along the Credit river west of Toronto and planted a 20-acre vineyard. In 1866, the country's first major winery Vin Villa was established at Canada's most southerly point, on Pelee island on lake Erie, by three gentlemen farmers from Kentucky who planted 20 acres/8 ha of ISABELLA vines. By 1890, there were 41 commercial wineries across the country, 35 in Ontario. In the Okanagan valley of British Columbia and along the St Lawrence river shoreline in Quebec, it was the Church rather than the regions' farmers which encouraged the planting of vineyards and fostered the art of wine-making.

PROHIBITION, which began in Canada in 1916, spurred the wine trade. Thanks to some fancy political lobbying by the grape-growers, wine was exempted from the general interdiction against alcohol. By the time the Great Experiment was brought to an end in 1927 (six years before Repeal in the United States), 57 winery licences had been granted in Ontario alone.

In that year, another experiment began, the creation of the provincial liquor board system, government MONOPOLIES which control the sale and distribution of all beverage alcohol sold in Canada and collect hundreds of millions of dollars in tax revenues. (By the mid 1990s, Alberta had privatized and British Columbia and Manitoba had some privately owned wine merchant stores competing with government monopolies.)

Until the mid 1970s, most Canadian wines were sweet, highly alcoholic products made from *labrusca* varieties and labelled Sherry or Port, depending on the colour.

The advent of the 'boutique' (small, usually owner-managed) winery was signalled in 1974 when Inniskillin, near Niagara Falls, was granted the first commercial licence since Prohibition. This coincided with a shift in public taste towards drier, less alcoholic, TABLE WINE. The wineries that followed in Ontario and British Columbia were dedicated to the proposition that *vinifera* grapes could be grown on appropriate sites in spite of the harsh winters and unpredictable springs.

In 1988, an APPELLATION system called Vintners Quality Alliance (VQA) was introduced, first in Ontario and then in British Columbia. See Wine laws below.

The Canadian wine industry has spawned a considerable number of estate wineries in which grape-growers are developing agritourism by offering events, attractions, bed and breakfast accommodation, and winery restaurants as well as wine.

Climate

Geographically, the major concentration of Canadian vineyards is on the same latitude as the LANGUEDOC and CHIANTI, but lower winter temperatures , the freeze–thaw–freeze cycle of early spring, and unpredictable weather at HARVEST rank Canada as a COOL CLIMATE wine region, with all the vintage variation and winemaking challenges that entails.

While some of Canada's vineyards may enjoy hotter summers than either Bordeaux or Burgundy, the growing season tends to be shorter. According to one estimate, average sunshine hours during the growing season are 1,500 in the Niagara peninsula, Ontario; 1,423 in British Columbia's Okanagan valley; and 1,150 in Dunham, Quebec—compared with 1,315 in Burgundy. A high proportion of grapes require CHAPTALIZATION. Drought can be a problem and some producers have installed irrigation systems.

Wine laws

Wine regulations vary from province to province. Most wine is retailed by provincial MONOPOLIES such as the Liquor Control Board of Ontario (LCBO).

The Vintners Quality Alliance Act in Ontario and similar legislation in BC establishes the legal framework for an appellation of origin system as well as minimum standards that must be met in order to obtain VQA approval. Compliance with the standards is legally enforced in Ontario and still voluntary in BC.

Minimum MUST WEIGHTS and limits to chaptalization are specified along with permitted grape varieties (not LABRUSCA).

Canadian wineries may also bottle wines which contain imported produce and which are not therefore entitled to the VQA designation. A wine labelled Product of Canada or Cellared in Canada usually contains a majority of imported grape juice or wine, particularly so after short domestic crops.

Ontario

Number of wineries: 130

Area under vine: 518 vineyards, 5,880 ha/ 14,700 acres vinifera, total 6,800 ha/17,000 acres including hybrids

Average wine grape production: about 40,000 tonnes

Ontario produces the majority of Canada's wine in three designated areas: the Niagara Peninsula, best known for the dramatic Niagara Falls, Lake Erie North Shore further to the south west, and Pelee Island, the most southerly point in Canada. Each of these areas is in the southern part of the province between the 41st and 43rd latitudes and within sight and influence of two of the Great lakes, lake Ontario and lake Erie, which temper the winter cold and the heat of summer (see LAKE EFFECT).

This cool climate growing region has a CONTINENTAL climate that is subject to extremes of very hot, often humid summers with occasional drought, to very cold winters where temperatures can fall below −20 °C. However, the median degree days (see CLIMATE CLASSIFICATION) during the growing season of 1426 °C are greater than Beaune, France (1315 °C), Hawkes Bay, New Zealand (1200 °C), and equal to that of Yakima, Washington. Long days and cool nights slow down fruit maturation while maximizing levels of acidity. More than 50 different varieties of wine grapes are grown in Ontario, where the rich ethnic mix of grape-growers is reflected in an unusually broad range including Viognier, Gewurztraminer, Zweigelt, Auxerrois, and Pinot Grigio.

Ontario is also the home to the Cool Climate Oenology and Viticulture Institute at BROCK University in St Catharines.

The **Niagara Peninsula**, the largest wine region in Canada (13,000 acres of vinifera, 16,000 total) is dominated by the moderating effect of its position between lakes Ontario and Erie. The proximity of the southern leg of the Niagara escarpment moderates air flow by acting as a passive barrier against continental winds. Climatically similar to Burgundy, the region regularly produces opulent Chardonnay, and Pinot Noir which has performed well enough to attract BOISSET of Burgundy to establish with VINCOR a JOINT VENTURE winery dedicated to the variety, designed by architect Frank Gehry, no less. Other Burgundian varieties such as Gamay Noir, Auxerrois, and Pinot Gris also thrive here.

Because of the length of the growing season, Niagara can produce elegant Rieslings. Late harvest wines, including Icewine, have gained international recognition. In warmer areas of the peninsula, Cabernet Franc, Merlot, Malbec, and Cabernet Sauvignon can ripen fully, and recent years have seen successes with the northern Rhône varieties Viognier and Syrah. FRENCH HYBRIDS such as Marechal Foch and Baco Noir, when taken seriously, have produced some of the most consistently successful reds, while Vidal is especially treasured for Icewine and other Late Harvest wines.

The Viticultural Areas (VAs) Lake Erie North Shore (42nd parallel) and Pelee Island (41st parallel) have the longest growing season and the highest number of heat units of any place in Canada but also the risk of WINTER FREEZE. Both areas continue to hold promise when scrupulous attention is paid to site selection and cultivars planted.

Pelee Island is the smallest VA and located in Lake Erie about 20 km from the shore with 243 ha/607 acres under vine. Marginally nearer the equator than Rome, it enjoys a longer growing season, often more than 30 days more, than the mainland. Canada's first commercial winery operation began here in 1866. **Lake Erie North Shore** in south western Ontario comprises a narrow band along the north shore over a large area but with only 142 ha/355 acres of mainly *vinifera* vines.

Wines carrying a viticultural designation must be made exclusively from *vinifera* grapes—except Icewine, which can also be made from Vidal. The fruit of *labrusca* vines, still grown in Ontario, is used primarily for juice and some inexpensive non-VQA sparkling wine. L.Br.

British Columbia
Number of wineries: 98
   Area under vine: (371 vineyards) 2,185 ha/ 5,462 acres
   Wine grape production: (2004) 18,000 tonnes
With only a quarter of Canada's vineyards in the country's extreme west, British Columbia produces a significant share of the best Canadian wines. European vines thrive in a largely disease-free terroir once believed too cold for *vinifera*. The province is currently divided into four APPELLATIONS. The smallest (28 ha/ 69 acres) is the **Fraser Valley** near Vancouver. Most coastal wineries are in the **Vancouver Island** and Gulf Islands (115 ha/285 acres) appellation. Because of the cool maritime climate, early-ripening varieties (Ortega, Pinot Noir, Pinot Gris) predominate. Most wineries here buy additional grapes from the Okanagan Valley (1850 ha/4,573 acres) and the nearby **Similkameen Valley** (84 ha/207.5 acres). These latter appellations, comprising 92 per cent of British Columbia's vineyards, are 400 km east of Vancouver, protected from coastal rains by two moderate mountain ranges. The season is hot and arid. With the lowest precipitation in southern Canada, vineyards must be irrigated. The dominant varieties include the major Bordeaux red varieties as well as Pinot Noir, Pinot Gris, Chardonnay, and Gewurztraminer.

The **Okanagan Valley**, one of the world's most northerly wine regions, is a superbly scenic glacial trench extending from the 49th parallel north for about 160 km. The defining feature is vast Okanagan lake, the largest of the valley's chain of lakes which tempers baking summer heat (see LAKE EFFECT). The southern part of the Okanagan is the northern extension of the Sonoran desert. Vineyards, on sand or well-drained sandy clay loam, are mainly on slopes.

The first vines in the Okanagan were planted in 1859 by a French Oblate priest, Charles Pandosy. The first important vineyards were developed from 1928 by a horticulturist who planted *labrusca* vines and sold grapes to the province's first wineries, which mushroomed in the 1960s.

Wineries would have preferred to import California grapes but the province insisted they also buy domestic grapes. Because local scientists opposed *vinifera*, new growers initially chose productive French and American HYBRIDS that were winter-hardy but yielded mediocre wine.

The quest for better wine led to *vinifera* trials. Inkameep Vineyards, established in the southern Okanagan by the Osoyoos Indian Band, planted Riesling, Ehrenfelser and Scheurebe in 1975.

The economic convulsion that swept away most second-rate wines was the free trade agreement concluded in 1988 between Canada and the United States. It stripped away the protections that domestic wines had enjoyed against competing imports. More than two-thirds of the Okanagan vineyards were pulled out after the 1988 harvest (18,400 tons, a record not equalled until the 2005 vintage).

The industry regrouped in 1990, forming the British Columbia Wine Institute and adapting the Ontario-developed Vintners Quality Alliance (VQA) program which imposed the first significant standards of wine quality and included mandatory tasting. Consumer confidence in the wines recovered, attracting new growers who from 1993 bought fallow vineyards or converted orchards.

British Columbia's largest producer is VINCOR, one of whose many JOINT VENTURES is Osoyoos Larose in partnership with Groupe Taillan, owner of Bordeaux's Ch Gruaud Larose, the first European producer to invest in British Columbia.

As a wine region, British Columbia is still defining itself. More than 60 grape varieties are grown and there are no restrictive appellation rules. Almost every style of wine is produced from sparkling wine to Icewine. The most successful are the BORDEAUX BLENDS, Chardonnay, and Pinot Gris, with credible Pinot Noir coming from selected sites. J.S.

Quebec
Number of wineries: 30
   Area under vine: 330 acres
   Production: 30,000 cases
Quebec is the least likely of all Canadian wine regions. The centre of the province's small but enthusiastic wine-growing zone is the old town of Dunham. The wineries, for the most part strung out along the American border, have to battle the elements to produce wine for the tourist trade. The vines need time-consuming WINTER PROTECTION. Average sunshine hours during the growing season in Dunham are approximately 1,150 (in Burgundy they are 1,315; Niagara has 1,500 and the Okanagan valley 1,423). Despite relatively low temperatures, topographical features create highly localized warm spots that allow the hardiest vines to survive, if not flourish. Quebec's cottage wineries produce mainly white wines, mostly very fresh SEYVAL BLANC, Vidal, Chardonnay, and Riesling. There is no appellation system in Quebec.

Nova Scotia
Number of wineries: 6
   Area under vine: 350 acres
   Average annual production: 600 tonnes
Midway between the equator and the North Pole, Nova Scotia has a notably short growing season which restricts the number of varieties that can be planted in the Annapolis valley and Northumberland strait. Plantings include local speciality L'ACADIE, Vidal, Seyval Blanc, Marechal Foch, and DE CHAUNAC. Earlier ripening clones are being sought. Like Quebec, Nova Scotia has no appellation system.

T.A. & L.Br.

Aspler, T., *Vintage Canada* (2nd edn, Toronto, 1995).
Bramble, L., *Discovering Niagara Wine Country* (Toronto, 2003).
Schreiner, J., *The Wineries of British Columbia* (Victoria, 1994).
——*The British Columbia Wine Companion* (Victoria, 1996).

Canaiolo, or **Canaiolo Nero**, red grape variety grown all over central Italy and, perhaps most famously, a permitted ingredient in the controversial recipe for CHIANTI, in which it played a more important part than SANGIOVESE in the 18th century. It has declined considerably in popularity since it was relatively difficult to graft in the wake of PHYLLOXERA, and suffered from poor CLONAL SELECTION. The decline in popularity of the GOVERNO wine-making trick has also hastened its decline since Canaiolo, without either the structure of Sangiovese or the scent of MAMMOLO, was most prized for its resistance to rot while being dried for *governo* use. Canaiolo of good quality does still exist in scattered spots in Chianti Classico, notably—and unsurprisingly—at the two RICASOLI properties of Castello di Brolio and Castello di Cacchiano in Gaiole in Chianti, in Barbarino Val d'Elsa (where the Castello della Paneretta and neighbour Isole e Olena both use Canaiolo in their Chianti Classico), and in the VINO NOBILE DI MONTEPULCIANO production zone. Efforts to salvage the variety by better clonal and MASS SELECTIONS are under way in Toscana, but there are few illusions that this will be accomplished either easily or quickly. Canaiolo is also grown, to an even more limited extent, in

LAZIO, SARDEGNA, and the MARCHE. Italy's total plantings of Canaiolo Nero have declined rapidly in recent years to well under 3,000 ha/ 7,410 acres.

A light-berried **Canaiolo Bianco** is also grown in Umbria, where, in ORVIETO, it is known as Drupeggio, but has also been declining in popularity.   D.T. & D.C.G.

Canandaigua, based in Fairport in the Finger lakes region of NEW YORK state, is a subsidiary of (and was the original name of) what is now the dominant American wine company CONSTELLATION.

Canary Islands, Spanish islands in the Atlantic ocean off the coast of Morocco which were famous in Shakespearian England, as witness Sir Toby Belch's call for 'a cup of canary' in *Twelfth Night*. The mediocre wines for the tourist trade are slowly being replaced by more interesting products, much subsidized by the regional government, including young reds from the LISTÁN NEGRO and NEGRAMOLL grapes and whites from LISTÁN Blanco, as well as the sweet MALVASÍAS from La Palma and Lanzarote islands. The number of denominated zones has ballooned, and by the mid 2000s included one for each of the islands of La Palma, El Hierro, Lanzarote, and Gran Canaria (with Monte Lentiscal as a named subregion), and no fewer than five for the island of Tenerife (Abona, Tacoronte-Acentejo, Valle de Güímar, Valle de la Orotava, and Ycoden-Daute-Isora). Bodegas Viñátigo in Tenerife island's Ycoden-Daute-Isora DO is one of the most effective producers, making varietal Listan, VIJARIEJO, MARMAJUELO, and Gual (which is the same as Madeira's Boal/BUAL).   V. de la S.

Canberra, the capital of AUSTRALIA, is ringed by wineries which together constitute a wine region called the Canberra District, even if, because freeholds are not granted in the Australian Capital Territory itself, they are all, bar one, over the border in the Southern NEW SOUTH WALES Zone. There is considerable site climate diversity due to variations in ALTITUDE from 500 m to 800 m (1,640–2,625 ft). Thus Riesling, Semillon–Sauvignon Blanc blends, Chardonnay, Pinot Noir, Shiraz Viognier (Clonakilla the star performer), and Cabernet blends can and do prosper in the correct site. Overall wine quality has improved markedly since the early 1990s.

cane, the stem of a mature grapevine shoot after the bark becomes tan-coloured at VERAISON and starts its overwintering form (see CANE RIPENING and CAMBIUM). After leaves have fallen, the canes of a vine display the total vegetative growth it made during the previous season (called the 'brush' in the US). The number of canes and their weight and average size are important guides to decisions about BALANCED PRUNING and CANOPY MANAGEMENT tactics. The canes are cut at winter PRUNING to

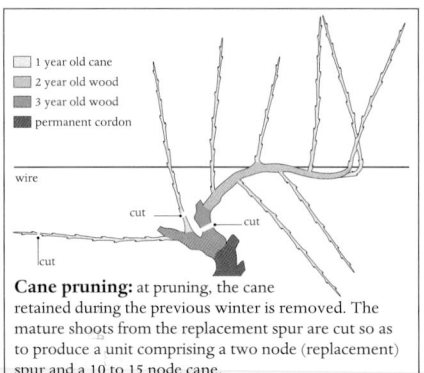

Cane pruning: at pruning, the cane retained during the previous winter is removed. The mature shoots from the replacement spur are cut so as to produce a unit comprising a two node (replacement) spur and a 10 to 15 node cane.

[legend:]
1 year old cane
2 year old wood
3 year old wood
permanent cordon
wire
cut
cut
cut

reduce the number of buds and to select their position. The cutting may be to SPURS or canes.   B.G.C.

cane pruning, a form of winter vine PRUNING in which the buds are retained on longer BEARERS called CANES, typically including six to 15 buds. This pruning system usually takes longer to perform by hand than the alternative SPUR PRUNING. Cane pruning is typically used for those varieties such as Syrah which have fewer FRUITFUL buds at the base of canes, but in many areas of the world where traditional attitudes dominate, it is used unquestioningly. However, the tendency in New World wine regions is to use spur pruning, which can be equally productive, requires less labour, and can be mechanized. For more details, see GUYOT pruning.   R.E.S.

cane ripening, or *aoûtement* in French, viticultural term used to describe a stage in the development of the shoot when the stem matures, and changes colour from green to yellow and thence to brown. The change involves the formation of corky tissue known as periderm and cellular changes including the accumulation of CARBOHYDRATE reserves, which collectively prepare the stem to withstand the cold of winter. The process begins at the base of the shoot and progresses upwards the tip, as does the dormancy status of its buds. VERAISON, the change in colour of the grapes, usually occurs at about the same time.   B.G.C.

Cannonau, sometimes spelt **Cannonao,** the SARDINIAN name for the widely planted red grape variety known in Spain as GARNACHA and in France as GRENACHE (see SARDEGNA). A high proportion of the grapes are grown on the east of the island to produce a varietal **Cannonau di Sardegna,** which comes in several forms, but most commonly as a full-throttle dryish red. Although the variety has lost ground since the mid 1990s, partly because as a BUSH VINE it is low-yielding and expensive to cultivate, about 6,300 ha/15,600 acres of Cannonau were recorded in the Italian vine census of 2000. The admirable Cannonau-

based Turriga made by the Argiolas winery near Cagliari, whose development was greatly aided by the work of consultant Giacomo Tachis (see ANTINORI), indicates that there is significant potential, yet to be exploited, for high-quality wine from the island's old Cannonau vines.   D.T. & D.C.G.

Canon-Fronsac, and **Côtes Canon-Fronsac,** underrated Bordeaux wine appellation, the heartland of Fronsac. See FRONSAC for more details.

canopy, that part of the vine above the ground, formed by the leaf and shoot system. It includes the trunk, cordon or canes, shoots, leaves, and fruit. See CANOPY MANAGEMENT.

canopy management, a portfolio of vineyard management techniques used to improve vineyard YIELD and wine quality, and to control VINE DISEASES, especially where vines are of high VIGOUR. Canopy management techniques aim to produce a desirable CANOPY MICROCLIMATE essentially by improving the exposure of leaves and fruit to the sun. The phrase became popular in many parts of the New World in the 1980s and early 1990s as part of a growing awareness of the way in which canopy microclimate affects vineyards. This awareness was not restricted to the New World. Considerable experimental work was also conducted in Europe, and the effects of canopy microclimate are now recognized as an explanation for the ability of distinguished vineyards to produce great wines (see TERROIR and VITICULTURE).

Some of the underlying principles of canopy management can be traced to early Roman writings. For example, 'BACCHUS loves hills' is partly explained by the fact that low-vigour vines growing on shallower soils on HILLSIDES have open canopies with good fruit and leaf exposure. In modern times, the principles were best formulated by the experimental work of Professor Nelson SHAULIS of Cornell University in New York state. During the 1960s, he showed that increased fruit and leaf exposure to sunlight improved both YIELD and GRAPE COMPOSITION AND WINE QUALITY. These early studies were also much involved with introducing MECHANICAL HARVESTERS and MECHANICAL PRUNING. Shaulis influenced researchers from other countries, who extended this work to VINIFERA vine varieties and also considered effects on wine quality. Studies in Bordeaux by Dr Alain Carbonneau demonstrated wine quality benefits of canopy manipulation in the mid 1970s. Other notable early studies were by Intrieri in Italy, Kliewer in California, Reynolds in Canada, and Smart in Australia and New Zealand.

Canopy management techniques are essentially aimed at producing an 'open' canopy microclimate, which is characterized by good leaf and fruit exposure to the sun and other climate elements, and therefore not much shade. The benefits of such a microclimate include improvements to wine quality and yield, and a significant reduction in diseases such as POWDERY MILDEW and BOTRYTIS BUNCH ROT. Interest in overcoming the common problems of excessively vigorous vines caused canopy management techniques to become popular. This was particularly marked in the New World, where a lack of experience to guide site selection and management practices resulted in some vineyards whose vines were so leafy and the fruit so shaded that it affected ripeness and wine quality. These problems were exacerbated by the widespread adoption of AGROCHEMICALS developed after the Second World War to control pests, diseases, and weeds, which, along with practices such as FERTILIZATION and IRRIGATION, stimulated shoot growth, often excessively. Canopy management techniques, especially trellis change, can offset the negative effects of vines with excess VIGOUR, but are not always necessary for low-vigour vineyards such as those found in most of the classic fine wine regions of Europe; see TERROIR.

A common feature of vineyards with a reputation for producing high-quality wines is that they are of moderate to low vigour, and that the canopy microclimate is characterized by good exposure of leaves and fruit to the sun, and little shade. Canopy management techniques can emulate this microclimate. For example, by altering TRELLIS SYSTEMS, it is possible to remove the fruit from the deep shade of the depths of the canopy to the outside of the canopy in the sun. Canopy management can also increase yield, which is reduced by densely shaded conditions. In particular, BUDBREAK and FRUITFULNESS are reduced by shade, no doubt an example of adaptive physiology which allowed WILD VINES to fruit only when they had climbed to the top of forest canopies. With increasing global concern about the use of agricultural chemicals, there is a swing towards using canopy management to help control FUNGAL DISEASES and reduce reliance on sprays (see INTEGRATED PEST MANAGEMENT). Not only is it difficult and wasteful to force sprays to penetrate to the centre of dense canopies, but shaded conditions also encourage diseases such as botrytis bunch rot and powdery mildew.

There is a range of canopy management techniques, the applicability of which varies from vineyard to vineyard. The simplest of these are TRIMMING, which cuts off excessive shoot growth in the summer, SHOOT THINNING which removes unwanted shoots early in the season, LEAF REMOVAL in the fruit zone, which allows more fruit exposure to sun and wind, and SHOOT POSITIONING, which makes trimming and leaf removal easy and effective. These more simple techniques of canopy management are quite traditional in many parts of the Old World and good examples may be seen in the neatly trimmed vineyards in many French regions. PRUNING also affects canopy density, as well as vine BALANCE. These practices may be termed 'Bandaid viticulture' in the sense that they overcome the problem only in the season during which they are applied, and need to be reapplied each year. More permanent solutions require changes to the trellis system, which affects the canopy shape, size, and density. The changes to the trellis usually involve increasing the canopy surface area and decreasing shading. For example, dense canopies in vineyards where rows are as much as 3.5 m/11.5 ft apart can be converted to a trellis system such as GENEVA DOUBLE CURTAIN, which effectively results in a canopy twice as long as the row. This is achieved by dividing the canopy into two curtains, thereby more or less doubling the canopy surface area. Other trellis systems such as the LYRE, SCOTT HENRY, and SMART-DYSON are also being widely used commercially, especially in New World vineyards.

There has been resistance to the extension of the ideas of canopy management, however, even within the US, where the technique was effectively born. There was a marked reluctance for academic and commercial acceptance of these ideas in California, and now paradoxically they are being taken up 30 years behind other regions, and seen to be imported from France, Italy, Australia, or New Zealand. This resistance stemmed partly from the fact that Shaulis's initial studies were made with the American grape CONCORD—even though it was proven quickly enough that VINIFERA varieties responded in the same way.

There is less scope in the Old World for canopy management since ROW SPACING is traditionally less, and trimming and leaf removal are used anyway. Centuries of trial and error have demonstrated the benefits of open canopies to improve wine quality and reduce vine diseases. However, in the Old World the benefits of canopy management are often not recognized as such by traditional viticulturists, many of whom ascribe the quality and disease effects solely to the associated lower yield or vigour, and more generally to the terroir. By the early 1990s, however, there were already examples in Old World commercial viticulture—in France, Italy, and Spain—where trellises had been altered for canopy management reasons. SPAIN's relaxation of laws prohibiting irrigation, together with proven performance of canopy management techniques in La Mancha, may mean that Spain will lead a revolution in use of New World viticultural technology in Europe. Contemporary thinking about canopy management suggests the optimal degree of leaf and fruit exposure might vary according to variety and region. There have been instances where excessive fruit exposure has had negative effects on quality. For example, in association with high temperatures it can lead to loss of colour, an effect sometimes called 'berry pinking'; and berries may shrivel if they are exposed to too much heat.   R.E.S.

Reynier, A., *Manuel de viticulture* (9th edn, Paris, 2003).

Smart, R. E., and Robinson, M., *Sunlight into Wine: A Handbook of Winegrape Canopy Management* (Adelaide, 1991).

canopy microclimate, the climate within and immediately around the grapevine CANOPY. This is the third level of climate definition (see also MACROCLIMATE, MESOCLIMATE) and in many ways the one of most relevance to contemporary viticulture because it can be so effectively manipulated, by CANOPY MANAGEMENT, to improve wine quality and yield and to reduce disease.

The canopy microclimate at the outside of the canopy is obviously affected by the macroclimate and mesoclimate, but that within the canopy depends on the way the canopy itself alters the climate. Bright SUNLIGHT falling on a dense canopy with few gaps in California's Napa valley may be considered as an example. Suppose a leaf facing the sun at midday receives 100 relative units of sunlight. The second leaf in the canopy will receive less than ten units and the third will receive less than one. So the second leaf in the canopy has a light climate like that of a northern European vineyard on an overcast day. In other words, the number of layers of leaves in the canopy can have even more effect on canopy microclimate than can vineyard location. This drastic reduction in sunlight levels in the canopy is caused by the vine leaves absorbing and reflecting more than 90 per cent of light falling on the upper surface; less than 10 per cent penetrates through to the lower surface.

This simple example illustrates the importance of canopy microclimate, and indeed how its effects can override those of regional CLIMATE, CLONE, ROOTSTOCK, and so on. (See VITICULTURE.) A feature of reputable vineyards, be they in the Old World or the New, is that they are typically of low to moderate VIGOUR and as a result the canopies are not dense or shaded. Many vineyards with an extended VINE AGE are also like this. Leaves and fruit are well exposed to the sun, so the microclimate in the centre of the canopy is not too different from that of the canopy outside. For vigorous and high-yielding vineyards, on the other hand, the canopy interior is a dark, humid, and cool place by day. Not only are the processes of fruit RIPENING slowed, but FUNGAL DISEASES such as BOTRYTIS BUNCH ROT and POWDERY MILDEW are encouraged. Canopy management techniques can be used to provide high-vigour vineyards with the same canopy microclimate as that of low-vigour vineyards.

Of the various climatological elements such as SUNLIGHT, HUMIDITY, TEMPERATURE, RAINFALL, EVAPORATION, and WIND, the canopy has greatest effect on sunlight, wind, and evaporation. The values of these three elements in the centre of a dense canopy can be less than one-tenth of those above the canopy, while temperature and humidity values are more similar to those outside the canopy. It is the leaves of the vine canopy that are responsible for creating the distinctive canopy microclimate. They strongly absorb sunlight and the energy (strictly, momentum) of the wind so that values below just one leaf are very different from those above it. Since evaporation depends on sunlight and wind, it is easy to appreciate that these values will also be reduced below the first leaf layer.

It is obvious therefore that the amount of vine leaf area has a significant effect on canopy microclimate. If most leaves and fruit are exposed, then the canopy microclimate values will not be too different from those above the canopy. If, on the other hand, the canopy is dense and the majority of leaves and bunches are not visible (and so are shaded), then it is fair to conclude that wine QUALITY and YIELD are both below the vineyard's potential. That a visual impression of the canopy can be so definitive in terms of the vineyard's ability to produce good-quality wines is the basis of a system of vineyard SCORING used to assess vineyard potential to produce quality wine.

It has often seemed paradoxical that exposed fruit would produce better wine quality, even in warm to hot climates where HEAT STRESS is anticipated. This is because grape bunches exposed to sunlight can reach temperatures 5 to 10 °C higher than what might already be higher than optimal air temperatures. Research in Washington state by Spayd and others has carefully separated light and temperature effects. They found a positive benefit of sunlight exposure on the fruit but this could be negated by high grape temperatures. Exposure to the ultraviolet part of sunlight also affected grape composition. They suggest exposing fruit to the morning rather than afternoon sun, to avoid the problems associated with high temperature such as depression of anthocyanins. This result reflects the practice common in Bordeaux, for example, of leaf removal on the eastern side of the canopy in the hottest part of the season and then on the western side only later in the season.   R.E.S.

Smart, R. E., and Robinson, M., *Sunlight into Wine: A Handbook of Winegrape Canopy Management* (Adelaide, 1991).

Spayd, S. E., Tarara, J. M., Mee, D. L., and Ferguson, J. C., 'Separation of sunlight and temperature effects on the composition of *vitis vinifera* cv. Merlot berries', *American Journal of Enology and Viticulture*, 53 (2002), 171–82.

cans. Ordinary wine is occasionally packaged in cans (usually 25cl), which have no harmful effect on wine destined for early consumption. The advantages are that cans are lighter and less fragile than BOTTLES, but the material from which they are made is not, unlike GLASS, inert. Cans are lacquered on the inside to give chemical resistance to the acid in the wine. However,

if there is the slightest pinhole in the lacquer, the wine attacks the aluminium, producing foul-smelling hydrogen sulphide, and the wine turns black.

cantina, Italian for a cellar, a wine shop (although the word ENOTECA is more promising), and a winery. A **cantina sociale** is a CO-OPERATIVE winery.

cap (*chapeau* in French), the layer of grape solids that floats on the liquid surface during red wine fermentation and requiring careful CAP MANAGEMENT. The cap usefully limits the amount of OXYGEN available to the YEAST, thereby encouraging the formation of alcohol, but has to be broken up and submerged in order to encourage the extraction of the desirable PHENOLICS which add colour, flavour, and longevity to a wine. See MACERATION, PUMPING OVER, DÉLESTAGE, and PUNCHING DOWN.

CAP stands for Common Agricultural Policy, a plank of EUROPEAN UNION policy which has had long-term effects on world wine production.

Cape, a euphemism for SOUTH AFRICAN, particularly during the apartheid era.

Cape Agulhas, a relatively new wine district in SOUTH AFRICA close to the southernmost tip of the continent.

Cape blend, a term increasingly used on labels in SOUTH AFRICA to describe a red wine in which PINOTAGE is one of the blending components.

Cape Riesling, misleading South African name for the French white grape variety CROUCHEN Blanc that is virtually extinct in its native France but was once grown in Australia as Clare Riesling. Also known as Paarl Riesling and South African Riesling, but much less distinguished than true RIESLING, which is also known as Weisser or Rhine Riesling in South Africa, Cape Riesling produces an unexceptional dry white, its popularity due to a combination of the name, its undemanding blandness, and reasonable price. Plantings are declining but there were still nearly 1,300 ha/3,200 acres planted in South Africa in 2003.

J.P. & M.F.

Cape Verde Islands far into the Atlantic produce minuscule amounts of wine. There is virtually no rainfall, but condensation from the huge volcano permits some vine-growing on the island of Fogo.

Capitolare, name given in 1993 by a group of producers in TOSCANA to a special group of wines previously described as Predicato. It means 'chapter' or 'classification', and refers to wines made from INTERNATIONAL VARIETIES using BARREL MATURATION. These wines have now been absorbed into the IGTs for Colli

della Toscana Centrale or Colli dell'Etruria Centrale.

capsule, French and occasional English name for the sheath over the top of a cork and bottle-neck, otherwise known as a FOIL, just as the **capsule cutter** is more widely known as a FOIL CUTTER. French wine released for sale within France, as opposed to export, must have its capsules embossed with a customs seal, known as a **capsule congé**. Traditionally LEAD or lead alloys were used to manufacture capsules, but in Europe these were found to be a major source of soil contamination in disposal sites, and lead contamination of wine was traced to this source, so the use of lead capsules has been phased out. Older bottles with lead capsules should be wiped carefully around the bottle-neck between pulling the cork and serving.

Caramany, named enclave in the area designated for Côtes du ROUSSILLON-Villages. All Carignan in the blend (which must be of at least three varieties with Carignan a maximum of 60 per cent) must be vinified by CARBONIC MACERATION, which technique was pioneered in the area by the Caramany CO-OPERATIVE.

carbamates, or **urethanes**, relatively simple organic compounds found in very low concentrations in some foods and wines. Ethyl carbamate, or ethyl urethane, is a naturally occurring component of all fermented foods and beverages. In the case of the YEAST *Saccharomyces cerevisiae*, ethyl carbamate is formed by the reaction between ETHANOL and urea, which in turn is produced by the degradation of the amino acid arginine, one of the main NITROGEN sources in grape juice and musts. In the late 1980s, ethyl carbamate was added to the growing list of compounds suspected of human carcinogenicity on the basis of animal tests.

Most wine types contain ethyl carbamate concentrations well below the limit suggested by US authorities of 10 mg per litre. High-alcohol, particularly sweet wines which have been heated during production (such as MADEIRA), are likely to be the wines with the highest levels of ethyl carbamate, and higher than average levels may be produced from grapes grown in vineyards given excess nitrogen FERTILIZERS. The level may also influenced by the yeast strain.   A.D.W. & J.Ha.

carbohydrates, organic compounds made up of carbon, oxygen, and hydrogen and which include sugars, starch, and cellulose. Of particular interest to the wine consumer are the simple sugar molecules GLUCOSE and FRUCTOSE, which together make up the SUGARS in grape juice, and which are subsequently fermented into the alcohol which distinguishes wine from grape juice. Sucrose is the sugar molecule made up of glucose and fructose and is manufactured in the leaves of plants, including vines, by PHOTOSYNTHESIS. Sucrose can be converted to all other forms of carbohydrates, such as starch, as a storage compound in the roots and trunks, and cellulose, which is present in all cells. Sucrose is also the basic plant biochemical building block, and can be converted to proteins, fats, and organic acids.

A vine's reserves of carbohydrates are an important factor in its ANNUAL GROWTH CYCLE. STARCH is the principal form of carbohydrate reserve which is stored in the woody vine parts in the autumn. The starch is converted into SUGARS which, via RESPIRATION, provide the chemical energy for growing shoots early the following spring. The reason perennial plants, such as vines, can grow to such a large size is this ability to store surplus chemical energy each growing season, which is then available for shoot growth the following season. This allows more rapid growth than for a plant starting out from a seed, which has limited food reserves.

At about VERAISON, when the fruit starts to ripen, the vine begins to replace carbohydrate reserves used earlier that growing season. Sugars are moved into the trunk, arms, and roots, where they are converted to the insoluble storage material starch. As shoots accumulate starch they change colour, from green to brown; this is called CANE RIPENING. Ideally there should be a period of warm, sunny weather after HARVEST during which the leaves can manufacture the sugars to provide the final topping up of starch reserves. However, this ideal state of affairs can be disrupted, for example by large crops of grapes or late-season shoot growth which slows ripening and limits the amounts of starch formed. Similarly, an autumn FROST which destroys leaves can interrupt the orderly build-up of reserves in the vine. High levels of carbohydrate reserves of sugars and starches make vines better able to withstand WINTER FREEZE, providing them with a sort of biological antifreeze mechanism. Although starch is the main carbohydrate storage compound, there are some other minor compounds such as AMINO ACIDS and carboxylic acids which show the same pattern of autumn accumulation and spring depletion.

Early shoot growth in spring is entirely dependent on these stored reserves, which are mobilized in the woody parts and moved to the developing shoots. If there are too many new shoots growing for the reserves available, new growth will be checked. The concept of BALANCED PRUNING ensures that the number of buds retained is proportional to the reserves available. The new shoots become independent of these reserves when the leaves reach about half their final size, and photosynthesis is sufficient to support further growth.

See also WOOD, in which the carbohydrate cellulose plays an important part.   R.E.S.

Winkler, A. J., et al., General Viticulture (2nd edn, Berkeley, Calif., 1974).

carbon, active. See CHARCOAL.

carbonation, the cheapest and least effective method of SPARKLING WINE-MAKING, involving the simple pumping of CARBON DIOXIDE into a tank of wine.

carbon dioxide, or CO_2, a naturally occurring atmospheric gas, commonly encountered as the sparkle in soft drinks, beers, and SPARKLING WINES. Its content in the atmosphere is only about 0.03 per cent; yet upon that small amount depends the growth of all living systems, including man, vines, yeasts, bacteria, all plants, and the existence of all fauna depending on them for food. Not least, it is the ultimate raw material of wine and, via a series of biochemical reactions involving the grapevine, yeast cells, and the consumer, results in carbon dioxide's being both assimilated and produced.

The cycle begins with the combination of carbon dioxide and water into sugars in the vine leaves by PHOTOSYNTHESIS; conversion in the leaves and berries of some of that sugar into a variety of compounds, including those directly or indirectly responsible for ACIDS, COLOUR, and FLAVOUR in the grapes and wine; and, as the final step, transformation of the grape juice into wine by FERMENTATION. Carbon dioxide is released in substantial amounts during fermentation. It returns whence it came with the metabolism of the alcohol and other wine constituents back to carbon dioxide and water, primarily in the liver of the wine drinker.

Carbon dioxide passes into vine leaves through small pores, or STOMATA. The greater the atmospheric concentration, the more can pass in, and the greater the potential growth and yield of the vine (provided that other factors such as water, light, temperature, or nutrients are not more directly limiting).

Carbon dioxide concentrations in the earth's atmosphere have increased by some 25 per cent since the beginning of the Industrial Revolution, largely through the burning of fossil fuels. By analogy, it seems certain that this has already helped to increase the yields of grapevines and, very possibly, grape and wine quality. Theoretical arguments have been advanced that it may also have tended to raise the optimum ripening temperatures for grape and wine quality.

With increasing awareness of CLIMATE CHANGE and rising atmospheric carbon dioxide levels, it is worth considering the wine industry's role in what may be the Earth's greatest environmental problem. Dr Damien Martin of HortResearch, New Zealand, has calculated that the activities of the world's wine producers typically lead to a net reduction in atmospheric carbon dioxide of 8 tonnes per ha of vineyard per year. The calculation estimates that for each ha almost ten tonnes are 'fixed' each year by photosynthesis, while each tonne of grapes produces 1.3 tonnes of carbon dioxide

during fermentation and a further 0.6 tonnes treating WINERY WASTE.   J.G. & R.E.S.

In wine-making

Carbon dioxide is used throughout the wine-making process to displace OXYGEN from contact with crushed grapes or wine. At some wineries, carbon dioxide is deliberately pumped over white grapes as they are received at the winery and pass through the destemmer in order to minimize OXIDATION. Draining tanks, presses, storage and blending vats, filters, and bottling lines are all locations where carbon dioxide may be applied by fastidious winemakers.

Carbon dioxide also plays an important role in the fermentation of all wines. Like humans, YEAST metabolizes starches and sugars to produce water and carbon dioxide. In the human case, carbon dioxide from muscle or brain activity dissolves in the blood, is transferred to the lungs and then to the atmosphere as exhaled breath. In the case of yeast's metabolic activity in six-carbon sugar solutions such as grape juice, the three main by-products are water, ETHANOL, and carbon dioxide. If excess oxygen is available, the yeast obtains more cell-building energy from the sugar by converting it to carbon dioxide and water. With only a moderate oxygen supply, the yeast produces carbon dioxide and the ethanol that distinguishes wine from grape juice.

As winery visitors during vintage time may discover, while wine is fermenting, substantial quantities of carbon dioxide are given off; while not being inherently toxic to humans, CO_2 displaces oxygen so that, in a confined space such as a FERMENTATION VESSEL, suffocation is all too possible. Winery workers must exercise particular caution in this respect.

In most still wines, this carbon dioxide is encouraged to dissipate leaving only very small amounts in the finished wine—although the more PROTECTIVE the wine-making, the more substantial these traces may be, as in, for example, many German and other light, aromatic, white wines. (Winemakers may, however, choose to remove carbon dioxide from such wines by SPARGING them with NITROGEN just before bottling.)

In sparkling wines, however, substantial quantities of dissolved carbon dioxide, between two and six atmospheres, are encouraged to remain in the bottle by one of the methods outlined in SPARKLING WINE-MAKING. Lesser quantities of carbon dioxide, between one and two atmospheres, may be encouraged in wines such as those labelled PERLANT, PÉTILLANT, or FRIZZANTE by inducing a second but less violent fermentation and preserving the carbon dioxide produced.

Since the 1960s, however, a number of winemakers in hotter, particularly New World, regions have pursued a deliberate policy of bottling wine, particularly white wine, with up to one atmosphere of carbon dioxide dissolved in it. This is because carbon dioxide, as it vaporizes from the wine, carries with it many ESTERS and thus tends to increase a wine's freshness and fruitiness, attributes which the winemaker may well wish to enhance. This is done by processing the wine at very low temperatures where carbon dioxide is much more soluble in wine, and bottling it early in order to preserve some of the gas given off during fermentation. The warmer the wine is served, the more obvious is the carbon dioxide to the taster.

While most tasters would be surprised and probably shocked to notice any carbon dioxide in a mature red bordeaux (in which case it could even be taken to be an unwelcome sign of FERMENTATION IN BOTTLE), it is not necessarily a fault in most types of white and rosé wines. Portugal's VINHO VERDE provides many examples of this deliberate wine style, as do many young whites from the MOSEL, and some Italian red wines contain a perceptible level of carbon dioxide, sometimes as a result of the GOVERNO practice of adding dried grapes to provoke a second fermentation.

Carbon dioxide also plays an essential role in CARBONIC MACERATION.   A.D.W.

carbonic acid is the acid formed when CARBON DIOXIDE is dissolved in water, H_2CO_3.

carbonic maceration, red wine-making process which transforms a small amount of SUGAR IN GRAPES which are uncrushed to ETHANOL, without the intervention of yeasts. It is used typically to produce light-bodied, brightly coloured, fruity red wines for early consumption, most famously but by no means exclusively in the Beaujolais region of France.

Louis PASTEUR observed in 1872 that grape berries held in air differed in flavour from those held in a CARBON DIOXIDE atmosphere (although he, wrongly, suspected that grapes held in carbon dioxide would produce wines for long ageing).

Carbonic maceration is not normally used with white grapes, as undesirable flavours are formed. When used to make red wines, whole bunches or clusters of grapes are deliberately placed, with care to ensure that the berries are not broken, in an anaerobic atmosphere, generally obtained by using carbon dioxide to exclude OXYGEN. An intracellular fermentation takes place within the intact berry and a small amount of ethanol is formed, along with traces of many flavourful aromatic compounds. All of these contribute to the distinctive aroma and flavour of the resultant wines. The maceration period in this anaerobic environment and phase, where these aromatic compounds are produced, depends on temperature, and can be from one to three weeks.

It is likely that the same metabolic pathways are involved in carbonic maceration as in normal alcoholic fermentation but the flavour differences suggest that other processes are also concerned. Michel Flanzy, whose work dates from 1936, and other French researchers have observed that ordinary grapes held intact for several days under a carbon dioxide atmosphere, then crushed and allowed to ferment, produce a wine which is much brighter-coloured, less tannic, and more distinctively perfumed than one made normally. Some find this very particular aroma reminiscent of bananas, others of kirsch.

Detailed studies suggest that whole grapes held under carbon dioxide lose about a fifth of their sugar, gain about 2 per cent in ALCOHOLIC STRENGTH, show a tenfold gain in GLYCEROL, lose about half of their harsh MALIC ACID, and show an increase in PH of about 0.25 units, all within the intact berry. These measurements exclude any changes in FLAVOUR COMPOUNDS. It is thought that the distinguishing volatile compounds include the volatile PHENOLS, benzaldehyde, vinylbenzene, ethyl cinnamate, ethyl vanillate, and methyl vanillate.

Under commercial wine-making conditions, it is almost impossible to produce a wine that depends wholly on carbonic maceration. The two key elements are the retention of whole berries, and an anaerobic atmosphere. While carbon dioxide is readily available to exclude oxygen, when whole bunches are poured into a tank, in practice the weight of the grapes breaks open those at the bottom, which begin to ferment in the normal way due to the action of indigenous YEASTS, derived either from the grapes or from the wine-making equipment or environment. Immediately above this exist whole grapes surrounded by juice; above this, whole grapes in an atmosphere of carbon dioxide. This upper layer will undergo true carbonic maceration. The grapes in the middle layer will undergo similar intracellular transformations, but at a much slower rate, and with the presence of yeast in the surrounding juice.

Even when a CRUSHER is employed in traditional red wine-making, a proportion of whole berries is retained, depending on the size and condition of the berries and the operation of the crusher. These berries undergo carbonic maceration as the fermenting MUST at the bottom of the vessel gives off carbon dioxide which excludes all oxygen above it. Thus, alcoholic fermentation and carbonic maceration would proceed simultaneously.

This also applies to some red burgundy made today using WHOLE GRAPE fermentations. Winemakers in other regions around the world, working with varieties other than Burgundy's classic PINOT NOIR, carefully adjust their crushers, pumps, and CAP management regime to maximize such flavour modification techniques.

The technique is open to much regional and personal modification (see SEMI-CARBONIC MACERATION as an example). Some winemakers allow one or two days' maceration in carbon dioxide while others (or the same individuals in different vintages), may prefer to leave the grapes a week or two under the gas. It is generally considered that the necessary period of maceration is longer when the fruit is less ripe because carbonic maceration reduces the concentration of malic acid, which tends to be higher in greener grapes.

Although Beaujolais is the most famous wine region where carbonic maceration is the most common wine-making technique, it is also widely used for the Beaujolais grape Gamay in other parts of France. It has also been turned to positive use in the southern Rhône, and it assists in making commercial reds from the sometimes tough Carignan grape to yield red wines for early drinking in the Languedoc-Roussillon in southern France—although there is an increasing tendency to blend these with traditionally made wines.

Its use in the New World has been limited to some novel products such as the Australian proprietary product of the 1980s, 'CabMac', which was that country's answer to Beaujolais.
                    P.L.

Ribéreau-Gayon, P., Dubourdieu, D., Donèche, B., and Lonvaud, D., *Traité d'Œnologie 1: Microbiologie du vin: Vinifications* (Paris, 1998), translated by Branco, J.M., as *Handbook of Enology 1: The Microbiology of Wine and Vinifications* (Chichester, 2000), 348–58.

Sneyd, T. N., 'Carbonic maceration: an overview', *Australian and New Zealand Wine Industry Journal*, 4 (1989), 281–5.

Carcavelos, one of just over 20 regions in PORTUGAL awarded DOC status, although the vineyards have almost been obliterated by the westward expansion of the capital city Lisbon along the Tagus estuary (see map under PORTUGAL). A cynic's view of Carcavelos is that it was created by the Marquis of Pombal, Portugal's autocratic 18th-century prime minister, because he had to do something with the grapes from his country residence at nearby Oeiras. He even flouted his own regulations and permitted Carcavelos to be blended with PORT. However, Pombal established the reputation of Carcavelos as a FORTIFIED wine which enjoyed a brief period of popularity in Britain in the early part of the 19th century (and see AUCTIONS for evidence of its renown even earlier). The wine may be made from a blend of up to nine different red and white grapes. It is usually fermented dry and fortified with GRAPE SPIRIT up to an ALCOHOLIC STRENGTH of 18 to 20 per cent. A small amount of *vinho abafado* (fermenting grape must preserved by the addition of alcohol) is added after FERMENTATION to sweeten the wine. Between three and five years' CASK AGEING give the wine a nutty character akin to a tawny port. Carcavelos was demarcated in 1908 but, of the land originally included, only Pombal's palace and two vineyards remain, totalling fewer than 10 ha/ 25 acres of vines.   R.J.M.

Cardinal, red TABLE GRAPE variety, a CROSS-ING of Flame Tokay × Ribier made in California in 1939. It has been grown quite widely in the south of France, Spain, Italy, Romania, and Bulgaria, and has more recently underpinned the wine industries of VIETNAM and THAILAND. *Cardinal* is also a—usually Burgundian—name for a red wine mixed with CASSIS.

Carema, almost alpine red wine zone of PIEMONTE in north west Italy, bordering on the Valle d'AOSTA, is the northernmost zone of Piemonte in which the great NEBBIOLO—present here in the Picutener and Pugnet clones, the approximate equivalents of the Lampia and Michet of the LANGHE—is cultivated (although see also VALTELLINA). Viticulture is not an easy task in this mountainous region, and the TENDONE-trained vineyards have been wrested from steep gradients by means of TERRACES.

The wine itself has a recognizably Nebbiolo character, with a higher ACIDITY and less body than the better wines of the Langhe or of GATTINARA, but interesting, perfumed, and pleasurable wines are regularly made in hot years. The total potential vineyard area is 120 ha/300 acres, although only 35 were planted in the early 2000s, and of these only 14 produced a DOC wine. The 14 ha are divided among over 40 growers, for most of whom viticulture is of course only a part-time activity at best; the resulting wines have been of variable quality in the past, although mastery of MALO-LACTIC FERMENTATION has resulted in better and more consistent wines from the local co-operative winery. The lengthy ageing periods (four years, of which two must be in barrel) imposed by the DOC rules, which hold the wine off the market long after competing products from the Langhe, have clearly been a commercial handicap. Producer Luigi Ferrando works hard at maintaining the wine's reputation, but his is a lone voice in a zone where production is declining.

D.T. & D.C.G.

Carignan, known as **Carignane** in the US, **Carignano** in Italy, and **Cariñena** in Spain, late-ripening black grape variety which could fairly be called the bane of the European wine industry, although old bushvines, as is their wont, are demonstrably capable of producing particularly concentrated wine. Carignan, distinguished mainly by its disadvantages, has dug its roots into so much of the southern French *vignoble* that even the most generous of EUROPEAN UNION bribes have had their work cut out to eradicate it. It is better than the ARAMON it replaced, however, and the produce of old vines on very poor soils such as at Domaine d'Aupilhac in MONTPEYROUX and Ch de Lastours in CORBIÈRES is exceptional—even if some would argue better in a blend than as a 100 per cent varietal.

Throughout the 1960s, it infiltrated the Midi, then rapidly trying to fill the void left in the national blending vat by the independence of ALGERIA, to such an extent that it was France's most planted vine variety from the mid 1960s until the end of the century, when it was overtaken by Merlot. Of all vines ripped out during the 1980s and 1990s under the EU's VINE PULL SCHEME, Carignan has quite rightly been the most common casualty but there were still 95,700 ha/236,480 acres of it in 2000—admittedly dramatically much less than the 1988 total of 167,000 ha.

Nowadays Carignan seems a very odd choice indeed, although presumably it seemed obvious to many *pieds noirs* returning from Algeria, where the wine industry depended at one time on its 140,000 ha/350,000 acres of Carignan. Its wine is high in everything—acidity, tannins, colour, bitterness—but finesse and charm. This gives it the double inconvenience of being unsuitable for early consumption yet unworthy of maturation. The vine is not even particularly easy to grow. It is extremely sensitive to POWDERY MILDEW, quite sensitive to DOWNY MILDEW, prone to rot, and prey to infestation by grape worms. Its diffusion has been extremely beneficial to the agrochemical industry. Its bunches keep such a tenacious hold on the vine that it does not adapt well to mechanical harvesting, but then the majority of Carignan is not trained on wires anyway but grows in gnarled old bushes that do not share the stability of GRENACHE.

There must have been some attribute which led to the almost exclusive dissemination of Carignan throughout the Midi in the 1950s and 1960s, and there was: yield. The vine can quite easily be persuaded to produce almost 200 hl/ha (11 tons/acre), ideal for a thirsty but not discriminating market. It also buds late, which gave it extra allure as a substitute for the much lighter Aramon, previously France's number one vine, which had been badly affected by the frosts of 1956 and 1963. It ripens late, too, however, limiting its cultivation to Mediterranean wine regions. About 70 per cent of France's total area of Carignan is in the two major Languedoc *départements* of the Aude and the Hérault. It is also the dominant variety in the Gard, only just less important than Grenache Noir in the Pyrénées-Orientales, and is planted in quantity all over south eastern France too. South west France has been saved from Carignan by its cooler, wetter autumns.

The regulations for the Languedoc-Roussillon's appellations have been forced to embrace the ubiquitous Carignan, but it is hard to argue that, for example, Minervois or Corbières are improved by their (continually reduced) Carignan component. Those wines that depend most heavily on the 'improving' varieties such as Syrah and Mourvèdre and least on Carignan are almost invariably the most successful.

Only the most carefully farmed old vines on well-placed, low-yielding sites can produce Carignan with real character. Elsewhere, the widespread introduction of CARBONIC MACERATION has helped disguise, if not exactly compensate for, Carignan's lack of youthful charm. The astringency of basic vin de table has owed much to this vine, although blending with Cinsaut or Grenache helps considerably.

The white mutation **Carignan Blanc** can still be found in some vineyards of the Languedoc and, in particular, Roussillon, and a total of almost 1,000 ha/2,470 acres of it still grew in France in 2000.

Although the vine (like Grenache) may have originated in Spain in the province of Aragón, it is not widely planted there today. Carignan is not even the principal grape variety in the wine that carries its Spanish synonym CARIÑENA. It is grown chiefly in Cataluña today although it was historically, as Mazuelo, a not particularly distinguished ingredient in Rioja. It also plays a major part in the wines of PRIORAT (where some of the finest Carignan-dominant wines in the world are to be found), COSTERS DEL SEGRE, PENEDÈS, TARRAGONA, and TERRA ALTA, so that Spain had total plantings of around 7,000 ha/17,300 acres in 2004.

The vine, gaining a vowel as Carignane, has been important in the Americas. Although it is rarely seen as a varietal, there were still about 5,000 acres/2,000 ha in California's hotter regions in 2004 for the vine's productivity and vigour are valued by growers, if not consumers. It is also grown (to a much lesser extent) in Mexico, Argentina, Chile, and Uruguay.

Because of its late-ripening habits, Carignan can thrive only in relatively hot climates. At one time it underpinned Israel's wine industry and it is by no means unknown in Italy. As Carignano it is grown in Lazio and most commonly in Sardegna (perhaps as a result of that island's long dominance by Aragón), where it makes strong and sometimes pleasing reds and rosés, notably some seriously toothsome Carignano del Sulcis.

And occasional bottlings of savoury old-vine Carignan have surfaced in South Africa.

Let some interesting old Carignan vines be treasured but let it not be planted.

www.carignans.com

Carina. See CURRANTS.

Cariñena, town in north east Spain which lends its name to both a denominated wine zone and a vine variety, widely grown in southern France as CARIGNAN. Although it is known to originate in the area, the vine (also called Mazuelo) has been widely abandoned in its native region in favour of GARNACHA, which seems better suited to the arid growing conditions in this, the largest of the four DO zones of the ARAGÓN region (see map under SPAIN). Until the 1980s, most of Cariñena's hefty red wines were sold in bulk for blending with lighter wines from other parts of Spain. Natural alcohol levels of 18 and sometimes 19 per cent were not uncommon. But Cariñena, like so many other regions of Spain, is trying to break with the past. The minimum ALCOHOLIC STRENGTH permitted by DO regulations for red Cariñena was reduced from 14 to 12 per cent in 1990, while some Garnacha vines are gradually being uprooted and replaced by Tempranillo and Cabernet Sauvignon. Among the white vine varieties that cover a fifth of Cariñena's total vineyard area, Macabeo and Garnacha Blanca have been joined by Parellada from Penedès. The CO-OPERATIVES, which produce over three-quarters of all the Cariñena's wines, are playing their part in a relatively slow modernization process. One positive development has been the creation of progressive private bodegas such as Solar de Urbezo.

V. de la S. & J.R.

Carmel Valley, California wine region. See MONTEREY.

Carmenère, sometimes spelt **Carménère** and **Carmenere**, is rarely acknowledged in the vineyards of Bordeaux today but was, according to Daurel, widely cultivated in the Médoc in the early 18th century and, with CABERNET FRANC, established the reputations of its best properties. He reports that the vine is vigorous and used to produce exceptionally good wine but was abandoned because of its susceptibility to COULURE and resultant low yields. Its name may well be related to the word 'carmine' and even today it yields small quantities of exceptionally deep-coloured, full-bodied wines and may even be, like PETIT VERDOT, the subject of a revival. (Ch Clerc Milon, PAUILLAC classed growth, admits to its presence in their ENCEPAGEMENT and the odd VARIETAL emerged on to the Bordeaux market in the early 2000s.)

Its new power base is CHILE, where, it was discovered in 1994, a substantial proportion of the vines previously believed to be Merlot are in fact this historic variety, presumably imported directly from Bordeaux in the late 19th century. It ripens even later than Cabernet Sauvignon and if yields are limited, by grafting on to low-vigour ROOTSTOCKS, for example, has the potential to make very fine wines, combining some of the charm of Merlot with the structure of Cabernet Sauvignon. Excessive herbaceousness can sometimes dominate its ripe tomato-like flavours but the Chileans had already acknowledged that at least 6,000 ha/14,825 acres of their vines were Carmenère by 2004. More than 4,000 ha of vines previously thought to be CABERNET FRANC in northern Italy have also been identified as Carmenère, which may not be produced as a varietal DOC, DOCG, or IGT wine but may be used for blending in Veneto, Trentino, and Friuli. Ca'del Bosco of LOMBARDIA make

a sturdy, robustly-priced varietal called Carmenero from it.

Daurel, J., *Les Raisins de cuve de la Gironde et du sud-ouest de la France* (Bordeaux, 1892).

Carmenet, a Médocain synonym for CABERNET FRANC which has also been adopted as the name of a winery in northern California.

Carmignano, historic central Italian red wine made 16 km/10 miles north west of Florence in a zone noted as one of TOSCANA's finest for red wine production since the Middle Ages. The vineyards are located on a series of low hills between 50 and 200 m (160–650 ft) above sea level, unusually low for the SANGIOVESE grape, which forms the base of the blend and gives wines with lower ACIDITY and firmer TANNINS than the wines of CHIANTI CLASSICO. The relatively low altitudes allow Sangiovese to ripen fully here in this relatively northern zone for the variety.

The wines were first given legal status by Cosimo III de'Medici—himself a major proprietor in the Carmignano zone at the villa of Artimino—who included them in his selection of four areas of superior wine production in an edict of 1716 which prohibited other wines from using the names of the selected areas. The granducal wines were sent regularly to Queen Anne of England, who apparently appreciated their quality. The wines were also praised by Giovanni Cosimo Villifranchi (1773) and Cosimo Ridolfi (1831), and began to be bottled and distributed on a national and international scale by Marquis Ippolito Niccolini and by the Fattoria di Artimino in the 19th century.

The report of the Dalmasso Commission in 1932 (see ITALY and TOSCANA) assigned Carmignano to the nearby zone of Chianti Montalbano, where cooler temperatures and higher altitudes result in Chianti wines of lighter body and higher acidity more suitable for drinking when young. Independent status was won in 1975, however, with the granting of a DOC for Carmignano, the only Tuscan DOC to require the inclusion of CABERNET SAUVIGNON (years before its use became common in Chianti). It was awarded DOCG status in 1990 (for the 1988 vintage). The DOCG law stipulates a minimum of 50 per cent of Sangiovese in the blend, together with up to 20 per cent of Canaiolo Nero and 10–20 per cent of Cabernet Franc and/or Cabernet Sauvignon. Bizarrely, a provision for up to 10 per cent white grapes remains.

The alleged tradition of Cabernet Sauvignon in the zone was of major assistance in detaching it from Chianti Montalbano. The vineyards of Ugo Contini-Bonacossi of Villa di Capezzana, the zone's major producer, were grafted with cuttings from Ch LAFITE in the 1970s. He claimed to be reviving a local tradition, for the Medici were great experimenters, and he is sure they had Cabernet Sauvignon

planted in their vineyards until PHYLLOXERA necessitated replanting in Carmignano in the 1920s and 1930s. As viticulture was hardly remunerative at the time, Cabernet was replaced with Sangiovese and Trebbiano.

Current production of DOCG wine is slightly under 2,700 hl/71,500 gal from the zone's approximately 110 ha/270 acres of vineyards. The DOC for younger wines, similar to Rosso di MONTALCINO, is Barco Reale (referring to the 'royal park', as distinguished in the Medici edict of 1716). A few producers have begun to experiment with oak BARRIQUES and bigger casks, although the phenomenon has not become generalized as it has in Chianti Classico.

D.T. & D.C.G.

Carmine, California crossing of Carignan × Cabernet Sauvignon with an intense Cabernet flavour and ageing potential.

Carnelian, black grape variety developed in and specifically for California by Dr H. P. Olmo of DAVIS. It is the result of crossing a 1936 crossing of Carignan and Cabernet Sauvignon with Grenache and was released in 1972. It was supposed to be a hot-climate Cabernet but too many of the Grenache characteristics predominate to make it easy to pick. Its California influence is limited, and restricted to the SAN JOAQUIN VALLEY, where the liberal produce of its 1,650 acres/660 ha goes into blends. Curiously, one of its loftiest expressions has come from a Texas vineyard, Fall Creek.

Carneros, also known as **Los Carneros**, a moderately cool, windy CALIFORNIA wine region, an AVA that spans the extreme south of both NAPA and SONOMA counties. Carneros sprang to public notice in and outside California in the mid 1980s, partly on the strength of some impressive Pinot Noirs and as much or more because of traditionally made SPARKLING WINES blended from Chardonnay and Pinot Noir grown in Carneros. Acacia, Buena Vista, Carneros Creek, and Saintsbury were important producers of still wines throughout the 1980s; Gloria Ferrer, Domaine Carneros, and Codorníu Napa were the pioneer sparkling wine producers following the lead of Domaine Chandon of Yountville (see MOËT & CHANDON), which first sourced grapes here.

In fact this is one of the state's older wine districts. Agoston HARASZTHY planted grapes in it before 1870. A property originally called Stanly Ranch was famous as a vineyard by 1880. However, persistent fog and wind made vine-growing difficult and, when PHYLLOXERA struck hard in the 1880s, there began a swift slide into a long night. The Stanly Ranch was bought and replanted in 1942 by wine producer Louis M. Martini, but the push that brought Carneros both fame and more than 3,000 acres/1,200 ha of vineyard did not begin until the 1970s.

Carneros sprawls across the last, low hills of the Mayacamas range before it slips beneath San Francisco bay. The larger part of the AVA lies within Sonoma county; grapes from that portion can also use the Sonoma Valley AVA. The smaller segment, in Napa county, is equally entitled to use Napa Valley as an AVA. In addition to Chardonnay and Pinot Noir, Carneros is gaining a reputation for Merlot and, to a limited extent, Syrah. Many wineries further north in Napa Valley either own vineyards or buy grapes, particularly Chardonnay, in the Carneros district in order to have a cooler climate blending component.

Growers and wineries within the AVA have banded together in a promotional body called the Carneros Quality Alliance, the seal of which appears on many wines from it.

carotenoids, important class of plant PIGMENTS whose red, orange, and yellow colours complement the green of chlorophyll and the blue and red of ANTHOCYANINS. They come from the chloroplasts in green grapes. Carotenoids are TERPENOIDS with 40 carbons and belong to the LIPID group of organic compounds. They include two main groups—xanthophylls and carotenes—which are prominent in grapes and provide the skin colour of so-called white grapes and are associated with vine leaf colours in autumn; carotenes also form a substrate for synthesis of many important regulatory and FLAVOUR COMPOUNDS and FLAVOUR PRECURSORS. Carotenoids serve as accessory pigments in the process of PHOTOSYNTHESIS. B.G.C.

Carso, DOC zone in FRIULI in north east Italy very close to Trieste and the border with SLOVENIA producing mainly red wines from the Terrano/Teran (REFOSCO) grape, and some whites from MALVASIA, which are not often exported. Like their colleagues in COLLIO, some producers have also been experimenting with barrel-fermented Chardonnay and Sauvignon Blanc, often with positive results.

Cartagène is the largely domestically produced strong, sweet aperitif of the Languedoc, made, rather like a VIN DE LIQUEUR, by adding grape spirit to barely fermenting grape juice.

Cartaxo, DOC in central southern Portugal. See RIBATEJO for more details of this subregion.

Carthage, ancient city on the north coast of Africa just east of modern Tunis, whose part in the history of viticulture was a curious and incidental one. It was most probably the early PHOENICIAN settlers at Carthage who introduced viticulture to that region of North Africa. A famous passage of the historian Diodorus (20. 8) paints a vivid picture of the country estates of the Carthaginian elite of the late 4th century BC, flourishing on the fertile soils around Carthage with a mix of farming, which included viticulture. However, at no

period did Carthaginian wine figure prominently in trade. It was eclipsed by North Africa's importance as a producer of corn and olive oil, most particularly in the period when it was part of the Roman empire. Still, there can be little doubt that Carthage's élite shared the same interest in viticulture as the rest of the Mediterranean world.

It was for them that a large work, written in Punic, of 28 books on agriculture was produced by a certain Mago. Nothing is known of the writer or of his date; but his work fits most easily into the great explosion of handbooks on agriculture written in the Hellenistic period, particularly in the 3rd and 2nd centuries BC. Like these other works, Mago's treatise is lost; our knowledge of its contents is entirely derived from references to it and quotations from it in the later writers. Of these the largest number are about vines, although it would be dangerous to infer from this very fragmentary selection that viticulture had particular prominence in his work. While Mago's work probably contained much that was taken from the earlier AGRICULTURAL TREATISES produced in the Greek world, it was not without information based on personal observation. As COLUMELLA (*De re rustica* 3. 12. 5-6) noted, Mago's advice to plant vines on north-facing slopes is particularly appropriate to Africa (see TOPOGRAPHY). Large extracts from Mago were translated into Greek and incorporated in a treatise on agriculture by Cassius Dionysius of Utica, near Carthage (VARRO, *De re rustica* I. I. 10). More surprisingly a decree of the senate ordered a translation of Mago into Latin (Columella, *De re rustica* I. I. 13). The most likely occasion for this must be in connection with one of the schemes for Roman settlement in North Africa in the period after Rome's destruction of Carthage in 146 BC. Columella was to call Mago 'the father of country matters', probably primarily because his work in its Latin version gave Romans convenient access to the vast literature on agriculture from the Hellenistic world.

The most famous Carthaginian of all is commemorated in the name of the co-operative and principal producer of CHÂTILLON-EN-DIOIS in the foothills of the French alps, the Cellier Hannibal. J.J.P.

Gsell, S., *Histoire ancienne de l'Afrique du nord* (Paris, 1951), iv. 1–169.

cartons, method of packaging wine in what are effectively cardboard 'bricks', sometimes known as tetrapacks, that has been particularly popular for everyday wines in Latin American countries such as CHILE. Once opened, the packaging cannot be resealed, so the wine needs to be consumed on the day of opening.

casa vinicola on the label of an Italian wine indicates a producer who buys in grapes or wine, like a French NÉGOCIANT.

case. BEER and milk may be sold in crates but, contrary to popular usage, wine is sold in cases. A case typically holds a dozen bottles, the basic trading unit in the fine wine trade and much of the wholesale wine trade. It is posited that the case contains 12 bottles because that is as many as a man can comfortably carry. Most cases are made of cardboard outers, with cardboard vertical or papier mâché horizontal dividers. Wine merchants truly dedicated to the mail-order business ensure that they use only particularly strong cases especially designed to minimize breakage. Most (but not all) fine wines designed for prolonged BOTTLE AGEING are dispatched from their producers in thick wooden cases, usually made of rough pine, branded with the name, and often logo, of the producer on the **case ends** (which can be attractive enough for future use as decoration or table mats). These cases are usually nailed down and can be opened only with a chisel or screwdriver and hammer, often breaking the wooden lid. Wine sold in unopened cases is presumed, in the fine wine market, to be worth sufficient premium that they are usually designated 'o.w.c.', or 'original wooden cases'.

The German wine trade has long sold wine in six-bottle cartons and as wine PRICES rise, an increasing proportion of top-quality and everday wine from around the world is offered in six-bottle cases. A **split case** may be one that is torn, but may be one that contains six bottles of each of two different wines, or four bottles of each of three different wines. One bottle of each of 12 different wines becomes a **mixed case.**

casein, the principal milk PROTEIN, is used by winemakers as a FINING agent particularly useful for removing brown colours from white wines. It is also used to a lesser extent in the general CLARIFICATION of young wines. Precipitated from milk by the addition of ACIDS, casein is chiefly used in the form of sodium or potassium caseinate. When this salt is added to cloudy wine, it reacts with some of the wine acid forming a curd which adsorbs and precipitates most of the very small particles, including the PIGMENTS causing discoloration. A.D.W.

cask, wooden container for wine, often used interchangeably with BARREL, a cylindrical container small enough to be rolled. The term is also used less precisely, however, for any form of COOPERAGE, i.e. wooden containers of any size, whether larger, immobile, storage containers such as the oval *Fuder* or *foudre* common in Germany and Alsace, or the *botte* of Italy, and also including quite large, immovable containers which may or may not be open topped.

In the 1970s, the Australian wine industry neatly, if misleadingly, coined the term **cask wine** for wine packaged in a bag packed inside a cardboard BOX, a wine type highly unlikely to have been either made or aged in wood of any sort (although OAK CHIPS could have played a part in some).

cask ageing, wine-making practice of ageing a wine after fermentation (see ÉLEVAGE) in a large wooden container usually too old to impart any OAK FLAVOUR. It may well, however, exert some WOOD INFLUENCE and help considerably to achieve natural CLARIFICATION and STABILIZATION. White wines subjected to cask ageing for several months include some of the great white wines of the LOIRE, GERMANY, and ALSACE. Red wines subjected to cask ageing, sometimes for several years, include many of the traditional wines of the RHÔNE, ITALY, SPAIN, PORTUGAL, and GREECE.

The alternatives, and possible supplements, to cask ageing are BARREL MATURATION, AGEING in inert CONTAINERS such as stainless steel tanks, BOTTLE AGEING, and BOTTLING almost immediately after FERMENTATION as in NOUVEAU wines.

casse, historic wine FAULT involving spoilage either by an excess of IRON or COPPER or PROTEIN precipitation.

cassis is French for blackcurrant and is used often as a tasting note for red wines, particularly red wines based on Cabernet Sauvignon grapes. Dry white wine mixed with some blackcurrant liqueur is known as both a **vin blanc cassis** and KIR (while red wine mixed with blackcurrant liqueur is sometimes called a *cardinal*).

Cassis, small, mainly white wine appellation in PROVENCE. The encroachment of Greater Marseilles on this old fishing village keeps total plantings to about 175 ha/430 acres in this sheltered amphitheatre, protected from the mistral by the Cap Canaille to the east, one of the highest cliffs in France.

Three-quarters of the wine is full, dry, herby white, made from increasing proportions of Clairette and Marsanne, together with some Ugni Blanc and Sauvignon Blanc grapes. The best producers such as La Ferme Blanche and Clos Sainte Magdelaine can make wines that age gracefully. A little red and rosé is also made, mainly from Mourvèdre (which ripens easily here—see nearby BANDOL), Grenache, and Cinsaut. Little Cassis is allowed to escape by the annual influx of summer visitors, however.

Castel, France's biggest wine company, claims the world's third highest turnover in wine but is also an important distributor of BEER, WATER, and wine-related machinery in France and Africa. Founded by four Castel brothers in 1949, the company is still family-owned and based in Bordeaux, where it owns at least a dozen CHÂTEAUX. Castel bought France's then second biggest wine company Vins de France in 1992, the Nicolas retail chain in 1998, Domaines Virginie in the Languedoc in 1999, and the British retail chain Oddbins

in 2002. It is also involved in a JOINT VENTURE for the production of Chinese wine and distribution of French wines in CHINA with Changyu, one of the country's largest wine companies.

Castelão, Portugal's most planted vine variety with a total of about 20,000 ha/50,000 acres planted in 2004 which makes varied red wines all over southern Portugal. Known variously as Periquita in Terras do Sado; **Castelão Francês** in the Ribatejo, João de Santarém in Oeste, Trincadeira in Dão, Mortágua or Moreto in the Algarve, and Santarém in the Douro, this versatile vine can produce fruity, relatively fleshy, even gamey red wines which can be drunk young or aged.

Castel del Monte, DOC in the far south east of Italy. For more details, see PUGLIA.

Castelli Romani, general term for the white wines of the VOLCANIC hills south east of Rome in the region of LAZIO (see map under ITALY) which stretch from just outside the city gates (some of the vineyards are in fact within the administrative borders of the city) into the province of Latina, south of the township of Velletri. Over 6,700 ha/16,750 acres of DOC vineyards fall within the zone and are divided into seven different appellations: Castelli Romani (1,400 ha of vineyard in the late 1990s); Colli Albani (1,115 ha), Colli Lanuvini (950 ha), FRASCATI (some 2,150 ha), Marino (1,000 ha), Montecompatri (12 ha), and Velletri (137 ha). The wines are made principally from MALVASIA grapes with usually at least 25 per cent TREBBIANO. BOMBINO (here also called Bonvino) and Bellone are also permitted in the blend, up to a maximum of 10 per cent, and can add a welcome note of complexity, but these vines are less suitable to the TENDONE training systems that have come to dominate the zone and are gradually being abandoned by growers. Malvasia di Candia is more widely utilized than Malvasia di Lazio, principally for its high productivity, although better producers prefer the quality level of the latter. A wide variety of different strains of Trebbiano are employed (Verde, Giallo, Toscano, Romagnolo, di Soave); the first of these, if theoretically more interesting, is not necessarily preferred in the vineyard. High YIELDS—ranging from the 98 hl/ha (6 tons/acre) of the Colli Lanuvini to the more than 115 hl/ha of the Colli Albani and Marino—make many of the discussions of blends and subvarieties purely nugatory; interesting wines from Malvasia and Trebbiano cannot be made at these yields. The wines of the separate DOCs tend to resemble one another closely, in fact, although Marino, with a more westerly ASPECT than most, can be somewhat fuller than its neighbours. Over three-quarters of the total production is in the hands of CO-OPERATIVES, the rest principally in the hands

of large commercial wineries. Both have followed a marketing strategy based on high volume and low prices, counting on the advantages of the proximity of the large Roman market and on the more extended recognition that has come from the millions of visitors who flock to the city each year and encounter the wines in the city's taverns and *trattorie*.

If the Castelli Romani wines are principally intended for the guzzling needs of their public, the character of the wines themselves has changed rather drastically, just as the vineyards have been transformed from GUYOT and CORDON training systems to tendone. Once fermented on their skins, these wines were golden in colour, full in flavour and aroma. The colour deepened as the Malvasia, a variety whose wines oxidize quite rapidly, began to age, and the aromas and flavours followed suit. The results were not always wines of great finesse, but they provided an excellent accompaniment to the flavoursome cuisine of Rome. Modern Castelli Romani wines, cold fermented off the skins, filtered, and stabilized, are a product without the defects of old. Given the grapes deployed, however, the wines without defects are inherently neutral.

Several avant-garde estates in Marino and Frascati are now producing interesting wines from Cabernet and Merlot, Chardonnay, and Sauvignon Blanc, and even more exotic varieties such as Viognier and Syrah. The results have demonstrated that the soil and climate of the Castelli Romani can indeed produce good-quality wines, but these new products, self-consciously detached from the history and traditions of the zone, do not seem to provide a key to resolving the area's viticultural problems, which, with a severe drop in demand for central Italy's standard Trebbiano-Malvasia wines in the mid 1990s, are becoming increasingly acute. This problem is exacerbated by high vineyard land PRICES, given that the hills are such an attractive place to live for Romans who want to distance themselves from the congestion of the city. For this reason, the amount of vineyard land has declined by 40 per cent in the past decade, and little—certainly not the quality of the wine—seems able to halt this decline.   D.T. & D.C.G.

Castets, almost extinct vine, probably selected from an escaped seedling in a forest in the Aveyron, SOUTH WEST FRANCE.

Castilla, **Castille** in English, old central Spanish kingdom divided by mountains into CASTILLA Y LEÓN, or Old Castile, in the north and CASTILLA-LA MANCHA, or New Castile, in the south.

Castilla-La Mancha, known as **Castile-La Mancha** in English (historically, Castilla la Nueva or New Castile), the lower, southern half of the plateau that makes up central SPAIN (see map under SPAIN). At altitudes between 500 and 700 m (1,650–2,300 ft) above sea level, this is Spain at her most extreme. Winters are long and cold with temperatures often falling below 0 °C/32 °F for days on end. In summer the heat is gruelling. The thermometer regularly rises above 35 °C, even 40 °C (104 °F), and little if any rain falls between May and September. The vast expanse of country which is green in the spring quickly turns to a shade of burnt ochre in July and August as all but the deepest river beds dry up completely. The locals say that they suffer 'nine months of winter and three months of hell'. Despite these fierce conditions, Castilla-La Mancha produces half of all the wine made in Spain. Around 700,000 ha/1.7 million acres of vineyard yield an average of 18 million hl/475 million gal of wine (averaging yields of just over 25 hl/ha (1.4 tons/acre)). One of Castilla-La Mancha's four DO regions, LA MANCHA itself, is planted mainly with the robust white wine vine AIRÉN.

There are an estimated 250,000 ha of Airén in the zone of La Mancha alone (less than half of them producing DO wine), making it the world's most widely planted vine variety. Cencibel (alias TEMPRANILLO) comes a fast-growing second with more than 50,000 ha in this region behind the DROUGHT-resistant Airén, but dominates in the Valdepeñas DO, while north west of Toledo, MÉNTRIDA produces rough and ready reds from overripe GARNACHA. Although the fourth DO, ALMANSA, belongs administratively to Castilla-La Mancha, the style of wine-making there is closer to that of the LEVANTE. MONASTRELL, Cencibel, and the red-fleshed Garnacha Tintorera produce big, alcoholic red wines.

The mountainous DO of MONDÉJAR east of Madrid produces largely undistinguished reds, but the Ribera del Júcar and MANCHUELA DOs further east are producing much more interesting reds from Tempranillo, Syrah, and such indigenous varieties as Bobal, Garnacha, and Monastrell, as well as possibly Spain's most fragrant renditions of Macabeo whites.

Until the 1970s, the wines from Castilla-La Mancha were mainly sold in BULK to be drunk by undiscerning palates in bars all over Spain. But in the 1970s and 1980s, parts of the region were quietly revolutionized. Attracted by the availability of grapes and low production costs, a number of large companies moved to the region bringing new wine-making technology with them. The large CO-OPERATIVES have similarly modernized their production, although much of their bulk wine from Airén still goes into subsidized distillation (see WINE LAKE). So a new generation of cleanly made and often inexpensive red, rosé, and white wine from Castilla-La Mancha is finding favour with buyers both at home and abroad.

Another development that contrasts strongly with centuries of bulk wine production has been a blossoming of distinguished single-estate wines that have vastly outgrown clichés about La Mancha wines, all of them inspired by the pioneering efforts of the Marqués de Griñón at his Dominio de Valdepusa. R.J.M. & V. de la S.

Castilla y León, Castile and León in English, is the largest of the 17 autonomous regions of SPAIN. This northern part of Spain's central plateau, rising to between 880 and 1,000 m (2,900–3,300 ft) above sea level, takes up about a fifth of the entire country. Centred on its capital, the university city of Valladolid, most of Castilla y León is thinly populated table land almost encircled by mountains. It is separated from the hub of Spain (MADRID and CASTILLA-LA MANCHA or New Castile) by the central mountain range which rises to over 2,000 m near Avila and Segovia (see map under SPAIN). To the north, the Cordillera Cantabrica, which peaks at over 2,600 m, deflects the maritime influence of the bay of Biscay.

The climate here is harsh. Short, hot summers are followed by long, cold winters when temperatures can drop to −10 °C/14 °F. Under often clear skies, temperatures drop quickly after sunset and, even in summer, nights are cool. FROST continues to be a threat until mid May. Rain falls mainly in winter and amounts to between 400 and 500 mm (15–19 in) a year. Much of the land is poor and unable to support anything other than nomadic flocks of sheep. However, the river Duero (known as DOURO in Portugal), which cuts a broad valley in the rather featureless plain, provides a natural water source. Grain, sugar beet, and vines are grown along its length.

A regional variant of the red TEMPRANILLO vine, variously called Tinta del País, Tinto Fino, Tinto Aragonés, and Tinta de Toro, is the chief good-quality grape variety in three of the five DO wine regions in Castilla y León. The largest of these is RIBERA DEL DUERO, which extends for about 100 km/60 miles either side of the river and is internationally known for its red wines. Downstream of Ribera del Duero, RUEDA made enormous progress in its white wine production in the 1980s, while TORO, straddling the Duero near the Portuguese border, is slowly improving its once heavy reds. CIGALES, north of Valladolid, specializes in rosé wine. BIERZO, abutting GALICIA in the north west, shows promise with its fragrant, characterful reds from the Mencía grape. There are also new Vinos de la Tierra (VdlT) areas, including the confusingly named Vinos de la Tierra de León and Vinos de la Tierra de Castilla y León. R.J.M. & V. de la S.

Castillon, Côtes de, is a dynamic, well-priced red wine appellation, effectively an eastern extension of ST-ÉMILION in BORDEAUX. With almost 3,000 ha/ 7,500 acres of vineyard on mixed soils, it is much bigger than its northern neighbour Côtes de FRANCS but produces similarly sturdy red wines based on Merlot grapes with generally better structure than regular red BORDEAUX AC. The 400 vine-growers here elected in 1989 to establish their own identity rather than depend on the name of Bordeaux. VINE DENSITY is 5,000 vines per ha and those vineyards closest to the river DORDOGNE tend to produce more supple wine than those at higher altitudes such as Ch de Belcier, one of the more important producers. The region is named after the town of Castillon-la-Bataille, the battle being that which brought an end to the HUNDRED YEARS WAR. Interesting, age-worthy wines are made at Ch d'Aiguilhe, Clos Puy Arnaud, Domaine de l'A, and others.

Cataluña, Catalonia in English, a proud and industrious region on the Mediterranean coast which encompasses a part of southern France and a part of north east Spain (see maps under FRANCE and SPAIN), some of whose inhabitants consider themselves neither French nor Spanish, and even those who do, think of themselves as Catalan first. The region has suffered a turbulent past, fighting for separation first from ARAGÓN to the west and then from CASTILLA and the national capital Madrid. Self-government was achieved in 1977, when Cataluña became one of Spain's 17 autonomous regions. Barcelona, the second largest city in Spain and the busiest port on the Mediterranean, became the Catalan capital. Centuries of political infighting have left Cataluña with a strong sense of independence. The Catalan language, akin to the French langue d'oc (see LANGUEDOC), often suppressed in the past in favour of Castilian Spanish, has now been restored as the official language and Cataluña (**Catalunya** in Catalan) is now officially bilingual (which leads to some confusion and anomalies in proper names). For details of French Catalonia, see ROUSSILLON.

Barcelona and its densely populated hinterland is a hive of enterprise and industry. A fifth of Spain's industrial output comes from the city alone. It is therefore no coincidence that Cataluña was at the vanguard of Spain's 20th-century wine-making revolution. The region began to stir in the early 1870s when José Raventos began making sparkling wine by the TRADITIONAL METHOD in the small town of San Sadurní de Noya (Sant Sadurní d'Anoia in Catalan). He founded the giant CODORNÍU firm, and his foresight generated the CAVA industry which earned its own Denominación de Origen (see DO) in 1986.

In addition to most of Spain's Cava, Cataluña produces an eclectic range of wines from traditional, powerful reds to cool-fermented dry whites. With Barcelona close at hand, wine producers have always found it relatively easy to raise finance and Cataluña was consequently the first region in Spain to introduce STAINLESS STEEL and its accompanying technology.

Much of the credit for the transformation of Cataluña's wine industry in recent years must go to the late Don Miguel Torres Carbó and his son Miguel A. TORRES, who imported INTERNATIONAL VINE VARIETIES to plant alongside indigenous varieties such as GARNACHA, MONASTRELL, and TEMPRANILLO (called Ull de Llebre in Catalan), and the Cava grapes, PARELLADA, MACABEO, and XAREL-LO.

The climate in Cataluña is strongly influenced by the Mediterranean. The coastal belt is warm and equable with moderate rainfall but conditions become progressively more arid and extreme further inland. There are nine DO regions: ALELLA, EMPORDÀ-COSTA BRAVA, CONCA DE BARBERÁ, COSTERS DEL SEGRE, MONTSANT, PENEDÈS, PLA DE BAGES, PRIORAT, TARRAGONA, and TERRA ALTA plus the new, controversial catch-all DO CATALUNYA. Of these, Penedès is the most important in terms of quantity, although most others, especially Priorat, have made great progress in quality.

Cataluña has long been an important centre of CORK production and is a particularly important source of corks for sparkling wines.

R.J.M. & V. de la S.

Catalunya, local Catalan name for the region of CATALUÑA and controversial DO created in the early 21st century for blends of wines made from anywhere in the region. The big bottlers such as TORRES were the chief proponents and are the chief beneficiaries.

Catarratto, Sicilian white grape variety that is the second most widely planted grape variety in Italy and, rather depressingly, the most popular white wine variety. In 2000, there were 43,000 ha/109,000 acres of **Catarratto Bianco Comune** (down from 60,000 ha in 1990) and nearly 7,500 ha of **Catarratto Bianco Lucido**, the latter, the superior in terms of wine quality, having given up ground to the former during the 1980s.

The variety is planted almost exclusively in the far western province of Trapani and has in the past been much used for the production of MARSALA. Today, it can be expected that much of the vine's produce is regarded as SURPLUS and is therefore either compulsorily distilled by the EUROPEAN UNION, or transformed into GRAPE CONCENTRATE. Despite its profusion, this variety is specified in the regulations of just three DOC zones; familiarity seems to have bred the usual contempt from locals. Visiting FLYING WINEMAKERS have learnt more respect for this grape and some fine, crisp but characterful table wines have been produced from it. See SICILIA for more details. California grape statistics recorded 300 acres/1,215 ha of it in 2004.

Catawba, deep pink-skinned LABRUSCA grape variety that was extremely popular in the 19th century and is still widely grown in NEW YORK state. Identified in North Carolina in 1802, even before CONCORD, it produces white and pink, still and sparkling wines from dry to very sweet.

catechin and its isomer **epicatechin** are PHENOLIC compounds (see also FLAVONOIDS) found mainly in grape seeds, but also in stems and berry skins. They contribute to bitterness in wines and are the constitutive units of TANNINS (see also PROANTHOCYANIDINS), which are responsible for astringency and increasing the stability of ANTHOCYANINS (see PIGMENTED TANNINS), leading to longer-lived COLOUR in wines. Because of the increased SKIN CONTACT involved during RED WINE-MAKING, catechin concentrations are usually higher in red wines than whites, but are involved in browning reactions in both red and white wine. Catechin may play a role in protecting vine parts from microbial attack as a pre-existing chemical barrier, but it is also produced by vines in response to DOWNY MILDEW infection.

Catechins, like other flavonoids, are antioxidant compounds that may contribute to the HEALTH benefits of moderate wine consumption. The study of catechins has been overshadowed by that of RESVERATROL and related STILBENES, which are present in wine in much lower concentrations. Perhaps this is because unlike resveratrol, these compounds are widely present in other fruits and vegetables and other beverages such as teas.

The concentrations of catechins vary with vine variety, with PINOT NOIR, then MERLOT, notably high among well-known red wine grapes, and SYRAH lowest. As with resveratrol, cool, damp climates seem to stimulate more catechin synthesis than do hot, dry ones.

G.L.C., R.E.S., & V.C.

Goldberg, D. M., Karamanchiri, A., Tsang, E., and Soleas, G., 'Catechin and Epicatechin. Concentrations of red wines: regional and cultivar-related differences', *American Journal of Enology and Viticulture*, 49 (1998), 23–34.

Mirabel, M., Saucier, C., Guerra, C., and Glories, Y., 'Copigmentation in model wine solutions: occurrence and relation to wine aging', *American Journal of Enology and Viticulture*, 50 (1999), 211–18.

cation exchange, see ION EXCHANGE.

cation exchange capacity (CEC), the amount of positively charged ions a soil can hold, is a significant factor in the degree to which SOIL NUTRIENTS are available to the vine. CEC is determined by SOIL TEXTURE, the amount of ORGANIC MATTER in the soil, and the amount and type of clay. Sandy soil has a low CEC. Fine-textured soil such as clay, with a high level of organic matter, tends to have a high CEC.

Cato, Marcus (234–149 BC), Roman statesman advanced as a writer on agricultural and viticulture matters, known as 'Cato the Elder' or 'Cato the Censor' to distinguish him from his great-grandson. He grew up on his father's farm near Reate, north east of Rome, then fought against CARTHAGE in the Second Punic War and afterwards had a distinguished political career. He became known as a strict moralist, castigating the 'new' extravagance, ostentation, and luxury and advocating a return to the 'old' virtues of austerity, honesty, and hard work. He wrote books on many subjects and published his speeches. PLINY the Elder praises him for the breadth of his learning (*Natural History* 25. 4), and COLUMELLA (*De re rustica* I. I. 12) and Cicero (*Brutus* 16. 61) honour him as the father of Latin prose. His only surviving work, *De agri cultura* ('Concerning the cultivation of the land'), also known as *De re rustica* ('Concerning country matters'), is important not only because it is the first lengthy prose work in Latin. *De agri cultura* is not divided into books or arranged systematically in any other way: Cato's remarks on viticulture and wine-making are scattered throughout the treatise. The advice he gives is of a severely practical kind. His prime concern is making farming, including wine-growing, profitable through hard work and careful management. For instance, he stresses that the grapes should always be thoroughly ripe when harvested, or one's wine will lose its good reputation. And in the making and storing of wine he was aware of the importance of HYGIENE to prevent the wine turning to VINEGAR. After the vintage, the wine jars should be wiped twice a day, each with its own broom. After 30 days, when FERMENTATION is complete, the jars should be sealed or the wine can be drawn off its LEES if desired as an alternative to LEES CONTACT. The type of estate he has in mind produces chiefly wine and olive oil: hence his extensive section on the construction of presses.

H.M.W.

Astin, A. S., *Cato the Censor* (Oxford, 1978)

Thielschen, P., *Des Marcus Catos Belehrung über die Landwirtschaft* (Berlin, 1963).

caudalie, French term for a unit of sensory measurement equal to one second's LENGTH of a wine's impact on the palate after swallowing or spitting.

Cava, Spanish SPARKLING WINES made using the traditional method of SPARKLING WINE-MAKING. The term Cava was adopted by the Spanish in 1970 when they agreed to abandon the use of the potentially misleading term Champaña. The word originates in CATALUÑA, which produces most but not all Cava, where it means 'cellar'. It was here in the town of San Sadurní de Noya that José Raventós, head of the family firm of CODORNÍU, made the first bottles of traditional method sparkling wine after a visit to France in 1872. Early growth in the industry coincided with the arrival of the PHYLLOXERA louse, which first appeared in Catalan vineyards in the 1880s. Vineyards that had once made sturdy red wines had to be uprooted and were replanted with MACABEO, PARELLADA, and XAREL-LO, the triad of grape varieties which is the mainstay of the Cava industry to this day. In 1889, the Raventos family were joined by Pedro Ferrer, who founded the firm of FREIXENET. Codorníu and Freixenet, both still family owned, are now two of the largest sparkling wine producers in the world, with their own winery outposts in CALIFORNIA.

Unlike any other Spanish DO, the Cava denominación is not restricted to a single delimited area. However, since Spain joined the EUROPEAN UNION in 1986, the EU authorities have insisted that Cava should be made from grapes grown in prescribed regions. As a result, the use of the term Cava is restricted to sparkling wines from a list of municipalities in CATALONIA, VALENCIA, ARAGÓN, NAVARRA, RIOJA, and the BASQUE country. Ninety-five per cent of all Cava is made in Cataluña, however, mostly in and around the town of San Sadurní de Noya. Total production amounts to over 1.2 million hl/31 million gal a year (about a third that of Champagne).

The somewhat neutral Macabeo (the Viura of Rioja) comprises about half of the blend for a typical Cava, its late BUDBREAK making it a popular choice for vineyards prone to spring frosts. The productive and indigenous Xarel-lo vine is the second most important, and its earthy aroma has been one of Cava's distinguishing features, although it thrives only at relatively low altitudes. Parellada performs better above 300 m/900 ft, where it produces finer wines relatively low in BODY. Plantings of the French vine CHARDONNAY, officially authorized for Cava in 1986, are increasing rapidly.

To qualify for the DO, Cava must be made according to the local, and in some respects less rigorous, adaptation of the champagne traditional method. The wine must spend at least nine months on its lees before DISGORGEMENT, achieve at least four atmospheres of pressure, and attain an ALCOHOLIC STRENGTH of between 10.8 and 12.8 per cent by volume. YIELDS, set at a maximum of 1 hl of must per 150 kg of grapes, are higher than those allowed in Champagne.

(The bitter competition between the two giants of Cava, Codorníu and Freixenet, produced a series of ugly court battles in the late 1990s, with Codorníu charging that its competitor's less expensive wines did not spend the minimum time on lees, and Freixenet counter-attacking with charges that its rival was using (then) illegal Pinot Noir grapes.)

Most REMUAGE is now carried out automatically in a *girasol* or GYROPALETTE, a Spanish invention which enables hundreds of bottles to be handled at a time. The best Cavas tend to be produced by the larger firms who control their own vinification rather than those producers who buy in ready-made base wine from one of the large but often outdated CO-OPERATIVES that continue to flourish all over Cataluña.

R.J.M. & V. de la S.

cave, French for a CELLAR or wine-making establishment and as close as the French language comes to an equivalent of a WINERY. A **caviste** is French for a specialist wine retailer, of which there are surprisingly few in France, presumably since so many consumers buy direct from the producer.

cave co-opérative, French for one of France's more than nearly 900 wine CO-OPERATIVES.

Cayetana, high-yielding Spanish white grape variety, grown on nearly 12,000 ha/ 30,000 acres in total, which produces low-acid, neutral-flavoured wines which oxidize easily. It is particularly popular in the EXTREMADURA region, especially in Badajoz province on the border with Portugal, where much of its produce is distilled into Brandy de Jerez. In Rioja it may be known as Cazagal, and Baladí is another synonym. Research in the early 2000s showed that this grape is the same as the JAÉN BLANCO of Andalucía and the CALAGRAÑO of Rioja. See also PARDINA.

Cayuga White, AMERICAN HYBRID with SEYVAL genes released in 1972 from Geneva in New York (see CORNELL). It is grown in the north east of the UNITED STATES and makes fruity white wines but is limited by being only moderately winter hardy.

Cebreros, wine zone in CASTILLA Y LEÓN in west central Spain, little known despite its outstanding feature, very old GARNACHA vineyards on steep slate slopes.

CEC. See CATION EXCHANGE CAPACITY.

cell, the structural unit of living organisms, the smallest unit capable of independent existence. YEAST and BACTERIA are examples of single cells while one grapevine has billions of cells. Each plant cell consists of a protoplast surrounded by a cell wall, but it can be differentiated into a host of forms. A cell in the flesh of a ripe grape berry, for example, can be 0.5 mm/ 0.02 in in length with a thin, wavy cell wall lined by an equally thin cytoplasm surrounding the vacuole, a 'sea' of water with dissolved sugars, acids, and hundreds of other solutes, otherwise known as grape juice. Other cells within the berry can be entirely different. A PHLOEM element aligns end to end with others to form a tube through which elaborated sap moves in a network throughout the plant. Adjacent fibre cells are long and slim with thick walls hardened by the wood polymer, lignin. The complex functioning of the leaf provides other examples of cell forms: STOMATAL cells function to allow carbon dioxide in and oxygen and water vapour out; others function as the 'carbohydrate factory'; and cells in its dense network of veins are designed to move water

and minerals up from the roots (in the XYLEM) and to move sugars and other elaborated organic nutrients out to the rest of the plant (in the phloem).

Despite this diversity, all cells of a plant have the same genetic information in their nuclei and, with some exceptions, may be separated and cultured as single protoplasts. By TISSUE CULTURE methods, these can then be used for the regeneration of another plant like the parent. The genetic material in each cell will therefore be 'tuned' for its differentiation and functioning by the dictate of its neighbours in that tissue and by its reaction to signals received from other tissues and organs.   B.G.C.

Taiz, L., and Zeiger, E., *Plant Physiology* (Redwood City, Calif., 1991).

cellar, widely used word that is roughly the English counterpart to CAVE, CANTINA, and BODEGA in French, Italian, and Spanish respectively. It can therefore be applied to both wine shops and wine-making premises, but is here considered only in its domestic sense, as a collection of wine and the place in which it is stored.

Location

Traditional underground cellars have the great advantages of being secure, dark, at a constant low temperature, slightly damp, and rarely disturbed. As outlined in STORING WINE, these constitute ideal conditions. Few modern dwellings have anywhere that enjoys all these advantages, and to re-create them it may be necessary to spend lavishly on specialist help in constructing or adapting quarters with low lighting levels and specially controlled temperature and humidity (and as few visitors as the expender of all this money and effort can bear). It is also possible to buy special cabinets which look like refrigerators and can be programmed to maintain certain temperature and humidity levels, but they are expensive relative to their capacity. Less expensive options include insulating a small room or large cupboard, insulating a space under some stairs, using a dark corner of a distant spare room or a closet against an outside wall, or a secure outhouse (although care must be taken that the TEMPERATURE never falls so low as to freeze the wine and push the corks out). It is important that any makeshift cellar is far from any heat source, even a hot water pipe and, especially, a boiler, but a constant medium temperature is less harmful than a place in which there are violent temperature swings. Those living on ground level can even excavate, and depend on a trapdoor.

Accessibility is an advantage or disadvantage depending on the cellar owner's personality and attitude towards the cellar. Paying for professional storage may be the only realistic option for some, but in this case cellar records (see below) are essential.

Design

Wine can be stored in the unopened CASES in which it is bought, but this is practical only for wines years away from being ready to drink, and very steady and sturdy shelves are needed if more than one layer of cases is to be stacked. A system which incorporates cases without lids on individual runners is particularly space-efficient. Wine racks take up more room but allow bottles to be kept horizontal (not strictly necessary for bottles with SCREW CAPS) and retrieved individually. Racks with slots for individual bottles offer the best access for very mixed cellars (metal and wood is the usual combination of materials used for these racks), even for bottles with alternative CLOSURES rather than CORKS, which need to be kept moist, but larger compartments, or BINS, can be used for larger quantities of bottles of the same wine.

It of course makes sense to keep the wines nearest MATURITY in the most accessible positions and vice versa (which dictates how wines may be kept in double-depth racks). There will be a slight temperature variation between the top and bottom of the cellar. Light levels are also likely to be higher at the top than the bottom, so there are at least two reasons why the fullest, least fragile, slowest maturing wines such as vintage port should be stored at the top and bottles as sensitive as, say, those containing sparkling wines should be stored close to floor level.

Contents

There is little point in devoting space and capital to storing wine unless it is difficult or expensive to replace, or will positively improve as a result of BOTTLE AGEING. It may therefore be worthwhile keeping the last bottle of nuptial champagne or holiday souvenir purely for sentimental reasons, but in general it is wise to be ruthless about cellar space, and accord it only to wines which are available only for a brief period (such as EN PRIMEUR rarities) or the wines recommended as worth AGEING. Space in wine books and magazines is often devoted to a concept called the 'ideal cellar' and the recommendations usually make interesting reading, but in truth there is no such thing and an individual's ideal depends entirely on his or her tastes and consumption patterns. Even the advice that NON-VINTAGE champagne is always improved by a year or so in a personal cellar may be questionable in an era of champagne glut.

Records

Cellar records are not necessary but they can add to the pleasure of wine COLLECTORS with a love of order and memorabilia. (The other school enjoys the twin elements of chaos and serendipity in plundering their wine cellars.) Traditional cellar records have a good-sized page for each case of wine acquired, stating price, supplier, and date of purchase. Below

this a dated tasting note for each bottle tasted can be inserted, together perhaps with details of the circumstances in which it was opened. The pages can be grouped by wine type (red bordeaux, for example) and individual bottles can be grouped appropriately together on pages. (Those using professional wine storage need, for obvious reasons, to keep full details of where and since when the wine has been stored.)

INFORMATION TECHNOLOGY can offer other, often more sophisticated and flexible, possibilities for cellar record-keeping but it is worth remembering that individual wines are usually kept for many years longer than a pc.

See also STORING WINE.

Thorn, J., *The Good Cellar Guide* (London, 1990).

cellar work, general term for all the processing steps requiring human intervention or monitoring in WINE-MAKING. In its most general sense it encompasses all operations included in wine-making. In the narrower human sense of what cellar workers actually do, apart from overseeing grape reception, DESTEMMING, CRUSHING, FERMENTATION, CLARIFICATION, FILTRATION, BLENDING, STABILIZATION, and BOTTLING, it generally entails operating PUMPS, adding FINING agents and other additions or processing aids, and almost constant cleaning (see HYGIENE). Cellars in which small barrels are used for both fermentation and maturation involve the most physical work, including filling, RACKING and moving barrels, TOPPING UP, and possibly STIRRING. See also ÉLEVAGE.

Celts, peoples who inhabited western Europe before the rise of Ancient ROME. Many of them were introduced to wine by the Romans, when some were already skilled COOPERS.

The first clear evidence that wine drinking with its attendant rituals was penetrating the courts of the prehistoric barbarian élites in western central Europe (eastern France, southern Germany, and Switzerland) appears in the archaeological record in the 6th century BC.

Griffon-headed cauldrons, CRATERS, jugs and strainers, and fine painted Attic cups, all of which would have been used at a Greek SYMPOSIUM, were shipped to Mediterranean ports such as Massilia (Marseilles). From there they were transported along the navigable RIVERS into the hinterland to be used in the complex systems of gift exchange which bound these peoples to the Greek and Etruscan traders of the south. Along with these trappings of civilization came wine. How much of it, if any, was at this stage Greek or Italian is difficult to tell. What is certain is that the large ceramic AMPHORAE in which the wine was transported inland were manufactured along the coast of southern France in the vicinity of Marseilles, suggesting, but not proving, that most of the wine consumed was locally manufactured.

The courts of the élite, places such as Mont Lassois on the main south–north trade route between Burgundy and Paris (where the celebrated Vix crater, a bronze vase 1.64 m/5.4 ft high and clearly made in Ancient GREECE, was found), and Heuneburg in Germany, lasted for a comparatively short time. They were flourishing in the 530s and 520s BC but had ceased to exist by the end of the next century as the old social order collapsed in a turmoil of unrest caused by migrating bands of Celts who were to thrust deep into Italy, Greece, and Turkey.

By the end of the 3rd century BC, a new order was beginning to emerge in the western Mediterranean. Rome was growing rapidly in power and had won a decisive victory over the CARTHAGINIANS in Spain, but their military involvement was to last for almost two centuries before the peninsula could be regarded as fully conquered. This meant a continuous movement of military detachments, supplies, and officials using the ports and the roads in southern France linking Italy and Spain. Inevitably the cities and the native tribes of Provence and Languedoc got used to this traffic and no doubt profited from it. So too did Roman entrepreneurs keen to exploit the new markets being opened up. For them the love of wine which the Celtic tribes of the interior so evidently possessed was a heaven-sent opportunity to offload, with profit, the considerable wine surpluses being generated by the large estates of northern and western Italy. As one contemporary writer somewhat incredulously remarked of the Celts of GAUL, 'They will give you a slave for an amphora of wine thus exchanging the cupbearer for the cup.' While this does not necessarily imply the actual exchange rate it shows which surpluses the two societies were prepared to exchange with each other for mutual benefit.

In the Celtic world it was important for those aspiring to power to host elaborate feasts to entertain their followers and others. The more exotic the commodities offered, the greater the status of the host. Wine from the south was in considerable demand and was avidly consumed. The drunken Celt who took his wine undiluted—something no civilized man would have done—was several times remarked upon by contemporary writers.

Wine was usually transported by sea in large ceramic amphorae made in distinctive styles and fabrics which can be quite closely dated and assigned to specific localities of manufacture. This means that it is possible to study the developing wine trade in some detail, and, since several of the estates produced amphorae with their own identifying stamps, individual marketing strategies can be identified. By studying the relative proportions of Italic and local amphorae in the successive levels of settlement sites in southern France, it is possible to show that throughout the 2nd century BC, when Provence and Languedoc were finally annexed by Rome, there is little trace in the archaeological record that local wine was drunk at all. In parallel with this, the number of shipwrecks containing amphorae found off the southern French coast increases noticeably, presumably reflecting the corresponding increase in the volume of trade.

Once offloaded at ports such as Massilia and Narbo (Narbonne), the amphorae were transported inland by road or river. En route a *portorium* (or transport tax) was charged at each settlement through which the wine passed, trebling the price charged by the time it eventually reached the native consumers. From the borders of Provincia of Ancient Rome, modern Provence, the wine penetrated the territory of the neighbouring tribes. At two locations, one just outside Toulouse and the other at Chalon-sur-Saône, substantial quantities of discarded Italian amphorae have been found. No precise count can now be made but estimates in the tens of thousands are unlikely to be far from the truth. These must surely be major transshipment points where wine was decanted into skins or BARRELS (for which the Celts of the CAHORS region were particularly famed) for the more arduous journeys by cart into the wild interior. Not all wine was decanted, however. Considerable numbers of amphorae have been recovered from major native *oppida* (towns) at Montmerlhe, Essalois, Jœuvres, and Mont-Beuvray between 20 and 100 km (12–62 miles) beyond the frontier. From here much of it passed into the hands of the local nobility to be consumed with relish in their lavish feasts.

The volume of wine imported into Gaul at this time is difficult to estimate in detail but a conservative assessment suggests that it may have reached 100,000 hl/2.6 million gal a year. When it is remembered that the largest trading system operating in pre-industrial Europe—the Gascon wine trade to Britain and Flanders in the 14th century (see BORDEAUX)—was 750,000 hl/20 million gal a year, the intensity of the Roman operation can be appreciated.

By the end of the 2nd century BC Italian wine was reaching all parts of France mainly along the navigable rivers but some, still in its amphorae, was being reloaded on to ships in the GIRONDE estuary to be transported along the Atlantic coast of France to Brittany. There much of it was consumed, but a small quantity was carried by Breton sailors on the last leg of its journey via Guernsey to the British port on Hengistbury Head, overlooking Christchurch harbour, constituting the earliest attested importation of wine to ENGLAND, or Britain. One wonders whether after such a journey it was even barely drinkable.

B.C.

Cuncliffe, B., *Greeks, Romans & Barbarians: Spheres of Interaction* (London, 1988).

Tchernia, A., *Le Vin de l'Italie romaine* (Paris, 1986).

——'Italian Wine in Gaul at the end of the Republic', in P. Garnsey, K. Hopkins, and C. R. Whittaker (eds.), *Trade in the Ancient Economy* (London, 1983).

Cencibel, synonym for the Spanish black grape variety TEMPRANILLO, especially in central and southern Spain, notably in LA MANCHA and VALDEPEÑAS, where it is the principal dark-skinned variety.

Central Coast, one of CALIFORNIA's umbrella AVAs, this sprawling wine region technically encompasses all of the land from San Francisco to Los Angeles, and inland from the coast almost to the CENTRAL VALLEY. In practice, the important and unique viticultural areas referenced by the name are concentrated in a mid-section of this too-broad appellation, the counties of MONTEREY, SAN LUIS OBISPO, and SANTA BARBARA.

Central Ranges Zone, Australian zone in NEW SOUTH WALES comprising the Cowra, Mudgee, and Orange regions.

Central valley. In CALIFORNIA, this great expanse is divided into the SACRAMENTO VALLEY in the north, which produces small quantities of wine, and the vast SAN JOAQUIN VALLEY in the south, which supplies the majority of the state's BULK WINE (and TABLE GRAPES and RAISINS). Plumbed by an extensive system of rivers out of the Sierra Nevada and IRRIGATION canals built since the 1920s, this large, fertile, sunny region is arguably the most productive farmland in the world with more agricultural output than the whole of China until 1990.

The Sacramento river from the north and the San Joaquin river from the south drain into the **Central Valley Delta**, which includes such AVAs as CLARKSBURG and, on slightly higher ground, LODI.

CHILE also has a Central Valley, an appellation commonly found on wine labels, and source of the majority of all Chilean wine.

Central Victoria, zone within the Australian state of VICTORIA comprising the Bendigo, Goulburn Valley, Heathcote, Strathbogie Ranges, and Upper Goulburn regions.

centrifugation, wine-making operation of CLARIFICATION using a **centrifuge**. Occasionally used to clarify white grape juice before FERMENTATION, the process is relatively expensive and slow. It is more effective when used to clarify new wines because of the greater difference in DENSITY between the yeast cells and the liquid than between the grape solids and the liquid.

While the force used in natural clarification is gravity, the centrifugal force used in centrifugation is 5,000 to 10,000 times greater and requires large amounts of electrical power and expensive specialist equipment to process only relatively small amounts of wine per hour.

A.D.W. & P.J.W.

Centurian, CALIFORNIA vine crossing with the same parentage as CARNELIAN but released three years later in 1975. The state's total acreage had fallen to around 300 acres/120 ha by the early 2000s, all in the central SAN JOAQUIN VALLEY. It has viticultural advantages over Carnelian but no organoleptic distinction.

cépage, French for VINE VARIETY. A VARIETAL wine, one that is sold by the name of the principal grape variety from which it is made (usually a VIN DE PAYS), is known as a **vin de cépage** within France, a term which has had some pejorative sense in comparison with a geographically named wine which qualifies as APPELLATION CONTRÔLÉE. High-quality vine varieties such as Syrah (as opposed to such traditional varieties as Carignan, Aramon, and Alicante Bouschet) are described as **cépages améliorateurs**, or 'improving varieties', in the south of France.

Cerceal, name of several white Portuguese grape varieties, whose Anglicized form is Sercial, a variety most commonly associated with the island of MADEIRA. See SERCIAL for more details.

Cerceal Branca is the official new name for **Cerceal do Dão**, a quite distinct ingredient in white DÃO.

Cercial is the official new name for **Cerceal da Bairrada**.

Cereza, pink-skinned grape variety of considerable importance in ARGENTINA which takes its name from the Spanish for cherry. Like CRIOLLA GRANDE, it is thought to be descended from the seeds of grapes imported by the early Spanish settlers, although it produces larger berries which result in paler wine than Criolla. It is declining in importance but there were still about 30,760 ha/76,000 acres of it in 2003, most notably in San Juan province and in eastern Mendoza. It produces mainly white and some rosé wine of extremely mediocre quality for early consumption within Argentina as well as being used for GRAPE CONCENTRATE.

Cérons, the least important sweet white wine appellation in the BORDEAUX region, on the left bank of the river GARONNE. Just north of BARSAC and SAUTERNES, it produces wines which rarely demonstrate either the finesse of the first or the concentration of the second of these two more famous appellations, possibly partly because YIELDS of 40 hl/ha (2 tons/acre) are allowed, as opposed to a maximum of 25 hl/ha in Barsac and Sauternes. In effect, Cérons is a buffer zone between Barsac and the GRAVES, and indeed it produces dry wines entitled to the Graves appellation as well as its own sweet wine which enjoys a long history (see BORDEAUX, history). The best bottlings from the likes of Clos Bourgelat can demonstrate real vivacity but apathy and depressed prices have discouraged many producers from making the investments of faith and equipment needed to make great sweet wine. Clay is slightly more common here than in Barsac and Sauternes and the generally flatter land may also play a part in reducing the likelihood of BOTRYTIZED WINES.

certified planting material, budwood, cuttings, or grafted plants which have normally been through a form of quality assurance to ensure trueness to type, freedom from known virus diseases, and typically designated clonal origin. Various bodies, often government controlled, offer such certification programmes around the world. See CLONE, CLONAL SELECTION, and VINE IMPROVEMENT.

Cesanese, the red grape variety apparently indigenous to LAZIO. For ancient historical reasons, and from an occasional modern wine produced near Anagni, one might expect great things from it. The superior **Cesanese d'Affile** (a minor ingredient in the cult wine Trinoro of southern Toscana) is more common but is losing ground and was planted on barely 1,000 ha/2,500 acres of vineyard in 2000. **Cesanese Comune** has larger berries and is also known as Bonvino Nero.

César, vine speciality of the far north of Burgundy, where it can contribute to such light, soft reds as IRANCY. DNA PROFILING at DAVIS suggested it is a progeny of PINOT and Argant.

Chablis is the uniquely steely, dry, age-worthy white wine of the most northern vineyards of BURGUNDY in north east France, made, like all fine white Burgundy, from Chardonnay grapes. Paradoxically, however, in the New World, particularly in North America in whose vineyards a wine as austere as Chablis is virtually impossible to produce, the name Chablis has been borrowed as a GENERIC name and abused so that it is more often used to describe a dry white wine of uncertain provenance and no specific grape variety bearing no resemblance other than its colour to true Chablis.

The appellation has increased considerably since the early 1990s and in 2004 included a total of 4,260 ha/just over 10,000 acres of Chardonnay vineyard around the small town of Chablis and 19 other villages and hamlets in the *département* of the Yonne, near the city of AUXERRE. Created in 1938, the Chablis appellation comprises four ranks, of which the top is grand cru Chablis, with seven named vineyards. Then come the premiers crus, including 40 vineyard names, then Chablis, by far the most common and infuriatingly variable appellation, and finally Petit Chablis, the lowliest. The best vineyard sites are on the south west facing slopes of the valley of the Serein, the small river that flows through the quiet town of Chablis to join the Yonne.

Chablis is quite separate from the rest of Burgundy, divided from the CÔTE D'OR by the hills of the Morvan, so that BEAUNE, for example, is over 100 km/62 miles to the south. In fact, the vineyards of Chablis are much closer to CHAMPAGNE and its southernmost vineyards in the Aube *département*, than to the rest of Burgundy, and until early in this century it was not unusual for wine from Chablis to find its way into the champagne makers' cellars in Rheims and Épernay.

History

Although it was the Romans who introduced vines to Chablis, as to so many other parts of FRANCE, it was the medieval church, notably the Cistercian MONKS of the nearby abbey of Pontigny, who firmly established viticulture as an essential part of the rural economy, possibly even introducing the Chardonnay vine. See BURGUNDY, history.

Towards the end of the 19th century, the Yonne as a whole was a flourishing wine region, with some 40,000 ha of vines. Vineyards lined the banks of the river Yonne, as far as Joigny and Sens. The best known of these Yonne wines was Chablis and the name was used to describe the ample quantities of dry white wine that was transported with great convenience along the rivers Yonne and Seine to satisfy the vast and thirsty Parisian market.

Three factors were responsible for the sharp decline in the vineyard area at the end of the 19th century: first POWDERY MILDEW, which appeared in Chablis in 1886, for which a cure had already been found, as had one for PHYLLOXERA, which first reached Chablis in 1887. However, many growers were reluctant to replant their vineyards, for the opening of the Paris–Lyons–Marseilles RAILWAY in 1856 considerably reduced their share of the Paris market. Thanks to the railways, Chablis lost its advantage of proximity to the capital and was simply unable to compete with the cheap wines of the MIDI, which could now be transported easily to the capital. Consequently the vineyard area gradually declined until it reached a mere 500 ha in the mid 1950s, before the fortunes of the appellation revived.

Climate

Climate has always played an important role in determining the success and quality of Chablis. Essentially the climate is semi-CONTINENTAL, with no maritime influence, so that the winters are long and hard and the summers often, but not always, fairly hot. There is all the climatic uncertainty, and therefore vintage variation, both in quality and quantity, of a vineyard far from the equator.

One of the key factors in determining how much wine will be produced is the possibility of spring FROSTS, which can cause enormous damage to the young vine shoots. Depending on how advanced the vegetation is, the vineyards are vulnerable from the end of March until well into May. Since the end of the 1950s, after a decade of vintages particularly badly affected by frost, various methods of protection evolved. Heaters, or SMUDGE POTS, may be lit in the vineyards; they are expensive but efficient. The alternative technique of using SPRINKLERS, or aspersion, to spray the vines with water from the moment the temperature drops to freezing point is also increasingly practised. Wind can seriously prejudice the effectiveness of aspersion, however. In the often parcellated vineyards of Chablis it can be all too easy to protect a neighbour's vines rather than one's own. Spraying must continue all the time the temperature is at 0 °C/ 32 °F or below. If there is any interruption, for any reason, such as a blocked pipe, then even more damage is caused to the vines than if no precautions had been taken in the first place.

However, both heaters and aspersion are sufficiently effective to make the difference in some years between a crop of reasonable quantity and virtually no crop at all. It is now perfectly possible to make a viable living from vines in Chablis, whereas in the 1950s, growers needed both eternal optimism and another crop, so that polyculture was common.

Vineyard expansion

It was the development of effective frost protection in the early 1960s that encouraged today's increase in the vineyard area of Chablis, which has not been without controversy. The seven CLIMATS of Chablis Grand Cru total just 100 ha and are all on one slope facing south west just outside the town. They are Les Clos, Blanchots, Bougros, Vaudésir, Valmur, Preuses, and Grenouilles. There is also, in true Burgundian fashion, an anomaly. The tiny vineyard of La Moutonne is partly in Vaudésir and partly in Preuses, but for some illogical and doubtless bureaucratic reason, an official INAO decree confirming its status as a grand cru has never been issued, even though its wines certainly demonstrate that it qualifies.

Much of the dispute over the vineyard expansion has centred on the premiers crus. By the early 21st century there were 40 in all, totalling 740 ha out of a delimited 750. Some are often seen on labels, while others are more obscure, and some such as Vaudevey came into existence only with the expansion of the appellation. Their protagonists argue that they are on slopes that were planted before the phylloxera crisis and that their TERROIR closely resembles that of the long-established premiers crus. Some of the lesser-known vineyards may use a better-known umbrella name, so that for example L'Homme Mort may be sold as Fourchaume, as follows, with umbrella names followed by their associated premiers crus:

Mont de Milieu

Montée de Tonnerre: *Chapelot, Pied d'Aloue, Côte de Bréchain*

Fourchaume: *Vaupulent, Côte de Fontenay, L'Homme Mort, Vaulorent*

Vaillons: *Châtains, Séchet, Beugnons, Les Lys, Mélinots, Roncières, Les Epinottes*
Montmains: *Forêt, Butteaux*

Côte de Léchet
Beauroy: *Troesme, Côte de Savant*
Vauligneau
Vaudevey: *Vaux Ragons*
Vaucoupin
Vosgros: *Vaugiraut*
Les Fourneaux: *Morein, Côte de Prés Girots*
Côte de Vaubarousse
Berdiot
Chaume de Talvat
Côte de Jouan
Les Beauregards: *Côte de Cuissy*

A full 2,860 ha of vineyard is now planted for AC Chablis, considerably more than was originally envisaged when the appellation was granted, with vines having been planted on much of the arable land. By 2004, 560 ha of a permitted 1,800 ha of Petit Chablis had been planted. There have been some moves to change the name of this category, for to some it sounds petty rather than petit, but for the moment its status and size are likely to remain substantially unchanged.

Soil is another significant factor in determining not only the unique flavour of Chablis, but also the vineyard area. Chablis lies on the edge of the Paris basin, where the rocks date back to the Upper Jurassic age, some 180 million years ago. On the other side of the basin is the Dorset village of Kimmeridge in southern England, which gives its name to the particular geological formation and period known as 'Kimmeridgean'. Basically the soil is what the French call *argilo-calcaire*, a mixture of limestone and clay, containing a multitude of tiny fossilized oyster shells. The next geological layer is Portlandien, which is very similar in structure to Kimmeridge, but is generally deemed not to give as much finesse to the wine. The grand cru vineyards are all on Kimmeridge while Portlandien constitutes most of the outlying vineyards of Petit Chablis.

Viticultural practices in Chablis are very similar to those in the rest of Burgundy, apart from the overriding need to protect the vines from frost.

The use of oak
In the cellar, as elsewhere in France, wine-making techniques improved enormously in the late 20th century, so that there is a better understanding of such elements as MALO-LACTIC FERMENTATION and the need for TEMPERATURE CONTROL during fermentation. The most interesting and controversial aspect of vinification in Chablis is the use of OAK. This is a most significant factor in influencing the taste of a Chablis, for it is where the winemaker can make the most impact. Chablis is the one fine wine area where Chardonnay is not automatically given some contact with oak.

Those who favour stainless steel want the purest flavour of Chablis, with the firm streak of acidity and the mineral quality that the French describe as *goût de pierre à fusil*, or gunflint. Louis Michel's is generally considered to be the epitome of this style, although others who employ it successfully include Jean Durup, Jean-Marc Brocard, A. Régnard, and Long-Depaquit.

Other producers, such as René and Vincent Dauvissat, and François and Jean-Marie Raveneau, have never completely abandoned their barrels. They may ferment their wine in vats and then, once the alcoholic FERMENTATION is finished, the wine goes into oak for a few months' BARREL MATURATION. Those who favour the use of oak barrels believe that the gentle process of oxygenation adds an extra dimension of complexity to the flavour of their wine. The proportion of new barrels in a cellar in Chablis can vary. Some producers buy very few each year, wishing to avoid the marked vanilla flavours that new wood can impart. Others such as William Fèvre (which belongs to BOUCHARD) regularly replace a third of their barrels. Some, such as Gilles Collet, Jean-Paul Droin, and Domaine Laroche for some crus, ferment in barrel; others just age their wine in oak, with annual variations according to the quality of the wine. Few wines other than grand cru and premie cru are matured in wood, however, for it is generally recognized that a wine needs a certain structure and extract to avoid being overwhelmed by the taste of oak. Paradoxically it is not unknown for a Chablis that has seen no wood, to take on, as it matures, a certain firm nuttiness that suggests some ageing in oak. Ultimately, as with all Burgundy, where vineyards and crus are split amongst several families, the choice of a bottle depends on the name of the grower and the estate on the label.

The Chablis market
Surprisingly perhaps until the early 1980s, Chablis was hardly appreciated in France itself as most of it was sold on the export market, usually through the large NÉGOCIANTS of Burgundy, based mainly in Beaune. Currently nearly a third of all Chablis is vinified by the local co-operative, La Chablisienne, which works well for its appellation. There are also five négociants based in the town, some with vineyards and some without. However, the trend of the last decade or two has been for an increasing number of producers, who originally sold their wine in bulk to négociants, to bottle and sell their wine themselves. Consequently the négociants have tended to decline in importance and the choice of Chablis producers has grown significantly.

Chablis has always been affected by significant variations in the size of the vintage. At times it seems that the swings between glut and penury can never be mastered, and prices fluctuate accordingly (much more dramatically, for example, than in the more regulated but climatically similar Champagne market).

However, some of the commercial instability has disappeared with the growth in the vineyard area, so that there is more Chablis available to satisfy world demand. Generally Chablis is a more prosperous appellation than it was in the 1970s, for with the possibility of frost protection the growers are much more certain of making a viable living from their vines than ever before.

Chablis remains one of the great white wines of the world. It is sometimes overshadowed by the greater opulence of a fine Meursault or Corton-Charlemagne, but it has an individuality of its own that sets it apart from the great white burgundies of the Côte d'Or. There is a unique streak of steely acidity, a firm flintiness, and a mineral quality that is not found elsewhere in Burgundy. Like all great white burgundy, it benefits from, but all too rarely receives, BOTTLE AGEING. A premier cru will be at its best at 10 years, while a grand cru could easily benefit from 15 or more years of maturation. A 1947 Côte de Léchet, not one of the best premiers crus, but from a great vintage, was still showing a remarkable depth of flavour with the characteristic *goût de pierre à fusil*, when it was 40 years old.   R.G. & J.R.

Bro, L., *Chablis, Porte d'or de la Bourgogne* (Paris, 1959).

Fèvre, W., *Le Vrai Chablis et les autres* (Chablis, 1978).

George, R., *Chablis* (London, 1984).

Chacolí. Castilian spelling of the Basque wine TXAKOLI. Chacolí **de Guetaria** is Getariako Txakolina, Chacolí **de Vizcaya** is Bizkaiko Txakolina, while Chacolí **de Alava** is Arabako Txakolina.

chai, French, and particularly Bordelais, term for a place where wine and occasionally brandy is stored, typically in BARREL. Thus a smart Bordeaux CHÂTEAU will have (perhaps) the château building itself with no direct wine-making function, a CUVERIE in which fermentation takes place, a first-year *chai* in which the most recent vintage's crop undergoes ÉLEVAGE, and a second-year *chai* to which it is moved at some point before the year end in order to make way for the next year's crop. The New World counterpart to the *chai* is sometimes called the barrel hall.

chalk, a soft and crumbly, highly porous (35 to 40 per cent) type of pure white LIMESTONE and a word often used erroneously as synonymous with it. Chalk-derived SOILS are valued in viticulture for their excellent DRAINAGE, combined with a capacity of the SUBSOIL to store substantial amounts of water. Because vine ROOTS can usually penetrate to chalk bedrock, continuity of moisture supply is assured regardless of short-term fluctuations in RAINFALL. Pure chalk is of low fertility, resulting in a rather low vine VIGOUR and naturally good CANOPY MICROCLIMATE.

True chalk is much less common under vineyards than most wine books suggest, chiefly because CALCAREOUS has been taken to mean chalky. Apart from some vineyards in southern ENGLAND, the principal wine region with chalk is CHAMPAGNE. Even here, the better vineyards are mostly on CLAYS, with only the longer roots reaching the underlying chalk. It is also widely believed that the SHERRY region around Jerez in south west Spain is on chalk, although the bedrock is not even pure limestone. The fact that Jerez, Cognac, and Champagne produce more or less exclusively white wines is one of the bases for the widely held misapprehension that there is a correlation between wine colour and SOIL COLOUR.

(See also DEACIDIFICATION for the use of chalk in wine-making.) J.M.H. & J.G.

Hancock, J., and Price, M., 'Real chalk balances the water supply', *Journal of Wine Research*, 1/1 (1990), 45–60.

Chalk Hill, California wine region and AVA north of Santa Rosa and south east of Healdsburg. See SONOMA.

Chalone, small California wine region and AVA in the mountains east of the Salinas valley. See MONTEREY.

Chalonnaise, Côte, red and white wine-producing region in the Saône-et-Loire *département* of BURGUNDY between the CÔTE D'OR and Mâconnais. The Côte Chalonnaise takes its name from the town of Chalon-sur-Saône, which had been an important CELTIC trading centre in Ancient GAUL. As well as generic BOURGOGNE Côte Chalonnaise, mostly red from the Pinot Noir grape, there are five village appellations: MERCUREY, which stands apart in both quality and price, produces mostly Pinot Noir with small quantities of white wine; GIVRY the same; MONTAGNY is exclusively a white wine appellation growing the Chardonnay grape; RULLY offers both red and white wines and is a centre for the sparkling wine industry in a small way; while BOUZERON has its own appellation exclusively for the Aligoté grape.

Although the soils in the Côte Chalonnaise are similar to those of the Côte d'Or, being based on limestone with a complex admixture of other elements, the vineyards are more scattered since there is no regular escarpment to provide continuity of suitable slopes.

Viticultural practices are broadly similar to those in the Côte d'Or. Vinification is sometimes carried out in barrels, although only the best producers use any new OAK. Bottling normally takes place in the summer before the new vintage.

Maximum yields for Mercurey are the same as those for VILLAGE WINES in the Côte d'Or, whereas the other appellations of the Côte Chalonnaise may produce an additional 5 hl/ha (0.3 tons/acre). Although cheerfully fruity while young, few wines from this region have enough body to age well. The Côte Chalonnaise is best served by such NÉGOCIANTS as Antonin Rodet and Faiveley, although growers such as Michel Juillot occasionally stand out. J.T.C.M.

Chambertin, Chambertin-Clos de Bèze, Chapelle-Chambertin, Charmes-Chambertin, Griotte(s)-Chambertin, Latricières-Chambertin, Mazis-Chambertin, Mazoyères-Chambertin, and Ruchottes-Chambertin, great red GRANDS CRUS in Burgundy's CÔTE D'OR. For more details, see GEVREY-CHAMBERTIN.

Chambéry, not a wine at all but a delicate, aromatic VERMOUTH made in the French alps. Of the huge volume of vermouth produced and assiduously marketed each year, the relatively rare Chambéry is one subtle enough to appeal to the wine drinker.

Chambolle-Musigny, village and appellation of particular charm in the Côte de Nuits district of Burgundy producing red wines from Pinot Noir grapes. A fine Chambolle-Musigny has a rich, velvety elegance which rivals the finesse of Vosne-Romanée or the power of Gevrey-Chambertin. There are two GRAND CRU vineyards, Le Musigny and Bonnes Mares (in part), and some exceptional PREMIERS CRUS worthy of promotion.

Le **Musigny** ranks with Romanée-Conti, La Tâche, Richebourg, Chambertin, and Chambertin-Clos de Bèze as one of the pinnacles of great burgundy (see DOMAINE DE LA ROMANÉE-CONTI, VOSNE-ROMANÉE, and GEVREY-CHAMBERTIN for details of these). The vineyard lies between the scrubland at the top of the slope and the upper part of CLOS DE VOUGEOT, on a slope of 8 to 10 per cent which drains particularly well through the oolitic limestone. The soil is more chalk than clay, covered by a fine silt, a combination which leads to the exceptional grace and power of Le Musigny, an iron fist in a velvet glove.

Of the 10.7 ha/26 acres of Le Musigny which is split between Musigny, Petits Musigny, and La Combe d'Orveau, seven are owned by Domaine Comte de Vogüé. Other significant producers are Barthod, the Château de Chambolle Musigny, Joseph Drouhin, Groffier, Mugnier, Jacques Prieur, and Roumier.

Adjacent to Le Musigny lies the premier cru Les Amoureuses, whose reputation and price suggest that this vineyard is worthy of elevation to grand cru. If a little less powerful than Le Musigny itself, the wines of Les Amoureuses demonstrate a very similar style. The next most sought-after premier cru, and the largest, is Les Charmes.

The other grand cru of Chambolle Musigny is **Bonnes Mares**, situated to the north of the village and overflowing into MOREY-ST-DENIS. The wines show more sturdiness than silkiness, are less graceful than Le Musigny but have evident power and structure. Bonnes Mares is noted for its ageing capacity. Ownership is spread over more than 30 proprietors, the largest being again Domaine Comte de Vogüé, a producer who also makes a very small quantity of white Musigny. Other notable producers based in Chambolle-Musigny include Groffier, Roumier, and Mugnier.

See also CÔTE D'OR, and map under BURGUNDY. J.T.C.M.

Chambourcin is a dark-berried FRENCH HYBRID commercially available only since 1963 and popular in the 1970s, particularly in the MUSCADET area, where it was still the third most planted variety, although a long way behind Melon and Folle Blanche. In 2000 French plantings still totalled 228 ha/653 acres. This extremely vigorous, productive vine produces better-quality wine than most hybrids, being deep coloured and full of relatively aromatic flavour, although in France it is not officially allowed even into the local VINS DE PAYS. It was successfully planted by Cassegrain in the warm, damp climate of Hastings Valley in NEW SOUTH WALES in Australia, a culture unfettered by anti-hybrid prejudice, and has since spread up and down Australia's east coast, including Queensland, with outbreaks elsewhere. It also looks promising in VIETNAM.

chambré, French word also used in English to describe a wine that has been deliberately warmed to room TEMPERATURE before serving (from *chambre*, 'room'). Most rooms nowadays are rather warmer than the ideal serving temperatures for most wines.

Champagne, name derived from the Latin term *campania*, originally used to describe the rolling open countryside just north of Rome (see CAMPANIA). In the early Middle Ages, it became applied to a province in north east France (see map under FRANCE). It is now divided into the so-called 'Champagne pouilleuse,' the once-barren but now cereal-growing chalky plains east of Rheims, and the 'Champagne viticole' (capital letters indicate the geographical descriptions, while lower case is used for the wine).

Champagne, with its three champagne towns Rheims (Reims in French), Épernay, and Ay, was the first region to make SPARKLING WINE in any quantity and historically the name champagne became synonymous with the finest, although Champagne is now responsible for less than one bottle in 12 of total world production of all sparkling wine. In common with other French regions making fine wines, notably Burgundy and Bordeaux, champagne formed the model for other aspiring winemakers, especially in Australia and the west coast of the United States, employing the same grapes, and the same SPARKLING WINE-MAKING method, as the French originals (known now as the traditional method). This form of imitation, while flattering, became decidedly awkward for the Champenois in the late 1980s. Their response was to tighten up the regulations regarding their own wines, and thus substantially increase the average quality—although they are unable to increase the 35,000 ha/86,500 acres devoted to vines to any significant extent for fear of diluting the quality of the wine.

History

Champagne was at the crossroads of two major trade routes, north–south between Flanders and Switzerland and east–west from Paris to the Rhine. Its position made it prosperous, but also ensured that it has been fought over many times in the course of the past 1,500 years. One of the most important battles in history was fought at Châlons-sur-Marne in AD 455, when Attila the Hun was finally repulsed. Subsequent battles included a savage civil war, the Fronde in the middle of the 17th century. As late as 1914 the famous 'Taxis de la Marne' brought French reinforcements from Paris to repulse the German invaders, who had (briefly) occupied Épernay and reached the outskirts of Rheims. But successive conflicts merely interrupted the progress of the vineyard.

Although there are numerous legends concerning earlier vineyards, the first serious mention is at the time of St Rémi at the end of the 5th century AD. For nearly eight centuries after Hugh Capet was crowned as king of France in Rheims cathedral in 987, the city's position as the spiritual centre of France naturally boosted its fame.

Vines had already been planted around the city, mainly by the numerous local abbeys and by the local nobility. But until the 17th century there was no generic 'vin de Champagne'. Since the 9th century, wines from the MONTAGNE DE REIMS south of the city had been known as 'vins de Reims', those from the Marne valley as 'vins de la rivière', or river wines. A number of villages, notably Bouzy and Verzenay on the Montagne, and Ay and Épernay in the Marne valley, were already being singled out for the quality of their wines. The wine trade was centred on Rheims and Châlons-sur-Marne, and the wines had the great advantage of immediate access to the Marne, which joined the Seine just east of PARIS (see RIVERS).

But the wines did not sparkle: they were light, pinkish still wines made from the Pinot Noir grape. In the last half of the 17th century, wine-making greatly improved, under the auspices of leading clerical winemakers, led by Dom PÉRIGNON, who transformed the Abbey of Hautvillers, above Épernay, into the region's leading centre of viticultural progress. The wines' fame grew greatly in the second half of the 17th century when they were introduced to the Court of Versailles, notably by the Marquis de Sillery, a large landowner in the region, and by the Marquis de St-Évremond, who introduced champagne to London society after he was banished to Britain in 1662.

In the cold winters normal in the region, the wines had a tendency to stop FERMENTATION and then to start refermenting in the spring. For a long time this was considered something of a nuisance, as the resulting release of CARBON DIOXIDE was often strong enough to break the flimsy bottles normal at the time. The development of stronger BOTTLES by British glassmakers permitted drinkers to enjoy the resulting sparkle. Indeed it was the café society of London, encouraged by St-Évremond, which probably first enjoyed true 'sparkling champagne' (see contemporary references in ENGLISH LITERATURE).

The habit was taken up by the licentious court round the duke of Orléans, who became regent of France after the death of Louis XIV in 1715, but serious winemakers (and their clients) continued to believe that sparkling champagne was inferior to the still wines of the region. Moreover even the stronger bottles could not reliably withstand the pressure generated by the SECOND FERMENTATION. So, throughout the 18th century, only a few thousand bottles were produced every year, and up to half of them would break.

The champagne business we know today was born in the first 40 years of the 19th century. The first notable step was taken by Madame (VEUVE) CLICQUOT. One of her employees developed the system of PUPITRES to assist in the REMUAGE process. CORKS were improved, and a corking machine developed. Understanding, and then mastering, the second fermentation took longer. The scientist and minister CHAPTAL had understood that 'sparkling wines owe their tendency to sparkle only to the fact that they have been enclosed in a bottle before they have completed their fermentation'. But it took a young pharmacist from Châlons-sur-Marne, André François, to enable winemakers to measure the precise quantity of sugar required to induce a second fermentation in the bottle without inducing an explosive force.

François died in 1838, shortly after he had published his formulae. But within a generation Champagne had become the home of the world's first 'wine industry', one dominated by a number of internationally famous brand names. Most of these were those of young entrepreneurs from the Rhineland, such as Messrs KRUG, BOLLINGER, and ROEDERER, who showed greater commercial nous than the local merchants, only a few of whom, apart from Madame Clicquot and Monsieur MOËT, survived.

But for over half a century, until well into the 1950s, Champagne suffered from a number of problems which clouded its earlier successes. The important RUSSIAN market collapsed in 1917, and two World Wars, separated by the slump, closed the export markets on which the region depended so heavily. The arrival of the PHYLLOXERA louse in Champagne in 1890 intensified competition from other sparkling wines, from Germany as well as from other French winemakers, and intensi-fied the fraudulent habits of some of the region's more unscrupulous merchants, who were wont to import juice and wine for bottling and sale as champagne.

The fraud compounded the misery caused by phylloxera to the region's growers and caused a near civil war in 1911. This was sparked off by the first attempts to define the region entitled to produce champagne. When the French Assembly included the Aube, a separate wine region 110 km/70 miles south east of Épernay, riots broke out in the Champagne region proper. Eventually the Aube was included as a separate 'second zone', although it was included in the main appellation when the boundaries were finally fixed in 1927.

The events of 1911 shook the whole wine-making community, and 25 years later the resulting desire for common action resulted in the combined group of growers and merchants known as the Commission de Châlons, set up in 1935 under the impetus of the remarkable Robert-Jean de Vogüé, head of Moët. At a time when growers were virtually giving away their grapes, the Commission provided them with some stability. Six years later, the desire for joint action led to the formation of the CIVC, the Comité Interprofessionnel du Vin de Champagne, the pioneering attempt, much copied elsewhere, to provide wine-making regions with an organization which represented all the interests involved.

Since 1950, the region has enjoyed unprecedented prosperity with sales quadrupling to well over 200 million bottles. Traditional export markets, such as Britain, the United States, Belgium, and Switzerland, took increasing quantities. Nevertheless the French market has long consumed far more champagne than all export markets and accounts for two-thirds of sales. This emphasis had important structural implications, since the traditional BRANDS were less dominant in the domestic market than outside France, where they still account for over 90 per cent of sales.

In the domestic market, nearly half total sales are made by individual GROWERS, CO-OPERATIVES, and co-operative unions. The first co-operatives in Champagne were founded just before the First World War. They grew rapidly in the early 1960s and by 1989 the region's 140 co-operatives represented over half the growers and a third of the area under vines. Some co-operatives merely press grapes, others make wine (much of which is returned to members for sale under their own label, a fact signified by the letters CM before the grower's code on the label; see LABELLING INFORMATION). Two or three co-operative unions, producing up to ten million bottles annually, became major forces, particularly in supplying buyers' own brands and subsequently uniting to promote their own brands.

The competition from the co-operatives added to the pressure on the, usually family-owned, MERCHANTS. In the 1960s and 1970s,

MOËT & CHANDON absorbed Mercier and Ruinart, the latter the oldest firm in the region, and after further acquisitions, including VEUVE CLICQUOT and KRUG, today represents by far the dominant grouping in Champagne. The growers' increasing power was reflected in a rapid rise of grape prices during the 1980s and by the inflexibility with which grapes were allotted to the merchants. In 1990, under the impetus of Moët, the market was freed. Since then price has been indicative, not legally binding. A number of firms, especially those without their own vineyards, experienced difficulties and were sold and resold a number of times. So the trade has become increasingly concentrated, with the seven biggest houses accounting for 70 per cent of the total.

Geography and climate

The region permitted to call its wines 'champagne' was strictly defined by the INAO in 1927. It sprawls from Charly a mere 50 km/30 miles east of Paris in the Marne valley to Rheims and south from Épernay along the Côte des Blancs and its southern extension, the Côte de Sézanne. A separate region is the Aube, 112 km south east of Épernay. Over the years, the acreage actually planted has varied widely, dropping to 11,000 ha/27,000 acres during the 1930s. In 2005, the appellation covered just over 30,000 ha in five *départements*—up from the 1993 total of 27,500 ha: 19,500 ha in the Marne; 2,500 in the Aisne (and Seine-et-Marne); and 5,500 in the Aube (and the Haute-Marne). Only a tenth of the vines are owned by merchants, who can now add to their holdings only under very strict conditions. The remainder is owned by nearly 20,000 growers, many of whom own less than a hectare of vines.

Much of the appellation (and Champagne is now the only major French region to have just one appellation), and all the better CRUS, are on the slopes of the hills typical of the region. The vines' roots dig deep into CHALKY depths, providing ideal conditions of DRAINAGE and HUMIDITY. The Champagne vineyard's exposure to the cold northern winter inevitably makes grape-growing a precarious operation, with the quality of the wines varying from year to year. As a result, champagne is traditionally a wine blended, not only from a number of different villages, but also from several vintages. The poverty of the soil requires constant addition of FERTILIZER, either the *cendres noirs*, the natural compost found on the region's hilltops, or, until the late 1990s, finely ground (and curiously multicoloured) household rubbish from Rheims, or even Paris.

The different qualities of grapes from the region's 301 widely spread CRUS has led to the establishment of a scale of prices. Originally the scale was from 50 to 100 per cent of the fixed price. Since a revision in 1985, it has been merely from 80 to 100 per cent, that top level allowed only to grapes from 17 'grand cru' communes. Grapes from a further 38 communes, called premiers crus, are sold at between 90 and 98 per cent of the maximum price.

There have long been proposals for a thorough reclassification of premiers and grands crus according to individual vineyards rather than a blanket award to all vines in a given commune.

Vine varieties

In the past, a number of grape varieties were planted in Champagne. But today almost the whole vineyard is planted with three:, Pinot Noir, Pinot Meunier, and Chardonnay. The Pinot Noir, which accounts for just over a third of the total acreage, is no longer as dominant as it was, but still provides the basic structure and depth of fruit in the blend. In Champagne, the Chardonnay, planted in a quarter of the vineyard, was traditionally grown on the east-facing slopes of the Côte des Blancs but has proved suitable in many other subregions, especially the Côte de Sézanne. In Champagne it grows vigorously and buds early, thus making it susceptible to spring FROSTS. It imparts a certain austerity and elegance to young champagnes, but is long lived and matures to a fine fruitiness. The remaining third is planted with Pinot MEUNIER, a variety widely grown only in Champagne, particularly in the Valley of the Marne. It provides many champagnes with an early-maturing richness and fruitiness. A little PETIT MESLIER is also grown and at least one varietal champagne is made from it.

Thanks to new CLONES and viticultural methods, the yield of grapes has grown greatly: from an average of 3,670 kg/ha in the 1940s to 9,910 in the 1980s (or from 24 to 66 hl/ha (1.3–3.7 tons/acre). The first limit was set in 1935. Since 1992, yields have been limited to 10,400 kg/ha (with the usual additional 20 per cent PLC in exceptional years). Since 1992, 160 (rather than the earlier limit of 150) kg of grapes are required to produce 100 l of juice, which means that the maximum permitted yield is 65 hl/ha.

VINE DENSITY is notably high, and vines are replanted after between 25 and 30 years. The grapes are picked in late September, on dates now fixed village by village. They cannot be harvested unless they contain that year's fixed minimum level of POTENTIAL ALCOHOL. But since the level can be as low as 8 per cent, sugar can be added to provide another degree and a half (see CHAPTALIZATION), and the second fermentation supplements the final ALCOHOLIC STRENGTH by up to another 2 per cent. Most champagne is about 12.5 per cent alcohol.

Wine-making

The pressing of the grapes is difficult, since the juice of what is to be a white wine must not be tainted by the skin of the mainly black grapes used. The traditional champagne PRESS was a vertical basket press, holding 4,000 kg/8,800 lb of grapes, a quantity known as a *marc* and a standard unit of measurement in the region. These presses are also called Coquard presses after the name of the manufacturer. A number of other types of press have since been introduced and the CIVC allows both hydraulic and pneumatic horizontal presses.

Since 1990, all pressing centres have had to comply with certain minimum standards. Traditionally 2,666 l/704 gal were extracted from every *marc*: the first 2,050 l were the cuvée, the next 410 l the *premières tailles*, while the final 205 l were the *deuxièmes tailles*. The total yield has now been reduced by 115 l to 2,550 l and the *deuxièmes tailles* abolished.

The juice is allowed to settle for between 12 and 48 hours, at a low temperature. A few firms use oak FERMENTATION VESSELS for some or all of their grapes, but the overwhelming majority of the grapes are fermented in STAINLESS STEEL vats holding between 50 and 1,200 hl (1,320–31,700 gal). The fermentation TEMPERATURE also varies, between 12 and 25 °C (54-77 °F). Most winemakers use a strain of YEAST specially developed by the CIVC.

Immediately after the first fermentation, most, but by no means all, champagnes now undergo MALOLACTIC FERMENTATION. The result is called *vin clair*. Traditionally champagne has been made from wines from a number of different vineyards within the appellation although large numbers of growers (and a few firms) make wines from a single commune or vineyard. Major firms use wines from between 50 and 200 communes for their blend. They also use between 10 and 50 per cent of *vins de réserve* from earlier vintages, generally stored in stainless steel or cement vats. Before the wine is bottled, a measured dose of bottling liquor (*liqueur de tirage*), a mixture of wine, sugar, and specially developed yeasts, is added to the wine. The bottles are then capped, usually with a crown cap lined with plastic. Following TIRAGE, LEES CONTACT, RIDDLING, and DISGORGEMENT, a sweetening DOSAGE is usually added before final corking. A few champagnes are sold without any added sugar at all; most are BRUT.

For more information, see in SPARKLING WINE-MAKING, traditional method.

Styles of champagne

In addition to their basic wine, their non-vintage brut, major firms also make single **vintage champagnes**, typically three or four in every decade. BLANC DE BLANCS are made exclusively from the Chardonnay grape while BLANC DE NOIRS are made exclusively from black grapes. Pink or **rosé champagne** is made either by adding a small proportion of red wine to the blend or, less usually, by letting the juice remain in contact with the skin of the grapes for a short time during fermentation. Until 1992, the Champenois could market as Crémant wines made under lower pressure: generally three atmospheres rather than the normal six. But today only wines made in other French wine-growing regions are allowed to use the term (see CRÉMANT). All the major firms have now followed the example of Roederer with their Cristal bottling and Moët & Chandon with Dom Pérignon and produce 'luxury', 'de luxe', or PRESTIGE CUVÉES to show their house styles at their best.

The small proportion of still wines made in the region are sold under the appellations Coteaux CHAMPENOIS and the rare pink ROSÉ DES RICEYS. RATAFIA is also made.   N.F. & J.R.

Bonal, F., *Le Livre d'or de Champagne* (Lausanne, 1984).

Faith, N., *The Story of Champagne* (London, 1988).

Juhlin, R., *4000 Champagnes* (Paris, 2005).

Stevenson, T., *Champagne* (London, 1986).

——, *World Encyclopedia of Champagne & Sparkling Wine* (London, 1998).

Zarifian, E., Coutant, C., Liger-Belair, G., *Bulle de Champagne* (Paris, 2005).

champagne method.
See SPARKLING WINE-MAKING for this, the most meticulous way of making a wine sparkle and the one employed throughout CHAMPAGNE. The term was outlawed in Europe in 1994 and replaced with TRADITIONAL METHOD. On labels it is generally referred to as Méthode Traditionnelle, Méthode Classique, Traditional Method, Classic Method, or Bottle Fermented (although this last is ambiguous and could be used of TRANSFER METHOD sparkling wines). The French equivalent was *méthode champenoise*.

Champenois, Coteaux.
Appellation used for the unusual still wines of CHAMPAGNE in northern France. For every one bottle of still white Coteaux Champenois produced, perhaps 20 of still red Coteaux Champenois are produced (in a good vintage), and 16,000 bottles of sparkling champagne. The wines of this cool region with their naturally high acidity and light body are much improved by dissolved CARBON DIOXIDE. It is difficult to justify the production of white Coteaux Champenois, from expensive Chardonnay grapes, but easier to understand why the Champenois like to be able to drink the odd bottle of local still red from time to time. The village of Bouzy on the MONTAGNE DE REIMS has a particular reputation for its red Coteaux Champenois, partly perhaps because of the appeal of the name Bouzy Rouge, as do Ay, Cumières, and Ambonnay. These red wines are of interest to outsiders only in the ripest vintages, while the whites and rosés serve only to compliment the Champenois on their wise decision to concentrate on sparkling wines.

See also ROSÉ DES RICEYS.

Chamusca,
subregion of RIBATEJO in central southern Portugal.

Chancellor,
productive red FRENCH HYBRID developed from two Seibel parents. For long it was known as Seibel 7053, but was named Chancellor in NEW YORK in 1970. See SEIBEL and UNITED STATES for more details.

Changins,
the federal viticultural research station in western SWITZERLAND near Nyon on Lake Geneva, is principally concerned with improving plant material, including CLONAL SELECTION; matching VINE VARIETY to specific TERROIR in both French-speaking Switzerland and Italian-speaking Switzerland; and developing viticultural techniques which reduce costs, improve wine quality, and minimize chemical inputs (see ORGANIC VITICULTURE). Areas of OENOLOGICAL research have included techniques for must SETTLING of white wines, red wine MACERATION, YEASTS, MALOLACTIC FERMENTATION, FILTRATION, and ENRICHMENT.

The research station's counterpart in German-speaking Switzerland is WÄDENSWIL. The two stations combined under the administration of Agroscope (ACW) in early 2006.

Chapoutier,
family-owned merchant-grower based at Tain-l'HERMITAGE in France's northern RHÔNE. One of the Rhône valley's great names, established in 1808 and owning some 230 ha/560 acres of vineyard, principally in the northern Rhône and notably 32 ha of Hermitage. More recent purchases have been made in Coteaux d'Aix-en-Provence, Banyuls, and 100 ha/247 acres in South Australia. The house used to be particularly well known for its white Hermitage, Chante Alouette, and for its Grande Cuvée wines, high-quality blends of one appellation but more than one vintage. During the 1980s, however, when Chapoutier's peers (GUIGAL and JABOULET, for example) and numerous small growers were catching the imagination of the wine world with the improving quality of their wines, Chapoutier wines stood out precisely because they seemed unexceptional by comparison. This situation changed dramatically when Max Chapoutier's sons Marc and Michel took over the running of the company full time in 1990. Michel now runs the company with a passion. All wines are now vintage dated, and great attention is paid to detail at every stage from vineyard management to bottling. The dynamic new image was briefly dented by highly publicized BOTTLE VARIATION in the 1993 Hermitage La Sizeranne, due to several BOTTLINGS at different dates. As a result, this practice, a hangover from the old regime, was discontinued in 1995. Viticulture is BIODYNAMIC, so that Michel Chapoutier now farms the largest area of biodynamic vineyard in the world. YIELDS are low, the wines are aged in OAK (new as appropriate) rather than old chestnut barrels, and the top reds are subjected to neither FINING nor FILTRATION. As a result, the wines have more concentration, polish, and distinction, and Chapoutier's Hermitage, CÔTE RÔTIE, and CHÂTEAUNEUF-DU-PAPE can compete with the very best from the region. In 1996, the firm

became the first wine producer to have labels in Braille.   M.W.E.S.

Livingstone-Learmonth, J., *The Wines of the Northern Rhône* (Berkeley, 2005).

Norman, R., *Rhône Renaissance* (London, 1995).

Chaptal, Jean-Antoine
(1756–1832), French chemist, statesman, and essential polymath who rose from humble beginnings to become Minister of the Interior under Napoleon. In 1799, he wrote the article on wine for the monumental *Dictionnaire d'agriculture* of the Abbé Rozier, but is better known for his *l'Art de faire le vin* (1807) and his support for the concept of increasing the ALCOHOLIC STRENGTH of wine by adding sugar to the must, the procedure now known as CHAPTALIZATION. Some winemakers throughout history sought to enhance either the quality or quantity of their product by adulterating the basic raw material, grapes, with other products. However, after the French Revolution of 1789, there was a considerable increase in the amount of poor-quality wine made in France. This provided the incentive for Chaptal to compile his famous *Traité théorique et pratique sur la culture de la vigne* (1801). Although he is best known for having introduced the metric system of weights and measures into France, as a practical scientist Chaptal was particularly concerned at the declining reputation of French wines, with increasing ADULTERATION AND FRAUD in the wine trade, and with the ignorance on the part of many French wine producers about the scientific advances that could help them. He was of the firm belief that it was perfectly natural, and desirable, to add sugar to wine in order to improve it. Although he encouraged farmers to use GRAPE CONCENTRATE, he recognized that sugar from cane or beet was also capable of having a similar effect. (Another of Chaptal's many achievements was his development of techniques for extracting sugar from sugar beet.) Chaptal's treatise synthesizing beneficial wine-making techniques current at the beginning of the 19th century marked a turning point in the history of wine technology. It was translated into Italian, Spanish, German, and Hungarian. Two American versions appeared and James BUSBY published a translation in Australia in 1825.   P.T.H.U.

Chaptal, J. A., *Traité théorique et pratique sur la culture de la vigne* (Paris, 1801).

Gough, J. B., 'Winecraft and chemistry in 18th century France: Chaptal and the invention of chaptalization', *Technology and Culture*, 39 (1998), 74–104.

Johnson, H., *The Story of Wine* (London, 1989).

Loubère, L. A., *The Red and the White: A History of Wine in France and Italy in the Nineteenth Century* (Albany, NY, 1978).

chaptalization,
common wine-making practice, named after its French promulgator Jean-Antoine CHAPTAL, whereby the final ALCOHOLIC STRENGTH of a wine is increased by the addition of sugar to the grape juice or must,

before and/or during FERMENTATION. Contrary to popular belief, Chaptal did not invent the process, which had been the subject of common experiment, not least by the innovative French chemist Pierre-Joseph Macquer.

Amelioration is a common English euphemism for chaptalization. The French sometimes call it *amélioration*; the Germans, who were introduced to the technique by the chemist Ludwig Gall in the mid 19th century, call it *Verbesserung*; while most southern Europeans consider it an appalling practice, chiefly because, thanks to their warmer climate, they have no need of it.

Although the practice is still commonplace, and is indeed the norm in northern Europe, potential alcoholic strength is increasingly raised by adding products other than beet or cane sugar (particularly grape products of which there is a surplus in many wine regions). The addition of sugar, grape must, concentrated grape must, and rectified concentrated grape must (RCGM) in order to increase a wine's alcoholic strength are collectively known as enrichment, the general term for chaptalization and all related techniques and that officially sanctioned in EUROPEAN UNION parlance. Within the EU, permission to chaptalize depends on the EU climatic zone in which an area falls. For example, it is permitted in Zone A, which includes the UK and northern Germany, but it is not permitted in Zone C IIIb, which includes southern Italy. A country's own regulations may also forbid the practice, as throughout Italy.

In 1993, the European Union, concerned about its wine SURPLUS, officially announced its disapproval of chaptalization and its intention to curb the practice because it tended to encourage higher YIELDS. Although this announcement made little difference to winemaking practices, chaptalization, once routine in northern Europe, is becoming less common, partly because grapes tend to be picked later and riper, perhaps partly because of CLIMATE CHANGE.

See ENRICHMENT for more details.

Gough, J. B., 'Winecraft and chemistry in 18th century France: Chaptal and the invention of chaptalization', *Technology and Culture*, 39 (1998), 74-104.

char. Term sometimes used of barrels. See TOAST.

Charbono is the name of two distinct black grape varieties, one in California, one in Italy. DNA PROFILING at DAVIS showed that the California variety is not the same as the DOLCETTO of Italy, as GALET once suggested, and established that it is identical to the virtually extinct Corbeau of the SAVOIE region in the French alps, which Galet also thought was one and the same as Dolcetto. (Douce Noire and Charbonneau are two of Corbeau's many synonyms.) According to ampelographer Anna

Schneider at Torino, the Italian variety Charbono is related neither to Corbeau nor to Dolcetto, and it is often cultivated in both Barbera and Dolcetto vineyards in Piemonte. The California variety clings to existence on a handful of acres on the North Coast, especially in the Napa Valley. As varietal wine (made chiefly by Inglenook) it can be difficult to distinguish from Barbera grown under similar circumstances. See also the Bonarda of ARGENTINA.   J.V.

Galet, P., *Dictionnaire encyclopédique des cépages* (Paris, 2000).

charcoal, absorbent material occasionally used in wine processing to remove COLOUR and COLLOIDS. Charcoal is an impure amorphous carbon obtained by the dry distillation of wood or some other material containing carbon (bones, peat, and plant debris have all been used). The sort of charcoal most frequently used in wine-making is generally known as **active carbon** and is much purer than the charcoal in common use as a fuel in 17th-century England.

Because of its very porous nature, charcoal has the particularly high ratio of surface area to weight required of an absorptive material. In wine-making it is used mainly to absorb the colloidal pigment polymers responsible for amber or brown colours in white wines, particularly in the manufacture of Pale Cream SHERRY. Off-flavours in wine are occasionally removed using a grade of active charcoal with a smaller pore size, transforming an unsaleable wine into a neutral one for use in a basic blend. Small amounts of active charcoal mixed with DIATOMACEOUS EARTH are sometimes used during final FILTRATION in the hope of removing unstable colloids which could potentially form a haze.   A.D.W.

Chardonel, recently named vine CROSSING of Seyval Blanc and Chardonnay made at New York State's Geneva experimental station (see CORNELL) in 1953. Originally tested in eastern US under the name GW3, it was named and released only in 1990. The variety is more resistant to POWDERY MILDEW and BOTRYTIS than Chardonnay, and in Missouri does not require GRAFTING. The wine is similar to Chardonnay and this appealingly named variety may be useful in warm to hot climates, like its famous parent.   R.E.S.

Smart, R, 'Chardonel, anyone?', *Practical Winery and Vineyard* (Jan/Feb 1998), 111-12.

Chardonnay, a name so familiar to wine lovers around the world that many do not realize that it is the name of a white grape variety. In its Burgundian homeland, Chardonnay has for long been the sole vine responsible for all of the finest white burgundy. As such, in a region devoted to geographical labelling, its name was known only to vine-growers. All this changed with the advent of VARIETAL labelling in the late 20th century, when Chardonnay virtually

became a BRAND. It is perhaps fitting that a variety so governed by the whims of FASHION should have seen considerable stylistic changes in the sorts of wine sought by its legion of fans. Until about the mid 1990s, rich, oaky varietals were the height of modishness but this has been followed by a trend towards leaner, more appetizing, and definitely less oak-dominated Chardonnays.

Chardonnay-mania reached a peak in the late 1980s and it was subsequently planted so widely that a glut was assured in the late 1990s, leading to a shortage of Chardonnay in the early 21st century in Australia. So popular is Chardonnay that synonyms are rarely used (although some Austrians in Styria persist with their name Morillon). The wine's relatively high level of alcohol, which can often taste slightly sweet, has probably played a part in this popularity, as has the obvious appeal of the OAK so often used in making Chardonnay. But it is not just wine drinkers who appreciate the broad, easy-to-appreciate if difficult-to-describe charms of golden Chardonnay. (The AUSTRALIAN WINE RESEARCH INSTITUTE's initiative, analysing the component parts of each major variety's flavour, found Chardonnay a particularly nebulous target, identifying flavour compounds also found in, among other things, raspberries, vanilla, tropical fruits, peaches, tomatoes, tobacco, tea, and rose petals.)

Vine-growers appreciate the ease with which, in a wide range of climates, they can coax relatively high yields from this vine (whose natural VIGOUR may need to be curbed by either dense planting, low-vigour ROOTSTOCKS or CANOPY MANAGEMENT). Wine quality is severely prejudiced, however, at yields above 80 hl/ha (4.5 tons/acre) and yields of 30 hl/ha or lower are usually needed for seriously fine wine. Growers' only major reservation is that it buds quite early, just after Pinot Noir, which regularly puts the coolest vineyards—those of Chablis, Champagne, and Chile's Casablanca Valley, for example—at risk from spring FROSTS. It can suffer from COULURE and occasionally MILLERANDAGE and the grapes' relatively thin skins can encourage rot if there is rain at harvest time, but it can thrive in climates as diverse as those of CHABLIS in northern France and Australia's hot RIVERLAND. Picking time is critical for, unlike Cabernet Sauvignon, Chardonnay can quickly lose its crucial acidity in the latter stages of ripening.

Winemakers love Chardonnay for its reliably high ripeness levels and its malleability. It will happily respond to a far wider range of wine-making techniques than most white varieties. The Mosel or Vouvray wine-making recipe of a long, cool fermentation followed by early bottling can be applied to Chardonnay. Or it can be treated to BARREL FERMENTATION and/or BARREL MATURATION, some of the highest-quality fruit being able to stand up to new oak. It accommodates each individual winemaker's policy on the second, softening MALOLACTIC FERMENTATION and LEES STIRRING without demur. Chardonnay is also a vital ingredient in most of the world's best SPARKLING WINE, not just in Champagne, demonstrating its ability to age in bottle even when picked early. And, picked late, it has even been known to produce some creditable BOTRYTIZED wines, notably in the Mâconnais, Romania, and New Zealand. Chardonnay blends happily with other less fashionable, cheaper varieties such as Chenin Blanc, Sémillon, or Colombard to meet demand or PRICE POINTS at the lower end of the market. But perhaps this is because its own character is, unlike that of the other ultra-fashionable white, Sauvignon Blanc, not too pronounced. Chardonnay from young or over-productive vines can taste almost aqueous. Basic Chardonnay may be vaguely fruity (apples or melons) but, at its best, Chardonnay, like Pinot Noir, is merely a vehicle for the character of the vineyard in which it is grown (see TERROIR). As in many other ambitious wines fashioned in the image of top white burgundy, its 'flavour' is often that of the oak in which it was matured, or the relics of the wine-making techniques used (see above). When the vineyard site is right, yields not too high, acid not too low, and wine-making skilled, Chardonnay can produce thrilling, savoury, dry, full-bodied wines that will continue to improve in bottle for one, two, or, exceptionally, more decades but—unlike RIESLING and the best, nobly rotten CHENIN BLANC and SÉMILLON—it is not a variety capable of making whites for the very long term.

Chardonnay's origins were long considered obscure, but DNA PROFILING has finally provided the answer to this mystery. Along with a host of other varieties common in north eastern France, it is the progeny of Pinot Noir and GOUAIS BLANC (see PINOT).

There is a rare but distinct pink-berried mutation, **Chardonnay Rose**, as well as a headily perfumed **Chardonnay Blanc Musqué** version, sometimes used in blends. Some of the 34 official French CLONES of Chardonnay have a similarly grapey perfume, notably 77 and 809, which have been quite widely planted and can add a rather incongruously aromatic note to blends with other clones of the variety. The arguably over-enthusiastic application of CLONAL SELECTION techniques in Burgundy means that growers can now choose from a wide range of Chardonnay clones specially selected for their productivity, particularly 75, 78, 121, 124, 125, and 277. Those seeking quality rather than quantity are more likely to choose 76, 95, and 96. Many New World wine regions began their love affair with Chardonnay on blowsy or inferior clones such as the Mendoza clone, only to find it rekindled by the introduction of better clones from Burgundy, sometimes known as Dijon clones.

Chardonnay's popularity in the late 1980s was sufficient to propel it to first or second place in terms of area planted in each of France, California, Washington State, Australia, and New Zealand by the early 1990s. It now occupies more of the world's vineyard, well over 175,000 ha/400,000 acres, than any white-berried variety other than Spain's widely spaced Airén—a remarkable feat for a vine credited with such nobility.

In France, for example, Chardonnay plantings virtually doubled from 1980 to reach 25,000 ha/62,000 acres by 1993 and by 2000 were 36,300 ha. This was initially due to the expansion of the Champagne vineyard, where Chardonnay now represents as much as a third of all vines planted, and of the Chablis zone (where the grape can achieve a lean steeliness and, in the best examples, considerable longevity). Improvements in frost protection techniques played a part in both these expansions. But since the 1980s, France, once home to sizeable tracts of dozens of local grape varieties, has become increasingly dominated by this paradigm of an INTERNATIONAL VARIETY. Only Ugni Blanc is a more commonly planted light-skinned grape in France, and Chardonnay covers more than twice as much vineyard as the third most-planted, Sémillon.

In the Burgundian heartland, the CÔTE D'OR, Chardonnay plantings increased by one-quarter in the 1980s to a grand total of 1,400 ha, and by a further third in the 1990s to a total of 1,866 ha by 2000. Although Chardonnay, occasionally called Beaunois or Aubaine in Burgundy, has gradually been replacing GAMAY and ALIGOTÉ, Pinot Noir vines still outnumber Chardonnay vines more than three to one on the Côte d'Or. Notably more Chardonnay is grown on the southern Côte de Beaune than on the Côte de Nuits. Famous white wine appellations with typical characteristics in brackets include, from north to south, Corton-Charlemagne (marzipan), Meursault (buttery), Puligny-Montrachet (fine and steely), Chassagne-Montrachet (hazelnuts), and any name that includes the word Montrachet (enormous concentration, and alcohol levels of 13 per cent and above).

In the CÔTE CHALONNAISE and the MÂCONNAIS to the south, plantings overtook those of Gamay in the 1980s so that there were 4,500 ha by 1988 and 6,200 ha by 2000. From the Côte Chalonnaise, the whites of Rully, Mercurey, and Montagny can offer economical, if slightly rustic, versions of the grander names of the Côte d'Or. The Mâconnais, where Chardonnay can take on a broad, appley character, produces not just white Mâcon with a range of geographical suffixes but also various Pouillys, most famously the full-bodied Pouilly-Fuissé. From further south still come the very similar St-Véran and Beaujolais Blanc. Although the regulations allow Aligoté into Beaujolais Blanc and Pinot Blanc into white wines labelled Bourgogne and Mâcon, most of these less expensive white burgundies are in practice made predominantly from Chardonnay. To the initial horror of the INAO, there has been an increasing trend towards slipping the word Chardonnay on to white burgundy labels to increase their appeal to non-French consumers.

Although nearly three-fifths of France's Chardonnay is still in either Champagne or Greater Burgundy, the variety has continued to conquer ever more land south and west of this base. It is embraced by an ever wider variety of appellations, and plantings can be found in Alsace, Ardèche, Jura, Savoie, Loire, and, especially, the Languedoc, where it was first planted to add international appeal to the lemony wines of Limoux. Official figures suggest that a total of more than 5,200 ha/13,000 acres was planted in the Languedoc-Roussillon between 1988 and 1993 and much of it is now used in varietal VINS DE PAYS d'Oc of extremely varying quality. By 2000 there were nearly 9,000 ha of Chardonnay in the Languedoc, 3,700 of them in the hot Hérault département, although this is essentially red wine country.

Few would have believed in 1980, when California had just 18,000 acres/7,200 ha of Chardonnay, that by 1988 the state's total plantings would overtake France's (rapidly increasing) total and that by 2005 California's Chardonnay area was expected to reach 100,000 acres/40,000 ha of Chardonnay. The rate of new plantings reached a peak in the mid 1990s, however, with the advent of a fashion for red wine. See under CALIFORNIA for more detail of the state's generally rich, heady style of Chardonnay.

Chardonnay, now North American for 'white wine', has been embraced with equal fervour throughout the rest of North America, from British Columbia in CANADA to Long Island in NEW YORK, although it is usually more restrained in character than in California. In 1990, Chardonnay overtook Riesling to become the most planted variety of any hue in WASHINGTON state with 2,600 acres/1,000 ha, and the 2004 total was about 7,000 acres/2,800 ha. Chardonnay is also popular, if not always desperately successful, in Oregon (where the introduction of DIJON CLONES has had a profound effect on quality), Virginia, and Texas. The scale of America's romance with Chardonnay in general and oak-aged Chardonnay in particular was reflected in the international COOPERAGE business in the 1990s.

Various South American countries have been seeking out cooler spots to imbue their Chardonnay with real concentration. Chile's ocean-influenced Casablanca valley and San Antonio and the high-altitude vineyards of Argentina's Uco valley are the most obvious examples and their best wines combine those New World virtues of accessibility and value. In Argentina, where the variety has shown impressive finesse, Chardonnay overtook Ugni Blanc, Chenin Blanc, Semillon, and Sauvignonasse in the 1990s to become the country's second most planted white wine grape after Torrentés. Total plantings were more than 4,600 ha by 2002. Chile has even more, 7,500 ha, making Chardonnay the country's most planted light-skinned grape variety.

The Australian wine industry's all-important export trade has been centred on its particularly user-friendly and frequently adapted style of Chardonnay. Rich fruit flavours, often disciplined by added acid and flavoured by OAK CHIPS, are available at carefully judged prices. Such was the strength of demand for Australian Chardonnay in the late 1980s that the area of Chardonnay vines increased more than fivefold during the decade so that in 1990, Chardonnay, with its 4,300 ha/10,600 acres, became Australia's most planted white wine grape variety (although 1,300 ha were too young to bear fruit). Plantings have continued even more bullishly throughout the 1990s so that by 2004 Chardonnay's total area was 28,000 ha, just less than Cabernet Sauvignon's and decisively less than Shiraz's. Meanwhile wine-making has become increasingly sophisticated. Wines vary from limey essences grown in cooler spots in Victoria and Tasmania to almost syrupy, smokey blends concocted from the hot irrigated vineyards of the interior. The average life expectancy of an Australian (and most other New World) Chardonnay is short.

Nor did NEW ZEALAND escape Chardonnay-mania. Throughout the 1990s and up to 2002, Chardonnay plantings outnumbered those of the country's more famous Sauvignon Blanc. New Zealand's Chardonnays, planted on an anticipated total of 4,000 ha in 2006, have perceptibly more natural acid than their trans-Tasman neighbours. The east coast of the North Island is its traditional Kiwi home but fine examples are made all over the country.

Chardonnay has had a chequered history in South Africa. Planting material in the late 1970s and early 1980s was frequently smuggled, and significant quantities of AUXERROIS contaminated the authenticity of 'Chardonnay' vineyards. However, changes in regulations governing plant importation have seen a significant improvement in planting material. By 2004, there were over 7,300 ha/18,000 acres of Chardonnay, making it the country's third most planted white wine grape, a long way behind Chenin Blanc and Colombard.

Although Chardonnay can thrive in relatively hot climates (such as Australia's irrigation zones), it has to be picked before acids plummet (sometimes before the grapes have developed much real character, although this is usually caused by excessively high yields) and it does require relatively sophisticated techniques, including TEMPERATURE CONTROL, in the cellar. This is why it is not especially well suited to hot Mediterranean wine regions and well-balanced Chardonnays with real interest from the likes of Greece, Israel, and the Lebanon tend to be exceptions.

The variety continues to be planted in an ever wider range of locations, but Italy has a long history of Chardonnay cultivation, especially on its subalpine slopes in the north. For decades, Italians were casual about distinguishing between their Pinot Bianco (PINOT BLANC, also known as Weissburgunder in the Italian Tyrol) and their Chardonnay (traditionally called Gelber, or Golden, Weissburgunder in the Italian Tyrol). Indeed the Italian agricultural census of 1982 failed to distinguish a single Chardonnay vine, while that of 2000 located more than 11,700 ha/29,000 acres, making it the country's fourth most planted light-skinned grape variety.

Alto Adige Chardonnay was the first Italian Chardonnay accorded DOC status, in 1984, although the vine has since been working its magic on producers all over Italy from Puglia to Piemonte and, of course, Aosta towards the French border.

Nowadays much of Italy's Chardonnay is produced, often without much distinction, in Friuli, Trentino, and, to a more limited extent, Veneto, where much of it is used as ballast for GARGANEGA. Some fine examples are produced in favoured sites in both Friuli and Trentino but a considerable proportion is siphoned off to become SPUMANTE, as it is in Lombardia, where it can add finesse to some fine fizz. Chardonnay gained ground rapidly in Italy in the 1990s, being planted in Tuscan spots where Sangiovese is difficult to ripen and in Piemonte replacing Dolcetto, which can be difficult to sell. Piemonte, cooler than Toscana, has, not unsurprisingly, had more overall success with the variety. See under these geographical names for more details of Italian Chardonnays.

Much less dramatic Chardonnay is also produced in Switzerland, particularly in Geneva, Valais, and Bündner Herrschaft (see map under SWITZERLAND). In Austria, a foreign vine known as Morillon in Styria and Feinburgunder in Vienna and Burgenland was not identified as the modish Chardonnay until the late 1980s. Austria's Chardonnays include relatively rich, oak-matured versions; lean, aromatic styles modelled on their finest Rieslings; and even sweet AUSBRUCH wines. See AUSTRIA.

Bulgaria had 2,300 ha of Chardonnay vineyard in the mid 2000s, mainly in the east, but, perhaps mainly for viticultural rather than oenological reasons, has only rarely been able to demonstrate real Chardonnay character in the bottle. There are limited plantings in Slovenia, Hungary, and Romania (whence Late Harvest Chardonnays have been exported) but it seems that the Soviet Union's political turbulence during the late 1980s may have saved it from the major Chardonnay invasion that took place almost everywhere else at that time. Official statistics in 1993, the most recent available, found that it had infiltrated only Moldova and Georgia, and played an extremely minor role relative to, for example, the white

grape varieties Rkatsiteli, Riesling, and Chardonnay's Burgundian rival Aligoté.

Germany was one of the last wine-producing countries to admit Chardonnay to the ranks of accepted vine varieties, in 1991 (although Schloss Reinhartshausen's had planted an experimental plot on a sandy island in the Rhine). This late, limited acceptance is perhaps not surprising since giving over one of Germany's favoured sites to a quintessentially French variety is inevitably viewed by some as a defeat for Germany's signal white variety Riesling. By 2003, however, total German plantings of Chardonnay had reached 890 ha/2,200 acres. The largest area is in the Pfalz, then in Rheinhessen and Baden, but this ubiquitous international variety can now be found throughout Germany, to the chagrin of proponents of Riesling and TRADITION.

Such is Chardonnay's fame and popularity that it is grown to a certain extent in climates as dissimilar as those of England, India, and Uruguay. In Spanish Cataluña, Chardonnay has added class and an internationally recognizable flavour to CAVA sparkling wines as well as producing some increasingly sophisticated still wines both here and in Costers del Segre, Navarra, and Somontano. Almost 3,000 ha of Chardonnay were registered in Spain in 2004. Portugal seems to have withstood Chardonnay-mania better than most.

Charitois, Coteaux. Vin de Pays in the Nièvre *département* in the upper LOIRE seeking VDQS status for its light whites.

Charlemagne, king of the Franks 768–814, crowned Holy Roman Emperor in 800, the man who ushered in civilization, order, and prosperity after the long Dark Ages, ruling a Christian kingdom based at Aachen (Aix-la-Chapelle) which included virtually all of France, Belgium, Germany, and Switzerland.

Charlemagne's name is associated by modern wine drinkers with one of the greatest white burgundies, Corton-Charlemagne (whose vineyards include a plot known as Le Charlemagne), produced on land he gave to the Abbey of Saulieu in 775 (see ALOXE-CORTON for more detail). Charlemagne's secretary and biographer Einhard tells us, however, that Charlemagne was a moderate man: he never drank more than three cups of wine with dinner, and he hated to see people drunk (*Life of Charlemagne*, ch. 24). Only a temperate man is truly interested in wine: when he renamed the 12 months of the year in his native language, he called October 'windume-manoth', the month of the wine harvest (Einhard, ch. 28)—which was presumably true of the vineyards then established in parts of northern Europe considered too cool for viable wine production today.

This Old FRANKEN name reflects the growing importance of wine in the Carolingian era, for under Charlemagne and his heirs more and more vines began to be grown. Viticulture had of course been long established in a large part of Charlemagne's empire. The Greek colonists had introduced wine-growing to Massilia (now Marseilles) from 600 BC onwards. When the Romans, under Julius Caesar, conquered Gaul in 51 BC, they gradually expanded the small-scale viticulture of the Gauls, who had drunk mainly BEER. The Roman settlers planted their first vineyards in southern Gaul, and by the 2nd century wine was grown extensively in most of Gaul. The Romans also planted vines in the Moselle valley, on the left bank of the Rhine, and in the areas we now know as Alsace, the Pfalz, and Rheinhessen.

The spread of Christianity was one reason for the expansion of viticulture that took place during Charlemagne's reign and continued for another two centuries afterwards. The Church needed a daily supply of wine to celebrate the EUCHARIST. Also, monasteries, many of which were new foundations, needed wine for the monks and their guests (see MONKS AND MONASTERIES) and vineyards were planted all over northern France and even southern Belgium.

The Rule of St Benedict permitted a modest daily ration of wine, and more on holy days and feast days; important guests who stayed at the monastery had to be suitably entertained, for they might one day repay the monks generously for their hospitality. Monasteries usually had their own vineyards, and often these had been donated by local landowners who hoped for a place in heaven. Bishops also wanted wine, not just for the day-to-day running of their households but as a status symbol to put themselves on a par with the nobility of the district. Bishops, like monks, had their own vineyards, and some bishops may even have moved their sees to be nearer vineyards: at least, this may explain why the bishopric of Langres moved south to Dijon (at the north of the CÔTE D'OR), that of Tongres to Liège in modern Belgium, and that of St-Quentin to Noyon north of Paris. Thus Christianity fostered the production of two grades of wine, wine for daily consumption and a superior kind that was designed to impress prestigious guests.

In 816, the Council of Aachen added a third category of ecclesiastical viticulture. The Council prescribed that a college of canons, living under monastic rule, should be attached to every cathedral and that the canons should grow wine. Often they tended vineyards adjacent to those of their bishops; collegiate churches could be founded elsewhere in the diocese as well, and they also acquired their own vineyards.

Unlike education, viticulture was not the preserve of the Church, however: laymen also grew wine. The factor that decided where they established their new vineyards was not TERROIR but ease of transport. If the enterprise was to be commercially viable, the area had to be near a navigable RIVER or within easy reach,

by road, of a major town or city. This is why so much wine was grown around PARIS, AUXERRE, and in CHAMPAGNE, despite the fact that it was too cold there for the vine to yield ripe and abundant fruit. If the summer had not been hot, there was nothing for it but to drink thin, acidic wine until the following autumn, unless one could afford to buy better wine from elsewhere. An interesting document from the last decade of the 8th century deals with the management of vineyards in secular ownership. It is known as the 'Capitulare de villis', or 'Concerning estates' (a capitulary being a collection of ordinances). Linguistic evidence and local references show that it was drawn up for Aquitaine, which was administered by Charlemagne's son Louis the Pious before he succeeded his father. The list of plants and herbs which it says must be grown in the estate's market garden owes more to the library than to real horticulture, but the advice it gives on wine-growing is sound and practical. Not only should the king's inspectors claim the portion of the vintage that is the royal household's due, they should also oversee hygienic procedures in the vineyard. Wine PRESSES should be clean, and grapes should not be trodden with the feet. Wine that is to be sent to the palace should be put into proper wooden BARRELS instead of leather wineskins. An inventory of the entire estate should be drawn up each Christmas, including the wine it has produced that autumn and any older wine left over.

The 'Capitulare de villis' has no connection with Charlemagne himself, and there is no solid evidence that he initiated the planting of any vineyard, although parts of France and the Rheingau were first planted in his day. Viticulture flourished, not because of a *dirigiste* policy but because political unity had brought prosperity. External threats, most importantly from the Moors and the Magyars, could not be prevented and had to be dealt with, but, within the frontiers of the Holy Roman Empire, peace reigned, and viticulture was so successful that there was a surplus of wine. Landowners had to resort to the right of 'banvin', by which none of their tenants was allowed to sell his wine until the lord had sold his own. In the south, wine was part of everyday life; in the north it was more of a luxury item but it could still be obtained readily.

How different things were in England! When the English scholar Alcuin, friend of Charlemagne and tutor to his court at Aachen, went back to his native country for a visit, he complained bitterly in a letter, dated 790, to a Frankish ex-pupil. The wine has run out, and his stomach aches with sour beer: please send wine. BEER has its uses, but it is not a civilized drink. In the 8th century, the Frankish kingdom was a better place for a wine drinker to be than Anglo-Saxon England.

See also GERMAN HISTORY.   H.M.W.

Bassermann-Jordan, F., *Geschichte des Weinbaus*, 3 vols., i (1907).

Dion, R., *Histoire de la vigne et du vin en France* (France, 1959; rpt 1977).

Duby, G., *Histoire de la France rurale*, 4 vols., i (1975).

Einhard and Notker the Stammerer, *Two Lives of Charlemagne*, tr. Lewis Thorpe (London, 1969).

Latouche, R., *The Birth of Western Economy* (London, 1961).

Charles Sturt University, one of Australia's foremost research and teaching institutions for grape-growers and winemakers. Courses started in 1976 within the Riverina College of Advanced Education, Wagga Wagga, New South Wales (NSW) to satisfy the need, within the rapidly growing wine industry, for a teaching institution in addition to ROSEWORTHY. In 1989, the College combined with other regional teaching institutions in NSW to form Charles Sturt University (CSU). The School of Wine and Food Sciences offers Bachelor of Applied Science degrees in either viticulture or wine science over three years full-time on campus or six years by distance education (DE). Initially a controversial option for the wine industry, DE is now the predominant means of learning, allowing students to continue in their current profession while studying. There is also a double degree in viticulture and wine science and a shorter Associate Degree in Wine Science (Winegrowing). CSU also offers its degrees through partner institutions in New Zealand and elsewhere in Australia.

In 1997, CSU joined the NSW Government's Department of Primary Industries and the NSW Wine Industry Association to form the National Wine and Grape Industry Centre, an alliance which conducts research and offers extension services to assist the wine industry in applying best practice. Deakin University joined the Centre in 2003.   N.B.

Charmat, the name of a bulk SPARKLING WINE-MAKING process which involves provoking a second fermentation in a pressure tank. Also called *cuve close* or tank method.

Charneco, Portuguese white wine, probably fortified, popular in England in the 16th and 17th centuries and mentioned by Shakespeare in *2 Henry VI*. It is probably the forerunner of BUCELAS.   R.J.M.

Charta (pronounced 'karta'), important organization of 30 RHEINGAU wine producers in Germany dedicated to making a traditional style of dry to off-dry RIESLING according to much stricter rules than those imposed by the GERMAN WINE LAW. Founded in 1983 by a small group of far-sighted producers, most notably the late Bernhard Breuer, the organization's then 50 members officially merged in 1999 with the Rheingau branch of the prestigious VDP growers' association. Charta distinguishes individual wines from each member estate that meet its standards. Charta wines must be made entirely of Rheingau Riesling grapes with minimum MUST WEIGHTS higher than prescribed by law. The RESIDUAL SUGAR cannot exceed TOTAL ACIDITY by more than 3 g/l. The goal is to produce concentrated, harmonious wines that go well with food and are suitable for ageing. Only after passing three blind-tasting tests and undergoing 12 months' BOTTLE AGEING are the wines released. Charta wines are sold in a tall brown bottle embossed with a double romanesque arch.

Charta labels bordered in black and depicting the same romanesque arches are reserved for wines classified Erstes Gewächs or FIRST GROWTH. These wines are made from hand-picked, non-BOTRYTIZED grapes from a (Charta-defined) classified top vineyard. YIELDS may not exceed 50 hl/ha (3 tons/acre). Such wines are offered EN PRIMEUR 12 months after the harvest but none is released until after 18 months in bottle.   K.B.S. & D.S.

Chasan, CROSSING of Palomino (known in France as LISTÁN) and Chardonnay vines made under INRA auspices by French AMPELOGRAPHER Paul Truel. The resulting wine bears a lightweight imprint of Chardonnay while the vine buds early. It is planted on a limited scale in the Midi, particularly in the Aude *département*, where the 2000 census records 538 ha/1,330 acres.

Chassagne-Montrachet, village in the Côte de Beaune district of Burgundy's Côte d'Or more famed for its white wines from the Chardonnay grape than for its equally plentiful red wines from Pinot Noir. Until the mid 1980s, the village produced more red wine than white, but the significant premium for white Chassagne led to considerable planting of Chardonnay, even on relatively unsuitable soils.

The better soil for Pinot Noir, limestone marl with a red gravel content, lies mainly on the south side of the village towards Santenay and incorporates most of the village appellation, although La Boudriotte and Morgeot, among the PREMIERS CRUS, make excellent red wines, as can Clos St-Jean to the north of the village. Red Chassagne-Montrachet tends to be somewhat hard and earthy when young, mellowing with age but rarely achieving the delicacy of truly fine red burgundy.

The fame of Chassagne rests with the white wines at village, premier cru, and especially GRAND CRU level. Chassagne shares the Le Montrachet and Bâtard-Montrachet vineyards with neighbouring Puligny and enjoys sole possession of a third grand cru, Criots-Bâtard-Montrachet (see MONTRACHET for more details). Among the premiers crus, the best known are Les Chenevottes, Clos de la Maltroie, En Cailleret, and Les Ruchottes. Suitable white wine soil tends to have more oolitic limestone and less marl in its make-up.

The white wines of Chassagne are noted for their steely power, less flattering than MEURSAULT when young, sometimes too similar to PULIGNY-MONTRACHET to tell apart. Good vintages from good producers such as Ramonet and the extended Gagnard family should age from five to ten years. A total of just over 300 ha was declared for the appellation in 1996.

See also CÔTE D'OR, and map under BURGUNDY.   J.T.C.M.

Chasselas, even if by no means the most revered white grape variety, is widely planted around the world and has a long, intriguing history. Some authorities cite Middle Eastern, even Egyptian, origins. Some point instead to the village of Chasselas in the Mâconnais in eastern France. Others suggest that Chasselas travelled to SWITZERLAND, where, as FENDANT, it certainly produces its finest wines today, from the famous Chasselas vine that was planted for the French king at Fontainebleau outside Paris in the mid 18th century. Others again, particularly the Swiss, argue that Chasselas's origins are Swiss and that the name Fendant, its common synonym in Valais, can be found in monastic records well before the 16th century.

In France, it is rather despised, not least because, as Chasselas Doré or Golden Chasselas, it is France's most common TABLE GRAPE. Total French plantings in 2000 were more than 3,000 ha/7,500 acres. The principal synonym of the Chasselas grown in France for wine production is **Chasselas de Moissac.** It is rapidly disappearing from Alsace, where it is regarded as the lowest of the low and is generally sold as Edelzwicker or under some proprietary name that excludes mention of any grape variety. Planted in the area responsible for Pouilly-Fumé, it makes the distinctly inferior white labelled Pouilly-sur-Loire and, as might be expected, approaches respectability only as it nears Switzerland, in SAVOIE. Here it is the main grape grown in the *département* of Haute Savoie on the south side of Lake Geneva in the Vin de Savoie CRUS of MARIGNAN, Marin, and Ripaille, and also for the separate appellation CRÉPY, where it has a long, sometimes noble, history. Best examples are from Château de Ripaille and Delalex in Marin.

On the shores of Lake Geneva, as on the other side of the lake in Switzerland, care has to be taken with the choice of ROOTSTOCK so as to avoid the variety's dangerous tendencies towards early budding and too much VIGOUR. But skilfully grown Chasselas can yield good quantities of fairly neutral, soft wine which achieves a peak of concentration in isolated sites such as the grand cru of Dézaley in the canton of Vaud. Chasselas/Fendant is by far Switzerland's most planted variety.

The variety's long history has enabled it to spread far and wide. In Germany, where it is known as Weisser GUTEDEL and is grown on more than 1,000 ha, it has been known since the 16th century. It was once revered in the PFALZ region. In Austria, it is known as Moster and Wälscher, but is not widely grown. It is reputedly grown in Romania, Hungary, to a limited extent in Moldova and Ukraine, in both the north and far south of Italy, around the Mediterranean including North Africa, in Chile, and was at one time curiously important in New Zealand.

château may be French for 'castle' but in wine parlance it usually means a vine-growing, wine-making estate, to include the vineyards, the cellars, often the wine itself, and any building or buildings on the property, which can range from the non-existent (as in the case of Ch Léoville-BARTON, for example), through the most rudimentary shack, to the sumptuous classical edifice called Ch MARGAUX. The term is most commonly used in BORDEAUX, where the 17th edition of the COCKS ET FÉRET guide lists more than 7,400 châteaux, although common use of the term developed only in the second half of the 19th century, when the owners of the great estates could afford to build grand lodgings to go with them. Only five of the original 79 properties in the Médoc, Graves, and Sauternes listed in the famous 1855 CLASSIFICATION, for example, are described as châteaux. Bordeaux proprietors soon learnt the value of a Château prefix, and have long adopted the policy of renaming properties almost at will, in particular suffixing their own surname as, for example, Ch Prieuré-LICHINE and Chx Mouton- and Lafite-ROTHSCHILD. The word château is by no means uncommon outside Bordeaux, however, mainly within but sometimes outside FRANCE (where it tends to lose its circumflex). According to current French law, the word château may be used only of a specified plot, or collection of plots, of land, which means that it is perfectly possible for CO-OPERATIVES, for example, to produce a wine labelled as Château Quelquechose (see CHÂTEAU BOTTLING). Some producers make a range of wines carrying the name of the property, but reserve the word château for their top bottlings.

château bottling, the relatively recent practice of BOTTLING the produce of a CHÂTEAU on that property. Such a wine is said to be **château bottled,** or *mis(e) en bouteille au château* in French, an expression used throughout France but particularly in BORDEAUX. (Its counterpart in BURGUNDY is DOMAINE BOTTLED, while in the NEW WORLD the term ESTATE BOTTLED is often used.)

Initially all wine was sold in bulk, and subsequently it was up to the MERCHANTS, whether in the region of consumption or production, to put the wine into bottle. Even as recently as the mid 20th century, the great majority of wine left the property on which it was produced in BARRELS. ADULTERATION AND FRAUD was therefore all too easy among less scrupulous merchants, and particularly tempting in the wake of the world wine shortages which followed POWDERY MILDEW and PHYLLOXERA at the end of the 19th century.

It was the young Baron Philippe de ROTHSCHILD who did most to promote château bottling when he took over Ch MOUTON-ROTHSCHILD in the early 1920s. He succeeded in persuading all the first growths (and Ch Mouton-Rothschild of course) of the wisdom of bottling all of their principal output, the so-called *grand vin*, on their own territory. This involved a certain amount of investment, but the resulting reliability and cachet more than compensated. Although Ch MARGAUX had to opt out for 20 years in 1930, the first growths set and maintained an example for quality-conscious wine producers everywhere.

Good bottling lines require a level of investment that is unrealistic for many a small wine property, however, so contract bottlers and mobile bottling lines are much in demand, and a producer may not be able to bottle at the precise time he or she would prefer. Others still bottle by hand, some with scant regard for HYGIENE and consistency. Such considerations mean that bottling at source is not necessarily superior to careful BULK TRANSPORT of the wine to a top-quality bottling plant.

Today, a producer of château bottled wine, described on the label as *mis(e) en bouteille au château*, is likely to care about quality. It is worth noting in addition that wines made from specific plots of land but vinified and bottled by CO-OPERATIVES may also be described as château bottled.

Château-Chalon,

extraordinary wine made in the JURA region of eastern France with its own small appellation named after the hilltop village where it is produced. Unlike other Jura appellations, Ch-Chalon must be a VIN JAUNE and must be made exclusively from SAVAGNIN grapes grown on the local limestone and, especially, MARL. (Other wines produced by local growers are entitled to the Côtes du Jura appellation.) It must reach a slightly higher POTENTIAL ALCOHOL than other Jura *vins jaunes*, 12 rather than 11.5 per cent (but in practice this is usually much surpassed). It must also be kept for at least six years and three months before bottling, most of this time spent in partially filled, untouched casks under the famous *voile*, or local benevolent FILM-FORMING YEAST. The resulting wine is exceptionally nutty, pale to deep golden brown, and long lasting. It must be bottled in a special *clavelin* bottle containing 62 cl/, supposedly the amount of wine that remains from a litre of wine kept in a cask in Ch-Chalon for six years. The result is a wine that shares many taste characteristics with SHERRY but is

more actively promoted as a gastronomic partner (especially with the local poultry of Bresse, also APPELLATION CONTRÔLÉE products) and as a candidate for BOTTLE AGEING. It is said to develop 'curry' flavours in bottle, thanks to the compound SOTOLON. In some years, producers nobly decide that the quality does not merit the production of any wine from the appellation. Production volumes therefore vary wildly from zero to around 2,000 hl/52,835 gal in a good year. Best producers include Jean Macle, Berthet-Bondet, Baud Père et Fils, and Philippe Butin.   W.L.

Château Grillet,

one of France's smallest wine appellations and one of the few with a single owner (although see also DOMAINE DE LA ROMANÉE-CONTI). Ch Grillet's few hectares of vineyard represent an enclave within the CONDRIEU zone in the north of the northern Rhône (see map under RHÔNE). A virtual amphitheatre carved out of the granite shelters the narrow terraces of VIOGNIER vines from the north winds which can so seriously prejudice both quantity and quality in Condrieu. Already appreciated by Thomas JEFFERSON in the late 18th century, Ch Grillet has always been in single ownership and, although the family name Neyret-Gachet appears on the label, André Canet, who married into the family, ran the property from the early 1960s (since succeeded by his daughter), extending the vineyard so that production from just 3.8 ha/ 9 acres in 1990, for example, was 15,800 l/ 4,200 gal, or nearly 2,000 cases of Ch Grillet's distinctive brown bottle, which was one of the last to grow from 70 to 75 cl.

Since the 1970s, the wine has maintained its high price more by its rarity than because it is obviously one of France's finest wines. The wine is usually more austere and less headily perfumed than the best Condrieu. It is kept in cask and is not usually bottled until well after the next harvest, considerably later than most Condrieu is bottled. The result is a restrained, taut, longer-living wine which, unlike Condrieu, may improve in bottle for a decade or even two. The potential of the vineyard is undoubted, as earlier eulogies testify.

Châteaumeillant,

small, isolated red and rosé wine VDQS zone in central France around the town of Châteaumeillant between ST POURÇAIN and TOURAINE (see map under FRANCE). Gamay and some Pinot vines are grown on fewer than 100 ha/250 acres of VOLCANIC soils. VIN GRIS is a local speciality, and one CO-OPERATIVE dominates production.

Châteauneuf-du-Pape,

the most important, and variable, appellation in the southern RHÔNE in terms of quality, producing mainly rich, spicy, full-bodied red wines which can be some of the most alluring expressions of warm climate viticulture, but can also be either impossibly tannic or disappointingly jammy.

About one in every 14 distinctively heavy and embossed Châteauneuf-du-Pape bottles contains full bodied white wine, which since the 1990s has been increasingly fresh and well made.

The wine takes its name, which means 'Pope's new castle', from the relocation of the papal court to Avignon in the 14th century, and in particular from the construction of summer quarters just north of the city in a village once known as Calcernier for its limestone quarry. It is now called Châteauneuf-du-Pape. The Gascon Pope Clément V (after whom Ch Pape-Clément in PESSAC-LÉOGNAN is named) arrived at Avignon in 1309 and is supposed to have ordered the planting of vines, but it was his successor John XXII who is credited with developing a papal vineyard in Châteauneuf-du-Pape.

The history of Châteauneuf-du-Pape as such is relatively recent, however. As Livingstone-Learmonth points out, the region's wine was known simply as *vin d'Avignon* in the 18th century, when it was shipped northwards up river. In the early 19th century, a wine called Châteauneuf-du-Pape-Calcernier emerges, but from JULLIEN's description it sounds a much lighter wine than the Châteauneuf-du-Pape of today. Châteauneuf-du-Pape's reputation steadily grew within France until the arrival of the PHYLLOXERA louse began seriously to affect wine production, in the early 1870s, before most other French wine regions.

Reconstruction of the vineyards was financially devastating, and the Châteauneuf-du-Pape vignerons were just some of those affected by the ADULTERATION AND FRAUD that were rife in the early 20th century. By 1923, the most energetic and well connected of their number, Baron Le Roy of Ch Fortia, had successfully drawn up a set of rules for the production of Châteauneuf-du-Pape, with the co-operation of his peers, which was the prototype for the entire APPELLATION CONTRÔLÉE system. Among what have now become the usual regulations, it involved the first geographical DELIMITATION of a table wine area, land being defined as suitable, by now in a much larger area, if it were so infertile and arid that thyme and lavender would grow on it. Another notable feature was the minimum specified ALCOHOLIC STRENGTH, at 12.5 per cent still the highest in France, and in the southern Rhône this must be achieved without the aid of external sugar addition, or CHAPTALIZATION. TRIAGE of picked grapes was mandatory and ROSÉ was outlawed (with a flick of the nose at the vignerons of TAVEL just across the river). When GIGONDAS drew up its own appellation rules, it incorporated many of these exigencies.

Perhaps it is because of the antiquity of Châteauneuf-du-Pape's wine regulations that quite so many VINE VARIETIES are theoretically permitted by the Châteauneuf-du-Pape appellation (because vines are such a long-term crop, appellation laws have to countenance the status quo to a certain extent). Three more varieties were added to the original ten in 1936. The Châteauneuf-du-Pape grape *par excellence* is GRENACHE and conversely Châteauneuf-du-Pape is its finest expression in France. Grenache dominates plantings in the Châteauneuf-du-Pape vineyards, and on their impoverished soils, with yields officially restricted to a base rate of just 35 hl/ha (2 tons/acre), it can produce wines which combine concentration with the usual sweet fruit of Grenache.

MOURVÈDRE also plays a part at many properties, although it needs the warmest MESO-CLIMATES to ripen fully, while SYRAH from the northern Rhône has also been planted by a number of producers who admire its TANNINS and structure, although, unlike Grenache and Mourvèdre, it needs care to avoid overripeness. CINSAUT is also grown, but to a declining extent. Of the other permitted red wine varieties, Muscardin, Vaccarèse, PICPOUL, TERRET Noir, and COUNOISE, only the last is grown to any significant extent, and has its admirers, particularly at Ch de Beaucastel, one of the most rigorous producers of Châteauneuf-du-Pape, and one of the few to cultivate all 13 permitted varieties. For white Châteauneuf-du-Pape, there is considerable variation in the proportions of Grenache Blanc, CLAIRETTE, BOUR-BOULENC, and ROUSSANNE planted, although Ch de Beaucastel have demonstrated that a VARIETAL Roussanne can be a worthy candidate for BARREL MATURATION. Picardan, which is not widely planted, produces light, relatively neutral wine.

The Châteauneuf-du-Pape appellation extends over more than 3,200 ha/7,900 acres of relatively flat vineyards at varying altitudes and expositions above the river in Châteauneuf-du-Pape and the neighbouring communes of Bédarrides, Courthézon, Orange, and Sorgues. The terrain is traditionally characterized by the large pebbles, or *galets*, some of them several inches across, which cover many of the more photographed vineyards, supposedly retaining heat and speeding the ripening process of the traditionally low-trained GOBELET vines. Soils in Châteauneuf-du-Pape are more varied than this, however, and those at the celebrated Ch Rayas, for example, are sandy CALCAREOUS without a *galet* in sight. On south-facing slopes, any reradiated night-time heat could well be too much, so, on very pebbly ground, the best vineyards may face at least partly north to moderate this.

Indeed, the key with red Châteauneuf-du-Pape in general is to balance the accumulation of SUGAR IN GRAPES, and therefore alcohol content, with the PHENOLICS, and tannins in particular. Traditionally DESTEMMING has been avoided, and fairly hot fermentations have been accompanied by frequent PUNCHING DOWN or PUMPING OVER, so that some wines have been tannic, although it is also easy for others to be too alcoholic without the flavour and structure to support it. Since the 1970s,

a number of producers have used CARBONIC MACERATION or SEMI-CARBONIC MACERATION to produce lighter, fruitier wines which can be drunk from about three years rather than from five or six. This is by no means a high-tech wine region, however. Some notable domaines include Ch de Beaucastel, Henri Bonneau (Réserve des Célestins), Chapoutier's Barbe Rac, Domaine de la Janasse, Domaine de Pegaü, Ch Rayas, and Domaine du Vieux Télégraphe but many more have established more recent reputations.

White Châteauneuf-du-Pape is a relative rarity, and may be made according to a wide range of formulas but overall quality has been steadily increasing. The wines are always full bodied and the less successful lack acidity and BOUQUET. They should usually be drunk young, although the all-Roussanne Vieilles Vignes bottling from Ch de Beaucastel can withstand several years in bottle.

See also RHÔNE.

Livingstone-Learmonth, J., *The Wines of the Rhône* (3rd edn, London, 1992).

Norman, R., *Rhône Renaissance* (London, 1995).

Parker, R. M., *The Wines of the Rhône Valley* (2nd edn, New York, 1997).

Châtillon-en-Diois, small appellation of about 60 ha/150 acres in area round DIE in the far east of the greater RHÔNE region in the cooler reaches of the Drôme valley for still wines: light, Gamay-based reds and light whites made from Aligoté and Chardonnay.

Chaume, or Chaume Premier Cru des Coteaux du Layon, appellation awarded in 2003, revoked in 2005, under appeal in 2006, to the superior LIQUOREUX Chenin Blanc sweet whites of COTEAUX DU LAYON on about 130 ha/320 acres of vineyard south of Angers. Grapes must be hand picked, with maximum yields of 25 hl/ha. QUARTS DE CHAUME is a much smaller, more demanding appellation.

Chautagne, named CRU in the upper Rhône valley north of Chambéry whose name may be added to the French appellation Vin de SAVOIE. Production is dominated by the CO-OPERATIVE, and some fine red wines are made, from Gamay, Pinot Noir, and, especially, the local Mondeuse.

Chaves, IPR in north east Portugal. See TRÁS-OS-MONTES.

Chelois, Seibel FRENCH HYBRID planted in the northeastern US. It tends to overcrop but responds well if VIGOUR is controlled. It is susceptible to WINTER FREEZE as well as berry splitting in wet harvest conditions.   D.F.

Chelva, leading Spanish TABLE GRAPE.

Chenanson, productive INRA CROSSING of Grenache Noir and Jurançon Noir planted on more than 600 ha/1,500 acres in southern France, presumably popular because it is

more productive and deeper-coloured than Grenache.

Chénas, the smallest of the ten Beaujolais CRUS in the far north of the region. Its 285 ha/700 acres of vines are divided between the villages of Chénas and La Chapelle de Guinchay. Hubert Lapierre is a reliable producer. For more details, see BEAUJOLAIS.

Chenin or **Chenin Blanc,** in its native region often called Pineau or Pineau de la Loire, is probably the world's most versatile grape variety, capable of producing some of the finest, longest-living sweet whites although more usually harnessed to the yoke of basic New World table wine production. In between these two extremes, it is responsible for a considerable volume of sparkling wine and, in SOUTH AFRICA, where it is by far the most planted vine, it is even used as the base for a wide range of fortified wines and spirits. Although, in its most common high-yield, New World form, its distinctive flavour reminiscent of honey and damp straw is usually lost, it retains the naturally high acidity that dogs it in some of the Loire's less ripe vintages but can be so useful in hot climates.

South Africa now has about twice as much Chenin planted as France's 2000 total of just under 10,000 ha/24,700 acres and the variety, still sometimes called STEEN, constitutes nearly 17 per cent of the country's entire vineyard. It was not until 1965 that the connection was made between Chenin and 'Steen', then the Cape's third most planted variety, prized for its productivity and good resistance to disease and wind. The vine may have been one of the original collection imported in 1655 by Jan van Riebeeck. In the late 1960s and early 1970s, it provided ideal material for new low-temperature, high-tech wine-making techniques so that a flood of off-dry, refreshingly crisp, but otherwise rather bland white washed over the South African wine market. In recent years, however, a dedicated band of Chenin Blanc specialists has emerged in South Africa. Their focus on the best sites and on restoring to high-quality production old vineyard blocks has produced something of a Chenin renaissance with the best examples attracting premium pricing and recognition from leading Loire producers.

In the 1980s, CALIFORNIA also had more Chenin planted than France, and still uses its remaining 13,000 acres/5,000 ha for much the same purposes as South Africa, as the usually anonymous base for everyday commercial blends of reasonably crisp white of varying degrees of sweetness, often blended with the even more widely planted French COLOMBARD. Both of these workhorse varieties are planted primarily in the hot, dry Central valley, a setting that might be described as the antithesis of Chenin's Loire homeland. (It also presumably helps extend quantities of, and add acidity to, cheaper wines labelled Chardonnay.) Only a handful of producers, notably Chappellet, take Chenin seriously enough to try to make wines worth ageing from it. In CLARKSBURG at the north end of the Central valley, it can take on a distinctive melony, musky flavour.

It is even rarer to find a Chenin made in the image of the great sweet Loire wine in California than in NEW ZEALAND, where plantings had fallen almost to 100 ha by 2004, mainly in the North Island. AUSTRALIA has over six times as much Chenin but treats it largely with disdain as low cost (high-yielding) blending material, usually extending Chardonnay, Semillon, and Sauvignon Blanc.

Chenin is widely planted throughout the Americas for no perceptible reason other than that it will obligingly produce a decent yield of relatively crisp wine. In 2002, there were 3,333 ha/8,2325 acres of Chenin in Argentina, whose heavily irrigated vineyards yield an even more blurred expression of the variety's character, as well as a tiny amount in Chile. In Mexico, Brazil, and Uruguay, it is more usually called Pinot Blanco, as it still is by some Argentine growers. It is also grown although not particularly popular in many North American states outside California. In Washington, for example, there were only about 200 acres left by 2005.

The variety was also exported to Israel to establish vineyards there at the end of the 19th century.

If Chenin appears to lead a double life—biddable workhorse in the New World, superstar in Anjou-Saumur and Touraine—it seems clear that the explanation lies in a combination of climate, soil, and yield. In California's Central valley, the vine is often expected to yield 10 tons per acre (175 hl/ha), while even the most basic Anjou Blanc should not be produced from vines that yield more than 45 hl/ha. It is hardly surprising that Chenin's character seems diluted outside the Loire.

GALET suggests that it may have been well established in Anjou as long ago as the 9th century and that it was exported to Touraine in the 15th. Rabelais certainly wrote about Chenin both as Chenin and under its already familiar synonym of Pineau, often Pineau d'Anjou. See also LA ROCHELLE. DNA PROFILING in Austria suggested in 1999 a possible parent–offspring relationship between Chenin and SAUVIGNON BLANC.

The vine is vigorous and has a tendency to bud early and ripen late, both of which are highly inconvenient attributes in the cool Loire valley (though hardly noticeable characteristics in the hotter vineyards of the New World). CLONES that minimize these inconveniences have been selected and six had been officially sanctioned in France by the 1990s.

About a third of all France's, which means the middle Loire's, Chenin was abandoned in the 1970s, often in favour of the red Cabernet Franc in Anjou-Saumur and Touraine and to make way for the temporarily more fashionable Gamay and Sauvignon de Touraine in the east of the middle Loire. It is today most planted in the heart of Anjou-Saumur and Touraine, as well it might be to judge from the superlative quality of the best wines of such appellations as ANJOU, BONNEZEAUX, Coteaux de l'AUBANCE, Coteaux du LAYON, JASNIÈRES, MONTLOUIS, QUARTS DE CHAUME, SAUMUR, SAVENNIÈRES (the grape's one definitively dry appellation), VOUVRAY, and CRÉMANT de Loire.

In most of the best wines, and certainly all of the great sweet wines, Chenin is unblended, but up to 20 per cent of Chardonnay or Sauvignon is allowed into an Anjou or a Saumur and even more catholic blends are allowed into whites labelled Touraine—although even here Chardonnay's pervasive influence is officially limited to 20 per cent of the total blend. If middle Loire white has any character at all it is that of Chenin, increasingly valued as the region's signature grape, in contrast to the widely planted Sauvignon Blanc and Chardonnay.

While basic Loire Chenin exhibits simply vaguely floral aromas and refreshingly high acidity (together with too much sulfur if made in one of the more old-fashioned cellars), the best have a physically thrilling concentration of honeyed flavour, whether the wine is made sweet (MOELLEUX), dry or demi-sec, together with Chenin's characteristically vibrant acidity level.

It is undoubtedly this acid, emphasized by a conscious distaste for MALOLACTIC FERMENTATION and concentrated in some years by BOTRYTIS, that helps preserve the finest Chenins for decades after their relatively early bottling. (In all of these respects, together with lateness of ripening and a wide range of sweetness levels that are customary, Chenin is France's answer to Germany's RIESLING.)

Chenin with its high acidity is a useful base for a wide range of sparkling wines, most importantly Saumur Mousseux but also Crémant de Loire and even some rich sparkling Vouvrays, which, like their still counterparts, can age beautifully. Treasured for its reliably high acidity, and useful perfume, it is also an ingredient, with Mauzac and, increasingly, Chardonnay, in the sparkling wines of LIMOUX.

Not before time, stricter controls are being enforced to ensure higher standards of dry and, especially, sweet Chenin in the Loire, and there are healthy signs of an increase in the amount of serious Chenin being produced elsewhere in the world.

Chenin Noir is a rarely used synonym for PINEAU D'AUNIS, a dark-berried grape variety.

Cheval Blanc, Château, very fine BORDEAUX property in ST-ÉMILION. In 1832, Henriette Ducasse married Libourne négociant Jean Laussac-Fourcaud, bringing with her 12 ha/30 acres of land including part of the narrow gravel ridge that runs through Figeac and neighbouring vineyards and reaches Ch PÉTRUS just over the border in POMEROL. This became Ch Cheval Blanc, which, in the International London and Paris Exhibitions in 1862 and 1867, won the medals still prominent on its labels. In 1892, Albert reversed the order of his double surname, and it remained in the Fourcaud-Laussac family until 1998 when it was sold to Bernard Arnault, chairman of LVMH, and Belgian businessman Albert Frère. Pierre, one of the young LURTONS, was made RÉGISSEUR in 1991.

The vineyard is of 41 ha, with 36 ha under vines: 55 per cent CABERNET FRANC vines, 45 per cent MERLOT, and no longer any MALBEC. The average production is about 8,000 cases; Petit Cheval is the second wine. The high percentage of Cabernet Franc, a variety felicitously originally favoured by Jean Laussac-Fourcaud which has proved particularly well-suited to the soils of Cheval Blanc, gives the wines a deep colour and a rich, concentrated blackcurrant bouquet and flavour. Although excellent wines were made towards the end of the 19th century and before the First World War, the property's international reputation was made with the 1921, which had enormous concentration and sweetness. Other very successful wines were made in the 1920s, and even in 1934 and 1937, but its more modern fame was achieved with the rich, porty 1947. Consistently good wines have been made with few exceptions ever since, although, like other St-Émilions and Pomerols, they usually do not last as long as the top red wines from the MÉDOC and the GRAVES.   E.P.-R.

Chevalier, Domaine de, important CHÂTEAU in Bordeaux producing top-quality red and particularly long-lived white wines. For more details, see PESSAC-LÉOGNAN.

Chevalier-Montrachet, great white GRAND CRU in Burgundy's CÔTE D'OR. For more details, see MONTRACHET.

Cheverny. The most important of the VDQS zones of the middle Loire was promoted to full APPELLATION CONTRÔLÉE status in 1993 and produces a wide range of wines in an enclave in the north east corner of TOURAINE near Blois (see LOIRE map). Light reds may be made from Gamay and Pinot Noir, while the Cabernets, Malbec, and Pineau d'Aunis are also allowed. Whites are as common as red Cheverny, and are usually keen, lean Sauvignons which can offer good-value northern ripostes to Sancerre and Pouilly-Fumé. Both Chenin Blanc and Chardonnay are also allowed in the 450-ha/1,100-acre appellation of Cheverny (some Chardonnay is even obligatory), and wines made from the local ROMORANTIN grape have their own 50-ha appellation **Cour Cheverny**.

Chian wine, from the island of **Chios**, was highly prized in both ancient and medieval times. See AEGEAN ISLANDS and DRIED GRAPE WINES for more details.

Chianti, the name of a specific geographical area between Florence and Siena in the central Italian region of TOSCANA, associated with tangy, dry red wines of very varied quality. The Chianti zone is first identified in documents of the second half of the 13th century which named the high hills between Baliaccia and Monte Luco 'the Chianti mountains'. The name was later applied to the townships of Castellina, Radda, and Gaiole that formed the nucleus of the medieval League of Chianti under Florentine jurisdiction. The earliest known recorded mention of Chianti the wine, in 1398, refers to a white wine (see TUS-CANY, history).

Oenological Chianti covers a much wider area than this historic zone. Eight zones of Toscana can call their wines Chianti: CHIANTI CLASSICO (7,142 ha/17,640 acres of vineyard); Chianti Montalbano (318 ha); the Florentine hills, Chianti Colli Fiorentini (905 ha); Chianti Montespertoli, part of Colli Fiorentini until 2002 (57 ha); CHIANTI RUFINA (745 ha); the hills of Siena, or Colli Senesi (3,553 ha); the Pisan hills, or Colline Pisane (154 ha); and the hills of Arezzo, or Colli Aretini (649 ha). There is also a further 10,324 ha of vineyard in the peripheral zones which can call their wines simply Chianti without an additional appellative.

The market for non-Classico Chianti was poor until the mid 1990s. The association of the wine with the straw flask, or *fiasco*, in the mind of the consumer was not a positive image, and the general quality of the wine did little to alter this perception. However, when the price of Chianti Classico rose rapidly in the mid 1990s, those producers able to produce forward, fruity wines that were appealing to drink, were able to make a market for themselves. This has grown, and good quality Chianti is now making a comeback. Production of basic Chianti in 2003 was about 650,000 hl. These wines are usually ready for drinking earlier than those from Classico or Rufina and this is reflected in the law which states that Chianti can be released onto the market as from 1 March following the vintage. Chianti from Colli Fiorentini, Rufina, and Montespertoli cannot be sold prior to 1 June following the vintage, while producers in Chianti Classico must wait until 1 October.

D.T. & D.C.G.

George, R., *Chianti and the Wines of Toscana* (London, 1990).

Chianti Classico, the heartland of the CHIANTI zone, was given its fundamental geographical DELIMITATION by the Medici Grand Duke Cosimo III in an edict of 1716, one of the first examples of such legislation, and was defined as the townships of Radda, Gaiole, and Castellina in addition to the township of Greve (including Panzano) as far as the hill of Spedaluzza 3 km/2 miles to the north of Greve. This area was expanded in the law of July 1932 (later to be confirmed by the DOC regulations of 1966) which established a legal framework for the various types of Chianti in Toscana; the zone was enlarged to the west to include parts of San Casciano Val di Pesa and Barberino Val d'Elsa and, more damagingly, to the north to include Chiocchio, Strada in Chianti, and San Polo in Robbiano. This last area allowed in substantial amounts of lighter wines, more similar to the wines of the Florentine hills (Colli Fiorentini), less suitable for ageing, which have not helped Chianti Classico's reputation for longevity.

Little is known of the precise varietal composition of the wines before the 19th century, although the work of Cosimo Villifranchi (1773) suggests that the wine was a blend of CANAIOLO in the largest part with lesser amounts of SANGIOVESE, MAMMOLO, and MARZEMINO. Modern Chianti can be said to have been invented in a certain sense by Baron Bettino RICASOLI, who, in a letter of 1872, synthesized decades of experimentation and recommended that the wine be based on Sangiovese ('for bouquet and vigour') with the addition of Canaiolo to soften the wine. Canaiolo, none the less, seems to have remained the basis for Chianti Classico until the end of the 19th century, reflecting how gradually Ricasoli's ideas were adopted in this most traditional region.

MALVASIA was suggested as appropriate for wines to be drunk young; its use was discouraged for wines intended for ageing. Villifranchi, however, had mentioned the use of both 'Tribbiano and San Colombano' as blending wines for Chianti. The DOC regulations of 1967, which canonized a mythical 'Ricasoli formula' which included between 10 and 30 per cent of the white grapes TREBBIANO and Malvasia, generous permitted YIELDS of 80 hl/ha (4.5 tons/acre), no limits on production per vine, no penalties for overcropping, and low minimum EXTRACT levels (from 20 g/l) were apparently designed to produce large quantities of rather facile wine.

More than 7,000 ha/17,300 acres of vineyard were planted between 1967 and 1972. This transformed not only the landscape, with mixed cultivation replaced by a monoculture of vines trained on wires, but also the quality of the grapes, for little attention had been paid to CLONAL SELECTION, ROOTSTOCKS, VINE DENSITY or proper considerations of SITE suitability (notably exposure). The overall result was a general lowering of the quality of the wine between 1965 and 1980, difficult economic conditions for producers, and a tendency for many houses to forgo DOC status for their better products and label them VINO DA TAVOLA (and later IGT). Production rose to 323,378 hl/

8.5 million gal in the late 1980s from hardly 7,000 ha of vineyards. In 2004, vineyard area remained the same, but production had dropped to 250,000 hl.

The zone is large and varied, stretching from the suburbs of Florence in the north to the outskirts of Siena in the south. Soil and aspect vary greatly within the zone. As a result, there are those who argue that the zone should be divided into subzones, or into communes, as in the MÉDOC. If this were the case, the wines from Castelnuovo Berardenga, the southernmost commune, would be the Pauillac of Chianti, for the wines have power, intensity and, at their best, great elegance and longevity. Those from Panzano, part of Greve but distinctly different thanks to the splendid position of its *conca d'oro* (golden shell), would be Margaux, for these are the finest wines in Chianti. The wines of Gaiole are muscularly intense yet nicely balanced, while those from Castellina and Radda tend to be more aromatic and less intense. To the north, the clay soils of Greve and the north eastern part of the zone produce less interesting wines, while San Casciano in the north west can produce attractively forward and plump wines. Such diversity makes the DOCG for a single zone a crass simplification.

The DOCG regulations of 1984, in addition to lowering the minimum requirement of white grapes to a cosmetic 2 per cent, lowered yield limits to 52.5 hl/ha with a maximum of 3 kg of fruit per vine, established 23 g/l as the minimum extract level, and forced producers to declassify the entire crop when yields exceeded legal limits by 20 per cent. A general improvement in the quality level has resulted from this stricter legal framework, as well as from greater willingness to experiment.

The 1984 regulations permitted the addition of up to 10 per cent of non-traditional grapes to the final blend, leading to frequent use of CABERNET SAUVIGNON (see VINO DA TAVOLA). MERLOT and SYRAH are also being used as minor ingredients in Chianti Classico blends, although to a lesser extent. Appellation regulations now permit Chianti Classico to be a 100 per cent Sangiovese wine, an obvious attempt to lure some of the more famous *vini da tavola* back into the DOC fold which is meeting some success. The law today stipulates that Chianti Classico must be made from a minimum of 80 per cent Sangiovese and a maximum of 20 per cent other recommended or authorized red varieties (including Cabernet, Merlot, etc.). White grapes are no longer permitted. A recent suggestion that Chianti's vineyards be planted with grapes such as Nero d'Avola or other southern varieties, on the spurious grounds that Chianti was historically made with a blending component from the south, seems to have been rejected. Some cynics have mused that this is a move to anticipate the day when gas chromatography can identify components in a wine that are not from Sangiovese or other permitted grapes; in other words, an admission that remedial blending is still widespread in Chianti Classico.

The use of small BARREL MATURATION for Chianti Classico and for Chianti Classico Riserva is standard practice for the top estates. New oak barriques are used for the Riserva or wines sold as IGT Toscana, and then used for the Chianti Classico which, being lighter, cannot sustain the same level of new oak. These small barrels, experimental in the 1980s, have supplanted the traditional large BOTTI of Slavonian oak.

The 1990s saw a return to using the Chianti Classico name for Riserva, single-vineyard wines and superior selections, perhaps inevitably given the dizzying plethora of fantasy names with no geographical precision used for SUPERTUSCANS. Price differentials between an expensive IGT and a Riserva from the same house were reduced if not entirely eliminated. Meanwhile the wines themselves, often marked with new oak, became increasingly 'international' in style, an uneasy balance between tradition and innovation.

D.T. & D.C.G.

Chianti Rufina, north eastern zone of CHIANTI, was first identified as an area of superior production in Cosimo III de'Medici's granducal edict of 1716, which names the zone Pomino after the famous estate of the Albizi family. Pomino, now owned substantially by FRESCOBALDI, has its own DOC, but the delimited zone of the DOC of 1967 followed to a substantial extent the territory first delimited by Cosimo III, with an extension of the zone to the west of the confluence of the Sieve and Arno rivers. This happens to be one case where the often contentious measure of enlarging the production zone was based on sound principles.

The soil of Rufina is remarkably similar to the clay and limestone marls of Panzano in Chianti; the vineyards, protected by a series of low mountains to the north, benefit from a warm, dry MESOCLIMATE. The vineyards are at a lower altitude than those of Classico, between 150 and 300m, but a pass in the Apennines to the north helps make this one of Toscana's finest wine-producing zones. Through this pass flows a cool maritime breeze that makes this zone much cooler than the Val d'Arno, which is only a few kilometers to the south. This moderating influence ensures an attractive aromatic character in the wines, and great longevity.

The Chianti produced here has always enjoyed an excellent reputation and has been cited for its superior qualities by Lapo Ricci, Cosimo Ridolfi, A. Bizzari, A. Brutini, and other authorities; Fernando Paoletti, in 1744, remarked upon the wine's outstanding longevity. Production levels have remained low, aided by an important proportion of old vineyards, with average YIELDS of little over 32 hl/ha

(1.8 tons/acre) from the 745 ha/1,860 acres of vineyards now classified DOCG.

Despite these advantages, the wines experienced the generalized obscurity attendant on all Chianti with the exception of Chianti Classico until the 1990s. Since then, however, prices have risen, but remain modest when judged against Chianti Classico estates. This increase in prices has led to a renewed interest in producing what can now be a remunerative wine, so vineyard area increased by about 50 per cent between the mid 1990s and mid 2000s. Frescobaldi is the largest producer in the zone, with close to 20 per cent of the vineyards, while Selvapiana has historically been one of the best.

D.T. & D.C.G.

Chiavennasca, synonym for the noble NEBBIOLO vine and grape in VALTELLINA.

Chignin, named CRU near Chambéry whose name can be added to the eastern French appellation Vin de SAVOIE. Most Chignin is a scented dry white made from the local JACQUÈRE grape variety. Technically a separate CRU, the rich, but dry **Chignin Bergeron** is made from the superior white ROUSSANNE grape, Bergeron being a local name for it.

Chile, long, exceptionally narrow country down the south west coast of SOUTH AMERICA that has become one of the world's prime resources of keenly priced VARIETAL wine. The Spanish conquistadores were responsible for the introduction of the wine-producing vine, *Vitis* VINIFERA, to Chile in the mid 16th century (see SOUTH AMERICA, history), but France was to have a greater influence on shaping the Chilean wine industry. The country is most famous viticulturally for being free of PHYLLOXERA, which frees vine-growers from the cost of GRAFTING young vines on to resistant ROOTSTOCKS. Chile's dry summers tend to yield exceptionally healthy fruit. In the 1990s, the wines exported from Chile were almost exclusively varietal, with a preponderance of fruitily uncomplicated CABERNET SAUVIGNON but new wine-making techniques and improvements in the vineyard have significantly broadened the range.

Chile's wine production fell considerably during the 1980s but while in 1991 2.3 million hl/60 million gal of wine were produced, that had risen to about 6 million hl/158 million gal by 2004. Chile produces about half as much wine as the vineyards of Argentina just over the Andes.

History

The *vinifera* vine, and deliberate cultivation of it for wine, was brought to the Americas by the Spanish (see SOUTH AMERICA, history). Cortés imported vine cuttings, or more probably seeds, directly from Spain to Mexico where the first successful American vintage

was produced, but it is not clear whether the vines first cultivated in the mid 16th century at Cuzco in PERU, the progenitors of the Chilean wine industry, came from Mexico or directly from Spain or Portugal. It is generally agreed, however, that Spanish settlers brought the vine to Chile some time in the 1550s, the vine probably arriving in the Central Valley with Juan Jufre et Diego Garcia de Cáceres in 1554. This was partly so that the early Spanish settlers could celebrate the EUCHARIST with its produce. Specific grape varieties mentioned by the Jesuit priest Alonso Ovalle include Muscatel, Torontel, Albilho, Mollar, and 'the common black grape' (presumably related to the PAIS).

Some early vineyards were ransacked by native Indians, notably in the far south of the country, but the capital Santiago has been associated with continuous wine production for more than four centuries. In the 17th century, Spain attempted to protect its export trade of wine to South America by banning new plantings of vineyards there, but with little success. Indeed in 1678, the Chilean governor recommended that not only should this ban be lifted but vineyards should be actively encouraged so that more farms, or haciendas, would be established. In the 18th century, Chile was known for the quantity and cheapness of wine it produced, much to the dismay of some Spanish wine producers.

The vine varieties grown and wine-making techniques of the early 19th century were well documented and fairly primitive by modern standards, the wines commonly being sweetened with boiled, concentrated must, for example. It was Chile's great good fortune that an energetic Frenchman, Claudio Gay, persuaded the Chilean government to set up the Quinta Normal, an experimental nursery for all manner of exotic botanical specimens, including European vines, as early as 1830. This meant that Chile had its own collection of *vinifera* cuttings safely banked in viticultural isolation before the onset of the world's late 19th-century vineyard scourges of POWDERY MILDEW and phylloxera, although it was private enterprise which, as so often, provided the spur to the nation's wine industry.

Now independent of Spanish domination, rich Chileans began to travel and experience a wider world, which included the fine wines of Europe, markedly different from the rustic produce of Pais and Moscatel grapes. One of these was Silvestre Ochagavía Echazarreta, who in 1851 personally imported, along with a French winemaker, a range of those vine varieties regarded today as the most classic and internationally respected. These cuttings were to form the basis of Chile's modern wine industry. A class of gentlemen farmers was emerging in Chile, some of whom had made their fortunes as a result of Chile's rich mineral deposits. Owning a vine-growing country estate on the fertile land outside Santiago, preferably

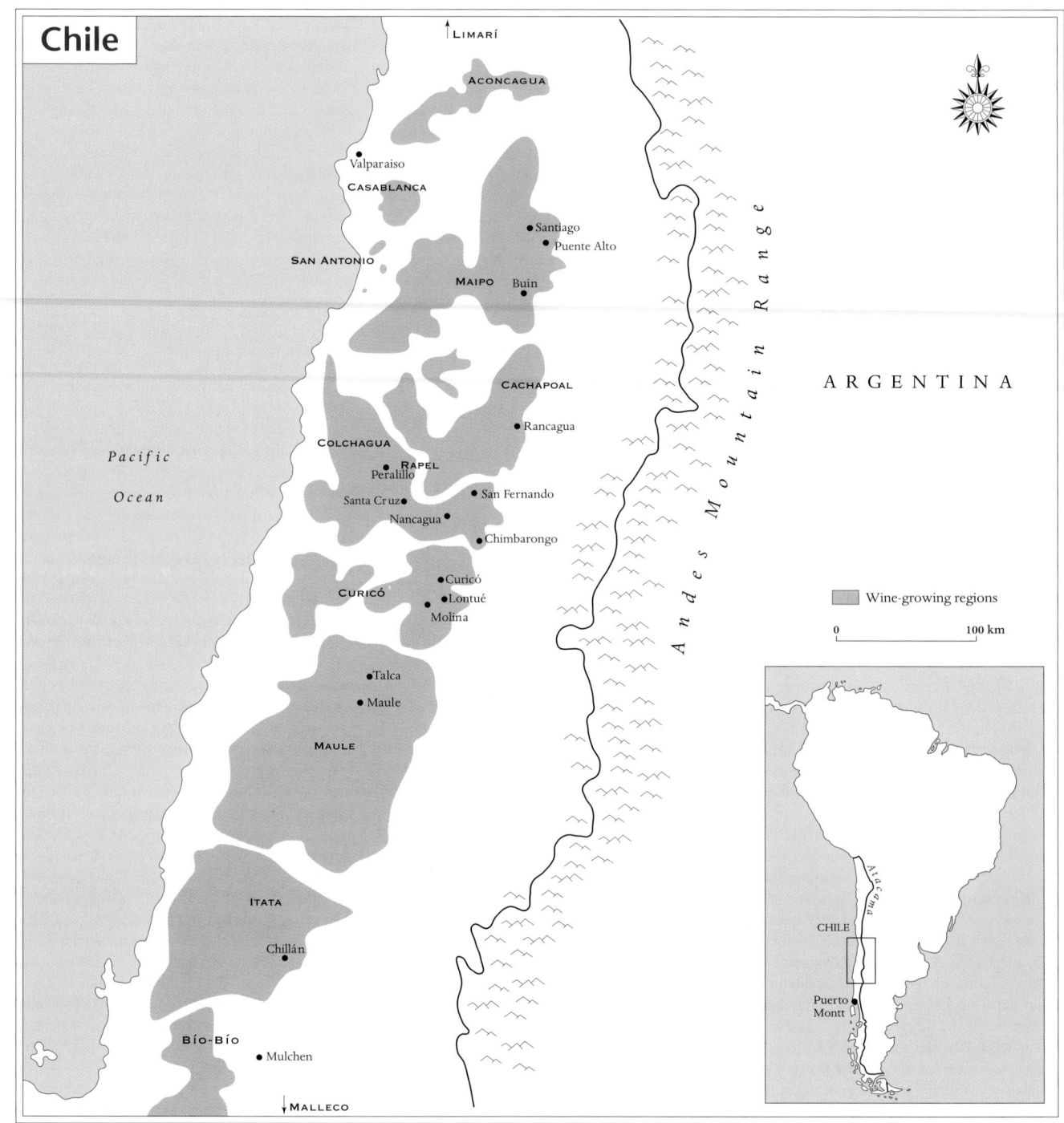

Chile

LIMARÍ

ACONCAGUA

Valparaiso

CASABLANCA

Santiago
Puente Alto

SAN ANTONIO

MAIPO Buin

Andes Mountain Range

ARGENTINA

CACHAPOAL

Rancagua

*Pacific
Ocean*

COLCHAGUA

RAPEL
Peralillo
Santa Cruz   San Fernando
Nancagua
Chimbarongo

Curicó
Lontué
Molina

CURICÓ

Talca
Maule

MAULE

Wine-growing regions

0   100 km

ITATA

Chillán

CHILE

BÍO-BÍO

Puerto
Montt

Mulchen

MALLECO

run by one of the many French refugees from phylloxera, was a sign of success in 19ᵗʰ-century Chile.

It was not long before Chile could boast the world's only healthy wine industry, both viticulturally and financially, run effectively by ten rich families (several of them of Basque origin) and their descendants. As almost every other wine-producing country succumbed to the successive ravages of mildew and phylloxera, the Chilean wine industry enjoyed the rudest of health. The industry, still (as today) substantially in private hands, was so profitable, and per capita wine consumption so high, that it was increasingly energetically taxed and constricted as the 20ᵗʰ century wore on.

Domestic demand for Chile's basic wines declined, and wine prices plummeted in the 1970s and early 1980s. About half of Chile's vineyards were pulled up, some of them in quite suitable locations. The unsettled nature of Chile's politics and economics provided a natural brake on the progress of this unique industry, until the successful establishment of free market policies and the return of democracy in the 1980s stimulated growth in this potentially important aspect of the Chilean economy. Between 1987 and 1993, more than 10,000 ha/25,000 acres of vineyard were planted with INTERNATIONAL VARIETIES, significant investments were made in new winemaking technology, and the focus of the wine industry switched completely from quantity for the domestic market to quality for export markets.

Geography and climate

With its 5,000 km/3,000 miles of coastline to the west, the Andes at heights of up to 7,000 m/23,000 ft to the east, extensive desert to the north, and Antarctic region in the south, Chile is unusually isolated, and this has undoubtedly played a major part in keeping phylloxera at bay.

The healthy fruit-growing climate of Chile, and ready access to ports (cf. Argentina), make the country an important exporter of TABLE GRAPES, with 52,685 ha /130,187 acres of vineyard dedicated to them, although by the early 21st century more than 110,000 ha were dedicated to wine production. In general it is the hotter, more northerly vineyards that produce table grapes. The two northernmost regions, Atacama and, especially, Coquimbo, produce far more table grapes than wine, and they also specialize in the production of Chile's own controlled appellation grapey spirit pisco, to which nearly 10,000 ha of vineyards were dedicated in the early 2000s.

The great majority of Chilean wine is produced between the latitudes of 32 and 38 degrees. A northern hemisphere counterpart of these latitudes might be North Africa and southern Spain, but in Chile temperatures are considerably mitigated by the influence of the Pacific and its cold Humboldt current. Chilean wine producers describe their climate as somewhere between that of California's NAPA valley and that of Bordeaux.

Although the coastal areas of Casablanca and San Antonio are being energetically developed, most of Chile's wine has traditionally come from the Central valley, a 1,000-km-long plateau which reaches as far south as Puerto Montt. The Central valley is separated from the Pacific ocean to the west by a relatively low coastal range whose peaks reach 300 to 800 m (1,000–2,600 ft) and is separated from the Argentine Mendoza wine region to the east by the Andes, which can reach altitudes of 6,000 m here. Vines will grow up to an ALTITUDE of 600 m on the western slopes of the Central valley, and 1,000 m on the sunnier eastern slopes of the valley on the foothills of the Andes. This Central valley is dissected by rivers which, during the growing season, carry torrents of melted snow from the Andes to the Pacific: IRRIGATION made easy.

Although there are distinct variations between individual regions and even subregions (see Maipo, Rapel, Maule), the climate in the Central valley is generally MEDITERRANEAN, with warm, dry summers, and rainfall, averaging between 300 and 800 mm (12–31 in) a year, restricted to the winter, thanks to the effect of the Pacific high-pressure area. Rainfall in the Central valley tends to increase both in the south and east, on the slopes of the Andes. On the western edge of the valley, summer temperatures average 15 to 18 °C (59–64 °F) and may rise to 30 °C/86 °F, with clear skies, strong sunlight, and relatively low humidity of just 55 to 60 per cent. On the eastern edge of the valley, however, under the influence of cold air drainage from the Andes at night, there is much greater TEMPERATURE VARIABILITY resulting in particularly good levels of ACIDITY and COLOUR in the ripe grapes.

Southern regions such as Bío-Bío and Malleco are also being developed for serious wine production. In carefully selected sites in places such as Mulchén and Traiguén, vines can yield good white wines, although frost and excessive rain may prejudice quality south of Temuco.

Regions and soils

The great bulk of Chile's wine is grown in the southern wine regions. Some wine is produced in the cooler, Pacific-influenced vineyards of the northerly Coquimbo region, which is in general so hot and dry that it is a much more important producer of table grapes and pisco. From north to south the main wine regions, with their most significant subregions, are (see map):

Coquimbo: Elqui, Limarí
Aconcagua: Aconcagua, Casablanca, San Antonio (including Leyda)
Central Valley: Maipo (including Santiago, Talagante, Pirque, Puente Alto, Isla de Maipo, Buin), Rapel (including Cachapoal, Colchagua), Curicó (including Teno, Lontué), Maule (including Talca, San Clemente, San Javier, Parral, Linares, Cauquenes)
Southern region: Itata, Bío-Bío, Malleco

In general, Chile's vineyards are planted on flat, fertile land where water is readily available either naturally or through irrigation, so that vine root systems are relatively shallow. Alluvial soils predominate in Aconcagua and are also present to the south in Maipo, although here there are loams and occasionally clay soils too. In both the Maipo region and the Cachapoal district of northern Rapel, there are mixtures of loam, clay, and sand, some of which may be subject to EROSION on slopes. Some TUFFEAU soils are found in southern Rapel and in Maule, while volcanic soils extend from south of Curicó to the Bío-Bío region, interrupted only by sand and sandy loam around Linares. Some parts of Cachapoal, Colchagua, and the Southern region suffer from relatively poor drainage, can be quite swampy, and may need no irrigation.

Coquimbo Chile's newest wine region is a good 600 km north of Santiago. Historically focused on table grapes and pisco, Viña Francisco de Aguirre started to produce exciting table wines only in the mid 1990s in the Limarí Valley, 20 km from the Pacific coast where the likes of Tamaya and Tabalí established themselves by the early 2000s. The cooling ocean influence plays an important part in delaying ripening in the Limarí and Elqui Valleys. Dry weather (annual RAINFALL only 100 mm) and clear skies allow healthy fruit-growing conditions.

Aconcagua Named after the river which bisects it, Aconcagua is made up of two very distinct zones. The interior of Aconcagua is one of Chile's hottest, driest wine regions. In the summer, clouds are rarely seen, and temperatures are often above 30 °C/86 °F. Soils are mainly alluvial and the region produces some good red wines. Errázuriz and von Siebenthal are two of the few important wine exporters to have their base in this region, at Panquehue in the much gentler intermediate region, cooled by coastal breezes. Towards the coast is San Antonio, a glamorous new subregion, with Leyda once considered a zone within it, where wineries such as Matetic, Casa Marín, Leyda, and Garcés Silva take advantage of the pronounced Pacific influence to create particularly fresh Sauvignon Blanc and some of the country's best Pinot Noir.

Casablanca One of the coolest and newest wine regions in Chile, on the coast close to Valparaiso. Officially part of the Aconcagua region, it is quite different from the vineyards to the north. Casablanca's vineyards are cooled to WINKLER Region I by cool morning fogs, the result of the Pacific's icy Humboldt current (which has a similar effect thousands of miles up the coast in CARNEROS in California). Frequent cloud slows ripening and reduces the average number of clear days per year to 180, as opposed to between 240 and 300 in the interior (mirroring the climatic contrast between Carneros and California's SAN JOAQUIN VALLEY). The first vines were planted in the cool Casablanca Valley in 1982 but by 2003 there were over 5,000 ha/12,350 acres of vines, thanks to extensive plantings, mainly of Sauvignon Blanc and Chardonnay vines, by both wine producers (notably Concha y Toro, Santa Rita, and Veramonte) and specialist grape growers. Spring FROSTS are a real hazard here.

Maipo The most famous wine region in Chile just south of the capital Santiago is not one of the largest. About 10,500 ha/30,000 acres of vines were recorded in 2003, with a clear predominance of red over white grapes, Cabernet Sauvignon and Chardonnay being the most widely planted according to official 2003 statistics, although Merlot, Carmenère, and Sauvignon Blanc are also important. Annual rainfall averages just 300 mm/12 in a year, most of it falling in the winter. Irrigation is common, although the water can be quite high in salt around the Maipo river from which the region takes its name. Potassium levels tend to be low throughout the region. Official subregions are Santiago, Pirque, Puente Alto, Buin, Isla de Maipo, Talagante, Melipilla, Alhué, and María Pinto. Although this is quantitatively not one of the most important wine regions in Chile, it is one often named on export labels, perhaps because, being closest to Santiago, it houses the headquarters of so many of the major companies, and also because it is famous for producing Chile's best Cabernet Sauvignon.

Rapel Wine region in Chile which had grown to more than 31,000 ha/76,000 acres of vineyard dedicated to wine production by 2003, the majority of which grow red grapes. The region is officially divided into the subregions Cachapoal and Colchagua although significant individual zones have already been identified within them. Apalta within Colchagua, for example, has a reputation for fine Merlot, Carmenère, and Syrah won, to a large extent by the French-owned winery Casa Lapostolle and by Viña Montes. Cabernet Sauvignon and Merlot are the most planted grape varieties, and the region has a particularly good reputation for full-flavoured red wines. Los Vascos winery, in which Ch LAFITE-Rothschild has an important stake, is at Peralillo. Large wineries such as Santa Emiliana, Santa Rita, Undurraga, and the smaller Viña Montes operation all made considerable vineyard investments in Colchagua in the 1990s.

Curicó Formed by the subregions Lontué and Teno, Curicó Valley was put on the international map when Miguel TORRES arrived there in 1979. According to 2003 statistics, the valley has 17,000 ha/42,000 acres planted, the most popular grapes being Cabernet Sauvignon with more than 6,000 ha and Sauvignon Blanc with 3,364 ha. Curicó has basically two different mesoclimates. Towards the east, around Molina and north of the Claro river, the climate is cooler thanks to the breezes from the Andes. To the west, the Coastal range minimizes the ocean influence and the climate is warmer, sometimes notably hot and dry. Even though the valley does not have any particular speciality such as Cabernet Sauvignon in Maipo or Sauvignon Blanc in Casablanca, the wide range of varieties planted reach a good general level of quality. The most recognized Curicó wineries, apart from Torres, are San Pedro, Valdivieso, Aresti, and Los Robles co-operative.

Maule Important wine region in Chile which includes the subregions of Talca, San Clemente, San Javier, Parral, Linares, and Cauquenes. According to official 2003 records, there were 30,250 ha/74,7200 acres of wine vines (hardly more than in 1997, unlike most other regions). Well to the south of Santiago, this is one of Chile's cooler and cloudier regions, thanks to the Pacific influence, although it is hotter and drier than Bío-Bío to the south. The rustic PAIS vine variety used to dominate plantings, especially in the rain-fed areas, but Cabernet Sauvignon has overtaken it to become the most planted variety. Vineyards in the rain-fed western areas often suffer from serious deficiencies of nutrients, especially NITROGEN and to a lesser extent potassium.

Thanks to new investment and viticultural practices, Maule is slowly changing its reputation of growing only bulk wine.

Southern region The vineyards of southern Chile totalled 13,800 ha/34,100 acres of vineyards split quite evenly between red and white grapes according to 2003 official statistics. Formed by Itata, Bío-Bío and the new Malleco subregion, this region is more open than Maipo and Rapel to the west, lacking the protection of a high coastal range, so that rainfall is higher and average temperature and sunshine hours are lower. By far the most planted vine variety is the humble PAIS, although Moscatel Alejandria (MUSCAT OF ALEXANDRIA) is also widely grown for basic wine to be consumed within Chile. Research in the early 1990s in the Chillán area, however, suggested that, with DRIP IRRIGATION and appropriate training systems such as the LYRE, some good-quality wine from the best-known INTERNATIONAL VARIETIES could be made here. The proof of that lies in the Mulchén and Negrete areas where wineries such as Cono Sur and Gracia are producing crisp Riesling and ripe Pinot Noir. The embryonic Malleco area showed its mettle with excellent Chardonnay made by French winery Aquitania.

Viticulture

IRRIGATION is essential in nearly half of all Chilean vineyards and, as in Argentina, is made possible by the melting snows of the Andes, diverted along a series of canals and channels. Drip irrigation was introduced only in the early 1990s. As a result of this ready and plentiful water supply, most vineyards have good access to water during the growing season. The irrigated vineyards are mainly in the north of the Central Valley, in the interior of the Aconcagua, Maipo, Rapel, Maule, and Curicó regions. On the slopes of the coastal range in the west of southern regions, rainfall is often sufficient, as it is in most of the Southern Region. The common PAIS vine is cultivated in these rain-fed wine regions.

FERTILIZERS are generally needed, but their use is regulated to avoid an excess of VIGOUR. Drip irrigation allows FERTIGATION in some of the more viticulturally developed areas.

Average YIELDS in Chile are about 70 hl/ha (4 tons/acre). Over-irrigated, high-yielding vines can experience difficulties in RIPENING. This is particularly true of varieties which ripen relatively late, such as Cabernet Sauvignon and Chile's speciality CARMENÈRE, or of high TRAINING SYSTEMS. There is a predictably rich cultural diversity of training and trellis systems in Chile. Some vines, particularly those dedicated to table grapes, are trained in variations on the TENDONE system in the high, arbour-like *parrón* trellis which encourages shade (like the *parral* of ARGENTINA).

The standard Spanish practice of growing unstaked vines as free-standing bushes,

trained into a GOBELET shape, has been common since the Spanish conquest but is today usually restricted to the País vine, notably in the south.

The Bordeaux post-PHYLLOXERA immigrants introduced row trellising to Chile at the end of the 19th century and this has evolved in two distinct ways. Low, narrow rows of vines that are traditional in Europe tend to be double GUYOT pruned or spur cordons, depending on variety, and used mainly to produce better-quality wines. More common for basic wine production are more widely spaced vines (sometimes with crosspieces, described as Californian), which permit the increasingly common phenomenon of vineyard MECHANIZATION. In the 1990s, most new plantings have been of long narrow rows between 2 and 2.5 m (6.5–8 ft) apart, with vines planted 1.2 to 1.5 m apart. Australian CANOPY MANAGEMENT techniques were introduced in some vineyards in the early 1990s.

HARVEST of wine grapes begins at the end of February for such early-maturing varieties as Chardonnay, continues through to the end of April for Cabernet Sauvignon, and can last well into May for Carmenère.

No Chilean vine-grower feels he needs to study ROOTSTOCKS since the country is free of phylloxera and the consequent need for grafting. Some FIELD GRAFTING has been undertaken, however, in the rush to increase the proportion of fashionable grape varieties planted. And such is the prevalence of NEMATODES in Chilean vineyards, because of *vinifera*'s low resistance to them relative to American vine species, that some authorities suggest using American rootstocks to combat this problem. Chile's vines are by no means free of VIRUS DISEASES.

Chile may be famously free of phylloxera, but POWDERY MILDEW and BOTRYTIS BUNCH ROT are annual and potentially extremely costly vine diseases, with VERTICILLIUM WILT another serious vine health hazard. And DOWNY MILDEW infections occurred in some areas for the first time during the heavily EL NIÑO-influenced 1997–8 growing season. The absence of summer rains means that SPRAYING is generally much less frequent than in many other wine regions, however.

Vine varieties

VINE IDENTIFICATION is a developing science in Chile. Conscious of its unique status as a wine-producing country as yet unravaged by phylloxera, Chile imposes a particularly strict QUARANTINE on imported plant material, which has helped to maintain certain aspects of its viticultural isolation. The quality and identity of the vines grown is the most dramatic example of this.

The majority of the vines called Sauvignon by the Chileans, for example, are almost certainly Sauvignon Vert, Sauvignonasse (or TOCAI Friulano) and occasionally Sauvignon

Gris, rather than the more familiar Sauvignon Blanc. Only a small but increasing proportion of Sauvignon Blanc, almost exclusively based on CLONES developed in California, had been planted by the early 1990s and even by the mid 2000s official statistics claiming 7,400 ha/18,300 acres of Sauvignon Blanc and just 200 ha of Sauvignon Vert probably did not reflect the true proportions of these two varieties.

Similarly, vines called Merlot are in fact a mixture, and sometimes a FIELD BLEND, of Merlot and the old Bordeaux variety CARMENÈRE, first identified as such in Chile in 1994. The vine identification required to distinguish Merlot from Carmenère is continuing and since the mid 1990s the word Carmenère has emerged on wine labels and is increasingly respected both as a varietal and, perhaps more suitably, an ingredient in a blend. Until the 1990s, the most commonly planted grape variety was the dark-skinned PAIS, found only in Chile and thought to be, like CRIOLLA CHICA of Argentina and the MISSION of California, a direct descendant of vine cuttings imported by the Spanish colonists. Official statistics recorded just under 15,000 ha/37,050 acres of Pais in 2003, more or less the same as in 1997 but half the area planted with the variety in the 1980s. The great majority is planted in the southern Maule and Bío-Bío regions.

The same survey found nearly 40,000 ha of Cabernet Sauvignon, now the most important variety by quite a margin (almost three times as much as seven years previously), almost 13,000 ha of 'Merlot' (a further 6,000 ha had already been identified as Carmenère), more than 7,500 ha of Chardonnay, almost 7,400 ha of 'Sauvignon', and just over 6,000 ha of Moscatel Alejandria (MUSCAT OF ALEXANDRIA). The early years of the century saw a dramatic increase in plantings of Syrah with almost 2,500 ha and Pinot Noir with more than 1,400 ha by 2003. In a fury of planting, at least 47,000 ha of vines went into Chile's rich soils between 1997 and 2003, with Merlot, Cabernet Sauvignon, Sauvignon Blanc, Chardonnay, Syrah, and Pinot Noir the most popular new varieties.

Such new plant material as is allowed in has come mainly from DAVIS, but European investors such as Miguel Torres, a couple from Chablis, and Ch Lafite-Rothschild are increasingly importing their own cuttings directly from Europe, under strict quarantine regulations.

Wine-making
Chile is undergoing possibly the most dramatic technological revolution in the wine world. Wineries were for decades underfunded as the domestic market could be satisfied with often oxidized white wines and faded reds made with the most traditional of equipment. All wines were made from grapes trucked,

often in very high temperatures with scant regard for OXIDATION, to wineries equipped with little in the way of temperature control, and made exclusively in vats made either of cement or the coarse local *raulí*, or evergreen beech, WOOD, usually coopered many decades previously. In the late 1980s, however, the wine industry made a commitment to the long-term future of Chile as a wine exporter and began to invest in the equipment necessary for that goal. Outside investors assisted the influx of both equipment and expertise, and since then the wineries of Chile have been invaded, at a pace usually determined by the enterprise's size and cash flow, by pneumatic PRESSES, oak BARRELS, STAINLESS STEEL, and modern filters. (One of the larger companies, Santa Rita, for example, views its purchase of 7,000 French and American oak barrels in 1988 as a milestone in its corporate history.) Often one of the most necessary improvements has been one of the technically least complicated: the provision of cool storage facilities.

Industry organization
Most of the big wine-exporting companies, many of them run by descendants of the wine dynasties of the mid 19th century, have their headquarters in Santiago or nearby in the Maipo region. Some of the biggest are Concha y Toro, Santa Rita, and San Pedro. Many own several wineries and many different vineyards, although it is also the norm to buy grapes from a wide range of growers. Estate wineries such as the historic Cousiño Macul, Los Vascos, Montes, Portal del Alto, and Santa Monica, for which practically all grapes used are grown by the owner/winemakers, are increasing in number. Foreign investment has come from California (MONDAVI), France (Chx Mouton- and Lafite-ROTHSCHILD and many others), Spain (TORRES), presumably attracted by the relatively low cost of land, vineyard establishment, and running costs in Chile, although this is offset by the need to import all sophisticated equipment and cooperage. In the mid 1990s, however, some of the larger Chilean wine companies invested in Argentina, tempted by lower land costs across the Andes.

Wine styles
Wines exported from Chile are, typically, extremely fruity and clean but did not until the early 1990s display the structure which can be imposed only by low yields and/or BARREL MATURATION. Yields are still relatively high, although there are some plots of very old vines which produce concentrated wine. Cabernet Sauvignon, Merlot-Carmenère, and Cabernet blends dominate Chile's red wine exports and can provide extremely good-value wines for drinking within two or three years, although an increasing proportion of wine capable of BOTTLE AGEING has been produced.

The new generation of white wines has been clean and well made rather than strongly char-

acteristic of any particular variety, although this was evolving dramatically in the early 1990s and it is now possible to find well-defined Chardonnay and Sauvignon Blanc, especially from cooler areas such as Casablanca and San Antonio. Pink and sweet wines are certainly made (Concha y Toro make a late harvest 'Sauterne'), and Alberto Valdivieso was the first to make sparkling wines using TRADITIONAL METHOD techniques, as early as 1879.

Table grapes may be vinified and sold as wine in Chile and the grape varieties Sultana and Ribier, or Alphonse Lavallé, are most commonly used for this purpose. Most of this wine is sold locally, or is exported in bulk. Wine made from a table grape variety sold locally should be labelled as such.

Although Chile is indubitably the Bordeaux of the southern hemisphere, for long it lacked a wine style to call its own but has now firmly dragooned Carmenère to be its answer to Argentina's Malbec, or Uruguay's Tannat.

J.R. & P.T.

Duijker, H., *Wines of Chile* (Utrecht, 2000).
Fielden, C., *The Wines of Argentina, Chile and Latin America* (London, 2003).
Tapia, P., *The Wines Of Colchagua Valley* (Santiago, 2001).
Waldin, M., *Wines of South America* (London, 2003).
www.winesofchile.org

China, vast Asian country with its own indigenous vine species (see VITIS) but a relatively short modern tradition of growing VINIFERA grapes to make wine. In a remarkably short time, however, it has emerged as a new global wine force, with the world's fifth largest vineyard area and seventh largest wine production level in 2004 according to the OIV. Consumption doubled between 1999 and 2004, and is overwhelmingly (more than 90 per cent) satisfied by domestic production.

Ancient China
Chinese literary accounts of the introduction of grapes to China have a strong legendary element, but it seems that grape seeds were brought back from Ferghana in modern UZBEKISTAN by General Chang Chien during the Han dynasty between 136 and 121 BC and planted in Xinjiang and Shaanxi (Xian). In the 2nd century AD, grape wine imported from the west was highly prized. It is possible that wine was made from grapes in China before the Tang Dynasty (AD 618–907), although the industry seems not to have been highly developed. But by the beginning of the Tang era it is well established that the Chinese were importing quantities of wine from the area of Tashkent in modern Uzbekistan. This central Asian wine was claimed to be drinkable for up to ten years. After the Chinese conquest of Turfan on the Chinese side of the Sino-Russian frontier in 640, Snake and Dragon Pearl and Mare's Teat (the former red and also known as Cabernet Gernischet, the latter a white table grape variety known as Maru in

Chinese) were imported and successfully cultivated in China. Thereafter viticulture prospered in China, especially in Gansu and Shanxi provinces in central China. Shanxi wine continued to be popular after the decline of the import trade following a break in relations with central Asia. It was not long before wine was being made also from a small native grape (*Vitis thunbergii*) which grows wild in Shandong province, north of Shanghai.

In earlier periods, two alcoholic beverages, *jiu* and *li*, were made from rice or wheat. Labelled wine jars indicate that 'wine' could be made from millet or other grains as well. Strictly speaking, however, these beverages are beers (brewed from cereals) rather than wines (fermented from fruits).

In the very earliest periods (pre-Han) the term used is *yin* 'drink', which includes alcoholic drink and water. In upper-class circles in the later Zhou Dynasty (12th century BC–221 BC), *yin* was drunk with meals, at which the procedures were extremely formalized. Archaeological excavations have revealed wine drinking cups made from bronze, pottery, lacquered wood, and bottle-gourds, and wine containers of bronze, pottery, and wood.   J.A.B.

Modern history

Viticulture continued in China (JULLIEN classified the wines of what he called Chinese Tartary). In 1892, Zhang Bishi, an officer in the Qing government, returned to China and established the Chang Yu winery in Yantai. He introduced 150 *vinifera* vine varieties from Europe, including Welschriesling, and apparently employed the then Austrian consul as his winemaker. Qingdao (formerly rendered as Tsingtao), the other winery established by Germans at that time, was first known as the Melco winery. Shang Yi winery (today's Beijing winery) was set up by French Catholics, and Tung Hua (Tonghua) winery at Jilin was managed by the Japanese. The wines produced by them were made mainly to cater for the foreign communities in China.

In 1949, the wineries were expanded by the government and, for reasons of economy, they generally blended grape wine with other juices, water, colouring, and fermented cereals. Because of this, the term 'wine' was until recently widely misunderstood in China. The relevant Chinese character 'jiu' literally means alcohol in any form, so it was difficult to distinguish wine from beer or spirits. Today's consumers take the trouble to specify grape wine (*putaojiu*).

Geography and climate

Most of China's 450,000 ha/1.1 million acres of vineyards are spread across provinces north of the Yangtze river, from the Xinjiang Uygur autonomous region in the extreme north west (where 18 per cent of vines are planted) to the coastal regions of Hebei (13 per cent), Shandong (12 per cent), Henan (5 per cent), and

Tianjin (2 per cent), and Liaoning (10 per cent) and Jilin (2 per cent) in the north east. Owing to the general lack of exposure to western wine culture and extreme continental conditions inland, production in all regions is still largely concentrated on TABLE GRAPES and DRYING GRAPES. China's 450 'alcohol manufacturing factories' (the literal translation of the word for winery) vinify only about one-sixth of the total grape harvest (an estimated 500,000 tons of grapes for wine from a total yield of around three million tons of grapes in 2005).

Temperatures in the coastal provinces of Shandong, Hebei, and Tianjin, which lie on the same latitude as California, are generally amenable to wine production. Cool Pacific breezes moderate humidity levels and temperatures range from 3 °C/37 °F in winter to 26 °C/79 °F in summer. Monsoons and typhoons which sweep in from the South China sea can prove hazardous, although monsoon winds rapidly aerate vines. Springs are generally dry, but summers and autumns can be muggy and wet, promoting FUNGAL DISEASES and ROT. Chinese peasants learnt, probably from the Soviet Union in the early 1950s, to establish their vineyards on flat land with fertile soil and to encourage high yields. Overcropping, poor drainage and ventilation on vineyards vulnerable to typhoons resulted in poor-quality fruit and therefore poor-quality wines.

A more suitable climate for advanced viticulture, with cooler inland temperatures, is in the centre of the Shandong peninsula at Pingdu. Here China's easterly range of mountains, the Dazashen, have south east-and south west-facing slopes with decomposed granite overlying limestone, low in nutrients, with free-draining soils.

In Xinjiang on tableland around the provincial capital Urumqi and the new industrial centre of Shiheze, where there has been most expansion since the late 1990s, natural rainfall is low but the vineyards tap the huge alpine water resource from the perennially snow-capped Tien Shan (Heavenly Mountains) range, through natural river systems and man-made canals. The soils are sandy loam over granite rock substructures. The region is relatively disease free and requires only minimal SPRAYING but, like most wine regions in China's interior, needs WINTER PROTECTION. For the moment there is no shortage of LABOUR.

Wineries

Jesuit MISSIONARIES are believed to have been the first to encourage the planting of vineyards here in the mid 19th century specifically to make wine. During the German and Japanese occupation of northern China at the turn of the century, the first two wineries at Yantai and Qingdao were established. However, still and sparkling wine production in the five largest state wineries—Qingdao, Yantai Chang Yu, Henan Min Chuan, Beijing Eastern Rural, and Jilin Tung Hua—remained very unsophisticated until 1978 when China opened again to the outside world.

After 1979, several moves were made to allow foreign investors to install a modern wine industry in north east China. In May 1980, Cognac giant RÉMY MARTIN set up the first joint venture winery, Sino-French Joint Venture Winery (Dynasty), with the Tianjin Agriculture Bureau. The Great Wall winery was also established in 1982 at Shacheng in Hebei Province by the monopolistic China National Cereals, Oils, Foodstuffs Import & Export Corporation with some technical assistance from the North American distiller Seagram. Both wineries applied modern wine-making techniques but produced relatively simple table wines from Dragon's Eye (Longyan) and other local table grapes. The Huadong (East China) winery, China's first 'château-style' wine estate to plant and produce VARIETAL and vintage-dated wines with an APPELLATION, Tsingtao, on the label, was established at Qingdao in 1985 and run by a British wine merchant from Hong Kong until 1990 when it was acquired and run by the multinational Allied Domecq, who abandoned it in 1999, since which time it has turned to mass production of inexpensive wine. Another multinational, PERNOD RICARD, set up the Beijing Friendship (Dragon Seal) winery in 1987 and an Italian venture set up the Marco Polo winery at Yantai in 1990. Other JOINT VENTURE wineries included Summer Palace, in which American distiller Seagram was involved. All ventures relied on imported advanced vinification equipment, European *vinifera* vine cuttings, and foreign OENOLOGISTS to produce the first 'western style' grape wines in China. State wineries followed their lead, among them, Chang Yu and Qingdao in Shandong.

In the mid and late 1990s, the Chinese government repeatedly encouraged the replacement of cereal-based spirits with fruit-based wines, motivated both by HEALTH concerns and by an acute grain shortage. Official recommendation of red wine as reducing the risk of cardiovascular disease sparked a wine boom throughout China. Thousands of cases of red wine from Europe were shipped in and rushed on to the market. Millions of litres of wine were shipped in BULK for local bottling. Distillers of traditional *baijiu* (white spirits) adapted their plants to make or bottle wines. Small wineries and bottling plants mushroomed all over China: more than 100 new wineries opened between 1996 and 2004.

By the mid 2000s, a number of large wine companies had established showcases with CHATEAU-style wineries surrounded by vineyard and offering some TOURISM facilities. Examples included the high quality Grace Vineyard of Shanxi province and in Hebei province Bodega Langes, a boutique winery

Mastroberardino, the most famous family wine company in the Campania region in the hinterland of Naples, have clearly mastered the art of decorating a barrel cellar.

and COOPERAGE owned by the Austrian owner of Norton in Mendoza, Argentina.

The traditional vineyard area of the burgeoning north west once centred on the Turpan Depression oases, which can be 154 m/500 ft below sea level. Production had been almost entirely devoted to raisin and table grapes with only a small proportion of Sultanine being made into unappetizingly sweet OXIDIZED dessert wines by Xinjiang's five state wineries, without any means of TEMPERATURE CONTROL. Xingjiang's first western-style winery, Lou Lan, was established there in the 1970s with a French winemaker and had made some promising Cabernet Sauvignon. The big move forward, however, came with the launch of the huge ViniSuntime wine venture in 1996. Suntime now rivals the traditional industry leaders in China—Chang Yu (its Chinese holding much diluted in the mid 2000s), CofCo Great Wall, and Dynasty—in terms of grape throughput with its 10,000 hectares of vines and several wineries.

Another new venture in Xinjiang is the Yanqi Xiangdu Winery, a Sino-French joint venture that launched its first wines in 2004 under the Champs d'Or label. Other big new wine ventures in the north west include the Xi Xia and Yuquan wineries in Ningxia Province and the Mogao winery in Gansu Province.

Grape varieties

China's wine boom has prompted considerable developments in viticulture. Thousands of native grape varieties exist in northern China, many from wild species (see VITIS), as breeding is a preoccupation of Chinese research institutions. The most widely planted table grapes, generally used for low-quality sweet table wines, are the cold-resistant Beichun (a HYBRID of V amurensis); high-yielding white Long Yan (Dragon's Eye); and Ju Feng Noir, also known as Jifeng (a hybrid of Japanese Koho and Jixiang developed by the Dalian Institute in 1973).

There are widespread plantings, typically introduced from Russia, of MUSCAT HAMBURG and RKATSITELI. Alongside large acreages of Italian Riesling (see WELSCHRIESLING), these varieties formed the initial backbone of China's modern wine industry. In the 1980s, classic European varieties were introduced by foreign investors and by 2005, plantings of vinifera vines specifically for 'western-style' wine-making had reached around 47,000 ha/116,000 acres. Red varieties dominate and, of these, Cabernet Sauvignon accounts for about 40 per cent, with Merlot and Cabernet Franc about 10 per cent each. Of the white varieties, Riesling (principally Welschriesling but also some true RIESLING) still dominates, accounting for around 40 per cent, although Chardonnay is increasingly popular, with 20 per cent. China's first vine NURSERY was established in the north of the Shandong peninsula in the early 2000s as a joint venture

with a French nursery by a subsidiary of CofCo, producers of Great Wall.

Viticulture

Until recently, vineyard development and grape supply were major problems for the wine industry. The grapes, supplied on contract through collective agencies, are grown on intensively subdivided lands. Individual farmers may work less than an acre each and are entitled to choose their own crop, often preferring less viticulturally risky table grapes. China's parallel systems of planned and market-driven economy and deep-rooted peasant traditions clearly hindered modernization. The traditional fan trellis system, dense foliage, excessive YIELDS, heavy summer IRRIGATION, peanut COVER CROPS, early picking to avoid ROT, and grape prices determined by weight alone are typical. Many vineyards planted in low-lying valleys alongside rice fields have high water-tables and a high risk of FLOODING.

The majority of the traditional vines are ungrafted, with no widespread PHYLLOXERA problem encountered to date. The strong summer rains, humidity levels over 85 per cent, and typically dense CANOPY encourage many vine diseases. ANTHRACNOSE, POWDERY MILDEW, DOWNY MILDEW, DEAD ARM, and WHITE ROT are commonplace, controlled by modern fungicides when available. Bitter rot (Greeneria uvicola) is also a major problem, as a low level of infection affects the wine. Viticulturists still find it difficult to impose a proper SPRAYING programme on farmers, and winemakers find it difficult to impose the right dates for HARVEST. With more and more wineries competing for grapes, and generally insufficient rewards to growers for waiting until full RIPENESS, grapes tend to arrive early and all at the same time, necessitating investment in extra PRESS capacity at some wineries. With cheap and plentiful LABOUR, all work is done manually with very limited mechanization. The low water-holding capacity and dry spring weather necessitate irrigation, controlled manually with pump and hose.

But the most eye-catching development in recent years has been in China's north west; particularly in the Xinjiang Uygur autonomous region (which already had the largest vineyard area in China but had produced little wine from it), and also in the neighbouring Provinces of Ningxia and Gansu whose dry, inland climate is proving suitable for ORGANIC viticulture, although there is a shortage of rainfall.   R.M.B. & D.G.

Cho Lee, J., 'Hidden dragon' and 'Out of the shadows', Harpers, Sept/Oct 2005.

Chinon, significant red wine appellation in the TOURAINE district of the LOIRE (see map) in which a small amount of rosé, and an even smaller amount of white wine from Chenin Blanc grapes, is produced from an area of

about 2,100 ha/5,200 acres in 2005. The vineyards extend south of the Loire on the banks of the Vienne, not far east of the fashionable red Saumur-Champigny, another product of mainly CABERNET FRANC grapes, here often called Breton. From 2000, up to 25 per cent of Cabernet Sauvignon grapes have been allowed, in theory anyway.

The region's most famous son, the early 16th-century writer Rabelais, did much to promulgate the wines of Chinon. In modern times, it is the gastronomic writers of Paris who have done much to increase demand for Chinon, and increase the extent of the vineyards that produce it (which had fallen to a few hundred hectares in the 1950s).

Two distinct styles of Chinon are made. A fuller, long-term BOURGUEIL-like wine comes from sites on the TUFFEAU limestone slopes and plateaux, most notably the south-facing slopes of Cravant-les-Coteaux, and the plateau above Beaumont. Lighter wines are made from sand and gravel vineyards near the river (in effect the old flood plains of the Loire and Vienne), with the most elegant examples coming from the gravel beds around Panzoult. These wines are closer to St Nicolas-de-Bourgueil in style.

Chinon is quintessentially a wine of refreshment, being light to medium bodied, often extravagantly scented (lead pencils is one common tasting note), and with an appetizing combination of fruit and acidity. The wines have become markedly richer and more satisfying as growers grass over their vineyards and use higher trellises, de-budding, and deleafing to ripen grapes more successfully. The best wines can benefit from BOTTLE AGEING, but that is not the point of the wine, which keeps the Chinon market free of foreign speculation on the part of COLLECTORS. Chinon is essentially a Frenchman's wine, and it takes some local knowledge to seek out the best, often artisanal, bottlings from the likes of Philippe Alliet, Bernard Baudry, the much-improved Couly-Dutheil, Charles Joguet, and Domaine du Roncée. A high proportion of the wine is sold to merchants, whose blends vary considerably in quality.

chip budding, a popular method for the BUDDING of vines, with a long history. It is known as the yema bud in Europe and California. During the first growing season of the ROOTSTOCK, a piece is cut from its original wood and a matching chip piece with a bud is cut from a scion cutting. The chip is inserted in the stock with CAMBIUM zones matching, then wrapped tightly with budding tape (see illustration on p. 170). Chip budding, which may take place at any time of year, may also be used for TOP GRAFTING.

See also FIELD BUDDING.   B.G.C.

Chiroubles, highest of the Beaujolais crus, producing some of the lightest but most

Sunlight catches the rows of tubing designed to administer **drip irrigation** to this vineyard in Paso Robles, San Luis Obispo, California. Vineyard owners can decide exactly how much water is administered to each vine and when.

Chip budding

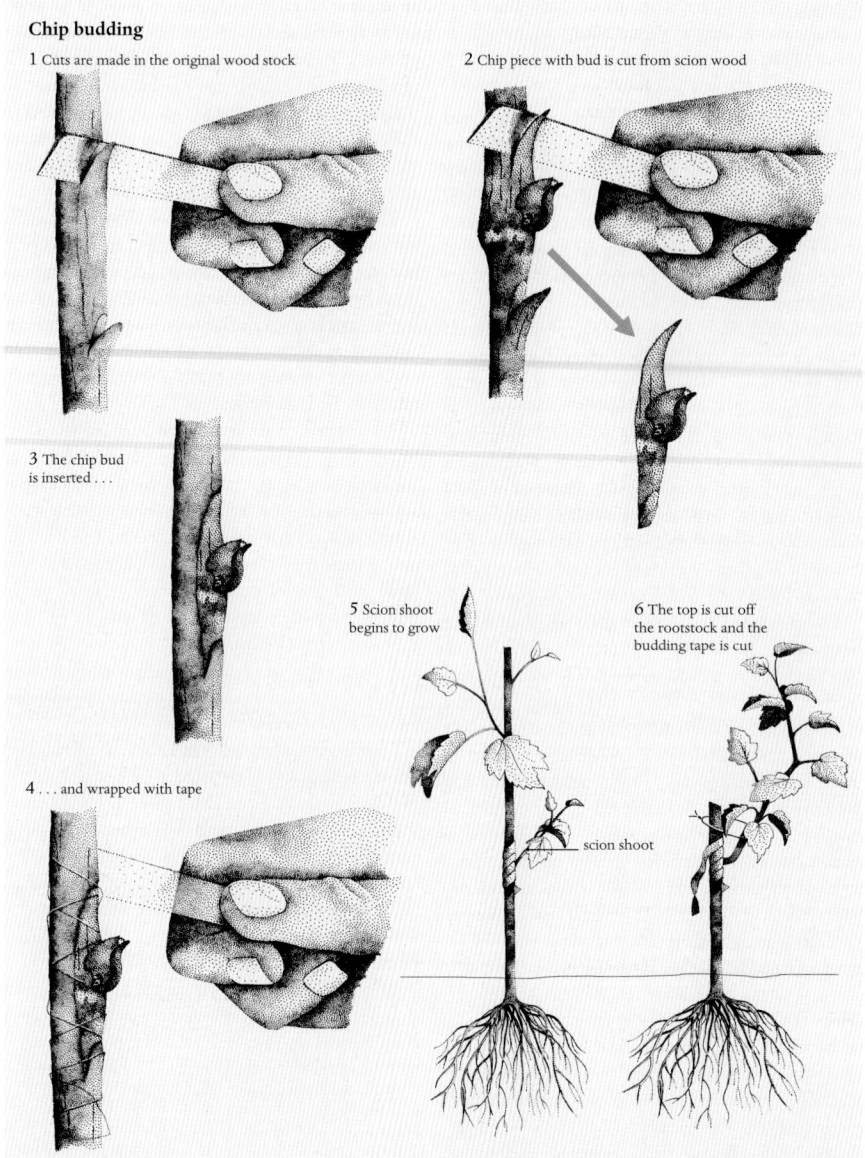

1 Cuts are made in the original wood stock

2 Chip piece with bud is cut from scion wood

3 The chip bud is inserted . . .

4 . . . and wrapped with tape

5 Scion shoot begins to grow

6 The top is cut off the rootstock and the budding tape is cut

scion shoot

---

genuinely refreshing wines. The soils are very similar to those of neighbouring FLEURIE and these wines are best drunk young. Perhaps the most archetypically Beaujolais of all the crus. There are more than 370 ha/910 acres. Domaines Cheysson and de la Rocassière are reliable. For more details, see BEAUJOLAIS.

Chitry, commune near AUXERRE whose name may be appended to that of BOURGOGNE.

chloroanisoles, group of compounds responsible, in most instances, for the musty odour of CORKED wine and one of which, TRICHLOROANISOLE, was the first identified as contributing to the problem. The formation of chloroanisoles in cork bark comes about in a stepwise process involving as the final step the methylation of chlorophenols by microorganisms. It is the earlier steps, i.e. those lead-

ing to the formation of the chlorophenols, which continue to elude understanding. It appears that the chlorophenolic precursors have multiple origins, including, among other possibilities, formation during chlorine bleaching of cork bark, the use of organochlorine biocides on cork trees in the forests, and perhaps even direct biosynthesis in cork tissue. Until the diverse origins of chlorophenols in cork bark are fully understood, the elimination of chloroanisoles, and hence their contribution to CORK TAINT, will remain a significant problem in cork production.   P.J.W.

chlorosis, vine disorder in which parts or all of the foliage turn yellow due to lack of chlorophyll. The most common and extreme chlorosis is that which is visible in spring and early summer and is caused by IRON deficiency, which is common on soils high in LIMESTONE.

Lime-induced chlorosis became a problem in parts of France as a consequence of PHYLLOXERA invasion at the end of the 19th century, since AMERICAN VINE SPECIES used as phylloxera-resistant ROOTSTOCKS were more prone to iron deficiency than were the original VINIFERA root systems. This problem, known in French as **chlorose calcaire**, has been largely overcome now by the selection of lime-tolerant rootstocks suitable for calcareous soils, such as 41 B or the newer Fercal. In Burgundy and Champagne, where soils tend to be high in limestone, it has been difficult to find rootstocks with sufficient lime tolerance for healthy vine growth. This sensitivity of early post-phylloxera rootstocks to lime-induced chlorosis may provide part of the explanation for an apparent drop in quality in post-phylloxera wines, according to some historical authorities.

Chlorosis is a common symptom of deficiencies of other nutrients such as NITROGEN, SULFUR, and MAGNESIUM. It can also be caused by some VINE DISEASES. The effect may be general, as for FANLEAF DEGENERATION virus, or more localized, as in, for example, the so-called oil spot on leaves due to DOWNY MILDEW infection.   R.E.S.

Chorey-lès-Beaune, village near (*lès* in old French) Beaune in Burgundy producing red wines from Pinot Noir grapes. Chorey lies in the plain below the main RN74 road, as do most of the appellation's vineyards. There are no vineyards of PREMIER CRU status, and much of the wine is sold as Côte de BEAUNE-Villages. Exceptional producers based here are Domaines Tollot-Beaut and Jacques Germain, which make some of the finest wines of the Beaune appellation. A good Chorey is similar to a village SAVIGNY-LÈS-BEAUNE or a lesser ALOXE-CORTON. A tiny quantity of white Chorey-lès-Beaune is made from Chardonnay.

See also CÔTE D'OR and map under BURGUNDY.   J.T.C.M.

Christianity and wine. See EUCHARIST, RELIGION, BIBLE, MONKS AND MONASTERIES, and MISSIONARIES.

Chusclan, the most famous of the Côtes du Rhône villages on the right bank of the river making fruity reds for relatively early consumption. As in nearby Tavel, its rosé is particularly appreciated.

Cienna, NEW VARIETY bred in Australia from the Spanish SUMOLL and Cabernet Sauvignon and released, with its sister variety Tyrian, in 2000. Both varieties have good sugar to acid ratios, low PH, good colour and flavour, and adequate yields. Both names were chosen after consultation with the Australian wine industry on their marketability.

Cigales, wine zone in northern Spain, north of Valladolid in CASTILLA Y LEÓN (see map under SPAIN). This DO has traditionally produced dry rosé wines made from Tinto del Pais (TEMPRANILLO) and some GARNACHA grapes, but an increasing number of dry reds show real potential and, so far, value.

R.J.M. & V. de la S.

Ciliegiolo, central Italian red grape variety of Tuscan origin named after its supposed cherry-like flavour and colour. It is declining in extent, although it can make some excellent wines, and could be a usefully soft blending partner for SANGIOVESE, particularly in CHIANTI. Unexpectedly, DNA PROFILING revealed that Ciliegiolo is one of the parents of Sangiovese. Some good VARIETAL Ciliegiolo from Umbria and Toscana, including one from the Rascioni and Cecconello estate in the MAREMMA, raised interest in the variety in the 1990s.

D.C.G. & J.V.

cincturing, viticultural practice involving removing, with a knife or special tool, a ring (3 to 8 mm (0.1–0.3 in) wide) of conducting tissue (PHLOEM) around a trunk, cane, or shoot, normally to improve FRUIT SET. Also called girdling or ringing in English and *incision annulaire* in French, the technique is more widely used for TABLE GRAPES than for wine production, which can rarely justify the necessary LABOUR cost. Cincturing stops both the upwards and downwards flow of nutrients and plant hormones, until the wound heals over.

R.E.S.

Cinsaut, sometimes written **Cinsault**, is a red grape variety known for centuries in the Languedoc region of southern France that has much in common with GRENACHE. Although it has good drought resistance and its best wines by far come from vines that yield less than 40 hl/ha (2.3 tons/acre), it can all too easily be persuaded to yield generously and unremarkably. The wines it produces tend to be lighter, softer, and, in extreme youth, more aromatic and charmingly fruity than most reds. Although prone to rot, it is particularly well adapted for rosé production and is widely planted throughout southern France, and Corsica, where it is the dominant vine variety. It differs from Grenache by virtue of its long history, its shorter growing season, and its easier adaptation to mechanical harvesting.

There was a threefold increase in French plantings in the 1970s, when Cinsaut was officially sanctioned as an 'improving' grape variety with which to replace ARAMON and ALICANTE BOUSCHET, mainly in the Aude and Hérault *départements*. Since then, the economic realities of quality's supremacy over quantity have slowed Cinsaut's fortunes and Languedoc producers have been much more likely to plant a variety with as much character and cachet as Syrah, Merlot, Mourvèdre, or Cabernet Sauvignon. Cinsaut is used almost exclusively to add suppleness, perfume, and immediate fruit to blends (typically of the ubiquitous but curmudgeonly Carignan), although all-Cinsaut rosés are increasingly common.

It is an approved but hardly venerated ingredient in the CHÂTEAUNEUF-DU-PAPE cocktail and is often found further east in Provence, as well as in the north of Corsica, where it has been widely pulled up in favour of more profitable crops.

Total French plantings of Cinsaut fell throughout the 1980s to less than 50,000 ha/123,500 acres (still more vineyard than Cabernet Sauvignon). The variety was most important in the 1950s and early 1960s when ALGERIA, then constitutionally part of France, was an important wine producer and depended particularly heavily on its healthily productive 60,000 ha of Cinsaut. Since Algerian wine was then used primarily for blending in France, notoriously for adding body to less reputable burgundies, some of this North African Cinsaut may still be found in a few older bottles of 'burgundy'. It is still the most extensively cultivated variety in MOROCCO and has long played an important part in the wine industry of the LEBANON, where it has formed the backbone of the wine industry for 150 years. In 2005, it still made up 40 per cent of Lebanese wine grapes but was in decline.

Cinsaut has in its time played a major part in South as well as North Africa (which makes it all the stranger that South Africa has had little ROSÉ culture). Having been imported from southern France in the mid 19th century, it was South Africa's most important red wine vine until the mid 1960s and was overtaken by Cabernet Sauvignon as the Cape's most planted red grape variety only in 1993. In 2004, it was South Africa's fifth most planted red wine grape with 3,000 ha in total. Cinsaut was once known carelessly as Hermitage in South Africa (although there is no Cinsaut in the northern Rhône). Thus South Africa's own grape variety speciality, a crossing of Pinot Noir with Cinsaut, was named PINOTAGE, now a much more respected South African vine variety than Cinsaut.

In both France and Australia (where its fortunes waned rapidly in the 1970s and 1980s), Cinsaut has occasionally been sold as a table grape under the name Œillade. In southern Italy, it is probably the same as the Ottavianello, planted around Brindisi and producing light, unremarkable red wines. Cinsaut can also be found in various corners of eastern Europe.

Cirò, the only DOC of any quantitative significance in the southern Italian region of CALABRIA.

citric acid, a common plant acid, abundant in some fleshy fruits such as lemons, but rare in grapes. The grape is unusual among fruits in that its major acid is TARTARIC ACID (and MALIC ACID), rather than citric acid, whose concentration in the juice of most grape varieties is only about one-twentieth that of tartaric acid.

Citric acid is also one of the ACIDS used in wine-making for the purposes of ACIDIFICATION. It is inexpensive but unsubtle and is used almost exclusively for inexpensive wines. It is always added after rather than before fermentation since it can be converted to ACETIC ACID by the yeast. It is produced commercially by fermenting SUCROSE solutions; very small amounts are recovered from processing citrus fruits. It is also used for cleaning. In the EUROPEAN UNION it is not permitted for acidification but it can be used to prevent iron casse if BLUE FINING is not possible. See also DIACETYL.

B.G.C. & A.D.W.

CIVC. Thanks to the **Comité Interprofessionnel du Vin de Champagne**, CHAMPAGNE is one of the most thoroughly organized wine regions in the world. The CIVC was established in 1941 as a co-operative organization grouping champagne GROWERS, CO-OPERATIVES, shippers, and houses under the auspices of the government (now represented by a commissioner appointed by the French Ministry of Agriculture). Growers/co-operatives and merchants/champagne houses each have a president to represent them. The CIVC is charged with organizing and controlling the production, distribution, and promotion of the wines of Champagne, as well as undertaking fundamental research for the region. Until 1990 it set a price for the grapes and still intervenes to regulate the size of the harvest and decide whether any of it should be 'blocked', or retained as juice rather than vinified and sold. The CIVC is financed by a levy on production and a tax on champagne sales.

But most importantly the CIVC is responsible for defending the Champenois's exclusive right to use the word 'champagne'. A notable victory was won in the English courts in 1959 and since then the name has achieved legal protection in most major markets, although not in the United States for established brands. The CIVC has fought a number of battles to ensure that the name Champagne is not used for other products, including a cigarette and a brand of perfume.

N.F.

Clairet, dark pink wine style that is a speciality of the BORDEAUX region, recalling the sort of red wines that were shipped in such quantity in the Middle Ages from Bordeaux to ENGLAND, and which originally inspired the English word CLARET. Dark-skinned grapes are fermented in contact with the skins for about 24 hours before fermentation of this lightly coloured wine continues to dryness. Small quantities of potentially refreshing wine are bottled to be sold under the appellation Bordeaux Clairet, and should be drunk as young as possible. It is said to have originated in Quinsac in the PREMIÈRES CÔTES DE BORDEAUX.

Clairette is a much-used name for southern French white grape varieties. **Clairette Ronde**, for example, is the Languedoc name for the ubiquitous UGNI BLANC, and various Clairettes serve as synonyms for the much finer BOURBOULENC. The French vine census of 2000 found 371 ha of pink-skinned **Clairette Rose**.

True **Clairette Blanche**, however, is a decidedly old-fashioned variety, producing alcoholic whites that MADERIZE easily, but it is allowed into a wide range of southern Rhône, Provençal, and Languedoc appellations, even lending its name to three (see below). Clairette is a traditional variety well suited to poor, dry soils, for long grown in what Galet calls 'the land of the olive tree'. It needs a non-vigorous rootstock to avoid COULURE and is susceptible to mildew and grape worms. Its small, thick-skinned grapes ripen relatively late, but can ripen dangerously fast at the end of the growing season. In the southern Rhône, it may be picked early to add aroma and acidity to a blend. Total French plantings fell to 3,000 ha/7,410 acres by the end of the 1990s. It is often blended with Ugni Blanc and Terret, one of the principal ingredients in many of the Languedoc's white VINS DE PAYS.

Its other common partner in the blending vat, and often vineyard, is the fatter GRENACHE Blanc. Clairette is widely distributed throughout the eastern Midi, especially in the Gard, where it produces CLAIRETTE DE BELLEGARDE and in the Hérault for CLAIRETTE DU LANGUEDOC, two of the Languedoc's earliest controlled appellations, presumably because these white wines were so unlike, rather than superior to, the typical produce of the Midi. Clairette is, strangely, the main grape of CRÉMANT DE DIE.

In previous eras, when consumers expected their whites to look pale brown and taste halfway to sherry, Clairette was clearly relatively important. With the more acid PICPOUL it formed the basis of PICARDAN, an extraordinarily popular wine exported in enormous quantities northwards from the Languedoc in the 17th and 18th centuries. It is hardly surprising that the variety spread far and wide in the 19th and early 20th centuries. At one time there were sizeable plantings in Algeria. It is known as Clairette Blanche in South Africa, where it was once as widely planted as in France. By the late 1990s, however, most of the vineyards had been grubbed up. It can still be found in tiny quantities in Australia's Hunter valley, where it was known as Blanquette. It is also planted in Romania, Israel, Toscana, and Sardegna, where it is a permitted ingredient in NURAGUS di Cagliari.

Clavel, J., *Vins et cuisine de terroir en Languedoc* (Toulouse, 1988).

Galet, P., *Dictionnaire encyclopédique des cépages* (Paris, 2000).

Clairette de Bellegarde is a small, 40-ha/100-acre enclave of exclusively white wine production in the south of the COSTIÈRES DE NÎMES appellation in the southern Rhône. Like CLAIRETTE DU LANGUEDOC, it is made entirely of the somewhat flabby CLAIRETTE grape and needs all the streamlining that modern vinification can impart to make this old-fashioned wine appeal to wine drinkers outside the region. Production is dominated by the Bellegarde co-operative. This wine demands to be drunk as young as possible.

Clairette de Die, sparkling white appellation centred on the town of DIE on the Drôme tributary east of the Rhône between Valence and Montélimar. According to PLINY, wine has been made here since Roman times. Die's gently fizzing wines may pre-date those of Champagne. Clairette de Die is a drink much more likely to refresh than either of the Languedoc's Clairettes (see above and below), but often despite rather than because of the CLAIRETTE grape. As well as a small quantity of still Clairette, a bit like CLAIRETTE DE BELLEGARDE but with the benefit of a slightly cooler climate, two very different sorts of sparkling Clairette de Die have been made, and one from Clairette plus at least 75 per cent MUSCAT BLANC À PETITS GRAINS grapes and the other from Clairette.

The more distinctive and more important is Clairette de Die Tradition, a refreshingly grapey fizz with Muscat flavours and an ALCOHOLIC STRENGTH of between 7 and 8 per cent, made by the *méthode dioise*, which should be signalled on the label. After pressing, the juice is filtered and kept at a sub-zero temperature before being fermented to about 3 per cent alcohol. It is then bottled and a second fermentation (see SPARKLING WINE-MAKING) is activated, unusually, by the inherent grape sugar rather than added sugar and yeast. After at least four months on the grapey lees of this process, the wine is decanted off and rebottled under pressure, leaving varying degrees of residual sweetness. No last-minute adjustments with DOSAGE are allowed.

CRÉMANT de Die is the more ordinary but usually well-made brut version made by the TRADITIONAL METHOD, mainly from Clairette grapes.

The local co-operative, geographically justified in calling itself the Cellier Hannibal, has been responsible for dynamizing the appellation and makes three in every four bottles carrying it. Perhaps it is significant that their top cuvée, and that of some smaller producers, contains no Clairette at all.

Other local still reds and whites may qualify as CHÂTILLON-EN-DIOIS.

Clairette du Languedoc is a slightly more important (90-ha/222-acre) appellation than CLAIRETTE DE BELLEGARDE, again exclusively from the overweight Clairette grape. It is one of the named subappellations of the southern French Coteaux du LANGUEDOC appellation. Clairette du Languedoc has suffered an extremely confused image as, despite its relatively small production, a wide array of different wine styles has been produced, and is officially sanctioned, within the appellation. The wine can be anything from an ultra-modern, early-picked, yellowish green, dry wine for drinking almost before the end of the year in which it was harvested, to a deep brown RANCIO sweet, alcoholic VIN DE LIQUEUR to suit French taste in aperitifs. The area qualifying for this confused appellation lies to the north east of Pézenas. The Adissan and Cabrières CO-OPERATIVES are the specialist producers.

Clape, La, named TERROIR within the Coteaux du LANGUEDOC in southern France which can be unfairly penalized for its name in Anglophone markets. La Clape was once an island off the busy Roman port of Narbo (Narbonne). Today it is a quintessentially Mediterranean coastal mountain just south of Narbonne which has one of France's highest average annual totals of sunshine. On the southern slopes of the mountain, the climate is heavily influenced by the sea. Altitudes of vineyards can vary by as much as 200 m/980 ft. La Clape is particularly well suited to growing BOURBOULENC, which must represent at least 40 per cent of the grapes used in the production of La Clape's sea-scented white wines such as those produced by Rouquette-sur-Mer, although these represent a distinct minority of the wine produced from about 1,000 ha/2,500 acres of vineyard within the appellation and most La Clape is full-blooded red, virtually indistinguishable from maritime CORBIÈRES with Ch de la Négly a notable producer. Some sweet wines are now made on the extensive l'Hospitalet domaine.

Clare Riesling. See CROUCHEN.

claret, English (not American) term generally used to describe red wines from the BORDEAUX region, or red bordeaux. Claret has also been used as a GENERIC term for a vaguely identified class of red table wines supposedly drier, and possibly higher in TANNINS, than those wines sold as generic burgundy (although, in the history of Australian wine SHOWS, it has been known for the same wine to win both claret and burgundy classes).

History

In medieval France, most red wine was the result of a short FERMENTATION, usually of no more than one or two days. The short period of contact with the grape skins meant that the resultant wines were pale in colour, and were probably very similar to the rosés of today. Such wines exported from Bordeaux were known as *vinum clarum, vin clar,* or

CLAIRET, and it is from the last of these that the English term claret is derived. Other much darker wines were also made by pressing the remaining skins, effectively the same as modern PRESS WINE, and these were known as *vinum rubeum purum*, *bin vermelh*, or *pinpin*.

Although the term *clairet* was widely used during the medieval period in France, the word claret does not appear to have been used at all extensively in England until the 16th century. In the second half of the 17th century, a new type of wine, of much higher quality and deeper colour, began to be produced in the GRAVES and on the sands and gravels of the MÉDOC to the north west of Bordeaux. These wines, the provenance of specific properties, where close attention was paid to grape selection, improved methods of vinification, and the use of new oak BARRELS, became known by the beginning of the 18th century as New French Clarets, and the earliest and most famous of them were HAUT-BRION, LAFITE, LATOUR, and MARGAUX (see BORDEAUX, history).

P.T.H.U.

Marquette, J., 'La Vinification dans les domaines de l'archevêque de Bordeaux à la fin du Moyen Âge', in A. Huetz de Lemps (ed.), *Géographie historique des vignobles*, i (Bordeaux, 1978).

Pijassou, R., *Un grand vignoble de qualité: le Médoc* (Paris, 1980).

Claret de Gers, probably the same as **Claret de Gascogne,** an almost extinct and undistinguished white grape of south west France also called Blanc Dame.

clarete is a Spanish term for a particularly Spanish hue of wine somewhere between a rosé (which the Spaniards would call *rosado*) and a light red. It is etymologically, though not oenologically, related to CLARET and derives from *claro*, the Spanish word meaning 'clear'. The term used to appear regularly on labels until it was prohibited following Spain's accession to the EUROPEAN UNION in 1986, but *clarete* is still sometimes used in Spanish as a descriptive term.

claret jugs. See DECANTERS.

Clare Valley, fine wine region in SOUTH AUSTRALIA with a strongly CONTINENTAL climate: warm summer days and cool nights. This combined with differences in soil, elevation, degree of slope and aspect, enables the region to produce Australia's finest Riesling as well as excellent Shiraz, Cabernet Sauvignon, and Malbec. While wines are sturdy and powerful, alcohol levels are generally lower than those of the Barossa Valley or McLaren Vale. Forty-three producers. J.H.

clarification, wine-making operation which removes suspended and insoluble material from grape juice, or new wine, in which these solids are known as LEES.

Clarification proper may be the removal only of insoluble solids such as the dead yeast cells and fragments of grape skins, stems, seeds, and pulp, but is frequently understood to encompass also the removal of dispersed COLLOIDS and other materials which exist in supersaturated concentration in the must or new wine, and in older wine that has not been stabilized. These latter substances include excess TARTRATES, pectins and gums, some PROTEINS, and small numbers of microorganisms such as YEAST and BACTERIA. Removal of all these substances, which are not visible to the unaided eye, is frequently called STABILIZATION, since no subsequent clarification is needed. Clarification has become more critical now that consumers have come to expect wines to be bright and clear.

Clarification can usually be accomplished naturally by simply holding the liquid in a storage tank until the larger particles settle (see SETTLING, or *débourbage*) and then siphoning, or RACKING, the clear upper layer from the compact layer of solids at the bottom of the tank. This takes time, however, especially if the wine is stored in small barrels where full clarification may take a year or two and several rackings.

Most winemakers, therefore, and certainly all concerned with high-volume production, choose to speed the process by intervening with one or more of FILTRATION, CENTRIFUGATION, FLOTATION, and the much cheaper process of FINING, the addition of agents which aid agglomeration and settling of colloids in the must or new wine.

One important white wine-making decision is the extent to which grape solids should be removed from the must before FERMENTATION. With Chardonnays, for example, it may be desirable to have a relatively high proportion of grape solids which produce various characters during fermentation. Winemakers may wish to eliminate most grape solids from the juice of more aromatic varieties in order to accentuate varietal fruit flavours. Juice for everyday white wines may be clarified before fermentation simply to speed and ease processing afterwards. This clarification can be done by simply holding the cooled and SULFUR DIOXIDE-treated juice in a tank for 24 hours or so. More often, pectin-splitting ENZYMES and fining agents such as BENTONITE will be added along with the sulfur dioxide in order to aid the clarification.

Flotation is a technique of must clarification borrowed from the ore refining and concentrating industry. It is based on the tendency of grape solids to adhere to rising bubbles. If very small bubbles of air are introduced at the bottom of a vat of must, easily oxidized PHENOLICS in the juice will react and some will be removed along with the other suspended solids which are carried to the tank top by the finely divided air bubbles. Oxidized phenolics, which are brown, not removed by

flotation will probably be adsorbed and removed with the lees after fermentation. (It is also possible to use compressed nitrogen instead of air.) The advantage of this technique is that the resultant wine resists further oxidative browning. However, there must be no yeast or fermentation activity in the must as this prevents flocculation. Flotation is best suited to large wineries where the process can run continuously.

For a long time neither centrifugation nor filtration was practical for removing solids from must. Centrifugation, which depends upon differing densities between the solids and the liquid, is impractically inefficient because of the high density of the sugar-laden juice. Before the development of ROTARY DRUM VACUUM FILTERS, the finely divided grape solids would quickly plug the small holes of a filter, making the process prohibitively expensive. Today, however, rotary filters may be used on lees which contain up to 15 per cent solids.

Red wines are not commonly clarified before fermentation because the skins are fermented with the juice in order to provide colour and flavour. In some cases, however, pectin-splitting enzymes are added to red must before fermentation to aid subsequent clarification and increase the eventual yield of FREE-RUN wine. Many everyday new red wines are processed in order to prevent the subsequent precipitation of tartrates and some will have the malic acid removed or reduced by a MALOLACTIC FERMENTATION to assure reasonable stability in bottle.

See also the similar but distinct processes associated with STABILIZATION. A.D.W.

Clarksburg, California wine region and AVA. Much of the AVA is composed of deep-soiled islands in the CENTRAL VALLEY delta from a point near Sacramento west beyond the town of Clarksburg. Though its position in the river channel leaves its vineyards open to the strongest summer sea fogs, the vast proportion of surrounding water retards overnight cooling when fogs are not afoot, so Clarksburg is far from being California's coolest vineyard district. Although a spectrum of varieties grows within the zone, only CHENIN BLANC truly distinguishes itself. Indeed, only here in all of California does Chenin Blanc become regionally identifiable. For all practical purposes it has swallowed up the Merritt Island AVA, which lies within its western end.

classed growth is a vineyard, estate, or château included in a wine CLASSIFICATION. The term is used almost exclusively in BORDEAUX for those châteaux included in the 1855 classification of the Médoc and Sauternes, the 1955 classification of Graves, and sometimes for those properties included in the regularly revised St-Émilion classification. The term is a direct translation of the French term CRU classé.

Classic, official German wine designation introduced in 2000 for dry-tasting wines (maximum 15 g/l RESIDUAL SUGAR) vinified from traditional grape varieties, harvested at at least 12 per cent potential alcohol (11.5 per cent in Mosel-Saar-Ruwer). See also GERMAN WINE LAW.

classical art, wine in. Wine was so deeply embedded in the culture of the classical world that it is inevitable that it would figure prominently in the art of that world. The vessels used for mixing and drinking wine (see CRATER, for example) were frequently decorated with scenes which played on the association with wine. So, most notably, the fine Attic Black and Red Figure pottery of the 6th and 5th centuries BC sometimes contain rural scenes of men harvesting grapes and treading them, as well as scenes from the *komos* (revels) and the SYMPOSIUM, in which the craters and cups are depicted in use. Sometimes it is possible to suspect an ironic commentary taking place. A famous Red Figure cup by the so-called Dokimasia painter has scenes of revelry around the outside with the awkward spaces under the handles filled by men crouched or crawling, the worse for drink, while inside the cup an old man is depicted being sick. Another playful irony is that nearly all these scenes can be found translated to another world, in which men are replaced by satyrs, uninhibited by the conventions of human society and presided over by the god DIONYSUS. Not surprisingly, Dionysus achieves a greater prominence in the art of the world of drinking than his place in the pantheon would suggest as his due. Feasting and banquets with wine also form the subject of some of the most memorable frescos from the tombs of the ETRUSCANS, where, for example, the Tomb of the Leopards at Tarquinia beautifully illustrates the funeral meal held near the tomb in honour of the dead.

Scenes of the vintage and the pressing of the grapes, with the role of humans frequently played by *amorini*, cupids, are found in great numbers at all periods throughout the Roman world, in paintings, sculptured reliefs, sarcophagi, decorated glass, and ivory plaques. Part of the explanation for the popularity of the themes, particularly on sarcophagi, is the obvious mystical symbolism of the vine and wine. Scenes of country life, including vines and the vintage, play a significant part in Roman painting from the 1st century BC onwards, and are most elaborately and impressively illustrated in mosaic. The vintage and tasks connected with viticulture, such as pruning and the cleaning and pitching of DOLIA, are often found in mosaics which illustrate the seasons or the tasks of the rural calendar. As a genre, these had a long history, which went back to the Hellenistic period in mosaic and may be connected with illustrated manuscript calendars. Fine examples in mosaic come from GAUL (St-Romain-en-Gal) and North Africa (the Maison des Mois at El Djem). From the 3rd century AD the élite of North Africa adorned their houses with mosaics which reflected the work of their estates. One of the most remarkable examples of realism in classical art must be the mosaic of the Labours of the Fields from Cherchel in Algeria, with men hoeing between TRELLISED vines.

The potential of the vine and wine as mystical symbols also explains why this was one of the themes of classical art which was most easily taken over by Christianity. A key monument is the church of Santa Costanza on the Via Nomentana in the north of Rome, a work of such rare beauty as to justify on its own a visit to that city. Santa Costanza was the mausoleum of Constantina, the daughter of Constantine, the first Christian emperor. Her huge porphyry sarcophagus has cherubs engaged in the vintage, a theme which is taken up by the remarkable mosaics which run round the ceiling of the ambulatory. The themes are traditional. Nothing is specifically Christian in these mosaics, but they are given a Christian connotation by the other, more overtly Christian, mosaics which would have adorned the dome.   J.J.P.

Berard, C., *et al.*, *A City of Images* (Princeton, NJ, 1989).

Dunbabin, K. M. D., *The Mosaics of Roman North Africa* (Oxford, 1978).

classical texts. The vine and the olive are the plants that characterize Mediterranean civilization. To grow them is the sign of a settled, not a nomadic, existence. Their products can be used as part of the daily routine, olive oil for cooking and washing, wine for drinking, or to mark a special occasion in the life of a community, when people would anoint their heads with fragrant oil and drink the best wine. In wine-producing countries wine can be an ordinary drink or a luxury item: classical literature reflects both.

This starts with HOMER (the end of the 8th century BC) and HESIOD (*c.*700 BC), the earliest Greek authors. Wine is mentioned frequently in the grander context. In Hesiod's *Works and Days* the cultivation of the vine is part of the order of nature as laid down by the gods: the secular and the religious were not distinct spheres. HERODOTUS' *Histories* (5th century BC) have many observations on wine and its uses among foreign nations. The Greeks had no books on agriculture, but THEOPHRASTUS (*c.* 370–*c.*287 BC) could be called the first systematic botanist. A very late Greek author, ATHENAEUS (fl. AD 200), is a good source of information on the wines of his day.

Among the Romans, VIRGIL (70–19 BC), HORACE (65–8 BC), and MARTIAL (*c.*AD 30–103/4) are the poets who display a particular interest in wine: Virgil chiefly in the *Georgics*, Horace throughout his poems, and Martial in many of his epigrams on the mores of his time. PLINY the Elder (AD 23/4–79) devoted an entire book of his *Natural History* to all aspects of wine. Other prose writers wrote treatises on agriculture: CATO (234–149 BC), VARRO (116–27 BC), COLUMELLA (1st century AD), and the derivative PALLADIUS (4th century AD).   H.M.W.

classical vine varieties. See ANCIENT VINE VARIETIES.

classical wines. See GREECE and ROME for general comments, as well as CAECUBAN, FALERNIAN, MASSIC, OPIMIAN, and SURRENTINE wines specifically.

classical world. See Ancient GREECE and Ancient ROME.

Classico, Italian term appended to the names of various DOC or DOCG wines to indicate that they have been produced in the historic zone which gave the wine its name, the zone which, at least in theory, offers the ideal conditions of soil and climate.

In reality, the name of the wine *without* the adjective Classico is usually applied to a significant expansion of the original production zone into areas which cultivate the same grape but in different, and usually less satisfactory, conditions. The origins of this practice, which occurred well before the establishment of the DOC system in the 1960s, lie in the regulation of the use of the name CHIANTI established by the Dalmasso Commission in 1932: large areas of Toscana, some far distant from CHIANTI CLASSICO, were permitted to use the name Chianti, while other historic areas of production of fine wine, Rufina and CARMIGNANO in particular, were obliged to add the word Chianti to their name. (Carmignano has since detached itself from the Chianti zone.)

This precedent was widely followed as the various DOCs came into being between 1967 and 1975, since when a significant number of Italy's historically important wines are now produced in both a Classico and a regular version. These include BARDOLINO, CALDARO, CHIANTI, CIRÒ, ORVIETO, SANTA MADDALENA, SOAVE, TERLANO, VALPOLICELLA, and VERDICCHIO.

The practice reflects a permanent tension in Italy's DOC system itself. Instead of choosing, like France, a geographical system of appellations, or choosing a VARIETAL system of nomenclature as California has done, Italy has, in effect, chosen to do both by giving an appellation name to a wine produced with the same grapes outside the original appellation; the geographical expansion of production zones under DOC regulation has been the chosen instrument for carrying out this policy.

More recently there have been keenly debated proposals in wine zones anxious for promotion to DOCG status that this should apply only to the Classico part of the zone.   D.T.

classification of various wine estates and vineyards is in general a relatively recent phenomenon, dictated by the increasingly sophisticated wine market of the late 19th, 20th, and 21st centuries. It has to a certain extent been superseded by the even more recent phenomenon of SCORING individual wines.

There were earlier instances of classifying individual vineyards, however. The vineyards of JURANÇON in south west France were officially evaluated as early as the 14th century. In 1644, the council of Würzburg in FRANKEN rigorously ranked the city's vineyards according to the quality of wine they produced (see GERMAN HISTORY). The vineyards of TOKAJ were classified in 1700, followed soon afterwards by a five-level categorization of all the vineyards of HUNGARY.

Bordeaux

BORDEAUX, with its plethora of fine, long-lasting wine from well-established estates and its well-organized market, is the wine region which has been most subject to classification of individual châteaux. The most famous wine classification in the world is that drawn up in 1855 of what became known as the CLASSED GROWTHS of the MÉDOC, and one GRAVES (see following pages). In response to a request from Napoleon III's 1855 Exposition Universelle in Paris (possibly so that dignitaries there should effectively know what to be impressed by), the Bordeaux BROKERS formalized their own and the market's ranking with a five-class classification of 60 of the leading Médoc châteaux plus the particularly famous and historic Graves, HAUT-BRION; and a two-class classification of SAUTERNES and BARSAC. This classification merely codified the market's view of relative quality as expressed by the prices fetched by individual estates' wines. (It also formalized previous informal lists of those wines widely regarded as the best by the likes of Thomas JEFFERSON, Wilhelm Franck, Alexander HENDERSON, and Cyrus REDDING.) The brokers issued the 1855 classification through the Bordeaux Chamber of Commerce, and were careful to explain that it was based on a century's experience. Within each of their classes, from FIRST GROWTHS, or PREMIERS CRUS down to fifth growths, or cinquièmes CRUS, the brokers listed châteaux in descending order of average price fetched. Thus, it is widely believed, LAFITE, the 'premier des premiers', headed the list because it commanded prices in excess even of LATOUR, MARGAUX, and Haut-Brion (although others have argued that the first growths were simply listed in alphabetical order). In the original classification, the term CHÂTEAU was rarely used.

The 1855 classification has endured remarkably well considering the many and various changes to the management and precise extent of individual properties since it was compiled, with only Chx MOUTON-ROTHSCHILD and Léoville-BARTON in the same hands. The vine-

yards of third growth Ch Desmirail, for example, have for long been subsumed into Ch Palmer, while another Margaux Ch Ferrière hardly exists as a third growth wine (although the label is used by the owners of Ch Lascombes), and Ch Dubignon-Talbot has not produced wine since the arrival of PHYLLOXERA in the late 19th century. Edmund PENNING-ROWSELL notes that Palmer's low ranking may have been influenced by the fact that the property was in receivership in 1855, and that Cantemerle, a property relatively new to the Bordeaux market, was added to the bottom of the list in a different hand. The only official revision of this much discussed list took place in 1973, when, after much lobbying on the part of Baron Philippe de ROTHSCHILD, Ch Mouton-Rothschild made the all-important leap from top of the second growths to become a first growth (although see also SUPER SECOND). It could be argued that such a classification contains an element of self-preservation in that highly classified properties are thereby able to command prices which sustain the investment needed to maintain their status, although the history of Ch Margaux in the 1960s and 1970s demonstrates that other factors may affect this hypothesis, and in the 1980s and 1990s many Bordeaux proprietors were driven by competition and ambition to invest, and in some cases price, at a level above that suggested by their official ranking. See Ch LÉOVILLE LAS CASES in particular.

The 1855 classification of Sauternes and Barsac is also printed on p. 177. Reflecting price and the *réclame* then attached to sweet wines, it elevated Ch d'YQUEM to premier cru supérievr, a rank higher even than any of the red wine first growths, and listed 11 châteaux as first growths and 14 as seconds.

Other than Haut-Brion's inclusion in the 1855 Médoc classification, the red wines of the GRAVES district were not officially classified until 1953. This one-class list, together with an official classification of the white wines made in 1959, appears on p. 177. It avoided some possible controversy by employing a democratically alphabetical order (Ch Haut-Brion Blanc was added in 1960). It should be said, however, that there is a wide differential between the prices commanded by Ch Haut-Brion and its close rival Ch La Mission-Haut-Brion, and those fetched by Chx Bouscaut and de Fieuzal, for example. The Graves district was subsequently divided into Graves and PESSAC-LÉOGNAN.

The classification of ST-ÉMILION, formally drawn up in 1955, is most frequently amended. Modifications were published in 1969, 1985, and 1996 and these are likely to continue on the basis of monitoring of wine quality, vineyard boundaries, prices, and the like (vineyards cannot be extended between reclassifications). St-Émilion classification's laudable topicality is mitigated by over-generosity in nomenclature, however. The top two properties Chx

CHEVAL BLANC and AUSONE are ranked, somewhat inelegantly, premiers grands crus classés A, while 11 properties qualify as premiers grands crus classés B. Below this are 55 grands crus classés, whose quality can vary considerably, and then in each vintage, on the basis of tastings, the deceptively grandiose rank of GRAND CRU (minus the classé) is awarded to scores of individual wines from properties below grand cru classé status. The 1996 classification is reproduced on pp. 176–7; a revision based on tastings of wines made between 1994 and 2004 is expected to be published in 2006.

POMEROL is the only important fine wine district of Bordeaux never to have been classified, although its star Ch PÉTRUS is conventionally included with Chx Lafite, Latour, Margaux, Haut-Brion, Mouton-Rothschild, Cheval Blanc, and Ausone as a first growth.

There have been regular attempts to revise and assimilate the various classifications of Bordeaux, most notably that drawn up by Alexis LICHINE in 1959. Most serious writers on bordeaux make their own revisions, more or less confirmed by the market.

See also CRU BOURGEOIS for those MÉDOC properties classified as just below the status of a fifth growth.

Burgundy

Burgundians were also well aware of the considerable variation in quality of the wines produced by different plots of land, or *climats*, as they are known in Burgundy. In 1855, Dr Lavalle published his influential *History and Statistics of the Côte d'Or* which included an informal classification of the best vineyards. This was formalized in 1861 by the Beaune Committee of Agriculture, which, with Lavalle's assistance, devised three classes. Most *climats* included in the first class eventually became grands crus when the APPELLATION CONTRÔLÉE system was introduced in the 1930s. See under BURGUNDY for a full list of Burgundian grands crus, and see under individual village names for details of their premiers crus.

Elsewhere

Few other regions of France have anything approaching an official classification, although see ALSACE for a list of those vineyards accorded grand cru status, CHABLIS for details of crus in this northern outpost of Burgundy, and CHAMPAGNE for some details of the classification of individual villages there.

There have been attempts, typically by WINE WRITERS, wine waiters or producers' associations to produce classifications of the best vineyards, or best wines, of many countries, notably Germany (see GROSSES GEWÄCHS) and Italy (see VERONELLI), but these have generally been too controversial to be widely adopted. With the exception of the DOURO, where individual vineyards have been classified for the

Bordeaux

The Official Classification of Médoc and Graves of 1855

First Growths (Premiers Crus)

	Commune	Appellation		Commune	Appellation
Ch Lafite-Rothschild	Pauillac	Pauillac	Ch Haut-Brion*	Pessac	Graves, now
Ch Margaux	Margaux	Margaux			Pessac-Léognan
Ch Latour	Pauillac	Pauillac	Ch Mouton-Rothschild**	Pauillac	Pauillac

Second Growths (Deuxièmes Crus)

	Commune	Appellation		Commune	Appellation
Ch Rauzan-Ségla	Margaux	Margaux	Ch Brane-Cantenac	Cantenac	Margaux
Ch Rauzan-Gassies	Margaux	Margaux	Ch Pichon-Longueville		
Ch Léoville Las Cases	St-Julien	St-Julien	(Baron)	Pauillac	Pauillac
Ch Léoville-Poyferré	St-Julien	St-Julien	Ch Pichon-Longueville,		
Ch Léoville-Barton	St-Julien	St-Julien	Comtesse de Lalande	Pauillac	Pauillac
Ch Durfort-Vivens	Margaux	Margaux	Ch Ducru-Beaucaillou	St-Julien	St-Julien
Ch Gruaud-Larose	St-Julien	St-Julien	Ch Cos d'Estournel	St-Estèphe	St-Estèphe
Ch Lascombes	Margaux	Margaux	Ch Montrose	St-Estèphe	St-Estèphe

Third Growths (Troisièmes Crus)

	Commune	Appellation		Commune	Appellation
Ch Kirwan	Cantenac	Margaux	Ch Cantenac-Brown	Cantenac	Margaux
Ch d'Issan	Cantenac	Margaux	Ch Palmer	Cantenac	Margaux
Ch Lagrange	St-Julien	St-Julien	Ch La Lagune	Ludon	Haut-Médoc
Ch Langoa-Barton	St-Julien	St-Julien	Ch Desmirail	Margaux	Margaux
Ch Giscours	Labarde	Margaux	Ch Calon-Ségur	St-Estèphe	St-Estèphe
Ch Malescot St-Exupéry	Margaux	Margaux	Ch Ferrière	Margaux	Margaux
Ch Boyd-Cantenac	Cantenac	Margaux	Ch Marquis d'Alesme Becker	Margaux	Margaux

Fourth Growths (Quatrièmes Crus)

	Commune	Appellation		Commune	Appellation
Ch St-Pierre	St-Julien	St-Julien	Ch La Tour-Carnel	St-Laurent	Haut-Médoc
Ch Talbot	St-Julien	St-Julien	Ch Lafon-Rochet	St-Estèphe	St-Estèphe
Ch Branaire-Ducru	St-Julien	St-Julien	Ch Beychevelle	St-Julien	St-Julien
Ch Duhart-Milon	Pauillac	Pauillac	Ch Prieuré-Lichine	Cantenac	Margaux
Ch Pouget	Cantenac	Margaux	Ch Marquis-de-Terme	Margaux	Margaux

Fifth Growths (Cinquièmes Crus)

	Commune	Appellation		Commune	Appellation
Ch Pontet-Canet	Pauillac	Pauillac	Ch du Tertre	Arsac	Margaux
Ch Batailley	Pauillac	Pauillac	Ch Haut-Bages-Liberal	Pauillac	Pauillac
Ch Haut-Batailley	Pauillac	Pauillac	Ch Pédesclaux	Pauillac	Pauillac
Ch Grand-Puy-Lacoste	Pauillac	Pauillac	Ch Belgrave	St-Laurent	Haut-Médoc
Ch Grand-Puy-Ducasse	Pauillac	Pauillac	Ch de Camensac	St-Laurent	Haut-Médoc
Ch Lynch-Bages	Pauillac	Pauillac	Ch Cos-Labory	St-Estèphe	St-Estèphe
Ch Lynch-Moussas	Pauillac	Pauillac	Ch Clerc-Milon	Pauillac	Pauillac
Ch Dauzac	Labarde	Margaux	Ch Croizet-Bages	Pauillac	Pauillac
Ch d'Armailhac***	Pauillac	Pauillac	Ch Cantemerle	Macau	Haut-Médoc

* This wine, although a Graves, was universally recognized and classified as one of the original four first growths.
** This wine was decreed a first growth in 1973.
*** Previously Ch d'Armailhaq, Ch Mouton-Baron-Philippe, and Ch Mouton-Baronne-Philippe.

The Official Classification of St-Émilion of 1955 (Reclassified 1996)
The 2006 classification was published too late for inclusion in this edition.

Premiers Grands Crus Classés

A. Ch Ausone   Ch Cheval Blanc

B. Ch Angélus   Ch Beau-Séjour Bécot   Ch Beauséjour-Duffaux la Garrosse   Ch Belair   Ch Canon   Clos Fourtet   Ch Figeac   Ch la Gaffelière
Ch Magdelaine   Ch Pavie   Ch Trottevieille

Grands Crus Classés

Ch l'Arrosée	Ch Bellevue	Ch Berliquet	Ch Cadet-Piola	Ch Cap de Mourlin
Ch Balestard-La-Tonnelle	Ch Bergat	Ch Cadet-Bon	Ch Canon-La Gaffeliere	Ch Chauvin

Ch Clos des Jacobins	Ch Dassault	Ch Haut-Corbin	Ch Pavie-Decesse	Ch La Tour-Figeac
Clos de l'Orátoire	Ch la Dominique	Ch Haute-Sarpe	Ch Pavie-Macquin	Ch la Tour du Pin Figeac
Clos St-Martin	Ch Faurie-de-Souchard	Ch Lamarzelle	Ch Petit Faurie de Soutard	(Giraud-Bélivier)
Ch la Clotte	Ch Fonplégade	Ch Laniote	Ch le Prieuré	Ch la Tour du Pin Figeac
Ch la Clusière	Ch Fonroque	Ch Larcis-Ducasse	Ch Ripeau	(Moueix)
Ch Corbin	Ch Franc-Mayne	Ch Larmande	Ch St-Georges-Côte-	Ch Troplong-Mondot
Ch Corbin-Michotte	Ch Grand-Mayne	Ch Laroque	Pavie	Ch Villemaurine
Ch la Couspaude	Ch Grand-Pontet	Ch Laroze	Ch la Serre	Ch Yon-Figeac
Couvent des Jacobins	Ch les Grandes Murailles	Ch Matras	Ch Soutard	
Ch Curé-Bon	Ch Gaudet St-Julien	Ch Moulin du Cadet	Ch Tertre-Daugay	

The Official Classification of Sauternes-Barsac of 1855

Superior First Growth (Premier Cru Supérieur)

Commune

Ch d'Yquem   Sauternes

First Growths (Premiers Crus)

	Commune		Commune
Ch La Tour-Blanche	Bommes	Ch Climens	Barsac
Ch Lafaurie-Peyraguey	Bommes	Ch Guiraud	Sauternes
Ch Clos Haut-Peyraguey	Bommes	Ch Rieussec	Fargues
Ch de Rayne-Vigneau	Bommes	Ch Rabaud-Promis	Bommes
Ch Suduiraut	Preignac	Ch Sigalas-Rabaud	Bommes
Ch Coutet	Barsac		

Second Growths (Deuxièmes Crus)

	Commune		Commune
Ch de Myrat	Barsac	Ch Naïrac	Barsac
Ch Doisy-Daene	Barsac	Ch Caillou	Barsac
Ch Doisy-Dubroca	Barsac	Ch Suau	Barsac
Ch Dolsy-Vedrines	Barsac	Ch de Malle	Preignac
Ch d'Arche	Sauternes	Ch Romer-du-Hayot	Fargues
Ch Filhot	Sauternes	Ch Lamothe-Despujois	Sauternes
Ch Broustet	Barsac	Ch Lamothe-Guignard	Sauternes

The Official Classification of Graves of 1959

Classified Red Wines of Graves

	Commune		Commune
Ch Bouscaut	Cadaujac	Ch La Tour-Martillac	Martillac
Ch Haut-Bailly	Léognan	Ch Smith-Haut-Lafitte	Martillac
Ch Carbonnieux	Léognan	Ch Haut-Brion	Pessac
Domaine de Chevalier	Léognan	Ch La Mission-Haut-Brion	Talence
Ch de Fieuzal	Léognan	Ch Pape-Clément	Pessac
Ch Olivier	Léognan	Ch La Tour-Haut-Brion	Talence
Ch Malartic-Lagravière	Léognan		

Classified White Wines of Graves

	Commune		Commune
Ch Bouscaut	Cadaujac	Ch La Tour-Martillac	Martillac
Ch Carbonnieux	Léognan	Ch Laville-Haut-Brown	Talence
Domaine de Chevalier	Léognan	Ch Couhins	Villenave d'Ornon
Ch d'Olivier	Léognan	Ch Haut-Brion*	Pessac
Ch Malartic-Lagravière	Léognan		

* Added to the list in 1960

quality of port they produce, the wine regions of Portugal and Spain are in too great a state of flux to submit satisfactorily to classification, like those of eastern Europe and the rest of the Mediterranean.

In the New World, Australia prefers to classify not vineyards but individual wines, often much blended between areas, by awarding them medals and trophies in their famous SHOWS. Langton's Classification of Australian Wine, produced periodically, distinguishes wines on the basis of track record and reputation at AUCTION. In North America, on the other hand, it seems that classification may never appeal to the democratic California wine industry.

See also CLIMATE CLASSIFICATION.

Caillard, A., and Langton, S., *Langton's Australian Fine Wine: Buying and Investment Guide* (4th edn, Sydney, 2005).

Markham, D., *1855: A History of the Bordeaux Classification* (New York, 1998).

Penning-Rowsell, E., *The Wines of Bordeaux* (6th edn, London, 1989).

Pitiot, S., and Servant, J.-C., *Les Vins de Bourgogne; Collection Pierre Poupon* (11th edn, Paris, 1992).

Claverie, white wine grape of south west France, sometimes called Chalosse Blanche, which once provided a wine sought out by the DUTCH but is now, even in its native Landes, virtually extinct.

clay, description of sediment or soil which is made up of particularly small particles. See SOIL TEXTURE, and GEOLOGY, for more details of this particular form of soil classification. The terms used in this classification are unrelated to the soil's mineral composition—although in general soils whose texture is described as clay tend to be dominated by clay minerals (a geological term with a technical meaning), while they may also contain considerable quantities of clay grade (particularly small particles of) quartz. To have a stable SOIL STRUCTURE, a soil must contain at least a moderate amount of clay. In viticultural terms, clay is especially celebrated as a vineyard SUBSOIL, often being more important than is obvious from the surface of the soils, as in parts of POMEROL, for example.   J.G.

cleanliness, an important quality in wine (a wine should not have any off-odours) and in wineries, for which see HYGIENE.

Clear Lake, California AVA. See LAKE COUNTY.

cleft grafting, a popular method for changing VINE VARIETY in the vineyard (see TOP GRAFTING). The severing of the trunk may be at ground level or just below the head; the latter is preferred because DESUCKERING is simpler, less vine training is required, and the extra wood of the trunk aids the rapid establishment of the new vine. The trunk is cut horizontally in early spring and the stump split

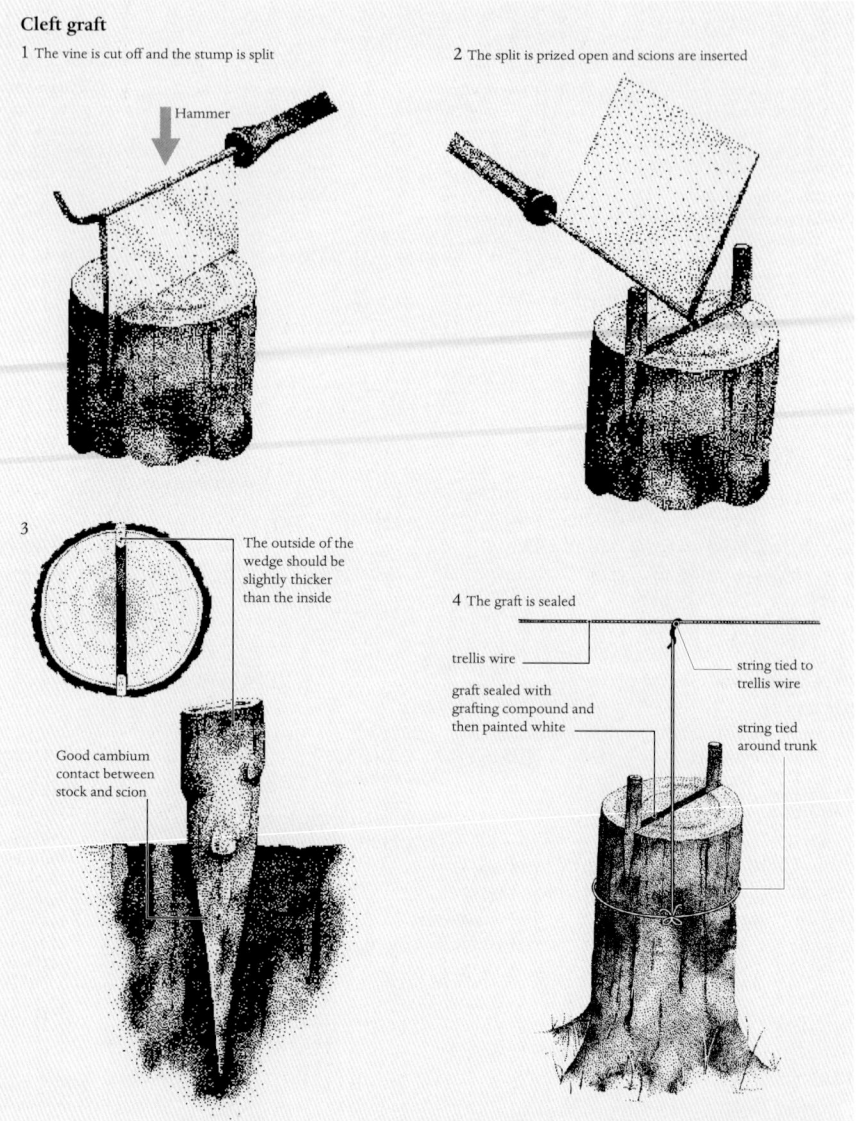

Cleft graft

1 The vine is cut off and the stump is split

Hammer

2 The split is prized open and scions are inserted

3

The outside of the wedge should be slightly thicker than the inside

Good cambium contact between stock and scion

4 The graft is sealed

trellis wire

graft sealed with grafting compound and then painted white

string tied to trellis wire

string tied around trunk

across the middle to about 5 cm/2 in depth. SCION pieces of one or two nodes are prepared from dormant canes with a long-tapered wedge. After the trunk is split and spread, the pieces are inserted one on each side so that CAMBIUMS of ROOTSTOCK and scion are matched to facilitate their bonding. The wounds are sealed with grafting mastic, then with paint. NOTCH GRAFTING is an alternative. See diagram.   B.G.C.

Clevner, grape variety, usually part of the PINOT family. In SWITZERLAND, the name is often applied to PINOT NOIR or Blauburgunder grown in the canton of Zurich. In ALSACE, Clevner or Klevner are usually synonyms for PINOT BLANC but see also KLEVENER DE HEILIGENSTEIN.

climat, French, particularly Burgundian, term for a specific vineyard site defined by, as the name suggests, all of its climatological as well as geographical characteristics, otherwise known as TERROIR. Thus the Burgundian grower uses the word *climat* interchangeably with 'vineyard'. A *climat* is generally but not always smaller than a specific appellation. The term *climat* may for example be used to refer to a grand cru such as Richebourg. To further complicate matters, most appellations have over the centuries been subdivided into small parcels of a few hectares, each with its own traditional name, known by local geographers as a LIEU-DIT.

climate, long-term WEATHER pattern of an area, and an extremely important variable in the wine-making equation. For more details, see MACROCLIMATE in particular, but also CLIMATE CLASSIFICATION, CLIMATE CHANGE, CONTINENTALITY, COOL CLIMATE, LATITUDE, MEDITERRANEAN CLIMATE, RAINFALL, SUNLIGHT,

TEMPERATE, TEMPERATURE, TEMPERATURE VARI-ABILITY, and, importantly, CLIMATE AND WINE QUALITY. For details of climate on a smaller scale, see MESOCLIMATE and MICROCLIMATE.

climate and wine quality.
Climate of course influences both the quality and styles of wine that an area can produce best. At the extremes, a climate can be so unsuitable for grape-growing that to produce good wines regularly is impossible or, at best, uneconomic. Cooler climates are best suited to producing light, delicate wines, while hotter climates are most suitable for FORTIFIED WINE production.

Temperature
Average mean TEMPERATURE during RIPENING strongly influences potential wine style. Defining grape maturity as that appropriate to making dry table wines, mean temperatures averaging above about 21 °C/70 °F in the final month to maturity lead to a rapid loss of MALIC ACID from the grapes, and to lower TOTAL ACIDITY and generally higher PH in the juice. Conversely, an average mean temperature below about 15 °C in the final month minimizes acid loss to the point that acid levels may be too high. There is also often a risk that the grapes will not ripen fully at all.

Average conditions during ripening cannot be estimated directly from raw climatic statistics, because they depend in part on when ripening occurs. That, in turn, depends on the heat requirements of individual VINE VARIETIES to reach maturity. Some are early maturing and have a relatively low total heat requirement. These will ripen successfully in cool climates, and in hot climates ripen very early. Late-maturing varieties need a long, warm growing season and a high heat total to ripen at all. Gladstones classifies the main wine grape varieties into eight maturing groups.

Beyond that, individual grape varieties differ in their optimum ripening temperatures for quality. Many of the early-maturing varieties are best when ripened under relatively cool conditions. The berries of some of them are very sensitive to heat, particularly red wine varieties such as Pinot Noir. Such varieties nevertheless need warmth during ripening to give enough colour and body for red wines, a contradiction which explains their limited and specialized climatic adaptations. Other equally early-maturing varieties, usually for white wine, can tolerate considerable heat during ripening and can give good quality across a wide range of climates. Chardonnay, Verdelho, and to a lesser extent Sauvignon Blanc are good examples. Late-maturing varieties such as Grenache, Mourvèdre, Carignan, and Muscat of Alexandria need not only high heat totals to reach maturity, but also moderately high temperatures during ripening for maximum wine quality.

Temperature variability
Whereas potential wine style depends broadly on average mean temperature during ripening, quality appears to be related at least as much to short-term temperature variability from day to day. It has yet to be established whether less variable (or more equable) ripening temperatures are likely to result in better wine quality but highly variable temperatures risk greater damage, both by frosts after budburst and by extremes of heat in summer. See TEMPERATURE VARIABILITY.

Sunlight
Contrary to common perception, cool viticultural climates are probably more limited by their low temperatures than by lack of SUNLIGHT. Heat as summed over the season determines which grape varieties, if any, reach a satisfactory degree of PHYSIOLOGICAL RIPENESS. Sunlight duration acts mainly by controlling sugar in grapes and therefore potential wine alcohol content at a given stage of physiological ripening. In practice, however, the relative contributions of sunlight and temperature are hard to distinguish, because low temperatures and low sunlight hours tend to go together. Poor seasons in cool climates are usually both sunless and cold.

Paradoxically, sunlight duration appears to limit wine style and (sometimes) quality fully as much in warm as in cool climates, even though their sunlight hours over the season are usually greater. The explanation lies in rates of RESPIRATION. Vines respire more sugar at high temperatures for their normal metabolism, but do not photosynthesize any faster; they therefore need more sunlight hours to generate a sugar surplus for ripening the fruit. It is why, for instance, Australia's often cloudy Hunter valley produces only table wines despite being very warm; and why mild to warm, but cloudy, regions of northern New Zealand such as Auckland produce predominantly light table wines. Similar factors appear to apply through much of central and northern Italy.

Regions with unlimited sunlight hours and intensity are nevertheless not necessarily at an advantage because they commonly suffer from excessive temperature variability (see above) and low relative humidities and WATER STRESS (see below). But in the absence of these adverse factors, ample sunlight does appear to be universally beneficial. A strong and constant sugar flow to the ripening berries assures not only their sweetness and sufficient alcohol in the wine, but also that colour, flavour, and aroma compounds are not limited by a lack of sugar substrate for their formation.

Timing of the sunlight is important. Studies such as that of Gadille in Burgundy show that the most critical period for quality is around the start of ripening (August in most European viticultural regions). Good conditions then assure an ample reserve of sugar in the vine, both for early conversion in the leaves and berries into flavour and aroma compounds, or their precursors, and so that sugar and flavour ripening of the berries can continue unabated under the cooler and less sunny conditions normally encountered later.

Rainfall
The general implications of rain for viticulture are discussed under RAINFALL.

Opinions differ as to optimum rainfall amounts during ripening. Most agree that any severe water stress at that stage is deleterious. On the other hand, heavy rain can lead to temporary juice dilution and sometimes to incomplete ripening, especially if accompanied by lack of sunshine. Wet ripening periods commonly signal poor vintages. Heavy rain close to maturity is especially damaging, because it can cause berry splitting and subsequent fungal infection of the bunches (see BOTRYTIS BUNCH ROT). This occurs most typically in certain varieties with tight bunches, such as Chenin Blanc and Zinfandel, and where the vines were under drought stress prior to the rain. HAIL at this time can be devastating.

Relative humidity and evaporation
Strong evaporative demands place the vines under water stress which, in extreme cases, can cause leaf loss and substantial collapse of vine metabolism. Obvious fruit damage often follows through excessive exposure to the overhead sun. Milder water stress can still reduce PHOTOSYNTHESIS and sugar production in the leaves, and hence reduce both quantity and fruit quality. Mechanisms are discussed more fully under EVAPORATION and HUMIDITY.

Virtually all of the world's acknowledged great table wines have so far come from regions with moderately high relative humidities and low evaporation. This is partly because of their lack of stress (see above) and through their usually restricted temperature variability.

Wind
The effects of WIND STRESS are largely on vine health and yield, via reduced disease incidence on the one hand, and closure of the leaf STOMATA and especially direct physical damage on the other. Dry winds may also reduce wine quality through increased evaporation, as explained above.

On the other hand, the daily alternating land and sea breezes of the summer months that occur with some regularity in coastal regions of the dry continents markedly benefit both vine physiological functioning and wine quality. They are especially important in Australia and west coastal United States, and are doubly advantageous. Dry land winds at night and in the early morning reduce the risk of FUNGAL DISEASES. Then mild, humid afternoon sea breezes reduce stresses on the vines and greatly improve day conditions for photosynthesis and ripening. The same applies on a reduced scale around inland lakes and rivers. See TOPOGRAPHY and TERROIR.

Summary

Two climatic types appear to offer the best compromises for both viticulture and wine quality. The first is that with cool to mild growing season temperatures and uniform to predominantly summer rainfall, such as is found in western and central Europe. Within that context, the best vineyard sites have specialized MESOCLIMATES with more than usual sunshine, warmth, and length of frost-free period.

The second broad climatic type, extending more or less contiguously from the first, comprises the cooler and more humid of the summer-dry MEDITERRANEAN CLIMATES, whenever summer heat is regularly moderated by afternoon sea breezes, and irrigation can be supplied in late summer if needed and permitted. Advantages over the uniform and summer-rainfall climates include more reliable summer sunshine and less risk of excessive rain and humidity during the ripening period.

The world's greatest table wines have traditionally come from the cool to mild temperate climates with uniform to summer-dominant rainfall. Partly this was because the limitations of frost and lack of warmth automatically confined viticulture there to the most equable mesoclimates, which happened also to have the best temperature regimes for wine quality.

For more detail, see TEMPERATURE, TEMPERATURE VARIABILITY, SUNLIGHT, RAINFALL, HUMIDITY, and WIND. See also COOL CLIMATE VITICULTURE and CLIMATE CHANGE.

J.G. & R.E.S.

Becker, N., 'Site climate effects on development, fruit maturation and harvest quality', in R. E. Smart *et al.* (eds.), *Proceedings of the Second International Symposium for Cool Climate Viticulture and Oenology: 11–15 January 1988, Auckland, New Zealand* (Auckland, 1988).

Gadille, R., *Le Vignoble de la Côte Bourguignonne* (Paris, 1967), cited by H. Johnson and J. Robinson, *The World Atlas of Wine* (5th edn, London and New York, 2001).

Gladstones, J., *Viticulture and Environment* (Adelaide, 1992).

Huglin, P., and Schneider, C., 1998. *Biologie et écologie de la vigne* (2nd edn, Paris, 1998).

climate change. Growing grapes for wine is a climatically sensitive endeavour, with narrow geographical zones providing the best production and quality characteristics. Therefore, the inherent uniqueness that wine region climates provide places the industry at greater risk from climate change than more broadly grown agricultural crops.

WEATHER and climate present three distinct spatial/temporal scales of risks and challenges to viticulture and wine production: first, individual weather events, which are mostly short term and localized (e.g. HAIL, WINTER FREEZES, FROST, and heavy rain); second, climate variability, which is measured on seasonal to

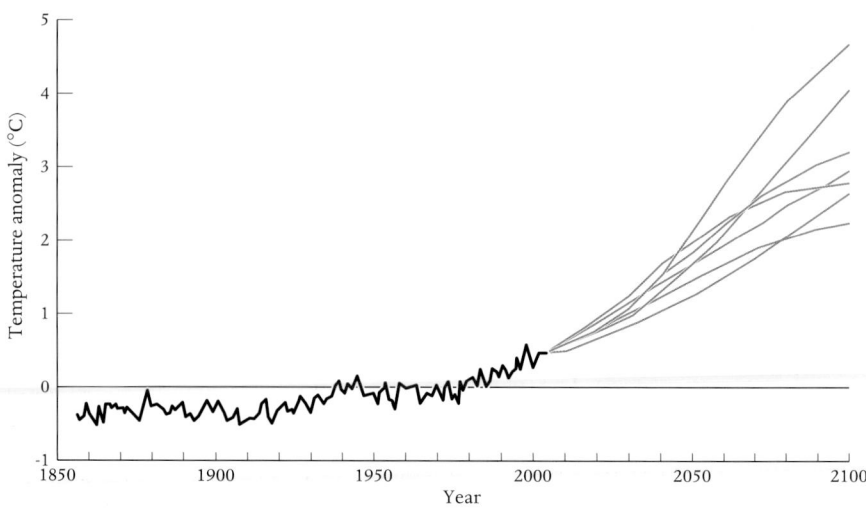

Climate change: observed and modelled global average temperature anomalies 1856–2100 as referenced to the 1961–90 base period. The observed temperatures (thick line) are from Jones et al. (2001). The modelled temperatures (grey lines) are General Circulation Model (GCM) output from the Intergovernmental Panel on Climate Change (Houghton et al.) and represent a range of predicted warming given various emission scenarios (Special Report on Emission Scenarios).

decadal time-scales and typically regionalized (e.g. DROUGHT or wet periods, warm or cold periods); third, climate change, which is recognized as long term and regional to global in scale (e.g. warming, cooling, changes in moisture regimes). In addition, one factor often influences and/or changes another—climate variability can change the frequency of individual weather events, or climate change can alter the nature of climate variability.

Historically climate change has been brought about by both internal and external natural processes such as volcanic events, ocean/snow/ice dynamics, solar variation, and meteoroid impacts. However, it appears that contemporary and future climate changes have become greatly influenced by human behaviour, through changes in atmospheric composition, deforestation, desertification, and urbanization. Probably the greatest concern for future climate change comes from increasing fossil fuel consumption and rising CARBON DIOXIDE (CO_2) levels in the atmosphere. While the magnitude of human influences on global climates is in debate, the unabated use of fossil fuels and a growing population will continue to alter the Earth's surface and atmosphere and the way they hold and distribute heat. To study climate change, scientists use empirical methods (based on observations and/or proxy data, such as tree rings), dynamic methods (based on complex three-dimensional, mathematical models of our Earth–atmosphere system), or a combination of the two. Although climate models are far from perfect representations of climate reality and are constantly scrutinized, they continue to improve as technology and knowledge increase; combined with obser-

vations, they provide the best tools for climate change studies.

Historical and contemporary climate changes

The grapevine is one of the oldest cultivated plants and, along with the process of making wine, has resulted in a rich geographical and cultural history (see ORIGINS OF VITICULTURE). History has shown that wine-grape growing regions developed when the climate was most conducive. In addition, records of dates of harvest and yield for European viticulture have been kept for nearly a thousand years, revealing large swings in growing season temperatures and productivity. For example, Pfister's historical research describes how during the medieval 'Little Optimum', roughly AD 900–1300, average temperatures were up to 1 °C warmer with vineyards planted as far north as the coastal zones of the Baltic sea and southern England. Recorded harvest dates for northern Europe from the High Middle Ages (12th and 13th centuries) show that fruit was ripening in early September as compared with late September to mid October today, and that growing season temperatures were roughly 1.7 °C warmer than today. However, during the 'Little Ice Age' (14th to late 19th centuries), temperature declines were dramatic, resulting in northern vineyards being abandoned and growing seasons so short that harvesting grapes in southern Europe was difficult.

Today our understanding of climate change and the potential effects on VITICULTURE and wine production has become increasingly important as changing levels of greenhouse gases and alterations in Earth surface characteristics bring about changes in the Earth's radiation budget, atmospheric circulation, and hydrologic cycle. Observed climate change during the 20th century shows that global mean surface temperatures have increased 0.4–0.8 °C (see figure). However, temperature changes have not been globally uniform, with some regions experiencing decreases, some not changing at all, and some increasing more dramatically. In addition, the warming trends have been found to be asymmetric with respect to seasonal and diurnal cycles, with greatest warming occurring during the winter and spring and at night (resulting in a smaller diurnal temperature range). For many locations, the 20th century's ten warmest years all occurred in the last 15 years of the century. Of these, 1998 was the warmest year on record. Other climate-related observations include: a decline in the coldest days (below frost level); decreasing snow cover extent in the northern hemisphere and floating ice in the Arctic ocean; sea level rising on average 8 cm/3 in over the past century; worldwide precipitation over land increasing by 5–10 per cent, but with some locations showing a greater frequency of drought; and the frequency of extreme rainfall events increasing throughout many regions.

While contemporary research shows that the impact of climate change on viticulture and wine has been less than on other crops, the results point to clear changes in both grapevine growth and wine quality parameters. Recent analyses have suggested that growing seasons in Europe should lengthen and that grape ripeness and wine quality in Champagne and Bordeaux should increase. Spatial modelling has also predicted potential shifts and/or expansion in regions suited to viticulture, with parts of southern Europe becoming too hot to produce high quality wines and northern regions becoming viable once again. Other studies examining the effects on specific varieties (Sangiovese and Cabernet Sauvignon) have found that climate change in Italy will lead to shorter growth intervals, more vegetative development with larger leaf areas, greater water consumption, decreases in yield, and increases in yield variability. A study of Napa and Sonoma in California found that higher yields and quality over the last half of the 20th century were influenced by asymmetric warming (at night and in the spring), where a reduction in frost occurrence, advanced initiation of growth in the spring, and longer growing seasons were the most influential factors. Numerous studies have detailed significant grapevine phenological changes for many wine regions. For example, in Bordeaux, the last 50 years of the 19th century saw earlier budding, flowering, and harvest driven by warmer and longer growing seasons. The changes in phenology in Bordeaux have been coupled with increases in vintage quality through better grape composition (mainly sugar and acid levels, which largely determine wine quality). Recent

research by Chuine and colleagues used contemporary grape harvest dates from Burgundy to reconstruct spring–summer temperatures from 1370 to 2003. While the results indicate that temperatures as high as those reached in the warm 1990s have occurred several times in the region since 1370, the extremely warm summer of 2003 appears to have been higher than in any other year since 1370. Jones and colleagues examined a 30–40-year record of vintage ratings for the majority of the world's high-quality wine-producing regions and found that vintage ratings during the last half of the 20th century increased, while year-to-year quality variability declined. However, their study revealed that vintage ratings in cool climate regions tended to be higher than those in warmer regions, where optimum climate-quality thresholds are being exceeded. Other studies of the effects of climate change on grape growing and wine production reveal greater pest and disease pressure due to milder winters and changes in sea level potentially altering the coastal zone influences on viticultural climates. In addition, researchers have found that increases in CO_2 will cause more vegetative growth in grapevines and increased water use efficiency; however the increased growth is likely to come at the expense of grape quality. Finally, an important indirect effect of increased CO_2 for the wine industry has also been identified: changes in the texture of oak wood may alter their suitability for wine barrel production.

Future predicted climate changes

Current climate modelling work, using a range of predictions with regard to CO_2 emissions, indicates that the globally averaged surface temperature will increase 2.0–4.5 °C over the period 1990–2100 (see figure). This level of change is 2–10 times greater than that which was observed during the 20th century. Recent focused research for the majority of the world's best wine regions reveals that growing season temperatures are projected to warm by 2.0 °C by 2050, with increased seasonal temperature variability. However, the warming rates vary: locations in the northern hemisphere are expected to warm more than those in the southern hemisphere. In addition, regions closer to the equator or inland are expected to warm more than those at higher latitudes or in coastal zones, respectively. Others have suggested that in Australia and California, this projected warming is likely to lead to a decrease in rainfall in most viticultural locations, leading to greater water stress and reductions in water resources in the future.

Future climate change of the magnitudes predicted will have numerous effects on society and natural ecosystems. Likewise, it presents numerous potential influences on, and challenges to, the wine industry, including additional changes in the timing of grapevine phenology, which is likely to result in a

disruption of balanced composition and flavour in grapes and wine. In addition, the changes are not likely to be uniform across all regions and varieties, but are likely to be related to climatic thresholds for optimum growth and quality. Furthermore, the warming will clearly force changes in the varieties grown and wine styles produced in particular regions: those that currently have a cool climate will have a greater choice of viable varieties, while in many of today's warmer regions, the future climates will be challenging for optimum grape growth and wine production. The warming is also predicted to produce poleward extensions in viable grape growing regions. Additional challenges will be found in the increased presence and/or intensity of pests and disease.

While the Earth's climate is always changing, as society develops we become more intertwined and fixed within our economic and cultural systems. This is never more evident than with wine production, where there are strong regional identities in terms of varieties and wine styles. Therefore, any future climate change has the potential to influence cultural change. To prepare for the future, the wine industry will most certainly need to integrate planning and adaptation strategies to adjust to changes in climate.   G.V.J. & H.S.

Chuine, I., Yiou, P., Viovy, N., Seguin, B., Daux, V., and Le Roy Ladurie, E., 'Grape ripening as a past climate indicator', Nature, 432 (2004).

Gladstones, J., Viticulture and Environment (Adelaide, 1992).

Houghton J. T. et al., Climate Change 2001: The Scientific Basis. Contribution of the Working Group I to the Third Assessment of the Intergovernmental Panel on Climate Change (Cambridge, 2001).

Jones, G. V., White, M. A., Cooper, O. R., and Storchmann, K.-H., 'Climate change and global wine quality', Climatic Change (2005).

Jones, P. D., Parker, D. E., Osborn, T. J., and Briffa, K. R., 'Global and hemispheric temperature anomalies—land and marine instrumental records', in Trends: A Compendium of Data on Global Change (Carbon Dioxide Information Analysis Center, Oak Ridge National Laboratory, US Department of Energy, 2001).

Pfister, C., 'Variations in the spring–summer climate of central Europe from the High Middle Ages to 1850', in H. Wanner and U. Siegenthaler (eds.), Long and Short Term Variability of Climate (Berlin, 1988), 57–82.

Schultz, H. R., 'Climate change and viticulture: a European perspective on climatology, carbon dioxide, and UV-B effects', Australian Journal of Grape and Wine Research, 6 (2000), 2–12.

climate classification, the description and grouping of climates for viticultural purposes.

History

Climate classification, particularly that of Köppen, has been commonly used in disciplines such as geography and ecology. While such approaches are helpful for a macroscopic view, specialized systems have been developed for viticulture. The first influential scientific study of viticultural climates was that of the French researcher A. P. de Candolle in the mid 19th century, a time when reliable climatic data were just starting to become available. De Candolle observed that the spring start of vine growth in European vineyards corresponded closely with the dates on which average mean temperature reached 10 °C/50 °F. On that basis he proposed that useful heat for vine growth and RIPENING could be measured by the amount that actual mean temperatures exceed 10 °C. A summation of the excesses for all individual days would give a measure of the total usable heat for the year.

Subsequent French research has paid surprisingly little attention to developing systematic methods, or models, for classifying viticultural climates (Seguin). Perhaps this is understandable, in that French viticulture is long established in its given environments. There is a need, however, for improved understanding of annual variations; a recent Burgundy study has shown a correlation between early harvest dates for Pinot Noir grapes with dry winters and warm springs. An interesting classification is proposed by Tonietto and Carbonneau. Some ideas on the role of day length at high latitudes, associated with researchers such as J. Branas and P. Huglin, are mentioned under LATITUDE. Huglin did some very extensive work on climate classification (see Huglin, and Huglin and Schneider). He compares climatic conditions with the amount of heat varieties need to ripen, concluding that great wines can only be made when grapes are just able to achieve ripeness, slowly and late in the season, in the local climate. See also TERROIR.

Leaving them aside, however, it is hardly surprising to find that the greatest interest in this field has been in the NEW WORLD, where the need for principles to evaluate potential new viticultural environments has been both pressing and obvious.

California heat summation
The first extensive practical use of de Candolle's method was in California, where AMERINE and WINKLER, in 1944, delineated five viticultural regions on the basis of their Fahrenheit temperature summations over 50 °F/ 10 °C. One advance over de Candolle was to confine the summations to an assumed vine growth and ripening season extending from 1 April to 31 October. The resulting comparisons are more relevant and reliable than those taking in all months of the year.

The California summations (like most others) are in practice calculated from monthly averages, each month's total being its average excess of the mean over 50 °F, multiplied by the number of days in the month. Amerine and Winkler's five regions, in terms of the total Fahrenheit 'degree days' for the seven months, are as follows:

Region I (the coolest) having less than 2,500 ° days F;
Region II, 2,500–3,000 ° days F;
Region III, 3,000–3,500 ° days F;
Region IV, 3,500–4,000 ° days F;
Region V, over 4,000 ° days F.

Regions I and II are found in general to produce California's best dry table wines, with light to medium body and good natural balance. Region III produces full-bodied dry and sweet wines. Region IV is reckoned to be best for FORTIFIED wines, with table wines mainly inferior. Region V, typified by the irrigated inland valleys, such as the hottest parts of SAN JOAQUIN VALLEY, is best for TABLE GRAPES and DRYING GRAPES, producing mainly low-quality table wines.

Although successful in California, Amerine and Winkler's system, sometimes called heat summation (or simply by Winkler's name), is not fully accepted elsewhere. We now know that it works well in California partly because temperatures there are quite closely correlated with other climatic factors possibly related to viticulture and wine quality: directly with TEMPERATURE VARIABILITY and total SUNLIGHT, and inversely with HUMIDITY (see also CLIMATE AND WINE QUALITY). Temperature alone thus gives an adequate index of all the relevant climatic variables. The correlations are much less close in most other environments. In some they are largely absent: in east coastal Australia and New Zealand, and in central and northern Italy, for instance. In these regions temperature alone is a poor indicator of their viticultural climates.

Some other systems based on temperature have been simpler. Prescott found that the average mean temperature of the warmest month gave essentially as good a climatic indication as the seasonal temperature summation. Average mean temperature for the whole seven months (see COOL CLIMATES) likewise gives a reasonable measure of growing season temperature regimes. All such indices, however, suffer from the same shortcomings as temperature summations.

An Australian alternative
More recent major proposals for viticultural climate classification have sought to place them on broader bases. The most widely used is that of Smart and Dry, developed for use in Australia. This involves five separate climate elements of temperature, sunlight, rainfall, evaporation, and humidity, but is still tolerably simple and workable. Following Prescott's earlier Australian work, Smart and Dry preferred to use the simple statistic of average mean temperature for January (July in the northern hemisphere) as a measure of usable heat. It is complemented by an index of CONTINENTALITY (the difference between mean summer and winter temperatures) to show the amplitude of swings in temperatures through the 12 months, together with indices of sun-

light, humidity, and water relations. The five elements of the classification are:

- average mean January (July) temperature (five categories);
- continentality (five categories);
- total seasonal sunlight hours (four categories);
- aridity, based on the difference between rainfall and 0.5 of measured EVAPORATION (four categories);
- relative humidity, as measured at 0900 hours (four categories).

The resulting five-way classification gives a reasonable overview of viticultural climates, and has been widely used for vineyard site selection. The index allows prediction of wine style and quality, most suitable varieties, irrigation requirements, and the likelihood of disease.

This writer's own proposal goes beyond simple categories, and is too complex to cover in full here. Briefly, a method to predict an average ripening date for any defined grape maturity type in any environment is developed. Like Amerine and Winkler's method (above) it employs growing season temperature summations over a 10 °C/50 °F base, but with refinements to improve the fit to known vine behaviour across existing viticultural environments. These entail:

- imposing an upper limit (19 °C) on the monthly average mean temperatures, beyond which no further increases are credited;
- a correction factor proportional to the average day length of each month (long days giving greater biological effectiveness for a given greater mean temperature; see LATITUDE);
- a correction for each month's average daily temperature range (a narrow range resulting in greater effectiveness, for a given mean).

Having arrived at a predicted ripening date, average conditions of temperature, sunshine, rainfall, and relative humidity for the final ripening month can be estimated. Conditions then are held to be those most influential in determining the quality characteristics of grapes and therefore of the potential wine (or at least to be sufficiently indicative of them for practical purposes). Calculated separately for each grape maturity group, the ripening month conditions become the direct basis for evaluating or comparing environments as to their likely grape variety adaptations, potential for wine quality, and most natural wine styles.   J.G.

Amerine, M. A., and Winkler, A. J., 'Composition and quality of musts and wines of California grapes', *Hilgardia*, 15 (1944), 493–575.

Gladstones, J., *Viticulture and Environment* (Adelaide, 1992).

Huglin, P., 'Nouveau mode d'évaluation des possibilités héliothermiques d'un milieu viticole', *Comptes Rendus de l'Académie d'Agriculture de France* (1978), 1117–1126.

——and Schneider, C., *Biologie et écologie de la vigne* (Paris, 1998).

Prescott, J. A., 'The climatology of the vine (Vitis vinifera). 3. A comparison of France and Australia on the basis of the warmest month', *Transactions of the Royal Society of South Australia*, 93 (1969), 7–15.

Seguin, B., 'Synthèse des travaux de recherche sur l'influence du climat, du microclimat et du sol sur la physiologie de la vigne, avec quelques éléments sur les arbres fruitiers', *Vignes & Vins*, special number *Agrométéorologie et Vigne* (Sept 1982), 13–21.

Smart, R. E., and Dry, P. R., 'A climatic classification for Australian viticultural regions', *Australian Grapegrower and Winemaker*, 196 (1980), 8, 10, 16.

Tonietto, J., and Carbonneau, A., 'Système de classification climatique multicritères (C.C.M.) géoviticole', in *3rd International Symposium Zonification Vitivinicola* (Tenerife, May 2000).

climate effects on vine diseases. The climate has a major effect on VINE DISEASES, and indeed is a major factor determining where grapes are grown worldwide. The most commercially important vine diseases are due to fungi, and these are normally encouraged by warm, humid, and rainy conditions. Such regions as a consequence produce wines of higher RESVERATROL content, with purported HEALTH benefits. Most of the world's viticulture is therefore carried out in regions with dry summers and less attendant risk of disease, the Mediterranean area being a classic example. However, as the risk of fungal disease decreases, the likelihood of DROUGHT increases and, in those parts of Europe where irrigation is prohibited (such as southern France), the effects of drought can be substantial. Some regions such as California, Chile, and Western Australia can be so dry during summer that DOWNY MILDEW, one of the worst vine fungal diseases, is not present at all.

Sometimes climate effects on vine disease are subtle and difficult to discern. A good example is the phytoplasma disease FLAVESCENCE DORÉE, which is known to occur in epidemics, with severity varying markedly from year to year. This is thought to result from climate-induced natural variations in population levels of the insect vector. While the insect population swings are dramatic, the weather perturbations responsible may indeed be so slight as to be barely distinguishable from the average. RAINFALL (and sometimes dew) has a major effect on diseases. Water is important for spore germination and dispersal by splashing, as for downy mildew and DEAD ARM, and so a rainy spring can cause epidemics of both these diseases. Rain near the time of harvest causes grape berries to split, and so many BUNCH ROT fungi and bacteria can gain entry and ruin the fruit. Many fungi spores such as those of BOTRYTIS BUNCH ROT and downy mildew germinate in high humidity. The fungal disease POWDERY MILDEW develops in the shade of dense vine canopies, and is also encouraged by overcast weather. Years of low rainfall mean that the effect of pests which damage roots such as PHYLLOXERA and NEMATODES are more evident.

TEMPERATURE is a major factor in disease development and spread, with temperatures of 20 to 27 °C favouring the germination of powdery mildew spores. Freezing winter temperatures can cause vine trunks to split, allowing the entry of the CROWN GALL bacterium.

WIND is important in spreading diseases: for example BACTERIAL BLIGHT is spread in wet, windy weather. Otherwise wind helps reduce disease by drying leaves and fruit after rain and dew.

Climate has a significant effect on wine quality because of disease, and there is no more important example than that of botrytis bunch rot. Intermittent rainy, humid, and warm weather near the time of harvest causes anguish to grape-grower and winemaker alike, because of the risk of losing both yield and quality. Yet, following infection, a change to dry weather can encourage the formation of NOBLE ROT. Furthermore, costs of grape production are higher when the weather induces disease. R.E.S.

Pearson, R. C., and Goheen, A. C., *Compendium of Grape Diseases* (St Paul, Minn., 1988).

Clinton, dark-skinned AMERICAN HYBRID, of *labrusca–riparia* origin. It is planted in Brazil and its wine has a pronounced FOXY flavour. It has also been known in Italian SWITZERLAND.

clonal selection, one of the two principal means of improving a vine variety (the other being the elimination of VIRUS DISEASES). Clonal selection is the practice of selecting a single superior plant in the vineyard and then taking cuttings from this vine for PROPAGATION. The selection is generally made with a particular attribute such as YIELD or fruit RIPENESS in mind. Clonal selection contrasts with MASS SELECTION.

New grapevines, in common with many other perennial crops, are produced by vegetative propagation, that is by using cuttings which are genetically identical. (This contrasts with agricultural field crops which are multiplied by seeds which are different one from another—although sexual reproduction leading to the production of seedlings is the means by which NEW VARIETIES are created.) In vegetative propagation, each bud from a so-called 'mother vine' essentially gives rise to a plant of the same CLONE (except for those very rare cases in which a bud mutation has taken place).

Clonal selection for vines was first demonstrated in 1926 in Germany, where it has been most widely practised. Other European countries have also developed clonal selection initiatives, but the practice is less well developed in some countries of the New World.

Clonal selection depends on the fact that adjacent vines in a vineyard may be different, sometimes discernibly different. More often the differences can be established only after some years of careful measurement. Differences on this scale would not normally be expected from soil variation. There are two possible explanations: the first being a difference in genetic make-up between the vines due to mutations; the second being a difference in the incidence of diseases in the vines.

Sometimes the disease is 'graft transmissible' and is carried from one vine generation to the next in CUTTINGS. The most common and commercially important transmissible disease agents are VIRUSES. Such disease agents are transmitted by careless selection of the BUDWOOD or ROOTSTOCK material used at GRAFTING (and thus a human influence), but it may also reflect the effect of viruses, VIROIDS, or PHYTOPLASMA transmitted by NEMATODES or INSECTS. In any event, infection, especially due to a virus, can have a major impact on yield, fruit ripening, and wine quality.

There has been disagreement between viticultural scientists working in this area as to the relative importance of genetic difference *vis-à-vis* virus diseases. Professor Helmut BECKER, an acknowledged authority on clonal selection based at the GEISENHEIM Institute in Germany, argued for the genetic difference principle, while the virologists led by Austin Goheen of the University of California at DAVIS believed that virus infection was the more important. (More recently the possibility has been raised that differing viroid incidence may be responsible for clonal variation.) Most workers in the field would now agree that both influences are important, but these views have had significant consequences. Some European centres had been slow to test for and eliminate virus diseases, whereas in California the emphasis had traditionally been on virus elimination, typically by THERMOTHERAPY, rather than on clonal selection and evaluation in the field. During the 1980s and 1990s this situation changed, although not necessarily in time for California's replanting programme necessitated in the 1990s by PHYLLOXERA. In countries such as Australia, New Zealand, and South Africa, efforts to improve vines acknowledge both viewpoints.

Importantly, whether the vine to vine difference in the field is due to mutation or a graft-transmissible disease, the effects can be passed on from generation to generation by the cuttings. This is the basis of the viticultural technique of clonal selection.

The process of clonal selection is necessarily long and requires considerable investment of resources. To make reliable field selections requires several years of records (up to nine are used in Germany) followed by comparative trials of many different clones of the one variety for evaluation. After waiting three years for the first harvest, five to ten more years are necessary to monitor yields and fruit ripeness. These trials are often conducted in several locations and with several rootstocks. Clonal selection should also involve making trial wine to assure trueness to VARIETAL type. Selected clones may not therefore be released until 15 or more years after the initial selection in the field. And, given the possibilities of both mutation and the spread of viruses by natural means, clonal selection should be an ongoing process. There has already been a release of second generation clones in Germany; fields originally planted to one clone have been selected again for 'clones of clones'.

There is no doubt that clonal selection has played an important part in improving both yield and wine quality from modern vineyards. When grafting became popular in the 1880s to overcome phylloxera, virus diseases were inadvertently spread. Many vineyards of both the Old World and the New World planted as late as the 1960s contained off-types, rogue vines, and virus diseases. As more healthy and true-to-type planting material becomes available as a result of clonal selection, then these problems disappear. Many reputable nurserymen worldwide will provide only plants propagated from clonally selected rootstocks and scions.

Mechanisms for clonal selection and propagation vary from country to country. Generally the studies are conducted by government-funded scientists (although it is not unusual for a leading Bordeaux château, for example, to be doing its own clonal selection from vines naturally adapted to that property). In France the extent to which planting material was infected by viruses up to the mid 1940s led to the formation of the Institut des Vins de Consommation Courante (IVCC). This organization and its affiliates test selected clones and supply CERTIFIED PLANTING MATERIAL. Certification in Germany was introduced voluntarily after the First World War, and the scheme later became law. The EUROPEAN UNION adopted guidelines for propagation material through the EU in the early 1990s. In Australia, South Africa, and New Zealand there are well-established VINE IMPROVEMENT programmes utilizing clonal selection as well as virus elimination. In California, the programme is conducted by the FOUNDATION PLANT SERVICES at the University of California at DAVIS. In South Africa, there is a Vine Improvement Association and a number of organizations specialize in heat treatment to eliminate viruses.

For many vine varieties, the differences in appearance and performance between clones with the same virus status is small. This suggests that genetic differences are generally minor and that the mutation rate is low. Some varieties, such as Pinot Noir, show extreme variation between clones, which suggests that multiple selections were initially made from the wild and/or a high mutation rate.

It is difficult to understand the effect of clonal selection on commercial wine quality since so many vineyards are planted with mixed clones. While most Old World countries have a wide range of clones available, sometimes, because of limited importations, a New World country might have only a few

for any one variety. An extreme example is Sauvignon Blanc in New Zealand, where all commercial plantings up until the early 1990s can be traced to a single clone imported from the United States. Some producers are critical of the limited availability of only improved clones from nurserymen. They argue that either mass selection or a range of clones produces better, more characterful wine than a single virus-free, high-yielding clone. Unfortunately, some clones were released on the basis of purely viticultural evaluation, which has fuelled suspicion about their effect on wine quality.   R.E.S.

clone in a viticultural context is a single vine or a population of vines all derived by vegetative PROPAGATION from cuttings or buds from a single 'mother vine' by deliberate CLONAL SELECTION.

Vine nurseries may sell a range of different clones of each vine variety, each with different attributes and characteristics and individually identified by numbers and/or names. In Germany, for example, there is a formal process of clonal evaluation and a systematic numbering system. Normally government agencies are involved in selection, evaluation, and distribution to nurserymen, and often the availability of clones and their acceptance varies regionally. Some clones are so outstanding that they become internationally distributed. Clones of Riesling from GEISENHEIM in Germany are examples of this. In the 1990s, there was considerable interest in Burgundian (sometimes called Dijon) clones; see particularly CHARDONNAY and PINOT NOIR.

By the late 1980s, many quality-conscious wine producers were wary of being dependent on a single clone of a particular variety—particularly Pinot Noir—deliberately seeking instead a mixture of clones or, less likely, vines from MASS SELECTION, for both viticultural and wine quality reasons.   R.E.S. & B.G.C.

Galet, P., *Dictionnaire encyclopédique des cépages* (Paris, 2000).

Marsh, S.A., 'The contribution of Pinot Noir clones to the vineyards of the Côte d'Or. An evaluation focusing on clones 114, 115, 667, 777' (MW dissertation, London, 2004).

Mullins, M. G., Bouquet, A., and Williams, L., *Biology of the Grapevine* (Cambridge, 1992).

clos is French for 'enclosure', and any vineyard described as a Clos should be enclosed, generally by a wall. This is a particularly common term in Burgundy, but is also used elsewhere. Similarly, the term *cuve close* refers to the sealed tank which gives its name to a bulk method of SPARKLING WINE-MAKING. The first new wave producers of PRIORAT adopted this term for their single-vineyard wines.

Clos de la Roche, leading red GRAND CRU in Burgundy's CÔTE D'OR. For more details, see MOREY-ST-DENIS.

Clos de Tart, Clos des Lambrays, and **Clos St-Denis,** red GRANDS CRUS in Burgundy's CÔTE D'OR. For more details, see MOREY-ST-DENIS.

Clos de Vougeot, also frequently known as **Clos Vougeot,** famous walled vineyard in BURGUNDY created originally by the monks (see MONKS AND MONASTERIES) of Cîteaux. Between the 12th and early 14th centuries the Cistercians purchased or received as donations the land, much of which needed clearing and planting, which subsequently became known as the Clos de Vougeot. By 1336, the 50-ha/120-acre plot was complete and enclosed by stone walls on all sides.

The Cistercians maintained ownership until the French Revolution, when all clerical estates were dispossessed, although Dom Goblet, the monk responsible for the vineyards and the wine, had a sufficiently fine reputation to retain his job in the short term. In due course, Clos de Vougeot was sold on to Julien-Jules Ouvrard in 1818, the year before he bought ROMANÉE-Conti, and remained in single ownership until 1889. Since then ownership has fragmented so that today there are over 80 proprietors.

A small chapel and rudimentary buildings, damaged during the religious wars, were rebuilt and enlarged in 1551, becoming the current Ch du Clos de Vougeot, a major tourist attraction. It is also home to the CONFRÉRIE des Chevaliers du Tastevin, a brotherhood which organizes copious feasts and the tastings for the Tastevinage. For this, producers submit wines to a jury; those selected are entitled to use the 'tasteviné' label, which should enable the wine to be sold more easily or at a higher price.

For more historical detail, see BURGUNDY, history. The vineyard and wines of Clos de Vougeot are described under VOUGEOT.
                                          J.T.C.M.

closures for wine containers are necessary to avoid harmful contact with OXYGEN and have changed remarkably little until recent times. CORKS are still the principal closures used for wine BOTTLES, just as they were more than two centuries ago and probably long before that, although alternative stoppers are increasingly common, thanks primarily to a rise in the incidence of CORKED wine as a result of cork taint since the mid 1980s.

History
Cork was certainly known in Ancient GREECE, where, as in Ancient EGYPT, great care was taken to provide AMPHORAE with a wide variety of airtight stoppers. Roman authors such as CATO, writing in the 2nd century BC, refer to the need to seal jars with cork and pitch when the fermentation was complete. However, this use of cork does not appear to have continued into the early medieval period, possibly because the main potential supply of European

cork was in southern Iberia, which had been conquered by the Moors in the 8th century. Medieval illuminations illustrate barrels generally sealed by wooden stoppers, with cloth frequently placed between the barrel and the stopper to provide a more airtight seal. Pitch and wax were also sometimes used to provide additional protection. In the long period during which wine was mainly stored in and served from the BARREL, the most common stopper was some form of BUNG.

With the development of glass bottles during the 17th century, it was necessary to devise new methods of stoppering. Glass stoppers, ground to fit individual bottles and tied to them with thread, were therefore introduced, and survived well into the 19th century. Indeed, as they are found in DECANTERS, they remain in use to this day, and are now also being introduced for bottled wine. However, such stoppers were expensive, and gradually from the beginning of the 17th century cork became the most frequent substance used to seal bottles. The use of corks also required the invention of another piece of equipment, the corkscrew or, as it was first called, the bottle-screw. The earliest corks were not pressed completely into the bottles, and so could be pulled out without excessive difficulty. However, by the end of the 17th century the introduction of CORKSCREWS enabled corks to be fully inserted into the necks of bottles.   P.T.H.U.

Johnson, H., *The Story of Wine* (London, 1989).
Simon, A. L., *Bottlescrew Days: Wine Drinking in England during the 18th Century* (London, 1926).

Modern closures

Modern technology, prompted by an increasing awareness of the extent of CORK TAINT and bottle-to-bottle variability, offers a range of alternatives to the traditional cork. To present a viable alternative to this natural substance they have to offer a reliable seal, present an inert substance to the wine, be easy to remove and reinsert, and be capable of being produced at a relatively low cost. Few have proved as successful as cork for long-term BOTTLE AGEING, however, and there is still considerable attachment on the part of many wine drinkers to the ritual of pulling a cork. For more details, see CROWN CAPS, SCREW CAPS, and SYNTHETIC CLOSURES.

Recent years have seen the development and marketing of a range of novel closures, such as Australia's Zork (which offers the convenience of a screw cap but pops like a cork) and ProCork (a natural cork sealed at both ends with a barrier membrane to protect the wine from oxygen and taint), and the glass Vino-Lok from Germany. These alternatives are likely to capitalize on the growing frustration with the variable performance of natural cork, but the field is still wide open to more acceptable, and more aesthetically pleasing, alternatives to a piece of bark.

See also CAPSULES.   J.A.G.

Goode, J. A., *Wine Science: The Application of Science in Winemaking* (London, 2005).

cloudy wine. See FAULTS and STABILIZATION.

Cloudy Bay, seminal winery in the Marlborough region of NEW ZEALAND, the brainchild of David Hohnen of Cape Mentelle in WESTERN AUSTRALIA. Its debut release of a moodily labelled varietal Sauvignon Blanc in 1985 on export markets created a reputation for Marlborough Sauvignon and a cult following for Cloudy Bay almost overnight, even though initially the grapes were bought in and the wine made under contract at another winery. The enterprise, based in its own premises, became a distant offshoot of the VEUVE CLICQUOT, and hence LVMH, empire in 1990. It also produces Chardonnay, Pinot Noir, and sparkling wine.

cluster, alternative, viticultural term for a BUNCH of grapes.

Coal River, wine region in TASMANIA.

Coastal, misleading, unregulated, and much-used term on California wine labels meant to, sometimes falsely, imply provenance cooler than the CENTRAL VALLEY.

Coastal Region, an important wine region in South Africa, home to several of the country's most important wine districts and wards, including Constantia, Durbanville, Franschhoek Valley, Paarl, Stellenbosch, Cape Point, Swartland, and Tulbagh. The name appears on many labels.

cochylis, a flying insect which can damage vines. See MOTHS.

Cockburn, port house which, in the second half of the 20th century, made the transition from bulk shipper to brand leader in the important British market. The house was founded in 1815 by Robert Cockburn and George Wauchope, who were joined in 1828 by Captain William Greig. A year later, Robert Cockburn's sons Archibald and Alexander joined the company and opened an office in London. In 1845, the brothers Henry and John Smithes joined the company, which became Cockburn Smithes and Co. John Smithes initiated an organized system of records for blending. He married Eleanor Cobb and both Smithes and Cobb families remained in the firm for many generations. The last family member Peter Cobb joined Cockburn's in 1960, became a director of the company in Oporto in 1980, and retired in 1999. In 1962, Cockburn's became an associate company of HARVEYS of Bristol and, subsequently, part of the Allied-Domecq conglomerate (until 2005). It is now part of a new American company, Beam Wine Estates. A year previously, Harveys

had bought Martinez Gassiot, transforming the two houses from fierce competitors to partners. Cockburn's most important brand is their reserve ruby Special Reserve. The house has taken some unconventional views on declaring vintage port: it released the lighter 1967 rather than 1966 against the popular vote (Martinez joined it) but decided against declaring 1977 and 1980 before releasing a 1983. In 1975, amid political turbulence in Portugal, Cockburn's made a major investment in land and buildings at Quinta de Santa Maria, near Régua. The house continued its tradition of using land in the higher reaches of DOURO with the purchase, in 1978, of 300 ha/ 750 acres of vineyards at Vilariça, where important viticultural experiments are being carried out, in particular trial of various clones of TOURIGA NACIONAL. This work was particularly useful when in 1989 the company acquired Quinta dos Canais, a 300-ha property on the north bank of the Douro, which has long provided the backbone of Cockburn's vintage port but which needed extensive renovation and replanting. A new winery has been built and a single-quinta vintage port is also produced here.   S.A., R.J.M. & J.R.

Cocks et Féret, important directory of Bordeaux châteaux which was first published in 1845 as *Bordeaux, its Wines and the Claret Country* by the Englishman Charles Cocks who died in 1854 (see LITERATURE OF WINE). It was translated into *Bordeaux et ses vins*, with the emphasis on classifying wines in order of merit, by Féret in 1850. A second edition appeared in 1868 and provides a useful historical record of the evolution of different properties' and districts' reputations. (The 1868 edition, for example, ranks Ch PÉTRUS as a mere CRU BOURGEOIS.) It continues, as just Féret in the 1990s, to this day.

Cocks, C., and Féret, C., *Bordeaux and its Wines* (17th edn, Bordeaux, 2004).

Cococciola, white wine variety native to the ABRUZZO where it is blended with TREBBIANO.

Coda di Volpe, ancient, full-bodied white grape grown near Naples in CAMPANIA.

Códega, Douro name for SÍRIA, Portugal's widely planted white wine grape.

Codorníu, the world's largest producer of bottle-fermented SPARKLING WINES made by the TRADITIONAL METHOD. The Codorníu group incorporates the Spanish CAVA brands Codorníu and Rondel, the still wine Masia Bach, and Raimat which makes both Cava and still wine (see COSTERS DEL SEGRE) but 65 per cent of its turnover is earned from sales of Cava. The history of Codorníu dates back to 1551, when the Codorníu family established their first winery in San Sadurní de Noya, PENEDÈS, in Spanish Cataluña. In 1659, the heiress to the Codorníu winery, María Ana Codorníu, married a member of the Raventós family. A direct descendant, Josep Raventós, decided to produce sparkling wine, uncorking the first bottle of Spanish wine made in the image of CHAMPAGNE in 1872. Within ten years, the style was popular across Spain, and, as a result, Codorníu can claim to be the wine on which the Cava industry was founded. The group's Cava is made from Parellada, Macabeo, and Xarel-lo grapes (no still wine is bought in) and 10 per cent of the blend is usually older reserve wine. A vintage premium Cava made substantially from Chardonnay was launched in 1992, named Anna de Codorníu after María Ana. Since then, Chardonnay has become a common ingredient in many Codorníu Cavas. In 1992, the group opened Codorníu Napa, a new winery in the CARNEROS district of California, since renamed Artesa. More than $50 million have been invested in a winery at Raimat. In 1997, Codorníu acquired the traditional Bodegas Bilbaínas firm in the RIOJA Alta, a major investment outside its Catalan base; then in 2000, it acquired a controlling stake in Cellers de Scala Dei, the oldest serious winery in PRIORAT. Also in 2000, the group built Legaris, a brand new winery in RIBERA DEL DUERO.   S.A. & V. de la S.

co-fermentation, the simultaneous fermentation of two or more varieties in the same vessel, is said to lift a wine's floral aromas, enhance its TEXTURE, and improve the brilliance and intensity of the colour.

The technique has its origins in the Old World, mostly notable in the CÔTE RÔTIE appellation in the northern Rhône. Here, the red variety SYRAH is co-fermented with the white variety VIOGNIER. Up to 20 per cent Viognier is permitted, but 5–10 per cent is more usual. This practice found increased favour in Australia and other parts of the New World from the early 2000s. Co-fermentation does not have to be a combination of red and white grapes—in the United States, for example, co-fermentation may originally have been a natural consequence of FIELD BLENDS such as ZINFANDEL and PETITE SIRAH. Another notable historical example is found in the CHIANTI region of Italy, where the primary red grape, Sangiovese, has traditionally been fermented with small amounts of the red variety Canaiolo Nero and the white varieties Trebbiano and Malvasia, although this practice is becoming less common.

Research by Dr Roger Boulton, Professor of Enology and Chemical Engineering at DAVIS, indicates that red varieties may contain low levels of co-factors (sometimes known confusingly as co-pigments), which are said to aid CO-PIGMENTATION and thus the formation of deeper and more stable colour in red wines. The addition of a variety with higher levels of co-factors may aid co-pigmentation, and co-fermentation may originally have been

adopted because it was seen to increase colour stability and intensity.

When Syrah, or Shiraz, and Viognier are co-fermented, there are many different techniques used to add the Viognier: whole fruit at the crusher; whole grapes, or pressed skins and grapes or just juice added to the crushed Shiraz must.

Differing harvest dates may put constraints on co-fermentation but these can be overcome by modern REFRIGERATION techniques. Further research is needed to ascertain the best combinations of varieties and the best proportions. Too many white grapes might simply dilute the colour of a red wine.   T.R.C. & J.Ha.

Boulton, R., 'The copigmentation of anthocyanins and its role in the color of red wine: a critical review', *American Journal of Enology and Viticulture*, 52/2 (2001), 67–87.

coffee houses. The traditional drink of Arabs, coffee was introduced to western Europe in the mid 17th century. Like tea and chocolate, it was soon to pose a serious threat to the popularity of wine.

The first English coffee house was reputedly opened in a room in the Angel Inn in Oxford's High Street in 1650 and within a couple of years the trend had taken hold in London. By the 1660s, coffee houses were challenging the traditional English tavern, and not only because they served this novel beverage which was very cheap and had the added advantage of not making you drunk. Samuel Pepys, among others, frequented these 'penny universities' in order to catch up on the city's gossip or join a political debate.

Some of the more popular ones survive as gentlemen's clubs, whilst coffee houses in Europe evolved into that ubiquitous institution, the café.   H.B.

Aubertin-Potter, N., and Bennett, A., *Oxford Coffee Houses 1651–1800* (Oxford, 1987).

Ellis, A., *The Penny Universities: A History of the Coffee Houses* (London, 1956).

Lillywhite, B., *London Coffee Houses* (London, 1963).

Colares, exceptional but now minuscule DOC wine region on the west coast of PORTUGAL just north of the capital Lisbon (see map under PORTUGAL). These vineyards were spared from the PHYLLOXERA pest in the 19th century (thanks to their sandy composition) but look unlikely to survive today's commercial pressures. RAMISCO, the Colares vine, is probably the only VINIFERA grape variety never to have been grafted. It is to be found planted only in a narrow strip of sand dunes on the clifftops above the Atlantic, its roots anchored in the clay below. It is ironic that the soils that saved Colares are making them today less and less viable. When a Colares vineyard is replanted, a trench 2 to 3 m deep has to be excavated to reach the clay. Owing to the tendency of the sides of the trench to collapse without warning, vineyard workers would

wear baskets over their heads to protect them against instant suffocation.

The region was badly hit by the collapse of the Brazilian market in 1930 and a year later the Lisbon government created the Adega Regional, a CO-OPERATIVE winery, which all growers were eventually obliged to join for their wine to be entitled to the Colares denomination. The Adega Regional was established in order to stamp out fraud, but standards slipped and the ruling had the effect of merely stifling initiative. In 1990, the EUROPEAN UNION forced the government to abolish the Adega Regional's monopoly (soon after a similar move in the Dão), but this was probably too late to save the wine from virtual extinction and by the mid 2000s just 22 ha/55 acres of vineyard remained (compared with over 1,800 ha in the 1930s). In 1999, the local municipality intervened and 8.5 hectares of traditional vineyard were placed in the hands of a charitable foundation. In theory, three different styles of wine are permitted to use the name Colares: two red and one white. The most highly prized comes from the sandy dune-like soils and the Ramisco grape must make up 80 per cent of the blend. A second red comes from the firmer ground away from the coast, although this has nothing like the same finesse. A small amount of white Colares is also made, principally from (unspecified) MALVASIA grapes.   R.J.M.

cold soak, MACERATION technique particularly popular for Pinot Noir.

colheita, Portuguese word meaning 'crop' or 'HARVEST' and, by extension, 'VINTAGE'. It is also the name of a style of PORT or MADEIRA from a single year aged in wood for at least seven or five years respectively before bottling.   R.J.M.

collage, French term for FINING.

collar rot, one of the FUNGAL DISEASES of the vine which particularly attacks young vines growing in cool, moist soil via the *Pythium* fungus. The vines are weakened and may die. Vines grafted on to Rupestris St George ROOTSTOCKS are most susceptible. Control is achieved by removing soil from the base of the trunk and reducing soil moisture.   R.E.S.

collecting wine became a popular hobby in the 1980s. Americans in particular have tended to call anyone who buys fine wine a **collector** rather than a wine enthusiast, connoisseur, or *amateur* (the French term), suggesting that the thrill lies in acquisition rather than in consumption. Ever since the development of cylindrical BOTTLES in the 1730s, when it first became possible to maintain a personal CELLAR, there have been individuals whose purchasing patterns amounted to building up a specific **collection** of certain wines. The rapid economic growth of the late 1970s and 1980s, however, together with a succession of good vintages to be bought EN PRIMEUR and the emergence of a truly international consumer wine press (see Robert PARKER, for example), resulted in the emergence of a significant group of serious wine collectors around the globe (notably in the United States, Germany, and ASIA). They communicate and trade with each other through the AUCTION houses and the specialist BROKERS, and for some of them the purpose of collecting is to enable occasional but usually sumptuous marathon TASTING events.

colli, also written **colline** and **collio,** is the Italian word for hills, and its use in a wine name indicates that the wine is produced on slopes of a certain altitude (it is an almost direct equivalent of France's CÔTE, Côtes, and Coteaux). Accordingly, articles about Colli Somewhere are listed not under Colli, but under S for Somewhere.

Elevation is obviously in the eye of the beholder, however, and the word *colli* is used to describe both mere knolls and near-mountainous viticulture at altitudes of over 500 m/1,600 ft. *Colli* and its variations can be found not only as the title of various DOCs but also as a part of their descriptive apparatus: CHIANTI, for example, is produced in the Colli Senesi and the Colline Pisane (Chianti dei Colli Senesi, Chianti delle Colline Pisane). The absence of the word does not imply that a given wine is produced in the flatlands; much of Italy's finest wine—BARBARESCO, BAROLO, BRUNELLO DI MONTALCINO, VINO NOBILE DI MONTEPULCIANO—is produced from HILLSIDE VINEYARDS without that fact being indicated in the wine's name.   D.T.

Collio, more properly **Collio Goriziano,** is a qualitatively important, predominantly white wine, DOC zone on the north eastern border of Italy with Slovenia. Collio did much in the early 1970s to increase Italians' confidence in their ability to make fine white wine.

Collio, a corruption of the Italian word for hills (see COLLI), is in the province of Gorizia (hence Colli Goriziano) and was reunified with Italy only after the First World War. Within the region of FRIULI, it is the fourth biggest DOC in terms of area planted and volume of production after GRAVE DEL FRIULI, ISONZO, and COLLI ORIENTALI del Friuli, but its fragrant and lively white wines, which account for 85 per cent of total production, have created an image of quality for Friuli throughout the world. Collio's red wines, overwhelmingly from MERLOT and CABERNETS SAUVIGNON and FRANC, tend to resemble LOIRE reds, at times with an identical vegetal quality underlined by a certain lightness of body and texture.

The territory itself extends across the hills from the Judrio river in the west—the former boundary between Austria and Italy and now Collio's boundary with the climatologically similar Colli Orientali—to the Slovenian border in the east. Vines are planted on a calcareous marl alternating with layers of sandstone called 'flysch of Cormons' after an important township in the heart of the zone.

The zone's current white wine style is relatively recent and was introduced not only to Collio but to all of Friuli by Mario Schiopetto, who had studied cold fermentation techniques in Germany. The strongly innovative character of his wines, coupled with their high quality and purity of varietal expression, gave direction to the entire zone and to the neighbouring Colli Orientali. The cellars of Collio and of the Colli Orientali tend to be extremely well equipped, with an abundance of REFRIGERATION units, pneumatic PRESSES, and all that is required for CENTRIFUGATION and STERILE BOTTLING. Relatively high yields (maximum permitted is 77 hl/ha, or 4.4 tons/acre) and formulaic wine-making can result in a certain blandness, simplicity, and monotony in the wines. Lower yields and better wine-making have produced cleaner, more pristine whites in recent years and this, allied to an attempt to inject a degree of complexity into the wines, either through the judicious use of oak or through a blend of one or more varieties, has returned Collio to the fore of Italian white wine-making.

The grape variety mix is very similar to that in the Colli Orientali to the immediate west. Since the mid 1990s, PINOT GRIGIO has overtaken TOCAI FRIULANO as the dominant variety of the DOC with 339 of the total 1,390 ha/3,475 acres planted in 2003. Tocai Friulano has also been surpassed by SAUVIGNON BLANC (252 ha), but is still more common than CHARDONNAY (129 ha) and PINOT BIANCO (89 ha). MERLOT accounts for 121 of the 245 ha of red grapes planted, with Cabernet Franc more common than Cabernet Sauvignon. The red wines from this zone seldom convince, as few of the vineyards are able to reach sufficient ripeness before the autumn rains set in.

See also SLOVENIA, which is capable of producing some extremely similar wines. Before the Second World War, Collio extended much further eastward, and many knowledgeable producers—some of whom have continued to own and farm vineyards across the border in Slovenia—claim that some of these positions are among the very finest of the entire zone.   D.T. & D.C.G.

Colli Orientali del Friuli, literally the eastern hills of the FRIULI region in north east Italy, is the region's second largest DOC. Its 2,300 ha/5,750 acres of vineyard give it 40 per cent more land dedicated to the vine than the COLLIO DOC between it and the Slovenian border, but the Colli Orientali have only a third as much vineyard acreage as GRAVE DEL FRIULI on the plain. It is the most versatile of the three, however, producing interesting white wines, high-quality dessert wines, and what are indisputably the finest, longest-lived red wines of Friuli. In a region known principally for its white wines, the Colli Orientali has 35 per cent of its vineyards planted to such red varieties as the international CABERNET and MERLOT as well as the renascent native varieties REFOSCO, SCHIOPPETTINO, and PIGNOLO. The area between Buttrio, Cividale, and Manzano has long been considered prime territory for superior reds, providing excellent growing conditions for all these varieties.

The territory of the DOC begins, as its name implies, to the east of the city of Udine and continues to the border of the province of Udine. The dividing line between the Colli Orientali and Collio is neither geological nor climatic, but simply historical: Udine and its province became part of Italy in 1866 while the neighbouring area of Collio, in the province of Gorizia, was not reunified with the rest of Italy until the end of the First World War. The contiguous zones in fact have the same sort of soil: the so-called 'flysch of Cormons', with alternating strata of calcareous marls and sandstone.

Wine has a documented history here, as in most parts of Italy, since the days of the Roman empire, but the zone first began to attract significant attention in the 1970s, when cold fermentation techniques began to produce here, and in the Collio DOC, significant quantities of fresh, fruity, and aromatic white wines, pioneering efforts for Italy. Significant development of red wines came in the 1980s as producers began to move away from lighter, fruitier styles towards a fuller, more structured style more worthy of ageing, a move that was frequently accompanied by the use of small oak barrels. A certain number of these more ambitious reds were released as an ambitiously priced VINO DA TAVOLA, because individual producers wanted either to distance the wines from their more facile antecedents, to make an unorthodox blend of varieties, or to emphasize their own name or that of Friuli. White wine, particularly from CHARDONNAY or PINOT BIANCO, was either fermented or aged in BARRIQUES; these wines were also marketed as vini da tavola to distinguish them from the fresher style of whites, which remained the backbone of production.

Current production is dominated by TOCAI FRIULANO among the white wine grapes, with 457 of the 1,480 acres planted to white varieties in 1996, followed by SAUVIGNON BLANC, PINOT GRIGIO, VERDUZZO, and Pinot Bianco. Small quantities of the sweet white PICOLIT are also made. Merlot is by far the most significant red variety, representing more than half of all red grape plantings, with Cabernet, Refosco, and minor quantities of PINOT NOIR and Schioppettino making up the rest. If the potential for fine wine is at least as high as in Collio, the wines themselves have been less consistent and significant quality fluctuations have not been uncommon even at the leading estates, partly perhaps because of their insistence on producing such a wide range of wine styles and grape varieties.   D.T. & D.C.G.

Collioure to tourists is one of the prettiest seaside villages on the Mediterranean coast just north of the Franco-Spanish border. To wine lovers it is a rare, particularly heady, deep red table wine whose aromas of overripe fruits and spice reflect the fact that Collioure comes from exactly the same area as BANYULS, or, more recently, a scented, particularly full white wine. The characteristics of the vintage determine what proportion of grapes become Collioure rather than Banyuls, but the grapes for Collioure are certainly picked before those destined to become VIN DOUX NATUREL, and generally represent less than a third of those destined to become France's answer to port.

The region's MOURVÈDRE is grown expressly for Collioure, however, as it, Syrah, and Grenache Noir must make up at least 60 per cent of the blend for the table wine. Cinsaut and Carignan are tolerated components. As in Banyuls, yields from these BUSH vines are some of the lowest in France, although 40 hl/ha (2.3 tons/acre) is decreed the official maximum. There is also, unusually, an official maximum alcohol level, 15 per cent, as well as a maximum RESIDUAL SUGAR level of 5 g/l—although many of these wines taste so ripe that they do give the impression of sweetness. Fine producers include Domaines du Mas Blanc, Clos de Paulilles, Domaine de la Rectorie, and La Tour Vieille, and a small amount of white wine and VIN GRIS are produced, mainly from various forms of Grenache.

colloid, substance consisting of ultramicroscopic particles, usually solids but occasionally liquids or gases. Wine colloids are very finely divided solids in particles with diameters ranging from about five nanometres to one micrometre. These are principally large organic molecules, most of which are polymers made of POLYSACCHARIDES including PECTINS, and of smaller molecules such as PHENOLICS, PIGMENTED TANNINS, and TANNINS (see POLYMERIZATION).

Colloids are major contributors to a wine's VISCOSITY, the extent to which the wine resists movement.

Colloids can be removed by FINING and FILTRATION. The fewer colloids are removed, the more BODY a wine will seem to have, the more astringent it may taste in youth, the slower it will mature, but the more complex it should taste when at its peak.   A.D.W. & P.J.W.

Colombard, which may be the offspring of GOUAIS BLANC and CHENIN BLANC, was originally a Charentais white grape variety used with Ugni Blanc (TREBBIANO) and FOLLE BLANCHE, but considered inferior to both, as an ingredient in cognac. As Colombard's star waned in France, almost half of total plantings being

pulled up in the 1970s, it waxed quite spectacularly in California, where, as FRENCH COLOMBARD, it became the state's most planted variety of all, providing generous quantities of reasonably neutral but reliably crisp base wine for commercial, often quite sweet, white blends to service the prevailing FASHION for white wine.

Its disadvantages of being quite prone to rot and POWDERY MILDEW are much lesser inconveniences in the hot, dry Central valley, where almost all of California's Colombard is planted (official statistics record just 43 acres/17 ha of the variety ever planted in the smart Napa Valley). And Colombard's disadvantages for the distillers of Charentes, that its wine is more alcoholic and less acid than that of the other cognac varieties, are positive advantages for consumers of the wine in its undistilled state (although Colombard is also used for California brandy).

The annual rate of planting of French Colombard in California slowed to a standstill towards the end of the 1980s and then picked up in the early 2000s so that by 2004 total plantings were about 32,000 acres (whereas Chardonnay's total was around 100,000 acres). Colombard is found in other American states, notably Texas.

It would take some sorcery to transform Colombard into an exciting wine, but pleasantly lively innocuousness is well within reach for those equipped with STAINLESS STEEL and TEMPERATURE CONTROL. In a nice example of transatlantic switchback, the producers of the Armagnac region set about duplicating California's modern wine-making transformation of the dull Colombard grape on their own varieties surplus to brandy production, thus creating the hugely successful VIN DE PAYS des Côtes de Gascogne. Colombard is the second most planted variety after Ugni Blanc in SOUTH WEST FRANCE and has been a prime ingredient in this much exported wine.

Between 1988 and 2000, total French plantings grew from 5,000 ha/12,300 acres to nearly 7,000 ha, mostly in cognac or, particularly, armagnac country, but also to a limited extent in Bordeaux's northern vineyards.

The variety, once important to the local brandy industry, is also popular for cheap, commercial off-dry white in SOUTH AFRICA. **Colombar,** as it is sometimes known there, is the country's third most important wine grape in the early 2000s with over 11,000 ha/ 27,000 acres under vine. As in Australia, it provides usefully crisp blending material with Chenin Blanc and the much more fashionable Chardonnay. Australia's total plantings were nerly 3,000 ha by the mid 2000s.

Colombia, South American country with a TROPICAL climate and a relatively short history of viticulture. For long Colombia depended on imported wines and spirits from Spain and developed a taste for sweet fortified wines such as

MÁLAGA. The initial output of the first vines planted here in the 1920s and 1930s was therefore directed towards aping this style of wine, as well as to the production of TABLE GRAPES. When wine imports from non-South American countries were punitively taxed in the mid 1980s, however, consumers became accustomed to the dry table wines of Chile and Argentina and in the early 1990s Colombia was beginning to produce small quantities of dry wines from VINIFERA vines—although by far the majority of vines grown, especially in the northern zone of Santa Marta, are HYBRIDS and table grapes. The main wine grape zone is in the south east of the country in the upper Cauca valley, where there are about 1,500 ha/3,700 acres of vineyards. Vines have to be defoliated by hand in order to provide a short period of DORMANCY (see TROPICAL VITICULTURE). A vine is in full production at just 15 months of age. Annual rainfall is 1,000 mm/ 39 in, although there are dry periods between December and March and between June and September. DOWNY MILDEW is the principal hazard. ISABELLA and Italia table grapes are grown in the main but there are experimental plantings of Cabernet Sauvignon, Chardonnay, and other INTERNATIONAL VARIETIES. The bulk of production is wine-based aperitifs and fortified wines and brandies, but a subsidiary of Pedro DOMECQ is at the forefront of experimentation with dry vinifera table wines.

Colorino, rare, deep-coloured dark grape variety used traditionally in Toscana for the wine-making GOVERNO technique. The late 1980s and early 1990s saw an upsurge in interest in Colorino as a sort of Tuscan version of PETIT VERDOT, capable of adding TANNINS and colour to firm up the structure of Sangiovese without the aromatic impact of the Cabernet Sauvignon adopted with such enthusiasm in Toscana. It lost ground after this early interest as many producers discovered that it was easier and cheaper to use deep-coloured blending wine to achieve the same results.

D.T. & D.C.G.

colour of wines. Wines are classified as red, white, or rosé but can vary widely in colour within these broad categories, sometimes with little obvious distinction between a light red and a dark rosé.

Red wines
Red wines derive their colour from the natural organic red/blue ANTHOCYANIN pigments, of which there are varying concentrations in the skins of darker-skinned grapes (only TEINTURIER grape varieties have red pulp). These concentrations depend on the VINE VARIETY, the RIPENESS of the grape, YIELD, and the weather conditions of the VINTAGE year. The amount of anthocyanins leached into the resulting wine depends on many factors including BERRY SIZE, homogeneity of berry ripeness,

length and temperature of the MACERATION of skins and new wine, together with the extent to which techniques to encourage EXTRACTION such as PUMPING OVER and PUNCHING DOWN are used. All these factors influence the intensity of colour in a young red wine.

The actual hue of a young red wine is influenced partly by the grape variety (Cabernet Sauvignon grape skins, for example, are blue-black, while those of Grenache are much more crimson), although much less than one might expect (see ANTHOCYANINS). A more important influence is the acidity of the grape juice. In low PH solutions, anthocyanins exist in bright red coloured forms, while as pH rises they change to a more colourless form. In general, therefore, the more acid the grape juice, the brighter the colour—although very high acid grapes may be unripe and deficient in available anthocyanins.

The anthocyanins as they occur in the grape are responsible for the colour of a red wine only in its very early life. In a red wine more than a few weeks old, the colour is due increasingly to products formed from anthocyanins, including PIGMENTED TANNINS, which are polymeric species resulting from reactions of anthocyanins with tannins. Pigmented tannins and other derived pigments have a wide range of colours, from orange to purple, but the purple species tend to be less stable so that brick red pigments gradually become predominant.

Red wines which undergo BARREL MATURATION also tend to have more stable colour than those which do not, because small amounts of OXYGEN promote the formation of the wine's pigmented tannins. During AGEING, reactions of the phenolics and anthocyanins continue, forming an ever increasing diversity of larger pigmented tannins. The larger ones aggregate and precipitate as sediment, depleting the wine of pigment.

The bleaching effect of SULFUR DIOXIDE (SO$_2$) on grape anthocyanins also means that red wines with a high level of free SO$_2$ tend to be paler than they would be with a lower level. However, most of the red pigments generated in wine by anthocyanin reactions are resistant to sulfite bleaching so that this effect decreases as the wine ages. Also, if red wines are bottled with high SO$_2$ levels, the normal chemical interactions among the phenolics and other wine constituents to generate BOUQUET are disrupted.

The colour of a young red wine can vary from blackish purple (as in a vintage PORT, for example) through many hues of crimson to ruby. With age, red wines take on brick and then amber hues, lightening with time. The colour at the rim of a glassful of wine can give the most telling indication of the hue and therefore age of a wine, while looking straight down through a glassful of wine from above can clearly indicate the intensity of colour (see TASTING).

During the 1990s, winemakers tended to make ever-deeper coloured red wines. This trend was encouraged by the increasing importance of large comparative tastings in JUDGING wine. Because many (though by no means all) of the world's best red wines are deeply coloured (particularly those based on Cabernet Sauvignon and Syrah grapes, for example), and because EXTRACTION may be associated with depth of FLAVOUR, there was a tendency among wine judges to favour deeply coloured wines. This led to a considerable increase in the number of red wines which owe their deep colour to over-extraction and/or colour added in the form of OENOCYANIN or some Teinturier wine but which are often otherwise undistinguished. See, for example, the notable increase in plantings of the red-fleshed RUBIRED in California, home of proprietary colouring agents such as Purple 8000 and Megared, which offer concentrated anthocyanins without tannins or RESIDUAL SUGAR.

See also RED WINE-MAKING and RED WINES for more information, including names for red wines in languages other than English.

White wines

Although red wines are red, white wines are not white. Very occasionally they are colourless, but they usually range from pale green, through straw, pale copper, and deep gold to amber.

The stems, skins, and pulp of the light-skinned grapes used for making white wines contain a large and complex mixture of phenolics similar to the red/blue-coloured anthocyanins except that they are not capable of the multiplicity of forms which result in pigment expression. The absorption of light by these white grape phenolics into white wine occurs mainly in the ultraviolet range, but extends into the visible range sufficiently to cause a light yellow colour in the wines we call 'white'. After CRUSHING of the grapes, these phenolics are exposed to oxygen and to the acids and other constituents of the grape juice, which causes a number of enzymatic and chemical reactions (including OXIDATION and polymerization) which result in changes of colour from light yellow to amber and eventually to brown.

Different 'white' grape varieties contain a slightly different array of phenolics, which results in differently coloured wines. Palomino and Pinot Blanc, for example, are particularly prone to oxidation and browning, while Riesling has traces of non-phenolic compounds which can cause a greenish tinge to the basic yellow.

Must browning is due to enzymatic oxidation and is highly dependent on the phenolic content (especially cinnamic acids) of the juice. During fermentation, yeast cells can absorb some of the brown polymerized materials which are then removed with the LEES. (Much the same phenomenon allows the use of quite

distinctly pale pink base wines from Pinots Noir and Meunier in the blend for bottle fermented sparkling wines which, after DISGORGEMENT, are white.) White wines may be made from dark-skinned grape varieties using minimum SKIN CONTACT and this phenomenon and/or CHARCOAL treatments. Some varieties used for white wines such as Gewürztraminer and Pinot Gris have greyish pink to purple skins and tend to result in deeply coloured wines with a strong pinkish yellow hue.

Careful protection from oxidation in pre-fermentation stages (for instance by addition of SO$_2$ or ASCORBIC ACID) reduces must browning but maintains a rather high level of phenolics in the wine, especially if some skin contact has led to extraction of CATECHINS or PROANTHOCYANIDINS. This may result in increased browning susceptibility of the wine and, under some circumstances, may produce a pink tinge to the basic yellow.

The names of the fundamental phenolics on which each group of complex compounds is built are the benzoic acid group, the cinnamic acid group, the flavan-3-ols, and the flavan-3, 4-diols (these last two are important to tannins).

With age, small amounts of oxygen act on these phenolic compounds to brown them and apparently deepen a white wine's colour. With extreme BOTTLE AGEING of many decades, a very old white wine can be the same medium intensity amber colour as a red wine of the same age.

White wine colour is also affected by the wine's levels of pH and SO$_2$; low pH and high SO$_2$ concentration has a bleaching effect—as has hydrogen peroxide, which is occasionally used to make wine look paler.

Wines made from grapes affected by NOBLE ROT tend to have a particularly deep golden colour. Those which have been given extended skin contact tend to brown relatively early, while young white wines subjected to BARREL FERMENTATION and LEES CONTACT tend to be markedly paler than those fermented in STAINLESS STEEL and then transferred to cask for barrel maturation because darker pigments are absorbed by the lees.

During the 1990s, white wines have in general become paler, as unintended oxidation becomes rarer, barrel fermentation has become more common, and barrel maturation has become more skilfully handled. See also WHITE WINE-MAKING and WHITE WINES.

Rosé wines

These wines, which vary enormously in hue and intensity, owe their combination of pink colour and white wine characteristics either to a very short skin contact with dark-skinned grapes, or, for some everyday wines and pink sparkling wines, to the BLENDING of red and white wines.

Wines that are pale bluish pink are likely to be the results of PROTECTIVE techniques, while those with an orange tinge may well have been exposed to some, possibly deliberate, oxidation. While a blindfolded taster can in some circumstances find it difficult to distinguish between low-tannin red wines and fuller-bodied white wines, it can be almost impossible on the basis of taste alone to distinguish a rosé wine from a white one.

See also ROSÉ WINE-MAKING, ROSÉ WINES, and AGEING.   J.R. & V.C.

Columella, Lucius Junius Moderatus, important but, for long, uncredited source of information on wine production in Ancient ROME. Little is known about his life except that he was born in Gades (Cádiz near JEREZ) and that he was an officer in the Roman army in Syria. He composed his treatise on farming, *De re rustica*, in AD 60–5. It is divided into 12 books, all in prose except the tenth, on gardens. This book was written in hexameter verse as an addition to VIRGIL's *Georgics*, which Columella admired. Columella's work shows by far the best grasp of technical detail of all the surviving Roman treatises on farming, and this is particularly clear in his treatment of VITICULTURE. Books 3 and 4, the most important of the treatise, deal with vine-growing, but much practical advice on wine-making is also contained in Book 12, which outlines the duties of the bailiff's wife. He discusses what grape variety to use in which type of soil; yield in relation to labour and capital outlay (he assumes that a well-managed vineyard will yield at least 20 AMPHORAE *per iugerum*, approximately 20 hl/ha (1.1 tons/acre), and possibly 30); planting; propagating; pruning; training and dressing; grafting (Books 3–4); the vintage, and wine-making (Book 12). Half of an earlier, shorter, work called *De arboribus* ('On trees') also survives: it has a section on vines which is much briefer than the corresponding sections of *De re rustica*.   H.M.W.

Martin, R., *Recherches sur les agronomes latins* (Paris, 1971).

White, K. D., *Roman Farming* (London, 1970).

Comité Interprofessionnel, body representing all interests concerned with the production of a certain wine and the French counterpart to the CONSORZIO of Italy and Spain's CONSEJO REGULADOR. The model for all such organizations was the CIVC of Champagne.

Commandaria, a dark dessert wine speciality of the island of CYPRUS with a honeyed, raisiny flavour and alcohol content usually around 15 per cent, produced from partially raisined grapes.

The name Commandaria dates from the Lusignan period of the island's history (1192–1489) and was derived from the Knights of St John of Jerusalem's chief feudal holding, called the Grand Commandery, within which lay the

vineyards producing the wine. This type of wine, however, was already well known centuries before the time of the Crusades. As long ago as 800 BC the Greek poet HESIOD described a sweet Cypriot wine, produced from sun-dried grapes. Cyprus Nama, the forerunner of Commandaria, was famed throughout the classical world (see DRIED GRAPE WINES).

In 1993, Commandaria became the first Cypriot wine to be granted full, legal protection covering both its geographical origin and production techniques. Commandaria must be produced within a strictly defined region comprising fourteen wine-producing villages on the Troodos foothills about 30 km/ 20 miles north of Limassol, from the Mavro (red) and Xynisteri (white) grape varieties, trained in the traditional low bush form. White grapes bring increased subtlety to Commandaria.

The vintage usually takes place in mid September. When picked, the grapes must be capable of giving juice with a minimum sugar level of 212 g/l for Xynisteri, and 258 g/l for Mavro. After picking, the grapes are dried in the sun for at least one week. At the end of this period the sugar content of the juice must lie within the range of 390 g/l to 450 g/l.

FERMENTATION, which must take place within the Commandaria region, stops naturally long before all the sugar is converted into alcohol, leaving a wine with considerable residual sweetness and a minimum ALCOHOLIC STRENGTH of 10 per cent. At this stage the wine is normally moved to one of the large wineries in Limassol to mature (rather as PORT is shipped down the Douro to Vila Nova de Gaia).

Once fermentation has been completed, the alcohol content of the wine may be increased by the addition of pure grape spirit (95 per cent alcohol) or wine distillate (at least 70 per cent alcohol), but the wine's actual alcohol must not exceed 20 per cent, while its total POTENTIAL ALCOHOL must be at least 22.5 per cent. Commandaria must be matured in oak casks for at least two years. In practice it is usually matured, in underground cellars, for considerably longer than this. Some producers use a three-tier SOLERA system. A small quantity of vintage Commandaria is also produced.

Though of limited commercial importance, even within Cyprus, Commandaria is one of the world's classic wines, and may well have the longest continuous history of any wine still in production. A premium version should be of real interest.   G.J.L.

Commanderie, common French term for a CONFRÉRIE.

commune, French for village or parish.

competitions, wine. Well-run reputable wine competitions can play an important part in the sales success of a wine producer, which is why some wine labels are adorned

with MEDALS and the like, and some wine merchants' lists are dotted with lists of awards. Care should be taken when studying these claims that the competition was a recent and respected one, and that the successful wine was exactly the same bottling as the one on offer. One of the most ambitious and successful international wine competitions is the International Wine Challenge held every May in London (at the same time as a newer rival event organised in London by *Decanter* magazine) and now in several other cities. It attracts many thousands of entries from around the world and most of its gold medal winning wines are of genuinely superior quality. The International Wine and Spirit Competition is an older British rival. Some of the more respected of the many wine competitions held regularly in the US are the Dallas Wine Competition, Los Angeles County Fair's Wines of the World, the Indy International in Indiana, Long Beach Grand Cru, Pacific Rim International, Riverside International, San Diego International, and the New York Wine and Food Classic for NEW YORK wines only. It should be remembered, however, that few of the world's most revered producers enter such competitions, and certainly none of those who produce very limited quantities. It is difficult to imagine there will ever be a wine competition which will identify the best, rather than the best of those who have something to gain by entering. In Australia they are known as wine SHOWS.

For more details of how competitions and wine shows work, see JUDGING WINE.

Completer, ancient white grape variety grown in Graubünden in eastern SWITZERLAND. The wine produced, pungent, acidic, and full bodied, is a speciality of Bündner Herrschaft. It was long thought to be identical to LAFNETSCHA of Valais in western Switzerland, but DNA PROFILING at DAVIS showed in 2004 that they are distinct varieties and that Completer is one of the parents of Lafnetscha. Subsequently, a few vines of Completer discovered among Lafnetscha vines supported this parentage and the unanticipated presence of Completer in Valais.   J.V.

Complexa, Portuguese red wine variety bred from Castelão, Tintinha, and Muscat Hamburg in the 1960s and introduced to MADEIRA as an experimental, deeper-coloured, softer alternative to TINTA NEGRA MOLE.   R.J.M.

compost, the name given to the product of microbial action on organic wastes under controlled conditions. Compost can be created from WINERY WASTE, typically MARC, and it may be mixed for example with animal manures which encourages microbial action and resultant high temperatures. Compost is applied to vineyard soils and, being rich in ORGANIC MATTER and NUTRIENTS, improves vine growth.

However, compost making and distribution requires handling large quantities of material, and for this reason most vine-growers around the world use manufactured FERTILIZERS. The use of compost and other organic soil amendments is, however, an integral part of ORGANIC and BIODYNAMIC VITICULTURE.   R.E.S.

computers. See INFORMATION TECHNOLOGY.

Conca de Barberá, small but promising wine zone in Spanish CATALUÑA, sandwiched in between PENEDÈS, COSTERS DEL SEGRE, and TARRAGONA (see map under SPAIN). At around 500 m/1,600 ft above sea level, this DO experiences cold winters, and hot summer days are tempered by cool winds from the sea. Miguel TORRES of Penedès recognized the grape-growing potential of the LIMESTONE country around the Castillo de Milmanda and some of his best CABERNET, PINOT NOIR, and CHARDONNAY grapes are sourced in the zone. Torres has been championing a federation between Conca de Barberá and Penedès 40 km/25 miles away. Some interesting rosé wines are also made from the local TREPAT vine, which is also the subject of interesting experiments in red wine vinification in CATALUÑA. Most of Conca de Barberá's grapes are used to produce CAVA, however, and consequently few wines carry the name of the DO on the label.   R.J.M. & V. de la S.

concentrated grape must. See GRAPE CONCENTRATE.

concentration, umbrella term for any wine-making operation which serves to remove volatile substances, mainly water, from grape juice or wine. Its most common application has been in the production of GRAPE CONCENTRATE but a range of more sophisticated concentration techniques is increasingly used on grapes and musts, often only on a certain portion of the total must, in order to produce more concentrated wines, notably in some of BORDEAUX's grandest cellars.

One component in a mixture can be concentrated using differences in boiling points, in freezing points, or in molecular size. The usual technique for making grape concentrate is to use differences in boiling points in a low-pressure, low-temperature evaporator. While very effective in concentrating sugar, this technique has the disadvantage of also removing volatile FLAVOUR COMPOUNDS.

A more recent and more sophisticated technique, used since 1989 in some parts of France as an alternative to ENRICHMENT, involves evaporating grape must under vacuum. Under vacuum, the water in the must evaporates at temperatures of about 20 °C/68 °F, no hotter than fermentation temperatures and therefore involving no dangerous loss of flavour. In practice, to achieve an acceptable rate of evaporation, temperatures rather higher have to be used, which can have a negative effect on the flavour of the final wine. The equipment needed (known in French as a *concentrateur sous vide*) is relatively expensive, but has the advantage of being able to handle unclarified grape must. Increasingly, though, vacuum concentrators are being superseded by REVERSE OSMOSIS machines.

Differences in molecular size have long been used to purify substances other than wine. The development of strong plastic membrane filters with very small pores of nearly uniform size means that the technique can be applied to purifying drinking water, and concentrating wine. However, filters with very small pores become easily clogged with grape must or wine. Reverse osmosis is an increasingly popular manipulation that makes use of a technique called tangential or cross-flow filtration to concentrate wine without clogging the filter because the flow of liquid is tangential to the membrane and at pressure.

Freeze concentration, using differences in freezing points, is used to make a range of sweet wines of varying qualities. The EISWEIN of Germany and Austria and the ICE WINE of Canada and elsewhere is made by picking frozen grapes from the vine, crushing them, and filtering the juice without allowing the mixture to thaw so that water is removed in the form of ice. Ice crystals are collected on the filter along with the more usual grape solids (skins, etc.) and the result is grape juice with a lower concentration of water, but a higher concentration of sugars, acids, and other soluble solids.

Natural freezing on the vine is replicated by producers in such different regions as SAUTERNES (where it is called CRYOEXTRACTION) and NEW ZEALAND. Freshly picked grapes may be frozen in special chillers prior to crushing and filtering. This technique is often practised selectively, not just for sweet white wines, but also on grapes destined to make dry white wines, not all of which are fully ripe. Since just-ripe grapes freeze at 0 °C/32 °F but fully ripe grapes freeze only at −6 °C or below, the mixture of grapes is chilled before crushing to an intermediate temperature so that it yields only the ripest juice (although it will yield nothing if there are no ripe grapes in the first place). The technique can only be practised on individual batches of grapes, however, so is relatively labour intensive.

One final method of concentrating grape must is also the oldest: desiccation. See DRIED GRAPE WINES.

Because in general these methods remove only water from the grapes or must, all other components are concentrated. An increased concentration of fermentable SUGARS results in a wine with a higher ALCOHOLIC STRENGTH. Increased concentrations of PHENOLICS in many cases result in wines with more BODY, potential for AGEING, and possibly more flavour. Increased ACIDITY, however, can result in wines that are aggressively tart, especially in less ripe years or in cooler wine regions. In some cases, particularly in cooler areas, musts which have been concentrated may have to be further subjected to DEACIDIFICATION, although in temperate climates TOTAL ACIDITY is usually only very slightly raised once TARTRATES have been precipitated.

Concentration is also used as a TASTING TERM.   J.R. & J.A.G.

Goode, J., *Wine Science* (London, 2005).

Concord, the most widely planted vine variety grown in the eastern United States, notably in NEW YORK state. It started life as a chance seedling and the majority of its genes clearly belong to the American vine species *Vitis labrusca*. The pronounced FOXY flavour of its juice makes its wine an acquired taste for those raised on the produce of VINIFERA vines. It was named after Concord, Massachusetts, by Ephraim W. Bull, who introduced it, having planted the seeds of a WILD VINE there in 1843. It is particularly important for the production of GRAPE JUICE and grape jelly, but it produces a wide range of wines, some KOSHER, often with some considerable RESIDUAL SUGAR. Viticulturally, the vine is extremely well adapted to the low temperatures of New York and is both productive and vigorous. Some Concord has also been grown in Brazil. See also VITIS and LABRUSCA.

Galet, P., and Morton, L. T., *A Practical Ampelography* (Ithaca, NY, and London, 1979).

Condado de Huelva, Spanish denominated wine zone in ANDALUCÍA, close to the city of Huelva between the JEREZ region and the Portuguese border (see map under SPAIN). Nowadays few of its wines, which have typically been FORTIFIED and made in the image of its neighbour SHERRY, are exported but the region has a long history (see SPAIN, history). In 'The Pardoner's Tale', Chaucer refers to the wines of Lepe, a small town just outside the modern Condado de Huelva DO and a notorious source of blending wine, and by the early 16th century the wines of Huelva were being exported to northern Europe and the emerging colonies in South America. But from the 17th century, much of Huelva's production was sold to Jerez, where it was blended anonymously into sherry SOLERAS. Huelva became a DO in its own right in 1964. The principal grape is the rather neutral ZALEMA along with a little PALOMINO (15 per cent of the vineyard area).

Three styles of wine are made. Condado Pálido is a pale, dry, fortified wine matured in a solera under a blanket of FLOR so that it resembles a coarse FINO sherry. Condado Viejo is a RANCIO style of wine aged in a solera and resembling a somewhat rustic Jerez OLOROSO. Vino Joven, on the other hand, is an unfortified dry table wine which now accounts for about half the regional production, and which can be a little fruitier than similar white wines produced in the Jerez area.

R.J.M. & V. de la S.

Condrieu, distinctive and fashionable white wine made in minuscule quantities in the northern RHÔNE. It is made exclusively from the VIOGNIER grape, whose successful wines manage the unusual combination of a pronounced yet elusive perfume with substantial BODY. The recent wave of Viognier planting all over the world was originally inspired by enthusiasm for Condrieu.

This small appellation encompasses seven right bank communes (which happen to span three *départements*, the Rhône, Loire, and Ardèche) just south of the red wine appellation CÔTE RÔTIE where the river turns a bend and the best vineyards are exposed to the south (see map under RHÔNE). The vine has probably been cultivated here for two millennia, since nearby Vienne was an important Roman city, although the total Condrieu *vignoble* fell to fewer than 10 ha/25 acres in the 1960s, when the wine was virtually unknown outside local restaurants, and when other fruit crops were much more profitable.

Since the 1970s, however, Condrieu's fame and price have risen steadily, and an increasing number of growers have been prepared to reconstruct small patches of vineyard on the steep, often granitic slopes, the best of which are traditionally said to have a topsoil of *arzelle*, or decomposed mica. The best sites should also be sheltered from the north wind, which can decimate the potential crop at FLOWERING, but little can be done to combat the inevitable SOIL EROSION. Average yields here are notoriously low (and very much lower than for Viognier planted further south), which is one reason why Condrieu is relatively expensive for a wine that is best drunk young, at between two and four years in general.

At one time, Condrieu was a sweet or medium sweet wine but almost all is made dry today. Vinification standards are extremely variable, particularly since some vignerons are relative newcomers (even if their grandfathers were experienced in making Condrieu). Two of the most experienced winemakers are Georges Vernay and GUIGAL, who now has a single-vineyard bottling La Doriane, but they have been definitively challenged by the likes of Cuilleron, Perret, and Villard. Policies on such fundamentals as the desirability of MALOLACTIC FERMENTATION and use of OAK vary considerably in Condrieu.

In 1990, there were 40 ha/100 acres of vineyard old enough to produce AC wine, but the total area under vine grew rapidly in the early 1990s so that by 1996 more than 100 ha qualified for the Condrieu AC but further expansion is hardly possible and growers have had to content themselves with producing a Viognier-based local Vin de Pays. CHÂTEAU GRILLET, France's other all-Viognier appellation, is an enclave within the Condrieu zone.

Conegliano, base of the main experimental viticultural station in the VENETO region of north east Italy. The Istituto Sperimentale per la Viticoltura was established in 1923. Six years later it expanded its operations to include OENOLOGY and one of its first directors was Professor Dalmasso, whose Dalmasso Commission made a significant report on the state of the Italian wine industry (see ITALY). His successor Professor Manzoni produced many crossings (see INCROCIO Manzoni) still cultivated today. In 1933, Conegliano became involved in combating ADULTERATION AND FRAUD in an area which was expanded in 1965 to include not just Veneto but also FRIULI. From 1986, the adulteration and fraud service became independent. At the same time, an experimental winery was established at Conegliano.

A 9-ha nursery for an ampelographical collection of vine varieties had been established in 1951, and another estate of 20 ha/50 acres was acquired nearby in 1963. From 1967, the institute's work was focused on viticulture, with four central units concerned with AMPELOGRAPHY and VINE IMPROVEMENT, biology and protection, PROPAGATION, and cultivation techniques. There are further units located around Italy and the institute is responsible for CLONAL SELECTION, research into ROOTSTOCKS, and an ampelographic collection of more than 2,000 VINE VARIETIES. Conegliano is home of the Italian national register for grape cultivars.

Conegliano's influence extends all over Italy, and not just because many of the country's better producers and consultant OENOLOGISTS have trained here. Important concerns include vine improvement (of TABLE GRAPES as well as scions and rootstocks), research into FUNGAL DISEASES and insect PESTS, propagating techniques, and environmental influences on grape quality and yield.

confréries, French 'brotherhoods' or associations, dedicated in particular to advancing the cause of various foods and drinks throughout France. More than 150 of them, most of them founded in the second half of the 20th century, are devoted to such various products as macaroons, jams, olives, and local shellfish. A high proportion of them, almost half, are based on specific wines and other alcoholic drinks. One of the most famous is the Confrérie des Chevaliers de Tastevin in Burgundy (see CLOS DE VOUGEOT). The Commanderie du Bontemps du MÉDOC et des Graves, founded in Bordeaux in 1949 by the energetic Henri Martin, is also well known and is the LEFT BANK answer to the oldest of these *confréries*, the Jurade de ST-ÉMILION. It dates its origins to the late 12th century, when the town councillors of this ancient town were given particular powers and responsibilities by the English crown, which then governed it (see BORDEAUX, history); it was reconstituted in 1947. These *confréries* are devoted to an annual programme of pageantry, feasting, and the *intronisation* (enthronement) of honorary converts to the cause.

connoisseurship of wine is a (disappearing) art in search of a less emotive name. The word **connoisseur** in English, and its counterpart *connaisseur* in French, conjures up a frightening vision of an elderly male so steeped in wine, wine knowledge, and wine prejudices as to be completely unapproachable. Much more attractive and widely acceptable terms are those which convey not just knowledge but an element of relish such as wine lover, wine enthusiast, or the common and attractive French term *amateur du vin*. None of these terms, incidentally, has any connotation of gender.

Whatever the drawbacks of the term, connoisseurship or wine expertise is an art that can give pleasure, and involves less an arid grasp of the precise ENCÉPAGEMENT of each vineyard and fermentation regimes for each vintage than an intelligent appreciation of how wines are likely to taste in a given environment, at a certain stage in their evolution, before or after other wines, and, importantly, with different foods. This is what consumers rather than producers are for. Experience can contribute to connoisseurship, but only if the consumer tastes with humility, attention, and an open mind. Mentors are useful but some newcomers to wine have an instinctive grasp of connoisseurship. A true connoisseur meets each wine halfway and tries to show it in the best possible light, in stark contrast to professional wine JUDGING. Too many wine drinkers seem determined to judge rather than enjoy wine. See wine TASTING, AGEING, SERVING, and FOOD AND WINE MATCHING. A connoisseur is not necessarily a wine BORE.

Consejo Regulador, Spanish term meaning 'regulating council'. Spanish wine law is administered through a network of Consejos Reguladores representing each and every DO. They comprise vine-growers, wine producers, and merchants who between them decide on the ground rules for their region.

Consorzio, Italian word for a consortium or association, notably of wine-growers dedicated to regulation. The most famous in Italian wine is the **Consorzio Chianti Classico**, which has been instrumental in promoting and defending the wines of CHIANTI CLASSICO. Its counterpart in France is the COMITÉ INTERPROFESSIONNEL; in Spain the CONSEJO REGULADOR.

Constantia, legendary, aromatic, concentrated 18th-century dessert wines from the Cape, SOUTH AFRICA, then a Dutch colony. Their fame was never matched by any other New World wines and at their height they commanded more prestige, more fabulous prices, and enjoyed more crowned patronage than the

---

Chardonnay grapes are picked at Chittering Estate near Perth, Western Australia, into relatively shallow plastic boxes, which minimize the likelihood of the bottom grapes' being squashed during **harvest** and starting fermentation prematurely.

most celebrated wines of Europe (with the possible exception of Hungarian TOKAJI). Constantia was even ordered by Napoleon from his exile on St Helena.

The Cape wines were grown at the 750-ha/1,850-acre Constantia Estate, founded in 1685 by an early Dutch governor Simon van der Stel just outside Cape Town, in the lee of Table Mountain. But it was Constantia's subsequent owners who achieved acclaim and prosperity, principally Hendrik Cloete, who purchased and restored it in 1778. Quality and fame gradually began to fade after the British occupied the Cape following the Napoleonic Wars. Initially sales picked up although from the mid 1820s a decline set in. In 1861, when the Gladstone government removed empire preferential tariffs, exports almost dried up and the twin disasters of POWDERY MILDEW and PHYLLOXERA brought to an end the golden era.

The sweet wines of Constantia, both red and white, the latter more expensive, were made principally from MUSCAT BLANC À PETITS GRAINS and its dark-berried mutation, probably including the lesser MUSCAT OF ALEXANDRIA together with the dark red PONTAC and CHENIN BLANC. Records show that slightly under 50 per cent of Constantia wine in the early 19th century was sold either as red or white Constantia without any varietal claim. Analyses of recently opened bottles (still perfumed with a tang of citrus and smoky richness) reveal they were unfortified although high in alcohol, apparently confirming records that the grapes were left on the vines long after ripeness to achieve shrivelled, but not BOTRYTIZED, concentration (see DRIED GRAPE WINES for more details of the technique). Other stories suggest the wines may have been fortified by shippers for protection on the long, rough, and hot journey across the equator to Europe.

An 18th-century Cape society diarist, Lady Anne Barnard, provides one of the most detailed reports of this era. 'What struck me most', she said after watching the pressing of the Constantia desserts of Hendrik Cloete, 'was the beautiful antique forms, perpetually changing and perpetually graceful, of the three bronze figures, half naked, who were dancing in the wine press beating the drum (as it were) with their feet in perfect time. Of these presses, there were four with three slaves in each.'

Groot Constantia has been a state-owned wine estate since 1885. In 1975, management of its activities passed into the hands of a control board and in 1993 into a trust, primarily to end the state's liability for the seemingly endless deficits. In recent times, Constantia has made sound, unexciting conventional wines. A neighbouring privately owned estate, Klein (Little) Constantia, a subdivision of the original farm, has been first to take up the challenge to re-enact the legend. It replanted vineyards of Muscat of Frontignan in the early 1980s and now produces naturally high-alcohol white dessert wines known as Vin de Constance (also without botrytis—in the manner of the old Constantia) to local and international acclaim.

See also SOUTH AFRICA, history.   J.P. & M.F.

Burman, J., *Wine of Constantia* (Cape Town, 1979).
Fridjhon, M,. *The Penguin Book of South African Wine* (Johannesburg, 1992).
Johnson, H., 'Groot Constantia', in *The Story of Wine* (London, 1989).
Leipoldt, C. L., *Three Hundred Years of Cape Wines* (Cape Town, 1952).

Constellation Brands, holding company of the increasingly important Constellation Wines, previously known as Canandaigua (still the name of its NEW YORK wine subsidiary). Based in Fairport, New York, Constellation Brands is one of the leading international producers and marketers of virtually all forms of alcoholic beverage and, thanks to consistent acquisition, became the world's largest wine business in 2004. It is also the third largest producer and marketer of distilled spirits in the United States; a leading producer and exporter of wine from Australia and New Zealand; and a major producer and independent drinks wholesaler in the UK. Some of its best-known brands include Almaden, Blackstone, Estancia Estates, Franciscan Oakville Estate, Inglenook, Mount Veeder, Paul Masson, Robert MONDAVI, Ravenswood, Simi, and Vendange in California; Columbia and Covey Run in Washington; Manischewitz (America's best-selling KOSHER wine) in New York; Veramonte in Chile; Alice White, Banrock Station, HARDYS, and Tintara in Australia; Drylands and Nobilo in New Zealand; Ruffino (40 per cent owned) in Italy; the Stowells range of BOX wines and Arbor Mist wine COOLERS. In 2006 it acquired VINCOR, Canada's dominant wine company.

H.G. & J.R.

consultants are used with increasing frequency in wine production, selling, and occasionally consumption. Consultant VITICULTURISTS are particularly useful since those who operate on an international scale can impart knowledge gleaned from a wide variety of different vine-growing environments, although strictly local specialists such as David Abreu in northern California can forge an international reputation. Like viticulturists, the more energetic consultant OENOLOGISTS can use their expertise in both hemispheres, although their work is necessarily limited by the timing of HARVEST. One of the first internationally famous consultant oenologists was Professor Émile PEYNAUD. Today his best-known successor from Bordeaux is Michel ROLLAND, although dozens of other highly respected consultants operate in Bordeaux alone and there are now hundreds of winemakers who travel the globe and offer, if not consultancy, then hard graft (see FLYING WINE-MAKERS). Consultants play an increasingly important role in wine production everywhere but have long been particularly important in Bordeaux, California, and Italy, where the likes of Riccardo COTARELLA are liberally used for marketing purposes. Many restaurateurs and hoteliers, most airlines, and even some wine retailers employ consultants in their wine selection. Some well-heeled COLLECTORS also take INVESTMENT advice from consultants.

consumption of wine throughout the world has fallen from a peak of around 285 million hl/7,500 million gal a year in the years 1976–80 to about 225 million hl in the early 2000s, a slight increase on the late 1990s level. Total world PRODUCTION is considerably more than this, resulting in a serious global wine SURPLUS that is most acute in Europe, the most important producer and consumer of wine. The main reason for the drop in global consumption has been sharp falls in average wine consumption by the world's two most important producers and consumers, France and Italy. The generation of Frenchmen and Italians who routinely consumed a litre of wine a day has been dying off. Wine consumption continues to grow, from a modest base, in many northern European countries, however—notably in Germany and the UK, the world's biggest importers of wine.

The countries with the highest per capita wine consumption in the early 21st century were still mainly the most important wine producers: in declining order of consumption, Luxembourg, France, Italy, Croatia, Portugal, Switzerland, Hungary, Spain, Argentina, and, the non-producing country with the highest wine consumption, Denmark. Of these, the only countries in which per capita wine consumption rose during the early 2000s were Switzerland, Hungary, and Denmark. Of anglophone countries, the most enthusiastic wine consumers are Australia (more than 21 l, or 28 bottles per capita a year), followed by New Zealand, the United Kingdom, Ireland, Canada, South Africa, and then the US (7.7 l, or more than 10 bottles).

National annual per capita wine consumption figures in litres according to the OIV are to be found in Appendix 2. See SURPLUS for statistics on global consumption since 1976 and see HEALTH for official medical advice on safe personal consumption levels of alcoholic drinks.

containers for wine are used at four main stages in a wine's life: during the FERMENTATION that creates it, during its MATURATION, for its TRANSPORT, and for SERVING it. Moreover, while wine containers have changed throughout history, they have also varied through space, with each wine-making region becoming characterized by vessels of different dimensions.

The **training system** of these Riesling vines is particularly distinctive with each plant trained up a single stake in the Ürziger Würzgarten vineyard on the slopes of the Mosel valley in northern Germany. The gradient is so steep that wires between vines would restrict vineyard workers' movements and make viticultural operations even more difficult.

History

A wide variety of materials were used for drinking and serving wine in the Ancient World, particularly CHINA. In prehistoric times in the eastern Mediterranean, wine was generally put in earthenware jars, or sometimes into WOODEN containers, soon after the grapes had been trodden or pressed, and this basic fermentation technology remained the norm until the 20th century, when VATS or tanks of concrete and STAINLESS STEEL were introduced. The basic receptacles used for storing and transporting wine in classical antiquity were pottery AMPHORAE, which varied greatly in size and shape but which could be sealed, thus preventing the potentially harmful access of OXYGEN. During the 11th century BC, experiments were also undertaken in transporting wine in large jars, known as *dolia*, anchored amidships, but their use did not persist. By the end of the 11th century AD, amphorae seem no longer to have been used, and most wine was transported long distance in wooden BARRELS. For short distances, numerous other vessels, in particular animal skins, were also used, especially in Iberia.

Throughout the medieval period, wooden barrels served as almost the only vessels used for maturing and transporting wine, and their sizes came to reflect local custom and requirements. The standard barrel size in England, for example, the BUTT or PIPE, was fixed by statute in the 15th century at 126 imperial gallons (572.8 l). However, in southern Italy at the same time, their wooden *botti* held about 454 l, while in Bruges the butt had a capacity of about 910 l; in Spain it varied from 454 to 477 litres. Meanwhile, it had been discovered in Germany that wines kept in larger barrels, providing they were not subjected to RACKING, lasted longer. This led to the construction of huge wooden tuns, containing thousands of litres, among the most famous of which were the Strasbourg Tun of 1472, and the Heidelberg Tuns of 1591 and 1663.

For serving wine, small jugs made of pottery were generally used during the medieval period. However, from the 16th century, glass BOTTLES became more frequently used, and by the second half of the 17th century, these bottles began to be used to store and mature wines. Bottle shapes evolved so as to allow extended BOTTLE AGEING and thus were born VINTAGE wines, and CONNOISSEURSHIP. Moreover, the use of bottles also enabled completely new types of wine, such as CHAMPAGNE and vintage PORT, to be produced.   P.T.H.U.

Allen, H. W., *A History of Wine: Great Vintage Wines from the Homeric Age to the Present Day* (London, 1961).

Peacock, D. P. S., and Williams, D. F., *Amphorae and the Roman Economy: An Introductory Guide* (London, 1986).

Unwin, P. T. H., *Wine and the Vine: An Historical Geography of Viticulture and the Wine Trade* (London, 1992).

Modern times

For details of containers used for fermentation, see FERMENTATION VESSELS, which may be either open topped or closed, and may have a capacity as big as 300 hl/7,925 gal. Wines are matured prior to bottling in closed containers (to avoid OXIDATION), either in tanks made from materials such as stainless steel or concrete, or in some form of COOPERAGE, from small, new oak barrels to large, old casks, or even in some cases in ceramic TINAJAS or glass BONBONNES. Wine may be blended in even larger tanks holding up to 15,000 hl. Wine is transported either in BULK, usually in food-grade 250-hl stainless steel tankers or disposable 'flexitanks', or, increasingly, in bottle, its final container before the wine GLASS, possibly after spending a short time in a DECANTER. Newer containers used in packaging wine include BOXES, CARTONS, and CANS.

When transport containers are used for shipping wine in bottle, care is taken by some fine wine merchants and some fine wine producers that the wine is shipped only in temperature-controlled containers, and sometimes only during cooler times of year. This is particularly important for wines which have undergone a minimum of FILTRATION. For more details, see TRANSPORT.

contaminants, potentially harmful substances found in wine, either as a result of air or water pollution, vineyard treatment RESIDUES, poor winery HYGIENE, ignorance, or ADULTERATION and FRAUD.

Of these, ignorance is possibly the most forgivable reason for contamination since the scope of what is regarded as, and can be measured as, a contaminant grows wider with the rapid progress of science and measuring techniques. LEAD, for example, which was deliberately added to wines by the Romans, is now known to be a serious neural toxin. CARBAMATES, on the other hand, have been regarded as contaminants only since the late 1980s. And it was only in the 1990s that the contaminating effect of some apparently innocuous treatments of wooden beams in some wine-making establishments became apparent (see TRIBROMOANISOLE).

Nowadays, contamination as a result of poor winery hygiene is extremely rare. Pollution is difficult to guard against. Wine producers are increasingly wary of some AGROCHEMICALS, however. Orthene, a fungicide used widely in the early 1980s, with no ill effects apparent during wine-making, produced a range of wines with an extremely unpleasant smell after several years' BOTTLE AGE. Many German wines made in the early to mid 1980s, particularly the 1983s, exhibited this particular contamination. The ST-ESTÈPHE property Ch Phélan-Ségur, a famous CRU BOURGEOIS, destroyed its entire 1984 and 1985 production because of Orthene contamination. And American authorities, in particular, have regularly applied stringent tests for traces of recently suspected contaminants, such as procymidone from agrochemical RESIDUES, to imported wines.

The wine trade, like every other commercial activity, has its villains, but they are increasingly rare. Fortunately, very few of the substances which the least scrupulous producers are tempted to add illegally to wine (SORBITOL, for example) are harmful—with the notable and horrifying exception of lethal doses of METHANOL added to one Italian producer's wines in 1987.

See also ADULTERATION, which sometimes involves the deliberate addition of contaminants.

continental climate is one with a high degree of **continentality**, defined for any place as the difference between the average mean temperature of its hottest month and that of its coldest month. Climates with a wide annual range are called continental; those with a narrow range, MARITIME. The former tend to be in the interiors of the larger continents; the latter, near oceans or other large water bodies.

The most continental viticultural climates are those of central and eastern Europe, together with inland northern America (see RUSSIA and CANADA, for example). The European west coastal and most Mediterranean viticultural regions rank as intermediate, while the most maritime viticultural climate of all is that of MADEIRA. All viticultural regions of the southern hemisphere, even those well inland, are classed (in this sense) as maritime. That is because the total land mass of the southern hemisphere is small relative to that of the oceans, which thus dominate temperatures.

The rapid autumn temperature drop in continental climates means that RIPENING can be precarious. VINTAGE variation therefore tends to be marked, and the effects of high YIELDS on ripening and wine quality are probably more evident than in maritime climates when autumn temperatures drop slowly, and ripening is relatively assured. Cool maritime climates, on the other hand, can result in viticultural problems due to insufficient warmth during FLOWERING and FRUIT SET.

European experience shows that ideal continental seasons can lead to superb wines when combined with appropriate cropping levels. Against that, maritime climates that are warm and sunny enough during flowering and setting can probably produce good quality more reliably, and thus have practical advantages for commercial viticulture.

See also CLIMATE AND WINE QUALITY and MEDITERRANEAN CLIMATE.   J.G. & R.E.S.

continuous method, SPARKLING WINEMAKING process developed in the USSR for SOVIET SPARKLING WINE and now used in Germany and Portugal.

contract wine-making. See CUSTOM CRUSH FACILITY.

controlled appellations, a method of LABELLING wine and designating quality that is modelled on France's APPELLATION CONTRÔLÉE system. It embraces geographical DELIMITATION and is the principle on which QUALITY WINE schemes such as the DOC of Italy and Portugal, the DO of Spain, and the AVA system of the United States are based. France has more than 400, Italy more than 300, Greece about 60, Spain over 60, and Portugal an ever-lengthening and much-revised list. Countries such as BULGARIA and HUNGARY have devised similar schemes, as have the UNITED KINGDOM and, most recently, BELGIUM. Controlled appellations were known even in Ancient GREECE; modern Greece has even adopted the French phrases used by the appellation contrôlée system in France for designating its better-quality wines. The French model of controlled appellations including not just geographical delimitation but also prescribed vine varieties and techniques, is increasingly called into question, with many wine producers, not just in the New World, arguing that it limits innovation and tends unquestioningly to maintain traditional practices and TRADITION. See Appendix 1 for a complete list of controlled appellations for which particular grape varieties are specified, with their permitted grapes.

cooking with wine. Good wine used in the kitchen adds depth and dimension to a dish that no other ingredient can. The recipes of Apicius, the most famous Roman chef, show that wine was commonly used in his sauces and it has found a place in the kitchen ever since.

Wine is an essential ingredient in many dishes and can be used in every stage of cooking from the preparation and tenderizing of meat to providing the final, often sweet, finish to a dessert. It is all the more curious, therefore, that so little research has been done into exactly what happens to wine during cooking, particularly as a result of the application of heat. Since the boiling point of ETHANOL is 78 °C/172 °F, considerably lower than that of water, however, it is reasonable to suppose that any wine used in cooking becomes progressively less alcoholic if heated to above 78 °C for any length of time. As a sauce is 'reduced' with wine, the other components in the wine such as any RESIDUAL SUGAR and, especially, its ACIDITY become even more marked. This is presumably why over-reduced sauces can taste so acid, and why they can have an almost caramelized appearance and taste. Other uses for wine in cooking do not involve changing the wine's composition by heating.

There is much debate about the necessary quality of **cooking wine**, some regarding the saucepan as the ideal repository for any wine considered too nasty to drink, others insisting that only the finest wine will do. Wine with an unpleasant flavour will not lose that flavour in the kitchen, and CORKED wine is not advisable. On the other hand, the complex BALANCE and full range of volatile FLAVOUR COMPOUNDS of a great wine will not survive the application of any fierce heat. The most important group of flavours the cook may want to extract from a wine are those of the fruit, which are then used to build sauces and slow-cooked dishes such as daubes; for this the wine must be well-made, and not too acidic, whether red or white.

The following are some of the most common ways in which wine is used in the kitchen.

Deglazing: pouring wine (or another liquid such as stock) into a pan in which something has been roasted or sautéed in order to dissolve the remnants of that operation in the liquid to make a sauce. Wine adds body and depth to the sauce. White VERMOUTH is often used.

Marinade: a method of imparting extra flavour, principally to meat and game, via a mixture based on carrots, shallots, onions, pepper, salt, vinegar, garlic, and red or white wine which takes the form of cooked and uncooked marinades. Instant marinades, using brandy, port, or madeira, are used for the ingredients of pâtés and terrines. After the meat has been removed, the marinade may be used for deglazing or for a more complicated sauce.

Stocks: wine is often used instead of, or as well as, water, to provide the essential base for soups and sauces. Red wine is used in game stock, white wine in chicken and fish stocks. (Wine features in many risotto recipes.)

Court-bouillon: a method of cooking fish, shellfish, or white meat in which herbs and spices are infused in white wine and water in which the food is subsequently poached.

Sauces: of the many which form the basis of classic French cuisine, *bordelaise* comprises red wine and shallots; *périgueux* uses madeira, veal stock, and truffles; *sauce Robert* is white wine, onion, and mustard; and *ravigote* is made with white wine and vinegar.

Stews and casseroles: wine, preferably from the same area as the dish, is an integral part of *coq au vin*, daube of beef, fish stew, *boeuf bourguignonne*, and many more classics of *la cuisine bourgeoise*. Acidic wine will detract rather than enhance.

Jellies: poached foie gras set in a Gewurztraminer jelly is an Alsace speciality. Sweet jellies can be made from Sauternes or any other sweet wine.

Desserts: wine has a surprisingly wide range of applications for sweet foods and patisserie. Red wine is used for poaching pears and macerating strawberries (a speciality of Bordeaux) while dessert wines such as Marsala and sherry are used in, respectively, zabaglione and English trifle. In Italy, strong, usually sweet, wines, typically VIN SANTO, are served with dry biscuits which are moistened in them.

J.R. & M.P.L.

Poussier, L., and Poussier, O., *Desserts and Wines* (London, 2004)

McGee, H., *On Food and Cooking* (New York, 1984).

cool climate viticulture, and **warm climate viticulture**, are indefinite terms, depending on the speaker's or writer's viewpoint, but are probably applied most usefully to the coolest and warmest thirds of the climatic or geographic range used successfully for growing wine grapes. Intermediate climate viticulture (see below) lies between, while true hot climate viticulture produces mainly TABLE GRAPES and DRYING GRAPES, and cannot, in general, produce high-quality wine grapes of any kind.

Major areas of cool climate viticulture would certainly include the northern half of France (the LOIRE, CHAMPAGNE, CHABLIS, BURGUNDY, and BEAUJOLAIS,): ENGLAND, LUXEMBOURG, GERMANY, SWITZERLAND, and AUSTRIA; in the US, the Lower Columbia valley of WASHINGTON and OREGON, and the coolest coastal strip of northern California (CARNEROS, ANDERSON VALLEY); the most southern vineyards of CHILE and SOUTH AFRICA; the South Island and southern North Island of NEW ZEALAND; and in Australia, the whole of TASMANIA, small areas of the higher Adelaide hills in SOUTH AUSTRALIA, and Drumborg in VICTORIA. Gladstones's data (table 183) show all these to have regional average mean temperatures for the growing season (April to October inclusive in the northern hemisphere, October to April in the southern hemisphere) of below 16.0 °C/60.8 °F. Jackson and Schuster (1987) and Casteel (1992) deal specifically with this type of viticulture.

The distinguishing characteristic of cool viticultural climates is that they will regularly ripen only early-maturing grape varieties such as CHASSELAS, MÜLLER-THURGAU, GEWÜRZTRAMINER, CHARDONNAY, PINOT NOIR, and GAMAY; and only in especially warm MESOCLIMATES can varieties such as RIESLING, which ripens early to mid season, be ripened. RIPENING also tends to take place under cool to mild conditions. The combination leads to wines which, at their best, are fresh, delicate, and aromatic. Most are white or only pale red, because full development of ANTHOCYANIN pigments and TANNINS in the grape skins needs greater and more prolonged warmth than does ripening of the flesh (see PHYSIOLOGICAL RIPENESS). Other, warmer viticultural climates will be examined here for the sake of comparison.

Intermediate climate viticulture is that with growing seasons long and warm enough for regular ripening of mid season grape varieties such as CABERNET FRANC, MERLOT, SYRAH (or Shiraz), and SANGIOVESE, and late mid season varieties such as CABERNET SAUVIGNON and

NEBBIOLO, to make mainly medium- to full-bodied red table wines. Typical regions are BORDEAUX and the northern RHÔNE valley in France; the RIOJA Alta in Spain; much of northern ITALY and TOSCANA; the intermediate and warmer coastal valleys of California, such as NAPA and SONOMA; the north and east coasts of the North Island of New Zealand; Margaret River and the south coast of WESTERN AUSTRALIA; the Barossa valley and hills, Padthaway, and Coonawarra in SOUTH AUSTRALIA; and much of central and southern VICTORIA. Average mean growing season temperatures are in the range 16.0 to 18.5 °C (60.8 to 65.2 °F).

Warm viticultural climates, if sunny enough, will ripen early and mid season grape varieties to high sugar contents and make the best sweet, fortified wines. They will also ripen late-maturing grape varieties such as MOURVÈDRE (Mataro), CARIGNAN, GRENACHE, TREBBIANO, and CLAIRETTE for making table wines. Examples are the south of France; the DOURO valley of Portugal and the island of Madeira; the Adelaide district and McLaren vale in SOUTH AUSTRALIA, the MURRAY DARLING regions of South Australia and Victoria, and the Hunter valley and Mudgee in NEW SOUTH WALES in Australia. Corresponding average mean growing season temperatures are in the range 18.5 to 21 °C.

Typical hot climate viticultural regions are those producing table and drying grapes in GREECE and TURKEY, and the San Joaquin valley of California. Growing season average mean temperatures are mostly 22 °C or higher. Subtropical and TROPICAL VITICULTURE for table grapes and wine, using mainly non-VINIFERA grape varieties, also falls into this temperature category.

Relationships of temperature, particularly during ripening, to wine qualities are discussed under CLIMATE AND WINE QUALITY.   J.G. & R.E.S.

Casteel, E. (ed.), *Oregon Winegrapes Grower's Guide* (4th edn, Portland, Ore., 1992).

Gladstones, J., *Viticulture and Environment* (Adelaide, 1992).

Jackson, D., and Schuster, D., *The Production of Grapes and Wine in Cool Climates* (Nelson and Melbourne, 1987).

coolers. There are two very different types of **wine cooler**. One is a blend of usually rather ordinary wine with fruit juice, water, carbon dioxide, and/or flavourings to produce a LOW-ALCOHOL drink designed to cool the drinker, and introduce him or her gently to the taste of wine. These products, only distantly related to wine itself, enjoyed a vogue in the mid 1980s, particularly in the United States.

The other sort of wine cooler was a large piece of domestic equipment designed to cool the wine in the days before domestic REFRIGERATION. A more recent and less cumbersome table top version with an acrylic double wall is now widely used but does no more than slow down the rate at which the wine loses its chill.

Coonawarra, important wine region in South Australia's Limestone Coast Zone and the most popularly revered area of AUSTRALIA for Cabernet Sauvignon, grown on its famous strip of TERRA ROSSA soil. Its cool, MEDITERRANEAN climate is very similar to that of Bordeaux; it is slightly warmer and has less growing season rainfall, but Cabernet Sauvignon is normally picked in the second half of April (or, in Bordeaux terms, the second half of October). For more detail, see SOUTH AUSTRALIA.

cooperage is a collective noun for wooden containers (as in 'small OAK cooperage') but has been more traditionally used for both the activities and workplace of **coopers**, those who make and repair small BARRELS and larger wooden VATS. At one time all wine or spirit producers of any size would have their own small cooperage, but today the craft is perpetuated almost exclusively by specialist cooperage businesses. The French term is *tonnellerie*.

History

Until relatively recently, coopers played an important role not only in the wine business but in myriad aspects of daily life. Almost all containers—buckets, barrels, tanks—were made by coopers from various woods (see BARRELS, history). Barrels were made to hold salted fish, flour, gunpowder, oil, turpentine, salt, sugar, butter, and many other household commodities since they retain liquids safely, keep the elements out, and are easy to manœuvre.

Coopers' guilds were already established by the end of the 9th century and, during the Middle Ages, laws relating to apprenticeships, master–apprentice relations, and guild memberships were codified throughout Europe (with nepotism already playing its part). At the end of the 18th century, there were approximately 8,000 coopers in Paris alone. It is still possible to meet coopers who are the last in a line of craftsmen dating back to the 17th century. Such men, who can probably make barrels with handtools alone, may well have served traditional apprenticeships that often involve extensive work in different regions of their own countries as well as abroad.

As Europeans colonized the New World, they inevitably took their coopering skills with them. John Alden, one of the more famous early North American colonists of Plymouth, Massachusetts, was a master cooper and by 1648 there were enough coopers to form a guild in this New England colony. America's important export trade of staves and logs to Europe began slightly later in the 17th century, when the Spanish controlled large parts of what is now the United States.

During the 19th century, coopering remained an important craft, but the advent of metal (and later plastic) containers ultimately reduced coopering to an adjunct of the drinks

business. More than 1 million barrels were made for salted herring in Britain in 1913, for example, but by 1953 the number had dropped to around one-tenth of this figure and now this business is virtually extinct.

American PROHIBITION had a dramatic impact on the sale of fine wines and spirits, and in turn on the cooperage business—particularly in the United States but also in the British Isles, where only those coopers working on beer barrels were unaffected. Before the Second World War, most beer barrels were made of wood and many breweries had their own cooperages, but by the early 1960s wooden barrels had been replaced by metal ones. In much of the wine industry, too, wood was replaced by concrete, stainless steel, and other neutral materials, particularly for larger tanks (see CONTAINERS).

Cooperage today

As wooden barrels are expensive to buy, use, and maintain, they tend to be used only for products whose sale price can justify such a major investment or, in the case of older containers, by those who have inherited them.

Cooperages are found wherever there is a wine or spirits business that needs barrels, notably in America, Scotland, and France but also in Italy, Spain, Portugal, Ireland, eastern Europe, Germany, Australia, and South Africa. They make new vats and barrels (see BARREL MAKING) and/or repair or maintain older barrels and vats (see BARREL MAINTENANCE and BARREL RENEWAL).

There are no serious industry analysts of the contemporary cooperage business, such as there are in the automotive or electronics industry, since it is effectively just a small part of the timber industry. Nor is there any official regulatory or inspection body as there is in the wine trade. Because of this, facts are few and rumour is rife. In the 1980s, it was rumoured that oak was being shipped from Slavonia to Spain, coopered there, and shipped to unsuspecting winery owners as French oak. In the 1990s, the rumour runs the opposite way: that Limousin oak is being sawn and shipped as Slavonian oak! Naturally all coopers maintain that their oak is the best wood, entirely hand split and seasoned in the open air but that their competitors cut corners. In the absence of facts, winemakers have to rely on results rather than rhetoric.

United States The great majority of wooden barrels traded today are made in the American Midwest for the ageing of bourbon whiskey. It is estimated that every year about 1,300,000 barrels are made there, primarily by two cooperages. Only between 60,000 and 80,000 of these so-called bourbon barrels go directly to wineries.

Nearly all American logs come from privately held forests located in the eastern half of the United States, notably in Minnesota, Wisconsin, Kentucky, Arkansas, Tennessee, the Virginias, the Carolinas, and Missouri. These logs are purchased by stave mill operators, some of whom also run cooperages. Cooperage use accounts for about 3 per cent of all American white oak harvested every year. Most American oak is used for furniture, construction, veneer, and pulp.

The logs are cut into appropriate lengths, quarter sawn, planed, and then sold to cooperages. Customers for American oak staves are found not only in bourbon country, but in cooperages in California, Australia—and Spain, where American oak has until recently been used almost exclusively for wine maturation, most notably in RIOJA and JEREZ, for the historical reasons outlined.

For whiskey to be called bourbon, it must, according to American government regulations that are a blessing to the cooperage business, be aged in a 'new, charred white oak barrel', so large quantities of used whiskey barrels are commercially available, many of them relatively new, even though distinctively charred and whiskey flavoured. An estimated 700,000 to 800,000 used bourbon barrels are sold each year to Spain, Scotland, Ireland, Japan, Thailand, India, Puerto Rico, Canada, and Taiwan, as well as to producers of other North American spirits. Most of them are used to mature spirits: various brandies, rums, and whiskies. The Scotch whisky industry is a particularly important consumer of American oak, at any one time using as many as 13 million casks in total. In some cases American oak barrels are sent to Jerez en route to Scotland, where some distillers still prefer to use casks infused with sherry flavours as was the norm in the 19th century, when sherry was shipped in cask to British wine merchants, who would then pass on these casks to the Scotch whisky industry. Now that sherry is no longer shipped in cask, some Scotch whisky distillers in Scotland have their barrels 'broken in' in Jerez with sherry.

France The French cooperage business is much smaller than its American counterpart but is much more important to the wine business. Between 150,000 and 200,000 French oak barrels were produced annually in the early 1990s, primarily in BORDEAUX, BURGUNDY, and Cognac, where most French cooperages are located. Although France remains the most important single customer for French oak barrels, slightly more than half of French annual production is exported, with the United States taking about half of all exports. The balance is shipped to 30 other countries, most notably Italy, Australia, New Zealand, South Africa, Chile, Argentina, and Germany. As well as selling to Bordeaux, Burgundy, Cognac, and Armagnac, French cooperages are also developing new 'export' markets selling to ambitious winemakers in French regions that had

abandoned new barrels. The RHÔNE, LANGUEDOC, ROUSSILLON, and SOUTH WEST FRANCE, as well as the LOIRE and to a much lesser extent ALSACE, have all become important purchasers.

In France about one-third of all forests are owned by local or national government. However, the sale of over 80 per cent of all lots, carefully delineated groups of trees, is administered by the National Forestry Office (ONF). In September and October, wood auctions are held all over France but for the buyer of oak destined to be turned into barrels and tanks the most important auctions are held in Nevers, Châteauroux, and Moulins.

A potential buyer bids on the trees in a delineated section, which should be at least 100 and preferably well over 120, sometimes 160, years old before providing suitable wood for casks. Buyers have the right to go into the forest, measure the trees, even to bore into them 30 cm/12 in to see how straight is the GRAIN. They must decide how much of each type of wood there is, how it can be used, and, of course, how much they should bid. The auction starts with a high price, which is lowered until somebody offers an acceptable bid.

As not every tree in an auction lot can be used for STAVES, French cooperages usually work with wood brokers who have other customers. The most valuable part of a tree is that with the tightest and straightest grains which can be used for panelling. The furniture and construction industries are important customers.

French barrels cost at least double those made of American oak. French logs are much more expensive because they must be hand split rather than machine sawn and demand more expensive drying methods. French cooperages also tend to be smaller and less automated than their American counterparts. But the special qualities of French oak ensure that it is the most sought after by modern winemakers and able to command a considerable premium.

As the use of French oak has become more widespread, staves are now shipped all over the world, notably to Australia, Italy, South America, South Africa, America, Spain, and Portugal, where they may be made up into barrels in local cooperages.

No system of APPELLATION CONTRÔLÉE limits the period of time French oak barrels may be used for any wine or spirit. Consequently the sale of used French oak barrels is not as organized as that for American barrels. In Burgundy, producers often use their new barrels for their grandest appellations and then use them for progressively lower-ranking wines. In Bordeaux, one proprietor will often own several châteaux and will treat his or her most prestigious property to the luxury of new oak before passing the barrels down the chain to a lowlier property. Alternatively, used barrels are sold to

wineries unable to command the sort of price that can support expensive new barrels, or where winemakers do not want the taste of new oak. In the New World, used barrels are often traded between wineries. Relatively young ones, especially those used for white wine, are highly valued, but barrels more than ten years old are usually sold to be cut in half for flower planters.

Italy In Italy, a relatively small but lively cooperage industry makes barrels and vats primarily with oak imported from France and Slavonia.

Spain Barrels have been important to the Spanish wine and sherry industries for centuries and the cooper's craft is sustained there. In Jerez, new barrels are spurned for the maturation of fine SHERRY and will probably be used at least three times for FERMENTATION before being used to mature a top-quality OLOROSO. The older a cask, the more expensive it is, and some bodegas boast casks (or butts as they are usually called here) that are more than 200 years old.

Portugal The demands of the port industry, and a ready supply of Portuguese oak, have kept the cooper's craft alive in northern Portugal so that French coopers have even imported Portuguese craftsmen.   M.K.

Kilby, K., *The Cooper and his Trade* (London, 1971).
Taransaud, J., *Le Livre de la tonnellerie* (Paris, 1976).

co-operatives, ventures owned jointly by a number of different members, are extremely important as wine producers and have the advantage for their members of pooling wine-making and marketing resources and costs. Collectively, they usually have access to a broad range of financial advantages, including subsidies in the EUROPEAN UNION, over individual producers. In most countries they also enjoy the commercial advantage of being able to describe their wines as bottled by the producer, using such reassuring phrases as MIS(E) EN BOUTEILLE *à la propriété* and ERZEUGERABFÜLLUNG more usually associated with much smaller, individually managed wine enterprises. The better co-operatives are becoming increasingly skilled not just at wine-making but also at marketing specific bottlings designed to look and taste every bit as distinctive as the individually produced competition. The worst co-operatives play almost exclusively with subsidies and politics. Co-operatives are at their strongest in areas where wine's selling price is relatively low and where the average size of individual holdings is small, although co-operatives are also quite significant in CHAMPAGNE and there are several in the MÉDOC, for example. The majority of wine co-operatives were formed in the early 1930s in the immediate aftermath of the Depression.

France

Since 1975, more than half of the wine produced in France has been produced by co-operatives, and the total area of vineyard owned by their members is also more than half the French total. The number of members, or *adhérents*, of France's *caves coopératives* (often referred to locally simply as *la cave*) represented almost half of all French vine-growers in the mid 1990s, but the average number of members of each co-operative is declining (down from 240 in the 1960s to 160 in the 1990s) as holdings are amalgamated and members were encouraged to grub up less suitable vineyards by the EU VINE PULL SCHEME. The total number of French co-operatives is declining too, although there were over 850 in the early 2000s. They are a particularly strong force in the LANGUEDOC and ROUSSILLON, the greater RHÔNE valley, PROVENCE, and CORSICA, where *la cave* can dominate local economic life. Although the co-operatives are being restructured and amalgamated into much bigger groupings, it is by no means unusual for a single village in Languedoc-Roussillon to boast two *caves coopératives*, typically distinguished by political orientation.

The co-operatives produce an impressive quantity of APPELLATION CONTRÔLÉE wine, nearly half of the country's total, and those which have established a reputation for particularly sound AC wines outside their own region include La Chablisienne of CHABLIS, the co-operative at Tain l'HERMITAGE, Mont Tauch in ROUSSILLON, the Plaimont co-operative organization in GASCONY, and a number of ALSACE co-operatives, notably that of Turckheim. The co-operatives' speciality, however, is VINS DE PAYS. Their combined output of these intensely local wines represents three-quarters of the national total, and is considerably more than their (fast declining) combined total output of wine at its most basic, VIN DE TABLE.

Co-operatives have been prime targets for FLYING WINEMAKERS. The average quality of wine made in French co-ops has improved since the early 1990s but their sales and marketing expertise has not in general, a major factor in France's CRISE VITICOLE.

http://www.ccvf.coop/sites/ccvf/

Germany

In GERMANY, the co-operative (known as *Winzergenossenschaft*, *Winzerverein*, *Winzervereinigung*, *Weingärtnergenossenschaft*, or *Weinbauernverband*) has played an increasingly significant role since 1869, when the first German wine co-operative was formally established in the AHR, where the great majority of the region's output is still processed by co-operatives. As outlined in GERMAN HISTORY, co-operatives offered smallholders the chance to compete in the newly quality-conscious German wine market of the late 19th and early 20th centuries.

Nearly two in every three German vine-growers today belong to the local co-operative, although their vineyards are often a small, part-time activity which therefore, cumulatively, represent almost a third of the total German area under vine. Many of the 13 wine regions of Germany have a central co-operative cellar, or ZENTRALKELLEREI, which is fed grapes, wine, or must by more localized co-operatives. In 2004, there were 231 co-operatives in Germany, of which 137 made wine on the premises.

The co-operative movement is particularly strong, and particularly successful, in the most southerly region of BADEN, where about 85 per cent of all wine produced from nearly 100 individual co-operatives is sold under the auspices of the giant central Badischer Winzerkeller at Breisach. This vast enterprise can today store 160 million l/42 million gal, and is therefore larger than any winery in France. The Baden co-operatives have been particularly active in transcending the co-operative image of quantity over quality by developing superior, small volume bottlings of distinctive wines. Co-operatives are also extremely important in the WÜRTTEMBERG region, where there are 68 co-operatives whose central cellar is at Möglingen in the PFALZ, and in Germany's four smallest regions, SAALE-UNSTRUT, AHR, HESSISCHE BERGSTRASSE, and SACHSEN. In the MOSEL-SAAR-RUWER region, the central co-operative cellar, Moselland of Bernkastel, processes about 20 per cent of the region's output, but in the other classic wine region, the RHEINGAU, the role of co-operative cellars is very much less significant.

Italy

In Italy, the *cantina sociale* is no less important, accounting for over 60 per cent of the country's production. EU policies have favoured co-operatives in the past, often as a result of wily or politically well-connected operators of them. As EU subsidies dwindle, however, the quality of the wine, and the ability to run the co-operative on a commercial basis, becomes increasingly important. One of the most respected Italian co-operatives, in the far north west, is the Produttori del BARBARESCO, whose origins are 19th century and which has a direct counterpart in the Terre del BAROLO. The influence of the *cantina sociale*, or *Kellereigenossenschaft* in German, is particularly strong in TRENTINO-ALTO ADIGE, where Cavit is perhaps the most exported name. In VENETO, co-operatives have traditionally been responsible for the bulk of production, particularly in Verona, where a large number of producers of Soave and Valpolicella either buy, or supplement their production through purchases, from the local co-op.

The co-operative Riunite of EMILIA-ROMAGNA was famous in the early 1980s for engulfing the United States, and other markets, in a tidal wave of LAMBRUSCO. Cantine Leonardo (from Vinci), the Cantine di Montalcino, and the

Cantina di Scansano are some of TOSCANA's improving co-operatives. Further south, quantity, and not necessarily quality, is the chief characteristic of the co-operatives that proliferate practically wherever the vine is grown. The Copertino co-operative in PUGLIA makes a good job of its eponymous red. The islands SARDEGNA and SICILIA are dominated by co-operatives, of which Settesoli in Sicilia and Santadi in Sardegna are models of quality.

Spain and Portugal

As in Italy, co-operatives are extremely important in Iberia, where grapes are so often grown alongside other crops. According to Metcalfe and McWhirter, more than 60 per cent of each vintage was delivered to one of Spain's 1,000 wine co-operatives or Portugal's 300 (see PORTUGAL, history) in the late 1980s and this has not changed substantially. However, the percentage of bottled wine sold by co-ops in Spain remains tiny—between 10 and 15 per cent of their total production, the rest being sold in bulk, with a substantial percentage going directly to distillation. Although the movement began in the early years of the 20th century, it substantially increased in importance in the 1950s, when the wine market was relatively depressed. One of the earliest wine co-operatives was in Olite in NAVARRA, where the movement is particularly powerful and where it can absorb as much as 90 per cent of grape production, although here, as elsewhere, links are being forged with individual producers to increase overall quality and technical expertise. It was only in the 1980s that many Iberian co-operatives even began to consider bottling wine, so much of their produce was sold off either for DISTILLATION or as BULK WINE.

Co-operatives are important in most Spanish wine regions (although in famed RIOJA they process only about 40 per cent of the region's grapes). In the vineyard vastness of La MANCHA, there are about 100 co-operatives of very varied quality, while YECLA and JUMILLA have export-minded co-operatives whose level of modern equipment and expertise is considerably above average. In the fortified wine regions of JEREZ, much of the rest of ANDALUCÍA, and the DOURO, co-operatives are less important than the long-standing links between vine-growers and individual wine producers. The 20th-century Portuguese table wine industry was revolutionized by the government's formation of co-operatives, however not always for the better (see DÃO).

Rest of the world

Practically wherever wine is made, co-operatives thrive, although the movement is not particularly strong in the UNITED STATES and has had its own variants in eastern Europe. Co-operatives have played a particularly important role in the development of the wine industry in SOUTH AFRICA (see also KWV). In the RIVERLAND of AUSTRALIA, the co-operative origins of Berri Renmano, now merged with the large family-owned producer HARDYS and one of the country's largest wine companies, date back to the 1920s.

Anderson, B., *The Wine Atlas of Italy* (London and New York, 1990).

Metcalfe, C., and McWhirter, K., *The Wines of Spain & Portugal* (London and New York, 1988).

Copertino, DOC for robust red wine made mainly from NEGROAMARO grapes in south east Italy. For more details, see PUGLIA. The co-operative winery of Copertino, directed by Severino Garofano, southern Italy's leading consulting OENOLOGIST, has attracted attention for its well-made wines at extremely reasonable prices.

co-pigmentation, a mechanism of colour stabilization, involving the interaction of ANTHOCYANIN pigments with another molecule (co-factor).

In aqueous media, anthocyanins are present under different forms in equilibrium, including red and violet pigment species and colourless hydrated forms. The latter predominate at mildly acidic PH values such as encountered in plant cell VACUOLES and in wine. However, the anthocyanin pigmented forms stack vertically with other species present in the solution (co-factors) to form complexes from which water is excluded. This results in enhanced colour intensity due to a shift of the balance from the colourless hydrated forms towards the dehydrated pigment forms involved in these stable complexes. The role of co-pigmentation in wine colour can be estimated by comparing red colour intensity before and after disruption of co-pigmentation complexes by dilution in a wine-like buffer. Co-pigmentation has been reported to account for 30 to 50 per cent of the colour of young red wines, on the basis of such measurements.

V.C.

Boulton, R., 'The copigmentation of anthocyanins and its role in the color of red wine: a critical review', *American Journal of Enology and Viticulture*, 52/2 (2001), 67–87.

Brouillard, R., and Dangles, O., 'Flavonoids and flower colour', in J. B. Harborne (ed.), *The Flavonoids. Advances in Research since 1986* (London, 1993), 565–88.

copita, special glass in which SHERRY is customarily served in Spain. It is designed to maximize the AROMA, and larger sizes can be used as a glass for general wine TASTING. See GLASSES.

copper, a trace element required in very small concentrations for healthy vine growth. Copper is toxic to plants except in very dilute concentrations. Reports of copper deficiencies in vineyards are rare, probably because of the very small requirements by the vines, but also because of the widespread use of FUNGICIDES containing copper. In acid soils, the copper from fungicide sprays can actually reach toxic

levels and some parts of the MÉDOC have been affected by copper toxicity. After the annual application of several kg of copper per ha, as in BORDEAUX MIXTURE, for about a century, the level of copper in the soil can be toxic and the vine growth became severely stunted. Generous applications of humus and lime will neutralize the effects of excess copper. See also CASSE.

R.E.S.

Corbeau. See CHARBONO.

Corbières, quantitatively significant appellation in the LANGUEDOC region of southern France producing some excitingly dense, herby red wines, a small amount of rosé, and a little increasingly well-made white wine from more than 12,000 ha/29,600 acres of vineyard in 2005. The terrain here in the Pyrenean foothills (see map under LANGUEDOC) is extremely varied, and so hilly that it is difficult to generalize about soil types and TOPOGRAPHY. In recognition of this, the appellation was in the 1990s subdivided into 11 so-called TERROIRS, although not without a certain amount of local dissent. The basic distinctions in this southernmost corner of the Aude *département* are between coastal zones influenced by the Mediterranean, the northern strip on the Montagne d'Alaric (some of which has more in common with MINERVOIS), the westernmost vineyards, which are cooled both by Atlantic influence and by ALTITUDE, and the rugged, mountainous terrain in the south and centre in which the FITOU appellation forms two enclaves.

Vineyards in the south west of the appellation are as high as 300 to 450 m (980–1,500 ft) above sea level, and HARVEST may not take place until well into October, while those in the Sigean area are right on the coast and can vary enormously in altitude but the high average temperatures and very low annual rainfall are partly compensated for by the marine influence. One of the most admired terroirs is that of Boutenac, which has particularly poor soils on a LIMESTONE base in what is known locally as Corbières' 'golden triangle'. In 2005, **Corbières Boutenac** was granted its own subappellation for wines that, unusually, contain at least 30 per cent Carignan and satisfy certain minimum ageing periods.

With terrain this extensive and this varied, it is perhaps hardly surprising that progress within the appellation can become enmired in local politics.

Carignan is still the dominant variety, representing well over half of all vines planted, although from the 2003 harvest the proportion of all the 'improving varieties' Syrah, Mourvèdre, Grenache, and Lladoner Pelut combined had to represent at least 50 per cent of the blend in all red wines. Some producers particularly value the spice and concentration of wine from old vines, which in Corbières effectively means old Carignan. Warmer parts of

Corbières can ripen Mourvèdre on a regular basis. Plantings of Cinsaut, useful along with Syrah for rosé, are more limited here than in neighbouring Minervois. Grenache, its relative Lladoner Pelut, Picpoul Noir, and Terret are also allowed in red and rosé Corbières.

White Corbières, a rare but often refreshing dry wine, is made principally from Bourboulenc, Maccabéo, and Grenache Blanc but Clairette, Muscat (sometimes vinified alone to make a dry wine), Picpoul, Terret, Marsanne, Roussanne, and Rolle or Vermentino are all also allowed, providing an interesting aromatic palette for the increasing number of producers prepared to experiment with superior white wine-making.

CO-OPERATIVES, Embrès-et-Castelmaure and Tuchan/Mont Tauch being particularly quality conscious, dominate the region, but there are many seriously ambitious individual estates too, including Clos de l'Anhel, Domaine du Grand Crès, Chx Haut-Gléon, de Lastours, Mansenoble, Domaine du Roque-Sestière, and Ch Voulte-Gasparets.

Simms, P. and S., *The Wines of Corbières & Fitou* (Toulouse, 1991).

Cordisco, occasional name for Italy's MONTEPULCIANO grape.

cordon, part of the vine's woody framework, arising from the top of the trunk and on which arms are borne (see diagram under PRUNING). Cordons can be at any angle but are generally trained along horizontal WIRES, or shallowly sloped wires as in some TENDONE trellises. The most common arrangement is a bilateral cordon in which two horizontal cordons are arranged in opposite directions from the top of the trunk, but any number of arrangements are possible. The unilateral cordon is common in some parts of Europe, and because of ease of training is being increasingly adopted in the New World. Usually the cordon is trained to its permanent position and remains there. See vine-TRAINING SYSTEMS.

B.G.C.

cordon de Royat, an old form of CORDON TRAINING used in France for wine grapes since the end of the 19th century (see illustration overleaf). The system was proposed by Lefebvre, director of the French agricultural school of Royat. The classic form is a unilateral CORDON on a short trunk (about 30 to 50 cm (12–20 in)), the term unilateral meaning that the cordon is trained only to one side of the trunk. The cordon extends mostly from one vine to another. The vines are normally SPUR PRUNED to two bud spurs. The number of spurs is limited for each variety under APPELLATION laws: in Burgundy, for example, to four spurs each for Pinot Noir and Chardonnay vines, and to eight for Gamay.

R.E.S.

cordon training, a form of VINE TRAINING in which the trunk terminates in a CORDON,

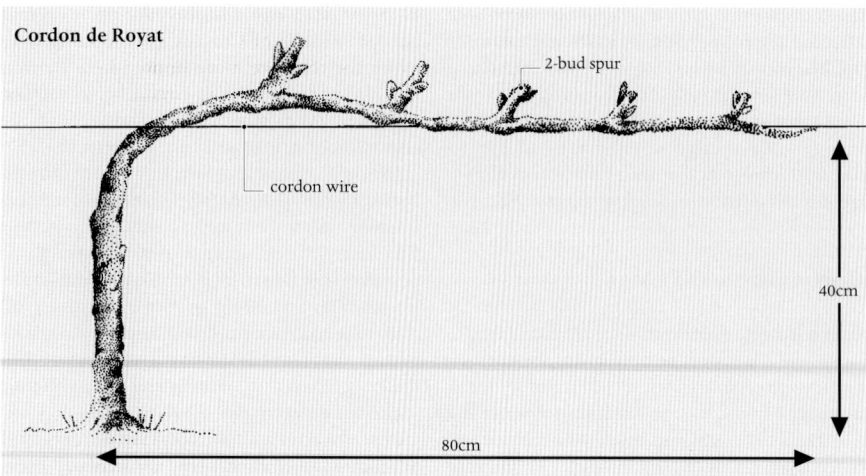

Cordon de Royat

2-bud spur

cordon wire

40cm

80cm

and the vine is then typically subjected to SPUR PRUNING. The alternative is HEAD TRAINING, where the vines are usually subjected to CANE PRUNING. The cordon is normally horizontal and can be unilateral (trained only to one side of the trunk) or bilateral (to both sides). See also CORDON DE ROYAT and PRUNING. R.E.S.

corkage, charge customarily levied in a restaurant for each bottle of wine brought in and consumed on the premises rather than bought from the restaurant's own selection (although see also BYO). The term is derived from the fact that the number of corks pulled represents the number of bottles consumed. There is considerable variation in the amount charged, and the grace with which the practice is accepted.

corked, pejorative tasting term for a wine spoiled by a cork stopper contaminated with CORK TAINT. This is one of the most serious wine FAULTS as in most cases it irrevocably imbues the wine with such a powerfully off-putting smell that it cannot be drunk with any enjoyment. The unpleasantly, almost mould-like, chemical smell is occasionally present in smaller doses that may initially be noticed only by noses particularly sensitive to it, but the odour usually intensifies with aeration and it is difficult for tasters to enjoy a wine once their attention has been drawn to its existence. A wine spoiled by cork taint may also be described as **corky** and the condition is known as **corkiness**. Even a low level of taint often results in a slight dulling effect on the bouquet and palate, and levels well below the threshold of most drinkers have been shown to suppress fruit characters significantly.

The problem of corkiness was perceived by the wine industry to have increased during from the 1980s, and in a 2003 article in the French journal *La Vigne*, Miriam Chastaingt noted that between 5 and 8 per cent of bottles distributed in the French market are likely to be corked. These developments have soured

relations between the wine and the cork industries and led to a marked increase in the use of alternative CLOSURES, particularly including SCREW CAPS and SYNTHETIC CLOSURES. At the start of the 21st century, the greatest competitor to cork in terms of performance appears to be the screw cap.

It is commonly, but erroneously, believed that a wine with small fragments of cork floating in it is 'corked'. This may be a SERVING fault but is certainly not a wine fault.

Chastaingt, M., 'Trop de vins sont bouchonnés, la grogne s'amplifie', *La Vigne*, 140 (Feb 2003), 28–33.

Stelzer, T., *Taming the Screw: A Manual for Winemaking with Screw Caps* (Brisbane, 2005).

corks, wine bottle stoppers, without which the appreciation of fine wine, and in particular BOTTLE AGEING, might never have evolved. Cork's unique combination of qualities have made it by far the most popular stopper for wine, but in the late 20th century the science of wine production bounded ahead of the science of cork production, to the detriment of relations between the two industries (see CORKED wine).

History
See CLOSURES.

The cork tree
The cork tree, *Quercus suber*, is a relatively young species of OAK and is unusual in that its bark is so thick and resistant that it can be stripped from the trunk and large branches without hurting the tree.

It grows in sandy soils free of chalk and prefers annual rainfalls between 400 and 800 mm (15–30 in), temperatures which never fall below -5 °C/23 °F, and an altitude between 100 and 300 m (330–1,000 ft). This effectively restricts cork oaks to the coast of the western Mediterranean, particularly Spain, North Africa, and much of Portugal, where cork plays a significant role in the economy. The cork industry was born in Cataluña but was disrupted by the Spanish Civil War. The commercial stability of

ALGERIA, another prime source of cork, was called into question in the 1960s, so that, in the early 21st century, Portugal is the centre of the world's cork business and cork is an important contributor to the Portuguese economy. Portugal's cork forests are today the most extensive, their 670,000 ha/1.6 million acres representing about 30 per cent of the world's cork trees, significantly assisted in the late 1980s by EUROPEAN UNION grants.

Spain has the next largest total area planted with cork oaks, about 480,000 ha, most of them now in the south and west of the country, from which a high proportion of the cork is shipped across the border for processing in Portugal's more temperate climate (although, in the north east, Cataluña is still an important supplier of corks, especially to France and particularly to Champagne). So entrenched is the modern cork industry in Portugal—many of the processing centres are located just south of Oporto and therefore close to the PORT trade—that it produces more than half of the world's total output of cork, helped by imports not just from Spain but also from North Africa. Algeria, Morocco, and Tunisia have between them as big an area of cork forest as Portugal but produce only one-fifth as much cork. As with wine, each cork region produces cork with different characteristics, although forestry management is the key to quality. Portugal's most prized cork region is Evora.

Cork trees, if not a cork industry, also flourish along the west coast of Italy, in Sicilia, Sardegna, and Corsica, and along the Mediterranean coast of France, particularly in Provence, but little is made of these plantations commercially. There have also been trial plantings of cork trees in countries such as the United States and Japan.

The bark of the cork tree is sufficiently thick to yield commercially useful cork in its 25th year, and cork trees are regularly stripped during the summer months, no more than every nine years by Portuguese law. On average, modern husbandry means that each hectare of cork forest yields 230 kg/500 lbs of cork; the older the tree the more cork it will yield. Although the average life expectancy of a cork tree is about 170 years, there is one 200-year-old tree in the Montijo region south east of Portugal's capital Lisbon which has yielded 1,200 kg of cork from a single stripping. Cork farming, an activity often administered by the state, is an even longer-term undertaking than growing vines, which have an active wine-producing life of around 30 years (and considerably longer in some instances).

The bark micro-structure is unique in that it consists of very small, closely packed, usually 14-sided cells which have undergone a process known as suberinization. This renders it light, elastic, inert, and relatively impermeable to gases and most liquids except particularly strong acids or bases. These qualities and its low conductivity make cork a useful and versatile commodity as an insulator, particularly for the automotive and construction industries, but the principal use for cork is still cork stoppers and, in particular, wine corks.

Cork processing

The modern cork processing operation has changed remarkably little over the past century. The strips of cork bark yielded by the annual stripping are stacked and left outside for seasoning (just as other woods are in BARREL MAKING) for at least six months. Still in large strips, the cork is then boiled for about 90 minutes, both to make it more flexible and in an effort to kill off any moulds and other contaminants. The planks are then left to rest in the warehouse of the cork processing plant for three weeks before being sorted by hand and cut into strips as wide as the length of the final cork stopper. Corks are then punched out of these strips, usually by hand-operated punches but using an increasing degree of mechanization. Maximizing yield is a significant factor since only about 40 per cent of all the commercially viable cork harvested is suitable for stoppers.

Corks are deliberately punched at right angles to the growth of the cork tree, so that any lenticels, occasional knots in the wood, remain transverse and the risk of possible leakage due to lenticels is minimized. The ends of the cork stoppers are then polished to present a smooth surface to the wine.

Various treatments then follow, with the twin aims of cosmetic appeal and hygiene. Bleaching, which has traditionally been done by immersing the corks in a bath of chlorine solution, makes the corks look less irregularly marked and also acts as a form of disinfectant. Unfortunately, however, there is evidence that this chlorine increases the likelihood of TRICHLOROANISOLE formation, and therefore the incidence of CORK TAINT. Hydrogen peroxide treatments have been offered as an alternative to chlorine bleaching by most cork processors since the mid 1980s but research work is now focused on other alternatives such as moisture-saturated heat treatments to destroy moulds and BACTERIA, but not cork's natural flexibility.

Corks are then graded on visual quality (the fewer markings the higher the grade), branded (most corks today are marked not only with the branding specified by the wine bottler, but also with an indication of the cork supplier), and often coated with some paraffin or silicon-based product that increases their extractability and, in many cases, eases their passage through high-speed BOTTLING lines.

Finally, corks are sealed into large plastic bags, typically with SULFUR DIOXIDE as a disinfectant, although irradiation and simple holes for aeration are used as respectively more and less sophisticated alternatives. Subsequent storage conditions are important to minimize possible contamination. Corks should ideally be stored in a ventilated, odour-free environment at a temperature between 15 and 20 °C (59–68 °F) in a humidity of 50 to 70 per cent. Poor cork storage conditions can dramatically increase the incidence of CORKED WINES.

The range available

Although the first cork stoppers were tapered, the development of CORKSCREWS made tightly fitting cylindrical corks the norm. Modern corks are available in varying lengths, from 25 to as much as 60 mm (1–2.3 in), according to the BOTTLE AGEING aspirations, or extravagant exhibitionism, of the wine producer. (GAJA of Barbaresco, for example, perhaps the most ambitious cork buyer, personally selects his 60 mm corks from a supplier in Sardegna.) The longer the cork, the longer it is likely to remain an intact and viable stopper (see RECORKING), although some oenologists argue that longer corks result in lower FILL LEVELS, which may prejudice AGEING. There is a limit to the length at which cork effectiveness can continue to increase, since most bottle necks allow only 50–55 mm of cork length to make contact with the glass. There is much less variation in diameter, however, with 24 mm being the norm, although corks 21 and 26 mm wide are not unknown, depending on the inside width of the necks of BOTTLES used.

The quality of the cork material itself also determines the price and potential life of the stopper, and corks may be graded into eight different quality levels. The cheapest form of cork, developed in 1891 by an American businessman, John Smith, is cork agglomerate, occasionally called 'agglo', reassembled crumbs of cork which can offer some of the benefits of intact cork itself. A more recent development is the 'technical' cork, such as the Altec and Diam closures from Oeno Bouchage (previously Sabaté), made from cork flour mixed with a synthetic component (the Diam version has been treated with supercritical CO_2, see CORK TAINT). Agglomerate corks with discs of natural cork at each end, such as Amorim's Twin Top®, are also very popular. The best-quality cork is that with the least markings. The longest, finest cork can cost five times as much as the cheapest, shortest agglomerate cork. However, since corks are graded on visual quality, this has no bearing on the likelihood of TCA or other taints.

Stopper corks with plastic tops are used for some wines, particularly FORTIFIED wines and some SWEET WINES, a single bottle of which may be consumed over an extended period.

Corks for SPARKLING wines, commonly known, with scant regard for appellation laws, as champagne corks, have to be made to very particular specifications. Initially cylindrical, they are much wider than normal corks, about 30 mm, and have to be (half) driven into the bottle-neck, forcing them into a mushroom shape. Champagne corks are held in place, against the force of the pressure of undissolved gas inside the bottle, by a wire muzzle. Because such corks are too wide to be punched whole from the bark of most cork oaks, and to moderate the cost of such a large cork, champagne corks are usually made from cork agglomerate with one, two, or occasionally three discs of natural cork stuck on to the end which goes into the bottle-neck and is in contact with the wine.

Clues from the cork

In general, the narrower and more misshapen a cork extracted from a bottle, the longer it has been there. This is a particularly useful clue to the likely age of a non-vintage sparkling wine, or at least to the time that has elapsed since DISGORGEMENT. It can also provide a clue to the likely age of any other non-vintage wine, or fine wine which has lost its label or, perhaps in the case of vintage PORT, never had one (although see also RECORKING).

Most fine wine corks are emblazoned with the name of the wine producer (if not the wine itself) and, often, the vintage. Different countries adopt different conventions. Italian corks, which fit particularly tightly into their narrow bottle-necks, are often marked with a two-letter regional code (UD for Udine on many FRIULI wine corks, for example). Most British wine bottlers brand their corks with a W followed by their own numerical code. The regular French message is simply MIS EN BOUTEILLE *à la propriété*.

A short agglomerate cork suggests that the bottler had little regard for the ageing ability of this wine, while a particularly long cork is indicative at least of ambition or optimism.

If a cork has crystals on the end that has been in contact with the wine (white in the case of a white wine and dyed dark red by a red wine), these are harmless TARTRATES. If a cork seems damp or mouldy at either end, this is not necessarily a sign of any wine fault. Some wine waiters are taught to smell the cork and present it to the customer as an essential part of wine SERVICE, but the state of a cork is no sure guide to the state of the wine it stoppered.

For alternatives to corks, including so-called 'plastic corks', see CLOSURES, CROWN CAPS, SCREW CAPS, and SYNTHETIC CLOSURES.

corkscrews, wide range of devices for extracting CORKS from the necks of wine BOTTLES.

It might be thought that cork extraction would prove an easy matter with any simple screw device, given the relatively soft, resilient nature of the stopper. However, there have been many hundreds of inventions since the middle of the 18th century with the aim of producing a better, more efficient corkscrew, and as yet none has been accepted as the perfect instrument. In particular, no corkscrew has yet been shown to be infallible with old PORT corks so PORT TONGS are sometimes employed instead. The extraction operation can vary considerably. Corks vary in length and, as they accommodate to the shape of the bottle-neck, they can also vary in shape. Furthermore, cork undergoes ageing in old bottles and may partially disintegrate on extraction. The necks of old port bottles, for example, usually have a slightly bulbous form, so that the lower part of the cylindrical cork is weakened where it ballooned out and became cone shaped. Italian wine bottles tend to be narrow at the neck, tightly compressing corks and making them relatively difficult to penetrate.

History

The free-blown, onion-shaped wine bottles (see BOTTLES, history) of the 17th century did not have a standard size of neck. Under these circumstances, tapered corks made a satisfactory stopper, especially as a portion remained proud of the bottle top, facilitating manual removal. The mould-made cylindrical glass bottle which evolved from about 1740 could be BINNED horizontally to keep the cork moist and at the same time to save space. This necessitated a driven cylindrical cork of standard diameter and the removal of such a cork required a special tool.

Simple corkscrews leave the operator to do the work of screwing in the worm and pulling out the cork unassisted. Various modifications of handle, shaft, and worm can increase the efficiency of these manœuvres: the handle should be formed to give a good pulling grip; the shaft can be fitted with a metal disc, or button, to obtain more complete contact with the cork; and the worm should be a steel helix 5.7 cm/ 2.2 in long, of good open pitch, and have an outer diameter of between 0.8 and 1 cm.

Although it is probable that simple corkscrews were in use by the mid 17th century in England, the earliest extant examples date from the 1690s.

Mechanical corkscrews are designed to reduce the amount of physical effort required during the three manœuvres of piercing, pulling, and disposing of the cork. Mechanical handheld corkscrews can never be used with the rapidity of an efficient wall- or bar-mounted mechanical instrument, although the modern hand-held **Lever Pull**, really a miniature barscrew in concept, can be used at remarkable speed.

National characteristics

Until fairly recently, the best corkscrews from the points of view of function, design, and quality of workmanship were made in wine-neutral Britain. The two-lever Italian corkscrew with a gimlet-like worm overcame the erstwhile problem of their short, tight corks.

The Germans rarely used other than the centre worm and often combined this with an inventive use of springs and ball bearings. In 1882, Karl Wienke of Rostock, Mecklenburg, conceived of using a knife-like handle as a lever. Known affectionately as the **waiter's friend**, it is still the essential tool of a SOMMELIER worldwide. The development of an articulated lever makes this model even easier to use as the cork is extracted in two stages, keeping it more upright and less likely to break.

The French were keen on nickel plating, contrasting with the bronzed finish of English pieces; well demonstrated by the lazy tongs models of both countries.

Americans printed the wooden handles with advertisements and became largely preoccupied with self-pullers and other models which used the frame of the corkscrew as a fulcrum and derived from the French *à cage* principle. **Screwpull**, invented in the 1970s by Herbert Allen, is the culmination of applying this principle using strong modern plastics and a teflon-coated helix. Many other manufacturers today use teflon-coated worms, copying the Screwpull principles.

A two-pronged extractor became jokingly known as the **butler's friend**, as it enabled the cork to be extracted and replaced without evident damage and, possibly, the wine to be replaced with one less fine. B.M.W. & R.N.H.B.

Watney, Bernard M., and Babbidge, Homer D., *Corkscrews for Collectors* (London, 1981).

cork taint. Although research results vary, around 5 per cent of all wines sealed under cork display a musty taint. This is caused by a number of potent organic compounds, the most significant of which is 2,4,6-trichloroanisole or TCA (see TRICHLOROANISOLE). These taint compounds are metabolic products of fungi naturally present in cork, or which have grown in the cork at various processing stages. Initially, the occurrence of this taint was ascribed to the washing of cork planks by chlorine-containing bleaches; these have since been replaced by peroxide, but the incidence of cork taint has remained the same. It seems that the structure of cork, which is permeated by fine pores (lenticels) to facilitate gas exchange, will always harbour fungi with the potential to produce taint compounds. A study by Duncan, Gibson, and Obradovic has demonstrated the presence of TCA in the bark of cork trees in a Portuguese cork forest. See CHLOROANISOLES. The effect of cork taint on the wine is often characterized as an off-putting, mouldy, wet cardboard or wet dog character. It suppresses fruit and shortens the length of finish of the wine. In its most subtle form, cork taint has a slight dulling effect on the bouquet and palate. At its extreme, high levels of cork taint render a wine quite unapproachable.

Only tiny amounts of TCA are needed to cause a taint problem since its aroma detection threshold in wine is about 3–4 ng/l. The cork industry has searched in earnest for methods to eradicate TCA from corks, and two new directions show promise. Sabaté's Diamant procedure, using supercritical carbon dioxide, has been almost 100% successful in stripping TCA from the cork flour used to make its popular Altec closure; however, it has yet to prove suitable for treating whole natural corks. Amorim's steam-based ROSA cleaning process removes most, but not all, of the TCA. OZONE is sometimes used as a preventive measure but its effectiveness is uncertain. The recent adoption by some cork producers of gas chromatography–mass spectrometry as a TCA detection tool should improve cork quality control measures but it seems unlikely that it will ever prove possible to completely eradicate taint compounds from cork. However, a recent AUSTRALIAN WINE RESEARCH INSTITUTE study has shown that cork may sometimes actually absorb TCA and other chloroanisoles from contaminated wine.

Research has identified the potential contribution of chemicals other than TCA to taint in wine. These include other chloroanisoles such as TeCA (see TETRACHOROANISOLE) and PCA (see PENTACHLOROANISOLE), as well as alternatives to chloroanisoles. MDMP (see METHOXY-DIMETHYLPYRAZINE) has recently been identified as a key compound responsible for a 'fungal must' taint in wines. Although its contribution to cork taint is yet to be established, some industry figures rate it as second only to TCA. TBA (see TRIBROMOANISOLE) also creates musty aromas in wine but is caused by contamination from the winery environment. This tallies with the observation that 'cork taint' can come from sources other than the cork: most notably from wooden structures in wineries that have been chemically treated, though the taint may still be transferred to the wine via the secondary contamination of the cork. But despite a few fairly high-profile instances of winery contamination, it seems that the cork is the culprit in the vast majority of cases. J.A.G., T.M.S., & P.J.W.

Capone, D., Sefton, M., Pretorius, I., and Høj, P., 'Flavour "scalping" by wine bottle closures', *Australian and New Zealand Wine Industry Journal*, 18/5 (2003), 16–20.

Chatonnet, P., Bonnet, S., Boutou, S., and Labadie, M.-D., 'Identification and responsibility of 2,4,6-tribromoanisole in musty, corked odors in wine', *Journal of Agricultural and Food Chemistry*, 52 (2004), 1255–62.

Duncan, B. C., Gibson, R. L., Obradovic, D., '2,4,6-trichloroanisole and cork production', *Australian and New Zealand Wine Industry Journal*, 12/2 (1997), 180–4.

Simpson, R. F., Capone D. L., and Sefton, M. A., 'Isolation and identification of 2-methoxy-3,5-dimethylpyrazine, a potent musty compound isolated from wine corks', *Journal of Agricultural and Food Chemistry*, 25 (2004), 5245–430.

Stelzer, T., *Taming the Screw: A Manual for Winemaking with Screw Caps* (Brisbane, 2005).

corky bark, virus-like disease and one of the few which can kill vines. It is one of a complex of diseases known as RUGOSE WOOD. Symptoms of the disease resemble another one of the VIRUS DISEASES, LEAFROLL VIRUS, in that, during autumn, leaves turn red or yellow and roll downwards. Vines infected with corky bark retain their leaves after they would naturally have fallen. Often the fruiting variety dies but the rootstock survives; this effect can sometimes be seen in old vineyards of Napa and Sonoma in northern CALIFORNIA. Corky bark posed a serious problem in Australia in the 1990s. The disease is usually spread by taking cuttings from infected vines. In Aguascalientes state in MEXICO the disease is spread naturally, possibly by an insect. There is no control for infected vineyards, and vine removal is the only solution if many vines are infected. The disease is detected by grafting to the indicator variety LN-33 (see INDEXING).

R.E.S.

Cornalin d'Aoste, ancient and almost extinct variety from AOSTA that was shown to be identical to HUMAGNE ROUGE in the Swiss Valais by DNA PROFILING. It is therefore an offspring of CORNALIN DU VALAIS, hence the need to distinguish each Cornalin.　　J.V.

Cornalin du Valais, rare Swiss red grape used to make deep-coloured red wines that need ageing. The vine demands a fairly warm climate, and it took the research institute at CHANGINS to induce some sort of regularity of yield. Today this distinctive speciality of VALAIS has many aficionados who were surprised to learn by DNA PROFILING at DAVIS that Cornalin du Valais is the progeny of PETIT ROUGE and Mayolet, two varieties from the AOSTA valley.

J.V.

Cornas, red wine appellation in the northern RHÔNE (see map) with the potential to provide serious challengers to HERMITAGE on the opposite bank to the north.

Cornas was renowned in the era of CHARLEMAGNE, and in the 18th century, but many of the terraced vineyards on its steep south-facing granite slopes fell into decline in the early 20th century. The appellation experienced a revival of interest in the late 1980s with the arrival of ambitious newcomers prepared to re-establish the TERRACES needed for high-quality vineyards, so that by the mid 2000s there were almost 100 ha/247 acres of vineyards in production. The consultant OENOLOGIST Jean-Luc Colombo established a base here and in the 1990s began making wine not only for himself, but also for the likes of Lionnet, employing such imports as new OAK and DESTEMMING, an anathema to Auguste Clape, the standard bearer during the lean years of the 1970s. Perhaps because Clape's very traditional wines demand considerable BOTTLE AGE, Cornas gained a reputation as a long-living wine, but the likes of Thierry Allemand, Domaine Courbis, Eric et Joël Durand, Vincent Paris, and Domaine du Tunnel are making a much more luscious style of Cornas.

Many of the best slopes such as Les Renards in the south are well sheltered from the cold north winds and enjoy some of the best positions in the northern Rhône. Cornas can provide some of the most satisfying red wine drinking, and offers a much more uniform and dependable quality level than the elastic ST-JOSEPH appellation to the immediate north.

Livingstone-Learmonth, J., *The Wines of the Northern Rhône* (Berkeley, 2005).

Cornell University has conducted viticultural research at its New York State Agricultural Experiment Station (NYSAES) in Geneva, NY, since the 1880s. Viticulturists have released 53 varieties of juice, table, and wine grapes since 1906.

As part of the breeding programme, disease-resistant and winter-hardy AMERICAN VINE SPECIES are crossed with VINIFERA as well as with Asian species of the VITIS genus. USDA-ARS Plant Genetic Resources Unit at Geneva makes 1,275 genotypes of cold-hardy *Vitis* germplasm available for grape breeding projects around the world.

The GENEVA DOUBLE CURTAIN training system, developed at Cornell by Herman Amberg, Donald Crowe, and Nelson SHAULIS, has been widely adopted in high-vigour sites, while the mechanical grape harvester developed by Shaulis, E. S. Shepardson, and James Moyer is used worldwide.

Oenology studies at Cornell began in the 1960s. CAYUGA WHITE, Cornell's first wine grape, was released in 1972, followed by Horizon (1983), Melody (1986), CHARDONEL (1990), Traminette (1996), and GR7 (2003). Studies on juice extraction, fermentation, flavour, and wine production are ongoing. Cornell's plant pathologists, grape physiologists, entomologists, and others develop technologies to enhance the TERROIR of New York's grapes and wines and to overcome infectious diseases and pests with minimal pesticide use.

Cornell instituted new undergraduate courses in oenology and viticulture in 2003, with teaching and research based in four departments at Geneva and on the main campus in Ithaca.

Cornifesto, minor dark grape in the DOURO.

Corse is the French, and therefore Corsican, name for CORSICA.

Corsica, mountainous Mediterranean island under French jurisdiction whose wines are improving in quality. Situated on the 42nd parallel, Corsica is actually much closer to Italy (83 km/50 miles) than to France (170 km/100 miles). The island, about 180 km long and 80 km wide, comprises a series of mountains around which runs a perimeter of capes, gulfs, and sandy beaches. The average altitude is 586 m/1,900 ft. Corsica produces many different types and styles of wine: red, white, rosé; still, sparkling; dry, sweet; APPELLATION CONTRÔLÉE, VIN DE PAYS, and VIN DE TABLE. The great majority of these are of relatively ordinary quality and are sold only on the island. Its most exported product is its single vin de pays, Vin de Pays de l'Île de Beauté.

History

The history of Corsica is closely related to that of Italy and this is reflected in the viticulture. Evidence suggests that vines were indigenous to the island and that their cultivation is one of the oldest in Europe, dating back to PHOENICIAN times and the settlement in 570 BC at Aleria on the east coast. Under Genoese rule in the 16th century, laws were enacted to control the harvest and tasting of wines; export of Corsican wines to destinations other than the republic of GENOA was banned. The English diarist James Boswell wrote in 1769, only a year after the Genoese ceded the island to France, of the excellence and diversity of Corsican wines. Napoleon was born in Ajaccio and Napoleonic laws still entitle the island to sell duty-free wines and tobacco.

The wine industry was revolutionized in the 1960s with the repatriation of many French *pieds noirs* from ALGERIA. Between 1960 and 1976 they imported and planted their own productive and often undistinguished vine varieties (see below) with such determination that the total vineyard area increased fourfold. MECHANICAL HARVESTERS were introduced to flatter vineyards to supplement more traditional methods and further the cause of quantity at the expense of quality.

In 1980, however, as EUROPEAN UNION subsidies favoured uprooting vines rather than producing yet more liquid to be poured into the European WINE LAKE, Corsican vineyards began to be restructured, with a more determined emphasis on quality. The total area under vine had dwindled to about 7,000 ha/ 17,300 acres by 2003. To a great extent the highly productive varieties have been replaced by nobler vines, both imported and Corsican.

Geography and climate

Four main soil types are present in Corsica: granite on the west side; schist in the north and the Cap Corse, the mountainous finger of land pointing Francewards in the far north; chalk and clay in Patrimonio immediately south of it; and marly sand and alluvial soils from Solenzara to Bastia on the east coast.

Corsica is sunnier than anywhere in mainland France with an annual average of 2,750 hours, and very little rain falls in the months of August and September. Due to the mountainous nature of Corsica, a jigsaw of MESOCLIMATES exists. The effects of ALTITUDE, latitude, maritime influence, and the winds vary considerably between vineyards. The average temperature is higher in the north of the island than in the south. The sea, by absorbing heat during the day and radiating it at night, plays a major role in diminishing the day-night TEMPERATURE VARIABILITY.

Viticulture

Vines are cultivated up to 300 m/1,000 ft in altitude. Traditionally vines were pruned in GOBELET form but pruning and training methods such as CORDON DE ROYAT and single GUYOT became more widespread with mechanization. The most common ROOTSTOCK is 110 R. The strong winds help to keep the vines free of disease, the main viticultural concerns being DOWNY MILDEW, POWDERY MILDEW, and FLAVESCENCE DORÉE provoked by cicadelle attack. Irrigation is prohibited, and VINE DENSITY is an average 2,500 vines per ha (1,000 per acre).

Vine varieties

NIELLUCCIO and VERMENTINO are the important indigenous Corsican varieties, while INTERNATIONAL VARIETIES now comprise almost a quarter of vines planted on the island, displacing the traditional varieties Cinsaut, Carignan, Grenache and Alicante Bouschet.

A host of more traditional Corsican varieties exist but few are planted in any significant quantity. CIVAM (Centre d'Information et de Vulgarisation pour l'Agriculture et le Milieu Rural de la Région Corse) is charged with researching and selecting Corsican varieties.

Nielluccio, planted on 1,600 ha/3,955 acres in 2003, is the most widely planted (even if its origins are probably Italian rather than Corsican), particularly in the north of the island, where it thrives on the chalky clay soils of Patrimonio. Nielluccio may be vinified as either a rosé or, if well vinified, an intensely coloured red with good, structured tannins and a balanced acidity. There was only just over 600 ha of SCIACARELLO, which is unique to Corsica, where it is most successful on the granitic south west coast between Ajaccio and Sartène, producing relatively crisp, peppery reds and rosés, light in colour but high in alcohol. It is often blended with Nielluccio or Grenache.

The only significant white native grape variety is also the best travelled. Vermentino, also known as Malvoisie on Corsica, and as Rolle by the host of growers planting it all over the south of France, is grown all over the island but performs best in the far north. It produces wines ranging from a pale, crisp version to a full-bodied golden wine with a ripe fruit flavour, depending on when it is picked. Although many of the wines are dry, sweet Vermentino wines are also produced. Codivarta, a white grape grown on the Cap Corse, is the only other uniquely Corsican variety cultivated to any appreciable extent. The deep pink-skinned BARBAROSSA, the Barbaroux of Provence, is also grown.

Vinification

Almost 70 per cent of all Corsican wine is made by CO-OPERATIVES, which, like some of the smaller wineries, have taken advantage of EUROPEAN UNION grants available for the installation of modern STAINLESS STEEL vats and REFRIGERATION equipment. White wines are usually therefore fermented at between 18 and 20 °C (64–8 °F), and clean-tasting rosés are made by SAIGNÉE and cool fermentation. MALOLACTIC FERMENTATION is usually suppressed for whites and rosés. Red wine-making is relatively traditional with fermentation temperatures regularly rising to 30 °C, followed by malolactic fermentation. The use of OAK was still relatively limited but increasing in the early 21st century, although Vermentino subjected to BARREL FERMENTATION and LEES STIRRING can yield good results, and wines such as the Cuvée des Gouverneurs from Orenga de Gaffory and Clos du Cardinal from Domaine Peraldi showed respectively that Nielluccio and Sciacarello respond well to ageing in oak.

The wines produced

Rosé is as important in Corsica as it is in its nearest mainland wine region PROVENCE, representing about 30 per cent of total production. White wine accounts for an increasing proportion of all wine produced but it is still only about 10 per cent.

In 2003, admittedly a year of small production, Corsica made 325,000 hl (over 8.5 million gal), a substantial decrease on the 1988 figure of just under 600,000 hl. The island's VINE PULL SCHEME has resulted in a dramatic drop in the amount of basic TABLE WINE produced, while the proportion of wine which qualified as VIN DE PAYS de l'Île de Beauté had increased to about two-thirds, almost all the remainder being AC wine.

Nine different appellations exist: Patrimonio, Ajaccio, Muscat de Cap Corse, Vin de Corse (Corsican wine), and Vin de Corse followed by either Coteaux du Cap Corse, Calvi, Sartène, Figari, or Porto Vecchio, the last four of these being specific towns or villages still in the process of establishing their own viticultural identity.

Patrimonio Patrimonio on the north coast was the first region in Corsica to gain AC status, in 1968. Red, rosé, and white wines are produced from around 440 ha of vines and YIELDS are restricted to 50 hl/ha (2.8 tons/acre). In the past, the wines of Patrimonio often included a mix of different imported grape varieties, notably Grenache, but from 2000, Nielluccio must account for 90 per cent of the blend in red wines and Vermentino for 100 per cent in the white. This has caused considerable controversy amongst the growers. Clos de Bernardi, one of the oldest estates reputed for its red, is situated in Patrimonio. Other growers such as Orenga de Gaffory, Gentile, Leccia, and Arena have also invested much time and money to make dramatic improvements in quality.

Ajaccio Some of Corsica's highest vineyards are in this extensive zone on the west coast which produces mainly red and rosé wines with a little white made from Vermentino. Sciacarello is the grape variety typical of the appellation and yields are set at 45 hl/ha. Domaine Peraldi, which overlooks the bay of Ajaccio, is one of the best producers.

(Vin de) Corse This generic AC is the dominant one on the island comprising the wines grown on the eastern plain where the largest estates were established in the 1960s. These tend to be Corsica's least distinguished AC wines, although Nielluccio, Sciacarello, and Grenache must represent at least 50 per cent of any red or rosé, while whites must be at least 75 per cent Vermentino.

(Vin de) Corse-Coteaux du Cap Corse The most northerly tip of the island, the Cap Corse, is renowned for its sweet Muscat and Rappu (a sweet MUSCAT-style red wine made from the ALEATICO vine variety). Some of Corsica's best dry white wines, such as Clos Nicrosi, are produced here.

(Vin de) Corse-Calvi Lower yields are required of this appellation in the north west of the island.

(Vin de) Corse-Figari comes from a small area in the south west of the island where Clos Canarelli is the leading producer.

(Vin de) Corse-Porto Vecchio is made in the far south east.

(Vin de) Corse-Sartène is a sub-appellation just north west of Figari.

Muscat du Cap Corse This VIN DOUX NATUREL from the northern tip of the island is made from MUSCAT BLANC À PETITS GRAINS grapes which were traditionally picked and left to dry in the sun in order to concentrate the sugars. Today they are picked at between 14 and 15 per cent POTENTIAL ALCOHOL and made, by the addition of alcohol at an early stage of fermentation, into a relatively elegant vin doux naturel.   J.E.M.

Dovaz, M., *Encyclopédie des vins de Corse* (Paris, 1990).
Mercurey, F.-N., *Vignes, vins et vignerons de Corse* (Ajaccio, 1991).

Cortese, Italian white grape variety most closely associated with south east PIEMONTE, where it was first mentioned in 1659 when the estate manager of the Castello dei Doria a Montaldeo wrote to the Marchee Doria: 'All vineyards were planted with Cortese vines and a few Vermentino. . .'. The AMPELOGRAPHICAL text of P. Demaria and G. Leardi published in 1870 testifies: 'Cortese is the white vine variety most widely cultivated in the province of Alessandria . . . where it is esteemed not only for its robustness and fertility but also for the exquisite excellence of its product.' Its most highly regarded wine is GAVI, produced initially to serve the fish restaurants of Genoa and the Ligurian coast not far to the south. The Cortese dell'Alto Monferrato a few miles west, like the Cortese grown on the Colli Tortonese, rarely achieves the ripeness, or wine-making proficiency, of Gavi. At its best, the wine is clean and fresh. The use of oak is usually misguided.

Cortese is also grown in the OLTREPÒ PAVESE in Lombardia and may be part of the blend in Veneto's Bianco di CUSTOZA. The wine produced is rarely complex and can be ineffably bland (unlike Piemonte's white ARNEIS and FAVORITA grapes) but sustains a good level of acidity through to full ripeness. Total plantings had fallen to about 1,500 ha/3,800 acres by 2000.   D.T. & D.C.G.

Corton and **Corton-Charlemagne**, respectively the great red and white GRANDS CRUS in ALOXE-CORTON in Burgundy's CÔTE D'OR.

Coruche, subregion of RIBATEJO in central, southern Portugal.

Corvina, or **Corvina Veronese**, the dominant and best grape variety of VALPOLICELLA and BARDOLINO in north east Italy, producing fruity, red wines with a characteristic sour cherry twist on the finish. Wines from the better Valpolicella producers who reduced yields in the 1980s and 1990s demonstrated that lack of BODY was not an inherent characteristic of Corvina. Since then, it has enjoyed great success as the best variety for AMARONE. Producers such as Allegrini have also illustrated that wines made solely or predominantly from Corvina can be serious, barrel-aged reds. Corvina, sometimes called Cruina, has traditionally been confused with CORVINONE. DNA PROFILING at SAN MICHELE ALL'ADIGE in 2005 supported a parent–offspring relationship with RONDINELLA. Italy's total plantings of the Corvina Veronese vine variety were down to about 2,500 ha/6,250 acres by the early 1990s.

Corvinone, red grape variety grown mainly in the VALPOLICELLA zone. It is so similar to CORVINA that it was long mistaken as merely a different CLONE of it. It is now highly regarded as a grape of specific use for such DRIED GRAPE WINES as AMARONE and RECIOTO as its loose bunches and large berries make it particularly suited to DRYING.

cosecha is Spanish for VINTAGE year.

Cossart Gordon, the oldest company to trade in MADEIRA wine. Cossart Gordon was established in 1745 by two Scotsmen, Francis Newton and William Gordon, who fled their homeland following the failure of the Stuart cause, with which they sympathized. In 1808, William Cossart, an Irishman of Huguenot descent, joined the firm. Cossart Gordon flourished on trade with the American colonies, at the time the most important market for Ma-

deira. The Cossart family has been among the most influential on the island for nearly two centuries. In 1953, Cossart, Gordon & Co. Ltd. became a partner in the important Madeira Wine Association, which had its origins in 1913 and which has since changed its name to the Madeira Wine Company Limited (see MADEIRA for more details). Cossart Gordon is controlled by the SYMINGTON family in partnership with the BLANDY family.   S.A.

Cossart, N., *Madeira: The Island Vineyard* (London, 1984).

Costers del Segre, small wine zone in north east Spain in semi-DESERT near the Catalan city of Lerida (see map under SPAIN). The climate is severe. The thermometer often dips below freezing point in winter and exceeds 35 °C/95 °F in high summer. RAINFALL barely reaches 400 mm/15 in in a year. The river Segre, a tributary of the Ebro after which this fragmented DO is named, is little more than a seasonal stream.

The history of Costers del Segre is really the history of one estate: Raimat, which covers 3,200 ha/7,900 acres of arid country 15 km/9 miles north west of Lerida. When Manuel Raventós, owner of CAVA producer CODORNÍU, first visited the property in 1914, he found infertile salt plains abandoned by farmers. An IRRIGATION artery, the Canal de Aragón y Cataluña, has since transformed the estate into an oasis but it took over 50 years of planting cattle fodder, pine trees, and cereals before the soil was fit for vines. Today the Raimat vineyard covers 1,250 ha, which amounts to a third of the Costers del Segre DO. A labyrinthine irrigation system starts automatically whenever the temperature rises above 35 °C, and provides FROST protection when the thermometer falls below 1 °C. As a result, imported vine varieties such as Cabernet Sauvignon, Merlot, Pinot Noir, and Chardonnay flourish alongside indigenous vines such as Tempranillo, Parellada, and Macabeo.

Elsewhere in the region, which splits into four separate subzones—Raimat, Artesa, Vall de Riu Corb, and Les Garrigues—other quality-conscious producers include Castell del Remei, Celler de Cantonella, Tomàs Cusiné, and L'Olivera.   R.J.M. & V. de la S.

Costières de Nîmes, the generally reliable and well-priced southernmost appellation of the RHÔNE. In French wine politics, it used to be considered part of the eastern LANGUEDOC but the climate, soil, topography—and wines—are closer to those just over the river in the southern Côtes du Rhône vineyards.

The relatively uniform soils are marked by large pebbles on gentle, typically south-facing slopes. A total of 25,000 ha/62,000 acres of land could qualify to produce wine for this appellation, and by the early 21st century about 3,300 ha were dedicated to the

production of appellation wine, about three-quarters of it red, and only a very small amount white. This is an important zone for the production of VIN DE PAYS. As in the nearby southern Rhône, Grenache is an important vine variety here, and must represent at least 25 per cent of any red; while Carignan is slowly being removed, it may still make up 40 per cent. Syrah and Mourvèdre are booming increasingly important in many of the best wines and must each total at least 20 per cent of the blend. This is an appellation in transition, not just geographically between the Languedoc and the Rhône, but temporally between a bulk wine producer and a source of genuinely characterful, well-made wines. CO-OPERATIVES are less important here than in most of the Languedoc and most of the development and experimentation is taking place on dynamic, smaller estates such as Chx de l'Amarine, de Beck, Paul Blanc/Mas Carlot, de Campuget, Mas de Bressades, Chx Grande Cassagne, Mas Neuf, Mourgues du Grès, and de Nages.

Côt or **Cot** is an important French synonym for the black grape variety of French origin also known as MALBEC and, in Cahors, Auxerrois.

Cotarella, Riccardo (1948–), one of Italy's most famous CONSULTANT oenologists, based in Umbria. Born in Orvieto, he graduated from the wine-making school in Conegliano in 1968 and started working for the Vaselli winery in Orvieto. Together with his brother Renzo (who is general manager for ANTINORI), he founded the Falesco winery at Montefiascone in 1979 with the aim of producing modern white wines to sell to the large bottlers. As the market for Italian wines began to change, Cotarella began to bottle his own wines. He leapt to prominence, however, with red wines from Umbria and Lazio based primarily on Merlot. Falesco's Montiano, first produced in 1993, became one of Italy's best known examples of this variety. His fame as a consultant was cemented when the 1993 Montevetrano, a red wine from Salerno in Campania, was released. He now consults to wineries as diverse as Morgante in Sicilia, Paola di Mauro in Lazio, Nottola and Castello di Volpaia in Toscana, Terra di Lavoro in Campania, and La Carraia, Lamborghini, and Sportoletti in Umbria. His wines are characterized by deep colour, richness, ripe fruit, low acid, and immense appeal. While his critics claim that he has been responsible for producing a more international style of wine, there is no doubt that he has improved quality in, and focused a great deal of attention on, previously unknown areas (not unlike Michel ROLLAND).   D.C.G.

Côte means literally 'slope' or 'hill' in French, **Côtes** is the plural, while **Coteau** (of which **Coteaux** is the plural) means much the same thing but possibly on a smaller scale. Since French vine-growers are great believers in the viticultural merits of HILLSIDES, all of these make suitable wine names. Thus, any index of French wine names contains long lists of Côte, Côtes, and Coteaux de, du, de la, and des various place-names, suggesting, often with reason, that the wine comes from the slopes above these places. Some of these prefixes are eventually dropped, however. Côtes de Buzet, for example, was renamed plain BUZET in the late 1980s, just as Côtes de Blaye in the Bordeaux region has become BLAYE.

For this reason, and to save readers having to remember whether a wine is, for example, a Coteaux de or a Coteaux du Somewhere, such an entry would be listed under S for Somewhere, rather than under Coteaux. Their Côte and Côtes counterparts are listed similarly. The only exceptions to this are names in which the Côte, Côtes, or Coteaux are integral. They follow.

Côte des Blancs, area of CHAMPAGNE on east-facing slopes south of Épernay noted for the quality of its Chardonnay grapes.

Côte d'Or, the heart of the BURGUNDY wine region in eastern France in the form of an escarpment supporting a narrow band of vineyards for nearly 50 km/30 miles southwards (and a touch west) from Dijon, capital of the *département* of the same name (see map under BURGUNDY). Although the name Côte d'Or apparently translates directly as 'golden slope', evoking its autumnal aspect, it may be an abbreviation of Côte d'Orient, a reference to the fact that the escarpment on which the vines flourish faces east. Viticulturally it is divided into two sectors, the Côte de NUITS, in which great red wines are made from the Pinot Noir vine, and the Côte de BEAUNE, where the reds are joined by the finest white wines made from Chardonnay.

The Côte d'Or represents the fault line separating the hills of the Morvan from the plain of the Saône, which, in the Jurassic period 195 to 135 million years BC, was an inland sea. The predominant rock is Jurassic LIMESTONE, which favours both Chardonnay and Pinot Noir vine varieties. However, the escarpment features many differing forms of limestone and other rocks. Oolitic limestone, which originated as a precipitation around marine debris of carbonate of lime from the seawater, is usefully porous, and provides good DRAINAGE compared with marlstone, which is made up of clay, sand, gravel, and marl, the result of decomposition of older mountains such as the Ardennes.

The escarpment is also broken up by streams—the Vouge in Vougeot, the Meuzin in Nuits-St-Georges, the Rhoin in Savigny, the Dheune and Avant-Dheune further south—running down from the hills eventually to join the Saône, and by dry valleys (*combes*)

such as the Combe de Lavaux in Gevrey-Chambertin. These breaks vary the orientation of the vineyards: thus Clos-St-Jacques and Corton are both exposed more to the south than east while much of Corton-Charlemagne actually faces south west. The streams also affect the composition of the soil by bringing down alluvial deposits.

A cross-section of the Côte reveals topsoil too sparse on the hilltop and too fertile in the plain to produce wine of any quality. The vineyard area begins to the west of the Dijon–Lyons railway line but only the most basic wines made from Aligoté and Gamay are produced here. Approaching the main Dijon–Chagny road, the RN74, the vineyards are still on flat, fertile land but Pinot Noir and Chardonnay are planted to produce BOURGOGNE Rouge and Bourgogne Blanc. These in turn give way to village APPELLATION vineyards; as the ground starts to slope upwards, drainage improves, and the soil is less fertile.

Where the slope becomes more pronounced and clay gives way to stonier topsoil, the vineyards are designated PREMIERS CRUS, reflecting the potential quality of the wines from land which drains well and enjoys greater exposure to the sun. The finest of these vineyards, in certain villages only, are classified as GRANDS CRUS (listed under BURGUNDY). The premier and grand cru vineyards are mainly at elevations between 250 and 300 m (800–1,000 ft) above sea level. Near the top of the slope, where the soil is almost too poor, there is usually a narrow band of village appellation vineyards providing fine but light wines.

Viticultural practices are relatively constant for both major grape varieties throughout the Côte d'Or. VINE DENSITY is notably high—about 10,000 vines per ha (4,000 per acre)—and vines are trained and pruned chiefly according to the single GUYOT system (although CORDON DE ROYAT is increasingly employed to restrict vigour in younger vines and those on overproductive rootstocks). Harvesting is still mostly manual, especially for Pinot Noir. Maximum yields are officially set at 40 hl/ha (2.3 tons/acre) for red wines at village and premier cru level, 45 hl/ha for whites. Maximum permitted yields for grands crus are mostly at 35 hl/ha for reds and 40 hl/ha for whites. In most vintages, a supplementary allowance (see PLC) of 20 per cent is allowed. Exceptionally in 1996 this was increased to 30 per cent in many villages.

There are no set rules for the production of great red burgundy, and every domaine or NÉGOCIANT house revels in its own idiosyncrasies. Principal options include DESTEMMING of the grapes (wholly, partly, or not at all); MACERATION period; fermentation TEMPERATURE; length of BARREL MATURATION; type of OAK barrels; FINING regime; and the extent to which FILTRATION is practised. The better wines of the Côte d'Or are all matured for at least a year, more often 18 months, in 228-l (59-gal)

oak BARRELS, a proportion of which are usually new. Before bottling, some producers fine and filter the wine; others prefer one treatment to the other; a few use neither in the belief that the wine thereby has more depth of flavour and capacity to evolve, even though it is less stable.

The qualities of great red burgundy are not easy to judge young, especially since the wine tends to be less deeply coloured than equivalent wines from Bordeaux or the Rhône. When young, a fine burgundy should show a bouquet of soft red fruit, ranging from cherries to plums depending on the vineyard and vigneron; complexity comes with maturity, the fresh fruit components giving way to more evolved aromas, often redolent of truffles or undergrowth (*sous-bois*, according to French palates).

Some wines are weighty, others intensely elegant, but all should have concentration. Style depends in part on the character of the village: GEVREY-CHAMBERTIN, VOUGEOT, NUITS-ST-GEORGES, CORTON, and POMMARD tend to produce robust, long-lived wines; CHAMBOLLE-MUSIGNY, VOSNE-ROMANÉE, and VOLNAY epitomize finesse and elegance. Within each village, different vineyards display their individual characteristics according to the exact SOIL STRUCTURE, ELEVATION, and TOPOGRAPHY.

Differences in annual WEATHER patterns are crucial in determining quality in the region. Burgundy is at a climatic crossroads, experiencing Atlantic, Mediterranean, and Baltic weather systems. A cool breeze from the north (*la bise*) is ideal to temper anticyclonic conditions in the summer; a southern wind brings heat but also danger; HAIL and thunder often result when the warm wind swings round to the west, the wettest direction. There is probably greater vintage variation in Burgundy than in any other wine region.

In some VINTAGES—1984, 1987, 1993, and 2001 for instance—most Pinot Noir grapes do not fully ripen, although growers who conscientiously restrict yields often produce excellent wines. The 1996 vintage, which produced fine wines for ageing, was unusual in that September sunshine ripened the grapes fully, judging by the sugar levels, yet cool nights maintained the acidity at levels normally associated with an unripe year. In other years, excessive rainfall can either swell the crop to produce dilute wines (as in 1982, 1992, and 2000) or encourage ROT (as in 1986 and 1994). Most difficult to judge are the hot vintages in which the fruit in the wine is either supported, or sometimes overwhelmed, by TANNINS (as in 1976 and 1983). Certain vintages, such as 1985, 1989, 1997, and 2003 produce fully ripe grapes and many wines which are attractive to taste throughout their lives. The greatest vintages of the past 30 years however have been 1978, 1990 and 1999.

Great white burgundy is produced in the Côte de Beaune, notably in the villages of MEURSAULT, PULIGNY-MONTRACHET, and

CHASSAGNE-MONTRACHET, along with a small enclave further north yielding the grand cru Corton-Charlemagne (see ALOXE-CORTON). The soils suited to Chardonnay production tend to be paler in colour than the iron-rich, redder soils on which the Pinot Noir thrives (see SOIL COLOUR). The Chardonnay vine is hardier than the Pinot, the grapes ripen more easily, and the wines require less delicate handling. It is easier to make good white burgundy than red but very little great white burgundy is made.

The grapes are pressed, usually without SKIN CONTACT, left to settle, then fermented in oak casks for up to a year (see BARREL FERMENTATION), although those with suitable cellars prefer to keep the wine for a second winter in wood. After the alcoholic FERMENTATION, the wines are racked into another set of barrels to remove the major deposits, the 'gross lees', but left on their fine LEES, which are regularly stirred up to nourish the wine (see LEES STIRRING) and avoid production of hydrogen sulfide.

Fine white burgundy, when young, is more likely to show the character of the oak in which it has been vinified than the grapes from which it came. Hallmarks of quality are fullness of BODY, balance of ACIDITY, and persistence of flavour. Only after two or more years of bottle age will a fine Meursault or Puligny-Montrachet start to show the quality of the fruit. This will deepen with age and, while vegetal tones will appear, they should not overwhelm the natural elegance of the wine. A village appellation wine should be at its best between three and five years old, a premier cru from five to ten years, while a grand cru worthy of its status needs a full decade of BOTTLE AGEING.

For more detail, see under names of individual villages or appellations. See BEAUNE, CÔTE DE and NUITS, CÔTE DE for a full list of the villages in each. To most of the villages and towns in the Côte d'Or was appended the name of their most famous vineyard, typically in the late 19th century. Thus, for example, Vosne became Vosne-Romanée and Puligny became Puligny-Montrachet. J.T.C.M.

Coates, C., *Côte d'Or* (London, 1997).

Hanson, A. D., *Burgundy* (2nd edn, London, 1994).

Norman, R. H., *The Great Domaines of Burgundy* (2nd edn, London, 1996).

Pitiot, S., and Poupon, P., *Atlas des Grands Vignobles de Bourgogne* (Beaune and Paris, 1985).

——and Servant, J.-C., *Les Vins de Bourgogne* (11th edn. of P. Poupon's original, Paris, 1992).

Côte Rôtie, one of the most exciting, if geographically extremely limited, red wine appellations in France, in the far north of the northern RHÔNE (see map under RHÔNE). In the 1970s, the area and its wines were somewhat moribund, a rather isolated outpost well north of Tain, where the major NÉGOCIANTS and the famous HERMITAGE vineyard are situated. One man, Marcel GUIGAL, is chiefly

responsible for the renaissance of this zone (helped by the adulation of another, the American wine critic Robert PARKER).

Côte Rôtie may be the site where the vine was first cultivated in GAUL, and vineyards have been sculpted from these, some of the steepest slopes of viticultural France, since at least the time when nearby Vienne was an important Roman settlement. The vines then grown were identified with the local tribe, the Allobroges (see RHÔNE, history).

Vine-growing brought so little reward in the 1960s and 1970s that total plantings were only about 70 ha/175 acres in the early 1970s; by the mid 1990s, however, plantings had reached 150 ha (rather less than the extent of the single biggest wine château in the MÉDOC) and by the early 21st century almost 200 ha of vineyards qualified for the appellation. Guigal's single-vineyard bottlings of La Mouline, La Landonne, and, later, La Turque reminded the wine-buying world of the potential majesty of wines hewn from the Côte Rôtie, or 'roasted slope'.

Because of the turn of the river here, the vineyards banked up the SCHIST behind the unremarkable town of Ampuis face directly south east, and are angled so as to maximize the ripening effect of any SUNLIGHT, while being sheltered from the cold winds. The slopes have traditionally been distinguished, with associated legend, either as Côte Blonde, supposedly producing alluring wines for relatively early consumption (often as a result of blending up to the permitted maximum of 20 per cent scented white VIOGNIER in with the mandatory SYRAH grape—see CO-FERMENTATION), or Côte Brune, associated with firmer, more durable, all-Syrah wines. The finest Côte Rôtie, local lore had it, was a blend of the two. More recently, the fame, and record prices, of wines flaunting specific vineyard sites has rather put paid to this theory, and the appellation is a hotbed of activity and ambition.

Syrah is trained particularly distinctively on these slopes (so steep in parts that winches have to be used), single GUYOT on single or double stakes. TERRACES are essential here, where they are known as *cheys* and have been in place for centuries. The theoretical minimum potential alcohol of these wines is 10 per cent, but most growers manage to achieve considerably more ripeness than this, and wines are made, with more or less new OAK (more *chez* Guigal), with considerable EXTRACTION and ambition, producing deep-coloured, relatively tannic, savoury wines which take ten years or more to develop one of the more rewarding BOUQUETS of the wine world, all undergrowth and ripe black fruits—although Côte Rôtie should always be more 'feminine' than Hermitage. Clusel-Roch, Jean-Michel Gerin, Jamet, René Rostaing, and Vidal Fleury also produce very fine Côte Rôtie.

Livingstone-Learmonth, J., *The Wines of the Northern Rhône* (Berkeley, 2005).

Cotnari, once-famous sweet white wine produced in wild, hilly countryside in the north Romanian Moldavia (see ROMANIA for geographical details). At one time it rivalled Hungarian TOKAJI as an elixir of FASHION sought after in the courts of northern Europe. It was still fashionable in Paris at the end of the 19th century, and it is clear that NOBLE ROT has played an important role here for several centuries, and continues to do so every three or four years today.

The wine may be made from any of the four white grape varieties grown in the region or as a traditional blend (containing a minimum of 30 per cent GRASĂ which provides the body and sugar). TĂMÂIOASĂ Românească provides its 'frankincense' nerve (and sugar without losing acidity in the Cotnari MESOCLIMATE), Frâncuşă the acidity (it must make up at least 30 per cent in a blend, although it can suffer from poor FRUIT SET), and Fetească Albă the aroma. Grasă ripens so dramatically that in 1958, for example, Grasă de Cotnari grapes reached a sugar level of 520 g/l. Cotnari, the finished wine, is made in various styles from dry to semi sweet, with minimum residual sugar levels specified within the DOC rules and an alcoholic strength of at least 11 per cent. Unlike TOKAJI, it is aged in WOOD for no more than a year, and is carefully protected from oxygen. Although golden, it retains a greenish tinge after many years in bottle.

Couchois, Bourgogne Côtes du, appellation created in 2001 for wines made from Pinot Noir grown around the town of Couches north west of the Côte Chalonnaise. See BOURGOGNE.

Couderc Noir, a HYBRID of a dark-berried RUPESTRIS-*lincecumii* and VINIFERA, is one of several productive but undistinguished hybrids that proliferated in the MIDI in the early 20th century (see BACO, CHAMBOURCIN, PLANTET, SEIBEL, SEYVE-VILLARD, VILLARD). Although not as popular as Villard once was, Couderc Noir was so widely planted that France's total area of Cabernet Sauvignon did not overtake that of Couderc Noir until well into the 1970s. By this time vigorous steps were being taken to eradicate this embarrassing legacy of another viticultural era, and the 1988 agricultural census found only about 2,500 ha/ 6,200 acres of each of Couderc Noir, Villard Noir, and the various Seyve-Villard varieties and by 2000 Couderc's total was just 300 ha. The wine produced can be aggressively non-*vinifera* in taste.

Coulanges-la-Vineuse, commune near AUXERRE whose name may be appended to that of BOURGOGNE.

coulure, French term, commonly used by English speakers too, for one form of poor FRUIT SET in grapes in which, soon after FLOWERING, the small berries, less than 5 mm/

0.2 in across, fall off. To a great extent, coulure is a natural and necessary phenomenon, since the vine cannot possibly ripen all the grapes if all flowers remained as berries. However, for some varieties in some years, coulure can be excessive and YIELD drastically reduced. Excessive coulure can have a disastrous effect on grape-growers' incomes, and can also affect grape supply and wine prices in certain years. GRENACHE vines are particularly susceptible to coulure, as are MALBEC, MUSCAT OTTONEL, and certain clones of MERLOT.

Coulure is caused by an imbalance in the levels of CARBOHYDRATES in vine tissue. Where these drop too low, the very small berries fall off because their stems shrivel. Weather conditions which reduce PHOTOSYNTHESIS will cause coulure, and thus periods of cloudy, cold, and wet weather around flowering can have devastating effects on yield for some varieties. This is known in France as **coulure climatique**. Coulure also happens where the total leaf area, and thus photosynthesis, is limited and unable to provide sufficient sugar levels for the vine tissue. This is how an unpruned vine regulates the amount of fruit to be ripened. Low plant sugar levels can also be due to excessively vigorous shoot growth, combined with warm temperatures which favour RESPIRATION. There are several known causes of this phenomenon, including very fertile soils, excessive application of FERTILIZERS, especially those high in NITROGEN, vigorous ROOTSTOCKS, and PRUNING too severely (see BALANCED PRUNING).

There is little growers can do to prevent coulure. It is not always possible to grow varieties which are not susceptible, as particular varieties may be required for a certain style or blend. CLONAL SELECTION can be effective in reducing susceptibility for some varieties, as for example with Merlot and Malbec. TRIMMING shoots, or more precisely the tips of shoots at exactly the right stage, can reduce coulure by stopping competition for sugars between actively growing SHOOT TIPS and very small berries. Later pruning may also help because a delayed BUDBREAK will increase the possibility of warmer weather at flowering. Some chemical GROWTH REGULATORS can reduce coulure by inhibiting shoot growth.   R.E.S.

Galet, P., *Précis de viticulture* (5th edn, Montpellier, 1988).

Huglin, P., *Biologie et écologie de la vigne* (Paris, 1986).

Counoise is one of the more rarefied varietal ingredients in red CHÂTEAUNEUF-DU-PAPE, easily confused in the vineyard with the much lesser southern Rhône variety AUBUN, with which it may sometimes be mingled in older vineyards. It is authorized as a supplementary ingredient for most red wine appellations around the southern Rhône, including Coteaux du LANGUEDOC (which allows Aubin as a synonym) but, although VARIETAL southern French versions are made, it is not widely

grown outside Châteauneuf-du-Pape. Total French plantings increased in the 1980s to around 900 ha/2,200 acres but were only 638 ha in 2000.

As a vine, it leafs and ripens late and yields conservatively. As a wine, it is not particularly deeply coloured or alcoholic but adds lift, a peppery note, and lively acidity to a blend. Enthusiasts such as the Perrin family of Ch de Beaucastel typically use about 5 per cent of Counoise in their red Châteauneuf-du-Pape and have disseminated it around California's Central Coast via their vine NURSERY there.

coupage, French and EUROPEAN UNION term for BLENDING. It means literally 'cutting' and retains a slightly pejorative overtone, tending to be reserved for wine blending at its least glamorous while the word ASSEMBLAGE is more commonly used for blending different lots of a fine wine. EU regulations prohibit the coupage of all sorts of different wines, including EU with non-EU wines, TABLE WINES with QUALITY WINES and different types of quality wines.

Courbu Blanc, Irouléguy speciality similar to PETIT COURBU but with darker young leaves, according to GALET. **Courbu Noir** is an almost extinct speciality of BÉARN.

court-noué, common French term for FANLEAF DEGENERATION, a virus disease of the vine.

Cova de Beira, large IPR region in central Portugal. Wines bearing the name are rarely seen on export markets. See BEIRAS.

cover crop, a crop of plants other than vines established in the vineyard, typically between the rows, generally for the benefit of the vineyard soil. Also known as a sward, or sod culture, it is an alternative to bare soil created by CULTIVATION. Sometimes cover crops are not deliberately planted but WEEDS are allowed to grow instead. Cover crops are normally mown during the vine-growing season, and may be removed by cultivation or HERBICIDE spray (but see ORGANIC VITICULTURE). Typical sown cover crops are grasses and legumes. The grasses used may be native to the area or specially introduced species such as rye grass, fescue, or bent grasses, although sometimes cereals such as barley or oats are used. Legumes planted as cover crops include clovers, medics, peas, and beans. Cover crop management is more difficult in high-density, narrow-spaced vineyards, such as Bordeaux's left bank and Champagne (see VINE DENSITY).

A common reason for sowing cover crops is to increase the ORGANIC MATTER in the soil and hence improve its structure and capacity to hold water. When this is the aim, the species sown should, like cereals, peas, and beans, grow quickly and produce plenty of bulk which can then be incorporated into the soil by shallow

ploughing. Cover crops with a deep tap root such as radish or hollow-stemmed such as oats maintain soil structure by facilitating water absorption and reduce the need for irrigation. The cover crop sward also reduces the amount EVAPORATION from the topsoil, even though some of this retained water will be used by the cover crop to survive. Vine roots are more likely to delve deeper into the soil where cover crops create competition for water and nutrients in the topsoil. Deeprooting vines are less susceptible to sucking up rain water near harvest, thus preserving colour, acid, and flavour in grapes, and maintaining thicker grape skins, which in turn are more likely to resist pests such as grape worm and vinegar flies.

Cover crops are also commonly planted to stop SOIL EROSION in areas with summer storms and are especially useful in sloping vineyards subject to alternate dry heat and sudden downpours, as in some parts of ALSACE. The roots of the cover crop bind the soil and resist the flowing water. Cover crops are also used to combat wind erosion, which can cause severe damage to young plants.

But perhaps the most important use of cover crops is to encourage earlier RIPENING and improve wine quality. Slight WATER STRESS hastens the ripening process, so cover crops, which compete with the vines for water and nutrients, especially NITROGEN, can help to generate this stress in areas of high summer rainfall. However, when winter legumes such as lupins, vetch, or beans are ploughed in during spring, they allow atmospheric nitrogen to be released into the soil. Legumes are much more efficient at doing this than most broadleaved weed species, which do provide nutrients but not in the amounts needed for most commercial wine production. In certain environments, this could have negative consequences for vine vigour. Some mowers throw the cover crop clippings under the vines, thus forming a MULCH.

Apparently weedy vineyards should not necessarily be dismissed as untidy; they may represent a deliberate ploy to improve wine quality. Deep-rooting crops such as mustard and chicory can be particularly useful to use up subsoil water which shallow-rooted grasses cannot reach.

Cover crops should be grown with caution during the vine's growing season. In spring, they make the vineyard more prone to FROST than if the soil is bare. The cover crop may play host to insects which spread diseases such as FLAVESCENCE DORÉE. In summer, the cover crop can use too much water or nitrogen and the vines can suffer as a result. Because of competition with vines for nitrogen, the use of cover crops can also cause STUCK FERMENTATIONS. These effects can be offset by close mowing or by killing the cover crop by ploughing or herbicides. Cover crops reduce the problems caused by dust from traffic on bare soil alleyways in the vineyard; dust can encourage MITES.   R.E.S. & M.W.

Cowra, well-established warm Australian wine region, best suited to Chardonnays, in NEW SOUTH WALES. The accent is more on yield than on quality, and most of the production goes to large wineries as a blend component in lower-priced VARIETAL or GENERIC wine styles.   J.H.

crater, big, deep bowl with a wide mouth used in Ancient GREECE for mixing wine, most often with water. The crater was characteristically 12 to 18 in (30–45 cm) high and could be either painted pottery or made of bronze. The most remarkable example is the huge bronze crater, over 5 ft/1.5 m high, probably of Spartan manufacture, which was found at Vix in France (see CELTS).   J.J.P.

Crato Branco, light-skinned grape speciality of Portugal's algarve, confirmed by DNA PROFILING in Portugal as identical to SÍRIA (and Roupeiro).

Cream, the sweetest, darkest style of SHERRY (with the exception of PX, which is even sweeter and darker) created expressly for the sweet-toothed British market by HARVEYS of Bristol. Bristol Milk was a style of sweet sherry sold successfully in the early 19th century by both AVERYS and Harveys. The story goes that a lady visitor to the cellars in 1882, on tasting Harveys' new, as yet unnamed, BRAND of sweet sherry observed, 'If that is Milk, then this is Cream.' Harveys Bristol Cream was thus named, and has become the most successful branded sherry in the world. This sweet style of sherry is eschewed by the Spaniards, for it is essentially the product of BLENDING not necessarily very distinguished sherries with sweetening and colouring wines. **Pale Cream** was another highly successful sherry style launched, with huge initial success, by CROFT in the 1970s. Most Pale Cream is essentially the same as Cream but with the colour removed, by CHARCOAL or other treatments, although it may also be sweetened FINO. Cream sherries generally have a RESIDUAL SUGAR content that is the equivalent of 4.5 to 6.5 °BAUMÉ.

Crémant, term used as France's shorthand for the country's finest dry sparkling wines made outside Champagne using the traditional method of SPARKLING WINE-MAKING. The term was adopted in the late 1980s, when the expression *méthode champenoise* was outlawed by the EUROPEAN UNION (and replaced by MÉTHODE TRADITIONNELLE). The principal provenances of modern Crémants are Alsace, Die, Jura, Bourgogne (Burgundy), Loire, Limoux, and Bordeaux, although others, such as Gaillac, are anticipated. The best sparkling wines of LUXEMBOURG are also called Crémant. (Crémant had previously been used to describe slightly less fizzy champagnes, with a pressure

of 2–3 atmospheres rather than the normal 5–6. KRUG, for example, produced a Crémant in the late 1970s.) Crémant de Saumur and Crémant de Vouvray were the first non-champagne sparkling wines to use the term, and in the mid 1970s the Crémant de Loire appellation was born, soon followed by Alsace and Bourgogne. Bordeaux and Limoux joined the official Crémant appellations, created under INAO authority, in 1990, and were followed by Die in 1993, and Jura in 1995.

Although grape varieties and TERROIRS vary from region to region, certain strict sparkling wine-making rules are imposed, including WHOLE BUNCH PRESSING; a maximum yield of 100 l per 150 kg of grapes (the same as CHAMPAGNE prior to 1993); a maximum SULFUR DIOXIDE content of 150 mg/l; a minimum of nine months' TIRAGE on the lees; and a compulsory tasting control.

Crémant d'Alsace
Sparkling wine-making using the traditional method in Alsace dates from the late 19th century and in the 1980s became an important commercial activity, representing about 10 per cent of the region's output. Only the grape varieties Pinots Blanc, Noir, and Gris, together with the related Auxerrois, and Riesling and such Chardonnay as is planted in Alsace, may be used (i.e. no Gewürztraminer or Chasselas), to a maximum yield of 80 hl/ha (4.5 tons/acre). The wines are well made, tend to have a particularly fine mousse, high acidity, and to be relatively light in BODY. Only if substantial proportions of Riesling are used do they acquire strong flavour. Production is in the hands of nearly 500 different small-scale producers whose blending capability is usually limited.

Crémant de Bordeaux
A small and declining amount of sparkling wine has been made in the BORDEAUX region since the end of the 19th century. Today production is controlled by a handful of companies who have not established a clear style or identity for the white and pink wines.

Crémant de Bourgogne
This appellation, created in 1975, replaced that of Bourgogne Mousseux (now used exclusively for sparkling red burgundy), under which name sparkling burgundy of all colours enjoyed considerable commercial success in the 1950s and 1960s. All grape varieties grown in BURGUNDY are allowed into Crémant, although Gamay may not constitute more than a fifth of the blend. Yields are limited to about 65 hl/ha. RULLY in the Côte Chalonnaise and AUXERRE in the far north of Burgundy are the principal sources of Crémant de Bourgogne (CÔTE D'OR grapes being in general worth considerably more when sold as still wine), and there can be considerable stylistic differences between their produce. Crémant from south-

ern Burgundy can be full and soft, a good-value alternative to bigger styles of champagne, while Crémant made in the north is usually much lighter and crisper.

Crémant de Die
Crémant de Die replaced the appellation Clairette de Die Brut in 1999 and is a dry wine made mainly from CLAIRETTE grapes, while Clairette de Die Tradition is the arguably more distinctive sweet sparkling wine made principally from MUSCAT BLANC. Maximum permitted yields are about 50 hl/ha (2.8 tons/acre). See CLAIRETTE DE DIE for more details.

Crémant du Jura
In 1995, this appellation effectively replaced CÔTES DU JURA, ARBOIS, and ETOILE Mousseux (though small amounts of these are still made) and has enjoyed considerable success so that by 2005 it represented more than 20 per cent of Jura's wine production. The wines may be white or rosé from any of the authorized JURA grape varieties, although the white must be at least half Chardonnay, and the rosé at least half Poulsard or Pinot Noir. In practice, few Crémants du Jura are made from anything other than these grapes, although some interesting white blends with Savagnin are available. All but the largest producers have their base wine made sparkling by one of two specialist companies who then return the finished wines to individual producers to market. The best wines offer excellent value for money. As Chardonnay is Jura's most planted variety, the Crémant appellation is particularly useful for underripe grapes in this relatively wet region and has a beneficial effect on the quality of still Chardonnay wines.

Crémant de Limoux
This appellation represents the increasing champenization of the ancient sparkling wines of LIMOUX in a particularly cool, high corner of the southern Languedoc. In 1990, Blanquette de Limoux became an appellation reserved for sparkling wines made principally from the MAUZAC grape grown traditionally in the region, while Crémant de Limoux contains Chenin Blanc (20 to 40 per cent) and Chardonnay; together they must comprise 90 per cent of the blend. The other two varieties allowed are Pinot Noir and Mauzac. A very high proportion is made by the CO-OPERATIVE, although the produce of nearly 300 growers is used to make this most southerly Crémant. Yields are restricted to 50 hl/ha.

Crémant de Loire
Crémant de Loire was created in 1975 and encompasses the Anjou-Saumur and Touraine regions. Most of the Loire's wide palette of grape varieties may be used to produce Crémant, with the notable and sensible exception of Sauvignon Blanc, whose aroma has yet to prove itself an attractive sparkling wine

ingredient. GROLLEAU grapes may not represent more than 30 per cent of any blend, and in practice Chenin Blanc is the most common dominant component, clearly distinguishing the flavour of most Crémant de Loire from Crémants made from Pinots and Chardonnay to the east. Yields are limited to 50 hl/ha. Levels of wine-making are generally high among the nearly 200 producers (including four co-operatives and several important NÉGOCIANTS) and an increasing level of complexity in the bottle is evident. Some producers have been Loire offshoots of Champagne houses, notably Langlois Chateau of BOLLINGER, Gratien & Meyer of Alfred Gratien, and the ambitious Bouvet-Ladubay of Taittinger.

Crémant de Luxembourg

Luxembourg has a long tradition of sparkling wine-making, and its particularly acid wines were at one time valued as base wines for SEKT. The Crémant de Luxembourg appellation was created in 1991, following the INAO rules laid down for French wines. Permitted grape varieties are Elbling, Pinot Blanc, Rivaner (Müller Thurgau), Auxerrois, Chardonnay, and Riesling for white wines, Pinot Noir for rosé.

Crépy, small wine appellation within the eastern French region of SAVOIE on the south eastern shore of Lake Geneva producing light, dry white wines from the CHASSELAS grape which would be difficult to distinguish from their Swiss neighbours in a BLIND TASTING. Most of the wine is drunk locally.

Crete, large island to the south of GREECE famous for the Minoan civilization (c.2000–1400 BC). Its wines were most famous in the Middle Ages when the island was known as Candia. See MALVASIA, MALMSEY, NAPLES, and VENICE.

crianza, Spanish term used both to describe the process of AGEING a wine and also for the youngest officially recognized category of a wood-matured wine. A crianza red wine may not be sold until its third (second for whites) year, and must have spent a minimum of six months in oak *barricas* (BARRIQUES). In RIOJA and other regions such as RIBERA DEL DUERO, where the term is most commonly used, the wine must have spent at least 12 months in oak casks. An increasingly frequent, albeit un-official, category now is **semi-crianza**, for wine aged in cask for less time than the crianza min-imum. With the term JOVEN fully accepted for fruity young wines without cask ageing, the slightly derogatory description *sin crianza* had all but disappeared by the late 1990s.

Crimea, peninsula off southern UKRAINE surrounded by the Black sea, whose south coast became an important holiday region for Russian aristocrats in the 19th century and centre for sanatoriums in the 20th century. Cyrus REDDING noted in 1833 that 'the Crimea wines are thought the best in the empire'. The wine-loving Count Mikhail Vorontsov, governor-general of that part of Russia which then included the Crimea, began to build the Alupka Palace and associated winery in the 1820s which still produces FORTIFIED wines in quantity, and also laid the foundations for the MAGARACH Institute for research into wine-making and viticulture. Vorontsov imported a wide range of grape varieties from Europe, but suffered many early wine-making failures, as did his successor as principal Crimean wine innovator, Prince Golitzin, in the early 1880s at his Novy Svet winery. Modern wine produc-tion on the south coast is chiefly under the control of the MASSANDRA central winery on the outskirts of Yalta. Average July temperat-ures of 24 °C/75 °F and annual sunshine of 2,250 hours at Yalta result in extremely ripe grapes best suited to the production of strong, sweet wines, most of them made like VINS DOUX NATURELS.

Criolla Chica is the Argentine name for the PAIS of Chile, the MISSION of California, and the Negra Corriente of PERU. It is thought to be descended from the seeds of grapes, presum-ably well raisined after their voyage under sail across the Atlantic, imported by the Spanish conquistadores, possibly as early as the 16th century (see SOUTH AMERICA). Criolla Chica is much less common in Argentina than the other pink-skinned grape varieties CRIOLLA GRANDE and CEREZA. Its wine is generally paler but slightly better quality.

Criolla Grande, the second most planted vine variety in ARGENTINA after CEREZA. Al-though the area planted with this coarse, pink-skinned grape has declined substantially, there were still nearly 24,000 ha/59,000 acres in 2003. Almost all Criolla Grande is in Mendoza province, where it is the most planted vine variety by far (covering 7,000 ha more than the red wine grape MALBEC, for example). Criolla Grande is a low-quality VINIFERA variety that was probably one of the first vines culti-vated in the Americas, and is much deeper skinned than CRIOLLA CHICA. The two Criollas, along with Cereza and Moscatel Rosada, form the basis of Argentina's declining trade in basic deep-coloured white wine sold very cheaply in litre bottles or cardboard cartons. Pink wine can also be made from Criolla Grande.

Criots-Bâtard-Montrachet, great white GRAND CRU in Burgundy's CÔTE D'OR. For more details, see MONTRACHET.

crise viticole, la, widely used phrase for France's wine crisis of the early 21st century re-sulting from her plummeting wine sales both at home and abroad. Sales stagnation affected not just the LANGUEDOC with its huge volumes of surplus VIN DE TABLE and VIN DE PAYS and its notoriously militant vignerons, but also APPEL-LATION CONTRÔLÉE wines from such prestigious regions as BORDEAUX and BURGUNDY. Only CHAMPAGNE seemed relatively unscathed, lead-ing to increased attempts to develop BRANDS of French still wines.

critters labels. See YELLOW TAIL.

Crljenak Kaštelanski, 'the red wine grape of Kaštela', an island off CROATIA, which turned out to be identical to ZINFANDEL.

Croatia, state south west of Hungary, is like its north western neighbour SLOVENIA in hav-ing two very different regions split by the ranges of hills which follow the coast.

The region of Inland Croatia (Kontinentalna Hrvatska) runs south and east from the eastern tip of Slovenia along the Drava tributary of the Danube, which marks the Hungarian border, down to the ill-fated town of Vukovar. Sub-regions are: Plešivica, Zagorje-Medjimurje, Prigorje-Bilogora, Moslavina, Pokuplje, Slavonija, and Podunavlje, each of which is fur-ther subdivided into several named districts. More than two-thirds of the country's and 90 per cent of inland Croatia's production is white. The dominant variety here is Laški Rizling or WELSCHRIESLING (here known by the more graceful name of Graševina). Other varieties planted include Gewürztraminer, various Pinots, Chardonnay, Riesling, Sauvi-gnon Blanc, Furmint (known as Moslavac in Croatia), Blaufränkisch (known as Frankovka), some Portugieser (Portugizac,) and some Müller-Thurgau (Rizvanac). The wines are gen-erally riper and more earthy in style than their Slovenian counterparts.

Coastal Croatia (the Primorska Hrvatska re-gion) is made up of Istria (Istra), the Croatian Coast (Hrvatsko Primorje), Northern Dalma-tia (Sjeverna Dalmacija), Central and Southern Dalmatia including their islands (Srednja i Južna Dalmacija), and the Dalmatian Hinter-land (Dalmatinska Zagora). Each of these also has subdivisions.

Istria has its fair share of Bordeaux red grapes such as Cabernet Sauvignon and Mer-lot as well as the local variety TERAN. The dom-inant white wine grape is Malvazija Istarska, which is considered indigenous and makes full bodied, dry wines with some minerality and a bitter almond finish. Gamay (here called Borgonja), Chardonnay, the Pinots and Mus-cat Blanc (Muskat Momjanski) are also grown in Istria. In the Hrvatsko Primorje subregion the local light-skinned variety Žlahtina is most important, with particularly popular light, fruity wines produced in a small part of the island of Krk.

But most of the rest of the coast boasts a whole selection of grape varieties which ap-pear to be native to this region. The PLAVAC MALI grape (see ZINFANDEL) is responsible for some potentially excellent red wines such as Dingač and Postup on the Peljesac peninsula, Zlatan Plavac, Ivan Dolac, and Faros on the island of Hvar. All of them tend to be heavy and very ripe, with a natural ALCOHOLIC STRENGTH of 14 to 15 per cent. Babić is another good-quality red grape grown on famously stony coastal vineyards near Šibenik. White grapes include Pošip and Grk on the island of Korčula, Vugava on the island of Vis, Bogdanuša on the island of Hvar, and Maraština grown all along the coast. Pošip and Bogdanuša can produce wines that are fresh, quite light, and herbal. The others make wines that are heavier, deeper coloured, full-bodied and indisputably from a warm climate. This Dalmatian coastal region stretches over the other half of the Croatian vineyard and produces 70 per cent red wine.

In addition to those specifically mentioned, more than 400 cultivars are grown, most of them native to their particular area, although a drastic erosion of indigenous CULTIVARS has occurred in recent years. International interest was stirred, however, by the discovery that the old Croatian variety Crljenak Kaštelanski (Tribidrag) is identical to California's Zinfandel. Malvasija Dubrovačka, an excellent white wine variety, may be found elsewhere around the Mediterranean under such names as Malvasia delle Lipari (off Sicilia), Greco di Gerace, Malvasia di Bosa (in Sardegna), Malvasia de Sitges (in Cataluña), and Malvasia di Lanzarote (in the Canary Islands).

Croatian viticulture dates back to several centuries BC when grapevines were probably introduced to the Adriatic coast by the ancient Greeks or Phoenicians. At the end of the 19th and the beginning of the 20th centuries, Croatia was a significant European wine producer with about 200,000 ha under vine, 90,000 ha in the Dalmatian region alone. According to 2005 statistics, about 59,000 ha/147,000 acres of vineyards remain. According to official data, there are 450 producers bottling more than 1,200 different labels, but Croatia has a long history of small, private producers too. The most famous Croatian wine producer internationally is Mike Grgich, who returned to his native Croatia from his successful eponymous winery in California's Napa Valley.   A.H.M., I.M., & E.M.

Croatina, red grape variety from the borders of the PIEMONTE and LOMBARDIA regions of northern Italy. The vine buds and ripens late but yields good quantities of fruity wine with a certain bite, designed to be drunk relatively young. Its common synonym is Bonarda, under which name it has an appetizing red VARIETAL DOC in the OLTREPÒ PAVESE zone of south west Lombardia. The variety is quite distinct from BONARDA Piemontese. Total plantings of Croatina are just a few thousand ha.

Croft, port and sherry shippers originally established as Phayre and Bradley in 1678. The first Croft, from York, became a partner in 1736 and since 1769, after several name

changes, the company has been known as Croft and Co. Croft's main property in the DOURO valley is the 109-ha/269-acre Quinta da Roêda near Pinhão, which produces the backbone for their vintage blends. In 1911, the firm was taken over by Gilbey's, and the majority shareholding eventually passed into the hands of the multinational corporation Grand Metropolitan, subsequently an integral part of Diageo. Port shipper Morgan Brothers was acquired in 1952 but when Croft was sold by Diageo to the FLADGATE PARTNERSHIP in 2001 it was a requirement of the sale that the Morgan brand name should no longer be used in deference to Diageo's Captain Morgan rum.

Croft expanded into the SHERRY business in the difficult era of the early 1970s. Croft invaded Jerez with energy and one novel idea: they launched an entirely new style of sherry, Pale CREAM, which could offer the beguiling combination of a pale, sophisticated appearance with the reassuring sweetness of a cream. It was an enormous and much-imitated success, necessitating almost immediate expansion for Croft Jerez, in the form of Rancho Croft, a series of ultra-modern bodegas an unparalleled 200 m/650 ft long. Croft's Jerez adventure ended in 2001, when Diageo, by then its parent company, sold the modern bodegas to GONZÁLEZ BYASS for 54 million euros. Some of its best old soleras were acquired by a new, quality-minded company, Tradición.

crop thinning, viticultural practice which, it is claimed, improves wine quality by encouraging fruit RIPENING. It is known as *éclaircissage* or *vendange verte* (green harvest) in French. Some bunches are removed from the vine and those remaining should in theory ripen more quickly with the benefit of improved LEAF TO FRUIT RATIO. Crop thinning is usually carried out by hand, and is therefore expensive. MECHANICAL HARVESTERS are occasionally used to thin crops, but here individual berries or parts of bunches are removed.

The YIELD is reduced more or less proportionately to the bunches removed (although any remaining berries may be slightly enlarged), which means that only those growers able to guarantee top prices for their produce can afford the operation. The technique became common in the early 1990s among the better wine producers in Bordeaux, where it had been practised at Ch PÉTRUS since 1973.

Crop thinning is normally carried out at VERAISON, when it is obvious which bunches are slow to ripen. It is cheaper if done earlier but there is a risk that the remaining bunches will become tight due to larger berries and so be prone to BOTRYTIS BUNCH ROT. Later bunch removal has more impact on yield, and earlier removal on fruit ripening.

Thinning is also appropriate when it is obvious that the vintage will be late, decreasing the chance of ripening a large crop.

The theory of crop thinning is that the remaining fruit ripens earlier, and so has better levels of SUGARS and ANTHOCYANINS for red varieties. However, many studies have shown that these benefits are small in magnitude, and that crop levels need to be greatly reduced for a small change in GRAPE COMPOSITION. For many vineyards where the yield is in BALANCE with shoot growth, and the leaves and fruit are well exposed, then there will be little benefit from crop thinning.   R.E.S.

Reynier, A., *Manuel de viticulture* (9th edn, Paris, 2003).

cross or **crossing,** the result of breeding a new variety by crossing two VINE VARIETIES of the same species, usually the European VINIFERA species. Thus MÜLLER-THURGAU, for example, is a cross. Crosses are different from HYBRIDS, sometimes called **interspecific crosses,** which contain the genes of more than one species of the VITIS genus.

Crouchen or **Cruchen,** white grape variety producing neutral wines in both South Africa and Australia. It originated in the western Pyrenees of France but is no longer grown there in any quantity, thanks to its sensitivity to FUNGAL DISEASES. There are records of its shipment to Clare Valley in SOUTH AUSTRALIA in 1850 and for long it was confused with Semillon, which Australians were wont to call Riesling. It was therefore known principally as Clare Riesling in Australia until 1976, when AMPELOGRAPHER Paul Truel identified it as this relatively obscure French variety. There were just over 100 ha planted by the mid 2000s. In 2004, the South Africans had about 1,300 ha/3,200 acres of the variety they confusingly call Cape Riesling. It may be sold simply as Riesling within South Africa (where true Riesling is known as Rhine or Weisser Riesling) and shares with that much greater German grape variety the ability to benefit from BOTTLE AGEING.

crown caps, small metal caps used on beer and soda bottles, have proved to be a very reliable closure for long-term wine bottle storage (see Helmut BECKER) and provide an extremely cheap and efficient closure for any sort of wine, but many wine drinkers find their association with what they regard as less sophisticated drinks unacceptable, particularly when it comes to wine SERVICE in a restaurant. The crown cap is also used nearly universally for closing SPARKLING WINE bottles during the TIRAGE process; DISGORGING is much more difficult if a cork has to be extracted. Some sparkling wines have been released under crown seal in Australia, to avoid the problems associated with cork closures.

crown gall, BACTERIAL DISEASE which occurs on over 600 plant species, including vines, particularly when grown where winters are so cold that vines can be damaged (see WINTER FREEZE). High incidence of the disease can make vineyards uneconomic. All VITIS VINIFERA varieties are susceptible, but some VITIS *labrusca* varieties are more tolerant, one reason why such species tend to be grown in very cold climates.

The disease, also known as black knot, is caused by *Agrobacterium tumefaciens*. The major symptom is the growth of fleshy galls (tumours) on the lower trunk which can girdle the trunk and portions of the vine above may die. At one time it was believed that the bacterium lived in the soil like its relative that causes galls on other plants. However, crown gall of vines lives inside the vine itself and so is spread at planting. Control of crown gall is difficult. Research in the early 1990s suggested that hot water treatment of dormant cuttings (50 °C/122 °F for 30 minutes) reduces the bacterium, and TISSUE CULTURE offers total elimination by producing nursery stock free of crown gall. Avoiding the disease can also help to reduce winter freeze injury to trunks. In the north eastern UNITED STATES, the growers train the vines with up to five trunks so that there is always a young healthy trunk to replace dead or dying ones. See TRAINING SYSTEMS.

In recent years, the crown gall bacterium has been the focus of intense research due to its application in GENETIC MODIFICATION in a wide range of plants other than vines. *Agrobacterium* has the ability to incorporate its own DNA (the genetic code) into the plant where it is combined with that of the host, and can thus be used to transfer new genes into the plant. Many new plants being created by modern plant scientists owe their origin to this otherwise harmful organism.   R.E.S.

Pearson, R. C., and Goheen, A. C., *Compendium of Grape Diseases* (St Paul, Minn., 1988).

Crozes-Hermitage,   the   northern RHÔNE'S biggest appellation, regularly producing about eight times as much wine as the much more distinguished vineyards of HERMITAGE which it surrounds, and still considerably more than the similarly priced, and similarly extended, appellation of ST-JOSEPH across the river. Like both these appellations, Crozes-Hermitage is usually red and made exclusively of the SYRAH grape, although a certain proportion, just over a tenth, of full-bodied dry white wine is made from the MARSANNE grape supplemented by ROUSSANNE. Up to 15 per cent of white grapes may theoretically be added to red Crozes at the time of FERMENTATION. Although some bottlers have treated the appellation with little respect for quality, a nucleus of excitingly ambitious producers such as Belle, Colombier, Graillot, Pochon, and Tardieu-Laurent emerged from the late 1980s to provide thoughtfully made Crozes-Hermitage of real distinction and mass. The best reds are rather softer and fruitier than Hermitage because the soils are richer (and because it is more difficult to justify BARREL MATURATION at Crozes prices), but they tend to share more of Hermitage's solidity

than average St-Joseph. A more typical red Crozes, however, exhibits the burnt rubber smell and sinewy build of overstretched Syrah, although the CO-OPERATIVE in the town of Tain l'Hermitage, two-thirds of whose production is Crozes-Hermitage, should not be underestimated. Les Chassis, between the *autoroute* south of Tain and the river, provides some of the finest red Crozes, including JABOULET's Domaine de Thalabert, which was for long the appellation's principal standard-bearer. Parts of Gervan just north of Tain enjoy a MESOCLIMATE very much closer to that of Hermitage than the flatter vineyards to the east, which are some of the few in the northern Rhône which can be harvested by machine. The clay-limestone alluvial soils of Crozes-Hermitage seem generally less well suited to white wine production, although there are some successful vineyards around Mercurol. The appellation, which dates from 1937, takes its name from a small village just north of Tain without any particular vinous claim. Total vineyard area in production expanded by about a quarter between 1990 and 2005 when it had reached almost 1,250 ha/3,000 acres by 2005. The best reds can be kept for five years or more (and in good years can happily survive for ten) but the average Crozes, red or white, is probably at its best drunk young.

Livingstone-Learmonth, J., *The Wines of the Northern Rhône* (Berkeley, 2005).

cru, French specialist term for a vineyard, usually reserved for those officially recognized as of superior quality. Such recognition was already known in Ancient ROME.

In English the word is often translated as 'growth'. PREMIERS CRUS, for example, are called FIRST GROWTHS in BORDEAUX, according to one of their official CLASSIFICATIONS. A cru that has been 'classified' is a **cru classé**, or CLASSED GROWTH. GRANDS CRUS can also have a very specific meaning, notably in BURGUNDY and ALSACE.

The top-ranked communes in BEAUJOLAIS are called crus, and their produce is Cru Beaujolais.

In SWITZERLAND, the first two vineyards to be officially awarded cru status were the neighbouring Dézaley and Calamin in Vaud.

In Italy there have been some attempts to define various superior vineyards as crus. The local dialect for such a site in PIEMONTE is SORI.

For the situation in Germany, see GROSSES GEWÄCHS.

cru artisan was recognized by the EUROPEAN UNION in 2002 as a 'traditional expression' reserved for AC wines from a particular category of wine estates in the Médoc, the Haut-Médoc, Margaux, Moulis, Listrac, St-Julien, Pauillac, and St-Estèphe. A cru artisan is more humble, and generally smaller, than a CRU BOURGEOIS.

cru bourgeois, a category of red wine properties, or CRUS, designated bourgeois, or a social stratum below the supposedly aristocratic crus classés. While the crus classés represent about 25 per cent of the Médoc's total wine production from 60 estates, the crus bourgeois represent a further 30 per cent. The properties can vary, however, from simple smallholdings to others such as Ch Larose-Trintaudon, the largest estate in the Médoc with its own vast château buildings, or Ch Clarke of Listrac, on which Baron Edmond de ROTHSCHILD lavished a large fortune.

In terms of wine quality, there is wide variation between the best and worst of the crus bourgeois. The best are producing wine that is seriously better, and occasionally more expensive, than that of the under-performing crus classés, while the worst make wine that is just slightly more exciting than red BORDEAUX AC. In general, however, this category can offer some of Bordeaux's best value and most accessible wines. They are made mainly from Cabernet Sauvignon grapes but often contain quite a high proportion of Merlot, usually supplemented by some Cabernet Franc. Some BARREL MATURATION is usually involved in the making of the most highly priced crus bourgeois, even if only a small proportion of new OAK is lavished on this wine category. However, viticulture and wine-making at the crus bourgeois exceptionnels (see below) is very similar to that practised by the crus classés. The wines are generally ready to drink at between four and eight years old but the best may be aged up to 15 years.

The description 'cru bourgeois' has been used orally for several centuries and appeared in an early edition of COCKS ET FÉRET in the mid 19th century but the First World War and then the dire state of the international wine market at the end of the 1920s called for a new impetus. A first CLASSIFICATION of the crus bourgeois of the Médoc was drawn up in 1932, and one can only imagine the difficulties of bestowing this supposed commercial advantage, ranked into three different classes, on a few hundred Médoc wine farmers. Thirty years later, when the Syndicate of Crus Bourgeois set about revitalizing itself, it was discovered that, of the 444 members registered in 1932, more than 300 had been absorbed into other estates, or converted their land from viticulture to another crop such as pines instead.

The lack of official recognition by the Minister of Agriculture when the list was first drawn up in 1932 was a constant source of difficulty and potential abuse of the title but the designation Cru Bourgeois was officially recognized in the EUROPEAN UNION labelling laws of 1979 on condition that its use be codified by the French government. Eventually, in 2003, a ministerial decree recognized the first classification of Médoc Crus Bourgeois (annulled in 2007). The vigorously contested selection comprised 247 châteaux from 490 candidates and was divided

Crus Bourgeois as at June 2003

Crus Bourgeois Exceptionnels (Exceptional Crus Bourgeois)

Château	Commune	Appellation
Château Chasse-Spleen	Moulis-en-Médoc	Moulis-en-Médoc
Château Haut-Marbuzet	Saint-Estèphe	Saint-Estèphe
Château Labegorce Zédé	Soussans	Margaux
Château Les Ormes-de-Pez	Saint-Estèphe	Saint-Estèphe
Château de Pez	Saint-Estèphe	Saint-Estèphe
Château Phélan Ségur	Saint-Estèphe	Saint-Estèphe
Château Potensac	Ordonnac	Médoc
Château Poujeaux	Moulis-en-Médoc	Moulis-en-Médoc
Château Siran	Labarde	Margaux

Crus Bourgeois Supérieurs (Superior Crus Bourgeois)

Château	Commune	Appellation
Château d'Agassac	Ludon-Médoc	Haut-Médoc
Château d'Angludet	Cantenac	Margaux
Château Anthonic	Moulis-en-Médoc	Moulis-en-Médoc
Château d'Arche	Ludon-Médoc	Haut-Médoc
Château Arnauld	Arcins	Haut-Médoc
Château d'Arsac	Arsac	Margaux
Château Beaumont	Cussac-Fort-Médoc	Haut-Médoc
Château Beau-Site	Saint-Estèphe	Saint-Estèphe
Château Biston-Brillette	Moulis-en-Médoc	Moulis-en-Médoc
Château Le Boscq	Saint-Estèphe	Saint-Estèphe
Château Bournac	Civrac	Médoc
Château Brillette	Moulis-en-Médoc	Moulis-en-Médoc
Château Cambon La Pelouse	Macau	Haut-Médoc
Château Cap-Léon-Veyrin	Listrac-Médoc	Listrac-Médoc
Château La Cardonne	Blaignan	Médoc
Château Caronne Sainte-Gemme	Saint-Laurent-Médoc	Haut-Médoc
Château Castera	Saint-Germain-d'Esteuil	Médoc
Château Chambert-Marbuzet	Saint-Estèphe	Saint-Estèphe
Château Charmail	Saint-Seurin-de-Cadourne	Haut-Médoc
Château Cissac	Cissac-Médoc	Haut-Médoc
Château Citran	Avensan	Haut-Médoc
Château Clarke	Listrac-Médoc	Listrac-Médoc
Château Clauzet	Saint-Estèphe	Saint-Estèphe
Château Clément Pichon	Parempuyre	Haut-Médoc
Château Colombier-Ponpelou	Pauillac	Pauillac
Château Coufran	Saint-Seurin-de-Cadourne	Haut-Médoc
Château Le Crock	Saint-Estèphe	Saint-Estèphe
Château Dutruch Grand Poujeaux	Moulis-en-Médoc	Moulis-en-Médoc
Château d'Escurac	Civrac	Médoc
Château Fonbadet	Pauillac	Pauillac
Château Fonréaud	Listrac-Médoc	Listrac-Médoc
Château Fourcas Dupré	Listrac-Médoc	Listrac-Médoc
Château Fourcas Hosten	Listrac-Médoc	Listrac-Médoc
Château Furcas Loubaney	Listrac-Médoc	Listrac-Médoc
Château du Giana	Saint-Julien-Beychevelle	Saint-Julien
Château Les Grands Chênes	Saint-Christoly-de-Médoc	Médoc
Château Gressier Grand Poujeaux	Moulis-en-Médoc	Moulis-en-Médoc
Château Greysac	Bégadan	Médoc
Château La Gurgue	Margaux	Margaux
Château Hanteillan	Cissac-Médoc	Haut-Médoc
Château Haut-Bages Monpelou	Pauillac	Pauillac
Château La Haye	Saint-Estèphe	Saint-Estèphe
Château Labegorce	Margaux	Margaux
Château de Lamarque	Lamarque	Haut-Médoc
Château Lamothe Bergeron	Cussac-Fort-Médoc	Haut-Médoc
Château Lanessan	Cussac-Fort-Médoc	Haut-Médoc
Château Larose Trintaudon	Saint-Laurent-Médoc	Haut-Médoc
Château Lestage	Listrac-Médoc	Listrac-Médoc
Château Lestage Simon	Saint-Seurin-de-Cadourne	Haut-Médoc
Château Lilian Ladouys	Saint-Estèphe	Saint-Estèphe
Château Liversan	Saint-Sauveur	Haut-Médoc
Château Loudenne	Saint-Yzans-de-Médoc	Médoc
Château Malescasse	Lamarque	Haut-Médoc
Château de Malleret	Le Pian-Médoc	Haut-Médoc
Château Maucaillou	Moulis-en-Médoc	Moulis-en-Médoc

Château	Commune	Appellation
Château Maucamps	Macau	Haut-Médoc
Château Mayne Lalande	Listrac-Médoc	Listrac-Médoc
Château Meyney	Saint-Estèphe	Saint-Estèphe
Château Monbrison	Arsac	Margaux
Château Moulin à Vent	Moulis-en-Médoc	Moulis-en-Médoc
Château Moulin de La Rose	Saint-Julien-de-Beychevelle	Saint-Julien
Château Les Ormes Sorbet	Couquèques	Médoc
Château Paloumey	Ludon-Médoc	Haut-Médoc
Château Patache d'Aux	Bégadan	Médoc
Château Paveil de Luze	Soussans	Margaux
Château Petit Bocq	Saint-Estèphe	Saint-Estèphe
Château Pibran	Pauillac	Pauillac
Château Ramage La Batisse	Saint-Sauveur	Haut-Médoc
Château Reysson	Vertheuil	Haut-Médoc
Château Rollan de By	Bégadan	Médoc
Château Saransot-Dupré	Listrac-Médoc	Listrac-Médoc
Château Ségur	Parempuyre	Haut-Médoc
Château Sénéjac	Le Pian-Médoc	Haut-Médoc
Château Soudars	Saint-Seurin-de-Cadourne	Haut-Médoc
Château du Taillan	Le Taillan-Médoc	Haut-Médoc
Château Terrey Gros Cailloux	Saint-Julien-Beychevelle	Saint-Julien
Château La Tour de By	Bégadan	Médoc
Château La Tour de Mons	Soussans	Margaux
Château Tour de Pez	Saint-Estèphe	Saint-Estèphe
Château Tour du Haut Moulin	Cussac-Fort-Médoc	Haut-Médoc
Château Tour Haut Caussan	Blaignan	Médoc
Château Tronquoy-Lalande	Saint-Estèphe	Saint-Estèphe
Château Verdignan	Saint-Seurin-de-Cadourne	Haut-Médoc
Château Vieux Robin	Bégadan	Médoc
Château de Villegorge	Avensan	Haut-Médoc

Crus Bourgeois

Château	Commune	Appellation
Château Andron Blanquet	Saint-Estèphe	Saint-Estèphe
Château Aney	Cussac-Fort-Médoc	Haut-Médoc
Château d'Arcins	Arcins	Haut-Médoc
Château L'Argenteyre	Bégadan	Médoc
Château d'Aurilhac	Saint-Seurin-de-Cadourne	Haut-Médoc
Château Balac	Saint-Laurent-Médoc	Haut-Médoc
Château Barateau	Saint-Laurent-Médoc	Haut-Médoc
Château Bardis	Saint-Seurin-de-Cadourne	Haut-Médoc
Château Barreyres	Arcins	Haut-Médoc
Château Baudan	Listrac-Médoc	Listrac-Médoc
Château Beau-Site Haut-Vignoble	Saint-Estèphe	Saint-Estèphe
Château Bégadanet	Bégadan	Médoc
Château Bel Air	Saint-Estèphe	Saint-Estèphe
Château Bel Air	Cussac-Fort-Médoc	Haut-Médoc
Château Bel Orme Tronquoy-de-Lalande	Saint-Seurin-de-Cadourne	Haut-Médoc
Château Bel-Air Lagrave	Moulis-en-Médoc	Moulis-en-Médoc
Château des Belles Graves	Ordonnac	Médoc
Château Bessan Ségur	Civrac	Médoc
Château Bibian	Listrac-Médoc	Listrac-Médoc
Château Blaignan	Blaignan	Médoc
Château Le Boscq	Bégadan	Médoc
Château Le Bourdieu	Valeyrac	Médoc
Château Le Bourdieu	Vertheuil	Haut-Médoc
Château de Braude	Macau	Haut-Médoc
Château du Breuil	Cissac-Médoc	Haut-Médoc
Château La Bridane	Saint-Julien-Beychevelle	Saint-Julien
Château des Brousteras	Saint-Yzans-de-Médoc	Médoc
Château des Cabans	Bégadan	Médoc
Château Cap de Haut	Lamarque	Haut-Médoc
Château Capbern Gasqueton	Saint-Estèphe	Saint-Estèphe
Château Chantelys	Prignac-en-Médoc	Médoc
Château La Clare	Bégadan	Médoc
Château La Commanderie	Saint-Estèphe	Saint-Estèphe
Château Le Coteau	Arsac	Margaux
Château Coutelin Merville	Saint-Estèphe	Saint-Esèphe
Château de Croix La	Ordonnac	Médoc
Château Dasvin-Bel-Air	Macau	Haut-Médoc
Château David	Vensac	Médoc
Château Devise d'Ardilley	Saint-Laurent-Médoc	Haut-Médoc
Château Deyrem Valentin	Soussans	Margaux

Château	Commune	Appellation
Château Dillon	Blanquefort	Haut-Médoc
Château Domeyne	Saint-Estèphe	Saint-Estèphe
Château Donissan	Listrac-Médoc	Listrac-Médoc
Château Ducluzeau	Listrac-Médoc	Listrac-Médoc
Château Duplessis	Moulis-en-Médoc	Moulis-en-Médoc
Château Duplessis Fabre	Moulis-en-Médoc	Moulis-en-Médoc
Château Duthil	Le Pian-Médoc	Haut-Médoc
Château L'Ermitage	Listrac-Médoc	Listrac-Médoc
Château d'Escot	Lesparre-Médoc	Médoc
Château La Fleur Milon	Pauillac	Pauillac
Château La Fleur Peyrabon	Saint-Sauveur	Pauillac
Château La Fon du Berger	Saint-Sauveur	Haut-Médoc
Château Fontesteau	Saint-Sauveur	Haut-Médoc
Château Fontis	Ordonnac	Médoc
Château La Galiane	Soussans	Margaux
Château de Gironville	Macau	Haut-Médoc
Château La Gorce	Blaignan	Médoc
Château La Gorre	Bégadan	Médoc
Château Grand Clapeau Olivier	Blanquefort	Haut-Médoc
Château Grandis	Saint-Seurin-de-Cadourne	Haut-Médoc
Château Granins Grand Poujeaux	Moulis-en-Médoc	Moulis-en-Médoc
Château Grivière	Blaignan	Médoc
Château Haut-Beauséjour	Saint-Estèphe	Saint-Estèphe
Château Haut-Bellevue	Lamarque	Haut-Médoc
Château Haut Breton Larigaudière	Soussans	Margaux
Château Haut-Canteloup	Saint-Christoly-de-Médoc	Médoc
Château Haut-Madrac	Saint-Sauveur	Haut-Médoc
Château Haut-Maurac	Saint-Yzans-de-Médoc	Médoc
Château Houissant	Saint-Estèphe	Saint-Estèphe
Château Hourbanon	Prignac-en-Médoc	Médoc
Château Hourtin-Ducasse	Saint-Sauveur	Haut-Médoc
Château Labadie	Bégadan	Médoc
Château Ladouys	Saint-Estèphe	Saint-Estèphe
Château Laffitte Carcasset	Saint-Estèphe	Saint-Estèphe
Château Laffitte Laujac	Bégadan	Médoc
Château Lafon	Prignac-en-Médoc	Médoc
Château Lalande	Listrac-Médoc	Listrac-Médoc
Château Lalande	Saint-Julien-Beychevelle	Saint-Julien
Château Lamothe-Cissac	Cissac-Médoc	Haut-Médoc
Château Larose Perganson	Saint-Laurent-Médoc	Haut-Médoc
Château Larrivaux	Cissac-Médoc	Haut-Médoc
Château Larruau	Margaux	Margaux
Château Laujac	Bégadan	Médoc
Château La Lauzette-Declercq	Listrac-Médoc	Listrac-Médoc
Château Leyssac	Saint-Estèphe	Saint-Estèphe
Château Lieujean	Saint-Sauveur	Haut-Médoc
Château Liouner	Listrac-Médoc	Listrac-Médoc
Château Lousteauneuf	Valeyrac	Médoc
Château Magnol	Blanquefort	Haut-Médoc
Château de Marbuzet	Saint-Estèphe	Saint-Estèphe
Château Marsac Séguineau	Soussans	Margaux
Château Martinens	Cantenac	Margaux
Château Maurac	Saint-Seurin-de-Cadourne	Haut-Médoc
Château Mazails	Saint-Yzans-de-Médoc	Médoc
Château Le Meynieu	Vertheuil	Haut-Médoc
Château Meyre	Avensan	Haut-Médoc
Château Les Moines	Couquèques	Médoc
Château Mongravey	Arsac	Margaux
Château Le Monteil d'Arsac	Arsac	Haut-Médoc
Château Morin	Saint-Estèphe	Saint-Estèphe
Château du Moulin Rouge	Cussac-Fort-Médoc	Haut-Médoc
Château La Mouline	Moulis-en-Médoc	Moulis-en-Médoc
Château Muret	Saint-Seurin-de-Cadourne	Haut-Médoc
Château Noaillac	Jau-Dignac-Loirac	Médoc
Château du Perier	Saint-Christoly-de-Médoc	Médoc
Château Le Pey	Bégadan	Médoc
Château Peyrabon	Saint-Sauveur	Haut-Médoc
Château Peyredon Lagravette	Listrac-Médoc	Listrac-Médoc
Château Peyre-Lebade	Listrac-Médoc	Haut-Médoc
Château Picard	Saint-Estèphe	Saint-Estèphe
Château Plantey	Pauillac	Pauillac
Château Poitevin	Jau-Dignac-Loirac	Médoc
Château Pomys	Saint-Estèphe	Saint-Estèphe
Château Pontac Lynch	Cantenac	Margaux
Château Pontey	Blaignan	Médoc
Château Pontoise Cabarrus	Saint-Seurin-de-Cadourne	Haut-Médoc
Château Puy Castéra	Cissac-Médoc	Haut-Médoc
Château Ramafort	Blaignan	Médoc

Crus Bourgeois—cont.

Château	Commune	Appellation
Château du Raux	Cussac-Fort-Médoc	Haut-Médoc
Château La Raze Beauvallet	Civrac	Médoc
Château du Retout	Cussac-Fort-Médoc	Haut-Médoc
Château Reverdi	Listrac-Médoc	Listrac-Médoc
Château Roquegrave	Valeyrac	Médoc
Château Saint-Ahon	Blanquefort	Haut-Médoc
Château Saint-Aubin	Saint-Sauveur	Médoc
Château Saint-Christophe	Saint-Christoly-de-Médoc	Médoc
Château Saint-Estèphe	Saint-Estèphe	Saint-Estèphe
Château Saint-Hilaire	Queyrac	Médoc
Château Saint-Paul	Saint-Seurin-de-Cadourne	Haut-Médoc
Château Segue Longue	Jau-Dignac-Loirac	Médoc
Château Ségur de Cabanac	Saint-Estèphe	Saint-Estèphe
Château Semeillan Mazeau	Listrac-Médoc	Listrac-Médoc
Château Senilhac	Saint-Seurin-de-Cadourne	Haut-Médoc
Château Sipian	Valeyrac	Médoc
Château Tayac	Soussans	Margaux
Château Le Temple	Valeyrac	Médoc
Château Teynac	Saint-Julien-Beychevelle	Saint-Julien
Château La Tonnelle	Cissac-Médoc	Haut-Médoc
Château Tour Blanche	Saint-Christoly-de-Médoc	Médoc
Château La Tour de Bessan	Cantenac	Margaux
Château Tour des Termes	Saint-Estèphe	Saint-Estèphe
Château Tour-du-Roc	Arcins	Haut-Médoc
Château Tour Prignac	Prignac-en-Médoc	Médoc
Château Tour Saint-Bonnet	Saint-Christoly-de-Médoc	Médoc
Château Tour Saint-Fort	Saint-Estèphe	Saint-Estèphe
Château Tour Saint-Joseph	Cissac-Médoc	Haut-Médoc
Château Trois Moulins	Macau	Haut-Médoc
Château Les Tuileries	Saint-Yzans-de-Médoc	Médoc
Château Vernous	Lesparre	Médoc
Château Vieux Château Landon	Bégadan	Médoc
Château de Villambis	Cissac-Médoc	Haut-Médoc

into three categories: **Cru Bourgeois** (9), **Cru Bourgeois Supérieur** (87) and **Cru Bourgeois Exceptionnel** (151). The selection was made on the basis of TERROIR, wine-making techniques, quality control, and history. Allegations that the jury members were biased (3 of the 18 jurors were themselves Cru Bourgeois owners) led to a legal decision annulling the original classification of the 78 châteaux whose proprietors disputed the results and calling for the Bordeaux Chamber of Commerce to re-examine their status. The full list is to be revised every 12 years. The Alliance des Crus Bourgeois du Médoc, created in 2003, is charged with guiding and controlling quality and promoting the image of its members.

The crus bourgeois are particularly important in MOULIS and LISTRAC, where they represent 85 and 66 per cent of these appellations' total production. In PAUILLAC and ST-JULIEN, on the other hand, the crus classés are much more important and the crus bourgeois represent just 10 and 15 per cent of total production.

'Non-classes attack nouvelle bourgeoisie', *Harpers* (London, 27 August 2003).

www.crus-bourgeois.com

Cruess, William Vere (1886–1968), biochemist, teacher, and author, was the link between work in wine research and teaching of the pre-PROHIBITION and post-Repeal eras in CALIFORNIA and thus had a central role in the restoration of the California wine industry. Professor of Food Technology at the University

of California at Berkeley, Cruess had done research on FERMENTATION before Prohibition. In the 'dry years' he studied such things as the production of grape syrup and other VINE PRODUCTS. Immediately upon Repeal he undertook to re-establish viticultural and oenological research at the University of California and did so with remarkable speed and efficiency. His *Principles and Practices of Wine Making* (1934) was the first work for the guidance of commercial wine-making published after Repeal.

Cruet, named CRU south east of the vermouth town of CHAMBÉRY whose name may be added to the eastern French appellation Vin de SAVOIE. Cruet is dominated by its CO-OPERATIVE, which makes a range of wines from such grape varieties as Gamay and the local Jacquère and Altesse.

Cruse, the most patrician and numerous of the merchant families who occupied the Quai des Chartrons, playing an important part in the BORDEAUX TRADE in wine. They originated in Schleswig-Holstein before the Prussians took it from the Danes in 1864. Hermann Cruse, born in 1790, came to Bordeaux in 1819 and opened his office in the Chartrons. As Cruse & Hirschfield, the firm did considerable business with north Germany. The family's fortune was made in 1848 and 1849, when Cruse made a vast speculation on the 1847 vintage, described by the BROKERS

Tastet & Lawton as 'very abundant, exquisite but not big'. Since 1848 was the year of revolution in France when Louis-Philippe fled to England, and revolutions broke out in Germany, wine prices slumped. Cruse bought no fewer than 13,650 TONNEAUX from 130 CRUS, nearly all MÉDOC and particularly CRUS BOURGEOIS for the German market.

In 1850, the firm was changed to Cruse et Fils Frères, and two years later Hermann Cruse bought Ch Laujac in the Bas-Médoc, still owned by the family. In 1865, he bought his biggest property, the first in a series of CLASSED GROWTH acquisitions, Ch Pontet-Canet in PAUILLAC. In the same year Edouard Cruse acquired Ch Giscours in MARGAUX, which they resold in 1913. In 1903, Frédéric Cruse inherited Ch Rauzan-Ségla in Margaux from his clergyman father-in-law, and this was sold in 1956. In 1945, Emmanuel Cruse purchased Ch d'Issan in a semi-derelict condition. It took many years to restore this fine, moated 17th-century château and its cellars.

After the beginning of the 1970s, wine prices in Bordeaux rose sharply and by 1973 had reached a point for generic red BORDEAUX AC that made it impossible for merchants to fulfil their contracts without substantial loss. A disreputable broker persuaded the Cruse company, then chiefly run by the younger generation headed by Lionel, son of Emmanuel, to buy TABLE WINE for resale as APPELLATION CONTRÔLÉE Bordeaux. No doubt other firms were involved, and certainly five were subsequently fined but their names were not published (a common practice in French wine fraud cases in order to avoid wholesale discredit to the wine region involved). Cruse was the most prominent merchant of Bordeaux at this time, however, and the authorities were refused entry to their premises in order to make a detailed inspection.

Accordingly, a much-publicized trial took place in 1974. The broker was sent to prison, and the Cruses received a suspended sentence together with a huge fine, substantially reduced on appeal. The firm never recovered from this and in 1979 was sold. In 1975 Ch Pontet-Canet was bought by Guy Tesseron, Emmanuel Cruse's son-in-law and a Cognac merchant who already owned Ch Lafon-Rochet. Ch d'Issan is still owned by the Cruse family and run by Lionel Cruse. The affair broadly coincided with the decline and sale, mostly to foreign concerns, of those houses that had formed the core of the Bordeaux trade, among whom the Cruses were for long the leaders.   E.P.-R.

Brook, S., *Bordeaux—People, Power and Politics* (London, 2001).

Faith, N., *The Winemasters* (3rd edn., London, 2005).

crush, mainly American term for the whole HARVEST season, named after one of the first processes in the winery (CRUSHING) rather than what happens in the vineyard.

crusher-destemmer, common combination of wine-making equipment which carries out the operations of both CRUSHING and DESTEMMING.

crushing (*foulage* in French), wine-making operation of breaking open the grape berry so that the juice is more readily available to the YEAST for FERMENTATION. Modern winery equipment that permits sufficiently thorough crushing has effectively speeded up the onset and completion of fermentation. The additional advantages of this are that the rapid accumulation of alcohol discourages any activity on the part of wild yeast and BACTERIA. The principal result is that an overwhelming proportion of grapes finish as attractive and balanced wines rather than as VINEGAR or unacceptably faulty wines.

Crushing was traditionally done by foot, by treading grapes thinly spread on a crushing floor slanted towards a drain and bounded by low walls to prevent the loss of juice. Foot treading is a relatively inefficient method of crushing, however, and extremely expensive in areas where LABOUR costs are more than minimal—which is why it persisted in the production of PORT in the DOURO.

Modern **crushers** operate on one of two general principles. One type uses intermeshed counter-rotating corrugated rollers spaced far enough apart to pass grape seeds (which exude bitter TANNINS and rancid oils if smashed) but smash anything larger. Such machines gener-

ally incorporate a stem-separating unit (see DESTEMMING) and are therefore known as **crusher-destemmers**, **crusher-stemmers** in the United States, *fouloir-égrappoirs* in France. The other general type also incorporates a destemmer but crushes the clusters by impacting them with paddles on a more rapidly rotating concentric shaft. Some machines are roller destemmers, while others are destemmer rollers, and many modern machines are sufficiently flexible for either the rollers or the destemmers to be left out.

It is to minimize the period over which grapes are crushed that the grapes are increasingly transported from vineyard to winery in shallow containers, ideally no more than 20 to 60 cm (8–23 in) deep, and why pressing stations are increasingly located close to the vineyard.   A.D.W.

crust, name for the SEDIMENT that forms in bottle-aged PORT, consisting of molecules that have become too heavy to stay in solution. **Crusted port** is a style of port created by British shippers in order to provide some of the qualities of vintage port in a shorter time, and therefore at a lower price.

cryoextraction (**cryo** referring to very low temperatures), French term for freeze CONCENTRATION, the controversial wine-making practice of artificially replicating the natural conditions necessary to produce sweet white ICE WINE. Since the late 1980s, the practice has been adopted by some SAUTERNES properties (notably Ch d'YQUEM) and has been used with increasing confidence there for less successful vintages. Freshly picked grapes are held overnight in a special cold room at sub-zero temperatures, -5 or $-6\,°C$ ($21\,°F$) for example, and then pressed immediately. The freezing point of grape must depends on its concentration of sugars, so only the less ripe grapes freeze. PRESSING the grapes straight out of the cold room therefore yields only the juice of the non-frozen, ripest grapes, whose chemical composition remains unchanged. The colder the grapes are kept, the less but richer juice is obtained, and vice versa. The wine producer can therefore manipulate how much wine of what quality is made (unlike ice wine, which is entirely dictated by natural conditions). The technique is particularly useful in wet vintages in which the health and ripeness of individual berries may vary, such as 1987 in Sauternes.

crystals in a bottle of white wine, on the underside of a cork, or on the inside of a vat, are harmless deposits. See TARTRATES for a full explanation.

CSIRO (**Commonwealth Scientific and Industrial Research Organization**), founded in 1926, is one of the world's largest and most diverse research institutions. Its charter covers research into areas of economic, envir-

onmental, and social benefit to AUSTRALIA. Early research focused on solving immediate problems relating to the adaptation of northern hemisphere practices, irrigation, and pest and disease control to the new Australian viticultural frontiers.

After the Second World War, CSIRO's viticultural research broadened to include nematology (see NEMATODES), IRRIGATION, hydrology, and basic VINE PHYSIOLOGY. In the 1960s, there was an even greater shift in emphasis to viticultural research. A new laboratory was opened in Adelaide to accommodate a group of plant (largely vine) physiologists. An early result of research in both centres was the introduction of the complementary management techniques of MINIMAL PRUNING and MECHANICAL HARVESTING.

Around this time, the grapevine germplasm collection was established at Merbein and now contains over 700 varieties of many species. VINE BREEDING and selection has yielded a number of new varieties such as TARRANGO, TAMINGA, TYRIAN, and CIENNA as well as successful table and drying grapes.

In the 1990s, CSIRO extended its research to encompass computer modelling of vine growth, water and nutrient application, and YIELD estimation. GENETIC MODIFICATION is an increasingly important avenue of research in viticulture worldwide, and CSIRO achieved the transformation of Sultana and Chardonnay grapevines in the late 1990s.

New CSIRO wine-grape research initiatives include a focus on flavour and aroma development in berries, understanding the management and genetics of grape flavour and aroma and links to final wine quality.

Results of CSIRO research have given Australian viticulturists access to improved varieties, ROOTSTOCKS resistant to salt and nematodes, and water and nutrient management strategies suited to different environments.   R.E.S.

Cuba. The ubiquitous Chardonnay is said to be grown on this Caribbean island in the tobacco-growing region of Pinar del Rio but most 'Cuban wine' is imported in bulk.

cultivar, term developed by professional botanists to mean a group of plants sharing common characteristics persisting under cultivation that have either been selected or otherwise genetically manipulated by humans. According to the rules of plant taxonomy, cultivar would be a more appropriate term than VARIETY but the term does not have a wide following outside professional botanists and horticulturists, except in South Africa, where it is widely and generally used. It has a major deficiency in that it has no adjectival form, and therefore no counterpart to VARIETAL.

cultivation, the vineyard process of ploughing the soil, normally to kill weeds.

The type of cultivation and its frequency vary from region to region around the world. Initially cultivation was by hand-held hoes. Animals were subsequently used to pull ploughs. For modern vineyards, tractor-mounted discs or tines disturb the topsoil and kill weeds. Cultivation within the vine row requires a special plough that will avoid trunks. Initially these were manually operated to dodge in and out; later, touch or electronic sensors were used to activate a hydraulic mechanism. Because of root and trunk damage, this practice was replaced in many vineyards by the use of undervine HERBICIDES. However, since the last two decades of the 20th century, growers in both the Old and New Worlds wishing to avoid the use of AGROCHEMICALS have returned to undervine cultivation. This has been assisted by the development of hoes which are more efficient and have more sensitive and accurate 'tripping' mechanisms, thus reducing damage to the vines.

Cultivation of the soil to control weed growth is particularly common in regions with irrigation or summer rainfall. A fastidiously cultivated vineyard is still regarded as a sign of good husbandry in some regions, but there is a growing recognition for many vineyards that cultivation damages SOIL STRUCTURE and can lead, for example, to problems of water infiltration. The planting of COVER CROPS or allowing volunteer plants to grow is becoming more common. R.E.S.

Winkler, A. J., *et al.*, *General Viticulture* (2nd edn, Berkeley, Calif., 1974).

currants, small, dark DRYING GRAPES made from the vine variety called **Zante Currant** (in Australia) or Black Corinth (in California). This dark-skinned variety originated in Greece, which is where most of the world's currants are produced, and takes its name from a corruption of the word Corinth. The bunches are long and cylindrical, and the berries very small and black with no seeds. FRUIT SET is poor without CINCTURING or the use of GROWTH REGULATORS. It is also occasionally used for wine-making in Australia, where a variant on it, CARINA, was bred in the 1960s. R.E.S.

Currency Creek, a cool, maritime region in the Fleurieu Zone of SOUTH AUSTRALIA producing BORDEAUX BLENDS (white and red), plus Shiraz. All are elegant. Three producers.

custom crush facility, American term for a winery specializing in vinifying grapes on behalf of many different vine-growers, typically those without their own wine-making equipment. The various wines are kept separate and marketed by the growers under their own labels. Such operations have played an important part in establishing ambitious new wine producers, as in CALIFORNIA and Long Island in NEW YORK, and indeed whole new wine

regions such as Marlborough and Central Otago in NEW ZEALAND, where new or small-scale growers can ill afford to build their own wineries.

Custoza, Bianco di, straightforward dry white wine produced in the VENETO region of north east Italy in a wide stretch of territory extending south westward from the city of Verona to the BARDOLINO zone on the shores of Lake Garda and the countryside immediately to the south of the lake. More than 1,400 ha/3,500 acres produce over 114,000 hl/3.0 million gal of wine each year. The substantial presence of TREBBIANO Toscano grapes (constituting 20 to 45 per cent of the blend), along with GARGANEGA (20 to 40 per cent), TOCAI Friuliano (five to 30 per cent) and a variety of other grapes (Riesling Italico or WELSCHRIESLING, PINOT BLANC, CHARDONNAY, MALVASIA Toscana), tends to yield a rather colourless, neutral wine on the fertile soils of this zone. Yields are high, and production is largely controlled by the two CO-OPERATIVES, one in Custoza, the other in Castelnuovo. The wine has historically fetched a higher price than basic Soave, but in recent years it has struggled to achieve this premium. D.T.

cut cane, Australian name for the viticultural technique designed to increase the sugar concentration in almost-ripe grapes to produce sweet wines. By cutting the canes almost at the time of HARVEST, water supply to the fruit is halted, and so the berries start to shrivel (as in the production of DRIED GRAPE WINES). Sugar concentration is elevated as water is lost through the berry skin and ACIDITY may also be increased. The technique, resulting in grapes known as PASSERILLÉS in French, has also been used to avert rain spoilage of DRYING GRAPES. R.E.S.

cuttings, cut lengths of canes used for vine PROPAGATION. Cuttings are the basis of propagation for commercial grape production, whether as own-rooted plants (see ROOTLINGS), or as scion varieties for GRAFTING on to ROOTSTOCK. Both methods are representative of asexual or vegetative propagation and the progeny are considered as CLONES of the source vines. In commerce, cuttings are cut from dormant vines in lengths of 30 to 45 cm (12–18 in). Once made, the cuttings are kept moist and planted in a nursery in spring for roots to form at the base, and a shoot to grow from the top bud. The plant is now called a rootling. It is lifted from the nursery and planted in its vineyard position the following year. B.G.C.

cutworms, the larvae of several species of moths, are one of the most serious pests of all sorts of crops worldwide. They hide in the soil or under the vine's bark during the day and emerge to feed and cause damage at night. Young vines are particularly prone to damage. When cultural practices, natural enemies, and

climatic factors do not keep cutworms to tolerable levels, there are highly effective chemical agents which can prevent major losses. DDT was once used, but there are now effective contact insecticides. M.J.E.

cuve is French for a vat or tank. Thus, a **cuverie** is the vat hall, typically where fermentation takes place. *Cuves* may be made of any material: wood, concrete, or, most likely, stainless steel.

cuve close, French for sealed tank, and a name for a bulk sparkling wine-making process (sometimes called Charmat) which involves provoking a second fermentation in wine stored in a pressure tank. For more details, see SPARKLING WINE-MAKING.

cuvée, French wine term derived from CUVE, with many different meanings in different contexts. In general terms it can be used to mean any containerful, or even any lot, of wine and therefore wine labels often carry relatively meaningless descriptions incorporating the word *cuvée*. **Tête de cuvée,** on the other hand, is occasionally used for the top bottling of a French wine producer, particularly in Sauternes.

In CHAMPAGNE and other environments in which traditional method sparkling wines are made, *cuvée* is a name for the first and best juice to flow from the press (see SPARKLING WINE-MAKING). The blend of base wines assembled for second fermentation in bottle is also known as the *cuvée*. Thus the term is often used in many champagne and sparkling wine names.

Elsewhere, particularly in German-speaking wine regions oddly enough, *cuvée* may be used to describe any ambitious blend, particularly of different vine varieties.

Cyprus, eastern Mediterranean island less than 100 km/60 miles from Syria to the east and Turkey to the north. The medieval Cyprus wine industry was commercially the most important in the Middle East, but for most of the 20th century, Cyprus wine languished in terms of quality. The 1990s saw investment leading to an improvement in production techniques and resulting wines, however.

History
Because of its position in the eastern Mediterranean, closer to the Middle East than to GREECE, Cyprus has changed hands many times. In antiquity, domination by various foreign powers alternated with brief periods of independence, and in 58 BC Cyprus became part of the Roman province of Cilicia in Asia Minor. Strabo (*Geography*, 7 BC) and PLINY mention the wine of Cyprus approvingly but it was not particularly famous. In AD 668 Cyprus was occupied by Arabs; when they were finally expelled in 965 Cyprus became an advance base of the Greek navy.

In 1191, in the course of the Third CRUSADE, Richard I, king of England, conquered Cyprus and sold it to the Templars, who soon gave it back to him, whereupon he presented it to the rejected king of Jerusalem, Guy de Lusignan. Guy de Lusignan imposed a feudal system on Cyprus and governed the island as a separate kingdom, which it remained until it became a colony of the then powerful VENICE in 1489.

The Crusaders and Venetian expansionism made the island part of the Latin west, which soon became fond of its wines. The earliest record of Cyprus wine being drunk in the west is dated 1178 when Count Baldwin of Guines offered it to the archbishop of Rheims. The wine is clearly a rare luxury, designed to impress an ecclesiastical magnate. In the next century it became more widely available. The Old French poem *La Bataille des vins* (see MEDIEVAL LITERATURE) awards the palm to *chypre*, Cyprus wine, because it is stronger and sweeter than any wine that is to be had in western Europe (FORTIFICATION and MUTAGE were as yet unknown). We do not know when the wines of Cyprus first reached the English market, but in the 13th and 14th centuries they, along with other sweet wines from the east and from Italy (see ENGLAND), fetched higher prices than the wines of GASCONY and LA ROCHELLE. The Venetians shipped them from Cyprus to Venice in their galleys, and from Venice they distributed them all over Europe.

A modern Cyprus wine, COMMANDARIA, preserves in its name a piece of crusading history. When the fall of Acre, in 1281, ended the Latin Christian presence in Palestine and Syria, the Knights Hospitallers moved their headquarters from Acre to Cyprus and thence to Rhodes. Like all religious orders, the Knights Hospitallers (or Knights of St John) acquired land on a large scale and grew wine. Their organization was strictly hierarchical, into priorates, then bailiwicks, and lastly commanderies. A commandery was a manor or group of manors under the authority of a commendator. Each commandery had its vineyard or vineyards: hence the name of the modern dessert wine from Cyprus. H.M.W.

Dion, R., *Histoire de la vigne et du vin en France* (Paris, 1959).

Simon, A. L., *The History of the Wine Trade in England*, 3 vols. (London, 1906–9).

Modern history

Ottoman rule (1571–1878) brought a steep decline in wine production, and in the importance of the wine industry, which remained in an underdeveloped state until the middle of the 19th century, the first of the modern wineries, Haggipavlu, not being founded until 1844. British administration of the island (1878–1960) saw a further revitalization of the industry, with Cyprus 'sherry', as this fortified wine was then allowed to call itself, becoming an important product for the first time. The invasion of northern Cyprus by Turkey in 1974, and subsequent political problems, hardly affected the wine industry, concentrated in the southern part of the island. Today, wine continues to play an important role in the agricultural economy of the Greek Cypriot, southern Republic of Cyprus.

Climate and geography

Commercial wine-growing is confined to the southern foothills and slopes of the Troodos mountain range at altitudes varying from 250 m to 1,500 m (800–4,900 ft) above sea level. The vineyard area is divided into six regions: Pitsilia (the highest), Marathasa, Commandaria, Troodhos South, Troodhos East, and Troodhos North. Three of the regions contain designated subregions: Madhari in the region of Pitsilia; Afames and Laona in Troodhos South; and Ambelitis, Vouni tis Panayias, and Laona Kathikas all within Troodhos East. Pitsilia and the northern (higher altitude) half of Commanderia have igneous soil and subsoil. Elsewhere soils are of sedimentary LIMESTONE with a particularly high free lime content.

The climate is typically MEDITERRANEAN: mild winters and hot summers with precipitation confined to the winter months. Rainfall is low: 500 mm/19 in per annum is the mean for the lower-altitude vineyards and 900 mm/35 in for the higher. Drip IRRIGATION is permitted.

The great variation in temperatures between low- and high-ALTITUDE vineyards (resulting in mean minimum summer temperatures varying from 9 to 20 °C/48 to 68 °F) results in one of the most extended vintage periods in the world. Picking usually starts in mid July and continues until early November. Climatic hazards are restricted to HAIL and, in higher-altitude vineyards, spring and autumn FROST. The lack of humidity means that DOWNY MILDEW is unknown but growers regularly spray against POWDERY MILDEW. BOTRYTIS is found only in grape bunches that have previously been attacked by eudemis MOTHS or other INSECTS. Since PHYLLOXERA has never reached Cyprus, vines are ungrafted. Almost all vines are BUSH trained, the exceptions being non-indigenous varieties where bud fertility near the trunk is poor, necessitating long fruiting canes supported by TRELLISING systems.

Vine varieties

The vast majority, almost three-quarters, of the Cyprus vineyard area is planted with the indigenous Mavro (black) grape variety. Only when cultivated at altitudes above 1,000 m/3,300 ft, where yields can be as low as 25 hl/ha (1.4 tons/acre), such as Laona, is Mavro capable of producing wine of quality and character. Elsewhere it gives high yields of very large grapes; 200 hl/ha (11 tons/acre) is by no means unknown. With its high juice to skin ratio, Mavro has a tendency to give pale, unattractive colours when vinified as a red wine. To counteract this problem, winemakers often remove up to 40 per cent of the juice prior to fermentation. The juice removed has commonly been used for 'Cyprus fortified wine' (as it must be labelled now that the Jerezanos have asserted their unique right to the name SHERRY), whilst the remaining pulp has a much better juice to skin ratio for the production of red table wines. Now that the FORTIFIED WINE trade is all but dead, much of the island's Mavro is turned into GRAPE CONCENTRATE, fruit juice, distillation base or bulk base for sangria, glüh-wein, and vermouth.

At its best, Mavro gives wine with a cherry or blackcurrant candy character when young, developing vegetal characteristics with three to five years' age. The wine rarely loses its faint iodine background flavour and is often high in alcohol.

The second most planted wine grape is the indigenous white grape Xynisteri, which, if picked before overripe and carefully vinified, has the ability to produce aromatic wines with a good balance of sugar, alcohol, and acids, and a tendency towards earthiness of flavour. In the better-quality wines, Xynisteri may be supplemented by PALOMINO—a variety imported with a view to improving Cyprus fortified wine—MALVASIA Grossa, and SULTANINA.

Fear of phylloxera has made the island's authorities particularly cautious about the introduction of non-indigenous grape varieties and heavy QUARANTINE regulations have been enforced, even if only in the southern part of the island. It was as recently as 1958 that the Ministry of Agriculture first imported new varieties for experimental purposes. Over the following ten years a series of trials was conducted to discover the varieties best suited to Cypriot conditions. In 1964, a further programme of experiments began aimed at finding the best MESOCLIMATE for each of the new varieties. The trials were completed in 1990 and, of imported varieties, CARIGNAN and GRENACHE have been most widely planted, with some CABERNET SAUVIGNON as well as some surprisingly successful RIESLING, some WELSCHRIESLING, and a small amount of CHARDONNAY also grown.

A renewed interest in the island's less planted indigenous varieties has developed, thanks to research conducted by the French ampelographer GALET at the invitation of one large Cypriot wine producer. Many of these traditional varieties have much greater quality potential than Mavro, but were less popular with growers because of cultivation difficulties. Promara can produce good-quality white wine when grown at high altitudes, Opthalmo produces red wines with better acidity than Mavro, but the native vine with perhaps the greatest potential for quality is the red Maratheftico—although it is unpopular with growers because of its sensitivity to powdery mildew. The vine is also difficult to grow commercially since it is one of the wine world's few non-hermaphrodite vines, and must be planted in vineyards of mixed varieties to ensure good POLLINATION. It is known as Pambakina or Pambakada in the Pitsilia region. Lefkada, with small bunches, producing deeply-coloured, very well-structured reds has considerable potential. Cabernet Sauvignon, Cabernet Franc, Syrah, Mourvèdre, Carignan, and Chardonnay were well established by the mid 2000s and commanded much higher grape PRICES than Mavro and Xynisteri.

With the exception of a very few estates owned by the commercial wineries or the Ministry of Agriculture, Cyprus vineyards are divided into thousands of smallholdings. Typically, the land is worked by the older generation. Children and grandchildren may be employed in the local tourist industry but are more likely to have moved to the towns to work in Cyprus's service and manufacturing industries, thus creating rural depopulation serious enough to be a significant social problem.

Wine-making

Until the late 1980s, almost all Cypriot wine was made in large wineries near the docks of Limassol or Paphos, but at considerable distance from the vineyards. Equipment was basic. In the 1990s, however, there was a marked change in the island's wineries. The large wineries have invested in much-improved equipment while some small, very well-equipped regional wineries have been built in the vineyard areas. The industry also started to employ foreign consultant winemakers, notably Australians, who have experience in making fresh, fruity wines in hot climates (see FLYING WINEMAKERS).

Organization of trade

Almost all Cypriot wine has been made by four large firms—SODAP, KEO, ETKO, and Loel. These firms not only own the large wineries of Limassol and Paphos but have also built a number of the regional wineries. SODAP is a CO-OPERATIVE while the others are public companies, with a substantial proportion of their shareholding owned by vine-growers. However, by the mid 2000s, around 15 per cent of Cypriot wine was made in more than 40 private wineries of varying sizes and this proportion was slowly growing.

The four large firms rely on exports for the majority of their sales since per capita wine consumption in Cyprus is extremely small. Beer, ouzo, and brandy are the principal alcoholic beverages drunk by Cypriots.

After the Second World War, the majority of the island's wine exports fell into four categories, tellingly reflecting the needs of different countries: large volumes of very basic wine for the eastern bloc countries; wine intended for industrial uses such as VERMOUTH, SANGRÍA, or, in German-speaking countries, commercially prepared GLÜHWEIN; grape concentrate

sent chiefly in the early 1990s to Japan, central and eastern Europe, and the United Kingdom where it was reconstituted and made into the ersatz BRITISH WINE; and Cyprus fortified wine.

The majority of Cyprus fortified wine is sweet, undistinguished wine, made by MUTAGE and matured in casks stored outside. The principal market for Cyprus fortified wine is the United Kingdom.

Healthy international demand for basic wine and grape products between the end of the Second World War and the collapse of the eastern bloc left the wine industry with little incentive to exploit the island's potential for quality. At harvest most grapes were transported in large, open lorries. Because picking took place in the morning, the movement of the grapes would start in the afternoon, at the hottest time of the day. Further problems resulted from the rural LABOUR shortage, which could mean that it took two days or more to fill one of the lorries, which would be parked in the open air, exposed to sun and heat. The small size of holdings, and the near universal use of bush training, make MECHANICAL HARVESTING almost impossible.

The early 1990s brought grave problems to the Cypriot wine industry. The economic difficulties affecting the eastern bloc after the collapse of communism (see GORBACHEV) drastically shrunk that market. Demand for Cyprus fortified wine was in steady decline, as was demand for fortified British wine, in which Cypriot grape concentrate had been such a significant ingredient. The island was also finding it increasingly difficult to compete on price with basic wine from Bulgaria, Chile, South Africa, and Languedoc-Roussillon.

The cost of supporting the ailing wine industry became an increasingly embarrassing problem for the Cypriot government. In 1992, a four-point plan to improve vine varieties and wine-making practices and to pull up vineyards in least favoured sites was issued by the government, and despite the scheme's cost, and the opposition of certain vine-growers, the area under vine has been reduced, to 18,000 ha in the early 2000s from 31,000 in the late 1980s, and the proportion of better-quality vine varieties, although still small, is increasing. The ambitious plan also incorporated the establishment of 'designation of origin' legislation, with Commandaria the first wine to be granted full legal protection in 1993.

In the mid 2000s, the problems were being brought to a head by imminent entry into the EU, which makes significant changes to how growers can be subsidized. Without subsidies, growing Mavro simply is not viable. The Cypriots are also updating their APPELLATION laws to bring them into line with the French model, even if what constitutes benchmark qualities and styles is not fully understood, and the laws themselves could be too restrictive to maximize the island's potential.

A further major decline in vineyard area looked highly likely.

See also COMMANDARIA. G.J.L. & A.H.M.

cytokinins, natural HORMONES in vines produced in the root tips and affecting the growth of other parts of the plant. Cytokinins favour cell multiplication and affect growth and development of shoots and INFLORESCENCES. Fewer cytokinins are produced in dry soils, and also in cold and wet soils, and this appears to be critical for BUDBREAK and early shoot growth.

Czech Republic, better known for its BEER, split from SLOVAKIA, the eastern part of what was Czechoslovakia, in the early 1990s. It took less than a third of the productive vineyard area, just over 40 per cent of wine production, and around two-thirds of the wine consumption of the original Czechoslovakia. Grapes, juice, and wine make their way over the border from Slovakia to satisfy this thirst, along with imports from other countries, notably HUNGARY and, more recently, MOLDOVA, AUSTRIA, MACEDONIA, and New World countries, mainly in BULK. In preparation for EU membership, in 1995 the Czech Republic passed wine laws modelled on the GERMAN WINE LAW, amending them in 2000 and 2004.

The republic and its vineyards divide into two distinct regions: the tiny, touristy vineyards of BOHEMIA such as at Karlštejn castle near Prague or on the banks of the river Labe (Germany's Elbe) in the north; and, quantitatively much more important, MORAVIA to the south along the Austrian and Slovakian borders.

The history, viticultural, and wine-making traditions of Bohemia, Moravia, and the wine regions of Slovakia are still marked by the communist era and the following observations apply to all of them.

The vast majority of vineyards were rationalized under the communist regime. Between 1950 and 1990, country dwellers were allowed 0.1 ha of private holdings per adult but the rest of the agricultural land was turned into farms, often mixed, sometimes with more than 1,000 ha/2,500 acres planted with long rows of vines that could easily be adapted to mechanical cultivation. The state-owned wineries, which made more than 80 per cent of Czecho-slovakian wine, were allocated farms to buy from. Both Moravia and Slovakia had a state winery office which consolidated and ran the major CO-OPERATIVES in each region . Within these regions, following the standard eastern European model, were several centralized bottling plants, each of which had its own wine production as well as satellite vinification centres. Consolidation among the big players is now underway, however, with the two largest companies Bohemia Sekt and Soare Sekt (both German-owned) leading the way in buying up their weaker competitors.

Czech Republic and Slovakia

Wine-growing regions

0   100 km

POLAND

LITOMĚŘICE   ●Mělník
            MĚLNÍK
        ●Prague

B O H E M I A

C Z E C H   R E P U B L I C

M O R A V I A
        Brno● VELKÉ
              PAVLOVICE
    ZNOJMO   SLOVÁCKO

GERMANY   MIKULOV   SKALIČA

                              SMALL
                              CARPATHIANS

        Danube
            Vienna●   ●Bratislava

A U S T R I A   SOUTHERN SLOVAKIA

                NITRA

S L O V A K I A   Košice●   EASTERN
                              SLOVAKIA

            CENTRAL SLOVAKIA   R
                                    U
                          TOKAJ   S
                                    S
                                    I
                                    A

H U N G A R Y

About two-fifths of the vineyards lie on gentle slopes, usually topped by woodland, while the rest are on undulating plains which fall away to the flatter Danube basin. The lower reaches tend towards clay and sand but the major influences on these vineyards are the relatively low ALTITUDE (between 100 and 250 m (330–820 ft) above sea level) and the CONTINENTAL CLIMATE. Rainfall here is relatively low, on average between a half and two-thirds of the annual rainfall in French vineyards on an equivalent latitude (Burgundy and Alsace).

Because of their position north of the Danube, most of the slopes face between south west and south east and are very protected by higher land in the north. The vines are trained like those of Germany and Austria. A problem here can be harvesting so late, sometimes as late as the end of November, that the crop gets frostbite.

Traditionally the most prized grape varieties were Cabernet Sauvignon, Pinot Noir, Sauvignon, Gewürztraminer (often known as Traminer or Tramin), (Rhine) Riesling, and Pinots Blanc and Gris but most are not widely planted as they did not reward Czechoslovakia's rather careless viticultural practices with generous yields. Apart from Ryzlink Rýnský (RIESLING) and Rulandské Bílé (PINOT BLANC), Ryzlink Vlašský (WELSCHRIESLING), MÜLLER-THURGAU, Veltlínské Zelené (GRÜNER VELTLINER), and Sylvánské Zelené (SILVANER) are the major white wine varieties, together with the Muscat-scented IRSAY OLIVER and the ultra-fashionable Chardonnay, whose international name survives intact. Modrý Portugal (BLAUER PORTUGIESER), Frankovka (BLAUFRÄNKISCH) and Svatovavřinecké (ST-LAURENT), during the previous regime referred to simply as Vavřinecké without reference to the saint, and ZWEIGELTREBE are the principal red wine varieties, which probably total no more than 35 per cent of the two nations' vineyard. Pinot Noir has a long and successful history in the Czech lands, and nowadays most winemakers feel obliged to supply the market with Cabernet Sauvignon and Merlot, often topped up with the legal maximum imported from countries such as Moldova to add body. Other popular varieties among whites include Frühroter Veltliner, Neuburger, Moravian Muscat (a cross between Muscat Ottonel and Prachttraube), and Kerner and the dark-skinned varieties André, Alibernet, Blauburger, Cabernet Moravia, Dornfelder, Neronet, and a host of newly developed CROSSINGS resistant to frost and fungal diseases, such as Agni, Bianca, Laurot, Lena, and those developed by the venerable professor Vilém Kraus and his disciples, such as Kofranka, Merlan, and Tintet.

Grape ripeness is at a premium here and is measured in °CNM (Czechoslovak normalized must weight measurement) similar to the KMW scale although 1 °CNM denotes 1 kg of sugar per 100 l of grape must, as opposed to 1 °KMW meaning 1 kg of sugar in 100 kg of must.

In the years leading up to EU membership, there was considerable investment in both planting and winery modernization, with cement tanks giving way to stainless steel and the introduction of BARREL MATURATION. Generous subsidies were on offer from the newly established Wine Fund for the planting of new vineyards that had to be completed before accession in May 2004. Total vineyard area grew from 11,000 ha/ 27,000 acres in 1998 to 18,666 ha/46,665 acres in 2004.

CHAPTALIZATION is allowed and frequently practised. MALOLACTIC FERMENTATION, LEES CONTACT, MICRO-OXYGENATION, TEMPERATURE CONTROL, CRYOEXTRACTION, REVERSE OSMOSIS, and other technological innovations are now well understood and exploited by all but the greatest dinosaurs. Unfortunately misplaced nationalism can get in the way of producing wines to compete with, say, the more adventurous Austrians. A long-held obsession with 'archiving' (cellaring) has also led to a culture of storing and drinking wines that were well over the hill after their first six months in bottle. And the wine laws, with their emphasis on must weight levels at harvest, do not help, having led many producers to pick far too late in the hope of achieving a superior special-attributes status with the consequent elevated price tags on 50cl or even 20cl bottles. Nevertheless a handful of small producers such as Dobra Vinice, Valihrach, Springer, and Reisten make consistently good wines that justify such prices as well as standing up to increasingly competitively priced imports. Some make excellent ICE WINE and STRAW WINE.

A.H.M. & H.K.B.

DAC, Districtus Austria Controllatus, a relatively recent appellation of origin concept in AUSTRIA in which a wine's origin is privileged over its grape variety, similar to AC (France). DAC wines are based on QUALITÄTSWEIN but express a typical regional style and flavour profile. The label shows only the DAC regional name and not the variety unless more than one variety is allowed. The Weinviertel was the first DAC granted, in 2003, for a typical, peppery Grüner Veltliner. The introduction of the DAC system in Austrian wine growing regions is preceded by the establishment of regional committees to determine marketing and production strategies. The goal is to establish clearly the profile of the wine growing region and its wines. There are currently five DACs (Weinviertel, Mittelburgenland, Traisental, Kremstal, Kamptal) with two more on the way.   R.Ho.

Dão, DOC wine region in north central PORTUGAL with the reputation of producing some of the country's best red wines (see map under PORTUGAL). There is no doubt that the region has great potential. Locked in on three sides by granite mountains and sheltered from the Atlantic, Dão benefits from long, warm summers and abundant winter rainfall. The sandy soils are well drained and the vineyards are stocked with a wealth of indigenous grape varieties. Over much of the last 50 years, however, the wines have rarely lived up to expectations.

Dão became a REGIÃO DEMARCADA in 1908 but since the 1940s it has suffered from heavy-handed government intervention. In a laudable attempt to impose some form of organization on the highly fragmented, largely subsistence economy in the north of Portugal, the Salazar government introduced a programme of co-operativization. Ten CO-OPERATIVES were built in Dão between 1954 and 1971 to much the same design. To make the programme work, the authorities passed legislation giving co-operatives the exclusive right to buy grapes. Private firms were effectively restricted to purchasing ready-made wine. The system served Dão badly. Wines became ever more standardized and, as co-operatives were poorly equipped and paid scant attention to HYGIENE, standards fell. This monopolistic legislation was felt to be incompatible with Portugal's membership of the EUROPEAN UNION and the law institutionalizing Dão's co-operatives was overturned in 1989. Some enterprising initiatives followed, led by SOGRAPE, who have built a huge new winery in the heart of the region. A number of promising single estates are also helping to revive the fortunes of one of Portugal's best-known wine regions.

About 80 per cent of Dão wines are red, with TOURIGA NACIONAL, TINTA RORIZ, JAEN, and ALFROCHEIRO PRETO having been indentified as the region's leading varieties. In theory, Touriga Nacional, one of the main PORT grapes which probably originated in Dão, should account for at least 20 per cent of

any blend but in reality usually accounts for much less. Although non-VINIFERA varieties have now largely been weeded out, there are still large quantities of such relatively inferior grapes as Bastardo, Tinta Pinheira, and Baga. Red Dão tends to be firm and tannic and, in the past, many wines suffered from excessively prolonged MACERATION with the stalks and protracted ageing in old casks or cement tanks. The new generation of producers is more meticulous and some have invested in new French and Portuguese OAK.

At one time white wines also suffered from being aged for too long, often tasting flat and OXIDIZED, but by the late 1990s, younger, fresher wines were being produced by modern, private wineries. ENCRUZADO, the best grape for white Dão, produces some crisp, fragrant wines but all too often it is blended with other less successful varieties such as Malvasia Fina and Bical, known here as Borrado das Moscas ('fly droppings').

In line with Portugal's other Regiões Demarcadas (RD), Dão became a Denominacão de Origem Controlada (DOC) in 1990.   R.J.M.

Mayson. R., *The Wines and Vineyards of Portugal* (London, 2003).

DAP, see DIAMMONIUM PHOSPHATE.

Davis, the usual abbreviation in the wine world for the influential wine-related faculties of the University of California at Davis, a small city 70 miles north east of San Francisco in California's Central valley. The city came to be known throughout the world as a centre for research and instruction in all aspects of agriculture because it was the home of the University Farm established in 1906.

Until the late 19th century, grape-growing and wine-making in California had been relatively haphazard, with numerous problems generally unrecognized. An act of state legislature in 1880 directed the nascent University of California to start research and instruction in VITICULTURE and OENOLOGY. The fact that Berkeley, the original site of the university, was too cold and foggy for grape-growing encouraged the establishment of the farm in the warm, inland climate of Davis.

The then Professor of Agriculture, Eugene Hilgard, soon recognized that grafting VINIFERA scions on to hybrid ROOTSTOCKS was the only practical solution to the world's PHYLLOXERA epidemic. He also recognized the importance of matching vine variety to soil and climate for fine wine production. Hilgard established early co-operation between ACADEME and practitioners.

PROHIBITION brought a temporary hiatus in Davis's wine-related activities. The Second World War subsequently closed the campus, effectively postponing the flowering of a newly organized research and teaching group until the late 1940s.

This powerful group included the late Albert J. WINKLER, famous for his DEGREE DAY/heat summation method of CLIMATE CLASSIFICATION; Harold P. Olmo, breeder of NEW VARIETIES; and well known oenologist Maynard A. AMERINE. The department was also responsible for the development of assays now routinely employed in wineries internationally. This work continues today.

Current research efforts are dedicated to understanding the impact of viticultural practices such as REGULATED DEFICIT IRRIGATION, YIELD, clonal variation, and SITE SELECTION on wine composition and perceived quality. In addition, modern molecular and genetic technologies are being developed and applied to the improvement of both scion and rootstock varieties with the aim of producing vines less susceptible to pests and diseases and increasing understanding of grape berry maturation and flavour and aroma development. Genomics technologies are being applied to further understanding of the yeast and bacterial fermentations of wine and to profile the presence and persistence of both wild and spoilage flora. The department is also playing an important role in defining the bioactive compounds of wines responsible for the health benefits of moderate consumption (see HEALTH). Sophisticated tools for the analysis of wine aroma, flavour, and ageability are also being pioneered and applied to the investigation of wine composition. Consumer preference profiling is being exploited to better understand the phenomenon of preference. Work continues on vine variety identification using DNA PROFILING. The Davis campus also houses the FOUNDATION PLANT SERVICES.

Davis continues to be the principal centre for teaching viticulture and enology in the Americas, and has trained numerous winemakers from around the world. It has become synonymous with a scientific approach to wine production and the understanding of wine quality as opposed to one informed solely by TRADITION and observation.   L.F.B.

day–night temperature difference, see TEMPERATURE VARIABILITY.

deacidification, wine-making process of decreasing the excessive ACIDITY of grape juice or wine made in cold wine regions or, in particularly cool years, in temperate wine regions. A number of techniques for making excessively acid wines more palatable have been developed and are usually strictly governed by local regulations.

Because poor summers result in low SUGARS as well as high ACIDS, the most common permitted correction is adding water to dilute the acidity (see HUMIDIFICATION) and, simultaneously, enough sugar to give a balanced wine after fermentation, effectively a combination of dilution and ENRICHMENT. MALOLACTIC FERMENTATION is another way of lowering acidity,

but it is difficult to persuade LACTIC ACID BACTERIA to work in very acid conditions.

Winemakers concerned about quality and cost generally prefer to rely on biological methods for reducing acidity but there are other forms of deacidification which rely on chemical processes, notably adding chemicals to MUST or wine that will precipitate significant amounts of acidity as insoluble solids that can be filtered or settle out. Calcium carbonate, or chalk, is the most satisfactory of these, since its addition results in insoluble calcium TARTRATES and the liberation of harmless CARBON DIOXIDE. In some very cool regions, where grapes have higher malic acid levels, the addition of calcium tartrate can lead to an imbalance in the proportion of malic to tartaric acid. Double salt deacidification resolves this by reducing the acidity in the juice and yet maintaining similar proportions of tartaric to malic acid. However, it is expensive and its use is generally limited to England, parts of Germany, and the eastern US.

Deacidifications are most effective after fermentation, partly because alcohol decreases the solubility of cream of tartar, thereby reducing some of the must acidity, and fermentation itself produces a better mix of flavour by-products in the more acid solution.

Deacidification is not the commonplace procedure that ACIDIFICATION is in warmer regions. It is practised in northern Germany, Luxembourg, the United Kingdom, Canada, New York state, Tasmania, and New Zealand's South Island in certain years.   A.D.W. & B.W.Z.

dead arm or **dying arm**, common names for several fungal diseases in vine wood that cause cankers and dieback. See EUTYPA DIEBACK, PHOMOPSIS, and BLACK DEAD ARM.

dead fruit. See SURMATURITÉ.

dealcoholized wine became popular as wine drinkers searched for a drink that tastes like wine but has none of the negative implications for HEALTH or subsequent activity such as driving. Such wines also have fewer calories than regular wine, fewer than 150 calories per bottle in many cases. They may broadly be divided into 'no-alcohol wines', with an ALCOHOLIC STRENGTH of less than 1 or at the most 2 per cent, and 'low-alcohol wines' with between 2 and 5.5 per cent alcohol.

Wine may be dealcoholized in several ways, all of which involve removing ALCOHOL from normally fermented wine, using either thermal or membrane techniques, yet retaining all other components. (See also REDUCED-ALCOHOL WINES, which are low-alcohol wines made by either dilution or partial fermentation.)

One method, particularly common in Germany, is a process of vacuum distillation, whereby wine, at extremely low pressures at normal room temperatures, is separated into

various fractions in a tall column. Under vacuum conditions the boiling point of alcohol is reduced and it literally 'boils' away at room temperature. The non-volatile wine compounds such as MINERALS, ACIDS, PHENOLICS, SUGARS, and VITAMINS are fully preserved. By avoiding high temperatures, there is no risk of 'cooked' flavours.

Another similar method, pioneered in France by UCCOAR, the large co-operative based in the Côtes de la MALEPÈRE region, working in conjunction with researchers at the local INRA station, and launched in 1988, involves evaporation under vacuum at low temperatures and under INERT GAS. The resulting wine has the colour and most of the taste characteristics of the original wine, but an alcoholic strength of less than 0.5 per cent.

REVERSE OSMOSIS can also be used, using osmotic pressure to separate, through an impermeable membrane, a solution of low concentration from one of higher concentration.

INRA at Narbonne have also developed another method of dealcoholizing wine called pervaporation. It depends on dense silicone membranes which at about 30 °C are particularly efficient at separating alcohol from water.

The SPINNING CONE COLUMN is being used increasingly, particularly in New World winemaking countries, as an alternative to vacuum distillation for the production of dealcoholized wines.

Taking the alcohol out of wine leaves it much less stable, so even higher standards of HYGIENE and STERILE BOTTLING conditions are necessary.

All of these methods of removing alcohol to produce no-alcohol or low-alcohol wines are expensive, however, relative to the methods of simply reducing alcohol.

By the mid 1990s, more than a dozen companies in France, Germany, Australia, and the United States were producing dealcoholized wine.

Escudier, J.-L., 'Les Nouveaux Produits de la Vigne', *Bulletin de l'OIV*, May–June (1993).

Debina, the sprightly white grape variety that is responsible for the lightly sparkling white wines of Zitsa in Epirus high in north west GREECE near the Albanian border. It seems likely that the variety is also cultivated in Albania. At these altitudes acidity levels remain high, and a tendency to OXIDATION has largely been checked by improved vinification methods.

débourbage, French term for SETTLING out solids from must or wine.

decanters, vessels, usually glass and stoppered, into which wine is poured during DECANTING.

The decanter as we know it today has changed form very little in the last 250 years, in that it is a handleless clear glass bottle with a

decanter jug *c.*1680   cruciform *c.*1720   shaft and globe *c.*1730-40   mallet *c.*1750

shoulder *c.*1760   taper *c.*1780   indian club *c.*1790   classic *c.*1810   pillar cut *c.*1825

Decanters

capacity of about 1 l and, normally, a stopper. The shape and the decoration have changed in line with fashion and as technology has allowed. Since the capacity is noticeably more than that of a standard 75-cl/27-fl oz bottle, it allows the wine to 'breathe' and develop (see AERATION).

History

The decanter's origins lie with the Roman serving bottle, which was typically square. Some Roman glass bottles may have been used for serving wine, but the Romans also used silver. After the collapse of the Roman empire, glass production went into a sharp decline until the revival of the glass trade in Renaissance Italy. By the 16th century, Venice had emerged as the principal centre of glass-making.

While the glass trade was expanding, other developments were afoot. Popular throughout northern Europe during the 16th and early 17th centuries were bulbous earthenware jugs with flat, small handles and short, narrow necks.

A more sophisticated finish, sometimes employed, was a saltglaze which produced a textured surface not unlike an orange peel. In addition, Chinese porcelain jugs were being imported for the most sophisticated of tastes, while some preferred their wine served in carved rock crystal. Whether the jug was saltglaze, tigerware, porcelain, or crystal, all the better-quality pieces were given silver or silvergilt mounts. For the grandest, gold was used.

Throughout the medieval period and well beyond, pouring vessels were also made in bronze and silver, but these media often gave way to glass once a centre of production became established in a country. The new glass serving vessels represented the latest in fashion and technology and were quickly adopted by society. For almost a century, England, which was an important wine market, relied on imports until George Ravenscroft started producing glass using lead oxide as a flux in the 1670s. This, together with his flint glass, allowed the production of usable jugs and glasses. His developments gave Britain a lead that lasted for about 100 years.

Contemporary with the jug, decanters were also made which took the same form as bottles but with a much greater sophistication of material, decoration, and workmanship.

With the exception of very early decanter jugs, decanters first acquired stoppers in the 1730s.

In the early 19th century, the introduction of steam-driven cutting tools produced a fashion for profusely cut decanters. By the 1820s decanter design was degenerating, the now-cylindrical bodies often cut with heavy pillars and panels and with abruptly squared shoulders.

The 1840s saw the return of the 'shaft and globe' shape that had been popular a century before. This form continued in fashion until the 20th century, gradually changing in proportion and weight of cutting. This period also saw acid-etched decoration of machine precision and other applications of mechanical and chemical technology which enabled decanters to be made in a variety of complex patterns. Some decanters from this time were raised on a foot, a new idea that remained popular for the remainder of the century.

Decanters were not the only vessels from which wine was served. Jugs were made in silver throughout the 18th century. Glass claret jugs were made during the 19th century and followed the pattern of decanters, the only difference being the addition of a handle and a modified rim to form a pouring lip.

Claret jugs of glass mounted with silver, silver plate, or gilt became popular in the 1850s. One favoured design, incorporating a globular body with a wide neck, closely imitated the jugs of the late 16th century.

The Arts and Crafts movement influenced some designs for claret jugs, as did art nouveau and late 19th-century interest in Japanese forms. Novelty jugs would also be made in the form of a duck, walrus, seal, or some other animal, with the body in glass and the head in silver or silver plate. All these forms were prevalent in the closing 30 years of the 19th century.

While it is not possible to describe every sort of decanter, there is one type which should not pass unmentioned. It has a conical body giving it a very wide base and it usually has neck rings. Many are plain but some have cut decoration. Their name may well be disputed because who in their right mind would take a decanter in a sailing ship? Nevertheless they are ship's decanters.   R.N.H.B.

Johnson, H., Janson, D. J., and McFadden, D. R., *Wine Celebration & Ceremony* (New York, 1985).

Modern decanters

Any container, a simple jug for example, can be used as a vessel for wine, so long as it is made of an inert material and can hold at least the contents of a bottle while, ideally, leaving a considerable surface area in contact with air. Some decanters, notably one designed in the late 1980s by the Ch LATOUR management, are shaped so that a bottle exactly fills them to their maximum width, thereby maximizing the potential for AERATION. Some decanters are designed specifically for magnums, or double-sized bottles. Others have handles, all manner of different shapes, engravings, shadings, and designs, including one to ensure circulation with a semi-spherical base that cannot be laid to rest other than in a special cradle by the host's elbow (see PASSING THE PORT). Wine need not be served from clear glass, or even glass at all, but most wine's COLOUR (whites as much as reds) can give great aesthetic and anticipatory pleasure.

See LEAD for details of the limited extent to which this toxic element may be leached from different sorts of decanters.

decanting, optional and controversial step in SERVING wine, involving pouring wine out of its bottle into another container called a DECANTER.

Reasons for decanting

The most obvious reason for decanting a wine is to separate it from any SEDIMENT that has formed in the bottle which not only looks unappetizing in the glass, but usually tastes bitter and/or astringent. Before winemakers mastered the art of CLARIFICATION, this was necessary for all wines. Today such a justification of the decanting process effectively limits it to those wines outlined in AGEING as capable of development in bottle, in most of which some solids are precipitated as part of the maturation process. Vintage and crusted PORTS in particular always throw a heavy deposit (since they are bottled so early in their evolution), as do red wines made with no or minimal FILTRATION. It is rare for inexpensive, everyday TABLE WINES to throw a deposit, and most large retailers insist on such heavy filtration that a deposit is unlikely (although not unknown in older, higher-quality reds). To check whether a wine bottle contains any sediment, stand it upright for an hour or more and then carefully hold it up to the light for inspection at the base (although some BOTTLES are too dark for this exercise to be effective).

Another, traditional but disputed, reason for decanting is to promote AERATION and therefore encourage the development of the wine's BOUQUET. Authorities as scientifically respectable as Professor Émile PEYNAUD argue that this is OENOLOGICALLY indefensible: that the action of OXYGEN dissolved in a sound wine when ready to serve is usually detrimental and that the longer it is prolonged—i.e. the longer before serving a wine is decanted—the more diffuse its aroma and the less marked its sensory attributes. His advice is to decant only wines with a sediment, and then only just before serving. If they need aeration because of some wine FAULT such as REDUCTION or MERCAPTANS, then the taster can simply aerate the wine by agitating it in the glass. His argument is that from the moment the wine is fully exposed to air (which happens when it is poured, but not to any significant extent during so-called 'BREATHING') some of its sensory impressions may be lost, and that decanting immediately before serving gives the taster maximum control.

It is certainly wise advice to decant fully mature wines only just before serving, since some are so fragile that they can withstand oxygen for only a few minutes before succumbing to OXIDATION. And it is also true that the aeration process of an individual glass of wine can be controlled by the person drinking out of it. However, there are certain types of wines, ultra-traditional BAROLO most obviously, which may not have been included in Professor Peynaud's experiments with decanting

regimes, which can be so concentrated and tannic in youth that to lose some of their initial sensory impressions is a positive benefit.

There is also the very practical fact that many hosts find it more convenient to decant before a meal is served rather than in the middle of it. There are also people who enjoy the sight of (perhaps both red and white) wine in a decanter so much that they are prepared to sacrifice the potential reduction in gustatory impact.

How to decant

Some authorities argue that bottles that have been STORED horizontally should be disturbed as little as possible before being decanted, so transfer them to either a DECANTING CRADLE or a (much more expensive) decanting machine. The alternative and more common method involves much more contact between the deposit and the clear wine, standing the bottle upright for as long as possible before opening, certainly a few hours for wines which have a great deal of sediment, to allow the sediment to fall through the wine to the base of the bottle. Whichever method is used, ensure that the decanter looks and smells absolutely clean, and find a strong light source against which the bottle can be held (a candle, flashlight, desk light, or unshaded table lamp will do). After opening the bottle, as gently as possible, and wiping the lip of the bottle clean, steadily pour the contents of the bottle into the decanter watching the lower shoulder of the bottle with the light source behind it. The sediment should eventually collect in the shoulder and the pouring action can be halted as soon as any sediment starts to spill into the bottleneck.

To extract maximum volume of liquid from a bottle with sediment, or if there is no time to let all the sediment fall to the bottom of the bottle, or if a cork collapses into fragments in the bottle during extraction, the wine can be filtered into the decanter through clean fabric such as muslin, or a paper coffee filter.

Peynaud, É., *The Taste of Wine* (London, 1987).

decanting cradles, bottle carriers, usually made of wicker or metal, which keep the bottle at a perpetually inclined angle with the bottleneck only slightly higher than the base of the bottle, so that the SEDIMENT does not have to fall through the wine to the base of the bottle between STORING horizontally and pouring.

Special **decanting machines** have also been constructed, designed to pour wine gently out of a bottle held horizontally so that the deposit hardly moves at all.

De Chaunac (Seibel 9549), early-ripening, productive, disease resistant, dark-skinned FRENCH HYBRID grown for a wide range of wine styles in NEW YORK's Finger lakes region and in Ontario in CANADA.

defoliation, loss of leaves, of a vine can be caused by various agents. If extensive and badly

timed, it inevitably adversely affects fruit RIPENING and wine quality, although the precise effects depend on the time of the year. Defoliation is, of course, a natural process and happens at the end of each growing season in the autumn. Normally it is caused by the first frost, but it may also be through mechanical damage or merely senescence. By this time the vines have lost most of the green colour from their leaves anyway and they are no longer effective at PHOTOSYNTHESIS. Providing the vine's reserves of CARBOHYDRATES are topped up by late-season photosynthesis, there is no negative effect of defoliation.

However, defoliation can occur at any time of the growing season due to climate, disease, or pests. FROSTS at any time in the growing season can partially or totally defoliate vines, but they typically remove the outermost leaf layers of a thick CANOPY. HAIL can also defoliate vines. A mild hailstorm may simply tear some leaves, but a severe hailstorm will rip off all the leaves, and cut shoots back to their thick stubs. FUNGAL DISEASES such as DOWNY MILDEW can also cause defoliation if left unchecked. Similarly, insect pests such as the western grapeleaf skeletonizer and GRASSHOPPERS can defoliate entire vines unless checked.

The vine responds to defoliation by producing new leaves on lateral shoots. However, this new growth will depend on stored carbohydrate reserves of the vine for a month or so, and so will weaken the vine until the new leaves are able to produce carbohydrates by photosynthesis and build up reserves again. While vigorous vines may be able to recover from a single defoliation, repeated defoliation can weaken the vine to the point of death.

Obviously, defoliation will have an impact on fruit growth and ripening. A low LEAF TO FRUIT RATIO causes a reduction in levels of fruit sugars (see SUGAR IN GRAPES), as well as in PHENOLICS, with an adverse effect on colour and flavour of the resultant wine. Note, however, that the vine can compensate for a lower than ideal leaf area by automatically increasing the rate of photosynthesis, so that practices such as LEAF REMOVAL and TRIMMING do not normally cause negative effects, as might be imagined. Good-quality wine can be made only from vines with a sufficient area of healthy leaves exposed to sunlight.   R.E.S.

dégorgement, French term for the DISGORGEMENT operations at the end of the traditional method of SPARKLING WINE-MAKING.

degree, or *degré* in French, the ALCOHOLIC STRENGTH of a wine, and identical to the wine's percentage of ETHANOL by volume. This has traditionally been regarded as the most vital statistic of all for everyday French VIN DE TABLE, whose price was traditionally quoted per *degré/hecto*, as though its only important characteristics were its potency and volume (although, at this quality level, wines with low alcohol levels tend to have been over-produced and to be vapid and low in fruit and concentration).

degree days. Unit devised to measure climate. See CLIMATE CLASSIFICATION for more details.

dehydration, wine-making process used in the production of DRIED GRAPE WINES—and a frequent consequence of extended HANG TIME. The dehydration process transforms grapes into RAISINS and has to be arrested before completion if appetizing wines are to be made from the results.

Dekkera, the sporulating form of the yeast genus BRETTANOMYCES which can cause off-flavours in wines, often described as 'mousy'. Like *Brettanomyces*, Dekkera is very sensitive to SULFUR DIOXIDE. In practice, Dekkera is used as a European, particularly French, synonym for *Brettanomyces*.

Delaware, dark pink-skinned VITIS *labrusca* vine variety that is quite popular in NEW YORK and, for reasons that are now obscure, is widely planted in JAPAN. Its early ripening is presumably an advantage in Japan's damp autumns. The wine is not as markedly FOXY as that of its great New York rival CONCORD. It was first propagated in Delaware, Ohio, in 1849.

délestage, or rack and return, is a CAP management procedure which both aerates the must and optimizes contact between must and solids during fermentation. When the cap has risen to the top of the tank, fermenting wine is taken from a bottom valve to a separate receiving vessel. The remaining POMACE is allowed to free drain for two or more hours. The wine is then gently pumped back over the top of the cap, using a low pressure pump or sprinkler system. This OXIDATIVE procedure, usually conducted daily, is designed to ensure optimum diffusion of tannins, pigments, and POLYSACCHARIDES from the fruit into the wine. It may also used to remove a proportion of the seeds and can thus reduce the extraction of bitter tannins from unripe seeds. See also MACERATION. B.W.Z.

delimitation, geographical. The central purpose of geographical delimitation of a wine area, typically into a CONTROLLED APPELLATION, is to establish a distinctive identity for the wines produced within it, and provide a means whereby the provenance of those wines can be guaranteed. It is based primarily upon the assumption that different environments give rise to wines of different character (see TERROIR).

Since classical antiquity, wines from certain regions tended to be called after the area of their production, with many gaining particularly high reputations (FALERNIAN, for

example), but the first legal vineyard delimitation was that introduced in the DOURO valley of northern Portugal in 1756 associated with the establishment of the Companhia Geral da Agricultura das Vinhas do Alto Douro. During the 18th century, there had been many disputes over the sources and qualities of wines exported from Oporto (see PORT), as well as conflicts between foreign wine shippers and the Portuguese growers, and the formation of the Companhia Geral with strictly defined areas of operation was designed to remedy the situation. At the heart of this legislation was the establishment of a specific area in the upper Douro valley from which farmers were able to obtain higher prices for their wines compared with those produced elsewhere.

During the 18th century in other parts of Europe, CLASSIFICATIONS of the different qualities of wine were becoming increasingly common, with Thomas JEFFERSON, for example, commenting on the various categories of wines from Bordeaux and Burgundy in 1787. In the 19th century, more formal classifications emerged, with the most famous of these being the classification of the wines of the Médoc, and Lavalle's classification of the wines of the Côte d'Or, both of which date from 1855. By the early 20th century, in the wake of the devastation caused by POWDERY MILDEW and PHYLLOXERA, there were two fundamental problems facing the wine industry: ADULTERATION AND FRAUD. Many wines contained a range of additives designed to mask their flavour; and wine purporting to come from a respected source frequently contained wines from elsewhere. In order to overcome these problems, some groups of growers, such as those in Chablis and Bordeaux, decided to form their own associations designed to guarantee the origin of their wines. National governments then began to concern themselves more formally with the geographical delimitation of areas of wine production, with the French taking a first step in 1905 towards the creation of a national system of wine control based on the delimitation of areas of origin. Through further laws, most notably those of 1919 and 1927, this eventually culminated in 1935 in the law creating the Appellations d'Origine Contrôlées, today's APPELLATION CONTRÔLÉE system.

Numerous systems were also developed in Germany, notably the GERMAN WINE LAW of 1930, but although this included the use of vineyard names, the perceived quality of Germany's wines has never been based primarily on geography but on MUST WEIGHTS (see GERMAN HISTORY).

Italian wine laws also include an element of geographical delimitation, as represented in the creation of the Denominazione di Origine Controllata (DOC) system in 1963 and most recently in the 1992 legislation with its specific reference to Indicazione Geografica Tipica (IGT).

The precise practical methods of geographical demarcation vary from country to country, but are usually based on the compilation of a detailed vineyard register and include varying degrees of political intrigue (see, for example, ALBANA DI ROMAGNA). Producers wishing to gain a certain status must satisfy regional and national committees of both the quality, origin, and distinction of their wines. One of the most rigorous systems of geographical delimitation is that adopted in France under INAO auspices. This requires that commissions of inquiry examine the relationships between such factors as GEOLOGY, SOILS, TOPOGRAPHY, DRAINAGE, slope, exposure, and wine quality. In BURGUNDY, for example, the geological origin of the soils is a determining factor in differentiating the GRAND CRU.

The central feature of geographical delimitation as it applies to wine is not just that it is intended to lead to improvements in wine quality, thus enabling the wines to be sold at a higher price, but also that it is a legislative procedure whereby a privileged monopolistic position is created for producers within a demarcated area. Whether a given vineyard falls within or outside the legal boundary of a delimited wine region can have important commercial consequences, which is why the much more recent demarcation of America's AVAs, South Africa's Wine of Origin, and some of AUSTRALIA's even newer GIs, many of them based more on political than geographical boundaries, can be such a contentious process.

The creation of geographically delimited areas remains highly controversial.   P.T.H.U.

Pomerol, C. (ed.), *The Wines and Winelands of France: Geological Journeys* (London, 1989).

Unwin, T., *Wine and the Vine: An Historical Geography of Viticulture and the Wine Trade* (London, 1991).

demi-sec, French term meaning 'medium dry' (see SWEETNESS). In practice, the term is used particularly for Chenin Blanc wines in ANJOU-SAUMUR and TOURAINE as well as for some SPARKLING WINES. See DOSAGE for official European Union sugar levels.

Denmark. Despite the far northern LATITUDE, vines have been grown here since the Middle Ages—mainly in greenhouses or against walls. Outdoor vine-growing was first seen in the 1980s, thanks to the development of NEW VARIEITES able to ripen in cool climates and survive cold winters. After decades of experimentation to find varieties best suited to the Danish climate and to producing good wine, growers now favour REGENT and RONDO for red wines and MADELEINE ANGEVINE and ORION for whites. Most Danish vineyards are small and amateur but by 2005 there were 10 professional growers, whose production was small and therefore very expensive. The Union of Danish Winegrowers has more than 1,000 members. B.G.

Génsboel, B., and Gundersen, J. M., *Vinavl i Danmark* (Winegrowing in Denmark), (Copenhagen, 1998).

Denominação de Origem Controlada, the name of a controlled appellation in PORTUGAL, which replaced the earlier Região Demarcarda when Portuguese wine laws were revised for EUROPEAN UNION entry. For more details, see DOC.

Denominación de Origen, Spanish controlled appellation. See DO.

Denominación de Origen Calificada, Spain's superior controlled appellation. RIOJA was the first DO to be promoted to this status. See DOCA.

density, a measurement of the concentration of matter in units of mass per unit volume. In wine it is usually expressed as g/cc, and occasionally as g/ml, at 20 °C/68 °F (which must be specified since wine's mass per unit volume decreases as its temperature increases). Wine is an interesting mixture because it contains dissolved solids (SUGARS, ACIDS, PHENOLICS, and MINERAL salts) which increase its density above that of pure water, but it also contains ALCOHOL, which is less dense than water. The result is that very dry wines can have densities near 0.8 g/cc while very sweet wines that are low in alcohol (such as some Italian MOSCATO, for example) can have densities around 1.03 g/cc.

A term closely related to density, and used in technical wine analysis, is **specific gravity**. The specific gravity is the ratio of the weight or mass of a volume of a liquid to the weight of an equal volume of water. It is thus a pure or unitless number which differs only slightly from density, according to temperature (since the density of water is only exactly 1 g/cc at a temperature of 3.98 °C).

Wine densities are also frequently reported in terms of one of the traditional scales used for measuring the sugar solution concentrations (see BALLING, BAUMÉ, BRIX, OECHSLE), which also measure wine density but in units other than g/cc. These scales all use different units (see MUST WEIGHT for equivalencies) from each other, with Oechsle bearing the most obvious relationship to specific gravity: a must with the specific gravity of 1.070, for example, is said to measure 70 °Oechsle. Density is usually measured with a HYDROMETER and while a range of alternative electronic density meters are available, hydrometers are the instrumental standard for this measurement. A.D.W.

deposit. See BOTTLE DEPOSIT and SEDIMENT.

derived pigments, see ANTHOCYANINS.

desert, an arid, treeless region. True deserts are not conducive to growing grapes for wine, even where IRRIGATION water is available. Low HUMIDITY and extreme temperature ranges place stresses on the vine which usually preclude good grape quality. With irrigation they can still be very suitable for TABLE GRAPES, especially early-maturing varieties, and for DRYING GRAPES, but wine grapes seldom rise above mediocre quality. See CLIMATE AND WINE QUALITY.

Some near-desert regions used extensively for viticulture include the SAN JOAQUIN VALLEY of California; the Bekaa valley of LEBANON; parts of ISRAEL; AZERBAIJAN on the west coast of the Caspian sea; the north west of CHINA; the lower Murray valley of SOUTH AUSTRALIA and VICTORIA; and the Little Karoo of SOUTH AFRICA. J.G.

designations. Within the EUROPEAN UNION, wine is broadly designated either a QUALITY WINE or a TABLE WINE. Within these broad categories there are more precise designations, usually CONTROLLED APPELLATIONS or categories such as VIN DE PAYS, IGT, LANDWEIN, or VINO DE LA TIERRA. Within the US, wines between 7 and 14 per cent alcohol are designated table wine while those over 14 per cent, whether sweet or dry, fortified or not, are designated dessert wine.

dessert wines usually mean SWEET WINES but according to American regulations they signify any wine between 14 and 24 per cent alcohol and thus includes an increasing proportion of dry, unfortified wines.

destalking. See DESTEMMING.

destemming, the wine-making process of removing the STEMS, or stalks, from clusters of grape berries. Known as *égrappage* or *éraflage* in French, it usually takes place immediately after and combined with the CRUSHING operation. Grape stems, and the attached BRUSH of pulp, contain TANNINS. If they are crushed or broken, these can be leached into the wine during FERMENTATION, making the wine taste bitter and astringent. Destemming also very slightly increases the resultant COLOUR and ALCOHOLIC STRENGTH because stems, if included, have a dilution effect. Fermentation is also likely to be slightly slower and cooler since including stems increases the interfaces between the fermenting must and air, or OXYGEN.

Although historically all wines were made without either crushing or stem removal, most white and the majority of black grapes are destemmed today. The exceptions are those white grapes subjected to WHOLE BUNCH PRESSING and black grapes used for CARBONIC MACERATION and those few employed in WHOLE BUNCH FERMENTATION. Some producers, notably in BURGUNDY and parts of the RHÔNE, believe in retaining a certain proportion of the stems to add structure, colour, and mid-palate weight, to improve TEXTURE, to ease the drainage of the juice through the CAP during MACERATION of red wines and during PRESSING of white wines.

Modern destemming machines, or **destemmers**, are usually based on the principle of straining or sieving larger stems from the crushed grape mixture which is fed into a horizontal rotating perforated cylinder. As the mass is tumbled, the juice, skins, and seeds pass through the perforations into a collector. The stems, which are long enough to bridge across the perforations, are carried to the open exit end where they are collected in a separate receiver. Stem fragments small enough to fall through the perforations in the cylinder go into the juice, which means that they remain in contact with the juice until after fermentation in the case of red wines but are removed along with the skins and seeds before fermentation in the case of white wines (see WINE-MAKING).

desuckering, the viticultural practice of removing unwanted young shoots. Known in most parts of France as *épamprage*, the practice is common to most vineyards of the world. Typically, the shoots removed are either on the TRUNK or in the HEAD of the vine, and grow in spring from buds surviving in the old wood. These shoots are termed WATER SHOOTS and for the majority of vine varieties have no bunches of grapes. Varieties differ in their production of water shoots; GEWÜRZTRAMINER, for example, produces many, while others produce few. The operation is carried out in spring, several weeks after BUDBREAK, when the water shoots are 10 to 15 cm (4 to 6 in) long. The work is relatively tiresome, as for many vineyards the shoots can be near the ground, although shoots can be removed from trunks mechanically with no damage to the trunk by mounting a rotating cylinder with rubber straps attached on the front of a tractor.

In California, desuckering is also carried out on CORDON-trained vines and so can alternatively be termed SHOOT THINNING. R.E.S.

Deutsche means literally 'German', thus the **Deutsche Weinstrasse** is a particularly famous route through the vineyards of the PFALZ region in Germany; **Deutscher Sekt** is that relative rarity, a SEKT or sparkling wine made in Germany that is actually made of German wine; and **Deutscher Tafelwein**, or DTW, means literally 'German TABLE WINE' and is distinct from EU TABLE WINE in that it is made exclusively from German grapes, such grapes failing to qualify for either QBA or QMP wine.

The **Deutsches Weinsiegel**, or German Wine Seal, is a significant award made to superior bottlings assessed by BLIND TASTING panels, but only after the wine has been awarded an official AP NUMBER. Award-winning bottles can be identified by a large, round paper seal on the bottle-neck: a yellow seal for dry wines, green for medium dry, and red for other styles. These awards, and a national competition, are held under the auspices of the **Deutsche Landwirtschafts-Gesellschaft**, or DLG, an agricultural society formed in the late 19th century to encourage quality and agricultural expertise. Prize-winning bottles carry gold, silver, or bronze strips across the neck.

dew, water which condenses on objects, such as leaves, when the air in immediate contact with them is cooled below dew point, the temperature at which the air becomes fully saturated by its current content of water vapour (see HUMIDITY). Dew contributes little directly to the water supply of the vine. However, the latent heat of vaporization that is released during condensation plays a positive role by slowing night-time temperature drop. The risk of FROST is appreciably reduced when the air contains enough water vapour to result in dew.

Dew has a major (mostly unfavourable) impact on the incidence of VINE DISEASES. It provides the necessary conditions for spore germination and the establishment of several fungal disease organisms, most notably those for DOWNY MILDEW (*Plasmopara viticola*), BLACK ROT (*Guignardia bidwellii*), and the malevolent form of botrytis bunch rot, GREY ROT (*Botrytis cinerea*), even in the absence of wetting rain.

Spreading bunch infection by the last of these after (but only after) normal maturity has been reached constitutes the benevolent form, NOBLE ROT, which is responsible for most of the world's greatest SWEET WINES. See CLIMATE AND WINE QUALITY and TOPOGRAPHY. J.G.

diacetyl, a product of MALOLACTIC FERMENTATION with a powerful butterscotch or butter aroma. The ability to detect diacetyl depends on its concentration and the wine type and style. The perception threshold varies from 0.2 mg/l for Chardonnay, 0.9 mg/l for Pinot Noir to 2.8 mg/l for Cabernet Sauvignon. At low concentrations, it may be perceived as nutty or toasty and add desirable complexity. In excess, as in some stereotypical NEW WORLD Chardonnays, it is perceived as distractingly obvious butteriness. The amount of diacetyl produced depends on the bacterial strain and the rate of progress of the malolactic fermentation as well as temperature, oxygen availability, sugar, the wine's pH, SO_2 content, and, importantly, CITRIC ACID concentrations. P.J.W.

Bartowsky, E. J., and Henschke, P. A., 'The "buttery" attribute of wine—diacetyl—desirability, spoilage and beyond', *International Journal of Food Microbiology* 96 (2004), 235–52.

Diageo, the world's largest drinks company, is very much more interested in spirits than wine, and BRANDS above all else. It owns Piat d'Or, Blossom Hill, Beaulieu Vineyard (now singular), and Sterling in California. It acquired the premium California-based Chalone Wine Group from Ch LAFITE-Rothschild in 2004 but has no obvious wine strategy. Its London fine wine merchant Justerini & Brooks is somewhat anomalous.

diammonium phosphate, or DAP, common YEAST nutrient added during FERMENTATION. The current EUROPEAN UNION limit is 1 g/l.

diatomaceous earth (DE), widely used in FILTRATION, is a naturally occurring, highly porous, chalk-like sedimentary rock mineral made mainly of silica and consisting of fossilized remains of diatoms, a type of hard-shelled algae. It is also known as Kieselguhr.

Die, town between the RHÔNE valley and the alps (see map under FRANCE) whose name features in the **Clairette de Die** and **Crémant de Die** sparkling wine appellations and **Coteaux de Die**, a light, still, dry white wine made from Clairette grapes. According to PLINY, the local tribe in Roman times, the Voconces, made a sparkling sweet wine, and practised an early form of TEMPERATURE CONTROL by plunging barrels full of fermenting must in the river. Most wines are sparkling and many of them are sweet and grapey. For more information, see CLAIRETTE DE DIE, CRÉMANT, and CHÂTILLON-EN-DIOIS.

diet, wine as part of. Medical research increasingly indicates that wine may be drunk for dietary reasons. Wine contains various VITAMINS and MINERALS but in such small concentrations that, for them to make any sufficient contribution to the human diet, excessive amounts of ALCOHOL would also have to be ingested. 'Moderate' wine consumption has been shown to have a beneficial effect for several medical conditions, however, and wine consumption clearly plays a part in the much-vaunted **Mediterranean diet** (see HEALTH).

No wine is 'slimming', but dry **dealcoholized wine** is usually lower in calories than most.

In Mediterranean countries it has always been natural to drink wine because it is abundant and relatively cheap. But wine forms part of our diet for reasons beyond necessity or ease of access.

Traditionally societies have wanted to drink wine because it tastes good. It was popular not least because of the dangers associated with drinking unclean WATER. Wine has also long been recognized as an important element in a healthy diet.

The concept of maintaining good health through diet can be traced back to Ancient GREECE and the Greek Hippocrates, in particular, although wine was included in the dietary laws of Moses 1,000 years earlier.

As late as the 1860s, doctors were still matching wines to lifestyles, as they would be termed today. For example, Dr Robert Druitt suggested CLARET 'for children, for literary persons, and for all those whose occupations are chiefly carried on indoors'. The fuller-bodied wines of BURGUNDY, the MIDI, and

GREECE he considered better suited to manual workers. H.B.

André, J., *L'Alimentation et la cuisine à Rome* (Paris, 1961).

Johnson, H., *The Story of Wine* (London and New York, 1989).

Tannahill, R., *Food in History* (2nd edn, London, 1988).

Dijon, town in northern BURGUNDY and the focus of the region's vinous ACADEME, the Institut Jules Guyot in the Université de Bourgogne (formerly the **Université de Dijon**). For some time OENOLOGY was taught by the charismatic vigneron René Engel, who was also a leading light in the Chevaliers de Tastevin, but Dijon was able to offer graduate diplomas in oenology from 1947. The course was further refined in 1955 when a viticultural research station and experimental winery were established in nearby MARSANNAY. Since then the station has worked in close collaboration with INRA.

From 1982, Dijon offered the four-year Diplôme National d'Oenologue. Research concentrates on five main areas: methods of micropropagation of vines; biological methods for controlling FUNGAL DISEASES; natural vine defences; physical and chemical oenological systems; and the adaptive responses of bacteria responsible for MALOLACTIC FERMENTATION.

Certain CLONES of Chardonnay, and PINOT NOIR clones such as 115 and 777, imported from Burgundy, are sometimes known as **Dijon clones**.

www.u-bourgogne.fr/IUVV

Dimiat, sometimes spelt **Dymiat**, Bulgaria's most planted indigenous white grape variety with 9,600 ha/23,720 acres in 2005, although RKATSITELI was planted on 11,700 ha. It is grown mainly in the east and south of Bulgaria, where it is regarded as a producer of perfumed everyday whites of varying levels of sweetness but usefully dependable quality. The vines yield copper-coloured grapes in great quantity. The wines should be consumed young and cool. Dimiat might also be a parent, with Riesling, of Bulgaria's MISKET VARNENSKI.

dining clubs, private societies of like-minded individuals who meet over meals. A high proportion of what are called dining clubs are in fact wining clubs devoted to the consumption and discussion of fine wines.

Dinka, very ordinary but widely planted white grape variety in HUNGARY and VOJVODINA. It is also known as Kövidinka and Kevedinka.

Dionysus, the classical god of wine, for whom Bacchus was the more common name among the Romans. However, grapes and vines are not his only attributes, and neither is wine the only aspect of his cult.

Although some scholars have argued that wine is a secondary element in his cult and the god Dionysus was a late importation from the east, he is a wine god, an Olympian, and an important influence on Ancient GREECE. The earliest festival known to be devoted to Dionysus, the three-day feast of the Anthesteria, is a wine festival. It gives its name to the spring month of Anthesterion and celebrates the broaching of the new wine (the wine of the most recent vintage, which was always kept until the next spring). Clay tablets dating from the late Bronze Age (*c*.1200 BC), connect Dionysus with wine, and thus provide further evidence for the early cult of Dionysus as a wine god.

Dionysus has been taken to be a non-Greek because he is a god of epiphanies. He appears suddenly, from outside, to strike people with madness, most famously represented in Euripides' tragedy *The Bacchae* (probably written shortly after 408 BC).

The Bacchae is about Dionysiac frenzy and, although the play praises Dionysus for his gift of wine which lessens the cares of mortals, the madness that he brings is not the result of excessive consumption of wine.

The essence of the cult of Dionysus is the surrender of personal identity. Hence one of Dionysus' symbols is the mask, and he is often depicted in VASE PAINTINGS of drinking ceremonies as a mask set up on a column draped in cloth. His other attributes are the thyrsus, a tall stick with a bunch of ivy leaves on top—ivy because it is evergreen and it produces its berries in the winter when the mountain ritual takes place and the vine is bare. He is also depicted with grapes or a wine cup, and often has an effeminate appearance with long flowing locks. He is frequently equated (especially by HERODOTUS in the 5th century BC) with the Egyptian god Osiris.

One well-known myth about Dionysus concerns the invention of wine. Dionysus discloses the secret of wine-making to the peasant Icarius and his daughter Erigone, with whom he had lodged as a guest, in return for their hospitality. Obedient to the god's command to teach the art to other people, Icarius shares his wine with a group of shepherds. At first they enjoy this delicious new drink, but as the unaccustomed wine overwhelms them they begin to suspect Icarius of having poisoned them. So they turn on him and batter him to death with their clubs. For a time his body cannot be found, but eventually Icarius' faithful dog Moera leads Erigone to the spot where he lies buried. Erigone hangs herself in despair. However, in death they receive their due rewards: Icarius becomes the star Boötes, his daughter the constellation Virgo, and Moera becomes Canis, or Sirius, the dog star. Boötes, also known in Greek as 'the grape-gatherer', rises in the autumn, at the time of the vintage, and in the warm climate of Greece the vintage may well have taken place some

time before the autumnal equinox, still under the constellation of Virgo. It is also interesting to note that PLINY the Elder recommends the rising of the dog star, 2 August, as the day when wine jars should receive their inside coating of RESIN to make them airtight in readiness for the vintage.

Dionysus is a god who strives against reason, calm and order. As such he is a god of the people, dangerous and subversive to those in authority. His cult attracts further suspicion because it is surrounded by secrecy.

Gradually Dionysiac orgies appear to have become orgies in the modern sense, and among the Romans the cult of Dionysus was a disreputable affair. Livy gives a lurid account of the banning of the Bacchanalia, but it should not be forgotten that Livy was a historian of conservative tendencies, an admirer of Augustus, who lamented what he considered to be the recent slide into luxury and immorality. Bacchus certainly played little part in the official religion of Ancient ROME; he was too dangerous a god. Among the Romans he survives in a sanitized version, jolly Bacchus the wine god, giver of wine and bringer of joy, who makes sorrow bearable. Satyrs and nymphs gambol about him harmlessly, and Silenus is a cheerful old soak. This is the Bacchus that survived into the Renaissance, familiar from the pictures of Titian and his contemporaries. The Romans reduced the complex god of the Greeks to little more than wine personified.

H.M.W.

Burkert, W., *Greek Religion*, trans. by John Raffan (Oxford, 1985).
Carpenter, T. H., *Dionysian Imagery in Archaic Greek Art* (Oxford, 1986).
Dalby, A., *Bacchus. A Biography* (Los Angeles, 2003).
Otto, W. F., *Dionysus: Myth and Cult*, trans. by Robert B. Palmer (Bloomington, Ind., and London, 1965).
Wilson, H., *Wine and Words in Classical Antiquity and the Middle Ages* (London, 2003).

direct producer, term used for a group of vines, also known as FRENCH HYBRIDS, bred from the late 19th century onwards in an effort to combine the pest and disease resistance of AMERICAN VINE SPECIES with the desirable fruit characters of the European VINIFERA species. They are called direct producers, and sometimes hybrid direct producers, or HDPs, because, unlike *vinifera* VINE VARIETIES, they do not need GRAFTING on to PHYLLOXERA-tolerant ROOTSTOCKS. They are not all sufficiently phylloxera tolerant, however, and added soil stresses such as drought or weeds can see them weakened by phylloxera. R.E.S.

direct shipping, cause célèbre in the US which, until a seminal Supreme Court decision in 2005 liberalizing direct shipments into New York state and Michigan, banned shipping of wine direct from winery to consumer in many significant states. See UNITED STATES, regulations for more detail of this long-awaited bypassing of the notorious 'three-tier system'.

disease-resistant varieties, semantically expedient term for grapevines introduced by the German Bundessortenamt (Plant Variety Rights Office) in 1995 that were bred specifically to produce wines that taste like VINIFERA yet meet consumer demands for reductions in AGROCHEMICAL use by incorporating some non-*vinifera* genes for resistance to various common vine diseases. The term replaces the previously pejorative terms HYBRIDS or INTERSPECIFIC HYBRIDS for some of their most promising results of VINE BREEDING.

There had been substantial bias against such new varieties, especially those including genes from AMERICAN VINE SPECIES, because of historical associations with poor wine quality and FOXY flavours. The bureaucratic hurdle of the EUROPEAN UNION's ban on non-*vinifera* vines for QUALITY WINE (designed initially to exclude the old AMERICAN HYBRIDS and FRENCH HYBRIDS) was bypassed by classifying these new disease-resistant varieties as VITIS *vinifera* subspecies *sativa*.

Merzling, the product of Seyve-Villard 5–276 and a cross Riesling × Ruländer, was the first variety so registered, and other German-bred varieties such as PHOENIX, RONDO, ORION, REGENT, Bronner, Johanniter, Primera, and Prinzipal have followed, all registered as *Vitis vinifera*. Thanks to this creative taxonomy, these disease-resistant varieties can be grown for quality wine production, though they still have to be registered for quality wine production in any given EU region. R.E.S. & J.R.

diseases, vine. See VINE DISEASES and individual diseases.

disgorgement, or *dégorgement* in French, an integral stage in the traditional method of SPARKLING WINE-MAKING entailing the removal of a pellet of frozen sediment from the neck of each bottle. Modern alternative techniques such as alginate beads may eventually render this cumbersome process superfluous though on a commercial scale they have not generally proved to be sufficiently economical or practical.

distillation, the separation of the constituents of a liquid mixture by partial vaporization of the mixture and the separate recovery of the vapour and the residue. When applied to wine, or any other fermented liquid, the result is a considerably stronger alcoholic liquid: brandy in the case of wine and other fermented fruit juices, calvados in the case of certain apples from northern France, whisky in the case of fermented barley.

distillation, compulsory. In an effort to curb, and dispose of, SURPLUS wine production, the EUROPEAN UNION authorities instituted a system in 1982 whereby any wine produced over a certain limit should theoretically be compulsorily bought, at a standard and not too attractive price, and distilled into industrial ALCOHOL (which policy resulted, perhaps inevitably, in an alcohol surplus). Average quantities distilled under this scheme in the 1980s were well over 30 million hl/790 million gal, or about a fifth of total European production. In 1993 the European Commission admitted that the scheme had done little to curb over-production, and announced stricter measures designed to offer less financial support to over-producers, and to curb abuse of the system more effectively. Between 1993 and 1996, the amount distilled was reduced to about 10 per cent of production, but the Commission decided to crack down and, in 1998, proposed introducing just one 'crisis distillation' measure instead of a multi-tiered system. The proposed new measure was intended to deal only with exceptional cases of market disturbance and serious quality problems, but continues to play an important part in the European wine market. Following further reforms of the Common Market Organisation for Wine in 1999, distillation was 'no longer an obligatory measure in the event of serious wine market crises' and it could be applied to quality wine. An EU report published in 2002 concluded that distillation was not an efficient way of eliminating structural surpluses and suggested alternative measures such as paying growers a premium for GREEN HARVESTING.

J.R., E.K., & J.Ha.

European Commission–DG Agriculture, 'Ex-post Evaluation of the Common Market Organisation for Wine: Final Report' (Rome, 2002).

diurnal temperature variation, see TEMPERATURE VARIABILITY.

divided canopy, group of vine-TRAINING SYSTEMS which involve separation of a leaf CANOPY into two or more subcanopies, sometimes called curtains. The expression was popularized by Professor Nelson SHAULIS in the 1960s and 1970s as part of his pioneering promotion of CANOPY MANAGEMENT. One of the most important divided canopy training systems is the GENEVA DOUBLE CURTAIN developed by Shaulis. The LYRE, SCOTT HENRY, and SMART-DYSON are more recent developments. The advantage of canopy division is that it increases the surface area of the canopy that is exposed to sunlight, while reducing canopy SHADE. Both yield and wine quality can increase as a result.

R.E.S.

DLG, source of German wine awards. See DEUTSCHE.

DMDC (dimethyl dicarbonate), a sterilant used by a number of producers of high-quality red wine outside of Europe to eliminate the risk of BRETTANOMYCES growth in bottle. DMDC works by deactivating enzymes in the spoilage yeast. Any remaining DMDC reacts principally with the water in the beverage. It

is currently approved in the United States, South Africa, and New Zealand for use in wine production. While it was originally developed for commercial wines, it has been accepted more widely by wineries at the top end of the market. While DMDC is a legal additive for fruit juice in the EUROPEAN UNION, it is not permitted in wine-making.

S.H.

DNA profiling, also known as **DNA typing**, **DNA fingerprinting**, or **DNA testing**, allows the unequivocal identification of any living individual. This technique was developed in 1985 in forensic science to confound criminals, and was first applied to grape CULTIVARS in 1993 by Australian researchers. Since a grape variety is made of CLONES reproduced asexually by VEGETATIVE PROPAGATION, it is genetically comparable to a human individual. The identification technique is based on small pieces of variable DNA called molecular markers, the most successful using repetitive pieces of DNA called **microsatellites**. They exist in any living organism and their length varies from one individual to another. The analysis of six to eight microsatellites is enough to obtain a unique 'genetic identity card', looking like a supermarket bar code, for every variety. This technique, for which data exchanges between laboratories is relatively easy, allowed, for example, identification of the enigmatic PETITE SIRAH in California and solved the long-standing mystery of ZINFANDEL's identity.

DNA profiling technique complements classical AMPELOGRAPHY and offers the advantage of unambiguously identifying grape varieties (as well as ROOTSTOCKS) from any part of the plant, independently of the factors potentially influencing the vine's morphology that can mislead ampelographers such as environmental conditions (e.g. drought), the development stage (e.g. woody canes used for trading, often impossible to identify visually), or sanitary state (e.g. viruses). There are about 10,000 grape cultivars in the world, for which about 24,000 names were recorded, thus the same grape often has several names (synonyms) in different regions. Inversely, the same name can be used for several distinct varieties (homonyms). DNA profiling can be very helpful in correcting misnomers and detecting synonyms (e.g. Zinfandel and Primitivo) and homonyms (e.g. the REFOSCO group), and is thus useful in managing important ampelographic collections. Although in 2002 DAVIS and Australia's CSIRO scientists independently found some microsatellite variations within a high number of Pinot, Chardonnay, and Primitivo clones, up to now neither DNA profiling nor any other molecular method has managed unambiguously to identify different clones of a grape variety.

Microsatellites follow the laws of heredity: half of them come from the mother and half of them come from the father. Much like paternity testing in humans, by looking at a

high number of microsatellites (30 to 50), it is possible with DNA profiling to reconstruct the parentage of a variety when both parents are still available. Researchers Carole Meredith and John Bowers at DAVIS were the first to uncover an unexpected parentage in 1997 when they surprised the whole wine world by announcing that CABERNET SAUVIGNON is the result of a (probably spontaneous) cross between Cabernet Franc and Sauvignon Blanc. Later on, in collaboration with Jean-Michel Boursiquot at MONTPELLIER, they revealed additional unexpected parentages such as those of CHARDONNAY and GAMAY (in 1999), and SYRAH (in 2000). A handful of additional parentages concerning less important varieties were then discovered by these scientists as well as by Austrian, Croatian, Italian, Portuguese, and German researchers, and in 2004, former Meredith collaborator José Vouillamoz and Italian researcher Stella Grando at SAN MICHELE ALL'ADIGE discovered the parentage of SANGIOVESE, Italy's most widespread variety.

Through DNA profiling, parent–offspring pairs can also be determined when one parent is missing, though it is impossible to infer the direction of the relationship. In 2005, the same researchers found several parent–offspring relationships among Italian varieties, e.g. TEROLDEGO, MARZEMINO, and REFOSCO DAL PEDUNCULO ROSSO, and reconstructed a complex pedigree of grape varieties across the Alps. Pedigree reconstruction makes available unprecedented information about history and migrations of grape cultivars, and provides a better understanding of the genetic events that led to today's range of cultivars.

DNA profiling has also been used to correctly identify fresh and dried grapes sold at market as well as the origin of free run juice from a winery.

Future studies will undoubtedly help to provide a clearer picture of the family trees of major grape varieties, but the 'holy grail' of reconstructing the exhaustive genealogical tree of all existing cultivars will almost certainly never be attained since many parents have disappeared because of frost, pests (e.g. PHYLLOXERA), or lack of interest.

J.V.

Bowers, J. E., Bandman, E. B., and Meredith, C. P., 'DNA fingerprint characterization of some wine grape cultivars', *American Journal of Enology and Viticulture*, 44/3 (1993) 266–74.
Bowers, J. E., and Meredith, C. P., 'The parentage of a classic wine grape, Cabernet Sauvignon', *Nature Genetics*, 16/1 (1997), 84–7.
Sefc, K. M., Steinkeller, H., Wagner, H. W., Glossl, J., and Regner, F., 'Application of microsatellite markers to parentage studies in grapevines', *Vitis*, 36/4 (1997), 179–83.
www.vitaceae.org

DO stands for Denominación de Origen, a Spanish CONTROLLED APPELLATION and the mainstay of SPAIN's wine quality control system. Each region awarded DO status is governed by a Consejo Regulador made up of representatives of the regional government (or the Ministry of Agriculture in the three multi-regional appellations Rioja, Jumilla, and Cava), vine-growers, winemakers, and merchants who earn their livelihoods in the region. The INDO (Instituto Nacional de Denominaciones de Origen, the Spanish equivalent of France's INAO) in Madrid no longer organizes DO regulations in single-region appellations. Now it is the regional government alone which decides on the boundaries of the region, permitted VINE VARIETIES, maximum YIELDS, limits of ALCOHOLIC STRENGTH, and any other limitations pertaining to the zone. Back labels or neck seals are granted by the Consejo to certify that a wine meets the standards laid out in the DO regulations. A Denominación de Origen Provisional (DOP) may be awarded to regions on their way to becoming full DOs. A superior category, Denominación de Origen Calificada (see DOCA), was created in 1991.

Rioja (promoted to DOCa status in 1991) became Spain's first DO in 1926 when its own Consejo Regulador was established. Jerez and Málaga had joined the ranks by the end of the 1930s and they were joined by several other regions immediately after the Civil War.

Spanish wine law has been subject to some criticism as the list of regions promoted to DO status continues to lengthen (see also PORTUGAL). The system has most often helped the newer, lesser-known DOs improve quality levels to no small degree, but some older, well-known Consejos Reguladores continue to uphold certain local quirks which may sometimes stifle enterprise and initiative among growers and winemakers, as INAO has been known to do in France.

See also VINO DE MESA and VINO DE LA TIERRA.

doble pasta, dark, full-bodied Spanish wine produced by running off a proportion of fermenting must after two days and adding more crushed grapes to refill the vat. The ratio of skin to pulp is effectively doubled, producing wines with a deep, black colour and very high levels of TANNIN. Doble pasta wines have traditionally been made in JUMILLA, YECLA, UTIEL-REQUENA, and ALÍCANTE, where they are used for blending but they are being superseded by GRAPE CONCENTRATE.   R.J.M.

DOC, initials which stand for Denominação de Origem Controlada in PORTUGAL and Denominazione di Origine Controllata in ITALY, those countries' counterparts of the French Appellation Contrôlée system of CONTROLLED APPELLATIONS. In both countries, DOC wines represent those regarded as QUALITY WINES by European wine law. A DOC system has also been in operation in ROMANIA since 1975, and is being streamlined for EU accession in 2007, despite French and Italian objections to the use of the term there.

Denominação de Origem Controlada

In Portugal, DOC stands for Denominação de Origem Controlada. On joining the EUROPEAN UNION in 1986, Portugal undertook revision of its wine laws to bring them into line with other European countries, most notably those of France. Each of the regions which had already been designated a REGIÃO DEMARCADA (RD) in earlier legislation (BUCELAS, CARCAVELOS, COLARES, DÃO, MADEIRA, SETÚBAL, VINHO VERDE. BAIRRADA, and DOURO) were subsequently designated as DOCs. The system equates roughly with the French APPELLATION CONTRÔLÉE and sets out permitted grape varieties, maximum yields, periods of ageing in bulk and bottle, and analytical standards for specified types of wine. Samples must be submitted to the local body controlling that region's wine industry, who grant numbered seals of origin to producers whose wines have satisfied the regulations.

For many years Portugal's wine laws have been a bureaucrat's dream and a winemaker's nightmare, stifling initiative in a number of wine regions (see DÃO and COLARES). Many of Portugal's best wines have traditionally been blends from more than one region (see GARRAFEIRA) and therefore excluded from the DOC legislation. A second tier of delimited regions, Indicação de Proveniencia Regulamentada (see IPR), was also introduced following Portugal's entry into the EU, along with a third catch-all category named VINHO REGIONAL roughly equivalent to France's VIN DE PAYS.   R.J.M.

Denominazione di Origine Controllata

Italy's viticultural production was given its first systematic regulation in 1963. A chosen few of its most famous wines had already been given legal recognition and protection during the 1930s well before the Italian parliament approved a framework law for the entire country and established a nationwide system of controlled appellations or *denominazioni*; DOC is simply the abbreviation of Denominazione di Origine Controllata, a direct translation of the French Appellation d'Origine Contrôlée. Also in 1963 legislators added another higher category, DOCG (Denominazione di Origine Controllata e Garantita) which added 'guaranteed' to 'controlled', a category which was intended to be reserved for the country's élite wines. The law, universally referred to in Italy as '930' (its number on the legislative calendar that year) was ostensibly inspired by French legislation and the French appellation system: individual production zones were mapped out and delimited; the VINE VARIETIES to be cultivated and fermented were defined (often in strict percentages); levels of ALCOHOL, TOTAL ACIDITY, and EXTRACT were established; ceilings placed on YIELDS; viticultural and wine-making practices regulated (although often in the haziest of terms: 'in conformity with existing practices' or 'so as to not change the nature of the wine' are frequent phrases in the rules of individual DOCs).

As the legal framework was fleshed out by the establishment of the various zones and the overall system of regulation went into effect, it became increasingly obvious that the Italian system bore only a superficial resemblance to the French one and was not succeeding in its fundamental purpose of guaranteeing QUALITY WINE to the consuming public. The 8.5 million hl/224 million gal DOC wine produced in an average Italian vintage are a mere third of the potential production of the existing DOC vineyard, confirming that producers in many DOC zones see no advantage in attaching the DOC name to their wines and deliberately choose not to label the wines as such.

Although over 300 separate DOC zones have been established and more than 1,200 DOC wines theoretically exist, only a small percentage of these wines have any real commercial vitality: 20 DOCs account for close to 45 per cent of the country's total DOC production, and 100 DOCs account for 80 per cent of the overall total; 300 DOC wines are produced in quantities less than 1,000 hl per year. The situation is particularly critical in Italy's south, which can be said to have collectively turned its back on the DOC system.

If producers have been sceptical of the advantages that DOC recognition would bring and are reluctant to classify their wines as DOC products, consumer disenchantment with the general quality of these wines has been even more accentuated and Italian consumers in particular, unlike their French counterparts, have refused to pay substantially higher prices for DOC wines than for non-DOC wines. For many years from 1975, an opposite phenomenon began to manifest itself: a refusal on the part of ambitious producers to label their best wines DOC and a policy of higher prices for many a VINO DA TAVOLA than for the DOC production of the same zones. The phenomenon began with the SUPERTUSCANS of TOSCANA but spread to EMILIA-ROMAGNA, FRIULI, PIEMONTE, SICILIA, and VENETO, and the apparent paradox of vini da tavola universally recognized as the best products of famous zones worthy of the highest prices threatened to become generalized.

What went wrong Various causes have been adduced for the general failure of law 930 to meet its expressed purposes, but the most common criticism has been of the overly strict and precise regulations established in the individual DOCs. With the benefit of hindsight, it is obvious that the DOC regulations enshrined in law the practices existing in the various zones in the 1960s, which represented the nadir of Italian wine; the first half of the 20th century saw prices plunge, so quality simply did not pay. As a result, high-yielding varieties and clones were planted, often in sites new to vines. These formed the base for the DOC laws, just at a time when both the market and the producers were beginning to change. As a result, the DOC laws quickly became irrelevant to many of the country's best producers.

These errors have been compounded by a lack of flexibility. The detailed prescription of such aspects as CASK AGEING and percentages of permitted grape varieties in individual zones has led many producers simply to ignore the laws. The very first Supertuscan, Tignanello 1970 (see VINO DA TAVOLA), was in fact released as a Chianti Classico despite its thoroughly illegal mere 3 per cent of white grapes, and in the 1980s many a prominent producer of Chianti Classico or VINO NOBILE DI MONTEPULCIANO had no qualms in publicly declaring that his wine was a far from orthodox 100 per cent SANGIOVESE. (The laws have since caught up with practice in both zones.)

The laws, based as they are on the APPELLATION CONTRÔLÉE system, adhere philosophically to the concept of GEOGRAPHICAL DELIMITATION but unfortunately, boundaries have been set as generously as permitted yields. Quite often, zones are carved out to coincide with political rather than geological boundaries, undermining the whole concept.

The coexistence of a superficially formal attempt at rigour with a laissez-faire approach to actual practice is a product of a national political culture whose improvisatory style to a certain extent reflects centuries of foreign domination. But law 930 principally reflects the period in which it was drafted, a period in which Italian producers had little knowledge of the wines outside their own regions let alone outside Italy. It also reflects the conviction of the time that the natural market for Italian wines was in the lower-medium price range (Italy, in 1963, was the poorest member of a Common Market, which had not yet admitted Spain, Portugal, or Greece) and that high-volume production was a necessity for economic survival. In this context it was probably inevitable that only those DOC wines with an established name, history, and reputation would draw any real benefits from law 930 and that the hundreds of 'invented' DOC wines, many of which were devised for political reasons and to satisfy local chauvinism, would attain no real public recognition and find few customers.

An attempt at reform Law 930 was modified by law 164 of December 1992, and the new legislation was drafted with the express purpose of giving Italy's DOC system credibility. Its main innovation was to introduce the principle of territorial subdivision by allowing larger DOC zones to be broken down into subzones, townships, hamlets, microzones, individual estates, and vineyards, and to give the entire structure a vertical and hierarchical basis: the new and smaller units more specific than DOC or DOCG zones have stricter production limits and criteria. Producers who wish to use a single-vineyard name for their DOC or DOCG wines have to register their vineyard and define its extent with the authorities, a reform aimed at curbing the multiplication of invented single-vineyard names (following the Italian FASHION for individual CRUS) with no real territorial basis.

Various DOCs or DOCGs may cover the same geographical limits, and producers have the option of declassifying their wines from a more restricted (and thus in a certain sense 'higher') to a more extended (and thus in a certain sense 'lower') DOC. Quality is thereby given a geographical basis by anchoring it in smaller, homogeneous areas with a real and proven aptitude for producing fine wines, instead of being attached to definitions such as SUPERIORE or RISERVA, which attempted, and failed, to link better quality with higher levels of alcohol and/or longer periods of ageing. All DOCG and DOC wines are required to undergo and pass ANALYSIS and tasting panels. And a new category of wines called IGT (Indicazione Geografica Tipica), intended as the approximate equivalent of the French VIN DE PAYS, was created in an attempt to bring all the renowned and high-quality wines selling as vino da tavola into the overall DOC system.

While many of these reforms are sensible and well intentioned, the loopholes in the legislation are only too obvious. Nothing has been done to curb the excessively generous yields of existing DOCs, and the lack of flexibility remains a problem. If, for instance, the percentages of permitted grape varieties were as strictly stipulated in the MÉDOC as in Chianti Classico, then every single CHÂTEAU there would have to have exactly the same ENCÉPAGEMENT.

Such dictates impede change. Even today, for example, many DOC zones cannot use SCREW CAP closures, as a majority of producers cannot be mustered to ratify the amendment. And even if they wanted to, producers in DOCG zones (such as Chianti or Gavi) cannot use screw caps, as a ministerial decree dating back to 1994 states that all DOCG wines must be sealed with natural cork. Such rigidity does little to allow individual producers to adapt to a fast-changing wine world. For this reason, the much more flexible IGT category has remained vibrant since it was introduced in 1994.

DOC zones, like Australian and New Zealand wine exporters, use chemical ANALYSIS and tasting panels in an attempt to ensure that any wine released is characteristic of that which it purports to be. In Italy, however, tasting panels have been notorious for their lack of rigour and reluctance to disqualify poorly made wines.

Law 164 did not simplify the system. In fact, it spawned an increasing number of individual DOCs. Initially only SASSICAIA in Toscana and Rosazzo in the Colli Orientali di Friuli were able to establish themselves as subzones of a larger DOC, while the DOC granted to PIEMONTE, which in theory established the entire regional production as DOC level, created the dangerous precedent of promotion by legislative fiat. Other regions were quick to claim similar treatment.

Perhaps the inevitable conclusion is that a wine industry interested only relatively recently in high quality is not currently suited for an appellation system like that of France, established to ratify, certify, and protect a long and settled tradition of fine wines, and not to create them from scratch. Italian wine production of the 1990s, marked by creative ferment and constant experimentation, was particularly ill-suited to a system of simple and stable rules.
D.T. & D.C.G.

DOCa, increasingly known simply as DOC (or DOQ in Catalan), Denominación de Origen Calificada, is the highest category in Spanish wine law, reserved for regions complying with certain conditions including above-average grape prices, and particularly stringent quality controls. RIOJA was the first Spanish region to be awarded DOCa status, in 1991, followed by PRIORAT in 2002.
R.J.M.

doce, Portuguese for sweet. See SWEETNESS and DOSAGE for official European Union sugar levels.

DOCG (Denominazione di Origine Controllata e Garantita) is a legal category established in ITALY in 1963 for its highest-quality wines, at the same time as its DOC was created, by law 930, as an Italian version of the French APPELLATION CONTRÔLÉE system. The express purpose of this category was to identify and reward the finest Italian wines, which were to be 'guaranteed' (the G), and not merely 'controlled'. If the DOC system did not enjoy general credibility because it was applied liberally and with little rigour, the DOCG title, in contrast, was conferred with admirable parsimony in its first years of existence. It was not even used until 1980, and by 1992, when the system was overhauled by law 164, only 11 wines had been deemed worthy of receiving the honour. The first five DOCGs to be conferred—BAROLO, BARBARESCO, CHIANTI, BRUNELLO DI MONTALCINO, and VINO NOBILE DI MONTEPULCIANO—are likely to be on everyone's short list of Italy's most important wines. The awarding of DOCG status to the undistinguished ALBANA DI ROMAGNA in 1986, however, widely regarded as political in inspiration and a violation of both letter and spirit of law 930 and, as such, a threat to the viability of the DOCG category itself, met such criticism that it was hoped that it would have prevented repetition of such an episode.

Subsequent DOCGs have included: TORGIANO Riserva, CARMIGNANO, GATTINARA, SAGRANTINO di Montefalco, TAURASI, VERNACCIA DI SAN GIMIGNANO, ASTI and MOSCATO D'ASTI, FRANCIACORTA, BRACHETTO d'Acqui, VERMENTINO di Gallura, GHEMME, GAVI, VALTELLINA,

GRECO di Tufo, FIANO di Avellino, RECIOTO di Soave, and MONTEPULCIANO d'Abruzzo Colline Teramane. The authorities found themselves in a similar situation to that of Albana di Romagna with the approval of DOCG for SOAVE, which, while merited in part of the zone, turned into a series of political compromises rather than a coherent attempt to define that which represented the best of Soave.

Political compromises apart, the greatest successes of DOCG have been to decrease YIELDS and promote an image of quality in virtually every zone to which it has been introduced.   D.T. & D.C.G.

doctors of medicine through the ages have displayed an uncommon affection for wine, and not just because of wine's uses as a MEDICINE and beneficial effects on HEALTH. Doctors have long been enthusiastic wine consumers (see Alexander HENDERSON, for example) and, more recently, producers. The WINE SOCIETY, an important wine-buying group founded in London in the late 19th century, regularly surveys the occupations of its members and the largest group is always made up of members of the medical profession, as are a number of the world's most serious wine COLLECTORS. There are numerous examples of vineyard owners who combine viticulture with practising medicine. Docteur Peste's slice of the CORTON vineyard is sold each year in the HOSPICES DE BEAUNE auction, itself a medical charity, for example. The MOSEL-SAAR-RUWER of Germany has an example of what might be called double-doctoring, in that the producer Dr Thanisch owns a portion of the world-famous Doctor, or Doktor, vineyard of Bernkastel.

Particularly strong medical connections can be traced in the history of AUSTRALIAN wine. During the transport of convicts and subsequent migrant trade of the 19th century, doctors became accustomed to using wine as medicine and many established their own vineyards on settling in Australia. More than 160 such cases can be cited, including the founders of what were for long Australia's three largest wine companies PENFOLDS, LINDEMANS, and HARDYS as well as those of labels such as Angove, Houghton, Stanley, and Minchinbury. Australia was founded in the rum age, developed in the beer age, and is now maturing in the wine age.

See also LITERATURE OF WINE.   J.R. & P.A.N.
Norrie, P. A., 'Australia's three leading wine doctors', *Journal of Medical Biography*, 3 (1995), 218–24.

dolce, Italian for sweet. See SWEETNESS and DOSAGE for official European Union sugar levels.

Dolceacqua, or **Rossese di Dolceacqua,** wine from the north western coast of Italy. For more details, see LIGURIA.

Dolcetto, an early-ripening, low-acid red grape variety cultivated almost exclusively in the provinces of Cuneo and Alessandria in the north west Italian region of PIEMONTE. The wines produced are soft, round, fruity, and fragrant with flavours of liquorice and almonds. Most are designed to be drunk in their first two or three years, although well-made bottles of Dolcetto d'Alba and Dolcetto d'Ovada can easily last at least five years. Dolcetto therefore plays an important role in the economy of various estates, providing a product which can be marketed early while the wines based on BARBERA or, particularly, NEBBIOLO grapes demand extended ageing in cask and bottle. Unlike Barbera, it is rarely blended with other varieties, chiefly because it is so rarely planted outside VARIETALLY minded Piemonte.

As a precocious ripener, ripening up to four weeks before the majestic Nebbiolo, Dolcetto also permits growers to exploit either higher or less favourably exposed vineyard sites and thus maximize the return on their holdings. In the precious BAROLO and BARBARESCO zones, for example, Dolcetto is rarely planted on a south-facing site unless the vineyard is too high to ripen Nebbiolo reliably. And in the zones of Dogliani, Diano d'Alba, and Ovada, Dolcetto is planted where other varieties may not ripen at all. There is a consensus amongst growers in the Dolcetto d'Alba DOC, source of much of the finest Dolcetto, that the variety prefers the characteristic white marls of the right bank of the Tanaro and cannot give maximum results in heavier soils.

If the grape is relatively easy to cultivate, apart from its susceptibility to FUNGAL DISEASES and a tendency to drop its bunches in the cold mornings of late September, it is far from easy to vinify. While low in ACIDITY, relative to Barbera at least, and therefore *dolce* (sweet) to the Piedmontese palate, Dolcetto ('little sweet one') does have significant TANNINS, which producers have learned to soften with shorter fermentations. So rich are the skins of Dolcetto in ANTHOCYANINS that even the shortest fermentation rarely compromises the deep ruby and purple tones of the wine. Like Barbera, it is prone to REDUCTION.

There are seven Dolcetto DOCs in Piemonte: Acqui, ALBA, ASTI (where little is planted, GRIGNOLINO being the young wine of choice), Diano d'Alba, Dogliani, Langhe Monregalesi, and Ovada. Alba, Ovada, and Dogliani are quantitatively the most significant, while the Langhe Monregalesi is a barely extant curiosity. Alba is generally considered to produce the finest quality, with good quality also being produced in what are virtually satellite appellations in Diano and Dogliani.

Ormeasco is LIGURIA's version of Dolcetto and is therefore the southernmost extent of Dolcetto territory in Italy. It grows just on the Ligurian side of the mountains that separate Piemonte from Liguria. In total, there were

7,336 ha/18,000 acres of Dolcetto planted in Italy in 2000.

Contrary to GALET's contention, DNA PROFILING at DAVIS showed that Dolcetto is not the same as the Douce Noire of SAVOIE, nor as the variety known as CHARBONO in California. A variety known as Dolcetto is known in Argentina but it is grown on an extremely limited scale.   D.T., D.C.G., & J.V.
Alcalde, A. J., *Cultivares Viticolas Argentinas* (Mendoza, 1989).
Galet, P., *Dictionnaire encyclopédique des cépages* (Paris, 2000).

Dôle, red wine made from mainly Pinot Noir with Gamay grapes grown in Valais in SWITZERLAND. A high proportion of Dôle lacks real interest and concentration but exceptions exist. **Dôle Blanche** is a lightly pressed, pale pink version. See also BOURGOGNE PASSETOUTGRAINS.

dolium, a large earthenware vessel used in the Ancient Roman period. Sometimes with a capacity of several thousand litres, they were often partly buried in the floor of a barn to act as a FERMENTATION VESSEL and provide storage for wine until it was transferred to AMPHORAE. In the late 20th and early 21st century, a number of Roman wrecks were discovered off the south coast of France in which the cargo space was largely taken up by up to 14 *dolia*, thus creating the ancient equivalent of a tanker for the transport of wine in bulk.   J.J.P.

domaine, French word for an estate, typically a vine-growing and wine-making estate in BURGUNDY.

domaine bottling, the relatively recent practice of BOTTLING the produce of a DOMAINE on the property which produced it (although bottling at least in the region of production was advocated as early as 1728; see LITERATURE OF WINE). Such wines are described as **domaine bottled,** or *mis(e) en bouteille au domaine* in French. The term is the BURGUNDY equivalent of Bordeaux's CHÂTEAU BOTTLING, whose history is mirrored by the practice of domaine bottling. Domaine bottling was even later and less common, however, since burgundy is generally produced in very much smaller quantities than bordeaux. Even today a high proportion of all burgundy is still sold in bulk to be blended for the NÉGOCIANTS' own labels. It was not until energetic wine merchants such as Frank SCHOONMAKER and Alexis LICHINE visited Burgundy in the second half of the 20th century that the better individual producers were encouraged, and in many cases subsidized, to bottle their own production, typically with the help of mobile BOTTLING lines. Poor standards of HYGIENE, and even faults in basic WINE-MAKING, can still dog some domaines and it is by no means the case that all domaine bottled burgundy is necessarily superior to one bottled by a négociant. A domaine bottled wine should, however, lack bland anonymity, and any Burgundian prepared to bottle his or her own wine shows signs of ambition. Now that so many Burgundian growers also have their own négociant business, the small print of bottling information may provide the only clue to the original provenance of the grapes: if the label states *mis en bouteille au domaine*, then the wine is made from fruit grown in their own vineyards. Otherwise the label is more likely to note: *mis en bouteille par . . .* followed by the producer's name.

See also ESTATE BOTTLED.

Domaine de la Romanée-Conti,

the most prestigious wine estate in Burgundy, based in Vosne-Romanée. 'The Domaine', as it is frequently called, is co-owned by the de Villaine and LEROY families and produces only GRAND CRU wines: one white, Le MONTRACHET, and six reds: Romanée-Conti and La Tâche (both MONOPOLES of the domaine), Richebourg, Romanée-St-Vivant, Échezeaux, and Grands Échezeaux. For more details of individual wines, see VOSNE-ROMANÉE and ÉCHEZEAUX. The Domaine is the exception to the law according to which no estate in Burgundy may be named after a specific vineyard. Its wines are notable for their richness and longevity.

History
What is now Romanée-Conti was identified by the monks of St-Vivant as Le Cloux des Cinq Journaux in 1512 and sold off, as Le Cros de Cloux, in 1584 to Claude Cousin. His nephew and heir Germain Danton sold again to Jacques Vénot in 1621. Vénot's daughter married a Croonembourg, which family retained the vineyard, now known as La Romanée (first mentioned in 1651), for four generations until it was sold to the Prince de Conti in 1760. The title Romanée-Conti was not used, however, until after dispossession by the revolutionaries and its sale by auction in 1794.

Romanée-Conti was bought by Julien Ouvard in 1819 and sold by his heirs to Jacques-Marie Duvault-Blochet 50 years later. Duvault-Blochet's eventual heirs were the de Villaine family. In 1911, Edmond Guidon de Villaine became director of what was now known as the Domaine de la Romanée-Conti, selling a half-share in 1942 to his friend Henri Leroy.

Over the years, Duvault-Blochet built up major vineyard ownership including part of Échezeaux, Grands Échezeaux, Richebourg, and the section of La Tâche known as Les Gaudichots. In 1933, the rest of La Tâche was bought from the Liger-Belair family, making a monopoly, and a small holding of Le Montrachet (0.67 ha/1.6 acres) was added in three slices between 1963 and 1980. The Domaine entered into a long-term contract to farm and produce the wines of Domaine Marey-Monge's holding of Romanée-St-Vivant

before eventually buying the land in 1988. This necessitated selling part of their Échezeaux vineyards and a slice of Grands Échezeaux, although they continue to farm the land and bottle the wines. Further vineyards owned by the Domaine in Vosne-Romanée and Bâtard-Montrachet are sold in bulk.   J.T.C.M.

The de Villaine–Leroy era
Henri Leroy provided the financial means, and the determination, firmly to cement DRC's position as the finest domaine in Burgundy. His NÉGOCIANT business, Société Leroy, was granted valuable distribution rights to DRC wines. Henri de Villaine, who succeeded his father in 1950, was critical of some of the comparative tasting activities of Henri Leroy's daughter 'Lalou' Bize-Leroy. In 1975, Lalou and Henri's son Aubert were appointed co-directors of this most famous estate, each representing the interests of their respective families. When Henri Leroy died in 1980, Lalou and her sister Pauline Roch-Leroy each had a 25 per cent share in the Domaine, while the de Villaine half was shared between about ten different family members.

Lalou's passion is tasting and wine-making, but her control of Société Leroy gave her power over both production and sales, which, together with the fact that in 1988 she set up her own Domaine LEROY including (like DRC) a portion of the Richebourg vineyard, resulted in her departure as co-director of the Domaine in 1993 when Aubert de Villaine and her sister Pauline decided to replace her with Pauline's son Charles Roch (soon to be killed in a motor accident and succeeded by his brother Henri Roch).

See also LEROY.

Mansson, P.-H., 'Behind the breakup at Domaine de la Romanée-Conti', *Wine Spectator* (15 Feb. 1993), 20–7.

Olney, R., *Romanée-Conti* (Paris, 1991).

Domecq,
JEREZ-based company, famous for its SHERRY and a pioneer of Spanish brandy. The firm's origins date back to the 1730s, when farmer Patrick Murphy came to Spain from Ireland and teamed up with Juan Haurie to manage vineyards. When Murphy died in 1762, Haurie took over the estates, by now well established in the finest sherry vineyards of Macharnudo and Carrascal. Pedro Domecq Lembeye inherited the company from his uncle in 1794. The company's rise to fame and fortune started in the early 19th century when the firm of Ruskin, Telford, and Domecq dominated the British sherry trade. Ruskin's son John preferred to write on art and architecture. When Pedro Domecq Lembeye died in 1839 he was succeeded by his brother Juan Pedro, who bought the Palacio de Aladro, which remained in the family for more than a century.

Juan Pedro died childless in 1869 and left the firm to his adopted son, also called Juan Pedro. A relative, Pedro Domecq Lustau, who was

born near Cognac, was responsible for pioneering the sale of 'Brandy de Jerez'. The family had been distilling it in small quantities for some time but it was Pedro Domecq who launched the Fundador brand in 1874, five years before the arrival of the PHYLLOXERA louse interrupted the supply of cognac in the Charentes and gave the Jerezanos a chance to supply world markets with their brandy.

The Domecqs also pioneered the production of Spanish-style brandy in Latin America. Indeed the Presidente brand, distilled in MEXICO, is one of the world's largest selling spirits.

Domecq owns about 1,000 ha/2,500 acres of vineyards in Jerez Superior. Its best-known sherry brand is the FINO La Ina and it also now controls HARVEYS and the world's biggest-selling sherry brand Harveys Bristol Cream. The family lost control in 1994 and the company was acquired by PERNOD RICARD from Allied Domecq in 2005.   S.A.

domestic wine production. See HOME WINE-MAKING.

Domina,
modern red GERMAN CROSSING planted on 283 ha/700 acres of vineyard. Its parents are Portugieser × Spätburgunder (Pinot Noir) and it combines the productivity of the first with the ripeness, tannins, and colour of the second, if not its finesse and fruit.

Dominio de Valdepusa,
Spanish DO created especially for the Marqués de Griñon estate near Toledo. See MÉNTRIDA.

Domitian,
Roman emperor (AD 81–96) who, in the words of the eulogy by the contemporary poet Statius (*Silvae* 4. 3. 11–12), restored 'to chaste Ceres the acres which had so long been denied her and lands made sober'. By a famous edict, possibly from AD 92, Domitian banned the planting of new vineyards in Italy and ordered the destruction of at least half of the vineyards in the provinces (Suetonius, *Domitian* 7). He may also have sought to ban the planting within cities of small vineyards, of the sort which have been found at POMPEII. His purpose was not, as some have supposed, an attempt to protect the price of Italian wine at a time of general over-production, but a heavy-handed attempt to divert investment into the production of cereals, the supply of which was a perennial problem for the large cities of the Roman empire. There was no way that Domitian could enforce such a ban and, following the protests which we know came from Asia, he did not persist with the measure. Hence the much later efforts of the Emperor Probus (AD 276–82) to encourage the planting of vineyards should not be taken as a sign that the ban lasted for centuries, as has often been thought.   J.J.P.

Dom Pérignon. See PÉRIGNON, DOM.

Doña Blanca, also known as **Dona Branca, Valenciana,** and Moza Fresca, GALICIAN variety grown in north west Spain, particularly in Monterrei, Bierzo, and to a much lesser extent Valdeorras, where it is known as Valenciana. In the mid 1990s, there were about 1,000 ha/2,500 acres and the slightly bitter white wines of Monterrei suggest there may be potential. It may be identical to MERSEGUERA.

Donnaz, red wine based on NEBBIOLO grapes made in Italy's Valle d'AOSTA.

DOQ, or Denominaciò d'Origen Qualificada, the Catalan equivalent of DOCA.

Doradillo, white grape variety, possibly of Spanish origin, but known today only in AUSTRALIA. It produces handsome quantities of entirely unremarkable wine more suitable for DISTILLATION or basic FORTIFIED wines than for bottling as a table wine. By 2004, there were barely 100 ha/247 acres of Doradillo planted, mainly in the hot, irrigated RIVERLAND of South Australia. In its time it has erroneously been called Blanquette and considered identical to the JAÉN of Spain.

Dordogne, river in SOUTH WEST FRANCE which rises on the Massif Central south west of Clermont-Ferrand, flows through the Corrèze *département* (whence the merchants of LIBOURNE came), flows through BERGERAC and related appellations, and in to the GIRONDE to form the more northerly of the two 'seas' referred to in the name of ENTRE-DEUX-MERS, with ST-ÉMILION, POMEROL, FRONSAC, and finally BOURG on its right bank. VIN DE PAYS de la Dordogne, typically a dry white wine made from Bordeaux grape varieties, may come from anywhere in the *département* named Dordogne, of which Périgueux is the principal town.

dormancy, sleep, the normal state of vines in winter. This period nominally starts with autumn LEAF FALL, although buds are in a state of so-called organic dormancy from VERAISON onwards. The period of dormancy ends with BUDBREAK in the spring. Pruning is carried out when the vines are dormant, and buds and CUTTINGS taken from the vines at this time are used in PROPAGATION. Tests on vines in winter show they are literally asleep or dormant, with minimal metabolic activity.   R.E.S.

Lavee, S., and May, P., 'Dormancy of grapevine buds—facts and speculation', *Australian Journal of Grape and Wine Research*, 3 (1997), 31–46.

Dornfelder, red GERMAN CROSSING, bred in 1956 by August Herold, who had unwisely already assigned his name to one of its parents, the lesser HEROLDREBE, and so Dornfelder owes its name to the 19th-century founder of the Württemberg viticultural school. A HELFENSTEINER Heroldrebe cross, Dornfelder incorporates every important red wine vine grown in Germany somewhere in its genealogy and happily seems to have inherited many more of their good points than their bad.

The wine is notable for its depth of colour (useful in a country where pigments are at a premium), its good acidity, and, in some cases, its ability to benefit from BARRIQUE ageing and even to develop in bottle. Producing wines that are velvety textured, slightly floral, and sometimes with just a hint of sweetness, Dornfelder is easier to grow than Spätburgunder, has much better resistance to rot than Portugieser, stronger stalks than Trollinger, better ripeness levels than either, earlier ripening than Lemberger (Blaufränkisch), and a yield that can easily reach 120 hl/ha (6.8 tons/acre) (although quality-conscious producers are careful to restrict productivity). It is hardly surprising that it continues to gain ground in most German wine regions, especially Rheinhessen and the Pfalz, where results are particularly appetizing. Germany's total plantings rose steadily throughout the 1980s and 1990s to reach a national total of 7,686 ha/19,000 acres by 2003.

dosage, the final addition to a SPARKLING WINE which may top up a bottle in the case of traditional method wines, and also determines the sweetness, or RESIDUAL SUGAR, of the finished wine. In French this addition is called the *liqueur d'expédition* and, in traditional method wines, usually comprises a mixture of wine and sugar syrup. Champagne is naturally so high in ACIDITY that even wines with relatively high residual sugar can taste bone dry. BOTTLE AGE or extended AUTOLYSIS are excellent substitutes for dosage, however, and, in general, the older the wine, the lower the necessary dosage to produce a BALANCED wine, and vice versa. Some champagnes are made with no, or zero, dosage. The table below gives the legal classification of sweetness levels for sparkling wine and champagne within the EUROPEAN UNION. This information must be included on the label.

double pruning, a viticultural technique in which the vines are pruned twice, which alters the timing of vine development (see PHENOLOGY). Double pruning may be carried out for one of two reasons: to delay BUDBREAK and hence reduce FROST hazard in cool climates; or to delay harvest and hence potentially increase wine quality in hot regions.

Since early winter pruning encourages earlier budbreak, frost injury risks are increased.

Pruning lightly in the beginning of the winter delays budbreak of basal buds; a second or double pruning can be done after the danger of frost is passed.

The related technique of double pruning in hot climates was developed by R. E. Smart and P. R. Dry at ROSEWORTHY in South Australia in the 1970s to delay fruit ripening from the heat of midsummer to cooler conditions of autumn. The vines are pruned normally in winter and then again in early summer just after flowering. Yields are reduced by this process but wine quality is much improved.   R.E.S.

Douce Noire. See CHARBONO.

douelle or **douve,** French for a STAVE.

Douro, Portuguese DOC named after the river which rises, as the **Duero,** in the hills far upstream of RIBERA DEL DUERO and flows for more than half its course in Spain until it turns south to form the frontier with PORTUGAL before turning west towards the Atlantic coast to cut a cleft through the hard, granite mountains of northern Portugal (see maps under PORTUGAL and SPAIN). The Douro valley is most famous as the source of the FORTIFIED wine PORT, although the Douro DOC is increasingly well known for the production of unfortified table wine. From the Douro's 38,000 ha/93,900 acres of vines, just over half the region's production is made into port.

The Douro valley was demarcated in 1756, making it one of the oldest delimited wine regions in the world (see DELIMITATION and PORTUGAL, history). The boundaries have since been modified but the irregular outline corresponds closely with an outcrop of pre-Cambrian SCHIST. Hemmed in by GRANITE, this schist runs either side of the river for nearly 100 km/63 miles from the Spanish frontier in the east to the village of Barqueiros in the west. For over two centuries, the demarcation applied only to the fortified wine port, but in 1979 it was extended to cover table wine (in the sense of unfortified wine) as well. Depending on the year, up to 55 per cent of the Douro's total wine production is not FORTIFIED but fermented out to make table wine, the proportion of the crop used to make port being increased only in years when grapes are in short supply. In the past, the best grapes were

EU classification of sweetness levels for champagne and sparkling wine (see DOSAGE)	
RS g/l	**Example descriptions**
< 3 with no sugar added after primary fermentation	brut nature/naturherb/bruto natural/pas dosé
0–6	extra brut/extra herb/extra bruto
< 15	brut/herb/bruto
12–20	extra dry/extra trocken/extra seco
17–35	sec/trocken/secco or asciutto/dry/seco
33–50	demi-sec/halbtrocken/abboccato/medium dry/semiseco
> 50	doux/mild/dolce/sweet/dulce

always used for producing port, but a number of port shippers and individual estates are now giving Douro red table wines much greater priority.

Under a complicated classification system, individual port vineyards are graded A to F (for more detail, see PORT). Properties in the Baixo Corgo (the most westerly and therefore the coolest and wettest subregion) as well as those in the hills close to the Douro's 650-m boundary are considered to be less suitable for making port than vineyards located in the heart of the region. Outlying farms, or QUINTAS, therefore qualify for lower grades. Under the system of licences administered annually by the Port Wine Institute, they are not permitted to fortify as much of their must to make port as those whose vineyards qualify for higher grades.

Unfortified wines are not new to the Douro. Until the early part of the 18th century, most of the wine exported from the region was fermented dry and shipped without the addition of spirit. At that time, however, the quality of many of these wines was so poor that merchants added brandy in order to stabilize them during shipment. Port, the sweet, fortified wine that we know today, evolved only in the 18th century, when shippers learned to arrest the fermentation leaving RESIDUAL SUGAR. After that time, table wines were for long largely neglected in favour of port, but Douro table wines have slowly been receiving more attention ever since the 1950s, when port shippers FERREIRA launched Barca Velha, a red wine made from grapes grown in the upper reaches of the Douro which established itself as one of Portugal's finest and most admired wines. Early experiments with making other Douro table wines were often hampered by a lack of technology, but an increasing number of winemakers are now investing in the skills and equipment that are necessary to make table wine in the extreme Douro climate.

The grape varieties used in making Douro wines are similar to those used to produce port, with over 100 different varieties officially sanctioned by the IVDP. TOURIGA NACIONAL and Tinta Roriz (TEMPRANILLO) are widely accepted as the best for red wines, many of which share the ripe, spicy, tannic character of a young port. Gouveio, Malvasia Fina, Rabigato, and Viosinho are the favoured white grapes. Wines made from grape varieties (including Cabernet Sauvignon, Syrah, and Chardonnay) which are not authorized under the DOC may be designated under the local VINHO REGIONAL, TRÁS-OS-MONTES-Terras Durienses. R.J.M.

Mayson, R., *Portugal's Wines and Wine Makers* (San Francisco, 1998).
—*The Wines and Vineyards of Portugal,* (London, 2003).
—*Port and the Douro,* (London, 2004).

Douro bake, traditional expression for the character imparted to wines, especially PORT, matured in the hot, dry climate of the DOURO valley (rather than the much cooler, damper atmosphere of VILA NOVA DE GAIA, where port has traditionally been matured by the shippers). Some wines matured in the Douro seem to develop faster, losing colour, browning, and sometimes acquiring a slightly sweet, caramelized flavour—although poor and sometimes unhygienic storage conditions often have a greater impact on wine quality than the climate, and many reputable shippers successfully age large stocks of port in the Douro.
R.J.M.

doux, French for sweet. See SWEETNESS and DOSAGE for official EUROPEAN UNION sugar levels.

Dow, important port shipper. See SYMINGTONS.

downy mildew, one of the most economically significant FUNGAL DISEASES affecting vines, often called peronospera in parts of Europe. It is a particular problem in regions with warm, humid summers such as many wine regions in northern Europe. The disease is caused by the organism *Plasmopara viticola*. This fungus is indigenous to eastern North America, and so some species of native AMERICAN VINES such as *Vitis cordifolia*, *Vitis rupestris*, and *Vitis rotundifolia* are relatively resistant. Commercially important varieties of VITIS VINIFERA, however, are highly susceptible.

The fungus caused havoc in the vineyards of Europe when it was accidentally introduced before 1878, probably on American vines imported as grafting stock to combat PHYLLOXERA. By 1882, the disease had spread to all of France. The famous BORDEAUX MIXTURE was first used as a preventive spray to control this disease.

The disease is now widespread around the world, but a few areas with low spring and summer rainfall are essentially free of it. These include Afghanistan, northern Chile, Egypt, and Western Australia. California was thought to be free of it but unseasonal rainfall caused sporadic outbreaks of it in the 1990s, while new vineyards in the south of Chile have also been unexpectedly affected.

Downy mildew attacks all green parts of the vine and young leaves are particularly susceptible. When severely affected, leaves will drop off. The loss of leaves reduces PHOTOSYNTHESIS and thus causes delays in fruit ripening and, typically, levels of fruit SUGARS, vine reserves of CARBOHYDRATES, and ANTHOCYANINS are depressed. BUDBREAK and early shoot growth can be delayed the following spring. Severe infections result in pale, puny reds and weak whites.

The symptoms of the disease are described quite aptly by the name. Leaves show patches of dense, white cottony growth on the undersurface. The earliest stage of the fungus is the so-called 'oil spot', easily seen on the upper leaf surface when it is held up against the light.

PETIOLES, TENDRILS, young INFLORESCENCES, and developing berries are also affected. The fungus spends the winter in fallen leaves and can sometimes survive in the buds. Spores germinate in the spring when temperatures reach 11 °C/52 °F and they are spread to the vine by rainsplash from the soil. Spores are further spread and germinated with high humidity (95 to 100 per cent relative humidity), warm temperatures (18 to 22 °C), and moisture. The most severe epidemics of the disease occur with frequent rainstorms and warm weather. The low yields of the French vintages of 1886, 1910, 1915, 1930, 1932, 1948, 1957, and 1969, all of them produced after wet growing seasons, were probably due to downy mildew.

There are two principal protection approaches. The first and most common is to use protective sprays which are often based on COPPER. However, the protection lasts for only ten days or so, especially when the shoots are growing rapidly in early spring. Curative fungicides which act against established infections became available in the early 1990s, but these are more expensive. A modern approach is to install a VINEYARD WEATHER STATION which can predict outbreaks by measuring the weather.

An alternative but less popular approach to the control of this disease is to plant DISEASE-RESISTANT VARIETIES. European vine breeders, especially at GEISENHEIM and GEILWEILERHOF in Germany, have been particularly successful in developing varieties which require no, or less, spraying against downy mildew, with native American vines contributing the resistant genes. Increased environmental awareness may encourage their use, but there is substantial consumer resistance to new varieties. R.E.S.

Emmett, R. W., Harris, A. R., Taylor, R. H., and McGechan, J. K., 'Grape diseases and vineyard protection', in B. G. Coombe and P. R. Dry (eds.), *Viticulture*, ii: *Practices* (Adelaide, 1992).
Galet, P., *Précis de viticulture* (5th edn, Montpellier, 1988).
Pearson, R. C., and Goheen, A. C., *Compendium of Grape Diseases* (St Paul, Minn., 1988).

drainage, free movement of water through the SOIL profile or across the land surface; or alternatively, the removal of surplus water by artificial means. The importance of good soil drainage for viticulture and wine quality cannot be overstated. For a detailed discussion, see Seguin. See also TERROIR and SOIL AND WINE QUALITY.

All good vineyard soils are well drained, whether naturally or by artificial drainage. Permanent waterlogging or prolonged waterlogging after the start of spring growth is lethal to vine roots. Even marginal waterlogging can be harmful, by causing restriction of root and soil microbial activity, and consequent starvation of the vine for nutrients and root-produced growth substances (see CYTOKININ). Soils that are cold and wet at the time of FLOWERING are a major factor in poor berry setting, or COULURE. However, if water-logging is temporary and the soil dries out at or just after flowering, with mild water stress before veraison, it is still possible to produce fine wines, especially on alluvial soils when sand or gravel is layered over finer sediment. Such waterlogging may reduce root depth but will not necessarily affect eventual wine quality.

Waterlogging confined to the SUBSOIL can still be a serious disadvantage, through killing or inactivation of the deeper roots. This can result in a vine with only a shallow effective root system, readily subject both to later DROUGHT after the surface moisture has evaporated or been used, and to excessive water uptake following rains during ripening. Seguin argues that such irregularity in the supply of SOIL WATER can be seriously detrimental to wine quality. Subsoils that are regularly waterlogged can be identified by their bleached, white or grey colour (see SOIL COLOUR) while well-drained subsoils are usually yellow to reddish, and mottled subsoils indicate intermittent waterlogging.

As a broad rule, light-textured and stony soils drain freely, while tight or heavy clay soils (see SOIL TEXTURE) restrict drainage. Subsoils composed of the latter type can result in water-tables 'perched' on top of them. These develop most commonly on gradients, where seepage of water down the slope through the surface soil is interrupted by barriers of rock, or of clay reaching or approaching the surface.

However, even heavy soils and subsoils can drain adequately if they have good crumb structure (see SOIL STRUCTURE). This depends on their chemical nature, including sufficient contents of CALCIUM and, in the upper layers, ORGANIC MATTER. Unstructured soils can easily pack down to form impermeable hardpans below the surface when subjected to trampling or wheeled traffic. Vineyards are commonly RIPPED before planting to facilitate drainage.

Several other management factors can influence soil drainage. Deeply tap-rooted green manuring or COVER CROPS, such as mustard or lupins, can help to create and maintain vertical channels which allow water to infiltrate freely into the deeper soil layers. The maintenance of an organic surface MULCH, whether applied or originating naturally from cover crops, attains the same effect through encouraging earthworm activity. These useful creatures also help to distribute surface organic matter and nutrients through the soil profile. Finally, the application of LIME or gypsum can help on some acid soils, by improving their crumb structure and permeability.

Artificial drainage, where required, can be of several types according to situation and need. Webber and Jones describe them in detail. All forms of artificial soil drainage are expensive, but, on otherwise valuable land for producing high-value grapes, they can be essential. Drain-age did, after all, transform the Médoc from a marsh to one of the world's most admired wine regions (see BORDEAUX, history).   J.G. & C.V.L.

Seguin, G., ' "Terroirs" and pedology of wine growing', *Experientia*, 42 (1986), 861–72.

Webber, R. T. J., and Jones, L. D., 'Drainage and soil salinity', in B. G. Coombe and P. R. Dry (eds.), *Viticulture*, ii: *Practices* (Adelaide, 1992).

draining (*égouttage* in French). In WHITE WINE-MAKING the operation usually takes place just after CRUSHING. Any juice run off without pressing is called drainings. The FREE-RUN juice is drained off the grape skins in a **draining tank** or **draining vat**, many of which incorporate special design features to assist the separation of liquids from solids. Similarly, in red wine fermentation, the red wine run off the skins may also be called drainings.

DRC, famous initials in the world of fine wine, standing for the DOMAINE DE LA ROMANÉE-CONTI.

dried grape wines, varied category of generally intense, complex, often sweet wines made from partially raisined grapes. The production technique, involving either leaving the grapes to raisin on the vine or picking and then drying them (on mats of straw or reed, racks of bamboo, or strung in bunches under the rafters), is associated with most of the celebrated wines of antiquity. This early CONCENTRATION technique continues one of the oldest traditions in the gastronomic world.

In the classical world this wine-making style may well have evolved because of problems of wine conservation, particularly for wines traded and consumed outside their area of origin, semi-dried grapes naturally resulting in sweeter, stronger and therefore more stable wines. (BOTRYTIZED wines and the technique of FORTIFICATION were developed many centuries later.) The dried grape tradition has proved particularly resilient close to its origins, notably in Italy.

Ancient history

The technique of twisting the stems of grape bunches to deprive them of sap, and leaving them to raisin on the vine, may have originated in CRETE, but vinification techniques for dried grapes were perfected in Ancient GREECE. The Ancient Greeks also learned from other inhabitants of the eastern Mediterranean, particularly the Hittites of Anatolia (see ASIA MINOR). The first description of how to make wine from dried grapes is provided by HESIOD, in the 8th century BC. His *Works and Days* describes how grapes should be dried in the sun 'for ten days and nights' and then in the shade for a further five, before fermenting the wine in jars.

Such methods were responsible for the famous wines of the islands (Chios, Lesbos, and Thasos) which were so highly prized by HOMER and succeeding writers. These wines were often noted as being at their best after many years' maturation, when they had 'lost their teeth': clear evidence of the longevity which only dried grape wines could provide before the invention of stoppered bottles. Sealed AMPHORAE may have been relatively airtight containers but long journeys in Mediterranean heat demanded exceptionally robust wines.

Coincidental with the rise of the Greek city states was the emergence of the most adventurous traders of the Mediterranean, those of PHOENICIA. They exported the wines of Lebanon (and the wine-making practices of CANAAN) along the littorals of North Africa and to Spain, Sardegna, and Sicilia. One of their colonies was CARTHAGE, founded in 814 BC, where in about 500 BC Mago wrote his seminal work on agriculture, now known only in the extensive quotations which survive in the works of succeeding classical authors, notably the Roman COLUMELLA. Redding quotes Mago in the following passage which summarizes the Graeco-Roman understanding of dried grape vinification:

Let the bunches of grapes quite ripe, and scorched or shrivelled in the sun, when the bad and faulty ones are picked out, be spread upon a frame resting on stakes or forks and covered with a layer of reeds. Place them in the sun but protect them from the dew at night. When they are dry (sufficiently shrivelled) pluck the grapes from the stalks, throw them into a cask and make the first must. If they have been well drained, put them, at the end of six days, into a vessel, and press them for the first wine. A second time let them be pounded (or trodden) and pressed, adding cold must to the pressing. This second wine is to be placed in a pitched vessel, lest it become sour. After it has remained twenty or thirty days, and fermented, rack it into another vessel and stopping it close immediately, cover it with a skin.

Other writers in Ancient ROME such as CATO, PLINY, HORACE, and VIRGIL add other details (such as storing these wines in the rafters, as with modern Tuscan VIN SANTO), but in general repeat the principles laid down by their Mediterranean forebears.

The Romans, like the Greeks, planted vineyards wherever they went—in Spain, France, Germany, and central Europe, perhaps even in England. Only in the last would the climate have been too austere for the production of *passum* (PASSITO) wines; elsewhere the practice became embedded in the complex strata of vinicultural history, a rich seam of vinous tradition to be mined in later centuries, after the long upheavals which followed the collapse of the Roman empire.

Evolution since the Middle Ages

Italy The *vinum reticum* of Verona praised by Pliny was presumably the ancestor of today's RECIOTO and AMARONE. It was relatively common for wines to be made from grapes dried on the vine cut off the flow of sap by having their stems twisted, or *torcolato* (the name of a modern white Recioto made by Maculan of

BREGANZE from partially dried, though not in fact twisted, VESPAIOLA grapes). The dried grape tradition was presumably enhanced in 1204 when Venice conquered Crete, the stronghold of this classical heritage. The result seems to have been a revival of dried grape wine-making throughout the growing Venetian empire, not just in Veneto but on the islands and coast of what is now SLOVENIA and CROATIA.

In early 14th-century PIEMONTE, such wines were in great demand and are mentioned again in the mid 17th century, but the tradition survives only as a curiosity today. In TOSCANA, however, VIN SANTO survives as an apparently unbroken tradition, practised by most of the best estates. Versions exist in other parts of Italy, notably in TRENTINO. Other survivals include the VERDUZZO of Ramandolo, the generally overrated PICOLIT of FRIULI, the remarkable Rosenmuskateller of TRENTINO-ALTO ADIGE, SFORZATO or Sfursat of VALTELLINA, ALBANA passito from Romagna, and SAGRANTINO passito from Umbria. In the south and islands, examples of this renascent tradition are too numerous to mention in detail but include a range of wines based on raisined MOSCATO, ALEATICO, MALVASIA, and Nasco grapes, not to mention Vecchio Samperi, the rare unfortified wine in the style of MARSALA from de Bartoli.

Elsewhere It is clear from REDDING that dried grape wines were much more common in early 19th-century France than today. He mentions the VIN DE PAILLE of Alsace, two types from Argentac in the Corrèze (way upriver of modern BERGERAC), one of them slightly sparkling, and what sounds like a magnificent example from the Sciacarello grape made at Sartène in CORSICA. He also makes clear that Muscat de RIVESALTES was then a true raisin wine, often the result of twisting grape stems on the vine, and not, as now, a fortified blend. In contemporary France, the tradition survives only in the vins de paille of Hermitage and the Jura, made as curiosities by two or three producers in each region, in quantities so tiny that they rarely reach the market.

In Spain, the classical traditions continued in muted form through the Muslim occupation and were revived thereafter. The most notable surviving derivatives are the Andalusian specialities SHERRY, MONTILLA, and MÁLAGA, whose richer styles have always been made with semi-dried grapes, but these are not pure dried grape wines because most (although not Telmo Rodriguez' Molino Réal Malaga) are now fortified. Elsewhere in Spain the tradition is almost extinct. In RIOJA there is evidence of an ancient local habit of using dried Moscatel or Malvasia grapes to produce wines which were variously described as *supurado*, *tostadillo*, *vino de paja*, or *vino dorado* (suppurating, toasted, straw wine, golden wine).

Surprisingly few dried grape wines can be found in modern Greece. The rich wines of Sámos date from the replanting of the island's vineyards in the 16th century but those of SANTORINI (Thíra of the ancients) are debased descendants of the classical prototypes, as is the now fortified COMMANDARIA of Cyprus.

There are records of straw wine (Strohwein) being made in FRANKEN in Germany; a rich red dried grape wine just over the border in Switzerland from Italy's VALTELLINA; a 'green' wine of remarkable strength produced near Cotnar on the borders of Moldova and Romania (see COTNARI); and of course the rather special case of TOKAJI in Hungary. The last survives; most of the others have vanished. The only notable additions to the once splendid roll-call of wines from the old Austro-Hungarian empire are a few straw wines and reed wines from AUSTRIA.

Redding mentions Shahoni, the 'royal grape' of the province of Cashbin in Persia, claiming that 'the grapes are kept over the winter, and remain on the vine a good deal of the time in linen bags', and also lists from Argentina a 'sweet wine, resembling Malaga, made at Mendoza at the foot of the Andes, on their eastern side' and the famous CONSTANTIA from South Africa, now being revived. In modern times there have also been tentative experiments with dried grape wines in California and Australia (see CUT CANE).

Modern production techniques

Grapes with maximum EXTRACT and SUGARS are required, which normally entails restricting YIELDS. Such grapes may be picked either before, at, or after full RIPENESS. Twisting the stalk was once practised in Veneto but most growers now prefer to dry their grapes off the vine.

Those who pick slightly before full maturation claim there is less risk of ROT, thicker skins, enhanced resistance during drying, and higher acidity, all of which favour aroma, freshness, balance, and longevity—and concentrate the grapes which remain on the vine.

Only the ripest, healthiest grapes are generally picked, which today means a pre-selection by experienced pickers (although see RECIOTO). Healthy grapes are vital since any incipient mould or rot soon spreads during the drying process. Skins must remain intact, to which end the grapes may well be laid in small trays for transport to the winery. The bunches should be *spargolo*, loose rather than compact, so that air circulates around the individual berries during the all-important drying process.

Sun drying is still practised in places such as the Sicilian island of PANTELLERIA off Tunisia, in southern PUGLIA, and the Greek island of SANTORINI. It can be up to eight times as fast as drying under cover, but this can result in excessive colour, caramelized flavours, and loss of aroma, bypassing some of the microbiological transformations which are the essence of fine dried grape wine. For the same reason, purists reject the use of drying ovens.

Most grape drying for commercial purposes happens in a winery loft, where windows may be opened to let in plenty of air (essential against the development of rot and mould). Bunches are hung up vertically (on hooks, or on long strings), or laid out horizontally on neutral, bone-dry materials. Straw is rarely used because of its attractions for mice, while oak slats can be expensive. Wire mesh, nylon nets, and fruit boxes were 20th-century developments; cane and rush mats and bamboo racks remain popular in much of Italy. Today, in zones where dried grapes constitute an important factor in the local wine economy, purpose-built grape-drying plants are being created complete with temperature control and wind machines.

The duration of the drying process is dictated by the grape variety, the type of wine required, and microclimatic conditions during drying. Sugar-rich Greek grape varieties such as Muscat, Aleatico, and Malvasia require less time than more northern varieties. Three weeks may suffice for a Muscat whereas a Veronese variety such as GARGANEGA for a white Recioto or CORVINA or CORVINONE for a red Recioto or Amarone will need three to four months, in some cases, for Recioto, even up to six months. Ideal conditions include considerable currents of dry air, and humidity is such a problem in some valley sites that drying facilities are being moved to higher altitudes. Excessive heat is generally regarded as negative, as is excessive cold.

The main effect of drying grapes is loss of water and the consequent concentration of sugars. The relationship between water loss and sugar gain is relatively direct so that a water loss of a third from grapes picked at $12°$ BAUMÉ would result in a wine of 16 per cent alcohol (if all the sugar were fermented out). Depending on the wine style desired, the loss of grape weight by evaporation varies between 10 and 60 per cent, with the norm for a PASSITO wine being somewhere in the region of 35 to 40 per cent, so the potential alcohol is raised by just over a third.

Other components behave less predictably. The TOTAL ACIDITY in grapes undergoing a 40 per cent dehydration rises not by 40 per cent but by around 25 per cent. These and other organic substances undergo various transformations, and there may be development of certain aromas and loss of others in the process. The longer the drying period, the greater the biological change of organic substances and resultant wine quality.

NOBLE ROT may develop on the grapes during dehydration but it is not desired by most practitioners, particularly those making the drier styles of dried grape wines such as Amarone. A further problem is insect infestation, particularly of bees, wasps, and hornets.

Crushing or pressing should ideally be as gentle as possible. Gravity, but certainly not CENTRIFUGATION, may be used to clarify white must, while in the case of red wines, stems may be totally or only partially removed.

The must of raisined grapes is so concentrated that it slows FERMENTATION, an effect accentuated in cooler climates, especially where the long drying period may mean that the grapes are crushed in midwinter and the ambient temperature is naturally low. In Italy, fermentation may therefore safely take place in wood, and may need to be started by heating or by adding specially cultured local YEAST. In traditional areas, the right yeasts have been in the atmosphere for centuries. *Saccharomyces uvarum* begins the job in Valpolicella, according to Masi, while *Saccharomyces bayanus* is able to work at higher temperatures and at the ALCOHOLIC STRENGTH of 16 per cent or more that is necessary for many Amarones.

Some producers allow the fermentation to stop and start for months or even, as in the case of Guiseppe Quintarelli, two to three years, and allow Nature to decide how sweet the final wine will be. Most, however, use RACKING and, increasingly, REFRIGERATION to stop fermentation.

The wine is then generally racked off its LEES and the lees sometimes used to enrich normal VALPOLICELLA, the process called RIPASSO. In CHIANTI, dried grapes may be added intact to a finished wine to achieve a similar effect, the so-called GOVERNO process.

Dried grape wines tend to be particularly high in VOLATILE ACIDS, a direct result of high sugar levels (accentuated if any BOTRYTIZED grapes have been included). The ACETIC ACID of such a wine may well exceed legal levels, sometimes entailing unacceptably high SULFUR DIOXIDE additions. Many argue that high levels of volatile acidity are essential to the quality of such wines, and some maintain that false 'passito' wines can be exposed precisely by improbably low levels of acetic acid.

Dried grape wines may be divided into two categories: those in which the fresh primary AROMAS are retained and those in which primary aromas are sacrificed to the development of a more complex BOUQUET. The former include most wines based on aromatic varieties such as Muscat, Brachetto, Aleatico, and Riesling, as well as sweet whites where the emphasis is on fruit, such as Recioto di Soave. These are subjected as far as possible to PROTECTIVE wine-making techniques.

Vin de paille and Vin Santo, with their RANCIO character, are the most notable examples of the OXIDATIVE style. Amarone and Recioto della Valpolicella of the traditional type are also treated oxidatively, the aim being to incorporate in the final tasting experience an evolution of aromas due in some measure to exposure to oxygen. Traditional Amarone and Recioto are, typically, the result of prolonged maceration, deliberately frequent racking, and ageing for years in large, old barrels. Strong, dry Valpolicella Amarone is a notable example, as is Vin Santo with the rancio

character encouraged by traditionalists. Since the 1980s, there has been a movement away from such classic styles, however, and modernist Amarone and Recioto producers are aiming for more FRUIT-DRIVEN wines.

In the early 1990s, an accelerated Eurotechnique was authorized experimentally by EUROPEAN UNION authorities, involving drying bunches in a single layer at between 30 and 35 °C (86–95 °F) under a current of warm air. Early results suggested an increase of 1 per cent POTENTIAL ALCOHOL in the first 12 hours. See AMARONE and RECIOTO.   S.P.D.L. & N.J.B.

Loftus, S., and Belfrage, N., *Dried Grapes* (Southwold, 1992).

Masi, Grupo Technico, *Amarone and Recioto; Historical and Technical Notes* (private communication, Verona, 1990).

Redding, C., *The History and Description of Modern Wines* (London, 1833).

Tachis, G., *Il Libro del Vin Santo* (Florence, 1988).

drinking, the activity for which wine was designed, now threatened by rising average ALCOHOLIC STRENGTH. TASTING is different.

drinking vessels. Before the development of glass-making enabled the production of GLASSES (the most common modern wine drinking vessels), a wide variety of drinking vessels were used for wine. Pottery cups were commonplace, and goblets made of a variety of metals, but even earlier than this wine was sucked through a reed, either from a bowl such as a CRATER, or possibly from a hollowed-out gourd or similar vessel provided by Nature. See Ancient EGYPT, INDIA, and ARMENIA.

Modern history

The majority of drinking vessels are glass but despite its use for thousands of years, glass has not always been available (see GLASS, HISTORY OF). In such times, the principal alternative was silver. There are other occasions when glass was too fragile for a particular environment. Clear drinking glasses were an expensive commodity beyond the means of most people in the 18th century, but then so was wine—at least in countries where wine was not produced.

Silver was most commonly used for wine drinking vessels until the Venetian glass industry burgeoned in the 16th century. Although glass became preferred, trade in it was limited and, but for exceptional grand occasions and settings, in each country wine was usually consumed from indigenous vessels.

The social history of drinking and eating habits and customs has inevitably played an important part in the history of drinking vessels. FASHIONS change and, for example, a plain tall narrow glass is now preferred for champagne over the cut saucer-bowl version that was in vogue in the mid 20th century. The first introduction of suites of glasses in limited sizes was in the late 18th century but the designated use for each size can only be conjectural.

It is often observed that many 18th-century drinking glasses are small, but they have to be considered in context. They were not placed on the table for the diner to quaff at will. Rather, they were brought by the footman to each diner when requested and were taken after

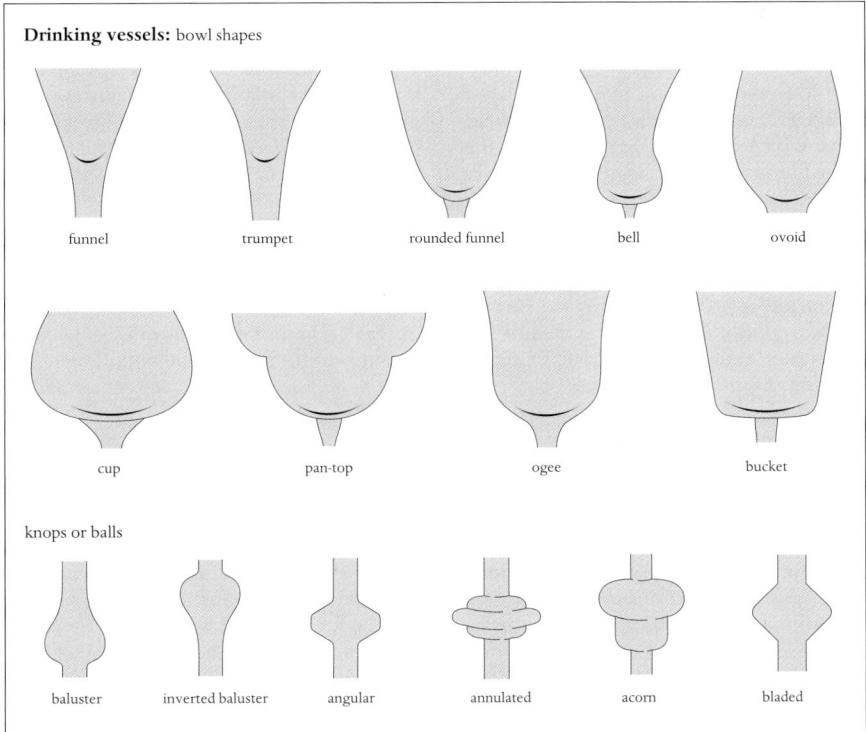

Drinking vessels: bowl shapes

funnel   trumpet   rounded funnel   bell   ovoid

cup   pan-top   ogee   bucket

knops or balls

baluster   inverted baluster   angular   annulated   acorn   bladed each draught to await another request. It may be speculated that the larger goblets were used by gentlemen after the servants had been dismissed towards the end of the meal.

By the mid 19th century, service *à la russe* had become fashionable, with its place settings of cutlery and glasses with which a diner today would be familiar. The 'new' arrangement dispensed with the need for a footman for each diner and it was the cause of the widespread use of long sets of glasses with each diner having up to six glasses for different wines, not to mention tumblers and finger bowls.

Glass Drinking vessels in both silver and glass were made by the Romans. The glass-making craft went into decline after the collapse of the Roman empire and, although glass was made in small quantities, it was not until the Renaissance that glass-making gained a prominent place in the decorative arts in Venice. By the 16th century, Venice was producing fine and elegant drinking glasses. The soda glass was almost colourless and very thin. The often-decorated baluster stems had elements of very narrow section.

Draconian attempts to prevent the secrets of glass-making from leaving VENICE were put in place in order that the city should retain its supremacy. However, a few of those with the knowledge left and small factories sprang up all over Europe in consequence. To raise revenue, the English monarch granted glass-making monopolies on payment of a fee and in 1574 Elizabeth I let a lapsed monopoly fall to Giacomo Verzelini. A few of his glasses, closely following Venetian models, sometimes dated, and usually engraved, survive. England and subsequently Britain became the dominant production centre.

In the early 17th century, wood-fired furnaces were outlawed in England, hence the setting up of glass houses in coal-producing areas—Newcastle, Stourbridge, and Bristol. As described in DECANTERS a major advance in glass technology was made in the 1670s by George Ravenscroft with the introduction of lead and flint glass and it was this which enabled British glass-makers to hold world supremacy for the ensuing hundred years. However, drinking glasses were still being made in Italy and in large numbers in what is now Germany and the Netherlands throughout the 17th century.

The earliest lead glass was frequently unstable and soon after manufacturers developed crizzling: a myriad of short cracks within the glass that gave it a milky effect. Ravenscroft soon improved the recipe and technique, enabling him to produce glasses of a rich weight and colour, quite unlike the light, pale products of Venice. The soda glass of Venice lent itself to thin and elegant shapes, often embellished with lattice designs in opaque white glass within the form or with coloured elements. The English lead glass, by contrast, was

heavy and dark, capable of being drawn into bold plastic forms.

The drinking glass can be divided into three parts: the bowl, stem, and foot. Made separately, the parts were put together during the final stages of production. The bowl can take a variety of shapes, each with a name recognized in the large glass-collecting fraternity. Trumpet, ovoid, bell, and bucket are obvious shapes, but rounded funnel, ogee, cup, and pan-top are also illustrated on p 239.

The stem of a wine glass is perhaps the element offering most opportunity for decorative treatment. The stem may be straight or with swellings called knops. The early examples were generally heavily knopped, the main element of the stem often of baluster outline but with other swellings above, or below, or both. The knops, like the bowls, have names such as acorn, bladed, baluster, annulated, and ball, all of which are more or less self-descriptive (see diagram).

Beneath the stem is the foot. Most wine glasses have a foot of a flattish conical section, some raising the stem 5 mm (0.25 in) or more away from the table, others by three times as much. Most glasses before the mid 18th century have an additional feature called a folded foot. Long before English glass became pre-eminent it was realized that if, when the foot was made, the rim was folded underneath (very rarely on top of) itself, a much sturdier glass was the result. Some glasses have a domed or tiered foot rather than a conical one.

During the 1670s and 1680s, wine glasses followed the Venetian forms, some of which had changed little over 100 years. By the 1690s, the particular qualities of lead-glass began to be appreciated and resulted in the manufacture of glasses of substantial weight and a solid form quite distinct from the Venetian tradition. Over the next 20 years, designs were refined to what many consider the zenith of glass-making, characterized by bold, pure, unadorned form. Many glasses were lightened by air bubbles or tears being blown within the stem and occasionally at the base of the bowl but the form remained substantial. These glasses are referred to as heavy balusters.

The heavy balusters became lighter as time progressed, partly perhaps because of taxation on the weight of glass. The bold designs became more fussy, with increased numbers of elements in the stem, and the stem itself became thinner. The heavy balusters had given way to light balusters and balustroids by the 1730s and 1740s. Some glasses had stems moulded of polygonal section; these are known as Silesian stems. During the 1740s and 1750s many glasses had stems that had inserted in them a series of small bubbles. When twisted and stretched these formed helices of air within the stem, or air twists. By this time, too, it was becoming fashionable for the stems to be straight sided and folded feet were at the end of their span.

A popular form in the 1760s was the result of twisting opaque white or coloured glass into the stem, instead of air bubbles.

The next phase of glass-making was the facet stem—quite simply the cutting of the stem with shield, diamond, or hexagonal facets. Traditionally air twists have been dated in the 1750s, opaque twists in the 1760s, and facet stems in the 1770s. It seems far more likely in view of the general shape and proportion of these styles that they were made more or less concurrently but, whatever the truth, it marked the end of the golden age for British glass collectors. Facet stems continued to be made to the end of the century, with the stems becoming shorter and the overall proportion degenerating.

During the 18th century, there were forms of embellishment other than pure shape. Wheel-engraving produced fine decoration in the 1730s and 1740s, sometimes being delicate bands of flowers and scrolls around the rim, while glasses engraved with Jacobite and Williamite symbolism had their enthusiastic followers. In the 1760s, the enamelled decoration of William and Mary Beilby of Newcastle enjoyed royal and other esteemed patronage while in the following decade the gilt decoration of James Giles drew its admirers, as did the stipple engraving of David Wolff.

The 19th century saw the fast decline of design, with many drinking glasses cut to match the cut decanters of the period. At this time, too, the idea of having glasses in different sizes and shapes for different drinks was becoming widespread, although this idea was not unknown in the 1780s. By the mid century, glasses could be ordered in large suites with sizes from goblet to liqueur matching the decanters, claret jugs, and finger bowls. Decoration was either cut or acid etched and in a variety of patterned styles.

The 20th century saw an interest in antiques and a large quantity of glass was made, much of it in the Georgian style. For the amateur it can be difficult to distinguish between a Georgian decanter of, say, 1815 and a copy made 100 years later. Wine glasses with green and cranberry-coloured bowls on clear stems also became popular at this time.

Silver During the 16th century and before, glass was a very highly prized commodity and wine would normally have been consumed from silver or silver gilt goblets. Early wine cups—often with a cover—were invariably heavily decorated and were considered status symbols. Many that remain are so large that their use must have been communal. Smaller cups for individual use date back to the Middle Ages but by the 1570s a standard pattern of a wide, shallow bowl on a baluster stem emerged. the making of silver drinking cups appears to have almost stopped by about the 1650s, probably due to the impact of Venetian glass and the subsequent burgeoning of glass-making in England.

There was a revival of silver drinking goblets in the 1780s which lasted for some 25 years. These were usually quite large, having ovoid bowls often made in prevailing styles during the 19th century in small numbers.

Other materials Drinking vessels were made in a variety of other media. Before long-distance maritime trade became frequent, ostrich eggs and coconuts were particularly prized for their exotic rarity and were mounted in silver as cups. At a more basic level, the horns of various animals were used for drinking, and wood was lathe-turned into cups and goblets. Antique cups of pottery and earthenware are also occasionally found.   R.N.H.B.

drip irrigation, a form of IRRIGATION in which water is applied literally as drops to each vine from a pressure-reducing plastic device (the dripper) attached to a plastic pipe. The technique was developed in Israel and Australia in the 1960s, and has been widely adopted wherever irrigation is permitted. Drip irrigation has transformed viticulture since it allows irrigation of vineyards on undulating land, and uses a limited water supply to maximum advantage. The technique requires extensive filtration of irrigation water and now FERTILIZERS can be added directly to it, a process known as FERTIGATION. Recent refinements include burying irrigation lines, which usefully reduces evaporation from the wet soil surface (and has obvious applications in regions where irrigation is prohibited).   R.E.S.

drosophila, an insect pest. See FRUIT FLY.

drought, a severe and prolonged deficit of RAINFALL, compared with that normally received. Its implications for viticulture depend on the region and its normal climate. In cool and wet viticultural regions, drought years often produce the best vintages, especially of red wines. This is because excessive vegetative growth, excess VIGOUR, is arrested; YIELDS are limited; BERRY SIZE remains small with a high ratio of the colour- and flavour-containing skin to juice; and sunshine and warmth are greater than average. Such effects are well known in Europe and New Zealand.

Such beneficial effects nevertheless depend on the drought's not being too extreme. Severe WATER STRESS is almost always detrimental to wine quality, especially if it occurs during ripening. Penning-Rowsell discusses the effects of individual Bordeaux seasons in some detail.

Most dry viticultural climates are regularly warm and sunny enough, and drought is nearly always detrimental: whether directly, in the case of DRYLAND VITICULTURE, or indirectly via a lack and/or reduced quality of IRRIGATION water. Drought in such climates drastically reduces growth and yield, and if very severe can disrupt the RIPENING process more or less com-

pletely. Drought in Australia as a consequence of EL NIÑO has had substantial effects on production.

See also CLIMATE AND WINE QUALITY.
                                                J.G. & R.E.S.

Drouhin, Joseph, one of the most respected NÉGOCIANTS and winemakers in Burgundy. Founded in 1880, the firm is based above historic cellars in the city of Beaune, dating from the 13th century. Joseph's son Maurice, who took over control of the firm in 1918, built up its reputation for quality and acquired a number of important vineyard holdings, starting with the Clos des Mouches (see BEAUNE). After the Second World War, exports of Joseph Drouhin wines increased considerably.

Robert Drouhin took over control of the house in 1957 and made many significant vineyard acquisitions, particularly on the CÔTE DE NUITS, including Musigny, Griotte-Chambertin, Bonnes Mares, and Grands Échezeaux. In 1968, an outpost in CHABLIS was established so that, of all Beaune merchants, Drouhin is the best placed in this northerly region with holdings in several grands crus and premiers crus. In the mid 2000s the firm's (increasingly organically cultivated) holdings totalled 71 ha/178 acres plus 3 ha recently acquired in Rully. The firm has also made and sold Marquis de Laguiche MONTRACHET since 1947.

The firm has its own NURSERY. At 12,500 plants per ha its VINE DENSITY is one of the highest in Burgundy (where the average is 10,000). Drouhin was one of the first firms to investigate and embrace the fundamentals of modern wine-making, although many traditional techniques are also used. Oenologist Laurence Jobard has been responsible for a succession of clean, rigorous wines that are never among Burgundy's richest but are serious expressions of each appellation. Today the firm is run by Robert's children Philippe, Véronique, Laurent, and Frédéric, who is manager.

Somewhat ironically in view of Maurice's stated aim that Joseph Drouhin should concentrate on burgundy exclusively, Robert Drouhin was the first Burgundian to make a significant investment in a wine region outside France. **Domaine Drouhin Oregon**, established in 1988, owns 60 ha in OREGON and 1989 was its first commercial vintage of Pinot Noir, made from bought-in fruit. Domaine Drouhin Oregon is produced by Véronique. In 1994, the firm was acquired by its Japanese distributor Snobrand but the Drouhin family bought back the majority in 2003.

Drumborg. See HENTY.

drunkenness and its history is inextricably entwined with that of wine, since one of the chief reasons wine has been cherished, and

prohibited, is its property to intoxicate. Excessive wine drinking has therefore always had moral or religious connotations, beginning with the 'shameful' intoxication of Noah after the Flood (see BIBLE).

Varying definitions of what constitutes excessive drinking have prevailed at different times and in different societies, with opinions sometimes diverging within that same society. It is also important to note that drinking has always accompanied festivity and ritual, and that societies have developed rules to contain it. The fear that these rules may be violated and society threatened is therefore apparent at almost every stage in the history of drunkenness.

Wine drinking is first documented in the ancient civilizations of the Middle East; the same is true of drunkenness (see SUMER and Ancient EGYPT). An early Mesopotamian tablet describes a man drunk from strong wine: 'he forgets his words and his speech becomes confused, his mind wanders and his eyes have a set expression.' The suggested hangover cure includes liquorice, beans, and wine, to be administered before sunrise and before he has been kissed. The request of an Egyptian woman living in the 17th Dynasty may have been typical: 'Give me 18 cups of wine, behold I should love drunkenness.' Other races were quick to point the finger of over-indulgence at the Egyptians.

Sources show that drunkenness was both tolerated and at times denounced in these ancient civilizations. Although wine played a part in all their religions, the voice of disapproval most frequently heard was clerical. The Ancient Jews also displayed a somewhat equivocal attitude towards wine drinking. The Old Testament contains many warnings against drunkenness alongside the positive benefits of temperate wine drinking. Some Jewish religious sects, such as the Nazarenes, chose to abstain altogether.

Society in Ancient GREECE also showed a marked ambiguity in attitudes towards wine drinking. On the one hand strict guidelines were laid down to curb any excess. Plato advised no wine before the age of 18 and moderation until 30. The all-male drinking party known as the SYMPOSIUM was, when properly observed, a strictly controlled ritual of drinking combined with poetry, entertainment, and debate. The aim was pleasant intoxication without loss of reason. See HERODOTUS for some more details.

On the other hand, some Greek wine drinkers drank specifically to lose their reason. The worshippers of the wine god DIONYSUS deliberately became intoxicated and indeed this was, in their eyes, a fundamental point of their religion. The authorities took fright at their wild behaviour, identifying drunkenness with a breakdown in social order. Despite attempts to ban the cult its popularity continued into Roman times.

Drunkenness in classical Rome earns its own special note below.

Attitudes toward drunkenness shifted somewhat after the Roman era. The Christian Church, whilst hallowing wine as a sacrament (see EUCHARIST), sought to dissociate itself from the riotous habits and heavy drinking of earlier religions. Behaviour reminiscent of the Dionysiac cult was met with excommunication. When St Bernard developed the Cistercian order in Burgundy he originally intended abstinence for his brethren; this was soon dropped. Monks earned a reputation for excessive drinking in the Middle Ages but this reflected their dominance in wine-growing as much as in wine consumption (see MONKS AND MONASTERIES).

There were periods in Ancient INDIA when drunkenness was considered a desirable state. Drunkards in the Middle East faced a formidable obstacle, however, in Muhammad's total prohibition on wine (see ISLAM). Wine drinking did not cease because of it, but had to be covert. Drinking among the upper classes of Persian society, for example, took place at secret parties reminiscent of Greek symposia with their strictly ritualized etiquette and emphasis on poetry and discussion (see ARAB POETS).

Meanwhile in Europe the scope for drunkenness was considerably increased with the discovery of DISTILLATION in the 12th century. Intoxication reached new heights as demand for this new liquor spread across the continent. The Dutch and Germans gained reputations throughout Europe for their drunkenness. In 17th-century Holland, drinking hours were applied to keep drinking in check. In Britain, too, drunkenness on the streets was increasingly blamed on spirits. By the 18th century wine was relatively expensive and only the middle and upper classes could afford this route to drunkenness.

The Victorians were not the first to confront the problem of drunkenness, but they put it on a new footing. Alcoholism was defined as a disease in the mid 19th century and came to be identified with degeneracy of race. In Britain, wine was not seen as the main culprit—indeed it was seen by many, including Prime Minister Gladstone, as the remedy against drunkenness. The new catchword was 'temperance', and, whilst in the minds of some this meant the encouragement of moderate wine drinking to combat the medical and social ills of addiction to spirits, to a growing band of (often religiously inspired) campaigners it denoted complete abstinence. The governments of Britain and the United States adopted differing interpretations. Gladstone lowered the duty on light table wines to improve the health and morals of the British whilst American states gradually voted themselves 'dry', culminating in full-blown PROHIBITION, which came into force in 1920. See also HANGOVERS. H.B.

Lucia, S. P. (ed.), *Alcohol and Civilization* (New York, 1963).

Sournia, A., *Histoire de l'alcoolisme* (Paris, 1986), trans. by N. Hindley as *A History of Alcoholism* (Oxford, 1990).

Vickers, M., *Greek Symposia* (London, 1978).

Roman drunkenness

Wine's power to intoxicate evoked forceful, and often contradictory, responses in the classical world, as in every society. The beneficial effects of wine were certainly not ignored. Indeed, a passage in Aristophanes' play *The Knights* deserves to rank alongside Falstaff's great eulogy of sherry ('Nothing is so conducive to living an effective life as wine. Do you not see? It is wine-drinkers who make money, clinch their business deals, win their legal cases, become happy, and help their friends', Shakespeare, *1 Henry IV*). People of all ages have taken to heart the practice ascribed to both the Persians and the Germans of considering serious decisions first when drunk, then the next day again when sober, and only acting on those that still seem right (Herodotus, *Histories* 1. 133, and Tacitus, *Germania* 22). Total abstention could be a source of criticism; Demosthenes' water drinking was derided by his political opponents. Further, the idea of 'in vino veritas' had a long history in the ancient world. Plato argued that drink could be a good test of a man's character, and ancient biographers were fascinated by the drinking habits of their subjects, believing that their true nature was revealed in their cups.

On the other hand, the bad effects of drink were also a ready subject for moralists. Undisciplined drinking, which flouted the conventions, was the core of the criticisms. It was not primarily how much you drank; the real issues were how and when you drank. First and foremost mixing wine with water was an essential mark of civilized behaviour. Only barbarians, Scythians, and Germans drank wine neat. Unmixed wine was supposed to have a deleterious effect on both physical and mental health. Even a half and half mix of wine and water was considered a heady brew. A sure sign of declining standards in ROME, according to many contemporary Jeremiahs, was the practice of beginning dinner and drinking ever earlier in the day and carrying on late into the night (see e.g. Suetonius, *Nero* 27). Pubs and snack-bars were open in the mornings; but no respectable person could afford to be seen staggering out of a bar at 11 a.m., as Cicero reminds his political enemy L. Piso—not even if your excuse was that you needed a drink as a medicinal pick-me-up (Cicero, *Against Piso* 13).

It is no accident that so many of Cicero's opponents are alleged to have been drunks. Rhetoric both in the courts and in the political arena frequently resorted to character assassination, concentrating on drink and sex to as great a degree as any modern tabloid journalist. Cicero claimed that his great enemy Mark Antony had a riotous home life, where drinking began by 9 a.m., and he never let anyone forget the unfortunate occasion when Antony threw up over the benches of the senate. Antony consistently denied the charges; but the mud stuck to such a degree that he was forced to publish a pamphlet *De ebrietate mea* ('Concerning my Drunkenness'), which Pliny wittily took to be his claim to the world drinking championship.

Whole peoples—normally those beyond the frontiers of the civilized Mediterranean world—could gain reputations for drunkenness. The Gauls' alleged passion for wine and their drunkenness was a theme to be found in writers from early to late antiquity. It was reinforced and renewed by Christian bishops and writers from the region, who came to count drunkenness alongside other sins. As Jerome said of one unfortunate, 'Sodom did not do him in, but the wine did.' J.J.P.

Athenaeus, *Deipnosophistae* 2. 35 ff.

Pliny the Elder, *Natural History*, trans. by H. Rackham (London, 1938), 14. 137 ff.

Drupeggio, name for the light-berried CANAIOLO Bianco that adds interest, with Trebbiano grapes, to Grechetto, Malvasia, and Verdello, in the ORVIETO wine of central Italy.

dry, adjective often applied to wines, usually to describe those in which there is no perceptible SWEETNESS. Such wines may have as many as 10 g/l RESIDUAL SUGAR, or even more in wines with particularly high ACIDITY (which tends to counterbalance sweetness). In this sense, virtually all red wines are dry, while white, rosé, sparkling, and fortified wines can vary considerably between **bone dry**, **dry**, **medium dry**, medium sweet, and sweet.

Some wines, particularly reds, are said to have a 'dry finish' if they are especially astringent.

For the technical definition of 'dry' as laid down in recent European Union labelling regulations, see SWEETNESS.

Dry Creek Valley, California wine region and AVA north west of Healdsburg. See SONOMA.

dry extract. See EXTRACT.

dry-farmed or **dry-grown.** See DRYLAND VITICULTURE.

drying grapes, which become **dried grapes**, second most common commercial use for viticulture, less important than wine but more important than TABLE GRAPES. Drying is a means of preserving grapes for eating (and precedes fermentation in the production of DRIED GRAPE WINES). Dried grapes are an ancient food supply. The low moisture content of the dried grape (10 to 15 per cent) and high sugar concentration (70 to 80 per cent) make the product relatively unsuitable for survival of food spoilage organisms.

Grapes have been dried since antiquity. Records of grape drying found in Egypt date back to 3000 BC, and records of dried grapes are found in biblical times. Aristotle in 360 BC referred to the seedless character of the Black Corinth grape, today's currant. Legend has it that Hannibal fed his troops with raisins during the crossing of the alps in 218 BC.

The common English name raisin comes from the French *raisin sec*, or dry grape. Three varieties dominate world trade in drying grapes: SULTANA (also known as Thompson Seedless in America, and Kishmish or Sultanina in Asia and the Near East); Zante CURRANT or Black Corinth (California); and MUSCAT OF ALEXANDRIA (Gordo Blanco in Australia and White Hanepoot in South Africa). In Australia and California, grapes usually destined for the dried grape industry have been diverted into wine at times of severe wine grape shortage.

In 2003, the biggest producer of dried grapes was the US, just ahead of Turkey, followed at some distance by Iran, Greece, Chile, South Africa, and Uzbekistan and world production was just over 1.2 million dried tonnes. Climate is a major factor determining where grapes are grown for drying. Temperatures should be high and there should be plenty of sunshine, while humidity and rainfall should be low. In such conditions, the evaporation rate is reliably high, but this usually means that the vineyards need IRRIGATION. Rainfall prior to harvest or during drying has catastrophic results, as the fruit can split and rot.

Harvested grapes are placed outside on wooden or paper trays, or concrete or clay slabs. After about 10 to 14 days, the bunches must be turned over to dry the other side. An alternative method widely used is to dip the grapes in solutions containing vegetable oils and potassium carbonate to speed their drying. In Australia and South Africa, special drying racks with roofs are used. These can help reduce rain damage, and allow drying solutions to be sprayed on the fruit.

Alternative methods of drying fruit on the vines have been developed in Australia and California. The canes supporting the bunches are cut at the base, but left on the trellis wires. (This is the derivation of the CUT CANE method of producing sweet wines in Australia.) The vines can be sprayed with the drying emulsion, and then mechanically harvested when dried. Dried grapes should not be packed with more than 13 per cent moisture, and sometimes grapes dried in the field need to be dried further.

Quality factors in raisins are size, hue, and uniformity of colour, surface condition, texture of both skin and pulp, and lack of any contamination. The highest-quality raisins are produced from the ripest fruit. See also CURRANTS, LEXIAS, MUSCATELS, SULTANAS, and RAISINS for specific sorts of dried grape. R.E.S.

Whiting, J. R., 'Harvesting and drying of grapes', in B. G. Coombe and P. R. Dry (eds.), *Viticulture*, ii: *Practices* (Adelaide, 1992).

dryland viticulture, viticulture relying entirely on natural RAINFALL, and a term used, sometimes as a sales pitch, only in regions where IRRIGATION is common.

There can be little doubt that some European areas with both uniform rainfall and MEDITERRANEAN climates, now practising fully dryland viticulture, could improve their wine quality if limited drip irrigation were allowed. Excessive WATER STRESS causes loss of PHOTOSYNTHESIS and eventually of the leaves themselves, and can seriously prejudice normal RIPENING.

On the other hand, even in New World regions where irrigation is widely practised, dryland vineyards are often prized for the quality of their fruit, for which some wineries will pay a premium, thereby allowing such vineyards to remain economical. J.G. & R.E.S.

DTW, DEUTSCHER Tafelwein.

Dubœuf, Georges (1933–), important producer and indefatigable promoter of BEAUJOLAIS, controlling more than 10 per cent of the wine produced in the region, with considerable interests outside it. Brought up in a winemaking family that has lived in the MÂCONNAIS since the 15th century, Dubœuf originally studied physical education in Paris, returning to POUILLY-FUISSÉ in 1953. He started selling to restaurants in the region, and subsequently became a contract bottler. In 1957, he grouped together 45 growers from the region under the title L'Écrin du Beaujolais (the Beaujolais Casket), but when the group fell apart three years later he branched out alone, taking some growers with him and establishing a base in Romanèche-Thorins. The Beaujolais boom, led by the Beaujolais NOUVEAU craze, is in no small part due to Dubœuf, who pioneered TEMPERATURE CONTROL, STAINLESS STEEL, and early BOTTLING, leading to a reliable, particularly fruity style of wine. He also encouraged DOMAINE BOTTLING, under the influence of Alexis LICHINE, who helped him set up in business. In the 1990s, he worked with 20 CO-OPERATIVES and over 400 growers, and virtually owned the village of Romanèche-Thorins. His company has an annual production of 24 million bottles, and although the famous floral Dubœuf label goes on bottles containing many styles of wine, it is Beaujolais, and white Mâconnais, for which he is best known. More than 4.5 million bottles of his production each year are Beaujolais Nouveau alone. Indeed, the Dubœuf name appears on the label of more than 15 per cent of all the Beaujolais sold anywhere. His early contacts in the important local restaurant trade have stood him in good stead, and Dubœuf now counts many Michelin-starred establishments among his best clients. A venture in California's Napa Valley in the 1980s failed to get off the ground, but in the late 1980s, Dubœuf had more success within France, expanding outside the

Beaujolais region to sell wines from the ARDÈCHE, RHÔNE, and LANGUEDOC. A huge museum of wine in Romanèche-Thorins is another achievement. Dubœuf's son Franck is closely involved with the family business.

S.A.

Dubœuf, G., and Elwing, H., *Beaujolais, vin du citoyen* (Poitiers, 1989).

Dubourdieu, a father and son of particular importance in the history of white wine-making in BORDEAUX. The father Pierre (1923–), owner—with son Denis—of Ch Doisy-Daëne in BARSAC, produced the first dry white wine in the SAUTERNES area and it is still made today. He was also instrumental in helping the Vaslin company improve the action of their grape PRESSES and he has clearly been an inspiration to his son Denis, with whom he has worked on many experiments.

Denis Dubourdieu (1949–) is a research scientist at the University of BORDEAUX, and owner and winemaker at Ch Reynon in the PREMIÈRES CÔTES DE BORDEAUX, Clos Floridène and Ch Haura in the Graves, and Ch Doisy-Daëne and Ch Cantegril in BARSAC. He and his research team have been a significant influence on white wine-making, not just in Bordeaux but throughout France and abroad. His early areas of research were into the nature of *Botrytis cinerea*, and in particular NOBLE ROT; earlier picking dates to enhance the AROMA of wines made from aromatic white grape varieties; and the influence of fermentation TEMPERATURES and selected YEAST on white wines. More recently he investigated AROMA COMPOUNDS in grape pulp and skins, identification of which can assist in the matching of vine varieties to soils, and in aspects of vinification strategy such as picking dates, fermentation temperatures, and—a favourite research area of his—the extent of prefermentation maceration (see SKIN CONTACT). In particular, he elucidated the chemical nature of the varietal aromas of SAUVIGNON BLANC wines and their odourless precursors located in the grapes; he has also demonstrated for the first time that yeast metabolism is involved in the transformation of FLAVOUR PRECURSORS into wine aromas. He has also clarified the significant REDUCTIVE and FINING properties of yeast LEES during BARREL FERMENTATION and BARREL MATURATION, rationalizing the ancient practice of BÂTONNAGE and also explaining why white wines fermented and aged in barrel are less oaky, oxidized, and astringent than those put into barrel only after fermentation and without lees. Most importantly to wine enthusiasts, his explanations of many of the phenomena of vinification have helped winemakers exploit them on a practical level. M.W.E.S.

Dubourdieu, D., 'Vinification des vins blancs secs en barriques', *Le Bois et la qualité des vins et eaux-de-vie* (Bordeaux, 1992).
Ribéreau-Gayon, P., Dubourdieu, D., Donèche, B., and Lonvaud, D., *Traité d'Œnologie* I: Microbiologie du vin: Vinifications (Paris, 1998), translated by

J.M. Branco, as *Handbook of Enology* 1: *The Microbiology of Wine and Vinifications* (Chichester, 2000).

——, Glories, Y., Maujean, A., and Dubourdieu, D., *Traité d'Œnologie 2: Chimie du vin: Stabilisation et traitements* (Paris, 1998), translated by Aquitrad Traduction as *Handbook of Enology 2: The Chemistry of Wine Stabilization and Treatments* (Chichester, 2000).

Ducellier, name associated with a special fermentation vat designed to extract, without electricity, maximum colour and tannins even in short fermentation periods. The system was devised for wine-making in ALGERIA but is now most commonly used to make PORT. See AUTOVINIFICATION.

Duché d'Uzès, Vin de Pays seeking VDQS status in 2005 for soft wines made in the east of the Gard *département*.

dulce, Spanish for sweet. See SWEETNESS and DOSAGE for official European Union sugar levels.

Dunkelfelder, dark-skinned GERMAN CROSSING notable mainly for the depth of its colour, a useful commodity in Germany's blending vats. It is increasingly popular with growers if not consumers. German plantings totalled 369 ha/910 acres in 2003, mainly in the Pfalz and in Baden.

Duras is perhaps the oldest vine variety still used in the once-famous red wines of GAILLAC. Its presence distinguishes them from the complex mosaic of other blending permutations that comprise the reds of SOUTH WEST FRANCE. It is not grown in the Côtes de Duras, nor anywhere else in any significant amount outside the Tarn *département*, where Gaillac is the chief appellation. In the Tarn, however, it has steadily gained ground, thanks to Gaillac's powerful internal lobby against incoming INTERNATIONAL VARIETIES, so that it was the most commonly planted of all Gaillac's traditional dark-berried grape varieties by the end of the 1980s, with more than 800 ha/2,000 acres in total (and nearly 1,000 ha by 2000). Duras, Fer, and Syrah are regarded as the principal red wine varieties and Gaillac growers are preparing to increase the proportion of Fer and Duras in their reds as the parvenu Gamay is gradually sent packing. The wine is deeply coloured, full bodied, and lively. Varietal Duras produced in Gaillac eloquently demonstrates a marriage of CÉPAGE to TERROIR well worth defending.

The vine buds inconveniently early but gives wines of particularly good structure and acidity. As Gaillac's producers turn increasingly from slightly fizzy white wines to solid red ones that express their rich varietal heritage, Duras is expected to be a beneficiary, replacing either MAUZAC or the popular non-appellation red wine varieties such as JURANÇON Noir and PORTUGAIS.

Duras, Côtes de, red and white wine appellation on the north eastern fringe of BORDEAUX which is regarded as one of the wine districts of SOUTH WEST FRANCE. It is bounded by Côtes du MARMANDAIS to the south, BERGERAC to the north, and ENTRE-DEUX-MERS and Ste-Foy-Bordeaux to the west. The town of Duras, with its impressive castle, marks the eastern extremity of the Entre-Deux-Mers plateau and the 1,760 ha/4,350 acres of vines are planted either on limestone hilltops, mainly for white wine grapes, or on slightly more sheltered limestone and clay slopes for red wine grapes. The vine varieties are essentially those of Bordeaux, and a specifically Duras character in the red wines is certainly difficult to discern (although more luxurious wine-making techniques such as BARREL MATURATION are increasingly employed). White Côtes de Duras can display originality, however, in fresh, dry Sauvignons and the sweet or MOELLEUX wines sometimes produced from the Bordeaux grape varieties Sémillon, Sauvignon Blanc, and Muscadelle together with the south western specialities ONDENC and MAUZAC. Some Chenin Blanc has also been imported from the Loire. Historically, the region was commercially penalized by the Bordelais as part of the HAUT PAYS, but the Huguenots who fled to the NETHERLANDS remained faithful to its wines.

Durbanville, an important ward in the Coastal Region in SOUTH AFRICA.

Durella, tart, white grape of VENETO.

Dureza, scarcely cultivated dark-berried vine of the Ardèche in the greater Rhône valley which has sometimes been confused with PELOURSIN, DURIF, and SYRAH. Its significance lies in the DNA PROFILING at DAVIS and MONTPELLIER that revealed it, and MONDEUSE BLANCHE, as parents of SYRAH.

Durif is a well-travelled black grape variety, revealed in 1999 as a crossing of PELOURSIN with SYRAH, propagated eponymously by a Dr Durif in south eastern France in the 1880s. Here it was useful for its resistance to DOWNY MILDEW but was unable to produce wines of high quality. It was tolerated but not encouraged by the French authorities in such regions as Isère and the Ardèche in the mid 20th century.

Today it has almost disappeared from France but it is still cultivated in both North and South America as a significant proportion of all vines called PETITE SIRAH.

Durif was for long grown in Australia's Rutherglen making a prodigiously inky, alcoholic wine of surprising quality. In the late 1990s and early 2000s, it has been enthusiastically planted by Riverina and Riverland winemakers, who have discovered it retains deep colour and strong flavour even when heavily cropped. More than 300 ha/740-acres were grown in Australia in the mid 2000s.

dusting, a vineyard practice designed to apply AGROCHEMICALS in dry powder form. Typical of such operations is the application of finely ground elemental SULFUR dust to control the fungal disease POWDERY MILDEW. Most vineyard agrochemicals are applied as a liquid formulation with water as the carrier, and applied by SPRAYING. R.E.S.

Dutch East India Company, powerful trading organization which played a seminal part in the wine history of SOUTH AFRICA. Founded in March 1602 by the amalgamation of four Holland and two Zeeland companies which had been set up between 1596 and 1602 to conduct trade in East Asia, the General United Chartered East-India Company in the United Netherlands (Vereenigde Oost-Indische Compagnie: VOC) dominated European trade with the Orient for the rest of the 17th century, with counters and outposts strung out along the extended sea routes which linked the Netherlands with southern Africa, India, Ceylon, Sumatra, Java, Borneo, and Japan. Apart from its participation in the bulk transport of fortified wines such as MADEIRA and spirits to the ends of its seaborne empire, it played a vital part in the Dutch penetration of southern Africa and in the establishment of viticulture on the Cape of Good Hope. See SOUTH AFRICA, history. A.J.D.

Dutchess, white AMERICAN HYBRID based on VITIS *labrusca* and possibly *aestivalis* and *bourquiniana* grown with limited success in New York state. First identified in 1868 at Marlboro, New York.

Dutch wine trade, a major influence on the history of international trade in wine. By the middle years of the 17th century, the Dutch republic had achieved a dominant position in the world trade in wines and spirits (and much else besides), greater, even, than that of ENGLAND, whose Navigation Acts in the 1650s were directed specifically at Dutch freight. John Locke recorded in 1678 that the Dutch conducted more trade through BORDEAUX than England. Amsterdam, Rotterdam, and Dordrecht were world emporia. Its geographical position, at the estuaries of three great RIVERS, Schelde (Scheldt), Maas (Meuse), and Rhine, made it a natural point of convergence for river-based traffic; its wealthy bourgeoisie created a consumer demand distributed throughout the region, in addition to that of the nobility; and, lastly, its relative proximity to long-established and highly productive wine-producing areas enabled it to become a major conduit for the highly prized wines of the Rhineland and Alsace (see GERMAN HISTORY).

The RHINE (and its distributaries Waal and Lek) was virtually a wine highway, linking Cologne with Dordrecht and Rotterdam. Moreover, Middelburg in Zeeland, on the island of Walcheren at the estuary of the Schelde, had been the principal port of call for a centuries-old and highly lucrative seaborne traffic which linked the Atlantic seaboard with Scandinavia and the lands of the Baltic; formerly the principal staple (official market) for the whole of the Netherlands and earlier still the out-port serving the Flemish and Brabançon cities of Bruges, Ghent, and Antwerp, it had been secured for the independent Netherlands after the rising against Spain in 1568.

Hanseatic League

Although merchants from the region had been handling wine from very early times, it was not until the late 13th century that the Dutch, principally Hollanders and Zeelanders, entered the thriving maritime commerce which linked the countries of the Atlantic seaboard with the Baltic, as associates of the German Hansa (the Hanseatic League). This powerful alliance of about 80 merchant towns had by that time established a virtual monopoly of Baltic and Scandinavian trade by organizing large fleets of merchant vessels to transport basic commodities in bulk. From 1237 they began to acquire rights in English markets; and from 1252 they acquired trading privileges in Flanders, with reduced customs in Bruges and its out-port Damme.

Thus they gained access to the Atlantic trade and the estuaries of the 'wine rivers' of Europe: Adour, Lot-Tarn-GARONNE, LOIRE, Seine, Schelde (Scheldt), Maas (Meuse), and Rhine-MOSEL, to which would later be added the Guadalquivir, for SHERRY, and the DOURO for PORT, or at least their prototypes. French wines, chiefly from Gascony and Poitou, French salt from the bay of Bourgneuf, English wool, and Flemish cloth constituted the major commodities traded for the produce of the northern lands. This was the commerce which enriched the cities of Ghent, Bruges, Ypres, Antwerp, and many others. Wine consumption was a mark of wealth in northern lands. At a time when a wage-earning man might have to spend a third of his income on bread, noble households devoted more than a third of their expenditure to wine, although cheap wine was readily available in taverns and inns, where it had to compete with locally brewed BEER and ale.

Zeelanders and Hollanders played an increasing role in the transportation of wines from Bordeaux and LA ROCHELLE to England, Flanders, and the Baltic from the last quarter of the 13th century onwards, gradually supplanting the Flemings and Brabançons, and they were joined in the course of the 14th century by mariners and traders from Dordrecht, Zierikzee, and Middelburg. In the first quarter of the 14th century, wine represented respectively 31 per cent and 25 per cent of imports into England and the Low Countries (Flanders, Zeeland), although this very high proportion was never equalled again. Much of this wine was re-exported: Gascon wine from England; Poitevin, Loire, and Rhine wines from Flanders and Zeeland.

The Dutch dominated the Bourgneuf salt trade during the 15th century, acquired a large share in the export of CLAIRET from Bordeaux and of the cheaper, white Poitevin wines from La Rochelle, and established a direct trade between Bourgneuf and the Baltic, carrying principally salt and wine, and returning to the Low Countries with fish, furs, and grain. The chief commercial centre was the thriving port of Middelburg, recognized by the Habsburg government in 1523 as the official French-wine staple for the whole of the Netherlands, where merchant ships of all countries transported their wares.

After England's loss of Gascony in 1453, before which wine was exported from Bordeaux to England and then re-exported by licence, the Dutch secured the lion's share of the direct trade out of Bordeaux so that Hanseatic and Dutch vessels shipped huge quantities of wine to Middelburg. The western French wines of Poitou, Saintonge, and Aunis were transported in Dutch and Breton ships. Expensive sweet Mediterranean wines (from the Peloponnese, Crete, Cyprus, and Rhodes) were carried by ships from GENOA and VENICE. Some Rhine wines also found their way to Middelburg, but the bulk of these highly favoured wines travelled down the Rhine by barge to Dordrecht. From Middelburg and Dordrecht wines could radiate by sea or pass by river to Antwerp, and thence to the rest of the region and beyond. The Dutch employed fleets of full-rigged ships of relatively large tonnage (up to 200 tons), which enabled them to undercut the freight charges of their competitors by a significant margin.

Expansion outside Europe

During the 16th century, three major changes, economic, religious, and political, contributed to the further expansion of Dutch commerce. The first was the fragmentation of the Hanseatic League itself, of which the Dutch were major beneficiaries and agents, and which enabled them to establish a virtual monopoly of Scandinavian and Baltic trade. The second, and much more dramatic, event was the undermining of Antwerp's commercial dominance by Spanish attempts to retain control of the Netherlands during the last third of the 16th century. The third was the declaration of independence from Spain made in 1581 by the seven northern provinces (Holland, Zeeland, Utrecht, Gelderland, Groningen, Friesland, Overijssel). Although the United Provinces did not secure final international recognition until the treaty of Westphalia in 1648, they were from the 1580s a formidable maritime force, opposed to Spanish hegemony on religious and political grounds. After Antwerp's capture by Spanish forces in 1585, the United Provinces blocked the entry to the river Schelde and so cut the principal artery which linked Antwerp to Middelburg and the North Sea. The Dutch economy was thus for the first time decisively detached from the rest of the Netherlands in terms of capital, shipping, and the expertise of refugee Jews, who had earlier fled Spain and Portugal and migrated north with their commercial knowledge and connections to Amsterdam, which grew to become the major commercial, maritime, and banking centre of the western world for the next century or so. Amsterdam, in north Holland, became heir to the Hanseatic League's Baltic trade and to Antwerp's international banking and commerce.

By the end of the 16th century, the Dutch fleet equalled the combined commercial fleets of Spain and Portugal, and far outstripped those of France and England. It was thus able to take advantage of Iberian colonial expansion in the Americas and participate in south east Asian commercial colonialism. The DUTCH EAST INDIA COMPANY was founded in 1602; the West India Company in 1621. These major enterprises, which transformed the Netherlands into a colonial power and a major competitor of the English, French, and Portuguese, were driven not by wine but by the desire to control as much as possible of the commerce of the New World and Asia: sugar, tobacco, calico, spices, and their manufactured products. But the handling of wine remained a significant part of the commercial interests of the independent Netherlands, whose fleets competed for markets around the globe. Wine, brandy, and vinegar constituted nearly 40 per cent of Dutch imports from France in 1645; most of the 224 ships which loaded wine at Bordeaux in 1682 were Dutch; and wines, fortified wines, and spirits were carried to the furthest corners of their trading empire, to North America, Surinam, the Caribbean islands, South Africa, Ceylon, and the Malay archipelago (Sumatra, Java, Borneo).

Influence on wine styles

Dutch interest in the transport of and trade in wines helped shape the evolution of wine production according to the dictates of changing taste and the requirements of the long-distance transportation of a perishable product by sea. Until the end of the 17th century, most wines could not survive from one vintage to the next, and many were spoiled and undrinkable within six months of the vintage, partly because they were transported in large oak casks, 'tuns' of 900 l weighing 1,000 kg, inclusive of the wood, which constituted the units of freight. Even before the creation of overseas colonies, wine destined for the Baltic had to overwinter at some convenient point. The grape harvest occurred too late in the year to permit immediate transportation to the northern lands, since the Baltic and White Seas often became impassable from November onwards. To overcome these disadvantages the

Dutch popularized *mistelles*, wines fortified by the addition of brandy to stop fermentation and prolong the life of the wine, and *vins pourris*, made from overripened grapes. They also introduced the French to the stabilizing effects of SULFUR candles (known in French as *allumettes hollandaises* for many years), and encouraged the production of distilled liquors, based on both grain and grape. Amsterdam and Rotterdam became the principal international markets for wines and brandy in the 17th century, sustained by regular and reliable supplies, bulk storage, and an international network of merchants. One effect was the increase in planting white grape varieties in western France, to satisfy the tastes of the Dutch market.

At the same time, they practised BLENDING wines from different areas to increase the bulk of more popular varieties, to improve the taste or increase the BODY of inferior wines, or simply to make them conform to the changing palates of consumers. From the 15th century, for example, the English came to prefer stronger and sweeter wines than formerly. Thus the weak *clairet* of Gascony was 'strengthened' by blending with CAHORS or Portuguese wines. When in the 16th century the English developed a liking for SACK, the white wines of southern Spain (exported through Seville and Cádiz), and when at about the same time the Canary islands and MADEIRA began producing sweet wines (malmseys and madeiras) from the MALVASIA grape (introduced from Crete), the Dutch entered that trade too, and made significant inroads into the rapidly growing trade in Portuguese wines (via Lisbon, Lamego, and Oporto). And, of course, it was the Dutch who had the technical skills with which to drain the marshes of the MÉDOC in the mid 17th century, thereby enabling production of what were to be recognized as some of the finest red wines in the world.

Dutch prominence in the wine trade in the 16th and 17th centuries was merely one aspect of their general primacy in all aspects of international commerce during that period. They were principally merchants and shippers, controlling all aspects of trade, purchase, transport, storage, and sale to local merchants and retailers. Their purchasing power enabled them often to dictate advantageous terms to the producers and the large tonnage of their ships enabled them to transport their wares at relatively low cost. Such was their access to the wine-producing areas of Europe that they were able to circumvent the English embargo on all French wines during the Anglo-French war of 1690–6 by passing them off as Spanish, Portuguese, or even Rhenish, and transporting them in the appropriate casks.

By the 1690s, however, this dominance was being seriously undermined by an aggressive trade war with England, culminating in the Franco-Dutch war of 1692–4, in which Holland's commercial enemies conspired with France against her. A combination of protectionist legislation in England, widespread piracy, the successful French invasion of 1692, and the rapid rise of English seaborne trade (especially from Bristol and London) marked the end of the Dutch supremacy, though not of Dutch involvement in the world trade in wines and spirits.

The Dutch also played the crucial role in dictating the style of modern MUSCADET.

A.J.D.

Craeybeckx, J., *Un grand commerce d'importation: les vins de France aux anciens Pays-Bas (xiii–xvi siècle)*, École Pratique des Hautes Études, section VI, Centre des Recherches Historiques (Paris, 1958).

Israel, J. I., *Dutch Primacy in World Trade 1585–1740* (Oxford, 1989).

James, M. K., *Studies in the Medieval Wine Trade* (London, 1971).

duty is levied on wine importation and movement into circulation from bond in many countries at an extremely variable level. In general, countries in which viticulture is an economically (and therefore politically) important activity, such as France and Italy, tend to have extremely low duties on wine, while almost non-producing countries, such as the UK, and/or those with restrictive policies on the sale of alcoholic drinks, such as Norway, tend to have high duties. Wine duty may be a flat rate per litre, as in the UK, or calculated ad valorem as in Hong Kong, where customs officials are issued with a set of current prices for all commonly encountered wines.

Wine is not often a good buy in so-called **duty-free** shops, however, as profit margins are rarely low enough to warrant the weight and breakability of wine bottles. In 1993, the relaxation of duty-free allowances when crossing borders within the EUROPEAN UNION led to widespread loss of trade to British wine merchants as consumers crossed the English Channel to take advantage of bulk buying in France (where the imposition of wine duty was proposed by the EU in 2005 but was considered a political impossibility because of the CRISE VITICOLE). For some historical background, see TAXATION.

Early Burgundy, California name for a grape once grown there in some quantity and eventually identified as the ABOURIOU OF SOUTH WEST FRANCE.

Early Muscat, bred in California as a TABLE GRAPE but has been successful on a small scale as a wine grape in Oregon.

Eastern Plains Zone, inland and north of **Central Western Australia Zone** encompassing 95 per cent of the state but still no wine producers in 2005.

eating grapes. See TABLE GRAPES.

échantillon, French for sample. See SAMPLING.

Échezeaux, GRAND CRU of the village of Flagey-Échezeaux in Burgundy's Côte de Nuits, producing red wines from Pinot Noir grapes (see map under BURGUNDY). While wines of VILLAGE or PREMIER CRU status in Flagey-Échezeaux are sold under the name of neighbouring VOSNE-ROMANÉE, the majority of the commune's vineyard land is shared between the two grands crus Échezeaux and Grands Échezeaux.

Échezeaux is perhaps fortunate to be rated grand cru, certainly in its entirety (37.6 ha/92.9 acres), as many of its wines are disturbingly light. The vineyard is made up of 11 LIEUX DITS ranging from Les Treux, which has a deep clay soil with indifferent drainage, to Les Échezeaux du Dessus, where the soil is shallower and chalkier and the wine correspondingly finer. It is not the equal, however, of neighbouring Grands Échezeaux (9 ha), which also abuts CLOS DE VOUGEOT.

There are 21 owners of Grands Échezeaux and over 80 of Échezeaux. Proprietors of both include DOMAINE DE LA ROMANÉE-CONTI, Domaine René Engel, and Domaine Mongeard-Mugneret.

See also CÔTE D'OR.   J.T.C.M.

éclaircissage. See CROP THINNING.

ecological viticulture. See ORGANIC and BIODYNAMIC VITICULTURE.

economics and wine, an important conjunction throughout the history of wine production. DOMITIAN's order to pull up half of the Roman Empire's vines planted outside Italy in the hope of holding back collapsing Italian wine (and vineyard) PRICES, was an early attempt to apply an economic principle in order to manage the wine supply side of the market—long before the study of 'economics' dawned in the midst of the Scottish Enlightenment (mid 18th to early 19th centuries). In 1817, emboldened by booming trade in textiles and wine between England and Portugal—METHUEN TREATY permitting—English econo-

mist David Ricardo blended wine into trade theory by using it to illustrate his compelling notion of '*comparative* advantage' (since upgraded to '*competitive* advantage') and to prove the benefits of free trade. But economic thinking started to be applied to wine in a systematic way only after a powerful combination of transport revolution (see RAILWAYS), trade liberalization, and the hasty reconstruction of European vineyards ravaged by PHYLLOXERA, sent wine prices crashing at the turn of the 20th century, triggering a severe crisis that lingered into the 1930s and an early return to trade protection, led by France.

Jean Milhau's 1935 *Etude économétrique du prix du vin en France* argued for containing wild variations in producer prices and incomes due to huge swings in harvest size while CONSUMPTION remained insensitive (inelastic) to price. Stabilizing prices within certain limits by regulating the volumes released from the wineries' stocks and by distilling SURPLUSES eventually became the cornerstone of France's new wine policy enacted in 1935, which also created a separate market organization for quality wines, now INAO. After the economic depression and the Second World War, research focused primarily on the planned integration of the EUROPEAN UNION's six disparate wine economies into a single market by 1970. Their common wine policy soon used compulsory DISTILLATION to support prices in order to stem the flow of cheaper wines from Italy into France and appease social unrest in the Languedoc Roussillon—the so-called 'wine wars' of the mid and late 1970s. Its main long-term achievement was to drive YIELDS up, quality down and customers away.

Peaking world demand and plunging domestic sales prompted INRA in Montpellier to take a fresh look at consumer behaviour in 1980, with the stunning finding that ordinary wine was often diluted with water and ultimately replaced by it. Wine drinking was becoming increasingly occasional and festive, making the markets in traditional countries more like the small but fast-growing new markets (often dominated by beer) opening up elsewhere. The higher elasticity of demand measured in Britain, for instance, led to repeated calls for a reduction in wine TAXATION in relation to that on spirits and beer, which the government sought to protect. In the US, wine demand had already fallen under academic scrutiny by the early 1960s, and in the following two decades major attempts were made—many at DAVIS—to build econometric models for California production, US consumption and trade. Consumers' valuation of a wine's attributes was one of the latest topics to draw the attention of a new wave of wine economists from America, Australia, and elsewhere.

To shoppers, a bottle of wine is a combination of attributes (e.g. colour, strength, grape variety/ies, vintage, origin, BRAND, packaging, and price) that benefit them later in a particular mood or on a particular occasion: give them pleasure, impress others, etc. Stark differences in attributes ensure that, except at the low, 'commodity' end of the market, wine is the most differentiated agricultural product with the highest value added to it (ESTATE BOTTLING aims to retain some of this locally), flowing both ways between producing countries who are also the world's main consumer markets. Freer trade gives consumers more choice and lower prices, but it also increases producers' exposure to riskier foreign markets and to overseas competitors at home. The winemaking/marketing revolution of the NEW WORLD, combined with GLOBALIZATION—the liberalization of agricultural trade since 1995 plus a sharp fall in transport and communication costs—has increased international wine trade, despite flat world demand, and diverted it gently away from its Mediterranean cradle towards the Pacific basin.   P.S.

> Milhau, J., *Etude économétrique du prix du vin en France* (Montpellier, 1935).
>
> Spahni, P., *The Common Wine Policy and Price Stabilization* (Aldershot, 1988).
>
> ——*The International Wine Trade* (2nd edn, Cambridge, 2000).
>
> See www.span-e.com/companion_bib for a short bibliography on wine economics.

Ecuador bottles a considerable quantity of wine (including a SCHEUREBE), but the extent of its vineyards is considerably more limited. Historically Ecuador was ruled by PERU and its viticulture followed a similar pattern, although concentrated on the coast and decidedly TROPICAL. Wine production was revitalized in 1982 when 200 ha/494 acres of vines were planted, mainly in the mountain provinces of Imbabura, Pinchincha, Cotopaxi, Tungurahua, Canar Azuay, and Loja, which are cool enough to permit vine DORMANCY and produce one vintage a year. The 50 ha planted on the coast produce three vintages a year. Principal vines planted are native varieties called Nacional Negra, and Moscatel Morado.

edel means 'noble' in German and thus **Edelfäule** is German for NOBLE ROT, **Edelkeur** is the brand name of one of the most successful sweet wines of SOUTH AFRICA, and EDELZWICKER is the name chosen to add lustre to a not particularly noble blend in ALSACE. Similarly, Gutedel is the German synonym for the not particularly noble CHASSELAS grape.

Edelzwicker, Alsace term, originally German, for what is usually a relatively basic blend. See ALSACE.

Eden Valley, wine region (High Eden is a subregion) abutting SOUTH AUSTRALIA's Barossa Valley, with a fine reputation for lime-juice-accented and long-lived RIESLING and elegant, medium-bodied Shiraz (Hill of Grace).

Edna Valley, California wine region and AVA on the ocean side of the coastal mountains. See SAN LUIS OBISPO.

education, wine. Education plays an important part in the production, sale, and enjoyment of a product as complex and, in many countries, as foreign as wine. Detailed knowledge of wine involves an appreciation of history, geography (inevitably including a host of foreign names), science, and technology, quite apart from the development of practical tasting skills.

Education for wine-producing professionals is discussed under ACADEME and is, naturally, concentrated in the world's wine regions. Some universities, such as BORDEAUX, offer courses, especially in tasting, that are open to wine merchants and the general public. There is even more overlap between wine trade education, courses designed specifically for the wholesale and retail trade, and consumer education; the most enthusiastic wine consumers may well want to know more about wine than the less academically inclined wine traders. The Institute of MASTERS OF WINE, for example, the leading international wine trade educational body which opened its notoriously stiff series of trade examinations to those unconnected with the wine trade in the early 1990s, admitted its first 'MW' without any connection with the wine trade, a Hollywood lawyer, in 1993.

While trade education is usually undertaken by this sort of professional body (the leading international organization is the London-based WINE & SPIRIT EDUCATION TRUST while the United States has its Society of Wine Educators), consumer education may be undertaken by professional lecturers and wine merchants. This can take the form of TASTINGS so informal as to constitute a party, tutored tastings, BLIND TASTINGS, or some form of wine TOURISM.

Other forms of wine education include wine articles (see WINE WRITERS), books (see the LITERATURE OF WINE), various forms of audiovisual instruction such as television and radio programmes, and software (see INFORMATION TECHNOLOGY). Interactive wine tasting is a way of combining the practical with the theoretical.

effeuillage. See LEAF REMOVAL.

Eger, much-disputed town in north east HUNGARY whose wines have been exported with success since the 13th century, although various Turkish incursions interrupted this trade. Eger's most famous siege was during the Ottoman occupation of the 16th century when, according to legend, the defenders of Eger were so dramatically fortified by a red liquid which stained their beards and armour that the Turks retreated, believing their opponents to have drunk Bikavér, or BULL'S BLOOD.

The town gives its name to a wine region on the foothills of the volcanic Bükk mountains where rainfall is low and spring tends to come late. As well as producing Egri Bikavér, currently being revived and rehabilitated, the region produces white wines, notably from LEÁNYKA grapes.

egg whites play a surprisingly important part in the production of fine red wines. Their particular albumin content makes them highly desirable FINING agents for red wines because they act relatively gently, adsorbing harsh and bitter TANNINS in preference to the softer tannins. Five egg-whites are usually sufficient to fine excess COLLOIDS from a 225-l/59-gal barrel of young red wine. The separation of yolks from egg whites can form an important part of CELLAR WORK in some seasons (and egg yolks can be a significant waste product of winemaking).

Egiodola, French 1954 vine CROSSING of Fer Servadou with Abouriou of which more than 300 ha grew in France in 2000.

> Galet, P., *Dictionnaire encyclopédique des cépages* (Paris, 2000).

égrappage, French term for DESTEMMING grapes meaning literally 'debunching'.

Egypt, North African country which continues to make small but increasing quantities of wine, about 42,000 hl/1.1 million gal a year from its growing 69,000 ha/170,000 acres of vineyard, which are mainly devoted to producing TABLE GRAPES. The Ancient Egyptians provide us with some of the oldest depictions of wine-making techniques, however.

Ancient Egypt

Remains of grapes have been found at First Dynasty (c.3100–2890 BC) and even prehistoric sites, but the vine is not part of the native flora of the country, and was probably introduced from CANAAN in Predynastic times, despite HERODOTUS' false claim (*Histories* 2. 77) that there were no vines in Egypt. The best grapes were considered to come from the Nile delta; only in the Ptolemaic Period (after 323 BC) was the vine taken further south. Vines, irrigated, and manured with pigeon droppings, were grown in walled gardens (where children acted as scarecrows), sometimes amongst other fruits such as olives, and trained over pergolas (see TENDONE) or allowed to form a natural canopy propped up by poles.

As in Ancient GREECE and Ancient ROME, there were two distinct wine-making operations: treading, or CRUSHING, to yield some FREE-RUN juice, and PRESSING the remainder with a sack-press. When harvested, grapes were trodden by foot by men who could hang on to overhead supports, or suspended ropes. The vat was deliberately shielded from the heat, and an offering of the must was made to the goddess Renenutet. Tomb paintings illustrate wine production amply, although the precise details are not always clear. After treading, the pressing was often carried out in a special sack-press with a pole fixed in a loop at either end of what was effectively a giant jelly bag. This was then twisted by several men in opposite directions and the liquid was collected in a vessel beneath. The liquid flowing out of the sack-press is always depicted as red, which suggests that the pressing took place only after some form of FERMENTATION. In Old Kingdom times (c.2686–2181 BC) the wine was transferred to AMPHORAE, which in this period were almost always vessels with spouts.

In scenes dating from the New Kingdom (c.1552–1070 BC), must flows from the trough along a small conduit into a receptacle. In the sack-press apparently only the skins would have been pressed. Probably the free-run juice and the PRESS WINE were fermented together, since differentiation of quality can hardly have been possible. Depictions show only the transfer of the must from the press into amphorae. In one illustration the contents of the press are transferred to large fermentation vats, then pressed in the sack-press and transferred into amphorae.

The actual alcoholic fermentation took place in the amphorae, from which the Ancient Egyptians would then deliberately exclude air, just like modern winemakers. The filled amphorae were covered with cloth or leather lids, smeared with Nile mud, and then sealed. Small holes to allow the continuing escape of CARBON DIOXIDE were later blocked up.

There is no evidence of white wine before the Graeco-Roman period, nor of the resination of wine jars to produce RESINATED WINES. Wine was also drunk for medicinal purposes, when it was sometimes flavoured with *kyphi*, a mixture of gums, resins, herbs, spices, and possibly other less pleasant ingredients such as the dungs of various animals and birds, and asses' hair.

Wine trade organization It is clear from the seals on amphorae and from the titles of certain officials that the manufacture and delivery of wine were already organized at royal level in the earliest periods. Wine is often shown in scenes on wall paintings. Lists from the Fifth Dynasty distinguish six types of wine according to its origin. 'Wine from Asia' and Canaan is also mentioned, and Canaanite wine amphorae are found in the New Kingdom. Inscriptions on amphorae of that period usually indicate year, vineyard site, owner, and chief winemaker (rather more information than is given on most modern wine labels). Most but not all centres of wine production lay on the western arm of the Nile delta.

Wine drinking Wine was drunk by gods, kings, and nobles, especially at feasts, and seems to have enjoyed a higher social cachet than BEER. Amphorae, often painted with vine leaves, are depicted on tables or resting on stands. The

wine was sieved as it was poured out. Servants would fill small beakers for serving, sometimes carrying a second small jug (possibly containing water to dilute the wine). The wine was drunk, occasionally through a reed-straw, from bowls or cups (which sometimes rested on stands). The king and his family are shown drinking at the royal capital Tell-el-Amarna (14th century BC). Priests received wine as part of their daily rations, likewise army officers and foreign mercenaries; but the workmen of Amarna received none, an indication of its value.

Religion and wine Wine is said to be the drink of gods, and also of the dead (along with milk). Thus it was important in cult worship and is frequently mentioned in lists of offerings, sometimes several sorts together. It was frequently offered as nourishment to deities by the king or private persons, also symbolizing purification. LIBATIONS of wine and water were made.

The goddess Hathor was the protectress of an important wine-producing area, and myths linked her to wine and DRUNKENNESS. When she was brought back to Egypt from the Nubian desert by command of Re (the sun god), she was still violent and savage in nature, and had to be appeased by music, dance, and the offering of wine. Wine was offered to her at the Feast of Drunkenness, and was interpreted as a symbol of the blood of the enemies of the enraged goddess.

Classical authors identified Osiris as the benefactor who bestowed wine on mankind, comparing him in this respect with the Greek god DIONYSUS. The grape certainly became a symbol of the dying and rising god. Vines depicted in tomb paintings symbolized the deceased's hope for resurrection. Other texts refer to wine as the perspiration of Re or as the eyes of the god Horus. His pupils are said to be grapes through which wine flows. In the later periods the term 'Green Eye of Horus' was used to refer to wine.

The god Thoth of Pnubs was the 'lord of wine, who drinks much', and the annual inundation, the beginning of which fell during the month named after him, led to a comparison between wine and the reddish colour of the Nile at that season.   J.A.B.

See articles 'Wein', 'Weinkrug', 'Weinopfer', and 'Weintrauben', in *Lexikon der Ägyptologie* (Wiesbaden, 1975–86), cols. 1169–92 (the standard scholarly reference work on the subject).

Modern wine production
The production and sale of wine in Egypt was controlled by the government between 1963 and 1998 when it was privatized. The leading winery is Gianaclis, about 75 km from Alexandria and, thanks to management bought in from Bordeaux, now equipped with TEMPERATURE CONTROL and some STAINLESS STEEL. Vines are planted mainly as BUSH VINES and IRRIGA-

TION is necessary (although drip irrigation is very rare). Varieties planted include THOMPSON SEEDLESS, CHASSELAS (here called Gazazi), Ezazi, Muscat Blanc, Kleopatra, and Talioni for white wines, and the late-ripening Rumi Red, CABERNET SAUVIGNON, MERLOT, and CARIGNAN for rosés and reds, which are sometimes made sweet. Harvest lasts from mid July to mid September and wines are sold, mainly to tourists, and drunk young. Vine planting in more suitable areas continues.

Platter, J. & E., *Africa Uncorked* (London, 2002).

Ehrenfelser is one of the better GERMAN CROSSINGS, a Riesling × Silvaner developed at GEISENHEIM in 1929. In this case the aim of producing a super-Riesling that would ripen in a wider range of sites was achieved and the crossing's only inherent disadvantages are that the wine is slightly too low in acidity for long-term ageing and that it cannot be called Riesling. Ehrenfelser, named after the Rheingau ruin of Schloss Ehrenfels, regularly ripens better and more productively than Riesling but is not nearly as versatile in terms of site as the more recently developed KERNER, which became a more obvious choice as a flexible Riesling substitute. Total German plantings of Ehrenfelser had fallen to just over 150 ha/370 acres by 2003, mainly in the Pfalz and Rheinhessen.

Einzellage, literally 'individual site' in the wine regions of GERMANY. Almost all of Germany's vineyards are officially registered as one of these approximately 2,600 **Einzellagen**, which can vary in size from a fraction of 1 ha to more than 200 ha/494 acres. The average size of an Einzellage is about 38 ha, about the same size as a typical BORDEAUX estate. As in BURGUNDY, for example, the vines may be divided among many different owners, who are allowed to put the name of the Einzellage only on QBA and QMP wines. Such names must usually be preceded by the name of the village in which they were produced; thus a wine from the Mandelring vineyard in the village of Haardt is called Haardter Mandelring. In the case of estates such as SCHLOSS JOHANNISBERG and Schloss Vollrads in the RHEINGAU, the name of the property itself suffices as provenance, and Scharzhofberger in the SAAR is considered so important that it dispenses with the prefix Wiltinger, but these cases are rare.

The same formula of town + vineyard name is also followed for so-called GROSSLAGEN, which are in reality collections of many individual sites in the vicinity of—but by no means always clustered around—the town in question. The result is one of the most misleading features of the German Wine Law, since unless the consumer knows that a designation such as Piesporter Michelsberg refers to a wide range of generally undistinguished sites, they will be deceived—by intention, sadly—into thinking that the wine in question was grown

on the steep slate terroir immediately around Piesport.
J.R. & D.S.

See also the Austrian term RIED.

Pigott, S., and Johnson, H., *The Wine Atlas of Germany* (London, 1995).

Eire. See IRELAND.

Eisacktaler, German for Valle Isarco, DOC in ALTO ADIGE producing pure, dry white wines.

Eisenberg, famous wine town in the Burgenland region of AUSTRIA, now part of the Südburgenland area, that produces excellent Blaufränkisch with an individual mineral character.

Eisheiligen, Germany's ICE SAINTS, those whose commemoration days fall between 11 and 14 May, including St Pancras and St Boniface. After 15 May, *Kalte Sophie* or St Sophie's day, the risk of spring FROST in the vineyards is deemed past.

Eiswein designates German wines produced from grapes frozen on the vine, and pressed while still frozen. The deliberate picking of Eiswein with any significant frequency seems to have originated in the 1960s, and from the 1980s the practice became routine at the majority of top estates, excepting those that farm vineyards not prone to deep frost. Freezing concentrates not just the SUGAR IN THE GRAPES, but also ACIDITY and EXTRACT, and Riesling Eiswein is routinely the highest in acid (as well as some of the highest-priced) of any German wines. For best results, a frost of at least −8 °C/18 °F is required, for which grapes are generally harvested between five and eight in the morning in the first sufficiently cold November or December days. Eiswein picked in January or even February is not uncommon, but is seldom of as high a quality. Such a wine is labelled for the calendar year of the growing season. Before 1971, Eisweine were frequently labelled for the date of picking or nearest Saint's Day (Nikolauswein, for example, designated a wine harvested December 6), but such information is currently not permitted on the label. Since 1982, Eiswein has been a separate Prädikat (see QMP) with the minimum must weight of a BEERENAUSLESE, namely 110–128 °Oechsle depending on the region and variety in question. The harvesting of Eiswein has become much more routine as a result of the widespread (if controversial) use of semi-permeable PLASTIC SHEETING spread over the vines to protect from birds and rain while waiting for a suitably deep frost. (Protection from wild boar is another matter, and more potential Eiswein is lost to these marauders than to any other cause.) While the classic concept of Eiswein for most growers is a wine from BOTRYTIS-free grapes, this is not a legal requirement, and the use of film in fact often promotes humidity and thus a low level of botrytis in the shrouded grapes. If the harvest

does not to achieve the requisite MUST WEIGHT or the character deemed appropriate to Eiswein by the individual vintner, the wine usually ends up being bottled as an AUSLESE or subsumed into another wine, even though this practice is technically legally questionable.

See also AUSTRIA and ICEWINE in Canada.
D.S.

Eiximenis, Francisc (?1340–?1409), Catalan Franciscan friar and author of *Lo Crestià* ('The Christian'), an encyclopedia of the Christian life. Thirteen books were planned but only four were finished. It is aimed at a popular, not a learned, audience, and hence it is written not in Latin but in the vernacular, Catalan. As a result it has had no influence on other European authors of the Middle Ages (see LITERATURE OF WINE).

Its third book, *Lo terç del Crestià*, dated 1384, is concerned with sin. The section on gluttony deals with DRUNKENNESS (chs. 350–9) and the etiquette of wine drinking (chs. 362–7, 393–5). Eiximenis is aware of the medical properties of wine, but his interest is in the moral aspects of drinking. Drunkenness, he says, leads to every conceivable vice, but, taken in moderation, wine is a good thing. All other nations, except perhaps the Italians, drink too much: only the Catalans have the art of sensible drinking. This means three cups at dinner, three at supper: one should never have more than four, and there is to be no drinking between meals. Although he disapproves of the fastidious habits of CONNOISSEURS, he does tell where the best wines are to be found. They are the strong, sweet wines of the Mediterranean, particularly MALMSEY (Malvasia), the Cretan Candia, and Picapoll from Mallorca (Majorca). He ranks Italian wines above French wines, and insists that strong wines (these do not include the wines of France) should be mixed with water, the stronger the wine the more water.
H.M.W.

Gracia, Jorge J. E., 'Rules and regulations for drinking wine in Francisc Eiximenis' *Terç del Crestià* (1384)', *Traditio*, 32 (1976), 369–85.

—— 'Francisc Eiximenis' *Terç del Crestià*: edition and study of sources, chs. 359–436' (Ph.D. thesis, University of Toronto, 1971).

Elba, Mediterranean island off TOSCANA. Viticulture played an important role in the economy of the island in the ancient world, and PLINY described Elba as '*insula vini ferax*' (an island with abundant production of wine). This continued until the late 19th and early 20th centuries, when a quarter of the cultivated surface was occupied by vines. Emigration from the island and the increasing attractions of the booming tourist industry have drastically reduced the role of wine in the overall economic picture, however, to the point where little more than 100 ha/250 acres of the Elba DOC are in production, with an annual yield of only 4,100 hl/108,000 gal, three-quarters of it white wine. The wines themselves are standard Tuscan products: SANGIOVESE with CANAIOLO

and/or white grapes for the reds; TREBBIANO (known locally as Procanico) for the whites. Elba's wines are correct but hardly inspiring, and rarely seen outside Toscana. Sweet red wines from ALEATICO grapes and dry whites from ANSONICA are the only two distinctive wine styles, but they are rarely seen off the island.
D.T. & D.C.G.

Elbling is an ancient, and some would say outdated, vine variety that has been cultivated in the Mosel valley since Roman times. At one time it was effectively the only variety planted in LUXEMBOURG and dominated the extensive vineyards of medieval Germany (see GERMAN HISTORY). Today it is increasingly unpopular in Luxembourg and in Germany, where only 712 ha/1,760 acres remained in 2003, most of it in the upper reaches of the MOSEL-SAAR-RUWER above Trier where chalk dominates slate and Riesling has difficulty ripening. Much of the Elbling grown here is used for SEKT. While the vine is distinguished for its antiquity and productivity, its wines are distinguished by their often searing acidity and their relatively low alcohol, making them an even tarter, lighter version of SILVANER traditionally ubiquitous in the less favoured MESOCLIMATES of other German growing regions. (Weisser Silvaner is one of Elbling's German synonyms.) MUST WEIGHTS are typically only about 60 °Oechsle, about 10° lower than Riesling. In the vineyard, Elbling can produce up to 200 hl/ha (11.4 tons/acre), but even at lower yields seldom expresses significant personality, much less charm. DNA PROFILING in Austria suggested a parent–offspring relationship with GOUAIS BLANC.

El Dorado, California county and AVA. See SIERRA FOOTHILLS.

electrodialysis, a sophisticated, electrically driven membrane filtration process which allows the removal of selected ions (electrically charged molecules), has been used since the 1960s to desalinate water and was adapted for use in the STABILIZATION of wine by INRA in the 1990s. In this context it is used to remove TARTRATES and bitartrates. Despite the relatively high capital costs of the technology, it is gaining acceptance in the wine industry because it uses 80 per cent less energy than cold stabilization, is much faster, and total running costs are up to 40 per cent lower. The volume of water used to extract the tartrate salt has been significantly reduced by the use of REVERSE OSMOSIS and there are said to be no adverse effects on wine quality. No further filtration is required to remove the potassium bitartrate crystals before bottling, though the wine does have to be filtered prior to electrodialysis to avoid clogging the mebranes. One of the greatest advantages of this process is that it allows great control over what and how much is removed from the wine.

Unlike ION EXCHANGE, which is far less selective, electrodialysis is permitted and widely used in the EUROPEAN UNION and most other wine-producing countries that regulate wine-making processes. There are a number of units in wineries in Italy, France, Germany, and Spain, and others in Australia, South Africa, and the US. Mobile units are in use in the EU, the US, Chile, Argentina, Australia, and New Zealand.

élevage, French word that describes an important aspect of wine-making but has no direct equivalent in English (other than the Anglicization 'elevage'). *Élevage* means literally 'rearing', 'breeding', or 'raising' and is commonly applied to livestock, or humans as in *bien élevé* for 'well brought up'. When applied to wines, it means the series of cellar operations that take place between FERMENTATION and BOTTLING, suggesting that the wine-maker's role is rather like that of a loving parent who guides, disciplines, and civilizes the raw young wine that emerges from the FERMENTATION VESSEL. The word *élevage* implies that all this effort is worth it, and is therefore normally applied only above a certain level of wine quality.

For details of the various stages of *élevage*, see RED WINE-MAKING and WHITE WINE-MAKING.

A.D.W.

elevation, the height either above sea level or above some local base altitude, such as that of a valley floor. Local elevation of vineyards above valley floors or flat land determines their air drainage and TEMPERATURE relations, including TEMPERATURE VARIABILITY and liability to FROST (see also TOPOGRAPHY; MESOCLIMATE; CLIMATE AND WINE QUALITY). Beyond such topographical effects are those of altitude *per se*. With comparable topography, average temperature falls by about 0.6 °C/1.1 °F for every 100 m/330 ft greater height. For more details, see ALTITUDE.

Elgin, cool, promising wine ward in the Overberg district in SOUTH AFRICA.

El Hierro, Spanish DO covering the whole of the eponymous island in the CANARY ISLANDS, with just 200 ha/500 acres of vineyards dominated by the white Vijariego grape, and producing undistinguished table wines.

ELISA, acronym for enzyme-linked immunosorbent assay, a serological test which can also be used to detect vine pathogens. First used in plant pathology in the mid 1970s, the technique is now used routinely to determine the presence of a wide range of vine pathogens, and test kits are available commercially.

R.E.S.

Weber, E., Golino, D., and Rowhani, A., 'Laboratory testing for grapevine diseases', *Practical Winery and Vineyard* (Jan/Feb 2002), 13–27.

ellagitannins. See OAK FLAVOUR and PIGMENTED TANNINS.

El Niño, anomalous seasonal ocean current along the coast of Peru, and part of a much larger atmospheric phenomenon called the 'southern oscillation', which can have a substantial impact on vineyard production in several countries where climate is affected by the Pacific ocean. The phenomenon recurs every two to ten years, and is associated with atmospheric pressure changes in the South Pacific; it can be predicted well in advance.

Typical effects were felt in 1998, which started with serious FLOODING in California and continued there throughout spring and early summer to retard the likely harvest dates. The Australian 1997–8 growing season on the other hand was generally affected by DROUGHT, decreasing quantity but greatly improving quality. There was a similar weather pattern in New Zealand. Chile's wine regions experienced a generally cooler, wetter growing season with DOWNY MILDEW in some areas for the first time. In Argentina around Mendoza, summer storms before vintage created BUNCH ROT problems.

R.E.S.

embotellado is Spanish for bottled.

Emerald Riesling, one of the earliest of the vine varieties developed at the University of California (see DAVIS) by Dr H. P. Olmo to emerge in VARIETAL (white) wine. It is a Muscadelle × Riesling cross and had its heyday in the late 1960s and early 1970s before slumping towards oblivion. About 250 acres/100 ha remained in the early 2000s, mainly in the very south of the SAN JOAQUIN VALLEY, and nearly all of the grapes disappear into generic blends. The purpose of the variety was to permit light, crisply acidic wines to be grown in warm inland climates. However, it performs best in the coastal counties, especially MONTEREY. It has also been tried in SOUTH AFRICA and is responsible for a particularly popular off-dry wine in ISRAEL.

Emilia. Western part of EMILIA-ROMAGNA.

Emilia-Romagna, Italian wine region which stretches across north central Italy from the eastern Adriatic coast to include vast tracts of inland Emilia in the west, which is quite distinct from coastal Romagna in the east (see map under ITALY).

Much of the region lies in the deep, alluvial plain of the Po river, and contains some of Italy's most fertile agricultural land. Its abundant agricultural output has created Italy's richest cuisine and a race of hearty eaters. It is no surprise, therefore, that the region's viticulture also produces abundantly, 6.5 million hl/172 million gal a year, slightly less than Italy's other most prolific wine regions PUGLIA, SICILIA, and VENETO.

Quantity, however, is in inverse proportion to quality in the case of Emilia-Romagna: only 15 per cent of the region's total output is DOC wine, and many of the DOC wines—TREBBIANO DI ROMAGNA and Emilia's LAMBRUSCO in particular—are hardly names to conjure with, falling more into the quaffing than the quality category. The region's inhabitants seem content to view wine merely as lubrication for their copious repasts and, at least in Emilia, are firm believers in the diuretic qualities of sparkling wine, both white and red; not only Lambrusco, but also the local MALVASIA, BARBERA, BONARDA, and the non-VARIETAL Gutturnio are as likely as not to be served foaming in the glass rather than as still wines.

The potential for good wine does exist, none the less, in the sub-Apennine strip on the region's southern border. Sangiovese has a long history in Romagna and certain areas to the south of Faenza and Forlì have demonstrated over the past decades that reasonable yields and careful vinification can give SANGIOVESE DI ROMAGNA wines that can compete with good, if not yet the best, Tuscan Sangiovese.

The hills to the south west of Bologna, a DOC zone known as Colli Bolognesi or Monte San Pietro, have given good results with the Bordeaux grapes SAUVIGNON BLANC, MERLOT, and CABERNET SAUVIGNON. If increasing output is a sign of success, then this is a highly successful DOC zone, for production more than doubled to 30,000 hl between the mid 1990s and mid 2000s. Most of this, however, is consumed in Italy, if not in the region.

The Colli Piacentini at the western edge of Emilia-Romagna are geologically and climatically similar to the contiguous OLTREPÒ PAVESE of Lombardy. Its best-known wine, Gutturnio, made from Barbera and CROATINA grapes, can reach the level of a good Oltrepò Rosso and has shown a certain affinity for wood ageing, including small BARREL MATURATION. In addition, the zone produces varietal Barbera, Bonarda (made from the Croatina grape), and refreshing white wines from Malvasia and Sauvignon Blanc grapes. The area's most interesting recent developments, however, have come from the subzone of Riverargo-Vigolzone, where important, age-worthy wines from CHARDONNAY, PINOT NOIR, and, especially, Cabernet Sauvignon indicate that the real potential of the Colli Piacentini, despite the significant size of its productions (over 200,000 hl a year), is yet to be discovered. These superior wines, just as in the case of the best Sangiovese of Romagna, have generally been marketed as IGT wines, indicating that the DOC label in Emilia-Romagna carries few, if any, connotations of quality or character.

D.T. & D.C.G.

Bastianich, J., and Lynch, D., *Vino Italiano: The Regional Wines of Italy* (New York, 2002).

Belfrage, N., *From Barolo to Valpolicella: The Wines of Northern Italy* (London, 1999).

Empordà-Costa Brava, DO in the extreme north east corner of Spanish CATALUÑA separated from ROUSSILLON only by the French border (see maps under SPAIN and FRANCE). The zone has a long history of wine production, which was nearly extinguished when PHYLLOXERA swept through the vineyards in the 1900s. Many of the TERRACES that climb the low foothills of the Pyrenees were never replanted. The climate is MEDITERRANEAN, although strong year-round winds protect the vineyards from FROST and VINE DISEASES, but can subject vines without WINDBREAKS to severe stress. Empordà-Costa Brava used to produce heavy RANCIOS, sometimes called Garnatxa, the Catalan name for the GRENACHE grape. This vine variety and Cariñena (CARIGNAN) still account for 80 per cent of production, although they are mostly turned into bulk rosé for the local market. Inspired by the quality-conscious Castillo de Perelada estate, a number of top-quality small producers significantly changed the perception of Empordà-Costa Brava from 1995. R.J.M. & V. de la S.

Enantio, also called LAMBRUSCO a Foglia Frastagliata, is a vine grown in TRENTINO to produce deep red wine. Recent DNA PROFILING at SAN MICHELE ALL'ADIGE revealed a likely parent–offspring relationship with NEGRARA Trentina. J.V.

encépagement, widely used French term for the mix of *cépages*, or VINE VARIETIES, planted on a particular property. These proportions (typically for a MÉDOC estate, for example, Cabernet Sauvignon 60 per cent, Cabernet Franc 20 per cent, and Merlot 20 per cent) do not necessarily correspond to the proportions of each grape variety in a given wine, partly because different varieties vary generally in terms of productivity, but also because factors such as FLOWERING and FROST may dramatically influence the yield from each variety in a given growing season.

Encostas d'Aire, IPR on the slopes of the Serra d'Aire in western Portugal. See ESTREMADURA.

Encruzado, Portuguese white grape variety most commonly planted in DÃO. It can yield well-balanced, full-bodied VARIETAL wine.

engarrafado, Portuguese for bottled.

England, the largest and warmest country in Great BRITAIN and the only one which produces wine in any quantity, albeit minuscule relative to most European wine-producing countries.

History
Perhaps the Romans introduced viticulture to England, but, whether they did or not, they cannot be held responsible for introducing the grapevine itself, because archaeologists have found prehistoric remains of the pollen of VINIFERA vines at Marks Tey in Essex, as well as seed at Hoxne in Suffolk (see PALAEOETHNOBOTANY).

Both these finds go back to the Hoxnian Interglacial, i.e. the period between the Second and Third Ice Ages, when summers were warmer than they are now. Grape seeds dating from the Hoxnian have also been found in the NETHERLANDS, north GERMANY, Denmark, and Poland. Since the British Isles were still part of continental Europe at the time (they did not become separated until after the Fourth Ice Age), this shows that VITIS *vinifera* had spread to regions of northern Europe which are now too cold for grapes. The seeds and pollen found in East Anglia are not accompanied by remains of cereals or other signs of agriculture. A more recent find at a Roman site at Wollaston in the Nene Valley near Wellingborough in the south Midlands is of what appear to be planting holes together with grape pollen, suggesting that this was the site of a vineyard.

Seeds have been found at Roman sites in London, Bermondsey, Silchester in Hampshire, and Gloucester, and stalks at a Roman villa near Boxmoor in Hertfordshire, but all without any evidence of cultivation, so these may be the remains of imported raisins. And even if grapes were grown in England, we cannot prove that they were made into wine. Wine was certainly imported from Italy, even before the Roman invasion of AD 43: remains of AMPHORAE testify to that. (See CELTS for evidence that a small quantity of wine was carried to Hampshire at the end of the 2nd century BC.) The earliest wine drinkers in Britain were the Belgae, a Celtic tribe that had invaded Britain in two waves, the first in 75 BC and the second in 20 BC, after the Romans had put down the Belgic rebellion in Gaul. The British Belgae kept in close contact with their kinsmen in Gaul, who were prodigious drinkers of Italian wine. In the reign of Cymbeline (Cunobelin), AD 10–40, galleys came up the river Colne to Camulodunum (one mile from Colchester in Essex).

Consumption of wine probably increased after the Roman invasion of Britain, for remains of amphorae and pottery drinking cups are common finds on the sites of Roman towns and country houses. Recent finds show that amphorae were manufactured at Brockley Hill, Middlesex, which appears to have been an important pottery centre, and also at other London sites. They are of a type that, according to archaeological evidence from southern France, were used as containers for locally produced wine; the London amphorae were probably the work of immigrant potters from France. The amphorae all date from AD 70–100: perhaps this short period could be explained by the edict issued by the Roman emperor DOMITIAN, which, by reducing the number of vineyards in the provinces, put a stop to the Romano-British wine industry.

Remains of imported amphorae are rare after AD 300 but it seems unlikely that the Romano-British were now producing enough wine to meet their own needs. In any case, from the 3rd century onwards wine began increasingly to be transported not in amphorae but in wooden BARRELS, which are perishable, so one would not expect to find many amphorae dating from the 4th century AD and certainly no wooden casks.

Our earliest conclusive evidence for wine-growing in Britain, then, must be Bede's *Ecclesiastical History*, which he finished in 731. It opens with a general description of Britain and Ireland, including geography, climate, agriculture, animals, nations, and languages. 'Britain', Bede says, 'is rich in grain and timber; it has good pasturage for cattle and draught animals, and wines are cultivated in various localities' (Book I, ch. I). Unfortunately, that is all he tells us about Anglo-Saxon viticulture–although in any case Bede has been shown to be a less than reliable source of information on viticulture in Ireland. As well as growing their own, the Anglo-Saxons certainly bought wine from the Franks. In the 8th and 9th centuries, Southampton was one of the largest ports of northern Europe and well placed for trade with northern France, especially Rouen (see PARIS). In return for animal hides, the merchants of Southampton obtained gold, silver, glass ware, and wine. However, as Viking pirates began to capture more and more ships, overseas trade was disrupted, and if imported wine was available at all it must have been a rare luxury item.

The Anglo-Saxons' daily drink was BEER, but they needed wine for the EUCHARIST: supply being erratic, it made sense for monasteries to have their own vineyards, as some had probably been doing since Bede's day (see MONKS AND MONASTERIES). A charter, dated 955, of King Edwy, great-grandson of King Alfred, grants a vineyard at Pethanesburgh, Somerset, to the monks of Glastonbury Abbey. But not all vineyards were owned by monks. The Laws of King Alfred regard viticulture as important enough to make it an offence for anyone to destroy a vineyard; no mention is made of monasteries here. An 11th-century document lists looking after the vineyard as one of the duties of the manager of a secular estate and, out of the 38 vineyards named in Domesday Book, only 12 were monastic. More importantly, if the figure is accurate—and William the Conqueror's surveyors did their work thoroughly—38 vineyards cannot possibly have produced a plentiful supply of wine for the whole of England. (According to the Bayeux Tapestry's depiction of William's invasion of England in 1066, he judged it as important to take wine as arms with him.)

Wine continued to be grown in England during the 12th and 13th centuries. There were vineyards as far north as south Yorkshire, and the praise lavished on the wines of Gloucestershire by the 12th-century chronicler William of

Malmesbury demonstrates that English wine was no thin, sour plonk. Worcestershire, too, was renowned for its wine. This golden age of English viticulture was the result of a long period of warm summer weather, which started in the mid 11th century (see CLIMATE CHANGE). It ended abruptly in the 14th century, when the ocean currents changed and summers became wet and cloudy. Moreover, when on his marriage to Eleanor of Aquitaine Henry II acquired Gascony, and when King John (1199–1216) granted the citizens of BORDEAUX numerous privileges in order to win their favour, Gascon wine became cheaper to buy for the English than any other wine, imported or home produced. Around 1,300 commercial vineyards were grubbed up all over England, and grapes made way for more profitable crops: this is how the Vale of Evesham, still famous for its plums and apples, came to be planted with fruit trees. Monastic viticulture continued for longer, but between 1348 and 1370 the Black Death carried off a third or more of the population, lay and ecclesiastic alike. Not only did many monks die, but the ensuing shortage of labour deprived the monasteries of their unsalaried workforce, the lay brothers. English viticulture did not cease altogether, but it was no longer commercially viable, even for the monks.

But with a wine-drinking Norman aristocracy, domestic production could never have satisfied demand. Via Rouen, then governed by the king of England, who was also duke of Normandy (until John lost Normandy), the English had ready access to the wines of the Île-de-France (see PARIS), which in 1200 were the most expensive on the English market, although people bought more of the wines of Poitou (see LA ROCHELLE) and Anjou (see LOIRE), and probably with reason, for they must have been less acidic. With the rise of Bordeaux, this changed, and until the end of the HUNDRED YEARS WAR the English bought more wine from Gascony than from anywhere else, with wine being second only to wool in importance for English trade at this time. Wine was shipped to England, principally to the port of Southampton, twice a year from Bordeaux, in the autumn and in the spring. Even if the vintage had been early, the new wine did not usually reach England before November; the wines that arrived in the spring were the wines 'of rack', so called because they were not racked off their LEES until the spring. The wines, 'of rack', an early form of SUR LIE, fetched higher prices. Since there was nothing better in which to keep the wine than wooden casks, OXIDATION was the norm and wine did not keep from one year to the next. The wine of the previous year was therefore sold off cheaply at AUCTION as soon as the new vintage appeared on the market in England. White wine was more expensive than red.

French wines were not the only wines to be drunk in 14th-century London. From the 1350s onwards, sweet wines from southern Europe began to be introduced (see VENICE, NAPLES, and GENOA), and they became the most expensive available. The most highly prized of these was 'vernage', the Italian VERNACCIA. Another favourite was 'malvesye', or MALMSEY, supplied mainly by Cyprus and Crete. Because of their additional strength and sweetness, these wines lasted longer than the thinner, drier wines that the English had been used to and were greatly prized. The wines of Alsace and the Rhine were highly valued because they were so brilliantly clear. Spanish wine, which was higher in alcohol than other wines, was regarded mainly as cheaper heady plonk, and better, more expensive, wines were often cut with it (see SPAIN, history).

Attempts were made to protect the consumer from ADULTERATION AND FRAUD, but their frequency suggests that they were not always successful. In 1321, a proclamation was made that in London all wines should be graded 'good' or 'ordinary' and the casks marked; everyone would have the right to see his wine drawn and maximum prices were fixed. Merchants and innkeepers refused to co-operate and were promptly fined. The marking of casks was probably abandoned, but the right to see one's wine being drawn is reiterated from one writ and proclamation to the next, and one even says that taverners should keep red wines and white in different cellars: a note of desperation is clearly creeping in. A London proclamation of 1371 makes clear what the unfortunate drinker was subjected to: overcharging, adulteration, and wine that was off. It makes one grateful for clearly labelled, tamper-free modern packaging: the glass BOTTLE and modern CLOSURES have improved the wine drinker's life almost beyond imagination.

H.M.W.

Dion, R., *Histoire de la vigne et du vin en France* (Paris, 1959).

James, M. K., *Studies in the Medieval Wine Trade* (Oxford, 1971).

Simon, A. L., *The History of the Wine Trade in England*, 3 vols. (London, 1906–9).

Modern English wine

English wine is an increasingly respectable drink, despite being produced at relatively high LATITUDES. Almost as much as the weather, nomenclature has dogged the fortunes of English wine. Too few consumers realize that English wine is quite distinct from BRITISH WINE: that it is the produce of freshly picked grapes grown outdoors in England and Wales and that British wine is the result of fermenting reconstituted, imported, GRAPE CONCENTRATE. The British government did little to encourage 20th-century English viticulture, for many years charging a lower excise duty on British wine than on the indigenous product.

It is clear that English viticulture did not cease entirely after the Middle Ages. Samuel Pepys's diaries of life in late 17th-century London record his consumption of wines made from vineyards around the city at Hatfield, Walthamstow, Greenwich, and Audley End. And, as outlined in the LITERATURE OF WINE, a number of 18th-century English publications referred to domestic vine-growing. William Speechly, gardener to the duke of Portland, wrote a *Treatise on the Culture of the Vine* (1790) which discussed both hothouse vines and vineyards, and the wines they produced. England's vines, however, remained only as specialities of well-tended aristocratic estates (such as the Great Vine of the royal palace at Hampton Court).

Major-General Sir Guy Salisbury-Jones established England's first commercial vineyard since the Middle Ages in the early 1950s at Hambledon in Hampshire, and over the next three decades was followed by a number of others, typically retired gentlefolk with little experience of viticulture or OENOLOGY. Since the early 1980s, however, the industry has become increasingly professional in its methods, and the total area under vine increased from about 400 ha/988 acres in the early 1980s to about 1,000 ha in the early 1990s. As many pioneer growers reached retirement, the total area in production declined to 756 ha in 2003, although the average English vinegrower is now rather more professional and dedicated to producing more diverse and interesting wines than was once the case.

Vineyards are concentrated in the warmest southern counties of Kent and Sussex, although in 2003 the 333 officially registered were all over, generally southern, England and Wales. Vineyards are planted in all but six counties of England, and the most northerly vineyard in the world is planted in Durham, near latitude 55°. Wine was made in 109 wineries, some of which make wine for dozens of vineyards.

The maritime influence and the Gulf Stream help to moderate the climate, but grape RIPENING so far from the equator is still hazardous, and grapes may remain on the vine until late October or even November. VINEYARD SITE SELECTION is critical in such a climate. The ideal site is a south-facing slope, with good DRAINAGE, protected from both FROST and WIND, with annual RAINFALL below 30 in/ 800 mm and an ALTITUDE of less than 350 ft/ 110 m above sea level. Spring frosts, poor FRUIT SET, and autumn ROT are constant problems in England's cool, wet climate. Only relatively early-ripening varieties are suitable, and good resistance to FUNGAL DISEASES is a great advantage.

The most planted varieties are, in declining order, SEYVAL BLANC, REICHENSTEINER, MÜLLERTHURGAU, and BACCHUS. Seyval Blanc's hybrid status presented a major stumbling block to introducing a QUALITY WINE scheme that meets with EUROPEAN UNION approval (see below). On the remaining 55 per cent of

English vineyard is grown a patchwork of dozens of other varieties, typically white GERMAN CROSSINGS, representing the frustrations of a nascent industry trying to coax RIPENESS from the English climate. SCHÖNBURGER, MADELEINE ANGEVINE, PINOT NOIR, HUXELREBE, and CHARDONNAY all have their devotees and there has been considerable recent interest in red wine-making in general, relying on varieties such as RONDO and DORNFELDER together with a few red-fleshed TEINTURIER varieties. Very occasionally, plastic tunnels (see PROTECTED VITICULTURE) are employed for additional ripeness. Plantings of the classic champagne varieties Chardonnay, Pinot Noir, and Meunier increased considerably recently, many prompted by the exceptionally warm 2003 vintage.

Total wine production can vary considerably, according to VINTAGE. In 2002, for example, only 9,385 hl/248,000 gal of English wine were produced as a result of spring frost, while more than 26,000 hl were made in 1996 because the previous summer was so warm. Average yields of well-managed vineyards are about 50 hl/ha (3 tons/acre) in a good year, and much lower on average. English wine's hallmark, high acidity, is useful for the traditional method SPARKLING WINE which may turn out to be England's finest vinous product. Increasingly sophisticated wine-making techniques are being introduced for still wines, however, such as MALOLACTIC FERMENTATION, BARREL MATURATION (or added OAK CHIPS), and even some BOTRYTIZED WINE.

In the 1980s, a high proportion of English wine was sweetened using (often imported) SWEET RESERVE, but a more typical current style is dry, aromatic, its acidity balanced by a certain amount of BODY, even if in cooler years considerably assisted by ENRICHMENT.

The average vineyard is just over 2 ha in size, and producers often lack marketing skills, relying heavily on tourist traffic (not unlike the other far northern wine industries of CANADA and upstate NEW YORK, with which England shares many features, although not their extremely low winter temperatures).

To fit into the European Union's requirements for nomenclature, still wine may be labelled either as United Kingdom (UK) TABLE WINE, increasingly English (or Welsh) Vineyards quality wine or, if it contains a HYBRID such as Seyval Blanc, English (or Welsh) Counties Regional wine. Wines that are labelled in the Quality and Regional wine categories all have to pass an analytical test, as well as a tasting panel, before they may be labelled. UK Table Wines, which do not have to be assessed before they are sold, may well therefore be of lower quality. Sparkling wines are usually labelled Quality Sparkling Wine, which indicates they are made by the TRADITIONAL METHOD, have a minimum pressure of 3.5 bars, a minimum alcohol level of 10 per cent, and have spent at least nine months in bottle on their

lees. Quality Sparkling Wines do not need to be tested and tasted before they go on sale.   S.S.

Skelton, S. P., *The Wines of Britain and Ireland* (London, 2001).

English literature, wine in.

References to specific wines in English literature are relatively common, and provide a useful record of FASHIONS in wine styles and the history of wine imports to the British Isles, from the time of Chaucer to the present day. Literary references to wine drinking are legion, presumably because it encouraged conversation, civilized, bawdy, or sometimes nonsensical. Generic 'wine' is mentioned too often to report, and more detailed and revealing references specifying wine type or provenance are scarce in English literature before the 17th century.

The first English writer to demonstrate a serious interest in wine was Geoffrey Chaucer (1345–1400), himself the son and grandson of a vintner. *The Canterbury Tales* are dotted with references to specific wines (see CONDADO DE HUELVA, for example). The Prologue details contemporary eating and drinking habits, while the 60-year-old knight in 'The Merchant's Tale' drank spiced wine in the form of 'ypocras, clarree, and vernage' (see VERNACCIA) for 'courage' in the bedchamber.

BORDEAUX was England's chief medieval wine supplier and it dominates wine references in the literature until long after Aquitaine was ceded to France. William Shakespeare's (1564–1616) 'good familiar creature' in *Othello* would undoubtedly have been bordeaux, although 'sherris SACK' was Falstaff's favoured drink in *1 Henry IV*, and Sir Toby Belch's call for 'a cup of CANARY' in *Twelfth Night* also demonstrates the increasing importance of Spanish wines. Shakespeare's contemporaries Robert Herrick, John Webster, and Burton certainly refer to wine, but only Robert Burton (1577–1640) mentions the evocative names of Alicant, Rumney, and Brown Bastard (respectively, wines from ALICANTE, sweet wines made in the Greek style, and a sweet blend from Portugal).

Samuel Pepys's (1633–1703) life seems to have been a succession of drinks if his diary provides an accurate record, with references to TENT, Canary, Rhenish (wine from the RHINE), and English wine from vineyards around London (see ENGLAND). Pepys also famously provides the first reference to New French CLARETS, and in particular that of 'Ho Bryan' (HAUT-BRION). Pepys mentions champagne, as does the comic playwright Sir George Etherege (?1634–91), who qualifies the reference with 'sparkling'. These, together with a brief note from Dean Swift (1667–1745), are the earliest mentions of what must have been a very new product (see CHAMPAGNE, history). Edward Ravenscroft (*fl.* 1671–97), the relatively obscure author of a rollicking farce *The London Cuckolds* (1682), is very forthcoming, with sack and PORT mentioned almost as many times as pretty women. John Gay (1685–1732) even published

in 1708 a rather indifferent poem entitled 'Wine' which mentions the mysterious drink 'Golorence'.

In the 18th century, the number of references to wine by English dramatists, novelists, and poets rises dramatically. R. B. Sheridan (1751–1816) insists about claret in *School for Scandal* that 'women give headaches, this don't', and champagne appears more than once in his *Paris Sketchbook*. David Garrick (1716–79) provides one of the first mentions of burgundy in English: 'rich Burgundy with a ruby tint'. As today, however, opinions about the relative merits of various wine regions are divided. The observation of Tobias Smollett (1721–77) in his *Travels through France and Italy* that 'the Wine known as Burgundy is so weak and thin' is a useful indication of the general derision of any wine region other than Bordeaux.

Samuel Johnson (1709–84) and Parson Woodforde (1740–1803) both give disquieting insight into the prodigious quantity of food and drink which then customarily appeared at table. Boswell reports Johnson's observation that 'few people had intellectual resources sufficient to forgo the pleasures of wine. They could not otherwise contrive how to fill the interval between lunch and dinner.' And during travels in Germany, 'I drank too much Moselle, imagining it to be a mere diuretic.' The next day he 'was uneasy from the Moselle'. There is a disparaging reference to Florence wine which 'neither pleases the taste nor exhilarates the Spirits'.

Jane Austen (1775–1817) admits to some of her characters drinking wine, although only in appropriate quantities of course. Among very few references to specific wines, the treasured South African CONSTANTIA is considered a suitable restorative for a young lady in *Sense and Sensibility*. Keats refers to claret frequently in correspondence but his most famous vinous reference is in 'Ode to a Nightingale' ('O, for a draught of vintage!' etc.). George Crabbe (1754–1832), whose works illustrate his somewhat grim sense of humour, describes the sorts and conditions of men who drink various wines in 'Champagne the courtier drinks the spleen to chase, the Colonel Burgundy, Port His Grace . . .' Crabbe's approver Lord Byron (1788–1824) is entertaining on the subject of wine and DRUNKENNESS, and recommends 'hock and soda-water' as a hangover remedy. He also turned wines into verbs, as in 'We clareted and champagned till two' in a letter to Thomas Moore. In his *Don Juan* VI. 607–8, one of the most misquoted pieces of literature (often confused with Keats), Byron eventually declares, 'If Britain mourn her bleakness we can tell her, the very best of vineyards is the cellar', an admirable sentiment.

The 19th-century writers indicate the increasing range of wines imported to the British Isles, and the widening appreciation and understanding of them. In *Melincourt*, Thomas Love Peacock (1785–1866) describes wine as both 'a hierarchical and episcopal fluid' and 'the elixir of life', and further references appear in *Crotchet Castle*. Peacock was clearly a burgundy *aficionado*, daring to suggest that 'an aged Burgundy runs an ageless Port'. George Meredith (1828–1909), who married the widowed daughter of Peacock, shares his interest in burgundy; precise references to Musigny and Romanée appear in *The Egoist* and *One of our Conquerors*. R. S. Surtees (1805–64), the master of comic fox-hunting novels, brings port, champagne, and 'tolerable St Julien doing duty for Ch Margaux' into such pieces as *Handley Cross* and *Mr Sponge's Sporting Tour*. He sagely advises against the excesses of the previous century, 'no side dishes, no liqueurs, only two or three wines'.

At a somewhat more elevated level, William Thackeray (1811–63) names Beaune and Chambertin and also refers to claret, sherry, and madeira, and comments, 'if there is to be Champagne have no stint of it . . . save on your hocks, sauternes, and moselles, which count for nothing'. This last quotation is from *Pendennis*, in which appears the character Captain Shandon, heavily based on William Maginn (1793–1842), who wrote under the pseudonym Sir Morgan O'Doherty, Bt. As a regular contributor to *Blackwoods Edinburgh Magazine* Maginn wrote many wonderful 'Maxims', many of which refer to or include wine and food: they are well worth searching out, as is the 'Spectator ab extra' of A. H. Clough (1819–61), an entire poem devoted to food and drink of which the first stanza has particular appeal for this writer:

Pass the bottle and damn the expense
I've heard it said by a man of sense
That the labouring classes could scarce live a day
If people like us didn't eat, drink and pay.

Henry James (1843–1916) is particularly descriptive about Burgundy and its vineyard in *A Little Tour of France*. Robert Louis Stevenson (1850–94) also enthuses over Burgundy in *Travels with a Donkey in the Cévennes*. His ill health led to frequent foreign journeys even as far afield as California: *The Silverado Squatters* is the first literary work to include reference to the vineyards there.

Other serious 19th-century writers who regularly included comments on wine are Robert Browning (1812–89), who clearly enjoyed Chablis; Charles Dickens (1812–70), whose novels, as one might imagine, mention punch more often than wine; and, most amusingly, Saki, or H. H. Munro (1870–1916), who delights in his many comments on wines and the manners of those who serve it, such as 'the conscious air of defiance that a waiter adopts in announcing that the cheapest Claret on the list is no more'. Finally, Edward Fitzgerald (1809–83), the erudite translator of the 11th-century ARAB POEM *The Rubáiyát of Omar Khayyám*, must be cited, as one particular passage has cut wine merchants to the quick ever since publication:

'I often wonder what the Vintners buy, one half so precious as the goods they sell.'

The 20th century sees further geographical extension of the wine regions mentioned in English literature, and a greater awareness of the variety and quality of the products available. Hilaire Belloc (1870–1953) wrote much in praise of all sorts of drink, notably 'Advice' full of vinous references, and his 'Heroic Poem in Praise of Wine', which expresses the sentiment, 'Dead Lucre: burnt Ambition: Wine is best'. The *Forsyte Saga* of John Galsworthy (1867–1933) abounds with references to hock, especially Steinberger. Aldous Huxley offers the somewhat jaded assessment that 'Champagne has the taste of an apple peeled with a steel knife', while Eric Newby in *Love and War in the Apennines* also paints a grim picture of the wine 'the Italians call *vini lavatori*'. But the balance is redressed by P. G. Wodehouse, whose characters' 'form' can often be restored by various vinous substances. Evelyn Waugh's diaries and letters inform us of his own serious wine-drinking habits, although only *Brideshead Revisited* among his works contains many specific wine references. He wrote a monograph *Wine in Peace and War* for wine merchants Saccone & Speed, and was paid, according to his son Auberon, at the rate of a dozen bottles of champagne per thousand words. More recent novelists whose work displays a deep understanding of wine include Sybille Bedford, and Dick Francis, who in one of his novels treats good wine extensively. Wine is one of several alcoholic drinks to figure largely in Kingsley Amis's work.

Are spy stories literature? Ian Fleming's James Bond has rather common tastes in champagne, and more than once Fleming mentions a vintage of Taittinger or Dom Pérignon which was never made. This usefully illustrates the way in which wine, mentioned by authors throughout the history of literature, is used more for illustrative purposes than anything else. In ingested form, however, wine has probably offered writers more inspiration than opium, and their references to it have helped us better understand the chronology of importation and imbibing of wine through the ages. See also MEDIEVAL LITERATURE. H.G.B.

engustment, word coined in the 1990s (from the Latin root *gustis* or taste) to denote that stage of berry RIPENING when aroma and flavour become apparent. Previously undefined, it is now clear that this important developmental phase (see VINE GROWTH CYCLE) involves compounds and metabolism distinct from those previously emphasized as part of berry ripening, e.g. sugars and acids (primary metabolites). Most AROMA COMPOUNDS develop in the berry in glycosylated form, and hence are secondary metabolites. These, and the free volatile forms, increase in concentration late in ripening. The verb is 'to engust'. See also FLAVOUR. B.G.C.

enologist is the American and South African spelling of OENOLOGIST, just as **enology** is the alternative spelling of OENOLOGY, the study of wine and, especially, wine-making.

enoteca, term used frequently in Italy for a wine shop with a significant range of high-quality wines, as opposed to a *bottiglieria*, a shop with a more pedestrian selection, and a *vineria*, run by a *vinaio*, more of a tavern, in which wine is sold by the glass as well as by the bottle. Various **enoteche** in Italy offer tasting facilities and some serve food to accompany the wines—from the mere appetite-stimulating to the most ambitious *haute cuisine*. The word comes from the same root as OENOTRIA, the Ancient Greeks' name for Italy, and *theke*, Greek for a case or receptacle. D.T.

Enotria, corruption of the Ancient Greek name for what is now Italy. See OENOTRIA.

en primeur, wine trade term, French in origin, for wine sold as futures before being bottled. It comes from the word PRIMEUR. En primeur sales are a relatively recent speciality, but not exclusivity, of CLASSED GROWTHS by the BORDEAUX TRADE (see BORDEAUX, history). Cask SAMPLES of wines have customarily been shown in the spring following the vintage and sales solicited, through BROKERS and NÉGOCIANTS, almost immediately. A particular property often releases only a certain proportion, or *tranche*, of its total production, depending on its need for cash and reading of the market.

This form of early sale has long been available to the wine trade, but was undertaken by wine consumers only in the late 20th century. It has been most popular in times of frenetic demand such as in the very early 1970s (when some wine was even sold *sur souche*, or on the vine before the grapes were picked) and throughout the 1980s, when a succession of good VINTAGES coincided with widespread economic prosperity and the accessibility of early VINTAGE ASSESSMENTS from the wine trade and press. The consumer pays the opening price as soon as the offer is made and then, up to two years later, having paid the additional shipping costs and DUTY, takes delivery of the wine after it has been bottled and shipped. The theory is that, by buying wine early, the consumer not only secures sought-after wines, he or she also pays less. This is by no means invariably the case, however, as outlined in INVESTMENT in wine.

En primeur purchases have many disadvantages in periods of economic recession. Not only do prices stagnate or even fall, but there is a much higher risk that one of the many commercial concerns in the chain between wine producer and wine consumer will fail, leaving the consumer with the possibility of having paid for the wine without any certainty of receiving it. There is also the important fact that en primeur purchases inevitably mean investing in an embryonic product. A third party's assessment of a single cask sample taken at six months is a poor justification for financial outlay on a liquid that is bottled only a year later (and is particularly hazardous for a wine as notoriously transient as red BURGUNDY), unless the wine market is extremely buoyant.

Buying en primeur may make financial sense only for the most authoritatively lauded vintages and the most sought-after wines, and then only in a rising market, although it can of course give a great deal of pleasure to those with a strong wine-COLLECTING instinct.

enrichment (*amélioration* in French, *Anreicherung* in German), wine-making operation whereby the fermentable sugars of grape juice or must are supplemented in order to increase the ALCOHOLIC STRENGTH of the resultant wine. This is traditionally and habitually done to compensate for natural underripeness in cool regions or after particularly cool summers in warmer regions. The original process, often generally called CHAPTALIZATION after its French promulgator CHAPTAL, involves adding sugar, whereas the wider term enrichment encompasses the addition of sugar, grape must, concentrated grape must, and rectified concentrated grape must, or RCGM, and is the term favoured in official EUROPEAN UNION terminology.

Enrichment is the wine-making counterpoint to ACIDIFICATION, which is the norm in hot wine regions. Most regions' wine regulations set limits for these processes and most of them, as in Bordeaux and Burgundy, for example, forbid the enrichment and acidification of the same batch of wine.

Geography

Enrichment is the norm in climates which cannot be relied upon to bring grapes to full ripeness every season: throughout northern Europe, for example, in the north eastern wine regions of the UNITED STATES, throughout CANADA, BRAZIL, in JAPAN, and in much of NEW ZEALAND, especially for red wines.

At the coolest limits of vine cultivation it is a prerequisite of wine production. The poorest summers in ENGLAND, for example, yield grape sugar levels in some varieties that have difficulty reaching the legal minimum POTENTIAL ALCOHOL level of 5 per cent. In regions as cool as England and Luxembourg, the so-called Zone A of the EU, musts may be enriched to a maximum increase in alcoholic strength of 3.5 per cent (4.5 per cent in particularly unripe years) for white wines, and an additional 0.5 per cent for red wines.

Many Burgundian winemakers, in Europe's Zone C where potential alcoholic strength may be raised by up to 2 per cent, and with a particularly variable climate, accustomed themselves to automatic enrichment, regardless of the characteristics of the growing season and ripeness of the grapes. This resulted in some unbalanced, excessively alcoholic wines in ripe vintages such as 1983 and 1989.

In Bordeaux, also in Zone C, chaptalization has also been the norm historically, and is thought to provide 'support' for wine's flavour, but some producers are developing alternative techniques for juice CONCENTRATION, a practice increasingly used elsewhere.

In principle, enrichment is forbidden for TABLE WINE produced within the EU, although there are local exceptions.

Enrichment is also much relied upon, especially for more commercial wines, in eastern Europe, Switzerland, Austria, and Germany. Indeed the major distinction between Germany's better-quality wine classified as QMP and ordinary QBA wine is that QmP wines may not be enriched by added sugar (although they may include SÜSSRESERVE of comparable ripeness added after fermentation for sweetening purposes). Similarly in AUSTRIA, sugar may not be added to wines of Kabinett quality or above.

In southern France, notably Languedoc-Roussillon, the southern Rhône, Provence, and Corsica, and throughout the rest of the south of the EU, chaptalization is expressly forbidden, but enrichment using concentrated must of various sorts is often permitted, and even encouraged, depending on the quality level of the wine and the characteristics of the VINTAGE. This sort of enrichment by adding concentrated must is commonplace in northern Italy, and has provided an end use for vast quantities of otherwise SURPLUS wine made in southern Italy (see Materials below).

Winemakers prohibited from practising enrichment tend to scorn the practice as artificial and manipulative (just as those in cooler regions, prohibited from adding acid, are wary of the practice of ACIDIFICATION).

There are wine regions, however, such as TASMANIA, the recently planted vineyards on the southern tip of SOUTH AFRICA, and even some of the higher vineyards of northern Italy, in which chaptalization is prohibited, to the detriment of wine quality in many seasons, simply because they belong to a political unit whose other wine regions are too hot to need it.

Materials

SUCROSE is the usual enrichment material used. In northern Europe this has normally been refined sugar beet, or occasionally cane sugar.

In an effort to help drain Europe's WINE LAKE, however, EU authorities have been trying to encourage the use of high-strength grape sugar syrups made from surplus wine, especially in Italy and southern France (see GRAPE CONCENTRATE and RECTIFIED GRAPE MUST for more details). Enrichment using grape concentrate is also permitted in Australia, but sugar may be added only to induce the second fermentation for sparkling wines.

Adding grape concentrate rather than sugar, however, has the effect of diluting flavour, as those determined to make only the very best German wines are well aware.

Technique

The enrichment material may be added before and/or during FERMENTATION. Both sugar and acid tend to inhibit yeast growth, however. Adding the enriching sugar when fermentation is already fully under way avoids the delay which could ensue if it were added to the unfermented must.

About 1.8 kg/4 lb of sugar is needed to raise the alcoholic strength of 1 hl of wine by one 1 per cent (slightly less for less dense white and rosé wine musts), which means that stacks of sugar sacks can be a regular sight in many large and not-so-large French wine cellars.

When conducted properly, enrichment increases the volume of the wine negligibly, has no tastable effect on the wine, and merely compensates for Nature's deficiencies in a particular growing season. Enriched wines certainly should not taste sweet, since all of the fermentable SUGARS should have been fermented into ALCOHOL; the wine should merely have more BODY and BALANCE than it would otherwise have done.

The non-wine-making observer may wonder, however, why in an age in which many consumers wish to curb their consumption of alcohol, and there is a global wine SURPLUS, the wine industry systematically and deliberately increases the alcohol content of so many of its products, in many cases to compensate for overcropped vines (see YIELD).

In recent years, concentration techniques such as vacuum evaporation and REVERSE OSMOSIS have become popular ways to enrich musts by removing water. In many ways, these subtractive techniques may be less 'unnatuaral' and open to abuse than additive techniques such as chaptalization. See also MANIPULATION.

Entraygues, or **Entraygues et du Fel**, **Vins d'**, miniature VDQS in SOUTH WEST FRANCE. Fewer than 10 ha/25 acres of vines around Entraygues on the river Lot in the Aveyron *département* were dedicated to the production of this wine in the early 1990s. Reds can be made from a wide range of south western vine varieties while the even rarer whites are made from Chenin Blanc and Mauzac.

Entre-Deux-Mers, large area of the BORDEAUX wine region between the rivers DORDOGNE and GARONNE; hence a name which means 'between two seas'. A high proportion of the vineyard land in this pretty, green region (which has much in common with BERGERAC to its immediate east) produces light red, often slightly austere wine made from MERLOT and

CABERNET grapes and sold as BORDEAUX AC. Indeed, since vine-growers converted their white wine vineyards to red varieties in the 1960s and 1970s, the Entre-Deux-Mers district has become the chief source of red Bordeaux AC. The Entre-Deux-Mers region contains a number of other appellations, some of them enclaves such as GRAVES DE VAYRES, STE-FOY, Bordeaux-Haut-Benauge (dry white wines which may also be sold as Entre-Deux-Mers-Haut-Benauge). The PREMIÈRES CÔTES DE BORDEAUX and its sweet white wine-making enclave lie between the Entre-Deux-Mers appellation and the river Garonne. Wines sold as Entre-Deux-Mers are dry whites made, with degrees of wine-making skill which vary from minimal to dazzling, mainly from SAUVIGNON together with SÉMILLON, MUSCADELLE, and UGNI BLANC grapes. After Bordeaux AC, this is the biggest dry white wine appellation in the Bordeaux region, producing a declining total that was almost 150,000 hl/3.96 million gal in 1996 but fell below 100,000 hl in 2000. Clay and sandy clay predominate and this is one of the few French wine districts to have adopted the LENZ MOSER system of high vine TRELLISING to any great extent. Most Entre-Deux-Mers should be drunk as young as possible. Chx Bonnet, Haut-Rian, Moulin de Launay, and Ninon make better wine than most but these are wines to be drunk young without great ceremony.

Matthews, T., *Village in the Vineyards* (New York, 1993).

enzymes, proteins present in all living systems that act as catalysts by inducing or speeding up specific biochemical reactions. Enzymes, named using the suffix -'ase', are characterized by both their substrate and the reaction which that they catalyse.

Enzyme activities of the vine are central to the life processes by which grape berries grow and develop. Enzymes in yeast cells, which are referred to as endogenous enzymes, are responsible for the changes brought about by FERMENTATION. In contrast, commercial or exogenous enzymes produced mainly by the fungus *Aspergillus niger* are used increasingly in modern wine-making to aid and improve the process.

Enzymes are very sensitive to their environment, functioning poorly at particularly high and low temperatures, which is one reason why vines show low rates of PHOTOSYNTHESIS at high and low temperatures. INVERTASE, for example, aids SUGAR storage in grape berries by converting SUCROSE to the invert sugars FRUCTOSE and GLUCOSE. Invertase in yeast cells also converts the non-fermentable sugar sucrose into fermentable sugars during CHAPTALIZATION.

PECTINS are structural molecules in the cell walls of fruits. In grape must, the structure and quantity of these molecules depend mainly on the grape variety, berry maturity,

and pre-fermentation grape handling processes. The large size of pectin molecules can affect the amount of juice yielded at PRESSING, ease of FILTRATION, CLARIFICATION, as well as extraction of ANTHOCYANINS and TANNINS from the grapes during wine-making. Grapes contain pectolytic enzymes (pectinases) that are responsible for softening the grape berries by changing the pectin structure during ripening. However, these pectinases are not active under wine-making conditions (pH level, SO_2, and alcohol). Therefore fungal pectinases are often added to white must to break up pectins, thereby decreasing the VISCOSITY of the juice, and speed up SETTLING. The addition of pectinases to red musts increases colour and tannin extraction.

Grapes affected by BOTRYTIS BUNCH ROT contain high concentrations of the enzyme laccase, which promotes very rapid OXIDATION and browning of the juice and young wine. At the end of fermentation, the combination of higher ALCOHOLIC STRENGTH, the tannins, and added SULFUR DIOXIDE reduce the laccase activity, thereby making the wine stable to enzymatic oxidation. If, however, the bunch rot is extensive, laccase activity may be so great that only heat treatment of the wine will inactivate the enzyme sufficiently to protect the wine from oxidation.

Commercial enzymes with glycosidase activity have been developed for particularly aromatic wines such as those based on Gewürztraminer and Riesling grapes, which, if added after fermentation, are able to free the TERPENE flavour compounds that are bound as GLYCOSIDES, thereby substantially increasing the AROMA of the resulting wine.

During wine AGEING, various oxidase enzymes may play a role in hastening the oxidation of PHENOLICS.   A.D.W., T.J., & P.J.W.

Lourens, K., and Pellerin, P., 'Enzymes in winemaking', www.winboer.co.za (Nov. 2004).

épamprage, French term for DESUCKERING.

epicatechin. See CATECHIN.

Épineuil, commune near AUXERRE whose name may be appended to that of BOURGOGNE.

éraflage, French term for DESTEMMING grapes.

Erbaluce, white grape variety, speciality of Caluso in the north of the PIEMONTE region of north west Italy. Most dry Erbaluce is relatively light bodied and acidic, although there are some fine examples. In the 1990s, significantly improved versions from the négociant houses of Orsolani and Bava indicated the wine is potentially as interesting as ARNEIS and fuller and richer than GAVI, Piemonte's two best-known white wines. Erbaluce's most famous, if rare, manifestation is the golden sweet Caluso PASSITO.

erinose mite. The grapevine is the only known host in the plant kingdom to the grape erineum mite, *Colomerus vitis*, sometimes called grape leaf blister mite. The mite is widely distributed, but usually causes only minor damage in commercial vineyards. The damage first appears as pinkish or reddish swellings or galls on the upper surfaces of the leaves. Beneath the gall, the concave portion of the leaf is lined with a felty mass of plant hairs or 'erinea'. This is one of the most unsightly grape pest problems, yet it has negligible effects on vine performance. Control is usually by preventive applications of SULFUR dust, and, as this is often applied to control POWDERY MILDEW, these mites are often incidentally controlled.

M.J.E.

Ermitage, alternative and historic name for HERMITAGE in the northern Rhône.

erosion. See SOIL EROSION, a severe problem in some steeply sloping vineyards.

Erstes Gewächs, Rheingau name for GROSSES GEWÄCHS.

erythorbic acid, alternative antioxidant to ASCORBIC ACID.

Erzeugerabfüllung, German word meaning literally 'producer bottled'. In theory, this word should indicate quality, and certainly all the finest wines of Germany qualify as *Erzeugerabfüllung*, but, as in France (see MIS EN BOUTEILLE), the term may be used by COOPERATIVES to describe blends of wines from many different member-producers over whose viticultural techniques the bottler exercises no control. One useful aspect of the term, however, in a country where wine label obfuscation is rife, is that it cannot be used by the giant mass-market bottlers (see GERMANY and, particularly, MOSEL-SAAR-RUWER), except for those vineyards they themselves own. The term GUTSABFÜLLUNG is officially defined in more restrictive terms, but is in practice seldom used.

esca, known since ancient times as a fungal disease of old vines and characterized by white rot and apoplexy (sudden death), today it is considered to be a complex of diseases that start with cuttings used in propagation. The Greek word *yska* signified both rotten grape wood and the spongy basidiomycete fungal bodies. The latter were used in the past—by the 5,300-year-old Alpine Ice Man, for example—to start fires and staunch bleeding. Enlightened by the taxonomic studies of Crous and Gams (1996, 2000), scientists now know that ascomycete micro-fungi are in fact the common link between the following reports: grapevine wood alterations following wounding (Petri 1912), black measles (Chiarappa 1959), esca (Larignon 1987, Mugnai 1996), slow vine decline (Ferreira 1994), black goo (Morton 1995), and young vine decline (Scheck 1998). The International Council of Grapevine Trunk Diseases, formed in 1998, meets biannually to bring together research on esca and other trunk diseases that points to future cures. Without such research, involving representatives from more than 20 countries, the longevity of vineyards worldwide will be severely limited and old-vine wines in very short supply.

Today, the esca disease complex includes brown wood streaking in newly grafted plants; PETRI DISEASE in young vines (less than ten years old), with symptoms of black goo and decline; young esca, with symptoms of black goo, tiger-striping of leaves, black measles dots on fruit, and decline; and esca proper, with all of the above symptoms plus white rot and apoplexy. Although there is currently no cure for the esca complex, research has shown the efficacy of stringent grapevine nursery sanitation, pruning wound protection, and stress avoidance in managing the problems.

L.M.

Relevant articles can be found in *Phytopathologia Mediterranea*'s special issue on esca and grapevine declines, 39/1 (2000). See especially those by K. Adalat, L. Chiarappa, P.W. Crous, L. Morton, P. Larignon, L. Mugnai, G. Surico (first authors). See the Mediterranean Phytopathological Union's website for list of titles: www.unifi.it/istituzioni/mpu/

Crous, P.W., and Gams, W., 'Phaeomoniella chlamydospora gen. et comb., nov., a causal organism of Petri grapevine decline and esca', *Phytopathologia Mediterranea* 39/1 (2000), 112–18.

Esgana Cão, and occasionally **Esganoso**, synonyms for the Portuguese white grape variety known on the island of Madeira as SERCIAL. Its full name on the mainland means 'dog strangler', presumably a reference to its notably high acidity. It can be found as an ingredient in VINHO VERDE, BUCELAS, and white PORT.

Espadeiro, red grape variety known, although not widely grown, in both the RÍAS BAIXAS zone of Galicia and Portugal's VINHO VERDE country. It can produce quite heavily and rarely reaches high sugar levels. The vine called Espadeiro grown near Lisbon may in fact be TINTA AMARELA.

espalier, a relatively unusual TRAINING SYSTEM, more desirable for aesthetic than commercial reasons, for vines or other fruit trees, by which the plant is trained to grow in a single plane to form a flat shape, for example against a wall (see diagram above). Espalier training leaves a trunk and one or two arms with several canes which are trained in the same plane with a trellis or wire for support. Different vines are trained to different heights in the French Espalier de Thoméry.

R.E.S.

Esparte, old Australian name for MOURVÈDRE.

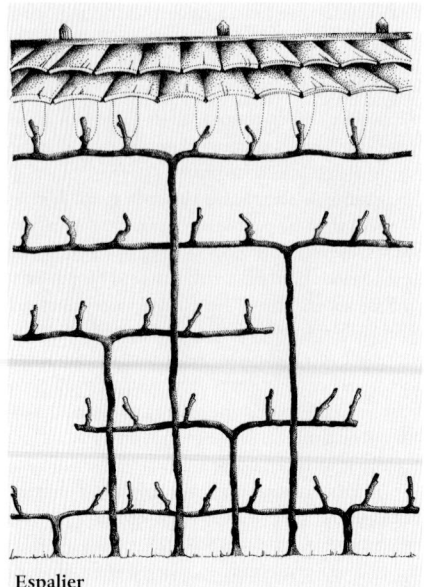
Espalier

espumoso, Spanish for sparkling. TRADITIONAL METHOD Spanish sparkling wine that is exported is labelled CAVA.

Esquitxagos, common grape with an uncommon name found around Tarragona in eastern Spain. It may be identical to MERSEGUERA.

Estaing, Vins d', miniature VDQS in SOUTH WEST FRANCE. Since the early 1990s, total plantings have grown, to more than 15 ha/37 acres of vines around Estaing up the river Lot from ENTRAYGUES in the Aveyron *département*. Reds can be made from a wide range of south western vine varieties. A very small quantity of white wine is made from Chenin Blanc and Mauzac. The climate here makes MARCILLAC look positively balmy.

estate bottled, term used on labels which has a very specific meaning in the United States, where an estate-bottled wine must come from the winery's own vineyards or those on which the winery has a long lease; both vineyards and winery must be in the geographical area specified on the label. This is the American counterpart of CHÂTEAU BOTTLED or DOMAINE BOTTLED.

estate wine, term in common parlance, but not in federal law, in the US that suggests loosely that the wine came entirely from grapes farmed on the winery's own property. 'Estate wine' may be casually construed conversationally to be exactly synonymous with ESTATE BOTTLED, which has legal status, but technically it is not.

In South Africa 'estate wine' is a specific term for a wine that was grown, made, and bottled on a single geographical unit registered with the Wine and Spirit Board.

esters, compounds formed by reaction of ACIDS with ALCOHOLS. The two most common forms of esters in wine are FERMENTATION esters, commonly found in the aroma of young white wine, and esters that are chemically formed during AGEING.

The fresh, fruity aroma of young wines derives in large part from the presence of the mixture of esters produced during fermentation, which is why it is usually called fermentation AROMA. The precise nature of esters formed during fermentation is strongly influenced by the fermentation temperature, as well as the YEAST strain and other factors. For more details, see TEMPERATURE.

Since wines contain much more ETHANOL than any other alcohol, and since the most common volatile organic acid is ACETIC ACID, it is not surprising that the most common ester in wine is ETHYL ACETATE, but many more combinations are possible from among the acids and alcohols present, and help to explain why wines differ so greatly in their aroma and, after years in bottle, BOUQUET. (See also ISOAMYL ACETATE.)

A number of esters that do not have a particularly marked odour are also present in wines. Among these are those resulting from reaction of the ethyl alcohol produced by fermentation with TARTARIC, MALIC, SUCCINIC, and other acids of the grape and wine, and such a process lowers the acidity and can mellow a wine.

When an acid reacts with an alcohol, water is produced in addition to the ester. This reaction is assisted or catalyzed by the hydrogen ion, a substance plentiful in acid (low PH) solutions such as wines. Hydrogen ions not only catalyse the formation of esters from acids and alcohols, they also function as catalysts for the splitting of esters into their acid and alcohol segments. The result of these two tendencies, formation and splitting, is that wines contain mixtures of the four participants in the reactions: organic acids, alcohols, the several esters from the possible combinations, and water. The relative amounts of the four participants in the two reactions is governed by their concentrations and the reaction rates for formation and splitting. Given enough time, a state will be reached in which the net formation of esters just balances the splitting of them. This is known as the equilibrium state. In practice, the equilibrium state in wines is not reached but merely approached, because the formation rates for some esters are extremely slow under wine storage conditions.

The fact that esters are formed at different rates, some of them reaching equilibrium only after decades, helps to explain the changes in wine aroma and bouquet during ageing.

A.D.W. & P.J.W.

Estremadura, VINHO REGIONAL in western Portugal sometimes known colloquially as Oeste (West). It covers a group of six wine regions north of Lisbon on the west coast of PORTUGAL: Encostas d'Aire, Alcobaça, Óbidos, Alenquer, Torres Vedras, and Arruda. With the exception of the first two, all had been recognised as DOCs in their own right by the mid 2000s (see map under PORTUGAL). Few consumers have heard of it, yet Estremadura produces more wine than any other part of Portugal. Henry VIZETELLY writing in 1880 reported that the 'neutral-tasting red wines' from the Oeste were exported in large quantities to France for mixing with the pale and poorer growths of the northern wine-growing departments. The rest was either drunk in Lisbon or distilled to make the grape spirit used to fortify PORT. Some wine continues to be sold for the manufacture of Portugal's national brands of VERMOUTH. All but 5 per cent of the wine from Estremadura's productive, maritime vineyards qualifies as Vinho Regional or Vinho de Mesa and much is still sold in returnable 5 l/1.3 gal flagons known as *garrafoes* that are to be found in taverns and restaurants all over the Portuguese-speaking world.

The region is dominated by 15 large CO-OPERATIVES which offer few incentives to quality. Consequently vine varieties have been chosen for their yield and resistance to disease in the warm, humid Atlantic climate. As many as 30 different varieties are officially permitted and, because of a tradition of making wine for DISTILLATION, white grapes outnumber red. Wine-making in Estremadura has begun to improve, however. With financial help from the EUROPEAN UNION, co-operatives have been installing more modern equipment. The most promising wines come from the DOC of Alenquer, where, sheltered from the Atlantic by the Serra de Montejunto, a number of single estates produce good red and white wines from vineyards on the predominantly limestone soils. Cabernet Sauvignon, Merlot, Syrah, and Chardonny have made inroads here alongside the likes of Touriga Nacional and Tinta Roriz.

R.J.M.

Vizetelly, H., *Facts about Port and Madeira* (London, 1880).

Mayson R., *The Wines and Vineyards of Portugal* (London, 2003).

—— *Portugal's Wines and Wine Makers* (San Francisco, 1998).

estufa, Portuguese word meaning 'hothouse' or 'stove', also applied to the tanks used to heat wine on the island of MADEIRA, thereby accelerating its development and maturation. The heating process itself is called **estufagem**. *Estufas* simulate the effects of the long tropical sea voyages in the 18th and 19th centuries when madeira (and SETÚBAL) was, at first accidentally and then deliberately, stowed in the hold of a ship to age prematurely as a result of the temperature changes involved in a round trip, or *torna viagem*, across the tropics.

R.J.M.

ethanal, synonym for ACETALDEHYDE.

ethanol, common name for ethyl alcohol, the most potable of the ALCOHOLS and an important, intoxicating constituent of wine and all other alcoholic drinks. Ethanol, often called simply 'alcohol', is colourless and odourless but can have considerable impact on how a liquid tastes.

Ethanol is the most potent component of wine (and the most obvious of those that distinguish it from GRAPE JUICE), but it is probably the least discussed by wine consumers (unless in the context of HANGOVERS). For although ethanol does not have a taste, it has an effect, not just on the human nervous system, but on how a wine tastes. The ethanol content in a perfectly balanced wine should be unfathomable, but wines that are slightly too high in alcohol can have a hot aftertaste.

Wines relatively high in ethanol—over 13 per cent for example (see ALCOHOLIC STRENGTH)—can taste sweet even if they contain practically no RESIDUAL SUGAR. Wines whose ethanol level robs them of their BALANCE may 'burn' or taste 'hot', especially in the aftertaste. Ethanol makes an important contribution to VISCOSITY so that, as a general rule, wines described as full bodied, or having considerable BODY, are high in ethanol while wines that are low in viscosity and body are low in ethanol. Ethanol may also play a role in wine conservation since low-alcohol wines may be prey to BACTERIAL attack. See ALCOHOLIC STRENGTH for ways in which the ethanol level may be manipulated.

Ethanol is produced in two ways, the most traditional and natural of which is by the fermentation by YEAST of solutions that contain SUGARS, such as that involved in wine production. It is required in huge volumes by industry, however, as a solvent for perfumes and as a raw material for the synthesis of products such as drugs, plastics, lacquers, polishes, plasticizers, and cosmetics. Most of the ethanol used by industry, other than that produced by distilling the European wine SURPLUS, is produced in factories by hydrating ethylene, a component of petroleum.

See ALCOHOLIC STRENGTH for the varied concentrations of ethanol to be found in different wines, HEALTH for the effects of alcohol consumption in the form of wine, and REDUCED-ALCOHOL WINES.

A.D.W.

Ethiopia produces quite respectable red wine and some white from vines grown at relatively high altitude, all vinified, along with imported grape products, in the country's lone winery, Awash, in Addis Ababa.

ethyl acetate, the most common ESTER in wine, and a natural organic compound present in most fruits, berries, other foods, and alcoholic drinks. Ethyl acetate is present in much higher concentrations than any other ester because it is formed by the reaction of the most common volatile organic acid in young wine, ACETIC ACID, with the most common alcohol produced by FERMENTATION, ETHANOL.

Ethyl acetate dominates the aroma of young wines, modified and varied by the different combinations of other chemical compounds present. Grape variety, weather, soil, and wine-making practices govern the types and concentrations of these other compounds and thus the AROMA and BOUQUET of the resultant wine. Present in moderate concentrations, ethyl acetate is perceived as contributing to the generally fruity character—although people vary in their sensitivity to the compound. The perception threshold is generally about 120 mg/l.

At higher concentrations, however, ethyl acetate can become unacceptably dominant and increasingly impart the character described as VOLATILE and, eventually, vinegary.

Wines exposed to oxygen first lose their fresh fruitiness and become vapid in smell and taste because of the ACETALDEHYDE resulting from the oxidation of ethanol. The OXIDATION goes further to yield acetic acid from the acetaldehyde intermediate and then, when some of this acetic acid reacts with ethanol, ethyl acetate is produced. By the time this stage is reached, the wine is no longer wine but wine vinegar, which combines the sharp, acid taste of acetic acid with the odour of ethyl acetate.

A.D.W.

ethyl alcohol, scientific name for ETHANOL, the alcohol most commonly encountered in wine and other alcoholic drinks.

Étoile, L'. See L'ÉTOILE.

Étraire de l'Adui, or **Étraire de la Dui**, historic vine grown before PHYLLOXERA on the fringes of the south east Rhône valley and Savoie. Similar to PERSAN.

Etruscans. The origins of viticulture in TOSCANA are as problematic as the origins of the Etruscan peoples who flourished in central north Italy from the 8th century BC until being absorbed by the Romans from the 3rd century onwards. However, at its height, Etruscan society was heavily influenced by the culture of the Greek colonies of southern Italy. They imported fine Greek pottery for use in the SYMPOSIUM and made their own copies. The dinner and drinking party was a favourite theme in the lavish paintings which adorned their tombs. Indeed, the Etruscans became a byword among Greek and Roman moralists for luxurious living and eccentric customs, such as allowing wives to participate in banquets. There are literary references to Etruscan wine from the late 3rd century BC, but much earlier, from the late 7th century, the wine was exported in a distinctive type of AMPHORA well beyond Italy to southern France. Various wines are attested throughout the region in the classical period, although none was universally recognized as of the highest class.

J.J.P.

Bouloumie, B., 'Le Vin etrusque', *Quaderni della scuola di specializzazione in viticoltura e enologia* (Turin), 7 (1983), 165–88.

Cerchiai, C., *L'alimentazione nel mondo antico: gli Etruschi* (Rome, 1987).

Heurgon, J., *Daily Life of the Etruscans* (London, 1964).

EU stands for EUROPEAN UNION.

Eucharist, wine in the.

The significance of wine in the Christian sacrament of Eucharist derives from the meanings of wine in the BIBLE and from the purposes of a variety of religious rituals. God's generous love of his people is symbolized by his gift of 'the fermented blood of the grape for drink' (Deut. 32. 14). The contrast of old wine and new wine is often used, new wine bursting its container, a proof of exuberance.

In Jewish sacrifices, wine to signify well-being and abundance, and animal blood to signify life itself, were both offered by being poured out as a libation, and so given back to God, in acts of thanksgiving, worship, and atonement for sin. Neither was consumed by the participants. In the celebration of the annual Passover supper, wine was drunk in joyful commemoration of the deliverance (redemption) by God of the whole people from enslavement to the Egyptians.

On the dark side, red wine is often compared with bloodshed. Contact with blood could be a defilement. Lapses into pagan ritual sacrifices involving human blood earned God's particular condemnation. Drinking from a cup and especially drinking it to the dregs was an expression indicating deep suffering rather than rejoicing, and the CRUSHING of grapes in the wine PRESS was a metaphor for the punishment of God. When Christ in spiritual agony in the garden of Gethsemane, anticipating his betrayal and death, prays for 'this cup' to be taken away from him (Matt. 26. 39–42), there is an echo of Isaiah's 'the stupefying cup', the cup of God's wrath (Isa. 51. 22), and Ezekiel's 'cup of affliction and devastation' that has to be drunk (Ezek. 23. 33).

In the light of this tradition, the words of Christ to his disciples would have been mysterious, even scandalous, yet evocative: 'If you do not eat the flesh of the Son of Man and drink his blood you have no life in you . . . for my flesh is real food and my blood is real drink. Whoever eats my flesh and drinks my blood lives in me and I live in that person' (John 6. 53–6). At his last supper before his crucifixion, Christ takes the cup and says, 'Drink from this all of you, for this is my blood, the blood of the new covenant poured out for many for the forgiveness of sins' (Matt. 26. 28). It was wine, so it should have been for rejoicing, but drinking from a cup could have the connotations of the cup of suffering, and as for drinking blood, that would be an inconceivable abomination. Yet his next words, 'From now on . . . I shall never again drink wine until the day I drink the new wine with you in the kingdom of my father' (Matt. 26. 29), suggest his joyful renewed presence with his followers at the messianic banquet that the Old Testament prophet Isaiah described when in the last times God would make for his people a feast of good things, including wine (Isa. 25. 6). Finally Christ commands his Church do this in memory of him.

So, the Eucharist of the risen Christ becomes the principal act of Christian faithfulness. In it the participants share in the redemptive death and resurrection of Christ through sacramental communion with his body and blood, signified by consuming consecrated bread and wine. By his blood shed on the cross the Eucharist has power to give peace and unity and continuously makes the Church into a unified, living body. It is called eucharist or thanksgiving since, at his last supper with his disciples, Christ pronounced over the wine (and bread) the traditional thanksgiving to God when he inaugurated a new covenant between God and his people in his own blood to be poured out in the sacrifice of the cross. Wine, in particular, would recall the blood shed by Christ whom some contemporaries greeted as the Lamb of God.

Controversy

Rites intended for unity tend paradoxically to be the focus of disunity, and the Eucharist is no exception. The eucharistic wine challenges the Old Testament tradition from which it originates. For the Jews, blood shed in animal sacrifice reconciled God and humans—it made atonement, literally, putting man and God 'at one'. Christ puts his own death in the place of that of the sacrificial animal. The Christian doctrine of drinking wine that has (sacramentally) become blood, even the blood of Christ the son of God, would be rejected as scandalous by Jews. Conversely, the Christian sacrifice of bread and wine in the Eucharist is a rejection of the shedding of blood in animal sacrifice.

After the Reformation, seemingly irreconcilable views about the Eucharist separated Protestants and Roman Catholics, notably about the exact meaning of the Eucharist as a 'memorial' of Christ's death and as a sacrifice, and about the sense in which the wine (and bread) become the body and blood of Christ. After the disputes of the Reformation there are now welcome signs of a reconvergence of views in which the emphasis is placed on the real presence of Christ in the Eucharist as a sacramental sign of his redemptive death.

A lesser controversy concerns receiving communion in the form of both bread and wine. In the course of centuries the Church had developed the practice of allowing the laity to take communion only under the form of bread, reserving communion under both species for the celebrant. The Church maintained that, since Christ is fully present under both species, this was only a matter of Church discipline and practical convenience—problems of hygiene with the cup and so on. All the great Reformers—Wyclif, John Huss, Luther, Calvin—campaigned for the restoration of communion wine for the laity, wishing to reduce the distinction between the celebrant and the congregation, and this has become universal in the Reformed tradition. In the 1960s, the Second Vatican Council allowed, subject to the local bishop's permission, communion under both kinds for the Catholic laity.

Sacramental signs are supposed to be 'natural', that is, unmistakable and able to be specified unambiguously. So the sacramental wine has to be fermented juice of the grape: it should not be turned to VINEGAR, nor heavily diluted with water; it must be real wine. But tradition fixes what the sacramental signs are and tradition varies. The fermented juice of the grape is what has always been meant by 'wine' in those parts of the world where Christianity arose. However, in spreading over the globe, Christianity encounters regions where the grapevine has never grown and where there never has been wine of the grape. The question arises in the world of MISSIONARIES whether the tradition could be modified to include rice 'wine', for example, or palm 'wine'.

There are other pastoral issues for sacramental wine. Christian missions among the urban poor in the 19th century were sensitive to the dangers of alcoholism. Was it right to put temptation in people's way? Was it even right to accord high ritual status to alcohol? John Wesley, the father of the Methodist tradition, took it for granted that the Eucharist should be celebrated with wine. In the second half of the 19th century, the alternative of celebrating with grape juice ('unfermented wine') gradually became common in the Methodist Church, under the influence of 'temperance' movements in both Britain and the United States.

A similar question was raised in relation to alcoholic priests in the Catholic Church. In 1974, bishops were authorized to grant to priests who had been treated for alcoholism permission to drink the unfermented juice of the grape instead of wine at the Eucharist. This authorization was revoked in 1983: in the Roman Catholic Church the symbolism of wine is recognized to be so central that even alcoholic priests are not now dispensed from taking at least a trace of wine when celebrating the Eucharist (by 'intinction', dipping the bread in the consecrated wine).

See also RELIGION and MONKS AND MONASTERIES.   J. & M.D.

Albert, J.-P., 'Le Vin sans ivresse: remarques sur la liturgie eucharistique', in D. Fournier and S. d'Onofrio (eds.), *Le Ferment divin* (Paris, 1992).

Jeremias, J., *Die Abendmahlsworte Jesu* (3rd edn, Göttingen, 1960), trans. as *The Eucharistic Words of Jesus* (London, 1966).

Tillard, J. M. R., *The Eucharist. Paths of God's People* (New York, 1967).

eudemis, a flying insect which can damage vines. See MOTHS.

eugenol. See OAK FLAVOUR.

European Union (EU), previously known as the **European Community**, group of 25 advanced western industrialized countries cooperating on both economic and political fronts. Twenty-one of the 25 members produce wine (of which seven only in marginal quantities), making the Union the world's leading wine economy, with an average of 70 per cent of world production and 60 per cent of world consumption.

The area under vines in the EU shrank to under 3.4 million ha/8.4 million acres in 1997 from almost 4 million ha in 1987. This represents 44 per cent of the total global vineyard area (a significant proportion of Asian vines produce DRYING GRAPES and TABLE GRAPES rather than wine).

In 2004–5, total EU production of wine was around 184 million hl/4,800 million gal (world production in 2002–3 was between 255 and 265 million hl, according to OIV statistics). Of this EU total, 41 per cent was QUALITY WINE and 55 per cent was TABLE WINE. The remaining 4 per cent is distilled into spirits such as cognac and armagnac.

Spain has the most extensive area under vines in Europe, and indeed the world, though France and Italy produce substantially more wine than Spain, which has the lowest-yielding vines in the EU. The other EU wine-producing countries are, in descending order of average wine production, Germany, Portugal, Greece, Hungary, Austria, Slovenia, Czech Republic, Slovakia, Cyprus, Luxembourg, Malta, the United Kingdom, and Belgium. (DENMARK, the NETHERLANDS, POLAND, IRELAND, and SWEDEN also produce a small amount of wine.)

Official figures for YIELDS in EU wine-producing countries averaged 53.7 hl/ha (3 tons/acre) in 2004–5. Luxemburg, Malta, and Germany reported the highest yields (115 hl/ha, 99 hl/ha, and 96 hl/ha respectively), and Portugal, Slovakia, and Cyprus the lowest (25 hl/ha, 24 hl/ha, and 17 hl/ha respectively).

Although the EU includes some of the most industrialized nations of the world, it is in Europe that wine production is of greatest social and economic importance. Wine accounts for an average of 5.3 per cent of the EU's agricultural production by value. In France, the proportion is 12.9 per cent, 10.7 per cent in Italy, 3.1 per cent in Spain, and 8.6 per cent in Portugal.

Wine produced within the EU is designated as either table wine or quality wine, the latter having to come from a specified, registered geographical region. Each country has its own precise system of definition. Wine imported into the EU, known as 'third country wine', must conform to European wine law and may not be blended with wine made within the EU.

The EU is an important net exporter of wine, and the trade was worth an average of 4.5 billion Euros for 2004, representing 13.8 million hl, about 7.6 per cent of production. Within the EU, Germany, the United Kingdom, and France are the three biggest importers of EU wines, accounting for 70 per cent of trade within the Union. The EU's imports from outside the Union averaged 11.6 million hl in 2004, worth 2.5 billion Euros. In 2004, the four top exporters to the EU were Australia, Chile, the United States, and South Africa, representing 81% of wine imports from outside the EU.

The EU's citizens drank an estimated 128 million hl of wine in 1996 (at that time only 15 member states), just over 34 l per inhabitant, considerably more than the 10 l world average for consumer countries. Between 1986 and 1996, consumption fell about 10 million hl. The decline slowed in the late 1990s, as consumers switched from basic table wine to higher-quality products of distinctive character. Figures for 2004 (for the 25 member states) show a consumption of 34.7 l per inhabitant, of which 15.6 l was quality wine, 15.4 l table wine and 3.7 l wine imported from outside the EU.

Mindful of its many vine-growing and wine-producing inhabitants, the Union has tried to curb output via its Common Agricultural Policy. In a first wave of measures launched in 1987, producers were offered premiums to grub up vines (see VINE PULL SCHEMES). More than 500,000 ha were pulled up between 1988 and 1997, notably in Spain and Italy. The wine policy accounts for between 3 and 5 per cent of total EU farm spending, and cost over 1 billion Euros in 1997.

In 1998, the European Commission, the EU's executive, launched proposals for a far-reaching revamp of the sector as part of its Agenda 2000 package of reforms. This aimed to maintain the improved balance between supply and demand on the EU market, while making producers more competitive in expanding markets.

The plan was to maintain a ban on planting vines for a transitional period, though the measure would operate flexibly to favour the expansion of production in wines for which there is expanding demand. Grubbing up continues to be encouraged, targeted at member states with regions persistently producing wines for which demand is poor. The 1999 reform of the Common Market Organisation introduced an aid for reconversion, adapting vineyards to produce marketable wines. The Commission introduced 'crisis' DISTILLATION to replace the previous complex multi-tiered system to deal with exceptional cases of market disturbance and serious quality problems. One of the aims of the 1999 reform has been to streamline EU legislation from the previous 23 Council Regulations down to a single new one. The budget available to achieve the reforms had been increased to 1.234 billion Euros. EU farm ministers, who resisted previous attempts at reform of the sector in the mid 1990s, have approved the 1999 regulation that has been applicable since 1 August 2000. Meanwhile, a new reform of the Common Market Organisation is being prepared. The 2006 reform aims mainly to improve the competitiveness of EU-produced wine, to reach a balance between supply and demand, to develop better knowledge and monitoring of the market, to simplify and clarify legislation, to ensure that wine production in Europe is sustainable, and to preserve the authenticity and character of the product.

The EU has specific LABELLING requirements, although individual EU countries may impose stricter national legislation. The European Commission negotiates bilateral agreements on trade in wine with third countries on behalf of EU member states. Up to 1993, it concluded agreements with Australia, Bulgaria, Hungary, and Romania. Since then, new bilateral agreements have been concluded with Switzerland, South Africa, Chile, and Canada. In 2005, a new draft wine agreement was renegotiated with Australia and an agreement with the United States of America was also negotiated. These agreements cover concerns such as: the mutual acceptance or recognition of oenological practices, the reciprocal protection and control of wine denominations (which implies the elimination of use of 'semi-GENERICS'), trade facilitations, consultations and arbitration procedures, tariff quotas, etc. Australia, for instance, has agreed to phase out the use of generic names such as Champagne and Chablis, while France and Italy agreed in 1993 to stop using the term Tokay, to be reserved for Hungarian wines.

The Agricultural Situation in the European Union 1996 Report (European Commission, 1996).

CAP Working Notes: Wine 1996/97 (European Commission, 1997).

Proposal for a Council Regulation on the Common Market Organisation of the Market in Wine COM(98) 370, July 1998.

PAC 2000 Situation et Perspectives—Vin (European Commission, 1998).

http://europa.eu.int/comm/agriculture/markets/wine/index_en.htm

European vines, much-used description for varieties of the common vine species VINIFERA of the VITIS genus, as opposed to AMERICAN VINE SPECIES and Asian vine species.

Euskadi. See BASQUE.

EU table wine is wine at its most basically European, a blend of TABLE WINES from more than one country in the EUROPEAN UNION. The constituents of an EU table wine tend to vary with the vagaries of the bottom layer of the European wine market. One of the most common blends, however, has been cheap white VINO DA TAVOLA from Italy, neutralized by extensive FILTRATION, CENTRIFUGATION, and, sometimes, CHARCOAL treatment, 'Germanized' by the addition of some German Tafelwein made from a heavily aromatic variety such as MORIO-MUSKAT, and sold as EWG TAFELWEIN. In France, EU table wine blends have included blends of French red VIN DE TABLE and much deeper coloured vino da tavola from southern Italy, and blends of French white vin de table with the much cheaper Spanish white VINO DE MESA. The market for such concoctions is, thankfully, shrinking.

eutypa dieback, one of the FUNGAL DISEASES which, by rotting the wood, can be very destructive and cause whole vineyards to be replanted. Sometimes it is known as dying arm, and is called **eutypiose** in France. Distribution is worldwide, over a wide range of climates. It is especially common in MEDITERRANEAN climates such as California, south eastern Australia, south west France, and South Africa. The disease became more widespread in southern France in the 1980s. Eutypa is caused by the fungus *Eutypa lata*, synonymous with the fungus *Eutypa armeniacae*. The fungus attacks many plants and it is a major disease of apricots. Symptoms rarely show in vineyards less than eight years old, but this can be several years after infection has occurred. In the mid 1990s, there was concern in France, for example, that the disease had spread beyond the Cognac region which had most obviously been attacked.

Young shoots are stunted and yellow with cupped leaves, thought due to a toxin produced in the infected trunks or arms. Old wood cut open reveals dead sapwood extending from an old PRUNING wound, the point of entry of the fungus. No vine variety is immune, but some such as Cabernet Sauvignon, Sauvignon Blanc, Ugni Blanc, and Grenache are more susceptible. Infection takes place with mild temperatures following rain. It is difficult to control the disease by removing infected vine parts as spores may blow in from other host plants. Studies in California suggest that spores may travel between 50 and 100 km (30–60 miles). Painting the fresh pruning wound with a paste of the FUNGICIDE Benlate is very effective in stopping infection. This disease does not affect wine quality, but it can have drastic effects on yield, as old vineyards degenerate long after the onset of the initial infection. Given the commercial interest in wine made from old vines (see VINE AGE), this disease is particularly regrettable. R.E.S.

Emmett, R. W., Harris, A. R., Taylor, R. H., and McGechan, J. K., 'Grape diseases and vineyard protection', in B. G. Coombe and P. R. Dry (eds.), *Viticulture*, ii: *Practices* (Adelaide, 1992).

Pearson, R. C., and Goheen, A. C., *Compendium of Grape Diseases* (St Paul, Minn., 1988).

Euvitis, considered by many botanists to be one of two sections of the genus VITIS (see BOTANICAL CLASSIFICATION), the other being MUSCADINIA. These two are considered to be two separate genera by others, since *Euvitis* and *Muscadinia* vines differ in chromosome number and in appearance. All of the commercially important wine, table, and drying grapes belong to the genus *Euvitis*. R.E.S.

Mullins, M. G., Bouquet, A., and Williams, L., *Biology of the Grapevine* (Cambridge, 1992).

Evans, Len (1930–2006), promoter, taster, judge, consumer, teacher, and maker of wine who did more to advance the cause of wine in AUSTRALIA than any other individual. Born in Felixstowe, England, he was an architect *manqué*, like his friend Michael BROADBENT, but in Evans's case the distraction was professional golf rather than wine. He emigrated to New Zealand in 1953 and arrived in Sydney, Australia, two years later, where his stepping stone into what was to become a lifetime's immersion in wine was working for the new Chevron Hilton Hotel. His energetic enthusiasm for wine was such that by 1965 he was the first National Promotions Executive for the Australian Wine Board. Evans was one of the few to see that the future lay in table wine rather than in the sweet fortified drinks in which Australia then specialized. A natural performer and publicist, Evans caused such a stir that Australians were apparently convinced that real men could indeed drink table wine, and since then table wine has become increasingly important to Australia's social life and economy.

By 1969 he was writing books and articles on wine, had left the Wine Board, and was starting up the Rothbury Estate in the HUNTER VALLEY and establishing his own restaurant-cum-dining club at Bulletin Place by Sydney Harbour. He collected people, preferably famous, with as much enthusiasm as seriously fine wine, but distinguished himself in his practical relish of both. He did not just transform BLIND TASTING into a competitive sport, but even oversaw the creation of a game predicated on it, the OPTIONS GAME, which was subsequently put to work raising substantial sums for charity under Evans's direction.

In the late 1970s, it seemed as though Evans, by now an intimate of the great and the good of the wine world, was about to take it over. Financed by a tax lawyer friend Peter Fox, he acquired properties in GRAVES, SAUTERNES, and the NAPA valley, with plans to staff them using an early version of the FLYING WINEMAKER concept. His exceptional tasting skills had also been recognized by his numerous invitations to judge at Australia's important wine COMPETITIONS, and by his appointment as chairman of judges (the first of many) at the Royal Sydney Show.

In 1981, Peter Fox was killed in a crash and the Evans Wine Company was thrown into turmoil. From the remains, Rothbury survived, as did the Petaluma winery in the ADELAIDE HILLS, with which Evans was involved from the start. Evans attempted to rusticate himself at his much embellished mud hut 'Loggerheads' overlooking Rothbury.

From then he continued to write, broadcast, and keep tables or halls full of people entertained, while reminding them that wine is for drinking. He was awarded an Order of the British Empire as well as numerous wine industry distinctions and was made a Chevalier de l'Ordre du Mérite Agricole in 1994.

In 1996, Rothbury, by now incorporating Saltram and St Huberts, was the subject of a hostile takeover bid from brewers Fosters, owners of Beringer Blass wines. Evans Family Wines and the establishment of Tower winery and luxurious lodge in the Hunter valley became his chief commercial preoccupations although he continued to the end to play an important part in educating those with clear potential in the Australian wine industry.

Oliver, J., *Evans on Earth* (Melbourne, 1992).

evaporation, conversion of water (or other liquids) from the liquid to the gaseous or vapour state, brought about by the input and absorption of heat energy. It has important implications for both growing vines and maturing wines.

Viticulture

There are three sorts of evaporation in the vineyard. First, there is evaporation from the soil, which is especially significant while the soil surface is wet. Then there is evaporation from the vine leaves, and lastly from other parts of the vine (bunches wet from rain, for example), which can have important disease implications.

The power of the atmosphere to evaporate water is related inversely to its HUMIDITY and directly to its temperature. Unfortunately the direct climatic records of evaporation, or potential evaporation, are sparse. The records are further confused by the fact that different countries use different instruments for measurement of evaporation. Nevertheless broad averages for regions can be estimated with fair accuracy, and these allow calculation of IRRIGATION requirements, for example.

Evaporation from the soil reduces the amount of water available to the vine and so can encourage WATER STRESS. It also creates humidity in the vineyard.

Evaporation out of grapevine leaves (a process known as TRANSPIRATION) takes place mainly through pores, or STOMATA, which form openings in the waxy leaf surface. It is regulated by opening and closing of the stomata, with closure taking place regularly at night. Transpiration from individual leaves is increased by their direct exposure to sunlight, which provides the energy needed for evaporation. The combined water loss from a vineyard is the sum of the evaporation from the soil and transpiration from the vines (and possibly a COVER CROP or weeds), and is called evapotranspiration.

Inadequate evaporation from wet leaves and bunches is, of course, a factor in FUNGAL

DISEASE infection. Vine-growers in many climates deliberately trim vines and remove leaves from the vicinity of the bunches, partly to allow in more light, but partly also to encourage evaporation, and thus avoid diseases such as BOTRYTIS BUNCH ROT (see CANOPY MANAGEMENT). J.G. & R.E.S.

Wine maturation
Evaporation also causes a loss of liquid stored in tight wooden containers, such as wine undergoing BARREL MATURATION. WATER, the principal component in wines, diffuses through small pores of OAK, eventually reaching the outer surface of the stave, where it evaporates into the atmosphere. ALCOHOL also diffuses through the stave, but at a rate considerably slower than that of water.

The atmosphere in contact with the barrel STAVE contains many molecules of water vapour (more when humidity is high, fewer in dry conditions) but relatively few molecules of alcohol. This diffusion–evaporation process means there exists a concentration gradient of water across the barrel stave which is determined by the relative humidity. Accordingly, high humidity slows the net transfer of water from the barrel interior to the atmosphere. Whilst the rate of alcohol transfer is not affected by high humidity, alcohol loss is enhanced relative to the decreased water loss. To summarize, wine subjected to barrel maturation in a high-humidity storage cellar will decrease in ALCOHOLIC STRENGTH whereas that stored in a dry cellar will increase.

This is why, in the low-humidity SHERRY bodegas of JEREZ, it is common practice to sprinkle water on the earth floors to raise the relative humidity and therefore prevent the alcoholic strength of the wine under FLOR film yeast from increasing to the point at which the yeast would be killed.

Evaporation makes regular TOPPING UP of a barrel necessary. The space left by evaporation is called the ULLAGE. A.D.W. & P.J.W.

evaporative perstraction is a membrane technique used as a means of ALCOHOL REDUCTION, as described in detail by Wollan.

Hogan, P.A., Canning, P.R., Peterson, P.A., Johnson, R.A., Michaels, A.S., 'A new option: osmotic distillation', *Chemical Engineering Progress*, 49 (July 1998).
Wollan, D., 'Controlling excess alcohol in wine', *Australia and New Zealand Wine Industry Journal*, 20/5 (Sept/Oct 2005), 48–50.

evapotranspiration, total loss of water from a vineyard. See EVAPORATION and TRANSPIRATION.

Évora, capital and subregion of the ALENTEJO in southern Portugal.

EWG Tafelwein, German term for EU TABLE WINE.

ex cellar(s), way of buying direct from wine producers and the price they quote.

excoriose. Vine disease. See PHOMOPSIS.

extract, or **dry extract**, or **total dry extract** (**TDE**), the sum of the non-volatile solids of a wine: the SUGARS, non-volatile ACIDS, MINERALS, PHENOLICS, GLYCEROL, glycols, and traces of other substances such as PROTEINS, PECTINS, and gums. Sometimes sugars are deliberately excluded to give sugar-free extract. Wines' extract, including sugars, usually starts at between 17 and 30 g/l but can vary considerably depending on the wine's SWEETNESS, COLOUR (red wines usually having a higher extract than whites, thanks to their greater phenolic content), and age, since some extract is precipitated as SEDIMENT over the years.

Historically, extract was determined by the simple but time-consuming expedient of evaporating a measured quantity of wine and weighing the residue, but this method is imprecise and has generally been replaced by using what is known as the Tabarié formula, techniques involving the measurement of ALCOHOLIC STRENGTH, the DENSITY, and the RESIDUAL SUGAR (if sugar-free extract is required).

To be high in extract, a wine does not necessarily have to be high in alcohol or BODY. Many fine German wines are high in extract, and yet are low in alcohol and are light bodied, especially low-yield Rieslings after dry summers. A.D.W.

extraction in a wine context usually refers to the extraction of desirable PHENOLICS from grape solids before, during and after FERMENTATION, although **over-extraction** is an increasingly common fault in an era when colour is associated with quality. Such wines lack FRUIT and BALANCE. See MACERATION for more details.

Extremadura, one of the 17 autonomous regions in SPAIN and, perhaps surprisingly, the country's fourth most important wine region. Spain's wild west is hardly ideal for growing grapes. Sheep are reputed to outnumber people in this semi-arid upland area between CASTILLA-LA MANCHA and PORTUGAL (see map under SPAIN). Most of the wine is sold in bulk for DISTILLATION and ends up as brandy de Jerez. Local names were beginning to appear on wine labels with increasing frequency in the late 1990s, however, following the trail blazed by Bodegas Inviosa in the Tierra de Barros ('land of mud') zone near the Portuguese border, which shares climate and soil features with neighbouring ALENTEJO.

The regional administration settled in the late 1990s for a single DO for the wine areas in Extremadura—RIBERA DEL GUADIANA. Cencibel, Garnacha, Graciano, and, increasingly, Cabernet Sauvignon and Syrah dominate amongst red grape varieties, and Pardina amongst white ones. With EUROPEAN UNION financing, a rapid overhaul of production methods has been taking place. CORK is an important crop here. R.J.M. & V. de la S.

Ezerjó, white grape variety widely planted in HUNGARY but scarcely known outside it. Most of the wine produced is relatively anodyne, but Móri Ezerjó produced from the vineyards near the town of Mór enjoys a certain following as a light, crisp, refreshing drink, and the Ezerjó grown, in quantity, in the far north west of Hungary can also yield lively dry whites for early consumption. It also produces strong, sweet wines, BOTRYTIZED in good vintages. Ezerjó means 'a thousand boons'.

F

Faber, or **Faberrebe**, like the much more popular SCHEUREBE, a German vine crossing bred by Dr Scheu at Alzey in Rheinhessen in the early 20th century. This crossing of Weissburgunder (Pinot Blanc) and Müller-Thurgau emerged in 1929. Faber, which will ripen easily in sites unsuitable for Riesling, is planted mainly in Rheinhessen. Germany's total plantings had dwindled to 970 ha/2,400 acres by 2003. Like so many 20th-century GERMAN CROSSINGS, its principal appeal lay in the ease with which it accumulated sugar, thus positioning it for a period of growth in the immediate aftermath of the OECHSLE-centric GERMAN WINE LAW of 1971. A little is also grown in England.

Factory House, handsome Georgian monument in OPORTO, standing on land granted in 1806 in perpetuity 'from this day and forever to the consul of the British nation and his corporation and their successors', is a testament to the historic role of the British in the port wine trade. The only surviving example of any Factory House, it is possibly the only actual building constructed as a meeting place for a 'factory', a body of traders or 'factors' buying and selling any commodity in a foreign country. The Portuguese were probably the first to establish such a factory, which they called a *feitoria*, in one of their earliest West African settlements. The first British factory was established by the East India Company near Bombay in 1613. By the beginning of the 18th century, British factories had been established in all major Portuguese ports, including of course Oporto, from which wine was an important export (see PORTUGAL). The Factory House, probably the first and only permanent meeting place for the Oporto factory, was begun in 1786 and finished, under the supervision of the consul John Whitehead, four years later. The cost of the land and the building was paid by the 'Outward Fund', voluntarily levied by the British shippers on their own exports of port.

The British factory's enjoyment of their grand, and determinedly exclusive, new clubhouse was cut short by the French invasion of Portugal in 1807. The official reopening of the Factory House took place at a dinner based on the number 11 on 11 November 1811. In the previous year, George III and the Prince Regent of Portugal had signed a commercial treaty that stipulated that there should be no more British factories in Portugal. The factory itself was therefore abolished and replaced by the British Association in Oporto as British port traders trickled back to enjoy a period of unparalleled prosperity.

The British Association is made up exclusively of members drawn from the British port shippers. By the early 21st century, the remaining British-owned port companies accounted for less than a third of all sales by volume but were still firmly entrenched in Oporto, as evinced by the city's Cricket and Lawn Tennis Club, the oldest British school in Europe, and an Anglican church.

The Factory House continues to be maintained for the exclusive use of the remaining British port shippers, although at such traditional Wednesday lunches as still take place, there are often more Portuguese (directors of the British companies and their friends) than British around the table.

Delaforce, J., *The Factory House at Oporto* (London, 1983).

fake wine. See ADULTERATION AND FRAUD and INVESTMENT.

Falanghina, or **Falanghina Greco**, very characterful ancient white grape which may have provided a basis for the classical FALERNIAN and is still grown on the coast of CAMPANIA north of Naples. About 300 ha/760 acres are now plantd in Campania, where it is the base for Falerno del Massico and Sannio DOCs. It produces attractive, unoaked, fragrant wines of real interest. Modern fermentation has enabled producers to preserve its aromas, which gave it a new lease of life from the mid 1990s.

D.C.G.

Falernian or **Falernum** was the most famous and most highly prized wine of Italy in the Roman period. It was produced on the southern slopes of Monte Massico, the range of hills which runs down to the west coast of Italy in northern CAMPANIA. With a precision which was unusual for the Romans, three distinct zones, or CRUS, were distinguished: Caucinian on the hilltops, Faustian on the slopes (probably in the region of present-day Falciano), and Falernian proper at the edge of the plain. Recent archaeological survey has revealed numerous Roman farms in this region and part of a vineyard of Roman date has been excavated. The vines were trained up trees and also on trellises on poles of willow.

Falernian was a white wine of at least two types, one relatively dry, the other sweeter. As with other Roman fine wines such as CAECUBAN and MASSIC, it was normal to age it considerably. It was considered drinkable between 10 and 20 years. Its distinctive colour, deep amber, was probably the result of MADERIZATION, which may also explain the references to 'dark' Falernian in one source. The frequent descriptions of the wine's 'strength' and 'heat' suggest a high ALCOHOLIC STRENGTH. One curious claim was that it was the only wine which could be set alight! Despite the concern of PLINY in the second half of the 1st century AD that the reputation of Falernian was being endangered by a commitment to quantity rather than quality, the wine remained in the front rank until at least the 4th century AD.

The contemporary revival is Falerno del Massico, produced in white, blended red, and all-PRIMITIVO grape versions in modern CAMPANIA. See also ATHENAEUS.

J.J.P.

Flood **irrigation**, seen here under parral-trained vines in Mendoza, Argentina, may lack the precision of the drip irrigation illustrated on p. 169 but is cheap and easy when copious quantities of meltwater from the Andes are available.

fanleaf degeneration, sometimes called **fanleaf virus,** one of the oldest known VIRUS DISEASES affecting vines. Records of it date back some 200 years in Europe and there are indications that it may have existed in the Mediterranean and Near East since grape culture began. Rather than being a single disease, it is in fact a complex of related diseases which include forms known as yellow mosaic and veinbanding. Shoot growth is typically malformed, leaves are distorted and asymmetric, and teeth along the edge are elongated. Shoots show abnormal branching with double nodes (see FASCIATION), short internodes, and zigzag growth. Leaves on infected plants look fanlike—hence the name. Bunches are smaller than normal, with poor FRUIT SET and many SHOT BERRIES. Sensitive varieties such as Cabernet Sauvignon can lose up to 80 per cent of potential yield and have a shortened productive life.

The disease can be detected by INDEXING using varieties of other species of VITIS such as Rupestris St George, or with other plants such as Chenopodium, or by serological tests using ELISA. The virus can be spread by infected planting material, and this reached widespread proportions in the late 1880s with the adoption of grafting vines on to ROOTSTOCKS resistant to PHYLLOXERA. A second means of spread was discovered in California in 1958. The NEMATODE *Xiphinema index* spreads the disease within a vineyard by feeding on the roots of infected plants and then healthy ones. Thus the symptoms of the disease spread slowly around an original infected plant.

There is no control for an infected vineyard and it must be removed. The virus particle can survive in root pieces for over six years. Nematode populations can be reduced by FUMIGATION. Current research aims to develop resistant rootstocks for planting in infested vineyards but has so far been only partly successful. The most successful method is to plant virus-free vines in a nematode-free soil. Fanleaf-free planting material is readily obtained by THERMOTHERAPY or TISSUE CULTURE. (See also NEPOVIRUSES.)　　　　R.E.S.

Bovey, R., et al., Virus and Virus-Like Diseases of Vines: Colour Atlas of Symptoms (Lausanne, 1980).

Pearson, R. C., and Goheen, A. C., Compendium of Grape Diseases (St Paul, Minn., 1988).

Fara, small red wine DOC in the Novara hills of eastern PIEMONTE in north west Italy. The wines are made from the NEBBIOLO grape. For more details, see SPANNA, the local name for Nebbiolo.

Far North Zone in SOUTH AUSTRALIA has a single (and recently arrived) region: Southern Flinders Ranges.

fasciation, a growth abnormality, of shoots in particular, in which growth is broadened and flattened as though there were several shoots fused side by side. It is relatively rare in grapevines, although some varieties seem to be prone. The cause is unknown but it is a common symptom of FANLEAF DEGENERATION infection.　　　　B.G.C.

fashion has played a part in wine consumption, and therefore eventually wine production, for at least two millennia. The wine drinkers of Ancient ROME favoured white wines, preferably old, sweet white wines (see FALERNIAN, for example). Indeed, throughout much of the modern age, sweet, heady wines have been prized above all others. In the early Middle Ages, the wine drinkers of northern Europe had to drink the thin, tart, sometimes spiced ferments of local vineyards because TRANSPORT was so rudimentary, and RHINE wines were considered the height of fashion. But when these consumers were introduced to such syrupy Mediterranean potions as the wines of CYPRUS and MALMSEY, wines traded energetically by the merchants of, for instance, VENICE, a fashion for this richer style of wine was established. By the 16th century, for example, light, white ALSACE wine was regarded as unfashionable by the German wine drinker (see GERMAN HISTORY), who was, as now, beginning to favour red wines. Many fashions were restricted to one particular district or region, particularly before the age of modern communications. It is clear that the wines favoured by the French court in the medieval period, for example, were considerably influenced by fashion and, possibly, more pragmatically political considerations (see MEDIEVAL LITERATURE and ST-POURÇAIN).

Towards the end of the Middle Ages, fashion seems to have begun to favour not just RESIDUAL SUGAR, but ALCOHOLIC STRENGTH too. Such wines as SACK and TENT from southern Spain were valued for their potency, although by the end of the 17th century, seafaring and exploration brought a new range of drinks to the trendsetters of northern Europe (see COFFEE HOUSES) which were very much more fashionable than any form of wine.

A new age demanded new products, and the most durable of these were the so-called New French Clarets (see CLARET and BORDEAUX, history), whose initial success was largely due to fashion. In the 18th century, however, no wines were more fashionable than a clutch of what a modern salesperson might call 'speciality items': Hungarian TOKAJI, South African CONSTANTIA, and Moldavian COTNARI. These were available in necessarily very limited quantities, but the wine styles created during or soon after this period illustrate the wine qualities regarded as fashionable then: PORT, MADEIRA, MÁLAGA, and MARSALA are all remarkable for their colour, alcohol, and often sweetness.

By the 19th century, much more detailed evidence of the wines then considered most fashionable is available, not just in the form of CLASSIFICATIONS and a number of books specifically comparing different wines (see LITERATURE OF WINE), but also in the form of price lists—for wine PRICES have reflected fashions in wine throughout history. It would surprise the modern wine drinker, for example, to see the high prices fetched by German wines compared with the classified growths of Bordeaux from the late 19th to the mid 20th centuries. The late 19th century was also a time when CHAMPAGNE was considered exceptionally modish in northern Europe, notably in St Petersburg.

In the 1920s and 1930s, wine in almost any form was extremely unfashionable. This was the age of the cocktail on one side of the Atlantic and of PROHIBITION on the other. These phenomena, together with the marked decline of traditional markets and a worldwide economic depression, threatened many small-scale vine-growers with penury (this was the era during which so many wine CO-OPERATIVES were established).

It was not until well after the Second World War, when some measure of real economic recovery and stability had returned, that wine slowly re-established itself as a fashionable drink (although of course it had long been a drink of necessity in wine-producing areas). As foreign travel became an economic possibility for the majority of northern Europeans, consumers in non-producing countries began to link wine with a way of life they associated with leisure, the exotic, and warmer, wine-producing countries.

By the late 1970s, wine CONNOISSEURSHIP itself was beginning to be fashionable, and the economic boom of the 1980s provided the means for a new generation of COLLECTORS. This led inevitably to a fashion for marathon 'horizontal' and 'vertical' TASTINGS of scores of bottles at a time. Buying wine EN PRIMEUR was particularly fashionable in this decade of superlative VINTAGES.

What has been most remarkable about fashions in wine consumption in the late 20th and early 21st centuries, however, has been how rapidly wine production has reacted to them, and in some cases created them (see wine BRANDS, ROSÉ WINES, pale cream SHERRY, LOW-ALCOHOL wine, and wine BOXES among others). The speed of producer reaction is doubtless related to the development of wine criticism, and its publication in the more immediate media of websites, newspapers, newsletters, magazines, radio, and television, rather than books (see WINE WRITING).

Perhaps the most significant fashion of the 1970s and 1980s was for VARIETAL wines, especially but by no means exclusively in the NEW WORLD. This led to a dramatic increase in the area planted with INTERNATIONAL VARIETIES—Chardonnay, Cabernet Sauvignon, and more recently Merlot, in particular. During a single decade, the 1980s, the world's total area planted with Chardonnay vines quadrupled, to nearly 100,000 ha/247,000 acres—and by the mid 2000s had surpassed 174,000 ha/

Vines at Suntory's Tomi-no-oka winery in Japan's Yamanashi prefecture are treated to individual wrapping to protect them against potentially fatal low temperatures in winter, and are trained horizontally on a **pergola** system to encourage air flow and minimize the danger of rot in the humid summers.

430,000 acres. There is hardly a country in which wine is produced that does not at least try to produce commercially acceptable Chardonnay in marketable quantities.

On a much more limited scale, the development of a cult following for the distinctive wines of CONDRIEU in the northern Rhône meant that VIOGNIER, the vine variety from which it is made, was introduced to wine regions as far afield as ROUSSILLON, South Australia, and California in the late 1980s and early 1990s. Viognier would feature again in the early 21st-century fashion for CO-FERMENTATION.

The 1990s saw an even more significant development, however, a dramatic shift in consumer taste away from white wines to red. Just as a high proportion of northern CALIFORNIA's post-PHYLLOXERA replantings and AUSTRALIA's ambitious new plantings were assigned to the then fashionable Chardonnay, it became clear that the wine drinker of the 1990s, particularly the new army of Asian wine consumers, would in fact prefer red—partly for heavily touted, perceived HEALTH benefits. A Chardonnay glut was forecast, and Merlot became the most fashionable wine in the United States by quite a margin. This led to imaginative sourcing of Merlot, any Merlot, imported in BULK from CHILE (where much of it may in fact have been CARMENÈRE) and the LANGUEDOC by North American bottlers.

In the vineyard, the most notable recent fashion has been to seek not just RIPENESS, but PHYSIOLOGICAL RIPENESS, resulting in a marked increase in average ALCOHOLIC STRENGTH, while in the cellar winemakers have reacted quickly to successive fashions for and then against obviously OAKY wines, both white and red.

Of course, fashions change rapidly and can be at least national if not parochial. What is fashionable in southern England, for example, may not be fashionable in Sydney or San Francisco. But for certain periods there are wine types and whole wine regions which can be said to be generally out of fashion outside their region or country of production. Obvious examples in the mid 2000s included lighter-bodied, higher-acid reds such as those of the Loire and Beaujolais, as well as sherry, which could hardly be accused of being light in body or high in acid. Such is the fickle nature of fashion.

fats, see LIPIDS.

fattoria, Italian for a farm, also used for a wine estate. A *fattoria* is generally bigger than a PODERE, which is often a small farm carved out of a larger property and designed to be just large enough to support a sharecropper/tenant and his family.

Faugères, reliable appellation in the LANGUEDOC in southern France. Almost 2,000 ha/4,900 acres of vineyard, mainly at relatively high altitudes (often well above 250 m/820 ft) on schistous foothills of the Cévennes, look down on the plains around Béziers, where vines are dedicated to VIN DE PAYS and VIN DE TABLE. The Faugères appellation vineyards are planted with quintessentially Mediterranean grape varieties to produce big, southern reds that taste like a cross between the spice of the southern RHÔNE and wild, rustic CORBIÈRES to the south west. The ubiquitous Carignan is gradually being replaced by Syrah, Grenache, and Mourvèdre (each of them mandatory in Faugères), and Cinsaut is still grown for fruit and rosés. As Carignan declines in importance, so CARBONIC MACERATION is expected to be replaced by more traditional vinification techniques. Carignan may represent no more than 40 per cent of the blend. Roussanne is encouraged in white Faugères, which has had its own appellation based on at least 30 per cent of this variety with Grenache Blanc, Marsanne, and Vermentino since 2004. Top-quality producers such as Abbaye de Sylva Plana, Alquier, Léon Barral, Estanilles, Fourrier, and La Liquière suggest that this is one of the Languedoc's most consistent appellations.

faults in wines vary, of course, according to the taste of the consumer. Some diners will quite wrongly 'send back' a wine (see SERVING WINE and SOMMELIER) simply because they find it is not to their taste. Taste varies not only according to individuals but also according to nationality. Italians are generally more tolerant of BITTERNESS, Americans of SWEETNESS, Germans of SULFUR DIOXIDE, the French of TANNINS, and the British of decrepitude (see MATURITY) in their wines, while Australians tend to be particularly sensitive to MERCAPTANS and most Americans view HERBACEOUSNESS as a fault rather than a characteristic. To winemakers, however, wine faults are specific departures from an acceptable norm, the least quantifiable of which may be a lack of TYPICALITY.

Visible faults

Faults in a wine's appearance are generally either hazes, clouds, or precipitates in the bottle. STABILIZATION is designed to avoid all these hazards. (In the past, BACTERIA sometimes affected a wine's VISCOSITY, but this problem is rare today.) Haze and cloud in bottled wines can have a variety of causes, of which the most common today is the growth of the microorganisms YEAST or bacteria. Mycoderma is a yeast-related fault which forms a film on the wine's surface (and so may be visible to winemakers, if not wine consumers). Clouds from heat-unstable PROTEINS and from heavy metal contamination do occur but they are much less frequent than they were in the era of copper and brass pipes and taps.

Precipitates, especially crystalline ones, are found from time to time and are usually the harmless result of excess potassium or calcium TARTRATES finally coming out of solution. (Tartrate stabilization usually prevents this.) From white wines, these may form as needle-like colourless or white crystals on the end of the cork in contact with the wine or in the bottom of the bottle, where they look misleadingly like fragments of glass. From red wine, tartrate crystals are usually dyed red or brown from the adsorbed PHENOLICS. See SEDIMENT.

Visible bubbles in a supposedly still wine are frequently viewed as a fault. Some wines, particularly off-dry whites, are deliberately bottled with a trace of CARBON DIOXIDE gas to make them taste more refreshing. Bubbles in a bottle of older wine, particularly a red wine, usually indicate unintentional FERMENTATION IN BOTTLE, however, and are definitely a fault.

While most consumers would agree that cloudy wines are faulty, there is much less agreement about COLOUR. Some wine judges in COMPETITIONS automatically disqualify rosé wines with a hint of amber, even though it is difficult to make a blueish-pink wine out of the GRENACHE grape variety, for example—and wines of all sorts and hues turn amber with age.

OXIDATION, which can brown wines prematurely, is a fault in young table wines but is best confirmed by the nose.

Smellable faults

Some wines smell so stale and unpleasant that the taster is unwilling even to taste them. The most likely explanation for this is a mouldy cork causing CORK TAINT. Such a wine is said to be CORKED, but a wine served with small pieces of cork floating in it indicates a fault in the SERVICE of the wine rather than a fault in the wine. Contact with fragments of sound cork does not harm wine.

Other off-odours can vary considerably. Oxidized wines (see above) smell flat and ALDEHYDIC. VINEGARY wines indicate the presence of ACETIC ACID due to microbiological activity by bacteria and yeast. ETHYL ACETATE, HYDROGEN SULFIDE, mercaptans, excess sulfur dioxide, and the smellable compounds generated by some bacteria can all be reasons for judging a wine faulty. (See also REDUCTION.) The picture is complicated, however, by the fact that we all vary in our sensitivities to most of these compounds (see TASTING), and some of them may be more acceptable in some sorts of wine than others. Acetaldehyde, for example, is the principal odorant of FINO sherries, but definitely indicates over-oxidation in white wines, and makes red wines taste vapid and flat. Although the average palate should not detect acetic acid on a fault-free wine, there are some much-admired, full-bodied red wines (such as some PORT, PENFOLDS Grange, and VEGA SICILIA) whose VOLATILITY is much higher than the norm. Many fine German winemakers at one time deliberately used relatively high concentrations of sulfur dioxide to preserve some of their best wines for a long life in bottle.

A wine may not smell clean because of the influence of one or several CONTAMINANTS such as agrochemical RESIDUES. If it smells of geranium leaves, there has probably been some bacterial degradation of SORBIC ACID, although this can easily be controlled by adding sulfur dioxide at the same time.

A wine may smell MOULDY either because of BACTERIAL SPOILAGE, or because it has taken on the smell of a less-than-clean container.

Another much-discussed microbiological fault, which can cause a wine to smell mousy, has been attributed to the action of yeasts of the BRETTANOMYCES genus, closely related to DEKKERA. More detailed studies on the causes of mousy off-flavour in wine have indicated that LACTIC ACID BACTERIA, including particular strains of *Lactobacillus*, and to a lesser extent *Oenococcus* and *Pediococcus*, are capable of producing the off-flavour compounds responsible for this most unpleasant fault. It cannot normally be smelled in wine unless it is alkalinized or rubbed in the palm of the hand (an action which neutralizes wine acidity). This mousy flavour is volatile only at neutral or high PH, which explains why it is not immediately apparent but builds up in the back of the mouth once a wine has been swallowed or expectorated, as the palate slowly returns to neutral pH through the buffering action of saliva.

See also TRIBROMOANISOLE, METHOXY-DIMETHYLPYRAZINE, and ISOBUTYL-METHOXY-PYRAZINE.

Tastable faults

Most faults are already obvious to the nose and need only confirmation on the palate (which is why in a restaurant it is, strictly speaking, necessary only to smell a sample of wine offered by the waiter). Some contaminations, notably from metal, are easier to taste than smell, however, and a wine that is excessively tannic or bitter (see BALANCE) will not display this fault to the eye or nose. See also CONTAMINANTS. A.D.W. & S.H.

Bird, D., *Understanding Wine Technology* (2nd edn, Newark, 2005).

Peynaud, É., *The Taste of Wine* (London, 1987).

Favorita, white grape of PIEMONTE in north west Italy, is cultivated near ALBA, both on the left bank of the Tanaro in the ROERO zone, and slightly less successfully on the right bank in the LANGHE hills. DNA PROFILING at Torino showed that Favorita is identical to both PIGATO and VERMENTINO from Liguria. Favorita was not widely planted in the mid 1990s, having lost ground to ARNEIS in the Roero and to the newly popular Chardonnay in the Langhe. In warmer sites such as Gagliardo has promoted it can have both minerality and a slightly salty note and can respond well to some BARREL MATURATION. D.T. & J.R.

Federspiel, the classical wines of the Wachau region in AUSTRIA which have an alcohol content between 11 and 12.5 per cent. The name originates from falconry, once a popular pastime in the Wachau. The falcon symbol exemplifies the racy elegance of these dry white wines made from grapes with a minimum ripeness of 83 °Oechsle or 17 °KMW. The must may not be chaptalized. See also STEINFEDER and SMARAGD.

Federweisser. See STURM.

feinherb, synonym for HALBTROCKEN used to describe a wine's sweetness level. The term was in general use in Germany in the first half of the 20th century and has been officially allowed on German wine labels since 2000, although the term has no legal definition or status.

Fendant, Valais name for the most planted grape variety in SWITZERLAND, the productive CHASSELAS. Fendant is therefore one of the most common Swiss VARIETAL wines, although the finest examples of Valais wines made from this grape variety tend to have some geographical designation on the label. See SWITZERLAND for more details.

Fer, alias **Fer Servadou** (and many other aliases), is a characterful black grape variety traditionally encouraged in a wide range of the sturdy red wines of SOUTH WEST FRANCE. In MADIRAN, where it is often called Pinenc, it is a distinctly minor ingredient, alongside Tannat and the two Cabernets. In GAILLAC, where it is known as Brocol or Braucol, it has also lost ground. It is technically allowed into wines as far north as Bergerac, but today it is most important to the red wines of the Aveyron *département*, ENTRAYGUES, ESTAING, and the defiantly smoky, rustic MARCILLAC. The iron-hardness of the name refers to the vine's wood rather than the resulting wine, although it is well coloured, concentrated, and interestingly scented. Fer has also been invited to join the already crowded party of varieties permitted in CABARDÈS.

French plantings totalled nearly 1,300 ha/ 3,250 acres in 2000.

There are about 1,000 ha/2,470 acres in Argentina of a variety known there as Fer which Galet claims is a clone of MALBEC.

Féret. See COCKS ET FÉRET.

fermentation, as it applies to wine, is the process of converting SUGAR to ETHANOL (ethyl alcohol) and CARBON DIOXIDE effected by the anaerobic (oxygen-free) metabolism of YEAST. It comes from the Latin word *fervere*, to boil; any mass containing sugar that has been infused with yeast certainly looks as though it is boiling, as it exudes carbon dioxide bubbles.

History

Before yeast's metabolic processes were properly understood, the word fermentation was also used to describe a much wider range of chemical changes that resulted in the appearance of boiling and in some of which carbon dioxide evolved. These have included the leavening of bread, the production of cheese, and the tumultuous reactions of acids with alkalis. Today such changes involving the intervention of yeast or BACTERIA in aerobic processes are not usually considered true fermentations.

By the middle of the 19th century, our understanding of science was such that opinions were divided about the nature of 'organized ferments' as opposed to 'unorganized ferments' in fermentation. Thanks to Louis PASTEUR, we now know that it is the organized ferments and their agents yeasts and bacteria that are primarily responsible for alcoholic fermentation. They act through their internal ENZYMES (enzymes were responsible for Pasteur's unorganized ferments), which, functioning as catalysts, mediate the series of reactions involved in the conversion of sugar into alcohol and carbon dioxide.

The net change during fermentation of one glucose molecule giving two alcohol and two carbon dioxide molecules expressed as a chemical equation is:

$$C_6H_{12}O_6 \rightarrow 2C_2H_5OH + 2CO_2$$

Many years and the research talents of several scientists, notably Embden, Meyerhof, and Parnas, have elucidated the successive steps in the apparently simple conversion of sugars to the metabolic end products, alcohol and carbon dioxide.

The complex process

The first steps in the process attach phosphate groups to the sugars. Next comes a series of steps in which the six-carbon sugar is split into two three-carbon pieces, one of which is then rearranged into the structure of the other. After some further rearrangements, this three-carbon molecule loses its terminal carboxylic carbon atom in the form of carbon dioxide gas. The residual part is the two-carbon compound ACETALDEHYDE, which goes next to alcohol if oxygen is lacking, or into another multi-step series of reactions eventually yielding energy, water, and more carbon dioxide if generous amounts of oxygen are available.

The net change when oxygen is present in excess is one glucose plus six oxygen molecules giving six carbon dioxide and six water molecules, as shown by this chemical equation:

$$C_6H_{12}O_6 + 6O_2 \rightarrow 6CO_2 + 6H_2O$$

Ideally for the yeast, therefore, the process should be carried out with generous quantities of oxygen available, for then much more cell-building energy is produced. For wine-making man, however, it is important that this process can be modified by limitation of the oxygen supply because then alcohol, rather than water, is produced along with carbon dioxide. Without the alcohol there would be no wine.

(It is interesting that this same series of steps in decomposition of sugar is employed by man during muscular activity, another form of fermentation. In man, and other mammals, the three-carbon compound PYRUVATE is converted to LACTIC ACID and supplies energy for muscular action.)

A number of intermediate compounds are involved. The biochemical reactions converting one compound into its successor in this series are not 100 per cent efficient, with the result that small amounts of certain of the intermediate compounds accumulate in the wine. These compounds and the products of their reaction with other substances in the mixture contribute to what is known as fermentation, or secondary, AROMAS. Included among these compounds are ACETALDEHYDE, ETHYL ACETATE, and numerous other ESTERS and FUSEL OILS.

Physical chemistry tells us that the reaction of six-carbon sugar to ethanol and carbon dioxide yields generous amounts of energy. A significant portion of this energy is captured during the process and used by the yeast for its own purposes. Another major portion of the energy, however, is not captured but appears as waste heat. Unless this waste heat is removed from the fermenting mass, its temperature will rise, reaching levels which damage or kill the yeast cells and stop the reaction, resulting in a STUCK FERMENTATION which can be very difficult to restart. Heat removal is not a major problem when fermentations are conducted in a small FERMENTATION VESSEL because the greater ratio of surface to volume furnishes sufficient radiation and conduction surfaces from which the heat can be dissipated. In a large container, however, the amount of heat liberated may be so large that it cannot all be radiated or conducted away and in such cases some REFRIGERATION system is needed.

Monitoring fermentation

Progress of a fermentation can be monitored in several ways. The most obvious is by simply observing activity in the fermentation vessel. As long as carbon dioxide is vigorously given off, the yeast are still working. Laboratory fermentations are sometimes followed by weighing the fermentation vessel at frequent intervals, thus obtaining a record of the weight of carbon dioxide gas lost and therefore, by calculation, the amount of sugar remaining. Chemical analyses of the unfermented sugar remaining, or of the alcohol produced, are accurate measures of the course of fermentation but are seldom used as they are complex and time consuming. The technique most commonly used in the operating cellar is a measurement of the DENSITY of a sample of fermenting juice.

Density can be determined quickly and with reasonable accuracy by floating a calibrated HYDROMETER in the juice. Although most hydrometers are calibrated to read the remaining sugar's percentage in weight, it must be remembered that this calibration is for a sugar in water solution. When alcohol, less dense than water, is added to the solution during fermentation, the hydrometer reading no longer gives a true reading of the sugar remaining. Indeed, when all of the fermentable sugar has been converted into alcohol, these hydrometers will give the apparently ridiculous reading of less than no sugar. The problem of deciding when the fermentation is complete matters because the presence of small amounts of sugar renders the wine susceptible to bacterial attack and necessitates different treatment after fermentation. Today there are quick, simple paper strips or pills which can reliably detect the presence of even very small amounts of fermentable sugars. Hand-held density meters are becoming increasingly common; these are faster and data can be downloaded directly into a computer. Larger producers may have tanks that monitor fermentation using in-line densitometers or pressure sensors, with readings automatically fed into the computer system.

Factors affecting fermentation

The time required for complete fermentation of white grape juice or crushed red grapes varies greatly. The TEMPERATURE maintained in the fermenting mass is the principal factor affecting duration of fermentation (as well as resultant character of the wine), more even than the initial sugar concentration (see MUST WEIGHT), YEAST type, the aeration of the MUST, and the quantity of micro-nutrients in the juice. In general, red wine fermentations are complete within four to seven days but white wines, which are frequently fermented at much lower temperatures, may require several weeks, occasionally months, and sometimes years in the case of extremely sweet musts (see DRIED GRAPE WINES, for instance).

Other factors which influence the course of a fermentation include agrochemical RESIDUES, ROT, and various chemical additions such as SULFUR DIOXIDE. In the most commercially minded wineries, fermentations may be deliberately hastened so that a single fermentation vessel may be used twice or even three or more times a season.

In the making of certain styles of wine, such as PORT, VIN DOUX NATUREL, and other VINS DE LIQUEUR, the fermentation may be arrested deliberately by the addition of alcohol, usually GRAPE SPIRIT.

The above is an outline of the most usual sorts of fermentation but there are many variants, including BARREL FERMENTATION, CARBONIC MACERATION, ROSÉ WINE-MAKING, and, quite distinct from the primary or alcoholic fermentation, FERMENTATION IN BOTTLE, MALOLACTIC FERMENTATION, and SECONDARY FERMENTATION.

See also MACERATION, the process that inevitably accompanies red wine fermentation, and also RED WINE-MAKING, WHITE WINE-MAKING, and SPARKLING WINE-MAKING. A.D.W.

Halliday, J., and Johnson, H., *The Art and Science of Wine* (London and New York, 1992).

Ribéreau-Gayon, P., Dubourdieu, D., Donèche, B., and Lonvaud, D., *Traité d'Œnologie* 1: *Microbiologie du vin: Vinifications* (Paris, 1998), translated by J.M. Branco, as *Handbook of Enology* 1: *The Microbiology of Wine and Vinifications* (Chichester, 2000).

fermentation in bottle plays an important part in SPARKLING WINE-MAKING. In most still wines, however, it is one of the wine FAULTS most feared by winemakers. It usually results from the presence of some RESIDUAL SUGAR together with live cells of either YEAST or BACTERIA under conditions which favour their growth. (High ALCOHOLIC STRENGTH and high levels of SULFUR DIOXIDE inhibit the growth of such micro-organisms.) It is also possible that a completely dry wine will start to ferment in bottle if it contains a high concentration of MALIC ACID since live LACTIC ACID BACTERIA may metabolize the malic acid causing a MALOLACTIC FERMENTATION in bottle.

The implications of a fermentation in bottle for the wine consumer can range from an inconsequential level of carbon dioxide in the wine to the generation of such large quantities of the gas that it explodes. This latter, potentially dangerous, occurrence is most likely if the wine contains significant amounts of fermentable sugar and is kept at warm room temperatures. If the fermentation is bacterial rather than by yeast, gas is usually produced, together with off-flavours, cloud, or haze (see BACTERIAL SPOILAGE).

A low level of gas in a wine, particularly a young white wine, is by no means necessarily a sign of unwanted fermentation in bottle. Many winemakers deliberately retain (from fermentation) or incorporate a low level of CARBON DIOXIDE to enliven some wines.

A.D.W.

fermentation vessel. The container in which FERMENTATION, and MACERATION in the case of red wines, take place can vary enormously in size, material, and design: from a small plastic bucket (in the case of some HOME WINE-MAKING) to an oak BARREL (in the case of white wines and a very few red wines undergoing BARREL FERMENTATION) to what is effectively a vast, computerized STAINLESS STEEL tower (for high-volume everyday wines). Stainless steel has the advantage that both cleaning and TEMPERATURE CONTROL are much easier than for wooden or concrete fermentation vessels and most modern white and rosé wines, and many reds, are fermented in stainless steel tanks.

Wooden fermentation vessels are still used by many winemakers, however. Traditional wine producers in Germany, Alsace, and the Loire may well use large, old, wooden CASKS which offer natural STABILIZATION and CLARIFI-CATION. Unless scrupulous attention is paid to cellar HYGIENE, however, harmful bacteria can linger in the staves of wooden casks.

Red wine may be fermented either in large wooden casks or open-topped wooden vats. An open top requires constant surveillance since BACTERIA can attack the floating CAP of skins, which will dry out and fail to achieve proper MACERATION without REMONTAGE or PIGEAGE. The cap may alternatively be kept submerged with a headboard or some other design feature.

Wooden fermentation vessels are particularly treasured by some traditionalists for red wine maceration, however, as they retain heat especially well, which favours the extraction process, and tend to have a much higher diameter to height ratio than stainless steel tanks, which favours the contact between wine and solids.

Modern stainless steel tanks, and design modifications of them such as various autovinifiers (see AUTOVINIFICATION), computer-controlled fermentation vessels, self-draining vessels, and Vinomatic automatic vinifiers, are closed at the top and automatically offer a high degree of hygiene.

Lined cement vats are also widely used for fermentation, even at such highly respected properties as Ch PÉTRUS in Pomerol, where stainless steel is regarded as more sensitive to temperature variation and offering less aeration.

fermented in bottle, legitimate description of a SPARKLING WINE made by the traditional, transversage, or transfer methods described in SPARKLING WINE-MAKING. Only traditional method wines could claim to be **fermented in this bottle,** however.

Fernão Pires, Portugal's most planted white wine grape, grown throughout central, southern PORTUGAL. Adaptable, it is the single most popular variety of any colour in the RIBATEJO, where it is now producing varietal wines. Known in BAIRRADA as Maria Gomes, Fernão Pires does well in a relatively warm climate producing large volumes of simple, honeyed, and sometimes slightly spicy, dry white wine.

Ferreira, one of the leading Portuguese port shippers, established in 1715. Dona Antónia Adelaide Ferreira, the *grande dame* of the DOURO valley, was perhaps one of the most dedicated personalities in the PORT industry in the latter half of the 19th century. Born in 1811 in Régua, Dona Antónia devoted her life to the Douro, ruling her vast estates as a benevolent dictator. She invested much of her considerable fortune in planting and improving her properties throughout this harsh terrain. The father of her first husband, also named António Bernardo Ferreira, founded one of the largest and most stately quintas in the Douro, the Quinta do Vesúvio, which the

family owned until its sale in 1989 to the SYMINGTONS. Today Ferreira own four properties in the Douro: Quinta do Seixo, Quinta do Porto, and Quinta do Caêdo near Pinhão and Quinta da Leda high up in the Douro, as well as buying in wine from other properties owned by the family. In the 1980s the properties were the subject of considerable research and investment, with the company pioneering the vertical system of planting whereby vine rows are aligned uphill rather than along contours. Until 1987, Ferreira was owned by descendants of Dona Antónia, but the company now belongs to SOGRAPE (alongside SANDEMAN and Forrester & Co., owners of the Offley brand). Ferreira is the leading brand of port in Portugal and pioneered the production of high-quality dry red wines in the Douro, of which their famous Barca Velha was the prototype in 1952.

Ferrón, or **Ferrol,** minor but characterful white grape variety of GALICIA.

fertigation, the viticultural practice of mixing FERTILIZERS with IRRIGATION water for direct application to vines. The technique is most often used with DRIP IRRIGATION systems, for which each vine has a water outlet. Fertilizers are placed in a tank through which the irrigation water passes, and so the vine is fed with appropriate amounts of water and nutrients as the growth proceeds. Some nutrients such as NITROGEN are readily available in a soluble form (urea); others such as PHOSPHORUS require a relatively expensive formulation to render them immediately soluble. Some vineyard additions such as gypsum and lime are quite insoluble and so require special formulations and injection machines.   R.E.S.

fertility, viticultural term for the FRUITFULNESS of buds or shoots, and also of vineyard soils, see SOIL FERTILITY.

fertilizers. Vines, in common with other plants, may require additions of fertilizers to overcome the deficiency in the soil of a particular nutrient (see SOIL NUTRIENTS). However, grapevines do not require such fertile soils as many other crops. Indeed, the vineyards most highly regarded in terms of the quality of wine they produce are grown on relatively infertile soils. While a modicum of nutrient stress may enhance quality, this is not to suggest that the fewer the soil nutrients the greater the wine quality. For example, a severe NITROGEN deficiency will cause a STUCK FERMENTATION and poor wine quality. Typically, a vineyard producing wine will receive less fertilizer than one producing table grapes.

Fertilizers are commercial formulations which are rich in plant nutrients. Typically they are manufactured (for example, superphosphate) but may be a mined natural product (for example, rock phosphate). COMPOST is not commonly used in commercial vineyards

because of its lack of cost effectiveness, but its use is encouraged from an ecological point of view (see ORGANIC VITICULTURE and BIODYNAMIC VITICULTURE). Animal manures are more widely used, but again, unless they are readily and cheaply available (as from the cattle deliberately kept at Ch MARGAUX, for example), then their use is restricted because of the relatively high cost of applying sufficient nutrients in this form.

The mineral elements most likely to be deficient in vineyards are nitrogen, POTASSIUM, PHOSPHORUS, ZINC, BORON, IRON, MANGANESE, and MAGNESIUM. The fertilizers commonly used to overcome some of these deficiencies are therefore urea, potassium or ammonium nitrate, potassium chloride or potassium sulfate, superphosphate; zinc sulfate; boric acid or borate; and magnesium sulfate. For the major nutrients of nitrogen, phosphorus, and potassium, where up to several hundred kilograms per hectare may be required, fertilizers are commonly spread on the ground. The so-called minor or trace elements are required in small amounts only, typically a few kilograms per hectare. Thus fertilizers compensating for deficiencies of the micro-nutrients zinc, boron, iron, and magnesium can be applied either mixed with other fertilizers to the ground, or sprayed onto the leaves.

The efficiency of fertilization varies with the type of fertilizer and the soil. For example, phosphate fertilizers are not readily available to plants grown in acid soils, so LIMING might increase growth because it makes more phosphorus available to the vine. Similarly, with high rainfall or irrigation, the nitrate form of nitrogen is leached so easily that it is lost to the vine roots unless they are very deep. The nitrate may end up contaminating groundwater, as has been the case in some parts of Germany, making fertilizer use in viticulture (and other forms of agriculture) the subject of scrutiny from environmentalists.

Fertilizer use can affect wine quality. Too much nitrogen can stimulate vine growth to such an extent that RIPENING is prejudiced and the resultant wines are thin, pale, and HERBACEOUS. Excessive use of potassium may also detrimentally increase wine PH.   R.E.S.

Coombe, B. G., and Dry, P. R. (eds.), *Viticulture*, ii: *Practices* (Adelaide, 1992).

Winkler, A. J., Cook, J. A., Kliewer, W. M., and Lider, L. A., *General Viticulture* (2nd edn, Berkeley, Calif., 1974).

Fetească, Fetiaska, or **Feteaska,** scented white grape variety grown widely in eastern Europe. ROMANIA, where the variety is the most widely grown vine by far, has two subvarieties, respectively white and royal: **Fetească Albă** and the exclusively Romanian **Fetească Regală,** which is a CROSSING of the GRASĂ of COTNARI and Fetească Albă developed in Daneş in Transylvania in the 1930s. There is also a dark-skinned variant, **Fetească Neagră,**

whose red wines show potential when well vinified and yields are severely restricted. Fetească is made into peachy, aromatic, almost MUSCAT-like wines with varying degrees of RESIDUAL SUGAR and, often, slightly too little ACIDITY. Fetească Regală was Romania's most planted grape variety in 2005 with around 14,000 ha/34,600 acres, when Fetească Albă was planted on more than 6,900 ha, and Fetească Neagră plantings totalled only about 1,300 ha.

Contrary to common belief, DNA PROFILING in Austria suggests that Fetească is not the same as LEÁNYKA. When cited on a label for export to Germany, the grape's name is often directly translated as Mädchentraube, or maiden's grape. (In Romanian, Fetească, meaning young girl's grape, contrasts directly with BĂBEASCĂ, grandmother's grape.)

FGL, see FOSTER'S.

Fiano, strongly flavoured classical vine responsible for CAMPANIA's **Fiano di Avellino** DOCG in southern Italy. Wines made from this variety lack the aromatic lift of GRECO DI TUFO but have an attractively waxy texture and subtle aromas. It is also planted in Puglia, where it is permitted as a component in the blend for Martina Franca DOC, in the Molise, where it is produced by Di Majo Norante as a VARIETAL as it is increasingly in western SICILIA. It is also planted in McLaren vale, SOUTH AUSTRALIA.   J.R. & D.C.G.

Fiddletown, California wine region and higher of the two AVAs in the SIERRA FOOTHILLS.

Fié, occasionally written **Fiét,** old Loire synonym for SAUVIGNON BLANC. This CLONE has largely been abandoned because of its remarkably low yield, but producers such as Jacky Preys of Touraine pride themselves on their richer versions of Sauvignon made from particularly old Fié vines.

Fiederweissen. See STURM.

Fiefs Vendéens, small, oceanic VDQS zone seeking full AC status in 2005, south of the Muscadet zone near the mouth of the Loire, qualified by one of the communes Mareuil, Brem, Vix, or Pissotte. Most wines are red, from Gamay and Cabernet, but there are rosés, and some whites made from varying combinations of Loire grapes, including Chenin Blanc, Sauvignon Blanc, and Grolleau Gris.

field blend, a mixture of different vine varieties planted in the same vineyard, as was once common. It is rare today but some of California's oldest vineyards are thus planted. See also CO-FERMENTATION.

field budding and grafting, viticultural operation of planting ROOTSTOCK rootlings in their vineyard position and inserting SCION buds. Many types of insertion may

be used but CHIP BUDDING is common. The success rate can be erratic, and careful attention is needed to watering, nutrition, and the tending of each vine. This method is therefore most suitable for small vineyards with good soils and a well-trained workforce.

(See TOP GRAFTING for details of the viticultural operation of changing VINE VARIETY in an established vineyard.)   B.G.C.

fifth growth. See the CLASSIFICATION of Bordeaux.

fighting varietal, term coined in CALIFORNIA in the mid 1980s for relatively inexpensive VARIETAL wines in 750 ml bottles (as opposed to JUG WINE). As varietal names gained currency in the US market, producers of low-priced wines began bottling Cabernet Sauvignon, Chardonnay, and other sought-after varieties from areas capable of producing large crops at low prices, and thus was born a replacement class of wines for old-fashioned GENERIC jug wines. Fighting varietals, though far from grand, improve upon what went before. In the new millennium the term 'fighting varietal' fell out of fashion to be replaced by VALUE BRANDS, a less expensive category of the same type of wines.

fill level, an aspect of individual bottles of wine which can be closely related to the condition of the wine. The lower the fill level when a wine is bottled, the more the space between the top of the wine and the bottom of the cork (the so-called ULLAGE) in which OXYGEN may be trapped in the bottle and may hasten the AGEING process. Most bottlers try to ensure that there is minimal ullage space in the bottle immediately after BOTTLING, a depth of 5–10mm/ 0.2–0.4 in to allow for expansion if ambient temperature ever exceeds the usual bottling temperature of 20 °C. Subsequent reductions in temperature cause a reduction in the wine's volume, thereby apparently lowering the fill level. For wines designed for early consumption, this is unlikely to make much difference, but fill levels are important indicators of the condition of a fine and, especially, mature wine, so that fill levels should always be specified by the AUCTION houses and other FINE WINE TRADERS. The lower the fill level, the more likely a harmful level of OXIDATION and therefore the lower should be the selling price. Despite this perception, experience shows many wines which age in bottle with substantial ullage exhibit no signs of oxidation. Some sorts of wine seem more resilient to low fill levels than others—vintage port and Sauternes are examples—and a low fill level can apparently, sometimes usefully, hasten the ageing process of an extremely TANNIC wine.

During long-term BOTTLE AGEING, some wine is likely to be absorbed by the CORK, resulting in a drop in fill level of perhaps 7 mm after ten years. (To reduce this absorption effect, Ch MOUTON-ROTHSCHILD adopted a policy

of using shorter corks from the 1991 vintage.) Some wine may also evaporate from the top of the bottle during this time, especially if some was trapped between the cork and the inside of the bottle-neck during bottling. Other reasons for a low fill level include poor control during bottling, wine being bottled at too high a temperature, and a faulty cork. In any event, it is always wise policy to pick bottles with the highest fill levels off the shelf, and to drink bottles of wine from the same case from lowest to highest fill level since the wine in bottles with the lowest fill level is likely to be the most evolved.

Note that the fill level in wine GLASSES should ideally be less than half the height of the glass and never more than two-thirds, in order to provide somewhere for the AROMA to collect.

Léon, P., 'On the Level', *Decanter* (Nov. 1993).

film-forming yeasts, sometimes called **film yeasts,** comprise a large group of several genera and many species of wild YEASTS, all of which require OXYGEN for their metabolism. For this reason they appear on the surface of wine in barrels or vats that are not kept completely filled. Some, such as FLOR, a strain of *Saccharomyces cerevisiae* and genetically very closely related to fermentation strains, can add desirable aromas and flavours, others produce off-flavours, while others are essentially inert.

The film-forming species of *Pichia*, *Hansenula*, and *Candida*, and other yeast genera have characteristics unfavourable to wine quality. These yeasts are widely dispersed in vineyard regions and are among the types encountered in spontaneous or wild yeast fermentations. When sugar is present, they are producers of alcohol and carbon dioxide, but have a low level of alcohol tolerance. Thus, while they are active in early stages of spontaneous fermentations, they become dominated by the more alcohol-tolerant *Saccharomyces* yeast, which finish the sugar conversion. These genera of yeasts in general form more ESTERS and ALDEHYDES than do *Saccharomyces*, which probably explains the fact that some winemakers favour their use in spontaneous fermentations.

Candida mycoderma, previously called *Mycoderma vini,* and now classified as *Candida vini* and *Candida valida,* are other yeast species that are responsible for the thin films that will form on top of wines in tanks or barrels that are not completely full. These yeasts require oxygen for film formation and thus act as a signal to the winemaker that a more frequent TOPPING UP regime is required. If wine has to be kept under ULLAGE, then maintaining a headspace of inert gas and an adequate concentration of sulfur dioxide in the wine will usually prevent film formation. For white wines, the ACETALDEHYDE produced is a negative factor, but for red wines, short exposure to a film of *mycoderma* does little damage.

Film-forming yeasts perform a vital function in the production of wines such as FLOR sherry, VIN JAUNE, and TOKAJI   A.D.W. & P.H.

filtration, fundamental but controversial wine-making process whereby solid particles are strained out of the wine with various sorts of filter. Filtration is a physical alternative to natural SETTLING and, like CENTRIFUGATION, requires more expensive equipment but much less patience. Basically, filtration speeds the wine-making process and allows better control, thereby lowering production costs.

There are two principal categories of filtration: depth filtration (further divided into earth and sheet or pad filtration) and surface filtration. **Depth filtration** involves the use of a relatively thick layer of a finely divided material such as DIATOMACEOUS EARTH, or pads made of cellulose fibres. As the cloudy wine passes through the layer, small particles are trapped in the tortuous channels and clear liquid passes through. **Surface filtration**, on the other hand, depends upon a thin film of plastic polymer material having uniformly sized holes which are smaller than the particles being removed from the solution. With tangential or cross-flow filtration, the liquid flows parallel to the filter surface, and thus keeps the filter membrane clear, avoiding clogging, the chief problem of surface filtration. The commonest form of surface filter, as used in many wineries, is the membrane filter. The membranes are usually made of spiral-wound, hollow-fibre, or tubular media but ceramic membranes, which last longer and are easier to clean, may also be used.

After FERMENTATION, as much as possible of the new wine is drained away from the solids and held in a settling tank. Soon afterwards, the wine is separated from the solids at the bottom of the tank by RACKING. At this point the new wine is often given a rough filtration as a start of the clarification and STABILIZATION process; depth filtration, with diatomaceous earth (DE) forming the layer through which the cloudy wine is passed, is commonly used for this (although there is growing concern about the health and safety issues related to working with DE). Subsequent depth filtrations use a finer grade of DE, or a tighter grade of cellulose pads to catch ever smaller particles.

Finally, just before bottling, the apparently clear wine may be passed through a synthetic polymer sheet which has holes of uniform size smaller than the cells of potentially hazardous YEAST or BACTERIA. This surface filtration, known as **microfiltration** or **sterile filtration**, should render the wine sterile but can only be done once a rougher filtration has cleared the wine of particles that would otherwise plug the holes in the plastic membrane. Sterile filtration is simple in comparison with the subsequent problem of getting the sterile wine into a stoppered bottle without any possible contamination from the atmosphere and bottling equipment. Only mastery of sterile filtration and STERILE BOTTLING has permitted the modern phenomenon of stable young white wines containing significant fermentable sugars (although added SORBIC ACID and SULFUR DIOXIDE can assist in controlling micro-organisms).

Carefully made fine red wine which has benefited from extended BARREL MATURATION should not need much if any filtration. Indeed many winemakers believe that even an early rough diatomaceous earth filtration should be avoided because all solids can contribute to flavour and that wine should be 'dirty' when it begins its maturation, even in small BARRELS. After months in wood a wine should be stable against any problems caused by PROTEINS, TARTRATES, and malates (MALIC ACID salts)—which is one of the great advantages of wood maturation for white wines too. It is also likely that yeast and bacteria populations are negligible.

Filtration of fine wines is a controversial issue. While it may be a necessity for ordinary commercial wines, it is widely thought that too heavy a filtration can indeed rob a fine wine of some of its complexity and capacity to age, not to mention some loss of colour, particularly a red wine as subtle as some fine red BURGUNDY. Some commentators and winemakers claim that filtration of any sort is harmful: it is not uncommon to see the term 'unfiltered' used as a positive marketing term. However, the possibile negative effects of filtration should be weighed against the very real risk of microbial contamination or instability, particularly where perfect storage or transport conditions cannot be guaranteed. An unfiltered wine throws a much heavier crust, or SEDIMENT, than one that has been filtered. Where wines are to be bottled unfiltered, an assay for viable micro-organisms is advisable.

Other specific filters or pieces of equipment used to separate solids from liquid include a **centrifuge decanter**, a **pressure leaf filter**, and a ROTARY DRUM VACUUM FILTER, which is an earth filter designed specifically for liquids with a very high proportion of solids such as LEES.   J.A.G. & D.B.

finca, Spanish for estate. Finca Élez is a Spanish DO created especially for the high altitude estate of Manuel Manzaneque.

Findling is a mutation of the German vine crossing MÜLLER-THURGAU grown to a limited extent in the MOSEL-SAAR-RUWER, where its higher must weights are treasured, even if its tendency to rot is not.

fine wine is a nebulous term, used by the AUCTION houses to describe the sort of wines they sell, which roughly coincide with those described in INVESTMENT. For example, within Bordeaux, a wine would have to be of CLASSED GROWTH level or equivalent to qualify as 'fine'.

The extent to which this category of wine coincides with the best wine the world produces has declined slowly but steadily since the 1970s. Buying from, selling to, and in many cases in direct competition with, the auction houses are the **fine wine traders**, a small group of wine merchants who specialize in servicing the needs of COLLECTORS and the like. See BROKERS for more details.

See also PHILOSOPHY OF WINE.

fining, wine-making process with the aim of CLARIFICATION and stabilization of a wine whereby a **fining agent**, one of a range of special materials, is added to coagulate or adsorb and precipitate quickly the COLLOIDS suspended in it. Fining (*collage*, or 'sticking', in French) is important because, by encouraging these microscopic particles to fall out of the wine, the wine is less likely to become hazy or cloudy.

Most young wines, if left long enough under good conditions, would eventually reach the same state of clarity as fining can achieve within months, but fining saves money for the producer and therefore eventually the consumer. Fining is most effective in removing molecules of colloidal size, which include polymerized TANNINS, PIGMENTED TANNINS, other PHENOLICS, and heat-unstable PROTEINS. (Other reasons for clouds, hazes, and deposits in bottled wines include TARTRATES and BACTERIA. See STABILIZATION for details of other methods of removing them.)

Over the centuries, a wide range of fining agents has doubtless been essayed, but scientific and technical advances have eliminated those (such as dried blood powder) that are dangerous to health and those (such as various gums) that are less than fully effective in improving the wine. Many fining agents, deriving variously from EGG WHITES, milk, fish bladders, and American BENTONITE clay deposits, may strike consumers as curious wine-making tools but it should be recognized that only insignificant traces, at most, of the fining agent remain in the treated wine. (Research by Cornelius Ough of DAVIS shows that very low levels of some of the proteinaceous fining agents such as egg whites may remain, but that when bentonite is used no detectable trace of it remains.) Nevertheless, in Australia and New Zealand, the use of any fining agent that is considered an 'allergenic substance' must be declared on the label (see LABELLING INFORMATION). It is important to distinguish between additives such as OENOLOGICAL TANNINS, that are intended to change the flavour of the wine, and processing aids such as Bentonite, which are used to improve stability and/or clarity.

Today two general classes of fining agents are used: pulverized solid or mineral materials, and complex organic compounds. Bentonite, an unusual form of clay, is particularly effective in adsorbing certain proteins and, to a limited extent, bacteria. SILICA functions similarly but somewhat less effectively. Kaolin, another type of clay, is even less effective than silica. Activated carbon (CHARCOAL) has been used to remove brown colours and is also effective in removing some off-odours. Potassium ferrocyanide may still be used as a fining agent for removing copper and iron (see BLUE FINING). All of these fining agents are inorganic chemicals.

Organic compounds used as fining agents include proteins such as the CASEIN from milk, albumin from egg whites, ISINGLASS, and GELATIN, which form insoluble complexes with the unstable pigments and tannins. There is a tendency to move away from animal-based products in the interests of VEGETARIANS AND VEGANS.

Everyday wines, both white and red, are normally fined earlier and to a greater extent than fine wines. Given the extra time accorded the making of fine wines, many of the potentially unstable components polymerize earlier and deposit without human assistance from man. In general, white wines need fining to preserve their lighter colour and to prevent heat-unstable proteins forming a cloud, while red wines need it for a reduction of astringent and bitter tannins. The fining operation removes components that are soluble but potentially subject to polymerization and cloud, or may precipitate with time.

See also FILTRATION, which cannot remove these soluble substances and acts only on particulates. A.D.W. & J.Ha.

fino, Spanish word with two related meanings in the SHERRY-making process. *Fino* is one of two types of wine made naturally in the sherry bodega (*oloroso* being the other). Fino is also a style of sherry, the commercial result of filtering and bottling a *fino*, the palest, lightest, and driest apart from MANZANILLA, and quintessentially the product of the *fino* type of sherry preserved and influenced by the film-forming yeast FLOR. It may be made in any of the three sherry towns, although Fino de Jerez is by far the most common, and that made in Puerto de Santa María is known as Puerto Fino. Most Fino sold in Spain has an alcoholic strength of about 15.5 per cent and is bone dry, and this is now also the norm for export brands. A freshly opened bottle of true, dry, light Fino is one of the most appetizing wines in the world, but the wine in an opened bottle loses its freshness and appeal as though it were a fragile low-strength wine. For more details, see SHERRY.

first growth is a direct translation of the French PREMIER CRU but its meaning tends to be limited to those BORDEAUX wine properties judged in the top rank according to the various CLASSIFICATIONS: Chx LAFITE, LATOUR, MARGAUX, HAUT-BRION, MOUTON-ROTHSCHILD, CHEVAL BLANC, AUSONE, d'YQUEM, together often with the unclassified but generally acknowledged star of POMEROL, Ch PÉTRUS. Just below these red bordeaux in terms of status are the so-called SUPER SECONDS.

Fitou, large red wine appellation in the LANGUEDOC in two enclaves in CORBIÈRES where it meets ROUSSILLON (see map under LANGUEDOC). When the boundaries of this, the first wine appellation of Languedoc, were drawn up in 1948, local politics prevailed and Fitou has remained with, apparently, a great tract of Corbières bisecting it. The clay-limestone soils of Fitou Maritime, i.e. coastal Fitou, are quite different from the arguably potentially more interesting schists of Fitou Montagneux, ie mountainous Fitou, 20 minutes' drive inland—although the purity in the wines of Domaine Bertrand-Bergé argue convincingly for the virtues of a maritime climate. The low-yielding vines on the 2,600 ha/ 6,400 acres of poor soils in these Pyrenean foothills are capable of great expression, but the appellation underperformed in the 1970s and 1980s. The region is even more in the grip of CO-OPERATIVES than its northern neighbour, with the Mont Tauch co-operative in Tuchan, the oldest in the Languedoc, responsible for half of all production and, since the mid 1990s, performing better than many individual producers. The Cave Pilote at Villeneuve-lès-Corbières, also in Fitou Montagneux, also raised its game in the early 1990s. The dominant vine variety is still Carignan, which must not constitute more than 70 per cent of the blend. It is supplemented by increasing amounts of Grenache, its relative Lladoner Pelut, Mourvèdre (in Fitou Maritime), and Syrah (in Fitou Montagneux). The territory demarcated for Fitou may also produce RIVESALTES.

fixed acids, those organic ACIDS of wines whose volatilities are so low that they cannot be separated from wine by DISTILLATION. The two main fixed acids of wine are TARTARIC ACID and MALIC ACID, but several other non-volatile acids are present in small amounts. Unfortunately, the distinction between fixed and volatile acids is not precise because there are some acids which have intermediate volatilities. Among these are LACTIC ACID and SUCCINIC ACID, both found in wine. The fixed acids are important in wines because they are the acids that give wine its refreshing tartness, as well as its natural resistance to bacterial attack. VOLATILE ACIDS, on the other hand, are more obviously smelly than fixed acids and generally produce fruity or, when present in excess, vinegary aromas. TOTAL ACIDITY, a standard wine measurement, is the sum of the fixed acids and volatile acids. A.D.W.

Fixin, appellation abutting Gevrey-Chambertin in the Côte de Nuits district of Burgundy, producing red wines of a similar style to its neighbour, though currently of lesser fame. Fixin wines have a similar sturdiness to Gevrey but have less powerful fruit and fragrance.

There are five PREMIER CRU vineyards: Les Arvelets and Les Hervelets (seemingly interchangeable; certainly wine grown in the former may be labelled the latter), Clos de la Perrière, Clos Napoléon, and Clos du Chapître. Dr Lavalle, writing in 1855, noted Le Chapître, Les Arvelets, and Clos Napoléon but he singled out Clos de la Perrière for special praise since at that time the Marquis de Montmort sold it at the same price as his Chambertin.

See also CÔTE D'OR and map under BURGUNDY. J.T.C.M.

fizziness, the property of a SPARKLING WINE to bubble, which may be measured as the pressure inside the stoppered bottle. A wine bubbles when the bottle is opened because the dissolved CARBON DIOXIDE in the wine moves from a stable to a meta-stable state once the pressure is reduced on opening. In a meta-stable state, the carbon dioxide comes out of solution in the form of bubbles, provided there are nucleation sites on the glass. Nucleation sites are minuscule pits and scratches naturally occurring in bottles or glasses. Carbon dioxide cannot simply leap out of the wine; it has to diffuse to a nucleation site and find a bubble that can then lift off from the glass and rise to the surface. A bottle of gently bubbling sparkling wine will take several hours to go flat, for all the carbon dioxide to be released in this way.

In a stoppered bottle, the cork maintains a pressure in the bottle so that there is an equilibrium between the dissolved carbon dioxide and the carbon dioxide above the wine. When the bottle is opened, the pressure above the wine drops to normal atmospheric pressure, one so-called atmosphere (the pressure at sea level at 20 °C/68 °F), and the wine is in the meta-stable state described above.

Most fully sparkling wines such as CHAMPAGNE are sold with a pressure of between five and six atmospheres, about three times that inside a tyre, which is the pressure which a normal champagne cork and bottle can withstand without undue risk. Such wines may be described as *mousseux* or CRÉMANT in French, *espumoso* in Spanish, SPUMANTE in Italian, and SEKT in German.

Many wines are somewhere between still and this level of fizziness, however. Wines with a gentle but definite sparkle may be described as PÉTILLANT in French, FRIZZANTE in Italian, and SPRITZIG in German, although many variations in nomenclature exist. European wine law defines a sparkling wine as any wine with an excess pressure of more than three atmospheres, while a semi-sparkling wine has a pressure of between one and 2.5 atmospheres. The amount of pressure can be controlled by the winemaker by varying the amount of sugar added during the TIRAGE stage in order to provoke the second fermentation or, in the case of carbonation, simply by controlling the amount of gas dissolved in the wine.

Some wines sold as still wines may fizz very gently, however. This could be a sign of a FAULT but is more likely to be a deliberate winemaking feature. See CARBON DIOXIDE for more details.　　　　　　　　　J.R. & T.J.

Jordan, A. D., and Napper, D. H., 'Some aspects of the physical chemistry of bubble and foam phenomena in sparkling wine', *Proceedings of the Sixth Australian Wine Industry Technical Conference* (1986).
Liger-Belair, G., *Uncorked: The Science of Champagne* (Princeton, 2004).

Fladgate Partnership. The Fladgate Partnership Vinhos S.A. was formed in 2001 when Taylor Fonseca Vinhos S.A. (see TAYLOR and FONSECA) purchased CROFT and Delaforce from DIAGEO. The group remains family owned and has 631 ha/1,558 acres of properties in the DOURO valley with over 1.2 million vines. Eschewing Douro table wines, its focus is premium PORT with a global market share of more than 30 per cent of this category.

flash détente, a technique originally used to extract flavour from fruit such as bananas and mangoes on Réunion, was successfully applied to wine by researchers at INRA in the early 1990s. A certain proportion of fully ripe and fully DESTEMMED grapes is rapidly heated and then immediately put under vacuum. This very fast method of first heating then cooling has been shown to break up the structure of the skin cells, thereby increasing the extraction of colour, POLYSACCHARIDES, and PHENOLICS by between 30 and 50 per cent. *Flash détente* has so far been authorized for use in certain appellations in southern France such as the Côtes du Rhône and units have been installed there, in Bordeaux, and even in Japan. Mobile units have been exported to Australia. See also THERMOVINIFICATION.

flavescence dorée, a PHYTOPLASMA disease (previously known as mycoplasma disease) of the vine which has the potential to threaten many of the world's vineyards. For more details, see GRAPEVINE YELLOWS.　　R.E.S.

flavonoids, a large group of PHENOLIC compounds that includes ANTHOCYANINS, CATECHINS, and the FLAVONOLS. More than 45,000 flavonoids from a wide variety of plant sources have been described. In wine, they contribute to COLOUR, ASTRINGENCY, BITTERNESS, and TEXTURE. Up to 90 per cent of the phenolic content in red wine is made up of flavonoids; in white wines the proportion may be lower because of less EXTRACTION from the skins, stems, and seeds. The antioxidant and cancer chemopreventive capacity of many flavonoids may contribute to the HEALTH benefits of moderate wine consumption.　　G.L.C.

flavonols, a group of PHENOLIC yellow PIGMENTS belonging to the FLAVONOID family. QUERCETIN, the most common flavonol in grapes, is abundant in vine leaves and present in skins and stems. Its concentration can be enhanced in grapes (and therefore in wine too) by exposing the berry cluster to the sun (see CANOPY MANAGEMENT). Indeed, Price and colleagues argue that the quercetin level in grape berries can be used as an index of the sun exposure they have experienced. Like CATECHIN, quercetin may enhance PIGMENT stability in young wines through CO-PIGMENTATION and has anti-oxidant properties similar to those of RESVERATROL (see HEALTH).
　　　　　　　　　　　　　B.G.C., P.J.W., & V.C.

Price, S. F., Breen, P. J., Valladao, M., and Watson, B. T., 'Cluster sun exposure and quercetin in Pinot Noir grapes and wine', *American Journal of Enology and Viticulture*, 46 (1995), 187–94.

flavour, arguably a wine's most important distinguishing mark. As outlined in TASTING, most of what is commonly described as wine's flavour is in fact its AROMA (or alternatively, in the case of older wines, its BOUQUET). This, the 'smell' of a wine, may be its greatest sensory characteristic, but is also the most difficult of its attributes to measure and describe. A wine's flavour could, in its widest sense, be said to be the overall sensory impression of both aroma (as sensed both by the nose and from the mouth), and the taste components, and may therefore incorporate the other, more measurable, aspects of ACIDITY, SWEETNESS, BITTERNESS, ALCOHOLIC STRENGTH, FIZZINESS, and ASTRINGENCY. It has, further, been proposed that the definition of flavour be enlarged to include not just how a wine smells, tastes, and feels (including, for example, the burning sensation associated with particularly alcoholic wines), but also individual tasters' psychological predetermination, the all-important factor of SUBJECTIVISM including personal preferences, expectations, and tolerances determined by individuals' cultural, regional, and psychological influences. (See PHILOSOPHY AND WINE.) In this book, however, the word flavour is used interchangeably with aroma. See also FLAVOUR COMPOUNDS and FLAVOUR PRECURSORS.

flavour compounds, imprecise and inclusive term for substances in wines that can be smelled or tasted (see TASTING), sometimes called aroma compounds. The term flavour compounds is used more particularly for the volatile compounds which are sensed olfactorily, by the nose, and which contribute to both AROMA and, later, BOUQUET, the flavour changing rapidly and markedly during the first few months of a wine's life and then more and more slowly as it matures. Certain compounds are associated with particular VINE VARIETIES although the exact chemical nature of compounds associated with varietal flavours is still the subject of study.

These volatile aroma compounds are in vastly smaller concentrations than those of the non-volatile taste compounds such as GLYCEROL or various ACIDS, some little more than one part per trillion. The flavour differences between varieties arises from differences in the types and amounts of volatile aroma compounds in their berries. It is commonly stated that these occur in the skins, but grape juice also contains significant amounts, and sometimes in different proportions from those found in the same grapes' skin.

Hardie and O'Brien propose that flavour compounds may be present in grapes because they fulfilled an evolutionary role in attracting insects to assist POLLINATION, defending the developing berry flesh against attack from insects and microbes, attracting birds and animals which would eat grapes and so disperse the seeds, and inhibiting germination of competitive plant species. In accordance with selection theory, the variation in flavour and aroma compounds between different VITIS groups of diverse origin is considered to reflect the range of ecological conditions existing during evolution.

The study of grape aroma has attracted scientific attention because of its importance in wine quality, long appreciated but methodologically difficult because of the abundance of candidate compounds, every one of which is potent but scarce. Research quickened in the 1980s as better measuring techniques emerged, notably gas chromatograph-mass spectrometers.

Some of the types of compounds so far identified among the aroma volatiles in the grape are as follows: *monoterpenes*, e.g. linalool, nerol, geraniol, found in floral grapes such as Muscat, Gewürztraminer, and Riesling; *norisoprenoids*, CAROTENOID-derived, e.g. damascenone (rose oil), megastigmatrienone (tobacco, spice), found in Chardonnay; *shikimate-derived*, e.g. raspberry ketone, vanillin, zingerone, found in Syrah/Shiraz; *nitrogen-containing*, e.g. methoxypyrazine (grassy), found in Cabernet Sauvignon and Sauvignon Blanc; *aliphatics*, some gamma LACTONES, an important component of OAK flavour. See METHOXYPYRAZINES and MONOTERPENES.

A large proportion of these compounds occur in grapes combined with SUGARS as GLYCOSIDES and as such are odourless FLAVOUR PRECURSORS. They revert to their aromatic form after hydrolysis of the glycoside by the action of ENZYMES or acids, a process that has been shown to be important in wine ageing.

Most recently, a series of volatile thiol compounds (see MERCAPTANS) has been found to be involved in the varietal aromas of Sauvignon Blanc, Scheurebe, Gewürztraminer, Pinot Gris, Riesling, Muscat, Sylvaner, Pinot Blanc, Petit Manseng, Sémillon, Cabernet Sauvignon, and Merlot. Importantly, these sulfur-containing compounds are present in grape juice and are released, in very low concentration, during fermentation by the action of yeast.

There is no doubt that increasing knowledge about flavour compounds, and their manipulation in the vineyard and winery (as, for example, by the addition of selected enzymes), represent the most important likely technological advances in the wine industry at the beginning of the 21st century. As emphasized above, our knowledge of this area is constantly expanding, especially as new measuring techniques are being developed (see GLYCOSYL-GLUCOSE ASSAY).

Although the chemical characterization of VARIETAL FLAVOURS is still in progress, it is instructive to consider the example of the methoxypyrazines studied by Allen *et al*. These remarkable compounds, associated with the 'green', herbaceous, or vegetative aromas in Cabernet Sauvignon and Sauvignon Blanc grapes, can be detected at one part per trillion in water (the equivalent of one grape berry in a million tons of grapes).

Contemporary studies of flavour compounds are beginning to provide important links between viticulture and wine quality such as the relationship between CANOPY MICROCLIMATE and the development of flavour compounds, which Allen *et al*. found can be increased tenfold using appropriate vineyard practices.

The above examples indicate the enormous effect that flavour chemistry is likely to have on our understanding and manipulation of wine quality, although it also raises the more sinister possibility of 'manufacturing' wines by the addition of traces of flavour compounds to neutral, low-quality wines. Concern about this issue has increased since the discovery in 2004 that illegal flavourings had been added to certain Sauvignon Blanc wines at a winery in South Africa to enhance the varietal character of the wine.

See PHENOLICS, AGEING, and BOTTLE AGEING.

R.E.S., B.G.C., & P.J.W.

Allen, M. S., *et al*., 'Contribution of methoxypyrazines to the flavour of Cabernet Sauvignon and Sauvignon Blanc', in P. J. Williams *et al*. (eds.), *Proceedings of the Seventh Australian Wine Industry Technical Conference* (Adelaide, 1990).

Dubourdieu, D., Tominaga, T., Masneuf, I., Peyrot des Gachons, C., Hardie, W. J., and Laure Murat, M., 'The role of yeasts in flavor development during fermentation: the example of Sauvignon blanc', in J. M. Rantz (ed.), *Proceedings of the American Society of Enology and Viticulture 50th Anniversary Annual Meeting, 19–23 June 2000* (Davis, 2001), 196–203.

O'Brien, T. P., 'Some considerations of the biological significance of some volatile constituents of grape (*Vitis* spp)', *Australian Journal of Botany*, 36 (1988), 107–17.

Williams, P. J., and Francis, I. L., 'Wine flavour research—experiences from the past offer a guide to the future', in J. M. Rantz (ed.), *Proceedings of the American Society of Enology and Viticulture 50th Anniversary Annual Meeting, 19–23 June 2000* (Davis, 2001), 191–5.

flavoured wines, somewhat amorphous category of wines whose basic wine grape flavour is modified by the addition of other flavouring materials. VERMOUTH is a flavoured FORTIFIED wine, while the Greek RETSINA is perhaps the most strikingly flavoured unfortified wine.

History

Spices have traditionally been added to wine (as they have to food) to provide some variety in taste, or, more likely, to hide any imperfections of taste. A wine that tasted like VINEGAR would have been much improved by such additions.

The ancient cultures of the Mediterranean added spices, herbs, and honey (and also drugs or resins such as myrrh) to their grape and date wines. Descriptions and recipes abound in ancient texts from MESOPOTAMIA to Ancient ROME. (See also Ancient EGYPT and Ancient GREECE.) The Greeks were reputed by the Romans almost never to drink their wines straight, and PLINY lists virtually everything from pepper to absinthe as wine flavourings.

Flavourings such as herbs and honey would not only cover off-flavours but would give appeal to light-bodied wines (see GERMAN HISTORY). There have long been local specialities of wines flavoured with herbs, spices, flowers, or nuts.

In medieval times, wine usually needed some improvement within a few months when it began to turn sour. This was often done at home and the most popular recipe was for 'hippocras', made with red or white wine. Sugar, honey, cinnamon, ginger, and pepper were the usual ingredients, and the name came from Hippocrates' sleeve, a reference to the muslin bag through which the infused wine was strained. Hippocras remained popular in England well into the 17th century, when it was enjoyed by Pepys, undergoing various changes of name and composition to emerge as punch, so beloved by the Victorians.

Meanwhile in Europe, spiced wines, often fortified with alcohol, evolved into the vermouths we know today. H.B.

Pliny the Elder, *Natural History*, trans. by H. Rackham (London, 1938), Book 14.

Younger, W., *Gods, Men and Wine* (London, 1966).

Modern variations

The category has been much expanded in recent years, however, by the emergence of flavoured, often low-alcohol wines—an attempt to persuade those who do not see themselves as wine drinkers to buy wine diluted and disguised as something else. They come in all degrees of alcoholic strength, sweetness, and fizziness and are popularly flavoured with fruits. Such products should be distinguished from FRUIT WINES, whose alcohol derives from the sugars of the (non-grape) fruit itself.

A.D.W.

flavourings are available to wine producers, and are used, illegally, to an unknown extent. Of the three sorts of flavourings available to the beverage industry—natural, nature-identical, and artificial—the last can be discounted because they are easily detectable, and natural and nature-identical flavourings are readily available, no more expensive, and extremely difficult to detect. Natural and nature-identical flavourings which impose the characteristics of a range of noble grape varieties such as CABERNET SAUVIGNON and SAUVIGNON BLANC are marketed. Their use is extremely difficult to detect but modern analytical techniques (see ANALYSIS) are able to detect additions at very low levels. In 2004, there was a successful prosecution in such a case. Since these flavourings are so intense, they can be effective at concentrations as low as 0.001 per cent and the addition of, for example, 100 ml/3.6 fl oz of essence to a 100-hl/2,640-gal vat is an operation which can be performed easily and discreetly. As with one of the most obvious wine flavourings, OAK ESSENCE, however, the apparent benefits of these flavourings are relatively short lived and they should be of interest to only the most cynical wine producer. G.T.

flavour precursors include GLYCOSIDES, or sugar derivatives, of compounds that would otherwise be flavour active. These flavourless compounds occur naturally in grapes (and many other fruits) as products of the normal metabolic activity of the fruit, and they are both numerous and more abundant than the free FLAVOUR COMPOUNDS. Their importance to wine comes from their ability to release and so augment the level of flavour compounds. In the case of glycosides, this release is by HYDROLYSIS. This may be a prolonged process during AGEING, for example, or one accelerated through the use of ENZYMES in the winemaking process. Both chemical and sensory studies at the AUSTRALIAN WINE RESEARCH INSTITUTE have demonstrated that flavour precursors are important in development of VARIETAL flavours and BOUQUET in wines. Because many flavour precursors are glycosides, quantification of this class of compound through measures of GLYCOSYL-GLUCOSE in grapes is being advocated as an indicator of grape quality.

A new category of grape flavour precursor, involving the coupling (or conjugation) of a volatile thiol compound to the AMINO ACID cysteine was discovered by Professor Denis Dubourdieu's research group at BORDEAUX University in 1998. The action of yeasts during alcoholic fermentation serves to free some of the highly potent thiol compounds from their S-cysteine conjugated precursor form. P.J.W.

Francis, I. L., Iland, P. G., Cynkar, W. U., Kwiatkowski, M., Williams, P. J., Armstrong, H., Botting, D. G., Gawel, R., and Ryan, C., 'Assessing grape quality with the G-G assay', in R. J. Blair, A. N.

Sas, P. F. Hayes, and P. B. Høj (eds.), *Proceedings of the Tenth Australian Wine Industry Technical Conference 1998* (Adelaide, 1999), 104–8.

Tominaga, T., Peyrot des Gachons, C., and Dubourdieu, D., 'A new type of flavour precursors in Vitis vinifera L. cv. Sauvignon blanc: S-cysteine conjugates', *Journal of Agricultural and Food Chemistry*, 46 (1998) 5215–19.

American Chemical Society, 'Hydrolytic flavor release in fruit and wines through hydrolysis of nonvolatile precursors', *Flavor Science: Sensible Principles and Techniques* (Washington, DC, 1993).

flavour scalping refers to the partial absorption from wine of some aroma and FLAVOUR COMPOUNDS by wine bottle CLOSURES and other types of packaging material (such as the bladders used in wine BOXES) during storage. This process mostly affects wine components that are the least water soluble. The extent of absorption is a function of time in bottle and the sorptive capacity of the closure, with SYNTHETIC CLOSURES having a much greater sorptive capacity than natural bark CORKS or technical closures made of processed cork bark. SCREW CAPS have little or no sorptive capacity. Bottles sealed with a particular closure will exhibit little bottle-to-bottle variation in this phenomenon. Flavour scalping does not necessarily diminish wine quality since some wine components can have an unfavourable impact on wine aroma; it does not affect all wines equally and, indeed, will not affect many wines at all.   M.A.S.

Capone, D., Sefton, M., Pretorius, I., and Høj, P., 'Flavour "scalping" by wine bottle closures', *Australian and New Zealand Wine Industry Journal*, 18/5 (2003), 16–20.

flétri, French term used to describe grapes which have been dried, or partially dried, before fermentation to increase the sugar content. It is used most commonly in SWITZERLAND and occasionally in the Valle d'AOSTA. See also DRIED GRAPE WINES.

fleuraison or **floraison**, French terms for FLOWERING.

Fleurie, one of the ten BEAUJOLAIS CRUS, and surely the appellation with the prettiest name in France. Fleurie includes more than 800 ha/1,976 acres of vines, has a particularly efficacious CO-OPERATIVE, and produces wines which, it is easy to believe, have a particularly floral perfume. Partly because of its name perhaps, Fleurie is one of the most expensive Beaujolais. Some of the more admired producers of Fleurie include Michel Chignard, Jean-Marc Després, Georges DUBŒUF, and Domaine de la Roilette.

Fleurieu Zone in SOUTH AUSTRALIA encompasses the regions of Currency Creek, Kangaroo Island, Langhorne Creek, McLaren Vale, and Southern Fleurieu.

flight, name for a series of different but related servings of wine, served in a bar or restaurant by the GLASS or as part of a TASTING.

Floc de Gascogne is the Armagnac region's answer to the PINEAU DES CHARENTES of Cognac. This strong, sweet VIN DE LIQUEUR, awarded APPELLATION CONTRÔLÉE status in 1990, is made by arresting the fermentation of local grape juice at an early stage by adding young armagnac, which in this case must have been produced by the same enterprise. The resulting liquid, of which about 17 per cent is alcohol, is aged for at least nine months (although not necessarily in wood, as for Pineau). It is usually drunk as an aperitif but is also much used by Gascony's famously resourceful chefs. A *pousse-rapière* (or rapier-pusher) is a blend of sparkling wine and Floc de Gascogne.

flooding of vineyards is normally a major inconvenience. Vines can be damaged if there is flooding while they are growing, but not if they are DORMANT. Floodwaters can also destroy TRELLIS SYSTEMS if debris catches in wires. EL NIÑO has made vineyard flooding in California commonplace but fortunately it is usually confined to the winter months.

Flooding (where feasible and controlled) was at one time one of the measures deliberately used in France, Argentina, and elsewhere to prevent or to minimize the effects of PHYLLOXERA, the root louse that devastated many of the world's vineyards in the late 19th century. Flooding when the vines are dormant can drown the lice but leave the vines unharmed, if not prolong their life expectancy. Unfortunately this treatment was also a factor in the abandonment of many of France's good HILLSIDE VINEYARDS, and replanting on flatland where the MESOCLIMATE and soils are inferior for wine quality (see LANGUEDOC in particular).

Natural winter flooding was used for vineyard IRRIGATION in antiquity, and is still so employed at Langhorne Creek in SOUTH AUSTRALIA, where the annual flood waters of the Bremer river are diverted across some of the vineyards each winter, bringing rich silt which tops up the soil fertility and water to recharge the reserve of moisture held throughout the deep, water-retentive soil profile. This gives the vines enough moisture to carry them right through the summer and results in high YIELDS, despite a summer-dry climate with only 500 mm/20 in of annual RAINFALL. However, new vineyards in the region use DRIP IRRIGATION.   J.G. & R.E.S.

flood irrigation. See IRRIGATION.

flor, or **flor yeasts**, are benevolent FILM-FORMING YEASTS which are able to form a film of yeast cells which floats on the surface of a wine. Flor yeasts are typified by those native to the JEREZ region of southern Spain which produce Fino and Manzanilla SHERRY. These yeasts have been assigned many names by different microbiologists over the years, including *Saccharomyces bayanus*, *S. capensis*, *S. cheriensis*, *S. fermentati*, *S. montuliensis*, and *S. rouxii*.

Flor yeasts are all capable of fermenting sugar in an anaerobic phase of their metabolism. In Jerez they are the active sugar-fermenting yeast. When all fermentable sugar has been consumed, these yeasts have the capacity to switch to another metabolic phase in which they use alcohol and oxygen from the atmosphere to produce a waxy or fatty coating on the cells' exterior which permits them to float on the wine's surface. The flor yeasts begin to form as small white curds on the surface of the wine, typically in the spring after fermentation as the ambient temperature begins to rise. These increase in size until the surface is completely covered by a thin white film which gradually thickens and browns. They also produce ACETALDEHYDE and other products which characterize the aroma of film or flor sherries.

Many studies have shown that these desirable yeasts will form films only in the narrow ALCOHOLIC STRENGTH range of 14.5 to 16.0 per cent. Below 14.5 the usual result is VINEGAR; above 16.0 the yeast struggles and dies, resulting in an *oloroso* style of sherry. Film sherry cannot be made in STAINLESS STEEL tanks because the yeast uses so much alcohol that the wine becomes watery and eventually acetifies. In wooden barrels such as the BUTTS of Jerez, in the area's low-humidity cellars, there is enough preferential EVAPORATION of water through the wood that the water loss just balances the alcohol used by the yeast, the end result being sherry.

Flor yeasts have been studied in detail by Fornachon in Australia, by Niehaus in South Africa, and by CRUESS in California, all regions hospitable to the flor yeast strains and the PALOMINO grape used for sherry, and where wines similar to sherry have been produced (although see also CYPRUS).

Flor or a similar film-forming yeast has been observed on wines in many and varied parts of the world, both ancient and modern.

Flor wines are made in MONTILLA, RUEDA, and Huelva (see CONDADO DE HUELVA) in Spain, and the ALGARVE in southern Portugal, where flor is also used to make a rather crude aperitif wine. See also JURA, whose VIN JAUNE is very similar to sherry, and TOKAJI in Hungary. Similar wines are also made in ROMANIA and, by Plageoles, in GAILLAC.   A.D.W.

Flora, CALIFORNIA aromatic white vine crossing. Perhaps the most delicately aromatic of Dr H. P. Olmo's DAVIS creations (see also CARNELIAN, EMERALD RIESLING, RUBY CABERNET, SYMPHONY), Flora deserves a rather better fate than it had endured by the early 1990s when acreage was too small for official statistics and Flora rarely appeared as varietal wine. A result of Gewürztraminer × Sémillon, it appears to

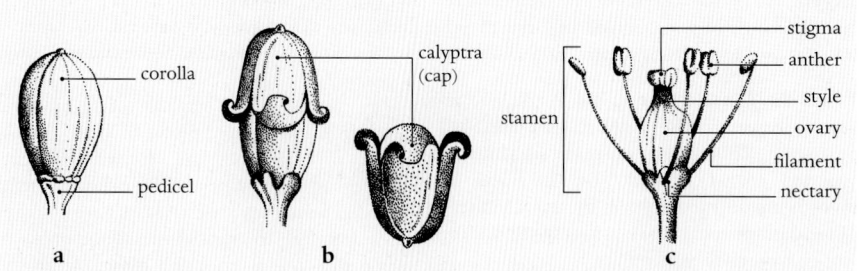

Bloom sequence of grape **flower**: (a) calyptra attached, (b) calyptra separating, and (c) open flower.

take after Gewürztraminer in cooler climates, Sémillon in warmer ones.

flotation. See CLARIFICATION.

flower cap of the vine is known as the CALYPTRA.

flowering, important event in the annual growth cycle of vines, the process preceding the fertilization of vine flowers and their subsequent development into berries. The sequence of events includes the opening of individual flowers, with the CALYPTRA (fused cap of petals) being shed, POLLEN being liberated, and ovules becoming fertilized. Fertilization leads to BERRIES being set (see FRUIT SET), the stage following flowering.

Compared with many other plants, the vine has unattractive small green flowers, and the flowering process in the vineyard is so notably unspectacular that it is likely to be missed by the casual observer. The vine-grower, however, is aware that this process is particularly important in the chain of events that leads up to HARVEST, and, with some varieties and some weather conditions, a poor flowering can mean financial disaster for the vineyard owner.

Flowering, or bloom, takes place about six to 13 weeks after BUDBREAK, the period being shorter for warm climates and early varieties. The vine FLOWER usually contains both male parts (STAMENS) and female parts (a pistil-containing OVARY). The flowering process begins as the cap falls away, exposing the stamens. POLLINATION is the process whereby pollen grains are shed and land on the moistened stigma surface where they germinate. They then penetrate the style and fertilize the ovary, leading to fruit set and the creation of a berry. The fertilized ovaries form SEEDS, with up to four per berry. The flower wall enlarges to form the SKIN and PULP of the grape berry. See diagram.

Most wine grape varieties have perfect, or hermaphroditic, flowers, that is with well-developed and functional male and female parts. Some varieties such as CURRANT, SULTANA, and Perlette, more suitable for DRYING GRAPES and TABLE GRAPES, have non-functional or defective female parts. Berries from such varieties are typically seedless or have small, poorly developed seeds, and therefore tend to be small because of a lack of HORMONES produced by normal seeds.

Cold, wet, and windy weather at flowering has a bad effect on flowering and fruit set. Studies in Europe (in CHAMPAGNE, for example) have shown that regional vineyard YIELD can be correlated with the concentration of pollen in the lower atmosphere, which in turn can also be correlated with weather conditions. Many studies have shown that the vine flower is probably self-pollinated, with insects and wind making little contribution; even flowers surrounded by a bag tend to set perfectly (although cross-pollination between flowers is possible). However, grape flowers do release a pungent, reputedly aphrodisiac, odour, from odour glands at the base of the pistil, which is known to attract insects. R.E.S.

Winkler, A. J., et al., General Viticulture (2nd edn, Berkeley, Calif., 1974).

flowers, vine. The grapevine flower is not showy, and has little attraction for birds, but it has the normal complement of sepals and petals surrounding the sexual parts: the male in the stamens and the female in the pistil. Flowers are grouped together on an inflorescence (see BUNCH). The five petals are locked together to form a cap or CALYPTRA and, at FLOWERING, they fall off, usually as a unit joined at the base; this is called 'capfall', an important PHENOLOGICAL stage. Once the caps are off, the STAMENS expand to their full length and the inflorescence begins to look fluffy. A wet, glistening coating covers the stigma at the top of the pistil when it is ready to receive large numbers of POLLEN grains lodged on this surface.

Different species and varieties of grapevine have one of three types of flower. The most common, and most FRUITFUL, are those with bisexual or hermaphrodite flowers, whose pistil and stamens are both functional. Some vine varieties (such as Ohanez) may have female or pistillate flowers, with a well-developed, functional pistil but with reflexed stamens which contain usually sterile pollen; with cross-pollination, using fertile pollen, these varieties become fruitful. And other varieties, particularly ROOTSTOCKS, may have male or staminate flowers (with functional stamens but no pistil) and therefore do not bear fruit. Most species of VITIS, in their native habitats, have male and female flowers on separate vines, which ensures cross-pollination and hence genetic diversity among the seedling progeny (see SEXUAL PROPAGATION). Commercial VINE VARIETIES are almost invariably bisexual and self-fruitful, and genetic diversity is avoided by VEGETATIVE PROPAGATION.

Flowering occurs in late spring when shoots have developed 17 to 20 visible internodes. This is a crucial stage in the reproductive development of the grape since a host of mishaps may lead to unsuccessful pollination or failure to develop into a berry (see FRUIT SET). B.G.C.

Mullins, M. G., Bouquet, A., and Williams, L. E., Biology of the Grapevine (Cambridge, 1992).

Pratt, C., 'Reproductive anatomy in cultivated grapes: a review', American Journal of Enology and Viticulture, 22 (1971), 92–109.

flowers in vineyards may be deliberately planted at row ends or even between rows as COVER CROPS. Rose bushes at row ends are commonplace in the Médoc and, increasingly, elsewhere, either for aesthetic reasons or because they may act as early indicators of a POWDERY MILDEW attack.

Flurbereinigung, a word of great significance to the landscape of GERMANY's wine regions meaning 'restructuring', a programme undertaken in the second half of the 20th century. Many of the slopes on which some of Germany's finest wines have been produced were relatively inaccessible, uneconomically steep, often terraced, vineyards and so, with national and local government assistance, more than half the landscape devoted to viticulture in western Germany has been physically reshaped, with improvements to access, drainage, and workability. In some cases land has also been reallocated between individual owners to lower their production costs. Outsiders can only guess at the number of parochial man-hours put into the organization of this substantial operation.

flying winemakers, term coined by English wine merchant Tony Laithwaite for a team of young Australian winemakers he hired to work the 1987 vintage in French CO-OPERATIVE wineries. The idea was to apply Australian hard work and technological expertise to inexpensive grapes, thereby producing a unique range of wines for his mail-order wine business. The concept was such a success that it has since been much imitated and developed into a phenomenon with a long-term impact on winemaking techniques and wine styles all over the world (see GLOBALIZATION) although the marked increase in local oenological training and skills is making the phenomenon less common.

The scheme originally depended on the fact that AUSTRALIA has a substantial number of highly trained winemakers (see ACADEME) who are relatively idle during HARVEST time in the northern hemisphere, where most of the world's wine is made. (Miguel TORRES had already capitalized on transhemispherical possibilities by investing in Chile from his base in Spain in 1978, about the same time as the Australian Len EVANS was investigating the possibilities of investment of capital and winemaking expertise in Bordeaux and California.) By the late 1980s, an increasing number of antipodeans were to be found using record amounts of WATER and working record hours in various European wineries. AUSTRALIAN INFLUENCE almost invariably played a part in the background of these flying winemakers, no matter what their nationality. They may have to import materials such as ENZYMES and sometimes mobile BOTTLING equipment, but their most notable import has often been human energy.

The scheme has since been developed into the creation of the flying winemaker, or rather 'international winemaker', since Laithwaite has registered his original name, as a longterm vocation. By the early 1990s, Australian-trained individuals such as Jacques LURTON and Hugh Ryman, son of an English Monbazillac producer, were running teams of winemakers around the globe, from MOLDOVA to Mendoza, often creating special wines or wine styles specifically to order from potential customers in northern Europe, typically quite different from the sort of wine traditionally made in that region.

This sort of bought-in OENOLOGY initially worked best in areas with a considerable quantity of relatively inexpensive grapes but whose technical potential was yet to be realized, thus excluding the classic wine regions and much of the NEW WORLD but decisively including southern France, much of Italy (especially Puglia and Sicilia) and Iberia, eastern Europe, some of the more open-minded South African wineries, and South America. More recently, flying winemakers have invaded some larger wineries in Germany, California, the eastern Mediterranean, and North Africa.

By the late 1990s, several teams of flying winemakers had developed from permanent bases in both France and Britain. INFORMATION TECHNOLOGY has enabled virtual wine-making from a distance of several time zones and many thousands of miles. And the commercial success of many of the products of flying winemaker activity has had a real effect on wine styles made and sold locally, too, sometimes to the detriment of individuality and regionality, in the short term at least. By the 21st century, the winemaker who had only ever made wine in a single location was almost the exception.

Williams, A., *Flying Winemakers: The New World of Wine* (Adelaide, 1995).

Foch, common North American name for the MARÉCHAL FOCH vine.

Fogoneu. See CALLET.

foil, alternative name for the CAPSULE which covers the cork and neck of a wine bottle. The term is most commonly used for bottles of sparkling wine because in this case it is almost invariably made of metal foil, whereas the 'foil' covering tops of bottles of still wine may be made from a wide range of materials. LEAD was once common but was prohibited in the US and the EUROPEAN UNION in 1993 because of both health and ecological concerns. Various plastics and tin are used, as is, increasingly, paper. Of the two most common types, one is made from polyvinyl chloride (PVC) with an aluminium top and is heat shrunk onto the bottle (alternatives made from more environmentally friendly polyethylene terephthalate (PET) are also available); the other is a polylaminate consisting of layers of polyethylene and aluminium which is spun into place. The foil is there largely for aesthetic reasons since the CLOSURE should provide an airtight seal and only a faulty one will allow any seepage of wine. Very occasionally, in the case of an oversight during bottling, a wine may be bottled with a foil but no cork; a tight foil has been observed to act as an effective bottle stopper in at least one case. The length and design of a foil is another purely aesthetic matter, although some clear identification on the top of the foil can be very useful in a CELLAR full of bottles on wine racks.

foil cutter, gadget for SERVING wine which helps cut the FOIL neatly just below the lip of the bottle with the advantages that this avoids unsightly and possibly dangerous torn metal edges, and that there is no likelihood of the wine's being poured over a foil which might taint it. Some foil cutters are blades incorporated into CORKSCREWS; others are separate prongs with small circular blades which cut the foil when rotated. Life without a foil cutter is quite feasible; living without one after being introduced to it is not.

Folgasão, early-ripening grape in northern Portugal and now the official name for TERRANTEZ.

Folle Blanche, white grape variety once grown in profusion along the Atlantic seaboard of western France, providing very acidic but otherwise neutral base wine for distillation by the largely DUTCH WINE TRADE. It never regained its position after PHYLLOXERA ravaged the vineyards of Europe in the late 19th century and France's total plantings of Folle Blanche continue to decline: from 12,000 ha/29,640 acres in 1968 to 2,600 ha in 2000, mainly for GROS PLANT production. It has also been grown to a very limited extent in California.

Folle Noire, occasional synonym for various French dark-berried grape varieties including JURANÇON and NÉGRETTE.

Fondillón, strong RANCIO wine from ALICANTE matured like an *oloroso* SHERRY.

Fonseca, common Portuguese surname associated with two important but unrelated wine producers in PORTUGAL.

Fonseca, or **Fonseca Guimaraens,** are PORT shippers, part of the FLADGATE PARTNERSHIP, founded by a Portuguese gentleman, Manoel Pedro Guimaraens, who acquired Fonseca, Monteiro, and Co. in 1822 and proceeded to place the company on a commercial footing. The Guimaraens took the original firm's name of Fonseca as their label and still ship all their vintage and other ports under this name. With the exception of the 1955 produced by Dorothy Guimaraens, every single Fonseca vintage port was made either by Frank Guimaraens or his great nephew Bruce between 1896 and 1991. Bruce's son, fifth generation David Guimaraens, took over in 1991 and was trained at ROSEWORTHY and worked in Australia before returning to Oporto. Fonseca Guimaraens was acquired by TAYLOR, Fladgate, and Yeatman in 1948 but the two houses maintain separate identities and styles of port. Fonseca owns two main QUINTAS, Cruzeiro and Santo António, located in the Val de Mendiz above Pinhão. Their total of 23 ha/57 acres of vines produce a substantial proportion of the blend for Fonseca's particularly rich vintage ports. In 1978, they acquired Quinta do Panascal, on the south side of the Douro, adding another 46 ha to the firm's vineyards. Fonseca's best-known wine is the superior ruby reserve port Bin 27; they also produce some excellent aged tawnies and Fonseca vintage ports, which, in blind tastings, can rank above all others. Fonseca Guimaraens is effectively used as a second label for their vintage ports, although their quality can be excellent.

José Maria da Fonseca Successores is a family company based in the south of the country at Azeitão in ARRÁBIDA on the Setúbal peninsula. Originally a producer of rich, fortified SETÚBAL, it is now more important as a producer of a wide range of unfortified Portuguese wines, notably Periquita made from Castelão grapes, designed for the international market from grapes from their own vineyards in the vicinity and beyond. See TERRAS DO SADO.

In the mid 1990s, José Maria da Fonseca Successores took over its sister company J. M. da Fonseca Internacional, which had been hived off as a separate business in the 1960s for the production of LANCERS.

food, wine as. See DIET.

food and wine matching is either an extremely complex, detailed subject, a set of rules embedded in one's national culture, or an activity only for gastro-BORES, according to one's point of view.

To the French, not surprisingly, wine is simply part of *gastronomie* in general, and few French people would dream of describing a wine without suggesting which dish or dishes it should be served with. France has traditionally looked to its chefs for expertise in tasting and selecting wine, and it was only in the late 1980s that wine began to be viewed as a distinct subject in its own right.

In the United States, food and wine matching became a subject of intense scrutiny in the 1980s as wine producers, under pressure from so-called neo-Prohibitionists, sought to distance wine from drinks consumed principally for their alcohol content by putting it firmly on the dining table.

For some of the most fanatical wine enthusiasts, food is an obstacle between palate and wine glass, whose flavours can get in the way of a decent wine-TASTING session.

It is certainly true that it is perfectly physically possible to drink any sort of wine with any sort of food. It is also true that 'white wine with fish and red wine with meat' is an absurd generalization built on a couple of sound maxims. There are also certain foods which have very specific effects on wine, and others which distort the PALATE to such an extent that wine tastes very odd or downright nasty in their wake.

But, as Hanni points out, wine and food matching is an ongoing process of sensory adaptation. If a sensory message to the brain is constantly repeated (such as the taste of sourness in food), then it will suppress our sensitivity to the source of stimulation, making the wine that follows taste less sour.

The following should be read in conjunction with the article on TASTING.

Some specific reactions

The wine merchant's maxim 'buy on an apple and sell on cheese' has a sound basis in gustatory fact. Fresh, uncooked apples, like most fruits high in both SWEETNESS and ACIDITY, make many wines taste thin and metallic; any wine that impressed when tasted with an apple must have been seriously good. Hard cheese such as cheddar, on the other hand, tends to make wines taste softer and fuller. Strongly acidic foods such as dishes containing lemon juice and VINEGAR were for long cast as villains in terms of serving with wine, but thanks to sensory adaptation can make a slightly too acid wine taste fuller and more agreeable (while reacting badly with top-quality wines). Raw garlic can react with water to produce a burning sensation in many palates, while an acidic drink such as wine (Provençal rosé with *aïoli*) neutralizes the garlic and refreshes the palate. Hanni has demonstrated that, to the majority of palates, freshly ground pepper is a sensitizing element that may ruin the nuances of a fine, old wine, but can flatter a young, light-bodied wine by making it taste stronger, fuller, and more complex.

Some wine-unfriendly foods

Globe artichokes and asparagus: A significant proportion of the population are sensitive to a substance in artichokes which has been dubbed 'cynarin' and which has the effect on them of making water taste sweet, and making wine taste metallic. McGee reports the evidence for this. A similar effect has been observed with fresh asparagus.

Some forms of chocolate are not only so sweet that it is difficult to find a wine sweeter than they are, they also coat the inside of the mouth. In this case a very strong, very sweet wine will overcome these disadvantages; lively young port, Australian Liqueur Muscat or Tokaji, and Málaga, seem to manage.

Some general rules

White wines generally (although not universally) taste more acid than red wines, so it makes sense to serve them with simple fish dishes which would normally call for the sort of acidity in lemon juice or vinegar.

Sweetness in food (which can be from as unexpected a source as tomatoes or balsamic vinegar) increases the perception of sourness, BITTERNESS, and ASTRINGENCY in wine, while making the wine appear less sweet, stronger, and less fruity.

Very acid foods (such as those dressed with vinegar or citrus juice) decrease our perception of sourness in wine, making the wine taste richer and more mellow. If the wine is at all sweet, it will taste sweeter.

Foods dominated by bitterness, sweetness, and UMAMI accentuate any bitterness in a wine.

Red wines high in TANNINS taste less tannic if served with heavily textured foods containing uncoagulated proteins for the tannin molecules to combine with, so it can make sense to partner a rare steak with a young wine based on Cabernet Sauvignon, Syrah, Nebbiolo, or Sangiovese.

Bitterness and astringency in wines can be muted by judicious use of salt in the food served with them.

Astringency in wine is suppressed by foods that are acid, salty, or fatty and accentuated by food that is sweet or spicy.

Salty foods may make sweet wines taste sweeter.

Full-bodied, aromatic white wines such as Gewürztraminer have traditionally been recommended with spicy foods, but contemporary Asians suggest that particularly those containing chili may well go best with lightly chilled, assertively fruity, possibly even tannic, reds.

Many cheeses are too pungent or greasy textured for very fine or mature red wine. Sweet wines, whether fortified or not, can be more flattered by the savoury, salty nature of cheese, and are less overwhelmed by it than, say, a mature red bordeaux.

All dry wines taste horrible with sweet foods, which seem to emphasize their acidity. Even quite sweet wines can taste very thin and nasty if served with dishes that are sweeter than they are themselves. It is therefore advisable to choose only relatively sweet, full-bodied wines with the sweet course. Germany's delicious sweet AUSLESEN are best sipped without food.

Clever use of lemon juice, vinegar, fresh pepper, and chewy meats can compensate for the shortcomings of ordinary wines. With very fine wine, however, it is probably safest to serve relatively neutral foods. A general observation in matching food and wine is that there are nearly always at least two ways of doing it: in one the wine completely parallels the food profile, in the other opposes and contrasts with it. For example, smoked eel can successfully be paired with, respectively, a creamy Chardonnay with heavy lees influence or a steely Riesling with green apple and mineral notes.

Some particularly successful combinations

Riesling and smoked salmon or other smoked fish.

Riesling (even medium sweet Riesling) with onion tart.

Chablis with oysters.

Cru Beaujolais with charcuterie, particularly *rosette de Lyon*.

Red bordeaux and lamb.

Red burgundy with feathered game.

Sauternes and Roquefort or other blue cheese.

See also ORDER OF WINES.

Hanni, T., *The Cause and Effect of Wine and Food* (St Helena, 1991).

——*The Components of Taste* (St Helena, 1998).

Lee, J. C., 'Some Prefer Red With Chili', *Wall Street Journal* (Nov 2004).

Poussier, L., and Poussier, O., *Desserts and Wines* (London, 2004).

McGee, H., *On Food and Cooking* (New York, 1984).

Roux, M., *Matching Food and Wine: Classic and Not So Classic Combinations* (London, 2005).

foot treading, traditional method of CRUSHING only rarely found outside Portugal's DOURO valley, where it is still used for the production of some of the finest ports. CHAPOUTIER of Hermitage and some BURGUNDY producers also use feet for breaking up the CAP of their top red table wines.

Forastera, common light-berried grape from the island of Ischia near Naples, also cultivated on the CANARY ISLANDS.

Forcayat, or **Forcalat**, almost extinct dark blending grape of VALENCIA making curious-smelling, light-coloured red wine.

forests, by supplying wood of a certain sort, have an important impact on the character and flavour of wine made using COOPERAGE made from that wood. See WOOD TYPES and, particularly, OAK for details of individual forest locations.

Forez, Côtes du. A range of hills between the upper reaches of the Loire and Lyons in eastern France give their name to light, vigorous red and rosé wines made, like BEAUJOLAIS, from the GAMAY grape. The wines, designed for early drinking, may taste reminiscent of those of the Côte ROANNAISE to the north. Both regions, part-granitic, have known greater glory. Full AC status was granted to Côtes du Forez in 2000. It is higher than the Côte Roannaise, has a slightly less dependable climate, and has taken an almost exclusively CO-OPERATIVE route. The Vignerons Foréziens co-operative is based in Boën-sur-Lignon and has won acclaim for its policy of developing quality through a series of different cuvées. Plantings have remained steady at around 200 ha/500 acres.

Fortana, tart dark grape, speciality of EMILIA, known as Uva d'Oro in neighbouring ROMAGNA.

fortification, the practice of adding spirits, usually GRAPE SPIRIT, to wine to ensure microbiological stability, thereby adding ALCOHOLIC STRENGTH and precluding any further FERMENTATION.

The principle behind this addition of alcohol is that most BACTERIA and strains of YEAST are rendered impotent, unable to react with sugar or other wine constituents, in solutions containing more than 16 to 18 per cent alcohol, depending on the strain of yeast.

The stage at which spirit is added has enormous implications for the style of fortified wine produced. The earlier it is added in the fermentation process, the sweeter the resulting wine will be. Vins de liqueur such as PINEAU DES CHARENTES, for example, are simply blends of sweet, hardly fermented grape juice with grape spirit. An even stronger charge of alcohol is added before fermentation to a significant proportion of the rich grape juice used in the production of Australia's LIQUEUR MUSCATS and Tokays. For most port-style wines (including the sweeter styles of madeira) and for all VINS DOUX NATURELS, fortification takes place during fermentation. Much of the natural grape sugar is retained by arresting fermentation before its completion, thereby boosting alcoholic strength to a pre-ordained level: usually between 18 and 20 per cent in port but between 15 and 16 per cent in most vins doux naturels. Spirit is added only at the end of fermentation, to dry, fully fermented wine, in the making of sherry, similar wines such as MONTILLA, and the drier styles of madeira. Any sweetness in such wines is usually due to a pre-bottling addition of sweetening agent, often itself a mixture of grape juice and spirit (see MISTELA, PX).

The spirit used for fortification comes from a variety of different sources and could be based on grapes, sugar beet, cane sugar, agricultural by-products, or even petroleum. Local regulations specify the types of spirit allowed for a given fortified wine and only grape spirit is allowed for fortified wines of any quality. The spirit used for fortifying port, however, is supplied by the Portuguese monopoly which has, in its time, been unable to provide grape spirit, without any perceptible damage to the final quality of the wines. Carbon dating usefully allows the immediate detection of petroleum-based spirit in any wine, however.

The method of DISTILLATION of the spirit plays a part possibly even more important than its source. The most neutral spirits are the products of a continuous still, which contain a minimum of flavour congeners (the impurities which contribute to the character of a spirit) and tend to be used in the fortification of wines that are designed for early consumption and deliberately exhibit the characteristics of the base wine (the MUSCATS of southern France, for example). Spirits produced by POT STILL distillation on the other hand are much more violently flavoured and are rarely added to fortified wines. A.D.W.

fortified wines are those which have been subject to FORTIFICATION and therefore include SHERRY, PORT, MADEIRA, VERMOUTH, MÁLAGA, MONTILLA, MARSALA, LIQUEUR MUSCAT, Liqueur Tokay, and several strictly local specialities (although liquids such as VIN DOUX NATUREL made by adding spirit to grape juice rather than wine are not, strictly, fortified wines). Practically all warm wine regions (see AUSTRALIA, CALIFORNIA, CYPRUS, SOUTH AFRICA, for example) make some sort of fortified wine, often in the image of port and sherry even if they are not allowed to use those protected names, within Europe anyway. It is an almost invariable rule that anywhere hot enough to produce good fortified wine is too hot to provide the ideal climate for its consumption.

Fort Ross, relatively new California AVA. See SONOMA.

Foster's, BEER-based Australian drinks group whose holding company FGL Wine Estates is increasingly important in wine (see GLOBALIZATION). The group's first wine acquisition was in 1996 with Mildara Blass, formed in 1991 when Wolf Blass Wines was merged with Mildara. In 2001, Foster's acquired Beringer of California to form the first major Australian-American wine corporation. But Foster's next acquisition, of a beleaguered Southcorp, the owner of LINDEMANS, PENFOLDS, Rosemount, and many other famous Australian brands, firmly established Australia as the centre of gravity for what they immediately styled 'the world's leading premium wine business'.

foulage, French for the wine-making operation of CRUSHING grapes.

Foundation Plant Services (FPS), a self-supporting service department of the University of California at DAVIS which produces, tests, maintains, and distributes disease-tested plant propagation material. It also provides plant importation, quarantine, and testing services.

fourth growth. See the CLASSIFICATION of Bordeaux.

foxy, usually deeply pejorative tasting term for the peculiar flavour of many wines, particularly red wines, made from AMERICAN VINES and AMERICAN HYBRIDS, vine varieties developed from both American and European species of the VITIS genus, particularly *Vitis labrusca*. (Wines made from many other hybrids—SEYVAL and NORTON, for example—are completely free of **foxiness**.) The CONCORD grape, widely planted in NEW YORK state, is one of the most heavily scented, reeking of something closer to animal fur than fruit, flowers, or any other aroma associated with fine wine, although the 'candy'-like aroma is, incidentally, quite close to that of the tiny wild strawberry or *fraise des bois*. It has long been considered that the juice component responsible is methyl anthranilate, but now there is another contender, o-amino acetophenone.

It has been discovered that earlier harvesting or long CASK AGEING reduces some of Concord's foxy characteristics. Aged New York sherry-style wines are a good example of wines that contain Concord that is virtually undetectable in their blends. Ironically, while often shunned at home, Concord grapes have delighted some California winemakers with their perfume.
H.L. & B.G.C.

fractional blending, prosaic English name for the labour-intensive SOLERA system of maintaining consistency of a blended wine, particularly SHERRY, over many years.

France, the country that produces more fine wine than any other, and in which wine is so firmly embedded in the culture that such French people as are interested in wine have a quasi-spiritual relationship with it. Per capita wine consumption in France has fallen dramatically, however, from over 100 l a year in 1977 to 50 l in the early 21st century, thanks to social changes, increased restrictions on advertising alcohol, and on driving with it in the bloodstream. By the end of the 20th century, wine export markets were also being shrunk by competition from other wine-producing countries with their own wine SURPLUSES, a strong euro, and a distinct lack of marketing skills, particularly a lack of BRANDS, on the part of the French wine industry. The result was *la CRISE VITICOLE*, the ongoing wine crisis.

The total area planted with vines shrank considerably (see EUROPEAN UNION and its VINE PULL SCHEME) particularly in the early 1990s: down from 1.23 million ha/3.04 million acres in the late 1970s to a total of 849,000 ha (including those vines dedicated to cognac,

France

BELGIUM

LUXEMBOURG

GERMANY

English Channel

CHAMPAGNE · VINS DE MOSELLE

Rheims
Bouzy
Château-Thierry · Châlons sur Marne
Épernay
Sézanne · Avize · Toul
Paris · CÔTES DE TOUL
Marne · Strasbourg
ALSACE
Bar sur Aube · Colmar
Les Riceys
Chablis
Auxerre
Vendôme · Orléans · Gien · St Bris
LOIRE · ORLÉANAIS · Dijon
Angers · Tours · Blois · CÔTE D'OR
Nantes · Saumur · Loire · BURGUNDY
Chinon · Nevers · CÔTE CHALONNAISE · Arbois · JURA · SWITZERLAND
VINS DU HAUT-POITOU
FIEFS VENDÉENS · Mâcon
Poitiers · Châteaumeillant · MÂCONNAIS · BEAUJOLAIS · Geneva
St-Pourçain-sur-Sioule · Seyssel · Annecy
La Rochelle · CÔTES LYONNAISES · SAVOIE
Saintes · Roanne · Lyons · Chambéry
CÔTES ROANNAISES
Angoulême · CÔTES CÔTES
COGNAC · D'AUVERGNE · DU FOREZ
Allier · Loire · Grenoble
Atlantic Ocean · RHÔNE · Valence
Blaye · Die
Bergerac · Dordogne · Massif Central · ITALY
BORDEAUX · Marcillac · Nyons
Bordeaux · Duras · Monbazillac · SOUTHERN RHÔNE
CÔTES DU MARMANDAIS · Cahors · Rodez · Avignon · Nice
BUZET · Agen
Fronton · Gaillac · Nîmes
ARMAGNAC · Montpellier · COTEAUX D'AIX EN PROVENCE
Tursan · Auch · Toulouse · LANGUEDOC · Aix en Provence · CÔTES DE PROVENCE
Bayonne · BÉARN · Béziers · Marseilles
Irouléguy · Pau · Madiran · Garonne · Cassis · Bandol
JURANÇON · Carcassonne
Pyrenees · Limoux · ROUSSILLON
Calvi · Patrimonio
Perpignan · Mediterranean Sea · CORSICA
VINS DE CORSE
Ajaccio
SPAIN · Sartène · Porto Vecchio

⬛ Wine-growing regions

0 ——————— 200 km

France

280

armagnac and TABLE GRAPES) in 2003, but France still has more land under vine than any country other than Spain. Average annual wine production fell from 65 million hl in the late 1980s to just over 50 million hl in the early 2000s.

There are few wine producers anywhere who would not freely admit that they have been influenced by the great wines of BORDEAUX, BURGUNDY, CHAMPAGNE, or possibly the RHÔNE (see map above). Other qualitatively significant wine regions, perhaps better appreciated

within France than abroad, include ALSACE (for historical details of which see GERMAN HISTORY), BEAUJOLAIS, CHABLIS, JURA, LOIRE, PROVENCE, SAVOIE, and SOUTH WEST FRANCE. France's most important wine region by far in terms of quantity, however, is the LANGUEDOC, and ROUSSILLON to the immediate south, whose output, and not just of VIN DE TABLE, still makes a contribution to the European WINE LAKE, but whose better-quality wines provide some of the world's best wine value. The Mediterranean island of CORSICA is also under

French jurisdiction, although it shares many characteristics with the Italian island of SARDEGNA.

Although the first instance of geographical DELIMITATION was in Portugal's DOURO valley, France is the birthplace of the widespread application of the notion that geography, or TERROIR, is fundamental in shaping the character and quality of a wine. This resulted in the early 20th century in the much-copied APPELLATION CONTRÔLÉE system. Its governing body is INAO. Appellation contrôlée, or AC, wines represent the wines of which France has traditionally been most proud, sold under the geographical name of the appellation rather than by vine variety, in contrast to the substantially VARIETAL wines of the NEW WORLD. AC wines represent an increasing proportion of all wine produced in France, more than 45 per cent by the early 2000s, and an increasing proportion of French vineyards is dedicated to their production each year. Vins Délimités de Qualité Supérieure, or VDQS wines, representing less than 1 per cent of French wine production, are those judged not (yet) up to AC standard. An increasingly significant category of French wine (and another that has been much copied elsewhere in Europe) is that represented by the VINS DE PAYS, or country wines. Rules governing vins de pays are much less constricting than the AC regulations: higher YIELDS and a wider range of vine varieties are generally allowed, and varietal vins de pays are common. By 2003, vins de pays constituted nearly 30 per cent of all French wine produced and the long-term aim is to upgrade even more of the production of the vast Languedoc-Roussillon region from vin de table to vin de pays.

Curiously, and perhaps because wine is so deeply entrenched in French history and culture, wine CONNOISSEURSHIP and to a certain extent the wine TRADE are not as evolved in France as, for example, in Australia, Belgium, Great Britain, Switzerland, and the United States. Although things are slowly changing, the average French citizen has bought and drunk little other than the wine produced closest to him or her, whether geographically or by virtue of family or friendship. This has tended to stifle the development of wine retailing, although the number of specialist wine MERCHANTS, known here as *cavistes*, has increased significantly since the early 1980s. As might be expected in a country associated with so many forms of gastronomic excellence, wine appreciation in France is closely tethered to the table. Wine is rarely drunk without food, and France's chefs and SOMMELIERS have been regarded as the rightful repositories of wine knowledge.

Although France is rivalled only by Italy as the world's principal wine exporter, it is also the world's third or fourth most important importer of wine after Germany, the UK, and sometimes the US. Wine has been imported ever since Massilia was settled by the Greeks (see below), but it was the development of the Languedoc as a virtual factory for particularly light red wines at the end of the 19th and the beginning of the 20th centuries that meant vast quantities of strong, deep-coloured red wines had to be imported for BLENDING (*coupage* in French), from North African colonies initially, and subsequently from southern Italy and, to an increasing extent, Spain. At the turn of the century, France was still importing more than 5.5 million hl/121 million gal of wine and

exported 15 million hl. (Its major source of imported wine, Italy, by contrast, imported about 0.56 million hl and exported 17 million hl.)

France is so important as a role model to the world of wine that many terms used internationally are French in origin (BLANC DE BLANCS, PIGEAGE, and VERAISON are just three varied examples). France is recognized the world over as a centre of wine research and ACADEME and has benefited ever since the time of Colbert in the late 17th century from the country's ability to identify and solve potential problems on a national level (see OAK). The OENOLOGICAL and viticultural faculties of the universities of BORDEAUX and MONTPELLIER have long enjoyed international prestige, and considerable viticultural research emanates from INRA stations.

One of France's great commercial strengths in recent years has been that it is the world's prime source of oak for top-quality wine and brandy COOPERAGE. France is an important exporter of barrels.

History

Around 600 BC, Greek immigrants arrived from Phocaea in ASIA MINOR and founded Massalia (Marseilles) as a Greek city (see Ancient GREECE). One of the colonists' importations was viticulture. In the 2nd century BC, the settlement, now known as Massilia, had become vital to the Romans, now a major power (see Ancient ROME), if they were to safeguard their trading route with Saguntum (modern Sagunto, near Valencia in Spain). When Massilia was attacked first by the Ligurians and then by the Celtic tribes of the Allobroges and the Arverni (of modern AUVERGNE), self-interest made the Romans take on the defence of the city. As a result they gained a new province, named at first Provincia (modern PROVENCE) and later, with the foundation of the Roman city of Narbo (modern Narbonne) in 118 BC, Gallia Narbonensis. Massilia remained Greek until 49 BC.

In the eyes of the Greek colonists, vines grew where olives and figs grew: the commercial exploitation of the three together had long been characteristic of Mediterranean agriculture, so it did not occur to a Mediterranean people that the vine could be cultivated further north than the olive and the fig. The wines of Massilia were available in Rome, but they were cheap and nasty. Even before Caesar's conquest of Gaul in 51 BC, the Gauls had consumed Italian wine in prodigious quantities, as the evidence from AMPHORAE found in France shows. The Greek geographer Strabo, who finished his *Geography* in 7 BC, said that Massilia and Narbo produced the same fruits as Italy, but that the rest of Gaul was too far north for the olive, the fig, and the vine (4. 2. 1). His statement may have been too sweeping, however, and in the 1st century AD good wine certainly did come from Gaul. PLINY tells us in his *Natural History* that in Vienna (modern Vienne in the RHÔNE valley)

the Allobroges produced RESINATED WINES which were a source of national pride and for which they charged high prices (14. 57). For more details, see GAUL.

Thus the first French wine of note was a Rhône wine. Yet at the same time or earlier the inhabitants of Gallia Narbonensis may themselves have taken the vine beyond the familiar territory of the olive and the fig, to GAILLAC in modern SOUTH WEST FRANCE. Archaeological evidence shows that in the second half of the reign of the Emperor Augustus (he was Imperator from 27 BC to AD 14), amphorae were being made in large numbers in workshops near Gaillac, and near Béziers in the LANGUEDOC. This suggests that they were needed for wine that was grown there and not imported. The RIVERS Tarn and GARONNE would have provided convenient transport to the Atlantic coast, where BORDEAUX was already a trading post. Since these wines are not mentioned by any classical author, they probably did not reach Rome, unlike the wines of Vienne.

Gaillac and Vienne are beyond the northern limit for olive trees, but they do sustain another tree that is considered characteristic of Mediterranean vegetation, the evergreen oak, QUERCUS *ilex*. Where the evergreen oak grows, the climate is hot enough to produce a good grape harvest every year, without fail. Yet viticulture advanced further north, away from the evergreen oak, to where the success of the vintage is no longer guaranteed. Bordeaux and BURGUNDY were next in line; by the 3rd century AD, wine was grown in both regions, despite the possibility of cold, wet summers when the grapes might not ripen fully. Yet even if the harvest failed occasionally, the demand for wine was such that the expansion of viticulture made economic sense.

The Romans had regarded the CELTS as drunks, and hence a source of great profit, immoderate fools who drank wine unmixed with water until they fell into a stupor, but when the drunken Celts started growing their own wine, its reputation was soon to surpass that of the Italian wines that they had once imported. After Bordeaux and Burgundy came the LOIRE and the Île-de-France (the PARIS basin including CHAMPAGNE). By the 6th century AD, even the west of Brittany had vines, and wine was grown further north than it is now, well north of Paris.

As the Roman empire disintegrated, Gaul ceased to be a Roman province and was overrun by Germanic invaders. The Visigoths, the Burgundians, and the Franks established kingdoms in Gaul; eventually, Aquitaine and Burgundy were subjected to Frankish rule. Under the Romans, the Gauls had been governed from the south; the Franks had come from the north, and Clovis, the first of the Merovingian kings (481–511), established Paris as the capital city of a kingdom that hardly extended further than the Île-de-France. Under

CHARLEMAGNE and his heirs, the royal court's principal seats were Aachen (Aix-la-Chapelle) and Paris. Hence political power, and the wealth that went with it, were concentrated in the north. In the Mediterranean, wine was part of everyday life, but in Paris and Aachen, on the northernmost limits of viticulture, wine was a luxury item, and from a luxury item it became a status symbol. Also, because Gaul was largely Christian by the 6th century, the Church's requirements added impetus to northern viticulture (see EUCHARIST). Monasteries and churches needed wine; local magnates, both lay and spiritual, wanted good wine.

Monastic influence

Monasteries had their own vineyards (see MONKS AND MONASTERIES and BURGUNDY), and so, often, did cathedrals. From the Carolingian era onwards, lay viticulture generally used the system of 'complant', which meant that a wine-grower would approach an owner of uncultivated land with an offer to plant it for him. Since it takes about five years for new vines to start yielding sufficient fruit, the grower would be given that length of time to work the vineyard; after that, half the land would revert to the owner, while the vines on the other half would become the possession of the grower, on condition that part of the harvest, or sometimes a monetary payment, be given every year in perpetuity. The Loire wine QUART DE CHAUME, for instance, owes its name to the complant mode of ownership and production: the *quart*, or fourth, being the share the vigneron owed the landowner (in 1440, the Abbey of Ronceray d'Angers); *chaume* meaning an uncultivated plot that is to be planted with vines. As labour grew more expensive, the conditions became more favourable to the grower: in the course of the 13th century, the owner would often no longer reclaim the half of his property, but the grower, and his children and his children's children after him, would continue to make their annual payments in wine or money. The system made it possible for wild country to be colonized and cultivated at no expense to the landowner: in this way, the new wine-growing region of Poitou (see LA ROCHELLE) was planted so efficiently in the 12th and 13th centuries. The advantage to the grower was that he was not a serf, tied to the land, but a free man, entitled to a large share of what he produced. It was therefore in his interest to make wine for which he could get a good price; nevertheless the owner exercised ultimate control, for the decision how and with what grapes to plant the vineyard was his, and he had the right to terminate the contract and evict the vigneron if the wine was not good enough.

In the Middle Ages, wine was France's chief export product, and the reasons why certain nations drink some wines in preference to others go back to this period. The English drink CLARET because BORDEAUX was at one time governed by the English crown and later remained the largest supplier of wine to England. The Scots drink claret because of the Auld Alliance with France against England. The Flemish and the Dutch have traditionally bought wines of Burgundy because Flanders and the southern part of the Netherlands were part of the dukedom of Burgundy and Burgundy's trade routes were mostly overland to the north. But transporting wooden BARRELS of wine along bumpy roads was difficult and expensive: whether a region exported a large share of its wine or produced wine mainly for its own consumption depended on its proximity to navigable rivers rather than on the quality of its wines. Apart from its trade with the north, which did not develop until the 15th century, Burgundy did not export much wine, whereas regions accessible by water, such as the LOIRE, the Île-de-France around PARIS, and GASCONY, did. The chief ports were Bordeaux, Rouen, and La Rochelle. Bordeaux served the Bordeaux area and the HAUT PAYS; Rouen served the Île-de-France; and La Rochelle served Poitou.

The ships used to transport wine before the 12th century were longboats like the Viking ships. But in the 12th century, the new ports of La Rochelle and Gravelines (on the English Channel near St-Omer), as well as the new Flemish ports of Nieuwpoort (near Ypres) and Damme (near Bruges), adopted a new type of ship, the cog. The cog was a broadly built ship, with a roundish prow and stern, more manœuvrable than the old kind and specifically designed for carrying freight. Its capacity was far larger than that of the old longboat, and soon all other ports started using it as a more efficient way of transporting wine. The cog doubled up as a warship if need arose.

The unit in which wine was measured, the TONNEAU, derived from Bordeaux. A tonneau, or wooden barrel, could hold 252 old wine gallons, or 900 l/238 US gal. A Paris tonneau was 800 l, but, because of the prominence of Gascon merchants in London and English merchants in Bordeaux, the Bordeaux measure became the standard. Many cogs could hold as many as 200 tonneaux; in practice, a barrel containing 900 l was too heavy to handle, and casks half or a quarter the size were used. Such was the importance of the medieval wine trade that, from being the space occupied by a tun of wine, a tonneau, or ton in English, became the unit in measuring the carrying capacity of any ship, whatever its load.   H.M.W.

Dion, R., *Histoire de la vigne et du vin en France* (Paris, 1959).

Duby, G. (ed.), *Histoire de la France rurale*, i (Paris, 1975).

Lachiver, M., *Vins, vignes, vignerons* (Paris, 1988).

Modern history

The social turmoil of the French Revolution at the end of the 18th century made few important changes to the patterns of wine production (although it did engender an entirely new class of consumers, and new styles of *restauration* for them). Until the middle of the 19th century, the vine was cultivated much more widely in France than it is today, and such abandoned areas as, for example, the Côtes d'AUVERGNE on the Massif Central, PARIS, and the MOSELLE were flourishing wine regions. As communications improved, the patterns of the wine trade changed, although Bordeaux continued to operate with a certain degree of autonomy, thanks to its geographical position and long-established trading links with northern Europe, first ENGLAND and then the DUTCH WINE TRADE. The 17th and 18th centuries saw an explosion of interest in wine production in the Gironde, and by the mid 19th century, when the world's most famous wine CLASSIFICATION was formalized at a magnificent exhibition in Paris, the great CHÂTEAUX of the MÉDOC were enjoying a period of prosperity that would not be rivalled until the 1980s. Wine continued to be important to the Burgundian economy, and French wine was recognized throughout the civilized world as one of the corner-stones of civilization itself. CHAPTAL had devised ways of improving overall wine quality (for the incidence of ADULTERATION AND FRAUD was high in the immediate aftermath of the Revolution), and France was beginning to produce its own wine experts such as the widely travelled and independently minded JULLIEN. A historian might say that a catastrophe to end this golden age was inevitable.

In fact there was a series of catastrophes, all viticultural, which had devastating effects on both the quantity and quality of wine produced. Oidium, or POWDERY MILDEW, was the first of a series of disastrous imports from North America, presumably the result of the 19th-century passion for collecting botanical specimens. Unlike European vines, most American vines are resistant to this FUNGAL DISEASE and so it was not until it had been imported to Europe that its effects, of reducing quantity, quality, and colour, were noted, in 1852. The 1854 vintage in France was disastrous, the smallest for more than 60 years. French vineyards were just returning to health, thanks to the development of SULFUR dusting, when another curious vine condition was noted: inexplicable debilitation and, eventually, death. The cause was a tiny louse, PHYLLOXERA, which was to ravage the vineyards of the world, but affected southern France first, causing the greatest commercial havoc there while a remedy was sought. Since phylloxera affects only the roots of vines, the only effective solution was eventually found to be to graft European vines on to resistant American ROOTSTOCKS. But the renewed importation of North American plant material seems to have brought with it two more deadly American fungal diseases, DOWNY MILDEW, whose effects on wine quality and quantity were first noted in 1878 and lasted until well into the 20th century, and BLACK ROT, which was evident from the mid 1880s.

It is hardly surprising therefore that French vignerons saw their salvation in planting HYBRIDS, vines with at least some genes from AMERICAN VINE SPECIES to provide a defence against these completely new and unforeseen hazards to one of France's greatest glories. First, after considerable debate, AMERICAN HYBRIDS were planted and then, in the early 20th century, so-called FRENCH HYBRIDS were developed which tasted more like the European VINIFERA vines' produce.

There was such a crisis in wine quality in the late 19th century that the great scientist PASTEUR was asked to look into the matter, and the result was a giant step forward for the science of wine-making, in which France has long been at the forefront of research (see University of BORDEAUX in particular).

By the turn of the century, the plains of the LANGUEDOC had been transformed into a great factory producing light red for drinkers in northern France, now commercially accessible thanks to the development of the RAILWAYS. These light wines were given weight, alcohol, and colour by the produce of new vineyards in ALGERIA and the economy of this North African colony was transformed.

Two World Wars left France's wine business in serious need of reorganization, and since the mid 20th century it has certainly been the world's most thoroughly and harmoniously organized, with the development of the powers of the INAO and increasing emphasis on the importance of the APPELLATION CONTRÔLÉE system for which it is responsible. Vigorous, and successful, efforts have been made to uproot hybrids from France's vineyards, to ensure that a sound standard of scientific training is available to France's thousands of vine-growers and winemakers, and that a thorough programme of research is dedicated to the concept of wine quality.

Thanks to falling sales both at home and abroad towards the end of the 20th century, the French wine business is experiencing a profound crisis of confidence in the early 21st century.

Geography and climate

France does not have the monopoly on fine wine production, but its geographical position is such that it can produce wine from an exceptionally wide range of grape varieties with a good balance of sugar and acidity. With wine regions lying between LATITUDES 42 degrees and 49.5 degrees, France can provide the two most suitable environments identified in CLIMATE AND WINE QUALITY for growing grapes. In the south, the MEDITERRANEAN CLIMATE can be depended upon to ripen grapes fully, but not so fast that they do not have time to develop an interesting array of FLAVOUR COMPOUNDS

and PHENOLICS. In the west, relatively high latitudes are tempered by the influence of the Atlantic's Gulf Stream. In the east, centuries of viticultural tradition have established what seem to be potentially perfect marriages between grape variety and particularly favoured terroir in the more CONTINENTAL climate of Burgundy, Alsace, and Champagne, France's most northerly wine region where, over the centuries, the ideal wine style has evolved to take advantage of the area's climate and special geology.

France also has a wide variety of SOIL TYPES, much charted and revered (although see GEOLOGY and SOIL AND WINE QUALITY for a discussion of the limited extent to which they may affect wine quality).

Vine-growing in modern France is concentrated in the south but there are vineyards in all regions other than the most mountainous and the most cloudy, which excludes most of the Massif Central, the high-altitude mass in the middle of the country, much of the alpine region on the south east, and the flat north western sector closest to Great Britain. See map on p. 280.

Vine varieties

France conducts a full agricultural census only every decade or so. The most recent was conducted in 2000 and published in 2002.

CARIGNAN was France's most planted vine variety for many decades, thanks to its ubiquity in France's largest wine region, the Languedoc-Roussillon, but by the turn of the century Merlot had assumed this role with a total of 101,000 ha/250,000 acres planted. GRENACHE was almost as widely planted as Carignan with 95,700 ha, while UGNI BLANC was France's fourth most planted variety with 90,000 ha. Fifth and sixth most planted varieties CABERNET SAUVIGNON and SYRAH were a long way behind with 53,400 ha and 50,700 ha respectively. Next most popular varieties CHARDONNAY and CABERNET FRANC could muster just over 36,000 ha each. But the picture overall is one of increasing domination of French vineyards by the INTERNATIONAL VARIETIES.

HYBRIDS, so widely planted in the mid 20th century, are all but a distant memory, although there were still more than 2,000 ha of BACO BLANC in Gascony. And there were still 9,000 ha of ARAMON—not a hybrid but a very poor quality red wine grape which dominated Languedoc vineyards before Carignan took its place.

One of France's strengths is her treasury of traditional local varieties, either imported as a result of shifting political power (most of France's most planted red varieties were originally Spanish), or the apparently indigenous likes of those still to be found in limited quantity in SOUTH WEST FRANCE. More than 100 different varieties are still planted to a significant extent, arguably a less varied palette

than Italy's but with a renewed enthusiasm for HERITAGE VARIETIES.

Viticulture

Most vineyards in France are immediately recognizably French. With its reliable RAINFALL and supply of soil water, northern France has the highest VINE DENSITY in the world, with up to 13,000 plants per ha, and the vines are typically planted in neat, low-trained rows, often using GUYOT systems of pruning and training (typically dictated by the detail of APPELLATION CONTRÔLÉE regulations). LEAF TRIMMING during the growing season is common. French vignerons have in general had centuries to match cultural practices to local conditions, although in the early 20th century many less suitable terrains were planted in an extension of classic zones. IRRIGATION is usually unnecessary in northern and western France, and strictly, if sometimes only theoretically, controlled in the south. The relatively humid climate of western France means, however, that frequent SPRAYING against FUNGAL DISEASES is often necessary. In the early 1990s, concern was increasingly expressed at the use of AGROCHEMICALS in many French wine regions, particularly Burgundy, where ORGANIC VITICULTURE is increasingly common. Other common viticultural hazards are FROST in the north, HAIL in Burgundy, and DROUGHT in the south. Crop levels can vary considerably since the weather during FLOWERING is by no means predictably fine, WINTER FREEZE has been known to kill a substantial proportion of vines, as in 1956, and spring frosts can seriously affect total national production, as in 1991. CLIMATE CHANGE may have been heralded by the abnormally high temperatures and low crop of 2003.

French viticultural research is of a high level, and co-ordinated nationally under the auspices of INRA, which has stations all over the country. Many of the world's vine-growers regard French NURSERIES as their prime source of planting material, and there has been considerable work on CLONAL SELECTION.

France's vine-growers are probably the most regulated and restricted in the world, however. For all wines other than VIN DE TABLE, dates of HARVEST are limited by regional annual decree, and YIELDS are minutely regulated. A low yield is generally regarded as the safest prerequisite for wine quality, but in the 1980s, the maximum basic yield allowed by appellation contrôlée regulations was routinely increased by a so-called *plafond limite de classement*, or PLC, supplement often as high as 20 per cent. Since the late 1980s, CROP THINNING has been the norm for many quality-conscious producers. The 1990s saw the introduction of SORTING tables and CONCENTRATION techniques with the aim of making ever more concentrated wines. MECHANIZATION was introduced to lowlier appellations in the late 1980s and 1990s.

PRECISION VITICULTURE techniques are currently being refined.

Wine-making

In many wine regions, TRADITION is as important as SCIENCE in determining wine-making techniques, although France's winemakers can and do draw on many centres of OENOLOGICAL academe for instruction and research (see ACADEME for a list of those described in further detail in this book).

Techniques vary enormously in France's hundreds of thousands of *caves* but in general, and in sharp contrast to the New World, PROTECTIVE JUICE HANDLING and an obsession with winery HYGIENE are relatively rare. Mastery of MALOLACTIC FERMENTATION and OAK AGEING, on the other hand, have long been taken for granted.

Part of French winemakers' easy relationship with BARREL MATURATION comes from the fact that France is the centre of the world's COOPERAGE industry, or at least that part of it of interest to winemakers.

France is also the birthplace of CHAPTALIZATION, and a high proportion of her wines have depended on some degree of ENRICHMENT although global warming suggests that France may need to introduce more widespread ACIDIFICATION too, forbidden for wines that have been chaptalized. Another wine-making practice once regarded as quintessentially foreign in France, the use of OAK CHIPS, is now tolerated for VINS DE PAYS and VINS DE TABLE.

Wine in France is red. Less than a quarter of all wine consumed in France is white, and in the hot summers of the south of France, rosé is more likely to be consumed than white, as a sort of red for high temperatures.

Wine quality categories

Of the average French harvest, wines from the most revered quality wine category APPELLATION CONTRÔLÉE now represent the most significant proportion (45 per cent of all French wine in 2003), while the most basic wine for direct consumption, that classified as VIN DE TABLE, is made in ever-decreasing quantities and, in 2003, for example, represented just over 9 per cent. The VIN DE PAYS category, distinctly superior to table wine, represented 28 per cent, while the VDQS wines waiting in the wings for promotion to full AC status represented less than 1 per cent. The remaining up to 20 per cent of an average year's French wine production is designed for DISTILLATION into brandy. France dominates the production of fine brandy with its cognac and armagnac.

For details of the history, climate, geography, vine varieties planted, and wines produced, see under regional, or even more geographically specific, names, including PARIS. For individual regions, see also ALSACE, BEAUJOLAIS, BORDEAUX, BUGEY, BURGUNDY, CHABLIS, CHAMPAGNE, CORSICA, JURA, LANGUEDOC, ROUSSILLON, LOIRE, PROVENCE, SAVOIE, RÉUNION, RHÔNE, and SOUTH WEST FRANCE. See also VIN and immediately following entries, as well as CRÉMANT for some of France's better-quality sparkling wines.

Bettane, M., and Desseauve, T., *Le Classement* (Paris, annually).

Jefford, A., *The New France* (London, 2002).

Johnson, H., *The Story of Wine* (London and New York, 1989).

—— and Robinson, J., *The World Atlas of Wine* (5th edn, London and New York, 2001).

Le Guide Hachette des Vins (Paris, annually).

Franciacorta, one of ITALY's newest areas for the production of high-quality red, white, and sparkling wines, extends across the hills of a series of townships to the south of Lake Iseo in the province of Brescia in LOMBARDIA. Since 1995 the name Franciacorta has applied solely to the DOCG sparkling wines made by the TRADITIONAL METHOD, while the zone's superior table wines may qualify for the DOC **Terre di Franciacorta**.

Although the zone presents a certain number of indisputable natural advantages—a mineral-rich soil of morainic origin, warm days and cool evenings in the summer, the latter assisted by the moderating influences of the lake—the wine had only a local reputation until the 1960s, when the SPUMANTE house of Berlucchi launched the first Franciacorta sparkling wines. The ensuing demand for the wines of this house gave national prominence to Franciacorta, a prominence which was rapidly exploited by a series of able entrepreneurs from Milan and Brescia.

Traditional method sparkling wine, made from CHARDONNAY, PINOT BLANC, PINOT NOIR, and PINOT GRIS grapes, still represents nearly half of the zone's production, but there was a significant development of French-style still wines in the 1980s, made at least partially from the classic red grapes of BORDEAUX and the red and white grapes of BURGUNDY, frequently given a full-blown international treatment including lavish amounts of new OAK ageing.

The producer's consortium adopted an admirable code of self-regulation for the sparkling wines while the DOC regulations were being revised, with a gradual reduction of yields (to 10 tonnes/ha); elimination of Pinot Gris; a minimum VINE DENSITY of 4,000 vines per ha; outlawing of TENDONE and GENEVA DOUBLE CURTAIN training systems; and fractional PRESSING of musts. Although Franciacorta made great progress in the 1970s and 1980s, the zone still suffers from an excessive variation in quality between the excellent products of such vanguard estates as Cà del Bosco, Bellavista, and Cavalleri and the more pedestrian efforts of younger houses, many of whose owners have invested more capital and enthusiasm than specific technical competence in the production process. The area under vines grew rapidly in the decade after the mid 1980s to reach almost 800 ha/2,000 acres by the early 21st century, producing about 44,000 hl/1.16 million gal of white wine (60 per cent of which is sparkling wine) and over 13,000 hl of red wine.

A revision of the DOC rules, approved in 1995, divided the zone's production into two categories: a DOCG, reserved for sparkling wines and called simply Franciacorta with the clear intention of identifying zone and a specific product as in CHAMPAGNE, and a DOC named Terre di Franciacorta for the still wines. The latter category consists of two types: a Burgundy-style Bianco based on Chardonnay and/or Pinot Bianco and a Bordeaux-style Rosso based on Cabernet (either Franc or Sauvignon, or both) and Merlot, with notably reduced percentages of Nebbiolo and Barbera compared with the previous DOC. Pinot Noir is permitted only in the zone's sparkling wines, as the possibility of a Burgundian-style still wine is not envisaged in the DOC despite the fact that two of the zone's leading estates have produced such a wine for over a decade.

D.T. & D.C.G.

Franconia, alternative English name for the German wine region FRANKEN, and a local name for the BLAUFRÄNKISCH grape variety in FRIULI in northern Italy.

Francs, village which gives its name to the small BORDEAUX CÔTES appellation **Côtes de Francs**, or **Bordeaux Côtes de Francs**, just north of CÔTES DE CASTILLON between ST-ÉMILION and BERGERAC. The original settlement took its name from a detachment of Franks sent there by Clovis after defeating the Visigoths (see FRANCE, history). The Côtes de Francs wine region has considerably more personality than regular BORDEAUX AC and its revival in the 1980s owed much to the Belgian Thienpont family (also associated with Le PIN and Vieux-Château-Certan). The vineyard area devoted to this appellation is a little more than 450 ha/1,125 acres. Vines are planted on high clay-limestone slopes, many of which enjoy a favourable west south west exposure. Almost all of the wine produced is well-structured red from CABERNET FRANC and MERLOT grapes, but a little sweet white is made in memory of a style once traditional for this area. Chx de Francs and Puygueraud are generally reliable. For more detail, see BORDEAUX.

Franc Noir de la Haute-Saône, vine speciality of the Aube in Champagne producing light, rather neutral red wine. It is a natural offspring of Pinot and Gouais Blanc (see PINOT).

Franken, known in English as **Franconia**, distinctive wine region in central GERMANY, with a total of 6,087 ha/15,041 acres of vineyard in the late 1990s. Until reunification in 1990, Franken formed the country's most eastern wine region. The sometimes severe winters and the risks of autumn and spring FROSTS have largely decided where vines should now be grown. Since the 1960s, the area under vine has nearly tripled, and old vineyards have been rebuilt and modernized (see FLUR-BEREINIGUNG). In some cases, the advantages of having more economically worked vineyards have been won at the price of an increased risk of damage from cold winds, no longer filtered by trees or hedges (see WINDBREAKS). No other region based on the Rhine or its tributaries has such wide variations in the size of its harvest, as was emphasized in 1985. In February, warm sunny days in the best south-facing sites above the Main were followed by temperatures down to −25 °C/−13 °F at night, with catastrophic results for the vineyard owners. The average yield in the following autumn was no more than 13 hl/ha (0.7 tons/acre). The dead vines had to be replaced, according to Bavarian regulations, by vines grown within the region, and three years were to pass before the NURSERIES could satisfy all the demands on their stocks.

During the first half of this century, SILVANER was the most widely grown vine in Franken. By 1964 it still covered over 50 per cent of the vineyard area and since 2004 its share has settled at around 21 per cent. Despite its modest share of total vineyard, Silvaner is still generally perceived as the region's noblest and most typical grape. As the wood of the vine is not very resistant to extremes of cold in winter, Silvaner needs to grow in the top-quality sites. It does especially well in the famous Würzburger Stein vineyard and on the slopes of the Steigerwald near Iphofen and Castell in the east of the region. MÜLLER-THURGAU grows in 36 per cent of the region's vineyards, and BACCHUS in 12 per cent. A further roughly 17 per cent of vineyard is devoted to such miscellaneous whites as Kerner, Riesling, Rieslaner, and Scheurebe, each of which is capable of highly expressive and distinctive results in Franken's calcareous and clay-rich soils. Müller-Thurgau, too, it must be emphasized, ought by no means to be overlooked or underestimated here.

In the mid 2000s, a mere 14 per cent of acreage was planted in red grapes (principally Spätburgunder), demonstrating that at least one German growing region has been (thus far at least) little influenced by the red wine boom that began in the 1990s. Those producers who sell their wine in bottle directly to the consumer often like to have a range based on different vine varieties, particularly if their vineyard holding is in only one site. The range of VINE VARIETIES planted is great and probably larger than necessary, and greater specialization in matching variety to site might result in higher average quality.

The best QUALITÄTSWEIN of Franken are sold in the flagon-shaped BOCKSBEUTEL, as are those of a few villages in neighbouring north BADEN. Its use within Germany is protected by law.

Most Franken wines come from a single vine variety. The German consumer's penchant for wines labelled TROCKEN has forced a return to regional tradition, and almost 60 per cent of Franken wine is now in this category. A further third is HALBTROCKEN, so wines with significant sweetness, save for the occasionally nobly sweet wine or EISWEIN, are rare.

Riesling does not play a leading role in Franken, Silvaner being the star performer in most of the region's sites, including those in and around Würzburg. But the quality of the best Rieslings from good estates is excellent and the style unique to the region. The Rieslings of the Stein and Innere Leiste vineyards at Würzburg, of Randersackerer Pfülben, Escherndorfer Lump, Iphöfer Julius-Echter-Berg, and of the (in part, somewhat run-down and almost 70 per cent steep) Homburger Kallmuth, can be quite splendid. Much cheap Franken wine is overpriced compared with wines from the PFALZ, but the best, although expensive, is good value.

The crossing Bacchus produces surprisingly elegant wine from the Steigerwald, when the yield is restricted to 60 or 70 hl/ha (4 tons/acre), reminding some of SAUVIGNON BLANC. The RIESLANER, a Silvaner × Riesling crossing from Würzburg, produces wines with high acidity, but seldom, at least in its home region, wine with the quality of Riesling. They can, nevertheless, be very impressive at AUSLESE level or above. Scheurebe, on the other hand, informs some intense and impressive dry wines as well as the occasional noble sweet variant.

The CO-OPERATIVE movement in Franken achieves on average some of the highest wine prices per litre of any co-operative cellars in Germany. The large cellar at Kitzingen receives the crop from nearly a quarter of the region's vines, and smaller co-operatives account for another 15 per cent. Most of the regional co-operative's customers are in south Germany and the quantities exported are small. The bulk of wine is sold locally, often through supermarkets, and the clear identity of Franken wine is emphasized by the Bocks-beutel. I.J. & D.S.

Breider, H., *Das Buch vom Frankenwein* (Würzburg, 1974).

Franken Riesling, occasional German name for SYLVANER.

Frankovka, synonym for the red BLAU-FRÄNKISCH grape used in Slovakia and Vojvodina.

Fransdruif, or just Frans, traditional Afrikaans name, meaning 'French grape', for the PALOMINO grape in South Africa.

Frappato, lesser Sicilian red grape variety, which can add fruit and freshness to the more powerful NERO D'AVOLA in the Cerasuolo di Vittoria DOC.

Frascati is both the most famous and quantitatively the most important of the CASTELLI ROMANI wines although production has declined rapidly recently. About 180,000 hl/4.75 million gal is made in favourable vintages from 2,600 ha/6,600 acres of vineyards. Its fame is less by virtue of its intrinsic quality—it differs little from the wines of its neighbouring DOC zones—than by virtue of its constant citation in the literature of Italy and in the accounts of the countless foreign visitors to Rome. The charms of the town of Frascati, with its beautiful villas, gardens, fountains, and cypress-lined boulevards, have doubtlessly contributed to the wine's cachet, as has the town's geographical proximity to Rome, a mere 24 km/15 miles away. Weekend and summer visitors from Rome have long been a significant factor in the town's economy, and Frascati had 1,022 taverns as long ago as 1450. The wine itself, the standard blend of Malvasia with Trebbiano of the Castelli Romani, is a sound, if rarely exciting, commercial product. A lightly sweet or AMABILE version with up to 10 g/l of RESIDUAL SUGAR also exists, as does a sweet DOLCE or *cannellino* version with 10 to 30 g/l. This latter wine is, at least in theory, obtained from grapes affected by NOBLE ROT, but any significant presence of BOTRYTIS fungus in the vineyards would result in much sweeter wines than these. Declining demand for white wine in general, and the central Italian Malvasia-Trebbiano blend in particular, put notable commercial pressures on the zone from the 1990s, inspiring much talk of a new commitment to quality. Neither the TENDONE vineyards nor the general mentality of the zone's quantity-oriented growers, however, seemed likely to provide rapid and painless solutions to these new problems. D.T. & D.C.G.

fraud, wine. See ADULTERATION AND FRAUD.

free-run is the name used by winemakers for the juice or wine that will drain without pressing from a mass of freshly crushed grapes or from a FERMENTATION VESSEL. Depending on the type of vessel used for DRAINING, it constitutes between 60 and 70 per cent of the total juice available and is generally superior to, and much lower in TANNINS than, juice or wine whose extraction depends on PRESSING. Most modern white wine is made from grapes that pass through a CRUSHER-DESTEMMER before going into a draining tank with a perforated bottom through which the free-run juice passes to the FERMENTATION VESSEL. In some wineries, free-run juice is collected by draining through specially designed, perforated-bottom screw or drag-link transfer conveyors which move the MUST directly from the crusher-destemmer to the PRESS, bypassing draining tanks completely. Many winemakers boast of using only free-run juice in the production of fine white wines, but PRESS WINE,

the wine produced by pressing what is left, may be useful as a BLENDING element.

In RED WINE-MAKING, the free-run wine is that which, after SETTLING, is drained or RACKED away from the LEES. In some wineries, free-run red wine is also recovered from specially designed transfer conveyors. Whatever remains goes into the press to yield press wine, which can be even more useful for its tannin concentration when making up blends of red wines.   A.D.W.

freeze. See WINTER FREEZE.

freeze concentration. See CONCENTRATION.

Freisa, or **Freisa Piccolo,** is a light red grape variety indigenous to the PIEMONTE region of north west Italy and, more specifically, to the provinces of Asti, Alessandria, and Cuneo in scattered vineyards which reach almost to the gates of the city of Turin.

The vine was known in Piemonte in 1799, and DNA PROFILING at DAVIS and Torino showed that Freisa has a parent–offspring relationship with NEBBIOLO. Freisa musts can be quite high in both ACIDITY and TANNINS even if, like Nebbiolo, it is relatively light coloured for the region, although its wines are coarser in terms of the tannins and flavours.

The wine exists as a VARIETAL in a range of styles, but traditionally as a slightly frothy wine from a SECONDARY FERMENTATION, which retains some unfermented RESIDUAL SUGAR to balance the slight bitterness from the LEES. Freisa's decisively purple colour and aromas of raspberries and violets tend to find favour much more readily than its flavours, which, with their combination of the bitter and the sweet, seem to arouse widely divergent reactions: from Hugh JOHNSON's 'immensely appetizing' to Robert PARKER's 'totally repugnant wine'.

It is DOC in both dry and sweet (*amabile*) styles in the following areas: the larger Freisa d'ASTI and the minuscule Freisa di Chieri, the LANGHE, the MONFERRATO, and the rare Pinerolese. As with Barbera, its popularity has declined rapidly in recent years in its native Piemonte.

Modern technology, in the form of pressurized tanks, now permits producers better control of both the residual sugar level and the amount of CARBON DIOXIDE in the wine, and this type of Freisa, which does not undergo a secondary fermentation in the bottle, tends to be distinctively drier and almost imperceptibly fizzy. Producers such as Aldo Vajra, Coppo, and Ascheri are experimenting with a more age-worthy, completely dry, and completely still type of Freisa aged in BARRIQUE. Several producers make a Freisa Nebbiolata, in which the wine is re-fermented on the skins of Nebbiolo used for BAROLO. Tannins abound in this style.

A larger-berried, quite distinct CLONE called **Freisa Grossa** or Freisa di Nizza is also grown on flatter vineyards but produces much less distinguished wine. A vine variety called Freisa is quite widely grown in Argentina, although total plantings are no more than a few hundred hectares.   D.T. & D.C.G.

Freisamer is a 20th-century German vine crossing (SILVANER × PINOT GRIS), originally called Freiburger after its birthplace. It reached a peak of popularity in the German wine region of Baden in the early 1970s but has all but disappeared in Germany. It is still grown in a number of north and central cantons in SWITZERLAND, however, and sweeter versions are a speciality of the Bündner Herrschaft in Graubünden.

Freixenet, the largest exporter of CAVA in the world, although not as strong on the domestic Spanish market as CODORNÍU. The brand was born at the beginning of the 20th century when Pedro Ferrer Bosch and his wife Dolores Sala Vivé decided to concentrate on sparkling wines. The company was named after an estate in Mediona, PENEDÈS, which had been in Pedro Ferrer's family since the 13th century, known as La Freixeneda, meaning a plantation of ash trees. His wife's grandfather founded the former Sala company, which started exporting wines to the USA in the second half of the 19th century. The company was initially keen to establish export markets, a policy which has paid off in the latter half of the 20th century. It now has four production centres in San Sadurní de Noya: Freixenet SA, Segura Viudas SA, Castellblanch SA, and Torrelavit SA, as well as wineries in a number of DO regions around Spain: Morlanda in Priorat, Fra Guerau in Montsant, Valdubón in Ribera del Duero, and Pazo de Bayon in Rías Baixas. The combined production of Cava alone is now more than 150 million bottles per year. Best-known brands are the medium dry Carta Nevada, launched in 1951, and Cordon Negro, a brut Cava in a distinctive black bottle. Freixenet's overseas interests include the Bordeaux négociant Yvon Mau, Henri Abelé in Champagne, the Wingara Wine Group in Australia, Gloria Ferrer in the CARNEROS district of California, and Finca Doña Dolores, a sparkling wine estate in MEXICO. The group has also invested in the Viento Sur venture in Argentina and has a JOINT VENTURE with Carrau in Uruguay.   S.A. & V. de la S.

French-American hybrids. See FRENCH HYBRIDS.

French Colombard, common California name for one of the state's most planted grape varieties, the French white COLOMBARD, now much more widely planted in California than in France. Originally brought from Cognac, Colombard is no longer often seen as a varietal wine. Most of it grows in the SAN JOAQUIN VALLEY for JUG whites and CHARMAT sparklers.

French hybrids, group of vine HYBRIDS bred in France in the late 19th and early 20th centuries, usually by crossing or hybridizing AMERICAN VINE SPECIES with a European VINIFERA variety (see VINE BREEDING). These are also known as direct producers, hybrid direct producers, HDPs, or, in French, *hybrides producteurs directs*. One early response to the invasion of the American PHYLLOXERA louse in Europe was to plant American varieties, since most had phylloxera tolerance. In Europe they proved to be both hardy and resistant to a wide range of FUNGAL DISEASES, but, because of the strange, often FOXY, flavour of the wine they produced, it has been illegal to plant the likes of ISABELLA, NOAH, Othello, Black Spanish (Jacquez), and Herbemont in France since 1934.

The aim of the early hybridizers was to combine the pest and disease resistance of the American species with the accepted wine quality of the European wine species *vinifera*. A group of French breeders such as François BACO, Castel, Georges COUDERC, Ferdinand Gaillard, Ganzin, Millardet, Oberlin, Albert SEIBEL, Bertille SEYVE, and Victor VILLARD, and, more recently, Joanny Burdin, Galibert, Eugene Kuhlmann, Pierre Landot, Ravat, Jean-François Seyve's sons Joannes and Bertille (who married Villard's daughter and developed the important Seyve–Villard series of hybrids), and Jean-Louis VIDAL, produced thousands of new hybrid varieties with such aims in mind. They used AMERICAN HYBRIDS as parents as well as American vine species. VITIS *aestivalis*, *rupestris*, *riparia*, and *berlandieri* were common parents because of their excellent disease and pest resistance, and a reduction in the strong fruit flavour associated with *labrusca*. Some of the ROOTSTOCKS used today were bred by these hybridizers, particularly Castel, Couderc, Ganzin, and Millardet. Active hybridizers in other countries included the Italians Bruni, Paulsen, Pirovani, and Prosperi.

These hybrids were widely favoured because of disease resistance and high productivity, so by 1958 about 400,000 ha/988,000 acres of French hybrids were planted in France, or about one-third of the total vineyard area. Wine quality was, however, often inferior, especially from the earlier French hybrids. With continued crossing and back crossing, the objectionable features in the taste of the wine could be reduced (see diagram for NEW VARIETIES). French planting regulations since 1955 have deliberately discouraged vine varieties associated with poor wine quality, however, both hybrids and *vinifera*, and so by 1988 there were fewer than 20,000 ha of hybrids. With the exception of Baco 22A, which may be used for armagnac, hybrids are being systematically phased out of French wine and brandy production, even though there were still sizeable plantings of Couderc Noir, various SEYVE–VILLARD hybrids, Villard Noir, CHAMBOURCIN, PLANTET, and Seibel for red wines and Villard Blanc and SEYVAL BLANC for white wines, according to the French vineyard census of 1988. Other hybrid varieties that are authorized, if not actually encouraged, in France include Baco I, Chancellor, Garonnet, Oberlin Noir, and Varousset for red wine and Rayon d'Or for white wine.

The French hybrids have been planted outside France and have made significant contributions at some time or other to the wine industries of the eastern UNITED STATES (see NEW YORK in particular), CANADA, ENGLAND, and New Zealand, where French hybrids were planted in the majority of vineyards into the 1960s, and used for FORTIFIED WINES. From the 1960s onwards, in almost all of these regions, these hybrids have been systematically replaced by *vinifera* varieties for reasons of wine quality, although in some sites in Canada and New York subject to WINTER FREEZE, only a hybrid such as Vidal will survive (and has produced some fine ICE WINE), while Seyval Blanc is still one of the most popular varieties in ENGLAND.   R.E.S.

Galet, P., *Précis de viticulture* (5th edn, Montpellier, 1988).

—and Morton, L. T., *A Practical Ampelography* (Ithaca, NY, and London, 1979).

French paradox,

term coined in the United States in 1991 to express the infuriating fact that the French apparently eat and drink themselves silly with no apparent ill effects on their coronary health. Immediately after this thesis was aired on prime-time television in the United States, and red wine consumption cited as a possible factor in reducing the risk of heart disease, sales of red wine quadrupled and GALLO had to put their leading branded GENERIC Hearty Burgundy on allocation. For more details, see HEALTH. A similar association between red wine consumption and health benefits played an important part in the 1990s wine boom in ASIA.

Frescobaldi,

one of Florence's most prominent noble families since the 13th century, are among the largest landholders in the central Italian region of TOSCANA with interests in a wide range of agricultural activities. Of their 4,200 ha (10,370 acres), 750 are under vine, which makes them the largest private owners of vineyards in the region (more important than, for example, the ANTINORI). The Frescobaldi holdings can be divided into three distinct blocks: the first, to the south west of Florence, produces light and refreshing white and red wines; the second, to the east of Florence, produces classic CHIANTI RUFINA from the Nipozzano estate and the distinctive red and white wines of Pomino, a high-altitude property with vineyards that rise to 700 m/

2,300 ft above sea level; the third block is Castelgiocondo in MONTALCINO, with 210 ha of vineyards in all, of which 150 is Brunello di Montalcino, its acquisition in the late 1980s having made the Frescobaldi the largest potential producer of Brunello. In 2004, the Frescobaldi acquired control of the Ornellaia estate in BOLGHERI, their first foray into what has been an Antinori fief.

Although the house's fame was created by its Nipozzano and Pomino wines, these two estates have belonged to the Frescobaldi for a relatively short time, having been acquired by marriage with the Albizi family in the late 19th century. The last of the Albizi, Vittorio, born into the French branch of the family near Auxerre, had a profound knowledge of the French viticulture of his time and rapidly decided, after returning to Toscana in the mid 19th century, that the higher portions of the Pomino estate could not ripen SANGIOVESE vines. He accordingly planted PINOT BLANC, CHARDONNAY, PINOT NOIR, CABERNET, and MERLOT vines, a decision which he explained and defended in the numerous writings and speeches that marked his career. His ideas were too far ahead of his time, however, and had no influence on his era. The Frescobaldi were, none the less, the first Italian producers of a BARRIQUE-aged white wine, beginning in the mid 1970s with the grapes from their Benefizio vineyard at Pomino. Their single-vineyard Chianti Rufina, Montesodi, was also among the first superior all-Sangiovese wines aged in small barrels. The house currently produces approximately 5.5 million bottles of wine each year.

In the mid-1990s, the Frescobaldi entered into a JOINT VENTURE with MONDAVI of California, producing two wines, Luce and Lucente, from the Sangiovese and Merlot grapes of the Castelgiocondo estate in Montalcino. After Mondavi's acquisition by CONSTELLATION in 2004, Frescobaldi became sole owners of this venture.   D.T. & D.C.G.

fresh grapes.

See TABLE GRAPES.

Fresno,

abbreviation for California State University, Fresno, located in the heart of the Central valley, where over 60 per cent of California wine grapes are grown. In 1997, it became home to the first licensed, bonded winery in a university in the US. The Department of Viticulture and Enology was formed in 2002 but these disciplines have been taught for over 40 years. Professors Carlos Muller and Ken Fugelsang have been at the heart of the oenology programme for 30 years. Students receive a very practical hands-on education and expertise is required in both disciplines. Professors Vincent Petrucci and Sayed Badr are renowned for their studies on raisins and table grapes respectively. Fresno State Winery has a 23,000-case capacity and production currently ranges from 15,000 to

20,000 cases. Fresno State wines, made exclusively by the students, have won 120 awards in open competition in six years.   R.T.

Friulano,

proposed new name for TOCAI Friulano.

Friuli,

or **Friuli-Venezia Giulia,** the north easternmost region of ITALY, borders on Austria to the north and SLOVENIA to the east and has long been a confluence of three distinct peoples and cultures: Italian, Germanic, and Slavic. (See map under ITALY.) Despite endorsements of local wines by the usual succession of popes, emperors, princes, and princelings, Friuli had little commercial history of distinctive wines until the late 1960s, when the introduction both of German wine-making philosophy and TEMPERATURE CONTROL—innovations usually credited to producer Mario Schiopetto—gave Italy's first truly clean, fresh, fruity white wines. This created a FASHION which has lasted to this day. This style of (predominantly white) WINE-MAKING is one of the characterizing features of the region's production; the other is the large number of wines produced by each single estate.

Friuli's geographical position on land successively disputed by Romans, Byzantines, Venetians, and Habsburgs, ensured that a large number of varieties would be available for planting. TOCAI Friulano, RIBOLLA, MALVASIA di Istria, VERDUZZO, PICOLIT, REFOSCO, SCHIOPETTINO, PIGNOLO, and the acidic red wine grape Tazzelenghe are considered indigenous (although see ROBOLA, for example). RIESLING, WELSCHRIESLING (here called Riesling Italico), TRAMINER, MÜLLER-THURGAU, and BLAUFRÄNKISCH (locally called Franconia) are imports from Austria. The French varieties PINOT BIANCO, PINOT GRIGIO, CHARDONNAY, SAUVIGNON, CABERNET, MERLOT, PINOT NERO were introduced during the 19th-century Habsburg domination (and greatly expanded during the replanting of Friuli's vineyards after the ravages of PHYLLOXERA), a domination which lasted until 1918 in the case of the province of Gorizia.

The result has been the multiplicity of single VARIETAL wines in each DOC: 17 for the 2,100 ha/ 5,200 acres of the COLLI ORIENTALI, 17 for the 1,500 ha of COLLIO. If the proliferation of DOC wines with varietal names attached to specific zones has created some confusion amongst consumers, the geography of Friuli's DOC structure is actually fairly easy to understand. Udine marks the northern border beyond which low temperatures make viticulture an impractical proposition in most cases: to the south of Udine exist two distinct bands of territory for the growing of grapes: the two hillside DOCs of Colli Orientali and Collio with calcareous MARL soils, and the ALLUVIAL plain with plentiful quantities of sand, pebbles, and rocks deposited by the various rivers—the Tagliamento, the Natisone, the

Judrio, the Isonzo—which criss-cross the plain. These flatlands are divided into five DOCs, moving from west to east: LISON-PRAMAGGIORE, LATISANA, GRAVE DEL FRIULI, AQUILEIA, and ISONZO. The HILLSIDE VINEYARDS give wines of much the greater personality, with Collio generally offering more delicacy and bouquet, Colli Orientali much body and length. The white, and red, wines of this latter zone have shown a real suitability for small BARREL MATURATION, a phenomenon much less widespread in Collio. Isonzo, which borders on Collio, stands out among the DOCs of the plain and, in the 1990s, began to produce wines which, from the best producers, challenge those of the hillsides.

The region's overall production averages a bit over 1 million hl/26.4 million gal per year, modest by Italian standards, but the percentage of DOC production, now over 50 per cent, is one of Italy's highest, surpassed only by that in the TRENTINO-ALTO ADIGE and more recently PIEMONTE.

Although Friuli enjoyed almost uninterrupted commercial success and expansion throughout the 1970s and 1980s, the formula of crisp and refreshing technologically sound wines is not difficult to copy, and the early 1990s saw increased competition and price pressure from other areas of Italy, particularly from the Trentino-Alto Adige.

For more details of notable specific wines, see also AQUILEIA, CARSO, COLLI ORIENTALI, COLLIO, GRAVE DEL FRIULI, ISONZO, LATISANA, LISON-PRAMAGGIORE, and see specific grape varieties PICOLIT, PIGNOLO, REFOSCO, RIBOLLA, SCHIOPPETTINO, TOCAI, and VERDUZZO.   D.T.

frizzante, Italian wine term for semi-sparkling wine (as opposed to SPUMANTE, which is used for fully sparkling wines). *Frizzante* wines generally owe their bubbles to a partial second fermentation in tank, a sort of interrupted CHARMAT process sparkling wine.

Fromenteau, name for several grape varieties, used as a synonym for both the ROUSSANNE of the Rhône and SAVAGNIN of the Jura. **Fromenteau Gris** is a synonym for PINOT GRIS.

Fronsac, small but once famed red wine appellation in the Bordeaux region just west of the town of Libourne on the RIGHT BANK of the river DORDOGNE (see map under BORDEAUX). The wooded low hills of Fronsac, and **Canon-Fronsac**, the even smaller and more famous appellation to the immediate south, constitute Bordeaux's prettiest countryside, and the region's altitude, unusual so close to the Gironde estuary, gave it great strategic importance. Fronsac was the site of a Roman temple, and then of a fortress built by CHARLEMAGNE, who is locally supposed to have taken a particular interest in this wine. The wine benefited further in the mid 17th century when the

Duc de Richelieu, also Duc de Fronsac and a man of considerable influence, replaced the fortress with a villa at which he entertained frequently. According to Enjalbert, the first great right bank wines were produced, around 1730, in Canon-Fronsac. Even well into the 19th century, the wines of Fronsac were much more famous than those of POMEROL on the other side of Libourne.

The low-lying land beside the river and any ALLUVIAL soils further inland from the Dordogne and its tributary the Isle are entitled to only the BORDEAUX AC, while the Fronsac and Canon-Fronsac appellations are concentrated on the higher land where LIMESTONE predominates and SANDSTONE is also characteristic. Merlot and Cabernet Franc (Bouchet) are the dominant grape varieties, supplemented by Malbec and, where it will ripen, Cabernet Sauvignon, densely planted on the land entitled to the Fronsac appellation and the more restricted area, mainly around the villages of St-Michel-de-Fronsac and Fronsac itself, which are entitled to the supposedly superior Canon-Fronsac appellation. The region with its cool soils performs particularly well in hot vintages.

Wines made in the 1960s and 1970s were often both austere and slightly rustic. The 1980s saw considerable refinement of techniques, and investment in wine-making equipment, notably some new barrels, so that Fronsac added suppleness to its density. It does not have the lush character of Pomerol but can offer a keenly priced alternative to more famous red bordeaux, with the juicy fruit of a St-Émilion and the ageing potential of a Médoc. The MOUEIX family, who owned Chx Canon-Moueix, La Dauphine, and Canon de Brem, as well as distributing several others, from the 1980s until the early 21st century, injected temporary confidence into the region. Other properties making superior wine include Chx Moulin Pey-Labrie and La Vieille Cure and Michel ROLLAND's Ch Fontenil. The largest and most picturesque property on the entire right bank is Ch de la Rivière. Total area planted, with red wine grapes only, is about 830 ha.

Enjalbert, H., *Great Bordeaux Wines: St Émilion, Pomerol, Fronsac* (Paris, 1983; Eng. trans. 1985).

Frontenac. Relatively new HYBRID grown experimentally, sometimes for port-style wines, in the Upper Plains and American Midwest. Usefully winter hardy, in the right hands it can produce wines reminiscent of very ripe Syrah.   D.F.

Frontignac, name used occasionally for grapey, sweet wine, particularly in SOUTH AFRICA, providing it has been produced from MUSCAT DE FRONTIGNAN. Australian synonym for MUSCAT BLANC À PETITS GRAINS.

Frontignan is the name of the wine for long called Muscat de Frontignan, the most

important of the Languedoc's four Muscats. Now a distinctly unglamorous town on the semi-industrial lagoon between Montpellier and Sète, Frontignan was famous for the quality of its MUSCAT for centuries. It was probably one of France's earliest vineyard sites, being close to the saltmarshes around Narbonne. PLINY the Younger singled out this particular 'bees' wine' for mention in his letters. ARNALDUS DE VILLANOVA, who is credited with the discovery of the process by which Muscat de Frontignan is made today (see VIN DOUX NATUREL), claimed that his daily ration of the wine, as advised by the then all-powerful Aragón monarch, made him feel years younger. It was popular in both Paris and London in the 17th and 18th centuries, doubtless with wider appeal then than the dry reds of south west France that were also shipped north. 'Frontiniac' was specifically praised by the philosopher John Locke in 1676, while both Voltaire and, even further afield, Thomas JEFFERSON were well-documented and enthusiastic purchasers. In the 18th and 19th centuries, Frontignan clearly made red as well as white wines which were compared with those of that other favourite of our sweet-toothed ancestors, CONSTANTIA. See also LANGUEDOC, history, for details of a claimed link between Frontignan and Ch d'YQUEM.

Muscat de Frontignan, despite being one of the first appellations, and certainly the first vin doux naturel appellation, to be officially recognized, fell into decline for much of the 20th century. Only the rather lighter Muscat de BEAUMES-DE-VENISE somehow escaped the malaise that affected the market for France's sweeter wines, until the 1980s, when the winemakers of Frontignan awoke as if from a deep sleep and started to produce a much higher proportion of more delicate, more refreshing, yet more characterful golden Muscats (although some dark, turgid, raisiny Frontignan can still be found). As in all Languedoc Muscats (see LUNEL, MIREVAL, and ST-JEAN-DE-MINERVOIS), only the finest Muscat variety, MUSCAT BLANC À PETITS GRAINS, should be used and the final wine must be at least 15 per cent alcohol with a sugar content of at least 125 g/l (sweeter than Beaumes-de-Venise's 110 g/l minimum). Cheaper Muscats made well outside the region but marketed vigorously to tourists do nothing for the image of this once-great appellation. Co-operatives dominate output, from a little over 800 ha/2,000 acres, but Ch de la Peyrade can take much of the credit for revitalizing wine-making in Frontignan, whose seaside vineyards may not be the Mediterranean's most picturesque but are at least reliably warm enough to maximize Muscat Blanc's potential.

A small proportion of Muscat de Frontignan is fortified so early it qualifies as a VIN DE LIQUEUR.

George, R., *The Wines of the South of France* (London, 2001).

The sediment remaining from the second fermentation deliberately provoked in bottles of Cavalleri's sparkling Franciacorta can be seen clearly here, after having been shaken by hand on to the **crown caps** habitually used in sparkling wine-making. See the alternative mechanical process on p. 457.

Fronton, formerly Côtes du Frontonnais, growing and dynamic appellation of more than 1,800 ha/4,500 acres of vines just north of Toulouse in SOUTH WEST FRANCE distinguished by its local red grape variety the NÉGRETTE, which must constitute 50 to 70 per cent of the appellation's reds, plus some rosés. Complementary grape varieties are usually Fer, Syrah, and the Cabernets and the character of the wines can vary considerably according to the exact TERROIR and ENCÉPAGEMENT. A little white is made from Mauzac. Soils on the gravelly terraces of the Tarn are particularly poor. The CO-OPERATIVE is an important producer (of table wine too) but there is considerable experimentation on the part of some relative newcomers to the region, although a high proportion of the wine is drunk without ceremony in Toulouse. Fronton has been producing wine since before the time of CHARLEMAGNE and in the 12ᵗʰ century the vineyard was already associated with 'négret'. The local VIN DE PAYS, used for white wines, is Vin de Pays du Comté Tolosan. Fine wines are made by Chx Bellevue La Forêt, Plaisance, and Le Roc.

frost, the ice crystals formed by freezing of water vapour on objects which have cooled below 0 °C/32 °F. Such frosts are known as white frosts, or hoar frosts. Black frosts cause freezing and extensive killing of plant tissue itself, without any necessary hoar formation. Frost is a major viticultural problem as it can damage and kill shoots and fruit, in spring, autumn, and winter. Frost control is expensive and not always effective; see FROST DAMAGE.

Frost frequencies are, in many studies, imputed arbitrarily from weather records. Temperatures as recorded in the standard Stevenson screen used by meteorologists, at 1.25 m/4.1 ft above the ground, are always higher than at ground level. A screen temperature of 2.2 °C/36 °F is normally assumed to indicate a light ground frost, and one of 0 °C a heavy ground frost. Temperatures at vine height of −1 °C or lower after BUDBREAK in spring will usually cause serious injury to the young shoots. Even 'light' frosts can often cause damage somewhere in the vineyard, because their incidence tends to be patchy, depending on TOPOGRAPHY. Geiger covers this aspect in detail.

Two main types of frost are distinguished: radiation and advection. Radiation frost occurs typically on still, dry, cloudless nights. Without cloud, mist, or much water vapour to absorb and trap heat radiated from the ground and plant tissues, heat escapes freely to space and rapid surface cooling results. Air in immediate contact with these surfaces then becomes cooled. The coldest air, being densest, remains or collects close to the ground and in hollows. Lowest air temperatures in the early morning on flat land are at 5 to 15 cm/2–5 in above ground, rising with height to a relatively warm 'inversion' layer, commonly some 15 to

30 m/100 ft above, beyond which temperatures gradually fall again with altitude. This pool of cold, dense air close to the ground is stable unless dispersed by wind, or unless it can flow away by gravity to still lower regions (see TOPOGRAPHY).

Advective frosts result from such flows of already chilled air from elsewhere. They can originate locally, or arrive from up to several hundreds or thousands of kilometres away, following valleys or other natural courses of AIR DRAINAGE.

The origins of frost point to logical methods of avoiding it. The first is to plant on hill slopes from which surface-chilled air can drain away freely. Free-standing and projecting hills are best, because they have no external sources of chilled air and what slips away must be replaced from the warmer atmosphere above (see TOPOGRAPHY).

A second method, employed on flat land subject to radiation frosts, is to use high TRELLIS SYSTEMS so that the main vine growth stands above the coldest air layer that settles close to the ground on still nights. (In practice, however, there is little difference in frost sensitivity of commercial trellis systems.) Plant cover between the rows also needs to be cultivated or slashed by the time of budbreak, so as to lower the effective cooling surface. The soil should preferably be firmed so that it most readily absorbs day heat to depth and reradiates it continuously through the night. STONES AND ROCKS in the soil surface assist in this.

WIND MACHINES have sometimes been employed to break up the sedentary cold air layer and mix in warm upper air just as HELICOPTERS and fog-creating machines have also been used to mix the inversion layer and to minimize frost damage. SMUDGE POTS and other burners can also create limited local heating which may help to promote convectional mixing of upper and lower air, together with smoke (by-laws permitting), which reduces further radiative heat loss from the soil. A new development in the battle against frost is the Lazo machine, which is a liquid propane gas powered burner towed behind a tractor on frosty nights. Hot air is blown by a fan out of the burner at 1000 °C but cools quickly so the vines are not burned.

In vineyards with sprinkler IRRIGATION, the SPRINKLERS can be turned on when temperatures fall to danger levels. This 'aspersion' technique both warms the vines and soil directly, and (if the soil was previously dry) improves its heat conductivity so that more warmth comes up from below. The release of latent heat as the water freezes on the vines protects the vine tissue from injury.

Spring frost damage to vines is by no means confined to cool viticultural climates. In fact it is not necessarily most characteristic of them. That is because the VINE GROWTH CYCLE is adapted to the general run of temperatures

experienced, with spring budbreak delayed in cool climates until the average mean temperature reaches about 10 °C, as described under CLIMATE CLASSIFICATION. More damaging is short-term TEMPERATURE VARIABILITY, such that an early spring warm enough to induce budbreak may frequently be followed by a return to killing frosts after growth has started. Paradoxically, such events can occur in otherwise hot vineyard regions, such as the high plains of TEXAS. This is because their early spring is often hot, which encourages early budbreak, but this may be followed by cold of arctic origin which can severely damage vines.

Planting on frost-prone sites is normally confined to grape varieties with naturally late budbreak, such as (where the growing season is long enough) CABERNET SAUVIGNON, CARIGNAN, MOURVÈDRE, CLAIRETTE, and TREBBIANO. RIESLING, SYLVANER, MÜLLER-THURGAU, and SAUVIGNON BLANC are classed as having mid season budbreak. Unfortunately some of the prime-quality varieties grown in COOL CLIMATES, such as PINOT NOIR and CHARDONNAY, burst early and are very vulnerable to spring frosts (see CHABLIS, for instance). The selection of individual sites with minimal frost risk is crucial for such varieties. The risk in any situation can be reduced to a small extent by late pruning, but this can only delay the effective time of budbreak by up to about a week or, at the most, ten days.

Frost has much more impact on yield than on wine quality, although if sprinkler irrigation is used before harvest to ward off autumn frost, it can have serious consequences for RIPENING. See also FROST DAMAGE. J.G.

Geiger, R., *Das Klima der bodennahen Luftschicht* (4ᵗʰ edn, Brunswick, 1961), trans. by Scripta Technicha, Inc., as *Climate near the Ground* (Cambridge, Mass., 1966).

McCarthy, M. G., Dry, P. R., Hayes, P. F., and Davidson, D. M., 'Soil management and frost control', in B. G. Coombe and P. R. Dry (eds.), *Viticulture*, ii: *Practices* (Adelaide, 1992).

frost damage occurs in vineyards mostly in spring but also in autumn and occasionally summer, when the air temperature drops below freezing (see also FROST). Ice forms in the plant tissue of buds which have begun to break, young shoots, leaves, and inflorescences, which may subsequently turn brown and die. The vine can respond by growing more shoots from BASAL BUDS, but these are typically less fruitful and the crop is reduced. Frost in the autumn causes DEFOLIATION, which is a problem if the fruit is not ripe and the vine's reserves of CARBOHYDRATES have not been restored.

Frost damage prevention can be difficult and expensive. VINEYARD SITE SELECTION is important, as is use of late-budding varieties. Late PRUNING can also delay BUDBREAK. Maintaining the soil as a firm, moist, weed-free surface helps encourage soil warming and nocturnal

The shiny face of modern wine-making seen here at Viña San Pedro near Molina, Chile. **Refrigerated** jackets keep the contents of these **stainless steel** tanks fresh and fruity even in the highest daytime temperatures of Chile's Central Valley.

reradiation, which will to some extent counter cold air temperatures.

Frost is so destructive that vineyard owners are forced to adopt extreme measures. Many vineyards rely on the application of SPRINKLER irrigation: the water freezes on the vines but stops the temperature dropping below 0 °C. More recent experiments, including the use of heated vineyard wires, blowing heated air through irrigation systems and traversing a gas heated blower through the vineyards, have not so far been widely adopted.

Typically cool climate regions are more prone to spring frost. For example, in 1991 frost damage was so great in western France, particularly for the earlier budding white grape varieties, that total French wine production, which averaged nearly 55 million hl in 1991–2000, was less than 43 million hl/1,135 million gal.

Note the distinction between frost and WINTER FREEZE, a related but different vine injury.

R.E.S.

Winkler, A. J., *et al.*, *General Viticulture* (2nd edn, Berkeley, Calif., 1974).

fructose

fructose is, with GLUCOSE, one of the two principal SUGARS of the grape and sweet wines. It is a six-carbon atom sugar, or a hexose. In solution, it rotates polarized light to the left, hence the original name levulose and its correct name, D(-)-fructose. Common table sugar, SUCROSE, is made up of one molecule of fructose and one of glucose.

The grapevine leaf in the presence of sunlight, water, and carbon dioxide makes sucrose by a complicated series of steps called collectively PHOTOSYNTHESIS. The sucrose is transferred in the plant sap from the leaf to the grape berry. There the sucrose is split into fructose and glucose, the forms in which it is stored in the berry. The vine is unusual among fruiting plants in the extent to which it is capable of concentrating the two sugars fructose and glucose in its berries; sugars routinely represent between 18 and 25 per cent of grape juice weight, while 12 per cent is the norm in apple and pear juice.

Fructose accumulates in the grape berry along with glucose but at lower concentrations during the early stages. However, at RIPENESS, and especially when grapes are overripe, fructose levels often exceed glucose. The glucose–fructose ratio is thus an indicator of grape ripening (roughly 1:5 at veraison but less than 1 at full ripeness). This is important because fructose is remarkable in that it has between 1.3 and 1.8 times the sweetening power of either glucose or sucrose (which has led to its manufacture in large quantities for use in so-called diet foods).

During FERMENTATION of grape juice, both fructose and glucose are consumed. Furthermore, in the acid and enzymic environment of grape juice, any sucrose present is split into its constituent parts, fructose and glucose, and

will consequently be fermented. With selected strains of wine yeasts, nearly all the fructose and glucose are converted to alcohol and carbon dioxide, leaving the wine with only traces of fermentable sugars.

A.D.W. & B.G.C.

früh is German for 'early'. Thus, for example, Früher Roter Malvasier is early red MALVASIA.

Frühburgunder, Blauer, increasingly highly regarded, small-berried mutation of Spätburgunder (Pinot Noir) which ripens a good two weeks before it. There were 176 ha/435 acres in southern Germany, particularly on the red sandstone soils around Miltenberg and, historically, Bürgstadt in FRANKEN, in 2003. Low-yielding examples can taste of black fruits.

Frühroter Veltliner, or **Früher Roter Veltliner,** 'early-ripening, red-skinned VELTLINER', is a white wine grape variety most commonly encountered in Austria, where there were still about 600 ha/1,500 acres planted, mainly in the Weinviertel district of Lower Austria. The wine produced is often less distinguished than that made from Austria's most common grape variety GRÜNER VELTLINER, being notably lower in acidity in many cases. Yields are also generally lower. DNA PROFILING in Austria showed that Frühroter Veltliner is not related to Grüner Veltliner at all but is a spontaneous cross between ROTER VELTLINER and SILVANER. It makes rather neutral wine and is well suited to producing white wines in a NOUVEAU style.

In Germany, it was rare but known in Rheinhessen, as **Frühroter Malvasier** or occasionally Roter Malvasier. Small plots may still be encountered in older vineyards of ALTO ADIGE in Italy (where it is known as Veltliner) and SAVOIE (where it may be known as Malvoisie Rouge d'Italie).

fruit. To a VITICULTURIST, fruit is a synonym for GRAPE, and details of grape ripening are to be found under RIPENING. To an OENOLOGIST or wine taster, fruit is a perceptible element essential to a young wine. Young wines should taste fruity, although not necessarily of grapes, or any particular grape variety. During BOTTLE AGEING, the fruity FLAVOUR COMPOUNDS in a good wine evolve into more complex elements which are described as BOUQUET; in a less good wine, the fruit simply dissipates to leave a non-fruity wine sometimes described as 'hollow'. The word **fruity** is sometimes used in wine descriptions concocted for marketing purposes as a euphemism for 'sweet'.

fruit driven, a TASTING TERM used to convey the fact that a wine has a dominance of grape-derived fruit flavour. For a wine to merit this description, the dominance of fruit overrides flavours in the wine that originate from other processes or treatments which the wine has undergone such as BARREL FERMENTA-

TION, BARREL MATURATION, LEES CONTACT, MALOLACTIC FERMENTATION, or, in the case of a sparkling wine, the influence of yeast AUTOLYSIS. Wines described as fruit driven are, typically, NEW WORLD reds which contrast with classic European wines. Traditionally, the latter exhibit complex OXIDATIVE flavours, together with prominent aromas of both primary and secondary FERMENTATION, but with less fruit evident. However, by the mid 2000s, a significant and increasing proportion of European wines could be described as fruit driven.

P.J.W.

fruit fly, vinegar fly, jack, and pomace fly are all names applied to various species of *Drosophila*, in particular *Drosophila melanogaster*. *Drosophila* feed and reproduce in fermenting fruits of all kinds and can frequently be found in the domestic fruit bowl. The major damage they cause in grapes, with a drastic reduction in wine quality, is the spread of BUNCH ROTS. *Drosophila* multiply rapidly—with a period of only six to eight days from egg to egg in hot climates—which explains why this fly has been used so much for the study of genetics. They are also a common problem in wineries during vintage, when insects can contaminate wine by spreading harmful BACTERIA. Control is difficult, and includes destruction of breeding places, such as piles of rejected fruit and POMACE.

Mediterranean fruit fly, *Caratitis capitata*, can be a grape pest in some areas such as parts of Australia and South Africa. Infestations of grapes are often due to a build-up in other soft fruits such as figs, apricots, peaches, nectarines, or citrus. Where Mediterranean fruit fly is a potential problem, bait should be laid six weeks before picking.

M.J.E.

Buchanan, G. A., and Amos, T. G., 'Grape pests', in B. G. Coombe and P. R. Dry (eds.), *Viticulture*, ii: *Practices* (Adelaide, 1992).

fruitfulness, viticultural term describing the number of bunches of grapes on each shoot. It can also be used to describe the potential productivity of buds. A shoot of low fruitfulness will have zero or one bunch only, while a **fruitful** one may have two or three or, very rarely, four. Some varieties are known to be very fruitful, an example being the so-called FRENCH HYBRIDS, no doubt due to their American parentage. At the other end of the fruitfulness spectrum is SULTANA, which has notoriously low fertility of buds at the base of canes. Many of the commercially important wine grape varieties fall between these two extremes and two bunches per shoot is most common. Where fruitfulness is low, the vine-grower must prune to CANES as opposed to SPURS, as shoots which arise from short spurs will typically be of lower fruitfulness, arising as they do from BASAL BUDS.

Interestingly, potential fruitfulness is determined at about the time the vines flower, as the buds are developing on the growing shoot. This process is known as INITIATION and is encouraged by warm, sunny weather and an open CANOPY that allows the sunlight to penetrate to the developing buds and adjacent leaves. By late summer it is usually possible to estimate the potential number of bunches which will be produced the following year by dissection and microscopic examination of the buds. The vine-grower anxiously assesses fruitfulness just as soon as the small bunches are evident on the developing shoots in spring. Normally, the higher the bunch number the higher is the potential yield of that season, although of course there are many other critical stages, especially FRUIT SET, before the harvest is brought in. R.E.S.

Winkler, A. J., *et al.*, *General Viticulture* (2nd edn, Berkeley, Calif., 1974).

fruit set, known as *nouaison* in French, an important and delicate stage of the vine's development after FLOWERING which marks the transition from flower to grape berry. The setting period of about a week is a critical one for the vine-grower, since it is a major determinant of the size of the crop, yet the grower can do little to change the course of events. Only 'set' or fertilized flowers grow into the berries from which wine is made; the others fail to grow and eventually fall off. Fruit set occurs immediately after FLOWERING, and is the result of successful POLLINATION achieving fertilization of the ovules and the development of seeds. The GRAPE SEED contains an embryo, formed by the union of the sperm cells from the POLLEN and the egg cell of the OVARY. Most wine grape varieties contain up to four seeds. The more seeds there are, the larger is the berry.

Not all flowers set, or form berries, and normally only about 30 per cent of flowers become berries, although the range can be from almost zero to 60 per cent. Those flowers that do not set fall from the bunch in a process called 'shatter' in English. It is not clear whether fruit set is more influenced by organic nutrition or HORMONES, but the crucial role played by the weather during this period is beyond dispute.

At one extreme, common in hot DRYLAND regions, high temperatures, low humidity, and attendant WATER STRESS can reduce fruit set, as can hot, dry winds. On the other hand, cold, cloudy, and rainy weather at flowering in the classical, cooler wine regions commonly reduces fruit set, and such conditions can cause widespread yield losses. Strategies for avoiding poor set include using BALANCED PRUNING to avoid rapid shoot growth, ensuring balanced VINE NUTRITION and water supply, TOPPING shoots during flowering, or, in extreme circumstances, CINCTURING vine trunks at flowering.

There are various forms of abnormal fruit set. Except in parthenocarpic (seedless) berries, poor pollination and fertilization of the ovules, or non-functional ovules which preclude the development of seeds, lead to poor fruit set, or COULURE, which leaves few berries per bunch, and much of the bunch stem empty. This can be due to the variety, vine VIGOUR, climatic conditions, or disease. MILLERANDAGE is when a high proportion of berries have no seeds and so remain small while normal-sized grapes grow on the same bunch.

Fruit set can also affect wine quality, especially when millerandage produces many small berries, offering an improved skin to juice ratio (see BERRY SIZE). R.E.S. & B.G.C.

Huglin, P., *Biologie et écologie de la vigne* (Paris, 1986).
Winkler, A. J., *et al.*, *General Viticulture* (2nd edn, Berkeley, Calif., 1974).

fruit wines, made by the FERMENTATION of fruits other than grapes, include cider and perry, but not beer or sake, since they derive their fermentable sugars from hydrolized starch. They are particularly common in cool climates such as in North America and Scandinavia.

A wine-like beverage can be made from almost any fruit, berry, or other plant material containing sugar. Most of these sources contain so little fermentable sugar, however, that it is usually necessary to add sugar from another source (a form of ENRICHMENT) to obtain sufficient ALCOHOL for stability (see STABILIZATION). Table sugar, or SUCROSE, is usually used, and most fruits other than grapes have excessive concentrations of ACIDS that split the sucrose into fermentable GLUCOSE and FRUCTOSE. Yeasts also contain a natural ENZYME which will convert sucrose to its component glucose and fructose.

In most cases, acid levels are so high that it is necessary to dilute the crushed fruit to reduce tartness in the resulting wine. In most fruits other than grapes, much of the acid mixture is CITRIC ACID (which predominates in the citrus fruits), although in apples and a few others it is MALIC ACID. (Grapes are distinguished by their high levels of TARTARIC ACID, which is more resistant to attack by BACTERIA.)

Lack of YEAST nutrients is a further problem in persuading fruits other than grapes to ferment. Commercial preparations made from autolysed yeast together with sufficient nitrogen, phosphorus, and potassium to make up the fruit's natural deficiency are commonly available to those who practise HOME WINEMAKING.

Very few fruit wines improve with BOTTLE AGE. Characteristic fruit flavours fade very rapidly and most are best consumed well within a year of bottling. A.D.W.

Fuder, German for large wooden BARREL, typically one with a capacity of 1,000 l/264 gal used in the MOSEL-SAAR-RUWER region. (The STÜCK is more commonly used in Rhein regions.) A **Halbfuder**, longer than a Halbstück, contains 500 l and was traditionally used for transporting wine from the Mosel.

full. A wine is described as full, or **full bodied**, if it is high, but not excessively high, in ALCOHOL and VISCOSITY. See BODY for more details.

Fumé Blanc is the curious descendant of the Loire synonym BLANC FUMÉ for the white grape variety SAUVIGNON BLANC. In the early 1970s, California's famous ideas man Robert MONDAVI had one of his most famous inspirations, that of renaming his unfashionable Sauvignon Blanc, Fumé Blanc, thereby imbuing it with some of the glamour of imported French Pouilly-Fumé. He also gave it some OAK ageing and a dark green bordeaux-shaped BOTTLE (both entirely alien to Pouilly-Fumé). This less-than-authentic formula proved a runaway success and Fumé Blanc became the highly successful name of a wine type in America, New Zealand, and elsewhere, even if there is little agreement about what exactly that wine type is.

fumigation, the viticultural practice of fumigating vineyard soils with the aim of killing soil-borne VINE PESTS or VINE DISEASES. It is usually carried out before planting. The earliest example of viticultural fumigation was the use of carbon bisulfide in France to combat PHYLLOXERA in the 1880s. Approximately 68,000 ha/167,960 acres were treated, requiring the painstaking insertion of about 30,000 holes per ha (12,000 per acre). Phylloxera is now controlled by GRAFTING, and today fumigation is used primarily to control the NEMATODE vector *Xiphenema index* of the virus disease FANLEAF DEGENERATION, but also for ARMILLARIA ROOT ROT, CROWN GALL, and occasionally squirrels and gophers.

Fumigation is difficult since it requires deep injection and a volatile chemical or gas which will permeate every pore to kill effectively. The exercise is most effective if the soil is porous and is not too wet. Newly fumigated vineyards in environmentally conscious areas such as California are covered with a large plastic sheet to prevent the fumigant being lost to the atmosphere. Some fumigants were banned in the early 1990s since they were found to contaminate groundwater. Methyl bromide, a soil sterilant, was phased out in 2005, and it has been suggested that it can be replaced by INTEGRATED PEST MANAGEMENT strategies. R.E.S.

Fumin, dark-berried vine speciality of the Valle d'AOSTA whose produce is usually used for blending.

fungal diseases, very large group of vine diseases which are caused by small, mostly microscopic, and filament-shaped organisms. Since fungi lack chlorophyll they need to live on other organisms to obtain nourishment. Fungal diseases have been of major significance in affecting grape production over centuries, with important consequences for both quantity and quality. Today they receive little public attention since they can successfully be controlled by a wide range of agricultural chemicals. In fact the famous fungicide BORDEAUX MIXTURE was used commercially to control DOWNY MILDEW in 1885 and for 50 years was the most important control of other fungal and bacterial plant diseases. Fungal disease epidemics are commonly related to weather conditions; examples are downy mildew and BOTRYTIS BUNCH ROT, both of which are favoured by warm, wet or humid weather, while POWDERY MILDEW is favoured by overcast weather.

Many of the economically important fungal diseases originated in America and therefore common varieties of the European *Vitis* VINIFERA species have no resistance. Thus, when powdery mildew was introduced in 1847, and then downy mildew in 1878, French *vinifera* vineyards were devastated. Fungal diseases can attack shoots and leaves but also developing bunches and ripe fruit. Some fungi such as *Armillaria* and *Verticillium* attack roots.

Botrytis is the fungus with which wine consumers are probably most familiar. In its benevolent form (see NOBLE ROT), it contributes to a high proportion of the most famous SWEET WINES. The more common malevolent form (see GREY ROT) causes substantial yield and quality losses, on the other hand.

Common fungal diseases are ANTHRACNOSE, ARMILLARIA ROOT ROT, BLACK ROT, BOTRYTIS BUNCH ROT, BUNCH ROTS, COLLAR ROT, DEAD ARM, DOWNY MILDEW, ESCA, EUTYPA DIEBACK, POWDERY MILDEW, TEXAS ROOT ROT, VERTICILLIUM WILT, WHITE ROT. Other groups of vine diseases include BACTERIAL DISEASES, PHYTOPLASMA diseases, and VIRUS DISEASES.

R.E.S.

Emmett, R. W., Harris, A. R., Taylor, R. H., and McGechan, J. K., 'Grape diseases and vineyard protection', in B. G. Coombe and P. R. Dry (eds.), *Viticulture*, ii: *Practices* (Adelaide, 1992).
Pearson, R. C., and Goheen, A. C., *Compendium of Grape Diseases* (St Paul, Minn., 1988).

fungi, a group of small and often microscopic multicellular or filamentous organisms which derive their energy living as saprophytes on dead plant or animal tissue, or as pathogens on living tissue. Fungi include YEASTS important in fermentation and many organisms causing vine FUNGAL DISEASES.

fungicide, type of pesticide that is effective against FUNGAL DISEASES in vineyards. The first of the modern fungicides used for any crop was the BORDEAUX MIXTURE used on grapevines against DOWNY MILDEW in 1885. Fungicides are applied by SPRAYING at times which are deemed effective to control the fungal disease. Fungicides are generally classified as protectants, eradicants, or systemics. Protectant fungicides are applied before the fungus infects the vines and they prevent infection by inhibiting fungal development on the plant surface. For ex-

ample, copper ions (from copper oxychloride) are toxic to the zoospores of grapevine downy mildew, thus preventing infection. Most protectant fungicides are non-specific, and are effective against a number of fungal diseases. Examples used in viticulture include copper compounds (such as copper oxychloride and Bordeaux mixture), dithiocarbamates (such as mancozeb), and SULFUR preparations.

Eradicant fungicides are effective when applied after the infection has occurred. They can either inhibit or kill fungi present on or in the vine, thus preventing these fungi from further disease development. A significant characteristic of eradicants is their ability to penetrate plant tissues, most being systemic (see later). Some eradicant fungicides can be applied one week or more after infection and still be very effective.

Systemic fungicides have the ability to infiltrate and move within plants. Movement may be relatively localized, such as from one side of a leaf to the other, or extensive, via the vine's vascular system. Systemic fungicides used in viticulture include the benzimidazoles (benomyl, for example), acylanilides (metalaxyl), dicarboximides (procymidone), and sterol inhibitors (fenarimol).

Mixtures of active ingredients may be used in formulations for different purposes, and may take advantage of synergistic effects: copper oxychloride and zineb mixtures, for example, or to create mixtures of protectant and eradicant fungicides, as for copper oxychloride and metalaxyl. Some fungicides may be used against more than one fungal pathogen: mancozeb is effective against both downy mildew and ANTHRACNOSE, for instance, whereas others have a narrow range of action.

It is important to keep levels of fungicide RESIDUES below limits specified for toxicological reasons. For wine grapes, there is an additional consideration: residues of some fungicides will inhibit yeast activity, thus affecting fermentation and resultant wine quality. The use of fungicides such as chlorothalonil, therefore, must cease well before harvest.

As with other pesticides, the potential for development of resistance to fungicides varies according to the type of fungicide. Fungicides can be grouped according to their mode of action as either multi-site or specific-site inhibitors. Multi-site inhibitors are potentially toxic to all fungal cells and the chance of developing resistant strains by mutation is therefore low. This group includes the protectant fungicides, which have been widely used in viticulture for decades without any significant decrease in efficacy. Specific-site inhibitors have more specific toxicity and, because they only inhibit one or a few steps in fungal metabolism, the chance of resistant strains arising is much greater. Most of the newer, systemic fungicides fall into this group. Strategies that delay or prevent the development of resistant strains include restrained use, the use of mixtures

of multi- and specific-site inhibitor fungicides, and alternation of multi- and specific-site inhibitors during the season. Over recent decades, resistance to fungicides used for POWDERY MILDEW and BOTRYTIS BUNCH ROT has developed. See also AGROCHEMICALS.

P.R.D.

Emmett, R. W., Harris, A. R., Taylor, R. H., and McGechan, J. K., 'Grape diseases and vineyard protection', in B. G. Coombe and P. R. Dry (eds.), *Viticulture*, ii: *Practices* (Adelaide, 1992).

furfurals. See OAK FLAVOUR.

Furmint, fine, fiery white grape variety grown most widely in Hungary, just over the Slovakian border from Tokaj, and in Slovenia as Sipon. It has also been grown in Austria's Burgenland, where it may be called Mosler. DNA PROFILING at Zagreb has shown that it is identical to Moslavac in Croatia and that Furmint probably has a parent–offspring relationship with GOUAIS BLANC.

Furmint is the principal ingredient in TOKAJI, one of the world's most famous dessert wines. The grapes are particularly sensitive to NOBLE ROT, yet the wine is characterized by very high acidity, which endows the wine with long ageing potential, high sugar levels, and rich, fiery flavours. In Tokaji it is usually blended with up to half as much of the more aromatic grape variety HÁRSLEVELŰ, and some Sárga Muskotály (MUSCAT BLANC À PETITS GRAINS) is also sometimes included in the blend.

Furmint can easily produce wines with an ALCOHOLIC STRENGTH as high as 14 per cent, and sturdy, characterful dry Furmint can be a delicious wine, even when drunk very young. Furmint is planted quite widely in Hungary, and in Somló in particular it makes extremely concentrated dry wines. The vine buds early but ripening slows towards the end of the season and the BOTRYTIZED (*aszú*) grapes may not be picked until well into November in some years.

The vine is so well established in Hungary that there is little concrete evidence for its geographical origins. It may have been brought by the wine-making immigrants encouraged by King Bela IV in the 13th century (see HUNGARY, history). Furmint's traditional stronghold was in Austria's Burgenland just over the border from Hungary's Sopron. It was habitually used here for AUSBRUCH wines until more commercially reliable varieties such as WELSCHRIESLING were introduced in the late 19th and early 20th centuries. Furmint is currently being revived in Austria, especially in the small town of RUST.

The variety was also grown in CRIMEA when Tokaji found such favour at the imperial court that the tsars wished to make their own version, it may be the 'Tokay' of ALBANIA, and it is still grown to a limited extent in South Africa, where it was imported in tandem with the other Tokaji grape Hárslevelǔ. See also GRASĂ.

fusel oils, a general collective term for the complex, unpleasant-smelling, and varied mixtures of natural organic chemicals that are separable as wine is distilled into brandy in a continuous still.

Fusel oils are of only minor importance to the wine drinker since they represent such a small proportion of wine, except in the case of some red wines made from Cabernet Sauvignon and Zinfandel grapes in which a hint of isoamyl alcohol can sometimes be detected (aromas sometimes likened to whisky or malt or described as burnt).

The fusel oil alcohols are predominantly by-products of the nitrogen metabolism of the YEAST during fermentation.   A.D.W.

futures in wine, wine bought before it is bottled and therefore long before it can be delivered. See EN PRIMEUR and INVESTMENT.

Gaglioppo, predominant red grape variety in CALABRIA in the far south of Italy. Possibly of Greek origin, it thrives in dry conditions and reaches high sugar levels which result in robust, if rarely subtle, wines. It is also grown in Abruzzo, the Marche, and Umbria. Italy's total plantings of the variety were less than 5,000 ha/12,500 acres in 2000.

Gaillac, dynamic, variegated wine district in SOUTH WEST FRANCE that is also of considerable historic importance. As outlined in the history of FRANCE, archaeological evidence suggests that Gaillac may have been one of the first viticultural centres of ancient GAUL, with wine production well established in the early years of the 1st century AD, probably after the Romans established the first vineyards of the LANGUEDOC around Narbonne, but possibly before then if those who contend that vine-growing pre-dated the Roman conquest are correct.

Gaillac certainly seems to have been producing wine long before BORDEAUX, the port through which its wines would have been shipped after being transported down the RIVERS Tarn and GARONNE. Barbarian invasions then curbed wine production until it was revived by MONKS at the Abbey of St-Michel-de-Gaillac in the 10th century and Gaillac wines were highly prized both locally and in northern Europe, especially ENGLAND, in the Middle Ages. Gaillac's export trade was thwarted, however, by the merchants of Bordeaux, who imposed stiff tariffs and conditions on the more robust wines of Gaillac and other 'high country' or HAUT PAYS wines made in the warmer, more dependable climate up river.

The wines may be called Gaillac after the small town at the centre of the production zone, but the most important settlement in the region by far is Albi just up river, with its extraordinary brick cathedral, a monument to the strength of religious belief. The Albigensian Crusade and the religious wars of the 12th and 13th centuries inevitably disrupted trade, although there is evidence that the English were once more buying Gaillac with enthusiasm in the 16th century, and the region, along with 'Limouth' (LIMOUX), was already associated with SPARKLING WINE production in 1680 (locals claim precedent over CHAMPAGNE).

The powerful, deeply coloured red wines of Gaillac continued to be prized by blenders in the early 19th century when ADULTERATION AND FRAUD were rife, but the arrival of the PHYLLOXERA louse towards the end of the century drove many local farmers to exploit crops other than the vine.

Today Gaillac's rolling fields are put to many uses, but the area devoted to AC wine production has grown from about 1,600 ha/3,900 acres of vines in the early 1990s to around 2,700 ha by the mid 2000s. (There has been a certain influx of aspirant wine producers from outside France, perhaps because land is relatively inexpensive.) The district is distinguished by its rich heritage of local VINE VARIETIES, and by its unusual diversity of wine styles.

The most distinctive local white grape variety is MAUZAC (which is also characteristic of Limoux), whose wines have a strong apple peel aroma and sometimes a certain astringency. LEN DE L'EL is another strictly local variety whose wine can lack acidity; appellation regulations insist on at least 15 per cent of Len de l'El and/or SAUVIGNON BLANC (although iconoclasts such as Robert Plageoles happily ignore these and produce a range of VARIETAL Gaillacs in an extraordinary range of styles). Some well-made Sauvignon is produced among dry whites, and the quality of still Mauzac has improved greatly. The other two white Bordeaux varieties SÉMILLON and MUSCADELLE are also grown but the indigenous ONDENC is also being revived, notably for sweet wines.

Some of Gaillac's finest wine is BARREL MATURED sweet white made from Mauzac, Muscadelle, Len de l'El, and the recently resurrected Ondenc, distinguished either as **Gaillac doux** or, if grown on certain demarcated LIMESTONE slopes, as **Gaillac Premières Côtes** (which may also produce whites that are dry, or sec). Yields for these last two appellations must be below 45 hl/ha whereas 60 hl/ha (3.4 tons/acre) is allowed for regular Gaillac. Some of these wines, such as Domaine Rotier's Cuvée Renaissance and Les Secrets de Ch Palvié can be very luscious indeed, BOTRYTIZED in some years.

Red wine, which can be an exciting south western ambassador, with the structure of a good bordeaux but more spicy flavours, is Gaillac's most common product, however, with DURAS as the intriguing local vine speciality. Its combination of colour, fruit, and BODY suggests that it may well have been largely responsible for Gaillac red wines' past reputation. FER Servadou, called locally Braucol, may also have added structure in the form of TANNINS, and the mandatory proportion of these two varieties together in red Gaillac is 40 per cent. A relatively recent arrival GAMAY was imported to provide Gaillac vignerons with income from PRIMEUR wines. SYRAH, however, is encouraged to add its concentration to that of the local varieties, while the Cabernets and Merlot of Bordeaux are tolerated complementary ingredients. The APPELLATION CONTRÔLÉE regulations of Gaillac hint at thousands of man-hours of local political manœuvre.

About a third of all white grapes, and much of the Mauzac, is vinified as a slightly sparkling wine sold as **Gaillac Perlé**, most notably by one of the two important CO-OPERATIVES in the region. More interesting and artisanal, however, are the medium sweet, lightly sparkling wines made by the *méthode gaillacoise*, a close relation of the *méthode ancestrale* (see SPARKLING WINE-MAKING), sold by some with the sediment still in bottle.

G

Plageoles also makes a VIN JAUNE style of wine sold as Vin de Voile, the *voile* or veil being that of the FILM-FORMING YEAST responsible. Other notable producers include Domaines de Causse Marines, d'Escausses, and de Gineste.

Gaja, the most renowned producer of high-quality, estate-bottled wines in PIEMONTE, traces its origins to 1856 when the Gaja family opened a tavern in its home town of BARBARESCO and began serving its own wines to accompany the food. By the end of the 19th century, the wines were already being bottled and supplied to the Italian army in Abyssinia, a highly unusual development in their home district of the Langhe, where a tradition of bottled wine assumed real significance only from the 1960s. The firm became an important force after the Second World War under the direction of Giovanni Gaja, who began an important series of vineyard purchases in what is now the Barbaresco DOC zone, a strategy that has given the house an important dimension both in terms of total vineyard area (currently 81 ha/200 acres, dwarfing all other Barbaresco houses) and an excellent selection of superior vineyard positions in the zone. Another significant influence on the firm's activities was that of Clotilda Rey, the mother of Giovanni Gaja, educated at Chambéry in French SAVOIE and a firm believer both in high quality to attract a selected clientele and in high prices to ensure that the house's efforts and philosophy were concretely reflected in a form that would further increase the prestige of the wines.

Gaja wines have gained worldwide recognition under Giovanni's son Angelo Gaja, who took over the direction of activities in the late 1960s; trained at the oenological school of Alba and at MONTPELLIER, an indefatigable traveller in the world's major viticultural areas, and a tireless and charismatic champion of his native region and its wines, he has given a new international perspective and a new elegance to the traditionally robust and powerful Piedmontese red wines, pioneering small BARREL MATURATION of both Barbaresco and BARBERA, and introducing international grape varieties—CABERNET SAUVIGNON, CHARDONNAY, and SAUVIGNON BLANC—to the vineyards of Piedmont (his Cabernet Sauvignon is called Darmagi, Piedmontese for 'what a shame', supposedly his father's reaction). He also acquired land in nearby BAROLO, with the 1988 Barolo Sperss marking a return to the zone from which the Gaja family made a wine from purchased grapes until 1961.

In the 1990s, Gaja expanded his horizons even further, purchasing the Pieve di Santa Restituta estate in Montalcino, where the first BRUNELLO DI MONTALCINO produced under his supervision was made in 1993, and, more recently, the development of the Ca' Marcanda estate in BOLGHERI on the Tuscan coast.

D.T. & D.C.G.

Steinberg, E., *The Vines of San Lorenzo* (New York, 1992).

Galego Dourado, white grape grown on the Atlantic coast of Portugal and known for its high-alcohol wines.

Galen, Greek physician whose work in the 2nd century AD was influential in Greece, Rome, and beyond. He identified the antiseptic properties of wine. See ATHENAEUS and MEDICINE.
Galen: *Selected Works*, tr. P. N. Singer (Oxford, 1997).

Galestro, the Italian name for the friable rock of the MARL-like soil that characterizes many of the best vineyard sites in CHIANTI CLASSICO, and also the name with which a Tuscan white wine based on TREBBIANO grapes was baptized when it was born at the end of the 1970s. Created to soak up the surplus of white grapes that developed when producers began to reduce the amount of Trebbiano used in their Chianti, Galestro the wine must contain from 60 to 85 per cent Trebbiano Toscano from central Toscana, together with a number of other varieties, both local and international: MALVASIA, VERNACCIA di San Gimignano, CHARDONNAY, PINOT BLANC, and RIESLING. Championed by a consortium founded in the late 1970s by the dominant NÉGOCIANT houses of Toscana—ANTINORI, FRESCOBALDI, RICASOLI, Ruffino, and others—it failed to make a lasting impact on the market, and is fast fading away. D.T. & D.C.G.

Galet, Pierre (1921–), father of modern AMPELOGRAPHY based in MONTPELLIER. Galet was born in Monaco and his upbringing in the Mediterranean climate of southern France undoubtedly helped to prepare him for a life spent outside surrounded by vines. Galet's working life was devoted to the science of describing and identifying VINE VARIETIES on the basis of minute botanical observation—an expertise he perfected while hiding from German occupation authorities in the international *Vitis* collection in the grounds of the Department of Viticulture at Montpellier. From 1946 to 1989, Galet was part of an elite teaching group that included Jean Branas, Denis Boubals, and François Champagnol at ENSA Montpellier, regarded as the national, if not international, centre of viticultural ACADEME. He taught thousands, including Paul Truel, whose own work based at Montpellier has been of worldwide significance, and Jean-Michel Boursiquot, who has succeeded him. Other accolytes include Lucie Morton, who translated some of his work into English for successful publication in the United States, Umberto Camargo in Brazil, Erika Dettweiler in Germany, and Anna Schneider in Italy.

His most tangible achievements, however, have been as author (and publisher, he has consistently published and sold his own books). His four-volume *Cépages et vignobles de France* came out between 1956 and 1964, and battered

copies are still circulated although he has since updated it to include handsome separate volumes with colour illustrations on American and French varieties, published in 1988 and 1991 respectively. His two-volume work on *Maladies et parasites de la vigne* came out in 1977 and 1982, while the fifth edition of his invaluable handbook *Précis de viticulture* appeared in 1988. In 2000, Hachette published his 936-page international dictionary of vine variety names and their synonyms.

Beyond teaching, much of his work involved vine identification for the practical purpose of, for example, settling a legal dispute, or advising a wine region on which varieties were actually growing in some of its old vineyards. This sort of work took him all over the Americas, North Africa, Cyprus, Afghanistan, Nepal, Thailand, and South Korea (Truel inspected the vineyards of Australia and Portugal). Able to identify hundreds of vine varieties at a glance, he was made an Officier de l'Ordre du Mérite Agricole and won many important awards, including a prize in 1983 from the OIV for the entirety of his published work. Few individuals embody such concentrated expertise. The reprint pamphlet cited below gives some of the flavour of this expert who had little patience with those not prepared to get their shoes dirty in the vineyard J.R. & L.M.
Galet, P., 'La Culture de la vigne aux États-Unis et au Canada', *France viticole* (Sept–Oct 1980 and Jan–Feb 1981).

Galicia, Spain's wet, Atlantic north west and one of the country's 17 autonomous regions encompassing the DO wine regions of RÍAS BAIXAS, RIBEIRO, RIBEIRA SACRA, MONTERREI, and VALDEORRAS. Separated by mountains from CASTILLA Y LEÓN, Galicia has developed in isolation from the rest of Spain, the region being geographically and culturally closer to northern Portugal than to Madrid (see map under SPAIN). The locals, many of whom are of Celtic descent, speak Gallego, a close relative of Portuguese. The wines also used to share an affinity with the light, acidic VINHO VERDE produced south of the Miño (Minho in Portuguese), the river that divides this part of Spain from Portugal, but they have become fuller and more substantial with the recovery of old native grape varieties and the use of modern wine-making techniques.

Wines were exported from Galicia as early as the 14th century, but northern European merchants quickly moved on in search of fuller-bodied wines from the DOURO in northern Portugal. The progressive fragmentation of agricultural holdings left the region with a subsistence economy and in the 19th century the countryside suffered from depopulation as people moved away to find work. Many of the magnificent TERRACES in the PORT vineyards of the Douro were constructed by itinerant labour from Galicia. Since Spain joined the EUROPEAN UNION in 1986, however, Galicia has benefited from a massive injection of funds which has transformed its wine industry.

Galicia is one of the wettest parts of Iberia. On the coast, RAINFALL averaging more than 1,300 mm/50 in a year is compensated for by an annual average of over 2,000 hours of sunshine. Vines flourish in these humid conditions and YIELDS in excess of 100 hl/ha (5.7 tons/acre) are unequalled anywhere else in Spain. Most of the vineyards are to be found towards the south in the provinces of Orense, Pontevedra, and also in Lugo to the east. Rías Baixas, with its prized ALBARIÑO grape, is the fulcrum of the Galician rebirth and its vibrant, dense wines can command high prices. But success has also meant, in the case of some producers, excessive yields and an abusive reliance on such techniques as the use of selected yeasts. On the Miño river, wines are often blends of Albariño, Loureira, and Caíño. Inland, the Ribeiro DO is making slow progress, almost all of it through the efforts of small producers such as Arsenio Paz, Emilio Rojo, and Viña Mein.

Local whites are based on complex blends, dominated by Treixadura and Torrontés, while reds from native varieties are making a timid comeback. In the inland Valdeorras and Ribeira Sacra DOs, light reds from the Mencía grape are prevalent, but the appley, white Godello grape is their main asset. The newest DO, Monterrei, has historic significance but only modest current activity.

R.J.M. & V. de la S.

gallic acid, a measurement of TANNIN.

Gallo winery of Modesto, CALIFORNIA, the largest family-owned wine-making operation in the world, was overtaken in overall size only in 2004 by the publicly owned CONSTELLATION. Gallo was developed by the brothers Ernest (1909–) and Julio (1910–93) from the vineyards of their father, who shipped grapes for HOME WINE-MAKING during PROHIBITION. On the eve of Repeal in 1933, the brothers obtained a licence to manufacture and store wine, and on the demise of Prohibition at the end of that year began the rapid expansion of their business. The received story is that they had only a couple of pamphlets published before Prohibition to guide their first wine-making efforts, but their father and uncle had been associated with the wine business before Prohibition, and wine-making in some form went on in the CENTRAL VALLEY, where the Gallos lived and grew grapes, throughout Prohibition. They perhaps knew more than a good story later would allow for.

Nevertheless, Ernest Gallo's success in establishing a national distribution network, first, while still in his teens, as a grape broker, and then for wine, stands as an extraordinary feat, particularly in view of the business milieu of the era, still dominated by the thuggish outlaw element nurtured by Prohibition.

Julio's special charge was production. By 1935, just two years after Repeal, the winery was producing 350,000 gal/13,300 hl of wine, and in 1936 the brothers built a new facility with a capacity of 1.5 million gal. The new winery's design showed their concern for the highest level of technical efficiency, as its capacity showed their determination in pursuing new and larger markets. In common with most large California wineries, the Gallos at first sold largely in bulk to bottlers; in 1937 they began to promote their own label and to devise their own marketing methods. The development of the firm thereafter was as a completely self-contained enterprise: it either owned its own vineyards or signed growers to long-term contracts; it built its own glass factory, maintained its own sales force, acquired control over distributorships, operated its own research department, its own print shop, and its own transport company.

By 1950, Gallo had the largest wine-production capacity in the United States. By 1967, it held first position in sales, and has continued to do so. Storage capacity at its four wine-producing facilities in 1992 was 330 million gal/12.5 million hl, many times more than that of Europe's largest wineries. In the process of its growth, Gallo has encouraged the planting of superior vine varieties, the use of modern crop management methods, and the best available wine-making technology. It has thus been involved in improving the basic standards of the California wine industry.

Moreover, Gallo's sales and marketing operation was long considered the academy for such functions in America. At one time, almost all the top wine sales executives in the US had at least a short stint with Gallo on their resumés. In the 1950s and 1960s, Gallo so revolutionized concepts of wine retailing in America that it was said that Gallo salesmen knew more about a store's inventory than its owner. No wonder Gallo has been accused of having a domineering influence over the rest of the industry, particularly, through its sheer size, in the councils of the trade organization the Wine Institute.

Known from the beginning for sound, inexpensive wines of every kind, including FLAVOURED WINES, wine coolers and FRUIT WINES, brandy, and bulk process SPARKLING WINES, Gallo inevitably became synonymous with 'pop' wine and JUG WINE, i.e. PLONK, generally recognized in the US by their screw cap bottles. Since 1977, however, Gallo has made a determined effort to associate its name with premium wines, in the US understood to be VARIETAL wines sold in bottles stoppered with a CORK. In the 1970s and early 1980s, Gallo was already the largest purchaser of grapes in the Napa Valley. In 2002, they even purchased Louis Martini Winery, one of Napa's most venerable institutions. By the end of the 1980s, Gallo had become the largest vineyard owner in Sonoma county. Two of Julio's grandchildren, Matt and Gina, run a winery in Dry Creek valley estimated to have a capacity of 7 million gallons. It is also estimated that they own 5,000 acres of vineyard spread all over Sonoma county, although even at this size, Gallo-Sonoma accounts for only a small percentage of the company's total volume. The company's estate wines are sold under the name Gallo Sonoma while names such as Anapamu, Rancho Zabaco, and Indigo Hills are used for wines made from grapes purchased from Monterey, Sonoma, and Mendocino respectively. Less expensive wines sold under other Gallo brands such as Carlo Rossi and Livingston Cellars are made in Modesto. The firm is wholly owned by the family and is notoriously secretive. Ernest Gallo's first on-the-record interview took place well after his eightieth birthday.

The Gallo brothers became as jealous of their own name as producers in the CHAMPAGNE region, prohibiting CHIANTI CLASSICO producers from using their traditional symbol of the black cockerel, or Gallo Nero, in the US and even preventing their own younger brother Joseph from using his own name on the cheese he produced.

Gallo, E. and J., *Our Story* (New York, 1994).

Hawkes, E., *Blood and Wine: The Unauthorized Story of the Gallo Wine Empire* (New York, 1993).

Gamaret, red grape CROSS bred in Switzerland by André Jaquinet at CHANGINS from Gamay and Reichensteiner. The variety, which has good rot resistance, was the third important variety grown in the canton of Geneva by 2005. In 2001, 45 ha/110 acres where planted; by 2007, 100 ha are expected. Gamaret generally produces dark purple wine with the aroma of spices and blackberries and subtle tannins. Initially Gamaret was developed for French western Switzerland while GARANOIR, with the same parents, was created for the German western part.

Gamashara, dark grape speciality of AZERBAIJAN.

Gamay, French red grape variety solely responsible for the distinctive, evolving and unfairly unfashionable wines of BEAUJOLAIS. Galet cites 30 different Gamays, many quite unrelated to the Beaujolais archetype, many of them particular CLONAL SELECTIONS of it, and many more of them red-fleshed TEINTURIERS once widely used to add colour to vapid blends. Red-fleshed versions can still be found, particularly in Mâconnais and Touraine, and France grew almost 300 ha/740 acres each of the teinturiers **Gamay de Bouze** and **Gamay Chaudenay** at the turn of the century. The 'real' Gamay is officially known as **Gamay Noir à Jus Blanc** to draw attention to its noble pale flesh, and is a natural offspring of Pinot and Gouais Blanc (see PINOT).

The introduction of Gamay to the vineyards of the CÔTE D'OR in the late 14th century was viewed as scandalous by those whose livelihood did not personally depend on rearing productive vines, and great efforts were made to retain PINOT NOIR at the expense of the less noble newcomer.

The vine is a precocious one, budding, flowering, and ripening early, which makes it prone to spring FROSTS but means that it can flourish in regions as cool as much of the Loire. It can easily produce too generously and the traditional GOBELET method of training is designed to match this aptitude to the granitic soils of the better Beaujolais vineyards.

Although today an increasing proportion of Beaujolais, particularly from the CRUS, is vinified like red burgundy with full BARREL MATURATION, Gamay juice for long tended to be vinified in a hurry, not least because of strong market pressure in the 1970s and 1980s for Beaujolais NOUVEAU; if Gamay-based wines were cellared for more than two or three years, it was usually by mistake. As a wine, Gamay tends to be paler and bluer than most other reds, with relatively high acidity and a simple but vivacious aroma of freshly picked red fruits, often overlaid by the less subtle smells associated with rapid, anaerated fermentation such as bananas, boiled sweets, and acetone. In France and Switzerland, it is often blended with Pinot Noir, endowing the nobler grape with some precocity, but often blurring the very distinct attributes of each.

Gamay and Beaujolais are entirely interdependent. No wine region is so determinedly *monocépagiste* as Beaujolais; in 2000 all but 225 ha of the Rhône *département*'s nearly 22,000 ha/54,360 acres of vines were Gamay Noir. Vinification techniques vary but most common is a local variant on CARBONIC MACERATION. Similar, often lighter and arguably truer, wines are made from the Gamay grown in the small wine regions of central France, particularly those around Lyons and in the upper reaches of the Loire such as CHÂTEAUMEILLANT, Coteaux du LYONNAIS, Coteaux du GIENNOIS, Côtes d'AUVERGNE, Côtes du FOREZ, Côtes ROANNAISES, and ST-POURÇAIN.

Outside Beaujolais, and perhaps because its wines have been seen as too different from the intense, fashionable norm, the Gamay vine has been losing ground. In the Côte Chalonnaise and Mâconnais between Beaujolais and the Côte d'Or, the Gamay was displaced as principal grape variety by Chardonnay during the 1980s, and Pinot Noir plantings had surpassed those of Gamay by the 21st century. The unexcitingly muddy quality of Gamays made here is expected to continue this trend. Gamay took up just 275 ha of the Côte d'Or's valuable vineyard in 2000. With a total of 34,500 ha in 2000, Gamay was France's sixth most planted red wine grape variety.

Gamay is the most planted red wine variety in SAVOIE, grown especially in the cru of Chautagne. It is also grown all over the Loire, especially in the Loir-et-Cher *département* upstream of Tours, but is not glorified by any of the Loire's greatest appellations. Gamay de Touraine can provide a light, sometimes acid, but usually cheaper alternative to Beaujolais, but it is most widely grown west of Touraine, alongside Sauvignon, for such light, lesser-known names as CHEVERNY and Coteaux du VENDÔMOIS. Gamay also provides a sizeable proportion of all of the Loire's important generic red Vin de Pays du Jardin de la France.

Outside France there has been even less incentive to develop this under-appreciated variety. (One notable California grower who bothered in the early 1980s to import and vinify true Gamay was Charles F. Shaw, whose name acquired fame only when it had been acquired by Franzia and applied to a trend-setting wine retailed at $1.99 in the early 2000s, known colloquially as Two Buck Chuck.) Today just a few hundred acres remain of the less distinguished vine known in California **Napa Gamay** (see VALDIGUIÉ) and the variety there called **Gamay Beaujolais**, which is probably a lesser clone of Pinot Noir.

Gamay is also grown in small quantities in Canada and is confused on a grand scale with BLAUFRÄNKISCH throughout eastern Europe. It is grown to a certain extent in Italy, and plays a relatively important role in the vineyards of CROATIA, SERBIA, KOSOVO, and, to least effect, in MACEDONIA.

It is chiefly valued, however, outside Beaujolais, by the Swiss, who grow it widely and, often blending with Pinot Noir, take it seriously—although, like Beaujolais's least conscientious producers, they are apt to chaptalize the life out of it (see SWITZERLAND).

Galet, P., *Dictionnaire encyclopédique des cépages* (Paris, 2000).

Gamay Beaujolais, California name for a particular, and undistinguished, selection of PINOT NOIR.

Gamay Blanc Gloriod, light-skinned grape grown in the Haute Saône which is GAMAY Noir's brother, since it is also a natural offspring of Pinot and Gouais Blanc (see PINOT).

Gambellara, dry white wine from the VENETO region of north east Italy. Based on GARGANEGA grapes (a minimum of 80 per cent, with 20 per cent of TREBBIANO di Soave or Trebbiano Toscano permitted in the blend), it is produced in the townships of Gambellara, Montebello Vicentino, Montorso, and Zermeghedo, only a short distance from SOAVE but in the neighbouring province of Vicenza rather than that of Verona. The wines, made from the same exaggerated yields as their neighbour (98 hl/ha (5 tons/acre) is quite legal), share the blandness of the vast majority of Soave, without sharing the reputation or the instant consumer recognition that Soave enjoys. Gambellara has still to attract quality-minded pioneer producers to demonstrate the potential of Garganega in this particular zone.

D.T.

Gamé, Bulgarian name for BLAUFRÄNKISCH.

Gamza, name for KADARKA in BULGARIA.

garagiste. See MICROCHÂTEAU.

Garanoir, red grapevine CROSSING created at CHANGINS by André Jaquinet from Gamay and Reichensteiner. It makes less concentrated, lighter, fruiter wines than its sister crossing GAMARET and is planted to only a limited extent in both French and German Switzerland.

Garganega, vigorous, productive, often over-productive, late-ripening white grape variety of the VENETO region in north east Italy. Its most famous incarnation is SOAVE, in which it may constitute anything from 70 to 100 per cent of the blend, often sharpened up by the addition of TREBBIANO di Soave, but increasingly plumped up by CHARDONNAY and other imports. In the Soave CLASSICO zone, with yields kept well in check, and where it is allowed to ripen fully, it can produce the fine, delicate whites redolent of lemon and almonds which give Soave a good name. Naturally high in acid, it can give balanced yet steely wines that have an alluring, delicate spiciness. The vine is also responsible for GAMBELLARA—indeed Garganega di Gambellara is its most important subvariety—but Garganega has such a long history in Veneto that it has developed myriad, if rarely particularly interesting, strains, clones, and subvarieties. Other wines in which it plays a major part include Bianco di CUSTOZA, Colli Berici, Colli Euganei, and it is also grown to a more limited extent in both FRIULI and UMBRIA. It is Italy's sixth most important white grape variety, and was planted on more than 11,637 ha/29,500 acres in 2000.

Garnacha is the Spanish, and therefore original, name for the increasingly fashionable grape known in France and elsewhere as GRENACHE. Its most common and noblest form is the dark-berried and light-fleshed **Garnacha Tinta**, sometimes known as **Garnacho Tinto**. As this variety, ubiquitous in much of Spain, is being re-evaluated from weed to asset (partly in response to the RHÔNE RANGER phenomenon but mainly because of PRIORAT's huge success), VARIETAL versions are becoming more common, as are blends with the firmer TEMPRANILLO, and the word Garnacha is increasingly seen on wine labels.

Even after extensive grubbing up in the 1980s and 1990s, when the variety was underappreciated, a total of 82,300 ha/203,300 acres made Garnacha Tinta Spain's second most planted red wine grape after Tempranillo in 2004. It is grown particularly in north and east, being an important variety in such wine regions as Rioja, Navarra, Priorat, Empordà-Costa-Brava, Campo de Borja, Cariñena, Costers del Segre, Madrid, La Mancha, Méntrida, Penedès, Priorat, Somontano, Tarragona, Terra Alta, Utiel-Requena, and Valdeorras. In Rioja it provides stuffing and immediate charm when blended with the more austere Tempranillo. The cooler, higher vineyards of Rioja Alta are reserved for Tempranillo, while Garnacha is the most common grape variety of the warm eastern Rioja Baja region where the vines can enjoy a long ripening season. The juiciness apparent in these early maturing riojas can be tasted in a host of other Spanish reds and, especially, rosados. Grenache has been adopted with particular enthusiasm in Navarra, where it has been the dominant grape variety and dictates a lighter, more obviously fruity style of red and rosado than in Rioja. In many other areas Garnacha is typically dry-farmed as an old bushvine (average vine age is high) so that the wines can be quite concentrated and tannic.

Perhaps the most distinctive, and certainly the most expensive, Spanish wine based on Garnacha Tinta (often incorporating some **Garnacha Peluda**, or 'downy Garnacha', known as LLADONER PELUT in Languedoc-Roussillon), is Priorat, the concentrated Cataluñan cult wine in which the produce of old Garnacha vines may be modernized by blending it with young Merlot, Cabernet, or even Syrah fruit.

Garnacha Blanca is the light-berried GRENACHE BLANC of which in 2004 there were about 3,000 ha/7,410 acres in Spain, where it plays a role in north eastern whites such as those of Alella, Priorato, Tarragona, Rioja, and Navarra.

Garnacha Tintorera, synonym for the red-fleshed ALICANTE BOUSCHET, Tintorera being Spanish for 'dyer' or TEINTURIER. Spain grew 22,200 ha/54,800 acres of this variety in 2004, more than a quarter as much as GARNACHA TINTA.

Garonne, river that rises south of Toulouse in SOUTH WEST FRANCE and flows north west towards the Atlantic and on which the city of BORDEAUX is situated. The confluence of the Garonne and the DORDOGNE, between MARGAUX and BOURG, marks the southern end of the GIRONDE estuary. The Garonne was an important trade route through south west GAUL in the era of Ancient ROME and continued to play a vital role in the medieval wine trade, where there was particular commercial rivalry between the wines produced up river in the HAUT PAYS, either on the Garonne or on its tributaries the Lot and the Tarn, and those produced in the immediate vicinity of Bordeaux.

Today the Garonne links the isolated but promising VIN DE PAYS du Comté Tolosan (represented by the ambitious and internationally targeted vins de pays of Domaine de Ribonnet) with, travelling north west down river, FRONTON, LAVILLEDIEU, Côtes du BRULHOIS, BUZET, Côtes du MARMANDAIS, GRAVES, PREMIÈRES CÔTES DE BORDEAUX, and Bordeaux's sweet white wine areas SAUTERNES and BARSAC.

garrafeira, word used by winemakers, wine bottlers, and wine collectors in PORTUGAL meaning a 'private wine cellar' or 'reserve'. The term was once widely used on wine labels to denote a red wine from an exceptional year that has been aged for at least 30 months before sale, including at least 12 months in bottle. White and rosé garrafeira wines, which are now fairly rare, must be aged for at least 12 months, including at least 6 months in bottle, to qualify. The law states that both red and white DOC wines must have an ALCOHOLIC STRENGTH at least 0.5 per cent above the legal minimum for the DOC region. Traditionally most garrafeiras were blends of wines from different parts of the country, labelled with the name of the merchant who bottled them. Under legislation introduced in the early 1990s, all garrafeiras must display their region of origin.

R.J.M.

Garrido, minor speciality of the CONDADO DE HUELVA region in southern Spain.

Garrut is a CATALUÑAN synonym for Monastrell or MOURVÈDRE.

Gascony, proud region in SOUTH WEST FRANCE which today comprises armagnac country and such wines as MADIRAN and JURANÇON. Its name appears on labels of the highly successful VIN DE PAYS des Côtes de Gascogne. In the Middle Ages it was incorporated into Aquitaine and was therefore, like BORDEAUX, under English rule for nearly 300 years from the middle of the 12th century.

Gattinara, historically the most celebrated, and certainly the most focally situated, of the sometimes intense red wines based on NEBBIOLO grapes, here known as SPANNA, in the cluster of hills which span Vercelli and Novara provinces in the PIEMONTE region of north west Italy. In the 19th century, these hills were far more widely planted with Nebbiolo than the LANGHE, and the wines were more highly prized than either Barolo or Barbaresco. The long decline of viticulture here was halted when Gattinara was awarded DOCG status in 1990. The Vercelli hills on the west bank of the Sesia river and the Novara hills on the east are showing once again that they are capable of producing some of the most serious rivals to the great BAROLO and BARBARESCO. It is traditional here to add a small softening portion of local BONARDA and/or VESPOLINA grapes, a ploy needed particularly in less ripe

vintages when Nebbiolo grown well to the north of the Langhe can seem austere rather than majestic. Of the seven Spanna zones, Gattinara should produce the most long-lived wines, and the most substantial are given extended ageing in cask.   D.T.

Gaul, part of western Europe closely approximating to modern France which existed before the rise of classical ROME. The élites of the CELTIC communities beyond the alps were large-scale consumers of wine, long before they were producers. The accoutrements of the Greek and Roman dinner party are frequently found amid the grave goods of Celtic chieftains. Their passion for wine was even claimed as the motive for the Gallic invasions of the Mediterranean world from the 4th century BC onwards (see e.g. Livy, 5. 33). The widespread ready market in Gaul for wine, as well as the slaves who were offered in exchange, was a major stimulus for exports from Italy, particularly in the last century BC (Diodorus, 5. 26). The cultivation of vines arrived with Greek settlers at Massilia (Marseilles) about 600 BC. From them the Gauls 'got used to living by the rule of law, and to pruning the vine, and planting the olive' (Justin, 43. 4. 1). But the real impetus came with the arrival of Roman settlers from the end of the 2nd century BC. By the end of the 1st century BC southern France and the RHÔNE valley (Gallia Narbonensis) were planted with all the fruit that Mediterranean visitors expected. But beyond the Cévennes was a world where 'no vine, olive, or fruit grew', as the great scholar VARRO (De re rustica, 1. 7. 8) noticed while on campaign there. The reasons for this were part sociological and part ecological. Some tribes banned the drinking of wine and even massacred traders, in the belief that it undermined their manliness and was the explanation of their defeats by Julius Caesar's armies. More significant was the need for vines which were resistant to FROST. The 1st century AD was a time of considerable development in the south, including wines from Baeterrae (Béziers) and around Vienne (see CÔTE RÔTIE), where the Allobrogica vine was noted for producing a wine with a natural resinated taste. Wines from this region competed in the markets of Italy and the western Mediterranean, as the finds of the distinctive local AMPHORAE confirm. Elsewhere in Gaul it is more difficult to trace the introduction of viticulture. The GARONNE was an important trade route from an early date; so it is highly likely that the BORDEAUX region was developed in the 1st century AD. On the other hand, the first references to vineyards in BURGUNDY, on the MOSELLE, and in the area of PARIS belong to the 4th century AD. However, recent archaeological finds suggest that viticulture may have developed considerably earlier in many regions than the inadequate literary sources suggest. For example, the discovery of kilns producing amphorae for wine from the late 1st century AD onwards on the LOIRE and its tributaries is testimony to the presence of viticulture in an area for which there is no other evidence. The scale of production should not be exaggerated. The modern map of wine production in France owes less to the Romans than to the Christian Church in the post-Roman period (see CHARLEMAGNE and MONKS AND MONASTERIES). J.J.P.

Dion, R., *Histoire de la vigne et du vin en France des origines au XIXe siècle* (Paris, 1959).

Ferdière, A., *Les Campagnes en Gaule romaine*, ii (Paris, 1988).

Gavi, renowned Italian dry white DOCG zone of about 1,100 ha/2,700 acres and the most interesting expression of the CORTESE grape in PIEMONTE. It is produced around the town of Gavi in a strip of land 15 km/9 miles long and no more than 5.5 km wide in the south east of the province of Alessandria. Cortese appears to be indigenous to this province being first noted for its quality in 1659. The red DOLCETTO grape was also important here until PHYLLOXERA devastated the vineyards.

At its best, Gavi is fruity and aromatic, occasionally with mineral notes and a tangy, citric finish; comparisons to white burgundy on the part of its more fervent admirers seem farfetched. Thanks partly to the high quality achieved by the pioneering La Scolca estate in Rovereto di Gavi, the wine enjoyed great commercial success in the 1960s and the early 1970s, first in the Italian market and subsequently abroad, before the emergence of FRIULI as an important source of fresh white Italian wine. Total production has grown to about 55,000 hl/1,452,000 gal a year.

Increasing competition in its category from TRENTINO, and ALTO ADIGE, as well as from Friuli, has subsequently put Gavi under a certain commercial pressure as a wine that had reached significant price levels, and estates in the zone seem uncertain as to where to position their production: as a medium-quality, medium-priced wine or as a wine with higher quality and price aspirations. The generous yields (over 70 hl/ha (4.2 tons/acre)) permitted by the DOCG regulations, coupled with often careless cellar techniques, have led to the production of a certain amount of bland Gavi. With care in the vineyard and cellars, the delicate flavours of the Cortese grape, retained thanks to the moderating MARITIME influence due to its proximity to the Ligurian coast less than 70 km/40 miles way, can yield pleasurable wines that are easy to drink, D.T. & D.C.G.

GDC, vine-TRAINING SYSTEM. See GENEVA DOUBLE CURTAIN.

Geelong, cool wine region in the Port Phillip Zone of the Australian state of VICTORIA that is especially good for complex, intense Pinot Noir and Chardonnay. Shiraz also does well. Thirty producers, most of which are small, family-owned and operated.

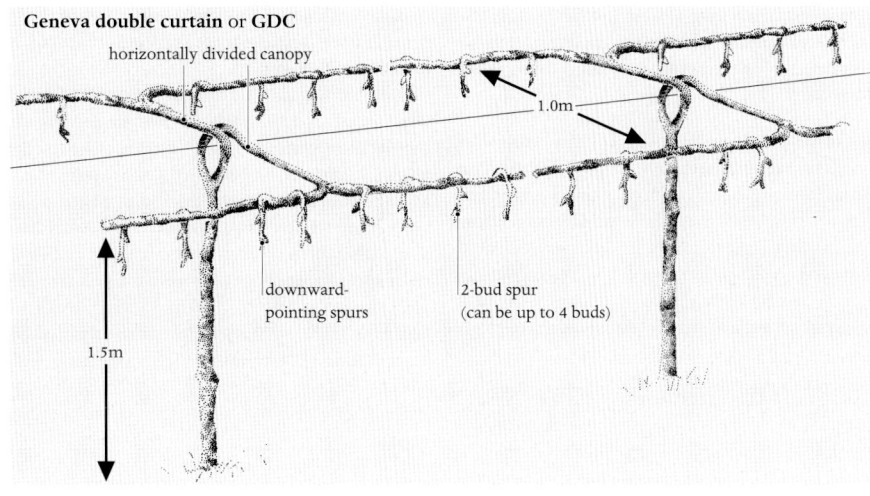

Geneva double curtain or GDC

horizontally divided canopy

1.0m

downward-pointing spurs

2-bud spur (can be up to 4 buds)

1.5m

Geilweilerhof, viticultural research station at Siebeldingen in the Pfalz region of GERMANY specializing in breeding vine varieties which combine resistance to FUNGAL DISEASES with superior wine quality. As early as 1926, Peter Morio and later Professor Husfeld were working on combining the desirable characteristics found in AMERICAN VINE SPECIES with the wine quality produced by VINIFERA varieties. Today some Asian species of the genus VITIS are also explored. Much of the focus of research is on improving VINE-BREEDING efficiency, with particular reference to pest and disease resistance, frost and drought resistance, eventual wine constituents (particularly aroma and phenolic compounds), the genetic resources of *Vitis*, grape genomic research, and biotechnology, including GENETIC MODIFICATION. Some of the most famous varieties from Geilweilerhof are MORIO-MUSKAT, BACCHUS, OPTIMA, and DOMINA. In the early 1990s, the successful breeding work of Professor Alleweldt led to the release of the first fungus-resistant varieties such as PHOENIX (1992), and a host of other new DISEASE-RESISTANT VARIETIES such as Sirius, Orion, and REGENT (1994). By 2004, Regent was planted on more than 2000 hectares in Germany, representing a breakthrough in the acceptance of NEW VARIETIES. Other new cultivars were released in 2004: Castell and Felicia (white), and Calandro and Reberger (black). Geilweilerhof provides three grapevine databases on its website. The journal *Vitis* has been published by the Geilweilerhof Institute of Grape Breeding since 1957. See also GEISENHEIM.

www.bafz.de/

Geisenheim, viticultural research institute named after the small town in the Rheingau region of Germany where it is sited. It was founded in 1872 by Eduard von Lade to improve the science of growing fruit, particularly apples, and has continued a tradition of combining education with applied research ever since then. In 1876, Professor Müller-Thurgau joined Geisenheim as a biologist and in 1882 developed the crossing MÜLLER-THURGAU, which later became the most planted in Germany.

Today research in viticulture and oenology is divided into six broad subjects: Environmental stress effects on grapevine physiology and fruit maturation, with particular emphasis on the possible effects of CLIMATE CHANGE on viticulture and on biotic stresses such as diseases, developing new biological and technological strategies to minimize the use of pesticides in both organic and conventional viticulture. Secondary metabolites formed during fruit development, focusing on aromatic precursors and phenols and their dynamics during fruit processing and wine-making. Water stress and the use of new technologies to guide irrigation for grapes and horticultural crops. Molecular and traditional genetics, including grapevine breeding for disease resistance, clonal selection for improved quality and vine health, plant regeneration *in vitro*, research on the adaptation of rootstocks to different soil and climate conditions, the genetics of phylloxera resistance and of yeast and bacteria, and the detection of genetically modified organisms. Steep slope viticulture and the development of new technologies for mechanization and increased efficiency such as REMOTE SENSING, GLOBAL POSITIONING systems in machine guidance, and efficient soil water management, as well as an economic evaluation of holistic approaches to vineyard management under these conditions. New technologies in juice and wine production, focusing on the interaction between maturity and nutritional status of the fruit, grape processing, microbiology, and must and wine composition.

In the past, wine-making research dealt with minimizing chemical input in the vineyard and winery (see ORGANIC WINE) in order to reduce off-flavors and to increase wine quality. Today the main focus is the investigation of traditional versus new oenological practices in a national and global context. Other areas of activity include identifying and describing objective parameters for wine quality as well as developing criteria for cork and alternative CLOSURES.

gelatin, the gel familiar in jelly and jello, used by winemakers as a FINING agent. This animal product (of which very small traces, unfortunately, remain in the wine after the fining operation) is particularly useful for precipitating excess TANNINS as large insoluble molecules which can be removed by FILTRATION. Gelatin is deliberately avoided by those making VEGETARIAN AND VEGAN WINES.

Gelber Muskateller, name for MUSCAT BLANC À PETITS GRAINS used in Austria. Production is less than half a percent of the national total but the variety is popular in Styria for light, dry wines and in the town of RUST, where botrytized AUSBRUCH wines are made from it.

gemischter Satz is a term used in Austria to refer to a mix of grape varieties that are vinified together to make a blended wine, often a basic pouring wine. This was much more common in the past, when varieties were interplanted in the vineyard, then harvested and fermented together. See also EDELZWICKER and BOURGOGNE PASSETOUTGRAINS.

generic wine, one named after a wine type (and usually borrowed European place-name) as opposed to a VARIETAL, named after the grape variety from which the wine was made. The term has been used particularly in AUSTRALIA and the UNITED STATES. Under American law, wines labelled as generics may be made from any grape variety or blend of varieties, and called either after their colour (red, white, rosé) or after places. With nothing else to call their results, early CALIFORNIA wineries borrowed European place-names shamelessly. Before PROHIBITION one could buy, not just St-Julien and Margaux made in the state, but wines named after particular châteaux. After Prohibition, stricter laws limited the borrowings to a handful of so-called **semi-generic** names, most commonly Burgundy, Chablis, Champagne, Chianti, Rhine, Sauterne (sic), Sherry, and Port, but did nothing to demand even the faintest approximations of the original in terms of grape varieties or style. Chablis could and can be just as sickly sweet as Rhine, and both can be made from THOMPSON SEEDLESS or any other white grape. Burgundy, Chianti, and Claret could all come from the same tank, and admittedly have done. Towards the end of the 1980s, Red Table Wine, White Table Wine, and Rosé began to replace place-names on many of the more reputable labels. However, Chablis, Burgundy, and other borrowed names remain in widespread use by a number of large-volume producers, giants GALLO foremost among them. A wine agreement between the US and EU finally drafted in 2005 permitted the continued use of these semi-generic terms on established BRANDS for an unspecified period.

Generic names can still be found on many wine labels, particularly in non-exporting or developing wine regions. No third-country wine entering the EUROPEAN UNION may carry a geographical name recognized as a European wine name. Thus, for example, the Australian company PENFOLDS had to change the name of their most famous wine from Penfolds Grange Hermitage to Penfolds Grange and, more fatuously, EU officials have objected to established New World place-names incorporating the word Port.

Outside Europe, CHAMPAGNE is still widely used as a generic name for SPARKLING WINE, although not usually for the best-quality products.

generoso is a Spanish and Portuguese term for a FORTIFIED wine.

genetic modification, sometimes called **genetic manipulation** or **genetic engineering**, modern approach to breeding which involves transfer of genes between organisms. This new technology has applications in both VITICULTURE and OENOLOGY.

A proposed benefit of genetic modification is the ability to insert foreign genes, carrying a particular desirable characteristic, into the genetic material of traditional VINE VARIETIES such as Cabernet Sauvignon, without altering the genes concerned with their other characteristics. There are hopes of introducing resistance to FUNGAL DISEASES and VIRUS DISEASES as well as to INSECT PESTS by the use of this technique, as well as improving berry ripening and quality. Whether such genetically modified vines can retain the same variety name remains to be legally tested. Research groups in both New and Old World wine countries have produced genetically modified vines; since the late 1990s and early 2000s, field trials have been in progress in Germany, Italy, Australia, and the US with the aim of improving fruit quality and disease resistance. Many governments have introduced strict testing procedures for genetically modified organisms and consumer resistance in parts of Europe has been considerable. It is expected that the commercial availability of genetically modified vines will depend on market acceptance of wines derived from these plants.

See also TISSUE CULTURE and INTERNATIONAL GRAPE GENOME PROJECT.

Mullins, M. G., Bouquet, A., and Williams, L., *Biology of the Grapevine* (Cambridge, 1992).

Geneva double curtain, often abbreviated to **GDC**, a vine-TRAINING SYSTEM whereby the CANOPY is divided into two pendent curtains, trained downwards from high CORDONS or CANES. The system was developed by Professor Nelson SHAULIS of Geneva Experiment Station in upstate New York in the early 1960s. The vines are planted in about 3-m/10-ft rows and the trunk divided at about 1.5 m height to form two parallel cordons about 1.3 m/4 ft apart. The foliage is trained downwards from these cordons, forming the so-called double curtains. This training system was one of the first examples of a DIVIDED CANOPY developed in the New World and, by reducing shade, it increases both yield and grape quality (see CANOPY MICROCLIMATE). While initially developed for the American variety CONCORD, the system has been applied to VINIFERA wine grapes, especially in Italy. It is one of a number of TRELLIS SYSTEMS advocated as part of CANOPY MANAGEMENT in the 1990s. The GDC system is particularly useful for wide row spacing vineyards of high VIGOUR. While most wine grape varieties have more erect shoots than the American vines it was developed with, it has been found suitable for use in many vineyards, and some notable increases in yield and wine quality have resulted from use of the system.   R.E.S.

Smart, R. E., and Robinson, M., *Sunlight into Wine: A Handbook for Winegrape Canopy Management* (Adelaide, 1991).

Genoa, north west Italian port and the principal city of the LIGURIA region. After the fall of Ancient ROME and the barbarian invasions, Genoa was occupied by the Lombards, a Germanic tribe, in 642. Under the Lombards, the region disintegrated economically, and the old Roman highways across the Apennines and along the coast were not maintained. It took Genoa until the early 11th century fully to recover from the effects of Lombard rule.

Genoa was therefore initially at a grave disadvantage compared with the city that was to become its deadly rival, VENICE. The Genoese navy had fought to protect its ships from Saracen sea power in the two centuries before the CRUSADES, together with Amalfi, Pisa, and Venice, and Genoa had established trading posts in the Byzantine empire, although it was nowhere near as successful in this as Venice. Nevertheless, Genoa's rise, like Venice's, was at first based on its eastern trade, and by the time of the Crusades it was battling with Venice, and occasionally Pisa, for economic control of the eastern Mediterranean. The Latin kings of Jerusalem were dependent on Venetian, Genoese, and Pisan naval power for their protection, and so they granted these cities trading areas in their ports. Whereas Venice continued to trade mostly with Constantinople and the Near East, Genoa's interests centred largely on Palestine and Syria. Along with sugar, glass, and textiles, it shipped wine from vineyards there, many of which had been planted by Christian settlers, to Italy, where these strong, sweet wines were accounted a luxury and bought by rich merchants for their own consumption.

Along with luxury goods acquired in the East, Genoa also began to export cheap bulky goods such as grain, salt, oil, alum (for dying woollen cloth), and wine to western and northern Europe. The overland route was prohibitively expensive, and so from the 13th century onwards Genoa organized regular sailings to Bruges and Southampton in galleys, which used their oars to get into and out of ports swiftly, regardless of the prevailing winds. The voyage still took several months, and only strong, sweet wines such as VERNACCIA ('vernage'), produced mainly in Liguria, and the MALMSEYS of the Aegean had any chance of arriving in drinkable condition. The Venetians did not follow the Genoese galleys until 40 years later. In the late 14th century, Genoa abandoned its galleys in favour of the much larger cogs, which had a capacity of 700 to 800 tons and could travel from Genoa to Southampton with only one stop on the way, at Cádiz (see SPAIN).

See also NAPLES and ITALY.   H.M.W.

Lopez, R. S., 'The trade of mediaeval Europe: the South', *The Cambridge Economic History of Europe*, 7 vols. ii: *Trade and Industry in the Middle Ages* (Cambridge, 1987).

Melis, Frederigo, 'Produzione e commercio dei vini italiani nei secoli XIII–XVIII', *Annales cisalpines d'histoire sociale*, 1/3 (1972), 107–33.

Geographe, moderately cool, gently hilly wine region in the South West Australia Zone of WESTERN AUSTRALIA. Eighteen producers.

geographical delimitation and **geographical designation**. See DELIMITATION, GEOGRAPHICAL.

Geographic Indications, the result of Australia's geographical DELIMITATION. See Labelling laws in AUSTRALIA for more about these so-called GIs.

geographical information system (**GIS**), database which can store, analyse and display in map form geographically related data such as soil type, climate, elevation, and crop history. GIS is an essential tool in PRECISION VITICULTURE.   R.G.V.B.

geology, mainly the study of the Earth's crust, may have been overestimated in its importance in shaping wine quality and flavour, and some geological remarks in popular wine books are nonsense. In its potential influence on wine, geology includes not only the ROCKS underlying vineyards, but the SOILS at the surface and variations in the slopes on which many vineyards grow (see TOPOGRAPHY), as well as how water drains through a vineyard. Some wine flavours are given names which may sound geological, such as 'earthy' or 'flinty', but these bear no relation to the associated geology. While geology may have an influence on a wine, it is generally less than the influence of weather, vine variety, viticultural

methods, and wine-making technique (see CLIMATE AND WINE QUALITY, VINE VARIETIES, VITICULTURE, and WINE-MAKING).

Geology is clearly of importance to the vine-grower because it affects the growth of vines and their production of suitable grapes in ways that are similar for many other long-lived plants: influences on the air temperature around the vines; controls on supplies of water to the roots; and provision of soil nutrients. See SOIL AND WINE QUALITY for more detail than appears below.

It is not difficult to establish the general, if not the precise, geology of a vineyard. The most widely available geological maps chart the geological system of the region (Devonian or Miocene, for example). To discover the lithology, the actual sort of rock and its mineral composition, geological maps at a scale of 1:100,000 or greater are usually needed. Some of these small-scale maps show only the bedrock geology, above which there may be superficial sediments of another composition, possibly several metres thick, and on top of this a layer of soil. However, maps of Quaternary geologic deposits often provide detailed information about the superficial sediments. The Quaternary deposits and the soil about them strongly influence the all-important DRAINAGE structure.

The classification of SOILS, especially under the system used in Europe, may seem obscure and difficult to understand. However, any grower who takes the time and effort to study the nomenclature will be rewarded with a wealth of information about what can be grown and how it should be grown. For example, some soils are generally linked with poor wine quality: podsols, for example, are very ACIDIC, while gley has poor drainage. Others are generally recognized as having great potential: redzinas have good structure and drainage due to their high calcium content. In the United States, the terminology is more logical and easier to understand. American soils have been extensively mapped, and many winegrowers have familiarized themselves with the soils in their vineyards and use the subtle differences to improve the quality of their grapes and wines.

It is also common for vineyard soils to be classified in terms of their texture (see SOIL TEXTURE). All soils considered as sediments are clastic, that is, composed of fragments. If the majority of fragments are pebbles (more than a few millimetres across), the sediment is a conglomerate (which is more common in vineyards than in the countryside in general). If the majority of the soil particles are between 0.05 and 2 mm (0.08 in), then it is SAND; particles between 0.002 and 0.05 mm make up SILT; and particles less than 0.002 mm across constitute CLAY. LOAM is a mixture of clay, silt, and sand. Many soils described as clay are actually relatively rich in silt. However, the distinction between and clay and loam is very

important in viticulture since some notable wines (such as Chx PÉTRUS and d'YQUEM), are produced on clay whereas few are produced on silty soils.

The above classification seems unrelated to the soil's mineral composition, but in general 'clay' as sediment is dominated by clay minerals which have strong powers to absorb water and metallic ions, or charged atoms, the charge allowing metals to go into solution in water (K^+ for POTASSIUM and Ca^{2+} for CALCIUM, for example). Silts and sands are usually dominated by the mineral quartz, which is chemically largely inert. Some sandstones contain significant quantities of feldspars (see Effect on vine nutrition below). The pebbles in conglomerates may also be of quartz, as they are in Châteauneuf-du-Pape, but in vineyards are often lumps of the underlying hard rock such as the limestone in Chablis.

LIMESTONES, in vineyard terms, may be normal rocky limestones or chalk, the first being much more common and its drainage properties rather variable. CHALK is much softer and has better drainage properties, but is rare in vineyards outside CHAMPAGNE and parts of southern ENGLAND. If a soil contains a substantial quantity of fragmented limestone, it can be described as calcareous, or *calcaire* in French, which has often been wrongly translated as chalk in English wine literature. Similarly, the French word *schiste* means SLATE as well as schist, and is sometimes used loosely to mean SHALE, and its direct translation as schist has caused further confusion. (The word 'limy' is sometimes used by writers instead of calcareous, but should more properly be limited to those soils whose PH is greater than about 7.6.)

Effect on temperature

The main effect of geology on soil temperature is related to water-holding capacity (see SOIL WATER). Water has a high specific calorific capacity and heating it requires a considerable amount of energy. Thus dry soils are warmer than wet soils.

In addition, general air temperatures around vines are modified by the TOPOGRAPHY, itself largely a product of geology, in two ways: by controlling the amount of radiant heat from the sun which reaches the grapes; and by varying the quantity of heat reradiated from the ground on to the vines and grapes. The physiological significance of the latter is discussed in CLIMATE AND WINE QUALITY.

In vineyards in which the ground is kept clear of WEEDS and COVER CROPS, the effects of reradiation can be considered in terms of bare soils. The albedos (the diffuse reflectivity) of most soils and rocks are in the range of 0.1 to 0.3. In other words, 10 to 30 per cent of radiation from the sun is reflected back. Sandy soils have higher albedos than clays; dry ground has a higher albedo than damp. Hence a dry, sandy soil reflects back about twice as much radiation as a damp clay.

Rock type	Porosity %	Matrix permeability (mD)	Mass permeability (mD)
Sandstone and conglomerate	20–40 seldom below 5	35–400	50–3,000
Clay and shale	8–20	0.05–0.3	10–10,000
Limestone:			
Regular	less than 5; occasionally up to 25	typically under 0.1	100 but very variable
Chalk	30–45	2–3	30–3,000
Granite	very low	very low	high

Effect on water balance

A balanced supply of water to the vines' roots is needed to produce high-quality wine grapes. The capacities of soils to supply this are discussed under SOIL WATER and SOIL AND WINE QUALITY. Underlying rocks can also play a significant role in vine–water relations because of the exceptional depth reached by some vine roots.

The ideal ground (soil and bedrock) for water balance has a high porosity for storing water; a sufficiently low matrix-permeability to stop it draining away too fast; but a high mass-permeability to ensure good drainage. Permeability is a measure of the ease with which a liquid passes through a sediment. The passage of water from one microscopic pore to another between the particles is known as the matrix permeability. Most rocks and soils are traversed by cracks along which water can flow much more easily. The total possible rate of flow is known as the mass permeability.

Some examples of common vineyard rock types are given in the table above, together with very approximate typical values of porosity in percentages, and permeabilities in millidarcys in fresh rock.

Of the rocks listed in the table, the ideal is chalk. The values given in this table are for fresh rock; in many vineyards there may be a thick cover of weathered and broken-up rock which, for water balance, behaves as an unconsolidated sediment. On the GRANITES of Beaujolais, for example, there are often several metres of material that behave like an unconsolidated sand in terms of both porosity and permeability. And regions which are indicated as limestone on a simple geological map, may actually have sufficient clay interbedded with the limestone or along joint planes to hold adequate supplies of water. Sandstones and conglomerates, which dry out easily, may have lenticular patches out of sight below the surface, with much lower matrix permeabilities which can hold reserves of water during periods of DROUGHT. Examples include the finer sand with its low matrix permeability in the Méric conglomerate of the Médoc, lenticles of silt beneath the conglomerates of the central Torres vineyards in Penedès. Very approximately, permeabilities increase with the square of the grain size, but the subject as a whole is complicated.

Effect on vine nutrition

Even in vineyards with some soil, vine roots usually extend below it into the underlying rock. The mineral composition of the rock as well as the soil affects the nourishment of the vine. Vines do best with the slow but regular supply of potassium ions from the breakdown by weathering of primary potassium-bearing minerals, although no direct correlation can be made between soil content and wine quality. Indeed excess potassium has been shown to have a negative effect on wine quality (see POTASSIUM for further details).

A significant proportion of the world's famous wines are from vineyards whose underlying rock contains potassium feldspar (a group of minerals), or is rich in illite (a clay mineral visible only with an electron microscope). Examples include the feldspar and illite-bearing Méric conglomerate of the Médoc; the potassium feldspar in the granites beneath Beaujolais and Hermitage; the illitic clays within the limestones of the Côte d'Or; the feldspathic sandstones of the Rotliegend formation west of Nierstein in Rheinhessen and some of the grands crus vineyards in Alsace; the muscovite-illite rich phyllites of parts of the Upper Mosel; the feldspar porphyry of Schlossböckelheim in the Nahe; and the alluvial sediments in the Napa valley derived from volcanic and pyroclastic rocks lining the sides of the valley.

For more detail, see SOIL, SOIL AND WINE QUALITY, ROCK, TOPOGRAPHY, TERROIR, and for details of specific soil and rock types, see under their individual names. J.M.H., C.V.L., & K.V.

Bibliographical note: There is a growing body of general literature on the relationships between geology and wine. A pioneering work was by P. Wallace, *International Geological Congress 24* (Canada, 1972) 6, 359–65. A more recent and lavishly illustrated book is C. Pomerol (ed.), *Terroirs et vins de France* (Paris, 1984–6), trans. as *The Wines and Winelands of France* (London, 1989), but, apart from the chapters on Burgundy and Jura, it lacks critical information on geological controls. Much more informative is E. Berry, 'The importance of soil in fine wine production', *Journal of Wine Research*, 1/2 (1990), 179–94. A book with considerable geological detail is H. Enjalbert, *Les Grands Vins de St-Émilion, Pomerol et Fronsac* (Paris, 1983), trans. as *Great Bordeaux Wines* (Paris, 1985). J. Swinchatt and D. Howell published *The Winemaker's Dance* (California, 2004) which argues that the array of wines produced in the Napa valley is due to the

diversity of the underlying geology. An introduction to general geology is H. H. Read and J. Watson, *Introduction to Geology*, i (2ⁿᵈ edn., London, 1970). Simple geological maps are available from national surveys of wine-producing countries.

Van Leeuwen, C., and Chéry, P., 'Quelle méthode pour caractériser et étudier le terroir viticole: analyse de sol, cartographie pédologique ou étude écophysiologique?', in *Un raisin de qualité: de la vigne à la cuve*, n° Hors Série du *Journal International des Sciences de la Vigne et du Vin* (2001), 13–20.

Wilson, J. E., *Terroir* (London, 1998).

Geoponika, a compilation of advice on agriculture put together about AD 950 at the behest of the scholarly Byzantine Emperor Constantine VII Porphyrogenitus, as part of a grand scheme of digests of knowledge. It may have been based on a compilation of some three centuries earlier by Cassianus Bassus. Of the 20 books, the largest section, Books 4–8, consisted of a long list of precepts on viticulture and wine-making. It survives in part. The information is of variable quality. Much can be traced back to the Roman AGRICULTURAL TREATISES but it includes material from authors, particularly of the Hellenistic period, whose work is otherwise unknown to us. J.J.P.

Georgia, independent state of the former Soviet Union between the Black sea and the High Caucasus. One of the world's great and historic centres of both wild and cultivated vines, it contains the Republics of Abkhazeti, Achara (Ajaria), and South Ossetia.

History

See ARMENIA for some details of the important role played by this part of the world in the ORIGINS of viticulture. Wine is integral to the culture of Georgia, a small country whose history is a succession of struggles for independence from such empires as the Assyrian, Roman, Persian, Byzantine, Osmanli, and, latterly, the Soviet Union. Throughout all these struggles, Georgia retains a strong identity, including its own language, customs, Christian religion, and a national reverence for wine which persisted for more than 5,000 years. Archaeology provides ample evidence that viticulture was long an important occupation of the Georgian people and wine drinking an integral part of their culture. Grape seeds, special knives for vine pruning, stone presses, crushers, clay and metallic vessels for wine, and jewellery depicting grape bunches and leaves dating back to between 3000 and 2000 BC have all been unearthed in Mtskheta, Trialeti, Pitsunda, in the Alazan valley, and elsewhere. Rich ornaments of fruited vines are found on the walls of ancient temples in Samtavisi, Ikalto, Zarmza, Gelati, Nikortsminda, and Vardzia. According to Apollonius of Rhodes (3ʳᵈ century BC) the Argonauts in the 14ᵗʰ century BC, having arrived in the capital of Kolkhida-Aia (nowadays Kutaisi), saw twining vines and a fountain of wine in the shade of the trees.

Georgian legends and folklore bear witness to that people's love of the grapevine. Georgia adopted Christianity in the 4th century, and the first cross was made of vines to show that the Christian faith and the vine were the most sacred treasures of the nation.

The Middle Ages were Georgia's golden age of wine. For many centuries, viticulture was of great agricultural and economic importance to the country. In the second half of the 19th century, vineyards covered 71,200 ha/176,000 acres, but FUNGAL DISEASES and PHYLLOXERA had reduced the total vineyard area to 37,400 ha by the beginning of the 20th century. In order to restore vineyards destroyed by phylloxera, the country had to import phylloxera-resistant ROOTSTOCKS.

The 20th century was the era of Soviet wine-making; during this time, a number of Georgian terroirs were identified and developed but quality was routinely, and efficiently, sacrificed for the vast quantities required by the Russian market. GORBACHEV's anti-alcohol campaign of 1985–7 dramatically reduced the market for Georgian wine although it mainly affected the state vineyards since no Georgian farmer would be willing to pull out his own vines. In 1990, the total area of the vineyards was 133,000 ha/279,000 acres. By the collapse of the Soviet Union in the late 1980s, the official total was 85,000 ha. Viticultural investment was sorely needed. By 2005, the total was 70,000 ha, of which almost 10,000 were of very young vines.

Viticulture and vine varieties

Vines in Georgia (unlike those in RUSSIA) do not need WINTER PROTECTION, and new vineyards are planted to grafted seedlings. Vineyards mostly use TRELLIS SYSTEMS and various TRAINING SYSTEMS such as cordon systems, fan-shaped systems with numerous canes, Georgian systems with canes trained in one or two directions, and pergolas.

WILD VINES are widely distributed in Georgia, where *Vitis vinifera silvestris* can still be seen. By both natural and artificial selection, they have given rise to more than 500 identifiable indigenous grape varieties. Thirty-eight grape varieties are officially allowed for commercial viticulture in Georgia including SAPERAVI and RKATSITELI, the two most widely planted varieties, plus Tsolikouri, Tsitska, Chinuri, Goruli Mtsvane, Kakhuri Mtsvane, Odzhaleshi, Orbeluri Odzhaleshi, Aladasturi, Obchuri Dzvelshavi, Aligoté, Pinot Noir, Chardonnay, Cabernet Sauvignon, as well as the following uniquely Georgian high-quality varieties: Usakhelouri, Alexandrouli, Mudzhuretuli, Otskhanuri Sapere, Krakhuna, Chkhaveri, Tetra, and Khikhvi. These last do not yield generously and so were largely ignored in the Soviet era. One of the difficulties Georgia currently faces in exporting wines is that for-eign consumers are so unfamiliar with the flavours of these traditional Georgian grape varieties.

Climate and geography

Georgia's topography and geology are complex. Mountains of the High Caucasus in the north account for about 30 per cent of its total area. The peculiarities of the relief determine a great diversity in the country's soil and climatic conditions, which, in turn, influence grape culture. The climate varies from moderate to subtropical. The annual rainfall is 300 to 600 mm (23 in) in the east and 1,000 to 4,000 mm (156 in) in the west. HAIL is a perennial threat.

Georgia has five viticultural zones: Kakheti, Kartli, Imereti, Racha-Lechkhumi, and the humid subtropical zone.

Kakheti, which grows 70 per cent of Georgia's wine and brandy grapes, is Georgia's richest agricultural land in the south east of the country in the Alazani and Iori valleys. The climate here is moderate, with an active temperature summation of 3,800 to 4,000 °C/6,800 to 7,200 °F and an annual rainfall of 400 to 800 mm (32 in). Cinnamonic forest and calcareous soils, some of them alluvial, are found in the zone.

In terms of mesoclimatic conditions and types of wines produced, Kakheti can be subdivided into three macroregions and more than 25 microregions (Tsinandali, Kvareli-Kindzmarauli, Manavi, Napareuli, Akhmeta, etc.). The most important for wine production include Telavi, Sagaredzho, Gurdzhaani, Kvareli, Akhmeta, and Signagi. The principal grape varieties in Kakheti are Saperavi and Cabernet Sauvignon for reds and Rkatsiteli and Kakhuri Mtsvane for whites. Alongside more modern technologies, these regions produce the distinctive Kakhetian wines, made peculiarly tannic by FERMENTATION in special earthenware jars (*kvevri*—not unlike the *tinajas* of VALDEPEÑAS) followed by an extended MACERATION of three or four months, very much as wines were made thousands of years BC. It is in this region that Georgians and foreign investors have invested most of their hopes for the future of Georgian wine.

Kartli is the heart of Georgia, inspired the original name for the country Sakartvelo, and occupies a vast territory in the Kura valley, the Gori and Mukhran lowlands included. These wines are the most European and the region produces materials for sparkling wines (especially) and brandy that account for 15 per cent of Georgia's wine and brandy production. The zone is moderately warm, with hot and dry summers; vineyards have to be irrigated because of the low rainfall (350 to 500 mm (19 in) per year). Main grape varieties are Chinuri, Goruli Mtsvane, Aligoté, and Chardonnay for whites and Pinot Noir, Tavkveri, and others for reds. The capital of Georgia, Tbilisi, where wineries producing sparkling wines and brandy are located, is in this zone. Tbilisi's oldest winery, founded in 1897, has a unique collection of ancient wines.

Imereti is the 'stomach' of Georgia, its gastronomic capital and keeper of national traditions, not least Georgia's famous hospitality. In the first half of the 19th century, Imereti's capital Kutaisi was the centre of Georgian wine-making and wine-trading. Imereti is in the eastern part of west Georgia, in the basins and in the gullies of Rioni, Kvirila, and other rivers. The most important grape varieties are Tsitska, Tsolikouri, and Krakhuna for whites and Aladasturi, Dzelshavi, Mgaloblishvili, and Otskhanuri Sapere for reds. Nowadays the most important Imereti wine regions are Zestaphoni, Terdzhola, Vani, and Bagdati. As well as modern European methods, Imereti also uses a very particular wine-making technique, similar to Kakheti's except that grape skins (*kvevri*, here called *churi*) are added to the clay jars during fermentation, a little like Italy's GOVERNO, and this is followed by a maceration of six to eight weeks. The vine variety particular to this region is Tzitzka.

Racha-Lechkhumi is Georgia's smallest wine region but one of the country's most important wine-making centres. It consists of two subregions, Ambrolauri and Tsageri, north of Imereti, on the banks of the Rioni and Tskhenistskali rivers. Moderate rainfall (1,000 to 1,300 mm (50 in) a year), southern exposed soils, and the assortment of local vine varieties such as Tetra, Tsitska, Tsolikouri for whites and Alexandrouli, Mudzhuretuli, Usakhelouri, Orbeluri Odzhaleshi, and Saperavi for reds encourage grapes with a sugar content as high as 30 per cent. The region is famous for its natural semi-sweet wines such as Khvanchkara.

The humid subtropical zone is a vast territory which contains Abkhazeti, Achara, Guria, and Samegrelo, all known for both semi-sweet and dry wines.

The future for Georgia

Georgia may lack the modern technology of many countries but has an enviably strong wine culture, national belief in its wines, and no shortage of historically established TERROIR such as Kakheti's Tsinandali, Teliani, Napareuli, Vazisubani, Mukuzani, Akhasheni, Gurdzhaani, Kardenakhi, Tibaani, Kindz-marauli, Manavi, Kvareli, Gremi, Eniseli, and Akhmeta; Imereti's Sviri, Sazano, Obcha, Vani; and Racha-Lechkhumi's Khvanchkara, Tvishi, Okureshi, and Orbeli. Wines from these terroirs are in great demand in modern Russia and other states of the former Soviet Union. Meanwhile, Georgia endeavours in many ways to move closer to Europe.   S.K. & N.C.

Foreigners have invested in the Georgian wine industry since the mid 1990s, and the European Bank for Reconstruction and

Development (EBRD) has provided some funding for this. In particular, the Dutch Royal Cooymans, an affiliated company of PERNOD RICARD, set up Georgian Wines and Spirits in 1994, initially to export Georgia's wines and brandies for bottling in the Netherlands. By 2000, they fully owned the Achinebuli winery in Telavi.   P.H.T.U.

See http://www.gws.ge/eng/company.php for further info;

for EBRD see http://www.ebrd.com/projects/psd/psd1999/6267.htm

Ampelography of the USSR (Moscow, 1946–70).

geranium, pejorative TASTING TERM for the smell of crushed geranium leaves that is given off by wines in which LACTIC ACID BACTERIA have reacted with the fungistat (a chemical that prevents fungi from growing) SORBIC ACID. This geranium smell, which occurs in very varied concentrations and for which the compound 2-ethoxyhexa-3,5-diene is responsible, first appeared in wines during the 1970s, when sorbic acid use became common. Its formation can be prevented by adding SULFUR DIOXIDE at the same time as the sorbic acid to prevent the growth and activity of the lactic acid bacteria responsible.   A.D.W.

German crossings, an important group of VINE VARIETIES that are the result of VINE BREEDING, an activity that was particularly vigorous in the first half of the 20th century but which continues to this day, most notably at GEISENHEIM and GEILWEILERHOF.

The man who bred Germany's first commercially successful modern crossing was in fact Swiss, Dr Hermann Müller (see MÜLLER-THURGAU), whose eponymous vine variety was to become the most planted in Germany in the second half of the 20th century, almost 100 years after it was developed. A succession of new crossings followed in the 20th century, notably from research institutes at Geisenheim, Geilweilerhof, Alzey, Würzburg, and Freiburg, producing a large number of NEW VARIETIES usually designed to achieve the high MUST WEIGHTS encouraged by the GERMAN WINE LAW. The most successful white wine varieties, in descending order of area planted in Germany at the beginning of the 21st century, are KERNER, BACCHUS, SCHEUREBE, FABER(REBE), HUXELREBE, ORTEGA, MORIO-MUSKAT, REICHENSTEINER, EHRENFELSER, SIEGERREBE, OPTIMA, and REGNER. Others include PERLE, NOBLING, WÜRZER, KANZLER, SCHÖNBURGER, FREISAMER, FINDLING, RIESLANER, JUWEL, ALBALONGA, and, more popular in England than Germany, GUTENBORNER and PHOENIX. Few of these crossings make distinctive, attractive, and characterful wines, although Kerner, Ehrenfelser and, particularly, Scheurebe and Rieslaner can make fine wines if sufficiently ripe. More typically, the vines have been planted to yield good quantities of high must weight wines.

Successful German crossings for red wine include DORNFELDER, HEROLDREBE, and

HELFENSTEINER, bred by Dr August Herold in the 1950s, as well as a host of others bred usually for their COLOUR, often using red-fleshed TEINTURIERS, including REGENT, DOMINA, Deckrot, Rotberger, Carmina, Sulmer, and Kolor. RONDO has proved very popular in England.

See also DISEASE-RESISTANT VARIETIES.

German history. This article encompasses the history of wine production not just in GERMANY but also in ALSACE.

The origins of viticulture to AD 800
Although the WILD VINE *Vitis vinifera silvestris* may be traced back to prehistoric times on the upper Rhine, the cultivated, wine-yielding vine species *Vitis* VINIFERA—and with it viticulture in Germany—almost certainly owe their origins to the Romans (see Ancient ROME).

Although archaeological discoveries have unearthed curved pruning knives near the sites of Roman garrisons on the left bank of the Rhine which can be dated to the 1st century AD, we cannot be sure they were used for

vines. Emperor PROBUS (276–82) is traditionally regarded as the founder of viticulture in Germany but firm literary evidence only occurs with the tract *Mosella*, written around 370 by the Roman author Ausonius of Bordeaux, who lyrically describes the steep vineyards on the banks of the river.

Continuity of viticulture is suggested by the use of typically Roman forms of TRELLIS SYSTEMS on low and high frames (*Kammer(t)-*, and *Lauben-* or *Rahmenbau*), which survived in parts of the Palatinate as late as the 18th century. Evidence of wine-growing under the Merovingians can be seen in the pious donations of their kings: Dagobert I (622–88) gave vineyards at Ladenburg on the Neckar (in what is now the most northerly, Oberrhein district of BADEN) to the church of St Peter in Worms. This grant is especially significant, since it offers one of the earliest pointers to vines on the right bank of the Rhine.

Until the era of CHARLEMAGNE, nevertheless, wine-growing was concentrated west of the Rhine: from Alsace down river into the Palatinate (the modern German wine regions

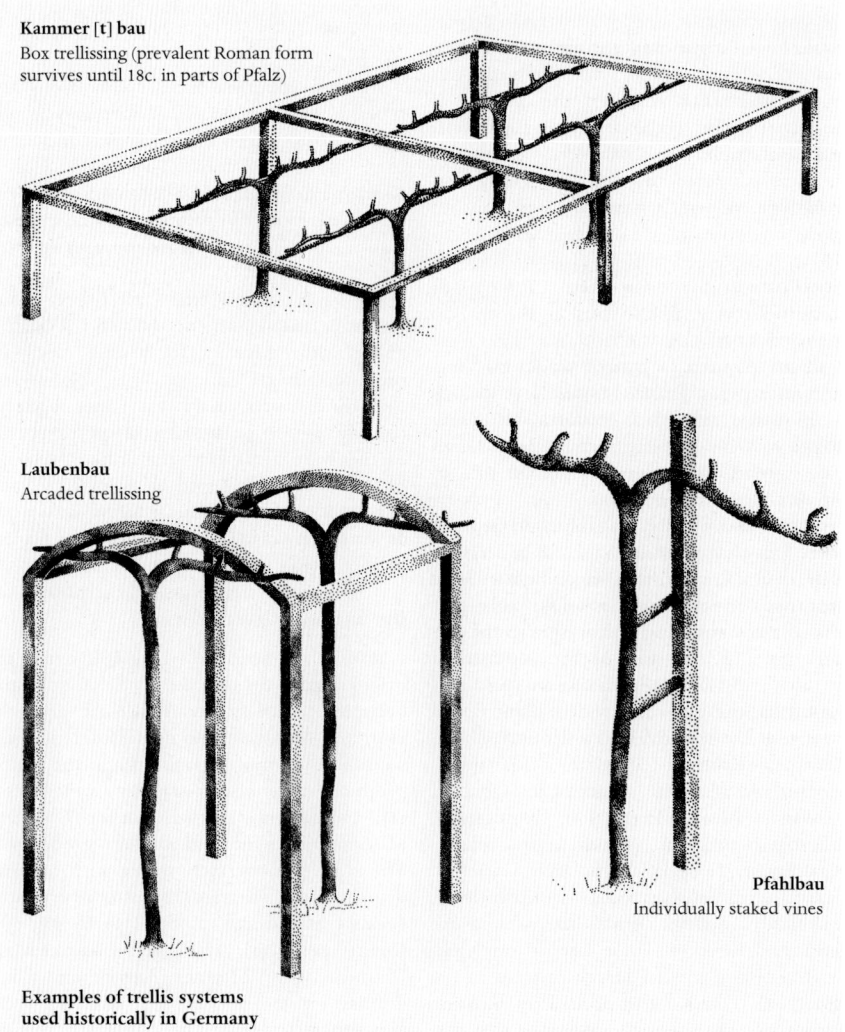

Kammer [t] bau
Box trellissing (prevalent Roman form survives until 18c. in parts of Pfalz)

Laubenbau
Arcaded trellissing

Pfahlbau
Individually staked vines

Examples of trellis systems used historically in Germany

of PFALZ and RHEINHESSEN), and thence downstream along the middle Rhine as far as Koblenz. Wine-growing extended up three left bank tributaries: the NAHE valley down to Bingen, where wine-growing is securely documented from 750; the Mosel (with its own tributaries, the SAAR and RUWER), where the tradition of Roman viticulture was vigorously maintained by monastic foundations such as St Maximin and St Martin in Trier; and the most northerly European wine-growing district, the AHR valley south of Bonn, where vines had been planted on sheltered slopes from at least the 3rd century AD.

East of the Rhine, in the districts beyond the frontier of Roman occupation, the spread of viticulture went hand in hand with the missions of Christian monks such as St Kilian in Franken and St Columban in Bavaria.

Apart from the existence of red wines, cited by the north Italian poet Venantius Fortunatus around 570, next to nothing is known about grape varieties and the quality of wine in this period.   T.S.

Scott, T., 'Medieval viticulture in the German-speaking lands', *German History*, 20 (2002), 95–115.

Viticulture's importance in the Middle Ages
From the foundation of the Carolingian empire, the history of German wine can be traced with greater confidence. CHARLEMAGNE's numerous capitularies (law codes, relating particularly to landholding) contain instructions to his officials to plant vines. His true significance, however, lay in the support he gave to the spread of Christianity, for churches and convents were the principal cultivators and consumers of quality wine (see MONKS AND MONASTERIES).

Many vineyards still famous today originate in monastic settlements of the High Middle Ages. In the RHEINGAU, Archbishop Ruthard of Mainz (1088–1109) founded a Benedictine abbey on the slopes above Geisenheim, the Johannisberg, later known as SCHLOSS JOHANNISBERG. In 1135, his successor, Archbishop Adalbert, gave the Steinberg vineyard above Hattenheim to the Cistercians, whose KLOSTER EBERBACH remains the informal headquarters of the German wine industry to the present. On the river MOSEL, Archbishop Baldwin of Trier founded the Carthusian priory of St Alban in 1335, which was endowed with vineyards at Eitelsbach on the Ruwer, the Karthäuser Hofberg. In FRANKEN (Franconia), too, the bishops of Würzburg actively encouraged viticulture along the river Main.

Elsewhere, secular princes played a leading part, especially in the Palatinate, where the count-electors had promoted Bacharach on the Rhine as the entrepôt for wine from their many territories on both banks of the river.

Although viticulture was dominated by the Church and the aristocracy, bourgeois ownership of vineyards was common, too, either corporately by city councils or by individual merchants and investors.

The rapid expansion of viticulture after the millennium, which only came to a halt in the 16th century, can largely be attributed to the recovery in population and the rise of towns as centres of consumption and exchange: 'a wine landscape is an urban landscape' ran the medieval tag. But the spread of vineyards into the higher valleys, often far from urban centres, can only be explained by the foundation of the new ascetic religious orders, Cistercians and Carthusians, who established their houses from the 12th century at a deliberate distance from civilization. In Alsace, for example, vineyards followed convents into the remote valleys of the Vosges. Apart from the heartlands of medieval viticulture in Alsace, the Palatinate, and the Mosel valley, all of which witnessed the further intake of land for vineyards up to 1500, wine-growing had spread by 1300 to the Rheingau, and throughout BADEN (with vineyards on Lake Constance from the 8th century), WÜRTTEMBERG, and Franken.

By 1500, even the rolling uplands of Swabia and the heavily afforested valleys of northern Franken had been cleared for vines. There viticulture reached its greatest extent in the 15th century, covering perhaps four times the area under vines today (see map of Western Germany and Alsace *c*.1500).

In eastern Germany, the Ottonian emperors promoted viticulture in their Saxon dynastic lands from the late 9th century. Vines were planted on the Elbe around Dresden and Meissen, and on the Saale and Unstrut, especially around Freyburg (see SAALE-UNSTRUT). Even in Brandenburg around Berlin and Jessen, east of Wittenberg, vines were grown on a commercial basis from the 14th to the 16th centuries.

The sites chosen for planting were by no means those on which wines still thrive today. Low-lying level sites were preferred; in Alsace, acknowledged as producing the best wines of medieval Germany, vineyards stretched across the plains from the Ried down to Mulhouse. From the 10th century, vines were at last being planted on slopes in TERRACES, with low walls to prevent SOIL EROSION. The famous slopes

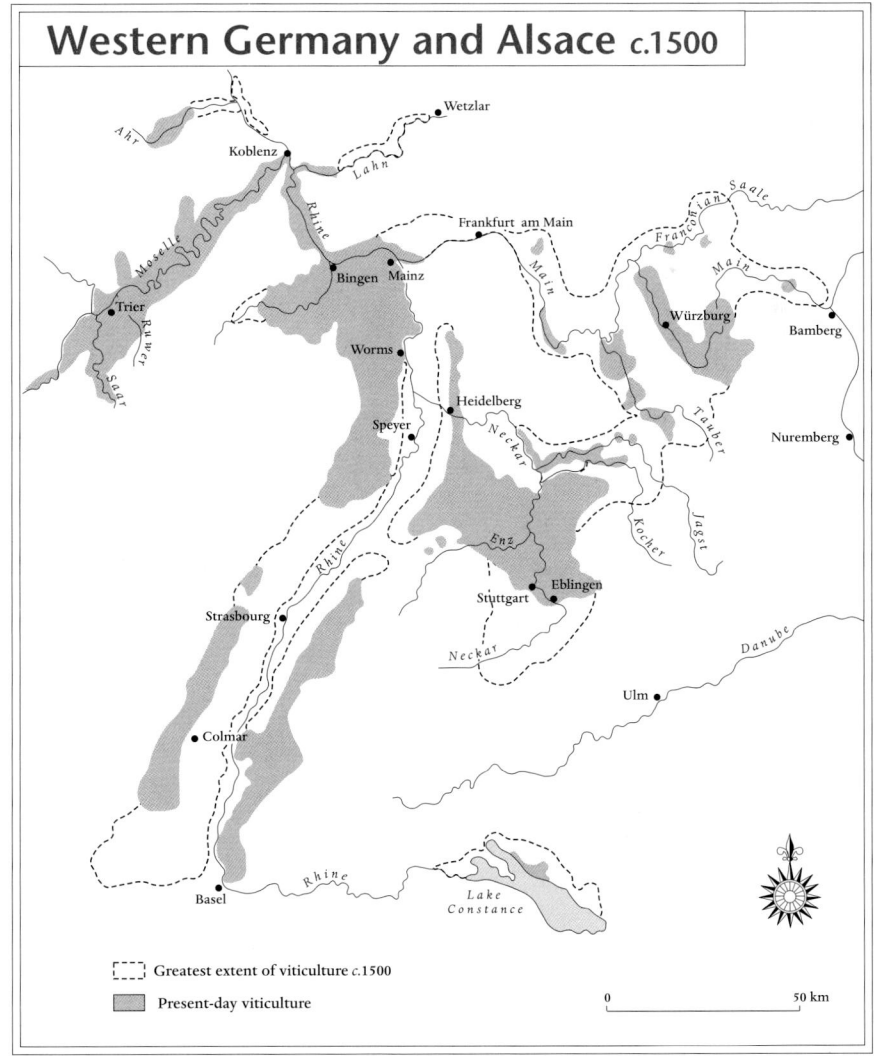

Western Germany and Alsace c.1500

Wetzlar · Koblenz · Frankfurt am Main · Bingen · Mainz · Würzburg · Bamberg · Trier · Worms · Heidelberg · Nuremberg · Speyer · Stuttgart · Eblingen · Strasbourg · Colmar · Ulm · Basel · Lake Constance

Ahr · Lahn · Rhine · Moselle · Ruwer · Saar · Main · Fränkische Saale · Tauber · Neckar · Enz · Kocher · Jagst · Danube · Rhine

☐ ⌐ ⌐ ⌐ Greatest extent of viticulture *c*.1500

▨ Present-day viticulture

0   50 km

of the Rheingau were initially planted in the 11th century: first the Rüdesheimer Berg, then in the 12th century the Johannisberg and Steinberg, with the slopes of Rauenthal not planted until the 13th.

Vine varieties Workaday wine was made everywhere from the ELBLING grape, by far the commonest medieval variety, with RÄUSCHLING widely planted in Baden. SILVANER, too, was extensively grown, but rarely as a high-quality grape in its own right: before 1800 it was normally blended with other varieties. Of the better grapes, MUSCAT (red and white) was grown on the Rhine and in Alsace, TRAMINER chiefly in the latter. RIESLING is first documented at Rüsselsheim on the river Main just east of the modern Rheingau in 1435, though a century earlier a vineyard in Kinzheim in Alsace was known as 'zu dem Russelinge'. The variant orthography of these early references, however, make it difficult to determine whether the Riesling or the Räuschling grape is meant. There is every likelihood that Riesling had been established and recognized as a high-quality grape much earlier than the sources suggest, for in 1477 Duke René of Lorraine, in praising the red and white wines of Alsace, mentioned in particular its Riesling.

In the Middle Ages, many Alsace wines were fortified (see FORTIFICATION) or spiced (see FLAVOURED WINES) in order to compete with the fuller bodied Mediterranean wines such as SACK and MALMSEY. Red wine was made from the Blauburgunder (PINOT NOIR) grape on the upper Rhine in Alsace and Baden (where Affental had already acquired a reputation by 1330). In Württemberg, by contrast, where much of the production, then as now, consisted of light red wines, the TROLLINGER grape already predominated. The Ahr valley may have been planted with red grapes, but they cannot have included the Pinot Noir, which was not introduced there until the 18th century.   T.S.

Scott, T., 'Medieval viticulture in the German-speaking lands', *German History*, 20 (2002), 95–115.

The wine trade in the Middle Ages

Although the quantity of wine harvested in medieval Germany never approached that of France, Italy, or the Iberian peninsula, production on the left bank of the Rhine always exceeded local consumption, so that commerce in wine became an economic necessity. Until the rise of towns, the wine trade was largely in the hands of the Church. Because the best vineyards lay along the Rhine and its tributaries, shipments of wine could pass easily down one of the great arteries of European trade to northern Germany, the Low Countries, Scandinavia, and England. Ease of transport, however, was offset by the numerous tolls which local lords levied on cargoes shipped down the Rhine.

Cologne and Frankfurt dominated Germany's medieval wine trade, a point tellingly illustrated by the decision of Kloster Eberbach, the important abbey in the rural depths of the Rheingau, to acquire its own cellars in Cologne in 1162 and in Frankfurt 50 years later. But their pattern of trade differed.

Throughout the Middle Ages, Cologne's trade with the Baltic, Scandinavia, and England was far more extensive than Frankfurt's. The city's wine trade reached its peak in the late 14th and early 15th centuries. Cologne continued to play a major role in the export of the best German wines, but its trading area was increasingly exposed to the rise of BEER as the everyday drink of northern Germany. It was Frankfurt's merchants who increasingly specialized in Alsace wines, although their popularity was challenged during the 15th century by wines from the Palatinate and the Rheingau.

Although German wines were firmly established in northern Europe during the Middle Ages, there were limits to their share of the market. In the southern Low Countries 'Rhine wine' was consumed, but it had to compete with the heavier wines of Burgundy, Auxerre, and also Bordeaux. In England, too, German wines faced a stiff challenge from France, as the trade with Gascony flourished from the 12th century. But German wine was not confined to northern markets. Alsace wines were extensively exported to southern Germany, Switzerland, and central Europe.   T.S.

Scott, T., 'Medieval viticulture in the German-speaking lands', *German History*, 20 (2002), 95–115.

Crisis and decline, 1500–1650

The Thirty Years War, which ravaged Germany in the early 17th century, left few viticultural regions unscathed, but the real problem arose from the loss of manpower through the casualties of war. The decline in exports of ALSACE wines is symptomatic of the difficulties. Wine consumption was dictated by FASHION, and by 1500 taste was moving away from the often spiced (see FLAVOURED WINES) white wines of Alsace towards those of the PALATINATE and the RHEINGAU, as well as to the lighter wines of FRANKEN. At the same time, demand for heavier red wines was increasing, so that Alsace found itself having to plant more PINOT NOIR vines together with 'Lampersch' (a red wine variety from Lombardia in Italy) to compete with imports from France and the Mediterranean.

The excessive expansion of vineyards up to 1500 brought about a slump in the land market by 1540, with a consequent collapse in the price of wine, much of it in any case of dismal quality, having been grown on sites quite unsuitable for viticulture.

It is no coincidence that the widespread agrarian rebellion of 1525 known as the German Peasants' War was concentrated in the wine-growing areas, where the peasantry had been exposed to the fluctuations of the market, demands by lords for higher taxes on its crop,

and the need to subdivide holdings into unprofitably small parcels by the laws of partible inheritance (see BURGUNDY, history), and yet was compelled to cling to its foothold in commercialized viticulture for want of alternative employment.

Throughout the century, viticulture retreated from the cooler, more remote valleys; poor-quality vineyards in the plains were abandoned in favour of slopes with better exposure and drainage. As the century wore on, the demand for grain for bread and brewing swelled, so that corn prices outstripped wine prices, and much land reverted to tillage. Nevertheless, on the eve of the Thirty Years War around 350,000 ha/865,000 acres of land in Germany were still under vines, over four times the extent of viticulture today. The 16th century also saw greater emphasis on better-quality white varieties.

A first classification Although the use of individual site names to distinguish quality (as opposed merely to identifying different vineyards) was largely unknown before 1800, there is one striking instance of ranking by quality in this period. In 1644 the council of Würzburg in FRANKEN classified the city's vineyards into four groups.   T.S.

Bibliographical note: There is no reliable survey in English. Readers of German may consult F. von Bassermann-Jordan, *Geschichte des Weinbaus*, 3 vols. in 2 (4th edn, Landau, 1991); R. Weinhold, 'Winzerarbeit an Elbe, Saale und Unstrut', *Akademie der Wissenschaften der DDR. Zentralinstitut für Geschichte: Veröffentlichungen zur Volkskunde und Kulturgeschichte*, 55 (Berlin, 1973); K. H. Schröder, 'Weinbau und Siedlung in Württemberg', *Forschungen der deutschen Landerkunde*, 73 (Remagen, 1953).

Recovery and improvement, 1650–1800

The recovery of German viticulture after the depredations of the Thirty Years War was slow and painful. Only FRANKEN (Franconia), which had been the scene of fierce fighting in the 1630s, experienced a swift recuperation in vineyards and wine prices in the 1650s. In the PALATINATE, viticulture was not fully restored until the 1710s. There many growers, despairing of making a decent living, emigrated to America in the early 18th century. The region was further afflicted by the wars of Louis XIV of France from 1674 to 1700, as indeed were districts on the left bank of the Rhine as a whole, including the MOSEL.

The vineyards of BADEN and WÜRTTEMBERG, which had suffered least the previous century, may have declined by as much as 80 per cent by the end of the 18th century. In ALSACE, however, the loss of manpower was partly compensated for by policies to encourage immigration from France, Lorraine, and Switzerland.

Efforts to improve viticulture from the late 17th century onwards pursued a double strategy: to encourage the planting of better-quality grape varieties, often on selected new sites, while at the same time prohibiting the clearing of land for vines where only poor quality could be expected. In what is now the MOSEL-SAAR-RUWER, for instance, the Abbey of St Maximin had been replanting at Grünhaus on the RUWER since 1695; as many as 100,000 new cuttings, it has been reckoned, were put down. But at the other end of the scale, more land was constantly being taken in by small growers, so that the prince-archbishops of Trier issued an edict in 1720 banning the clearing of forest for new vineyards.

In 1750, another decree enjoined the production of natural, unsugared ('naturrein') wines, and in 1786 the last archbishop-elector, Clemens Wenceslas (r. 1768–1801), a keen champion of viticulture, ordered that inferior grapes be grubbed up and replaced with the RIESLING vine. At Bingen, the archbishop of Mainz decreed in 1697 that the famous Scharlachberg ('scarlet slope', perhaps because it once grew red wines) be planted exclusively with Riesling.

Likewise in the Rheingau, Constantine, prince-abbot of the ancient Hessian convent of Fulda, which had acquired the site and castle of Johannisberg (see SCHLOSS JOHANNISBERG), ordered the replanting of the vineyards with Riesling and 'Orléans' vines in the 1760s. In this period, the sources begin to distinguish the quality of Rhine wines according to village or, on occasion, site.

Vine varieties In Alsace, improvement owed nothing to the French crown, everything to local initiatives by institutions such as the Jesuit College at Sélestat, which began to plant Riesling in 1756 in place of lesser vines. Alsace saw the development of two new varieties in the 18th century. In 1756, Johann Michael Ortlieb of Riquewihr pioneered an early-ripening clone of RÄUSCHLING, the Kleiner (small) Räuschling (also known as Ortlieber or, in Alsace, as KNIPPERLÉ). In 1740, the mayor of Heiligenstein by Barr, Erhard Wantz, introduced a new variety under the name of KLEVENER.

In much of southern Germany, Silvaner was displacing ELBLING, but the real innovation was the development of PINOT GRIS by Johann Seger Ruland in Speyer around 1711. It has nothing to do with the Hungarian wine TOKAJI. Although it spread quickly, the Ruländer suffered a rapid decline because its early ripening meant that its harvest could not be held back until the later maturing Riesling, so that peasant growers preferred to let it rot rather than gather it early only to have to deliver up a fine wine as a tithe to their feudal lords. Not until tithing was abolished in the wake of the French Revolution did Ruländer establish its rightful place among German wines of distinction.

The 17th and 18th centuries also saw the first attempts to make specially selected or late-picked wines. The term CABINET to indicate a wine of reserve quality is first encountered at Kloster Eberbach in the Rheingau in 1712. The picking of individual ripe berries off the stalks (*Abrappen*) was also deployed, particularly with Traminer grapes, to make what were in effect AUSLESEN, although the wines were relatively short lived. Nevertheless, the potential of picking grapes affected by NOBLE ROT was well recognized by the early 18th century.

Despite these advances, the period up to 1800 was a troubled one for German wine in export markets. Cologne and Frankfurt maintained their leading role in overseas trade, and the 18th century witnessed the first wine AUCTIONS of quality wines. Cologne's merchants were proud of their adherence to the oenological equivalent of the brewing purity laws (*Reinheitsgebot*), which forbade blending Rhine wines with those from the south, especially France and Italy. Yet their stranglehold on the market in Rhenish wines was challenged in the 1670s when English merchants began to buy at source. T.S.

> Bibliographical note: There is no reliable survey in English. For readers of German, Bassermann-Jordan, cited above, remains an indispensable guide but some information may be gleaned from O. W. Loeb and T. Prittie, *Moselle* (London, 1972).

The rise of modern viticulture, 1800–1900

The French Revolution and its aftermath wrought profound changes in German viticulture. During the Revolution itself, the PALATINATE was invaded and occupied, although in the succeeding Napoleonic Wars it was barely affected. The whole of Germany on the left bank of the Rhine was ceded to France, which proceeded to reorganize the region's administration into four departments.

On the MOSEL, these political upheavals led to around one-fifth of the vineyards, many of them owned by the Church, changing hands, and once the estates of the empire had agreed upon the abolition of all ecclesiastical principalities at the diet of Regensburg in 1803, another 25 per cent came under new ownership.

Although after the fall of Napoleon the Church regained some of its estates, a new and substantial class of peasant and bourgeois vineyard proprietors had been created. On the right bank of the Rhine in the RHEINGAU, Johannisberg (see SCHLOSS JOHANNISBERG) passed through several hands, including Napoleon's general Marshal Kellermann, before it fell to Austria at the Congress of Vienna in 1815 and was bestowed upon the then Foreign Minister Prince Metternich, in whose family it still remains. On the Main, the estates of the prince-bishops of Würzburg in FRANKEN, or Franconia, were acquired after a short interlude by the Bavarian crown in 1816.

In ALSACE, however, the repercussions of the Revolution were quite different. Once it had become part of the French customs area, growers hastened to increase production in order to capitalize upon a huge internal market. The result was the renewed planting of inferior vine varieties on low-lying sites. Moreover, the imposition by France of tolls on foreign wines hurt Alsace in particular, since it elicited reprisals from Baden, Württemberg, and Switzerland, all still important customers for Alsace wines.

At the Congress of Vienna, the political map of Germany was redrawn. The Mosel became a province of Prussia; RHEINHESSEN (west of the Rhine) was absorbed into the grand duchy of Hesse-Darmstadt; the Rheingau fell to the dukes of Nassau; and what remained of the Palatinate, the Pfalz proper, was reunited with Bavaria. From 1805/6 Saxony (see SACHSEN) and WÜRTTEMBERG had been elevated to kingdoms, BADEN to a grand duchy. The regulation of customs dues between these independent states became a matter of urgent necessity.

When Bavaria and Württemberg joined Prussia to create the general customs union (Zollverein) of 1834, followed by Baden and Hesse-Darmstadt the next year, all the major wine-growing districts were in open competition with each other. As a result, the better wines prevailed, and the market in lesser wines collapsed, although at least the Zollverein enabled German wines to compete on more favourable terms in the domestic market with French wines, especially those from BORDEAUX, which had begun to reach the north German cities in huge quantities in the 1820s. Baden and Württemberg were the worst hit by the new competition. In Baden the tithe was abolished in 1833, but the area under cultivation constantly receded, and many vignerons emigrated to ALGERIA or VENEZUELA.

The development of the transport network, above all the RAILWAYS, allowed rapid and easy distribution of the better wines from the more favoured regions, so that Württemberg's production declined by 40 per cent in the 19th century. Franken, too, suffered because of Bavaria's link with the Palatinate; the area under vines shrank by 60 per cent between 1850 and 1900.

Only the foundation of the German empire in 1871, however, put an end to all internal customs barriers. Yet the reabsorption of Alsace and Lorraine in that year brought little relief to wine-growers there. Alsace may have constituted 26 per cent of German vineyards yielding 39 per cent of production after 1871, but its wines were threatened by imports of cheap wines from France, sweetened wines from across the Rhine, and preferential trade treaties signed by Germany with Austria and Italy in 1891 and with Spain in 1893.

Quality in the ascendant Quality of production became the central concern of German vinegrowers and administrators after 1800. The beginnings of quality DELIMITATION can be traced to the 1830s. Wine ordinances in the German states began to prescribe that grapes of different levels of ripeness should be harvested separately. Their measurement was greatly facilitated by systems for weighing the must to achieve a specific MUST WEIGHT, refined in the 1830s by the Pforzheim physicist Ferdinand OECHSLE, whose system is still in use today.

Growers' associations for the improvement of wines and viticulture were founded in many German territories. The state authorities, moreover, played a vital role by establishing schools of viticultural research and teaching. Württemberg was the pioneer in 1860 with its academy at Weinsberg, followed by Prussia's establishment of the institute at GEISENHEIM in 1870, after it had annexed the Rheingau from Nassau in 1867. The Hessian wine academy at Oppenheim dates from 1885; in 1899 citizens of Neustadt an der Weinstrasse founded a wine school to serve the Palatinate; and the Nahe acquired a Prussian academy in 1902. These endeavours were underpinned by the creation of state domaines. The earliest was set up by Baden at Meersburg on Lake Constance in 1802, followed shortly thereafter by the Bavarian state domaine in Würzburg. After its acquisition of Nassau, Prussia formed a state domaine at Eberbach, the Kloster Eberbach, from its abbatial estates throughout the Rheingau. At the end of the century, Prussia established further state domaines: on the Moselle at Avelsbach in 1896, with estates on the Saar at Ockfen, and on the Nahe at Niederhausen in 1902.

The emphasis on quality, however, placed the smaller peasant growers in a quandary. Without the capital to invest in better vines and wine-making equipment, they were left with inferior grape varieties on poorer sites in a shrinking market. The only solution, albeit imperfect, was to seek safety in numbers by banding together in CO-OPERATIVES. The first such growers' union was formally established on the river AHR in 1869.

Towards the end of the century, viticulture fell victim to Germany's late industrialization, which sucked LABOUR into the cities. In terms of marketing, the industry was torn between the lure of the controlled addition of sugar, pioneered by the chemist Ludwig Gall (the German counterpart to Jean CHAPTAL in France), which helped to make thin, sour wines from sun-starved soils saleable (see CHAPTALIZATION), and the reputation which attached to untreated, 'naturrein' wines. The first national Wine Law of 1892 had permitted controlled sugaring, but the Imperial Wine Law of 1909 restricted sugaring to 20 per cent of the undiluted wine.

One answer was to turn the more acidic vintages into sparkling wine, known in German as SEKT With some good vintages in the 1860s, Sekt had become a highly popular drink in Germany by the late 19ᵗʰ century.

The true threat to German viticulture, however, lay in VINE PESTS and VINE DISEASES— DOWNY MILDEW in particular and the PHYLLOXERA louse (*Reblaus* in German), which first appeared in German vineyards in the Ahr valley in 1881.   T.S.

The 20ᵗʰ-century wine industry

The first half of the 20ᵗʰ century was a period of deep recession in the German wine industry. The area under vines shrank still further, from around 90,000 ha/220,000 acres in 1914 to less than 50,000 ha/123,000 acres in 1945. Both World Wars placed severe strains on Germany's domestic economy and caused considerable dislocation in its export markets. Exports had reached a peak of 190,000 hl/5 million gal by 1914, but in the aftermath of the First World War the situation was bleak.

The major growing regions on the left bank of the Rhine were occupied by France until 1929. In the PFALZ region, moreover, the activities of separatist groups severely disrupted civilian life up to 1924, which hit the wine industry in particular. The raging inflation of the Weimar period brought economic hardship to many growers, especially the smaller proprietors. A flood of imports from France and Luxembourg, as specified by the Versailles Treaty, undercut the prices which German producers could charge; many growers faced bankruptcy, and by 1928 exports had collapsed to no more than 39,000 hl/1 million gal per annum.

The Nazi era helped to revive domestic consumption of German wine, but the National Socialist policy of subordinating all private associations to state control (*Gleichschaltung*) meant, for the wine industry, that all independent professional bodies were abolished and replaced by a single Union of Viticulture under one president, thereby destroying the enterprise and initiative of individual growers and regional wine associations. The end of the Second World War heralded the return of some of the consequences of the First. German growers faced a shortage of labour but an abundance of cheap imports from France, Algeria, and Hungary. In their zone of occupation in the Pfalz, the French requisitioned wine on a grand scale. They retained control of the Saar until it was returned to Germany by plebiscite in 1956.

The parlous state of exports in the 1930s persuaded some merchants, principally those trading to the United Kingdom, to try to increase sales by marketing BRANDS, which could contain more than one grape variety, were sourced from more than one region of production, and were usually sweetened. This is the origin of LIEBFRAUMILCH.

Undoubtedly the most significant step forward for German viticulture in the first half of the century was the Wine Law of 1930, which went far towards rectifying the deficiencies of the 1909 law. It provided a clear definition of what constituted a natural, as opposed to a sweetened, wine, forbade the blending of red and white, and of German and foreign, wines, and outlawed the planting and sale of wines made from HYBRIDS.

Viticulture Between 1950 and 1990 German viticulture underwent a dramatic transform-

ation. The area under vine once again expanded steadily, and by 1997 was well over 100,000 ha/250,000 acres. But the most startling development was the increase in YIELDS. At the beginning of the century the average of 20 hl/ha (1.1 tons/acre) was no more than what might have been expected of an abundant vintage in any preceding century. By 1950 that had doubled to 40 hl/ha, and by the 1980s frequently exceeded 100 hl/ha (5.7 tons/acre), although today's more discriminating growers cropped less heavily.

From the 1950s there was a radical restructuring of German vineyards, known as FLURBEREINIGUNG. The number of individual sites has been substantially pruned, and since the GERMAN WINE LAW of 1971 a new vineyard register has been compiled and average wine quality has improved immensely. Despite these advances, the outlook for German wines is still uncertain while they remain largely unfashionable.   T.S.

Hallgarten, S. F., *German Wine* (London, 1976).
Langenbach, A., *German Wines and Vines* (London, 1962).
Loeb, O. W., and Prittie, T., *Moselle* (London, 1972).
Pigott, S., *The Mosel and Rheingau, including the Ahr, Nahe and Pfalz* (London, 1997).

German Wine Law was until recently a source of pride for German wine producers. In its fifth generation, however, it was an animal bred with particular care in 1971 that grew fairly rapidly into a monster which many of the best wine producers in GERMANY have since done their best to amend or ignore. The German Wine Law of 1971 substantially updated the 1930 Wine Law (see GERMAN HISTORY), particularly in vineyard rationalization, and was precipitated by the demands of the EUROPEAN UNION wine regime. Compared with the anarchic chaos of Italy's wine-labelling habits, and the convoluted geography of France's APPELLATION CONTRÔLÉE (AC) system, the German Wine Law of 1971 was a marvel of precision. Each vineyard is delineated and registered (see EINZELLAGE) and its produce can be used to make wine at any quality level, depending not on YIELDS but on the ripeness, or MUST WEIGHT, of the grapes.

The least ripe grapes qualify as Deutscher TAFELWEIN, or table wine, which in the mid 2000s represented just 3 per cent of all wine produced in a typical German vintage (and averaged less than 1 per cent in the period 1988–97). All the rest is graded as QUALITY WINE according to the generous terms of the German Wine Law, and in EU terms is therefore seen as the equal of France's AC wine. German officials make much of the fact that every quality wine is analysed and tasted and has to earn its AP NUMBER, but the failure rate is so low as to cast doubt on this highly bureaucratic 'control'.

The bottom layer of Germany's quality wine is made from grapes whose ripeness qualifies for QBA status, a 'quality wine from a specified region'. This is the category under which most German wine is usually sold. Wines made from riper grapes, however, are qualified as QMP, 'quality wine with distinction': the riper the grapes, the higher the official PRÄDIKAT or distinction (and selling price), rising from KABINETT through SPÄTLESE, AUSLESE, BEERENAUSLESE, TROCKENBEERENAUSLESE, to EISWEIN. This category varies tremendously according to the weather. A mere 7 per cent of the 1984 harvest qualified for QmP status, while in the exceptional vintages of 1976 and 2003 the proportion was 83 and 64 per cent respectively. The ten-year average for 1994–2003 is over 49 per cent and reflects a remarkable series of ripe VINTAGES. This emphasis on must weights was understandable in a country where the perennial challenge is to ripen grapes fully, but did little to encourage real quality and harmony in Germany's wines (see GERMANY and GERMAN HISTORY). Many quality-conscious producers themselves declassify wines from one Prädikat to a lower one, or from QmP to QbA, because the wine does not reach their own personal evaluation of what constitutes, say, an Auslese.

The German Wine Law has been substantially amended since 1971. The little-used LANDWEIN category was introduced in 1982 as a German answer to France's VIN DE PAYS, and at about the same time Eiswein, with its entirely different production technique, was admitted as a Prädikat in its own right alongside Beerenauslese and Trockenbeerenauslese.

In 1989, the German parliament agreed to comply with EU regulations to limit yields, but a measure of how much progress was still to be made was that the maximum yield proposed for the noble RIESLING vine in the supposedly noble wine region MOSEL-SAAR-RUWER was 120 hl/ha (6.8 tons/acre) (more for other grape varieties).

During 1993, much more stringent amendments were proposed, for enactment in time for the 1994 vintage. The maximum permitted yields are to be calculated for each grower strictly on the basis of the actual area in production rather than, as in the past in some regions, on the basis of the area owned, and were instituted for QbA wines at no more than average production for the previous ten years. There are additional controls on SURPLUS wine and greater enforcement of compulsory DISTILLATION, although individual growers can elect to produce nothing but Deutscher Tafelwein, in which case there are no yield controls other than those imposed directly by EU authorities. Impatient with the lack of legal progress in yield reduction, the prestigious VDP growers' association successfully instituted reasonably stringent limitations for their members.

More significantly, the minimum MUST WEIGHTS required for various Prädikats in the Ahr, Mittelrhein, Mosel-Saar-Ruwer, Saale-Unstrut, and Sachsen were raised, and

there were moves, albeit limited, to substitute a much clearer labelling system whereby the consumer could tell at a glance whether a wine comes from a single site or Einzellage, or a collective site signalled on the label either as one of the old GROSSLAGEN, or as one of the newer URSPRUNGSLAGEN.

Two new legal categories of wine quality, CLASSIC and SELECTION (both spelt with a *c* even in Germany) were introduced in 2000, with more fanfare in the German market than abroad. The intention was to set qualitative standards for dry-styled wines utilizing only regionally typical varieties. Unlike Prädikat wines, these may be CHAPTALIZED and the RESIDUAL SUGAR can exceed the threshold for TROCKEN. In the case of Selection, however, YIELDS are more stringent (60 hl/ha maximum) and MECHANICAL HARVESTING is outlawed.   I.J. & D.S.

Germany,

Germany, the most distinctive major wine producer in Europe with both wines and problems quite unlike those of anywhere else. Grape growing in Germany is a small but prestigious part of the whole country's farming industry. Germany's expected 2004 crop of 10.5 million hl/277 gal from about 100,000 ha/ 247,000 acres make her Europe's fourth biggest wine producer. Unlike France and Italy, however, Germany makes about as much wine as she consumes, while also being the largest importer of wine in the EU. The financial turnover represented by wine is a little greater than that of cut flowers or eggs, but considerably less than the figure for sugar beet. Whilst a small part of the grape harvest results in wines of exquisite finesse, unique in style to Germany, over half the crop is sold on price, and not on quality. There are individual vineyard sites, EINZELLAGEN, in the majority of which high-quality grapes can be harvested from traditional vine varieties nearly every year, but the trail that leads to the best German wines is discovered most easily through the name of the producer. In the relatively cool weather of northern Europe (see CONTINENTALITY), the cheapest wines can be made according to a more or less unchanging recipe, but producing fine wines in Germany requires not only a good site and technical ability, but also imagination and a dedication to excellence. Most unfortunately, undistinguished bulk wines have since the 1970s routinely been allowed to benefit from both the GERMAN WINE LAW and the reputations of top-flight vineyards, thus threatening to debase both.

History
See GERMAN HISTORY.

Geography and climate
Over the centuries, the German vineyard has expanded and contracted, often in response to the price and availability of grain. See GERMAN HISTORY and map there. Many of Germany's

best vineyards are on the steepest slopes, quite unsuited to anything other than the vine. Overlooking the rivers RHINE, Neckar, Main, Nahe, Ahr, MOSEL and its tributaries, their high cost of cultivation is justified only by the quality of the wine they can produce. In the steep vineyards, three times as many man-hours are spent tending the vine as is the case on flat or gently sloping terrain, where the natural position of the vine-grower is on the seat of a tractor.

Several other factors limit MECHANIZATION in the vineyards, amongst which are the smallness of the holdings and the tradition of selective harvest. Vine-growing in Germany was once the work of peasants, controlled by the Church and the nobility. Statistically, it has now become a mainly female, mainly part-time occupation, based on an average holding of 1.3 ha/ 3.2 acres. In the 21st century, picking is generally done by 'guest workers' from eastern and southern Europe, among whom Poles are preeminent. Most German growers do not make wine but supply grapes to merchants or, more likely, to the CO-OPERATIVE cellars which receive the crop from about 30 per cent of the total German vineyard. For more geographical detail, see map of Germany and Alsace overleaf; see also entries under the names of individual wine regions which are, in declining area of total vineyard, RHEINHESSEN, PFALZ, BADEN, MOSEL-SAAR-RUWER, WÜRTTEMBERG, FRANKEN, NAHE, RHEINGAU, MITTELRHEIN, SAALE-UNSTRUT, AHR, HESSISCHE BERGSTRASSE, and SACHSEN. Most German wine labels carry the name of the region in which the wine was produced.

Viticulture
The vine-growing regions of the EUROPEAN UNION are divided into climatically different zones. In Germany, Baden shares Zone B with a number of French regions including Alsace, Champagne, and the Loire valley. Although the remaining German regions are all in Zone A, their MACROCLIMATES and MESO-CLIMATES are perhaps the most varied of all the world's vineyards. Mesoclimatic variations within a single site or EINZELLAGE can result in simultaneous pickings of the same variety which exhibit significant differences in potential alcohol and flavour. According to research at GEISENHEIM, the average alcohol content of wine of the same vineyard can vary from one vintage to another by over 6 per cent. The degree of LATITUDE, TOPOGRAPHICAL features such as a favourable exposition to the sun, shelter from frequent cold winds or damaging FROSTS, and the ALTITUDE are some of the factors which dramatically influence the quality of its viticulture.

Some 7 per cent of Germany's vines are individually supported by POSTS, a system followed mainly in the Mosel-Saar-Ruwer region where tight spacing between vines on steep slopes is the norm. Elsewhere, they are trained

Germany and Alsace

BELGIUM

LUXEMBOURG

FRANCE

SWITZERLAND

AUSTRIA

Bonn

AHR

Ahr

Rhine

MITTELRHEIN

Lahn

Koblenz

Mosel

Cochem

MOSEL-SAAR-RUWER

Zell

Wehlen

Piesport

Bernkastel

Ruwer

Trier

Saarburg

Saar

Nahe

NAHE

Bad Kreuznach

Lorchhausen

MITTELRHEIN

Wiesbaden

Frankfurt

RHEINGAU

Rüdesheim

Bingen

Johannisberg

Mainz

Hochheim

Geisenheim

Nierstein

Oppenheim

Worms

RHEINHESSEN

HESSISCHE BERGSTRASSE

Main

FRANKEN

Würzburg

Tauber

Neckar

Heidelberg

Neustadt

PFALZ

WÜRTTEMBERG

Stuttgart

Baden-Baden

Black Forest

Strasbourg

Barr

Ribeauvillé

Sélestat

Riquewihr

Turckheim

Colmar

Eguisheim

Breisach

BADEN

Offenburg

Kaiserstuhl

Freiburg

Thann

A L S A C E

Rhine

Rhine

Bodensee

A

SAALE-UNSTRUT

Saale

Unstrut

Naümbürg

B

Elbe

SACHSEN

Dresden

A   B

Germany

310

Wine-growing regions

0 _____ 50 km

on WIRES in rows, often with wide spacing. Nearly 5 per cent of all vines grow on their own roots, without having been grafted on to resistant ROOTSTOCKS. Partly through the replanting involved in modernization programmes (see FLURBEREINIGUNG), only 18 per cent of the vines at the start of the 1990s were over 20 years old. Among growers whose aim is to produce top-quality fruit, PRUNING is usually to six to eight buds per square metre, depending on the variety. To produce a more concentrated must, excess bunches of grapes are removed in the months following the FLOWERING in June (see CROP THINNING). The aim in VINE TRAINING in recent decades has been not just to harvest healthy grapes, but sometimes also to reduce costs by facilitating MECHANICAL PRUNING and MECHANICAL HARVESTING.

Except in instances of unusually cool or hot summers, ripeness—particularly of Riesling—varies from one bunch to another as well as within the cluster. For 200 years, German vintners have practised the selective picking of individual clusters, or occasionally even individual grapes, at the moment when they have reached a desired condition of ripeness. Frequently, this involves the segregation of grapes influenced by BOTRYTIS so as to achieve rot-free dry wines and nobly rotten sweet wines. This process of selection (literally AUSLESE) cannot be other than the most manual of labour, quite beyond the scope of a mechanical harvester. On a good estate, wines from these chosen grapes are individually vinified, matured, and bottled, to form the higher-priced echelon of a year's collection. The scrupulous attention to viticultural issues—increasingly including environmental awareness (see SUSTAINABLE VITICULTURE)—and rigour of selection exercised at harvest by leading German vintners since the 1980s has played a significant role in improving quality and minimizing the number of vintages in which Riesling fails to ripen adequately. In addition, Nature itself contributed an utterly unprecedented sequence of warm growing seasons from 1988 to 2003.

Wine-making

The aim of good, modern German WINE-MAKING is wine that is true to its region and vine variety. At smaller estates, more care and individual attention can be given to wine-making than is possible in much larger establishments. PRESSES are set to work at not more than two atmospheres and must SETTLING in many cellars is left to the gentle force of gravity. An increasing number of vintners favour spontaneous fermentation with ambient YEASTS or the propagation of yeast cultures specific to their vineyards, as opposed to inoculation with commercial strains. Temperature during white wine FERMENTATION is often kept below 20 °C/68 °F. SKIN CONTACT during fermentation has traditionally been associated exclusively with the production of red wines,

but in recent years many quality-conscious German vintners have experimented successfully with brief pre-fermentative skin contact for whites. The significance of extended LEES CONTACT of young white wines has been increasingly appreciated by Germany's vintners as has the general rule to minimize pumping or otherwise handling the young wine. While Germany has been a leader in wine-making technology as well as viticultural research—the GEISENHEIM Institute, for example, has had enormous international influence—a movement toward minimal intervention and rediscovering traditional methods is a significant part of today's German wine scene.

The use of SÜSSRESERVE or unfermented grape juice to sweeten wine is no longer so common in the cellars of private estates as it was in the 1970s and 1980s. If their wines have a little RESIDUAL SUGAR, it is often the result of low cellar temperatures, judicious application of SULFUR, and STERILE BOTTLING FILTRATION to arrest fermentation. Great sweetness and finesse combine in AUSLESE, BEERENAUSLESE, and TROCKENBEERENAUSLESE wines produced from grapes that have been attacked by *Botrytis cinerea* that has developed into NOBLE ROT. Such grapes may be gathered at any time during the harvest, and are nowadays as likely to result from early, selective picking as from picking late. (In 1989, the PFALZ estate of Bürklin-Wolf gathered a Riesling Trockenbeerenauslese as early as 27 September.) A similar sweetness, though usually without the flavour or complexity of noble rot, is achieved by gathering grapes when they are frozen on the vine, to produce EISWEIN. The artificial freezing of grapes or wine (for example, the CRYOEXTRACTION employed on some Sauternes estates) is not allowed in Germany.

CHAPTALIZATION, or the adding of sugar to increase ALCOHOLIC STRENGTH, is permitted for TAFELWEIN and QBA. The category known as QMP, by contrast, guarantees that a wine has not been chaptalized. DEACIDIFICATION of must or young wine is allowed but quality-conscious growers generally eschew these practices or limit them to vintages of extreme acidity or manifestly deficient ripeness. ACIDIFICATION has traditionally been forbidden, although an exception was made for the torrid 2003 vintage in which it was widely practised. Concentrating grape must through the removal of water—whether via REVERSE OSMOSIS, cryoextraction, or any other means—is forbidden, although these practices became topics of heated discussion in early 21st-century German wine circles in view of their widespread use in other EU countries. BARREL MATURATION in casks of varying sizes is nowadays practised for only a minority of German white wines other than those made from Weissburgunder and Grauburgunder grapes. The use of small new barrels for maturing red wines or whites from Burgundian varieties is becoming

increasingly fashionable in Germany, just as elsewhere.

Since the 1980s, German consumers and vintners have overwhelmingly come to favour dry wines labelled as TROCKEN. While significantly less than half of the wine produced in Mosel-Saar-Ruwer, the Nahe, and Rheinhessen is trocken—thus reducing the national percentage of dry wine to 36 per cent—the majority of off-dry or conspicuously sweet wine from these growing regions is exported. This 'drying out' of German wine taste has had profound effects on the stylistic and qualitative evolution of German vintners. On the one hand, the bottling of white wine, and particularly Riesling, undisguised by sweetness has led to a recognition that low yields, long ripening, selective harvest, and immaculate vinification are needed in order to achieve balanced, expressive, and site-typical wine. On the other hand, many traditional devotees of German Riesling—particularly non-Germans—would characterize the majority of trocken Rieslings as jarringly conspicuous for their lack of residual sugar. There is no lack of polemic in German wine circles about what constitutes good taste or TRADITION.

Germans' self-professed abhorrence for residual sugar has accelerated the trend towards the consumption and production of more red wine as well as more wines—red and white—from the Pinot family. The warmer, drier regions, notably Baden and the Pfalz, have benefited as a result. Red wine varieties' share of total plantings increased from just under a quarter in 1999 to more than a third in 2003. While many of the grapes and vineyards implicated in this red wine boom have yet to prove themselves, the quality of the best German reds—above all those from the traditional Spätburgunder (Pinot Noir)—has risen undeniably, at times to international stature.

Vine varieties and yield

As most vine varieties approach their climatic limits, a steep decline in wine quality is expected. With RIESLING, the classic German wine, matters run differently. Near the northern edge of the vineyards in the Mosel-Saar-Ruwer, Rheingau, and Nahe, Riesling sheds all unnecessary fat. What remains is style, and structure—the analogy to an elegant, slim fashion model may be banal but it is accurate. Before the concept of quality in wine started to spread from the estates of the Church and the nobility in the 18th century, different vine varieties were not grown separately in the vineyard but mixed together in the hope that at least some would produce a crop. In these circumstances, the question of grape RIPENESS was less important and, until the early 19th century, many harvests were gathered before their time, to avoid the risk of uncontrollable ROT. The attraction of Riesling was its performance in the vineyard rather than its wine. Amidst the chaos and competition of a mixed plantation, Riesling made a mark, sufficient for large estates to start growing it as a single vine. As the value of late and selective harvesting became understood, the reputation of Riesling wine rose above that of all other white grape varieties.

Germany's 1971 Wine Law, however, significantly disadvantaged Riesling in the market place. Levels of wine quality were defined by MUST WEIGHT alone, i.e. by the concentration of SUGARS in the grape juice measured in degrees OECHSLE. Such a system may have some validity when applied to a single vine variety growing in a narrowly defined area but, given a broader application, it becomes increasingly unreliable, as the consumer eventually discovered. Achieving certain minimum must weights is scarcely a guarantee of quality, and a host of GERMAN CROSSINGS propagated towards precisely that end virtually guaranteed the debasement of the 1971 Wine Law's purported distinctions of PRÄDIKAT, not to mention that of late-ripening Riesling. Since the late 1990s, the pendulum has swung back towards Riesling, even in areas of the Pfalz and Rheinhessen previously dominated by crossings.

Among the many factors insufficiently emphasized in the current German Wine Law is YIELD. The VDP growers' association and certain local organizations have attempted to impose voluntary production limits, even though quality and BALANCE in vine and wine cannot be quantified in hl/ha. Germany's average yields have long been the highest of any significant wine-producing country and are almost invariably well over 80 and sometimes over 100 hl/ha.

Since the mid 1990s, RIESLING has strengthened its lead over its offspring MÜLLER-THURGAU, Germany's second most planted vine variety. Less welcome to many self-styled traditionalists has been the decline of the third white grape, SILVANER. Meanwhile, plantings of red varieties have increased dramatically, with SPÄTBURGUNDER (Pinot Noir) now Germany's third most planted variety overall with more than half as much acreage as Riesling. DORNFELDER is Germany's fourth variety.

While accounting for under 20 per cent of total vine acreage, Riesling is still not just the quantitative German number one, but also her historical claim to fame and—again today as was the case a century ago—her international visitors' card. Riesling still accounts for more than half of total plantings in the Mosel-Saar-Ruwer, more than two-thirds of the Mittelrhein, and over three quarters of the Rheingau.

Other varieties planted to a significant extent include, in declining order, KERNER, PORTUGIESER, GRAUBURGUNDER, Weissburgunder (PINOT BLANC), Trollinger, BACCHUS, Schwarzriesling (Pinot MEUNIER), and SCHEUREBE.

Wine labelling

The official EUROPEAN UNION category of table wine is TAFELWEIN and quality wine is QUALITÄTSWEIN. The latter is subdivided into simple quality wine QBA, and quality wine with distinction QMP, which embraces Kabinett, Spätlese, Auslese, Beerenauslese, and Trockenbeerenauslese wines, as well as Eiswein. Each of these 'predicates' is determined by a minimum must weight and represents very approximate differences in style and total alcohol content. Within the range offered by one producer, a Spätlese wine would normally be superior to a Kabinett wine, and be priced accordingly. However, a QbA from a top estate at DM8 per bottle will be a far better wine than a Spätlese bottled for a supermarket and sold at less than half the price.

Whereas a Beerenauslese, Trockenbeerenauslese, or Eiswein is almost inevitably bottled with a high level of residual sugar, designation of a wine as Kabinett, Spätlese, or Auslese bears no direct relation to the sweetness of the finished wine. Among wines not labelled as TROCKEN (dry), FEINHERB or HALBTROCKEN (medium dry, see SWEETNESS for the official European Union classification of such terms), an Auslese will generally, though not always, taste noticeably sweeter than a Spätlese, which will in turn taste sweeter than a Kabinett.

All German quality wines (which represent 95 pert cent of a typical harvest) are analysed by officially approved laboratories and tasted BLIND. Any serious technical faults, or deviation from the regional style recognized by the official tasting panel, obvious at the time of examination will prevent a wine from receiving a control number (see AP NUMBER) and being sold as quality wine. The system is certainly open to criticism for being too lenient in its judgements, but no other EU member except arguably Austria offers any more stringent standards of national oversight.

The tradition of picking parcel by parcel and even selectively within parcels, combined with what many Germans would claim is a national passion for minutiae, can make for dozens of different bottlings at a given wine estate. And German Riesling is arguably capable of more stylistic diversity than any other combination of place and variety. The resulting multiplicity of bottlings, combined with the divided ownership of individual sites, has made it very difficult for vineyard names (other than those of a few hundred or so) to have any widely recognized associations of flavour, bouquet, or style. Reacting to this, some bottlers have abandoned the use of the names of individual sites or even of Prädikat in favour of their own estate-internal categories, and the most prestigious growers' association, the VDP, advocates both simplification of labelling and the association of renowned vineyard names with a specific, recognizable style.

The German Wine Law has in recent decades added new layers of terminology while adapting but not jettisoning the old. The results can be bewildering and many growers and consumers would argue that the very foundation of the 1971 Wine Law, so single-mindedly rooted in ripeness as measured by sugar at harvest, is itself rotten, and not nobly.

A CLASSIFICATION of German estates similar to that of the Médoc had prominent proponents among journalists and growers in the late 1980s. From the mid 1990s, momentum gathered for a system of classifying vineyards, with the sites at the apex of a qualitative pyramid being designated a GROSSES GEWÄCHS (great growth). The VDP membership has voluntarily bound itself to such a system, but unresolved conflicts with the federal German Wine Law had precluded the use of the term on labels by the mid 2000s. Since 2000, when strictures against including non-mandated information on the label were eased, a variety of winery-internal designations including star-ratings and the equivalent of informal LIEUX-DITS have appeared on labels, somewhat counter to the avowed VDP aim of simplification.

The VDP's well-intended attempts at a classification of superior vineyard sites, combined with the German Wine Law's ongoing layering and loosening, can hardly be said to have solved Germany's perennial dilemma of unintelligible wine labels and consumer confusion. Nor is it clear at what point either the vicious cycle of over-production and depressed prices from nugatory flatlands, or the attrition of excellent, steep vineyard land for lack of farmers, will see an end. But there are also propitious signs as German vintners enter the 21st century. The international reputation of their revered Riesling is higher than at any time in a century. Unprecedented levels of technological sophistication are meeting their equal in quality aspirations, responsibility to the environment, and the rediscovery of ancient viticultural wisdom. And a reaction has set in both against the stylistic straitjacket of German consumers' and opinion makers' fanaticism for dry wine and against the threat of global gustatory uniformity, promising German wines and vintners an opportunity to flourish with that dazzling stylistic diversity of which they are uniquely capable.

See also AHR, BADEN, FRANKEN, HESSISCHE BERGSTRASSE, MITTELRHEIN, MOSEL-SAAR-RUWER, NAHE, PFALZ, RHEINGAU, RHEINHESSEN, SAALE-UNSTRUT, SACHSEN, and WÜRTTEMBERG.

I.J. & D.S.

Bassermann-Jordan, F. von, *Geschichte des Weinbaus* ('History of viticulture') (Frankfurt, 1907).
Payne, J. and Diel, A., *The Guide to German Wines/ German Wine Guide* (London/ New York, 2005).
Pigott, S., *Life beyond Liebfraumilch* (London, 1988).
— and Johnson, H., *The Wine Atlas of Germany* (London, 1995).

Gevrey-Chambertin, small town in the Côte de Nuits producing some of Burgundy's most famous red wines from Pinot Noir grapes. The area allowed the appellation was sharply reduced in the late 1990s to exclude some less favoured land towards the plain, but with about 400 ha/1,000 acres under vine, including an overflow of vineyards into neighbouring Brochon, which does not have its own APPELLATION, this is still the largest viticultural source in the Côte d'Or. In 1847, Gevrey annexed the name of its finest vineyard, Chambertin, somewhat tediously dubbed the king of wines and wine of kings (although it was in fact the Emperor Napoleon's favourite wine).

Gevrey-Chambertin wines are typically deeper in colour and firmer than their rivals from Vosne-Romanée and Chambolle-Musigny. Good examples may take time to develop into perhaps the richest and most complete wines of the Côte d'Or. Sadly, owing to the ease with which a famous name sells, there are too many underachievers, both at VILLAGE WINE level and amongst the GRANDS CRUS. Among traditionalists, Rousseau is an exception, however, while Denis Mortet dazzles in a more modern way.

In all, Gevrey boasts eight grands crus, the pick of which are Chambertin and Chambertin-Clos de Bèze. The latter, comprising 15.4 ha/38 acres, may equally be sold as Le Chambertin. It is hard to differentiate between the two qualitatively although Clos de Bèze is slightly further up the hill than Chambertin, with a less deep soil, giving wines which are fractionally less powerful but full of sensual charm.

Le Chambertin, 12.9 ha (plus the 15.4 of Clos de Bèze), is the flagship. Theoretically the most powerful vineyard of them all, Chambertin has tended to suffer from over-production since the appellation commands such a high price. None the less, Chambertin has always been regarded as the most complete vineyard of the Côte d'Or: if not quite as sumptuous as Musigny or Richebourg, or as divinely elegant as La Tâche or Romanée-St-Vivant, Chambertin is matched only by Romanée-Conti (see VOSNE-ROMANÉE) for its completeness and its intensity.

Two other grand cru vineyards, Mazis-Chambertin and Latricières-Chambertin, lie on the same level as Chambertin and Clos de Bèze; one, Ruchottes-Chambertin, is to be found a little higher up the slope, while Charmes-Chambertin, Griotte-Chambertin, and Chapelle-Chambertin are further downhill.

Mazis-Chambertin (12.59 ha), also written Mazy-, is usually regarded as being next in quality to Chambertin and Clos de Bèze. The flavours are just as intense, the structure perhaps just a little less firm. Latricières (6.94 ha) is less powerful, although the wines are explosively fruity when young, with an entrancingly silky texture. Ruchottes (3.50 ha), thanks to a particularly thin calcareous soil, is lighter in

colour, angular in style, but again impressively intense. The wines are finer than those of Chapelle-Chambertin (5.39 ha), which also tends to lightness of colour.

Griotte-Chambertin (5.48 ha), which owes its name to the grill-pan shape of the vineyard rather than the griottes cherry aromas which the wine seems to have, produces wines which are better than those of neighbouring Chapelle- or Charmes-Chambertin. The latter, at 31.6 ha, is the largest grand cru in the village and, as with Clos de Vougeot and Échezeaux, its size precludes homogeneous quality. Some of the vineyard, such as the part stretching down to the main road, the RN74, should perhaps not be classified as grand cru, although a good Charmes is one of Gevrey-Chambertin's most seductive, fragrant wines when young.

Some of the grands crus are matched, if not surpassed, by the best of the premier cru vineyards, especially those with an ideal south eastern exposition such as Les Cazetiers and Clos St-Jacques. Indeed, Domaine Armand Rousseau, the famous name in Gevrey thanks to the eponymous Armand's pioneering DOMAINE BOTTLING in the 1930s, charges significantly more for Clos St-Jacques than for several grands crus in an impressive range of wines.

See also CÔTE D'OR, and map under BURGUNDY.   J.T.C.M.

Gewürztraminer, often written **Gewurztraminer,** is a pink-skinned grape variant of TRAMINER responsible for particularly pungent, full-bodied white wines. Gewürztraminer may not be easy to spell, even for wine merchants, but is blissfully easy to recognize—indeed many wine drinkers find it is the first, possibly only, grape variety they are able to recognize from the wine's heady perfume alone. Deeply coloured, opulently aromatic, and fuller bodied than almost any other white wine, Gewürztraminer's faults are only in having too much of everything. It is easy to tire of its weight and its exotic flavour of lychees and heavily scented roses, although ALSACE's finest Gewürztraminers are extremely serious wines, with an occasional savoury note reminiscent of bacon fat in some of the most complex examples, capable of at least medium-term ageing.

This by now internationally famous vine variety's genealogy is both ramified and fascinating. The variety which truly deserves the name Traminer, like Gewürztraminer but with pale green berries and much less scent, is the original variety, first noted in the village of Tramin or Termeno in what is now the Italian Tyrol (see ALTO ADIGE) around AD 1000. It was popular here until the 16th century, when the much more ordinary, but more prolific VERNATSCH or Schiava supplanted it. DNA PROFILING in Austria showed a parent–offspring relationship between Pinot and TRAMINER (hence Gewürztraminer), connecting two of the oldest grape varieties in Europe.

True Traminer has also been known in Alsace since the Middle Ages (see GERMAN HISTORY), although it is said to be cuttings imported much more recently from the PFALZ, the German wine region in which it was widely grown and prized for its richness, that encouraged its spread in Alsace. DNA profiling at Milan has vindicated GALET's opinion that the SAVAGNIN so vital to the VIN JAUNE of the JURA is none other than Traminer, both varieties being famous for their ripeness levels, depth of flavour, and ability to age.

Traminer, like its parent PINOT, mutates easily, however, and Gewürztraminer is the name adopted in the late 19th century for the dark pink-berried MUSQUÉ mutation of Traminer (and adopted as its official name in Alsace in 1973). Although much has been read into the direct German translation of *gewürz* as 'spiced', in this context it simply means 'perfumed'. Traminer Musqué, Traminer Parfumé, and Traminer Aromatique were all at one time French synonyms for Gewürztraminer. As early as 1909, the AMPELOGRAPHER Viala acknowledged Gewürztraminer as an accepted synonym for SAVAGNIN Rosé, and this aromatic, dark-berried version is known as Roter Traminer in German and Traminer or Termeno Aromatico, Traminer Rosé, or Rosso in Italy. Its long history in Alsace means that it is occasionally known as some sort of KLEVNER, particularly in this case Rotclevner.

Gewürztraminer has become by far the most planted variant of Traminer. The grapes are certainly notable at harvest for their variegated but incontrovertibly pink colour, which is translated into very deep golden wines, sometimes with a slight coppery tinge. Winemakers unfamiliar with the variety have been known to be panicked into extracting colour and flavour. Gewürztraminers also attain higher alcohol levels than most white wines, with over 14 per cent being by no means uncommon, and acidities can correspondingly be precariously low. MALOLACTIC FERMENTATION is almost invariably suppressed for Gewürztraminer and steps must be taken to avoid OXIDATION.

If all goes well, the result is deep golden, full-bodied wines with a substantial spine and concentrated heady aromas whose acidity level will preserve them while those aromas unfurl. In a lesser year or too hot a climate the result is either an early-picked, neutral wine or an oppressively oily, flabby one that can easily taste bitter to boot.

Viticulturally, Gewürztraminer is not exactly a dream to grow. Relative to the varieties with which it is commonly planted, it has small bunches and is not particularly productive, although the Germans have predictably selected some high-yielding CLONES. Its early budding leaves it prey to spring frosts and it is particularly prone to VIRUS DISEASES, although the viticultural station at Colmar has developed such virus-free clones as those numbered 47, 48, and 643.

Since Gewürztraminer has been seen as a second-rank variety in terms of international popularity and saleability, few winemakers outside Alsace have expended real energy on making great Gewurz. For the moment, the finest examples still came almost exclusively from this region in eastern France, where Gewürztraminer, Riesling, and PINOT GRIS are considered the only 'noble' white grape varieties.

Of these three, Gewürztraminer is the second most planted in Alsace as a whole, and (just) the most widely planted in the more famous vineyards of the Haut-Rhin *département*, with a total of 2,700 ha/7,400 acres in 2000. It is particularly successful on the richer clay soils of the Haut-Rhin and has inspired a raft of late harvest examples labelled VENDANGE TARDIVE or even SÉLECTION DE GRAINS NOBLES in sunnier years. The variety easily attains must weights well in excess of Riesling at comparable ripeness levels and regulations take account of this. Such late harvest Gewürztraminers may not last the same number of decades as their Riesling counterparts but many last longer than their first decade. The trick for winemakers is to achieve BALANCE in these potentially heavyweight wines.

Earlier-picked Alsace Gewürztraminer should be intriguingly aromatic yet dry and sturdy enough to accompany savoury food but too many examples are simply scented fly-by-nights, lightweight wines produced from heavily cropped vines that taste as though they have been aromatized by a drop of MUSCAT OTTONEL. In these lower ranks, it can be difficult to distinguish a poor Alsace wine labelled Gewürztraminer from one labelled Muscat. Producers with a particularly fine reputation for their Gewürztraminer include Léon Beyer of the bigger houses and Zind-Humbrecht and Cattin among the grower/bottlers.

Germany relegates its (Roter) Traminer to a very minor rank, well behind Riesling, with just over 800 ha in total, including some plantings of the non-aromatic sort which is very occasionally bottled separately. The variety needs relatively warm sites to avoid spring frost damage and to assure good FRUIT SET so that in northern Germany Riesling is usually a more profitable choice. Almost two thirds of Germany's Traminer is planted in Baden and the Pfalz, where it can produce wines of discernible character but is too often associated with somewhat oily sickliness. At Rhodt in the Pfalz, a Traminer vineyard said to be nearly 400 years old styles itself the world's oldest.

There is almost as much Traminer planted in AUSTRIA as in Germany but here too it has been consigned to the non-modish wilderness, even though some examples, particularly later-picked semi-sweet wines from Styria and botrytized sweet wines from Burgenland can exhibit an exciting blend of race and aroma and can develop for many years in bottle.

The variety is grown, in no great quantity but usually distinctively, throughout eastern Europe, called Tramini in Hungary; Traminac in Slovenia; Drumin, Pinat Cervena, or Liwora in the Czech Republic and Slovakia; occasionally just Rusa in Romania; and Mala Dinka in Bulgaria. Most of the vines are the aromatic mutation and demonstrate some of Gewürztraminer's distinctive perfume but often in extremely dilute, and often sullied, form, typically overlaying a relatively sweet, lightish white. Hungarians are particularly proud of their Tramini grown on the rich shores of Lake Balaton. It is grown by the Romanians in Transylvania, by the Bulgarians in the south and east, and also, as Traminer, in Russia, Moldova, and Ukraine, where it is sometimes used to perfume Soviet sparkling wine.

It is grown in small quantities, sometimes called Haiden or HEIDA, in Switzerland and in ever smaller quantity in Luxembourg. In Iberia, Torres grow it in the High PENEDÈS for their Viña Esmeralda and it is essentially a mountain grape even in Italy, where Traminer Aromatico is grown almost exclusively, and decreasingly, in its seat, ALTO ADIGE. The less scented and less interesting Traminer is also grown to a limited extent, and Italian wine-making together with vineyard altitude do nothing to emphasize Gewürztraminer characteristics in the resulting wines, although the international nature of the variety may encourage a small renaissance of popularity.

In the New World, Gewürztraminer presents a challenge. Many wine regions are simply too warm to produce wine with sufficient acidity, unless the grapes are picked so early (see HARVEST, timing), as in some of Australia's irrigated vineyards, that they have developed little Gewürztraminer character. Australia's 'Traminer' vine population of about 750 ha, concentrated in some of the less exciting corners of South Australia and New South Wales, has made a modest recovery in the early years of this century, its wine typically used to perfume and sweeten Riesling in commercial blends.

The variety has been more obviously successful in the cooler climate of NEW ZEALAND, although even here total plantings are not much more than 200 ha, despite some lively examples from Gisborne on the east coast of the North Island. This, incidentally, was one of the earliest identifications of varietal/geographical matching in the southern hemisphere.

Another happy home for Gewürztraminer is in the Pacific Northwest of America, particularly in Washington and Oregon, although the variety has been losing ground to Riesling in Washington and to Pinot Gris in Oregon. Washington had 600 acres in 2005 and could demonstrate some appetizing life in several well-vinified examples, even if too many were too sweet. In Oregon, too, the smoky fume of Alsace is apparent in some bottlings, generally

of late harvest or ICE WINES, although rot can be a problem in this wetter climate.

Gewürztraminer remains a relatively minor variety in California, however, whose 1,300 acres/530 ha, almost half of them in Monterey, too often bring forth oil rather than aroma (see CALIFORNIA for more on the wines). There are a few hectares of Traminer in Argentina, and some increasingly convincing bottlings from Chile, but generally South America relies on TORRONTÉS and MOSCATEL to provide aromatic whites. Limited plantings in South Africa have so far yielded sweetish wines but some of the right aromas.

It seems likely that serious Gewürztraminer will remain an Alsace speciality for some years yet.

Galet, P., *Dictionnaire encyclopédique des cépages* (Paris, 2000).

G-G. See GLYCOSYL-GLUCOSE ASSAY.

Ghemme, red wine DOCG, promoted in 1997, high up in the subalpine Novara hills in the north of the PIEMONTE region of north west Italy. Like GATTINARA across the river Seisa in the Vercelli hills with its satellites LESSONA and BRAMATERRA, Ghemme is made from the NEBBIOLO grape leavened with BONARDA and VESPOLINA. Other Novara DOCs are BOCA to the north and the rather lighter SIZZANO and FARA to the south. For more details, see SPANNA, the local name for Nebbiolo.

GI or **GIs**, AUSTRALIA's abbreviation for GEOGRAPHIC INDICATIONS.

gibberellins, naturally occurring plant HORMONES which regulate vine growth as for other plants. Isolated in 1941 from a rice fungus, they have been much studied since. In the vine they are formed in growing tissue in the leaves, roots, and berries. Many thousands of hectares of Thompson Seedless (SULTANA) vines are treated by spraying with gibberellins during FLOWERING and shortly afterwards, and this results in larger berries suitable as TABLE GRAPES. Other seedless varieties respond similarly to this treatment. Trials at GEISENHEIM and Oppenheim in Germany involving the application of gibberellic acid to seeded grapes during full bloom, causing berry shatter (see FRUIT SET), resulted in a substantial reduction in both BOTRYTIS infection and the development of sour rot. The technique is already in commercial use in northern Italy.   R.E.S. & H.R.S.

Winkler, A. J., *et al.*, *General Viticulture* (2nd edn, Berkeley, Calif., 1974).

Giennois, Coteaux du, once known as **Côtes de Gien,** appellation (since 1998) which extends on both banks of the Loire to the north of POUILLY-FUMÉ in the upper Loire to the town of Gien. Although the zone is quite extensive, and encompasses both calcareous and flint soils, it comprised fewer than 200 ha/495 acres in 2002. Most of the wines are light reds made from Gamay and Pinot Noir, while crisp, pale whites are made exclusively from Sauvignon Blanc. Joseph Balland-Chapuis is one of the most dedicated producers in this region, where spring FROSTS are a perennial threat.

See also LOIRE, including map.

Gigondas, good-value red and rosé wine appellation in the southern RHÔNE. From about a third of the total area, the best wines are remarkably similar to good red CHÂTEAUNEUF-DU-PAPE, and overall wine standards are high, even if Gigondas wine-making can sometimes be more rustic than high-tech. Gigondas can taste delightfully untamed (even if inappropriate in the heat of a typical Gigondas summer's day). Gigondas shares Châteauneuf's low maximum YIELD, 35 hl/ha (2 tons/acre); high minimum natural ALCOHOLIC STRENGTH, 12.5 per cent; and a compulsory TRIAGE to eliminate imperfect grapes.

The total *vignoble* is about 1,300 ha/3,200 acres of rugged, herb-scented vineyard just below the much-painted rocks, the Dentelles de Montmirail. For red wines, Grenache grapes must account for no more than 80 per cent of the total blend, while Syrah and/or Mourvèdre make up at least 15 per cent. The varieties permitted for Côtes du Rhône, except Carignan, may be used for the rest. Neither Syrah nor Mourvèdre are mandatory in the rosés, however.

The district has been noted for its wine since Roman times. Later a significant proportion of the land under vine formed part of the estates of the princes of Orange. In the 20th century, however, lacking a Baron Le Roy of its own (see CHÂTEAUNEUF-DU-PAPE), it laboured under the commercial disadvantage of qualifying merely for the Côtes du Rhône appellation for several decades. In 1966, it was elevated to Côtes du Rhône-Villages, and in 1971, won its own appellation. The best wines can repay BOTTLE AGEING for a decade or more. Over-achieving producers include Domaines du Cayron, Les Goubert, and St-Gayan.

Gippsland Zone, vast, relatively cool zone east of Melbourne, VICTORIA, noted for Pinot Noir and Chardonnay. So far it has no regions simply because production has not reached the critical 500 tonne mark. Depending on one's view, there are either three (east, west and south) distinct climates, or six (the latter view propounded by Phillip Jones, the elusive proprietor of Bass Phillip, regarded by many as Australia's best PINOT NOIR).

girasol, name for GYROPALETTE, the mechanized riddling crate invented in CATALUÑA in the 1970s. They are now widely used in CHAMPAGNE, ITALY, and elsewhere. *Girasol* is Spanish for sunflower, which also turns during a 24-hour period.

girdling, making an incision round a vine trunk, cane, or shoot, usually to improve fruit set. For more details, see CINCTURING.

Girò, red grape used for fortified wines on SARDEGNA.

Gironde, the estuary which separates the MÉDOC from BLAYE and the south western extreme of cognac country gives its name to the *département* in which the city of Bordeaux and the BORDEAUX wine region is to be found. The rivers DORDOGNE and GARONNE flow into the Gironde (see map under BORDEAUX).

GIS. See GEOGRAPHICAL INFORMATION SYSTEM.

Givry, famous as the preferred wine of King Henri IV (perhaps because it was the birthplace of his mistress Gabrielle d'Estrées), produces mostly red wine in the Côte CHALONNAISE district of Burgundy. The rare white wines, a tenth of the total production, are often particularly interesting with a soft bouquet reminiscent of liquorice. The reds have more structure and ability to age than those of neighbouring RULLY, but less depth than Mercurey. About one-sixth of the vineyard area is designated PREMIER CRU, including Clos Marceaux, Clos Salomon, and Clos Jus.

J.T.C.M.

glass, history of. For more than 3,000 years, glass has played a unique role in the history of wine, in terms of both serving (GLASSES, DRINKING VESSELS, and DECANTERS) and storage (BOTTLES).

Glass vessels were known in the Ancient world (first appearing in EGYPT *c.*1500 BC) and became common during Roman times, when the techniques of glass-blowing spread throughout the Roman empire. Wine was sometimes drunk from glass tumblers and surviving examples show astonishingly intricate craftsmanship. Glass bottles were used as decanters for carrying wine to table, but not for storage because they were too fragile.

Glass-making continued after the collapse of Roman power. By the time of the Renaissance, VENICE had become the centre of luxury production. Venetian glassware was exported throughout the known world and Italian craftsmen settled across Europe setting up new workshops. In Tudor England, aristocrats preferred Venetian-style glasses to silver (which was considered too common) but glass was so expensive that several diners were expected to share each beaker.

Glass bottles at this time were used by apothecaries rather than wine merchants, although the wines produced around Florence were sometimes transported in *fiaschi* wrapped in straw. The problem with glass was that it was too light and therefore too fragile to withstand either transport or storage. The most common CONTAINERS for wine were BARRELS for bulk, and leather, tin, or stoneware bottles.

A turning-point in the history of glass (and the history of wine) came early in the 17th century, when a timber shortage led to the introduction of coal-fired furnaces in England. Hotter furnaces made possible the production of bottles that were not only darker and heavier, but stronger. At first these dark, onion-shaped bottles were used mainly as decanters and for personal use, but by the beginning of the 18th century they were used for the long-distance transport of wine. Initially the French had to rely on English imports, but by 1790, there were five factories around Bordeaux (still an important centre of glass production) producing 400,000 English-style bottles.

This development was revolutionary because it made possible the ageing of wine. The necessary corollary was the CORK, whose use became common at this time. The advantages of BOTTLE AGEING were most noticeable in PORT, a staple drink in Georgian England. As the practice of BINNING wine became more common, the shape of wine bottles evolved towards the taller cylindrical shape (*c.*1760) we know today.

Meanwhile a revolution in drinking glasses had emanated from the two southern English workshops of George Ravenscroft, who in 1675 had discovered how to make LEAD crystal. This gave rise to a whole new style of English glassware quite distinct from intricate Venetian fashions. Increasingly, different glasses were designed and produced to be used specifically for certain wines, and by the end of the 18th century the concept of a uniformly decorated glass service was well established throughout Europe.

H.B.

Klein, D., and Lloyd, W., *The History of Glass* (London, 1984).

glass, wine by the. In many of the world's restaurants and bars, particularly in the United States, wine is served by the glass. This is especially useful for those who want to drink less than a half or full bottle, or want to taste as many different wines as possible in a FLIGHT of different small servings, or want to practise focused FOOD AND WINE MATCHING in a group that has ordered a wide range of different dishes. When carefully administered, with a high level of professional service and due attention to LEFTOVERS in opened bottles, possibly using special storage systems involving INERT GAS, this is an admirable service to the consumer (and occasionally producer; part of the mythology of Opus One, the luxury Napa Valley Cabernet that resulted from the Mondavi-Mouton JOINT VENTURE, is that it was both launched and commercially saved by extensive by-the-glass serving programmes). The practice is still in its infancy in many countries, however, notably in Britain where wine by the glass is too often the dregs from a badly kept bottle of very ordinary wine served in a pub. This despite, or perhaps because of, the fact that there is strict UK legislation ordaining that wine must be served in measures of 125 ml, 175 ml, or occasionally 250 ml.

glasses, not just the final CONTAINER for wine but an important instrument for communicating it to the human senses (see TASTING). Wine can be drunk from any DRINKING VESSEL but clean (and only clean) GLASS has the advantage of being completely inert and, if it is clear, of allowing the taster the pleasure (or in the case of BLIND TASTING the clues) afforded by the wine's appearance: colour, clarity, and so on.

For this reason, wine professionals and keen amateurs prefer completely plain, uncoloured, unengraved, uncut glass, preferably as thin as is practicable to allow the palate to commune as closely as possible with the liquid. Thin-rimmed glasses are particularly highly valued.

The ideal wine glass also has a stem—indeed Americans call wine glasses 'stemware'—so that the wine taster can hold the glass without necessarily affecting the wine's TEMPERATURE (a critical element in wine tasting). The stem also enables a glass to be rotated easily (although it takes a certain knack); rotation, as explained in TASTING, is essential for maximizing AROMA or BOUQUET. This rotation process also means that the ideal wine glass narrows towards the rim, to minimize the chance of spillage during rotation, and to encourage the volatile FLAVOUR COMPOUNDS to collect in the space between the surface of the wine and the rim of the glass.

Individuals have their own aesthetic preferences, but any glass which fits the above criteria will serve as a wine glass, including some relatively inexpensive examples. There is a sensual thrill to be had, however, in really thin crystal. This is usually expensive, although central Europe, and BOHEMIA in particular, has a long tradition of producing fine glasses at good prices.

For many households, a single wine glass model will do, perhaps supplemented by smaller glasses for FORTIFIED wines and an elongated one for SPARKLING WINES. Purists, however, use slightly different glasses for different sorts of wine, conventionally (although not particularly logically) a smaller glass for white wines, and traditionally Germanic shapes for German and Alsace wines.

In this respect there is no greater purist than Georg Riedel, an Austrian glass-maker who is unusual for his wine CONNOISSEURSHIP. He has designed a series of different glasses not just for young red bordeaux and mature red bordeaux, but also, for example, different glasses for vintage port and tawny port, for Brunello di Montalcino and for Chianti. These designs are all based purely on analysing how different taste characteristics are optimized on the nose and palate by minute variations in glass design. Those determined to take full advantage of all Riedel permutations may need to give up a room or two to accommodate the necessary number of glasses, however, and in practice most people content themselves with just two or three possible glass types, often chosen as much on appearance as on efficacy.

Special glass types

Over the centuries, various specific glasses have come to be associated with different wine types.

CHAMPAGNE and other sparkling wines were for long drunk in a flat, saucer-like glass called a **coupe**, but this has been abandoned in favour of the tall **flute**, which preserves the wine's MOUSSE. This has evolved into a slightly more bulbous **tulipe**, which combines height with narrowing towards the rim.

In Spain, SHERRY has traditionally been served in the **copita**, and tastes infinitely better in a part-filled glass in this elongated tulip shape than it does brimming over a cut-glass thimble as it is so often served elsewhere.

The ideal PORT glass is not so very different from the copita, although it is usually rather bigger in order to allow maximum appreciation of the complex bouquet of a vintage port. Glasses like this are ideal for almost all fortified wines, which, for obvious reasons, are conventionally served in smaller quantities than table wines.

BURGUNDY, particularly red burgundy, has come to be served in glass balloons, sometimes so large they resemble fish-bowls. The idea, apart from lusty exhibitionism, is that a good burgundy can offer such a rich panoply of aromas that they should be given every chance to escape the wine and titillate the taster. Most wine connoisseurs use the shape on a reduced scale.

The wines of ALSACE and GERMANY are sometimes served in particular forms of glass such as the **Rohmer**, often with green or brown glass stems, mainly for traditional reasons. There are still those who teach wine SERVING who regard serving these wines in standard white wine glasses as an intolerable aberration.

See also SERVING WINE.

glassy winged sharpshooter, LEAFHOPPER insect of great significance in some American wine regions as it is the vector of PIERCE'S DISEASE.

Glenrowan, historic Australian wine region in North East VICTORIA ZONE (see VICTORIA), famous for Ned Kelly, fortified wines, and full-bodied reds. See LIQUEUR MUSCAT.

globalization of the world's wine markets has never been as dramatic nor as comprehensive as in the past two decades. Until the late 20th century, it involved little more than the exporting of CUTTINGS and traditional expertise. Most wine was consumed in the country of production, and those countries were mostly in Europe. But since the 1980s, with the fall in TRANSPORT and communication costs, the wine industry has embraced new modes of internationalization that have added to and complemented technology transfer, notably cross-national mergers and acquisitions of wine companies (see below), and the emergence of FLYING WINEMAKERS and VITICULTURISTS.

Globalization has also brought changes to the demand for wines. Deregulation of wine retailing in Britain and elsewhere allowed the emerging supermarket chains to compete with traditional sellers of wine. Those chains responded to the new consumers' preferences by sourcing robust, fruity wines that are more approachable and affordable than FINE WINE but better than basic European TABLE WINE. For national advertising to be profitable for those chains, and for wineries seeking to build BRANDS, large quantities of homogenous wine are needed year after year. It became clear that producers in the New World were more adept at responding to that new demand and the results included *la* CRISE VITICOLE.

The share of global wine production exported, which had always been below 15 per cent and mostly intra-European, reached 30 per cent by the mid 2000s. And the New World's share of global wine exports rose from 3 per cent in the late 1980s to 25 per cent (if sparkling wine is excluded) by 2004. Recognizing their poor performance, Europe's producers began belatedly in the mid 2000s to adapt their practices to compete. Simultaneously, New World producers are seeking to expand their exports of more expensive wines to complement their lower-end products. The next phase of wine's globalization therefore may involve a convergence whereby both groups produce TERROIR-driven super-premium wines alongside affordable bottles of blended commodity branded wines, while cheap basic bulk wines continue their demise.

Mergers and acquisitions accelerated from the mid 1980s when Louis Vuitton bonded with Moët-Hennessy to form LVMH and Bacardi with Martini. It also brought UK-based Grand Metropolitan (now DIAGEO) to invest in California wineries and Paris-based PERNOD RICARD to add Jacob's Creek to its portfolio of brands via Orlando Wyndham. Global drinks companies' interest rests mainly with sparkling wines, brandies and vermouths, however, which have lent themselves much more easily to global branding than still wines. Seagram and Pernod had both entered the mass market before, only to leave it to wine-focused operators such as Canandaigua (now CONSTELLATION) and CASTEL; Diageo would do the same in the mid 1990s. Pernod Ricard signalled a return to the fray by acquiring MONTANA and other main wine brands in Allied Domecq's 2005 break-up.

A second phase of international consolidation drew Australian producers closer to the American market with the merger of California's Beringer with Australian brewers FOSTER'S subsidiary Mildara Blass in 2001, and the acquisition of HARDY by Constellation in 2003. At about the same time, the carve-up of Seagram between Diageo and Pernod added some wine-specific assets to Castel and Allied Domecq. The latter's failed attempt in 2003 to add an Australian—Peter Lehmann—to its portfolio, after eventually acquiring Montana of New Zealand, exposed the vulnerability of premium wineries to hostile takeovers by acquisitive global players. (Allied's chief rival for Montana, Asian brewers Lion Nathan, went on to acquire the Australian Petaluma group of wine brands.) Canadian company VINCOR added British and South African acquisitions to its international range of producers in 2004 and KENDALL-JACKSON of California is also a serious if smaller international player. Companies such as ANTINORI, GALLO, MONDAVI, and Southcorp (once Australia's leading wine company but bought by Foster's in 2005) have been involved in a changing roster of JOINT VENTURES which have also helped to globalize wine.

The emergence of large international wine companies and brands, built on economies of scale, and the ease with which technology and know-how can be transferred, have raised fears of significant shifts of production from western Europe to the globe's cheapest wine regions. But globalization is bound by terroir and the need for companies to offer differentiated wines—one of the main reasons why the largest wine companies control only a fraction of the world market. Even the biggest drinks company Diageo is not among the world's 100 biggest companies overall. See also BRANDS.

P.S. & K.A.

Anderson, K. (ed.), *The World's Wine Markets: Globalization at Work* (Cheltenham, 2004).

Spahni, P., *International Wine Trade* (2nd edn., Cambridge, 2000).

—— 'ONE World' (www.span-e.com, 2005).

Wittwer, G. and K. Anderson, *The Global Wine Statistical Compendium, 1961 to 2003* (Australian Wine and Brandy Corporation, 2005)

global positioning system (GPS), a satellite-based navigation system which allows detailed mapping of specific vineyard features to a positional accuracy of 1 m/3 ft through the use of differential corrections. Differential GPS (dGPS) is an essential component of PRECISION VITICULTURE.

R.G.V.B.

global warming. See CLIMATE CHANGE.

gluconobacter, a genus within the acetic acid bacteria family associated more with grapes than wine because of its high sugar tolerance. Like ACETOBACTER species, gluconobacter species are capable of spoiling wine by converting it into vinegar.

glucose is with fructose one of the two principal SUGARS of the grape and of sweet wines. Like fructose, it is a six-carbon atom sugar, or a hexose. In solution, it rotates polarized light to the right, hence the original name dextrose and its correct name, D(+)-glucose.

The two major sugars that accumulate in grapes occur in about equal amounts; at the beginning of RIPENING, glucose exceeds fructose (up to fivefold), but in overripe grapes there is less glucose than fructose. Glucose also serves a very important function as the major sugar used by the vine for forming GLYCOSIDES (see also FLAVOUR COMPOUNDS). Common table sugar, sucrose, is made up of one molecule of glucose and one of fructose. See FRUCTOSE for details of the unusual relationship between these sugars and the grape.

B.G.C. & A.D.W.

Glühwein, German for 'glow wine', seems a particularly apt name for the MULLED WINE that has cheered many an alpine skier. Premixed wine, sugar, and spices are also available under this name.

glutathione, or **glutathion,** sulfur-containing compound found in grape juice and an important antioxidant which has been shown to play a significant part in the ageing of wines. It also has an important role in stabilizing the volatile sulfur compounds which characterize the aroma of Sauvignon Blanc and possibly some other white grape varieties.

glycerol, or **glycerine**, member of the chemical class of polyols and a minor product of alcoholic fermentation. The name derives from the Greek word for sweet and glycerol does indeed taste slightly sweet, as well as oily and heavy. It is present in most wines in concentrations ranging from about 5 to 12 g/l, although BOTRYTIZED wines frequently have concentrations up to 25 g/l.

Glycerol does have a slight effect on the apparent sweetness of a wine but, contrary to popular conception, glycerol makes only a very minor contribution to the apparent VISCOSITY of a wine, and bears no relation to the TEARS observed on the inside of many a wine glass. Whereas sensory tests have demonstrated that glycerol imparts sweetness at a threshold of about 5.2 g/l in white wine, a level of more than 28 g/l would be needed before any difference in viscosity were noted.

A.D.W. & T.H.L.

glycolosis. See YEAST.

glycosidase, see ENZYMES and FLAVOUR PRECURSORS.

glycosides are naturally occurring molecules made up of two parts joined by a glycosidic linkage; one of the parts is a sugar, frequently GLUCOSE, and the other may be a non-sugar, called an aglycone. Common aglycones are phenolic compounds, for example ANTHOCYANINS, although TERPENOIDS and a number of other compound types are found glycosylated in many plant tissues, including fruits. Glycosides present in wines come from the grape and here the sugar is usually glucose, although it too may be connected to a second, non-glucose sugar residue. Formation of a glycoside changes the physical and chemical properties of molecules that are glycosylated. Glycosides are usually more water soluble, and invariably much less volatile than the aglycones from which they were derived. It is still not clear why they form in plants but glycosylation is presumed to aid detoxification and the transport of aglycones, or to make plant tissues rigid. Plants and fruits often have a higher concentration of glycosides than aglycones. The sensory properties of flavour-active aglycones are profoundly diminished by glycosylation and such glycosides, known as FLAVOUR PRECURSORS, are a reserve of FLAVOUR and contributors to VARIETAL flavour expression (as opposed to aspects of flavour that arise from vinification) and BOUQUET in wines. Following the recognition of glycosides as flavour precursors, a recent development is the determination of this class of compound in grapes and wines through measures of GLYCOSYL-GLUCOSE.

P.J.W.

glycosyl-glucose assay, or G-G assay, is a recent and experimental measure of grape and wine composition complementing, and additional to, those already available (see GRAPE COMPOSITION AND WINE QUALITY and GRAPE QUALITY ASSESSMENT). The basis of the G-G assay is the recognition of the role of GLYCOSIDES as FLAVOUR PRECURSORS of varietal wine flavour. The assay as applied to a grape, juice, or wine sample involves (a) isolation of the glycosides, (b) their complete hydrolysis to yield glucose, and (c) quantification of the glucose. The results are expressed as the amount of glycosides in micromoles, either per litre or per berry as appropriate. The G-G assay has been applied to both light- and dark-skinned grape varieties, at early stages of berry development through to harvest, to musts and juices during fermentation, and to wines before, during and after AGEING. Accordingly, the assay allows the viticulturist and oenologist to relate the glycoside component of grape composition, obtained before harvest, to the glycoside concentration of a wine, irrespective of its style, years after its vinification. It has revealed the decrease in G-G in wines with ageing as glycoside HYDROLYSIS progresses, the range in glycoside concentration in juices of the same varieties grown in different regions, and the different rates of increase in glycoside concentration in fruit grown under different conditions. In the late 1990s, the assay was advocated as a valuable new tool to viticulturists wishing to investigate the influence of vine-growing practices on grape composition. As such it holds promise of an objective measure of fruit composition pertinent to wine quality.

P.J.W.

Whiton, R. S., and Zoecklein, B. W., 'Evaluation of glycosyl-glucose analytical methods for various glycosides', *American Journal of Enology and Viticulture*, 53 (2002) 315–17.

Williams, P. J., and Francis, I. L., 'Wine flavour research—experiences from the past offer a guide to the future', in J. M. Rantz (ed.), *Proceedings of the American Society of Enology and Viticulture 50th Anniversary Annual Meeting, 19–23 June 2000* (Davis, 2001), 191–5.

GM 6494. See RONDO.

gobelet, or **goblet**, a form of vine-TRAINING SYSTEM, used since Roman times, whereby the spurs are arranged on short arms in an approximate circle at the top of a short trunk, making the vine look something like a goblet drinking vessel. The vines are free standing (apart from a small supporting stake when young) and the system is best suited to low-VIGOUR vineyards in drier climates. This is a form of HEAD TRAINING and is generally subject to SPUR PRUNING. The trunk is short, typically 30 to 50 cm (12–19 in), and the foliage is unsupported by WIRES.

The gobelet is widespread in France, from Beaujolais southwards, although it is now less common than it was because it is generally more economical to train vines on trellis systems rather than have them free standing. The traditional spacing was 1.5 by 1.5 m (5 ft), but the distance has been increased to allow tractor access and the vineyards are typically cultivated in both directions. Sometimes the vines are trained with several trunks. With low-vigour vineyards the foliage can be relatively erect, but shoots may trail on the ground in high-vigour vineyards, and there can be substantial SHADE. Grape yield and quality may suffer as a result. The system is used widely in many Mediterranean countries. In Italy, the system is called *alberelli a vaso*, in Spain *en vaso*, and in Portugal *en taça*. In many New World countries such as Australia, South Africa, and California, the traditional and low-vigour gobelet-trained vineyards were often called bush vines; they have increasingly

A **gobelet** or **bush** vine

been replaced by vines with some form of trellising to accommodate the improved vigour of newer vineyards. R.E.S.

Galet, P., *Précis de viticulture* (5th edn, Montpellier, 1988).

goblets. See DRINKING VESSELS.

Godello, fine white grape variety native to north west Spain and northern Portugal. As Godello it is most successful in VALDEORRAS, where plantings are increasing once more, although it is also known as Verdello in other parts of northern Galicia. Spain had 880 ha/2,200 acres planted in 2004. It is known as GOUVEIO in northern Portugal.

Goldburger, Austrian gold-skinned grape variety, a crossing of WELSCHRIESLING and Orangetraube. About 300 ha/740 acres of this vine are planted, almost all of them in BURGENLAND, where it reaches high MUST WEIGHTS but rarely produces exciting wines. This early-ripening variety, Austria's answer to many GERMAN CROSSINGS, is mainly used for sweet wines.

Goldkapsel. Some producers in GERMANY deliberately give their finest bottlings a gold CAPSULE over the cork. The practice largely arose after the promulgation of the 1971 GERMAN WINE LAW, which on the one hand stipulated a very broad band of minimum MUST WEIGHTS—particularly on the Mosel-Saar-Ruwer—between the levels of Auslese and Beerenauslese, and on the other hand forbade further qualifications of the Prädikat (such as fein, feinste, CABINET, hochfeinste, etc.) from appearing on the label. Goldkapsel bottlings are usually available in very small quantities and command a considerable premium, although there are no legal controls over their use. The VDP group of top estates reserve Goldkapsel for particularly good SPÄTLESE or AUSLESE wines that are offered for sale at the association's auctions. The position is further complicated (or enriched, depending on your budget) by the fact that some producers use gold capsules of two different lengths, thus their very finest bottlings qualify as **lange Goldkapsel**. Even more than the designations of Prädikat themselves, therefore, designations of gold capsule or long gold capsule are in practice based on subjective, estate-specific, internal criteria set by each vintner. J.R. & D.S.

Goldmuskateller, German name for the golden-berried MOSCATO Giallo grape speciality in ALTO ADIGE.

gold rushes have played a significant role in the development of New World wine production through their influence both on demand for alcoholic beverages and also on LABOUR supply. In CALIFORNIA, commercial viticulture had emerged during the 1830s, and with the discovery of gold in 1848 there was

a massive increase in demand for all types of alcohol in the gold-mining counties of Amador, Calaveras, El Dorado, Nevada, Placer, and Tuolumne. However, by the 1850s, once the first flush of gold fever was over, a number of the immigrants, seeking to profit from the rising price of wine, turned to grape-growing and wine-making as a more reliable source of income. By 1857 it is estimated that there were some 1.5 million vines in California, and only three years later, after the enactment of legislation in 1859 which exempted vineyards from taxation, this total had risen to some 6 million.

Viticulture had been introduced into AUSTRALIA on the establishment of the new colony in New South Wales in 1788. Its subsequent spread followed the increasing pace of colonization and settlement, with new vines being planted almost as soon as each new colony was founded. During the first half of the 19th century, however, despite the activities of proponents such as James BUSBY, wine-making remained a minority interest. The gold rush of 1851 changed this by attracting numerous immigrants to VICTORIA, with large numbers coming from France, Switzerland, Italy, and Germany, countries which had long traditions of viticulture and wine-making. Many, failing to make a success of prospecting, turned to farming, and in particular to viticulture, with the result that the pattern of vineyards in Victoria closely reflected the scattered distribution of the gold. In particular, during the 1870s and 1880s, the gold-mining areas of Ballarat, Bendigo, Great Western (now Grampians), and the Murray river all became important wine regions. P.T.H.U.

Halliday, J., *The Australian Wine Compendium* (London, 1985).

Pinney, T., *A History of Wine in America: From the Beginnings to Prohibition* (Berkeley, Calif., 1989).

González Byass, the largest producer of sherry, still run by the family that founded the house. In 1835, 23-year-old Manuel María González Angel set up business as a shipper in JEREZ in southern Spain. Within months he had joined forces with D. Juan Dubosc to make their first large shipment to London: 48 hogsheads and a quarter cask, sent to Robert Blake Byass, who was to become their UK agent. In 1844, the company purchased its first vineyards, and in 1846 the first wines were bottled in Jerez. The FINO brand Tio Pepe was born in 1849, named after Manuel's uncle José Angel y Vargas (*tío* being Spanish for uncle), who helped his nephew establish the SOLERA. In 1855, Robert Blake Byass became a shareholder in the business, but it was not until 1870, when his sons and the sons of the founder entered the firm that it became González Byass & Co. The company remained in the hands of the two families until, in 1988, the González family financed the purchase of the 45 per cent of shares held by the Byass family, later placing most of these with IDV, the British drinks subsidiary of the conglomerate Grand Metropolitan. The family bought the shares back from IDV in 1997, also the year in which Mauricio González Gordon, from the fourth generation of the family to work in the company, retired as chairman. His successors were Chon Gómez-Monche, another fourth-generation family member in the company and, from 2001, family friend Carlos Espinosa de los Monteros.

The company owns 550 ha/1,300 acres of vineyards, and controls a further 450 ha owned by independent farmers. In the mid 1990s, the company began releasing expensive vintage-dated dry sherries, renewing a Jerez practice from the days before the solera system was adopted. The company also produces brandy; RIOJA at Bodegas Beronia; CAVA at Castel de Villernau/Jean Perico; and spirits and liqueurs under the name Alcoholera de Chinchón. In 2001, the company acquired the Spanish interests of CROFT. The UK remains the company's most important export market.   S.A. & V. de la S.

González Gordon, M., *Sherry: The Noble Wine* (3rd edn, London, 1990).

Gorbachev, Mikhail (1931–), last President of the Soviet Union (1985–91) and significant in the history of wine because of his 1985–8 national campaign against alcohol abuse. Measures were energetically directed not just against vodka consumption but also against the production and importation of wine. The immediate domestic effect was that the total vineyard area in the Soviet Union (which until the fall of communism included such wine-producing republics as MOLDOVA, UKRAINE, the CRIMEA, UZBEKISTAN, RUSSIA, AZERBAIJAN, GEORGIA and, producing very much less wine, ARMENIA, KYRGYZSTAN, TAJIKISTAN, KAZAKHSTAN, and TURKMENISTAN) fell by a third between 1980 and 1990 to the 1960 level of just over 1 million ha/2,471,000 acres. In 1990, the Soviet Union still accounted for 12 per cent of the world's total area of vineyard and 5 per cent of the wine produced. By 1996, according to OIV statistics, those same countries accounted for 11 per cent of the world's vineyard but only 3 per cent of the wine produced.

The effects of Gorbachev's anti-alcohol campaign were equally dramatic in countries from which the Soviet Union had been importing huge quantities of wine; see BULGARIA, ROMANIA, HUNGARY, and CYPRUS. These countries suddenly had to find new customers for an important proportion of their annual grape harvest—customers who would certainly be more demanding than their Soviet predecessors—or simply abandon vines and wine production to a significant degree.

Wine produced within the old Soviet Union, on the other hand, was viewed by some of the newly independent republics as a potential earner of hard currency, by others as useful barter. As individuals struggled for economic survival in the new free market economies, the markets were flooded with alcohol substitutes, cheap vodkas, brandies and wines from central and western Europe. For more detail, see under the names of individual republics.

Gordo or **Gordo Blanco**, originally Spanish synonyms for MUSCAT OF ALEXANDRIA since adopted by Australia.

Gouais Blanc, light-skinned grape variety commonly planted in central and north eastern France in the Middle Ages which produced very ordinary, acid wine, while the more highly valued Pinots were planted on more favoured sites. DNA PROFILING at DAVIS and MONTPELLIER has shown that Gouais Blanc and Pinot had a great number of important progeny in Northern France (see PINOT). Following that discovery, researchers became more interested in this ancient variety and realized that, besides its numerous synonyms in France, Gouais Blanc is also identical to BELINA DROBNA and Heunisch Weiss or Weisser Heunisch in Eastern Europe, and to Liseiret and Preveiral in Italy. Moreover, dozens of additional possible parent–offspring relationships have been suggested between Gouais Blanc and French or European varieties, including RIESLING and FURMINT. Gouais Blanc has been called a 'key variety' for grape diversity in Europe by some researchers, and some others have even nicknamed it the 'Casanova of grapes'. Varietal Gouais Blanc is produced by Josef-Marie Chanton of Visp in Switzerland's Valais under the name Gwaess.   J.V.

Goulburn Valley, long-established temperate wine region in Australia's Central VICTORIA Zone (see VICTORIA). Nagambie Lakes is a subregion with Tahbilk and Mitchelton its leading wineries.

goût, French noun for TASTE in all its senses. Some wines, particularly old CHAMPAGNES, are described as suiting the **goût anglais**, or English taste (supposedly for wine necrophilia). Sweet champagne was described as to the **goût russe** in the days of the imperial court. A wine made from fruit adversely affected by HAIL, for example, might be described in French as having a **goût de grêle**. Another much discussed and loosely applied TASTING TERM is **goût de terroir**, sometimes used about those aspects of flavour deemed to derive from the TERROIR rather than the grape variety but sometimes erroneously used synonymously with the term 'earthy'.

(The late 19th-century Champenois defined champagne sweetened to satisfy the *goût russe* as one with 273 to 330 g/l of RESIDUAL SUGAR, as opposed to the *goût anglais* of 22 to 66 g/l.)

Gouveio, adopted as the principal name for the estimated 400 ha/988 acres total plantings of the particular Verdelho that is grown in the Alentejo and Dão regions of PORTUGAL (not the VERDELHO of Madeira or Australia). This is the vine variety known in Spain as GODELLO.

governo, also known as *governo alla toscana*, since it is most closely associated with TOSCANA, is a wine-making technique once widely used in the various CHIANTI production zones, and occasionally in UMBRIA and the MARCHE. The technique consisted of setting aside and drying grapes from the September and October harvest, pressing them in mid to late November, and introducing the resulting unfermented grape juice into young wines which had just completed their alcoholic FERMENTATION, thereby restarting the fermentation. This practice led to a slight increase in the ALCOHOLIC STRENGTH of the wines, but its principal and most desirable effect was to encourage the MALOLACTIC FERMENTATION, which was not always easy in the cold cellars of the past, with wines made from a grape as high in ACIDITY as SANGIOVESE. A side-effect was to increase the level of CARBON DIOXIDE in the wine, some of which inevitably remained in young Chianti, bottled and marketed in the spring after the harvest. One of the precise purposes of the *governo* was to make the wines marketable at an earlier date by accelerating the malolactic fermentation.

Today *governo* is much less widely used as producers have striven to transform Chianti's image from quaffing wine to a serious candidate for BOTTLE AGEING. The technique was also used in the VERDICCHIO production zone in the Marche, to add fizz and a slight sweetness—from the high sugar content of the dried grapes—to counteract Verdicchio's occasionally bitter finish. It has virtually disappeared here now.   D.T.

GPS. See GLOBAL POSITIONING SYSTEM.

Graciano, sometimes called **Graciana**, is a richly coloured, perfumed black grape variety once widely grown in Rioja in northern Spain. It had fallen from favour because of its inconveniently low yields, thereby depriving modern Rioja of an important flavour ingredient, but by 2004 plantings totalled almost 1,000 ha/2,500 acres, from which some VARIETAL bottlings are made in Rioja and Navarra, and there were experimental plantings as far afield as Toledo. This is Portugal's TINTA MIÚDA and it has also been certified through DNA PROFILING that the Tintilla de Rota grape of Jerez is Graciano.

The vine buds very late and is prone to DOWNY MILDEW but can produce wine of great character and extract, albeit quite tannic and notably acidic in youth. Known as Morrastel in France, it was popular in Languedoc-Roussillon until the middle of the 19th century, when Henri BOUSCHET stepped in to provide growers with a more productive, more disease-resistant, but wildly inferior crossing of Morrastel with Petit Bouschet, **Morrastel-**

Bouschet which in time replaced virtually all of the original Morrastel in French vineyards. True Morrastel, or Graciano, is still grown in southern France in minute quantities and Languedoc's viticultural archivists have recently shown interest in it.

There is ample possibility for confusion since Spaniards have used the name Morrastel as a synonym for their very different, and widely planted, variety Monastrell (MOURVÈDRE). Even today in North Africa the name Morrastel is used for both Graciano and Mourvèdre.

The variety known as Xeres in California, which has also been planted on a similarly limited scale in Australia, is probably Graciano, as is Graciana, the variety of which there are small plantings in Mendoza, Argentina.

Galet, P., *Dictionnaire encyclopédique des cépages* (Paris, 2000).

Alcade, A. J., *Cultivares Viticolas Argentinas* (Mendoza, 1989).

Graciosa, IPR on the Azorean island of the same name making small quantities of white wine.

grafting, the connection of two pieces of living plant tissue so that they unite and grow as one plant, has been a particularly important element in growing vines since the end of the 19th century, when it was discovered that grafting on to resistant ROOTSTOCKS was the only effective weapon against the PHYLLOXERA louse.

History

The grafting of vines as a means of PROPAGATION was well known in Ancient ROME, and it is referred to as early as the 2nd century BC by CATO in his treatise *De agri cultura*. Knowledge of grafting survived through the medieval period, but it was in the 19th century that it came into particular prominence as the only method of satisfactorily ensuring the continued production of wine in the face of the threat posed by phylloxera. European varieties of VITIS VINIFERA had little resistance to phylloxera. It was only through the grafting of *vinifera* cuttings on to American species of *Vitis*, which had some phylloxera resistance, that traditional European grape varieties could continue to be cultivated, and thus wine with the commercially acceptable taste thereof could still be made. Early experiments to counter phylloxera had generally centred on chemical treatments or flooding, but during the 1870s, those, such as Laliman, who had been advocating the use of AMERICAN VINE SPECIES gained increasing support. Eventually, at the 1881 International Phylloxera Congress in Bordeaux, it became generally accepted that grafting of French scions on to American rootstock was the best solution, and this led to much experimentation to identify the best rootstocks for particular soil types. On a regional scale, however, widespread adoption of grafting awaited the efforts of people such as Gustave Foëx, director of the agricultural school at MONTPELLIER, who in 1882 produced a small booklet recommending the use of American vines, written in a clear style specifically designed for the small wine producers of the Languedoc. Traditionally grafting was done by hand, either in the field (FIELD BUDDING) or indoors (BENCH GRAFTING), using such techniques as the whip and tongue method. Today, however, most grafting in Europe is done by machines which join together scion and rootstock, usually in an omega-shaped cut. In California and to a lesser extent South Africa, field grafting is still common.

P.T.H.U.

Foëx, G., *Instruction sur l'emploi des vignes américaines à la reconstruction du vignoble de l'Hérault* (Montpellier, 1882).

Laliman, L., *Études sur les divers travaux phylloxériques et les vignes américaines* (Paris, 1879).

Ordish, G., *The Great Wine Blight* (London, 1972).

Paul, H. W., *Science, Vine and Wine in Modern France* (Cambridge, 1996).

Winkler, A. J., *et al.*, *General Viticulture* (Berkeley, Calif., 1974).

Modern viticultural practices

Vines are grafted or budded to take advantage of the desirable properties of the rootstock variety. Foremost is resistance or tolerance to soil-borne pests and diseases, especially phylloxera and NEMATODES. Other properties are tolerance to soil SALINITY, to high LIME levels, to SOIL WATER logging or DROUGHT, and an ability to modify VIGOUR or to hasten or delay RIPENING. If conducted in the vineyard, as FIELD BUDDING AND GRAFTING, the practice offers a method of changing a VINE VARIETY. If conducted indoors, before planting, it is called BENCH GRAFTING, which may in warm climates be complemented by NURSERY grafting.

The uniting of the SCION with the rootstock is achieved by a slow growth process: a mass of undifferentiated cells, the CALLUS, develops at each cut edge of the respective CAMBIUMS (zones of dividing cells), so it is important to position the two cambiums opposite each other and close together. Thereafter, the scion piece is part of the whole plant vascular system.

A number of factors determine success or failure in grafting, in addition to the skill involved in cutting and matching of cambiums. The first is that the graft needs specific environmental conditions such as warm temperatures (24–30 °C/75–86 °F) and high humidities (90–100 per cent) around the union. The second is the compatibility of the scion/stock combination. The third, and probably the most serious, is that some rootstocks are difficult to root (see ROOTLING), which can affect the overall success of grafting.

Particular forms of graft include CLEFT GRAFTING, NOTCH GRAFTING, WHIP GRAFT. See also GREEN GRAFTING.

B.G.C.

grafting machine, a device used in GRAFTING by making cuts through the vine rootstock and scion pieces with mirror-image shapes that permit snug fitting. Shapes used include castellate and omega. Grafting machines are an essential part of the factory-like methods used for BENCH GRAFTING, but innovative growers have used modified machines for NURSERY grafting and FIELD (BUDDING AND) GRAFTING.

B.G.C.

Graham, important port shipper. See SYMINGTONS.

grain, an important aspect of any wood, particularly OAK, used for wine COOPERAGE. French oak is classified by winemakers and coopers as either tight grained or wide grained. STAVES used in BARREL MAKING are essentially cuts of wood fashioned from transversal sections of the tree. The ends of each stave therefore reveal growth rings from the life of the tree.

castellate cuts made with revolving saw

cuts made with fixed knife blades

staples inserted to make firm graft

Two types of machine **grafting** used for bench grafts

Tight-grained, less porous wood can be separated from wide-grained wood by a glance at the end of the stave.

The slower the growth of the tree, the tighter the grain of the wood. Alternating bands of dark and light wood reveal spring and summer growth. Growth in spring, the most important growing season for oak, is often rapid and is marked by large XYLEM vessels, cells with large openings for conducting water. Much smaller vessels mark growth in the summer. Of course, as with grapes, trees reflect soil and climate conditions, as well as the differences between species. For example, within the same region, minor differences in soil and climate may mean that one stand (delineated grouping) of trees grows straight and tall, and therefore has tight grains, while a few kilometres away another stand of trees may grow out, with wider grains. Within a single tree, the side of a tree furthest from the equator grows slightly slower than its opposite. Trees on the edge of a forest will also tend to grow out rather than up, while the reverse is generally true of trees growing in the depths of a forest.

Quercus robur (see OAK) usually gives wide-grained staves, which is to say that there are at least 3 mm/0.1 in between growth rings. Between the growth rings a gradual shift from spring to summer growth can be seen. For *Quercus robur*, spring growth is usually more than a quarter of the total annual growth. *Quercus petraea* on the other hand usually provides wood with less than 3 mm between the growth rings, and a sharp division between spring and summer growth can be seen. With *Quercus petraea*, spring growth usually amounts to less than a quarter of the total annual growth. There is considerable cross-fertilization between species, however.

Limousin oak tends to be wide grained. In the Limousin forests trees are wider apart than they are in the forests of central France, where trees must grow up, rather than out, for sunlight. Furthermore the Limousin forest appears to be dominated by *Quercus robur*. Consequently Limousin staves reveal greater spring growth and hence, more annual growth. Because of the greater percentage of large xylem vessels, these oaks are more porous.

Wider-grained wood tends to be more tannic than tight-grained wood because of the larger vessels. Analytically wide-grained wood is about 10 per cent TANNINS; tight-grained around 7 per cent. Thus wide-grained wood needs longer air drying (see BARREL MAKING) lest the wine aged in it be too bitter.

Although most coopers divide wood by forest so that tight- and wide-grained woods are worked together, others may divide wood into tight- and wide-grained woods.

See also WOOD INFLUENCE. M.K.

Graisse, also known as Plant de Graisse, minor white grape variety grown in the Armagnac region.

Grampians, temperate Australian wine region formerly known as Great Western in the Western Victoria Zone (see VICTORIA). Top-class Shiraz.

Granaccia or **Granacha,** Italian names for GRENACHE.

grand cru means literally 'great growth' in French. In Burgundy's CÔTE D'OR a grand cru is one of 34 particularly favoured vineyards (see BURGUNDY for list), a decided notch above PREMIER CRU. In Alsace, grand cru is a recent, elevated appellation accorded several dozen specific vineyards (see list under ALSACE). In Bordeaux, the words grand cru usually apply to a specific property or château and depend on the region in which it is located (see CLASSIFICATION).

Grande Rue, La, red burgundy GRAND CRU vineyard in VOSNE-ROMANÉE.

grandes marques, obsolete, self-imposed term for some of the major firms or BRANDS of CHAMPAGNE. The original Syndicat des Grandes Marques was founded in 1882 but was disbanded in 1997. This outdated term means literally 'big brand' in French.

grand format, bottle size larger than the standard 75 cl size and of particular interest to COLLECTORS and INVESTORS (provided it is filled with FINE WINE).

Grand Noir de la Calmette hardly deserves a name that suggests it is the great black grape variety of the BOUSCHET experimental vine-breeding station, Domaine de la Calmette. Bred from Petit Bouschet and the common ARAMON, it has a very high yield and, from its TEINTURIER parent, red flesh (although not as red as Alicante Bouschet's). Often known simply as **Grand Noir**, it was widely planted in France until the 1920s and is now almost extinct there. See also GRAN NEGRO.

Grand Roussillon, little-used ROUSSILLON VIN DOUX NATUREL appellation used effectively for declassified RIVESALTES. It also comes in RANCIO form.

Grands Échezeaux, red GRAND CRU in Burgundy's CÔTE D'OR. For more details, see ÉCHEZEAUX.

grand vin, name current in BORDEAUX for the main wine produced by a CHÂTEAU (as opposed to a SECOND WINE or *second vin*).

granite, a coarse-grained, visibly crystalline plutonic rock, composed of QUARTZ and feldspar as well as other minerals. Bereich Ortenau, a subregion of BADEN in south west Germany, has soils composed mainly of crumbled granite. The MOULIN-À-VENT vineyards of Beaujolais in France are made from grapes grown on shallow soils of decomposed granite,

and granite is the dominant element in the soils of the northern RHÔNE to the immediate south. Many of the vineyards of SARDEGNA are on granite soils, as are the vines producing the table wines of the lower DOURO, MINHO, and neighbouring DÃO (but not the vineyards producing PORT). Granitic soils are often of low fertility and this fact combined with typical rapid DRAINAGE makes such soils favoured for viticulture. See entries prefixed SOIL.

M.J.E.

Granite Belt, the first established wine region in the extreme south of QUEENSLAND, Australia, cooled by its high ALTITUDE. Sirromet, Robert Channon, and the tiny Boireann can produce wines of international quality.

Granja-Amareleja, subregion of ALENTEJO adjacent to the Spanish border in one of the most arid parts of southern Portugal.

Gran Negro or **Grão Negro,** rustic red-fleshed grape grown to a limited extent in northern Spain, particularly Valdeorras. Probably identical to GRAND NOIR DE LA CALMETTE, it was introduced after the PHYLLOXERA invasion.

Gran Reserva, Spanish term for a wine supposedly from an outstanding VINTAGE which has been subject to lengthy AGEING, the exact period varying from DO to DO, before release. Rioja produces the great majority of all Gran Reservas and here red wines must spend a minimum of two years in OAK. The wine may not leave the BODEGA until the sixth year after the vintage. White wines must spend a total of at least four years in cask and bottle, including at least six months' CASK AGEING, to qualify. For much of the 20th century, Gran Reservas represented Spain's finest and most expensive wines, but many of the country's most celebrated winemakers are nowadays concerned to preserve FRUIT in their top bottlings and do not necessarily equate quality with time spent in wood.

See also RESERVA.

granvas, Spanish term for sparkling wine made by the tank or Charmat SPARKLING WINE-MAKING method.

grape, the berry or fruit of the grapevine, or VINE, whose juice is the essential ingredient in WINE. A grape is *raisin* in French, *uva* in Italian and Spanish, and *Rebe* in German. The grapes produced by commercial viticulture are sold either as TABLE GRAPES or DRYING GRAPES, or crushed and processed into wine or GRAPE JUICE, GRAPE CONCENTRATE, or RECTIFIED GRAPE MUST. Wine production is, however, the most important use, accounting for some 80 per cent of the world's grape production. The solids, including stems, skins, seeds, and pulp, left after these juicing processes are called grape POMACE. There are several hundred grapes to a BUNCH for wine grape varieties, and berries are individually relatively small.

The form and appearance of grape berries varies hugely between VINE VARIETIES. Their shape varies from flattened, through spherical and oval, to elongated and finger-like; colour from green to yellow, pink, crimson, dark blue, and black; and size from as small as a pea (as in CURRANT, for example) to the huge, egg-like berries of some recently bred table grape varieties which may weigh as much as 15 g/0.5 oz each. The majority of wine grapes, however, are spherical to short oval, 1–2 g in weight, and are coloured yellow (called 'white' by vine-growers) or very dark purple (called 'black' or 'red').

Grape berries are borne on the end of a stalk, the PEDICEL, which in turn is borne on the BUNCHSTEM, or peduncle. At the end opposite the pedicel is a small stub of dead tissue which is the remnant of the style and stigma (see FLOWER). Some varieties, for example Riesling, have corky lenticels scattered over the skin. When cut open (see diagram below), the grape is seen to have two units (carpels) side by side, each enclosing a space (a locule) in which are the seeds. When the berry enlarges, the space becomes compressed by encroaching flesh. The significant parts of a berry are the flesh, skin, and seeds.

Flesh or pulp

The flesh or pulp (*pulpe* in French) is the bulk of the berry or PERICARP. The pulp contains the juice in the VACUOLES of pericarp cells. A sec-tion across the flesh shows that there are about 40 large parenchyma cells from beneath the skin to the single cell layer that is the inner lining. A central core of vascular strands con-nects to a mesh of veins that encircles the outer edge of the flesh like a chicken-wire cage and provides the vascular connection with the rest of the vine; the veins contain the XYLEM, which transports water and minerals from roots, and PHLOEM, which is the all-important pathway for sugar from the leaves. Another zone with a different texture is the so-called BRUSH, which is the lighter coloured part of the flesh near the junction with the pedicel.

The pulp and the juice are the most import-ant part of the grape to the winemaker, and the wine drinker, for they contain the main com-ponents of the finished wine. Because the juice of all grapes (apart from the specialist TEINTURIER varieties) is a pale grey, whatever the colour of the grape's skin, white wine can be made from grapes of all colours, so long as the juice is not left in contact with dark skins. Red wines can be made only by leaching col-our from such skins, while pink wines can be made either from short contact with dark skins or more prolonged contact with pink or red skins.

Skin

The grape's skin (*pellicule* in French) is the tough, enveloping layer around the grape that holds it together. The outside layer, or bloom, consists of wax plates and cutin, both of which resist water diffusion and hence water loss from the berry. They also impede pene-tration of fungal spore growths and other biological infections. This waxy layer forms the grape's typically whitish surface, called the BLOOM. The fatty acids and sterols from the bloom supply important nutrients for the growth of YEAST, either added or ambient yeast in the atmosphere, during FERMENTATION.

Below the wax and cutin are the cell layers that form the skin; the first is the true epider-mis, below this are about seven cell layers forming the hypodermis in which are concen-trated most of the berry PIGMENTS, yellow CAROTENOIDS, and xanthophylls, and the red and blue ANTHOCYANINS important in the mak-ing of red wine. As well as some TANNINS, a significant amount of a grape's FLAVOUR COM-POUNDS are also associated with the skin layers. There may well be differences in the precise locations of the PHENOLICS (pigments, tannins, and flavour compounds). Those compounds located closest to the pulp are presumably ex-tracted first.

There are other differences in the chemical composition of skin compared with the under-lying flesh: besides phenolics, they are rich in POTASSIUM. Skins constitute between 5 and 12 per cent by weight of a mature grape berry, depending on the vine variety. The thickness of grape skin can vary from about 3 to 8 μm.

Seeds

Seeds, *pepins* in French, of grapes vary in size and shape between varieties; for example, those in MUSCAT BLANC À PETITS GRAINS are about 5 mm long while those in the table grape Waltham Cross are nearly 10 mm. Their num-ber per berry tends to be a characteristic for each variety with one or two predominating. Four is possible since each carpel bears two ovules; however, some freak Ribier berries with double the number of carpels may have eight seeds. Often, incompletely developed seed structures occur, called stenospermic (thin-seeded), alongside fully developed seeds. The greater the number and amount of seed devel-opment, the larger the berry; this relationship is largely a reflection of differences in amount of cell division in the pericarp. The plant hormone GIBBERELLIN may substitute for the berry-enlarging effect of seeds, as it is when Sultana is grown for the table, for example.

Seeds are only of minor importance in wine-making although if they are crushed, as those who eat seeded grapes know, the bitter tannins they contain are released. Unlike the stems, which are relatively easy to separate from the berries, seeds always accompany the juice and skins into the draining tanks or press for white wines, or into the fermentation vessel for red wines. In WHITE WINE-MAKING, the contact time between juice and seeds and absorption of tan-nins from the seeds is minimal. In RED WINE-MAKING, on the other hand, the prolonged contact between the seeds and an increasingly alcoholic solution means that tannins are very

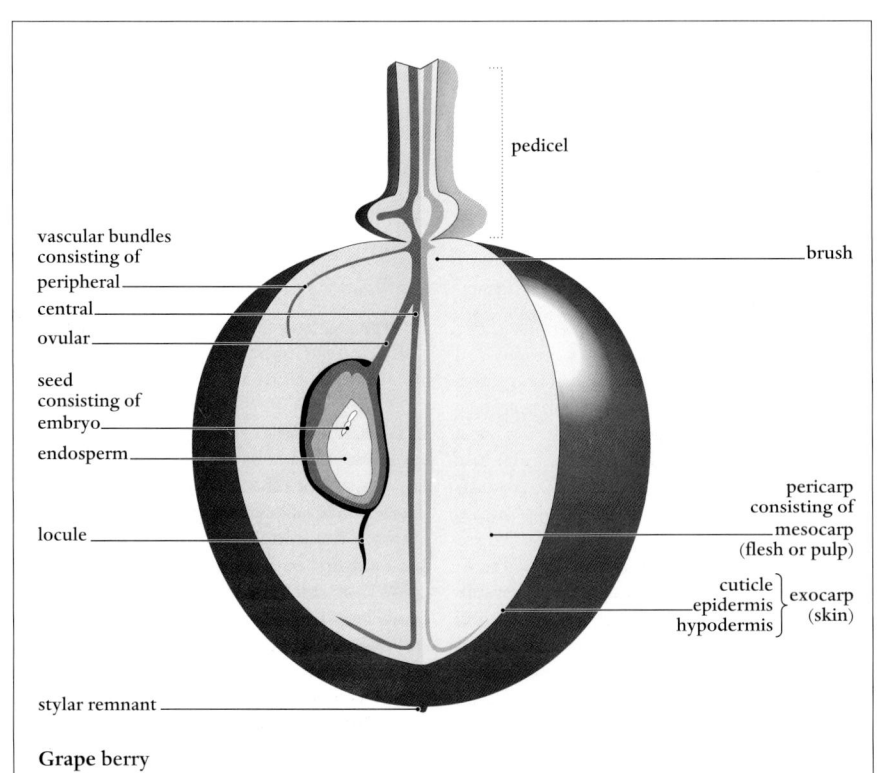

vascular bundles consisting of
peripheral
central
ovular

seed consisting of
embryo
endosperm

locule

stylar remnant

pedicel

brush

pericarp consisting of
mesocarp (flesh or pulp)

cuticle
epidermis } exocarp
hypodermis } (skin)

Grape berry

likely to be dissolved. Grape seeds have served as a source of edible or industrial oil.

See also GRAPE COMPOSITION AND WINE QUALITY, GRAPE QUALITY ASSESSMENT, and RIPENING. (For other parts of the vine plant, see VINE MORPHOLOGY.) B.G.C. & A.D.W.

Coombe, B. G. 'Research on development and ripening of the grape berry', *American Journal of Enology & Viticulture*, 43 (1992), 101–10.

grape composition and wine quality.

Grape composition is the essential basis of wine quality, and knowledge of grape composition is critical for those winemakers interested in making the appropriate wine style. The concentrations of all component chemical groups play a part. Grape SUGARS, for example (see MUST WEIGHT), determine the possible potential ALCOHOLIC STRENGTH of the wine. ACIDS and nitrogenous compounds (see NITROGEN) affect the course of FERMENTATION and exert their own effects on flavour. POTASSIUM salts have effects on PH and thus on microbiological activity and oxidative STABILITY. PHENOLICS contribute to levels of COLOUR and TANNINS. A multitude of volatile compounds alter aroma (see ACIDITY, AMINO ACIDS, FLAVOUR COMPOUNDS, SUGARS).

Grape composition is constantly changing during RIPENING. A central factor in grape ripening is the steady increase in sugar concentration after sugar accumulation has been triggered at VERAISON. Another feature is that acidity declines, due mainly to the RESPIRATION of malate but also to dilution by berry growth and the formation of salts, especially with potassium, which increases concurrently with sugar. Colour and tannins increase in skins early during ripening. Less is known about the timing of the increase in aroma compounds because until recently they have been difficult to measure, but in some varieties intensity appears to develop late in the ripening process, after sugar concentration has levelled (see ENGUSTMENT and GRAPE QUALITY ASSESSMENT). Monitoring the GLYCOSIDE concentration in ripening grape berries is now possible through analysis of GLYCOSYL-GLUCOSE. This allows a relatively easy measurement of the increase in these components, including the important FLAVOUR PRECURSORS of the fruit. Quality epitomizes the integration of these chemical groups in such a way that there is a balance between individual components, coupled with an intensity of VARIETAL character. B.G.C. & P.J.W.

grape concentrate

is what is left when the volatile elements are removed from fresh grape juice. Rarely used to produce really fine wine, it can provide a useful supply of grape SOLUBLE SOLIDS for use long after the HARVEST. Grape concentrate is the main ingredient, for example, in so-called MADE WINES produced without the benefit of freshly picked grapes (see BRITISH WINES and HOME WINE-MAKING).

Grape concentrate can also be used in BLENDING to soften and sweeten dry wines of everyday commercial standard made in cooler regions. It is widely used in Germany, for example, where it is called *Süssreserve*. For more details of grape concentrate used for sweetening purposes, see SWEET RESERVE. Grape concentrate is also in some circumstances used for ENRICHMENT, increasing the eventual alcohol content of a wine (it is a permitted prefermentation additive in Australia, for instance, although sugar is not). It is also used to sweeten some other fruit juices and foodstuffs, and is sometimes used as an alternative to honey. Concentrate is also used to produce a small category of high-intensity red and purple colourants, used to enhance colour and add body to wines.

Historically, winemakers made a form of grape concentrate by simply boiling grape juice until the volume was reduced by at least one-half. This resulted in a liquid with a strong cooked, caramel flavour, however, and such an additive is used exclusively for sweet, dark, strong wines such as rich SHERRY, MÁLAGA, and MARSALA. In Spain it is known as *arrope*.

Today, the caramelizing effect is avoided by CONCENTRATION of the grape juice under very low temperatures in vacuum evaporators. Modern low pressure concentrators represent a heavy investment for a winery selling anything other than the most expensive wine. They therefore tend to be operated by specialists who may use them to concentrate other fruit juices at other times of year. Most grape juice is subject to CLARIFICATION and is reduced in TARTRATES before concentration so that the solids precipitated are minimal when water is removed.

Red grape concentrate may be made by first heating the grapes to extract PIGMENTS into the juice before concentration. A.D.W.

grape juice

is a sweet, clear, non-alcoholic liquid. Winemakers generally use the term to refer to MUST that has undergone CLARIFICATION and STABILIZATION. Preserved by holding at temperatures so low that any YEAST or BACTERIA are inhibited, such juice was often used in commercial wine-making to soften or sweeten new, dry wines. Since the development of efficient juice concentrators, however, it has generally been supplanted in wine-making by GRAPE CONCENTRATE, which can be stored much more cheaply, is inherently stable against microbiological attack, and dilutes the wine much less.

A certain amount of grape juice is bottled and sold as a drink, however, although grape juice is a minor beverage compared with juices of other fruits such as citrus and apple. Since it so readily ferments, it needs to be protected from yeast contamination. This is usually done by PASTEURIZATION and/or ULTRAFILTRATION and heavy additions of SULFUR DIOXIDE. Many VINIFERA varieties lose their pleasant,

fresh taste after pasteurization, and the American grape juice industry uses the non-*vinifera* CONCORD variety. The juice from grapes harvested at optimum ripeness for wine has a rather cloying sweetness which can overshadow the refreshing ACIDITY. Interestingly, it is very difficult to distinguish VARIETAL character in most grape juices, other than such conspicuous flavours as those associated with MUSCAT and Concord grapes. Wine drinkers generally find grape juice bears disappointingly little relation to wine. A.D.W.

grape juice composition.

The relative proportions of the compounds that make up grape juice are constantly changing as the berries ripen, so the time of HARVEST greatly affects composition. Most of the sugary solution that results when grapes are squeezed or crushed derives from the contents of the VACUOLES of the cells of the pulp or flesh, although heavy crushing and pressing adds further solution from vacuoles of the skin and vascular strands, thereby mixing many different compounds into the must. Thus the composition of the juice that issues when berries are crushed changes with the pressure and time of crushing; the first, FREE-RUN juice has fewest suspended solids and skin extracts; further pressing yields juice with more PHENOLICS and POTASSIUM salts, and hence lower TOTAL ACIDITY.

Fermentation of juice with skins present, as in red wine-making, yields still more FLAVOUR COMPOUNDS and PIGMENTS that are enriched in the cells of the skin. See GRAPE.

See also ACIDITY, AMINO ACIDS, ANTHOCYANINS, ASCORBIC ACID, CAROTENOIDS, CITRIC ACID, FRUCTOSE, GLUCOSE, GLYCOSIDES, LIPIDS, MALIC ACID, MINERALS, PECTINS, PROTEINS, SOLUBLE SOLIDS, STARCH, SUCROSE, TANNINS, TERPENOIDS, VARIETAL character, VITAMINS, and the all-important SUGAR IN GRAPES. B.G.C.

grape quality assessment

is needed by winemakers for long-term strategic planning and, in the short term, for the planning of each vintage, especially in fixing HARVEST dates. Assessment is often a matter of combined judgement by grape-growers and winemakers, using experience of the performance of previous vintages as the main guide, supplemented by tasting of berries and by measurements of GRAPE COMPOSITION (see SAMPLING and ANALYSIS). In some regions, sugar content (see MUST WEIGHT) is sufficient to indicate forthcoming wine quality, especially in cool regions (unless, of course, major catastrophes such as disease intervene). In warm to hot regions, sugar alone is an unreliable guide to quality and additional measurements are needed: TOTAL ACIDITY and PH of the juice are useful, as well as some measure of the colour of skins in some red grapes. The importance of aroma is increasingly recognized, but it is difficult to measure. Valuable information can be obtained by collecting and storing juice samples at intervals during grape development and running comparative 'sniffing tests', but these are costly and difficult because of their subjective nature. An experimental technique, GLYCOSYL-GLUCOSE ASSAY, was developed in the late 1990s to supplement these methods. This gives a measure of the total GLYCOSIDE concentration in grapes, which include FLAVOUR PRECURSORS of varietal FLAVOUR COMPOUNDS. More recently, the use of near infrared (NIR) spectroscopy for the determination of red grape colour, expressed as the concentration of total ANTHOCYANINS, is a further development in grape quality assessment.

Many other characteristics of the harvest contribute to the assessment of its quality. Foremost is the amount and type of berry ROT which has been quantified in wineries in many countries. Other factors are the presence of broken skins due to heavy RAINFALL, HAIL, or physical damage. The extent of berry shrivel, evenness of ripening, contamination with leaves, clods, and other non-grape material, and BERRY SIZE are other important factors. Careful vine-growers will also take account of the appearance of the vineyard, the state of the CANOPY, condition of the leaves, and the general vineyard management.

See also ACIDITY, ANTHOCYANINS, FLAVOUR COMPOUNDS, GRAPE COMPOSITION AND WINE QUALITY, PHENOLICS, SUGARS.   B.G.C.

grape sorting. See TRIAGE.

grape varieties. This term is often used interchangeably with vine varieties since different varieties of vine have predictably different grapes or berries. The effect of grape varieties on wine quality is discussed under VINE VARIETIES. Different varieties of vine produce grapes with very different and distinct characteristics (many of them outlined under the names of individual varieties). Wines made predominantly from a single grape variety, usually specified on the label, are called VARIETAL wines. The wine consumer is thus familiar with the names of many popular varieties such as CHARDONNAY, CABERNET SAUVIGNON, MERLOT, PINOT NOIR, RIESLING, SAUVIGNON BLANC, and SYRAH/SHIRAZ.

See under the names of individual varieties. Specialized varieties are listed for both TABLE GRAPES and DRYING GRAPES.

grapevine, an alternative name for the plant on which most of the world's wine trade depends. It is known by most wine producers and consumers as the VINE.

grapevine yellows, generic term for a group of related PHYTOPLASMA diseases of grapevines which pose a serious threat to vineyards in many wine regions of the world because there is no known control. The best-known of these diseases, FLAVESCENCE DORÉE, can kill young vines and makes old vines

uneconomical. It is spread by infected plants from the nursery and further spread by insects called LEAFHOPPERS, to which many common vineyard WEEDS are alternative host plants. The disease occurs sporadically in epidemics, and varieties vary in their sensitivity to it.

Flavescence dorée, the first recorded phytoplasma grapevine disease, appeared in the Armagnac region in south west France on the vine variety BACO 22A in 1949. It spread rapidly throughout France towards the end of the 20th century. In 1982, only isolated vineyards in Armagnac were affected by flavescence dorée, as well as a very restricted area in the Languedoc. By 1987, this disease had spread to Cognac, throughout Languedoc and to the northern and southern Rhône, and by 1992 to the Loire valley, Bordeaux, and the Côtes du Rhône. Several variants have also been noted, including Bois Noir in north eastern France, Bordeaux, and Switzerland, Vergilbungskrankheit in Germany, leaf curl and berry shrivel in New York state, and a form known as Australian grapevine yellows. A similar disease has been described in Romania, Israel, Chile, and Italy, and more recently in Slovenia, Croatia, Hungary, and Spain. That these diseases are more or less related has been shown by a form of DNA PROFILING called polymerase chain reaction. These diseases are related to phytoplasma diseases which attack many other crops and native plants such as, for example, some which affect pawpaw and tomato in Australia.

The first sign of grapevine yellows can be delayed BUDBREAK and very slow shoot growth until FLOWERING. Later, shoots on infected vines stop growing while leaves yellow and curl downwards. Later in the season, shoots droop as though made of rubber. When affected early in the season, bunches fall off. Otherwise, the berries shrivel and taste bitter. The disease can kill young vines, and old vines do not recover completely from infection. Symptoms seem to vary from year to year, and crop levels fluctuate. During epidemics, as for example in northern Italy in 1995, yields of some vineyards dropped to one-tenth of a normal crop. The Australian experience is that vineyards with well-established infections yield at about half the rate of healthy vineyards.

Different species of leafhopper seem to be associated with the spread of different forms of grapevine yellows. Flavescence dorée is transmitted in the field by *Scaphoideus titanus*. Originally native to the eastern United States and Canada, this insect was apparently introduced to Europe after the Second World War. The German form is spread by the leafhopper *Hyalesthes obsoletus*, and in Australia the vector is currently unknown but *Scaphoideus titanus* is suspected.

Other plants can furthermore act as reservoirs of the disease in that insects spread the disease to and from them and grapevines. These so-called host plants include many

broadleaf weeds and COVER CROPS such as nettles, mallow, chicory, dandelion, thistles, bindweed, deadly nightshade, and many clovers. The infection spreads rapidly when the appropriate insect vector and host plants are also present in or around the vineyards, which phenomenon is increasing as vineyard CULTIVATION is practised less frequently and cover crops and weeds are more common (see ORGANIC and BIODYNAMIC VITICULTURE). Disease epidemics in France and Italy have been associated with the natural fluctuations in leafhopper populations, and this is probably the case everywhere.

There is no effective control of grapevine yellows diseases. Insecticide sprays can reduce the leafhopper populations—especially of *Scaphoideus*—and reduce the spread of the disease. The removal of broad leaf cover crops and weeds reduces insect levels and opportunities for feeding on host plants. However, if the vineyards are small and are surrounded by native vegetation then this can be impractical. The disease can be spread by infected planting material. Young plants can be dipped in hot water before they leave the nursery (typically 50 °C for 30 to 45 minutes when fully dormant) which will kill phytoplasma as well as some other diseases, but regrettably not all nurseries follow this practice.

Chardonnay and Riesling are among the most susceptible VINIFERA varieties, followed by Grenache, Tannat, Pinot Noir, and Pinot Gris. Some AMERICAN VINE SPECIES are tolerant. Grapevine yellows diseases may eventually be more destructive to the world's viticulture than was PHYLLOXERA, because they are widespread, are spreading even further, and cannot be controlled with resistant ROOTSTOCKS. Wine quality does not appear to be affected, but the supply of grapes, especially of Chardonnay, can be.   R.E.S.

Bovey, R., *et al., Virus and Virus-like Diseases of Vines: Colour Atlas of Symptoms* (Lausanne, 1980).

Pearson, R. C., and Goheen, A. C., *Compendium of Grape Diseases* (St Paul, Minn., 1988).

Grapput, or Synonym for the rapidly declining French grape variety BOUCHALÈS.

Grasă, the 'fat' white grape of COTNARI in ROMANIA, where it is grown exclusively, on a total of about 450 ha/1,100 acres of vineyard in 2005. It can reach extremely high MUST WEIGHTS but needs the balancing acidity of grapes such as TĂMÂIOASĂ Românească in a blend. In 1958, Grasă grapes in Cotnari reached a sugar concentration of 520 g/l. The vine is usefully sensitive to NOBLE ROT and is said to have been grown in this part of western Moldavia since the 15th century. Some believe that this is the same variety as the FURMINT of Tokay.

Graşevina, Croatian name for the republic's most planted vine variety, WELSCHRIESLING. The name **Grassica** may also be used.

grasshoppers, insects of the families *Acrididae* and *Tettigoniidae* which can feed on the vine. Reductions in vineyard leaf area impair grape RIPENING, with potentially severe effects on wine quality. In California, for example, the devastating grasshopper (*Melanoplus devastator Scudder*) is particularly harmful to vineyards, causing damage by defoliation, usually in mid to late summer. In eastern Australia, the Australian plague locust (*Chortoicetes terminifera*) can be a major pest. Dense swarms can build up in pasture areas, and descend very quickly on vineyard areas, especially when pastures dry out. Control where necessary is usually by insecticides.   M.J.E.

Buchanan, G. A., and Amos, T. G., 'Grape pests', in B. G. Coombe and P. R. Dry (eds.), *Viticulture*, ii:, *Practices* (Adelaide, 1992).

grassy, TASTING TERM usually used synonymously with HERBACEOUS.

Grau, German for grey or *gris*.

Grauburgunder, German synonym for PINOT GRIS used for the increasingly popular dry wines made from this grape in Germany. Sweeter wines are normally labelled RULÄNDER. Its success in producing spicy, full-bodied dry wine accounts for the steady increase in total area planted with the variety in Germany: its 3,400 ha/8,400 acres by 2003 making it the country's fifth most planted white wine grape. It needs a good site with deep, heavy soils to maximize the impressive level of extract of which it is capable. It is a particularly popular speciality of the warm BADEN region, although there are several hundred hectares in both RHEINHESSEN and the PFALZ.

Grave del Friuli, vast DOC zone in the FRIULI region of north east Italy which sprawls across the southern portion of the provinces of Pordenone and Udine (with the largest portion in the former). This is flatland whose GRAVEL- and sand-based soil has been deposited over the millennia by the many rivers and streams that cross the territory before adding their waters to the Adriatic. It owes its name to the same root as the gravelly GRAVES region of Bordeaux in France.

Over 6,500 ha/16,000 acres of vineyards produce light, fruity reds and fresh, aromatic whites. MERLOT, with just under 2,000 ha/5,000 acres in the mid 2000s, is the dominant vine variety here, as in the neighbouring LISON-PRAMAGGIORE DOC to the west. Various CABERNETS (close to 800 ha) and REFOSCO dal Peduncolo Rosso (just under 200 ha), plus minuscule quantities of PINOT NERO, bring the total area of red varieties to virtually 3,500 ha, more than half the total, making this, the largest DOC, something of an anomaly in Friuli.

As elsewhere in the region, TOCAI Friulano's domination has been challenged by Pinot Grigio, each variety being planted on about 850 ha of vineyard. Significant plantings of PINOT BIANCO (450 ha), SAUVIGNON BLANC (more than 400 ha), and VERDUZZO (300 ha) also produce white wine. Sauvignons of marked character are produced here, with an aromatic intensity that appeals to lovers of the powerfully herbaceous. Some attempts—often unconvinced and unconvincing—at more structured reds have been made since the mid 1980s but the Merlots and Cabernets of Grave del Friuli seem intrinsically lighter than the better reds from the COLLI ORIENTALI, Friuli's second most important DOC.

                         D.T. & D.C.G.

gravel, a soil or unconsolidated rock in which pebbles are the most obvious component, known in French as *graves*, from which the two appellations below, and the DOC above, take their names. Gravel is the most distinctive soil type of Bordeaux's so-called LEFT BANK wine regions. It is said that glaciers, slowly moving down to the Atlantic coast from the distant Pyrenees, followed the course of the nearby river, pushing back its high right bank. When glaciers melted, the pebbles remained near the surface. The vineyards of the GRAVES are, not surprisingly, characterized by their gravelly surface and gravel is nowhere so prevalent as at Ch HAUT-BRION, where in places it is 16–20 m/50–65 ft deep. Such soils offer excellent DRAINAGE, imposing on the vine the slight WATER STRESS favoured for wine quality. See VINE PHYSIOLOGY and SOIL AND WINE QUALITY.

Gravel soils are also highly prized for quality wine production on the plateau of ST-ÉMILION, in CHÂTEAUNEUF-DU-PAPE, GRAVE DEL FRIULI, and in the Gimblett Road region of Hawkes Bay in NEW ZEALAND. However, many gravel areas may well be used for viticulture simply because they are too difficult to work and too infertile for any other form of agriculture. It is notable that Chx Haut-Brion and La Mission-Haut-Brion are now viticultural oases in the southern suburbs of Bordeaux, indicating that the land is more valuable for housing than for vines.

See entries prefixed SOIL.

                         M.J.E., R.E.S., & J.M.H.
Enjalbert. H., *Great Bordeaux Wines: St Émilion, Pomerol, Fronsac* (Paris, 1983: Eng. trans. 1985).

Graves, French for gravelly terrain, and a term at one time used for many of Bordeaux's wine districts, but now the name of one particular large region extending 50 km/30 miles south east of the city along the left bank of the river GARONNE (see map under BORDEAUX). Graves is Bordeaux's only region famous for both its red and white wines, although its aristocratic, mineral-scented, Cabernet-dominated red wines are made in much greater quantity than its dry whites. In the early 1990s, about 1,800 ha/4,500 acres were planted with red wine grapes, while about 950 ha produced dry white Graves. By 2004, a total of almost 3,100 ha of vines were dedicated to the Graves appellation. **Graves Supérieures** is another growing appellation, this time reserved for sweet wines, to which about 500 ha were dedicated in 2004, producing wines very similar to, but generally coarser than, those from the enclave entitled to the CÉRONS appellation.

The Graves, and in particular the outskirts of Bordeaux, the Grabas de Burdeus, is the birthplace of CLARET. In the Middle Ages, much of the light CLAIRET dispatched in such quantity to England was grown in these vineyards within easy distance of the quayside; the Médoc was largely marshland (see BORDEAUX, history). Ch Pape-Clément is Bordeaux's first named château, while HAUT-BRION was the first New French Claret noted in London, by Samuel Pepys, in 1663. Thomas JEFFERSON noted that in the late 18th century 'Grave' wines were considered the finest Bordeaux had to offer. It was presumably this historic fame which had Ch Haut-Brion, Graves's most famous property, included with the finest Médoc châteaux in the famous CLASSIFICATION in 1855.

For centuries Graves encompassed all the vineyards south of the border with the MÉDOC in a great sweep around the city and upstream along the Garonne as far as Langon, with the exception of the enclaves for sweet white wine appellations BARSAC, CÉRONS, and SAUTERNES. In 1987, the separate appellation of PESSAC-LÉOGNAN was formed, a slice of the original Graves appellation which includes all of its most famous properties, and the southern suburbs of Bordeaux itself. For more details of the wines produced there today, see PESSAC-LÉOGNAN.

The creation of this new premium appellation had the effect of somewhat declassifying the historic name Graves, although some excellent wines are conscientiously made within the modern Graves appellation on the varied GRAVEL terraces which have been deposited there over the millennia. The reds, which can truly taste like country cousins of their more urbane neighbours in Pessac-Léognan, can often be good value, and mature earlier than their Médoc counterparts. It is in this area that some serious barrel-fermented, or at least oak-aged, dry whites are made, from Sauvignon and Sémillon grapes in varying proportions, at properties such as Clos Floridène and Chx Chantegrive, La Grave, St-Robert, du Seuil, and Vieux Ch Gaubert (although better value can sometimes be found on the opposite bank of the Garonne; see PREMIÈRES CÔTES DE BORDEAUX and ENTRE-DEUX-MERS).

Parker, R., *Bordeaux* (4th edn, New York, 2003).

Graves de Vayres, a small BORDEAUX district, named after the historic town of Vayres, which has nothing to do with GRAVES but is just across the river DORDOGNE from the town of Libourne. From about 600 ha/1,480 acres of, not surprisingly, gravelly soil, with patches of sand, the appellation produces mainly light red wines made substantially from MERLOT grapes, although many of them are sold under the simple BORDEAUX AC. White wines, both sweet and dry, were once more important. Today the white is usually dry, occasionally given BARREL MATURATION, and constitutes the minority of wine sold as Graves de Vayres.

Greater Perth Zone, WESTERN AUSTRALIA, encompassing the Peel, Perth Hills, and Swan District regions.

Great Southern, high-quality, cool climate wine region in the extreme south west of WESTERN AUSTRALIA, including subregions Albany, Denmark, Frankland River, Mount Barker and Porongurup. Each has its own TERROIR and climate dictated in part by the distance from the south coast of Western Australia.

Great Western. See GRAMPIANS.

Grecanico Dorato, Sicilian white grape variety whose total vineyard area increased from less than 3,000 ha in 1980 to 5,172 ha/13,100 acres in 2000. The name suggests Greek origins and the wines currently made may not be maximizing its full aromatic, rather SAUVIGNON BLANC-like potential.

Grechetto, sometimes **Greghetto,** characterful central Italian white grape variety most closely associated with UMBRIA. It is an ingredient in ORVIETO and in the whites of TORGIANO and the Colli Martani DOC. The grapes' thick skins provide good resistance to DOWNY MILDEW, making it sufficiently sturdy to produce good VIN SANTO. It is typically blended with Trebbiano, VERDELLO, and MALVASIA. In ANTINORI's most admired white wine Cervaro, it has played a supporting role to CHARDONNAY, and this type of wine is now being copied by other ambitious producers in Umbria. Grechetto di Todi is probably even more widely planted than Grechetto Spoletino. Intrinsically more interesting than either Trebbiano or DRUPEGGIO, it is expected to have a much larger role in Umbrian white wines, particularly Orvieto, in the future. Occasionally called **Greco Spoletino** or **Greco Bianco di Perugia,** it is by no means identical to GRECO BIANCO, although it is presumed to share its Greek origins.

Greco Bianco, name of one or perhaps several, usually noble, white grape varieties, assumed to be of Greek origin, currently grown in southern Italy. Plantings totalled less than 1,000 ha/2,500 acres in the early 2000s. DNA PROFILING has shown at least one Greco Bianco to be identical to ASPRINIO.

In CAMPANIA, it produces the respected DOCG dry white **Greco di Tufo** around the village of Tufo. With better vinification, its delicate aromas, which put some people in mind of good Viognier, have come to be better appreciated. Blended with FALANGHINA and BIANCOLELLA grapes, it makes a contribution to the inconsequential dry whites of the island of Capri. It is also used in the blend of Gravina DOC of Puglia, where the high altitude of the vineyards, bordering on Basilicata, brings out the variety's aromatic character.

The oenologist Severino Garofano believes another CLONE is responsible for the sweet **Greco di Bianco** made from semi-dried grapes called Greco grown around the town of Bianco on the south coast of CALABRIA.

Greco Nero, the most widely planted Greco vine variety in Italy with 3,200 ha/7,900 acres, mainly in Calabria, where it is often blended with GAGLIOPPO.

Greece, renascent Mediterranean wine producer with a particularly rich history of wine made in classical times from the 7th century BC and on in the Roman era (see Ancient ROME). Early Greek colonization led to the vine being taken to all parts of the Mediterranean, thus laying the foundations for viticulture and the whole later development of wine in this area. In modern Greece, about 130,000 ha/321,000 acres are devoted to vines, only about half of them producing grapes for wine, DRYING GRAPES and TABLE GRAPES being important to the agricultural economy. About 70 per cent of the annual wine production of between 3.5 and 4 million hl (about 100 million gal) is of white wine.

Ancient Greece

Origins Wine was important in Greek society from the earliest times, forming part of the Greek cultural identity. The Ancient Greeks were aware that other societies, such as the Babylonians in MESOPOTAMIA and the inhabitants of Ancient EGYPT, made and drank wine, but for them it was a luxury, and they normally drank BEER (a drink disparaged by Greek writers as inferior and fit only for foreigners) or else 'wine' made from dates or lotus. Complete ignorance of viticulture was the mark of savages; so too was the drinking of undiluted wine, which was associated with northern barbarians such as the Scythians (in modern CRIMEA).

The vine was initially domesticated in Greece in the late neolithic, and widely cultivated by the early Bronze Age. Wine was clearly a significant element in the culture of Minoan CRETE before 2000 BC: remains of grapes and of installations for wine production (treading floors and spouted vats) have been found by archaeologists at palaces and villas, and it is probable that some of the large storage jars found in the palace complexes contained wine rather than olive oil; an ideogram for 'wine' has been identified in the early script Linear A, and artistic evidence suggests the use of wine in ritual contexts. Given the links between Crete and Egypt in this period, the Minoans might be expected both to have learned viticulture from their neighbours and to have exported to supply the demand there and elsewhere in the Near East. In turn, Crete will have influenced contemporary Thíra (modern SANTORINI), where vines and grapes are depicted on painted pottery.

Mycenae There is no doubt of the importance of wine in Mycenaean culture (c.1600–1150 BC), which followed and developed on the mainland from Minoan culture: evidence from Mycenae, Tiryns, and Sparta includes grape pips and residues of wine, as well as the seal of a jar bearing the impression of vine leaves, while the palaces have revealed many storage jars, including a complete cellar at Pílos which contained at least 35 large jars, some labelled as containing wine. The evidence of the Linear B script, preserved on clay tablets fired hard in the destruction of the palaces, confirms that wine was important: the palace records contain many references to it, and include words for 'wine', 'vineyard', and, apparently, 'wine merchant', not to mention allusions to the god DIONYSUS. Finds of Mycenaean pottery abroad imply that they were exporting wine and oil to Syria, Palestine, Egypt, Cyprus, Sicilia, and southern Italy, while the discovery of a few small CANAANITE jars (the earliest AMPHORAE) at Mycenae may suggest that connoisseurs were also importing foreign wines; certainly wine appears to have been a luxury item largely restricted to the élite.

Early Greek literature In the poetry of HOMER and HESIOD, the earliest Greek literature, wine is an essential part of life. It is naturally drunk by Greek and Trojan heroes at their feasts, but also used in the rituals of sacrifice, prayer, and burial, to solemnize agreements, and for therapeutic purposes; it is also the human drink, whereas gods drink nectar. A depiction of the vintage, in an enclosed vineyard, is part of the encapsulation of human life on the shield which Hephaestus makes for Achilles (*Iliad* 18. 561 f.). Wine is the touchstone of civilization: even the Cyclopes in the *Odyssey* drink it, but without cultivating the vine, unlike the pleasure-loving Phaeacians, and, when offered the fine wine of Maron, Polyphemus swigs it neat until he falls into a stupor. Homer implies that the vine was widespread in Greece in his time, describing a number of places as 'rich in vines' (including Phrygia: in this as in other respects the Trojans are as civilized as the Greeks), and he gives us our earliest reference to specific wines, Pramnian and Ismarian, while Hesiod mentions Bibline. Advice on viticulture forms part of Hesiod's *Works and Days*: he mentions pruning and the harvest, including drying the grapes before vinification to make early forms of DRIED GRAPE WINES.

The extent of viticulture In the classical period, vines were grown throughout Greece, and, through colonization, the Greeks carried viticulture to Sicilia and southern Italy (which the Greeks called OENOTRIA, 'land of trained vines'), southern France, and the Black Sea. Some producers operated on a large scale, with extensive estates: we can infer the existence of vineyards of 8 to 10 ha and 30 ha/74 acres on the island of Thásos in the northern Aegean in the late 5th century BC and of one of about 12 ha in Attica in the middle of the 4th century, and Diodorus records a cellar at Acragas in Sicilia with a storage capacity of 12,000 hl/317,000 gal and a vat holding 400 hl/10,500 gal (*Library of History* 13. 83). However, most viticulture was probably on a small scale, part of the normal peasant system of polyculture, which in Greece was founded on grain, vines, and olives; vines require more labour than cereals, but wine and grapes clearly played an important part in the Greek diet.

Trade Viticulture was also important to the economy of many cities, as is shown by the number of states whose coinage bears wine-related designs. Greek wine was traded within Greece, with Athens, the largest and richest city, offering the best market, and exported throughout the Mediterranean world, especially to Egypt, the Black Sea, Scythia, and Etruria (modern TOSCANA). Soon the colonial cities began to produce and export their own wine. (See CELTS for archaeological evidence of the geographical extent to which Greek wine and drinking rituals were adopted.) Amphorae from Marseilles are found along the southern coast of France and up the RHÔNE valley, while in the CRIMEA archaeology has revealed extensive estates, their vineyards protected from the prevailing winds by low walls and planted with indigenous vines which were gradually domesticated, rather than with imported varieties.

The scale of the Greek wine trade can be inferred from the widespread finds of amphorae and the seals which indicate their origin. The richest evidence is from the island of Thásos, which took elaborate precautions to regulate its wine trade, both to maximize tax revenues and to prevent fraud which would damage its reputation; amphorae were required to be of standard sizes and were sealed with the name of an annual magistrate, which acted as a guarantee of authenticity; other states also used this system. Thásos also protected her commerce by forbidding her citizens to import foreign wine.

Viticultural practices No vine grown today can be confidently traced back to any Ancient Greek variety, although we know the names of 50 or more, some of which were cultivated in Italy in Roman times, and names such as GRECO, GRECHETTO, and AGLIANICO (i.e. Helleniko) reflect popular traditions of continuity (although recent research suggests that these are more romance than reality). Roman writers noted that the YIELDS of Greek varieties were low, although their qual-

ity was good. In the 4th century BC, the botanically expert THEOPHRASTUS was aware of the need to match varieties to soil type and MESOCLIMATE, and recommended PROPAGATION by cuttings or suckering. A variety of VINE-TRAINING regimes was used: often vines were supported by forked props or trained up trees, but a few varieties naturally formed bushes, and sometimes plants were simply left to trail on the ground; training on trees meant climbing up, or using trestles, to pick the grapes. PRUNING was known to have an important effect on yields and quality, and land leases sometimes specify that the lessors be allowed to oversee it towards the end of a lease, as well as regulating the use of manure as fertilizer.

Vinification The HARVEST was, as in modern Greece, early by European standards: Hesiod recommends early September. Vase paintings suggest that, in many cases, pressing took place near the vineyard: the grapes were trodden inside a handled wicker basket which in turn stood in a wooden trough with low legs, from which the juice ran through a spout into an earthenware vat sunk in a hole in the ground; sometimes a sieve was placed over the mouth of the vat. As pickers brought grapes in, they were added to the basket, while the treader held on to the basket handles or a ring or rope overhead (or a convenient vine) to keep his balance, and worked at CRUSHING in time to a flute. There are also scenes of treading in the vat itself, in which case the skins and pips will not have been strained out, and the wine will have taken colour from the skins, an early form of PIGEAGE. In either case, the vats will then have been covered and the juice taken for FERMENTATION in jars of larger capacity (*pithoi*); these could be 3 m/10 ft high, with a mouth a metre across. Larger and more specialized establishments had permanent stone treading floors rather than wooden ones, but otherwise the process was the same; although the beam PRESS was normally used for olives, there is little evidence for its use in wine production in classical Greece, and the screw press probably appeared only in Roman republican times. Small-scale producers may well have employed more primitive forms of pressing such as torsion in a fabric container, but no evidence for these survives.

References to the drying of grapes in Hesiod and the *Odyssey* (see DRIED GRAPE WINES) suggest that this was the early norm, but in later times practices varied: a Lesbian wine, Protropon, was made from FREE-RUN juice, while in other cases grapes were deliberately harvested unripe to produce a wine with high ACIDITY (Omphakias); fresh MUST itself was sometimes drunk, as was boiled must. Finally, the solids left after treading could be moistened with water and trodden again to yield a low-quality PIQUETTE called Deuterias or Stemphulites.

Although wine was often transferred from the fermentation vessels once fermentation was over, it is clear that it had not been subjected to proper RACKING or FINING since a sieve or strainer through which to pour the wine is a standard feature of the SYMPOSIUM, and although Theophrastus may refer to the addition of gypsum, which was later used for the purposes of both CLARIFICATION and ACIDIFICATION, he describes this as an Italian practice. References to 'strained wine' suggest that it was unusual, and the straining may have been done at the point of sale, rather than during production.

Common additives The basic wine could be 'improved' by various additives: the use of a small percentage of seawater or brine seems to have begun in the 4th century BC, apparently as a flavouring, although it probably also had preservative qualities, and the technique was associated with particular areas of production, notably the island of Kós, and marked a shift in taste during antiquity. We also hear of the addition of aromatic herbs, to produce a sort of VERMOUTH, and of perfume being added both in production and by the consumer, as well as of the use of boiled must and, on Thásos, of the addition of a mixture of dough and honey to produce a special CUVÉE for consumption on state occasions. BLENDING of different wines was also practised: Theophrastus gives one example, a mixture of hard but aromatic wine from Heraclea with soft Erythraean (a salted wine) which lacks BOUQUET, and says that there are many other blends known to experts (see TASTING, ancient history). There is some evidence, mainly in the Bronze Age, for the deliberate addition of pine or terebinth resin, but it is likely that storage (below) was normally a more significant cause of such flavours.

Containers for wine Finished wine was normally stored in AMPHORAE lined with resin or pitch (see RESINATED WINES) to limit porosity, which will have affected the taste to some extent, and pitch was also used to secure the stopper, which was usually of pottery, although the use of cork was known. Amphorae of the classical period held between 20 and 75 l (5–20 gal), depending on their origin, and added 5–15 kg (11–33 lbs) to the total load. These commercial amphorae are, of course, to be distinguished from the much smaller painted pots, also called amphorae, which were used to present the wine when it was drunk. In the *Odyssey* (2. 340 f.), Telemachus had wine drawn off from the big *pithoi* in which it had been ageing into amphorae for his journey abroad. Homer also refers quite frequently to wine kept in wineskins, but in classical times skin bags were probably mainly filled for rapid consumption; despite being lighter and, perhaps, less fragile, they will have flavoured the wine, being usually made from the skin of a sheep or goat.

Selling wine In Athens, wine was bought mainly from wine sellers for immediate consumption: after the purchaser had sampled the wine, the required amount was ladled or siphoned from the amphora into a jug or small amphora which the purchaser usually provided: wealthier customers, however, and those holding parties, will have bought an amphora at a time. Evidence on price is scanty, but for imported wine of good quality, such as Chian or Mendean, in Athens in the 4th century BC a *chous* of about 3.25 l cost between a quarter of a drachma and 2 drachmas (a drachma being a day's wage for a craftsman). Of course, these were luxury wines, with prices to match: one Athenian, urged to improve his morals by the Areopagus, the Council of Elders, cited drinking Chian, along with keeping a mistress, as evidence of a life of blameless hedonism appropriate to a gentleman. See also MERCHANTS, ancient history.

Specific wines Some idea of the leading wines of classical Greece can be obtained from references in literature, particularly lyric poetry and the Athenian comic poets; these make it clear that in Athens, at least, there was a degree of CONNOISSEURSHIP, different poets singing the praises of different wines while disparaging their rivals. The most frequently praised wines are those of Thásos, Lésvos, Mende, and Khíos (especially one called Ariousian), while those of Ismaros (in Thrace), Náxos, Peparethos (modern Skópelos), Acanthos and, from the 4th century, Kós were also admired.

This makes it clear that, although other areas had their admirers, the regions which produced the best wines were, by general consent, the AEGEAN ISLANDS, particularly to the east, and Chalkidike (modern Khalkhidhikhi near Ch Carras, see below) and Thrace on the northern mainland.

Two other much-praised wines, Pramnian and Bibline, are problematic. Pramnian, whose name goes back to Homer, is associated with a number of places—Lésvos, Smyrna, and the island of Ikaros (modern Ikaría, in the Dodecanese)—and indeed, according to ATHENAEUS, some considered it a generic name for dark wine, or long-lived wine; however, there was also a vine variety called Pramnian, and it seems most likely that Pramnian, which perhaps originated on Ikaría, came to be used as the name of wine of the style of the original, 'neither sweet nor rich, but dry, hard and unusually strong', whether or not made from the original vine.

In the case of Bibline, the problem is a confusion of names, since there was also Bybline wine, from Byblos in PHOENICIA, which is highly praised for fragrance by the 4th-century BC gastronome Archestratus; Bibline, however, took its name from a region in Thrace where it originated, and came from a vine called Bibline, which was apparently subsequently introduced elsewhere. Since scribes were prone to confuse the two, allusions cannot always be reliably attributed to one or the other, but it is plain that both had excellent reputations. On these interpretations, both Pramnian and Bibline will also fall within the top zone outlined above. In all cases, wines are praised in terms of their origins; we never hear of particular estates or producers as being superior.

What was Greek wine like? First, it could be of three colours, white, black or red, and tawny, the last being less frequently mentioned; Homer's wine is always dark. Greeks were sensitive to aromas, and often speak of wines being fragrant; more specifically, they refer to wine as 'smelling of flowers', an expression often almost equivalent to our BOUQUET, although the way in which the comic poet Hermippus talks of a mature wine 'smelling of violets, roses and hyacinth' shows that it was not always metaphorical; the same passage attributes a scent of apples to Thasian wine. The sweetest wines were said to lack bouquet, which could, according to Theophrastus, be supplied by blending, spicing, or perfuming.

In taste, wine is often praised as sweet, honeyed, ripe, and soft, and this must have appealed to the Greek palate, to judge from the production of PASSITO, or dried grape wines, and even sweet wine further concentrated by boiling. Given the likely ripeness of the grapes, the limitations of natural YEASTS, and, perhaps, the risk of STUCK FERMENTATION without TEMPERATURE CONTROL, sweetness must have been the most frequent outcome, and is often assumed by Greek writers: Aristotle distinguishes among heavy drinkers between drunkards and the sweet-toothed. However, this was not always the case: as noted earlier, grapes were sometimes picked unripe, and some varieties, like Pramnian, were naturally more austere; one vine was allegedly called 'smoky' because the wine was so sharp as to bring tears to the eyes, like smoke. Medical writers discussing the qualities of wines class them as dry or sweet white; and dry, sweet, or medium red/black, so there was obviously a wide range of styles.

Wine ageing Given the vagaries of vinification, much Greek wine will not have lasted long, succumbing either to OXIDATION, which medical and scientific writers noticed and discussed as a form of decomposition, or to spoilage due to inadequate storage, the risk of which was noted by Aristotle. It is not surprising that the people of Thásos traded in VINEGAR as well as wine, and that sour wine was a regular cheap drink, especially since the risk of oxidation must have increased as a large jar was emptied.

Nevertheless, some wines clearly aged, since old wine was highly regarded by the Greeks: 'praise old wine, but the flowers of new songs,' said the poet Pindar, and comic poets noted that women preferred old wine but young men. The old wine praised by Hermippus (above) was described as *sapros*: literally, 'rotten' or 'decomposed', but obviously referring in the case of wine to the production of secondary flavours through AGEING; older wine was also described as having 'lost its bite'. We never find discussion of particular VINTAGES (unlike Roman wines and specific vintages such as OPIMIAN wine mentioned by Roman writers), and there is little reliable evidence as to how long good wine might keep: Theocritus speaks of drinking four-year-old wine, perhaps from Kós, in the early 3rd century BC, and in the same era Peparethian wine was regarded as a slow developer in requiring six years to reach maturity, while the elder PLINY (in the 1st century AD) considered all foreign wines middle-aged at seven years old; comparisons with the wines of Ancient ROME, which evidently matured more slowly, might allow one to guess that few Greek wines lasted more than ten years, a good age for a wine in the heroic age (*Odyssey* 3. 390–2), but not a very long time by modern standards, especially when we remember that the CONTAINERS were very much larger than modern ones, so that the rate of development should have been proportionately reduced.

The uses of wine Wine had many uses for the Greeks. It was of course important as a food and drink (it was doubtless often safer than water), and the SYMPOSIUM, which centred around the drinking of wine, was one of the most important Greek social forms. Wine was almost always drunk diluted with water: the ratio varied, normally ranging between 2 : 3 and 1 : 3, which would give a range in ALCOHOLIC STRENGTH of about 3 to 6 per cent and generally at the lower end of this range (roughly the same as British draught beer). Weaker mixtures are disparaged in comedy (and even 1 : 3 called for a good wine), but 1 : 1 was considered by some dangerous to the health, and the regular drinking of unmixed wine, a habit confined to barbarians, was believed by some Spartans to have caused the insanity and death of their King Cleomenes. The mixed wine was also normally cooled, sometimes in special pottery coolers; the very rich added snow.

The medical uses of wine were numerous, and much discussed by medical writers. Its advantages as a pick-me-up, tonic, and analgesic were obvious, and by experience it became clear that certain wines were nourishing, diuretic, good for the digestion, and so on, but the qualities of different types were also discussed in terms of the four essential qualities (hot, cold, wet, dry) in order to decide how they should be used to correct imbalances in the bodily humours.

There are occasional references to procedures for making wine-based medicines, either by adding drugs to the wine or by treating the vines with an appropriate agent, although these usually seem to be closer to folklore than science; certain wines also had the reputation of producing medical side-effects: those of Troizen (just across the Saronic Gulf from Athens), for example, were said to render the drinker sterile. The Greeks were also well aware of the hazards of consuming wine to excess, and Athenaeus mentions popular remedies for a HANGOVER.

After social aspects, however, the most important aspect of wine was its place in religion. A LIBATION (*sponde*) of wine was offered whenever wine was drunk as a sort of first fruit (at the symposium different gods were invoked for each bowlful) and drink offerings were part of the formula for prayers; hence treaties and truces were referred to as *spondai*, because they were sanctified by prayers and libations. Wine was used to quench the burning offerings on the altar at a sacrifice, and was one of the liquids poured on the ground as an offering to the dead.

More than this, however, wine was directly associated with a particular divinity: DIONYSUS was the patron god and the symbol of wine, as Demeter was of cereals, and one of the 12 major divinities (a further indication of the basic importance of wine to the Greeks). R.B.

Wine festivals

For the Athenian of the 5th century BC, festival days in honour of the gods at set times of year gave the sort of relaxation now provided by weekends. Many of them were associated with wine drinking, vine-growing, and the HARVEST. The most important of these, the Anthesteria, in honour of DIONYSUS, celebrated the opening of wine jars in February to test the new wine. It included processions and ritual wine drinking contests and was probably closest to the modern idea of a wine festival. None the less, at the heart of the festival was the serious business of the dedication of the new wine to Dionysus.

Other festivals included the Oschophoria, a vintage celebration in September which seems to have been restricted to aristocratic families: two young men led a procession carrying vine branches with the grapes still on them (*oschoi*) in honour of Dionysus. The Apatouria in the same month was the festival when young males were registered in their *phratries*, or clans, and there was much associated pouring of wine. The last day of this festival was called Epildon and came to mean 'the morning after'. Strangely, there does not seem to have been a particularly important festival at the time of the grape harvest. At the country Dionysia celebrated in the country around Athens, a jar of wine and a vine headed the procession.

The great festivals of Athens, the Panathenaia and the City Dionysia, were dominated by the vine (perhaps because they were held further from the vineyards) but there is no doubt that wine was enjoyed at them. H.H.A.

Bibliographical note: There is no modern book specifically on Greek wine, works on ancient wine (cited under Ancient ROME) tend to pass rapidly on to Rome, where the evidence is much fuller; however, Roman sources are not necessarily reliable evidence for Greek practice 500 years earlier. Of the ancient sources, ATHENAEUS' *Deipnosophistae* collects much classical literary material (especially Books 1–2, 25e–40f) and Theophrastus' *Enquiry into Plants and On the Causes of Plants* (especially 3. 11–16) contains a lot of botanical lore; all are accessible in translation in the Loeb Classical Library, the first two with good indexes. On Athenaeus, see Brock, R., and Wirtjes, H., 'Athenaeus on Greek wine', in D. Braund and J. Wilkins (eds.), *Athenaeus and His World* (Exeter, 2000), 455–65, 587–8 with further general bibliography. The Minoan and Mycenaean periods are discussed in McGovern, P. E., Fleming, S. J., and Katz, S. H. (eds.), *The Origins and Ancient History of Wine* (Luxembourg, 1995), chs. 15–18. Grace, V., *Amphoras and the Ancient Wine Trade* (2nd edn, Princeton, NJ, 1979), is a good general introduction to AMPHORAE; see also Koehler, C., in McGovern, Fleming, & Katz, ch. 20. Sparkes, B. A., 'Treading the Grapes', *Bulletin Antieke Beschaving*, 51 (1976), 47–64, collects and discusses the pictorial evidence for the vintage. Wilson, H., *Wine and Words in Classical Antiquity and the Middle Ages* (London, 2003), is mainly concerned with the literary, social, and religious uses of wine but also deals with AGEING.

Medieval history

In the medieval Greece that was part of the Byzantine empire, wine was grown by private individuals and by monasteries (see MONKS AND MONASTERIES). Monasteries were foremost among the great landowners because, as in western Europe, they received donations and bequests from the laity. In the 8th and 9th centuries, agriculture was exceptionally profitable; its chief products were wine and fruits and also cotton and medicinal herbs. As in antiquity, the best wines came from the AEGEAN ISLANDS, Khíos first of all, and Thásos and Crete. The wines of THRACE and ASIA MINOR (Cappadocia in particular) were ranked second to these. Evidence from shipwrecks shows that wine was still transported in amphorae in the 7th century, whereas wooden BARRELS were commonly used in western Europe from the 3rd century AD. After the 7th century, the Greeks, too, started using wooden casks, which are lighter and easier to handle than amphorae.

In the 12th century, Constantinople (on the site of modern Istanbul) was the centre of the Byzantine empire's wine trade. Wines were shipped to Constantinople from the Aegean islands, from Thebes, and also from near Monemvasia, a port on the southern Peloponnese, which gave its name to MALVASIA and its English corruption MALMSEY. Monasteries were exempted from customs duties and were therefore at an advantage compared with private growers and traders: the monasteries of Patmos and Mount Áthos, for instance, made large profits from selling their wines in Constantinople.

But the private growers and wine merchants of Greece faced a much greater problem than unfair competition from monks. In 1082, the Emperor Alexius I Comnenus had granted VENICE trading facilities at Constantinople and in 32 towns without payment of taxes of any kind. As a result so much money disappeared to the west that Byzantium was economically ruined. Wine producers and wine merchants suffered badly. With no duties to pay, the Venetians were able to sell wine much more cheaply than any Greek could. Often this was imported Italian wine, but most of the wine came from Crete, known then as Candia, which was a colony of Venice (and which was to remain one until the mid 17th century). Worse still, many taverns in Constantinople were owned by Venetians so, in Constantinople at least, they controlled the retail trade as well.

It took until the middle of the 14th century for the Byzantine government at least to try to protect the empire's own trade. After earlier failed attempts, the Venetians agreed in 1361 to accept a distinction between wholesale and retail trade and to impose a tax on their own, with the proceeds of course going to Venice, on taverns run by Venetians. In the 15th century, tax was finally levied on wine imported by Venetians, but by then it was too late, for Byzantium's wine trade was no longer viable. Crete and CYPRUS, under Venetian ownership, continued to produce the strong, sweet wines that were capable of surviving the long sea voyage to western Europe, but the harbour of Monemvasia, close to Byzantium's own supply of Malvasia wines, was now too small to take the larger ships that the west had increasingly come to adopt. Monemvasia had been an entrepôt for ships from Cyprus and Crete bound for the west; from the late 14th century onwards, it lost out to Cyprus and Crete as a port and the south west Peloponnese declined as a producer of export-quality wine. All trade in Greek wine ceased in the late 15th century, when, after the fall of Byzantium, the Ottoman Turks occupied the Peloponnesian shore and drove out its inhabitants. H.M.W.

Kazhdan, A. P. (ed.), *The Oxford Dictionary of Byzantium*, 3 vols. (Oxford, 1988).

Lambert-Gócs, Miles, *The Wines of Greece* (London, 1990).

Nicol, Donald M., *Byzantium and Venice* (Cambridge, 1988).

Modern history

The centuries of domination by the Ottoman Turks were to blight Greek viticulture and wine-making until well into the 20th century. Wine-making was not normally forbidden to the Christian population, but communication difficulties resulted in a localized peasant industry viewed by the Turkish rulers as a useful means of raising revenue through TAXATION. Thus, while FRANCE, for example, was developing fine wine regions and their markets, Greece remained in what might be termed the vinous Dark Ages.

The battle for independence was prolonged and tortuous, and the exhausted and impoverished modern Greek state, founded in 1913, had preoccupations more important than the creation of a fine wine industry. It was not until well after the two World Wars and the subsequent bitter civil war that Greece began to modernize its fragmented wine industry, widely regarded as a source of cheap, often poorly made wines suitable only for the domestic market.

The Vine Institute of Athens, which experiments with wine-making techniques and advises winemakers, was founded in 1937, and some of the major modern wine companies had been established in the late 19th century, but were then chiefly concerned with DISTILLATION, bulk wine sales being a subsequent addition. Only in the 1960s was any significant proportion of Greek wine sold in bottle rather than directly from the barrel.

Since the 1960s, however, there has been considerable investment in modern technology, and its results have been evident since the early 1980s with the emergence of Greece's first generation of trained OENOLOGISTS (although it is to the Greek language that we owe the very term OENOLOGY). Such is their enthusiasm that, although in strict commercial terms the big companies Achaia Clauss, Boutari, Kourtakis, and Tsantalis still dominate the market, an increasing number of small, quality-minded estates is emerging. Most modern Greek wine finds a ready market within Greece, where the appreciation of good wine has increased considerably. Some fine wines have been exported from the likes of Antonopoulos, Domaine Carras, Ktima Gerovassiliou, Gaia, Oenoforos, and the Sámos co-operative, however.

Geography and climate

There are vineyards in all parts of Greece. At latitudes of between 34 and 42 degrees north, they constitute some of the world's hotter wine regions, although some vines are deliberately planted at relatively high ALTITUDES.

The climate is generally predictably MEDITERRANEAN, with short winters and very hot summers in which DROUGHT can be a serious threat in some years, particularly in the south. There can be considerable variation between the CONTINENTAL-influenced cooler vineyards in the mountains, whether on the plateau of Mantinia in the Peloponnese or in Epirus and Macedonia, where grapes may not even reach full RIPENESS, and the intense heat of Pátras or islands such as Crete and Rhodes on which some grapes may be picked in July.

Most of the vineyards are sufficiently close to the sea for maritime breezes to moderate temperatures, but lack of water, particularly on the islands and in the south, is a major problem. Although some rain does fall in the autumn, the first three months of the year are generally the wet months, and many wine areas have no rain at all for six months, which can make the establishment of young vines extremely difficult. IRRIGATION is not generally permitted but may be used to establish new vineyards.

Most of Greece is extremely mountainous. Vines can be found growing on flat land near sea level, such as at Ankhíalos; on foothills as at Rapsani on the lower slopes of Mount Olympus; and at altitudes as high as 800 m/2,600 ft on the highest slopes in Neméa. Vines are often planted on north-facing slopes in the hottest areas in order to slow ripening.

There are many soil types in Greece but the soil is generally of low fertility. Subsoils on the mainland tend to be limestone, while on the islands they are mainly volcanic. Clay, loam, schist, and marl are all found, as well as sandy clay and chalk.

Viticulture

The Greek land tenure system means that much of the vineyard area is in the hands of smallholders. Little by little, the large companies which buy in the great majority of their grapes have been working more closely with these vine-growers and spreading more modern viticultural techniques. Grape PRICES were for long determined by sugar levels, which too often resulted in dangerously low levels of ACIDITY, but these problems have been largely resolved by the big commercial concerns and the more modern CO-OPERATIVES. The more ambitious of the small estates are introducing modern farming practices.

Traditionally most vines were left to grow as BUSH VINES, but almost all new vineyards have been designed with TRELLIS SYSTEMS on wires, except for those on very windy sites such as are common on the island of SANTORINI. CORDON systems of pruning and training are more common than GUYOT.

Viticultural knowledge lags behind wine-making practice and the small Vine Institute in Athens for some time concentrated its work on varieties suited to TABLE GRAPES and DRYING GRAPES. VIRUS DISEASES of the vine are common in some vineyards, and the wine industry might profit from research into improving ROOTSTOCKS, particularly for hotter areas. The most common rootstocks are 110 R or 41 B.

Vine varieties

Greece is a still underdeveloped source of indigenous, ancient grape varieties of which more than 300 have been identified. Many of them are used solely for the important table grape or dried fruit industries, however, and many others are used in tiny quantities on a purely local basis. There is still considerable work to be undertaken in VINE IDENTIFICATION, not just in rediscovering classical varieties, but in discovering the relationships between Greek varieties and those grown elsewhere, in ITALY, CYPRUS, TURKEY, ALBANIA, MONTENEGRO, KOSOVO, CROATIA, and MACEDONIA in particular.

The specifically Greek wine grape varieties can offer unique characters and flavours. Although, for example, Debina remained a speciality of Epirus in the north west, and Xinomavro of Macedonia in the north east, Greek vine-growers are increasingly experimenting with varieties in areas far from their traditional homes as their value in blends is being recognized.

The most important Greek white grape varieties are ASSYRTIKO, RHODITIS, ROBOLA, SAVATIANO, MOSCOPHILERO, VILANA, DEBINA, and both MUSCAT BLANC À PETITS GRAINS and the slightly less important MUSCAT OF ALEXANDRIA. The Greek port of Monemvasia also gave its name to the MALVASIA grape. Among Greek red grape varieties, the most important to the modern Greek wine industry have been AGHIORGHITIKO, LIMNIO, MANDELARIA, and XINOMAVRO. See regional details below for more local grape varieties.

In addition to these native varieties, a number of INTERNATIONAL VARIETIES have been imported, particularly from France, which some estimates put at around 15 per cent of total plantings. These include Chardonnay, Sauvignon Blanc, and Ugni Blanc among whites and both Cabernet Sauvignon and Cabernet Franc, a little Merlot, Grenache, Cinsaut, and Syrah among red grape varieties. Some Greek wines may be VARIETAL versions of these, but it is far more usual to find these foreign varieties playing a minor role in blends with Greek varieties. Indeed, there is a strong lobby within Greece which argues that Greek wine should not be made from international varieties, and any new wine applying for appellation status is likely to encounter difficulties if the principal grapes used are not Greek in origin.

Wine-making

Since the mid 1980s, almost all Greek wineries have had some sort of REFRIGERATION and the sort of HYGIENE afforded by the use of STAINLESS STEEL vats. Only the oldest co-operatives had yet to make such investments in the mid 1990s. Enterprising small wineries have more recently introduced grape refrigeration prior to pressing.

As in other Mediterranean areas, early picking and cool fermentations enabled by temperature control resulted in clean but characterless white wines of about 11.5 per cent alcohol. Such techniques as SKIN CONTACT, slightly later picking, and deliberate OXIDATION of the must prior to fermentation were used by some of the more daring producers from the early 1990s to develop more interesting wines.

Better-quality red wines have traditionally been matured in large, old casks, but imported French BARRIQUES are increasingly used for the

Greece

BULGARIA

MACEDONIA

ALBANIA

Vardar

Drama

THRACE

GOUMENISSA

AMYNDEO

MACEDONIA *Strimon*

NÁOUSSA

Thessalonika

Epanomi

Vermion Mts.

Aliakron

LEMNOS

Mt.▲ Olympus

CÔTES DE MELITON

ZITSA Metsovo

RAPSANI

CORFU

Ioánnina

EPIRUS

Pinios

AEGEAN ISLANDS

THESSALY

Vólos

Akheloos

ANKHÍALOS

Aegean Sea

IONIAN IS.

CEPHALONIA

Thebes

ATTICA

Andros

SÁMOS

Gulf of Corinth

Pátras

PÁTRAS

Corinth Canal

Corinth

Athens

Tinos

ZAKYNTHOS

NEMÉA

MANTINIA

Alfíos

CYCLADES

PÁROS

PELOPONNESE

Ionian Sea

Monemvasia

SANTORINI

RHODES

Mediterranean

CRETE

Sea

ARCHANES

DAPHNES PEZA

SITEAIA

TURKEY

■ Wine growing regions

0   100 km

BARREL MATURATION of reds and even some whites.

Wine laws

Greek wine laws were drawn up in the early 1970s and refined in the early 1980s as Greece prepared to join the EUROPEAN UNION. It is hardly surprising, therefore, that the laws conform strictly to EU guidelines, often even employing the use on the label of the French terms Appellation d'Origine Contrôlée and VIN DE PAYS (for which, as in France, a wider variety of grape varieties may be used than for full APPELLATION CONTRÔLÉE wines).

Wines which qualify as QUALITY WINES according to EU law are either sweet wines,

from Mavrodaphne or Muscat grapes, described as Controlled Appellation of Origin (OPE) with a blue seal over the cork, or dry wines described as Appellation of Superior Quality (OPAP), with a pink seal. The words Réserve or Grande Réserve indicate superior wines with extended AGEING.

Vins de pays, of which there were 80 in 2005, may be made in a wide variety of specified areas, nearly always from a range of vine varieties which includes both Greek and foreign grape varieties. Commercially the most important vin de pays areas are Attica, Drama, Epanomi, and Thívai (or Thebes).

The large TABLE WINE category includes wine BRANDS that were Greece's most successful

wines, as well as some more interesting wines made outside the appellation regulations. The Greeks have also used the term CAVA to indicate high-quality table wine which is made only in small quantities and which has been subject to prolonged ageing.

The official list of Greek wine appellations was drawn up in the 1950s, although some more recent wine areas, such as the Côtes de Meliton on the Khalkhidhikhi peninsula (see Ancient history above), were subsequently grafted on to the official list. Of the 28 appellations in Greece's widely differing regions, some are produced only in tiny quantities. Some are in danger of extinction and one, Kantza, is no longer made at all. Many are rarely seen outside their area of origin while some are well known and thriving.

Wine regions

Wine is made all over Greece, often on a very small, traditional scale. The following includes those quality wine regions which have established their own identity within Greece and sometimes abroad; see map.

Northern Greece The regions of Macedonia and Thrace are noted mainly for their red wines, although wines of all hues are made there today. Náoussa, home of red wine from Xinomavro grapes, is on the south eastern slopes of Mount Vermio, at altitudes of between 200 and 350 m (660–1,150 ft), where there is usually no serious lack of rain and winters are cool enough for vine dormancy. Náoussa must be aged for at least a year in OAK, traditionally in old wooden casks, but there has been considerable experimentation with new, small barriques. A system of defining the better slopes and awarding them GRAND CRU status has resulted in two categories of Náoussa: young wine from the lighter, sandy soil and more age-worthy wine from clay and limestone soils.

Xinomavro is also grown in this area to produce Goumenissa, where it is blended with Negoska grapes, and to make Amyndeo, which lies on the opposite, north western slopes of Mount Vermio from Náoussa but at altitudes as high as 650 m/2,100 ft. Sparkling rosé is made here as well as red wine.

Perhaps the most famous appellation in northern Greece is its most recent, the Côtes de Meliton on the slopes of Mount Meliton in Sithoniá. This is the appellation specially created by Domaine Carras, a wine estate developed with the well-publicized assistance of Professor Émile PEYNAUD of Bordeaux. Here both white and red wines are made with a mixture of Greek and French vine varieties, notably Cabernet Sauvignon. It is significant, however, that, as the domaine extends its vineyards, many of the new vines planted are Greek varieties, including the recently rediscovered and elegant indigenous white MALAGOUSIA.

Also in Thrace is an area around Drama where some good-quality vins de pays are made from a mixture of Greek and French grape varieties.

Central Greece Not far from the town of Ioánnina and near the border with ALBANIA lies Zitsa, which produces a dry or medium lightly sparkling white wine from the local Debina grape variety. To the immediate south west, in the mountains round Ioánnina, are Greece's highest vineyards at Metsovo (900 m/3,000 ft), which yield the popular vin de pays Katoi from locally grown Cabernet Sauvignon grapes blended with Aghiorghitiko grapes grown in Neméa.

On the east coast in Thessaly, Rapsani is produced on the foothills of Mount Olympus

from Xinomavro (here grown at its most southerly point) blended with Krassato and Stavroto grapes and given CASK AGEING. This appellation is undergoing much-needed revival but old vintages suggest that the potential for long-lived, concentrated reds is there. Thessaly's other appellation is Ankhíalos, a dry white wine made from Rhoditis with some Savatiano grapes grown near Vólos at sea level.

Peloponnese This dramatically formed, large southern peninsula has the greatest number of Greek wine appellations, as well as some interesting vins de pays and table wines. On the plateau of Mantinia in Arcadia, at altitudes of about 600 m/2,000 ft, the Moscophilero grape produces a fresh, dry, aromatic, slightly spicy white appellation, while the same grape can be vinified, with extended MACERATION, to yield a simple but fruity rosé.

At Neméa, not far from the Corinth canal, which separates the Peloponnese from mainland Greece, the Aghiorghitiko grape is grown on marl and deep red soil. If yields are not too high, it can produce intense, fruity red wine from three different zones whose altitude varies between 250 and 800 m. Grapes from the lowest vineyards frequently lack acidity and can be used to make a sweet wine, but the finest, dry wine is said to come from vineyards between 450 and 700 m above sea level. As in Náoussa (see above), barriques are increasingly used for the maturation, and SEMI-CARBONIC MACERATION has even been used to make a sort of Neméa NOUVEAU. Since the late 1990s, Neméa has seen, more than any other Greek region, a flurry of investment in high-tech wineries. Leading vineyards have been replanted with a higher VINE DENSITY.

The vineyards around Pátras on the north coast are responsible for four different appellations. Pátras itself is a dry white wine made from Rhoditis grapes grown on the slopes around the town. Muscat of Pátras is a dessert wine made strong and sweet like a VIN DOUX NATUREL from Muscat Blanc à Petits Grains grapes, as is Rion of Pátras, which is almost extinct owing to the encroachment of buildings on the vineyard area. Mavrodaphne of Pátras is a very popular appellation, on the other hand, consisting of a blend in which Mavrodaphne makes up the majority but may be supplemented by the locally grown Korinthiaki (Corinth or CURRANT) grape grown mainly for DRYING GRAPES. Fermentation is arrested when alcoholic strength has reached about 4 per cent (as in making PORT) and the wine, like tawny port, is then aged in wood. Examples aged for 10–12 years in cask can be delicious.

The islands Among the Ionian islands off the west coast, Cephalonia is best known for its wine, particularly the powerful dry white Robola. Vines here were individually trained on high, stony land, and mainly ungrafted (although PHYLLOXERA's arrival in the late

1980s presumably signals an end to this). A varietal dry, unfortified red table wine from Mavrodaphne is also made. Mavrodaphne and Muscat dessert wines, similar to those of Pátras, are also produced on the island.

From the Cyclades come the wines of Páros, SANTORINI, and, more recently, Tinos. Páros is a powerful, quite tannic red made from a curious blend of grapes in which the deep colour of the Mandelaria is lightened by the addition of half as much of the white grape called Monemvasia (see MALVASIA). Rainfall is low but the maritime location helps raise humidity. Vines are trained on low bushes as protection against the strong winds. Strong winds are also a characteristic of Santorini. Rainfall on this volcanic island is also very low, but the porosity of the calcareous subsoil helps to retain overnight humidity. The Santorini appellation is for a fine, mineral-scented, dry white made from Assyrtiko grapes blended with a little Athiri and Aïdani, but a sweet DRIED GRAPE WINE, Visanto, is also made.

The island of Rhodes has been an important producer of wine since classical times. Today there are three appellations: one for a sweet Muscat made in very limited quantities, one for a dry white from Athiri grapes, and another for a red from the Mandelaria, here known as Amorgiano. Only grapes grown on the higher reaches of the north or north eastern slopes qualify for appellation wines. The Rhodes cooperative, the CAIR, also makes a considerable quantity of improving sparkling wine.

Two of Greece's most famous wines are made among the Aegean islands. Lemnos was the original home of the Limnio grape, which is still grown there, but the appellation wines are both Muscats. The dry version is rarely seen off the island, but the VIN DE LIQUEUR Muscat of Lemnos is widely admired, being surprisingly delicate.

Muscat of Sámos can claim to be Greece's most famous wine (after retsina). Muscat Blanc à Petits Grains is grown up to 800 m/ 2,600 ft above sea level, often on TERRACES on the island's steep hillsides, and the vintage can last a full two months, depending on vineyard altitude. Muscat of Sámos comes in several forms: Sámos Doux is a MISTELA-type vin de liqueur, while Sámos Vin Doux Naturel is made by stopping the fermentation later. Potentially finest of all, however, is Sámos Nectar, an unfortified dried grape wine made from grapes dried in the sun so that they are capable of being fermented into a wine of 14 per cent alcohol, which is then given three years in cask. France is the single largest market, importing more than half of the island's annual production.

The last of the appellation wines of any commercial importance comes from Crete from a variety of grape varieties unique to the island, together with Mandelaria. The pale red Liatiko reaches high alcohol levels and ripens very early, sometimes as early as August, while the powerful, deep-coloured Mandelaria produces particularly robust red wines. The most important local white grape is Vilana. Local red wine appellations for dry and sometimes sweet wines are Archanes, Daphnes, and Siteaia, while Peza, the most common wine appellation on the island, may be either dry red or white. The vineyards, which tend to be on the north of the island, protected from the hot winds from North Africa by the mountain range, are in the process of being replanted after phylloxera was discovered on the island in the late 1970s.

See also RETSINA, a FLAVOURED WINE speciality of Greece which can claim direct descent from the RESINATED WINES of later classical times.   M.McN. & N.M.

Lambert-Gócs, M., *The Wines of Greece* (London, 1990).

Lazarakis, K., *The Wines of Greece* (London, 2005).

Manessis, N., *The Illustrated Greek Wine Book* (Corfu, 2000).

green, pejorative tasting term for a wine made from grapes that did not reach full RIPENESS.

green grafting, viticultural term for BUDDING and GRAFTING in the vineyard or nursery using green stem tissue. Green grafting offers less flexibility in timing than CHIP BUDDING and T-BUDDING because the ROOTSTOCK shoots must be green, and so it must take place in late spring or early summer. As with T-budding, the SCION pieces to be inserted may be from stored winter cuttings or the current season's green shoots.   B.G.C.

green harvest, see CROP THINNING.

greenhouse effect and viticulture. See CLIMATE CHANGE.

Grenache, increasingly fashionable vine variety that was in the late 20th century the world's second most widely planted, sprawling, in several hues, all over Spain and southern France but has been overtaken by Merlot and Cabernet Sauvignon. It probably owes its early dispersal around the western Mediterranean to the strength and extent of the ARAGÓN kingdom, but this would make a rewarding subject for an AMPELOGRAPHICAL historian. As GARNACHA, it probably originated in Spain in the northern province of Aragón before colonizing extensive vineyard land both north and south of the Pyrenees, notably in Roussillon, which was ruled by Spain, and more particularly by the kingdom of Aragón, for four centuries until 1659. From here Grenache presumably made its way east and was certainly well established in the southern Rhône by the 19th century. It is also known today that Grenache was not planted in Rioja before phylloxera struck in 1901. The productive, resistant Grenache then practically replaced native varieties in Rioja Baja and made significant inroads in Alta and Alavesa. Grenache is un-

doubtedly, however, the same grape variety as Sardegna's CANNONAU, which the Sardinians claim as their own, advancing the theory that the variety made its way from this island off Italy (where it is also known as Granaccia and Tocai Rosso) to Spain when Sardegna was under Aragón rule, from 1297 until 1713.

Whatever its origins, Grenache has been uprooted to such an extent in Spain (total area down from 170,000 ha/420,000 acres in the late 1980s to 82,3000 ha in 2004) that France has the world's largest Grenache presence, or at least had 95,700 ha planted accordig to the last vine census in 2000—more than any variety other than Merlot and Carignan. For a vine that covers so much terrain, it has until recently been a name rarely encountered by name by the wine drinker, much of it being blended with other varieties with more colour and backbone. Grenache produces essentially very fruity, rich, sweet-tasting wine, with varying degrees of tannin depending on the degree of WATER STRESS.

With its strong wood and upright growth, Grenache Noir is well suited to traditional BUSH VINE viticulture in hot, dry, windy vineyards. It buds early, can be prone to COULURE and ripens relatively late (after Cabernet Sauvignon). In regions allowing a relatively long growing cycle it can achieve heady sugar levels. The wine produced is, typically, paler than most reds (although low yields tend to concentrate the pigments, and tannins, in Spain and some Châteauneuf-du-Pape vineyards), with a tendency to oxidize early, a certain rusticity, and more than a hint of sweetness. If the vine is irrigated, as it has tended to be in the New World, it may lose even these taste characteristics. If, however, as by the most punctilious Châteauneuf-du-Pape producers, it is pruned severely on the poorest of soils and allowed to reach full maturity of both vine and grape, it can produce excitingly dense reds that demand several decades' cellaring. The rediscovery of Rhône reds in the late 1980s (see RHÔNE RANGERS for example) encouraged some New World producers to invest more effort in their own Grenache, even though its sturdy trunk has made it less widely popular in the modern era of MECHANICAL HARVESTING.

See GARNACHA for details of the variety in Spain.

In France, the majority of Grenache is planted in Languedoc-Roussillon, where it is second in quantity only to Carignan and is widely blended with that 'old' variety and Cinsaut the newer Syrah and Mourvèdre, but its greatest concentration is in the far eastern Languedoc where it meets the windswept southern Rhône. Here seas of Côtes du RHÔNE of varying degrees of distinction are produced alongside smaller quantities of CHÂTEAUNEUF-DU-PAPE, GIGONDAS, and the like. Although blending has been the watchword here, notably with the more structured Syrah, older vintages of such monoliths as the famously

concentrated Châteauneuf-du-Pape Ch Rayas show what can be done by Grenache and determination alone. The variety's kingdom spreads north to the Drôme *département*, where it also dominates, on nearly 10,000 ha. Grenache is responsible for much of southern France's fruitiest, fullest rosé, most obviously and traditionally in Tavel and in neighbouring Lirac, but also much further eastwards into Provence proper. In Languedoc-Roussillon, Grenache plays a generally unsung supporting role, together with its downy-leaved close relative Lladoner Pelut, which is also habitually cited in the APPELLATION CONTRÔLÉE regulations for red wines. In Roussillon, Grenache Noir, Gris, and Blanc are valued not only for their dry wines but are the vital ingredient in such distinctive vins doux naturels as BANYULS and MAURY.

Grenache Noir is being uprooted in Corsica but in Sardegna, as Cannonau, it plays a dominant role in the island's reds, which can achieve daunting levels of natural ripeness, whether in deep, dark dry reds, which can easily reach 15 per cent natural alcohol, or dessert wines. The vine is also grown in Calabria and Sicily.

Grenache's ability to withstand drought and heat made it a popular choice with New World growers when FASHION had little effect on market forces. Extensive historic acreage in the central San Joaquin valley, and some in Mendocino, constituted the majority of the almost 8,500 acres/3,400 ha of it planted in California in 2004. The wine typically made from these old vines—cheap, sweet, gimmicky Grenache Rosé or 'White Grenache'—had done little for Grenache's image in California but the state's RHÔNE RANGERS are rescusitating it with new plant material imported straight from the Rhône valley in their Central Coast vineyards.

Grenache was Australia's most planted black grape variety until the mid 1960s. Shiraz (Syrah) overtook it in the late 1970s but it was not until the early 1990s that Australia's Cabernet Sauvignon output overtook that of Grenache. Since then all red Rhône varieties have once more returned to FASHION and the total area planted with Grenache in Australia has remained relatively static, high-yielding vines in Riverland having been pulled out while more cosseted vines have been planted in McLaren vale and Barossa valley.

Grenache Noir is also grown in Israel, where it was exported at the end of the 19th century, to a limited but increasing extent in South Africa, and still, to a much greater degree, in North Africa, where it was once an important element in the usefully soupy reds of Algeria and in some fine Moroccan rosés.

Grenache Rose and **Grenache Gris** are also commonly encountered in southern French whites and some pale rosés.

Galet, P., *Dictionnaire encyclopédique des cépages* (Paris, 2000).

Grenache Blanc, the white-berried form of GRENACHE NOIR, is discreetly important in France, where it was overtaken by Sauvignon Blanc as fourth most planted white grape variety (after Ugni Blanc, Chardonnay, and Sémillon) as recently as the late 1980s. Although in decline, the variety is grown on a total of more than 6,000 ha of France, half of them in Roussillon, where it produces full-bodied whites that vary from fat and soft to nervy, terroir-driven cellar candidates of the upper Agly valley. It can also be an important ingredient in the paler Rivesaltes.

Grenache Blanc is also often encountered—with the likes of Marsanne, Roussanne, Viognier, and Rolle—in the blended white wines of Languedoc-Roussillon, to which it can add supple fruit if not longevity. It need not necessarily be consigned to the blending vat, however. If carefully pruned and vinified, it can produce richly flavoured, full-bodied varietals that share some characteristics with Marsanne and can be worthy of ageing in small oak barrels. It is also an ingredient in white Châteauneuf-du-Pape.

See GARNACHA BLANCA for details of the variety in Spain.

Grés de Montpellier, appellation within the Coteaux du LANGUEDOC in southern France created in 2005 for red wines made with at least 70 per cent of Syrah and Mourvèdre combined and at least 20 per cent of Grenache Noir in 46 communes in the hinterland of the city of Montpellier.

grey rot, sometimes known as **grey mould** and sometimes just **rot,** the malevolent form of BOTRYTIS BUNCH ROT and one of the most harmful of the FUNGAL DISEASES that attack vines. In this undesirable bunch rot form, the *Botrytis cinerea* fungus rapidly spreads throughout the berry flesh and the skin breaks down. Other fungi and bacteria then also invade the berry and the grapes become rotten. Badly infected fruit develops off-flavours; badly infected vineyards themselves have a characteristic mouldy and often vinegary smell. Wines produced from such fruit smell mouldy and red wines look pale and grey-brown. When the *Botrytis cinerea* fungus attacks healthy, ripe, white wine grapes and the weather conditions are favourable, it results in so-called NOBLE ROT, which can produce some of the world's finest sweet wines. If the grapes are dark-skinned, unripe, or damaged, or the weather is unremittingly humid, the fungus wreaks so much damage that it is called grey rot.

Grignolino, very localized, curiosity of a grape variety of the PIEMONTE region in north west Italy sold almost invariably as a pale red VARIETAL wine with an almost alpine scent and a tangy ACIDITY. Grignolino is a native of the MONFERRATO hills between Asti and Casalese and serves the same function as DOLCETTO in the province of Cuneo: that of providing a wine that can be drunk young with pleasure while the brawnier wines of the zone are shedding their youthful asperity—although Grignolino is more difficult to match with food than the fuller Dolcetto. The light colour and relatively low alcohol (11 to 12 per cent) can be deceptive; the wine draws significant TANNINS from the abundant pips of the Grignolino grape and takes its name from *grignole*, the dialect name for pips in the province of Asti.

Although Piemonte's producers have been regularly predicting a breakthrough for Grignolino that would transform it into Italy's answer to BEAUJOLAIS, the wine remains an unquestionably local taste and, with its rather odd combination of pale colour, perceptible acidity, and tannins, somewhat *sui generis*. In recent years, its popularity has declined quite rapidly, with a number of producers grubbing up vineyards as even local markets turn away from this variety. The two DOC areas, Asti and Monferrato Casalese, are rather large, the former having been extended to the south and the latter to the north of the historic areas of Grignolino cultivation, but they produce fewer than two million bottles a year between them; Grignolino del Monferrato Casale is much the better and more characterful of the two.   D.T. & D.C.G.

Grillet, Château. See CHÂTEAU GRILLET.

Grillo, Sicilian white grape variety once used as the base for the best MARSALA. Grown on bush vines, it produced potent, full-bodied base wines that were supplemented by a proportion of the more aromatic INZOLIA. Grillo's decline has mirrored that of Marsala, and it has been replaced in many vineyards by the more vigorous CATARRATTO. At its best, it gives full-bodied wines of real interest, although they lack the aromatic intensity that has made Inzolia's transformation from fortified to dry white wine variety so much easier. See SICILIA for more details.   D.C.G.

Gringet, synonym for SAVAGNIN.

Groenekloof, cool, promising wine ward in the Darling district in South Africa.

Grolleau or **Groslot,** is the everyday red grape variety of TOURAINE. It produces extremely high yields of relatively thin, acid wine and it is to the benefit of wine drinkers that it is so systematically being replaced with Gamay and, more recently, Cabernet Franc. Total French plantings have fallen steadily so that they totalled only 2,200 ha/5,500 acres in 2000. The status of the variety is such that it is allowed into the rosé but not red versions of APPELLATION CONTRÔLÉE wines such as ANJOU, SAUMUR, and Touraine. It has played a major part only in Rosé d'Anjou, in which it is commonly blended with Gamay, which ripens just before it.

Grolleau Gris, planted on just 800 ha/2,000 acres of France in 2000, is the pink-skinned version of GROLLEAU which produces innocuous white wines, mainly used for blending the Loire's hugely successful VIN DE PAYS du Jardin de la France, although if yields are restricted (which can be difficult), it can produce wines of real character.

Groppello Gentile, red grape variety grown to a limited extent in the Italian wine region of LOMBARDIA.

Groslot is a common synonym for the Loire's rather commonplace red vine variety GROLLEAU.

Gros Manseng, Basque white grape grown on about 2,000 ha/5,000 acres of SOUTH WEST FRANCE to produce mainly drier versions of Jurançon and various Béarn wines. It is also allowed into Gascony's Pacherenc du Vic-Bihl. The vine looks similar to but is distinct from the rarer PETIT MANSENG. It yields more generously and produces discernibly less elegant, less rich, but still powerful wine. Unlike the smaller-berried Petit Manseng, it is not sensitive to COULURE. Gros Manseng, unlike Petit Manseng, is rarely used for sweet wines.

Gros Plant, or, to give it a name that is more of a mouthful than the wine usually is, **Gros Plant du Pays Nantais,** is the country cousin of MUSCADET. Made from FOLLE BLANCHE vines, called Gros Plant here, grown in a wide arc east but mainly south of the city of Nantes on the Loire, Gros Plant is one of the most acidic-tasting wines made anywhere, and Gros Plant's aggressively dry style serves only to accentuate its inherent tartness—exacerbated by the grapes' tendency to rot here before they ripen. The Folle Blanche vine responsible was introduced to this region by the DUTCH WINE TRADE, and outnumbered the Muscadet vine until the ravages of PHYLLOXERA in the late 19th century. Gros Plant qualifies as a VDQS and is the single most extensive VDQS vineyard. About a third as much Gros Plant is made as Muscadet, although a much smaller proportion ever leaves the region. A small amount of sparkling Gros Plant is also made.

Gros Rhin, Swiss synonym for SILVANER, to distinguish it from Petit Rhin, or Riesling.

Grosser Ring, or, as it is officially called today, **Grosser Ring VDP Mosel-Saar-Ruwer,** is an association of some of the finest estates in the MOSEL-SAAR-RUWER region of GERMANY, constituting the local branch of the prestigious VDP growers' association. Founded in 1908 by the mayor of Trier, and still based in that Roman city on the Mosel river, it consolidated several local groups of renowned estates that traditionally sold their so-called

NATURREIN wines at auction. The Grosser Ring conducted its IIIth AUCTION on its 90th anniversary in September 1998. In addition, the association holds tastings and events throughout Germany and abroad to promote the wines of its members (30 in 2005). The Grosser Ring is axiomatically devoted to the RIESLING grape by virtue of its location, and is distinguished by its willingness to expel under-performing members, who must have holdings in top vineyard sites; cultivate at least 90 per cent Riesling; be full-time wine-growers; and produce more QMP than average.

Grosses Gewächs (in the Rheingau known as **Erstes Gewächs**) represents the apex of a qualitative pyramid for classifying German wines that has been operative since 2002 within the membership of the VDP winegrowers' association. Wines so designated (but not necessarily so labelled, as the terminology was not recognized by the GERMAN WINE LAW as recently as 2005) are from traditional grapes and vineyard sites classified (by the VDP) as having demonstrated their historical superiority. The sites in question may be entire EINZELLAGEN or portions of Einzellagen. The category Grosses Gewächs also stipulates that the fruit be cropped at no more than 50 hl/ha, hand harvested, at no less than the MUST WEIGHT required for SPÄTLESE, and the wine be subject to sensory review. Besides attempting to classify, protect, and promote the best vineyard CRUS of Germany, the VDP regulations for Grosses Gewächs were also intended to stipulate a recognizable style of wine. Grosses Gewächs would have either RESIDUAL SUGAR comparable with TROCKEN or the lower permissible end of HALBTROCKEN, or else be nobly sweet wines of AUSLESE or above. Few growers in the Mosel-Saar-Ruwer were enthusiastic about these stipulations, which effectively eliminated the category of tasteably sweet Spätlese from the top echelon of German wine. In 2005, the VDP regulations had still not been finalized nor embraced by law. Grosses Gewächs wines were therefore typically bottled in glass embossed with a logo featuring a grape cluster and the numeral 1 with a 'front' label designating only the site and vintage. The wines also carried an official label designating Prädikat and generally noting that the wine is trocken.   D.S.

Grosslage, literally a 'large site' in GERMANY, is in wine terms a collection of individual sites (EINZELLAGEN) and a decidedly opportunistic geographical device which has enabled some very ordinary wines to be labelled as though they were from a single vineyard. About 150 Grosslagen were created by the GERMAN WINE LAW of 1971, each of them given a popular name. The average size of a Grosslage is about 600 ha/1,500 acres, while the average size of an Einzellage is just 38 ha. Wines produced anywhere within the Grosslage, all of which fall within individual wine regions, may use the Grosslage name. Thus in RHEINHESSEN, for example, the Krötenbrunnen Grosslage covers 1,800 ha of flat land which includes 27 individual vineyards, or Einzellagen, in 13 different villages. Since the name of one of these villages, Oppenheim, is the most famous, wine from anywhere in the Grosslage area may be sold as Oppenheimer Krötenbrunnen. Lawmakers may know that there is at the very least a quantitative difference between an Oppenheimer Krötenbrunnen and, for example, an Oppenheimer Kreuz from a single vineyard on the elevated RHEINTERRASSE, capable of producing really concentrated wines of distinction, but the average consumer does not.

Some of the most commonly exported combinations of village name and Grosslage name (a village name must always be prefixed) are, in the MOSEL-SAAR-RUWER, Zeller Schwarze Katz, Kröver Nacktarsch, Bernkasteler Badstube, Bernkasteler Kurfürstlay, Piesporter Michelsberg, Klüsserather St Michael, Wiltinger Scharzberg; in the NAHE, Binger Schlosskapelle, Rüdesheimer Rosengarten; in Rheinhessen, Niersteiner Gutes Domtal, Oppenheimer Krötenbrunnen; and in the PFALZ, Forster Mariengarten.

There have been repeated moves since the early 1990s to abandon Grosslagen altogether and replace them with more rigorously defined URSPRUNGSLAGEN. This has so far been fiercely resisted by those merchants who find Grosslagen so commercially convenient, although members of the VDP abandoned the use of Grosslagen from the 1998 vintage.

The wine areas of AUSTRIA have also been divided into Grosslagen, or collective sites. Some of them, such as Retzer Weinberge in the Weinviertel, encompass a vast vineyard area, but none of them has any reputation outside Austria.

Pigott, S., and Johnson, H., *The Wine Atlas of Germany* (London, 1995).

Gros Verdot, an unusual Bordeaux variety without the concentration or interest of PETIT VERDOT. May be grown in South America.

grower, the all-important producer of the raw material for wine-making. This individual may be called a grape-grower, more precisely a vine-grower, possibly even a wine-grower if he or she also vinifies. Terms in other languages include *vigneron* and *viticulteur* in French, and *vignaiolo* in Italian. Wine producers who grow their own grapes and vinify them into wine but on a limited scale are often referred to somewhat carelessly and often inaccurately as **small growers**. A significant proportion of all vinegrowers produce only grapes, however, which they sell to CO-OPERATIVES, merchant-bottlers (see NÉGOCIANT), or larger wine operations.

growth cycle of the vine. See VINE GROWTH CYCLE.

growth regulators, synthetic substances which act on vines like HORMONES to regulate their growth and development. A synthetic AUXIN, 4-CPA, has for example been used to improve FRUIT SET, as has the growth retardant CCC (2-chloroethyl trimethylammonium chloride). Synthetic GIBBERELLINS have been used to increase berry size, especially for the seedless SULTANA, and a synthetic ethylene-releasing compound termed ethephon can be used to hasten grape maturity and enhance colouration in particularly cool climates. More recently applied to viticulture, hydrogen cyanamide encourages early and complete BUDBREAK, which can be useful for TROPICAL VITICULTURE. These chemicals are mostly used for TABLE GRAPES and their application to both table grapes and wine grapes is regulated by rules governing the use of AGROCHEMICALS. Some hormones effective on grapevines—ABSCISIC ACID and CYTOKININS, for example—have not been produced commercially for use in the vineyard.   R.E.S.

Grumello, subzone of VALTELLINA in the far north of Italy.

Grüner Veltliner. The most commonly planted vine variety in AUSTRIA is grown elsewhere in eastern Europe and is increasingly respected worldwide. This well-adapted variety is planted on more than a third of Austria's 48,500 ha/119,800 acres of vineyard, particularly in Lower Austria, where it represents more than half of total white grape production, and in the Vienna region, where it comprises about a third of all plantings. DNA PROFILING in Austria showed that Grüner Veltliner is not genetically related to ROTER VELTLINER or FRÜHROTER VELTLINER.

The vine can be productive and is relatively hardy, but ripens too late for much of northern Europe. Yields of 100 hl/ha (5.7 tons/acre) are possible, invariably using the LENZ MOSER system of vine training, in the least distinguished vineyards of the Weinviertel in Lower Austria and the resulting wine is inoffensive if unexciting. However, at its best, arguably in the Wachau, Kamptal, Kremstal, Weinviertel, Donauland, and in the hands of some of the most ambitious growers in Vienna, Grüner Veltliner can produce wines which combine perfume and substance. The wine is typically dry, full-bodied, peppery, or spicy, and with time in bottle can start to taste positively Burgundian. Grüner Veltliner can produce a variety of wine styles from base wines for Austrian SEKT, simple wines served at HEURIGER, popular medium-bodied peppery wines to very opulent, concentrated wines. Grüner Veltliner may be regarded as Austria's biggest asset and is now so popular on restaurant wine lists that we may expect to see the variety planted in a much wider range of countries. It is difficult for non-German speakers to pronounce so is often abbreviated to 'Gruner', 'GV', or even 'Gru-Ve'.

The variety has long been grown just over Lower Austria's northern border in the CZECH REPUBLIC, where it is known as Veltlin or Veltlínské Zelené and in the Sopron vineyards of HUNGARY as Zöldveltelini. It is also (just) known in Germany's Rheinhessen but by early 2005 it was already being tried in Central Otago in New Zealand.

Guarnaccia, a strain of GRENACHE local to the island of Ischia off Naples.

Guenoc Valley, California AVA. See LAKE COUNTY.

Guigal, family-owned merchant-grower based at Ampuis, CÔTE RÔTIE, in the northern RHÔNE. Although established as recently as 1946 by Étienne Guigal, Établissements Guigal is the most famous of any of the Rhône valley's merchants or growers with COLLECTORS and INVESTORS. This is very largely due to the efforts of its manager since 1961, Étienne's only son Marcel, a man of exceptional modesty and a gifted, meticulous winemaker. Guigal owns slightly more than 20 ha/50 acres of prime vineyard in Côte Rôtie, and it was the wines made from three of its best parcels, extravagantly praised by influential American wine writer Robert PARKER in the early to mid 1980s, that first drew international attention to Marcel Guigal. It would be fair to say that the quality of Guigal's top wines, along with Parker's persistent enthusiasm for them among many other Rhône wines, spearheaded a resurgence of interest in the whole region.

Guigal's so-called CRU wines (La Mouline, La Landonne, and La Turque) are dark, dramatic, mouth-fillingly rich and oaky expressions of the SYRAH grape (supplemented by up to 11 per cent of co-planted VIOGNIER in the case of La Mouline); made from low yields of very ripe, late-picked fruit aged for three and a half years in 100 per cent new oak, and bottled without FINING or FILTRATION. They are particularly impressive when young and their quality is beyond question, but opinions are divided about their style; purists in particular feel that their character is masked by excessive oak. Reputation and rarity combined (only 400 to 700 cases of each are made each year) have also made them extremely expensive and therefore game for criticism, fair or not. More recent offerings include the more plentiful Côte Rôtie Ch d'Ampuis, La Doriane, a special CONDRIEU, and, from the 2000 vintage, Ermitage Ex Voto. Because of the ballyhoo over his top wines, it is easy to overlook the fact that Guigal's NÉGOCIANT wines, made

substantially from bought-in grapes, are also very good and deservedly popular.

In 1984 Guigal bought and revitalized the firm of Vidal Fleury, the company where Étienne Guigal worked for 15 years before founding his own. Vidal Fleury is run quite independently of Guigal although Marcel, helped increasingly by his son Philippe, makes its Côte Rôtie wines. M.W.E.S.

Parker, R. M., *Wines of the Rhône Valley* (2nd edn, New York, 1997).

Gumpoldskirchen, wine centre in lower AUSTRIA famous for its fiery, full-bodied whites made from ZIERFANDLER (or Spätrot) and ROTGIPFLER grapes. Now part of the district known as Thermenregion.

Gundagai, small wine region in SOUTHERN NEW SOUTH WALES ZONE. Makes ripe, fleshy Shiraz and soft, peachy Chardonnay.

Gutedel, meaning 'good and noble' in German, is not the most obvious synonym for CHASSELAS today but Germany still grows more than 1,100 ha/2,720 acres of Weisser Gutedel, almost all of them in the Markgräflerland, southern Baden, which along with neighbouring areas of Alsace and Switzerland, is sometimes referred to as the Gutedel Triangle on account of this variety's ubiquity and continued popularity. The wines, generally juicy and straightforward, may have notes of almond and hay in the better examples, and particularly old vines in calcareous sites can evince both distinction and minerality. A dark-berried form, **Roter Gutedel,** is also known in Baden.

Gutenborner is a very minor white-berried GERMAN CROSSING bred from Müller-Thurgau × Chasselas Napoleon which has had some success in sheltered sites of ENGLAND. Its main attribute is its ability to ripen in cool climates.

Gutsabfüllung. See ERZEUGERABFÜLLUNG.

guttation, botanical term applied to vines losing water through small pores at the leaf margin, due to root pressure. It can be seen early in the morning for vines in wet soil under cool conditions. See also BLEEDING.

Gutturnio, red wine from EMILIA-ROMAGNA in Italy.

Guyot, Jules, respected 19th-century French scientist with a particular interest in viticulture and wine-making whose name lives

Simple single **Guyot** vine training

on in the system of CANE PRUNING which he promulgated. His practical treatises on growing vines and making wine were translated into English in the second half of the 19th century and are enthusiastically followed by NEW WORLD vignerons.

Although cane pruning had been used in France for a very long period, it was promoted by Dr Guyot in 1860. The basic principle of Guyot pruning is to leave six- to ten-bud canes and for each a single two-bud spur at the base; shoots from this spur form the cane the following year (see PRUNING). The **Guyot simple** form, also known as single Guyot, has one cane and one spur. The length of the cane (in French *long bois* or *aste*), or at least the number of buds thereon, may be fixed by APPELLATION laws. **Guyot double,** or double Guyot, the most common vine-TRAINING SYSTEM in Bordeaux, has two canes and two spurs, and the canes are trained to each side. Sometimes the canes are arched, as in the Jura. Galet lists regional variations of the Guyot. R.E.S.

Galet, P., *Précis de viticulture* (5th edn, Montpellier, 1988).

gyropalette or **girasol,** special metal crate holding many dozen inverted bottles of traditional method sparkling wine in a remote-controlled, movable frame. This is the mechanized form of RIDDLING and was developed in Cataluña in the 1970s. For more details, see SPARKLING WINE-MAKING.

HACCP. See QUALITY ASSURANCE.

hail, frozen raindrops or ice bodies built up by accretion, typically falling in thunderstorms. To the normal ill effects of heavy summer RAINFALL is added direct physical damage to the vines and fruit. That to the vines ranges from ripping and stripping of the leaves to bruising and breaking of the young stems: effects which can carry over to the following season or even much longer. Damage to young bunches may destroy or at best reduce the crop, although compensatory growth of the remaining berries may minimize the effects on final YIELD. Hail damage while berries are ripening, on the other hand, is invariably a disaster. Smashed berries are prey to ROT and ferment on the vine, rendering even undamaged parts of the bunches unusable. BURGUNDY is particularly prone to hail damage, as is Mendoza in ARGENTINA.

Hailstorms characteristically follow irregular but well-defined pathways through an area, sometimes devastating parts of a vineyard but leaving other parts untouched. Local TOPOGRAPHY may result in a tendency for the storms to follow preferred pathways, but largely their incidence is unpredictable. Various devices have been tried for warding them off, such as explosive rockets fired into thunderclouds, or towers charged with static electricity to divert them. More recently vines have been covered with netting, which reduces the impact of hailstones. The technologies can hardly be described as proven, but have found supporters among vine-growers understandably desperate to protect their hard-won crops.

J.G.

hail disease. See WHITE ROT.

halbsüss, literally 'half sweet' in German. Used on labels in AUSTRIA to designate wines whose RESIDUAL SUGAR is between 9 and 18 g/l.

halbtrocken, term used to designate German wines with between 10 and 18 g/l RESIDUAL SUGAR. A wine with more than 12 g/l qualifies for this designation only if the residual sugar level is not more than 2 g/l greater than its TOTAL ACIDITY and thus has integrated, harmonious residual sugar but nevertheless tastes dry. Because the concept was unpopular with so many vintners, the GERMAN WINE LAW was loosened in 2000 to permit optional designations on labels, and the term FEINHERB quickly came into widespread use as an alternative indication of wine that tastes dry or nearly-dry but is not legally trocken.

A sparkling wine produced within the EU can be described as halbtrocken if it contains between 33 and 50 g/l residual sugar and, therefore, tastes perceptibly sweet. See also DOSAGE.

In AUSTRIA, halbtrocken signifies a residual sugar level of no more than 12 g/l.

See also SWEETNESS.

Hammurabi (end of 18ᵗʰ century BC), king of BABYLONIA responsible for uniting MESOPOTAMIA with its capital Babylon. His law code survives on baked clay tablets and contains the earliest references to wine shops and wine sellers.

Hanepoot, traditional Afrikaans name for SOUTH AFRICA's most planted Muscat vine variety, MUSCAT OF ALEXANDRIA. It is often sold as a FORTIFIED WINE, for which demand has declined steadily since the late 1980s.

hangover, one of wine's least welcome effects, normally following some DRUNKENNESS or certainly excessive consumption. Drinking wine with or after food and drinking at least as much WATER as wine can lessen the likelihood of a hangover. Homeopathic prophylactics include milk thistle extract (silymarin) and nux vomica. There is no evidence that wine hangovers are different from those caused by any other form of ALCOHOL, although inexpensive wine, non-organic wine, wine consumed with grain-based alcholic drinks, and bottle-aged PORT have all been accused of increasing the risk of hangover. The only indisputably effective control is moderation.

hang time, American expression that strictly applies to the entire growing season, or total period between FLOWERING and HARVEST, but has come to be associated with the fashionable practice of extending hang time beyond traditional ripeness to achieve so-called PHYSIOLOGICAL RIPENESS. This is a controversial practice which can result in overripe flavours and such high alcoholic strength that musts need dilution. Very ripe, dehydrated grapes weigh less than those picked at conventional ripeness, resulting in lower payments for growers paid by weight.

Haraszthy, Agoston (1812–69), early CALIFORNIA wine-grower and promoter, frequently but wrongly identified as the 'father of California wine'. Born in Austro-Hungary, he went to the United States in 1842 and to California in 1849, where he engaged in multifarious activities, including politics, horticulture, and gold-refining. In 1856, he bought a SONOMA county vineyard and established the Buena Vista winery, still extant today. In 1861, as a member of the state commission on viticulture, he travelled to Europe and sent back many thousands of vine cuttings to California. His account of this trip and of his work as a wine-grower in California, *Grape Culture, Wines, and Wine-Making* (1862), first brought California as a wine state to the attention of the nation and is Haraszthy's main claim to importance in the history of wine in America.

After losing control of the Buena Vista winery he migrated to Nicaragua, where he died in mysterious circumstances, perhaps devoured by an alligator. In the years after his death it came to be believed that Haraszthy was the

first to show the possibilities of wine-growing in the state, the first to introduce superior grape varieties into California, and in particular the first to introduce the ZINFANDEL vine. None of this is true, but the story has become legendary and difficult to dislodge.　　T.P.

Pinney, T., *A History of Wine in America* (Berkeley, Calif., 1989).

hard, TASTING TERM applied to wine that is high in astringent TANNINS and apparently lacking in FRUIT. See TEXTURE.

Hardys, formerly **BRL Hardy,** important wine company in AUSTRALIA owned by the American giant CONSTELLATION since 2003 and the result of a 1992 merger between the family-owned Thomas Hardy & Son and the RIVERLAND Berri Renmano CO-OPERATIVE group. Thomas Hardy began making wine at Chateau Reynella in McLaren Vale, SOUTH AUSTRALIA, in 1850 and was the country's biggest wine producer by 1894 (making mainly 'claret' and 'chablis'). Hardys' progress mirrored that of New South Wales-based LINDEMANS, both of them winning international acclaim at the Bordeaux Great Exhibition of 1882 and investing in vineyard in Padthaway in the late 1960s. In 1976, the UK-based Emu Wine Co was acquired, and along with it Houghton of WESTERN AUSTRALIA. Stanley, Leasingham, and Clarevale co-operative became part of the Hardy Group in 1988. In 1990, Hardys broke new, if cripplingly expensive, ground for an Australian company, by buying La Baume, then a decrepit winery in the LANGUEDOC, and the much more substantial Chianti estate of RICASOLI, which was not included in the 1992 merger. A renovated La Baume was sold to Grands Chais de France in 2003 and a JOINT VENTURE in Chile (Mopocho) was abandoned in the late 1990s. In Australia, Hardys bought Yarra Burn winery in the YARRA VALLEY in 1995, and now own Brookland Valley winery in MARGARET RIVER outright, having added some vineyard land in TASMANIA to its holdings. The company has invested substantially in vineyards in the new, cooler wine regions of South Australia and in developing vineyards, and a new tourism/winery project, in CANBERRA. Banrock Station and Stamp of Australia are important export labels.

Harriague, name for TANNAT in Uruguay. Inspired by a viticultural pioneer.

Hárslevelű, white grape variety, whose name means 'linden leaf', which is most widely grown in HUNGARY, where it produces characteristically spicy, aromatic white wines. This is the variety which brings perfume to the FURMINT grapes that make up the majority of the blend for the famous dessert wine TOKAJI, although it is widely planted elsewhere in Hungary and produces a range of VARIETAL wines which vary considerably in quality and provenance. Good Hárslevelű is typically deep

green-gold, very viscous, full, with the powerful flavour of linden honey. In Somló, it produces a less aromatic wine with some minerality while in Villány-Siklós it gives a softer, more perfumed wine.

The variety is popularly associated with the village of Debrö in the Mátra foothills (although much of the wine sold as Debröi Hárslevelű has been a much less specific and less distinguished off-dry blend).

The variety is also grown over the border from Hungary's Tokaji region in SLOVAKIA, and in South Africa.

harvest, both the process of picking ripe grapes from the vine and transferring them to the winery (or field pressing station), and its occasionally festive, if frenetic, duration.

This transition period in the wine-making cycle from vineyard to cellar is also known as VINTAGE (crush in much of the New World), and RÉCOLTE or *vendange* in France, *vendemmia* in Italy, *Ernte* in Germany, COSECHA in Spain, and *vindima* in the DOURO and *colheita* in the rest of Portugal.

Timing

The single most critical aspect of harvest is its timing, choosing that point during the grape RIPENING process when the grape is physiologically mature and the balance between its natural accumulation of SUGARS and its decreasing tally of natural plant ACIDS is optimal (see SAMPLING, grapes).

Typically this is a frenzied period, especially in hotter climates where warm, dry weather can rapidly accelerate ripening, causing different varieties to ripen at the same time, and sometimes putting pressure on available FERMENTATION VESSEL space. In cooler climates, the threat of humid weather and possible ROT, heavy RAINFALL making vineyard access difficult, HAIL damage, or even FROST can also put unwelcome pressure on picking schedules. ACIDIFICATION and ENRICHMENT are respectively the most common rescue operations in the case of grapes picked slightly after or before ideal maturity. MICRO-OXYGENATION may also help reduce the HERBACEOUSNESS resulting from slightly unripe fruit.

Timing of the harvest is additionally complicated by the fact that the fruit in different parts of a single vineyard may vary in ripeness, and the picking of a single plot may take several days.

Although the timing of harvest depends on fruit RIPENESS, it also depends on the region, the grape variety, and the type of wine required (Pinot Noir grapes destined for sparkling white wine are invariably picked much earlier than they would be for a still, red wine, for example). Harvest typically takes place in autumn (see VINE GROWTH CYCLE): September and October in the northern hemisphere and March and April in the southern hemisphere. In very hot climates harvest may start in mid-

summer, however, while at the coolest limits of vine cultivation grapes may be picked when all the leaves have fallen from the vine and there is snow on the ground.

Harvest can, at least theoretically, take place somewhere in the world in every month of the year. Some German EISWEIN is not picked until the January following the official year of harvest (which it must by law carry on the label, no matter when it was picked). New vineyards have been planted in western NEW SOUTH WALES and may be picked on 1 January, making the first wine of the new year. The common vintage period for most southern hemisphere wine is March and April. In very cool southern hemisphere vineyards such as Central Otago in NEW ZEALAND, grapes may remain on the vine until early June.

By July the harvest has usually begun in the earliest regions of the northern hemisphere, the warmest vineyards of CYPRUS and the vineyards of the south eastern states of the UNITED STATES, for example. In August, grapes for the production of California sparkling wine are usually picked. For the majority of wine regions in the northern hemisphere, September and October are the harvest months, with the cooler and later regions and varieties extending into November. Northern hemisphere fruit may still be on the vine in December, particularly for Eiswein production. Very hot southern hemisphere vineyards have been known to pick particularly precocious grapes before the end of December.

Manual harvesting

The traditional method of harvesting, by hand, consists of cutting the stem of individual bunches (peduncle) and putting the bunches into a suitable container. This method, as opposed to MECHANICAL HARVESTING, can be employed regardless of terrain, row spacing (see VINE DENSITY), and precise vine-TRAINING SYSTEM. It also allows pickers to select individual bunches according to their ripeness and to eliminate unhealthy fruit affected by ROT or DISEASE.

Occasionally individual berries are harvested, in the case of bunches affected by BOTRYTIS, an operation that is possible only with a high LABOUR input. This is most famously practised at Ch d'YQUEM and in other vineyards specializing in botrytized sweet wines in SOUTH WEST FRANCE, Austria, and Germany (see AUSLESE, BEERENAUSLESE, and TROCKENBEERENAUSLESE) but the technique may also be employed in the production of (necessarily expensive) dry wines when the vineyard has been attacked by less noble rot.

The cost of manual harvesting increases dramatically when yields are low, for particularly widely spaced vines, or on particularly steep vineyards as in the MOSEL.

The efficiency of hand picking, as opposed to mechanical harvesting (see below), depends on vineyard conditions. If the fruit is at a convenient height and the crop heavy, an experienced picker can harvest up to 2 tonnes a day. Output is reduced by worker fatigue, or in regions where the fruit is at a less convenient height: close to the ground as in traditional Bordeaux vineyards, for example; or grapes trained on the overhead TRELLIS SYSTEMS of southern Italy, northern Portugal, Argentina, and Chile. Light crops are also particularly expensive to pick by hand, where bunches are small because of the grape variety (GEWÜRZTRAMINER, for example) or because of poor fruit set (see COULURE). In such circumstances, even an experienced picker may have less than 500 kg/1,100 lb to show for a day's work.

Manual harvesting requires little equipment. The stems are cut by small secateurs or hooked-tip knives. The fruit is put into a small container holding perhaps 5 or 10 kg of fruit. This was traditionally, and still is in parts of Europe, a wooden trug, cane basket, or leather hod strapped on to the pickers' backs, but nowadays it is most likely to be an unromantic but lighter and easier-to-clean plastic container which may be emptied at intervals into a larger container for transport to the winery, or field pressing station, typically by tractor. These larger containers, often called 'gondolas' in the New World, holding between 500 kg and 2 tonnes, are passed down the row before being towed to the winery. In many vineyards, the fruit is simply emptied into the back of a trailer, although the shallower the depth of fruit, the less damage it will suffer, and so containers full of grapes are increasingly stacked on trailers for transport to the grape reception area.

The harvest workforce varies from region to region. In much of Europe, picking teams include both experienced locals and casual workers, often students and itinerant workers. Iberia traditionally supplied picking teams that would systematically work their way northwards through Europe from region to region as they successively reached ripeness. Similarly, Australian vineyards of the 1950s and 1960s were traditionally picked by the large numbers of itinerants who moved between the sugar-cane-fields of northern Australia and the vineyards of the south. But increased mechanization in the sugar-cane industry has necessitated increased mechanization of the Australian wine industry. In the western United States, the typical grape-picker is Mexican. Wine farms in South Africa enjoy access to relatively inexpensive labour although since 1994 regulatory protection for rural employees has been strengthened. When in the late 1980s the Iron Curtain was torn down and EUROPEAN UNION membership raised wages in Spain and Portugal, eastern Europe became an important source of itinerant labour for vineyard owners in northern Europe.

Providing this annual influx with accommodation, sustenance and, often, transport is an increasingly onerous task each harvest. It is said that in many wine regions mechanical harvesting is the direct result of protest by the spouses of vineyard owners, to whom much of this annual work-load has traditionally fallen.

See also MECHANICAL HARVESTING.

R.E.S. & A.D.W.

Coombe, B. G., and Dry, P. R. (eds.), *Viticulture*, ii: *Practices* (Adelaide, 1992).

Loftus, S., *Puligny-Montrachet: Journal of a Village in Burgundy* (London, 1992).

harvest traditions celebrate the culmination of a year's hard work in the vineyard and, in areas which have not yet succumbed to MECHANIZATION, encourage the pickers in their back-breaking task.

France

Harvest traditions are at their strongest in France.

The church plays a role in many European villages, where a symbolic bunch of grapes is blessed before the harvest and a thanksgiving service held at the end (see also RELIGION). (New World producers such as Robert MONDAVI of California have emulated this tradition.)

Vineyard owners and other members of their families try to be present for the harvest even if they usually work in a distant city. At the end of the harvest a certain amount of horseplay almost inevitably accompanies the picking of the last rows, and one or two pickers end up being thrown into the sticky mass of grapes (a tradition endangered by the increasing use of shallow plastic containers to transport grapes to the cellar).

Traditionally, the tractor pulling the final load is decorated with flowers before it drives, horn blaring, to the cellar. On some estates the pickers still offer a bouquet of flowers to the owner and speeches are made. Large or small, almost all estates celebrate the end of harvest with a party and some regions have their own name for this: *la paulée* in BURGUNDY, *la gerbebaude* in BORDEAUX, and *le cochelet* in CHAMPAGNE.

Most harvest traditions are gastronomic, however, and the major events in a picker's day are the three meals which punctuate it (or four if the *casse-croute*, a second breakfast normally taken in the vines, is counted). In France, the women who run the kitchens during the harvest are usually part of a family team, helped by local women who may work in the vines during the rest of the year. For 11 months these women cook only for their families and friends, but for one month they must turn themselves into restaurateurs of a special kind. Working in often rudimentary kitchens, they must feed demanding pickers both well and economically. Soups, rabbit dishes, and dishes such as *pot-au-feu*, *coq au vin*, and *blanquettes* are often requested by pickers nostalgic for an era when long, slow cooking was the norm. A harvest would not be a harvest in Burgundy without a *bœuf bourguignon*, for example, and in Bordeaux the bonfires of *sarments*, or vine shoots, on which are grilled steaks and sausages, may be kept blazing to form the focus of informal dancing and singing after dinner.

The harvest cook's work is regularly interrupted to administer first aid, and when the cook's long day ends, she (and it is still usually she) is likely to be kept awake by pickers at play. Small wonder that there is something of a revolt among the younger generation of vine-growers' spouses, who may anyway have full-time jobs elsewhere. Caterers are increasingly used, and high unemployment has in some cases substituted for students in search of a good time local people who would rather increase their earnings by forgoing lunch. These developments, together with an increase in the paperwork involved in being even a temporary employer, have contributed substantially to the substitution of MECHANICAL HARVESTERS for human pickers, and therefore to the death of harvest traditions.

The menus for each day, handwritten in notebooks every year, enlivened by anecdotal remarks, together with the photograph albums kept on many estates, may eventually be the only record of harvest traditions. R.H.

Rest of Europe

Harvest traditions are most likely to survive where vineyards are picked by approximately the same people each year, which is why few survive in Italy and Germany, where grapes are increasingly picked by immigrants with no tradition of grape-picking in their families. As mechanization invades a wine region, so harvest traditions retreat, presumably until revived as a public relations exercise. This means that harvest traditions are more likely to survive where LABOUR costs are relatively low.

A prime example of this has been the DOURO valley, where PORT is made, although even here rural labour shortages are having an effect. Even in the early 21st century, however, it was still just possible to associate a genuine sense of folk tradition and celebration with the harvest, as some local pickers invade the QUINTAS at which they and their families have traditionally worked every September for decades. The increasingly depopulated TRÁS-OS-MONTES region has supplied many of the teams, or *rogas*, of pickers who brought noise, chatter, and traffic to a region marked by its silence the rest of the year.

At a few properties in the Douro, pickers' feet were still expected to provide a more bucolic, gentler, and more effective alternative to the mechanical CRUSHER, or robotic lagar (see FOOT TREADING). The *roga*, or sometimes only its male members, is expected not only to pick the grapes, but to make the wine as well. Donning shorts, and with their arms around each others' shoulders, they march methodically backwards and forwards across the granite LAGARES, often thigh-high in sticky purple grapes, to a chant or beat of a drum. Once a floating CAP of skins has visibly been separated from the juice beneath, *liberdade* (liberty) is declared and the march evolves into dancing, traditionally to the sound of an accordion but nowadays, more often than not, to recorded music from a stereo system.

Traditionally the leader of the *roga* would present the owner of the farm or winery, the *patrão*, with a decorated vine branch at a final celebratory vintage feast.

New World
Such traditions as have evolved around the harvest, or crush, in the New World tend to be the direct result of having large numbers of people, often from very different backgrounds, doing work unfamiliar to many of them, in the open air. The weather conditions, especially the temperature and sunshine, have greatest effect on worker comfort, and indirectly on the development of traditions. In many parts of the New World, harvest can be a time of heavy physical work for moderately low pay under trying conditions. Where the weather is hot, the harvest can start early in the morning, and meal breaks are short as there is often little opportunity to relax in a hot, dusty, vineyard with little available shade.

Many of the social aspects of harvest are changing with use of the mechanical harvester. One harvester and operator can pick as much in three shifts during the 24 hours as could hundreds of human pickers during the day.

Hanson, R., *Recipes from the French Wine Harvest* (London, 1995).

Harveys of Bristol, once-powerful force in the British wine trade in the mid 20th century and owners of the world's most significant brand of sherry, Harveys Bristol Cream, and thereby creators of an entire style of sherry (see CREAM). In 1822, the first in a long line of John Harveys entered the wine trade, working with his uncle in wine cellars in Denmark Street in the west of England port of Bristol. The third John Harvey pioneered the use of advertising by the wine trade in the early 20th century. It was only in the 1930s, after the Repeal of PROHIBITION in the US, that the company's sales of sherry outstripped its port business. By the 1950s, Jack Harvey built up an export business for Harveys' sherries, particularly in North America (although the firm had no production base in Spain).

In 1946, the firm had taken on Harry WAUGH, a talented wine buyer, salesman, and teacher, to vitalize Harveys' fine wine business, and to rival that of their neighbours AVERYS. During the 20 years that Waugh and chairman George McWatters, a member of the Harvey family, were there, Harveys was to take the wine trade lead in training, in sponsorship of the arts and other activities, and in presen-

tation of its wares to an increasingly discerning public.

In 1960, Harveys acquired the port shippers COCKBURN, and its ports became as internationally successful as Harveys' sherries; so successful in fact that, after a fierce takeover battle, the firm was acquired by the Showerings group, famous for cider, perry, and BRITISH WINE, in 1966. Two years later, Showerings merged with the giant Allied Breweries Group (later to become Allied-Lyons) and in 1970 Harveys acquired their first ever production base in JEREZ and, through takeovers of de Terry and Palomino y Vergara, developed their substantial new footholds in Jerez and Puerto de Santa María so that, from 1989, all Harveys sherries were, for the first time, bottled in Jerez. A decline in the sherry market forced substantial rationalization so that by the early 1990s, Harveys were concentrating on their fortified wine BRANDS Harveys Bristol Cream and Cockburn's Special Reserve.

These activities were run in parallel with, but at an increasing distance from, Harveys' fine wine business, which declined considerably in prestige after the Showerings takeover, even though in 1963 the firm had acquired a quarter share in the Bordeaux first growth Ch LATOUR. The parent company Allied-Lyons acquired a majority holding in the château before selling it in 1993, taking over the sherry firm DOMECQ the following year. Both Harveys and Cockburn have been owned by the American company Beam Wine Estates since the break-up of Allied Domecq in 2005.

Hastings River, warm and humid wine region on the north coast of NEW SOUTH WALES. Mildew-resistant hybrid Chambourcin is an important red variety. Many other grapes are sourced from more reliable regions. TOURISM is the principal rationale for the region.

Haut, French for 'high'. See the rest of the name if there is no relevant entry under H.

Haut-Brion, Château, the most famous property in the GRAVES district in BORDEAUX producing both red and white wines, today, after years of fierce competition, run in tandem with Ch La MISSION HAUT-BRION. Haut-Brion has a special reputation as the first of the wines which were designated PREMIERS CRUS in the famous 1855 CLASSIFICATION of Bordeaux wines to be mentioned in extant records. The cellar records of the English King Charles II mention no fewer than 169 bottles of the 'wine of Hobriono' [*sic*] served to guests of the royal table. The wine was praised by Samuel Pepys. The London diarist recorded for 10 April 1663 that he 'drank a sort of French wine called Ho Bryen that hath a good and most particular taste I never met with'. Thomas JEFFERSON also praised it on his visit to Bordeaux in 1787 as American minister in France. The property was then owned by the Pontac family,

very rich members of the *noblesse de la robe*, and prominent in the Parlement of Bordeaux. But when in 1694 François-Auguste de Pontac died childless, the estate was divided between two of his family, and the two parts were not reunited until 1840, by the latest of a number of owners, Eugène Larrieu, whose family held it until after the First World War. After a further series of not very successful owners in a very difficult time, the château was bought in 1935 by Mr Clarence Dillon, an American banker. Today the property is run by his grandson Prince Robert of Luxembourg with his mother, the Duchess de Mouchy. In 2004, Jean-Philippe Delmas became estate manager when his innovative father, Jean-Bernard, retired.

Partly, no doubt, owing to its historic reputation, Haut-Brion was the only non-MÉDOC to be included in the famous 1855 classification of the wines of Bordeaux. Enclosed in the Bordeaux suburb of Pessac, the château building dates from the 16th century, and the 45 ha/111 acres of vineyards are composed of 45 per cent CABERNET SAUVIGNON vines, 18 per cent CABERNET FRANC, and 37 per cent MERLOT. Average production is 13,000 cases, including a SECOND WINE, **Ch Bahans-Haut-Brion**, since 1976 sold with a vintage date. About eight TONNEAUX a year of the property's rare dry white wine, **Haut-Brion Blanc**, is made from about 63 per cent SÉMILLON and 37 per cent SAUVIGNON BLANC vines planted on 2.7 ha.

E.P.-R. & J.R.

Hautes Côtes de Beaune and **Hautes Côtes de Nuits**, sometimes known collectively as the **Hautes Côtes**, vineyards dispersed in the hills above the escarpment of the Côte d'Or in Burgundy. Most of the production is red wine from Pinot Noir, with some white wine made from Chardonnay or occasionally Pinot Blanc or Pinot Gris, but at ALTITUDES reaching 500 m/1,640 ft the grapes do not ripen easily. This is also suitable ground for BOURGOGNE ALIGOTÉ, especially as the blackcurrant bushes needed for the production of CASSIS can often be seen growing alongside.

Forty-seven communes are included in the Hautes Côtes appellations. The most prolific villages include Meloisey, Nantoux, and Échevronne above the Côte de Beaune and Villars-Fontaine, Magny-lès-Villars, and Marey-lès-Fussey above the Côte de Nuits. There is a good CO-OPERATIVE for the Hautes Côtes wines located just outside Beaune and an enjoyable restaurant and tasting area, the Maison des Hautes Côtes, at Marey-lès-Fussey. Many leading growers in the Côte de Nuits such as Bertagna, the Gros family, and Jayer Gilles now also offer affordable wines from the Hautes Côtes.

See also CÔTE D'OR, and map under BURGUNDY. J.T.C.M.

Haut-Médoc, the higher, southern part of the Médoc district of Bordeaux which includes the world-famous communes of MARGAUX, PAUILLAC, ST-ESTÈPHE, and ST-JULIEN, as well as the less glamorous ones of LISTRAC and MOULIS. Red wines made here outside one of these appellations usually qualify for the appellation of Haut-Médoc. For more details, see MÉDOC.

Haut Pays, French term meaning 'high country' which was used in the Middle Ages to describe the area upstream of BORDEAUX which produced wines (and presumably had done for longer than Bordeaux since at the beginning of the Christian era wine-making seems to have spread north west from Narbonne towards the Atlantic). This included GAILLAC, BERGERAC, Quercy (modern CAHORS), and Nérac (BUZET). Their more dependable climate often produced wines stronger than the light, thin wines then made in the Bordeaux region itself and were seen as a serious commercial threat. The port of Bordeaux penalized them by taxing them heavily and barring them from the port until the region had exported its own wines. See also HUNDRED YEARS WAR.

Haut-Poitou, VDQS zone almost due south of SAUMUR in which about 500 ha/1,200 acres of vines on limestone and marl produce a range of VARIETAL wines, marked by clean, fruity acidity. Almost equal quantities of reds and whites are produced from the usual middle Loire range of Bordelais, Burgundian, and Loire vine varieties. SAUVIGNON and GAMAY can be particularly successful, as can CABERNET (a blend of both Sauvignon and Franc) in particularly ripe vintages. The CO-OPERATIVE at Neuville dominates production.

Hawaii, chain of islands in the Pacific ocean and one of the 50 UNITED STATES. It produces mainly FRUIT WINES, notably a sparkling pineapple wine, as well as some grape wines, on the island of Maui.

head, or crown, of a vine is the top of the TRUNK where CORDONS branch, or where a group of arms are placed for new CANES in cane pruning.

head space, that space in a container holding a liquid that is not taken up by that liquid. In wine containers it is often called the ULLAGE, or ullage space. In large, modern wineries, the head space of stainless steel tanks is often deliberately filled by an INERT GAS as a preservative measure.

head training, a form of VINE TRAINING whereby the trunk has a definite head, or knob, consisting of old wood rather than arms of a CORDON. Head trained vines are normally subject to CANE PRUNING, but may, after SPUR PRUNING, be described as GOBELET. The head may be anywhere between 40 cm/1.25 ft and 1 m/3.3 ft from the ground. The GUYOT system is a common cane-pruned form of head training. R.E.S.

health, effects of wine consumption on. Until the 18th century, wine played a central role in medical practice, not least because it was safer to drink than most available water, as outlined in MEDICINE. Other health benefits historically ascribed to wine were unproven and mostly optimistic. In the 1970s and early 1980s, wine drinking, like all forms of alcohol consumption, was targeted by some health campaigners, and warning labels proliferated on wine bottles (see LABELLING). Wine contains alcohol, and alcohol is toxic. Its contribution to liver damage, brain damage, and accidents is well known. Less well known is that the incidence of many cancers, nerve and muscle wasting, blood disorders, raised blood pressure, strokes, skin infections, psoriasis, and infertility increases with high intake, and the babies of mothers who drink heavily during pregnancy may have abnormal facial features and low intelligence (so-called fetal alcohol syndrome).

Since the early 1990s, however, a substantial and increasing body of research has shown that modest drinkers have lower mortality than heavy drinkers or non-drinkers, suggesting that alcohol consumption (and perhaps especially wine consumption) can have a net beneficial effect on health. So convincing is the evidence to date that the link between moderate wine consumption and reduced risk of heart disease has now attracted federal research funding in the United States.

Coronary heart disease

The most beneficial effect of wine is its contribution to reduced mortality from coronary heart disease, the western world's major killer. This strikes when plaques of cholesterol build up in the arteries supplying the heart muscle. These furred-up arteries cannot supply the heart muscle with enough oxygen, resulting in the pain of angina. Heart attacks happen when blood clots block these narrowed arteries completely, cutting off the oxygen supply. Heavy drinkers develop increased cholesterol levels as well as raised blood pressure, weakened heart muscle, and a susceptibility to potentially fatal abnormal heart rhythms. Given this record, it was not just the temperance movement which believed that moderate drinking must surely be doing some harm. Yet there is now a mass of evidence that those who drink moderately are less likely to develop coronary heart disease and to die from it than either those who drink heavily or those who have never drunk alcohol. Furthermore, it is the alcohol in alcoholic drinks which has been identified as the single most important ingredient in prevention of cardiovascular disease.

Alcohol, it seems, moderates the level of inflammatory blood chemicals called cytokines which adversely affect blood cholesterol and blood-clotting proteins. Blood carries LDL (low-density lipoprotein) cholesterol, which forms the plaques which block arteries, and HDL (high-density lipoprotein) cholesterol, which mops them up. Moderate alcohol consumption improves the balance between the harmful and beneficial forms of cholesterol. Blood clots are formed by platelets—small shards of old cells which float harmlessly in the blood until they are chemically triggered to stick together in a tangle of threads of fibrin protein. Alcohol has two anticoagulant effects which make blood less likely to clot in the wrong place. It makes the platelets slightly less sticky, and it reduces the level of fibrin available to form a clot. An added benefit for moderate drinkers is increased vascular elasticity, enabling a more rapid flow of blood through the arteries and lowering risk of cardiovascular disease.

The anticoagulant effect of alcohol lasts less than 24 hours. This may explain why the risk of a heart attack is reduced during the day following a couple of drinks. The traditional wine drinker's glass or two with the evening meal provides a steady, safe level of alcohol. In contrast, the beer or spirit drinker's Saturday night binge leaves him or her temporarily over-anticoagulated (and at increased risk of a stroke due to bleeding) until he or she has metabolized the alcohol, then at increased risk of heart attack until the next night out. Unfortunately, there is increasing evidence of binge drinking of wine, particularly amongst young European women, which carries the risks of the same negative health consequences as for any other alcoholic drink.

But alcohol is not the only compound of cardiovascular significance in wine. Red wine, much more than white, is rich in PHENOLICS, which have antioxidant properties. There are hundreds of phenolic compounds in wine, but attention has focused on RESVERATROL, possibly due to its known and potent beneficial health properties. In the laboratory it inhibits not only the oxidation reaction by which LDL-cholesterol is formed, but also inhibits reactions which make platelets more sticky and the lining of blood vessels liable to promote a blood clot. It is thought that red wine or red grape juice, although not white wine, increases the level of resveratrol in the blood and its antioxidant activity.

A growing number of studies conclude that the way alcohol is consumed—the pattern of drinking—is key to potential health benefits. An Italian study showed that drinking with meals significantly reduced the risk of a heart attack (three or more drinks a day appeared to halve the risk), but there was no such relationship seen in those drinking the same amount outside mealtimes.

It is therefore likely that it is the combination of alcohol, the usual consumption pattern of wine (versus that of other alcoholic drinks), and antioxidant content that makes wine the superior drink for cardiovascular health. These factors may explain the FRENCH PARADOX. See also FLAVONOLS.

Cancer

Awareness of the influence of lifestyle on cancer risks has stimulated research into the relationship between drinking and cancers. As antioxidants are thought to be part of the body's defence against cancer, the phenolics in red wine could plausibly bolster that defence. Indeed, in the laboratory, resveratrol protects cells from cancerous change. Resveratrol in wine is absorbed from the digestive tract into the body, but so is alcohol, which causes damage, so wine's rich mixture of chemicals has potential for harm as well as benefit.

Sadly, the news so far from studies on wine and cancer is largely bad. Alcohol consumption is a risk factor, albeit minor, for cancer of the digestive tract. The association is strongest for cancer of the oesophagus (gullet) and becomes progressively weaker for stomach cancer and cancer of the colon. Studies in several countries of the incidence of breast cancer show that even modest consumption of alcohol is associated with an increase in risk. This is especially relevant for women under 60, most of whom are more at risk from breast cancer than from heart disease and who thus benefit less from wine's cardioprotective effects. More positive news on red wine's anticancer properties is emerging from a number of studies showing associations between moderate consumption and reduced risk of ovarian, prostate, and lung cancers, but there is clearly still much to be learned about wine and cancer.

Respiratory problems

Very heavy drinkers are prone to pneumonia, but three to four drinks a day appear to protect non-smokers from the effects of the common cold virus. Recent research has shown that the antioxidant resveratrol may help to fight chronic bronchitis and emphysema by reducing the amount of chemicals in the lungs that cause the diseases.

Some asthmatics experience an adverse reaction to wine. A variety of constituents may be responsible. SULFITE can irritate the airways, triggering wheeze in sensitive people. Sulfur levels in wine are being reduced and many countries insist that the presence of sulfite is indicated on wine labels. TANNINS have also been implicated as red wine is more often a problem than white, and an allergic reaction due to the HISTAMINE in some red wines is the culprit for a few.

Headaches

Some migraine sufferers identify red wine as a trigger. Their downfall is likely to be the phenolics, which in the test tube liberate from cells the chemical messenger 5-hydroxytryptamine (serotonin) which plays a part in the initiation of migraine. Red wines may also contain histamine, which can induce headache in susceptible subjects. As antihistamines can interact with alcohol, choosing a wine low in histamine may be the best strategy for avoiding the problem.

Dementia

The intoxified brain does not function well (whatever its owner may temporarily believe), and the deleterious effect on intellectual function of long-term assault with heavy alcohol is well known. It comes as a pleasant bonus to find that moderate wine drinkers are less likely to develop various dementias, including Alzheimer's, than their non-drinking or heavy-drinking compatriots. Wine appears to be of greater benefit than other drinks in this respect.

Vision

A common cause of declining vision in old age is macular degeneration—wearing out of the light-sensitive cells at the back of the eye. An American study published in 1998 showed that the visual cells of moderate wine drinkers are 20 per cent better preserved than those of non-drinkers and drinkers of beer and spirits. As with heart disease, wine's anticoagulant and antioxidant properties may be responsible.

Bones

Very heavy drinkers are prone to fracture their bones; a consequence of the effects of too much alcohol on their bone structure and on their lifestyle. Laboratory work shows that alcohol has a damaging effect on the cellular bone-forming mechanism. However, some population studies show an association between moderate drinking and improvement in bone density. Those such as postmenopausal women at risk of osteoporosis may find a glass of wine a day beneficial rather than harmful.

Diabetes mellitus

Although diabetics are obliged to watch carefully what they eat and drink, alcohol taken with a meal does not substantially alter their blood sugar. Non-insulin diabetes mellitus, the form of diabetes which usually develops in middle age, is due not so much to lack of insulin but to decreased response to it. This is another effect of cytokines, so may explain Italian research showing that moderate drinkers are more sensitive to insulin than non-drinkers, and an American study which found that moderate drinking is associated with a significantly lower risk of developing non-insulin-dependent diabetes.

Peptic ulcers and stomach upsets

Ulcer sufferers have traditionally been advised to avoid alcohol lest it irritate the lining of the stomach. This advice is now less often needed.

Gastritis, peptic ulcers, and stomach cancer are now known to be strongly associated with infection by the bacterium *Helicobacter pylori* and a short course of treatment designed to eradicate *H. pylori* is saving many former sufferers a lifetime of treatment. Furthermore, a study in Germany in 1997 showed that moderate wine and beer drinkers were significantly less likely to be infected with *H. pylori* than non-drinkers, possibly due to the antimicrobial effects of alcohol. If moderate drinkers are less likely to have *H. pylori* infection, they should have fewer ulcers, a deduction supported by evidence from America. Recent research suggests that more regular, moderate consumption may reduce the chances of infection with *H. pylori* more strongly than occasional consumption of large amounts of alcohol.

Gallstones are another cause of upper abdominal misery. There is some evidence that moderate drinking reduces gallstone formation. The major component of most gallstones is cholesterol, so the benefit is probably due to wine's effect on cholesterol metabolism.

St Paul's advice to 'use a little wine for thy stomach's sake' proves to have been wise on another count. Wine is more active against the bacteria which cause travellers' diarrhoea than bismuth, another traditional and distinctly less palatable prophylactic. Wines appear to become more effective as they age although their antibacterial potential declines after about ten years.

Sensible drinking

Health authorities in many countries have disseminated 'sensible drinking levels', suggested maxima for personal consumption of alcohol usually expressed in 'units', or STANDARD DRINKS, of alcohol, though there is wide variation between what constitutes a unit and how many of them may safely be consumed.

These limits are at best only a rough guide as individuals' reactions to alcohol must always be taken into consideration when assessing recommended consumption levels. Sex, age, build, genetic make-up, state of health, drinking with or without food, drug intake all affect the way alcohol is metabolized. For instance, glass for glass, women, regardless of their weight or size, absorb relatively more alcohol than men because of differences in levels of stomach enzymes, their lower body water content meaning that alcohol is more concentrated in their tissues and, if they are also taking the contraceptive pill, more slowly eliminated. This may explain why women who drink in excess of the recommended daily units experience significantly greater risks of poor health outcomes than men who do likewise. Conversely, it appears that the relationship between moderate consumption and better general health is stronger for women.

Aside from any specific health benefits, it emerges that self-reported health—a good predictor of all-cause mortality—is best for moderate drinkers, and especially for wine drinkers.   J.H.H. & B.B.

Augustin, L.S.A., *et al.*, 'Alcohol consumption and acute myocardial infarction: a benefit of alcohol consumed with meals?', *Epidemiology*, 15 (2004) 767–69.

Doll, R., 'One for the heart', *British Medical Journal*, 315 (1997), 1664–8.

——, *et al.*, 'Alcohol, tobacco and breast cancer—collaborative reanalysis of individual data from 53 epidemiological studies, including 58 515 women with breast cancer and 95 067 women without the disease', *British Journal of Cancer*, 87 (2002), 1234–45.

Gronbaek, M., *et al.*, 'Mortality associated with moderate intakes of wine, beer or spirits', *British Medical Journal*, 310 (1995), 1165–8.

Kuepper-Nybelen, J., *et al.*, 'Patterns of alcohol consumption and *Helicobacter pylori* infection: results of a population-based study from Germany among 6545 adults', *Alimentary Pharmacology and Therapeutics*, 21 (2005), 57–64.

Renaud, S., and de Lorgeril, M., 'Wine, alcohol, platelets, and the French paradox for coronary heart disease', *Lancet*, 339 (1992), 1523–6.

Truelsen, T., *et al.*, 'Amount and type of alcohol and risk of dementia', *Neurology*, 59 (2002), 1313–19.

Heathcote, exciting (Shiraz) Australian wine region, once part of Bendigo, VICTORIA. More producers emerging every day.

heat stress affects vines when air temperatures are high. Very high daytime temperatures, of more than 40 °C/ 104 °F, cause the vine to 'shut down', or virtually cease PHOTOSYNTHESIS, as the ENZYMES responsible can no longer work. High temperatures also lead to WATER STRESS, especially when accompanied by bright sunshine, low humidity, and strong, dry winds. High temperatures cause fast RESPIRATION in vines and this leads to, for example, low levels of MALIC ACID in mature fruit in hot regions. VARIETAL character and red COLOUR in grapes are also depressed by high temperatures. Some researchers claim that more moderate daytime temperatures, in excess of only 25 °C, can depress colour formation and varietal flavour expression.   R.E.S.

Spayd, S. E., Tarara, J. M., Mee, D. L., and Ferguson, J. C., 'Separation of sunlight and temperature effects on the composition of *vitis vinifera* cv. Merlot berries', *American Journal of Enology and Viticulture*, 53 (2002), 171–82.

heat summation, a computation that forms part of many systems of CLIMATE CLASSIFICATION.

heat-treated vines, vines which have undergone **heat treatment**, or THERMOTHERAPY, to eliminate disease.

hectare, common agricultural measurement of area equivalent to 10,000 sq m, or 2.47 acres.

hedging, see TRIMMING.

Heida, or **Païen** in French, Swiss synonym for TRAMINER and a speciality of Visperterminen.

Helfensteiner is famous principally as a parent of DORNFELDER, a successful German red wine crossing. It is itself a crossing of FRÜHBURGUNDER × TROLLINGER and is essentially a product of Württemberg, where its ability to ripen earlier than Trollinger is valued but its susceptibility to COULURE is causing its decline from a small flurry of popularity in the early 1970s.

helicopters are more expensive than fixed-wing aircraft, which limits their application to viticulture. Their manœuvrability is a bonus, however. They are particularly useful for crop SPRAYING, and the turbulence created by the rotors helps the spray to penetrate (although there are the usual problems where individual landholdings are small). They may be used as airborne WIND MACHINES to stir up cold, dense air just above the vineyard surface with warmer air above to prevent spring FROST damage. It is not uncommon in New Zealand, for instance, to have helicopters on standby when the risk of frost is high. On occasion they have been used in an attempt to dry excess moisture off vine leaves and bunches immediately after heavy RAINFALL at HARVEST.

Henderson, Dr Alexander (1780–1863), Scotsman who qualified as a doctor and then moved to London and contributed to a wide range of publications, including the *Encyclopaedia Britannica*. After visiting the wine regions of France, Germany, and Italy, he wrote *The History of Ancient and Modern Wines*, which was published in 1824 (eight years after JULLIEN but nine years before REDDING). Some of the most useful aspects of his book perhaps reflect some aspects of his medical training: his observations on the art of wine TASTING.

Henriques, Justino, the largest single shipper of MADEIRA, bottling under a variety of names including Cruz, the largest single BRAND of madeira (and PORT) in France. Established in Funchal in 1870, Justino Henriques operates from modern industrial premises outside the city. The company is now controlled by the French import and distribution group La Martiniquaise.

Henty (including Drumborg), particularly cool Australian wine region in the Western Victoria Zone (see VICTORIA) used as a source of grapes for sparkling wines; also fine table wines.

herbaceous, TASTING TERM for the leafy or grassy aroma of crushed green leaves or freshly cut grass. **Herbaceousness** is generally considered a defect only when present in excess (although American tasters are much less tolerant of it than, for example, the British).

Wines made from the produce of SAUVIGNON BLANC, SÉMILLON, CABERNET SAUVIGNON, CABERNET FRANC, or MERLOT vines which failed to ripen fully are often excessively herbaceous. In general, the younger the vines, the greater their VIGOUR, and the earlier the grapes are picked, the more pronounced the herbaceousness. One cause of vegetative herbaceous aromas, particularly in wines of Sauvignon Blanc and Cabernet Sauvignon, is the presence of METHOXYPYRAZINES originating from the grape; see also FLAVOUR COMPOUNDS. Another source of herbaceousness is six-carbon atom LEAF ALDEHYDES.

Numerous investigations have shown that they, and the corresponding six-carbon atom ALCOHOLS, derive from linoleic and linolenic, which are both fatty acids found in plant leaves and in the fruit. These decompose rapidly once the grape berry is crushed to yield hexanal, hexenal, and the related unsaturated alcohols, all six-carbon atom compounds which can react further during FERMENTATION to produce a wide range of flavour compounds which are responsible for the aroma called herbaceous. Another reason why a wine may taste herbaceous is from vine leaves inadvertently picked with the grapes. Early MECHANICAL HARVESTERS were particularly prone to do this, and the grapes were often so mangled that it was impossible to separate the wet leaves from them. Wines made from such a blend would also not surprisingly be high in leaf aldehydes and taste distinctly leafy or herbaceous, a problem accentuated when such mechanical harvesters are used on relatively young vineyards. More sophisticated machine harvesters have reduced leaf contamination considerably.

                                    A.D.W. & P.J.W.

Herbemont, dark-skinned *aestivalis-cinerea-vinifera* HYBRID grown in Brazil because of its resistance to FUNGAL DISEASES.

herbicides, chemicals applied to vineyards to control the growth of WEEDS. They may be either pre-emergent (or residual) or post-emergent (knockdown). The latter group comprises two types, contact and systemic herbicides. Residual herbicides act against germinating seedlings of the weeds, while post-emergent herbicides damage live plant tissue. Typically, herbicides are applied only to the strip of ground directly under the vine, and weeds growing between the rows are controlled by cultivation or mowing. Herbicides are used even between rows in some vineyard regions, though there can be risks of soil erosion or loss of water infiltration without the organic matter produced by COVER CROPS in this zone.

In areas of winter rainfall, a contact or systemic spray is typically used in late autumn to early winter, followed by a pre-emergent herbicide in the early spring. In regions with summer rainfall, or irrigated areas, further contact or systemic sprays may be needed to control weeds that grow during the growing season. Most herbicides used in vineyards are low-hazard chemicals which present no danger to the operator (see AGROCHEMICALS). Many of the knockdown chemicals are inactivated by soil, and so leave no soil RESIDUES.

Continued use of some herbicides leads to the increased presence of so-called 'escape' weeds, however, which were previously suppressed by competition from other weeds. Varying the type of herbicides used can sometimes control these, otherwise mechanical removal is essential. Some herbicides can even damage vines, either by wetting vine leaves inadvertently, or when herbicides are leached into the root zone, as can happen with young vines, sandy soils, and irrigation.

Concern about environmental pollution as a result of herbicide use has been growing (see ORGANIC and BIODYNAMIC VITICULTURE), and more and more vine-growers are substituting undervine ploughing for herbicide use—helped by the increasing sophistication of machinery for this type of cultivation. See WEED CONTROL. Although the use of herbicides is relatively inexpensive, it does encourage the vine roots to go to the more fertile soils nearer the surface.   R.E.S.

heritage varieties,

heritage varieties, expression for VINE VARIETIES that are intensely local to a particular area and have a relatively long tradition of being grown there. Typically they have been rescued from near-extinction. An example would be PETIT COURBU and ARRUFIAC of Gascony, or such specialities of Valais in Switzerland as HUMAGNE ROUGE.

Hermitage,

Hermitage, the most famous northern RHÔNE appellation of all, producing extremely limited quantities of seriously long-lived reds and about a third as much full-bodied dry white wine. Although the appellation is only the size of a large Bordeaux estate, Hermitage was one of France's most famous wines in the 18th and 19th centuries when the name alone was sufficient to justify prices higher than any wine other than a FIRST GROWTH bordeaux (which were sometimes strengthened by the addition of some Hermitage until the mid 19th century). The origin of the name Hermitage is not so much shrouded in mystery as obscured by many conflicting legends, most of them concerning a hermit, *ermite* in French. Not least of the puzzles is how and when Ermitage acquired its H (dropped for some modern bottlings), although there was no shortage of English-speaking enthusiasts of the wine in the 18th century (including Thomas JEFFERSON). The first recorded mention of Hermitage in English was in Thomas Shadwell's 1680 play *The Woman-Captain*, 'Vin de Bon, Vin Celestine, and Hermitage, and all the Wines upon the fruitful Rhône'. These 'manly' wines were also a great favourite with the Russian imperial court, but the economic upheavals of the first half of the 20th century affected Hermitage as much as any Rhône appellation. While the surrounding appellation CROZES-HERMITAGE has, like most of the Rhône valley, seen considerable changes over the last 20 years, Hermitage is a constant, give or take a wine-making tweak or two.

The wine comes from an almost unenlargeable 132 ha/326 acres of particularly well-favoured vines on the extraordinary hill of Hermitage, a south-facing bank of granite, thinly covered with extremely varied and well-charted soil types, which almost pushes the town of Tain l'Hermitage into the river Rhône just as it turns sharp left (see map under RHÔNE). Wines produced here in the Roman town of Tegna were already known to writers such as PLINY and MARTIAL.

The combination of heat-retaining granite and a reasonably steep southern exposition do much to encourage grape RIPENING here. It is not surprising that such a celebrated vineyard has been for long divided into various CLIMATS, all with their own soil types and reputations for wine types. Professor Pierre Mandier, a geologist at Lyons, has charted the hillside in considerable detail. The most famous *climats* are at the western end of the hill, which benefits from the highest temperatures. Les Bessards has a topsoil of sandy gravel on granite and produces some of the sturdiest wines. Le Méal produces more aromatic wines from a soil with more limestone, and bigger stones towards the top of the slope, where l'Hermite is crowned with a small stone chapel owned by Paul JABOULET Aîné and has more sand and fine LOESS. Clay predominates in the lower *climats* of Les Gréffieux and Les Diognières. Other famous *climats* include Beaume(s), Maison Blanche, Péléat, Les Murets, Rocoule, La Croix, and Les Signeaux in the extreme east. Although white and red grapes are planted all over the hill, some of the finest white Hermitage comes from the higher vineyards, and clay-limestone soils are considered the best suited.

Producers such as Gérard Chave, the modest master of Hermitage, delight in blending the produce of holdings all over the hill to produce a complex, well-balanced expression of each vintage. Producers with less diversified holdings may produce less complex wines, some of them labelled with a single *climat*.

Unlike CÔTE RÔTIE upriver, red Hermitage is in practice made from the SYRAH vine alone (although the AC regulations permit the addition of up to 15 per cent white grapes); indeed Hermitage has laid claim to be the cradle of Syrah, while white Hermitage may be made from the robust MARSANNE or the nervier, and less common, ROUSSANNE.

SOIL EROSION is a frequent problem here, the result as much of exposure as of gradient, although the hill is steep enough in parts for TERRACES to be necessary, and some retaining walls are used as advertising sites for the merchant houses of CHAPOUTIER and Jaboulet, based in and near Tain respectively.

The appellation regulations limit yields to a basic 40 hl/ha (2.3 tons/acre) but ENRICHMENT may be allowed in some vintages, so long as the ALCOHOLIC STRENGTH of the resultant wine is no more than 13.5 per cent for reds and 14 per cent for whites.

Wine-making philosophies vary here, but are essentially traditional. Red wines are the result of relatively hot FERMENTATIONS matured in often quite old COOPERAGE of varied capacity, according to vintage characteristics. Red Hermitage should be very deeply coloured and headily perfumed. They can evolve for two or three decades after which they may be mistaken for great red bordeaux. Some of the finest red wines of Hermitage come from Chave, Le Pavillon from Chapoutier, La Chapelle from Jaboulet, and Le Gréal from Sorrel.

White wines are possibly even more varied, according to the blend of grape varieties used, RIPENESS, whether MALOLACTIC FERMENTATION has taken place, and whether WOOD is used for fermentation and/or AGEING. Almost all white Hermitage is notably full in BODY, and some of the more serious examples such as Chave's and Chapoutier's Chante Alouette are among the longest-living dry white wines of France.

In very ripe years, some of Hermitage's white grapes may be transformed into VIN DE PAILLE so long as the must is not enriched and the yield is no more than 15 hl/ha. This sweet white Hermitage is delicious but all too rare.

Hermitage has also been used as a synonym for SHIRAZ in Australia, where, for example, PENFOLDS Grange was originally called Penfolds Grange Hermitage. Hermitage was also the historic South African synonym for CINSAUT and is sometimes used in Switzerland for Marsanne.

Livingstone-Learmonth, J., *The Wines of the Northern Rhône* (Berkeley, 2005).
Norman, R., *Rhône Renaissance* (London, 1995).
Parker, R. M., *Wines of the Rhône Valley* (2nd edn, New York, 1997).

Herodotus,

Herodotus, prolific Ancient Greek writer. The *Histories* of Herodotus (490/480–425 BC), a native of Halicarnassus in Asia Minor, are not a history in the modern sense: the Greek word *historia* means 'an investigation'. Herodotus' main subject is the conflict between the Greeks and the Persians, and as such his book is history; but it is also an investigation into the geography and anthropology of the east in Herodotus' own day, for as a young man he had travelled widely in the Greek-speaking world and in Egypt and Africa.

Forming part of Herodotus' descriptions of the customs of foreign nations are some intriguing observations about wine and DRUNKENNESS. He says that the Assyrians use palm-wood casks to transport wine, in boats built in Armenia, down the Euphrates (1. 194).

In fact, Herodotus' curiosity concerns the construction of the boats: their cargo is mentioned in an aside and he expresses no surprise at the Assyrians' use of palm-wood BARRELS instead of AMPHORAE. He has just told us that the date palm supplies the people with food, honey, and wine and that Assyria is the world's largest producer of grain. The country does not grow vines (1. 193) but, as we know from other sources, Babylon imported wine from ARMENIA. This is probably what the casks contained: with date palms growing all around, transporting fermented date juice would not have made sense. See also MESOPOTAMIA.

All of Book 2 and the beginning of Book 3 are taken up with Herodotus' description of Egypt before he goes on to relate the Persian conquest of that country. He states that the Egyptians have no wine but drink a wine made from barley (2. 81). This cannot be true, for we know that the vine was grown there in the 5th century BC. Egyptian wine may have been too scarce, however, for Herodotus to have come across it on his travels. Egypt certainly imported wine from Greece and PHOENICIA, as Herodotus mentions (3. 8). He says that it came in earthenware jars, and that when the wine had been finished the mayor of the town had to collect the empty jars and send them to Memphis, where they would be filled with water and sent to the Syrian desert. This system was devised by the Persians immediately after they had conquered Egypt so that they could reach Egypt through the Syrian desert without risking death through thirst.

When the Persians have subjugated the Egyptians, the king, the megalomaniac Cambyses, marches against the Ethiopians. The expedition is a disaster, and the Ethiopians recognize the Persians' superiority in one respect only: they have wine, and that is the reason for their longevity (3. 23). But Cambyses is too fond of it, and when he is told so by a court official he wrongly deduces that the Persians regard this as the cause of his madness (3. 35). His madness and cruelty seem to have been congenital (3. 38). Wine can cause madness, though: Cleomenes, king of Sparta, went mad and died as a result of drinking wine unmixed with WATER, a nasty habit he had picked up from those notorious drunkards the Scythians (6. 85). Only a barbarian would drink unmixed wine. The Persians are all great drinkers of wine, and their frequent drunkenness explains one of the strangest of their customs. The sensible part is that any decision they take when they are drunk they reconsider when they are sober. But the opposite also holds: any decision taken when they are sober has to be reconsidered when they are drunk (1. 135). Far from regarding drunkenness as undesirable and immoderate behaviour, the Persians, if Herodotus is to be trusted, view it as an altered state of consciousness that is as valuable as sobriety. H.M.W.

Herodotus, *The Histories*, trans. Aubrey de Sélincourt, rev. A. R. Burn (Harmondsworth, 1972).

Heroldrebe is the marginal dark-berried GERMAN CROSSING to which the prolific breeder August Herold of the Weinsberg in Württemberg put his name. This PORTUGIESER × LEMBERGER crossing yields regularly and prolifically, about 140 hl/ha (8 tons/acre), but it ripens so late that it is suitable only for Germany's warmer regions, particularly the Pfalz. Total area planted was less than 200 ha/500 acres by 2003. It spawned DORNFELDER.

Herzegovina. See BOSNIA AND HERZEGOVINA.

Hesiod (*c*.700 BC), the earliest agricultural writer of Ancient GREECE, wrote *Works and Days*. Most of this is homely advice for the farmer: 'Be sparing of the middle of the cask, but when you open it, and at the end drink all you want; it's not worth saving dregs.' He is the first writer to tell of simple rustic pleasures: 'I love a shady rock and Bibline wine [from BYBLOS], a cake of cheese, and goat's milk, and some meat of heifers pastured in the woods, uncalved, of first-born kids. Then I may sit in the shade and drink the shining wine, and eat my fill, and turn my face to meet the fresh west wind, and pour three times an offering from the spring which always flows, unmuddied, streaming down, and make my fourth LIBATION one of wine.' Hesiod gives the time for the grape HARVEST as 'when Orion and the dog star [Sirius] move into the mid sky'.
H.H.A.

Hessische Bergstrasse, one of the smallest wine regions in GERMANY (see map under GERMANY). The northern vineyards on the western slopes of Germany's Odenwald have formed a separate region since 1971. They comprise just 454 ha/1,122 acres, of which just over half was planted in RIESLING by 2003. The best produces distinguished wine, comparable with that of the RHEINGAU. The area devoted to red grapes, particularly SPÄTBURGUNDER, was nearly 10 per cent by 2003. Of the 850 or so growers, approximately 620 deliver their grapes to a large regional CO-OPERATIVE cellar at Heppenheim, which sells 70 per cent of its stock in litre bottles within the region. Only a small and decreasing amount of the co-operative's wine is sold by supermarkets, and sales directly to the consumer and to the wine trade are increasing (although Hessische Bergstrasse wines are rarely seen outside Germany). The state of Hesse is the largest vineyard owner with 38 ha/94 acres under vine, based on at Bensheim. The region is particularly well known for its Riesling EISWEIN, but the wines from other vine varieties are also very elegant, and compare well with those from elsewhere in Germany. All but 11 per cent of Hessische Bergstrasse wines are dry: TROCKEN, or HALBTROCKEN. I.J. & D.S.

Heuriger is an Austrian wine speciality. *Heurig* literally means 'this season's' but Heuriger has come to mean both wine from the most recent vintage and the place where the wine is offered for consumption by its producer. A winemaker's right effectively to set up his own wine bar was established in the time of CHARLEMAGNE, officially recognized by Emperor Josef II in 1784, and has continued as a tradition throughout AUSTRIA. These small, often family-run, wine taverns, can be found throughout Austria's wine regions but are a particularly popular tourist attraction in the suburbs of VIENNA and in the Thermenregion south of the capital. Food is generally served alongside the owner's wine, usually crackling new Heuriger wine but sometimes supplemented by old, or *alte*, wines. The wine of the new vintage officially becomes Heurige on St Martin's Day, 11 November. Before that it may have been sold at the unfermented MUST (*Most*) stage, as partially fermented STURM, or as still cloudy new wine (*Staubiger*). Local by-laws determine when a Heurige may sell its new wine, which period it signals by hanging out a bush of pine twigs above the entrance. Some top producers such as Wieninger of Vienna or Lalger in Spitz in the Wachau offer their top wines at reasonable prices for immediate consumption. See also PRIMEUR, the French counterpart, minus the hospitality.

higher alcohols. See FUSEL OILS.

hillside vineyards. Even in Ancient ROME it was said *Bacchus amat colles*, or BACCHUS loves the hills, suggesting that hillside vineyards have long been regarded as a source of high-quality wine.

This is partly because hillside soils are typically shallow, so that vineyard VIGOUR is relatively low, a factor commonly associated with high wine quality. Over millions of years soil tends to be washed down the hillsides and accumulates on the valley floors. Vines planted there will typically be more vigorous as the

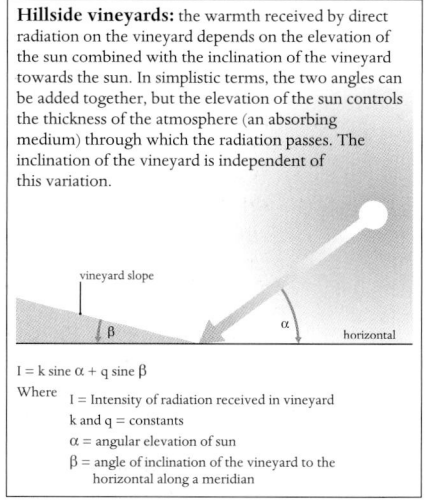

Hillside vineyards: the warmth received by direct radiation on the vineyard depends on the elevation of the sun combined with the inclination of the vineyard towards the sun. In simplistic terms, the two angles can be added together, but the elevation of the sun controls the thickness of the atmosphere (an absorbing medium) through which the radiation passes. The inclination of the vineyard is independent of this variation.

vineyard slope

β   α   horizontal

$I = k \sin \alpha + q \sin \beta$

Where I = Intensity of radiation received in vineyard
k and q = constants
α = angular elevation of sun
β = angle of inclination of the vineyard to the horizontal along a meridian

soils are deeper and the roots will be able to reach more water and nutrients.

Vines may also be planted on hillsides for reasons of MESOCLIMATE, as hillsides are less prone to FROST because cold air can drain freely away at night (see AIR DRAINAGE and TOPOGRAPHY). If the slopes face the equator, they receive more sunshine during the day and can reradiate at night or during cloudy weather the heat absorbed during the day. In warmer regions, some vineyards may be planted on hillsides to take advantage of cooler temperatures at higher ALTITUDES and therefore extend the growing season. Since the early 1980s, there has been an increasing tendency to plant elevated sites in Australia, Argentina, South Africa, and California, for example, in order to produce a more COOL CLIMATE style of table wine.

Hillside vineyard sites have their drawbacks. SOIL EROSION is an obvious example, and in California's NAPA valley there are strict regulations to avoid erosion. Working on steep slopes is particularly tiring, productivity is affected, and the costs are higher. In most vineyards of the world, rows run up and down the slopes. Where the slopes are too steep for tractors, as in the CÔTE RÔTIE, parts of the MOSEL valley, and SWITZERLAND, everything must be done by hand, or by machines winched down into the vineyards. Where rows run across the slopes, the vineyard is normally laid out in TERRACES, as in Portugal's DOURO valley or France's hill of HERMITAGE.   R.E.S.

Hilltops, moderately cool, high altitude wine region in NEW SOUTH WALES, Australia. Provides elegant, medium-bodied Shiraz, Cabernet Sauvignon, and Merlot from moderately low-yielding vineyards. Also fine, slow-developing Chardonnay.

hippocras, popular medieval FLAVOURED WINE.

histamine, the amine involved in a range of allergic reactions in humans, was once thought the cause of some people's allergy to red wine. Improved methods of wine ANALYSIS have demonstrated that the amounts of histamine in wine are at least an order of magnitude below that required to cause an allergic reaction in the great majority of people. However, a few people have low levels of the enzyme which breaks down histamine, so histamine levels in their blood rise high enough to cause allergic reactions after drinking wine with even low levels of histamine. One ADELAIDE research project found levels of between 2 and 9.9 mg/l of histamines in wine, while another at DAVIS found an average of 1.8 mg/l in 253 California wines, with higher concentrations in fortified wines. See also LACTIC ACID BACTERIA and ALLERGIES.   A.D.W. & J.H.H.

Hochgewächs, one of a number of label clues to one of GERMANY's better wines, launched in the late 20th century and virtually

extinct by the 21st, to supplement those provided by the GERMAN WINE LAW.

hock, traditional generic English term for (white) Rhenish wines, from the RHINE regions of GERMANY, sometimes for the wines of Germany in general. It is a contraction of hockamore, an English rendering of the adjective Hochheimer, denoting wines from Hochheim on the river Main just west of Frankfurt (see RHEINGAU).

The earliest firm reference in English occurs in Thomas D'Urfey's play *Madam Fickle; or, The Witty False One* in 1676: 'Here's a glass of excellent old Hock.' The *Oxford English Dictionary* gives a first reference in 1625 in John Fletcher's play *The Chances*, but this depends on a corrupt reading of hock for hollock, a light red wine. However, it is likely that the term was already current in England by the 17th century, for its use is closely linked to the growth in popularity of Rhenish and Main wines, which began to supplant the wines of ALSACE in export markets after 1500 (see GERMAN HISTORY).

At the outset, hock appears to have described only wines from the middle Rhine: in an address to the Royal Society in 1680, Anthony van Leeuwenhoeck, the inventor of the microscope, spoke of 'vinum Mosellanicum, vinum Rijncoviense and vinum Rhenanum, quod vulgo hogmer dicitur' (called 'hogmer' in the vernacular). In 1703, Johann Valentin Kauppers in his *De natura . . . vini Rhenani* could still distinguish between 'Rhine wines' and wines from the Rheingau, but in the course of the 18th century hock became the general designation of German wines sold in Britain.   T.S.

In modern commerce, a wine labelled 'Hock' is likely to be a simple QBA wine from a German Rhine wine region such as RHEINHESSEN or possibly the PFALZ. It has been by no means uncommon for the same wine to be offered as Hock to a gentlemen's club and LIEBFRAUMILCH to a supermarket buyer. Hock has also occasionally been used for non-German wines as a GENERIC term.

Holland, see NETHERLANDS.

Homer, writer(s) in Ancient GREECE of the two epic poems: the *Iliad* (telling the story of Achilles and the Trojan wars) and the *Odyssey* (the return of Odysseus from Troy to his home, Ithaca, and his adventures on the way). Homeric poems are usually dated to the 8th century BC and wine features regularly in both books. See also CLASSICAL TEXTS.

home wine-making, small-scale domestic activity indulged in either for fun, to save money, or both. Because such wine attracts no DUTY, it is especially popular in countries with high excise duties. Some countries with no or minimal viticulture such as Britain have a long tradition of making FRUIT WINES and wines based on other plants.

Home wine-making was especially popularity in the United States during PROHIBITION, when vinifying an annual allowance of 200 gal/ 7.5 hl of fruit juice (a limit that still applies in the US) was the only legal way the average American household could procure alcoholic drink. While technology was primitive, and exploding bottles were common, the pursuit was so popular that vineyard acreage in California doubled between 1919 and 1926. After Repeal, home wine-making continued, mainly in the hands of European immigrants with strong wine-making traditions.

In Great Britain, the hobby peaked in the late 1980s, with GRAPE CONCENTRATE the usual raw material, producing MADE WINE which lacks the fresh fruitiness of wine made from the juice of freshly picked grapes. In the US, home wine-making grew relatively slowly, with less than half a million Americans making roughly 2.5 million cases of wine a year in the early 1990s, mainly from grapes grown in California and shipped by rail to the rest of the country, but also from juice or grape concentrate.

Wine-making kits, based on canned grape juice concentrate, were introduced in the 1950s but the North American boom in home wine-making was largely due to the introduction in the 1980s of a new type of kit by Canada's Brew King. Using a combination of concentrates and flash PASTEURISED fresh grape juice and including much of the necessary equipment, it encouraged many new recruits.

The introduction in the Canadian provinces of Ontario and British Columbia of 'Wine On Premise', where customers could go to a shop and vinify an unlimited amount of wine for personal use, free of any tax, led to kits' capturing more than 20 per cent of the total wine market in Canada within 10 years.

Today the world's major wine kit manufacturers are all based in Canada but distribute throughout Canada, the US, Europe, Iceland, and Southeast Asia. Together, they sell enough wine kits to produce more than 10 million cases of wine per year, using internationally sourced grape material.   J.R. & T.V.

homoclimes, geographical term meaning 'similar climate'. It has been a popular approach to VINEYARD SITE SELECTION in the New World to search for homoclimes of classical French regions. Homoclimes were determined using overlay techniques of climate maps, but can be found more efficiently and accurately with digitized maps and GEOGRAPHICAL INFORMATION SYSTEMS. For example, Tamar Ridge Vineyards has used this approach to identify new vineyard regions in Tasmania with the same climate as distinguished the MARLBOROUGH region of New Zealand.   R.E.S.

Hondarrabi, family of Spanish BASQUE vine varieties. **Hondarrabi Zuri,** of which 364 ha/900 acres were identified in Spain's official vine statistics in 2004, is light berried and more common in Getariako TXAKOLI than the dark-berried Hondarrabi Beltza, which is more common in Bizkaiko Txakoli around Bilbao. DNA PROFILING at Madrid suggested that Hondarrabi Zuri could be a hybrid between Vitis VINIFERA and another VITIS species.

Horace (Quintus Horatius Flaccus) (65–8 BC), the Latin poet, did not write a systematic guide to viticulture but wine does figure prominently in his work, and reflects his Epicurean philosophy of enjoying its pleasures in moderation. He tells us that at the Sabine farm which his patron Maecenas gave him he does not grow wine (*Epistles* I. 14), but as a token of his gratitude he serves Maecenas the local wine, laid down by the poet himself in the year that his patron had recovered from a serious illness (*Odes* I. 20). This matching of the wine to the guest and the occasion is a constant feature of Horace's invitation poems, and other poems about drinking: see also *Odes* I. 9 and 4. 2 (simple wines for intimate occasions), 3. 21 (a wine from the year of the poet's birth for an honoured guest), I. 37 (a grand old CAECUBAN to celebrate the defeat of the monstrous Cleopatra), 3. 14 (a wine that goes back to the Social War, 91–88 BC, to celebrate Augustus' return), 3. 28 (Caecuban of Bibulus' consular year, 59 BC, in honour of Neptune).

Horace cannot afford the very best wine, old FALERNIAN: to spend a feast day drinking that would be the greatest happiness (*Odes* 2. 3). Note that to Horace good wine is always old wine: the Romans (and the Greeks) preferred old wine to the wine of the current vintage. *Epistles* I. 19 is Horace's contribution to the debate about poetic inspiration. Callimachus (*c*.310/05–*c*.240 BC) first raised the question of whether water, symbol of the purity of poetic labour, or wine, which brings poetic frenzy, is the better drink for a poet. On the authority of Cratinus (*c*.520–*c*.423 BC), Horace sides with the wine drinkers, for were not Homer and Ennius (see Ancient GREECE), the fathers of Greek and Latin epic respectively, wine bibbers? 'Laudibus arguitur vini vinosus Homerus', Horace asserts: 'in his praises of wine, wine-bibbing Homer betrays himself.' To the modern reader, Horace seems to have more in common with today's civilized wine enthusiast than any other classical writer. H.M.W.

Commager, S., 'The function of wine in Horace's Odes', *Transactions of the American Philological Association*, 88 (1957), 68–80.

Griffin, J., *Latin Literature and Roman Life* (London, 1985).

Wilson, H., *Wine and Words in Classical Antiquity and the Middle Ages* (London, 2003).

horizontal trellis. See TENDONE system of VINE TRAINING.

hormones, natural substances present in trace concentrations in vines and other plants which move from one organ or part of the plant to another to regulate growth and development. Synthetic GROWTH REGULATORS may have similar chemical structures, and a similar mode of action. There are three groups of hormones which promote growth, these being AUXINS, GIBBERELLINS, and CYTOKININS, and two groups which inhibit growth, ABSCISIC ACID and ethylene. R.E.S.

Hospices de Beaune, charity auction which has taken place in BEAUNE annually since 1851 on the third Sunday in November, a key feature of the Burgundian calendar. The beneficiaries are the combined charitable organizations of the Hôtel Dieu, founded in 1443 by Nicolas Rolin, chancellor of the duchy of Burgundy, and the Hôpital de la Charité.

The produce of vineyard holdings donated by benefactors over the centuries is auctioned at prices usually well in excess of current commercial values. Nevertheless, the results serve as some indication of the trend in bulk wine prices for the new vintage.

The cuvées sold are named to commemorate original benefactors such as Nicolas Rolin and his wife Guigone de Salins or more recent ones such as de Bahèzre de Lanlay, an inspector of aerial telegraphs. The Hospices de Beaune also provides the occasion for 'Les Trois Glorieuses', the three great feasts held over the weekend at CLOS DE VOUGEOT on Saturday night, in Beaune on Sunday night, and in MEURSAULT for the extended lunchtime bottle party that is the Paulée de Meursault on Monday.

The Hospices de Nuits also holds a charity wine auction; see NUITS-ST-GEORGES.

See also AUCTIONS. J.T.C.M.

hot bottling. See PASTEURIZATION.

hot pressing. See THERMOVINIFICATION.

Howell Mountain, California wine region and AVA east of St Helena, defined by elevation of about 1,400 ft/425 m. See NAPA valley.

Hugel, one of the best-known and oldest wine producers in Alsace, having been established in 1639. The family business is run today by the 12th and 13th generations. The Hugels, based in Riquewihr, make fine wines from their own 26 ha/65 acres of vineyard around the village planted mainly with Riesling and Gewürztraminer, together with a little Pinot Gris and Pinot Noir. Their Tradition range can be excitingly full and the Jubilee range masterful. The Hugel family also pioneered the resurrection of Alsace's late harvest wines and were instrumental in drawing up the rigorous requirements for these VENDANGE TARDIVE and SÉLECTION DE GRAINS NOBLES wines. They are arch exponents of these styles themselves, and produce them, and the Jubilee range, exclusively from their own ALSACE GRAND CRU vineyards. The Hugel family, of which six family members worked in the Riquewihr wine business in the mid 2000s, have long been champions of maximizing quality in Alsace's finest wines, and are vociferous opponents of the Alsace Grand Cru appellation, which they feel is no guarantee of quality. The Hugels buy in grapes, never wine, for their basic generic range of wines from about 120 ha/300 acres of vineyard under contract from more than 300 growers. Marc Hugel is in charge of wine-making.

Humagne Blanche, Swiss Valais white grape which, unexpectedly, is not related to HUMAGNE ROUGE. The wine produced is fairly neutral relative to PETITE ARVINE but supposedly contains particularly high levels of iron. DNA PROFILING at DAVIS recently showed that Humagne Blanche is the parent of LAFNETSCHA. J.V.

Humagne Rouge, relatively rare red wine grape of the Swiss Valais region whose wines are wild, rustic, and relatively high in TANNINS. They are particularly recommended with venison. DNA PROFILING at CHANGINS and Aosta showed that this variety is identical to CORNALIN D'AOSTE of the Valle d'AOSTA and confirmed that it is not related to HUMAGNE BLANCHE. Additional DNA profiling at DAVIS revealed that Humagne Rouge (or Cornalin d'Aoste) is a progeny of CORNALIN DU VALAIS. J.V.

humidification, euphemism for the (sometimes illegal but increasingly common) wine-making operation of adding water.

humidity, or moisture content, of the atmosphere has considerable implications both for vine growth and for the STORAGE of barrels and wine, whether in bulk or bottle. Humidity is normally measured as per cent relative humidity (% RH): the amount of water (in true gaseous, or uncondensed, form) a given volume of air holds, as a percentage of the maximum it could hold without condensation at the same temperature. (The latter amount increases with temperature, so the RH of air containing a constant amount of water vapour falls as temperature rises, and vice versa.) The difference between a given air body's water vapour content and what it could hold when saturated at the same temperature is called its saturation deficit, which is a direct measure of evaporative power. Actual EVAPORATION is further influenced by WIND and SUNLIGHT.

Relative humidity follows a regular daily cycle, normally being highest in the early morning, when temperature is lowest, and lowest in the early to mid afternoon, when temperature is highest. Broadly speaking, high humidity is conducive to the spread of FUNGAL DISEASES, especially when combined with high temperatures. The early morning figure is more critical for certain fungal diseases, however, which need water condensation on the vine or fruit for their spore germination and growth (see DEW). The afternoon figures, together with temperature and wind, dominate in determining evaporation, and therefore the likelihood of WATER STRESS. The contrast between morning and afternoon relative humidities tends to be greatest inland, and least near coasts which have alternating dry morning winds from the land and humid afternoon breezes from the sea (see WIND).

Although high relative humidities encourage fungal diseases, Gladstones argues that such levels are also conducive to high wine quality, provided that there is enough sunlight and diseases are absent or controlled. The critical humidities in this respect are those in the afternoon. Where the vines suffer little water stress, PHOTOSYNTHESIS is relatively continuous and there is maximum production of SUGAR IN GRAPES and its derivatives in the form of berry colour, flavour, and aroma. Moreover, because the yields are attained with least TRANSPIRATION (water throughput and evaporation), there will be less uptake of certain minerals into the vines and fruit, including POTASSIUM. Must and natural wine PH should therefore be lower, with benefits for brightness of wine COLOUR, freshness of wine flavour and aroma, and greater resistance to OXIDATION and BACTERIAL SPOILAGE.

Viticultural regions of the world with high afternoon relative humidities during the fruiting period include all those of Germany, Switzerland, Austria, and Hungary; Burgundy, Alsace, Champagne, the Loire valley, Bordeaux, and the Mediterranean coastal strip of France; marginally central and northern Italy, and the upper Rioja region of Spain; Madeira and some exposed coastal areas of Portugal; most of the coolest parts (Region I: see CLIMATE CLASSIFICATION) of the coastal valleys of California, Oregon, and Washington; the Cape Town/Constantia area in South Africa; Margaret River and the south coast of Western Australia; coastal Victoria; and all of Tasmania and New Zealand.

Typical areas of intermediate humidity include the southern Rhône valley of France; most inland table wine-producing areas of Portugal, such as Dão, and of Spain; Bulgaria; intermediate and warmer parts of the coastal valleys of California, such as the Napa and Santa Clara valleys; Stellenbosch and Paarl in South Africa; the Western Australian west coast and hills; Barossa, Adelaide hills, Langhorne creek, and Coonawarra in South Australia; Grampians and other parts of the Great Dividing range in Victoria; and the Hunter valley and marginally Mudgee in New South Wales.

Viticultural regions with low afternoon relative humidities are nearly all hot as well, and tend to have high TEMPERATURE VARIABILITY. Such regions include the middle and upper Douro valley of Portugal (to a moderate degree); the Central valley of California; the Little Karoo in South Africa; and the Murray and Murrumbidgee valley areas of South Australia, northern Victoria, and southern New South Wales.

The tendency for more humid wine regions to have higher quality reputations is evident from the above list, but compelling evidence for this based on VINE PHYSIOLOGY is yet to be presented.

For details of humidity and barrels, see EVAPORATION. For details of humidity and wine storage, see STORING WINE.   J.G.

Gladstones, J., *Viticulture and Environment* (Adelaide, 1992).

Hundred Years War. The sporadic fighting between the kings of England and France known as the Hundred Years War (1337–1453) changed both the political map of Europe and the nature and volume of the medieval wine trade. Both crowns claimed ownership of the wine regions of western France, which, through the wealthy port of BORDEAUX, supplied England with almost all her wine.

The hostilities themselves had a marked effect on the wine trade. First the large and commercially successful vineyards of the HAUT PAYS, or 'high country', upstream from Bordeaux (GAILLAC, BERGERAC, BUZET, CAHORS) were for the most part under French control. This increased English reliance on the lesser vineyards of Bordeaux and its environs, encouraging their expansion.

Secondly, the ships carrying wine back to England faced the risk of greater piracy. Convoys organized for their protection proved expensive. Reduced supplies and greater freight costs led to a dramatic rise in the price of wine in England.

After Bordeaux's surrender at CASTILLON in 1453, England remained a major market for her wines, although the overall volume of this trade was not to reach the pre-war peak for many centuries. English merchants became more willing to look beyond western France for their wine imports while Bordeaux attracted a wider clientele of merchants from northern Europe.

See also BORDEAUX, history.   H.B.

Dion, R., *Histoire de la vigne et du vin en France* (Paris, 1959).

James, M. K., *Studies in the Medieval Wine Trade* (Oxford, 1971).

Renouard, Y., *Études d'histoire médiévale* (Paris, 1968).

Hungary, important central European wine-producing country with its own particularly distinctive range of vine varieties and wines. Hungary usually produces less wine than its eastern neighbour Romania, but considerably more than, for example, Austria and Bulgaria. About 65,000 ha/160,000 acres were devoted to vines in the early 2000s, and about 70 per cent of them produced white wines. Total Hungarian wine production has been decreasing and is now usually below 4 million hl (105 million gal) a year, of which about a fifth is exported.

History

Vine-growing and wine-making have been practised in what is modern Hungary since at least Roman times, when it was part of the Roman province of Pannonia. The Magyar tribes who arrived here at the end of the 9th century found flourishing vineyards and familiarity with wine-making techniques. Under Bela IV (1235–70), the king who rebuilt Hungary after the Mongol invasion of 1241, wine production was given such priority that immigrants from areas with particular expertise in vine-growing and wine-making were deliberately invited to rebuild the devastated areas, and by the end of his reign wines from the two towns of SOPRON and EGER were being exported in relatively large quantities. Hungary's most famous wine, TOKAJI, is first mentioned in records in the late 15th century, although it was almost certainly dry at this time.

Following the defeat and death of Louis II at the battle of Mohács in 1529, much of the country was under Muslim rule for a century and a half, during which wine production survived, but did not thrive (see ISLAM).

The most important development in the 17th century was the emergence of especially rich Tokay Aszú. As early as 1641, a Vine Law for the entire Tokaj-Hegyalja district was drawn up which regulated VINEYARD SITE SELECTION, the construction of TERRACES, IRRIGATION, manuring, and hoeing (which had to be done for the last time on 20 August before the official harvest date of 28 October). By 1570, NOBLE ROT was recognized, and the laws for Aszú formulated. For more details, see TOKAJI.

In 1686, the city of Buda was liberated from the Turks, followed within the next few years by all of the rest of Hungary, which then became part of the vast Habsburg empire. A bid for independence led by Ferenc Rákóczi failed in 1711, but had the effect of spreading the fame of Tokay wines to the court of the French king, Louis XIV, to whom Rákóczi had wisely sent sample bottles as gifts. This was the beginning of Tokay's formidable international reputation.

The vineyards of Tokay were some of the first to be submitted to CLASSIFICATION, in 1700, and the first national vineyard classification anywhere, a five-level rating, was undertaken in Hungary in 1707–8 as part of general appraisal of the country's resources.

PHYLLOXERA struck Hungary in the 1870s, devastating the southern vineyards at Pancsova initially but eventually spreading to the Northern Massif and Tokaj-Hegyalja. Replanting on phylloxera-resistant ROOTSTOCKS began in 1881, but scientific proof that the phylloxera louse could not thrive in sandy soils had just been published, encouraging the planting of new vineyards in the

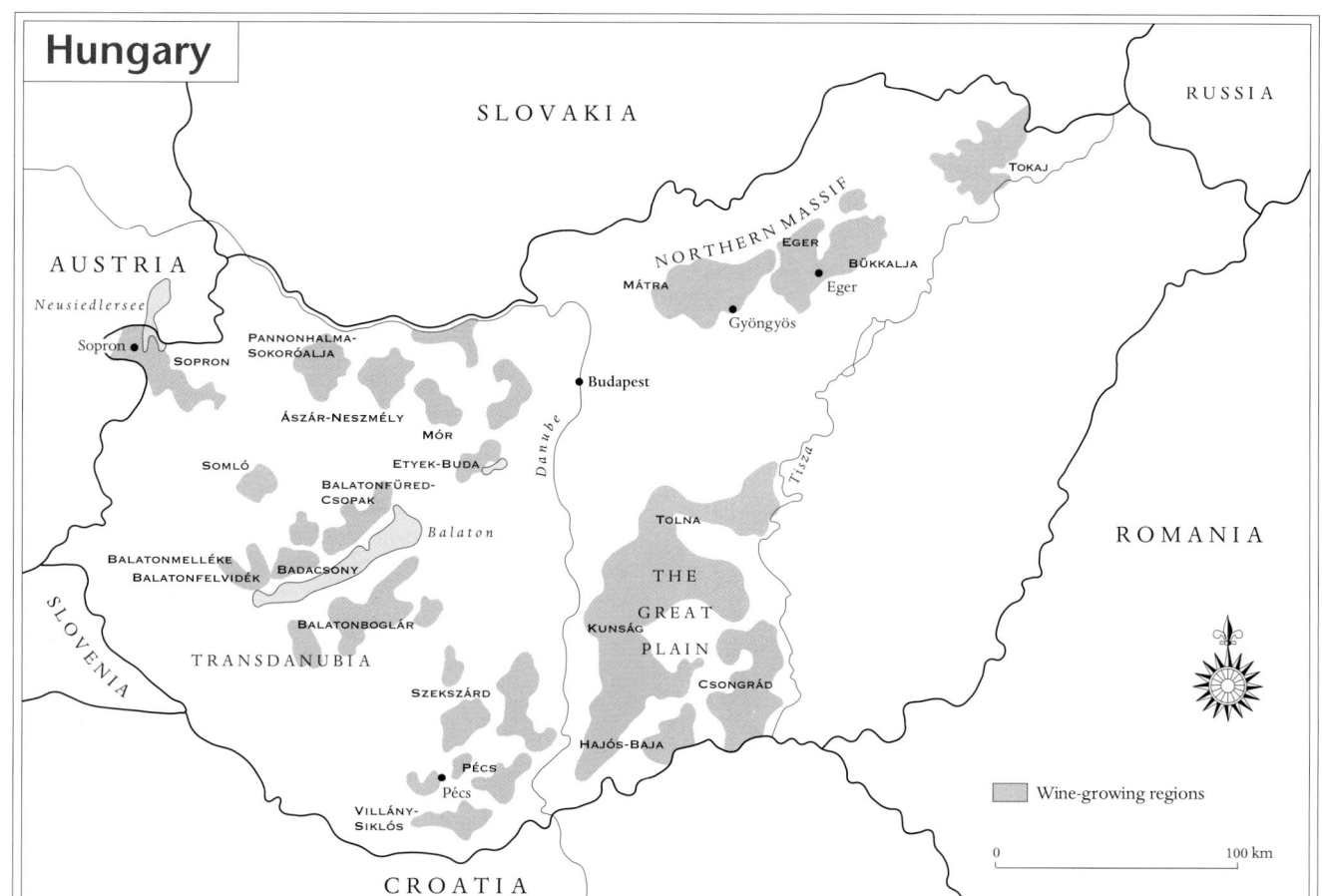

Hungary

SLOVAKIA

RUSSIA

AUSTRIA

Neusiedlersee

NORTHERN MASSIF

Tokaj

Sopron ● ■
SOPRON

PANNONHALMA-
SOKORÓALJA

EGER
MÁTRA   BÜKKALJA
Eger
● Gyöngyös

● Budapest

Danube

Tisza

ÁSZÁR-NESZMÉLY
MÓR

ETYEK-BUDA

SOMLÓ
BALATONFÜRED-
CSOPAK

Balaton

TOLNA

ROMANIA

BALATONMELLÉKE   BADACSONY
BALATONFELVIDÉK

THE
GREAT
PLAIN

SLOVENIA

BALATONBOGLÁR

Kunság

TRANSDANUBIA

SZEKSZÁRD

CSONGRÁD

HAJÓS-BAJA

● Pécs
PÉCS

VILLÁNY-
SIKLÓS

Wine-growing regions

0   100 km

CROATIA

Great Plain, where vines were also discovered to be particularly suitable plants for stabilizing the shifting sands.

Zsigmond Teleki (1854–1910) bred the famous 5 BB Teleki rootstock which proved perfectly suited to producing high-quality grapes even when planted in the desolate, intensely calcareous hillsides of Villány. When Teleki died in 1910, his sons Andor and Sándor continued the NURSERY business with great success until World War II, maintaining subsidiaries in six countries. Ironically, Franz Kober in Oppenheim eventually collected most of the recognition by subjecting Teleki's clones to further selection and indeed the rootstock is more commonly known today as 5 BB Kober. Móricz Preysz (1829–77) was the pioneer of PASTEURIZATION, publishing his work on the technique, needed then to stabilize Tokaji, in 1861, two years before Louis PASTEUR developed pasteurization.

In 1947, the National Association of Hungarian Vine-Growers, Wine Trades and Wine-Growing Communities, which had originally been founded in 1830 to promote co-operation and study for the benefit of all in the wine industry, was forced to suspend its activities when the communist state monopoly took control. An era of state farms and state wineries followed, during which all wine exports were funnelled through the state-controlled trading company Monimpex (and half of all production at one point handled by just two state wineries designed to export huge quantities of very ordinary wine to the USSR). Unlike the similarly organized BULGARIAN wine industry, that of Hungary suffered a period of stagnation and generally low technology during this era, which stultified the development of Hungarian wine until the somewhat complicated return of a free market economy and private enterprise in the late 1980s. A considerable proportion of all Hungarian vines had remained in private hands in the communist era, and this has enabled Hungary to adapt production to the more stringent requirements of western importers more quickly than other ex-Comecon countries.

In the post-communist division of vinicultural spoils (see below), there was no shortage of western interest in the unique Tokaji wines, and technology in other areas benefited from temporary invasion by foreign—typically antipodean (see AUSTRALIAN INFLUENCE)—winemakers.

Geography

Hungary, which lies between the latitudes 45 and 50 degrees north, is land-locked but includes Europe's largest lake, Balaton. The river Danube (called Duna in Hungary) flows through it from north to south, dividing the country in almost equal halves. To the west lies Transdanubia, while to the immediate east of the river is the Great Plain. North east of the capital Budapest are the volcanic hills which constitute the Northern Massif, whose south-facing slopes are particularly well suited to vine-growing. In the extreme north east of the country is the Tokaj (formerly Tokaj-Hegyalja) region, which borders SLOVAKIA. See TOKAJI for more details.

Soils are very varied. The Great Plain is mainly sand and loess, while the area around lake Balaton is of complex basalt volcanic rock with clay and sandstone. Other soils include limestone and slate, particularly around Balatonfüred. In Tokaj, the soils are volcanic with a topsoil of decayed lava. The best wines often come from volcanic soils, producing full, well-structured wines rich in minerality.

See below and SZEKSZÁRD, TOKAJI, and VILLÁNY-SIKLÓS for details of individual wine regions.

Climate

Hungary's climate is essentially continental and central European, involving fairly predictably cold winters and hot summers (see CONTINENTAL). The relatively northerly latitude (on a par with Burgundy) makes it ideally situated to produce aromatic and semi-aromatic varieties such as Sauvignon Blanc and Gewürztraminer, while its continentality allows full ripening of such red varieties as Cabernet Sauvignon, especially in the south. The sun shines for a high average of about 2,000 hours a year, and the total heat summation during the vegetative ripening period is approximately 2,500 °C. Prolonged, sunny autumns which favour the development of noble rot are by no means rare, however.

Vine varieties

Wine labelling in Hungary is largely VARIETAL so that wine producers and consumers have a keen appreciation of specific vine varieties. Hungary had a particularly rich selection of indigenous vine varieties, many of which were largely abandoned when phylloxera invaded the country's vineyards in the late 19th century. A potentially exciting selection of localized white grape varieties can still be found, although some such as KÉKNYELŰ, found almost exclusively in Badacsony on the north shore of Lake Balaton, and JUHFARK, known mainly in Somló, are dangerously close to extinction. The aromatic Sárfehér is also valued as a TABLE GRAPE.

Indigenous varieties which are relatively widely planted include the EZERJÓ, a light speciality of the Mór region west of Budapest; FURMINT, which is widely grown but is the most characteristic ingredient of Tokaji; HÁRSLEVELŰ, which is usually a lesser Tokaji ingredient and is also widely grown throughout Hungary. Kövidinka, or DINKA, produces ordinary wines in quantity on the Great Plain, as it does across the southern border with VOJVODINA. New crossings such as the Muscatlike IRSAI OLIVÉR and the spicy Cserszegi Füszeres (a crossing of Irsai Olivér and Gewürztraminer) are now being more widely planted for their own intrinsic character and quality. Other light-berried crossings include ZEFIR and ZENIT. Hungary's most characteristic red grape variety is KADARKA, although PORTUGIESER (once known as **Kékoportó**) can also make some appetizing wines here.

The usual range of central European vine varieties is grown: Olaszrizling (the Hungarian name for WELSCHRIESLING), Leányka, Zöldveltelini (Austria's GRÜNER VELTLINER), Cirfandli (Austria's ZIERFANDLER, a speciality of Pécs); and, for red wine production, KÉKFRANKOS (along with Nagyburgundi, the Hungarian name for BLAUFRÄNKISCH), and Austria's ZWEIGELT.

A wide range of vine varieties have been imported into Hungary from western Europe, however, including Chardonnay, Sauvignon Blanc, Sémillon, Riesling (sometimes called Rajnai Rizling or Rheinriesling), Gewürztraminer (Tramini), Muscat Ottonel and Yellow Muscat, the deeper hued Muscat Blanc à Petits Grains (both of which are sometimes called

Muskotály), Silvaner (Zöldszilváni), Müller-Thurgau (Riesling Silvaner or Rizlingszilváni), and Pinot Gris, whose distinctively Hungarian synonym is Szürkebarát. Red wine varieties imported from the west include Merlot and, to a much lesser extent, Cabernet Sauvignon and Cabernet Franc and a small amount of Pinot Noir and Syrah.

The 1997 wine law permitted a wider range of grape varieties in each region. Since the mid 2000s, permitted grape varieties have been determined by county rather than by wine region and revisions to the regulations within each region are in progress.

Wine regions

According to Hungarian law, there are 22 Hungarian wine regions (see map on p. 349), but the following may be considered pre-eminent today: Badacsony, Balatonboglár, EGER, Etyek-Buda, Somló, SOPRON, SZEKSZÁRD, Tokaj (for details of which see TOKAJI), and VILLÁNY-SIKLÓS. Names such as Gyöngyös, Csopak, Pannonhalma, and Ászár may also be familiar from export labels. The wine regions fall into three major geographical groups, as outlined below.

Transdanubia This western part of Hungary, between the Austrian border and the Danube, contains 14 of the designated wine regions which are increasingly bringing their own marked characteristics to the wines. The area is heavily influenced by the waters of lake Balaton, the Neusiedlersee in AUSTRIA, and the Danube itself.

Traditionally the northern side of lake Balaton was the vine-growing area, with the famous Badacsony area on the volcanic slopes at the south west end. The surface area of water in the lake has a considerable ameliorating effect on the MESOCLIMATE (see TOPOGRAPHY) and the wines tend to be full and powerful. This is home to the ancient Kéknyelű, but also makes fine Pinot Gris (Szürkebarát), as well as Olaszrizling. Balatonfüred-Csopak also lies on the northern shore, on slate, and produces a range of western varieties and Olaszrizling.

On the slopes of an extinct volcano north west of lake Balaton is the once historic wine region of Somló, whose wood-aged, blended wines once enjoyed a similar reputation to those of Tokay. Juhfark was once prized here, along with Furmint, but today Olaszrizling, Hárslevelű, and Traminer are in the ascendant. The small wine region of Somló is attracting increasing investment as its potential for elegant, age-worthy wines with a distinctive mineral character becomes evident.

On the south shore of the lake is a relatively new area, Balatonboglár, where the fertile soils include sand and loess. Important grapes grown here are Olaszrizling, Királyleányka, Zöldveltelini, Irsai Olivér, Chardonnay, Muscat, Merlot, and Pinot Noir.

Sopron, the most westerly wine region of northern Transdanubia and effectively a continuation of Neusiedlersee-Hügelland, AUSTRIA's most revered source of sweet white wine, is dominated by ambitious growers of Austro-German extraction. Sopron is mainly a red wine region and the principal vine varieties are Kékfrankos, Cabernet Sauvignon, Cabernet Franc, Merlot, and Pinot Noir. Its Sauvignon Blanc and Syrah are also gaining a good reputation.

In the north are two increasingly important white wine areas. Ászár-Neszmély is now as well known for its exceptionally modern Hilltop winery at Neszmély as for its Sauvignon Blanc, Pinot Gris, Irsai Olivér, and Olaszrizling. Mór, between Sopron and Budapest, is better known for the tart Ezerjó, Leányka, and aromatic Gewürztraminer.

Southern Transdanubia has three important wine regions close together in the far south of the country just west of the Danube. Villány-Siklós is most famous for the saddle of land in the Villány hills which manages to produce highly prized reds even in difficult years. Several producers are exploiting these natural advantages. Cabernet is most successful here, although Kékfrankos, Merlot, and Zweigelt are also good. More and more good Pinot Noir and Syrah is also produced.

Szekszárd has traditionally been associated with Kadarka, which it has managed to ripen more healthily than most regions, owing to its long, warm summers but only 60 ha remain. This native red variety has been supplanted by vigorous Kékfrankos, Merlot, and Cabernet. The area around Bátaszék, 15 km/9 miles to the south, is also producing some particularly good Sauvignon Blanc.

Pécs, Hungary's warmest wine region, is at constant risk of drought. A wide range of vine varieties is cultivated here, often on very small estates. They include Olaszrizling, Chardonnay, Kadarka, Cabernet, Merlot, and Pinot Noir.

The Northern Massif This range of hills running north east from Budapest along the border with Slovakia contains four wine regions, the Mátra, Eger, Bükkalja, and Tokaj (for details of which, see TOKAJI).

In the foothills of the Mátra mountains, the soils are mainly volcanic and most of the wine produced is white. Muscat, Olaszrizling, and Királyleányka predominate. In western Europe at least, the area is well known for the German-owned Gyöngyös Estate on which modern Chardonnay, Sauvignon Blanc, and Sémillon have been made for export.

Just to the east of the Mátra foothills, in the foothills of the Bükk mountains, is the wine region named after the historic town of EGER. Spring often comes late here and the rainfall is low. Some white wines are made, principally from Olaszrizling, Leányka, and Chardonnay but the region is best known for age-worthy red wine, notably Egri Bikavér or, on export markets, BULL'S BLOOD. Once one of the most famous wine BRANDS, this blend represented a triumph of marketing although quality varied considerably towards the end of the communist era. Eger is once again making fine wine. At one time the blend depended heavily on Kadarka, but as elsewhere this troublesome native variety was replaced by Kékfrankos, supplemented by Cabernet, Merlot, and Portugieser (Kékoportó). The Bükkalja region generally favours white wines.

In the past, only Tokaji, made even further east, has rivalled Bull's Blood for recognition outside Hungary, although the situation has been changing rapidly as wine-making and exporting skills have passed into private, and often non-Hungarian, hands.

The Great Plain This vast, flat expanse (known as Alföld in Hungary) south of Budapest and between the Danube and Hungary's second river the Tisza accounts for nearly half the country's vineyards. The plain was heavily planted after the phylloxera invasion because of phylloxera's intolerance of sandy soils, and because vines were better at stabilizing the soil than the fruit trees planted earlier.

MECHANIZATION is easy on this flat land, but the DROUGHT in summer and FROST in both late spring and early autumn are a perennial threat, and the combination of sandy soil and high summer temperatures means that soil temperatures can be very high indeed.

Most of the wide variety of vines planted here are the western, INTERNATIONAL VARIETIES or Olaszrizling, Rajnai Rizling (RIESLING), and Ezerjó, although some Kadarka is planted.

The three official wine regions of the Great Plain are Csongrád, Hajós-Baja, and Kunság but wine quality is generally indifferent. The best producers are more likely to seek out grapes from areas where viticultural technique has progressed more noticeably.

Structure of the trade

Prior to the reintroduction of a capitalist system in the early 1990s, the Hungarian wine industry was under the control of the state. All wine exports were under the control of the state trading organization Monimpex.

In the early 1980s, Hungary was the principal central European wine exporter, shipping out more than 3 million hl/79 million gal, or 60 per cent of production, notably very ordinary quality wine in bulk to the USSR and East Germany. These markets shrank abruptly at the end of the 1980s, leading to sudden over-supply and extreme uncertainty among vine-growers and winemakers.

Under government policy, the state farms and state wineries were offered for sale, often in a state of perilous financial health. Foreign investment was actively sought, with some degree of success, particularly in Tokaj, where the

famous name of Tokay attracted capital from France, Spain, Germany, Britain, and the Netherlands. The monolithic Hungarovin organization was sold to the German SEKT giant Henkell, and the famous Italian firm of ANTINORI, for example, made an investment in the Tolna region.

The state of flux of the early 1990s, caused partly by uncertainty over property rights and exact boundaries, was followed by a far more stable economic and political environment. The influx of western European capital enabled much-needed investment in modern winery equipment, resulting in a marked improvement in quality for all wines but particularly for flavoursome dry whites.

With a new lease of life for Tokaji, Chardonnay and Sauvignon Blanc increasingly rivalling those of New Zealand, and Pinot Gris and Gewürztraminer challenging those of Alsace, Hungary is poised to become one of the finest, and certainly best-value, producers of characterful white wines in the world.

D.J.G., G.R., & G.M.

Liddell, A., *The Wines of Hungary* (London, 2003).

Rohály, G., *Rohály's Wine Guide: Hungary* (Budapest, annually).

Rohály, G., *et al.*, *Terra Benedicta*, (Budapest, 2003).

Hunter Valley Zone, historic NEW SOUTH WALES wine zone within striking distance of Sydney in which **Hunter** is a region and Broke Fordwich a subregion with other subregions pending.

Huxelrebe is an early 20th century German vine CROSSING that enjoys some popularity both in Germany and, on a much smaller scale, in ENGLAND. Although like SCHEUREBE and FABER it was actually bred by Dr Georg Scheu at Alzey, this crossing takes its name from its chief propagator, nurseryman Fritz Huxel. It was bred in 1927 from GUTEDEL (Chasselas) and Courtillier Musqué (which is also an antecedent of the popular hybrid MARÉCHAL FOCH). The crossing is capable of producing enormous quantities of rather ordinary wine—so enormous in fact that the vines can collapse under the strain. If pruned carefully, however, and planted on an average to good site, it can easily reach Auslese MUST WEIGHTS even in an ordinary year and produce a fulsome if not exactly subtle wine redolent of honey, musk, and raisins for reasonably early consumption. In England, its ripeness is a useful counterbalance to naturally high acidity. In Germany, it is grown almost exclusively in the Pfalz and Rheinhessen and, although it is losing ground, there were still 876 ha/2,163 acres in 2003. Günter and Wittmann manage to spin gold from it.

hybrids, in common viticultural terms, the offspring of two varieties of different species, as distinct from a CROSS between two varieties of the same species. (See VITIS for details of the various species of the vine genus.) EUROPEAN

UNION authorities prefer the somewhat cumbersome term 'interspecific cross' to the word hybrid, which has pejorative connotations within Europe.

Hybrids can occur naturally by cross-pollination, as happened, for example, in early American viticulture (see AMERICAN HYBRIDS). More commonly, however, hybrids have been deliberately produced by man (see NEW VARIETIES and VINE BREEDING) to combine in the progeny some of the desirable characteristics of the parents. This viticultural activity was particularly important in the late 19th century, when European, and especially French, breeders tried to combine the desirable wine quality of European VINIFERA varieties with AMERICAN VINE SPECIES' resistance to introduced American pests and diseases, especially the PHYLLOXERA louse, which was devastating European vineyards (see FRENCH HYBRIDS).

Grafting European vines on to American ROOTSTOCKS proved the eventual solution, and many of today's commercially important rootstocks are hybrids. Early rootstocks were often pure varieties of a single American vine species chosen for their resistance to phylloxera. It was subsequently found, however, that hybrid rootstocks with combinations of genes from several American vine species allowing tolerance of various soil conditions and diseases, were more successful in the nursery.

Different species of *Vitis* contain genes with natural tolerance or resistance to winter cold, lime-induced CHLOROSIS, SALINITY, DOWNY MILDEW, POWDERY MILDEW, BOTRYTIS BUNCH ROT, CROWN GALL, PIERCE'S DISEASE, NEMATODES, WINTER FREEZE injury, and phylloxera. It is logical, therefore, to explore the possibilities of new hybrid varieties for wine production in an age of increasing concern about the AGROCHEMICALS which are used to control some of these. Vine breeders such as those at GEILWEILERHOF have proved that new hybrids, now called DISEASE-RESISTANT VARIETIES, may, without recourse to agrochemicals, produce useful quantities of wine which, in controlled tests, cannot be distinguished from that of their pure *vinifera* counterparts. As a result, EU authorities now allow such varieties as RONDO, REGENT, PHOENIX, and ORION (all new hybrids) in to QUALITY WINE.

Hybrids can yield good wine with no recognizably non-*vinifera* characteristics; see SEYVAL BLANC in England's cool climate, CHAMBOURCIN in summer rainfall areas such as parts of NEW SOUTH WALES, and some AMERICAN HYBRIDS.

The pedigree of many modern hybrids can involve seven or eight generations of crosses so that their ancestry is typically complex and includes *vinifera*, American varieties, possibly Asian varieties, and also early released French hybrids. R.E.S.

Galet, P., and Morton, L. T., *A Practical Ampelography* (Ithaca, NY, and London, 1979).

Huglin, P., *Biologie et écologie de la vigne* (Paris, 1986).

Mullins, M. G., Bouquet, A., and Williams, L., *Biology of the Grapevine* (Cambridge, 1992).

hydrogen sulfide, or H₂S, is the foul-smelling gas, reminiscent of rotten eggs, which even at very low concentrations (parts per billion) is easily recognized in wine because it is highly volatile and has a very low detection threshold. Although it can form at any stage of wine production, H₂S forms most commonly during alcoholic FERMENTATION, either in the active early to middle vigorous phase or towards the end. The formation of higher levels of H₂S during the vigorous phase, which coincides with rapid yeast growth, is associated with a deficiency in the amount of NITROGEN in the grape must or juice. Addition of nitrogen, typically in the form of diammonium phosphate (DAP), usually suppresses the appearance of H₂S. Grape berries of some varieties (e.g. Riesling, Chardonnay, and Syrah) tend to have a low level of yeast assimilable nitrogen (YAN), depending on soil type, nutrient status, and vineyard management conditions. The amount of H₂S produced by some yeast strains can also be affected by SULFUR DIOXIDE added to the must shortly before inoculating with YEAST. (Some producers consider it unwise not to add sulfur dioxide to must before fermentation, since it suppresses indigenous populations of yeast and bacteria, which can have a negative affect on fermentation and wine quality.) Certain yeast strains have a greater tendency to form H₂S from sulfate and sulfur dioxide when deprived of nitrogen, in a futile attempt to make sulfur-containing AMINO ACIDS needed for protein synthesis and cell growth. The addition of nitrogen stops H₂S accumulating in the wine during fermentation, not by stopping its formation in the yeast cell but by allowing the yeast to make amino acid precursor compounds that react with the H₂S to form sulfur-amino acids. Hot climate reds, which are prone to rapid fermentations in higher TEMPERATURES, use more nitrogen and tend to develop sulfidic smells. These are commonly described by the tasting term 'REDUCTION'. Choosing a yeast that has a low tendency to form H₂S and to correct nitrogen deficiency in musts and juices provides a useful means to lowering the incidence of H₂S formation during fermentation.

Small amounts of SULFUR used as vineyard fungicide can easily be reduced to H₂S by the highly REDUCTIVE conditions generated by yeast. Reducing or eliminating sulfur residues by ceasing sulfur applications several weeks before HARVEST can help. Recent research suggests that the role of sulfur RESIDUES as a source of H₂S in wine is overstated. In rare instances, usually when the juice has been stored for some time, a deficiency of VITAMINS can also cause H₂S to be formed. H₂S can also form through direct contact of wine with certain metals such as zinc and even the layer of manganese sulfide which can form on the surface of stainless steel. Iron and aluminium also serve as catalysts for the formation of sulfides.

Even traces of hydrogen sulfide can spoil the aroma of some wines. Fortunately, however, hydrogen sulfide is very volatile and can usually be removed by the stripping action of CARBON DIOXIDE produced during fermentation. However, H₂S formed towards the end of fermentation or, worse still, after fermentation is completed is of greater concern to the winemaker. If allowed to remain in the wine, it can react with other wine components to form MERCAPTANS (i.e. thiols), and disulfides (see SULFIDE), which have pungent garlic, onion, or rubber aromas. The smell of rotten eggs is always a FAULT in a finished wine but acceptance of the presence of trace amounts of mercaptans and disulfide is more controversial. Hydrogen sulfide and thiols can usually be removed from the new wine by a small addition of copper sulfate, or in the case of robust wines (especially reds) by AERATION, traditionally achieved by simple stirring, or by RACKING. A process of racking in association with temporary removal of yeast lees has been shown to be particularly effective in the removal of hydrogen sulphide.

A.D.W. & P.H.

Feuillat, M., 'Les capsules à vis pour le bouchage des vins: des essais faits en Bourgogne il y a 40 ans', *Revue des Oenologues*, 114 (Jan. 2005).

Henschke, P. A., and Jiranek, V., 'Hydrogen sulfide formation during fermentation: effect of nitrogen composition in model grape must', in J. M. Rantz (ed.), 'Nitrogen in Grapes and Wine', Proceedings of the International Symposium, Seattle, June 1991', *American Journal of Enology and Viticulture* (1991), 172–84.

Rauhut, D., 'Yeasts: production of sulfur compounds', in G. H. Fleet (ed.), *Wine Microbiology and Biotechnology* (Chur, 1993).

hydrolysis, a chemical reaction with, or involving water and often catalyzed by the hydrogen ions of acids. Hydrolysis is the reaction whereby an ESTER is split into its acid and alcohol components and GLYCOSIDES into their sugar and aglycone parts. The reaction is of great importance to the AGEING of wine when slow hydrolysis affects the FLAVOUR PRECURSORS releasing aroma-active aglycones from their flavourless glycosides. P.J.W.

hydrometer, an instrument used for measuring the soluble solids, sugar content, or MUST WEIGHT of juice and wine, consisting of a closed glass tube with a bulbous base, weighted so that it floats upright. The floating depth is inversely proportional to the DENSITY of the solution and is read by matching the bottom of the meniscus against a scale within the stem. This scale may be calibrated as for BAUMÉ, BRIX/Balling, or OECHSLE. As with all such density measurements, correction for the TEMPERATURE of the solution is necessary. B.G.C.

hygiene, an essential discipline in modern cellar management, involving cleanliness of wine-making premises and equipment, and a great deal of WATER.

History

Winery hygiene was clearly already regarded as important in Ancient ROME, as suggested by writers such as CATO and references in classical literature to SULFUR.

At the heart of the transformation from traditional mouldy cellars to their spotlessly clean counterparts has been a desire by winemakers to obtain much greater control over the processes of vinification and the maturation of wine, primarily through an emphasis on hygiene. While the pace of scientific research on the microbiology and biochemistry of wine-making has quickened appreciably since 1945, its origins lie in the middle of the 19th century with the experimental work of Louis PASTEUR. Until then, the precise reasons why pressed grapes would ferment into wine, and would then become unpalatable if left open to the air for any length of time, were unknown. Practical experience had convinced Roman winemakers of the need to use chemicals such as sulfur to help prevent spoilage, and by the late 15th century in Germany it was recognized that wine kept in large barrels that were subjected to regular TOPPING UP would last longer than wine kept in small barrels which were left on ULLAGE. However, it was Pasteur who first reported in western Europe that wine deteriorated mainly as a result of the actions of micro-organisms, and that these could be killed by heating the wine in the absence of oxygen (although see HUNGARY history).

Much of the impetus for the recent changes in winery hygiene has come from the New World, and in particular from institutions such as the Department of Viticulture and Enology at the University of California, DAVIS, where the driving mentality during the 1950s and 1960s was towards the eradication of poor-quality wine. This, it was argued, could best be achieved through tight control of the fermentation process, excluding the chance interference of a range of micro-organisms. More recently, innovative research at the AUSTRALIAN WINE RESEARCH INSTITUTE has also played a significant part in advancing the importance of winery hygiene. Above all, greater hygiene has enabled the adverse effects of ACETOBACTER and other spoilage micro-organisms such as BRETTANOMCYES to be avoided.

P.T.H.U.

Current practice

Hygiene is regarded as vital by modern winemakers (although it is still ignored by some traditional or peasant winemakers, several of whom somehow manage to produce top-quality wine). Old cellars, while usually more picturesque, are almost impossible to keep clean and free of BACTERIA and wild YEASTS.

Most modern wineries, on the other hand, are designed with sanitation and hygiene in mind. STAINLESS STEEL tanks can be easily cleaned and sanitized; hard floors are designed to drain dry; and all equipment is sited and mounted so that it can be cleaned thoroughly around, above, and below the unit. Vast quantities of water are used, together with non-foaming detergents and sterilizing agents, by carefully trained staff. In many wineries, all places where finished wine is exposed to the atmosphere are in separate, essentially sterile rooms, and care is taken particularly during BOTTLING, to its limit in STERILE BOTTLING. See also WINERY WASTE.

Some local wine-making traditions supposedly rely on cellar moulds (see TOKAJI in Hungary, for example).

Hygiene, or sanitation, is also important where the grapes are received, as overripe and damaged fruit can easily attract insects, particularly FRUIT FLIES *Drosophila melanogaster*. Piles of POMACE and stems should also be distanced from the winery as these can also become a breeding ground for insects.   A.D.W.

Amerine, M. A., 'The fermentation industries after Pasteur', *Food Technology*, 19/5 (1965), 75–90.

Paul, H. W., *Science, Vine and Wine in Modern France* (Cambridge, 1996).

Winkler, A. J., *Viticultural Research at University of California, Davis, 1921–1971* (Davis, Calif., 1973).

hyperoxidation. See WHITE WINE-MAKING.

IBMP, or **2-isobutyl-3-methoxypyrazine,** see ISOBUTYL-METHOXYPYRAZINE.

Ice Saints, saints whose commemoration days fall on the last spring days on which FROST is regarded as a danger; a local tradition in northern wine regions. See EISHEILIGEN and SAINTS GLACES.

ice wine, direct Anglicization of the German EISWEIN, sweet wine made from ripe grapes picked when frozen on the vine and pressed so that water crystals remain in the press and the sugar content of the resulting wine is increased. This sort of true ice wine is a speciality of CANADA, where it is written ICEWINE (see below). It is also increasingly made elsewhere including AUSTRIA, LUXEMBOURG, OREGON, and Michigan in the UNITED STATES. The term has also been used in other English-speaking, wine-producing countries for wines made by artificial freeze CONCENTRATION, or CRYOEXTRACTION.

Schreiner, J., *Icewine—The Complete Story* (Toronto, 2002).

Icewine, made in British Columbia, Québec, and particularly Ontario, is CANADA's version of EISWEIN and the crown jewel of its wine industry. In 1993, 72,000 half-litre bottles of Icewine were produced but by 2004 annual production had grown to more than 800,000 half-litre bottles, routinely retailing at more than C$50 each. The word Icewine has been trademarked by VQA Canada which imposes the world's most stringent standards on the production of ICE WINE. In Ontario, grapes for Icewine must have reached temperatures as low as −8 °C/18 °F before being harvested (as for Germany's Eiswein) but sugar levels must reach at least 35 °Brix, considerably higher than the minimum requirements in Germany and Austria. (See opposite p. 481.) From the 1997 vintage, all grapes used for VQA Icewine had to be processed by VQA member wineries or Ontario grape growers who have registered as VQA processors, and strict monitoring systems are in place. All Icewine must be VARIETAL and made from VINIFERA grapes or the French hybrid VIDAL. Grapes must be grown and pressed within a recognized Viticultural Area. Residual sugar at bottling must be at least 125 g/l. No SWEET RESERVE may be added. L.Br.

icon wine, an expression favoured by marketing people for highly priced wine. Icons are generally regarded as ultra-premium wines, which cost more than super-premium wines, which are in turn more expensive than premium wines. The rest is all but undrinkable.

Idaho, state in the PACIFIC NORTHWEST of the UNITED STATES which, as a wine region, has more in common with its neighbour eastern WASHINGTON than with western Oregon. With vineyards at an altitude of around 2,500 ft/ 762 m, however, it is close to if not beyond the normal viticultural fringe. Its diurnal temperature variation (see TEMPERATURE VARIABILITY) is even greater than that of eastern Washington, with the effect of a paradoxical combination in grapes of high acid and high sugar. This posed interesting challenges for both grape-grower and winemaker in the past. In recent years, however, major developments in the vineyard—lower yields, drip irrigation, open canopies and, above all, planting in warmer localities—have had a dramatic influence on wine quality. In few places has GLOBAL WARMING been more of a blessing. Winters can still be severe but rarely as devastating as they were in the 1970s and 1980s. Regarded then as a marginal climate, primarily noted for wines from hardier white varieties such as Riesling, Gewurztraminer, Chenin Blanc, and Chardonnay, Idaho now grows notable wines from Merlot, Cabernet Sauvignon, and Syrah. It is no surprise to find successful Rieslings, from off dry to ICE WINES.

The industry has been dominated by Ste Chapelle Winery, one of the Northwest's largest (fifth in size in the Pacific Northwest) and more successful wineries, situated in the Snake River valley to the west of Boise, in an area renowned for its cherries, apples, and peaches, always an indication of wine grape potential. Ste Chapelle was Idaho's first winery, controlling over two-thirds of the state's 1,000 or so acres/400 ha of vineyards (in 2005). In recent years it has had a leading role in improving grape-growing techniques. The University of Idaho's experimental vineyard at the research station in Parma is actively exploring other grape varieties that might find ideal expression in the region. There is substantial cross-border traffic in wine and grapes between Idaho and Washington. L.S.H. & D.L.

Gregutt, P., McCarthy, D., Prather, D., *Northwest Wines* (Seattle, 1996).

Hill, C., *Northwest Wines & Wineries* (Seattle, 1995).

Perdue, A., *Northwest Wine Guide* (Seattle, 2003).

IFOAM, International Federation of Organic Agriculture Movements. See ORGANIC VITICULTURE.

IGT stands for **Indicazione Geografica Tipica,** a category of wines created in ITALY by law 164 in 1992 as an approximate equivalent of the French VIN DE PAYS. EU law compelled Italy to bring its myriad esteemed, and often extremely expensive, wines selling as a VINO DA TAVOLA under some sort of control since TABLE WINES are not technically allowed to show vintage, variety, or name of estate on the label. IGT was developed as a convenient haven for these rebels. It has also provided lesser vini da tavola with a marketing vehicle for their wines. This has been of benefit, and IGT is now seen as a qualified success, providing both control and flexibility in a relatively intelligent manner. The most common IGTs tend to be regional:

Toscana, Umbria, and Sicilia, for example. For more details, see DOC. D.T. & D.C.G.

Île de Beauté is VIN DE PAYS language for CORSICA and, along with the Loire's similar denomination as 'Jardin de la France', one of the most alluring vin de pays names.

imbottigliato is Italian for bottled.

impériale. See BOTTLE SIZES.

Imperial Tokay, historical name used for wine produced on the vineyard properties of the Austrian Habsburg emperors in the TOKAJ-Hegyalja region of Hungary, especially during the 19th century. The Habsburg holdings were concentrated in the village of Tarcal, particularly the highly respected Szarvas vineyard that had been confiscated from the rebellious Prince Ferenc Rákóczi II in 1711. The term became widely known in western Europe following the creation of the Austro-Hungarian Monarchy in 1867. However, Imperial Tokay was usually misunderstood either as being necessarily far superior to all other Tokaji wines, or as being an alternative term for Eszencia.

M.L.-G.

INAO, the **Institut National des Appellations d'Origine**, is the organization in charge of administering, regulating, granting, and protecting the French APPELLATIONS CONTRÔLÉES, not just for about 470 different wines and spirits, but for more than 40 different cheeses and a range of other foods including meat, poultry, and olive oil. As such, and since VIN DE TABLE production is fast declining, it controls an increasing proportion of all French wine, more than 50 per cent of volume and nearly 60 per cent all vineyards in the mid 2000s. Nearly 75,000 vine-growers therefore depend on its rules, its undoubted restrictions, its protection, and its efforts to continue France's reliance on geographically based wine names. The organization is based in Paris but run by regional committees and administrative centres.

INAO was founded in 1935 and, since for much of the 20th century France's leading role in the world of wine was undisputed, it provided a role model for the administration of more embryonic CONTROLLED APPELLATION schemes in other countries. During the 1980s, however, commercial competition from non-French wines, and even from some French VINS DE PAYS on export markets, encouraged a reexamination of the role of INAO. The result was an even stronger INAO, given additional powers in 1990, fiercely dedicated to the notion of controlled, geographically determined appellations, empowered to protect them against imitation both in France and abroad, and determined that France's viticultural future in particular depended on her ability to trade on her uniquely well-established wine names.

Falling sales called INAO's one-time policy of removing all VINE VARIETY names from wine labels, on the premise that French wines express TERROIR rather than mere fruit flavour, into question. (Certain vin de pays producers positively relish their freedom to sell VARIETAL wines, or *vins de cépages* as they are known, and often despised, within France.) Indeed, now that AC wines constitute the majority of French wines, some critics have called the denomination meaningless, others have called for a super-category.

Any group of wine producers can apply to INAO to establish an appellation, possibly of VDQS status initially. They have to prepare a dossier by giving reasons for the request, proof of the traditional use of the name of the proposed appellation, full details of the terroir and how it affects production, and economic details concerning markets, sales, prices, and comparative prices of similar products.

incrocio, Italian for vine CROSSING. A wine made from **Incrocio Manzoni** grapes, for example, is made from one of Signor Manzoni's many crossings of one VINIFERA variety with another. His Incrocio Manzoni 6.0.13, Riesling × Pinot Blanc, often known simply as Manzoni Bianco, is the most widely planted, on a total of almost 10,000 ha/24,700 acres in 2000, mainly in north east Italy. Incrocio Manzoni 2.15 is Prosecco × Cabernet Sauvignon. Incrocio Terzi No 1 is a Barbera × Cabernet Franc cross grown in Lombardia.

indexing, method of testing vines for VIRUS DISEASES and PHYTOPLASMA diseases and their like. Sap from the plant to be tested is exposed to so-called indicator plants which show typical symptoms if the disease is present. Sap from the two plants can be mixed by abrading leaves or by grafting. Cabernet Franc, for example, is used as an indicator vine variety to test for LEAFROLL VIRUS. Indexing tests are now being replaced by serological methods; see ELISA. R.E.S.

Weber, E., Golino, D., and Rowhani, A., 'Laboratory testing for grapevine diseases', *Practical Winery and Vineyard* (Jan/Feb 2002), 13–27.

India, large Asian country where wine consumption and production are increasing fast, despite the general unsuitability of most of the country for conventional wine-growing.

History

The vine was probably introduced into north west India from Persia as early as the 4th millennium BC, during the Indus civilization, but wine may not have been made from its fruit for many centuries. The gradual invasion of Aryan tribes from central Asia during the 2nd millennium BC produced the Vedic period (broadly c.2000–800 BC), a blossoming of culture in north west India. The Aryans enjoyed gambling, music, and intoxicating drink, and in the four Vedas, the world's oldest religious

texts, two drinks are mentioned: *soma*, a milky drink ceremoniously prepared immediately before a sacrifice and probably containing hallucinatory hemp; and *sura*, a potent secular drink made from either barley or paddy (rice) fermented with honey.

While praising the favourite Aryan god, the rowdy and hard-drinking warrior Indra, the Vedas clearly condemn the effects of drinking. Later Hindu, Buddhist, and Jain texts reveal similar dichotomies. While the fifth of the Ten Precepts of Buddhism forbade alcoholic drinks, the Buddha (d. 483 BC) himself is said to have regarded alcohol as less reprehensible, merely an 'opening for the swallowing up of wealth'. The remarkable Kautilya, chief minister under the Mauryan King Chandragupta (ruled c.324–300 BC), partly or wholly wrote the Arthasastra, a text on statecraft in which he condemns alcohol and yet chronicles the king's drinking bouts and mentions *madhu* (wine) of various varieties and qualities, some home produced. This is the first documentation of wine made from grapes in India.

Down the centuries, wine has maintained its status in India as a drink of the Kshatriya caste of aristocrats and warriors rather than of the masses, who have preferred more potent alcohol prepared from the staple local agricultural crops of wheat and barley in the north, paddy in irrigated areas, and millet in dry zones.

The contradictory attitudes towards intoxicating drinks continue into modern times. The Muslim (see ISLAM) Mughal emperors' royal vineyards were in the Deccan; the alcoholic emperor Jehangir (who ruled 1605–27) would drink himself insensible on double- and triple-distilled wine (brandy), violating the Qur'ān's command not to lose one's sensibilities through intoxication.

Secular independent India's Constitution, adopted on 26 January 1950, states as one of its aims total prohibition of alcohol. Several states have enforced total prohibition in the past; even one of the most important wine-producing states Andhra Pradesh repealed prohibition as recently as 1997. There are orthodox Indians of all faiths who still abstain but since 1998 when the northern state of Haryana repealed its prohibition laws, Indians everywhere are free to consume wine and other alcohol if they choose.

Under the influence of Victorian Britain, whose upper classes expected to consume wines of all sorts in quantity, Indian viticulture was encouraged in the 19th century. Vineyards were established in Kashmīr, Bārāmati, Surat, and Goalkonda. A number of Indian wines were exhibited at the Great Calcutta Exhibition of 1884 and elicited favourable comment. But in the 1890s, Indian vineyards, like their European counterparts, succumbed to PHYL-LOXERA.

Since Independence in 1947, wine production has increased very slowly as it requires long-term investment and, ideally, a strong local market. The Indian government promoted viticulture as an agri-industry but it was hardly taken up by co-operatives and remained largely in the private sector. Goa continued to produce low-quality fortified wines made in the image of port, an industry initiated by Portuguese colonists in the 16th century. L.N.

Prakash, O., *Food and Drinks in Ancient India* (Delhi, 1961).

Viticulture

India's 60,000 ha/148,000 acres of vineyards produce about 1.6 million tons of grapes a year, of which only about 10 per cent are used for wine while the bulk is used as TABLE GRAPES and RAISINS. Established vineyards can be found in the temperate north west of the country in the state of Punjab , and as far south as the state of Tamilnadu on the southern tip of the subcontinent. Two-thirds of the country's area under vine, however, is in the three south-central states, also in the tropics, of Mahārāshtra (30,000 ha/74,100 acres), Karnataka (12,000 ha/29,600 acres), and Andhra Pradesh (6,000 ha/15,000 acres). In Mahārāshtra, cultivation is concentrated around Pune, Nāsik, Baramati, Sangali, and Sholhāpur on the west of the Deccan Plateau, about 300 km/180 miles in length and 60 km in width, 135 km inland from Mumbai. The remainder of southern India's plantings are at Karnataka near Bangalore, and in Andhra Pradesh around Hyderābād.

Plantings range from altitudes of 300 m/ 984 ft on the Deccan in Mahārāshtra and 200 m/660 ft in Karnataka and a few at 800 m/2,600 ft on the slopes of Sahyadri together with a few terraced vineyards at 1,000 m/ 3,300 ft in Kashmir. With India's hot summer and heavy monsoon, temperatures in growing areas range from 8 °C/46 °F in winter to 45 °C in summer, 625–1,500 mm (25–60 in) of rain falling between June and August depending on the region. There is little unseasonal rain. Humidity levels are high particularly during the monsoon, moderated only by the afternoon winds. Eastern regions suffer most from humidity and extreme heat.

Indigenous table grapes such as Arkavati, Arkashyam, and Anabeshahi are grown for the local market on very small holdings. Bangalore Blue (ISABELLA), Gulabi (MUSCAT HAMBURG), and Perlette are also widely grown (collectively on about 20 per cent of the vineyard area) and used mostly as table grapes with a small proportion for low-quality sweet wines for the domestic market. But THOMPSON SEEDLESS/SULTANA and its various mutations is by far the most widely planted variety, accounting for over half the total vineyard area.

Vines are trained high on wire and bamboo with wide ROW SPACING to retain SOIL WATER, prevent SUNBURN, and maximize aeration of the vines, minimizing the risk of FUNGAL DISEASES. Since the early 1980s, DRIP IRRIGATION

has been used throughout the growing season and YIELDS are high, up to 700 or 900 hl/ha (40 or 50 tons/ha). Pruning takes place in April and September with harvest (always manual in India) in February and March. In warmer regions, particularly Andhra, Karnataka (Bangalore), and Tamilnadu, there are normally two harvests a year. See TROPICAL VITICULTURE.

The contemporary wine industry

Until the 1990s, the small Indian wine industry went virtually unnoticed outside the country, partly because of the quality of the wine, which was typically sweet, alcoholic, and MADERIZED and made by rudimentary village operations, with the exception of a large winery and distillery established in Hyderābād in 1966 by the Shaw Wallace group. Even within India, the prevailing religious and official attitude towards alcohol hardly encouraged a wine industry.

The current renaissance of Indian viticulture began with the establishment of Chateau Indage in 1984 near Pune in Maharashtra state and of Grover Vineyards in 1988 north of Bangalore in Karnataka state, both of which set themselves the highest standards and the goal of exporting. Chateau Indage planted Chardonnay, Ugni Blanc, Pinot Blanc, Pinot Noir, Cabernet Sauvignon, and Merlot at an altitude of 800 m on the south-facing LIMESTONE slopes of Sahyadri mountain at Nārāyangaon, 150 km from Pune. These vines were grafted on to specially imported ROOTSTOCKS with resistance to phylloxera and NEMATODES. Chateau Indage imported French equipment and expertise from Champagne to establish India's most sophisticated winery, producing a surprisingly elegant sparkling wine sold under the names Omar Khayyam and Marquise de Pompadour. Grover Vineyards trialled 35 vine varieties initially and settled principally on Cabernet Sauvignon and Clairette, which grow on PERGOLAS. The first wine was released in 1992 and in 1996 the champagne house Veuve Clicquot took a minority stake in the company.

A third contender emerged when former Silicon Valley engineer, Ranjeev Samant, returned to his home country to establish Sula Wines at Nashik in 1996. Sula overtook Grover in 2005 as India's second largest wine bottler following the opening of a new winery. Sula produced India's first Chenin Blanc, Sauvignon Blanc, and Zinfandel wines.

Thanks to the more liberal government policy and improved economic conditions, a prosperous, wine-drinking middle class has emerged in India. Demand for wine has been growing at 20 to 30 per cent a year, and total consumption was just under six million l in 2005. R.M.B. & D.G.

Indicação de Proveniencia Regulamentada,

the second tier of designated

wine regions in PORTUGAL. For more information, see IPR.

indicator. See INDEXING.

Indonesia had three wineries by 2005, all on the resort island of Bali. The pioneer, and still the largest wine-making enterprise, is Hatten Wines, founded in 1994. It operates from an old rice wine factory at Sanur Beach on the southern tip of the island but most of the grapes are grown around the villages of Seririt and Lovina, a few miles from the city of Singaraja, at the northern extreme of the island (8 °latitude). Here, the ELEVATION provides some modest respite from the relentless TROPICAL heat and humidity but climatic conditions are such that the vines crop almost continuously. These vineyards were planted originally for TABLE GRAPES with the French VINIFERA table grape Alphonse Lavallée (Ribier) growing on overhead PERGOLAS. MUSCAT varieties were planted more recently and Shiraz and Chambourcin are being trialled for more robust reds. The winery crushed 250 tonnes in 2004 and makes a wide range of wine styles. Indico Wines is a more recent venture producing a range of wine styles from the grape it calls Isabella, but which is almost certainly Alphonse Lavallée. Wine of the Gods produces wine in Bali from grape juice imported from Western Australia. D.G.

inert gas, a gas used to protect wine from OXIDATION by the air, such as NITROGEN or CARBON DIOXIDE.

inert gas mixture, mixture of gases that does not include OXYGEN. Traditionally, such mixtures have been composed of NITROGEN and CARBON DIOXIDE but more recently argon is being included in these mixes, either in place of, or along with, nitrogen. Such mixtures are used in wine storage processes in lieu of NITROGEN because the greater density of carbon dioxide and argon causes them to layer and so more efficiently exclude oxygen. Inert gas mixtures may not have been used in winemaking as often as nitrogen because the carbon dioxide fraction dissolves in wine, possibly leaving a higher than desirable residual concentration of this gas. Argon, like nitrogen, has a very low solubility in wine and inert gas mixtures of either or both of these two with carbon dioxide can, with modern metering equipment, be selected to leave a residual level of dissolved carbon dioxide that is optimal for the style of wine under storage. A.D.W. & P.J.W.

Inferno, subzone of VALTELLINA in the far north of Italy.

inflorescence, the structure that bears the flowers (see BUNCH for more details). At FLOWERING, the grape flower becomes a BERRY and the inflorescence a bunch.

information technology has revolutionized the world of wine as much as any other. Computers are now used throughout the production process. In the vineyard they can schedule and control IRRIGATION, for example, or measure weather and predict and even control SPRAYING regimes. They can assist VINEYARD SITE SELECTION by analysing and mapping data on CLIMATE, SOIL, VIGOUR, and TOPOGRAPHY. In the winery, they can weigh and sample grapes, control CRUSHING and PRESSING operations, ensure the most vigilant TEMPERATURE CONTROL, and oversee BOTTLING. They cannot, yet, oversee the progress of wine in individual barrels.

Thanks to information technology, wine ANALYSIS is today much more sophisticated than could have been imagined even a decade ago, and there have even been attempts to mechanize the process of TASTING. Information technology has greatly assisted such techniques as DNA PROFILING in vine variety identification, and the possible new technique of 'fingerprinting' a vineyard by analysis of its MINERALS.

Those who sell wine, whether to consumers or in BULK to the trade, can use information technology to administer all aspects of TRANSPORT, STORAGE, stock control, and retailing, as well as being able to present their wares directly to potential customers via the Internet—which can be an advantage when selling a commodity as tightly regulated as an alcoholic beverage. The Internet has spawned a new generation of independent, often very small, online wine merchants while online wine AUCTIONS were well established by the turn of the century.

As well as offering wine consumers a new market place, for both buying and selling, and a new medium for wine information and EDUCATION via myriad WEBSITES, the Internet has provided them with an unprecedented forum for discussion, not just about the wines themselves but also about WINE WRITERS, a new sort of consumer power, even if one that tends to attract wine BORES.

Those who keep detailed cellar records and TASTING NOTES have reason to be grateful for the flexibility and sorting ability of personal computers.

As Internet technologies develop, the international wine market will be revolutionized. For example, we will be able to dispatch 'personal agents', smart pieces of software programmed with our tastes in wine, across the Internet in search of the precise wines we want according to parameters such as PRICE, VINTAGE, PRODUCER, VARIETY, and APPELLATION.

Eventually, the price of computing microchips is likely to fall to such an extent that every BOTTLE and CASE of wine will be networked with a chip costing a fraction of a penny. It is no fantasy to believe that long before 2020, our mobile phones will be able to scan bottles in a store and provide tasting notes and comparative pricing information

on nearby retailers, and the uncorking of the last bottle in a case will automatically send an order to a local retailer for a refill.

J.R. & R.S.L.

initiation, botanical term for the start of the vine's fruiting when the first signs of bunches are evident as small pieces of tissue in the developing bud. These buds are themselves developing beside the leaf stalk on the shoots as they grow in spring. Initiation happens during the FLOWERING stage of the growing season. Warm, sunny weather conditions at this time favour initiation, with one, two, occasionally three, or very rarely four bunches initiated. When this shoot bursts the following year, it will be termed FRUITFUL.

Part of the annual variation in vineyard YIELD is thus due to weather conditions affecting initiation during the year previous to the crop being harvested. The time when the vines are flowering is the most critical period for bunch initiation. To most vine-growers, a 'light crop year' often refers in an oblique way to weather conditions which affected initiation a little over 12 months previously, although other factors can affect yield.   R.E.S.

Huglin, P., *Biologie et écologie de la vigne* (Paris, 1986).
Winkler, A. J., *et al.*, *General Viticulture* (2nd edn, Berkeley, Calif., 1974).

injection, alternative name for CARBONATION, the cheapest and least effective method of SPARKLING WINE-MAKING involving the simple pumping of CARBON DIOXIDE into a tank of wine.

inner staves, or **inserts**, planks of wood, usually oak, placed in a stainless steel tank and held in position by a metal framework, are a way of imparting oak flavour to wine more cheaply than by fermenting or ageing in barrels since the staves are easily replaced. Inner staves are sometimes used in conjunction with MICRO-OXYGENATION to mimic the use of barrels for fermentation or maturation without the cost of barrels, a barrel cellar, and barrel cellar workers. See also BARREL INSERTS.

INRA (**l'Institut National de la Recherche Agronomique**), the French specialist organization for agronomic research. Founded just after the Second World War in 1946, it is funded by the government, a larger proportion of its budget coming from the Ministry for Scientific Research than from the Ministry of Agriculture.

There are 22 separate research centres in France; the one in Montpellier has specialist units in OENOLOGY and VITICULTURE which actively co-operate with MONTPELLIER University. INRA Bordeaux specializes in viticulture.

Advances in viticulture since INRA's creation have been enormous. The Institute's most significant contribution has been the introduction of CLONAL SELECTION in France to help combat VIRUS DISEASES and thus

improve quality and YIELDS. INRA's current viticultural and oenological research priorities focus on vine–environment interaction, vine resources (at the Domaine de Vassal, see below), quality control, and technological innovation.

There has been success in establishing the best use of FERTILIZERS on high-quality vineyards, and current research aims to reduce the use of FUNGICIDES, whose extravagant use in the 1970s and 1980s led to an urgent need for more sophisticated control regimes. This development, known as *la lutte raisonnée* ('the rational struggle') in France, aims at the minimal, and only carefully considered, use of products rather than a predetermined programme of regular applications. As the ill effects of the last generation of AGROCHEMICALS become clearer, particularly in respect of COPPER toxicity, this is expected to become the area of greatest viticultural change. INRA's Domaine de Vassal on the Mediterranean coast, home to more than 7,000 VINIFERA varieties and HYBRIDS is a centre for the analysis, preservation, and management of biodiversity, especially with regard to pest and disease resistance and wine quality. The soils are free of both PHYLLOXERA and the nematode *Xiphinema index*. Some NEW VARIETIES, CHASAN for example, have also been developed here and, thanks to the work of AMPELOGRAPHERS such as Paul Truel, Domaine de Vassal has become a worldwide focus for vine identification

The importance for eventual wine quality of the grapes' condition at HARVEST has long been recognized by both viticulturists and oenologists, and INRA is also studying the effects on wine quality of various vine-TRAINING SYSTEMS. More basic research is concentrated on the exact nature of grape RIPENING, which is still not fully understood. Research priorities include: organoleptic properties of PHENOLIC compounds, wine stability, biology of wine yeasts, and control of fermentations.

INRA's experimental unit Unité Experimentale de Pech Rouge (UE Pech Rouge) is dedicated to the development and transfer of technology. Its mission is to provide experimental ideas and resources for the research unit at Montpellier and for professional partners, to disseminate technological innovation, and to contribute to the training of oenologists.

In 1991, the Institut d'Oenologie de Bordeaux (see University of BORDEAUX) and INRA, Bordeaux, formed a Pôle de Recherche Scientifique sur la Vigne et le Vin with a view to working more closely together in the two areas in which scientific research can improve the quality of wine.   W.B. & J.Ha.

insecticides. See PESTICIDES.

insect pests. A wide variety of insects attack grapevines. Injury may occur as a result of direct feeding action, where reductions in leaf amount or leaf health can delay RIPENING with serious implications for wine quality, or by carrying (vectoring) a particular VIRUS DISEASE or PHYTOPLASMA disease.

Alternatively the vine root system can be attacked, which leads to development of WATER STRESS and restricted VINE NUTRITION. While minor stress may enhance wine quality (see VINE PHYSIOLOGY), the more likely outcome of root damage by insects such as PHYLLOXERA (the most destructive of all insect pests) is severe stress or vine death. Some insect pests, such as phylloxera, attack only grapevines, while many attack a range of different plants.

Different insect pests attack grapes and vines in different parts of the world, and in different districts, and what may be an important pest in one area may be unimportant or non-existent in another. The most important insect pests in European vineyards are the BEETLES *écrivain* and *cigarier* and the MOTHS pyrale, cochylis, eudemis, and eulia, and MITES. Mediterranean FRUIT FLY can be a pest in some areas of Australia, but is not present in the United States, while LEAFHOPPERS are serious pests in California but not Australia. Other insects, such as CUTWORM and GRASSHOPPERS, are general agricultural pests worldwide.

Insect pests which affect only the appearance of grapes concern growers of TABLE GRAPES but not growers of wine grapes, who are more likely to be concerned with effects on YIELD or wine quality. Grape RIPENING can be seriously delayed, for example, when the WESTERN GRAPELEAF SKELETONIZER reduces leaf area and thus reduces PHOTOSYNTHESIS; vineyards can be destroyed as young plantings by cutworms, or when mature by MARGARODES and phylloxera. Perhaps more insidiously, insects such as fruit fly can carry spores associated with BUNCH ROTS, and MEALY BUG can transmit LEAFROLL virus. Leafhoppers spread the serious GRAPEVINE YELLOWS and PIERCE'S DISEASE and make such disease notoriously difficult to control.

In general, insect pests are relatively easy to control in vineyards, although insecticides (see PESTICIDES) are among the more dangerous AGROCHEMICALS for operators to apply. Modern approaches to viticulture are more environmentally aware than previously, and so persistent chemicals such as DDT are no longer used and INTEGRATED PEST MANAGEMENT, designed to reduce insecticide use, is becoming increasingly common (see also ORGANIC and BIODYNAMIC VITICULTURE). For example, predatory mites are encouraged, to control levels of damaging mites.

See also entries for the specific pests APHIDS, BEETLES, BORERS, CUTWORMS, ERINOSE MITE, FRUIT FLY, GRASSHOPPERS, LEAFHOPPERS, LEAF ROLLERS, LOCUSTS, MARGARODES, MEALY BUGS, MITES, MOTHS, PHYLLOXERA, SCALE, THRIPS, WESTERN GRAPELEAF SKELETONIZER.

M.J.E. & R.E.S.

Buchanan, G. A., and Amos, T. G., 'Grape pests', in B. G. Coombe and P. R. Dry (eds.), *Viticulture*, ii: *Practices* (Adelaide, 1992).
Flaherty, D. L., *et al.* (eds.), *Grape Pest Management* (2nd edn, Oakland, Calif., 1992).

integrated pest management, or **IPM**, a term which dates back to the mid 1970s in Europe. Initially developed for insect pests, IPM now encompasses the control of diseases, weeds, and physiological vine disorders and has the potential to increase economic returns for the grower and improve environmental and human safety by reducing, limiting or even eliminating the use of AGROCHEMICALS.

IPM is considered by conventional growers as a form of SUSTAINABLE VITICULTURE but most IPM management systems differ from ORGANIC VITICULTURE because they tolerate the use of industrially synthesized products such as HERBICIDES, PESTICIDES, and FERTILIZERS. However, IPM aims to stop the regular, calendar-based spraying of chemicals in a wasteful, unthinking manner and instead to apply such treatments in a more accurately timed way and targeted to specific threats. IPM is often seen as a first step towards organic or BIODYNAMIC viticulture.

Thus IPM takes account of the environment, particularly weather phenomena, the occurrence and life cycles of pests, and the incidence of natural enemies and alternative host plants. It requires a knowledge of the biology of the pest, monitoring the occurrences of the pest and any natural predators, recording environmental conditions, and then integrating all this information into a decision-making process.

A number of VINE PESTS and diseases have been studied under the aegis of IPM philosophy. For example, the European grape berry MOTHS *Lobesia botrana* and *Eupoecilia ambiguella* can cause extensive damage, and studies have shown that their population levels can be limited naturally by VIRUS DISEASES and protozoan diseases. Similarly, MITES which can cause damage to vines can be controlled by other species of predatory mites, and sometimes this effect can be limited by the application of pesticides, in particular some FUNGICIDES. Indeed, the increased use of some agrochemicals has altered the balance of predator to pest mites. R.E.S. & M.W.

Cavalloro, R., *Integrated Pest Control in Viticulture* (Rotterdam, 1987).

integrated production, or **IP**, European system of viticulture aimed at reducing environmental degradation in vineyards while at the same time maintaining economic viability of viticulture. It is similar in philosophy to SUSTAINABLE VITICULTURE. As the name suggests, it has its roots in INTEGRATED PEST MANAGEMENT, or IPM.

IP was developed as a concept in 1974, and major development has come from France,

Germany, and, especially, Switzerland. Integrated production emphasizes a holistic approach to viticulture, by considering the vineyard as an 'agro-ecosystem'. The reduction of chemical inputs, especially nitrogen FERTILIZER and broad spectrum INSECTICIDES, is a first step. Where rainfall is sufficient, COVER CROPS are established, ideally to include legumes. CANOPY MANAGEMENT is also important to reduce SPRAYING against BOTRYTIS and POWDERY MILDEW. Some spraying is permitted, with restrictions more on frequency than on type of spray material. ORGANIC and especially BIODYNAMIC approaches might be described as more absolute integrated production systems since industrially synthesized chemicals are prohibited and accreditation and inspection are administered by independent assessors.

R.E.S. & M.W.

Jordan, D., 'Sustainable viticulture: development of a scheme for New Zealand', in T. Henick-Kling, T. E. Wolf, and E. M. Harkness (eds.), *Proceedings of the Fourth International Symposium on Cool Climate Enology & Viticulture*, III (Rochester, 1996), 44–6.
Smart, R. 'Integrated production: new buzz words in viticulture?', *Practical Winery and Vineyard* (Jan/Feb 1996), 66–8.

International Grape Genome Project (IGGP), a framework for multinational collaborative grapevine research, with an emphasis on grapevine genomics. See GENETIC MODIFICATION.

international varieties, loose term for those VINE VARIETIES with an international reputation for their VARIETAL wines. They are planted in almost every major wine region in which they stand a chance of ripening. Foremost among them are the red wine variety CABERNET SAUVIGNON and the white wine variety CHARDONNAY (which many consumers take to be either a place or, more usually, a BRAND). Other strong candidates as international varieties are MERLOT, PINOT NOIR, and, especially, SYRAH/SHIRAZ among reds and SAUVIGNON BLANC, RIESLING, MUSCAT, GEWÜRZTRAMINER, VIOGNIER, PINOT BLANC, and PINOT GRIS among whites. As winemakers and wine consumers constantly search for new excitement, the list of possibilities grows longer. MOURVÈDRE, TEMPRANILLO, SANGIOVESE, and NEBBIOLO could already be said to have joined this elite.

International Wine & Food Society (IWFS), the oldest and most cosmopolitan of the gastronomic societies for consumers rather than professionals. Initially simply the Wine & Food Society, it was founded in London in 1933 by André SIMON and like-minded friends. Its aim, other than providing a readership for a journal *Wine and Food* which Simon planned to edit, was to promote the highest quality of raw materials and an appreciation of how they could best be served and consumed. An early motto was 'Not much, but the best'. Launched in full economic depression (partly as a reaction to the culinary decline which resulted from it), the society attracted its fair share of criticism initially, and might well have withered had not the Repeal of PROHIBITION opened up North America to the proselytizing of M. Simon. Soon there were branches all over the United States and today two-thirds of the membership live in North America; although the IWFS remains based in London, fewer than a quarter of its members live in Britain. There are over 7,000 members of 140 branches in about 30 countries, all organizing their own programmes of lunches, dinners, tastings, lectures, and gastronomic tourism depending on the inclinations and aspirations of local branch members. The Society, now much imitated, is a non-profit-making concern and has always taken a particular interest in wine. André Simon and his early colleague A. J. A. Symons launched the first pocket VINTAGE CHART in 1935 and it is annually revised by a special committee of the IWFS to this day, providing useful income through sales to publishers of diaries and the like. The journal was published regularly between 1934 and 2000 and was at one stage edited by Hugh JOHNSON.

Internet. See INFORMATION TECHNOLOGY.

internode, the part of the stem between NODES (see illustration on p. 591). The internode length in vines varies between different VINE VARIETIES and with growing conditions. It is shorter with weak roots, low temperatures, WATER STRESS, mineral deficiencies (especially of NITROGEN), and the position along the shoot (with the nodes closest together at the base and the tip). Shoots on vigorous vines have long internodes, and are large in diameter. Measured lengths vary from about 1 mm to 350 mm/13.6 in but commercially used cuttings usually have internode lengths between 50 and 150 mm. B.G.C.

interspecific hybrid denotes the result of sexually crossing more than one grapevine species, while a CROSS of varieties of the same species is **intraspecific**. See HYBRID and VITIS for some background.

invecchiato, Italian for aged.

invertase, an important ENZYME in the vine for converting the larger molecule SUCROSE to its constituent molecules of GLUCOSE and FRUCTOSE in the ripening fruit so that sugar develops (see SUGAR IN GRAPES). The enzyme was first discovered in yeast in 1846, and is sometimes also called saccharase, sucrase, and Beta-fructosidase. The name invertase comes from the so-called 'invert' sugars of glucose and fructose. The reaction of this enzyme differs from that of other enzymes in that it is not reversible. This is one of the most widespread enzymes in the plant kingdom, and

indeed one of the most efficient. It can metabolize 1 million times its own weight of sucrose with no loss of activity. The enzyme is located in the vacuole of berry cells, where it functions readily in the acidic environment. R.E.S.

investment in wine is the acquisition of wine for gain, whether as a means of making money or financing consumption or a combination of the two.

'This crisis is perfectly rational. It was even foreseeable. The day I saw in *Time* magazine a photograph of a bank vault with a bottle of Lafite in it, I assembled my staff and told them: "the crisis has started". Indeed from the moment when you start to think of wine as an investment and not as something to be drunk, that's the end' (Baron Elie de ROTHSCHILD of Ch LAFITE-Rothschild, quoted in *The Winemasters* by Nicholas Faith).

The principal object of wine investment is to make a profit on wine which has increased in value as it matures. The essential premise on which wine investment is based is that demand for the wine in question exceeds supply, a premise that is often hard to gauge accurately. Such investment may be made purely for financial gain or to purchase wines with a view to financing consumption. In the latter instance, the investor's prime objective is to secure wines of limited availability or high FASHION that may not appear again on the market.

Wine investment is not an activity confined to private individuals or investment companies outside the wine trade. Buying 'earliest, cheapest, lowest' is usually available to those in the know or with solid contacts. Indeed, historically, the wine trade itself, with its inside knowledge, has been known to 'take a position' on a vintage, buying grapes on a speculative hunch. This practice, known as buying *sur souches*, i.e. while the grapes are still on the vine, was referred to in Roman times by Pliny the Younger (8. 2) and became part of the folklore of the BORDEAUX TRADE, as discussed below.

Speculation and buying for consumption need not be mutually exclusive. Indeed, spreading the risk by buying mixed portfolios of wine with both disposal and consumption in mind makes sound sense and is normally advised by companies dealing in wine investment. The benefits can make wine investment an attractive proposition. As a wasting asset with a life expectancy for tax purposes of less than 50 years, wine does not generally attract Capital Gains Tax in the UK. There may, however, be circumstances in which tax officials would regard wine investment as a business and tax it accordingly. Vintage PORT, in particular, with a life expectancy of 50 years or more, is liable not to be regarded as a wasting asset for tax purposes. The popularity of wine as an investment has led to the creation of one or two offshore schemes regulated by the Financial Services Authority, unlike those

of wine merchants whose main aim is to move stock.

But wine investment is inevitably a gamble, especially for anyone under the mistaken impression that making money from it is simply a question of holding on long enough to one's stock. Speculation in wine tends to be especially risky because wine is subject to both the vagaries of the weather and the unpredictable fluctuations of market forces. Buyers' and sellers' markets come and go and wine PRICES are as liable to go down as up. BORDEAUX, for reasons discussed below, is the principal medium of wine investment. The name Bordeaux is virtually synonymous with wine investment and its turbulent past bears witness to fortunes made and unmade in the name of wine.

In more recent years, the wine investment scene has embraced a wider portfolio of wine regions including Burgundy, Italy, Spain, California, and Australia. It has also attracted unscrupulous wine brokers who have manipulated secondary wine market data and extrapolated media reports to build a case for wine investment. Promises of high returns have often not been fulfilled because of fat broker margins, high storage costs, weakening currency exchange markets, and shady dealings. Counterfeit or forged wine accounts for a minute proportion of the fine and rare wine market, but in periods of high speculation and expectations, some fraudsters have attempted to circulate wine of questionable provenance, especially in emerging Asian markets and notably DRC, Sassicaia, Chx Pétrus and Mouton-Rothschild, and Penfolds Grange.

Bordeaux: cyclical history
The first great boom in Bordeaux resulted from a period of prosperity which coincided with shortages caused by POWDERY MILDEW, or oidium, in the 1850s. The canny merchant Hermann CRUSE had struck the first speculative blow already, when, in 1848, he had bought up vast quantities of the 1847 vintage, only to release his hoard at undisclosed prices following Napoleon III's imperial accession. British Chancellor of the Exchequer (later to be Prime Minister) Gladstone's reduction of duty on French wine following the 1860 Anglo-French Commercial Treaty and the Single Bottle Act of 1861 (which paved the way for the off-licence, and thus a retail trade in alcoholic drinks) further fuelled demand for red bordeaux.

Following the fine vintages of 1864 and 1865, prices doubled. Two successive lean years then led to speculative buying of the hard and slow-maturing 1868 vintage, *sur souches*. Chx Lafite and Margaux offered their 1868 to the Bordeaux market, achieving record prices which were not to be surpassed for another 58 years. But this was already the beginning of the end. The Bordeaux merchant Edouard Kressmann mirrored Hermann Cruse's earlier coup with his successful speculative purchase of the fine 1870 vintage harvested during the Franco-Prussian War. The 1875 vintage marked the end of this first golden era, however, as the imminent plagues of DOWNY MILDEW and PHYL-LOXERA cast a blight over the vineyards of Bordeaux (see BORDEAUX, history).

History was to repeat itself nearly a century later. During the post-war period of economic regeneration, the turning-point came in 1959 when, following two devaluations of the French franc, the Americans first decisively entered the market for fine Bordeaux wines. The 1959 vintage was hailed as the vintage of the century, a term which subsequently came to be applied *ad nauseam* to almost any vintage of note (usually revealing more about the ability of the Bordelais to feed speculation than about the quality of the vintage at issue). The clamour increased for the small but spectacular vintage of 1961. Between 1958 and 1961, the prices of the FIRST GROWTHS, on which most of the speculative activity was focused, more than quadrupled. By 1961, they had widened the gap between themselves and the other CLASSED GROWTHS to such an extent that their reputation as blue chip investment wines became even more firmly established.

Towards the end of the decade, the devaluation of the French franc in 1969 and the rivalry between Chx LAFITE and MOUTON-ROTHSCHILD contributed to a fresh climate of speculation that was to grip Bordeaux in the early 1970s. An opening price battle between the first growths heralded the start of a boom, underpinned by a widespread feeling that demand would outstrip supply for the foreseeable future. A flood of foreign investment capital washed into Bordeaux to lap up the 1970 and 1971 vintages. Extortionate prices were asked—and paid—for the 1972 vintage, even though it turned out to be lean and mean.

A market develops
As inflation soared, red bordeaux became an investors' haven. The AUCTION houses Christie's and Sotheby's, whose new wine departments were established in, respectively, 1966 and 1970, provided the ideal forum for acquisitions and disposals. During the same period, numerous investment schemes were established to attract corporate finance, while wine merchants such as Justerini & Brooks set up their own schemes to cater for the speculative appetites of consumers. (Such schemes were to be the precursors of the government-backed Business Expansion Schemes set up in the British economic boom of the mid 1980s in the wake of a fresh outbreak of speculation fever.)

Rising oil prices and the collapse of American financial hegemony already signalled impending disaster by the spring of 1973. Tastings of the 1972 vintage coincided with the prospect of a large 1973 vintage, which turned out to be unexceptional in quality. An East Anglian wine merchant, writer Simon Loftus, was offered—

and refused—£1 million by a respectable City finance house to buy 1972 vintage wines. Circumstances were aggravated by a scandal in which the Bordeaux house of CRUSE was charged with—and subsequently convicted of—fraud. By 1975, Chx Lafite and Mouton-Rothschild had buried the hatchet and offered surplus stocks through Christie's.

Speculation fever was rekindled by the *annus mirabilis* of 1982, when an exceptional red Bordeaux vintage coincided with a relatively weak French franc and a strong American dollar. Opening prices of the first growths, FF170, were more than double those of the 1980s. The fashion for buying EN PRIMEUR, boosted by the superb 1982 vintage, created a new wave of populist investment fervour. The momentum for this new form of speculative buying was buoyed by a succession of fine vintages during the 1980s, and by, for the first time, accessible press comment on the relative merits of individual, if embryonic, wine samples (see WINE WRITING). A typical good investment from the 1982 vintage would have been a case of the ST-ESTÈPHE Ch Cos d'Estournel, which could be bought for less than £100 in the spring of 1983 and was fetching £1,000 at auction 20 years later.

But in the early to mid 1990s, despite particularly fine crops in 1985, 1986, 1989, and 1990, the market took a downward turn, largely because the unfulfilled promise of increasing consumption was further aggravated by an embarrassing surplus of fine bordeaux. A case of the PAUILLAC Ch Grand Puy Lacoste 1986 offered in June 1987 for £118 excluding all duty and taxes could be bought at auction seven years later for £130, excluding buyer's premium.

How to minimize the risks
The lessons of the 1980s and the earlier booms demonstrate that, in order to fulfil the promise of any investment, timing, knowledge, and skill (not to mention a measure of luck) are all essential preconditions for would-be investors, whether individuals or companies. Timing requires knowledge both of market conditions and of the potential of a wine for maturing. The finer the wine, generally speaking, the longer it takes to reach its peak, and the longer it remains on a plateau of maturity. It takes knowledge and skill to be aware of and interpret the likely future trends of individual properties and vintages, taking into account their real and perceived qualities. (One of the best ways to acquire such knowledge is to keep abreast of the pronouncements of the most influential wine critics, notably Robert PARKER, but anyone buying for investment would be well-advised to read a range of expert opinions on any particular wine or vintage and keep track, month by month, of price indices such as those in *Decanter* magazine.)

At the same time, investors need to be aware of less immediately obvious features of wine

investment such as the importance of optimum STORAGE conditions, the costs involved, and the disposal options. The better the guarantee of storage in ideal conditions, the more attractive the proposition for the vendor. At the commercial auction rooms of Christie's and Sotheby's in London, the vendor can expect to receive the current auction market price on disposal. At the same time, vendors should be aware of the requirement to pay a vendor's premium, or, if a disposal is effected through a specialist wine BROKER or FINE WINE TRADER, of commission on the disposal.

Investors need also to take full account of the buying options. If the conditions are right, the simplest and most attractive method of purchasing is buying en primeur, as buying futures is known in the French wine trade.

Wine may also be bought at auction, in which case care should be taken to ensure that the wine has been properly stored and that the initial outlay is not prohibitive. For both reasons, any such purchase should be made at a commercial auction house holding regular, professionally run sales, such as Christie's, Sotheby's, Zachys, or Langton's. And wine should ideally be bought in complete, original CASES offered in BOND, to avoid the additional expenses of paying duty and any value added tax.

Suitable wines for investment
The factors that make wine a worthwhile investment are numerous and complex. For one thing, political and economic auguries, specific market conditions, and likely future trends need all to be taken into account. Purchasing is always best done in a buyer's market when conditions allow investors to take advantage of low prices such as occurred in the mid 1970s following the Bordeaux crisis, or during a glut as occurred at the end of the 1980s. A period of relatively high inflation, too, in contributing towards the creation of demand and putting pressure on supplies, such as occurred at the end of the 1960s and early 1980s, may also help bring about the desired preconditions for investing in wine. The emergence of new secondary fine wine markets can also promote capital growth in wine.

Wine purchased for investment must be available at a price attractive enough to give the purchaser, after a reasonable period of holding on to stock, a return on his or her initial outlay that is at least comparable with other forms of investment. It follows that the type and format of wine chosen must be intrinsically capable of increasing sufficiently in value over a period of time. Generally speaking, investment wines should be capable of ageing for a good 20 years or longer so that investors are able to hold on to the wines and sell when the market is right (although the fine wine market today seems to prefer young wines to old). Investment wines must either have an established reputation or, where the investor is

Cedar Creek vineyards on the shores of lake Okanagan in British Columbia, **Canada**, are sprayed with water, a relatively wasteful and imprecise technique compared with drip irrigation. Summers can be hot and dry here.

in a position to evaluate likely trends, be lesser-known wines with the potential to gain in value. And, where appropriate, wines should come from a good, preferably great, vintage and should be capable of being easily traded. Account should be taken of the fact that magnums and LARGE FORMAT bottles are popular with COLLECTORS.

Only a handful of wines fulfil these limited but strict criteria. Beyond wines with established reputations, the market for investment becomes too highly specialized for any but the best-informed insiders to dabble in with any degree of confidence or measure of success.

'At one moment the example of a fashionable person will make a wine held in very little estimation before and perhaps worthless in reality the prime wine of a table for a season. In England it is the fashion, or accident, which frequently makes the demand considerable for a particular species' (Cyrus Redding).

See also AUCTIONS, EN PRIMEUR, and PRICE.
A.H.L.R.

Faith, N., *The Winemasters* (2nd edn, London, 1999).
Penning-Rowsell, E., *The Wines of Bordeaux* (6th edn, London, 1989).
Redding, C., *A History and Description of Modern Wines* (3rd edn, London, 1851).

Inzolia, sometimes spelt **Insolia**, white grape variety grown mainly in Sicilia and to a much more limited extent in Toscana, where it is known as Ansonica. It was planted on a total of nearly 9,500 ha/24,100 acres of Italian vineyard in the early 2000s, although total plantings were declining. It is grown mainly in western Sicilia, where it was valued as a relatively aromatic ingredient, with Grillo, in top-quality MARSALA. Today it is more often encountered as a VARIETAL, or blended with the much more common CATARRATTO, in dry white table wines. The best examples show a certain nuttiness, the worst could do with more acid and more flavour. It may be related to the Ghirghentina of MALTA.

ion exchange, chemical process used in, for example, water softening which has useful applications in wine-making, particularly for TARTRATE stabilization, but it has the serious disadvantage of increasing the sodium content of wine and also alters the taste and aroma of wines so much that the practice is banned in the EUROPEAN UNION. It is however permitted in the manufacture of RECTIFIED CONCENTRATED GRAPE MUST.

Bird, D., *Understanding Wine Technology* (2nd edn, Newark, 2005).

IPR stands for **Indicação de Proveniencia Regulamentada**, a second-tier designated wine region in PORTUGAL. In theory, once the region has its own regulatory body, it is a candidate for promotion to DOC. Most had made the grade by the mid 2000s and a number of smaller neighbouring IPRs have merged into one DOC. Portugal's IPRs are an approximate,

if proportionately more significant, counterpart to the VDQS wines of FRANCE, with specified grape varieties, minimum alcohol content, and maximum yields.
R.J.M.

Iran, large country in the Near East once known as PERSIA, under which title details of Iran's important vinous history are to be found. Alcoholic drinks of all sorts are officially prohibited in modern Iran (see ISLAM). According to OIV statistics, total vineyard area had increased to 285,000 ha/700,000 acres by 2004, and in 2002 Iran was the second most important Asian producer of DRYING GRAPES, after Turkey.

Irancy, small Burgundy appellation near AUXERRE created in 1999 for light reds from Pinot Noir with up to 10 per cent of the local CÉSAR grapes.

Iraq, Middle Eastern country with about 52,000 ha/128,000 acres of vines planted in the late 1990s grown chiefly for DRYING GRAPES and TABLE GRAPES. In ancient times it was part of MESOPOTAMIA, where there was a thriving trade in wine. See also BAGHDAD for evidence of early medieval viticulture, and ISLAM for an explanation of Iraq's modern relationship with wine.

Ireland, or **Irish Republic**, country with several small vineyards (not dissimilar to those of ENGLAND). Ireland may well have been a more faithful customer of GASCON wines than England. Several Irishmen have played a part in the history of Bordeaux wine: the BARTONS provide one example, and the Lynch of PAUILLAC's Ch Lynch-Bages was also Irish.

iron, a mineral element essential for healthy vine growth in trace amounts. Normally enough iron is taken up from the soil to meet the plant's needs, but iron deficiency in leaves can cause lime-induced CHLOROSIS, the well-known disorder of the vine when it is grown on wet, alkaline soils. Leaves turn yellow; this occurs because iron is unavailable for the manufacture of chlorophyll. In alkaline soils (rich in LIMESTONE), iron is in a chemical form which makes it unavailable to the vine roots. Soils can be measured for their ability to provide sufficient iron to the vine (see SOIL ALKALINITY).

Fertilizer containing iron cannot simply be added to the soil as it will in turn be made unavailable by the soil alkalinity; the answer is to add iron in a protected form, such as a chelate, a form in which iron is bound in an organic complex preventing it from oxidation. Although expensive, such chelate forms can be both applied to the soil and sprayed on the leaves. Most commonly, however, lime-induced chlorosis is overcome by using a suitable ROOTSTOCK.
R.E.S.

Champagnol, F., *Éléments de physiologie de la vigne et de viticulture générale* (St-Gely-du-Fesc, 1984).

Irouléguy, unique and isolated French wine appellation in BASQUE country in the extreme south west of the country fuelled almost entirely by national pride. The language and lettering used on labels here are distinctively Basque, with a heavy sprinkling of Xs. These vineyards of lower NAVARRA and the Spanish TXAKOLI are the last officially recognized vestiges of what was once a thriving wine industry (which can now be traced as far as URUGUAY). Although there were 470 ha/1,160 acres of vines in 1906, vines were almost abandoned until the late 20th century. An APPELLATION CONTRÔLÉE was granted in 1970, and by the early 1990s, the vineyard area was once again expanding. About 190 ha of scattered vineyards on soils including limestone, schist, red clay, and gravel are now cultivated by about 60 vine-growers (one of them the winemaker at Ch PÉTRUS, no less) in rolling pastoral countryside in the far western Pyrenees, up to more than 400 m/1,300 ft above sea level, under heavy Atlantic climatic influence in the west. The vines are protected from north winds and enjoy more sunshine than most French wine regions. The local Tannat grape is blended with Cabernet Sauvignon or Cabernet Franc for light, crisp reds and much of the wine produced is a fragrant, relatively substantial rosé. Domaines Brana and Arretxea are two of the most renowned producers outside the CO-OPERATIVE, making distinctively fragrant white wine from PETIT COURBU, GROS MANSENG, and PETIT MANSENG.

irrigation, the application of water to growing plants such as vines, effectively a man-made simulation of RAINFALL, which can be useful in drier regions. Few vineyard practices are more maligned than irrigation.

In its commonly visualized form, irrigation is carried out in hot, arid regions, and employs heavy furrow or sprinkler irrigation to maximize yield for TABLE GRAPES, DRYING GRAPES, and BULK wines. That is the background for the widely held view, especially in France, that only DRYLAND VITICULTURE can produce outstanding wines, and that irrigation inevitably reduces quality.

Widespread adoption of drip (or trickle) irrigation since the 1960s has now greatly blurred the distinction. Although originally developed for and used in true arid climates, such as in ISRAEL, the technique has found its major viticultural use for supplementary watering. That is, the vineyards rely mainly on natural rainfall, and irrigation is used to make up deficits. It is extensively used in MEDITERRANEAN CLIMATES which are regularly dry during the critical ripening period; or else in climates with more uniform rainfall but which might periodically suffer from DROUGHT. In both of these climates the capacity to avoid severe WATER STRESS potentially improves grape and wine quality, provided that irrigation does not excessively stimulate vine growth and yield. See also SOIL AND WINE QUALITY; SOIL WATER.

Irrigation is one of the oldest agricultural and viticultural techniques and was clearly practised, for example, in Ancient EGYPT, and in Ancient ARMENIA too. The need for irrigation depends entirely on CLIMATE. Where EVAPORATION is high and rainfall low, vines suffer water stress. Many of the world's vineyards are in Mediterranean climates where the rain falls mostly over the winter, and the summers are dry and hot. Water stress in the vineyard during the summer depends on how much of the winter rain can be stored in the soil. Soils such as sand and gravel can hold only limited amounts of water, silts and clays much more. Vines with only shallow roots because of restricting soil conditions also experience water stress. On the other hand, some soils are able to store so much water that vines can grow without significant water stress, despite long periods without any rain. Typically these are deep loamy or silt soils, and are commonly found on valley floors. Some of the deeper soils of California's Napa valley are representative, and these may be found side by side with shallower soils where there is a need to irrigate.

While a modicum of water stress is desirable to encourage fruit RIPENING and enhance wine quality, excessive water stress has serious implications (see WATER STRESS). In these circumstances, irrigation applied in a restricted fashion can actually improve quality (see PARTIAL ROOTZONE DRYING and REGULATED DEFICIT IRRIGATION).

It is easy to understand irrigation's notoriety, however. When vines have access to generous supplies of water they grow rapidly, producing long shoots, big leaves, big berries, and where YIELD is increased, then ripening is delayed. All of these are features of vineyards which produce poor-quality wine grapes. Yield is also greatly increased; depending on the severity of the water stress, irrigation may improve yield by 300 per cent or more.

Irrigation is widely practised in the New World but less frequently in the Old (although irrigation is commonplace in some of the oldest vineyards in the world in the Near East and central Asia). In principle it is banned in much of the EUROPEAN UNION other than for young vines, but this is a restriction which is easy, if initially quite expensive, to flout. While some still believe that irrigation is intrinsically inimical to wine quality, and there are many examples of deliberate over-irrigation, some of those who deliberately install irrigation systems in southern Europe are motivated by the desire to make better wine (see COSTERS DEL SEGRE, for example). The modern view is that excessive water stress can be as damaging to quality as can excessive irrigation and that in drier regions carefully controlled irrigation can be a useful technique for maximizing yield and/or quality.

The mechanics

Soils vary in their ability to store water. The 'field capacity' is the maximum amount of water a thoroughly, deeply wetted soil will retain after normal drainage. The driest moisture content at which vines can extract water from the soil is called the 'permanent wilting point'. At this point, the plant will not recover if water is applied. Between these two limits is the amount of available water in a soil. The ability to store water is highest for silt soils and lowest for coarse sands and gravels. The latter soils are preferred for fine wine production as there is less likelihood of excessive water supplies to the vine following rainfall.

The irrigation strategy employed by a vine-grower depends on his or her ambitions for quality and yield. For maximum yields the vines are not allowed to experience water stress at any stage of the growth cycle, and vines are irrigated to maintain moisture levels near field capacity. Such strategies are common for bulk wine production, which is often undertaken in hot, dry climates. Irrigation amount is measured as a depth of water applied: for unrestricted irrigation in a hot climate, up to 800 mm/31 in of water can be applied during the growing season. Smaller quantities of water are applied to vines producing better-quality wine. The regions in which they are grown are typically cooler and more humid, so the evaporation is less, and also the rainfall is often higher. Further, it is desirable to have the vines experience a little water stress, so application amounts can be as low as 100 mm/4 in, or in some years even zero, depending on the weather.

There are several ways of deciding when to irrigate. In desert regions where the climate is relatively constant, such as much of Argentina, California, and inland Australia, irrigation is generally done by the calendar. The interval between irrigations can be longer in the early spring and late autumn, but the vineyards are irrigated most often in midsummer, when evaporation is highest. Weather stations, now commonly seen on many vineyards, are used to measure evaporation. In areas with more rainfall, and especially where it is irregular, irrigation has to be much more carefully timed according to measurements of either the soil moisture or, less frequently, the plant water stress.

Soil moisture can be measured in several ways. The appearance and feel of the soil can be a useful guide, but while the surface is dry the subsoil can be still wet. Tensiometers are ceramic cups connected to a water column which creates a vacuum as water is extracted into the dry soil. Gypsum blocks contain an electrode; as the soil dries the electrical resistance changes. Neutron moisture meters are a recent irrigation aid by which an aluminium tube is placed permanently in the soil, and a neutron source lowered into it. The meter measures the spread of neutrons from a source, which depends on soil moisture. More recent equipment and methods such as capacitance probes and time domain reflectometry, developed in the 1990s, allow easier and more accurate measurement of soil moisture. Data may be logged in the field or transmitted by telemetry to the viticulturist's computer.

Plant stress can be measured by the experienced viticulturist observing stress symptoms such as drooping shoot tips, tendrils, and leaves. Leaf temperature can also provide a guide since, as vines become water stressed, leaves facing the sun are heated significantly above air temperature. This temperature difference can be determined by feel, or by a remote sensor which can measure routinely and non-destructively, but not in wind or cloud. Water stress can also be measured by the so-called PRESSURE BOMB, which is common in California. See WATER STRESS for this and other methods of measurement.

The amount of water applied depends on many factors. Water supplies are limited in many vineyard areas, so water is used sparingly and only to avoid the worst effects of severe water stress. Where water is not limited and maximum yield is the aim, then sufficient water should be applied to bring the vine root system back to field capacity. This can be calculated by measuring either evaporation or soil moisture. Much more difficult is to apply a limited amount of water so that a desired level of vine water stress is maintained to promote ripening and improve quality. However, this is the common aim of vine-growers interested to maximize wine quality.

Methods of irrigation vary considerably. The ancient method, still used in some desert areas for bulk wine production, is **flood irrigation**. Water fed from a supply canal is run down the rows and is soaked up by the dry ground. For this to work, the vineyard floor must be flat and the rows not too long. Furrow irrigation (see ARGENTINA) is similar but allows greater control. More recent developments have been **sprinkler** and DRIP IRRIGATION (also known as trickle irrigation). Sprinklers are typically about 20 m/65 ft apart and span several rows. Dripper supply lines, usually long plastic tubes, are placed down each row, usually with one dripper at each vine. Both sprinkler and drip irrigation are capable of delivering exact amounts of water fairly uniformly over a vineyard. Even a well-operated flood system is less accurate.   R.E.S.

Coombe, B. G., and Dry, P. R. (eds.), Viticulture, ii: Practices (Adelaide, 1992).

Van Leeuwen, C., Choné, X., Tregoat, O., and Gaudillère, J.-P., 'The use of physiological indicators to assess vine water uptake and to manage vineyard irrigation', The Australian Grapegrower & Winemaker, 449 (June 2001), 18–24.

www.fao.org/docrep/004/Y3655E/y3655e11.htm

Irsay Oliver, aromatic, relatively recent white vine CROSSING grown in SLOVAKIA and also popular in the CZECH REPUBLIC and HUNGARY as **Irsai Olivér**. This eastern European cross of Pozsony × Pearl of Csaba was originally developed in the 1930s as a table grape. It ripens extremely early and reliably (although it is prone to POWDERY MILDEW) and produces relatively heavy, but intensely aromatic, wines strongly reminiscent of MUSCAT.

Isabella, sometimes **Isabelle**, widely distributed and widely planted VITIS *labrusca* AMERICAN HYBRID of unknown origin. It is said to have been named after a southern belle, Mrs Isabella Gibbs, and to have been developed in South Carolina in 1816. It can withstand tropical and semi-tropical conditions and has been planted all over Portugal, Ukraine, Japan, and the southern hemisphere, notably in BRAZIL, where it is by a substantial margin the most common vine variety. In New York state, it was one of the first hybrids to be planted after PHYLLOXERA's late 19th-century devastation but it has largely been replaced by CONCORD. New plantings were banned in France in 1934. The vine is high yielding but the wines are very obviously FOXY.

Ischia, island and tourist destination in the bay of Naples in the Italian region of CAMPANIA (see map under ITALY) which has managed to preserve a small part of the vineyards which once covered a significant part of the island. The DOC Ischia wine, produced from 50 ha/ 125 acres of vineyards, exists in both red and white versions: the former from GUARNACCIA grapes plus some PIEDIROSSO and a little BARBERA, the latter from Forastera with Biancolella and others. A Bianco Superiore, with at least 50 per cent Biancolella, is also produced with both lower yields and more alcohol. D'Ambra, the island's principal producer, also makes 100 per cent VARIETAL wines from Forastera, Biancolella, and Piedirosso (the last of which is called by its local name Per'e Palummo); originally marketed as VINO DA TAVOLA but now DOC wines, they showed marked improvement in the 1980s and indicate that Biancolella and Piedirosso have an interesting future.   D.T. & D.C.G.

isinglass, a particularly pure PROTEIN obtained from the bladders of sturgeon and other freshwater fish that has been used for FINING wine for centuries. As early as 1660, King Charles II of England regulated the use of isinglass by merchant VINTNERS.

Like GELATIN, isinglass reacts with the excess TANNINS in harsh young red wines. Although expensive, and difficult to prepare, isinglass is also occasionally used in the CLARIFICATION of white wines to be bottled without a final polish FILTRATION, as it has about the same clarifying property. However, there is a noticeable trend away from the use of animal-derived products for fining, mainly in the interests of VEGETARIANS AND VEGANS.   A.D.W.

Islam, the Muslim religion founded by the Prophet Muhammad (spelt variously Mohammed, Mohamet, etc.) in the 7th century AD, has had, and continues to have, the most profound effect on the history of wine. The consumption of any alcoholic drink was prohibited by Muhammad so that wine is neither officially consumed nor enthusiastically produced in most of the Near and Middle East, some of North Africa, and parts of Asia. Wine is therefore no longer produced in much of the land most closely associated with the ORIGINS OF VITICULTURE, and the rise of Islamic fundamentalism in the late 20th century represents a considerable constraint on the world's wine consumption.

Muhammad's prohibition

Wine (in Arabic *khamr*) was not prohibited from the outset of the Prophet Muhammad's preaching (between 610 and 632). Islam, both dogma and practice, emerged initially as the product of continuous revelation (the Qur'ān, often spelt Koran) during the Prophet's lifetime and his responses to the vicissitudes of the early Islamic community (these are recorded in the *hadīth* literature and constitute the second most substantive source of Islamic law). There are four verses in the Qur'ān which refer to wine; the first is quite positive (*Sūra* 16, verse 69): 'We give you the fruit of the palm and the vine from which you derive intoxicants and wholesome food.' The following two verses are cautionary but are not considered by Muslim jurists to enjoin abstinence from alcohol (Sura 2, verse 216, and Sura 4, verse 46): 'They will ask you concerning wine and gambling. Answer, in both there is great sin and also some things of use unto men, but their sinfulness is greater than their use.' 'Believers do not approach your prayers when you are drunk, but wait till you can grasp the meaning of your words; nor when you are polluted—unless you are travelling the road—until you have washed yourself.'

There is consensus amongst medieval Muslim jurists, however, that the fourth verse, which came in response to disturbances in the community, was tantamount to an injunction (although it is not couched in the same language as the prohibition on other dietary items, such as pork) (Sura 5, verse 92) 'Believers, wine and games of chance, idols and divining arrows are abominations devised by Satan. Avoid them so that you may prosper. Satan seeks to stir up enmity and hatred among you by means of wine and gambling and to keep you from the Remembrance of Allah and from your prayers.'

Although this verse was understood universally to articulate prohibition, there was dissension when it came to establishing the precise nature of forbidden wine. *Khamr*, the word used in the Qur'ānic verses, is the Arabic generic term for wine. There were, however, many types of fermented beverages known to pre-Islamic and later Arabs. The second caliph,

'Umar ibn al-Khattāb, is reported in the *hadīth* literature to have settled the question: 'Wine has been prohibited by the Qur'ān; it comes from five kinds of fruits: from grapes, from dates, from honey, from wheat and from barley; wine is what obscures the intellect.' The issue remained whether beverages prepared in a way different from wine were prohibited. For example *tilā'* appears to have been allowed by 'Umar; this was a kind of syrup made from grape juice which was cooked until two-thirds of it evaporated. However, the same source relates that 'Umar punished a man who became drunk on this concoction.

Another tradition quotes the Prophet stipulating the kinds of vessels in which fruit juice beverages could be made or stored: '. . . I forbid four things: *dubbā'* (a gourd), *hantam* (glazed wine jars), *muzaffat* (a vessel smeared with pitch) and *naqīr*.' When asked about the nature of *naqīr* he answered: 'It is a palmtrunk which you hollow out; then you pour small dates into it and upon them water. When the process of fermentation has finished, you drink it with the effect that a man hits his cousin with the sword.' The community was, therefore, enjoined to store fruit beverages in leather skins that prevented fermentation.

Nabīdh, date wine, is the drink about which there has been the most controversy. Several traditions state that this beverage was amongst the drinks prepared by Muhammad's wives and drunk by him: 'Aisha said: 'We used to prepare *nabīdh* . . . in a skin; we took a handful of dates or a handful of raisins, cast it into the skin and poured water upon it. The *nabīdh* we prepared in this way in the morning was drunk by him in the evening; and when we prepared it in the evening he drank it the next morning.' Despite this, three of the four Sunni schools of law as well as the Shiah prohibit *nabīdh*. The Hanafi school allows it when used in moderation, although intoxication is still prohibited.

Most jurists now consider discussions about types of wine to be secondary casuistry. What is deemed crucial, on the basis of *hadīth*, is that any beverage which intoxicates should not be consumed.

Despite the Qur'ānic injunction, even those types of wine recognized to be *harām* continued to be imbibed in many periods of Islamic history; this is best reflected in the rich tradition of Bacchic poetry which had its roots in pre-Islamic Arabia but flowered as a poetic genre in the early Abbasid period (see ARAB POETS). This canon of literature is largely mimetic and most certainly reflects the drinking habits of a significant sector of the Islamic community, notably—in some cases—the caliph and his entourage.

The wines consumed

Both Arabic poetry and other sources such as agricultural works tell us much about wine as a product. Although wine was produced in al-Tā'if in the Hijaz (156 km/97 miles south east of Mecca) from pre-Islamic times, it was imported mainly by Jewish and Christian merchants from SYRIA and MESOPOTAMIA. With the expansion of Islam, Arabs were introduced to finer wines grown mostly in the Christian monasteries of Iraq. 'Ana in upper Mesopotamia is only one of many areas that were known for viticulture. It was in the taverns around monasteries and in the monasteries themselves that most wine was consumed, as well as some of the outlying towns of Baghdad, districts of Baghdad itself (especially al-Karkh), and not infrequently in the caliphal court at the very heart of the Islamic community.

The most lauded of beverages were four types of wine—white, yellow, red, and black—made from both red and white grapes, from a variety of vine varieties whose names are preserved in medieval agricultural books (Heine gives details of 21 of them, including KIŠMIŠ). In poetry, the date wine *nabīdh* was despised (cf. above). Grape wine was always mixed with water before drinking (one-third wine to two-thirds water, about the same dilution as in Ancient GREECE). The poets were fascinated by the bubbles which this mixing produced; although wine was celebrated as an ancient product ('It has aged since the time of Adam'), it may be that it was often very young and thus still fermenting when consumed. There were three classes of age: young wine, which was less than a year old, low in alcohol, and had little bouquet; middle-aged, which was a year old; and old wine, which one source claims was usually sour. P.K.

Heine, P., *Weinstudien, Untersuchungen zu Anbau, Produktion und Konsums des Weins im arabisch-islamischen Mittelalter* (Wiesbaden, 1982).
'Khamr', *The Encyclopaedia of Islam*, vol. iv (new edn, Leiden, 1978).
Kueny, K., *The Rhetoric of Sobriety: Wine in Early Islam* (Albany, NY, 2001).

Effect of Islam on wine history

In the Middle Ages, Muslim conquest by no means outlawed wine production, however. Muhammad's caliph successors were based in Damascus and, subsequently, in BAGHDAD, which had its own local wine industry. Wine production continued in Moorish Spain (the Alhambra built by the Moors in 14th century Granada has its Puerta del Vino), Portugal, North Africa, Sicilia, Sardegna, Corsica, Greece, Crete, and other eastern Mediterranean islands, usually under the heavily taxed auspices of Jews or Christians, even though they were ruled by Muslims. The Ottoman Turks made repeated raids on various eastern European wine regions in the Middle Ages, and, if the TOKAJI legend is based on fact, could therefore be said to have been indirectly responsible for the discovery of BOTRYTIZED WINES. For some more details, see SPAIN, GREECE, and CYPRUS.

It is because of the dissemination of Muslim techniques associated with alchemy that the art of DISTILLATION is said to have spread through western Europe. Indeed the words ALCOHOL is of Arab origin.

isoamyl acetate is an ESTER present in all fermented beverages. At higher concentrations, it is sometimes associated with banana-like aromas, and is often found in cool-fermented whites wines and red wines that have undergone CARBONIC MACERATION. Research suggests that this ester may have an influence on the varietal aroma of certain wines such as PINOTAGE and on the aftertaste of certain young Alsace wines.

Francis, I. L., and Newton, J. L., 'Determining wine aroma from compositional data', *Australian Journal of Grape and Wine Research*, 11 (2005), 114–26.

isoamyl alcohol. See FUSEL OILS.

isobutyl-methoxypyrazine, more properly, **2-isobutyl-3-methoxypyrazine,** or **IBMP,** smells of green or bell peppers and grass and is found in all green matter. The perception threshold in red and white wines is 6 ng/l and the concentration is higher in unripe grapes with low sun exposure because it is very sensitive to UV light. This is why it is more often found in late-ripening varieties such as Cabernets Sauvignon and Franc and Carmenère. 6 ng/l is very common in Sauvignon Blanc, where it is not generally considered a fault. It is possible to distinguish between natural IBMP and similar tasting artificial flavourings using isotope analysis but not if the additive is an exact copy of the natural compound. Such tests are very expensive and a huge amount of wine is needed to produce enough compound for testing.

Isonzo, small DOC in the extreme north east of Italy in the FRIULI region. The plain to the south of the COLLIO hills formed by the Isonzo river on its way to the Adriatic is, from a geological point of view, split in two. The left bank of the Isonzo river, the part closest to the sea, is like GRAVE DEL FRIULI a mixture of gravel and soil formed by fluvial and glacial deposits. The subzone on the right bank, inland towards COLLI ORIENTALI, is a less fertile red gravel, and produces Isonzo's finest wines. This distinction has been recognized in the DOC regulations since 2003, with wines from the right bank being entitled to put Rive Alte on the label, while those from the left bank can use the subzone Rive Giare.

The zone includes just over 1,300 ha/ 3,210 acres of vineyard. TOCAI Friulano (220 ha/ 545 acres in 2005), PINOT GRIGIO (200 ha), SAUVIGNON BLANC (150 ha), and PINOT BIANCO (120 ha) are the significant white varieties; MERLOT (210 ha) and CABERNET (185 ha, with a dominance of CABERNET FRANC) are the important red grapes planted. As in the rest of Friuli, the wines tend to be produced as VARIETALS. The whites are generally fresh, simple and fruity, while the reds are soft and forward.

The flat plains of Isonzo, encircled by mountains to the north and east and running into the sea in the south, have long persuaded outsiders that the zone is little different from its southern neighbour, Grave del Friuli. However, the good DRAINAGE provided by the gravel soils, and a gap in the mountains to the north east, through which flows a cool moderating breeze, sets it apart from Grave. The zone at its best, in the Rive Alte subzone, is capable of producing grapes as good as those from Collio and Colli Orientali. In the past, some of the region's top producers have bought grapes in Isonzo. The high prices paid for the grapes held back the emergence of the zone's producers, but today the likes of Vie di Romans, Lis Neris, Pierpaolo Pecorari, Ronco del Gelso, Mauro Drius, Borgo San Daniele, and I Feudi di Romans are producing wines that rival the best from the rest of Friuli.

D.T. & D.C.G.

isopropyl-methoxypyrazine (IPMP). See METHOXYPYRAZINES.

Israel, the biblical land of milk and honey (see CANAAN), lays claim to being the cradle of the world's wine industry. In the eastern Mediterranean on the shores of the Levant, it leapt to international prominence only since new, cooler vineyards were planted in the disputed territory of the Golan Heights in the early 1980s and the Upper Galilee in the 1990s. According to 2002 OIV statistics, Israel had about 7,000 ha/17,300 acres of vineyard in total and was producing about 60,000 hl/1,585,000 gal of wine.

History

The fruit of the vine was economically important in the Holy Land and was designated one of the seven blessed species of fruit specified in the book of Deuteronomy (see BIBLE). The dangers of immoderate wine consumption were fully recognized, and excess strictly forbidden. Vine-growing continued under Christian rule, even after the destruction of the Second Temple in Jerusalem, until AD 636, when the spread of ISLAM brought about destruction of the vineyards. The CRUSADERS temporarily restored wine production between AD 1100 and 1300, but with the exile of the Jews, vine-growing ceased.

At the end of the 19th century, Jews returned to the Holy Land from the Diaspora, and 1882 saw the beginning of the modern era with the support of Baron Edmond de ROTHSCHILD. His massive benefaction made viticulture an important part of the agricultural resettlement programmes. French experts provided expertise. Two wineries with deep underground cellars were built, Rishon Le Zion in 1890 and Zichron Ya'acov in 1892, which remain the largest wineries in Israel. The Société Co-operative Vigneronne des Grandes Caves was founded in 1906, trading under the name Carmel. The

Rothschilds owned the wineries until 1957, when they were donated to the co-operative. The industry grew and thrived, exporting KOSHER wine to Jewish communities throughout the world for over 100 years.

The quality revolution began in the 1980s: planting vineyards with noble varieties in cooler, higher altitude areas, combined with internationally trained winemakers and expertise, originally from California, had dramatic effects. Yarden wines from the Golan Heights Winery and those of Domaine du Castel first won internation acclaim in the 1980s and 1990s respectively.

Climate

The vine thrives in Israel's MEDITERRANEAN conditions. The seasons divide in two: the winter with rain from October to March (with occasional snow on higher vineyards), and the hot, humid summer with virtually no precipitation from April to October. DRIP IRRIGATION is essential to nourish the vines, which are pruned to provide maximum shade for the grapes from the harsh sunlight. Much harvesting is mechanical, the white varieties being picked mainly at night to minimize temperatures.

Geography

The area dedicated to vines has increased rapidly to 4,000 ha/10,000 acres, with the cost and scarcity of WATER together with a booming wine market encouraging many fruit growers to switch to vines.

Israel's viticulture is divided into five regions: Galilee in northern Israel is the best quality region, including the Upper and Lower Galilee and the Golan Heights. The Shomron covers the coastal region south of Haifa, including Mount Carmel, and the Sharon Plain is the largest wine region. The Samson region comprises the central coastal plain and the Judean foothills. The Judean Hills stretch from the mountains north of Jerusalem southwards to the Yatir Forest. The Negev, the southern, desert area of Israel, includes Ramat Arad and central Negev. More than 80 per cent of vineyards lie in the Shomron, Samson and Galilee regions, although many of the newer vineyards are being planted in the Upper Galilee and Judean foothills.

Soils vary from sandy and TERRA ROSSA on the coast, limestone and chalk on the stony hills, and volcanic in the north.

Vine varieties

Cabernet Sauvignon, Merlot, Sauvignon Blanc, and Chardonnay have been planted with considerable success. As elsewhere, Syrah is the coming variety. Cabernet Franc, Pinot Noir, Gewurztraminer, Riesling and Muscat Canelli are also grown. There are no indigenous varieties although EMERALD RIESLING has enjoyed exceptional commercial success in Israel, and Muscat of Alexandria is planted in

Medterranean areas. Local crossing ARGAMAN is used mainly in inexpensive blends. The high-altitude vineyards tend to produce much more elegant wines than those made in the coastal areas, where acid levels tend to be low.

Modern wine production

Less than 15 per cent of modern wine production is of the sacramental wines which gave Israeli and kosher wines a bad name for so long.

The dominant and historic producer remains Carmel, with nearly 50 per cent of production, followed by Barkan Wine Cellars and Golan Heights Winery. These three wineries control over 80 per cent of the domestic market, although there are about 20 commercial wineries in total. In addition, the 1990s saw the burgeoning of well over 100 much smaller enterprises, few of them producing kosher wines. Since 2000, the largest wineries responded. Carmel built three new boutique wineries near key vineyards. Barkan bought Segal Wines, opened a new winery and was then taken over by the country's largest brewery, while the Golan Heights Winery built a new winery in the Upper Galilee.

Most Israeli wines exported are produced by either Carmel or Golan Heights, followed by Barkan. Other, smaller wineries exporting high-quality wines include Dalton, Galil Mountain, Recanati, and Tishbi and the finest of the BOUTIQUE wineries Domaine du Castel, Flam, Margalit, Saslove, and Yatir. The US is the biggest export market.

See also KOSHER (although by no means all Israel's wine is kosher). A.S.M.

Ben Yosef, M., *The Bible of Israel Wines* (Moshav Ben-Shemen, 2002).

Gal-Cohen, T., *The Wine Route—A Tour Of Israel's Wineries* (Tel Aviv, 2003) (Hebrew only).

Rogov, D., *Rogov's Guide to Israeli Wines 2005* (London, 2004).

www.israelwines.co.il

Italia, TABLE GRAPE from which wine has sometimes been made in Australia. DNA PROFILING at CONEGLIANO confirmed it is a crossing between Bicane and MUSCAT HAMBURG.

Italian Riesling, or **Italian Rizling**; sometimes **Italianski Rizling**, white grape variety. See RIESLING ITALICO and WELSCHRIESLING.

Italy, with FRANCE one of the world's two mammoth wine producers, sometimes producing as much as 60 million hl/1,584 million gal a year. Italy has more land under vine than any other country other than France and SPAIN, although thanks to the European VINE PULL SCHEME, the total has been reduced from close to 1.4 million ha/3.4 million acres in the early 1990s to a forecast 856,000 ha/2.1 million acres by 2004. Italy routinely exports more wine than any other country, including

France—much of it inexpensive wine for BLENDING in and possible re-export from France and Germany.

Unlike either France or Spain, however, the vine is cultivated virtually everywhere in the Italian peninsula, from the alps in the north to islands that are closer to the coast of North Africa than to the Italian mainland (see map overleaf). Viticulture impinges on the national consciousness, on the national imagination, and on daily life in a way that is hardly conceivable to those not accustomed to the Mediterranean way of life and its dietary trinity of bread, olive oil, and wine; until the late 1980s, it was unthinkable for Italians to sit down and eat without wine on the table.

The Italian's relationship to wine is not necessarily a hedonistic one. The average Italian is far from a connoisseur of fine bottles, but is rather the heir of thousands of years of vineyard cultivation and wine-making. There are few Italians without some conception—though the conception itself may be naïve, foolish, banal, or simply wrong-headed—of how grapes are grown and transformed into wine.

The result is what might be called the Italian paradox: a country with a plurimillennial tradition of wine, a country whose Roman legions spread viticulture to a large part of western Europe, a country where wine is omnipresent in the nation's life and customs, is also a country where wine is, for the most part, taken for granted in the national consciousness. While France and Germany played a major role from the beginning of the age of modern wine—an era in which wine circulates in bottles with labels which identify both its provenance and its maker—wine in most of Italy, with the exception of Piemonte, Toscana, and a few other scattered areas, was sold in bulk until well after the Second World War. Little of the country's better wine was exported until the 1970s, and a significant part of the export trade was in important volumes of wine for the large colonies of Italian emigrants in northern Europe, in the United States, and in South America (Argentina, for example, was a major market for Barolo immediately after the Second World War). Knowledge of non-Italian viticulture and OENOLOGY was virtually non-existent in Italy, and circulation of foreign wines was confined to a tiny élite in the country's major cities. Luigi VERONELLI's book at the end of the 1950s was the first general treatment of Italian wines in over 350 years, since Andrea Bacci's opus of 1595. And even in the early 1990s, wine appreciation was an activity of very little significance to Italians.

To consider the history of wine in Italy is to consider the history of Italy itself, however; wine and Italian civilization are virtually synonymous. The Ancient Greek name for much of Italy already acknowledged the importance of viticulture to the peninsula: OENOTRIA, or 'land of trained vines'. D.T.

Italy

SWITZERLAND

AUSTRIA

HUNGARY

Alps

Alps

VALLE
D'AOSTA

TRENTINO-
ALTO ADIGE
Bolzano •

FRIULI

SLOVENIA

Novara •
Vercelli •

LOMBARDIA

Trento

Udine •

Milan
Pavia •

VENETO

Gorizia •

Turin •

Verona •

Venice •

Trieste •

CROATIA

Asti •
Alba •

Piacenza •

Po

PIEMONTE

LIGURIA

EMILIA-
ROMAGNA

Bologna •

Genoa •

Ligurian

Sea

SAN
MARINO

Florence •

Bolgheri •

TOSCANA

Apennines

Ancona •

MARCHE

BOSNIA AND
HERZEGOVINA

Adriatic Sea

CORSICA

Siena •

Montalcino •

Perugia •

UMBRIA
Orvieto •

Elba •

LAZIO

ABRUZZO

Rome •
Frascati •

MOLISE

SARDEGNA

Oristano •

Naples •
Ischia

CAMPANIA

Bari •
PUGLIA

BASILICATA

Taranto •

Cagliari •

Capri

Tyrrhenian

Sea

CALABRIA

Lipari •

Mediterranean Sea

Palermo •

Marsala •

SICILIA

TUNISIA

Pantelleria

0   200 km

Italy, Magna Graecia, and Roman Italy

The pastoral past of the tribes of Italy may be reflected in the use of milk in LIBATIONS rather than wine (see PLINY, *Natural History*, 14. 88), but viticulture and wine will have made an early impact as part of GREEK and ETRUSCAN culture (see ORIGINS OF VITICULTURE for more details). SICILIA may have played a key role in the development of viticulture on the mainland. The Sicilian Murgentina grape, which flourished in volcanic soils, was successfully transplanted near POMPEII on the slopes of Vesuvius, where it was called locally the Pompeian grape. This in turn was introduced further north around Clusium (Chiusi) in Etruria, where it proved particularly prolific. Again, the Eugenia, the high-quality grape from Tauromenium (Taormina in Sicilia), successfully found a home in the Colli ALBANI south of Rome, but was a failure elsewhere.

Incidental mentions by the historians suggest that by the time that Hannibal invaded Italy in the late 3rd century BC, vines could be found throughout the peninsula, from beyond the Po valley, down the Adriatic coast, and in CAMPANIA; but little wine was of particular note before the middle of the 2nd century BC according to Pliny (*Natural History*, 14. 87). It was Pliny, too, who in a key passage (*Natural History*, 14. 94 ff.) made a very acute observation. He noted that OPIMIAN wine of the year when Opimius was consul (121 BC) was accepted as one of the greatest vintages, but that this applied generally to wine in that year, not to any particular CRUS. An edict of the censors of 89 BC imposing a price limit on costly wines refers only to wine made from the Aminnean grape (see ANCIENT VINE VARIETIES), not to any estates.

The creation of the grands crus of Roman Italy belongs to the 1st centuries BC and AD. This fact is more or less confirmed by ARCHAEOLOGY. The expansion of villas connected with wine production and overseas trade, as evidenced by the AMPHORAE, may have begun in the late 3rd or 2nd centuries, but the real growth is later. Three factors were involved in this development. First there was the exceptional growth of the city of ROME, which created a huge market for wine. Secondly, there was the opening up of trade routes to GAUL and SPAIN, which stimulated the growth of vineyards in the areas immediately behind ports; and finally there was the interest of the Roman aristocracy with an ever-increasing level of wealth to invest. So it is no accident that the areas in which the great wines of Roman Italy developed were LAZIO and Campania, regions within easy reach of the Roman market and where the Roman élites had their country homes. In the Colli Albani, the mainly sweet wines of Alba itself were highly prized, as were those of Velletri. The Emperor Augustus gave a boost to the wines of Setia (Sezze) by favouring them above all others. Beyond Terracina, CAECUBAN, produced in the marshes around the Lago di Fondi, was in the very front rank

of wines. The wines from the slopes of Monte Massico, particularly the various types of FALERNIAN, long remained the most favoured. In northern and central Campania, the wines of Cales, along with Gauranum (from Monte Barbaro, overlooking the northern end of the bay of Naples) had reputations which were close to that of Falernian. Then on the bay of Naples itself were the noted vineyards of Pompeii and the Sorrento peninsula. The very light, white wine of this region, SURRENTINUM, made from the Aminnean Germana Minor grape, enjoyed very high status in the 1st century AD, although it did not win universal approval ('high-quality vinegar' was the view of the Emperor Tiberius).

Few wines outside Lazio and Campania ever approached the status of these wines and none exceeded it. On the north western side of Italy, Etruria (TOSCANA) had a great variety of wines, but only those of Luni and Genoa in Liguria made much impact. In Magna Graecia (southern Italy), a number of areas produced wines of some note, including Tarentine (from Taranto). The Adriatic coast of Italy presents an interesting test case. It would be difficult to guess at the importance of the wines of this area simply from the rather limited literary evidence. But the evidence of amphorae shows that PUGLIA and Ancient Calabria and, perhaps, areas further up the east coast exported wine to all the countries round the Adriatic and to the Greek world from the 2nd century. Brindisi certainly was the focus for a flourishing export trade. Further north, Hadrianum, the wine of Atri, and the adjoining Praetuttian vineyards (roughly the northern area of Montepulciano d'ABRUZZO) achieved a high reputation in the 1st century AD. A significant development is to be associated with the time of the first Roman emperor, Augustus (31 BC–AD 14); this was the increasing prominence of northern wines from the Po valley and beyond. The distinctive type of amphora which carried the wines of this region was sometimes stamped with the names of men who rose to prominence in the entourage of Augustus and had estates in the region. These amphorae doubtless carried Praetuttian, the wines of Ancona, of Ravenna, and of the towns along the Via Aemilia. VIRGIL, Augustus' court poet, reflected the emperor's liking for the wines of Verona (see VENETO), made from the Rhaetic grape (although, because of its distance from the sea, it is unlikely this area's wines achieved more than a passing prominence). Augustus' wife Livia did her bit to promote the wines of the FRIULI region, by publicly ascribing her longevity to an exclusive diet of the wine of Pucinum, beyond Aquileia.

Archaeology has combined with history to give us this picture of viticulture in Roman Italy, which differed in significant ways from the current scene. It should always be remembered that, as now, there would be an enormous consumption of undistinguished, local

wines, which never travelled, and are rarely to be identified in the historical record.   J.J.P.

Pliny, *Natural History*, trans. by H Rackham (Loeb Classical Library, 1945), Book 14.

Tchernia, A., *Le Vin de l'Italie romaine* (Rome, 1986).

Medieval history

The fall of the Roman empire did not put an end to viticulture in Italy, but barbarization and economic collapse meant the disappearance of the market for fine wines. With Goths, then Lombards, in Rome and most of the north, and the remains of the empire administered precariously from Ravenna, Falernian, and Caecuban had become distant memories. Yet the Italian diet remained based on bread, olives, and wine, and so wine continued to be grown as one of the necessities of Mediterranean life.

The Dark Ages were a period of economic stagnation; except for the importation of luxury goods from the Near East, trade was local. We know little about the wine that was grown until the 11th century, when population, production, and exchange increased, and Italy, particularly northern Italy, became politically and economically the most important part of Europe (see GENOA and VENICE). Between the 11th and the 14th centuries, the population of Italy doubled to between 7 and 9 million inhabitants. People of all social classes migrated to the towns, including members of the nobility. As a result, urban communes came to govern the countryside. South of Toscana, however, the aristocracy lived near the land and the feudal system, with its lack of distinction between trade and agriculture persisted.

One of the reasons for the strength of the Italian economy was that it had monopolized the trade in luxury items and their distribution throughout Europe. These included the strong, sweet wines of Crete, Cyprus, and other parts of the Aegean (see MALMSEY), but also goods produced in Italy itself, such as high-quality wool and silk (from Lucca and Florence). When it became possible to transfer credit throughout the Mediterranean and western Europe (instead of having to carry and exchange actual coins), Florence became the banking capital of Europe. The Florentine house of ANTINORI is a good example of several of these developments. The Antinoris were, and still are, a noble Tuscan family that moved from the country to the city; having made their money in banking, they diversified into selling wine and also used their capital to buy up land to grow their own wine.

The rich merchants of the cities became a new market for fine wines. Good wine became a sign of affluence and a source of profit: it is no coincidence that the merchant dynasties of Bardi and FRESCOBALDI should have gone into wine-growing, buying up land for the purpose. All over Italy, the usual way to improve land was to deforest it and plant it with vines. When there was enough moisture, the vines were raised on trees, stakes, or trellises (see TENDONE), in the Roman way, to increase yields by exposing the grapes to the sun. Thus sown and planted crops could be raised in the same fields. In the drier regions, particularly in the south (with the exception of CAMPANIA), the vines were left to grow unsupported, as BUSH VINES, or left to trail on the ground in vineyards or at least in separate plots.

Vine-growing as well as wine-making in medieval Italy were much as they had been in the days of the classical writers on agriculture, and in one crucial respect things were worse: since AMPHORAE and other impermeable earthenware vessels were no longer available, wine was kept in wooden BARRELS, which were hard to clean and were not airtight. Unless a vine contained high proportions of two natural preservatives, sugar and alcohol, it would not last out the year.

The Roman VINE VARIETIES seem to have disappeared. In his treatise on agriculture (1303) PETRUS DE CRESCENTIIS, who had read the classical authorities and often repeats their advice, does not mention any of the famous Roman CÉPAGES. He lists some 37 contemporary Italian varieties, but he makes no attempt to relate those to the grapes he encountered in his classical predecessors. The list he gives is mostly concerned with the northern half of Italy, and especially his own city of Bologna. The list is not a great help to the modern scholar, because his descriptions are too brief for identification and most of the names are unrecognizable. 'Sclaua' is the variety he praises most highly; in the Middle Ages it was grown in the Po valley. This must be the same name as modern SCHIAVA, except that the modern variety is red, whereas Petrus' is white. Other varieties with recognizable names are 'graeca' (like the modern GRECO) and 'uernacia' (VERNACCIA), both of which Petrus says make good wines but have low yields, and 'muscatellus' (MUSCAT), which is better for eating. 'Tribiana' (TREBBIANO?) has small berries, takes long to start producing, and makes good wine that keeps well. 'Albana', a white grape that is characteristic of Romagna, may well be the parent of the modern grape of that area (see ALBANA). However, a familiar name is no guarantee of identity. Modern Trebbiano (Ugni Blanc) is also sometimes known as Greco, so Petrus' 'graeca' and his 'tribiana' may in fact be the same grape. 'Graeca' is unlikely to be Greco di Tufo, which is now grown in Campania and may well be a genuine and very ancient Greek import. Also, since the grapevine mutates relatively easily, modern grape varieties may be very different from their medieval ancestors. None of Petrus' 17 red varieties has a familiar name, and Petrus does not devote much space to them. Like most medieval drinkers, he preferred white wines to red.

From the 13th century onwards, wine was medieval Italy's most profitable cash crop. Share-cropping was traditional throughout the country, with the land owner taking half the wine or more if production was high. Sometimes a contract was drawn up for a longer period at a fixed rent. Smallholders survived in the highlands, but in Toscana and the northern plain they could not afford to stay on the better land. Peasants occasionally retailed their wine, but usually the landowners regulated sales to the towns. Consumption was high (the figure for Florence, c.1338, is a gallon a week for every man, woman, and child, but estimates for Milan and Venice are very much higher), yet production more than met demand, particularly in Campania.

Italy is mountainous and has few navigable RIVERS, which made internal transport costly and difficult before the coming of the RAILWAYS. Also, because Italy was not a political unity, there were obstacles in the form of tolls, duties, and differences in coinage, weights, and measures. Transport by sea was cheap and export to other countries no more laborious than much internal trade, so merchants in northern Italy or near the sea readily turned to foreign markets. The northern districts sold wine in Switzerland and Germany, the Marche exported to the Levant via Venice, which enjoyed tax privileges in Constantinople, and Genoese ships took the wines of Liguria to Spain, Flanders, and England. Nevertheless, the volume of Italy's international wine trade was merely the surplus production of a fertile vine-growing country. The Italians could afford not to deprive themselves of any of the *vin ordinaire* or fine wine they wanted to drink and still make money out of what remained.

See also GENOA, NAPLES, VENICE, and TOSCANA.

H.M.W.

Jones, P. 'Italy', in *The Cambridge Economic History of Europe*, 7 vols., i: *The Agrarian Life of the Middle Ages* (Cambridge, 1966).

Marescalchi, A., and Dalmasso, G. (eds.), *Storia della vite e del vino in Italia*, 3 vols. (Milan, 1993).

Modern history

That the revival of Europe's trade in the early Middle Ages began in the Mediterranean is by now universally accepted. It is therefore no surprise that specific references to what were to become some of Italy's most important grapes and wines can be found as early as the late 13th and early 14th centuries. Barbera was already mentioned during this period, and Nebbiolo, Trebbiano, and Garganega were specifically named by PETRUS DE CRESCENTIIS in his *Liber ruralium commodorum* of c.1304. The country's chronicles, both civic and monastic, of the 14th and 15th centuries abound with descriptions of the leading wines of their day—at times identified by grape variety, at times identified by their production zone. Many of them coincide, at least nominally, with the current wines of these same zones.

English records seem to indicate that wines such as Vernaccia, Trebbiano, and Greco were all known as such at this time. Sante Lancerio, cellarmaster to Pope Paul III, recounted the wines of his day in an account of papal travels in 1536, describing, criticizing, and praising the prominent products of his epoch, amongst which we find Aglianico, Aleatico, and Greco from the south, Vino Nobile di Montepulciano, Trebbiano di Romagna, Sangiovese di Romagna from the centre, and Cinqueterre from the north. And in Andrea Bacci's work we find a full-fledged treatise on Italy's wines, an attempt to deal with and describe the country's viticultural production on a national basis and in a national context, a surprising phenomenon inasmuch as Italy was far from being a nation in the modern sense in the late 16th century.

But it was precisely at this time—in the 17th, and then in the 18th, centuries—that the development of Italian viticulture and wines began to diverge from those of her neighbours. This critical period, which saw the rise of modern wine in BOTTLES stoppered with CORK and from specific producers, left Italy virtually untouched. Old bottles from this period are non-existent, nor is there any evidence of a long history of bottled wine from individual properties. Although some of Toscana's leading NÉGOCIANT houses trace their history back to the Middle Ages (see ANTINORI and FRESCOBALDI), they, and the few Piedmontese houses which can trace their history to the late 18th century, sold bulk rather than either bottled wine or estate wines until relatively recently.

Any overall evaluation of the quality of Italian wine in the 18th century is impossible, but signs of deterioration do exist. The 'Florence' wines so greatly appreciated in the late 17th and early 18th centuries by Lady Sandwich, by Swift, and by Bolingbroke are described as 'disagreeably rough' by Sir Edward Barry in 1775, and there is good reason not to dismiss his words as a mere subjective reaction. Pietro Leopoldo, grand duke of Toscana, during an inspection tour of his realm in 1773, reported a significant loss of viticultural commerce with England due to the lessened quality of the wines of Chianti. More importantly, Italy's wines, including many of its most famous ones, did not assume their current form until quite recently: Barolo and Barbaresco were sweet wines until the middle and end of the 19th century, respectively; Chianti did not become a predominantly Sangiovese wine until the late 19th century; Brunello di Montalcino did not even exist as a wine until the end of the 19th century; Orvieto and Cinqueterre were predominantly sweet wines until the modern epoch; the best-known wines of central Italy such as Orvieto, Verdicchio, Frascati, and the other white wines of the Castelli Romani were regularly fermented on their skins until the 1970s. The INTERNATIONAL VARIETIES which today play so important a role in the viticulture of Italy's north east—Trentino-Alto Adige, Veneto, and Friuli—began to assume a significant role only after the replanting of the country's vineyards in the wake of the ravages of PHYLLOXERA in the early 20th century. The crisp and refreshing white wines of Friuli are entirely a post-Second World War phenomenon; Sicilia's first dry table wines, in contrast to the better-known sweet wines or blending wines of the island, were created only in 1824, by Duke Edoardo di Salaparuta.

Cyrus REDDING's observation that 'Italian wines have stood still and remained without improvement, while those of France and Spain . . . have kept pace to a certain extent with agricultural improvement and the increasing foreign demand' testifies to two and half centuries of marking time, of neglect, and probably of deterioration of quality.

The reasons for this period of stagnation, which in Italian historical literature is often called the period of Italy's *decadenza*, are not difficult to determine. The country experienced an extended domination by foreign powers, first by the Spanish Habsburgs both in the north and the south, then by Spanish Bourbons in the south and Austrian Habsburgs in the north. Meanwhile the increased influence—both temporal and spiritual—of Counter-Reformation Catholicism effectively removed the country's destiny from its own hands. Even more significant was the general shift of trade and commerce from south to north, from the Mediterranean to the Atlantic, which transformed Italy's geographical position for the first time in two millennia from that of a central to that of a peripheral power. Italy was on the fringes of a Europe in which the most prosperous and progressive areas, the northern markets, were virtually inaccessible to her, and were increasingly dominated by the fine wines of France and Germany.

The unification of Italy in 1861, and a slow but steady period of economic growth, did much to reverse the decline of the previous two and a half centuries, although economic growth and modernization were neither unfaltering nor swift. It was only the economic boom after the Second World War which allowed the Italians to attain a truly European standard of living. It also created a class of consumers with both an interest in wine and the means to purchase it, which gave Italian wine producers the essential confidence in their own capacities and their own products which are the only real basis for making good-quality wine. Thus wine began to be transformed from a daily beverage and a source of calories (see DIET) to a source of pleasure based on the concept of choice. Even in the Italy of the 1990s, these two conceptions of wine survive in an uneasy state of coexistence.

Major developments in the recent history of Italian wine are described under DOC, DOCG, IGT, and VINO DA TAVOLA.

Geography and climate

Generalizations about a peninsula 1,200 km/ 750 miles long extending through about 10 degrees of LATITUDE are not easy. The dominant geographical feature of the 'boot' is the Apennines, which begin close to the border with France and then form the central ridge, the national spinal column, down the peninsula to the 'toe' in Calabria. In the far north are the alps; in Sicilia, the Madonie form yet another chain of central mountains. Good-quality viticulture is almost entirely a HILLSIDE phenomenon in Italy; there are no Italian equivalents of the *vignoble* of Bordeaux, and the Grave del Friuli and other flat viticultural areas of Friuli do not produce wine at the same quality level as the higher nearby districts of Collio and Colli Orientali. Unlike that of France, Italian agriculture has always been organized vertically instead of horizontally: instead of growing grapes in certain given areas and other crops in different areas, Italians have used the richer soils of the valley floors for the cultivation of grain and vegetables and for the grazing of cattle, reserving the hills of the same areas for the cultivation of the vine and the olive.

A significant number of the country's most admired wines come from CALCAREOUS soils. Piemonte, Toscana, the hillside zones of Friuli, and the Salento in Puglia all provide examples of this. The other dominant soil type is VOLCANIC, present in such zones as Soave, the Castelli Romani to the south west of Rome, the interior of Campania and Basilicata, and Sicilia.

Climate is inevitably affected by ALTITUDE. Latitude is not a sure guide to temperature and further south is not always synonymous with hotter temperatures. Altitude, exposure, wind currents, TOPOGRAPHY, soil composition, and proximity to the sea are other relevant factors. If Cabernet Sauvignon can be grown at 46 degrees 30 minutes of latitude (north of Bordeaux), it is due to the narrow, heat-trapping alpine valleys of Alto Adige. Umbria is generally cooler than Toscana albeit further to the south; a wide span of central Italy—Umbria, the Marche, Lazio—is more renowned for its white wines than for its reds, while Piemonte, in the far north on the French and Swiss border, is principally a producer of powerful, dense red wines. Even Sicilia confirms the rule that, in the case of Italy, geography is not destiny: the island as a whole produces considerably more white wine than red, and the western part of the island, in particular the province of Trapani in the extreme south west of the island, produces almost exclusively white wine.

While the climate of the far north of Italy may be CONTINENTAL, that of central and southern Italy is MEDITERRANEAN. Italy's indigenous red grape varieties—with the exception of Dolcetto—are almost invariably later ripeners. Nebbiolo, Barbera, Refosco, Corvina, Sangiovese, Sagrantino, Aglianico, Negroamaro, and Nero d'Avola all require sustained heat throughout the summer and early autumn to ripen properly and lose their tannic and acidic asperity, and successful ripening is therefore far from automatic. Poor VINTAGES are by no means a strange or inexplicable phenomenon in Italy, and in a typical decade there are usually at least two vintages of unacceptable quality.

Viticulture

Two distinguishing features mark Italian viticulture: first, the late development of vineyards as such and a significant presence until relatively recently of polyculture in grape-growing areas; second, the current dominance of vine-TRAINING SYSTEMS created expressly for high YIELDS and easy MECHANIZATION. Polyculture was a common phenomenon throughout Europe at one time. What is distinctive about Italy is the extent to which this practice lasted into the modern epoch. Grain was planted between rows of vines even in Barolo and Barbaresco until the 1950s, and central Italy was dominated by an almost standard type of mixed culture in which vines, planted amidst olive groves and rows of grains, were trained up trees to prevent the grapes from being eaten by the animals allowed to roam freely in the fields. Some modern vineyards, planted exclusively with vines in regular rows, did exist, particularly in Italy's north west, but viticulture in general was merely part of a general system of agriculture, one cash crop among many. It is no surprise, therefore, that when Italy's vineyards were replanted in the 1960s and 1970s, frequently with the assistance of EUROPEAN UNION funds, vineyards were generally adapted to the new exigencies of mechanization and productivity. Whereas in France the practicalities of mechanization were adapted to the existing low trained-trained vines and high VINE DENSITY with their proven ability to give high-quality grapes, Italian vineyards were redesigned when they were replanted, in a way that would make them compatible with the new large TRACTORS and other machines which were then becoming generally available. The result was spacings of up to 3 m/10 ft between the rows and high training systems. This low-density viticulture, with an average of between 2,500 and 3,300 vines per ha, coupled with the large yields that were common in the initial period of Italy's DOC epoch (roughly 1965–80), had as their inevitable result the very high yields per vine, often as much as 5 kg/11 lb of grapes, and a reduction in vine longevity.

The higher training systems, while offering improved protection against FUNGAL DISEASES, reduced the amounts of reradiated heat and often resulted in less ripe grapes with higher acidity, rougher tannins, and lower levels of EXTRACT. In the 1980s, there was renewed interest in higher VINE DENSITY and lower yields per vine. Initial experiments with planting densities in central Italy have shown greatly improved results from densities of 7,500 to 10,000 per ha and little if any improvement with yet higher densities. Expansive vine-training systems such as TENDONE or even more extreme horizontal systems such as Sylvoz, Casarsa, and other accentuatedly productive CORDON systems are no longer as popular, and there is a visible return to more quality-orientated systems, GUYOT or CORDON DE ROYAT in particular, the latter being popular for the ease with which it adapts to mechanization.

CLONAL SELECTION aimed at identifying and reproducing qualitatively superior clones of native vine varieties and the most appropriate ROOTSTOCKS to graft them on to is a relatively recent activity, although important research programmes were already under way for Sangiovese, Nebbiolo, and other indigenous varieties in the early 1990s. The popularity of Kober 5 BB and other very productive rootstocks, a feature of the planting period from 1965 to 1980, is unlikely to be repeated.

Wine-making

If Italian viticulture has tended to follow its own course, with little attention paid to the practices of other countries, the same cannot be said of its OENOLOGY and wine-making practices. Indeed, substantial investments in cellar equipment have made Italian wine-making facilities some of the most modern in Europe, and Italians make equipment such as BOTTLING LINES that is some of the best, and most exported, in the world. Chaptalization is forbidden but ENRICHMENT with concentrated grape must is permitted in some areas and within certain limits.

Wooden FERMENTATION VESSELS have, for better or for worse, been eliminated and, although cement vats and tanks are still widely in use for both fermentation and storage, stainless steel tanks are very much more common. TEMPERATURE CONTROL is widely accepted, for the production of both red wines and white wines, and the PUNCHING DOWN of the cap of red wines has been generally replaced by regular PUMPING OVER during the period of fermentation. The lengthy fermentations and MACERATIONS of the past, sometimes up to six weeks, have been shortened, substantially by most and slightly less so by avant-garde producers seeking the highest quality. DESTEMMING has long been an integral part of modern Italian wine-making since the vigorous tannins of most of Italy's major red varieties make fermenting with the stems far from advisable.

WHITE WINE-MAKING techniques, on the other hand, changed drastically in the 1970s and 1980s, with the introduction of cool fermentations, FILTRATION, and CENTRIFUGES. The most fundamental change of all, however, has been the end of the practice of fermenting white wines on their skins, which was once widely practised in Friuli and throughout central Italy. Gains in lightness and freshness have been obvious, even if at the price of a certain

standardization. Producing white wines of more character without sacrificing the newly achieved crispness and cleanliness is the current challenge for Italian white wine-making.

Fermentation may have evolved considerably in the second half of the 20th century, but ÉLEVAGE underwent more profound modifications during the same period. Large casks, usually oval rather than upright, have always been the preferred containers for AGEING red wine in Italian cellars; long ageing periods, particularly for what were considered the grandest wines, were an almost unvarying rule; wood of a certain age was generally preferred to new wood (although this may often have been for financial rather than qualitative reasons). Current practice favours smaller casks, with 15- to 50-hl (395- to 1,300-gal) containers replacing the 100- to 150-hl sizes of the past; ageing periods have been diminished, but many of Italy's most renowned red wines have tannins which need a considerable time in cask to soften and round, and periods of two years in cask (for Chianti Classico Riserva, Barolo, and Vino Nobile di Montepulciano), or even three years in cask (for Brunello di Montalcino and Barolo Riserva), are by no means uncommon, even though only Brunello was, until 1998, still legally obliged to age for a full three years. Regular replacement of excessively old wood has been accepted as an integral part of correct cellar techniques.

OAK has generally been the preferred wood for casks, much of it from Slavonia or elsewhere in central Europe. In the south of Italy, in areas such as Basilicata and Sicilia, where chestnut forests abound and there are no local sources of oak, the traditional chestnut cooperage is gradually being replaced by oak casks to achieve a more international style and to avoid the bitterness which old chestnut casks can impart. French oak became increasingly popular, if controversial, in the 1980s, initially in the form of BARRIQUES to be supplemented by larger casks. Sangiovese and Barbera were the first varieties to be widely aged in new small oak barrels, and the generally positive results have led to widespread use of BARREL MATURATION in many zones of Italy, albeit only by the most ambitious producers. Their use for such international varieties as Cabernet, Merlot, Pinot Noir, Chardonnay, and Sauvignon Blanc is also a recent phenomenon which has yielded both excellent results and some heavily over-oaked wines.

General inexperience in modern wine-making techniques is a chronic problem in Italy, where fine wine is such a recent phenomenon. This led to a major boom, particularly in the 1980s and 1990s, in the employment of consulting OENOLOGISTS in Toscana, Piemonte, and Friuli, the three most important fine wine regions, a practice which was to spread to Umbria and the Marche. Media coverage of the exploits of individual consultants threatened to overshadow the significance both of

specific estates and of individual TERROIRS (increasingly acknowledged within Italy). Italy's training institutes in oenology and viticulture are still woefully inadequate to its future needs (although see CONEGLIANO and SAN MICHELE ALL'ADIGE), with tertiary educational faculties of agriculture devoting little time and few resources to sound, professional oenological training. This suggests that the authorities have yet to realize the enormous economic potential of Italy's myriad distinctive grape varieties and viticultural environments.

Vine varieties

Despite the recent appearance of widely acclaimed wines from INTERNATIONAL VARIETIES, Italian viticulture as a whole remains firmly wedded to traditional, indigenous varieties, whose number has been estimated as over 2,000. Of the country's 20 most widely planted grapes, a group which includes all varieties with over 10,000 ha/24,700 acres planted, only Merlot, with some 48,000 ha, is an obvious import. According to an agricultural census conducted in 1990, Sangiovese was by far the most planted variety in Italy with 86,000 ha planted (albeit in strains of varying distinction), followed by the Sicilian white grape Catarratto, the central Italian white Trebbiano Toscano, Piemonte's Barbera, Merlot, Puglia's Negroamaro, the central and southern red Montepulciano, Trebbiano Romagnolo, Primitivo of the south, and white Malvasia. See articles on individual regions and zones for the names of other Italian vine varieties.

Large-scale plantings of international varieties—principally French, although there is also some Riesling and Gewürztraminer—are on the whole confined to the country's north east (which, in many cases, was under either direct Austrian rule or strong Austrian influence until 1919). They are planted in an arc stretching from Franciacorta, in the eastern part of Lombardia, through Trentino-Alto Adige, the northern part of Veneto (the provinces of Vicenza and Treviso), and Friuli. Scattered plantings of international varieties exist throughout the rest of the country, but had not established significant toeholds in any one zone or subzone by the mid 1990s. There was little generally accepted identification of variety with terroir, and even in Alto Adige and Friuli, no single international variety dominated, with Schiava by far the most significant vine planted in the former, TOCAI in the latter.

Plantings of international varieties have tended to follow international FASHION: various members of the Pinot family in the 1970s; Chardonnay, Sauvignon Blanc, and Cabernet in the 1980s; Syrah and Viognier in the 1990s. Central Italy, with only the late-ripening Sangiovese an important red grape and with the relatively uninteresting Trebbiano as its major white grape, is likely to see expanded plantings of international varieties in the coming decades. The high costs of viticulture in its important hillside zones make it imperative to obtain a higher return from the vineyards, an objective which may be realizable only with non-native varieties and which may lead to neglect of the less well-known native varieties with a significant potential such as MONTE-PULCIANO D'ABRUZZO, COLORINO, and GRE-CHETTO.

Organization of trade

Italy's wine trade resembles those of its European neighbours in terms of a division of labour between individual properties, commercial and NÉGOCIANT houses, and CO-OPERATIVE wineries. What distinguishes Italy is the overwhelming importance of the latter two categories, a dominance which is the direct result of the extreme fractioning of vineyard property. Close to 40 per cent of the country's agricultural properties grow grapes and the average size of their 'vineyards' is 0.8 ha. Middlemen for the marketing of the wines, be they négocians or co-operatives, are thus indispensable links in the distribution chain which connects growers to consumers. Private estates of a certain size are an important reality only in Toscana and, to a lesser extent, in Friuli, while the recent development of a significant number of prestigious small 'domaines' in the finest zones of Piemonte might be considered a miniature, but embryonic, version of Burgundy. It is no coincidence that these are the three regions producing Italy's best wines.

Large commercial houses were a relatively late development in Italy, virtually all of them having been founded after the unification of the country in 1861 and thus being a century younger than comparable houses in France, Spain, and Portugal. The reasons for their late foundation and slow growth are far from mysterious: Italy was not a country prior to her unification and the movement of merchandise across the borders of the many small states which existed in the peninsula was a costly and cumbersome procedure. REDDING cites 'a vexatious system of imposts' as a major cause of Italian viticultural backwardness in the 19th century, a backwardness which was commercially, as well as technically, penalizing. There was very little in the way of a national market, and little knowledge of even the finest products outside of their specific production zones. Even today, négociant houses are a major presence only in Toscana, Veneto, and Sicilia, while co-operative wineries play a more significant role in other Italian regions.

Co-operatives became the dominant force in the production and distribution of Italian wine in the late 20th century, a logical development considering the political dominance of the Christian Democratic party in the country's various governments and the favour shown to co-operative movements in the social doctrine of the Roman Catholic church. Income maintenance has been as significant a concern as the products themselves; this objective has entailed large volumes, which, thanks to ample subsidies, could be marketed at low prices. Quality has not always been the strong point of the resulting wines, although individual co-operatives, particularly in the north, have always been responsive to the market and conscious of the need to create products that would please consumer palates. Italy enjoyed particular success in the 1970s and 1980s with its exports of the Riunite co-ops' LAMBRUSCO.

As EUROPEAN UNION and national subsidies are reduced, Italian wines will have to respond more readily to free market economics. The creation of the European Economic Community and the opening of neighbouring markets to large quantities of low-priced Italian wine can be seen as merely postponing the day of reckoning. Rapidly falling wine consumption (in Italy alone, per capita consumption fell more than 50 per cent between 1960 and 1990) signals that a fundamental modification of Italy's production philosophy is only a matter of time.

There can be few doubts that Italy's new prosperity and the worldwide popularity of the 'Mediterranean diet' (a shorthand, in most cases, for Italian cooking) have changed prospects and possibilities for Italian wine and created a new viewpoint amongst the country's producers. And there can be even fewer doubts that admirers and enthusiasts of Italian wine have never had such an embarrassment of riches at the beginning of the third millennium AD.

For details of individual regions, see ABRUZZO, ALTO ADIGE, PUGLIA, BASILICATA, CALABRIA, CAMPANIA, EMILIA-ROMAGNA, FRIULI, LAZIO, LIGURIA, LOMBARDIA, MARCHE, MOLISE, PIEMONTE, SARDEGNA, SICILIA, TRENTINO, TOSCANA, UMBRIA, Valle d'AOSTA, and VENETO.

For details of terms to be found on Italian wine labels, see CLASSICO, DOC, DOCG, IGT, RISERVA, and VINO DA TAVOLA.   D.T. & D.C.G.

Bastianich, J., and Lynch, D., *Vino Italiano: The Regional Wines of Italy* (New York, 2002).
Belfrage, N., *From Barolo to Valpolicella: The Wines of Northern Italy* (London, 1999).
—— *From Brunello to Zibibbo: The Wines of Southern Italy* (London, 2001).
Cernilli, D., and Petrini, C. (eds.), *Italian Wines* (Rome and New York, annually).

IVDP, Instituto do Vinho do Douro e do Porto, which governs the production of both PORT and DOURO wine.

Izsáki, low-quality, late-ripening light-skinned grape, sometimes called White Kadarka, grown to a decreasing extent on the Great Plain of Hungary.

J

Jaboulet Aîné, Paul, important RHÔNE valley merchant and wine producer, whose most famous wine is Hermitage la Chapelle. The house was founded in the early 19ᵗʰ century by Antoine Jaboulet and takes its name from the older of his twin sons. Jaboulet's own vineyard holdings in production, which provide between a quarter and a third of the firm's needs, totalled more than 95 ha/235 acres, in every northern Rhône appellation but Côte Rôtie in the late 1990s. Recent acquisitions included additional holdings in Hermitage and Crozes-Hermitage, a stake in Condrieu (first vintage 1996), Domaine St-Pierre in Cornas (1994), and most of Domaine Raymond Roure in Crozes-Hermitage (1996). Of the raw materials bought in, from 150 growers the length of the Rhône valley, two-thirds is wine rather than grapes, and in the late 1990s quality was notably variable. The firm was based in its old cellars in Tain l'Hermitage from 1834 until 1984 when a modern winery and warehouse was built in La Roche de Glun just south of the town. Jaboulet sell a range of more than 20 different wines, most of them in the firm's own deep-PUNTED bottle, and the best are their own special cuvées. Their CROZES-HERMITAGE, Domaine de Thalabert, was some of the earliest proof offered to wine drinkers outside France that this appellation could produce serious, age-worthy wine. The firm's top red cuvées are CHÂTEAUNEUF-DU-PAPE, Les Cèdres, CÔTE RÔTIE, Les Jumelles, and most notably HERMITAGE, La Chapelle, with La Chapelle 1961 an acknowledged classic. The white Hermitage, Chevalier de Stérimberg demonstrates the late Gérard Jaboulet's admiration for the ROUSSANNE grape. In 2005, after years of under-performance, the company was sold to the owner of Ch La Lagune in Bordeaux, an investor in Champagne Billecart Salmon.

Livingstone-Learmonth, J., *The Wines of the Northern Rhône* (Berkeley, Calif. 2005).

Norman, R., *Rhône Renaissance* (London, 1995).

Jacob's Creek, leading wine BRAND of PERNOD RICARD, France's share of the Australian wine boom. The Reserve range is impressive.

Jacquère is the common white grape variety in SAVOIE, where it produces high yields of lightly scented, essentially alpine dry white. Plantings increased in the 1980s to reach a steady level of about 1,000 ha/2,470 acres from 1990. It has also been successfully grown in some CONDRIEU vineyards even though it is not permitted by the APPELLATION CONTRÔLÉE regulations.

Jadot, Louis, merchant-grower based in BEAUNE, dealing exclusively in Burgundy and owners of some 50 ha/122 acres of vineyards in the CÔTE D'OR and 35 ha/86 acres in BEAUJOLAIS. The company has been owned by the Kopf family since 1985. Founded in 1859 by the eponymous Louis Jadot, the company was run from 1962 to 1992 by André Gagey, who joined the firm as an assistant in 1954. When Louis-Alain Jadot, last of the family line, died prematurely in 1968, Gagey was asked by the family to become general manager, and he has now been succeeded by his son Pierre-Henry. Jadot's success has been very much due to the combined talents of André Gagey and winemaker Jacques Lardière. Both red and white NÉGOCIANT wines, made from bought-in fruit, are thoroughly reliable, but the firm's reputation is based on the high quality of its domaine wines. Jadot's holdings increased during the 1980s with the acquisition of the cream of the Clair Daü vineyards, followed by substantial purchases in Beaujolais in the 1990s: Ch des Jacques and Ch des Lumières. The company also manages and vinifies the Côte d'Or vineyards of Domaine Gagey (7 ha) and Domaine Duc de Magenta (13 ha). A large, beautiful, and flexible new winery was accordingly built on the Jadot premises in 1997. Among the reds, the Côte de Beaune wines stand out, with the MONOPOLE Beaune, Clos des Ursules, being especially fine. The domaine whites are wines of concentration, class, and distinction. Never over-oaked, they are a clear expression of their TERROIR and wines such as their Puligny-Montrachet Les Folatières, Corton-Charlemagne, and Chevalier-Montrachet Les Demoiselles, are regularly among the best bottles of white burgundy to be had.   M.W.E.S.

Jaen, red wine grape in Portugal's DÃO region, where it ripens early to produce deep-coloured wines that are notable for their lack of acidity. Occasionally seen as a VARIETAL, it is normally stiffened with Touriga Nacional and Alfrocheiro. The vine, planted on a total of 3,400 ha/8,398 acres in Portugal's BEIRAS region, is identical to Galicia's MENCÍA.

Jaén Blanco, Andalucian white grape that was shown in the early 2000s to be identical to CAYETANA Blanca. It is also said by some to be Portugal's AVESSO.

Jahrgang, German for VINTAGE (as in the year rather than the HARVEST process, for which the word is *Ernte*).

Japan. Grape-growing and, to a lesser extent, wine production have a long history in this Far Eastern country, even though wine drinking on any appreciable scale is a relatively recent phenomenon. Between 1993 and 1998, wine consumption doubled but since then has remained relatively stable, at just under 4 l per capita—low by European standards, but by far the highest in Asia. There are now 175 domestic wineries in 36 of the 44 prefectures and sales under domestic labels accounted for 36 per cent of total wine sales in Japan in 2004.

History

Legend has it that grape-growing began at Katsunuma, in Yamanashi prefecture of

Japan

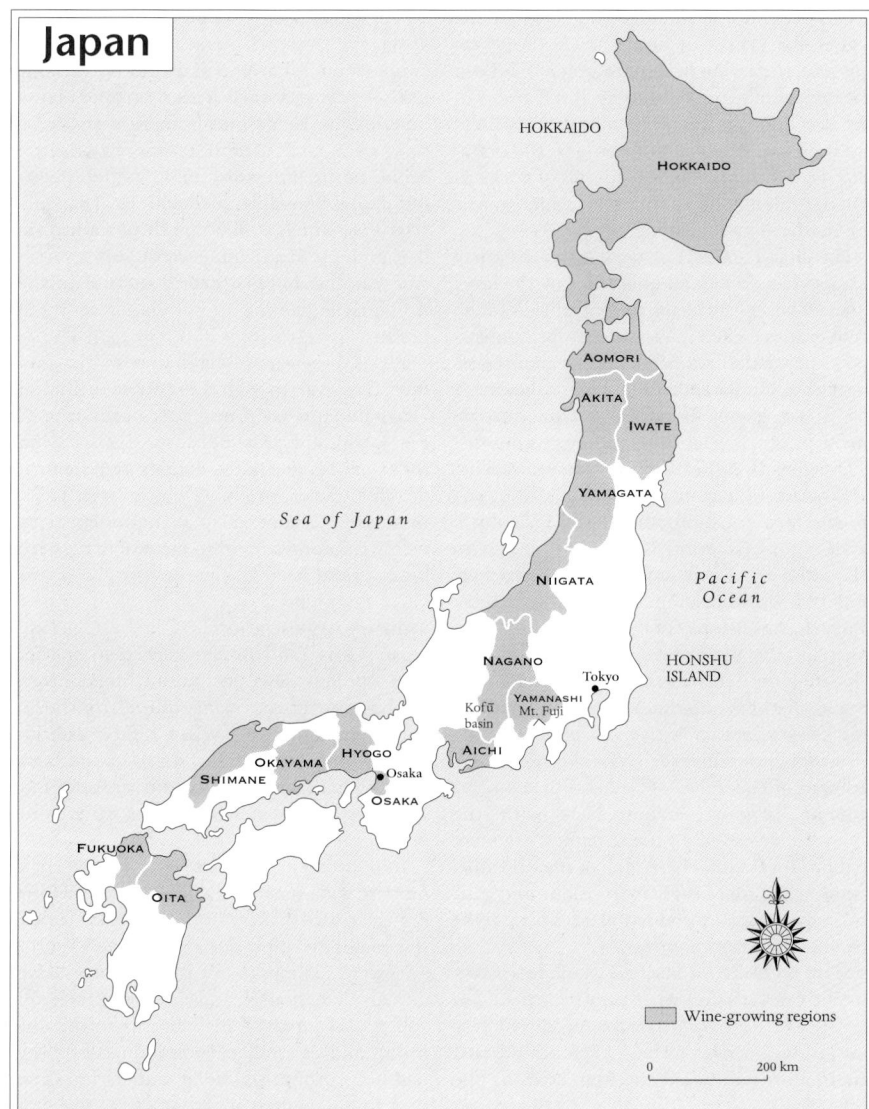

HOKKAIDO
HOKKAIDO

AOMORI
AKITA
IWATE
YAMAGATA

Sea of Japan

NIIGATA

Pacific Ocean

NAGANO
Tokyo
Kofū basin
YAMANASHI
Mt. Fuji
HONSHU ISLAND

OKAYAMA
HYOGO
AICHI
SHIMANE
Osaka
OSAKA

FUKUOKA
OITA

Wine-growing regions

0   200 km

of Yokohama drinking wine set out to make a substitute from local grapes. The early product was not good, but the effort was enough to convince local authorities to permit the import of European VINIFERA and AMERICAN VINES as the basis for a new industry.

Today, the viticultural industry is modest, but entrenched—and still focused mostly on producing TABLE GRAPES, rather than on providing top-quality raw material for WINE-MAKING.

Geography and climate

Grapes are now grown in 46 of the 47 prefectures, the exception being tropical Okinawa.

Three prefectures (Yamanashi, Yamagata, and Nagano) on the main island, Honshu, however, account for almost 40 per cent of the 19,200 ha/47,420 acres under vine throughout Japan.

Production is in the order of 230,000 tonnes of grapes per year, although only one-tenth of these grapes is used for wine-making. The bulk of the production is for the table and the grape varieties under cultivation and viticultural practices reflect this.

Japan's climate is not naturally suited to viticulture and successful grape-growing has always been a struggle.

In Yamanashi prefecture, where a fifth of Japan's grapes are grown and where half of the active wineries are located, a monsoonal climate presents a serious problem of excess water and HUMIDITY. Here, and in most of the prefectures of Honshu, vines traditionally have been trained on to overhead wires or platforms (*budodana*) so that the bunches will hang lower than the foliage and be more freely exposed to circulating air. This TENDONE method of cultivation, known as *tanazukuri*, was developed as a defence against FUNGAL DISEASES and has been reasonably effective. VINE DENSITY is notoriously low: in some places there may be only two or three vines generating foliage to cover 100 sq m/120 sq yds. The demands made on the vine to support this practice, combined with the excess RAINFALL and the tendency of growers to maximize YIELDS in any case, robs the grape of the character necessary for robust wines.

Grapes from the district of Katsunuma, with about 15 per cent of the prefecture's vines, are those generally preferred by winemakers. Katsunuma fares considerably better climatically than districts lower down in the Kofu basin. Rainfall is lower, it has better DRAINAGE because of its higher ELEVATION, gets a refreshing breeze which helps control rot and mildew, has a wider diurnal temperature variation (see TEMPERATURE VARIABILITY) and better ripening conditions for wine grapes generally.

Nagano and Yamagata, the prefectures where most of the recent growth in the industry has been concentrated, do better again but conditions are still far from ideal. Nagano had 25 wineries and Yamagata 11 in the mid 2000s.

central Honshu. As the story goes, in the year 718 the Buddha Nyorai passed vines to a holy man by the name of Gyoki, who planted the vines at Katsunuma, where he built the Daizenji Temple.

It was the grape itself, rather than wine, in which the Japanese were initially interested. The monks taught that grapes had medicinal value. The statue of Nyorai, which Gyoki had carved in his honour and which is still housed in the temple today, was named Budo Yakushi (*budo* meaning grape; and *yakushi* meaning teacher of medicine) by pilgrims to the temple.

Wine may, perhaps, have been made from local grapes in Katsunuma in earlier times but wine consumption in Japan had not been documented until the arrival of Portuguese MISSIONARIES in the 16th century. The Jesuit missionary St Francis Xavier carried wine as gifts for the feudal lords of Kyushu in southern Japan whom he visited in 1545. Others who followed him continued the practice so that the

locals acquired a taste for wine and began to import it regularly.

They called the wine *tintashu*, combining the Japanese word for sake (*shu*) with a derivative of the Portuguese word for red (TINTO). (The word lives on today, incidentally, as the brand name for a port-style wine produced by Suntory, the brewing and whisky giant.)

During the Tokugawa shogunate of the 17th century, the missionaries were expelled, Christians persecuted, and practices associated with Christianity, such as drinking wine, condemned. Ironically, however, the choice of Edo as the Tokugawa capital (on the site of modern Tokyo) was a boost for the farmers of nearby Yamanashi: their grapes quickly came to be prized for the tables of the shogun's court.

Eventually, in 1875, the first attempts at commercial wine-making were undertaken in Yamanashi, where grape-growing had begun over a millennium before. An enterprising merchant who had seen foreigners at the port

In the 1960s, a second frontier of the modern Japanese industry was opened up in an even more unlikely location, in central Hokkaido, Japan's northernmost island. This is an extremely cold environment for grape-growing. Average temperatures rise to only about 23 °C/73 °F in July, August, and the early part of September. By the end of September, average temperatures are about 15 °C and, by October, below 10 °C. Vineyards are covered in deep snow for most of the winter and vines are given WINTER PROTECTION by being buried in heaped soil to avoid damage. In Hokkaido, canes are trained low along horizontal wires, in contrast to the *tanazukuri* technique.

Japanese vineyard soils are in general very acid.

Vine varieties

History, the dominant demand for TABLE GRAPES, and the climatic vagaries with which growers have had to contend over the years, have combined to result in the rather exotic range of grape varieties which form the basis of viticulture in Japan.

Strictly speaking, there are no VINIFERA vines truly native to Japan. There are several introduced *vinifera* vines which have evolved here uniquely, however, and these are now regarded justifiably as Japanese varieties.

The most significant of these, and the undoubted sentimental favourite of the Japanese, is the Koshu. This is the descendant of the vines carried along the Silk Road to Japan 1,200 years ago and, in the public eye at least, is virtually synonymous with the industry of Katsunuma, which has over 90 per cent of the total Koshu vineyard area.

Koshu has survived as an important variety because it has adapted to the difficult growing conditions in Yamanashi prefecture and because it is supported by long tradition. It is a heavy-bearing vine producing big, round, pink-tinged berries. It is most suitable as a table grape, but is also used to make a wine which is almost colourless and, as might be expected, without a great deal of BODY. Interestingly, however, the Kizan winery in Yamanashi has produced some respectable brandy from Koshu grapes, which may herald a new role for Koshu.

Koshu is the most visible of the modest *Vitis vinifera* presence in Japanese viticulture. Neo-Muscat, a variety developed from a crossing of Koshu Sanjaku with MUSCAT OF ALEXANDRIA, is also *vinifera* and is now, in fact, more widely planted than Koshu, but is less well known. Another Koshu cousin, Ryugan (also known as Senkoji, and probably the same as the Longyan of CHINA), is grown only in tiny quantities, chiefly in Nagano prefecture in central Honshu. As with Koshu, Neo-Muscat and Ryugan produce grapes which are best suited to the table, but which are also made into light and generally sweetish wine.

In Hokkaido, a vine growing wild in the region for centuries and known locally as *yamabudo* (literally, mountain grape) has been the subject of a great deal of research and genetic development since the 1960s. The variety has been identified as belonging to the oriental, cold-resistant *amurensis* species of VITIS originating along the Amur river, which forms the border between China and Siberia.

The first commercial wine of this variety was produced in small quantities by the large Tokachi winery at Ikeda, in central Hokkaido, from grapes picked in the wild by local townsfolk. The small black berries make an interesting, although unconventional, red wine with a distinctive gamey bouquet and an austere, earthy palate. It is labelled, simply, Amurensis.

Drawing on earlier work on the species done at a research station in Kharbarovsk in the former Soviet Union, the Ikeda Viticulture and Enology Experimental Station sought to adapt and cross this local vine to breed NEW VARIETIES which are a match for the extreme climatic conditions of Hokkaido and are more suitable for commercial viticulture and wine-making. Crossings with a SEIBEL clone delivered the best outcomes. The first result of this programme, a variety that was named Kiyomi, is now thought to be the result of a crossing of two types of Seibel. But a second attempt, crossing Kiyomi back with the *amurensis*, delivered a variety, named Kiyomai, that produces larger berries than the wild vine, and that are more regular in colour and general appearance. An added attraction is that the vine does not require.

More recent work has been done by viticulturists on Honshu with another *yamabudo* strain (*Vitis coignetiae*) that has produced very promising wines. The Yamanashi-based Sawanobori family led the way, crossing the local *coignetiae* with a Russian and a Himalayan strain of the wild grape to produce a new variety, called Shokoshi, that ripens easily and delivers naturally the richer colours and flavours not attainable from the native strains. Another new variety, called Yama Sauvignon, from a crossing of *yamabudo* with Cabernet Sauvignon, is also delivering attractive wine.

However, the vines which are by far the most widely planted throughout Japan, accounting for almost 80 per cent of the total area under vine, are HYBRIDS based on *Vitis labrusca*, most of which were introduced directly from the United States.

They have generally performed well in the difficult local growing conditions and, most importantly, have provided the best commercial results for growers attuned primarily to the table grape market. In particular, as the highest prices are attracted by the first fruit onto the market each season, the fact that many of them are early-ripening varieties has been very attractive to growers.

Kyoho, a local hybrid of the American variety CONCORD, is now the most widely grown in Japan, comprising 35 per cent of the vineyard area.

DELAWARE follows with 20 per cent. Campbell's Early was once a clear second, but is now fourth. Kyoho has been further bred to produce a rash of minor varieties aimed at achieving better-quality table grapes, including Pione (possibly identical to Thailand's POKDUM), which is now the third ranked variety and produces quite creditable VARIETAL rosé. Another popular hybrid is Muscat Bailey A, which is gaining in popularity as a wine grape.

All of these varieties actually find their way into wine, even though the vines were not bred originally, nor are grown specifically in modern Japan, for this purpose. Grapes which for some reason fail to satisfy requirements as table grapes, or those which ripen late in the season, often end up at the wineries, providing the domestic component of many of the lower priced local labels.

Industry organization

Japan's first (and much-vaunted in Europe) 'wine boom' saw per capita consumption double during the 1980s, albeit from a low base. Consumption levelled off towards the end of the decade but a second wine boom quickly gathered momentum around 1993, when a strong yen encouraged a surge in imports.

Initially they had focused on investment in modern wine-making equipment and on training their winemakers in the methods used in the major wine-producing nations (Suntory even went so far as to buy the ST-JULIEN classed growth Ch Lagrange, and the 1980s saw several substantial Japanese investments in the California and Australian wine industries). They had hoped that this, along with various practices in the winery aimed at extracting more flavour and body from the flimsy local fruit base, would be sufficient to match the competition from the foreign producers whose attention to the Japanese market had been attracted by its rapid growth, by the potential associated with 127 million affluent people, by favourable exchange rates, and by the relaxation of import barriers.

The domestic industry has also tried to hold its ground by using imported BULK WINE, GRAPE CONCENTRATE, MUST, and even imported grapes to extend the quantity and improve the quality of its own base material. Labelling laws have allowed considerable leeway for producers in this regard and some wines sold under domestic BRANDS are known to contain the barest minimum of genuine domestic material. In 2002, for example, Japan imported 24 million l/6.3 million gal of bulk wine for bottling or blending into domestic brands. But imports of bulk wine have dropped by almost two thirds since their peak in 1998 as local companies abandon, or else have lowered priorities for, import-dependent brands and, instead, concentrate on lifting the quality of their domestic wines.

The increasing sophistication of the Japanese consumer and the persistence of the European and New World producers have resulted in major inroads into the domestic industry's hold on the market over the years. In 1982, domestic labels accounted for three-quarters of the bottled wine market in Japan; by 2004 this share had fallen to just over one-third.

Furthermore, the extent to which even this reduced market share depends on imported product is more readily evident because of a voluntary labelling code, adopted by the Japan Wineries Association under pressure from the Ministry of Finance, which has removed some (but sadly not all) of the ambiguity regarding the origin of wine bottled under domestic labels.

Wine bottled under domestic labels is to be declared either as *kokunai san* (domestic wine) or *yunyu san* (imported bulk wine). If imported bulk wine and domestic wine are blended, the larger portion is to be specified first; but the exact proportions are rarely indicated and neither is the country, or countries, of origin of the imported portion revealed. If imported grape concentrate or must is used, this is not likely to be indicated. One of the best known premium labels preserves total ambiguity by revealing no origin information whatsoever.

Genuine domestic wine can command a significant premium and serious producers increasingly make a feature of this on their labels when they can, declaring that the wine is made using 100 per cent domestic grapes (*kokusan budo* 100%), grown, fermented, and bottled in Japan. The winemakers of Katsunuma have taken this one stage further with a certificate of origin seal for the district's top ranked wines. Nagano prefecture introduced a similar regional certification system in 2003.

In turn, this will require major alterations to vineyard practices. If the existing vine varieties are to continue to be the basis of the winemakers' raw material, then, at the very least, yields must be substantially reduced and grapes should be grown specifically for wine-making.

But the structure of the industry militates against rapid progress. There are an estimated 80,000 grape-growers. The average vineyard size is around 0.25 ha in Yamanashi, and not much bigger elsewhere. Even in Hokkaido, where the scale of viticulture is greatest, the average vineyard is only slightly more than 0.5 ha/1 acre.

Price maximization is essential to maintain a viable income for small grape-growers and when table grapes can command a price four or five times the price winemakers are prepared to pay, it is hard to imagine that the bulk of the existing growers will change their ways. Vineyards dedicated solely to producing wine grapes are the answer but there are still too few of them.

The large domestic wine producers rely overwhelmingly on bought-in grapes. Most of them do also have vineyards, but these are small and primarily for experimental purposes. On these vineyards, and with a small band of collaborating contract growers, they are testing new varieties of wine grapes, new approaches to SOIL MANAGEMENT and DRAINAGE, different methods of PRUNING and TRAINING SYSTEMS, new approaches to leaf and CANOPY MANAGEMENT, and alternative ways of treating the fruit. The fruit from these experimental vineyards is, of course, made into wine and some of it is very good, but it is generally not available in sufficient quantities to make any appreciable difference to the quality of their mainstream labels and is usually sold to a small group of aficionados in small quantities as individual bottlings. Long overdue modifications to laws severely limiting corporate ownership of farming land are providing some hope for the future but they have been slow in coming and are very limited in scope.

However, both large and small producers have recently accelerated their efforts to expand the small area of land planted to superior European *vinifera* varieties. Cabernet Sauvignon and Cabernet Franc have been planted in the west of Yamanashi prefecture with some reasonable results; Chardonnay and Merlot look fairly well suited to Nagano; and northern European varieties such as Müller-Thurgau, Zweigelt, and particularly Kerner, have done well in Hokkaido.

Together, however, the European varieties comprised little more than 1 per cent of the total area under vine in the mid 2000s and, with the exception of a few hectares of Cabernet Sauvignon, almost all have been planted since the 1970s.

In contrast to the fragmentation of the grape-growing industry, wine-making is extraordinarily concentrated. Over 300 establishments are licensed to make fruit alcohol and, of these, 175 are wineries regularly making commercial grade wine from grapes, 68 of them in Yamanashi prefecture.

Five giant, diversified beverage conglomerates account for half of the total sales of domestic wine (including locally bottled imported bulk wines and blends). Mercian, in top position, accounted for 17 per cent of all sales under domestic labels in 2004. Suntory was second, with 13 per cent, followed by Sapporo (Polaire), Manns Wine (subsidiary of soy sauce maker Kikkoman, main labels Solaris, Manns), and Asahi (Ste Neige), who together account for another 15 per cent of sales. Each of the top five has premium domestic wine labels that are growing in volume and improving steadily in quality. The Japan National Wine Competition, launched in 2003, now provides the market with an objective indicator of relative quality. In the 2005 competition, with 446 entries, seven of the 13 gold medals awarded were taken by Mercian and Manns

Wine. But, clearly, some of the best wines in Japan are still to be found among the much smaller family-owned or city-owned wineries. In Yamanashi, benchmark Koshu is produced by Marufuji (Rubaiyat label), Katsunuma Jōzō, and Grace wineries. Some of the better examples of Cabernet Sauvignon, Merlot, and Chardonnay are found among this group too. Other small wineries with a reputation for quality include Hayashi Noen, Izutsu, and Obuse Domaine Sogga (all in Nagano prefecture), Takeda (Yamagata), Okuizumo (Shimane), Coco Farm (Tochigi), Kuzumaki specialising in *yamabudo* varieties and hybrids (Iwate), and Tsuno (the southernmost winery in Japan, in Miyazaki prefecture).　　D.G.

Jardin de la France is the cleverly evocative name devised for the Loire, 'garden of France', as a vast VIN DE PAYS regional entity. It has been one of the most successful vins de pays, typically a red made from Gamay and Grolleau, although one bottle in every three is a white, which may be made from Sauvignon Blanc, Chardonnay, and/or Chenin Blanc. Gamays and even Sauvignons are sometimes sold as PRIMEUR wines.

Jasnières, white wine appellation of just 50 ha in an enclave within the less favourably exposed Coteaux du LOIR district in the northern Loire. The appellation all but expired in the 1950s but Joël Gigou at Domaine de la Charrière and others such as Domaine Renard-Potaire have injected new passion into the making of these traditionally dry wines from the Chenin Blanc grape. Locals see Jasnières as 'the SAVENNIÈRES of Touraine', so dry and steely are these traditional wines in their youth, and so well do they respond to BOTTLE AGEING. In particularly ripe vintages since the late 1980s, however, extraordinarily rich, appley, BOTRYTIZED wines have been fashioned, either dry or sweet according to the extent of NOBLE ROT infection. The soils are characterized by their high flint content, on the south-east-facing slopes on the north bank of the Loir. Annual production of Jasnières is about double that of white Coteaux du Loir.

The local VDQS is Coteaux du VENDÔMOIS. See also LOIRE, including map.

Jefferson, Thomas (1743–1826), third president of the United States, a wine lover whose interest in wine and hopes for American wine-growing typified the early Republic. As a Virginia farmer, Jefferson grew grapes from all sources, native (see VITIS, AMERICAN VINE SPECIES) and VINIFERA, at his estate Monticello for 50 years with uniform lack of success: no Monticello wine ever materialized, but the hope never died. His vineyard at Monticello has now been restored to the form it had in 1807.

As ambassador to France (1784–9), Jefferson made himself expert in wine, travelling to all the major French wine regions as well as to those of Germany and Italy. He tasted, discussed, and bought largely, and acted also as agent and adviser for his friends in the selection and purchase of wines. The record of this activity contained in his papers is a small encyclopedia of pre-Revolutionary wine and wine production. As president (1801–9), Jefferson was celebrated for the variety and excellence of his cellar at the White House in Washington, which abounded in CHAMBERTIN, MARGAUX, HERMITAGE, YQUEM, and TOKAY. Bottles of late 18th century wines such as Ch LAFITE, supposedly ordered by Jefferson, in the late 20th century fetched record-breaking prices at AUCTION.

After his retirement from public life, living on a much-reduced scale, Jefferson turned to the wines of the south: the reds of BELLET and MONTEPULCIANO, for example, and the Muscat of RIVESALTES. He spared no effort to ensure a good supply from good sources. At all times, Jefferson was eager to assist the many efforts to solve the riddle of successful wine-growing in America: he gave land next to his Virginia estate to support Philip Mazzei's Italian Vineyard Society, an ambitious effort to grow wine by importing Italian vines and vineyard workers; he encouraged such neighbours as James Madison and James Monroe in their viticultural experiments; it was in his administration that land on the river Ohio in Indiana was granted to Swiss-born J. J. Dufour for the enterprise that resulted in the first successful commercial wine production in the UNITED STATES.

By such assistance, and by minimizing wine TAXATION, Jefferson hoped to make the US a wine-drinking country. He could be extravagant in his optimism: a wine from the native Alexander grape he called equal to Chambertin; a sweet SCUPPERNONG from North Carolina he thought would be 'distinguished on the best tables of Europe'. The US, he affirmed, could 'make as great a variety of wines as are made in Europe, not exactly of the same kind, but doubtless as good', even though his own experience contradicted the proposition.

Jefferson's personal pleasure in wine was clear: 'Good wine is a daily necessity for me,' he wrote. He also saw wine as an element in his vision of a nation of independent yeomen: 'no nation is drunken where wine is cheap,' hence wine should be the nation's drink. Despite his failures in practical vine-growing, Jefferson is the great patron of the idea that the US should be a wine-growing nation.						T.P.

A number of bottles of 1784 and 1787 FIRST GROWTH bordeaux, engraved with the initials Th.J. and apparently unearthed by the German wine collector Hardy Rodenstock, constitute the controversial Jefferson bottles, some of which have been offered at auction (see PRICE for details of the most expensive bottle ever sold).

de Treville Lawrence, R. (ed.), *Jefferson and Wine* (2nd edn, The Plains, Va., 1989).

Gabler, J. M., *Passions: The Wines and Travels of Thomas Jefferson* (Baltimore, 1995).

jerepigo or **jerepiko**, unfermented dessert 'wines' in South Africa, the Cape's version of MISTELLE or VIN DOUX NATUREL produced by adding alcohol before fermentation to ripe, very sweet grape juice, usually MUSCADEL. Such products are often labelled Muskadel or Muscadel Jerepigo. Usually about 17 per cent alcohol, often with intense ripe fig and muscat flavours, these traditional, warming wines, once popular in South African winters but now sold in ever-declining volumes, probably derive their name from the Portuguese term JEROPIGA.						J.P.

Jerez, or **Jerez de la Frontera**, city in ANDALUCÍA, south west Spain, that is the centre of the sherry industry. Jerez is also the name of the DO which produces sherry. In Spain the wine is known as *vino de Jerez* (or simply *Jerez*), and sherry is an English corruption of the Spanish word (while in France the town and drink are known respectively as Xérès and *xérès*). The town owes its full name to the fact that in the Middle Ages it was on the frontier between Christian and Moorish Spain. For more details of Jerez's history and organization, see SHERRY.

jeroboam. See BOTTLE SIZES.

jeropiga, Portuguese term for grape must prevented from fermenting by the addition of grape spirit. *Jeropiga* is often used to sweeten FORTIFIED wines. (*Vinho abafado*, on the other hand, is partially fermented before spirit is added; see CARCAVELOS.)

João de Santarém, name used for the widely planted CASTELÃO red wine grape in parts of the RIBATEJO region of Portugal.

Johannisberg, Valais name for fuller-than-average dry white wine made from SILVANER grapes in SWITZERLAND.

Johannisberg Riesling, sometimes abbreviated simply to **JR**, common synonym for the great white RIESLING grape variety of Germany, notably in California. There is no direct connection with the famous SCHLOSS JOHANNISBERG in Germany's RHEINGAU region except that both the famous castle and the region's reputations are founded on Riesling.

Johnson, Hugh (1939–), world's best-selling wine author. Johnson's passion for wine began when he was at Cambridge University, where he read English. One of the great stylists of the LITERATURE OF WINE, he was immediately taken on as a feature writer for Condé Nast magazines on graduation. As a result of his close friendship with André SIMON,

the founder of the International Wine & Food Society, he became General Secretary of the society and succeeded the legendary gastronome as editor of its magazine. At the same time he became wine correspondent of the *Sunday Times* and embarked on his first book *Wine*, whose publication in 1966 established him as one of the foremost English gastronomic writers of the time. More than 750,000 copies have been printed, in seven languages.

His next book was even more successful, even though it allowed only limited scope for Johnson's matchless prose. *The World Atlas of Wine* represented the first serious attempt to map the world's wine regions, and first appeared in 1971. More than four million copies in a total of 14 languages have been sold of this and subsequent editions in 1977, 1985, 1994, and the fully updated 2001 edition, co-written with Jancis Robinson.

Pausing only to write a best-selling book on trees, *The International Book of Trees*, inspired by his acquisition of an Elizabethan house in 12 acres of Essex countryside, he went on to devise and write a best-selling annual wine guide, *The Pocket Wine Book*, which has sold more than eight million copies in a dozen languages, including Mandarin, since its first edition in 1977.

The more expansive *Hugh Johnson's Wine Companion* followed in 1983 and was revised in 1987, 1991, 1997, and 2003. It sold widely in the US as *Hugh Johnson's Modern Encyclopedia of Wine* and in France as *Le Guide mondial du connaisseur de vin*. This prolific output, encouraged by Johnson's publishers Mitchell Beazley, was supplemented by *The Principles of Gardening*, another best seller, and a succession of co-authored and less serious wine books (including even a 'pop-up' version).

Johnson's most distinctive work, however, did not appear until 1989. *The Story of Wine* is a *tour de force*, a single-volume sweep through the history of wine in which Johnson's literary skills and breadth of vision are headily combined. The book was written to coincide with an ambitiously international 13-part television series, *Vintage: A History of Wine*, written and presented by Johnson. In 1992, he co-authored *The Art and Science of Wine* with Australian James Halliday. *A Life Uncorked* (2005) is his most reflective and autobiographical work.

Between 1986 and 2000 Johnson sold the Hugh Johnson Collection, glassware and other wine-related artefacts, with notable success in Japan, where he was a consultant to Jardines Wines and Spirits. He has also served (1986–2001) on the administrative council of first growth Ch LATOUR, as a consultant to British Airways, and has been president of the Sunday Times Wine Club since its inception in 1973. In 1989, Johnson co-founded The Royal TOKAJI Wine Company, a reflection of his interest in wine history. Other activities include regular journalism on and indulgence in gardening. In 2004, none too hastily one might argue, the French made him a Chevalier de l'Ordre National du Mérite.

Johnson is one of the most vocal opponents of SCORING wine, and his writing has been characterized more by a sensual enthusiasm for wine in all its variety than by the critical analysis of individual wines which characterizes writers such as the American Robert PARKER. His daughter Kitty has followed him in to wine writing.

Johnson, H., *Wine: A Life Uncorked* (London, 2005).

joint venture, increasingly common phenomenon in the world's wine business whereby two enterprises with very different strengths combine to produce a wine or wines. The modern prototype was that announced in 1979 between Baron Philippe de ROTHSCHILD of Bordeaux and Robert MONDAVI of California to produce Opus One, the luxuriously priced Napa Valley Cabernet Sauvignon, combining Mondavi's knowledge of and holdings in the Napa Valley with the prestige and wine-making expertise associated with Baron Philippe's first growth Pauillac Ch MOUTON-ROTHSCHILD. Most joint ventures are designed to justify a premium over the other wines made *in situ* by virtue of a much-heralded connection with a glamorous outsider. Both Mondavi and the Mouton team embarked on subsequent joint ventures but they have been joined by dozens of other companies attracted by the global nature of today's wine business (see GLOBALIZATION). Joint ventures are particularly well suited to new wine regions such as those in CHINA and INDIA, for example, where the wine-making expertise of an established wine producer blends well with an enterprise which can offer local knowledge and contacts.

Jongieux, named CRU in the upper Rhône valley just north of Chambéry whose name may be added to the French appellation Vin de SAVOIE. Vineyards allowed this special appellation produce a range of still wines from such varieties as Mondeuse, Pinot Noir, Gamay, Jacquère, Altesse, and Chardonnay. Within Jongieux is the separate Marestel cru, which may append its name to ROUSSETTE DE SAVOIE.

Jordan, Middle Eastern country which produces a small amount of wine each year from an increasing total vineyard area of about 4,000 ha/10,000 acres, which is mainly dedicated to TABLE GRAPES.

Joubertin, occasionally **Jaubertin**, now almost extinct but once widely planted, productive dark-berried vine originally from Savoie in south east France.

joven, Spanish for young. Some wines destined for early consumption are sometimes sold as a Vino Joven.

Juan García, crisp, lively, local dark-skinned vine speciality of the Fermoselle-Arribes zone west of TORO in north west central Spain, where it is usually mixed in the vineyard with other, lesser vines. A total of about 2,500 ha/6,000 acres are planted and, on rocky hillside sites, it can produce highly perfumed if relatively light reds.

Juan Ibáñez, dark-berried vine grown to a limited extent and mainly in mixed vineyards in Cariñena in north east central Spain. Known as Miguel del Arco in Calatayud.

judging wine, an activity that most wine drinkers undertake every time they open a new bottle, but also a serious business on which the commercial future of some wine producers may to a certain extent depend. For details of domestic, amateur wine judging, see TASTING.

The judging process at a more professional level can vary from a gathering of a few friends, a few bottles, and much hot air, to a COMPETITION in which wines have been carefully categorized by wine type, style, and possibly price and are tasted BLIND, in ideal conditions, without any consultation until a possible final discussion of controversial wines. Back-up bottles are always needed in case of CORKED bottles, and to verify whether any other FAULT is confined to a single bottle. SCORING systems vary but typically involve awarding a specific allocation of points for various different aspects such as appearance, nose, palate, perhaps TYPICALITY, and overall quality. MEDALS and trophies are often awarded as a result. Wine SHOWS, often part of much broader annual agricultural shows, are particularly important in Australia, where to be invited to act as a judge, or even associate judge, is a great honour. Wine judges usually wear white coats, work in silence, and may be expected to evaluate as many as 200 wines a day.

For the results of professional wine judging on an individual or small group basis, see WINE WRITING.

jugs for serving wine. See DECANTERS.

jug wine, term used in CALIFORNIA for the most basic sort of wine, an American counterpart to VIN ordinaire or PLONK. After PROHIBITION was repealed in 1933, most inexpensive California GENERIC table wine was bottled in half-gallon and gallon (1.9- and 3.9-l) glass jugs or flagons with SCREW CAPS to satisfy a demand largely made up of thirsty immigrant labourers from the Mediterranean and eastern Europe. As this market segment has aged and died without direct replacement, newer generations have turned to wine sold in BOXES, FIGHTING VARIETALS and their cheaper, 'value' successors, and jug wines have waned.

Juhfark, distinctive but almost extinct white grape variety once widely grown in HUNGARY.

After the PHYLLOXERA invasion it never regained its importance and is today found almost exclusively in the Somló region, where it can produce wine usefully high in acidity which ages well. The vine, whose name means 'ewe's tail', is inconveniently sensitive to both frost and mildew.

Juliénas, one of the ten BEAUJOLAIS crus in the far north of the region. About 600 ha/1,500 acres of vines can produce wines with real backbone, although most should be drunk within two or three years of the vintage. Reliable producers include Jean-François Perraud and Michel Tête.

Jullien, André (1766–1832), seminal wine writer, Parisian wine merchant, and one of the first explorers of the *world* of wine, venturing even as far as 'Chinese Tartary' in order to discover and assess all international wine regions and their produce. His was an extraordinary outlook, and it must have been a demanding journey, in an era when his peers barely ventured beyond the threshold of their wine shops. He had clearly read the contemporary LITERATURE OF WINE, which, until that point, concerned itself almost entirely with the details of how to grow vines and how to make wine (see CHAPTAL, for example). His aim was to discover and categorize the characteristics of as many different CRUS as he could find, travelling throughout eastern Europe, along the Silk Road to Asia, as well as discovering the vineyards of Africa. There can be few contemporary wine writers who are as well travelled. The result was the publication in Paris in 1816 of *Topographie de tous les vignobles connus*, a substantial volume full of useful detail which includes the most comprehensive wine CLASSIFICATION (into five classes according to quality) ever undertaken. Much of it was translated into English and published, in abridged form, as 'a manual and guide to all importers and purchasers in the choice of wines' in London in 1824. In effect, Jullien's work set the style for a high proportion of modern wine writing.

For more details of Jullien's classification, see the LITERATURE OF WINE.

Jumilla, denominated wine region in the LEVANTE north of Murcia in central, southern Spain (see map under SPAIN) producing mainly strong red wines. The climate is arid, with RAINFALL amounting to just 300 mm/11.7 in a year. The principal grape variety in this DO is the red Monastrell (MOURVÈDRE), which ripens in the summer temperatures of around 40 °C/104 °F to produce wines that can reach a natural ALCOHOLIC STRENGTH of 18 per cent. Average YIELDS of 12 to 15 hl/ha (0.7–0.8 tons/acre) have been uneconomically low, but more recent planting of GRAFTED vines has improved prospects.

About half of the region's much-reduced total area of 33,000 ha/81,510 acres lies in

Castilla-La Mancha and the rest in the region of Murcia. For this reason, Jumilla is one of the three DOs in Spain regulated by the Agriculture Ministry and not by regional authorities.

Much of the wine from Jumilla was traditionally produced by the DOBLE PASTA method and used for blending with lighter wines from other parts of Spain. The vast San Isidro CO-OPERATIVE dominates the region's production, although since the mid 1980s a number of smaller, private producers such as Agapito Rico, Casa Castillo, Finca Luzón, and Hijos de Juan Gil have been striving, with some success, to tame Monastrell, often by blending it with Tempranillo or Merlot. That a big northern company such as TORRES has invested in the region is significant. The Merseguera grape produces rather fat, bland, hot country white wine.   R.J.M. & V. de la S.

Jura, far eastern French wine region, between Burgundy and Switzerland, that is sufficiently isolated to have retained TRADITION, some unique grape varieties, and such unusual wine types as VIN JAUNE and the occasional VIN DE PAILLE, as well as the local VIN DE LIQUEUR, Macvin du Jura, and a certain amount of MARC du Jura. Henri Maire is the dominant wine company.

Although this was once an important wine region, with nearly 20,000 ha/49,400 acres planted in the early 19th century, there are only about 1,600 ha of vineyards today, on slopes mainly at ALTITUDES of between 250 and 400 m/820–1,310 ft on the first upland between the Bresse plain and the Jura mountains. The chief town is Lons-le-Saunier, although ARBOIS is deemed to be the wine region's capital. The lower land may be flat CLAY while there is LIMESTONE on higher ground (mirroring that of the CÔTE D'OR on the other side of the Saône) and vineyards with outcrops of MARL are considered the best. Some slopes are steep enough for SOIL EROSION to require annual treatment. Vines have to be trained high, usually in double GUYOT, in order to avoid autumn frosts, for the harvest here can continue until well into late October, so late do some varieties ripen. The climate here is even more CONTINENTAL than in Burgundy and winters can be very cold.

Five grape varieties are of importance in modern Jura (although more than 40 played a role at the end of the 19th century). PINOT NOIR and CHARDONNAY, occasionally known here proprietorially as Melon d'Arbois, have been borrowed from Burgundy, although they have been grown in the Jura vineyards since the Middle Ages. Chardonnay has been increasing in importance here as elsewhere, and had reached 45 per cent of total plantings by the early 21st century. Its early ripening and good sugar levels make it popular with growers, even if it can hardly be said to provide the definitive expression of the region. Quality has improved however with the growing popularity of CRÉMANT DU JURA for which underripe or young-vine Chardonnay may be used, leaving the best for the still wines. Pinot Noir is increasingly valued either as a varietal wine or to add useful colour and sometimes structure to local red wine varieties. POULSARD, often called Ploussard, grown particularly in Arbois-Pupillin makes light reds or deep-coloured rosés, often with an orange tint, sometimes described as *corail*. Poulsard may account for as much as 25 per cent of total vine plantings in Jura and is also used for vin de paille. Another local red wine grape variety, TROUSSEAU, needs the additional warmth of gravelly soils to ripen and is grown chiefly in Arbois, where some producers are capable of fashioning it into a deep-flavoured VARIETAL wine.

Jura's really distinctive grape variety, however, is the white SAVAGNIN, also called Naturé here, which is probably an antecedent of TRAMINER and hence GEWÜRZTRAMINER. Grown to a limited extent all over the region, it is a permitted ingredient in all of its white wines but is especially known as the sole permitted variety for the extraordinary, nutty, long-lived vin jaune, sold in the distinctive 62 cl *clavelin* squat bottle. (Other Jura wines are mainly sold in another specially shaped bottle with the word Jura stamped on the shoulder.) See VIN JAUNE and CHÂTEAU-CHALON, which specializes in this unusual drink, France's answer to top-quality dry SHERRY.

See also the more varied appellation ARBOIS which, like Côtes du Jura, makes red, pink, or white still wine along with vin jaune and vin de paille. The appellation L'ETOILE is reserved for these last two while Château-Chalon is reserved for vin jaune only. Crémant du Jura, sparkling wines which are generally white and occasionally rosé, may be produced anywhere in the region.

Wine-making techniques are generally traditional, and CHAPTALIZATION is as common as one would expect of a region sited between Burgundy and Switzerland. Unusually, most reds are matured in tank rather than wood, and bottled early, while white wines are often aged in small or large oak barrels and bottled later.

The wines are distinctive, particularly those which contain the local grape varieties, but remain a mainly local treat. At their worst they taste like thin burgundy; at their best they are particularly good candidates for FOOD AND WINE MATCHING. **Côtes du Jura,** the region's second most important appellation, after Arbois, includes a wide area although fewer than 700 ha/1,750 acres of vines, and wines may be red, white, or dark pink; still or sparkling; vinified normally or matured slowly into vin jaune. About a third of the wine produced is still red or pink. Notable producers in this appellation include Alain Labet, Baud Père et Fils, Pignier, and Ch d'Arlay, whose history testifies to Jura's varied past under Burgundy and Spanish domination. An increasing proportion of varietal wines are made, from any of Jura's five varieties.   J.R. & W.L.

Friol, J.-P., and Bertaud, M., *Jura, les vins authentiques* (Nantes, 1997).

Jurançon is a name closely associated with SOUTH WEST FRANCE, of a distinguished white wine both dry (Jurançon Sec) and sweet (labelled simply Jurançon), of a relatively important, if undistinguished, dark-berried vine variety, and of an entirely unimportant light-berried vine.

The wine
This fashionable, tangy, distinctive white wine has been celebrated and fiercely protected since the Middle Ages, and Jurançon was one of France's earliest APPELLATIONS CONTRÔLÉES. In the 14th century, the princes of BÉARN and the parliament of NAVARRA introduced the concept of a CRU by identifying and valuing specific favoured vineyard sites. Locals claim this as France's first attempt at vineyard CLASSIFICATION, just as they claim the drop of Jurançon with which the infant Henri IV's lips were rubbed at his baptism in 1553 was responsible for most of his subsequent achievements. The Dutch were great enthusiasts for this wine and there was also a flourishing export trade across the Atlantic until PHYLLOXERA almost destroyed the wine. Jurançon's reputation was further advanced in the early 20th century by the enthusiasm of the French writer Colette.

PETIT MANSENG, GROS MANSENG, the local PETIT COURBU, and a little local Camaralet and Lauzet vines are grown on about 820 ha/2,000 acres of vineyards in this hilly, relatively cool corner of southern France near Pau at the relatively high average ALTITUDE of 300 m/984 ft. Spring FROSTS are such a threat that many vines are ESPALIER trained, but the Atlantic influence ensures sufficient RAINFALL. Vineyards on a mixture of limestone, sand, clay, and stones are protected by the Midi d'Ossau mountain. While the wines from Monein tend to be particularly rich in traditional style, those from the Coteaux (Chapelle-de-Rousse) tend to be crisper and more mineral.

Gros Manseng is chiefly responsible for Jurançon Sec, the more common dry but strongly flavoured version of this wine, for which yields of 60 hl/ha (3.4 tons/acre) are allowed. Petit Manseng, with its small, thick-skinned berries, is ideal for the production of Jurançon's real speciality, long-living sweet Jurançon made from grapes partially dried on the vine (see PASSERILLÉ) which in some years may not be harvested until December, at a maximum yield of 40 hl/ha but often much less. If several TRIES are made through the vineyard (two are mandatory), the results may be bottled separately. OAK is used to increasing effect. These MOELLEUX wines, whose green tinge seems to deepen with age, serve well as aperitifs and with a wide range of foods. One of

France's best-value SWEET WINES is made particularly successfully by the likes of Bru-Baché, Cauhapé, and Clos Uroulat.

The vine varieties

Vines called Jurançon have in their time been cultivated in practically every region of south west France, other than Jurançon itself. The black- or red-berried version was once the high-yielding ARAMON-like workhorse of this part of France and more than 1,200 ha/ 3,000 acres were still in production at the turn of the century, even though this **Jurançon Noir** could only be sold as VIN DE PAYS. Some south western appellations still sanction Jurançon Noir in their red wines, but its inclusion is today usually theoretical. **Jurançon Blanc** was once quite widely planted in Gascony but is nearly extinct.

Juwel, white grape variety and one of the GERMAN CROSSINGS. A few vines linger, mainly in RHEINHESSEN.

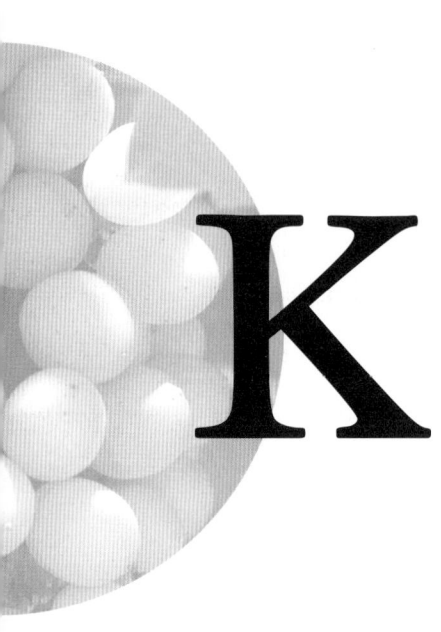

K

Kabinett, one of six so-called PRÄDIKATS applying to German wine that has not been chaptalized, and designating—depending on growing region and grape variety—must weights between 67 and 82 °Oechsle. As such, Kabinett designates the lightest end of the German wine spectrum, and Mosel Kabinetts that have RESIDUAL SUGAR are often as low as 7 or 8 per cent alcohol. The term Kabinett, like the pegging of quality designations to minimum must weights itself, is entirely a product of the 1971 GERMAN WINE LAW. The name was chosen for its association with the English word CABINET, widely used in Germany prior to 1971 as a general term of approbation for wines in all styles.

See also AUSTRIA.　　　　　　　　　D.S.

Kadarka is the most famous red wine grape of HUNGARY, largely because of the important role it once played in BULL'S BLOOD, but the variety is in marked decline and has been substantially replaced by the viticulturally sturdier KÉKFRANKOS, and by PORTUGIESER in Villány. It is still cultivated on the Great Plain and in the Szekszárd wine region just across the Danube to the west but its tendency to GREY ROT and its habit of ripening riskily late limit it to certain favoured sites. The vine is also naturally highly productive and needs careful control in order to produce truly concentrated wines, ideally trained as BUSH VINES. Fully ripened Szekszárdi Kadarka can be a fine, soft, full-bodied wine worthy of ageing but is produced in minuscule quantities. Kadarka is too often over-produced and picked when still low in colour and flavour and is no longer the backbone of Hungary's red wine production.

Kadarka's origins are obscure, but some believe it is related to the variety known as Skadarsko, from Lake Scutari, which forms the frontier between ALBANIA and MONTENEGRO.

Today it is grown on a very limited scale over the southern border in Vojvodina, and in Romania, where it is called Cadarca, and, most importantly, in Bulgaria, where it is called Gamza and is widely planted in the north, where it can produce wines of interest in long growing seasons if yields are restricted.

Because of its—largely historic—fame, this is a variety which is often included in any large NURSERY collection of vine varieties.

See also IZSÁKI.

Kalterer or **Kalterersee,** German for the TRENTINO and ALTO ADIGE zone known as Caldaro or Lago di Caldaro in Italian.

Kangaroo Island, unique, cool, maritime region (fauna, flora, etc.) south of Adelaide in SOUTH AUSTRALIA. Bordeaux-based FLYING WINEMAKER Jacques Lurton has established a vineyard and winery (The Islander), the leading product an eclectic blend of Sangiovese, Cabernet Franc, and Malbec.

Kanzler is a modern GERMAN CROSSING that has already fallen from grace. A Müller-Thurgau × Silvaner cross bred at Alzey in 1927 and always essentially a Rheinhessen variety, it reaches high MUST WEIGHTS but needs a good site and, fatally, does not yield well.

Kazakhstan, independent central Asian, once Soviet, republic. This large area south of Russia and bordering China is subject to great extremes of climate. Its capital in the far south east is Alma-Ata. Less than 4 per cent of Kazakhstan offers favourable soil and climatic conditions for commercial grape culture.

History

Evidence of grape culture in Kazakhstan dates back to the 7th century AD. The Turkestan area of the Chimkent region (where the grapevine was imported from the Samarkand and the Fergana regions of UZBEKISTAN) and the Panfilov area of the Taldy-Kurgan region (where grapevines are popularly believed to have come from CHINA's western Xinjiang province) are the country's most ancient viticultural areas.

At the end of the 19th century, grapes were grown on a small scale by private farms. The development of commercial grape culture began in the 1930s, when the first fruit- and wine-growing state farms such as Issyk in the Alma-Ata region, Uch Bulak in the Dzhambul region, and Juvaly and Kaplanbek in the Chimkent region were established. Viticulture developed rapidly after 1957. Vineyards occupied 4,997 ha in 1958, and 22,311 ha/ 55,130 acres in 1976. Twenty-six specialized fruit- and wine-growing state farms in the south and south east of the country owned 85 per cent of the total vineyard area with the rest divided between collective farms and individuals.

Modern viticulture

According to OIV figures, Kazakhstan had 13,000 ha/32,120 acres of vines in 2002 producing 236,000 hl/over 6.2 million gal of wine. The climate of the country is very CONTINENTAL. The active temperature summation varies from 1,800 °C in the north east to 4,500 °C in the south, and winters can be very cold. The annual rainfall is 700 to 1,000 mm/27–39 in in the Zaili and Talas Alatau but is as little as 100 to 150 mm (4–6 in) in some areas of the Gur'yev and the Aktyubinsk regions.

Commercial vine culture is principally located in the Chimkent, the Alma-Ata, the Dzhambul, the Kzyl-Ordin, and the Taldy-Kurgan regions with southern areas concentrating on dessert wines. IRRIGATION is the norm, and most vineyards also need WINTER PROTECTION.

More than 40 grape varieties are allowed for commercial culture, of which 24 are for TABLE GRAPES, an important crop here. Wine varieties include RKATSITELI, RIESLING, PINOT NOIR, SAPERAVI, ALIGOTÉ, ALEATICO, Bayan Shirey, Kuljinski, Maiski Cherny, CABERNET FRANC, CABERNET SAUVIGNON, Rubinovy Magaracha, Hungarian Muscat (probably MUSCAT OTTONEL), and Muscat Rosé.

Kazakhstan has the potential to become one of the main suppliers of wines and especially grapes to eastern portions of Russia.   V.R.

kék means 'blue' in Hungarian and, as such, can be a direct equivalent of BLAU in German or even NOIR in French.

Kékfrankos, Hungarian name for the red grape variety known in Austria as BLAUFRÄNKISCH (of which it is a direct translation). This useful variety, which produces lively, juicy, peppery, well-coloured reds for relatively early consumption, is grown widely in HUNGARY. It is most successful in Sopron near the Austrian border although it can also produce full-bodied wines in Villány. On the Great Plain its wines can be relatively heavy.

Kékmedoc, formerly called Medoc Noir, is the Hungarian name for a dark-skinned grape variety which produces aromatic, medium-bodied red wine for early consumption which smells like MUSCAT. It was brought into Hungary by Mathiasz János, and is grown to a limited extent in Eger. Some think it is identical to ALEATICO; Galet suggests the French variety Mornen Noir.

Kéknyelű, revered but rare white grape variety grown in HUNGARY and named after its 'blue' stalk. Once widely planted, it was becoming rare even in its last stronghold Badacsony on the north shore of lake Balaton by the mid 1990s. The vine itself is so sensitive that yields are extremely low and so it began its fall from favour in the 1970s, when wine-making philosophy in Hungary was to produce large quantities of ordinary wine for export to other Comecon countries. True, well-made Kéknyelű can be aromatic and exciting but some very ordinary blends have been label led Badacsony Kéknyelű. Recent plantings there bode well, however.

Kékoportó, former name of PORTUGIESER in HUNGARY.

Keller is German for a cellar, even a small domestic cellar, while **Kellerei** is used in much the same way as the word CAVE in French, for any sort of wine-producing premises whether above or below ground. A German wine specifying a Keller rather than a WEINGUT on the label is usually the produce of a merchant rather than an estate. In ALTO ADIGE, the Italian Tyrol, **Kellereigenossenschaft** is a common name for one of the many wine CO-OPERATIVES. **Kellermeister** is German for cellarmaster, a position very similar to MAÎTRE DE CHAI in France.

Kendall-Jackson, original brand name of the winery and vineyard empire begun by Jess Jackson (Kendall was his former wife's maiden name) in Lake county, California, during the mid 1970s. By the early 1990s, expansion and acquisition had resulted in such a proliferation of brand names that the formal title of the umbrella company was changed to Artisans & Estates, but in US trade jargon 'K-J' is still used for the whole collection, as well as for the Kendall-Jackson labels specifically.

In many ways, Jess Jackson exemplifies the entrepreneurial nature of the CALIFORNIA wine industry as well as the go-go climate of the 1980s.

Most prominent players in the world of wine started with a significant viticultural or financial inheritance. Jackson did not, which adds grist to popular conjecture about his personality. Born in 1930, Jackson grew up poor and put himself through college and law school at UC Berkeley working as a police officer and a longshoreman. He made his own financial stake over thirty years as an attorney in San Francisco.

He entered the wine industry almost accidentally in 1974 when he purchased a small pear and walnut ranch on the western side of Clear lake as a weekend retreat. He planted grapes, but had trouble selling them for a decent return, so he began to investigate converting them to wine. By 1998, estimates valued his family-owned wine venture at more than $1 billion, selling 3.5 million cases a year with annual revenue around $325 million and 1,200 employees. Artisans & Estates own 10,000 acres/4,045 ha of vineyards in Santa Barbara, Monterey, Sonoma, Napa, and Mendocino counties as well as in Lake. They also own Villa Archeno wine estate in Toscana, Viña Calina in Chile, and a cooperage in France.

In the 1980s, Kendall-Jackson happily disregarded the California industry's movement toward vineyard designations, concentrating instead on blending from various regions to achieve certain taste characteristics. To say this strategy worked would be a grave understatement. Jackson's first wines were put together under the auspices of CONSULTANT Ric Forman in 1982, then continually improved under the hand of winemaker Jed Steele, who arrived in 1983. The hallmarks of K-J's blended Chardonnays were refreshingly strong ACIDITY, creamy oak vanillins (see OAK FLAVOUR), exotic pineapple fruit flavour, and softness and immediate drinkability from just-perceptible RESIDUAL SUGAR. Classically inclined show JUDGES put up token resistance to the residual sugar, but consumers had no such reservations.

Speculation is that a dollop of Muscat-based SWEET RESERVE is the mystery ingredient driving this successful recipe. Verification is not available because Jackson went to court in 1992 to prevent Jed Steele from revealing what he claimed were 'trade secrets', on his departure from K-J. Despite a noteworthy

historical precedent in the California wine industry of shared information, Jackson prevailed. In 1992, Kendall-Jackson overtook MOËT & CHANDON to become the top revenue-producing premium wine brand in the US.

In 1987, Jackson acquired 1,000 acres in Santa Barbara county and opened the first of his additional winery labels, Cambria Winery and Vineyard. Since that time, acquisitions have been so frequent that any book is obsolete on the subject long before publication. Particularly notable was the 1993 purchase of Vinwood Cellars, a 500,000-case former CUSTOM CRUSH FACILITY in Alexander valley; the 1994 purchase of Robert Pepi Winery in Napa valley; and the 1995 purchase of the 1,800-acre Gauer Estate vineyards in Alexander valley. Matanzas Creek was added later. Other important A & E brands included: Hartford Court (Russian River Pinot Noir and Zinfandel), Edmeades (Mendocino old-vine Zinfandel), La Crema, Kristone (Central Coast sparkling wines), Atalon, and Cardinale. Several of these portfolio brands represent a marked departure from the Kendall-Jackson brand philosophy in that they are sold with a marketing story which attempts to capitalize to some extent on REGIONALITY. There has also been a significant move towards SUSTAINABLE VITICULTURE and HILLSIDE VINEYARDS.   B.C.C.

Kenya, African country virtually on the equator, with a very limited production of wines. Since the mid 1980s, *vinifera* vines have been cultivated and have been harvested every eight months, providing three vintages every two years, chiefly from vineyards around lake Naivasha (see TROPICAL VITICULTURE). Rainy seasons are March to May and October to December and some producers may revert to one growing season from June to September. The best white wines have been made from Sauvignon Blanc grapes together with some experimental Chardonnay, Colombard, and Chenin Blanc, while some decent red wine has been made from Ruby Cabernet with some Carnelian, and even a Pinot Noir. The pioneer growers were John and Guy d'Olier of Lake Naivasha Vineyards. Until the early 1990s, wine was bottled and marketed exclusively by the Kenya government.   J.P.

Platter, J. & E., *Africa Uncorked* (London, 2002).

Kerner—at least to judge from its 5,000 ha/ 12,350 acres in Germany in 2003—is the great success story of modern German vine breeding. Released for commercial use only in 1969, after such GERMAN CROSSINGS as SCHEUREBE and around the same time as FABER and HUXELREBE, the reliable ripener Kerner has since the 1990s jockeyed, with the ancient SILVANER, for position as Germany's third most planted light-berried vine. As with most of these crossings, the bulk of Germany's Kerner is planted in Rheinhessen and the Pfalz, but it is still popular in Württemberg, where it was bred from a red parent TROLLINGER

(Schiava Grossa) × Riesling. The large white berries produce wines commendably close to Riesling in flavour except for their own leafy, sometimes candied and mawkish, aroma and slightly coarser texture. It is a crossing which does not need to be subsumed in the blending vat but can produce respectable VARIETAL wines, up to quite high PRÄDIKAT levels, on its own account. Of the 20th-century *vinifera* crossings, only the more capricious EHRENFELSER tastes as Riesling-like, both crossings having the ability to age, thanks to their high acidity. Kerner is popular with growers as well as wine drinkers because of its late budding and therefore good FROST resistance. It is so vigorous, however, that it needs careful summer trimming. It ripens slightly later than Müller-Thurgau, about the same time as Silvaner, but can be planted in almost any vineyard site and regularly achieves MUST WEIGHTS and acidity levels 10 to 20 per cent above the dreary Müller-Thurgau. As with BACCHUS, many of the best examples of Kerner come from the clay-limestone soils of FRANKEN.

Kerner, which takes its name not from any vine breeder but from a local 19th-century writer of drinking songs, has also been planted in England, quite successfully in JAPAN, and to a very limited extent in South Africa.

Kevedinka, ordinary white eastern European grape variety. See DINKA.

kir, alternative name for a *vin blanc cassis*, dry white wine and blackcurrant liqueur, named after a hero of the Burgundian resistance movement during the Second World War, Canon Kir, who was also mayor of Dijon. The CÔTE D'OR is an important grower of blackcurrants and most of the best-quality blackcurrant liqueurs, or *eaux-de-vie de cassis*, are made here. The typical base wine is the relatively acid Bourgogne ALIGOTÉ and to most palates a dash of full-strength liqueur is all that is needed. In a French bar, however, the *cassis* may make up to a fifth of the mix. A **kir royal** is made with sparkling rather than still white wine.

Királyleányka, meaning 'princess', Hungarian light-skinned grape variety, lightly perfumed and with refreshing ACIDITY. It is sometimes known as Dánosi Leányka after its geographical origins in Transylvania. Balatonboglár is its chief home in modern Hungary but there are also fine examples from Eger and Mátra.

Kişmiş, Kismis, Kishmish, Middle Eastern synonyms for the common SULTANA.

K-J. See KENDALL-JACKSON.

Klein Karoo, inland wine region in SOUTH AFRICA also known as Little Karoo.

Klevener de Heiligenstein is an Alsace oddity, a vine speciality of the village of Heiligenstein introduced in 1740 by its mayor Erhard Wantz, possibly from Chiavenna in the Italian alps. It is a locally adapted TRAMINER, occasionally known as Clevner de Heiligenstein, which is increasingly popular. Around 55 ha/135 acres were planted in and around the commune of Heiligenstein in the late 1990s. See also ALSACE and GERMAN HISTORY.

Klevner, like CLEVNER, is, and more particularly was, used fairly indiscriminately in Alsace and other German-speaking wine regions for various vine varieties, notably but not exclusively for various members of the PINOT family. References to Klevner in Alsace in the mid 16th century are common.

Klöch, wine centre in Styria in AUSTRIA, now part of the Süd-Oststeiermark district and known for Traminer wines grown on volcanic soil.

Kloster Eberbach, monastery in the RHEINGAU region of Germany with a tradition of viticulture; now seen as the cultural wine centre of the Rheingau. Kloster Eberbach was founded in 1135 by Bernard of Clairvaux. Throughout the Middle Ages, Cistercian monks produced wine at the monastery, and made its name as one of the most important wine estates of its time. Through viticultural enterprise, the monastery became extremely powerful, owning a fleet of ships which sailed the Rhine.

Kloster Eberbach is now the home of the educational organization the German Wine Academy and the Rheingau Wine Society. It also provides a regional centre for wine auctions, trade fairs, and seminars. The Lay Brothers' Refectory houses a collection of historic wine presses, dating back to 1668. The Steinberg vineyard, planted by monks 700 years ago next to the monastery, is still producing highly rated wines.

See also MONKS AND MONASTERIES.　S.A.

Klosterneuburg, city on the Danube west of Vienna in AUSTRIA whose Augustinian monastery has since the 11th century been a substantial vineyard owner and wine producer and has, since 1860, been the country's centre for viticultural and OENOLOGICAL research. Austria's standard measurement of grape ripeness or MUST WEIGHT is the KMW, or Klosterneuburger Mostwage, which is equivalent to about 5 °OECHSLE. It is sometimes known as Babo after August Freiherr von Babo, who developed the system. Stift Klosterneuburg, the winery's total vineyard holdings, spread over the districts of Vienna, Thermenregion to the immediate south of the capital, and Donauland-Carnuntum, of which the abbey is in effect the wine capital, constitute the country's largest estate with more than 100 ha/247 acres. Klosterneuburg

wines are made by a company owned by the monastic order, and are partly bottled in their own special squat bottle. The cellars also house the Austrian State Wine Archive and there is both a quality control centre and an oenological school. Research activity is wide ranging but centred on developing vine CROSSINGS as well as pest control and general oenological and viticultural matters. In the 1920s, Dr Zweigelt developed several successful vine variety crossings at Klosterneuburg which are widely planted in modern Austria (see ZWEIGELT).

KMW, measure of MUST WEIGHT in AUSTRIA. See KLOSTERNEUBURG.

Knights Valley, inland California wine region and AVA between the northern end of Napa valley and the southern end of Alexander valley. See SONOMA.

Knipperlé is now almost a relic, a dark-berried vine once much more popular as the base of light white wine in Alsace. This early-ripening variety was introduced in 1756 by Johann Michael Ortlieb and it was therefore alternatively known as Ortlieber (see GERMAN HISTORY). Occasional bottles can still be found but this variety, relatively popular as a high yielder and early ripener at the end of the 19th century, is too prone to rot to be of more than historical interest. It is a natural offspring of Pinot and Gouais Blanc (see PINOT).

Korea, rugged, mountainous peninsula on the Asian mainland, between China and Japan, for long a producer of TABLE GRAPES but of wine only since 1977, when the large beverages group, DooSan Baekwha, launched its Majuang label, which still accounts for about 80 per cent of all Korean wine produced. The first wine was a substitute for imported SACRAMENTAL WINE for the Korean Catholic Church but its ultimate goal was to reach local consumers with an affordable alternative to costly imported table wines. Wine consumption in Korea soared in the 2000s but the market is almost entirely reliant on imports. DooSan's earlier rivals have mostly abandoned their local wine ventures. Recent entrants Chateau Mani and Kenneth Kim Vineyards have mounted a limited challenge and the tiny East of Eden Winery has attracted attention with its sweetish red wine made from the exotic wild mountain grape (literally *sanmaoru*)—VITIS *amurensis*.

Viticultural conditions are far from ideal, due principally to extremely cold winters and rainy and humid summers. Vineyards are scattered throughout the country but those attached to wine-making operations are either in the south east of the peninsula in the provinces of North and South Gyeongsang on sandy or stony sedimentary soils, and favoured by a milder MARITIME climate, or in the provinces of Gyeonggi and Chungcheong in the north west. The main varieties grown for the table are the hybrid Campbell Early, comprising two thirds of the total vineyard area, and Kyoho. The varieties grown specifically for wine are Riesling, Seibel, White Muscat (MUSCAT BLANC À PETIT GRAINS) and Muscat Bailey A. There are, however, no substantial plantings of the wine varieties. In fact, the total of DooSan's corporate vineyards is only 140 ha/350 acres. Beneath the appearance of a substantial local industry, therefore, is the reality that, like that of JAPAN, the Korean domestic wine industry is heavily dependent on wine imported in bulk. To the credit of the producers and the regulatory authorities, this information is declared on the label—all in Korean, of course. D.G.

kosher (meaning 'pure') wine satisfies strict rabbinical production criteria that make it suitable for consumption by religious Jews. However, whereas the kashrut (dietary laws) of food depends on the food's source, the kashrut of wine depends more on the handler. Wine has always played an important part in Jewish ritual, is mentioned frequently in the BIBLE, and was produced in Palestine, as attested by archaeological excavations, until the Muslim conquest of AD 636, when all alcoholic beverages were banned (see ISLAM).

Rabbis encouraged moderate wine consumption as good for HEALTH. Wine has been a constant thread through Jewish festivals; it is sipped as the sabbath starts (kiddush) and again when it ends (havdala) with a blessing: 'Blessed are You, Lord our God, King of the universe, who creates the fruit of the vine.'

Kosher wines worldwide can be made from any suitable grapes, with no restrictions on styles. To be considered kosher, a wine must be handled by orthodox religious Jews only. OENOLOGISTS who are not themselves sabbath-observing may instruct observant Jews to carry out the necessary physical operations in the winery. All substances used in the process must be kosher. Examples of forbidden FINING agents include gelatin (an animal derivative), casein (a dairy derivative), and isinglass (which comes from a non-kosher fish). Kosher wines may be suitable for vegetarians (and, if egg whites are not used, for vegans too).

Wines described as 'kosher for Passover' have not come into contact with bread, dough, or grain. Otherwise normal wine-making procedures are followed. Wine need not be inferior because it is kosher.

Kosher wine produced in ISRAEL must conform to biblical agricultural laws, dating from when the land of Israel was an agrarian society.

1. No wine may be produced from a vine until its fourth year.
2. The vineyard, if within the biblical lands, must be left fallow every seven years, though in practice vineyards are symbolically sold to a non-Jew to allow production to continue.
3. Only vines may be grown in vineyards: no other fruits or vegetables are allowed.

4. There must be a symbolic ceremony in which just over 1 per cent of production is poured away in remembrance of the 10 per cent tithe set aside for Levites and priests in the days of the Jerusalem Temple.

Sweet, heavy sacramental reds such as Manischewitz and Palwin, known as kiddush wines, have given kosher wines a bad name. In America, kosher wines became sweet because CONCORD grapes, the principal variety available to immigrants in the New York area, were acidic and its wine needed sweetening to become palatable. Jews are also permitted to use pure, natural kosher grape juice for the kiddush blessing instead of a sacramental wine.

The tradition of sweet wines began to be eroded in the 1980s when top-flight dry Israeli VINIFERA wines and their American counterparts came into play. Today, Jews can make blessings while using increasingly good table wines from Australia, California, France, Italy, Israel, and Spain which are perfectly respectable wines that happen to be kosher. Most wine-producing countries produce kosher wine, some of the best of which include Israel's Yarden from the Golan Heights and Carmel's single-vineyard and Yatir wines, Royal Wine Corporation's Herzog brand in California, and Ch Valandraud from St-Emilion.

Strictly religious Jews may demand wine (or must) that is flash PASTEURIZED so that the wine then becomes *yayin mevushal*. This term translates literally and rather unfortunately as 'boiled wine'. Mevushal wine, which remains kosher even if served by someone non-observant or a non-Jew, is required by kosher caterers and many kosher restaurants. This does affect quality and ageing potential but new flash pasteurization techniques lessen the damage. Most higher quality kosher wines are not Mevushal.

Not all wines produced in Israel are automatically kosher, although some producers who make non-kosher wines (which allow them freer creative rein as winemakers) contract with others to produce kosher bottlings for their portfolios. H.G. & A.S.M.

Kosovo, small region within SERBIA between MACEDONIA and MONTENEGRO (see map of former YUGOSLAVIA). Until the onset of civil war in the 1990s, its 10,000 ha/24,700 acres of vineyards in spectacular inland mountain and valley settings were largely devoted to the production of Amselfelder branded wine for sale in Germany. Trainloads of light red were sent in bulk to Belgrade for STABILIZATION, sweetening, and shipment. The light aromatic fruit of the PINOT NOIR was certainly the inspiration behind this brand. CABERNET FRANC, MERLOT, PROKUPAC, and GAMAY are also part of the region's production.

Kosovo is a poor region and its dependence on exports of Amselfelder became a serious liability when Yugoslav turmoil made the

German importers realize how easily other eastern European vineyard areas could copy the style. A.H.M.

Kotsifali. Generous, spicy, if soft wines are produced from this red grape speciality of the Greek island of Crete, planted on about 550 ha/1,350 acres. They are best blended with something more tannic such as MANDELARIA.

Kövérszőlő, one of the oldest grape varieties in TOKAJ, also called Fehérszolo, 'white grape', and revived in the late 1990s. It ripens two weeks earlier than FURMINT and is particularly suitable for high-quality aszú wines.

Kövidinka, ordinary white eastern European grape variety. See DINKA.

krater. See CRATER.

Kratosija, relatively important grape in Macedonia and Montenegro.

Krems, important, medieval wine town in lower AUSTRIA, now part of the Kremstal area and home to one of Austria's largest producers, the co-operative Winzer Krems.

Krug, small but important Champagne house founded in Rheims in 1843 by Johann-Joseph Krug, who was born in Mainz, Germany, in 1830. By 1893 the firm occupied its current modest cellars, around whose courtyard the Krug family still live. Krug does not make an ordinary NON-VINTAGE champagne but specializes exclusively in PRESTIGE CUVÉES, of which the multi-vintage Grande Cuvée is the flagship. Consistently producing champagne that is among the most admired in its region of origin, Krug is the only house to persist in BARREL FERMENTATION of its entire production of base wine, in old 205-l/54-gal casks. Wines from at least six and sometimes nine different vintages make up the blend for Grande Cuvée, one of the most distinctive and long lived of champagnes. Grande Cuvée, with new packaging and a special bottle, succeeded the rather fuller-bodied Private Cuvée as Krug's most important product in 1979. In 1971, Krug acquired and replanted the Clos du Mesnil, a walled vineyard of less than 2 ha/5 acres. Its Chardonnay grapes provide one of Champagne's very few single-vineyard, or CRU, wines of which the 1979 vintage was the first. Small quantities of the finest vintage Krug are released, as Krug Collection, about ten years after their initial release. Although the firm is run by members of the fifth and sixth generation of champagne-making Krugs, it has been owned by LVMH since 1999.

Arlott, J., *Krug: House of Champagne* (London, 1976).

Krug, Charles (1825–92), German-born American wine producer, came to San Francisco in 1852 as a newspaper editor. After vineyard ventures in San Mateo and SONOMA, perhaps at the urging of HARASZTHY, Krug settled in the NAPA valley in 1860, founding a winery near St Helena in 1861. Krug was not the first Napa valley winemaker but he soon became the most eminent of his day and inevitably came to be called the 'father of Napa wine'. His success came in part because he understood public relations and because he developed his own sales organization. The winery he founded was acquired by the MONDAVI family in 1943 and is still notable among Napa valley establishments, although Robert Mondavi left to set up on his own in 1965 after an acrimonious dispute with his brother Peter.

Although Charles Krug did not come from a German wine region (he was born near Kassel), he exemplifies the important contribution to pioneer wine-growing made by Germans in all parts of the US where the vine was successfully cultivated.   T.P.

Kuč. See TRBLJAN.

KWV, the South African Co-operative Wine Growers' Association, or Ko-operatiewe Wijnbowers Vereniging van Zuid Afrika, is the mainly export wine producer which emerged from the transformation in 1997 of South Africa's grape grower body from co-operative to company. Until its conversion, it combined the functions of producer, marketing body, and statutory government control board, only gradually releasing its tight grip on the country's wine industry in the early 1990s.

It was established in 1918 after years of glut and grower bankruptcy. One of its statutory functions was to enforce production quota limits to prevent unmanageable surpluses. It also fixed annual minimum wine prices. Its powers—weighted in favour of producers rather than consumers and often oblivious to market forces—were criticized by free-marketeers and some producers who, even if non-members, were subject by law to KWV regulations. The KWV argued it spared government the embarrassment of the direct grower subsidies. Grower benefits, however, have been indirect. Wine CO-OPERATIVES and farmers enjoyed Land Bank credit terms well below commercial interest rates, opportunities that were not available to non-whites until the end of the apartheid era. Such was KWV's political influence in pre-democratic South Africa that wine, alone among alcoholic drinks in South Africa, was exempt from excise duty for many years.

In the mid 1990s, the newly structured KWV was relieved of all the statutory functions previously performed by the 4,600-strong growers' co-operative. Nevertheless, the organization still exerts considerable influence. As a shareholder in the major national wholesaler, as the most important supplier of bulk brandy

to the country's spirit producers, as the proprietor of grape juice concentrating facilities, through domination of many of the industry organizations and as a major supplier of goods, plant material, and services to the country's grape farmers and wine producers, the KWV's position remains largely unassailed.

Its conversion from co-operative to company was not without controversy. The process was challenged by the Minister of Agriculture, who cited the statutory void which would result from the process and a concern about the real ownership of some of the organization's assets as grounds for his intervention. Resolution was reached through an out-of-court settlement in which the KWV undertook to pay a sum of 370 million rand (equal at the time to $77 million) into a wine industry trust (see SOUTH AFRICA) to redress inequalities of the past and to assist in the management and promotion of the industry. In 2004, with the consent of trustees appointed by the next Minister of Agriculture, a significant percentage of this fund was set aside to allow a black consortium to buy 25 per cent of KWV's shares.

The export boom which followed South Africa's first democratic elections in 1994 saw an end to wine SURPLUSES for the first time since the 1950s. By 1996, South Africa was importing GRAPE CONCENTRATE, bulk table wine, and wine for DISTILLATION. The strong domestic brandy market takes up about 25 per cent of the annual grape crop, while less than a third of the harvest is consumed locally as wine. The tenfold increase in exports from 1993 to 2003 proved too great for the wine-producing capacity of the industry, forcing the country's major brand owners to blend BULK imports, mainly from Argentina, into some of their table wines to make up the shortfall. New planting programmes however have ensured that this is a temporary problem and by 2005 the cyclical swing from shortage to glut was already evident.

Meanwhile, just over half the annual harvest of about 1.2 million tons becomes table wine. The 66 co-operative wineries still crush a significant proportion of each vintage although much of their production is destined for brandy and other distilled products. The KWV produces a wide range of table wines and still markets many FORTIFIED WINES made in port and sherry styles.

Most top-quality South African table wine, however, comes from private producers and a few wholesaler-producers. The biggest wholesaler, Distell (the result of a merger between Stellenbosch Farmers' Winery and Distillers Corporation) together with the KWV (which remains a significant shareholder in the merged entity) still controls the great majority of South Africa's vine-related alcohol products, as it has since 1979.

The KWV and organizations which are nominally independent but which were formally part of KWV (and which now generally fall under the South African Wine and Brandy Company) still fulfil functions which include research, vine PROPAGATION, advisory services, and administration of the WINE OF ORIGIN system.   J.P. & M.F.

Fridjhon, M., and Murray, A., *Conspiracy of Giants* (Johannesburg, 1986).
South African Wine Industry Directory (Paarl, annually).

Kyrgyzstan, mountainous central Asian republic of the CIS on the border between KAZAKHSTAN and China of only minor wine-producing importance.

Kyrgyzstan, whose capital is Bishkek, has a CONTINENTAL climate and three zones favourable for viticulture: the Chuia and the Talas valleys, the south of the country, and the Issyk-Kul depression. Commercial viticulture is developed in the first two zones.

The country's grape and wine industry specializes in the production of TABLE GRAPES and DRYING GRAPES although about 44,000 hl of wine, mostly strong and sweet, was produced from the country's suspiciously steady 8,000 ha/20,000 acres of vineyard in 2002, according to OIV statistics.

The Issyk-Kul depression is at an altitude of 1,600 to 1,800 m, around lake Issyk-Kul. This viticultural region does not experience large temperature fluctuations. Because the July average daily temperature is 18 °C and that of January is 3 °C, no WINTER PROTECTION is needed. The central part of this region, on the south and north banks of lake Issyk-Kul, is particularly favourable for viticulture and the production of dessert wines and base materials for sparkling wines (see also CHINA).

Practically all vineyards in Kyrgyzstan have some form of IRRIGATION.

Forty-five grape varieties are recognized, including 23 wine varieties such as RKATSITELI, PINOT NOIR, Bayan Shirey, Kuljinski, CABERNET SAUVIGNON, RIESLING, SAPERAVI, Budeshiru Tetri, Mairam, Mourvèdre Kirghizski, Hungarian Muscat, and Black Muscat. Table varieties include CINSAUT, and MADELEINE ANGEVINE.   V.R.

In 1999, the ANTINORI family of Italy undertook a small vineyard development north of Lake Issyk-Kul, together with an experimental winery, with the aim of demonstrating to an essentially nomadic population the virtues of stable, long-term agriculture. Eight hectares of spur-pruned cordon-trained Chardonnay, Riesling and Pinot Noir yielded their first crop in 2002. The growing season is relatively short but serviceable wines have been made for Russian and Chinese markets.

First growth **Château Margaux** is not only the most important wine made in the commune of Margaux, it is also the grandest and most photographed château building in Bordeaux, built by Louis Combes for the Marquis de la Colonilla in the early 19th century.

labels, the principal means by which a wine producer or bottler can communicate with a potential customer and consumer (although see also BOTTLES, CASE, FOIL).

Wine labels are a relatively recent development, which awaited the widespread sale of bottled wine, and use of glues strong enough to stick to glass in about 1860. Before then wines were sold unlabelled and stacked in BINS, and served in decanters, so BIN LABELS and DECANTER LABELS are the precursors of today's wine bottle label. For many years, wines were identified by branded CORKS rather than by paper labels, a habit that persisted longest for vintage PORT.

Every wine in commercial circulation has to have a main label, as its passport quite apart from its function as a sales aid. Many wines also have a **neck label**, typically carrying the VINTAGE year so that the producer need not have new main labels printed for each new vintage (although labelling requirements can change so rapidly that in practice this sometimes seems necessary). See LABELLING INFORMATION for details of the information available on a main label. As wine consumers have become ever more sophisticated and curious, however, an increasing proportion of bottles carry a **back label** giving additional background information. This can vary from a genuinely useful outline of grape varieties used, vintage conditions, approximate SWEETNESS level, and serving advice, to a collection of fine-sounding words involving the 'finest' grape varieties picked at 'perfect ripeness' in 'optimum conditions' and vinified according to the 'highest standards', but which contain no genuine information whatsoever. Now that the amount of mandatory information required on wine labels is so considerable, some design-conscious bottlers try to beat the system by conveying all of this detail on what is obviously meant to be the back label, while applying to a second label (which the retailer, but not the labelling inspector, is meant to treat as the main label) a dramatic design statement without all the clutter of the mandatory information.

Labels matter to lawyers and officials, and they matter enormously to the retail wine trade, in which they communicate far more effectively with many consumers than any recommendation or award, but they are relatively unimportant to wine sales from a list, such as by mail or in the hotel and restaurant industry. The efforts of some new wine producers to design a really distinctive label may often be partly wasted, although they may be appreciated. The Italians have been as innovative in label design as in that of bottles, and some NEW WORLD designs can be arresting, effective, innovative, and sometimes all three. ARTISTS' LABELS have a certain following. Producers of established wines have usually inherited a label and rarely do anything more than slightly modify it (although even most of the estab-

lished Bordeaux CLASSED GROWTHS have incorporated some design modification into their labels in the last ten years). The fact that the label of Ch PÉTRUS would win no design award seems to do little to hinder sales. The label design of wine BRANDS, however, is an extremely important factor in their success. One of the most evocative labels is that used for MATEUS Rosé, depicting a beautiful palace in northern Portugal, which has nothing whatever to do with the wine.

Labels are usually, but not always, applied straight after BOTTLING as part of the same mechanized process. Some small-scale producers still apply their labels by hand with pots of glue. Producers of champagne and other sparkling wines take particular care to use strong, water-resistant adhesive in applying their labels since their bottles are likely to spend their last hours in public circulation immersed in a bucket of water.

Wine labels have such a fascination of their own, and can help recollection of the circumstances of their consumption, that wine **label collecting** is a recognized activity. Some of those who practise it call themselves vintitulists.

labelling information. The amount of information required on wine LABELS seems to increase dramatically each year. The following are the main categories of usually mandatory information, with national or international minimum criteria (which may be stricter on a local or regional basis).

Wine designation: wines made within the EUROPEAN UNION have to be identified as to whether they qualify as TABLE WINE, QUALITY WINE, or one of several specific intermediate categories such as France's VIN DE PAYS or Germany's LANDWEIN. They will accordingly carry one of the descriptions listed under these headings (Appellation Contrôlée, or Vino de Mesa, for example). Labels on wines made outside the European Union have to carry the telltale word 'wine' when travelling within Europe. In the United States, no DESIGNATION is required on the label.

Geographical reference: this may take the form of the name of a country (as in Greek table wine, for example), or the name of an AVA or any other state or smaller region in the United States, or could be the name of a tiny controlled appellation (such as BOCA in north west Italy, for example). In France, this is often written Appellation X Contrôlée, where X is the name of the geographical reference, or even Appellation d'Origine X Contrôlée. Within Europe, if a geographical zone is cited on the label, all the wine should usually come from this zone. In the United States, if a country, state, or county is listed on the label, 75 per cent of the grapes in the wine must come from that area, and if an AVA is stated on the label, then 85 per cent should come from that area. Eighty-five per cent of an

L

Disaffection with natural corks because of the increased perception and incidence of wines tainted by **trichloroanisole** (TCA) led to a dramatic increase in sales of **synthetic closures** such as these made by SupremeCorq in the late 20th century, although screw caps have since gained ground.

Australian wine must also come from the region specified whereas in South Africa it must be 100%. Exported wine has to carry the name of the country of origin.

Volume of wine: this is most likely to be 75 cl/25 fl oz but must, quite rightly, be stated on all labels. See BOTTLE SIZES and BOXES.

Alcoholic strength: this is usually stated as a percentage followed by '% vol' but may be expressed in degrees (°) or, in Italy in particular, as *gradi*. See ALCOHOLIC STRENGTH. Tolerances vary considerably and can be as high as 2 per cent alcohol in the US.

Vintage year: within Europe, a vintage may not be stated for a TABLE WINE, and, wherever it is stated, at least 85 per cent of the wine should be the produce of that year. See VINTAGE and NON-VINTAGE. In America, Australia, and South Africa, at least 85 per cent must be from the vintage stated.

Name and address of producer or bottler: this is usually provided in a fairly straightforward fashion, although, within Europe, an address which happens to incorporate the name of a controlled appellation cannot be used on the label of a table wine, or even a vin de pays, so some sort of postal code is usually substituted.

Bottling information: the relationship between the source of the grapes and the producer or bottler is indicated by exactly how this is expressed. See BOTTLING INFORMATION for more details.

On a CHAMPAGNE label, the following codes printed next to the registered number of the bottler are useful:

NM: *négociant-manipulant*, one of the big houses/firms/négociants;

RM: *récoltant-manipulant*, a grower who makes his or her own wine;

CM: *coopérative de manipulation*, one of the co-operatives;

RC: *récoltant-coopérateur*, grower selling wine made by a co-op;

MA: *marque d'acheteur*, buyer's own brand;

SR: *société de récoltant*, a small family company (rare);

R: *récoltant*, very small-scale growers (very rare).

Varietal information: this is entirely optional, but, if a variety is specified on a label of wine in Europe, then it must comprise at least 85 per cent of the wine. In the United States, it must comprise at least 75 per cent (or 51 per cent in the case of some particularly FOXY native varieties: see NEW YORK). In Australia, it must comprise at least 85 per cent of the stated variety.

Allergen labelling: in most countries, including the US, South Africa, Australia, and New Zealand, it is obligatory to state on the label that a wine contains SULFITES if it contains more than 10 mg/l of SULFUR DIOXIDE. Changes to EU regulations in 2004 concerning ALLERGENS meant that any wine made or sold in the EU must also comply with this ruling, using the words 'contains sulphites' or 'contains sulphur dioxide'. SO_2 is used to a certain extent in the making of virtually all wine and is a by-product of FERMENTATION, therefore virtually all wine contains this level of sulfites. In Australia and New Zealand, the list of potential allergenic substances that must be mentioned is longer and includes fish, milk, egg or nut products used as processing aids. The mention must be in the form of a description plus a numerical code, for example, 'contains antioxidant (300) and preservative (220)', 300 and 220 being the respective codes for ASCORBIC ACID and SULFUR DIOXIDE, or the label may state the actual substance name. Currently, these products are provisionally excluded from EU labelling requirements on the grounds that they are 'not likely, or not very likely, to cause adverse reactions in susceptible individuals'. See also VEGETARIAN AND VEGAN WINES.

Gratuitous government interference: in some countries, wine labels have to carry other 'warnings', usually as a result of some scientifically vague but much-publicized connection between wine and ill HEALTH. In the United States, labels on all wine have to warn that pregnant women and those in charge of heavy machinery are ill advised to consume any or much of it.

Sweetness: see SWEETNESS.

Fizziness: see FIZZINESS.

labour. Viticulture, unlike wine-making, has long required a substantial input of labour. The Romans used slaves while MONKS AND MONASTERIES played an important part in medieval vine-growing. A peasant class was long necessary to maintain viticulture in Europe, and increasingly vineyard labour was paid for by leasing part of the vineyard to the labourer, share-cropping or, in French, MÉTAYAGE. The close association between vine-growing and humans began to alter towards the end of the 20th century, however, mainly because of changes in technology.

There have traditionally been three levels of labour input to viticulture: man alone, man plus draught animal, and man plus machines. In ancient vineyards, all work was done by man, which consisted of ploughing (see CULTIVATION), PRUNING, TRIMMING, DESUCKERING, LAYERING, and HARVESTING. The labour input was high, and vineyards on the plains required between 70 and 80 man-days per hectare per year. This means that any one person might tend about 3 ha/7 acres, with due allowance for using other labour at times of peak demand such as harvesting and pruning. The YIELD from such vineyards was not high compared with modern standards. A generous 33.5 hl/ha (2 tons/acre) meant that one man's labour might produce a maximum of about 15 tonnes of grapes. For HILLSIDE VINEYARDS, one man might tend only about 100 sq m of vineyard, although this was not necessarily full-time work, with a likely output of tens of kilograms of grapes per person per year. Such vineyards relying totally on manual labour are increasingly rare, as the price of labour has increased much more than the price of wine, but some may be found all around the Mediterranean.

Intensive labour input continued for many vineyards up until the mid to late 19th century, when the invasion of POWDERY MILDEW, DOWNY MILDEW, and PHYLLOXERA led to the need for SPRAYING, and ROOTSTOCKS. Previously many vineyards had been planted haphazardly without rows, and with high density, almost like a field of wheat. As need be, unhealthy vines were replaced by layering from adjacent vines. With the need to spray, and also for ploughing, draught animals became more common, not only horses but also mules and oxen. Indeed, milk cows were also used; in France's Auvergne, for example, cows provided meat, milk, and labour. Vines then needed to be planted in rows to make easy the passage of the animal, and there were typically many fewer plants per hectare because of the cost of GRAFTING plants on rootstocks. One horse was able to work 7 ha, and one man was needed for every 3 ha. A typical family farm consisted of about 7 ha of vines, one horse with two drivers, and one labourer.

Since the Second World War, the pattern of viticulture has changed in France and elsewhere with the widespread introduction of MECHANIZATION. This was no simple matter, as there were conflicts between generations of farmers about replacing horses with TRACTORS, and substantial changes in the support services in rural villages. Mechanics and fuel salesmen replaced blacksmiths and fodder merchants. In the end, economic necessity determined the future; one man and a tractor was now able to tend 30 ha of vineyards, although with manual labour including pruning, trimming, and harvesting, 1 ha still required 43 days' work throughout the year.

In the 1960s, the mechanization revolution intensified. Ploughing had been largely replaced by HERBICIDES, and then there was the introduction of MECHANICAL HARVESTING followed by MECHANICAL PRUNING. Some sprays were even applied from the air, using aeroplanes or HELICOPTERS. There are some vineyards in south eastern Australia where the total annual labour input is less than 50 man-hours per hectare: all operations are carried out mechanically including harvesting and pruning; spraying is conducted from the air; and weed control is by herbicides. On large estates, one worker is required for each 30 ha with this degree of mechanization, and the output can be more than 500 tonnes of wine grapes. This figure, compared with less than 15 tonnes per person about a century earlier, demonstrates how productivity has increased through mechanization. A counter-trend, albeit on a small scale in Australia, is the move towards ORGANIC and BIODYNAMIC grape growing, although the latter in particular requires considerable human input.

Australian examples are relevant because of the acute rural labour shortage here and in

New Zealand, although recent Asian immigrants were providing some solutions in the mid 2000s. The wine industries of South America and, especially, South Africa have never known a labour shortage while in California and elsewhere on the West Coast of the US, Mexico has provided an exceptionally skilled viticultural labour force.

Future developments are not obvious. It is unlikely that robots will replace vineyard labour to any significant extent, although a robot capable of pruning vineyards was developed in France in the 1980s. The variability of vineyards, of terrain, and of the weather make the task of robot development more difficult than for the factory floor.

It seems likely however that an increasing proportion of vineyard tasks will be mechanized, even in countries where labour resources are not necessarily limiting or expensive. Mechanization is seen to offer benefits of timeliness as well as of economics which encourage its further adoption. However, on a few estates where the slopes are too steep for mechanized ploughing, or where there is a wish to avoid compaction of the soil, notably in ALSACE and BURGUNDY, a few producers have returned to using ploughs pulled by draught animals such as horses.

Once the grapes have been delivered to the winery, wine-making requires relatively little labour. A WINEMAKER is required to make decisions and, increasingly, program a computer which may control such operations as TEMPERATURE CONTROL and RACKING wine from one container to another (see INFORMATION TECHNOLOGY).

Only BARREL MATURATION and, particularly, LEES STIRRING require much manual labour (see CELLAR WORK). Otherwise, cleaning is the chief manual operation.   R.E.S. & J.R.

Coombe, B. G., and Dry, P. R. (eds.), *Viticulture*, ii: *Practices* (Adelaide, 1992).

Galet, P., *Précis de viticulture* (5th edn, Montpellier, 1988).

labrusca, species of the *Vitis* genus native to North America. The juice of its grapes, and wine made from them, usually have a pronounced flavour described as FOXY. See VITIS.

Labruscana, North American, especially New York state, term for a native vine variety with mainly *Vitis* LABRUSCA but some VINIFERA genes, for example CONCORD.

L'Acadie. See ACADIE.

laccase, a powerful oxidative ENZYME particularly associated with BOTRYTIS BUNCH ROT which turns grape must brown.

La Clape. See CLAPE.

Lacrima di Morro, fast maturing, wild strawberry-scented red grape speciality of Morro d'Alba in the MARCHE.

Lacrima Nera is sometimes used as a synonym for GAGLIOPPO.

lactic acid, one of the milder ACIDS in wine, present in much lower concentrations than either MALIC ACID or TARTARIC ACID. Lactic acid, named after *lactis*, Latin for milk, is most frequently encountered as the principal acid in yoghurt, sour milk, pickled cucumbers, and sauerkraut. Lactic acid is a common participant in both plant and animal metabolic processes. It is the end-product of intense muscular activity in animals (see ACIDS); a by-product of the alcoholic FERMENTATION process in wines and beers; and the end-product of the metabolic action of the many LACTIC ACID BACTERIA.

In wine, lactic acid can be produced by bacteria both from traces of sugar and from malic acid. The function of the second MALOLACTIC FERMENTATION which a high proportion of red wines and some white wines undergo is to transform harsh malic acid into the much milder lactic acid.   A.D.W.

lactic acid bacteria, or **LAB,** an abbreviation of **lactic acid producing bacteria,** known by some winemakers simply as **lactics,** are some of the few BACTERIA that can survive in such an acidic solution as wine. They all produce LACTIC ACID. Those of importance to wine-making can be subdivided into the three genera *Oenococcus* (of which the best known species is *Oenococcus oeni*, formally called *Leuconostoc oenos*), *Lactobacillus*, and *Pediococcus*. They are involved in the production of pickles, sauerkraut, and yoghurt as well as being the agents of MALOLACTIC FERMENTATION in wines, by which the harsh MALIC ACID is effectively decomposed into the milder lactic acid.

Lactic acid bacteria function best in environments that contain very small amounts of OXYGEN, which is why their growth in grapes is limited. Lactic acid bacteria inhabit wooden vats and barrels in traditional wineries and can be deeply embedded in the wood fibres that even the highest standards of HYGIENE are unable to remove them. They can have the positive effect of precipitating malolactic fermentation in wines with an excess of malic acid. In newer wineries, lactic acid bacteria may need to be deliberately introduced to achieve this effect. Unfortunately, however, many strains of lactic acid bacteria can generate off-flavours and turbidity in wines. This is most likely to happen when traces of sugar remain as nutrients in the wine. Some species of LAB can also produce biogenic amines, notably HISTAMINE, tyramine, and putrescine. A recent Spanish study found ranges of 1–13 mg/l and showed differences between grape varieties and LAB species. Low PH prevented biogenic amine formation. Malolactic fermentation and short storage periods in bottle (3–6 months) showed increases in histamine concentration, whereas longer periods

of storage led to a general decrease in histamine. Some countries have legal limits on these amines but the levels are higher than those normally found in wine. In Switzerland, for example, the legal limit for histamine is 10mg/kg. See also ALLERGIES.

Fortunately, however, lactic acid bacteria are very sensitive to SULFUR DIOXIDE and are much easier to control than ACETOBACTER, the other group of bacteria of wine-making importance. Lactic acid bacteria grow best in very weakly acidic solutions and at temperatures near those of the human body. Bacteriologists regard them as 'fastidious' in that they require a wide range of micro-nutrients. They are also intolerant of high concentrations of ETHANOL.

Their effect on new wine can therefore be limited by sulfur dioxide, low temperatures, and frequent RACKING so as to eliminate the possibility of providing micro-nutrients from the YEAST decomposition products in the LEES.
                A.D.W.

Landete, J. M., Ferrer, S., Polo, L., and Pardo, I., 'Biogenic amines in wines from three Spanish regions', *Journal of Agricultural and Food Chemistry*, 53 (2005), 1119–24.

lactones, see OAK FLAVOUR.

Lado, native white grape variety that is an important component of blends in the Arnoia valley in RIBEIRO, north west Spain.

Ladoix, the appellation from the village of **Ladoix-Serrigny** in the Côte de Beaune district of Burgundy's Côte d'Or producing mostly red wines from Pinot Noir grapes. They are more frequently sold as Côte de Beaune-Villages (see BEAUNE, CÔTE DE). Although there are now 24 ha/59 acres of Ladoix PREMIERS CRUS, a further 8 ha of the best-placed vineyards are sold as Aloxe-Corton premier cru. Furthermore, 6 ha of Corton-Charlemagne and 22 ha (out of 160) of Le Corton, including part of Le Rognet and Les Vergennes, are actually sited in Ladoix (see ALOXE-CORTON for more details).

As well as the Corton-Charlemagne, a tiny amount of white Ladoix-Serrigny is made from Chardonnay or Pinot Blanc.

See also CÔTE D'OR, and map under BURGUNDY.   J.T.C.M.

ladybirds, see ASIAN LADY BEETLE.

Lafite, Château, subsequently **Ch Lafite-Rothschild,** FIRST GROWTH in the MÉDOC region of BORDEAUX. The vineyard, to the north of the small town of PAUILLAC and adjoining Ch MOUTON-ROTHSCHILD, was probably planted in the last third of the 17th century. Inherited in 1716 by the SÉGURS, who also owned Ch LATOUR, it was sold in 1784 to Pierre de Pichard, an extremely rich president of the Bordeaux Parlement who perished on the scaffold. The estate was confiscated and sold as public property in 1799 to a Dutch consortium which in

1803 resold it to a Dutch grain merchant and supplier to Napoleon's armies, Ignace-Joseph Vanlerberghe. When he fell on hard times, he resold it to his former wife in order to avoid its falling into a creditor's hands. Perhaps for the same reason, or to avoid splitting it up under French inheritance laws, in 1821 she apparently sold it to a London banker, Sir Samuel Scott, for 1 million francs. He and then his son were the nominal owners for over 40 years. But when the real proprietor Aimé Vanlerberghe died without issue in 1866, the family decided to sell it and pay the fines owed because of the concealment. In 1868, after a stiff contest with a Bordeaux syndicate, it was knocked down to Baron James de ROTHSCHILD of the Paris bank, for 4.4 million francs, including part of the Carruades vineyard. Baron James died in the same year and the château has remained in the family ever since. Baron Eric de Rothschild took over direction of the property from his uncle Baron Élie in 1975. In the famous 1855 CLASSIFICATION, Lafite was placed first of the premiers crus, although there is controversy as to whether the order was alphabetical or by rank. Yet, as Christie's AUCTIONS in the 1960s and 1970s of 19th-century British country mansion cellars showed, in Britain Lafite was nearly always the favoured first growth.

The château itself is a 16th-century manor. The vineyard, one of the largest in the Haut-Médoc, was 103 ha/255 acres in 2005 with an ENCÉPAGEMENT of 71 per cent Cabernet Sauvignon, 3 per cent Cabernet Franc, 25 per cent Merlot, and 1 per cent Petit Verdot. Annual production is about 45,000 cases, of which about a third may be the SECOND WINE, called Carruades de Lafite but not restricted to wine produced on the plateau in the vineyard known as Les Carruades. See ROTHSCHILDS for other wine investments made by the owners of Ch Lafite.   E.P.-R. & J.R.

Penning-Rowsell, E., *The Wines of Bordeaux* (6th edn, London, 1979).

Lafnetscha, rare Swiss Valais white grape often mistaken for COMPLETER. In fact, DNA PROFILING at DAVIS showed in 2004 that Lafnetscha is an offspring of HUMAGNE BLANCHE of Valais and Completer of Graubünden in Switzerland.   J.V.

Lafões, IPR in central northern Portugal making light, dry white wines similar to those of neighbouring Vinho Verde, sometimes referred to as *verdascos*. Red wines are more similar to those of nearby DÃO.   R.J.M.

lagar, term used in PORTUGAL for a low-sided stone trough where grapes are trodden and fermented. Most have now been replaced by conventional fermentation vats except in the DOURO valley, where some of the best PORTS continue to be foot-trodden in *lagares*. In the late 1990s, stainless steel 'robotic lagares' were introduced in the Douro by the SYMINGTON

family and have become an important factor in the making of premium quality port. See PORT for more detail.

Lagoa, DOC centred on one co-operative winery in the ALGARVE, southern Portugal.

Lagorthi, rare Greek white grape whose aromatic produce may save it from extinction.

Lagos, fishing port, holiday resort, and DOC in southern Portugal. See ALGARVE.

Lagrein, red grape variety grown on only about 300 ha/750 acres in ALTO ADIGE. Although often over-produced, it can produce **Lagrein Scuro** or **Lagrein Dunkel**, somewhat tannic reds of real character, as well as fragrant yet sturdy rosé called **Lagrein Rosato** or **Lagrein Kretzer**. Lagrein can be slightly bitter on the finish and its presence, valued for both TANNINS and colour, can at times be detected as an element in other wines of the zone, particularly Pinot Nero and Schiava. According to Burton Anderson, this variety, whose name suggests origins in the Lagarina valley of Trentino, was mentioned as early as the 17th century in the records of the Muri Benedictine monastery near Bolzano in Alto Adige. In 2004, DNA PROFILING at SAN MICHELE ALL'ADIGE revealed a parent–offspring relationship between Lagrein and TEROLDEGO, another deeply coloured and ancient variety from Trentino. Wine-making techniques have changed in recent years, as younger producers have shortened maceration times and used barriques to achieve rounder, less aggressive flavours.

Anderson, B., *The Wine Atlas of Italy* (London and New York, 1990).

Lairén, southern Spanish name for the white grape variety AIRÉN.

Lake county, smallest viticultural district among CALIFORNIA'S NORTH COAST counties and also the least understood. In this warm inland district east of Mendocino county and north of Napa county, a vigorous but short-lived 19th-century industry died out with PROHIBITION, leaving scant historic guidance to the growers who restored vineyards to the region during the 1970s. The county's 5,000 acres/2,000 ha of vines and its small population of wineries are concentrated in the Clear Lake AVA. Further south is the much smaller Guenoc Valley AVA.

Clear Lake AVA

Nearly all of the AVA's vineyards nestle between steep hills to the west and the lake, the largest entirely within California, to the east. By the early 1990s, the district, north of NAPA and east of MENDOCINO, had grown some excellent Sauvignon Blanc and pleasant, early-maturing Cabernet Sauvignon. Zinfandel may be well adapted, although evidence remains scant. Although several wineries (especially

the original KENDALL-JACKSON facility) are located near the town of Lakeport, a fair proportion of the region's grapes go to wineries in Napa, Mendocino, and SONOMA counties.

Guenoc Valley AVA

Inland wine region and AVA promoted by Orville Magoon's Guenoc winery. North of Napa valley and east of Alexander valley.

lake effect, the year-round influence on vineyards from nearby large lakes which permits vine-growing in areas such as the north east UNITED STATES and Ontario in CANADA despite their high LATITUDE. In winter, the large lakes provide moisture to the prevailing westerly winds, which creates a deep snow cover, protecting vines from WINTER FREEZE even in very low temperatures. The lake eventually freezes. In spring, the westerly winds blow across the frozen lake and become cooler. These cooler breezes blowing on the vines retard BUDBREAK until the danger of FROST has passed. In summer the lake warms up. By autumn/fall, the westerly winds are warmed as they blow across the lake. The warm breezes on the vines lengthen the growing season (balancing the late start to the growing season) by delaying the first frost.   H.L.

Lalande-de-Pomerol, appellation to the immediate north of POMEROL that is very much in the shadow of this great red wine district of Bordeaux. It includes the communes of Lalande-de-Pomerol and Néac and produces lush, Merlot-dominated wines which can offer a suggestion, sometimes a decidedly rustic suggestion, of the concentration available in a bottle of fine Pomerol but at a fraction of the price. Including about 1,100 ha/2,700 acres of vineyards, the Lalande-de-Pomerol appellation is much bigger than that of Pomerol, and its soils are composed of well-drained gravels, particularly in the south, where it is divided from the Pomerol appellation only by the Barbanne river. At one time, the Barbanne separated that part of France which said *oc* for yes (see LANGUEDOC) from that part which said *oil* and spoke the *langue d'oil*. Because land here is so much cheaper than in Pomerol, recent years have seen investment from those who already own properties in St-Emilion and, particularly, Pomerol. Obvious examples include La Fleur de Boüard, co-owned with Ch Angelus, and La Chenade and Les Cruzelles, co-owned with Ch l'Eglise Clinet.

La Mancha. See MANCHA.

Lambrusco, central Italian VARIETAL wine based on the eponymous red grape variety, enormously popular with the mass market in the US and northern Europe in the early 1980s.

The several different vines called Lambrusco are grown principally in the three central provinces of EMILIA—Modena, Parma, and Reggio nell'Emilia—although significant plantings can be found across the river Po in the province of Mantova, and occasional plantings can be found as far afield as PIEMONTE, TRENTINO, and even BASILICATA. This robust variety, of which there are at least 60 known subvarieties, has long been known for its exceptional productivity, and CATO described it as *trecenarie* by virtue of the 300 AMPHORAE that each *jugero* (two-thirds of an acre) yielded.

Modern Lambrusco, a frothing, fruity, typically red wine meant to be drunk young, is produced principally by the CO-OPERATIVES of Emilia in four separate DOCS: **Lambrusco di Sorbara** (from the varieties Lambrusco di Sorbara and, the most planted, Lambrusco Salamino); **Lambrusco Grasparossa di Castelvetro** (85 per cent of which must come from the variety of the same name); **Lambrusco Reggiano** (produced principally from Lambrusco Marani and Lambrusco Salamino, with Lambrusco Maestri and Lambrusco Montericco permitted although they are gradually disappearing); and **Lambrusco Salamino di Santa Croce** (which should include 90 per cent of the synonymous variety whose small bunches are thought to resemble a 'small salami'). The Lambrusco Grasparossa, Sorbara, and Salamino tend to be dry or off-dry wines with a pronounced ACIDITY, which, together with its bubbles, are reputed to assist the digestion of Emilia's hearty cuisine.

Lambrusco Reggiano, on the other hand, tends to be AMABILE or slightly sweet, the sweetness generally being supplied by the partially fermented must of the ANCELLOTTA grape, which DOC rules permit (up to a maximum of 15 per cent) in the blend. (It is notable that, according to the Italian agricultural census of 1990, total plantings of Ancellotta were 4,700 ha/11,600 acres, more than of any single Lambrusco subvariety, a reflection of producers' desire to add colour from the deep-tinted Ancellotta grape to their various Lambrusco grapes.) This is the wine that took America by storm in the late 1970s and early 1980s, when the Cantine Riunite of Reggio nell'Emilia, a consortium of co-operatives, succeeded in exporting up to 3 million cases per year to the UNITED STATES. So successful has Lambrusco been on export markets that special white, pink, and light (LOW-ALCOHOL) versions have perversely been created, the colour and alcohol often being deliberately removed.

Most Lambrusco made today is a fairly anonymous, standardized product made in industrial quantities by co-operatives or large commercial wineries using the Charmat or bulk method of SPARKLING WINE-MAKING, together with heavy FILTRATION, STABILIZATION, and, frequently, PASTEURIZATION. 'Proper' Lambrusco, whose SECONDARY FERMENTATION takes place in the bottle, has become something of a relic of the past, although occasional artisan Lambruscos of this type can be found in the production zones themselves. The dis-

tinctive qualities of the different clones and different zones have tended to disappear with large quantities and industrial techniques but, in theory, Lambrusco Grasparossa is the fullest and most alcoholic and Lambrusco di Sorbara, in its combination of balanced fruit and acidity, is precisely that classic accompaniment to Emilian egg pasta and charcuterie which made the name of the wine. Although it is still possible to find good bottles of Lambrusco from small producers in the various DOC zones, conferring a generalized superiority on a given zone or a given type would be a risky business indeed in current circumstances. Lambrusco Reggiano, with an annual production of about 250,000 hl/6.6 million gal, is the most common, followed by Lambrusco di Sorbara with 115,000 hl, Lambrusco Grasparossa with 65,000 hl, and Lambrusco Salamino with 55,000 hl.

There are also several hundred hectares of a red grape variety known as **Lambrusco Maesini** in Argentina.   D.T. & D.C.G.

Lancers, BRAND of medium sweet, lightly sparkling wine made by the firm of J. M. da FONSECA at Azeitão, near SETÚBAL in PORTUGAL. The brand was created in 1944, when Vintage Wines of New York saw that American veterans of the Second World War were returning home from Europe with a taste for wine. Lancers, initially sold in a stone crock, continues to be moderately successful in the United States, whereas MATEUS Rosé, created two years earlier, tends to be better known in Europe. A fully sparkling Lancers, made by the CONTINUOUS METHOD, was introduced in the late 1980s.
                                                        R.J.M.

Landot, or **Landot 4511**, very vigorous, cold-hardy FRENCH HYBRID of increasing interest for red wine in the northeastern United States.

Landwein, rarely seen category of dry or medium dry table wine, or TAFELWEIN, in German-speaking countries. In GERMANY, Landwein must have an ALCOHOLIC STRENGTH of at least half a per cent more than the minimum level for German table wine. It does not enjoy the reputation of its French equivalent VIN DE PAYS.   I.J.

In AUSTRIA, Landwein is slightly more common. It must be dry, with no more than 6 g/l RESIDUAL SUGAR, and reach at least 14 °KMW (68 °OECHSLE), which is considerably riper than the German minimum, reflecting the warmer climate.

Langenlois, important wine town in Lower AUSTRIA, part of the Kamptal area.

Langhe, plural of **Langa**, name given to the hills to the north and south of the city of Alba in the province of Cuneo in PIEMONTE. The soils, composed of clay marls, are the classic ones for the NEBBIOLO grape, and produce the Langhe's most famous wines BAROLO and

BARBARESCO, although they can also yield BARBERA and DOLCETTO of excellent quality. The hills gradually rise in altitude to the south of Monforte d'Alba, creating a climatic limit to the cultivation of Nebbiolo; to the south of Dogliani, where altitudes of over 600 m/1,970 ft are reached, the cultivation of grapes of any sort virtually ceases. Langhe is also the name of a regional DOC for Piemonte, used for non-traditional grape varieties (Langhe Chardonnay or, for Sauvignon Blanc, Langhe Bianco) or as a lower DOC category into which more geographically limited DOC wines can be declassified, Dolcetto d'Alba becoming Langhe Dolcetto, for example, and Barbera d'Alba becoming Langhe Rosso.   D.T.

Langhorne Creek, productive wine region in SOUTH AUSTRALIA cooled by lake Alexandrina and the nearby Southern ocean. It has an unusual ability to produce large yields of medium-bodied red wines which achieve sensory ripeness (an important ingredient in Orlando Wyndham's red JACOB'S CREEK) in its temperate climate. Smaller wineries which limit yields on estate vineyards are producing high-quality Shiraz, Cabernet Sauvignon, and blends thereof.

language of wine. Wine-talk is a problem: 'When trying to talk about wine in depth, one rapidly comes up against the limitations of our means of expression . . . We need to be able to describe the indescribable. We tasters feel to some extent betrayed by language,' comments Émile PEYNAUD.

Wine-talk is triply disadvantaged: first, people TASTE and smell wine differently from each other; second, a partially obscure conventional vocabulary has arisen: the wine flavour described as gooseberry, for example, does not taste very much like gooseberries; third, the need to impress customers in a cut-throat market has led to ear-catching and sometimes bizarre descriptions: 'a fascinating old, old smell of unswept floorboards', 'old tarpaulin fringed with lace', 'Wham bam thankyou mam red, all rich, gooey, almost treacly fruit-dark plums and prunes awash with liquorice and chocolate and cream'.

In many ways, wine descriptions are in their linguistic infancy, parallel to the days when linguistic sounds could be described only by comparison to other sounds: in the 16th century, English *a* was described as like 'the balling of the sheepe when she feedeth', for example. Phonetics now has an International Phonetic Alphabet, with agreed parameters, but this is still far from true of wine terminology.

Descriptive terms should be distinguished from expressive or evaluative ones, it is sometimes argued. Yet even this proves to be difficult for wine: even the most straightforward descriptions are bizarre by the standards of 'normal' usage. An English speaker asked to describe the colours red and white is likely to mention blood versus snow, yet a red wine is typically reddish-purple and a white one pale straw, each with a range that goes beyond the usual boundaries for red and white. Other wine colour terms are equally odd: black, as in Greek Mavrodaphne 'black-daphne' or the old 'black wine' of Cahors, refers simply to a hue darker than is usual for wines.

Yet colours illustrate one useful way in which wine terms can be partially analysed, by looking at the internal structure of the wine vocabulary. Red and white are opposites on a scale with rosé in the middle. Such antonyms are an anchor-point in descriptions. Possibly for this reason, the terms sweet versus dry are the first technical terms to be widely understood, and are now regularly found in supermarket classifications, even though, outside a wine context, the average person would oppose sweet to sour, and dry to wet.

Technically, antonyms such as sweet versus dry are gradable, in that sweet means 'sweet in relation to a norm', even though the norm is far from clear. Further opposites/scales have not generally caught on, though some recur in descriptions, as young vs. mature, light vs. heavy, crisp (nicely acidic) vs. flabby—though a basic problem is that a word such as flabby tends to be used as a general derogatory term, so is also found in opposition to terms such as hearty, sturdy, meaty, which indicate a wine with BODY.

Synonyms are also useful in understanding vocabulary structure, and words for wines with 'body' abound: beefy, big, broad, chunky, powerful, robust—though none has yet won out over others.

As the above examples show, most wine descriptions involve adjectives, though ones with a somewhat specialized interpretation. Adjectives depend for their meaning on the words to which they are attached: an old wine will be younger than an old house, but possibly older than an old friend, who may well not be aged. Many wine adjectives consist of a noun plus ending -y, as buttery, chalky, chocolatey, earthy, flinty, flowery, fruity, grapey, herby, meaty, nutty, oaky, peppery, silky, spicy, sugary, velvety.

Readers of wine columns sometimes get the misleading impression that 'anything goes'. Yet the majority of wine flavour descriptions cover a fairly narrow range, mostly of other food words, as appley, gamey, grapefruity, minty, peachy, plummy, raspberry—though these are often 'code' terms, in that a wine described as grapefruity or minty does not (to the uninitiated) taste very much like either. Terms that move outside these food flavours relate easily only to a small portion of wine qualities, as with the power terms listed above for wines with body. A further set relate perceived smoothness to fabrics, so wines may be velvety, silky, satiny—though even here, the range of fabrics is limited: a wine may be soft, though is not normally woolly. Shape and TEXTURE terms tend to be applied to wines with a high degree of acidity, as angular, austere, flinty, steely. The AROMA (nose) is perhaps the aspect of wine that has caused the greatest controversy in recent years, and seems to be hardest to convey: cat's pee, pencil shavings, sweaty saddles, tobacco had relatively little attention paid to them, yet fury erupted when a serious critic referred to a wine as smelling of hamster cages. Any successful metaphor must achieve cultural resonance, and avoid cognitive dissonance: it must fit in with existing traditions and preconceptions or risk being rejected.

Yet in many cases, wine descriptions are unclear only out of context or when single words are used. Humans often think about word meanings in terms of 'prototypes' or typical examples. Prototypes are bundles of characteristics: so a robin, a prototypical bird, has a red breast, is fairly small, has wings, slender legs, and so on. Similarly, a bunch of features characterize particular wines, some of them accurate, some evocative: a Sauvignon Blanc, for example, popularly referred to as 'cat's pee on a gooseberry bush' is spoken of as acidic, clean, refreshing. However, increasingly, wines are acquiring shorthand labels for these bundles of characteristics: some Chardonnays, such as those produced in Meursault, are labelled buttery for a fairly rich white wine—a description accepted even by those that love Meursault wines, but dislike butter. A Rioja is recognized and labelled oaky, even by those who have no idea why this tag is used.

All of this suggests that wine knowledge is becoming increasingly sophisticated. A future hope is that a more sophisticated classification system of the vocabulary of wine can match the knowledge of its drinkers.

See AROMA WHEEL, TASTING, TASTING TERMS, and PHILOSOPHY OF WINE.   J.A.

Lehrer, A., *Wine and Conversation* (Bloomington, Ind., 1983).

Peynaud, E., *The Taste of Wine* (Paris, 1983; London, 1987).

Languedoc, France's best-value, most fluid wine region and certainly its most important in terms of volume of wine produced, and in terms of the importance of viticulture to the region's economy. The Languedoc takes its name from a time when its inhabitants spoke Occitan, the language in which *oc* is the word for 'yes', hence *langue d'oc*. It comprises the three central southern *départements* of the Aude, Hérault, and Gard, a sea of little other than vines just inland from the beaches of the Mediterranean (see map opposite and FRANCE).

For administrative purposes, the Languedoc is often bracketed with the region to its immediate south, as in **Languedoc-Roussillon**, although the ROUSSILLON has a perceptibly different character, and is better equipped to replace vines with the other fruit crops it has for long cultivated.

Between them they had a total of nearly 32,000 vignerons cultivating about 214,000 ha/ 528,000 acres of vineyard in the early 2000s, exactly a quarter of all French vines. It had represented a third a decade earlier but strenuous EUROPEAN UNION-inspired VINE PULL SCHEMES aimed at reducing Europe's wine SURPLUS were specifically targeted at France's deep south.

Despite its quantitative importance (with a third as much vineyard again as Australia), Languedoc-Roussillon produces only just over 10 per cent of France's AC wines. For many years, the Languedoc's only appellation was Fitou, but in 1985 Corbières, Minervois, and the catch-all appellation Coteaux du Languedoc were elevated from VDQS to AC status and others have followed. A high proportion of the vast area technically included in these AC zones is dedicated to non-appellation wine, however, either because the ENCÉPAGEMENT is outside the appellation specifications, or because the vigneron continues to be more interested in quantity than quality. The Languedoc is still by far the principal producer of VIN DE TABLE, as well as producing nearly 60 per cent of France's intermediate category VIN DE PAYS, much of it labelled regionally as Vin de Pays d'Oc. In a very real sense the Languedoc is France's most anarchic wine region. Not only is it the only one in which vignerons still take direct and often violent action in protest at the organization of their sector of the wine business, a phenomenon all too visible in the 2000s, it is also the one in which wine producers are most obviously dissatisfied with the detail of the, admittedly relatively recent, appellation laws. Some important producers ignore the AC system completely and put most of their effort into making high-quality vins de pays. In 2005, there were proposals to institute a sort of super-appellation **Languedoc** for wines made anywhere within Languedoc or Roussillon with less Carignan and lower maximum yields than more specific appellations such as Corbières and Minervois.

Only about 13 per cent of the Languedoc-Roussillon's wine output was white in the early 2000s. See ROUSSILLON for more detail on whites made there but the best Languedoc whites, after a decidedly OAKY phase, have become increasingly fine and interesting. The small proportion of dry rosé is mainly for local consumption. A substantial quantity of VIN DOUX NATUREL is made (see MUSCAT), and LIMOUX is the Languedoc's centre of SPARKLING WINE-MAKING. The Languedoc is still principally a source of red wine, however, a typical representative being no longer a thin, pale remnant of the region's past as a bulk wine supplier but a dense, exciting, increasingly supple ambassador of some of France's wildest countryside.

History

There is some debate about whether the CELTS cultivated vines before the Roman, or even

Appellations of Languedoc-Roussillon

Greek, invasions of GAUL, but the first French vineyards about which all historians can agree were planted around 125 BC on the hills near the Roman colony of Narbo, modern Narbonne, which today produce Corbières, Minervois, and Coteaux du Languedoc. Narbonne was then an important Roman port, protected by what was then the island of La Clape. Cargoes would be taken up river as far as Carcassonne and then transported overland to join the GARONNE and thence to the Roman legions in Aquitaine. The hinterland of Narbonne and Béziers came to produce so much wine that it was exported to Ancient ROME, although the edict of DOMITIAN was designed to put a stop to this.

It was not until the Middle Ages, under the auspices of the Languedoc's MONKS AND MONASTERIES, that viticulture once again thrived (although today only the Abbaye de Valmagne retains its wine-producing role). Already the University of MONTPELLIER was established and ARNALDUS DE VILLANOVA oversaw several important developments for wine and spirit production there. The development of greatest potential significance for the Languedoc and its wines was the late 17th-century construction of the Canal du Midi, which connected the Mediterranean with the Atlantic. The Bordelais were by now so experienced at protectionism, however (see HAUT PAYS, for example), that the wine producers of the Languedoc failed to benefit substantially from this new distribution network until the end of the 18th century.

Much more profitable were the efforts of the DUTCH WINE TRADE in the late 17th century to develop northern European markets for *picardan*, a sweet white wine made from Clairette and Picpoul grapes that was well known in Holland by 1680, and subsequently for eaux-de-vie. The port of Sète was established in 1666 and became particularly important for exports to ENGLAND and the NETHERLANDS, Narbonne having long since silted up. Sweet wines were also produced, notably a DRIED GRAPE WINE made from Muscat grown at FRONTIGNAN, whose inhabitants insist that it was as a result of a visit by a Marquis de Lur-Saluces to Frontignan after the great frost of 1709 that Ch d'YQUEM became a sweet wine property, and that their straight-sided bottle was adopted for bordeaux.

By the mid 19th century the vineyards of the Languedoc could be divided into the HILLSIDE VINEYARDS, vines planted on gravelly terraces at mid altitude (these two roughly approximating to the modern Languedoc appellations), and vines, mainly Aramon and Terret grapes, planted on the plains for distillation into brandy.

In 1855, the Languedoc's fortunes were to change for ever, as a result of its first RAILWAY connection, via Lyons, with the important centres of population in the north. A link via Bordeaux was opened the next year. Between 1850 and 1869, average annual wine production nearly quadrupled in the Hérault. The arrival of PHYLLOXERA could hardly have been worse timed, but, thanks to feverish experimentation and the eventual adoption of GRAFTING, as well as HYBRIDS and some of the new BOUSCHET crossings, the Languedoc vineyard was the first to be reconstituted after the devastations of this American louse. By the end of the 19th century, the Languedoc became France's principal wine supplier, producing 44 per cent of the entire French wine production, from 23 per cent of the country's total *vignoble*.

This superficial success was at some cost, however. Dr GUYOT had in 1867 warned against the increasing influence of VINE VARIETIES and practices designed to produce quantity rather than quality, and against the over-industrialization of the Languedoc wine trade. By the turn of the century, the plains of the Languedoc, the Hérault particularly, were being milked of thin, light, pale red that needed blending with the much more robust produce of new colonial vineyards in ALGERIA to yield a commercially acceptable drink. France had sown the seeds of her (continued) dependence on wine imports. Such was the extent of commercial interference in the French table wine market, including widespread ADULTERATION AND FRAUD, that prices plummeted and France's social crisis of 1907 provoked what were merely the first in a long series of wine-related riots.

Since then the vignerons of the Languedoc, typically but by no means always members of one of the region's hundreds of CO-OPERATIVES, many of them formed in the 1930s and most now part of a larger group, have been some of the world's most politicized. Their sheer number has given them political power, but the fall in demand for VIN DE TABLE and difficulty in selling even the keenly priced VIN DE PAYS, which has taken its place as the Languedoc's principal product, has led to increasing frustration among growers.

Land here is relatively inexpensive, which has drawn a wide range of new investors, both producers with an established record in a more famous wine region or complete outsiders keen to set up LIFESTYLE WINERIES.

Geography and climate

The great majority of the Languedoc's vines (and virtually all of those which have been grubbed up recently) are planted on flat, low-lying alluvial plain, particularly in the southern Hérault and Gard. In the northern Hérault and western Aude, however, vines may be planted several hundred metres above sea level, in the foothills of the Cévennes and the Corbières Pyrenean foothills respectively, sometimes at quite an angle and on very varied soils which can include gravels and limestone.

The climate in all but the far western limits of the Languedoc (where Atlantic influence is apparent) is definitively MEDITERRANEAN and one of the major viticultural hazards is DROUGHT. Annual rainfall can be as little as 400 mm/15.6 in by the coast. July and August temperatures often exceed 30 °C/86 °F; such rain as does fall tends to fall in the form of localized deluges. WIND is common throughout the growing season, with the *tramontane* bringing cool air from the mountains.

Viticulture

The Languedoc is the land of the proud peasant farmer. The size of the average holding is small, and usually much divided between parcels inherited from various different branches of the family. Basic, straggling BUSH VINES still predominate, although an increasing proportion of vines, especially the newer INTERNATIONAL VARIETIES, are being trained on WIRES. IRRIGATION is theoretically permitted only within strictly specified limits, and in practice only the best and the worst producers tend to have any form of available irrigation system. The flatter, larger vineyards lend themselves to MECHANICAL HARVESTING but their parcellation has slowed the inevitable invasion. The region is by no means free of FUNGAL DISEASES and some sprayings are usually necessary.

Vine varieties

The dominant vine variety is CARIGNAN, which is declining but still accounted for more than a quarter of all vines at the turn of the century,

despite considerable incentives to plant better-quality varieties, known as *cépages améliorateurs*, such as GRENACHE (the second most planted variety, of which about 10,000 ha/25,000 acres were also pulled out during the 1990s), CINSAUT (useful for rosés), and especially SYRAH (third most planted variety), and the much rarer MOURVÈDRE. Other varieties have made substantial inroads in the region since the mid 1980s. Fourth and sixth most planted varieties Merlot and Cabernet Sauvignon may be outlawed for the production of APPELLATION CONTRÔLÉE wines but are used to produce VIN DE PAYS, about 70 per cent of which are sold as VARIETAL wines. Vestigial Cinsaut, good for rosés, is fifth most planted, while Chardonnay, used for both vins de pays and the sparkling wines of Limoux, is by far the most planted white wine variety. Aramon preceded Carignan as the Languedoc's workhorse variety but 'traditional' (pre-phylloxera) Languedoc vine varieties included Aspiran, Bourboulenc, Clairette, Maccabéo, Œillade, Picpoul, Ribarenc, and Terret, which was planted on 2,700 ha in 2000—almost as much land as Sauvignon Blanc and considerably more than Viognier or other increasingly popular white varieties such as Rolle, Roussanne, and Marsanne.

Wine-making

Winery equipment and techniques are still relatively unsophisticated in the Languedoc, where selling prices have rarely been high enough to justify major investment. DESTEMMING equipment, for example, was widely regarded as a luxury until recently, and new oak BARRELS beyond the means of most producers. (In any case, the fruit is so intense in many red wines that they do not necessarily benefit from oak.) The great majority of Languedoc wine is made in one of the co-operative cellars whose will to make good-quality wine varies considerably. Fermentation and ÉLEVAGE typically take place in large concrete *cuves*, although stainless steel is slowly invading the region. Partly in an effort to tame the natural astringency of Carignan, full or partial CARBONIC MACERATION was for long the most common red wine-making technique. BOTTLING usually takes place at a merchant's cellar rather than on the premises where the wine was made. The wine container most frequently seen by the consumer in the region is probably the road tanker (a high proportion of the locals buy their wine in bulk rather than bottle). There is increasing experimentation with SWEET WINE-MAKING of various sorts (see MINERVOIS Noble, for example) but the results have to be labelled 'Moût partiellement fermenté, issu de vendanges passerillés' because the term VENDANGE TARDIVE is officially restricted to Alsace.

For more specific information, see the individual appellations CLAIRETTE DE BELLEGARDE, CLAIRETTE DU LANGUEDOC, CORBIÈRES,

FAUGÈRES, FITOU, LIMOUX, MINERVOIS, ST-CHINIAN, Coteaux du LANGUEDOC, CABARDÈS, Côtes de la MALEPÈRE, and also the vin de liqueur CARTAGÈNE, and various MUSCAT vins doux naturels, plus FRONTIGNAN.

Clavel, J., and Baillaud, R., *Histoire et avenir des vins en Languedoc* (Toulouse, 1985).

Marcillaud, L., and Rivière, P., *Grands Vins du Languedoc-Roussillon* (Castelnau-le-Lez, 1997).

www.languedoc-wines.com

Languedoc, Coteaux du, varied and probably too extensive appellation whose zone includes some of France's best-value vineyards and most of the land suitable for growing vines above the coastal plain in a swathe through the Hérault *département* from Narbonne towards Nîmes. This territory was once known as Septimanie and is in effect a giant south-facing amphitheatre, although of course there are many local variations in TOPOGRAPHY. As elsewhere in the Languedoc, much of the land technically included within the appellation is used for other purposes (other crops or VIN DE PAYS, for example). The total vineyard area dedicated to producing Coteaux du Languedoc by 2000 was about 10,000 ha/24,799 acres, a considerable increase on the 6,500 ha declared in the early 1990s.

Although much of the zone qualifies for the basic Coteaux du Languedoc appellation, a number of subappellations, CRUS, or specific TERROIRS have been identified and are allowed to append their own name to that of the appellation on labels. Of these, CLAIRETTE DU LANGUEDOC, FAUGÈRES, and ST-CHINIAN were long ago allowed to break free and establish their own independent identity. Other subappellations waiting with particular impatience for independent existence are La CLAPE, PICPOUL DE PINET, PIC-ST-LOUP, MONTPEYROUX, and ST-SATURNIN. GRÉS DE MONTPELLIER and TERRASSES DU LARZAC were given subappellation status in 2005. Others, some of which produce relatively little wine of distinction, are CABRIÈRES, Coteaux de la MÉJANELLE, QUATOURZE, Coteaux de ST-CHRISTOL, DRÉZÉRY, the historically celebrated St-Georges-d'Orques, and Coteaux de VÉRARGUES. With the exception of Picpoul de Pinet and Clairette de Languedoc, which are white wines, most of the wine produced under these names is a full-bodied blend of southern red wine grape varieties, supplemented by some crisp, light rosé, often made from Cinsaut.

On the schists of the highest sites such as St-Saturnin and Montpeyroux, yields are particularly low but the wines can be powerful, concentrated, long-lived essences of the Languedoc. Well-drained gravelly limestone can yield more forward, fruity wines. La Clape, on the other hand, produces wines from vineyards heavily influenced by the Mediterranean.

The appellation regulations have been concerned to diminish the proportion of Carignan and Cinsaut permitted for red wines, currently

40 per cent maximum apiece. Grenache, its relative Lladoner Pelut, Syrah, and Mourvèdre are the principal varieties encouraged for the appellation's red wines. Grenache Blanc, Clairette, Picpoul, and Bourboulenc are the principal white grape varieties and white Coteaux du Languedoc must contain at least two of them. The late 1990s saw a significant increase in the number of seriously interesting white wines, typically made from blends including at least two of Grenache Blanc, Bourboulenc, Roussanne, Rolle, and Viognier, although this last is not officially sanctioned by the appellation regulations.

Producers making fine wines with the simple Coteaux du Languedoc appellation include Mas Cal Demoura, Mas Jullien, La Sauvageonne, Domaine Peyre Rose, Prieuré de St-Jean de Bébian, and Ch St-Martin de la Garrigue.

For more information, see under the increasing number of individual subappellation names.

George, R., *The Wines of the South of France* (London, 2001).

Marcillaud, L., and Rivière, P., *Grands Vins du Languedoc-Roussillon* (Montpellier, 1998).

www.coteaux-languedoc.com

Lanuvini, Colli, white wines from the hills south east of Rome. For more information, see CASTELLI ROMANI.

Lanzarote, Spanish DO including the whole of this black-soiled, volcanic, but relatively flat island in the CANARY ISLANDS. Vineyards still cover 2,500 ha/6,000 acres, with a clear domination by the white Malvasía grape, as on LA PALMA. The technically up-to-date El Grifo winery has been a pioneer in the development of modern dry Malvasía of some originality, and the overall quality of the other producers, led by Los Bermejos and La Geria, has advanced significantly.   V. de la S.

La Palma, Spanish DO including the entire eponymous island in the CANARY ISLANDS. Current vineyard surface reaches 1,600 ha/ 3,840 acres, planted at varying heights (200 to 1,400 m/4,600 ft above sea level) on the volcanic island. A large range of grape varieties are cultivated, but La Palma's most distinguished wine is traditional sweet Malvasías, almost forgotten in recent years but whose reputation, as Canary SACK, goes back to Elizabethan England.   V. de la S.

large format, bottle size larger than the standard 75 cl size and of particular interest to COLLECTORS and INVESTORS (provided it is filled with FINE WINE).

La Rochelle, port on the Atlantic coast about 160 km/100 miles north of BORDEAUX in the *département* of Charente-Maritime. In the Middle Ages, La Rochelle was a New Town, having been founded in 1130, in an age of economic expansion. The climate at La Rochelle is hot and dry enough for the winning of sea salt, and salt was initially the basis of La Rochelle's economy. Merchants came from the north to buy salt, but they also wanted wine, and it was in response to that demand that the people of La Rochelle turned to viticulture. Because of its favourable climate, Poitou was a more reliable producer than the Seine basin (see PARIS), Rheims (see CHAMPAGNE), BURGUNDY, or the RHINE. Hence the English and the Flemish turned more readily to the wines of Poitou, all the more so because these wines were less acidic than those of Rheims and Paris. La Rochelle also exported its wines to Normandy, Scotland, Ireland, and even Denmark and Norway. In 1199, Poitou was the wine the royal household bought most of, with the wines of ANJOU and the Île-de-France coming second and third. But in 1224, when La Rochelle fell to the French, it had to cede its position of best-selling wine to Bordeaux, although the wines of La Rochelle remained popular with the English in the 14th and 15th centuries.

The grape varieties were probably those of Burgundy and the Paris region: MORILLON, which was an early form of PINOT NOIR, and Fromenteau, thought to be the ancestor of PINOT GRIS. In documents of the 13th and 14th centuries, a third cépage appears: it is called Chemère, Chemière, Chenère, or Chenère Blanche, and it is likely to have been the parent of CHENIN BLANC. In accordance with medieval preference, most of the wines that Poitou made were white.

See also DUTCH WINE TRADE and HAUT-POITOU.   H.M.W.

Dion, R., *Histoire de la vigne et du vin en France* (Paris, 1959).

Laški Rizling, the name current in SLOVENIA, VOJVODINA, and some other parts of what was Yugoslavia for the white grape variety known in Austria as WELSCHRIESLING (under which name more details appear). The vine is cultivated most successfully in the higher vineyards of Slovenia (just over the border from the spirited Welschrieslings of STYRIA), and Fruška Gora in Vojvodina, where it can produce equally crisp and delicately aromatic wines. Few of these superior examples have been exported, however, whereas for decades in the second half of the 20th century a Slovenian BRAND, Lutomer Riesling (eventually renamed Lutomer Laški Rizling after German lobbying), was the best-selling white wine in the UK, its heavily sweetened style conveying little of the intrinsic character of the variety. The Rizling Vlassky is the variant known in the CZECH REPUBLIC.

lateral shoot, sometimes called simply a **lateral**, secondary shoot that grows from the axil of a leaf on the main shoot. Its origin on grapevines is linked with the complex development of the BUD. At most nodes, especially on weak vines, the lateral shoot is short (less than 20 mm/0.8 in), fails to become woody, and drops off in autumn leaving a prominent scar at the side of the bud. But on more vigorous shoots, especially at the middle nodes or at the end where vigorous shoots have been topped or trimmed, the lateral shoot grows in the same way as a primary shoot producing hardened permanent wood. Sometimes, lateral shoots are fruitful (see SECOND CROP). Laterals that develop on secondary shoots are called tertiaries; quaternaries have even been seen on extremely vigorous vines.

B.G.C.

Latin America. See SOUTH AMERICA and MEXICO.

Latisana, a DOC of the FRIULI region in north east Italy whose unchallenging wines are rarely exported.

latitude, angular distance north or south of the equator, measured in degrees and minutes. The main northern hemisphere viticultural regions extend between 32 and 51 degrees north, and most of those in the southern hemisphere between 28 and 42 degrees south. Extreme poleward limits are at about 52 degrees north in ENGLAND (and Ireland), and just over 46 degrees south in Otago, NEW ZEALAND. Some vines are also cultivated for wine production in tropical highlands or irrigated desert conditions as close to the equator as eight or nine degrees. See TROPICAL VITICULTURE.

Comparisons between hemispheres based purely on latitude are misleading. Northern hemisphere vineyards are on average warmer during the growing season at given latitudes, a fact partly related to their greater CONTINENTALITY. But even over the whole year, the northern hemisphere is on average warmer than the southern hemisphere at similar latitudes, partly because of the greater land mass and its disposition around the North Pole, and partly (in the case of western Europe) because of warming by the Gulf Stream.

When wine regions with equal average mean temperatures during the growing season, or equal temperature summations (see CLIMATE CLASSIFICATION), are compared, grapes tend to ripen more fully when grown at high latitudes, i.e. further from the equator. Alternatively, later maturing grape varieties can be ripened. The reasons for this phenomenon of great significance for wine quality remain unproven, but two main mechanisms have been proposed.

First, compared with low latitudes, the summers at high latitudes have longer days, with given totals of SUNLIGHT hours more spread through them. One can argue, on physiological grounds, that this should be used more efficiently for PHOTOSYNTHESIS and sugar production than the same sunlight duration concentrated in a shorter day. In the latter case, the rate the vines can use the sugar, or transport it away from the leaves, may itself become a limitation to further photosynthesis. Also, it seems likely that the high-latitude summer and autumn days will have more hours of weak sunlight, not intense enough to register as bright sunlight by the standard recording methods, but still intense enough to support photosynthesis. Huglin and earlier European researchers favour these explanations.

The second (and probably complementary) explanation is that the conventionally used monthly average mean temperatures (i.e. for each month, the average of its maximum temperatures plus that of its minima, divided by two) do not accurately reflect the actual average temperatures experienced by the vines (McIntyre *et al.*). Where summer days are longer, it seems likely that a greater proportion of the 24 hours is in the upper half of the temperature range. The day's mean, which is strictly half-way between its maximum and minimum temperatures, then underestimates its true average. With shorter summer days at low latitudes this is less marked, so that higher mean temperatures are needed to achieve the same temperature averages and rates of vine and fruit development; and thence earliness and completeness of PHYSIOLOGICAL RIPENING, or flavour ripening. (Accumulation of SUGAR IN GRAPES, on the other hand, could be expected to be more directly related to effective sunlight duration, as described above.) Further, in high-latitude continental climates, calculation from monthly average mean temperatures close to or below 10 °C/50 °F at the beginning and end of the vine-growing season fails to credit up to several weeks of true growing conditions above 10 °C in the warmer parts of those months.

Finally, it can be noted that high-latitude viticultural climates tend to have higher relative HUMIDITIES and less day-to-day TEMPERATURE VARIABILITY during the growing season than those at low latitudes (apart from where the latter are coastal). Both factors have likely implications for ripening and for grape and wine quality. See CLIMATE AND WINE QUALITY, HUMIDITY, TEMPERATURE VARIABILITY, and map under WORLD PRODUCTION. J.G.

Gladstones, J., *Viticulture and Environment* (Adelaide, 1992).

Huglin, P., 'Possibilités d'appréciation objective du milieu viticole (Possibilities of objective evaluation of the viticultural environment)', *Bulletin de l'OIV*, 56 (1983), 823–33.

McIntyre, G. N., Kliewer, W. M., and Lider, L. A., 'Some limitations of the degree day system as used in viticulture in California', *American Journal of Enology and Viticulture*, 38 (1987), 128–32.

Latium, Anglicized version of the Italian wine region LAZIO.

Latour, Château, famously long-lived FIRST GROWTH in the MÉDOC region of BORDEAUX. The originally square tower from which the château takes its name was one of a defensive line against ocean-going pirates. Vines were already planted here in the late 14th century and at least a quarter of the land was vineyard by 1600. At the end of the 17th century, a number of smallholdings were accumulated into one ownership under the de Mullet family. The New French Clarets they produced made their first publicized appearances in AUCTIONS in London COFFEE HOUSES early in the 18th century. Owned from 1677 by the Clauzel family, it passed by marriage to the powerful SÉGURS, who also owned LAFITE, MOUTON, and Calon-Ségur. On the death in 1755 of the Marquis Nicolas-Alexandre de Ségur, 'Le Prince des Vignes', his properties passed to his four daughters, three of whom in 1760 acquired Latour. Their male descendants owned the château, which in 1842 became a private company, until its purchase by the British Pearson family in 1963, with 25 per cent acquired by HARVEYS of Bristol, and a diminishing minority remaining in the hands of the French families. The property was greatly improved, with STAINLESS STEEL tanks controversially installed as FERMENTATION VESSELS in time for the 1964 vintage, partly on the advice of director Harry WAUGH. In 1989, the estate was sold to multinational corporation Allied-Lyons, already owners of Harveys, for the equivalent of £110 million. In 1993, Allied-Lyons sold their 94 per cent share of the property to French businessman François Pinault (who acquired the London AUCTION house of Christie's in 1998), when Latour was valued at £86 million.

The estate of 77 ha/190 acres of vineyard (11 ha were acquired in 2005) consists of 75 per cent Cabernet Sauvignon vines, 24 per cent Merlot (increased from 15 per cent in the 1980s), and a very small amount of Cabernet Franc and Petit Verdot, with an average annual production of 30,000 cases of the three wines made there. In 1966 was first produced a SECOND WINE, Les Forts de Latour, made from the produce of young vines and from three plots on the other side of the St-Julien–Pauillac road. A third wine is also bottled and sold as Pauillac. Latour's wines generally require much longer to develop than those of the other first growths, and they often have greater longevity. Latour is also known for its ability to produce good wines in lesser vintages.

It also possesses better archives, back to the 14th century, than any other wine estate in Bordeaux and so has spawned an unusual and useful array of monographs. E.P.-R. & J.R.

Faith, N., *Latour* (London, 1991).

Higounet, C. (ed.), *La Seigneurie et le vignoble de Château Latour* (Bordeaux, 1974).

Penning-Rowsell, E., *Château Latour: A History of a Great Vineyard 1331–1992* (London, 1993).

Latour, Louis, one of Burgundy's most commercially astute, and oldest, merchants. Jean Latour first planted vines in Aloxe-Corton, then called simply Aloxe, in 1768; his family had grown vines on the plain to the east of Beaune since the 16th century. Jean's son was the first in a long line of Louis Latours and enlarged the domaine considerably and it was not until the late 19th century that the family added wine brokering to their vine-growing activities.

With an eye to the developing export markets, the third Louis Latour bought the Lamarosse family's NÉGOCIANT business in Beaune's historic Rue des Tonneliers in 1867, and was so successful that in 1891 he was able to buy Ch Corton-Grancey in Aloxe-Corton. With this acquisition came one of the most handsome, and most photographed, houses in the Côte d'Or, together with extensive wine-making premises, and some notable vineyards around the hill of Corton to add to the Latour family holdings, which already included some Chambertin; Romanée-St-Vivant, Les Quatre Journaux; and Chevalier-Montrachet, Les Demoiselles.

It was the third Louis Latour who is reputed to have realized the hill of Corton's potential for great white wine when he replanted some of the hill now designated Corton-Charlemagne with Chardonnay vines after PHYLLOXERA had laid waste vineyards originally planted with Pinot Noir and Aligoté.

Innovations of succeeding Louis Latours include a succession of 'new' and increasingly daring white wines. What was then known as Grand Pouilly, and subsequently became known as Pouilly-Fuissé, was introduced to the United States in the 1930s, immediately after the Repeal of PROHIBITION. A wine known as MÂCON-Lugny was introduced as a respectable alternative to CÔTE D'OR white wines in close co-operation with the Lugny CO-OPERATIVE. Louis Latour also pioneered the planting of Chardonnay vines in the relatively unknown ARDÈCHE in the early 1980s. The firm has 350 ha of vines under contract to local growers, whose produce is vinified at Latour's winery in Alba. In the late 1980s, Louis Latour bought land in the Var *département* in PROVENCE, planting the Beurot selection of Pinot Noir to produce gentle red wines sold as Pinot Noir, Domaine de Valmoissine.

The house enjoys a solid reputation for its white wines, but has incited controversy over its endorsement of PASTEURIZATION of even its finest red wines. In 1997, they celebrated the bicentenary of the négociant business and the firm is currently run by the seventh generation Louis-Fabrice Latour.

Latour-de-France, like CARAMANY, is a small village singled out for special mention as a suffix to the appellation Côtes du Roussillon-Villages. It may have been accorded this distinction less because of the superior quality of the wine than because the name had been successfully promoted to the French wine consumer by wine merchants Nicolas, who once bought the majority of production. For more details, see ROUSSILLON.

Lauzet, almost extinct and not especially exciting vine allowed into JURANÇON.

Lavilledieu, Vins de, almost extinct VDQS (just 30 ha left) in SOUTH WEST FRANCE on terraces between the GARONNE and Tarn rivers north of FRONTON. Lavilledieu has a long history, dating back to the pre-Christian era and revived by monks (see MONKS AND MONASTERIES) who cleared the forest of Agre and replaced trees with vines in the 12th century, but its wine production today is minuscule. A wide variety of south western vine varieties are allowed (notably the NÉGRETTE of Fronton).

law impinges on wine principally in the areas of penalizing ADULTERATION AND FRAUD of all sorts; regulating wine DESIGNATIONS, CONTROLLED APPELLATIONS, and LABELLING INFORMATION; and controlling the sale and service of any alcoholic drink as, for example, in state liquor laws or licensing laws. In the UNITED STATES, the consumption of any alcoholic drink is restricted to those over 21, for example, and DIRECT SHIPPING of wine to consumers in many states has been forbidden.

layering, known as *marcottage* in French, is an ancient method of vine PROPAGATION which involves taking a long cane from one vine and training it down to the soil, then burying a section to normal planting depth but with the end bent up and emerging in a desired position. This is a useful method of filling empty spaces in established vineyards, a task that is difficult by normal planting methods, but only if the new roots survive in that soil, and so only in areas without PHYLLOXERA, NEMATODES, and other soil-borne pathogens (such as BOLLINGER's Vieilles Vignes vineyard, the Nacional vineyard at QUINTA DO NOVAL or COLARES in Portugal, and parts of Australia and Chile). The foster vine may be left connected to the parent or may be separated after it has reached normal size. B.G.C.

laying down wine is an English expression for holding wine as it undergoes BOTTLE AGEING. Thus most people lay down wine in their (however notional) CELLARS. Considerable quantities of red bordeaux are **laid down** by COLLECTORS all over the globe, for example.

Layon, Coteaux du, large appellation, for generally medium sweet (much richer from the best independent vignerons) white wine made from the Chenin Blanc grape, in the ANJOU district of the Loire. Three small areas within the area produce wines of such quality that they have earned their own appellations, BONNEZEAUX, QUARTS DE CHAUME, and premier cru CHAUME. They, and most of the best vineyards of the Coteaux du Layon, are on the steep slopes on the right bank of the Layon tributary of the Loire. TERROIR is all here, for Coteaux du Layon should be an intense wine made ideally from several TRIES through the vineyard, selecting BOTRYTIZED grapes, or those that have begun to raisin on the vine. Producers such as Claude Papin of Ch Pierre Bise vinify grapes picked on slate, schist, clay, and sandstone separately to demonstrate the variation in style and potential longevity. Other fine producers include Vincent Ogereau and Philippe Delesvaux, but this variable appellation is also a hotbed of ambition. Yields vary enormously according to the conditions of the vintage, but are officially limited to 30 hl/ha (1.7 tons/acre), and 25 hl/ha for wines produced in the clay soils around Chaume and sold as **Chaume Premier Cru des Coteaux du Layon**. The villages Beaulieu-sur-Layon, Faye d'Anjou, Rablay-sur-Layon, Rochefort-sur-Loire, St-Aubin-de-Luigné, and St-Lambert-du-Lattay can append their name to that of Coteaux du Layon, or sell it as **Coteaux du Layon-Villages**, provided the wines have a POTENTIAL ALCOHOL of 13 per cent, and an actual ALCOHOLIC STRENGTH of 12 per cent rather than the 11 per cent minimum demanded of the rest of Coteaux du Layon. After a period in the late 1990s when maximum possible sugar levels were sought at all costs, growers today tend to pick between 18 and 23 per cent potential alcohol, producing wines with RESIDUAL SUGAR of around 100 g/l, perhaps up to 200 from the finest *tries*, which are sweet but not too rich to drink with gusto. In favourable vintages, some great wine is produced in this appellation, but producers are dogged by the depressing effect on selling prices of a substantial quantity of extremely ordinary just-sweet wine sold under the name Coteaux du Layon. Wines may be sold as DEMI-SEC, MOELLEUX, and, sweetest of all, LIQUOREUX. In the mid 2000s, about 1,400 ha/3,400 acres were devoted to the appellation that includes the seven village crus and is spread along about 20 km of slopes, in an extremely narrow strip of vines concentrated on those south-west facing slopes above the Layon and on a few slopes around St-Lambert.

See also LOIRE, including map.

Lazio, the region known as Latium in English, the ancient homeland of the Latins (see ITALY, history), and the seat of Italy's government and administration in the capital, Rome (see map under ITALY). The region also has a significant but declining viticultural production, its approximately 100,000 ha/247,000 acres of vineyards yielding annual totals of 2.7 million hl/71 million gal of wine, making it sixth among Italy's regions behind Sicilia, Puglia, Veneto, Emilia-Romagna, and Abruzzo. Only 15 per cent of the total Lazio vineyard is dedicated to making DOC wine. White wines, almost exclusively from MALVASIA and TREBBIANO grapes, represent over 85 per cent of it, with the wines of the CASTELLI ROMANI representing by far the majority. Malvasia and Trebbiano blends are also produced in some quantities in the DOC zones of Cerveteri, Est!Est!!Est!!!, and in that small portion of the ORVIETO zone which spills over the Umbrian border into Lazio. Lazio has no significant red DOCs although an occasional Cabernet–Merlot blend of significant quality—from the lauded Montiano from Falesco, the Boncompagni Ludovisi estate near Rome, the Di Mauro estate in Marino, and the newer Castel De Paolis estate in Grottaferrata, for example—suggests that the soil and climate are well suited to red wine production, even if no real tradition exists in the region. Merlot was planted this century in the DOC zone of Aprilia by the settlers from Veneto who drained the Pontine marshes, but the 14 tonnes/ha allowed by the DOC rules are hardly compatible with quality. The CESANESE grape has its proponents in its home province of Frosinone, but most Cesanese is neither well made nor interesting (despite the example set by a blend of Cesanese, Merlot, and Cabernet produced at the Colacicchi estate in Agnani during the 1960s and 1970s). A number of fine red wines made in the mid 1990s suggests a new consciousness of the region's potential, possibly partly inspired by neighbouring UMBRIA's success. But the TENDONE training systems and the firmly established regional tradition of high YIELDS mean these are still exceptions rather than the rule.

D.T. & D.C.G.

Le. For anything prefixed Le, see under the next letter of the name.

lead, one of the familiar and widely dispersed heavy metals which occurs naturally in trace amounts in all plants, therefore in grapes, and therefore, usually in microgram per litre quantities only, in wines. This ubiquitous element, which has no known biological function in plants or animals, is now known to be a neural toxin of particular danger to children. This has resulted in the reformulation of many products, particularly petroleum products, so as to exclude lead.

History

Lead has been associated with wine since the time of Ancient ROME. The Romans recognized that lead not only prevented wines from turning sour (and rescued those that already had) but also made them taste sweeter (see PLINY). What they did not know, however, is that, even when taken in only very small quantities over a long period, lead is a poison.

Its dangers were understood from the end of the 17th century when a German doctor, Eberhard Gockel of Ulm in Württemberg, noticed that the symptoms suffered by some of his wine-drinking patients matched those observed in lead miners. Gradually legislation was passed in Europe banning the use of lead in wine but the practice continued. At last, in 1820, the campaigner Frederick Accum complained that 'the merchant or dealer who practises this dangerous sophistication, adds the crime of murder to that of fraud'.

Poisoning could result not only from the wilful addition of lead to wine. The Romans heated grape juice in lead vessels in order to produce *sapa*, a sweet concentrate used as a wine additive and in cooking, and even in the 19th century wine BOTTLES were cleaned with lead shot, thereby contaminating the wine.

H.B.

Viticultural aspects

Grapes containing lead may produce wine containing lead. Recent health concerns about lead in wine have led to studies of lead in grapes. There are two principal sources of lead. One is from lead-rich automobile exhaust particles settling on both grapes and soil. This is a problem for roadside vineyards in particular, but one which is declining as the use of unleaded fuels increases. The other source is from prior use of the now-banned chemical insecticide lead arsenate, which has contaminated many vineyard soils, especially where SOIL ACIDITY is high.

R.E.S.

Lead in modern wine

Most of the traces of lead from grapes are precipitated out with the LEES during winemaking. However, as analytical methods continue to improve, microgram quantities per litre are likely to be found in most wines.

The equipment used in modern wineries should not result in any lead contamination. The few wines which contain lead in milligram per litre concentrations derive it principally from capsules or FOILS which contain lead, or from lead-crystal DECANTERS. (Modern bottles are made of lead-free glass.) Seepage of wine around the cork can corrode the foil and, if the lip of the bottle is not thoroughly cleaned before pouring, the wine may be contaminated by some of the lead salt. To protect those who do not clean obvious lead salts from a bottle lip before pouring, however, the use of lead capsules or foils is now declining or prohibited in many regions.

Lengthy storage of wines in lead-crystal decanters provides time for the wine acids to leach some lead from the glass, but keeping a wine in a lead-crystal glass or decanter for the usual period of no more than a few hours is too short for dangerous amounts of lead contamination. One study found a lead concentration of around 5 mg/l in port left in a lead-crystal decanter for four months, so that 10 l of it would have to be consumed in a short time for a potentially toxic human intake of lead! The amount of lead leached from glassware is determined by the raw materials used to make it and research reported in the *Lancet* suggests that lead concentrations in wine increased by 50 per cent after one hour in a low-quality Yugoslavian decanter, but by only 15 per cent after three hours in better-quality decanters.

Analyses of thousands of representative samples of wine suggest that the lead content of wines is decreasing in general but in the early 1990s ranged from 0 to 1.26 mg/l, with the average lead content being 0.13 mg/l, values well below any legal maximum.

An Australian study found that there was minimal uptake of lead from wine when it was consumed with food.   A.D.W. & J.R.

Accum, F., *Treatise on Adulteration of Food, and Culinary Poisons* (London, 1820).

Eisinger, J., 'Early consumer protection legislation: a 17th-century law prohibiting lead adulteration of wines', *Interdisciplinary Science Reviews*, 16/1 (1991), 61–8.

Gulson, B. L., *et al.*, 'Contribution of lead in wine to the total dietery intake of lead in humans with and without a meal: a pilot study', *Journal of Wine Research*, 9/1 (1998), 5–14.

McWhirter, K., 'Lead-free lessons', *Wine & Spirit* (Nov 1993).

Pliny the Elder, *Natural History*, trans. H. Rackham (London, 1938), book 14.

leaf (*feuille* in French). Vine leaves range in size up to that of a dinner plate but are normally the area of a human hand (100 to 200 cm²). Their individual area correlates with shoot VIGOUR and also varies with vine variety (Merlot has large leaves, for example, while Gewürztraminer has small leaves). The vine is a leafy plant with sometimes many hectares of total leaf area per hectare of vineyard. A proportion of these leaves will be shaded and therefore not PHOTOSYNTHETIC. The total leaf and shoot system of a vine is known as the CANOPY.

The green, flat zone of the leaf connected to the stem by the PETIOLE is known as the leaf blade, or lamina. The lamina of a grape leaf expands to nearly its full area in six or more weeks, growing to a shape and form characteristic for each VINE VARIETY. The arrangement of the five lobes, the shape of the 'teeth' at the edge of the leaf, the size and shape of the sinuses, and especially the angle and lengths of the main veins are features that are measured (ampelometry) for vine variety identification by AMPELOGRAPHERS.

Leaf colour is responsive to VINE NUTRITION, becoming yellow all over with deficiencies of nitrogen and sulfur, or patterned with yellow or red and/or dead zones with most other deficiencies. Similarly, yellow and dead areas on leaves occur with some virus infections and as a result of herbicide contamination, although usually in different patterns. With the onset of autumn, leaf colour changes naturally from green to yellow or red, depending on the vine species and the presence of certain VIRUS DISEASES. See LEAFROLL VIRUS.   B.G.C.

leaf aldehydes make wines taste HERBACEOUS.

leaf fall, the process which occurs naturally in autumn, often after the first frost, which marks the end of the VINE GROWTH CYCLE. Ideally this is some time after HARVEST, so that the vine has been able to build up its reserves of the CARBOHYDRATES important for growth the following spring. See also DEFOLIATION.   R.E.S.

leafhoppers, members of the insect family Cicadellidae which can cause both direct and sometimes serious indirect damage to vineyards. In California, both the grape leafhopper, *Erythroneura elegantula*, and the closely related and biologically similar variegated grape leafhopper, *Erythroneura variabilis*, cause damage to grapes. They begin to feed on grapevine foliage as soon as it appears in spring, and do so by sucking out the contents of leaf cells. As injury progresses, heavily damaged leaves lose their green colour and PHOTOSYNTHESIS is much reduced. TABLE GRAPES are spoilt by spots of leafhopper excrement. The damage caused is in direct proportion to the numbers. When there are 20 or fewer leafhopper nymphs per leaf, no control is required.

There are, however, a number of natural enemies of leafhoppers, the most important being a tiny wasp, *Anagrus epos*. Low leafhopper populations do not need treatment, especially if this parasite is found to be active. Leafhoppers appear to develop resistance to insecticides quickly, so these may have to be changed every few years.

Some other leafhopper pests do not cause direct damage but spread important grape diseases. PIERCE'S DISEASE of the Americas is spread by so-called sharpshooter leafhoppers (subfamily Cicadellinae). The bacteria that cause Pierce's disease inhabit the XYLEM of the plants, and xylem sap-feeders can transmit the bacteria from plant to plant. FLAVESCENCE DORÉE is caused by a bacterium (phytoplasma) that inhabits the PHLOEM and appears to be transmitted exclusively by the leafhopper *Scaphoideus littoralis* after a latent period of several weeks, during which the phytoplasmas multiply and circulate within the insect to finally reach the insect vector's salivary glands to be introduced into the plant during feeding.

M.J.E., R.E.S., & A.H.P.

Flaherty, D. L., *et al.* (eds.), *Grape Pest Management* (2nd edn, Oakland, Calif., 1992).

Pearson, R. C., and Goheen, A. C., *Compendium of Grape Diseases* (St Paul, Minn., 1988).

leaf removal, vineyard practice aimed at helping to control BOTRYTIS BUNCH ROT and other BUNCH ROTS, and at improving GRAPE COMPOSITION and therefore wine quality. Typically the leaves are removed around the bunches to increase exposure to the sun and wind. The bunches dry out more quickly after dew and rain so that moulds are less likely to develop. Increased exposure to sunlight helps the berries produce more of the PHENOLICS important in wine quality. Grape SUGARS are also increased and MALIC ACID reduced, both of which contribute to improved wine quality.

For optimal effects on wine quality, leaves should be removed several weeks before VERAISON, although it is more usual to remove them at its onset. In Europe it is common to remove leaves nearer to the time of harvest, primarily to reduce the risk of botrytis bunch rot. Leaf removal is also used to improve the colour of black and red TABLE GRAPES. Traditionally leaf removal has been done by hand, requiring about 50 hours of labour per hectare (2.5 acres), but machines which take less than five hours per hectare to remove leaves by suction and/or cutting have been developed.

Recent studies around the world have questioned excessive leaf removal in warm to hot climates, because there can be negative effects on fruit composition and wine quality. This is due to the bunches being heated by the sun, leading to undesirably high temperatures within the grape berries in the afternoon when air temperature is also higher. The alternative is to do less removal on the western side of the canopy.

Decreasing dependence on AGROCHEMICALS in the vineyard has led to renewed interest in leaf removal in both Old and New Worlds. As well as making the fruit less prone to FUNGAL DISEASES by improving aeration, leaf removal can also increase the effectiveness of such chemicals as may be applied to protect the fruit. R.E.S.

Smart, R. E., and Robinson, M., *Sunlight into Wine* (Adelaide, 1991).

leaf rollers, also called **leaf folders**, insects which cause damage to vines at the caterpillar stage (and nothing whatever to do with LEAFROLL VIRUS disease). As the name suggests, they form the leaf into a roll, and feed on the edge of the leaf inside the roll. The roll restricts the exposed leaf surface, and the feeding reduces the leaf area. In California, both the grape leaf roller (*Desmia funeralis*) and the omnivorous leaf roller (*Platynota stultana*) are serious vineyard pests. In Australia, a native leaf roller, the light brown apple moth (*Epiphyas postvittana*), is the country's most serious insect pest, feeding on a wide range of native and imported plants, including grapevines. As well as feeding on young shoots, the larvae cause damage by feeding on berries, resulting in yield reductions of up to 10 per cent, and allowing the entry of BOTRYTIS and other BUNCH ROTS. Control of leaf rollers can be by selective or by broad spectrum insecticides, but some predators are active against some species, which can help to control low populations. Biological control has proved ineffective in vineyards, though successful in orchards.

See also BEETLES for a European insect which causes leaf rolling. M.J.E.

Buchanan, G. A., and Amos, T. G., 'Grape pests', in B. G. Coombe and P. R. Dry (eds.), *Viticulture*, ii: *Practices* (Adelaide, 1992).

Flaherty, D. L., *et al.* (eds.), *Grape Pest Management* (2nd edn, Oakland, Calif., 1992).

leafroll virus, virus disease that is widespread in all countries where grapes are grown. The disease is now thought to be due to a complex of different viruses which can be differentiated. Of all the VIRUS DISEASES of vines, it can have the most serious effects on wine quality. These dramatic effects are not understood by the many appreciative TOURISTS in wine regions who marvel at the attractive autumnal colours of vineyards. Few realize that these colours often indicate the presence of a serious disease, although other factors may contribute to autumnal colours. Leafroll virus causes yield to be reduced by as much as 50 per cent. Wine quality is also affected because of delayed RIPENING. Thus wines from infected vines are lower in alcohol, colour, flavour, and body. The disease does not kill vines, so they are infrequently removed. Yet removal is the only known treatment to overcome the effects of the virus.

Characteristic symptoms are downwards rolling of the leaf blade in autumn. The area between the leaf veins turns red for black-fruited varieties, and yellow for white-fruited varieties—hence the attractive colours at the end of the season. Some varieties such as Cabernet Franc and Chardonnay show the classic symptoms; others such as Riesling and most ROOTSTOCKS show no symptoms at all. Infected vines may be stunted but this is hardly sufficient for diagnosis.

Leafroll probably originated in the Near East along with VITIS VINIFERA and was carried along with grape cuttings. The disease is spread chiefly by humans, using cuttings or buds from infected vines. Cuttings for budwood are taken when the vines are dormant and no leaves are present to show symptoms, making it impossible to distinguish healthy from infected plants. Once infected planting material is used, then the new vineyard is immediately infected, and will perform at below its potential for its lifetime.

There are however a few recorded instances where natural spread of the virus has been confirmed, including New Zealand and South Africa. An insect vector (MEALY BUG) is implicated.

This virus disease, like many others, has become more widespread as GRAFTING on to PHYLLOXERA-resistant rootstocks has become more commonplace because grafting increases the chances of using infected material. Thus, many Old World vineyards planted early in the 1900s show the virus. Some tasters believed that grafting to phylloxera-resistant rootstocks from the 1880s onwards led directly to a decline in wine quality. In fact this supposed drop in quality may have been an effect of increased spread of leafroll virus due to grafting.

Because there is no control for this disease, growers should ensure that they plant only

material that is tested free of the virus. The University of California at DAVIS led the world in developing a 'clean stock' programme, now known as FOUNDATION PLANT SERVICES, with the result that vineyards planted in California since the early 1960s are generally virus free. In addition, this virus-tested planting stock has been exported and, for example, many of the vineyards of Australia and New Zealand are planted with such material. The virus is detected by INDEXING, or by using immunoassays such as ELISA, or by electron microscope searches for the virus particles. Healthy planting material is produced by eliminating viruses using THERMOTHERAPY or heat treatment or, more reliably, by TISSUE CULTURE. Propagation is recommended from these 'clean' mother plants. R.E.S.

Emmett, R. W., Harris, A. R., Taylor, R. H., and McGechan, J. K., 'Grape diseases and vineyard protection', in B. G. Coombe and P. R. Dry (eds.), *Viticulture*, ii: *Practices* (Adelaide, 1992).

Pearson, R. C., and Goheen, A. C., *Compendium of Grape Diseases* (St Paul, Minn., 1988).

leaf to fruit ratio, viticultural measurement which indicates the capacity of a vine to ripen grapes. The ratio of vine leaf area to fruit (grape) weight determines just how well a vine can mature grapes and how suitable they will be for wine-making. Although it is less understood and discussed, it can have an even more important effect on wine quality than YIELD.

This ratio indicates the vine's ability to manufacture compounds important for grape RIPENING. If most leaves are exposed to the sun, then the leaf area is proportional to the ability of the vine to make SUGARS by PHOTOSYNTHESIS. Against this should be set the weight of grapes to be ripened. Some studies, however, show that photosynthetic rate can somewhat adjust to a low leaf to fruit ratio, and so the effect of over-severe LEAF REMOVAL in the fruit zone, for instance, may not be as detrimental to ripening as anticipated.

A low value of leaf to fruit ratio, for example 5 sq cm per g grape weight, indicates that the fruit will ripen sluggishly, and so levels of SUGAR IN GRAPES will increase slowly along with PHENOLICS and FLAVOUR, but PH will be relatively high for the corresponding sugar level. The other extreme of, say, 30 sq cm per g grape weight suggests a very leafy vine with a small crop of grapes, but one which will ripen quickly and completely, and so produce better wine quality than for the low leaf to fruit ratio. Such low yields, however, may be uneconomic, and so most vine-growers would aim to manage their vineyards with a sufficient but not excessive leaf to fruit ratio (see vine BALANCE). A value of between 10 and 15 sq cm per g grape weight is considered adequate for ripening of most vine varieties, although higher values are considered necessary by some for PINOT NOIR and perhaps MERLOT. Also, high leaf to fruit ratios must be carefully managed in the vineyard, so as to avoid any negative effects on wine quality due to canopy SHADE.   R.E.S.

Champagnol, F., *Éléments de physiologie de la vigne et de viticulture générale* (St-Gely-du-Fesc, 1984).

leafy, tasting term usually used synonymously with HERBACEOUS.

Leányka, meaning 'maiden', originally from Transylvania and long considered a Hungarian name for the white grape variety called **Fetească** in Romania, but Austrian scientists say that DNA PROFILING does not support this synonymy. Varietal Leányka has long been produced in EGER and Sopron has produced some excellent examples. It can produce good-quality wine if yields are restricted, and is suitable for ageing in exceptional vintages. A particularly aromatic strain is grown on the south shore of lake Balaton. For more details, see HUNGARY.

Leatico, synonym for ALEATICO.

Lebanon, one of the oldest sites of wine production, incorporating some of the ancient eastern Mediterranean land of CANAAN and, subsequently, most of PHOENICIA. In Baalbek, the ancient Greek city in the Bekaa valley which is the vine-growing centre of Lebanon, is the temple of BACCHUS, built in the middle of the 2nd century AD and excavated, displaying much of its former glory, in the early 20th century. In 2002, about 150,000 hl, nearly 4 million gal, of wine were produced from a shrinking total of about 15,000 ha/37,500 acres of vineyard (most of it dedicated to TABLE GRAPES and DRYING GRAPES) according to OIV statistics.

In the Middle Ages, the rich wines of Tyre and Sidon were particularly treasured in Europe, and were traded by the merchants of VENICE, to whom these ports belonged for much of the 13th century. In 1517, what is now Lebanon was absorbed into the Ottoman Empire and wine-making was forbidden, except for religious purposes. This allowed Lebanon's Christians, mainly Maronites and Greek and Armenian Orthodox, to produce wine and in 1857 the Jesuit missionaries of Ksara introduced new vine varieties and production methods from French-governed Algeria, laying the foundations of the modern Lebanese wine industry.

The French administration that governed Lebanon between the wars created unprecedented demand for wine, while Lebanon's post-independence role as a cosmopolitan, financial hub allowed the new wine culture to take hold. It lasted until 1975 when the country descended into a 15-year civil war that stunted the development of the sector. Although only two harvests were lost to the fighting, only Chateau Musar, which recognized the need to penetrate new markets if it was to survive, genuinely thrived during this turbulent period. With peace came new opportunities

and growth. The success of Chateau Kefraya, which began producing wine in 1979 after decades of supplying grapes to others, and the popularity of New World wines, galvanized Lebanon's few established wineries and inspired a new generation, many of whom were producers of arak, the aniseed-flavoured brandy which is still so much more popular in Lebanon than wine, to exploit the potential of the Bekaa valley's formidable terroir.

Apart from some experimental vineyards in Bhamdoun, Kfifane, Richmaya, Jezzine, and parts of the eastern Bekaa, the overwhelming majority of wine grapes are grown in the western Bekaa and Zahleh, where, at an impressive altitude of around 1,000 m/3,280 ft between the Lebanon and Anti-Lebanon mountain ranges, they enjoy dry summers, cool nights, and consistent rainfall so that the grapes rarely ripen before the middle of September (considerably later than some southern French vineyards, for example). Minimal vineyard treatments are needed today and almost half of all vines for wine production are trained on WIRES rather than sprawling in vigorous BUSH form. Average yields are around 5 tonnes/ha.

French influence on the country is still apparent in the grape varieties most commonly planted—Cinsaut, Carignan, Cabernet Sauvignon, Merlot, Mourvèdre, Grenache, Syrah, Ugni Blanc, and Clairette—although since the early 1990s some other fashionable INTERNATIONAL VARIETIES have been planted. It is also evident in the name and aims of the national wine association, the Union Vinicole du Liban, formed in 1997 with the eventual aim of creating a system similar to France's APPELLATION CONTRÔLÉE.

That said, the Hochar family's distinctively Levantine red Chateau Musar is still Lebanon's most celebrated wine, a gamey blend of 50 to 80 per cent Cabernet Sauvignon fleshed out with Cinsaut and Carignan. It has been both fêted as a work of genius and dismissed as an anachronism, flawed with excessive VOLATILE ACIDITY and hype, but its fans around the globe are legion. Influenced by a close relationship with the BARTONS of Bordeaux in the early 1960s, the Hochars introduced DESTEMMING and MATURATION in new French OAK BARRELS. Musar also produces small quantities of an equally full-bodied, oak-aged white, primarily from the indigenous OBAIDEH grape with Merweh, or Meroué, thought to be Sémillon, and even smaller quantities of rosé.

Lebanon's biggest producer is Chateau Ksara, sold to a consortium of Lebanese businessmen in 1973 and now responsible for more than a third of all the wine sold in Lebanon, including most notably its top Bordeaux blend Cuvée du Troisième Millénaire.

Chateau Kefraya, Lebanon's second biggest winery, was founded in 1979 and claims to use grapes only from its own 300 ha vineyards in the village of Kefraya. Its Cabernet–Syrah blend Comte de M 1996 convinced the outside

world that there was more to Lebanese wine than Chateau Musar. The majority shareholder is the colourful Druze politician Walid Jumblat.

If one winery can be said to have lit a fuse under what was, until the mid-1990s, a sector that lacked a competitive edge, it is Massaya, a Franco-Lebanese alliance formed in 1997 between the Lebanese Ghosn brothers and a heavyweight French triumvirate from Bordeaux and Châteauneuf-du-Pape. Clos St Thomas and Domaine Wardy wineries also produce respected wines by French-trained Lebanese winemakers and have the connections to make inroads abroad. These are necessary as Lebanon is unlikely to become a serious wine-drinking nation itself.   M.R.K.

Karam, M., *Wines of Lebanon* (London, 2005).

lees, old English word for the dregs or sediment that settles at the bottom of a container such as a FERMENTATION VESSEL. Wine lees are made up of dead YEAST cells, grape seeds, pulp, stem and skin fragments, and insoluble TARTRATES that are deposited during the making and ageing of wine.

In the production of everyday wines, clear wine is separated from the lees as soon as possible after FERMENTATION, to ensure that yeast AUTOLYSIS is avoided and to begin clarification and stabilization. Some wines, both red and, especially, white, may be deliberately left on some of their lees, the so-called **fine lees** (as opposed to the coarser **gross lees**, from the French *grosses lies*, off which most wines are racked early in their life if greater complexity and reduction of MALIC ACID are desired), for some months in order to gain greater complexity of flavour. This is called LEES CONTACT.

Fine wines left on lees for a considerable time usually require much less drastic processing than more ordinary wines that were separated early from the lees, because the semi-stable colloidal PHENOLICS and tartrates gradually precipitate during this AGEING period.

Deposits of FINING agents used in CLARIFICATION such as bentonite, silicic acid, and casein are also referred to as lees. They are usually simply settled to permit the recovery of as much wine as possible, but in some large wineries are processed by ROTARY DRUM VACUUM FILTRATION to salvage a bit more wine with a strong lees flavour.

Once the maximum amount of good wine has been recovered, usually by RACKING after prolonged SETTLING, or by the harsher process of FILTRATION, the lees are valuable only for their potassium acid tartrate (cream of tartar) and small amounts of alcohol. After the recovery of tartrates and alcohol, lees are usually returned to the vineyard, where they serve to add some NITROGEN to the soil. Care should be taken when otherwise disposing of lees as they contain organic matter which may rot and cause environmental POLLUTION.   A.D.W.

lees contact, increasingly popular and currently fashionable wine-making practice known to the Ancient Romans (see CATO) whereby newly fermented wine is deliberately left in contact with the LEES. This period of lees contact may take place in any container, from a bottle (as in the making of any BOTTLE-FERMENTED sparkling wine where yeast AUTOLYSIS produces desirable flavour compounds) to a large tank or vat—although a small oak BARREL is the most common location for lees contact. It may take place for anything between a few weeks and, in the special case of some sparkling wines, several years (see SPARKLING WINE-MAKING). Most commonly, however, lees contact is prolonged for less than a year after the completion of FERMENTATION.

Lees contact encourages the second, softening MALOLACTIC FERMENTATION because the LACTIC ACID BACTERIA necessary for malolactic fermentation feed on micro-nutrients in the lees. This has the effect of adding complexity to the resultant wine's flavour. Many producers, particularly those of white BURGUNDY and other wines based on CHARDONNAY grapes, try to increase the influence of the lees on flavour by LEES STIRRING, or *bâtonnage*, as this practice is known in French. Both lees contact and lees stirring also enhance the structure and MOUTHFEEL of a wine since the POLYSACCHARIDES released from the dead yeast cells can significantly reduce astringency and increase body.

White wines made with deliberate lees contact are sometimes described as SUR LIE, a description commonly used to differentiate one type of MUSCADET from another, although in this case small barrels rarely play a part in the process. Lees contact even in BULK STORAGE is increasingly used as a way of increasing flavour in everyday white wines—South Africa's Chenin Blanc, for example.

Red wines, with their more robust flavours, gain less benefit from lees contact, but, for many red wines, the added complexity of the malolactic fermentation, which is encouraged by lees contact, is very valuable. There is an increasing trend to leave red wine on the lees.

Wines left in contact with a layer of lees more than 10 cm/4 in thick for more than a week or so, however, are very likely to develop HYDROGEN SULFIDE, disulfide, or MERCAPTAN odours. This is because, as the YEASTS start to autolyse, or digest themselves, they produce strongly REDUCING conditions. Any fungicide residues of SULFUR, SULFUR DIOXIDE, or even the sulfur-containing amino acids of the yeasts, are likely to be reduced to the foul-smelling SULFIDE. This is why it is important to rack new wine from its gross lees (see LEES) so that the lees level does not become too thick.

lees stirring, or *bâtonnage*, as it is called in French, is the wine-making operation of mixing up the LEES in a barrel, cask, tank, or vat with the wine resting on them. It is an optional

addition to the process of LEES CONTACT and is often employed, particularly for whites which have undergone BARREL FERMENTATION. As the French name suggests, such stirring is usually done with a stick, although some racking systems allow the barrel itself to be rotated in situ.

Lees stirring is done partly to avoid the development of malodorous HYDROGEN SULFIDE. Unless a thick layer of lees is stirred, oxygen does not reach the bottom layer and strong enough REDUCING conditions develop to change any small amounts of SULFUR into hydrogen sulfide (see LEES CONTACT).

Stirring up the lees in the barrel also affects OAK FLAVOUR, however. If the lees are stirred, they act as an even more effective buffer between the wine and the wood, limiting the extent to which wood TANNINS and PIGMENTS are extracted into the wine. Wines subjected to lees stirring therefore tend to be much paler and less tannic than those whose lees are not stirred.

Regular lees stirring also stimulates the release of MANNOPROTEINS, thereby improving the MOUTHFEEL and stability of the wine.

left bank, an expression for that part of the BORDEAUX wine region that is on the left bank of the river GARONNE. It includes, travelling down river, GRAVES, SAUTERNES, BARSAC, PESSAC-LÉOGNAN, MÉDOC, and all the appellations of the Médoc. The most obvious characteristic shared by the red wines of these appellations, as distinct from RIGHT BANK appellations, is that the dominant grape variety is Cabernet Sauvignon rather than Merlot and Cabernet Franc, although there are many other distinctions.

leftover wine in an opened container such as a half-empty bottle is prey to OXIDATION and steps must be taken in order to prevent it turning to VINEGAR—which could happen within hours or even minutes for a very old wine, within two or three days for most young table wines, and FINO and MANZANILLA sherry, and most bottle-matured PORT, within a few weeks for a robust wood-matured port such as common or garden Ruby or Tawny or OLOROSO sherry, or within months for most MADEIRA.

Because OXYGEN is the villain in this piece, the easiest way to avoid spoilage of leftover wine is to decant it into a smaller container, perhaps a half-bottle, which approximates as closely as possible to the volume of wine left. There are also patent devices for filling the ULLAGE in a bottle or decanter with INERT GAS, by pumping or spraying, or an attempt can be made to create a vacuum with a pump device. Leftover wine, no matter what the container or colour, is best stored cool to slow the reactions involved in its deterioration.

The most satisfactory way of disposing of wine leftovers is surely to drink them, and

the leftovers of some wines, particularly concentrated young red wines, can taste better, and certainly softer, after a day or even two on ullage (see AERATION and DECANTING).

Leftover wine can also be used quite satisfactorily as COOKING wine or to make vinegar. See also RECORKING.

legno riccio, Italian name for the RUGOSE WOOD complex of vine VIRUS DISEASES.

legs, outmoded tasting term and alternative name for the TEARS left on the inside of a glass by some wines.

Lemberger, also known as **Blauer Lemberger** and occasionally **Limberger**, is the German name for the black grape variety much more widely grown in Austria as BLAUFRÄNKISCH and in Hungary as KÉKFRANKOS. Germany has very much less of the variety planted, but like all red varieties it has become increasingly popular so that by 2003 there were 1,438 ha/3,552 acres in all, almost exclusively in WÜRTTEMBERG, where both climate and consumers are tolerant of pale reds made from late-ripening vines. The wine, often blended with TROLLINGER to produce a light red suitable for early drinking, has a better colour than that of most Germanic red wine varieties. The likes of Ernst Dautel of Bönnigheim are starting to make wines with the same spiced black fruit flavours and density as the better Austrian and Hungarian renditions.

About 120 acres/48 ha are also grown in WASHINGTON state where it is a popular VARIETAL in tasting rooms in Yakima valley. Its relatively low acidity is no disadvantage in this climate and Lemberger has an increasing number of fans among winemakers.

Len de l'El and **Len de l'Elh** has, like MANSENG, been a beneficiary of proud regionalism in SOUTH WEST FRANCE. It was once a major and is now a compulsory minor ingredient in the white wines of GAILLAC. The wine is powerful, characterful, but can be flabby. Its name is local dialect for *loin de l'œil*, or 'far from sight'. This vigorous vine needs a well-ventilated, well-drained site if it is to escape rot in lesser years. French plantings totalled 730 ha/1,800 acres in 2000.

length or persistence of flavour is an important indicator of wine quality. See the tasting term LONG.

Lenz Moser, biggest wine producer in AUSTRIA. In the 1920s, Dr Lenz Moser III developed a new TRAINING SYSTEM employing wider rows (about 3.5 m/11.5 ft) and higher trunks (1.3 m) than had previously been the norm, thereby reducing VINE DENSITY. Lenz Moser's ideas influenced Professor Nelson SHAULIS, who developed the GENEVA DOUBLE CURTAIN.

The Lenz Moser system found favour in parts of Europe in the mid 20th century because it decreases LABOUR and therefore production costs, without any need for special machinery. French and German studies found reductions in fruit quality, however, probably because of SHADE in the fruit zone and it is now much less common even in Austria. It is also known as high culture, or *Hochkultur* in German.   R.E.S.

León, wine zone in north west Spain. See CASTILLA Y LEÓN.

Léoville Las Cases, Château, the flagship wine of ST-JULIEN and one run as though it were a FIRST GROWTH (down to the pricing policy) by Jean-Hubert Delon. It is perhaps the most obvious candidate as a SUPER SECOND.

The biggest of the three parts into which the extensive original Léoville estate was divided after the French Revolution was awarded to the original owners, the Abbadie-Léoville family, represented by the Marquis de Las Cases. From 1900 it was run by Théophile Swawinski, a distinguished Médoc viticulturist who also administered Ch Pontet-Canet for the CRUSE family. From him it passed to his son-in-law André Delon, grandfather of Michel Delon, Jean-Hubert's late father, who with his father Paul acquired majority ownership of the property in 1930. In 1994 the Delons succeeded in buying out the remaining minority shareholders, descendants of the Las Cases family. Unlike the BARTON family, who acquired the pretty Ch Langoa at the same time as the Léoville-Barton vineyards, the Delons have no magnificent château building, but, perhaps more importantly for them and for the world's wine drinkers, the Las Cases vineyard is made up substantially of one, well-placed contiguous plot rather than the more intertwined parcels of Léoville-Barton and Léoville-Poyferré.

The Delon policy is admirably strict in terms of viticulture, wine quality, and longevity. These firm, deep-coloured, Cabernet-based wines are supported by a strict selection process which can make Clos du Marquis one of Bordeaux's finest SECOND WINES, similar to Les Forts de LATOUR in that a particular 40 ha of land, outside the original Léoville estate, are always designated for this fine wine; definitely not a dump bin for less satisfactory *cuves*.

A further 60 ha are devoted to Ch Léoville Las Cases, comprising 60 per cent of the original estate, currently planted to 65 per cent Cabernet Sauvignon, 19 per cent Merlot, 13 per cent Cabernet Franc, and 3 per cent Petit Verdot. The Delons' policy is to release EN PRIMEUR prices very late, typically after the first growths and at a level far closer to them than those of their fellow second growths. In the early 1990s, the Delons, already owners of Ch Potensac in the MÉDOC, also acquired the POMEROL property Ch Nénin.

Leroy, famous name in French wine, not just because **Baron le Roy** of CHÂTEAUNEUF-DU-PAPE was instrumental in the development of the APPELLATION CONTRÔLÉE system, but also in the CÔTE D'OR. The NÉGOCIANT house **Maison Leroy** was founded in the small village of Auxey-Duresses in 1868 and its extensive warehouses there still house substantial stocks of fine, mature burgundy. Henri Leroy joined the family firm in 1919 and made his fortune exporting fortified wine from the Charentes to Germany between the two World Wars. This enabled him to buy a half share in the world-famous DOMAINE DE LA ROMANÉE-CONTI (DRC), a share inherited equally by his two daughters Pauline Roch-Leroy and **Lalou Bize-Leroy** on his death in 1980.

Lalou, a prodigious taster, rock climber, and glamorous dresser, had been co-director of the Domaine since 1975 and contributed considerably to its wine-making policy of quality above all. She also ran Maison Leroy, but Burgundy's steady move towards DOMAINE BOTTLING made her job of buying the finest raw materials for her négociant skills of ÉLEVAGE increasingly difficult. In 1988, helped by an £8 million investment from her Japanese importers Takashimaya, she succeeded in buying the Domaine Noëllat of VOSNE-ROMANÉE, an already fine canvas on which to paint her vision of the perfect domaine, soon renamed **Domaine Leroy**. This domaine now comprises more than 22 ha/54 acres of some of the Côte d'Or's finest vineyards, including a total of nearly 7 ha in nine different GRANDS CRUS.

This effectively entailed setting up in competition with DRC, since the Domaine Leroy is based in the same village and, like DRC, has holdings in the grand cru RICHEBOURG. Unfettered by the commercial considerations of the dozen or so shareholders in DRC, Lalou was able to institute fully BIODYNAMIC VITICULTURE, almost uneconomically low YIELDS, and to invest in every possible wine-making luxury. The wines, which come from a much broader range of (mainly red wine) appellations than those of DRC, are extremely concentrated, expressing as definitively as possible their exact geographical provenance, as well as considerable oak sometimes.

Independently of her sister Pauline, Lalou owns the Domaine d'Auvenay, another biodynamically farmed enterprise founded in 1988, with total holdings of around 4 ha, including small plots in four different grands crus.

A sales company, **Société Leroy**, enjoyed the exclusive distribution rights to DRC wines, some of the most highly priced in the world, in all markets except the US and UK until a bitter dispute in 1992 which ousted Lalou from co-directorship of DRC. Today, only Domaine Leroy prices rival those of DRC.

Les Baux. See BAUX.

Lesquerde, subappellation of Côtes du ROUSSILLON-Villages.

Lessona, small but historically important red wine district in the Vercelli hills in the subalpine north of the PIEMONTE region of north west Italy. Nebbiolo grapes, here called Spanna, make up the majority of the wine although some Bonarda or Vespolina may be added to produce a slightly less austere wine. Sella is the only producer of note, although Paolo De Marchi of Isole e Olena, one of Chianti Classico's better producers, is attracting attention with wines from his revitalized family estate, Villa Sperino. See SPANNA for more details.

See also the nearby BRAMATERRA and GATTINARA, also in Vercelli, and BOCA, GHEMME, SIZZANO, and FARA in Novara.

L'Étoile, small, rarely exported appellation in the JURA region of eastern France which specializes in traditional, OXIDATIVE white wines aged in part-filled barrels. These may be pure Chardonnay or Chardonnay blended with the local SAVAGNIN grape. It also produces VIN DE PAILLE, CRÉMANT DU JURA, and the extraordinarily nutty VIN JAUNE.

Levante, the collective name for four Mediterranean provinces of SPAIN forming two autonomous regions officially known as Comunidad Valenciana and Murcia. The Levante encompasses five DO wine zones: ALICANTE, UTIEL-REQUENA, VALENCIA in the Valencian autonomy; and BULLAS, JUMILLA, and YECLA in Murcia (see map under SPAIN). The climate becomes progressively extreme away from the coast with summer TEMPERATURES reaching 45 °C/113 °F in places and annual RAINFALL amounting to less than 300 mm/ 12 in. Most of the wines are correspondingly coarse but progress has been made in Jumilla, Yecla, and Alicante. The port of Valencia itself is one of the largest wine entrepôts in the world with five huge firms handling millions of litres of bulk wine from all over south and central Spain, although this trade has been declining since the early 1990s.   R.J.M.

Leverano, DOC for robust red wine made mainly from NEGROAMARO grapes in south east Italy. For more details, see PUGLIA.

lexias, DRYING GRAPES produced principally from the MUSCAT OF ALEXANDRIA variety in Australia, named after a contraction of Alexandria. A similar product, which also requires deseeding, is called *valencias* in Spain.

Liatiko, ancient Cretan vine producing relatively soft wine, usually blended with the stronger MANDELARIA and KOTSIFALI to make sweet reds, exported in great quantity by Venetian merchants in medieval times. The name suggests the Tuscan vine ALEATICO but there is no evidence of a relationship.

libation, the pouring out of wine (and occasionally other liquids: water, oil, honey) as a religious act. The practice of offering a libation to a god was universal in the Greek and Roman world. Whenever wine was drunk in formal gatherings, such as symposia, a libation was poured while a prayer was said to invoke a chosen god. Libations also regularly accompanied prayers and sacrifices on all sorts of occasions. The origins of the practice are to be found in the offering of the first fruits to gods; but libation should also be seen in the context of the way in which social intercourse between humans (and by analogy between humans and gods) was maintained by the mutual exchange of gifts. Libations poured on the ground were also specifically seen as a gift for the dead. 'The souls are nourished by libations', as Lucian says.   J.J.P.

Burkert, W., *Greek Religion* (Oxford, 1985).

Libourne, small port on the RIGHT BANK of the Dordogne in the Bordeaux region. It is now the commercial centre for the right bank appellations, although it was established in the 13th century, much later than ST-ÉMILION's port Pierrefitte, and was at the time considered a parvenu in comparison with FRONSAC. In modern history, its wine trade is much more recent than the Chartronnais of the BORDEAUX TRADE in the great city across the Garonne, and its more modest traders concentrated initially on selling in northern mainland Europe rather than in the British Isles. Of merchants based here on the banks of the river Dordogne, J. P. MOUEIX is the most important. For more details, see POMEROL, the wine region on the eastern outskirts of the town.

The wines St-Émilion, Pomerol, and especially Fronsac are sometimes referred to collectively as **Libournais**.

Lichine, Alexis (1913–89), was born in Russia but, unlike André TCHELISTCHEFF, another Russian who was to shape the American wine industry, he and his family left before the Revolution, and he was educated in France.

After the Repeal of PROHIBITION, Lichine sold wines, first in a shop in New York and subsequently for the gifted American wine importer Frank SCHOONMAKER. After the Second World War, in which he served with distinction, he returned to finding French and German wines from individual estates and selling them in an America where wine was all but unknown.

His success in doing this was considerable and came from a flair for seeing and recounting the romantic side of wine and winemaking, as well as appreciating the pleasures wine can bring.

During the 1950s, he became a major figure in the French wine world, setting up his own company, Alexis Lichine & Co., to sell only CHÂTEAU BOTTLED and DOMAINE BOTTLED wines, for the most part from major properties.

He sold this company to British brewers Bass-Charrington in 1964, and gradually left the commercial world to make wine and write books.

His first book, *The Wines of France*, was an excellent primer to the subject and his second, the ambitious *Alexis Lichine's Encyclopedia of Wines and Spirits*, was a great success with enthusiasts anxious to learn. For more detail, see the LITERATURE OF WINE.

Lichine assembled a group of investors to buy and renovate the MARGAUX second growth Ch Lascombes in 1952, and ran the property with great success before selling it, again to Bass-Charrington, in 1971.

He also bought in 1951 the fourth growth Ch Prieuré at Cantenac just outside Margaux. He officially renamed this property, based on an old Benedictine priory, Ch Prieuré-Lichine in 1953 and it was at this property, typically one of the first to welcome passing visitors, that he died in 1989. His son Sacha ran the property until its sale in 1999.   W.B.

licoroso, Portuguese sweet FORTIFIED WINE (as opposed to a GENEROSO, which may be dry or sweet).

lie or **lies**, French for LEES.

Liebfraumilch,   quintessentially mild white wine from GERMANY known almost exclusively in export markets where it has weaned many a potential wine drinker off soft drinks. In its heyday in the 1980s, it accounted for an extraordinary, some would say horrifying, 60 per cent of all German wine exported. It is a 'traditional declaration' which can be used for QBA from any one of the following regions: RHEINHESSEN, PFALZ, NAHE, and RHEINGAU, of which the first two account for the overwhelming majority of production. Liebfraumilch must contain not less than 18 g/l RESIDUAL SUGAR and contain at least 70 per cent of RIESLING, SILVANER, MÜLLER-THURGAU, or KERNER grapes, although in practice Müller-Thurgau usually dominates the blend. Until the early 19th century, Liebfraumilch (or **Liebfrauenmilch**) was the name given to the wine (principally from Riesling) of the vineyard in Worms in Rheinhessen surrounding the collegiate church of Our Lady, the Liebfrauenkirche. In 1908, the Worms wine trade agreed to rename it Liebfrauenstift (later changed to Liebfrauenstift-Kirchstück) and the designation Liebfraumilch became a broad, regional appellation. Well-known BRANDS include Madonna, BLUE NUN, and Black Tower.

lieblich, used on labels in AUSTRIA to designate wines whose RESIDUAL SUGAR is between 12 g/l and 45 g/l.

Liechtenstein. The principality's 26 ha/ 64 acres of vineyard are concentrated on the capital Vaduz, above and at some distance from the river RHINE, where the climate is strongly influenced by the warming föhn effect of the wind from the south. The largest vineyard owners, the domaine of the Fürst von und zu Liechtenstein, produces good-quality wine in the style of eastern SWITZERLAND, from Blauburgunder (PINOT NOIR) and from a small plantation of CHARDONNAY. Seventy per cent is sold directly to local consumers.   I.J.

Ospelt, M., and Müller, W., *Weintradition Liechtenstein* (Triesen, 2004).

lieu-dit, French term used quite generally to refer to the local, traditional name of a small area of land, usually defined by topography or history. Such locally given names are also used more specifically, especially in Burgundy, to refer to a plot of land or vineyard within a larger appellation. In practice these names are used on labels for vineyards below PREMIER CRU in rank, for example Les Tillets in the commune of Meursault.

lifestyle winery, term coined in NEW ZEALAND for a small winery established and run, typically by an educated young to middle-aged couple who have access to funds generated by another career, more for its bucolic appeal than as a strictly commercial proposition.

lifted, tasting term for a wine with a high but not excessive level of VOLATILE ACIDITY. Such a wine may also be said have **lift** conferred on it.

light. A wine is described by wine tasters as light, or **light bodied**, if it is low in ALCOHOL and VISCOSITY. See BODY for more details.

lightning, a climatic phenomenon which may strike a vineyard and, by travelling along a wire, damage vines around the point of contact. Most vines recover after a lightning strike, however.

Liguria, the crescent-shaped strip that runs along Italy's Mediterranean coast from the French border to the edge of Toscana, is Italy's third smallest region after the Valle d'Aosta and Molise. See map under ITALY and see GENOA, VERNACCIA, and ITALY for some historical detail. The extremely rugged terrain—the Apennines descend virtually all the way to the sea—combined with the microscopic size of individual properties make agriculture in general and viticulture in particular a marginal activity, and the greater economic possibilities offered by the thriving tourist industry, commercial flower-growing, and olive-growing have drained manpower from the region's vineyards at a steady pace ever since the Second World War. Total Ligurian wine production is less than 300,000 hl/7.9 million gal, and DOC wines, from 500 ha of vineyard, represent just 8 per cent of this figure.

A crossroads of trade and traffic between Italy, France, and Spain, Liguria has long cultivated a multitude of different vine varieties, and a census of the province of Imperia in 1970 revealed no fewer than 123. Many of these have since been abandoned, however, and, although the undistinguished Albarola is the region's most planted variety, the region is concentrating its efforts on the white varieties VERMENTINO (PIGATO) and the less characterful Bosco, and the red varieties ROSSESE, SANGIOVESE, and DOLCETTO (the last of these called Ormeasco in Liguria). Ormeasco, Pigato (now proved identical to Vermentino), Rossese, and Vermentino each have their own DOC within the Riviera di Ponente zone, a wide stretch of territory between Genoa and the French border.

Liguria's most renowned wine, the white Cinqueterre, is perhaps most famous for its vertigo-inducing vineyards perched on TERRACES sculpted into cliffsides high above the Ligurian sea. The wine itself, made from Bosco plus Albarola and/or Vermentino, rarely rises above the thirst-quenching level. The once-renowned Sciacchetrà, a sweet Cinqueterre made from raisined grapes, has virtually disappeared.

Production of Vermentino is concentrated in Castelnuovo Magra, to the south of La Spezia in the Colli di Luni DOC zone, and in Diano Castello and Imperia in the province of Imperia, although better expressions of the variety now come from the Tuscan coast, SARDEGNA, and some BELLET made across the French border. Production of Pigato is concentrated in Ranzo and Pieve di Teco, to the north of the city of Imperia. Ormeasco (Dolcetto) is produced almost exclusively in Pornassio and Pieve di Teco. The Rossese grape, of minor significance in the Riviera di Ponente DOC, has its own DOC near Ventimiglia, Rossese di Dolceacqua or simply Dolceacqua. The wine has its fanatical admirers, who have found in it blackcurrants and roses, power and delicacy, and cite Napoleon's admiration for Dolceacqua (although the terms of the praise—a comparison to CHÂTEAU-CHALON—are peculiar in and of themselves). Since an annual production that rarely exceeds 2,000 hl is divided between 100 growers, finding a representative bottle of wine that could serve as a yardstick of quality is no easy task.

D.T. & D.C.G.

lime, in the forms of slaked lime (calcium hydroxide) or ground limestone (calcium carbonate), is sometimes added to soils to neutralize SOIL ACIDITY. It is fairly immobile in the soil, except in light sands, and must therefore be incorporated deeply and thoroughly to be fully effective. **Liming** is therefore most appropriately used, if likely to be needed, before vine PLANTING. It is easy to achieve in the topsoil but very difficult in the subsoil (below 50cm/20 in). The CALCIUM in lime or limestone also helps to give the soil greater crumb structure and friability (see SOIL STRUCTURE). Gypsum (calcium sulfate) can be used for the latter purpose

on soils where acidity is unlikely to become excessive. One common problem of over-liming when soils are moist is lime-induced CHLOROSIS (iron is involved in photosynthesis and deficiency results in yellowing of leaves). The ferrous (Fe^{2+}) form is oxidised to the ferric (Fe^{3+}), which is unavailable to plants. This is less likely to occur where soils are not moist.   J.G.

limestone, a rock made of the mineral calcite (calcium carbonate); in dolomitic limestone there is some admixture of calcium-magnesium carbonate. Limestone is *calcaire* in French.

Common limestones differ from CHALK (a special type of limestone) in being hard and not readily penetrated by plant roots, except through cracks. The soils formed over limestones are often much richer in clay than the underlying limestone, although pebbles of the limestone may be common in the vineyard, especially on slopes. Some limestone soils, such as the Mediterranean TERRA ROSSA, are red-brown in colour; these are moderately alkaline and have a good clay-loam texture and structure. Leaching of the calcium carbonate from sandy limestones will leave the soil relatively sandy.

Some limestone soils overlie substantial reservoirs of SOIL WATER, of high quality for IRRIGATION. The longer roots of well-established vines may be able to reach these reservoirs, especially if deep RIPPING to shatter and crack the hard limestone has been carried out before planting. Limestone-derived soils are in general valued most highly in cool viticultural regions. The great wines of BURGUNDY come from vines grown on the slopes of the CÔTE D'OR escarpment, where Jurassic limestone is the predominant rock but not the only type of limestone found there.

The red limestone-derived terra rossa of Coonawarra in SOUTH AUSTRALIA similarly produces some of Australia's best red wines from Cabernet Sauvignon and Shiraz, both vine varieties being close to the cool limit for their reliable ripening.

In warm climates, however, such as those of the south of France, and the Riverland of South Australia, limestone soils are not regarded as superior, or even necessarily as suitable for viticulture (see SOIL AND WINE QUALITY).   J.G., R.E.S., & J.M.H.

Limestone Coast Zone, moderately cool, high-quality wine area in SOUTH AUSTRALIA encompassing Coonawarra, Mount Benson, Padthaway, and Wrattonbully regions. The zone is much greater in extent, with the districts of Bordertown, Robe, Penola, and Mount Gambier candidates for official recognition as regions in the coming years. Bordertown, the furthest north, is the warmest area (robust Shiraz, Cabernet Sauvignon, etc.). Mount Gambier, to the extreme south, is the coolest, best suited to Pinot Noir and Chardonnay.

Limnio, dark grape variety native to the island of Lemnos in GREECE, where it can still be found. It has also transferred successfully to Khalkhidhikhi in north east Greece, however, where it produces a full-bodied wine with a good level of acidity. It is mentioned, as Limnia, in the Onomastikon by Polidefke.

Limousin, old French province centred on the town of Limoges, and a term encountered most frequently in the wine world as a term for the region's OAK.

Limoux, small town and appellation in the eastern Pyrenean foothills in southern France. For centuries it has been devoted to the production of white wines that would sparkle naturally after a second fermentation during the spring. They became known as Blanquette de Limoux, Blanquette meaning simply 'white' in Occitan. Locals claim that fermentation in bottle was developed here long before it was consciously practised in CHAMPAGNE, dating the production of cork-stoppered sparkling wines at the Abbey of St-Hilaire from 1531. (Limoux is just north of CATALUÑA, a natural home of the CORK oak.)

The region's vineyards are so much higher, cooler, and further from Mediterranean influence than any other Languedoc appellation (even Côtes de la MALEPÈRE to its immediate north) that many are Atlantic-influenced even though they are just inland from the CORBIÈRES hills. Within the region there are distinctly different zones, according to factors such as altitude, soil types, and the influence of the Atlantic or Mediterranean.

The grape used traditionally was the MAUZAC, called locally Blanquette, but increasing amounts of Chardonnay and, to a lesser extent, CHENIN BLANC have been planted so that in the 1980s the Limoux vineyards were much valued as one of southern France's very few sources of CHARDONNAY grapes from mature vines. Still wines made from them were therefore in great demand, especially for export markets. This international success was cleverly capitalized upon by Toques et Clochers, an annual charity AUCTION of different Chardonnay barrel samples, inspired by the famous HOSPICES DE BEAUNE auction but embellished by the involvement of some of France's most famous chefs. These often lean, oak-aged Chardonnays regularly fetched prices far in excess of their then classification as VINS DE PAYS so the Limoux appellation was thoroughly overhauled in 1993. It now encompasses still whites made mainly from Chardonnay (although Chenin Blanc may be included and at least 15 per cent of Mauzac must be included), with, unusually, compulsory WHOLE BUNCH PRESSING and BARREL FERMENTATION.

In 2005, a red wine Limoux appellation was added, with Merlot compulsorily making up at least 50 per cent of the blend, Carignan constituting no more than 10 per cent, and Carignan, Côt, Syrah, and Grenache constituting at least 30 per cent. Cabernet Sauvignon and Cabernet Franc may play a part—truly an Atlantic and Mediterranean blend. Such (relatively light) wines used to be sold as Vins de Pays de la Haute Vallée de l'Aude.

But Limoux is essentially a sparkling wine town. Blanquette de Limoux is the region's most famous product, sparkling wine containing Mauzac, Chardonnay, and Chenin Blanc. The CRÉMANT de Limoux was devised in 1990 for less rustic, more internationally designed sparkling wines made mainly from Chenin and Chardonnay (together a maximum of 90 per cent), plus Mauzac and a maximum of 10 per cent Pinot Noir.

Limoux's distinctly marginal speciality is Blanquette Méthode Ancestrale (see SPARKLING WINE-MAKING), a sweeter, often slightly cloudy, less fizzy sparkling wine made exclusively from Mauzac left to ferment a second time in bottle without subsequent disgorgement of the resultant sediment. Like the GAILLAC Mousseux made from Mauzac by the *méthode gaillacoise* with similar regard for tradition and disdain for technology, these hand-crafted wines are low in alcohol, high in Mauzac's old apple-peel flavours, and can taste remarkably like a superior sweet cider.

Limoux's sparkling wine business is dominated by the dynamic local CO-OPERATIVE, which sells a range of bottlings under such names as Aimery and Sieur d'Arques. The most notable individual estate in the region is Domaine de l'Aigle, set up by the area's more notable individual, now independent of it, Jean-Louis Denois.

Lincoln University Centre for Viticulture and Oenology, research and teaching institution at Lincoln, Canterbury, in the South Island of NEW ZEALAND. Research focuses specifically on the growth and production of Pinot Noir and Sauvignon Blanc, in particular how cool-climate growing conditions, such as those in New Zealand, affect the flavours, aromas, MOUTHFEEL, PHENOLICS, and TANNINS of these grape varieties. Lincoln is a general university with a traditional agricultural science background, from which the viticulture and oenology programme grew in 1989. Lincoln is the largest wine training facility in New Zealand with three different courses, a one-year graduate diploma; a three-year programme and the post-graduate Bachelor of Viticulture and Enology Honours programme. The four-year Bachelor of Viticulture and Oenology Honours degree introduced in 2005 emphasizes the integration of grape growing and wine-making and its importance in the production of a quality wine. The focus is on such aspects of wine production as site selection, planting material, vine management, harvest parameters, grape handling, fermentation control, and wine finishing as well as vine physiology and fermentation chemistry. J.T.

www.lincoln.ac.nz

Lindemans, for long a rival of PENFOLDS but since the late 1980s part of the same group, now owned by FOSTER'S. Lindemans' origins lie in the Hunter valley, where former Royal Naval surgeon Dr Henry John Lindeman arrived in 1843 and planted 40 ha/100 acres with Semillon (then called Hunter River Riesling), Verdelho, and Shiraz. The name was first drawn to international attention in 1882 when it won a prize at the Great Exhibition in Bordeaux. The company still owns Australia's biggest vineyard, 596 ha at Padthaway in VICTORIA as well as over 200 ha in Coonawarra in SOUTH AUSTRALIA and holdings in Mildura, Victoria, which is home to the company's major winery, Karadoc, which routinely processes 1,500 tonnes of grapes a day. Lindemans was among the first to exploit Padthaway's potential, establishing a vineyard there in 1970. Lindemans Padthaway Chardonnay, BARREL FERMENTED in French oak, played a key role in establishing the region's reputation in the early 1980s, being the first Australian Chardonnay to win an international trophy. Lindemans Bin 65 Chardonnay, made in vast quantities at Karadoc, is Australia's biggest-selling single VARIETAL wine and has become one of the world's most successful, and consistent, wine BRANDS.

Lindenblättrige, German synonym for Hungary's light-berried HÁRSLEVELŰ grape.

linguistics. See LANGUAGE OF WINE.

lipids, a group of chemicals that includes oils, fats, and waxes. Lipids are distinctive in plants because, despite the plant's watery environment, they are not soluble in water, which is also the basis of their important roles. They make up the membranes of plant CELLS which keep apart entirely different zones of metabolic activity, often with large differences in ACIDITY on either side of the membrane. They make energy-rich reserves of food as in seeds, grapeseed oil being a good example. Also they coat the surface of the plant with a water-impermeable layer of waxy cutin which stops desiccation. A host of other compounds have lipid-like structures, including important plant pigments such as chlorophyll and CAROTENOIDS. B.G.C.

Lipovina, Czech synonym for Hungary's light-berried HÁRSLEVELŰ.

Liqueur Muscat and **Liqueur Tokay** are two of AUSTRALIA's great gifts to the world: sumptuously hedonistic dark, sweet, alcoholic liquids that taste something like a cross between madeira and Málaga. They are made from, respectively, a very dark-skinned strain of MUSCAT BLANC À PETITS GRAINS, called here Brown Muscat, and MUSCADELLE, traditionally known as Tokay in Australia. The centre of production is a hot north eastern corner of the state of Victoria around the towns of Rutherglen and Glenrowan. Grapes are semi-raisined on the vine, partially fermented, and then FORTIFIED with grape spirit before being subjected to an unusual wood-ageing programme that resembles a cross between a sherry SOLERA and, under many a hot tin roof, a Madeira ESTUFAGEM. The results can be uncannily fine quality, are bottled when they are ready to drink, and do not change with BOTTLE AGE. These wines are quite sweet enough to serve with virtually any dessert. In the late 1990s, the wine-makers of Rutherglen joined forces to create a four-tier nomenclature for Muscat (and, by extension, Tokay). At the bottom is Rutherglen Muscat; next is Classic; then Grand; and finally Rare. It is a voluntary, self-regulated system, but is a very real guarantee of style, which becomes progressively richer and more complex with each tier. Rare is released in tiny quantities each year, limited by the maintenance of a very old solera base.

liquoreux, French term meaning 'syrupy sweet', used for very rich, often BOTRYTIZED, wines that are markedly sweeter than MOELLEUX wines.

liquoroso, Italian for a strong, usually FORTIFIED, wine.

Lirac, large and growing (more than 700 ha/1,700 acres in the mid 2000s) appellation on the right bank of the southern RHÔNE producing mainly full-bodied reds and rosés, and a small amount of sometimes heavy white wine. The rosés can offer good-value alternatives to nearby TAVEL, made in very similar conditions and from the same sort of grape varieties, while the reds generally resemble a particularly soft, earlier maturing Côte du Rhône-Villages, although there are one or two notably more ambitious exceptions such as Domaines du Joncier and de la Mordorée and some of the better producers in CHÂTEAUNEUF-DU-PAPE across the river who also make a Lirac. The appellation includes three communes other than Lirac, of which Roquemaure was an important port in the 16th century from which wines would be shipped as far north as England and Holland (see RIVERS). In the 18th century, Roquemaure was a much more important wine centre than Châteauneuf-du-Pape.

Modern red and rosé Lirac must contain at least 40 per cent Grenache with Mourvèdre, Syrah, Cinsaut, and occasionally Carignan, while white wines contain Clairette, Bourboulenc, and Grenache Blanc with other southern white grapes and Ugni Blanc. Quality has increased considerably.

See map under RHÔNE.

Lisbon, capital city of PORTUGAL which formerly produced a red fortified wine to rival the PORT shipped out of Portugal's second city, Porto (Oporto). The wine is no longer produced but the name can still be found on the silver decanter labels made to adorn decanters in the 19th century. See also CARCAVELOS.

R.J.M.

Lison-Pramaggiore, DOC mainly in the VENETO region of north east Italy created in 1986 by the fusion of two previous DOCs, the CABERNET di Pramaggiore and TOCAI di Lison. Other grapes are grown in the zone, however, and each of CHARDONNAY, PINOT GRIGIO, Riesling Italico or WELSCHRIESLING, SAUVIGNON BLANC, VERDUZZO, MERLOT, and REFOSCO is entitled to DOC status as a VARIETAL wine. Tocai is the workhorse grape amongst the white, with close to 20,000 hl/528,00 gal produced each year, but Merlot, with an annual production of more than 20,000 hl, has surpassed Cabernet (predominantly Franc rather than Sauvignon) amongst the red wine varieties.

The vineyards themselves are in the wide plain created by the Piave river as it descends from the hills of Conegliano and Montello towards the Adriatic and, as such, can be considered an eastward continuation of the PIAVE DOC zone, extending into the Pordenone province of FRIULI. The wines are fresh and pleasurable, if not memorable, with Cabernet regularly giving the most interesting results. Cooler vintages, together with the high percentage of Cabernet Franc and high yields in the vineyards (84 hl/ha), tend to bring out an aggressive herbaceousness which is perhaps more appealing to local markets than to international ones.

D.T.

Listán, synonym for PALOMINO, the white grape variety that can produce superb sherry around JEREZ, but results in dull, flabby white table wines almost everywhere else. Official Spanish vine statistics of 2004 listed 10,200 ha/25,000 acres of Listán, the name by which the variety is known in most of Spain, notably on the Canary Islands (see below) plus 18,000 ha of Palomino Fino. The French vine census of 2000 still found 400 ha of **Listan**, mainly in the western Languedoc and in the Armagnac region.

The vine's productivity and hardiness made it a popular choice when large parts of north western Spain were replanted after PHYLLOXERA struck. Listán/Palomino (often known as Jerez in Galicia and Rueda) has also been grubbed up there, however, at an increasing pace since the mid 1970s. It is usually replaced by native varieties, from VERDEJO to GODELLO, that had been on the verge of extinction. However, Listán has found one last refuge on the CANARY ISLANDS' volcanic soils, where it can produce table wines of much greater individuality and distinction than on the Spanish mainland.

The rebirth of Canary wines in the 1990s thus gave this much-maligned variety a new lease on life.

V. de la S.

Listán Negro, recently appreciated grape which dominates wine production on the island of Tenerife in the CANARY ISLANDS, planted on several thousand hectares. CARBONIC MACERATION has managed to coax exceptional aromas out of this medium-bodied wine. The grape may also be called Almuñeco.

Listrac, or Listrac-Médoc, one of the six communal appellations of the Haut-Médoc district of Bordeaux. In relation to the other five (MARGAUX, ST-JULIEN, PAUILLAC, ST-ESTÈPHE, and even MOULIS, with which it is often compared), Listrac seems the least well favoured. It is, just, the furthest of them all from the Gironde estuary and the vineyards are planted on about 650 ha/1,600 acres or so of mainly clay-limestone on a gentle rise which, at an altitude of about 40 m/131 ft, constitutes some of the highest land in the Médoc. Although the Merlot grape is increasingly widely planted, the wines can be relatively austere in youth and their chief characteristic is their reliable density even in lighter vintages. The most cosseted property is probably the late Baron Edmond de ROTHSCHILD's Ch Clarke, given extra ballast by oenologist Michel ROLLAND, while the similarly renovated Ch Fourcas-Hosten has a reputation as solid as its wines. Yields of 45 hl/ha (2.6 tons/acre) are officially tolerated here, whereas the limit is 40 hl/ha in Moulis and other Haut-Médoc village appellations.

For more information, see MÉDOC and BORDEAUX.

Parker, R., *Bordeaux* (4th edn, New York, 2003).
Penning-Rowsell, E., *The Wines of Bordeaux* (6th edn, London, 1989).

Listrão was grown on Madeira as a table grape and is planted on nearby Porto Santo where it makes a flabby dry white wine and a fortified wine known as Listrão de Porto Santo.

R.J.M.

literature of wine. The literature that concerns wine specifically, as opposed to references to wine in more general writing (for which see ENGLISH LITERATURE), is a complicated tapestry that has been woven from a broad variety of strands from classical times to the present day. Most writers concern themselves with how and where grapes are grown, how and where wine is made, and how individual wines taste, but their methods vary considerably and there are works on wine which are also works on travel, on history, on medicine, on agricultural matters, and on gastronomy.

Early works and agriculture

Many early works are richer in references to the effects of drinking wine (see DRUNKENNESS) than to the wine itself. CLASSICAL TEXTS constitute the earliest known literature of wine (although see also Ancient MESOPOTAMIA). While Mago of CARTHAGE clearly inspired many subsequent writers, his text does not survive and the first known classical writers to concentrate on wine and wine-making were probably CATO (234–149 BC) and VARRO (116–27 BC). Cato, particularly, was keen on the profit motive in wine-making and his instructions appear mainly to have been aimed at quantity rather than quality, even suggesting, at one point, how Coan wine (from Kós, one of the AEGEAN ISLANDS) could be faked from Italian grapes.

Much more modern in his outlook towards the production of wine was COLUMELLA (2 BC–AD 65), whose family, based near Cádiz in southern Spain, may well have owned vineyards. His *De re rustica* gives detailed advice on such matters as CLONAL SELECTION, the planting of vineyards, and the need for wines to be as natural as possible. 'The wine is clearly the best which can solely give pleasure by its own nature.' PLINY the Elder (AD 23–79) was the last great classical writer on wine and wine-making, although he was clearly influenced by Varro. The works of all these three, and the more derivative PALLADIUS in particular, were translated and used as textbooks throughout Europe until the end of the 16th century.

In these books, viticulture was treated merely as a part, albeit a major part, of the broader subject of agriculture. This tradition was continued by such writers as PETRUS DE CRESCENTIIS (1230–1310), an Italian lawyer who was forced to leave his own country and spent 30 years in exile in Spain and France. One volume of his monumental *Liber ruralium commodorum* dealt specifically with wine-growing and making. The work was translated into French on the instructions of Charles V.

The first French writer to attempt to classify wines in any way was Charles Étienne (1504–64). His *Vinetum . . .* first appeared in Lyons in 1536. This was subsequently translated into French and incorporated in *L'Agriculture et maison rustique des maistres Charles Étienne et Jean Liebault*, 1564 (Liebault was Étienne's son-in-law). This was a best seller and was translated into English by Richard Surflet in 1606. It was followed in due course by the *Nouvelle Maison rustique* by Louis Liger of AUXERRE, which appeared in many editions throughout the 18th and early 19th centuries. While this book deals with a broad selection of rural topics, the sector on wine is particularly fascinating with its details of the then popular wines of Orléans, Burgundy, and Champagne. The characteristics are also given of 50 different VINE VARIETIES grown in France both as table grapes and for wine-making, of which 'morillon noir' is today's PINOT NOIR and 'gamet' is today's GAMAY. More than 15 varieties of MUSCAT are mentioned, but CABERNET SAUVIGNON is notably absent (DNA PROFILING explained why in the late 1990s).

In some ways, an English equivalent was Philip Miller's *Gardeners' Dictionary*, which first appeared in 1731. Here, under the headings Vitis and Wine, are detailed articles on such subjects as grape varieties, Burgundy, Champagne, and English vineyards, although he says of these last, 'There have of late years been but very few vineyards in England, tho' they were formerly very common.'

As wine was the everyday drink throughout much of Europe, in parallel with the books on the agricultural aspects of wine there were others devoted, perhaps only in part, to its keeping and serving. In England the anonymously written *Mystery of Vintners* appeared in 1692 and *L'Art d'améliorer et de conserver les vins* (1781) was first published in Paris, under the title *Dissertation sur les vins*, in 1772. Further editions came out in Liège and Turin soon afterwards. The information they gave was often plagiarized and adapted to appear in such general books as *The Laboratory*, or *School of Arts* (1799).

Wine as medicine

The role of wine in the world of MEDICINE had been important from the earliest of times. It was used widely as a medium for the infusion of medicinal herbs and many wine-based remedies were given in such books as *The Secrets of Alexis of Piedmont*, which appeared in a number of languages from 1555 onwards.

Indeed the first book specifically on wines in English, *A New Book of Wines* (1568), was written by William Turner, who studied medicine at Cambridge. He warned of the danger of drinking the sweet, heavy wines of the Mediterranean as opposed to the healthy, light wines of the Rhine.

This medicinal tradition was adapted by the wine merchant Duncan M'Bride in his *Choice of Wines . . .* (1793) which included general discussion about the wines that were available at the time and their potential application for various medical conditions. Particularly recommended was Toc-kay de Espagne (*sic*), of which only M'Bride knew the source.

A much later sequel is *Wine is the Best Medicine* (1974, updated 1992) by the Frenchman Dr E. A. Maury. This has a more rational approach to the subject, with a variety of individual French wines being recommended for everything from flatulence to cystitis.

DOCTORS have always had a major role to play in English wine literature. Sir Edward Barry was a Bath physician whose *History of Classical Wines* appeared in 1775. He has been criticized for relying too closely on the work of the 16th-century papal medical adviser Barrius, but he also includes an appendix on modern wines and viticulture in England.

Doctors were also responsible for the first two 'modern' books to deal with wine in depth. Whilst the title of *A Practical Treatise on Brewing, Distilling and Rectification*, by R. Shannon, MD (1805), might put off the oenophile there is 'A Copius Appendix on . . . Foreign Wines, Brandies and Vinegars'. This work is particularly strong on the wines of Portugal and Spain, but does not hesitate to lift, unattributed, from Miller on the wines of Burgundy.

Dr Alexander HENDERSON's *The History of Ancient and Modern Wines* (1824) is perhaps the first book in English to attempt to give descriptions of a broad range of wines, based upon his own travels to France, Germany, and Italy. It is also the first book to try to analyse the science of TASTING.

The golden age

In the number of wines it talks about, Henderson's book is overwhelmed by what must be the most remarkable book on wine ever published, the *Topographie de tous les vignobles connus* (1816) by André JULLIEN, a Parisian wine merchant who was born in Burgundy. In this are rated all the wines, not just of France, but of all known wine regions of the time including California, South America, South Africa's Cape, and 'Chinese Tartary'! He forecasts (or perhaps helps to shape) the 1855 CLASSIFICATION in Bordeaux by rating as first-class wines Lafitte (*sic*), Latour, Ch-Margaux, and Haut-Brion.

Outside Europe, his favourites all seem to be dessert wines, including TOKAJI, CONSTANTIA, COMMANDARIA, and COTNARI. Both his first-hand experience and his reading must have been gargantuan for him to compile such a work of reference. He followed this up with another classic *Manuel du Sommelier* (1822). Cavoleau's *Oenologie française* was a similar work to the *Topographie*, but limited to French wines, which came from the same publisher 11 years later.

The 19th century was a golden age for wine writing in Britain. Shannon and Henderson were followed by Cyrus REDDING (1785–1870), a journalist whose interest in wine was stimulated during five years based in Paris. An avid traveller, he wrote *A History and Description of Modern Wines* (1833) as a result of first-hand observation of the ADULTERATION and FRAUD which were then prevalent in the wine trade.

Many of the books were written by wine merchants, often criticizing the practices of their colleagues, or vaunting their own specialities. Perhaps the most enjoyable to read is Thomas Shaw, whose *Wine, the Vine and the Cellar* (1863) is an agreeable blend of reminiscences, knowledge, and simple advice. He was convinced even then that 'in wine tasting and wine talk there is an enormous amount of humbug'. Another of his campaigns was against excessive DUTIES on wine and this led to the famous Gladstone budget in 1862 in which they were considerably reduced.

Charles Tovey was a wine merchant in Bristol in south west England and in the introduction to *Wine and Wine Countries* (1862) he says that 'there can be no question that the Wine Trade is losing its position by the introduction into it of unscrupulous traders'. He drew heavily upon his 50 years' experience in denouncing and describing their deceits.

This same theme was continued by his London colleague James L. Denman, who wrote copiously on wine adulteration. His more particular interest, however, both commercial and literary, was the wines of Greece.

Another doctor to write on wines was John Thudichum, who had come to London from Germany, where his father had written technical books on wine. One of his particular hobby-horses was the adding of gypsum to SHERRY, but his credibility within the trade was compromised by extensive research that he had carried out in Jerez, trying to produce AMONTILLADO by purely chemical means. His *Treatise on Wines* (1872), written with another doctor, A. Dupré, does, however, give a clear picture of viticulture and vinification at that time.

Specialist books

While all these books give a general idea of the wines of Europe and, in some cases, the world, some specialist books on individual regions had also begun to appear. One of the first of these was published in London as early as 1728. This was the *Dissertation sur la situation de Bourgogne* by the French tutor to the son of a Mr Freeman. Arnoux, in this brief book, describes the various wines of Burgundy and how they are made. He also makes a plea for them to be imported into England in bottle rather than in cask. This book must have met with some success, for it was soon translated into English and was subsequently used by Philip Miller in his *Gardeners' Dictionary* and by Robert Shannon.

It was more than a century until the next two classic books on the vineyards of Burgundy appeared and coincidentally it was in the same year, 1831. Morelot's *Statistique de la vigne dans le département de la Côte d'Or* is largely what its title suggests, although the second half of the book deals with both viticulture and vinification in the region. The *Histoire et statistique de la vigne et des grands vins de la Côte d'Or* by Lavalle is a more readable book, for it gives many historical details concerning Burgundy and its wines, as well as more details of the characteristics of the wines from the various villages and ownership of the vineyards. Later editions have etchings of vineyard scenes.

In Bordeaux, the first book of significance was the *Variétés bordelaises* of Abbé Beaurein (1784–5), which noted that the English were at last showing interest in the wines of the Médoc. The first major book dealing solely with the wines of Bordeaux, however, was the *Traité sur les vins du Médoc* of William Franck (1824), which ran into several editions. In many ways this was the forerunner of Charles Cocks's book *Bordeaux, its Wines and the Claret*

Country (1845), which was translated into French five years later and became the classic reference work on Bordeaux wines, known after its original authors as COCKS ET FÉRET. An interesting independent view of the region is also given by the Paris merchant Charles Pierre de Saint in *Le Vin de Bordeaux* (1855).

Writing on Portuguese wines was dominated by the English. In 1787, John CROFT wrote *A Treatise of the Wines of Portugal* and this was followed by the many works of James Forrester (1809–61), who, from his position in the trade, took a strong position against the many adulterations that were taking place.

The 19th century saw the rapid expansion of vineyards in the New World and guidance was sought in Europe as to how to make the finest wines. From this came two interesting works. The first was the *Journal of a Tour through some of the Vineyards of Spain and France* by James BUSBY, which was published in Sydney in 1833. This is a fascinating account of a three-month trip, mainly by stagecoach, to find the right vine varieties for planting in Australia. The interpretation of what he learned appeared in two further books. The journey, almost 30 years later, by Agoston HARASZTHY, one of the pioneers of California viticulture, was largely by train. Perhaps because of his origins, he spent more of his time in the various states of Germany and none at all in France. His *Grape Culture, Wines and Wine-Making*, a journal of this tour, appeared in New York in 1862 and did much to establish the reputations of both Haraszthy and California wine.

A third, and earlier, New World traveller to have left his memories of vineyard visiting is Thomas JEFFERSON, later to become president of the United States. During his five years as minister to France (1784–9) he took advantage of his situation to visit many of the vineyards of Europe, and his diaries leave a fascinating picture of a layman's perception of the world of wine as it then was.

One final wine writer of Victorian times was the journalist and publisher Henry VIZETELLY. His books on champagne, port, and sherry are notable for their many illustrations. These works, with their beautiful engravings, many used by modern publishers, are the forebears of the lavishly illustrated wine books published today.

Technical literature

Parallel with this growth in books on the vineyard regions and their wines, there was a considerable body of work on VITICULTURE and WINE-MAKING. In France at the end of the 18th century the Burgundian Béguillet and Maupin, from Paris, both wrote detailed works which were widely read.

In England, William Speechly, gardener to the duke of Portland, wrote a *Treatise on the Culture of the Vine* (1790) which went into three editions. This dealt with both hothouse and open-air vines in ENGLAND and discusses some of the vineyards which were then planted there and the wines they produced.

Three French writers of the 19th century whose names live on in the world of wine are Jean-Antoine CHAPTAL (1756–1832), Dr Jules GUYOT, and Louis PASTEUR (1822–95). Chaptal was the essential polymath, rising from humble beginnings to become Minister of the Interior under Napoleon. In 1799, he wrote the article on wine for the monumental *Dictionnaire d'agriculture* of the Abbé Rozier, but is better known for his *L'Art de faire le vin* (1807) and his support for the concept of increasing the alcohol strength of wine by adding sugar to the must, the procedure now known as CHAPTALIZATION.

Jules Guyot was instructed under the Second Empire to carry out a survey of the vineyards of France and to make recommendations as to how viticulture might be improved. His three works on viticulture in north and central France (1860), the east (1863), and the west (1866) give a vital picture of France before the arrival of PHYLLOXERA. His name lives on as a method of vine TRAINING. It is largely to him that we owe the parade-ground look of today's vineyards in place of the rabble-like appearance of vines subjected to the traditional practice of LAYERING.

Louis Pasteur's *Études sur le vin* (1866) deal with the question of vinification and particularly the advantages of the heat treatment, or PASTEURIZATION, of wine. His is also the first detailed work on the role that YEASTS have to play in FERMENTATION. Another important work on the techniques of vinification was *Le Vin* (1867), by the Burgundian Comte de Vergnette-Lamotte.

Modern wine writing

The 20th century has seen a great resurgence in wine writing, particularly in Britain. Much of the credit has been laid at the door of Professor George SAINTSBURY, whose vinous reminiscences, *Notes on a Cellar-Book* (1920), were written when he was 75 years old. While this erudite miscellany of thoughts is an enjoyable read, there are many who consider it overrated despite its commercial success. (It was reprinted twice within four months and has run through many editions since.)

What it did prove, however, was that there was a demand for books on wine and authors soon appeared to satisfy that demand. In the main, they fall into two fields, the reminiscent and the relevant. One of the finest of the former is H. Warner Allen, a journalist with a deep love for wine and its history. Much of his work is memories of bottles of vintages long past. His *A History of Wine* (1961) is, however, necessary reading for any wine enthusiast. Others who might be said to be in this group were Maurice Healy and Stephen Gwynn. All of them were highly educated men, for whom drinking fine wines was a part of everyday life.

The relevant school was nobly fronted by André SIMON (1877–1970), even if much of his work is also reminiscent. His early writings were largely on the history of the wine trade and he was, all his life, passionately interested in wine books, compiling a number of bibliographies on food and drink (see below). As a member of the wine trade, he introduced a degree of accuracy to his work that is missing from some of the 'gentlemen' wine writers cited above. In all he wrote more than 100 works in which his knowledge is matched by his readability.

Contemporary wine writing in Britain continues this parallel, with works coming from writers who have taken to wine and wine professionals who have taken to writing. While the choice might seem to be between elegance and erudition, the distinction is not always so straightforward.

From the British wine trade have come such as Tommy Layton, a prolific writer on the wines of Loire, Alsace, Spain, and Italy; his one-time office boy Michael BROADBENT, whose *Great Vintage Wine Book* and *Vintage Wine* are unrivalled collections of tasting notes on thousands of wines going back to the 17th century; Clive Coates on the wines of Burgundy and Bordeaux; Anthony Hanson on Burgundy; Serena Sutcliffe on Champagne; John Radford on Spanish wines; Gerald Asher, now based in the United States; Steven Spurrier; and many others. Kermit Lynch is perhaps the most accomplished writer to have emerged from the wine trade in the US.

Representing the world of the professional writer are the biographer and founder of the Good Food Club, Raymond Postgate, whose *The Plain Man's Guide to Wine* proved so successful that it went through 16 editions in 26 years; Edmund PENNING-ROWSELL, whose frequently revised book on the wines of Bordeaux was a masterpiece of research; the polished journalist Cyril RAY; John Arlott, whose enjoyment of wine and the pleasure it brings shone through his writing; Julian Jeffs, the genial patent lawyer; and Pamela VANDYKE PRICE, particularly strong on the wines of France.

The late 20th century saw something new in the world of wine books: writers deliberately writing for their customer, the reader, rather than for their own pleasure, their work often embellished with ambitious illustration. The most successful and innovative of these has undoubtedly been Hugh JOHNSON, with *Wine*, *The World Atlas of Wine*, and *The Story of Wine*. That there is a broader demand for wine knowledge was borne out by the interest shown in the subject by other media such as television. This undoubtedly widened the market for such writers as Jancis Robinson, Oz Clarke, and Andrew Jefford.

In the rest of Europe, much of the wine literature was originally written in English, although the Dutch writer Hubrecht Duijker, with a series of heavily illustrated and highly instructive works on Bordeaux, Burgundy, Rioja, and other wine regions, achieved a broad international readership. Few French writers are read outside France, although each region has had its specialized writers such as Pierre Poupon, Pierre Forgeot, and Jean-François Bazin in Burgundy, René Pijassou in Bordeaux, and there is also the eclectic Bernard Ginestet. An exception, for the technically minded, is Pierre GALET's work on AMPELOGRAPHY, which is a worthy successor to the larger book on the same subject by Pierre Viala. The works of Émile PEYNAUD on wine-making and wine tasting have also been widely read outside France. In Spain, José Peñín leads the growing number of writers on wine, as VERONELLI did in Italy.

In the United States, wine writing became a boom industry in the late 20th century. This was led by Alexis LICHINE, who before the Second World War joined the wine trade with Frank SCHOONMAKER, himself a successful writer on wine. During the war he served as social aide-de-camp to General Eisenhower and afterwards bought vineyards in Bordeaux and Burgundy, eventually writing two highly successful and informative books, *Wines of France* and *Alexis Lichine's Encyclopedia of Wines and Spirits*.

Other effective American writers on wine include Alexis Bespaloff, who worked for the Alexis Lichine wine company, Joseph Bastianich, Matt Kramer, Karen MacNeill, Ed McCarthy and Mary Ewing Mulligan MW, Kevin Zraly and, the most powerful wine writer of all, Robert PARKER, whose personal tastes and system of SCORING WINE out of 100 points has won him both followers and critics, and has influenced wine-making styles, particularly in Bordeaux, where he is at his strongest. The mainly technical works coming from the wine faculty of the University of California at DAVIS, particularly those of Maynard AMERINE, have also played a major role in the education not just of the American winemaker, but also of the American consumer.

Wine writing in Australia was led by Len EVANS followed by the even more prolific James Halliday. These vineyard owners have been followed by a host of career wine writers such as Max Allen and Peter Forrestal.

The end of the 20th century saw a dramatic increase in interest in wine, which has led to a corresponding increase in the number of wine books available. It is easy to chart through wine literature the change in public perception of wine, from élitist to populist, a move encouraged by wider travel and higher disposable incomes. Publications on wine are less often now literary works than a manual, a newsletter, a website, or, increasingly, a buyer's guide such as Bettane & Desseauve's on French wines, Peñín's on Spain, Platter's on South Africa, Gambero Rosso on Italy, and many, many more.

The literature of wine is infinite and, as appreciation of wine spreads around the world, so will the demand for words on wine. From Cato the Censor to Robert Parker is a long road, but the road is far from being at its end.

See also LANGUAGE OF WINE, MEDIEVAL LITERATURE, WINE WRITING, and INFORMATION TECHNOLOGY. C.C.F.

Useful bibliographies:

Amerine, M. A., and Borg, A. E., *A Bibliography on Grapes, Wines, Other Alcoholic Beverages and Temperance: Works Published in the United States before 1901* (Berkeley, Calif., 1996).

Gabler, J. M., *Wine into Words: A History and Bibliography of Wine Books in the English Language* (Baltimore, 1985).

Simon, A., *Bibliotheca vinaria* (London, 1913, and facsimile: London, 1979).

Vicaire, G., *Bibliographie gastronomique* (Paris, 1890, and facsimile: London, 1978).

Little Karoo, wine region in SOUTH AFRICA.

little leaf, a symptom of ZINC deficiency of vines. An associated symptom is a PETIOLAR sinus that is wider than normal.

Livermore Valley, California wine region and AVA east of San Francisco bay. Livermore hides behind hills high enough to screen out nearly all of the sea fogs common on the bay itself. It is therefore warm and—a passage between the cool, marine air of the bay and the hot, rising air of the CENTRAL VALLEY—windy, as evinced by thousands of turbines blanketing the hills of Altamont Pass at the eastern edge of the valley.

If the gods had got it all right, Sauvignon Blanc and Semillon would dominate the 1,400 acres/566 ha planted to vines in Livermore Valley in the early 1990s, for no other grape does half so well in this small bowl in Alameda county east of San Francisco bay. Those two grape varieties, linked by their history in Bordeaux, first came with French emigrants during Livermore's first great blossoming in the 1870s and 1880s (see CALIFORNIA, history). These original growers believed in the virtues of its stonier-than-GRAVES soils. Today the difficulty of selling Semillon to Chardonnay-besotted Americans has begat changes. Zinfandels and Petite Sirahs have emerged as the best quality wines; Chardonnay is widely planted and promoted. For 30 years, vine acreage has been under severe pressure from urbanization but scions of pioneer Wente winery have crafted a land-use compromise with the political authorities which is an important example for California: 10 acres of land are set aside for open space or agricultural uses whenever permits are issued for an acre of home or business development. An immediate result has been two prime golf courses surrounded by vineyards and homes. B.C.C.

Livinière, La. Commune in the hilly far north of MINERVOIS in the south of France which has successfully campaigned hard and justifiably for a special subappellation for its 200 ha/500 acres.

Lladoner Pelut or **Lledoner Pelut,** a black grape variety also known as GRENACHE Poilu or Velu in the south of France and GARNACHA Peluda or Lledoner Pelut in Spain. Both vine and wine closely resemble Grenache Noir except that the underside of the leaves is downier. It is officially and widely sanctioned in Languedoc-Roussillon, often being specified in appellation regulations alongside Grenache, and has the advantage of being less susceptible to rot. In 2000, France grew a total of 564 ha/1,400 acres, largely in Roussillon, as befits its Catalan name, and it is also grown in Spanish Cataluña.

Galet, P., *Dictionnaire encyclopédique des cépages* (Paris, 2000).

loam, the ideal soil for the growth of most plants, consisting of a balanced mixture of clay, silt, and sand (see SOIL TEXTURE). With enough ORGANIC MATTER, loams have a friable, crumby structure (see SOIL STRUCTURE). These desirable characteristics are enhanced where CALCIUM is prominent among the ions bonded to the clay particles and organic matter, i.e. where the soil is not acid. A good loam has a high capacity to store water and plant nutrients but, unlike stiff clay, is not close textured enough to impede the free DRAINAGE of water. Rich, loamy soils can encourage excessive VIGOUR in vines, however, particularly in cool to mild climates with ample RAINFALL, so loams (which exist in almost all regions) are not always ideal for viticulture. J.G.

locusts can damage vines. See GRASSHOPPERS for more detail.

lodge, term used by British shippers of PORT and MADEIRA for a building where wine is stored and matured, especially in Vila Nova de Gaia in OPORTO and Funchal in Madeira respectively. It is derived from the Portuguese word *loja* meaning 'shop' or 'warehouse'. The Portuguese themselves tend to use the term ARMAZÉM. R.J.M.

Lodi, town in the CENTRAL VALLEY of California that also gives its name to an AVA. Cooler than either the northern or southern halves of the valley, this prolific farming region was populated from the late 19th century by largely German smallholders who formed large COOPERATIVES to sell their grapes to large marketing companies such as CANANDAIGUA, Sebastiani, and JFJ Bronco in the late 1970s and early 1980s. The deep, rich-soiled valley floor was built up by alluvial deposits from rivers running out of the Sierra Nevada then pooling before running out to the Pacific through the Central valley delta and San Francisco bay. Lodi is inland from, less watery, and thus warmer than the CLARKSBURG AVA to the north west, but much less warm than

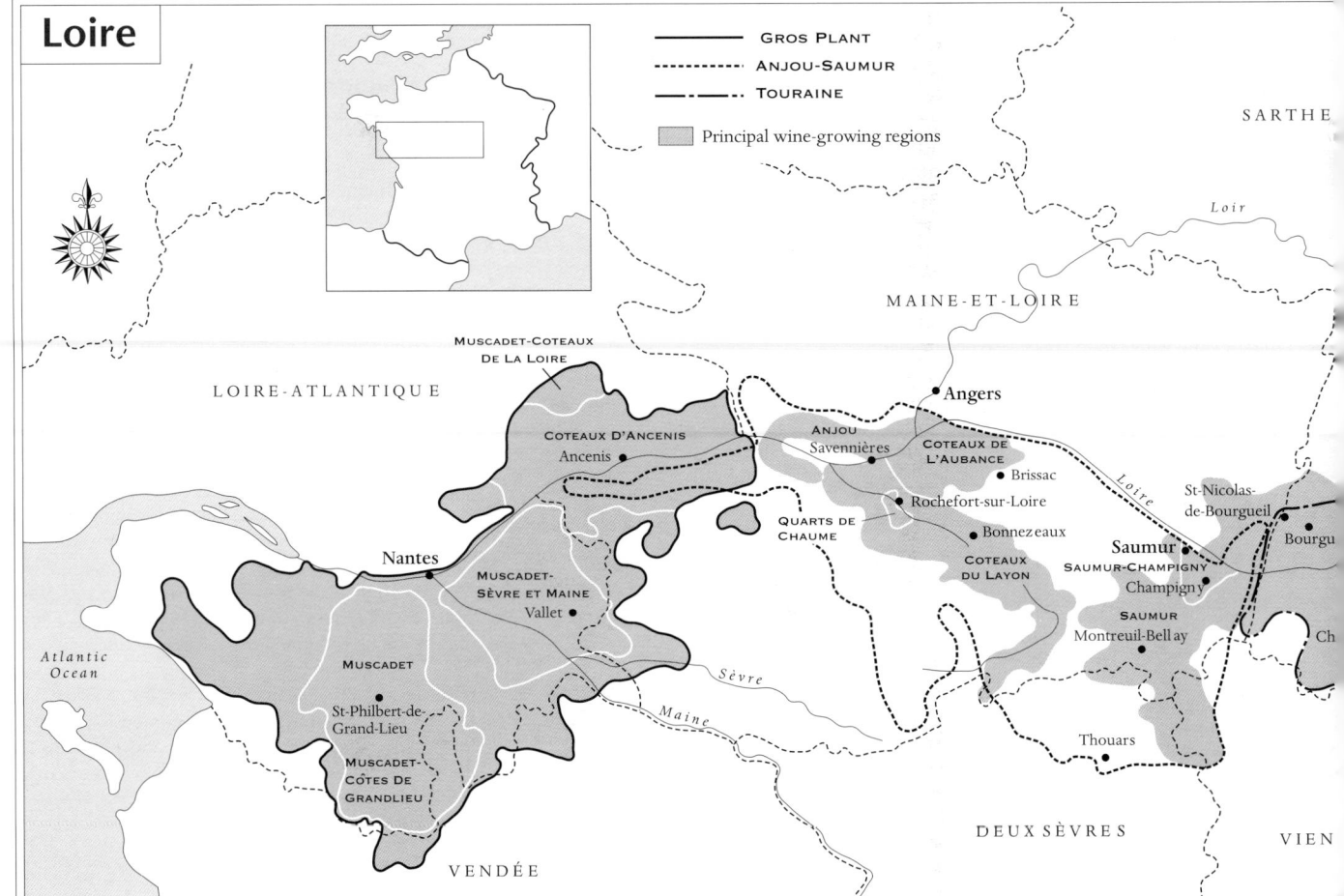

Loire

SARTHE

Loir

MAINE-ET-LOIRE

MUSCADET-COTEAUX
DE LA LOIRE

LOIRE-ATLANTIQUE

•Angers

COTEAUX D'ANCENIS
Ancenis•

ANJOU
Savennières•

COTEAUX DE
L'AUBANCE
•Brissac

Rochefort-sur-Loire•

Loire

St-Nicolas-
de-Bourgueil•

•Bourgu

QUARTS DE
CHAUME

•Bonnezeaux

Saumur•
SAUMUR-CHAMPIGNY
Champigny•

Nantes•

MUSCADET-
SÈVRE ET MAINE
Vallet•

COTEAUX
DU LAYON

Ch

SAUMUR
Montreuil-Bellay•

*Atlantic
Ocean*

MUSCADET

Sèvre

St-Philbert-de-
Grand-Lieu•

Maine

•Thouars

MUSCADET-
CÔTES DE
GRANDLIEU

DEUX SÈVRES

VIEN

VENDÉE

loess
408

Madera, Fresno, and other districts further south in the San Joaquin valley.

Zinfandel and Ruby Cabernet have shown the greatest adaptability to Lodi's growing conditions, and Zinfandel commands nearly 12,000 acres/5,000 ha. Zinfandels from here tend to cluster at the fleshy, plummy, ripe end of the spectrum but represent good value in today's market place. Since the mid 1980s, Chardonnay and Merlot plantings have increased substantially but high YIELDS tend to reduce their distinctiveness beyond recognition. Somewhat surprisingly, Viognier produces nicely fragrant examples from Lodi, inexpensively priced, and there are hundreds of acres planted.   B.C.C.

loess, a light-coloured, fine-grained accumulation of CLAY and SILT particles that have been deposited by the wind. An essentially unconsolidated, unstratified CALCAREOUS silt, it is usually homogeneous, permeable, and buff to grey in colour, containing calcareous concretions and fossils. It is found particularly in some vineyards in AUSTRIA and GERMANY.

Loir, Coteaux du, northerly wine outpost of the greater LOIRE region on the confusingly

named but usefully warming Loir tributary about 40 km/25 miles north of Tours in the Sarthe *département*. Viticulture seriously declined here, but enthusiasts such as Joël Gigou at Domaine de la Charrière have invested in a bright future for the varied wines of this small, 70-ha/173-acre area, of which JASNIÈRES is the most famous appellation. Bright reds, occasionally the product of BARREL MATURATION, are being made from Gamay, which does well on the clay-limestone sectors of the appellation. In ripe years such as 1997, 2002, and 2003, Pineau d'Aunis can be good enough to shine in a VARIETAL wine but acidity can be very high in less ripe years. Cabernet Franc and Cot (Malbec) are also allowed for reds, and Grolleau may be used in its light, dry rosés. Dry white wines are made from Chenin Blanc (Pineau de la Loire also permitted), but red wines predominate.

The local VDQS is Coteaux du VENDÔMOIS. See also LOIRE, including map.

Loire, France's most famous river and name of one of its most varied wine regions whose wines are greatly appreciated locally and in Paris, but—with the famous exceptions of Sancerre and Pouilly-Fumé—are still widely

underrated outside France. This may be partly because the Loire's best red wines are often distinguished by their delicacy rather than by their weight and longevity, and because so many of its finest white wines are made solely from Chenin Blanc, a grape variety associated with very ordinary wine outside the middle Loire: Anjou-Saumur and Touraine.

History

We know little about the early history of viticulture in the Loire valley, but recent archaeological discoveries suggest that it was extant at least in the upper Loire in the 1st century AD (see GAUL), and it was certainly well established by the 5th century. In a letter to a friend, probably prepared for publication *c*.469, Sidonius Apollinaris (*c*.430–*c*.480), who was born in Lyons but spent a large part of his life in the Auvergne, praises the country of the Arverni (the Auvergne) for its landscape, its fertile fields, and its vineyards. In 475, ROME was forced to cede the Auvergne to the Visigoths, but the depredations of the barbarians left vine-growing safe.

In the next century, Gregory of Tours (*c*.539–94) makes frequent mention, in his *History of the Franks*, of viticulture in the Loire region. As

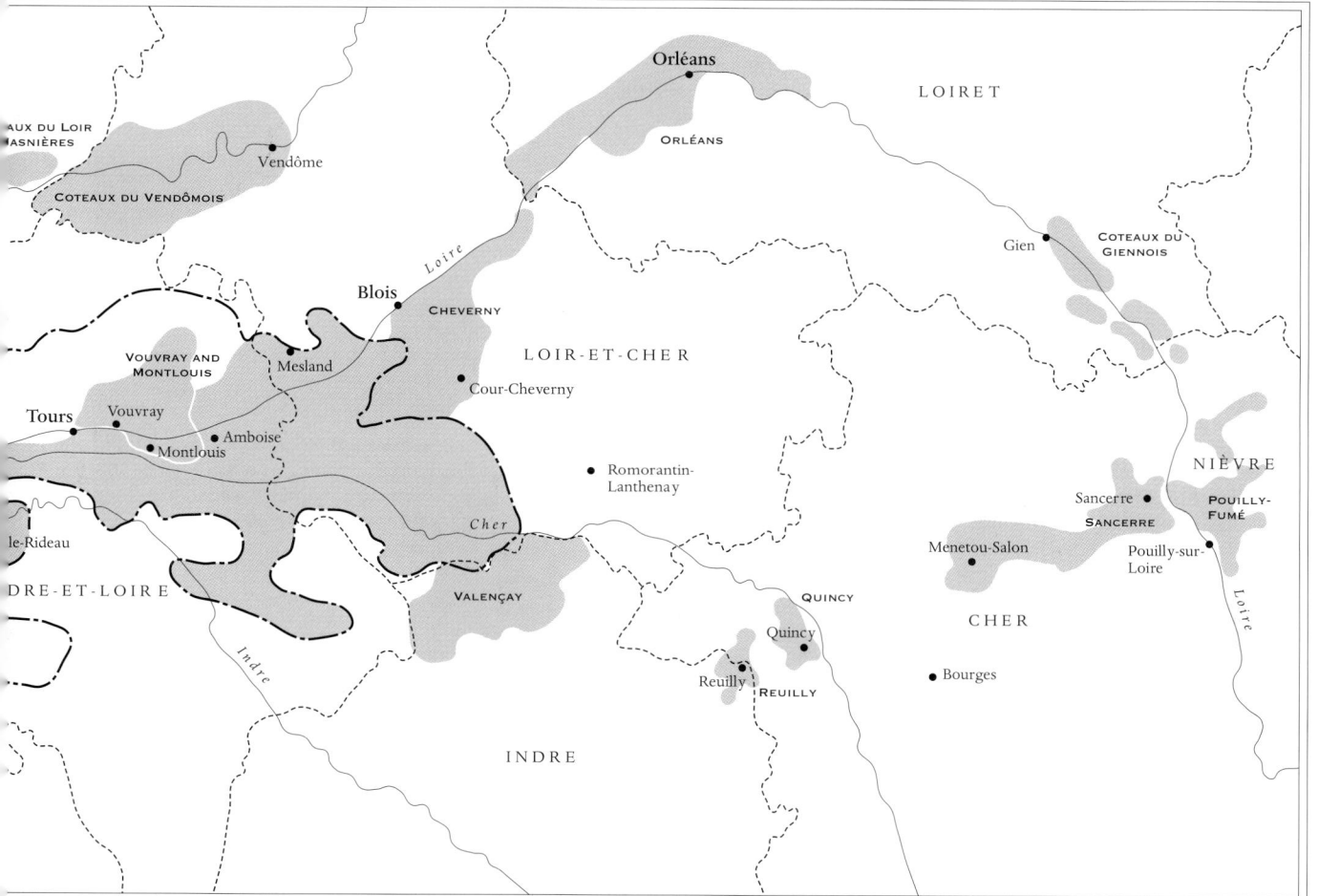

bishop of Tours, he took a great interest in the wine of his diocese (modern TOURAINE). He tells us that, in 591, drought was followed by rain so that the grain harvest was ruined but the vines yielded abundantly. He also tells in detail of the Bretons' often successful attempts to seize the vineyards and/or grapes of the Nantes region (modern MUSCADET) in the 6th century.

The wines of the Loire continued to be held in high regard, and not only by the Bretons, who gave up plundering and bought the wines they wanted. The inhabitants of west Brittany had grown some wine themselves, but in the 13th century they gave up viticulture in favour of growing grain and instead purchased their wines from Nantes. Like Nantes, Touraine produced wine of export quality, and by the end of the 11th century the wine of SANCERRE was already well reputed. In the 12th century it was exported to Flanders and sold via Orléans.

From the late 11th century onwards, the aspiring bourgeoisie of the newly rich Flemish cities wanted more and more of its chief status symbol, which was wine (see DUTCH WINE TRADE). With its excellent river connections, the Loire region was especially well placed to meet this growing demand. Some of its wine

was shipped to Flanders, or further north, or to England: some of it was carried to PARIS by river to be consumed there or sold on. Angers in particular grew rich on the Flemish guildsmen's desire for social advancement, and vines were planted even just outside its city walls. The count of ANJOU granted Angers the monopoly of carrying wine on the rivers Maine and Loire as far as the Breton port of Ingrandes; in addition, merchants could not buy their wines direct from the vineyards but had to buy them at Angers. These two privileges put the producers of SAUMUR at a disadvantage. The wines of Saumur were not fashionable in France, and Saumur was badly placed for overseas trade. In England in the late 12th century, before the rise of BORDEAUX, Anjou was the only wine to rival Poitou, shipped from LA ROCHELLE, in popularity. Anjou remained highly esteemed in England throughout the Middle Ages.

In France itself, the Loire wine that was most prized was one that has now all but disappeared from public regard: ST-POURÇAIN, made on the river Sioule in the Loire basin. King Louis IX served it at a banquet in Saumur to celebrate his brother Alphonse's 21st birthday. St-Pourçain fetched high prices during

the 14th century and was a favourite with the papal court at Avignon. The wines of the Coteaux de LAYON did not become famous until the 15th century.

For more historical detail, see entries under individual wine names.   H.M.W.

Dion, R., *Histoire de la vigne et du vin en France* (Paris, 1959).

Geography and climate

So long is the extent of the viticultural Loire that generalizations are impossible. The Loire's vineyards vary from the CONTINENTAL climate which produces Sancerre and Pouilly-Fumé, to the Muscadet region warmed by the Gulf Stream. Loire wine regions represent today, however, the north western limit of vine cultivation in Europe (with the exception of ENGLAND's vineyards). Spring FROST can be a serious problem, as it was in 1991, when it destroyed up to 90 per cent of the crop in some of the Loire's wine regions. The character of Loire wines can vary considerably from VINTAGE to vintage, since in a cool summer the grapes may struggle to reach full RIPENESS, while a particularly hot year such as 1989, 1990, 1997, and 2003 may result in some exceptional sweet white wines, some of them BOTRYTIZED in the middle

Loire, but can rob the Loire's dry white Sauvignons of their nerve, and leave some Muscadet dangerously limp.

The region is sufficiently far from the equator, however, that few of its red wines can be accused of being TANNIC, and the naturally high acidity associated with these latitudes, and some of its grape varieties, make much of the Loire's produce ideal base wine for sparkling wines.

Viticulture

The Loire is essentially a region of increasingly consolidated family holdings; the average holding has increased from 10 to 25 ha in recent years and many farmers have abandoned their other crops to concentrate on viticulture. In the middle Loire, rainfall is relatively low, but SPRAYING against FUNGAL DISEASES is still frequent elsewhere. VINE DENSITY is relatively high, between 4,000 and 5,000 plants per ha (1,600–2,000 per acre) on average, and up to 10,000 plants per ha in some Sancerre vineyards. Excess VIGOUR was a problem in the late 1980s and early 1990s, and resulted in HERBACEOUS flavours in many of the red wines, although CANOPY MANAGEMENT seems to have resolved this in many cases. COVER CROPS have long been the norm, and CROP THINNING was introduced in the early 1990s. MECHANICAL HARVESTING is relatively common, but cannot be used for the sweet white wines of the middle Loire, where successive TRIES through the vineyards are needed to select only the ripest grapes.

Wine-making

White winemakers of the Loire traditionally followed very similar principles to their counterparts in Germany, assiduously avoiding MALOLACTIC FERMENTATION and any new OAK influence, preferring instead to ferment and store wines in inert containers, and to bottle wines early, possibly after some LEES CONTACT in the case of Muscadet. For years, Loire reds suffered from a lack of EXTRACTION.

The result of the particularly competitive wine market of the 1980s and a drop in demand for sweet wines in the late 1990s, however, was to stimulate a rash of experimentation in cellars along the length of the Loire. BARREL MATURATION and in some cases BARREL FERMENTATION were introduced for reds and whites (see ANJOU, specifically). Some producers encouraged their white wines to go through malolactic fermentation, while red winemakers worked hard to extract greater colour and TANNINS from their red wine musts, by the use of prolonged SKIN CONTACT, TEMPERATURE CONTROL, and PUMPING OVER regimes. (It should be said that, in many a Loire autumn and winter, temperature control is just as likely to include heating the must as cooling it.) SKIN CONTACT prior to fermentation was also introduced for some white wines, especially Sauvignons.

CHAPTALIZATION is the norm in the Loire, for both reds and whites, and is usually done to a maximum of an additional 2.5 per cent ALCOHOLIC STRENGTH of the finished wine except in exceptionally hot vintages.

Vine varieties

At the mouth of the Loire, MELON de Bourgogne and FOLLE BLANCHE predominate. The upper Loire is, in the early 21st century anyway, the terrain of Sauvignon Blanc for white wines and Pinot Noir for reds and rosés. The majority of the most successful sites in the middle Loire have proved themselves suitable for either CABERNET FRANC or CHENIN BLANC, but in the thousands of hectares of vineyard planted around them, there is a greater diversity of vine varieties than anywhere else in France, including a mix of CABERNET SAUVIGNON, MALBEC, GAMAY, MEUNIER, PINOT GRIS, CHARDONNAY, and of course seas of Sauvignon and Pinot Noir. This is usually explained in terms of spheres of Bordeaux and Burgundy influence, but it indicates that, outside its most famous appellations, the regions of the Loire have been searching for their own wine identities. The vineyards of the Loire were particularly badly hit by PHYLLOXERA. The heavily calcareous soils in many regions meant that CHLOROSIS was a common problem when vines were replanted grafted on to resistant ROOTSTOCKS. The Loire, with its relatively cool climate, persisted with a higher proportion of HYBRIDS longer than any other French wine region. The maximum proportion of 20 per cent Chardonnay written into the rules of so many Loire appellations shows that the authorities at least are aware of the danger of the Loire losing its own identity (although Cabernet Sauvignon plantings are increasing and in the mid 2000s there were moves afoot to allow a proportion of Merlot in to wines such as Saumur-Champigny). Those varieties that are exclusive to the Loire such as PINEAU D'AUNIS, GROLLEAU, ARBOIS, ROMORANTIN, and Meslier-St-François are in retreat.

Wines produced

Of all French wine regions, the Loire produces the greatest diversity of wine styles: from still through all types of sparkling wine, including the generic CRÉMANT de Loire; from bone dry and searingly tart to unctuous LIQUOREUX (although still with a high degree of acidity); and all hues from water white to (quite) deep purple. Rosés are a speciality of the Loire, whether the various VINS GRIS made well upstream, the famous Rosé d'Anjou, various pink Cabernets, or the generic ROSÉ DE LOIRE.

Travelling upstream, the major districts, with each appellation for which there is a separate entry, are (see map):

Pays Nantais: MUSCADET; GROS PLANT du Pays Nantais; Coteaux d'ANCENIS; FIEFS VENDÉENS.

ANJOU: SAVENNIÈRES; Coteaux du LAYON; QUARTS DE CHAUME; BONNEZEAUX; Coteaux de l'AUBANCE.
SAUMUR.
TOURAINE: CHINON; BOURGUEIL; VOUVRAY; MONTLOUIS; CHEVERNY; VALENÇAY.
Upper Loire: REUILLY; QUINCY; MENETOU-SALON; SANCERRE; POUILLY-FUMÉ.
Northern outposts: Coteaux du LOIR; JASNIÈRES; Coteaux du VENDÔMOIS.
On the bend: ORLÉANS; Coteaux du GIENNOIS.
Southern outposts: Vins du THOUARSAIS; HAUT-POITOU; CHÂTEAUMEILLANT; ST-POURÇAIN; Côtes d'AUVERGNE; Côtes ROANNAISES; Côtes du FOREZ (although some of these are very far from the Loire and its climatic influence).

Friedrich, J., *A Wine and Food Guide to the Loire* (New York, 1996, and London, 1997).

Lombardia (**Lombardy** in English), the largest and most populous region of ITALY, and the driving force behind the country's post-Second World War economic boom, the dynamo which has given Milan and its hinterland one of Europe's highest standards of living. Visitors driving across the great Lombard plain of northern Italy between the Ticino of southern SWITZERLAND and the river Po (see map under ITALY) get little sense of a thriving agriculture, but the region is a viticultural centre of some importance: its annual production of just over 1.1 million hl/28 million gal (with DOC wines accounting for more than a third of the total) is larger than that of such famous wine regions as FRIULI, TRENTINO-ALTO ADIGE, UMBRIA, or the MARCHE, areas whose more bucolic landscapes suggest a greater significance for the vine.

Lombardia's centres of viticulture are off-centre geographically—in the far north, in the far south, and in the far east—all well off the region's main axis of communication. And the fact that each of Lombardia's three major viticultural areas cultivates different grapes and makes wine in a completely different style from the others does little to clarify the image of Lombardia wine: the region has neither a key grape nor a key wine to make it better known, and its sheer size and disparity are marketing handicaps. This is compounded by the fact that most of the region's wine is consumed (not wholly critically) by the denizens of Milan and its environs, which means that there is little pressure from the more competitive export markets to buy the wines. Good wine is none the less produced in VALTELLINA, OLTREPÒ PAVESE, and FRANCIACORTA.

Other DOCs include LUGANA, whose Trebbiano-based white wines are produced to the south of lake Garda. Botticino and Cellatica are red blends (the former with a slight suggestion of sweetness) from SCHIAVA, BARBERA, and MARZEMINO grapes grown in the province of Brescia and served with the local versions of *pot-au-feu* or wine-laced stews. Garda and Garda Bresciano, introduced in the late 1990s, cover a wide range of varietal whites (Pinot Grigio, Chardonnay, Garganega, Tocai,

Lombardia

410

etc.) and reds (Merlot, Cabernet Sauvignon, Corvina, Marzemino, and others). The wines tend to be light but pleasant, especially if consumed overlooking lake Garda.

For more detail on specific notable wines see BONARDA, CROATINA, as well as Colli BOLOGNESI and Colli PIACENTINI. D.T. & D.C.G.

Belfrage, N., *Barolo to Valpolicella—The Wines of Northern Italy* (London, 1999).

long, much-derided tasting term for wines whose impact on the PALATE is particularly persistent. A wine that is long is usually of high quality. On the basis of studies in other food systems, it is assumed that wine COLLOIDS have a role to play in lengthening the palate of a wine. This occurs through interaction of various FLAVOUR COMPOUNDS with particular colloids resulting in some or all of the wine's flavour compounds being retained in the mouth, along with the associated polymers, after the wine has been swallowed. Delayed release of the flavour compounds then accounts for the persistent or long palate of the wine. See also TASTING and CAUDALIE. P.J.W.

Los Carneros. See CARNEROS, wine region and AVA of California.

lot marking, a requirement within the EUROPEAN UNION since the early 1990s that all packaged wine should be marked with a lot number unique to an individual batch so that the packaging circumstances can be identified in the event of any complaint or recall. The mark is usually an L followed by a coded date of packaging.

Loupiac, sweet white wine appellation on the right bank of the GARONNE in the BORDEAUX region sandwiched between CADILLAC and STE-CROIX-DU-MONT. The wines of Loupiac were first cited in the 13th century (the Loupiac region was once much bigger), although in much of the 20th century the wines failed to fetch the prices necessary to justify truly meticulous wine-making. The best vineyards are on clay-limestone slopes overlooking the river and are well situated to benefit from NOBLE ROT, provided producers are prepared to take the necessary risks. Good Loupiac such as that produced at Domaine du Noble and Chx du Cros and Loupiac-Gaudiet is generally deeply coloured and noticeably full bodied; the use of new OAK became gradually more common from the late 1980s (see SAUTERNES for more details).

Loureiro, occasionally **Loureira**, fine, 'laurel-scented', white grape variety that is the most planted in VINHO VERDE country in northern Portugal and also grown in RÍAS BAIXAS in north west Spain. Plantings total about 6,000 ha/15,000 acres in Portugal but just 460 ha in 2004 in Spain, where ALBARIÑO is much more important. It has often been blended with TRAJADURA (Treixadura in Spain)

but can also be found as an aromatic VARIETAL wine. It can yield quite productively in the north of the Vinho Verde region and produces its best quality, usually quite low in alcohol, around Braga, Ponte de Lima, and the coast.

low-alcohol wine is usually REDUCED-ALCOHOL WINE but may also be, like NO-ALCOHOL WINE, regular wine from which alcohol has been deliberately removed, usually but not necessarily with harmful effects on flavour and quality. Such wines are usually reduced to an ALCOHOLIC STRENGTH which excludes them from DUTY, reducing their price. See also COOLERS, and DEALCOHOLIZED WINE.

Low Countries, historical region of north west Europe including the NETHERLANDS, BELGIUM, and LUXEMBOURG, which once played an important part in the wine and spirit trade. See DUTCH WINE TRADE.

Lower Austria. See Niederösterreich.

Lower Murray Zone in SOUTH AUSTRALIA, has a single but very important region, the Riverland.

low-input viticulture, an alternative to conventional viticulture with the aim of minimizing all inputs to the vineyard. This may be of AGROCHEMICALS, with the aim of improving the environment (see ORGANIC and BIODYNAMIC VITICULTURE), or of inputs such as LABOUR, with the aim of improving the vineyard's profitability.

Luberon, Côtes du, wines made on the fashionable slopes of the Luberon, where vineyards add colour and bucolic allure to one of the more sought-after corners of Provence. The appellation, which comprised more than 3,700 ha/9,130 acres of vineyard in the mid 2000s, is a sort of buffer state between the RHÔNE and PROVENCE, or more precisely between the Côtes du VENTOUX appellation and that of Coteaux d'AIX-EN-PROVENCE (although French officialdom places it firmly in the Rhône).

The appellation was created only in 1988 and produces significant quantities of all three colours of wine, although single VARIETAL wines must be sold as VINS DE PAYS du Vaucluse. All reds contain some Syrah, augmented by Grenache, possibly Mourvèdre and Cinsaut, and no more than 20 per cent Carignan. Those who try hard, such as old-timers Chx de Mille and de l'Isolette and the more recent Domaines d'Antonin and de Mayol and Chx Val Joanis and La Canorgue, can produce herb-scented reds with some concentration and ageing potential. Whites are made from Grenache Blanc, Clairette, Bourboulenc, Ugni Blanc, Vermentino, and possibly some Marsanne and Roussanne. The region's rather cooler nights (and winters) than in most Côtes du Rhône vineyards help to produce some of

the crisper, more interesting white wines of the southern Rhône. Rosés may incorporate up to 20 per cent of white grapes, and have particular allure when drunk locally to the sound of cicadas.

Lugana, dry white Italian wine based on the eponymous grape previously known as Trebbiano di Lugana, the same as TREBBIANO DI SOAVE, so akin to Verdicchio produced to the south and south west of lake Garda in the province of Brescia, straddling the provinces of Lombardia and Veneto. Over 700 ha/1,730 acres produce more than 45,000 hl/1.3 million gal of wine per year. The flat glacial plain, its climate moderated by cooling breezes from lake Garda, can produce wines of real richness and perfume such as those from Ca' dei Frati and the merchant Zenato. Most, however, is produced with an eye on the tourists who flock to the lake during the summer. D.T. & D.C.G.

Lunel is the centre of the Muscat de Lunel appellation for sweet golden VIN DOUX NATUREL made from MUSCAT BLANC À PETITS GRAINS grapes grown on potentially interesting infertile inland soils between Montpellier and Nîmes. Yields are low and vinification techniques improving although many local vine-growers have been more interested in developing lower alcohol, dry vins de CÉPAGE or wines that qualify as COTEAUX DU LANGUEDOC. A single CO-OPERATIVE is responsible for almost all the wine produced, which, as any geographer might suspect, tastes like a cross between the Muscats of FRONTIGNAN and ST-JEAN-DE-MINERVOIS. Lunel's historical claim to fame is less convincing than Frontignan's: its Muscat was dispatched to console Napoléon on the island of St Helena. The town does call itself the Cité du Muscat, however.

Lunel is also the occasional Hungarian name for a yellow-berried form of Muscat Blanc à Petits Grains grown in the TOKAJI region.

Lurtons, ramified family of property owners and winemakers in BORDEAUX, owning more wine estates in the Bordeaux region than any other single family. The original Lurton property is the modest Ch Bonnet in the ENTRE-DEUX-MERS, which belonged to Léonce Recapet, François Lurton's father-in-law. Although he and François acquired Ch Brane-Cantenac in MARGAUX in 1925, the current extent of the Lurton empire is largely due to the efforts of the brothers André and Lucien, both of whom bought numerous properties during the 1960s and 1970s. The elder brother André, who now owns Ch Bonnet and whose estates are mainly in the GRAVES (Chx La Louvière, Couhins, Rochemorin, Cruzeau), was a particularly potent force in the renaissance of the Graves region during the 1980s. A man of vision, energy, and a flair for promotion, he led the campaign for the new appellation of PESSAC-LÉOGNAN and became the first president of its Syndicat Viticole. He led by example, reconstituting the vineyards of the properties he bought and considerably improving the standards of both red and white wine-making.

The younger brother Lucien was the owner of ten properties (among them Chx Brane-Cantenac, Durfort-Vivens, and Desmirail in Margaux, Bouscaut in Pessac-Léognan, and Doisy-Dubroca and Climens in Barsac) before passing them on to his ten children. He too did much to improve the estates he owned, but, in marked contrast to André, Lucien did very little in the way of public relations. If his red wines were sometimes thought to be not quite up to the potential of their vineyards, Ch Climens has been, year in, year out, one of the finest Barsacs. The younger generation of Lurtons seem likely to continue to be a significant presence in Bordeaux and beyond and the great majority of them work in the wine business. André's sons Jacques and François started a worldwide wine-making service in 1988, advising and installing FLYING WINE-MAKERS in France, Spain, Italy, South America, and at one time South Australia and Moldova. In 1991, Pierre Lurton (son of Dominique who is brother to André and Lucien) became the estate manager at Ch CHEVAL BLANC, the St-Émilion first growth and, later, Ch d'YQUEM for LVMH. In 1994, Lucien's daughter Brigitte sold her stake in Climens to found Belondrade y Lurton in the Spanish white wine district of RUEDA but this is now run by her ex-husband while she is a hotelier in Bordeaux.

M.W.E.S. & J.R.

Lawther, J., 'Wine in the Blood', *Decanter* (Mar 1998), 38–43.

Lussac-St-Émilion, satellite appellation of ST-ÉMILION in Bordeaux.

Lutomer, known as **Ljutomer** in SLOVENIA, small town in the far east of the country which lends its name to a popular British BRAND, most famously of LAŠKI RIZLING.

lutte raisonnée, literally 'reasoned struggle', is an approach to viticulture which tries to minimize the application of AGROCHEMICALS so that they are used only when absolutely necessary and not as a matter of routine. See also SUSTAINABLE VITICULTURE.

Luxembourg, or **Luxemburg,** was for long the European Union's smallest and coolest wine producer before being rivalled in both respects by ENGLAND. The rarely exported wines produced are relatively dry and, depending on grape variety, reminiscent of those of Alsace or England in style. With the exception of an increasing number of light reds and rosés made from Pinot Noir vines, the wines made on the western, Luxembourg bank of the river MOSELLE are white. In 2004, there were 1,290 ha/

3,200 acres of vineyard—roughly the same as in England but producing in some vintages ten times as much wine. Average YIELDS have been decreasing but the official limits of 140 hl/ha (8 tons/acre) for Elbling and Rivaner and 120 hl/ha for other vine varieties suggest near-Germanic production levels. Except in very ripe years such as 1995, 1996, 1997, 2002, and 2003, CHAPTALIZATION is a necessity here and the wines can be marked by relatively high acidity (although DEACIDIFICATION may be practised by some producers). A national law passed in 1996 was designed to encourage higher-alcohol wines, a tendency encouraged by global warming (see CLIMATE CHANGE).

History

The German Mosel, below Trier, and the Luxembourg Moselle above it, had to surmount the same problems—cool climate and political change—for centuries but since the First World War the two regions have adopted different solutions. After the war, during which the grand duchy remained neutral, Luxembourg was required to break the free tariff agreement that had been made with Prussia in 1842. Thus a ready market for Luxembourg's sharp whites made from the Elbling grape evaporated and Germany looked elsewhere for base wines for SEKT and suitable blending material for the Rheinpfalz's flabbiest wines. The Champagne house Mercier opened up an offshoot in Luxembourg in the late 19th century. A new economic agreement with Belgium signed in 1921 did little to soak up the surplus; Belgian taste is for the richness of Pomerol, the vinous antithesis of Elbling. Thus Elbling has been replaced by nobler, or at least softer, varieties.

Geography and climate

Luxembourg's vineyards are in two of the grand duchy's eastern cantons, Remich and Grevenmacher. On the alluvial plain of Remich, the heavier soils tend to produce less aromatic, heavier, earlier-maturing wines from such villages as Remich, Wintrange, and Schengen. Parts of the narrower valley of Grevenmacher to the north have been reshaped by terracing, as in the Mosel across the German border, but yields are lower, calcareous soils predominate, and wines such as the village of Ahn's fine Rieslings are particularly slow maturing.

Luxembourg, at the northern limit of vine cultivation in Europe, suffers a wide range of cool climate problems such as spring frosts, hail, and COULURE, so that yields can vary substantially.

Vine varieties

Most Luxembourg still wines are varietal wines and are almost invariably labelled as such.

Rivaner This, Luxembourg's own strain of MÜLLER-THURGAU, so effectively replaced Elbling in the 20th century that by the early

1980s it covered as much as half of the grand duchy's total vineyard, being relatively easy to ripen whatever the local conditions. Its ability to yield obligingly high quantities was so abused by many growers, however, that it became synonymous with mediocrity and is now in decline. In 2004, it was planted on less than 400 ha/1,000 acres of the country's vineyard.

Auxerrois This has higher status in Luxembourg than anywhere else in the world (and certainly higher than in Alsace, where ten times as much is planted). Its low acidity is a positive attribute this far from the equator and when yields are curbed, barrel-aged Auxerrois can produce smoky, full-bodied wines worth ageing. See AUXERROIS.

Pinot Gris is also highly regarded in Luxembourg where it accounted for 13 per cent of all vines in 2004, again for its low acidity and its weight, as are, for much the same reasons, is **Pinot Blanc** (10 per cent).

Riesling Not the most sought-after wine in Luxembourg, it nevertheless accounts for about one-eighth of Luxembourg's vineyards—the same proportion as in the early 1990s.

Elbling may have been a Luxembourg speciality since Roman times but consumers exposed to softer, fuller, and more aromatic wines rejected it in favour of various members of the PINOT family so that it slid from second to sixth most planted variety between 1997 and 2004.

Chardonnay has also been planted, mainly for sparkling wine production. **Gewürztraminer** is even rarer.

Appellations

Luxembourg's answer to the APPELLATION CONTRÔLÉE system of France is highly individual and would be difficult to apply to a bigger wine industry. There is just one appellation, Moselle Luxembourgeoise, which is allowed to practically all wines, both still and sparkling, although they are all submitted to analysis and a tasting. Superior wines may be ranked as Vins Classés, Premiers Crus, or even Grands Premiers Crus. This generous system, which ignores geographical differences and the influence of TERROIR, has attracted some criticism and a rival organization in the form of Domaine et Tradition, which encourages local variation and expression and imposes a maximum yield of 85 hl/ha (4.8 tons/acre). (The maximum yield allowed on the French MOSELLE is 60 hl/ha.)

Since 1993, there has been some limited experimentation with ICE WINES and other sweet wines, with official regulation in 2001. Pinots Blanc and Gris and Riesling picked at −7 °Celsius with a MUST WEIGHT of at least 120 °Oechsle may be labelled **Icewine** (*sic*). The same regulations allow Auxerrois, Pinot Blanc, Pinot Gris, and Gewürztraminer with 105 °Oechsle and Riesling with 95 °Oechsle to be sold as **Vendange Tardive**, while the appellation **Vin de Paille** may be used for Auxerrois, Pinot Blanc, Pinot Gris, and Gewürztraminer with at least 130 °Oechsle.

For details of Luxembourg's appellation for traditional method sparkling wines, see CRÉMANT de Luxembourg.

Industry organization

As in the German Mosel, the average vine-holding is extremely small—2.76 ha/6.8 acres in 2004—although it has gradually increased as more and more of the smallest holdings are sold to larger landowners. The number of growers more than halved during the 20 years up to 2004, to 471. About 20 per cent of vines are grown by independent domaines which make wine themselves. Several wine CO-OPERATIVES together function as Vinsmoselle and represent about 60 per cent of the grand duchy's wine production.   J.R. & A.D.

LVMH, scrupulously even-handed acronym for Moët Hennessy-Louis Vuitton, the French luxury goods conglomerate which has a dominant interest in the CHAMPAGNE industry, not least through its subsidiaries, which include MOËT & CHANDON, KRUG, and VEUVE CLICQUOT, and a substantial position in Cognac through HENNESSY. Its distribution, and production, companies throughout the world play an important part in the international wine and spirits trade. In 1987, LVMH acquired a 12 per cent stake in the Guinness Group, which rose to a 24 per cent stake in 1990. In 1997, LVMH exchanged its shares in Guinness and Grand Metropolitan for 11 per cent in the newly created DIAGEO amalgamation of the two, thus becoming the largest shareholder in this dominant drinks group. In 1998, LVMH acquired a substantial stake in Ch d'YQUEM, while its chief executive Bernard Arnault became co-owner of Ch CHEVAL BLANC. For more details of LVMH's champagne interests, see MOËT & CHANDON.

Lyonnais, Coteaux du. Light red wines made chiefly from Gamay grapes grown in the hills both north and south west of the city of Lyons, and drunk mainly by its inhabitants.

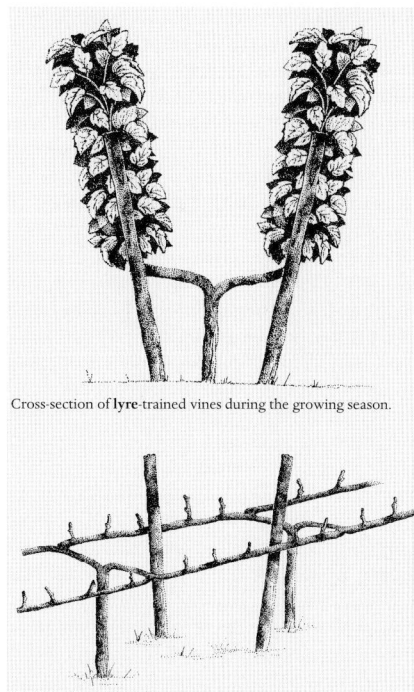

Cross-section of **lyre**-trained vines during the growing season.

Vine training to the **lyre** system showing spur pruning (cane pruning can also be used).

The red wines can be every bit as good as nearby BEAUJOLAIS, although the appellation was granted only in 1984. A small amount of white wine is also made, from Chardonnay and Aligoté. The CO-OPERATIVE at Sain-Bel vinifies three-quarters of production.

lyre, a vine-TRAINING SYSTEM whereby the CANOPY is divided horizontally into two curtains of upward-pointing shoots and which resembles a lyre in shape (see illustration). The system was developed in Bordeaux in the early 1980s by Dr Alain Carbonneau, now Professor of Viticulture at MONTPELLIER. Carbonneau was much influenced by the pioneering studies of Nelson SHAULIS in CANOPY MANAGEMENT. The lyre system improves the CANOPY MICROCLIMATE and leads to improvement in yield and wine quality because of better leaf and fruit exposure to sunlight. Either SPUR PRUNING or CANE PRUNING can be used. Further use

of this system has been delayed by the unavailability of mechanical harvesters. The system is being adopted in New World vineyards in particular, especially in California, and to a lesser extent in Australia, New Zealand, Chile and Uruguay.

The lyre system is essentially an inverted GENEVA DOUBLE CURTAIN, with the two adjacent curtains of foliage trained upwards rather than downwards. Both systems are used to reduce the shading of dense canopies. The lyre system is typically recommended for medium-vigour vines, whereas the GDC can harness higher vine vigour. The lyre system has shown substantial improvements in wine quality where it has been evaluated in Europe.   R.E.S.

Coombe, B. G., and Dry, P. R. (eds.), Viticulture, ii: Practices (Adelaide, 1992).

Smart, R. E., and Robinson, M., Sunlight into Wine: A Handbook for Winegrape Canopy Management (Adelaide, 1991).

lyric poetry. There are many references to wine in the lyric poets of Ancient GREECE. Archilochos, writing in the middle of the 7th century BC, describes the comfort brought by wine on a long sea journey:

Along the rowers' benches bring your cup
And lift the lids of the big wine jars up
And drain the good red wine: we can't, 'tis clear
Be sober all the time we're watching here.

Fifty years later, Alkaios of Lesbos (who knew and admired the poetess Sappho) has many references to wine, often in vigorous verse: 'Wet your lungs with wine; for the dog star is coming round, and everything is thirsty with heat.' In an early variant of not waiting for the sun to be over the yard-arm, he writes: 'Drink! Why wait for the lamps? The day is almost done!'

The curmudgeonly Theognis, writing at the same time, probably from Megara on the isthmus of Corinth, extols the value of wine and the dangers of DRUNKENNESS. 'Stand by ready to pour for those who want to drink. We cannot have a party every night. Still because I am moderate in my use of honeyed wine, I reach my house before I think of soothing sleep, and I make clear how divine a beverage for man is wine.'   H.H.A.

Macabeo is northern Spain's most planted white grape variety, on nearly 32,000 ha/ 80,000 acres in 2004, and, as **Maccabéo** or **Macabeu**, has become so popular in ROUSSILLON that it has been France's eighth most planted white grape variety since the end of the 1980s with a total of 5,200 ha in 2000.

In early-picked form, in Côtes du Roussillon it is either a fairly characterless white, a useful ingredient in rosé, or, as in Spain, a common lightener of potent reds in which it is officially sanctioned up to 10 per cent of the total blend (up to 30 per cent in rosé). Later picked, it may be an ingredient in, or even sole constituent of, one of Roussillon's distinctive VINS DOUX NATURELS. In the LANGUEDOC, in the white wines of Minervois and Corbières, it may be blended with BOURBOULENC, GRENACHE BLANC, and a host of other southern white varieties.

Macabeo spread to southern France from Spain but Odart claims that its origins are Middle Eastern. It is a vigorous vine that buds conveniently late for regions prone to spring FROSTS and can be quite productive so long as autumns are dry and the possibility of ROT is minimized. Well established at one time in North Africa, the vine can tolerate hot, dry conditions.

The wine produced tends to have a vaguely floral character and relatively low acidity unless the grapes are picked so early that the floral character is even more difficult to discern, but it has the advantage, unlike other, more traditional RIOJA varieties, of withstanding OXIDATION well. Perhaps this is one of the reasons why it was so enthusiastically embraced by the growers of Rioja, where, as Viura, it all but displaced Malvasía and Garnacha Blanca after its post-phylloxera introduction to represent more than 90 per cent of all white varieties planted.

Macabeo is also grown widely in PENEDÈS and, especially, CONCA DE BARBERÁ, where, with Parellada and Xarel-lo, it makes up the triumvirate of CAVA varieties, as well as being found throughout eastern Spain as far south as MANCHUELA and YECLA.

Odart, A., *Traité des cépages* (3rd edn, Paris, 1854).

McDowell Valley, California AVA. See MENDOCINO.

Macedonia, state to the north of Ancient Greece famous as the home of Alexander the Great and his father Philip, who had conquered Greece by 346 BC. Alexander went on to defeat all the empires of the east before his early death aged 33 in 323 BC. In 167 BC, Macedonia collapsed and became part of the Roman empire. The members of the Macedonian royal family were notorious as heavy drinkers of wine. Macedonia is now split: half in what was Yugoslavia and half a province of modern GREECE.

Ex-Yugoslavian republic

Squeezed into an enclave surrounded by BULGARIA, SERBIA, KOSOVO, ALBANIA, and Greece, the republic is hot and mountainous and is also prone to earthquakes. The climate here is extremely favourable to vine cultivation and its estimated 30,000 ha/74,100 acres of total vineyards grow TABLE GRAPES as well as including 22,400 ha/55,330 acres devoted to producing red wine in great quantity and a little white. Total wine production of 1.8 million hl in the mid 1990s had shrunk to 447,000 hl in 2002 according to OIV figures.

Macedonia has some good modern vineyards, 80 per cent of which are planted with red wine grapes, by far the most important of which is the indigenous VRANAC but there is also the local Kratosija, as well as some Cabernet Sauvignon and Merlot. White grapes are mainly SMEDEREVKA and Laški Rizling (WELSCHRIESLING) with some Chardonnay, Sauvignon Blanc, and a little ZILAVKA.

The three vine-growing regions are the central and most important Povardarie region around Skopje, the eastern Pcinja-Osogovo region on the Bulgarian border and the western Pelagonija-Polog region around Lake Ohrid and the Albanian border. The climate is MEDITERRANEAN to CONTINENTAL and soils are relatively fertile. A.H.M. & J.R.

Macedon Ranges, very cool, sparkling and fine table wine region in the Port Phillip Zone in the Australian state of VICTORIA.

Maceratino, increasingly rare white grape grown on Italy's Adriatic coast, possibly related either to GRECO or the local VERDICCHIO.

maceration, ancient word for steeping a material in liquid with or without a kneading action to separate the softened parts of the material from the harder ones. This important process in RED WINE-MAKING involves extraction of the PHENOLICS (TANNINS, colouring materials, or ANTHOCYANINS, other GLYCOSIDES, including FLAVOUR PRECURSORS, and nonglycosylated FLAVOUR COMPOUNDS) from the grape skins, seeds, and stem fragments into the juice or new wine. Some maceration inevitably takes place in the FERMENTATION VESSEL. It is governed by TEMPERATURE, contact between the solids and liquid and the degree of agitation, time, and by the composition of the extracting liquid, in this case the grape juice as it becomes wine. Although everyday red wines are made simply by a rapid fermentation lasting just two or three days, many winemakers encourage an additional maceration period after fermentation has been completed, particularly for long-lived wines such as red BORDEAUX. If fermentation is slow to start, possibly due to the low temperature of the grapes and/ or the use of ambient yeast, the winemaker may take advantage of the 'accidental maceration' that results.

The maceration process can never extract all of the phenolics from red grapes, however, because the enclosed membranes of individual

CELLS within the skin layer containing the phenolics are not broken by the CRUSHING operation that breaks open the berry. The diffusion of anthocyanins through these membranes is slow, and the maceration process is further complicated by the fact that reactions progressively occur among the compounds newly released from their confining cells leading to the formation of PIGMENTED TANNINS. Winemakers must use trial and error, often over many years, to decide which are the optimum maceration conditions for each grape variety and season. Rapid laboratory analyses can help to estimate colour and tannins (and Ferré has shown in his *Traité d'œnologie bourguignonne* that extraction reaches a maximum of 80 per cent of the grapes' available colouring matter on the sixth day of maceration), but the winemaker's eye and palate often prove surer guides.

Both heat and alcohol encourage the extraction of desirable compounds, which is fortunate since both are produced by fermentation. As fermentation continues, heat is produced and the increasingly alcoholic liquid becomes a better and better solvent for the organic compounds to be extracted.

But the grape solids (mainly skins) have to be encouraged to make sufficient contact with the liquid for optimal extraction. Air entrained with grape skins in the crushing operation tends to make them float to the surface in the fermentation vessel to form a layer known as a CAP. This tendency is accentuated by the bubbles of CARBON DIOXIDE gas generated by fermentation within the lower liquid layers. Without human intervention, a thick and drying layer of grape skins will be buoyed up by this stream of carbon dioxide and the extraction of desirable skin components will cease.

For generations, wine-making ingenuity has been harnessed to devising methods of breaking up and submerging the cap and keeping the skins mixed with the fermenting liquid. Keeping skins and liquid in contact is relatively simple with small batches of fermenting grapes (see PUNCHING DOWN). With larger batches, a system of either grids or coarse mesh screens must be devised to keep the cap submerged, or liquid from the bottom of the tank must be pumped to the top and sprayed over the skins (see PUMPING OVER and DÉLESTAGE).

Several proprietary systems have been devised to extract the desirable organic compounds from the grape skins into the fermenting wine. Some of these use a quick high-temperature phase to disrupt the cells containing anthocyanins and liberate the desirable organic compounds (see THERMOVINIFICATION and FLASH DÉTENTE); others use mechanical stirrers or rotating tanks (see ROTOFERMENTERS) which keep the skins and liquid in contact; or some form of AUTOVINIFICATION. In general, heat and mechanical agitation systems are used for ordinary wines, while the more sensitive techniques of punching down

or pumping over are preferred for finer wines, although care must be taken that any pumps used are relatively gentle. The shape of the vat also influences the behaviour of the cap.

Along with temperature, liquid composition, and intimacy of contact, the fourth factor influencing colour, tannin, and flavour extraction is time of contact, a factor, albeit less than perfectly understood, over which winemakers can have total control (provided they have access to sufficient vat space). In general the longer the solids and liquids are in contact, the greater the degree of extraction. It has been shown, however, that the extraction of the desirable compounds slows down considerably after the new wine approaches 10 per cent alcohol and is at its height during the earlier phases of fermentation. The total maceration time varies according to the phenolic content of the skins (itself a function of grape variety and weather) and according to the desired style of wine. Within certain limits, the greater the degree of extraction, the longer the life expectancy of a wine—although care must be taken to avoid extracting the harshest phenolics. In red wine-making, maceration usually lasts at least as long as fermentation does, but may be prolonged for a further week to three or even four weeks afterwards. Care must be taken to avoid the increased risk of high levels of VOLATILE ACIDITY. Some musts, naturally low in tannins, may be heated after the completion of fermentation to encourage the extraction of phenolics.

Some wine producers favour a prefermentation **cold maceration** of red grapes rather than maceration of skins in an alcoholic liquid. This optional wine-making operation involves the maceration of grape skins with juice while the mass is held at a low temperature. In theory each of the extractable compounds in the skins has its own temperature coefficient governing the extraction rate, and the theory of cold maceration is that a more favourable combination of phenolics is extracted by water and added SULFUR DIOXIDE than is obtained with an alcoholic solution. The Lebanese oenologist and consultant Guy Accad was an influential proponent of this technique in Burgundy in the 1970s and 1980s. He recommended very high levels of sulfur dioxide to maximize colour and tannin extraction prior to the onset of fermentation. There is still much debate about his methods and the resulting wines, especially their long-term development.

See also BARREL FERMENTATION for an outline of a red wine-making option which dispenses with post-fermentation maceration altogether.

In WHITE WINE-MAKING, maceration is usually actively discouraged by separating the juice from the skins as soon as possible in order to avoid extraction of tannins, since no colouring matter is required and the resultant astringency is viewed as a fault in white wines.

Some winemakers deliberately allow a certain period of SKIN CONTACT for white grapes before they are crushed, however, and in the late 1980s this technique (known as **macération pelliculaire** in French) was encouraged by Denis DUBOURDIEU among others in order to produce more flavourful dry white bordeaux. Sauvignon and, particularly, Sémillon grapes are held for between four and eight hours at about 18 °C/64 °F, resulting in juice higher in flavour compounds, tannins, POTASSIUM salts, and POLYSACCHARIDES, and wines with more BODY and a slightly higher PH.

A quite different red wine-making technique is CARBONIC MACERATION, practised particularly in Beaujolais and for other red wines designed for early consumption.

Maceration is also important in the production of fruit-flavoured spirits such as the *crème de cassis* used in making a *vin blanc cassis* or KIR which is the aromatic and deeply coloured product of blackcurrants macerated in alcohol.   A.D.W. & P.J.W.

macération carbonique. French term for CARBONIC MACERATION.

macération pelliculaire. French term for the prefermentation maceration of white grapes described in MACERATION and known elsewhere as SKIN CONTACT.

maceration préfermentaire. French term for prefermentation MACERATION.

McLaren Vale, intensively planted, historic SOUTH AUSTRALIAN wine region especially noted for rich reds. These have a distinctive and often useful dash of dark chocolate in their make-up. More controversial is their level of alcohol: seldom less than 14.5 per cent and sometimes in excess of 15.5. The winemakers' response is that they are not seeking high alcohol, simply waiting for the right flavour development.

Mâcon, important commercial centre on the river Saône and capital of the **Mâconnais** dynamic district of BURGUNDY which produces considerable quantities of white wine and some red. Unlike in the Côte d'Or to the north (see map under FRANCE), vineyards on the rolling limestone hills of the Mâconnais are interspersed with land dedicated to livestock and arable farming. Côte d'Or producers as renowned as Leflaive and Lafon are investing in this southerly region.

The climate and ambience of the region differ from the Côte d'Or however: southern tiles are used for roofs, cicadas can be heard in summer, and the vineyards benefit from more sun, less rain, and little risk of frost. BEAUJOLAIS is to the immediate south of the Mâconnais.

Viticultural practices are broadly similar to those in the CÔTE D'OR, except for the widespread use of LYRE training systems, although yields may be a little higher, up to a permitted

55 hl/ha (3 tons/acre). Vinification is sometimes carried out in barrels, although only the best producers use new OAK. Bottling normally takes place in the summer before the next vintage.

The appellations of Mâconnais, in approximately ascending order of quality are, for white wines made from Chardonnay: **Mâcon**; **Mâcon Supérieur**; **Mâcon-Villages** or **Mâcon** followed by a particular village name (for more details of which, see MÂCON-VILLAGES); ST-VÉRAN; Pouilly-Vinzelles, Pouilly-Loché, and Pouilly-Fuissé (for more details of which, see POUILLY-FUISSÉ). Wines may occasionally be found carrying the appellation **Pinot Chardonnay-Mâcon**. Red wine appellations are **Mâcon**, **Mâcon Supérieur**, and **Mâcon** followed by a particular village name. Almost all these red wines are made from the Gamay grape since, although Pinot Noir is permitted, such wines may be sold as BOURGOGNE Rouge at a higher price than Mâcon fetches.

In 1998, the village of Viré and the adjacent hamlet of Clessé were given their own single appellation VIRÉ-CLESSÉ. This may promote a spate of individual appellations from other leading villages such as Lugny, which have habitually appeared on labels as a suffix to the name Mâcon (see MÂCON-VILLAGES).

Leading producers include the Bret Brothers, Guffens-Heynen and his négociant company Verget, Merlin, Vincent, and Thévenet.

J.T.C.M.

Mâcon-Villages, appellation covering the great majority of the white wines of MÂCON. The wines may be sold either as Mâcon-Villages or as Mâcon followed by the name of the particular village. Viré and Lugny have been the best known by virtue of their CO-OPERATIVES. The full list of 43 villages with the right to the appellation is: Azé, Berzé-la-Ville, Berzé-le-Châtel, Bissy-la-Mâconnaise, Burgy, Bussières, Chaintré, Chânes, La Chapelle-de-Guinchay, Chardonnay (whence the grape may have taken its name), Charnay-lès-Mâcon, Chasselas, Chevagny-lès-Chevrières, Clessé, Crèches-sur-Sâone, Cruzille, Davayé, Fuissé, Grévilly, Hurigny, Igé, Leynes, Loché, Lugny, Milly-Lamartine, Montbellet, Péronne, Pierreclos, Prissé, Pruzilly, La Roche-Vineuse, Romanèche-Thorins, St-Amour-Bellevue, St-Gengoux-de-Scissé, St-Symphorien-d'Ancelles, St-Vérand, Sologny, Solutré-Pouilly, Vergisson, Verzé, Vinzelles, Viré, and Uchizy.

Most Mâconnais wines are vinified in stainless steel or glass-lined concrete vats for early bottling and consumption within a year or two of the vintage. A handful of growers are producing significantly finer wines through low yields followed by BARREL FERMENTATION and BARREL MATURATION. Jean Thévenet has also made a speciality of an extraordinary late-picked and sometimes BOTRYTIZED sweet white Mâcon.

J.T.C.M.

macroclimate, also called regional climate, means a climate broadly representing an area or region on a scale of tens to hundreds of kilometres (Dry and Smart). Unlike the more precise terms MICROCLIMATE and MESOCLIMATE, macroclimate approximates to what is normally meant by the word 'climate'. It is usually taken from a long-established recording station within the region. While easy enough to define, the concept is subject to problems in practice, however. Most climate-recording stations with long enough histories to be reliable over time are sited in towns and cities; they therefore potentially suffer from two defects. First, urban growth around them has in many cases led to a spurious warming trend in the records; mainly in the minimum temperatures, due to retention of the day's heat by roads and buildings, and in cities by industrial and domestic energy input. Secondly, the sites are likely to be disproportionately on flat land or in valleys. They therefore tend to be unrepresentative, not only of the landscape as a whole, but even more so of the better vineyard sites (see TOPOGRAPHY).

Macroclimatic data have to be used with caution when applied to viticulture. Informed adjustments are nearly always needed for differences in ALTITUDE, LATITUDE, slope, aspect, and even SOIL type, before worthwhile estimates can be made for the mesoclimates of actual vineyards. This is especially so in cool regions, where small differences in effective temperature can make big differences in time and completeness of RIPENING.

J.G.

Dry, P. R., and Smart, R. E., 'Vineyard site selection', in B. G. Coombe and P. R. Dry (eds.), Viticulture, i: Resources (Adelaide, 1988).

macro-oxygenation, an umbrella term for the deliberate exposure of wine to OXYGEN that contrasts with the very specific technique of MICRO-OXYGENATION. See AERATION, PUMPING OVER, DÉLESTAGE, RACKING, BARREL FERMENTATION, and BARREL MATURATION.

Macvin du Jura, powerful VIN DE LIQUEUR made in the JURA in eastern France by arresting the fermentation of grape juice by adding local MARC. This sweet but curiously earthy drink should be served cool as an APERITIF or with sweet dishes. It has been made since at least the 14th century and was awarded its own APPELLATION CONTRÔLÉE, the 400th created by INAO, in 1991.

Madagascar, large tropical island off the east African coast which was a French colony between 1896 and 1960 and has a wine industry that has since been run largely by Chinese immigrants. The island produces about 88,000 hl/2.3 million gal of wine a year (about as much as LUXEMBOURG) from about 2,000 ha/ 4,940 acres of mainly HYBRID vines in the central *hauts plateaux* area grown at altitudes of between 750 and 1,350 m. Swiss settlers encouraged the Betsileo farmers to apply their expertise growing rice on high terraces to viticulture in the 1960s. About 700 vine-growers, with an average of 2 ha of vineyard each, are centred on Fianarantsoa and Ambalavo. See TROPICAL VITICULTURE.

Platter, J. & E., *Africa Uncorked* (London, 2002).

Mädchentraube, German synonym for FETEASCĂ.

Madeira, Atlantic island belonging to Portugal, nearly 1,000 km/625 miles from the Portuguese mainland and 750 km off the coast of North Africa, now a DOC for fortified wines and a VINHO REGIONAL (see TERRAS MADEIRENSES) for unfortified wines. Of these, the FORTIFIED **madeira**, probably the world's most resilient and longest living wine, is much the most famous. This volcanic island rising steeply from the ocean is an unlikely place to find such an exciting and individual wine. But Madeira flies in the face of generally accepted wine-making norms.

History

Like PORT, madeira seems to have begun as an unfortified wine. There are few early records but Madeira's strategic position in the middle of the Atlantic put the island at an advantage and the island's capital Funchal became a natural port of call for ships en route to Africa, Asia, and South America. By the end of the 16th century (less than 200 years after the discovery of the island), there is firm evidence that Madeira's wine industry was well established. However, the early madeira wines were unstable and many deteriorated long before they reached their destination. Alcohol (probably distilled from cane sugar) was therefore added to some wines in order to help them survive a long sea voyage, although FORTIFICATION did not become general practice until the middle of the 18th century.

In the second half of the 17th century, ships en route to India (including many of the DUTCH EAST INDIA COMPANY fleet) called regularly at Funchal to pick up casks of wine termed pipas or PIPES. It was soon found that madeira somehow tasted better after pitching and rolling across the tropics in the hull of a ship. With this came a fashion for *vinho da roda*, wines that had benefited from a round trip, as opposed to *vinho canteiro*, wine which matured on the island, called after the trestles (*canteiros*) on which the pipes rested in the madeira LODGES. Wines continued to undergo long, tropical sea journeys to induce this special flavour until the 1900s, when the practice became impractical. Over the preceding century most shippers turned to using ESTUFAS, rooms or tanks in which the wine could be artificially heated to simulate the rapid maturation brought about by a long sea journey—although the finest madeiras continue to be aged naturally on *canteiros* (see Wine-making below).

With the colonization of North America in the 17th century, Madeira established an important export market on the east coast. By the end of the 18th century, the new North American colonies were buying a quarter of all the wine produced on the island. Madeira was held in such high esteem that it was used to toast the Declaration of Independence in 1776. Colonial troops returning to Britain opened up a new market for madeira there, but high-quality madeira is still much appreciated in the United States. The Madeira Club of Savannah survived PROHIBITION and continues to meet regularly over a quarter of a millennium after the first pipes of madeira were landed on the coast of Georgia.

As well as being extremely fashionable in Britain and the United States, the drink was also popular with Portuguese settlers in Africa, and in Brazil, and demand began to outstrip supply.

In 1851, however, the first of a series of crises struck the island's wine industry. Oidium or POWDERY MILDEW reached the island (in the same year as it was first identified in BORDEAUX) and quickly spread through the dense vineyards, almost wiping out production in just three years.

The industry revived after it was found that oidium could be controlled by dusting the vine leaves with SULFUR but shortly afterwards the PHYLLOXERA louse struck, leaving the island's wine-based economy in ruins. From the mid 1870s, vines all over the island were uprooted and replaced by sugar cane. Wine shippers abandoned Madeira and many vineyards were never replanted.

Phylloxera-resistant AMERICAN VINE SPECIES were introduced a decade or so later but many farmers, seeking a rapid return to prosperity, cultivated VITIS *labrusca*, *riparia*, *rupestris*, and hybrid vines rather than using them merely as ROOTSTOCKS onto which Madeira's traditional Vitis VINIFERA varieties could be grafted.

Madeira's wine industry returned to normal levels of production at the beginning of the 20th century and shipments to traditional markets were restored. But the island's economy was dealt another blow, first by the Russian Revolution in 1917, and immediately thereafter by the introduction of Prohibition, in the United States. Many firms were forced to close, but a number chose to amalgamate to form the Madeira Wine Association, renamed as the Madeira Wine Company in 1981.

Although at the end of the 17th century there were about 30 wine shippers operating on Madeira, by the mid 2000s there were just six exporters of madeira, of which Justino Henriques is now much the largest wine producer on the island, although the best known is probably the Madeira Wine Company comprising BLANDY, COSSART GORDON, Leacock, and Rutherford & Miles among more than 20 brand names. In 1988, the SYMINGTON family of OPORTO took a stake in the company,

which subsequently became a controlling interest, and thoroughly overhauled the winemaking practices and equipment.

France, Germany, and the Benelux countries are the largest markets for modern madeira, although most of the wine destined for these countries is of very basic quality and bought for cooking rather than drinking. The United States, Japan, and the United Kingdom are the main markets for better-quality madeira.

Viticulture

Madeira is a difficult place to grow grapes. Nearly all the island's vineyards are planted on tiny step-like terraces called *poios*, carved from the red or grey basalt bedrock. Although some of the newer vineyards are CORDON-trained, most vineyards are planted on low trellises (known as *latada*) similar to those of the VINHO VERDE region on the Portuguese mainland. These serve to raise the CANOPY above the ground, making the grapes less vulnerable to the FUNGAL DISEASES that thrive in this damp, subtropical climate. With a mean annual temperature of 19 °C/ 66 °F and high rainfall, powdery mildew and BOTRYTIS BUNCH ROT are constant threats.

Viticulture at this latitude is only made possible by altitude. Madeira rises to over 1,800 m/ 5,900 ft and the mountains are almost perpetually covered in cloud as moisture in the warm oceanic air is forced to condense. Annual rainfall on the island's summit reaches nearly 3,000 mm/117 in, over three times the total in the island's capital Funchal on the south coast, where EVAPORATION is high. The network of IRRIGATION channels called *levadas* now extends to over 2,000 km/1,200 miles, supplying the 2,000 growers farming around 1,800 ha/ 4,500 acres of piecemeal vineyard. MECHANIZATION is rendered impossible by both the terracing and the small size of the vineyard plots. As a result, cultivation costs are rising and many vineyards on the south of the island have fallen prey to property speculation.

Vine varieties

The most planted variety by far is the red-skinned TINTA NEGRA MOLE, which has been the principal *vinifera* variety on the island since phylloxera arrived at the end of the 19th century. Its name means 'black, soft' and it is often denigrated, somewhat unfairly in view of its versatility. Along with the recently introduced COMPLEXA grape, it can make good madeira, but wines based on Tinta Negra Mole rarely have the keeping qualities of those based on the so-called 'noble' varieties. Plantings of the traditional varieties SERCIAL, VERDELHO, BUAL, MALVASIA, and the almost extinct Terrantez, are slowly increasing once again since their rout as a result of phylloxera. Other varieties planted are principally disease-resistant AMERICAN HYBRIDS such as Cunningham and Jacquet, although they are no longer permitted as ingredients in madeira and

should be used exclusively in the production of the island's rustic table wine. Small quantities of ARNSBURGER and Cabernet Sauvingon are planted on the north side of the island for the production of unfortified wine. LISTRÃO is planted on the nearby island of Porto Santo where they make a small quantity of their own fortified wine for the local market.

Wine-making

Madeira is made in a number of different ways and methods of production vary enormously according to the market and the price that the wine commands. Production revolves around the use of the ESTUFA system and its natural alternatives.

The *estufagem* process has been much improved in recent years with concrete tanks having been largely replaced by stainless steel (*cubas de calor*) ranging in size between 20,000 and 50,000 l/13,200 gal and most widely used for large-volume production. Hot water circulates either through a stainless steel coil in the middle of the tank or a jacket, heating the wine to a maximum temperature of 55 °C/130 °F for at least 90 days. The process is carefully monitored by the wine industry's controlling body, the Instituto do Vinho da Madeira (Madeira Wine Institute, or IVM).

A second type of *estufagem* (used exclusively by the Madeira Wine Company) takes place in 600-l/158-gal wooden casks or lodge pipes which are stored in warm rooms (*armazens de calor*) heated by the nearby tanks or by steam-filled hot water pipes. Temperatures usually range between 30 °C and 40 °C and the wines develop over a longer period, usually six months to a year. This is a gentler process than the bulk method generally used, and is used for higher-quality (see below).

The very finest madeiras are produced without any artificial heating at all. Some of the smaller shippers and stockholders (*armazenistas*) refuse to resort to the *estufa* to age their wines. These madeiras are left to age naturally in 600-l pipes stowed under the eaves of lodges in Funchal, heated only by the sun. These *vinhos de canteiro* mature in cask for at least 20 years, although some may remain in this state for a century or more before bottling, and are usually destined for vintage lots.

One of Madeira's most pressing problems is a lack of good-quality base wine caused by a shortage of grapes from *vinifera* vine varieties. The white Sercial, Verdelho, Malvasia, and Terrantez varieties, which are classified as 'noble' by the ruling Madeira Wine Institute, are in short supply (see below). Most madeira is therefore made from the versatile Tinta Negra Mole.

Traditionally, shippers bought unfermented MUST direct from the growers, who trod the grapes by foot in LAGARES. Today few winemakers use *lagares* and the main shippers buy grapes rather than must, from farmers all over the island. Most firms ferment in

25,000-l/6,600-gal vats made from stainless steel but a few still use lined cement or even ferment small quantities of wine in cask. The noble varieties are usually pressed and fermented separately from Tinta Negra Mole. Malvasia and Bual are traditionally fermented on their skins while Sercial and Verdelho musts are separated from the grape skins before fermentation.

Higher-quality wines (usually those made with a high percentage of the more expensive noble grapes) are made by arresting the fermentation with 95 per cent strength grape spirit to produce a wine with an ALCOHOLIC STRENGTH of between 17 and 18 per cent. Wines made from Malvasia and Bual are fortified early in the FERMENTATION process, leaving up to 7 °Baumé (see MUST WEIGHT for conversions into other scales of measurement) of RESIDUAL SUGAR in the wine. Verdelho and Sercial are fermented until they are practically dry, although they may be sweetened at a later stage with either *vinho surdo* or *abafado*. *Surdo* is an intensely sweet MISTELA fortified to an alcoholic strength of 20 per cent, often before fermentation has begun, while *abafado* is a drier wine arrested at a later stage.

Producers of cheaper wines prefer to ferment all wines dry, leaving the fortification until after the wines have passed through the *estufa*. This saves on the cost of valuable alcohol, a few degrees of which are lost through evaporation during *estufagem*. The wines are sweetened after fortification according to style and are often adjusted with caramel.

The wines' age is counted from the point at which *estufagem* has been completed. Until 2002 the most basic wines were generally shipped in bulk (*granel*) but this practice has now been suspended.

Styles of madeira
The quality of even the most basic madeira improved greatly in the late 1990s and early 2000s. Inexpensive wines which used to smell cooked and taste coarse and stewed are now much fresher and cleaner, even if they are not as fine and incisive as cask-aged examples. Finer wines are distinguished by their high-toned RANCIO aromas and searing ACIDITY. Madeira varies in colour from pale gold to orange-amber to deep mahogany brown with a yellow-green tinge appearing on the rim of well-aged examples.

Standard blends Madeira's wines were traditionally named after the principal noble grape varieties grown on the island: Sercial, Verdelho, Bual (or Boal), and Malvasia (or MALMSEY), these names denoting increasingly sweet styles of madeira. But since phylloxera destroyed many of Madeira's best vineyards at the end of the 19th century, much of the island's wine has in reality been made from either AMERICAN HYBRIDS or the basic local *vinifera* variety Tinta Negra Mole. The use of

American hybrids has technically been illegal since 1979. From the beginning of 1993, Madeira has been made to conform to the EUROPEAN UNION requirement that a VARIETALLY named wine must contain at least 85 per cent of wine made from the specified grape variety. Insufficient quantities of the noble varieties resulted in renaming most standard blends simply 'Dry', 'Medium Dry', 'Medium Sweet', 'Medium Rich', and 'Rich' or 'Sweet'.

Sercial Among the noble grapes, Sercial is usually grown in the coolest vineyards, at heights of up to 800 m/2,640 ft or on the north side of the island. Many growers erroneously believe that the variety is related to Germany's RIESLING grape but it is in fact the same as the ESGANA CÃO (meaning dog strangler) which grows on the Portuguese mainland, the grapes exhibiting the same ferocious levels of ACIDITY. At high altitudes, Sercial ripens with difficulty to make a 10 per cent base wine which is dry, tart, and astringent when young. With fortification and ten or more years' ageing in cask, a good Sercial wine develops high-toned, almond-like aromas with a nervy character and a searing dry finish. The Sercial wines range in residual sugar from 0.5° to 1.5 °Baumé.

Verdelho Verdelho, which also tends to be planted on the cooler north side of the island, ripens more easily than Sercial and therefore lends itself to producing a medium dry wine with Baumé readings of between 1.5° and 2.5° after fortification. With age, the wines develop an extraordinary smoky complexity while retaining their characteristic tang of acidity.

Bual Bual, or Boal in Portuguese, is grown in warmer locations on the south side of Madeira. It ripens to achieve higher sugar levels than either Sercial or Verdelho and, after fortification to arrest the fermentation, Bual wines range from 2.5 to 3.5 °Baumé. These dark, medium rich, raisiny wines retain their acidic verve with age.

Malmsey The MALVASIA grapes which produce malmsey are usually grown in the warmest locations at low altitudes on the south coast, especially around Câmara de Lobos. Subvarieties include Malvasia Candida and Malvasia Babosa, which ripen to produce the very sweetest madeira wines, gaining richness and concentration with time in cask. Sugar readings in a malmsey range between 3.5 and 6.5 °Baumé, but the wines are rarely cloying as the sweetness is balanced by characteristically high levels of acidity. Like all high-quality madeira made from noble varieties, malmseys are some of the most resilient in the world and will keep in cask and bottle for a century or more.

Historic styles Madeira's unparalleled ability to age means that styles of wine long abandoned by the island's wine shippers may still be found, and enjoyed. Rainwater is a light,

medium dry style of madeira named after wine which was supposedly diluted by rain during shipment to the United States. Rainwater madeira is still made in small quantities, although the law is vague on what exactly constitutes the style. Two other styles of madeira based on the noble TERRANTEZ and BASTARDO grapes are rarely made since both varieties are almost extinct on the island, although Terrantez is making a modest comeback. Intensely sweet wines made from three types of Moscatel (MUSCAT) grape, usually produced for blending, are occasionally bottled on their own.

Qualities of madeira
A generally accepted hierarchy (from the youngest and most basic to the oldest and most distinguished) parallels the different styles of madeira as follows.

Bulk wine (*granel*) accounted for between 30 and 40 per cent of the island's production until shipments were suspended in 2002. Only denatured wines (usually spiced with salt and pepper for culinary use) may now be exported in bulk.

Three Year Old, sometimes designated 'Finest', blended wines, bottled after *estufagem* and ageing in tank, rarely in wood. All are based on the Tinta Negra Mole and Complexa grapes.

Five Year Old Reserve madeira is a blended five-year-old wine, some or all of which will have undergone *estufagem* in tank. A proportion of the blend is likely to have been aged in cask. Most are made from the Tinta Negra Mole and Complexa grapes but some are made from the noble varieties (see above). The use of the term 'Reserve' is complicated by the fact that one shipper, Pereira d'Oliveira, bottles *frasqueira* (vintage) wines as 'Reservas'.

Ten Year Old Special Reserve is a wine in which the youngest component in the blend will be around ten years old, having aged in cask, usually without recourse to *estufa* tanks. These wines are mostly made from the noble grape varieties and labelled accordingly.

Extra Reserve is a category which is rarely seen but the term is used to denote a blended, 15-year-old wine.

Solera wines were made using the SOLERA system more commonly associated with SHERRY. This blended style began in the 19th century but is now prohibited for madeira by EU law. Some old bottlings of solera wine can still be found.

Colheita or '*Harvest*' wines are from a single year, or harvest, bottled after spending at least five years in ageing in cask. These are effectively early bottled *frasqueira* or 'vintage' wines which share the individuality if not the concentration or the complexity of a wine aged for a minimum of twenty years (see below).

Frasqueira is the official term which denotes 'vintage' madeira: wine from a single year which, unlike vintage PORT, must age in cask for a minimum of 20 years. Many wines spend considerably more time in wood than the legal minimum and are sometimes aged in 20-l/ 5-gal glass carboys, or *garrafoes*, before bottling. The wines are extremely resistant to OXIDATION and may be kept in bottle for many years. Vintage madeira, especially Sercial, is capable of many decades' BOTTLE AGEING. Shippers carrying stocks of old vintages are so confident of madeira's ability to withstand oxidation that they keep the bottles standing upright so that there is no risk of a poor or tainted cork spoiling the wine.

Serving madeira

Madeira is probably the most robust wine in the world. Little can harm the wine after it has gone through the *estufa*, or been aged for twenty or more years in cask. Most shippers storing bottles upright RECORK their most venerable vintages, say, once every 20 years. All wines tend to throw a deposit with age, but madeira throws less than most. Decanting is therefore recommended for older, vintage wines but is not always necessary. Such wines should be left to breathe for a short time before serving simply to allow any BOTTLE SICKNESS to dissipate. Drier Sercial and Verdelho styles benefit from being served 'cellar cool' rather than iced. Sweeter Buals and Malmseys should be served at room temperature. Once opened, a bottle of madeira has the advantage of lasting for many months.   R.J.M.

Cossart, N., *Madeira: The Island Vineyard* (London, 1984).

Huetz de Lemps, A., *Le Vin de Madère* (Grenoble, 1989).

Liddell, A., *Madeira* (London, 1998).

Mayson, R., *The Wines and Vineyards of Portugal* (London, 2003).

Madeleine Angevine, early-ripening

vine variety used for TABLE GRAPES in KYRGYZSTAN. This crossing of Précoce de Malingre and MADELEINE ROYALE was made by Vibert in Angers in 1859 and is now seldom grown but it was used as parent or grandparent in breeding such GERMAN CROSSINGS as Siegerrebe, Reichensteiner, Forta, and Noblessa. Confusingly, it is also the official name in the UK for a crossing more correctly known as **Madeleine × Angevine 7672**, a freely pollinated seedling of Madeleine Angevine which was first sent to the UK from Alzey research institute in Germany in 1957. In 2004, it accounted for 6 per cent of the UK vineyard area.

Madeleine Royale, TABLE GRAPE variety

grown from a Chasselas seedling by Moreau-Robert in Angers in 1845.

maderization, occasionally madeirization,

is the process by which a wine is made to taste like MADEIRA, involving mild OXIDATION over a long period and, usually, heat. Such a wine is said to be **maderized**. Although this tasting term is occasionally applied pejoratively to mean that a wine is OXIDIZED, it should properly be applied only to wines with a high enough ALCOHOLIC STRENGTH to inhibit the action of ACETOBACTER, which would otherwise transform the wine into VINEGAR. Very few maderized wines are made today by simply ageing the wine at cellar temperature (although this was once a technique practised for making fuller sherry styles outside Jerez); the oxidation process is instead hastened by heating or 'baking' the wine as on the island of Madeira. Oxidation reactions, like most organic chemical reactions, can be roughly doubled in speed by a temperature rise of 10 °C/18 °F. For example, a wine requiring ten years at a cellar temperature of 20 °C to develop a maderized character could manifest approximately, although not exactly, the same character after about two and a half years at 40 °C or 15 months at 50 °C. Maderized wines are normally amber to brown in colour and have a distinctive cooked or mildly caramelized flavour. Wines processed at excessively high temperatures may taste burnt and harsh. Most such wines and especially those made from AMERICAN VINES or AMERICAN HYBRIDS are fortified and sweetened before being marketed. Madeira and similar wines such as early sherry-style wines made in California were particularly popular in the 18th and early 19th centuries but have since fallen out of FASHION. See also RANCIO wines.   A.D.W.

made wine, somewhat inelegant name for

wine made not from freshly picked grapes but from reconstituted GRAPE CONCENTRATE. The advantages for producers are that it can be made throughout the year, and that grapes can be sourced wherever they happen to be cheapest. CYPRUS has been an important source, as has Spain more recently. BRITISH WINE is one of the most commercially successful made wines, but made wines have also been produced in notable quantity in JAPAN and eastern Europe. The produce of many HOME-WINEMAKERS is made wine.

Madiran, dynamic red wine appellation in

SOUTH WEST FRANCE which has remodelled its concentrated, traditionally tannic wines, GASCONY's signature red.

There are said to have been vineyards here in Gallo-Roman times, and certainly the wines of Madiran were appreciated in the Middle Ages by pilgrims en route for Santiago de Compostela. About 1,400 ha/3,460 acres in the south of the ARMAGNAC region produce Madiran. Soils are mainly clay and limestone with so-called *grebb*, or *grip*, granules and pebbles strengthened with iron and manganese oxide from Pyrenean glacial alluvial deposits. The climate in Madiran is softened, and often moistened, by the Atlantic to the west, but autumn is usually dry.

The traditional grape variety is TANNAT, its very name hinting at the naturally astringent character of its high TANNIN level. The AC regulations stipulate that vineyard proportions should be 40 to 80 per cent of Tannat with Cabernet Sauvignon, Cabernet Franc, and Pinenc (FER) but many top cuvées depend heavily on Tannat. The wine traditionally needed long BOTTLE AGEING but some of Madiran's most dynamic winemakers have been experimenting with ways of softening the impact of Tannat (DESTEMMING is mandatory), including hand-picking only the ripest grapes, gentle handling, new oak, and MICRO-OXYGENATION to produce wines which have density, potential for ageing, but considerable charm in youth. Madiran can taste like a classed growth claret given the sort of Gascon twist needed to cope with *magret de canard*. The leader of the appellation has been Alain Brumont, who produces both Montus and Bouscassé. Other reliable producers include Ch d'Aydie, Domaine Berthoumieu, Domaine Capmartin, Ch Laffitte-Teston, and Patrick Ducournau, who pioneered micro-oxygenation.

From the same area comes white PACHERENC DU VIC-BILH.

Madrid, Vinos de. The Spanish capital

Madrid is much less well known as the name of a wine denomination. The DO Vinos de Madrid forms a semicircle around the southern suburbs. Of the three officially recognized subzones, the most important is round the town of Arganda del Rey to the east of Madrid. White wines are made from the Malvar and AIRÉN. Reds are produced from Tinto Fino (TEMPRANILLO), also known (in east central Spain, but not in Madrid) as Tinta Madrid, Garnacha (GRENACHE) and, increasingly, Cabernet Sauvignon, Syrah, and Merlot. A handful of prdoucers have risen above mediocrity, but their wines rarely stray further than city bars and cafés.   R.J.M. & V. de la S.

Magarach, wine research institute at Yalta

in the CRIMEA, founded in 1828, more than 50 years before DAVIS or the Institute of Oenology at the University of BORDEAUX. Although its activities have been unusually wide ranging (including some innovative by-product recycling), the Institute Magarach has been particularly distinguished in developing CROSSINGS and special vinification techniques.

Its three experimental vineyards cover nearly 2,000 ha/5,000 acres and include a collection of vines with more than 3,000 varieties. Some of the most successful of 30 vine varieties designed to combine quantity with quality are **Magarach Ruby** or Roubinovyi Magaracha (CABERNET SAUVIGNON × SAPERAVI), **Magarach Bastardo** or Bastardo Magarachski (BASTARDO

× Saperavi), and Ranni Magaracha. A newer generation of DISEASE-RESISTANT VARIETIES has since been developed with specific resistances to various pests and diseases.

At one time much of Magarach's effort was directed towards producing convincing copies of various classic wine styles (Magarach Malmsey, for example). The institute's own cellar harbours nearly 20,000 sample bottles, some of them containing wine from the mid 19th century.

Specific research avenues tend to have a particularly practical aspect, involving hundreds of patents.

Magliocco Canino, dark-berried vine variety of CALABRIA in southern Italy where a few hundred hectares are planted. Librandi have been making efforts to revive it as a varietal but it is also often blended with GAGLIOPPO.

magnesium, mineral element essential for healthy vine growth. It is an essential element in the chlorophyll molecule, and so CHLOROSIS is a common symptom of magnesium deficiency. The most conspicuous symptom is coloration between the main veins of the leaf, which becomes particularly noticeable around VERAISON. This zone is yellow for white varieties, and red for dark fruit varieties. This deficiency can be severe in some situations, reducing YIELDS, and slowing fruit RIPENING. Magnesium deficiency may be associated with BUNCHSTEM NECROSIS, in which the bunch stems and berries shrivel before ripening. Maturity is affected and wine quality suffers.

Soils high in POTASSIUM encourage magnesium deficiency. Similarly, some ROOTSTOCKS such as SO 4 and Fercal are incapable of taking up sufficient magnesium and tend to show deficiency symptoms. Magnesium deficiency is overcome by applying fertilizers to the soil or by spraying leaves.   R.E.S.

Champagnol, F., *Éléments de physiologie de la vigne et de viticulture générale* (St-Gely-du-Fesc, 1984).

magnum, large BOTTLE SIZE containing 1.5 l/ 54 fl oz, or the equivalent of two bottles. It is widely regarded as being the ideal size for BOTTLE AGEING fine wine, being large enough to slow the AGEING process, but not so big as to be unwieldy, or unthinkably expensive (unlike some other LARGE FORMATS).

Mago, influential classical writer on agricultural, including viticultural, matters. See CARTHAGE for more details.

maître de chai, term often used in France, particularly in Bordeaux, for the cellarmaster, as opposed to the RÉGISSEUR, who might manage the whole estate, or certainly the vineyards. It means literally 'master of the CHAI'. As SCIENCE and ACADEME invade wine-making, the wine-making decisions are increasingly made by an OENOLOGIST.

Majarcă Albă, Romanian white grape, possibly originating in the former Yugoslavia where it is known as Slankamenka.

Majorca, known as **Mallorca** in Spanish and Catalan, Spanish Balearic island in the north west Mediterranean which was once the seat of the kings of ARAGÓN. In the 19th century, the island was famous for its sweet MALVASÍA wines, which all but disappeared when the vineyards fell victim to PHYLLOXERA. Of the 2,500 ha/6,175 acres of vines currently in production on the island, 400 belong to the BINISSALEM, Spain's first offshore DO wine region on the island's central plateau, with good, original reds from the local MANTO NEGRO grape. A second DO in the south eastern part of the island, Pla i Llevant, was added in the late 1990s. See also the CALLET grape.

Mala Dinka, occasional Bulgarian name for GEWÜRZTRAMINER.

Málaga, city and Mediterranean port in ANDALUCÍA, southern Spain (see map under SPAIN), which lends its name to a denominated wine zone producing rich, raisiny FORTIFIED wines. Since the 1960s, Málaga has become more famous as the tourist gateway to the Costa del Sol, but its wine industry has a long and distinguished history dating back to around 600 BC, when the Greeks first planted vines in the area. The Moors continued to make wine, calling it *xarab al Malaqui*, or Málaga syrup, probably to remove any reference to alcohol but also evoking the extraordinary sweetness of the grapes growing in the hills above the city. In the 17th and 18th centuries, Málaga, often spelt **Malaga,** was exported worldwide and by the mid 19th century there were over 100,000 ha/247,000 acres of vineyard, making Málaga Spain's second largest wine region. Exports of Mountain, as the wine became known in Great Britain and North America, totalled between 30,000 and 40,000 BUTTS (as much as 220,000 hl/5.8 million gal) a year.

In the mid 19th century, Málaga was dealt a double blow, first by POWDERY MILDEW, then, in 1876, by the arrival of PHYLLOXERA. Málaga was the first wine region in Spain to be affected by the louse and its effect on the local economy was devastating. The terraced vineyards, then covered with Muscat grapes, to the north and east of the city were abandoned and many families emigrated to South America. Málaga never really recovered until the 1960s, when tourism became Málaga's major industry. From a peak immediately prior to the arrival of phylloxera of 113,000 ha/279,000 acres, the region's vineyard area was only 1,200 ha in the early 21st century, making Málaga one of Spain's smallest DOs. Where there were once over 100 BODEGAS near the port in the centre of the city, the number of producers had risen from two in the late 1990s to 14 by 2003.

Málaga's vineyards are still split into four zones, the most important of which is the Antequera plateau 50 km/30 miles north of the city of Málaga itself. The principal grape variety nowadays is PEDRO XIMÉNEZ, which gives high sugar levels in the hot, dry climate (although considerable amounts of the more productive AIRÉN vine were also planted in the 1980s). In the cooler mountain zone immediately north of the city, Moscatel de Alejandría (MUSCAT OF ALEXANDRIA) is the dominant vine, and is grown mainly for the production of RAISINS in the two coastal zones to the east and west of Málaga. In order to compensate for the lack of grapes in the region, Pedro Ximénez may also be imported from MONTILLA-MORILES, which abuts Málaga to the north, although according to regulations it may not exceed 10 per cent of the volume.

Traditionally, Malága was a DRIED GRAPE WINE made by leaving the grapes in the sun on grass mats for between seven and 20 days to concentrate the natural sugars. Today the wines are made using a number of different methods. The sweetness is normally obtained by arresting the fermentation with grape spirit (as for MISTELA), although some grapes are still dried and can be fermented to 18 per cent alcohol leaving considerable RESIDUAL SUGAR. A third way of adjusting the sweetness is with *arrope*, unfermented grape must that has been boiled down to 30 per cent of its normal volume. This may be added either before or after fermentation.

Wherever the grapes are grown, Málaga wines must be aged in the city of Málaga itself to qualify for the DO (although see SIERRAS DE MÁLAGA). The wines mature in different sizes of oak COOPERAGE arranged into SOLERAS. The Consejo Regulador recognizes 16 different types of wine ranging from sweet to dry with an ALCOHOLIC STRENGTH between 15 and 23 per cent. Most wines are deep brown, intensely sweet, and raisiny, some tasting slightly burnt through the addition of too much *arrope*. Dry wines are paler with a rather undistinguished nutty character. The most common styles are as follows:

Lágrima: intensely sweet wine made from FREE-RUN juice without any mechanical pressing.
Moscatel: sweet, aromatic wine made exclusively from Moscatel de Alejandría grapes.
Pedro Ximénez (occasionally labelled Pedro Ximen): sweet wine made exclusively from Pedro Ximénez grapes.
Solera: sweet wine from a dated solera.

R.J.M. & V. de la S.

Peñín, J., *Guía Peñín* (Madrid, annually).
Radford, J., *The New Spain* (2nd edn, London, 2004).

Malaga Blanc, dominant grape variety in THAILAND, where it is used mainly as a TABLE GRAPE but also produces relatively soft white wine. Originally from the south of France, where it is named Panse de Provence, it is believed that this grape was introduced to

Thailand in 1685 by the first Embassy of the King Louis XIV of France to King Narai the Great of Siam. The grapes' thick skins make them usefully resistant to heavy rain.

Malagousia or sometimes **Malagoussia**, elegant white grape variety rediscovered and identified only recently in modern GREECE. It may be related to Malvasia and yields similarly full-bodied, perfumed wines.

Malbec, black grape variety once popular in Bordeaux, still the backbone of CAHORS, but given a new lease of life by its obvious success in ARGENTINA. It has many synonyms, of which Galet cites as the true name Côt, or Cot as it is known in much of western France, including the Loire, where it was once quite widely grown. In Argentina, it was often called Malbeck (until Argentina joined the rest of the wine world), in the Libournais Pressac, and in Cahors, suggesting origins in northern Burgundy, Auxerrois. Galet's complete list of synonyms runs to several thousand words, however, for the variety has at one time been grown in 30 different *départements* of France.

Malbec has been declining in popularity in France—and by 2000 was planted on a total of only 6,100 ha/15,000 acres of French vineyard—for it has many of the disadvantages of Merlot (sensitivity to COULURE, frost, DOWNY MILDEW, and rot) without as much obvious fruit quality. Indeed it can taste like a rather rustic, even shorter-lived version of Merlot, although when grown on the least fertile, high, rugged, limestone vineyards of Cahors it can occasionally remind us why the English used to refer to Cahors as 'the black wine'. Cahors APPELLATION CONTRÔLÉE regulations stipulate that 'Cot' must constitute at least 70 per cent of the wine. Other appellations of SOUTH WEST FRANCE in which Malbec may play a (smaller) part are Bergerac, Buzet, Côtes de Duras, Fronton, Côtes du Marmandais, Pécharmant, and Côtes du Brulhois. It is also theoretically allowed into the Midi threshold appellations of Cabardès and Côtes de la Malepère but is rarely found this far from Atlantic influence.

At one time, especially before the predations of the 1956 frosts, Malbec was quite popular in Bordeaux and is still permitted by all major red bordeaux appellations, but total Bordeaux plantings fell from 4,900 ha/12,100 acres in 1968 to 1,400 ha by 2000 (very similar to the level in 1988). It persists most obviously in Bourg, Blaye, and the Entre-Deux-Mers region but is being systematically replaced with varieties whose wines are more durable.

Blended with Cabernet and Gamay, it is also theoretically allowed in a wide range of mid Loire appellations—Anjou, Coteaux du Loir, Touraines of various sorts, and even sparkling Saumur—but has largely been replaced by Cabernets Franc and Sauvignon.

It is in Argentina that Malbec really holds sway, planted on more than 20,000 ha/

50,000 acres of vineyard in most of Argentina's wine regions, making it the country's most important serious wine grape. Varietal Argentine Malbecs have some perceptibly Bordelais characteristics, of flavour rather than structure. The wines are generally much more ripe and lush than their French counterparts, although they are similarly capable of extended AGEING here. For more detail, see ARGENTINA.

The commercial success and clear appeal to modern wine drinkers of Argentine Malbec has spawned a new fashion for the variety elsewhere, not least in Chile, where varietal bottlings increased considerably in the early 21st century. Chile's version tends to be more tannic than Argentina's and may be blended with the other Bordeaux grapes which Chile grows in such profusion. Viu, Chile's Malbec specialist, and others blend it with Cabernet Sauvignon.

Australians have so far shown no great respect for their Malbec and had been uprooting it systematically until the early 1990s, although poor clonal material was probably partly to blame. Plantings totalled just over 500 ha in the mid 2000s and some Clare Valley producers have made fine wine from it. Californians had even less planted (although Malbec was quite significant before PROHIBITION) but 1,000 acres/250 ha of Malbec were planted between 1995 and 2003, raising total acreage by a factor of seven. Most but by no means all of today's California Malbec is added to MERITAGE style bordeaux blends.

A small amount of Malbec, Malbech, or Malbeck is also planted in north east Italy.

Goldin, C., *The Secrets of Argentine Malbec* (Buenos Aires, 2004).

Malepère, Côtes de la, shares many of the wine characteristics of CABARDÈS, another small wine region where the Midi and Aquitaine meet near Carcassonne in the south west of France. The wines, mainly red, are made up of a blend of Bordeaux and Languedoc varieties but in the case of Malepère, with its wetter, more Atlantic climate, it is the Bordeaux varieties that predominate. The main varieties listed in the regulations are Merlot, Cot (Malbec), and Cabernet Franc. Secondary varieties, all of these tested and developed at the region's important viticultural research station at Alaigne, include Cabernet Sauvignon, Grenache, Lladoner Pelut, and Cinsaut (in the east of the region). In contrast to Cabardès, Carignan is not allowed. The region, awarded VDQS status relatively late, in 1983, has been working actively towards full APPELLATION CONTRÔLÉE recognition just like Cabardès to the north, although it belongs climatically even more definitively to south west France than to the LANGUEDOC, from which it is geographically protected by the Hautes Corbières peaks. The vineyards, mainly clay and limestone, are immediately north of those responsible for Blanquette de LIMOUX.

Wine production is dominated by several large CO-OPERATIVES, of which the determinedly *océanique* Cave du Razès is responsible for almost two-thirds of the region's entire production.

Mali Plavac. See PLAVAC MALI.

malic acid, one of the two principal organic acids of grapes and wines (see also TARTARIC ACID). Its name comes from *malum*, Latin for apple, the fruit in which it was first identified by early scientists. Present in nearly all fruits and berries, malic acid is now known to be one of the compounds involved in the complicated cycles of reactions by which plants and animals obtain the energy necessary for life. One of these cycles of reactions is known as the citric acid, Krebs, or tricarboxylic acid cycle and its elucidation was one of the outstanding triumphs of biochemistry.

Another, which comes into play during the final stages of RIPENING in many fruits, including grapes, causes the decomposition of malic acid. When all of the malic acid has been used up in this latter series of reactions, the fruit becomes overripe, or senescent. The malic acid decomposing reaction is much more rapid in hot summer temperatures, probably because of the more rapid RESPIRATION of malate in the berry. This is, at least in part, one reason for the lower total acid concentrations in grapes grown in warmer regions. It accumulates in young grape berries reaching high levels at about VERAISON—sometimes as high as 20 g/l—but, as ripening progresses, the level of malate declines to concentrations of between 1 and 9 g/l when the grapes are ripe. This large range in ripe grapes is an important source of variation in quality and style.

Tartaric acid, the other main grape acid, does not participate in several of the reaction pathways in which malic acid is an essential component, which is why the hotter the summer, the lower the likely proportion of malic acid in the grapes. Malic acid's different chemical structure allows it to participate in many more of the enzymatic reactions involved in living systems than tartaric acid because it can be pumped across plant membranes serving as a transportable energy source. Because the concentrations of tartaric acid are relatively and desirably stable, attention is given to the tartrate/malate (T/M) ratio, which varies from about 1 to 6 and is characteristic for each grape variety. High malate varieties, with a low ratio, are desirable for hot districts and examples are SYLVANER, COLOMBARD, BARBERA, and CARIGNAN.

Malic acid is lost not just through the citric acid cycle, and through other reaction cycles during grape ripening, but also in many cases as a result of MALOLACTIC FERMENTATION of wines either during or after alcoholic FERMENTATION. Just as high temperatures favour the loss of malic acid in grapes, they encourage the lactic organisms responsible for malolactic fermentation. The winemaker can exercise some control over this loss of malic acid if necessary, however, since the growth and activity of these organisms can be slowed or inhibited by moderate concentrations of SULFUR DIOXIDE. In addition, since the LACTIC ACID BACTERIA responsible for malolactic fermentation require many micro-nutrients (vitamins, growth factors, nitrogenous compounds), early and thorough separation of the new wine from its LEES can inhibit bacterial activity and preserve malic acid.

Malic acid is available commercially for use in acidifying foods and beverages and in numerous industrial processes. At one time it was isolated from fruits and other plant tissues but is more usually synthesized from another organic acid today.   A.D.W. & B.G.C.

Malmesbury, ward in the Swartland region of SOUTH AFRICA making some good quality wines.

malmsey, English corruption of the word MALVASIA, derived from the port of Monemvasia which was important in Ancient GREECE. The word was first used for (probably a wide range of) the unusually sweet, rich wines of Greece and the islands of the eastern Mediterranean, particularly Crete, then called Candia (see GREECE, medieval history). Sweet white wines were prized in the Middle Ages, particularly but not exclusively by northern Europeans, who regarded their own wines as thin, and admired the longevity of these liquids, very possibly DRIED GRAPE WINES, so sturdily high in sugar and alcohol. The acute merchants of GENOA, NAPLES, and VENICE were able profitably to capitalize on this stability in their trading links between east and west.

As European temperatures fell as a result of CLIMATE CHANGE, these richer wines held even more allure. Venetians in particular created a demand for malmsey in 15th-century England. George, duke of Clarence and younger brother of England's King Edward IV, was popularly believed to have been drowned in a BUTT of malmsey in the Tower of London in 1478.

Malvasia vines came to be planted all round the western Mediterranean (even today, Malvasia and MALVOISIE are two of the most commonly used synonyms for various, often quite unrelated, VINE VARIETIES). Malmsey, which originally denoted any strong, sweet wine, was eventually used specifically for the sweetest style of MADEIRA, particularly that made from Malvasia grapes.

malolactic fermentation, occasionally abbreviated to **MLF** or, in French, 'la **malo**', conversion of stronger MALIC ACID naturally present in new wine into LACTIC ACID (which has lower ACIDITY) and CARBON DIOXIDE. It should more accurately be called malolactic conversion as it is not literally a fermentation process, though the release of carbon dioxide may initially give that impression. It is accomplished by LACTIC ACID BACTERIA, which are naturally present in most established wineries but may have to be cultured and carefully introduced in newer establishments where malolactic fermentation is desired. This process is unrelated to and almost never precedes the main, alcoholic FERMENTATION, for which reason it is sometimes called a secondary fermentation. Nevertheless, it is not uncommon for malolactic fermentation to be complete by the end of the alcoholic fermentation.

It is written chemically thus:

$$COOH\text{-}CHOH\text{-}CH_2\text{-}COOH \rightarrow COOH\text{-}CHOH\text{-}CH_3 + CO_2$$

malic acid→lactic acid + carbon dioxide

Malolactic fermentation is desirable in wines which have excessive ACIDITY, particularly red wines produced in cooler climates. It can also add flavour and complexity to both red and white wines, as well as rendering the wine impervious to the danger of malolactic fermentation in bottle. Recognition and mastery of malolactic fermentation (which would traditionally happen as if by accident when temperatures rose in the spring) was one of the key developments in winemaking in France and elsewhere in the mid 20th century. By the early 1990s, most fine red wines, many sparkling wines, and a small but increasing proportion of the world's white wine involved full or partial malolactic fermentation. In hotter climates or warmer years in cooler areas, some winemakers deliberately suppress malolactic fermentation in some or all batches of a wine in order to maintain the wine's acidity. Some grape varieties seem to have a greater affinity with malolactic fermentation than others. Among white grapes, Chardonnay is a generally successful candidate for the process, while most producers of Riesling and Chenin Blanc deliberately avoid it, despite the high natural acidity in these latter two. Malolactic fermentation may reduce the acidity of a particularly ripe wine unduly, and care must be taken that the amount of the buttery-smelling DIACETYL produced by the process is not unpleasantly excessive, as it has tended to be in early experiments with malolactic fermentation in some white wines. Malolactic fermentation's effect on decreasing TOTAL ACIDITY is often most marked on those wines which were highest in malic acid before it took place, that is the products of particularly cool growing seasons. In some cases, the winemaker may even have to ACIDIFY after malolactic fermentation.

Like most BACTERIA, lactic acid bacteria grow best in very weakly acidic solutions and at temperatures near those of the human body (which is why malolactic fermentations traditionally took place without encouragement as temperatures rose in the spring, especially if cellar doors were opened). Malolactic fermentation is therefore strongly influenced by the wine's PH: if it is less than 3.1, it is practically impossible, if more than 4.5, considerably retarded. Lactic acid bacteria are 'fastidious' in that they require a wide range of micro-nutrients. They are also intolerant of even moderate concentrations of SULFUR DIOXIDE and high concentrations of ETHANOL. Malolactic fermentation can therefore be encouraged by adding lactic acid bacteria to the MUST soon after alcoholic fermentation has started. At this point conditions are ideal for the lactic acid bacteria—the solution is warm, its alcohol content is low, the sulfur dioxide added before fermentation has already been volatilized, and the dying yeast cells, or LEES, provide the necessary micro-nutrients. Alternatively, immediately after alcoholic fermentation has been completed, the new wine can be transferred to an old wooden vat in which successful malolactic fermentations have already been completed and in which there will almost always be a sufficient population of lactic acid bacteria. However, it is very important to know what was in the barrels before so that no form of spoilage is encouraged. Or it can be transferred to an inert tank or vat, or to small barrels (an increasingly common practice for wines that are judged in their youth such as fine red bordeaux), and inoculated with a commercially available culture of lactic acid bacteria. In general, old wooden COOPERAGE will carry a heavy enough population of bacteria so that no inoculation is needed. The winemaker must be careful to discard cooperage harbouring any undesirable bacteria, but save those casks with a good record for malolactic fermentation. A malolactic fermentation which occurs during alcoholic fermentation is particularly efficient since it advances the winemaking schedule and because it is easier to start when the alcohol level is lower than after full alcoholic fermentation has been completed. See also OAK CHIPS.

Malolactic fermentation may well be regarded as undesirable in wines to be bottled and sold young, most white wines, mass-market bottlings of any hue, for example, together with light reds such as Beaujolais and Dolcetto. In this case, care is taken to avoid any contact with vats infected with lactic acid bacteria and to rack the new wine off the lees and their micro-nutrients quickly. Sulfur dioxide additions and cool cellar temperatures can also stun any lactic acid bacteria into inactivity. Such techniques as sterile FILTRATION, STERILE BOTTLING, and PASTEURIZATION can insure against the commercial embarrassment of malolactic fermentation's taking place in bottle. If a bottled still wine starts to fizz, this is the most likely cause and is most commonly encouraged by the combination of heat and residual lactic acid bacteria. See FAULTS IN WINE for more.   A.D.W.

Henick-Kling, T., 'Malolactic fermentation', in G. H. Fleet (ed.), *Wine Microbiology and Biotechnology* (Amsterdam, 1993), 289–326.

Lonvaud-Funel, A., 'Understanding wine lactic acid bacteria. Progress and prospects in controlling wine quality', paper presented at the ASEV 50th anniversary annual meeting, Seattle (Washington, 2000).

Malta, the central Mediterranean island, has a small wine industry that can trace its history back to Phoenician times, but it was the arrival of the Knights of St John in 1530 that laid the foundations of today's wine industry. Viticulture in Malta flourished until the arrival of the British in 1800, when many vineyards (and olive groves) were uprooted in favour of cotton. By the end of the 19th century, when demand for Maltese cotton had diminished, a replanting programme of sorts was started and in spite of the outbreak of PHYLLOXERA in 1919, viticulture flourished once again. By the 1950s 1,000 ha/2,470 acres were under vine.

The majority of vines planted were TABLE GRAPE varieties which produced wines so low in sugar and acid that considerable adjustments were needed in wineries rarely equipped for high-quality wine production. The most popular were Gellewza, which makes soft, fleshy reds and aromatic, fruity dry rosés, while Gennarua and the superior Ghirghentina (which may be related to Sicilia's INZOLIA) make weighty white wines. Most of these indigenous vines are grown as BUSH VINES without IRRIGATION and harvested at the end of August. By the mid 1980s, area under vine was just 320 hectares.

Some 1950s experiments with Muscat and Trebbiano were relatively successful but it was not until the 1970s that another serious attempt was made with wine grape varieties, this time Cabernet Sauvignon planted by Marsovin at Wardija in the north of the island. During the 1990s, many new vineyards were planted and with the help of drip irrigation and French and Italian expertise, various other VINIFERA varieties were planted.

Grapes and musts have long been imported in quantity from Italy to satisfy local and tourist demand. Only when Malta joined the EU in 2004 were labels required to distinguish between wines made from domestic and imported grapes. The EU is also funding 1,000 ha of new vineyards which should eventually make the island self-sufficient. A quality control system along Italian lines was also planned. Of dozens of different varieties so far planted on the island, Syrah and Cabernet Sauvignon so far show most promise.

Land holdings vary from 0.1 to 20 ha. Most small farmers sell their grapes under contract to either Deicata, Marsovin, or the much newer, French-inspired Camilleri, the island's three main wineries. Meridiana is another important winery part owned by ANTINORI dating from the late 1980s. INTERNATIONAL VARIETIES

are grown mainly at Ta'Qali in the centre of Malta. A number of ambitious projects are in the pipeline, including Montekristo which plans to reclaim old quarries and turn them into vineyards, with native varieties a speciality. Ta Betta has a high altitude site in Siggiewi in the south of the island.

Vineyards typically have relatively shallow, poor, loamy topsoil on sand, limestone and clay with richer and more fertile clayey soils in the north. Some alluvial soils can be found in the valleys. The climate is Mediterranean with hot, dry summers and cool, rainy winters. The average mean temperatures vary from 12.8 °C in January to 25.6 °C in July. Average rainfall is 575mm but is so concentrated in the winter months that irrigation is generally needed, although some vintages benefit from summer rainfall. M.T.

Malvar, white grape commonly grown around MADRID producing slightly rustic wines but with more body and personality than the ubiquitous AIRÉN. Plantings totalled about 2,500 ha/6,200 acres in the mid 1990s.

Malvasia, name used widely, especially in Iberia and Italy, for a complex web of grape varieties, typically ancient and of Greek origin and producing characterful wines high in alcohol and, often, RESIDUAL SUGAR. Most are deeply coloured whites but some are, usually light, reds. Malvasia is widely disseminated, even if it is not grown in enormous quantity anywhere nowadays.

Malvasia is the Italian corruption of Monemvasia, the southern Greek port which, in the Middle Ages, was a busy and natural entrepôt for the rich and highly prized dessert wines of the eastern Mediterranean, notably those of Crete, or Candia (see GREECE, history). Most Malvasia, which, like the somewhat similar MUSCAT, exists in many guises and hues, is more or less related to Malvasia Bianca, with the exception of **Malvasia di Candia**, which is a distinctly different variety. So important was Malvasia during the time of the Venetian republic that wine shops in VENICE were called *malvasie*.

The French corruption of Malvasia has been used particularly loosely; for more details, see MALVOISIE. The word was also corrupted into MALMSEY in English, which was for long an important style of MADEIRA, traditionally based on the Malvasia grape. The Germans call their various though rare forms of Malvasia **Malvasier**.

Malvasia, in its various forms—white and red, dry and sweet—has in its time been one of Italy's most widely planted grapes, with a total of close to 50,000 ha/123,500 acres being cultivated in the early 1990s in regions as distant and disparate as Basilicata and Piemonte. A 2000 survey found only 8,800 ha of **Malvasia Bianca di Candida** throughout Italy however, frequently grown in combination with various

types of Trebbiano, forming what might be called the standard central Italian white blend. This type of wine lost considerable ground in Toscana, and then Umbria, from the 1970s, as producers replaced both Malvasia and Trebbiano with INTERNATIONAL VARIETIES. Varietal Malvasia wines are rare in central Italy, but pioneering efforts began to appear in the CASTELLI ROMANI zone in the early 1990s.

The finest dry white VARIETAL Malvasia is made in Friuli, where two DOCs—COLLIO and ISONZO—cultivate what is called locally **Malvasia Istriana** and which, according to local tradition, was carried to these vineyards from Greece by the fleets of VENICE. About 53,000 hl/1.4 million gal a year are also made as a DOC wine in the Colli Piacentini, where a slight sparkle is quite common. Lightly sparkling dry to demi-sec Malvasia is frequently encountered in Emilia, where it is referred to as *champagnino* or 'little champagne', and where local trenchermen consider it the perfect accompaniment and *digestif* for the rich local fare.

Sweet white Malvasia, normally a PASSITO and once considered one of Italy's finest dessert wines, underwent a major loss of consumer favour and an even more significant contraction in acreage after the Second World War, so that its very existence seemed threatened. Lazio's **Malvasia di Grottaferrata** and Sardegna's **Malvasia di Bosa** and **Malvasia di Planurgia** have become almost extinct, although an occasional bottle can still be found in the production zones themselves. **Malvasia delle Lipari**, which seemed destined to share their fate, was revived in the 1980s by artist Carlo Hauner, and the survival of this distinctive sweet orange relic from the volcanic Aeolian Islands, sometimes called the Lipari Islands, off the north east tip of SICILIA seems assured, at least in the short run, although current quantities are a mere fraction of the more than 100,000 hl/2.6 million gal produced annually before the arrival of PHYLLOXERA. BASILICATA has its own version of sweet Malvasia, produced in the same zone as Aglianico del Vulture, and local producers, buoyed by the new interest in their red wine, are attempting to capture the market's favour with their Malvasia, which also exists in dry and spumante versions.

Red Malvasia, also known as **Malvasia Nera**, is most commonly used in conjunction with other grapes: as the minority partner of Negroamaro in the standard red blend of the provinces of Lecce and Brindisi in PUGLIA, and as a useful supplement to Sangiovese in Toscana, where it adds both colour and perfume. The introduction of the even more aromatic and deeply coloured Cabernet Sauvignon to Sangiovese-based Tuscan blends in the 1970s and 1980s (see TOSCANA) has led to a distinct loss of favour for Malvasia Nera and uncertain long-term prospects.

Piemonte is the only significant producer of varietal Malvasia Nera wines, with two DOC zones: **Malvasia di Casorzo**, in both a dry and sweet version, and **Malvasia di Castelnuovo Don Bosco**. Total area planted is less than 100 ha/250 acres, however.

On the French island of CORSICA, most growers believe that their Malvoisie is identical to VERMENTINO, which may be related to the greater Malvasia family.

Malvasia is planted to a declining extent in northern Spain, notably in RIOJA and NAVARRA, although the less interesting Viura (MACABEO) has been gaining ground. Malvasia is also planted on the CANARY ISLANDS, where it makes distinctive sweet wines on La Palma and Lanzarote. Spain grew a total of 5,500 ha of Malvasia in 2004—about the same as both Verdejo and Albariño.

Myriad Malvasias are also grown in PORTUGAL, with official registers listing no fewer than 12 different Malvasias including Malvasia Fina, Malvasia Rei, Malvasia Candida, and **Malvasia Grossa.**

Malvasia Fina, also known as **Boal**, Arinto do Dão, Boal Cachudo in Ribatejo, Assario Branco in Dão, is grown in higher vineyards in the Douro and can be a crisp contribution to the blend for a white PORT. Portugal grew a total of about 7,500 ha of Malvasia Fina in 2004.

Malvasia Rei is a much less distinguished grape, PALOMINO, grown on about 5,900 ha of Portuguese vineyard in 2004 which tends to make rather flabby wines in the Douro, Beiras, and Estremadura, where more than half the vines were grown.

Malvasia Candida, a local corruption of Malvasia di Candia, is the variety which gave its name to MALMSEY and is slowly being replanted on the island.

Malvasia Corada is a Douro synonym for VITAL.

Malvasia da Trincheira is a Douro synonym for FOLGASÃO, or Terrantez.

In California, there are more than 1,800 acres/720 ha of Malvasia Bianca, the most substantial plantings being in Tulare county at the very southern end of the SAN JOAQUIN VALLEY. The potential for California Malvasia Bianca has been demonstrated in appetizing white table wines made by Randall Grahm of Bonny Doon.

The variety is grown to a very limited extent in modern Greece, mainly on the Aegean islands of Paros and Syros, but **Malvazia** is extensively planted in what was once Yugoslavia. See also CROATIA. D.T. & J.R.

Malvoisie is one of France's most confusing vine names, perhaps because, like PINEAU, the term was once used widely as a general term for superior wines, notably those whose origins were supposed to be Greek. There is no single variety whose principal name is Malvoisie, but it has been used as a synonym for a wide range of, usually white-berried, grape varieties producing full-bodied, aromatic whites. Despite the etymological similarity, Malvoisie has rarely been a synonym for the famous MALVASIA of Greece and Madeira. Malvoisie is today found on the labels of some Loire and Savoie wines made from such plantings of PINOT GRIS as remain, as Malvoisie du Valais is a common synonym for, usually sweet, Pinot Gris in Switzerland. It is also sometimes used for BOURBOULENC in the Languedoc, and occasionally for MACCABÉO in the Aude, for CLAIRETTE in Bordeaux, and for TORBATO in Roussillon. VERMENTINO, which may in fact belong to the Malvasia family, is sometimes called Malvoisie in Iberia and is known as Malvoisie de Corse in Corsica.

Malvoisie Rose and **Malvoisie Rouge** are occasionally used as synonyms for FRÜHROTER VELTLINER in Savoie and northern Italy, while the **Malvoisie Noire** of the Lot in south western France may be TROUSSEAU.

Galet, P., *Dictionnaire encyclopédique des cépages* (Paris, 2000).

Mammolo, heavily perfumed red grape variety producing wines which supposedly smell of violets, or *mammole*, in central Italy. This, a permitted ingredient in CHIANTI, is relatively rare today, although a small amount is also grown in the VINO NOBILE DI MONTEPULCIANO zone.

Mancha, La. Europe's largest single demarcated wine region in the heart of Spain (see map under SPAIN). By the mid 2000s, the vineyards of the DO La Mancha had reached a total of 192,000 ha/474,000 acres of arid table land from the satellite towns south of Madrid to the hills beyond VALDEPEÑAS nearly 200 km/125 miles to the south. Vineyards not registered for the DO brought the total area of La Mancha devoted to the vine to 400,000 ha/990,000 acres in the late 1990s. The Moors christened it Manxa, meaning 'parched earth', and that is an apt description of the growing conditions in southern Castile, CASTILLA-LA MANCHA. RAINFALL is unreliable, with annual totals averaging between 300 and 400 mm/16 in. Summers are hot with temperatures rising to over 40 °C/104 °F, while winters are bitterly cold with prolonged FROSTS.

The doughty AIRÉN vine seems to be well suited to these extreme conditions and is therefore popular among La Mancha's 18,000 smallholders. It was planted on a grand total of about 280,000 ha of La Mancha, and about 70 per cent of all land dedicated to the DO. It is planted at the remarkably low VINE DENSITY of between 1,200 and 1,600 vines per hectare (485–650 per acre) because of the very dry climate. FUNGAL DISEASES are almost unknown in La Mancha's dry growing season and cultivation is therefore relatively easy. YIELDS of between 20 and 25 hl/ha (1.4 tons/acre) seem puny by international standards, and, despite limited MECHANIZATION, production costs remain low. LABOUR costs were low in central Spain, but vineyard workers began to be recruited from Morocco in the early 1990s. The flat, brown, alcoholic white wines, poorly made without TEMPERATURE CONTROL in earthenware TINAJAS, commonplace even in the 1970s, have now completely vanished.

Technological development has given La Mancha a new lease of life and opened new and more discerning markets for the region's fresh, inexpensive, if rather neutral dry white wines. Red wines, made increasingly from Cencibel (TEMPRANILLO) grapes, have also improved enormously and a number of enterprising growers are experimenting with other grape varieties, including CABERNET SAUVIGNON and CHARDONNAY, now admitted and even encouraged by DO regulations. Of the 2 million hl/53 million gal produced annually, a large part is still distilled into industrial alcohol or sent to JEREZ to make brandy de Jerez.

R.J.M. & V. de la S.

Manchuela, one of Spain's newest wine regions, granted a DO in 2000, with vineyards totalling more than 70,000 ha/173,000 acres (although less than 5,000 ha of these were registered for DO wines in 2005) on the eastern border of CASTILLA-LA MANCHA, straddling Cuenca and Albacete provinces. This is the home of the Bobal grape, which is mainly used for rosés and unoaked young reds, with Tempranillo growing in importance for oak-aged reds. At least one private estate was making a name for itself by adapting Syrah to the local clay-limestone TERROIR and making blends with the best local varieties Monastrell, Garnacha, and Bobal. The white Macabeo also produces very drinkable fragrant whites in northern Albacete. Overall, this high plateau, which reaches an altitude of more than 1,000 m/3,280 ft in western Cuenca shows great potential but has lacked the investment required to develop it. V. de la S.

Mandelaria, sometimes **Mandelari**, powerful speciality of various Greek islands, including Crete, where it is often blended with the much softer KOTSIFALI. It is probably Greece's third most planted red wine variety. The grapes have thick skins and therefore the wine produced is deep coloured and notably high in TANNINS. It can produce harmonious dry reds such as Peza, or even sweet reds. Known as Amorghiano on Rhodes.

manganese, a soil nutrient essential for vine growth but in very low quantities. Manganese deficiency causes leaf yellowing, and is found most commonly on alkaline soils high in LIMESTONE. Acid soils (see SOIL ACIDITY) which are poorly drained and high in manganese can cause toxicity, reducing both vine growth and YIELD. R.E.S.

manipulation, a slightly pejorative term referring to a range of interventions made by winemakers. Wine is unusual among alcoholic drinks in that once the grapes have been picked and put into a container, it can more or less make itself. However, winemakers almost always intervene in a variety of ways in order to achieve particular quality or stylistic goals. These range from traditional techniques such as DESTEMMING, CRUSHING, SAIGNÉE, CHAPTALIZATION, BARREL FERMENTATION, LEES STIRRING, AGEING in barrel, RACKING, CLARIFICATION, and FILTRATION to more modern steps such as the use of ENZYMES, cold MACERATION, CRYOEXTRACTION, cultured YEASTS, REVERSE OSMOSIS, MICRO-OXYGENATION and OAK CHIPS—or, more likely, a combination of these methods. Many of these practices are controlled by regulations in most wine-producing countries. In general, those that have been practised for many years (such as chaptalization) are less controversial, even though they may be more interventionist and open to abuse than modern equivalents (such as REVERSE OSMOSIS). J.A.G. & J.Ha.

Goode, J., *Wine Science* (London, 2005).

mannoproteins are POLYSACCHARIDES released from YEAST cells during FERMENTATION and by AUTOLYSIS during LEES ageing. Their release is generally considered beneficial and is encouraged by slightly higher fermentation temperatures. Firstly, mannoproteins can interact with aroma compounds and thus potentially change the sensory properties of a wine. Secondly, they have the potential to protect white and rosé wine from protein haze. Thirdly, they can improve TARTRATE stability. Finally, it is thought that they can bind with TANNINS to reduce astringency and improve MOUTHFEEL. E.W. & J.Ha.

Lubbers, S., Voilley, A., Feuillat, M., and Charpentier, C., 'Influence of mannoproteins from yeast on the aroma intensity of a model wine', *Lebensmittel-Wissenschaft und -Technologie*, 27 (1994) 108–14.

Moine-Ledoux, V., Perrin, A., Paladin, I., and Dubourdieu, D., 'First results of tartaric stabilisation by adding mannoproteins (Mannostab™), *Journal International des Sciences de la Vigne et du Vin*, 31 (1997), 23–31.

Waters, E. J., Alexander, G., Muhlack, R., Pocock, K. F., Colby, C., O'Neill, B. N., Høj, P. B., and Jones, P. R., 'Preventing protein haze in bottled wine', *Australian Journal of Grape and Wine Research*, 11 (2005), 215–25.

Manseng, Basque vine variety responsible for the exceptional tangy rich white wines of JURANÇON in the western foothills of the French Pyrenees. See GROS MANSENG and PETIT MANSENG.

Manseng, usually Petit Manseng, can also be found in Uruguay, where it, like TANNAT, was taken by Basque settlers in the 19th century.

Manto Negro, most common grape on MALLORCA, producing scented but light reds which tend to age and even OXIDIZE early. It may be best blended with a more structured grape such as CALLET.

Mantonico Bianco, ancient light-berried vine, probably of Greek origin, grown on just over 1,100 ha/2,700 acres in CALABRIA. A **Mantonico Nero** is also known.

manzanilla, a specially refreshing style of SHERRY that is made quite naturally in the seaside sherry town of SANLÚCAR DE BARRAMEDA. Like FINO, it is a very pale, light, dry style of wine that is heavily influenced by FLOR yeast, but manzanilla is made in the particularly humid, maritime air of Sanlúcar, which tends to result in a thicker layer of flor, a slower maturation process, lower alcohol content, and slightly higher acidity—especially since grapes are often picked slightly less ripe than for *fino*. As the wine matures, and the flor dies, a manzanilla may develop into a **Manzanilla Olorosa** and then a **Manzanilla Pasada**, which is a Sanlúcar equivalent of a fino amontillado. Most manzanilla is now shipped at its natural strength of barely 15 per cent alcohol. For more details, see SHERRY.

Manzoni. See INCROCIO.

Maranges, the southernmost VILLAGE WINE appellation in the Côte de Beaune district of Burgundy, produces medium-bodied red wines of some charm when young. The vineyard stretches across the three villages of Cheilly, Dezize, and Sampigny, each of which takes Les Maranges as a suffix. Formerly the wines were sold either under the village name or, much more frequently, as Côte de Beaune-Villages. Since 1988, such wines may be called Maranges or **Maranges Côte de Beaune**. White wines are permitted but are scarcely made.

See also CÔTE D'OR, and map under BURGUNDY. J.T.C.M.

marc, the general French term both for grape POMACE and, more widely, for pomace brandy. It is used to distinguish the product from a *fine*, which may be made by distilling local wine. Most traditional wine regions make marc from the pomace, grape skins, and pips left after pressing. This was rarely for financial gain but often because peasant wine-growers hate to see anything they have grown go to waste.

Marche (**Marches** in English), the easternmost region in the central belt of Italy stretching from TOSCANA through UMBRIA to the Adriatic coast (see map under ITALY). It shares a variety of characteristics with these neighbours to the west: a TOPOGRAPHY shaped by land rising from the coastal plains to rolling hills and, westward, to the central spine of the Apennines; Mediterranean vegetation of cypress, umbrella pine, olive, and vine; and a TEMPERATE climate that, though it is marked by hot, dry summers, is not as uniform as its western neighbours. In the northern part of the region around Ancona, the climate is CONTINENTAL, while in the south near Ascoli Piceno it

is MEDITERRANEAN. This has an impact on the grape varieties that perform best in the north and south of the Marche. Viticultural characteristics are shared with Toscana and Umbria: CALCAREOUS soils from the sea which once covered an important part of central Italy; HILLSIDE VINEYARDS; and substantial plantings of SANGIOVESE and TREBBIANO vines, although Sangiovese does not perform as well here as it does in Toscana, perhaps because the climate is wetter or the CLONES inferior. The Marche has been the last of the three regions to realize its potential for good-quality wines, however, partly because the region is off Italy's main commercial axis of Milan–Bologna–Florence–Rome–Naples, and partly because of the lack of any urban centre more important than Ancona. The region experienced remarkable economic growth between 1960 and 1990, but was relatively impoverished before the Second World War, and the lack of a discerning local clientele has been an undoubted handicap in the improvement of wine quality. (Cesare MONDAVI, who laid the foundations of one of the most famous wine producers in the world, emigrated from this region in the early 20th century.)

Total current production of wine has averaged over 1.9 million hl/50 million gal per year in the 1990s, with about 17 per cent qualifying for one of 11 regional DOCS. VERDICCHIO in its two versions—from the Castelli di Jesi and from Matelica—dominates this DOC production with close to 200,000 hl produced in an average year. The better wines of these appellations are now demonstrating that Verdicchio is one of the few central Italian white varieties with character and personality, a fact which has been obscured by the large yields permitted by the DOCs (13–14 tons/ha) and high-trained vineyards planted with a mere 2,000 vines per ha (800 per acre). Bianchello del Metauro, and Bianco dei Colli Maceratesi are bland and anonymous white wines, the first from the local Bianchello grape variety, the latter based on Trebbiano.

The greatest potential in the region, however, is represented by the outstanding red variety MONTEPULCIANO, far superior to any of the local white varieties grown. Both of the major red DOCs, Rosso Conero and Rosso Piceno, are made with varying percentages of Montepulciano. The better the wine, the higher the amount of Montepulciano in the blend; the lighter the wine, the more the blend is dominated by Sangiovese. Rosso Conero, taking its name from Monte Conero, which towers over the city of Ancona to the south, is produced from Montepulciano along with a maximum 15 per cent of Sangiovese, while Rosso Piceno is produced from a minimum of 60 per cent Sangiovese and a maximum of 40 per cent Montepulciano in a large part of the region's hill country in the southern Marche. The better producers in Rosso Piceno have been increasing the proportion of

Montepulciano in their blends to such an extent that a change in the law is likely. A Rosso Piceno CLASSICO heartland does exist in the province of Ascoli Piceno, but does not constitute a real guarantee of superior quality and is virtually irrelevant in terms of labels on the market. Maximum permitted YIELDS, at close to 100 hl/ha (5.7 tons/acre) in both DOCs, are excessively generous; wine-making is frequently slipshod and haphazard, and it is far easier to find a poor bottle of Rosso Conero or Rosso Piceno than a genuinely interesting one. The data concerning the Rosso Piceno DOC are starkly illustrative of the region's commercial problems: of the annual potential of 465,000 hl, from 4,800 ha/11,860 acres of vineyard, less than 30,000 hl/790,000 gal are declared most years. Despite these obstacles, however, a general rise in the overall quality level was observable in the 1990s, partly due to renewed interest in distinctive wines from local rather than INTERNATIONAL VARIETIES. The rapid rise in the price of first Tuscan, and then Umbrian, wines created commercial opportunities for the less expensive wines of the Marche, a fact which alert estates were quick to capitalize on. The new presence in the region of some of the most famous—and expensive—names among Italy's consulting OENOLOGISTS was a sign of both a commitment to higher quality and an awareness that local technique needs help to satisfy international consumers.

See also VERDICCHIO.   D.T. & D.C.G.

Bastianich, J., and Lynch, D., *Vino Italiano: The Regional Wines of Italy* (New York, 2002).

Belfrage, N., *From Brunello to Zibibbo: The Wines of Southern Italy* (London, 2001).

Marcillac, isolated, small, but growing AC in SOUTH WEST FRANCE whose vigorous red wines can have real character. This is the liveliest wine district of the Aveyron *département* (although see also the Vins d'ENTRAYGUES and d'ESTAING), but it can be hard to preserve the viticultural tradition here in the harsh climate of the Massif Central at altitudes up to 600 m/ 2,000 ft. Although there were several thousand hectares of vines here in the late 19th century, today there are only about 150 ha/370 acres of VINIFERA vines dedicated to the appellation (many growers responded to the PHYLLOXERA crisis by planting HYBRIDS). Marcillac, usually red and sometimes rosé, must be made of at least 90 per cent FER, here often called Mansois, a hard-wooded vine capable of making peppery, aromatic mountain wines with excellent structure. BARREL MATURATION has been introduced to temper the high acidity of wines which, unlike many of the Bordeaux duplicates produced in the south west, are highly distinctive. The local CO-OPERATIVE at Valady is an important producer, as is Le Vieux Porche.

marcottage, French term for the LAYERING method of vine propagation in the vineyard.

Maréchal Foch, red wine grape variety named after a famous French First World War general. This FRENCH HYBRID was bred by Eugene Kuhlmann of Alsace, who cited the VINIFERA variety Goldriesling as one parent. It has good winter hardiness and ripens very early. It was once widely cultivated in the Loire and is still popular in CANADA and NEW YORK, where it is spelt **Marechal Foch**, is sometimes called simply Foch, and may be vinified using CARBONIC MACERATION. It produces fruity, non-FOXY wines which can stand on their own two feet.

Maremma, long, loosely defined strip of TUSCAN coastline south of Livorno (Leghorn) extending southward through the province of Grosseto. (Lazio also has its part of the Maremma, between Civitavecchia and the border with Toscana, but this is not a viticultural zone.) The Alta Maremma, or upper Maremma, corresponds to that part of the province of Livorno south of the Cecina river and includes the now famous production zone of BOLGHERI.

In etymological terms, the word Maremma derives from the Latin *mare*, or sea, and is related to the French *marais*. Like the MÉDOC in Bordeaux, the low-lying parts of the Maremma were swampy or marshy for much of their history with chronic problems of malaria. Baron Bettino RICASOLI of Brolio attempted to found a wine estate near Grosseto in the mid 19th century but was forced to give up as a result of the high mortality rate among the workers sent there. Poverty and banditry were generalized phenomena until the draining of the swamps and the elimination of malaria in the 20th century.

Production of bottled wine is consequently a recent phenomenon and quality wine can be said to date from the first bottles of SASSICAIA in the 1970s, although the zone of Morellino di Scansano, high and relatively malaria free, enjoyed a certain reputation in the past. Prior to the 1980s, however, it was more highly prized as a blending wine to add muscle to some of the more attenuated Sangiovese-based wines produced from high-yielding vineyards in better known zones. Bolgheri continued to develop in the 1980s, but the late 1980s and 1990s saw the emergence of important wines in other parts of the Maremma as well, and three specific zones can now be said to exist in addition to a variety of single, and at times isolated, estates. Suvereto, a village in the Val di Cornia, 12 km/7 miles to the south east of Bolgheri but further towards the interior and with a different soil, has become a centre of production not only of high-level Cabernet and Merlot but also of Sangiovese and Montepulciano.

Sangiovese, Cabernet, and Syrah have shown very good results further to the south near the city of Massa Marittima in the province of Grosseto. In what is the Maremma's classic zone for Sangiovese, Morellino di Scansano has improved considerably, thereby confirming the observations of Giacomo Barabino in 1884: 'the wines of Magliano, Pereta and Scansano'—three towns in the current DOC zone—'are excellent and in few other places is so exquisite a wine produced'. The zone itself is a large one, with HILLSIDE VINEYARDS that begin at an altitude of 150 m/500 ft near the sea and rise to 500 m near Scansano itself. Some of the vineyards are on acidic soil, somewhat unusual for Sangiovese, which in central Toscana has always given superior results on alkaline soils. The mid 1990s saw a boom in investment in the zone, with many of Toscana's most prestigious high-quality wineries purchasing properties and vineyard land, attracted both by the potential shown in the better wines and the relatively low vineyard land PRICES compared with other, better-known central Tuscan DOCs. They were also attracted by the earlier ripening engendered by the temperate climate, something that in turn enables them to pick before the autumn rains in eight out of ten years, a luxury seldom afforded growers in the central Tuscan hills.

The large investments made in the 1980s and 1990s left many a producer with a large hole in their bank account. The market for these big, burly, and decidedly expensive wines has not turned out to be as big or receptive as many people had hoped. The economic downturn in the early part of the new century was not foreseen by the business plans put together by the early pioneers, and some interesting bargains were to emerge from the lesser known parts of the Maremma. The wines may be full, forward and muscular, but they lack the pedigree of the best from Bolgheri or the central Tuscan hills. Bolgheri apart, the Maremma has not turned out to be the promised land it appeared to be in the mid 1990s, although it should in future be a source of some excellent wines from vineyards planted with the right technology, clones, and varieties.   D.T. & D.C.G.

Margaret River, most important wine region in WESTERN AUSTRALIA, air conditioned by the warm Indian ocean. First class Chardonnay (Leeuwin Estate) and Cabernet–Merlot (Cullen *et al.*).

margarodes, otherwise known as ground pearls, are a serious insect pest in some vineyards, although they are, fortunately, found only in certain restricted regions. Margarodes weaken and kill vines with a similar action to PHYLLOXERA, and afflicted vines normally die about four years after a decline in VIGOUR is noted.

While many species of margarodes occur on a wide range of host plants worldwide, the most damaging to vines is the *Margarodes vitis* of South America. There are ten species of margarodes in South Africa, five of which infest vine roots, with *Margarodes prieskaensis* being one of the most damaging. The pre-adult insect is a round cyst which attaches itself to the roots, and is covered by a hard, waxy covering. The insects are conspicuous by their foul odour.

The mature cysts can remain inactive in the soil for many years. Winged male and female forms mate above the soil surface and eggs are laid in the vicinity of vine roots in early summer. There are no sources of resistance to ground pearls within the VITIS genus which includes vines, so control by grafting on to resistant ROOTSTOCKS seems unlikely. Many attempts to control margarodes with chemicals have failed, but recent studies in South Africa with hexachlorobutadiene have been successful.   R.E.S.

de Klerk, C. A., 'Chemical control of *Margarodes prieskaensis (Jakubski) Coccoidea: Margarodidae* on grape-vines', *South African Journal for Enology and Viticulture*, 8 (1987), 11–15.

Winkler, A. J., *et al.*, *General Viticulture* (2nd edn, Berkeley, Calif., 1974).

Margaux, potentially the most seductive communal appellation of the Haut-MÉDOC district of Bordeaux. At their stereotypical best, the wines of Margaux combine the deep ruby colour, structure, and concentration of any top-quality Médoc with a haunting perfume and a silkier texture than is found to the north in ST-JULIEN, PAUILLAC, and ST-ESTÈPHE. Mid 20th-century vintages from its two finest properties Ch Margaux (see below) and Ch Palmer certainly demonstrated this and helped to develop a cliché conception of Margaux that can be of little help in BLIND TASTING today, when so many wines up and down the Médoc seemed to be designed to maximize BODY and EXTRACT, often at the expense of inter-communal distinctions.

Margaux is the most southerly, most isolated, and most extensive of the Médoc's communal appellations (see map under BORDEAUX). Although it is made of several non-contiguous parcels of the best portions of vineyard land, inferior parcels qualifying merely as Haut-Médoc, the appellation takes in not just the substantial village of Margaux, but also the neighbouring communities of Cantenac, Soussans, Labarde, and Arsac.

In total more than 1,400 ha/3,460 acres qualified for the Margaux appellation in the mid 2000s, and within its boundaries there are inevitably considerable variations in both topography and soil type. Within the apellation is limestone, chalk, clay, and sand, but most of the finest wines should come from gentle outcrops, or *croupes*, where gravel predominates and DRAINAGE is good—although properties here are particularly parcellated and intermingled with one estate often comprising very different, and often distant, plots of land. Ch Margaux, for example, has vineyards in both Cantenac and Soussans.

Margaux has in the past enjoyed enormous *réclame*, and more Margaux properties were included in the 1855 CLASSIFICATION of the Médoc and Graves (more than 20) than from any other appellation. The appellation clearly still has great potential, but in the 1970s, 1980s, and even 1990s a curious number of châteaux failed to keep pace with the substantial improvements in wine quality achieved in the other three major appellations of the Médoc. Revival is now in the air.

Ch Margaux itself, the FIRST GROWTH standard-bearer as well as name-bearer for the appellation, was revived only in 1978 after more than a decade of disappointing vintages (see below for more details). Of the five second growths within the appellation, Chx Rauzan-Ségla, Rauzan-Gassies, Durfort-Vivens, Lascombes, and Brane-Cantenac, the first was seriously revived only when the owners of the couture house Chanel bought it in 1994 (restoring the 'z' in its name), and the second and third have been some of the most notable under-performers in the whole Médoc. Among the original ten third growths, Desmirail, Ferrière, and Dubignon-Talbot were practically abandoned for years, the last apparently for ever. Only Ch Palmer, officially a third growth, could be said to have represented the appellation with any glory and consistency in the second half of the 20th century. Ch Palmer, part owned and managed by the late Peter A. SICHEL, produced a wine that could without hyperbole be described as legendary in 1961.

Rauzan-Ségla and Rauzan-Gassies were originally one estate and, according to Penning-Rowsell, probably the first other than the first growths to establish a reputation abroad. Rausan-Ségla (as it was then spelt), the larger part, or rather many different parts, was for long owned by the CRUSES and since then passed through several corporate hands, the last of which installed effective new winemaking equipment in the mid 1980s before the sale to the Wertheimer family of the fashion house Chanel.

Ch Lascombes passed from Alexis LICHINE to a British brewer in 1971 and is now run, with considerable RIGHT BANK influence, by an American-led consortium. The large Ch Brane-Cantenac estate, like Durfort-Vivens owned by a LURTON, has been producing lighter wines than its status in the 1855 classification suggests.

Of Margaux's many third growths other than Palmer, Kirwan has been improving; Issan is arguably more famous for its romantic moated château than its modern wines (see CRUSE); Giscours has experienced a renaissance under new ownershop; Cantenac-Brown has been run by AXA; Malescot St-Exupéry, originally called St-Exupéry, is slowly taking on more flesh; Boyd-Cantenac is too often dull; while Marquis d'Alesme-Becker, originally called Becker, can be uncomfortably lean.

More care has recently been lavished on Ch Prieuré-Lichine than on Margaux's other fourth growths Chx Pouget and Marquis de Terme, although the latter is much improved since the mid 1980s. Chx Dauzac and du Tertre are Margaux's often somewhat dreary fifth growths, and such unclassified growths as Chx d'Angludet (a Sichel property), Bel Air Marquis d'Aligre, La Gurgue, Labégorce-Zédé, Monbrison, and Siran can often provide more excitement, wine-making integrity, and particularly value.

One of the Médoc's most famous white wines is made here, even though it qualifies only as BORDEAUX AC (see below).

Duijker, H., and Broadbent, M., *The Bordeaux Atlas* (London, 1997).

Ginestet, B., *Margaux* (Paris, 1984).

Parker, R., *Bordeaux* (4th edn, New York, 2003).

Penning-Rowsell, E., *The Wines of Bordeaux* (6th edn, London, 1989).

Margaux, Château, exceptional building and the most important wine estate in the village of MARGAUX in the Bordeaux wine region, and a FIRST GROWTH in the 1855 CLASSIFICATION. There is much potential for confusion since both Ch Margaux and GENERIC wine from the commune of Margaux are colloquially referred to as 'Margaux', but the former is likely to cost many times more than the latter.

Ch Margaux was one of the four New French Clarets captured in the Anglo-French wars at the beginning of the 18th century, and sold in the COFFEE HOUSES of the City of London (see BORDEAUX, history). Thomas JEFFERSON on his visit to Bordeaux in 1787 picked it out as one of the 'four vineyards of first quality'. Sequestered in the French Revolution after the execution of the owner, it was bought by the Marquis de la Colonilla in 1804 and rebuilt in the First Empire style, by L. Combes, as we know it today—the grandest CHÂTEAU of the Haut-MÉDOC. After passing through several hands, shares were bought by a Bordeaux wine merchant, Fernand Ginestet, in 1925, and the family share was slowly increased to give his son Pierre Ginestet complete ownership in 1949. Also a merchant, he was badly hit by the 'energy crisis' in the early 1970s and had to seek a buyer. The French government refused to allow the American conglomerate National Distillers to buy it, but in 1977, the château was acquired by the French grocery and finance group Félix Potin, headed by the Greek André Mentzelopoulos, domiciled in France. A great deal of money was spent on restoring the neglected vineyard, *chais*, and mansion and Émile PEYNAUD was taken on as consultant. André Mentzelopoulos died suddenly in December 1980, and first his wife Laura and then his daughter Corinne took over control, assisted by Paul Pontallier, the young director who joined the estate in 1983 (coincidentally one of the property's most successful vintages). In 1992, in a complicated international deal involving Perrier mineral water, the Italian Agnelli family of Fiat motor cars became involved in ownership of the estate, but Corinne Mentzelopoulos remained in charge and took a personal stake in the property.

The 82 ha/203 acres of dark grape varieties are planted with roughly 75 per cent CABERNET SAUVIGNON grapes, 20 per cent MERLOT, and 5 per cent of CABERNET FRANC and PETIT VERDOT. Average total red wine output is about 30,000 cases, of which the resurrected Pavillon Rouge de Ch Margaux is the excellent SECOND WINE. A hitherto somewhat uninspiring white wine Pavillon Blanc was transformed into an ambitious dry wine. It is made in a new and separate temperature-controlled cellar, with BARREL FERMENTATION, exclusively from SAUVIGNON BLANC grapes planted on 12 ha of separate vineyard.   E.P.-R. & J.R.

Faith, N., *Château Margaux* (London, 1980).

Maria Gomes, Bairrada and Vinho Verde synonym for the Portuguese white grape variety FERNÃO PIRES.

Maria Ordoña. See MERENZAO.

Marignan and **Marin** are both named CRUS on the south eastern shore of Lake Geneva whose name may be added to the French appellation Vin de SAVOIE. The wine is typically a light, dry white made from the Chasselas grape.

Marino. See CASTELLI ROMANI.

maritime climate, the opposite of a CONTINENTAL climate, has a relatively narrow annual range of temperatures. Places with a maritime climate tend to be near oceans or other large bodies of water (see LAKE EFFECT, for example). For the effects on wine quality and style, see CLIMATE.

marl, the crumbly combination of LIMESTONE and CLAY which is often added to soils lacking limestone (see LIME). Many of the finest wines of the CÔTE D'OR are from grapes grown on predominantly CALCAREOUS marl with some limestone. Whitish marl is found naturally to some extent in the vineyards of BEAUNE and POMMARD. It assumes more importance in MEURSAULT, where it forms the best soil for grapes grown for white wines. There is pebbly marl in the JURA region of France, and TAVEL in the southern RHÔNE has soils which are predominantly Cretaceous marl. In the German region of RHEINHESSEN, the soil is partly derived from marl. See entries prefixed SOIL.
                    M.J.E.

Marmajuelo (also known as Bermejuela), rare but outstanding white grape variety grown on the CANARY ISLANDS.

Marmandais, Côtes du, Bordeaux satellite wine district in SOUTH WEST FRANCE on either side of the river GARONNE, elevated from VDQS to full AC status in 1990. The town of Marmande, on the Garonne, gave it its name and provided a ready means of transporting the wines to Bordeaux and then to northern Europe, especially the NETHERLANDS, from the Middle Ages until the early 19th century. The arrival of the PHYLLOXERA louse caused many farmers to abandon viticulture, however, and vines are just one of many crops in these gentle Marmandais hills. Geographically the region is simply an extension of eastern GRAVES in the south and ENTRE-DEUX-MERS in the north. Bordeaux grape varieties CABERNET SAUVIGNON, CABERNET FRANC, and MERLOT predominate, and the cooler climate here upriver tends to result in light versions of red, and some rosé, bordeaux. But these varieties may not exceed three-quarters of production, and Côtes du Marmandais's distinction is in the local variety ABOURIOU, which, with FER, GAMAY, and SYRAH, must make up the rest. Total vineyard area increased sharply in the 1990s but declined to 1,460 ha/3,600 acres by the mid 2000s. Only a small proportion is planted with the white wine varieties SÉMILLON, UGNI BLANC, MUSCADELLE, and, increasingly, SAUVIGNON BLANC, which is the principal white variety.

Much of the increasingly sophisticated wine production is in the hands of CO-OPERATIVES but Elian Da Ros has provided much-needed glamour as an ambitious individual producer, and Ch de Beaulieu is reliable.

marque. French for BRAND.

Marqués, occasional name for LOUREIRO.

Marsala, town in western SICILIA and the FORTIFIED wine produced around it. For over 200 years one of Sicily's, and Italy's, most famous products, Marsala has fallen on hard times as declining quality, evaporating markets, and plunging production levels have called into question the very survival of the wine, or at least of its better types.

History

Although the province of Trapani, where the wine is produced, has always been a centre of Sicilian viticulture, Marsala can said to have been born with the arrival in Marsala in 1770 of John Woodhouse, an English merchant and connoisseur of PORT, SHERRY, and MADEIRA, who noted a striking similarity between the wines of the subzone of Birgi and these fortified wines of Spain and Portugal. Woodhouse 'invented' Marsala in 1773 by adding 8 1/2 gal of grape spirit to each of the 400-l/105-gal barrels which he shipped to England, and proceeded to open a warehouse and cellars in the township of Marsala in 1796. The victualling of Nelson's fleet in 1798 doubtlessly assisted in spreading the name of the wine, and Woodhouse was followed by another Englishman, Benjamin Ingham, who founded a Marsala firm in 1812 and contributed greatly to improving the area's viticulture. The largest Marsala house, Florio, whose premises once occupied a full km of seafront, was founded by Vincenzo Florio from CALABRIA in 1832. Marsala's production and marketing has always been dominated by large commercial houses, although there has been little continuity over time. These three pioneering houses failed to survive the 1920s and were absorbed by the vermouth house of Cinzano in 1929, and of the various Italian houses founded in the 19th century only Rallo, Pellegrino, and Vito Curatolo Arini remain today, with the last being the only producer still run by descendants of the founding family.

Wine-making and viticulture

Marsala has always been a fortified wine, but production techniques have changed over the decades and modern Marsala, as codified in the DOC regulations of 1969, can be fortified only by adding grape spirit. Alcohol levels will also be slightly increased by MUTAGE, creating a sweet so-called *sifone* by adding 20 to 25 per cent of pure alcohol to a must of late-picked, overripe grapes. The viticulture of the zone has been considerably modified. Vines are trained on either WIRES or TENDONE systems rather than the traditional gobelet, and the traditional superior grapes of the region, GRILLO and INZOLIA, have been supplanted by the higher yielding CATARRATTO. This and enthusiastic IRRIGATION has led to significant increases in yield (the DOC rules allow an excessively generous 10 tons/ha) and a corresponding drop in the grapes' sugar levels. All these factors have led to poorer base wines, which has led to more routine sweetening and a loss of the intrinsic character of the wine itself, at its best when a dry Marsala Vergine.

The ageing of the better categories of Marsala (Superiore and Vergine) in ancient and poorly maintained casks has done little for the quality of these wines, which, in theory, should be the standard-bearers of the zone. What has been most damaging to Marsala, however, has been the multiplication of the types produced, obscuring the fact that Marsala Superiore and Marsala Vergine (made by SOLERA) are the only true descendants of the historic tradition of Marsala.

Modern Marsala now comes in three different colours—Oro (golden), Ambra (amber: the colour coming from *mosto cotto*, which also serves as a rather poor quality sweetener of other wines), and Rubino (ruby)—and each colour comes in a Secco (a maximum of 40 g/l of RESIDUAL SUGAR), a Semisecco (40 to 100 g/l), and a sweet (over 100 g/l) version. There are, in addition, five further types, depending on the CASK AGEING that the wines receive: one year for Fine, two years for Superiore, four years for Superiore Riserva, five years for Vergine, ten years for the Stravecchio version of Vergine.

Consumers in the past were just as likely to encounter Marsala in its various *speciale* forms, sweet, cloying, and flavoured with coffee, chocolate, strawberries, almonds, eggs, all of which enjoyed a DOC status equal to the real wine from 1969 to 1984, helping to create the impression that Marsala is best kept in the kitchen. The revision of the DOC in 1984 banned the use of the name Marsala for these *speciale* forms, and also banned the use of *mosto cotto* in Marsala Oro and Marsala Rubino. *Mosto cotto* is regrettably still required for Marsala Ambra, and represents a foolish attempt to create the impression of a cask-aged wine by deepening its colour with concentrate. The almost extinct Vergine version, however, the purest and most interesting type of all, cannot be made with concentrate

Production figures show a wine virtually on its death-bed. It is hardly an encouraging sign that Marco de Bartoli, the most innovative producer in the zone, makes no reference to Marsala on the label of his Vecchio Samperi, a prototypical and high-quality Marsala Vergine, preferring to call it a VINO DA TAVOLA.

D.T. & D.C.G.

Marsannay, northernmost appellation of the Côte de Nuits district of the CÔTE D'OR (see map under BURGUNDY). It is unique in Burgundy for having APPELLATION CONTRÔLÉE status for red, white, and pink wines. The vineyards of Couchey and Chenove are included with those of Marsannay. Prior to 1987, the wines were sold as generic BOURGOGNE followed by the specification Marsannay or Rosé de Marsannay. The latter style of wine is a speciality of the village pioneered in 1919 by Joseph Clair and taken up by the local CO-OPERATIVE. Leading producers are Audoin, Charlopin, and Bruno Clair.

The small white wine production has yet to show particular character. The red wines are attractive and fruity, if lighter than those of neighbouring FIXIN. There are no PREMIER CRU vineyards.

J.T.C.M.

Marsanne, increasingly popular white grape variety worldwide, making full-bodied, scented white wines. Probably originating in the northern RHÔNE, it has all but taken over here from its traditional blending partner ROUSSANNE in such appellations as ST-JOSEPH, ST-PÉRAY, CROZES-HERMITAGE, and, to a slightly lesser extent, HERMITAGE itself, where wines such as CHAPOUTIER's Chante Alouette show that the variety can make exceptionally good wines for ageing. The vine's relative productivity has doubtless been a factor in its popularity, and modern wine-making techniques have helped mitigate Marsanne's tendency to flab. It is increasingly planted in the south of France, where, as well as being embraced as an ingredient in most appellations, it is earning itself a reputation as a full-bodied, characterful VARIETAL, or a blending partner for more

aromatic, acid varieties such as Roussanne, VIOGNIER, and ROLLE. The wine is particularly deep coloured, full bodied with a heady, if often heavy, aroma of glue, sometimes honeysuckle, verging occasionally on almonds. It is not one of the chosen varieties for Châteauneuf-du-Pape, in which CLAIRETTE supplies many of Marsanne's characteristics, but France grew a total of 1,200 ha/3,000 acres of the variety at the beginning of the 21st century. It is known, as **Marsana**, in north east Spain.

California's RHÔNE RANGERS have also been generating interest in the variety, although acreage was minuscule in the mid 2000s. Australia has some of the world's oldest Marsanne vineyards, notably in the state of Victoria, and a fine tradition of valuing this Rhône import and the hefty wines it produces, which have sometimes developed relatively fast in bottle. There were just 240 ha planted in the mid 2000s, however. In Switzerland, as Ermitage Blanc, it produces both light, dry and complex sweet wines in Valais.

Marselan, new CROSSING of Cabernet Sauvignon and Grenache Noir made by INRA and authorized for Vins de Pays in 1990. The variety was developed specifically for the LANGUEDOC, where is copes with both wet and dry growing seasons, is resistant to FUNGAL DISEASES and COULURE, and is small-berried. It can offer respectable levels of both colour and flavour.

Martial (Marcus Valerius Martialis) (*c.*AD 40–103/4), born in Bilbilis, in Spain; he was poor and wrote Latin poetry for a living. In his *Epigrams*, in 15 books, more than 1,500 short poems in all, he writes about the vices he sees around him in Ancient ROME but he prudently uses pseudonyms to disguise the names of those he satirizes: e.g. 'Hesterno fetere mero qui credit Acerram, fallitur in lucem semper Acerra bibit' (1. 28). ('He who thinks that Acerra reeks of yesterday's wine is wrong. Acerra always drinks until daybreak.') Since snobbery and pretentiousness are two of his main targets, he often mentions wine. Misers and the *nouveaux riches* drink OPIMIAN wine (1. 26, 3. 82, 9. 87, 10. 49), and when Martial satirizes the classical cult of old wine (old wine was always preferred to new and was known by its consular year), he invents a wine that has not even got a consular year, because it was laid down before the Republic (13. 111). He generally presumes detailed knowledge about wine on the reader's part, as for instance in 2. 53, 4. 49, 3. 49. The reader needs to know which wines were good and which were not in order to get the point of the epigram. At the end of Book 13 (106–25) is a series of epigrams listing 21 types of wine. Martial expresses his opinions of certain wines tersely, as in the following (13. 122), 'Acetum' (Vinegar):

Amphora Nilliaci non sit tibi vilis aceti
esset cum vinum, vilior illa fuit.

(Don't think an amphora of Egyptian vinegar is mean stuff. When it was wine, it was meaner still.)

H.M.W.

Griffin, J., *Latin Literature and Roman Life* (London, 1985).

Marzemina Bianca, rare northern Italian white grape variety.

Marzemino, interesting, late-ripening red grape variety grown in northern Italy, from Lombardia to Friuli. DNA PROFILING at SAN MICHELE ALL'ADIGE revealed parent–offspring relationships with both TEROLDEGO and REFOSCO DAL PEDUNCULO ROSSO, thus anchoring the genetic roots of this variety in northern Italy. Once much more famous than now, it does not have particularly good resistance to FUNGAL DISEASES, and is often allowed to overproduce, but it can yield lively wines, some of them lightly sparkling. There is some evidence it was an ingredient in CHIANTI at one time. For more details, see TRENTINO and LOMBARDIA.

J.R. & J.V.

mas, southern French term for a domaine.

The most famous wine-producing *mas* is **Mas de Daumas Gassac**, established by outsiders to the world of wine just south east of MONTPEYROUX in the Languedoc in the 1970s. Aimé Guibert was the first to prove that a French non-appellation wine, labelled merely VIN DE PAYS de l'Hérault, can be an extremely serious, long-living red which can fetch the same sort of prices as a Bordeaux CLASSED GROWTH. Mas de Daumas Gassac also makes some rosé and some ambitious white, from a blend of unusual but trend-setting grape varieties including VIOGNIER, PETIT MANSENG, PETIT COURBU, PETITE ARVINE, AMIGNE, and NEHELESCHOL.

Mackenzie, A., *Daumas Gassac: The Birth of a Grand Cru* (London, 1995).

Masdeu, strong red wine made on and named after an exceptionally well-maintained estate near Perpignan in ROUSSILLON which found a market via London wine merchants and salerooms in the middle of the 19th century as a cheaper alternative to port.

Shaw, T. G., *Wine, the Vine and the Cellar* (London, 1864).

Massandra, winery built to extremely high specifications on the outskirts of Yalta in the CRIMEA in the 1890s to supply Livadia, the tsars' summer palace. Miners had to be imported from GEORGIA to tunnel into the rock to excavate three layers of cool, damp cellars. Prince Golitzin (see CRIMEA) was the first winemaker and was succeeded by the first of the Yegorov family, members of which made wine at Massandra for almost a century from 1898. The most successful wines are strong and sweet, many of them VINS DOUX NATURELS as well as FORTIFIED. The modern installation at Massandra is used not for wine-making, but for AGEING and BOTTLING. Massandra staff oversee production in a number of satellite wineries from the 2,500 ha/6,175 acres of vines under Massandra control. Grapes grown on the southern hillsides and in mountain valleys are responsible for such unique dessert wines as White Muscat of the Red Stone, White Muscat Livadia, Rosé Muscat Yuzhnoberezhny, Black Muscat Massandra, Tocay Yuzhnoberezhny, Pinot Ai-Danil, and Kokur Surozh.

The **Massandra Collection** was begun by Prince Golitzin and its oldest member is an 18th century wine made in the image of SHERRY, but it is today made up substantially of the best Crimean wines. Approximately 10,000 bottles have been added each year and some wines in the collection are decades old. The Collection was carefully evacuated during the German occupation of Yalta 1941–4, some as far as to Georgia, but was back in place in time for the historic Yalta peace conference in 1945. In the early 1990s Sotheby's offered two consignments of strong, very sweet, durable wines from the Massandra Collection at AUCTION in London as part of the auctioneer's trading arrangements with the disintegrating Soviet Union. A further sale was held in 2004.

Massic, a white wine which was among the most famous wines of Roman Italy and was much praised by the Roman poets. The type of grape is unknown. The wine was produced on Monte Massico, the line of hills which runs down to the sea on the west coast of Italy between the rivers Garigliano and Volturno. This zone is adjacent to the territory which produced FALERNIAN and some writers treat Massic as a subtype of that famous wine. The wine was transported to Sinuessa on the coast, where there were numerous kilns producing the AMPHORAE in which the wine was exported.   J.J.P.

mass selection, viticultural technique used to provide large quantities of buds for the propagation of vines. Field vine selection can be either by mass selection, when many vines are selected to provide budwood, or by CLONAL SELECTION, in which a single mother vine is selected to provide CLONES. In mass selection, the identity of individual vines is not maintained.

Mass selection can be either negative or positive. If negative, then undesirable vines in a vineyard are marked so that cuttings are not taken from them. These vines might include those with low yield, poor fruit maturity, virus disease symptoms, higher than average incidence of fungal diseases, or off-types (MUTATIONS). Negative mass selection is also a good opportunity to mark 'rogue vines' (those of another variety) to ensure that mixed plantings do not occur in the future. Positive selection identifies the best vines, for example those

with good fruit set, larger and looser bunches, good fruit maturity, and so on.

Usually the vineyard assessment is made several times over the season. For example, rogue vines and NEPOVIRUS symptoms are easier to pick out in the spring, whereas differences in grape ripening are obviously best determined just before harvest. Vines are commonly marked by paint on the trunk. In winter, cuttings are taken from marked vines in positive mass selection, whereas marked vines are avoided in negative mass selection.

Since there is not the same detailed recording and selection of individual vines, the gains in yield or quality from mass selection are typically less than for clonal selection, but the resultant wine, made from vines with a mixture of different characteristics, may be more interesting than one made from a single clone. The benefits to be had from mass selection will depend on how heterogeneous was the field from which the selection is made. Obviously there will be little benefit of mass selection if the vineyard is quite uniform, but if there is a high proportion of rogue vines, off-types, or virus diseases, then the nurseryman might expect substantial benefits.

Unfortunately, in many viticultural regions of the world, cuttings are taken in winter from vineyards which have not benefited from even the most cursory inspection in the preceding summer. In the winter all vines appear similar, and so mistakes of mixed plantings, off-types, and virus diseases are spread unwittingly from one vineyard to the next generation by propagation.   R.E.S.

Coombe, B. G., and Dry, P. R., *Viticulture*, i: *Resources in Australia* (Adelaide, 1988).

Galet, P., *Précis de viticulture* (5th edn, Montpellier, 1988).

Masters of Wine, those who have passed the examinations held every year by the **Institute of Masters of Wine** (**IMW**), the wine trade's most famous and most demanding professional qualification. The Institute had its origins in the British wine trade in the early 1950s, when a counterpart to the qualifying examinations for other professions was devised by a group of wine merchants in conjunction with the VINTNERS' COMPANY. The first examination was held in London in 1953 and six of the 21 candidates were deemed to have qualified as Masters of Wine. The Institute of Masters of Wine was formed in 1955. The examinations consist of four (once five) written papers and three 'practical' (i.e. wine tasting) papers. The examinations are distinguished by the breadth and depth of their scope. University courses (see ACADEME) offer more detailed instruction in the OENOLOGY or VITICULTURE of a particular country or region, while the MW examinations test knowledge of both subjects on a worldwide basis, as well as of such varied subjects as ÉLEVAGE, BOTTLING, transport, QUALITY CONTROL, marketing,

commercial aspects of the wine trade, the effects of wine consumption on HEALTH, and general wine knowledge. Each tasting paper requires candidates to describe, assess, and, often, identify up to 12 wines served BLIND. These wines, including sparkling and fortified wines, may come from anywhere in the world. Since 1999 candidates have also been required to prepare an original dissertation.

Despite a notoriously low pass rate (although it has risen markedly in recent years and candidates have always been allowed to pass practical and theoretical parts in separate years), by 1978 the number of Masters of Wine had reached 100, including two women. In 1982 the Institute held its first, relatively academic, symposium, at Oxford, but also lost four of its members and realized that some expansion would be necessary for its survival (it had no executives and no premises until 1987). In 1983 it relaxed its entry requirements and allowed candidates from the fringes of the wine trade, such as WINE WRITERS, to take the examinations. In 1987 the examinations were opened up to those outside the United Kingdom and the next year the first overseas candidate, an Australian, passed the examinations, at this stage still held in London. In 1990, two Americans qualified as Masters of Wine and since 1991 examinations have been held, on the same dates, in London, Sydney, and North America. By 2005 there were 250 Masters of Wine (including 59 women) of 18 different nationalities, and several MWs with no professional connection with wine at all; 79 members live and work outside the UK.

Numbers of candidates have increased just as markedly as numbers of Masters of Wine. The examinations are increasingly demanding as the wine world expands, and the standard of preparation offered by the Institute was raised considerably in the mid 1990s and early 2000s.

The aims of the Institute have at times been less clear than the status of its members, and for many years it offered examinations but remarkably little education although this is changing, thanks to annual residential courses, regular seminars, tastings, and a mentoring scheme. According to the Institute's Mission Statement, it aims to promote the highest standards of quality and excellence in wine alongside the 'highest standards of conduct within the wine industry'.

Mastroberardino, historically the most important producer of TAURASI in the southern Italian region of CAMPANIA. The family split in 1994, with one branch retaining the vineyards but setting up under the Vignadora label, and the other branch retaining the name but seeking grapes elsewhere. Today, both have been superseded, in quality terms, by I Feudi di San Gregorio and Vesevo.

Mataro is one of the many synonyms of MOURVÈDRE used primarily in Australia, sometimes in Roussillon, and, by those who do not realize how fashionable Mourvèdre has become, in California (see RHÔNE RANGERS).

Mateus. The Palace of Mateus near Vila Real just north of the DOURO valley in northern Portugal lent its name to **Mateus Rosé**, a medium sweet, sparkling rosé that has become one of the world's most famous wine BRANDS. It was created in 1942 by Fernando van Zeller Guedes, whose family owned a property producing VINHO VERDE. Inspired by these naturally pétillant red and white wines which were already popular in Portugal and Brazil, Guedes produced a sparkling rosé which was sweetened to make it more appealing to the developing North American and northern European markets. Production began at the end of the Second World War (at very much the same time as that of its rival LANCERS) in a winery built close to the Mateus Palace. The property did not belong to the Guedes family and its owners opted for a single payment in return for the use of the name and a picture of the palace on the LABEL, rather than a royalty on each bottle sold.

In the 1950s and 1960s, sales grew rapidly and by the late 1980s, Mateus, by then supplemented by a white version, accounted for over 40 per cent of Portugal's total table wine exports with worldwide sales amounting to 3.25 million cases. A small quantity of Mateus Rosé is still made at Vila Real but most of the wine is produced at Anadia in BAIRRADA. Faced with falling sales of Mateus in the early 1990s, SOGRAPE, the Guedes family firm which owns the Mateus brand and is the largest wine producer in Portugal, has diversified into other areas of the Portuguese wine industry, including PORT, and in 2005 launched Mateus Rosé Tempranillo made in VALENCIA.

R.J.M.

Matrassa, dominant, dark-berried vine of AZERBAIJAN. It is found in other central ASIAN republics and may also be called Kara Shirei and Kara Shirai. Sometimes spelt Matrasa.

maturation of wine. See AGEING.

mature, tasting term for a fine wine that seems to have enjoyed sufficient AGEING for it to have reached the peak of its potential. In practice, it is also used by the most polite, or determinedly optimistic, tasters to describe wines that are past that point. Any hint of orange at the rim of a red wine suggests MATURITY.

maturity, desirable state in a wine when it is consumed. In a sense, the most basic wine designed for early drinking is mature almost as soon as it is bottled, but mature when applied to a wine carries with it the implication that the maturity is the result of a certain amount of BOTTLE AGEING. Such a (red) wine is deemed fully mature when it has dispensed with its

uncomfortably harsh TANNINS and acquired maximum complexity of flavour (sometimes described as BOUQUET) without starting to decay. The period of maturity varies considerably with wine type, but is probably longer than most wine consumers believe. A wine that has been followed since its youth and begins to taste mature may continue to delight, and possibly evolve for the better, for a decade or more. For more details of the process, and of the difference between individual wine types, see AGEING.

Robinson, J., *Vintage Timecharts* (London and New York, 1989).

Maury is one of ROUSSILLON's famous VINS DOUX NATURELS, a cousin from the hilly, SLATEY hinterland of seaside BANYULS, which is actually produced in greater quantity even if it is less famous. Like Banyuls it is produced predominantly from Grenache Noir with a maximum yield of 30 hl/ha (1.7 tons/acre) and is almost invariably strong, sweet, red, and possibly RANCIO, having been aged in a variety of containers (cement, wood, glass) in a variety of conditions (hot, cold, humid or not). Maury is on high inland schist at the northern limit of the Côtes du Roussillon-Villages area in the Agly valley. The ruins of the Cathar castle of Quéribus, a constant reminder of the area's harsh natural environment, dominate the village of Maury. Maury is particularly tannic in youth and often has a deeper colour than Banyuls. The CO-OPERATIVE, Les Vignerons du Maury, dominates production but other producers manage to surface too, notably Mas Amiel and Domaine de la Préceptorie. The wines serve much the same purpose as Banyuls but more insistently demand ageing. The highly distinctive table wines produced here are sold mainly as Vins de Pays des Côtes Catalanes (see ROUSSILLON for more details).

Mauzac, or more properly **Mauzac Blanc**, is a declining but still surprisingly important white grape in SOUTH WEST FRANCE, especially in GAILLAC and LIMOUX, where it is the traditional and still principal vine variety. It produces relatively aromatic wines which are usually blended, with Len de l'El around Gaillac and with Chenin and Chardonnay in Limoux. France grew a total of 3,200 ha/8,000 acres of Mauzac in 2000.

Thanks to energetic winemakers such as Robert Plageoles, since the late 1980s there has been a revival of interest in Gaillac's Mauzac, which comes in several different hues, sweetness levels, and degrees of fizziness. During the 1970s and 1980s in Limoux, total plantings of Mauzac rose but had fallen again to 1,600 ha by the end of the century as the appellation, for both still and fizzy wines, was invaded by Chardonnay.

The vine, whose yields can vary enormously according to site, buds and ripens late and

grapes were traditionally picked well into autumn so that musts fermented slowly and gently in the cool Limoux winters, ready to referment in bottle in the spring. Today Mauzac tends to be picked much earlier, preserving its naturally high acidity but sacrificing much of its particular flavour reminiscent of the skin of shrivelled apples, before being subjected to the usual SPARKLING WINEMAKING techniques. Some gently sparkling Gaillacs are still made by the traditional *méthode gaillacoise*, however, just as a small portion of Limoux's Blanquette is made by the *méthode ancestrale*.

Mavro means 'black' in Greek and is the common name of the dominant but undistinguished grape on the island of CYPRUS.

Mavrodaphne, dark-skinned grape variety grown particularly round Pátras in the Peloponnese in GREECE, where it is the foundation of a port-like dessert wine, **Mavrodaphne of Pátras**, which responds well to extended CASK AGEING. This aromatic, powerful variety, also grown to a much more limited extent on the island of Cephalonia, is occasionally vinified dry but only for use as a blending component. Various relationships with the similarly named Mavro of CYPRUS and MAVRUD of Bulgaria have been posited but Mavro is simply Greek for black, and Mavrodaphne means 'black laurel'.

Mavro Neméas, alternative name for the dominant Neméan dark-skinned vine AGHIORGHITIKO.

Mavroud, almost extinct Greek vine which, it is tempting to believe, may be MAVRUD.

Mavrud, indigenous Balkan grape variety most closely associated with BULGARIA, capable of producing intense, tannic wine if allowed to ripen fully. Grown in central southern Bulgaria and a speciality of Assenovgrad near Plovdiv, it is small berried, low yielding and has a long vegetative period. The robust wine produced responds well to oak ageing, although it tends to age rather faster than Bulgaria's other noble indigenous vine MELNIK. Mavrud is also grown in ALBANIA.

Mazuelo and **Mazuela,** RIOJA name for CARIGNAN.

MDMP. See METHOXY-DIMETHYLPYRAZINE.

mead, a fermented alcoholic drink, called *hydromel* in France and *Honigwein* or *Met* in Germany, made from honey, which, it is claimed, pre-dates either wine or beer. Monks kept bees for candlewax and any surplus honey was fermented into mead. The dissolution of the monasteries meant the virtual demise of mead-making in Britain. Since the Second World War, some larger companies have marketed a mixture of wine and honey as mead, but the tradition of genuine mead-making persists. Grape mead is grape juice mixed with honey before fermentation.

mealy bugs, small, white insects of the family Cicadellidae which suck vine sap. Young mealy bugs infect new growth in the spring, typically the undersurface of leaves at the base of the shoot. They also can feed on the fruit, canes, and trunk, and one species, the vine mealy bug *Planococcus ficus*, can feed on roots. Mealy bugs become mature and reproduce in early summer, and there can be three or more generations a year. Mealy bugs prefer a humid environment, and so are mostly found in a dense vine CANOPY.

The vine mealy bug, first identified in California's Coachella valley in the early 1990s, is now widespread in the San Joaquin valley and the Central Coast, where it is regarded as a serious problem. It is spread by infected new plantings and can be controlled by dipping the dormant plants in hot water.

Mealy bugs do not cause significant commercial damage by their sap-sucking action alone, but there can be two indirect effects. First, they produce copious quantities of a sugary, sticky liquid called honeydew, which collects over the bunches and foliage, and on which fungus grows, often giving it a sooty appearance. Grapes affected by this impart a distinctive and undesirable taste to wine, and the fruit may be fit only for DISTILLATION. Mealy bugs of the genera *Planococcus* and *Pseudococcus* have been implicated in the spread of LEAFROLL VIRUS, which has serious implications for the loss of vineyard yield and grape quality. Mealy bugs have been confirmed as spreading leafroll virus in South Africa, Israel, the US, and New Zealand.

Where mealy bug infestations are serious, a schedule of preventive sprays is necessary, but the waxy covering of the insect and the sheltered locations make control difficult.

M.J.E. & R.E.S.

Buchanan, G. A., and Amos, T. G., 'Grape pests', in B. G. Coombe and P. R. Dry (eds.), *Viticulture*, ii: *Practices* (Adelaide, 1992).

Golino, D.A., Sim, S.T., Gill, R., and Rowhani, A., 'California mealybugs can spread grapevine leafroll disease', *California Agriculture* 56 (2002), 196–201.

measles, as it affects vines, see ESCA.

mechanical harvesting, harvesting by machine in place of the traditional manual HARVEST. Undoubtedly one of the greatest changes from ancient to modern vineyards has been the adoption of machine harvesting, which was first introduced commercially in the 1960s. Whereas manual grape harvesting required literally hordes of pickers to descend on vineyards and complete the harvest, now the vintage may be completed by just one harvester driver, perhaps with a supporting driver and vehicle to receive the harvested grapes.

Depending on the YIELD and vineyard TOPOGRAPHY, to harvest a vineyard by hand requires between one and ten man-days per hectare, as opposed to less than five man-hours per hectare by machine.

Mechanical harvesting has been adopted for different reasons in different parts of the world. In some of the earliest developments instigated by SHAULIS in New York state, a major consideration was potential cost savings. In Australia, the availability of LABOUR was important, and welfare payments were another factor. In France, the increasing bureaucracy and costs involved in employing people even temporarily added allure to machine harvesting in the 1980s and 1990s. The net effect was that seasonal workers were more difficult to find, demanded higher wages, and were also perhaps less reliable, all of these factors promoting machines over man at vintage time. Machine harvesting may have been developed in the United States, but the technology was rapidly refined in France.

History

Mechanical harvesting can either increase the efficiency of manual labour, or virtually replace it. Early attempts at mechanization emphasized the first approach, but it has been the second approach which has been the more successful, by developing machines which essentially replace most of the manual operations.

Many forms of integrated machine harvesters have been developed and evaluated, although by the early 21st century, most machines worked by striking the CANOPY to remove fruit and catching it with horizontal conveyor belts. The early New York development was the 'vertical impactor', which used a metal finger to strike the vine cordon; the shock dislodged the berries. However, the most common form of harvesting now is the 'horizontal slapper' which uses fibreglass rods to strike the foliage and dislodge the fruit, sometimes as single berries, sometimes as bunches.

Effect on wine quality

The effect of machine harvesting on wine quality has been the subject of much scientific study and commercial experience. The majority of studies have shown that sophisticated mechanical harvesting has no negative effect on wine quality, and some have even argued that there is a positive effect. Certainly most forms of machine harvesting damage some grapes so that parts of berries and bunches are mixed with the juice of broken berries. However, the juice can be protected from OXIDATION by SULFUR DIOXIDE addition, especially if moved quickly in a closed container to the winery. This problem can be minimized by harvesting at night, a practice widely adopted in hotter wine regions where grapes harvested by day can arrive at the winery at over 40 °C/

104 °F. Indeed, in these circumstances, machine picking is a bonus for wine quality.

Another disadvantage of machine harvesting is that there can be excessive SKIN CONTACT, which, depending on its duration, usually dictated by transport times, can lead to white wines becoming too high in PHENOLICS. The skin contact involved in transporting mechanically harvested white grapes to a winery can also cause a significant increase in the concentration of PROTEINS in the wine, necessitating higher rates of BENTONITE fining. Long distances between the winery and vineyard may make a mechanical harvest for delicate white wines an impossibility. Machine-harvested grapes can also contain leaves and petioles (see MOG), which may cause taints. Despite much evidence in favour of machine harvesting, some producers will remain with hand harvesting. The gentler nature of hand harvesting (which can also involve some degree of selection) is preferable for many top-quality wines, especially sparkling wines, for which WHOLE BUNCHES may be pressed without first crushing.

R.E.S.

Coombe, B. G., and Dry, P. R. (eds.), *Viticulture*, ii: *Practices* (Adelaide, 1992).

Galet, P., *Précis de viticulture* (5th edn, Montpellier, 1988).

mechanical pruning involves using machines for PRUNING vines in winter. Viticulture is a very traditional form of agriculture and many who tend the vines regard the annual winter pruning as their prime opportunity to interact physically with each vine. Because of this, and because they feel that mechanical pruning cannot offer the precision of manual pruning, many vine-growers oppose mechanical pruning, even at the expense of hours of back-breaking labour in cold and sometimes wet weather.

Early experiments in mechanical pruning were carried out in Australia and New York state in the mid 1970s. The machinery was not as elaborate as that for MECHANICAL HARVESTING, which was undergoing simultaneous development. The pruning machines were simply reciprocating cutters or flails mounted on a tractor. In Australia circular saws were widely used, and sometimes these were mounted on a machine harvester with the picking head removed.

Machine pruning is simple in the extreme, as the vine canes are trimmed back leaving typically a SPUR with two or more buds (CANE PRUNING cannot, of course, be mechanized). Early commercial experiments followed mechanical pruning with hand pruning to tidy the vines' appearance, by thinning out spur numbers and cutting them to a uniform two-bud length. This is known as mechanical pre-pruning, and cuts pruning time in half. Encouraged by early experiments in Australia, however, most vines have since been left untended after machine pruning. Although they look ugly in late winter, soon after BUDBREAK they cannot be distinguished from hand-pruned vines. Because more buds are left on the vine (up to fivefold) the YIELD usually increases for the first year or so, but many studies show no significant effect on wine quality.

Mechanical pruning is now widespread in Australia, especially in the hotter wine regions. Other parts of the world have been much slower to embrace mechanical pruning, however, especially those where LABOUR is plentiful and relatively inexpensive. Mechanical pre-pruning is becoming more widespread for the extensive vineyards of southern France. In cooler regions such as northern Europe, mechanical pruning is less useful because machine pruning leaves too many buds, tending to increase yield and slow RIPENING.

The 100 to 150 hours per hectare required for hand pruning can be reduced to less than ten hours per hectare with mechanical pruning. Some of the substantial cost savings associated with this reduction may be lost if too extensive hand pruning follows. The logical extension of mechanical pruning is not to prune at all, so-called MINIMAL PRUNING.　　　　　R.E.S.

Coombe, B. G., and Dry, P. R. (eds.), *Viticulture*, ii: *Practices* (Adelaide, 1992).

Winkler, A. J., *et al.*, *General Viticulture* (2nd edn, Berkeley, Calif., 1974).

mechanization. Most WINE-MAKING operations other than TASTING and overseeing individual barrels can be fully mechanized, but mechanization has been much slower to invade the vineyard. Robotic technology is used, for example, in the production of PORT, in the movement of pallets around the winery, and in the preparation of grape samples. For more details of viticultural mechanization, see MECHANICAL HARVESTING, MECHANICAL PRUNING, and, most importantly, LABOUR.

medals from wine COMPETITIONS and other JUDGINGS are coveted by many wine producers. There is a certain hierarchy of medals, however. State and national wine shows are important to the wine trade in AUSTRALIA, but a Hobart gold medal may be reckoned less glamorous than a Canberra silver. In France, medals awarded by the fairs in Paris and Mâcon are usually indications of real quality, as are those awarded in Germany by the Deutscher Landwirtschaft Gesellschaft, or DLG.

medical aspects of wine consumption. See HEALTH.

medical profession. See DOCTORS.

medicine, wine in. From ancient times to the 18th century, wine enjoyed a central role in medicine (see LITERATURE OF WINE). The earliest practitioners of medicine were magicians and priests who used wine for healing as well as religious purposes (see RELIGION). Receipts for wine-based medicines appear in papyri of Ancient EGYPT and the tablets of SUMER in about 2200 BC, making wine man's oldest documented medicine.

The beginnings of systematized medicine are commonly attributed to the Greek Hippocrates (*c*.450 BC), who recommended the use of wine as a disinfectant, a medicine, a vehicle for other drugs, and as part of a healthy DIET. He experimented with different wines in order to discover how each might be most appropriately used—whether diluted or not, for example—to cure a specific ailment, from lethargy or diarrhoea to easing difficult childbirth.

The most famous physician of Ancient ROME was GALEN (2nd century AD), whose medical experience was shaped by treating injured gladiators in Asia Minor, although Aurelius Cornelius Celsus (25 BC–AD 37) had already written extensively about the medical uses of various wines from different regions of Greece and Italy. Galen learned (like the Good Samaritan of the BIBLE) that wine was the most effective means of disinfecting wounds, even soaking exposed abdominal contents in wine before returning them to the abdominal cavity in the case of severe stomach wounds. His post as imperial physician involved tasting the emperor's wines in order to select the best and most healthy.

Ancient Jewish civilization prized wine for its medicinal properties. In the Talmud it is stated that: 'Wine is the foremost of all medicines: wherever wine is lacking, medicines become necessary.'

The Koran presented Arab doctors with a dilemma. The likes of Avicenna (11th century AD) recognized the importance of wine in healing, but since its consumption was forbidden throughout the world of ISLAM had to be careful to prescribe it as a dressing only (although he noted boldly that 'wine is also very efficient in causing the products of digestion to become disseminated through the body'). Arabs studied medicine from Greek sources then transmitted it back, slightly amended, to the west. The works of Galen, for example, reached medieval Europe partly via the great medical school of Salerno in Italy, where they were translated from Arabic to Latin, and partly through direct translation from Greek. It was then that the notion of wine as an essential element in a healthy diet gained ground.

The medicinal use of wine continued throughout the Middle Ages, in MONASTERIES, hospitals, and universities. The earliest printed book on wine is by a doctor, one ARNALDUS DE VILLANOVA of the University of MONTPELLIER, who had written at the beginning of the 14th century. Building on the observations of his classical forebears, he offers not only remedies for curing human ailments with appropriate wines, but also recipes for curing 'sick' or bad wines too.

A new dimension was added to the role of wine in medicine with the introduction of DISTILLATION in the western world in the 12th century. Hieronymus Brunschwig, the German pharmacologist, wrote in the 15th century that '*Aqua vitae* [the water of life, or ALCOHOL] is commonly called the mistress of all medicines', but warned, 'it is to be drunk by reason and measure'.

Medicinal attitudes towards wine began to change in the latter half of the 19th century—although wine was still being added to sterilize water as late as the 1892 cholera epidemic of Hamburg (vindicated by modern research indicating that wine contains substances which make it a more effective anti-bacterial agent than pure alcohol), and strong, sweet wines such as PORT were still being prescribed as aids to recuperation in the early 20th century. Alcoholism was defined as a disease and the injurious side-effects of excessive drinking studied. The appearance of temperance societies, sometimes supported by the medical establishment, caused many to re-evaluate the role of wine in DIET and medicine.

One further aspect of the conjunction of wine and medicine is the great influence that DOCTORS have had since ancient times, not just as wine consumers (and producers) but also in promoting or damaging the commercial potential of certain wines. Undoubtedly Roman connoisseurs took note of the recommendations of Galen and others, while in 17th-century France the commercial battle between wine regions reached new heights when Louis XIV's physician prescribed burgundy in preference to champagne. Other examples of vinous prescriptions abound.

For a modern view of the medical effects of wine consumption see HEALTH.　　H.B. & P.A.N.

Darby, W. J., 'Wine and medical wisdom through the ages', in *Wine, Health and Society* (San Francisco, 1982).

Lucia, S. P., *A History of Wine as Therapy* (New York, 1963).

Sigerist, H. E., *The Earliest Printed Book on Wine* (New York, 1943) (contains Villanova's *Tractatus de vinis*).

medieval literature. The only medieval successor to the Roman AGRICULTURAL TREATISES is PETRUS DE CRESCENTIIS' *Liber ruralium commodorum* of *c*.1304; otherwise there are few medieval authors who wrote specifically on wine.

One of these is Henri d'Andely, whose *Bataille des vins* dates from just after 1223 and it belongs to the genre of the medieval debate poem. The king of France, Philip Augustus, wants to know which is the best wine: his preference is for whites. Some 70 wines are tasted and the crown of victory passes all the French wines by, for it goes to the wine of CYPRUS.

Another Old French poem about wine is *La Disputoison de vin et de l'iaue* ('The Debate between Wine and Water'), written some time between 1305 and 1377, when the papal court was at Avignon. The debate reflects the changing FASHIONS of the time, including those for the wines of BEAUNE, GASCONY, LA ROCHELLE, ST-POURÇAIN-sur-Sioule, and PARIS.

Of the Middle English poets, Chaucer is the one who displays most knowledge of wine, although he tends to mention different wines only briefly. Chaucer's father and grandfather were among the most important VINTNERS in London and held the office of deputy to the king's butler, who was the person responsible for the collection of taxes on imported wines. Jugs of MALMSEY ('malvasye') and VERNACCIA ('vernage') are, for example, the extravagant presents that the monk in 'The Shipman's Tale' gives his friend the merchant, whom he is about to cuckold.

Wine is just wine in the medieval drinking songs, too. Most of them are in Latin, and they are not so much in praise of drinking as of DRUNKENNESS. The 9th-century poem about Adam, abbot of Angers, for example, has an address to BACCHUS as its refrain. One of the *Carmina Burana*, 'Potatores exquisiti' (*CB* 179), asks all serious topers to banish moderate drinkers from parties and to drink until speech becomes impaired and walking impossible. Even when one is on one's own, the object of drinking should be inebriation.   H.M.W.

Hanford, J. H., 'The mediaeval debate between wine and water', *Publications of the Modern Language Academy of America*, 28 (1913), 315–67.

Raby, F. J. E., *The Oxford Book of Medieval Latin Verse* (Oxford, 1959).

Waddell, H., *Medieval Latin Lyrics* (London, 1933).

Wilson, H., *Wine and Words in Classical Antiquity and the Middle Ages* (London, 2003).

Mediterranean, famous sea, wine-producing climate, diet, and many other things besides. By classical times, vines were grown for wine in almost all the countries bordering the Mediterranean sea and on many of the islands; from Spain in the west to Byblos in the east, from northern Italy to Egypt, the vine made inexorable progress, with AMPHORAE of wine traversing the sea regularly. Historically, the Mediterranean was the focus of viticulture, and most wine was produced in MEDITERRANEAN CLIMATES. In the Middle Ages, particularly when temperatures rose overall (see CLIMATE CHANGE) and when consumers were accustomed to very light, acid wines, viticulture spread much further north than the shores of the Mediterranean (see PARIS, ENGLAND, and GERMAN HISTORY, for example).

Mediterranean climate, a climate type characterized by warm, dry, sunny summers and mostly mild, wet winters. It occurs throughout the Mediterranean basin, on the west coast of the United States, in Chile, southern and south western Australia, and the Cape Province of South Africa. The autumn and spring seasons range from mostly dry on the hot, equatorial fringes bordering deserts, to wet at the poleward fringes, where Mediterranean climates merge into those with a more or less uniform rainfall distribution as in central and western Europe.

It was in the MEDITERRANEAN region that viticulture and wine-making developed, as an adjunct (some might say, an essential component) to western civilization as we know it. Yet the Mediterranean is no longer the place most readily associated with fine wine. Why is this so?

The most famed and esteemed wines of classical times were undoubtedly sweet and strong: made from very ripe grapes, fermented to the limit of natural fermentation, and then left with considerable RESIDUAL SUGAR. The warm, sunny climates typical of the Mediterranean are well suited to this style of wine, but late 20th-century consumers are more likely to seek wines that are fruity, dry, and not too high in alcohol. These are the natural characteristics of wines made in cooler and perhaps less sunny climates, where grapes ripen at lower sugar levels and with higher ACIDITY (see CLIMATE AND WINE QUALITY and COOL CLIMATE VITICULTURE).

For all that, a renaissance is now taking place in Mediterranean climate viticulture around the world. With appropriate SITE SELECTION, Mediterranean climates have some distinct advantages for viticulture over uniform or summer-rainfall climates, provided that supplementary IRRIGATION can be given as needed. Sunshine is mostly more reliable and generous. There is less risk of excessive rainfall during ripening. As a result of both, the risk of FUNGAL DISEASES is generally lower. And to the extent that many Mediterranean climates have the disadvantages of low HUMIDITY and high TEMPERATURES during the ripening period, precise VINEYARD site selection can help to minimize these disadvantages, by seeking out coastal or high-altitude sites, for example.

Further favouring Mediterranean climates is the fact that some of the main advances in both vineyard management and wine-making technology have particular application there. DRIP IRRIGATION in a summer-dry climate allows a degree of control over SOIL WATER availability and vine VIGOUR, and permits the use of MESOCLIMATES and soils (see SOIL AND WINE QUALITY) that were too dry for viticulture before. Improved CANOPY MANAGEMENT has at least as great an application as in other climates.

In the winery, control of TEMPERATURE and BACTERIA, YEAST nutrition, and careful ACIDIFICATION now make it possible to use fully ripe grapes more safely than under previous, more primitive wine-making regimes, and thereby to capture regularly the attractive fullness of fruit flavour that ripening under warm, sunny conditions can give.   J.G. & R.E.S.

Médoc, the most famous red wine district in Bordeaux, and possibly the world. The Médoc stretches north west from the city of Bordeaux along the left bank of the Gironde estuary, a virtually monocultural strip of flat,

unremarkable land sandwiched between the *palus*, or coastal marshes, and the pine forests which extend for miles south into the Landes. The vineyard strip is about 5 to 12 km/3 to 8 miles wide, and runs northwards, with various intermissions for scrub, pasture, polder, and river bank, more than 70 km/50 miles from the northern suburbs of Bordeaux to the marshes of the lower, more northerly part of the Médoc, the so-called Bas-Médoc (see map under BORDEAUX). Wines produced in the Bas-Médoc use the **Médoc** appellation, while those on the higher ground in the south eastern section are entitled to the **Haut-Médoc** appellation, although many of them qualify for the smarter individual village, or communal, appellations. From south to north, these are MARGAUX, MOULIS, LISTRAC, ST-JULIEN, PAUILLAC, and ST-ESTÈPHE.

As outlined in BORDEAUX, history, the Médoc is a relatively recent wine region. Before the Dutch diligently applied their drainage technology to the polders of the Médoc in the mid 17th century, the region was salt-marsh, of interest for grazing rather than vine-growing. The ditches were so effective, and Bordeaux merchants so keen to supply vinous rivals to GRAVES and the powerful Portuguese wines that had been shipped in great quantity to the important British market, that New French Clarets were born, and great estates established in the Médoc on the back of their commercial success. In the mid 19th century, the Médoc enjoyed a period of prosperity unparalleled until the 1980s.

The climate on this peninsula is Bordeaux's mildest, moderated both by the estuary and by the Atlantic ocean just over the pines. These forests protect the vineyard strip from strong winds off the ocean, and help to moderate summer temperatures, but it is only in the Médoc and the Graves district further south that Bordeaux vignerons are confident of ripening Cabernet Sauvignon grapes with any frequency. The Médoc is also Bordeaux's wettest region, which makes ROT a constant threat and SPRAYING a habit.

A typical estate, or CHÂTEAU, in the greater Médoc district hedges its viticultural bets and grows at least three different grape varieties: a majority of Cabernet Sauvignon, supplemented principally by Merlot, together with some Cabernet Franc with, perhaps, a little late late-ripening Petit Verdot and occasionally some Malbec. However, Merlot often predominates in the damper, cooler soils of the Bas-Médoc as it is easier to ripen in lesser vintages, and Cabernet Sauvignon comprises only about half of all the vines planted in the district.

While the Médoc possesses few distinctive geographical features, many man-hours have been spent charting the subterranean Médoc. It has long been argued that its great distinction is its soil, in particular its GRAVEL. Many a geological theory has been employed to explain exactly how, and whence, these gravel deposits arrived in the Médoc, and efforts have been made to correlate exact soil and rock types with the quality of wine produced from vines grown on them. The work of Dr Gérard Seguin of the University of BORDEAUX, however, indicates that the soil's physical attributes may well be very much more important than its mineral composition, and that one of the most important soil attributes is good DRAINAGE (see SOIL AND WINE QUALITY). The gravels of the Médoc are ideal in this respect, and are particularly important in such a damp climate—although in hotter vintages mature vines can benefit from the extensive root systems encouraged by the gravel. The gravels of the Médoc are also good at storing valuable heat, thereby promoting RIPENING.

It is traditionally said that the best vines of the Médoc are those which grow within sight of the Gironde, and certainly this is true of all the district's FIRST GROWTHS. Some argue that this is because the gravels deposited here are younger and more effective for vine maturation, others that the MESOCLIMATES of coastal vineyards tend to be slightly warmer, others that vines on higher ground have to establish more complex root systems.

A total of about 1,500 vine-growers farm this land, about a quarter of which forms part of one of the classed growths ranked in the famous 1855 CLASSIFICATION of the Médoc (and Graves).

The Haut-Médoc appellation

The landscape of the Haut-Médoc may not be remarkable but it is peppered with grandiose château buildings erected and embellished with the money to be made from selling CLASSED GROWTH red bordeaux. Certainly the Haut-Médoc today is nothing if not stratified, thanks largely to the effects of the 1855 classification of its most famous estates, which recognized scores of them as first, second, third, fourth, and fifth growths, commercial and social positions from which none but Ch MOUTON-ROTHSCHILD has so far been able to escape.

Most of these classed growths are entitled to a village appellation such as Pauillac or Margaux (see map under BORDEAUX), but five of them are in communes without their own appellations and qualify merely as Haut-Médoc. The most highly ranked of these is the third growth Ch La Lagune in Ludon just outside the city, a property which has retained its reputation for robust, concentrated wines. Just north of this well-run property is the fifth growth Ch Cantemerle. The commune of St-Laurent, inland from ST-JULIEN on the main road through the forests of the Médoc, boasts the improving fourth growth Ch La Tour-Carnet and two improving fifth growths, Chx Belgrave and Camensac.

The area classified as Haut-Médoc as opposed to any more specific commune grew very slightly to 4,600 ha/11,360 acres by 2004.

Many of these vineyards are CRUS BOURGEOIS offering some of the best value to be found in Bordeaux. The best wines share the deep colour, concentration, tannins, and ageing potential of the classed growths, and are made in a very similar fashion except that the basic YIELD allowed is 43 hl/ha (2.4 tons/acre) rather than the 40 hl/ha permitted for the Médoc's four important village or communal appellations, and a leap of faith and selling price is needed to justify the use of new BARRELS. From 1994, the AC regulations specified a VINE DENSITY of between 6,500 and 10,000 vines per ha (as opposed to 5,000 to 10,000 for the Médoc appellation). Some other particularly ambitious properties include Chx Beaumont, Bernadotte, Cambon La Pelouse, Citran, Coufran, Lamothe-Bergeron, Lanessan, Sénéjac, Sociando-Mallet, and Tour du Haut-Moulin.

The appellation Médoc

The total area qualifying for the basic Médoc appellation increased dangerously fast in the 1990s and early 2000s and reached nearly 5,700 ha/14,000 acres by 2004, 1,000 ha more than in 1996 and considerably more than that of the generally finer Haut-Médoc. Growers were encouraged by what they thought would be a steady increase in worldwide demand for red bordeaux. They were wrong and many found themselves in severe financial difficulties by the mid 2000s. The basic limit to yields was increased from 45 to 50 hl/ha in 1994, and a high proportion of the wines are dominated by Merlot. Much of the wine produced on these lower, less well-drained, heavier soils is solid if uninspiring claret sold in bulk to CO-OPERATIVES or to the BORDEAUX TRADE for blending into GENERIC Médoc, if the growers are lucky. Estates on which an effort is made to produce something more distinctive than this, usually by restricting yields, include Chx Les Grands Chênes, Les Ormes Sorbet, Potensac (run particularly fastidiously by the owners of Ch LÉOVILLE LAS CASES of St-Julien), Preuillac, La Tour de By, Tour Haut-Caussan (one of Bordeaux's rare ORGANIC WINES), and Vieux Robin. Goulée is a particularly concentrated blended Médoc made by the owners of Ch Cos d'Estournel.

For more details, see BORDEAUX.

Duijker, H., and Broadbent, M., *The Bordeaux Atlas* (London, 1997).

Parker, R., *Bordeaux* (4th edn, New York, 2003).

Penning-Rowsell, E., *The Wines of Bordeaux* (6th edn, London, 1989).

Méjanelle, Coteaux de la, sometimes called **Méjanelle**, named TERROIR within the Coteaux du LANGUEDOC in southern France, just outside the city of MONTPELLIER. Unlike the rest of the Coteaux du Languedoc, this is a historic zone of individual estates, most notably Ch de Flaugergues. Syrah, Grenache, and Mourvèdre dominate in these particularly Mediterranean vineyards, at a much lower

altitude than much of the rest of the Coteaux du Languedoc.

Melnik, powerful indigenous late-ripening Bulgarian red grape variety that is grown exclusively around the ancient town of Mělnik close to the Greek border in what was Thrace. It may therefore have been cultivated here for many centuries (see GREECE, Ancient) and its wines certainly taste more Greek in their extract, tannin, and alcohol than typical of modern Bulgaria. Its full name is Shiroka Melnishka Losa, or 'broad-leaved vine of Melnik', and its berries are notably small with thick, blue skins. Some wines have the aroma of tobacco leaves, another local crop. Oak ageing and several years bring out a warmth and style not unlike a NEBBIOLO. This is probably the Bulgarian wine with the greatest longevity, but see also MAVRUD. An early ripening clone, Ranna Melnishka Losa, yields wines with rounder fruit and softer tannins. With total plantings of 4,700 ha/11,610 acres in 2004, it accounted for over half of all vines in Bulgaria's Struma Valley region.

Melon, or **Melon de Bourgogne**, French white grape variety planted on more than 13,000 ha/32,000 acres in 2000, famous in only one respect and one region, MUSCADET. As its full name suggests, its origins are Burgundian (see PINOT), Melon having been outlawed just like Gamay at various times during the 16th and 17th centuries. Unlike its fellow white Burgundian Chardonnay, several of whose synonyms include the word Melon, it is not a noble grape variety but it does resist cold well and produces quite regularly and generously. It had spread as far as Anjou in the Middle Ages according to Bouchard and so it was natural that the vine-growers of the Muscadet region to the west might try it. It became the dominant vine variety of the Loire-Atlantique in the 17th century, when DUTCH traders encouraged production of high volumes of relatively neutral white wine, in place of the thin reds for which the region had previously been known, as base wines for Holland's enthusiastic distillers.

Melon's increasing importance today rests solely on MUSCADET, although it is also grown to a limited extent in Vézelay in northern Burgundy.

Many of the older cuttings of the variety called PINOT BLANC in California are in fact Melon.

Bouchard, A., 'Notes ampelographiques rétrospectives sur les cépages de la généralité de Dijon', *Bulletin de la Société des Viticulteurs de France* (1899).

Galet, P., *Dictionnaire encyclopédique des cépages* (Paris, 2000).

Mencía, increasingly valued red grape variety grown so widely in north west Spain that plantings total over 9,100 ha/22,500 acres, notably in BIERZO, RIBEIRA SACRA, and

VALDEORRAS (see map under SPAIN). DNA PROFILING has laid to rest the once-popular theory that Mencía and Cabernet Franc were related. In addition, the rediscovery by young winemakers of old, low-yielding hillside plots of Mencía has dispelled the notion that this variety necessarily produces light reds since wines of great concentration and complexity have emerged from these forgotten vineyards on deep schists and produced a PRIORAT-like revolution in the region. It was the fertile plains on which Mencía was replanted after PHYLLOXERA, with resulting high yields, that gave the variety its reputation for dilution.

Mencía is identical to Portugal's JAEN.

Mendocino,

one of CALIFORNIA's largest and climatically most diverse counties. All of its 15,000 acres/6,000 ha of vineyards are in the southern half. Even there, the meteorological range between the coastal Anderson Valley AVA and the interior McDowell Valley AVA beggars the imagination.

Isolation from San Francisco kept its 19th-century vineyards small, and delayed their impact outside the county. The same isolation kept wine for surreptitious resale there throughout PROHIBITION. Most of the plantings flank the town of Ukiah, near the headwaters of the Russian river. Although the districts of Redwood valley, Ukiah, and Hopland are fairly well defined, only Redwood Valley has its own AVA. The others use the blanket Mendocino AVA because of its wider consumer recognition.

Mendocino AVA

The coverall AVA in Mendocino county includes the more specific Anderson Valley, Yorkville Highlands, Mendocino Ridge, McDowell Valley, and Potter Valley AVAs, as well as the county's most substantial vineyard plantings along the Russian river course from Redwood valley southward through Ukiah to Hopland and on south into Sonoma county's Alexander valley. Cabernet Sauvignon and Sauvignon Blanc have been reliable in the large zone along the Russian river. Zinfandel and Petite Sirah from third-generation Italian–American growers on the benchlands can reach great heights in the hands of an artisan wine-maker. Chardonnay from vineyards such as Lolonis has been surprisingly fine. Fetzer is the dominant winery by size; Frey is notable as a producer of good-quality organic wine.

Anderson Valley AVA

Scouts for Louis ROEDERER of Champagne say they hunted in California until they found somewhere with weather as bleak as Roederer's home in north eastern France, and that Mendocino county's coast-hugging Anderson Valley fitted their requirement perfectly. Visually, scores of scenes sluiced out by a short, swift river, the Navarro, make landscape painters lunge for canvas and brushes. Close framed by steep hills, the valley has only a couple of patches that might pass for floor and, unusually for California's valley vineyards, only one or two of the 20 or so are flat. Anderson Valley is hardly 10 miles end to end, but a steady rise in elevation from 800 to 1,300 feet combines with a rising wall of hills to make the inland end at Boonville warmer and sunnier than the oft-befogged area between Philo and Navarro, where most of the vines grow.

Following redwood logging, sheep and apples reigned here until grapes came, a little wave of them in the 1970s, a bigger one in the 1980s, and then a spate of celebrity weekend homes in the 1990s. A couple of extraordinary Gewürztraminers have come from Anderson Valley AVA. Some of its Rieslings and Chardonnays have been memorable. Ridgetops to the west have yielded a succession of wonderfully oak-ribbed Zinfandels from a scattering of tiny patches. Greenwood Ridge, Handley, and Navarro vineyards are the mainstay wineries for table wine production. Duckhorn's Goldeneye operation was a later arrival. However, from 1984, first Roederer then Scharffenberger threw the region's weight behind traditional method sparkling wines from Chardonnay and Pinot Noir, which many critics think may be America's best so far. Sharffenberger was subsequently sold to Pommery, which changed the name to Pacific Echo.

McDowell Valley AVA

In practice this is a one-winery AVA located in a small, upland valley east of the town of Hopland in southern Mendocino county. Bill Crawford of McDowell Valley Vineyards has become a repository of Syrah clonal research catalyzed by his discovery that he owns a small plot of mixed red varieties, including the true Syrah, first planted in 1913. B.C.C.

Mendoza. See ARGENTINA.

Menetou-Salon

is just west of, and very much smaller than, the much more famous SANCERRE, near the city of Bourges, producing a not dissimilar range of red, white, and rosé wines which can often offer better value. Sauvignon Blanc grown here is capable of making wines every bit as refreshingly aromatic as Sancerre. Soils in the appellation are mainly LIMESTONE and can be very similar to those in the more famous zone to the east, although Menetou's vineyards are flatter and less compact, resulting in a less favourable mesoclimate. The best zone is around the village of Morogues, a name used on the labels of producers such as Henry Pellé. The village of Parassy also has a high concentration of vineyards. Sauvignon represents about 60 per cent of the appellation's total production, while Pinot Noir grapes are responsible for scented, light reds and pinks for early consumption, this lightness owing much to a permitted yield of 68 hl/ha for Pinot—yet more evidence of the similarity between Sancerre and Menetou-Salon.

See also LOIRE, including map.

Méntrida,

Spanish town and wine zone south west of Madrid in CASTILLA-LA MANCHA (see map under SPAIN) producing robust red wines from GARNACHA grapes. It is by no means clear what the winemakers in the hills around the town have done to deserve DO status. The one producer who is making high-quality wine in this part of Spain, Marqués de Griñon, grows CABERNET SAUVIGNON, CHARDONNAY, SYRAH, and PETIT VERDOT in his vineyard at Malpica de Tajo, which used to be just outside the denomination but has now been incorporated within it. He spurned the opportunity to jump rank from VINO DE MESA de Toledo to DO by countenancing an extension of the boundary, thereby initiating a fashion for superior non-DO wines sometimes called super-Spanish, after Italy's SUPERTUSCANS. He was rewarded in 2002 with his own single-estate DO, Dominio de Valdepusa.

R.J.M. & V. de la S.

Menu Pineau,

synonym for the ARBOIS vine.

Meranese,

or **Meraner** in German, red wines from around the town of Merano in ALTO ADIGE.

mercaptans,

or thiol compounds, are a group of usually potent and often foul-smelling chemical compounds formed by YEAST reacting with SULFUR in the LEES after the primary alcoholic FERMENTATION. If not removed from the new wine (which can usually be achieved by simple AERATION, by prompt RACKING, for example, or by the addition of a small amount of copper sulfate), less volatile and even more unpleasant compounds tend to be formed.

At extremely low concentration, some mercaptans can have less undesirable and even pleasant odours. An example of this phenomenon is to be found in the mercaptans recently discovered as important contributors to the varietal aroma of Sauvignon Blanc and other wines, see FLAVOUR COMPOUNDS and FLAVOUR PRECURSORS. Professor Denis Dubourdieu and his group at the University of BORDEAUX, who have extensively investigated the role of mercaptans in wine aroma, have also found that benzyl mercaptan contributes to the empyreumatic aroma, i.e. reminiscent of smoke or 'gun flint', of Chardonnay, as well as some Sauvignon Blanc and Sémillon wines. Even OAK FLAVOUR is affected by mercaptans, and furfuryl mercaptan, a compound with a powerful coffee aroma, can be released into wines during maturation in barrels with toasted STAVES. While the detailed chemical and biological mechanisms responsible for the formation of mercaptans in wines are not known in every case, Professor Alain Maujean has recently reviewed and discussed the known chemistry of sulfur in winemaking. P.J.W.

Blanchard, L., Tominaga, T., and Dubourdieu, D., 'Formation of furfurylthiol exhibiting a strong coffee aroma during oak barrel fermentation from furfural released by toasted staves', *Journal of Agricultural and Food Chemistry*, 49 (2001), 4833–5.

Maujean, A., 'The chemistry of sulfur in musts and wines', *Journal International des Sciences de la Vigne et du Vin*, 35 (2001), 171–94.

Tominaga, T., Guimbertau, G., and Dubourdieu, D., 'Contribution of benzenemethanethiol to smoky aroma of certain Vitis vinifera L. wines', *Journal of Agricultural and Food Chemistry* 51, (2003), 1373–6.

merchants are almost as important to the wine world as producers and consumers, and may have been for at least four millennia. Three very different types of wine merchant are considered below, but they share a dependence on the vine and the attractions its produce has for the consumer.

Ancient Greece

As outlined in the ancient history of TASTING, specialized wine merchants already existed as a class in Ancient GREECE. They developed the art of wine tasting which, with cunning, could be applied to the art of selling wine, as recorded in detail by the 3rd-century AD writer Florentinus (preserved in the *Geoponica* 7. 7):

Purchasers of wine should be offered a taste when the north wind blows [when, as he has already explained, wines taste at their best]. Some people try to trick their customers by using an empty cup which they have dipped in very good wine with a great aroma. The quality of the wine leaves its trace for some time, so that the bouquet seems to belong to the wine now poured in the cup, and in this way they deceive the customer. More unscrupulous dealers put out cheese and nuts in the shop, so as to tempt the customers who come in to eat something; the aim is to prevent them from tasting accurately. I record this not as a suggestion for us to follow, but so that we shall not suffer from these practices. The farmer will often need to taste the wine, both new and old, to detect wine which is about to deteriorate. N.G.W.

Modern Britain

The British wine merchant is, almost necessarily, an importer, or a customer of one. Wine merchants were important in medieval England and Gascony, when they were known as VINTNERS in English. Even today, a wine merchant in Britain enjoys a social standing perceptibly higher than that of, for example, a grocer. This is somewhat ironic since the majority of the wine sold in Britain has been sold by grocers, as opposed to specialists, since at least 1987. This was largely due to the efforts of the licensed supermarkets to improve the range and quality of wines they sell, although it is also simply a function of the fact that so many Britons pass through a supermarket

at some point every week. The independent specialist wine merchant has to struggle to compete with the low margins funded by the sheer quantity of wine a chain of supermarkets can sell. They do so by offering personal service, advice, sale or return facilities, credit, mail order, glass loan, and so on, with the supermarkets and such specialist chains as have survived the onslaught of competition from supermarkets hot on their heels.

France

The French term most often translated as merchant is *négociant*, most often a producer/bottler rather than a specialist retailer (known as a *caviste* in French and still a relatively rare phenomenon), since so many wine purchases in France have been made direct from the producer (*vente directe*) or, increasingly, at the supermarket (*grande surface*). See NÉGOCIANT and BORDEAUX TRADE for more details.

See also wine TRADE.

Mercurey, most important village in the Côte CHALONNAISE district of Burgundy. While most of the production is in red wines made from Pinot Noir, a small quantity of unusually scented white wine from Chardonnay is also made. With 650 ha/1,600 acres under vine, Mercurey produces almost as much wine as the other Côte Chalonnaise appellations Givry, Rully, and Montagny combined. The appellation, including the commune of St-Martin-sous-Montaigu, includes 29 PREMIER CRU vineyards making up 20 per cent of the total.

The red wines tend to be deeper in colour, fuller in body, more capable of ageing, and half as expensive again as those of the neighbouring villages. Maximum yields for Mercurey are the same as those for VILLAGE WINES in the CÔTE D'OR, whereas the other appellations of the Côte Chalonnaise may produce an additional 5 hl/ha (0.3 tons/acre).

Mercurey is said to have been the favourite wine of Gabrielle d'Estrées, although her lover Henry IV preferred neighbouring Givry. The leading producers are Ch de Chamirey, Faiveley, Juillot, Lorenzon, and Raquillet. J.T.C.M.

Merenzao, red grape speciality of the VALDEORRAS region in north west Spain, sometimes known as María Ordoña, María Ardoña, or Bastardo. Some recent experiments suggest it has real potential. It is not yet known whether it is identical to the Portuguese variety of the same name.

Merille was once widely planted in SOUTH WEST FRANCE, where there were still 130 ha/320 acres of it in 2000. It produces undistinguished red wine and is not permitted by any local appellation such as Buzet or Côtes du Marmandais.

meristem culture. See TISSUE CULTURE.

Meritage (rhymes with heritage), name coined in 1981, by the winner of a competition in the *Los Angeles Times*, for American wines made from a blend of grape varieties in the image of BORDEAUX, devised to distinguish these wines from VARIETAL Cabernet Sauvignon, Merlot, etc., most usefully on wine lists. This trade-marked name is legally available on labels only to American wineries that agree to join the Meritage Association and uphold the following requirements of the wine labelled Meritage: made exclusively from Cabernet Sauvignon, Cabernet Franc, Merlot, Malbec, Petit Verdot grapes for red wines, and Sauvignon Blanc, Sémillon, and Muscadelle for whites; produced in quantities of no more than 25,000 cases a year; one of the two most expensive wines produced by the winery. Nearly but not all of the members are in CALIFORNIA. B.C.C.

Merlot or **Merlot Noir,** black grape variety originally associated with the great wines of St-Émilion and Pomerol but now so popular worldwide that it competes only with Cabernet Sauvignon as the most planted dark-skinned grape variety overall. Its recent increase in popularity may be most readily associated with consumption in the United States, but in reality total American Merlot plantings lag behind those of Cabernet Sauvignon by quite a margin and it is in Bordeaux, and in France overall, that Merlot is so decisively the most planted red wine grape with a total of more than 101,000 ha/250,000 acres planted to the variety in 2000 (as opposed to 53,000 ha of Cabernet Sauvignon). DNA PROFILING by Austrian researchers provided evidence that Merlot is likely to be the progeny of CABERNET FRANC, the other parent being unknown. In consequence, Merlot turns out to be the probable half-brother of CABERNET SAUVIGNON, which helps to explain why Merlot-dominant red bordeaux can taste so like Cabernet-dominant red bordeaux.

Although Merlot has become the red (and therefore fashionably scorned) answer to Chardonnay, few of those who order it in such quantity—typically by the GLASS in the United States—would be able to describe its flavour with any precision. One thing they would be agreed on though is that it is 'smooth'. If any single wine promoted TEXTURE rather than flavour to the front rank of concerns for American winemakers it is Merlot, 'Cabernet without the pain' (cf. ASTRINGENCY). Indeed one of its flavour characteristics in France, a fragrance bordering on HERBACEOUSNESS, is seen as a positive drawback by many American tasters.

Throughout Bordeaux and SOUTH WEST FRANCE and, increasingly, much of the rest of the world, Merlot plays the role of constant companion to the more austere, aristocratic, long-living Cabernet Sauvignon. Its early-maturing, plump, lush fruitiness provides a more obvious complement to Cabernet

Sauvignon's attributes than the CABERNET FRANC that often makes up the third ingredient in the common BORDEAUX BLEND. It also provides good viticultural insurance in more marginal climates as it buds, flowers, and ripens at least a week before Cabernet Sauvignon (although this makes Merlot more sensitive to frost, as was shown dramatically in 1991 when some RIGHT BANK properties hardly produced any wine at all). Its early flowering makes it particularly sensitive to COULURE, which weaker ROOTSTOCKS can help to prevent. Merlot is not quite so vigorous as Cabernet Sauvignon but its looser bunches of larger, notably thinner-skinned grapes are much more prone to ROT. It is also more sensitive to DOWNY MILDEW. (Spraying can be a particularly frequent phenomenon in the vineyards of Bordeaux.) Merlot responds much better than the late-ripening Cabernet Sauvignon to damp, cool soils, such as those of St-Émilion and Pomerol, that retain their moisture well and allow the grapes to reach full size. In very well-drained soils, dry summers can leave the grapes undeveloped. Unlike Cabernet Sauvignon, Merlot is extremely sensitive to the timing of HARVEST, and acid levels can be dangerously low if picking is delayed too long. Merlot arguably reaches its apogee in the finest wines of Pomerol such as Ch PÉTRUS and Le PIN.

For the vine-grower in anything cooler than a warm or hot climate, Merlot is much easier to ripen than Cabernet Sauvignon, and has the further advantage of yielding a little higher to boot. It is not surprising therefore that, in France and northern Italy, total Merlot plantings have for long been greatly superior to those of Cabernet Sauvignon.

This is particularly marked in Bordeaux, where Cabernet Sauvignon dominates Merlot only in the famously well-drained soils of the Médoc and Graves—and even here Merlot plantings increased considerably in the late 1990s, typically at the expense of Cabernet Franc. Elsewhere, not just in St-Émilion and Pomerol but also in Bourg, Blaye, Fronsac, and, importantly, those areas qualifying for basic Bordeaux or the rest of the so-called BORDEAUX CÔTES appellation, Merlot predominates.

According to the 2000 French vine census, Merlot represented two-thirds of all black vine varieties in the Gironde while Cabernet Sauvignon covered only 27 per cent of vineyard dedicated to red wine.

It was already documented as a good-quality vine variety in the Libournais in 1784 according to the historian Enjalbert, and in 1868 was noted by A. Petit-Laffitte as the Médoc's premier variety for blending with the much younger grape variety Cabernet Sauvignon. But it is clearly in St-Émilion and, especially, the clay soils of Pomerol that the variety produces its more glorious wines (see under ST-ÉMILION and POMEROL for more detail).

Even here, however, except for notable exceptions such as Ch PÉTRUS, Merlot produces wines perceptibly lower in colour, acid, and, especially, tannin than left bank red bordeaux dominated by the thicker-skinned Cabernet Sauvignon. The relatively early-maturing, easy-to-appreciate Merlot is a wine with distinct advantages over Cabernet Sauvignon in times of inflation.

Merlot is also more widely planted than either sort of Cabernet in the rest of SOUTH WEST FRANCE. Wherever in this quarter of France the APPELLATION CONTRÔLÉE regulations sanction Cabernet Sauvignon (see CABERNET SAUVIGNON for details), they also sanction Merlot, although the latter is favoured in the Dordogne while the Cabernets are preferred in Gascony.

With Syrah, Merlot has been a major beneficiary of the Languedoc's replanting with 'improving' grape varieties. Total plantings in the Languedoc more than doubled between 1988 and 1998 to reach 18,500 ha and were 25,300 ha by 2000. Most of this is destined for VINS DE PAYS for the only Languedoc appellations to sanction Merlot within their regulations are CABARDÈS and Côtes de la MALEPÈRE. Merlot has been a much more successful import here than Cabernet Sauvignon and can produce some good-value, fruity wines for drinking young, many of which were shipped to the United States in the mid 1990s to satisfy American demand for this most fashionable of wines.

The Merlot of northern Italy was pressed into similar duty when California's new plantings in the wake of PHYLLOXERA were still too young to be productive. The variety is important in Italy, even if total plantings have fallen from more than 30,000 ha/74,000 acres in 1990 to 25,600 ha in 2000. It is planted particularly in the north east, often alongside Cabernet Franc, where vast quantities of the wine called there 'Merlott' are grown on the plains of both GRAVE DEL FRIULI and PIAVE, even if better, more concentrated wines come in smaller quantities from higher vineyards. In FRIULI indeed, where Merlot performs perceptibly better than most CABERNET, there is even a Strada del Merlot, a tourist route along the Isonzo river. Individual denominations for Merlot abound in FRIULI, VENETO, and TRENTINO-ALTO ADIGE. Merlot is also planted on the Colli BOLOGNESI in Emilia-Romagna. The variety is planted in 14 of Italy's 20 regions. In general, little has been expected from or delivered by the sea of light, vaguely fruity Merlot from northern Italy, which makes it all the more remarkable that the variety is being taken seriously by a handful of producers in Toscana and Umbria and, more recently, in Friuli itself.

Ornellaia in BOLGHERI and the Fattoria di Ama in CHIANTI CLASSICO were some of the first to show that Italy could provide something more in the mould of serious Pomerol. Significant quantities of Merlot are likely to be produced in Toscana and central Italy in the near future, some vinified on its own but an even larger proportion used to supplement Sangiovese. Many producers have come to prefer the variety to Cabernet Sauvignon, both for ripening more easily and for being a less dominant blending component with native Italian varieties.

Merlot is vital to the wine industry of Italian SWITZERLAND and is made at a wide range of quality levels, including some very fine wines indeed.

Merlot has also been popular over Italy's north eastern border in SLOVENIA and all down the Dalmatian coast, where it can be attractively plummy when yields are restricted. It is also known in HUNGARY, notably around Eger in the north east and Villány in the south. It is also the most widely planted red wine variety in ROMANIA, where there may be as much as 7,300 ha/18,000 acres. Merlot is the second most planted variety in, particularly southern, BULGARIA after Pamid and ahead of Cabernet Sauvignon, with which it is often blended. It is also planted widely in MOLDOVA.

Outside these traditional strongholds, Merlot was until the early 1990s taken up much more slowly than the world-famous Cabernet Sauvignon. The fact that it is slightly lower in acidity as well as international *réclame* may have hindered its progress in some warmer climates such as Iberia and most of the eastern Mediterranean, where it is not generally as common as the more structured Cabernet Sauvignon. For example, in 2004, Spain grew more than 10,000 ha of the latter and 8,700 ha of Merlot, most successfully in Penedès.

A lift in Merlot's reputation was already apparent, however, by 1990, most obviously in North America. Merlot was suddenly regarded as 'the hot varietal' in the Cabernet-soaked state of California, and demonstrated decisively that it had a particular affinity with the conditions of Washington state and those of Long island in NEW YORK state.

In 1985, California had a total of hardly 2,000 acres/800 ha of Merlot. This had already risen to about 8,000 acres by 1992 when the faddish American mass market discovered the variety as softer and milder than the state's Cabernet Sauvignons, and demand soared. By 2003, there were 52,000 acres in the ground in California. In the late 1990s, quality suffered. Half of the red grapes planted to replace PHYLLOXERA-infected vines in Napa during 1996 were Merlot, but a similar area of Merlot (about 1,500 acres in each region) was also planted in the less glamorous Central valley counties of Merced, King, Madera, and San Joaquin. The immediacy of faddish demand far outstripped the rapidity with which vines could be planted and start producing. This situation tempted many growers to stretch their crops by irrigating to increase yield. As demand levelled off and supply began to catch up after 2000, growers were no longer tempted to over-water and quality once again began to rise. See CALIFORNIA for more detail of the wine style.

Merlot has had little success in Oregon's vineyards, where the much cooler climate makes coulure too grave a problem, but in Washington's sunny inland Columbia basin, Merlot has produced consistently fine, fruity, well-structured reds about which there are more details under WASHINGTON. Merlot was the state's most popular black grape variety with over 1,500 acres by 1991, an increase of more than 100 per cent in just three years, and there were nearly 8,200 acres by 2005—although Merlot's susceptibility to WINTER FREEZE proved disastrous in 1996. Merlot is also grown increasingly in other North American states, notably in NEW YORK's Long Island.

In South America, Merlot has become extremely important to Chile's prolific wine exports. Vines called Merlot have done particularly well in the damper soils of the more southerly wine regions in Chile's Central valley, although by no means all of the country's recorded 12,900 ha/31,800 acres in the early 21st century are true Merlot Noir. An increasing proportion has been identified as another old Bordeaux variety CARMENÈRE—and some is even sold as such. See CHILE for more detail. It is also planted to a more limited extent in URUGUAY (where it can blend well with the local TANNAT), BRAZIL, and BOLIVIA.

California's relatively late but almost demented enthusiasm for Merlot has been mirrored in AUSTRALIA, where plantings have skyrocketed since the early 1990s and there were nearly 11,000 ha by 2004, a third as much as total Cabernet Sauvignon plantings. There is great potential for Merlot in cooler regions, whether produced as a straight varietal or blended with Cabernet Sauvignon *et al*.

Merlot clearly has potential in New Zealand, too, particularly Hawkes Bay, and plantings had reached 1,590 ha by 2006, making it the country's fourth most planted grape variety. Originally used mainly for filling in the flavour holes of the more angular Cabernet Sauvignon, it is now more commonly bottled on its own. South Africa has produced some interesting varietal Merlots as well as using it to good effect in various BORDEAUX BLENDS. Between 1996 and 2002 plantings increased fourfold and Merlot is now the fourth most popular red wine variety in South Africa.

Enjalbert, H., *Les Grands Vins de St-Émilion, Pomerol et Fronsac* (Paris, 1983).

Merlot Blanc, white wine grape which, unexpectedly, is not a white MUTATION of MERLOT Noir; still grown on 176 ha of France in 2000, mostly in Bordeaux.

Merseguera, lacklustre Spanish white grape variety (Esquitxagos in Penedès) widely grown in ALICANTE, JUMILLA, and VALENCIA. The vine ripens relatively early and has compact bunches of large grapes.

Meslier St-François is, like ARBOIS, a white grape variety that is a local speciality of the Loir-et-Cher *département* in the westward bend of the Loire but has been disappearing at an even faster rate. DNA PROFILING at MONTPELLIER and DAVIS revealed in 2000 that Meslier St-François is a progeny of GOUAIS BLANC and CHENIN BLANC.

mesoclimate, a term of climatic scale, intermediate between regional climate or MACROCLIMATE, and the very small scale MICROCLIMATE. It encompasses the more specific terms TOPOCLIMATE and SITE CLIMATE, and has largely replaced both in specialist usage (although the word microclimate is widely and incorrectly used by non-specialists for mesoclimate). The usual scale of a mesoclimate is in tens or hundreds of metres, so one speaks correctly of the mesoclimate of a particular vineyard or potential vineyard site.

The full definition of a mesoclimate (or site climate) requires detailed on-the-spot records, but these are seldom available over the long periods (conventionally 30 years or more) needed to iron out short-term climatic fluctuations, and thus to be fully representative. The process can be considerably shortened if site records can be calibrated continuously against those of a nearby and reasonably comparable older station. The differences, once established as consistent over a number of seasons, can be applied to the longer-term records of the latter.

In the absence of any local temperature measurements it is still possible to make fair estimates by interpolating within known regional trends, and then allowing for differences in altitude at the rate of 0.6 °C/1.1 °F per 100 m/330 ft. Following that, individual mesoclimates can be approximated more closely still by allowing for features of TOPOGRAPHY such as slope and aspect, and even soil type, as discussed in general terms by Geiger.

J.G.

Geiger, R., *Das Klima der bodennahen Luftschicht* (4th edn, Brunswick, 1961), trans. by Scripta Technica, Inc., as *Climate near the Ground* (Cambridge, Mass., 1966).

Gladstones, J., *Viticulture and Environment* (Adelaide, 1992).

Mesopotamia. In ancient Mesopotamia, which lay in the fertile land between the rivers Tigris and Euphrates and is often thought of as the cradle of civilization, the most widely consumed alcoholic drink at all periods was probably BEER. However, grape wine is already mentioned in cuneiform texts preserved on clay tablets from Ur dating to approximately 2750 BC. Vines do not grow so well in the lowlying and humid south of Mesopotamia, and wine seems to have been imported from the more mountainous north. This is probably the origin of the poetic Mesopotamian name for wine, 'liquor of the mountains'.

By the first millennium BC, wine was as widely used as beer, at least in privileged circles. Unfortunately, little information is available about the methods of production. Some wines, such as the so-called 'bitter wine' of Tupliash, an area lying to the east of the river Tigris, seem to have been drunk FLAVOURED with herbs.

But from the beginning of the first millennium BC, it appears that wines were more commonly identified by their place of origin than by their type. These are mostly regions in the north or north west of Mesopotamia (in modern northern Iraq and northern Syria), but also including Suhu (a region in modern Iraq on the middle course of the river Euphrates, downstream from the modern Syrian border). In an inscription detailing offerings made to the god Marduk in his temple at Babylon, King Nebuchadnezzar II (r. 604–563 BC) mentions 'liquor of the mountains', 'clear wine', and the wines of eight different named regions.

A few documents (in the form of clay tablets) survive from the early 8th century BC from the Assyrian capital Kalhu (modern Nimrud). These are the remnants of a once vast archive detailing the administration of wine rations to the 6,000-strong palace household, from the king and queen down to assistant cooks and shepherd boys. The wine magazines were lined with great wine jars and archaeologists have estimated that one magazine stored at least 151 hl/4,000 gal. The basic daily ration was quite modest: 0.184 l, with 0.306 l for a skilled craftsman. Nobles received considerably more.

Wine and beer were frequently offered, among many other foods and drinks, to deities as part of the cult, and the practice of LIBATION was widespread in temple ritual.

Among the Babylonians and Assyrians, wine was widely used, as was beer, for medicinal purposes (see MEDICINE), especially as a vehicle for various concoctions often of rather dubious, if not frankly revolting, ingredients.

See also Ancient SUMER, and see HERODOTUS for details of the earliest recorded mention of the use of BARRELS for transporting wine, down the Euphrates.

J.A.B.

Bottéro, J., 'Getränke' ('Drinks'), *Reallexikon der Assyriologie und vorderasiatischen Archäologie* (the standard reference work on the subject, 1st pub. in Berlin, 1928, and still being completed).

Kinnier Wilson, J. V., *The Nimrud Wine Lists* (London, 1972).

metabisulfite, often added to freshly picked grapes to prevent OXIDATION of the must. See SULFUR DIOXIDE.

metals. See MINERALS.

metatartaric acid. See TARTRATES.

métayage, French word for a system of sharecropping particularly common in the CÔTE D'OR whereby a vine-grower, or *métayer*, rents a vineyard or, more likely in Burgundy, part of a vineyard, and pays rent in the form of wine or grapes.

methanol, another name for **methyl alcohol**, also known as wood alcohol, is the member of the chemical series of common ALCOHOLS with the lowest molecular weight. Methanol, which is moderately toxic, has unfortunately been confused with ETHANOL on occasion, with serious results to the health and even life of the unwary consumer. The immediate risk of ingesting any quantity of methanol is blindness, but consumption of between 25 and 100 ml (4 fl oz) can be fatal. As recently as the mid 1980s, some Italian wines were found to have been contaminated with methanol (see ADULTERATION).

Wines naturally contain very small quantities of methanol: about 0.1 g/l, or less than one-hundredth of the normal concentration of ethanol. Some methanol is naturally present in grapes and further traces are formed during FERMENTATION but most is formed by demethylating the pectin materials that are naturally present in the grape (see COLLOIDS and ENZYMES). Red wines, and particularly those subjected to prolonged MACERATION, are likely to have higher methanol concentrations than average. Brandy in general has rather higher levels of methanol than wine because the DISTILLATION process concentrates it. And wines and brandies made from fruits other than grapes tend to have higher methanol concentrations because grapes have fewer pectins than most other fruits. It would be impossible to ingest a dangerous level of methanol from such drinks, however, without ingesting a fatal amount of ethanol long beforehand.

Methanol is often encountered in everyday life because it is a common solvent for household products as well as being used as fuel for chafing dishes. A.D.W.

méthode ancestrale, sometimes called **méthode artisanale** or **méthode rurale**, very traditional SPARKLING WINE-MAKING method used chiefly in Limoux, resulting in a lightly sparkling, medium sweet wine, sometimes complete with sediment.

méthode champenoise, French term for the traditional method described in detail in SPARKLING WINE-MAKING. This description was once a valuable aid to the consumer in distinguishing the most meticulously made sparkling wines from those made by less complicated methods. From 1994 this description was outlawed by EUROPEAN UNION authorities, however, in favour of one of the following: 'fermentation en bouteille selon la méthode champenoise'; 'méthode traditionnelle'; 'méthode classique'; 'méthode traditionnelle classique'. English-language equivalents are 'fermented in this bottle' and TRADITIONAL METHOD.

méthode classique, term for the traditional method of SPARKLING WINE-MAKING approved by the EUROPEAN UNION.

méthode dioise, SPARKLING WINE-MAKING process used for CLAIRETTE DE DIE.

méthode gaillacoise, GAILLAC's version of the MÉTHODE ANCESTRALE. See SPARKLING WINE-MAKING.

méthode traditionnelle and **méthode traditionnelle classique,** alternative terms for the traditional method of SPARKLING WINE-MAKING that are approved by the EUROPEAN UNION. See MÉTHODE CHAMPENOISE.

methoxy-dimethylpyrazine, more properly **2-methoxy-3, 5-dimethylpyrazine,** or MDMP, exists in cork and becomes a taint in wine at concentrations above the perception threshold of approximately 2–4 ng/l in red and white wines. This compound is identified by aromas of fresh cork, woody, and dusty smells.

An AUSTRALIAN WINE RESEARCH INSTITUTE study in 2004 isolated this compound and confirmed that it is responsible for a taint described in Australia as 'fungal must'. It has been suggested that this may prove to be second only to TCA as a cause of CORK TAINT in Australian wine.

Simpson, R. F., Capone, D. L., Duncan, B. C., and Sefton, M. A., 'Incidence and nature of "fungal must" taint in wine corks', *Australia and New Zealand Wine Industry Journal*, 20/2 (Jan/Feb 2005), 26–31.

methoxypyrazines, FLAVOUR COMPOUNDS which result in HERBACEOUSNESS. They contain nitrogen and are secondary products of AMINO ACID metabolism. Three methoxypyrazines have been identified for Cabernet Sauvignon and Sauvignon Blanc grapes: ISOBUTYL-METHOXYPYRAZINE (IBMP), secbutyl-methoxypyrazine (SBMP), and isopropyl-methoxypyrazine (IPMP). Sensory evaluation has confirmed the contribution of IBMP, which has a very low threshold of 2 ng/l in white wine, to the aroma described as characteristic of capsicum or bell pepper and green gooseberries. It is generally the most dominant of the three. IPMP, the most abundant of the three, has a more earthy aroma, characteristic of cooked or canned asparagus (found in some New Zealand Sauvignon Blanc).

Related studies have demonstrated that the levels of IBMP and IPMP compounds in grape berries matches what is known commercially about the herbaceous wine character. First, the berry concentrations of IBMP drop markedly during ripening, as does the herbaceous character, and more so with increased sun exposure. Secondly, concentrations of IBMP are higher for grapes grown in cooler climates; Australian samples have been found to have much lower levels of IBMP than French or New Zealand samples, for example. IBMP is generally higher in Cabernet Sauvignon than in Sauvignon Blanc, suggesting that other compounds may play a part in contributing to the complex Cabernet Sauvignon flavour,

masking the methoxypyrazine flavour to a certain extent. In wine, methoxypyrazines are particularly stable against OXIDATION, but levels can be lowered during CLARIFICATION; their sensory impact may also be influenced through binding with other wine components.

Allen, M. S., *et al.*, 'Contribution of methoxypyrazines to the flavour of Cabernet Sauvignon and Sauvignon Blanc', in P. J. Williams *et al.* (eds.), *Proceedings of the Seventh Australian Wine Industry Technical Conference* (Adelaide, 1990).

Lacey, M. J., Allen, M. S., Harris, R. L. N., and Brown, W. V., 'Methoxypyrazines in Sauvignon blanc grapes and wines', *American Journal of Enology and Viticulture*, 42/2 (1991), 103–8.

Marais, J., 'Effect of grape temperature, oxidation and skin contact on Sauvignon Blanc juice and wine composition and wine quality', *South African Journal of Enology and Viticulture*, 19/1 (1998), 10–16.

Roujou de Boubée, D., Cumsille, A. M., Pons, M., and Dubourdieu, D., 'Location of 2-methoxy-3-isobutylpyrazine in Cabernet Sauvignon grape bunches and its extractibility during vinification', *American Journal of Enology and Viticulture*, 53/1 (2002), 1–5.

Methuen Treaty, accord signed between Britain and Portugal in 1703 which gave Portuguese goods preferential treatment in Britain and encouraged the imports of Portuguese wine, at the expense of wine from the rest of Europe, notably France, at a time when PORT was evolving into the strong, sweet drink we know today.

metodo classico and **metodo tradizionale,** Italian terms for SPARKLING WINES made by the traditional method.

Meunier is one of France's dozen most planted black grape varieties but neither it nor its common synonym **Pinot Meunier** are often encountered on a wine label. Meunier is an early, particularly downy, MUTATION of the famously mutable PINOT NOIR. It earns its name (*meunier* is French for miller) because the underside of its downy leaves can look as though they have been dusted with flour. In Germany, it is known as Müllerrebe (miller's grape) as well, misleadingly, as Schwarzriesling.

Meunier is treasured in Champagne, as it was in the once-extensive vineyards of northern France, because it buds later and ripens earlier than the inconveniently early budding Pinot Noir and is therefore much less prone to COULURE and more dependably productive. Acid levels are slightly higher although alcohol levels are by no means necessarily lower than those of Pinot Noir. Meunier is therefore the popular choice for Champagne's growers, especially those in cooler north-facing vineyards, in the damp, frost-prone Vallée de la Marne, and in the cold valleys of the Aisne *département*. In fact, so commercially reliable is Meunier for Champagne's powerful vine-growers that it is Champagne's most popular variety by far, covering 10,500 ha/26,000 acres, or almost 40 per cent of the region's vineyards, although plantings of Pinot Noir and Chardonnay have recently increased at a greater rate than those of Meunier.

Common wisdom has it that, as an ingredient in the traditional three-variety champagne blend, Meunier contributes youthful fruitiness to complement Pinot Noir's weight and Chardonnay's finesse. Few producers boast of their Meunier, however (with the honourable exception of KRUG), and few preponderantly Meunier growers' champagnes have great weight or staying power. Meunier is generally lower in pigments than Pinot Noir, and one of its common French synonyms is Gris Meunier.

It has largely disappeared elsewhere in northern France although it is still technically allowed into the rosés and light reds of Côtes de TOUL, wines of MOSELLE, and, in the Loire, TOURAINE and ORLÉANS.

As Müllerrebe or Schwarzriesling, a selection of Meunier is relatively, and increasingly, popular in Germany, where the majority of its more than 2,500 ha/6,180 acres are now grown in the WÜRTTEMBERG region. It is also grown in German-speaking SWITZERLAND, and to a much lesser extent in Austria.

Curiously, in Australia, Meunier has a longer documented history as a still red varietal wine (at one time called Miller's Burgundy) than Pinot Noir, notably at Great Western (now called Grampians) in VICTORIA. New-found enthusiasm for authentic replicas of champagne saved the variety from extinction in Australia and there have been some new plantings in cooler spots so that the national total was more than 150 ha in the early 2000s.

It was also with an eye to producing 'genuine' replicas of champagne that growers in California sought Meunier cuttings in the 1980s so that the state's total acreage of the variety, still about 200, is almost exclusively in CARNEROS.

Meursault, large and prosperous village in the Côte de Beaune district of Burgundy's CÔTE D'OR producing mostly white wines from the Chardonnay grape (see map under BURGUNDY). Although Meursault contains no GRAND CRU vineyards, the quality of white burgundy from Meursault's best PREMIERS CRUS is rarely surpassed.

The finest vineyards are Les Perrières, Les Genevrières, and Les Charmes. Between them and the village of Meursault are three more premiers crus, Le Poruzot, Les Bouchères, and La Goutte d'Or. Another group by the hamlet of BLAGNY are sold as Meursault-Blagny if white or Blagny premier cru if red. while, at the other end of the village, Les Santenots is sold as Meursault Santenots if white and Volnay Santenots if red, as it usually is. Apart from Les Santenots, and the lean but fine red wines of Blagny, the other red wines of Meursault tend to be grown low on the slope and do not feature among the best of the Côte de Beaune.

Les Perrières was cited as a 'tête de cuvée' vineyard in the original CLASSIFICATION of 1861 and might well have been classified as a grand cru. Its character derives from the quantity of stones, after which the vineyard is named, which reflect the sun back onto the vines. If Les Perrières is regularly the richest wine in Meursault, Les Genevrières comes close, producing particularly elegant wines. Les Charmes is the biggest of the three major vineyards and produces the most forward wines, seductive even in their youth.

Meursault also enjoys a wealth of good wines from other named vineyards such as Chevalières, Tessons, Clos de la Barre, Luchets, Narvaux, and Tillets. These are frequently more interesting than the village wines of PULIGNY-MONTRACHET, where the water table is higher. Furthermore, it is possible to dig cellars significantly deeper in Meursault, which enables many growers to prolong BARREL MATURATION through a second winter, which improves the depth, stability, and ageing potential of the wines. Meursault is made from 371 ha/910 acres of white wine vineyard, of which 100 are designated premier cru, and 15 ha of Pinot Noir.

Meursault also hosts one of the three glorious feasts of Burgundy during the third weekend in November (see TROIS GLORIEUSES). On the Monday after the HOSPICES DE BEAUNE sale, some 600 local growers and guests gather at noon for the Paulée de Meursault, an end-of-harvest feast revived in the 1920s by Comte Jules Lafon. Everybody brings their own bottles to share with other tables. The occasion slightly belies the local proverb that he who drinks only Meursault will never be a drunkard. Comte Lafon is still one of the finest producers of Meursault, along with Coche Dury and Guy Roulot.   J.T.C.M.

Meuse, Côtes de. Vin de Pays in the far north east of France seeking elevation to VDQS status for its featherlight whites and *vin gris*.

Mexico, the Americas' oldest wine-producing country, had 41,000 ha/101,000 acres under vine in 2002, although only about 10 per cent of this land is designed to produce wine, the great majority having been planted after the early 1960s in response to huge domestic demand for brandy. This demand was fuelled by protectionist import taxes on both wines and spirits, which also encouraged foreign investment from the likes of Martell and DOMECQ, brandy producers who have done much to build on the efforts of indigenous wine producers such as Casa Madero, L. A. Cetto, and Santo Tomás. The OIV records an annual wine production of about one million hl/26.4 million gal.

Mexico's history of wine production dates from 1521, just a year after the arrival of the Spanish conquistadores, who had no intention of forswearing wine in this new continent (see SOUTH AMERICA, history). Cortés issued an edict three years later ordering all new Spanish settlers to plant 1,000 vines for every 100 natives on the land they had been granted. In 1531, King Carlos V commanded that every vessel headed for the New World should carry vines for cultivation, which made the country self-sufficient in wine (and curbed exports from Andalucía) by the end of the 16th century. The first commercially produced wine in the oldest winery in the Americas was made in 1597 at the Mission of Santa Maria de las Parras in what is now the Casa Madero winery. Father Juan Ugarte is credited with spreading viticulture northwards from mission to mission into what is now the state of CALIFORNIA. The notable growth of Mexican viticulture and wine-making came to an abrupt end in 1699 when King Charles II of Spain's protectionist edict prohibiting wine production in Spain's new colonies was applied with particular vigour in Mexico. Only SACRAMENTAL WINE was allowed.

Thanks to PHYLLOXERA, Mexico's vineyard was but a few hundred hectares at the beginning of the 20th century but in 1948 the National Association of Winemaking was established by 15 producers and a fragile domestic market for wine began to develop in the 1960s. The country's total vineyard area doubled in the 1970s, although there is enormous variation in characteristics between the various vineyard regions. Average annual wine production was about 2 million cases in the 1980s but, thanks to a 1989 free trade agreement with the EUROPEAN UNION and a flood of cheap imports from Germany, dropped considerably in the 1990s.

The five Mexican states producing wine are Querétaro, Aguascalientes, Zacatecas, Coahuila, and, by far the most important and promising, Baja California in the north west of the country. Baja California's principal wine regions are Valle de Guadalupe, Valle de Calafia, Valle de Santo Tomás, Valle de San Vicente, and Valle de San Antonio de las Minas. Annual rainfall is only about 10 in/250 mm but vines can thrive in the MEDITERRANEAN climate, not unlike Napa and Sonoma's with its Pacific influence, wherever IRRIGATION water can be found. Vine varieties are a mix of INTERNATIONAL VARIETIES with PETITE SIRAH, ZINFANDEL, COLOMBARD, and CHENIN BLANC from California, plus NEBBIOLO, BARBERA, and TEMPRANILLO.

The most important wineries are: Monte Xanic, Vinos Bibayoff, Cavas Valmar, Casa de Piedra, Viñas Liceaga, and the Bordelais Chateau Camou, all established in the 1980s and 1990s; the much older L.A. Cetto, Casa Pedro Domecq, Bodegas Ferriño, and Santo Tomás (now working with Wente of California); and

GARAGISTES Adobe Guadalupe and Mogor Badan. FREIXENET of Spain also established Finca Doña Dolores in 1983 near Cadereyta to produce Sala Vivé sparkling wine. The early 21st century saw a dramatic increase in quality and ambition among the best Mexican wine producers and more foreign investment is likely.

Mexico's own influence on New World wine has also been considerable, if indirect. Without Mexicans as the prime LABOUR source for vineyard work, California's late 20th-century wine industry might have developed quite differently.   E.S.M. & B.T.A.R.

Michigan, Midwestern state in the UNITED STATES whose vineyards between the Great lakes of Superior, Michigan, Huron, Erie, and the diminutive lake St Clair, enjoy a slightly less harsh climate than the state's neighbours, a slight difference that is enough to make viticulture viable. The industry is well-developed with over 40 wineries, several doing robust business, although they were dealt a severe blow in 2005 when the Michigan legislature voted to outlaw wine shipping within the state (see UNITED STATES, regulations). Wineries such as Bel Lago, Black Star Farms, Chateau Grand Traverse, Fenn Valley, Good Harbor, Old Mission Cellars, Peninsula Cellars, Raftshol, St Julian (delicious sherry styles), Tabor Hill, and L. Mawby with its excellent sparkling wines, are likely to persevere. Aromatic varieties are best here, with Pinot Blanc, Pinot Gris, Riesling, Gewurztraminer, and Chenin Blanc consistent producers. Pinot Noir has so far been best used for sparkling wine.   D.F.

microbes, or **micro-organisms**, extremely small living beings, a few of which are capable of causing VINE DISEASES and FERMENTATION. Those affecting wines and vines are usually referred to as YEASTS and BACTERIA. **Microbiology** is the study of such micro-organisms, which need **micro-nutrients** as well as nutrients for growth.

microbullage, French term for MICRO-OXYGENATION.

microchâteau, unofficial name for a relatively recent phenomenon on Bordeaux's RIGHT BANK, miniature wine estates producing ultra-modern wines, deep-coloured, early-maturing, often sweet, oaky, flattering reds typically produced in quantities of a few hundred cases from low YIELDS, careful SELECTION, fairly warm and short FERMENTATIONS, short MACERATION, MALOLACTIC FERMENTATION in barrel, 15 to 18 months of 100 per cent new BARREL MATURATION, minimal FILTRATION, and, often, Michel ROLLAND as consultant oenologist. Le PIN in Pomerol was the archetype, and is the only one to experience sustained demand. As its PRICES soared, a host of micro-

châteaux appeared in St-Émilion (where there is more available land) in the late 1990s. The microchâteau owners are often referred to as *garagistes*, a reference to the fact that their output is so small that it can be made in a garage. Ch Valandraud was one of the first and most successful, establishing the model of drawing fruit from several quite separate vineyards. Others include Le Dôme, La Gomerie, La Mondotte (produced by the owner of Ch Canon La Gaffelière), Quinault L'Enclos, and Rol Valentin, although demand for such wines waned considerably in the 21st century and prices continued to slide in the mid 2000s.

Echikson, W., *Noble Rot* (New York, 2004).

microclimate, widely misused term meaning strictly the climate within a defined and usually very restricted space or position. In viticulture, it might be at specified positions between rows of vines, or distances above the ground.

Common use of the term microclimate to describe the climate of a vineyard site, hillside, or valley is clearly wrong. The correct term for these is usually MESOCLIMATE, or possibly site climate or topoclimate.

CANOPY MICROCLIMATE is that within and immediately surrounding the vine canopy, or green parts of the vine. There are microclimates on or close to the surfaces of individual leaves, grape bunches, or even berries. Microclimates exist at various positions or depths within the soil. All these distinctions are important in understanding vine responses to environment.

Microclimate is potentially influenced by management practices, such as vine TRELLISING, VINE TRAINING, and TRIMMING; vine VIGOUR and the factors affecting it; and SOIL MANAGEMENT and mulching. In this respect it differs in important ways from climatic definitions of wider embrace, such as MACROCLIMATE and MESOCLIMATE, which are wholly or largely uninfluenced by management.

Microclimate distances are normally measured in millimetres to a maximum of a few metres; those of mesoclimate, in tens or hundreds of metres.   J.G. & R.E.S.

micro-oxygenation, also known by the French term *microbullage*, is a vinification technique initiated in 1990 by winemaker Patrick Ducournau in MADIRAN to control the AERATION of wines in tank. The method was authorized by the European Commission in 1996 and is used mainly but not exclusively on red wines. Its guiding principle is that all wines require OXYGEN to a greater or lesser extent, its aim being to enable the winemaker to deliver precise and controlled levels at various stages in the WINE-MAKING process. It also addresses the issue of wine storage, effectively transforming large inert storage vessels into selectively permeable containers of infinitely variable dimensions.

Micro-oxygenation can be used during the early stages of alcoholic FERMENTATION to build a healthy YEAST population and help avoid a STUCK FERMENTATION. It also helps to maintain yeast viability, thus minimizing the production of sulfides, which may later cause REDUCTION problems. When used after fermentation, it can aid rapid and complete CLARIFICATION and STABILIZATION, thus reducing the need for FILTRATION. Injections of oxygen during ÉLEVAGE can also help counter the problem of REDUCTION. But, proponents believe, its chief attribute is that it mirrors the effects of oxygen on wines treated to BARREL MATURATION: wines in barrel are exposed to oxygen passively and continually, whereas wines stored in tank are exposed to significant amounts of oxygen only during RACKING and somewhat violently. Used in conjunction with OAK CHIPS or INNER STAVES, the technique can provide an efficient, cost-effective alternative to oak barrels. Micro-oxygenation seems to favour POLYMERIZATION of tannins and the retention of PIGMENTED TANNINS resulting respectively in a softer taste and more stable colour. Some Bordeaux producers use micro-oxygenation on new wine during maceration before PRESSING as a way to begin this process while the must has all its constituents available. Proponents claim that it is also an effective remedy for GREEN or vegetal characters due to slightly underripe fruit. It has been suggested that the introduction of oxygen in this way appears to accelerate the ageing process but this is contested by those who make the equipment and promote its use.

The micro-oxygenation apparatus consists of a system of two chambers and valves connected to a cylinder of oxygen. The gas is moved into a first chamber that is calibrated to the volume of wine. It then moves into a second chamber and is delivered into the wine, a timer controlling the periodic injection of a predetermined dose. The gas passes through a small polyamide tube into the tank and diffuses through a porous ceramic stone hung near the bottom of the vessel. A typical dosage rate is between 0.75 and 3 cc of oxygen per litre of wine per month and the treatment might take four to eight months. In the absence of good scientific studies on the effects of this technique, micro-oxygenation is still largely an art. There are no firm guidelines for how much micro-oxygenation a wine can take; winemakers have to guess this and monitor the process carefully by regular tasting.

The technique was first developed as a response to the fierce TANNINS of Madiran's TANNAT grape and seems particularly well suited to tannic grape varieties. It has also been used on wines high in tannin but relatively low in ANTHOCYANINS, some SANGIOVESE, for example.

Micro-oxygenation does not necessarily preclude barrel maturation. A variation on this technique is used in barrel as a gentler alternative to racking, and one which binds less SULFUR DIOXIDE, for example. A measured amount of oxygen is injected into the wine in barrel, again with a small ceramic stone. This 'punctual' micro-oxygenation has been dubbed *cliquage*. The wine is otherwise aged conventionally in barrels, which allow continuous micro-oxygenation due to the structure of the wood and produce big, rich red wines that remain relatively supple, the epitome of FASHION in fact.

By the beginning of the 21st century, approximately 2500 micro-oxygenation units were in use throughout France, particularly in BORDEAUX, where it is used on a property as grand as Ch Canon La Gaffelière, the St-Émilion grand cru classé (see CLASSIFICATION), and in at least 11 countries on five continents. Perhaps its largest take-up, however, has been in Chile, where it is particularly appreciated for its ability to moderate the greenness and vegetal character found in some Chilean red wines. Results so far suggest the technique is particularly suitable for fashioning wines for short- to medium-term consumption from tannic or potentially reductive grape varieties.

L.F. & J.Ha.

Lemaire, T., 'La micro-oxygénation des vins', École Nationale Supérieure Agronomique (Montpellier, 1995).

Moutouneti, M., Ducournau, P., Chassin, M., and Lemaire, T. (ed. Allan, D.), 'The Technological Significance of Micro-Oxygenation for Wines', *Air liquide*, 22 (Mar 1998).

Midi, common name for the south of France. Like 'Mezzogiorno' in Italy, it means literally 'midday' and refers to regions where midday is a time of extreme heat and inactivity, at least in summer. Midi is often used synonymously with LANGUEDOC-ROUSSILLON, although strictly speaking the Midi encompasses PROVENCE as well.

mildew. See DOWNY MILDEW and POWDERY MILDEW.

Milgranet, rare vine speciality of French vineyards north and west of Toulouse producing particularly firm red wine.

Millau, Côtes de, small, 40-ha zone in the Gorges du Tarn in SOUTH WEST FRANCE, promoted to VDQS status in 1994, making reds and some rosés mainly from a blend of Gamay and Syrah. The Aguessac CO-OPERATIVE dominates production.

millerandage, abnormal FRUIT SET in the vine which is shown by the joint presence of large and small berries in the same bunch. This mixed berry size is due to differences in seed number, with the small berries being seedless. They may be known as 'hen and chicken' or 'pumpkins and peas'. The condition is due either to inclement weather at FLOWERING, which affects some varieties, Gewürztraminer,

for example, more than others, or alternatively to BORON deficiency, or FANLEAF DEGENER-ATION. The cause of millerandage is poor fertilization of the OVARY by POLLEN.

Millerandage can cause a major loss of YIELD, especially where the proportion of small berries is high. Winemakers have, however, been known to welcome the condition, as there is a widely held view that small BERRY SIZE makes better-quality wine. A common New World example of this belief is the Chardonnay CLONE developed at DAVIS which is known as both 1A and Mendoza. This clone is subject to millerandage with cool flowering, but is appreciated for its beneficial effect on wine quality by some winemakers in New Zealand, Australia, and California.

R.E.S.

Galet, P., *Précis de viticulture* (5th edn, Montpellier, 1988).

millésime is French for VINTAGE. A vintage-dated wine is therefore said to be **millésimé**.

minerals and **mineral elements**, the dissolved non-organic salts in grapes and wine. Many are elements essential for vine growth. These can vary enormously between different vineyards and production methods but in grapes would typically include—in addition to the elements carbon, hydrogen, and OXYGEN, which are essential for growth—in declining concentrations, POTASSIUM, NITROGEN, PHOS-PHORUS, SULFUR, MAGNESIUM, CALCIUM (at 200 to 2,000 mg/l in grape juice), followed by BORON, MANGANESE, IRON at 20 to 50 mg/l, and then COPPER, ZINC, and molybdenum at less than 5 mg/l. Analyses also show the presence of many other elements—sodium, chlor-ine, rubidium, silicon, cobalt, LEAD, arsenic, and others—each with unknown or nil function. (Notable is wine's high ratio of potassium to sodium, as advocated for cardiac patients' diets, and the relatively low concentration of iron, despite the traditional view that wine is an important source of this particular mineral.)

Concentrations of minerals in wine can vary between low parts per million to fractions of parts per billion and may reflect the substances present in the soils, whether naturally or as a result of FERTILIZERS or PESTICIDES (although see VINE NUTRITION and SOIL AND WINE QUALITY for more detail of the relationship between minerals in soil and minerals in wine).

The mineral content of wine can be measured in fractional parts per billion by modern methods of ANALYSIS such as atomic absorption spectroscopy and mass spectrometry. This has resulted in the establishment of legal limits for components that were undetectable as recently as the 1970s.

Recent studies in British Columbia indicate that wine element 'fingerprints' can be determined, specific to an individual vineyard and virtually unaffected by vintage, grape variety, or wine-making techniques. As few as six

elements can distinguish a vineyard, although up to 25 elements can be used to establish a vineyard of origin's 'fingerprint'. This technique offers a check against fraudulent labelling.

A.D.W., B.G.C., & R.E.S.

Greenlough, J. D., Longerich, H. P., and Jackson, S. E., 'Element fingerprinting of Okanagan Valley wines using ICP-MS: Relationships between wine composition, vineyard and wine colour', *Australian Journal of Grape and Wine Research*, 3 (1997), 75–83.

mineral vine nutrition. See VINE NUTRITION.

Minervois, improving western LANGUEDOC appellation for characterful reds, generally suppler than those from CORBIÈRES to the south, together with some rosé and white, produced on more than 4,000 ha/9,880 acres of varied inland terrain in the Aude and eastern Hérault *départements* (see map under LANGUE-DOC). The appellation takes its name from the village of Minerve, scene of one of the bloodiest sieges of the Cathar sect in the 13th century. There is considerable archaeological evidence that the Romans practised viticulture here. Cicero records the dispatch of wine to Rome from the *pagus minerbensis*, and La Livinière, the first Minervois village to be accorded its own appellation, **Minervois-La Livinière**, is said to take its name from *cella vinaria*, Latin for 'wine cellar'. More recently, the vineyards of Minervois were invaded first by PHYLLOXERA and then by the CARIGNAN vine, whose influence is being successively reduced.

Since 1985, when Minervois was granted AP-PELLATION CONTRÔLÉE status, strenuous efforts have been made to upgrade overall quality, and a number of both CO-OPERATIVES and individual wine producers have made considerable investments both in winery equipment and in planting better vine varieties. Mourvèdre and Syrah must account for at least 20 per cent of the blend, with Grenache, Lladoner Pelut, Carignan, Cinsaut, and other traditional Languedoc varieties. Various combinations of Bourboulenc, Rolle (Vermentino), Maccabéo, Roussanne, Marsanne, and Grenache Blanc are responsible for the varied quality and character of white Minervois, the first two being best suited to the south eastern part of the appellation closest to the Mediterranean, while the last two perform best in western, Atlantic-influenced sites. White Minervois is increasingly aromatic and sophisticated. Some producers are reviving a local SWEET WINE-MAKING tradition in **Minervois Noble**, a golden, sweet wine made from Minervois white wine grapes which reach at least 17 per cent POTENTIAL ALCOHOL either by NOBLE ROT or, more commonly, PASSERILLAGE. The maximum permitted yield is 15 hl/ha.

For red wines, most Carignan is vinified using full or partial CARBONIC MACERATION for five to 12 days, while other red wine varieties are given longer in the fermentation vat, with frequent pumping over or punching down to encourage EXTRACTION of PHENOLICS. DESTEMMING is increasingly common, and red wines have traditionally been given at least a year in cement tanks or large old casks. Small barrel maturation is becoming more common, but there are constraints on investment in a region whose selling prices have been relatively low.

The appellation can be divided into five climatic zones: Les Côtes Noires in the far north west on the coolest, most Atlantic-influenced foothills of the Montagne Noire; La Clamoux on alluvial terraces and flatter land in the south west towards Carcassonne; La Zone Centrale in the middle of the appellation at an altitude of around 400 m; La Causse on high land and poor, dry soils in the north east where yields are lowest; and Les Serres in the warmest, most MEDITERRANEAN south east.

In the extreme north east of the region, some of France's rarest and most delicate VIN DOUX NATUREL is produced: MUSCAT DE ST-JEAN-DE-MINERVOIS, whose best exponents are Domaines de Barroubio and Montahuc. Other reliable producers include Domaine des Aires Hautes, Borie de Maurel (Cuvée Sylla), Clos Centeilles, Ch Coupe Rose, Ch Laville-Bertrou, Ch d'Oupia, Domaines Piccinini and Jean-Baptiste Senat, and Chx La Tour Boisée and Villerambert Julien.

Minho, VINHO REGIONAL (formerly called Rios do Minho) in north west Portugal named after the Minho province, itself named after the river (called Miño in Spain with which it forms the boundary—see map under PORTUGAL). The boundaries of the region are the same as those for the VINHO VERDE DOC but producers are allowed to use different grape varieties and make wines with higher levels of alcohol than the usual Vinho Verde maximum of 11.5 per cent. Wines bearing the name Minho are rarely found outside Portugal.

R.J.M.

minimal pruning, also known as zero pruning, viticultural technique developed by the CSIRO in Australia whereby the vines are essentially left without any form of PRUNING from one year to the next. The technique has particular application to higher-yielding, low-cost vineyards in warmer areas but is also being used in some cooler regions producing high-quality wines, especially Australia's COONAWARRA region.

The technique was developed and popularized in the late 1970s and 1980s but its scientific interest can be traced back to a difference of opinion between two eminent viticultural scientists in the late 1960s. When Professor Nelson SHAULIS of CORNELL University in New York state was visiting the CSIRO at Merbein in Victoria, Australia, he debated with Dr Peter May and Allan Antcliff whether an unpruned vine might die. To settle the question a

SULTANA (Thompson Seedless) vine was left unpruned; to general surprise, it produced a large crop that ripened satisfactorily. At this time there was interest in MECHANICAL PRUNING, and in many ways minimal pruning is a natural extension of that method. The technique has now been extensively evaluated for vine varieties for both wine production and DRYING GRAPES and in both hot and cooler climates.

One might imagine that an unpruned plant would exhaust itself and die if its growth and cropping were not controlled by pruning. Interestingly, the opposite is true. The production of Sultana vines, which have now not been pruned for almost forty years, has continued to be satisfactory. Although vines are not killed by pruning, it has been shown to have a weakening effect on them. Furthermore, zero winter pruning is what vines experience in their natural state, and primitive vines survived in the wild for millions of years before they were first cultivated by man and pruned. A feature of unpruned, or minimally pruned, vines is that there are many short shoots, whereas a pruned vine has fewer shoots which in turn grow more vigorously. A minimally pruned vine typically produces more fruit than one conventionally pruned, especially in the first year or so of minimal pruning.

Ripening of this increased crop can be delayed, and if RIPENING is inadequate, due to cool weather for example, then wine quality can be reduced. In hot regions a harvest delay of a week or so is of little consequence, but in cooler climates the delay may be disastrous.

Minimally pruned vines look extremely wild and untidy compared with vines pruned by hand. After several years, old wood builds up in the centre of the thicket that is an unpruned vine, and this can exacerbate the threat of pests such as MEALY BUG. During the growing season, however, the vine's appearance may not be too different from that of normally pruned vines. Where minimal pruning is practised in hotter, dry climates, shoots stop growing quite early in the summer, and so the CANOPY can be relatively open with good fruit exposure, a requirement of a good CANOPY MICROCLIMATE. Where the climate is cooler and more humid and the vines are growing in fertile, moist soil, however, shoots may continue to grow, and the bunches of grapes may effectively be buried under several layers of leaves. This shaded canopy may then result in reduced colour and flavour in the grapes and eventual wine. R.E.S.

Coombe, B. G., and Dry, P. R. (eds.), *Viticulture*, ii: *Practices* (Adelaide, 1992).

Miousat, light-berried vine rarity of GASCONY which has been rescued from oblivion but is still grown in very limited quantities. The wines can smell of peach brandy and are relatively astringent.

Mireval is the large village that gives its name to Muscat de Mireval, the sweet golden

VIN DOUX NATUREL appellation that adjoins and is somewhat overshadowed by FRONTIGNAN to the west of it. Production, from about 260 ha/640 acres of Muscat Blanc à Petits Grains, has been almost exclusively in the hands of the CO-OPERATIVE, called La Cave de Rabelais in honour of the only well-known writer to have mentioned it. The wine is virtually indistinguishable from Frontignan and to those who live outside Mireval there seems little justification for Muscat de Mireval's independent existence, although soils here may be a little more calcareous than those of Frontignan.

mis(e) en bouteille is French for bottled. A wine that is **mis(e) en bouteille au château** is CHÂTEAU BOTTLED, while **mis(e) en bouteille au domaine** is DOMAINE BOTTLED. **Mis(e) en bouteille du château/domaine** is a term used by CO-OPERATIVES for their bottlings of wines they vinified from the grapes of individual properties. The BOTTLING operation is often referred to as **la mise.**

Misket Varnenski, Bulgarian grape-scented, pink-skinned grape variety that, despite its name, has no member of the MUSCAT family in its antecedents. It may be a crossing of the native DIMIAT with Riesling and is a speciality of the sub-Balkan region, especially Sungurlare (see BULGARIA). **Misket Cherven,** or Red Misket, is used for simple but perfumed everyday white wines. Official figures recorded a total of nearly 5,000 ha of Red Misket in Bulgaria in the mid 2000s.

Mission, the original black grape variety planted for sacramental purposes by Franciscan MISSIONARIES in MEXICO, the south west of the UNITED STATES, and CALIFORNIA in the 17th and 18th centuries. Mission was presumably of Spanish origin, imported to America by the conquistadores, and is important as a survivor from the earliest VINIFERA vine varieties to be cultivated in the Americas. It is identical to the PAIS of Chile and CRIOLLA CHICA of Argentina. It was an important variety in California until the spread of PHYLLOXERA in the 1880s and there were still about 600 acres/240 ha grown in the early 2000s, mainly in the south of the state, and used for sweet wines. The wine made from Mission is not particularly distinguished but the variety has enormous historical significance.

Pinney, T., *A History of Wine in America* (Berkeley, Calif., 1989).

missionaries have doubtless played a role in the establishment of viticulture all over the world and, particularly, in documenting these achievements. Missions and missionaries had a particularly profound effect, however, on the history of wine production in much of Latin America, in California, in New Zealand, and, to a certain extent, in Japan.

Soon after European colonization of South and Central America, missionaries, particularly Jesuit missionaries, established missions alongside more commercial ventures and, whatever the commercial interest in establishing viticulture, the missionaries grew vines to provide some wine for the EUCHARIST (although see SOUTH AMERICA, history). Both Argentina and Chile date their wine industries from the first successful attempts to cultivate the vine at missions in the foothills on either side of the Andes in the late 16th century, and by the 17th century, Peru's viticulture, which probably pre-dated that of both Chile and Argentina, was concentrated around Jesuit missions in coastal valleys. Mexico, however, is the Americas' oldest wine-producing country, and grape seeds were planted almost as soon as Cortés had landed there. Jesuit missionaries are believed to have been the first to cultivate vines for the specific purpose of wine-making in Baja California (northern Mexico) in the 1670s. It was not until the late 18th century that they established their series of missions up the west coast of what is now the American state of CALIFORNIA, and brought with them the so-called MISSION grape from Mexico.

Two centuries earlier, in 1545, Portuguese Jesuit missionaries had introduced wine to the feudal lords of southern JAPAN, who developed a taste for wine and continued to import it. Much more recently, it was Jesuit missionaries who sowed the seeds of the modern wine industry in CHINA.

At much the same time or even earlier, in the early 19th century, French Marist missionaries played a significant role in New Zealand's wine history by introducing vine cuttings from Europe, brought expressly to provide sacramental wine. The first Catholic bishop of the South Pacific, from Lyons, arrived with cuttings in 1838 and by 1842 they were reported to be performing well. The Mission winery in Hawkes Bay, founded by Catholic priests in 1851, is still in production and run as an adjunct to a Marist seminary.

See also RELIGION and MONKS AND MONASTERIES.

Cooper, M., *The Wine and Vineyards of New Zealand* (Auckland, 1984).

Seward, D., *Monks and Wine* (London, 1979).

Mission Haut-Brion, Château La.

Important GRAVES wine estate now under the same ownership as its long-standing rival Ch HAUT-BRION. Two other GRANDS CRUS are made here: **Ch La Tour-Haut-Brion** red and a full, waxy white wine **Ch Laville-Haut-Brion**. La Mission itself usually contains considerably more Merlot than Haut-Brion, and very much more than Ch La Tour Haut-Brion. The property was revitalized by the Woltner family, who acquired it in 1919 and in many subsequent vintages managed to make even more concentrated, long-lived wines than their FIRST GROWTH neighbour, typically fermented at much lower temperatures than Ch Haut-Brion. In 1983, however, La Mission

was sold to the Dillons, so that both these famous estates, the flagships of the newer PESSAC-LÉOGNAN appellation (although much of La Mission is in fact in the Bordeaux suburb of Talence rather than Pessac), are run, retaining their quite distinct premises and characters, by the same team. Of the varied total vineyard, 20.9 ha/51.6 acres is classified as La Mission, 4.9 ha as La Tour, and 3.7 ha is planted with slightly more Sémillon grapes than Sauvignon to produce Laville.

Missouri, Midwestern state in the UNITED STATES which has played an important part in the country's wine history. In the 1860s, Missouri made more wine than CALIFORNIA and NEW YORK combined. Wine production blossomed under a heavy influx of Germans in the Missouri river valley, west of St Louis, and today this area is billed to its many wine TOURISTS as 'the Rhineland of Missouri'.

When the AVA system was initiated in the 1980s, Missouri's Mount Pleasant rushed its application through the process, and America's first AVA was therefore Augusta, the site of many of Missouri's best vineyards today. It remains one of America's top ten wine-producing states and enjoys robust support from the state government, with agricultural stations, experimental wineries and talented researchers, marketers, and consultants. Several of Missouri's nearly 40 wineries (such as Adam Puchta, Augusta, Crown Valley, Montelle, Mount Pleasant, St James, and, especially, Stone Hill) are remarkably successful in national wine COMPETITIONS. HYBRIDS and AMERICAN VINE varieties comprise nearly all plantings and VARIETAL Seyval Blanc, Vidal Blanc, Chambourcin, Vignoles, and Norton have set a standard for these varieties in other states.   D.F.

mistela is the Spanish term and **mistelle** the French for a mixture of grape juice and alcohol. The FERMENTATION process is arrested by the addition of alcohol, leaving a sweet, stable, alcoholic liquid arguably less complex than an equivalent wine that owes its alcohol content to fermentation. It was the commercially vigorous and adaptable Dutch who developed this sort of drink, so much more stable over long journeys than wine (see DUTCH WINE TRADE). In Spain, such usefully stable sweetening agents are used in blending wines such as SHERRY and MÁLAGA, but are also sometimes sold, like France's PINEAU DES CHARENTES, for drinking as an aperitif. Other examples of wines that either comprise or may include *mistelle* are all those that qualify as VIN DE LIQUEUR, some VIN DOUX NATUREL, Australia's LIQUEUR MUSCAT, and Liqueur Tokay.

mites, minute insects which feed on leaf surface cells and which can be an important grapevine pest worldwide. Those that feed on the leaves include grape (or grapeleaf)

rust mite (*Calepitrimerus vitis*); Pacific spider mite (*Tetranychus pacificus*), which is the most destructive; two-spotted spider mite, which is only occasionally found on grapes; and Willamette mite (*Eotetranychus willametti*). Mite feeding slows PHOTOSYNTHESIS and can reduce grape RIPENING.

In Europe, red mite (*Panonychus ulmi*) and two types of yellow mite (*Eotetranychus carpini* and *Tetranychus urticae*) cause the most damage. They feed on green parts of the vine and can affect FRUIT SET and CANE RIPENING, as well as reducing LEAF health.

Predatory mites often keep these mites sufficiently under control, although it is important not to destroy them with other sprays. Sulfur sprays applied for erinose or POWDERY MILDEW are effective on some types of mite. White oil applied before BUDBREAK or miticides during summer can control mites. See also ERINOSE MITE.   M.J.E.

Mittelrhein, small and shrinking wine region in GERMANY better known to the outside world for its cliffs and castles than its Rieslings, which however can be outstanding. Most of the vines of Germany's 500-ha/1,250-acre Mittelrhein region grow within sight of the river RHINE, often looking down upon it from a considerable height (see map under GERMANY). The first commercial vineyards start about 8 km/5 miles south of Bonn and none is found on the west bank of the river until Koblenz is reached, 58 km/36 miles upstream. Thereafter, they climb both sides of the Rhine gorge, wherever site, the MESOCLIMATE, and much hard work make vine-growing a more or less viable exercise. The temperature is raised by the large volume of water in the Rhine (see TOPOGRAPHY), and in summer there is usually enough rain to maintain the health and strength of the vines on their porous, steep, heat-trapping slate and quartzite slopes. Most winters are mild, and spring, arriving early, starts a growing season which, for the RIESLING vine, lasts into late autumn.

Riesling is planted on 69 per cent of the area under vine. At its best, the wine is characterized by ripe, firm ACIDITY, and about 79 per cent is dry (TROCKEN or HALBTROCKEN). The greatest amount of good wine comes from south of Koblenz, at neighbouring Spay and Boppard (the Hamm vineyard), and further south at Bacharach, whose most notable vineyards are Hahn, Posten, Wolfshöhle, and St Jost. At their best, Mittelrhein Rieslings combine the minerality and tension of the Mosel-Saar-Ruwer and Nahe Rieslings with tropical fruit flavors. SPÄTBURGUNDER—which accounts for just 8 per cent of Mittelrhein acreage—can also yield serious quality in and around Bacharach.

The Mittelrhein vineyard is shrinking, dramatically so in many towns, with largely barren slopes, giving way in the north of the region to urban development and in the south to easier and more lucrative ways of earning a living. Little wine is exported, or even leaves the region, but a cadre of quality-conscious growers, five of them members of the VDP association, are striving to publicize the high quality of the best Mittelrhein Riesling and stem the tide of vineyard abandonment.

About a quarter of the harvest is processed by CO-OPERATIVE cellars at Bacharach and six other towns, and grape-growing is generally a part-time occupation, or simply a weekend hobby. Costs are most likely to be covered if the producer sells directly to tourists. The Rhine gorge is spectacular in parts, and deeply involved in the story of Germany, both mythical and real. Its admirers keep the local wine industry in business. I.J. & D.S.

MJT, mean January/July TEMPERATURE.

moelleux, French term meaning literally 'like (bone) marrow', or 'mellow'. Wines described as *moelleux* are usually medium sweet; very rich BOTRYTIZED wines may be described as LIQUOREUX.

Moët & Chandon, Champagne house producing the single most important champagne BRAND in the world, and part of the vast LVMH group. The Champagne house was founded by Claude Moët, born in 1683 to a family which had settled in the Champagne district during the 14th century. He inherited vineyards and became a wine merchant, establishing his own firm in 1743. He was succeeded by his son Claude-Louis Nicolas and his grandson Jean-Rémy Moët, who used his impressive connections to open up international markets for his wine. Jean-Rémy was a close personal friend of Napoleon Bonaparte, and was awarded the cross of the Légion d'Honneur in the final years of the emperor's rule. In 1832, Jean-Rémy handed over the firm to his son Victor and his son-in-law Pierre-Gabriel Chandon. At the same time, the company acquired the Abbey of Hautvillers and its vineyards. In 1962, Moët & Chandon's shares were quoted for the first time on the Paris Stock Exchange, leading to a period of considerable expansion. First, Moët bought shares in Ruinart Père et Fils, the oldest Champagne house, in 1963. Five years later, it acquired a 34 per cent stake in Parfums Christian Dior, increasing this to a 50 per cent stake shortly afterwards. In 1970, Moët took control of Champagne Mercier, a popular brand in France, and capped it all by buying out Dior and merging with HENNESSY in 1971 to form the holding company Moët Hennessy. The acquisitions continued unabated, including, in 1981, a stake in the American importers Schieffelin, which incorporated a 49 per cent share in H. SICHEL Söhne in Germany, producers of BLUE NUN, until the Sichel family bought it back in 1992. At one stage this American investment also involved the Simi winery in Sonoma,

Moët having established Domaine Chandon, a seminal sparkling California wine-making establishment in the Napa Valley, in 1973.

This was by no means the company's first venture into the New World. Bodegas Chandon was established in Argentina in 1960, and Provifin, now Chandon do Brasil, followed in 1974, both companies making considerable amounts of wine for the domestic market, much of it sparkling. In Germany, too, a SEKT business had been established in the form of Chandon GmbH in 1968. In 1985, the group founded Domaine Chandon, Australia, to make a premium sparkling wine sold as Domaine Chandon in Australia and Green Point in the UK, and in 1987 established a company in Spain for the production of a CAVA although the winery and vineyard associated with Masía Chandon were subsequently sold to FREIXENET.

In 1987, Moët Hennessy merged with the Louis Vuitton Group, makers of luxury leather goods and then owners of Champagne houses VEUVE CLICQUOT, Canard-Duchêne, and Henriot, and Givenchy perfumes. The LVMH group's composition continues to evolve but in 2005 it owned five Champagne houses: Moët & Chandon, Mercier, Ruinart, Veuve Clicquot, and Krug (having once also owned Pommery, and Lanson briefly while stripping it of its extensive vineyard holdings before selling it on). Of these, Moët & Chandon and Mercier are run most closely in tandem.

Moët, the brand, continues to sell at over twice the rate of its nearest competitors and claims that one in four bottles of Champagne exported comes from the house. It is the leading brand of champagne in most world markets with a share of the champagne market in the United States that can be as high as 50 per cent.

The house prestige cuvée is named after Dom PÉRIGNON, the legendary figure of the Abbey of Hautvillers, and broke new ground in terms of packaging, pricing, and qualitative ambitions when it was launched in 1928. S.A.

MOG, or material other than grapes, refers to leaves, canes, vines, and other debris picked inadvertently with the grapes at harvest. The amount of MOG is increased by MECHANICAL HARVESTING.

Moldavia See MOLDOVA.

Moldova may be one of the geographically smallest states of the former Soviet Union but it has more vineyard, 108,000 ha/267,000 acres in 2002 according to the OIV, than any other apart from Ukraine and the TABLE GRAPE producer Uzbekistan. It has the greatest potential for wine quality and range, thanks to its extensive vineyards, temperate CONTINENTAL CLIMATE, and gently undulating landscape sandwiched between eastern ROMANIA and UKRAINE. Moldova, the Romanian

name for what was known as Moldavia when it was part of the Soviet Union, was the name adopted on independence in 1991 since Romanians constitute 65 per cent of the population, and Romanian is the national language.

History

Archaeological evidence—of leaves of *Vitis teutonica*—confirms that the vine was widely grown in this area, Bessarabia, millions of years ago. Grape seeds dating back to 2800 BC have been found, as well as AMPHORAE, and the well-documented voyages to this region by the Greeks and then Romans can only have encouraged this particular branch of agriculture. HERODOTUS visited the colonies of Ancient GREECE at the mouth of the rivers Dnepr and Dnestr in the middle of the 5th century BC and reported that wine drinking was already common there.

After the feudal state of Moldova was formed in the second half of the 14th century AD, trade was established with RUSSIA, UKRAINE, and Poland, and Moldovan viticulture developed rapidly, reaching a high point in the 15th century during the era of Stephan the Great.

The Turkish occupation of Bessarabia (or Bogdan as it was known in the Ottoman empire) was a severe blow to Moldovan wine production (see ISLAM), and it was only after the country was annexed to Russia in 1812 that the industry was revived. By 1837, vineyards totalled 14,500 ha/35,750 acres and total wine production was more than 100,000 hl/2.6 million gal. Moldova, with neighbouring Wallachia, formed the basis for independent Romania in the middle of the 19th century. In 1891, Moldova's vineyard totalled 107,000 ha, much of it planted with vine varieties imported from France, but was severely ravaged by PHYLLOXERA and OIDIUM until GRAFTING was adopted in 1906. The tsars provided incentives to grow European vine varieties, which still predominate. By 1914, the province of Bessarabia (the part of Moldova between the rivers Prut and Dnestr) was Russia's most important source of wine. In 1940, the country was annexed by Russia and the vineyards were once again devastated, by the effects of the Second World War. The post-war period revival period saw energetic reconstruction and the spread of INTERNATIONAL VARIETIES so that by 1984 Moldova's vineyard area reached a peak of 258,000 ha.

Since then, GORBACHEV's anti-alcoholism campaign, and the effects of land privatization after independence, have seen Moldova's vineyard total fall to a local estimate of 148,000 ha in 2005: about 110,000 ha of plantings on an industrial scale to produce commodity grapes and 38,000 ha in private hands.

Climate and geography

Much of Moldova is low and hilly, rarely rising above 350 m/1,150 ft above sea level and with a gradual descent towards the Black sea in the south. The climate is ideal for viticulture, with average summer temperatures of around 20 °C/68 °F. Spring (and occasionally winter) FROST can be a problem but the active temperature summation is between 2,700 °C in the north and 3,400 °C in the south. Annual rainfall is between 400 and 600 mm/23 in. The main rivers are the Dnestr, Prut, and Reut. The country's four agricultural zones are: Northern, Central, Southern, and Southeast, but about 90 per cent of all vineyards are in the Southern and Central zones. Significant wine regions include Romanesht, Chumai, Khinchesh, Krikova, Mileshtii Mich, and Purkar.

Although at the end of the 20th century much of the vineyard was controlled by state farms, today most vines are tended by private farmers with the tractor work being done under contract for groups of these owners. The work on some big farms has been contracted out completely. Only one or two collective farms remain. Some completely new, privately owned vineyards were planted in the 2000s, with the Moldovan Prime Minister boasting in 2005 that over 6,000 ha had been replanted in the previous two to three years.

Viticulture
Unlike the wine regions of Russia to the north east, Moldova is able to grow the great majority of its vines, 70 per cent, without WINTER PROTECTION against frost damage and most vines are CORDON trained on medium height trellises. Very few of Moldova's 148,000 ha of vines (in 2005) are irrigated and there is a high level of MECHANIZATION, reflecting grapes' importance to the Moldovan agricultural economy. Most vines are grafted, with the most common ROOTSTOCK being SO 4. AGROCHEMICALS have been virtually unknown. Much of the vineyard as at 2005 was run down and under-producing, with an apparent lack of the viticultural expertise needed to renew the cordons. The new plantings should gradually remedy this situation but vines planted in the 1970s and 1980s are likely to continue to suffer neglect.

Vine varieties
Moldova has a more European range of grape varieties than any other state of the former Soviet Union. About 80 per cent of all vines planted in Moldova are European varieties such as Aligoté, Feteasca, Rkatsiteli, Sauvignon Blanc, Chardonnay, Riesling, Silvaner, Muscat Ottonel, Pinot Gris, Roter Traminer for white wines and Cabernet Sauvignon, Merlot, Malbec, Gamay Fréaux (a TEINTURIER), Pinot Noir, and Saperavi for reds. New varieties specially bred for their resistance to pests and diseases account for 20 per cent of plantings and include Onitscanschii Belii, Riton, Luminitsa, Legenda, Muscat de Ialoveni, Bianca, and Hibernal for white wines, Negru de Ialoveni, and Rubin Tairovschii for reds. There remain some plantings of such traditional varieties as Serecsia and Plavai.

Wines produced
Acid levels are good to high, CHAPTALIZATION rare, MALOLACTIC FERMENTATION haphazard, and winery hardware and HYGIENE lag behind what the West has come to regard as the norm. PASTEURIZATION has been regarded as a panacea. Potential is exciting, however, especially since commercially popular vine varieties are in place. The republic's total wine production has remained unusually constant for an ex-member of the Soviet Union, about 1 million hl/26.4 million gal. Moldova continues to make some FORTIFIED WINES notably Cagor, a 16 per cent, partially fermented red, often based on Cabernet. Most saleable of Moldova's wines are probably those based on Chardonnay, Sauvignon Blanc, and Cabernet Sauvignon although some excellent Pinot Gris and Pinot Noir has been made. Reds made in the early 1960s such as Negru de Purkar and Roshu de Purkar were exported to and acclaimed in Britain as the Soviet Union was breaking up.

Industry organization
Despite its excellent natural resources and potential, Moldova is still battling to make a significant impact in western Europe, although there is considerable export to Russia, Belarus, Ukraine, and Kazakhstan. Although the official standard of living and infrastructure, especially transport systems, remain poor, Russian and American capital has flowed in to the country's wine industry and in 2004 there were no fewer than 20 JOINT VENTURES, and six wine companies were entirely foreign-owned. Of Moldova's 153 wine companies in 2005, 70 concentrated on grape processing, 17 on storing and bottling, and 66 engaged in both activities. All except ten of them were privately owned. Successful exporters include Acorex, Cricova, DK Intertrade/Aur Vin, and Lion Gris. The old Purkhar Estate is also being restored and marketed.   F.K.

Molette is a common white grape variety used particularly for the sparkling wines of SEYSSEL in SAVOIE. The base wine produced is neutral and much improved by the addition of some ALTESSE.

Molinara, red grape variety grown in the Veneto region of north east Italy, particularly for VALPOLICELLA. Its wines tend to be high in acidity, light in colour, and prone to OXIDATION, so the variety is losing ground to CORVINA, RONDINELLA, and INTERNATIONAL VARIETIES in the zone.

Molise, after the Valle d'AOSTA, Italy's smallest and least populated region, is a poor and mountainous area situated south of ABRUZZO in the south east of Italy. Poor, and further impoverished by a continuous emigration of manpower for almost a century, the region has only 9,500 ha/23,465 acres of vineyards with an annual production of 400,000 hl/10.5 million gal, a mere twentieth of the production of neighbouring PUGLIA. Production is almost entirely in the hands of CO-OPERATIVE wineries, which sell virtually all of the wine in BULK.

The proximity of Abruzzo—to which the Molise was joined administratively until the 1960s—has left its mark on Molise's viticulture: the two predominant vine varieties are MONTEPULCIANO d'Abruzzo and TREBBIANO d'Abruzzo. There have been attempts to diversify, however, with the planting of grape varieties from southern Italy such as FIANO and GRECO DI TUFO and of more internationally famous varieties such as CHARDONNAY, RIESLING, SYLVANER, and PINOT BLANC. The region has a mere two DOCs, and the only one of any significance is Biferno, which may be red, rosé, and white, and is produced in the uplands of the regional capital of Campobasso. Reds and pinks are based on Montepulciano grapes with some red AGLIANICO and white TREBBIANO TOSCANO; Biferno Bianco is based on Trebbiano Toscano, with additions of BOMBINO and MALVASIA.

The best wines of the region, produced by the De Majo Norante winery, have chosen the IGT route in response to the world's lack of interest in Molise's DOCs, although the wines themselves are strictly made from southern Italian varieties.   D.T.

Bastianich, J., and Lynch, D., *Vino Italiano: The Regional Wines of Italy* (New York, 2002).

Belfrage, N., *From Brunello to Zibibbo: The Wines of Southern Italy* (London, 2001).

Moll, robust but potentially interesting white grape grown on the Spanish island of MALLORCA, also known as Prensal.

monasteries. See MONKS AND MONASTERIES.

Monastrell is the main Spanish name for the black grape variety known in France as Mourvèdre and also as Mataro. See MOURVÈDRE for more details.

Monbazillac, increasingly serious sweet white wine appellation within the BERGERAC district in south west France immediately south of the town of Bergerac on the left bank of the DORDOGNE. Monbazillac has a long history of sweet wine production, which here seems to pre-date the influence of the DUTCH WINE TRADE (one property's label still boasts 'Réputé en Hollande depuis 1513').

Like SAUTERNES, it is made from Sémillon, Sauvignon, and, particularly successful here, Muscadelle grapes and the vineyards lie on the left bank of an important river close to its confluence with a small tributary, in this case the Gardonette. This environment favours autumn morning mists and the development of NOBLE ROT, particularly on north-facing slopes, and an increasing number of producers are willing to take the risks involved in trying to produce fully BOTRYTIZED wines. In a determined quest for quality, MECHANICAL HARVESTING was banned from 1993 and successive TRIES through the vineyard insisted upon. The top-quality botrytized wines offer exceptional value. Basic maximum permitted yields here are 40 hl/ha (2.3 tons/acre), as opposed to the 25 hl/ha in Sauternes, but in a good vintage such as 1996, the average yield in Monbazillac was 26 hl/ha (as opposed to Sauternes' 22.5 hl/ha). Just under 2,000 ha/5,000 acres of vineyard are dedicated to Monbazillac, considerably more than Sauternes, where picking generally takes place earlier so vintage characteristics can be very different.

The POTENTIAL ALCOHOL must be at least 14.5 per cent. The most conscientious producers have quite rightly relied on nature for the richness of their often markedly orange-tinged wines. In the past, too much Monbazillac was simply a sweetened, heavy wine, sometimes redolent of SULFUR DIOXIDE, blended and bottled by a NÉGOCIANT with little passion for the possibilities that exist within this region. Since 1993, there has been a clear distinction between serious sweet Monbazillac and early-picked dry white wine which is sold as Bergerac Sec. The leading property by far is Ch Tirecul La Gravière, which makes extremely intense, rich nectar, but fine wines are also made by the likes of Chx Bélingard and La Brie.

Mondavi, important family in the recent history of CALIFORNIA wine, with Robert Mondavi (1913–) in particular doing more than anyone to raise awareness of the civilizing influence of wine in general and of California as a source of top-quality wine in particular.

Robert's father Cesare came to the US in 1906 from the MARCHE on Italy's east coast. He and his Italian wife Rosa ran a boarding house for miners in Minnesota before moving to LODI in California's San Joaquin valley in 1922, whence, throughout PROHIBITION, they shipped grapes back east to America's temporarily swollen band of HOME WINEMAKERS. Immediately after Repeal, Cesare turned to winemaking and was joined in the late 1930s by his sons Robert and Peter.

As early as 1936, the Mondavis made their crucial move out of the hot Central valley (leaving GALLO to build up the world's largest winery there) into the cooler NAPA valley where they were determined to make table wines, rather than the then much more popular dessert wines. Robert's first job in the wine industry was at the Sunny St Helena winery, then called Sunnyhill, part-owned by Jack Riordan, a friend of his father. The Mondavis acquired the nearby Charles KRUG winery in 1943. Robert Mondavi's obsession with constant fine tuning of wine quality grew here, inspired by old bottles from the Inglenook winery, and guided by

oenologist André TCHELISTCHEFF. During the 1950s, he became increasingly fascinated by the CABERNET SAUVIGNON grape and in 1962 visited BORDEAUX for the first time, a seminal visit which was to convince him of the necessary conjunction between fine wine and gracious living.

This led to disputes with his younger brother Peter which were exacerbated by Cesare's death in 1959 so that by 1965 Robert was excluded from the Charles Krug winery, where Peter remained, and won compensation only after a long and bitter lawsuit. The opening of the Robert Mondavi winery on the Oakville highway in 1966, strikingly Californian, in the mission style, thanks to architect Cliff May, marked the beginning of a new chapter not just for the Mondavis but for California wine. Just as Baron Philippe de ROTHSCHILD had signalled a new era for Bordeaux when he took over at Ch MOUTON-ROTHSCHILD in the 1920s, so the Robert Mondavi winery was at the forefront of developing VARIETAL wines based on Europe's most famous vine varieties (each, innovatively, made differently); continual experimentation with different BARRELS, TOAST, FINING, and FILTRATION regimes; special Reserve bottlings; comparative tastings with France's most famous wines; wine TOURISM; and cultural events associated with the winery and its wines. It was therefore no surprise when in 1979 a JOINT VENTURE was announced between Robert Mondavi and Baron Philippe: Opus One, with its own lavish winery since 1992, is a Napa Valley Cabernet-based wine made jointly by Tim Mondavi and Mouton's winemaker. Also in 1979 the company bought a co-operative in Lodi which, producing the high-volume, lower-priced range of Woodbridge FIGHTING VARIETALS, has been its single most profitable venture by far.

During the 1990s, Robert Mondavi extricated himself from day-to-day operations, which then also included: a Chilean venture with Eduardo Chadwick producing Caliterra varietal wines and the highly priced Seña; a joint venture in Italy with the FRESCOBALDI family producing wines called Luce and, much later, controlling Ornellaia in BOLGHERI (see ANTINORI); a venture in the Languedoc producing French wines sold under the name Vichon; and the Byron winery in the Santa Maria valley.

Although the Robert Mondavi winery had considerable assets in the form of 1,500 acres/607 ha of prime Napa valley vineyard, and annual production of Napa valley wine peaked in the early 1990s at about 500,000 cases (more than any other producer), borrowings and the prospect of significant inheritance taxes forced this family-owned winery to make a public share issue in 1993. In 2004, the board voted to sell the company and it was purchased by CONSTELLATION Brands, which has disposed of many of the joint ventures, although not Opus One.

Mondavi, R., *Harvests of Joy* (New York, 1998).

Mondéjar, denominated wine zone in northern Castilla-La Mancha, Spain, near Guadalajara, created in 1996 and producing table wines of modest distinction. Tempranillo is the main variety in the 3,000 ha/7,200 acres of vineyards.

Mondeuse, one of the oldest and most distinctive red grape varieties of SAVOIE, bringing an Italianate depth of colour and bite to the region in contrast to the softer reds produced by the Gamay imported only after PHYLLOXERA. The juicy, peppery wines are powerfully flavoured and coloured and are some of Savoie's few to respond well to careful oak ageing (although when grown prolifically on Savoie's more fertile, lower sites Mondeuse can easily be a dull wine too, which may explain why the variety has been underrated). DNA PROFILING at SAN MICHELE ALL'ADIGE has shown that Mondeuse is not identical to the REFOSCO DAL PEDUNCULO ROSSO of FRIULI, as advanced by some authorities because the wines are so similar.

Total French plantings of Mondeuse Noire fell sharply in the 1970s and were barely 200 ha/500 acres in 2000 but there is a small 21st-century renaissance in this characterful variety, most of whose produce is sold as a varietal Vin de Savoie, unusually capable of ageing. It is also grown in the Vin du BUGEY region.

Mondeuse Blanche is a light-berried vine found in Savoie, particularly in BUGEY, producing a dry, relatively soft white wine. DNA PROFILING has shown that it is not a white MUTATION of MONDEUSE Noire, and that Mondeuse Blanche and DUREZA from Ardèche are the parents of the classic SYRAH.

Monferrato in historical terms is a series of hills to the east of Turin in PIEMONTE extending eastwards towards the Po river flatlands. In viticultural terms, it corresponds to the grape-growing zones of the provinces of Asti and Alessandria. Monferrato assumed a new significance with the overall reorganization of Piemonte's DOC structure in the 1990s. Barbera del Monferrato is still a light and simple product, frequently fizzy and definitely intended to be drunk young. But important red wines from blends of native and INTERNATIONAL VARIETIES, as for example Barbera and Cabernet or Pinot Noir, can now be sold as a Monferrato Rosso DOC, as can varietal wines from these non-native grapes. Either Chardonnay or Sauvignon can be labelled Monferrato Bianco, without the name of the variety, and for this reason many producers, who can utilize Piemonte Chardonnay as an alternative DOC, have chosen it in preference to Monferrato Bianco.   D.T.

Monica, red grape variety grown in great quantity on SARDEGNA, where some varietal Monica di Sardegna is thus labelled. It is thought to have originated in Spain (although it is not known in modern Spain). Its wines are generally undistinguished and should be drunk young, although more recent wines from the Santadi co-operative suggest that with YIELDS lower than the current 15 tonnes/ha, Monica could be a pleasurable, if not always memorable, wine.

monks and monasteries. Wine has always had spiritual and religious significance (see RELIGION AND WINE), and monks and monasteries have long been regarded as playing a crucial part in wine history.

While wine and the vine played a prominent role in most religions of the eastern Mediterranean during antiquity, it was in Christian religious symbolism and practice that it achieved particular significance, as an essential element of the EUCHARIST. Such Christian symbolism built on earlier Jewish beliefs in which the vine or vineyard was used as one of the favourite symbols for the nation of ISRAEL in the Old Testament. The adoption of Christianity as the state religion of the Roman empire during the 4th century AD (see Ancient ROME) meant that wine was to attain a position of the utmost ideological prominence in European society. This religious significance of wine is widely regarded as of particular importance at two stages in its history: first, in ensuring the survival of viticulture following the collapse of the western Roman empire; and secondly in the introduction of viticulture and wine-making to the Americas.

It has generally been argued that Christian communities' need for grape-based wine with which to celebrate the Eucharist was one of the main factors enabling viticulture and wine-making to survive in western Europe following the fall of Rome in AD 476. It is assumed that when transport was difficult, it was easier for isolated Christian communities in northern Europe to cultivate their own vines rather than import wine. Moreover, monks are widely regarded as the only individuals capable of nurturing viticultural and wine-making traditions.

There is, however, little firm evidence for this hypothesis. The Germanic tribes which overran the western Roman empire were known to be fond of wine, and there is little reason to suppose that they consciously destroyed vast expanses of European vineyards. This is supported by the evidence of surviving elements of the Gallo-Roman aristocracy, who recorded the continued cultivation of vines during the second half of the 5th century in areas of GAUL such as Clermont-Ferrand. Bishops and monks certainly did own vineyards and organized the production of wine throughout the period from the 6th to the 10th century, but it is significant that in most instances they appear to have gained their vineyards mainly as grants from royalty or the secular nobility. This implies that substantial non-monastic vineyards survived and were developed in the aftermath of the Germanic invasions of the 5th century. The real role of monasteries therefore seems not so much to have been in the preservation of a tradition of viticulture following the collapse of Rome, but rather in building up substantial holdings of vineyards, and thus in being among the most important winemakers of medieval Europe (see also CHARLEMAGNE).

During the Middle Ages, monastic houses came to possess some of the most renowned vineyards of Europe. The Benedictines (who, like the Carthusians, are now popularly associated with a high-quality liqueur based on distilled wine) thus owned extensive vineyards. In BURGUNDY the monks of Cluny owned most of the vines in what is now GEVREY-CHAMBERTIN, while the abbey of St-Vivant owned vineyards in what is now called VOSNE-ROMANÉE. Along the Loire, the Benedictine abbey of St-Nicolas held vineyards in what is now ANJOU, and Benedictine monasteries at BOURGUEIL and La Charité also produced quantities of wine. Further south, the Benedictine abbey at ST-POURÇAIN produced what was one of the most renowned wines in medieval France. In CHAMPAGNE, the Benedictines held six monasteries in the diocese of Rheims, while in the RHÔNE they held vineyards at both CORNAS and ST-PÉRAY. In BORDEAUX, they owned such properties as Ch Prieuré in Cantenac (now carrying the suffix of a more recent owner, Alexis LICHINE) and Ch Carbonnieux in GRAVES. In Germany, the abbey at St Maximin in the RUWER was producing about 9,000 l/2,370 gal of wine a year towards the end of the 8th century. Although they also owned many German vineyards, especially in RHEINHESSEN and FRANKEN, the Benedictines' best known German wine estate was SCHLOSS JOHANNISBERG in the RHEINGAU (see GERMAN HISTORY).

The more ascetic Cistercians likewise owned numerous important vineyards throughout Europe. The abbey of Clairvaux had extensive vineyards in CHAMPAGNE, and the Cistercians of Pontigny are reputed to have been the first to plant the CHARDONNAY vine in CHABLIS. Their most famous vineyard, however, was the extensive, walled CLOS DE VOUGEOT, and their other holdings in Burgundy included vineyards in MEURSAULT, BEAUNE, and POMMARD. Cistercians also produced fine wines in SANCERRE and PROVENCE. Their most important wine-producing abbey in Germany was KLOSTER EBERBACH in the RHEINGAU, but there were many others, notably at Himmerod and Machern in the MOSEL and Maulbronn in WÜRTTEMBERG. As major landowners throughout Europe, other monastic orders also owned extensive vineyards; the Carthusians, for example, had particular interests in CAHORS, SWITZERLAND, and Trier in the Upper Mosel. (See also PRIORAT.)

The second main viticultural role widely attributed to the monks was their influence on the development of vineyards in the Americas. In the 17th century, the Jesuits were major wine producers on the coastal plain of PERU, and in the 18th century, with the expansion of Spanish interests in CALIFORNIA, the Franciscans, particularly under the leadership of Júnipero Serra, played an important part in introducing viticulture and wine-making to Alta California. Most of the missions established in California during the 1770s and 1780s thus cultivated vines and made wine, with the Mission of San Gabriel becoming particularly famous for its wines, although the majority of mission vineyards nevertheless remained very small.

In the 20th century, monastic wine-making continues, despite the earlier effects of the Reformation in northern Europe. Benedictine monks at the abbeys of Gottweig in AUSTRIA, St Hildegard above Rüdesheim in the German Rheingau, and Muri-Gries near Bolzano in ALTO ADIGE in Italy are all currently producing wine, as are Cistercian monks at Heiligenkreuz in Austria and in Spain's NAVARRA, and the Augustinian canons at KLOSTERNEUBURG, also in Austria.

Quite apart from the general role played by monastic orders in the history of wine, certain individual monks and monasteries enjoy vinous fame on their own account. The classic example of this is the work of Dom PÉRIGNON in improving the quality of the wines of Hautvillers in CHAMPAGNE at the end of the 17th century.

See also MISSIONARIES.   P.T.H.U.

Cushner, N. P., *Lords of the Land: Sugar, Wine and Jesuit Estates of Colonial Peru, 1600–1767* (Albany, 1980).
Goodenough, E. R., *Jewish Symbols in the Greco-Roman Period*, vols. v and vi (New York, 1956).
Seward, D., *Monks and Wine* (London, 1979).
Unwin, T., *Wine and the Vine: An Historical Geography of Viticulture and the Wine Trade* (London, 1991).

monopole, Burgundian term for wholly owned vineyard or CLIMAT.

monopolies. State, province, or national exclusive controls over the sale, and occasionally production, of all alcoholic drinks have a long history. In INDIA, the manufacture of the sort of wine drunk in the immediately pre-Christian era was a state monopoly. In countries such as ALGERIA and, to a lessening extent, EGYPT, the state controls wine production as well as distribution. The administrators of many ancient civilizations saw the economic and social advantages of exercising a monopoly over the distribution of wine and beer (the only alcoholic drinks known in antiquity). State monopolies on selling alcoholic drinks have been features in many Scandinavian countries, Pennsylvania in the UNITED STATES, and much of CANADA, although some of these monopolies were broken in the 1990s. The disadvantage for consumers can be a restriction of choice, and in many cases severe restrictions on places and conditions of sale whereby wine is sold with all the safeguards and ignominy associated with the distribution of dangerous drugs. The advantage for producers can be that a sale to a monopoly represents a relatively high-volume order. Bulk sale to the Swedish monopoly, for example, was for long an important factor in the export business of PENFOLDS and other Australian companies. The most important monopoly on wine sales is held by the Liquor Control Board of Ontario (LCBO) in Canada.

monoterpenes have ten carbon atoms and are members of the group of natural products called TERPENOIDS. Monoterpenes are major contributors to the characteristic flavour properties of MUSCAT grapes and wines, and responsible for the floral aromas of many non-Muscat wines such as RIESLING. Individual monoterpenes that are found in grapes and contribute to the attractive flavour properties of wines include the ALCOHOLS geraniol, nerol, linalool, and citronellol, although more than 40 have now been reported. Monoterpenes were amongst the first grape and wine FLAVOUR COMPOUNDS to be elucidated, and the first to be discovered in glycosylated form (see GLYCOSIDES) as FLAVOUR PRECURSORS.   P.J.W.

Strauss, C. R., Wilson, B., Gooley, P. R., and Williams, P. J., 'Role of monoterpenes in grape and wine flavor', in *Biogeneration of Aromas*, American Chemical Society (Washington, DC, 1986).

Montagne de Reims, the 'mountain of Rheims', or the forested high ground between the CHAMPAGNE towns of Rheims and Épernay. Its lower slopes are famed for the quality of PINOT NOIR base wine they produce.

Montagne-St-Émilion, the largest satellite appellation of ST-ÉMILION in Bordeaux. Chx Faizeau and Maison Blanche are two of the more admired properties.

Montagny, the appellation for white burgundy produced in the communes of Montagny-lès-Buxy, Jully-lès-Buxy, Buxy, and St-Vallerin in the Côte CHALONNAISE. The wines have a little more body and more acidity than other whites from this region. Previously, all vineyards could be designated PREMIER CRU on condition that the wine had an ALCOHOLIC STRENGTH of 11.5 per cent. Now Montagny has been brought into line with other appellations, though a high proportion of vineyards (199 out of 298 ha) have been classified as premier cru. Much of the production passes through the excellent CO-OPERATIVE founded in 1929 at Buxy, which boasts the motto 'with the good wines of Buxy everyone sings and everyone laughs'.   J.T.C.M.

Montalcino, town in TOSCANA in central Italy famous for its long-lived red BRUNELLO DI MONTALCINO.

Montana, dominant producer and exporter of NEW ZEALAND wine, responsible for about half the country's production. In the mid 2000s, the company owned 3,100 ha/7,660 acres of vineyards in every region except Central Otago and Nelson and wineries in Auckland, Gisborne, Hawkes Bay, and Marlborough. It was founded in 1934 when Ivan Yukich planted a vineyard in the Waitakere Ranges west of Auckland. His sons, Frank and Mate, adopted the vineyard's name, Montana, when they founded a wine company 30 years later. Montana helped drive, and greatly profited from, New Zealand's rapid rise in wine consumption from the early 1970s.

Increased wine production was originally achieved with the help of contracted grape growers, particularly in Gisborne and later in Hawkes Bay. In 1973, the North American wine and spirit giant Seagram bought 45 per cent of Montana, the additional capital and expertise allowing the company to invest heavily in vineyards, specifically pioneering grape-growing in MARLBOROUGH. In all, 1,200 ha/3,000 acres were purchased at an average price of NZ\$1,121 per ha (it would cost around NZ\$100,000 per ha in 2005). Had it all been planted with grapevines, it would have trebled the size of the national vineyard. Initially 265 ha were planted although 60 per cent of the vines died during a record drought. Irrigation solved the problem when it was installed in 1979.

In the mid 1980s, Montana produced a TRADITIONAL METHOD sparkling wine with Champagne Deutz: Deutz Marlborough Cuvée. It also enlisted the help of Bordeaux NÉGOCIANT Cordier to help refine red wine-making at the company's Hawkes Bay winery, Church Road. Seagram sold its share in the company in 1987.

In 2000, Montana acquired Corbans Wines, New Zealand's second largest wine producer. Between 2001 and 2005, the company, renamed Allied Domecq Wines (NZ), was the jewel in the crown of the wine division of the eponymous British conglomerate before being acquired by PERNOD RICARD. BRANDS marketed in Europe include Montana, Stoneleigh, Church Road, Lindauer, and Timara. Brancott, Lindauer, and Stoneleigh are the principal brands targeted at the US and Canada to avoid confusion with the American state of Montana.   R.F.C.

Montecarlo, zone near Lucca in north west TOSCANA which was one of the first to produce modern dry red and white wines, blending the ubiquitous TREBBIANO and SANGIOVESE with a host of more interesting grape varieties. These were brought directly to the zone from France in the mid 19th century by the scion of the noble Mazzini family, still producers of wine in the zone. Good Chardonnay, Pinot Blanc, Syrah, and Cabernet–Merlot blends began to appear with some regularity in the

1990s, indicating that this northerly part of Toscana is capable of producing much better wines than it has in the past.

Montefalco. See SAGRANTINO.

Montenegro, comparatively small southern coastal region immediately north of ALBANIA, formerly part of YUGOSLAVIA (see map in that article) and now in a loose federation with SERBIA. Montenegro, with 4,000 ha/9,880 acres of low-yielding vineyard, has been most famous for VRANAC, a red grape which gives intense, deeply coloured VARIETAL wine capable of developing a velvety texture and intense flavours if aged for three or four years in bulk and then bottle. In the early 1990s, the main producer here began to use an element of new oak, which lent a fashionably soft, spicy edge to the wines.   A.H.M.

Montepulciano, name of a vigorous red grape variety planted over much of central Italy (30,000 ha/75,000 acres in 2000, about the same as in 1990), and the name of a town in TOSCANA in central Italy at the centre of the zone producing the highly ranked red wine VINO NOBILE DI MONTEPULCIANO (which is not made from this grape variety, but is made around the town of the same name).

The grape variety is recommended for 20 of Italy's 95 provinces but is most widely planted in ABRUZZO, where it is responsible for the often excellent value **Montepulciano d'Abruzzo**, and in the MARCHE, where it is a principal ingredient in such reds as Rosso Conero and Rosso Piceno. It is also grown in MOLISE and PUGLIA. At its best, it produces wines that are deep in colour with ripe, robust tannins. Both the colour and the tannins make it a favoured blending ingredient with producers looking to boost their more feeble efforts. Unfortunately, high yields, often abetted by official advice in the 1970s and 1980s that producers should train their vines high, and a tendency to REDUCTION in the wines, have ensured that general quality is not as high as it should be. DOCG for Montepulciano d'Abruzzo Colline Teramane, for Montepulciano grown in the hills in the area around Teramo in the northern part of Abruzzo, came into effect with the 2003 vintage, perhaps an attempt to promote future, rather than to recognize current, quality.

The variety ripens too late to be planted much further north, although Montepulciano has recently shown it can yield dependable quantities of deep-coloured, well-ripened grapes with good levels of alcohol and extract in UMBRIA and the Tuscan MAREMMA. It is sometimes called Cordisco, Morellone, Primaticcio, and Uva Abruzzo.

Monterey, one of the major agricultural counties south of San Francisco in CALIFORNIA, with a reputation as 'America's salad bowl'. In this exceptionally picturesque region, beauty and grinding toil continue to coexist, very much as described in John Steinbeck's novels, notably *The Grapes of Wrath*.

As a wine region, Monterey is not cut from the normal cloth. Rainfall is so low that grapes cannot be grown there without IRRIGATION. Water supply is ample, however, from the underground Salinas river, which defines the large valley so open to the Pacific ocean that sea fogs cool and darken its northern end so that few or no grape varieties will ripen there. Into this contradictory situation came an army of would-be growers who, between 1968 and 1975, took Monterey from one isolated vineyard to the most heavily planted county on the American west coast, with a peak of 37,000 acres/ 14,980 ha. Nearly every year from 1975 to 1995 saw a steady reduction in vine acreage with vines increasingly concentrated in the southerly warmest and sunniest parts of the Salinas valley. That trend has since reversed, with acreage increased from 20,000 to over 40,000 between 1995 and 2004. The first Monterey wine successes came from near the towns of Soledad and Greenfield and that area, now the Arroyo Seco AVA, remains near the forefront, although it has since been eclipsed by the Santa Lucia Highlands, a more recent AVA that flanks Arroyo Seco and reaches further north along the western foothills.

Monterey AVA

The blanket AVA for Monterey county encompasses Arroyo Seco AVA, Carmel Valley AVA, San Lucas AVA, Hames Valley AVA, Chalone AVA, and all other vineyards not included in these more specific regions. The San Lucas AVA was sponsored by the vast Almaden Vineyards when it owned large acreages in them; it has not been actively used on labels since Almaden left the region although it contains a hefty percentage of Monterey's total acreage in vines. The borders of the AVA are overlapped by the largest contiguous vineyard in the world, San Bernabe's 13,000 acres owned by Delicato of the Central valley. Both Hames Valley and San Lucas would be considered hot by the overall standards of Monterey county.

Arroyo Seco AVA

A fairly coherent district within the vastness of Monterey county's Salinas valley has its anchor point at the scruffy farm town of Greenfield. Most of its vineyards lie to the west of that town, on either bank of the dry wash for which it is named in Spanish, but some range east and north to the even scruffier precincts of Soledad. Chardonnay is the mainstay for most of the wineries who draw upon it, but some cleave resolutely, and less successfully, to Cabernet Sauvignon. Rieslings from the area, with their reliable aroma of nectarines, can be of great interest. The earliest plantings here came in the early 1960s.

Carmel Valley AVA

The only seaward-facing wine district in Monterey county, with a much more affluent, less agricultural population than Salinas valley. It has a handful of small wineries and vineyards draped across steep slopes in the drainage area of the Carmel river, 10 to 12 miles/19 km inland from Carmel bay. Bernardus leads in terms of quality.

Chalone AVA

Chalone's reputation was made by the winery of the same name set high in the Gavilan mountains, on the east side of Monterey's Salinas valley, notably with Chardonnay, Pinot Blanc, and Pinot Noir. Although Chalone looks directly down to the Arroyo Seco AVA, it remains worlds apart in climate (being above the fog) and soils, which for Chalone are crystal laden and CALCAREOUS.   B.C.C.

Monterrei, relatively new DO in southern Galicia, on Spain's border with Portugal. Most of the wine is still sold in bulk, and the recovery of local grape varieties is less developed than elsewhere in Galicia. This is still more a project based on distant glories, than a current reality.   V. de la S.

Monthelie, a village producing red and occasionally white wine in the Côte de Beaune district of Burgundy's CÔTE D'OR (see map under BURGUNDY). It is so dominated by wine production that local saying has it that a chicken in Monthelie is likely to die of hunger at harvest time.

The wines resemble those of VOLNAY but are neither quite as rich nor as elegant, although they age well and are more powerful than those of AUXEY-DURESSES, the neighbouring appellation to the south with which the PREMIER CRU vineyard Les Duresses is shared. The other premier cru vineyards of Monthelie such as Meix Bataille and Champs Fulliot lie adjacent to Volnay. Some Chardonnay was planted in the 1980s, for Monthelie also borders the white wine village of MEURSAULT.   J.T.C.M.

Montilla-Moriles, southern Spanish denominated wine zone in ANDALUCÍA, 40 km/ 25 miles south of Cordoba (see map under SPAIN), producing both FORTIFIED and unfortified wines in the style of SHERRY, usually known simply as **Montilla**. For many years wine from the country around the towns of Montilla and Moriles found its way into sherry SOLERAS. The practice largely ceased in 1945 when the area was awarded a separate DO, although wines made from the PEDRO XIMÉNEZ grape, some of them very fine, are still legally exported to JEREZ and neighbouring MÁLAGA for blending. Since it became a region in its own right, Montilla has had to contend with a popular image as an inferior, cheap alternative to sherry.

The soils in the centre of the region associated with lower YIELDS and better wines resemble the chalky ALBARIZA of Jerez, although most of Montilla-Moriles is SANDY and parched. The climate is relatively harsh with summer temperatures rising to 45 °C/113 °F and short, cold winters. The Pedro Ximénez vine, which accounts for over 70 per cent of production, seems to thrive in the hot conditions, yielding extremely sweet grapes. The wines therefore achieve ALCOHOLIC STRENGTHS between 14 and 16 per cent without FORTIFICATION. Other grape varieties include the Lairén (AIRÉN) and MUSCAT OF ALEXANDRIA, which tend to produce lighter wines for blending. The PALOMINO vine, which is the basis for most sherry, has not been successful in Montilla.

Wine-making practices in Montilla parallel those for sherry. Pale, dry FINO and AMONTILLADO style wines are made from FREE-RUN juice, while heavier styles similar to OLOROSO are made from the subsequent pressings. (The terms Fino, Amontillado, and Oloroso are permitted on Montilla labels within Spain but may not be used in other European Union countries, where they are restricted to sherry. Pale Dry, Medium Dry, Pale Cream, and Cream are the styles most commonly found on labels outside Spain.)

Pale Dry Montilla matures under a film of FLOR, initially in cement or earthenware TINAJAS, then in a solera similar to those in Jerez. However, in the hot climate of Montilla-Moriles, far removed from the cooling winds of the Atlantic, the flor is usually less thick than in Jerez and the wines tend to have less finesse as a result (see SHERRY). Heavier oloroso styles are fortified and aged for longer in soleras, where they become dark and pungent. Around half the region's wines are not fortified, which puts them at an advantage in certain markets where duties are levied on alcoholic strength. These usually disappear into inexpensive commercial blends, many of which are heavily sweetened with concentrated must for export.
                      R.J.M.

Montlouis, overshadowed white wine appellation in the TOURAINE district of the Loire that exists across the river from the much larger and more famous VOUVRAY, although it has its own characteristics. As in Vouvray, the CHENIN BLANC grape is grown exclusively for Montlouis, which is made in all degrees of sweetness, according to each VINTAGE's peculiarities.

Although TUFFEAU also forms a base from which many a house and cellar is hewn, topsoils here on the south bank just downstream of Touraine-Amboise are lighter and sandier than in Vouvray, and the wines are less sharply defined, tending to mature considerably earlier (which can be a great advantage). About a third of the wine produced from Montlouis's 400 ha/1,000 acres of Chenin Blanc is the usefully sturdy and characterful **Montlouis**

Mousseux. A little **Montlouis Pétillant** is also produced. François Chidaine, and Jacky Blot of Domaine de la Taille aux Loups are the leading producers.

Montmélian, named CRU just south of Chambéry whose name may be added to the eastern French appellation Vin de SAVOIE. It is dominated by a CO-OPERATIVE and most wine is light white from the JACQUÈRE grape.

Montpellier, University of.
L'École Nationale Supérieure Agronomique (ENSA), now know as Agro.M, was created in 1872 as a response to the viticultural crises caused by POWDERY MILDEW, DOWNY MILDEW, and especially PHYLLOXERA in southern FRANCE.

The first Professor of Viticulture was Gustave Foëx, who established the first important repository of French and American vine varieties and it remains the world's most comprehensive, with more than 3,000 in total (although see also MAGARACH). He experimented with phylloxera-resistant ROOTSTOCKS and published a guide to American vines which went into six editions. Ever since the Foëx era, AMPELOGRAPHY has been a speciality of Montpellier.

Pierre Viala was Professor of Viticulture at the end of the 1880s, when he went to the United States expressly to collect vine varieties species suitable for CALCAREOUS soils. Thanks to his efforts, VITIS berlandieri was used to obtain rootstocks such as 41 B, which allowed the replanting of the Cognac and Champagne regions. From 1890, Viala worked at the Institut National Agronomique in Paris, where he published a treatise on vine diseases and then, with Jean Vermorel, the classic seven-volume *Ampélographie* between 1902 and 1910.

Viala's successor in Montpellier was Louis Ravaz, who had created Cognac's viticultural research station and specialized in research into BLACK ROT and downy mildew. He also published an important work on American vines, extended Montpellier's vine collection, and was to become the first vine physiologist. With Viala, he founded the *Revue de Viticulture*, which appeared from 1894 to 1949, and also helped to create the magazine *Le Progrès Agricole et Viticole*.

From 1930, Jean Branas occupied the Chair of Viticulture and was particularly interested in VINE NUTRITION and VIRUS DISEASES. Together with certain ex-pupils, he undertook control of French vine nurseries and began a CLONAL SELECTION programme in the sandy, NEMATODE-free soils of La Petite Camargue (Le Grau du Roi) on the nearby Mediterranean coast.

Since 1946, INRA has provided the financial support as well as the personnel needed to develop viticultural research at Montpellier. Branas had the vine collection transferred to the Domaine de Vassal, also on the Mediterranean coast (see INRA).

Denis BOUBALS succeeded Branas in 1975 as Professor of Viticulture. His work was much concerned with the causes and heredity of resistance to powdery and downy mildews, to phylloxera, and to *Xiphinema index*. He created the experimental Domaine du Chapître at Villeneuve-lès-Maguelonne and has published numerous works on viticulture and, especially, ampelography. His two main collaborators were the vine physiologist François Champagnol and Pierre GALET. The current Professor of Viticulture is Alain Carbonneau, well known for his studies on canopy MICROCLIMATE and the development of the LYRE training system. He is also Director of the Institut des Hautes Etudes de la Vigne et du Vin (IHEV).

The Unité Mixte de Recherche (UMR) Sciences pour l'Oenologie is the centre for oenological research at Montpellier. This research unit works in collaboration with the Unité Expérimentale de Pech Rouge at Gruissan near Narbonne (see INRA).

Research covers three main areas: the structural analysis and physico-chemistry of POLYPHENOLS in relation to flavour, stability, and the prevention of some diseases; the physiology and genomics of commercial YEASTS adapted to specific wine conditions; and the development and maturation of the grape with particular attention to polyphenol biosynthesis.

Montpeyroux,
the highest named CRU within the Coteaux du LANGUEDOC in southern France and, with nearby PIC-ST-LOUP, the most exciting. It produces mainly but not exclusively red wine together with some interesting VIN DE PAYS. Although Syrah, Grenache, Mourvèdre, and Cinsaut are fast taking over, Carignan has been the dominant vine variety and a small plot of 50-year-old vines is responsible for some exceptionally masterful examples from Domaine d'Aupilhac, which pioneered old-vine Carignan. Other fine estates busy putting the Languedoc on the world wine map include Domaines Font Caude and L'Aiguelière. DROUGHT is a common summer problem and yields on these rocky slopes are notably low.

Montrachet,
or **Le Montrachet**, the most famous GRAND CRU white burgundy, the apogee of the Chardonnay grape produced from a single vineyard in the Côte de Beaune district of the CÔTE D'OR. Claude Arnoux, writing in 1728, could find no words in either French or Latin to describe its qualities, though he noted that it was very expensive and that you needed to reserve the wine a year in advance. Dr Lavalle's view (see BURGUNDY, history), expressed in 1855 and not necessarily valid today, was that whatever the price for a good vintage of Le Montrachet, you would not have paid too much.

Le Montrachet covers a whisker under 8 ha/20 acres straddling the borders of Puligny and Chassagne, two communes which have annexed the famous name to their own (see PULIGNY-MONTRACHET and CHASSAGNE-MONTRACHET). Part of the secret lies in the LIMESTONE, part in its perfect south east exposition, which keeps the sun from dawn till dusk. Curiously, the vines in the Puligny half of the vineyard run in east–west rows, those in Chassagne north–south, reflecting the contours of the land.

The principal owners and producers of Le Montrachet are the Marquis de Laguiche, Baron Thénard, DOMAINE DE LA ROMANÉE-CONTI, BOUCHARD Père et Fils, Domaines Lafon and Prieur in Meursault, and Domaines Ramonet, Colin, and Amiot-Bonfils in Chassagne. In 1991, Domaine Leflaive of Puligny purchased a smallholding. The largest slices belong to the Marquis de Laguiche, whose wine is made by Joseph DROUHIN, and Baron Thénard, whose wine is made by the NÉGOCIANT Remoissenet.

Four more grands crus are associated with Le Montrachet: Chevalier-Montrachet, Bâtard-Montrachet, Bienvenues-Bâtard-Montrachet, and Criots-Bâtard-Montrachet.

Chevalier-Montrachet (7.36 ha) is situated directly above the Puligny section of Le Montrachet, on thin, stony soil giving wines which are not quite as rich as the latter. Particularly sought after are the Chevalier-Montrachet, Les Demoiselles, from Louis LATOUR and Louis JADOT, emanating from a section of the vineyard which was incorporated from what was previously the premier cru Les Demoiselles.

Bâtard-Montrachet (11.86 ha), on the slope beneath Le Montrachet, also spans the two communes, producing rich and heady wines not quite as elegant as a Chevalier-Montrachet. In the Puligny section of Bâtard is a separate enclave, **Bienvenues-Bâtard-Montrachet** (3.68 ha), while an extension of the Chassagne section is the rarely seen **Criots-Bâtard-Montrachet** (1.57 ha).

See CÔTE D'OR for details of viticulture and wine-making.   J.T.C.M.

Arnoux, C., *Dissertation sur la situation de Bourgogne* (Dijon, 1728).

Ginestet, B., *Montrachet* (Paris, 1988).

Loftus, S., *Puligny-Montrachet* (London, 1992).

Montravel,
mainly dry white wine appellation in the extreme west of the BERGERAC district in SOUTH WEST FRANCE just over the boundary of the GIRONDE *département* with the DORDOGNE, and thus close to Bordeaux's Côtes de FRANCS, which also has a tradition of sweet white wine-making. The main grape variety is Sémillon, with obligatory Sauvignon Blanc and often some Muscadelle. The overall quality of these dry wines increased considerably in the late 1980s, with a certain amount of BARREL MATURATION having been introduced, but they are chiefly a local phenomenon. Chx Masburel, Pique-Sègue, and Puy-Servain have made some international impact.

The appellations **Côtes de Montravel** and **Haut-Montravel** are used for small quantities of sweet wines, with the former generally denoting a MOELLEUX and the latter, a description rarely used, for an even sweeter version. The appellation was extended in 2001 to red wines made from Bordeaux grape varieties.

Montsant, DO created in CATALUÑA in 2001 which used to be known as the Falset sub-region of the TARRAGONA DO. Its 2,000 ha/4,950 acres of vineyards were given their own identity in order to highlight its superior quality. It largely lacks the schist soils of its neighbour PRIORAT but otherwise its old Garnacha and Cariñena vineyards on steep slopes enable it to produce wines of very similar style and quality.   V. de la S.

Montù, also known as **Montuni**, black grape indigenous to the plains of EMILIA in Italy.

Moravia, eastern, wine-producing part of the CZECH REPUBLIC whose wine region lies just north of the Weinviertel of Austria.

    Moravia is also the name of a common dark-skinned grape planted in central Spain. It produces rustic wines, particularly in south eastern La Mancha.

Morellino di Scansano, see MAREMMA.

Morellone, occasional name for Italy's MONTEPULCIANO grape.

Moreto, undistinguished red grape variety that is widely planted in Portugal, notably but not exclusively in the ALENTEJO, where there were 1,600 ha/4,000 acres in the early 2000s. It is also used as a synonym in the Algarve for the (unrelated) CASTELÃO.

Morey-St-Denis, important village in the Côte de Nuits district of Burgundy producing red wines from Pinot Noir grapes (see map under BURGUNDY). Morey suffers, perhaps unfairly, in comparison with its neighbours CHAMBOLLE-MUSIGNY and GEVREY-CHAMBERTIN because its wines are usually described as being lighter versions of Gevrey or firmer than Chambolle, according to which side of the village they are located. Indeed, in the past, the wines were often sold under those names. Geologically there is no need for Morey-St-Denis to feel inferior as the same stratum of LIMESTONE runs from the Combe de Lavaux in Gevrey through Morey to the Combe d'Antin in Chambolle.

There are four GRAND CRU vineyards, moving southwards from the border with Gevrey-Chambertin: Clos de la Roche (16.9 ha/42 acres), Clos St-Denis (6.6 ha), Clos des Lambrays (8.8 ha), Clos de Tart (7.5 ha), plus a small segment of Bonnes Mares overlapping from Chambolle.

Although Morey chose to append St-Denis to its name in 1927, Clos de la Roche is probably

the finest vineyard. The soil is rich in MARL, giving greater depth, body, and ageing ability than most other vineyards.

Clos St-Denis, sandwiched between Clos de la Roche and the village itself, may be the quintessential wine of Morey-St-Denis—a touch lighter than Clos de la Roche, with a trace of austerity, but the pinnacle of finesse.

Excellent examples of both Clos de la Roche and Clos St-Denis have been made by Domaine Ponsot, Domaine Dujac, and the Lignier cousins. While Domaine Ponsot was one of the first to bottle their own wines in Burgundy, Domaine Dujac is the comparatively recent creation (since 1968) of Jacques Seysses, an inspirational grower whose example significantly influenced the generation taking over their family domaines in the 1980s.

Clos des Lambrays is all but a monopoly of the Saier brothers, who bought the run-down vineyard and winery from the Cosson family in 1979. At that time, Clos des Lambrays was classified as PREMIER CRU but the Saiers won promotion to grand cru on the grounds of the vineyard's potential, as indicated by its TOPOGRAPHY and GEOLOGY. As yet, despite major renovation and great attention to detail, it is not certain that wines comparable with Clos St-Denis or Clos de la Roche are being made.

Clos de Tart has always been a MONOPOLE: founded by the Cistercian sisters of Notre Dame de Genlis in 1250, it remained in their hands until the French Revolution, when it was auctioned in one piece. In 1932, one of the Marey-Monge family sold it to the current owner, Mommessin. Clos de Tart makes a fine, silky wine which does not always seem to have quite the power and concentration expected of a grand cru—although Dr Lavalle singled it out in 1855 as the only 'tête de cuvée' vineyard in Morey.

Successful premier cru vineyards in Morey-St-Denis include Les Ruchots, Clos de la Bussière (*monopole* of Domaine Georges Roumier), Les Millandes, Clos des Ormes, and Les Monts Luisants. Domaine Ponsot also produces a rare and curious white wine from the last, a proportion of which is made from Pinot Noir vines which have mutated into a type of Pinot Blanc.

    See also CÔTE D'OR.   J.T.C.M.

Morgon, important BEAUJOLAIS cru which encompasses about 1,100 ha/2,717 acres of vines around the commune of Villié-Morgon. The wines produced are considered notably denser and longer lived than most Cru Beaujolais and the appellation has even been used as a verb, as in describing the process by which a young Beaujolais becomes more like a Pinot Noir-dominated red burgundy with time in bottle: *il morgonne*. Soils here are more weathered and the total ripeness is likely to be greater than in most crus, although some consider that only the wines made on the slope known as Côte de Py just south of Villié-

Morgon have the real depth traditionally associated with Morgon. DUBŒUF's Cuvée Jean Descombes is one of the best.

Morillon is an old north eastern French name for PINOT NOIR and is still a common name for the powerfully aromatic CHARDONNAY of STYRIA in southern Austria. It was a widely used Burgundian vine variety name in the Middle Ages and was, for example, an old name for Chardonnay in Chablis country.

Morio-Muskat is Germany's most popular MUSCAT-like vine variety by far, although it is quite unrelated to any Muscat. Somehow Peter Morio's Silvaner × Weissburgunder (Pinot Blanc) crossing is almost overwhelmingly endowed with sickly grapiness that recalls some of Muscat's more obvious characteristics, even though its parents are two of the more aromatically restrained varieties. It was particularly popular with the eager blenders of the PFALZ and RHEINHESSEN in the late 1970s, when its total German area reached 3,000 ha/7,410 acres, and demand for LIEBFRAUMILCH was high: a drop of Morio-Muskat in a neutral blend of Müller-Thurgau and Silvaner can cheaply Germanize it. Total plantings are falling fast, however, and Germany had only 680 ha in 2003 as this aggressively blowsy crossing has undoubtedly had its day. If allowed to ripen fully, it can produce reasonably respectable VARIETAL wines but this is not one of Germany's finest specialities and it needs at least as good a site as Silvaner to achieve this. MUST WEIGHTS of Morio-Muskat are naturally low, although acidity is medium to high. The grapes can rot easily and ripen a week after Müller-Thurgau, which means that BACCHUS can be a better alternative for Germany's cooler northern wine regions.

Moristel, light, loganberry-flavoured speciality of SOMONTANO in northern Spain. The vine is relatively frail and the light red wine produced oxidizes easily. It may be better in a blend than as a VARIETAL.

Mornington Peninsula, maritime, cool climate wine region south east of Melbourne in the Australian state of VICTORIA and a summer playground for rich and poor alike. Site climate and soil type varies widely across this long east–west peninsula, and the differences are apparent in the wine styles.   J.H.

Morocco, with its high mountains and cooling Atlantic influence, has arguably the greatest potential for producing good-quality wine in North Africa. Viticulture, which existed in the Roman era, was probably introduced by Phoenician settlers. But it was the French colonists who brought large-scale wine production so that Morocco played a significant part in the world's wine trade in the 1950s and 1960s, although it never produced as much sheer quantity as neighbouring

ALGERIA. At independence in 1956, Morocco had 55,000 ha/135,850 acres of carefully husbanded vineyard. With the departing French colonists went wine-making expertise, capital, and a large proportion of domestic consumption. This was compounded in 1967 by new EEC (now EU) quotas which literally decimated Morocco's exports. Frozen out of European markets and faced with stiff competition from other over-producing Mediterranean countries, most producers grubbed up their vineyards and replaced them with cereal crops. Between 1973 and 1984, the great majority of vineyards were taken over by the state, which by 1984 had also established a firm grip on the sale of wine, including grape price-fixing regardless of quality.

By the early 1990s, only about 13,000 ha of the nation's 40,000 ha of vines were planted with wine vines, over half of them, many virused, were 30 years old or more and therefore economically unproductive. The average production was just 350,000 hl—the exceptionally low average yield of well under 30 hl/ha (1.7 tons/acre) betraying a certain carelessness in viticulture. The state had a virtual monopoly of the domestic market. The only independent producer to prosper in this postcolonial climate was Brahim Zniber, now head of North African wine giant Les Celliers de Meknès and also owner of its main domestic competitor, Thalvin-Ebertec (since 2001), as well as of Sincobar, so that today the Sniber group has a 90 per cent share of the domestic market. Zniber, who bought his first vineyards from departing French producers in the 1950s and started bottling wines in 1976, encouraged the introduction of an appellation system and pioneered varietal wines.

In a bid to revive Morocco's rural economy, the late King Hassan II successfully attracted foreign investment in viticulture during the 1990s. Several large Bordeaux groups, including CASTEL, William Pitters, and Taillan, took up the offer of long leases on prime vineyard land from the state holding company SODEA. This policy of seeking inward investment, continued by King Mohammed VI, had a galvanizing effect on the industry from the mid 1990s. Thousands of hectares have been replanted with better quality grape varieties by foreign investors, Celliers de Meknès, and a few smaller entrepreneurs so that vineyards totalled 50,000 ha by the early 21st century. State-of-the-art bottling and vinification plants have been built by Celliers de Meknès and Castel, with the refrigeration necessary for TEMPERATURE CONTROL and oak barrels. Although SODEA was by far the largest grower and owner of vineyard land, a gradual break-up and privatization of the company was already underway in 2005. In the meantime, virtually all of its wine is sold to Les Celliers de Meknès for blending and bottling.

Well over 75 per cent of wine is red. Historically the uninspiring Carignan dominated the Moroccan *vignoble* although there was a later wave of planting Cinsaut (still the country's most planted variety accounting for almost 40 per cent of the total), which can produce agreeable VIN GRIS. With rosé, this pale orangey-pink wine accounts for almost 20 per cent of total wine production. Alicante and Grenache are also important but the proportion of 'improving' grape varieties such as Cabernet Sauvignon, Syrah, and Merlot, which together account for about 15 per cent of Moroccan production, is increasing rapidly. White grape varieties such as Clairette and Muscat tend to produce heavy, often musty, non-aromatic white wines which in 2005 comprised barely 3 per cent of total production. There have been experiments with July-picked, cool-fermented Chenin Blanc, Sauvignon Blanc and, inevitably, Chardonnay.

Morocco's appellation system, modelled on the French APPELLATION CONTRÔLÉE, is called Appellation d'Origine Garantie. AOG rules delimit the geographical area of production and set maximum yields but do not dictate grape varieties. The system has yet to achieve any real significance in terms of guaranteeing quality—Thalavin-Evertec make some of the country's best wines and do not even use it—but the following 14 AOG zones, mostly in the cooler, fertile regions of the north, have at least the stamp of official recognition by the EU.

The East: Beni Sadden, Berkane, Angad
Meknès/Fès region: Guerrouane, Beni M'tir, Saiss, Zerhoune
The Northern Plain: Gharb
Rabat/Casablanca region: Chellah, Zemmour, Zaër, Zenatta, Sahel
El-Jadida region: Doukkala

The Meknès region of the Middle Atlas, where vines are planted at an altitude of around 600 m/1,968 ft, and Berkane (once famous for its Muscat VIN DOUX NATUREL) have traditionally enjoyed the finest reputation but there are vast new plantings around Benslimane and Beni Mellal. Some of the best modern wines come from grapes grown in the Zaër highlands, closer to the capital Rabat. Thanks to the Atlantic influence, good wines are also produced further south along the coast: in the Doukkala, where Castel's Boulaouane domaine produces the wine for France's leading foreign wine brand; and—more improbably—near Essaouira, where Charles Melia from Châteauneuf-du-Pape makes wines from Rhône varieties.

Although Morocco is often described as having a semi-arid MEDITERRANEAN climate, the Atlas mountains and Atlantic ocean combine to create cool mesoclimates in the north. Nevertheless, summer temperatures can reach 35-38 °C; rainfall between May and October is very low; and drought cycles are worsening. Another problem can be the strength of the prevailing WINDS from the Atlantic of up to 65 km/40 miles per hour. Vine TRELLISING and careful row orientation have become more common, and all main producers now practice DRIP IRRIGATION.

With a current annual output of less than 400,000 hl, Morocco's wine production remains modest. Although huge quantities of very poor wine are still produced, the wine industry is now dominated by private companies, all of which make consistently palatable—if, as yet, unexceptional—wines. Perhaps the most innovative of these is Thalvin-Ebertec, which has experimented successfully with white grapes such as Chenin Blanc and Viognier, as well as the little-known red grape, ARINARNOA. The local market for good quality Moroccan wine is buoyed by strong demand from the developing tourist industry and the country's affluent urban elite, as well as by the high duties on imported wines. Moroccan law prohibits the sale of alcohol to Muslims, but in practice the law is seldom if ever applied. Alcohol is freely available in all the main cities outside the holy month of Ramadan. Not everyone approves of this permissive approach—least of all Morocco's growing Islamist movement, which seeks to ban or limit alcohol consumption.

See also CORKS, of which Morocco is a relatively important producer. R.H.N.J.

Joy, R., *A Survey of Moroccan Wine* (ESC Dijon, 2003).
Platter, J. & E., *Africa Uncorked* (London, 2002).

morphology. See VINE MORPHOLOGY.

Morrastel is the main French synonym for Rioja's GRACIANO. It is also, confusingly, one of Spain's synonyms for MOURVÈDRE, although Monastrell is the more common Spanish name for Mourvèdre. Morrastel is the name used for the Graciano still grown in the central Asian republic of UZBEKISTAN. See also the TINTA MIÚDA of Portugal.

Morrastel-Bouschet, a much lesser CROSSING, is sometimes called simply Morrastel in southern France, where it was grown in considerable quantity in the mid 20th century, most notably in the Aude and Hérault *départements*. See GRACIANO for more details.

Mortágua, western Portuguese synonym for the red wine grape known as Camarate, for TRINCADEIRA in Torres Vedras, and, occasionally in Dão and Setúbal, for TOURIGA NACIONAL.

Moscadello, sometimes **Moscadelleto,** name for the MUSCAT OF ALEXANDRIA grown in and around MONTALCINO in central Italy. Moscadello was the major wine of Montalcino for centuries, being cited by English travellers in the 17th and 18th centuries, long before anyone even noted the presence of important reds. The firm Villa Banfi made an important investment in selling this sweet grapey, fizzy white wine in the 1980s, and other producers of BRUNELLO DI MONTALCINO followed their lead.

There is also a decisively sweet late-harvest version, notably from Col d'Orcia, which appears to have more commercial potential than the regular Moscadello, which has not so far been able to compete successfully against better-known wines such as MOSCATO D'ASTI.

Moscatel, Spanish and Portuguese for MUSCAT. The term may be applied to both grape varieties and wines. Thus **Moscatel de Grano Menudo** is none other than MUSCAT BLANC À PETITS GRAINS, while **Moscatel de Alejandría** and **Moscatel Romano** are MUSCAT OF ALEXANDRIA. **Moscatel Rosado**, on the other hand, may be a South American speciality (see below). **Moscatel de Málaga** has been identified as a local speciality of southern Spain. Most of the vines known simply as Moscatel in Spanish- and Portuguese-speaking countries are Muscat of Alexandria, although northern Spain has some of the superior small-seeded variety.

Inexpensive wines called simply Moscatel abound in Iberia and are in general simply sweet and grapey.

See also Moscatel de SETÚBAL.

Moscatel de Alejandría, Spanish name for MUSCAT OF ALEXANDRIA.

Moscatel de Austria, the principal grape variety used in the production of pisco, Chile's aromatic brandy, and almost certainly the same as Argentina's TORRONTÉS Sanjuanino. This russet-coloured, neutrally flavoured variety has compact bunches of large, thin-skinned, grapes, making it susceptible to ROT in damp weather. It needs a hot climate to ripen properly.

Moscatel Rosada, quantitatively important but qualitatively very unimportant pink-skinned grape grown in ARGENTINA and to a much lesser extent in Chile, for common table wine and TABLE GRAPES. It is not apparently related to any known Muscat.

Moscato, Italian for MUSCAT.

Moscato Bianco, sometimes called **Moscato di Canelli**, is the finest Muscat grape variety MUSCAT BLANC À PETITS GRAINS and is that most commonly encountered in Italy, making it the country's fourth most planted white grape variety with more than 13,000 ha/ 32,110 acres planted in 2000, cited in 17 DOCs. **Moscato Giallo** and **Moscato Rosa Trentini** (both found in ALTO ADIGE, often called Goldmuskateller and Rosenmuskateller respectively) are distinct and different varieties with golden and pink berries respectively. **Moscato di Alexandria** is the Italian synonym for the lesser white grape variety MUSCAT OF ALEXANDRIA.

Like MALVASIA, Moscato Bianco is ancient, versatile, and enjoys a geographical distribution that covers virtually the entire peninsula. Wines called Moscato are produced all over the country and are usually made from Moscato Bianco grapes. In the south and, especially, the islands, they are typically golden and sweet.

Few of Italy's regions do not have their own Moscato-based wines, and Luigi VERONELLI's *Reportorio dei vini italiani*, published in 1990, listed over 50 different types of Moscato. The majority of these are low in alcohol and at least lightly sweet, ideal accompaniments to fruit and fruit-based desserts. The best known and most widely popular of these wines— almost the national prototype for Moscato— is the Moscato planted in the Asti region in its two different forms: the sparkling ASTI version and the more lightly fizzy and less alcoholic MOSCATO D'ASTI. Wines that are comparable, in style if not in quality, are also produced in significant quantities in the OLTREPÒ PAVESE and Colli Euganei DOC zones, while attempts to launch—or, perhaps more accurately, revive—the production of Moscato in the Brunello di Montalcino zone (as MOSCADELLO di Montalcino) has proved to be a commercial fiasco. A drier, crisper, but still aromatic style of Moscato is produced in TRENTINO, and the better bottles can approach the quality of an average ALSACE Muscat.

Italy's south, in particular SICILIA, was once renowned for its Moscato wines, including the mythical Moscato di Siracusa and Moscato di Noto, which by now have virtually vanished into the land of legend, although attempts to revive **Moscato di Noto** are now under way. Small quantities of Moscato-based wines are still produced in SARDEGNA (**Moscato di Cagliari, Moscato di Sorso Sennori**), in BASILICATA (**Moscato del Vulture**), and in Puglia (**Moscato di Trani**), but the most significant southern Moscato is **Moscato di Pantelleria**, a PASSITO wine from the Muscat of Alexandria grape, considerably more alcoholic and more lusciously sweet than the better-known Moscato d'Asti. The revived popularity of Moscato di Pantelleria in the 1980s coincided with, and perhaps influenced, new attempts to achieve a more luscious style of Moscato in Piemonte, and a new category of passito wines, far sweeter than Moscato d'Asti and frequently given BARREL MATURATION, began to emerge in the late 1980s. Small quantities of Moscato passito have long been made in the Valle d'AOSTA, principally near the township of Chambave.

Moscato wines come in colours other than white in Italy: a pink Moscato Rosa, redolent of roses, is produced in Alto Adige and, to a much lesser extent, in Trentino and Friuli, while red Moscato, aromatic to the point of decadence but not always particularly well made, is produced near Bergamo in the **Moscato di Scanzo** DOC zone. D.T.

Moscato d'Asti, fragrant and lightly sweet, gently fizzy, dessert wine made in the PIEMONTE region of north west Italy now of DOCG status. It is produced from MOSCATO BIANCO, Italy's version of the aristocratic MUSCAT BLANC À PETITS GRAINS, whose production in and around the town of Asti increased sixtyfold in the 20th century. A mere 15,000 tonnes of Moscato Bianco were harvested in an average late 19th century vintage, but this was before the establishment of the ASTI sparkling wine industry headquartered in Canelli. Santo Stefano Belbo is considered the cradle of Moscato in Piemonte, and at the end of the 19th century almost 80 per cent of all Moscato was grown in the calcareous soils of Canelli, Santo Stefano Belbo, Calosso, Castiglione Tinella, and Cassinasco. Strevi, Riccaldone, and Acqui Terme in the province of Alessandria, then and now a source of excellent Moscato, produced another 5 per cent of the total. These are still considered the classic zones for fine Moscato, although the later expansion of the growing areas has revealed a real vocation for Moscato on the slopes of Cossano Belbo, Mango, Neviglie, and Trezzo Tinella. Moscato d'Asti is therefore something of a misnomer, since an important part of the production is not in the province of Asti at all but in the province of Cuneo (stretching as far as Serralunga Alba in the eastern part of the BAROLO zone), and a significant part is in the province of Alessandria.

As a wine, Moscato d'Asti is often lumped together with ASTI, although the two wines are, in fact, quite different. With a maximum of 1.7 atmospheres of pressure in the bottle, a third that of Asti, Moscato d'Asti is only slightly frothy while Asti is fully sparkling. Its ALCOHOLIC STRENGTH is considerably lower (5.5 per cent as opposed to Asti's 7–9.5 per cent), the less powerful aromas and flavour of Asti frequently give a sweeter sensation on the palate even if the RESIDUAL SUGAR level is normally slightly lower than those of Moscato d'Asti.

The ripest, and best, MOSCATO grapes are used to produce Moscato d'Asti. By law, the minimum potential alcohol of grapes selected for Moscato d'Asti must be 10 per cent, while for Asti the minimum is 9 per cent. The 'wine' is classed as 'partially fermented grape must', for the juice is chilled and filtered immediately after pressing and fermented only when required in order to ensure that the beguiling aromas of the Moscato grape are not lost. Fermentation is stopped when the wine reaches 5.5% alcohol; the unfermented sugar lends a hedonistic grapey character to the wine, and helps to exalt the Moscato's heady perfumes.

A vanguard minority of producers has begun to press in recent years for a lowering of the minimum alcohol requirement from its present level of 5.5 per cent, claiming that the wine would become both more fragrant and, as a slightly sweeter wine, a more suitable accompaniment to desserts. Moscato d'Asti will never be a classic dessert wine, however, its chief virtues being its delicacy, its intensely musky aromas, a sweetness that is as much suggested as forthrightly declared; its definition as 'the perfect breakfast wine' contains a nugget of jocular truth.

If Moscato d'Asti remains a relative drop in the overall scheme of things (3 million bottles compared with the 75 million bottles of Asti) and has known a significant commercial development only in the 1970s and 1980s as small producers who had previously sold either grapes or wine to the larger Asti Spumante houses began to bottle Moscato d'Asti under their own name, it has by now gained a secure niche as a classic and unusually refreshing expression of one of the world's most important and popular grape varieties.　　　D.T. & D.C.G.

Moscato di Sardegna, relatively new and as yet relatively unrealized DOC for light, frothy, sweet white wines made in SARDEGNA in the image of ASTI.

Moscato di Strevi, fine, lightly fizzy MUSCAT made in the hills around Strevi in the east of the ASTI zone. As it is usually riper in flavour than most MOSCATO D'ASTI due to Strevi's warmer MESOCLIMATE and steep vineyards, it has been granted subzone status in the Asti DOCG zone.

Moscato Spumante, the most basic form of light, fizzy, Italian white wine made in the style of ASTI but usually with the most basic, industrial ingredients. Not to be confused with the infinitely superior MOSCATO D'ASTI.

Moscophilero, vine variety with deep pink-skinned grapes used to make strongly perfumed white wine in GREECE, particularly on the high plateau of Mantinia in the Peloponnese, where conditions are sufficiently cool that harvest is often delayed until well into October. Its name, like that of Italy's VESPAIOLO, indicates the extent to which insects are drawn to these ripe grapes. There are strong flavour similarities with fine MUSCAT but the origins of this distinct vine variety are as yet obscure. Small quantities of fruity light pink wine are also made from this spicy variety, which is also increasingly used for sparkling wines.

Mosel and **Moselle,** the German and French names respectively for the river which rises in the Vosges mountains of France, forms the border between LUXEMBOURG (in which it plays a key part in wine production) and Germany, and joins the river Rhein or Rhine at Koblenz in Germany, 545 km/340 miles later.

France
The name Moselle is still part of today's French wine nomenclature in the VDQS **Moselle,** which, together with Côtes de TOUL, constitute what the French call their *vins de l'est* or 'wines of the east', the last remnants of what was once an important and flourishing Lorraine wine industry. Extensive vineyards around Metz supplied PINOT NOIR grapes to Champagne in the 19th century and subsequently provided base wine for SEKT when the region became German after the Franco-Prussian war of 1870. PHYLLOXERA arrived late here and the region was relatively unaffected until 1910. The poor-quality HYBRIDS chosen for replanting, together with increasing industrialization (see RAILWAYS) and the proximity of the First World War battlefields, hastened the decline of this wine region. White Auxerrois and Müller-Thurgau are the most common varieties and most wines are light, crisp, white, and aromatic, a small proportion being made sparkling.

George, R., *French Country Wines* (London, 1990).

Germany
In Germany 'Mosel' describes a subregion for table wine (see TAFELWEIN) within the MOSEL-SAAR-RUWER region. Colloquially, apart from indicating the river and the valley, Mosel describes the wine from the whole of the Mosel-Saar-Ruwer region, regardless of quality; it is often used in this way by the world's wine trade.

As a result of its success in the English-speaking world, Moselle became a GENERIC name for any light, medium dry, faintly aromatic wine. In the middle of the 19th century, Sparkling Moselle was a popular partner to Sparkling Hock (see HOCK).

Mosel-Saar-Ruwer, once the official name of GERMANY's best-known wine region which appends to the name of the river known in Germany as MOSEL and in France as MOSELLE the names of two of its viticulturally important tributaries (see map under GERMANY). It is now known simply as **Mosel.** The wines produced are typically white, low in alcohol, and some of the most refreshing and underrated in the world. Theirs is a style which no other wines can even emulate.

Thanks partly to the world's relative indifference, the total area planted has been declining slowly and in 2003 was 9,500 ha/26,000 acres, of which over half are on slopes whose angle of inclination is more than 26 per cent. Many vineyards rise almost immediately from the banks of the Mosel or, less directly, from those of the SAAR and RUWER and a few are in the smaller side valleys which feed the larger river with water from the Hunsrück plateau or the volcanic hills of the Eifel. Just downstream of Trier are the Mosel's first, steep vineyards, which continue with little interruption, on one bank or the other, all the way to Koblenz. As the river twists and sometimes retraces its route, the vineyards are at their steepest on the outer edge of the curve. Those on the flatter inner edge are frequently planted with grapes other than Riesling on land more suited to agriculture than to viticulture. TOPOGRAPHY is all important here.

Downstream from Cochem, the Mosel straightens out but, for much of the way, it still flows through a gorge, deep below the surrounding countryside. SLATE has been used in the region for hundreds of years as a building material, and where it has not been present in sufficient quantity in the soil it has been added to feed the vine with MINERALS and to retain warmth. Some of the vineyards between the almost vertical spurs of rock could be created only with the aid of explosives, as far back as the 16th century, a dangerous operation when there was a wine village below. Vineyards have been modernized but more recently and to a much lesser extent than in the regions of BADEN or WÜRTTEMBERG (see FLURBEREINIGUNG). Production costs in the steep Mosel vineyards remain among the highest in Germany.

The Mosel-Saar-Ruwer normally has a warm but by no means hot summer with an average temperature in the hottest month of July of 18 °C (64 °F). The MESOCLIMATE is of rather more significance and here there are considerable variations. In some Saar and Obermosel (upstream from Trier) vineyards, there is a risk of FROST damage particularly in spring, but also in late autumn and winter. Even in relatively gentle winters, there are usually a few very cold nights for EISWEIN production.

The Mosel-Saar-Ruwer region is divided into six districts, or *Bereiche*, of which the Bereich Bernkastel is the only one whose name appears with any frequency on bottles sold outside Germany. About a third of the region's production is offered under GROSSLAGE (collective site) names, such as Piesporter Michelsberg, Klüsserather St Michael, Zeller Schwarze Katz, or Bernkasteler Kurfürstlay. There are some 500 or more single-vineyard (EINZELLAGE) names, of which only 60 or so have real significance in terms of the quality of wine they produce. Too often with the simple QBA quality wines from less-than-meticulous vintners, vineyard characteristics are so diluted by over-production, and hidden by added SÜSSRESERVE, that the vineyard name loses its meaning.

In the 18th century, many villages produced red wine, particularly those in what we now know as the Bereich Zell (see GERMAN HISTORY). By the early 19th century, white wine had taken the lead and the ELBLING vine covered nearly two-thirds of the vineyard area. It still predominates in the Bereich Obermosel, where, as in LUXEMBOURG, it supplies a clean, fresh, rather rustic wine from yields in copious vintages that once were as high as 220 hl/ha (12.5 tons/acre) or more. Riesling, grown in over 90 per cent of all vineyards in 1954, now occupies just 57 per cent of plantings but is once more gaining ground. In the 1960s and 1970s, MÜLLER-THURGAU was increasingly grown in what had previously been farmland. It was also planted in vineyards where the chances of Riesling ripening consistently to the level required by the GERMAN WINE LAW of 1971 were doubtful. Unlike Riesling and Elbling, Müller-Thurgau

It is a happy accident for wine lovers that Kevin Judd, winemaker at keep **Cloudy Bay**, producer of the world's most popular Sauvignon Blanc, is also a keen photographer and blessed with many a view as stunning as this in his home region of Marlborough, New Zealand.

and other GERMAN CROSSINGS which were introduced in the 1960s have not produced wines with pronounced regional characteristics. Today the name Riesling on the label is the first clue in finding a good wine from the Mosel-Saar-Ruwer.

The greater amount of alcohol in wines from warmer climates can hide flaws. With a cheap Mosel, RESIDUAL SUGAR in the bottled wine can have a similar effect. Higher up the quality scale, these wines, usually so light in alcohol, have to be grown and vinified with particular care if their lack of BODY is not to count against them. The key to a fine Mosel-Saar-Ruwer Riesling is its backbone of fruity-tasting TARTARIC ACID, which balances any residual sugar present. A low-alcohol Mosel Riesling often tastes merely off-dry although it has more than 30 g/l residual sugar. As TROCKEN or HALBTROCKEN wines are increasingly made in this region just as elsewhere in Germany, one ought not to assume that all Mosels are light. Nevertheless, even if some Auslese Trocken is sold with over 12 per cent of natural alcohol, the quintessential Mosel remains for many non-Germans the delicate, fresh Kabinett wine, only slightly stronger in ALCOHOLIC STRENGTH, about 9 per cent, than a dark, double bock beer from Munich. Mosel Kabinett at its best is unique, and one of the glories of the world of wine. Perhaps its only rival is a wine of similar quality from the NAHE.

Other than at Trier and Koblenz, with about 100,000 inhabitants apiece, the Mosel-Saar-Ruwer and its surrounding countryside are lightly peopled. In the absence of alternative jobs, much of the local population earns a living or a part-time income from wine. Nearly three times as many hours are spent per hectare per annum in the steep Mosel vineyards than is necessary in the more easily worked land of the PFALZ region. Unfortunately, the difference in price in the Mosel bulk wine market between high-yielding Müller-Thurgau from a second-rate site, and a Riesling from a good vineyard, does not encourage the production of less and better wine. For fine Riesling one should turn to the very large number of private estate bottlers. They are a surer guide to a good Mosel than are the names of the famous villages, or of the best-known single-vineyard sites. Even that of a vineyard as prestigious as the Wehlener Sonnenuhr is not a guarantee of a high-quality wine, unless it is one of the best estate bottlings, labelled ERZEUGERABFÜLLUNG.

Lower Mosel

The district with the highest percentage of Riesling vines on the river Mosel starts at the confluence of the Rhine and Mosel at Koblenz and continues upstream until shortly after the narrow town of Zell, from which the Bereich Zell takes its name. It has many small, steep vineyards which can be maintained only by hand, and the lowest percentage of flat or gen-

tly sloping sites workable by tractor. The individual holdings are not as large as those of the Bereich Bernkastel and their sheer incline and rockiness as well as their relative isolation in a narrow, steeply walled valley have traditionally put them at a commercial disadvantage relative to their neighbours upstream. During the 1980s and 1990s, the Deutsches Eck growers' association had some success in raising commercial consciousness as well as wine quality for these villages jointly with those of the neighbouring MITTELRHEIN region, their close cultural and geological cousins. More recently, the name Terrassenmosel is being used as a way of distinguishing, and of creating a quality image for, these steepest of Mosel vineyards, nearly all of them planted on terraces dating back many centuries. The stony, relatively dry MESOCLIMATE here, as well as the frequent convergence of blue Devonian slate, red slate, and quartzite, can result in fascinating and distinctive wines, as a few of the top growers—some beginning to enjoy international attention—are proving.

The precipitous walls of slate outside Koblenz at Winnigen—most notably the Uhlen vineyard—are regaining a reputation for high ripeness and excellence that was essentially lost and forgotten for nearly a century.

Up river from Winningen, in Kobern, Lehmen, and Pommern, private estates sell good Riesling wines directly to the consumer, and upstream of the busy but attractive Cochem, the villages of Ediger and Eller are important wine producers. At Bremm, the terraced Calmont rises 200 m/656 ft from the river. With a 65 per cent incline, it is one of the steepest vineyards in Germany and, like others in the area, is enjoying a revival at the hands of young, quality-conscious vintners and through the use of monorails permitting secure vineyard access. After Neef and Bullay, the Mosel forms a characteristic oxbow, passing the town of Zell and leading into the Bereich Bernkastel.

Middle Mosel

Of the fewer than 100 vineyards with outstanding potential on the Mosel-Saar-Ruwer, over half are in the Bereich Bernkastel. Travelling upstream, a roster of towns and their top sites begins with the blue and red slate sites of Enkirch, (Batterieberg, Steffensberg), Wolf (Goldgrube), and Kinheim (Rosenberg). The red slate of Erden (Treppchen and Prälat) generates some of the Mosel's most celebrated Rieslings, with a prominent and luscious citric undertow. Neighbouring Ürzig, virtually all of whose top vineyards are united under the name Würzgarten, gives the best Erdeners a run for their money with frequently spicy and strawberry- or kiwi-scented Rieslings. The top vintners of Ürzig all have holdings in Erden as well.

Below Ürzig the Mosel inscribes one of its periodic, tight turns and then enters a

straight stretch whose south-facing slopes enjoy international fame: Zeltingen (Himmelreich, Schlossberg, Sonnenuhr), Wehlen (Sonnenuhr), Graach (Himmelreich, Domprobst), and Bernkastel. Flavours of orchard fruits, vanilla and nut oils typify many of the wines from these sites, and in the case of Bernkastel, a characteristic note of black cherry. In a departure from usual German practice, the names of the best individual sites at Bernkastel, with the exception of the famous Doctor, are—partly on account of their diminutive size—less prestigious and well known than is their collective identity as the Grosslage Badstube. Put another way, Badstube is one of the few if not only German Grosslagen made up entirely of first-rate terroir. After another twist, the river flows past Lieser (Niederberg Helden) and a side valley at Mühlheim; the most prominent vintners of both towns are reclaiming a reputation for excellent TERROIR. Next comes Brauneberg (Juffer, Juffer-Sonnenuhr) whose unusually well-watered walls of southeast-facing slate were responsible for their pre-eminent position in the Mosel pecking order during the 19th century, and earn high praise again today for stunningly rich yet refined Rieslings. Nor do Kesten (Paulinsberg) or Wintrich (Ohligsberg) any longer want for conscientious vintners to prove that their Rieslings have more than historical interest.

Astride a tight loop in the Mosel hang the amphitheatrical slopes of Piesport, whose Goldtröpfchen site is among the region's best and internationally best-known. Honied richness and tropical and black fruit flavours characterize the best of these wines, but sadly many growers trade too easily on the site's name, and the use of the Grosslage name Piesporter Michelsberg for wine from uninspiring surrounding vineyards brings the name of this historic wine village into disrepute. Nearby Dhron (Hofberg) lacks star status but can produce distinctively excellent Riesling as well.

One of the Mosel's narrowest switchbacks and most vertiginous walls of blue slate occurs upstream from Piesport at Trittenheim (Altärchen, Apotheke) and neighboring Leiwen (Laurentiuslay), wines from the former being characteristically richer and from the latter sleeker and more distinctly mineral. Thanks to a bevy of wine-growing talents, the reputation of these sites is now in the ascendant. Upstream Thörnich (Ritsch), Detzem (Maximiner Klosterlay), and Pölich (Held) offer in the hands of a few vintners glimpses of their potential greatness. The same is true of vineyards just below Trier at Longuich (Maximiner Herrenberg), where the abbey of St Maximin, arguably the pre-eminent medieval viticultural institution of the Mosel, established its main press house and planted a forest that has served successfully as a hail shield for five centuries.

McDowell Valley vineyards in Mendocino county, northern California, where vines have traditionally been planted much further apart than in Europe to allow space for conventional tractors between the rows and because the vines tend to be much leafier, or more **vigorous**.

In hot summers with insufficient rain, estate owners sometimes report that wines from their less good sites have been more successful than those from the best vineyards, where intense heat and WATER STRESS can slow down the accumulation of SUGAR IN GRAPES. Fine Mosel is a highly individual wine, which is never available in large quantities. To meet the needs of supermarkets and chain stores for large volumes of inexpensive labels, much ordinary wine, almost certainly not from Riesling, is sold under collective site (Grosslage) names. These include the names of famous villages such as Piesport or Bernkastel.

Saar and Ruwer

The vineyards of the Saar and Ruwer rivers form two districts together making up 11 per cent of the Mosel-Saar-Ruwer region, but their reputation is out of proportion to their surface area. As every additional 100 m/328 ft above sea level results in a drop in average temperature of over 0.5 °C/0.9 °F, the extra height of the Saar, Ruwer, and the upper reaches of the Mosel renders them cooler than the Bereich Bernkastel. In good vintages, the wines are a joy to taste with an abundance of flavour and wonderful acidity, but in poor years it can be difficult for the grapes in many vineyards to reach RIPENESS.

The main Ruwer vineyards begin near the village of the same name, and end some 10 km/6 miles upstream. Sole ownership of the Eitelsbacher Karthäuserhofberg and of the Maximin Grünhaus vineyards in neighbouring Mertesdorf by two outstanding estates in recent years ensures that top-quality Ruwer wines reach international markets. A few other excellent local estates as well as some leading Mosel producers also have holdings at Eitelsbach and Kasel. There are variations on both blue and red slate soils along the Ruwer. Generally, the best wines tend to favour flavours of red fruits and brown spices. The percentage of well-balanced trocken Rieslings—or at least their success within the German market—has arguably been greater than that of corresponding wines from the valley of the Mosel proper.

The vineyards of the Saar form the Grosslage Scharzberg, playing on the name of the Saar's most famous single vineyard, Scharzhofberg at Wiltingen. Scharzhofberg itself has become almost synonymous with the estate to which most of the site nowadays belongs, that of Egon Müller. But there are other excellent Wiltingen vineyards including the Braune Kupp (a Müller MONOPOLE) and Gottesfuss, as well as several choice morsels that despite their 19th-century renown no longer enjoy legal recognition as Einzellagen. Among the other most significant Saar wine villages and their best sites—travelling upstream—are Filzen (Herrenberg), Kanzem (Altenberg), Mennig (Euchariusberg), Oberemmel (Hütte), Wawern (Herrenberg),

Schoden (Saarfeilser Marienberg), Ockfen (Bockstein, Herrenberg), Ayl (Kupp), Saarburg (Rausch), and Serrig (Schloss Saarsteiner).

Above Trier, and upstream of the confluence with the Saar at Konz, the character of the Mosel changes, becoming entirely rural again. The pretty rolling vineyards face those of LUXEMBOURG, a few hundred metres across the river. This area cannot adequately ripen Riesling, but remains almost the last bastion of ELBLING, a grape dating back to Roman times.

The Mosel and commerce

The Moselland co-operative based in Bernkastel processes about one-fifth of the average Mosel-Saar-Ruwer harvest and exports some 40 per cent of its production. Its 2,700 grower-members represent nearly half of the region's declining number of growers, most of them farming fewer than 5 ha of vines, only just enough to provide an adequate, sole source of income for its owner.

Of the region's wine sold in bottle, the majority is bottled by wine merchants, who, although they are customers of the co-operative cellars for bulk wine, are also their competitors.

Bulk prices on the Mosel have been indirectly dictated by the supermarkets at a level at which quality is irrelevant. As the number of bottling growers continues to decrease and the German thirst for red wine dramatically increases—particularly since the mid 1990s—so has the vulnerability of small Mosel growers to predatory pricing. Many of them began planting red vines, notably Dornfelder, whose bulk price, however, has not been sustained.

As an escape from the difficulties of the cheap wine market, SPARKLING WINE can be an interesting alternative. The Saar-Mosel Winzersekt (a producers' association) concentrates on sparkling wines based on Riesling from the Mosel, Saar, and Ruwer and Elbling from the Obermosel. But their wines must compete with locally powerful German BRANDS of SEKT made from the least expensive wine imported in bulk.

While the standing of Mosel wine in Germany has been debased by over-production and price warfare, not to mention by the legal adoption of names of famous villages and vineyards to designate Grosslagen, there remains a small upper tier of excellent estate-bottled wine. There may be more talent concentrated among the vintners of the Mosel than anywhere else in Germany today. The tendency since the 1990s has been for the best vineyards to be consolidated in ever-fewer but more adept wine-making hands. There is still no shortage of cheap and often dull wine but there is also at last a new generation of innovative, talented, and quality-oriented vintners who strive to offer excellent value.

I.J. & D.S.

Payne, J., and Diel, A., *The Guide to German Wines/ German Wine Guide* (London/New York, 2005).

Pigott, S., and Johnson, H., *The Wine Atlas of Germany* (London, 1995).

Mossel Bay, South African wine region now known as RUITERBOSCH.

Moster, occasional Austrian synonym for CHASSELAS.

mother vine, an identified, preferred individual vine from which CUTTINGS or other vegetative propagation materials are taken. They can be labelled as CLONES, which are the basis of CLONAL SELECTION and VINE IMPROVEMENT programmes. B.G.C.

moths, flying insects which damage grapevines in the larval stages. The four most important types in France are pyrale (*Sparganothis pilleriana*), cochylis (*Eupoecilia ambiguella*), eudemis or European grape moth (*Lobesia botrana*), and eulia (*Argyrotaenia pulchellana*). The pyrale larvae attack young leaves and grapes, whereas the cochylis, eudemis, and eulia develop several generations in the grape bunch after the initial invasion, from which grubs attack the developing grapes and encourage BOTRYTIS BUNCH ROT. Control of these pests is difficult because the attacks, which may be severe, are irregular. INSECTICIDES can be used, as can feeding traps and PHEROMONES; such pests are also the subject of INTEGRATED PEST MANAGEMENT strategies using natural predators.

The grape berry moth (*Polychrosis viteana*) causes damage to developing bunches in many parts of America but not California. The Orange Tortrix moth (*Argyrotaenia citrana*) damages buds, leaves, and bunches in California. In Australia and New Zealand, the grapevine moth (*Phalaenoides glycine*) feeds on a range of plants, and the caterpillars do most damage to the leaves. It is controlled by insecticides and also a predatory shield bug. The light brown apple moth larvae infestations of the bunch are also an important means of spreading botrytis. See also LEAF ROLLERS. R.E.S.

Winkler, A. J., *et al.*, *General Viticulture* (2nd edn, Berkeley, Calif., 1974).

Moueix, important family in the BORDEAUX TRADE, notably, but by no means exclusively, in ST-ÉMILION and POMEROL. The Moueix family came from the Corrèze, a severe district in central France, noted for its hard-headed men. Jean Moueix (1882–1957) bought Ch Fonroque in St-Émilion in 1930, and his son Jean-Pierre (1913–2003) joined him that year, with the purpose of selling only the hitherto somewhat neglected wines, nearly all red, produced on the RIGHT BANK of the Dordogne, from the Côtes de CASTILLON downstream to BLAYE. In 1937, Jean-Pierre formed Établissements Jean-Pierre Moueix on the quay in LIBOURNE. Increasingly successful in the post-war period, it became from 1970 the major NÉGOCIANT there selling the finer châteaux wines, at a time when the traditional merchants were failing.

In 1956, the 70-year-old firm of Duclot in the city of Bordeaux was acquired to deal mainly with the 'left bank' districts (MÉDOC, GRAVES, etc.), as well as selling direct to private customers in France. As Bordeaux Millésimes it is prominent in the export trade. From 1968 both were headed by Jean-Pierre's elder son Jean-François (b. 1945). Fonroque was inherited by Jean-Antoine Moueix (1908–57), and then by his son Jean-Jacques (b. 1935), a director of the Libourne firm, now retired.

In 1970, the younger son, Christian (b. 1946), became a director, with special responsibilities, along with the firm's OENOLOGIST Jean-Claude Berrouet, for the 17 estates owned or farmed by the firm. In 1982, Christian started a JOINT VENTURE in Yountville, NAPA VALLEY, with two daughters of John Daniel, former owner of Inglenook, before buying them out in 1994. From a 50-ha/124-acre vineyard and an architectural landmark winery opened in 1998, a Bordeaux-style wine named Dominus is produced. He now runs the Libourne négociant.

In the 1950s, Jean-Pierre Moueix began to acquire châteaux on the right bank: Trotanoy (1953), La Fleur-Pétrus (1953), Lagrange (1959), La Grave (Trigant de Boisset) (1971), and Certan-Giraud, renamed Hosanna (1999), in Pomerol; and Magdelaine (1954) in St-Émilion.

In the 1970s and 1980s, the firm expanded into FRONSAC, acquiring Canon, Canon de Brem, La Croix-Canon, and Canon-Moueix in the superior Canon-Fronsac appellation and La Dauphine in Fronsac. These properties were sold en masse in 2000.

A number of other properties are farmed on behalf of their owners, including Chx Lafleur-Gazin and Latour-Pomerol in Pomerol. However, much the most important acquisition was a half-share of Ch PÉTRUS in 1964. Moueix had had the exclusive selling rights since 1945, and when the owner, Mme Loubat, died in 1961 she left it to her nephew and niece and the former sold his share to M. Moueix. The Moueix family now own it all, with Jean-Francois as *gérant* and Christian as *directeur*.

Jean-Pierre Moueix, a man of great probity and courtesy, was a notable collector of art and books, and the château in which he lived beside the river Dordogne on the edge of Libourne is full of the works of such leading modern artists as Picasso and Francis Bacon.

E.P.-R. & J.R.

mouldy, pejorative tasting term used for wine spoiled by the growth of minute fungi on grapes or winery equipment. Many different types of mould grow on grapes in the vineyard, depending on region and vintage conditions but ROT is the most common. For more details, see FUNGAL DISEASES.

Mouldy COOPERAGE can also cause this sort of aroma. Empty barrels are difficult to keep clean and free of mould for the humid conditions inside them are ideal for the growth of these organisms. Once spores of mould become embedded in the pores of a wooden vessel, it is almost impossible to remove them completely. See BARREL MAINTENANCE. Mouldy, along with musty, is also used to describe a wine that is affected by CORK TAINT. A.D.W.

Moulin-à-Vent means 'windmill' in French and is the name of one of the most famous of the BEAUJOLAIS crus, named after a local windmill. The area includes delimited vineyards within Chénas and Romanèche-Thorins. Of all the wine produced in the Beaujolais region, Moulin-à-Vent is expected to last the longest, taste most concentrated, and therefore, in a way, to be the least typical. With time, the wines begin to taste more like old Pinot Noir than Gamay, and some 50-year-old Moulin-à-Vent can be quite a satisfying drink, even if an atypical Beaujolais. It has also generally been the most expensive. The area planted increased in the 1980s and remains at around 640 ha/1,580 acres in the mid 2000s. Ch des Jacques, bought by Louis JADOT, is a notable name.

Moulis, or **Moulis-en-Médoc,** smallest of the six communal appellations of the Haut-Médoc district of Bordeaux (the others being MARGAUX, ST-JULIEN, PAUILLAC, ST-ESTÈPHE, and neighbouring LISTRAC). Although it includes only about 600 ha/1,500 acres of vineyards, there is considerable diversity of TERROIR in Moulis, in terms of both topography and soil composition. Countryside that is positively rolling by Médoc standards, and soils that include various gravels, clays, and limestone, result in wines as varied as the occasionally brilliant Ch Chasse-Spleen, the good-value Ch Maucaillou, and a host of properties whose names include the word Poujeaux. The finest of these is usually long-lived Ch Poujeaux itself. Like Listrac, this is not CLASSED GROWTH country. Perhaps because of this, the best Moulis wines can offer good value, being as well structured as any Haut-Médoc, often with some of the perfume of Margaux to the east. Yields are more restricted in Moulis than in Listrac.

For more information see MÉDOC and BORDEAUX.

Parker, R., *Bordeaux* (4th edn, New York, 2003).
Penning-Rowsell, E., *The Wines of Bordeaux* (6th edn, London, 1989).

Mountain, 19th-century English term for MÁLAGA, which is indeed flanked by mountains. The name is no longer used but is commonly found on DECANTER LABELS produced before PHYLLOXERA devastated the Málaga region in 1876.

Mount Barker, cool subregion of the Great Southern region, Western Australia, with a strongly CONTINENTAL climate especially suited to Riesling, Shiraz, and Cabernet Sauvignon.

Mount Benson, relatively new seaside wine region in the Limestone Coast Zone of SOUTH AUSTRALIA. Two distinguished residents are CHAPOUTIER of the Rhône valley and (via a large modern winery) G&C Kreglinger, relatives of the Thienponts who own Vieux Château Certan and Le PIN in POMEROL. The region makes elegant, light to medium bodied wines.

Mount Lofty Ranges Zone, encompasses the Adelaide Hills, Adelaide Plains, and Clare Valley wine regions in SOUTH AUSTRALIA.

Mount Veeder, California wine region and AVA in the mountains between Napa and Sonoma. See NAPA valley.

Moura, subregion of ALTENTEJO in southern Portugal.

Mourisco Tinto, lesser PORT grape variety which produces red wines relatively light in colour in northern Portugal. Favoured by a few for light tawny ports, it is nonetheless the Douro's fourth most planted variety.

Mourvèdre, warm climate red grape variety whose fortunes are declining in Spain, where it is the fourth most planted red wine grape, as it has become markedly more fashionable elsewhere. The Spaniards grew 63,000 ha/155,000 acres of the vine they call Monastrell in 2004 while in France, where it is enjoying a resurgence of popularity in the south, there were 7,600 ha overall in 2000. In California and Australia it was often called MATARO but has been enjoying a new lease of life as either varietal Mourvèdre or in a blend with Grenache and Syrah/Shiraz, sometimes called GSM.

The origins of the variety are almost certainly Spanish. Murviedro is a town near Valencia (Mataro is another near Barcelona). It is certainly easier to grow in Spain than in the cooler reaches of southern France for it buds and ripens extremely late, a week later even than Carignan according to Galet. Provided the climate is warm, the upright, vigorous Monastrell adapts well to a wide range of soils and recovers well from spring frost. (It is sensitive to low winter temperatures, however.) It is susceptible to both DOWNY and POWDERY MILDEWS, which are of course much less prevalent in hot Spanish vineyards than in much of France.

The wine produced from Monastrell's small, sweet, thick-skinned berries tends to be heady stuff, high in alcohol, tannins, with a somewhat gamey, almost animal, flavour when young and well capable of ageing provided both OXIDATION and REDUCTION, to which it is particularly prone in southern France, is carefully avoided in the winery. It is especially common in the Murcia, Alicante, Albacete, and Valencia regions and all over the LEVANTE. It is the principal black grape variety in such DOS as ALICANTE, ALMANSA, JUMILLA, VALENCIA, and YECLA.

Mourvèdre needs France's warmest summers to ripen fully. It dominated Provence until the arrival of PHYLLOXERA and the search for productive vines to supply the burgeoning market for cheap table wine. For many decades it marked time in its French enclave BANDOL but is now regarded as an extremely modish and desirable 'improving variety' throughout the Languedoc and Roussillon, especially now that clones have been selected that no longer display the inconveniently variable yields that once resulted from degenerated vine stock. As recently as 1968, total French plantings were as little as 900 ha, spread between Provence, the southern Rhône, the Languedoc, and Roussillon.

In southern France, Mourvèdre produces wines considered useful for their structure, intense fruit, and, in good years, perfume often redolent of blackberries. The structure in particular can be a useful foil for Grenache in Provence and Cinsaut further west. In Bandol, it is typically blended with both of these, and the statutory minimum for Mourvèdre is now 50 per cent. Mourvèdre is condoned in a host of APPELLATION CONTRÔLÉE regulations all over the south of France from Coteaux du Tricastin to Collioure, including Châteauneuf-du-Pape and environs. Although it usually plays a useful supporting role, being fleshier than Syrah, tauter than Grenache and Cinsaut, and infinitely more charming than Carignan, varietal Mourvèdres from the Languedoc have met with commercial success.

Somewhat belatedly, Australia realized it had all the wherewithal to produce authentic Rhône blends, despite the loss of precious old-vine Grenache and Mourvèdre in South Australia in the late 1980s (due to an ill-advised VINE PULL SCHEME). Old-vine Grenache–Shiraz–Mourvèdre (or any combinations thereof) proliferated since the 1990s as resources have been moved from fortified to table wine production. Plantings of Mourvèdre, still called Mataro in official statistics, were more than 1,000 ha in the mid 2000s.

Although grown at least since the 1870s, California's unfashionable Mataro was fast disappearing until the RHÔNE RANGERS made the connection with Mourvèdre and pushed up demand for wine from these historic stumps, notably in Contra Costa county between San Francisco and the Central valley, where there were considerable new plantings in the early 1990s thanks to demand from the likes of Bonny Doon and Cline Cellars. By the

mousse

460

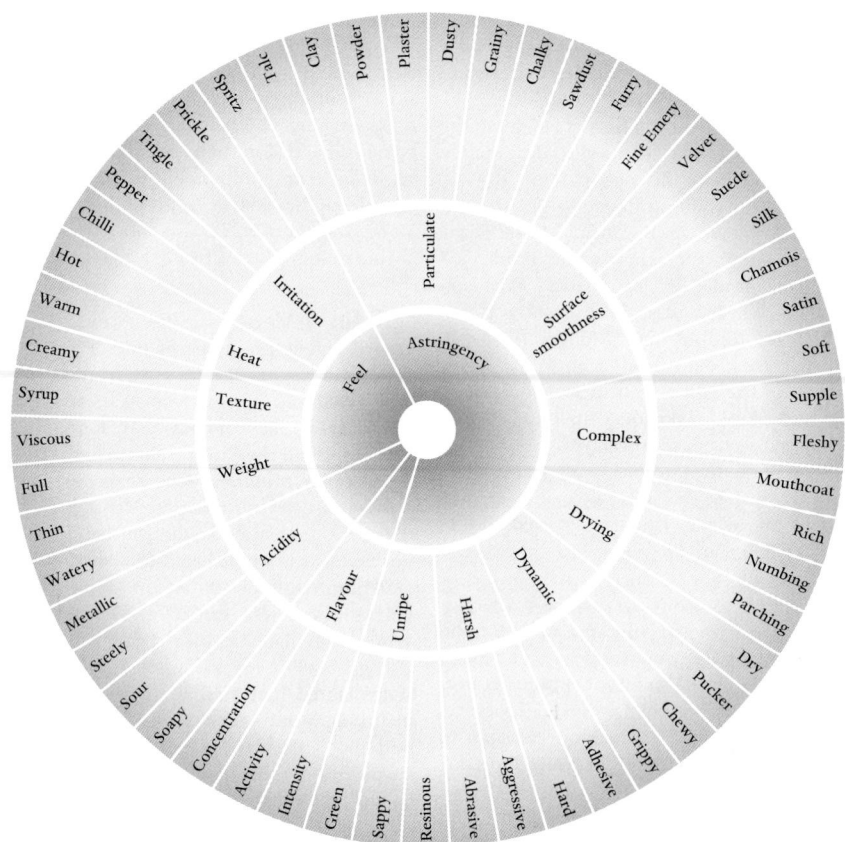

Partly in response to the AROMA WHEEL, the Australian Wine Research Institute developed this **mouthfeel** and astringency wheel in 1998.

mid 2000s, the state's total plantings had risen again, to 650 acres/260 ha.

Galet notes that there may be some Mourvèdre in Azerbaijan, although that is not what it is called.

Galet, P., *Dictionnaire encyclopédique des cépages* (Paris, 2000).

mousse. French term for FIZZINESS.

mousseux, French for sparkling. Some *mousseux* wines are made by the traditional method (see SPARKLING WINE-MAKING) while others may be made by the much less painstaking CHARMAT process.

mousy, TASTING TERM commonly associated with the wine FAULT caused by BRETTANOMYCES yeasts and some bacteria, including some, but not all, LACTIC ACID BACTERIA. Although the exact mechanism of mousy taint formation is not totally clear, for example why some wines are spoiled and others are not despite the presence of micro-organisms capable of producing the fault, it is evident that low levels of SULFUR DIOXIDE, high PH, and exposure to OXYGEN render a wine vulnerable to this spoilage. Mousiness is usually apparent only after a wine has been swallowed or expectorated. Once detected, the taint renders the wine undrinkable.   P.J.W.

Grbin, P. R., Costello, P. J., Herderich, M., Markides, A. J., Henschke, P. A., and Lee, T. H., 'Developments in the sensory, chemical and microbiological basis of mousy taint in wine', in C. S. Stockley, *et al.* (eds.), *Proceedings of the Ninth Australian Wine Industry Technical Conference: 16–19 July 1995* (Adelaide, 1996).

mouthfeel, non-specific tasting term, used particularly for red wines, to indicate those textural attributes, such as smoothness, that produce tactile sensations on the surface of the oral cavity (see diagram above). For more detail, see TEXTURE.

Mouton Cadet, the most successful Bordeaux BRAND, began life in 1927, a poor vintage in which Baron Philippe de ROTHSCHILD created what was effectively a SECOND WINE called Carruades de Mouton for Ch MOUTON-ROTHSCHILD. Penning-Rowsell notes that it was not a success, and its successor in 1930 was named Mouton-Cadet, since Philippe was the *cadet*, the youngest, of the family. Eventually, as Mouton Cadet, it developed a prosperous life of its own, and demand was so great that the flexibility of the BORDEAUX AC appellation was needed. Today Mouton Cadet is available in red and white versions, having been repackaged and re-blended in 2004 to rely more on Merlot and Sauvignon

Blanc respectively with tighter control over its many suppliers all over Bordeaux.

Penning-Rowsell, E., *The Wines of Bordeaux* (6th edn, London, 1989).

Mouton-Rothschild, Château, important wine estate in PAUILLAC in the BORDEAUX wine region and the only one ever to have been promoted within the 1855 CLASSIFICATION, to FIRST GROWTH.

Originally part of the LAFITE estate with which it is intermingled, it became in the middle of the 18th century a separate entity, owned by the de Brane family. In the first half of the following century, Baron Hector de Brane (or Branne) became known as 'the Napoleon of the vines' for his work in developing the Médoc vineyards, and, in company with his neighbour Armand d'Armailhacq, in supposedly introducing the CABERNET SAUVIGNON vine. In 1830, he sold Mouton to a M. Thuret and retired to his Ch Brane-Cantenac in the commune of MARGAUX. At this time, Mouton had little international repute, and the first entry in a Christie's AUCTION catalogue was in 1834. In 1853, Thuret sold it to Baron Nathaniel de ROTHSCHILD, of the English branch of the family, two years before the 1855 classification which placed Mouton-Rothschild at the top of the second growths, a position unsatisfactory to the family, but not seriously contested until Baron Philippe de Rothschild took over the running of it from his father in 1922. He startled Bordeaux by employing a poster artist, Carlu, to design an art deco label, including the Rothschild arrows, for the 1924 vintage, and then proposing CHÂTEAU BOTTLING of all the first growths (and Mouton-Rothschild). He also instigated what was initially a SECOND WINE, called MOUTON CADET.

On his return in 1945 after the Second World War, Baron Philippe initiated the series of ARTIST'S LABELS, each year designed by a well-known artist, including Cocteau, Braque, Dali, Bacon, and Henry Moore. He also began a campaign to elevate Mouton to first growth status, which he achieved in 1973. He and his American wife Pauline created a magnificent Musée du Vin, or wine museum, filled with *objets d'art* and open to the public since 1962 on application.

The 80-ha/200-acre vineyard is planted with 77 per cent CABERNET SAUVIGNON grapes, 12 per cent MERLOT (much increased in the late 1990s), 9 per cent CABERNET FRANC, and 2 per cent PETIT VERDOT. Average production is about 20,000 cases. A second wine, Petit Mouton, was introduced in 1994 and a dry white AC Bordeaux Aile d'Argent in 1991. The wine is famously concentrated and intensely aromatic in good vintages. See ROTHSCHILDS for details of other wine investments and JOINT VENTURES. E.P-R. & J.R.

Herman, S., and Pascal, J., *Mouton Rothschild, The Museum of Wine in Art* (Paris, 2003).

Ray, C., *Mouton-Rothschild* (London, 1974).

moût partiellement fermenté, issu de vendanges passerillés, term used on labels of French SWEET WINE since Alsace has sole rights to VENDANGE TARDIVE.

Mouyssaguès, ancient vine of the Aveyron in the harsh uplands of SOUTH WEST FRANCE. The wine produced can be dark crimson and tough, and the vine has been widely abandoned because it is not particularly suitable for GRAFTING.

Moza Fresca, Valdeorras name for the Spanish grape DOÑA BLANCA.

Mudgee, relatively isolated and well-defined wine region in NEW SOUTH WALES, associated with generous, smooth reds.

mulch, materials put on the vineyard soil surface to assist vine growth. Mulch is useful because it keeps soil damp and also stops it getting too hot. Mulches also hinder the growth of weeds, and those composed of ORGANIC MATTER provide nutrients for the vine's growth as the mulch decomposes.

Animal manure and straw were common mulches of the past but in many modern vineyards these have been replaced with thin plastic film. Young vines are planted through holes in the plastic. The response of young vine growth to plastic is often remarkable, especially for vineyards which rely on rainfall rather than IRRIGATION for their water. The film controls weed growth, stops water evaporating from the soil surface, and in spring it warms the soil, promoting root growth. The appearance of a vineyard with plastic film under the vines does not please all wine TOURISTS, nor those who favour more 'natural' means of vine establishment.

A major disadvantage to straw mulch has been the cost of placing a sufficiently deep mat below each vine. This cost can be reduced by modern techniques of mechanically unrolling bales of hay, or alternatively throwing the straw under the vine as the COVER CROP is mown.

So-called organic vineyards use mulches of living plants as well as dead material. The main disadvantage of living mulches for the young vines is that there may be too much competition for water and nutrients, and so the living mulch may need to be killed off. However, when a thick plant mulch breaks down, then nutrients are released and the soil is improved. Either living or dead organic mulches can cause problems because of INSECTS and FUNGI which can be harboured in the litter around the vine trunk. R.E.S.

mulled wine is wine that has been heated with sugar and spices and also, sometimes, slices of fruit and even brandy. This was a particularly common way of serving wine in the Middle Ages, since honey and spices helped to compensate for any shortcomings in wine quality (which were likely to be considerable as the months since the HARVEST wore on in this age when wine was served directly from the barrel). The verb 'mull' was current at least from the beginning of the 17th century. Recipes vary and quantities are not critical. Red wine is almost invariably used, and cinnamon and cloves are common. Slow simmering retains the ALCOHOL; fast boiling dissipates it. Sugar or honey should be added to taste, and fruit peel can impart bitterness. Whole oranges stuck with cloves are often used. It is far less difficult to make good mulled wine than to find DRINKING VESSELS that retain the heat but are not uncomfortably hot to hold. See also GLÜHWEIN.

Müllerrebe, which translates from German as 'miller's grape', is the common, and logical, name for Germany's increasingly planted selection of Pinot MEUNIER. SCHWARZRIESLING is the official German synonym. See also SAMTROT.

Müller-Thurgau, white grape variety which could fairly be said to have been the bane of German wine production but which is at long last on the wane there. This crossing was developed in 1882 for entirely expedient reasons by a Dr Hermann Müller, born in the Swiss canton of Thurgau but then working at the German viticultural station at GEISENHEIM. His understandable aim was to combine the quality of the great RIESLING grape with the viticultural reliability, particularly the early ripening, of the SILVANER. Most of the variety's synonyms (Rivaner in Luxembourg and Slovenia, Riesling-Sylvaner in New Zealand and Switzerland, Rizlingszilvani in Hungary) reflect this combination. Since then some authorities have argued that he actually crossed two strains of Riesling rather than, as he thought, Riesling with Silvaner, but late 20th-century DNA PROFILING by researchers at GEILWEILERHOF established that the variety is actually Riesling × MADELEINE ROYALE, a TABLE GRAPE obtained from an artificial but still unknown crossing made in 1845. The variety is all too short on Riesling characteristics, typically smelling vaguely peachy with a fat, flaccid mid-palate, too often with a slight suspicion of rot, to which its rather large, thin-skinned berries are prone.

The vine certainly ripens early, even earlier than Silvaner. Unlike Riesling, it can be grown anywhere, producing prodigious quantities (sometimes double Riesling's common yield range of 80 to 110 hl/ha (4.6–6.3 tons/acre)) of extremely dull, flabby wine.

Müller-Thurgau was not embraced by Germany's growers until after the Second World War, when the need to rebuild the industry fast presumably gave this productive, easily grown vine allure. In the early 1970s, it even overtook the great Riesling in total area planted (having for some time produced far more wine in total) and remained in that position throughout the 1980s, although by the end of that decade there were already signs of disaffection with the grape. Typically blended with a little of a more aromatic variety such as MORIO-MUSKAT and with a great deal of SÜSSRESERVE, Müller-Thurgau was transformed into oceans of QBA sugarwater labelled either LIEBFRAU-MILCH or one of the internationally recognized names such as Niersteiner, Bernkasteler, or Piesporter (see GROSSLAGE). By the late 1990s, Riesling was once again Germany's most planted grape variety but with 2003 plantings standing second only to Riesling at more than 16,000 ha/ 39,500 acres, Germany's Müller-Thurgau is still (too?) significant.

The wood is much softer than Riesling's and can easily be damaged by hard winters. The grapes rot easily (as can be tasted in a number of examples from less successful years), and the vine is susceptible to DOWNY MILDEW, BLACK ROT, and, its own bane, ROTBRENNER, but it will continue to flourish while there is a market for cheap German wine.

Outside Germany it can be much more exciting. In northern Italy's ALTO ADIGE, where extensive acreage of ancient vines testifies to the promotional success by early proponents of Dr Müller's crossing, bottlings from easily a score of today's best domaines and grower co-operatives testify to the refinement, minerality, complexity and sheer refreshment value that is possible with Müller-Thurgau—just not, it seems, in Germany. Most of the best Alto Adige wines are grown on very steep, stony, high altitude sites of which Tiefenbrünner's Feldmarschall is an extreme example. It is also increasingly planted in FRIULI and is grown as far south as EMILIA-ROMAGNA. This foreign-sounding variety, sometimes called Riesling-Sylvaner, has its followers among Italy's fashion-conscious connoisseurs.

The variety thrives all over central and eastern Europe. It is planted, appropriately enough, in SWITZERLAND, playing an increasingly important role in the vineyards of the German-speaking area in the north and east. In AUSTRIA (sometimes called Rivaner) it constitutes 6.5 per cent of total plantings and is responsible for PRIMEUR style wines that are rarely of much intrinsic interest. Across Austria's southern border, it is also grown in SLOVENIA and is even more important to the east and north of Austria in the CZECH REPUBLIC and HUNGARY. As Rizlingszilvani, it covers thousands of hectares of vineyard around Lake Balaton and produces lakesful of flabby Badacsonyi Rizlingszilvani.

Müller-Thurgau was planted enthusiastically by New Zealand grape growers on the recommendation of visiting German experts as a preferable substitute for the HYBRIDS that were all too prevalent in the country's nascent wine industry of the 1950s and 1960s. Chardonnay

overtook the crossing's total area (1,300 ha/ 3,210 acres) as long ago as 1992, however, as it is a far more valuable crop. It would be difficult to argue that New Zealand's 'Riesling-Sylvaner' is ever a very complex wine but it does usually display a freshness lacking in German examples, despite its traditional similar reliance on *Süssreserve* or SWEET RESERVE.

Elsewhere in the New World, most growers are not driven by the need for early-ripening varieties (and would find the flab in the resultant wine a distinct disadvantage), although some Oregon growers have experimented successfully with it, and credible examples have been produced in the Puget sound vineyards of western Washington state.

Northern Europe's two smallest and coolest wine producers, ENGLAND and LUXEMBOURG, depend heavily on Müller-Thurgau, which is the most planted variety in Luxembourg (where it is called Rivaner) and third most planted in the UK.

Munson, T. V.

Munson, T. V. (1843–1913), Texan credited with putting PHYLLOXERA-resistant roots on French vines, and saving Europe's vineyards from devastation. Thomas Volney Munson was a lifelong student of viticulture, especially AMERICAN VINE SPECIES. At Kentucky University he became interested in TEXAS and its grapes and travelled tens of thousands of miles in 40 states gathering WILD VINE specimens, and studying soils and climates. He travelled by horseback and train, hunting from rail cars and jumping off to collect specimens whenever the train stopped. In 1876, Munson settled on the Red river near Denison in Texas, which he described as a 'grape paradise' because of the six or eight species of wild vines there. He developed a vineyard and nursery business as well as becoming the authority on the wild grape species of North America. Munson's passion was for VINE BREEDING, and he produced about 300 varieties using local VITIS species *lincecumii, champini,* and *candicans*. None however became commercially important.

Being aware of phylloxera's predations in Europe, Munson began GRAFTING European vines to American species as ROOTSTOCKS to grant resistance. He passed on the results of his research to Viala, Planchon, and other French experts. In the 1880s and 1890s, French growers accordingly imported huge quantities of American species for use as rootstocks, especially from Texas and Missouri. The French government made Munson a Chevalier du Mérite in 1888, only the second American to have achieved this honour (Thomas Edison being the first).   R.E.S.

Murray Darling

Murray Darling, large Australian wine region straddling the Darling river and both sides of the Murray river in VICTORIA and NEW SOUTH WALES. While totally dependent on irrigation (the soils have little water-holding capacity and there is negligible growing season

rainfall) and high yields of low-cost grapes, international competition is leading to higher standards of fruit quality being demanded by the big companies which purchase the massive annual grape production.

Muscadel

Muscadel or **Muskadel**, South African name for MUSCAT BLANC À PETITS GRAINS, the term being generally used only for very sweet versions made by adding spirit to the juice of this grape (as for MISTELLE). The white grape variety that was, with its darker-berried mutation, chiefly responsible for the famous 18th-century CONSTANTIA dessert wine was called Muscadel.

The total area planted in South Africa had fallen to below 300 ha/737 acres by the early 21st century, much of it in the inland regions of Robertson and Worcester (see SOUTH AFRICA, regions). With the exception of Vin de Constance from Constantia, which is unfortified, the wines it produces are not the most fashionable.

Muscadelle

Muscadelle is the famous also-ran third grape variety responsible, with SÉMILLON and SAUVIGNON BLANC, for the sweet white (and duller dry white) wines of Bordeaux, and Bergerac where it truly flourishes. A total of 2,000 ha/5,000 acres were planted in France in 2000, 1,200 ha in the Gironde, where the majority of Muscadelle vines are not in the great sweet white wine areas of SAUTERNES, but in the unfashionable and vast ENTRE-DEUX-MERS, including such lesser sweet white appellations as PREMIÈRES CÔTES DE BORDEAUX, CADILLAC, LOUPIAC, and STE-CROIX-DU-MONT. Muscadelle is relatively more important to Bergerac than to Bordeaux and it is valued as the finest ingredient in some of the best MONBAZILLAC.

The variety, unrelated to any member of the MUSCAT family, shares a vaguely grapey aroma with them but has its origins in Bordeaux. The usefully productive Muscadelle leafs late and ripens early and has rarely demonstrated great subtlety in the wines it produces. The occasional VARIETAL Muscadelle can demonstrate a certain tang but its use is almost exclusively in blends, adding the same sort of youthful fruitiness to south western sweet whites as MEUNIER does to the north east sparkling whites called champagne.

The variety is grown widely but not substantially in eastern Europe but in only one obscure corner of the wine world does Muscadelle produce sensational varietal wine, the LIQUEUR TOKAY of AUSTRALIA. For years Australians thought the grape they called Tokay, which produced these dark, syrupy, wood-matured concentrates for after-dinner drinking, was Hungarian, but the French AMPELOGRAPHER Paul Truel identified it as Muscadelle in 1976. It had dual usage in Australia: to produce lesser quality table wine from vines grown in the Riverland and elsewhere (plantings which have now been removed) and in North East Victoria to produce fortified wine (where plantings are stable at around 175 ha/432 acres).

Muscadet, one of France's dry white commodity wines currently undergoing revolution. The Muscadet region extends mainly south east of Nantes near the mouth of the Loire, on about 13,000 ha/32,000 acres of gently rolling, Atlantic-dominated countryside where hundreds of wine farmers maintain family vine holdings, increasingly consolidated and devoted to one grape variety. The white MELON de Bourgogne, a reliable but relatively neutral variety, was introduced to the region in the 17th century by the DUTCH WINE TRADE, who were in need of distilling material for their brandewijn and had the means to transport it. The terrible winter of 1709 killed a high proportion of the red wine grapes previously grown here and transformed it into a predominantly white wine region.

The most significant, and varied, appellation by far, representing more than three-quarters of production, is **Muscadet-Sèvre et Maine**, named after two small rivers which flow through this, the most monocultural part of the Pays Nantais south and east of Nantes. Indeed, more Muscadet-Sèvre et Maine is produced every year than in any other Loire appellation. Particularly ambitious wines are made on the clay soils of Vallet, while those from the schist and granite slopes around St-Fiacre are also much admired. The appellation known as **Muscadet-Coteaux de la Loire** is in the north and **Muscadet-Côtes de Grandlieu** is in the south west of the region. **Muscadet** is the basic appellation, not made in great quantity and usually less exciting.

According to stricter regulations drawn up in the late 1990s, basic Muscadet is excluded from that substantial proportion of the wines that are matured SUR LIE, their flavour at least theoretically enriched by LEES CONTACT. So neutral is the Melon grape that Muscadet producers have long been able to store their wines over the winter without RACKING them off the lees, and without the risk of picking up off-flavours. This leaves the wines with rather more flavour and a small amount of CARBON DIOXIDE before bottling, which must be done where the wine was made and either during the spring or autumn following the harvest.

At its worst, Muscadet is an anodyne, watery, dry white with or without a little sparkle, but at its best it captures the essence of France's north Atlantic coast and provides an authentic, light, tangy, almost salty foil for its seafood. (It is the only French unfortified wine for which the authorities specify a maximum ALCOHOLIC STRENGTH, 12 per cent.) Since the mid 1980s, producers have been experimenting with such techniques as BARREL FERMENTATION and LEES STIRRING and since the late 1990s

those producers seeking maximum ripeness levels have also employed pre-fermentation SKIN CONTACT. Muscadet can no longer be dismissed as a simple, homogeneous wine. Top producers include Guy Bossard at Domaine de l'Ecu, Domaine Guindon, and Sauvion.

Other wines produced in the Pays Nantais are GROS PLANT, Coteaux d'ANCENIS, and FIEFS VENDÉENS. See also LOIRE, including map.

Friedrich, J., *A Wine and Food Guide to the Loire* (New York, 1996)

Muscadinia, a section of the botanical genus VITIS, although some botanists have suggested that it should be considered a separate genus rather than a section of *Vitis*. *Muscadinia* includes the three genera *rotundifolia*, *munsonia*, and *popenoei*, according to Galet. *Vitis* contains the true grapevine, as outlined in BOTANICAL CLASSIFICATION. *Muscadinia* and *Vitis* differ in chromosome number and morphology.

Members of the *Muscadiniae* occur only in the south eastern UNITED STATES, MEXICO, and (according to the Institute MAGARACH) in UKRAINE, but seem related to *Vitis ludwigii* found as fossil seeds in Tertiary sediments of northern Europe. There is speculation that *Muscadinia* can be regarded as transitional between the temperate genus *Vitis* and *Ampelocissus*, which is adapted to tropical climates. Species of the three genera have similar characteristics.

The **Muscadines**, as they are called, typically have small bunches of large, thck-skinned berries. The three species included in *Muscadinia* are found in America and Mexico. The best known is *Vitis rotundifolia* of which a number of varieties, most notably SCUPPERNONG, are grown commercially. The very thick skins and musky flavour of Muscadines produce fruit and wine quite different from that of European VINIFERA vines. Scuppernong's cluster has only a few berries which ripen unevenly and drop off when ripe. The large berries have a thick, slippery pulp that is difficult to press and excessive pressure brings bitterness from the skins. Muscadines are typically low in sugar concentration, and usually require CHAPTALIZATION.

A few thousand hectares of Muscadine grapes are grown in the cotton belt in the south eastern United States.

The Muscadines have natural resistance to PIERCE'S DISEASE and can therefore be planted in some areas unsuitable for VITIS species and HYBRIDS of them. They are also usefully resistant to PHYLLOXERA, NEMATODES, DOWNY MILDEW, and POWDERY MILDEW, which makes Muscadine germplasm valuable in VINE BREEDING. For long the different chromosome numbers of *Vitis* (2n = 38) and Muscadines (2n = 40) proved a barrier to breeding, since progeny were typically infertile. However, recent advances have allowed Muscadine germplasm to be incorporated into VINE IMPROVEMENT programmes. R.E.S.

Galet, P., *Précis de Viticulture* (4th edn, Montpellier, 1983).

Lu, J., Schell, L., and Ramming, D.W., 'Interspecific hybridization between Vitis rotundifolia and Vitis vinifera and evaluation of the hybrids', *Acta Horticulturae*, 528 (2000), 479–86.

Mullins, M. G., Bouquet, A., and Williams, L., *Biology of the Grapevine* (Cambridge, 1992).

Pinney, T., *A History of Wine in America from the Beginnings to Prohibition* (Berkeley, Calif., 1989).

Muscardin, light red grape variety allowed in to CHÂTEAUNEUF-DU-PAPE.

Muscat, one of the world's great and historic names, of both grapes and wines. Indeed Muscat grapes—and there are at least four principal varieties of Muscat, in several hues of berry—are some of the very few which produce wines that actually taste of grapes. MUSCAT HAMBURG and MUSCAT OF ALEXANDRIA are raised as both wine grapes and TABLE GRAPES (although it has to be said that Hamburg is much better in the second role). MUSCAT BLANC À PETITS GRAINS is the oldest and finest, producing wines of the greatest intensity, while MUSCAT OTTONEL, paler in every way, is a relative parvenu. See also various MOSCATELS and MOSCATOS.

Muscat grapes were probably the first to be distinguished and identified and have grown around the Mediterranean for many, many centuries. With such strongly perfumed grapes (thanks to a particularly high concentration of MONOTERPENES), described in French as MUSQUÉ as though they were actually impregnated with musk, Muscat grapes have always been attractive to bees and it was almost certainly Muscat grapes that the Greeks described as *anathelicon moschaton*, and PLINY the Elder as *uva apiana*, 'grape of the bees'. Some even theorize that Muscat derives its name from *musca*, the Latin for flies, also attracted to these scented grapes.

Muscat wines, carrying many different labels including Moscato (in Italy) and Moscatel (in Iberia), can vary from the refreshingly low-alcohol, sweet and frothy ASTI SPUMANTE, through Muscat d'ALSACE and other bone-dry Muscats made for example in Roussillon, to sweet wines with alcohol levels between 15 and 20 per cent, usually by MUTAGE (as in the VINS DOUX NATURELS of southern France and Greece). Since a high proportion of the world's Muscat is dark-berried, and since a wide variety of wood-ageing techniques are used, such wines can vary in colour from palest gold (as in some of the more determinedly modern Muscats de FRONTIGNAN) to deepest brown (as in some of Australia's LIQUEUR MUSCATS).

Most Muscat vines need relatively hot climates (although see MUSCAT OTTONEL and GERMAN HISTORY in which the medieval cultivation of both light- and dark-berried Muscat vines is documented). There either are or have been many famous Muscats around the Mediterranean. See MOROCCO, GREECE, SICILIA, and SARDEGNA.

Muscat Bailey A, white grape HYBRID used to make wine in the Far East.

Muscat Blanc à Petits Grains is the cumbersome but descriptive full name of the oldest and noblest variety of Muscat with the greatest concentration of fine grape flavour, hinting at orange-flowers and spice. Its berries and seeds are, as its name suggests, particularly small, and they are round as opposed to the larger, oval berries of MUSCAT OF ALEXANDRIA—in fact another synonym for this superior variety is Muscat à Petits Grains Ronds. But its berries are not, as its principal AMPELOGRAPHICAL name suggests, invariably white. In fact there are pink-, red-, and black-berried versions (although the dark berries are not so deeply pigmented that they can produce a proper red wine) and some vines produce berries whose colour varies considerably from vintage to vintage. Many synonyms for the variety include reference to the yellow or golden (*gallego, giallo, gelber*) colour of its berries. And Brown Muscat is one of Australia's names for a Muscat population that is more dark than light, and resembles South Africa's Muskadel in that respect (thereby providing more evidence of early viticultural links between these two southern hemisphere producers). Other names for the variety in its many different habitats include Muscat of Frontignan, Frontignac, Muscat Blanc, Muscat d'Alsace, Muskateller, Moscato Bianco, Moscato d'Asti, Moscato di Canelli, Moscatel de Grano Menudo, Moscatel de Frontignan, Muscatel Branco, White Muscat, Muscat Canelli, and Muskadel (in South Africa). Any Muscat with the words Alexandria, Gordo, Romain, Hamburg, or Ottonel in its name is *not* this superior variety.

This particular Muscat may very well be the oldest known wine grape variety, and the oldest cultivated in France, having been established in Gaul around Narbonne, notably at FRONTIGNAN, by the Romans—and possibly even before then brought to the Marseilles region by the Greeks. Muscat Blanc has clearly been established for many centuries round the Mediterranean, where its early budding poses few problems. It was certainly already widely esteemed in the vineyards of ROUSSILLON by the 14th century, and dominated them until the 19th century (apparently pre-dating the arrival of MALVASIA from the east). This is the predominant Muscat of CORSICA. It is Piemonte's oldest documented variety. That it is recorded as growing in Germany, as Muskateller, as early as the 12th century, and is the first documented variety grown in Alsace, in the 16th century, suggests that spring frosts may have been less common then, for the variety has now been replaced by the more accommodating Muscat Ottonel in Alsace and, as Gelber MUSKATELLER, has all but disappeared from a Germany that has apparently been in thrall to the flashily ersatz MORIO-MUSKAT crossing. As Gelber Muskateller, this variety is currently limited to 100 ha/250 acres in Germany, largely in the Pfalz, but there are signs of a comeback, particularly due to the influence of Müller-Catoir, whose distinctively pungent dry wines from this variety have earned a keen following.

Muscat Blanc also yields more conservatively than other Muscats and is sensitive to a wide range of diseases, which has naturally limited its cultivation—although it has travelled for so long and so widely that it is particularly widely distributed.

As Moscatel de Grano Menudo it is still grown in Spain but to a limited extent. Most Spanish wines labelled Moscatel are made from Muscat of Alexandria.

Muscats of various sorts are grown widely in the former SOVIET UNION, particularly MUSCAT OTTONEL and the variety described as Muscat Rosé, the pink-skinned form of Muscat Blanc. Muscat of some sort is grown in UKRAINE, MOLDOVA, KAZAKHSTAN, UZBEKISTAN, TAJIKISTAN, and TURKMENISTAN. Early 20th-century bottles labelled White Muscat and Pink Muscat from the extraordinary MASSANDRA Collection, produced in the CRIMEA, have demonstrated the potential for great sweet wines made here.

Muscat Blanc is also grown in ROMANIA, where it is known as TĂMÂIOASĂ Alba, and its Russian name is Tamyanka.

In the heart of Habsburg country, Muscat Ottonel has held sway until recently, although Gelber Muskateller is more revered for the quality of wine produced. Dry, racy Muskatellers from Styria and occasionally the Wachau have been particularly popular in Austria.

In Hungary, too, Ottonel, simply known as Muskotály, dominates except in the TOKAJI district, where a particularly golden-skinned Muscat Blanc, there called Muscat Lunel or Sárga Muskotály (Yellow Muscat) is grown. Some varietal Muscats of sweet Aszú quality are made from the few hundred hectares that supplement the Furmint and Hárslevelű that are the main ingredients in this extraordinary wine.

If anywhere could be said to be Muscat's homeland it is Greece and here, although it is today grown alongside Muscat of Alexandria (which is the prime Cypriot Muscat), Muscat Blanc à Petits Grains is accorded the honour of being the only variety allowed in Greece's most rigidly controlled Muscats such as those of Sámos, Pátrai, and Kefallinía. For the moment, Greek Muscat, like its many variations on the MALVASIA theme, is almost invariably sweet, alcoholic, and redolent of history, but drier versions more suited to drinking with food are now made on Lemnos. See GREECE for more details.

This is the Muscat that, as MOSCATO, predominates in Italy. It was planted on over 13,000 ha/32,000 acres in 2000, notably underpinning the sweet sparkling wine industry. The light, frothy ASTI, the subtler MOSCATO D'ASTI, and other spumante and frizzante all over north western Italy demonstrate another facet of the variety's character. Various forms of Moscato can be found throughout Italy with some particularly delicious and flirtatious bottlings in TRENTINO-ALTO ADIGE but most of its produce in the south and islands belongs to the richer, Mediterranean school of wines.

This school represents the traditional face of Muscat Blanc in France but, contrary to almost all other white grape varieties, this Muscat has been gaining ground and was planted on almost 7,000 ha/17,500 acres in 2000, chiefly because of the development of dry Muscat unfortified wine in the Languedoc and Roussillon and the development of a virtually CLAIRETTE-free grapey (Tradition) version of the Rhône's fizzy CLAIRETTE DE DIE.

Muscat Blanc has also been supplanting the still more widely planted Muscat of Alexandria in Roussillon, however, where it is the superior Muscat ingredient in the many and various north Catalonian VINS DOUX NATURELS such as MUSCAT DE RIVESALTES. In the Languedoc and southern Rhône, too, its increasing area of vineyard reflects increased demand for the golden sweet Muscats of BEAUMES-DE-VENISE, FRONTIGNAN, LUNEL, MIREVAL, and ST-JEAN-DE-MINERVOIS, in which it is the exclusive ingredient.

In the New World, the variety grows most gloriously, as Brown Muscat and Frontignac with all manner of colour of grape skins, in Australia, where it is capable of the great LIQUEUR MUSCATS. Official grape variety statistics distinguished between about 300 ha of dark-skinned grapes and nearly 200 ha of light-skinned fine Muscat (as opposed to the most common Muscat Gordo, or Muscat of Alexandria). In South Africa, this Muscat produces wines of varying strength and sweetnesses, including Klein Constantia's well-known Vin de Constance. Muscat of Alexandria is very much more important than this finer Muscat in California, where most of Muscat Blanc's 900 acres/360 ha are in the central SAN JOAQUIN VALLEY. Once variously called Muscat Frontignan and Muscat Canelli, it is now officially called Muscat Blanc and distinguished from ORANGE MUSCAT.

Galet, P., *Dictionnaire encyclopédique des cépages* (Paris, 2000).

Muscat d'Alsace is an Alsace synonym for the vine variety MUSCAT BLANC À PETITS GRAINS. For more details of what to expect of a wine labelled Muscat d'Alsace, see ALSACE.

Muscat de Beaumes-de-Venise is the often delicate VIN DOUX NATUREL from the southern Rhône village of BEAUMES-DE-VENISE under whose name there are more details.

Muscat de Frontignan is the old name for the once internationally famous wine of FRONTIGNAN. It is also a synonym for the grape variety solely responsible for it, MUSCAT BLANC À PETITS GRAINS. This is the most common Muscat VIN DOUX NATUREL of the Languedoc. Ch de la Peyrade produces finer wine than most.

Muscat de Lunel. See LUNEL for details of this southern Languedoc VIN DOUX NATUREL. It is yet another synonym for the grape variety solely responsible for it, MUSCAT BLANC À PETITS GRAINS.

Muscat de Mireval. See MIREVAL for details of this relatively unimportant southern Languedoc VIN DOUX NATUREL.

Muscat de Rivesaltes is the most important appellation of the Rivesaltes region in Roussillon and is by far the biggest Muscat appellation in France. Unlike the four Muscat VINS DOUX NATURELs listed above, and the one listed below, it is made from MUSCAT OF ALEXANDRIA with some MUSCAT BLANC À PETITS GRAINS. Much of it is of decidedly ordinary quality, although Domaine Cazes and Domaine de Chênes produce some superior bottlings. For more details, see RIVESALTES.

Muscat de St-Jean-de-Minervois is the golden VIN DOUX NATUREL speciality of ST-JEAN-DE-MINERVOIS in the northern Languedoc and is produced in very limited quantities.

Muscat du Cap Corse, Corsican VIN DOUX NATUREL. See CORSICA.

Muscat Hamburg is the lowest quality of the wine-producing Muscats. Recent DNA PROFILING at CONEGLIANO showed that it is a crossing between MUSCAT OF ALEXANDRIA and TROLLINGER (also called SCHIAVA Grossa). It comes exclusively in black-berried form and is far more common as a TABLE GRAPE than a wine grape. Its chief attribute is the consistency of its plump and shiny dark blue grapes, which can well withstand long journeys to reach consumers who like black-skinned Muscat-flavoured grapes. In France it was grown on almost 4,000 ha/9,880 acres in 2000 and was the most important table grape. It is also relatively important as a table grape in Greece, in eastern Europe, and Australia. It was extremely popular as a greenhouse grape in Victorian England, where it occasionally took the name of Snow or Venn, two of its more successful propagators.

In the world of wine production, its importance is limited but it does produce a fair quantity of light, grapey red throughout eastern Europe, and in CHINA, crossed with the indigenous VITIS *amurensis*, it has spawned a generation of varieties adapted for wine production.

Muscat of Alexandria is a Muscat almost as ancient as MUSCAT BLANC À PETITS GRAINS but its wine is distinctly inferior. In hot climates it can thrive and produce a good yield of extremely ripe grapes but their chief attribute is sweetness. (In cooler climates, its output can be seriously affected by COULURE, MILLERANDAGE, and a range of FUNGAL DISEASES.) Wines made from this sort of Muscat tend to be strong, sweet, and unsubtle. The aroma is vaguely grapey but can have slightly feline overtones of geranium rather than the more lingering bouquet of Muscat Blanc.

Some indication of its lack of finesse as a wine producer is the fact that a considerable proportion of the Muscat of Alexandria grown today is destined for uses other than wine: California for example uses most of its 4,000 acres/1,600 ha for RAISINS; Chile distils most of its Muscat of Alexandria to make pisco; it is even grown under glass in Britain and the Netherlands to provide grapes for the fruit bowl.

As its name suggests, Muscat of Alexandria is thought to have originated in Egypt and was disseminated around the Mediterranean by the Romans, hence its common synonym Muscat Romain. Its southern Italian synonym is Zibibbo.

Today it is most important to wine industries in that old arc of maritime history Iberia, South Africa, and Australia, where it may be known respectively as Moscatel, Hanepoot, and Muscat Gordo Blanco or Lexia, a particularly Australian contraction of the North African port.

Spain had 9,000 ha/22,500 acres of it planted in 2004, but it is not known how much of this serves the wine industry, typically with sweet MOSCATELs of various sticky sorts. Muscat of Alexandria's various Spanish synonyms include Moscatel de España, Moscatel Gordo (Blanco), and most importantly Moscatel de MÁLAGA, which is probably a close relative.

In Portugal, its most famous incarnation is Moscatel de SETÚBAL but Portugal's Muscat of Alexandria grapes have also been harnessed to produce aromatic, dry, much lower alcohol Muscats. This is the fate of the majority of Australia's 2,400 ha of Gordo Blanco, once used mainly for fortified wines, although from cooler vineyards it can produce sound, unfortified wines that are sweet because late picked. Dry wine produced from the Gordo Blanco grown in Australia's irrigated Riverland is typically used for blending with, and often softening, more glamorous grape varieties.

Muscat of Alexandria is the dominant Muscat in South Africa—HANEPOOT is its traditional Afrikaans name—and was the country's fourth most planted white wine variety in the late 1990s, but by the early 2000s it was in marked decline and only 2,800 ha remained. For years it provided sticky, raisiny wines for FORTIFICATION, as well as everything from GRAPE CONCENTRATE to RAISINS. Today some drier, lighter wines are also made from it.

As Moscatel de Alejandria it is also extremely important in Chile, where its 6,000 ha make it the country's third most planted pale-skinned grape, after the mixture known as 'Sauvignon' and Chardonnay. It is also grown to a relatively limited extent in Argentina, Peru, Colombia, Ecuador, and even Japan.

Although Muscat Blanc is more important in GREECE, Muscat of Alexandria is grown widely there and is the Muscat that predominates in Turkey, Israel, and Tunisia, although in much of the Near East nowadays these grapes are eaten rather than drunk. The rich, dark Moscato di Pantelleria is geographically closer to Tunisia than Sicilia which administers it and is made from Muscat of Alexandria, or ZIBIBBO, as it is known in much of Italy. In fact this is the only wine with even a modicum of international renown that is made remotely near to the city the variety is named after.

In France, total plantings of Muscat d'Alexandrie, or Muscat Romain, have remained at about the same level , just over 3,000 ha, almost exclusively in Roussillon, since the 1960s. Although Muscat Blanc is catching up, this is still the dominant Muscat in this most Spanish corner of France, where at one time its grapes were left to raisin on the vine before adding their distinctive flavour to the highly prized local wines. It is most obvious in Muscat de RIVESALTES but is also blended into other varieties, chiefly GRENACHE of all hues, to produce the *département*'s other VINS DOUX NATURELS.

Muscat of Frontignan is a common synonym for MUSCAT BLANC À PETITS GRAINS and this is the Muscat variety that is solely responsible for the VIN DOUX NATUREL of the same name. See also FRONTIGNAN for details of the wine that justifies this synonym.

Muscat Ottonel is the palest of all the Muscats, both in terms of the colour of wine produced and in terms of its character. Its aroma is altogether more vapid than the powerful grapey perfumes associated with MUSCAT BLANC À PETITS GRAINS and MUSCAT OF ALEXANDRIA. It was bred as recently as 1852 in the Loire, probably as a table grape from CHASSELAS and the distinctly ordinary Muscat de Saumur, according to Galet.

Its tendency to ripen earlier than these other two Muscats has made it much easier to cultivate in cooler climates and nowadays Muscat Ottonel is the dominant Muscat cultivated, on a few hundred hectares, in ALSACE. This low-vigour vine, which does best in deep, damp soils, is also grown in eastern Europe, notably in AUSTRIA, where it is planted in Burgenland and used mainly for Prädikatswein. It may well be that it is at its best as a late harvest wine, for there are some fine, apparently long-living examples from both HUNGARY and ROMANIA (where the variety is often known, respectively, as Muskotály and TĂMÂÎIOĂSA Ottonel). Romania had 6,000 ha/14,820 acres of Muscat Ottonel in the early 1990s. In Alsace, however, VENDANGE TARDIVE Muscat tends to remain a theoretical possibility. One of the most widely planted Muscats in the former Soviet republics is Ottonel, often known as Hungarian Muscat. In BULGARIA, it is known as Misket Ottonel. It is planted in CRIMEA, UKRAINE, MOLDOVA, KAZAKHSTAN, UZBEKISTAN, TAJIKISTAN, and TURKMENISTAN.

> Galet, P., *Dictionnaire encyclopédique des cépages* (Paris, 2000).

Muscat Romain, or Roman Muscat, is a common name for MUSCAT OF ALEXANDRIA in Roussillon, where it has for long been the most commonly planted Muscat.

muscatels are DRYING GRAPES produced by sun drying large-berried, seeded grape varieties, usually MUSCAT OF ALEXANDRIA.

mushroom root rot, vine disease. See ARMILLARIA ROOT ROT.

Musigny, Le, great red GRAND CRU in Burgundy's CÔTE D'OR. For more details, see CHAMBOLLE-MUSIGNY.

Muskateller, German for MUSCAT, almost invariably the superior MUSCAT BLANC, or some mutation of it. **Gelber Muskateller**, for example, is the gold-skinned version which is increasingly recognized as superior to MUSCAT OTTONEL in Austria, where it is particularly popular in STYRIA. In Germany, homeland of MORIO-MUSKAT, Gelber Muskateller is a distinctly minority interest, and there is even less of the red-skinned **Roter Muskateller**.

Muskat-Ottonel is what Germans call their minuscule plantings of MUSCAT OTTONEL.

Muskat-Silvaner or **Muskat-Sylvaner** was once, tellingly, the common German-language synonym for SAUVIGNON BLANC used in Germany and Austria.

Muskotály, name used in HUNGARY for Muscat, usually MUSCAT OTTONEL but also occasionally a yellow-berried form of MUSCAT BLANC À PETITS GRAINS, here called Muscat Lunel or Sárga Muskotály.

musqué is a French term meaning both 'perfumed', as in musky, and 'muscat-like'. Many vine varieties, including CHARDONNAY, have a Musqué mutation which is particularly aromatic and may add to the variety's own characteristics a grapey scent reminiscent of MUSCAT.

must is the name used by winemakers for a thick liquid that is neither GRAPE JUICE nor WINE but the intermediate, a mixture of grape juice, stem fragments, grape skins, seeds, and pulp that comes from the CRUSHER-DESTEMMER that smashes grapes at the start of the wine-making process. The French equivalent is *moût*, the Italian and Spanish is *mosto*, and the German is *Most*, but the word 'must' has been used in English for at least a thousand years with several small nuances of specific meaning. All refer to the mixture of crushed, chopped, or smashed fruit being prepared for, or undergoing, FERMENTATION.

A.D.W.

must chilling, important white wine-making operation, particularly in the NEW WORLD, which delays the onset of fermentation until after pressing, and helps prevent OXIDATION. See REFRIGERATION and TEMPERATURE. France's first MUST CHILLER was installed, by Australians, in the Languedoc, in the early 1990s.

must weight, important measure of grape RIPENESS, indicated by the concentration of dissolved compounds in grape juice or must. Since about 90 per cent of all the dissolved solids in grape juice are the fermentable SUGARS (the rest being acids, ions, and a host of other solutes), any measurement of these solids gives a reliable indication of the grapes' ripeness, and therefore the POTENTIAL ALCOHOL of wine made from them (see FERMENTATION).

Must weight may be measured approximately in the vineyard before harvest using a REFRACTOMETER, or in the winery, using a refractometer or a HYDROMETER, calibrated according to one of several different scales used in different parts of the world for measuring the concentration of dissolved solids. This variation is not so surprising when one considers how crucial this statistic is to the wine-making process and therefore how early in the evolution of each country's wine industry a scale will have been adopted. Each scale merely requires a different calibration of the hydrometer, usually with a reading of zero indicating that the DENSITY of a solution is exactly one, as in pure water.

BAUMÉ is the scale most commonly used in much of Europe, including France, and in Australia. The number of degrees Baumé indicates the concentration of dissolved compounds in a solution calibrated so that it indicates, usefully, the potential ALCOHOLIC STRENGTH of a wine made by fermenting the must to dryness. A must of 11 °Baumé, for example, will yield a dry wine with an alcohol content of 11 per cent.

In the United States, and increasingly in Australia, ripeness is most commonly measured in degrees BRIX, also sometimes called Balling, both terms borrowed from the sugar-refining industry. The Brix reading simply indicates the percentage of solids (of which about 90 per cent are sugars) by weight.

Winemakers in Germany most commonly use the OECHSLE scale, which simply indicates

Baumé (degrees)	Brix/Balling (degrees)	Oechsle (degrees)	Potential alcohol (% vol)
10	18.0	75	10
11	19.8	84	11
12	21.7	93	12
13	23.5	101	13
14	25.3	110	14
15	27.1	119	15

the density of the juice: a grape juice with a specific gravity of 1.085 is said to be 85 °Oechsle. This scale is much discussed since the GERMAN WINE LAW has tended to equate quality with degrees Oechsle. Austria has its own, similar scale, devised at KLOSTERNEUBURG, which measures ripeness in degrees KMW (or Babo).

Since it takes about 16.5 g/l (0.6 oz/1.76 pt) of sugar to produce 1 per cent alcohol by fermentation (in white wines, closer to 18 g/l in reds, depending on the efficiency of the YEAST strain), it is possible to calculate approximately the potential alcohol using any of these scales. All of these must weight measurements can be roughly converted among themselves, with Baumé values about five-ninths of Brix/Balling values, and 14.7 °Brix/Balling = 60 °Oechsle. Some equivalences are outlined in the table above, although, according to published scales, the relationship between the different measurements is not a strict one. See nomograms in Hamilton and Coombe.

A typical dry wine is made from grapes which measure between 11.1 and 13.3 °Baumé, between 20 and 24 °Brix or Balling, and between 83 and 104 °Oechsle. Grapes grown in ENGLAND in particularly cool years, however, may reach a natural must weight of less than 50 °Oechsle, while some grape varieties in the SAN JOAQUIN VALLEY of California can easily reach 30 °Brix, as they gradually dehydrate under the intense heat. One German wine harvested at Nussdorf in the PFALZ in 1971 was picked at 326 °Oechsle and was still fermenting 22 years later, having reached just 4.5 per cent alcohol.

B.G.C. & A.D.W.

> Hamilton, R. P., and Coombe, B. G., 'Harvesting of winegrapes', in B. G. Coombe and P. R. Dry (eds.), *Viticulture*, ii: *Practices* (Adelaide, 1992).

mutage is the process of stopping a MUST from fermenting, sometimes by adding SULFUR DIOXIDE but usually by adding alcohol, thereby creating an environment in which yeasts can no longer work. Mutage transforms fermenting must into a **vin muté** such as a VIN DE LIQUEUR or a VIN DOUX NATUREL. The alcohol may be added before or after the grape juice has been separated from the skins. Mutage plays a crucial part in making PORT, although the term is not used.

mutation, spontaneous change to genetic material occurring during cell division in organisms such as grapevines. Since so many VINE VARIETIES are of ancient origin, they have accumulated a substantial load of mutations. ANCIENT VINE VARIETIES were invariably dark-skinned; light-skinned varieties are the result of mutation. Generally mutations are deleterious, but man has had many centuries in which deliberately to select those vines which perform best (a process now formalized as CLONAL SELECTION), so beneficial mutations have been maintained.

Mutation is particularly common among certain black-berried vine varieties that degenerate easily such as PINOT NOIR, CARIGNAN, ASPIRAN, GRENACHE, and TERRET. Most of these have forms called variously Noir (black), Gris (grey), Blanc (white), Rose (pink), Vert (green), Rouge (red), and sometimes more.

Galet lists the types of mutations commonly seen in vines, which include leaf and berry colour, including albinism, absence of hairs on shoots and leaves, deeply lobed leaves, cauliflower-like growths on shoots, fasciations on shoots, very large inflorescences, and absence of inflorescences. Mutation can also cause polyploidy (multiple sets of chromosomes), which leads to 'giant' plants and berries. The two Gamay TEINTURIERS, Gamay

Fréaux and Gamay de Chaudenay, are thought to be mutations of Gamay de Bouze. A mixture of normal and mutant tissue is known as a chimera, and the varieties Pinot Noir and (Pinot) Meunier are partners in a so-called periclinal chimera. Such plants are essentially composed of a mutant 'skin' enclosing a 'normal' interior. Meunier is essentially similar to Pinot Noir, with the exception of white hairs on the shoot tip and young leaves.

Mutation can be induced by chemicals such as colchicine and by ionizing radiation. A form of genetic variation known as somaclonal mutation is induced during TISSUE CULTURE, and it is thought that this will be a useful means of increasing clonal variation among existing varieties.   R.E.S. & J.R.

Galet, P., *Dictionnaire encyclopédique des cépages* (Paris, 2000).
—*Précis de viticulture* (5th edn, Montpellier, 1988).
Mullins, M. G., Bouquet, A., and Williams, L., *Biology of the Grapevine* (Cambridge, 1992).

muzzle, the wire which holds a SPARKLING WINE cork in place. Known in French as a **muselet.**

MW, abbreviation for MASTER OF WINE.

Myanmar (formerly Burma), tropical Southeast Asian nation, bordered by THAILAND, Laos, CHINA, INDIA, and Bangladesh, with a single viticulture and wine-making venture that had its first commercial vintage in 2004. Myanmar Vineyard Estate has elevated vineyards (1,300 m/4,265 ft) on LIMESTONE slopes at the southern extension of the Himalayan ranges, west of the Shan state capital Taunggyi. It aims to be producing 300,000 bottles a year under the Aythaya and Konbosa labels for local and export markets by 2007. Shiraz, Cabernet Sauvignon, Sauvignon Blanc, and Muscat are the initial staple varieties. Dornfelder, Tempranillo, Chenin Blanc, and Sémillon vines had been established by 2005 when Pinot Noir, Gewürztraminer, Chardonnay, and Barbera were being trialled.   D.G.

mycoderma. See FILM-FORMING YEASTS.

mycoplasma. See PHYTOPLASMA.

Nagyburgundi, occasional Hungarian synonym for BLAUFRÄNKISCH although Kékfrankos is more common.

Nahe, wine region in GERMANY of 4,200 ha/ 10,400 acres of vines, a slight decline since the 1990s, scattered over a wide area on either side of the river Nahe (see map under GERMANY). Vineyards begin upstream at Martinstein, with Monzingen being the first famous and ancient wine village, mentioned as early as 778. The region was defined in anything like its current form only as part of the GERMAN WINE LAW of 1971, bringing together three geologically and climatically distinct areas.

First there is the by turns bucolic and geologically dramatic stretch of the river between Monzingen and Bad Münster am Stein. Here many of the vineyards have been modernized and reconstructed where necessary and practical (see FLURBEREINIGUNG), and steep, often terraced slopes produce world-class RIESLING on a geologically complex mix including SANDSTONE, porphyry, melaphyr, and SLATE. A single vineyard, such as the tiny Oberhäuser Brücke (a MONOPOLE of the Nahe's foremost vintner, Helmut Dönnhoff), can incorporate four fundamentally different soil types, and it does not seem to be mere imagination that such geological complexity is mirrored in the taste of the wines. The general climatic tendency is to warm as the Nahe meanders downstream. Excellent ventilation, low precipitation, and balmy autumnal temperatures, in addition to the steep, southward inclination of vineyard slopes, offer ideal circumstances for late-ripening Riesling.

The foremost wine villages (with their most notable vineyards) along this stretch of the Nahe, travelling downstream are Monzingen (Frühlingsplätzchen, Halenberg), Meddersheim (Rheingrafenberg), Schlossböckelheim (Felsenberg, Kupfergrube), Oberhausen (Brücke), Niederhausen (Hermannshöhle, Kerz), Norheim (Dellchen, Kirschheck), and Traisen (Bastei, Rotenfels). Wines of pronounced, often pungent spice and mineral inflection with frequent red fruit notes are characteristic for many of the best vineyards in this area. The state domaine of Niederhausen-Schlossböckelheim founded by the state of Rheinland-Pfalz in 1902 (and privatized in 1998) established any international reputation that Nahe Riesling had managed to enjoy prior to the 1980s.

The second outstanding area, also famous for its Rieslings, lies on the northern outskirts of Bad Kreuznach, immediately adjacent to the city. Here the vineyards are LOESS and CLAY, heavier and on gentler slopes than those elsewhere along the Nahe, producing relatively substantial wines. Viticulture around Bad Kreuznach was traditionally dominated by large landholders who also had important holdings in the Middle Nahe. Foremost among these were two branches of the Anheuser family and the Reichsgraf von Plettenberg, each of which made contributions from the 1930s—but particularly after the Second World War—to the gradual recognition of what is today known collectively as Nahe wine. Best-known among Bad Kreuznach's vineyards are the Brücke, Kahlenberg, and Krötenpfuhl but this region's declining significance is reflected in its lack of representation among VDP members.

The third area of particular distinction is the Lower Nahe near the confluence with the Rhine at Bingen, 116 km/72 miles from the source of the Nahe. Here, steeply terraced vineyards on a slate and quartzite base resemble those of the nearby MITTELRHEIN. Flavours of citrus, stone fruits, and salty or wet stone mineral notes typify the Rieslings of this subregion where Scheurebe, Weissburgunder, and traditional Silvaner can also succeed. Top sites include a trio along the Troll-Bach at Dorsheim just west of the Nahe: Burgberg, Goldloch, and Pittermännchen; as well as two sites along similar tributary streams at Münster-Sarmsheim: Dautenflänzer and Pittersberg.

The three aforementioned areas by no means exhaust the historic or current sources of excellent Nahe wine. These include the Alsenz near its confluence with the Nahe at Bad Münster (notably the Altenbamberger Rotenberg and Ebernburger Schlossberg), as well as a number of villages located several miles north and west of the Nahe, notably Roxheim, Sommerloch, Wallhausen, and Bockenau. The last two boast, respectively, the towering Johannisberg and Felseneck vineyards.

MÜLLER-THURGAU was the most widely grown vine variety for a time, but its area has declined dramatically in recent decades to a current 16 per cent of all vineyard. Among the best producers, Riesling represents 75 per cent or more of their vines. Its current share of 25 per cent of the region's total vineyard area has varied little in the last 15 years, which suggests that any site offering good conditions for Riesling already has the vine growing in it.

In 1960, SILVANER was grown on more than half the Nahe vineyards but today it accounts for less than 10 per cent, and its share continues to dwindle. Silvaner is a reliable vine whose wine in the Nahe is sound, solid, and usually unremarkable, except from some good sites of the Lower Nahe.

Plantings of the PINOT varieties Grauburgunder and Weissburgunder are increasing, not least because they are versatile in terms of FOOD AND WINE MATCHING, and examples of considerable complexity and refinement now abound among the offerings of the Nahe's best vintners. Since 1990, the area devoted to red grapes has more than quadrupled, and accounted for 23 per cent of Nahe vineyards in the mid 2000s. Nearly half of this is DORNFELDER, with SPÄTBURGUNDER and PORTUGIESER the other main varieties.

Until the mid 20th century, the Nahe enjoyed scant national let alone international reputation, in large part due to its wine being subsumed anonymously into RHINE blends. Even today, when nearly half of all Nahe wine is sold in bottle directly to the consumer, much inexpensive Nahe wine is blended to suit the needs of German supermarkets and grocery chains. CO-OPERATIVES have never had the importance here that they enjoy in other German growing regions. For wines of finesse one must turn to the private estates, nine of which are members of the prestigious VDP association. Among them, in keeping with current German fashion, the proportion of dry wines has increased since 1980 but in the mid 2000s was still barely a quarter. Non-TROCKEN Riesling can be racy and refreshing, as in MOSEL-SAAR-RUWER, without tasting noticeably, let alone tiresomely, sweet.

Good Nahe wine at all quality levels had for long been underpriced in Germany but by the late 1990s the leading estates could command prices on a par with the RHEINGAU. In the mid 2000s, there are also some worrying signs. Significant tracts of potentially top-flight vineyard land have been abandoned due to lack of vintners ambitious—or perhaps foolhardy—enough to try to make a living from the steepest slopes, and entire subregions such as the Alsenztal, a monocultural sea of vines less than a century ago, are threatened with extinction. D.S.

Payne, J., and Diel, A., *The Guide to German Wines/German Wine Guide* (London/New York, 2005).

Pigott, S., and Johnson, H., *The Wine Atlas of Germany* (London, 1995).

Namibia has one wine producer at Omaruru north west of Windhoek and a newer planting of Shiraz near the Etosha National Park to the north.

Platter, J. & E., *Africa Uncorked* (London, 2002).

nanofiltration, a membrane separation technique closely related to REVERSE OSMOSIS. See ALCOHOL REDUCTION.

Wollan, D. 'Physico-chemical tuning of wine composition', presentation given at the 12th Australian Wine Industry Conference (Adelaide, 2004).

Napa, small town north of San Francisco in CALIFORNIA that gives its name to **Napa county** and, California's most famous wine region and now an AVA, the **Napa Valley**. Although Napa was one of the last of California's coastal counties to receive the vine, the Napa valley has earned the state's wine most of its fame both inside and outside the UNITED STATES in both the 19th and 20th centuries. In America if not the wine world, 'the Valley' is Napa valley. Natural beauty and proximity to San Francisco have attracted, not just willing investors, but owners and winemakers with aggressive desires to make names for themselves in this most gentlemanly of pursuits. The first generation of them began the climb to prominence

between 1880 and 1919. The third spurred Napa out in front of the pack during the boom times between 1966 and the early 1990s. The fourth is today threatening to turn Napa into a parody of conspicuous consumption. But it was an undervalued interim group that kept the flame alive through the lean years between 1933 and 1966, when California wine was at its ebb. Six companies, Beaulieu Vineyard, Beringer Vineyards, the Christian Brothers, Inglenook Vineyards, Charles KRUG, and Louis M. Martini, pursued fine wine under their own labels when most districts sold commodity products in bulk (see CALIFORNIA, history). Their vineyards provided half the model that attracted the dizzying investments of the 1970s and 1980s, when vineyard acreage tripled and the number of Napa wineries shot from fewer than 20 to more than 200. The other half of the attraction model was provided by the original 'boutique wineries' Mayacamas and Stony Hill, which had sprung up from this fertile ground in the late 1950s. The oldtimers inspired such prominent wineries as the Robert MONDAVI winery, Trefethen, Freemark Abbey, Chateau Montelena, and Sterling Vineyards, while the small artisan model begat smaller operations such as Heitz, Stag's Leap Wine Cellars, Diamond Creek, Caymus, and Schramsberg.

The Napa valley proper is a long, lazy arc with its foot in San Francisco bay and its head on the western shoulder of mount St Helena. Like most of the north–south valleys around San Francisco bay, it has a cool end at the bay (in the south) and a warm one away from it (in the north), although it is barely more than 40 miles/64 km end to end, and sometimes less than a mile wide. With more than 40,000 acres/16,000 ha of vineyard in the Napa Valley AVA, the main valley has little more land to plant, although a succession of smaller valleys in hills to the east such as Chiles and Pope valleys offer some room for expansion.

Napa's magic is derived in no small part from a magnificent diversity of exposure, climate, and soil, which has led to several sub-AVAs within the generously drawn main AVA. In the early 1990s, growers proposed dividing the Napa valley floor into communes much as the Haut-MÉDOC is divided. The scheme has more or less succeeded with sub-AVAs in the middle of the valley from south to north being Oak Knoll, Yountville, Oakville, Rutherford, St Helena, and Calistoga. Several growers in outlying valleys who had historically sold their grapes to wineries in the centre of Napa valley demanded inclusion in the Napa Valley AVA. The oldtimers meanwhile resisted dilution of the great franchise enjoyed by the name. So now, by regulation, both the name Napa valley and the subappellation names appear on labels simultaneously. Distinctions among the wines makes even greater refinement of internal boundaries seem

inevitable. With or without diversity, Napa has been such a congenial home to Cabernet Sauvignon that one could argue a case for Napa's having caused its popularity, not the other way around. Versatile growing conditions give Napa growers the options of Chardonnay, Sauvignon Blanc, Zinfandel, Syrah, and, most notably among recent replantings in the wake of PHYLLOXERA, Merlot.

The following are the most significant subappellations.

Howell Mountain AVA

Howell Mountain won its pre-PROHIBITION fame for Zinfandel, but the current generation of growers and winemakers, led by Dunn Vineyards and La Jota, has turned sharply towards Cabernet Sauvignon as the variety of choice. The district ranges upward from 1,400 ft/430 m elevation in Napa's east hills, and has as its anchor the Seventh Day Adventist community of Angwin.

Mount Veeder AVA

Mount Veeder stretches out along ridgetops that separate the Napa and SONOMA valleys immediately west of the town of Napa, and is centred on the peak from which its name comes. Its oldest winery is Mayacamas, its largest the Hess Collection. Most of the plantings in it are Cabernet Sauvignon and Chardonnay.

Oakville AVA

This is one of the most prestigious wine-growing districts in America. Stretching across the valley floor and piedmont areas just north of the Yountville hills, it encompasses famous historic vineyards such as ToKalon and Martha's, cult Cabernets such as Harlan (on the western hills) and Screaming Eagle (on the eastern side), as well as a long list of highly successful wineries such as Groth and Opus I. As with most districts in Napa, there is a range of soils, drainage characteristics, and exposures. In general the weather is somewhat warmer than Yountville or Stags Leap because of the way the hills baffle winds off the bay. But most commentators would consider Oakville a bit cooler than Rutherford, thus lending an elegant nuance to Cabernets by comparison.

Rutherford AVA

With Oakville, the name of Rutherford was put before BATF (see TTB) during 1991 as part of the grower plan to divide all of the Napa valley into community-based sub-AVAs. The original petition would have further divided Rutherford into Rutherford and Rutherford bench, but that refinement was dropped before hearings began. Before AVAs, Rutherford bench was an innocently coined name meant to distinguish the long, snaky alluvial band stretching along the Napa valley's west side, from St Helena down to Yountville, from the valley floor closer to the Napa river. Rutherford bench has become a source of equal parts of mirth and ire in Napa. It ain't a bench, it ain't only at Rutherford because it extends through Oakville, it shuts out too much good vineyard, say the wrathful. Whatever, the west side of this middle stretch of valley holds many of California's premier patches of Cabernet Sauvignon, including Beaulieu Vineyard Nos. 1 and 2, Staglin, Niebaum-Coppola's Rubicon, Bella Oaks, Bosche, Sycamore, To Kalon, and more.

Stags Leap District AVA

Well south and on the eastern side of the valley, Stags Leap District (shunning the apostrophe) celebrates Cabernet Sauvignon and Merlot, and virtually nothing else. All of its fame rests on varietals from those grapes. Other varieties grow well, but not with enough regional distinctiveness to call attention to themselves. The hallmarks of its Cabernets are a greater emphasis on sour cherry flavours than in counterparts from other parts of Napa, and suppler TANNINS. Curiously, it was little planted to Cabernet before 1970. It takes its name from a basalt palisade north east of Napa city, under the towering wall of which its vineyards lie, and from which deer were reputedly driven by indigenous hunters. Clos du Val and Stag's Leap Wine Cellars were the pioneers, since joined by Chimney Rock, Pine Ridge, Shafer, Silverado Vineyards, Sinskey, and others.

Oak Knoll AVA

This relatively cool AVA created in the early 2000s is mostly on the valley floor, south of Yountville and Stags Leap but north of the town of Napa. Trefethen is one of its oldest wineries; Biale and Lewis are also notable. Merlot grown here is promising.

See also CALIFORNIA, including map.   B.C.C.

Sullivan, C., *Napa Wine: A History from Mission Days to Present* (San Francisco, 1994).

Lapsley, J. T., *Bottled Poetry: Napa Winemaking from Prohibition to the Modern Era* (Berkeley, Calif., 1996).

Naples, large south Italian port and capital of the CAMPANIA region. The area around Naples had once produced all the greatest wines of Ancient ROME, not only FALERNIAN, but also CAECUBAN, MASSIC, and SURRENTINE, but in viticultural terms it was never to be that famous again. With the fall of the Roman empire and the economic decline of Italy, the market for fine wines collapsed.

Its oriental trade, which dates from Naples's medieval period under Byzantine rule, included the strong sweet MALMSEY of Crete, but PUGLIA produced similar wines itself, mostly for consumption in southern Italy. Naples also traded in the VERNACCIA of Liguria, which it sold to Sicilia, Majorca, and PARIS. These wines were known collectively as *vini grechi*, because like the wines imported from the Aegean they were high-quality sweet wines, capable of surviving a long sea voyage.

The wines of Campania, which were not in the Greek style but dry, were called *vini latini*. They were considered inferior and were not long lived enough to be sent overseas to northern Europe. The highest regarded of the *vini latini* were those of Mount Vesuvius, which were sold to other parts of Italy by the merchants of Naples and Salerno. In addition, Naples sold CALABRIAN wines to Aragón and the Balearic islands.

All this made Naples the most important Mediterranean wine-trading port in the 14th century, yet, because of its many changes of regime and its severance from Sicilia in 1282, Naples never became a political or economic power to match the northern city states. Geographically it was far better placed than VENICE and GENOA to conduct the lucrative trade in Aegean wines and other luxury goods with northern Europe, but by the late 13th century, when Genoa began to send its galleys to Southampton and Bruges, Naples was no longer in a position to compete.

See ITALY.   H.M.W.

Lopez, R. S., 'The trade of mediaeval Europe: the South', in *The Cambridge Economic History of Europe*, 7 vols., ii: *Trade and Industry in the Middle Ages* (Cambridge, 1987).

Melis, F., 'Produzione e commercio dei vini italiani nei secoli XIII–XVIII', *Annales cisalpines d'histoire sociale*, 1/3 (1972), 107–33.

Nardo, DOC for robust red wine made mainly from NEGROAMARO grapes in south east Italy. For more details, see PUGLIA.

Nasco, ancient light-berried vine making soft white wines around Cagliari in SARDEGNA.

nature when applied to a French wine usually means 'still'. Nature, with a capital N, is viewed by wine producers as friend or enemy and everything in between depending on whether they are, respectively, TRADITIONALISTS or technocrats.

Naturwein (known as **Naturrein** in the mid 20th century), German wine to which no sugar had been added for the purposes of ENRICHMENT of its alcoholic strength. The term was abolished by the 1971 GERMAN WINE LAW, which established as QMP all wine which would have qualified as Naturwein. See GERMAN HISTORY.

Navarra, known in English as **Navarre**, autonomous region in north east SPAIN which also lends its name to a denominated wine zone. The kingdom of Navarra once stretched from BORDEAUX to Barcelona but today this extensive denomination is overshadowed by the neighbouring DO zone RIOJA, a small part of which extends into the province of Navarra (see map under SPAIN). The wines share a common history.

Pilgrims en route to Santiago de Compostela fuelled the demand for wine in the Middle Ages. Later, in the mid 19th century,

both Rioja and Navarra benefited greatly from their proximity to France after the arrival of the PHYLLOXERA louse. Because northern Spain was affected considerably later than south west France, vineyards here were expanded and large quantities of Navarran wine were sold to producers in France until phylloxera arrived in Navarra itself in 1892. The region recovered fairly quickly but the area under vine in 1990 was less than a third of that a century before.

The region splits into five subzones according to climate, from the cooler slopes of the Baja Montaña close to the Pyrenean foothills and the slightly warmer Valdizarbe and Tierra Estella districts in the north of Navarra, to Ribera Alta in the centre of the region, and Ribera Baja round the city of Tudela in the south. Rainfall totals range between 600 mm (23 in) in the north and 400 mm in the south and east, while summer temperatures become correspondingly warmer. With over 30 per cent of Navarra's vineyards, Ribera Baja has traditionally been the most important of the five subzones, although most of the new planting in the late 1980s and early 1990s took place in the cooler north.

The Garnacha grape (see GRENACHE) has dominated Navarra's vineyards but plantings of TEMPRANILLO increased considerably in the 1990s. Garnacha lends itself to good, dry rosé, which Navarra continues to make in large quantities. Red wines improved by leaps and bounds in the 1990s through much more careful wine-making and frequent blending of Tempranillo, Cabernet Sauvignon, Merlot, and even Syrah with Garnacha. White wines account for less than 10 per cent of the region's production and have traditionally been made from the neutral Viura, or MACABEO, grape. Chardonnay, however, has been extensively planted. The new varieties and technical improvements have been largely promoted by the oenological research station, EVENA, set up at Olite by the CONSEJO REGULADOR and the regional government.

R.J.M. & V. de la S.

NDVI. See NORMALIZED DIFFERENCE VEGETATION INDEX.

Néac, small red BORDEAUX appellation to the immediate north east of Pomerol.

Nebbiolo, great black grape variety responsible for some of the finest and longest-lived wines in Italy. It is native to the PIEMONTE region in the north west, and is its most distinctive and distinguished vine. The quality of wines such as BAROLO and BARBARESCO inspires hopeful planting of the variety all over the world.

Italian Nebbiolo

It has been hypothesized that PLINY the Elder's citation of Pollenzo (just north west of the current Barolo zone) as a source of outstanding wine referred to wines made from this grape. Documents from the castle of Rivoli dating from 1235 have also been taken as a description of Nebbiolo. Canale d'Alba in the Roero district provides the first unmistakable historical reference in 1303: 'une carrata (barrel) de bono puro vino nebiolo'. PETRUS DE CRESCENTIIS *Liber ruralium commodorum* in 1304 made an unambiguous link between the 'Nubiola' grape, which he termed 'delightful', and 'excellent wine'. The communal statutes of La Morra of 1431 furnish further evidence that the variety's exceptional qualities were understood and appreciated at an early date: substantial fines were levied against those guilty of cutting down a Nebbiolo vine, and recidivists could be punished with the loss of their right hand or even hanging. Some have postulated that the name derives from *nobile*, or noble, but a more likely derivation is from *nebbia*, or fog, a frequent phenomenon in Piemonte in October when the grape is harvested.

Modern Piemonte has shown its respect for Nebbiolo in a more concrete, if less poetic, way by restricting its planting to a few selected areas: the total production of wines from the grape rarely exceeds 125,000 hl/3.3 million gal, or just 3 per cent of the region's production, less than one-fifteenth of the annual production of BARBERA. Nebbiolo is always the first variety to bud and the last to ripen, with harvests that regularly last well past the middle of October, and the variety is accordingly granted the most favourable HILLSIDE exposures, generally south to south west. Perhaps as important as the vineyard site, however, are the soils: Nebbiolo has shown itself to be extremely fussy and has in the past century given best results only in the calcareous marls to the north and south of Alba on the right bank of the Tanaro in the DOCG zones of BARBARESCO and BAROLO respectively. Here Nebbiolo-based wines reach their maximum aromatic complexity, and express a fullness of flavour which balances the relatively high ACIDITY and substantial TANNINS which are invariably present. Historically, much more Nebbiolo was planted in the Novara and Vercelli hills, but vineyard area declined rapidly during Italy's industrial revolution in the 1950s.

Good Nebbiolo wines are once again being produced in varying soil types in the hills on the left and right banks of the Sesia river in the province of Novara (see BOCA, GHEMME, SIZZANO, FARA) and in the Vercelli hills (see LESSONA, BRAMATERRA, GATTINARA). Here Nebbiolo is called SPANNA and is usually blended with softer VESPOLINA and/or BONARDA grapes.

NEBBIOLO D'ALBA, a tamer, less savage version of the grape, only suggests the heights which the variety can gain in more choice positions. The ROERO district on the left bank of the Tanaro has predominantly sandy soils which

produced better and better wine throughout the 1990s, although without the classic aromas of tar found in Barolo and Barbaresco.

Nebbiolo, often called Picutener, also plays the leading role in the postage stamp-size DOC of CAREMA on the border of the Valle d'Aosta, in the neighbouring and equally Lilliputian DOC of Donnaz in the Valle d'AOSTA itself, and in Lombardia in VALTELLINA, where it is known as Chiavennasca—the only sizeable zone where Nebbiolo is cultivated outside Piemonte. The latter three areas, subalpine in latitude and definitely cool during the growing season, produce a medium-bodied style of Nebbiolo in which the fruit must frequently struggle against the grape's tannic asperity and acidic sharpness; the added ripeness of warmer vintages is even more valuable here.

These zones apart, Nebbiolo is hardly known in Italy, although it is an ingredient in the FRANCIACORTA cocktail, and the innovative VENETO winemaker Giuseppe Quintarelli makes a RECIOTO version of Nebbiolo, a modern reminder of what may have been Piemonte's legion of DRIED GRAPE WINES.

Three principal CLONES of Nebbiolo are conventionally identified: Lampia, Michet, and Rosé. The last of these is disappearing because of the pale colour of its wines, while Michet is Lampia afflicted with a virus which causes the vine's canes to fork. More importantly, however, this clone, while producing smaller bunches and YIELDS and particularly intense aromas and flavours, does not adapt itself to all soils. Most producers, mindful of the relatively embryonic state of clonal research, prefer to rely on a careful MASS SELECTION in their vineyards rather than staking their future on a single clone. More systematic clonal research in the 1990s has only confirmed that Nebbiolo has serious problems with VIRUSES, what might be called the genetic equivalent of excessive inbreeding in a variety so concentrated on a relatively small area, a fact which is hampering the multiplication of the better clones which have thus far been identified.

The total area planted with Nebbiolo has declined in recent decades to under 5,000 ha/ 12,700 acres by 2000.   D.T. & D.C.G.

Genetic relationships

Through DNA PROFILING, researchers in Anna Schneider's laboratory at Torino and José Vouillamoz at DAVIS found that **Nebbiolo Rosé** is not a clone of Nebbiolo but is a distinct variety. Furthermore, Nebbiolo Rosé turned out to have a parent–offspring relationship with Nebbiolo. Several additional parent–offspring relationships were discovered between Nebbiolo and traditional varieties from Piedmont (FREISA, VESPOLINA, and Bubbierasco) and Valtellina (Negrera and Rossola). While the complete pedigree of Nebbiolo is still unknown, these relationships indicate that Nebbiolo probably has its roots in Piedmont and/or Lombardia. In addition, a

possible parent–offspring relationship was suggested between Freisa and VIOGNIER, so that Nebbiolo and Viognier are likely to be cousins.   J.V.

Outside Italy

Vine-growers all over the world are experimenting with Nebbiolo. The results often lack the haunting aromas that characterize the variety but isolated examples in regions as far apart as Oregon, Washington state, and Australia's King valley in Victoria suggest the quest may not be fruitless. Nebbiolo has so far somewhat reluctantly accompanied Barbera to both North and South America. In California, Sangiovese has proved much more successful. High yields have tended to subsume the variety's quality in South America. The few hundred hectares planted in Argentina are mainly in San Juan province.

Nebbiolo d'Alba is an Italian DOC red produced from NEBBIOLO grapes grown on 556 ha/ 1,370 acres of vineyard in 32 townships surrounding the city of Alba in the PIEMONTE region and is, to all extents and purposes, a satellite appellation to BAROLO and BARBARESCO. Seven of the townships are partially inside the Barolo DOCG zone, although the areas which can produce Nebbiolo d'Alba—the southern sections of Monforte d'Alba and Novello, the north eastern tip of La Morra, all but a western slice of Diano d'Alba, the northern parts of Verduno, Grinzano Cavour, and Roddi—have been carefully and intelligently excluded from the Barolo zone. Most of the vineyard land is on the northern bank of the river Tanaro in the Roero hills, on sandier soils that yield wines that are softer, less intense, and faster maturing than a Barolo or a Barbaresco, more generically 'Nebbiolo' and less pointedly characterful.   D.T. & D.C.G.

Nebbiolo delle Langhe, formerly a VINO DA TAVOLA of the PIEMONTE region in north west Italy.

A few leading Barolo producers—Aldo Conterno and Elio Altare in particular—pioneered special CUVÉES for small oak BARREL MATURATION in the 1980s. These wines, which commanded a much higher price and enjoyed an entirely different prestige from the average Nebbiolo delle Langhe, carried the same classification on the label. The approval of an overall regional DOC for Piemonte in 1995 remedied this situation by creating a new DOC called Langhe Nebbiolo into which producers in Barolo, Barbaresco, Nebbiolo d'Alba, and Roero may declassify their wines.   D.T.

necrosis, a term used to describe death of tissue. For example, necrotic spots of leaf tissue caused by DOWNY MILDEW appear blackish brown. For many vine foliar diseases and disorders, the yellowing of leaf sections, or CHLOROSIS, precedes necrosis.

négociant, French term for a MERCHANT and one used particularly of wine merchants who buy in grapes, must, or wine, blend different lots of wine within an APPELLATION, and bottle the result under their own label. Making a perfectly balanced blend from a number of imperfect parts is a potentially noble calling, but one that once provided so many opportunities for ADULTERATION AND FRAUD that it brought the entire profession into question, if not ill repute, at least until the late 1980s. Nowadays, with the bureaucracy involved in the APPELLATION CONTRÔLÉE system, cheating requires real ingenuity.

The role of the négociant is particularly worthwhile in BURGUNDY, where the oldest négociants, traditionally concentrated in Beaune, have been joined by a new breed of smaller operation, often run alongside a grower's own DOMAINE. So many individual growers produce tiny quantities from each of a number of different appellations that it can make sense to make up commercially more significant quantities and bottle them together. Many of the larger Burgundy négociants have significant vineyard holdings of their own. BOUCHARD PÈRE ET FILS and BOISSET, for example, are two of the CÔTE D'OR's most subtantial vineyard owners. Louis LATOUR, Louis JADOT, and Joseph DROUHIN are other important Burgundian négociants. The term **négociant-éleveur** implies that the négociant oversees the ÉLEVAGE of the wine it sells.

Like all important French wine regions, Bordeaux also has a great concentration of négociants, many of which own CHÂTEAUX (while some of the FIRST GROWTH châteaux also own a négociant business). For more details, see BORDEAUX TRADE.

Negoska, Greek red grape which is a softening ingredient, making very fruity, alcoholic wines, with XINOMAVRO, in the wines of Goumenissa.

Negra de Madrid, synonym for the GRENACHE grape around Madrid.

Negra Mole and **Negramoll,** Iberian dark-skinned grape variety. See TINTA NEGRA MOLE.

Negrara, name related to the colour of the berries (*negra* meaning 'black'), and corresponding to a group of several distinct CULTIVARS in northern Italy. **Negrara Trentina** is the most common variety, and recent DNA PROFILING revealed a parent–offspring relationship with ENANTIO. J.V.

Négrette, black grape variety special to the vineyards north of Toulouse in SOUTH WEST FRANCE. In FRONTON, it must dominate the blend and in Vins de LAVILLEDIEU it must constitute at least 35 per cent. Wine made from Négrette is more supple, perfumed, and flirtatious than that produced from the more famous south western black grape variety TANNAT,

and is best drunk young, with its fruit, sometimes described as having a slightly animal, or violet, flavour, unsuppressed by heavy oak ageing. The variety is inconveniently prone to POWDERY MILDEW and BOTRYTIS BUNCH ROT and is therefore better suited to the hot, dry climate of Toulouse than to many other wine regions. Total French plantings were 1,300 ha/ 3,200 acres in 2000.

Negroamaro, often written **Negro Amaro,** dark-skinned southern Italian grape variety that fell victim to the EU VINE PULL SCHEMES with total area planted falling from 31,000 ha/76,500 acres in 1990 to 16,760 ha in 2000. It is particularly associated with the eastern half of the Salento peninsula, in the provinces of Lecce and Brindisi, where it forms the base, blended with small proportions of Malvasia Nera and (not necessarily legally) Primitivo, for DOCs such as Salice Salentino, Copertino, Brindisi, Leverano, and Squinzano. It is later ripening than Primitivo, with chunkier tannins. It is also used to produce some lively rosé. For more details, see PUGLIA.

Negroamaro is thought to have been brought to Puglia by the colonizing Greeks in the 8th and 7th centuries BC. While one school feels that its name derives from its colour (*negro*) and character (*amaro*, or bitter), Californian winemaker Mark Shannon, who now lives in Puglia, holds that the name derives from Latin and Greek roots for its dark colour; *nigra* in Latin and *mavro* in Greek, citing one of the grape's synonyms, Nigramaro, as evidence. D.C.G.

Neheleschol, extremely ancient Middle Eastern light-berried vine with enormous bunches, planted experimentally at MAS de Daumas Gassac in the Languedoc.

nematodes, microscopic roundworms generally found in soil which can seriously harm vines. Some feed on bacteria or fungi and are part of the normal vineyard ecosystem. Others, however, feed on grapevine roots and thus reduce both the size and efficiency of the root system. Although the vines do not necessarily die, they suffer WATER STRESS and deficiencies in VINE NUTRITION and grow weakly. Some species of nematodes are important because they transmit VIRUS DISEASES. The viruses spread by nematodes are called NEPOVIRUSES. They can be spread throughout the vineyard from just one infected plant by nematode feeding. Often they show up as a few yellow vines in the vineyard.

The fact that nematodes damage vines was first established in about 1930, in California. Because of characteristic and visually striking root damage, the root knot nematode, *Meloidogyne* species, was considered most important. However, in 1958 it was discovered that FANLEAF DEGENERATION was spread by nematodes of the species *Xiphenema index*.

This milestone discovery in plant pathology was made by Hewitt and colleagues of the University of California at DAVIS. It had been established in France as long ago as 1883 that fanleaf degeneration spread through the soil, and some French authorities believed until the 1950s that the PHYLLOXERA louse was responsible for the spread.

Root knot nematodes occur mainly in sandy soil. Their presence is visible to the naked eye since the knots (swollen tissue or galls) on the roots formed in response to their feeding resemble a string of beads. One female can lay up to 1,000 eggs, and with up to ten generations a year in warm climates they can spread rapidly. The root lesion nematode *Pratylenchus* also damages vines by feeding on their roots.

The so-called dagger nematode, *Xiphenema index*, is especially important in spreading a number of virus diseases (see FANLEAF DEGENERATION). Other *Xiphenema* species spread other virus diseases. Virus particles can survive for many years in root fragments after an infected vineyard is removed. Replanting a new, 'virus-free' vineyard can lead to disappointment, as reinfection with nematode feeding can follow.

At one time vineyards in which nematodes were previously present were subjected to FUMIGATION with injected chemicals before planting, but the nematicide DBCP, which was considered capable of controlling all nematodes, is now banned. Methyl bromide and 1,3-dichloropropene are highly effective and can kill nematodes surviving on old root pieces but they may also be banned because of environmental concerns. In California, for example, products such as methyl bromide have been phased out of commercial viticulture in favour of ORGANIC alternatives.

Nematode diseases are often spread on infected planting material or by the movement of infected soil on cultivation implements or by irrigation water. Infected nursery plants can be freed of nematodes by dipping them in hot water. Biological control using ROOTSTOCKS is possible and generally preferred. Some VITIS species (*solonis, champini,* and *doaniana*) show resistance to nematodes. Among the most nematode-resistant rootstocks are Couderc 1613, Ramsey, Schwarzmann, Harmony, and Dog Ridge. R.E.S.

Hardie, W. J., and Cirami, R. M., 'Grapevine rootstocks', in B. G. Coombe and P. R. Dry (eds.), *Viticulture,* i: *Resources* (Adelaide, 1988).

Winkler, A. J., *et al.* (eds.), *General Viticulture* (2nd edn, Berkeley, Calif., 1974).

Nepal, tiny mountain kingdom in the Himalayas lying between India and Tibet, home to the highest vineyard in the world (2,750 m/9,000 ft). Two hectares of VINIFERA vines were planted in 1992 at Jonsom in the Anapurna region by a local politician keen to foster a new industry in this remote corner of the world. D.G.

nepoviruses, group of 13 VIRUS DISEASES which are spread from plant to plant by the feeding of NEMATODES (microscopic worms) on roots. They also have in common a polyhedral structure, hence the name 'nepovirus': 'ne' for nematode and 'po' for polyhedral. Such diseases can be very destructive and almost impossible to control. This is because the virus can survive for years in nematodes and root fragments even after all infected vines have been removed. So, even if a new, supposedly virus-free, vineyard is planted, it will quickly become infected by the nematode feeding. Among the important virus diseases in this group are FANLEAF DEGENERATION, tomato ringspot, and tobacco ringspot.　　　R.E.S.

Pearson, R. C., and Goheen, A. C., *Compendium of Grape Diseases* (St Paul, Minn., 1988).

Nerello, important Sicilian red grape variety. **Nerello Mascalese** is more widely planted than **Nerello Cappuccio** and is concentrated in the north east of the island. The wines produced tend to lack the concentration of NERO D'AVOLA although they are usually high in alcohol. Most of the wine is used for blending. For more information, see SICILIA.

Nero d'Avola, increasingly reputable red grape variety that is one of the best in Sicilia and is also known as Calabrese, suggesting origins in Calabria on the mainland. It is also, fortunately, Sicilia's most widely planted red wine grape, planted on about 14,000 ha/ 34,600 acres. Quality-minded producers on the island value the body, deep colour, and ageing potential which Nero d'Avola can bring to a blend. VARIETAL Nero d'Avola has shown itself a fine candidate for BARREL MATURATION. Like Syrah, Nero d'Avola requires a good site, warmth, and low VINE TRAINING to succeed. At its best, it produces deep coloured wines that have a wild plum and chocolate character, high levels of tannins, and decent acidity. Avola itself is in the southern part of the province of Siracusa, and nearby Pachino, on the extreme south eastern tip of the island, is particularly reputed for the quality of its Nero d'Avola grapes. For more information, see SICILIA.

Netherlands, north European country more often referred to as Holland, whose inhabitants are known as the Dutch. In the 17th century particularly, they played a dominant role in the world's wine and spirit trade (see DUTCH WINE TRADE), and played a key role in draining the MÉDOC lowlands bordering the Gironde. For a long time, Holland was the world's largest importer of SHERRY—until 1997, when it was surpassed by the British Isles.

The country also has its own small, indigenous wine industry with an impressive history, despite the coolness of the climate. There are records of wine-producing vines growing in Limburg in southern Holland in 1324 and vine-growing around Maastricht ceased only in the early years of the 19th century, discouraged by a series of cold summers and the economic turbulence of the Napoleonic era. It was not until 1967 that the Netherlands became a wine producer once more when Frits Bosch created his Slavante vineyard of just 800 sq m. There are more than 100 active vinegrowers, although only about 30 have more than a hectare of vines, many of them producing only minuscule amounts. The largest producers in the southern part of the country, around Maastricht, are medal winners Apostelhoeve, Hoeve Neekum, and Wijngoed Fromberg in Ubachsberg. In Noord-Brabant, De Linie and Domaine d'Heerstayen also enjoy a considerable reputation. In this part of the country mainly VINIFERA varieties such as Riesling, Müller-Thurgau, Auxerrois, Sylvaner, and Pinot Gris are grown for white wines while Pinot Noir and Gamay produce light reds. Wine-growing in more northerly and eastern parts of the country has grown considerably since the introduction of new DISEASE-RESISTANT VARIETIES such as Regent and Rondo for reds and Johanniter, Merzling, and Solaris for white wines. Notable producers here are Wijngaard Wageningse Berg, Wijnhoeve De Colonjes at Groesbeek, and Wijngaard Hof van Twente, Bentelo. Further growth is expected because wine is a more profitable crop than most, and offers TOURISM possibilities.　　　N.McG. & R.d.G.

nets can literally save a grape crop. See BIRDS.

Neuburger, sometimes distinguished white grape variety grown almost exclusively in AUSTRIA. DNA PROFILING in Austria showed it is a crossing, quite possibly an accidental crossing, of ROTER VELTINER × SYLVANER, which makes nutty wine that tastes like an even fuller-bodied Weissburgunder. It ripens relatively early and achieves a higher MUST WEIGHT than GRÜNER VELTLINER, Austria's most popular vine. It is grown mainly in Wachau, Thermenregion, and Burgenland in Austria, and in Transylvania in ROMANIA.

Neusiedlersee, wine area and shallow lake in the Burgenland region in the far east of AUSTRIA around which most of the country's best sweet white and red wines are made. The LAKE EFFECT on autumn temperatures and the resultant humidity are important factors in the regular development of BOTRYTIS for the famous sweet wines.

Nevers is the town that gives its name to the central French *département* of Nièvre, most famous in the wine world for the wines of POUILLY-FUMÉ and for its OAK.

New Latitude Wines, term coined by Thai wine writer Frank Norel in 2003 for wines made in the TROPICAL fringes of the global wine map, although it could equally well apply to those from high latitudes where viticulture has recently been encouraged by CLIMATE CHANGE. See LATITUDE.

New South Wales, AUSTRALIA's most populous state, consumes far more wine than it produces, but its wine geography is developing rapidly.

The **Hunter Valley** (now an official wine zone), 130 km/80 miles north of Sydney, has always had a special hold on the affections (and wallets) of Sydneysiders. It is also one of the internationally known regions, notwithstanding its relatively small contribution (less than 3 per per cent) to the country's total crush, and its perverse climate. That climate is abnormally hot for a fine wine district, although the heat is partially offset by high HUMIDITY, by afternoon cloud cover, and by substantial rainfall during the growing season—less beneficially in the years in which most of the rain falls during harvest.

Out of this climatic witches' brew comes exceptionally long-lived dry SEMILLON, the best peaking somewhere between ten and 20 years of age and assuming a honeyed, buttery, nutty flavour, and texture which suggests it has been fermented or matured in oak, when (traditionally) none was used. Most remarkable is the ALCOHOLIC STRENGTH, often as low as 10 per cent. Since 1970, CHARDONNAY also has proved its worth: Australia's first Chardonnay of note were made in the Hunter Valley by Tyrrell's. Here the lifespan is usually much shorter, but there are exceptions. Whether young or old, Hunter Chardonnays are generous and soft, with peachy fruit and considerable VISCOSITY.

SHIRAZ was the traditional red counterpart to Semillon in the Hunter, making extremely distinctive, moderately tannic, and long-lived wines with earth and tar overtones, sometimes described as having the aroma of a sweaty saddle after a hard day's ride. At 20 to 30 years of age, the best acquire a silky sheen to their texture and move eerily close to wines of similar age from the RHÔNE valley in south east France.

CABERNET SAUVIGNON is another relatively new arrival, planted for the first time this century at Lake's Folly winery in 1963. By and large, Hunter Valley wines tend to be more regional than varietal in their statement, a tendency which becomes more marked with age.

Riesling, Sauvignon Blanc, and Pinot Noir are among prominent varieties which have been tried and found unsuited to the climate and TERROIR. VERDELHO has made a remarkable comeback (highly regarded in the 19th century, then all but forgotten) as a soft, flavoursome wine requiring neither oak nor patience to show its wares.

Overall, the Hunter Valley produces better white wines than it does red, with Semillon its one unique contribution. If one is to differentiate the Upper Hunter, a separate viticultural region well to the north, from the Lower

Hunter, the bias towards white wine becomes more acute in the former. Rosemount has enjoyed acclaim for its Chardonnay, although the Semillon in particular lacks the concentration and longevity of its Lower Hunter Valley counterpart.

Nowhere in Australia is the rate of change and the pace of growth more apparent than it is in New South Wales. The development of viticulture along the entire length of the western (or inland) side of the Great Dividing range could not have been foreseen at the start of the 1990s, but by the end of the century it was making a significant contribution to the national crush.

The principal zones are the Central Ranges Zone and the Southern New South Wales Zone, providing two and a half times as much as the Hunter Valley. The former takes in the regions of Mudgee, Orange, and Cowra; the latter takes in the regions of Hilltops, Canberra District, Gundagai, and Tumbarumba.

Of these, **Mudgee** is by far the oldest, with an unbroken history of viticulture and wine-making stretching back to 1858. It is first and foremost red wine country, however well the ubiquitous Chardonnay does here. Indeed, Mudgee was the source of a precious VIRUS-free clone of Chardonnay almost certainly brought to Australia in the early 19th century. As with the Hunter Valley, Mudgee has never been attacked by PHYLLOXERA.

The climate is as hot as that of the Hunter Valley, but the summer rainfall is significantly lower, and it is rare for harvest rain seriously to interrupt proceedings. The red wines—Shiraz and Cabernet Sauvignon—are deeply coloured and intensely flavoured, and are ideal blend components for the products of the Hunter Valley's frequent wet vintages. ORLANDO WYNDHAM, which moved the centre of its wine-making operations from the Hunter Valley to Mudgee in the late 1990s, closed its New South Wales wine-making operations altogether in 2004, and brought them back to South Australia.

ELEVATION is as important as LATITUDE in shaping the climate (and the ensuing wine style) of the regions south down the Great Dividing range to **Orange**. With most of its vineyards established on hillsides forming part of the extinct volcano mount Canobolas at altitudes of between 600 and 900 m, Orange is the coolest of these regions (apart from the southern outpost of Tumbarumba in the Australian Alps). Zesty, lively Chardonnay and mid-weight Cabernet Sauvignon, Merlot, and Shiraz with clearly articulated varietal character are the order of the day. Here, as in the **Hilltops** region (which produces wines of slightly fuller style and weight), warm but not excessively hot summer days and cold nights are followed by a cool, dry autumn which assists in the slow ripening and relatively late harvest dates.

McWilliam's has thrown its lot in with the Hilltops region, while HARDYS has chosen **Canberra District** in a move which surprised most observers. Here most of the wineries have been small, clustered just outside the border of the Australian Capital Territory, but relying heavily on tourist (and local resident) trade to promote cellar-door sales. The climate is not dissimilar to that of Orange and Hilltops: strongly CONTINENTAL with warm to hot days, cold nights, and a dry summer. Riesling, Chardonnay, Pinot Noir, Shiraz, and Viognier need site selection, but with appropriate matching can be truly excellent.

Cowra (and nearby Canownindra) is significantly warmer, basically because the vineyards are at a lower altitude. Here broad acre farming is made easy by the flat plains, and yields (with the aid of IRRIGATION, of course) are substantial. Softly fleshy Chardonnay is the mainstay, with soft Cabernet Sauvignon, Shiraz, and Merlot seldom achieving enough concentration and structure to match the quality of Chardonnay.

The Big Rivers Zone, encompassing Riverina, Perricoota, and the New South Wales side of the Murray Darling and Swan Hill regions, which it shares with Victoria (they fall on both sides of the Murray river, the border between the two states), produces 75 per cent of the state's grape crush.

Riverina (sometimes called the Murrumbidgee Irrigation Area, or MIA) is centred around Griffith 450 km/275 miles south west of Sydney. With the notable exception of BOTRYTIZED Semillon (made in a SAUTERNES style), the wines are on a par with those produced in the Perricoota, Murray Darling and Lower Murray regions. Replanting in the late 1990s and early 2000s put increasing focus on Chardonnay, Shiraz, Merlot, and Cabernet Sauvignon, but substantial quantities of MUSCAT GORDO BLANCO and the multipurpose SULTANA are still harvested. High yields are sought, and under normal conditions Chardonnay is the best variety. It takes a cool year such as 2002 for the red varieties to rise above pedestrian quality as they emphatically did in that year.

Overall the wines reflect the very warm climate and the quasi-hydroponic growing regimes. The technical excellence of the wineries assures clean, fault-free, mildly fruity wines well suited to the drinker of cask wine (in BOXES), and to the requirements of overseas BULK markets such as the own brands of the British supermarket chains.   J.H.

Halliday, J., numerous works including *The Wine Atlas of Australia and New Zealand* (2nd edn, Sydney, 1998); *Australia Wine Companion* (Sydney, annually).

new varieties, somewhat loose and relative term used to describe VINE VARIETIES specifically and deliberately developed by man, which effectively means developed since the late 19th century (although it is sometimes used parochially to describe varieties new to a region).

There is interest in breeding new varieties which are resistant, for example, to environmental stresses, fungal and bacterial diseases, and nematodes and insects (see VINE BREEDING). Of these, the major goals are varieties tolerant of the fungal diseases DOWNY MILDEW, POWDERY MILDEW, and BOTRYTIS BUNCH ROT or resistant to PIERCE'S DISEASE. Unfortunately, new varieties, especially HYBRIDS but even some CROSSES, suffer from the stigma of the poor wine quality of the early French hybrids. The uptake of newly developed grape varieties has been further hindered by consumer preference for traditional varieties, particularly the INTERNATIONAL VARIETIES, a consequence in part of VARIETAL labelling.

The early French hybridizers mentioned in FRENCH HYBRIDS were not the only French vine breeders to have developed new varieties. Louis BOUSCHET and his son Henri used controlled pollination from 1824 to create a range of seedlings which after selection became known as the Bouschet crosses. Of these the TEINTURIER variety ALICANTE BOUSCHET is the most important and indeed is the only one to be officially recommended for planting in France. Another early and successful VINIFERA vine breeder was Hermann Müller, whose variety MÜLLER-THURGAU was once the most planted in Germany. A succession of new crossings followed, notably from research institutes at GEISENHEIM, GEILWEILERHOF, Alzey, Würzburg, and Freiburg. For details of these, see GERMAN CROSSINGS.

Other new varieties such as Zweigelt, Blauburger, and Neuburger were bred in Austria, the first two at KLOSTERNEUBURG. The emphasis in RUSSIA has been on breeding varieties with cold tolerance as well as disease tolerance, and there are substantial areas, not just in Russia but in other ex-Soviet republics, planted with varieties such as Saperavi Severny, Stepniak, Fioletovy Ranni, and Cabernet Severny. In NEW YORK state and CANADA, the emphasis also has been on developing varieties with cold and disease tolerance, often relying on the French hybrids for resistant genes. Recent releases such as CAYUGA WHITE, Melody, CHARDONEL, and Traminette are being more widely planted. The names of the last two varieties, incorporating those of their respective *vinifera* parents, may make them more acceptable to consumers.

New varieties in France, most of them developed in association with the University of MONTPELLIER, have been *vinifera* crosses such as PORTAN, CALADOC, Chenanson, Ganson, Gramon, Monerac, CHASAN, Arriloba, Odola, and Perdea, as well as EGIODOLA and ARINARNOA developed by INRA at Bordeaux. In France, new varieties must first be registered with the Comité Technique Permanent de la Sélection des Plantes Cultivées (CTPS) as a prelude to their recognition in the EUROPEAN UNION.

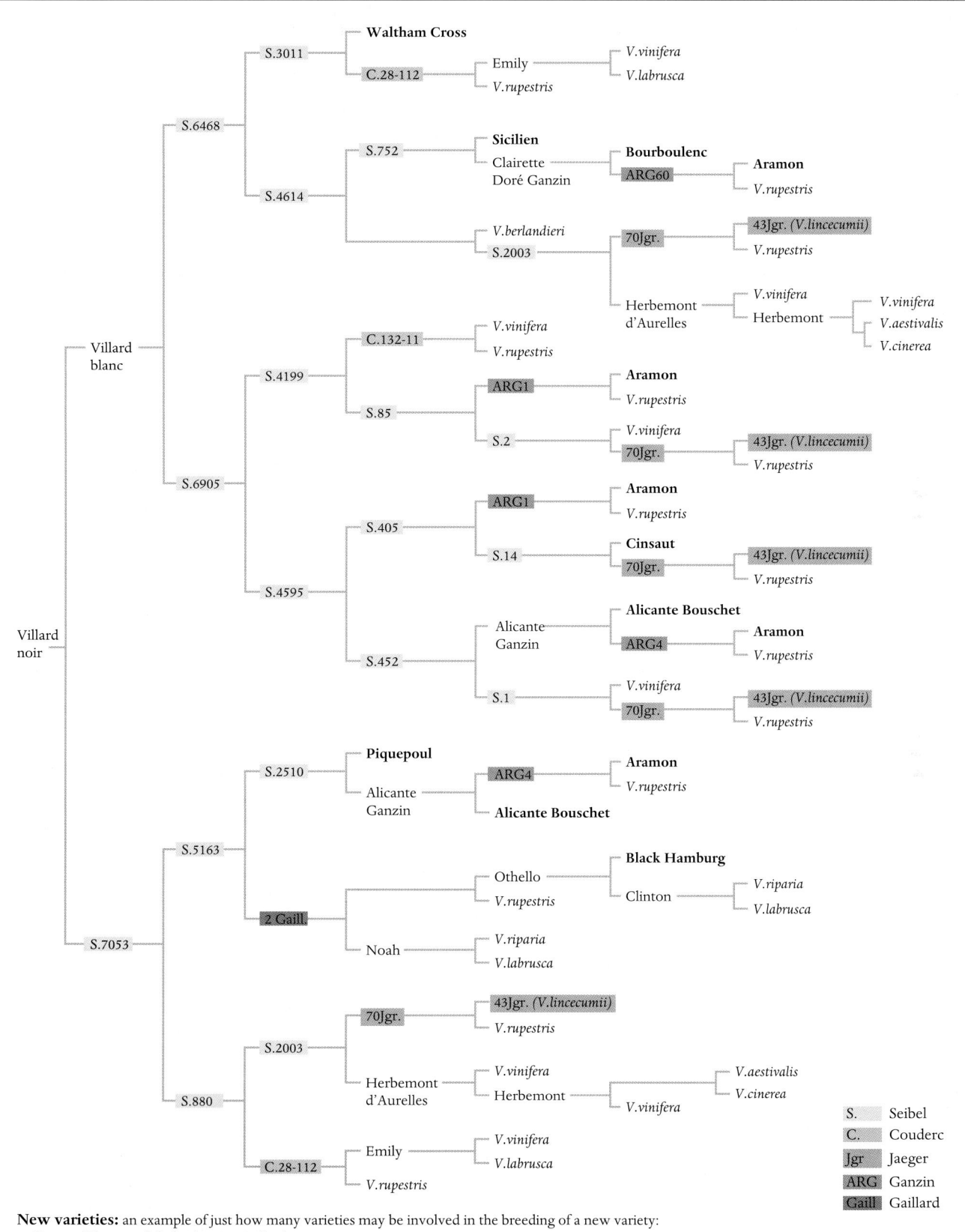

S.		Seibel
C.		Couderc
Jgr		Jaeger
ARG		Ganzin
Gaill		Gaillard

New varieties: an example of just how many varieties may be involved in the breeding of a new variety:
pedigree of the French hybrid variety Villard noir.

Australia has a vine-breeding programme designed to produce varieties suitable for hot climates, and Goyura, TARRANGO, Tullilah, TAMINGA, TYRIAN, and CIENNA have all been released. In California such new varieties as CARNELIAN, RUBY CABERNET, EMERALD RIESLING, SYMPHONY, and FLORA have all enjoyed popularity at some point while RUBIRED, unlike similarly red-fleshed ROYALTY, is widely planted to add colour to blends.

New varieties of particular interest today are interspecific hybrids because of the opportunities they offer for natural disease resistance with much reduced use of AGROCHEMICALS. These DISEASE-RESISTANT VARIETIES have complex genealogies which may include, not just *vinifera* genes, but also those of various AMERICAN VINE SPECIES, French hybrids, and even Asian vine species.

A full account of vine breeding and the inheritance of characteristics is given by Huglin. See also VINE BREEDING. R.E.S.

Huglin, P., *Biologie et écologie de la vigne* (Paris, 1986).
Mullins, M. G., Bouquet, A., and Williams, L., *Biology of the Grapevine* (Cambridge, 1992).
Smart, R. E., 'Chardonel, anyone?', *Practical Winery and Vineyards*, (Jan/Feb 1998), 111–12.

New World, term much used in the wine world, initially somewhat patronizingly but with increasing admiration over the past quarter-century as the New World's share of global exports rose from 3 to 23 per cent, to distinguish the colonies established as a result of European exploration, beginning with some of the longer voyages in the 15th century. As such it contrasts with the OLD WORLD of Europe and the other Mediterranean countries where the vine was widely established by the 4th century. Most of the differences between the Old and New Worlds of wine are being systematically eroded as those in the Old World increasingly adopt technical innovation and those in the New World are increasingly exposed to some of the better aspects of TRADITION.

History
The new colonists needed wine for religious reasons (see EUCHARIST), and the planting of the vine was a matter of high priority when the conquistadores invaded SOUTH AMERICA. Cortés was already arranging to plant vines in MEXICO by 1522. By 1530, vines were cultivated in both Mexico and JAPAN, and by the 1550s in PERU, followed soon after by CHILE. The New World's oldest winery in continuous use is Casa Madero at San Lorenzo in north eastern Mexico where the first vintage in the Americas was made, from VITIS *aestivalis*, in 1597.

The European settlement of SOUTH AFRICA followed a decision by the DUTCH EAST INDIA COMPANY soon after 1640 to establish a victualling post at the Cape of Good Hope, to serve the growing Batavia trade. Dutch settlement

began in 1652 and the first vines were planted in 1655.

British settlers planted the first vines in the UNITED STATES of America in Virginia in 1619; thus began a series of unsuccessful attempts to establish European or VINIFERA vine varieties on the east coast of America. Settlers there were dismayed that they could not cultivate this sort of vine when local wild vines, AMERICAN VINES, grew in profusion in the forests. At that time they were not to know the nature of the pest and disease scourges which were attacking their plantations, and were subsequently to invade Europe (see DOWNY MILDEW, POWDERY MILDEW, and PHYLLOXERA). PIERCE'S DISEASE presumably also played a role in the devastation of these European vines on some sites. Added to these problems in many areas were those of much colder winters than *vinifera* varieties can withstand.

There were not the same problems in Baja California, where Spanish-Mexican Jesuit MISSIONARIES established vineyards in the 1670s. Although prone to summer drought, this region was free of both FUNGAL DISEASES and PHYLLOXERA and European vines flourished here. Gradually plantings were made further north—in Los Angeles in the 1820s and NAPA and SONOMA in the 1850s (see CALIFORNIA, history).

Vines were introduced to AUSTRALIA by Captain Arthur Phillip in 1788 as part of the first British colony at Sydney. As this large country was invaded by the British, so the culture of the vine spread also. Viticulture was well established in all modern wine-producing states by the 1850s. Samuel Marsden, a missionary from Australia, is acknowledged as bringing the first vines to NEW ZEALAND in 1819.

Viticulture
New World viticulture is a phrase used to differentiate the viticultural practices in the New World from those of the Old World. It is difficult but not impossible to generalize about the viticultural practices of countries as diverse as the United States, Australia, New Zealand, South Africa, and the countries of South America as opposed to those more usual in Europe.

A common difference is in planting distances, or VINE DENSITY, with a particularly marked contrast between the 1 m by 1 m (3 ft by 3 ft) high-density planting of the MÉDOC and the 3.7 m by 2.5 m (12 ft by 8 ft) planting pattern common in California and Australia. But no difference is absolute or constant. In some parts of the Old World, there is a trend towards wider spacings for reasons of economy, while some growers in the New World are planting more densely in a search for higher quality. POSTS characterize New World vineyards rather than the STAKES of the Old World.

The VINE VARIETIES planted in the New and Old Worlds are increasingly similar, as are the ROOTSTOCKS onto which they are grafted, usually because the New World has concen-

trated on the INTERNATIONAL VARIETIES made famous in the Old World. Old World methods are more traditional, and many aspects of modern viticultural technology, especially MECHANIZATION, have been developed and first used in the New World. MECHANICAL HARVESTING and MECHANICAL PRUNING, for example, were first developed in America, but by the early 1990s there was a high degree of acceptance, of the former at least, in Europe. Some vineyard sites in the Old World have been used for viticulture for hundreds of years, but there are still many potential new vineyard regions to be discovered in the New World (see VINEYARD SITE SELECTION).

Technological advance is by no means the sole prerogative of the New World, however. The development and application of new technology in Europe is the equal of anywhere in the world, as evidenced by work there on CLONAL SELECTION, VINE BREEDING, and CANOPY MANAGEMENT. R.E.S.

Wines and wine-making
If New World wines can be said to have a style of their own it is that they are much more likely to be VARIETAL both in how they are described on the label and in how they taste. Only a (growing) minority of New World wines are made with the clear intention of expressing their geographical provenance (see TERROIR), but the great majority seen on export markets at least are designed to express the fruit of the vine varieties from which they are made. FRUIT DRIVEN is an essentially New World wine description.

New World wine-making, particularly in CALIFORNIA, has been subject to ever more rapid changes of direction and swings of FASHION than its Old World counterpart. This has been possible because both viticulturists and winemakers in the New World are much more willing, and much freer, to experiment. (Those in the Old World are more likely to be restrained by local regulations such as the APPELLATION CONTRÔLÉE laws.)

In the Old World, with its centuries of winemaking tradition, Nature is generally regarded as the determining, guiding force. In much of the New World, however, it may be regarded with suspicion, as an enemy to be subdued, controlled, and mastered in all its detail, thanks to the insights provided by SCIENCE. Most of the world's best wines are made by those who incorporate aspects of both these approaches.

New World winemakers are rather more likely to adopt PROTECTIVE WINE-MAKING methods, attempting to shield grapes, juice, must, and wine from OXYGEN throughout the wine-making process, especially for white wines and light reds. This may involve BLANKETING and MUST CHILLING, using only fully enclosed PRESSES, and careful use of INERT GAS.

Obsession with HYGIENE is generally more marked in the New World than the Old, with the consequence that WATER use is much higher. Rubber boots are not essential for most Old World winemakers.

In general, target TEMPERATURES throughout wine-making are lower in the New World than in the Old. This is especially true for FERMENTATION. Use of wild and/or ambient YEASTS is still relatively rare in the New World—although it is gradually becoming rarer in the Old World too.

The Old World red wine-making practice of following fermentation with an extended MACERATION in the fermentation vessel is increasingly replaced in the New World by RACKING some red wines into barrel before they have completed their first fermentation, in the belief that this, together with MALOLACTIC FERMENTATION in barrel, results in a softer, fuller, earlier maturing wine.

ENZYMES, both for settling and for releasing flavours, are a more common wine-making addition in parts of the New World than in the Old.

New World wines tend to be immediately appealing on release, whereas some Old World wines may be positively off-putting to taste for their first year or two in bottle. In general, however, Old World wines are capable of more extended BOTTLE AGEING than their New World counterparts—although the proportion of exceptions to this rule is steadily increasing as New and Old Worlds move inexorably closer towards each other.

Some Old World observers identify three phases in the development of New World wine production. In the first, the technology phase, producers put all their faith in cellar techniques and technology. In the second, the viticulture phase, the importance of grape quality is acknowledged and techniques such as canopy management are introduced to the vineyard. In the third, terroir phase, producers introduce VINEYARD SITE SELECTION, cooler climates, reduced irrigation, and may eventually seek distinguished sites capable of producing distinctive single-vineyard wines. See also NEW LATITUDE WINES.

New York, north eastern state of the UNITED STATES of America, between the Atlantic and the Great Lakes, historically an important source of wine but now third to CALIFORNIA and WASHINGTON as a US wine-producing state, as measured by acreage planted and annual tonnage (although its LABRUSCA-based products boost its wine volume total above that of Washington). Its inland wine regions share some characteristics with those of Ontario across the border in CANADA. The market for wine in the New York city metropolitan region is one of the world's most competitive and demanding.

History

After unsuccessful trials with VINIFERA around Manhattan Island in the first days of settlement, nothing more is heard of viticulture in New York until the early 19th century. Vine-growing then developed in three regions across the state. The work with native grapes (see AMERICAN VINE SPECIES) of the Long island nurseryman William Robert Prince led to plantings along the Hudson river from which wine was produced in small quantities by the 1840s.

The second region was the Finger lakes district of central New York, where significant plantings of AMERICAN HYBRIDS began in the 1850s. From these a large industry developed, centred on the towns of Hammondsport, Penn Yan, and Naples, and specializing in white wines, both still and sparkling. By the end of the 19th century, there were 24,000 acres/ 9,700 ha of vines in the Finger lakes region.

In western New York, along the lake Erie shore, a 'grape belt' developed after the Civil War. A part of the region's grapes went into wine, but the vineyards were increasingly planted to CONCORD for GRAPE JUICE.

After PROHIBITION, vine-growing in New York was dominated by a few large wineries in the Finger lakes, which continued the traditional trade in still and sparkling white wines from native grapes, but also used neutral blending wine from California. A special niche in New York is the production of sweet KOSHER wine from the Concord grape, as well as dry kosher table wines from other grape varieties.

The new interest in wine that emerged in the 1970s had important results in New York. The Farm Winery Act of 1976 made it economically feasible for financially depressed grape growers to own and operate a small winery by allowing direct sales to consumers. First FRENCH HYBRIDS, then VINIFERA vines, began to be planted more and more widely; new wineries, mostly small, grew up; one entirely new region, the eastern end of Long island, was successfully developed; the large established wineries of the Finger lakes passed through repeated changes of ownership, saw their traditional markets shrink under new competition, and fell into decline. By 2005, New York had 210 wineries, more than 190 of them established since the Farm Winery Act, and produced 40 million gal/1.5 million hl of wine.   T.P. & H.G.

Geography and climate

New York's grape and wine industry preserves from property developers about 31,400 acres/ 12,700 ha of vineyards, and is a significant part of the state's agricultural economy. The industry provides thousands of jobs, generates millions of dollars in sales, contributes millions of dollars in taxes, and attracts over a million TOURISTS each year. About 33 per cent of all grapes grown in the state are destined for wine production, while most are used for grape juice, jellies and jams, and TABLE GRAPES.

New York state has four distinct wine regions which represent eight American Viticultural Areas, or AVAs. The four regions are Finger Lakes (which is itself an AVA and includes Seneca Lake and Cayuga Lake AVAs) in the central part of the state; Lake Erie at the western border; Hudson River, which begins about 40 miles/64 km north of New York City; and Long Island (itself an AVA and including The Hamptons and North Fork AVAs), whose vineyards in the East End are at least 78 miles east of NYC. In spite of frequent low winter temperatures, the growing season has from 2,000 to 2,700 DEGREE DAYS. Its glacier-altered TOPOGRAPHY, strategic bodies of water, and deep, well-drained soils also encourage viticulture. The greatest viticultural hazard is sudden temperature changes; on Christmas Day 1980, for example, temperatures dropped 50 °F/28 °C, killing many vines (see WINTER FREEZE).

Finger lakes The picturesque Finger lakes district is the oldest, and has been the centre of the New York wine industry, with grape-growing and wine production dating back to the 1820s. While Finger lakes is the second largest wine-grape-growing area in the state, 90 per cent of the state's wine is produced there in 83 bonded wineries. The narrow, deep lakes, so named because they look like the fingers of a hand, were carved by Ice Age glaciers, which deposited shallow topsoil on sloping shale beds above the lakes. This combination of steep slopes and deep lakes provides good AIR DRAINAGE and DRAINAGE of water, and fewer extremes of temperature in winter and summer. Since the lakes retain their summer warmth in winter, any cold air sliding down the steep slopes is warmed by the lake and rises, permitting more cold air to drain from the hillside. Conversely, in spring, the now cold water of the lake retards budding until the danger of FROST is past (see LAKE EFFECT). The lakes significant to the wine industry are Canandaigua, Keuka, Seneca, and Cayuga, which are big enough to moderate the climate. The official Finger Lakes AVA was established in 1982, with Cayuga Lake being granted its own AVA in 1988, since local wineries could demonstrate that its lower altitude and greater lake depth created a MESOCLIMATE suitable for the *vinifera* varieties most recently planted there. Cayuga now has 20 bonded wineries. Riesling does exceptionally well in this cool climate, and is attracting consumer attention. Recent plantings of Pinot Noir and Cabernet Franc have also made successful wines. Lake Seneca is emerging as an important wine-producing area with 43 wineries spread around the lake's perimeter. Most of Finger lakes' ESTATE WINE production is sold locally.

Lake Erie Lake Erie is one of the Great lakes, and is the one that provides the most protection against extremes of weather to western New York, since it is lower in latitude and downwind from the Arctic air masses that prevail over lakes Superior and Huron. (Lake Michigan provides similar benefits to the states around its southern tip.)

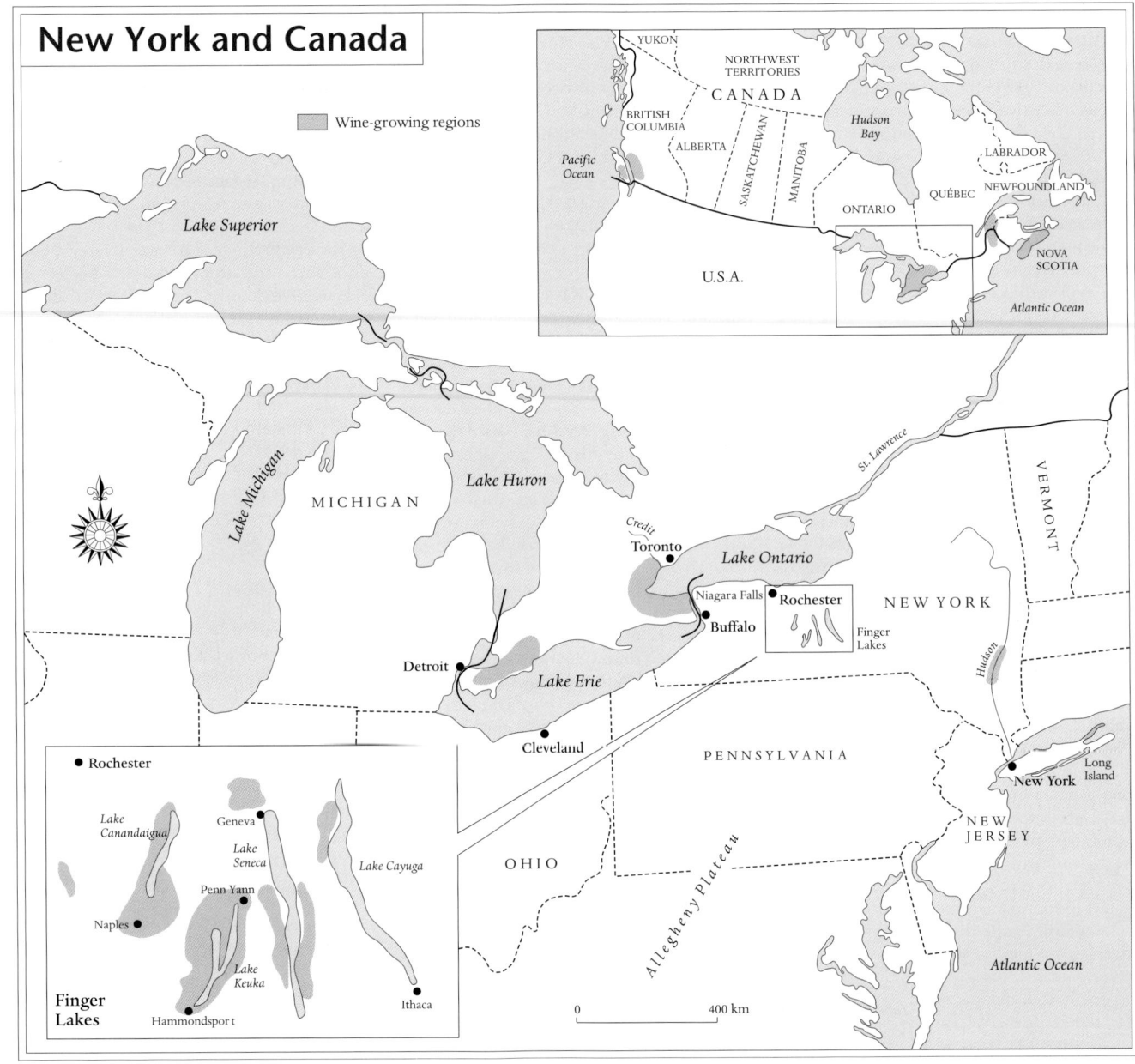

New York and Canada

Wine-growing regions

Finger Lakes

Furthermore, besides the beneficial effects of the lake itself, the 3-mile wide Allegheny plateau, which runs parallel to lake Erie, extends the lake's moderating influence. The Lake Erie AVA was established in 1983, and includes three states: New York around Chautauqua, Pennsylvania, and Ohio, with counties that border on the lake. About 19,000 acres/ 7,700 ha are planted, giving Lake Erie the largest acreage in NY, but it has only nine wineries to date since most of the grapes planted in the region are for grape juice and table grapes—a result of pressure from Prohibitionists in the early 19th century.

Hudson river Wine has been made along Hudson river continuously for the past 300 years,

and it contains the oldest winery in the United States still in operation: Brotherhood America's Oldest Winery Ltd, established in 1839. Hudson River Region became an AVA in 1982. There are wineries on both sides of the Hudson river, but the moderating effects of the river on the local climate are seen as less important than the steep palisaded valley which acts as a conduit for maritime air and weather generated by the Atlantic ocean. Glaciers have deposited shale, slate, schist, and limestone throughout the region. Among the region's 24 wineries is Royal Kedem Wine Corporation, one of the world's largest KOSHER wineries. Seven wineries are nearby in non AVA areas. Seyval Blanc is a prominent white French hybrid and many *viniferas* also dowell.

Long Island The eastern Long Island region consists of three AVAs. The Hamptons, Long Island, itself an AVA, had almost 3,000 acres/ 1,215 ha in 2004. The North Fork of Long Island AVA (1986) has 20 wineries. The Hamptons, Long Island AVA (1985) has three bonded wineries. Overall the East End has 39 producers, some of them using an apparently prospering CUSTOM CRUSH FACILITY. North Fork of Long Island is a peninsula surrounded by Long Island sound on the north, Peconic bay to the south, and the Atlantic ocean to the east. These bodies of water make the area temperate, sending breezes that moderate heat and cold, extending the periods when frost is not a threat, reducing daily temperature swings, and increasing winter precipitation. Local growers feel that the Atlantic's MARITIME influence is similar to its influence on BORDEAUX. Long Island's greatest viticultural hazard, however (apart from BIRDS), is the threat of ocean hurricanes, and some vineyards on the South Fork shore have been sprayed by salt water (see SALINITY). The growing season is at least three weeks longer than other wine regions in New York state, which means that dark-skinned *vinifera* varieties, especially Merlot and Cabernet Franc, predominate for they may be ripened fully almost every year. The North Fork soils have less silt and loam than those on the South Fork, and require IRRIGATION because of their reduced water-holding capacity. The first pioneers to buy potato fields and replant them with vines were Alex and Louisa Hargrave, who founded Hargrave Vineyard (now Castello di Borghese), the first commercial *vinifera* vineyard on Long Island in 1973. The Hamptons is also a peninsula, south of North Fork of Long Island. Thus, Peconic bay now forms the northern edge, and the Atlantic ocean washes the east and south. The Atlantic ocean provides the same benefits to this area as it does to North Fork. Spring fogs keep the area cool and prevent premature BUDBREAK. The soils are deep and have a higher percentage of silt and loam, which makes for better water-holding capacity, requiring less irrigation. Eastern Long Island, with its desirability as a vacation area, enjoys increasingly strong sales of its wines to summer visitors.

Niagara escarpment, possible new AVA bordering lake Ontario's southern shoreline, for which the owner of Warm Lake Estate was campaigning in 2005 with three other wineries constituting the Niagara Wine Trail on this benchland under the escarpment, a LIMESTONE bluff. Pinot Noir does best.

Vine varieties and wines

New York has more vinous diversity than any other major US wine state because it grows AMERICAN VINES, AMERICAN HYBRIDS, FRENCH HYBRIDS, and VINIFERA varieties (see VITIS).

American vines and hybrids The indigenous vines originally grown were *Vitis labrusca* and were valued for their resistance to PHYLLOXERA and their winter hardiness, although the early settlers found the grapes quite different in flavour from those of their European homelands. These native vines often hybridized by chance with other *labruscas* or even other American vine species, and produced a second generation of native grapes commonly grown today, of which the blue-black-skinned CONCORD is the most planted variety. These formed the backbone of the early New York wine industry, although they are often derided today for their FOXY flavour. (So pronounced is this flavour that such varieties were exempted when the US laws on VARIETAL labelling increased the minimum permitted percentage of the cited grape variety from 51 to 75 per cent.)

The major red-pink native varieties are CATAWBA and DELAWARE, both of which are winter hardy and vigorous. Since Catawba has been used in CHARMAT process sparkling wines, it is often subjected to THERMOVINIFICATION, or given limited SKIN CONTACT to yield pink juice. Delaware, on the other hand, is prized for use in fine sparkling wines, and it is fermented cold in stainless steel tanks without skin contact. It has higher sugars and lower acids than Catawba. Both grow in the Finger Lakes and Lake Erie regions.

The white native varieties currently grown include NIAGARA, DUTCHESS, Elvira, and Moore's Diamond, but only Niagara has a bright future in New York state. The others are declining due to susceptibility to disease, poorer tolerance to cold temperatures, limited use for table grapes, grape juice, and wine, and low grape prices, as well as the state's accelerating VINIFERA revolution. Any remaining acreage of these is in the Finger Lakes. Niagara, however, is vigorous, winter hardy, and productive, and has a large following among those who enjoy its decidedly foxy flavour. It is grown mostly in Lake Erie and the Finger Lakes, but there is also a little in the Hudson valley. It is fermented cold, and finished with some RESIDUAL SUGAR to balance its intense aroma.

Of dark-skinned native varieties, Concord is widely planted, being grown in every area of New York except Long Island, and is highly productive. It has low sugars and high acids, and the wine is invariably sweetened, resulting in residual sugar ranging from 1 per cent for table wines to more than 10 per cent for DESSERT WINES. Thermovinification is used to extract colour for sweet red wines, or grapes may be pressed without skin contact when used in sparkling wines. Other red grapes include Fredonia, which was developed in the early 1900s at New York State Agricultural Experiment Station (NYSAES) in Geneva (see CORNELL). Fredonia is similar to Concord, but ripens a useful two weeks earlier. Today it is planted mostly in Lake Erie, and used as a table grape or for juice. Ives is used similarly to Concord, and is planted mostly in the Finger lakes. ISABELLA, which used to be very popular, has been largely replaced by other varieties.

Traditional vine spacing for native varieties is 10 ft by 6 ft (3 m by 2 m) with vines trained to wires for maximum SUNLIGHT interception. William Kniffen developed the widely used umbrella, four cane, and double Kniffen vine-training systems in the 1850s. CHAPTALIZATION is permitted and is usually necessary here, while ACIDIFICATION is forbidden and usually unnecessary. DEACIDIFICATION is often practised, and MALOLACTIC FERMENTATION is increasingly encouraged.

French hybrids French hybrids represent the majority of acreage devoted to dry table wines. Most were developed by French hybridizers, working intensively from 1880 to 1950, to create new varieties that were hardy and disease and pest resistant. Newer hybrids (and some CROSSINGS) have been bred at NYSAES. The most important white hybrid is SEYVAL BLANC, which grows in every New York wine region except Long Island, and which, much to the confusion of some consumers, can be made clean and fruity in STAINLESS STEEL, or can be the much more complex result of BARREL FERMENTATION and malolactic fermentation. VIDAL BLANC and, particularly, VIGNOLES both lend themselves to making late harvest, dessert wines, Vignoles sometimes being beneficially affected by NOBLE ROT. AURORE, once the most widely planted white hybrid grape in New York, has given way to the prestige of Seyval Blanc. Two New York white hybrids, developed at NYSAES and released commercially in 1982, are Cayuga GW3 and Melody. Both of these are vigorous, resistant, and productive, and make fruity off-dry wines. Wine made from Melody is reminiscent of its Pinot Blanc parent. A third white, Traminette (1996), echoing Gewürztraminer, is promising. The red French hybrids are declining in acreage. The most famous are BACO Noir and CHAMBOURCIN, which are vinified in all styles from NOUVEAU to PORT-like; MARÉCHAL FOCH, which can also make a good nouveau using CARBONIC MACERATION; DE CHAUNAC; CHANCELLOR, which needs some OAK ageing to add complexity; and Chelois (Seibel 10878), which works well in blends, especially with Baco Noir.

Vinifera In the 1950s, Charles Fournier, winemaker at Gold Seal winery in the Finger lakes and former winemaker at VEUVE CLICQUOT in Champagne, hired Dr Konstantin Frank, a *vinifera* expert from UKRAINE, to make experimental plantings of ROOTSTOCKS and *vinifera* varieties in a cold climate. By the early 1960s they had produced commercial *vinifera* wines. The most adaptable varieties were brought from Europe and, in descending order of total acreage in 2005, the state's white *vinifera* varieties were Chardonnay, Riesling, Gewürztraminer, Pinot Blanc, and Sauvignon Blanc. The first four are grown successfully in all of New York's regions, but Sauvignon Blanc grows well only on Long Island, where the growing season is long enough to ripen it. Of the red *vinifera* varieties grown in New York—Cabernet Sauvignon, Merlot, Cabernet Franc, and Pinot Noir—Merlot and Cabernet Franc show particular promise. They both ripen earlier and give greater yields than Cabernet Sauvignon, are adaptable to different soil types, and can make fine varietal wines as well as blending well with other red Bordeaux varieties. Cabernet Sauvignon does best on Long Island, needing its long growing season to ripen, while the maritime climate of Long Island has proved too moist and warm for Pinot Noir, which performs better in the warmer areas of the Hudson valley and Finger Lakes. *Vinifera* plantings are increasing, as is VINE

DENSITY, sometimes as close as 3 ft × 5 ft. In the warmer Long Island region, the open LYRE training system is gaining favour. In colder areas, especially the Finger Lakes, a multi-trunk FAN system is preferred to provide insurance against WINTER FREEZE of some canes.

H.L. & H.G.

Cass, B. (ed.), *Oxford Companion to the Wines of North America* (Oxford and New York, 2000).

DeVito, C., *East Coast Wineries: A Complete Guide From Maine to Virginia* (Rutgers, NJ, 2004).

Hedricks, U. P., *The Grapes of New York* (Albany, NY, 1908).

Miller, M., *Wine: A Gentleman's Game* (New York, 1984).

Palmedo, P. F., and Beltrami, E., *The Wines of Long Island: Birth of a Region* (Great Falls, Va., 1993).

New Zealand, southern Pacific islands 1,000 miles/1,600 km away from the nearest land mass, AUSTRALIA, has an agricultural economy that is far more dependent on sheep and dairy products than it is on wine. Vines were first planted in 1819 but it took more than 150 years for New Zealanders to discover that their country's cool, MARITIME climate was suitable for high-quality wine production. Although production is small by world standards (one-tenth of Australia's relatively small wine output), vines are now grown on about 20,000 ha/49,400 acres in nine regions spanning 1,200 km/720 miles, almost the full length of the country's North and South Islands.

History

MISSIONARIES were responsible for New Zealand's first grapevines, planted by an Englishman, the Reverend Samuel Marsden, at Kerikeri on the far north east coast of the North Island in 1819. There is no record of Marsden making wine. That honour belongs to the first British resident, James BUSBY, who established a vineyard at nearby Waitangi in 1836 and subsequently sold his wine to the British troops.

New Zealand's early English working-class settlers preferred BEER to wine, their thirst founding and sustaining a substantial brewing industry. (The country's annual per capita consumption of beer still exceeds 70 l/18 gal per capita, while that of wine is well below 20 l.)

The wine industry has experienced a roller-coaster ride during its relatively brief history. Nature has played a part in its fortunes, thanks to pests such as PHYLLOXERA and diseases such as POWDERY MILDEW, but government policy has had by far the most significant impact. Economic peaks include the growth years 1890–1910, when New Zealand wine managed to capture 25 per cent of the country's total wine consumption (imports, especially from Australia, have long dominated); the Second World War years when visiting American troops offered a new and affluent market; and the period ever since 1958 after the government raised the duty on beer, spirits, and imported wine, and restricted the importation of wine.

New Zealand

Significant developments in wine quality include the era of New Zealand's first government viticulturist, Romeo BRAGATO, who made improvements between 1895 and 1909 despite the ravages of phylloxera; the gradual replacement of AMERICAN HYBRIDS with European VINIFERA varieties from the late 1960s; the first vines planted in the Marlborough region in 1973; the founding of the official trade body the Wine Institute of New Zealand (now NZ Winegrowers) in 1975; the prohibition of wine dilution (as recently as 1983); and the Closer Economic Relations agreement with Australia which, from 1990, forced New Zealand winemakers to compete against wines imported from Australia without the protection of tariffs.

Troughs in the economic fortunes of the wine industry are as common as peaks. Low points have included the damaging effect of the temperance movement between 1910 and 1919. New Zealand voted for national PROHIBITION by a narrow margin in 1919 but the votes of returning servicemen tipped the balance. The post-war economic depression had a predictably adverse effect on the wine industry. As one winemaker put it, 'We had to sell the grapes to get the money to buy the sugar to make the wine' (see CHAPTALIZATION). From 1945 to 1958 a flood of imports severely affected the viability of local wine-making and encouraged the industry to band together and lobby the government for relief, a move which ultimately resulted in significant protection. The rapid expansion of vineyards and a large harvest in 1983 led to a wine surplus, and heavy discounting in 1985 and 1986. The government

For many wine lovers, this is the most appetizing sight of all—long-aged bottles of fine wine, in this case red Burgundy made during the First World War still unbroached in the cellars of Louis **Jadot** in Beaune.

Gevrey Chambertin
1er Cru
1915

intervened with a sponsored VINE PULL SCHEME in 1986, which meant that one-quarter of the country's vines were uprooted.

Troughs in national wine quality occurred after powdery mildew first appeared in 1876, and after the identification of phylloxera in 1895. In most of the rest of the world, vine-growers chose immunity from this voracious root louse by grafting European grape varieties onto American phylloxera-resistant ROOT-STOCKS. Their counterparts in New Zealand chose a second option: they simply planted phylloxera-resistant American hybrids. In 1960, the American ISABELLA vine, nicknamed Albany Surprise, was New Zealand's most widely planted grape variety.

Until 1881 wineries were not able to sell wine directly to the public but had to channel their produce through hotels, the country's only liquor outlets. Both hotels and wineries had to sell a minimum of 9 l/2.4 gal to every customer. From 1955, specialist wine shops were allowed to sell single bottles of New Zealand table wine, although the allocation of licences was carefully controlled. In 1960, restaurants were allowed to sell wine. A BYO licence was introduced in 1976 to allow diners to take their own wine to restaurants. Supermarkets were granted a licence to sell local and imported wine (but not beer or spirits) from 1990. Beer has been sold in supermarkets since 1999.

Geography and climate

New Zealand grows the world's most southerly grapes and, less significantly, the world's most easterly, thanks to an adjacent dateline. A parallel is sometimes made between the southern latitudes of New Zealand's wine regions and those of famous European regions. If New Zealand were in the northern hemisphere, the country would stretch from North Africa to Paris but the moderating influence of the Gulf Stream on European vineyards results in hotter growing conditions than in the vineyards of equivalent southern LATITUDES.

A broad climatic distinction can be made between the warmer North Island regions and those in the cooler South Island, although significant climatic differences exist within the five to six degree latitude span of each island. Under the imperfect HEAT SUMMATION measure of the daily average temperature above 10 °C/50 °F during the vine-growing season, New Zealand qualifies as Region I (along with BORDEAUX and BURGUNDY). This system ignores diurnal and seasonal TEMPERATURE VARIABILITY, however, and the largely MARITIME climate of New Zealand is very different from the CONTINENTAL climate of Burgundy. Bordeaux, with its proximity to the sea, is a closer match, in climate at least, to the North Island region of Hawkes Bay, which happens to produce New Zealand's finest Cabernet Sauvignon.

New Zealand is a green and pleasant land thanks to an abundant RAINFALL throughout most of the country. Plentiful rain promotes good pastures but it can have a negative effect on wine quality, particularly during the critical RIPENING period. Excessive moisture, through poorly drained soils or heavy rainfall, encourages leaf and shoot growth. Dense vine CANOPIES tend to shade innermost leaves and grape bunches to produce green, HERBACEOUS flavours, to delay ripening, and to promote FUNGAL DISEASES. Excessive vine VIGOUR was one of New Zealand's major viticultural hindrances until Dr Richard Smart (this book's viticulture editor) preached the gospel of CANOPY MANAGEMENT during his tenure as government viticulturist between 1982 and 1990. As a result, many winemakers with vines that had produced excessively vegetal Cabernet Sauvignon reds and Sauvignon Blanc whites were able to make higher-quality wines within a single vintage of applying canopy management techniques. Some growers in the Marlborough region claimed that their HARVEST had been advanced by as much as seven days. Dr Smart's canopy management techniques made by far the greatest contribution to improved New Zealand wine quality during the 1980s.

Chief preoccupation of New Zealand vine-growers in the 1990s was VINEYARD SITE SELECTION. New Zealand viticulture was for many years centred on the principal city of Auckland, an important market with one-third of the country's population. Between 1960 and 1983, wine production rose from 4.1 million l to 57.7 million l (15.2 million gal). New Zealand, it was claimed, had the fastest growing wine production in the world. In the late 1960s and early 1970s, the flat, fertile Gisborne river valley usurped Auckland's status as New Zealand's largest wine region. High yields of often relatively lowly grapes such as MÜLLER-THURGAU helped satisfy the nation's thirst for fresh, fruity, and slightly sweet table wine. Later, as PHYLLOXERA devastated Gisborne's grape crop and as demand for higher-quality wines increased, Hawkes Bay became the country's leading wine region. In 1990, Marlborough overtook Hawkes Bay and 15 years later had more than twice Hawkes Bay's productive vineyard area.

Viticulture

New Zealand's remote location has not, as it has done in CHILE, provided a barrier against the importation of vineyard pests and diseases. Phylloxera still threatens around one-tenth of the country's vines which are planted on their own, ungrafted root while FANLEAF DEGENER-ATION and LEAFROLL VIRUSES have a detrimental effect on both the quality and quantity of the country's grape crop. Both are symptoms of an industry which has grown faster than the availability of grafted rootstock and virus indexed vines. Strict QUARANTINE is of course enforced, and easily enforceable, on imported plant material.

As explained above, New Zealand has come to be regarded as a cradle of knowledge about canopy management techniques, and New Zealand VITICULTURISTS, like their wine-making colleagues, are able usefully to spend the New Zealand winter in northern hemisphere wine regions during their growing season. New Zealand's harvest generally takes place from February to May (and sometimes as late as June in parts of Central Otago).

New Zealand's vine-growers are free to IRRIGATE and there are no restrictions on PRUNING or YIELDS, which average about 70 hl/ha (3.6 tons/acre) nationally.

Much of the viticultural equipment has to be imported from Europe, but New Zealand technicians have even developed their own specialist equipment such as the Gallagher leaf-plucking machine (see LEAF REMOVAL). As increasing attention is paid to the selection of vineyard sites (and land in New Zealand is relatively inexpensive), the wine industry may begin to reach its full potential. Flatlands viticulture is the norm in a country where land is plentiful and wine PRICES are only beginning to justify the additional expense and trouble involved in establishing HILLSIDE VINEYARDS. Most New Zealand vine-growers regard the vineyards of the MOSEL-SAAR-RUWER or DOURO valleys with awe and disbelief.

Vine varieties

Sauvignon Blanc, the variety for which New Zealand established an international reputation, is the country's most planted variety with Chardonnay a distant second. Pinot Noir overtook Cabernet Sauvignon in 1997 to become the country's most planted red variety, although a significant percentage of the Pinot Noir crop is destined for sparkling wine production. Plantings of Riesling, the sixth most planted variety, continue to grow slowly as the often slightly sweet and frequently very good wine made from it battles to lose its unfashionable image in the local market place. Other varieties planted on a total of more than 100 ha/250 acres are Muscat Dr Hogg (a bulk grape used to give extra fruitiness to basic Müller-Thurgau), Chenin Blanc, Müller-Thurgau, Gewurztraminer, Merlot, Sémillon, Syrah, Cabernet Franc, Malbec, and a rapidly expanding acreage of Pinot Gris. All vine materials are screened for VIRUS DISEASES by an official government-run agency, and the number of CLONES available from the country's nurseries is considerably more limited than, for example, in Europe.

Wine-making

The youthful and dynamic New Zealand wine industry has been greatly influenced by Australia's ADELAIDE University, which provided training, and personnel, for many New Zealand winemakers. In recent years, however, local universities and technical institutes have begun to offer courses in viticulture and

Icewine, sweet wine made from frozen grapes such as this bunch of Vidal on Ontario's Niagara Peninsula, is the Canadian wine industry's pride and joy, although **climate change** is having an effect even here.

oenology. These include LINCOLN Unviersity, Blenheim Poly-Tech, Massey University, Hawkes Bay Poly-Tech, and Gisborne Poly-Tech. Auckland University now offers an MSc in Wine Science. Traditional wine-making techniques from benchmark European wine regions have also been adopted, however. The country's southern hemisphere location has had a positive effect on the development of wine styles and wine-making techniques. Many young New Zealand winemakers choose to work a second annual vintage in Europe and gain a wider perspective on the world of wine (see FLYING WINEMAKERS). A reverse migration of mostly young French winemakers has a similar effect.

The country's isolation does have disadvantages, however, such as adding to the cost of importing highly fashionable new oak BARRIQUES from France (or at the very least from the nearest cooperage in Australia). An efficient domestic STAINLESS STEEL industry, however, developed to serve New Zealand's dairy industry, has provided economy and ingenuity in winery tank design.

Winemakers in New Zealand operate relatively free from regulatory constraint, with ACIDIFICATION, DEACIDIFICATION, and ENRICHMENT all permitted. It is a remarkable tribute to the ambitions of the industry, especially abroad, that overall wine quality is as high as it is.

In 2001, a small number of winemakers adopted the SCREW CAP as a closure instead of traditional cork. They created an organization The Screwcap Initiative to assist members with any technical aspects of application and to promote the new seal to an often sceptical market locally and in export markets. Four years later, more than two-thirds of all New Zealand wine bottles were sealed with a screw cap.

New Zealanders have so far tended to worship the winemaker rather than the vineyard. This NEW WORLD phenomenon is in direct contrast to the French view of the primacy of TERROIR. A decade or two will no doubt reveal the ephemeral nature of winemakers and the permanence of geography, but until that time, New Zealand winemakers will continue to be revered by an adoring domestic public.

Industry organization

The industry is dominated by MONTANA, the Villa Maria/Vidals/Esk Valley group, and the Nobilo Group, which is part of CONSTELLATION. Only the smaller wineries do not rely on fruit bought in from the country's grape-growers although many do supplement their own grapes with grapes grown under contract.

As in other New World wine-producing countries such as ARGENTINA and AUSTRALIA, many wineries have traditionally been located far from vineyards, and the development of South Island wine regions, separated from many winery headquarters by the treacherous Cook strait, has only exacerbated this phenomenon in New Zealand. Increasing attention to field CRUSHING facilities, and the construction of wineries, or at least PRESSING stations, closer to the vineyards, was a notable development during the 1990s.

Every winery and grape-grower must belong to NZ Winegrowers, the statutory body formed in 1975 as the Wine Institute of New Zealand, and re-named in 2002 when it combined its membership with that of the New Zealand Grapegrowers Council Inc. NZ Winegrowers collects a production-based fee from its members. It has had an enormous influence on the development of the image and quality of local wine and has overseen New Zealand's substantial export attack on the United Kingdom, which, as shipments to the US increase substantially, now imports less than half of all the wine exported from New Zealand.

Wine regions
See map.

Gisborne This east coast North Island region based on the town of the same name has shaken off its image as a BULK wine region and has largely recovered from phylloxera with massive replantings. By the mid 2000s, 93 per cent of Gisborne vines (as compared with 92 per cent of Hawkes Bay vines, and 98 per cent of Marlborough vines) were GRAFTED on to phylloxera-resistant rootstocks. Replanting also improved the mix of varieties in Gisborne. Müller-Thurgau, the dominant variety before replanting began in earnest, now represents only 10 per cent of the Chardonnay acreage. Gisborne vine-growers and winemakers have given their region the rather contentious title Chardonnay Capital of New Zealand. Gisborne Chardonnay is certainly the country's most distinctive regional example of the variety, with soft and charming fruit flavours that often resemble ripe peach, pineapple, and melon. Gewürztraminer is Gisborne's other claim to vinous fame.

Montana established a large winery in Gisborne, chiefly to process grapes for bag-in-BOX packaged blends which accounted for nearly 60 per cent of the nation's wine sales by the late 1990s but now account for less than 30 per cent. In contrast to these large-scale, high-tech production facilities are the small batch presses and BARRIQUES used to make limited edition, premium Chardonnay. At the other end of the production scale are many small LIFESTYLE WINERIES that make only premium bottled table wine or traditional method sparkling wines. They include Millton Vineyards, New Zealand's first certified ORGANIC winery, which now produces grapes and wine according to the principles of BIODYNAMISM. Most Gisborne grapes are grown by farmers who sell them to wineries under long-term contract, or to the highest bidder. Several Auckland wineries regularly buy Gisborne grapes, which are mechanically harvested before being transported for nine hours by road in covered dump trucks. Varieties of grapes that are low in PHENOLICS, such as Müller-Thurgau, appear to suffer few ill effects and may even gain flavour from this period of compulsory SKIN CONTACT, but Sauvignon Blanc and Gewürztraminer can suffer as a result.

Hawkes Bay (strictly, Hawke's Bay) around the town of Napier is one of New Zealand's older wine regions and certainly one of the best. Complex soil patterns and MESOCLIMATES make it difficult to generalize about the wines of such a diverse region, particularly when they are made by such an eclectic group of winemakers. Situated on the east coast of the North Island, 215 km/130 miles south of Gisborne and 323 km/194 miles north of Wellington, Hawkes Bay frequently records the country's highest sunshine hours. The terrain varies from coastal ranges that rise to 1600 m/5,300 ft to wide, fertile plains consisting of alluvial and gravelly soils. A high water table and fertile soils can result in excessive vine vigour over much of the plains. In other parts of the region, deep, well-drained gravel soils encourage WATER STRESS and many vines require irrigation during long, dry periods. In pursuit of wine quality, vineyards were established on free-draining soils of lower fertility, at least from the mid 1980s. For ease of cultivation, vines have been almost exclusively planted on flat land, despite the allure of nearby limestone hills which may offer superior aspect and DRAINAGE. A collective of local grape growers and winemakers has identified an approximate 800 ha of deep shingle soils as an ideal area for the production of high-quality wines, particularly Syrah, Cabernet Sauvignon, and Merlot. The defined area has been named Gimblett Gravels, a district name that now appears on some of Hawkes Bay's better red wines.

Chardonnay and Merlot are the most planted Hawkes Bay varieties. The best Hawkes Bay reds are a blend of Merlot and Cabernet Sauvignon, often with Cabernet Franc and/or Malbec playing a supporting role. They have intense berry and cassis flavours, often with a gently HERBACEOUS reminder of their moderately COOL CLIMATE origin and, sometimes, strong OAK influence from up to two years' maturation in new French BARRIQUES. By 2005, the exalted status of BORDEAUX BLENDS was being tested by a small but rapidly expanding volume of Syrah, which at its best can perform with distinction. Hawkes Bay Chardonnay may lack the seductive charm of the Gisborne equivalent but the best have intense citrus flavours and a brooding elegance that are seldom matched by the wines of other regions. Hawkes Bay Sauvignon Blanc is a softer, fleshier wine than the better-known Marlborough Sauvignon Blanc. It often has a nectarine or stone fruit character, a useful indicator of regional identity.

Marlborough Marlborough is the biggest of New Zealand's big three wine regions. Industry giant Montana planted the first vines in Marlborough when it established the South Island's first commercial vineyard in 1973. At the time it seemed an enormous gamble but after the vines reached full production Montana's investment returned a handsome dividend in terms of quality and profit. Other producers soon followed to establish wineries in the region or to secure a supply of grapes for the 18-hour journey north to Auckland or Gisborne. The single wine that put Marlborough Sauvignon Blanc on the international map was CLOUDY BAY, in 1985. Since 1989, winemakers based outside the region have been able to use the services of a growing number of CUSTOM CRUSH FACILITIES to process grapes into juice or wine which can then be transported in bulk with less risk of extracting astringent PHENOLICS from grape skins. The availability of contract wine-making facilities has encouraged an increasing number of vine-growers to process part or all of their crop into wine for sale under their own label.

Marlborough, at the north eastern tip of the South Island, consists of a large, flat, river valley with deep deposits of silt and gravel. A number of soil patterns are found throughout the valley and even within single vineyards, leading to significant variations in quality and style depending on the grape source. Shallow, stony soils, which aid DRAINAGE and limit fertility, are favoured for high-quality wine production. Surface boulders help reflect the sun's rays and retain warmth during Marlborough's cool, clear, summer nights. Irrigation is widely used throughout the valley to establish vines in the sometimes arid, free-draining soils and to relieve vine stress during the typically dry Marlborough summer. Many of Marlborough's best wines are made from irrigated grapes, which, it is claimed, would have suffered a loss in quality if the vines were forced to rely on a natural supply of ground water. Since the temptation to over-irrigate is greater for contract grape-growers who are paid by the ton than for winemakers whose reputation relies on the quality of their wines, most wine producers try to build quality incentives into grape payments (see PRICE), but they acknowledge the difficulty involved in assessing grape quality. Grape SUGARS, ACIDS, and even dry EXTRACT levels can be quantified, but all fail to distinguish grapes that can make good wine from those that have the potential to make truly great wine. It is undeniable that many of New Zealand's best wines are made from grapes that are grown in winery-owned vineyards where the winemaker assumes total responsibility for wine quality.

Sauvignon Blanc is Marlborough's best-known and most planted variety. These pungent, aromatic wines that blend tropical fruit flavours with gooseberry and capsicum herbaceousness are probably the closest thing that New Zealand has to a national wine style (however much the country's winemakers would prefer to build their international reputation on more prestigious wines, such as Chardonnay or Pinot Noir). Marlborough Pinot Noir has overtaken Chardonnay to become the region's second most planted grape variety, and a small but growing proportion of the Marlborough Pinot and Chardonnay crop is used in traditional method SPARKLING WINE production. Riesling is another very successful Marlborough vine variety; it reaches its apogee as a sweet, luscious, botrytis-affected dessert wine. BOTRYTIZED wines can be produced here most years although the results vary considerably with vintage conditions.

Northland Northland, at the very northern tip of the country, was the birthplace of New Zealand wine. The region's warm, wet, temperate climate has proved to be a barrier to good-quality wine production, particularly on the wetter west coast. Modern viticultural methods and careful site selection have allowed several producers to establish relatively rot-resistant varieties such as Cabernet Sauvignon and Syrah with promising results.

Auckland Auckland, the largest city, gives its name to the one New Zealand wine region where winery visitors can be assured of finding wines made from grapes grown as far south as Canterbury in the South Island, and are more likely to be offered wine from Marlborough and Hawkes Bay than the product of a local vineyard. Auckland viticulture declined during the rapid growth of Gisborne, Hawkes Bay, and Marlborough through the 1970s and 1980s but began to grow in the 1990s as grape-growers adopted canopy-thinning techniques to correct vine vigour. New subregions, including Waiheke Island, Clevedon, and Matakana, are now producing high-quality and highly fashionable reds which have helped raise Auckland's profile and esteem as a wine region.

Wairarapa Wairarapa, which includes the **Martinborough** region, is at the southern end of the North Island about one hour's drive from the nation's capital, Wellington. In 2004, Wairarapa had less than 4 per cent of the country's vines but 11 per cent of its winemakers. They are typically small-scale, LIFESTYLE producers with a quality-at-all-costs attitude to wine-making and a passionate faith in their region's potential. Wairarapa winemakers argue over whether the region is more suitable for Pinot Noir (Ata Rangi, Dry River, Martinborough Vineyards) or Cabernet Sauvignon (Benfield & Delamere), but there is ample evidence that both varieties perform well. In their quest to make great wine, most producers crop their vines so that YIELDS are considerably below the national average, a significant factor in the region's success. In terms of topography, climate, and soils Wairarapa might easily be considered a miniature Marlborough, were it not for the region's ability to make top-quality reds on a regular basis.

Nelson Nelson is the South Island's most northerly wine region, nearly two hours' drive across high ranges from Marlborough. The rolling hills of Nelson rise from a scenic coastline to form a beautiful setting for the region's 15 wineries. Sauvignon Blanc has overtaken Chardonnay to become the region's main grape variety, thanks to world demand for this varietal. Pinot Noir and Chardonnay are second and third respectively with Riesling a distant fourth. The varied topography of Nelson makes it difficult to generalize about weather and soils, although records show that the region is slightly cooler and wetter than the Marlborough average.

Canterbury Canterbury, around Christchurch on the central east coast of the South Island, has three subregions: **Waipara** in North Canterbury, the plains west of Christchurch, and Banks Peninsula to the east of the city. The region is cool and dry with a moderate risk of October and April FROSTS. Low rainfall and light soils of moderate fertility help control vine vigour and canopy here. Viticultural research at LINCOLN has had a considerable influence on selecting suitable vine varieties for the local growing conditions and in assisting local growers with viticultural techniques. It is no surprise, given Canterbury's cool climate, that Chardonnay and Pinot Noir are the region's most planted varieties, with Riesling in third place and Pinot Gris fourth.

Central Otago Central Otago grows New Zealand's, and the world's, most southerly grapevines, some of them cultivated south of the 45th parallel. It is New Zealand's only wine region with a CONTINENTAL climate, providing greater diurnal and seasonal TEMPERATURE VARIABILITY than any other. Most Central Otago vines are planted on HILLSIDE VINEYARDS to give better sun exposure and reduce frost risk. No other New Zealand wine region is as dependent on a single grape variety. In 2006, Pinot Noir represents nearly 75 per cent of the region's vines. The growth in vineyard area, and development of new districts within the larger region, have been extraordinary. The now crowded valley at Gibbston was, with Wanaka, one of the original areas to be planted with vines as recently as the early 1980s. Bannockburn is widely regarded as the most successful district although recent vineyards in the Cromwell/Bendigo and Alexandra districts may challenge Bannockburn's crown. Central Otago's often voluptuous and intensely fruity Pinot Noir has helped put New Zealand red wine on the world map. The wines from this youthful and very experimental area have evolved rapidly in quality with potential for further gain. Pinot Gris is in very distant second place with Chardonnay and Riesling close behind.

Waitaki on LIMESTONE in North Otago was rapidly being developed in the mid 2000s.

R.F.C.

The New Zealand Vineyard & Wine Industry Review (Hamilton, 2005).

Cooper, M., *Wine Atlas of New Zealand* (Auckland, 2002).

Courtney, C., *Wine in New Zealand* (Auckland, 2003).

Thompson, J., *Celebrating New Zealand Wine* (Auckland. 2004)

Neyret, or **Neiret**, rare, dark-berried vine still found in PIEMONTE at the foot of the Alps. DNA PROFILING at Torino established that it is identical to the French Chatus of south east France.

Niagara, American hybrid grown successfully in NEW YORK state. This VITIS *labrusca* variety is vigorous, productive, and withstands low temperatures well. Known as the white answer to CONCORD, one of its parents, it makes wines with a strong FOXY flavour. The other is Cassady, mainly *labrusca* with some VINIFERA genes. It was created in Niagara, New York, in 1872. See also CANADA.

Niederösterreich, Lower Austria, the most important wine region in AUSTRIA, in the far north east of the country.

Nieddera, promising Sardinian red wine grape.

Nielluccio, planted on 1,600 ha/4,000 of the island in 2000, is CORSICA's most planted indigenous grape variety, although it was probably brought there from the Italian mainland, presumably by the GENOESE who ruled the island until the late 18th century, as it is ampelographically identical to the SANGIOVESE of Toscana. In 1988, however, it represented only 14 per cent of all Corsican vines, thanks to the domination of the coarser varieties imported by French immigrants from North Africa in the 1960s and 1970s. Often blended with the, arguably more interesting, other major indigenous red wine variety SCIACARELLO, it constitutes an increasing proportion of the island's APPELLATION CONTRÔLÉE reds and, particularly, rosés, for which it is especially suitable. It is the principal ingredient in Patrimonio, on whose clay-limestone soils it thrives. It buds early and ripens late and is therefore susceptible to late frosts in spring and rot during the harvest.

Nincusa, minor dark-berried grape grown on the coast of CROATIA.

nitrogen, mineral element and inert colourless, odourless, tasteless gas that is extremely useful in both grape-growing and wine-making. Nitrogen makes up 78 per cent of air and, as an inert constituent, it dilutes air's highly reactive constituent OXYGEN, thereby moderating the rate at which RESPIRATION and burning occur. In its combined forms, nitrogen is an essential element in AMINO ACIDS, PROTEINS, and ENZYMES, without which life as we know it could not exist. In its combination with hydrogen as ammonia, nitrogen is vital to plant growth and is the essential element in most FERTILIZERS.

Viticulture

Nitrogen has a major impact on vineyard VIGOUR, and potentially on wine quality. Nitrogen is essential for vine growth and is one of the three major elements, along with POTASSIUM and PHOSPHORUS, needed most for plant growth. It is an important component of proteins, and also of chlorophyll. The most common symptoms of nitrogen deficiency, which can be expected on sandy soils low in organic matter, are reduced vigour and pale green or yellow leaves. Soil and plant tests can be used as a guide to the use of nitrogen fertilizers.

Much more caution is needed with vines than most other plants in applying nitrogen fertilizers, or large amounts of manure, or planting in soils naturally rich in nitrogen. COVER CROPS containing clover and other legumes should also be monitored carefully as they might add excessive nitrogen to the vineyard soil.

Whatever the origin, too much nitrogen in a vineyard results in excessive vegetative vine growth, termed high vigour. Such vineyards typically show reduced YIELD and quality owing to the SHADE effects. CANOPY MANAGEMENT procedures may be used to overcome some of these effects, but will not eliminate them completely. Vineyards with excessive nitrogen supplies are also prone to poor FRUIT SET (COULURE, for example) and are more susceptible to BOTRYTIS BUNCH ROT. Excessive nitrogen is also considered to have a direct and negative effect on wine quality, reducing SUGARS, COLOUR, and PHENOLICS, and increasing ACIDITY. High nitrogen levels in the soil also lead to increased wine levels of urea, ethyl CARBAMATES, and HISTAMINES. In some parts of Europe such as Germany, excessive nitrogen fertilization of vineyards has led to pollution of water supplies with nitrates which pose hazards to human health.

A feature of vineyards producing high fruit quality is that they have a restricted supply of nitrogen. Along with WATER STRESS, this is one of two important checks on vine growth which result in the vine BALANCE that is essential for premium wine quality. Sometimes all grass cover crops are grown to use up soil-rich supplies of nitrogen, and so make it less available to vines.

On the other hand, severe nitrogen deficiency is equally disadvantageous to quality, especially for white wines. Fruit from nitrogen-deficient vineyards can be lower in fermentable SUGARS and may also result in STUCK FERMENTATIONS, with the concomitant risk of forming SULFIDES. See also ATYPICAL AGEING.

R.E.S.

Wine-making

In combination with phosphorus and potassium, nitrogen can serve as a critical factor in YEAST growth and therefore FERMENTATION, notably in HOME WINE-MAKING of FRUIT WINES. Ammonium ions, primary amino acids, and small peptides, but not the secondary amino acids proline and hydroxyproline, are the principal forms of nitrogen present in grapes that can be used by yeast; these nitrogen components constitute what is often referred to as yeast assimilable nitrogen (YAN). Simple tests have only recently been developed for measuring YAN so that a deficiency of this essential yeast nutrient can now be easily determined. Nitrogen can also affect wine composition: in high concentrations it is associated with intensified AROMAS, while low concentrations favour the formation of HYDROGEN SULFIDE.

Obtained by fractional DISTILLATION of liquid air, nitrogen in both gaseous and liquid forms is a major commercial product used in a wide range of industrial activities. As ammonia, it is the starting material for most fertilizer mixtures. In liquid form, it has myriad uses in REFRIGERATION. In pure gas form, it is used to prevent a wide range of sensitive products from coming into contact with oxygen. Wine is just one of these.

Nitrogen as an inert gas is extremely useful to the winemaker in filling the head space in closed stainless steel tanks and bottles (see SPARGING and LEFTOVER WINE). Experiments in northern Italy have shown that if a bladder PRESS is enclosed in nitrogen, white wines are fresher and more fragrant, require less SULFUR DIOXIDE, and have higher levels of antioxidants (see wine and HEALTH). Nitrogen is more expensive but more effective than INERT GAS MIXTURE at preserving wine from potential harmful contact with oxygen.

A.D.W.

Champagnol, F., *Éléments de physiologie de la vigne et de viticulture générale* (St-Gely-du-Fesc, 1984).

Peyrot des Gachons, C., Van Leeuwen, C., Tominaga, T., Soyer, J.-P., Gaudillère, J.-P., and Dubourdieu, D., 'The influence of water and nitrogen deficit on fruit ripening and aroma potential of *Vitis vinifera* L. cv Sauvignon blanc in field conditions', *Journal of the Science of Food and Agriculture*, 85/1 (2005), 73–85.

Rantz, J. M. (ed.), 'Nitrogen in grapes and wine', Proc. Int. Symposium, Seattle, June 1991, *Amer. Soc. for Enol. and Vitic.* (Davis, Calif., 1991).

Winkler, A. J., *et al.* (eds.), *General Viticulture* (2nd edn, Berkeley, Calif., 1974).

NMR, see NUCLEAR MAGNETIC RESONANCE.

Noah, seminal figure in the history of wine according to the BIBLE. See also ORIGINS OF VITICULTURE.

Noah is also the name of a relatively undistinguished AMERICAN HYBRID white grape variety first propagated in 1869 in Illinois. It is particularly hardy and has been widely grown in France and eastern Europe but is of declining importance.

no alcohol wine is a term sometimes used for wine with an ALCOHOLIC STRENGTH of less than 1 or 2 per cent. For more details, see DEALCOHOLIZED WINE.

Noble Joué, occasional synonym for PINOT vines. See also TOURAINE.

noble rot, also known as *pourriture noble* in French, *Edelfäule* in German, *muffa* in Italian, and sometimes simply as botrytis, is the benevolent form of BOTRYTIS BUNCH ROT, in which the *Botrytis cinerea* fungus attacks ripe, undamaged white wine grapes and, given the right weather, can result in extremely sweet grapes which may look disgusting but have undergone such a complex transformation that they are capable of producing probably the world's finest, and certainly the longest-living, sweet wines. Indeed, the defining factor of a great VINTAGE for sweet white wine in areas specializing in its production is the incidence of noble rot. The malevolent form, which results if the grapes are damaged, unripe, or conditions are unfavourable, is known as GREY ROT.

Ideal conditions for the development of noble rot are a TEMPERATE CLIMATE in which the humidity associated with early morning mists that favour the development of the fungus is followed by warm, sunny autumn afternoons in which the grapes are dried and the progress of the fungus is restrained. In cloudy conditions in which the humidity is unchecked, the fungus may spread so rapidly that the grape skins split and the grapes succumb to grey rot. If, however, the weather is unremittingly hot and dry, then the fungus will not develop at all and the grapes will simply accumulate sugar rather than undergoing the chemical transformations associated with noble rot, so the result is less complex SWEET WINE.

In favourable conditions, the botrytis fungus *Botrytis cinerea* spreads unpredictably from grape to grape and bunch to bunch in different parts of the vineyard, penetrating the skins of whole, ripe grapes with filaments which leave minute brown spots on the skin but leave the skin impenetrable by other, harmful microorganisms. The grapes turn golden, then pink or purple, and then, when they are in a severely dehydrated state, they turn brown, shrivel to a sort of moist raisin, and may seem to be covered with a fine grey powder that looks like ash (to which the word *cinerea* refers). It is almost incredible that such unappetizing-looking grapes can produce such sublime wine, and there have been many instances in which nobly rotten grapes have been discarded, or at least unrecognized, in wine regions unfamiliar with the phenomenon.

These visible changes are an outward sign of the extraordinary changes that occur inside the grape. More than half of the grape's water content is lost due either directly to the action of the fungus or to loss by evaporation as the skins eventually deteriorate. Meanwhile, *Botrytis cinerea* consumes both the SUGAR IN GRAPES and, especially, ACIDS, so that the overall effect is to increase the sugar concentration, or MUST WEIGHT, considerably in an ever-decreasing quantity of juice. The fungus typically reduces a grape's sugar concentration by a third, but reduces the TARTARIC ACID by five-sixths and the usually less important MALIC ACID by a third.

While it metabolizes these sugars and acids, the fungus forms a wide range of chemical compounds in the grape juice, including GLYCEROL (quite apart from that formed by alcoholic fermentation), ACETIC ACID, gluconic acid, various ENZYMES especially LACCASE and PECTINASE, as well as the yeast-inhibiting glycoprotein dubbed 'botyticine', which limits yeast growth and increases the production of acetic acid and glycerol during fermentation. The PHENOLICS in the grape skins are also broken down by the fungus so that the TANNIN content of the juice is significantly reduced. In sum, botrytized grape juice is very different from regular grape juice, and not just because of its intense levels of sugar.

It is unusual for all grapes on a vine, or even on a single bunch, to be affected in exactly the same way, to exactly the same effect, and at exactly the same speed, which is why the HARVEST of a botrytis-affected vineyard can necessitate several passages, or TRIES, during which individual bunches, or parts of them, are picked at optimum infection level, and grapes affected by grey rot may have to be eliminated.

Weather conditions other than alternating early mists and warm afternoons can result in a satisfactory noble rot infection. In cold, wet weather, noble rot may form at a reasonable rate on fully ripe grapes, and grey rot be kept at bay. Wind can help to dehydrate the grapes and concentrate the sugars.

See SAUTERNES for details of common weather patterns there. See BOTRYTIZED WINES for details of where and how they are made, and their history.

Olney, R., *Yquem* (London, 1986).

Ribéreau-Gayon, P., Dubourdieu, D., Donèche, B., and Lonvaud, D., *Traité d'Œnologie* 1: *Microbiologie du vin: Vinifications* (Paris, 1998), translated by J. M. Branco, as *Handbook of Enology* 1: *The Microbiology of Wine and Vinifications* (Chichester, 2000).

Tregoat, O., Gaudillère, J.-P., Choné, X., and Van Leeuwen, C., 'Étude du régime hydrique et de la nutrition azotée de la vigne par des indicateurs physiologiques. Influence sur le comportement de la vigne et la maturation du raisin (*Vitis vinifera* L. cv Merlot, 2000, Bordeaux)', *Journal International des Sciences de la Vigne et du Vin*, 36/3 (2002), 133–42.

Nobling is a 1939 crossing of Silvaner × Gutedel (Chasselas) that has declined in importance even in Baden, where there were more than 100 ha/250 acres in the early 1990s. It can achieve good MUST WEIGHTS and yet retain acidity but it needs a relatively good site that can be used more profitably for more fashionable or productive varieties.

node, the part of a plant's stem at which a leaf is attached. In the grapevine, this zone is swollen and bears the leaf winter BUD and LATERAL SHOOT. TENDRILS or INFLORESCENCES are also borne at nodes on the side opposite to the bud.   B.G.C.

Noilly Prat, not a wine at all but a dry white French VERMOUTH particularly useful for COOKING. Of the huge volume of vermouth produced and assiduously marketed each year, Noilly Prat has sufficient character to appeal to the wine drinker (although see also CHAMBÉRY).

Noir, French for black and therefore a common suffix for dark-berried vine varieties.

Noirien is, most commonly, the name given to the PINOT family of grape varieties found primarily in eastern France that are related to or closely associated with Pinot Noir: Pinot Gris, Pinot Blanc, Auxerrois, and Chardonnay. In addition, Noirien is a synonym for Pinot Noir and, more misleadingly, Noirien Blanc is used as a synonym for Chardonnay.

non-vintage, often abbreviated to NV, a blended wine, particularly champagne or sparkling wine, which may contain the produce of several different VINTAGES, although in champagne-making practice it is usually substantially based on the most recent vintage, to which some additional ingredients from older years, often called 'reserve wines', may be added.

Within the EUROPEAN UNION, basic TABLE WINE may not be sold with a vintage year on it and is in practice often a blend made throughout the year so that the first blend of the winter season, typically, may contain a mixture of wine from both the new and last year's vintages.

normalized difference vegetation index (NDVI) is the most widely used indicator of plant biomass in agriculture. In viticulture, NDVI provides a relative measure of canopy size and condition and therefore correlates with VIGOUR. It is calculated from measures of reflected light at wavebands corresponding to red and infrared light. See also REMOTE SENSING.   R.G.V.B.

Hall, A., Lamb, D. W., Holzapfel, B., and Louis, J., 'Optical remote sensing applications in viticulture—a review', *Australian Journal of Grape and Wine Research*, 8 (2002), 36–47.

North Coast, general CALIFORNIA umbrella region and AVA implying north of San Francisco but technically not including Marin county because so few grapes are grown there. It does include all vineyards in LAKE, MENDOCINO, NAPA, and SONOMA counties and has rather more homogeneous growing conditions than many suspect. The name appears on some relatively prestigious wines assembled from, especially, Napa and Sonoma and also on some pretty ordinary blends.

North East Victoria Zone, wine zone in the Australian state of VICTORIA incorporating the wine regions of Alpine Valleys, Beechworth, Glenrowan, King Valley, and Rutherglen.

Northern Rivers Zone, on the north coast of NEW SOUTH WALES in Australia with one region, Hastings River.

Northern Slopes Zone, Australian wine zone parallel with NORTHERN RIVERS ZONE but on the western (inland) side of the Great Dividing range. Developing rapidly up to and after the turn of the 21st century, in part supplying its own wineries, and in part selling to QUEENSLAND wineries, particularly in the Granite Belt.

North West Victoria Zone comprises the high-yielding, irrigated vineyards of the Murray Darling and Swan Hill regions falling on the VICTORIA side of the Murray river in Australia.

Norton, arguably the only variety of AMERICAN VINE SPECIES origin making a premium quality wine. Little known and little grown outside the eastern and midwestern UNITED STATES, Norton is undoubtedly underrated because of entrenched bias against non-VINIFERA varieties. In Arkansas and MISSOURI, it was the mainstay of an extremely important wine industry. Leon D. Adams calls Norton 'the best of all native American red-wine grapes' and praises it for its wines' lack of FOXY character.

The origin of this dark-skinned variety is uncertain, but it takes its name from Dr D. Norton of Richmond, Virginia, a pioneer grape-grower. Most agree it is a vine of the species VITIS *aestivalis* although there are indications of *Vitis labrusca* parentage also. Many argue it is identical to Cynthiana, also grown in Missouri, Arkansas, and Virginia from the 1850s onwards.

Norton is tolerant of BUNCH ROTS, and other fungal diseases such as BLACK ROT, ANTHRACNOSE, DOWNY MILDEW, and POWDERY MILDEW, and its roots are tolerant of PHYLLOXERA. The vine is vigorous, and requires a long growing season. The grapes are acidic, but the wine is indistinguishable by taste from wine made from *vinifera* grapes. Grapes are very dark coloured and full flavoured, and Norton reliably

produces healthy fruit in places with high summer rainfall even without SPRAYING.

R.E.S. & J.R.

Adams, L. D., *The Wines of America* (3rd edn, New York and London, 1985).

nose, the most sensitive form of TASTING equipment so far encountered, the sense of TASTE being so inextricably linked with the sense of smell. When the nose is blocked, whether by a cold or by mechanical means, the ability to taste either food or drink is seriously impaired—so much so that cold sufferers have to resort to decongestants if the need for their tasting skills is serious.

Nose is also used as a synonym for the smell, AROMA, or BOUQUET of a wine, as in wines having 'a nose of raspberries', 'a raspberry nose', or even 'raspberries on the nose'.

Nosiola, the only remaining white grape variety native to TRENTINO in northern Italy. It is grown principally on the hills around the village of Pressano, where is produces dry wines, and in the Valle dei Laghi to the west of Trento, where it is used to produce Vino Santo (see VIN SANTO). Only about 100 ha/250 acres are planted, yet interest in the variety has been revived in recent years as several producers, notably Cesconi, have demonstrated that it can, when made with care, produce fragrant, zippy whites of real interest. About 4,500 hl/118,800 gal of varietal Nosiola are made under the Trentino DOC each year. It is an ingredient in the much rarer Trentino Sorni Bianco and can also be used as part of the grape mix in the Valdadige DOC. Recent DNA PROFILING at SAN MICHELE ALL'ADIGE revealed a surprising parent–offspring relationship with the Swiss RÈZE, a very ancient alpine variety. D.C.G.

notch grafting, a method of GRAFTING vines that resembles CLEFT GRAFTING. It differs in that the cut trunk is not split across, but instead the scion pieces are cut to fit a V-shaped notch made on either side of the trunk to a length of about 3 cm/1 in. The scion pieces are often tacked into place. Notch grafts are not as secure as cleft grafts. A related method is the bark graft done later in spring when the bark lifts freely, but again the union is sometimes weak. B.G.C.

nouveau, French for new, and a specific style of wine designed to be drunk only weeks rather than months or years after the HARVEST. The most famous and successful nouveau is BEAUJOLAIS Nouveau, which, at its peak, in 1988, accounted for more than 800,000 hl/21 million gal, or 60 per cent of all Beaujolais produced. The Beaujolais producers themselves are keen to point out that their Nouveaux are not simply *un phénomène 'marketing'*, but that they owe their origins to the 19th century, when the year's wine would complete its fermentation in cask while en route to nearby Lyons, where the new wine provided a direct

link with village life in the Beaujolais hills. The phenomenon originated in a group of villages just west of Villefranche whose wines seemed to mature earliest. After the constraints of the Second World War, the Beaujolais producers were gradually allowed to release an increasing proportion of new wine. The original term was PRIMEUR, meaning 'young produce', and from 1951 the Beaujolais producers were allowed to release their primeurs from 15 December. These young, refreshing wines enjoyed great success in the bistros of Paris in the 1950s and 1960s, and by the end of the 1960s the phrase *Le Beaujolais Nouveau est arrivé* had been coined. (One British wine merchant was already importing Beaujolais Nouveau in barrel in the early 1960s.) In the 1970s, the phenomenon spread outside France, thanks to energetic work on the part of producers such as Georges DUBŒUF and his agents around the world, and Alexis LICHINE in the United States. By the end of 1974, Beaujolais Nouveau had reached Great Britain to such an extent that the first Beaujolais Nouveau race (of bottles of purple ink to London) had been run. Eventually the Nouveau was flown, with inexplicable haste and brouhaha, to markets around the world: the craze reaching Australia in 1982 and Japan and Italy in 1985. Initially the release date was fixed at 15 November, but was eventually changed to the third Thursday in November, for the convenience of the wine trade and the media, who for much of the late 1970s and 1980s were apparently fascinated by this event.

The immense commercial success of Beaujolais Nouveau inevitably spawned other (much less successful) Nouveaux—infant wines from other regions of France, notably Gamays made in TOURAINE and the ARDÈCHE, a range of wines made in the LANGUEDOC and ROUSSILLON, and many VINS DE PAYS, particularly Côtes de Gascogne. Vin de Pays Primeur or Nouveau may be released on the third Thursday of October following the harvest, a full month before Beaujolais Nouveau.

Italy produces a range of similar wines, described as **novello**, and Austria's HEURIGE could be said to be a version of the phenomenon. Many southern hemisphere producers have tried to sell their own early releases as 'Nouveau' because they carry the same year on the label and are available many months before the appearance of Beaujolais Nouveau (which has somewhat diluted the novelty that used to attach to bottles carrying the current vintage year).

Wine-making techniques have to be adapted to produce wines that are ready to drink so early. The majority of Nouveau wines are red and many of them are produced, like Beaujolais, by CARBONIC MACERATION or SEMI-CARBONIC MACERATION, which yields particularly fruity, soft, aromatic red wines suitable for drinking young and slightly cool, typically involving a fermentation of only about four days, and fairly brutal STABILIZATION. Those winemakers who do not or cannot practise any form of carbonic maceration may ferment the grapes traditionally but at lower temperatures than usual (in the low 20s °C (*c.*70 °F)) and allow only the briefest of MACERATIONS. White grapes, for which carbonic maceration is not suitable, are generally fermented very cool, at 15 to 20 °C, and boiled candy aromas typically result.

The great attraction of Nouveau wines for producers is that they produce a financial return so quickly. As one taster remarked, their characteristic aroma is the scent of cash flow. Their appeal for the wine drinker is that they are a refreshing and stimulating reminder of the passing of the seasons, a sort of liquid HARVEST TRADITION. Nouveau wines do not deteriorate in bottle substantially more rapidly than non-Nouveau wines, but their lifespan is inevitably shorter.

Nouvelle, vigorous South African mid 20th-century CROSSING of Sémillon and Crouchen Blanc which became popular from the mid 1990s for its ability to add obvious METHOXYPYRAZINE aromas to Cape Sauvignon Blanc. The first varietal version was made in 2005.

novello, Italian for new, and therefore a name applied to Italian NOUVEAU wine.

nuclear magnetic resonance, NMR, or, more specifically, Site Specific Natural Isotope Fractionation by Nuclear Magnetic Resonance (SNIF-NMR), was in the mid 1990s the most powerful analytical tool for the authentication of alcoholic drinks. It is therefore an important weapon, and deterrent, against ADULTERATION AND FRAUD (see also MINERALS).

It was developed during the 1980s by Professor Gérard Martin of Nantes University in north west France and is officially approved as an analytical method both by the EUROPEAN UNION and, more internationally, by the OIV. This powerful research aid has been patented and marketed on a worldwide basis by the EU-funded Eurofins enterprise.

Its strength is that it can examine the precise structure of the ETHANOL molecule in such a way that it drastically reduces the potential for fraud. The principle is based on deuterium, the stable natural isotope of hydrogen, and its distribution in the ethanol molecule. There are three distinct sites of deuterium and NMR can differentiate between these sites, showing the abundance of deuterium in each of them.

The isotopic content of each site is linked to both the origin of the molecule and the conditions prior to the production of alcohol, i.e. FERMENTATION showing the degree of CHAPTALIZATION (where the wine was enriched with sugar cane, sugar beet, or GRAPE CONCENTRATE, for example).

One obvious application is proving chaptalization in excess of legal limits. Another, much more far-reaching, long-term application has been the establishment of databanks based on the analysis of representative sample wines from each wine area. (This is already well advanced for many European wine areas.) This application, based on each region's unique deuterium ratios, should be able to provide an absolute guarantee of geographical authenticity. While it may never be sufficiently detailed to distinguish a Ch LAFITE from a Ch LATOUR, it can easily distinguish between a BORDEAUX and a BERGERAC.   G.T.

Nuits, Côte de, named after the principal town of Nuits-St-Georges, this is the northern half of the escarpment of the CÔTE D'OR, producing the greatest red wines of Burgundy, from the Pinot Noir grape, and very occasional white wines. The principal villages, from north to south, are GEVREY-CHAMBERTIN, MOREY-ST-DENIS, CHAMBOLLE-MUSIGNY, VOUGEOT, VOSNE-ROMANÉE, Flagey-ÉCHEZEAUX, and NUITS-ST-GEORGES. See also MARSANNAY. The soils on the lower part of the slope tend to be much more fertile than the main parent rock because more immature soil has been incorporated.

Wines from FIXIN, Brochon, Prémeaux, Comblanchien, and Corgoloin may be sold as **Côte de Nuits-Villages**. These are usually but not exclusively red wines.

See also BEAUNE, CÔTE DE, and the map under BURGUNDY.   J.T.C.M.

Nuits-St-Georges, small market town in Burgundy giving its name to the Côte de Nuits, the northern half of the Côte d'Or. Nuits-St-Georges has remained fully independent of BEAUNE to the south and Dijon to the north, with numerous NÉGOCIANTS making their headquarters here. The town also boasts its own charity auction, the Hospices de Nuits, held in March, when the wines can be better judged than those of the HOSPICES DE BEAUNE in November.

The appellation Nuits-St-Georges lies both sides of the town which straddles the small river Meuzin and incorporates the vineyards of neighbouring Prémeaux-Prissey to the south. While all the wines of Nuits-St-Georges are sturdy and long lived, those abutting Vosne-Romanée to the north show the most fruit and elegance. The finest wines are normally held to come from the vineyards south of the Meuzin, where the ground is stonier and the wines are the fullest and longest lived of them all. There is more clay in the soil of the Prémeaux vineyards, making wines which are fat but a touch less fine.

Whereas the Intendant Bouchu noted in 1666 a preference for Nuits, 'where the wine is excellent', over Prémeaux, 'where the wine is of good quality', the king of Saxony specif-

ically ordered in 1780 'the wine of Prémeaux, the colour of the stained glass windows of La Sainte Chapelle'.

Nuits boasts 27 PREMIER CRU vineyards but no GRANDS CRUS, perhaps because the town's leading vigneron, Henri Gouges, was too modest when the CLASSIFICATIONS were agreed in the 1930s. However, the eponymous Les St-Georges vineyard, first singled out as early as the 11th century, has always been cited as of the highest quality. Also particularly fine in the southern Nuits-St-Georges sector are Les Cailles and Les Vaucrains, both adjacent to Les St-Georges, while Les Murgers and Les Boudots on the Vosne-Romanée side and Les Argillières, Clos l'Arlot, and Clos de la Maréchale in Prémeaux have good reputations.

Some white wine is also made from the Chardonnay grape, as in the Clos l'Arlot, and from the Pinot Blanc grape in Domaine Gouges' premier cru Les Perrières.

Top producers include Henri Gouges, Robert Chevillon, Domaine de l'Arlot, Patrice Rion, and growers in neighbouring VOSNE-ROMANÉE such as Arnoux and Grivot.

See also CÔTE D'OR and BURGUNDY map.   J.T.C.M.

numbers and wine, a combination that has assumed increasing importance as WINEMAKING has become more scientific, and as consumers, faced with a bewildering choice of wines, seek easily appreciated assessments of wine quality. As recently as the 1970s, winemakers had only the vaguest grasp of their wines' vital statistics; and the only numbers of significance to most wine drinkers were those of VINTAGE, PRICE, and, among more sophisticated connoisseurs of bordeaux, the numerical rankings associated with wine CLASSIFICATION.

Numbers are increasingly used for identification, however. Australian wine producers such as PENFOLDS have for decades exhibited a penchant for incorporating BIN numbers into the names of their wines. Individual CLONES of various VINE VARIETIES can be so numerous that they are usually identified by individual numbers, as are CASKS and individual BARRELS in some larger wineries.

As the growing of grapes and the making of wine becomes more scientific, however, numbers as measurements play a key role, as they do in all scientific thinking (see in particular SCORING vineyards).

Consumers, as well as producers, have an interest in measurements taken at all stages of wine production, from SOIL to finished liquid. These measurements, such as PH, level of TANNINS, or the ALCOHOLIC STRENGTH which appears on most wine labels, cannot be used on their own as a measure of how a wine will taste. Scores attempt to measure quality, however, whether in the vineyard or tasting room.   J.R.

A statistician's view

Scores for individual wines use number as a measurement of the quality of a wine. When tasting wine, the nuances of COLOUR, AROMA, FLAVOUR, and taste, the interplay of ALCOHOL, ALDEHYDES, ESTERS, and ACIDS, the location, temperature, even one's companions, have such complicated effects that, whilst providing much of the enjoyment of wine, they make the idea of describing a wine numerically seem over-simplified at best, ridiculous at worst. Yet we all accept the numerical description that is price. Reputation, age, and availability, apart from the quality of the wine, all play a part; nevertheless, price gives some indication of quality.

Respected attempts have been made by experts to provide numerical measures of quality, free from the other factors that influence price. Robert PARKER in the United States, and other wine critics and publications including the influential *Wine Spectator* magazine in the US and many more worldwide, use a scale from 50 to 100. Michael BROADBENT in Britain uses one from 0 to 5, expressed in stars rather than numbers. Many tastings described in the press report numerically, sometimes just describing quality, sometimes rating value. In many countries, professional wine judges (see JUDGING) employ a 20-point system.

There are two reasons for wanting to apply numbers to wine. First, a number is precise: the number 17 means the same to everyone, whereas words used by tasters, such as 'earthy', although very useful, are difficult to recognize or describe. Secondly, and more importantly, numbers combine easily. For example, we can take the average of the numerical values given to a wine by several tasters to obtain an improved measure. More complicated combinations can be devised to extract further information from a tasting (see Amerine and Roessler). Much criticism of numerical measures derives from the critic's inability to understand how to use the numbers, rather than from the numbers themselves; whereas words are more familiar. A similar deficiency rests with the consumer, who is misled by the precision of number to think that a wine rated 91 by Parker must be obviously better than a 90, whereas, for a reason outlined below, it need not be.

Ideally a numerical measure of a wine's quality should be reproducible. If a desk is measured to be 1 m long, then any trained person will reproduce 'one metre' on measuring it. Ideally, when Parker quotes 85, others should agree. Unfortunately they do not. The evaluation of wine is too SUBJECTIVE, and the wine itself too variable, for this to be possible. This does not rule out the usefulness of numerical measures, but it means that one has to be more careful in using them. For example, if all trained tasters gave wine A a mark in the 80s, and wine B one in the 70s, it is clear, despite the variability within the decades, that wine A is better than wine B.

Many factors may affect the variability. Wines can vary enormously at different, often quite close, stages of evolution. There is also the common phenomenon of BOTTLE VARIATION, common not just from case to case, but from bottle to bottle, especially but not exclusively with older wines stored in different conditions. Tasting conditions, particularly TEMPERATURE and exposure to air, influence the judgement. The tasting of one wine may be affected by the immediately previous tasting of another, with a carry-over effect from one experience to the next. There are obvious differences between judges' abilities and partialities. Judges tire easily and many cannot fairly assess more than 20 wines in a single session. These difficulties are not insuperable. A preliminary tasting to disqualify poor judges is a fine idea, if understandably unpopular, especially when it happens that some tasters are good with some wines, but inexperienced with others. A careful design of the tasting, accompanied by a rigorous analysis of the results, can produce judgements of real value. It may often be necessary to provide two numbers, one of which acts like a Parker–Broadbent value, the other providing a measure of variability. Thus two wines may be reported as (75 ± 2) and (75 ± 5) respectively, indicating that both were rated 75 on average, but that the latter produced more disagreement than the former. The first was rather consistent, whereas the second was more variable. A more sophisticated approach can use two numbers that characterize two different aspects of the wine's quality. Some tastings reported in the wine press may be misleading, either because the tasting has not been performed with sufficient care, or because the results have not been analysed competently. It is rare for the press report of a tasting to contain enough information for a reader to assess the value of the tasting, despite the abundance of words of doubtful precision.

Much of the joy of wine comes from its enormous variety. Numbers will not destroy this variety nor lessen the appreciation, merely help to put it on a firmer basis. To do this requires more carefully organized, comparative wine TASTINGS, and better analyses of the data obtained from them. See also wine SCORING and WINE WRITING.   D.V.L.

Amerine, M. A., and Roessler, E. B., *Wines: Their Sensory Evaluation* (Davis, Calif., 1983).

Ashenfelter, O., *Liquid Assets* (Princeton, NJ, various issues).

Nuragus, white grape variety grown principally to produce the unremarkable varietal Nuragus di Cagliari on the island of SARDEGNA.

nursery in viticultural terms is either a place set aside for nurturing young vines, or a name for a GRAFTING establishment. Open-ground vine nurseries are where CUTTINGS are planted to develop roots and become ROOTLINGS. Cuttings are taken in winter, stored in a cold room, then CALLUSED by burying them in moist sand, often on heated beds, until young roots form at the base (after six to eight weeks). In spring they are planted in rows in the nursery, where the first-year shoots develop. Nursery soils need to be deep, friable, and well drained, free of pathogens and with a good water supply. In the following winter or spring, they are lifted, shoots and roots are trimmed, and the vines planted out in the vineyard. For grafted vines, the products of BENCH GRAFTING are callused in a humid room before planting in a nursery.   B.G.C.

nursery budding and **nursery grafting**, methods for the PROPAGATION of grafted vines that complement BENCH GRAFTING, used in warm climates. Great flexibility is possible in the type of SCION wood used and in the timing of grafting. Inserted scions are tied tightly with budding tape and, after the inserted bud has started to grow, the rootstock foliage is shortened back and later removed.   B.G.C.

nutrients. All living things, including vines and yeasts, need NITROGEN, PHOSPHORUS, and POTASSIUM, along with CARBON, hydrogen, OXYGEN, and other MINERAL ELEMENTS as nutrients. Lack of nutrients in must can lead to STUCK FERMENTATION.

For more details of **nutrition** of the vine, see VINE NUTRITION.

NYSAES, New York State Agricultural Experiment Station in Geneva. See CORNELL.

NV. See NON-VINTAGE.

oak is a hard, supple, and watertight WOOD, which has the simple advantage over other WOOD TYPES used for COOPERAGE of displaying a natural affinity with wine, imparting qualities and flavours that today's consumers appreciate as enhancing or complementing those of many wines. Oak in general is one of the strongest of the common hardwoods of the temperate northern hemisphere. As well as being particularly good at holding liquids, oak is also physically easy to work; it encourages clarity and stability in red wines and adds new layers of complexity to many white wines.

There are hundreds of species of oak, all of which can be broadly separated into two categories, red and white. The red oaks are porous and cannot therefore be relied upon for watertight cooperage. For wine, three sorts of white oak are most important, one American and two European, all of them belonging to the botanical genus QUERCUS:

1. *Quercus alba*, also known as American white oak. This general name is also applied to the American oak species *Quercus bicolor*, swamp white oak; *Quercus lyrata*, overcup oak; *Quercus durandii*, Durand oak; *Quercus michauxii*, swamp chestnut oak; *Quercus macrocarpa*, bur oak; and *Quercus prinus*, chestnut oak. Some of these species can hybridize with each other.
2. *Quercus petraea*, once also known as *Quercus sessiliflora*, or *Quercus sessilis*, and as *chêne sessile* in France.
3. *Quercus robur*, once known as *Quercus pedunculata*, also called pedunculate or variously English, French, and Russian oak, *chêne pédonculé* in France.

In such forests as TRONÇAIS, *Q petraea* and *Q robur* grow promiscuously together but are not systematically differentiated as far as timber quality is concerned, although the trees are fairly easy to tell apart (see below).

The anatomy of different oaks has implications for barrel making. A trunk can be thought of as a bundle of tubes or vessels and fibres running parallel to the trunk with groups of fibres called rays running radially from the outside towards the centre of the trunk. Oak is non-storeyed; the longitudinal tubes and fibres overlap so as to give strength. (In a soft wood such as pine, the tubes and fibres are stacked, making the wood much less resistant to pressure.) It is also ring-porous; there are distinct bands of large and small pores or tubes laid down at different times of the year (see GRAIN).

Oak is rich in tyloses, which are structures that plug the tubes. This is what makes it particularly good for holding liquids, as the path of the liquid through the wood is blocked by these tyloses. American white oaks, *Quercus alba*, are the richest in these tyloses, which is why American barrel STAVES can be sawn into shape without risk of leakage. With European oaks there are fewer tyloses so the wood is more porous and must be split to follow the

Country (excluding ex-Soviet Union)	Growing stock (millions of cu m)
United States	767
France	467
ex-Yugoslavia	178
Hungary	105
Bulgaria	79
Turkey	75
Germany	72
Poland	64
ex-Czechoslovakia	56
Portugal	52
Japan	47
Great Britain	34
Greece	21
Sweden	16
Switzerland	5
Netherlands	3
Ireland	2
Total	1,927

tubes and then bent so that all the tubes are parallel to the stave, thus minimizing leakage.

American oak generally has a more obvious flavour, vanillin in character, and can be more astringent than the smoother, subtler oaks of Europe. Vital to barrel quality is not just the source of the oak, however, but its seasoning (see BARREL MAKING for more details).

World oak resources

All statistics regarding the amount of standing timber in a given country should be read with some caution. The figures in the table above, many of them based on a report of the United Nations Economic Commission for Europe, are the most recent available but should be read with caution (a more recent estimate put Hungary's total at 79 million cu m, for example).

According to the same UN report, a little over half of Portuguese oak is CORK oak (*Quercus suber*), but the statistics are clearly incomplete as no oak was recorded as growing in Spain.

Ages of the oak forests are given but not species. In Poland, for example, approximately 75 per cent of the stands are less than 80 years old, as they are in Hungary. Cooperage quality oak should be at least 80 years old and preferably much older.

According to research done by Backman and Waggener of the University of Washington (US) in 1988, the former Soviet republics had approximately 9.7 million ha/24 million acres of oak, of which around 3.1 million are located in the far eastern region, close to the Pacific ocean. This is *Quercus mongolica*, not a species used for cooperage. About 1.7 million ha are in Ukraine and are said to add up to around 233 million cu m. Most of the balance, about 4.7 million ha with 763 million cu m/8,180 million cu ft of oak, is in European Russia, where the North Caucasus, the Urals, and Povolzhsk regions have the highest proportions of oak in their forests. If these estimates are correct,

the former Soviet republics have the greatest oak resources in the world, even though they may have suffered from poor forestry management for many decades (see below). According to some estimates, Romania also has substantial, if poorly managed, oak forests.

American oaks

In 1987, according to a report published by the US Forestry Service in 1989, there were 24,497 million cu ft/698 million cu m of commercially important selected white oaks in the eastern United States, although only a certain proportion of this would be suitable for cooperage, where the quality criteria are much higher than for pulp and veneer. *Quercus alba* covers most of the eastern United States, extending east from Minnesota, Iowa, Missouri, and Arkansas, north of Mexico, and south of Canada and Maine.

There is no general agreement as to which American regions provide the best oak for wine or whiskey barrels. Some people feel that oak from Minnesota and Wisconsin is best for wine barrels; others feel that it is too tannic. Wood from the more southerly parts of the US is condemned by some for being too sappy. Oregon white oak, *Quercus garryana*, which grows about 50 to 90 ft (15–27 m) tall, and around 24 to 40 in (60 cm–1 m) in diameter, has also been used experimentally for wine barrels, and began to be used on a limited scale for commercial production in the mid 1990s. There are approximately 6,000 million cu ft of various species of oak in California, Oregon, and Washington, but, other than Oregon oak, little is suitable for barrels. In the US alone, an estimated 150,000 to 200,000 American oak barrels are sold to producers each year, about 15 per cent more than those made of French oak, not least because they are less expensive.

American oak is also used widely by the wine industries of Spain, North and South America, and Australia. Because American oak generally has a more powerful flavour than European oak, it was for long used mainly for relatively powerful red wines such as RIOJA and other Spanish reds, Australian SHIRAZ, and warmclimate CABERNET SAUVIGNON, but cooperage techniques improved so considerably in the 1990s that it is now routinely used on a much wider range of wine styles. See COOPERAGE, history.

European oaks

These oaks grow throughout Europe, as far east as the Urals, as far south as Sicilia, as far west as Ireland, France, and Portugal, and as far north as southern Norway.

Quercus patraea can reach a height of 25 m/82 ft and can live over 300 years. Branches form high up the relatively straight trunk. Wood from this tree is usually tight grained (see GRAIN). This species grows well in sandy, silty soil with good drainage, but thrives in a variety of soils. In Europe it is found throughout the United Kingdom and from France east to Poland and the Baltic states and as far south as Italy and ex-Yugoslavia.

Quercus robur, thought of as English or French oak, also grows to over 25 m in height and can live over 300 years. Its branches spread out to provide more shade than *Quercus patraea* and it tends to produce wide-grained wood. It prefers fertile soils where there is plenty of water. As *Quercus robur* tolerates a wider range of growing conditions, it is more widespread in Europe than *Quercus patraea*. It extends further north into the Scandinavian countries, further south into Turkey, Georgia, and Portugal, and east as far as the Urals. Although wood from this species tends to have wider grains than *Quercus patraea*, the two species can be positively distinguished only by examination of leaves and acorns. The acorn of *Quercus robur* is attached via a long PEDUNCLE whereas that of *Quercus patraea* is attached directly to the twig. There is so much cross-fertilization that there are many hybrids of these two species, however.

Coopers do not usually distinguish the two species in their workshops. Like winemakers, they tend to pay more attention to geographical provenance and grain size than oak species. And, as winemakers increasingly understand, details of BARREL MAKING can have an even more significant effect on wine quality than exact forest location.

France Although Baltic and Slavonian oak were the most admired oaks in the 19th century, French oak has since become the standard by which all other oaks are judged. Thanks to sound forestry management, French oak is available in viable commercial quantities and can add to wine flavours that appeal to modern consumers.

Almost a quarter of France, or nearly 14 million ha/34 million acres, is forest, constituting more than 40 per cent of all forest in the European Union. About one-third of this forest land is oak. There are 4.13 million ha of *Quercus petraea* and *Quercus robur*, according to the French Office National des Forêts.

France is the world's major source of European oak, by quite a margin. According to Vivas, around 2 million cubic m of oak are harvested in France each year, whereas annual growth is around 10 million cubic m. At least 200,000 French oak barrels are made and sold every year, it is estimated, of which the majority are sold to the US.

Since 1947, around 2 million ha/5 million acres of France have been reforested. Unlike many other countries, France has done a good job of managing its forests since the Second World War. Supplies of French oak—barring unusual circumstances such as dramatic CLIMATE CHANGE—should remain abundant.

Concern about the condition of the French forests dates back to at least 1291, when scholars note the mention of 'maistre des fôrets' in the Royal Ordinances. The most famous of these Ordinances was written during the regime of Colbert in 1669. Colbert is commemorated in the Tronçais forest, where he ordered systematic replanting of oak trees for use in shipbuilding.

Sylviculture is actively practised in France so that trees in government-owned forests are not allowed to grow wild, but are carefully farmed to yield suitable wood, just like any other crop. Trees are encouraged to grow tall and straight, yielding grains appropriate for barrel making, for example, by a variety of physical techniques.

The following forests all over northern France provide oak for wine and brandy barrels:

Western Loire and Sarthe: woods from forests in the western LOIRE, from the *départements* of Indre, Cher, and Indre-et-Loire, and in the Sarthe near Le Mans, have tight grains and are highly prized.

Limousin: woods from the following regions in France: the eastern part of the *département* of Deux-Sèvres, Vienne, Haute-Vienne, the northern part of the Corrèze, the Creuze, the eastern part of the Charente and the southern part of the Indre, the northern part of the Dordogne. These oaks tend to have wide grains and are usually grouped together as Limousin. Soils here tend to clay-limestone or granite. These woods are more TANNIC than the right-grained woods and are more popular with brandy makers than winemakers.

Nièvre and Allier: woods from these two central *départements* just south of SANCERRE go by many names. Sometimes this wood is sold under the name of the specific forest. Tronçais, for example, is a government-owned forest north of Moulins, while Bertranges is a forest near Nevers. This sort of oak may also be sold under the name of the region, such as Allier and Nevers. To many French winemakers, however, all of this wood is regarded simply as *bois du centre*, wood from the centre of France. However these forests are named, the wood is usually tight grained and is popular for both brandy and wine. Soil here tends to silica and clay. As stands are planted with close spacing, the trees tend to grow up, rather than out; hence the tighter grains.

Vosges: wood from the Vosges forests in ALSACE-Lorraine became popular with winemakers outside the region in the early 1980s. This wood is usually tight grained and resembles the oak from Nièvre and Allier. Oak experts say they can identify this wood by its 'clear' or 'white' colour. The character of Vosges woods varies according to the altitude of the stand.

Jura and Bourgogne: just to the east of BURGUNDY are forests which traditionally supplied Burgundy with oak. These forests are still important and supply wood mainly to Burgundian wine producers.

Argonne: located near CHAMPAGNE, this forest provides a small amount of oak for the cooperage business, principally for those few champagne producers who still ferment in barrel. Sometimes the wood is sold as Vosges.

According to L'Office Nationale des Forêts, the most important French *départements* for oak are, in declining order of importance, Haute-Saône, Nièvre, Yonne, Côte d'Or, Haute-Marne, Dordogne, Cher, Allier, Moselle, Saône-et-Loire, Loire-et-Cher, l'Orne, l'Eure, and la Sarthe.

There is no APPELLATION CONTRÔLÉE and much confusion of nomenclature in the world of oak. This means not only that winemakers are suspicious about proclaimed wood origins but that people use different definitions for the same name. Some would include wood from the western Loire in the category of 'bois du centre' while others would exclude anything but Nevers and Allier. Others will classify wood around Nevers with wood from the Yonne and CÔTE D'OR as 'Bourgogne'.

Eastern Europe Historically, the forests of eastern Europe were extremely important sources of oak, mainly *Quercus robur* and *Quercus petraea*. In the 19th century, Baltic oaks were prized by the French and British, although it is not clear exactly how much oak suitable for cooperage is left in Lithuania, Latvia, and Estonia. Before the Second World War, Polish, Russian, and Baltic oaks were important in both the beer and wine industries and in the 1990s coopers were scouting east keenly in search of good-quality wood that could be bought more cheaply than French oak. Political changes in eastern Europe in the late 1980s immediately resulted in Hungarian and Moravian oak being offered to winemakers in the west. Some coopers have conducted successful trials of wines matured in eastern European oak and, although there is still much to be learnt about making barrels with these woods, between 6,000 and 10,000 such barrels were sold, at keen prices, in the US alone in 1997—roughly 5 per cent of French oak barrel sales but growing fast.

SLAVONIA, BOSNIA AND HERZEGOVINA, and SERBIA have been a useful source of oak for the large casks and oval vats used by Italy's wine producers (who often called them simply Yugoslavian, or Slavonian). It is said these oaks are too tannic for French grape varieties but work well with Italy's NEBBIOLO and SANGIOVESE, but this could be a reflection of wood preparation or TERROIR. Much of this wood was sawn, rather than hand split (see BARREL MAKING) and the result was porous barrels that provided astringent flavours. These forests have been managed poorly, too many trees have been cut down, and access to these woods has been restricted for internal political reasons.

Portuguese oak Oak grown in the far north of Portugal can, if well seasoned, be of use to Portugal's winemakers, being more subtle than the locally used chestnut and much cheaper than oak imported from France.

See also OAK FLAVOUR, WOOD INFLUENCE, BARREL, BARREL FERMENTATION, BARREL MAINTENANCE, BARREL MATURATION, BARREL RENEWAL, BARREL TYPES, BARREL INSERTS, INNER STAVES, OAK CHIPS, and OAK ESSENCES. M.K.

Backman, C. A., and Waggener, T. R., *Soviet Timber Resources and Utilization: An Interpretation of the 1988 National Inventory* (Seattle, 1991).

Burns, R. M., and Honkala, B. H. (eds.), *Silvics of North America*, ii: *Hardwoods* (Washington, DC, 1990).

Chang, S. J., 'The demand and supply situation of the world's oak timber', *International Oak Symposium Proceedings* (San Francisco, 1993).

Vivas, N., *Manuel de tonnellerie à l'usage des utilisateurs de futaille* (2nd edn, Bordeaux, 2002).

Waddell, K. L., Oswald, D. C., and Powell, D. L. (eds.), *Forest Statistics of the United States 1987* (US Dept. of Agriculture, 1980).

oak ageing, the process of AGEING a wine in contact with OAK. This typically involves BARREL MATURATION, ageing the wine in a relatively small oak container, although the phrase may also be used for CASK AGEING in a larger oak container, and can even be used for wines exposed to the influence of OAK CHIPS or INNER STAVES. Wines thus treated may be described as **oak aged, oak matured,** or **oaked.** (**Oaky** is a tasting term usually applied to wines too heavily influenced by OAK FLAVOUR, which smell and taste more of wood than fruit, and may be aggressively tannic and dry.)

oak alternatives, common term for a group of materials and techniques, including the use of OAK CHIPS, BARREL INSERTS, INNER STAVES, and sometimes MICRO-OXYGENATION, which are, strictly, alternatives to BARRELS rather than oak.

oak chips, useful if ersatz wine-making tool, an inexpensive alternative to top-quality BARREL MATURATION which imparts OAK FLAVOUR and aroma and may improve mouthfeel and colour stability though the resultant wine may be less complex and have poorer ageing potential.

Oak chips vary considerably both in the provenance of the OAK (from subtle Limousin to harsher American oak) and in the size of the chip (from pencil shaving to the more common cashew nut size). Oak chips, just like BARRELS, are also subjected to different degrees of TOAST. The quality of the oak, the method and duration of seasoning, and the degree and duration of toast are far more significant than the shape of the chip or shaving.

Oak chips are used either instead of barrel maturation or to supplement the oak flavour imparted by a used barrel. The average dose of chips is about 1 g/l, or 5 lb per 1,000 gal, typically added prior to fermentation. Chips offer considerable savings over new cooperage: a sufficient quantity of American oak chips to impart some degree of oak flavour could cost less than a twentieth of the cost of a new American oak barrel (and an even smaller fraction of the cost of a new French barrel). They are most effective when added during FERMENTATION, when presumably a combination of heat and enzymatic activity combine to generate the most favourable flavour EXTRACTION. Such wines sometimes have such an overpoweringly oaky flavour that they must be blended with unoaked wine. In addition to cost savings, chips have other advantages over barrels: less oak is needed because of the greater surface area in contact with the wine, there is less oak wastage compared with producing barrel staves, the toast is more even, their aromatic potential is always equivalent to a new barrel since they are not re-used, and they take up far less space in the winery.

Research by Wilkinson *et al.* has shown that the oak character imparted by the chips may intensify after the chips have been removed. This is because the formation of certain oak lactones (see OAK FLAVOURS) takes longer than the period during which the chips are in contact with the wine.

It is possible to buy oak chips impregnated with LACTIC ACID BACTERIA immobilized at the stage immediately prior to exponential growth so that they can be used to encourage MALOLACTIC FERMENTATION but these are not widely used because of the additional costs involved.

Many wine producers are coy about admitting to using oak chips although, unlike OAK ESSENCE, oak chips may be used perfectly legally in many wine regions. A wine description which mentions 'oak maturation' or 'oak influence' without actually mentioning any form of cooperage is a good clue.

The **oak shavings** which can result from BARREL RENEWAL may similarly be used, and larger **oak cubes** in a perforated bag are sometimes put into older barrels to impart oak flavour.

See also BARREL INSERTS and INNER STAVES.

G.T. & J.Ha.

Wilkinson, K. L., Elsey, G. M., Prager, R. H., Pollnitz, A. P., and Sefton, M., 'Rates of formation of *cis*- and *trans*-oak lactone from 3-methyl-4-hydroxyoctanoic acid', *Journal of Agricultural and Food Chemistry*, 52 (2004), 4213–18.

oak essences or **oak extract,** usually illegal wine-making additive (unlike OAK CHIPS) which can inexpensively substitute, at least in the short term, for some of the OAK FLAVOUR imparted by BARREL MATURATION in expensive new oak. Various powders and liquids are marketed based on extractions from different woods. In some cases, specific TANNINS are targeted and extracted so as to add structure as well as flavour to a wine (see OENOLOGICAL TANNINS).

Doses of powdered oak extracts can vary between 5 and 20 g/hl but powders are more difficult to use than liquids because of potential problems with CLARIFICATION. The usual dose of a liquid extract is about 0.01 per cent and, since most liquids are based on ETHANOL or brandy, they can be extremely difficult to detect analytically. However, their ability to sustain a wine through BOTTLE AGEING is questionable.   G.T.

oak flavour. The wood in which a wine is fermented and/or aged has a profound and often complex effect on its characteristics and flavour (see WOOD INFLUENCE). Certain substances present in wood may also be directly extracted and absorbed into the wine, however. Those extractable substances identified in OAK, the most commonly used wood, are listed below.

Lactones These compounds, responsible for what is generally called the aroma of oak, or 'oakiness', are derived from lipids in the oak. They are more coconut-like at higher concentrations and can easily overpower a wine's inherent AROMA. Higher concentrations are found in American oak. Toasting of the oak (see TOAST) may increase this flavour; open-air seasoning of the STAVES prior to BARREL MAKING generally decreases the lactones. The specific compounds are the cis and trans isomers of p-methyl-g-octalactone. The former is more aromatic and imparts an earthy, herbaceous character; the latter imparts more spiciness and has a higher threshold value in wine. Seasoning affects the ratio of cis to trans isomers.

Phenolic aldehydes VANILLIN, a product of lignin degradation, is the best-known member of this group. Toasting increases the level of these (although they decrease at high toast levels), as does seasoning in the open air. BARREL FERMENTATION reduces their level because yeast metabolism reduces, for example, aromatic vanillin to odourless vanillic alcohol.

Volatile phenols These too are the product of lignin degradation and are not present in non-toasted wood. They impart a spice-like roasted character, ranging from clove to smokiness. These decrease with seasoning of the oak. The main volatile phenol associated with wood is eugenol (clove-like). Others include guaiacol and 4-methylguaiacol (smoky, charred aromas), which may increase at higher levels of toasting, and 4-vinylguaiacol (reminiscent of carnations).

Terpenes These essential oils important in fruit, tea, and perfume are found in American oak and to a lesser degree in some French oak. It is likely but as yet unproven that they have flavour effects. This was a particularly active area of wine research in the early 1990s.

Carbohydrate degradation products This is a large and complex group that includes furfurals, which are produced from toasting wood sugars and have a bitter almond flavour. Maltol and cyclotene are also produced from the toasting process and not only have caramel-like flavours of their own, but also act as flavour potentiators. Like monosodium glutamate with food, these potentiators increase the perception of other flavours.

Tannins and other phenolics TANNINS and other PHENOLICS give colour and astringency but more importantly act as a reservoir to balance the oxidative/reductive reactions of the wine, protecting it from OXIDATION and lessening the chance of unpleasant REDUCTIVE aromas. Hydrolysable tannins derived from oak lignin are known as ellagitannins. Their concentration decreases with heavy toasting. It is worth noting that wine in the barrel is biologically active. The YEASTS that effect the FERMENTATION of sugars to alcohol also transform some of these directly extracted oak compounds into other compounds with flavours different from the original. The furfurals, for instance, which have a bitter flavour when originally extracted and are derived from hemicellulose, are transformed by the yeasts into compounds which have a range of flavours from smoked meat to leather. Furfural levels increase with the duration of the toasting. BACTERIA are also active in wine and, in the case of white wines, the barrel contributes compounds which bacteria can transform from relatively flavourless to highly aromatic ones reminiscent of smoke, cloves, and coffee.

Those who cannot afford to extract their oak flavour from new BARRELS may use OAK CHIPS, BARREL INSERTS, INNER STAVES, or even OAK ESSENCE. Some winemakers believe that the use of chips and inserts gives them better control over the type and amount of oak flavour extracted, so use of these products is no longer simply due to economics. Used carefully and in combination with MICRO-OXYGENATION, these products have allowed some wineries to achieve flavour effects in tank very similar to those promoted by barrel ageing, and for a fraction of the cost.   L.B. & J.Ha.

oak influence. See WOOD INFLUENCE.

Oak Knoll. See NAPA.

oak root rot, vine disease. See ARMILLARIA ROOT ROT.

Oakville, important source of top quality NAPA Valley Cabernet.

Obaideh, hardy, vigorous, workmanlike indigenous grape of LEBANON, high in sugar, low in acidity, used extensively in the making of arak (local spirit), sacramental wines, and white Chateau Musar. The Obaideh was once believed to be a strain of Chardonnay, but without any DNA PROFILING of Lebanese CULTIVARS, it is difficult to determine its exact origins.   M.R.K.

Óbidos, DOC in western Portugal. See ESTREMADURA.

ochratoxin A (OTA) is a mycotoxin, i.e. a toxin produced in very small quantities by certain moulds, found in a range of food and beverages such as cereals, beer, coffee, cocoa, and wine. It has been shown to be carcinogenic and nephrotoxic (causing kidney damage) and has been reported in grapes and grape products since the mid 1990s. Studies have identified *Aspergillus carbonarius* and *Aspergillus niger* as the main synthesizers of OTA on grapes. (See also BUNCH ROTS and SOUR ROT.)

EUROPEAN UNION regulations were tightened in 2005 and the limit is currently 2 μg/l for wine and grape juice. Surveys conducted since 1999 have shown that warm climate wines, e.g. from the Mediterranean region, are more likely to be affected by OTA than wines from other regions. Healthy vineyards and good hygiene in the winery are the most important factors in limiting OTA.

Ochratoxin A is removed from wine at various stages of wine-making when solids are removed, particularly during FILTRATION, RACKING, CLARIFICATION, and FINING, but it is relatively stable and not destroyed by fermentation or maturation conditions.

Leong, S. L., 'Wine and fungi: implications of vineyard infections', in J. Dijksterhuis and A. Samson (eds.), *New Challenges in Food Mycology* (New York, 2005).

Oechsle, scale of measuring grape sugars, and therefore grape RIPENESS, based on the DENSITY of grape juice. Grape juice with a specific gravity of 1.075 is said to be 75 °Oechsle. This is the system used in Germany and it has its origins in a system of weighing grape must developed first by the Württemberg scientist J. J. Reuss, but much refined in the 1830s by the Pforzheim physicist Ferdinand Oechsle (see GERMAN HISTORY).

Like other scales used elsewhere (see BAUMÉ and BRIX), it can be measured with a suitably calibrated REFRACTOMETER or HYDROMETER. A similar scale, devised at KLOSTERNEUBURG, is used in Austria.

Each scale of sugar measurement relates to the others. For example, a grape juice of 14.7 °Brix has a specific gravity of 1.06 and an Oechsle value of $(1.06 - 1.0) \times 1000 = 60$. According to published scales, these relationships are not strict ones; see nomograms in Hamilton and Coombe.

For more details, see MUST WEIGHT.   B.G.C.
Hamilton, R. P., and Coombe, B. G., 'Harvesting of winegrapes', in B. G. Coombe and P. R. Dry (eds.), *Viticulture*, ii: *Practices* (Adelaide, 1992).

œil-de-perdrix, French for 'partridge's eye', used as a name and tasting term for pale pink wines made from Pinot Noir, especially in the Neuchâtel canton of SWITZERLAND.

Œillade, occasional synonym for CIN-SAUT, especially when it is sold as a TABLE GRAPE, and also an almost extinct local, earlier-budding Cinsaut-like vine speciality of the greater southern RHÔNE valley.

oenocyanin, a TANNIN product extracted from the skins of black grapes, comprising a mixture of PIGMENTED TANNINS, some ANTHO-CYANINS, and other PHENOLICS. Marketed as a food colourant, oenocyanin is a valuable source of natural pigments available from POMACE. Even though it is a tannin derived from grapes, and therefore of a composition more similar to the natural tannins of wine than many OENOLOGICAL TANNINS, regulations in most countries forbid the use of oenocyanin in RED WINE-MAKING because it is classed as a colouring agent.   P.J.W.

oenological tannins, or commercial tannins, are products made by extraction of tannin from oak, chestnut, or birch woods and other suitable plant sources, including grape seeds. These have long been used (and are approved additives in many wine-making regulations) to improve the AGEING character-istics, TEXTURE, depth of colour, and colour stability of red wines. (The addition of oeno-logical tannins encourages the flocculation of PROTEINS, for example.) Our understanding of the way in which oenological tannins achieve these often desirable outcomes is no less partial than our understanding of wine tannin chemistry in general, but many winemakers have discreetly built up considerable practical experience in using these materials.   P.J.W.

oenologist, or, in the United States and South Africa, **enologist,** one who practises OENOLOGY. A CONSULTANT oenologist is likely to concentrate on the activities traditionally considered WINE-MAKING but increasingly con-cerns himself or herself with what happens in the vineyard as well as in the cellar. In general usage, an oenologist is either a scientifically qualified employee or a roving consultant, as opposed to a fully employed practitioner who may or may not have scientific training, the WINEMAKER. In California, certain winemakers are so adept and so modish that their input alone can be enough to double or treble PRICES and transform them into a CALIFORNIA CULT wine. Most famous of them is Helen Turley, and others include Heidi Peterson Barrett, Mia Klein, Philippe Melka, Merry Edwards, and Andy Erickson.

oenology, or **enology,** the knowledge or study of wine, derived from the Greek *oinos* meaning 'wine'. The French and Italian terms are, respectively, *oenologie* and *enologia*.

Oenology has been used as synonymous with WINE-MAKING and distinct from VITICUL-TURE, which is concerned with vines. There is a general tendency towards including the study of viticulture as well as wine production

in the term, however, as more people accept that wine is made to a great extent in the vine-yard. See also OENOLOGIST.

Oenotria, name given to southern Italy when Greek colonists first arrived in the 8th century BC or soon after. The Greeks may have found the indigenous inhabitants already producing wine and using stakes to support the vines, and it is possible that they adopted a word meaning 'stake' (*oinotron*) as a name for the inhabitants. But this word is very rare; a different word (*kharax*) is used in most dialects of classical Greek; so it may be that Oenotria was the name already used by the local popu-lation and the similarity between it and the word meaning 'stake' is purely coincidental.
                              N.G.W. & H.M.W.

oidium, much-used French name for POW-DERY MILDEW.

OIV stands for **Organisation** (formerly **Of-fice) International de la Vigne et du Vin,** the Paris-based intergovernmental body which represents the interests of vine-growers, and the wine, DRYING GRAPE, and TABLE GRAPE in-dustries of its members, about 45 different countries (five new members since 1993), in-cluding all the important wine producers. It was established in 1924, during PROHIBITION in the United States, charged with demonstrat-ing the beneficial effects of wine consumption, as well as co-ordinating research and nomen-clature and upholding high standards of pro-duction. It continued its work, with the benefit of diplomatic immunity, uninterrupted dur-ing the Second World War. Today it is more concerned with the wide spectrum of scien-tific, technical, economical, and social prob-lems involving the vine and all its products. The OIV co-ordinates research, gathers statis-tics, and publishes books, papers, and journals, including the important *Bulletin de l'OIV*, not just on VITICULTURAL and OENOLOGICAL mat-ters, but also on legal and economic aspects of wine production. The OIV also co-ordinates conferences to discuss the issues regarded as most pressing by the world's wine producers. In the late 1980s and early 1990s, topics in-cluded the possibility of increasing commer-cial controls as an indirect result of HEALTH concerns, and the increasing importance of ecological concerns. Since 1986, the OIV's edu-cational branch has offered an International Diploma in Management of Wine and the Vine, a master's degree taught in English and French while travelling around the world of wine.

Olasz Rizling or **Olaszrizling,** is the most common name in HUNGARY for the white grape variety known in Austria as WELSCHRIESLING (under which more details appear). The variety is extremely popular in Hungary, although introduced less than a century ago. The Olaszrizling produced around lake Balaton,

Somló, and Eger is particularly prized and, in general, the warmer climate imbues Hun-garian versions of this variety with more weight than their counterparts in Austria, or those in SLOVENIA, where it is commonly known as LAŠKI RIZLING, from the same root as Olasz, possibly meaning Vlach, or 'from Wallachia' in ROMANIA.

old vines are reputed to produce grapes which make better quality wine. See VINE AGE for a discussion of this common assertion.

old wine. See AGEING and MATURITY.

Old World is Europe and the rest of the Mediterranean basin such as the Near East and North Africa. The term is used solely in contrast to the New World, the Old World hav-ing little sense of homogeneity. In very general terms, Old World techniques in vineyard and cellar have relied more on TRADITION and less on SCIENCE than in the New World but this is changing as more and more wine producers travel freely between Old and New Worlds, ex-changing ideas and techniques. The notion of TERROIR is an important and well-established one in much of the Old World, especially France, Germany, and Italy. To typical Old World producers, geography is considerably more important than technology.

For more details of what characterizes the Old World, see NEW WORLD.

Olifants River, wine region in SOUTH AFRICA.

oloroso, Spanish word with two related meanings in the sherry-making process, *oloroso* being the stronger, richer type of wine made in the bodega (as opposed to *fino*), Oloroso being one of the commercial styles of sherry. Pure Oloroso is a dry, dark, nutty wine that is ba-sically bottled *oloroso*, and is often labelled Dry Oloroso. In some foreign markets, however, the term Oloroso is applied to any commercial sweet, dark blend of basic sherry plus colour-ing and sweetening wine that falls somewhere between AMONTILLADO and CREAM. Oloroso may have an alcoholic strength anywhere be-tween about 18 and more than 20 per cent. See SHERRY for more details.

Oltrepò Pavese, LOMBARDIA's most size-able viticultural area, administratively part of PIEMONTE from 1741 to 1859, extends across the hills of a series of townships in the province of Pavia south of the Po river where the land be-gins to rise towards the Ligurian Apennines (the name means 'beyond the Po, in the Pavia region'). Over 16,000 ha/39,520 acres of vineyards, with a potential production of ap-proximately 1.2 million hl/31.6 million gal of DOC wines, were planted in the mid 1990s, although annual production was less than 450,000 hl. This apparent discrepancy is partly explained by the significant quantities of grapes, PINOT NOIR in particular, that are sold to be vinified outside the production zone: the large SPUMANTE houses of Piemonte have long relied on this neighbouring zone of Lombardia for useful varieties not cultivated in their own region. Significant amounts of BULK wine have always been sold in nearby Milan, a practice which has encouraged abundant production at extremely low prices; the quality of Oltrepò wines has thus gained little from its proximity to Italy's largest and most affluent urban market. The small size of the properties (1.8 ha per grower) and the significant role played by CO-OPERATIVES have also tended to reward quantity over quality.

If the vast majority of the Oltrepò's production is not particularly interesting, there is no doubt that good, and occasionally very good, wine can be made in this zone. The most interesting is the blended red Oltrepò Rosso, which is based on BARBERA grapes to which CROATINA adds spice and BODY (it can sometimes have a RHÔNE-like pepperiness) and UVA RARA gives sweetness and aroma. Regrettably this blend accounts for less than 5 per cent of the total DOC production. Barbera (frequently sharply acidic and not helped by the generous yields of 12 tonnes/ha permitted by the DOC rules) is more than five times as common, and Bonarda, produced from the Croatina grape and less interesting on its own than when combined with other varieties, is more than three times as common. (Confusingly, Bonarda is a grape variety in its own right, but in the Oltrepò, the Croatina grape, a generally superior variety, has always been called Bonarda.) The bland Riesling Italico (see WELSCHRIESLING) is the most significant white grape, accounting for over 15 per cent of total production. Oltrepò MOSCATO, which normally bears little resemblance to the elegant and perfumed wines produced in the bordering Piedmontese province of Alessandria, supplies another 8 to 9 per cent of the total. Pinot Noir is principally used for spumante, most of whose production is controlled by the co-operatives and most of which is correct but hardly inspiring. An occasional good bottle of Oltrepò spumante and an occasional bottle of still Pinot Noir, given a Burgundian treatment and aged in OAK, indicate that the variety has real, if as yet unrealized, potential in the zone.   D.T.

Omar Khayyám (d. AD 1132) was a Persian poet, made famous in the English-speaking world by Edward Fitzgerald's translation (and adaptation) of the *Rubáiyát* ('Quatrains') in 1859 (2nd edn, 1868). In his own life, he was known as a philosopher and a scientist, and was remembered for a long time, both in the Middle East and Europe, as one of the greatest mathematicians of medieval times. His quatrains would scarcely have been deemed original in his own society (see ARAB POETS). In a time of strict orthodoxy, this genre of occasional verse, which was popular in PERSIA in the

11th and 12th centuries, was the best medium for expressing dangerous personal doubts to a close circle of friends.

Khayyám's own quatrains are the outpourings of a non-conformist intellectual who was opposed to religious fanaticism; they range from a pious outlook to the extremes of scepticism. Wine is an important theme in this poetry. Given the ISLAMIC prohibition against wine, many of the *rubáiyát* may seem heretical; however, the defiant anti-Islamic stance of Bacchism in the 8th and 9th centuries had by the 12th century been transformed in significance by Sufism (Islamic mysticism). Some commentators have, therefore, viewed the *rubáiyát* as a mystical genre, with wine forming part of a sensitive allegory. More recently it has been accepted that wine merely serves to express religious scepticism and provides solace from existential anguish; Omar Khayyám sought to drown the world's sorrows in wine and thus rejected 'the hope of a diviner drink' offered by Islam. Khayyám's was a humanist protest that scorned sectarianism and intolerance: 'If I'm drunk on forbidden wine, so I am! | And if I'm a pagan or idolater, so I am! | Every sect has its own suspicions of me, | I myself am just what I am . . . To be free from belief and unbelief is my religion.'

Although Persian wine poetry was largely influenced by Arabic poetry, the range of Bacchic expression in the *rubáiyát* is far more limited than what we find in the detailed, sometimes exuberant, descriptions of wine amongst the earlier Arab poets.

See also PERSIA and ENGLISH LITERATURE, WINE IN.   P.K.

Avery, P., and Heath-Stubbs, J. (trans.), *The Rubáʿiyat of Omar Khayyam* (London, 1979).

Ondarrabí. See HONDARRABI.

Ondenc was once an important vine variety in GAILLAC and all over SOUTH WEST FRANCE but has fallen from favour because it yields poorly and is prone to rot. During the 19th century, when it was much more popular in the greater Bordeaux region, Ondenc must have been taken to Australia, where it was identified, called Irvine's White at Great Western in Victoria and Sercial in South Australia, by visiting French AMPELOGRAPHER Paul Truel in 1976. Since then it has all but disappeared from Australian vineyards too, although rot is much less of a problem here.

ONIVINS, the public organization charged with overseeing regulations for viticulture and wine-making in France, analysing market developments and implementing national and EUROPEAN UNION support for the French wine industry, was enlarged and renamed VINI-FLHOR in 2006.

opening the bottle is an important and potentially difficult operation for bottles sealed with a cork. A wide range of CORKSCREWS

is available for opening bottles of still wine. See CLOSURES for details of alternatives to CORK, most of which are much easier to remove.

If the cork proves too recalcitrant for a corkscrew, the cork should simply be pushed in, if possible, and the wine poured out of the bottle, possibly into a jug, while the cork is held down with a long, thin instrument of some sort. See PORT TONGS for one way of opening bottles with very old corks.

But before the cork can be extracted any FOIL or wax seal has to be broached. A knife blade or FOIL CUTTER is the simplest way to cut a foil neatly, just below the lip of the bottle, which should be wiped of any residue from the foil, especially if it is an old one and contains LEAD. Wax seals are more difficult to penetrate and call for a sharp knife, or foil cutter, and tolerance of a certain amount of mess.

Opening a bottle of SPARKLING WINE is potentially extremely hazardous, as the pressure inside the bottle can expel a cork so fast that it can inflict grave injury. The bottle should be held at 45 degrees (to maximize the wine's surface area) with the cork pointing in the least dangerous direction (and certainly not at anyone, or at anything precious or fragile). The wire MUZZLE should be untwisted and discarded, while holding the cork in the bottle, usually with the top of the thumb. The bottle should then be very gently screwed off the cork with one hand while the cork is held in place with the other. The cork should be allowed to escape the bottle very slowly and the wine poured from the 45-degree angle, perhaps with a thumb in the punt (see BOTTLES). The racing driver technique of giving champagne a good shake and prising off the cork with two thumbs is about as dangerous as motor racing.

See SERVING wine for the timing of opening a bottle.

Opimian wine is the wine of the consular year of Lucius Opimius, 121 BC. It owes its fame to the conjunction of an exceptionally hot summer and a momentous historical event, the assassination of C Gracchus, which temporarily ended the movement for social reform.

Writing in 46 BC, Cicero states that the Opimian vintage is already too old to drink (*Brutus* 287), and PLINY the Elder describes it as 'reduced to a kind of bitter honey' but still recognizably wine and exorbitantly expensive (*Natural History* 14. 55–7). Petronius (*Satyricon* 36) and MARTIAL (*Epigrams* 1. 26, 3. 82, 10. 49, etc.) treat Opimian as a literary commonplace rather than a real wine: drinking Opimian in large quantities is what the *nouveaux riches* do to flaunt their wealth, but this is satire, not fact.

To have lasted this long, the wines were almost certainly DRIED GRAPE WINES.   H.M.W.

Oporto, Portugal's recently much-modernized second city and the commercial centre, known in Portuguese as Porto, which gave its name to PORT. Grapes grown in the harsh conditions up river of Oporto in the DOURO valley would be crushed and vinified before being shipped to port shippers' LODGES across the Douro from Oporto in the suburb known as VILA NOVA DE GAIA. Oporto has long had a substantial population of British merchants, whose meeting place the FACTORY HOUSE survives to this day.

The PORTUGIESER red grape is sometimes known as Oporto in Romania.

Optima is a 1970 GERMAN CROSSING, of a Silvaner × Riesling with Müller-Thurgau. It ripens very early indeed, sometimes more than ten days before Müller-Thurgau, and can notch up impressive ripeness readings, even if the wines themselves are flabby and undistinguished. It will grow on some of the poorest of sites and is therefore used, mainly in the Mosel and Rheinhessen, as a useful but ignoble booster of PRÄDIKAT level in a blend, like the more widely planted ORTEGA. Its late budding makes it popular in the Mosel-Saar-Ruwer and it is also grown in Rheinhessen. Germany's plantings of Optima reached a peak of 420 ha/1,037 acres in 1990 but had declined, unlamented, to 126 ha by 2003.

options game, BLIND TASTING game which in practice allows novice tasters almost as great a chance of winning as professionals. Developed by Australian Len EVANS, it requires an informed quiz-master who presents players with a series of increasingly precise options for the identity of the wine. A typical series of options might be: 'Australia, California, or Bordeaux?', 'left or right bank?', 'St-Estèphe, Pauillac, St-Julien, or Margaux?', 'pre-1980 or post-1979?', 'first or fifth growth?', 'Latour, Lafite, or Mouton?'. Players remain in the game only by choosing the correct successive options.

Orange, cool high ALTITUDE, promising Australian wine region in one of the cooler parts of NEW SOUTH WALES.

Orange Muscat, white grape variety with MUSCAT characteristics apparently unrelated to MUSCAT BLANC À PETITS GRAINS. There were slightly more than 160 acres/64 ha planted in California in the mid 2000s and a little in Oregon.

Orange River, wine region in SOUTH AFRICA.

order of wines to be served. This can affect how individual wines taste quite considerably. The general convention is a wise one for maximizing pleasure: dry before sweet, young before old, ordinary before fine.

A sweet wine can make dry wines taste acidic and unpleasant if they are tasted afterwards, so it makes sense to serve wines in an increasingly sweet sequence (which matches the usual sequence of foods during a meal, although serving the sweet course before cheese can upset things).

Old wines are generally more complex than callow young ones and so it generally flatters all wines if the oldest in the sequence are served last. This is not infallible, however. Many young wines are so overwhelmingly robust in comparison to a delicate old wine that they overpower it, and increasing levels of average ALCOHOLIC STRENGTH with each vintage also provides an argument in favour of tasting from (weaker) old to (more powerful) young. For this reason, many tasters approach large tastings of PORT, especially vintage port, from the oldest to the youngest wine. Some wine producers, particularly but not exclusively in newer wine regions, also prefer to show their wines in chronological order of progress from old to young. And those planning particularly generous meals may find that the nuances of the oldest, finest wine they serve last may be lost on some palates already soaked in too many younger wines.

Similar considerations apply to serving wines in an upward sequence of quality.

Oregon, one of the UNITED STATES known by wine lovers for its PINOTS and part of the PACIFIC NORTHWEST. Oregon lies between CALIFORNIA and WASHINGTON state but is markedly different from both. Its propensity for ripening grapes is the most marginal of the three, significant to those who hold that grapes which struggle to ripen achieve greater complexity, and fundamental therefore to the view that it may be from the Northwest—and Oregon in particular—that the best wines of the US will ultimately emerge. While Oregonian viticulture can be traced back for five generations, the growth of its wine industry has been a much more discreet affair than that of California and can hardly yet be considered mature. Underfunded and somewhat shy by instinct, the Oregon wine industry was slow to find a native, high-profile spokesperson to project it on the wide international screen, although that may be changing. Oregon historically cultivated an image of rustic charm and natural simplicity as opposed to glamour or sophistication, although its producers are stubborn individualists rather than simple peasants. However, the lure of wine-making in the state has attracted increasingly moneyed producers (including wine guru Robert PARKER and the relatively vast King Estate, as well as the LIFESTYLE seekers with their bags of gold).

History

VINIFERA vine varieties arrived in the late 19th century. A census of 1860 revealed Oregon's wine production was some 2,600 gal/98 hl. Twenty years later, Jackson county alone was producing 15,000 gal and a post-PROHIBITION boom saw 28 wineries making a million gal by 1938, even if much of that was FRUIT WINE. Little progress was made in the next 25 years as California dominated the market.

Oregon's modern era dates from 1961, when Hillcrest Vineyard was established near Roseburg (well south of today's concentration of grape-growing) by Richard Sommer, a refugee from the University of California at DAVIS, where he had been firmly advised that *vinifera* grapes could not be grown in Oregon.

The Pinot Noir era dates from 1965. California refugee Charles Coury planted a wide range of Alsace varieties—including Pinot Noir—on the exact site in Washington county of an alleged 19th-century vineyard. But it is David Lett of the Eyrie Vineyard who is most frequently referred to as 'Papa Pinot', having first rooted Pinot Noir cuttings near Corvallis while researching a permanent vineyard site. In 1966, he replanted them in the north end of the Willamette valley in the Dundee hills—now the epicentre of Oregon's wine industry—convinced that Burgundian varieties could be grown better in Oregon than in California. He was followed by Dick Erath of Knudsen-Erath (now known as Erath Vineyards) among about six other true believers in those early years. The majority of the pioneers had done time in California before deciding that it was the wrong sort of place for their preferred style of wine.

Lett was to make the breakthrough that proved Davis wrong. It was his 1975 Eyrie Vineyard Pinot Noir that put Oregon under the spotlight with an eye-catching performance in a French-sponsored 1979 tasting comparing top French wines with their New World emulators: the Eyrie was placed second. Beaune merchant Robert DROUHIN staged a follow-up which served only to confirm the result. Drouhin eloquently endorsed it by purchasing land and building a state-of-the-art winery within a stone's throw of Lett's own vineyards in the Dundee hills.

By the mid 2000s, over 13,700 acres/5,547 ha of vines were planted with more than 300 wineries in production. In vineyard and volume terms, Oregon remains significantly smaller than WASHINGTON to its immediate north, but it achieved a good deal more publicity throughout the 1980s—almost certainly because the state focused its attention on PINOT NOIR, the red grape variety that had proved so difficult to please outside BURGUNDY.

Geography and climate

While almost all Washington state vines are planted in the rain shadow and semi-desert east of the Cascade mountains, most Oregon vines are directly exposed to the marine airflow of the Pacific ocean, giving milder winters but cooler and wetter summers than Washington. Oregon is notoriously wet, yet in most years the majority of the rain falls between October and April, not during the crucial part of the growing season. In a late-ripening year, however, rain during HARVEST can cause ROT and dilution, while flocks of migrating BIRDS can ravage a vineyard within hours.

Weather patterns in the early years of the 21st century however have at least temporarily adjusted Oregon's cool climate image. Heat and drought from 2000 to 2005 resulted in stressed grapes and more alcoholic wines. Climatologists have predicted that these La Niña and El Niño weather patterns run in cycles, so a return to a more CONTINENTAL climate for Oregon is expected.

Promoters of Northwest wine are fond of pointing to the similarities in LATITUDE between this area and Bordeaux and Burgundy. Such a comparison can be misleading, however, since it takes no account of the influence of TOPOGRAPHY. Where latitude does have an important influence is in the annual ration of SUNLIGHT, vital for PHOTOSYNTHESIS, but often overlooked by those preoccupied by temperature (see DEGREE DAYS).

In any marginal ripening climate, the choice of VINE VARIETY and selection of growing site take on added importance. Oregon's best-known wine district (and AVA) is the **Willamette Valley** (pronounced with the emphasis on the *a*), which stretches along the west bank of the Willamette river 150 miles/240 km from Portland in the north to Eugene in the south. Its vineyards lie on the foothills of the Coast range that forms the western edge of this broad valley, specifically in the Red hills of Dundee, so called for their ruddy-coloured clay-like Jory loam soils. Similar sites and soils, equally promising, can be found in the Eola hills between McMinnville and Salem, and the area just north of the Dundee hills known as Ribbon ridge with its prized Willakenzie soil mixture. (Dundee Hills, Red Hill Douglas County, and Ribbon Ridge are all AVAs.) It is reasonable to assume at least equal potential in many hitherto unexploited areas.

Contrary to common belief, Oregon vineyard soils owe little to volcanic origins and are not exceptionally fertile. Even as recently as the early 1990s, however, most vines were planted on their own roots, leaving them prey to PHYLLOXERA (although its spread has been slowed, though not halted, by the scattered distribution of the state's vineyards). By the mid 1990s, though, the new Dijon CLONES (grafted onto phylloxera-resistant ROOTSTOCKS) had gained popularity both as replacement vines and new plantings. Vineyard elevations are commonly between 250 and 750 ft/110–330 m. Frost is rarely a problem. Summer temperatures show little consistency, and harvest dates can vary from early September to late November. Wine characteristics differ accordingly. Pinot Noir ripened well in most of the 1980s vintages but, as in Burgundy, individual skill, or lack of it, has often been the greater influence on final wine quality. By the 1990s, wine-making skill had improved across the board, but a succession of rainy, difficult

harvests from 1995 to 1997, and the heat-stressed 1994, 1998, and 2003 vintages, challenged even the most conscientious winemakers. As a result, recent years have seen great VINTAGE variation among the wines.

There are also significant wine districts south of the Willamette valley: the **Umpqua Valley AVA** (which includes the **Red Hills Douglas County AVA**), the **Rogue Valley AVA**, the warmer and drier **Applegate Valley AVA**, and the **Illinois valley** just north of the California border and cooler and wetter by virtue of its proximity to the Pacific. The potential of south west Oregon is interesting and underdeveloped. Its main drawback may be commercial rather than climatic, for it lacks a major population centre. Its newest AVA is simply **Southern Oregon**, a blatant effort to distinguish itself from the cooler, more northerly Willamette valley.

The wineries of the northern Willamette valley (as well as the Columbia gorge area) received an additional seven new AVAs in the early 2000s in an effort to distinguish among and between the geographic differences, primarily for marketing purposes: **Ribbon Ridge**, **Chehalem Mountains**, **McMinnville**, **Eola-Amity Hills**, **Yamhill-Carlton**, **Dundee Hills**, and the previously mentioned **Columbia Gorge**, which straddles both Oregon and Washington.

Grape varieties

Pinot Noir has passed the test with many wines of commendable depth and complexity. PINOT GRIS followed (again first planted by David Lett of Eyrie Vineyards), achieving growing popularity in a crisp, dry style of characterful white showing more flesh than Pinot Grigio and more acidity than Alsace versions. CHARDONNAY was initially widely but not wisely planted, but from the mid 1990s the produce of Dijon clones began a new chapter in the history of Chardonnay in Oregon. RIESLING is commercially useful and is increasingly fashionable, while GEWÜRZTRAMINER works but is hard to grow and even harder to sell. ICE WINES made from Riesling and Gewürztraminer have been more obviously successful.

Among red wine grapes other than Pinot Noir, GAMAY Noir has seen success, mostly vinified the same way as Pinot Noir to produce generally bigger wines than light, fruity Beaujolais. MERLOT is rare since FRUIT SET usually fails, while CABERNET SAUVIGNON finds most of Oregon too cool, although fine examples have started to emerge from the south of the state. Syrah is planted primarily in the south (with some limited plantings in the upper Willamette valley, surprisingly) and has become a very popular variety with Pinot-focused wineries.

Wine-making today

Oregon is a sympathetic home for any vine which does not like too much heat (although

Pinot Noir grapes which ripen too fast may have to be picked before they reach full maturity in a particularly hot year). Increasingly mature vineyards and greater experience will reveal the extent to which the pioneers are justified in their hopes.

The economies of scale necessary for the production of cheap wine are not a feature of the Oregonian wine industry, which is therefore motivated by a need for quality rather than quantity. Crop YIELDS are small and the vines are mostly CANE pruned rather than CORDON pruned, thus demanding more time, care, and skill from the grower.

Some of Oregon's typically high prices softened in response to the American recession following September 11, 2001. Many wineries added a lower priced Pinot Noir to their line up, sometimes from their own vineyards, and occasionally produced from purchased wine. The role of the independent négociant also has blossomed, with producers such as A to Z and Big Fire cleverly buying oversupplied wines and blending them into well-priced bargains. These négociants can only exist as long as there are bulk wines available. With the growth of planting in Oregon over the first five years of the 2000s, there looks to be a secure supply at least through the first decade of the century.

The biggest issues of the 1990s were YIELD and CLONE choices. The lower yielding, earlier ripening Dijon clones promise potentially more complex Pinot Noir and Chardonnay. Many producers are deliberately reducing yields in an effort to produce superior, more concentrated wines. Oregon's wine producers are currently preoccupied by aspects of viticulture: the differing merits of ORGANIC, BIODYNAMIC, and merely SUSTAINABLE viticulture, this last best defined by the popular LIVE movement (a monitored Low Input Viticulture and Enology programme based on a Swiss model known as Vintura). It has been estimated that at least half of Oregon's vines are now at least effectively (if not necessarily certified) organic, and the number of converts to biodynamism was rising fast in the early years of the century.

A typical Oregon winery both owns vineyards and buys in fruit from specialist growers. Most wineries are relatively small, with an annual production of between 2,500 and 20,000 cases the norm. Most are proud to be run personally and relatively idiosyncratically. ACIDIFICATION is necessary only in the hottest vintages; and although CHAPTALIZATION may be practised, wines with a natural ALCOHOLIC STRENGTH of at least 12 per cent are easily achieved.   L.S.H.

Cass, B. (ed.), *Oxford Companion to the Wines of North America* (Oxford and New York, 2000).

Doerper, J., *Compass American Guides: Oregon Wine Country* (New York, 2004).

Haeger, J. W., *North American Pinot Noir* (Berkeley, 2004).

Hall, L. S., *Wines of the Pacific Northwest* (London, 2001).

www.WinesNorthwest.com

Orémus, former name for ZÉTA.

organic matter, the CARBON-containing matter left in the SOIL from the rotting of plant, animal, and microbial residues.

Normally most organic matter is in the top 20 cm/8 in of the soil, with some deeper as a result of deeply penetrating ROOTS and distribution by earthworms and other burrowing animals. On undisturbed soils, much of the store of readily available plant nutrients is associated with the surface layer and its organic matter, having been extracted from the SUBSOIL over the millennia and deposited at the surface in plant residues and those of grazing animals. This applies especially to the less soluble nutrients such as PHOSPHORUS and most of the trace elements, which do not appreciably leach down the profile except in very sandy soils.

Fresh organic matter reflects the composition of the plant and animal materials from which it was formed but, as decomposition proceeds, the more soluble elements are progressively leached away, unless quickly taken up again by plant roots. The end point of decomposition is a largely inert organic material called humus. Although fairly low in NITROGEN, this is still very important in helping to give the soil a desirable crumb structure and friability (see SOIL STRUCTURE). It also provides a framework for the absorption and further storage of both water and free nutrients, in states of varying bondage and accessibility to plant roots.

The total result in undisturbed soils is a constant recycling of nutrients and their steady availability to plants. Importantly, it is at rates which broadly match the favourable conditions for plant growth, and plant nutrient requirements. Sound viticulture aims, if necessary, first to build up soil organic matter content and that of associated MINERAL nutrients, and then to maintain them at a level just high enough to ensure soil health and a steady supply of nutrients appropriate to the needs of the vines. On initially infertile soils, this may necessitate a substantial use of FERTILIZERS or, in the case of ORGANIC and BIODYNAMIC VITICULTURE, of imported plant materials or animal wastes to make good any mineral element deficiencies. Only then is it possible to ensure vigorous growth of the green manure and COVER CROPS needed for the build-up or permanent maintenance of organic matter. At all stages, the increase or maintenance of soil organic matter demands that CULTIVATION, if any, be kept to an absolute minimum.

Viticulture for high-quality wine-making nevertheless demands that soil organic matter content and fertility be just high enough to ensure a suitable BALANCE between fruiting and moderate vegetative growth. Higher levels tend to be associated with excessive vegetative vigour and poor CANOPY MICROCLIMATES. Seguin discusses organic matter levels in relation to the top CRUS of Bordeaux. J.G.

Seguin, G., ' "Terroirs" and pedology of wine growing', *Experientia*, 42 (1986), 861–72.

organic viticulture, a system of grape-growing broadly defined as shunning man-made (industrially synthesized) compounds such as FERTILIZERS, FUNGICIDES, and PESTICIDES, as well as anything that has been GENETICALLY MODIFIED. It contrasts with 'conventional', sometimes even called 'industrialized' or 'chemical' viticulture, by utilizing naturally occurring substances. For instance, elemental sulfur and the salt copper sulfate (see BORDEAUX MIXTURE) are used to control POWDERY MILDEW and DOWNY MILDEW respectively. Both these treatments and others commonly used in organic vineyards (e.g. soap, plant oils, and powders such as BENTONITE) are contact or barrier sprays which, unlike chemically produced systemic sprays, do not enter either the vine's sap or the grape pulp and so are less likely to produce RESIDUES in the wine. Organic growers, especially those in damp, humid climates, are often criticized for relying too heavily on Bordeaux mixture, leading to copper toxicity in the soil, yet organic rules significantly restrict the amount used compared with the amount allowed in conventional vineyards (to one-third in France, for example).

Organic growers must therefore take the 'prevention rather than cure' approach to farming in general and to GREY ROT (BOTRYTIS BUNCH ROT) in particular by employing CANOPY MANAGEMENT techniques to open up the canopy and reduce the risk of rot. Organic growers argue that although such techniques can result in higher labour costs, which may have to be passed on in the price of the wine, they eliminate costs to the wider community such as cleaning up by local authorities of groundwater polluted by anti-rot sprays. They also argue that the emphasis on manual labour provides employment opportunities in communities suffering rural depopulation due in part to increased MECHANIZATION.

The primary concern for all organic farmers is soil health, for without a healthy, living soil in which to grow, the vine will struggle and the grower may become more reliant on chemical intervention. Organic growers regard the soil as having three essential properties: its physical structure and thus its capacity to hold nutrients and water, its chemical state (soil PH, for example, affects how well plants can take up nutrients), and crucially its biology or the prevalence of microbial life.

The primary route to soil health in organic vineyards is through the application of organic fertilizer in the form of COMPOST. This feeds the soil, rather than directly feeding the vine itself, allows the slow release of mineral NUTRIENTS, and encourages living organisms such as worms, beneficial bacteria, and fungi in the soil. Man-made or so-called chemical fertilizers provide nutrients but do not promote the intrinsic life in the soil. The principle of feeding the soil and not the plant also means that foliar feed fertilizers—those applied to the leaves of the vine—are prohibited under organic norms.

Growers who switch from conventional to organic soil management claim that vine shoots need much less frequent trimming as vine VIGOUR is reduced. This makes yields less erratic and reduces the risk of attack by fungal diseases, which are most attracted to nitrogen- or potassium-rich vegetative growth.

Weed management in organic vineyards tends to look quite different from that performed in many conventional vineyards, as the tidiness of a vineyard's appearance is seen as having no direct bearing on wine quality. Organic growers are generally tolerant of native plant growth between the vines, but taller weeds will be mowed by tractor, eaten by ruminants (usually sheep), burnt, or ploughed. Some organic growers are experimenting with spraying natural plant resins as a means of discouraging weed growth.

Weeds can also be suppressed by sowing COVER CROPS between the vine rows, usually in spring and/or autumn. Cover crops also benefit organic vines by encouraging beneficial fauna into the vineyard and helping to maintain biodiversity, creating polyculture out of the traditional vine monoculture. However, care must be taken in the choice of crop since some cover crops grown as companion plants can act as hosts for noxious pests: for example, flax grown as a renewable resource to tie down pruned vines in Chile acts as a host for MEALY BUGS.

Obtaining certified organic seed from a local source is often problematic. Forthcoming EU legislation which will make organic seed a prerequisite for certified organically grown seed crops should gradually increase the availability of seeds for cover crops such as oats and barley.

Bought-in cover-crop seed mixes raise concerns over the issue of air miles (see SUSTAINABLE VITICULTURE). An alternative is to manually collect seeds from selected native plants growing around the vineyard, as practiced at the Viñedos Organicos Emiliana (VOE) vineyard in Chile's Colchagua valley.

Organic pioneers in California are reducing the number of cover-crop sowings by mowing the cover crops only after they have set seed in situ. This reduces both the need to buy in seed and to plough. Minimal CULTIVATION preserves topsoil structure; it also means that the vineyard becomes a beneficial 'carbon-sink' rather than the cause of the release of carbon and dust into the atmosphere, both of which may contribute to global warming and, in the case of dust, encourage certain vine MITES.

Cover crops and organic compost also promote humus formation, which is especially vital for perennial crops such as vines, where no crop rotation is possible. Humus-rich soils are also more likely to hold vital water and nutrients than impoverished ones, and to promote the growth of mycorrhiza (symbiotic fungi) on vine roots, organisms which allow vine roots to penetrate deep into the soil and encourage the uptake of trace elements, both of which are said by some to make wines taste more TERROIR-specific or 'mineral' and thus more complex.

Cover crops can also have pesticidal properties; for example, mustard roots release compounds into the soil that NEMATODES find noxious. Some growers in California claim that a combination of selected cover crops, reduced irrigation requirements, and a switch from conventional fertilizer to organic compost has resurrected vineyards otherwise condemned as overly susceptible to attack from PHYLLOXERA.

History

The origins of the organic agriculture movement are European, and date from the 1920s when the green movement was closely intertwined with reactionary cultural and political phenomena such as National Socialism in Germany. After the Second World War, the organic movement provided a counterpoint to the increasing industrialization of agriculture necessitated by austerity and rapidly rising populations. However, whereas industrial food conglomerates found GLOBALIZATION both necessary and desirable, organic activists in Europe and North America were slower to form international bonds, and hence risked accusations of parochialism. The formation in 1972 of the International Federation of Organic Agriculture Movements (IFOAM) to oversee both the setting of the majority of the world's organic standards and the certification bodies has helped change this perception.

However, although the first organic vineyards date from the post-war period (in France at least), it took until the mid 1980s for wines produced from organically grown grapes to begin to shake off a reputation for earnest amateurism and increased costs.

One broad motor for change was increased public unease at the effects of industrialized farming, notably in the UK, where the food scandals of the mid 1990s and early 2000s involving BSE and foot and mouth disease provoked widespread public debate. Concern about the perceived threat that genetic modification might have on our food and wine stimulated greater interest in the alternatives. Genetically modified organisms (GMOs) are banned under every organic norm worldwide.

More particularly though, growers themselves began adopting organics in greater numbers, because they felt it would save money in the long term, by preserving and enhancing vineyard soils, and by giving the wines an organoleptic and marketing edge. Others, especially in Europe, were tempted by generous subsidies, paid over the period of organic conversion, usually a minimum of three and a maximum of five years. Subsidies have proved most attractive to growers in warmer, drier climates such as in southern France, southern Italy, Spain, and latterly Greece, where organic farming can occur almost by default, although the bureaucratic costs of, and fees for, organic certification have acted as a disincentive to some growers. Conversely, a few producers pay for organic certification but choose not to market their wines as organically grown, or practise organic methods but do not seek certification. In Chile, the move to organics since 2000 seems to have been spurred in part by concerns over worker safety and the previous mishandling of vineyard chemicals.

Conford, P., *The Origins of the Organic Movement* (Edinburgh, 2001).

Organic certification and terminology

Some scientists argue that all forms of existing viticulture are technically organic in the sense that grapevines are living organisms; an 'inorganic vineyard' is thus an oxymoron. Nevertheless, to be described as 'organic' a vineyard and/or its wine (see ORGANIC WINE) must, in most markets, have third party certification, usually from a non-governmental organization overseen by a ministry of agriculture or its equivalent.

It is important to distinguish between 'wine made from organically grown grapes' and 'organic wine', with the former being far more common. Indeed, 'wine made from organically grown grapes' is the only acceptable definition in the EU, since its organic directive covers practices in the vineyard alone and not in the winery. Organic certification is granted after a three-year conversion period as wine grapes are a perennial crop (conversion takes two years for annuals such as potatoes and carrots). Wine-making restrictions on the use of additives such as SULFUR DIOXIDE, processing aids such as FINING agents, and other agents such as yeast and enzymes, plus mechanical processes such as centrifugation and FILTRATION, are essentially left to individual certification bodies. Permitted levels of sulfur dioxide are generally at least 30 per cent lower than those tolerated for wines from conventionally grown grapes.

Most European certification bodies overseeing vineyards operate at the EU's baseline standards, although vineyard-specific bodies in Germany such as Eco-Vin are stricter, as are the (non-wine specific) Austrian Ernte für das Leben ('harvest for life') and Switzerland's IMO (Institute for Market Ecology), especially over the issue of buffer zones between conventional and organic plots.

In Australia and the USA, growers have the choice of producing 'wine from organically grown grapes' along the European model as well as ORGANIC WINE. The American system has been streamlined since October 2002 when the US Department of Agriculture launched its National Organic Progam (NOP). Previously each state had its own certifying agency and regulatory controls could vary widely from state to state. New Zealand's organic winegrowers have drawn up their own grapegrowing and wine-making standards under the Certified Organic Winemakers of New Zealand (COWNZ) banner. In France, Italy, and Spain, a set of standards designed to take account of regional rather than national factors would make more sense—ACIDIFICATION may be viewed as acceptable in Sicily but not in Champagne, for example. See also ALTERNATIVE VITICULTURE, BIODYNAMIC VITICULTURE, and SUSTAINABLE VITICULTURE.

Organic viticulture worldwide

Despite recent increases in organic vineyard conversions, notably in Argentina, Chile, and Australia, less than two per cent of the world's vineyard was expected to be certified organic by 2007. The major concentrations of organic vineyards are in the south of France (c.1.7 per cent of France's national vineyard is certified), Spain (1.5 per cent), Italy (3.4 per cent), Germany (2 per cent), Austria (1.8 per cent), and California (1.3 cent of the state). In most countries, the majority of organic vines belong to estate growers although in Spain and Argentina a significant number of organic hectares belong to CO-OPERATIVE growers. Statistics from Italy are patchy and hard to decipher as vineyards are often polycultural landholdings where vines, olives, and other fruits are interplanted. Flagship northern European regions such as Champagne struggle with organic viticulture in such an unfavourable climate and because the internal grape market there has tended to reward quantity above quality. Alsace, which is drier and influenced by Germany's green movement, has been Europe's most notable region for organic conversions since 1995 and, if current rates are maintained, around 50 per cent of the region will be certified by 2010 (although a cut in conversion subsidies from Paris may slow growth). California growers, especially those selling grapes rather than making estate wines, seem to dip in and out of certification with perplexing ease although the world's biggest producer of wines from organically grown grapes, Fetzer Vineyards, now farms all its own vineyards to certified organic standards (800 acres/325 ha or one-sixth of its grape needs), and has asked all its contracted growers to work towards organic certification.

See also ORGANIC WINE, BIODYNAMIC VITICULTURE. M.W.

Dutel, G. H., 'The viticultural and oenological aspects of organic wine production', *Journal of Wine Research*, 1/3 (1990), 225–30.

Rousseau, J., 'Wines from organic farming', *Journal of Wine Research*, 3/2 (1992), 105–21.

organic wine, wine produced from grapes produced by ORGANIC VITICULTURE and without the addition of SULFUR DIOXIDE during wine-making. The term is legally defined in only a very few countries such as the USA and Australia. In the EUROPEAN UNION, the directive covering organic viticulture does not cover the production or labelling of organic wine. Thus in the USA and Australia, a distinction is made between 'wine produced from organically grown grapes' (to which SO_2 has most likely been added during wine-making) and 'organic wine' (made without the addition of SO_2). However, in these countries, less than 1 per cent of wines produced from organically grown grapes are made and labelled as 'organic wine' due to concerns that the wine risks rapid BACTERIAL SPOILAGE, especially at bottling or during shipping. It may be that some varieties and wine styles, such as hefty tannic Zinfandels, are better suited to ageing under a non-sulfur ('sulfite-free') regime than delicate, aromatic whites such as Sauvignon Blanc or Riesling, for example.

The monitoring organizations which set and enforce standards for the production of 'wine made from organically grown grapes' do forbid the use of most other chemical additives, while allowing sulfur dioxide, usually at levels up to but no more than two thirds of the amount permitted for conventional (non-organic) producers. The one FINING agent which is universally forbidden is PVPP, although others are allowed, so that wines labelled in some way as organic may be unsuitable for VEGETARIANS AND VEGANS. (It is a common misconception that organic also equals vegetarian- or vegan-friendly.) It is also usually suggested that physical treatments (such as FILTRATION, THERMOVINIFICATION, and PASTEURIZATION) be kept to a minimum, although any restrictions on the latter are based on the need to conserve energy (fossils fuels) rather than on any scientific rationale. Rules governing wine-making for wines produced from BIODYNAMIC grapes are much stricter with regard to wine-making additives, the types of cleaning agents used on tanks and presses, and physical treatments. Organic and biodynamic wines are likely to remain a tiny part of the market because such wines usually taste best when sold direct from vat or barrel, at the farm gate, and to consumers who are willing to drink them almost immediately.   M.W.

origins of viticulture. Unlike brewing, WINE-MAKING is a natural process which does not strictly require any human intervention—in fact, apes often seek out fermenting fruits. To make wine, all that is needed is for the juice of a ripe grape to come into contact with airborne YEAST. Wine-making, then, was not 'invented' by mankind: humanity's role is a more modest one, to refine and guide.

Grape juice ferments quickly, so as long as grapes are available, from WILD VINES, wine can be made in little more than a day or so. Agriculture is therefore not a precondition of wine production. Nomadic tribes, who do not grow grain or pulses because they do not spend enough time in one place, can make wine. This makes it impossible to date the beginning of wine-making, and the only safe assumption is that, given the behaviour of apes, wine-making is at least as old as humanity itself, provided that mankind had access to grapes.

But what kind of grapes? Modern wine is commonly made from VINIFERA grapes, but other species of vine are capable of producing wine as well. From prehistoric times, wine could be made wherever people and grapes coincided. Yet there is little doubt that, of all the VITIS species, *Vitis vinifera* is the most suitable for wine. *Vitis vinifera* is believed to have originated south of the Black Sea in Transcaucasia, now GEORGIA and ARMENIA, since this is the area that still has the greatest variability of grape varieties and is therefore where humans were most likely to have started using it.

It is remarkable how close to this region is Mount Ararat, where, according to the account in the BIBLE, the Ark landed after the Flood and NOAH planted the first vineyard and became the first winemaker. The details of the biblical account cannot be right. Just as wine-making was not the invention of a single person, it was unnecessary to plant a vineyard in order to make wine. Planting a vineyard presupposes a fully sedentary way of life, which is a far more advanced state of civilization than that of the nomadic tribes or even of the earliest farmers, who were no more than subsistence farmers: sheep and goats require little care, and grain and pulses, which in the Near East can be harvested a few months after sowing, are not labour-intensive crops. After the harvest the farmer can move on with his animals. Archaeologists assume that by 7000 BC previously nomadic farmers in the Near East had taken up grain-farming and stock-breeding.

Domesticating fruit trees involves a different kind of existence. The first wild fruits to be domesticated in the Near East were the fig, the date, the olive, and the vine. Fruit trees have to be planted, grafted, and pruned, and they take years to reach maturity. The vine and the fig start producing fruit after three years, the date after five, and the olive tree needs five or six years to start producing but 25 to come into full bearing. Unlike grain and pulses, orchard crops will benefit generations of farmers living on the same land. Deliberate cultivation of fruit trees such as the vine therefore presupposes a fully sedentary way of life and a complex social and economic system, with one generation leaving property to the next. This stage was probably reached in the 4th millennium BC or possibly the 5th.

While collecting berries from the wild and making wine out of them is a casual activity, systematic viticulture demands time, careful thought, and technical skill. In order to produce good wine, and lots of it, the farmer presumably wanted the highest-yielding vines with the largest, sweetest berries. In the wild, fruit trees are raised from seed, but when they are domesticated they need to be propagated by taking CUTTINGS and GRAFTING. Wild populations are allogamous, i.e. they need other members of the same species in order to reproduce. As a result, their progeny varies, and this variation is not desirable for the fruit grower, who wants grapes (or other fruit) of a consistent size and taste. Hence CLONAL SELECTION and propagation, which allows farmers to select the kind of fruit they want, and to continue producing from this preferred type.

The wild grape, which botanists now generally class as a subspecies, *silvestris*, of *Vitis vinifera*, has smaller, more acid berries. *Silvestris* grapes also differ from cultivated grapes in the shape of their pips, which tend to be more globular than those of cultivated grapes. They are also smaller and have a stalk or beak at the attachment to the main body of the pip (see PALAEOETHNOBOTANY). These differences have enabled archaeologists who study plant remains to determine whether a population is wild or cultivated. But the evidence needs to be treated with caution, because the differences are slight. Yet when remains can be identified beyond reasonable doubt as exclusively *vinifera*, we can conclude that the people in the area were orchard farmers who cultivated the grapevine and did not just gather berries from the wild.

Unfortunately not many remains have been found, but carbon dating of those that we have suggests that *Vitis vinifera* was cultivated in the 4th millennium BC; there is no physical evidence of earlier cultivation. These finds are from Ancient EGYPT (Omari) and Syria (Hama) in what was then MESOPOTAMIA. The earliest remains of *vinifera* found around the Aegean Sea (Ancient GREECE and the islands) have been dated c.2500 BC.

However, cultivation of *Vitis vinifera* is not necessarily the same thing as wine-making. Grapes can be eaten as whole fruits, they can also be pressed, and the juice can be made into wine. Archaeologists have found remains of PRESSES dating from the Bronze Age (i.e. c.3000 to 1050 BC). Finds of empty grape skins together with pips and stalks at Myrtos, Crete, from the early Minoan period (i.e. c.3000 BC) are proof of wine-making as opposed to the production of table grapes.

Yet the earliest piece of evidence is not a grape skin or a stalk or a pip at all: it is a wine stain. In the 1970s, a Persian AMPHORA dating from 3500 BC was found at Godin Tepe, IRAN. Recent chemical analysis of the red stain inside has shown that it contains both TANNINS and TARTARIC ACID, suggesting that the amphora must have had wine in it.

Taken together, these pieces of evidence show that the vine was domesticated for the purpose of producing wine first in the region between and to the south of the Black sea and the Caspian sea at least as early as the 4th millennium BC and that subsequently cultivation spread west in the following millennium to Egypt and the Aegean belt. Less evidence for the prehistoric period is available west of here: there are remains of *Vitis vinifera* but none that suggest viticulture. The exception is southern Spain: finds include vine stem cuttings (from the Cueva del Monte de la Barsella north of ALICANTE), which point to cuttings as a method of propagation in the 3rd millennium BC. At other sites, fragments of stem and pips go back to the 4th millennium BC. Whether the early development of viticulture in southern Spain was a consequence of contact with the Levant we do not know.

Archaeological research in the early 1990s finally proved that viticulture was not introduced to Italy by the Greeks. The ETRUSCANS, who occupied the western half of central Italy between the Arno and the Tiber and whose civilization flourished from the 8th century BC until they were conquered by the Romans in the 4th century BC, cultivated *Vitis vinifera* which had been growing wild in Italy for thousands of years. This does not rule out the possibility that Greek VINE VARIETIES were introduced at various stages of Italy's history. In the south and in SICILIA, Greek varieties came over with the Greek colonists (from the 8th century BC), but they may also have used wild specimens of *vinifera* which they found in their new territories. The Roman authors of AGRICULTURAL TREATISES testify, from the 1st century BC, that Greek vine varieties were imported into Italy by Roman farmers, presumably because they wanted to improve their wines by experimenting with the new varieties.

As for France, the Greek colonists who founded Massilia (modern Marseilles) around 600 BC introduced viticulture there. Like their counterparts in Italy, they probably brought their own vine cuttings over with them, but they may have used vines growing wild in Massilia as well.

Viticulture was subsequently spread throughout much of Europe from Ancient ROME (see also CELTS), within Gaul from Massilia and Narbo (Narbonne) in the 1st and 2nd centuries BC. See FRANCE for more details.

See also PALAEOETHNOBOTANY AND THE ARCHAEOLOGY OF WINE. H.M.W.

McGovern, P. E., *Ancient Wine* (Princeton and Oxford, 2003).

—— Fleming, S. J., and Katz, S. H. (eds.), *The Origins and Ancient History of Wine* (New York, 1995).

Nuñez, D. R., and Walker, M. J., 'A review of palaeobotanical findings of early *Vitis* in the Mediterranean and of the origins of cultivated grapevines', *Review of Palaeobotany and Palynology*, 61 (1989), 205-37.

Renfrew, J., *Palaeoethnobotany: The Prehistoric Food Plants of the Near East and Europe* (London, 1973).

Wilson, H., *Wine and Words in Classical Antiquity and the Middle Ages* (London, 2003).

Orion, modern vine crossing, a DISEASE-RESISTANT VARIETY, which produces crisp, aromatic white wine not unlike SEYVAL BLANC, notably in England.

Orléans, VDQS for wines produced around the city of Orléans where the river Loire turns west, and Burgundian influence is evident in the choice of grape varieties. At one time this was an important wine region but the development of the RAILWAYS changed all that and today only about 100 ha/250 acres of vineyards remain. They are too close to Paris to be of much practical interest to wine drinkers outside France, for the pale and fragrant reds, and rosés, made from MEUNIER grapes, here called Gris Meunier, have many devotees in the French capital. Reds and rosés may also be made from Pinot Noir or, in the case of reds from gravelly soils, Cabernet Franc. Light white wines, which are very much in the minority, are made from Chardonnay and Pinot Gris, here sometimes called Auvernat Blanc and Gris respectively. About 100 ha/250 acres of vineyard are dedicated to Orléans while **Orléans-Cléry** is an even smaller VDQS zone south west of the city for Cabernet-based reds.

See also LOIRE, including map.

Ormeasco, local name for DOLCETTO on the north western coast of Italy. For more details, see LIGURIA.

Ortega is popular as an OECHSLE booster in German wines, especially with the blenders of Rheinhessen. This CROSSING of Müller-Thurgau and Siegerrebe produces extremely full-flavoured wines that often lack acidity but can reach high MUST WEIGHTS, if not quite as high as the equally early-ripening but less widely planted OPTIMA. Varietal wines are made, and QMP Ortega is a distinct possibility even in less good vintages, but a little goes a long way. The vine does not have good disease resistance, however, and its susceptibility to COULURE leaves Optima the more obvious choice for the Mosel-Saar-Ruwer. Germany's total plantings dropped from around 1,200 ha/2,960 acres in the the late 1980s to 805 ha in 2003. The variety is also quite popular in ENGLAND, for obvious reasons.

Ortrugo, white grape grown in the hills around Piancenza in EMILIA, often blended with Malvasia.

Orvieto, dry, medium dry, and sometimes—although increasingly rarely—sweet white wine produced near the medieval hill city of the same name, an important artistic centre during the late Middle Ages and Renaissance, is one of Italy's historically renowned white wines and by far the most important DOC in UMBRIA. The production zone is divided into a CLASSICO zone of over 1,700 ha/4,300 acres, extended by 600 ha of regular Orvieto. Production figures reflect the relative size of these zones, with Orvieto Classico accounting for around 80 per cent of the 147,500 hl/3.9 million gal produced in an average year.

The historic Orvieto, described by Gabriele d'Annunzio as 'the sun of Italy in a bottle', was a lightly sweet wine, often concentrated by some NOBLE ROT obtained by storing the harvested grapes in the humid caves and grottoes that dot the TUFFEAU soil of the zone. Modern Orvieto is based on 40 to 60 per cent of TREBBIANO TOSCANO blended with 15 to 25 per cent VERDELLO, the remainder being made up of GRECHETTO, CANAIOLO DRUPEGGIO, and/or MALVASIA. It is overwhelmingly a dry wine, the sweet or amabile version accounting for less than 5 per cent of total production. Like most blends with a Trebbiano base produced in substantial quantities—YIELDS of up to 11 tonnes/ha are permitted by the DOC rules—dry Orvieto tends to be a bland, pedestrian product. The 1980s saw attempts to develop a richer, more luscious style of sweet Orvieto more dependent on NOBLE ROT. Some interesting wines resulted but those made from Sauvignon Blanc or Riesling had to be marketed as VINO DA TAVOLA since the DOC rules for Orvieto did not foresee this development.

Commercial difficulties in the 1990s led many producers to conclude that a substantial modification of the formula for the Orvieto blend was needed, with a large increase in the overall percentage of Grechetto at the expense of Trebbiano and Drupeggio. (Such Trebbiano as remains may well be largely Procanico, a subvariety with significantly smaller berries and bunches.) The emergence of superior red wines IGT wines from Orvieto, however, in many cases made from Sangiovese, Merlot, and Cabernet, and of lusciously sweet dessert wines based on INTERNATIONAL VARIETIES, have further complicated the picture, revealing a potential that has little relation to the wines which gave the zone its name and reputation. D.T. & D.C.G.

Osey, variously spelt **Oseye** and **Osaye,** fortified wine from PORTUGAL drunk in England in the 15th century, thought likely to have originated from vineyards near Lisbon, the name being an English corruption of the locality of Azóia northwest of Lisbon. See also CARCAVELOS and SETÚBAL. R.J.M.

Mayson, R., *The Wines and Vineyards of Portugal* (London, 2003).

osmosis. See CONCENTRATION.

Österreicher strictly means 'Austrian' in German and is also an old synonym for one of SILVANER's parents.

Ottavianello, Puglian name for the French red grape variety CINSAUT.

ouillage, French word meaning both ULL-AGE and TOPPING UP.

ovary, the ovule-containing part of the pistil of a FLOWER which, in the grapevine, develops into the grape berry. After FLOWERING, the ovary becomes a berry and the ovules become seeds (see GRAPE). B.G.C.

overcropping, a vine condition which reduces grape RIPENING and wine quality. It is associated with low LEAF TO FRUIT RATIOS. Overcropping can be due to PRUNING to many buds with some fruitful varieties, or to a loss of leaf area as a result of INSECT PESTS or FUNGAL DISEASES. If climatic conditions are limiting for PHOTOSYNTHESIS, as with low temperatures or very limited sunlight, then vines may be considered overcropped. The grapes of overcropped vines are typically lower in sugar, colour, and flavour, and have an increased PH. Wines made from such fruit are typically termed thin.

Overcropping is a term which is also used emotively in arguments against high vineyard yields. Provided that the vine is in BALANCE and good health, even high yields can be properly ripened with good weather. See also YIELD. R.E.S.

overripeness. See SURMATURITÉ.

o.w.c. stands for 'original wooden case' and is frequently used as a description in the sale of FINE WINE. See CASE.

oxidation, wine fault resulting from excessive exposure to OXYGEN (as opposed to AERATION, which is deliberate, controlled exposure to oxygen). Wines spoiled by oxidation are said to be **oxidized**.

Oxidation is a threat as soon as the grape is crushed, which is why high-quality grapes are transported to the winery as fast as possible in shallow containers, and why field pressing stations sited as close as possible to the vineyard are increasingly common. When the grape is crushed, unless special precautions are taken to exclude oxygen, it immediately starts to react with the liberated juice compounds. The most obvious change is the browning of the juice resulting from the oxidation of PHENOLICS catalysed by an ENZYME (polyphenol oxidase, also known as laccase) present in grapes and thus referred to as enzymatic oxidation or enzymatic browning. The presence on the grapes of moulds associated with ROT introduces additional oxidative enzymes which accelerate reactions with oxygen, especially those involved with browning. Small amounts of SULFUR DIOXIDE are therefore usually added at the time of crushing to inactivate enzymes and counter the oxidation of phenolics. See PROTECTIVE JUICE HANDLING for the techniques involved in minimizing the risk of oxidation.

Some winemakers, however, deliberately encourage a certain amount of prefermentation oxidation of grape varieties such as Chardonnay in order to develop a range of flavours other than those associated with primary fruit AROMA. Sometimes known as hyperoxidation, this also enhances enzymatic oxidation of phenolics and their conversion to insoluble polymers, which are then removed by CLARIFICATION treatments. As a result, the wine contains lower amounts of phenolic compounds that may generate brown pigments and haze through non-enzymatic oxidation reactions (see below) and is thus more stable. See WHITE WINE-MAKING for more details.

The last step of FERMENTATION, the REDUCTION of ACETALDEHYDE to ETHANOL, is coupled with the oxidation of the co-enzyme NADH, as shown in this equation:

$$CH_3CHO + NADH + H^+ \rightarrow$$
$$CH_3CH_2OH + NAD^+$$

Note that no new oxygen is involved in this reaction, but that the essence of the reduction is the transfer of electrons from the co-enzyme to the acetaldehyde. Most oxidation–reduction reactions involved in growing grapes and making wine are of this type.

In wine itself, however, exposure to oxygen in the presence of an organism such as ACETOBACTER could result in a reversal of the above reaction, with alcohol being oxidized to acetaldehyde. The NADH produced by oxidizing alcohol is, in turn, oxidized by oxygen from the air. When this happens, the wine loses its fresh, fruity aroma and becomes vapid and flat smelling. Further exposure to oxygen converts the acetaldehyde to ACETIC ACID, the acidic component of wine VINEGAR, the winemaker's bête noire.

Oxygen reacts with the phenolics in both white and red wines through complex chemical oxidation processes that may also promote oxidation of ETHANOL to ACETALDEHYDE. In whites, the COLOUR changes from light yellow to amber and ultimately brown, and at this last stage the quality of a table wine is usually seriously impaired. In reds, with their greater complement of phenolics (ANTHOCYANINS, TANNINS, and PIGMENTED TANNINS), the colour change is much less apparent and a red wine can accommodate, and indeed benefit from, considerably greater exposure to oxygen than a white wine. While the natural formation of stable pigmented tannins in a red wine is a process requiring oxidation, other products of the reaction of the wine's phenolics with oxygen bring about highly desirable changes in the sensory properties of the wine. An appropriate level of oxygen exposure is usually accomplished through PUMPING OVER, DÉLESTAGE, RACKING, TOPPING UP, and the usual transfer operations imposed on a red wine.

To produce table wines attractive in aroma and colour, and certainly those designed to be drunk young, the winemaker generally restricts the exposure of must and wine to oxygen as much as is technically feasible (see PROTECTIVE WINE-MAKING for more details).

Some wines, however, such as *oloroso* SHERRY, tawny PORT, and MADEIRA, owe their character to deliberate exposure to oxygen. And those who make wines of all sorts are constantly experimenting with various aspects of controlled oxidation, often motivated by the role played by oxygen in AGEING. See WHITE WINE-MAKING, RED WINE-MAKING, and MICRO-OXYGENATION.

The term MADERIZATION is sometimes used interchangeably with oxidation, although it should theoretically also involve excessive exposure to heat.

See also OXYGEN. A.D.W. & V.C.

oxidative wine-making contrasts with PROTECTIVE WINE-MAKING in that the winemaker deliberately exposes the wine to oxygen at various stages in the wine-making process in order to encourage certain reactions and achieve a particular style of wine—*oloroso* SHERRY being an extreme example. See also OXYGEN, AERATION, BARREL MATURATION, and HYPEROXIDATION.

oxygen, colourless, odourless, tasteless gas that makes up nearly 21 per cent of the atmosphere. It is essential to all animal life forms and for many other living systems. Unlike NITROGEN, which makes up a much higher proportion of air and is inert, oxygen is highly reactive. Oxygen interacts with grape juice, must, and wine in both good ways (see AERATION) and bad ways (see OXIDATION).

Handling juice

A small amount of oxygen (about as much as dissolves in must as it comes from the CRUSHER) is required for the multiplication of the YEAST that will conduct the alcoholic FERMENTATION. Larger amounts may well be detrimental by oxidizing PHENOLICS. The aim of PROTECTIVE JUICE HANDLING is to minimize oxidation.

Making wine

During fermentation, the CARBON DIOXIDE given off by the nascent wine prevents exposure to oxygen, but, when fermentation ceases, the wine must be protected from access to oxygen if it is to remain wine. Early winemakers learned that, with very few exceptions, wines had to be kept in full containers at all times lest they change into VINEGAR.

Modern winemakers have equipment which allows most steps in making wine to exclude oxygen. One of the most effective has been the STAINLESS STEEL tank in which ULLAGE space can be filled with INERT GAS to exclude oxygen. Wooden vats, casks, and barrels are not sufficiently impervious for this blanketing technique. Some tanks have lids that can be raised or lowered depending on the volume of liquid in the tank. In older wineries, the oxidation of wine was minimized by frequent small additions of SULFUR DIOXIDE, which, although it is needed less frequently as an antioxidant in modern wine-making, is still used to inhibit microbial activity. ASCORBIC ACID has also been used to a certain extent as an antioxidant, but it must be employed in conjunction with sulfur dioxide (see ERYTHORBIC ACID too). REFRIGERATION of wine in storage slows all reactions, including oxidation, but it has the danger that oxygen solubility increases at low temperatures. The aim of PROTECTIVE WINE-MAKING is to minimize oxidation, although see WHITE WINE-MAKING for alternative approaches.

Oxygen plays a positive role during RED WINE-MAKING, when the small doses of oxygen which the wine receives during the inevitable operations of filling, RACKING, and TOPPING UP

deepen and stabilize COLOUR, soften and intensify flavour, and assist natural STABILIZATION and CLARIFICATION by encouraging the precipitation of the less stable PHENOLICS.

See also OXIDATION, AERATION, MICRO-OXYGENATION, and SERVING WINE.

A.D.W. & P.J.W.

ozone is a form of OXYGEN having three instead of the usual two oxygen atoms per molecule. It is formed in the upper atmosphere by the action of ultraviolet light on normal oxygen; and, by being opaque to further incoming ultraviolet light, happily prevents most of the potentially very damaging ultraviolet wavelengths from reaching the earth's surface.

Some man-made molecules such as the chlorofluoro carbons, used in REFRIGERATION, can, if released into the atmosphere, add to the

effects of natural gases from volcanoes, etc. to destroy ozone. This occurs only at very low temperatures, such as occur over the poles in winter, but is nevertheless a matter of concern.

Some ozone is also released into the lower atmosphere as an industrial pollutant, and can cause a recognizable 'stippling' of vine leaves close to industrialized areas. Its significance to viticulture has been studied in California and New York state, but the economic effects remain uncertain.

In a wine-making context, ozone has been advocated as a sanitizing agent for the maintenance of HYGIENE in a winery and for use, for example, on stainless steel tanks, bottling equipment, and barrels. Ozone is sometimes used in cork manufacture as a preventive measure to retard microbial growth, though its effectiveness is uncertain.   J.G. & P.J.W.

Paarl, important wine district in SOUTH AFRICA.

Paarl Riesling. See CAPE RIESLING.

Pacherenc du Vic-Bilh, defiantly Gascon name for tangy white wines made in the MADIRAN region from a mixture of intensely local grape varieties and an import: PETIT COURBU and PETIT MANSENG, which must make up at least 60 per cent, ARRUFIAC (also known as Arrufiat and Ruffiac), Gros Manseng, and Sauvignon, the last making up no more than 10 per cent of the blend. The deep yellow wine can be either dry or more probably sweet, depending on the VINTAGE, and tastes like a slightly more alcoholic (thanks to Petit Courbu) version of JURANÇON, which is made further south. More than 220 ha/540 acres are dedicated to this keenly priced wine, which may be picked as late as December. The sweet wines, made from PASSERILLÉ grapes, can last ten years or so in bottle. The Plaimont co-operative has access to some excellent fruit.

Pacific Northwest, self-conscious region in the far north west of the UNITED STATES. A beautiful and unspoilt landscape and some fine regional products, including food and wine, have brought a sense of pride to the states of WASHINGTON, OREGON, and IDAHO. Comparisons with CALIFORNIA, the state to the immediate south, are habitually made.

packaging of wine most often involves BOTTLING, but alternative packages for wine include BOXES, CANS, and CARTONS.

Padthaway, a significant, moderately cool, primarily grape-growing (rather than wine-making) region in the south east of SOUTH AUSTRALIA. While all the mainstream varieties are grown in the region, and while grape quality is, as elsewhere, sensitive to yield, Shiraz is a regional specialty, and can produce long-lived wine of high quality.

Pagadebit, occasionally **Pagadebito** or **Pagadebiti,** is sometimes used as a synonym for the BOMBINO BIANCO of Puglia, but it is also a distinct variety which is enjoying a certain revival in Romagna in north central Italy, and also grown across the Adriatic in the former Yugoslavia. The name refers to the vine's reliable yields which, in theory, should allow growers to pay their debts. It is also known as Debit.

pago, Spanish term for a vineyard, used particularly in JEREZ and CASTILLA Y LEÓN.

Païen. See HEIDA.

País, the second most common grape variety in CHILE (having been overtaken this century by Cabernet Sauvignon) although it is not used for wine of export quality. It is most common in Maule and Bío-Bío in the south and is also sometimes known as Negra Peruana. There were about 15,000 ha/37,000 acres in Chile in the early 2000s.

Pakistan. According to OIV statistics, the total area of vines in this Asian ISLAMIC republic grew from 3,000 ha/7,400 acres in the late 1980s to 13,000 ha in the early 2000s. They are dedicated to the production of TABLE GRAPES and DRYING GRAPES, but VINIFERA wine may occasionally be made from WILD VINES growing in the high valleys along the Silk Road, where one of the richest resources of ancient, genetically varied plant material may still be found.

palaeoethnobotany and the archaeology of wine. The study of the botanical remains of grapes and wine residues found in archaeological excavations is something of a detective story in which small pieces of evidence are put together to build up a picture of the development of mankind's use and, later, domestication of grapes.

The botanical evidence consists of the remains of vine LEAVES, BERRIES, STEMS, and SEEDS or pips; sometimes even the roots, or the hollows left by them, may subsist too. Their recovery is the result of painstaking examination of archaeological deposits. Usually the finds of grape remains form a very small proportion of the total botanical material recovered, the bulk of which is usually the seeds of annual crops such as cereals, pulses, and oilseeds.

The most common remains of grapes found are grape pips and they usually subsist because they have become charred at the time of deposition. Once converted to charcoal, they will subsist in recognizable form for many thousands of years buried in the ground. On other archaeological sites they may be preserved in damp or wet soils in a waterlogged condition. Elsewhere, where there is a high concentration of calcium in the groundwater, they may become mineralized or semifossilized. Sometimes stray pips were incorporated in handmade clay pots and when the pots are fired, they burn out leaving a small hole the exact size and shape of the pip.

Occasionally, complete fruits survive in charred form, as when grapes were thrown on to a funeral pyre as part of the ritual, e.g. at Salamis and Athens. Exceptionally, finds of skins of fruits (possibly remains of pressings) survive, for example at early Minoan Myrtos, Crete (see Ancient GREECE).

Finds of burnt fruit stalks (PEDICELS) are exceptional but can be taken to indicate the presence of domesticated vines (the stems of bunches of WILD VINES are very strong and robust and do not come away with the fruit in the way that those of cultivated vines do). They have been recovered from the Greek prehistoric sites of Sitagroi and Myrtos.

The Greek prehistoric potters of the early Bronze Age developed the habit of standing

their pots on upturned vine leaves to dry in the sun before firing. This resulted in the veins on the underside of these leaves being finely impressed and then baked on the bases of these pots. In some places—the Cyclades, for example—these are the only evidence that grapes were present on these islands at that time. Vine leaves were also used on clay sealings of Bronze Age pots, such as at Menelaion near Sparta. If vine leaves were being used in these ways by the Bronze Age Greeks, they may also have been used for cooking, as they are in Greece today.

The critical question in examining all this palaeoethnobotanical material is how can one tell whether it is derived from wild or cultivated sources. Apart from the fruit stalks, just discussed, it is the size and shape of the pips which give us the clue: the pips of wild grapes are spherical with a short stalk or beak and a small, round chalazal scar on one side, and two divergent grooves on the other side of the pip. The pips of cultivated grapes are usually larger and pear shaped. The stalk is usually longer, the chalazal scar larger and often oval in outline, and the grooves on the back of the pip parallel to each other. These features can be seen on the archaeological material, however it is preserved.

The domestication of grapes seems to have first taken place around 4000 BC in the region between the Black and Caspian seas. The domesticated grapevine provides fresh fruit, dried raisins, sultanas and currants (according to the VINE VARIETY), wine, vinegar, grape juice, and a light salad oil obtained by crushing the pips. The most significant product, however, was wine, which was greatly valued.

Finds of wild grape pips in archaeological contexts go back to the earliest palaeolithic sites in Europe, for example at Terra Amata in the south of France (c.350000 BC), where the fruits appear to have been eaten. There are a number of sites from the mesolithic period (12th–9th millenium BC) with finds of wild grape seeds: from Belma Abeurader, France, to Grotte del Uzzo in Sicilia, the Frangthi Cave in southern Greece, Çayönü in Turkey, Tell Abu Heureya, Syria, and Jericho in Jordan. The earliest finds of pips from domesticated grapes come from the neolithic site of Shulaveris-Gora in Georgian Transcaucasia, dated c.6000 BC. From this site too comes a residue of resinated wine in a pot: the earliest find of wine to date. Another site which has yielded traces of neolithic wine is Hajji Firuz Tepe in northern Iran. Here a kitchen was excavated dating to 5400–5000 BC. In it were six jars set into the floor with their lids nearby. Chemical analysis has shown that they contained wine resinated with resin from the terebinth tree. It is not clear whether this wine was made from wild or cultivated grapes (wild grapes still grow close to the site today). If all these jars had contained wine they would have held around 50 litres, sug-

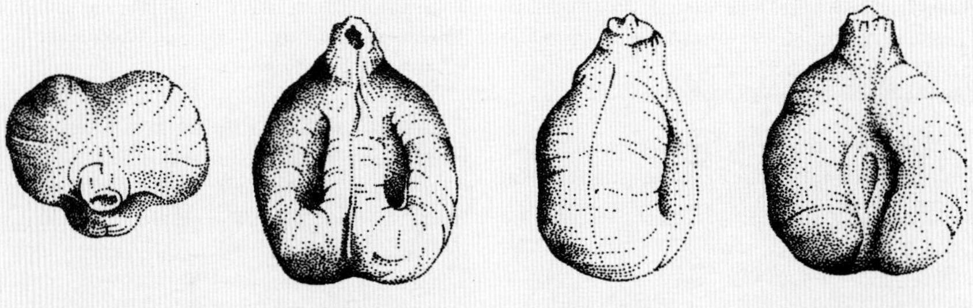

Fig 1. seed (pip) of wild vine *Vitis silvestris*

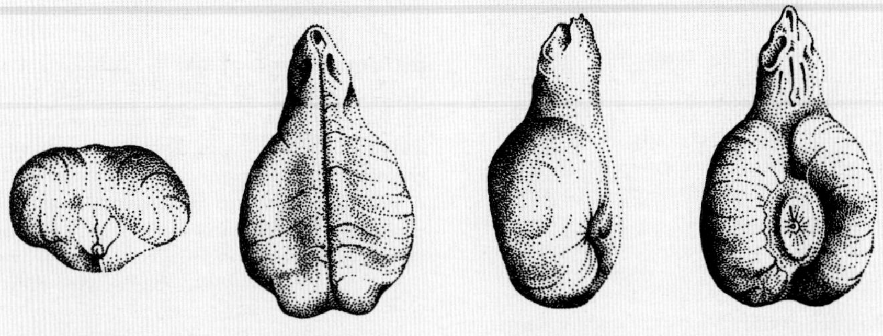

axial view · ventral (inner) view · lateral view · dorsal (outer) view

Fig 2. seed of cultivated vine *Vitis vinifera*

axial · ventral · lateral · dorsal

The exact shape of ancient grape pips helps **palaeoethnobotanists** determine whether the pips came from wild or cultivated vines.

gesting large scale wine production at a very early date.

It is not essential that vines were domesticated before WINE-MAKING was invented. What appears to be necessary is having a suitable container in which to store the wine during and after the FERMENTATION process. All the ingredients—the sweet, juicy fruit, and airborne YEAST—are available for wild fruits. Thus, it is possible that the finds from palaeolithic sites (Old Stone Age) in the Mediterranean region of wild grape pips could indicate that wine-making had begun using leather bags even before the beginnings of agriculture.

The finds of grape remains such as pips, stalks, and skins in circumstances suggesting wine production are rare. One exceptional find comes from Kurban Huyuk in eastern Turkey, where masses of grape pips, stem and vine fragments were found together with cakes of pressed fruits in a mid to late 3rd millennium BC pit. In prehistoric GREECE, they occur associated with spouted vessels on the early Bronze Age sites of Áyios Kosmas, Attica, and Myrtos in Crete. Remains of wine presses also occur occasionally as at Minoan Vathypetro in Crete, and there are a great number of drinking vessels made from exotic materials from Bronze Age sites suggesting that drinking wine was a special activity.

Analysis of residues found in the bottom of pottery containers has been undertaken by Patrick McGovern of MASCA in the University Museum, Philadelphia, using infrared, liquid chromatography and other chemical techniques to identify traces of tartaric acid, calcium tartrate and terebinth resin indicating the residues of wine. The actual residues in the bases of pithoi of wine have not been found very often (partly because the analysis of residues found in pottery vessels is still comparatively new in archaeology). Apart from identifying the earliest finds of wine residues, detailed above, these analyses have also given evidence of the earliest trade in wine. This dates back to 3500 BC at Godin Tepe, IRAN, where a reddish deposit turned out to be formed from TARTRATE crystals (similar to those which form on the bottom of wine corks today). Godin Tepe lies on a well documented trade route through the Zagros mountains to lowland Mesopotamia. Even stronger evidence of trade comes from the earliest finds of wine residues in Egypt from the royal tomb of Scorpion I at Abydos dating to 3100 BC. Here three rooms in the tomb formed a kind of wine cellar filled high with about 700 amphorae arranged in three or four layers one on top of another. They were stoppered with clay sealings bearing fine seal impressions. Deposits of crusty yellow residues inside the amphorae turned out to be of a resinated wine. In addition, 47 of them contained grape pips and several had raisins, stalks, skins, pips, and dried pulp intact. Eleven of the jars also contained the remains of sliced sycamore figs which had been strung together and suspended in the wine. Analysis of the clays from which the amphorae were made indicated that they probably came from various regions in the southern Levant. Viticulture was firmly established in the delta region of Egypt and in some of the western oases by the Sixth Dynasty (*c.* 2323 BC). Processes of wine-making are shown in paintings and engravings on the walls of tombs from the Old Kingdom onwards, for example in the tomb chapels at Beni Hasan, especially nos. 15 and 17.

One of the most romantic finds of labelled wine jars must be that from Tutankhamun's tomb. They were sealed with clay and their contents were reduced to dried residues. The 26 wine jars have labels indicating the location of the vineyard, the year of the vintage (the majority belonging to the years 1345 BC, 1344 BC, and 1340 BC), the ownership of the vineyard and the name of the chief vintner. Most of them came from the western delta, one from the eastern delta, and one from the El Kharga oasis. Two of the vintners had Syrian names; four of the jars were labelled 'sweet wine'.

Analyses have also shown that sometimes wine was mixed with other alchoholic beverages. It appears that this was the case in Minoan Crete, where a number of residue analyses have shown that wine was mixed with barley beer and honey to form what McGovern has called 'Geek grog'. This was also the case in the finds from Midas' tomb at Gordion in Turkey (*c.*700 BC), where the funeral feast consisted of a tasty lamb and lentil stew washed down with an intoxicating beverage made from mixing wine, barley beer, and honey mead.

Other early residues of wine are known from 7th century BC CYPRUS, and from the contents of AMPHORAE in a Roman shipwreck off the southern coast of France, near Marseilles. There is a Roman glass BOTTLE containing what is claimed to be Roman wine in the museum in Speyer, Germany.

From apparently insignificant remains of grape pips, stalks, pulp, and leaves, and the analyses of dried up residues in the bottom of pots, found by chance to subsist in sediments on archaeological sites, and extracted with painstaking care, it is possible to begin to understand the ORIGINS OF VITICULTURE and its development. J.M.R.

Ancient biomolecules

In 2003, scientists at the Botanical Garden of Geneva, Switzerland, were able to analyse for the first time by DNA PROFILING a tiny amount of DNA from waterlogged and charred grape pips recovered from archaeological sites in France (Iron Age and Greek period, 5th century BC) and Hungary (Roman times, 2nd to 4th centuries AD). These remains could not be matched to any modern cultivar, but they could be assigned to their most likely geographic origin. DNA profiling of additional grape remains from archaeological sites as well as comparison between wild and cultivated grapes throughout the distribution

of VITIS VINIFERA in the future might shed some new light on the place and time of the first domestication(s) event(s) of grapes. J.V.

McGovern P. E., Fleming, S. J., and Katz, S. H. (eds.), *The Origins and Ancient History of Wine* (New York, 1995).
—— *Ancient Wine* (Princeton and Oxford, 2003).
Renfrew, J., *Palaeoethnobotany: The Prehistoric Food Plants of the Near East and Europe* (London, 1973).
Sandler, M., and Pinder, R. (eds.), *Wine, A Scientific Exploration* (London and New York, 2003).

palate, term used when describing TASTING as a process and an ability. It is generally used to describe the combined human tasting faculties in the mouth and, sometimes, NOSE. The impact of a wine on the mouth may be divided chronologically, and somewhat loosely, into its impact on the front, middle, and back palate. The word may also be used more generally as in describing a good taster as 'having a fine palate'.

Palatinate, originally territory under the jurisdiction of a local authority with sovereign powers, the term came to be used for that part of Germany which today includes both Rheinhessen and the PFALZ wine regions. It has been used as an alternative English name for the German wine region Pfalz. See also GERMAN HISTORY.

Palette, miniature appellation of barely 35 ha/86 acres in PROVENCE in the hills east of Aix-en-Provence. The appellation is a relatively old one, created in 1948 in recognition of a distinctive LIMESTONE outcrop here. A single property, Ch Simone, produces most of the wine, and for many years has been responsible for all the most serious wine of the appellation. For seven generations, Ch Simone has been in the Rougier family, who continue to respect the traditional wine-making techniques, involving very old vines, prolonged fermentation, and BARREL MATURATION using very little new wood. FIELD BLENDS of southern vine varieties make extremely dense, long-lived reds, full-bodied rosés, and white wines which belie modern white wine-making philosophy.

George, R., *The Wines of the South of France* (London, 2001).

palissage, French term for VINE TRAINING.

Palladius (4th century AD). Next to nothing is known about the life of this agrarian writer of Ancient ROME. He is the author of a treatise called, like Varro's earlier work, *De re rustica*, in 15 books. The first book is a general introduction to farming; the last two comprise a guide to veterinary medicine and an account of GRAFTING. The remaining 12 books deal with the tasks to be carried out throughout the agricultural year, one book for each month; Palladius has more to say about the vine than about any other crop. What he says, however, is sound but not original: he relies heavily on earlier authors, especially COLUMELLA (and,

to a lesser extent, PLINY and VARRO). Unlike CATO, Varro, and Columella he was well known in the Middle Ages and in the early Renaissance: he is quoted by Albertus Magnus, Vincent of Beauvais, and PETRUS DE CRESCENTIIS, and an anonymous Middle English translation of his work, connected with Humphrey, duke of Gloucester, survives. There is no direct evidence for his influence on medieval English wine producers, however. H.M.W.

Palmela, DOC on the Setúbal peninsula in southern Portugal. See TERRAS DO SADO for more details.

Palo Cortado, a traditional and fully natural style of sherry based on a fluke of nature. This is a wine that was originally pre-selected to become a *fino* or, later, an Amontillado, i.e. a wine of greater finesse than those pre-selected to become *olorosos*, which are aged in OXIDATIVE fashion from the start. Yet some examples of these more delicate wines never develop the protective veil of FLOR yeast they need to become an Amontillado and end up ageing in *oloroso* fashion. As a result, such wines have an intermediate style—the elegance of the Amontillado with the power and body of the Oloroso. This is the rarest category of sherry, yet some of the greatest dry sherries are Palos Cortados. For more details, see SHERRY. V. de la S.

Palombina. See PIEDIROSSO.

Palomino, white grape variety most closely associated with the making of SHERRY around JEREZ in southern Spain and generally declining in importance elsewhere. It is almost certainly of Andalucian origin, supposedly named after one of King Alfonso X's knights. **Palomino Fino,** which once grew exclusively around Sanlúcar de Barrameda (see MANZANILLA), has been adopted as the most suitable variety for sherry production, as distinct from the lowlier Palomino Basto or Palomino de Jerez once widely used.

The vine is relatively susceptible to DOWNY MILDEW and ANTHRACNOSE and responds best in warm, dry soils. Its loose, generous bunches of large grapes make it suitable for TABLE GRAPES as well as wine. Its yield is relatively high and regular, about 80 hl/ha (4.5 tons/ acre) without irrigation, and the wine produced is, typically, low in both ACIDITY (as low as 3.5 g/l expressed in tartaric acid) and fermentable SUGARS. This suits sherry producers who pick Palomino grapes at about 19 °Brix (see MUST WEIGHT) and find Palomino must's tendency to oxidize no inconvenience, but for this very reason the variety tends to make rather flabby, vapid table wines, unless substantially assisted by ACIDIFICATION.

Of Spain's 28,000 ha/69,000 acres or so of Palomino Fino, the great majority is in sherry country around Jerez but it has also been planted in CONDADO DE HUELVA, where it is edging out ZALEMA. It was also once planted in Galicia and Rueda but is being uprooted there in favour of local varieties. In the increasingly vinously significant CANARY ISLANDS, it is the main white variety and notably successful.

Outside sherry country, as in France, it is often known as Listán, or Listán de Jerez. See LISTÁN for details of the declining fortunes of this variety in France. It is commonly thought to be the Perrum of the Alentejo in southern Portugal.

The country with the most Palomino planted outside Spain has been SOUTH AFRICA, but the variety, known as Fransdruif in Afrikaans and White French in English, has been losing ground fast and is generally distilled or used for blending into basic table wines.

California's acreage of the variety, once wrongly identified as Golden Chasselas, is also falling, from just over 1,000 acres/400 ha to about 650 acres during the mid 2000s, almost all of them in the SAN JOAQUIN VALLEY, where the wine produced is used chiefly for blending. In Australia, total plantings had fallen to fewer than 100 ha/247 acres by 2004, much of it grown in SOUTH AUSTRALIA and used for making sherry-style FORTIFIED wines. New Zealand once also grew a surprising amount of Palomino considering its hardly ideal climate but the vines have been systematically replaced with more suitable varieties. Argentina has limited planting of the variety but PEDRO GIMÉNEZ predominates. CYPRUS has imported the Palomino vine because of its dependence on producing inexpensive copies of sherry.

Pamid, Bulgaria's most widely planted and least interesting indigenous grape variety producing rather thin, early-maturing red wines with few distinguishing marks other than a certain sweetness. It does not play a major role in bottles bound for export. It is also planted quite extensively (4,800 ha/1185 acres in 2005), as Roşioară, in Romania.

Pampanuto, also known as **Pampanino,** minor Puglian white grape which is invariably blended with more acid wine.

Pansa Blanca, synonym for the Spanish white grape variety XAREL-LO, used in ALELLA. A **Pansa Rosado** is also known.

Pantelleria, VOLCANIC island at the extreme southern limit of Italy and closer in fact to Cape Bon in TUNISIA than to the southern coast of SICILIA, to which it belongs administratively. Moscato di Pantelleria is one of Italy's finest dessert wines, made from the ZIBIBBO (MUSCAT OF ALEXANDRIA). The wine has enjoyed a certain reputation since the 1880s, when the MARSALA house of Rallo began to market it, and it was awarded a medal at the Paris Exhibition of 1900. It was placed on the official list of Italy's 'typical' wines in 1936 and the accompanying description, with due allowance for hyperbole, has an undeniable correspondence to a good bottle of Moscato di Pantelleria today: 'velvety, sweet, caressing, and generous'. The viticulture of the island is unusual: vines are GOBELET trained but buried in a hole (called a 'crater' by local growers) to protect them from the fierce winds that sweep across the island.

Moscato di Pantelleria comes in two different versions. The first is the regular Moscato, with a minimum alcohol level of 8 per cent and 40 g/l of RESIDUAL SUGAR, although many of the better producers raisin the grapes for 10 to 12 days to achieve a higher total alcohol level and a greater quantity of residual sugar (see DRIED GRAPE WINES); wines with a POTENTIAL ALCOHOL of 17.5 per cent can be called *vino naturalmente dolce*. The second version is lusher and richer and is true dessert style, which made the wine's reputation. This Moscato Passito di Pantelleria must have at least 14 per cent alcohol and 110 g/l residual sugar, although a current trend is to seek a more decadently sweet style, raisining the grapes for up to 30 days and arriving at close to 140 g/l of residual sugar. This search for power comes at a cost: the Moscato perfumes tend to be destroyed by the very high level of VOLATILE ACIDITY that results from prolonged drying under the hot sun. A PASSITO with a potential alcohol of 23.5 per cent and one year of ageing can theoretically be called Extra, although the term is rarely encountered on labels.

After a period of neglect and decline, Moscato di Pantelleria seemed in the early 1990s to experience a period of revived popularity and recognition in Italy, with an undeniable increase in the overall quality level and some interest in the product on the part of the commercial houses of Marsala, who have begun to market the wine once again.   D.T.

Paraguay in SOUTH AMERICA produces 60,000 hl of wine a year, according to OIV figures.

Pardina, light-skinned grape grown in EXTREMADURA shown by DNA PROFILING in 2005 to be a clone of CAYETANA Blanca.

Parellada, highly regarded Catalan white grape variety grown on 10,000 ha/25,000 acres in 2004 and widely used, with MACABEO and XAREL-LO, for the production of CAVA. It is the least planted of these three varieties in PENEDÈS, the region most closely associated with these Spanish sparkling wines. Parellada can produce a fine, high-quality wine when grown in relatively poor soil and in cooler conditions, but has a tendency to over-produce lower-quality wine in fertile soils. It has large, loose bunches of large grapes which have good resistance to BOTRYTIS BUNCH ROT. It has been blended successfully with both Chardonnay and Sauvignon Blanc, most notably in some BARREL-AGED examples from TORRES. It is also an important variety in COSTERS DEL SEGRE.

Paris, capital of FRANCE, once the centre of a thriving wine region and still one of the few capital cities in which vineyards of any size may be found (although see also VIENNA). Rueil, Suresne, Nanterre, Coulombe, and Argenteüil were all renowned for their wine in the 17th century. Today there are still several suburban vineyards, and even a small vineyard on the slopes of Montmartre, whose meagre produce, from 2,000 vines originally densely planted in 1933, is auctioned for charity.

History

Wine was grown around Paris in the 4th century, and its fame as a wine-growing area dates from long after the Roman empire. Clovis, king of the Franks 481–511, made Paris the capital of his kingdom and from the 8th century onwards Frisian, Saxon, and English merchants sailed up the river Seine to Paris to buy wine. Under the Merovingians and the Carolingians, Paris was an important centre of trade, and much of the wine sold there would have been produced locally.

A document from the beginning of the 9th century shows that viticulture was a major part of the local economy. The Roll of Irminon, named after the abbot of St-Germain-des-Prés who instigated this survey of his monastery's lands, is the only document of its kind dating back to the time of CHARLEMAGNE. Vineyards at Rambouillet, Dreux, Fontainebleau, Sceaux, and Versailles were cultivated not only by monks but also by laymen, and it is clear from the amounts produced that there must have been a surplus to sell on the open market. Documents from the Abbey of St-Denis, near Paris, show that St-Germain-des-Prés was not unique in this respect. In the 9th century, St-Denis had vineyards in the abbey precincts and possessed wine-growing estates in the Île-de-France, as the Paris basin was known; many smaller monasteries in the area also produced wine for sale (see MONKS AND MONASTERIES).

In the 10th century, Paris was well established as a centre of the wine trade. The main trade route was down the Seine to Rouen (today an important wine BOTTLING centre for northern European markets) and thence overseas. In the late 10th century, merchants from England, Ireland, Flanders, and Picardy visited Rouen, and later Henry II (king of England, including Normandy, 1154–89) gave Rouen the monopoly of transporting wine to England. The other, later (from the 13th century onwards), trade route from Paris was down the Seine or up the Oise as far as Compiègne, where the wine would be loaded on to carts and carried to Flanders by road. By then the merchants of Paris had managed to acquire for themselves privileges similar to those of their Gascon counterparts (see BORDEAUX). In an edict of 1190, Philip Augustus, king of France, declared that only the merchants of Paris, who were themselves usually wine producers as well (see CLIMATE CHANGE for details of the warmer MACROCLIMATE prevailing then), had the right to sell wine in Paris. They were able to prevent the sale of any wine they wished: thus they regulated the import of wines from outside the region and they controlled the quality of the wines sold as 'vins de France'. The wines of AUXERRE, CHABLIS, and Tonnerre had to pass through Paris before they were permitted to be transported further, and wines from other regions were not to be offered for sale before the 'vins de France' had all been sold. The wines of the LOIRE were also put on the market in Paris.

The 'vins de France' included not only the wines of Paris up to Vernon in Normandy but also those of CHAMPAGNE (Rheims, Épernay, Châlons-sur-Marne): this usage continued among wine producers until just after the French Revolution. The Capetian kings of France, who reigned from 987 to 1498, were particularly fond of the wines of Paris, but some of what they drank must have been from Champagne, since no distinction was made. In those days the region grew more than it could drink. Some of it was sold to the neighbouring areas of Normandy, Picardy, and Artois; the principal foreign export markets in the Middle Ages were England and Flanders. The 'vins de France' were highly esteemed both at home and abroad: in 1200 they fetched higher prices in London than the wines of ANJOU.   H.M.W.

Dion, R., *Histoire de la vigne et du vin en France* (Paris, 1959).

Lachiver, M., *Vins, vignes et vignerons* (Paris, 1988).

Parker, Robert M., Jr (1947–), extremely influential American wine critic whose most obvious contribution to the LITERATURE OF WINE has been the concept of applying NUMBERS to wine. His scores, followed slavishly by some COLLECTORS and even more INVESTORS, have a demonstrable effect on individual wine PRICES.

Robert Parker was born in farming country near Baltimore and both trained and worked as a lawyer there. He discovered wine at the age of 20 on his first trip to France. By the mid 1970s, at the height of active consumerism, Parker became frustrated by the lack of truly independent and reliable wine criticism, and began to think about launching his own consumer's guide to wine buying.

The first, complimentary, issue of his bimonthly newsletter the *Wine Advocate* appeared in 1978, and by 1984 he felt confident enough of its success to retire from the law and concentrate on the punishing schedule of tastings and travel on which it is based. By then he had made a name for himself with his enthusiastic, and unusually detailed, endorsement of

the 1982 vintage in Bordeaux, and subscriptions grew rapidly with the American market for wine FUTURES. By 1998, when a French language edition was launched, the *Wine Advocate* had more than 45,000 subscribers, mainly in the United States but in more than 35 other countries. There are no advertisements and little background, but hundreds of TASTING NOTES and assessments of individual, usually fine, wines. His judgements have had a significant effect on market demand and the commercial future of some producers.

Parker's was by no means the first American consumer wine newsletter, but it was the first to use scores between 50 and 100 for individual wines quite so obviously. This system was easily and delightedly grasped by Americans familiar with high school grades, even though Parker himself urges caution, asking readers to use the numerical ratings 'only to enhance and complement the thorough tasting notes, which are my primary means of communicating my judgments to you'. Wine salesmen have been less circumspect and use Parker's ratings mercilessly, while the notion of SCORING wine at all came under attack from some other wine authorities, notably Hugh JOHNSON, whose view is that wines themselves vary with time and conditions of tasting, and that wine tasting is an intrinsically subjective process. Parker's own view, stated on the cover of every issue of the *Advocate*, is that 'wine is no different from any consumer product. There are specific standards of quality that full-time wine professionals recognize.'

Parker's diligence in recording the impressions of his hard-worked palate (he regularly tastes more than 100 wines a day) has provided the ingredients for several lengthy books, and not just the annual *Wine Buyer's Guides*, which are essentially *Advocate* compendia. *Bordeaux* (originally subtitled 'The Definitive Guide to the Wines Produced since 1961') first appeared in 1985 and enjoyed considerable success in the United States, in Britain in 1987, and in France in 1989. The fourth, fully revised, and more modestly subtitled ('A Consumer's Guide to the World's Finest Wines') edition appeared in 2003. *The Wines of the Rhône Valley and Provence*, which appeared in 1987, reflected Parker's other great passion (he was instrumental in establishing the reputation and ambitious pricing policy of Côte Rôtie's GUIGAL). A second edition, entitled *Wines of the Rhône Valley*, appeared in 1997. *Burgundy* (1990), with its complex mosaic of appellations, producers, and vintages, and its less predictable wines, succumbed less easily to being 'Parkerized'. He has since taken on a Burgundy specialist assistant, Pierre-Antoine Rovani; Daniel Thomases, the orginal Italian contributor to this work, reports on Italian wines; and David Schildknecht reports on Germany, Austria, eastern Europe, and the eastern US.

Parker is recognized as a fervent, if critical, admirer of French wines. He was the first

non-Frenchman to write a wine column for *L'Express* magazine, and was made a particularly emotional Chevalier de l'Ordre du Mérite National in 1992. The Légion d'Honneur followed in 1999.

With a few notable and sometimes voluble exceptions, most agree that Parker is a gifted taster and diligent reporter. But his success has won a degree of power over the wine market so great that it is dangerous, in that such a high proportion of producers, particularly red wine producers, seem deliberately to be adapting the style of their wines to suit this one, compelling palate regardless of their own personal tastes.

Langewiesche, W., 'The million-dollar nose', *The Atlantic Monthly*, 286/6 (2000) 42–62.

McCoy, E., *The Emperor of Wine* (New York, 2005).

Parraleta, interesting, fragrant red wine grape rescued from extinction in Spain's SOMONTANO region.

partial rootzone drying, or PRD, Australian vineyard IRRIGATION technique designed to control vine VIGOUR and maintain wine quality with minimum interference to YIELD. It also requires less irrigation water than many conventional techniques. PRD was developed by scientists Dry and Loveys from the University of ADELAIDE and CSIRO, after observation of basic vine physiology in response to WATER STRESS. Using vines with divided root systems, they discovered that when only a portion of a vine's root system was drying, shoot growth was slowed. The hormone ABSCISIC ACID was found to be produced by drying roots, and to subsequently cause reduced shoot growth.

Field experiments with Cabernet Sauvignon showed that it was possible to control shoot vigour and reduce the amount of water needed while maintaining yield and quality. This was achieved with two DRIP IRRIGATION lines per row, used alternately for irrigation while the other part of the root system was drying. Commercial evaluation of PRD began in the mid 1990s.

The results from these studies can be used to interpret some of the known beneficial effects of water stress, especially for red wine quality. It is also possible that such findings will explain the acknowledged TERROIR effects on wine quality (Professor Seguin in Bordeaux having shown the importance of some vine roots drying near the surface while the vines continue to draw water from much deeper levels). See also REGULATED DEFICIT IRRIGATION.
                                                      R.E.S.

Kriedemann, P. E., and Goodwin, I., *Irrigation Insights* 4: *Regulated Deficit Irrigation and Partial Rootzone Drying* (Canberra, 2003).

Loveys, B. R., Stoll, M., and Davies, W. J., 'Physiological approaches to enhance water use efficiency in agriculture: exploiting plant signaling in novel irrigation practice', in M. A. Bacon (ed.), *Water Use Efficiency in Plant Biology* (Oxford, 2004), 113–142.

McCarthy, M. G., Loveys, B. R., Dry, P. R., and Stoll, M., *Water Reports 22: Regulated Deficit Irrigation and Partial Rootzone Drying as Irrigation Management Techniques for Grapevines* (FAO, 2002).

Pascal Blanc, almost extinct Provençal light-berried vine variety, very sensitive to POWDERY MILDEW and ROT.

Pascale di Cagliari, Sardinian dark grape speciality.

Paso Robles, very large California wine region and AVA on the inland side of the coastal mountains. See SAN LUIS OBISPO.

passerillage, French word for the process by which **passerillé** grapes are DRIED, shrivelled, or raisined on the vine, concentrating the SUGAR IN GRAPES—an alternative to wines whose sugars have been concentrated by BOTRYTIS.

Passerina, Marche name for BIANCAME.

Passetoutgrains. See BOURGOGNE PASSETOUTGRAINS.

passing the port. One of the wine trade's most cherished traditions is the rule that PORT, particularly a decanter of vintage port, must be passed round a table from the right to the left of diners. No single satisfactory explanation has ever been advanced, although so fiercely held is the custom that a miniature railway was constructed to transport decanters across an inconvenient fireplace in the Senior Common Room of New College Oxford.

Howkins, B., *Rich, Rare & Red* (London, 1982).

passito, Italian term for DRIED GRAPE WINE.

Pasteur, Louis (1822–95), a scientific genius and gifted scholar, has left a body of work which impinges on physics, chemistry, microbiology, agronomy, and medicine. On the centenary of his birth in 1922, the Institut Pasteur in Paris published a monograph on his principal discoveries listed under the following headings:

1847: Molecular disymmetry
1857: Fermentations
1862: Supposedly spontaneous generations
1863: Study of wines
1865: Silkworm diseases
1871: Study of beers
1877: Virus diseases
1880: Viral vaccines
1885: Rabies protection

Pasteur's original work on what were supposedly spontaneous generations, or transformations, led him to interpret the process of alcoholic FERMENTATION and to demonstrate that this, far from being spontaneous, was the result of intervention by living cells, YEAST, using sugar for their own nutrition and transforming it into ALCOHOL and CARBON DIOXIDE. 'The chemical act of fermentation is

essentially a phenomenon which correlates to a vital act . . . Now what for me constitutes this chemical division of sugar (into alcohol and carbonic gas), and what causes it? I admit that I have no idea' (*Œuvres de Pasteur*, ii. 77). With something approaching genius, Pasteur understood the phenomenon without being able to provide a precise explanation; contemporary biochemistry was able to explain in detail the different stages of the chemical fermentation mechanism only in the first half of the 20th century.

During his career as a scientist, Pasteur must have devoted only three or four years to the study of wine. Yet in this time he achieved as much as a good specialist researcher would have been delighted to achieve in an entire lifetime. Not only did he apply his theories to fermentation and ensure the mastery of the basics of vinification and conservation of wines, he also perfected the art of adding TARTARIC ACID, demonstrated the presence of SUCCINIC ACID and GLYCEROL, and made valuable suggestions about the role of OXYGEN in wine AGEING.

But it was above all in the field of microbiological diseases of wine that Pasteur's work has been most valued. One of the early problems assigned to Pasteur was to explain and prevent the vinegar spoilage of red wines shipped in barrel from Burgundy to England, as well as to try to explain some of the many FAULTS in French wine which had become apparent at the time. He identified the following transformations in various wine constituents:

mannitic acid: degradation of sugars
'tourne': degradation of tartaric acid
bitterness: degradation of glycerol
'graisse': production of a polysaccharide

From his discovery of the various micro-organisms which caused different wine maladies, such as the ACETOBACTER which turn wine into vinegar, came the whole science of bacteriology. He suggested that the application of heat (now called PASTEURIZATION) would destroy these micro-organisms and prevent microbial development, with beneficial effects on the quality of wine. The demonstration of the existence of these BACTERIAL DISEASES was extremely fruitful for the science of OENOLOGY; it resulted in the progressive reduction in VOLATILE ACIDS in wine which was an important factor in raising overall quality. Pasteur's research work on wine, and beer, also gave rise to his remarkable studies on the cause and prevention of infectious diseases in humans and animals.

From a drop of faulty wine, characterized by the presence of micro-organisms which could be seen with the aid of a microscope and by faults which could be tasted, Pasteur could contaminate a perfectly healthy wine. He expressed his thoughts thus: 'When one observes beer and wine experiencing fundamental changes because these liquids have given asylum to microscopic organisms which were

introduced invisibly and fortuitously to them, where they since proliferated, how could one not be obsessed by the thought that similar things can and must sometimes happen to humans and animals?' (1866)

Whatever the undoubted merits of Pasteur's work, to which we owe the basis of wine microbiology, with all its practical consequences for vinification and wine conservation, it should be noted that he did not understand the positive role that LACTIC ACID BACTERIA could have in degrading MALIC ACID. Because of this it was particularly difficult to grasp the principles of MALOLACTIC FERMENTATION, which, in 1930, Jean RIBÉREAU-GAYON elucidated as a bacterial transformation which could be of great benefit to a wide range of wines. It was not until the 1970s that the rest of the wine world was convinced. Not without reason, Émile PEYNAUD has written, 'the evolution of oenology would certainly have been very different if Pasteur, instead of leaving us the basis of a perfect method of adding tartaric acid, had taught us to add malic acid'.

For Pasteur 'yeast make wine, bacteria destroy it'. Pasteur truly created the science of wine-making; if today oenology is a discipline in so many universities throughout the world, it is to Pasteur that we owe this achievement.

P.R.-G.

pasteurization, process of heating foods, including wines, to a temperature high enough to kill all micro-organisms such as YEAST and BACTERIA. It is named after Louis PASTEUR, the French scientist who discovered that micro-organisms were alive and the cause of much wine spoilage.

Heat sterilization techniques have improved greatly since the early versions of pasteurization, which often resulted in burnt or cooked flavours in wines treated, particularly those that had not been subjected to complete CLARIFICATION. Wines are pasteurized by rapid heating to about 85 °C/185 °F for one minute, quick cooling, and return to storage tank or bottling line. Keeping the wine longer, for up to three days, at about 50 °C/122 °F is used to coagulate heat-unstable proteins and to speed ageing in low-quality red dessert wines. **Flash pasteurization** may also be effected by heating to temperatures as high as 95 °C for a few seconds, followed by rapid cooling. Some wine is **hot bottled** (at about 55 °C) and allowed to cool slowly or, for utmost effectiveness, closed bottles of wine are occasionally heated to about 55 °C and cooled to room temperature under a water spray. These techniques are relatively brutal, however, and are used only on ordinary wines which have no potential for improvement after BOTTLE AGEING. A.D.W.

Patrimonio. See CORISCA.

Pauillac, small port and communal appellation in the Médoc district of Bordeaux which has the unparalleled distinction of boasting three of the five first growths ranked in Bordeaux's most famous CLASSIFICATION within its boundaries—Chx LAFITE, LATOUR, and MOUTON-ROTHSCHILD—as well as a bevy of other CLASSED GROWTHS rivalling them (and each other) with increasing insistence. For all the importance of its wines, Pauillac gives the impression of being the only settlement in the Haut-Médoc to have an existence independent of wine—an impression reinforced by its size and nearby industrial installations.

This, however, is Cabernet Sauvignon country *par excellence*, and while there is considerable variation between different properties' TERROIRS and wine-making policies and capabilities, certain expressions recur in Pauillac tasting notes: cassis (blackcurrant), cedar, and cigar box (the last two sometimes a reflection of the top-quality French oak cooperage which the selling prices of Pauillac permit). A high proportion of the Médoc's most concentrated wines are produced here.

About 1,200 ha/3,000 acres of vines produce this famous appellation in an almost continuous strip between Pauillac's boundary with ST-JULIEN to the south and ST-ESTÈPHE to the north, separated from the waters of the Gironde estuary by only a few hundred metres of *palus* too marshy for serious viticulture (although very suitable for grazing Pauillac's famous *agneaux présalés*, saltmarsh lamb). This strip of vines, 3 km/2 miles wide and more than 6 km long, dedicated to the production of the world's most famously long-lived red wine, is divided into two by the small river Gaët, whose banks are also unsuitable for vines. As elsewhere in the Médoc, the layers of GRAVEL here provide the key to wine quality, offering excellent DRAINAGE, aided by the almost imperceptibly undulating topography and a series of *jalles* or streams running water off the gravelly plateau and into the Gironde.

The stars of the northern sector of Pauillac are undoubtedly the two ROTHSCHILD properties Chx Lafite and Mouton-Rothschild, whose plots of vineyard are intermingled on the plateau of Le Pouyalet, reaching the considerable (for the Médoc) altitude of 30 m/100 ft at its highest point. Clustered around them are their satellite properties, whose wines benefit from the first-class wine-making ability of their owners. Ch Duhart-Milon is Lafite's fourth growth, made in the town of Pauillac. The fifth growths Ch Clerc-Milon and Ch d'Armailhac (the latter called Ch Mouton Baron Philippe and then Ch Mouton Baronne Philippe between 1956 and 1989) are made, to an often very high standard, close to Mouton itself. Other classed growths on this plateau just a stream away from St-Estèphe are the fifth growths Chx Pontet-Canet and the generally much less exciting Pédesclaux.

Throughout the 1970s, much was made of the inter-Rothschild rivalry in the northern half of Pauillac, resolved by the next generation. In the mid 1980s and early 1990s, the extreme south of the appellation around the village of St-Lambert was a battleground for wine supremacy, between first growth Ch Latour and, particularly, its near neighbours the two Pichons. All three of these have made considerable investments in their vineyards, *chais*, and more cosmetic aspects of their property, and the Pichons have demonstrated that, just like first growth Latour, they are capable of making sublime wine at the St-Julien end of Pauillac. The Pichon-Longueville estate was originally one, but had already been divided into a smaller 'Baron' portion and a larger Comtesse de Lalande portion by the time the 1855 classification ranked them in the bottom half of the second growths (a much lower position than they merit today). In the early 20th century, Pichon-Baron, as it was known, was highly regarded. By the early 1980s, Pichon-Longueville-Lalande had decisively overtaken it in reputation. By the early 1990s, however, Pichon-Baron had been lavishly renovated by AXA Millésimes and renamed, confusingly, Pichon-Longueville, once more offering a perennial challenge to its neighbours.

In the hinterland of this southern extreme of Pauillac are neighbouring fifth growths Chx Batailley and Haut-Batailley, whose wines can challenge those of fifth growth Ch Grand-Puy-Lacoste to the immediate north, which is run impeccably by Xavier Borie and can offer some of Pauillac's best value. A dozen of the 18 fifth growths are in Pauillac, and none has been more successful than the Cazes family's flamboyantly styled Ch Lynch-Bages (the name betraying the original Irish connection), whose standing and fame suggest a considerably higher ranking. Chx Lynch-Moussas, Croizet-Bages, and Grand-Puy-Ducasse have rarely merited the limelight, although Grand-Puy-Ducasse was extensively renovated in the 1980s. Ch Haut-Bages-Libéral, between Chx Latour and Lynch-Bages, has produced fine vintages.

Two of Pauillac's most distinctive products do not feature in the 1855 classification. Les Forts de Latour, the SECOND WINE of Ch Latour, is regularly one of its most successful wines (and it is priced as such), while the co-operative at Pauillac is a particularly important one, selling some of its considerable produce under the name La Rose Pauillac.

For more information see MÉDOC and BORDEAUX.

Coates, C., *Grands Vins* (London, 1995).

Duijker, H., and Broadbent, M., *The Bordeaux Atlas* (London, 1997).

Parker, R., *Bordeaux* (4th edn, New York, 2003).

Penning-Rowsell, E., *The Wines of Bordeaux* (6th edn, London, 1989).

pays. French for country. See VIN DE PAYS.

PCA, or **2,3,4,5,6-pentachloroanisole**, see TETRACHLOROANISOLE.

PCD. See PLANT CELL DENSITY.

PCR, abbreviation for **polymerase chain reaction**, a laboratory method based on DNA analysis used to detect vine pathogens. This technique has helped in determining strains of VIRUS, for example, and the INSECTS responsible for their spread.

Weber, E., Golino, D., and Rowhani, A., 'Laboratory testing for grapevine diseases', *Practical Winery and Vineyard* (Jan/Feb 2002), 13–27.

pearls or **pearl glands**, small, spherical nodules that develop on the surface of vine stems, PETIOLES, and the underside of leaves along the large veins. They form under warm humid conditions, such as in a glasshouse, and when the vine's growth is exuberant. They are a multicellular outgrowth of the epidermis, even to the extent of an occasional STOMA, but collapse to a rusty colour and disappear when the humidity drops.   B.G.C.

Pécharmant, expanding red wine appellation within the BERGERAC district in SOUTH WEST FRANCE. Almost 400 ha/1,000 acres of vines were dedicated to the appellation by the mid 2000s, planted on gravelly, south-facing slopes just east of the town of Bergerac. The wines are some of Périgord's longest-lived reds, made from Bordeaux grape varieties, especially MERLOT. Little of it escapes the region, however. Within the zone, some sweet white wine is made in the much smaller ROSETTE appellation.

Pecorino, vine speciality of the Marche and Abruzzo on Italy's east coast making a slow comeback because of its firm, dry, minerally white wine that compares well with the local Trebbiano.

pectinase, an ENZYME used to break up grape PECTINS and thus speed up SETTLING. It is also used to promote juice and flavour extraction during SKIN CONTACT.

pectins, carbohydrate polymers made up of galacturonic acid units which have the important function of 'gumming' plant cells together. The group is diverse and includes pectic acid, hemicelluloses, and gums; the associated sugars are galactose, mannose, and arabinose. The pectin content of grapes increases steadily throughout ripening, reaching levels of about 1 g/l. Pectin is an important contributor to COLLOIDS. For the importance of pectin hydrolysing enzymes to winemaking, see ENZYMES.   B.G.C.

Pedernã, white wine grape grown in the MINHO in Portugal. See ARINTO for full details.

pedicel, the stalk of an individual flower which, on a bunch of grapes, becomes the short stem bearing each berry. Its length varies with vine variety, from 5 to 15 mm (0.5 in), and its diameter varies with variety and BERRY SIZE.

After FLOWERING, pedicels are liable to develop a separation layer at their base causing the flower to drop; the remainder adhere and can develop into berries (as in FRUIT SET). When berries of certain vine varieties ripen, the pedicels may develop a corky abscission at their top, at the junction with the berry. If this does not happen, then pulling off the berry tears the skin and leaves behind a chunk of pulp on the end of the pedicel that is called the BRUSH.   B.G.C.

Pedro Giménez, declining but still quite important white grape variety in ARGENTINA, where, along with the coarse and declining CRIOLLA and CEREZA, it is one of the vines underpinning the country's substantial production of everyday wine for domestic consumption. It is mainly planted in Mendoza but is also found in Chile's pisco region. AMPELOGRAPHERS in Argentina believe there is no connection between this variety and the PEDRO XIMÉNEZ of Spain.

Alcalde, A. J., *Cultivares vitícolas argentinas* (Mendoza, 1989).

Pedro Luis, white grape of Andalucía once known as False Pedro in South Africa.

Pedro Ximénez, Pedro Jiménez, or just **Pedro,** white grape variety traditionally associated with ANDALUCÍA in southern Spain, especially in MONTILLA-MORILES, where it accounts for about 70 per cent of all plantings, but also in southern Cataluña, VALENCIA, EXTREMADURA, and the Canary Islands. Producers in JEREZ and MÁLAGA routinely import the super-ripe wines made from Pedro Ximénez grown in Montilla-Moriles. PALOMINO Fino, which is more productive and less disease-prone than Pedro Ximénez, is now the grape of Jerez and by 2004 Pedro Ximénez was grown on a total of fewer than 10,000 ha/25,000 acres of vineyard. The other common fate of these thin-skinned grapes, which were traditionally dried in the sun to produce sweetening wines for fortified blends, is to produce rich, raisiny, sweet fortified VARIETAL wine (see PX).

In Australia, Pedro Ximénez was once quite widely grown but its total area had fallen to well under 100 ha/247 acres by 2004. Although once used to bulk out inexpensive blends there, it has been known to shine, most particularly in BOTRYTIZED form to produce the rich, deep golden McWilliam's Pedro Sauterne (*sic*) made in irrigated vineyards near Griffith in NEW SOUTH WALES.

A vine called PEDRO GIMÉNEZ is extremely important in ARGENTINA but AMPELOGRAPHERS believe that it is not the Pedro Ximénez of Spain.

peduncle. See BUNCHSTEM.

Peel, warm coastal region just to the south of Perth in WESTERN AUSTRALIA with CHENIN BLANC and SHIRAZ its best wines.

Pelaverga, pale, rare, red grape of Piemonte making slightly fizzy, strawberry-flavoured wines.

Peloursin, obscure southern French red grape variety. There are some Peloursin vines, with Durif, in north east Victoria in Australia. In the late 1990s, DNA PROFILING identified the vines known as PETITE SIRAH in California as a FIELD BLEND of Peloursin, some true SYRAH, and mainly Durif, which turns out to be a crossing of Peloursin and Syrah.

Penedès, sometimes spelt **Penedés,** the largest and most important denominated wine zone in CATALUÑA in north east Spain (see map under SPAIN), producing an innovative range of wines. With its proximity to Barcelona, Penedès has always had a ready outlet for its wines. In the 19th century, it was one of the first regions in Spain to begin mass production and France, stricken by PHYLLOXERA, became an important market. The phylloxera louse reached Penedès in 1887, by which time José Raventós had laid the foundations of CODORNÍU and the CAVA industry. Vineyards that had once produced strong, semi-fortified reds were uprooted in favour of white grapes for sparkling wine. Cava has subsequently developed a separate nationally organized DO.

Penedès underwent a second radical transformation in the 1960s and 1970s largely because of Miguel Torres Carbo and his son Miguel A. TORRES, wine (and brandy) producers in the heart of the region at Vilafranca del Penedès. They were among the first in Spain to install TEMPERATURE CONTROL and STAINLESS STEEL tanks. Miguel Torres, Jr, who studied OENOLOGY in France, also imported and experimented with such revolutionary vine varieties as Cabernet Sauvignon, Chardonnay, Sauvignon Blanc, Merlot, Pinot Noir, Riesling, and Gewürztraminer, which were planted alongside and blended with native varieties. Other growers followed in the Torres family footsteps and Penedès was in the 1980s one of the most dynamic and varied wine regions in Spain. By the late 1990s, however, the region was failing to confirm the high hopes placed in its red wines, which were increasingly overshadowed by those of PRIORAT.

Penedès rises from the Mediterranean like a series of steps and divides into three distinct zones. Bajo, or Low, Penedès reaches altitudes of 250 m/825 ft away from the tourist resorts of the Costa Dorada. This is the warmest part of the region which traditionally grew Malvasía and Moscatel de Alejandría (MUSCAT OF ALEXANDRIA) grapes for sweet FORTIFIED wines. With the expansion of the resort towns and declining sales of such wines, these vineyards have either been abandoned or replanted with GARNACHA, CARIÑENA, or MONASTRELL making sturdy reds. The second zone, Medio Penedès, is a broad valley 500 m/1,600 ft above sea level, separated from the coast by a ridge of hills.

This is the most productive part of the region providing much of the base wine for the sparkling wine industry at San Sadurni de Noya (see CAVA). MACABEO, XAREL-LO, and PARELLADA are grown for Cava, together with increasing quantities of Chardonnay and red varieties such as TEMPRANILLO (often called here by its Catalan name Ull de Llebre) and Cabernet Sauvignon. Penedès Superior, between 500 and 800 m above the coast on the foothills of Spain's central plateau, is the coolest part of the region where some of the best white grapes are grown. The native Parellada is the most important variety here, but Riesling, Muscat of Alexandria, Gewürztraminer, and Chardonnay are also successful.   R.J.M. & V. de la S.

Peñín, J., *Guía Peñín* (Madrid, annually).
Radford, J., *The New Spain* (2nd edn, London, 2004).

Penfolds, makers of Australia's most famous fine wine **Penfolds Grange,** now owned by FOSTER'S. Penfolds' first vineyard was founded in 1844 at Magill, South Australia, by Dr Christopher Rawson Penfold. For more than 100 years, Penfolds, in common with most Australian wineries, concentrated on producing FORTIFIED wines and brandy, much of which was exported to the UK. In 1950, Max Schubert, then chief winemaker, visited Europe, primarily to observe the making of sherry in Spain, but detouring on the way home to visit Bordeaux, where he was taken in hand by Lionel CRUSE. This inspired him to adopt an entirely new approach to fermentation techniques and the use of new oak, the aim being simultaneously to protect the varietal flavour of Shiraz while adding a level of complexity previously unknown in Australia. Schubert's ambition was to create a red that would rival the finest wines of Bordeaux for both quality and the potential to improve with age for up to 50 years. This he achieved with **Penfolds Grange** (known as Penfolds Grange Hermitage until EUROPEAN UNION authorities objected to this misappropriation of a French place-name), now widely acknowledged to be Australia's greatest wine. The first vintage of Grange, named after Dr Penfold's cottage in Magill, was 1951; all early vintages were made from Shiraz grapes grown at Magill and Morphett Vale, Adelaide, and the wine was matured in new American oak for 12 months. So intense did the first vintages seem that they were rejected as maverick 'dry port'. In 1957, Schubert was ordered to cease production of Grange; instead he took the operation underground, emerging three years later when maturing vintages began to fulfil their promise. In fact, fine vintages of Grange improve for up to 30 years and beyond (in the mid 2000s, the 1952 and 1953 vintages were still magnificent), and the wine became the first NEW WORLD wine to become an internationally acknowledged collectable. Fruit from Kalimna in the Barossa Valley was introduced in 1961, boosted by grapes from the Clare and Koonunga Hill vineyards. Small amounts of Cabernet Sauvignon are included in most vintages of Grange, and the wood-ageing period has been lengthened to between 18 and 20 months. The wine is not released for at least four years after the vintage.

A string of award-winning red wines from Penfolds followed, many identified by BIN numbers which originated in the winery stock-keeping system. Of particular note is Bin 707 Cabernet Sauvignon. In April 1998, Penfolds released a long-awaited super-premium white wine Yattarna Chardonnay.

S.A. & J.H.

Hooke, H., *Max Schubert, Winemaker* (Alexandria, 1994).

Read, A., *The Rewards of Patience* (5th edn, Sydney, 2004).

Penicillium, one of a group of FUNGI commonly found on rotten grapes. See BUNCH ROTS.

Peninsulas Zone, This Australian wine zone takes in the Southern Eyre Peninsula and the Yorke Peninsula on either side of SOUTH AUSTRALIA's Spencer Gulf.

Penning-Rowsell, Edmund (1913–2002), English wine writer with a scholarly interest in the history and wines of Bordeaux in particular. Educated at Marlborough College and a lifelong socialist, he was a journalist on the *Morning Post* from 1930 until 1935, when he began a career of almost 30 years as a book publisher. He was introduced to the pleasures of wine when his wife's employer at the BBC gave her as a leaving present (only unmarried females were then regarded as suitable employees) some non-vintage Moulin-à-Vent. Correspondence and eventual friendship with Bristol wine merchant Ronald AVERY was another formative influence.

The traditional but non-profit-making ethos of the co-operative buying group the WINE SOCIETY suited him perfectly and he joined the Society soon after his marriage in 1937. In 1959 he was elected to its Management Committee and served as its chairman from 1964 until 1987, a record length of time.

In 1949 he had reviewed wine books for the *Times Literary Supplement* and in 1954 wrote his first wine article for the magazine *Country Life*. After 1964, soon after his publishing career came to an end, he became wine correspondent of the *Financial Times*, scrupulously refusing to mention the Wine Society during his chairmanship. His wine primer *Red, White and Rosé* was published in 1967, and a second edition appeared in 1973, but his great gift to the LITERATURE OF WINE is *The Wines of Bordeaux*, which was first published in 1969 and whose sixth edition appeared 20 years later.

Until his sight failed him, he meticulously recorded the facts of his remarkable cellar in a series of cellar books and, typically, in his characteristic green ink. This unique archive included details of every purchase, every souvenir from his annual round of visits to the wine regions (continued into his ninth decade), and impressions of every bottle sampled.

A perennial figure in Bordeaux at vintage time and at the HOSPICES DE BEAUNE auction, Penning-Rowsell was made a Chevalier de l'Ordre du Mérite Agricole in 1971 and a Chevalier de l'Ordre du Mérite National in 1981.

Loftus, S., 'Purple prose: the wine writers', in *Anatomy of the Wine Trade* (London, 1985).

pepper, a tasting term for two very different aromas commonly found in red wines. **Bell peppers**, or **green peppers**, is used characteristically in the US of underripe CABERNET SAUVIGNON. A freshly sliced green pepper or capsicum liberates the chemical compound 2-methoxy-3-isobutylpyrazine (see METHOXYPYRAZINES), a vegetable-like or HERBACEOUS aroma to which most tasters have a very low threshold (see FLAVOUR COMPOUNDS). Young wines made from the SYRAH grape, on the other hand, particularly if it does not reach full maturity, can smell of **black peppercorns**.

Per'e Palummo. See PIEDIROSSO.

pergola, a form of overhead VINE TRAINING. Where the canopy is horizontal, the pergola can alternatively be called TENDONE. Pergola trellises can be either one or two armed, depending on whether the vines are trained on one or both sides of the row. If the trellis is joined overhead it is called a closed pergola.

The pergola is widely used in Italy, where the canopies vary but are often inclined rather than horizontal (in Trentino, for example, the slope is 20 to 30 degrees). In Emilia-Romagna the **pergoletta** system is used, while the **pergoletta Capucci** was developed by the eponymous Bologna professor. The **pergoletta a Valenzano** is very similar to the GENEVA DOUBLE CURTAIN. Where the vines have marked VIGOUR, the bunches which hang below the leafy canopy are in SHADE, with predictable negative effects on wine quality. R.E.S.

pericarp, the 'fruit wall' forming the bulk of a plant's ovary, consisting of sugary flesh and highly coloured skin attractive to animals, especially BIRDS, with the result that the SEEDS are spread. In the grape berry, the whole fruit except for the seeds (both the skin and the flesh) constitutes the pericarp. See GRAPE for more details.

Pérignon, Dom (1639–1715), Benedictine monk who has gone down in history as 'the man who invented champagne'. The title is the stuff of fairy-tales: the transition from still to sparkling wine was an evolutionary process rather than a dramatic discovery on the part of one man. The life of Dom Pérignon was in fact devoted to improving the still wines of Champagne, and he deserves his place in the history books for that reason.

Brother Pierre Pérignon arrived at the Abbey of Hautvillers, north of Épernay, in 1668. His role was that of treasurer, and in the 17th century that meant being in charge of the cellars. He collected tithes from surrounding villages in the form of grapes and wine, fermenting and blending until he created wines that sold for twice as much as those of the abbey's rivals. Dom Pérignon introduced many practices that survive in the process of modern wine production, among them severe pruning, low yields, and careful harvesting. He also experimented to a great extent with the BLENDING process, and was one of the first to blend the produce of many different vineyards. Dom Pérignon produced still white and red wines, favouring black grapes because a SECONDARY FERMENTATION was less likely. Ironically, he was often thwarted in his endeavours by the refermentation process, which produced the style of wine that was eventually to prove so popular. His fame as the 'inventor' of champagne probably spread after his death, embellished by Dom Grossard, the last treasurer of the abbey, which closed at the time of the French Revolution. More modern champagne producers have jumped on the bandwagon, promoting the idea of a founder figure. Eugene Mercier registered the brand name Dom Pérignon before MOËT & CHANDON acquired it and used it to launch the first champagne marketed as a PRESTIGE CUVÉE, a 1921 vintage launched in 1928.

See also CHAMPAGNE. S.A.

Faith, N., *The Story of Champagne* (London, 1988).
Johnson, H., *The Story of Wine* (London, 1989).

Periquita, Portuguese word meaning 'parakeet' applied to both a usefully versatile red grape variety grown all over southern Portugal (see CASTELÃO) and a branded red wine from José Maria da FONSECA Successores.

Perlan, traditional name of the CHASSELAS grape in the canton of Geneva in SWITZERLAND, rarely seen on labels now that the name Chasselas de Genève is preferred.

perlant, French term for a wine that is only slightly SPARKLING. **Perlwein** is the German equivalent. See FIZZINESS.

Perle is, like WÜRZER, a GERMAN CROSSING of Gewürztraminer and Müller-Thurgau; in this case Gewürztraminer's rosy-hued grapes have been inherited but its extravagant perfume is more muted. It is declining in popularity but has been particularly useful in FRANKEN since its late budding protects it from spring frost damage. Hardly 100 ha remain for the vine's compact bunches make it an easy target for GREY ROT.

Pernand-Vergelesses, village in the Côte de Beaune district of Burgundy's Côte d'Or producing red and white wines. The former, made from Pinot Noir, are somewhat angular in style and do not always appear fully ripe as Pernand is set back from the main sweep of the Côte and many of its vineyards have a westerly, even north western exposition, which can retard RIPENING.

Pernand chose to suffix the name of its best red wine vineyard, east-facing Les Vergelesses, which it shares with neighbouring Savigny-lès-Beaune, although the most sought-after wines are the whites on the Pernand side of the hill of Corton (see ALOXE-CORTON). Seventeen of the 72 ha/178 acres entitled to the GRAND CRU appellation Corton-Charlemagne lie within Pernand-Vergelesses. White Pernand wines have a hard but attractive flinty character which develops well during BOTTLE AGEING. As it ages, BOURGOGNE ALIGOTÉ from this area is said to resemble white Pernand-Vergelesses; and white Pernand to approach the quality of Corton-Charlemagne.

The most successful producer based in Pernand-Vergelesses is Bonneau du Martray, one of the top names in Corton-Charlemagne. See also CÔTE D'OR, and map under BURGUNDY.

J.T.C.M.

Pernod Ricard, owner of the Jacob's Creek brand and, since its acquisition of Allied Domecq in 2005, the world's second largest spirits company after DIAGEO. Founded in 1975 with the merger of Pernod and Ricard pastis empires, it is still headquartered in France but owns leading spirits brands produced in such countries as Scotland, Ireland, Poland, and Cuba. Its first significant wine acquisition, in 1989, was the Australian-based Orlando Wyndham Group, and hence Jacob's Creek and Wyndham Estate, which claims to be the first commercial grower in Australia of SHIRAZ. Richmond Grove and Poet's Corner were also part of the group.

Outside Australia, Pernod Ricard acquired Etchart in Argentina in 1992, began to produce Old Tbilisi and Tamada wines in GEORGIA in 1993, established the Long Mountain South African wine brand in 1994, and bought Framingham in New Zealand in 2004. The acquisition of most of Allied Domecq in 2005 brought, in addition to considerable spirits brands, Montana, Corbans, and Stoneleigh in New Zealand, major production facilities in Spain including the Campo Viejo Rioja brand, Balbi in Argentina, several wineries in California, and Mumm and Perrier-Jouet champagnes. See GLOBALIZATION.

peronospera, European name for the very important VINE DISEASE more usually called DOWNY MILDEW.

Perricone, SICILIAN red grape variety planted on hardly more than 1,000 ha/2,500 acres of the island. Soft varietal wines are sometimes called by its synonym Pignatello.

Perricoota, large, sparsely populated, region bordering the Murray river in NEW SOUTH WALES to the east of Australia's Murray Darling region and south of the Riverina.

Perrum, Portuguese white grape variety producing rather ordinary wines in the Alentejo.

Persan, now rare Savoie red grape which can produce wines worth ageing.

Persia, Near Eastern country officially known as IRAN since 1935, which has known the consumption of wine since ancient times.

Ancient Persia

Much of this area was also known as MESOPOTAMIA in classical times. There had been vines in the area from earliest times, but it was only from 550 BC that Cyrus the Great and Darius extended Persia's power to cover all the lands from the west end of the Mediterranean to the river Indus in the east, incorporating the old empires of BABYLONIA and Assyria, which were overwhelmed and extended.

Persia may be the site of one of the earliest ever wine-related archaeological discoveries (see ORIGINS and PALAEOETHNOBOTANY). A large earthenware jar stored on its side in a room at the archaeological site of Godin Tepe (dated to about 3500 BC) in central western Iran was found to have a dark stain inside, closely akin to TARTARIC ACID, which occurs at high levels in wine.

More detailed evidence is available from the era of the Achaemenid Dynasty, which ruled Ancient Iran from c.559 to c.331 BC. Dating from the period just before Persia and Greece became embroiled in the Persian Wars, an enormous archive of documents written on clay tablets in the Elamite language preserves detailed records of the administration of the Achaemenid royal capital Persepolis from 509 to 494 BC. Here there are records concerning the distribution of large quantities of (grape) wine and *sawur*, another (probably weaker) sort of wine. Sometimes the wine was stored at, or issued from, the ancient city of SHIRAZ, whose name is now associated with so many wines. Wine was normally released in monthly amounts, although in certain cases the issue was daily. One *marrish* (a measure of 10 quarts) of wine was valued at one shekel.

Such 'rations' often amounted to far more than one person could consume: perhaps they would be better described as salaries. Some were given to important women with households of their own to support: these received 30 quarts per month. King Darius writes in one order that 100 sheep and 500 gal of wine should be issued for the royal princess Artystone, no doubt in order for her to give a lavish banquet at her own court. Persian royal ladies were very independent and maintained their own establishments and dependants.

Generally wine was not given to boy and girl workers (who did, however, receive other rations including sometimes beer), except according to one document where some boys received one-third of a quart daily for 156 days. Otherwise the general allowance was 10 or 20 quarts monthly for men and 10 for women. Some labourers received a good deal less.

Presumably in an effort to increase the proletarian population available for large-scale labour, special wine rations were provided under the Achaemenid dynasty as a reward for women labourers who had just given birth to children: women who bore sons received 10 quarts, and those who bore daughters 5 quarts. The issue was sometimes spread out over the entire subsequent year.

Important caravans of diplomatic visitors accompanied by élite guides travelled from as far afield as Kandahar, India, Sardis, and Egypt. Those due to arrive at the capital Persepolis during the cooler months of the year (November to May), when the king and his entourage were in residence, were issued with travel rations to ease their arduous journey at the various stations at which they put up on the Royal Road. The records indicate that these, naturally, included generous amounts of wine.

On occasions wine was issued, along with grain and beer, for the benefit of the royal horses, perhaps when they were used for long journeys. The amounts issued varied from half a pint to 10 pints per animal per month. *Sawur* wine was even made available to the king's camels as an occasional concession.

In the 5th century BC, HERODOTUS noted that the Achaemenids would make important decisions in a drunken state, then confirm these decisions when sober, and vice versa. The Persian empire was finally split up after the death of Alexander the Great in 323 BC. J.A.B.

Hallock, R. T., *Persepolis Fortification Tablets* (Chicago, 1969).

Shiraz as wine capital

The consumption of wine survived through the Sassanian Period, from the 3rd to the 7th centuries AD, influenced in part by Zoroastrian rite, and continued after the subsequent ISLAMIC conquest of the country.

Shiraz, a city rebuilt 50 km/30 miles from the site of Persepolis by the Arabs in the 8th century and the home town of Hāfiz, Persia's most famous mystic Bacchic poet (see ARAB POETS), had acquired a reputation by the 9th century for producing the finest wines in the Near East.

Thanks principally to the work of Edward Fitzgerald in the 19th century, the medieval polymath and poet OMAR KHAYYÁM has become famous in the west for poetry in which wine plays an important part.

From the diaries of 17th-century English and French travellers and especially the writings of C. J. Wills in the 19th century, we gain a picture of the excellence of some Persian wines. Tavernier (17th century) wrote: 'the wine of Shiraz has by far the greatest foreign as well as native celebrity, being of the quality of an old sherry and constitutes an excellent beverage.' In the same century, Thomas Herbert commented: 'No part of the world has wine better than Shiraz.'

The wine most often described and praised was white, made from thick-skinned, pip-filled grapes grown on terraces round the village of Khoullar, four days' camel ride away from Shiraz (those grown in the immediate vicinity of the city produced watery wine, thanks to excessive IRRIGATION). C. J. Wills describes a 19th-century replication of the traditional Shiraz wine-making process in some detail. The wine, fermented on the skins with regular PUNCHING DOWN, was made either sweet and fruity for long keeping, the stems being removed immediately after fermentation in used jars, or dry and rich in PHENOLICS for drinking in its first year or so. A form of FILTRATION through coarse canvas bags was practised. Wills describes the wine as 'like a light BUCELLAS' when young, to be avoided on account of the headaches it induces. After five years, however, it attains a 'fine aroma and bouquet' and 'nutty flavour'.

See also DRIED GRAPE WINES, for the Persians were certainly in the habit of drying their grapes.   P.K.

Hugh Johnson paints a fascinating and vivid picture of the export of wine from Shiraz to India by European merchants, in 1677 (already in BOTTLES 'wrapped in straw and packed in cases . . . swaying down to the Gulf Coast on mule back. There is scarcely any earlier instance of the regular use of bottles for shipping wine.' Tavernier notes that the 1666 vintage was so bountiful that the Persian king gave permission to export as much wine to the French, English, Dutch, and Portuguese trading companies as was retained by himself and his court. Wine was measured in 'mans', units of weight rather than volume.

For an outline of modern viticulture, see IRAN.

Johnson, H., *The Story of Wine* (London and New York, 1989).

Planhol, X., 'Une rencontre de l'Europe et de l'Iran: le vin de Shiraz', in D. Boidanovic and J. L. Bacque-Grammont (eds.), *Iran* (Paris, 1972).

Tavernier, J.-B., *Voyages en Perse* (Geneva, 1970).

Wills, C. J., *The Land of the Lion and the Sun* (London, 1891).

—— *Persia as it is* (London, 1886).

Perth Hills, picturesque, rapidly growing warm region just west of Perth in WESTERN AUSTRALIA. The region has moved from one of rustic, cottage craft to more polished winemaking in the wake of the recent arrivals Millbrook Winery and Western Range Wines.

Peru, the first country in SOUTH AMERICA to have encouraged systematic viticulture. Under orders from the famous conquistador Francisco Pizarro, the first Peruvian vineyard was planted in about 1547. Specific VINE VARIETIES were imported from Spain and by the 1560s Peru is thought to have had 40,000 ha/99,000 acres under vine, producing so much wine that it was exported to other South American countries and even, according to one document, as far as Spain. One of the several ways by which viticulture spread to Argentina was from Peru, with Nuñez de Prado, in 1550.

The arrival of the PHYLLOXERA louse in 1888 heralded the start of a serious decline in Peruvian viticulture, which was halted as recently as 1960. Only in the 1970s was progress made on establishing suitable planting material and there are now NURSERIES at Ica, Chincha, Moquegua, and Tacna, as well as a national wine research centre.

Today about 11,000 ha/27,200 acres of Peru is planted with vines, yielding many TABLE GRAPES but also 127,000 hl of wine in 2002 according to the OIV. Almost all vines are on the central coast around Pisco (which gives its name to the national drink, a grape brandy) and, particularly, Ica to the south, where winemaking and distillation investment is concentrated. (Elsewhere, both techniques and equipment tend to be extremely primitive.) Winter temperatures are so high that full vine DORMANCY is usually impossible, and two crops a year can be harvested from the same plant (see TROPICAL VITICULTURE). Summer temperatures are also high, between 24 and 33 °C (75–91 °F) in the hottest month, and rainfall is low, but IRRIGATION water is readily available from the Andes. Yields often reach 20 tons per ha (8 tons/acre).

Vine varieties planted include ALBILLO, ALICANTE BOUSCHET, BARBERA, CABERNET SAUVIGNON, GRENACHE, MALBEC, MOSCATEL, SAUVIGNON BLANC, TORONTEL, as well as the table grapes Italia, Negra Corriente (thought to have been imported from the Canary islands in the 17th century and possibly identical to MISSION), Quebranta, and a variety called Borgoña, which is in fact ISABELLA.

Some of the less 'international' vine varieties are also planted along the coast to the north and south, in the mountains up to an altitude of 1,500 m/5,000 ft, in the dry, temperate climate of the valleys of Ayacucho, Hunaca, and Abancay. Tacama is the best-known producer.

Pessac-Léognan, important BORDEAUX red and dry white wine appellation created in 1987 for the most celebrated part of the GRAVES district immediately south of the city (and often still referred to as Graves). It takes its somewhat cumbersome name from its two vinously most important communes, and includes all of the properties named in the 1959 CLASSIFICATION of Graves, and many other fine châteaux too. This is Bordeaux's most urban wine area—indeed the vineyards of its most famous property Ch Haut-Brion and its neighbour and stablemate Ch La Mission-Haut-Brion are today surrounded by suburban development, including the campus of the University of BORDEAUX, on the boundary of the suburbs of Pessac and Talence. It is hardly surprising that Bordeaux's earliest wine estates were developed here, although the wines of Chx HAUT-BRION, LA MISSION-HAUT-BRION, and Pape-Clément justify the properties' existence on grounds far more solid than mere geographical convenience. Further from the city, vineyards are carved out of the pine forests which extend south west into the Landes. In all, about 1,300 ha/3,200 acres of vineyard within Pessac-Léognan produce red wine, and the total area devoted to white wine grapes was about 260 ha by 2004.

Soils here have particularly good DRAINAGE, being made up of gravel terraces of very different eras. The ENCÉPAGEMENT for red wines is very similar to that of the MÉDOC to the immediate north, being mainly Cabernet Sauvignon grapes with some Merlot and Cabernet Franc, but the wines can be quite different. It is not fanciful to imagine that the best wines of Pessac-Léognan have a distinct aroma that reminds some tasters of minerals, some of smoke, others even of warm bricks. Ch Haut-Brion is the most obvious exponent of this genre (see HAUT-BRION for details of the red and white wines of this property and those of La Mission-Haut-Brion). Other current over-achievers include Chx Pape-Clément and Smith Haut-Lafitte, while Chx de Fieuzal, Haut-Bailly, and La Louvière can provide some of Bordeaux's better value.

White wines made here can be some of the most characterful dry white wines in the world, made from Sauvignon (which must comprise at least a quarter of the blend) and Sémillon grapes grown generally on the lighter, sandier parts of the vineyard, and often produced with considerable recourse to BARREL FERMENTATION and BARREL MATURATION. The most admired, Domaine de Chevalier and Chx Haut-Brion and Laville-Haut-Brion, can develop in bottle over decades, and the dry white wines of Ch Malartic-Lagravière, for example, demand a decade in bottle at the very least. More recent, and more modern if still long-lasting, fine white wines are made at Ch Couhins-LURTON.

Duijker, H., and Broadbent, M., *The Bordeaux Atlas* (London, 1997).

Parker, R., *Bordeaux* (4th edn, New York, 2003).

Penning-Rowsell, E., *The Wines of Bordeaux* (6th edn, London, 1989).

pesticides, substances or mixtures of substances applied to vineyards which are used to prevent, destroy, repel, or reduce the harmful effects of FUNGI, BACTERIA, INSECTS, NEMATODES, or other undesirable organisms regarded as VINE PESTS. Pesticides are made up of AGROCHEMICALS and are usually classified according to their principal use as, for example, fungicides, bactericides, insecticides, nematicides, miticides, etc. Many pesticides have more than one mode of action and may be effective against more than one type of pest. For example, SULFUR is both a fungicide and a miticide in vineyards.

Most pesticides consist of an active chemical constituent in a concentrated form that is suitable for use after mixing with a diluent (water or oil). Less often, pesticides are formulated as dusts, granules, or fumigants and require DUSTING rather than SPRAYING. Mixtures of active ingredients may be used to create formulations with greater efficacy or versatility: two chemicals may be mixed, for example, to produce a DOWNY MILDEW fungicide with both protectant and eradicant properties. For convenience, two or more pesticides may be combined in a spray mixture. However, problems due to chemical incompatibility may arise when different pesticides are mixed.

Pesticides are, to varying degrees, toxic chemicals, and their potentially harmful effects on humans, other animals, and non-target organisms in the environment must be recognized. Since the 1990s, increasing attention has been paid to the safety of vineyard workers and the environment with chemicals classified according to toxicity and workers taught safe handling practices. Recycling spray machines are increasingly used to minimize drift onto the environment. See also RESIDUES.

The following factors should be taken into consideration when developing strategies for pesticide use in vineyards: use patterns, rates, the potential development of pesticide resistance, and potential effects on non-target organisms. Use patterns may involve routine application schedules or more flexible strategies that rely on pest warning services and/or the monitoring of pest activity, as in INTEGRATED PEST MANAGEMENT. Such flexible strategies are often adopted to minimize pesticide use.

The continuous use of some pesticides may result in a dramatic increase in the proportion of individuals in a pest population that are able to survive exposure to the pesticide. An example has been the development of resistance by the BOTRYTIS fungus to the fungicide Benomyl and also to the dicarboximide group of fungicides. A serious outcome of the development of pest resistance is the so-called 'treadmill effect': as resistance to a pesticide increases, the pesticide is used in increased dosages or, more frequently, until such time that pesticide treatment becomes ineffective or uneconomic. Even more serious is the development of resistance to a group of related (cross-resistance) or dissimilar (multiple-resistance) chemicals. Pesticides which use strategies that delay or prevent the development of pest resistance are designed to avoid long-term exposure of the pest to a single pesticide or group of pesticides with similar mode of action.

See also FUNGICIDES and INSECTICIDES.

P.R.D.
Emmett, R. W., Harris, A. R., Taylor, R. H., and McGechan, J. K., 'Grape diseases and vineyard protection', in B. G. Coombe and P. R. Dry (eds.), Viticulture, ii: Practices (Adelaide, 1992).

pests of vineyards. See VINE PESTS.

pétillant, French term for a lightly sparkling wine, somewhere between PERLANT and MOUSSEUX.

petiole, the stalk of a plant's leaf which supports the leaf blade or lamina. Petioles are stem tissue and branch from the main stem of the shoot having similar anatomical features. At both ends of the petiole are swellings that alter the position of the leaf blade according to such stimuli as water stress and low light. Samples of petioles taken at FLOWERING are used as a basis for assessing a vine's status in terms of VINE NUTRITION.

The characteristics of petioles vary with vine variety and growing conditions, being longer on vigorous vines. Between varieties, petiole length varies from 5 to 20 cm (2–8 in), petiole colour varies from green to red, and petioles may vary from smooth to hairy. These features help in the identification of varieties (see AMPELOGRAPHY). B.G.C.

petit, 'small' in French and therefore often encountered in wine and grape names.

petit château. See PETITS CHÂTEAUX.

Petit Courbu, ancient, rescued white grape variety of GASCONY capable of adding body and quality to the wines of BÉARN, IROULÉGUY, JURANÇON, and PACHERENC DU VIC-BILH as well as those of Côtes de ST-MONT. See also COURBU.

Petite Arvine, the finest of the grape specialities of Valais in SWITZERLAND. Wines tend to be nervy with considerable EXTRACT and, often, a vague suggestion of grapefruit and salt. Wines vary in sweetness between dry, mi-FLÉTRI, and downright sweet.

Petite Sirah, name common in both North and South America, and first mentioned in California wine literature in the early 1880s, for a related group of black grape varieties. DNA PROFILING techniques suggested in the late 1990s that the name had been applied in California vineyards to no fewer than four different vines: DURIF, true SYRAH of the Rhône, PELOURSIN (an obscure French vine which turned out to be Durif's parent), and even PINOT NOIR.

Petite Sirah is relatively important in a wide range of warm wine regions, especially in both California and South America. In California, acreage declined until the mid 1990s but then began to climb again, reaching 4,400 acres by 2003, mostly in the Italian-American enclaves of Sonoma, Paso Robles, Amador, Mendocino, and Napa. Accurate acreage assessment is difficult because so many of the old Italian vineyards were planted with a mixture of different varieties. (Almost all Petite Sirah vines are much older than the state average.)

Although Petite Sirah has been valued as a relatively tannic, well-coloured blending partner for blowsier Zinfandels, it has been somewhat eclipsed by the fashionable true French Syrah. It has nevertheless carved out a place for itself in California, for it makes dark, well-balanced, sturdily tannic red wine of agreeable if not highly distinctive flavour. As such, it has been essential as a backbone for some everyday red blends: useful when rain-weakened Cabernet Sauvignon needed shoring up, or Pinot Noir went too pale and soft in a sunny vintage. Sonoma and Mendocino counties seem to grow Petite Sirah best, especially the dry-farmed, elderly HILLSIDE VINEYARDS within the Russian river drainage from Redwood valley down through Healdsburg and out towards Guerneville. Louis J. Foppiano and Guenoc have long produced polished, supple varietal examples. Ridge, Lava Cap, and J. C. Cellars take the varietal wine to its dark, tannic limits. California producers started a new promotional push for the grape in 2004 called P.S. I Love You.

Argentina grows a vine called Petite Sirah (and at one time, misleadingly, Sirah). It is also well known in Brazil's semi-tropical climate as Petite Sirah or Petite Syrah and has produced respectable sturdy red in MEXICO.

Petit Manseng, top-quality white grape variety originally from SOUTH WEST FRANCE which is the superior form of MANSENG. Petit Manseng, which is much more suitable for sweet wines than GROS MANSENG, has particularly small, thick-skinned berries which yield very little juice (sometimes less than 15 hl/ha, although up to 40 hl/ha (2.3 tons/acre) is allowed for both JURANÇON and PACHERENC) but can withstand lingering on the vine until well into autumn, or even December, so that the sugar is concentrated by the shrivelling process known as PASSERILLAGE. The variety is however sensitive to both sorts of MILDEW. In 2000, France grew a total of just over 600 ha/1,500 acres of Petit Manseng, less than a third the total of Gros Manseng.

The variety is now being planted in the LANGUEDOC and California, already indicating that Petit Manseng is following VIOGNIER in terms of popularity with those groups who follow vine variety FASHION.

Petit Meslier, ancient and almost extinct white variety cultivated in Champagne. It used to produce fruity wines, but it has fallen out of favour because of its naturally low yields. DNA PROFILING at DAVIS showed in 2000 that Petit Meslier is a progeny of GOUAIS BLANC and

SAVAGNIN. An unusual 1998 varietal champagne suggested a certain green leafy character and a powerful aroma.

Petit Pineau, synonym for the ARBOIS vine variety.

Petit Rhin, synonym for the great RIESLING grape of Germany used mainly in Switzerland.

Petit Rouge, fine red grape variety indigenous to the Valle d'AOSTA.

petits châteaux, the French term meaning literally 'small castles' has a very specific meaning in the BORDEAUX wine region. These thousands of properties are modest not so much in their extent as in their reputation and price. A CLASSED GROWTH is emphatically not a petit château, no matter how few hectares it encompasses. The greatest concentration of petits châteaux is in the appellations BORDEAUX, BOURG, and BLAYE, although they are found throughout the region. Some of Bordeaux's best wine value is to be found at the most conscientious petits châteaux.

See also CHÂTEAU.

Petit Verdot is one of Bordeaux's classic black grape varieties, no longer planted in any great quantity but enjoying a small revival in some quality-conscious vineyards. The vine ripens even later than Cabernet Sauvignon and is equally resistant to rot. It shares Cabernet Sauvignon's thick skins and is also capable of yielding concentrated, tannic wines rich in colour. When it ripens fully, which in most Bordeaux properties happens only in riper vintages, its rich, age-worthy, sometimes rather spicy wines can make a valuable contribution to some of the best wines of the Médoc. Its inconveniently late ripening encouraged many producers to abandon it in the 1960s and 1970s so that total French plantings were just over 300 ha/740 acres in 1988, increased to more than 400 ha, virtually all in the Gironde, by 2000. As its qualities are recognized, there has been a revival elsewhere, notably in AUSTRALIA, where the variety has performed exceptionally well in VARIETAL form in the irrigated Riverland and by the mid 2000s there was a national total of more than 1,600 ha planted. In California, where the state's total plantings had reached 900 acres/360 ha by 2003, mainly in Napa and Sonoma, it has so far been used mainly as an ingredient in MERITAGE blends.

In Chile, there were a few hectares of 'Verdot' and 137 ha of Petit Verdot in 2003. The 'Verdot' of which there were 190 ha in Argentina's Mendoza in 2002 is probably the coarser, probably unrelated, Gros Verdot variety.

Petri disease, a decline affecting young vines and named after Italian plant pathologist Lionello Petri (1875–1946), who in 1912 first reported brown wood streaking and dark gummy sap (see BLACK GOO) in declining

American rootstock mother vines. Propagation material infected with the fungi *Phaeomoniella chlamydospora* and *Phaeoacremonium* sp. can lead to early plant failures and a greatly reduced stress tolerance.   L.M.

Pétrus, Château, the most famous wine of POMEROL and today the most expensive in BORDEAUX.

In the heart of the small Pomerol plateau, Pétrus was partly bought in 1925, by Mme Loubat, wife of the owner of the Hotel Loubat in Libourne. By 1949, it consisted of 6.5 ha planted with 70 per cent MERLOT vines and 30 per cent CABERNET FRANC. In 1969, 5 ha were purchased from the adjoining Ch Gazin, and gradually the balance between the two vine varieties was altered until it was 95 per cent Merlot and 5 per cent Cabernet Franc.

Although it won a gold medal at the 1878 Paris International Exhibition, and the London-based WINE SOCIETY listed the 1893, Pétrus received little international attention until the remarkable, tiny crop of 1945, and the much more widely distributed 1947. Its exceptional concentration of colour, bouquet, and richness of flavour derives from a pocket of clay in the middle of the vineyard and the subsoil which affords exceptionally good DRAINAGE. Average production is 2,000 to 3,500 cases.

However, its fame is largely due to M. Jean-Pierre MOUEIX of the Libourne merchants, who started his business before the Second World War. He took over the sole distribution of Pétrus in 1945, and, when Mme Loubat died in 1961, he acquired 50 per cent of the shareholding, while Mme Loubat's niece Mme Lily Lacoste inherited the other 50 per cent, which was acquired by Jean-Pierre's elder son Jean-François Moueix in 2001. Jean-François inherited his father's half in 2003. The property is managed by the négociants J. P. Moueix of Libourne with their distinguished OENOLOGIST Jean-Claude Berrouet in charge of winemaking. The limited size of the property, and the availability of the Moueix team of pickers, mean that all the grapes can be harvested, at optimum ripeness, in half a day.

FERMENTATION VESSELS are neither wood nor stainless steel, but mundane cement.

There is no official CLASSIFICATION of Pomerol, but Pétrus is unofficially recognized as a PREMIER CRU, and is distributed only through Moueix, with exclusive agents in the UK and restricted ones in the US. It tends to fetch a much higher price than any other red bordeaux (although see Le PIN), and at AUCTION achieves even higher prices relative to the rest. In 2005, a rather grander building superseded Pétrus's modest farmhouse.

E.P.-R. & J.R.

Petrus de Crescentiis (1230–1310), Italian author whose writings on wine were much

read in the Middle Ages (see LITERATURE OF WINE). Petrus de Crescentiis finished his *Liber ruralium commodorum* ('Book on agriculture') *c.*1304. Only part of his book, Book 4, is concerned with wine. He knows and quotes from the classical writers on agriculture (mainly PLINY, COLUMELLA, and VARRO) but he is no mere slavish follower of his authorities, for he has a great deal to say about medieval WINEMAKING practice and his advice is reliable.

The ancients loved old wine, but Petrus knew that medieval wine was a different matter; if wine was kept in a wooden BARREL instead of an impermeable earthenware AMPHORA, it would not last long. Most medieval wine was drunk within a year of the vintage, but sweet or highly alcoholic wines, as some Mediterranean wines were, kept longer. Petrus divides wines into three categories: new (under a year); old (four years); and between new and old. New wine, he says, has no digestive or diuretic properties but inflates the belly. Old wine is bitter and can be off; unless it is mixed with water, it goes to the head. Two-year-old wine is best. Petrus also points out that TOPPING UP casks of wine is essential in order to stop the wine turning into vinegar; alternatively, a layer of olive oil can be floated on the surface of the wine. He also explains how to achieve the RACKING of a wine from one cask into another.

Given the soundness of his advice and the clarity of his prose style, it is not surprising that Petrus's book should have been popular. It survives in many manuscripts and early printed editions. By the end of the 15th century, it had been translated into German, French, and Italian.   H.M.W.

Marescalchi, A., and Dalmasso, G. (eds.), *Storia della vite e del vino in Italia*, 3 vols. (Milan, 1933).

Savastano, L. G., *Contribute allo studio critico degli scrittori agrari italiani* (Acireale, 1922).

Peurion, yellow-berried, ROT-prone vine variety much cultivated in north east France before the arrival of PHYLLOXERA. It is a natural offspring of Pinot and Gouais Blanc (see PINOT).

Peynaud, Émile (1912–2004), Bordeaux oenologist whose work had a profound and worldwide impact on wine-making and wine appreciation in the second half of the 20th century. After the Second World War, Peynaud worked with Jean RIBÉREAU-GAYON before joining him at BORDEAUX University's Institut d'Oenologie, while employed by the house of Calvet. It was here, in the late 1940s, that he began to advise numerous BORDEAUX châteaux on their wine-making. Because this CONSULTANCY work was the activity for which he later became best known, it is perhaps easy to forget his achievements as a taster, scientist, and teacher.

Peynaud wanted to understand the detail of the wine-making process, to eliminate its hitherto haphazard nature, and to produce consistently clean-tasting and healthy wines. Many of the practices that now seem unexceptional in wine-making were by no means axiomatic in the 1950s, and they are rooted in changes resulting from his wide-ranging scientific research. Among these were the complete control of MALOLACTIC FERMENTATION, the understanding that quality starts in the vineyard with good-quality grapes, that red grapes should be fully ripe when picked, that dark grapes' skins (containing the PHENOLICS so crucial to red wine aromas and textures) should be treated more gently with softer CRUSHING, better-controlled fermentation temperatures, shorter MACERATION, and more moderate PRESSING of the skins for the PRESS WINE. Each technique aimed at improving the flavour and texture of the resulting finished wine.

Taste became the arbiter in wine-making decisions, and it underlay his other cardinal principle: selection. Select only healthy grapes when picking, vinify the produce of plots of vines of markedly different age or quality separately, choose only the best vats to be incorporated in the principal wine, and so on. Peynaud himself describes his method as 'monitoring the whole process of wine-making from grape to bottle' and this is the subject of his first book, *Connaissance et travail du vin*.

Peynaud considered the ability to taste accurately as essential to good wine-making as a thorough grasp of OENOLOGY. He says in his second book, *Le Goût du vin*, 'I am not sure whether I have contributed most by making tasting an introduction to oenology or oenology an introduction to tasting.' *Le Goût du vin* is as comprehensive and lucid on tasting wine as his first book was on making wine. It aimed to educate the palates not only of winemakers but of wine drinkers too. He was acutely aware of their symbiotic relationship.

As with his pupil Michel ROLLAND, critics used to complain that his wine-making methods so marked the wines that they were losing their individuality, but mature bottles tended to show genuine distinction and individuality.

Peynaud would have left his mark on the wine world had his gifts been limited to scientist, technician, and possessor of a refined palate; that his influence has been so widespread is due to his additional great gift as a teacher and communicator.   M.W.E.S.

Parnell, C., 'Émile Peynaud, Man of the Year', *Decanter* (Mar 1990), 36–40.

Peynaud, É., *Connaissance et travail du vin* (Paris, 1981).
—— *The Taste of Wine* (2nd edn, New York, 1996).

Pfalz, until 1992 known as **Rheinpfalz,** is an important wine region in southern GERMANY in terms of both quantity and quality. The 23,400 ha/58,000 acres of vineyard follow the eastern edge of the Haardt range (a northern extension of Alsace's Vosges) for about 80 km/50 miles (see map under GERMANY) along the so-called Deutsche Weinstrasse, or German Wine Route, officially established in 1935 to link 40 villages. Viewed from a satellite, these vineyards would seem to reach in finger-like strips 8 km or so into the plain, which stretches a further 12 km to the Rhine. In some of the villages of the district in the southern half, the Bereich Südliche Weinstrasse, vines occupy nearly all the available land and viticulture has expanded greatly since the 1960s; only those parts of valleys at risk from cold air remain unplanted. The relatively sunny, dry Pfalz, long a mecca for German TOURISTS and, like Rheinhessen, long associated with the cheap and cheerful, has since the 1980s acquired a national and international reputation as an innovative and exciting wine-growing region.

The vineyards to the north of Neustadt, collectively known as the Mittelhaardt, are the best known in the Pfalz, in large part thanks to wine estates with such historic reputations as Bassermann-Jordan, Bürklin-Wolf, and von Buhl. The top sites of the Mittelhaardt villages largely nestle between the western edge of the villages and the lower slopes of the Haardt, on sandstone and volcanic soils. The reputations of Riesling-dominated villages (from south to north, with vineyards) Ruppertsberg (Nussbien, Gaisböhl, Hoheburg, Reiterpfad), Deidesheim (Leinhöhle, Hohenmorgen, Kieselberg, Mäushöhle, Grainhübel, Kalkofen), Forst (Ungeheuer, Pechstein, Jesuitengarten, Kirchenstück), Wachenheim (Gerümpel, Goldbächel, Rechbächel), Bad Dürkheim (Spielberg), Ungstein (Herrenberg, Weilberg), and Kallstadt (Saumagen) is secure. The resurgence of traditionally renowned growers, along with the maturation of vines in sites that were largely replanted in the FLURBEREINIGUNG (vineyard restructuring) of the 1980s, has resulted in increasingly impressive quality in recent years.

Villages in the immediate vicinity of Neustadt and its suburbs, while a little less well-known for most of the 20th century, have more than demonstrated their excellence in recent years in the hands of several of the Pfalz's most meticulous growers. Outstanding locations include Haardter Bürgergarten, Herzog, and Mandelring, Mussbacher Eselshaut, and Königsbacher Idig. The low rolling calcareous and sandy hills east of the Weinstrasse—notably at Laumersheim, Grosskarlbach, Freinsheim, and Herxheim—have also demonstrated their ability to generate memorable wines, and here the energy of young vintners and small family wineries has been a driving force for quality.

South of Neustadt, the so-called Südliche Weinstrasse long endured a reputation for high yields of indifferent grape varieties. Nowadays though, thanks above all to the ambitions of local vintners and a boom in dry wines from red, Grauburgunder (see PINOT GRIS) and Weissburgunder (see PINOT BLANC) grapes, this area has become increasingly fashionable inside Germany. Its less common but often exceptional Rieslings—from such villages as Birkweiler, Burrweiler, and Siebeldingen in soils that range from sandstone to slate—have also stepped onto the international stage. While this subregion of the Pfalz is warm and dry enough consistently to ripen Spätburgunder to above 13 per cent alcohol, it is still nearly 50 miles north of the northernmost significant Riesling vineyards of ALSACE.

High yields, mechanical harvesting, and a reliance on such crossings as Müller-Thurgau, Kerner, and Morio-Muskat were long associated with the Pfalz. But Riesling, always dominant in the prestigious towns of the Mittelhaardt, has staged a comeback throughout the Pfalz with more than 20 per cent of plantings by 2003. Red wine vines have gained ground rapidly, approaching 40 per cent of total plantings, whilst Kerner and the traditional Müller-Thurgau are the only white wine CROSSINGS that exceed 3 per cent of the total vineyard. Pinot Noir, Weissburgunder, and Grauburgunder represent collectively 10 per cent of Pfalz plantings, and each of these Burgundian varieties is increasingly common. Scheurebe may be statistically relatively insignificant, but there are signs of a revival, as with Rieslaner. Traminer, traditionally associated with the Pfalz, has failed in recent decades to mirror its success in neighbouring Alsace, or even to maintain more than a residual toehold, but the best examples, dry and sweet, can still be excellent.

Across the region, nearly half of all wines are now dry (TROCKEN), a reminder that the Pfalz is climatically well suited to producing the sort of fuller-bodied wines that the German market demands. Climate and taste also help explain why this region has been a leader in advocating the establishment of GROSSES GEWÄCHS full-bodied, dry wines (principally Riesling) from the best sites. The majority of non-dry Pfalz wine is nowadays destined for export.

Pfalz red wines are also fuller bodied today, with alcohol levels often over 13 per cent, and barrel maturation common. Pfalz Spätburgunder (Pinot Noir) is now attracting international attention. The older style of light Pfalz red wine, sometimes a little sweet, is still widely exemplified by PORTUGIESER, which still represents 10 per cent of plantings and is also the source of much pink WEISSHERBST. This undemanding vine is normally allowed to produce a high yield of reddish wine, but, on the rare occasions when the crop is limited, the improvement in concentration and quality is considerable, even if, unfortunately, less profitable. The success of the DORNFELDER crossing is particularly remarkable. Since 1990 the area planted has increased nearly five-fold to 2,800 ha/6,900 acres, or 12 per cent of the vineyard area. Even growers who lack the technical equipment of a red wine specialist can produce from Dornfelder a pleasant BEAUJOLAIS style wine. However, when MALOLACTIC FERMENTATION and OAK maturation come into play, Dornfelder yields stylish wines with greater depth, length of flavour, and ageing potential, rather like a good DOLCETTO or CHINON.

An increasing amount of Pfalz wine was made into sparkling wine in the 1990s (see SEKT). Technical specifications have been set high by an association of producers, with much attention being paid to the quality of the base wine, either from Riesling, Weiss-burgunder, or Spätburgunder. Only the FREE-RUN juice from unpressed grapes and that which flows from the first pressing is used. Others may work to less exacting standards (see SPARKLING WINE-MAKING).

Of the roughly 10,000 vine-growers in the region, over half deliver their grapes to co-operative cellars, producers' associations, or merchants' cellars. Some growers own small parcels of land in the best-known sites of the Mittelhaardt, where the standards and reputation of the local CO-OPERATIVES are high. In the Bereich Südliche Weinstrasse, the co-operative cellars are known for soft, inexpensive, off-dry wines for export, but here too production is moving in the direction of the dry, full-bodied style favoured by the majority of estate bottlers. An indication of the success of the best co-operative cellars is the growing percentage of wine that they sell in bottle, rather than on the depressed BULK wine market.

The wooded hills of the Pfalz forest, which rise to over 680 m/2,231 ft in parts, attract many visitors from such nearby cities as Mannheim, Ludswigshafen, and Karlsruhe, enabling much wine to be sold directly to the consumer. At the same time, dry Pfalz wines are increasingly prominent in the offerings of fine wine merchants throughout Germany.

I.J. & D.S.

Payne, J., and Diel, A., *The Guide to German Wines/German Wine Guide* (London/New York, 2005).

Pigott, S., and Johnson, H., *The Wine Atlas of Germany* (London, 1995).

pH, a scale of measurement of the concentration of the effective, active ACIDITY in a solution and an important statistic, of relevance to how vines grow, how grapes ripen, and how wine tastes, looks, and lasts. (The technical definition is that pH is the negative logarithm of the all-important hydrogen ion activity or concentration.) Low values of pH indicate high concentrations of acidity and the tart or sour taste that occurs in lemon juice, for example. Values near 7 are effectively neutral; drinking waters have pH values near 7. Values between 7 and 14 are found in basic or alkaline solutions such as caustic or washing soda. Grape must and wine are acidic, with pHs generally between 3 and 4. The scale is logarithmic so a solution with a pH value of 3 has ten times as much hydrogen ion activity as one whose pH value is 4.

Soils

The pH of soils is of some relevance to the resultant wine, although the effect is not direct. More important are effects on vine growth. Soils high in LIMESTONE tend to have high pH values, between 8 and 9, and in general limit plant growth, although the grapevine is one of the domesticated plants most tolerant of such inhospitable soils. Poorly drained soils high in ORGANIC MATTER tend to have acid pH values, between 5 and 6, which are also unfavourable to vine growth. IRRIGATION and soils high in NITROGEN encourage vines to produce excessively large crops and can yield grapes with lower concentrations of organic acids and therefore higher pH values. See also SOIL ACIDITY and SOIL ALKALINITY.

Grapes

The pH of grapes as well as wines can vary enormously since TEMPERATURE, RAINFALL, SOIL TYPE, viticultural practices, and VINE VARIETIES can all influence the different natural organic acids and minerals of mature grapes. In general, cool regions produce wines with low pH and hot regions produce wines with high pH. Part of the reason why white wines generally have a lower pH than red wines is that red wines have higher levels of POTASSIUM, which is extracted from the grape skin, where this ion is concentrated. See also GRAPE and ACIDITY.

The pH of grape juice is now well established as a factor affecting wine quality. In particular, high pH values are associated with high concentrations of potassium and low acidity, and red wine quality in particular is diminished (see below). Among factors known to affect the potassium concentration of grapes are potassium content of soils and SHADE within the canopy.

Wines

The pH range of most wines is between 2.9 and 4.2 (which incidentally, since the pH of the normal stomach is about 2, means that wines are 10 to 100 times less concentrated in the acid hydrogen ion than is the stomach interior). Wines with low pHs taste very tart while those with high pHs taste flat, or 'flabby'. Wines whose pH is between 3.2 and 3.5 not only tend to taste refreshingly rather than piercingly acid, they are also more resistant to harmful BACTERIA, age better, and have a clearer, brighter COLOUR (see below). Wines with pH values higher than this tend to taste flat, look dull, and are more susceptible to bacterial attack. In the last twenty years, average pH levels have risen considerably as a result of longer HANG TIME and a FASHION for riper wines. While it is possible to manipulate pH values, with grapes and wines it is difficult because of the wine's high 'buffer capacity', which roughly correlates with TOTAL ACIDITY. The pH can be increased by decreasing the concentration of hydrogen ions, however, and vice versa. (See ACIDIFICATION and DEACIDIFI-

CATION for discussion of the legal and practical aspects of these operations.)

The winemaker is interested in both the pH and the total acidity (the fixed and volatile acids) of both the grape juice and the resultant wine for several reasons. What one tastes in wines as the tart or sour sensation is influenced both by the total amount of acids present and by the concentration of hydrogen ions in the solution. Different YEASTS and bacteria have varying tolerances for hydrogen ion concentration and for the nature and concentration of the acid.

Finally, the resistance of the wine to changes of effective acidity (hydrogen ion concentration) during processing and STABILIZATION depends mainly on the total acid concentration. Keeping wine pH values low is of further importance because the hydrogen ion concentration of the wine controls the effectiveness of SULFUR DIOXIDE. Sulfur dioxide gas, when dissolved in wine, reacts with the water in the wine to form sulfurous acid, the form of the compound that is best at inhibiting bacteria and wild yeasts and countering OXIDATION. Sulfurous acid breaks down partially into hydrogen ions and bisulfite ions, a form having little effect on micro-organisms such as bacteria and wild yeasts. High hydrogen ion concentrations (low pH values) in the wine tend to combine with the bisulfite ions and thus keep more of the sulfur dioxide in the effective, anti-microbial form.

pH is also important in wine-making because the PIGMENTED TANNINS that colour red wines exist (like the monomeric ANTHOCYANINS from which they are formed) in several forms of different colours. At low pH values, the high concentration of hydrogen ions forces the pigment molecule into a form with a positive charge and a bright red colour. As pH increases (and hydrogen ion concentration decreases), the pigment molecules tend more and more to change through dull purple to blue, and ultimately greyish forms. The net result in the several pigments of red wine is a passage from bright to purplish red and finally to a dull brownish red as pH increases.

Measurement of pH is a familiar operation to those who maintain a garden, swimming pool, or aquarium. Probably the earliest measurement technique was the use of indicator solutions or papers dependent on the fact that many dyes change molecular form and colour as the hydrogen ion concentration, or pH, changes. More precise laboratory measurements use glass electrodes.

A.D.W., B.G.C., & P.J.W.

phenolic ripeness. See PHYSIOLOGICAL RIPENESS.

phenolics, sometimes called **polyphenolics** or **polyphenols,** very large group of highly reactive chemical compounds of which **phenol** (C_6H_5OH) is the basic building block. These include many natural colour pigments such as the ANTHOCYANINS of fruit and dark-skinned grapes, most natural vegetable TANNINS such as occur in grapes, and many FLAVOUR COMPOUNDS.

In grapes

These compounds occur in great profusion in grapes. They are particularly rich in stems, seeds, and skins but also occur in juice and pulp. The concentration of phenolics in grape skins increases if the berries are exposed to sunlight (see CANOPY MANAGEMENT).

Many hundreds of compounds belong to the phenolic category, and they can initially be classified as either non-flavonoid or FLAVONOID. The former include compounds derived from cinnamic and benzoic acids (one of the most abundant in grape juice is caftaric acid, the tartrate ESTER of caffeic acid) and stilbenes such as RESVERATROL. Flavonoids encompass CATECHINS and their polymers, called PROANTHOCYANIDINS or condensed TANNINS, which are an essential part of the taste and flavour of grapes and other fruits, and pigments, including FLAVONOLS such as QUERCETIN, and anthocyanins. With a few exceptions, such as the phenolic amino acid tyrosine that is a constituent of proteins, phenolics belong to the general group known as secondary metabolites, meaning that they are not involved in the primary metabolism of the plant. They are highly water soluble and are secreted into the BERRY vacuole, many as GLYCOSIDES, and some are FLAVOUR PRECURSORS.   B.G.C. & V.C.

In wines

Phenolic acids (especially cinnamic acids) are the major phenolics in grape pulp and juice, and thus in white wines made without skin contact. Anthocyanins are localized only in the skins, except in red-fleshed *teinturiers*, so that red wine-making requires a MACERATION phase to extract them into the juice. Flavonols, which are constituents of skins, stems, and leaves, as well as catechins and tannins, which are also present in seeds, are simultaneouly extracted. Alcohol, produced by FERMENTATION, greatly speeds up this extraction process. Additional phenolics (including gallotannins and ellegitannins as well as flavour compounds such as VANILLIN) may also be present in wine as a result of barrel ageing, the use of OAK CHIPS, or the addition of OENOLOGICAL TANNINS. Once extracted into the wine, the anthocyanins, catechins, and tannins are gradually converted to various types of derivatives, including PIGMENTED TANNINS. These reactions are responsible for the colour and taste changes observed during wine ageing.

Tannin polymers (see POLYMERIZATION) formed without anthocyanins, as they are in a white wine, taste bitter when they are of moderate size, while larger ones are responsible for the mouth-puckering astringency in young

wines. As the wine ages, tannins and their derivatives form larger and larger particles through aggregation and complexation with other molecules such as proteins and polysaccharides. This may result in the development of haze and sediments and other technological problems (e.g. clogging of filtration membranes, adsorption on tank surfaces).

A significant number of flavour precursors as well as FLAVOUR COMPOUNDS also have the phenol structure. Examples of these are VANILLIN, the key aroma compound of the vanilla bean, and raspberry ketone, the impact compound of raspberries. An ESTER, methyl salicylate, familiar as oil of wintergreen, is also a phenolic compound. These and many others are either grape constituents or are produced as trace components during alcoholic fermentation and by glycoside HYDROLYSIS during the subsequent processing and ageing phases. See also OAK FLAVOUR for details of the part played by the phenolics in new OAK.

A.D.W., P.J.W., & V.C.

As a tasting term

Phenolic is also sometimes used, imprecisely, as a pejorative tasting term, to describe (usually white) wines which display an excess of phenolics by tasting astringent or bitter.

As health benefit

It is in its high phenolics content that red wine is distinguished from white, and it is thought that it may well be the antioxidative properties of phenolics which reduce the incidence of heart disease among those who consume moderate amounts of red wine. See HEALTH.

Frankel, E. N., *et al.*, 'Inhibition of oxidation of human low-density lipoprotein by phenolic substances in red wine', *Lancet*, 341 (1993), 454–7.
Somers, T. C., and Verette, E., 'Phenolic composition of natural wine types', in H. F. Linskens and J. F. Jackson (eds.), *Wine Analysis: Modern Methods of Plant Analysis*, NS 6 (Berlin, 1988).

phenology, the study of the sequence of plant development (see diagram opposite). As applied to vines, it records the timing of specific stages such as BUDBREAK, FLOWERING, VERAISON, and LEAF FALL. Such studies indicate the suitability of VINE VARIETIES to certain climatic zones. See VINE GROWTH CYCLE.

pheromones are in a viticultural context synthetic products used in the biological control of vineyard INSECT PESTS. They work by causing sexual confusion (see INTEGRATED PEST MANAGEMENT).

philosophy and wine. Wine first played a part in the history of Western philosophy at the SYMPOSIUM of the early Greek philosophers where it enlivened and encouraged discussion. Later, during the Enlightenment, David Hume recommended drinking wine with friends as a cure for philosophical melancholy, and Immanuel Kant thought wine softened the

harsher sides of men's characters and made their company more convivial. In recent times, philosophers have turned their philosophical attention to wine as an object of perception, assessment, and appreciation. Their enquiries have focused on the relationship between wine and our experience of it, including its intoxicating effect on us (see DRUNKENNESS), and the meaning and value it has for us in our lives.

The issue of objectivity

To know the chemical WINE COMPOSITION and its method of VINIFICATION is not yet to know how it tastes. To know this, one must experience the wine itself by TASTING it. But in tasting a wine are we discovering properties the wine has or just noting our SUBJECTIVE responses to it? And is every response as good any other? Here we have a key philosophical question: how subjective are tastes and tasting? On one view, the only objective knowledge we can have of wine is that provided by scientific analysis: the chemist describes the way the wine is, the wine critic describes the way it tastes. The former is objective, the latter is merely subjective. But are the two unconnected? Winemakers rely on scientific analysis to achieve the taste they are aiming for, and experienced wine tasters rely on taste to identify and describe compounds of flavours or aromas that arise from fermentation. For this to be so, wine tasters must draw objective conclusions about a wine from their subjective responses to it, and wine makers must create conditions they hope will produce a certain taste for us. A revised view would be that while tasting is a subjective experience of individual tasters, *what* we taste, the TANNINS, or ACIDITY in a wine, are objective properties or characteristics of the wine itself.

Nevertheless, many of the qualities we value in wine such as finesse, BALANCE, and LENGTH can only be confirmed by tasting. And some philosophers would argue that these more complex properties depend on us and should be conceived as some kind of relation between the wines and our responses to them. The problem for this view is whether to treat all such responses as equally good. If we differ in opinion about whether a wine is round or balanced, does this mean there is no fact of the matter about who is right? Is it balanced for me but not for you? On such a subjectivist view, matters of taste are neither right or wrong: the conclusion is that *de gustibus non est disputandum*.

Tastes and tasting

Philosophers who reject this conclusion argue that taste properties, such as a wine's length or balance, *are* objective features of a wine and that under the right conditions, and with the right experience and training as tasters, they are revealed to us in experience. Tasting a wine involves the taster's subjectivity but verdicts based on those subjective experiences are not mere matters of opinion: so not subjective in

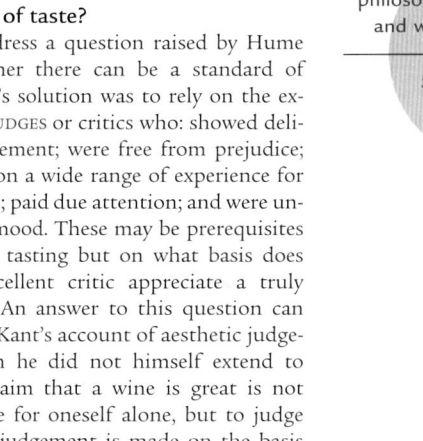

Phenology

1 winter bud, at rest

2 bud in a cocoon

3 green stage

4 leaf emergence

5 leaf elongation

6 bunch visible

7 bunches separate

8 flowers separate

9 flowering

10 fruit set

perceptual experience alone and that evaluation goes beyond what one finds in a description of its objective characteristics. According to these thinkers, something else is required to arrive at an assessment of a wine's merits. This may be the pleasure the taster derives from the wine, the valuing of certain characteristics, or the individual preferences of the taster. Is there room on such views for non-subjective judgements of wine quality?

To say that assessments of quality rest on interpretation is to say that one cannot recognize a wine's quality on the basis of perceptual experience alone. And yet according to some philosophers, a novice taster can recognize the merits of wine by taste without the expert knowledge of the wine critic. Moreover, expert knowledge may enable one to recognize a wine as an excellent example of its type but if that style of wine offers one no pleasure, could one, as a wine critic, still judge it to be or admire it as a great wine? Many philosophers would think not, but then on what basis does one judge something to be a great wine, and what could separate the experienced and the novice taster in evaluating wines? Is each taster's opinion equally good?

A standard of taste?

Here we address a question raised by Hume about whether there can be a standard of taste. Hume's solution was to rely on the excellence of JUDGES or critics who: showed delicacy of judgement; were free from prejudice; could draw on a wide range of experience for comparisons; paid due attention; and were unclouded by mood. These may be prerequisites for accurate tasting but on what basis does such an excellent critic appreciate a truly great wine? An answer to this question can be found in Kant's account of aesthetic judgement (which he did not himself extend to wine). To claim that a wine is great is not just to judge for oneself alone, but to judge for all. The judgement is made on the basis of pleasure but this is not a claim about what one finds personally pleasant or agreeable. It is a judgement about the pleasure the wine affords anyone suitably equipped to taste it. There is no such thing as a wine that is great *for me*. In claiming to recognize a great wine, I am claiming something about *the wine itself*, about how it will (and should) strike others. It is thus a universal claim about the delight all can take in it, and others would be mistaken were they not to judge it so. Kant's solution does not solve all problems of the objectivity of taste, however. Disagreements about a wine's qualities are still disagreements amongst ourselves, and not disagreements settled solely by the properties of the wine itself.

A further problem is created when two (or more) experienced, unprejudiced wine critics differ in their opinions regarding the excellence of a wine. Perhaps they agree in their

that sense. Certain experiences will be more accurate than others, some people will be better tasters then others, and judgements of a wine can be right or wrong. On this objectivist view, *tastes* are in the wine, not in us, and by improving the skills of *tasting* we can come to know them more accurately.

What is meant by 'fine wine'?

A related issue concerns the evaluation of wines and whether there is a clear separation between describing a wine and assessing its QUALITY. Part of this issue is how we should characterize FINE WINE. From the absence of a definition we should not infer there is no category of fine wine any more than our inability to define 'chair' satisfactorily should lead us to conclude that there are no chairs. Criteria for being a fine wine can be given, as when we can say that a fine wine is one whose complex, individual character rewards the interest and attention paid to it, and affords the degree of

discrimination we exercise in assessing its qualities and characteristics. But is a fine wine a wine that must be appreciated? Or can experienced wine tasters assess the qualities of a wine without enjoying it? The alternative view is that recognizing a wine's merits depends on the enjoyment, pleasure, or preferences of the individual taster. The dispute here concerns the ultimate nature of wine tasting and wine appreciation. Do we directly perceive the quality of a wine, or do we assess its quality on the basis of what we first perceive? Tasting seems to involve both perception and judgement. But does the perceptual experience of tasting—which relies on the sensations of touch, taste, and smell—already involve a judgement of quality? Is such judgement a matter of interpretation, and if it is, does assessment require wine knowledge in order to arrive at a correct verdict?

Some philosophers would claim that one cannot assess a wine's quality on the basis of descriptions of the wine's objective characteristics but diverge in evaluating its merits. If they merely point to divergent qualities, one can argue for pluralism about the qualities and tastes of a wine. However, if they genuinely conflict in judgement, but neither has overlooked any aspect of the wine's identifiable properties, and both agree in the terms they use to describe and classify wines, we may be tempted to conclude neither is right and neither is wrong. However, subjectivism about standards of taste can be resisted in this case by embracing relativism about matters of taste. According to relativist doctrine, both critics are right: both make true judgements about the wine in question. It is simply that the truth of each judgement is *relative* to a standard of assessment, or set of preferences, not shared by the other. Cultural differences could account for these divergences and there would still be a right answer according to one set of standards, or the other. In effect, this is to claim there can be more than one standard of taste, and each critic is right relative to a standard of assessment.

Finally, philosophers have stressed the meaning and value wine has in our lives as a celebration of our relationship with our natural surroundings. The place, culture, and history of a people that falls under the concept of TERROIR are celebrated and acknowledged in drinking a wine that reflects that terroir and the efforts of people to uphold and maintain the traditions with which they transformed soil and vine into grape, and grape into wine. The final transformation, according to philosopher Roger Scruton (Smith, 2006), occurs when we take wine into ourselves and through its intoxicating effects it transforms us and opens us up to one another.   B.C.S.

Hume, D., 'Of the standard of taste', *Essays Moral, Political and Literary* (Oxford, 1965), 231–55.

Kant, I., *The Critique of Judgement*, Sections 1–7 (Oxford, 1952).

Smith, B. C. (ed.), *A Question of Taste: Philosophy and Wine* (Oxford, 2006).

phloem, the principal food-conducting tissue of the vine and other vascular plants. Phloem is composed of a mix of CELL types which lie alongside the XYLEM, the water-conducting tissue, and the combination makes up a system of veins or vascular bundles. Despite their proximity, phloem and xylem are entirely different: phloem has thin-walled tubes containing a strongly sugared sap under positive pressure which moves along from areas of strong to weak concentrations, while xylem consists of large, strong-walled tubes through which a dilute mineral solution moves under negative pressure (tension) by forces generated by TRANSPIRATION. During the thickening of woody parts, the CAMBIUM produces cells on the outside that become the new season's phloem; in later years these cells are added to the bark of the vine. Phloem of grapevine

wood has the characteristic, unusual among deciduous trees, of reactivation after the next BUDBREAK and can remain functional for three to four years.

The vascular system permeates throughout the plant, but bundles of veins are particularly dense in the LEAF blade, as can be seen by holding it up to the light. This high density facilitates the loading of newly photosynthesized SUCROSE into the phloem tubes for its movement out of the leaf (see TRANSLOCATION).   B.G.C.

Phoenicia, ancient mercantile state covering modern LEBANON, extending slightly further north and slightly further south to encompass the cities of Ruad, Byblos, Beirut, Sidon, and Tyre. Vines and olives were grown on the rockier terrain, while the alluvial valleys were given over to grain. Independent Phoenician culture lasted from about 1400 BC to 322 (when Alexander the Great captured Tyre), but their greatest colony, CARTHAGE in modern Tunisia, survived until destroyed by the Romans in 146 BC.

Evidently the Phoenician colonists found in North Africa a fertile region ideal for viticultural development. The Graeco-Roman historian Diodorus Siculus describes the Carthaginian countryside as being (in the 4th century BC) full of vines, olives, and cattle, especially in the Bagradas valley and in southern Tunisia. The Carthaginian author Mago left an extensive treatise on agriculture, including instructions on viticulture. Unfortunately his work does not survive, but some citations from the Latin translation made by the Romans in 146 BC are preserved. The Roman agricultural writer COLUMELLA (1st century BC) quotes a recipe of Mago's for a DRIED GRAPE WINE or *passum* which he describes as *optimum* 'excellent—I myself have made it' (*De re rustica* 12. 39. 1).   J.A.B.

Harden, D., *The Phoenicians* (London, 1962).

Phoenix, one of GEILWEILERHOF's most successful DISEASE-RESISTANT VARIETIES, a crossing of SEYVAL BLANC and BACCHUS which produces attractive, herbaceous, elderflower-scented wine in England with a minimum of SPRAYING. Despite its parentage, it produces remarkably VINIFERA-like wine so has been registered as a *vinifera* variety. Consequently, it may used in the production of QUALITY WINE.

phomopsis, a fungal genus which leads to a number of disease conditions depending on the species. *Phomopsis viticola* causes phomopsis cane and leaf spot, also known as excoriose, dead arm, and Phomopsis Type 2. Symptoms include black lesions at the base of grape shoots, leaf petioles, and bunch stems; bleached patches on winter canes; death of affected fruit buds; stunted shoots; small black spots with yellow halos on deformed leaves; rot on infected berries. Although this disease

poses the greatest threat in early spring, especially in cool and rainy conditions, control measures to protect the fruit may continue into the summer in some regions. Because the fungus colonizes old wood, cane pruning and hand harvesting reduce pressure from this disease. There is ongoing research into other species. Studies in Australia, for example, have shown there that Phomopsis Type 1 (also called *Diaporthe*) does not harm the vine.   L.M.

Rawnsley, B., and Wicks, T., '*Phomopsis viticola*: pathogenicity and management', Final report to the Grape and Wine Research and Development Corportation, Project No. SAR 99/1 (2002).

phosphorus, one of the most important MINERAL elements required for vine growth, yet the amounts required are so small that for most vineyards, the supply from the soil is sufficient. There is only about 0.6 kg of phosphorus in a tonne of grapes (1.3 lb per ton). Phosphorus in the vine is an essential component of compounds involved in PHOTOSYNTHESIS and sugar–starch transformations as well as the transfer of energy. Phosphorus deficiency is rare, and found mostly on acid soils, sometimes in HILLSIDE VINEYARDS, but its symptoms are a gradual loss of VIGOUR and, sometimes, some red spots on the leaves.   R.E.S.

photosynthesis, a biochemical reaction which combines water and atmospheric carbon dioxide using the energy of the sun to form SUGARS in plants, including vines. Important in this process are the green chlorophyll pigments in leaves which capture the sun's energy. Photosynthesis is the essential first step in the wine-making process, as the sugars formed in photosynthesis, along with other chemical products derived from sugar, are transported to grape berries (see SUGAR IN GRAPES), and eventually fermented into ETHANOL to produce wine. (According to the neat laws of nature, humans eventually metabolize wine's ethanol back to carbon dioxide and water; see CARBON DIOXIDE.)

Photosynthesis can be summarized by this chemical equation:

$$6\,CO_2 + 6\,H_2O + \text{light energy} = C_6H_{12}O_6 + 6\,O_2$$

(carbon dioxide + water + sunlight = sugar + oxygen)

The process of photosynthesis maintains atmospheric supplies of OXYGEN, essential for animal life on earth. Since these reactions take place inside the vine leaf, carbon dioxide must be able to diffuse in and oxygen out. This takes place through minute pores called STOMATA on the underside of vine leaves.

Photosynthesis is affected by environmental and plant factors, all of which have an effect on grape RIPENING and hence wine quality. Light, temperature, and WATER STRESS are the three most important climatic controls. Photosynthesis is limited by low light levels, as, for example, under overcast conditions or, more commonly, for shaded leaves away from the canopy surface (see CANOPY MICROCLIMATE). Light levels of about 1 per cent of full sunlight are too low for photosynthesis. Leaves exposed to such light levels turn yellow and eventually fall off. Photosynthesis increases almost linearly with light up to about one-third full sunlight, and then is said to be light saturated, in that any further increase in sunlight intensity will not increase photosynthesis. So outside leaves on vine canopies are often light saturated in sunny conditions, and some sunlight is wasted.

Photosynthesis is highest with leaf temperatures from about 15 to 30 °C (59–86 °F), with a slight peak at about 25 °C. Photosynthesis is severely inhibited for temperatures below 15 °C and above 30 °C. During one day in hot DESERT regions, day–night TEMPERATURE VARIABILITY may be so great that vine leaf photosynthesis is inhibited by both low temperatures in the early morning and high temperatures in the afternoon. Low temperatures limit photosynthesis and hence grape ripening in cool climate wine regions such as those of northern Europe. High-quality vintages there are warm, sunny years when photosynthesis is highest.

Dry soil conditions will cause stomata to close, thus interfering with photosynthesis, but saving the vine from further desiccation. Such an effect of water stress on photosynthesis and grape ripening can be seen, especially towards HARVEST, in many of the world's wine regions, typically in MEDITERRANEAN CLIMATES. The vine can, however, tolerate a mild water stress with no negative effect on wine quality, indeed it will probably be enhanced. Wind can also cause stomata to close and interfere with grape ripening, as is common in MONTEREY in California, for example.

As a general rule, photosynthesis is enhanced by sunny conditions and mild temperatures. These conditions are known to give maximal sugar concentration in grapes and, conventionally, the best wine quality.   R.E.S.

Champagnol, F., *Éléments de physiologie de la vigne et de viticulture générale* (St-Gely-du-Fesc, 1984).

Jackson, R., *Wine Science: Principles, Practice, Perception* (San Diego, 2000).

Mullins, M. G., Bouquet, A., and Williams, L., *Biology of the Vine* (Cambridge, 1992).

Winkler, A. J., *et al.*, *General Viticulture* (2nd edn, Berkeley, Calif., 1974).

phylloxera. This small yellow root-feeding aphid has probably had a more damaging impact on wine production than any other VINE PEST, or any VINE DISEASE. It attacks only grapevines, and kills vines by attacking their roots. For many years after it first invaded Europe there was no known cure.

The effects of phylloxera were first noted in France in 1863, just as the country was recovering from another great scourge of 19th-century European viticulture: oidium, or POWDERY MILDEW, which was first noted in 1847. Like powdery mildew, and the other FUNGAL DISEASES yet to arrive (DOWNY MILDEW in 1878 and

BLACK ROT in 1885), the phylloxera louse was an unwelcome import from America which devastated European vineyards until appropriate control measures were found. In the history of agriculture it rivals the potato blight of Ireland as a plant disease with widespread social effects. In France, for example, almost 2.5 million ha/6.2 million acres of vineyards were destroyed, the aphid making no distinction between the vineyards of the most famous châteaux and those of humble peasants. For individual French vine-growers from the late 1860s, the sight of their vineyards dying literally before their eyes was particularly traumatic, although the epidemic soon spread elsewhere. Phylloxera invasion had a major social and economic impact, involving national governments and local committees, and requiring international scientific collaboration. For a while the very existence of the French wine industry was threatened. (See BURGUNDY, modern history, for example.)

Phylloxera has had several scientific names. Initially called *Phylloxera vastatrix* (the devastator) by the French scientist J.-E. Planchon, and also *Phylloxera vitifoliae* (A. Fitch), it is now more correctly known as *Dactylasphaera vitifoliae* (H. Shimer). See below for more detail.

Biology

The female phylloxera is yellow and about 1 mm/0.039 in long. Typically surrounded by

masses of eggs, it is barely visible to the naked eye as it feeds on the roots. There are four to seven generations in the summer, each producing females capable of laying more eggs. As the eggs hatch, so-called 'crawlers' move to other roots of the vine, and some climb the trunk and can spread to other vines, or even vineyards, by the action of wind or machinery dislodging them from the foliage. Because of the movement of the crawlers through soil cracks, phylloxera tends to spread in a circle from the original infected vine. Wind-blown crawlers create secondary infections downwind.

It has a complex life cycle, existing in both root-living and leaf-living forms, and causes damage to vines by injecting saliva to produce galls, by feeding on the sap, and by causing root deformities.

In humid regions, there is also an associated life cycle whereby the root-hatched nymph produces a winged form which can travel longer distances, and which lays male and female eggs. The hatching female in turn lays a winter egg which develops into the stem mother or fundatrix, which lays eggs in a leaf gall (these galls typically being produced only on the leaves of American vines). Nymphs hatching from leaf galls can begin new infections as egg-laying females on roots.

The principal agent for the spread of phylloxera is humans. It is most commonly

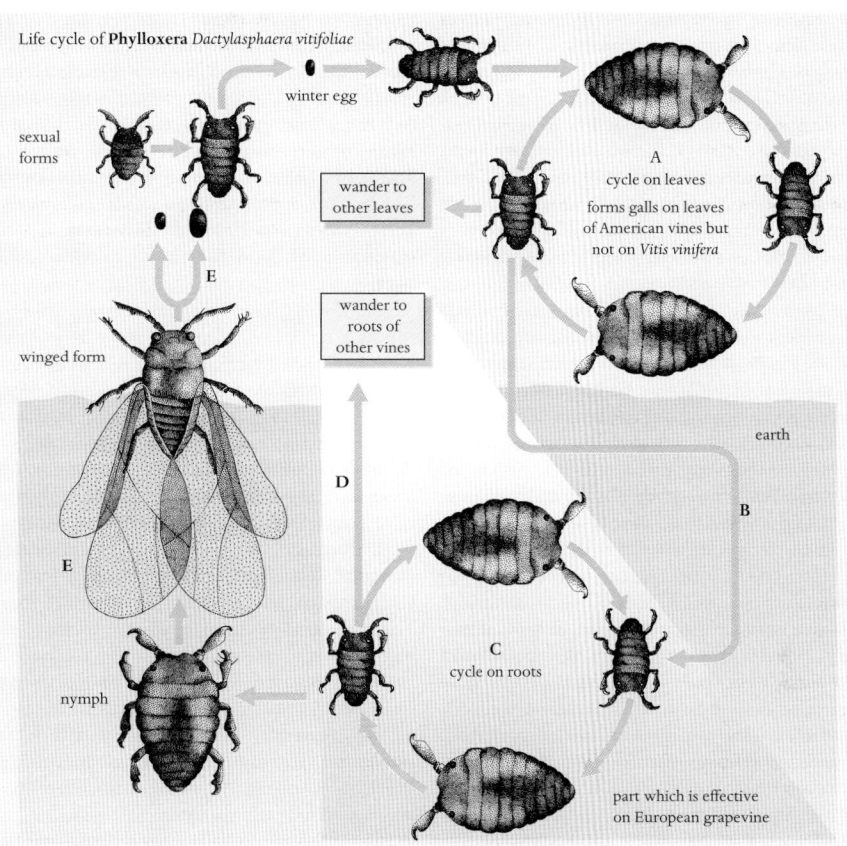

Life cycle of **Phylloxera** *Dactylasphaera vitifoliae*

winter egg

sexual forms

wander to other leaves

A
cycle on leaves
forms galls on leaves of American vines but not on *Vitis vinifera*

wander to roots of other vines

winged form

earth

E

D

B

nymph

C
cycle on roots

part which is effective on European grapevine

transported from one vineyard to another on the roots of ROOTLINGS (one-year-old dormant plants). However, phylloxera is easily moved in the soil that sticks to implements, and by irrigation water. Recent research by King and colleagues in New Zealand has shown that crawlers present in vine foliage lead to secondary spread over considerable distances; they are moved by machines such as foliage trimmers and harvesters which brush against foliage, and also by wind.

Phylloxera is native to the east coast of the United States, and so native AMERICAN VINE SPECIES have generally evolved with resistance. Studies have shown that the basis of resistance is the development of cork layers beneath the wound made by phylloxera feeding on the root. This stops the invasion of other microbes (bacteria and fungi) which eventually rot the root and kill non-resistant vines.

Phylloxera kills vines which have not developed this resistance, such as the European VINIFERA vine species from which most wine is made, by destroying the root system. When first present, the phylloxera numbers build up quickly on roots and there is little apparent root damage. After a few years, the root rot affects the top growth, shoot growth is stunted, and leaves lose their healthy green colour. Normally a vine dies within several years of the first infection. Vines which are struggling for other reasons are more susceptible to phylloxera and succumb quickly. Those growing on deep, fertile soil can continue to produce economic crops for many years after phylloxera attack. Phylloxera does not survive well in sandy soil, so vines planted in sand (such as on the Great Plain of HUNGARY, those planted by Listel on the French Mediterranean coast, or COLARES in Portugal) are immune from attack.

History

Attempts by early European colonists in North America to establish imported *vinifera* vines met with disaster, presumably substantially because of phylloxera, to which they had no resistance—although at this time phylloxera had yet to be identified, and other American vine diseases such as PIERCE'S DISEASE in Florida, downy and powdery mildew in all regions, and the very cold winters doubtless played a part. See UNITED STATES, history, for more details.

How did phylloxera come to Europe? In the mid 19th century there was considerable importation of living plants into Europe. This trade was supported by wealthy people who could afford elaborate gardens, greenhouses, and conservatories, and encouraged by the Victorians' keen interest in botany. Plants could be imported dormant, or kept alive and protected from salt spray by glass container mounted on the deck. In 1865 alone, 460 tons of plants worth 230,000 francs were imported into France, and this trade had grown to

2,000 tons by the 1890s. In 1875, 50 tons were imported from the US and much of this was vines. Jules Planchon, Professor of Pharmacy at MONTPELLIER University, noted that rooted American vines were imported in particularly significant quantities between 1858 and 1862, and sent to parts of Europe as far apart as Bordeaux, England, Ireland, Alsace, Germany, and Portugal. No doubt phylloxera was an unsuspected passenger on vine roots at the same time.

Just like the fungal disease powdery mildew, the first reporting of phylloxera was in England, in 1863, when Professor J. O. Westwood, an entomologist at Oxford University, received insect samples from a greenhouse in the London suburb of Hammersmith. Since the insects were in a leaf gall, the vine species was probably American, and these plants may even have been a source of introduction of the pest to England. In 1863, an unknown vine disease in France was being talked about, with two vineyards in the southern Rhône affected. The first printed report in France was a letter written by a veterinarian in 1867 about a vineyard planted in 1863 at St-Martin-de-Crau (only about 30 km/20 miles north east of the University of MONTPELLIER's modern phylloxera-free domaines on the Mediterranean coast, ironically), which developed unhealthy vines in summer 1866, failing to grow the following spring. It is likely that infection occurred several years beforehand. There were other reports from Narbonne in the Languedoc, and the Gard and Vaucluse *départements* in the southern Rhône in 1867, and from Bordeaux in 1869. (It was usually several years after the initial sighting that the louse's predations had a serious effect; the Médoc, for example, was not commercially compromised until the late 1870s.)

The first of many committees formed to resolve the phylloxera question was a Commission instigated by the Vaucluse Agricultural Society. On 15 July 1868 it began its investigation of affected vineyards in the southern Rhône. One member of the Commission was Jules Planchon, who had good training to work on phylloxera. He had spent a period at Kew Botanical Gardens in England, and subsequently became the brother-in-law of J. Lichtenstein, an amateur entomologist. Planchon noticed that dying vines had small yellow insects on their roots and noted the resemblance to an aphid *Phylloxera quercus* living on oak trees. He named the insect believed to be ravaging vineyards *Phylloxera vastatrix*. The form previously described by A. Fitch as living in the leaf galls of American vines was established by Planchon to be the same insect and therefore, according to the rules of priority, it became known as *Phylloxera vitifolii* (Fitch).

The Hérault Commission made its findings public in August 1868 but these caused little interest in any but the local newspapers. There was a marked reluctance to accept that this

little yellow insect could be causing such devastation. Other explanations current at the time were over-production, winter cold and other bad weather, weakening of the vineyards as a result of continued vegetative reproduction, soil exhaustion, and also God's wrath at contemporary vices. Even eminent scientists of the time misdiagnosed the problem. The distinguished entomologist V. Signoret thought phylloxera was an effect not the cause, and Dr GUYOT thought its presence was due to over-severe pruning (the opposite of overcropping)! The debate was ended by the 1869 Commission of the Société des Agriculteurs de France headed by L. Vialla, who gently but firmly debunked all false theories.

Total French wine production fell from a peak of 84.5 million hl/2,200 million gal in 1875 to a mere 23.4 million hl in 1889. But even by June 1873 the French government was sufficiently alarmed by the spread of phylloxera to offer a large prize (300,000 francs) for a remedy, which was to be verified by experimentation carried out by the School of Agriculture at Montpellier. Up to October 1876, 696 suggestions were forwarded to Professors Durand and Jeannenot at Montpellier and between 1872 and 1876 1,044 treatments were evaluated. Among the deluge of suggestions submitted were those verging on the ridiculous, which included burying a living toad under the vine to draw the poison, and irrigating the vines with white wine. Entries were received from other countries as different as Denmark and Singapore. All of this work, however, produced little benefit, as only two treatments based on the chemical application of various forms of SULFIDE appeared to show much advantage. Surprisingly, carbon bisulfide failed in the evaluation even though it was later used extensively.

Early attempts at commercial control of phylloxera included FLOODING, which was studied by the Commission in 1873. It was found that flooding in winter for weeks on end controlled the pest, but of course few vineyards were near enough to water supplies or sufficiently flat for this to be a widespread solution (although it is still used in parts of Argentina). Vineyards on sandy soils were noted to be immune, although this offered no control. The injection of the liquid carbon bisulfide was to become widespread, so that by 1888 some 68,000 ha/168,000 acres had been treated. The insecticidal properties of carbon bisulfide were found in 1854 on grain weevils, and Baron Paul Thénard evaluated it in Bordeaux in 1869. The first experiments used too high a dose, severely affecting the vines, but subsequently the practice of injecting it, mixed with water, into the soil, using about 30,000 holes per ha, became widespread.

By the time of the International Phylloxera Congress at Bordeaux in 1881, two distinct schools of thought on how the industry might be saved had emerged. The chemists considered salvation lay in carbon bisulfide or related chemicals, or in flooding. In opposition were the 'Americanists', who advocated grafting desired varieties on to American vine species used as ROOTSTOCKS. Gaston Bazille had suggested GRAFTING in 1869 and Leo Laliman of Bordeaux drew early attention to the resistance of these species to the phylloxera. Laliman had studied the resistance of American species to powdery mildew in a collection in his vineyards since 1840. (He subsequently tried to claim the prize for controlling phylloxera.)

Following successful demonstrations of the ability of American vines to withstand phylloxera, and the visit of Planchon to America in 1873, where his study was guided by the noted scientist C. V. Riley, state entomologist of Missouri, the use of grafted vines began, rising from 2,500 ha in 1880 to 45,000 ha in 1885. It was Riley who positively identified the unknown French insect as identical to the American one, a critical step in its eventual control; he was one of the first to suggest grafting European varieties to American rootstocks, and his authority and expertise on phylloxera gave weight to the suggestion. Riley referred French experts to the nurserymen of Missouri, who provided most of the rootstocks that saved the vineyards of France and ultimately Europe. Millions of rootstock cuttings were shipped to France, especially between 1873 and 1876. Fortunately in Missouri there were many native American VITIS species: *labrusca* was found to lack resistance, but *aestivalis*, *rupestris*, and *riparia* were found to be most effective. Another American who helped the French by providing expertise and rootstock was one of the fathers of American viticulture, T. V. MUNSON of Texas.

All was not plain sailing, however. Many American species could not tolerate the CALCAREOUS soils of France (see CHLOROSIS), the amount of grafting to be done was almost overwhelming, and also there was a concern that the use of these foreign rootstocks (whose own wine is so often reviled for its FOXY flavour) might affect wine quality. The latter objection is voiced by the uneducated even today, and in Burgundy the importation of American vines was prohibited until 1887, although the clandestine activities of growers anxious to save their vineyards forced its repeal.

Eventually rootstock use became the established method for the control of phylloxera and this has had a dramatic effect on vine NURSERY operations worldwide. There was a period in the late 19th century, however, when it was thought that breeding HYBRIDS of European with American vine varieties might produce vines with sufficient phylloxera resistance not to need grafting, whose wines were not marked by the undesirable foxy flavour of some American grapes. The class of varieties so created is loosely termed FRENCH HYBRIDS or DIRECT PRODUCERS. These efforts were generally unsuccessful, however, in that the vines

had inadequate phylloxera tolerance and produced lower-quality wine, although they became popular with growers because of their high yields and their tolerance of FUNGAL DISEASES. Nevertheless, many of the rootstocks used today (see ROOTSTOCKS for a detailed list) were bred in this period—although hybrids with *vinifera* as one parent have been generally found to have insufficient tolerance to phylloxera (see below).

Geography

Phylloxera is now widespread around the world, having been found in California (1873), Portugal (1871), Turkey (1871), Austria (1872), Switzerland (1874), Italy (1875), Australia (1877), Spain (1878), Algeria (1885), South Africa (1885), New Zealand (1885), and Greece (1898). There are few parts of the world free from the pest, although these include parts of Australia (on which a strict QUARANTINE is imposed), parts of China, Chile, Argentina, India, Pakistan, and Afghanistan, and some Mediterranean islands such as Crete, Cyprus, and Rhodes. And phylloxera cannot survive at particularly high ALTITUDES.

There are also small sandy vineyards in otherwise affected wine regions (see BOLLINGER and COLARES) which have never been affected by phylloxera either because of isolation or because of the soil composition.

For much of the late 20th century, phylloxera has not been regarded as a serious problem, either because it was not known in a region, or because a wide range of rootstocks are available which are suited to different varieties, soil, and climate conditions along with tolerance to other pests such as NEMATODES. About 85 per cent of all the world's vineyards were estimated in 1990 to be grafted onto rootstocks presumed to be resistant to phylloxera.

Phylloxera has been noted in the 1980s, however, on ungrafted vines in parts of Greece, England, New Zealand, Australia, Oregon, and, most dramatically, on grafted vines in California where the so-called 'biotype B' strain of phylloxera was identified. The widely used rootstock AXR1 (see ROOTSTOCKS for details) was found to offer insufficient phylloxera tolerance, and a significant proportion of grafted vineyards in Napa and Sonoma succumbed to phylloxera and were replanted in the 1990s.

Phylloxera is known to occur naturally as a number of related strains or 'biotypes'. King and Rilling exchanged phylloxera and vine cuttings between New Zealand and Germany, and confirmed evidence of the biotype differences between the two countries. Interestingly, the AXR1 rootstock was found not to be affected by phylloxera found in New Zealand, but it was affected by German phylloxera. New Zealand probably obtained phylloxera from California in 1885, which suggests that the biotype of phylloxera originally in California did not affect AXR1. With the introduction

of other biotypes, probably on rooted vines imported from eastern American states at a time of nursery shortages in California, the demise of AXR1 began.

No doubt one of the most important effects of the phylloxera invasion of the world's vineyards was the inadvertent spread of VIRUS DISEASES. As grafting became widespread towards the end of the 19th century, virus diseases were also spread as a common result of grafting, because virus-infected cuttings were used in grafting. A virus originally present only in the rootstock would spread to the fruiting *vinifera* variety after grafting. Rootstocks do not show virus symptoms, and virology in viticulture was not well understood until the 1950s. With known effects on fruit ripening (see LEAFROLL VIRUS), perhaps it was virus diseases more than grafting which led to the debate as to the relative merits of 'PRE-PHYLLOXERA' and 'post-phylloxera' wines. R.E.S.

Boubals, D., 'La Realité internationale relative au phylloxera', *Progrès agricole et viticole*, 108 (1991), 494–6.

Buchanan, G. A., and Amos, T. G., 'Grape pests', in B. G. Coombe and P. R. Dry (eds.), *Viticulture*, ii: *Practices* (Adelaide, 1992).

Campbell, C., *Phylloxera—How Wine was Saved for the World* (London, 2004).

King, P. D., and Rilling, G., 'Further evidence of phylloxera biotypes: variations in the tolerance of mature grapevine roots related to the geographical origin of the insect', *Vitis*, 30 (1991), 233–44.

Ordish, G., *The Great Wine Blight* (2nd edn, London, 1987).

Pinney, T., *A History of Wine in America* (Berkeley, Calif., 1989).

Winkler, A. J., et al., *General Viticulture* (2nd edn, Berkeley, Calif., 1974).

physiological ripeness, or sometimes **physiological maturity**, fashionable terms loosely used by some winemaker, especially in the New World, to contrast with RIPENESS measured by the normal analytical measures of MUST WEIGHT, ACIDITY, and PH. The terminology is imprecise because all grapes undergo physiological ripening irrespective of how it is assessed.

The concept of physiological ripening arose when winemakers realized that in many, particularly warmer, wine regions, these chemical measures were not sufficient to predict the optimum HARVEST date for wine quality. In its simplest form, the concept includes aspects of the berry's maturation which are not measured (but could often be) and which describe changes in a ripening grape berry important to eventual quality. These include skin colour, berry texture including skin and pulp texture, seed colour and ripening, flavour, and phenolic changes, often accompanied by lignification of the berry stem. The aim is to pick at as near optimum values of as many of these parameters as possible. Wine quality is thought to suffer if only a few parameters are at optimal value when the fruit is harvested; factors such as weather conditions, site, and viticultural technique can unbalance these relationships. A common example is the relatively faster rate of sugar increase in warm to hot climates compared with phenolic development, flavour increase, and acid decrease. The resulting wines tend to be high in alcohol without necessarily being accompanied by ripe fruit aromas. On the other hand, VARIETAL flavour appears to increase more quickly relative to sugar in cooler climates.

A likely important aspect of physiological ripeness which is overlooked in conventional RIPENING considerations is that of the condition of the grape skin. There is empirical evidence that wine quality can be affected, even though other aspects of fruit condition seem similar.

There is an increasing tendency to encourage growers to leave grapes longer and longer on the vine. The aim of this prolonged HANG TIME is riper tannins and phenolics but this is often achieved at the cost of excessively high sugar levels. As a consequence, winemakers may resort to adding WATER to the must, where local regulations allow, or the use of equipment such as the SPINNING CONE to reduce the ALCOHOLIC STRENGTH of the finished wine.

At the start of the 21st century, many wine producers were trying to find ways of encouraging physiological ripeness to coincide with optimal sugar accumulation. These included research into YEASTS specifically designed to result in lower alcohol levels, precisely timed IRRIGATION regimes, and slowing sugar accumulation by careful reduction of the LEAF TO FRUIT RATIO. Z.L., J.R., & J.Ha.

physiology of the vine. See VINE PHYSIOLOGY.

phytoalexins, compounds produced by plants in response to bacterial or fungal attack. They are not normally present in significant quantities until a plant is invaded by disease. In grapevines, phytoalexins belong to a class of PHENOLICS called stilbenes (see RESVERATROL). When a fungus such as DOWNY MILDEW or BOTRYTIS invades the vine, resveratrol is synthesized and accumulates very rapidly near the infection point. At sufficient concentrations, resveratrol can slow or even stop the growth of the disease. Some grape varieties that are known to be resistant to fungi (Castor, for example) also have a high potential for stilbene production. Resveratrol was discovered in vines in 1976, and a related compound viniferin was discovered in 1977. This phytoalexin was studied with renewed interest when it was discovered also to be a constituent of the Asian medicinal herb *Polygonum cuspidatum*. The gene for resveratrol synthesis, stilbene synthase, has been cloned from VINIFERA vines and inserted into tobacco. The resulting transgenic plants were more resistant to BOTRYTIS infection, showing the value of resveratrol as a natural

defence against fungi. However, botrytis and possibly other pathogenic fungi manufacture a LACCASE, which can detoxify stilbenes and allow infection to proceed, but phenolics such as CATECHIN can inhibit this enzyme's activity, thus cancelling out the fungi's defence. G.L.C. & R.E.S.

Goetz, G., Fkyerat, A., Me'tais, N., Kunz, M., Tabacchi, R., Pezet, R., and Pont, V., 'Resistance factors to grey mould in grape berries: identification of some phenolics inhibitors of *Botrytis cinerea* stilbene oxidase', *Phytochemistry*, 52 (1999), 759–67.

Langcake, P., 'Disease resistance of Vitis spp. and the production of the stress metabolites resveratrol, ε-viniferin, α-viniferin and pterostilbene', *Physiological Plant Pathology*, 18 (1981), 213–26.

Siemann, E. H., and Creasy, L. L., 'Concentration of the phytoalexin resveratrol in wine', *American Journal of Enology and Viticulture*, 43 (1992), 49–52.

phytoplasma, once known as mycoplasma, small and sometimes microscopic organisms similar to BACTERIA associated with vine diseases of the PHLOEM, transmitted by insects and grafting. The most serious diseases caused, GRAPEVINE YELLOWS, may well have widespread implications for the world's wine industry in the 21st century. The relentless spread of various forms of phytoplasma continues in many European grape-growing regions, Slovenia and Hungary among others. R.E.S.

Piacentini, Colli, diverse DOC zone centred on the hills of Piacenza in Emilia in north central Italy. See EMILIA-ROMAGNA for more details.

Piave, mainly red wine DOC in the hinterland of Venice in north east Italy. Like the neighbouring LISON-PRAMAGGIORE, the Piave DOC embraces vineyards in the plain of the Piave river, and is demarcated by the Conegliano and Montello hills to the north and the flatlands of the river's Adriatic delta to the south. Unlike Lison-Pramaggiore, however, it is entirely in the provinces of Venezia and Treviso in VENETO. This is overwhelmingly MERLOT territory (84,000 hl of varietal Merlot out of the zone's average 175,000 hl/4.6 million gal total vintage), with CABERNET (principally Franc) accounting for an additional 34,000 hl/ 898,100 gal; VERDUZZO (18,000 hl) and TOCAI (11,000 hl) account for the bulk of the white wine production. The wines, at their best, are fruity, fresh, and unpretentiously appealing; with yields of 90 hl/ha (5 tons/acre) for Merlot and over 80 hl/ha for Cabernet and Tocai from the rich soil, they seem destined to remain that way. See also RABOSO, another local vine variety and varietal DOC. D.T. & D.C.G.

picardan, white wine, often sweet, developed from LANGUEDOC raw materials by the DUTCH WINE TRADE in the late 17th and 18th centuries. Picardan is also the name of one of the most neutral white grape varieties allowed in CHÂTEAUNEUF-DU-PAPE.

picking grapes is apparently romantic but in practice back-breaking work for humans. For more details, see HARVEST and LABOUR. J.M.

Pico, IPR on the island of the same name in the Azores, an autonomous region of PORTUGAL. The vineyards, mostly planted with VERDELHO, are protected by a network of volcanic stone walls and now form a World Heritage Site. A small amount of fortified wine is produced and drunk locally. Rising to a height of 2,300 m (7,500 ft), Pico is the highest point in Portugal. R.J.M.

Picolit, also written **Piccolit** and **Piccolito** in the past, fashionable and audaciously priced sweet white VARIETAL wine made in the FRIULI region of north east Italy, one of the more commercially successful of the DRIED GRAPE WINES. The grape variety derives its name from the small, or *piccolo*, quantity of grapes it produces, thanks to its exceptionally poor pollination rate in the vineyard.

The wine was already famous in the 18th century when Count Fabio Asquini, with a sizeable production of over 100,000 bottles, exported Picolit to the courts of England, France, Austria, Holland, Russia, Saxony, and Toscana. A letter of Monsignor Giuseppe de Rinaldis of 1765 indicates that it was greatly appreciated by the papal court as well.

Rosazzo in the COLLI ORIENTALI appears to be the variety's original home, and it is certain that Picolit owes its survival to the efforts of the Perusini family of the Rocca Bernarda of Ipplis, which laboured throughout the 20th century first to identify and then to reproduce hardier CLONES with a reduced failure rate.

Some better estates still make the wine much as it was in the past—Fabio Asquini left copious notes on his working methods—with the bunches, harvested late in mid October, left to dry and raisin on mats before pressing. Other producers have opted for a late harvest style, with the grapes left even longer in the vineyard, picked with higher MUST WEIGHTS, but not raisined after picking. The use of small oak BARREL MATURATION is an innovation introduced in the mid 1980s. Although Picolit is generally considered a dessert wine, it is not luscious and is best considered a VINO DA MEDITAZIONE, a wine to be sipped alone in order to appreciate its delicate floral aromas and its light sweetness which suggests peaches and apricots.

The wine became the object of a cult enthusiasm in Italy in the late 1960s and 1970s, fetching extremely high prices that non-Italian connoisseurs find difficult to understand or justify; the Picolit boom has also resulted in frequent and illegal blending of the wine with the more neutral VERDUZZO, which has stretched the quantities available but has done no service to the wine's reputation. D.T.

Picpoul or **Piquepoul** is an ancient Languedoc grape variety that is commonly encountered in Blanc, Noir, and Gris versions with the white being the most planted today, although they have frequently been mixed in the vineyard in their long history in the Midi. Piquepoul meaning 'lip-stinger', signifying the high acidity of its must, was cited as a producer of good-quality wine as early as the beginning of the 17th century and, with CLAIRETTE, formed the basis of PICARDAN, exported northwards in vast quantites in the 17th and 18th centuries. Its susceptibility to FUNGAL DISEASES, however, together with its unremarkable yield, reduced its popularity considerably after PHYLLOXERA arrived. In the early 20th century, the variety's good tolerance of sand made it a popular choice for the coastal vineyards that serviced the then flourishing VERMOUTH industry. Today many of those vineyards are tourist campsites and vermouth is an Italian phenomenon. See PICPOUL DE PINET.

Picpoul Noir produces alcoholic, richly scented, but almost colourless wine that is best drunk young. Although it is allowed as a minor ingredient in CHÂTEAUNEUF-DU-PAPE and Coteaux du LANGUEDOC, it is rarely seen.

Picpoul Blanc, on the other hand, is increasingly popular and was grown on 1,000 ha of French vineyard by 2000. It can provide usefully crisp blending material in the Languedoc but it is most commonly encountered as PICPOUL DE PINET.

Picpoul de Pinet, one of the more dynamic named CRUS of Coteaux du LANGUEDOC producing green-gold, full-bodied, lemon-flavoured white wine exclusively from PICPOUL Blanc grapes. This curious speciality in the deep south of France, one of the country's few VARIETALLY named AC wines, has in the post-modern age of vinification attracted new interest. Millions of tourists each summer see the well-signposted CO-OPERATIVE at Pinet, the most important producer of this distinctive wine and clearly visible from the main *autoroute* along the Mediterranean coast. The co-operative at Pomerols and some individual domaines such as Félines Jourdan have made some good examples.

Pic-St-Loup, one of the most successful named CRUS within the Coteaux du LANGUE-DOC in southern France and the least dependent on CARIGNAN grapes or CO-OPERATIVES. The zone includes 12 communes around the eponymous and dramatic peak north of Montpellier (including one called Claret—although the robust red wines made here much more closely resemble southern Rhône than any bordeaux). About 5,000 ha/12,300 acres of vineyard could in theory produce appellation wine, but only about 500 ha are planted with the Syrah, Grenache, and Mourvèdre vines which must comprise 90 per cent of plantings for Pic St-Loup. Much of the wine produced within the zone is VIN DE PAYS or VIN DE TABLE. Among many fine domaines are

Ch de Cazeneuve, Domaine de l'Hortus (which also makes very fine white Vins de Pays), Ermitage du Pic St-Loup, Ch de Lancyre, Ch de Lascaux, and Mas Bruguière.

Picutener, local strain of the NEBBIOLO grape in and around the Valle d'AOSTA.

pièce, size and shape of barrel conventionally used in Burgundy. See BARREL TYPES for more details.

Piedirosso, Italian red grape variety planted in CAMPANIA, particularly on the islands of ISCHIA and Capri. It is also known as Per'e Palummo and Palombina. Plantings halved during the 1980s so that there were hardly more than 1,000 ha/2,500 acres left by 1990.

Piedmont, Anglicized name for PIEMONTE.

Piemonte, qualitatively outstanding and highly distinctive wine region in north west ITALY whose principal city is Turin (see map under ITALY). This subalpine part (its name means 'at the foot of the mountains') of the former kingdom of Savoy was the driving force behind Italian reunification in the 19th century and led the initial phases of Italy's industrial revolution. Its geographical position both isolated and protected it during the period of Habsburg, Bourbon, and papal domination which marked Italian life between 1550 and 1860, while its proximity, both geographical and cultural, to France (the kingdom's court and nobility were Francophone until well into the 19th century) gave it both an openness to the new ideas of the European enlightenment and relative prosperity—in stark contrast to the poverty of much of the rest of the peninsula. It is no surprise, therefore, that Piemonte's viticulture is the most stable and evolved in Italy and has made the greatest progress both in identifying the proper areas for growing its own individual VINE VARIETIES and in the proper techniques for fermenting and ageing them. In the late 1990s, total annual wine production averaged over 3 million hl/79 million gal, with 40 per cent at DOC level until recently.

NEBBIOLO is Piemonte's noblest grape and is, with the Sangiovese of Toscana, the grape responsible for most of Italy's greatest wines. Although there are 12 Nebbiolo-based DOCs or DOCGS, only the world-famous BAROLO and BARBARESCO supply significant amounts of wine. GATTINARA, for example, which is the largest of the Nebbiolo DOCs outside the LANGHE hills, encompasses a mere 102 ha/250 acres. Piemonte's workhorse grape, supplying the region's everyday red wines (and an increasing number of smart ones), is BARBERA, grown virtually everywhere there are vineyards in the provinces of ALBA, ASTI, and Alessandria. Robust and warming, if at times rather rustic and sharply acidic, it has suffered in the

past from overcropping and indifferent wine-making, but the 1980s and the 1990s saw significant improvement in quality. Luxury cuvées of Barbera, aged in new oak, now challenge the price levels of fine Barolo and Barbaresco. DOLCETTO, Piemonte's fruity red wine for young drinking, also demonstrated major improvement in the 1980s as more careful vinification mitigated its inherent bitterness, and more careful AGEING reduced the problems of REDUCTION and off-odours.

White grapes, with the exception of the MOSCATO used extensively for various SPUMANTE and FRIZZANTE (most notably ASTI), used to be a virtual afterthought in Piemonte, but the region's production of white wine rose from a mere 10 per cent of the regional total to 25 per cent during the 1980s. Part of this surge is due to the increasing popularity and commercial success of Asti and the emergence of MOSCATO D'ASTI as a significant wine in its own right, but wines based on CORTESE such as GAVI and those from the Colli Tortonesi and Alto Monferrato have also become increasingly popular. Native Piemontese varieties such as ARNEIS and FAVORITA, mere curiosities in the early 1980s, were planted on 430 and 100 ha of vineyards respectively by the early 1990s. But perhaps the most surprising development of the 1980s was the arrival and rapid acceptance in Piemonte of CHARDONNAY. Younger wine producers also experimented with PINOT NOIR, SYRAH, SAUVIGNON BLANC, and, especially, CABERNET SAUVIGNON, but these other INTERNATIONAL VARIETIES have yet to establish a real foothold here.

Vines are planted at ALTITUDES which can vary from about 150 m to above 400 m (490–1,150 ft), with the best, south-facing sites typically devoted to Nebbiolo, while the coolest positions are planted with Dolcetto (or Moscato in the zones in which it is grown). Barbera is widely planted in between. Average summer temperatures and rainfall are very similar to those in Bordeaux.

In 1995, a systematic revision of the entire DOC system of Piemonte produced Italy's first overall regional DOC. The territory was divided into six broad zones: Piemonte, LANGHE, MONFERRATO, Colline Novarese (the province of Novara), Coste della Sesia (the Colline Vercellesi), and Canavese (the CAREMA and ERBALUCE di Caluso zones to the north of Turin). Each of the region's cultivated varieties can be used either for a smaller, more geographically restricted DOC or DOCG or declassified into a large, more general, and hence 'lower' DOC. The Nebbiolo of Barolo, for example, can become either a Barolo DOCG or Langhe Nebbiolo DOC; the Barbera cultivated in the province of Asti can be used either for the Barbera d'Asti, Monferrato Rosso, or Barbera Piemonte DOCs. 'Lower' appellations allow both higher yields and lower alcoholic strength. The new system, in theory, allows all of Piemonte's wine to achieve DOC status. While a laudable aim, many producers regret the lack of flexibility, and look in envy at how IGT is used in other parts of Italy. What has not been accomplished yet is the creation of recognized subzones or CRUS in the more renowned and important DOCs such as Barolo, Barbaresco, Barbera d'Alba, Barbera d'Asti, and Moscato d'Asti—despite a long tradition of recognizably superior wines from certain areas within these DOCs.

For more details of individual wines, see ALBA, ARNEIS, ASTI, BARBARESCO, BARBERA, BAROLO, BRACHETTO, CAREMA, CORTESE, DOLCETTO, ERBALUCE, FAVORITA, FREISA, GATTINARA, GAVI, GRIGNOLINO, LANGHE, MOSCATO, NEBBIOLO, ROERO, RUCHÈ, SPANNA.

D.T. & D.C.G.

Bastianich, J., and Lynch, D., *Vino Italiano: The Regional Wines of Italy* (New York, 2002).

Belfrage, N., *From Barolo to Valpolicella; The Wines of Northern Italy* (London, 1999).

Pierce's disease, or **PD**, is one of the vine BACTERIAL DISEASES most feared around the world as it can quickly kill vines and there is no cure. The disease, along with FLAVESCENCE DORÉE, is a principal reason for QUARANTINE restrictions on the movement of grape cuttings and other plants between countries. In common with many other economically significant vine diseases, it originates on the American continent. The disease is a principal factor limiting grape-growing in the gulf coastal plains of the UNITED STATES (see TEXAS) and southern CALIFORNIA. The disease was first described in 1892 in southern California as Anaheim disease, but was later named after the Californian researcher Pierce. By 1906, the disease had destroyed almost all of the more than 16,000 ha/39,500 acres of vines, and there was another epidemic in the 1930s in the Los Angeles basin, which never recovered as a viticultural area. Pierce's disease has continued to cause chronic problems in coastal northern California (Napa and Sonoma) in isolated hot spots near riparian vegetation and in the Central valley near insect vector breeding habitats such as pastures and hay fields. The disease is today found across the southern United States and throughout Mexico and Central America. It has also been reported in Venezuela.

Leaves develop marginal discoloration that advances to dead tissue. This progressively enlarges until only the PETIOLE remains attached. Vines die within one to five years after infection, depending on grape variety, vine age, and climate. Originally believed to be a virus, the disease is now known to be caused by a bacterium named *Xylella fastidiosa*. This bacterium lives in a wide range of host plants, and causes damage also to almonds and alfalfa (lucerne). Various strains of the bacterium differ from one another in their ability to multiply within, and cause disease to, certain plant species. For example, grape strains do not multiply in sweet orange, but orange strains (now in South America) cause disease in grape. The disease is spread by insects called sharpshooters (see LEAFHOPPERS), which transmit the bacterium from host plants to the vineyards during feeding. In coastal California, vectors originally fed and reproduced in natural vegetation along streams, and the largest numbers of infected vines were therefore typically within 100 m/330 ft of a vineyard edge. Only the spring infections of vines (April–May) establish chronic Pierce's disease; later infections do not survive until the following year.

However, the introduction of the glassy winged sharpshooter into southern California in the 1980s has led to far more widespread damage. This leafhopper also spreads the bacterium, and, significantly for vineyards, it can fly further and more frequently. Vineyards near Temecula, for example, were destroyed by an outbreak spread by this new insect vector. It has moved northwards in the Central valley, and vigorous quarantine efforts are protecting vulnerable Napa and Sonoma counties for the moment. Since Pierce's disease exists in these counties, but the insect vector is limited, a new insect vector could have major implications.

There are no resistant VINIFERA varieties, and some varieties such as Chardonnay and Pinot Noir are especially susceptible. Varieties developed from MUSCADINE grapes or other wild grape species native to south eastern USA and Mexico have natural resistance or tolerance and are the only ones to be grown where the disease is endemic. In California, growers are advised to avoid planting near hot spots or use less susceptible varieties. There is no satisfactory chemical control of the bacterium.

Despite some scares in Europe, Pierce's disease has not become established there although it has been reported in Kosovo. Cold winters appear to limit where the disease occurs in North America and could do the same in northern Europe. In southern Europe, the failure of Pierce's disease to establish itself may be due to the lack of vectors that overwinter as infective adults since these are the only ones that could establish chronic infections in the spring. However, this situation could change if Europe were to be invaded by new vector species able to overwinter as adults. Climate studies indicate that both the bacterium and glassy winged sharpshooter if introduced might develop in European, South American, South African, and Australasian vineyard regions to a greater or lesser extent. FLAVESCENCE DORÉE is already quite widespread in Europe, however, and could perhaps pose a greater global threat to vineyards than Pierce's disease.

A.H.P. & R.E.S.

Goodwin, P., and Purcell, A. H., *Pierce's disease. Grape Pest Management* (2nd edn, California, 1992), 76–84.

Hoddle, M. S., 'The potential adventive geographic range of glassy-winged sharpshooter, *Homalodisca coagulata*, and the grape pathogen *Xylella fastidiosa*: implications for California and other grape growing regions of the world', *Crop Protection* 23 (2004), 691–9.

Pearson, R. C., and Goheen, A. C., *Compendium of Grape Diseases* (St Paul, Minn., 1988).

Pieroth, known as **PRP** in the US, commercially important German-based truly international company specializing in selling a wide range of wines, usually with exclusive labels so that price comparisons are difficult, and often in customers' homes.

Pierrevert, Coteaux de, zone in the alpine foothills of northern PROVENCE representing some of the highest vineyards in France, promoted to AC status in 1998. The appellation extends over a large area east of the Côtes du LUBERON but a declining area, 210 ha/520 acres in the late 1990s, is dedicated to making this wine. Wines of all three colours are produced and, thanks to the relative harshness of the climate, they are usually marked more by acidity than body. Grenache and Syrah are the dominant grapes. Tourism in the Hautes Alpes de Provence is such that there has been little need to seek export markets.

Pigato, characterful white grape variety producing distinctively flavoured varietal wines in the north west Italian region of LIGURIA. DNA PROFILING showed that Pigato and VERMENTINO, both long-established in Liguria, and FAVORITA cultivated in Piemonte, are all identical.

pigeage, French term for PUNCHING DOWN the CAP of grape skins and other solids. For more details, see MACERATION.

pigmented tannins, also called **polymeric pigments**, are responsible for the colour of red wines, together with ANTHOCYANINS, which are the phenolic red PIGMENTS of dark-skinned grapes. Pigmented tannins comprise a great diversity of molecular species formed by the reactions of anthocyanins with non-pigmented CATECHINS, PROANTHOCYANIDINS (i.e. condensed tannins from grapes), and ellagitannins (i.e. hydrolysable tannins extracted from barrels or added as components of some OENOLOGICAL TANNINS), under the influence of acids and oxygen. Their formation begins in the course of MACERATION, and then progresses throughout the AGEING of a red wine, so that the grape anthocyanins as individual molecular species make only a transitory and ever-diminishing contribution to the colour of a red wine.

Although this process has been known for over thirty years, some of the structures postulated for pigmented tannins have only recently been shown to form in wine, owing to progress in the development of analytical techniques, whereas others have not yet been confirmed. Besides, several so far unsuspected reaction processes and products have been unravelled in the last few years. Formation of pigmented tannins occurs through both direct addition reactions between anthocyanins and tannins and reactions involving fermentation products such as ACETALDEHYDE and pyruvic acid. The nature and amounts of the resulting products depend on the nature and proportions of the phenolics present and the relative kinetics of the various reactions. Physico-chemical parameters such as pH and temperature and the presence of oxygen, of yeast metabolites, and of co-factors, such as metal ions, also affect the type and/or kinetics of the reactions.

Colour changes, from the purple nuance of young wines towards the red-brown tint of mature wine, are classically ascribed to the conversion of anthocyanins to pigmented tannins. However, pigmented tannins cover a wide range of colours, from orange to purple and blue. Besides, anthocyanin reactions also yield lower molecular weight orange pigments which are not pigmented tannins. Reactions of tannins under OXIDATIVE conditions also lead to brown-orange pigments that do not derive from anthocyanins. Most of these pigments show increased colour stability with respect to hydration and sulfite bleaching compared with anthocyanins but this property is neither characteristic of nor specific to pigmented tannins. Known pigments account for only a small proportion of wine colour, meaning that most pigmented tannins are of analytically intractable nature, due to their multiplicity and diversity of structure and the transient nature of individual molecular species as they equilibrate among each other.

There is also conjecture about interactions of pigmented tannins with PROTEINS and POLYSACCHARIDES and the influence of such putative interactions on the properties (particularly taste properties—see below) of the pigmented tannins.

Experience has also shown that the formation of pigmented tannins, as well as conferring stability on the colour of a red wine (for decades, in favourable circumstances) also modulates the ASTRINGENCY of the very high concentration of phenolics of the wine, improving its TEXTURE and other taste properties. The desirable effects of pigmented tannins on mouthfeel are well illustrated by a comparison of the taste properties of a red wine with those of a white wine made, like a red wine, with extensive maceration. Such highly tannic white wines are not just unattractive, but crude and coarse on the palate; furthermore, they do not improve with age but remain tannic and undrinkable. In contrast, the pigmented tannins of the red wine make it palatable and soft with good ageing characteristics, and this despite the fact that their presence increases further the phenolic and tannin polymer content of the red wine relative to that of its macerated white wine counterpart.

Changes in astringency taking place during red wine ageing are usually attributed to an increase of tannin molecular weight as a result of the of formation of co-polymers with anthocyanins since larger polyphenolic species have been claimed to be insoluble and thus non-astringent. However, recent studies have shown that tannin solubility does not decrease with molecular weight and that astringency in fact increases with the tannin size. Besides, tannin reactions in wine do not only yield larger polymers but also lead to lower molecular weight species. The latter reactions may contribute to the decrease of astringency observed during wine ageing. Nevertheless, the taste of pigmented tannins and the effect of incorporating anthocyanin units in a tannin structure on its astringency remain to be investigated. P.J.W. & V.C.

Fulcrand, H., Atanasova, V., Salas, E., and Cheynier, V., 'The fate of anthocyanins in wine: are there determining factors?', in A. L. Waterhouse and J. A. Kennedy (eds.), *Red Wine Color: Revealing the Mysteries. ACS Symposium Series 886* (New York, 2004), 68–88.

pigments, inclusive name for the compounds which impart colour. Colour results from the presence in these compounds of structures or functional groups that absorb light of particular wavelengths. Young red wines get their colour from the ANTHOCYANINS and PIGMENTED TANNINS, with the former decreasing in concentration and the latter reciprocally increasing and making the dominant contribution to colour as the wine ages. In contrast to the broad understanding of the pigments (and their chromophores) responsible for red wine colour, the yellow to amber colours of white wines are less well understood. PHENOLICS present in the white grapes are evidently involved, and some limited oxidation of these is assumed to play a role in desirable white wine colour development. Brown polymers, resulting from excessive OXIDATION of white wine CATECHINS, are known to be responsible for the browning of oxidized wines. See AGEING and COLOUR. P.J.W.

Pignatello, synonym for the Sicilian red grape variety PERRICONE.

Pignerol, old Provençal white grape once grown in BELLET.

Pignola Valtellinese, red grape speciality of the Valtellina zone of Lombardia in northern Italy. DNA PROFILING revealed a parent–offspring relationship with Rossolino Nero.

Pignoletto, lively, crisp white grape grown around Bologna in northern Italy on an area totalling almost 7,000 ha/17,300 acres according to the 2000 vineyard census.

Pignolo, promising red grape variety native to the FRIULI region of north east Italy, probably first cultivated in the hills of Rosazzo in the COLLI ORIENTALI. It is mentioned by the Abbot Giobatta Michieli in his 'Bacchus in Friuli' in the late 17th century, and its 'excellent black wine' was appreciated by the monks of the Abbadia di Rosazzo a century later. The variety, whose Italian name means 'fussy', is a very shy bearer and it was generally ignored by local growers who preferred other, more productive grape varieties until, like SCHIOPPETTINO, it was given a new lease of life by a EUROPEAN UNION decree of 1978 authorizing its use in the province of Udine. Production is still on a very small scale but the results suggest encouragingly high quality. The rich, full, deep-coloured wines have shown a real affinity for BARRIQUE ageing.

D.T.

Pin, Le. The original MICROCHÂTEAU consisted of just one hectare of vines within sight of Ch PÉTRUS, the traditional holder of the crown in POMEROL. This gentle, south-facing slope of gravel and sand, with about 10 per cent clay, was bought for a million French francs in 1979 by three members of the Thienport family, Belgian NÉGOCIANTS who also own nearby Vieux-Château-Certan in Pomerol and properties in the Côte de FRANCS. The vineyard had previously been farmed by a grower in Lalande-de-Pomerol *en* MÉTAYAGE, and its produce had for years been vinified there and sold as Le Pin, but not as a CHÂTEAU BOTTLED wine. When the Thieponts bought it, a third of the vines were only a year old. The first commercial vintage was 1981, and until the mid to late 1980s the wine was quite a hard sell. Jacques Thienpont, who commuted between Belgium and Bordeaux, managed to buy out his two co-investors in 1988 and, by adding a further hectare in three contiguous plots, now owns and manages the grand total of about 5 acres. The vines are mainly Merlot, supplemented by about 4 per cent Cabernet Franc. The wine was always distinctive, deep, and luscious with an almost Burgundian richness, absolutely in tune with the FASHION for early-maturing, sensual wines, typical of Michel ROLLAND, in fact. Le Pin was the first red bordeaux to have its MALOLACTIC FERMENTATION completed in 100 per cent new oak barrels (no great investment when the total production of the property averages 600 cases). Demand for this rarity escalated towards the end of the 1980s and the price of the fashionable 1982 vintage reached a peak of £2,500 a bottle in 1997, just before the ASIAN boom began to falter. It is Le Pin's success which can truly be said to have inspired the rash of new, small, luxury RIGHT BANK estates.

Pineau, a word widely used in France as a synonym for the PINOT family of grape varieties. It seems to have been a portmanteau word for any better-quality vine in medieval France (probably a reference to the pine-cone shape of so many bunches of grapes) but is today a word associated primarily with the Loire. It is the first word of a wide range of vine synonyms, sometimes various forms of Pinot but often CHENIN, most notably as **Pineau de la Loire**.

Pineau d'Aunis, sometimes called Chenin Noir, is a historic Touraine variety making light red wines once sought by the kings of both France and England according to Galet. France grew a total of 431 ha/1,000 acres of it in 2000, mainly around Tours in the Loire valley. The variety is one of the many sanctioned for the red and rosé appellations of Touraine and Anjou but is used only to a limited extent, mainly to bring peppery liveliness and fruit to rosés, although in ripe years it can yield a fine red, too, notably in Coteaux du LOIR. See also Coteaux du VENDÔMOIS.

Galet, P., *Dictionnaire encyclopédique des cépages* (Paris, 2000).

Pineau des Charentes or **Pineau Charentais** is the VIN DE LIQUEUR of the Cognac region and has enjoyed some *réclame* in France as a strong, sweet aperitif more likely to be the product of an artisan than of big business. It is made by adding at least year-old cognac, which in practice usually means year-old cognac, straight from the cask to must that is just about to ferment, thereby producing what is effectively a mixture of grape juice and brandy. These somewhat disparate elements must then be matured together in cask at least until the July following the harvest, although anything labelled Vieux Pineau should have spent at least five years in cask. The final alcohol level is usually between 17 and 18 per cent. This alternative use for the many superfluous vines of the two Charentes *départements* has been most useful, and the authorities have been careful to control quality with tasting panels and specially numbered paper seals on every bottle. The product has been embraced by French *restauration* in all its glory and much effort expended on the essential business of matching various dishes to various styles of Pineau. The style most often encountered outside France is pale gold, decidedly sweet, and with young spirit much in evidence but there are many subtler examples, including soft, fruity rosé styles made from the same grapes as red BORDEAUX. See also FLOC DE GASCOGNE.

Pineau Menu, synonym for the ARBOIS grape.

Pinenc, local name for the FER Servadou red wine grape variety in Gascony, SOUTH WEST FRANCE.

Pinot is the first word of many a French vine variety name and is thought to refer to the shape of Pinot grape bunches, in the form of a pine (*pin*) cone. Pinot is considered one of the most ancient grape varieties, and Galet cites no fewer than 100 different sorts of Pinot, although most of them are CLONES or SEEDLINGS. Among the better known, PINOT BLANC, PINOT GRIS, MEUNIER, and PINOT NOIR are all clones of Pinot. CHARDONNAY is still occasionally called Pinot Chardonnay. The father of modern vine identification GALET stoutly maintained that Chardonnay was not a member of the Pinot family, but DNA PROFILING analysis in 1999 showed that the following varieties are the progenies of Pinot and the obscure and rather ordinary variety GOUAIS BLANC: ALIGOTÉ, AUBIN Vert, AUXERROIS, BACHET Noir, BEAUNOIR, CHARDONNAY, FRANC NOIR DE LA HAUTE-SAÔNE, GAMAY BLANC GLORIOD, GAMAY Noir, KNIPPERLÉ, MELON, PEURION, ROUBLOT, and SACY. Furthermore, independent DNA analysis in Austria revealed a parent–offspring relationship between Pinot and TRAMINER, and between Pinot and the Austrian red grape ST-LAURENT.

In German, members of the Pinot family frequently have the word Burgunder in their German names (see SPÄTBURGUNDER, Weisser Burgunder, and GRAUBURGUNDER). There was a marked increase in the popularity of these grape varieties throughout the 1980s as tastes changed in favour of drier, fuller German wines.

Galet, P., *Dictionnaire encyclopédique des cépages* (Paris, 2000).

Pinotage, hardy and, depending on fashion, sometimes popular red grape variety that is South Africa's contribution to the history of the VINIFERA vine. In 1925, STELLENBOSCH University viticulturist A. I. Perold crossed Pinot Noir and Cinsaut, then commonly called Hermitage in South Africa, hence the contraction Pinotage. In vineyard and bottle, this crossing disguises its parentage well. Not until 1961 did a Pinotage label appear in South Africa, on a 1959 Lanzerac. Although sometimes scorned, even in the Cape, as a coarse red with a flamboyantly sweetish paint-like pungency (from ISOAMYL ACETATE), it has increasingly produced rich, long-lasting, deep-coloured wines whose wild fruitiness has been tamed by time and good oak.

Pinotage is a good vineyard performer, with intensely coloured grapes, easily attained ripeness by mid-vintage, and good fixed acidity. It is a substantial bearer, producing as much as 120 hl/ha (6.8 tons/acre), although its best wines tend to come from older, lower yielding BUSH VINE vineyards with yields of around 50 hl/ha. By the 1990s, some producers began treating Pinotage more carefully, experimenting with prolonged and cooler fermentations as well as the opposite in an attempt to dispel the volatile ESTERS which have always limited the VARIETAL's appeal. French and more recently American oak has added an extra dimension, while more managed yields and careful handling in the cellar has shown that Pinotage can deliver dense fruit for accessibly early drinking.

In 1992, Pinotage was the second cheapest red grape in South Africa; in 1997 old-vine Pinotage commanded higher prices than any other grape. Ever the victim of fashion, Pinotage saw its prices start to ease by 2003 and producers were looking to blending strategies involving the likes of CAPE BLENDS to optimize the volumes available. Notwithstanding the efforts of the Pinotage Producers Association, formed partly to manage this transformation, it is clear that Pinotage does not have the cachet of Australian Shiraz or Argentina Malbec. Between 1992 and 1996, South Africa's area of Pinotage increased by half to reach 3.3 per cent of the national total. By 2002, it had reached 6.4 per cent, or 6,660 ha/16,450 acres.

Pinotage is also grown, to a much more limited extent, in Brazil, California, New Zealand, and Zimbabwe. M.F. & J.P.

Pinot Beurot, ancient Burgundian synonym for PINOT GRIS.

Pinot Bianco, common Italian name for the white PINOT BLANC grape of French origin and much, much more widely grown than the French original in France. Introduced there as Weissburgunder well before the mid 19ᵗʰ century when the region was under Austrian rule, it was once very popular in north eastern Italy. By 2000, however, with total plantings of just over 5,000 ha/12,500 acres, it had been decisively overtaken by Chardonnay and Pinot Grigio.

It is grown particularly in TRENTINO-ALTO ADIGE, VENETO, FRIULI, and LOMBARDIA although, as in Alsace but not in Germany or Austria, Pinot Grigio enjoys higher esteem here. Pinot Bianco is prized in Alto Adige, however, and has produced this region's finest white wines. It was first noted in Italy in Piemonte in the early 19ᵗʰ century and until the mid 1980s the name Pinot Bianco was used to describe Pinot Blanc, Chardonnay, or a blend of the two. Even today, there are vineyards in which both varieties grow side by side. Italians generally vinify Pinot Blanc as a high-acid, slightly SPRITZIG, non-aromatic white for early consumption, and often coax generous yields from the vine. In Lombardia, the high acid and low aroma are particularly prized by the SPUMANTE industry. Good Pinot Bianco from Alto Adige from low-yielding vineyards, fermented and aged in oak barrels, indicate that Pinot Bianco could give much better results in Italy if it were treated with more respect.

Pinot Blanc, French white vine variety, member of the PINOT family and particularly associated with ALSACE, where most of its French 1,300 ha/3,200 acres in 2000 were to be found. It was first observed in Burgundy at the end of the 19th century, a white mutation of PINOT GRIS, which is itself a lighter-berried version of PINOT NOIR. Although its base is Burgundian, today it is found all over central Europe.

For many years no distinction was made between Pinot Blanc and CHARDONNAY since the two varieties can look very similar. No Pinot Blanc is notable for its piercing aroma; its scent arrives in a cloud. Most wines based on Pinot Blanc are also relatively full bodied, which has undoubtedly helped reinforce the confusion with Chardonnay, not only in Burgundy but also in north east Italy, where it is known as PINOT BIANCO. Although Chardonnay dominates white burgundy, Pinot Blanc is technically allowed into wines labelled BOURGOGNE Blanc and into some white MÂCON, but is no longer grown in any quantity in Burgundy.

Even in Alsace, Pinot Blanc's French stronghold, it is less important in terms of total area planted than Riesling, Silvaner, or even the white AUXERROIS with which it is customarily blended in Alsace, to be sold as 'Pinot Blanc'. In LUXEMBOURG, on the other hand, the higher acidity of Pinot Blanc makes it less highly regarded than Auxerrois.

While in Alsace it is regarded as something of a workhorse (and sometimes called Clevner or Klevner), it has been generally held in higher esteem by the Germans, who have a much greater area planted, 3,100 ha in 2003, than the French (although just less in total than they have of the Pinot Gris they call Grauburgunder). Under the fashionable name Weissburgunder, it remains Germany's sixth most planted white wine CULTIVAR, with vinous personalities ranging from the full, rich examples of Baden and the Pfalz to relatively delicate, mineral-inflected variations along the Nahe and Mosel-Saar-Ruwer, and with quality aspirations ranging from a workaday norm to occasional brilliance. It is popular with growers seeking food-friendly wines that are softer than Riesling and can show local characters.

As PINOT BIANCO it is a popular dry white in Italy but it is in Austria that, as Weissburgunder, the variety reaches its greatest heights, and certainly its greatest must weights. Accounting for about 6 per cent of the country's total vineyards, it is grown in all regions. As a dry white varietal, Weissburgunder is associated with an almond-like scent, medium to high alcohol, and an ability to age, but it has achieved its greatest glory in Austria in ultrarich, botrytized TROCKENBEERENAUSLESE form, often blended, typically with WELSCHRIESLING (acting out the respective parts of Sémillon and Sauvignon Blanc in Sauternes, according to top practitioner Alois Kracher of Burgenland).

Pinot Blanc is widely disseminated over eastern Europe. In Slovenia, Croatia, and Vojvodina, it is widely grown and may be called Beli (White) Pinot. It is also grown in the Czech Republic, Slovakia, and is widely used in Hungary to produce full-bodied, rather anodyne dry whites more suitable for export than indigenous vine varieties.

Vine-growers in the New World recognize that Pinot Blanc has lacked Chardonnay's glamour but there were still 700 acres/280 ha in the mid 2000s of a variety called Pinot Blanc in California, mainly in Monterey, where it is sometimes treated to barrel ageing and the full range of Chardonnay wine-making tricks, to creditable effect. Older vines bearing this name are almost certainly not Pinot Blanc but the Muscadet grape MELON (now proven to be another member of the extended Pinot family).

Elsewhere in the New World, Pinot Blanc is largely ignored in favour of the most famous white wine grape.

Galet, P., *Dictionnaire encyclopédique des cépages* (Paris, 2000).

Pinot Blanco, common misnomer for CHENIN BLANC in Latin America.

Pinot Chardonnay is an old synonym for CHARDONNAY, the classic white grape of Burgundy. It was adopted at a time when Chardonnay was believed to be a white mutation of PINOT NOIR (correctly, as it turned out—see PINOT). **Pinot Chardonnay-Mâcon** has been an appellation recognized by INAO as virtually interchangeable with MÂCON Blanc but is not often seen.

Pinot de la Loire, misleading occasional synonym for CHENIN BLANC in the Loire.

Pinot Grigio is an immensely popular VARIETAL wine and the common Italian name for the French vine variety PINOT GRIS and, as such, is probably the name by which the variety is best known to many wine drinkers. There were about 3,500 ha/8,600 acres of Pinot Grigio vineyard in Italy in 1990 (much less than the area planted with PINOT BIANCO, for example) but so great has been demand for Pinot Grigio that its plantings had overtaken those of Pinot Bianco to reach 6,700 ha by 2000. Most of these plantings were in the north east. The best and richest wines are produced in Friuli, while those produced in Alto Adige can be particularly aromatic. The bulk of Pinot Grigio produced today comes from Veneto, where large volumes are produced by growers for their local CO-OPERATIVES, and then sold to the large bottlers. These Veneto versions tend to be rather neutral and, at their best, inoffensive, the high yields diluting any true Pinot Grigio character. The variety is also grown widely in LOMBARDIA although there is less fastidiousness here about distinguishing it from other hues of PINOT, especially when supplying grapes for the sparkling wine industry. Pinot Grigio is planted as far south as EMILIA-ROMAGNA and as far north as ALTO ADIGE.

Pinot Gris is a widely disseminated, increasingly fashionable vine variety that can produce soft, gently perfumed wines with more substance and colour than most whites, which is what one might expect of a variety that is one of the best-known mutations of PINOT NOIR. If Pinot Noir berries are purplish blue and the berries of the related PINOT BLANC are greenish yellow, Pinot Gris grapes are anything between greyish blue and brownish pink—sometimes on the same bunch. In the vineyard, this vine can easily be taken for Pinot Noir for the leaves are identical and, especially late in a ripe year, the berries can look remarkably similar. At one time, Pinot Gris habitually grew in among the Pinot Noir of many Burgundian vineyards, adding softness and sometimes acidity to its red wine. Even today, as Pinot Beurot, it is sanctioned as an ingredient in most of Burgundy's red wine appellations and the occasional vine can still be found in some of the region's famous red wine vineyards. It was traditionally prized for its ability to soften Pinot Noir musts but older CLONES have a tendency to yield very irregularly.

There also remain small pockets of the variety in the Loire, where it is often known as Malvoisie (although even in such a small appellation as Coteaux d'ANCENIS both Malvoisie and Pinot Beurot are officially allowed as a suffix). It can produce perfumed, substantial wines in a wide range of different sweetness levels. It is also known as Malvoisie in Valais in SWITZERLAND, where it can also produce full, perfumed, rich whites.

But, within France, Alsace is where Pinot Gris (here traditionally but mysteriously known as Tokay, see GERMAN HISTORY) is most familiar—albeit on just a few hundred hectares of vineyard—and most revered, with good reason. It may be less commonly planted than the other members of Alsace's noble triumvirate, Riesling and Gewürztraminer, but it is gaining ground and fulfils a unique function as provider of super-rich, usually dry, wines that can be partnered with food without the distraction of too much aroma. For more on the wines, see ALSACE.

As with Pinot Blanc, however, much more Pinot Gris is planted in both Germany and Italy than in France. (See PINOT GRIGIO for details of Italian Pinot Gris.) In Germany, it has generally been known as RULÄNDER but, when vinified dry as it increasingly is, it is known as GRAUBURGUNDER (or occasionally Grauer Riesling, Grauer Burgunder, or even Grauklevner), under which name are more details on German, and Austrian, wines made from this variety.

The variety, like Pinot Blanc, is widely planted not just in Austria but in Slovenia, Moravia, and particularly ROMANIA, where, on almost 1,000 ha/2,500 acres of eastern vineyard, it is known both as Pinot Gris and Ruländer. In Hungary, it is revered as SZÜRKEBARÁT, although varietal versions may often be exported as the more familiar Pinot Gris, or even the more marketable Pinot Grigio. Pinot Gris is also grown in MOLDOVA.

Pinot Gris's impact on the New World has so far been limited but is perceptibly increasing. The variety has been one of OREGON's most successful, having overtaken Chardonnay in 2000 to become the state's most planted and produced white variety and, with a total of almost 4,200 acres/1,700 ha, Oregon's second most popular vine after Pinot Noir. There has also been a dramatic increase in plantings in California, mainly Monterey and Napa, since the late 1990s so that by 2003 it had overtaken Sauvignon Blanc to become the wine state's second most planted white grape variety after Chardonnay. And improved CLONAL SELECTION has precipitated a renewal of enthusiasm in New Zealand (where plantings were expected to triple to 530 ha between 2000 and 2006) and Australia, where there were more than 300 ha in 2004 (and the wine is sometimes labelled Pinot Grigio).

The variety is also much admired for its weight and relatively low acidity in LUXEMBOURG.

Pinot Liébault, unusual and slightly more productive Burgundian selection of PINOT NOIR, first identified in GEVREY by A. Liébault in 1810, according to Galet.

Galet, P., *Dictionnaire encyclopédique des cépages* (Paris, 2000).

Pinot Meunier. See MEUNIER.

Pinot Nero is Italian for PINOT NOIR. The variety is quite widely planted in the north east of the country and in LOMBARDIA, and it doubled its area to a total of about 3,500 ha/8,600 acres in the 1980s, but few examples show great intensity of flavour. Much of the Pinot Nero planted is used by the upper reaches of the SPUMANTE industry but a few producers—Hofstatter, Haas, and Gottardi—are making a name for the variety in Alto Adige.

Pinot Noir is the grape variety wholly responsible for red burgundy and gives its name to the NOIRIEN family of grape varieties. Unlike Cabernet Sauvignon, which can be grown in all but the coolest conditions and can be economically viable as an inexpensive but recognizably Cabernet wine, Pinot Noir demands much of both vine-grower and winemaker (see CLIMATE AND WINE QUALITY, for example). It is a tribute to the unparalleled level of physical excitement generated by tasting one of Burgundy's better reds that such a high proportion of the world's most ambitious wine producers want to try their hand with this capricious and extremely variable vine. Although there is relatively little consistency in its performance in its homeland, Pinot Noir has been transplanted to almost every one of the world's wine regions, except the very

hottest, where it can so easily turn from essence to jam.

If Cabernet produces wines to appeal to the head, Pinot's charms are decidedly more sensual and more transparent. The Burgundians themselves refute the allegation that they produce Pinot Noir; they merely use Pinot Noir as the vehicle for communicating local geography, the characteristics of the individual site, the TERROIR on which it was planted. Perhaps the only characteristics that the Pinot Noirs of the world could be said to share would be a certain sweet fruitiness and, in general, lower levels of tannins and pigments than the other 'great' French red varieties Cabernet Sauvignon and Syrah. The wines are decidedly more charming in youth and evolve more rapidly, although the decline of the very best is slow.

Part of the reason for the wide variation in Pinot Noir's performance lies in its genetic make-up. It is a particularly old vine variety, in all probability a selection from WILD VINES made by mankind at least two millennia ago. There is some evidence that Pinot existed in Burgundy in the 4th century AD. Although Morillon Noir was the common name for early Pinot, a vine called Pinot was already described in records of Burgundy in the 14th century and its fortunes were inextricably linked with those of the powerful medieval monasteries of eastern France and Germany (see BURGUNDY and GERMAN HISTORY).

Clearly Pinot Noir has for long been grown in Burgundy but it is particularly prone both to mutate (as witness PINOT BLANC, PINOT GRIS, and Pinot MEUNIER) and degenerate, as witness the multiplicity of Pinot Noir CLONES available even within France. Galet notes that no fewer than 50 Pinot Noir clones (as opposed to 25 of the much more widely planted Cabernet Sauvignon) are officially recognized within France, with the most popular being one of first generation of virus-free Burgundy clones 115, followed by the productive Champagne clones 375 and 386. Marsh surveyed top Côte d'Or producers in the early 2000s and found second generation clone 677 marginally more admired for wine quality than the more widely planted 777 or 828. It is possible to choose a clone of Pinot Noir specially for the quality of its wine, its productivity, regularity of yield, resistance to rot, and/or for its likely ripeness (which can vary considerably). A major factor in the lighter colour and extract of so much red burgundy in the 1970s and 1980s was injudicious CLONAL SELECTION, resulting in higher yields but much less character and concentration in the final wine. The most reputable producers of all tend nowadays to have made MASS SELECTIONS from their own vine population. The clone called Pommard is well distributed in the New World, especially in North America, as has been one named after the WÄDENSWIL viticultural station in Switzerland. More sought after now are Burgundian, or 'Dijon'

clones. In general the most productive clones, which have large-berried bunches, are described as Pinot Droit for the vines' upright growth, while Pinot Fin, Pinot Tordu, or Pinot Classique grows much less regularly but has smaller berries with thicker skin.

In as much as generalizations about a vine variety with so many different forms are possible, Pinot Noir tends to bud early, making it susceptible to spring FROST and COULURE. Damp, cool soils on low-lying land are therefore best avoided. Yields are theoretically low, although too many Burgundians disproved this with productive clones in the 1970s and early 1980s. The vine is also more prone than most to both sorts of mildew, rot (grape skins tend to be thinner than most), and to viruses, particularly FANLEAF and LEAFROLL. Indeed it was the prevalence of disease in Burgundian vineyards that precipitated the widespread adoption of clonal selection there in the 1970s.

Pinot Noir generally produces the best-quality wine on LIMESTONE soils and in relatively cool climates where this early-ripening vine will not rush towards maturity, losing aroma and acidity. In Burgundy, for example, where it is typically cultivated alongside the equally early-ripening Chardonnay, Pinot Noir may ripen after Chardonnay in some years, before it in others. There is general agreement, however, that Pinot Noir is very much more difficult to vinify than Chardonnay, needing constant monitoring and fine tuning of technique according to the demands of each particular vintage. A vogue in Burgundy for ROTOFERMENTERS was followed in the late 1980s by one for cold MACERATION before fermentation as a way of leaching more colour and flavour out of these relatively thin-skinned grapes. See RED WINE-MAKING.

Pinot Noir is planted throughout eastern France and has been steadily gaining ground from less noble varieties so that by 2000 its total area of French vineyard was 26,300 ha/65,000 acres, up from 22,000 ha in 1988. This is still less than the total planted with Burgundy's other red vine variety GAMAY because of the vast extent of Beaujolais in comparison with the famous Côte d'Or.

The CÔTE D'OR was once the wine region with the biggest single area of Pinot Noir, but the extension of the Champagne region in the 1980s meant that, by the end of this decade, more Pinot Noir went into champagne than into red burgundy. Even in the greater Burgundy region, Pinot Noir is rarely blended with any other variety, except occasionally with Gamay in a BOURGOGNE PASSETOUTGRAINS and, increasingly, to add class to a MÂCON. At one time, Pinot Gris would be planted randomly in the same vineyard as Pinot Noir and the varieties would be vinified together. The red wines of Burgundy can vary from deeply coloured, tannic, oak-aged mouthfuls that demand long bottle age to acidic dark rosés that should be drunk as young as possible. The best GRANDS CRUS are intense, fleshy, vibrant, fruity wines with structure but oak influence that is never obvious. See under individual village names specified for the CÔTE D'OR for more detail on individual wines.

Pinot Noir is also gaining ground in the Côte CHALONNAISE and, to a lesser extent, MÂCONNAIS, typically at the expense of Gamay, which is in decline in both of Burgundy's subregions between the Côte d'Or and Beaujolais. During the 1990s, Pinot Noir definitively overtook Gamay plantings in the Saône-et-Loire *departement*. Pinot Noir is the favoured black grape variety in northern Burgundy too. In the Yonne *département*, dominated by its 5,000 ha (3,000 ha in 1988) of Chardonnay for Chablis production, there were also 688 ha of Pinot Noir by 2000, used for such wines as IRANCY and particularly northern versions of BOURGOGNE. It is cultivated even further north east for the light reds and VIN GRIS of Lorraine such as Côtes de TOUL and the wines of MOSELLE.

Although plantings of Pinot Noir have increased throughout France (and indeed the world) since the 1980s, the greatest increase was seen in Champagne, where it is used, as it is in the production of a wide range of sparkling wines made around the world in champagne's image, as a still, very pale pink ingredient in the base blend of still wines. The grapes are pressed very gently and any remaining pigments tend to agglomerate with the dead yeast cells during the champenization process. In such a blend, Pinot Noir is prized for its body and longevity, as well it might be for that small proportion of champagne made exclusively from Pinot Noir is usually memorably substantial. In Champagne, only a tiny quantity of Pinot Noir is used for still red Coteaux CHAMPENOIS and ROSÉ DES RICEYS.

Pinot Noir is also planted, to a limited but increasing extent, in the most easterly vineyards of the Loire and its tributaries, most notably to make red and pink SANCERRE but also in MENETOU-SALON and ST-POURÇAIN, and is technically allowed in an array of the Loire's VDQS wines. It was taken to the vineyards of the JURA and SAVOIE from Burgundy centuries ago and is increasingly offered as a VARIETAL wine. It is rarely encountered in the south or west of France, the domains of Syrah and Cabernet Sauvignon, but there are limited plantings in the Languedoc with some intriguing, if atypical, results in cooler sites, notably LIMOUX.

Pinot Noir has become increasingly well made, and desirable, in all areas where German is or was spoken. In Alsace, where it has been an important vine since the early 16th century (see GERMAN HISTORY), it is effectively the only black-berried vine variety planted, with a total area of nearly 1,400 ha in 2000. Pinot Noir is capable of producing quite deep-coloured, perfumed, sweet reds in the ripest vintages.

In cooler years, it produces deep pink wines, often with a similar smoky perfume to a white Pinot Blanc or Pinot Gris, that can be reminiscent of old-fashioned German Spätburgunders, even down to the whiff of rot in the wettest vintages. See ALSACE for more.

Germany's rediscovered interest in CONNOISSEURSHIP of the 1980s and 1990s resulted in a marked increase in demand for the nation's noblest red. See SPÄTBURGUNDER for more details.

It is fair to say, however, that, whereas Cabernet Sauvignon is often associated with the flavours of oak, Pinot Noir is often encountered with more than its fair share of sweetness, especially in inland Europe, as though over-chaptalization had been adopted as an alternative to true ripeness. In Austria, Pinot Noir is sometimes called Blauburgunder but is not widely planted. Some highly respected examples are made in Vienna and Burgenland, although others can taste sweet and oddly viscous. There is some similarity of style with the much more common local Austrian variety ST-LAURENT.

Pinot Noir is spread widely, if not in great quantity, in the vineyards of eastern Europe, where its name is usually some variant on the local word for Burgundian. There are plantings of Burgundac Crni in parts of CROATIA, in SERBIA, where it can be quite successful, and in much paler form in KOSOVO. It is also grown to a limited extent in the CZECH REPUBLIC, SLOVAKIA, HUNGARY, BULGARIA, ROMANIA, MOLDOVA, GEORGIA, AZERBAIJAN, KAZAKHSTAN, and KYRGYZSTAN. Romania has more than 600 ha planted, not as much as the variety known there as BURGUND MARE.

Elsewhere in Europe, the finicky nature of the Pinot Noir vine has set a natural limit on its spread. In Iberia, there has been some successful experimentation in SOMONTANO and CATALUÑA in Spain, where plantings, mainly for CAVA, totalled 400 ha in 2004, and even in the RIBATEJO in Portugal. The vine is relatively important in SWITZERLAND, particularly, as Blauburgunder, in eastern, German-speaking Switzerland. In French Switzerland, it is blended with Gamay to make the ubiquitous Dôle. There have been some noble experiments in some cooler Italian wine regions, notably LOMBARDIA, where it is used for sparkling wine production; see PINOT NERO. See also Valle d'AOSTA, BREGANZE, TRENTINO, ALTO ADIGE (where it is called Blauburgunder), COLLIO, and FRIULI, as well as OLTREPÒ PAVESE, where the rather neutral Pinot Noir is valued as an ingredient in classically made sparkling wine.

It was wine producers in the New World, however, who turned the full heat of their ambitious attentions on Pinot Noir in the late 1980s and early 1990s. Some even relocated their wineries many hundreds of miles in order to be closer to sources of suitably cool climate Pinot Noir fruit. OREGON's wine reputation has so far rested almost entirely on its

fine, fruity Pinot Noirs, grown on 18,780 acres/7,600 ha, more than half the total vineyard area. Although for many years this Pacific Northwestern state, with its often miserably cool, wet climate, was popularly supposed to provide America's answer to red burgundy, the number of seriously fine Pinot Noirs that emerged from CALIFORNIA in the late 1980s redefined the more southerly state's reputation for Pinot, especially but not exclusively in regions such as the Russian river district of Sonoma, Carneros, Chalone, the Gavilan mountains of San Benito, and, especially, Central Coast districts most affected by the Pacific. The state's total acreage remained steady into the 1990s but then took off so that by the mid 2000s there were about 24,000 acres/9,600 ha of Pinot Noir, notably in Sonoma. The Central Coast and Anderson valley in Mendocino county have also seen significant increases, with Carneros, where the variety is also valued as an ingredient in champagne-like sparkling wines, one of Pinot Noir's most important uses in the New World, also relatively important for Pinot.

The variety called **Pinot St George** in California, now in sharp decline, is unrelated to any known Pinot and is probably in fact NÉGRETTE, while that called Gamay Beaujolais (of which more than 450 acres/180 ha remained in 2003) is a clone of Pinot Noir, although not one embraced by the most ambitious producers of California Pinot Noir.

Outside California and Oregon (where Pinot Noir is sometimes picked a good six weeks after it is in California), the variety has no established American outpost of great reputation, although there were plantings in many of the UNITED STATES including NEW YORK, IDAHO, Pennsylvania, and Arizona, and the vineyards around lake Michigan. Washington state persists with it only on its southern border with Oregon. There are pockets of Pinot Noir in CANADA, however, and they are producing increasingly successful wines in both Ontario and British Columbia.

As Pinot Negro, it is known in most Argentine provinces where vines are grown but except at the highest altitudes of Tupungato, the climate is too hot and irrigation too commonplace to produce wines of real quality, as in most of the rest of South America, although Chile had almost 1,500 ha planted in cooler spots such as Chimbarongo, Casablanca, and San Antonio in the early 2000s and the quality of wine produced was promising.

Across the Atlantic in SOUTH AFRICA, on the other hand, at least one producer, Hamilton-Russell, had managed to coax convincingly Burgundian flavours from Pinot Noir vines grown in a particularly cool southerly spot and this has since acted as a spur to others, including neighbours Bouchard Finlayson, and Clos Cabrière—even if the quantity of true Pinot Noir planted is still minute compared with the total area of its progeny,

South Africa's signature black grape variety PINOTAGE.

Plantings of Pinot Noir in Australia and New Zealand on the other hand rose substantially in the early 1990s, with notable success in the latter country. New Zealand had 3,754 ha/9,535 acres of Pinot Noir by 2006, eight times as much as in 1996, with the most impressive results coming from Martinborough, Canterbury, and rapidly growing Central Otago. New Zealand has already established itself as one of the New World's most successful producers of this fickle variety. See NEW ZEALAND for more details.

Fine Pinot Noir has been more elusive in Australia, where total plantings climbed from 1,100 ha in 1991 to 4,400 in 2004. Areas with proven success as producers of good-quality red wine (as opposed to useful ingredients for the sparkling wine business) include Geelong, Gippsland, Macedon Ranges, Yarra Valley, and Mornington Peninsula, all relatively cool areas around Melbourne in Victoria, as well as Tasmania. See AUSTRALIA for more details and more potential areas of exciting Pinot Noir production.

Wherever there is a wine producer with a palate, there will be experimentation with Pinot Noir.

Barr, A., *Pinot Noir* (London, 1992).

Galet, P., 'La Culture de la vigne aux États-Unis et au Canada', *France viticole* (Sept–Oct 1980 and Jan–Feb 1981).

—— *Dictionnaire encyclopédique des cépages* (Paris, 2000).

Marsh, S. A., 'The contribution of Pinot Noir clones to the vineyards of the Côte d'Or. An evaluation focusing on clones 114, 115, 667, 777' (MW dissertation, London, 2004).

Pinot St George, California red grape identified as NÉGRETTE and now difficult to find.

pipe, wine trade term, adapted from the Portuguese *pipa* meaning 'barrel', for a large cask with tapered ends, the traditional measure of PORT as well as of MADEIRA, other Portuguese wines, and MARSALA, although the volume can vary around the country. In the DOURO valley, where port is produced, the yield of each vineyard is measured in pipes of 550 l/145 gal, while downstream in VILA NOVA DE GAIA, the suburb of Oporto where port is matured, a pipe may vary in size between 580 and 630 l, but is usually taken as 620 l. For shipping purposes, however, a pipe of port is 534.24 l, divided into 21 measures of 25.44 l called *almudes*, while pipes of madeira and Marsala are 418 and 423 l respectively. Gentlemen in Victorian England traditionally laid down a pipe of port for their sons and godsons, but inflation and changing consumption patterns have made this generosity exceptional.

Pipers Brook, wine region in TASMANIA.

pips. See grape SEEDS.

piquette, thin, vinous liquid made by adding water to the grape POMACE. Throughout history, from the time of classical GREECE and ROME to the mid 20th century, it has been given to slaves or low-paid workers. (See ancient PRESSES for details of *lorca*, the Roman version.) In the early 21st century, with its wine SURPLUS, LABOUR shortage, and concentration on quality, few employers would dare to offer even the most lowly worker such a drink.

Piros Szlanka. See PAMID.

pisco, aromatic brandy made in Peru, Chile, and Bolivia, mainly from Moscatel (MUSCAT) grapes, rather like Bolivia's singani.

Pla de Bages, denominated wine region north west of Barcelona in Spain with just over 500 ha/1,200 acres under vine. Grape varieties are similar to those in neighbouring PENEDÈS, with foreign varieties such as Merlot and Cabernet Sauvignon planted rapidly during the 1990s.   V. de la S.

Pla i Llevant, small but thriving DO on the Spanish island of Mallorca.

Planalto-Mirandes, IPR in north east Portugal. See TRÁS-OS-MONTES.

plank, term used occasionally for STAVES when they are used to add OAK FLAVOUR to wine.

Planta Fina or **Planta Fina de Pedralba,** grown in Valencia, south east Spain, to make sturdy, aromatic white wines. DNA PROFILING at Madrid suggests it is identical to VERDEJO.

Planta Nova, another undistinguished white Spanish grape variety planted in Valencia and Utiel-Requena.

plant cell density (PCD) is the most commonly used REMOTELY SENSED indicator of vine vigour or canopy size in Australian viticulture. Like NDVI, it is calculated from measures of reflected light at wavebands corresponding to red and infrared light.   R.G.V.B.

Plantet, 5455 SEIBEL, once the Loire's most popular FRENCH HYBRID, has been more successfully eradicated from the French vinescape than some others (see BACO, COUDERC, VILLARD). France had 26,000 ha/63,000 acres planted in 1968 but just 200 ha in 2000. Its chief attributes are its productivity and its ability to crop regardless of the severity of the winter and spring frosts (although New York state winters have proved too harsh for it).

planting a vineyard ostensibly constitutes that vineyard's birth, but this viticultural operation can be undertaken only after a wide range of decisions have been taken. The potentially long process of VINEYARD SITE SELECTION is followed by SOIL PREPARATION and the choice

of CLONES of both VINE VARIETY and ROOTSTOCK. Decisions must also be made about VINE DENSITY. Following delivery from the NURSERY, the young plants must be prevented from drying out before they are finally planted.

The planting operation is normally carried out in winter or spring. It consists of simply digging a small hole sufficient to take the normal dormant ROOTLING, or occasionally a CUTTING or, increasingly frequently, a growing plant. The hole can be dug by spade or post hole auger, but care must be taken, particularly in heavy clay soils, that holes dug by machine do not have such dense sides that roots cannot grow through them. In dry conditions, a high-pressure water jet can help to create a planting hole and at the same time provide moisture to assist early growth. For large estates, a planting machine adapted from forestry can be mounted behind a tractor to allow workers to put plants into a pre-formed furrow which is then filled in as the machine passes.

A cardinal rule of establishing grapevines, as for other plants, is to press the soil firmly in around the newly planted vine to avoid air pockets. Dry soil conditions around the roots of the young plant should be avoided.   R.E.S.

planting density. See VINE DENSITY.

plastic corks, a widely used but inaccurate term for SYNTHETIC CLOSURES.

plastic sheeting can be used in the vineyard to modify the climate. Studies in Canada have shown that transparent sheets suspended either side of the cordon will raise temperatures and advance vine development, helpful in cool climates. It has also been used experimentally on the ground in some vineyards to protect the vines from rain towards the end of the ripening period, thus allowing grapes to ripen fully but keeping vegetative growth to a minimum. However, when Michel ROLLAND first trialled this method in 1999 in Fronsac, the French regulatory body INAO judged it to be a modification of the soil and the wine had to be sold as a VIN DE TABLE. Plastic sheeting or patches can be used to keep weeds down and retain soil moisture around young plants (see MULCH). It can also be used on vines to protect grapes destined for EISWEIN from birds and rain.   R.E.S. & J.Ha.

Plavac Mali, grape variety with an interesting genetic history producing dense red wines all along the Dalmatian coast and on many of the Adriatic islands in CROATIA. Mali means 'small' and a white grape variety called simply **Plavac** is also known, and results in equally heady wines. Both varieties thrive on sandy soil. Plavac Mali produces wines high in tannins, alcohol, and colour which can, unusually for red wines from what was Yugoslavia, age well. Postup and Dingač are two of the better-known reds made from Plavac Mali. DNA

PROFILING at DAVIS provided evidence that Plavac Mali, once suspected of being identical to ZINFANDEL, is a natural crossing between it and Dobričić, an obscure and ancient Croatian variety cultivated near Split.

Plavai, late-ripening white VINIFERA grape variety native to MOLDOVA and widely planted throughout eastern Europe and the ex Soviet republics. In Moldova, it is also known as Belan and Plakun; in Romania, it is called Plavana; in Hungary, Melvais; in the Krasnodarski region of Russia, Belan or Oliver; in Ukraine, Bila Muka or Ardanski; and in Central Asia, Bely Krugly.

Plavina, red grape grown in northern CROATIA which may also be called Brajdica. Sometimes also erroneously used as a synonym for PLAVAC MALI. DNA PROFILING at SAN MICHELE ALL'ADIGE and Zagreb suggested parent–offspring relationships with VERDECA cultivated in Puglia as well as with ZINFANDEL.

PLC, important abbreviation for the official French *plafond limite de classement*, a mechanism whereby the maximum YIELD permitted within an APPELLATION CONTROLÉE is regularly increased by up to 20 per cent.

Pliny (AD 23/4–79). Gaius Plinius Secundus is known in English as 'Pliny the Elder' to distinguish him from his nephew, also a man of letters and Pliny the Elder's adoptive son. Of Pliny the Elder's many works, the only one to survive is the *Natural History*, 37 books, dedicated to the Emperor Titus and published posthumously. Book 14 is devoted exclusively to wine, while Book 17 provides important information on the techniques of viticulture, and the beginning of Book 23 is devoted to the medicinal properties of wine (see MEDICINE). Although most of the *Natural History* is based on earlier authors rather than on scientific observation, and his information, invaluable as much of it is, must be used with discrimination, the fourteenth book, on wine, seems in large part to be the product of independent enquiry. It contains practical advice as well as literary and historical learning. Its most interesting part ranks Italian wines according to quality, and sweet wines seem to be favoured (although see also ATHENAEUS). The best wine used to be CAECUBAN, but in Pliny's day it is FALERNIAN, particularly Falernian of the Faustinian CLOS. Setine is also a wine of the first rank. The next best wines are Alban, SURRENTINE, and MASSIC; Pliny awards third prize to Mamertine, of Messina in Sicily. An early proponent of TERROIR, he concludes that it is the country and the soil that determine quality, and not the vine variety; in any case, people's tastes differ. Pliny died during the eruption of Vesuvius when his extraordinary curiosity got the better of his common sense. In his much-quoted writings on wine, he drew on VARRO's *De re rustica*; PALLADIUS' treatise on husbandry is indebted to Pliny.

H.M.W. & J.J.P.

André, J., *Pline l'Ancien: histoire naturelle, livre XIV* (Paris, 1958).
Beagon, M., *Roman Nature: The Thought of Pliny the Elder* (Oxford, 1992).
Pliny the Elder, *Natural History*, trans. by H. Rackham (London, 1945).

plonk, vague and derogatory English term for wine of undistinguished quality, is a term of Australian slang that has been naturalized in Britain. During the First World War, the French *vin blanc* with its un-English nasal vowels was adapted in various fantastic ways, from 'von Blink', which sounded like a German officer, to 'plinketty plonk', which suggested the twanging of a banjo. This was shortened to 'plonk', which coincidentally was also British soldiers' slang for 'mud'. By the Second World War this had given rise to 'A/C Plonk' for aircraftman 2nd class, the lowest of the low in the RAF and hence parallel to plonk in the glass.

Despite its etymology, plonk need not be white; and if the word suggests any kind of wine in particular it is cheap red served at a party. For this reason, colour-blind theories have sometimes been proposed, such as that it mimics the sound of a cork being withdrawn from a bottle. But it has no more to do with this sound than with the unceremonious plonking down of glass. L.H.-S.

ploughing. See CULTIVATION and LABOUR.

Ploussard. See POULSARD.

podere, Italian for a farm, usually smaller than a FATTORIA and usually a subdivision of a fattoria, intended to supply enough land for the subsistence of a sharecropping family.

points out of 100, common method of SCORING wine promoted notably by American writer Robert PARKER. See also NUMBERS.

Pokdum, dark-skinned vine variety named after the Thai grape grower Nong Pok who propagated this particular mutation of a CROSSING of Golden Queen and MUSCAT BAILEY A in the Pak Chong area of Nakhon Ratchasima province in the early 1980s. It accounts for almost 10 per cent of THAILAND's vines and is thought to be identical to Pione in JAPAN.

Poland. Perhaps partly thanks to CLIMATE CHANGE, vines are now grown commercially in Poland, as far north as 200 km north of Warsaw in the Mazury lakes region. Varieties grown include the usual early ripeners Leon Millot, Ortega, Regent, Rondo, Seyval Blanc, Siegerrebe, and one called Sibera Bianca.

politics and wine. While wine-making and TERROIR affect how wines taste in the glass, politics determines how and which wines make it to consumers. The relations that wine producers have with the state and with each other vary across wine-making and wine-consuming countries. This variation affects the quality, price, export profile, and availability of wine to consumers.

In France, where grapevines predated Roman times, wine and the state have had as cosy a relationship as the vines and the terroir. Indeed, the Church and aristocrats, key political allies of the monarchy, held many vineyards in feudal times and it was Emperor Napoleon III who commissioned the famous 1855 CLASSIFICATION of the wines of Bordeaux. Crisis struck in the late 19th century as the PHYLLOXERA louse devastated large swathes of vineyards, threatening the voluminous tax receipts from wine and the livelihood of a large number of citizens engaged in its production. The state came to the aid of the growers by organizing a major campaign to pool scientific knowledge and treatments and, eventually, tamed the pest.

With the resolution of the phylloxera blight, some regions developed an addiction to state aid that took decades to break, if it ever was broken. The wine boom that preceded phylloxera, the subsequent bust, and an early 20th-century boom so devastated producers of low-end TABLE WINES that they convinced the state to guarantee them a minimum price. But the market fluctuations led to other problems for better quality producers, notably ADULTERATION AND FRAUD. Underscoring the importance of wine in France, the strong French state delegated the power to set quality standards for superior producers through the formalization of the APPELLATION CONTRÔLÉE system in 1935. This system continues to this day with an ever-increasing number of qualifying regions. However, the tight historic relationship between French wine producers and the state appears to be weakening at the beginning of the 21st century as strict drink–driving laws and bans on alcohol advertising have contributed to declining domestic consumption.

The politics of wine in the UNITED STATES could not be more different. Despite the best early personal and policy intentions of King James I during the colonial period and of Thomas JEFFERSON during the republic, the land proved inhospitable to vines suitable for wine-making until the mid 19th century in California. Even international recognition of some of California's best wines in the 1890s was not enough to propel the industry to success since wine fell victim to political shifts hostile to the industry.

The temperance movement was consolidating as a political force. So abhorrent was its view of any type of alcohol and so strong were its supporters that they succeeded in officially banning alcohol throughout the country for 13 years under PROHIBITION. Although no policy enshrined in the Constitution has ever been so quickly repealed, the damage to the wine industry was severe. During Prohibition, vineyard acreage paradoxically expanded through a loophole that permitted HOME WINE-MAKING. Yet the quality of the vines plummeted to such an extent that it took the California wine industry three decades to recover.

An even longer lasting effect was that at Repeal in 1933, the states were left to regulate the distribution and sale of alcohol within their boundaries. This has left a patchwork of laws and a system that often prohibits wineries from selling directly to consumers (online for example) since most states mandate the intervention of a distributor, which can raise prices to consumers and limit choice. Ironically, in a country that prides itself on free markets, the wine industry is arguably even more heavily regulated than that of France.

The success of AUSTRALIA lies in part in overcoming a problem of collective action. With a small domestic market and tremendous productive potential, industry participants realized the importance of export markets. Yet the exported wine had for decades been mostly mediocre bulk wine. In the 1970s and accelerating in the 1980s, the industry participants and the state coordinated an upgrading of the country's international reputation through setting standards for export and initiating successful marketing campaigns. The relatively low number of producing, or at least exporting, firms made this coordination easier. Other countries seeking to emerge on the world wine stage have typically sought to emulate this Australian example, with varying degrees of success.

Changes in the national political regime can revolutionize the wine industry, as the example of SOUTH AFRICA vividly demonstrates. With the collapse of the apartheid regime in 1994, South Africa's international isolation ended as the numerous countries that had trade embargoes in place lifted them. Practically overnight, the number of outlets for South African wines expanded exponentially. Investment flowed in and increasingly high-quality wines flowed out to the rest of the world. A similar political opening has also made for a global market in the wines from Central and Eastern Europe, although their export potential has not yet reached the levels of South Africa.

Because wine is an important product in world trade, international politics play a role in structuring the wine. Certainly wine policy is most advanced at the international level within the EUROPEAN UNION, which now has the final say on many wine regulations and subsidies in the region and often negotiates the laws of the World Trade Organization for European producers. Perhaps just as important is the symbolic role of wine in international diplomatic and trade disputes, particularly as wine is so strongly associated with France. Indeed, when the French ruffle

diplomatic feathers, whether testing nuclear devices in the South Pacific or threatening a veto in the United Nations Security Council, it is often their wine producers who pay an inordinate price as their wines are then targeted by tariffs or boycotts.

Future political struggles in the wine world will almost certainly also provide support for the adage 'all politics is local'. The issues of environmental responsibility, SUSTAINABLE VITICULTURE, and land use have recently appeared on the agendas of wine-growing communities from Napa to Bordeaux and are likely to remain there for the foreseeable future.

T.C.

pollen, collective term for pollen grains which carry the male gametes in sexual propagation for the vines as for other plants. Pollen develops within sacs of the ANTHER. Mature grains have a sculptured surface typical for each species. See FLOWERING. B.G.C.

Pollera Nera, ancient dark-berried vine of Liguria and north west Toscana.

pollination, the transfer of pollen from the anther to the receptive stigmatic surface. If the transfer is to a flower of the same genotype, the process is called self-pollination; when to other genotypes, it is called cross-pollination. Transfer may be by insects or birds (biotic), or by wind, water, or rain (abiotic). In grapevines, pollination appears to happen as a result of self-pollination of nearby flowers aided by some insects, although some pollination occurs before the CALYPTRA have fallen. Fertilization occurs two or three days after pollination depending on the ambient temperature (see FLOWERING).

See also POLLEN. B.G.C.

pollution. Air pollution can damage grapevines in many parts of the world. Air pollutants arise from industrial gases and particles, exhaust gases including LEAD, and AGROCHEMICALS. Principal pollutants are hydrogen fluoride, sulfur dioxide, and OZONE, and in restricted areas phenoxy herbicides such as 2,4-D (see AUXINS) applied to nearby crops. Hydrogen fluoride has reduced vineyard yields in many countries. While the leaves can accumulate high levels of fluoride, it is not translocated to the fruit. Mourvèdre is particularly sensitive to this type of pollution, while Carignan is tolerant.

Controls on wineries to reduce environmental pollution as a result of their operations are increasing. See also WINERY WASTE. R.E.S.

Pearson, R. C., and Goheen, A. C., *Compendium of Grape Diseases* (St Paul, Minn., 1988).

Pol Roger, Champagne house founded in Épernay in 1849 and still in family hands. The founder's sons changed their surnames to Pol-Roger by deed poll, Pol being a champenois variant of Paul. The wines rank high among

the top champagne houses for quality, although it is one of the smaller GRANDES MARQUES. Pol Roger owns 85 ha/210 acres of vineyards on prime sites in the Vallée d'Épernay and on the Côte des Blancs and latterly on the Montagne de Reims. Particularly deep cellars house 6.5 million bottles, representing five years' supply. Sir Winston Churchill was a devotee of the house, even naming his racehorse Pol Roger. The compliment was repaid after his death, when all non-vintage labels exported to Britain were edged in black for 25 years. The Sir Winston Churchill Cuvée was launched in 1984 as Pol Roger's PRESTIGE CUVÉE. The company has been managed by the great-grandsons of the original Pol Roger, Christian Pol-Roger and Christian de Billy (who retired in 1998), and the son of the latter, Hubert de Billy. S.A.

polymeric pigments, see PIGMENTED TANNINS.

polymerization, the molecular process in which smaller molecules combine to form very large molecules. In all living material, the simple amino acids combine, or **polymerize**, in very large chains to create the PROTEINS, some of which function as enzymes. In AGEING wines, simpler PHENOLIC molecules combine to form larger TANNIN **polymers** and PIGMENTED TANNINS which eventually grow so large that they fall from the solution as SEDIMENT.

A.D.W.

polyphenols and **polyphenolics.** See PHENOLICS.

polysaccharides, carbohydrates composed of several simple sugar molecules bonded together, are found in all wines. They can be grouped into three categories according to their origin: grape polysaccharides (e.g. PECTINS), fungi polysaccharides (most notably glucans from *Botrytis cinerea*, see BOTRYTIZED wines), and yeast polysaccharides (ρ-glucans and MANNOPROTEINS). The amount of polysaccharides released depends to a great extent upon the yeast strain but also on fermentation temperature.

polyvinylpolypyrrolidone. See PVPP.

pomace, a word used for centuries by English cider-makers (it comes from the Latin *pomum* meaning 'apple') meaning the debris of fruit processing. In WHITE WINE-MAKING, the pomace is the sweet, pale brownish-green mass of grape skins, stems, seeds, and pulp left after PRESSING. In RED WINE-MAKING, the pomace is a similar mass of grape debris coloured blackish red left after the FREE-RUN wine has been drained. Because red wine pomace is what is left after FERMENTATION rather than before, it also includes dead yeast cells and contains traces of alcohol rather than sugar.

In larger wineries, the significant amount of sugar which remains in white grape pomace may be washed out of the solid mixture and fermented to produce material for DISTILLATION into pomace brandy. Similarly, the smaller amounts of alcohol in red grape pomace may in large wineries be recovered by distillation. OENOCYANIN, a food colouring agent, is also recovered from red wine pomace, particularly in Italy. In some regions the solids from several wineries may be amalgamated for processing to recover TARTRATES and, occasionally, grapeseed oil.

The French call both pomace that has been drained dry and pomace brandy MARC. Some English speakers called this dry pomace the **press cake**.   A.D.W.

Pomerol, small but distinctive wine region in Bordeaux producing opulent and glamorous red wines dominated by the Merlot grape. Although they are now challenged by their counterparts in its much larger neighbour ST-ÉMILION, Pomerol's most successful wines are some of the world's most sought after, but the glamour attaches to the labels rather than the countryside.

Pomerol is produced from a constant 780 ha/1,930 acres of vineyard on a plateau immediately north east of LIBOURNE that is as geographically unremarkable as the MÉDOC, but without even any buildings or historical landmarks of note. A confusing network of narrow lanes connects about 150 smallholdings, most of which produce only a few thousand cases of wine a year in one of the world's most monocultural landscapes.

Vines were intermittently grown on this inhospitable, unfertile land from Roman times, but viticulture was abandoned during the HUNDRED YEARS WAR and the vineyards not re-established until the 15th and 16th centuries. For hundreds of years afterwards, Pomerol was regarded merely as a satellite district of neighbouring St-Émilion to the east, and it was not until the late 19th century that the wines began to be appreciated, and then only in France. In the early 20th century, they became known in northern Europe, notably in BELGIUM, whose wine merchants would import the wines in bulk; Belgian-bottled Pomerols of this period attract high prices at AUCTION. A succession of hard-working middlemen from the impoverished inland *département* of Corrèze made Libourne their base and developed markets for RIGHT BANK wines in such markets as Paris, Belgium, and Holland, leaving the traditional BORDEAUX TRADE to provide the British market with Médoc, Graves, and Sauternes. Such famous and well-educated British connoisseurs as George SAINTSBURY do not even mention Pomerol. It was not until the 1950s that British merchants Harry WAUGH and Ronald AVERY 'discovered' Pomerol, and its most famous property Ch PÉTRUS.

The most successful of the Libourne merchants is Jean-Pierre MOUEIX, whose fortunes have been interlinked with those of Pomerol. After establishing a reputation for the appellation, the firm acquired a number of properties, as well as contracts to manage other properties, including Ch Pétrus, and still sells a significant proportion of the Pomerol made in each vintage.

The success of Ch Pétrus in particular, whose wines regularly fetch prices far above those of the Médoc FIRST GROWTHS, is mirrored by worldwide demand far in excess of supply for the wines of similarly minuscule properties such as Chx Lafleur, Le PIN, L'Église-Clinet, and La Fleur de Gay.

Pomerol's finest wines are in general made on the highest parts of the plateau, which is predominantly layers of gravel interleaved with clay, becoming sandier in the west, where rather lighter wines are made. The subsoil here is distinguished by a local iron-rich clay, the so-called *crasse de fer*, of which Ch Pétrus has a stratum particularly close to the surface.

Apparently as important in fashioning wines that are plump, voluptuous, and richly fruity enough to drink at less than five years old and yet which can last for as long as many a great Médoc are VINE AGE and low yields. (At Ch Pétrus, for example, the wine produced by vines less than 12 years old is usually excluded from the ASSEMBLAGE.) Yields here are often the lowest for red bordeaux and are zealously restricted at the best properties. The early flowering of the Merlot grape, and the fact that a single vine variety accounts for about 80 per cent of plantings in the appellation, unusual in Bordeaux, means that in VINTAGES such as 1984 and 1991, the majority of the crop can be lost to, for example, poor weather at flowering or spring frosts.

Pomerol is also unusual in being the only one of Bordeaux's great wine districts to have no official CLASSIFICATION. The scores of properties are in general humble farmhouses with little to distinguish one from another, and only Ch de Sales has a building of any pretensions to grandeur, and an extent of more than 40 ha. The most sought-after wines, depending on the vintage, include Chx Pétrus, Lafleur, Le Pin, La Conseillante, Trotanoy, Certan de May, La Fleur de Gay, L'Église-Clinet, Clinet, L'Évangile, Latour-à-Pomerol, and Vieux-Ch-Certan.

See also LALANDE-DE-POMEROL.

Coates, C., *Grands Vins* (London, 1995).
Duijker, H., and Broadbent, M., *The Bordeaux Atlas* (London, 1997).

Pommard, prosperous village in Burgundy producing the most powerful red wines of the Côte de Beaune district of the Côte d'Or, from the usual Pinot Noir grapes. Until the 1980s, lesser wines were often sold under this popular designation while at other times Pommard has suffered from a dearth of sufficiently

conscientious producers and a perception that it offers poor value. However, a fine Pommard will be darker in colour than neighbouring VOLNAY, deeper in flavour, more tannic in structure, less charming when young but capable of developing into a rich, sturdy wine of great power after ten years in bottle. Claude Arnoux noted in 1728 that Pommard lasted longer than Volnay, only in those days he meant 18 months rather than 12.

Pommard stretches from the border of Beaune to the edge of Volnay. On the Beaune side, the finest vineyards are Les Pézerolles and Les Épenots, including the Clos des Épeneaux MONOPOLE of Comte Armand. Towards Volnay, the most impressive PREMIER CRU vineyards include Les Chanlins, Les Jarolières, Les Fremiers, and, in particular, Les Rugiens. The lower section of the latter, Les Rugiens Bas, has the potential to make the richest wines of all in Pommard, and is frequently mentioned as being worthy of elevation to GRAND CRU status. Clos de la Commaraine, Le Clos Blanc, and Les Arvelets have also been cited in the past as good sources for Pommard. Particularly high achievers are de Courcel, Comte Armand, and many of the best growers in Volnay such as de Montille and Lafarge.

See also CÔTE D'OR, and map under BURGUNDY.   J.T.C.M.

Arnoux, C., *Dissertation sur la situation de Bourgogne* (Dijon, 1728).

Histoire et chroniques du village de Pommard en Bourgogne (Pommard, 1995).

Pompeii, ancient Roman settlement at the centre of an area of thriving viticulture which stretched round the southern bay of Naples from the slopes of Vesuvius to Sorrento and was at one time an important wine port. There was a Pompeian wine ('headache-inducing' according to PLINY (*Natural History* 14. 70)) and a local vine, the Holconia, which carried the name of one of the most prominent Pompeian families. The eruption of Vesuvius on 24 August AD 79 which destroyed Pompeii and its surrounding territory also preserved detailed evidence of all the processes involved in the production, sale, and consumption of wine. There are the farm-villas outside Pompeii, mainly excavated in the 19th century, which contained press rooms, and elaborate piping systems for running the must off into large DOLIA set in the ground in yards where fermentation took place. There is the more recent discovery of market vineyards within the walls of Pompeii. Then there are the incidental details: in the House of the Vettii one dining room has a painted frieze in which cherubs are engaged in what were doubtless the businesses of the owners, including working a wine press and the presentation of wine to be tasted by a prospective buyer. The local wine was widely exported in AMPHORAE. Finally there are the numerous inns, bars, and eating places, clustered significantly mainly around the gates of the town and in the busy public areas around the Forum. Once again our imagination can be fuelled by lively scenes of inn-life painted on their walls.   J.J.P.

Pontac, distinctive red-fleshed (see TEINTURIER) grape variety known only in SOUTH AFRICA, probably imported to the Cape from SOUTH WEST FRANCE in the late 17th century. Pontac may even have been named after the de Pontac family, whose Bordeaux wines were then well known (see BORDEAUX, history). It produces wines dark in colour, with strong though not coarse TANNINS and smoky berry flavours which emerge only after several years' BOTTLE AGEING. Widely planted until PHYLLOXERA devastated the Cape's vineyards between 1866 and the 1880s, Pontac was superseded by higher-yielding and more fashionable varieties. Low yields, VIRUS infection, colour instability, and limited commercial prospects seemed destined to ensure its extinction. However, since the 1980s a few dedicated growers have obtained virus-free vines and the Cape now has a direct link to its first years of VINIFERA production. In 2003, there were just 6.25 ha.   M.F.

port, a FORTIFIED WINE made by adding brandy to arrest fermenting grape must which results in a wine, red and sometimes white, that is both sweet and high in alcohol. Port derives its name from OPORTO (Porto), the second largest city in PORTUGAL, whence the wine has been shipped for over 300 years, notably by English merchants. Port production varies considerably from year to year but by the late 1990s averaged about 90 million l/24 million gal.

Fortified wines are made in the image of port in places as far apart as SOUTH AFRICA, AUSTRALIA, and CALIFORNIA but, within the EUROPEAN UNION, EU law restricts the use of the term port to wines from a closely defined area in the DOURO valley of northern Portugal (one of the first examples of geographical DELIMITATION). See map under PORTUGAL.

History
Port originates from 17th-century trade wars between the English and the French. For a time, imports of French wines into England were prohibited, and then, in 1693, William III imposed punitive levels of TAXATION which drove English wine merchants to Portugal, a country with whom the English had always shared good relations. At first they settled on the northern coast but, finding the wines too thin and astringent (see VINHO VERDE), they travelled inland along the river Douro. Here merchants found wines that were the opposite of those they had left behind on the coast. Fast and furious FERMENTATION at high temperatures produced dark, astringent red wines that quickly earned them the name 'blackstrap' in

London. In a determined effort to make sure that these wines arrived in good condition, merchants would add a measure of brandy to stabilize them before shipment.

The discovery of the wine-making technique which results in port is credited to an Englishman, a Liverpool wine merchant who, in 1678, sent his sons to Portugal in search of wine. At Lamego, a town in the mountains high above the Douro, they found a monastery where the abbot was adding brandy to the wine during rather than after fermentation, killing off the active yeasts and so producing the sort of sweet, alcoholic red wine that port was to become.

British trade with France ceased altogether in the early 18th century with the outbreak of the War of the Spanish Succession. By this time, a number of port shippers were already well established and in 1703 England and Portugal signed the METHUEN TREATY, which laid down further tariff advantages for Portuguese wines. By the 1730s, however, the fledgling port industry was blighted by scandal. Sugar was being added and elderberry juice being used to give colour to poor, overstretched wines. Unprincipled over-production brought about a sharp fall in prices and a slump in trade. Prompted by complaints from British wine merchants, the port shippers contacted the Portuguese prime minister of the day, the marquis of Pombal. Partly to create a lucrative Portuguese monopoly on port production, in 1756 he instituted a series of measures to regulate sales of port. A boundary was drawn around the Douro restricting the production of port to those vineyards within it. Vineyards outside the official wine region, in BAIRRADA for instance, were summarily grubbed up by the authorities.

Geography and climate
Pombal's demarcation, modified a number of times since 1756 (see DOURO), corresponds closely to an area of pre-Cambrian SCHIST surrounded by granite. From the village of Barqueiros about 70 km/40 miles upstream from Oporto, the region fans out either side of the river stretching as far as the frontier with Spain. It is referred to by the port shippers as 'the Douro'. The vineyards are shielded from the influence of the Atlantic by the Serra do Marão, a range of mountains rising to an altitude of 1,400 m/4,600 ft. Inland, the climate becomes progressively more extreme. Annual rainfall, which averages 1,200 mm/47 in on the coast, rises to over 1,500 mm on the mountains and then diminishes sharply, falling to as little as 400 mm at Barca d'Alva on the Spanish border. Summer temperatures in the vineyards frequently exceed 35 °C/95 °F. It is hard to imagine a more inhospitable place to grow grapes. The topsoils in this mountainous region of Portugal are shallow, stony, and low in NUTRIENTS. Over a period of 300 years, however, the land has been worked to great advantage.

The valley sides are very steep but TERRACES hacked from the schist, often with little more than a shovel and crowbar support, give vines a metre or two of soil in which to establish a root system. The bedrock fractures vertically, however, and, once established, vines root deeply in search of water and nutrients.

The Douro region divides into three officially recognized subzones. The Baixo (Lower) Corgo is the most westerly of the three and covers the portion of the region downstream from the river Corgo, which flows into the Douro just above the small city of Régua. This is the coolest and wettest of the three zones and tends to produce the lightest wines suitable for making inexpensive ruby and tawny ports (see Styles of port below). Upstream from the river Corgo, the Cima (Higher) Corgo is the heart of the demarcated region centred on the town of Pinhão. Rainfall is significantly lower here (700 mm as opposed to 900 mm or more west of Régua) and summer temperatures are, on average, a few degrees higher. All the well-known shippers own vineyards or QUINTAS here and this is where most of the high-quality tawny, Late Bottled Vintage, and vintage port is made. Much of the Douro Superior, the most easterly of the three subregions, is still pioneer country. Although it has long been a part of the demarcated zone, the country is remote and sparsely populated and in past centuries little headway was made in planting vineyards due to the impossibility of navigating upriver beyond the former rapids of Cachão da Valeira. The Douro Superior is also the most arid part of the region with average temperatures at least 3 °C higher than at Régua 50 km downstream. But rising LABOUR costs are forcing producers to consider planting the flatter land close to the Spanish border which is more suitable for MECHANIZATION and has considerable potential for high-quality port.

Viticulture
Viticulture in the Douro altered radically in the 1970s and 1980s, perhaps more than at any time since PHYLLOXERA swept through the region at the end of the 19th century, leaving many hillsides abandoned. The most noticeable change is the river itself, which was progressively dammed in the 1960s to form a string of narrow lakes.

Methods of cultivation have also changed the Douro landscape. Faced with an acute shortage of LABOUR at the end of the 1960s, along with escalating costs, growers began to look for alternatives to the tiny, step-like terraces built with high retaining walls in the 19th century. The first bulldozers arrived in the late 1970s to gouge out a new system of terraces called *patamares*. Inclined ramps bound together by seasonal vegetation replaced the costly retaining walls and, with wider spacing between the vines (resulting in a VINE DENSITY of 3,500 vines per ha (1,420 per acre) as opposed to 6,000 on some traditional terraces), small caterpillar tractors can circulate in the vineyards.

At much the same time, some growers pioneered a system of planting vines in vertical lines running up and down the natural slope. This 'up and down' planting has been a qualified success, although access and SOIL EROSION are problems where the gradient exceeds 30 degrees. In the 1980s, there was a flurry of new planting under a World Bank scheme which provided farmers with low-interest loans. The traditional, labour-intensive terraces, still impeccably maintained by some growers, now stand alongside the newer *patamares* and vine rows planted vertically up the hillside, both of which allow limited MECHANIZATION.

Most of the Douro's vineyards used to be pruned according to the French GUYOT system and were trained on wires supported by stakes hewn from local stone, but now all but the very old vines are spur pruned and VSP-trained on wires supported by wooden stakes. Most vines used to be GRAFTED *in situ* but now most are bench grafted. IRRIGATION is essential for young vines. July and August are generally dry and SPRAYING against FUNGAL DISEASES is necessary only in the early summer or in exceptionally wet years. Aside from the usual vineyard PESTS, most of which can be controlled by spraying, wild boar eat grapes and may occasionally damage new vineyards.

The Douro HARVEST usually starts in late September and lasts for around three weeks. The steeply terraced vineyards come alive as gangs of pickers descend from outlying villages for the duration of the harvest (see also HARVEST TRADITIONS). Yields in the Douro are amongst the lowest in any wine region in the world, with 500 to 750 g per vine from old vines the norm. From younger plantings, those up to 20 years old, 1.5 kg is the average production per vine in the best vineyards.

Vine varieties

More than 80 different grape varieties are authorized for the production of port but few growers have detailed knowledge of the identity of the vines growing in their vineyards. All old vineyards contain a mixture of grapes, often with as many as 20 or 30 different varieties intermingled in the same plot. But research conducted in the 1970s (mostly by COCKBURN and Ramos Pinto), identified the best varieties and all new plantings since then have been more orderly. TOURIGA NACIONAL, TINTA BARROCA, TOURIGA FRANCA, Tinta Roriz (Spain's TEMPRANILLO), and TINTO CÃO are the favoured five black-skinned varieties, although varieties such as SOUSÃO, TINTA AMARELA, and MOURISCO find favour with certain growers. GOUVEIO, MALVASIA Fina, and VIOSINHO are generally considered among the best varieties for white port.

Port wine-making

Rapid EXTRACTION of COLOUR and TANNINS is the crux of the various vinification methods used to produce red port. Because FERMENTATION is curtailed by fortifying spirit after just two or three days, the grape juice or must spends a much shorter time in contact with the skins than in normal RED WINE-MAKING. The MACERATION process should therefore be as vigorous as possible.

Until the early 1960s, all port was vinified in much the same way. Every farm had a winery equipped with LAGARES, low stone troughs, usually built from granite, in which the grapes were trodden and fermented. Some are still in use, mainly at the small, privately owned quintas, and some of the finest ports destined for vintage or aged tawny blends continue to be trodden in *lagares*. The human foot, for all its many unpleasant associations, is ideal for pressing grapes as it breaks up the fruit without crushing the pips that would otherwise release bitter-tasting PHENOLICS into the wine.

Lagares would be progressively filled over the course of a day, and trodden by the pickers themselves, thigh high in purple pulp, in the evening. Most *lagares* hold 10 to 15 PIPES (about 5,500 to 8,250 l (2,180 gal)) although a number of the larger quintas have *lagares* with a capacity of up to 30 pipes. As a rule of thumb, between one and two people per pipe are needed to tread a *lagar*. Fermentation begins as a result of the action of ambient YEASTS on the grapes' sugar. The alcohol produced, and the increasing TEMPERATURE of the mass of purple skins, juice, and stems, encourages the extraction of the phenolics vital for the character of port. After about two or three hours of hard, methodical treading, the CAP of skins and stalks starts to float to the surface. Regular PUNCHING DOWN of the cap was traditionally performed with long, spiked sticks from planks run across the top of the *lagares* which ideally need some form of cooling.

After 24 to 36 hours, the level of the grape sugar in the fermenting must declines from 12 or 13 °BAUMÉ to between 6 and 8 °Baumé. Depending on the intended sweetness of the wine, the wine would be run off the *lagar* into a vat, already about one-fifth full with grape spirit whose ALCOHOLIC STRENGTH is 77 per cent. As the spirit is mixed with the wine, the yeasts are killed and the fermentation is arrested. At this stage the must becomes young, sweet, fiery port with an alcohol content of 19 or 20 per cent.

In the 1960s and 1970s, treading grapes in *lagares* became much less widespread. The Douro valley and the remote TRÁS-OS-MONTES region which traditionally supplied LABOUR at harvest time have suffered from marked emigration and the port shippers were forced to look for other, less labour-intensive, ways to make wine.

Most port producers abandoned *lagares* altogether. Many isolated properties were without electricity and shippers set about building central wineries to which grapes from outlying farms could be delivered. Most of these were equipped with AUTOVINIFICATION tanks, which required no external power source and have proved to be a successful alternative to treading in *lagares*. The resulting wine is fortified just like foot-trodden young wines were.

In the late 1990s, a new generation of winemakers started to experiment with more novel ways of making port as the labour shortages in the region worsened. Two key types have emerged: cap plungers as introduced by the FLADGATE PARTNERSHIP and automated treading machines or 'robotic lagares' as designed by the SYMINGTON family. Both systems seem to be successful and are likely to become widely used for the making of premium quality ports. These sophisticated systems are too expensive to be used to make the large volumes of standard quality ports.

Many wineries are equipped with PRESSES and the mass of grape skins and stems that remains after treading or crushing is forked into a press to extract the last of the juice. This deeply coloured, astringent wine is run off and fortified separately. It may be blended back at a later stage or used to bolster a lighter wine.

White port is made in much the same way as red with SKIN CONTACT during fermentation. White grapes used to be trodden in *lagares* but nowadays most wines are fermented on the skins in cement or stainless steel vats without recourse to autovinification. Most quality-minded producers are now fermenting in temperature-controlled conditions, having first separated the must from the skins. This results in a cleaner, fresher, lighter, and less astringent style of white port, some of which has a lower alcoholic strength of 16.5 or 17 per cent (see below).

The fortifying grape spirit for port used to be distilled from wine made in Portugal, mainly from the ESTREMADURA region north of Lisbon, although in recent years most of the spirit has been imported, and is distilled from the Europe's WINE LAKE. Until 1992, this spirit had to be purchased from the Casa do Douro (see Organization of the industry, below), which set a fixed price and controlled distribution. This monopoly was broken by the EU and producers have since been free to purchase any spirit they choose provided that it complies with the 77 per cent norm of alcoholic strength and is approved by the Port Wine Institute.

See VIN DOUX NATUREL for a comparison of port wine-making techniques with those in the production of French counterparts such as Banyuls.

Organization of the industry

At the turn of the 21st century, a total of just over 33,000 growers farmed 38,000 ha/ 93,900 acres of vines in the Douro, mostly in the Baixo Corgo, nearly a third of which is under vine. In common with most of the north of Portugal, the region is fragmented into tiny holdings of which 140,000 were registered with the Casa do Douro, the official body set up in 1932 to represent the growers. Over 80 per cent of these holdings are less than 0.5 ha/ 1.2 acres in size and a mere 0.01 per cent have an area greater than 30 ha/74 acres.

Vineyards in the Douro are graded according to a complicated points system and classified into six different categories rated A to F. Twelve different physical factors including site, aspect, exposure, and gradient are taken into consideration, each of which is allocated a numerical score. In theory, a vineyard could score a maximum of 2,031 points but a property with more than 1,200 points is awarded an A grade. A vineyard with less than 200 points is given an F grade. On this basis, the annual *beneficio* authorization (the total amount of port that may be made that year) is distributed to individual farmers. This is calculated annually by the port industry's regulating authority, the Instituto dos Vinhos do Douro e do Porto (Douro Port Wine Institute, or IVDP).

Permits are then distributed to farmers detailing the amount of grape must that they may fortify to make port. The amount varies according to the year but, typically, A and B grade properties may make 550 to 600 l of port per thousand vines, while F grade properties are rarely allowed to make port at all. The surplus is usually made into unfortified wine with its own denomination (see DOURO) but most of this sells for a much lower price than port.

This quality control system, instituted in 1947, served the port industry well for four decades, but pressure for its reform intensified when in 1990 the independence of the Casa do Douro was severely compromised by its purchase of shares in Royal Oporto, then one of the largest port shippers. After a period of instability, in the mid 1990s the Casa do Douro had most of its regulatory powers withdrawn and these were transferred to an independent interprofessional body representing both growers and shippers, the CIRDD, Commissão Interprofessional da Região Demarcada do Douro. This in turn was absorbed by the IVDP. The Casa do Douro continues to represent the farmers.

After vinification, the bulk of the new wine stays at the QUINTA or farm until the spring after the harvest when it is trucked downstream to the shippers' LODGES in VILA NOVA DE GAIA across the river Douro from Oporto, where the shippers have traditionally been based. The cooler climate and markedly high humidity near the coast are thought to be beneficial for slow CASK AGEING but QUINTA DO NOVAL for one deliberately matures its wines in purpose-built air-conditioned cellars in the Douro. See DOURO BAKE for the effect on port of maturing it upstream in the Douro valley.

Both growers and shippers have to submit to the authority of the IVDP. This government-run body employs inspectors to check the movement of stock. It ensures that shippers adhere to the so-called *lei do tergo* (law of the third), which restricts shippers from selling more than a third of their stock in any one year. The IVDP is also empowered to analyse and taste a sample from each port shipment before issuing the guarantee seal which is stuck to the neck of every bottle of port leaving the region.

The market for port has altered dramatically since the Second World War. The so-called 'Englishman's' wine that used to be drunk everywhere from gentlemen's clubs to street corner pubs became the Frenchman's wine when France's imports of *le porto* (largely inexpensive wood ports; see Styles of port below) overtook those of the United Kingdom in the early 1960s. The British market is still highly coveted by port shippers, however, especially those of British descent such as COCKBURN, CROFT, SANDEMAN, TAYLOR, and the SYMINGTONS who control shippers such as Dow, Graham, and Warre. In the late 1990s, the United States' imports of vintage port overtook Britain's.

Styles of port

There are two broad categories of port, fortified wines whose style is shaped by either CASK AGEING or BOTTLE AGEING. Wood-matured ports, often called simply wood ports, are aged either in wooden casks or, sometimes, cement tanks, and are ready to drink straight after FINING, FILTRATION, and BOTTLING. Ports designed to mature in bottle, however, are aged for a short time in wood and are bottled without filtration. It may then take up to 20 or 30 years before such a wine is ready to drink. Within these two general categories there are many different styles of port. The official legislation governing the different categories of port was tightened up considerably in 2002 and the following are now permitted.

Ruby. This is one of the simplest and least expensive styles of port. Aged in bulk for two or three years, it is bottled young while the wine retains a deep ruby colour and a strong, fiery personality. Young wines from more than one vintage are aged in all sorts of vessels (wood, cement, and occasionally stainless steel) before being blended, filtered, and bottled. PASTEURIZATION is sometimes applied to stabilize such wines and can result in 'stewed' flavours, but good ruby with its uncomplicated berry fruit aromas and flavours is often a good, warming drink. When the British FASHION for ruby port and lemonade faded in the 1960s, many shippers dropped the name ruby on the labels of such ports in favour of their own, self-styled brands.

Premium ruby, a wine with more colour and depth, may be bottled as *Reserve* or *Reserva*.

This category has now replaced 'vintage character', a misleading term which was largely used in English-speaking markets.

Tawny. The word tawny is applied to a confusingly wide range of very different styles of port. In theory, tawny implies a wine which has been aged in wood for so much longer than a ruby that it loses colour and the wine takes on an amber-brown or tawny hue (see AGEING). In practice, however, much of the tawny port sold today is no older than the average ruby and may therefore be found at the same price. The difference between a commercial ruby and its counterpart labelled 'tawny' is that, whereas ruby is made from a blend of big, deep-coloured wines, tawny is often produced from lighter wines grown in the cooler Baixo Corgo vineyards where grapes rarely ripen to give much depth or intensity of fruit. Vinification methods may also be adapted to produce paler coloured wines, and the colour of the final blend may be adjusted further by adding a proportion of white port so that the wine ends up with a pale pink hue rather than tawny brown. Many bulk tawnies are left up-river for longer than other wines for the heat to speed up the maturation (see DOURO BAKE). The resulting wines often display a slight brown tinge on the rim but tend to lack the freshness and primary fruit character normally associated with young port. The French typically drink inexpensive, light, tawny-style wines as an aperitif and supplying this market has become the major commercial activity for many of the larger port shippers.

Aged tawny. Port that has been left to age in wooden casks for six or more years begins to take on a tawny colour and a soft, silky character as the PHENOLICS are POLYMERIZED (see AGEING). Most of these tawnies are bottled with an indication of age on the label, although a new category of *Tawny Reserve* or *Tawny Reserva* may be applied to wines that have spent at least seven years in wood. The terms 10, 20, 30, or Over 40 years old seen on labels are, however, approximations as tawny ports are blended from a number of years' produce. The legislation is deliberately vague and most aged tawnies are a blend tasted and approved by the IVDP as conforming to the character expected from the age claimed on the label. Aged tawnies are made from wines of the very highest quality: wines set aside in undeclared years that might have otherwise ended up as vintage port (see below). They mature in cask in the cool of the lodges at Gaia until the shipper considers that they are ready to blend and bottle. Labels on these wines must state that the wine has matured in wood and give the date of bottling, which is important since aged tawny port may deteriorate if it spends too long in bottle. Once the bottle has been opened, younger aged tawnies may be subject to quite rapid OXIDATION, losing their delicacy of fruit if left on ULLAGE for more than a few days. (Very old tawnies and colheita ports are usually more robust.) Port shippers themselves often drink a good aged tawny, chilled in summer, in preference to any other. The delicate, nutty character of a well-aged tawny suits the climate and temperament of the Douro better than the hefty, spicy character of vintage port, which is better adapted to cooler climes.

Colheita. Meaning 'harvest' or 'crop' and therefore by extension 'vintage' in Portuguese, colheita ports are in fact very different from vintage ports (below). Colheitas are best understood as tawny ports from a single year, bottled with the date of the harvest on the label. The law states that colheita ports must be aged in wood for at least seven years, although most are aged for considerably longer. The wines take on all the nuances of an aged tawny but should also express the characteristics of a single year. All colheita ports carry the date of bottling and most wines should be drunk within a year or so of that date. (MADEIRA may also use the word 'colheita'.)

Vintage port. The most expensive style of port is one of the world's simplest of wines to make. Vintage port accounts for hardly 1 per cent of all port sold, yet it is the wine which receives the most attention. British shippers, in particular, have built vintage port into a flagship wine, 'declared' in an atmosphere of speculation when the quality of the wine, the quantity available, and the market are judged fit. Wines from a single year, or VINTAGE, are blended and bottled after spending between two and three years in wood. Thereafter, most of the wine is sold and the consumer takes over the nurturing for up to 30 or more years, although an increasing proportion is being drunk much earlier, especially in the US. Vintage port is distinguished from other ports by the quality of the grapes from which the wine is made. Only grapes grown in the best, usually Cima Corgo, vineyards, picked at optimum ripeness following an outstanding summer, are made into vintage port. Even then, nothing is certain until at least a year after the harvest when shippers have had time to reflect on the characteristics of the wine and the market. The vintage may be declared only after the IVDP has approved samples and proposed quantities in the second year after the harvest. With the steady improvement in vinification methods since the mid 1980s, some wine of vintage port potential is now made at the best quintas in most years. But a shipper will declare a vintage only if there is sufficient quantity and if it is felt that the market is ready to support another vintage (1931 being a classic example of a qualitatively superb vintage undeclared by most shippers for entirely commercial reasons). Vintage declarations may be very irregular but very roughly three vintages have been declared in each decade. Because they should be bottle aged for longer than almost any other style of wine, vintage port bottles are particularly thick, dark, and sturdy. The wines,

extremely high in phenolics in their youth, throw a heavy DEPOSIT and need especial care when DECANTING and SERVING.

Single-quinta vintage. Just as wine-producing CHÂTEAUX evolved in France in the 18th and 19th centuries, the single, wine-making QUINTA is developing in Portugal, and many of the better-known Douro quintas belong to a particular port shipper. Single-quinta ports are made in much the same way as vintage port, aged in wood for two or three years without filtration so that they throw a sediment (and should therefore be decanted before serving). A number of significant differences distinguish single-quinta vintages from declared vintage ports, however. First of all, shippers' single-quinta ports tend to be made in good (but not outstanding) years which are not declared. In years which are declared for vintage port, many of these wines will be the lots that make up the backbone of the vintage blend and are not therefore available for release as wines in their own right. Secondly many single-quinta ports are kept back by shippers and sold only when the wine is considered to be ready to drink, perhaps eight or ten years after the harvest. Single quintas or individual vineyards in the Douro were given a fillip in 1986 when the law requiring all port to be exported via Vila Nova de Gaia was relaxed, opening the way for a number of small vineyard owners who, before, had been restricted to selling their wines to large firms.

LBV. Late Bottled Vintage port is a wine from a single year, bottled between the fourth and sixth years after the harvest. Three different styles of LBV wines have evolved, however. First there are LBVs bottled without any filtration or treatment so that, like a vintage port, they need to be decanted before serving. These wines, once designated with the word 'traditional' tend to be made in good but undeclared years and are ready to drink earlier than vintage port, four to six years after bottling. Since the revision of the legislation in 2002, unfiltered LBV may also be sold as Envelhecido em Garrafa or 'bottle matured', provided the wine in question has been aged in bottle for a minimum of three years prior to release on the market. Many of these wines share much of the depth of a true vintage port.

A third style of LBV is the most common. These are wines which have been fined and sometimes filtered and cold stabilized before bottling to prevent the formation of sediment. That in itself is no bad thing (decanting has always been awkward for restaurateurs) but the size of some of the blends and heavy-handed filtration conspire to strip much of the character from the wine. Many filtered LBVs are therefore a poor substitute for the intensity and concentration of fruit in a traditional unfiltered LBV.

Crusted port. This port is so called because of the 'crust' or DEPOSIT that it throws in bottle.

In spite of its rather crusty, establishment name, it is the fairly recent creation of British shippers, notably the SYMINGTON group. It is designed to appeal to vintage port enthusiasts, even though the coveted word 'vintage' does not appear on the label (because crusted ports are not wines from a single year or vintage but blends from a number of years bottled young with little or no filtration). Like vintage port, the wines continue to develop in the bottle, throwing a sediment or crust, so that the wine needs to be decanted before it is served. Rather like traditional LBVs, many crusted or crusting ports offer an excellent alternative to vintage port, providing the port enthusiast with a dark, full-bodied wine at a much lower price. It may be exported from Oporto three years after bottling.

Garrafeira. The word GARRAFEIRA, meaning 'private cellar' or 'reserve', is more commonly associated with Portuguese table wines than with port. Until 2002 it did not form part of the IVDP's officially authorized lexicon but was a style produced by a single shipper, Niepoort. Now a port may be designated as a garrafeira if it comes from a single year and is aged for a minimum of seven years in glass demi-john before bottling (like some MADEIRA). In practice the wines age in 5- or 10-l demi-johns for considerably longer than the minimum. After 20, 30, or even 40 years in glass, the wine is decanted off its sediment and rebottled in conventional 75-cl bottles. The wines combine depth of fruit with the delicate, silky texture associated with tawny port. Three dates appear on the label: date of harvest, date of bottling (i.e. when the wine was transferred to demi-john), and date of decanting (i.e. decanted from the sediment that has formed in the demi-john and transferred to a 75cl bottle).

White port. Ernest COCKBURN remarked in the early 20th century that 'the first duty of port is to be red'. Nevertheless a significant proportion of white grapes grow in vineyards in the Douro and all shippers produce a certain amount of white port. White port is made in much the same way as red except that MACERATION during fermentation is much shorter, or non-existent. Most white ports have a certain amount of RESIDUAL SUGAR, even those labelled 'dry' or 'extra dry'. Intensely sweet wines, made mainly for the domestic market, are labelled *lagrima* (tears) because of their VISCOSITY (see also MÁLAGA). Another, drier style of white port, described as *leve seco* (light dry) is made by some shippers. These are wines with an alcoholic strength of around 16.5 or 17 per cent, rather than the usual 19 to 20 per cent. Most commercial white ports are aged for no more than 18 months, generally in tanks made of cement or stainless steel. Wood ageing lends character to white port, turning it gold in colour and giving the wine an incisive, dry, nutty tang. White port is sometimes used by shippers for blending cheaper tawnies.

Moscatel. One of over 30 different grape varieties used for making white port, Moscatel is occasionally used on its own to make a sweet fortified VARIETAL white wine with the grape aroma characteristic of MUSCAT. The village of Favaios on the north bank of the Douro makes a speciality of moscatel.

See also articles on individual port shippers COCKBURN, CROFT, FERREIRA, FONSECA, QUINTA DO NOVAL, SANDEMAN, SYMINGTONS, and TAYLOR.
R.J.M.

Bradford, S., *The Story of Port* (2nd edn, London, 1983).
Mayson, R., *The Wines and Vineyards of Portugal* (London, 2003) .
—— *Port and the Douro* (London, 2004).
Suckling, J., *Vintage Port* (New York, 1990).

Portalegre, DOC subregion of the ALENTEJO in central, southern Portugal with its own distinctive terroir. On the lower slopes of the predominantly granite Serra de São Mamede, these vineyards are the highest and therefore the coolest in the province. With TRINCADEIRA the leading variety, Portalegre has the capacity to produce wines with considerably more finesse than in the hotter more arid regions to the south.

Portan, like CALADOC and CHASAN, is a crossing made by French AMPELOGRAPHER Paul Truel at the INRA station at Domaine de Vassal. In this case he crossed Grenache Noir and Portugais Bleu (Blauer PORTUGIESER) to develop a Grenache-like variety that would ripen even in the Midi's cooler zones. It is grown to a strictly limited extent, on a total of 367 ha/906 acres according to the French vine census of 2000, but is allowed into Vin de Pays d'Oc.

Portimão, fishing port and DOC in Portugal's ALGARVE.

Porto, Portugal's second city (Oporto in English) which has lent its name to PORT wine, Vinho do Porto.

Port Phillip Zone, Australian wine zone surrounding Melbourne, VICTORIA, and encompassing the Geelong, Macedon Ranges, Mornington Peninsula, Sunbury, and Yarra Valley regions.

port tongs, rare instrument for opening a bottle of vintage PORT so old that the cork is likely to crumble under the impact of a CORKSCREW. The specially shaped tongs are heated in a flame and applied to the neck of the bottle, which is then immediately cooled with a cold, damp cloth. The sudden temperature change should result in a clean break. Tongs can be used on other venerable bottles.

Portugais, or **Portugais Bleu,** is the French manifestation of the more commonly Germanic black grape variety Blauer PORTUGIESER. Its influence is only slowly declining in France, where there were still more than 200 ha/

495 acres in 2000 and it was once one of the most planted varieties in the Tarn *département*, in some cases at the expense of the nobler varieties responsible for red GAILLAC.

Portugal. Among European wine-producing nations, Portugal has been something of a paradox, arguably discussed in the greater world of wine more because of the CORK of which it is by far the dominant producer than for its wines. Sitting on the western flank of the Iberian peninsula, this seafaring nation which discovered so much of the NEW WORLD has long clung firmly to the Old—at least in terms of its tradition of myriad indigenous vine varieties. Secluded both geographically and, for much of the 20th century until it joined the EUROPEAN UNION in 1986, politically as well, Portugal has developed in isolation from other countries, including neighbouring SPAIN. However, the sizeable wine industry that has grown up in this small country owes much to foreign trade. Total area under vine has declined from 385,000 ha/951,000 acres in the late 1980s to just over 240,000 ha producing just over 7 million hl by the mid 2000s. The Portuguese rival the French and Italians in terms of per capita wine consumption. See map.

History
The British have always enjoyed an amicable relationship with the Portuguese. As early as the 12th century, wines were being shipped to England from the MINHO in north west Portugal. In 1386, the Treaty of Windsor set the seal on a friendship that has persisted, virtually uninterrupted, to the present day. When England went to war with France in the 17th century, Portugal was therefore the natural alternative source for wine. PORT, often called 'the Englishman's wine', originated from this conflict. By the time England and Portugal signed the METHUEN TREATY in 1703, which laid down tariff advantages for Portuguese wines, a thriving community of English and German wine shippers was already well established in OPORTO. Out in the Atlantic, the island of MADEIRA, an important trading post for passing ships, began exporting wine to the newly colonized state and yet-to-be UNITED STATES of America, an important market on the East Coast which survives to the present day. Renewed conflict between Britain and France over the French invasion of the Iberian peninsula in 1807 rekindled demand for Portuguese wines. BUCELAS, CARCAVELOS, and a red wine simply called 'Lisbon' were popular in Britain until the 1870s.

In the last 30 years of the 19th century, PHYLLOXERA devastated Portuguese vineyards as severely as those elsewhere in Europe. Some Portuguese wine regions never really recovered. Many growers resorted to planting high-yielding DIRECT PRODUCERS, which still predominate in some of the smallholdings of north and central Portugal. For much of

the 20th century, Portugal turned her back on the outside world. Following 20 years of political and economic turmoil, the demure son of a DÃO smallholder, Antonio de Oliveira Salazar, became prime minister in 1932. His regime, which lasted for over 40 years, fostered a corporate, one-party state. Portugal's chaotic wine industry was thoroughly reorganized. The Junta Nacional do Vinho (JNV) founded in 1937 initiated a programme of co-operativization. Over 100 winery CO-OPERATIVES were built, mostly in northern Portugal, in less than 20 years. At the time they represented a significant advance but, all too often, the system imposed by central government was too inflexible and wine-making standards deteriorated.

It is paradoxical, however, that, against this background of self-imposed seclusion, Portugal should give birth to one of the greatest international wine success stories of modern times: medium sweet, lightly sparkling rosés called MATEUS and LANCERS.

In 1974, Portugal was once again thrown into turmoil by a military-led revolution. But after two years of upheaval the soldier politicians returned to barracks and subsequent democratically elected governments eventually returned Portugal to the European mainstream. Portugal's winemakers have benefited enormously from European Union entry in 1986. Monopolistic legislation was overturned and, thanks to EU policies of supporting agricultural underdogs, money poured in to help update the wine industry, much of which was hidebound by a lack of investment in modern technology. The relaxation of the state bureaucracy and the availability of grants and low-interest loans has encouraged a number of single estates, or quintas, to cut their links with local co-operatives and make and market their own exciting and distinctive wines. Since the 1990s, Portugal's wine industry has been undergoing a steady transformation and regions like Dão and the Alentejo now boast some of the most modern wine-making facilities in southern Europe. The transformation in the vineyard has been slower but a considerable amount of research is being undertaken into Portugal's unique array of native grape varieties (see below).

Geography and climate
For such a small country, Portugal produces a remarkable diversity of wines. Roughly rectangular in shape, it is under 600 km/360 miles long and no more than 200 km wide. The wines produced on the flat coastal littoral are strongly influenced by prevailing Atlantic westerly winds. Rainfall, which reaches 2,000 mm/78 in a year on the mountain ranges north of Oporto, diminishes sharply to less than 500 mm in some inland wine areas. The temperate MARITIME CLIMATE, with warm summers and cool, wet winters, becomes more extreme towards the south and east. An average

Portugal

Monção

Minho

Bragança

Viana do Castelo

CHAVES

Braga
Barcelos
Guimarães

VALPAÇOS

Miranda
do Douro

VINHO VERDE

TRÁS-OS-MONTES

PLANALTO-
MIRANDES

Vila Real

Oporto

Pinhão

Baião • *Douro*

DOURO

TÁVORA-
VAROSA

BEIRAS

BEIRAS

Aveiro

Viseu

DÃO

Guardã

BAIRRADA

Buçaco

Coimbra

BEIRAS

Atlantic Ocean

ENCOSTAS D´AIRE

Castelo Branco

Leiria

ALCOBAÇA

TOMAR

Tagus

ÓBIDOS

SANTARÉM

CHAMUSCA

PORTALEGRE

CARTAXO

Santarém

Portalegre

TORRES VEDRAS

ALMEIRIM

ALENQUER

ARRUDA

BUCELAS

RIBATEJO

CORUCHE

COLARES

Lisbon

BORBA

CARCAVELOS

Palmela

ALENTEJO

ÉVORA

REDONDO

SETÚBAL

Évora

Setúbal

ARRÁBIDA

REGUENGOS

SPAIN

TERRAS
DO SADO

GRANJA-AMARELA

VIDIGUEIRA

MOURA

Beja

0   100 km

ALGARVE

Madeira

PORTIMÃO

LAGOA

Funchal

LAGOS

TAVIRA

Faro

annual temperature of around 10 °C/50 °F in the northern hills compares with more than 17.5 °C on the southern plains, where, in summer, temperatures frequently exceed 35 °C/95 °F.

Reflecting these contrasting climatic conditions, no two wines could be more dissimilar than VINHO VERDE and PORT, which are produced in adjoining regions. There are pockets of viticulture all over Portugal. Only the very highest mountain peaks of the central and northern mountain ranges are unable to support viticulture.

Vine varieties

Portugal's vineyards have evolved in isolation. Only a handful of varieties have crossed international frontiers, leaving Portugal like a viticultural island with a treasure trove of indigenous grape varieties. Since the end of the 19th century until very recently, however, little research had been undertaken, and Portugal's haphazard vineyards remained *terra incognita*, not just to outsiders but to the vine-growers themselves. But a number of studies have been undertaken since Portugal joined the EU, in order to identify the country's most promising VINE VARIETIES, and many individual growers have also conducted their own research. Among whites, LOUREIRO and ALVARINHO (in Vinho Verde), BICAL (in Bairrada), ENCRUZADO (in Dão), ARINTO (in Bucelas and throughout southern Portugal), and Antão in the ALENTEJO are showing potential. Among Portugal's best and most distinctive red grapes are TOURIGA NACIONAL (in the Douro and Dão) and Spain's TEMPRANILLO (known as Tinta Roriz in the Douro and Aragónez in the Alentejo), BAGA (in Bairrada), CASTELÃO (once better known as Periquita), and TRINCADEIRA (in the Alentejo). INTERNATIONAL VARIETIES such as Cabernet Sauvignon and Chardonnay have made few inroads, although SYRAH is now making progress in the south of Portugal.

Wine laws

Portugal's wine law pre-dates that of most other European countries (although see also TOKAJI in Hungary). In 1756, the then prime minister, the Marquis of Pombal, drew a boundary around the vineyards of the Douro valley to protect the authenticity of port, one of the wine world's first examples of geographical DELIMITATION. Bucelas, Colares, Carcavelos, Dão, Madeira, Setúbal, and Vinho Verde were all awarded REGIÃO DEMARCADA (demarcated region) status between 1908 and 1929, followed by Bairrada, Algarve, and Douro (for table wine) in 1979 and 1980. Since Portugal joined the European Union, the Regiões Demarcadas or RDs have been redesignated Denominação de Origem Controlada (DOC). A second tier of Indicação de Proveniencia Regulamentada (IPR) wine regions has also been introduced, with a third tier of larger regions producing VINHO REGIONAL. Under-

pinned by the VINHO de mesa (TABLE WINE) designation, this brings Portugal's wine law roughly into line with that of other EU countries.

For details of Portugal's extremely varied viticultural techniques, wine-making practices and expertise, and individual regions, see also ALENTEJO, ALGARVE, BAIRRADA, BUCELAS, COLARES, CARCAVELOS, DÃO, DOURO, ESTREMADURA, MINHO, RIBATEJO, SETÚBAL, TERRAS DO SADO, TRÁS-OS-MONTES, VINHO VERDE, and, most importantly, PORT. The viticulturally important Atlantic islands of MADEIRA and the AZORES are autonomous regions of Portugal.

R.J.M.

Mayson, R., *The Wines and Vineyards of Portugal* (London, 2003).
— *Port and the Douro* (London, 2004).

Portugieser or **Blauer Portugieser,** black grape variety common in both senses of that word in both Austria and Germany, its name suggesting completely unsubstantiated Portuguese origins. The vigorous, precocious vine is extremely prolific, easily producing 120 hl/ha (almost 7 tons/acre), thanks to its good resistance to COULURE, of pale, low-acid red that, thanks to robust ENRICHMENT, can taste disconcertingly inconsequential to non-natives.

Blauer Portugieser is synonymous with dull, thin red in lower AUSTRIA, where it is particularly popular with growers in Pulkautal, Retz, and the Thermenregion. It covers five times as much vineyard area as Blauburgunder (Pinot Noir) and is the country's third most planted dark-berried vine variety after Blauer ZWEIGELT and Blaufränkisch. Such wines are rarely exported, with good reason, and are only rarely worthy of detailed study.

Brought from Austria in the 19th century, Germany's everyday black grape variety Portugieser overtook even SPÄTBURGUNDER (Pinot Noir) in the 1970s in terms of total plantings, thanks to the prevailing German thirst for red wine regardless of its quality. Portugieser's total area has remained steady at around 5,000 ha/12,400 acres, half of them in the PFALZ, where a high proportion of Portugieser is encouraged to produce vast quantities of pink WEISSHERBST.

The variety is so easy to grow, however, that it has spread throughout central Europe and beyond (as PORTUGAIS Bleu it was once grown widely in south western France). It was ingeniously named Oportó or Kékoportó (*kék* meaning 'blue') in ROMANIA and HUNGARY, where it is now known as Portugieser. It produces well-coloured, lively red wine not unlike that of KÉKFRANKOS but with a little more body and possibly a better aptitude for cask ageing. It is grown in the red wine region of Villány, where it can yield wines of real concentration, is an ingredient in BULL'S BLOOD, and is also grown, with slightly less success, on the Great plain. It is also grown in northern Croatia as Portugizac Crni, or Portugaljka.

post, substantial support for wires and vines which is common in NEW WORLD vineyards and usually made from wood, and driven into the ground at intervals down the row. Other materials used include concrete, steel, and plastic. Woods used for such posts are soft woods such as pine, treated to withstand insect and fungus attack, or naturally resistant hardwoods. A common spacing of about 6 m/20 ft between posts is close enough to stop the wire sagging. Smaller-diameter posts placed one beside each vine are called STAKES and these are more common for Old World vineyards.

R.E.S.

potassium, one of the three major elements required by the vine for healthy growth, along with NITROGEN and PHOSPHORUS. It constitutes about 3 per cent of the vine's dry weight, and is an important component of grape juice. Potassium (K) deficiencies show up first in older leaves as CHLOROSIS, which may become a marginal burn when severe. Potassium-deficient leaves are often shiny. Severe deficiencies can inhibit growth, yield, and sugar content. They can be confirmed easily by analysing for potassium levels in leaves or petioles, and 1.0 to 1.5 per cent K is the optimal range. Potassium deficiency is more evident during drought or in cold soils in spring, both of which reduce the roots' uptake of potassium.

Potassium is widely regarded as the most important element directly affecting wine quality. This is because high potassium levels in grape juice cause high PH, which adversely affects wine quality. Juice potassium levels are influenced by soil potassium levels, although this is not always a straightforward relationship. (Delas and colleagues in Bordeaux have shown positive linear correlations between plant K levels and juice K, but this was for vines with K contents up to and exceeding three times the optimal value.)

ROOTSTOCKS also have an important effect on juice K, with lower-vigour rootstocks giving lower juice K. This effect has been shown both in France and Australia. Part of the explanation may be that more vigorous rootstocks tend to result in SHADE in the canopy, which is known to increase both juice K and pH. In hot climates with low humidity, must potassium and juice pH are high, which may be the result of the high TRANSPIRATION rate of vines growing in such an environment (see CLIMATE). It seems that distribution of potassium in the plant is important, and that shade causes accumulation in the leaves, which subsequently migrates to the fruit. CANOPY MANAGEMENT techniques which reduce shade can therefore be effective in reducing must K and pH. While skins are only about 10 per cent of the berry weight, they contain 30 to 40 per cent of grapes' potassium.

R.E.S.

Champagnol, F., *Éléments de physiologie de la vigne et de viticulture générale* (St-Gely-du-Fesc, 1984).

Delas, J., Molot, C., and Soyer, J. P., 'Fertilisation minérale de la vigne et teneur en potassium des baies, des moûts et des vins', in P. Ribéreau-Gayon and A. Lonvaud (eds.), *Actualités oenologiques 89: comptes rendus du 4ᵉ Symposium International d'Oenologie, Bordeaux, 15–17 juin, 1989* (Paris, 1989).

Smart, R. E., and Robinson, M., *Sunlight into Wine: A Handbook for Winegrape Canopy Management* (Adelaide, 1991).

potential alcohol, measurement of a wine or must which equates to its total ALCOHOLIC STRENGTH if all the sugar were to be fermented out to alcohol. Thus, a Sauternes might have an alcoholic strength of 13 per cent, but a potential alcohol of 20 per cent if all the RESIDUAL SUGAR were fermented into alcohol.

Pouilly-Fuissé, important white wine appellation which commands the highest prices in the MÂCONNAIS district of Burgundy. The appellation, restricted to the Chardonnay grape, includes about 850 ha/2,100 acres in the communes of Fuissé, Solutré (which includes the hamlet of Pouilly), Vergisson, and Chaintré (see also MÂCON VILLAGES). The richest wines are said to come from Fuissé and Solutré, those of Vergisson being a little lighter but elegant. There is no concept of PREMIER CRU vineyards in this appellation but Pouilly-Fuissé may be followed by the name of a specific vineyard.

The grapes are grown in sun traps beneath the two impressive crags of Solutré and Vergisson which mark the end of the LIMESTONE plateau on which all burgundy save Beaujolais is grown. A popular myth is that the soil beneath the crags was enriched by the remains of animals driven from the top of the cliff by Stone Age hunters. The wines are full bodied and ripe but do not usually attain the elegance of the finer wines from the Côte de Beaune. Normally bottled after a year's BARREL MATURATION, they are capable of ageing well thereafter, particularly Vincent's wines at the Ch de Fuissé and those of Guffens-Heynen (the family domaine associated with the NÉGOCIANT Verget). Prices can vary enormously depending on the demands of major export markets in a given year.

The small village of Pouilly also lends its name to two adjacent lesser appellations, POUILLY-VINZELLES and POUILLY-LOCHÉ.

J.T.C.M.

Pouilly-Fumé, also known as **Pouilly Blanc Fumé** and **Blanc Fumé de Pouilly,** one of the Loire's most famous wines, perfumed dry whites that epitomize the SAUVIGNON BLANC grape (along with nearby MENETOU-SALON, QUINCY, REUILLY, and, most notably, SANCERRE). Sauvignon here is often called Blanc Fumé, because wines made from this variety when grown on the predominantly LIMESTONE soils, with some flint (*silex*), supposedly exhibit a 'smoky' flavour, or whiff of gunflint (*pierre à fusil*). The wines are certainly perfumed, sometimes almost acrid, and it takes extensive local knowledge reliably to distinguish Sancerres and Pouilly-Fumés in a blind tasting of both. Pouilly-Fumé is arguably a more homogeneous appellation than Sancerre, which is not surprising since less than half as much Pouilly-Fumé is made as white Sancerre. Unlike that of Sancerre, the Pouilly-Fumé appellation applies only to white wines. The best Pouilly-Fumé (such as the range produced by Didier Dagueneau) is perhaps a denser, more ambitiously long-lived liquid than Sancerre, for drinking at two to six years, for example, rather than one to four (although there are, as always with wine, exceptions). At the most historic estate, de Ladoucette's magnificently turreted Ch du Nozet, are bottles which prove that Pouilly-Fumé can last for decades, although whether it actually improves is a matter of taste. Some producers began experimenting with OAK for both fermentation and maturation in the mid 1980s and the wines of the region have become more complex. The appellation takes its name from the small town of Pouilly-sur-Loire on the right bank of the Loire in the Nièvre *département*. The name **Pouilly-sur-Loire** is given to the zone's less distinguished VDQS wine, a usually thin and short-lived liquid made in very much smaller quantities from the CHASSELAS grape, grown here in the 19ᵗʰ century for the tables of Paris. Pouilly-sur-Loire's official minimum ALCOHOLIC STRENGTH is 9 per cent, as opposed to Pouilly-Fumé's 11 per cent. In the 1970s and 1980s, Pouilly-Fumé was much favoured by FASHION, and the total area planted with Sauvignon increased considerably. In the mid 2000s, it totalled about 1,000 ha/2,500 acres. Some of the finest vineyards are on the slopes above the Loire north of Pouilly between it and the village of Sancerre.

See also LOIRE, including map.

Friedrich, J., *A Wine and Food Guide to the Loire* (New York, 1996, and London, 1997).

Pouilly-Loché. See POUILLY-VINZELLES.

Pouilly-Vinzelles. Borrowing the prefix from its more famous neighbour in southern Burgundy POUILLY-FUISSÉ, the village of Vinzelles has its own small appellation of 51 ha, most of which forms a steep, east-facing slope overlooking the valley of the Saône. The best vineyard is Les Quarts and the leading producer Domaine de la Soufrandière. Otherwise most production is in the hands of the local co-operative, as is the case also for **Pouilly-Loché,** an even smaller appellation of 29 ha which may be sold under the name of Pouilly-Vinzelles (but not vice versa).

Poulsard, sometimes called **Ploussard,** is a relatively rare speciality of the JURA, planted on less than 300 ha/750 acres in 2000, one of the region's dark grape varieties adapted over the centuries to its very particular climate and soils. It does particularly well in the northern vineyards of the Jura, especially at Pupillin near Arbois, self-proclaimed capital of Ploussard. Its large, long, thin-skinned grapes give only lightly coloured wine that is distinguished by its perfume. Its delicate pigment makes it much prized for adding colour to VIN DE PAILLE. It also makes unusual very pale reds, which may be left on the skins for as long as a week without tainting the wine too deeply, and are sometimes confusingly sold as rosé. It may also be blended with TROUSSEAU and Pinot Noir. It is also grown to a very limited extent in BUGEY, mainly for the semi-sweet sparkling CRU Cerdon.

W.L.

pourriture, French for ROT. *Pourriture noble* is NOBLE ROT. *Pourriture grise* is GREY ROT, or malevolent BOTRYTIS BUNCH ROT.

powdery mildew, also called oidium, the first of the vine FUNGAL DISEASES to be scientifically described, in 1834 in the United States. It is native to North America, where it causes minor damage on native grapes. The fungus was given the name *Oidium tuckerii* after the gardener, a Mr Tucker, who first noted it in Europe, in Margate, England, in 1845 (one source says 1831/32). Today the fungus is more widely known as *Uncinula necator*. The disease was first noted in France in 1847, where it soon spread and caused widespread havoc to vineyards and wine quality. Today the disease is spread worldwide. There is a difference in susceptibility between different vine species, with many native AMERICAN VINES being very resistant.

Varieties of the European vine VITIS VINIFERA are generally very susceptible, although some variation is noted. For example, Aramon, Pinot Noir, Malbec, Merlot, and Riesling are noticeably more tolerant than Carignan, Colombard, Chardonnay, and Cabernet Sauvignon.

All green parts of the vine are attacked and the infection is very visible. A fine, translucent, cobweb-like growth spreads around the spot where the fungus first penetrates. After one to two weeks, grey-white ash-like spores are produced on short, upright stalks. The infection looks powdery, leading to the common name. Spores are spread by wind and, with favourable conditions, new infections rapidly occur. The fungus survives over winter inside buds or on the surface of the vine. If bunches are infected before flowering, then FRUIT SET and yield may be considerably reduced and berry RIPENING delayed. Yield can be further reduced if berries are infected before they reach full size. Surface cells are killed so that the berries never grow to full size. Fruit of coloured varieties also fails to colour properly.

Fruit infected with powdery mildew is universally avoided in wine-making, yet there has been surprisingly little research into the effects on wine quality. Studies in New York state and Australia agree on the following points: wine made from infected bunches loses its fruity aromas, to be replaced by mouldy, wet fur, and earthy characters; wines are described as 'oily' and 'viscous'. The greater the infection, the more obvious the effects.

The disease develops and spreads most rapidly in warm weather, 20 to 27 °C (68–80 °F). Unlike all other fungal diseases of vines, this one is little affected by humidity, making climate conditions which favour it different from those which favour many others. Powdery mildew is favoured by dense, shaded CANOPIES. In fact, bright sunlight inhibits the germination of spores. Fortunately the control of this disease was discovered soon after it appeared in Europe. Mr Tucker noted the similarity between this vine disease and that affecting peach trees which could be controlled by a mixture of SULFUR, lime, and water. Dusting with sulfur was accepted after the disastrous French vintage of 1854, the smallest since 1788. This same technique is still used today.

In dry climates, sulfur dust is used; wettable powders are used in higher rainfall regions; and organic fungicides have been developed more recently. Cultural practices such as maintaining a non-shaded canopy (see CANOPY MICROCLIMATE) help prevent development of the disease. Recent developments in vine breeding have produced varieties with natural resistance and acceptable wine quality. These DISEASE-RESISTANT VARIETIES use the natural tolerance of native American species somewhere in their pedigree.   R.E.S.

Galet, P., *Précis de viticulture* (5th edn, Montpellier, 1988).

Ordish, G., *The Great Wine Blight* (2nd edn, London, 1987).

Pearson, R. C., and Goheen, A. C., *Compendium of Grape Diseases* (St Paul, Minn., 1988).

Stumner, B. E., Francis, I. L., Markides, A. J. and Scott, E. S., 'Powdery mildew and grape and wine quality', *The Australian & New Zealand Grapegrower & Winemaker*, 464 (Sept. 2002), 68–74.

Prädikat, in GERMANY a wine 'distinction', awarded on the basis of increasing grape ripeness or MUST WEIGHT: either KABINETT, SPÄTLESE, AUSLESE, BEERENAUSLESE, EISWEIN, or TROCKENBEERENAUSLESE. According to the GERMAN WINE LAW, a QMP wine is a Qualitätswein mit Prädikat, or 'quality wine with distinction', now officially known as a Prädikatswein.

In AUSTRIA, **Prädikatswein** excludes Kabinett wine but includes, at increasing minimum must weight levels, Spätlese, Auslese, Strohwein (or 'straw wine', see VIN DE PAILLE), Eiswein, Beerenauslese, AUSBRUCH, and Trockenbeerenauslese.

Pramaggiore. See LISON-PRAMAGGIORE.

PRD, see PARTIAL ROOTZONE DRYING.

precipitates, solids which are deposited on the bottom of barrels, casks, tanks, or vats by wine stored in them.

Technically, precipitates are solids which deposit from solutions because of reactions or temperature changes, and differ from SEDIMENTS, which are suspensions of solids which settle from the mixture when agitation ceases. Technically, therefore, the stem, pulp, and skin fragments and the seeds and dead yeast cells which settle after fermentation as gross LEES are not precipitates, while subsequent deposits of TARTRATES and oxidized PHENOLICS are. Practical winemakers, however, tend to classify both groups as precipitates, along with COLLOIDS.   A.D.W.

precision viticulture is an approach to wine-grape production which recognizes that the productivity of vineyards, and even of blocks within vineyards, can be inherently variable. Thus, vineyard management is targeted rather than implemented uniformly over large areas. Research in Australia suggests that grape yield within a single vineyard under conventional uniform management will typically vary 10-fold (ie 2–20 tonnes/ha), generally because of variation in soil conditions and TOPOGRAPHY.

Critical to this approach to viticultural management is the collection and use of large amounts of data relating to vine performance and the attributes of individual production areas (vineyards, blocks, sub-blocks, zones, etc.) at a high spatial resolution. This approach relies on a number of key enabling technologies including the GLOBAL POSITIONING SYSTEM (GPS), GEOGRAPHICAL INFORMATION SYSTEMS (GIS), REMOTE SENSING, and YIELD MONITORS, which, when used in conjunction with the GPS, enable geo-referenced records of yield to be collected 'on-the-go' during harvest. Such technologies, and the data derived from them, enable precision viticulture (PV) practitioners to manage vineyards by 'zones' rather than by blocks using targeted management to tailor production according to expectations of vineyard performance, and desired goals in terms of both YIELD and/or GRAPE COMPOSITION AND WINE QUALITY. This is feasible given recent research which has shown that patterns of spatial variation in vineyard performance tend to be constant from one vintage to another, which in turn lends itself to the adoption of ZONAL VITICULTURE and selective harvesting, and the use of data collected in previous years to predict likely performance in subsequent years.

Targeted management may mean the timing and rate of application of water, fertilizer, ameliorants such as MULCH or sprays, or the use of machinery and labour for a range of vineyard operations such as pruning, shoot or crop thinning. Selective harvesting is another kind of targeted management and involves split picking of fruit according to different yield/quality criteria in order to exploit observed variation within a vineyard. Different parts of the same vineyard block are

harvested into separate bins, either during a single operation or at different times, in order to maximize the uniformity of fruit parcels delivered to the winery. See ZONAL VITICULTURE.

In early 2005, yield monitors were the only 'on-the-go' sensing technologies available for attachment to existing vineyard machinery, but methods to simultaneously predict yield and assess grapevine canopy conditions and grape composition are under development.
                    R.G.V.B.

Bramley, R. G. V., 'Understanding variability in winegrape production systems. 2. Within vineyard variation in quality over several vintages', *Australian Journal of Grape and Wine Research*, 11 (2005), 33–42.

—and Hamilton, R. P., 'Understanding variability in winegrape production systems. 1. Within vineyard variation in yield over several vintages', *Australian Journal of Grape and Wine Research*, 10 (2004), 32–45.

— and — 'Hitting the zone—making viticulture more precise', in R. J. Blair, P. J. Williams, and P. B. Hoj (eds.), *Proceedings of the 12th Australian Wine Industry Technical Conference* (Adelaide, 2004).

Predicato, name selected in the 1980s by a group of quality-minded producers in TOSCANA in central Italy for their new range of wines made substantially or exclusively from INTERNATIONAL VARIETIES in an attempt to impose order on the chaotic and ungoverned spread of VINO DA TAVOLA. Since the introduction of IGT in 1994, Predicato (or Capitolare, as it was later called) has faded from the scene.

premier cru, or **premier cru classé**, is a CRU judged of the first rank, usually according to some official CLASSIFICATION. The direct translation of the French term *premier cru*, much used in the context of BORDEAUX, is FIRST GROWTH. A **premier grand cru** (**classé**) or **premier cru supérieur** may, as in the case of ST-ÉMILION and Ch d'YQUEM, be a rung higher even than this. In Burgundy, scores of vineyards are designated premiers crus, capable of producing wine distinctly superior to VILLAGE WINE but not quite so great as the produce of the GRANDS CRUS. See BURGUNDY in general and each of the villages on the CÔTE D'OR in particular. See also ERSTES GEWÄCHS and CHAUME.

Premières Côtes de Bordeaux, qualitatively important member of the BORDEAUX CÔTES group of appellations. The Premières Côtes extend for 60 km/40 miles from north of the city of Bordeaux as far as Langon in a narrow strip along the south western edge of the ENTRE-DEUX-MERS appellation (although the alluvial land immediately bordering the GARONNE river qualifies only as BORDEAUX AC). The soils here are very varied, with the *coteaux* rising from the river bank offering the most valuably gravelly or CALCAREOUS terrain. Clay predominates on the plateau between the *coteaux* and the Entre-Deux-Mers boundary. The name of the commune may be appended to the name of the appellation on the label.

The land dedicated to the appellation increased considerably during the first half of the 1990s to reach 3,500 ha/8,750 acres by 1996 (at which level it remained for the next 10 years), planted mainly with red grape varieties, particularly MERLOT, but the region is also the only one of the Bordeaux Côtes appellations to produce significant quantities of sweet white wines, known in the south as **Cadillac** and in the north as **Premières Côtes de Bordeaux**, from Sémillon, Sauvignon Blanc, and Muscadelle. Dry whites are sold as AC Bordeaux. There is a recognizable band of seriously ambitious producers here, especially of quite concentrated red wines which may lack the ageing potential of Bordeaux's more famous examples but can offer good value for drinking at three to five years old. Particularly successful properties include Chx Carignan, Carsin, Haut Rian, Lezongars, Parenchère, and Reynon. See BORDEAUX for more detail.

The appellation Bordeaux-St-Macaire (see BORDEAUX AC) is effectively a south eastern extension of the Premières Côtes de Bordeaux.

premium wine, debased and virtually meaningless term, not unlike RESERVE. See ICON WINE.

Prensal. See MOLL.

pre-phylloxera, term used to differentiate European, and especially French, wines made from vines before the arrival of the devastating phylloxera louse towards the end of the 19th century from those made from the vines GRAFTED on to phylloxera-resistant American ROOTSTOCKS which replaced them. In the first half of the 20th century, there was much understandable discussion about the relative merits of pre- and post-phylloxera wines with, perhaps inevitably, overall agreement that the earlier generation of wines were distinctly superior. As pointed out at the end of PHYLLOXERA, however, it was probably not the grafting itself which resulted in an apparent drop in quality, but the effects of the VIRUS DISEASES, particularly LEAFROLL, imported into European vineyards along with all this phylloxera-resistant plant material from across the Atlantic.

pre-pruning. See MECHANICAL PRUNING.

press, in a wine context usually means **wine press**, a particularly ancient piece of wine-making equipment, used for the PRESSING operation of separating grape juice or wine from solids. Wine presses or their remains provide some of the longest-surviving evidence of the ORIGINS OF VITICULTURE. In ancient times, the design of presses was varied and ingenious. See Ancient EGYPT and GREECE for more details.

Ancient history

CATO (De agricultura 18–19) in the 2nd century BC provided the first detailed description of a press room. He describes a beam or lever press. This would be constructed on an elevated concrete platform with a raised curb, which formed a shallow basin, which sloped gently to a run-off point. On this was constructed the press, which consisted of a long, heavy horizontal beam, which slotted into an upright at the back and ran between two uprights at the front. The front end of the beam was attached by a rope to a windlass. The grape solids were put under the beam and pressure applied by winding down the end. As the pulp compacted, so wedges were hammered into the slot at the pivot end to lower it. Over time various refinements were introduced. Most notably, according to PLINY (Natural History 18. 317), a 'Greek-style' press was introduced in the late republic or early empire, in which the windlass was replaced with a vertical screw thread, sometimes with a heavy counterweight. There is ample archaeological evidence from Italy, and elsewhere, for the use of presses. All the Roman AGRICULTURAL TREATISES, apart from the writings of Palladius, assume the use of a press in their descriptions of wine-making. However, the press was an elaborate and comparatively expensive piece of equipment and its use was far from universal. Some farmsteads have large tanks for treading the grapes in, but no evidence of a press. It is not clear whether the must from the treading was always kept separate from that from the pressing. The grape pulp could be subject to a second pressing; but this was carefully kept separate. The pressed grape skins could even be soaked in water to produce *lorca*, a drink to be given to the farm hands (VARRO, De re rustica I. 54), a forerunner of PIQUETTE.   J.J.P.

Rossiter, J. J., 'Wine and oil processing at Roman farms in Italy', *Phoenix*, 35 (1981), 345–61.

White, K. D., *Farm Equipment of the Roman World* (Cambridge, 1975), 112–15.

Presses today

Wine presses have evolved over the last thousand years or more into the relatively complicated machines used today. The **basket** presses used during the Middle Ages by religious orders were large devices built of wood in which grapes were squeezed by a horizontal wooden disc which just fitted into a cylindrical basket made of wooden staves bound into the cylinder shape by encircling wooden hoops. The juice from the crushed berries escapes through the spaces between the basket staves and flows into a tray below. Some of these traditional presses, usually depending on a giant lever for pressure, still exist and are occasionally used in Burgundy and parts of Italy. Similar, usually smaller versions of the basket press reliant on hand or hydraulic power can be found in many of the Old World's less mechanized wineries today and most producers of CHAMPAGNE and SAUTERNES still rely on variations on this vertical pressing theme,

demanding though they are in terms of time and manpower.

In modern **horizontal** presses, the basket press principle has been turned on its side. They can be divided into either batch or continuous presses, the latter almost never used for fine wines. Most batch presses depend upon squeezing a charge of crushed grapes or POMACE against a perforated screen. Pressure may be applied by a moving press head as in the old basket press or, more gently in theory, by having an airbag, or **bladder**, expand to squeeze the pomace against the inner wall of a perforated cylinder. The firm Vaslin makes a high proportion of the horizontal basket type, while the names Willmes, Bucher, and Pera are often associated with the bladder type. Many of these horizontal batch presses are called **tank** presses because they are fully enclosed, in order to reduce the exposure of the pomace and juice to air. (See also NITROGEN.)

Continuous presses are much harsher and usually worked either by a screw or a belt. The screw press usually resembles a giant domestic food chopper. The decreasing pitch of an Archimedes screw subjects the pomace to increasing pressure as it is moved along within the perforated cylindrical housing. The juice obtained, especially near the exit end, is very cloudy and rich in PHENOLICS but the juice from the crushed grape or pomace entry point is much clearer. Belt presses are much rarer and function by pressing intact berries between two perforated moving belts arranged so that the clearance between them decreases. Juice from belt presses is much clearer and better quality than that from screw presses, but the screw press allows faster throughput and is therefore the cheapest form of press. Both screw and belt presses can also be enclosed. The belt press was really more of an alternative to the crusher since it was still necessary to drain the juice and press the skins further in some other form of press.

Many modern presses are controlled by a computer program designed to optimize the pressing cycle for each grape variety and wine type. The screw press is the most common in large commercial wineries while some form of tank press is increasingly common for fine wine production.   A.D.W.

Pressac, Bordeaux RIGHT BANK name for the red grape variety Cot or MALBEC.

pressing, wine-making operation whereby pressure is applied, using a press, to grapes, grape clusters, or grape POMACE in order to squeeze the liquid out of the solid parts, known as *pressurage* in French. Historically, intact grape clusters were probably pressed, but it cannot have been long before someone realized that more juice could be obtained more quickly by smashing the clusters before pressing.

Timing of pressing depends on wine type. The great majority of wines today are made by CRUSHING and DESTEMMING before the pressing operation, but see also WHOLE BUNCH PRESSING whereby cooled grapes may be pressed even before crushing to avoid the extraction of unwanted PHENOLICS from the grape skins, although in some circumstances such SKIN CONTACT is considered desirable.

Grapes for red wines are usually pressed either after or during FERMENTATION, when sufficient extraction of COLOUR and TANNINS from the skins has taken place. Grapes for white wines are pressed before fermentation. Pressing of the sweet white grape pomace immediately after crushing is difficult because the skins are still slimy and slick, while after fermentation and maceration most of the slippery gums have been removed from the skins, making pressing much easier and quicker.

See also PRESS, PRESS WINE, and FREE-RUN.

A.D.W.

pressure bomb or **pressure chamber**, a device for measuring water potential in plants developed by the American plant scientist Scholander in the 1960s. Since then it has been used for studies in grapevine physiology, and more recently in California as a guide to the timing of vineyard irrigation. The blade of the leaf is placed in an airtight chamber. Pressure is increased until XYLEM fluid exudes from the cut PETIOLE end. However, water potential of the grapevine can vary from minute to minute, depending on sunshine, temperature, humidity and soil moisture content so it is difficult to interpret this dynamic value as an irrigation guide. R.E.S.

Smart, R. E., 'Do not blow up your irrigation schedule with the pressure bomb!', *Practical Winery & Vineyard* (Nov/Dec 2001), 80–1.

press wine, dark red wine squeezed from POMACE (grape skins, stem fragments, pulp, dead yeast) in a wine PRESS. Press wine is generally inferior in quality to FREE-RUN wine, and certainly more astringent, although some presses are capable of exerting pressure in controlled stages so that the product of the first, gentle pressing is very close to free-run in quality. Continuous screw presses in particular often exert such pressure that the product is excessively bitter and astringent. A certain proportion of press wine may be usefully incorporated into the free-run wine, especially if it lacks TANNIN. Otherwise it is used for a lesser bottling or, traditionally, given to workers at the establishment which produced it.

All white wine except for the free-run juice is effectively press wine, although its quality and characteristics are shaped considerably by how gently the white grapes were pressed. See also the TAILLE produced in CHAMPAGNE. A.D.W.

prestige cuvée, one of several names given to a CHAMPAGNE house's highest-quality wine. At one time the houses saw their NON-VINTAGE wine as their greatest expression. Vintage-dated champagne was added to the range and a premium usually charged for it. ROEDERER's Cristal bottling and MOËT & CHANDON's named after Dom PÉRIGNON scaled new heights, however, and today most of the major champagne firms offer one product available, at a price and, often, in a specially created bottle, in limited quantity at the top of their range.

price is probably the single most important aspect of a wine to most consumers, just as the price of grapes is one of the most important variables of the viticultural year to most grape-growers. The price of vineyard land is not directly proportional to the price fetched by grapes grown on it, however. See below.

Grape prices

Wine grapes are an important item of commerce throughout the world, and the economic fortunes of many rural communities rise and fall with local wine grape prices. Although many wine consumers have the impression that most wine grapes are grown on estates which also process them into wine, nothing could be further from the truth. The majority of the world's wine grapes are sold in the form of fresh fruit, to be vinified quite independently of the grape-grower, whether by commercial wineries or CO-OPERATIVES.

The means to determine prices for wine grapes varies from region to region. Prices are normally fixed annually, taking into account supply and demand as well as individual VINTAGE characteristics. A buoyant wine market bolsters grape prices, whatever the size of the crop, with some wineries attracting fruit away from others by paying higher prices. When the market is depressed it is not unusual to see fruit left on the vine (as in Australia in the mid 2000s, for instance), since the cost of harvesting can be more than the potential income. In many areas, notably Europe and South Africa, surplus grapes are distilled into alcohol, which in turn often becomes SURPLUS to requirements.

Normally grapes are bought and sold according to VINE VARIETY and sugar content. In most European regions, there is some sort of representative body which oversees grape prices. For example, in Bordeaux, the Conseil Interprofessionnel du Vin de Bordeaux (CIVB) has a board made up of wine producers and NÉGOCIANTS which seeks to organize the market for grapes and wine. As well as documenting wine sales, the CIVB may enter the market place in its own right and, for example, buy wine stocks for ageing in years of high supply. The regional organization in Champagne is the oldest of the French regional associations, and has powers and services which extend beyond grape price determination. The Comité Interprofessionnel du Vin de Champagne (CIVC) has in its time determined grape prices by means of a relatively complex series of calculations (see CHAMPAGNE).

For many European producers, grape prices are set by co-operatives, and although the formulas may not be so rigid as those traditionally employed in Champagne, they must take into account the same factors concerning supply, demand, and intrinsic quality. In much of the New World, the majority of grape-growers sell their produce to wineries. In Australia, there are statutory bodies which are involved in setting minimum prices. In the United States of America, individual growers negotiate freely with individual wineries, even though they may voluntarily join an association which will set recommended prices. The US government does, however, report on prices paid after each vintage.

A basic problem in buying and selling wine grapes is that their true value is not known until they are made into wine, and indeed until that wine is sold. Concentration of SUGAR IN GRAPES is the most common measure which can be related to grape quality. This is particularly important for grapes grown in cool climates, where better-quality wines are invariably made from grapes with higher MUST WEIGHTS. However, in warm to hot climates it is not difficult to reach the desired sugar level, and other aspects of GRAPE COMPOSITION are better related to quality. Increasingly, progressive wineries are implementing grape quality assessment schemes to reward growers for producing high-quality fruit. These schemes can be related to the vineyard site as well as to rootstock and clone, vineyard management methods, and also perhaps to a detailed chemical ANALYSIS of the fruit. Some wineries keep wine batches from different growers separate, and so are able to pay a bonus based on performance, but a lack of understanding of and agreement on vineyard factors which affect wine quality is likely to hamper widespread application of wine grape quality bonus systems. Some enlightened wine producers pay growers per ha/acre and effectively manage grape quality themselves. R.E.S.

Vineyard land prices

Wine is acknowledged as a natural product, and there is a widespread acceptance that the region or even vineyard of origin has a major effect on wine quality (see CLIMATE AND WINE QUALITY, SOIL AND WINE QUALITY, and VITICULTURE). Needless to say, those vineyards with a reputation for high wine quality attract high land prices. Perhaps the clearest examples are to be found in the Bordeaux region, where, thanks partly to several important CLASSIFICATIONS of individual châteaux, land prices are also clearly stratified. In the mid 2000s, for example, the price of planted vineyard entitled to the basic Bordeaux appellation had fallen to very roughly 25,000 euros per ha (it was about 200,000 francs per ha in the late 1990s) while one of the most celebrated properties might cost the equivalent of 1.5 to 3 million euros per ha (very much less than Gérard Perse offered AXA MILLESIMES in 2001 for Ch Petit Village in Pomerol, only to rescind the offer).

In Burgundy, a region in which geographical delimitation is even more precise, land prices vary in a similar fashion, particularly where appellation boundaries are in place. For example, land within the MEURSAULT appellation in Burgundy can cost several times as much as land just over the border in ST-AUBIN. In the mid 2000s, a vineyard with a village appellation cost between 150,000 and 500,000 euros per ha while a grand cru appellation could cost the equivalent of more than 2 million euros per ha.

Vineyard land prices in Spain, which were as high as 100,000 euros per ha in the late 1990s for unplanted land with the necessary EU planting rights, began to fall by as much as 30 to 40 per cent in the early 21st century as over-production and falling wine prices took some of the glow from viticultural extension. Land prices in the mid 2000s in the NAPA valley in California routinely exceeded US$100,000 per acre (US$250,000 per ha) for good sites, planted on a ROOTSTOCK other than AXR1, and some land has sold for more than US$500,000 per acre. Nearby unplanted land without Napa valley's reputation however might sell for under US$20,000 per acre. In Australia, suitable vineyard land on the famous TERRA ROSSA soil of COONAWARRA was sold in 1998 at up to A$100,000 (£37,000) per ha with established vineyard, whereas adjacent land without the terra rossa soil may sell for as little as A$2,000 per ha (as pasture).

Interestingly there are extensive tracts of land which have suitable soils and climate to grow quality grapes economically which are yet to be 'discovered' and planted to vineyards. As such, they have the value only of their existing land use. In many instances this might be low-value grazing. In HAWKES BAY, New Zealand, many of the vineyards are planted in soils which have alternative horticultural uses, and so are valued relatively highly, with 2005 prices at NZ$100,000 (£40,000) per ha, although land in fashionable Marlborough was meanwhile selling for NZ$150,000 per ha.

To the south are extensive areas of low fertility, stony soils which are not well regarded for grazing as they are drought prone, and yet are very well suited for viticulture. Before this was recognized in the mid 1980s, their value was as low as NZ$5,000 per ha. Similar phenomena can be observed in other countries such as Chile and Argentina where vineyard plantings are moving to non-traditional areas.
R.E.S. & J.R.

Wine prices

The price of a wine is a function of the price of the grapes, the price of LABOUR, the price of a winery or the debt outstanding on it, pricing policy on the part of the producer, pricing policy on the part of any merchants involved in selling it, the cost of TRANSPORT, BOTTLING, LABELLING, and marketing, quite apart from any DUTIES and TAXATION. The interest for the wine producer must be to maximize his or her return on capital, without acquiring a reputation for profiteering.

GLOBALIZATION continues to give bigger retailers increasing power to dictate prices and PRICE POINTS, which has had a generally deflationary effect on retail prices, if hardly an inflationary one on absolute value. See also ECONOMICS AND WINE.

The interesting question for the consumer, however, is the extent to which retail wine prices, which can vary more than a thousandfold, reflect wine quality. The answer is, of course, not very closely. All sorts of factors can depress the price of a wine to make it a bargain relative to the competition. Some national economies offer particularly low production costs (such as PORTUGAL and some of South America) when translated into the currencies of many potential importers. Currency movements in general have far more (upward) impact on wine prices than most wine drinkers realize (merchants do not always pass on the benefit to consumers of downward movements). The enormous surge in demand for 1982 Bordeaux in the United States was partly the result of the strength of the American dollar relative to the French franc in 1983 when EN PRIMEUR purchases were made. Other political events can also affect wine prices. The fall of communism and the effect of GORBACHEV's anti-alcohol policies on eastern Europe left SURPLUS production in countries such as BULGARIA, HUNGARY, and ROMANIA, which used to ship enormous quantities to the Soviet Union, and these emerging economies' desire for hard, western currency led them to export goods such as wine at extremely keen prices, or as part of barter deals. Specific countries may also benefit from preferential import tariffs.

Pricing policy in general may be geared to gaining a foothold in a new market, as SOUTH AFRICA needed to do after the lifting of sanctions in the early 1990s. Or it may have the result of bolstering prices in the belief that high prices automatically buy respect and prestige, a phenomenon associated with some aspirant CALIFORNIA CULT wines.

The above considerations relate to the prices of wine when it is first offered for sale. Serious wine COLLECTORS and those considering investing in wine are interested in what happens to the price of FINE WINE over time. As detailed in INVESTMENT and AUCTIONS, this depends on the precise wine and the time, and also on the rarity value of a given wine, its provenance and condition, and the general state of the market.

Most ordinary wine drinkers took a certain comfort in the story of what happened to the world's most expensive bottle of wine sold, at Christie's for £105,000 in 1985: this particular bottle of Ch Lafite 1787, supposedly once the property of Thomas JEFFERSON, was stood upright on display under warm lights by its owner Malcolm Forbes so that, unnoticed, the cork dried out and dropped into the bottle, rendering the wine OXIDIZED and undrinkable.

Not least because of the ASIAN economic boom, the late 1990s saw the prices of the most sought-after fine wines, the so-called TROPHY WINES, draw away from those of other wines, making such wines seem even poorer value than ever. It is ironic perhaps that at a time when the difference in quality between wines at the top and bottom ends of the market has never been narrower, the price difference has never been greater. But presumably this reflects the substantially increased number of affluent wine consumers, and the significant position that wine now holds in a number of cultures round the world.

price points, the supposedly particularly significant retail prices that increasingly dominate wine selling, whether by producer to retailer or by retailer to consumer. Mass market wines are typically offered by the producer at a proposed retail price of x.99. Bigger retailers impose a carefully planned timetable of retail discounts and promotions on their main suppliers, thereby sometimes entailing artificially inflated base price points from which these 'reductions' can be made.

Prieto Picudo, unusual, musky, Spanish medium-red grape grown in a large area totalling almost 5,000 ha/12,500 acres, mainly around the city of León in north central Spain. These red wines are light in colour but very distinctive, even if they are not officially embraced by the DO system.

Primaticcio, occasional name for Italy's MONTEPULCIANO grape.

primeur, French word for young produce which has been adapted to mean 'young wine'. French AC rules allow all of the following to be released on the third Thursday of November following the harvest: Beaujolais, Côtes du Rhône, Coteaux du Tricastin, Côtes du Ventoux, Coteaux du Languedoc, Gamays from Touraine, Anjou, and Gaillac, Coteaux du Lyonnais, Côtes du Roussillon, Mâcon Blanc, Tavel Rosé, Rosé d'Anjou, Cabernet d'Anjou, Cabernet de Saumur, Bourgogne Blanc, Bourgogne Aligoté, Bourgogne Grand Ordinaire Blanc, Muscadet, and Gaillac Blanc. For more details of this style of wine, see NOUVEAU.

See also EN PRIMEUR for details of fine wines offered for sale as futures before they are bottled.

Primitivo, Italian name for a red grape variety grown principally in PUGLIA. Once highly prized for blending, in the 1990s it fell victim to the same EU VINE PULL SCHEME as NEGROAMARO. Its total vineyard area fell from 17,000 ha/42,000 acres in 1990 to just under 8,000 ha in 2000, despite the fact that it has become much better known to the consumer as a variety in its own right. This commercial success as a VARIETAL (rather than as a blending ingredient) has staunched the loss of vineyards in the 21st century.

It might have remained relatively obscure had not its similarity to California's ZINFANDEL been noted, and DNA PROFILING established that both varieties are identical to the ancient Croatian variety Crljenak Kaštelanski. It was presumably brought across the Adriatic sea from Croatia to Puglia in the 18th century. Its name derives from the latter part of the 18th century, when a priest in Gioia del Colle selected vines from promiscuous old vineyards and noted that fruit from these vines matured earlier than those from other vines. As a result, he called the variety *primativo*, from the Latin *primativus*, or 'first to ripen'. In 1799, he planted these cuttings in a vineyard in Liponti, just outside Gioia del Colle.

Historically, it has suffered from a poorly conceived DOC in Manduria: a minimum alcohol level of 14 per cent for the regular production and higher alcohol for the *liquoroso* versions (both sweet and dry) which reach a leg-wobbling 17.5 to 18 per cent. It was highly prized as a high strength blending ingredient by many producers of AMARONE.

It is also DOC in its original homeland of Gioia del Colle. As an IGT Salento wine, it has enjoyed a boom since the late 1990s, where careful selection and modern vinification resulted in wines of great appeal and value. A move to limit the use of the name Primitivo solely to DOC wines was rebutted by producers in 2005. Growers will be grateful, for the success of IGT Primitivo has meant that higher prices are now being paid for the grapes. This in turn has ensured that the variety is being replanted after years in which it was only grubbed up, as the backbreaking work involved in cultivating the gobelet-trained vines was not remunerative. D.C.G.

Prinç, Moravian synonym for TRAMINER.

Priorat, one of Spain's most inspiring red wines made in an isolated DO zone in CATALUÑA a inland from Tarragona (see map under SPAIN). (Its Spanish rather than native Catalan name is **Priorato**.) In the 1990s, a true revolution engulfed the region, where production methods for Priorat had barely altered since the 12th century when the Carthusian MONKS first established the priory after which the wine is named. Priorat is one of the world's few first-class wines to be made from Garnacha (GRENACHE), together with some of the unfashionable Cariñena (CARIGNAN). The age of the vines and concomitantly extremely low yields, which average just 5 or 6 hl/ha (0.3 ton/acre), undoubtedly contribute to the

intensity and strength of Priorat. Under the hot Mediterranean sun, grapes ripen to a POTENTIAL ALCOHOL of up to 18 per cent, although in the 1990s this was steadfastly reduced.

Poor, stony soils derived from the underlying SLATE and QUARTZ, called locally *llicorella*, support only the most meagre of crops. MECHANIZATION is almost impossible and many steeply terraced smallholdings had been abandoned in recent years as the rural population left to find work on the coast. The success of new-wave Priorat is slowly reviving the vineyards, however.

The region is dominated by CO-OPERATIVES but there is an increasing number of well-equipped estates, traditionally led by Scala Dei, while De Müller makes some good *generoso*. In the 1980s, René Barbier, the scion of the Franco-Spanish wine-making family (whose eponymous firm in Penedès is now the property of FREIXENET), recognizing Priorat's potential for top-quality red wines, located some particularly promising vineyard sites, renamed CLOS. Such French vine varieties as Cabernet Sauvignon, Merlot, Syrah, and some Pinot Noir were planted. A group of private growers took over. The wines of René Barbier (Clos Mogador), Costers del Siurana (Clos de l'Obac), Álvaro Palacios (Finca Dofí, L'Ermita), Mas Martinet (Clos Martinet), and Clos & Terrasses (Clos Erasmus) had won worldwide acclaim by the late 1990s. Complex blends including small proportions of French varieties, careful wine-making, and ageing in new French oak barrels were the key innovations. Scala Dei, which also produces dry white and rosé wines, joined in this quality drive, with other small estates jumping on the bandwagon by the mid 1990s. By the mid 2000s there were more than 50 bodegas in Priorat. The wines must reach a minimum alcoholic strength of 13.5 per cent to qualify as Priorat. R.J.M. & V. de la S.

proanthocyanidins, oligomers and polymers of flavanols. Proanthocyanidins are PHENOLICS belonging to the FLAVONOID group, also called condensed TANNINS. The term proanthocyanidin refers to the reactivity of these molecules that release red anthocyanidin pigments (i.e. anthocyanin aglycones) when heated in an acidic medium, still commonly used for their analysis.

Several classes can be distinguished by the differing nature of the anthocyanidin released. The most common proanthocyanidins are PROCYANIDINS, which are the only proanthocyanidins in grape seeds, whereas tannins of grape skins and stems consist of both procyanidins and prodelphinidins. V.C.

Probus, Marcus Aurelius (AD 232–82), Roman emperor (276–82) who employed troops in the planting of vineyards in GAUL and along the Danube. (See GERMAN HISTORY.) This positive encouragement of viticulture was

in marked contrast to the earlier Emperor DOMITIAN.

Procanico, Umbrian and possibly superior subvariety of TREBBIANO.

procyanidin, a specific type of PROANTHOCYANIDIN based on CATECHIN and epicatechin units which releases cyanidin when heated in acidic media. V.C.

procymidone, a systemic FUNGICIDE used to combat BOTRYTIS.

production of a particular vineyard is normally measured as YIELD. The world's production of wine still totals between 250 and 300 million hl (6,600 million–7,900 million gal) annually, and is considerably in excess of CONSUMPTION, leading to continued SURPLUS, but there is wide variation according to VINTAGE. The 1991 vintage, for example, was particularly low because in many of the significant European wine regions production was seriously affected by spring FROSTS while the 2004 vintage was boosted by an exceptionally successful FLOWERING in most of Europe, the continent that is responsible for about 70 per cent of the world's production, with the Americas and then Asia being the next most important continental producers. Production is falling in Europe (Spain up but France and Italy down—and see EUROPEAN UNION initiatives), North Africa, and in the Americas (US and Chile up, Argentina down) but is tending to rise elsewhere. The tables in Appendix 2 show the world's significant wine-producing countries and OIV estimates of their total area of vineyard, annual wine production, and per capita consumption.

Many wine-producing countries of what was the eastern bloc produced much less wine during the early 1990s than previously, but are now increasing production again, and now face mixed fortunes. (Note that a considerable amount of wine may be produced in Belorussia and northern former states of the Soviet Union such as Estonia and Lithuania even though they have no vines, according to OIV statistics. Similarly, Russia's wine output is boosted by substantial imports of grapes, must, and unfinished wine.) Some of the most marked increases in wine production have been in Australia, Japan, and, particularly, China. (See map under WORLD PRODUCTION for the location of different countries' wine regions.)

Prohibition in common parlance most often means a prohibition on the consumption of alcohol (which suggests the importance generally attached to the possibility of intoxication). Prohibition has officially been in force throughout the world of ISLAM for 12 centuries, and elsewhere there have been periods throughout history (usually just after a period of particularly heavy consumption) during which the arguments for Prohibition have seemed convincing. One of these periods was the early 20th century, when Prohibition was enforced in parts of Scandinavia, was put to a referendum in New Zealand, and was enforced most famously in the United States.

Prohibition in the US

'Prohibition' is generally considered the period in the United States, 17 January 1920–5 December 1933, during which, according to the language of the 18th Amendment to the Constitution, the 'manufacture, sale, or transportation of intoxicating liquors' throughout the country was prohibited. The passage of the 18th Amendment crowned a movement going back to the early 19th century.

Beginning with local, voluntary organizations concerned to foster temperance in a hard-drinking country, the movement then undertook to pass restrictive legislation on a local or state basis (Maine went 'dry' in 1851). As the movement increased in vigour and confidence, total prohibition of alcohol consumption rather than temperance became the object. By the last quarter of the 19th century, the aim was to secure a complete national prohibition by means of a constitutional amendment. The work of propaganda to this end was in the hands of organized reformers, especially the Woman's Christian Temperance Union (1874) and the Anti-Saloon League (1895); they had the support of many Protestant churches, especially in the south and midwest. By the time the 18th Amendment was passed, 33 of the then 48 states were already dry.

The working out of the amendment was provided for by the National Prohibition Act (October 1919), usually called the Volstead Act: it defined 'intoxicating liquor' as anything containing 0.5 per cent alcohol, so extinguishing the hope that wine and beer might escape under a less stern definition. Some uses of wine were, however, allowed under the act: it could be used in religious ceremonies; it could be prescribed as medicine; and it could be used as a food flavouring or in other 'non-beverage' applications. All of these provisions could be and were greatly abused, and the act had to be amended and supplemented as experience showed the problems of enforcement.

The popular conception of Prohibition is that speakeasies abounded, gangsters and bootleggers of all sorts flourished, and every American gladly flouted the law. The reality is harder to determine, but there can be no question that the consequences for the American wine industry were disastrous. A number of American wineries, by obtaining licences to manufacture wine for the permitted uses, managed to continue a restricted operation (the apparent needs of communicants, for example, soared during this period). Effectively, however, the industry was wrecked. In 1919, the production of wine in the US was 55 million gal/2 million hl; by 1925 it had sunk to just

over 3.5 million gal. Winemakers received no compensation. Most wineries simply went out of business and their establishments were broken up.

The Volstead Act permitted the heads of households to manufacture up to 200 gal/7 hl of fruit juice annually and, by a benevolent inconsistency, this provision was construed to allow HOME WINE-MAKING. In consequence, vineyard acreage in CALIFORNIA shot up to unprecedented size to meet the national demand for fresh grapes: the 300,000 acres/121,000 ha of vineyard in 1919 had nearly doubled by 1926. Most of the new planting was in very inferior grape varieties, however (THOMPSON SEEDLESS and ALICANTE BOUSCHET, for example), and the degradation of the California vineyards thus induced by the conditions of Prohibition had seriously damaging effects on California wine long after Repeal. Nor can the quality of the average home-made wine have done much to enhance national CONNOISSEURSHIP.

The first efforts of the opponents of Prohibition were to achieve 'modification' of the terms of the Volstead Act. They tried for example to alter the definition of 'intoxicating liquor', or to allow individual states to make regulations different from those of the act. These efforts got nowhere; in consequence, the 'Wets' concentrated on achieving Repeal by constitutional amendment. Aided by the economic collapse of 1929 (invalidating the argument that Prohibition was economically sound) and by the adoption of Repeal as a political question (the Democratic party made Repeal a plank in its platform for the 1932 elections), the repeal movement succeeded: in December 1933 the 21st amendment, repealing the 18th, was ratified. Unfortunately, the amendment left to the separate states the entire regulation of the 'liquor traffic' within their borders, with the result that US liquor laws—including local and state prohibition—remain a crazy quilt of inconsistent and arbitrary rules, another lastingly destructive effect of national prohibition.

The forces that achieved prohibition in the US remain potent, and protean. National prohibition in the simple terms of the 18th amendment is not likely to come again; but liquor—wine very much included—continues to be an object of punitive taxation, of moral disapproval, and of obstructive legislation in the United States today. See UNITED STATES for more details.   T.P.

Asbury, H., *The Great Illusion* (New York, 1950).

Krout, J. A., *The Origins of Prohibition* (New York, 1925).

Sinclair, A., *Prohibition: The Era of Excess* (London, 1962).

Prokupac, red grape variety grown all over SERBIA, where the strong wine it produces is often blended with more international vine varieties. It is also grown in KOSOVO and MACE-

DONIA. Within its native land, it is often made into a dark rosé. Its stronghold is just south of Belgrade, where some argue it is identical to SYRAH.

proles, three categories of VINE VARIETIES of the VINIFERA species, grouped according to their geographical origin and, to some extent, their common end use (see BOTANICAL CLASSIFICATION). The classification is the work of Negrul in 1946. The differences between these groups may not only be a matter of response to environment, but also partly due to human selection for particular features related to end use, such as berry size for table grapes. Detailed observation of vine characteristics can reveal particularly close relationships which indicate that they are likely to have come from the same area. Thus are linked, for example, the CABERNET SAUVIGNON, CABERNET FRANC, MERLOT, PETIT VERDOT, and FER varieties.

Proles occidentalis: varieties native to western Europe, which were selected mostly for winemaking use. Most of the important wine grape varieties are in this group—RIESLING, CHARDONNAY, Cabernet Sauvignon, and so on—and they have common features of small bunches with small, juicy berries.

Proles pontica: the oldest varieties, and those native to the Aegean and Black seas, which have shoot tips and leaf undersurfaces covered with dense, white hairs. Examples of varieties in this group are CLAIRETTE, FURMINT, HÁRSLEVELŰ, and Zante CURRANT.

Proles orientalis: varieties originating in the Middle East, Iran, and Afghanistan. These varieties were selected mainly for TABLE GRAPES, and so tend to have large, oval berries in straggly bunches. The berries are often crisp, with less juice and sugar. This group of vines includes most varieties for DRYING GRAPES as well as most table grape varieties, such as SULTANA and MUSCAT OF ALEXANDRIA, but also the wine grape CINSAUT.   R.E.S.

propagation, the reproduction of a plant, whether by sexual or asexual means. Sexual propagation means reproduction by seed and involves the combination of two separate sets of chromosomes, one from the male (pollen) and the other from the female (the egg cell inside the ovule); their fusion during fertilization produces an individual with a set of genes different from its two parents. Asexual or vegetative propagation means reproduction without seed, by taking vegetative bits of the parent plant and getting them to form shoots and roots; the progeny are genetically identical to the parent and are called CLONES.

For details of micropropagation, see TISSUE CULTURE. For more details of specific propagation methods, see SEXUAL PROPAGATION and VEGETATIVE PROPAGATION. See also LAYERING.   B.G.C.

Prosecco, white grape variety native to the VENETO region in north east Italy. It is responsible for a popular wine of the same name, the DOC for which is Prosecco di Conegliano Valdobbiadene, made west of the township of Conegliano near the Piave river, where 5,000 producers cultivate 4,300 ha/10,600 acres of vineyard. Outside this zone, it is also produced as an IGT Colli Trevigiani. Prosecco wines exist in still, but mainly fizzy and sparkling, versions. The production zone, in the province of Treviso but near the border with the alpine province of Belluno, is quite cool. The variety is rather neutral, a factor accentuated by extremely high yields in the vineyards. The harvest starts in mid-September, and all the wines are fermented dry. This base wine is then turned into either FRIZZANTE or SPUMANTE wines using the Charmat process of SPARKLING WINE-MAKING. The finished wines are light and frothing, their neutrality and defects too often masked by over-generous additions of sugar. Of the 28 million bottles produced in an average year, approximately 1 million are of still wine, 7 million of frizzante or fizzy wine, and 20 million of spumante. The subzone of Cartizze, even cooler than the rest of the zone, comprises 106 ha of vineyard, and one million bottles of Prosecco which is held to be superior to the normal DOC production.

The variety is also known, to a very limited extent, in Argentina.   D.T. & D.C.G.

protected viticulture, a form of vine-growing where the vines are protected from climatological excesses to avoid stress. In a conventional agricultural sense, this would involve protection from low temperatures using glass or plastic houses or cloches; such structures are rare in commercial wine grape vineyards because of the prohibitive costs although they can be seen in the cool climate of ENGLAND or even in parts of California to protect some Chardonnay vines from poor FRUIT SET. Protected viticulture is more usual for TABLE GRAPES, as in northern Europe, Japan, and New Zealand.

Vines may also be protected from the wind by WINDBREAKS, and from frost by various techniques, and from drought by IRRIGATION.
                                                                    R.E.S.

protective juice handling, grape and must processing techniques with the aim of minimizing exposure to OXYGEN and therefore the risk of OXIDATION. This is regarded as especially important for white wines since, once grapes are crushed and juice liberated from the berry, the PHENOLICS react rapidly with oxygen to produce amber to dark-brown polymers (see POLYMERIZATION). Some ordinary wines are made encouraging this oxidation, the brown pigments being removed subsequently by FINING. Most better-quality wines result from minimal oxygen exposure, saving the phenolics for later contribution to AROMA and BODY.

(Some ambitious winemakers experimented with deliberate prefermentation oxidation of the must in the early 1980s but this is uncommon today.) The introduction of tank PRESSES has aided protective juice handling during the lengthy PRESSING operation enormously. See also NITROGEN. Grapes for red wines are far less vulnerable to damage from oxygen since they contain much greater concentrations of TANNINS and PIGMENTS.

See also SKIN CONTACT.   A.D.W.

protective wine-making, wine-making philosophy founded on the need to minimize exposure to OXYGEN and concomitant risk of OXIDATION. It usually incorporates PROTECTIVE JUICE HANDLING. White wines are then fermented in closed top tanks to exclude oxygen as much as possible while allowing for the escape of CARBON DIOXIDE from fermentation. All subsequent operations are then conducted as far as possible in closed equipment and small amounts of SULFUR DIOXIDE are added if exposure to oxygen occurs. Storage and processing at low temperatures favours the retention of some of the carbon dioxide, which has the effect of sweeping out any accidentally dissolved oxygen. Red wines, because of their greater PHENOLIC content, are much less sensitive to exposure to oxygen. Indeed, if they undergo BARREL MATURATION, some exposure to oxygen during TOPPING UP contributes to the wine's maturation. See AGEING.   A.D.W.

protein profiling, a recently developed technique which uses mass spectrometry to identify the grape variety or varieties in unfined juice or wine. Varieties are differentiated by the PROTEINS which are synthesized in the grapes following VERAISON. Unlike DNA, these proteins are relatively stable in juice and wine.

Research by the AUSTRALIAN WINE RESEARCH INSTITUTE on haze-forming proteins has led to this potentially useful tool for checking the varietal integrity of bought-in juice and wine, as long as the proteins have not been removed by FINING. The technique has been well proven for light-skinned grapes but further research is needed for dark-skinned grapes. The analysis requires sophisticated instrumentation and specialist staff so is not yet practical for everyday use at the weighbridge.

Hayasaka, Y., Baldock, G., Pocock, K., Waters, E. J., Pretorius, I., and Høj, P., 'Varietal differentiation of grape juices by protein fingerprinting', *Australian and New Zealand Wine Industry Journal*, 18/3 (2003), 27–31.

proteins, very large polymers of the 20 natural AMINO ACIDS. Proteins are essential to all living beings.

In grapes
Proteins may be water soluble and function as ENZYMES, or water insoluble and function as storage reserves (as in grape seeds and vine wood). While all functions are important,

the enzymatic properties of proteins are the basis of all reactions within living systems. The most abundant enzyme on earth, nicknamed 'rubisco', catalyses the trapping of carbon dioxide during PHOTOSYNTHESIS in plants.
                                                                    B.G.C.

In wines
Proteins from the grape remain in solution in all white wines but in some (notably those vinified from MUSCAT, GEWÜRZTRAMINER, SAUVIGNON BLANC, and SÉMILLON grapes), the concentration is often so high that the proteins coagulate to form an unsightly haze or cloud. Such haziness, which can be initiated when the wine is warmed, is irreversible. To avoid this happening after bottling, which renders the wine unstable, the heat-unstable proteins are removed by BENTONITE fining as part of normal wine-making STABILIZATION procedures. Research at the AUSTRALIAN WINE RESEARCH INSTITUTE has shown that the troublesome, heat-unstable proteins of white wines belong to a particular group from the grape known as pathogenesis-related or PR proteins. PR proteins are made by the grapevine as part of its natural defence against fungal attack and stress, although it appears that some PR proteins are present at background levels even in fruit that is free of, and never suffered from, FUNGAL DISEASES. The unique properties of PR proteins—their stability in acid conditions and resistance to degradation by proteolytic ENZYMES—means that fermentation and the other processes of wine-making selectively eliminate other proteins of the grape leaving the PR proteins as virtually the sole survivors.

This knowledge of PR proteins could hold the key to varietal differentiation of wines. While DNA PROFILING can permit the identification of different vine varieties, the technique cannot easily be extended to wine because the action of nucleases during fermentation destroys most of the grape DNA. However, the PR proteins appear to be characteristic for the classic varieties of *Vitis vinifera* and small differences among PR proteins can be distinguished by mass spectrometry. Accordingly, by applying mass spectrometric analysis to the PR proteins of a wine, it appears that the long held ambition of identifying the grapes from which the wine was vinified is achievable. See also PROTEIN PROFILING.

The greater concentration of PHENOLICS in red wines means that much of the protein is removed in the LEES as an insoluble tannin–protein complex, and haze formation is not normally a hazard in bottled red wines. Nevertheless, an alternative instability problem, BOTTLE DEPOSIT which involves proteins, can still beset a red wine.   P.J.W.

Hayasaka, Y., Adams, K. S., Pocock, K. F., Baldock, G. A., Waters, E. J., and Høj, P. B., 'Use of electrospray mass spectrometry for mass determination of grape (*Vitis vinifera*) juice pathogenesis-related proteins: a potential tool for varietal differentiation', *Journal of Agricultural and Food Chemistry*, 49 (2001), 1830–9.

Waters, E. J., Alexander, G., Muhlack, R., Pocock, K. F., Colby, C., O'Neill, B. N., Høj, P. B., and Jones, P. R. 'Preventing protein haze in bottled wine', *Australian Journal of Grape and Wine Research*, 11 (2005), 215–25.

Provence, region with considerable potential in the far south east of France (see map under FRANCE) whose associations with tourism and hedonism have perhaps focused too much attention on its relatively expensive rosés.

The precise period during which viticulture was introduced to the region is disputed. Certainly it appears unlikely that the Phocaeans, Greeks from Asia Minor, found vines when they founded Massilia (Marseilles) in about 600 BC. It is likely, however, that the Provincia of Ancient GAUL produced its own wines under the influence of classical ROME (although it is not certain that it preceded Narbo, or Narbonne, in the LANGUEDOC as a wine producer). See FRANCE for more details.

The region was much fought over, being under the influence in successive eras of the Saracens, Carolingians (see CHARLEMAGNE), the Holy Roman Empire, the counts of Toulouse, the Catalans, René of ANJOU, and the House of SAVOY. For much of the 19th century it belonged to SARDEGNA. At the end of the 19th century, Provençal viticulture was nearly killed by the PHYLLOXERA louse, but was given a new lease of life by the arrival of a RAILWAY link with northern Europe.

As a result of its rich cultural heritage, Provence enjoys a particularly distinctive range of vine varieties, which show various historical influences from Italy, notably Sardegna. No fewer than 13 varieties are allowed in Côtes de Provence, for example, including CARIGNAN, CINSAUT, GRENACHE, UGNI BLANC, and CLAIRETTE, but also MOURVÈDRE, TIBOUREN, the indigenous dark-berried Calitor (known in Provençal as Pécoui Touar), Barbaroux (Italy's BARBAROSSA), ROLLE (Vermentino), and SÉMILLON. Grenache is by far the most planted variety in Provence, followed by Carignan, then Syrah and Cinsaut.

The climate here is France's most MEDITERRANEAN, with an average of 3,000 hours of sunshine a year, and less than 700 mm/27 in annual RAINFALL, which is concentrated in spring and autumn. Winters are mild, but usually allow full vine DORMANCY. The greatest climatological threat is WIND, in particular the famous *mistral*, a cold wind from the north. Proximity to the sea and careful vineyard siting on southern expositions can offer some protection. It has the advantage of minimizing the risk of FUNGAL DISEASES, and Provence is particularly suitable for ORGANIC VITICULTURE.

The magic attached to such names as the Côte d'Azur, St-Tropez, and Provence in general may have increased urban development, and pushed up land prices in habitable parts of the region, but it has also attracted outsiders prepared to make significant investments in vine-growing and wine-making, thereby raising standards overall.

Côtes de Provence

This area of about 20,000 ha/50,000 acres is by far the most significant appellation in Provence, although the vineyard sites vary enormously. The appellation applies to a large part of the Var *département* (other than the enclave entitled to the Coteaux Varois appellation) from the subalpine hills above Draguignan, cooled by the influence of the mountains to the north, to the coast at St-Tropez, the epitome of a Mediterranean wine zone. But it also includes pockets of hotter terrain between Cassis and Bandol, and land immediately south and east of the Palette appellation near Aix-en-Provence. The appellation even encompasses a tiny isolated area of vines at Villars-sur-Var high up in the mountains 40 km/25 miles north of Nice in the Alpes-Maritimes.

About four-fifths of production is of pale pink dry rosé, which seems to find a growing local market almost regardless of quality. There is renewed interest in producing 'serious' rosé, however, with a distinctive new style combining flavour with a fashionably pale hue, and some producers even using a limited amount of OAK maturation. The best really do seem to have a special affinity with the garlic- and oil-based cuisine of Provence, particularly *aïoli*. Much of it is sold in a special 'skittle' bottle; all of it should be consumed as young and as cool as possible. Cinsaut and Grenache are typically used particularly for rosé, but Tibouren can add real interest to a blend. Rosés must contain at least 20 per cent of SAIGNÉE wine (as opposed to 30 and 50 per cent respectively in the rosés of Coteaux d'Aix-en-Provence and Les Baux de Provence).

The focus of attention for a new generation of serious wine producers in this appellation, however, is red wine, which accounts for just 15 per cent of production. Great efforts have been made to replace the prolific Carignan vine with the more recent 'improving varieties' Syrah and Cabernet Sauvignon to add structure to the suppler permitted ingredients. The varieties Grenache, Syrah, Cinsaut, and Mourvèdre and Tibouren (both of which have a long history here) must comprise at least 70 per cent of any blend in red and rosé Côtes de Provence (80 per cent by 2015).

There is considerable experimentation with different forms of ÉLEVAGE, including the use of new OAK for some of the most ambitious cuvées, typically dominated by Cabernet Sauvignon and/or Syrah, although the former may represent no more than 30 per cent of the total blend.

An increasing number of producers, especially in the coastal sector, are paying as much attention to their white wine output. Rolle in particular is enjoying renewed interest.

Special subappellations include Fréjus, Ste-Victoire, and, unconfirmed in 2005, La Londe.

Domaines de la Courtade, Gavoty, Ott, Ch Real Martin, Domaines Richeaume, du Rimauresq, and St André de Figuière are some of the most successful producers. See also the individual Provence appellations of Coteaux d'AIX-EN-PROVENCE, BANDOL, Les BAUX DE PROVENCE, BELLET, CASSIS, PALETTE, and Coteaux VAROIS.

George, R., *The Wines of the South of France* (London, 2001).

Parker, R. M., *The Wines of the Rhône Valley and Provence* (2nd edn, New York, 1987).

PRP, see PIEROTH.

Prugnolo Gentile, synonym for SANGIOVESE in VINO NOBILE DI MONTEPULCIANO

pruners, devices used for winter PRUNING of grapevines. From ancient times until the 19th century, a pruning hook or knife was used. In modern times, pruning is normally carried out using hand-held SECATEURS. These were developed in the mid 19th century, and came into widespread use in the latter half of the century. Secateurs cut with a scissor action, and there are various forms available (including power-assisted versions). Sometimes pruning saws may be needed to remove old CORDONS or ARMS. Vineyard winter pruning is now being mechanized with tractor-mounted machines doing most of the cutting, as described in MECHANICAL PRUNING. R.E.S.

pruning of vines involves cutting off unwanted vegetative parts in the form of canes in winter. For details of cutting off unwanted vegetative growth in the form of excess SHOOTS in early spring and shoot tips in summer, see SHOOT THINNING and TRIMMING respectively. **Summer pruning** is another term for trimming.

Winter pruning is a vineyard practice developed primarily to produce fewer but larger bunches of riper grapes and is particularly important in cooler climates. More than 85 per cent of each year's shoot growth may be removed. There is an important relationship between vine pruning and VINE TRAINING, as the pruning method used depends on the training system employed.

Vines growing in their natural state, as in the WILD VINES of America and the Middle East, are of course not pruned. At the top of such vines, many of which grow up trees, and on other parts of the vine exposed to the sun, are many small bunches of grapes. While the vine may have had thousands of buds present in winter which could have produced shoots and fruit, only a small proportion will burst in spring. This reduced BUDBREAK is the principal means by which unpruned vines in their

Head trained vine with cane pruning

cane — replacement spur

Bilateral cordon trained vine with spur pruning

arm
spur

cordon — head or crown

trunk

Pruning alternatives

natural state avoid OVERCROPPING, which may weaken the vine and shorten its life. The wild vine is much branched, with many shoots growing apparently haphazardly.

History

It is not known when mankind began to prune vines but vine pruning was certainly known in Ancient EGYPT and was already a well-established practice by the beginning of the Roman era, described in detail by such writers as PLINY and VIRGIL. There are also numerous references to vine pruning in the BIBLE. For example, 'a Sabbath of rest unto the land, a Sabbath for the Lord: thou shalt neither sow thy field, nor prune thy vineyard' (Lev. 25. 4). Vine pruning also figures in the description of the Last Days (Mic. 4. 3): 'and they shall beat their swords into ploughshares, and their spears into pruning hooks.'

Aims of pruning

Among the early aims of vine pruning as practised by the Ancient Egyptians would have been to increase the size of individual berries and bunches, an important consideration even today in the production of TABLE GRAPES. A vine which is lightly pruned has many buds and will produce numerous bunches with small berries.

Another aim of vine pruning is to establish or maintain a shape of vine, which makes all other vineyard operations easier. For example, keeping vines pruned back to a more or less constant structure means they can easily be neatly trained in rows. Otherwise, vines would sprawl and quickly cover the space between rows.

But perhaps the most important aspect of pruning is that it regulates the next season's YIELD by controlling the number of buds which can burst and produce bunches of grapes. The number of buds retained after winter pruning may be influenced by TRADITION, local CONTROLLED APPELLATION regulations, the scien-

tific principles behind BALANCED PRUNING, or greed.

Timing

Pruning is carried out in winter, normally once the first frost causes the leaves to fall, thereby exposing the woody CANES, but the precise timing of winter pruning is not generally critical. In most viticultural regions, however, winter pruning should be completed by the time of budbreak in spring, as the PRUNERS can damage emerging shoots as they work. Some early-budding varieties may be pruned very late in an effort to delay budbreak and minimize FROST DAMAGE. Vines lose water (see BLEEDING) from pruning wounds just prior to budbreak. In regions with warm winters, such as tropical and subtropical regions, the vines may not become completely dormant, and vines may have to be pruned when they are covered in leaves. See TROPICAL VITICULTURE.

Two basic options

The basic principles of pruning have changed remarkably little since classical times, although the French viticulturist GUYOT in 1860 introduced firm suggestions as to the length and position of canes, formalizing some of the old ideas.

Along the canes, which were green, soft shoots during the previous growing season, are buds which are arranged on alternate sides of the cane about 8 cm/3 in or so apart. Basically there are two types of vine pruning: either to SPURS, or to CANES.

Spur pruning Spurs are cut to retain only two buds, while canes are longer, typically with five to 15 buds. In the spring, each bud on the two-bud spur normally produces one shoot. In autumn, these shoots become woody. During winter pruning the cane growing from the uppermost bud on the spur is removed, and the cane from the bottom bud is cut back to two buds, creating the new spur. The vine's physiology determines that, when a cane is cut, the last two buds will burst. This is the reason for the common two-bud spur. If spurs were left with three buds, the bottom bud would often not produce a shoot, and so the spur position would move further and further from the cordon or head as the years passed.

Spur pruning is commonly used with free-standing vines, such as are widely seen in Mediterranean wine regions. The GOBELET-trained vines in the south of France are typical. Gobelet vines are free standing with short trunks rarely more than half a metre high. The spurs arise from the trunk or from short arms on the trunk. This is of course a very simple form of vine training, requiring no supporting POSTS or WIRE; it is therefore among the oldest forms prevailing and was already known to the Roman writers COLUMELLA and PALLADIUS. This vine training is particu-

larly common in the Old World. In Languedoc and Roussillon, for example, the great majority of vineyards are still pruned and trained in this basic way. It is common in the lower-rainfall areas of Spain, Italy, and Portugal, such vineyards being of lower VIGOUR, to which the system is best suited. Some of the older New World vineyards, for example in California, Australia, and South Africa, also have such vines, here often described as head trained.

Another spur-pruned form which is more common with higher-vigour vineyards is cordon training. Here the spurs arise from one or more horizontal arms or CORDONS. Known in France as CORDON DE ROYAT, this pruning method has been used for wine grapes since the end of the 19th century. The cordons are trained along a wire, and this method is particularly common in New World vineyards. Of all pruning methods, this one lends itself most readily to MECHANIZATION since all of the canes to be pruned are more or less in the one plane (see MECHANICAL PRUNING).

Cane pruning Cane pruning became common after the 1860 studies of the Frenchman Dr Guyot. In traditional French vineyards each vine is typically pruned to one cane with six to eight buds and one spur with two buds. During winter pruning the cane from the previous year is cut off and a new one laid down, using one of the canes arising from the spur. The number of buds on the cane depends on regional tradition and the small print of the APPELLATION CONTRÔLÉE laws. For example, eight buds may be left on Syrah canes in the Côtes du Rhône; eight on all major varieties in Burgundy; in Bordeaux seven buds is the maximum for Sémillon in Sauternes, six for Muscadelle, but eight for Merlot Blanc. These small bud numbers per cane (and hence cane length) contrast greatly with those used for wine grapes in other regions where vine vigour is higher. For example, in vigorous irrigated vineyards in Australia it is not uncommon to see up to ten canes, each with up to 15 buds, left on a single vine after winter pruning. Of course, these vines are planted further apart than their Old World counterparts, as discussed in NEW WORLD.

A common observation with cane pruning is that buds in the middle of the cane often do not burst. There are often a few shoots growing near the head of the vine (at the base of the cane), and the last two shoots at the cut end of the cane will invariably grow. Where the cane was growing in shade the previous year the budburst is invariably poor, as outlined in CANOPY MICROCLIMATE.

In France, the colloquial name for canes varies regionally: *courgée* in Jura, for example, *aste* in Bordeaux, *baguette* in Burgundy, *archet* or *archelot* in Beaujolais, and, appropriately enough in view of the region's notoriously high yields, *pisse-vin* in the Languedoc.

Pedro Ximénez grapes have to be painstakingly picked by hand from these sprawling **bush vines** in the Montilla-Moriles wine region of Andalucía, southern Spain, where they are often dried further and their juice used to produce particularly dark, sticky, syrup-sweet wine called PX.

Controlling yield

A fundamental question in relation to vine pruning is how many buds to leave on each vine at winter pruning. Does it matter? For many vignerons in the world this first question is never posed, as TRADITION or APPELLATION laws dictate how the vines are to be pruned. The winter pruning period can be a time when the mind is put into neutral, and the body is braced to survive long days spent outdoors, often in unpleasant and cold weather. Quite often, traditional pruning practices are followed, and vigorously defended against any suggestion of change.

When vines are pruned to just a few buds, most of them burst successfully, and the shoots will typically grow vigorously. They will be very long, with large leaves and many LATERAL SHOOTS. Early shoot growth is stimulated by the vine's food reserves in the trunk and roots being spread around only a few shoots. A low-vigour vine which has limited reserves of CARBOHYDRATES must therefore be pruned to few buds only compared with one of higher vigour which contains more reserves.

A vine that is very lightly pruned, to scores or even hundreds of buds, will produce many more shoots and bunches of grapes. Individual shoots will be shorter, and the number and size of berries will be reduced. However, the total yield of grapes will be greater, and the grapes will take longer to ripen. This may cause no problems in warm and sunny climates, but can be disastrous in cooler climates, where it can be a struggle to ripen the grapes anyway before autumn chill and frosts stop the ripening process.

There is therefore more concern about pruning levels in cooler climates than in warmer ones. In Germany, for example, the common rule is to leave about ten buds at winter pruning for each square metre of vineyard land surface. In New York state, Professor Nelson SHAULIS has developed balanced pruning guidelines for pruning which rely on the vine's growth as assessed by PRUNING WEIGHT (the weight of annual growth as canes removed at pruning); about 35 buds should be retained per kg of pruning weight. Having weighed a few vines, the grower can assess the pruning weight by eye as part of his pruning decision. For more vigorous vines with higher pruning weights, more buds are retained.

For high-vigour vineyards it may not be sufficient just to prune lightly, as this will lead to crowding of shoots in the vine CANOPY. Recognition of this problem has led to the development of CANOPY MANAGEMENT strategies to avoid dense canopies for vigorous vineyards. Similarly, yield cannot be limited by pruning high-vigour vineyards to just a few buds. The yield will still be considerable, as will BERRY SIZE (undesirable for wine quality). Bunches will be tight, increasing the risk of BUNCH ROT and there will be considerable shoot and leaf growth, which is likely to result in SHADE rather than vine BALANCE.

Mechanization

Up until the 1960s, winter pruning was labour intensive, but increases in labour costs and reductions in labour supply in Australia led to experimentation with and eventual development of MECHANICAL PRUNING. Tractors equipped with circular saws or reciprocating cutter blades were able to speed the laborious process of hand pruning without serious effects on wine quality in warm regions. This in turn has led to the even more iconoclastic option of MINIMAL PRUNING, or not pruning at all, although the latter is now viewed with increasing disfavour.

By the early 1990s, a full spectrum of vine-pruning practice was evident, from the hand pruning of a lower-vigour vine in a traditional vineyard to less than 10 buds, to one essentially unpruned following the passage of a machine, with thousands of buds remaining.

The time taken to prune a vineyard depends on how the vineyard is trained, the VINE DENSITY, and the pruning method. Pruning times can be up to 200 hours or more per ha for high-density cane-pruned vineyards. For wide-row, spur-pruned vineyards trained to cordons the figure may be as low as 50 hours per ha, and in combination with mechanical pre-pruning this may be reduced even further to less than 20 hours per ha.

Care must be taken to avoid the fungal disease EUTYPA DIEBACK, of which spores may be transferred on pruners, infecting the pruning wounds following large cuts. R.E.S.

Coombe, B. G., and Dry, P. R. (eds.), *Viticulture*, ii: *Practices* (Adelaide, 1992).

Galet, P., *Précis de viticulture* (5th edn, Montpellier, 1988).

Winkler, A. J., *et al.*, *General Viticulture* (2nd edn, Berkeley, Calif., 1974).

pruning machines. See MECHANICAL PRUNING.

pruning weight, a measure of vine VIGOUR, or, more strictly, capacity, obtained by weighing the canes removed from a vine at winter PRUNING. This is the most useful and common measure of vine growth. The value may be used, for example, to assess how many buds might be left at winter pruning to achieve the best vine performance, using concepts of BALANCED PRUNING. Similarly, the ratio between the weight of prunings and the fruit produced is a good indication of BALANCE.

Puerto de Santa María, one of the three towns making and maturing SHERRY. **Puerto Fino** is the name given to a FINO matured in Puerto de Santa María.

Puglia, Italian name for what is known by English speakers as Apulia, the long (350 km/ 210 mile) and fertile region along the Adriatic coast in Italy's extreme south east (see map under ITALY) which has long been of major importance for the production of wine and TABLE GRAPES. A MEDITERRANEAN CLIMATE and a predominance of soils well suited to grape-growing (a CALCAREOUS base from the Cretaceous era overlain by topsoils rich in iron oxide from the Tertiary and Quaternary eras) have created an ideal viticultural environment. Its name derives from the Roman *a-pluvia* or 'lack of rain'. It has about 100,000 ha/ 250,00 acres of land dedicated to the vine, and an average annual wine production of just over 7 million hl/185 million gal, but in the 1980s it was sometimes 13 million hl. Today it rivals Sicilia for second place in Italy's league of most productive regions, but both are now well behind Veneto. Many growers have taken subsidies from the EUROPEAN UNION to grub up their vineyards but, unfortunately, many of these were of low-yielding bushvines, while those remaining tend to be high-cropping inferior varieties planted on fertile soils.

A large part of the region's viticultural production is utilized, now as in the past, as anonymous ingredients in BLENDING that are usefully high in alcohol, as a base for VERMOUTH, or is either compulsorily distilled or transformed into GRAPE CONCENTRATE for ENRICHMENT as part of efforts to drain the European WINE LAKE. Production of DOC wines in Puglia rarely exceeds 2 per cent of the regional total, and less than a quarter of the regional production is ever sold in bottle. Although Puglia is fortunate in its topography, with a virtual absence of the hard-to-cultivate rocky, arid hills and mountains which dominate neighbouring CAMPANIA, MOLISE, and BASILICATA, over 70 per cent of vineyards are in the plains, where evenings and nights offer little relief from the torrid daytime TEMPERATURES. High YIELDS are the rule, and a significant number of DOCs have lost credibility with excessively tolerant production limits: 98–105 hl/ ha (6–7 tons/acre) in the Castel del Monte DOC, 98–126 hl/ha in many of the various DOCs where NEGROAMARO, Puglia's most interesting native variety, is cultivated. Even the Primitivo di Manduria DOC, with a more reasonable limit of 63 hl/ha, seems to hold little attraction for local producers. Of a potential total declaration of more than 24,000 hl/633,600 gal from the 540 ha/ 1,330 acres designated for this DOC, fewer than 2,000 hl/52,800 gal are declared in a typical vintage.

Viticulturally, the region can be divided in three: in the north, on the flatlands around Foggia, large volumes of undistinguished wine are churned out from tendone-trained TREBBIANO, SANGIOVESE, and MONTEPULCIANO; in the central part, inland from the sea around Barletta, where the UVA DI TROIA can produce some decent wines under the Castel del Monte DOC, and where Montepulciano is showing

Vines in autumn on Waiheke island near Auckland in New Zealand's North Island. The brilliant possible **sunlight** and unpolluted atmosphere of New Zealand is thought to contribute to the wines' bright fruit and pungent flavours.

promise; in the south, the flat Salento peninsula produces many of Puglia's best wines from NEGROAMARO and PRIMITIVO.

The Salento peninsula, the heel of the boot, is home to eight DOCs based on Negroamaro: Alezio, Brindisi, Copertino, Leverano, Matino, Nardò, Salice Salento, and Squinzano. Negroamaro is found predominantly in the eastern half of the Salento peninsula, in the provinces of Lecce and Brindisi. When grown on GOBELET-trained vines in the narrow Salento peninsula, where the proximity of both the Adriatic and the Ionian seas brings a welcome cooling at night (see TOPOGRAPHY), it gives rich, spicy wines of considerable interest.

On the western side of Salento, the PRIMITIVO grape is dominant, with DOCs in Manduria and in its original homeland of Gioia del Colle. As an IGT Salento wine, it has enjoyed a boom since the late 1990s, where careful selection and modern vinification has resulted in wines of great appeal and value.

The Uva di Troia grape, used in several DOCs (the large one of Castel del Monte and the small ones of Rosso Barletta, Rosso Canossa, Rosso di Cerignola, Cacc'e Mmitte di Lucera) is considered by many a variety with real potential, so far ignored by producers deterred by its relatively low productivity.

Puglia was with Toscana one of only two regions to have its IGTs registered by the agreed date and it has six: Salento, Tarantino, Valle d'Itria, Daunia, Le Murge, and Puglia. This has resulted in an increase in VARIETAL wines such as Negroamaro del Salento and Uva di Troia di Puglia, many of them made by FLYING WINEMAKERS, sometimes using OAK.

CO-OPERATIVES are responsible for 60 per cent of Puglia's production. Some of them have experienced serious financial difficulties, but others have benefited from flying winemaker input. Meanwhile, many small growers have been persuaded to accept EU-funded VINE PULL SCHEMES and plant alternative crops.

D.T. & D.C.G.

Puisseguin-St-Émilion, satellite appellation of ST-ÉMILION in Bordeaux.

Puligny-Montrachet, village in the Côte de Beaune district of Burgundy's Côte d'Or producing very fine wines from CHARDONNAY and a tiny amount of less exalted red. Puligny added the name of its most famous vineyard, the GRAND CRU Le Montrachet, in 1879 and has benefited from the association ever since.

Puligny contains two grand cru vineyards in their entirety, Chevalier-Montrachet and Bienvenues-Bâtard-Montrachet, and two which are shared with neighbouring Chassagne: Le Montrachet itself and Bâtard-Montrachet. Below this exalted level, yet still among the finest of all white wines of Burgundy, are the PREMIER CRU vineyards. There are at least 13 of these, more if subdivisions

are counted. At the same elevation as Bâtard-Montrachet lie Les Pucelles (made famous by the excellence of Domaine Leflaive's version), Le Clavoillon, Les Perrières (including the Clos de la Mouchère), Les Referts, and Les Combettes, which produces the plump wines to be expected of a vineyard adjacent to Meursault-Perrières.

A little higher up the slope, at the same elevation as Le Montrachet, lie Les Demoiselles, Le Cailleret, Les Folatières (including Clos de la Garenne), and Champ Canet. Part of Les Demoiselles is classified as grand cru Chevalier-Montrachet but a very small slice remains as premier cru, being regarded, along with Le Cailleret, as the finest example.

Further up the slope, where the terrain becomes rockier and the soil almost too sparse, are Le Champ Gain, Les Truffières, Les Chalumeaux, and the vineyards attached to the hamlet of BLAGNY, which are designated as Puligny-Montrachet premier cru for white wines, and Blagny premier cru for reds.

The VILLAGE WINES of Puligny-Montrachet are less impressive, perhaps because the water-table is nearer the surface here than in neighbouring MEURSAULT, for example. This phenomenon also means that the deep cellars ideal for AGEING wine are rare in Puligny, and few of the village's growers can prolong BARREL MATURATION for more than about a year. Although the Leflaive and Carillon families can both trace their origins as vignerons back to the 16th century, there are surprisingly few domaines in Puligny and a substantial proportion of its produce is contracted to the NÉGOCIANTS of Beaune. Sauzet is a third fine family producer.

In centuries past, Puligny, though less noted than Chassagne for its red wines, grew a significant amount of Pinot Noir grapes. Little is now grown.

See also MONTRACHET, CÔTE D'OR, and map under BURGUNDY.   J.T.C.M.

Loftus, S., *Puligny-Montrachet* (London, 1992).

pulp, viticulturally, the soft tissue of grape berries inside the skin (also called the flesh or PERICARP) which is the source of the juice of the grape. The word may also be used by winemakers to refer to the solid matter that settles from the juice after must SETTLING. For more detail of grape pulp, see GRAPE.

B.G.C.

pumping over. Wine-making operation involving the circulation of fermenting red wine through the CAP created by the grape skins and other solids. The French term is REMONTAGE. This has the important effect of AERATION, avoiding the build-up of dangerous REDUCING CONDITIONS. It also prevents drying out of the cap and encourages the EXTRACTION of the skins' valuable colouring matter and TANNINS into the wine. It may be done either in a closed or open top vat, between one

and three times a day depending on the fermentation rate. The mechanical systems involved include some adaptation of the AUTO-VINIFICATION system, ROTOFERMENTERS, and tanks which incorporate automatic PUNCHING DOWN. See also DÉLESTAGE and MACERATION.

pumps, mechanical devices for **pumping,** moving liquids such as wine and suspensions of solids such as grape juice from one location to another. The most traditional—and some of the most modern (see WINERY DESIGN)—wineries depend on gravity, and the first generation of pumps required considerable manpower. Most modern pumps, however, are driven by electricity and come in a range of different designs and sizes which should be matched to the fluid to be moved.

MUST from the CRUSHER-DESTEMMER is usually moved to the DRAINING tank or FERMENTATION VESSEL by means of a diaphragm or off-centre helical screw-type pump because this type performs particularly well with solid suspensions, including LEES. Cloudy juice from the draining tank might well be moved by means of a centrifugal pump to the fermentation tank, and most of the semi-clear and clear wines being processed are also moved using these types of pump.

Misuse of pumps can easily lead to OXIDATION, and centrifugal pumps operated at very high speeds can lead to the shearing of some of the larger COLLOIDS, which results in a diminution of apparent BODY in a fine wine, but pumps have in general terms reduced wine costs and increased wine quality. Some modern pumps can move as much wine, as gently, in an hour as 100 men could do in a day, and with much less exposure to OXYGEN.

A.D.W.

punching down, the wine-making operation of breaking up and submerging the CAP of skins and other solids during red wine fermentation to stop the cap from drying out, to encourage the EXTRACTION of colour and TANNINS, and to encourage useful AERATION in the making of a deeply coloured red wine. Keeping skins and liquid in contact is relatively simple with small batches of fermenting grapes. In tanks filled to a depth of 1–1.5 m/3–4 ft, a person can physically mix the floating solids into the fermenting grape juice using a wooden punch, stick or paddle, or even his or her feet. The cap may also be punched down by special metal devices, either by man or mechanically. It is usually done between one and three times a day depending on the fermentation rate. The French term is PIGEAGE. See also MACERATION and DÉLESTAGE.

punt, optional indentation in the bottom of wine bottles, particularly common in bottles of sparkling wine. See BOTTLES for more details.

pupitre, French name for a hand riddling rack, traditionally used for RIDDLING sparkling wines by hand. For more details, see SPARKLING WINE-MAKING.

PVPP, polyvinylpolypirrolidone, a synthetic material used as a FINING AGENT and sometimes also used to remove pink or brown colours from white wines.   D.B.

PX, common abbreviation for the Spanish grape variety PEDRO XIMÉNEZ, and particularly for the dark, STICKY, ultra-sweet varietal FORTIFIED WINE made from it that is so fashionable in Spain and increasingly so elsewhere. MONTILLA-MORILES is the usual source and top-quality wines can be almost as dark and viscous as molasses.

Pyrenees, hilly Australian wine region in the Western Victoria Zone sandwiched between the Grampians to the west and Bendigo to the east, named after the mountains separating France from Spain.

pyruvate, three-carbon compound formed by YEAST at a midway stage in the complex FERMENTATION process. Depending on the amount of oxygen available, it is converted either to carbon dioxide and water or, preferably for wine-making, to ACETALDEHYDE and then ETHANOL.

pyruvic acid plays a key role in the fermentation and metabolism of carbohydrates, and is one of the FIXED ACIDS of wine. Unlike the main fixed acids, pyruvic acid is a relatively minor constituent and comes predominantly from the primary FERMENTATION and, in those wines in which it occurs, the MALOLACTIC FERMENTATION. Although pyruvic acid is usually present in such low concentration that it would have little effect on the overall acidity or flavour of a wine, nevertheless its formation during fermentation, and presence in wine, is of importance for two reasons. Firstly, because of the capacity of pyruvate to bind with SULFUR DIOXIDE: after ACETALDEHYDE, pyruvic acid is a major binding agent of sulfur dioxide, thus limiting the activity of the latter as an antioxidant and antimicrobial agent. Secondly, pyruvic acid, in common with acetaldehyde and a select few other wine constituents, has the capacity to react with ANTHOCYANINS to form low molecular weight derived pigments in red wines. When the major anthocyanin of *Vitis vinifera* red grapes is involved in this reaction with either acetaldehyde or pyruvic acid, the derived pigments known as the vitisins are formed. These derived pigments are of significance to red wine colour because of their stability, resistance to bleaching by sulfur dioxide, and their enhanced colour properties.   P.J.W.

QbA, or **Qualitätswein bestimmter Anbaugebiete**, is Germany's largest wine category, effectively the lower ranks of so-called QUALITÄTSWEIN, or 'quality wine'. The chief requirement of a QbA wine is that, as the direct translation suggests, all the wine in the bottle comes from only one of Germany's 13 specified wine regions (although see also LIEBFRAUMILCH). The grapes should also reach certain minimum ripeness levels in terms of MUST WEIGHT. These are carefully specified for each grape variety and for each region. The classic grape variety Riesling, for example, need reach a must weight of just 51 °OECHSLE (a potential alcohol of about 6.1 per cent, less than 15 °Brix) in the Ahr, Mittelrhein, and Mosel-Saar-Ruwer, while Roter Traminer and Ruländer must reach 72 °Oechsle in the southernmost wine region of Baden.

The wines also have to be made from recommended grape varieties and have to earn an AP NUMBER, but this is hardly very challenging. Unlike QMP wines, QbA wines may have their alcohol content increased by ENRICHMENT.

This category therefore includes the great majority of wines exported from Germany, all Liebfraumilch, and the sea of anonymous medium dry blends carrying such GROSSLAGE names as Piesporter Michelsberg and Niersteiner Gutes Domtal. In addition, many top wine producers make one or several QbA blends depending on the vintage, and there is an increasing tendency among quality-conscious growers to declassify to this category wines that would officially qualify by must weight as Kabinett or even Spätlese. Sometimes this is done in reaction to the often misunderstood or misleading meaning of the Prädikat terms and more often because the grower believes the wine will be better balanced for having been judiciously chaptalized.

The proportion of each vintage which qualifies merely as QbA rather than QmP can vary from less than 30 per cent in a very ripe VINTAGE such as 1997 (even less than in 2003), to 80 per cent in the unripe year of 1984.   J.R. & D.S.

QmP, or **Qualitätswein mit Prädikat**, now officially known as PRÄDIKATSWEIN, is Germany's category of usually superior wines. It means literally 'quality wine with distinction' and the PRÄDIKAT can qualify as one of six distinct subcategories, determined by the grapes' MUST WEIGHT, as specified below, together with certain stipulations as to how and when the grapes are picked. Unlike QBA wines, a QmP wine cannot have sugar added to it for the purposes of ENRICHMENT. Since the late 1980s, it has also been common for the best producers to choose to set themselves higher minimum must weights for each Prädikat than the official minima, or to choose to declassify wine for marketing reasons.

The proportion of the total German harvest which qualifies as QmP wine varies enormously with the weather conditions of each

Prädikat	Minimum °Oechsle/ potential alcohol (%)	
	Riesling in Mosel-Saar-Ruwer	Spätburgunder in Baden
Kabinett	67/8.6	85/11.4
Spätlese	76/10.0	95/13.0
Auslese	83/11.1	105/14.5
Beerenauslese, Eiswein	110/15.3	128/18.1
Trockenbeerenauslese	150/21.5	154/22.1

year. The cool weather of 1984 yielded a harvest of which only 7 per cent qualified as QmP, while the hot 1976 summer ripened 83 per cent of the entire crop to at least Kabinett level. Most of Germany's finest wines are QmP wines, one exception being some of the more experimental wines, notably some of those aged in BARRIQUE, which may have been refused an AP NUMBER on the ground that they lack TYPICALITY, as experimental wines are wont to do.

Precise OECHSLE levels are specified by law for each combination of grape variety and region. The table above gives the official minima for combinations at opposite ends of the spectrum.

See KABINETT, SPÄTLESE, AUSLESE, BEERENAUSLESE, TROCKENBEERENAUSLESE, and EISWEIN (which has the same must weight requirements as Beerenauslese but is produced from naturally frozen grapes) for more details.

Qualitätswein, German for 'quality wine'. In GERMANY, this bloated category encompasses about 95 per cent of each German vintage, including some very ordinary blends indeed, and excludes only TAFELWEIN and LANDWEIN. GERMAN WINE LAW recognizes two sorts of Qualitätswein: Qualitätswein bestimmter Anbaugebiete or QBA, often called simply Qualitätswein, and, usually recognizably superior, Qualitätswein mit Prädikat or QMP, now officially shortened to PRÄDIKATSWEIN.

In AUSTRIA, Qualitätswein is the category between Landwein and Prädikatswein, and it includes not only wine officially designated Qualitätswein, but also Austria's Kabinett wine. Qualitätswein must reach at least 15 °KMW (73 °Oechsle) and must refer to a wine area. Maximum yield is 9,000 kg/ha and the wine has to pass an analytical and sensory test. Qualitätswein may be chaptalized.

quality assurance is a general concept covering the way in which a business is organized so that the quality of the product is assured at all stages. As applied to a wine business, good quality assurance will ensure that the original potential of the grapes and wine is not lost on the way to the bottle. Quality assurance is the totality of all the management actions and procedures that set out to achieve this high standard, and therefore incorporates QUALITY CONTROL.

An internationally recognized standard of quality management is ISO 9001:2000. This standard imposes a discipline that demands a uniformity of action throughout the business every time, all of the time.

Another useful though simple tool is Hazard Analysis and Critical Control Points (HACCP). The manufacturing process is divided into its basic stages, then each stage is examined to determine the problems that could occur at each one (hazard identification). Each hazard is then assessed for its potential danger to the process (the hazard analysis). Those that constitute the greatest danger are identified as the critical control points, to which the maximum attention is given. This procedure is now considered so important that it is mandatory throughout the EUROPEAN UNION for anyone involved in food and beverage handling, and is gaining worldwide recognition. D.B.

Bird, D., *Understanding Wine Technology* (2nd edn, Newark, 2005).

quality control, the series of analyses and tests that verify a wine's palatability, stability (see STABILIZATION), compliance with regulations, TYPICALITY, and freedom from FAULTS and CONTAMINANTS. Most large wineries maintain laboratories capable of conducting all but the most difficult of the required analyses (see ANALYSIS), while smaller wine enterprises send samples to an independent commercial laboratory. For complete quality control, a chemical analytical laboratory, a microbiological laboratory, and a statistically controlled tasting panel are required. See also QUALITY ASSURANCE. See also SAMPLING. A.D.W.

quality in wine. The concept of quality is regularly used in connection with wine, both for marketing purposes and as a marker of personal evaluation. It is also widely used as an element in JUDGING in wine SHOWS. Nevertheless it is notoriously hard to pin down its precise nature. Even wine professionals comment at times that 'it is a matter of personal taste'. There are many—including Émile PEYNAUD—who argue that the denotation of quality is essentially the subjective enjoyment of pleasure, and others who claim that it exists only relative to other factors, such as PRICE or the circumstances of consumption. It is certainly true that our response to wine is in part idiosyncratic, dependent on varying physiological responses and the drinker's cultural background (see WINE AND PHILOSOPHY and TASTING) but that has not precluded a number of ways of trying to define quality. Whether wine quality has a SUBJECTIVE or objective nature is complex, as is the relationship of quality to preference. Arguably it is possible to assess a wine as high quality without actually liking it.

Some wine professionals believe that quality can be precisely measured. Certainly there are means such as GLYCOSYL-GLUCOSE ASSAY to evaluate grape quality, but Somers, formerly of the AUSTRALIAN WINE RESEARCH INSTITUTE, argues that, for red wines at least, it is possible to predict a wine's quality by using its ultraviolet absorbance to measure its PHENOLIC concentration. A more marketing-focused perspective is that a high-quality wine is one that is fit for its purpose, but given the complex motivations for drinking wine, this raises the question of precisely what the purpose is. The American oenologist Maynard AMERINE believed that wine is an aesthetic object and that its evaluation therefore calls for the use of aesthetic criteria.

Some commentators have suggested quality can be measured by such intrinsic indicators as a wine's BALANCE, LENGTH, intensity, harmony, varietal purity, and complexity. Such concepts are used in assessing wine throughout the world, although without any consistent application. Other means of grading quality, extrinsic to the drink itself, have also been used. These include the relationship of wine to the price it fetches, as in the best-known CLASSIFICATIONS. This does not however guarantee the actual organoleptic 'quality' of the drink as measured by critical or popular response.

Charters and Pettigrew suggest that drinkers consider that wine quality has a number of dimensions. Some of these are extrinsic to the wine, such as how it has been made; others are intrinsic, and include how the wine tastes (involving subdimensions such as concentration, balance, smoothness, drinkability, and interest), its capacity for AGEING, and its TYPICALITY. However, the most important quality dimension for consumers is the amount of pleasure afforded by the wine. Thus one can argue that for most drinkers quality has two components: a series of dimensions which catalyse quality and a sense of pleasure in the product which is the end result of those catalytic dimensions.

They also suggest a way out of the objective vs subjective quality conundrum. Employing a paradox which mirrors the sociological concept of intersubjectivity, it can be noted that wine drinkers often hold both perspectives simultaneously. Thus quality is partly objective, measured by external criteria which depend on a broad commonality in our response to the components of a wine (such as its balance and intensity) and subject to debate and agreement between drinkers. It is also partly personal, and related to the consumer's individual preference.

Charters, S., and Pettigrew, S., ' "I Like it But How do I Know if it's Any Good?": Quality and Preference in Wine Consumption', *Journal of Research for Consumers* (5), 2003.

—— and —— 'The Intrinsic Dimensions of Wine Quality: An Exploratory Investigation', *3rd Australian Wine Marketing Colloquium* (2003).

Somers, C., *The Wine Spectrum: An Approach Towards Objective Definition of Wine Quality* (Adelaide, 1998).

Country	Quality wine
France	VDQS, APPELLATION CONTRÔLÉE*
Italy	DOC*, DOCG
Spain	DO*, DOCa
Portugal	DOC
Germany	QbA*, QmP
Greece	OPE, OPAP* (see GREECE)
United Kingdom	Quality wine (see ENGLAND)
Luxembourg	Appellation contrôlée (see LUXEMBOURG)

* indicates the more important category, in terms of the amount of wine likely to carry the designation.

quality wine is not only an expression widely and loosely used for any wine of good quality, it is an official wine DESIGNATION throughout the EUROPEAN UNION, and therefore throughout most of Europe. The EU recognizes quality wine as the higher of its two general categories of wine: quality wine (which must be produced in a specified region—an indicator of European reverence for geography) and TABLE WINE. In English, it may be referred to as Quality Wine PSR, in French as VQPRD, or Vin de Qualité Produit dans les Régions Délimitées. Each member country has a different system to describe this designation, but most are based on a system of CONTROLLED APPELLATIONS (although the German system depends more on the level of natural, unaugmented SUGAR IN GRAPES, or ripeness).

The quality of the wine in each of these categories varies widely, as does the proportion of a typical vintage which qualifies as 'quality wine' in each country. Germany is notorious in classifying more than 95 per cent of every vintage as quality wine, while in France the proportion is slightly more than 50 per cent. Quality wine represents an increasing proportion of wine throughout Europe, approximately 25 (55 if IGT wines are included), 33, and 30 per cent respectively of the total wine production of Italy, Spain, and Portugal.

quarantine of imported plant material plays an important part in international viticulture, and can put a (necessary) brake on certain aspects of its development. Like any form of agricultural quarantine, it can annoy travellers but is designed to protect farmers from the ravages which may be caused by the introduction of pests and diseases from other countries or regions (see the history of DOWNY MILDEW, POWDERY MILDEW, and PHYLLOXERA). Most of the devastating pests and diseases of the vine species used commonly for wine production, *Vitis* VINIFERA, have in fact been spread from America, AMERICAN VINE SPECIES having developed a tolerance to these diseases which the European *vinifera* lacks.

Quarantine systems for viticulture are in place at national borders, and also sometimes at regional levels. Most wine-producing countries maintain strict quarantine on vine imports in an attempt to keep out the likes of

PIERCE'S DISEASE, and FLAVESCENCE DORÉE, both of which could ravage a region's viticulture if they were to spread. Quarantine would appear less effective for flavescence dorée than for Pierce's disease, as the former is now found in most grape-growing countries and is continuing to spread. Quarantine also works to reduce the spread of other fungal, virus, and BACTERIAL DISEASES as well as insect and nematode PESTS which might not be lethal but may cause significant commercial damage. Licences issued for importation are typically restricted to a few cuttings which are subjected to disease testing. The quarantine delays can be up to two years, but new diagnostic tests such as ELISA developed in the 1980s have reduced this period. Smuggling of vines is not unknown, especially when producers believe that they are disadvantaged by not having access to better varieties or CLONES. In a reference to the popular luggage manufacturers, smuggled vine importations are popularly known as 'Samsonite vines' (see Chardonnay in SOUTH AFRICA, for example).

Sometimes there are quarantine areas within national boundaries, such as those that exist in South Australia in an attempt to avoid the further spread of phylloxera. Some countries and regions are free of major pests or diseases. CHILE, for example, has remained free of phylloxera, even though it is present in Argentina just over the Andes. Increasing international competition in the wine market makes the possibility of sabotage from another region or nation by introduction of a pest or disease less fanciful. The economic health of many of the world's viticultural regions depends on effective vine quarantine being maintained, and continuing vigilance and community support are essential.   R.E.S.

Quarts de Chaume, extraordinary small enclave within the Coteaux du LAYON appellation producing, only in the best vintages and usually only as a result of NOBLE ROT infection, sweet white wines from BOTRYTIZED Chenin Blanc grapes or, increasingly, such grapes DRIED on the vine. Total annual production can often be as little as a few thousand cases, from just over 30 ha/74 100 acres of vineyard, supposedly the finest quarter, or *quart*, of the Chaume part near Rochefort-sur-Loire of Coteaux du Layon (see FRANCE, history, for details). The vineyards here have the advantage of a southerly exposition within a sort of amphitheatre. The brown SCHIST and carboniferous soils are distinctive and result in powerful wines, particularly since the average VINE AGE is high—with a maximum permitted YIELD of only 22 hl/ha (1.2 tons/acre), which is rarely achieved, few new investments are being made in this minuscule but potentially glorious appellation. The naturally high acidity of the Chenin Blanc grape endows these wines, very similar to those of nearby BONNEZEAUX, with impressive longevity. Domaine des

Baumard and Ch Pierre Bise make particularly fine examples.

quartz, a hard glossy mineral consisting of silicon dioxide in hexagonal crystalline form, which is present in most rocks, especially sandstone and granite. Flint is a form of quartz. Predominantly quartz soils are typically infertile but often have good drainage. See GEOLOGY.

Quatourze, one of the named CRUS within the Coteaux du LANGUEDOC appellation in southern France. Production of appellation wine in this small windswept zone just west of Narbonne is small and dominated by Ch Notre-Dame du Quatourze.

Queensland. Australia's northern state appointed a Minister for Wine in 2004, a portfolio which even South Australia does not duplicate. The reason is that in 2001 there were 39 wine producers; but by 2005 there were more than 140. This rate of growth outstrips every other state, and has forced a re-evaluation of the potential for viticulture on the eastern (coastal and adjacent ranges) side of the state.

Paradoxically, in the senior region of the **Granite Belt**, the rate of growth is less frenetic, a mere doubling in numbers to 48. Humidity and summer rainfall are less of an issue than spring frost, for this is a high altitude (700 m to 1,000 m) inland region with warm days and cold nights. Its principal white varieties are (in order of size) Chardonnay, Semillon, and Sauvignon Blanc (and 14 others), the red varieties Shiraz, Cabernet Sauvignon, and Merlot (likewise 14 others). The varietal pattern tells one that this is a normal region in climatic terms, with a two-thirds red, one-third white wine ratio. The state's largest winery, Sirromet, has its 100 ha of vineyards here, although its high-tech 800-tonne winery is on the coast south of Brisbane. It and several smaller wineries have made wines which have won gold medals at home and abroad and deserve to be taken seriously.

South Burnett was the first region to gain formal recognition as a GEOGRAPHIC INDICATION. In a remarkably short time, it has significantly surpassed the Granite Belt in size, crushing 80 per cent more. Here too several large wineries, notably Barambah Ridge with a crush capacity of 500 tonnes (much of it for other producers), Clovely Estate, and Stuart Range, all make wines of genuine quality.

Another 30 or so wineries are scattered along the Queensland coast and hillsides; although here the focus is fairly and squarely on the general LIFESTYLE tourist trade, there are more than a few wineries producing creditable wine as well as providing a host of scenic and other attractions.

Finally, there are wineries along the **Darling Downs** and further west, with historic Jimbour Wines at the northern end making

seriously good wine, and Lilyvale Wines, at the southern end in the nascent southern Darling Downs region abutting the New South Wales border, making fine Semillon.   J.H.

Halliday, J., numerous works including *The Wine Atlas of Australia and New Zealand* (2nd edn, Sydney, 1998).

Australia Wine Companion (Sydney, annually).

quercetin, also spelt **quercitin,** a yellow dystuff belonging to the FLAVONOL family, originally extracted from the bark of black oak (QUERCUS), now synthesized.

Quercus is the botanical genus to which oak belongs and is therefore the most important family of plants to wine after the vine genus VITIS since it provides both CORK and wine's most classic storage material (OAK). It is subdivided into two subgenera, *Cyclobalanopsis*, and *Equercus*, to which all oaks used for wine containers and corks belong. The species most commonly used for BARRELS are the American white oak *Quercus alba*, and the European oaks *Quercus robur* and *Quercus petraea*. For more details, see OAK.

The species whose bark is stripped to provide cork is *Quercus suber*.

Quercy, Coteaux du, VDQS between Cahors and Gaillac in SOUTH WEST FRANCE for reds and rosés made from Cabernet Franc and other Bordeaux grape varieties.

Quincy, rapidly expanding, historic white wine appellation in the greater Loire region producing racy dry wines from Sauvignon Blanc grapes from about 170 ha/420 acres of sand and gravel on the left bank of the Cher tributary. Its long history (it was the second APPELLATION created, after Châteauneuf-du-Pape) and early popularity owe much to its proximity to RIVER transport (especially in comparison with the much smaller nearby appellation REUILLY). The wines tend to be a little more rustic, less delicate, than those made in Menetou-Salon and Sancerre to the east.

See also LOIRE, including map.

quinta, Portuguese word meaning 'farm', which may also refer to a wine-producing estate or vineyard. Single-quinta ports are those made from a single year and from a single estate in the Douro valley; see PORT.

Liddell, A., and Price, J., *Port Wine Quintas of the Douro* (London, 1992).

Mayson, R., *Port and the Douro* (London, 1999).

Quinta do Noval. Founded in 1813, Noval is the name of both the estate and the leading Portuguese, and unusually vineyard-based, PORT shipper. Quinta do Noval was owned by the firm António José da Silva, who in 1973 changed their name to Quinta do Noval-Vinhos, because Noval represented their finest wine (and they also wanted to avoid confusion with all the other da Silva companies in

OPORTO). The estate of Quinta do Noval, in the Pinhão valley, enjoyed a heyday in the mid 20th century when run by Luiz Vasconcellos Porto, before being inherited by the Van Zeller family. The firm's vineyards produce well over 30 per cent of their needs, with the remainder being bought in from other properties in the DOURO valley. Noval's most prestigious wine is Nacional, produced from 2.5 ha/5 acres of vines which are not GRAFTED on to PHYLLOXERA-resistant American ROOTSTOCKS and are therefore 'national'. These vines yield particularly small quantities of fruit, so that a Nacional vintage port is made only in exceptional years. The wines these ungrafted vines produce are amongst the most concentrated of all vintage ports, however, with a deeper colour and much fuller texture than others. This results in these ports commanding high prices on the market, with the Nacional 1931 VINTAGE (which Noval was virtually alone in declaring) enjoying almost legendary status as the most expensive port ever sold (for $5,900 in 1988 in the Bahamas). Quinta do Noval has continued to age its wines in air-conditioned lodges in the Douro valley rather than in VILA NOVA DE GAIA and continues to ship its wines direct from a new warehouse built at Alijo in the 1990s.

In 1993, the firm was acquired by the French insurance company AXA, and its winery, vineyards, and reputation have since been fully restored with more than three-quarters of the vineyard area having been replanted, mainly with Touriga Nacional and Tinto Cão, innovatively retaining the original vineyard TERRACES while adapting them for modern cultivation wherever possible. A third vintage port Silval, made from bought-in grapes, was introduced in 1995.

R

Rabo de Ovelha, white grape variety grown in Portugal, particularly the Alentejo, taking its name from the 'ewe's tail' shape of its bunches. Noted more for alcohol than subtlety. Also known as **Rabigato** (cat's tail) in Vinho Verde country and the Douro. Total plantings were 2,700 ha/6,700 acres in 2004.

Raboso, tough red grape variety grown in the VENETO region of north east Italy, notably as Raboso Piave, sometimes called Friulano, on the flat valley floor of PIAVE. Raboso Veronese is grown in the provinces of Padova (Padua), Treviso, Venezia, and Rovigo. The name is thought to derive from the Italian *rabbioso*, or angry, presumably a reference to consumer reaction to the uncompromisingly high ACID-ITY and rough TANNINS which characterize the grape and its wine. This is a grape variety which has excellent resistance to disease and rot, but which makes CABERNET SAUVIGNON look rather mellow. Unfortunately Raboso is not notably high in the ALCOHOL which might compensate for its astringency and can therefore taste extremely austere in youth. Stalwart defenders of the variety insist that with prolonged FERMEN-TATION, oxygenated by frequent PUMPING OVER, and lengthy CASK AGEING, the grape could give distinguished wines, Veneto's answer to the Nebbiolo of Piemonte or the Sangiovese of Toscana. The reputation and price level of Raboso make it difficult to justify this kind of investment, and vineyard plantings, which continue to decline, reflect this fact. Raboso is a permitted VARIETAL of the Piave DOC but only just over 2,300 hl/5,800 gal are made each year.

Raboso is also planted, to an extremely limited extent, in Argentina, presumably taken there by Italian immigrants.   D.T. & D.C.G.

rack and return, see DÉLESTAGE.

racking, the wine-making operation of re-moving clear wine from the settled SEDIMENT or LEES in the bottom of a container. The verb to **rack** has been used thus at least since the 14th century.

Racking is usually achieved by pumping or siphoning the wine away from the sediment into an empty container but special large **rack-ing tanks** are used by some large wineries (and breweries). They are equipped with drain lines, the lower ends of which can be adjusted to just clear the sediment layer and permit more rapid and more complete wine removal from the solids.

Racking, or *soutirage* as it is known in French, forms an important part of the annual cycle of cellar work, or ÉLEVAGE, in the production of most fine wines matured in small BARRELS. Racking from barrel to barrel is very LABOUR intensive and, with the cost of the barrels themselves, one of the chief economic argu-ments against BARREL MATURATION. Each racking inevitably involves a barrel that needs cleaning.

According to classical *élevage*, the first rack-ing takes place soon after FERMENTATION and the ensuing MACERATION to separate the new wine from the gross LEES. In cooler regions, the second racking typically takes place just after the first frosts of winter have precipitated some of the TARTRATES, while in many cellars there is a third in spring and a fourth before the full heat of the summer. Wines may be racked once or twice during a second year in barrel. New World winemakers have tended to rack less frequently.

Racking is not only part of the CLARIFICA-TION process, it also provides AERATION, which, in the case of red wines, is essential to the for-mation of PIGMENTED TANNINS and is beneficial to the sensory properties of the wine. Aeration also discourages REDUCTION of any excess SUL-FUR to malodorous HYDROGEN SULFIDE.

rack, wine. Common storage for wine bot-tles. See CELLAR.

Raffiac, sometimes **Raffiat**, alternative names for ARRUFIAC.

railways. Until the arrival of a railway in their region, wine producers were almost to-tally dependent on water-borne means of transport. Without access to the sea or a nav-igable RIVER or canal, transport was too diffi-cult and expensive for all but the finest and rarest wines. This gave an overwhelming ad-vantage to regions such as BORDEAUX, which were served by a major port, or CHAMPAGNE, with access to the river system of northern France.

The construction of the railways enabled a number of wines previously unknown outside their region to be exported. In some cases—notably CHIANTI in central Italy and RIOJA in northern Spain—this enabled high-quality wines to achieve their deserved recognition for the first time. The construction of a railway line between the town of JEREZ and the coast in the mid 19th century greatly encouraged ex-ports of SHERRY.

The railways also facilitated the transport of inferior wines. They allowed the late 19th-century development of the mass-production vineyards of the LANGUEDOC and ROUSSILLON in the south of France, whose rough wines were transported in vast quantities to northern France and Belgium, thus ruining such mar-ginal northern European vineyards as those around ORLÉANS and, to a lesser extent, those of the French MOSELLE. The railways in ARGEN-TINA were also crucial in establishing Mendoza as an important wine region so far from the capital Buenos Aires. During the 15 years of PROHIBITION in North America, efficient rail transport of fresh grapes from California to the suddenly numerous HOME WINEMAKERS in the eastern states played a part in maintaining a wine-making tradition in the United States.

          N.F.

rainfall, a component of climate which affects grapevines in many and conflicting ways.

For vines depending directly on rainfall (see DRYLAND VITICULTURE), there needs to be enough rain, at the right times, to promote adequate growth and to avoid severe WATER STRESS during ripening. On the other hand, more than enough rainfall can lead to excessive vegetation growth and a poor CANOPY MICRO-CLIMATE, especially on soils high in nitrogen. It can also cause waterlogging on soils prone to it (see DRAINAGE).

The effects of irregular rainfall are moderated to the extent that the soil has sufficient depth and water-holding capacity, and is well enough drained for the vine roots to survive at depth (see SOIL WATER, SOIL DEPTH, TERROIR).

Alternatively, insufficient rainfall and/or insufficient soil water-holding capacity can be overcome by IRRIGATION. This is especially important in MEDITERRANEAN CLIMATES where the summer is dry. Under all these regimes the practical minimum annual rainfall for commercially adequate yields is somewhere around 500 mm/20 in in cool viticultural climates, rising to about 600–750 mm/24–30 in in warm to hot climates.

Hot regions with full irrigation typically have 300 mm/12 in of annual rainfall or less, and mostly depend on rivers, aquifers, or wells to provide water for their supply. The normal unreliability of what rainfall they do get means that full wetting of the soil profile seldom occurs naturally, and frequent heavy watering is usually needed throughout the growing and ripening season.

No particular upper limit of rainfall is apparent for viticulture, provided that the soils are well drained, leached SOIL NUTRIENTS can be replaced, SUNLIGHT is enough, and HUMIDITY is not so high that FUNGAL DISEASES cannot be controlled. Some successful viticultural areas, such as the VINHO VERDE region in northern Portugal, and parts of southern SWITZERLAND, have annual rainfall totals exceeding 1,700 mm/67 in.

Heavy rain close to and at vintage is nevertheless nearly always detrimental to wine quality, especially if it follows water stress. The berries then swell suddenly and often split, resulting in fungal and bacterial infection of the bunches (see BUNCH ROT). At a minimum, the juice and its flavour are diluted. HAIL at this time is especially disastrous. J.G.

Raisin Blanc, white grape variety planted to a very limited extent in South Africa. It is the southern French variety known as Servin or Servan.

raisins, alternative generic name for DRYING GRAPES, from its direct French translation *raisins secs*, but also used specifically for relatively large, dark, dried grapes, particularly in California, where raisins are as important a viticultural crop as grapes for wine.

Grapes which have dried either on the vine or have been dried after picking, to produce either dried fruit or DRIED GRAPE WINES, are often described as fully or partially **raisined**.

Rajinski Rizling and **Rajnai Rizling,** various eastern European names for the true RIESLING grape of Germany.

Ramandolo. See VERDUZZO.

Ramisco, red grape variety grown exclusively in the shrinking COLARES region of Portugal and therefore probably the only VINIFERA vine variety never to have been GRAFTED. It can produce wines of real character that are extremely tannic in youth but the decline of the region has made them a rarity.

rancio, imprecise tasting term used in many languages for a distinctive style of wine, often FORTIFIED WINE or VIN DOUX NATUREL, achieved by deliberately MADERIZING the wine by exposing it to OXYGEN and/or heat. The wine may be stored in barrels in hot storehouses (as for some of Australia's LIQUEUR MUSCATS and Liqueur Tokays), or immediately under the rafters in a hot climate (as for some of ROUSSILLON's vins doux naturels), or in glass BONBONNES left out of doors and subjected to the changing temperatures of night and day (as in parts of Spain). The word rancio has the same root as 'rancid' and the wines which result have an additional and powerful smell reminiscent of overripe fruit, nuts, and melted, or even rancid, butter.

Key flavour compounds identified in aged vin doux naturel wines arise by Maillard reaction of sugars with amino acids and by oxidation. These compounds are known to be present in, and responsible for, the characteristic flavour of other sweet food products. Thus, for example, furaneol, cyclotene, maltol, sotolon, which are known contributors to the flavour of honey and caramelized sugar products, have been found in these wines along with several lactones that are important to the flavour of dried fruits.

This richness emerges in a complex series of sensations on the nose and palate. 'Rankness, a special character of fullness and richness', was the unflattering description given by Charles Walter Berry, the wine merchant who was Britain's leading cognac connoisseur between the World Wars (rancio can often be found in oak aged brandies). This richness, allied to a certain mild cheesiness in the nose, reminds some tasters of Roquefort cheese. But the richness, depth, and diversity of rancio can remind others of rich fruit cakes with their flavours of candied fruits, apricots, sultanas, almonds, and walnuts. N.F., J.R., & P.J.W.

Cutzach, I., Chatonnet, P., and Dubourdieu, D., 'Study of the formation mechanisms of some volatile compounds during the aging of sweet fortified wines', *Journal of Agricultural and Food Chemistry*, 47 (1999), 2837–46.

random oxidation, also known as sporadic post-bottling oxidation, describes the premature browning that occurs in some white wines some months after bottling. The problem is common enough for some industry figures to refer to it as the 'new CORK TAINT'. Wines are protected against oxidation through the addition of SULFUR DIOXIDE (SO_2) at bottling but if the level of free SO_2 falls too low, the wine is unprotected, and browning can occur. The main explanation is oxygen transfer through the cork, which seems to be highly variable. However, some scientists suspect that random oxidation may be caused by as yet poorly understood chemical reactions independent of the closure. It has been suggested that the addition of the antioxidant ASCORBIC ACID during wine-making to keep white wines fresh may have the paradoxical effect of rendering the added SO_2 less effective, and making some wines susceptible to oxidation. Another proposed cause is poor procedure or intermittent failure on the bottling line, allowing some wines to have much higher levels of dissolved oxygen from the outset. Random oxidation is mainly a problem with white wines: while oxygen ingress through the closure will certainly damage red wines, they are more resistant to oxidation because of their high PHENOLIC content. Oxidation is also more likely to be spotted in white wines because of the dramatic colour change that accompanies it.

Ranina, Slovenian synonym for the BOUVIER grape.

Rasteau, one of the more successful Côtes du Rhône villages in the southern RHÔNE making some wines to rival Châteauneuf-du-Pape. Its heady, typically very concentrated red, white, and rosé table wines have been sold as Côtes du Rhône-Villages, increasingly with the name Rasteau as a suffix, but a separate AC is being sought for its table wines. Some of the best producers are Domaines des Buisserons, Gourt de Mautens, La Soumade, and du Trapadis.

Wines sold as Appellation Rasteau Contrôlée have been for many years all VINS DOUX NATURELS, sweet mixtures of just-fermenting grape juice and pure grape spirit in various shades of brown and red. They are essentially alcoholic Grenache juice (90 per cent of the grapes must be GRENACHE Noir, Gris, or Blanc) treated to a range of AGEING processes which may vary from the negligible through various forms of CASK AGEING (usually in relatively ancient cooperage) to the sort of deliberate exposure to heat and oxygen that results in sticky brown liquids which can be sold as Rasteau RANCIO. Although Rasteau is the chosen name for this variable drink, the grapes may be grown anywhere in the communes of three Côtes du Rhône villages: Rasteau, Cairanne, and Sablet.

ratafia is an old, usually domestically produced wine made in the French countryside by drying grapes to a raisin-like state and then moistening and fermenting them in the spring. Ratafia de Champagne was the VIN DE LIQUEUR of Champagne, made by adding young grape spirit to hardly fermenting grape juice. Today however there are more profitable ways of selling the juice of Champagne grapes.

ratings, scores applied to individual wines. See NUMBERS AND WINE and SCORING.

Ratti, Renato (1934–88), industrious and dedicated winemaker based at La Morra in BAROLO in the north west Italian region of Piemonte. He did much to revolutionize winemaking techniques to make wines from the Nebbiolo grape drinkable at a much earlier stage in their evolution. As head of the local winemakers' association, he energetically promulgated the notion of TERROIR, and hastened the recognition of individual vineyards, or CRUS, in the LANGHE hills.

Räuschling, white grape variety today most commonly planted in German-speaking SWITZERLAND, where it can produce fine, crisp wines. In the Middle Ages, it was widely cultivated in Germany, particularly Baden (see GERMAN HISTORY). DNA PROFILING in Austria revealed a parent–offspring relationship with GOUAIS BLANC.

Ravat, French vine breeder who gave his name to a number of FRENCH HYBRIDS.

Ray, Cyril (1908–91), English war correspondent turned wine writer, famous more for his style and punctiliousness than for an obsession with wine itself. During the Second World War, he was a war correspondent, receiving several commendations for his courage and scrupulous accuracy in reporting. It was his service throughout the Italian campaign that aroused his first definite interest in wine—both the ordinary peasant wines and those of the highest quality served at more aristocratic celebrations of the liberation.

In 1956, he edited the first of what were to be perhaps his most lasting contribution to the LITERATURE OF WINE, 16 volumes of *The Compleat Imbiber*, compilations of stories, comments, and verses, although the 'pirate' edition, produced in later years without his seeing the proofs, provoked a special outburst of his famous rage against publishers. He also became wine correspondent of the *Observer* newspaper, *Punch* weekly magazine (where he was also a consultant to their purchases of wine), and the *Spectator*. Although he wrote on many different subjects, his wine columns greatly influenced sales. He was seldom interested in tasting young wines himself, however, his preferred drink often being Guinness stout.

Cyril Ray founded the British organization the Circle of Wine Writers and was its first president. He received a succession of awards and prizes for his wine writing including Commendatore, Italian Order of Merit, 1981, and Chevalier, French Order of Merit, 1985. Among his books were strongly historical monographs on LAFITE-Rothschild, WARRE, BOLLINGER, MOUTON-ROTHSCHILD, Langoa- and Léoville-BARTON, Ruffino Chianti, and, one of the last, Robert MONDAVI. His son Jonathan has followed him in to WINE WRITING.   P.V.P.

raya, Spanish word meaning 'stripe' or 'streak' and a term for the symbol used to classify SHERRY must. A *raya* is also a coarse style of OLOROSO used in blending medium dry sherry.

RDI, see REGULATED DEFICIT IRRIGATION.

Rebe, German for vine. **Rebsorten** are vine varieties.

Rebula, Slovenian name for RIBOLLA.

Recioto, distinctive category of north east Italian DRIED GRAPE WINES, a historic speciality of VENETO. The word derives from the Italian for ear, *orecchio*, because the wine was originally produced only from the ripest grapes in the bunch, from the upper lobes, or ears, although selected whole bunches have long been substituted. The most common forms of Recioto are sweet red Recioto della VALPOLICELLA and the much rarer sweet white Recioto di SOAVE.

Recioto della Valpolicella, like its dry counterpart AMARONE, is produced from 40 to 80 per cent CORVINA, the great native grape of Valpolicella, and 5 to 30 per cent RONDINELLA, with up to 15 per cent of other red grapes authorized to be planted in the province of Verona; like Amarone, these grapes need to be raisined in special drying rooms during the late autumn and winter months after the harvest; like Amarone it is produced in the Valpolicella DOC zone which has been divided into a CLASSICO subzone and a larger zone whose wines are simply called Recioto. As for Amarone, DOCG status was achieved in 2009. The wine is a decisively sweet one as the grapes need by law to be dried for at least a month longer than those used for Amarone. The earliest date at which the grapes for Amarone can be crushed is 1 December, while for Recioto it is the 1 January following the vintage. A certain development of NOBLE ROT has been virtually inevitable, given the damp climate of Valpolicella during the months of raisining, but producers are seeking to eliminate it today as it lends an OXIDIZED character to the wine. Some producers are also experimenting with new barrels of 400- to 500-l/132-gal capacity in place of the traditional, considerably larger casks of old Slavonian oak.

Recioto represents a very small proportion of Valpolicella's total production: 4,000–5,000 hl/105,000–132,000 gal in recent years. About 1,800 hl of Recioto di Soave DOCG are produced. This sweet white wine is made almost exclusively from dried Garganega grapes. Most producers encourage the development of NOBLE ROT during this drying process, which lasts until March.   D.T. & D.C.G.

récolte, French for HARVEST. A **récoltant** is therefore a GROWER. In CHAMPAGNE, a **récoltant-manipulant** (identified by 'RM' on the label) is a grower who also makes his or her own champagne, of whom there are more than 2,000 in the region, as opposed to a **récoltant-coopérateur,** who sells champagne made by a CO-OPERATIVE, of whom there are slightly fewer.

recorking, a hazardous exercise conducted by some top wine producers and some fine wine traders. The aim is to prolong a wine's potential longevity after extended BOTTLE AGEING may have weakened the cork. Ch LAFITE occasionally sends its MAÎTRE DE CHAI on recorking tours which have doubled as public relations exercises. With plenty of advance notice, bottles can be assembled from various CELLARS and COLLECTORS. He eases the old cork out and, ideally, tops up the bottle as necessary with the same, and certainly similar, vintage of Lafite. Some documentary evidence of this operation is provided. The FINE WINE market became suspicious of recorking in any circumstances other than the most public in the late 1980s, however, as it potentially offers too much possibility for ADULTERATION AND FRAUD. PENFOLDS were the first New World wine producer to offer a recorking service, for their Grange South Australian red.

rectified grape must, or **RGM**, is preserved GRAPE JUICE that has been rectified, processed to reduce the concentration of solids other than SUGARS. It is generally further treated by removing water to yield **rectified concentrated grape must,** or **RCGM**, which is a common commodity used principally in Europe for ENRICHMENT. The EUROPEAN UNION authorities have been keen to promote its use in place of sugar as a way of helping reduce the European WINE LAKE. Many winemakers who need to use it in northern Europe have a natural antipathy to introducing a product made from what they view as inferior grapes. There are several major producers of RGM in Europe who absorb SURPLUS grape production from areas such as the LANGUEDOC, SICILIA, and PUGLIA. They submit it to such modern technological processes as ION EXCHANGE and REVERSE OSMOSIS together with super-efficient FILTRATION and evaporators to produce what is in effect a concentrated invert sugar (GLUCOSE and FRUCTOSE) solution from grape juice. See also CONCENTRATION.

Redding, Cyrus (1785–1870), England's answer to the great wine explorer of France, André JULLIEN. Redding came from an old Cornish family and, after publishing several biographies and histories when working as a young journalist in London, was sent to Paris in 1814, where he was based for five years. It was during this time that he was introduced to wine regions and a wine-producing culture. Jullien's book was published two years after his arrival in Paris and Redding's most important work, *A History and Description of Modern Wines*, takes full account of both Jullien and CHAPTAL's previous publications, but Redding seems to have been independently inspired by the disparity between the wines then available in the British Isles and what he tasted in cellars all over Europe (see ADULTERATION). Like Jullien, he was an intrepid traveller and his book includes observations not just on European wines but on those of Asia, Africa, and both North and South America. His emphasis on the word Modern owes much to his criticism of earlier writers such as Sir Edward Barry and Alexander HENDERSON (see LITERATURE), whose reverence for CLASSICAL WINES he felt was misplaced. The first edition of *A History and Description of Modern Wines* was written when Redding had returned to England in 1833; modern facsimile editions have also appeared, so useful, fresh, and unpretentious are Redding's observations to this day.

Redondo, subregion of ALENTEJO in southern Portugal with a large co-operative winery.

redox potential, or oxidation–reduction potential, is a measure of the summation of all of a wine's components' potentials to oxidize. Since wine is made up of components that are either oxidized or reduced (see OXIDATION and REDUCTION), it is a system composed of many joined redox pairs. Oxidation reactions are always coupled to reduction reactions. Electrons made available from an oxidation are taken up by the compound being reduced until an equilibrium is established. The reaction with the most positive value (in which electrons are most easily accepted) will occur at the expense of reactions with lower values. Thus an equilibrium is reached from all the redox pairs and a net redox potential can be determined.

Redox potentials are of only limited value to even the most scientific winemaker, however, since they do not express how rapidly the various reactions will occur. They reveal only the potential situation that will obtain given unlimited time. Redox potentials can also prove to be difficult to measure in practice. A determination of the concentration of dissolved OXYGEN in a given wine can often

prove to be of more value in guiding the winemaker in his or her choice of cellar treatments.

A.D.W.

Zoecklein, B., 'Understanding oxidation: redox potential', *Vineyard & Winery Management* (Nov–Dec 1989), 32–3.

reduced-alcohol wines are those with a lower than normal ALCOHOLIC STRENGTH, generally less than 5.5 per cent.

The easiest and cheapest way to produce these low-alcohol products is simply to dilute wine using water (to make a SPRITZER-type drink), natural or flavoured fruit juices, or even GRAPE JUICE to make an all-vinous product. See wine COOLERS.

Another method is to arrest fermentation before it is complete by refrigeration, resulting in a sweet, low-alcohol, often lightly sparkling drink. This is a particularly common technique in Italy and is conducted at all sorts of quality levels, from the finest MOSCATO D'ASTI to partial fermentation of LAMBRUSCO must stored throughout the year at low temperatures and transformed into relatively industrial 'Lambrusco Light' as required.

See also DEALCOHOLIZED WINE.

reduction, chemical reaction that is in effect the complement of OXIDATION and one in which an element or compound gains electrons. The essential feature of an oxidation is that electrons are transferred from the component being oxidized to the one being **reduced**. The reaction cannot be isolated; to have a reduction, something else must be oxidized. A reduction is simply the passing of electrons from one substance to another. Common reduction reactions are those of iron ore to iron the metal, or the reduction of ACETALDEHYDE to ETHANOL as happens in the final stage of alcoholic FERMENTATION. Wine in a stoppered bottle or other airtight container is said to be in a **reductive** state because any reaction that takes place within it reduces the possibilities for further change by using up some of the available OXYGEN.

Reducing conditions such as these are desirable towards the end of fermentation (unlike at the beginning when oxidizing conditions encourage yeast growth) in order that alcohol is produced along with the carbon dioxide from the acetaldehyde. Reducing conditions continue to be generally preferable throughout ÉLEVAGE of wine in the cellar, especially for white wines, which can withstand oxidation much less well than reds with their higher content of PHENOLICS.

Wines, especially red wines held in the absence of oxygen, may suffer from excess reduction, resulting in the slow POLYMERIZATION of TANNINS and PIGMENTED TANNINS. **Reduction** is also used as a convenient, but rather inaccurate, term to describe the formation of sulfur compounds such as HYDROGEN SULFIDE, MERCAPTANS, and thiols, which tend

to form under reducing conditions. Typical descriptors for such compounds include rotten eggs, garlic, struck flint, cabbage, rubber, and burnt rubber. Such reduction is usually considered to be a wine fault, although sulfur compounds can add complexity at lower levels, depending on the wine style. In some cases, reduction faults can be cured by AERATION, perhaps careful RACKING, an operation which introduces some oxygen, an oxidizing agent strong enough to prevent the reduction of most sulfur compounds.

Reduction has become a much-debated topic in the wine trade since the more widespread adoption of tin-lined SCREW CAPS as closures. These make a near-impermeable seal and some commentators have suggested that the reductive conditions they create may discourage the loss of an aroma of struck flint, attributed to reduced sulfur compounds in some wines. The extent of this phenomenon is currently unclear because it is not unique to wines bottled with screw caps and because the gas impermeability of a very good cork has been shown to be equivalent to that of a screw cap. What is clear is that reductive characters can appear in a wine regardless of the closure, unless these characters have been prevented or removed during the wine-making process. See also REDOX POTENTIAL.

A.D.W., P.J.W., & J.A.G.

Goode, J., *Wine Science* (London, 2005).

red wine-making, the production of wines with reddish to purple colours. The great majority of red wines made today depend on CRUSHING and DESTEMMING of the grape clusters or bunches as a first step in their production (although see also WHOLE BUNCH FERMENTATION and CARBONIC MACERATION).

The mixture of skins, seeds, and some stem fragments, along with the juice, then goes into a FERMENTATION VESSEL, where YEAST converts SUGARS into ALCOHOL. The natural ANTHOCYANIN pigments, which are contained in the skins of black grapes, along with FLAVOUR COMPOUNDS, FLAVOUR PRECURSORS, and large amounts of PHENOLICS (the latter originating from both the skins and seeds) are extracted into the fermenting wine by the alcohol produced by yeast during FERMENTATION and MACERATION. Without some maceration of juice and skins, wine made from dark-skinned grapes is merely pink (as described in ROSÉ WINE-MAKING). Duration of this EXTRACTION process can be anything from a fast two- or three-day fermentation for an everyday wine to a week-long fermentation followed by a further one, two, or even three weeks' maceration for a full-bodied red wine that is designed to age.

Red wine fermentations are almost always conducted at TEMPERATURES higher than those used for white wines. Red wines fermented at lower temperatures tend to be lighter in colour and body and to display the fruitier range

Red wine-making

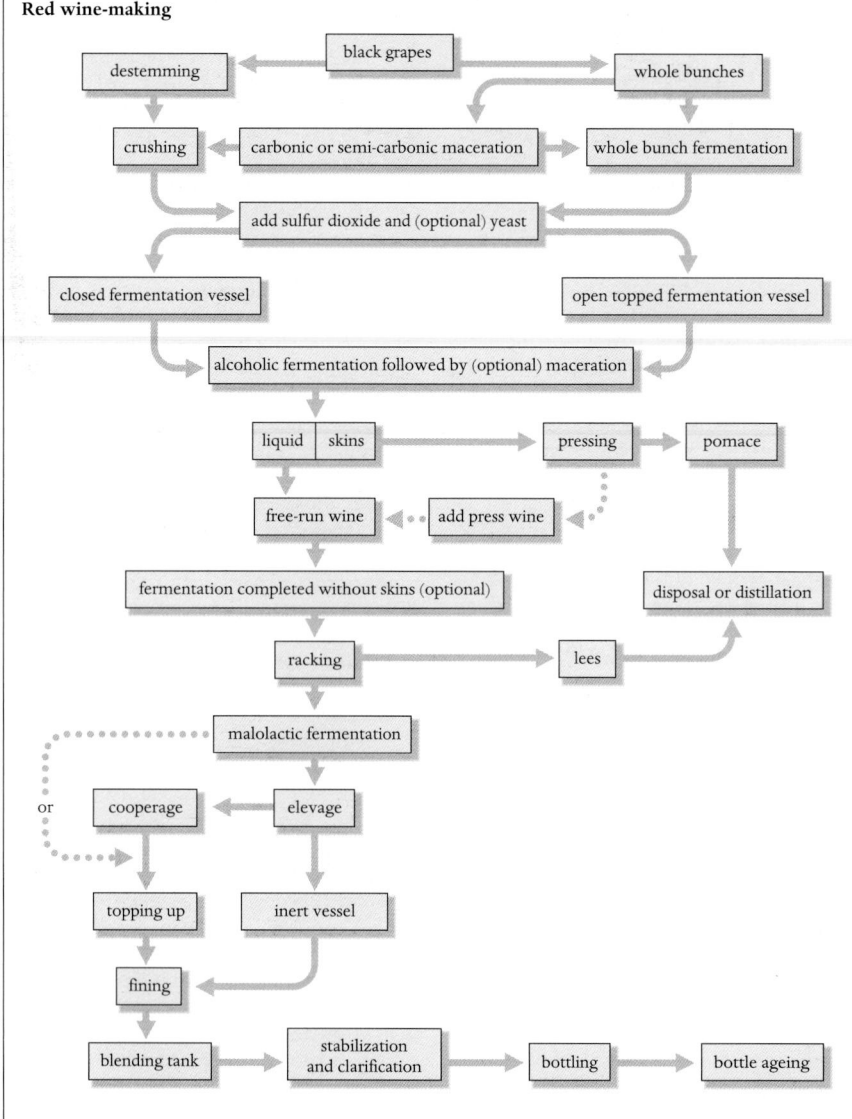

of ESTERS. There is usually some producer somewhere in the world deliberately fashioning light reds in this style to be consumed chilled.

Red wine-making differs from white wine-making not only in terms of skin–juice contact and temperature but also because some exposure to OXYGEN is more generally desirable than with white wines, and BARREL MATURATION, or at least CASK AGEING, is also more common for red wines than white. Because red wine-making extracts many flavour compounds and GLYCOSIDES from the grape skins, and phenolics from both the seeds and skins, red wines contain a higher concentration and wider range of compounds than white wines and are thus capable of developing a complex BOUQUET after prolonged storage in bottle. The phenolic compounds extracted from skins, seeds, and stem fragments react more or less slowly with oxygen dissolved in the wine to

form PIGMENTED TANNINS and these, together with the colourless TANNINS that were extracted directly or formed during the maceration, contribute to the TEXTURE of the wine.

During barrel maturation, when the oxygen supply to the wine is restricted to that introduced during TOPPING UP, a further range of flavour compounds is introduced. Both the substances produced in the earlier reactions between grape phenolics and oxygen and those derived by HYDROLYSIS of the wood lignin and cellulose, as well as extraction of the wood phenolics, interact and contribute an entirely new range of flavours (see OAK FLAVOUR).

Further reactions of the grape- and wood-derived phenolic constituents, and augmentation of the grape-derived flavour compounds by hydrolysis of flavour precursors all progress during BOTTLE AGEING. The abundance and great diversity of compounds available in a

red wine are the reasons that AGEING assumes particular importance for fine red wines. See also WINE-MAKING.   A.D.W. & P.J.W.

red wines actually vary in COLOUR from dark pink to almost black, with an enormous variation in the amount of blue or yellow to be seen at the rim. Their colour depends on the grape varieties used, the vintage characteristics, the health of the grapes, the wine-making methods (in particular the extent of MACERATION), the wine's PH, and the amount of time it has spent in tank, barrel, and bottle. A red wine that has suffered OXIDATION or is many decades old may be the same deep tawny colour as a very old white wine.

Red wines are produced in virtually all of the world's wine regions, although the proportion of red wines produced at the cool limit of wine production is low, since it can be difficult to develop sufficient pigmentation of most grapes' skins to produce a proper red wine (although see also TEINTURIERS).

French for red is *rouge*, Italian is *rosso*, Spanish and Portuguese more expressively *tinto*, Russian is *cherny*, and German is *rot*. Spain divides her red wines into those which really are *tinto* and lighter ones called CLARETE.

It has been only since the development of BOTTLES suitable for AGEING wine that red wines have been seen in any sense superior to white (see Ancient GREECE, ROME, medieval ITALY, and FASHION).

reflection from soils and in some cases from water is considered by some to influence wine quality. Very white soils, such as the ALBARIZA soils of JEREZ, do indeed reflect high proportions of sunshine, and can add to the heating of vines growing on them. This is easy to demonstrate by calculation. More difficult to prove is the theory that sunlight reflected from rivers may benefit nearby vineyards, as in the Mosel valley. While the eye can behold the silvery sheen of water at low sun angles (specular reflection), it is unlikely that this can have any thermal effect on adjacent vineyards.
                                                              R.E.S.

Refosco is a group of distinct red varieties cultivated in north east Italy, Slovenia, and Croatia, most of them being related to the Slovenian Refošk (also called TERAN in Croatia) and producing very similar wines. The finest variety is known in Friuli as REFOSCO DAL PEDUNCULO ROSSO.   J.V.

Refosco dal Peduncolo Rosso, named after its red stem, is a member of the REFOSCO group of red grape varieties that makes usefully vigorous wine in the FRIULI region of north east Italy. It has a long history in the area, apparently praised by PLINY the Elder and reputedly producing the favourite wine of Livia, the second wife of Augustus Caesar, cited in the *Annals of Friuli* of Francesco di Manzano in 1390. DNA PROFILING at SAN MICHELE

ALL'ADIGE recently revealed a parent–offspring relationship with MARZEMINO, another ancient variety of Northern Italy.

This vine is cultivated both in HILLSIDE VINEYARDS and in flatter parts of Friuli and gives a deeply coloured wine with plummy flavours and a hint of almonds, a medium to full body, and a rather elevated ACIDITY which can be difficult to control or moderate, the variety being a notoriously late ripener. Refosco has the advantage of good resistance to autumn rains and rot.

There was a significant return of interest in Friuli's Refosco in the 1980s, and much greater care was taken in its cultivation and vinification in an effort to improve the wine's quality, including variable experiments with small barrels. The combination of new oak and high acidity is not always successful.

The most promising zone for Refosco is COLLI ORIENTALI and the Koper district in SLOVENIA. Others include GRAVE DEL FRIULI, LISON-PRAMAGGIORE (outside Friuli), Latisana, and Aquileia.   D.T. & J.V.

refractometer, an instrument for measuring refractive index, which is related to the amount by which the angle of a light wave is changed when passing through the boundary between two media. The amount of refraction is a convenient way to measure solute concentration of a solution and is widely used in viticulture and wine-making to follow the ripeness of grapes (by measuring MUST WEIGHT) and changes during vinification. Refractometers may be precision laboratory instruments or pocket versions that can be used in the vineyard. In either case, TEMPERATURE correction or control is important for accuracy.   B.G.C.

refrigeration, cooling process that has had a profound effect on how and where wine is made and how it tastes (see TEMPERATURE), enabling the winemaker to have a much greater degree of control than was possible before mechanical refrigeration became the norm for all but the least sophisticated wineries in the second half of the 20th century. More than any other factor, refrigeration has permitted warm and hot regions to produce wine of internationally acceptable quality.

Making wine
The essence of refrigeration is the transfer of heat from the body being refrigerated to some other place. The most obvious winery application of refrigeration is in the TEMPERATURE CONTROL of FERMENTATION—although refrigeration also allows winemakers to delay the processing of freshly picked grapes or must (see MUST CHILLING) until convenient, even in hot areas, where the use of chilled rooms to cool and store grapes prior to pressing is increasing. The energy generated by the conversion of sugar to alcohol, carbon dioxide, and water is only partly used by the YEAST in building

cells and by-products. The rest appears as heat, which, above a certain temperature, risks killing the yeast and therefore arresting the fermentation process. The amounts of heat generated by fermentation are large. Ten hl/ 260 gal of grape juice containing 20 per cent sugar will generate about 3.6 million kilocalories, or enough to melt 45 tons of ice.

Not all the heat generated has to be removed by refrigeration, however. Because heat moves naturally by conduction from hotter bodies to cooler ones with which they are in contact, warm fermenting wine loses heat to the walls of the FERMENTATION VESSEL and from the outside of the wall to the atmosphere. Some of the fermentation heat will be removed by radiation from the outside of the fermenting vessel too, provided its temperature is higher than that of the objects in its vicinity. Heat may also be lost by radiation if open-topped fermentation vessels are used, or by volatilization of some of the water and alcohol in the wine.

All of these natural heat removal processes that function independently of refrigeration occur at the surfaces of the fermenting mass. Heat production, on the other hand, occurs throughout the entire volume of the mass. The amount of heat removed from a fermenting mass therefore depends on the surface to volume ratio of the fermentation vessel. A 225-l/59-gal BARRIQUE, for example, will probably lose enough generated heat for the temperature to remain within an acceptable range for fermentation. A typical large tank, on the other hand, which might contain several hundred hectolitres, will certainly need active heat removal to keep the temperature of the fermenting mass below danger point.

The development of mechanical refrigeration in the early 20th century at least made cooling a possibility in areas where insufficient naturally cold water was available. Early efforts to control temperature, used in France as recently as the 1970s, included the simple addition of blocks of ice to the fermenting wine (with concomitant dilution). More mechanical early systems of refrigeration cooled the wine by running cold water through metal tubes suspended in the tank. The development of more efficient PUMPS permitted systems which moved wine from the tank through coils immersed in cold water and then back into the tank.

In modern wineries, however, wines are seldom moved for cooling purposes. STAINLESS STEEL tanks with cooling devices, usually coils, incorporated in the external walls are now standard wine equipment. Temperature-sensing probes in tanks signal a computer system which controls the supply of refrigerant to the coils to a level predetermined for each tank by the winemaker.

Refrigeration has become increasingly important in other wine-making processes, however. Some producers, notably in Australia,

store grape juice in refrigerated conditions for several months before fermentation. Others prior to fermentation, notably in parts of North America, New Zealand, and SAUTERNES, may apply heavy refrigeration to emulate the conditions necessary to produce EISWEIN (see freeze CONCENTRATION). The Burgundian vogue for cold MACERATION occasionally calls for refrigeration too. In warmer wine regions, some degree of refrigeration may be needed during wine maturation, and refrigerated tanks are routinely used for everyday wines to ensure that TARTRATES are not precipitated in bottle (see STABILIZATION).   A.D.W.

Serving wine
Refrigeration plays a part, and all too often a villainous part, in the SERVING of wine. Long before the advent of mechanical refrigeration, and its domestication, wine was deliberately chilled prior to serving (see Ancient GREECE, for example). It was fashionable to chill both red and white wines before serving at least from the 16th century. A wide range of wine coolers was used to achieve this until the 20th century, when mechanical refrigeration was domestically available. The modern successors of these large containers for both ice and bottles are the single-bottle wine coolers known as ice buckets and the gel-filled flexible sleeves kept frozen ready for use.

See also TEMPERATURE.

Regent, dark-skinned DISEASE-RESISTANT VARIETY bred at GEILWEILERHOF in Germany and first registered in 1989. This crossing of SILVANER × MÜLLER-THURGAU with CHAMBOURCIN has good colour and moderate acidity. It is grown to a limited extent in Germany and shows promise in the UK.

Região Demarcada, a demarcated region (RD) of PORTUGAL, although the expression is no longer seen on labels. See Denominação de Origem Controlada (DOC) for more details.

regionality, increasingly used New World term for the concept, now fully accepted there, that the location of a vineyard plays an important part in shaping the character of the wine produced from it. It is less geographically precise and, importantly, less French, than the term TERROIR.

More and more wines in, for example, California and Australia, where this new word was coined, are labelled and marketed on a geographical as well as VARIETAL basis, although many producers are wary of the restrictions that would ensue from CONTROLLED APPELLATIONS.

régisseur, French term used particularly of the director or manager of a Bordeaux estate.

Regner, declining, light-skinned German CROSSING made in 1929 from a white table grape Seidentraube and Gamay. Fewer than 90 ha/225 acres remained in 2003, mainly in Rheinhessen. Like OPTIMA and ORTEGA, it buds and ripens very early and can reach impressive must weights, even if at the expense of acidity. This is not generally a wine to drink as a VARIETAL (although tests in England's cool climate have been successful).

Régnié, the most recently created BEAUJO- LAIS cru (in 1988), is a tribute to communal spirit, or at least the spirit abroad in the neigh- bouring communes of Régnié-Durette and Lantignié, whose vignerons lobbied for years to be allowed to join the other nine crus. The 750 ha/1,850 acres of vines are some of the highest and most westerly of the crus immediately east of Beaujeu.

Reguengos, subregion of ALENTEJO in southern Portugal with a large and very suc- cessful co-operative winery.

regulated deficit irrigation (RDI), an IRRIGATION scheduling technique which uses mild WATER STRESS at key stages of fruit devel- opment to reduce vegetative growth and im- prove berry ripening and thus improve grape quality.

RDI was first applied on peach and pear orchards in Australia in the 1980s. Research showed that it restricted SHOOT growth with- out significantly affecting YIELD. It is now common practice in many vineyards in Austra- lia, especially in those planted to black grape varieties, due to the greater benefits to grape colour.

The main benefits of this strategically man- aged water stress are less competition between berry ripening and vegetative growth, better water conservation, and, especially with some varieties such as Syrah, reduced berry size. It requires very careful monitoring of SOIL WATER content and typically results in slightly lower yields. It is most effectively applied through DRIP IRRIGATION.

RDI is more stressful to the vine than PAR- TIAL ROOTZONE DRYING and its use in hot re- gions can cause problems if its application is followed by a spell of hot weather: vines with limited soil moisture can suffer extremes of water stress, which may, for example, lead to rapid loss of leaves. This situation can be alle- viated by carefully monitoring of weather fore- casts and applying some irrigation.

Water deficit is generally applied variably between fruit set and a month or so after veraison but is generally avoided in the later stages of berry ripening. The timing of the deficit still needs further evaluation. For ex- ample, experiments in Australia have shown that reduced irrigation prior to veraison causes a greater reduction in berry size than does less irrigation after veraison. However, the role of berry size in affecting wine quality is contentious.   R.E.S. & J.Ha.

Kriedemann, P. E., and Goodwin, I., *Irrigation In- sights 4: Regulated Deficit Irrigation and Partial Rootzone Drying* (Canberra, 2003).
McCarthy, M. G., Loveys, B. R., Dry, P. R., and Stoll, M., *Water Reports 22: Regulated Deficit Irrigation and Partial Rootzone Drying as Irrigation Management Techniques for Grapevines* (FAO, 2002).

Reichensteiner is a white grape variety whose creator Helmut BECKER maintained it was the first EUROPEAN UNION crossing, with French, Italian, and German antecedents. In 1978 he developed this crossing of Müller- Thurgau with a crossing of the French table grape MADELEINE ANGEVINE and the Italian Early Calabrese. Its antecedents are hardly noble and both wine and vine most closely re- semble its undistinguished German parent, but Reichensteiner with its looser bunches is less prone to rot and well-pruned plants stand a good chance of reaching QMP must weights in good years. There are fewer than 200 ha in Germany with more than half, as is so often the case with the newer crossings, in Rheinhessen. The variety, named, like EHRENFELSER, after a Rhineland castle, has been planted to a limited extent in New Zea- land and in ENGLAND, where it is the second most planted variety after SEYVAL BLANC.

religion and wine. Wine is a wonder- working substance, and is therefore linked to metaphysics and to ritual. At the heart of the miraculous qualities of wine is the ALCOHOL it contains, and its capacity for quickly chan- ging people's feelings, for better or worse.

Wine itself, however, has a quite specific history and geographical distribution (see ORIGINS OF VITICULTURE). It is associated with the peoples who live round the Mediterranean sea, in Europe, the Near East, and North Africa; and within this huge Circum-Mediterranean super-region the place of wine in the local values has been affected by the major revolu- tion in the area whereby the old order, which was apparently partly monotheistic, partly polytheistic, and which presumably dated back into prehistory, was replaced by Chris- tianity and ISLAM, rooted in the values of Ju- daic monotheism.

The different parts of the Circum- Mediterranean emerged from prehistory at different times, the western end of the Medi- terranean basin far later than EGYPT and the Levant, for example, while northern and east- ern Europe, outside the wine-producing area, acquired their first written records even later, and from Christian MISSIONARIES. A careful reading of the books of the Old Testament (see BIBLE) reveals the repeated emphasis on wine as a symbol of prosperity.

At a time when wine was so important to the prosperity of the human population, these people also saw it as a suitable offering to the superhuman authorities. Along with animal sacrifices, and offerings from other crops, LIBATIONS of wine were poured out to

the gods by Italians and Greeks, and there were similar practices in the Levant. Although Israel, in the form of its remnant, the Jews, became, by reason of its monotheism, increas- ingly distinctive within the context of its neighbours, yet its rituals retained a main- stream familiarity. The offerings which were required in the temple in Jerusalem have been recorded, at least in part, in some of the books of the Old Testament, and they included cattle, sheep, and goats, which were ritually killed, together with cereal products, olive oil, and wine.

There was, however, another aspect to wine which probably had no Jewish counterpart, and this was obligatory, or almost obligatory, ritual DRUNKENNESS. In the Greek-speaking areas it was apparently normal to get drunk at the seasonal feasts of the god DIONYSUS, and his true devotees, presumably, felt bound to be drunk more often than that. In the same way, in Ancient ROME at the dark-of-the-winter festival of the Saturnalia, drunkenness was part of the general licence, and the reversal of normal sober (in every sense) behaviour. These examples emphasize the ambiguous na- ture of wine's effects. It can make you have a wonderful time, and it can make you danger- ously irresponsible, as can the gods. (Indeed the gods themselves also get drunk—see, for example, SUMER.) Presumably, the Bacchanalia (see BACCHUS) and the Saturnalia were never fully respectable, but they were legal, because they emphasized the normality, and even value, of mundane daily life.

The period from prehistory to the revolu- tion referred to above runs from *c.*3000 BC through to the opening centuries AD. The revo- lution itself began slowly and quietly. Accord- ing to the prophetic critics of Israel, it is clear that Israel's abandonment of the various gods and spirits, most of them unrespectable (capricious, unpredictable, badly behaved), was a long, slow, bumpy, and incomplete pro- cess of conversion to the worship of God Almighty alone. However, by the time that some of them returned from the Exile in MESO- POTAMIA, in the 6th century BC, many were com- mitted to devotional monotheism and to the sense of being the chosen people and the pre- cious vine or vineyard of God's cultivation. This process initially made them peculiar, a minority among their neighbours, but it also led on later to the great crisis of the 1st century AD when the Jews split in two, and the Chris- tian section set out on a world mission of evangelization.

The Christian achievement of banishing the multiplicity of gods from the Mediterranean area was reinforced by the Muslims, from the 7th century AD onward. There was a progressive impact on wine. Jews took wine for granted for secular use and for religious ritual, but rejected drunkenness as irresponsible. The early Chris- tians accepted the Jews' position, apparently without debate, but rejected drunkenness at 'the Lord's table' as particularly disgraceful (see EUCHARIST). The Muslims rejected wine absolutely, and they still do (see ISLAM). Their response to its ambiguity has been that it is too dangerous, not worth the cost. Much later, during the modern period, some Christian groups in the northern half of Europe have independently followed the Muslims into total abstention, but they were stimulated into reaction not so much by wine as by distilled spirits. It was these various attitudes from northern as well as from southern Europe which were carried by colonists to the NEW WORLD, resulting in the most famous example of PROHIBITION, in the United States in the early 20th century.

See also MONKS AND MONASTERIES. J.D.K.

Fournier, D., and d'Onofrio, S. (eds.), *Le Ferment Divin* (Paris, 1992).

remontage, French word for various systems of PUMPING OVER, circulating liquid in the fermentation vessel through the CAP of grape solids during red wine fermentation.

The term may also be used in French for soil replacement after EROSION of vineyards.

remote sensing is the detection and/or measurement of features on the earth's surface using sensors mounted on satellite or aircraft platforms. Its application in viticulture is almost entirely confined to the inference of VIGOUR and canopy condition (although research suggests that it has potential for estimating canopy leaf area and certain aspects of fruit quality). This is achieved by sensing the amount of light that is reflected from a vineyard in the visible (blue, green, red) and near infrared parts of the electromagnetic spectrum and calculating indices between them. Commonly used indices in viticulture are the NORMALIZED DIFFERENCE VEGETATION INDEX (NDVI) and PLANT CELL DENSITY (PCD). Research has shown VERAISON to be the optimal time to acquire remotely sensed imagery of vineyards, especially with respect to its use in PRECISION VITICULTURE or ZONAL VITICULTURE.

R.G.V.B.

Hall, A., Lamb, D. W., Holzapfel, B., and Louis, J., 'Optical remote sensing applications in viticulture—a review', *Australian Journal of Grape and Wine Research*, 8 (2002), 36–47.

Johnson, L. F., 'Temporal stability of and NDVI-LAI relationship in a Napa Valley vineyard', *Australian Journal of Grape and Wine Research*, 9 (2003), 96–101.

Lamb, D. W., Weedon, M. M., and Bramley, R. G. V., 'Using remote sensing to map grape phenolics and colour in a cabernet sauvignon vineyard—the impact of image resolution and vine phenology', *Australian Journal of Grape and Wine Research*, 10 (2004), 46–54.

remuage is French for the RIDDLING process, an integral stage in the traditional method of making SPARKLING WINES. It means literally 'shaking', a reference to the need to dislodge the deposit left in a bottle after a second fermentation has taken place inside it.

Modern alternative techniques may eventually render this cumbersome process superfluous. A person or machine that performs *remuage* is a **remueur**. For more details, see SPARKLING WINE-MAKING.

rendement, French for YIELD, usually expressed in hl/ha.

rendzina, a dark, interzonal type of soil found in grassy or formerly grassy areas of moderate rainfall, on limestones, especially in chalklands. It is characterized by a brown to black, friable surface and a light grey or yellow, soft underlying horizon. Such soils are associated with TERRA ROSSA soils of Coonawarra in SOUTH AUSTRALIA. See GEOLOGY.

research into grape-growing and wine production is officially and principally in the domain of academe, although some individual viticulturists and winemakers are more prone to experimentation and more subject to the rigour of SCIENCE than others. For a list of important wine research institutions, see ACADEME.

Reserva, term used in both Spain and Portugal to distinguish wines from a supposedly good vintage. In Portugal, a Reserva is a wine from a good vintage with an alcohol level at least half a per cent above the regional minimum. In Spain, a red wine labelled Reserva will have had at least three years' AGEING in cask and bottle, of which a year must be in oak cask. The wine may not be released until the fourth year after the harvest. Spanish white wines labelled Reserva must spend a total of at least two years in cask and bottle to qualify, with at least six months of this period in OAK.

See also GRAN RESERVA. R.J.M.

Reserve is a term liberally used by wine producers for various bottlings. It should be quite literally reserved itself, for superior wines, but, unlike RESERVA and RISERVA, the English term Reserve has few controls on its use. Some wineries release several bottlings, all of which may incorporate the word in their names (Proprietor's Reserve, Estate Reserve, Reserve Selection, Private Reserve, Vintner's Reserve, and the like). The French term is **Réserve** and there are moves to control the use of terms such as Cuvée de Réserve. In CHAMPAGNE, reserve wines are those held over from a given year for future blending, typically into the NON-VINTAGE cuvée.

residual sugar, occasionally **RS**, the total quantity of SUGARS remaining unfermented in the finished wine. This may include both fermentable sugars, mainly GLUCOSE and FRUCTOSE, which have for some reason remained unconverted to alcohol during FERMENTATION, and small amounts of those few sugars which are not readily fermented by typical wine YEAST.

Some, but by no means all, residual sugar is tasted as SWEETNESS.

Residual sugar in wine is usually measured in grams of total sugars per litre of wine and can vary between about 1 g/l (0.1 per cent) and 25 g/l (2.5 per cent) or more. Wines with a residual sugar content of less than 2 g/l, such as the great majority of red wines and many white wines that do not taste at all sweet, are generally described as 'dry' (but see SWEETNESS for some more specific definitions). It is rare to find a wine with much less than 1 g/l residual sugar because some sugars are almost invariably impervious to the action of the yeasts. On the other hand, many wines with a residual sugar level even as high as 25 g/l may taste dry because the sweetness is offset by high ACIDITY or possibly bitterness from TANNINS. Some ordinary wines (usually white) that are naturally high in acids may have sugars (usually the particularly sweet fructose), sweet GRAPE JUICE, or sweet RECTIFIED GRAPE MUST added deliberately to increase their palatability or commercial appeal (see SWEET RESERVE).

Exceptionally sweet wines may be produced either in extraordinarily ripe years or by unusual wine-making techniques such as those involved in freeze CONCENTRATION, BOTRYTIZED, or DRIED GRAPE WINES. The sweetest form of the unique Hungarian sweet wine TOKAJI, for example, must have a minimum residual sugar of 250 g/l—the 1947 vintage of Tokay Essencia managed 488 g/l.

Sugar levels in grapes are measured as MUST WEIGHT by various different scales, of which BAUMÉ, BRIX, and OECHSLE are the most common.

One German wine harvested at Nussdorf in the Pfalz in 1971 was picked at 326 °Oechsle, or about 870 g/l sugar, and had reached only 4.5 per cent alcohol in a particularly slow fermentation 20 years later, producing a wine with about 480 g/l residual sugar.

In theory, 100 g of sugar should yield 51.1 g of alcohol, but numerous practical experiments show that only 47 to 48 g of alcohol are obtained. Between 16 and 17 g/l of sugar are required to produce 1 per cent of alcohol in white wines (up to 18 g/l in reds, depending on the yeast strain).

There are many reasons why fermentable sugars may remain unfermented: yeasts vary enormously in their potency, especially their tolerance of higher sugar and higher alcohol concentrations; grape musts vary in their micro-nutrient and growth factor content; low TEMPERATURES and chemical additions can also arrest fermentation.

Residual sugar presents no great danger in a wine that is yet to be processed in bulk, but in a bottled wine the presence of such sugars may cause FERMENTATION IN BOTTLE. Small amounts of sugar are furthermore readily used by BACTERIA to produce unwanted ACETIC ACID, off-flavours, and, sometimes, CARBON

DIOXIDE gas. The winemaker therefore must ensure either that a wine is effectively free of fermentable sugars or, in the case of most sweet and medium dry wines, that the wine undergoes full STABILIZATION against the risk of further microbiological activity. This can be achieved by heavy FILTRATION followed by STERILE BOTTLING, by PASTEURIZATION, or by a technique called yeast nutrient depletion, which effectively removes the micro-nutrients from the wine before bottling, but is impractical for wines aged for less than three years.

A great sweet wine such as a fine SAUTERNES or a BEERENAUSLESE remains stable because of the action of noble rot. Both the very high residual sugar and the trace materials secreted by the BOTRYTIS into the juice inhibit fermentation. Because of this, many fine sweet German wines are stable despite their high sugar levels and low alcohol levels. A.D.W.

residues. Residues of AGROCHEMICALS, the commercial preparations used in vineyards for the control of pests, diseases, or weeds, are that portion which is found on the grapes or in wine. Residues in viticulture and wine are typically different from those in other forms of agriculture and food processing. There are usually long 'withholding periods' between application and harvest so that the agrochemical is degraded. Most of any remaining agrochemical is also likely to be eliminated with the skins during PRESSING, and more is removed during juice CLARIFICATION, FERMENTATION, and subsequent FILTRATION.

PESTICIDES may leave deposits or by-products that persist in plant or animal tissues or in soil, water, or air. Some pesticides are rapidly inactivated after application; others (or their by-products) may persist for years in a biologically active form. Such residual contamination may affect human or livestock health, subsequent crop growth, and pollute the environment. Excessive or illegal pesticide residues in wine may lead to rejection on domestic and/or international markets, perhaps as a result of the use of inappropriate pesticides, incorrect application methods, or application too close to harvest. Residue effects on non-target organisms should also be considered. Useful insects such as bees or natural parasites and predators of pests may be affected by pesticide residues.

FUNGICIDE residues may inhibit fermentation by yeast, as discussed by Lemperle, but extensive trials have shown that the proper use of fungicides has no adverse effect on the taste or smell of wines. The COPPER contained in some fungicides can even improve wine quality by reducing SULFIDE, although residues of elemental SULFUR used to prevent fungal disease in the vineyard can be transformed, in REDUCING conditions, into foul-smelling HYDROGEN SULFIDE.

So-called maximum residue limits (MRLs) are established by governments for particular agrochemicals or their metabolites (breakdown products) in particular foodstuffs. Consumer health is not the only basis for such action. MRLs have, unfortunately, become important as a potential trade barrier for protectionist purposes. This can happen, for example, in cases where the importing country is free of certain vine diseases and therefore has no established MRLs for the relevant agrochemicals and can set zero MRLs for imported wines. See also AGROCHEMICALS. R.E.S. & P.R.D.

Lemperle, E., 'Fungicide residues in musts and wine', in R. E. Smart, R. J. Thornton, S. B. Rodriguez, and J. E. Young (eds.), *Proceedings of the Second International Symposium for Cool Climate Viticulture and Oenology; 11–15 January 1988, Auckland, New Zealand* (Auckland, 1988).

resinated wines. Of the earthenware vessels in which the ancient Greeks and Romans kept their wines (see AMPHORAE) only the very best were airtight. Normally they were porous, and it is clear from the Roman writers on agriculture that the insides of jars were therefore coated with resin. It was therefore probably as a purely practical measure that resin was initially used. But soon people must have discovered that the wine would keep even better if they added resin to the wine itself. COLUMELLA deals at length with the different kinds of resin that can be employed in this way (*De re rustica* 13. 20–14), but he emphasizes that the best wines should not have resin put into them. Yet many people came to like the taste of resin and used it not only as a preservative but also as a flavouring agent. PLINY recommends that resin should be added to the fermenting must (*Natural History* 14. 124) and he discusses which kinds of resin are best: resin from mountainous regions has a more pleasant smell than resin from low-lying areas (16. 60).

The Romans abandoned amphorae in favour of wooden casks in the 3rd century AD because BARRELS were lighter and easier to handle. Wooden casks do not need an inside coating of resin, and this saved the winemaker time and money. Thus the Romans ceased to make resinated wines. Winemakers in Transalpine Gaul, most of whom did not have pine trees nearby, and those of Cisalpine Gaul, Illyria, and the alpine region, where the climate is cooler and wood does not crack so easily, had started using wooden casks in the 1st century AD. Unlike the west, however, Byzantium did not lose its taste for resin when it was no longer needed as a preservative. The pine forests of the eastern part of central Greece and of Euboea still provided the resin to enhance the flavour of some Greek wines after the 7th century.

This was very much not to the taste of one western visitor to Constantinople. In 968 Liudprand, bishop of Cremona, was sent there to arrange a marriage between the daughter of the late Emperor Romanos and the son of his own patron, Otto I, the Holy Roman Emperor. The mission was not a success. The Emperor Nicephorus treated Liudprand rudely and kept him a virtual prisoner. Liudprand's *De legatione Constantinopolitana* ('The mission to Constantinople') was his revenge. He has not a good word to say for the Byzantines in general and Nicephorus in particular. We are dealing with a masterpiece of invective, and since Liudprand's purpose is satirical, we should not believe his every word. But his observations on the food and wine he had are interesting. Horrified, he relates how he was given goat stuffed with onions, garlic, and leeks, swimming in fish sauce. Worst of all, and mentioned in his very first chapter, is the wine: undrinkable because it is mixed with resin, pitch, and gypsum. Like the fish sauce, not in the least remarkable to an Ancient Roman, but not a thing to serve a modern Lombard. Liudprand may have had perfectly decent, unresinated, wine at times during his enforced stay, but it would have spoilt his story to tell us about that.

For not all Greek wine was resinated in the Middle Ages. The strong, sweet wines that reached the markets of western Europe were not, but pilgrims travelling to the Holy Land say that some local wines were. The account of Pietro Casola, who sailed to Jerusalem in 1494, stopping off frequently on the way, is particularly valuable because he takes pains to describe the customs, the food, and the wines of every region. He often speaks of the excellent sweet wines in Greece, but in Modone, on the south-western tip of the Peloponnese (near Monemvasia which gave its name to MALVASIA), he is given a wine that has had resin added to it during fermentation in order, he explains, to preserve it. He objects to its strong unpleasant odour, but he goes on to describe the fine malmsey, muscatel, and rumney of Modone. Of Cyprus he says that he loves everything about it except the wine, which has resin in it. He must have been unlucky not to have tasted the famous sweet wines that Cyprus exported, but an earlier account by an anonymous French cleric, *Le Voyage de la Saincte Cyte de Hierusalem* of 1480, confirms what he observes about Cyprus and Modone.

See RETSINA for details of modern resinated wine. H.M.W.

Newett, M. M., *Canon Casola's Pilgrimage to Jerusalem in the Year 1494* (Manchester, 1907).
The Works of Liudprand of Cremona, trans. by F. A. Wright (London, 1930).

resins used in wine-making are natural or synthetic materials usually composed of long chains of simpler molecules that are capable of POLYMERIZING. Gum acacia is a natural resin used to stabilize the PIGMENTS in red wine. Another natural resin is Aleppo pine resin, which is used in the preparation of RETSINA.

Synthetic resins, manufactured by polymerization processes, have several uses in wine-making. One of the commonest is epoxy resin, which can be used in the form of a two-part paint for coating the inside of concrete vats, producing an inert and easily cleaned surface. Epoxy-resin compounds are also used for surfacing floors in wineries and bottling halls, being much more resistant than concrete to the acids in wine.

Silicone resins are used in the manufacture of BUNGS for wooden BARRELS; they have the flexibility of rubber but are taint-free and non-perishable.

ION EXCHANGE resins can be used in some countries for TARTRATE stabilization. They are prepared in the form of small beads which are packed into a vertical cylindrical tank known as a column, through which the wine is passed. The particular property of these resins is their ability to exchange the ions which are loosely held on their surface with ions in the liquid phase.   D.B.

Bird, D., *Understanding Wine Technology* (2nd edn, Newark, 2005).

respiration, biochemical process in animals and plants, including vines, which provides the chemical energy required for other reactions and for growth. Respiration may be considered the opposite of PHOTOSYN-THESIS in that OXYGEN is consumed and CARBON DIOXIDE and energy released, according to the following formula:

$$H_{12}O_6 \text{ sugar} + 6O_2 \rightarrow 6CO_2 + 6H_2O + \text{energy}$$

In addition to SUGARS, other compounds such as STARCH, fats, AMINO ACIDS, organic ACIDS, and other substances may be broken down to release energy.

In plants, temperature has a major effect on respiration rate. The rate of respiration approximately doubles for each 10 °C/18 °F increase in temperature. Of particular interest to wine drinkers is the respiration of MALIC ACID, which takes place in the grape during RIPENING. This reaction depends on temperature, an important reason why acidity levels are higher in wines from cooler climates.

(Respiration is also the name given to the metabolism of foodstuffs in humans; following ingestion of wine, the primary energy source, alcohol, is metabolized in the liver.)   R.E.S.

Winkler, A. J., *et al.*, *General Viticulture* (2nd edn, Berkeley, Calif., 1974).

resveratrol, PHENOLIC compound produced by grapevines (and other plants such as peanut and eucalyptus trees), particularly in response to microbial attack (see PHYTOALEXINS) or artificial agents such as ULTRAVIOLET RADIATION. It is one of a number of compounds (including CATECHIN and QUERCETIN) found in wine thought to contribute to HEALTH aspects of its moderate consumption. Resveratrol is also found in other grape products such as juice and raisins. Resveratrol belongs to a class of compounds called stilbenes. In grapevines this also includes its derivatives, piceid, pterostilbene, and the viniferins. Woody parts of the vine normally contain large amounts of stilbenes, principally viniferins, which are thought to protect against wood decay. In the vineyard, leaves and berries produce resveratrol only in response to some action, such as fungal attack, where its subsequent accumulation may slow or stop the infection. There are numerous factors in the growing of grapes and vinification that can affect resveratrol concentration in the finished wine. Species, variety, clone, and rootstock influence potential stilbene production. For example, wines made from MUSCADINIA grapes or from PINOT NOIR tend to have high levels of resveratrol, whereas CABERNET SAUVIGNON has lower levels. Wines produced in cooler regions or areas with greater disease pressure such as Burgundy and New York often have more resveratrol, while wines from hot, dry climates such as Australia and California frequently have lower resveratrol concentrations.

Wine-making procedures have a great effect on resveratrol concentration in the final product. Red wines have a much higher resveratrol content, usually about ten times, than that found in whites. This is not necessarily because white grapes manufacture less resveratrol, but because stilbenes are manufactured in the grape skins and MACERATION, integral to the production of a red wine, encourages the extraction of these compounds. YEAST strain, LACTIC ACID BACTERIA, use of FINING agents, and handling procedures can also influence resveratrol concentration to some extent. Much of the interest in resveratrol in the 1990s and early 2000s came from its suspected connection to wine's HEALTH benefits. It was known to play a part in herbal remedies for many years, but it was not until 1992 that New York researchers Siemann and Creasy made the link between it, wine, and its possible contribution to the FRENCH PARADOX. Resveratrol has been reported to reduce serum platelet aggregation, cholesterol levels, liver lipids, and act as a cancer chemopreventative agent. As part of the phenolic milieu in wine, its moderate consumption can contribute to good health.   G.L.C.

Goldberg, D.M., Yan, J., Ng, E., Diamandis, E.P., Karumanchiri, A., Soleas, G., and Waterhouse, A. L., 'A global survey of trans-resveratrol concentrations in commercial wines', *American Journal of Enology and Viticulture*, 46 (1995), 159–65.

Siemann, E. H., and Creasy, G. L, 'Concentration of the phytoalexin resveratrol in wine', *American Journal of Enology and Viticulture*, 43 (1992), 49–52.

retsina, modern form of RESINATED WINE that is extremely common in GREECE, and a potent catalyst of taverna nostalgia outside it. Modern retsina is made like any other white (or rosé) wine, except that small pieces of resin from the *Pinus helepensis* pine are added to the must and left with the wine until the first RACKING separates the finished wine from all solids. Major producing areas are Attica, Euboea, and Boeotia, all in the southern part of central Greece close to Athens, but retsina is also made for local consumption all over the country. SAVATIANO is usually the principal grape, often enlivened with some RHODITIS or occasionally ASSYRTIKO, but a wide range of local grape varieties are also used, and an interesting ATHIRI retsina is made on the island of Rhodes.

Retsina is protected by the EU as a traditional appellation. It is rarely made outside Greece and southern Cyprus, where local palates are accustomed to its distinctively pungent flavour, and visitors expect it. A South Australian version has been essayed.

M.McN. & N.M.

Reuilly, small but expanding French appellation so far inside the bend of the Loire that it is often described as coming from central France. Its most useful manifestation is as a less expensive and sometimes purer version of the SANCERRE appellation to the east made from Sauvignon Blanc grapes in one of the riper vintages. Considerable amounts of red and rosé wine are made, mainly from Pinot Noir and Pinot Gris respectively (the local Gamay is sold as VIN DE PAYS). Pale pink Reuilly has its devotees. Unlike nearby QUINCY, Reuilly is not just a sleepy viticultural centre, but the best wines yielded by its 150 ha/370 acres of vineyards scattered on the LIMESTONE base around the village of Reuilly can be finer, especially from the likes of Claude Lafond. This Loire appellation (which consisted of just 30 ha in the early 1990s) is not to be confused with that of RULLY in the Côte Chalonnaise.

See also LOIRE, including map.

Réunion. This French island in the Indian ocean, once mainly planted with ISABELLA, now produces small quantities of respectable red and white from French varieties.

reverse osmosis is an increasingly popular though rather controversial wine-making intervention or MANIPULATION based on the principle of cross-flow or tangential membrane filtration. In standard FILTRATION procedures, the liquid flows perpendicularly to the filter surface, making clogging a major problem. In cross-flow filtration, the liquid flows parallel to the filter membrane so that it helps scour the surface and prevent clogging. The liquid flows at pressure, and it is this pressure that causes water and some salts to pass through the membrane filter. Cross-flow filtration is highly promising for many wine-making applications but it is quite slow and expensive compared with traditional filtration techniques.

It is currently used chiefly for two distinct purposes: ALCOHOL REDUCTION and must CONCENTRATION. In the former, a portion of a high alcohol wine is passed through a reverse osmosis installation, which removes a colourless permeate that consists almost entirely of water and alcohol, and returns the retentate (the rest of the wine) to the tank. The alcohol may then be removed from the permeate by distillation and the water returned to the wine, to produce a wine of reduced alcohol content. This low alcohol wine can then be used as a blending component to produce a final wine of the desired alcohol level. An advantage of this technique is that only a portion of the wine need be subjected to this potentially intrusive manipulation, typically less than one-quarter.

In the case of must concentration, reverse osmosis is used to remove water from the unfermented grape must, achieving a similar result to vacuum evaporation. It has been widely adopted in Bordeaux, where many producers regard it as an insurance policy against the negative effects of a rainy harvest. Controversially, some have seen it as a way of producing more concentrated, denser wines of the sort that appeal to influential critics and the modern market place. In some countries, principally Australia, the main use of reverse osmosis is on finished wines, where the selective removal of water and alcohol concentrates all other components.

Another important use for reverse osmosis is the reduction of excessive levels of VOLATILE ACIDITY. Stuck fermentations are sometimes coupled with high levels of acetic acid and some commentators have suggested that it is the volatile acidity that is arresting the fermentation. This view is supported by the fact that where volatile acidity is reduced by the use of reverse osmosis and anion exchange (to remove selectively the acetic acid), three-quarters of these fermentations resume.

More recently this technique has been proposed as a way of removing negative flavour compounds that result from BRETTANOMYCES spoilage in red wines. In 2005, work was underway to apply similar membrane techniques as a means of removing sugar from grape musts in order to reduce alcohol levels in wine—a possible alternative to HUMIDIFICATION.   J.A.G. & J.Ha.

Rèze, very rare Swiss Valais white grape responsible for the sherry-like *vin des glaciers*. Most of it is planted in Haut-Valais. In the 1960s, eminent French ampelographer Louis Levadoux and linguist Jacques André speculated that Rèze corresponds to *Uva raetica*, a grape described by PLINY the Elder and widespread in northern Italy in Roman times. In 2005, DNA PROFILING at SAN MICHELE ALL'ADIGE revealed that Rèze has parent–offspring relationships with NOSIOLA and Groppello di Revò in Trentino and CASCAROLO in Piemonte. Although there is still no evidence, this is consistent with the *Uva reatica* hypothesis. In Switzerland, the area of cultivation fell from

400 ha at the beginning of the 20th century to less than 1 ha at the beginning of the 21st century because Rèze and other VALAIS grapes were superseded by CHASSELAS to produce FENDANT.   J.V.

Rhamnales, the order of the plant kingdom which includes the family Vitaceae, in turn including the genus VITIS, the grapevine. See BOTANICAL CLASSIFICATION.

Rhein, German name for the river RHINE.

Rheingau, for generations the most economically successful wine region in GERMANY and still one of its most famous abroad. The Church and nobility provided the discipline and organization necessary for a solid business in wine, which survived the unrest and secularization in the early 19th century (see GERMAN HISTORY). The region now includes 3,160 ha/7,800 acres, over 90 per cent of which lie on the right bank of the RHINE, between Wiesbaden and the MITTELRHEIN boundary at Lorchhausen (see map under GERMANY). The remainder of the Rheingau vineyards are near Hochheim (the origin of the word HOCK) on the banks of the Main, shortly before its confluence with the Rhine at Mainz.

The vineyards at Hochheim and in the central part of the region are mostly on gently rolling or flat land, but from Rüdesheim downstream to Lorchhausen the terrain is much steeper. The Rheingau soil is very varied throughout. As part of the practice of good husbandry, many Rheingauers have recorded in detail the weather conditions over the centuries. Through the telescope of hindsight, excessively cold winters seem to have been frequent, and the Rhine froze often. In spite of this and within the context of the whole of the German vineyard, the region has a favoured MESOCLIMATE. With its southern ASPECT, it is marginally warmer than much of Rheinhessen to the south, and its annual RAINFALL of a little over 600 m/23 in means that there is an adequate supply of water for the RIESLING vine to ripen its grapes long into the autumn. The vines of today can tolerate extremes of weather better than those of the past, as years of research have much improved their quality and strength.

At GEISENHEIM, the Rheingau has one of the world's leading viticultural institutes, but it has not been invaded by newer GERMAN CROSSINGS to the same extent as other German regions such as RHEINHESSEN and the Pfalz. The climate and exposition of its vineyards, and the structure of its trade and its traditions, have called for the Riesling vine, which, since 1990, represents 78 per cent of vineyard, by far the largest share in any German growing region. To produce consistently the high-quality wine expected of Riesling from some of Germany's best-known vineyards, a relatively low YIELD is essential. Most good Rheingau

estate bottlers aim for 70 to 80 hl/ha (4–4.5 tons/acre)—low for Germany.

No German wines have ever achieved higher international standing (or prices) than did the Rieslings of the Rheingau in the late 19th century, and even in the mid 20th century prices were much higher than those of many of Bordeaux's CLASSED GROWTHS. The record of the late 20th century has been mixed. Under the stylistic inspiration of the late Bernard Breuer of Rüdesheim and the late proprietor of Schloss Vollrads, Graf Matuschka-Greiffenclau, this region led Germany in producing ever drier Rieslings, purporting to be closer to a late 19th century model and inherently more adaptable to late 20th-century cuisine. The Rheingau CHARTA organization and the local VDP association were early activists in the promotion of low YIELDS, of a consistently TROCKEN (dry) style of Riesling, and of the CLASSIFICATION of top vineyards as Erstes Gewächs or FIRST GROWTHS (see GROSSES GEWÄCHS).

The state of Hesse, with 147 ha/363 acres of vineyard in various parts of the region, uses the 12th-century Cistercian monastery KLOSTER EBERBACH for numerous promotional functions, including courses, conferences, and a famous AUCTION held each year. Proximity to the metropolitan markets of Mainz, Wiesbaden, and Frankfurt has further helped Rheingau wines re-establish high reputations and prices. But all of this has not been enough to secure the continued fortunes of many of the large, formerly noble, estates, several of which have in recent years been sold, closed, or continue to struggle economically. The Rheingau has also had stiff competition within Germany from the increasingly fashionable and predominantly dry wines of the dynamic, warmer BADEN and PFALZ regions.

While Riesling rules the Rheingau, its consort is the equally noble SPÄTBURGUNDER (Pinot Noir), brought here already in the Middle Ages by the Cistercians around the same time that they were founding the famous CLOS VOUGEOT in Burgundy. Pockets of high-quality Spätburgunder—which accounts for 13 per cent of total vineyard area—abound in the Rheingau. But the most important sites for Pinot Noir are at opposite ends of the region: on the CALCAREOUS soils of Hochheim on the Main, and on the steep SLATE terraces of Assmannshausen, which has enjoyed a singular reputation as a red wine town since the mid 18th century. For much of the 20th century, Rheingau red tended to be pale and rather sweet but today's reds, often given BARREL MATURATON, are much richer, darker, and stronger. The best of them command prices concomitant with their world-class quality.

The principle of picking selected bunches of grapes, AUSLESEN in German, was understood in the 18th century, but that of the widespread picking of grapes affected by NOBLE ROT dates, in the Rheingau, from about 1820.

Almost 60 per cent of Rheingau wine today is bottled trocken, and a further 27 per cent HALBTROCKEN. In spite of modern trends (or as many Rheingauer would claim, a return to dry wine TRADITION), all would probably agree that it is in rich, sweet, BOTRYTIZED WINES of Auslese quality and upwards in a great vintage that Rheingau Riesling still reaches a peak of possible quality.

In the Rheingau, seven co-operative cellars receive grapes from slightly less than 10 per cent of the harvest. Their role is thus a relatively minor one, compared with that of the private and state-owned estates. Other than at the region's two famous castles, SCHLOSS JOHANNISBERG and Schloss Vollrads, most such larger estates have vineyard holdings in numerous, not always contiguous, villages. Many properties date from the 18th century and a few can trace their wine-making history to a much earlier period. Part-time growers account for nearly one third of Rheingau acreage, and an encouraging late 20th-century trend has been the emergence of some top-quality wines from part-time vintners.

At Lorch at the westernmost limit of the Rheingau, the local wine is made mainly in the village, and ripening Riesling on steep slate slopes is more of a struggle than elsewhere in the Rheingau. Immediately upstream at Assmannshausen, Pinot Noir dominates proceedings, above all in the south-facing Höllenberg. Upstream of Rüdesheim, the Rhine runs east–west, exposing on the so-called Rüdesheimer Berg the first of the Rheingau's famous progression of south-facing slopes. The steep, stony slate and quartzite-dominated Berg Schlossberg, Berg Roseneck, and Berg Rottland sites, all directly overlooking the Rhine, can generate Rieslings of peachy richness, spiciness, and depth even in difficult vintages. The progression of small villages and top-class vineyards continues with Geisenheim (Kläuserweg, Rothenberg), Johannisberg (Hölle, Schloss Johannisberg), Winkel (Jesuitengarten, Schloss Vollrads), and Oestrich (Doosberg, Lenchen). All are capable of producing Riesling wines of a high order, but many would argue that they are surpassed by the best Rieslings from Hattenheim (Pfaffenberg, Nussbrunnen, Wisselbrunnen), and Erbach (Marcobrünn, Siegelsberg, Schlossberg). Soils of loess, sand, and marl alternate in these central Rheingau villages, and parcels further from the river are generally later-ripening and more ventilated due to their elevation. In hot summers, the wines of Hallgarten (Steinberg, Schönhell), Kiedrich (Gräfenberg), and Rauenthal (Baiken, Gehrn, Rothenberg), which lie on higher, stony, phyllite ground some distance from the Rhine, can be quite outstanding, with a flavour with seems to last for ever. At lower elevations near the eastern edge of the Rheingau, the towns of Eltville (Sonnenberg) and Walluf (Walkenberg), while never quite rivalling the best Rieslings of the region, can still be memorable. On gentle slopes down to the river Main, Hochheim produces more corpulent Rieslings quite distinct from those grown elsewhere in the Rheingau yet equally complex.

D.S.

Payne, J., and Diel, A., *The Guide to German Wines/ German Wine Guide* (London/New York, 2005).
Pigott, S., and Johnson, H., *The Wine Atlas of Germany* (London, 1995).

Rheinhessen, large, growing, and varied wine region in GERMANY (see map under GERMANY). On the eastern edge of this 26,200-ha/ 64,500-acre region, the red soil of sloping vineyards such as Nierstein's Roter Hang group produces wine that is internationally recognized as of the highest quality. A third of the region's stock of RIESLING vines grows in this privileged area known as the Rheinterrasse. It stretches from Bodenheim, a little south of Mainz, to the outskirts of Worms. Its most famous vineyards are those in the so-called *Rotliegenden* (Permian red shale) of Nierstein—including Hipping, Oelberg, Orbel, and Pettental—and the Rothenberg in neighbouring Nackenheim. A string of communes immediately south of Nierstein—Oppenheim, Dienheim, and Ludwigshöhe—also boast excellent eastern exposure on the edge of the Rhine. The region as a whole is protected from winds and excessive rain by the hills on its western border, which rise to over 600 m (nearly 2,000 ft). The temperature in the vineyards nearest the river RHINE is warmer throughout the year than that of the rolling country away from the river, and in severe winters they avoid the worst effects of FROST. Aromas of peach, citrus, and a distinctive smoked meat pungency characterize wines grown on the red soils of the Rheinterrasse. LOESS, SAND, and CALCAREOUS soils in each of these villages can also yield distinctive wines from the traditional varieties Riesling and Silvaner.

The north of Rheinhessen has its best vineyards at Ingelheim (known in Germany over many years for its SPÄTBURGUNDER, or PINOT NOIR), at Bingen in the Scharlachberg site, and in the region's highest vineyards, the so-called 'Rheinhessian Switzerland' immediately southeast of Bad Kreuznach. In the south, the wine villages of Flörsheim-Dalsheim, Weinheim, Westhofen, Bechtheim, and Osthofen have begun to attract international attention thanks in large part to the efforts of a handful of ambitious young vintners. A significant number of Germany's pioneers in ORGANIC and BIODYNAMIC viticulture have come from the ranks of Rheinhessen growers, helping to attract attention to the region.

There are over 400 individual vineyard sites in Rheinhessen, most of which have little meaning in terms of the style and quality of wine they produce. Over half of the region's wine is sold as BRANDS or under the name of a GROSSLAGE, most notorious of which is Niersteiner Gutes Domtal (a designation virtually guaranteeing that the wine does not originate in Nierstein vineyards). A quarter of all Rheinhessen wine is exported.

For much of the second half of the 20th century, this region was dominated by GERMAN CROSSINGS designed to be hardy, high-yielding, and above all capable of maximal must weights, in accordance with the diktats of the 1971 GERMAN WINE LAW. Among the eventual results was a surfeit of undistinguished grocery store 'Spätlesen', and ever-cheaper white wine on the bulk market.

Since the mid 1980s, more and more growers have recognized the need to limit yields and achieve real quality, rallying around the traditional Silvaner and Riesling grapes of the region—each of which accounts for 10 per cent of local acreage—but also increasingly planting red varieties. While Müller-Thurgau continues to be the most widely grown grape in Rheinhessen, the red Dornfelder is nowadays in second place, and well over one third of total acreage is now devoted to red varieties. Quality-conscious Rheinhessen vintners have launched more than one promotional venture in the German market in recent years to promote Silvaner.

Three-quarters of Rheinhessen wine is sold in bulk. Nearly half of the region's wine is bottled by merchants elsewhere and supplies the lower end of the market. This high volume of inexpensive wine destined for export helps explain the relatively small (28 per cent) proportion that is bottled as TROCKEN. A great many CO-OPERATIVES are active, but they struggle with the vicious cycle of high yields and low prices that plague other contributors to the European WINE LAKE.

D.S.

Rheinpfalz, German wine region. See PFALZ.

Rhein Riesling, or **Rheinriesling**, common synonym in German-speaking countries for the great white RIESLING grape variety of Germany.

Rheinterrasse, admired wine district in Germany. For more details, see RHEINHESSEN.

Rhenish, description of wines in common use in the Middle Ages which usually encompassed most of the wines then produced in what is GERMANY today and also those of ALSACE.

Rhine, English name for the river known in German as the **Rhein** and French as the **Rhin** (where it lends its name to the two ALSACE *départements* Haut-Rhin and Bas-Rhin). The German 'Rhein' describes a table wine (see TAFELWEIN) subdistrict identical to the quality wine regions AHR, HESSISCHE BERGSTRASSE, MITTELRHEIN, NAHE, PFALZ, RHEINGAU, and

RHEINHESSEN. On some wine lists in the English-speaking world, all German wines, other than those regarded as MOSEL (or often 'Moselle'), appear somewhat imprecisely under the heading 'Rhine'. A German white table wine from either Riesling or Silvaner grapes, or their derivatives (of which nearly 50 are registered varieties), entitled to bear the name 'Rhein' may also be known as HOCK. See also SWITZERLAND and LIECHTENSTEIN.

'Rhine' is used colloquially by Australians as an abbreviation for Rhine Riesling, their synonym for the RIESLING grape variety. The word Rhine has been incorporated into a host of names associated in the English-speaking world with white, usually medium dry, but not necessarily at all Germanic, wines.   I.J.

Rhine Riesling, synonym for the great white RIESLING grape variety of Germany, once common in Australia.

rhizopus, vine disease and one of a group of fungi commonly infecting grapes with rot. See BUNCH ROTS.

Rhoditis, slightly pink-skinned grape variety traditionally grown in the Peloponnese which was much more important in the GREECE of the pre-PHYLLOXERA era. The vine is particularly sensitive to POWDERY MILDEW. It ripens relatively late and keeps its acidity quite well even in such hot climates as that of Ankhíalos in Thessaly in central Greece, although it can also ripen well in high-altitude vineyards in Greece. It is often blended with the softer SAVATIANO, particularly for RETSINA.

Rhône, one of the most important wine RIVERS, linking a range of vineyards as dissimilar as those of CHÂTEAUNEUF-DU-PAPE in southern France, sparkling SEYSSEL, and Fendant du Valais in SWITZERLAND.

In wine circles, however, the term Rhône usually means the fashionable wines made in the Rhône valley in south east France which themselves vary so much, north and south of an almost vine-free 50-km/30-mile stretch between approximately Valence and Montélimar, that they are divided into two very distinct zones (although the regional appellation Côtes du Rhône encompasses the less ambitious wines of the north as well as a large area of the south). The Rhône regularly produces more APPELLATION CONTRÔLÉE wine than any region other than Bordeaux, about 95 per cent of the nearly 4 million hl/105 million gal produced each year being red and usually high in alcohol relative to other French wines.

The greater Rhône valley is divided into four wine districts, of which the **southern Rhône** (*Rhône méridionale* in French) is by far the most important in terms of quantity. The overwhelming majority of the more than 2 million hl/53 million gal of wine that qualifies as **Côtes du Rhône** or **Côtes du Rhône-Villages** comes from the southern part of the Rhône valley.

The most important Rhône district in terms of the prestige of its wines is the **northern Rhône** (*Rhône septentrionale* in French), which includes the appellations of Hermitage and Côte Rôtie, representing serious rivals to the great names of Bordeaux and Burgundy in the quality and, especially, longevity of their best wines. The northern Rhône is quite different from the southern Rhône in terms of climate, soils, topography, and even vine varieties.

A third small but extremely ancient district about 64 km/40 miles east of Valence up the Drôme tributary comprises the Diois appellations, named after the town of Die, of CHÂTILLON-EN-DIOIS, CLAIRETTE DE DIE, CRÉMANT de Die, and Coteaux de DIE.

And finally there are the outlying appellations that are on the eastern borders of the southern Rhône and the northern borders of PROVENCE. See Coteaux du TRICASTIN, Côtes du LUBERON, Côtes du VENTOUX, and Côtes du VIVARAIS.

It should be noted that COSTIÈRES DE NÎMES, for long considered part of the LANGUEDOC region, is effectively a western extension of the southern Rhône.

History

Finds of AMPHORAE show that the inhabitants of the Rhône valley drank wine from Baetica, the eastern province of Roman-occupied SPAIN, in the 1st century BC. In the 1st century AD, the Romanized élite of the Rhône valley drank FALERNIAN. From the 1st century BC onwards, wine was carried up the Rhône: Chalon-sur-Saône was a river port for the Gauls (see Côte CHALONNAISE). In his *Geography*, completed in AD 7, Strabo emphasized the importance of good RIVER connections for trade in Gaul. From the Mediterranean one can get to the Atlantic ocean and the Channel by river (*Geography* 4. 1. 2).

Strabo asserted categorically that viticulture was impossible beyond the Cévennes, which was north of the territory of the evergreen oak, *Quercus ilex*, and hence too cold for the vine, which he assumed needed a MEDITERRANEAN CLIMATE. He was proved wrong by the GAULS, who even in his day had probably discovered that the Côte Rôtie and the hill of Hermitage were superb sites for vineyards. They were certainly making wine by AD 71, when PLINY said that in Vienne the Allobroges were producing an excellent wine, still unknown in VIRGIL's day (*Natural History* 14. 18). There were three CRUS, Taburnum, Sotanum, and Helvicum. Pliny's observation that they tasted naturally of resin cannot be correct, for wine was stored and transported in earthenware vessels which were covered with resin on their insides in order to make them impermeable, so any wine, and particularly a wine that had come from afar or was old, would have tasted of resin (see RESINATED WINES).

Pliny calls the vine that the growers of Vienne used Allobrogica. It has black grapes and is resistant to cold (*Natural History* 14. 26–7). Given the latter, Allobrogica is unlikely to be SYRAH—unless Pliny, like Strabo, thought that the Rhône valley's climate was inclement and decided therefore that any vine variety growing there must be able to withstand the cold. The Allobroges are proud of their wines, which fetch a high price (*Natural History* 14. 57). Elsewhere, Pliny remarks that the Gauls have mastered the art of grafting and improved on CATO: the Romans in turn have learned from them (*Natural History* 17. 116). The Allobroges exported their wines not only to Rome but also to Britain.

We do not know for certain where the two vine varieties that are characteristic of the Rhône, Syrah and VIOGNIER, came from. Some authors claim that the name Syrah equals Shiraz, the wine-growing city in PERSIA, and that the Phocaeans brought the vine from Persia after they had established their Greek colony at Marseilles (Massilia) around 600 BC. The vine must then have made its way up the Rhône and disappeared from the region of Marseilles. A second theory is that Syrah derives its name from Syracuse, from where the legions of the Roman Emperor PROBUS carried it to the Rhône valley after AD 280. If this is right, Pliny's Allobrogica cannot be Syrah. Because there is no AMPELOGRAPHICAL evidence for either of these theories, a third one has been proposed: the Syrah vine had established itself in the Rhône valley long before the advent of systematic viticulture and grew wild there. Probus' legions have been held responsible for the introduction of Viognier as well: the hypothesis is that Probus' soldiers brought the Viognier vine with them from Dalmatia, which was a wine-growing area when it was part of the Roman empire. There is in Dalmatia (but mainly on Vis, an island off the Dalmatian coast) a vine called Vugava, which bears some resemblance to Viognier in that it produces a strong, dry, and highly aromatic wine. It is an appealing, but uncomfortably complicated, theory, and again we have no ampelographical proof (see SYRAH).

The people living in the Rhône valley doubtless carried on making wine after the Romans left, but we have hardly any records at all until the late Middle Ages. Medieval wine merchants eagerly bought and sold the wine of Bordeaux, Gaillac, La Rochelle, the Île-de-France, and the Loire, but there was no trade in Rhône wines until the 14th century. This cannot have been because they were bad wines, for when Pope Clement V moved the papal court to Avignon in 1309 his entourage was quick to discover the local wines (see CHÂTEAUNEUF-DU-PAPE). Some three-quarters of the wines consumed at the papal court came from the Rhône valley, although the court was fond of Burgundy, too. When Urban V went back to Rome for three years from 1367 to 1370, he had a vine from the Côtes du Rhône planted there.

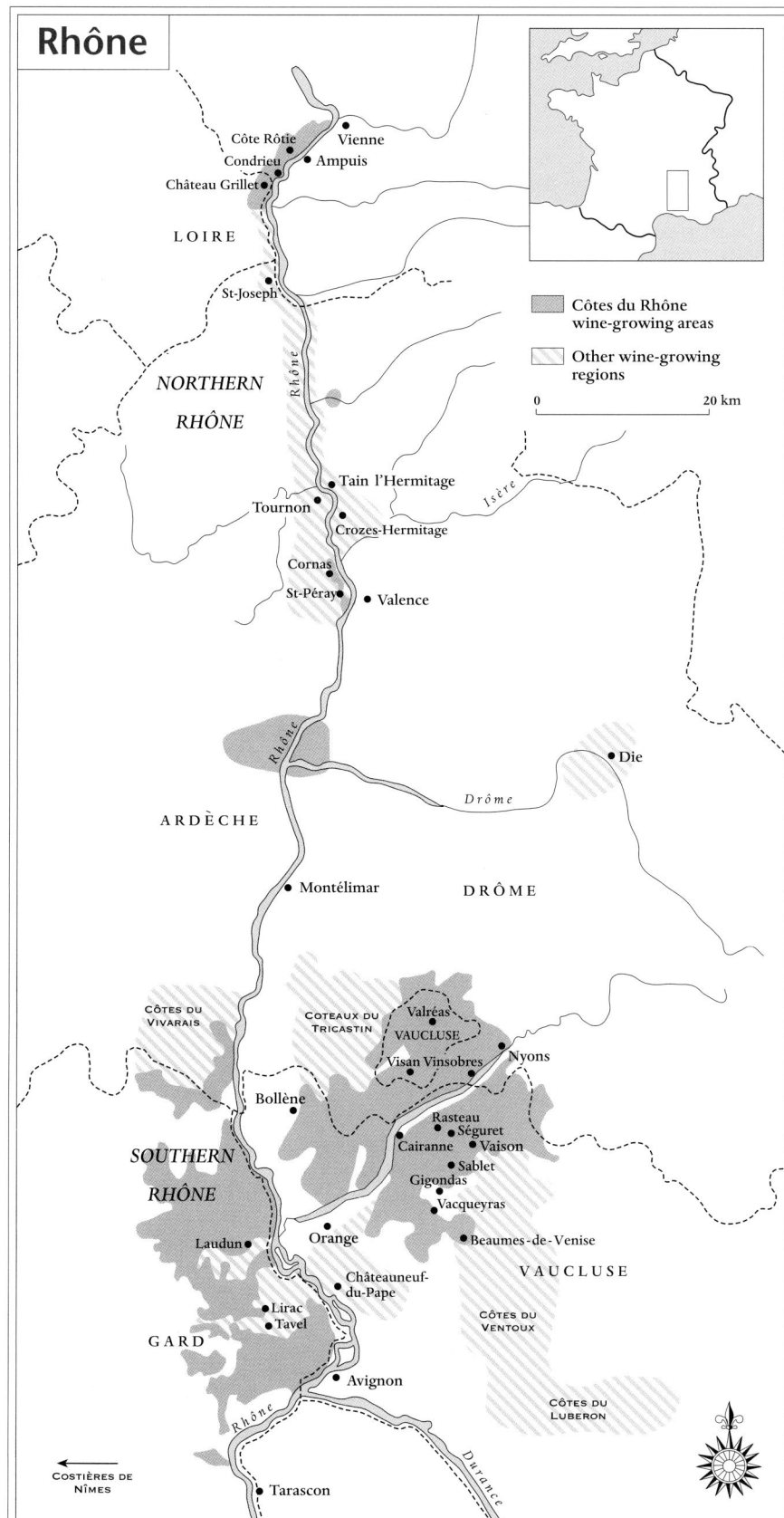

Rhône

Côte Rôtie • Vienne
Condrieu • Ampuis
Château Grillet •

LOIRE

Rhône

St-Joseph •

NORTHERN RHÔNE

Isère

Tain l'Hermitage •
Tournon •
Crozes-Hermitage
Cornas •
St-Péray • **Valence**

Rhône

• Die

Drôme

ARDÈCHE

• Montélimar

DRÔME

CÔTES DU VIVARAIS

COTEAUX DU TRICASTIN

Valréas
VAUCLUSE
Visan Vinsobres • Nyons

• Bollène

Rasteau
Séguret
Cairanne • **Vaison**
Sablet
Gigondas
Vacqueyras

SOUTHERN RHÔNE

Laudun • **Orange** • **Beaumes-de-Venise**

VAUCLUSE

Châteauneuf-du-Pape

CÔTES DU VENTOUX

• **Lirac**
• **Tavel**

GARD

• Avignon

Rhône

CÔTES DU LUBERON

Durance

← COSTIÈRES DE NÎMES

• Tarascon

Côtes du Rhône wine-growing areas

Other wine-growing regions

0   20 km

It was his hatred of political infighting, not his love of French wines, that drove Clement back to Avignon. After his successor Gregory XI returned to Rome for good in 1377, the pope and his Roman household continued to drink the wines of the Rhône.

Châteauneuf-du-Pape owes its name to a new castle built by John XXII, a summer residence in the hills 16 km/10 miles north of Avignon. It was destroyed by German bombers in the Second World War.

The name Hermitage La Chapelle has its origins in medieval legend. When the Crusader Gaspard de Stérimberg returned from the Holy Land, he gained the permission of Blanche of Castille, queen of France and regent during the minority of her son Louis IX (1226–70), to build a chapel and dedicate it to St Christopher; there he lived as a hermit for 30 years until he died. JABOULET's white Hermitage Chevalier de Stérimberg is named after this knightly recluse on the hill of Hermitage.

It was not only the Rhône which benefited from the extravagant habits of the papal court at Avignon: BURGUNDY, too, saw demand for its wines soar. As Burgundy became a major wine-producing region, it realized the dangers of competition from the south, especially because the wines of the Rhône were heavier than its own and hence more likely to survive transport unscathed. The duchy of Burgundy was in a powerful position, for in order to reach the markets of Paris and the north of France the wine of the Rhône had to be carried up the Saône through Burgundian territory. The solution was simple: Burgundy imposed severe restrictions on the entry and transit of all non-Burgundian wines. In 1446, the city of Dijon banned wines from Lyons, Vienne, and Tournon altogether, for the spurious reason that they were '*très petits et povres vins*'. While these measures remained in force, from the 14th to the 16th centuries, they were successful. The wines of the Rhône valley were excluded from the trade with England and the Low Countries, and they were not available in Paris until the 17th century, when transport overland had become less expensive and merchants could afford to carry their wines to the lower reaches of the Loire by ox-drawn cart and then ship them down the Loire.   H.M.W.

Dion, R., *Histoire de la vigne et du vin en France* (Paris, 1959).

Livingstone-Learmonth, J., *The Wines of the Northern Rhône* (Berkeley, Calif., 2005).

Northern Rhône

The vineyards of the northern Rhône have probably been noticed by more tourists than any others, since so many millions of tourists are funnelled each year between northern and southern Europe down the narrow Rhône valley south of Lyons past Tain l'Hermitage. Here, high above the *autoroute du soleil*, TERRACES have been set to work as advertising hoardings for such producers as JABOULET and

CHAPOUTIER. For a few seconds, the vineyards of the northern Rhône make an impression, but their produce is aimed in the main at the fine wine connoisseur rather than at the mass market. The total production of the northern Rhône is less than 5 per cent of total Rhône valley wine, with Crozes-Hermitage alone representing well over half of all wine produced in the north.

At the southern limit of that part of Europe where CHAPTALIZATION is allowed, the northern Rhône is under the influence of a CONTINENTAL climate, with hard winters and summers whose effect on the grapes can be exaggerated by the steep slopes to which many of the better northern Rhône vineyards cling, although SOIL EROSION is a constant threat. The steep banks of this now heavily industrialized river naturally limited vine cultivation for many centuries, and the best wines are produced on inclines which are expensive to work and help to maximize the effect of the available SUNLIGHT (see TOPOGRAPHY). Since the 1980s, however, when the better wines of the Rhône were recognized as offering some of the best fine wine value (and wine-making recognized as a potentially noble way of earning a living), there has been considerable expansion, particularly on the flatter land in such appellations as St-Joseph and Crozes-Hermitage, but also in, and especially around, more restricted appellations such as Cornas and Condrieu. Most appellations are based on the right bank of the river, but the left bank vineyards of Crozes-Hermitage, and especially Hermitage, are particularly well exposed to afternoon sunshine.

This is the prime territory of the SYRAH grape, which is the only red grape permitted in northern Rhône red wines. Fashionable VIOGNIER is the defining grape variety of the white wines Condrieu and Château Grillet, while other white northern Rhône wines are made from the robust MARSANNE given nerve by the more delicate ROUSSANNE grape.

Most wine-making and all vine-growing is in the hands of individuals working a family holding. About half of all wines are bottled by merchants, of which Jaboulet, Chapoutier, Delas, and GUIGAL are some of the best known. Guigal's single-vineyard bottlings and distinctive, if controversial, use of new OAK did much to raise international awareness, and prices, of the northern Rhône in the 1980s. The district has benefited from an influx of wine-making perfectionists, whose hero is often Gérard Chave. A notable consultant OENOLOGIST based in the northern Rhône, in Cornas, is Jean-Luc Colombo, and one of a new breed of NÉGOCIANTS is Tardieu-Laurent, the Laurent being Dominique Laurent of Beaune. There are very few CO-OPERATIVES, although the one at Tain l'Hermitage is remarkably effective.

For more details, see the specific appellations CHÂTEAU GRILLET, CONDRIEU, CORNAS, CÔTE RÔTIE, CROZES-HERMITAGE, HERMITAGE, ST-JOSEPH, and ST-PÉRAY.

Livingstone-Learmonth, J., *The Wines of the Northern Rhône* (Berkeley, Calif., 2005).

Southern Rhône

The southern Rhône has only the river in common with the northern Rhône. The countryside here in the flatter, southern part of the valley is definitively southern, almost Provençal, with both houses and vegetation demonstrating the influence of a MEDITERRANEAN climate. Many other fruits are grown here, and one of the chief hazards is the sometimes cold WIND that can blow down the Rhône valley. Most vines are GOBELET trained, although Syrah grapes are usually trained on wires in a single GUYOT system. If drought persists, some IRRIGATION is permitted.

Most wines are blends rather than made from a single vine variety. Although Syrah is increasingly widely planted to endow red wines with longevity, four times as much GRENACHE is grown in the southern Rhône. It can in theory be supplemented or seasoned by a wide range of other local varieties, but in practice only CARIGNAN, CINSAUT, MOURVÈDRE, and Syrah are planted to any extent. Similarly, UGNI BLANC is in reality still the most planted white grape variety, even though it, like Carignan, may make only a limited contribution to a blend.

CO-OPERATIVES are very important in the southern Rhône, making about 70 per cent of total production. The NÉGOCIANTS of the northern Rhône also have a long tradition of buying wine here for blending and bottling en route to the north. But there is also a host of individual estates, especially in Châteauneuf-du-Pape, keen to etch their own stamp on a particularly accessible appellation. Wine-making techniques here are extremely varied, including everything from full-blown CARBONIC MACERATION to fly-blown ancient, open, wooden fermenting vats of uncertain age and certain lack of HYGIENE. New oak has been treated with suspicion but is increasingly common even here.

The southern Rhône is the only part of France other than the LANGUEDOC and ROUSSILLON to have a tradition of making sweet VIN DOUX NATUREL: a golden Muscat version in BEAUMES-DE-VENISE, RANCIO tawny, and ruby red in RASTEAU.

For more details, see also CHÂTEAUNEUF-DU-PAPE, COSTIÈRES DE NÎMES, GIGONDAS, LIRAC, TAVEL, and VACQUEYRAS.

Côtes du Rhône

This expression is sometimes used for the entire Rhône valley, but the specific appellation, granted in 1937, has almost become French for red wine. With BEAUJOLAIS and BORDEAUX AC, Côtes du Rhône has almost become a commodity, which must be discouraging for the increasing number of seriously quality-minded producers of it. The great majority of Côtes du Rhône comes from the flatter, arid, often windswept vineyards of the southern Rhône, typically a light fruity red wine made, using full or SEMI-CARBONIC MACERATION, by one of the many co-operatives in the region.

A significant proportion of this wine is released as a PRIMEUR, in competition with Beaujolais Nouveau. Notable independent estates include Domaines Gramenon, de la Janasse, la Réméjeanne, and St-Estève, and Chx du Grand Moulas and de Trignon but the two most age-worthy and exceptional red Côtes du Rhônes available are Coudelet de Beaucastel and the extraordinary Domaine de Fonsalette, produced respectively as adjuncts to two of the most famous estates in Châteauneuf-du-Pape, Chx de Beaucastel and Rayas. About 2 per cent of Côtes du Rhône is white, but a considerable quantity of rosé is made, specifically for summer drinking in the region.

The total area of vineyard dedicated to the appellation is about 42,000 ha/103,000 acres, a vast proportion of viticultural France matched only by the generic Bordeaux appellation. The area which qualifies for the appellation includes the fringes of smarter northern Rhône appellations as well as huge tracts of both the left and right banks of the southern Rhône. Most of the northern Rhône NÉGOCIANTS blend and bottle their own Côtes du Rhône, and that of Guigal can show the marked Syrah character of the northern Rhône.

The great majority of grapes used for Côtes du Rhône, however, are southern, which means officially those allowed in CHÂTEAUNEUF-DU-PAPE plus the scented white Viognier, and Carignan. Grenache tends to dominate.

Côtes du Rhône-Villages

This useful appellation represents a distinct step up in quality, and often value, from generic Côtes du Rhône. The basic maximum permitted YIELD is 42 rather than 50 hl/ha (2.4 tons/acre), and the appellation has adopted the Châteauneuf-du-Pape's minimum alcoholic strength of 12.5 per cent for red wines. The possibility for promotion to a specific appellation exists for each named village: first GIGONDAS then VACQUEYRAS, and in 2005, BEAUMES-DE-VENISE and VINSOBRES escaped the relative anonymity of the Villages appellation. RASTEAU is also seeking such recognition. Eighteen villages are allowed to append their name to the appellation Côtes du Rhône-Villages (and very cumbersome wine names some of them make too): Rochegude, St-Maurice-sur-Eygues, Rousset-les-Vignes, and St-Pantaléon-les-Vignes in the Drôme *département*; Cairanne, Rasteau, Roaix, Séguret, Valréas, Visan, Sablet, Massif d'Uchaux, Plan de Dieu, and Puyméras in

Vaucluse; and Chusclan, Laudun, St-Gervais, and Signargues on the right bank of the river Rhône in the Gard. Of these, Cairanne with such fine producers as Domaines Alary, Brusset, de L'Oratoire St-Martin, and Marcel Richaud has long been considered ripe for promotion. Many more communes, including some as far north as the ARDÈCHE, are allowed to submit wine for the appellation, though they may not append their village name. The total area of vineyard supplying wine for this appellation was more than 5,700 ha/ 14,000 acres in the late 1990s, about one-eighth of that producing generic Côtes du Rhône. Some of the most energetic and thoughtful wine producers of France are based within this appellation.

Livingstone-Learmonth, J., *The Wines of the Rhône* (3rd edn, London, 1992).
—— *The Wines of the Northern Rhône* (Berkeley, 2005).
Norman, R., *Rhône Renaissance* (London, 1995).
Parker, R. M., *Wines of the Rhône Valley* (New York, 1997.)

Rhône Rangers, loose affiliation of CALIFORNIA wine producers who, led by Bob Lindquist of Qupé winery and Randall Grahm of Bonny Doon, decided in the 1980s to produce wines in the image of the reds and, increasingly, whites of the RHÔNE valley in France. Such wines provided a useful outlet for the produce of old GRENACHE and Mataro (MOURVÈDRE) vines which had previously languished out of favour. It also resulted in a dramatic increase in plantings of such vine varieties as SYRAH (whose total California plantings grew from 2,000 acres/800 ha prior to 1995 to over 17,000 acres/6,800 ha in 2003) and VIOGNIER (500 acres/200 ha prior to 1995; over 2,100 acres/840 ha in 2003). Joseph Phelps of NAPA was an early exponent, Bonny Doon of SANTA CRUZ a later but noisier one. The movement was regarded by some as providing welcome alternatives to the usual California diet of unblended Cabernet Sauvignon, Merlot, and Chardonnay, by others as an act of treachery against the state's own wine styles and vine varieties (PETITE SIRAH was only gradually accepted into the Rhône Rangers' blending vats).

Rías Baixas, the leading DO wine zone in GALICIA, north west Spain (see map under SPAIN), producing some of the country's most sought-after dry white wines. Named after the flooded coastal valleys, or *rías*, that penetrate up to 30 km/19 miles inland, the zone's reputation is based on the white ALBARIÑO grape, which has been accorded cult status in Spain. Wines were exported to northern Europe in the 16th and 17th centuries but, after the ravages of PHYLLOXERA, many of the traditional vine varieties were abandoned, and by the 1900s the region's vineyards were largely planted with high-yielding HYBRIDS and by Jerez's PALOMINO, producing poor-quality wine. The revival began in the late 1970s, when growers were

encouraged to replant native vine varieties and producers were given incentives to invest in modern wine-making equipment. The metamorphosis gathered pace with the application of EUROPEAN UNION funds following Spain's accession to the EU in 1986.

Rías Baixas has five separate subzones, all within the province of Pontevedra. Many of the purest Albariño wines come from Val do Salnés zone centred on the town of Cambados on the west coast. The two further subzones, O Rosal and Condado do Tea, are on the northern slopes of the river Miño facing the VINHO VERDE region in Portugal on the opposite bank. A fourth, small subzone, Soutomaior, was admitted in the late 1990s, to be joined by Ribeira do Ulla in the far north. All five zones share the same GRANITE-based subsoils and relatively cool, damp, MARITIME climate. The Atlantic influence is strongest in Val do Salnés, where annual RAINFALL averages 1,300 mm/50 in. Vines were traditionally cultivated on pergolas (see TENDONE) to protect grapes from the constant threat of FUNGAL DISEASES, although modern vineyards are planted on a more practical local variant of the GENEVA DOUBLE CURTAIN vine-training system.

Twelve different vine varieties are officially permitted in Rías Baixas although Albariño accounts for 90 per cent of the vineyard area. Other white grapes which may be blended with Albariño according to local regulations include CAIÑO BLANCO, as well as TREIXADURA, and Loureira (see LOUREIRO; locally known as Marqués), both of which are found in the Vinho Verde region. (TORRONTÉS and GODELLO are also permitted.) On its own, Albariño produces a fragrant, intensely fruity, dry white wine with a natural minimum alcohol often above 12 per cent. Yields used to be low, which made the wines expensive, but abusive yield increases began to occur in the 1990s, sometimes aggravated by over-reliance on selected, aroma-enhancing YEASTS. There have been experiments with OAK. The six permitted red grapes, including MENCÍA, ESPADEIRO, and Caiño Tinto, are relatively unimportant.

R.J.M. & V. de la S.

Ribatejo, DOC and VINHO REGIONAL (known as Ribatejano) in central southern Portugal corresponding to the province of the same name on both sides of the river Tagus (Tejo) inland from the capital Lisbon (see map under PORTUGAL). Fertile ALLUVIAL soils yield ample supplies of fruit and vegetables for the urban population around the river estuary. The Ribatejo province is therefore one of the wealthier parts of rural Portugal, although north and west of the river the land tends to be divided into the sort of smallholdings which characterize the adjoining ESTREMADURA region. The river is roughly the dividing line between these modest properties in the north and the vast estates of southern Portugal. Vines planted on the flood plain are naturally

irrigated most winters by the swollen river so that yields as high as 100 hl/ha (5.7 tons/acre) are common here. The Ribatejo is second only to Estremadura in the amount of wine it produces each year although less than 5 per cent qualifies as DOC. Much is made in the co-operatives and sold to the undemanding local market.

The best wines come from the less fertile soils away from the river and since the mid 1990s vineyards have increasingly been transferred from the flood plains. The Ribatejo was for many years the anonymous source of some of Portugal's best red wines, the GARRAFEIRAS aged for at least three years and sold under the name of a merchant rather than that of the region. Many of the larger estates are now making and marketing their own predominantly red wines from CASTELÃO and TRINCADEIRA alongside international varieties such as Cabernet Sauvignon, Merlot, Syrah— and even a small amount of Pinot Noir. However white varieties still predominate in the Ribatejo with FERNÃO PIRES still accounting for over 40 per cent of the vineyard area. The Ribatejo DOC is divided into six subregions: Almeirim, Cartaxo, Chamusca, Coruche, Santarém, and Tomar. Of these, Almeirim and Cartaxo, each dominated by a large co-operative winery, are the most important.

R.J.M.

Mayson, R., *The Wines and Vineyards of Portugal*, (London, 2003)

Ribeira Sacra, growing Spanish DO, created in 1996. It is the only GALICIAN region specializing in red wines, from the MENCÍA grape, with some whites from Godello and Albariño.

V. de la S.

Ribeiro means 'river bank' or 'riverside' in the Galician language and is the name of a red and white wine zone in GALICIA, north west Spain (see map under SPAIN). Ribeiro spans the valleys of the river Miño and its tributaries and Arnoia downstream from Orense. The region became a DO in 1957 but this has had little impact on exports (although in the 16th and 17th centuries wines from Ribeiro had been exported as far afield as Italy and England). PHYLLOXERA put paid to the region's prosperity at the end of the 19th century. As in RÍAS BAIXAS, for example, farmers, seeking a quick return to profit, replanted their holdings with the sherry grape PALOMINO. Over recent years, growers have been encouraged to uproot this productive but unsuitable variety in favour of TREIXADURA, TORRONTÉS, and LADO, white grape varieties which perform well in the damp MARITIME climate of north west Iberia. Both varieties can be made into aromatic, crisp white wines. The deeply coloured, light-bodied red wines, mainly from red-fleshed Garnacha Tintorera (ALICANTE BOUSCHET) grapes, are of no great interest, but such growers as Arsenio Paz have reintroduced red wines made from indigenous varieties. With help from EUROPEAN UNION funds, wineries have been updated and the traditional, labour-intensive pergolas (see TENDONE) are being replaced by lower vine-TRAINING SYSTEMS.

R.J.M. & V. de la S.

Ribera del Duero, important wine zone in CASTILLA Y LEÓN in north central Spain strongly challenging RIOJA as the leading red wine-producing region in Iberia with nearly 19,000 ha/47,000 acres of vineyard, almost a third as much as Rioja, planted in the mid 2000s. Ribera del Duero spans the upper valley of the river Duero (known as DOURO in Portugal), starting some 30 km/18 miles east of the city of Valladolid (see map under SPAIN). Although Bodegas VEGA SICILIA on the western margin of the denomination has been producing one of Spain's finest wines since the mid 19th century, the region was awarded DO status only in 1982. Since then more than 50 private estates have emerged.

At first sight, the Duero valley is not the most congenial place to grow grapes. At between 700 and 850 m/2,800 ft above sea level, the growing season is relatively short. FROST, commonplace in winter, continues to be a threat well into the spring. Temperatures, which can reach nearly 40 °C/104 °F in the middle of a July day, fall sharply at night—a phenomenon associated with wine quality elsewhere (see TEMPERATURE VARIABILITY).

The potential was recognized by Alejandro Fernández, who played a key role in the considerable development of the region in the 1980s. Pesquera, his wine vinified from grapes growing around the village of Pesquera del Duero a short distance upstream from Vega Sicilia, was released in the early 1980s to international acclaim. Other growers (many of whom had previously sold their grapes to the CO-OPERATIVES) were thereby encouraged to make and market their own wines, soon challenging Rioja's traditional hegemony inside Spain. In the 1990s, consumption of top-quality Ribera wines soared within Spain, causing deepening concern in Rioja. Several Ribera producers attained quality levels not much below those of Vega Sicilia and Pesquera. The leading challengers included Dominio de Pingus, Alión, Pérez Pascuas, Pago de los Capellanes, Emilio Moro, Aalto, Hermanos Sastre, Dominio de Atauta, Hacienda Monasterio, and Cillar de Silos. Several of these growers are in the east of the region, near Aranda de Duero, where a tradition of cheap rosés had previously inhibited production of top-quality reds.

The region's principal vine variety, the Tinto Fino (also called Tinta del País), is a local variant of Rioja's TEMPRANILLO. It seems to have adapted to the Duero's climatic extremes and produces deep-coloured, occasionally astringent, firm-flavoured red wines without the support of any other grape variety. White wine made from the ALBILLO, a white variety enjoyed as a table grape by the locals, is not entitled to the DO but may occasionally be blended into the intense red wine to lighten the load and add glycerine content. Cabernet Sauvignon, Merlot, and Malbec, introduced by Vega Sicilia 130 years ago, are now allowed throughout the denomination. Garnacha is used in the production of rosé.

R.J.M. & V. de la S.

Peñín, J., *Guía Peñín* (Madrid, annually).

Radford, J., *The New Spain* (2nd edn, London, 2004).

Ribera del Guadiana is the chosen name for a single denominated zone encompassing about 22,000 ha/54,000 acres of vineyards in Spain's EXTREMADURA region. The DO, awarded in 1998, includes such well-known areas as Tierra de Barros. The autonomous Extremadura government is actively encouraging the planting of INTERNATIONAL VARIETIES and improvements in wine quality but the results have been slow in coming.	V. de la S.

Ribera del Júcar, promising Spanish DO in the Cuenca province of CASTILLA-LA MANCHA whose first vintage was 2003.

Ribéreau-Gayon, dynasty of important OENOLOGISTS closely associated with the history of the Institut d'Oenologie at the University of BORDEAUX .

Ribolla, white grape variety also known as **Ribolla Gialla** to distinguish it from the less interesting **Ribolla Verde**, best known in FRIULI in north east Italy but also grown, as Rebula, in SLOVENIA, and almost certainly the Robola of the island of Cephalonia in GREECE.

Ribolla's first historically documented appearance in Friuli is in a notarial contract of 1289. The city of Udine demonstrated its respect for the wine by specifically legislating against its adulteration in 1402. That the wine had its admirers from an early date is demonstrated by Boccaccio's inclusion of Ribolla in a diatribe against the excesses of gluttony, an opinion confirmed by Antonio Musnig towards the end of the 18th century, when he rated it the finest white wine of Friuli. The grape lost ground steadily in the 19th and 20th centuries, however, in the wake of the PHYLLOXERA epidemic and Friuli's subsequent enthusiasm for non-native (French) varieties when vineyards were replanted. In the mid 1990s, Ribolla accounted for less than 1 per cent of all the white DOC wines of Friuli. Rosazzo and Oslavia are generally considered the two classic areas for Ribolla Gialla. The wine is light in body, floral, not without delicacy, but high in acidity and without a particularly strong personality. Some attempts at new oak ageing have been made in recent years, particularly in Oslavia, where the wines are frankly presented as an attempt to assert a Slavic identity which has been stifled by an indiscriminate enthusiasm for INTERNATIONAL VARIETIES.

Ribolla Nera is the SCHIOPPETTINO grape.

D.T.

Ricasoli, one of the oldest and most powerful noble families of TOSCANA in central Italy, important landholders between Florence and Siena for over a thousand years. The vast size of their holdings led the medieval republic of Florence to bar them from holding public office lest the combination of territorial dominion and civic position create a threat to republican liberties. Bettino Ricasoli (1809–80), a dominant figure in the political life of his time and the second prime minister of the newly united Italy in 1861, a dedicated agricultural experimenter and reformer, played a fundamental role in the revitalization of the viticulture of his time and invented what came to be the standard varietal formula for the production of CHIANTI: Sangiovese and Canaiolo for wines meant to be aged; Sangiovese and Canaiolo plus Malvasia for wines to be drunk young. The formula itself was significantly modified in the 20th century with the introduction of Trebbiano into the blend and a generalized use of white grapes in all Chianti wine, without the original distinction between the different styles of Chianti.

Perhaps even more important than the formula that he promulgated were Ricasoli's efforts in organizing the production and marketing of the wines of Chianti. A firm believer in a division of LABOUR in which the peasantry—virtually all share-croppers at the time—would grow the grapes and large commercial houses—principally controlled by the Tuscan nobility such as ANTINORI and FRESCOBALDI)—would age and distribute the finished wines, he founded the Ricasoli NÉGOCIANT firm, which would assume a position of leadership in Toscana for the better part of a century; André SIMON could still write after the Second World War that 'the most reliable brand of Chianti is that of Baron Ricasoli'.

The more recent past has been less kind to the fortunes of the house: a partnership with American distillers Seagram in the négociant part of the business in the 1960s led to huge expansion of production and a general lowering of quality, and the marketing of Ricasoli wines in supermarkets and other mass distribution centres was extremely damaging to their image. More damaging yet was an apparent obliviousness to modern ideas in Tuscan and Italian OENOLOGY, as the house missed both the 1980s trend to fruitier wines for younger drinking and fuller, more complex wines for cellaring. After a brief encounter with the Australian family wine producers HARDYS, the négociant operations were repurchased by the Ricasoli family in early 1993.

Another Italian **barrel** cellar, decorated with no less effort but in a more determinedly 20th-century style than Mastroberardino's, by Bellavista of Erbusco, Lombardia.

Following a large replanting programme in the vineyards, which are in some of the best sites in the southern part of the zone, a revitalized Castello di Brolio has once more joined the ranks of Chianti Classico's best producers. The Ricasoli label is reserved for the well-chosen négociant wines. D.T. & D.C.G.

rich is a tasting term for, generally, a red wine that gives an appealing impression of power and sweetness even though it has negligible RESIDUAL SUGAR. It may also be found as a label description on bottles of relatively sweet CHAMPAGNE (see DOSAGE).

Richebourg, great red GRAND CRU in Burgundy's CÔTE D'OR. For more details, see VOSNE-ROMANÉE.

riddling, an integral stage in the traditional method of making SPARKLING WINES, known as *remuage* in French. It involves dislodging the deposit left in a bottle after a second fermentation has taken place inside it and shaking it into the neck of the inverted bottle. It can be achieved either by hand or, more speedily, by machine (see GYROPALETTE). Modern alternative techniques may eventually render this cumbersome process superfluous. A **riddling rack** is English for a PUPITRE. For more details, see SPARKLING WINE-MAKING.

Ried, term used in AUSTRIA for single-vineyard sites.

Rieslaner, increasingly rare, late-ripening Silvaner × Riesling crossing that is grown to a very limited extent in Germany's FRANKEN region, where, provided it can reach full ripeness, it can produce wines with race and curranty fruit.

Riesler, confusing old Austrian synonym for WELSCHRIESLING.

Riesling has for long been arguably the world's most undervalued, and certainly most often mispronounced grape. ('Reeceling' is correct.) Riesling is the great vine variety of Germany and could claim to be the finest white grape variety in the world on the basis of the longevity of its wines and their ability to transmit the characteristics of a vineyard without losing Riesling's own inimitable style; in this sense it is very much more like Cabernet Sauvignon than Chardonnay (although DNA PROFILING in Austria in 1998 revealed a parent–offspring relationship with GOUAIS BLANC, a parent of Chardonnay, Pinot Noir *et al.*; see PINOT). Riesling has suffered, in an era when oak and heft have been considered the height of FASHION, because it is no friend of BARRIQUES, and its wines tend to be relatively low in alcohol. In the 1960s and 1970s, the name Riesling was debased by being applied to a wide range of white grape varieties of var-

ied and often doubtful quality, the ultimate backhanded compliment.

In the late 19th and first half of the 20th centuries, German Riesling wines were prized, and priced, as highly as the great red wines of France. Connoisseurs knew that, thanks to their magical combination of ACIDITY and EXTRACT, these wines could develop for decades in bottle, regardless of ALCOHOLIC STRENGTH and RESIDUAL SUGAR. Riesling is made at all levels of sweetness, and it is indubitable that the high proportion of late 20th-century German wines that have been far too low in extract and, for many consumers, too high in residual sugar has damaged Riesling's reputation. The average residual sugar of Riesling made everywhere has been declining fast, but the variety will surely always be distinguished for its ability to produce great sweet wines, whether they be the cold weather speciality EISWEIN or ICE WINE, or the BOTRYTIZED, Beerenauslese and Trockenbeerenauslese and their counterparts outside Germany. Riesling's high natural level of TARTARIC ACID provides it with a much more dependable counterbalance to high residual sugar than, for example, the Sémillon grape of Sauternes.

Riesling wine, wherever produced, is also notable for its powerful, rapier-like aroma variously described as flowery, steely, honeyed, and whichever blend of mineral elements is conveyed by the individual vineyard site. This distinctive aroma, usually experienced in conjunction with Riesling's natural raciness and tartness, is particularly high in MONOTERPENES, 10 to 50 times higher, for instance, than WELSCHRIESLING, a quite unrelated white grape variety prevalent in central Europe which, much to German fury, borrowed the word Riesling for many of its aliases (RIESLING ITALICO, for example). An important contributor to the bottle-aged bouquet of Riesling wines is the norisoprenoid hydrocarbon 1,1,6-trimethyl-1,2-dihydronaphthalene (TDN). At or just above the detection threshold it adds to the complexity of these wines. It can sometimes be found in relatively high concentrations, particularly in wines that have been in bottle for two or more years, and in excess, TDN can impart an undesirable kerosene-like flavour.

Viticulturally, true Riesling (often called **Weisser**, **White**, **Rhine**, or **Johannisberg Riesling**) is distinguished by the hardness of its wood, which helps make it a particularly cold-hardy vine, thus a possible choice for relatively cool wine regions, even if it needs the most favoured, sheltered site in order to ripen fully and yield economically. So resistant is it to FROST that winter pruning can begin earlier than with most other varieties. Its growth is vigorous and upright, and this is a top-quality variety which seems able to produce yields of 60 or 70 hl/ha (4 tons/acre), without any necessary diminution of quality. (Maximum yields allowed by the French INAO

authorities are higher in Alsace, France's Riesling enclave, for example, than for any other comparable fine wine.) Its compact bunches of small grapes make it relatively prone to BOTRYTIS, and COULURE can be a problem, but its chief distinction in the vineyard is its late budding. Riesling ripens early relative to most INTERNATIONAL VARIETIES, but late relative to most other varieties planted in Germany such as the GERMAN CROSSINGS. In cool vineyards in the northern hemisphere, it is often not picked until mid October or early November (and sometimes even later). Riesling can ripen so early in warmer regions, however, that its wines can taste dull; a long, slow ripening period suits Riesling best and manages to extract maximum flavour and EXTRACT, while maintaining acidity. Thus, many of Germany's (and therefore most of the world's) most admired Rieslings are grown on particularly favoured sites in cooler regions such as the MOSEL-SAAR-RUWER, whose crackling, light-bodied style of Riesling is unique.

Germany

As outlined in GERMAN HISTORY, Riesling is by no means the oldest documented vine variety grown in Germany (including, as it did for so long, Alsace). ELBLING and SILVANER were widely grown throughout the Middle Ages, while RÄUSCHLING was the speciality of Baden in the south. An invoice dated 1435, from a castle in the extreme south east of the Rheingau on the river Main, mentions '*riesslingen in die wingarten*', presumably Rieslings in the vineyard. Early spellings of words like Riesling have to be treated with care, since the similarly named Räuschling was so much more common then than today, but 1,200 'Ruesseling reben' (*reben* being German for vines) were bought by the Jacobshospital in Trier in the upper Mosel in 1464 and 'Ruesslinge' are documented near Worms in Rheinhessen in 1490. The Latin text of Heironymus Bock's herbal in 1552 provides the first known instance of Riesling spelt as it is today. Riesling seems to have been recognized as a top-quality variety from the late Middle Ages and was planted throughout the Rhine and Mosel from the middle of the 16th century.

Riesling is first mentioned in connection with Alsace as one of its finer products in 1477 by Duke René of Lorraine, even if we have to wait until 1628 for the first documentary evidence of its actually being planted there.

In the 18th century, various prince-bishops and other ecclesiastical authorities did their utmost to encourage Riesling plantings at the expense of other lesser varieties, notably in the Mosel. But the habit of picking grapes earlier than is today customary did the late-ripening Riesling no favours and by 1930 the Rheingau region, supposedly the classic Riesling heartland, had only 57 per cent of its vineyards planted with the variety (as opposed to 80 per cent today).

Hail is a perennial threat in the vineyards of Mendoza, Argentina, and all the foliage on these high-trained vines has been stripped by a particularly severe summer hailstorm. Many producers use nets to protect their vines against hail.

This provided a stimulus to Germany's burgeoning viticultural researchers (see GEISENHEIM) to select and develop top-quality CLONES of the variety. Today, partly thanks to the efforts of a special centre for the CLONAL SELECTION of Riesling at Trier, the German vine-grower can choose from more than 60, of which one of the more controversially perfumed is the N90 used by such innovative growers in the Pfalz region as Müller Catoir and Lingenfelder. (French-certified clones of Riesling still numbered precisely one, 49, in the mid 2000s, on the other hand.)

Much of the work of these viticultural institutes was also focused on developing the famous GERMAN CROSSINGS, designed to produce high yields of grapes with high MUST WEIGHTS but without the viticultural inconveniences of Riesling. In the second half of the 20th century, with their country awash in new money and an ocean of high sugar grape juice, many Germans gave up wine-growing, or at least the steep slope cultivation of the demanding Riesling vine, trends which sadly continue. In 1980, Riesling represented less than 20 per cent of German vineyard area, and even amid signs of a Riesling renaissance among sophisticated wine drinkers, its share of area has barely increased since. Along the Mosel-Saar-Ruwer, still home to more than a quarter of Germany's Riesling area, Riesling fell from 80 per cent of surface area in 1964 to 57 per cent in 2003—a total of 20,770 ha/51,300 acres.

Undeniably, though, the top vintners and sites not just of the Rheingau and Mosel-Saar-Ruwer, but also of the Nahe, Mittelrhein, Rheinhessen, and the Pfalz, are largely devoted to Riesling despite—in fact, precisely because of—its precarious, slow ripening in the face of climatic challenge. In these growing areas, Riesling is selected for the sunniest hillsides, steepest slopes, most sheltered rocky crenellations, and pockets of reflected heat. In such spots, Riesling shows dazzling diversity. It can be as delicate as a 7 per cent alcohol Mosel Kabinett that is somehow satisfyingly complete—or it may occasionally reach double that strength yet remain refreshing. It may be bone dry, off dry, or unabashedly sweet, sparkling or still.

Riesling's showcase is the northerly Mosel-Saar-Ruwer, home to more than one-quarter of all Germany's Riesling. The finest estates here are without exception dedicated to Riesling and plant the variety on their best sites to the exclusion of all else. Many of them, such as the famous names Haag, Müller, Prüm, and von Schubert, belong to the GROSSER RING association. Some would argue that Riesling finds its greatest expression on the steep banks of the Mosel and its Saar and Ruwer tributaries, ideally with a 30 per cent gradient to attract maximum ripening SUNLIGHT. For the same reason, all the best Mosel sites face south (which is why the best vineyards may be on either side of this meandering river).

The site should also be sheltered from wind and its ripest grapes are likely to come from vines neither so close to the river that morning mist slows ripening, nor above about 200 m/660 ft. The easily warmed red and blue SLATE soils typical of the region can also help late-season ripening. The result is wines unique in the world for their combination of low alcohol (often only about 8 per cent, although stronger, drier styles have become increasingly popular), striking aroma, high extract, and delicacy of texture. No other variety planted here can achieve as much subtlety.

The geological and microclimatically diverse NAHE is planted only around one quarter to Riesling, yet it is capable of superb feats of balance, its wines combining richness and tension. With the establishment of the state domaine of Niederhausen–Schlossböckelheim in the early years of the 20th century, and the subsequent degree of perfection achieved by its wines (and by some other large landholders) in the late 20th century, the Nahe was setting stunning qualitative standards—particularly with late and selective harvest wines—yet was hardly known abroad. Today Helmut Dönnhoff, farming some of the same sites as the former state domaine, has set standards that are rapidly bringing the Nahe to international attention and setting the pace for other family-owned estates.

The RHEINGAU and its steep-sided downstream neighbour the MITTELRHEIN are the only German growing regions dominated by Riesling, with 78 and 69 per cent respectively of their total area devoted to it. Some of the world's most complex variations on Riesling—both in dry and residually sweet forms—come from the slopes of the Main and Rhine rivers between Hochheim and Rüdesheim. A few leading Rheingau growers, notably Robert Weil, are today re-establishing both the lustre and the high prices of yore.

The historical as well as contemporary stylistic significance of Riesling in the PFALZ is out of proportion to its 20 per cent share of vineyard area. The Bassermann-Jordans, von Buhls, Bürklins, and Deinhards who established vine roots in the Mittelhaardt in the first half of the 19th century all followed the example of the Rheingau in planting Riesling in their best sites, thus establishing this variety as the future touchstone of local vinous quality. Pfalz Riesling typically ripens to over 12 per cent alcohol and has on that account been taken by most vintners today as particularly suitable for vinification to completely dry, relatively corpulent Rieslings such as those from particularly significant sites of Dr Bürklin-Wolf (see GROSSES GEWÄCHS). Müller-Catoir's long-serving cellarmaster Hans-Günter Schwarz in particular influenced two generations of Pfalz vintners in the pursuit of ripe fruit capable of making clear, pure wines.

Although almost one-fifth of WÜRTTEMBERG's area is devoted to Riesling, the result-ant dry wines are consumed almost entirely within that growing region. By contrast, the exceedingly small percentage of area devoted to Riesling in RHEINHESSEN, has a significance—above all in export markets—quite disproportional to its size. The Rieslings grown on red sandstone along the Rhine at Nackenheim and Nierstein, and to a lesser extent in nearby Bodenheim, Oppenheim, and Dienheim, are distinguished by their aromatic meld of citrus, peach, and smoked meats, as well as for their track record of ageability. Estates such as Fanz Karl Schmitt and Freiherr Heyl zu Herrensheim of Nierstein, and in recent decades particularly Gunderloch in neighbouring Nackenheim, have set qualitative benchmarks for Riesling quality in export markets. Even in the hinterlands where workaday crossings predominate, Riesling can shine in stony hillside sites at Bingen am Rhein and immediately east of Bad Kreuznach in villages such as Siefersheim, as well as wherever small pockets of red sandstone (e.g. in Weinheim) emerge.

Elsewhere

For many wine drinkers, Riesling is acceptable only in its French form, a wine from ALSACE, the only part of France where this German vine is officially allowed—a cause of some frustration with the strictures of INAO. Alsace's plantings of the variety wine producers there view as their most noble increased steadily, passed the 3,000-ha mark in the late 1980s, and were just over 3,400 ha in 2000. What is needed to produce Alsace Riesling of real class is, as in Germany, a favoured site of real interest such as many of Alsace's famous grands crus vineyards.

The hallmark of Alsace has been dry wines from aromatic grapes such as Riesling and certainly the great majority of Alsace Rieslings follow the variety's alluring perfume with a taste that is fairly alcoholic (easily 12.5 per cent) and bone dry. The dry climate of Alsace minimizes the risk of rot and makes extended ripening a real possibility, however, often resulting in the prized late harvest wines which qualify as VENDANGE TARDIVE or, even sweeter, SÉLECTION DE GRAINS NOBLES, the richest, most sumptuous ripeness category of ALSACE wines.

To the north, about 12 per cent of the LUXEMBOURG vineyard is planted with Riesling, which tends to produce dry, relatively full-bodied wines (thanks to CHAPTALIZATION), closer in style to those of Alsace than to those of the Mosel-Saar-Ruwer, which is just over the German border.

In AUSTRIA, Riesling (sometimes called **Rheinriesling** and formerly Weisser Riesling to distinguish it from the more widely planted WELSCHRIESLING) is quantitatively not especially important, planted on just over 1,600 ha/4,000 acres of vineyard, but is regarded as one of the country's finest wines when made on a favoured site. The most hallowed Austrian Rieslings are dry, full-bodied, concentrated, and aromatic, and a high proportion of them come from the terraced vineyards of the Wachau in Lower Austria. Certain favoured sites in neighbouring Kamptal such as the Zöbinger Heiligenstein vineyard near Langenlois and those just over the border from the Wachau in Kremstal also enjoy a high reputation for their aristocratic, whistle-clean Rieslings. Riesling is a relatively important variety in the vineyards of Vienna, especially those of Nussberg and Bisamberg.

Not surprisingly, Riesling works well in the continental climate of the CZECH REPUBLIC and SLOVAKIA (where Egon Müller of the Saar valley in Germany makes fine Riesling) to the immediate north of Austria's vineyards, where relatively light wines have real crackle and race. Most of SWITZERLAND is too cool to ripen Riesling properly, with the exception of some of the more schistous soils and warmest vineyards of Valais around Sion.

Although practically unknown in Iberia (*pace* TORRES in Spain's high Penedès), Riesling has infiltrated the far north east of Italy. It is grown with real enthusiasm in the high vineyards of ALTO ADIGE, where it produces delicate, aromatic wines quite unlike most Italian whites. It is also grown quite successfully in FRIULI, where it is known as **Riesling Renano**; and over the border in SLOVENIA, delicate **Renski Rizling** is produced in **Podravje**. Riesling, known as **Rizling Rajinski** and variants thereof, is also planted southwards in CROATIA and, less distinctively, in VOJVODINA.

It is planted throughout the rest of eastern Europe in Hungary and Bulgaria and to a much more limited extent in Romania but in each of these countries the climate can be too warm to coax much excitement from the variety and Welschriesling tends to reign supreme.

The country which had more Riesling planted than any other, even Germany, in the mid 1980s was what was then the USSR. If official statistics were to be believed, the Soviet Union grew 25,000 ha/61,700 acres of true Riesling before GORBACHEV'S VINE PULL SCHEME. It seems unlikely that the communist system encouraged the long wait for Riesling to ripen, so Soviet Riesling wines were presumably not the fullest, but it is easy to see why the variety would be popular in the cold winters of RUSSIA and UKRAINE, which has by far the biggest area planted with the variety. Rhine Riesling is also grown in MOLDOVA and, reputedly, in most of the central Asian republics: KAZAKHSTAN, UZBEKISTAN, TAJIKISTAN, KYRGYZSTAN, and TURKMENISTAN.

In the New World, true Riesling is most widely grown in AUSTRALIA, where it was the most planted white wine grape variety of all until Chardonnay caught up with its nearly 4,000 ha/10,000 acres in 1990. Total plantings had fallen to 3,400 ha by 1997 but revived a little to 4,250 ha by the early 2000s. After a period in the wilderness, Riesling is at last having its long-promised renaissance. Plantings are moving to the Eden and Clare valleys, Tasmania, and Great Southern, all producing wines with a minerally raciness underlying the tangy, lime-accented fruit. The wines are less phenolic than those of Alsace, and less alcoholic than Alsace or Austria. They also richly repay cellaring for up to, or even beyond, 20 years.

NEW ZEALAND began to produce convincing wines from its 725 ha/1,840 acres of Riesling in the early 21st century, notably when some producers addressed themselves to making scintillating late harvest sweet wines. Today, the Rieslings of Marlborough, where the variety is the third most planted white wine grape after Chardonnay and Sauvignon Blanc, are made at all sweetness levels. Nelson has also proved an excellent source of late harvest bottlings.

Riesling (of some sort) is cultivated far more widely in South America than one might imagine. Both Argentina and Chile have a few hundred hectares and some of Chile's is grown in the far south to good effect.

Riesling's progress in North America has been hampered simply by consumer demand for anything *but* Riesling, although certain producers with a reputation such as Wollersheim of Wisconsin soldier on (see UNITED STATES). California's total acreage of what is occasionally known as **White Riesling** remained at around 4,000 (1,600 ha) throughout the 1980s but declined to 1,850 acres by 2003. With the exception of Stony Hill's age-worthy wines and the Alsace-like offerings from Claiborne-Churchill, the variety is rarely made bone dry in California, and can command a decent price only if very sweet and described as Select Late Harvest (the equivalent of a German BEERENAUSLESE) or somesuch. Recognition and mastery of NOBLE ROT came only after 1973 when Jerry Luper produced one at Freemark Abbey, and in the late 1980s there were still some grape-growers willing to sell BOTRYTIZED grapes for a song, believing them beyond redemption. Such wines have trouble hanging on to their acidity and tend to brown after five years or so in bottle. Riesling is planted all over the state and has enjoyed some success in SANTA BARBARA (Firestone), MONTEREY (Ventana), and MENDOCINO (Navarro and Greenwood Ridge). Certain very high vineyards such as Madroña in El Dorado county have also enjoyed success with Riesling.

WASHINGTON state claims a special affinity for Riesling, even organizing the world's first truly international conference on the subject. The state's total area planted declined in the late 1980s but climbed to 2,800 acres/1,130 ha in the early 21st century. As in Oregon, the variety has suffered from consumer passion for other varieties rather than from any inherent viticul-tural disadvantage, but has enjoyed a modest renaissance since 1999 in both Washington and Oregon. Washington Riesling is conveniently winter hardy, and some of its wines can be delightfully delicate.

Because of its winter hardiness, Riesling tends to be treasured in the coolest wine regions of North America. In CANADA, Riesling is cultivated with particular success in Ontario, making fine, delicate ICEWINES just over the border from the Finger lakes region of NEW YORK state, where it is also increasingly respected. The sheer quality of New York Riesling has contributed to a revived interest in the grape and wine in New York and worldwide.

Pigott, S., *Riesling* (London, 1991).
Price, F., *Riesling Renaissance* (London, 2004).

Riesling Italico, or **Riesling Italianski,** white grape variety which Germans would like to see called RIZLING Italico to distinguish it from true RIESLING, known as Riesling Renano in Italy. In Austria, it is called WELSCHRIESLING (under which more details can be found); in much of what was YUGOSLAVIA, it is called LAŠKI RIZLING, in the CZECH REPUBLIC, it is called Ryzlink Vlašský, and in HUNGARY, it is called OLASZ RIZLING. Riesling Italico (*sic*) was ROMANIA's third most planted variety in the early 1990s, and was often blended with other varieties such as Muscat Ottonel. Within Italy, it is most common in the far north east, in FRIULI just over the border from SLOVENIA. Provided its tendency to overcrop is curbed, it can produce delicate, crisp, mildly flowery wines, most in COLLIO. It is grown to a limited extent in ALTO ADIGE and, more successfully, in LOMBARDIA.

Riesling-Sylvaner is the flattering, and misleading, name for MÜLLER-THURGAU that is, curiously, preferred in SWITZERLAND, where the canton of Thurgau is to be found. It has also been widely used in NEW ZEALAND, where it was for some time the most planted variety, although EUROPEAN UNION authorities disapproved. (And now that the term is on the wane, the reputation of true New Zealand Riesling is in the ascendant.)

right bank, an expression much used of that part of the BORDEAUX wine region that is on the right bank, or north, of the river DORDOGNE. It includes, travelling down river, Côtes de CASTILLON, Côtes de FRANCS, ST-ÉMILION and its satellite appellations, POMEROL and LALANDE-DE-POMEROL, FRONSAC and Canon-Fronsac, BOURG, and BLAYE. The most obvious characteristic shared by these appellations, and distinct from LEFT BANK appellations, is that the dominant grape varieties are Merlot and Cabernet Franc rather than Cabernet Sauvignon. In recent years, much has been made of the rivalry between the established large estates of the left bank and the much smaller properties of the right bank (including many MICROCHÂTEAUX) with their more recent reputations.

rimage, Catalan word for VINTAGE used especially for BANYULS rather as COLHEITA is used for port.

ringing vines. See CINCTURING.

Rioja, the leading wine region of SPAIN, producing predominantly red wines in the north of the country. Named after the *río* (river) Oja, a tributary of the river Ebro, most of the Rioja wine region lies in the autonomous region of La Rioja in north east Spain, although parts of the zone extend into the neighbouring BASQUE country to the north west and NAVARRA to the north east. Centred on the regional capital Logroño, Rioja divides into three zones along the axis of the river Ebro. **Rioja Alta** occupies the part of the Ebro valley west of Logroño and includes the wine-making town of Haro. **Rioja Alavesa** is the name given to the section of the zone north of the river Ebro which falls in the Basque province of Alava. **Rioja Baja** extends from the suburbs of Logroño south and east to include the towns of Calahorra and Alfaro.

History

There is archaeological evidence that the Romans made wine in the upper Ebro valley (see SPAIN, history). Wine trade was tolerated rather than encouraged under the Moorish occupation of Iberia, but viticulture flourished once more in Rioja after the Christian reconquest at the end of the 15th century. The name Rioja was already in use in one of the statutes written to guarantee the rights of inhabitants of territory recaptured from the Moors. Rioja's wine industry grew around the numerous monasteries (see MONKS AND MONASTERIES) that were founded to serve pilgrims en route to Santiago de Compostela, and the region's first wine laws date from this period.

For centuries Rioja suffered from its physical isolation from major population centres, and the wines found a market outside the region only in the 1700s, when communications improved and Bilbao became an important trading centre. In 1850, Luciano de Murrieta (subsequently the Marqués de Murrieta) established Rioja's first commercial BODEGA in cellars belonging to the Duque de Vitoria and began exporting wines to the Spanish colonies. The Rioja region benefited unexpectedly, but substantially, from the all too obvious arrival of POWDERY MILDEW in French vineyards in the late 1840s. Bordeaux wine merchants crossed the Pyrenees in large numbers and in 1862 the Provincial Legislature in Alava employed a French adviser to help local vinegrowers. Shunned by smallholders who were concerned only with the requirements of the local Basque market, Jean Pineau was finally employed by the Marqués de Riscal, who set about building a bodega at Elciego along French lines. It was finished in 1868, four years before Murrieta built its own similar installation at Ygay.

When the PHYLLOXERA louse began to devastate French vineyards in the late 1860s, yet more merchants came to Spain in search of wine. French duties were relaxed and Rioja enjoyed an unprecedented boom which lasted for nearly four decades. New bodegas were established, among them the Compañía Vinícola del Norte de España (CVNE), López de Heredia, La Rioja Alta, and Bodegas Franco-Españolas, all of which were heavily influenced by the French. During this period the 225-l/59-gal oak *barrica*, or BARRIQUE, was introduced from Bordeaux, and these influential maturation containers are still sometimes referred to as *barricas bordelesas* in Rioja (although American OAK was the popular choice). Helped by a new rail link (see RAILWAYS), Rioja sometimes exported 500,000 hl/13.2 million gal of wine a month to France in the late 19th century.

Phylloxera did not reach Rioja until 1901, by which time Bordeaux had returned to full production with vines grafted onto phylloxera-resistant ROOTSTOCKS. Spain also lost its lucrative colonial markets and Rioja's wine industry declined rapidly. A number of new bodegas were established in the period following the First World War and Spain's first Consejo Regulador was established in Rioja in 1926, but the Civil War (1936–9) and the Second World War which followed put paid to further expansion. Recovery came in the late 1960s and 1970s, when, encouraged by growing foreign markets and the construction of a motorway connecting Logroño and Bilbao, a number of new bodegas were built in the region, many with the support of multinational companies, which later sold back the wineries to Spanish firms.

Sales on the domestic market continued to grow throughout the 1980s, while exports recovered strongly in the 1990s after significant price increases in the late 1980s cut them sharply. Rioja was promoted from DO to DOCA status in 1991.

Climate and geography

Rioja enjoys an enviable position among Spanish wine regions. Sheltered by the Sierra de Cantabria to the north and west, it is well protected from the rain-bearing Atlantic winds that drench the Basque coast immediately to the north. Yet Rioja's wine producers rarely experience the climatic extremes that burden growers in so much of central and southern Spain. It is difficult to make climatic generalizations, however, about a region that stretches about 120 km/75 miles from north west to south east. Indeed, Spanish critics argue that within this single DO there are several entirely different wine-producing regions.

The vineyards range in ALTITUDE from 300 m/984 ft above sea level at Alfaro in the east to nearly 800 m on the slopes of the Sierra de Cantabria to the north west. Average annual RAINFALL increases correspondingly from less than 300 mm/12 in in parts of Rioja Baja to over 500 mm in the upper zones of Rioja Alta and Rioja Alavesa.

Rioja Alta and Rioja Alavesa share a similar climate and are distinct from each other for mainly administrative reasons, although there are soil differences between the two. Many of the best grapes are grown here on the cooler slopes to the north west around the towns and villages of Haro, Labastida, San Vicente, Laguardia, Elciego, Fuenmayor, Cenicero, and Briones. These zones share similar CLAY soils based on LIMESTONE. Downstream to the east, the climate becomes gradually warmer with rainfall decreasing to less than 400 mm at Logroño. Where the valley broadens, there is a higher incidence of fertile, ALLUVIAL soils composed chiefly of SILT. Around Calahorra and Alfaro in Rioja Baja the climate is more MEDITERRANEAN. In summer, DROUGHT is often a problem here, and temperatures frequently reach 30 to 35 °C/ 95 °F.

Viticulture and vine varieties

Seven grape varieties (four red, three white) qualify for Rioja's Denominación de Origen and their distribution varies in different parts of the region. The most widely planted variety is the probably indigenous, black TEMPRANILLO, which ripens well on the clay and limestone slopes of Rioja Alta and Rioja Alavesa, where it forms the basis for the region's best wines and in the mid 2000s was planted on nearly 40,000 of the region's 62,000 ha/153,000 acres of vineyard.

Most Riojas are blends of more than one variety, however, and wines made from the GARNACHA vine, which after phylloxera superseded native varieties in the Rioja Baja, are often used to add BODY to Tempranillo, which can taste thin on its own in cooler VINTAGES. On its own, Garnacha produces hefty, alcoholic red wines. Rioja, like neighbouring Navarra, produces rosé entirely from Garnacha grapes. Two further red varieties, Mazuelo (Cariñena or CARIGNAN) and GRACIANO, are of relatively minor importance. Although Mazuelo is not especially prized for quality, the indigenous Graciano has great potential, contributing to the aroma and structure of the wine. Owing to its susceptibility to disease and its low productivity, Graciano fell from favour with Rioja's vinegrowers before a strong revival in the 1990s, when the area devoted to this variety grew back to 200 ha/500 acres and VARIETAL versions are no longer oddities.

The CABERNET SAUVIGNON vines which arrived with the French in the 19th century are allowed by special dispensation in vineyards belonging to the Marqués de Riscal. Several other companies have experimental plantings of this Bordeaux grape, and of white imports such as Chardonnay.

Historically, until PHYLLOXERA arrived, Rioja's chief white grape variety was MALVASÍA. On its own, it produced rich, alcoholic, dry white wines which responded well to ageing in oak. However, Viura (known elsewhere in Spain as MACABEO) took over as the most planted light-berried variety in the region and from the early 1970s, fresher-tasting, cool-fermented, early-bottled white wines were in FASHION all over Spain. By the 1990s, most white Riojas were made exclusively from Viura, and Malvasía vines were extremely difficult to find, although some of the traditional oak-aged whites and new barrel-fermented wines are blends of Malvasía and Viura. Verdejo, Sauvignon Blanc, and Chardonnay are also permitted.

Vineyards in Rioja tend to be small, especially in Rioja Alta and Rioja Alavesa, where vines are often interspersed with other crops. Vines used to be free-standing BUSH VINES trained into low goblet shapes (see GOBELET), but of the thousands of hectares of new vineyard which have been planted since the 1970s, most are trained on WIRES. This resulted in a marked and alarming increase in YIELDS in the region in the 1990s, even before IRRIGATION was legalized in the late 1990s. Official DO limits are 63 hl/ha (3.5 tons/acre) for white wines and 45 hl/ha for reds. In 1998, there were about 50,000 ha of authorized vineyards, producing an average of about 2 million hl/53 million gal of wine, of which about 80 per cent was red.

Wine-making

Grapes are usually delivered to large, central wineries belonging either to one of the CO-OPERATIVES or to a merchant's bodega. Most wineries in Rioja are reasonably well equipped with a modern STAINLESS STEEL plant and facilities for TEMPERATURE CONTROL.

Rioja wine-making is characterized not by fermentation techniques but by BARREL MATURATION, however, and the shape and size of the 225-l *barrica bordelesa* introduced by the French in the mid 19th century is laid down by law. The regulations also specify the minimum ageing period for each officially recognized category of wine. In Rioja, red wines labelled CRIANZA and RESERVA must spend at least a year in oak, while a GRAN RESERVA must spend at least two years. In common with other Spanish wine regions, American OAK has been the favoured WOOD TYPE for wine maturation. New American oak barrels give the soft, vanilla flavour that has become accepted as typical of Rioja, but a similar effect can also be achieved by slow, OXIDATIVE maturation in older barrels. French oak is used increasingly, however.

Over 40 per cent of all Rioja falls into one of the three oak-aged categories above (the rest is either white, rosé, or sold as young, unoaked JOVEN red, much of it within Spain), and the larger bodegas therefore need tens of thousands of casks. In the late 1990s, the largest producer of Rioja, Bodegas Campo Viejo, maintained a stock of over 45,000 *barricas*. Most bodegas renew their *barricas* on a regular basis; new oak use is on the increase and the number of traditional producers who pride themselves on the age of their casks is dwindling. Some new producers are also spurning the tradional categories and bottling their oak-aged wine with a basic, generic Rioja back label.

After the widespread adoption of cool fermentation techniques in the 1970s, the amount of oak-aged white Rioja progressively diminished. López de Heredia, Marqués de Murrieta, and only a few other bodegas upheld the traditional style by ageing their white wines in oak *barricas*. For whites labelled Crianza, Reserva, or Gran Reserva, the minimum wood-ageing period is just six months with a further year, two years, or four years respectively before the wines may be released for sale. By the mid 1990s, a large number of producers had switched to fashionable BARREL FERMENTATION, however, in effect reviving the region's traditional white wine vinification method.

Some reds as well as whites may occasionally need ACIDIFICATION.

Organization of trade

Rioja's vineyards are split among nearly 20,000 growers, most of whom tend their plots as a sideline and have no WINE-MAKING facilities of their own, although in Rioja Alavesa they have been financially encouraged by the Basque regional government to acquire them. Many growers have an established contract with one of the merchant bodegas, whose numbers rocketed from about 100 in the mid 1990s to more than 500 a decade later. Others belong to one of the 30 CO-OPERATIVES that serve the region and receive around 45 per cent of the grapes. Most co-operatives sell their produce, either as must or as newly made wine, to the merchant bodegas, who blend, bottle, and market the wine under their own labels.

In the 1980s, a number of bodegas bought up large tracts of land to plant their own vineyards, although few as yet have sufficient to supply their entire needs. A number of single ESTATES, such as Contino and Remelluri, have also emerged, with the distinction, rare for the region, of growing, vinifying, and marketing their own wines.

Like other Spanish DOs, Rioja is controlled by a CONSEJO REGULADOR. Based in Logroño, the Consejo keeps a register of all vineyards and bodegas and monitors the movement of stocks from the vineyard to the bottle.

The Consejo also maintains laboratories at Haro and Laguardia where tests are carried out on all wines before they are approved for export. After a long debate dating from the 1970s, Rioja was granted DOCA status in 1991. The qualifications have little to do with absolute quality, the single most important being that Rioja's grape prices are at least 200 per cent above the national average. The Consejo Regulador set itself the target of mandatory BOTTLING within the region, was defeated in the EUROPEAN UNION court in 1992, but finally won on appeal in 2000. R.J.M. & V. de la S.

Peñín, J., *Guía Peñín* (Madrid, annually).
Radford, J., *The New Spain* (2nd edn, London, 2004).
—*The Wines of Rioja* (London, 2004).

Ripaille, named CRU on the south eastern shore of Lake Geneva whose name may be added to the French appellation Vin de SAVOIE. The wine is typically a slightly sparkling white made from the Chasselas grape.

riparia, species of the VITIS genus native to North America much used in developing suitably resistant ROOTSTOCKS and HYBRIDS.

ripasso, Italian term meaning literally 're-passed', for the technique of adding extra flavour, and alcohol, to VALPOLICELLA by re-fermenting the young wine on the unpressed skins of AMARONE wines after these DRIED GRAPE WINES have finished their fermentation in the spring. While this undoubtedly adds body and character to a ripasso Valpolicella, the fact is that all the goodness has been extracted from the grapes during their first fermentation, so only bitter TANNINS are leached from the skins. Some producers, notably Allegrini, are therefore substituting grapes that have been dried (though not to the extent required for Amarone) for the fermented Amarone skins, although this technique is necessarily expensive. The technique is also used in South America. D.T. & D.C.G.

ripeness, term used to describe that stage of the continuous process of grape RIPENING or development which is chosen by the winemaker and/or grape processor as that desired at HARVEST. What constitutes the ideal chemical and physical composition of grapes at this point is a subjective judgement dependent on wine style, the winemaker's current belief about optimal ripeness, FASHION, and many other factors, so ripeness is a relative term which can have many different meanings. Grapes considered at perfect ripeness by one winemaker for one purpose may be considered overripe or underripe by different winemakers for other uses.

Ripeness is often related to MUST WEIGHT or grape sugar concentration. Being directly related to POTENTIAL ALCOHOL, the concentration of SUGAR IN GRAPES has a major impact on wine type. The commercial table (non-fortified) wines of the world fall between two extremes, both European. VINHO VERDE grapes grown in northern Portugal are traditionally harvested early to give bottled wines that are sparkling, refreshing, and low in ALCOHOLIC STRENGTH (about 8.5 per cent). At the other extreme are the BOTRYTIZED wines of the world which contain so much sugar in their raisin-like berries that yeast cannot ferment all of the sugar. So the alcohol concentration may approach 15 per cent and yet there is also substantial RESIDUAL SUGAR in the finished wine.

Sugar levels are not the only aspect of grape composition to affect what is considered ripeness. Especially in cool climates, ACIDITY levels can be closely monitored to determine the grapes' ripeness. The acidity in grapes declines with ripening, and must be below certain values (which differ for different wine styles) so that the resultant wine will not be too tart and unpalatable. In warm to hot regions it is more common that the acidity is too low and the PH is too high once sugars have reached the desired potential alcohol level.

Measures of sugar, acidity, and pH have been commonly used around the world to define grape ripeness and optimal harvest time, but growers and winemakers continue to search for better definitions of ripeness to improve wine quality. For red wine, measurements of grape PHENOLICS, including anthocyanins and tannins, are proving useful. For all grapes, a measure that indicates flavour is so eagerly sought that it may be said to be the grape researcher's holy grail (see PHYSIOLOGICAL RIPENESS). This is a particularly difficult measurement because of the huge diversity of potential FLAVOUR COMPOUNDS on the one hand, and their minute concentration on the other. Nevertheless, the development of a measure of FLAVOUR PRECURSORS plus other GLYCOSIDES through analysis of the GLYCOSYL-GLUCOSE concentration of grapes and wines is a valuable new approach to this problem.

Individual grapes' physical condition, especially skin thickness and integrity, is also considered as an aspect of grape ripeness relevant to wine quality.

See also GRAPE COMPOSITION AND WINE QUALITY, and GRAPE JUICE COMPOSITION.

R.E.S. & B.G.C.

ripeness measurement. See MUST WEIGHT, RIPENESS, RIPENING.

ripening, grape. The important process of grape development which is a prelude to HARVEST. Ripening begins when the berries soften at the stage called VERAISON and is concluded normally by harvest, which can occur at different stages for different wine styles. Ripening can be affected by many plant, pest and disease, and environmental factors, and is in many ways the most important vine process affecting wine quality since it is so crucially related to the chemical and physical composition of the harvested fruit, and so to eventual wine quality.

Following FRUIT SET, grape berries grow in size but are hard, green, and very acidic (see GRAPE). When almost half their final size, veraison, or the inception of ripening, occurs. The timing of this will depend on variety and climate, but it is normally 40 to 60 days after fruit set, longer for cooler climates. The period from veraison to harvest will obviously depend on the harvest stage of ripeness required, but for grapes destined for dry table wine the period varies from about 30 days in hot regions to about 70 days in cooler regions. For early-ripening varieties such as Pinot Noir and Chardonnay, the ripening period is shorter than for a variety such as Cabernet Sauvignon, which ripens relatively late.

Not all bunches on a vine nor berries on a bunch are at the same stage of development; the first flowers to open set the first berries which in turn go through veraison and ENGUSTMENT, and ripen first. During the latter stages of ripening when the sugar content is above 20 °BRIX, the berry skin may lose some water. So for very ripe grapes the increase in concentration of sugar for example in the berry is due to a loss of water rather than more movement into the berry.

It is relevant to consider ripening in terms of the various chemical compounds of most interest to the winemaker. Sugar, or more precisely SUCROSE, is the most important. It is moved from the leaves to the berries by TRANSLOCATION, and is broken down to the constituent molecules GLUCOSE and FRUCTOSE by the enzyme INVERTASE. Sucrose may originate from current PHOTOSYNTHESIS or from stored CARBOHYDRATE reserves in the woody parts of the vine such as its trunk, arms, and roots. Heavy crop loads slow the increase in concentration of SUGAR IN GRAPES, as also do factors slowing photosynthesis such as low or high temperatures and cloudiness. There can also be competition for the products of photosynthesis; if shoot tips are growing actively, for example, then fruit ripening is slowed (see VIGOUR).

The second major indicator of grape ripening is ACIDITY. The concentration of TARTARIC ACID falls during ripening, due to dilution effects associated with berry growth. The concentration of MALIC ACID falls more quickly than tartaric during ripening, and this is because of temperature-dependent RESPIRATION in addition to dilution. Grapes ripening in cool climates therefore tend to have higher acidity as less malic acid is respired. Juice PH rises throughout ripening due to the decreases in free acids and increases in POTASSIUM. In hot regions, alarmingly high juice pH can be a factor in the timing of harvest.

The skin colour of red grapes is due to ANTHOCYANINS; veraison is signalled as they replace the green colour of chlorophyll. Anthocyanin concentration rises during ripening and the value at harvest depends on both environmental and plant factors. Temperature and light have major effects; high temperatures and low light levels reduce skin coloration in many varieties. Grape TANNINS are distributed between the skins, seeds, and stems. They increase during ripening at a rate comparable to anthocyanins.

The most abundant minerals in the grape are POTASSIUM, CALCIUM, MAGNESIUM, and SODIUM, and they increase in concentration during ripening. Potassium is predominant and has a major effect on juice pH. Potassium is distributed between flesh and skins, and the potassium extracted from skins during fermentation is one reason why red wines have a higher pH than white wines.

Flavour compounds are all-important factors in wine quality, even if their measurement is many years away from becoming a universal practice (although see GLYCOSYL-GLUCOSE ASSAY). At the beginning of the 21st century, analytical techniques as well as knowledge about their role were still a developing science. See FLAVOUR PRECURSORS and FLAVOUR COMPOUNDS.

See also GRAPE JUICE COMPOSITION, GRAPE QUALITY ASSESSMENT, RIPENESS, and PHYSIOLOGICAL RIPENESS. R.E.S. & B.G.C.

Coombe, B. G., 'Research on development and ripening of the grape berry', *American Journal of Enology and Viticulture*, 43 (1992), 101–10.
Hamilton, R. P., and Coombe, B. G., 'Harvesting of wine grapes', in B. G. Coombe and P. R. Dry (eds.), *Viticulture*, ii: *Practices* (Adelaide, 1992).
Tregoat, O., Gaudillère, J.-P., Choné, X., and Van Leeuwen, C., 'Étude du régime hydrique et de la nutrition azotée de la vigne par des indicateurs physiologiques. Influence sur le comportement de la vigne et la maturation du raisin (*Vitis vinifera* L. cv Merlot, 2000, Bordeaux)', *Journal International des Sciences de la Vigne et du Vin*, 36/3 (2002), 133–42.

ripping is a viticultural operation conducted in many parts of the world before PLANTING a vineyard in order to to break up compact soils so that water can penetrate and roots can grow to a greater depth. Normally bulldozers or heavy tractors are used.

Ripping also provides the opportunity to incorporate FERTILIZERS and soil amendments (see SOIL AMELIORATION) such as phosphates, forms of potassium or lime, as they will not readily leach through the soil.

Ripping dense clay soils allows roots to penetrate to greater depths and so the vines are able to access more water and nutrients. This will increase the vineyard VIGOUR and likely YIELD. Unless steps are taken to manage these more vigorous vines correctly, then SHADE may reduce both yield and quality. Ripping is a procedure, like IRRIGATION, which can modify some important properties of the soil affecting wine quality; see TERROIR.

R.E.S.

Coombe, B. G., and Dry, P. R. (eds.), *Viticulture*, ii: *Practices* (Adelaide, 1992).

ripping out vines is known as *arrachage* in France, where it became a common practice as part of the EUROPEAN UNION'S VINE PULL SCHEME. In the late 1980s and early 1990s, smallholders in the south of both France and Italy in particular took advantage of substantial financial inducements to abandon viticulture on all or part of their land in an effort to drain the European WINE LAKE. About 300,000 ha/741,000 acres of French vineyard and about 400,000 ha of Italian vineyard were ripped out between the late 1970s and 1991. France's total vineyard was reduced by a further 80,000 ha and Italy's by about 150,000 ha between 1991 and 1996, while a further 284,000 ha were ripped out in Spain and 126,000 in Portugal. There was also substantial ripping out of vines in Argentina in recognition of its SURPLUS of poor-quality vine varieties.

The more traditional reason for ripping out a vineyard is that the VINE AGE is so high and the average YIELD so low that the vineyard is no longer economic (although the prestige associated with old vines, or VIEILLES VIGNES, may retard this process).

A vineyard may also be ripped out because its owner wishes to change VINE VARIETY or CLONE, although this may be achieved by TOP GRAFTING, or field grafting onto, the existing trunks and root systems. Vineyards are normally ripped out when invaded by a pest as deadly as phylloxera (as thousands of acres were in northern California in the late 1980s), and a disease such as LEAFROLL VIRUS, ESCA, or GRAPEVINE YELLOWS may damage production to such an extent that ripping out is the only option.

If the vineyard is to be replanted, care must be taken that the soil is free of pests and disease. FUMIGATION may be necessary; see also NEMATODES.

Riserva, Italian term usually denoting a wine given extended AGEING before release and one with a higher minimum ALCOHOLIC STRENGTH, by one or half a per cent, than the non-Riserva version. In this latter respect, there is a certain overlap with the SUPERIORE designation. Some Riserva wines, unlike Superiore wines, are obliged to undergo a certain minimum ageing period in wood in order to qualify as a Riserva; the regular bottlings of such wines are not normally aged in wood. The Riserva bottlings of the most famous Italian wines—BARBARESCO, BAROLO, BRUNELLO DI MONTALCINO, CHIANTI CLASSICO, VINO NOBILE DI MONTEPULCIANO—are today not necessarily aged for a longer period in wood, however, but are simply required to have been aged longer overall, either in wood or in bottle, before release. (Chianti Classico Riserva, in fact, does not require any wood

ageing whatsoever.) Producers are not required to declare a Riserva or set aside given quantities of wine as a Riserva before the commercial release of their production, but may simply decide which wines are Riserva on an *ad hoc* basis. This latitude has allowed a certain number of houses simply to reclassify their unsold inventory as Riserva in an effort to obtain a higher price, prompting some calls for the abolition of the entire category.

D.T.

Rivaner, another name for MÜLLER-THURGAU, used in LUXEMBOURG, where it is the most planted grape variety, and, increasingly, elsewhere. Rivaner sounds more appetizing.

Riverina, major Australian wine region on the Murrumbidgee river in southern NEW SOUTH WALES. Home to Casella and the new millennium YELLOW TAIL phenomenon. Griffith is an important wine production centre but most wines made here are described coyly as coming from South Eastern Australia.

Riverland, the most productive wine region in AUSTRALIA, a sprawl of vineyards irrigated by the river Murray mainly in the state of SOUTH AUSTRALIA. The same market forces as described in MURRAY DARLING are forcing grape growers to improve the quality, and also to ensure they have the right varietal mix in an ever-changing market place. South Eastern Australia is the catch-all description usually found on labels.

rivers have played an important role throughout the history of wine, both as arteries of trade and also through their action in helping to shape valley slopes particularly well suited to the cultivation of the vine. More recently they have provided valuable IRRIGATION water.

A river is crucial to the earliest detailed account of the wine trade. HERODOTUS, writing in the 5th century BC, records how in MESOPOTAMIA wine in palm-wood casks was loaded onto boats in the upper reaches of the river Tigris, and then sailed down to Babylon, where the boats were broken up because of the impossibility of paddling them upstream against the current.

During the Roman era, rivers continued to play a vital role in the transport of bulky items such as wine. There were two main trade routes in GAUL: a western one from Narbonne to Toulouse and then along the river GARONNE to Bordeaux and the Atlantic; and a northern one up the RHÔNE to Lyons, and thence along the Saône, before cutting across country to the MOSEL and the RHINE, and eventually reaching the North sea. These routes witnessed the transport of thousands of AMPHORAE of wine, but they were also a highway along which the idea of vine cultivation and wine-making passed. By the 1st

century AD, viticulture was thus well established along the Rhône and the Garonne, and gradually vineyards came to be cultivated along most of the other major river valleys of Gaul such as the LOIRE and the Seine (see PARIS).

By the year 1000, although vineyards were relatively widely established throughout southern Europe, in the north they were found most frequently in river valleys. The main reason for this was the high cost of overland transport, which gave those with easy access to the main fluvial transport routes a distinct competitive advantage. Environmental factors were also important, with the south-facing slopes of such valleys providing ideal sites because of the extra exposure to the sun that they afforded (see VINEYARD SITE SELECTION). This is particularly evident in the development of vineyards in the cool Mosel–Rhine area, where most of those established before 1050 were in close proximity to rivers.

Coastal transport became increasingly important during the later medieval period, but rivers also maintained their role as arteries of the wine trade, and, with the opening up of eastern Europe, rivers such as the Dnestr, the Vistula, and the Danube came to play as significant a role as did the Garonne, Loire, Seine, Rhône, and Rhine in the west.

In the 19th and 20th centuries, with the development of the RAILWAYS and, subsequently, efficient road transport, it is the environmental factors that have been most important in determining the location of vineyards along the slopes of river valleys. Above all, these locations provide additional sunshine, generally alleviate the problems associated with FROST and excess humidity (see HILLSIDE VINEYARDS), and frequently have soils well suited to vine cultivation (see TOPOGRAPHY). Moreover, in some special locations, as in SAUTERNES and along the Rhine, the proximity to water provides the ideal conditions for NOBLE ROT, which can result in some of the world's greatest sweet wines.

In the New World, certain rivers have been crucial to the development of several wine regions. The Murray river in Australia, for example, is responsible for the existence of that country's extensive RIVERLAND vineyards, California's CENTRAL VALLEY depends on riverwater, and most of the vineyards in WASHINGTON state depend on water from the Columbia river.

P.T.H.U.

Postan, M. M., and Miller, E. (eds.), *The Cambridge Economic History of Europe*, ii: *Trade and Industry in the Middle Ages* (2nd edn, Cambridge, 1987).

Pounds, N. J. G., *An Historical Geography of Europe 450 BC–AD 1330* (Cambridge, 1973).

Schenk, W., 'Viticulture in Franconia along the river Main: human and natural influences since AD 700', *Journal of Wine Research*, 3/3 (1992), 185–204.

Rivesaltes, town north of Perpignan in southern France that gives its name to two of the biggest appellations of ROUSSILLON,

Rivesaltes and **Muscat de Rivesaltes**, both of them VINS DOUX NATURELS. Muscat de Rivesaltes, which represents about 70 per cent of France's total Muscat production, can in fact be produced throughout most of Roussillon's recognized wine-producing area, together even with some sections of the Aude *département* to the north (including much of the FITOU appellation). The Rivesaltes production zone is similarly generous but specifically excludes those vineyards that produce BANYULS.

The Muscats of 'Perpinyà' and 'Clayrà' (Claira is the next town to Rivesaltes) were already sought out by 14th-century wine buyers from as far away as Barcelona and Avignon. Their sweetness was originally concentrated by leaving the grapes on the vine to shrivel, as was still the custom in the 19th century (see DRIED GRAPE WINES), and may even have been enhanced by adding honey, for which the region is still famous. Today Muscat de Rivesaltes is the only Muscat vin doux naturel which may be made from MUSCAT OF ALEXANDRIA as well as the finer MUSCAT BLANC À PETITS GRAINS, which was once unpopular for its degeneration and unreliable yields; but new clones are being replanted. Average yields of these low-trained vines, often on difficult-to-work dry terraces, can be as little as 22 hl/ha (1.3 tons/acre) (the official upper limit is 30 hl/ha). Since the 1980s, more skilled vinification has helped improve quality, despite the domination of Muscat of Alexandria. Techniques include SKIN CONTACT and MUTAGE *sur marc*, i.e. on the skins. Muscat de Rivesaltes is already on sale the spring after the harvest and should be drunk as young and cool as possible, either as an aperitif or with fruit or creamy desserts.

The even more common Rivesaltes, on the other hand, has the potential, not often realized, to be a more complex vin doux naturel, made in all conceivable colours and styles. These sweet, heady, wines can be made from any permutation of Grenache Blanc, Noir, and Gris, Maccabéo, and to a much lesser extent Torbato (here called Malvoisie du Roussillon), and the two Muscats allowed for Muscat de Rivesaltes. Varietal Rivesaltes are permitted, from a golden Maccabéo to a Grenache Noir that can be anything from crimson to deep chocolate brown, depending on its ÉLEVAGE. These tests for FOOD AND WINE MATCHING may be vinified 'en blanc', like white wines without any contact with the skins, or may be macerated for weeks in an effort to leach maximum colour, tannin, and flavour into the wine. They may be fermented in stainless steel and bottled young or fermented and aged in wooden casks of all ages and sizes, sometimes according to some sort of SOLERA. Some wines are made to taste deliberately RANCIO and, while some producers deliberately expose the maturing wine to the punishing heat and light of a Roussillon noon, others may include a period in glass BONBONNES in

the ageing process. No Rivesaltes can be released until 16 months after the harvest. If the overall quality is more varied and less exciting than that of Banyuls or MAURY, it is improving, largely thanks to the efforts of Domaine Cazes. Rivesaltes may taste of raisins, coffee, chocolate, fruits, or nuts and the most concentrated can, like Banyuls, be some of the few wines that happily partner chocolate.

Riviera di Ponente, or **Riviera Ligure di Ponente**, wine from the north western coast of Italy. For more details, see LIGURIA.

Rizling, term for the white grape variety known variously in central Europe as WELSCHRIESLING, OLASZ RIZLING, LAŠKI RIZLING, and RIESLING ITALICO. The Germans disapprove of any name for this inferior grape variety which suggests a relationship with their own noble RIESLING vine, but will accept Rizling as a suitably distinctive alternative.

Rkatsiteli, Georgian white grape variety which is probably planted much more extensively than most western wine drinkers realize, on as many as 127,000 ha/314,500 acres according to one global estimate. It was by far the most planted grape variety in the SOVIET UNION and was much more widely grown before President GORBACHEV'S VINE PULL SCHEME. It is still the most planted vine variety in the ex-Soviet republics, however, being grown in all of its wine-producing independent republics with the exception of TURKMENISTAN. It is widely grown throughout eastern Europe and there are pockets of the variety in China and the United States as well.

Much is demanded of this variety and it achieves much, providing a base for a wide range of wine styles, including fortified wines and brandy. The wine is distinguished by a keen level of ACIDITY, easily 9 g/l even when picked as late as October, and by good sugar levels too. It is also the most-planted white grape variety in BULGARIA (11,700 ha in 2005), and there are more than 600 ha of it in ROMANIA.

In CHINA, it is known as Baiyu and has been an important source of neutral white wine for the nascent Chinese wine industry.

Roannaise, Côte, hand-crafted, lightish reds and some rosés made chiefly from locally adapted GAMAY grapes, called St-Romain à Jus Blanc here, using Beaujolais cellar techniques, usually SEMI-CARBONIC MACERATION. The south east-facing slopes of the upper Loire, on which vines are grown on a granitic base, are only one range of hills west of the BEAUJOLAIS region. Direct RIVER and canal links with Paris gave the region's wines relative fame and popularity in the 19th century so that annual production was almost 800,000 hl/21.1 million gal at the beginning of the 20th century. Production was down to 4,000 hl by 1994 when APPELLATION CONTRÔLÉE status was won but has been stead-

ily increasing with about 200 ha of vineyards in production in the mid 2000s. Wine quality is in the hands of more than a score of individual winemakers (unlike Côtes du FOREZ to the south), egged on by the Troisgros family at their famous restaurant in the town of Roanne.

Robertson, important wine-producing district within the Breede River Valley region in SOUTH AFRICA.

Robola, wine and grape variety for which the Ionian island of Cephalonia in GREECE is most famous. The distinctively powerful, lemony dry white is made entirely from Robola grapes, which are cultivated exclusively on the island, except that the vine is almost certainly the Rebula of SLOVENIA, and the RIBOLLA which has been grown in FRIULI in north east Italy since the 13th century. The wine made from these early-ripening grapes is high in both acidity and extract and is much prized within Greece.

robotic lagares, see PORT.

Rochelle, La. See LA ROCHELLE.

rock. Those who study GEOLOGY take a very broad view of this word. Any of the natural solid constituents of the Earth's crust are MINERALS. Any natural assemblage of minerals is a rock (although it may also contain liquids and/or gases), whether it is hard or soft, at the surface of the Earth or far beneath it. From this it follows that 'rock' in its widest sense includes soil, and SUBSOIL. There are some geologists whose research is devoted to soils, particularly ancient ones.

For more information about rock types, see SOIL and SOIL TYPES. J.M.H.

Rockpile, relatively new California AVA. See SONOMA.

Roditis Kokkinos, sometimes written **Rhoditis**, referring to the island of Rhodes, is a slightly pink-skinned Greek grape variety traditionally grown in the Peloponnese, especially before PHYLLOXERA struck Greek vineyards. The vine is particularly sensitive to POWDERY MILDEW. It ripens relatively late and keeps its acidity quite well even in such hot climates as that of Ankialos in Thessaly in central Greece, although it can also ripen well, and makes very much more interesting wine, in high-altitude vineyards. It is often blended with the softer Savatiano, particularly for RETSINA.

Roederer, Louis, family-owned Champagne house known both for its early links with the Russian court and for its extensive vineyard ownership. The original company was founded by a M. Dubois around 1776; Louis Roederer joined in 1827, becoming owner in 1833. By the second half of the century, RUSSIA had become the major market for Champagne Louis Roederer: 666,386 bottles out of a total company production of 2.5 million were exported there in 1873. In 1877, the special Cuvée Cristal Louis Roederer was commissioned by Tsar Alexander II, who wanted his champagne in clear glass crystal bottles so that it would stand out. The bottles were so strong that they did not need a PUNT. The creation of Cristal (sold in clear glass bottles without a punt to this day) strengthened links with the imperial court, but in 1917 the Russian Revolution brought an immediate 80 per cent loss of its market. Camille Orly-Roederer, widow of the great-nephew of Louis, rebuilt the company after this blow, in particular by strengthening Roederer's vineyard holdings at a time when other houses were selling, a move many later regretted. By the mid 1990s, 180 ha/444 acres supplied 80 per cent of Roederer's requirements, thereby allowing the house to remain unusually independent. Mainly thanks to these vineyard holdings, Roederer produces far more vintages of Cristal than is usual for a PRESTIGE CUVÉE. The best cuvées of almost every harvest are blended to make a vintage Cristal, except in notably poor years such as 1968 and 1972. In 1993, the house acquired 60 per cent of the capital of the holding company of Champagne Deutz. The company diversified into ST-ESTÈPHE in Bordeaux in the 1990s, acquiring Ch Beauséjour in 1992 and Ch de Pez in 1994. Outside France, the company briefly owned Heemskerk Vineyards in TASMANIA and has invested with considerable success in the Anderson Valley, near the MENDOCINO coast. Roederer Estate, one of California's finest sparkling wines, was first released in 1988. Camille Orly-Roederer's grandson Jean-Claude Rouzaud runs the company today.

S.A.

Roero, increasingly important sandy hills on the left bank of the river Tanaro in the PIEMONTE region of north west Italy which takes its name from the villages of Montaldo Roero, Monteu Roero, and Santo Stefano Roero to the north west of Alba. Significant quantities of red BARBERA and white ARNEIS are also grown in the conical hills, whose TOPOGRAPHY is strikingly different from that of the LANGHE hills directly to the east on the right bank of the Tanaro.

Rolland, Michel (1947–), the most famous CONSULTANT oenologist, responsible in several ways for the current FASHION for superripe, deep-coloured, supple red bordeaux. He and his wife Dany have since 1973 run a laboratory in POMEROL on which many local growers depend for ANALYSIS, and they own Chx Le Bon Pasteur in Pomerol, Bertineau St-Vincent in Lalande de Pomerol, Rolland-Maillet in St-Émilion, and Fontenil in Fronsac

and farm Ch La Grande Clotte in Lussac-St-Émilion. The Bordeaux RIGHT BANK enterprises to which he is consultant are too numerous to list (although they include L'Angélus, Beau-Séjour Bécot, Clinet, Clos l'Église, La Dominique, La Gaffelière, Grand Mayne, Larmande, Pavie, Pavie-Decesse, and Troplong-Mondot). In the Médoc and Graves they include many properties managed by négociants Dourthe and Chx Fieuzal, Kirwan, Léoville-Poyferré, Malescot St-Exupéry, Pape-Clément, Smith Haut Lafitte, and La Tour Martillac. He has also made wine for Skalli of the Languedoc, the arch-promulgator of VIN DE PAYS. But it is his consultancies outside France that set him apart from all but a handful of his countrymen in the breadth of his experience: Simi, Newton, Merryvale, Cuvaison, St-Supéry, and Harlan in California; Marqués de Cáceres, Bodegas Palacio, Marqués de Griñon in Spain; Ornellaia in Italy (after TCHELISTCHEFF); Trapiche in Argentina; Casa Lapostolle in Chile; Pajzos in Hungary; Grover in India; and many more, bringing his total number of clients to more than 100. The Rollands and their two daughters also have holdings in Bonne Nouvelle in South Africa, Campo Eliseo in Toro, and Clos de los Siete, Val de Flores, and Yacochuya in Argentina. He studied oenology at the University of BORDEAUX during the PEYNAUD era and has continued to declare his philosophy that wine should give maximum pleasure, although he has been criticized for a certain uniformity of style.

Rolle, the white grape variety traditionally most closely associated with BELLET, is now increasingly grown in the Languedoc and, especially, Roussillon, where it is frequently blended with southern French varieties such as Viognier, Roussanne, Marsanne, and Grenache Blanc. It is aromatic and usefully crisp for warm wine regions and is accepted by French authorities as identical to the VERMENTINO of Corsica, Sardegna, and the Tuscan coast although some Italian authorities dispute this. Its relationship to the variety called Rollo in Liguria is still unclear.

Romagna. Eastern part of EMILIA-ROMAGNA.

Romanée, Romanée-Conti, Romanée-St-Vivant, great red GRANDS CRUS, for more details of which, see VOSNE-ROMANÉE. See also DOMAINE DE LA ROMANÉE-CONTI.

Romania, sometimes spelt **Roumania** or **Rumania**, is eastern Europe's quantitatively most important wine producer with enormous unrealized potential. In 2004, there were 193,150 ha/477,000 acres of vineyard, of which almost 180,000 ha were wine grapes according to Romanian industry data, athough this is a steep fall from the almost 230,000 ha/568,000 acres devoted to wine production according to OIV figures for 1996. Romania has

powerful historical and cultural links with MOLDOVA, which became an independent, Romanian-speaking republic in 1991.

History

The coastal region of what is now Romania (modern Dobrogea or Dobrudja) was settled by the Ancient GREEKS in the 7th century BC and they may have introduced viticulture. The Geto-Dacian tribes were eventually defeated by the Romans around AD 106 and vine-growing appears to have become well established in Târnave, Odobeşti, and Drăgaşăni when this region was part of the Roman province of Dacia. Some archaeological evidence suggests that Romania may have a 6,000-year-old tradition of vine-growing.

The region was overrun by successive cultural influences, including Hungary, the Ottoman Turks (and, later, Russians and Austrians), but vine-growing seems to have continued uninterrupted. Romania's existence as a united political unit comprising the old principalities of Wallachia and Moldavia dates only from 1861, and Transylvania and Banat did not join Romania until after the First World War. The total vineyard area grew from 95,000 ha in the 1860s to 150,000 ha/370,500 acres by 1884, when the PHYLLOXERA louse began its devastation of Romanian vineyards. As a result, resistant HYBRIDS dominated wine production in 1930.

Between 1947 and 1989, Romania was a socialist republic and in the 1950s and 1960s, in an effort to increase productivity, the total vineyard area was expanded, to more than 340,000 ha by 1972. Vine material was also selected for quantity and frost resistance rather than quality. Immediately prior to the revolution of December 1989, this figure had decreased, largely as a result of uprooting hybrids, to about 275,000 ha. During the communist period, the state gradually increased its direct share of vineyard holdings to about 30 per cent of the total by the end of the 1980s. About 60 per cent was owned by state-owned CO-OPERATIVES, leaving just 10 per cent in private hands, and those of the state-funded viticultural institutes. Most wine was produced by state-owned Vinalcool wineries.

Romania has a Latin culture with a Romance language and wine has strong cultural role. White wine accounts for approximately two-thirds of Romanians' robust wine consumption, with by far the majority being at least a little sweet. Romanian wine exports were just 11 per cent of production in 2004, mainly to Moldova and Germany.

In the early 1990s, the state's official exporting body became a private company incorporating western European interests and a limited number of shareholding wineries. Privatization in the 1990s took several forms, including the dismantling of agricultural production co-operatives and restitution of land

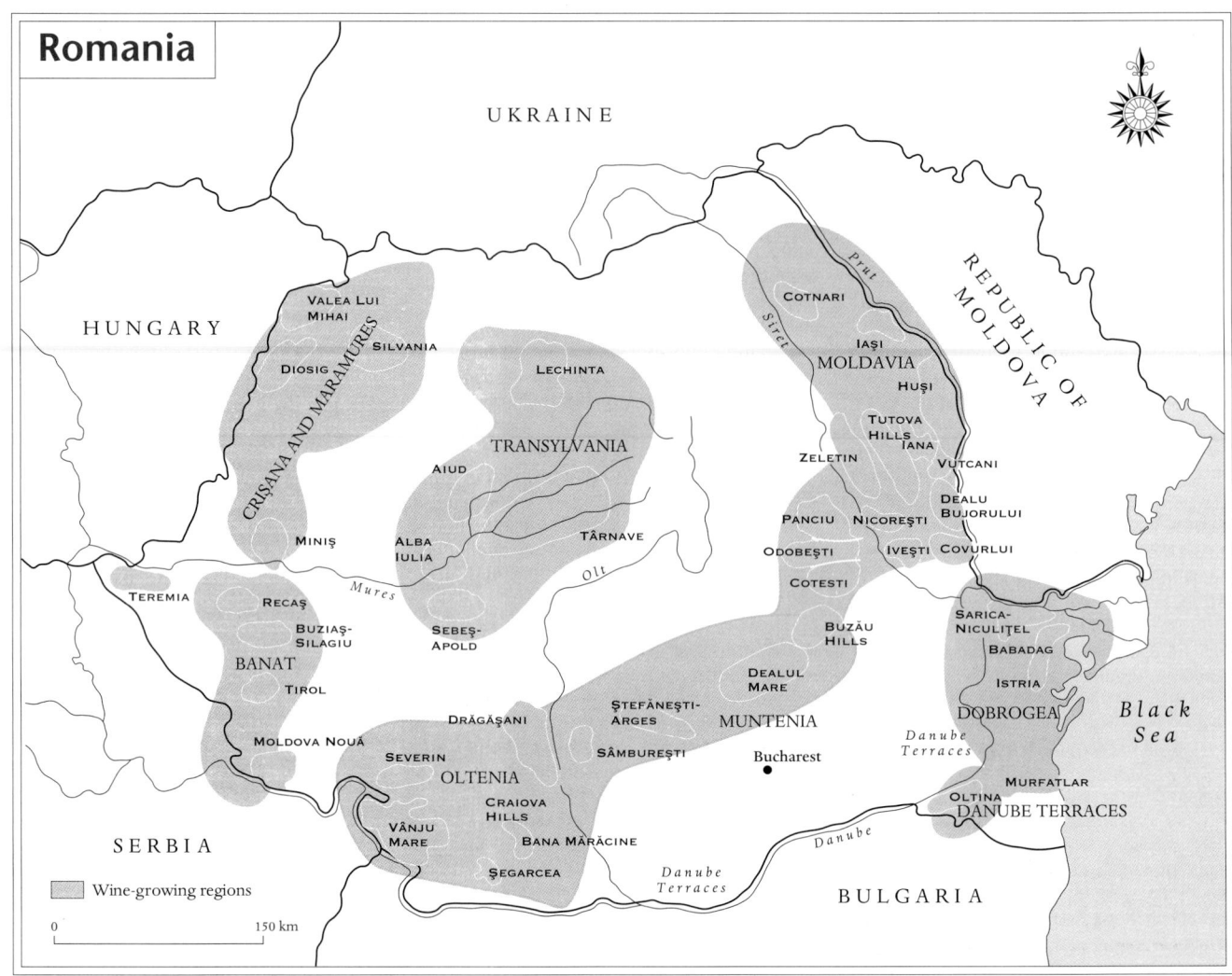

Romania

to former private owners. Around 180,000 ha of vineyard were handed back in plots of under less than 1 ha, resulting in very fragmented land holdings. Since privatization of wineries, which was largely completed by the late 1990s, western investment has been accelerating with British, German, French, Italian, Moldovan, and Dutch involvement. A group of leading wineries established a professional body in 2002 (Wine Exporters and Producers Association, WEPA). Investment and industry reforms such as revised wine laws and anti-fraud measures, are expected to continue ahead of EU membership due in 2007. Romania has agreed to remove all its hybrid vines by 2014.

Geography and climate

Although there is a coastal plain on the Black sea coast, the country is dominated by mountains, the north–south eastern Carpathians and the east–west Transylvanian alps, whose average altitude is *c*.1,000 m/3,280 ft. The Wallachian plain stretches south to the river Danube and Bulgaria, while the Pannonian

plain lies between the hills and Hungary to the west. Romania's wine regions are widely dispersed throughout the country, in a wide range of different conditions.

Romania lies on much the same latitudinal span as France, although its climate is much more CONTINENTAL yet the Black sea influence helps to moderate winter temperatures in Dobrogea by the coast. Temperatures are high but rarely excessive in the growing season, and rainfall during the harvest is unusual in most wine regions. Average July temperature is 23.5 °C and average annual rainfall is 540 mm/21 in.

Viticulture

Vine-TRAINING SYSTEMS used here traditionally were mainly GOBELET or single, double, or multiple bows, as in the MOSEL. From the late 1950s, a state plan to raise foreign currency by export-funded research has resulted in today's impressive predominance of neatly wired rows using concrete posts and mainly GUYOT and CORDON training. Planting density is typically low, although new vineyards

can have as many as 4,500 vines per ha. MECH-ANICAL HARVESTING was still a novelty in the mid 2000s but LABOUR is increasingly difficult to find.

Officially recorded yields are low, ranging from a recent low of 3.9 tonnes/ha in 2003 to 5.4 tonnes/ha in 2004. This national figure hides considerable local variation depending on the region, condition of the vineyard, and widespread planting of hybrids for home production. The bigger commercial wineries are investing in vineyards and introducing VSP as far as possible to gain control over both quality and cost of grapes. In 2004, VINIFERA vines accounted for around 90,000 ha/222,300 acres of vines expected to produce 3.3 to 3.5 million hl.

IRRIGATION is permitted but rarely used, even in the drought year 2003, and would normally only be of benefit in two years out of ten so the expense is largely unjustified. However, the German-owned Carl Reh winery plans a major drip irrigation project for 2006.

Winters can be very harsh in parts of Romania, although many of the longest-established wine regions have MESOCLIMATES which offer some protection. Trees act as naturals WINDBREAKS in new areas such as Ştefăneşti-Arges. Some particularly FROST-prone valley floor vineyards are being up-rooted, and higher vine-training systems are used to protect against frost in other areas. Other viticultural hazards include both POWDERY and DOWNY MILDEW, as well as GREY ROT, particularly in fragmented vineyards where vines may be left untreated due to the cost of SPRAYING. Another potential problem for grape growers is theft of fruit, requiring larger operations to employ full-time security guards and dogs near to harvest time. Concern about crop loss also discourages smaller growers from waiting for optimum ripeness.

Wine-making

Ahead of EU accession, Romania is benefiting from the SAPARD (Special Accession Program for Agricultural and Rural Development) investment programme which funds 51 per cent of investments retrospectively but has a huge burden of bureaucracy. In effect, therefore, only the bigger, already better funded, wineries can benefit. Nonetheless, a considerable amount of modern vinification equipment has been installed, including temperature control, stainless steel, new presses, and water treatment. Limited vinification capacity was before this a problem across Romania forcing wineries to use short macerations for reds and technology such as special ROTOFERMENTERS designed in conjunction with the University of Craiova.

Traditionally, wine was aged in old Carpathian casks, if it saw any oak, and high VOLATILE ACIDITY and OXIDATION were common problems. Today new, often Hungarian, OAK barrels are increasingly widespread. Some wineries are starting to work with both Romanian oak chips and barrels, although the best producers are co-financing oak maturation to ensure it is sufficiently seasoned before use. Bottling facilities are improving, although not all wineries have their own facilities. Locally made glass is of poor quality so many producers buy in from Bulgaria and Italy, in spite of import taxes.

Vine varieties

Romania is notable for the number and scope of its grapevine collections. It has a wide range of vine varieties, including a significant proportion of AMERICAN VINES and HYBRIDS and a number of purely local specialities.

Industry data for 2005 showed that the most planted varieties by far are two white FETEASCĂS, Fetească Albă (9,800 ha/24,206 acres) and a 1930s crossing of it, Fetească Regală (17,700 ha), both of which can produce fresh, perfumed, dry white wines but are more often vinified with varying degrees of perceptible sweetness. The next most planted white variety is Riesling Italico, or WELSCHRIESLING, grown on 8,400 ha but usually marketed locally simply as 'Riesling'. A vine known as Banat Riesling around Recaş is regarded as the same grape variety, but elsewhere is called Creată (meaning 'curly'). Merlot is the most planted red wine variety with 9,800 ha of generally good CLONES. CABERNET SAUVIGNON was grown on 8,500 ha by 2005, significantly less than in neighbouring Bulgaria. There were plans to introduce some genuine Riesling to Transylvania in 2005. Other significant international varieties include SAUVIGNON BLANC, PINOT GRIS, RKATSITELI, MUSCAT OTTONEL, ALIGOTÉ, and GEWÜRZTRAMINER among white wine grapes. Pinot Noir is seen in certain export markets as Romania's signature grape variety, although estimates vary as to the amount of genuine Pinot Noir in the country. Officially it covered 1,750 ha in 2000, while 2005 data show 500 ha. It arrived in Romania around 1900, particularly for sparkling wine production. Chardonnay arrived at around the same time to be planted on calcareous soils near the Black sea coast. The area has proved too warm for sparkling wine of any quality, but a late harvest sweet Chardonnay from this area is locally popular.

Specifically Romanian varieties planted to a significant extent include the light-berried 'fat' GRASĂ and the aromatic 'frankincense' TĂMÂIOASĂ Românească grapes of COTNARI. Busuioaca is a violet-skinned Muscat making sweet wines of genuine character and quality, with typical aromas of peaches and honey, named after the Romania word for the herb basil busuioc. It is best known around Bohotin in Moldova, although less than 90 ha remain and there is also a little around Pietroasele. The Galbena vine of Odobeşti makes light, crisp whites—400 ha are officially registered—and the white Şarba is also found in this area. Of dark-berried varieties, Roşioară (Bulgaria's PAMID) is relatively common for everyday wine (4,800 ha planted), Băbească (6,300 ha) can produce light, fruity reds of moderate quality, and Fetească Neagră (1,300 ha) is capable of producing deep-coloured, age-worthy red wines. Other Romanian varieties planted to a limited extent include Majarca Albă, Mustoasa Maderat, Iordana, Zghihara, and Plavaie grown in Odobeşti. There is also some interest in reviving old varieties such as Crîmposie and Negru from Drăgaşani, which can produce long-lived reds and the deep coloured Novac.

There are also limited plantings of such varieties as Kékoportó (i.e. PORTUGIESER, more usually called simply Oporto), and a variety called Burgund Mare ('big Burgundian') which was previously believed to be Pinot MEUNIER, but is now accepted as synonymous with KÉKFRANKOS, or Blaufränkisch.

Romanian viticultural stations have been enthusiastic developers of vine CROSSINGS, including for example Columna, a crossing of Pinot Gris and Grasă, and the red wine grape Codana.

Wine laws

In 2002, Romania brought in new, EU-friendly wine laws. Wines, which must be made from authorized vinifera varieties, may be table wines (Vin de Masa), 'special wines' (including fortified and liqueur wines), or quality wines divided into:

Vin cu Indicatie Geografica for wines with recognized geographical description (equivalent to VIN DE PAYS); Vin de Regiune is a Romanian traditional expression, protected by EU and may also be used for this category.

DOC (Denumire de Origine Controlată): high-quality wines from a CONTROLLED APPELLATION of origin (minimum sugar levels at harvest are 180 g/l). Further subcategories of DOC are:

DOC-CMD wines harvested at full maturity (min 187 g/l sugar at harvest)
DOC-CT late harvest wines (min 220 g/l sugar)
DOC-CIB noble late harvest wines (min 240 g/l sugar at harvest and BOTRYTIZED)

DOC wines come from one of the seven major regions and usually show the name of the designated district where they were made. Some of the districts have subdivisions, often called after some local geographical feature such as a small river or valley.

Wine regions

The Romanian wine regions are usually divided into seven distinct zones (see map): the plateau of Transylvania in the middle of the country; the Pannonian plain on the Hungarian border in the old province of Crişana; the Moldavian hills on the eastern slopes of the Carpathians; the warm, central Muntenia region, including Odobeşti in the southern Carpathians; the Oltenia hills to the immediate west; the Banat hills towards the border with Serbia in the former Yugoslavia; the knolls of Dobrogea between the Danube and the Black sea; and the flatter Danube terraces.

Transylvania This high central region produces predominantly white wines. The total vineyard area in 2005 was 7,200 ha/17,790 acres including 6,000 ha of *vinifera*. The most important and oldest Transylvanian wine region is **Târnave**, also sometimes spelt **Tîrnave**, with its two main subdenominations of Jidvei and Blaj, plus the less well known Mediaş. These are some of Romania's coolest vineyards at ALTITUDES up to 300 m/984 ft on slopes which can approach those of the MOSEL in steepness. (The mainly white wines also have an appealing Mosel-like acidity; reflecting the medieval immigration of Saxon settlers from the Mosel valley to the region.) Some of the most common varieties are Fetească Regală, and the other Fetească. Welschriesling, Muscat Ottonel, and the Austrian NEUBURGER are also grown here. Traminer is particularly highly regarded. In general, wine styles are relatively Germanic. Some sparkling wines are also made, and Transylvanian wine was sold for more than £2 a case in London in the 1840s.

Other proposed DOC regions are Alba Iulia, Alba, Aiud, and Lechinta. In the **Alba Iulia** region vines are also grown on south-facing hills along the Mures river, and benefit from the usually rather warmer autumn weather here. **Aiud** is distinguished as the site of Romania's historic school of viticulture, and has a long history of producing fine white wines.

In the far south west of Transylvania is the **Sebeş-Apold** region, where the proximity of the southern mountains lowers overall temperatures slightly. Apold's Iordană vine makes high-acid, low-alcohol wine used mainly for Apold sparkling wines.

The **Lechinta** vineyards are Transylvania's northernmost, and dampest, though little commercial viticulture remains here.

Crişana and Maramures. There are two proposed DOCs within this region, **Silvania** and **Miniş**, and total vineyard area is around 9,000 ha/22,240 acres with 4,200 ha of *vinifera* vines. Two proposed 'table wines with geographical indication' are Dealurile Crişani and Viile Maramureşului. This region is so far west that parts of it are climatologically influenced by the Adriatic. Permitted white varieties include Fetească Albă and Regală, Welschriesling, Muscat Ottonel, Traminer, Furmint, Pinot Gris, and Sauvignon Blanc. Miniş grows these, as well as a traditional white variety, Mustoasă in the Maderat region, which makes light, crisp wine. Recommended reds are Cabernet Sauvignon, Cadarca, Merlot and Burgund Mare, while Pinot Noir and Oporto are also authorized. There are several foreign investments in vineyard land and replanting here. Springs can be so mild on the south- and south west-facing slopes on the foothills of the Zarand mountains that BUD-BREAK is usually earlier than in the rest of Romania, although EROSION can be a problem on the steeper slopes. Annual rainfall is about 650 mm/23 in, and averages 365 mm during the growing season. Soils vary considerably and include VOLCANIC, SHALE, and LIMESTONE together with some GRAVEL, CLAY, and iron oxide.

Moldavia (The eastern part of the old Romanian province of Moldavia is now the republic of MOLDOVA.) This eastern province of Romania is home to possibly the country's oldest, and certainly most famous, wine region COTNARI, whose golden nectar was at one time almost as sought after as those of TOKAJI and CONSTANTIA. For more details of this specific sweet wine, see COTNARI.

Moldavia lies north east of the Carpathians and is Romania's northernmost viticultural area at a latitude of 47°. It is also the largest viticultural region covering some 66,000 ha/163,090 acres of vines including 41,000 ha of *vinifera*. Vineyards are typically sited on the slopes of south- and south west-facing amphi-

theatres which protect the vines from the harsh north winds. Altitudes can vary from 200 m to almost 500 m. The region enjoys more than 2,000 hours of sunshine in an average year, and annual rainfall is only about 500 mm/20 in. Soil types include RENDZINA, chernozem, and podzols. Grasă is the variety responsible for most of the best sweet wines, supplemented by Tămâioasă, but Muscat Ottonel is also grown, together with Fetească Albă and Frâncusa, to produce dry and medium dry lesser wines. **Iaşi** is the historic capital of Moldavia and a major trading centre between east and west and the DOC will have the subregions of Copou, Uricani, and Bucium (the last of which can also be DOC in its own right). On the surrounding hills, the traditional Moldavian Fetească Albă is grown, mainly for light, everyday wines, together with the more recent Fetească Regală, Frâncusa, Welschriesling, Aligoté, and Sauvignon Blanc. A SPUMANTE style of wine is also made here from Muscat Ottonel. A range of red varieties, including Merlot, Cabernet Sauvignon, and Oporto, is also cultivated around Iaşi, where Băbească shows perhaps its finest form.

In the nearby **Huşi** vineyards, sweet, scented, deep-coloured wine is made from Busuioaca (a dark-skinned aromatic grape, probably from the Muscat family) grapes grown at Bohotin, sometimes fortified. Another local variety is Zghihara, which is closely related to Galbena but ripens earlier, and reaches higher sugar levels. Iana east of the city of Bacau and Dealurile Bujorului also become DOCs under the new proposal.

Odobeşti is one of the largest and oldest viticultural centres in Romania and may well date from the Roman era. The gentle south west-facing slopes are protected from the north by the Carpathians. Deep, fertile soils are mainly dedicated to everyday white table wine made from the local Galbena grape, but it is sensitive to both DROUGHT and GREY ROT. High-yield white wines are made from Fetească Albă, Welschriesling, and Şarba, a CROSSING of Welschriesling and Tămâioasă developed at the Odobeşti research station in 1972 which has a grapey aroma and good acidity. The local grape Plavaie is also grown here for light, high acid, low alcohol, everyday wines. In Panciu, to the immediate north of Odobeşti, winters are colder, winds stronger, and HAIL more frequent, but some good still white and sparkling wines are made. **Cotesti** just south of Odobeşti, on the other hand, is distinctly warmer and can produce some deep-coloured reds. Nicoresti, east of Panciu, is another red wine region, particularly well known for its Băbească.

Muntenia is often grouped with Oltenia and the two areas together cover 51,000 ha/126,000 acres, including 22,000 ha of vinifera. On south-facing foothills of the Carpathians

north of the capital Bucharest is the historic and extensive **Dealul Mare**, occasionally written Dealu Mare ('big hill'), region, best known for its red wines. Vineyards are at altitudes of between 130 and occasionally even 600 m/2,000 ft, protected from winter freeze by TOPOGRAPHICAL quirks and special local MESOCLIMATES. Annual rainfall averages around 640 mm. This is principally a red wine district with Cabernet Sauvignon, Merlot, some Pinot Noir, and Fetească Neagră grown in the Valea Călugărească, or 'valley of the monks'. Other subregions include Boldeşti, Urlaţi, Ceptura, Tohani, and Breaza. An outcrop of calcareous soil in the Pietroasa district is known for its lusciously sweet golden late harvest wines, especially Tămâioasă from Pietroasele, which may be BOTRYTIZED. Archaeological finds suggest a long history of wine production in Stefăneşti, possibly dating back to Alexander the Great. The area is noted for robust reds. The new DOC of **Dealu Bujorului** ('hill of the paeony') north of Galati is the site of the Valea wine institute.

Oltenia This region continues from Muntenia into the southern mountains west of Bucharest and include the historic and extensive vineyards of **Drăgaşani**, which are said to date from Roman times and stretch over 60 km/36 miles in the foothills of the Transylvanian alps ranging from 200 m to 500 m in altitude. Average rainfall is nearly 700 mm/28 in and hail is a frequent hazard. Welschriesling and Tămâioasă Românească are particular well regarded. Sambureşti is a much smaller wine region which specializes in Cabernet Sauvignon. Near the university town of Craiova lies the small DOC of **Bana Mărăcine**, with a small vineyard area based around the viticultural research station. About 20 km south of Craiova is the DOC Segercea, the site of a significant new winery investment and much new planting. The DOC **Vânju Mare** in the south west is notable for predominantly full-bodied reds and will have several subregions including **Severin**. This is the sunniest and warmest of the southern Carpathian wine regions and concentrates on red wine production. In the far south west, an outcrop of TERRA ROSSA around Oprisor in Mehedinti county may eventually produce some of Romania's best reds. The climate here is temperate continental with a Mediterranean influence. Sunshine hours are typically 2,400 to 2,600 and rainfall can be up to 800 mm per annum. Much of this area was substantially grubbed up in the 1980s and has only recently been replanted.

Banat While official statistics show nearly 2,800 ha/6,920 acres of vines in this area, the only remaining commercial winery at Recaş reports only 800 ha in reality, of which approximately 670 ha belong to Recaş winery itself. Historically the region was part of the Transylvanian province of the Austro-Hungarian

Empire and this influence is still clear in the varieties typically planted in the region: Cadarca, Italian Riesling, Furmint, Fetească Regală, Burgund (Kékfrankos), Muscat Ottonel, Oporto, together with communist era plantings of French varieties, substantial new vineyards have been planted with selected clones of more INTERNATIONAL VARIETIES as well as Fetească Neagră in the early 21st century. Banat has a moderate, Mediterranean climate, cooler than much of the rest of Romania, but warmer than most of Hungary.

Dobrogea This region on the Black sea coast comprises 16,000 ha/39,540 acres of vines, of which 12,300 ha are *vinifera*. It can have as many as 300 days of sunshine each year and rainfall between April and October averages only 150 mm to 200 mm. The climate is distinctly warm, although moderated by breezes from the Black sea. **Murfatlar**, with its two subregions of Medgidia and Cernavodă, is the most important wine region here, best known for whites. Late harvest wines, especially from Chardonnay, are a speciality here. Although BOTRYTIS is rare, the concentration of SUGAR IN GRAPES can reach 430 g/l some years. There are also substantial plantings of Pinot Gris, Welschriesling, Muscat Ottonel, and Sauvignon Blanc. Merlot and some Cabernet Sauvignon tend to be planted on north-facing slopes in an effort to prolong RIPENING. In the northern part of Dobrogea, the DOC region of **Babadag** has loess and chernozem soils and annual rainfall averaging 450 mm and is best known for reds. **Sarica Niculițel** is on hills overlooking Tulcea and the Danube just before it reaches the delta. The climate here is continental and semi-arid, although the emphasis is on whites, including Aligoté, both Feteascăs, and Welschriesling.

Danube Terraces Most vineyards here are devoted to TABLE GRAPES, and little wine of any quality is made. The only DOC is **Oltina**.

C.G.

www.wineromania.com

Roman Muscat, synonym for MUSCAT OF ALEXANDRIA.

Rome, classical. '*Vita vinum est*' ('Wine is life'), exclaimed Trimalchio to his dinner guests (Petronius, *Satyricon* 34).

Wine was deeply embedded in Roman culture at all levels; it was as much a staple for the poor as for the wealthy. So the evidence is particularly rich, detailed, and varied—as rich, indeed, as for any aspect of ancient society. There are the casual, but often illuminating, references in the poets, in letters, and even in the graffiti scratched on inn walls. All the AGRICULTURAL TREATISES, one of the largest bodies of technical literature to survive from antiquity, devote great space to detailed discussion of viticulture (see in particular CATO, *De agri cultura passim*, from the 2nd century BC, VARRO,

Roman Italy

De re rustica, Book 1, from the end of the 1st century BC, COLUMELLA, *De re rustica*, particularly Books 3–5, 12, and the separate work 'On trees' from the mid 1st century AD, and his contemporary PLINY, *Natural History*, Books 14, 17, and 23, and PALLADIUS from late antiquity). What these reveal is a lively debate, which has its modern counterpart, about CLIMATE, VINE VARIETIES, PLANTING and PRUNING techniques, technological developments, and the economics of viticulture. A more surprising source of information is Roman law; the sale of wine, particularly wholesale, raised considerable problems for the law of sale, when there was the question of what guarantee of quality the buyer might reasonably expect. The legal texts tell us much about the details of how wine was marketed. Equally interesting material comes from medical writers. Wine played an important role in medical treatment, and much of the information about the colour, quality, and effects of particular wines owes far less to the tasting books of Roman CONNOISSEURS than it does to the notes of the DOCTORS (see MEDICINE). Finally there is ARCHAEOLOGY, of which the most spectacular recent achievement, inspired by the underwater excavation of Roman wrecks, has been the identification of the types of AMPHORAE used to carry the wine and the recognition of the scale and pattern of the wine trade.

Both Pliny (*Natural History* 14. 21–39) and Columella (*De re rustica* 3. 2. 7–28) offer surveys of the main ANCIENT VINE VARIETIES. Columella's classification is the most revealing. His first class consists of the varieties used for the great Italian wines, most notably

the types of Aminnean. His second class is high-yielding vines, which nevertheless can produce wines which can be aged successfully. The final group is those prolific vine types used largely to produce *vin ordinaire*. This reveals that wine producers were aware of the great diversity in the markets for their wines and chose their vines accordingly.

'Classic wines can only be produced from vines grown on trees,' was Pliny's verdict (*Natural History* 17. 199). Although this was disputed by some agricultural writers, the most striking fact about Roman viticulture was that the great wines—CAECUBAN, FALERNIAN, etc.— nearly all came from vineyards in which the vines were trained up trees, usually elms or poplars. However, all the normal forms of VINE TRAINING were also known and described by agricultural writers, from the low, free-standing BUSH VINE to elaborate TRELLIS SYSTEMS. As in every age, the literature abounds with references to extraordinary YIELDS (for example, over 300 hl/ha (17 tons/acre), high but not unknown in modern terms); but Columella (*De re rustica* 3. 3) considers the economics of a vineyard on the basis of yields ranging from 21 to 63 hl/ha, which range may look familiar to modern vine-growers concerned with wine quality.

'Be the first to dig the ground . . . but the last to harvest the grapes' was the advice in VIRGIL's poem of the countryside (*Georgics* 2. 410). This is just one of many clues which suggest that the Romans sought to make their white wines—and nearly all the great wines were white—sweet.

The treading of the grapes was usually, but not invariably, followed by their PRESSING. The must obtained from the treading was sometimes kept separate, but more frequently added to that from the pressing. The grape pulp could be subject to a second pressing, or even, after being soaked for a day, a third, to produce a thin drink for slaves (see PIQUETTE). From the press room the must was run off to ferment in large DOLIA, which were frequently sunk in the ground. The wine could be racked off into amphorae at any stage from 30 days after being made, to various points through the winter and into the next spring. Many white wines of note were probably left SUR LIE, with the possible consequent enhancement of flavour and complexity. To those in the post-PASTEUR age of stainless steel vats, Roman wine-making must seem somewhat slapdash and uncertain. However, the accumulated wisdom and experience conveyed in all the agricultural treatises demonstrate a commitment to care (for example, in stressing the need for cleanliness at all stages) and sophisticated observation (as in the siting of the press room and *dolia* yard with regard to the ambient TEMPERATURE during fermentation).

'We consider the best wine is one that can be aged without any preservative; nothing must be mixed with it which might obscure its natural taste. For the most excellent wine is one which has given pleasure by its own natural qualities.' Columella's statement (*De re rustica* 12. 19) reflected current opinion. However, it is made at the beginning of a long discussion of additives for wine. Some of these are less objectionable to modern opinion than others. It was a normal practice to add boiled must to wine either during fermentation or soon after to act both as a sweetener and, so it was thought, a preservative. The addition of quantities of chalk or marble dust may be seen as attempts to modify the acidity of the wine (see DEACIDIFICATION). More surprising is the general advocacy of the addition of seawater or salt during fermentation. This was a distinctive Greek practice, taken over by the Romans. It was supposed both to 'enliven a wine's smoothness' (Pliny, *Natural History* 14. 120) (presumably increase acidity) and to prevent a mouldy taste (Columella, *De re rustica* 12. 23. 2). RESINATED WINE was common. So were FLAVOURED WINES with all kinds of herbal and plant additives, of which the primary effect was to disguise the inferior nature of the basic wine.

For Roman connoisseurs, the key to a good wine was AGEING. In Roman law the distinction between 'new' wine and 'old' was that the old had been aged for at least one year. Of course, vast quantities of wine were drunk within the first year. However, a higher price could be expected if the producer could hold back even for as short a period as the summer following the vintage. As for the great wines, both white and red, their key characteristic was their capacity to be aged for considerable periods. Falernian was considered drinkable after 10 years, but at its best between 15 and 20 years; SURRENTINE, another white wine, came into its own after 25 years. It may be that being sealed in an amphora which had an impermeable coating of resin meant that the ageing process was slowed. On the other hand, CATO recommends that air space should be left when amphorae are filled, which must have led to OXIDATION on a level which would be unacceptable now. The frequent mention of the darkening of the colour of the great whites suggests that MADERIZATION was normal and, indeed, desired. The final curiosity of Roman wines was the widespread practice of storing them in lofts over hearths, where they were exposed to smoke and heat. This was seen as a means of accelerating ageing, for which the nearest modern parallel may be the process of heating which MADEIRA is subjected to.

The heyday for Roman viticulture was the 1st century BC and the first two centuries AD. This was the time for the recognition and development of great wines in central ITALY which could compete successfully with those from the Greek world (see GREECE). It was a period of considerable experimentation and innovation, not least in western areas such as GAUL and SPAIN, which saw the creation of their own vineyards, often by Italian settlers after the areas had become part of Rome's empire. There was clearly a massive increase in the market for wine throughout the empire. Rome itself, with a fluctuating population of a million or more, sucked in imports from Italy and the provinces, while the process of the Romanization of the provinces included the stimulation of new markets for a commodity which was at the heart of Roman culture. The market for wine was a very diverse one, ranging from the élite's desire for great wine to the mass market for wines (for which the thousands of amphorae recovered from sites throughout the empire and beyond are ample testimony).

J.J.P.

Billiard, R., *La Vigne dans l'antiquité* (Lyons, 1913).
Purcell, N., 'Wine and wealth in Ancient Italy', *Journal of Roman Studies*, 75 (1985), 1–25.
Tchernia, A., *Le Vin de l'Italie romaine* (Rome, 1986).
Wilson, H., *Wine and Words in Classical Antiquity and the Middle Ages* (London, 2003).

Romorantin, a white, eastern Loire grape variety that is fast fading from the French *vignoble*. Cour CHEVERNY is an appellation especially created for Romorantin grown just west of Blois. DNA PROFILING at DAVIS showed it is a natural offspring of MEUNIER and GOUAIS BLANC.

Ronco, north east Italian term derived from the verb *roncare* (to clear land, particularly land which is either wooded or overgrown with underbrush), which has been used for over a century in a wide swathe of northern Italy to indicate a HILLSIDE VINEYARD. The first appearance on a wine label dates from the early 1970s, when it was used by Mario Pasolini in the province of Brescia in LOMBARDIA for his Ronco di Mompiano, a VINO DA TAVOLA from MARZEMINO and MERLOT grapes. More or less contemporary examples can also be found from the OLTREPÒ PAVESE, frequently with the diminutive form **Ronchetto**. The widest current use is in FRIULI, where the dialect form *ronc*. Examples can also be found in ALTO ADIGE and in ROMAGNA.

See also COLLI. D.T.

Rondinella, Italian red grape variety grown in VENETO, especially for Valpolicella. The vine yields profusely and is therefore extremely popular with growers but its produce is rarely sufficiently flavoursome to please consumers. Rondinella is not as widely planted nor as respected as CORVINA VERONESE, with which it is usually blended, although DNA PROFILING in the early 2000s established a parent–offspring relationship with it.

Rondo, once known as GM6494, red-fleshed DISEASE-RESISTANT VARIETY grown to a limited extent in such northern European countries as DENMARK, ENGLAND, NETHERLANDS, and POLAND, where it is treasured for its combination of early ripening and depth of colour. It was bred using some VITIS *amurensis* genes to withstand cold winters, has small berries and makes light, fruity wines. It can occasionally suffer POWDERY MILDEW, however. Despite its parentage, it produces remarkably VINIFERA-like wine so has been registered as a vinifera variety. Consequently, it may used in the production of QUALITY WINE.

root, one of the three major organs of higher plants, the others being leaves and fruits/seeds. Roots' main functions are anchorage of the plant, storage of reserves of CARBOHYDRATES, absorption of WATER and MINERALS from the soil, and synthesis of specific compounds such as reduced nitrogen compounds and such hormones as CYTOKININS.

The roots of a commercial vineyard originate from the roots that develop at the base of CUTTINGS, which are more divided than the tap-root style of a SEEDLING's root system. The position and number of the main framework roots, the 'spreaders' which extend out and down, are determined during the first three years. Although most vine roots occur in the top metre of soil (less if unfavourable soil horizons impede their penetration), there are many examples where roots have penetrated to 6 m/20 ft or more; often these examples are found in dry conditions such as the DOURO valley. The root framework supports a large number of fibrous roots which, by their continuing growth, comb the soil for minerals and water. Root density is highest in friable soil with continuing supplies of minerals, water, and oxygen.

Vine roots are much less dense than those of many other crop plants. Different species of VITIS have different root distribution and habits, a difference that is deliberately used in the breeding of ROOTSTOCKS. B.G.C.

Van Zyl, J. L., 'The grapevine root and its environment', Republic of South Africa, Department of Agriculture and Water Supply, Technical Committee 215 (Stellenbosch, 1988).

root growth, that part of a vine's annual growth cycle which takes place below ground. In most fruit trees, the spring flush of root growth occurs at the same time as BUDBREAK, but for the vine it is delayed. There are two peaks of root growth during the year. The first takes place at FLOWERING of the shoots in early summer, and the second coincides with the normal HARVEST period in autumn. There is an important correlation between the size, health, and activity of the vine's root system and the growth of shoots and leaves above ground. This is because the roots act as storage sites for the vine's crucial reserves of CARBOHYDRATES and also as the site for the production of HORMONES such as cytokinins and gibberellins. Vines with restricted or unhealthy roots have low VIGOUR and this is the basis of the principles of BALANCED PRUNING. Root growth also varies according to VINE AGE.   R.E.S.

root knot nematode. See NEMATODES.

root lesion nematode. See NEMATODES.

rootling, a one-year-old vine grown in a NURSERY, the most common material used for planting a vineyard. Generally it is a grafted rootling, with the fruiting variety, or SCION, grafted on to a rootstock. Most species of the vine genus VITIS, especially VINIFERA varieties, form roots readily on their CUTTINGS, but some rootstocks such as *Vitis berlandieri* and *Vitis champini* form roots poorly.   B.G.C.

rootstock, the plant forming the root system of a grapevine to which a fruiting variety, or SCION, is grafted. In most vineyards in the world, European wine-producing VINIFERA vines are grafted on rootstocks which are, with few exceptions, either varieties of one AMERICAN VINE SPECIES or more commonly HYBRIDS of several. See VITIS for details of the different species of this genus. Rootstocks are normally used to overcome soil pests or diseases, but may also be used for special soil conditions.

The use of rootstocks for grapevines became common around 1880 in France in order to combat the devastating root louse PHYLLOXERA, which attacked the roots of the European grapevine *Vitis vinifera*, and the control of phylloxera remains a major, but by no means the only, reason why rootstocks are used.

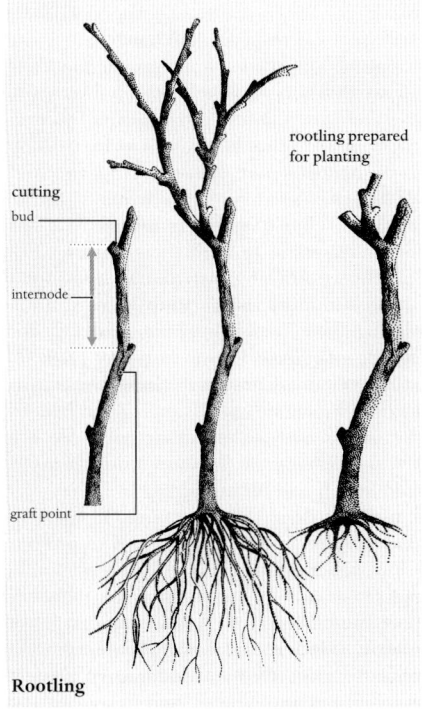

cutting
bud

internode

graft point

rootling prepared
for planting

Rootling

There are parts of the world where the choice of rootstock is more debated than the choice of the fruiting variety, since the latter might well be regulated by law or tradition. Even in the traditional viticultural regions of the Old World, the choice of rootstock tends to change with time, helped by long-term experiments and commercial experience. By contrast, in some parts of the New World, the use of rootstocks is relatively new, or prior use has been restricted to only a few locally available rootstock varieties.

While phylloxera has been present in California since 1873, for example, only a few rootstock varieties were used in more recently developed vineyards. The rootstock AXR1 (alternatively ARG1 or Ganzin 1) had been found so adaptable in California it was described in Winkler's textbook as 'the nearest approach to an all-purpose rootstock', and was the majority rootstock, despite Winkler's qualifying phrase that 'resistance to phylloxera is not high'. In the 1980s, AXR1 succumbed to phylloxera, and the choice of rootstocks for replanting has been largely based on guesswork, since there was only limited evaluation of other rootstocks under local conditions.

Choice of rootstock

Although at one time it was a common complaint that PRE-PHYLLOXERA wines are better than those since the invasion (perhaps partly because early rootstocks were not always ideally matched with soil types), more recent experiments have shown that little effect on wine quality can be attributed directly to rootstock. The effect of rootstock on wine quality is probably no greater than that of other factors such as soil, climate, fertilization, and irrigation. Certainly rootstocks can influence VIGOUR, and the high-vigour rootstocks such as Rupestris St George can produce canopies so dense that they affect wine quality (see CANOPY MANAGEMENT). Other studies indicate that the high-vigour rootstocks Harmony, Dog Ridge, Freedom, and Ramsey can result in high levels of POTASSIUM and PH in the resultant wine, but again this may be an indirect effect mediated through vigour and excessive canopy SHADE.

Any vigorous rootstock which stimulates vegetative growth late in the season will have a detrimental effect on fruit RIPENING and therefore on wine quality (see VINE PHYSIOLOGY). The use of rootstocks has also led to an increase in vine CHLOROSIS in those regions where limestone soils are common. Similarly, some rootstocks can induce MAGNESIUM deficiency, which, when severe, can inhibit PHOTOSYNTHESIS and ripening. Perhaps the most significant negative effect of all has been the impact of the universal adoption of GRAFTING on the spread of VIRUS DISEASES; rootstocks do not always show virus symptoms, and it can easily be shown that the spread of virus diseases is increased by grafting.

LEAFROLL VIRUS in particular delays ripening and can substantially reduce wine quality, and recent work on VINE IMPROVEMENT has concentrated on avoiding the inadvertent spread of virus diseases by grafting.

Rootstocks can have a dramatic effect on YIELD. In the absence of a rootstock, a vine grown on its own roots may not grow at all and die because of root damage from phylloxera or NEMATODES. Grafting onto a rootstock suitable to LIME conditions or DROUGHT can, on the other hand, increase yield dramatically.

Rootstock selection for any particular vineyard may be guided by known soil pests or diseases (especially nematodes and phylloxera), by suitability to the soil environment (especially lime content, fertility, drought incidence, and waterlogging), or by the effect on the performance of the scion variety that is desired, such as lower vigour or earlier ripening.

Rootstocks also differ in characteristics that are important to nurserymen. These include the ability of mother plants to produce plenty of wood, the ease with which cuttings root, and also the ease with which they can be grafted.

Rootstock characteristics

Phylloxera resistance The three most resistant AMERICAN VINE SPECIES are *V riparia, rupestris,* and *berlandieri,* and the most susceptible species is the European VINIFERA (see VITIS). Interspecific HYBRIDS containing genes from any of the first three species will therefore have satisfactory resistance, and those hybrids including *vinifera* will have suspect resistance. Rootstocks of *vinifera–rupestris* (including AXR1, and Couderc rootstocks 1202 and 93–5) and *vinifera–riparia* parentage should be avoided as possessing insufficient phylloxera tolerance. Interestingly, *vinifera–berlandieri* rootstocks such as 41 B and 333 EM generally have sufficient resistance. A few examples of rootstocks with high phylloxera resistance are Riparia Gloire, 101–14 Mgt, SO 4, and 5 BB.

Nematode resistance Two principal types of NEMATODES are present in vineyard soils. VITIS species having the most resistance to root knot nematodes are *V champini, longii,* and *cinerea.* Those having most resistance to the dagger nematode include *V candicans, longii,* and *rufotomentosa.* Vines of the MUSCADINIA section of the *Vitis* genus are resistant to both types of nematodes, which explains the interest in this group of vines for rootstock breeding. As for phylloxera, *V vinifera* is very susceptible to nematodes, so any one rootstock will not have resistance to all nematode species, nor indeed to all nematode races. Rootstocks commonly used for nematode tolerance include Ramsey, Dog Ridge, Harmony, 1613 C, 1616 C, SO 4, and Schwarzmann.

Lime tolerance Both *V. vinifera* and *V. berlandieri* contribute tolerance to the soils high in LIMESTONE common in Burgundy and Champagne. Rootstocks acknowledged to have the highest lime tolerance are 41 B, 333 EM, and the more recently bred Fercal.

Drought tolerance *Berlandieri–rupestris* hybrids are best able to tolerate drought, and these include 110 R and 140 Ru, followed by 1103 P and 99 R. *V riparia* species and hybrids have low drought tolerance.

Salt tolerance The chloride component of salty soils can be toxic (see SALINITY). The *V berlandieri* species is considered tolerant, but Australian research has found the *V champini* rootstock Ramsey to be quite tolerant. *V vinifera* is also tolerant.

Vigour The species *V champini*, *berlandieri*, and *rupestris* and their hybrids give the most vigour, and *V riparia* the least. Among the most vigorous rootstocks are therefore Rupestris St George, 99 R, and 110 R, while Riparia Gloire and 101-14 are among the least vigorous. Vigorous vines tend to delay fruit maturity and can substantially reduce red wine colour.

Some internationally important rootstocks

AXR1, otherwise called **ARG1** in France, Australia, and New Zealand, is a *vinifera–rupestris* hybrid made by Ganzin in 1879. The rootstock was initially popular in France but at the turn of the century it was found there and in South Africa to have insufficient phylloxera resistance. It is popular with growers because the vines are vigorous and yield well, and is favoured by nurserymen because it is easy to graft. It was found satisfactory in California until the 1980s, when it succumbed to a supposed new biotype of phylloxera.

Dog Ridge is a seedling from the species *V champini* which is suggested for use on light textured soils with high nematode contents. It is only moderately tolerant of phylloxera. This rootstock is extremely vigorous, so it should not be used in fertile soils, and vines need to be pruned lightly to achieve BALANCE. The rootstock is not suggested for high-quality vineyards.

Fercal is a relatively recent rootstock bred at INRA Bordeaux and developed especially for high lime soils. It is a result of crossing a *berlandieri* × Colombard hybrid with 333 EM. It is resistant to phylloxera, and grafts readily. Fercal is of moderate vigour, and more tolerant of chlorosis and drought than 41 B.

Harmony is a hybrid of open pollinated seedlings selected from *V champini* and 1613 C. It was selected at Fresno, California, in 1966, and is quite tolerant of root knot and dagger nematodes. Phylloxera tolerance is, however, low, and vigour moderate to high.

Riparia Gloire de Montpellier is one of the oldest rootstocks used against phylloxera in France. Of the several *riparia* crosses brought in at the time of the phylloxera crisis, this proved the best. It confers excellent phylloxera resistance and is of low vigour, providing for lower yields of improved-quality fruit and early ripening. It is widely used throughout Europe for the production of good-quality wine.

Rupestris St George is sometimes called **Rupestris du Lot** or **Rupestris-monticola**. It was another early introduction to France to fight phylloxera, and the exact origin is unknown. This is an extremely vigorous variety with a long growing season. It has excellent resistance to phylloxera, but vines grafted to it can easily overcrop or set poor crops because of extreme vigour. Because of high vigour, it is not used for high-quality vineyards.

Schwarzmann, a *riparia–rupestris* hybrid with high tolerance of phylloxera and nematodes but only moderate vigour. It is suited to deep, moist soils and is not as widely used as it might be.

SO 4, a *berlandieri–riparia* hybrid, is correctly known as **Selection Oppenheim de Teleki No. 4**, from the viticulture school at Oppenheim in Germany. This popular rootstock, used widely in France and Germany, shows excellent phylloxera resistance, and tends to favour fruit set and slightly advanced maturity. Vigour is moderate, as is tolerance to nematodes. SO 4 is not, however, suited to dry conditions, and is prone to magnesium deficiency.

5 BB Kober is sometimes called **5 BB Teleki**, and is a *berlandieri–riparia*. The seedling was raised by the Hungarian Sigmund Teleki from seeds produced by a French nurseryman. In 1904, some of the most interesting plants were sent to the Austrian Franz Kober, who selected 5 BB. This is quite a vigorous rootstock which is suited to more humid, clay soils. In many situations vigour is excessive. The rootstock 5 BB is widely used in Europe, especially in Germany and Switzerland.

5 C Teleki is a *berlandieri–riparia* hybrid selected in 1922 by Andre Teleki. The rootstock is similar to SO 4 in aptitude, and is mostly used in Germany.

41 B is an old rootstock obtained by Professor Millardet in 1882 at Bordeaux, and is a hybrid between the *vinifera* variety Chasselas and *berlandieri*. This rootstock has the advantage of being highly tolerant to lime and so it is widely used in Cognac and Champagne. Its tolerance of phylloxera is sufficient but not absolute. This rootstock is moderately tolerant of drought.

99 Richter is a *berlandieri–rupestris* hybrid created by Franz Richter in 1889. This vigorous rootstock should not be used in cool regions because it can delay ripening. Phylloxera resistance is high and nematode resistance moderate.

101-14 Millardet et de Grasset is a lower-vigour and early-maturing rootstock used in some of the higher-quality vineyards in France. The vine is a *riparia–rupestris* hybrid made by Professor Millardet and the Marquis de Grasset. It has high resistance to phylloxera but moderate nematode tolerance. The vine can tolerate only low lime content and has a shallow root system.

110 R is a relatively old rootstock resulting from a *berlandieri–rupestris* cross made by Franz Richter in 1889. This rootstock is noted for its high vigour and thus tends to delay maturity, especially if planted in fertile soils. 110 R has high phylloxera tolerance but low nematode tolerance. It is moderately lime tolerant and quite drought tolerant, and so is widely used in MEDITERRANEAN CLIMATES. Initially it was not used extensively because of poor rooting in the nursery.

140 Ruggeri is a hybrid produced in Sicilia by Ruggeri using *berlandieri* and *rupestris*. This vigorous rootstock is well suited to dry soils high in lime, and Mediterranean climates. This rootstock should not be planted on fertile, moist soils because of possible excess vigour.

161-49 Couderc, *riparia–berlandieri* hybrid obtained in 1888. This rootstock has high resistance to phylloxera but is susceptible to nematodes.

333 EM (École de Montpellier) is one of the few rootstocks used (with Fercal and 41 B) which has a *vinifera* parent. It was hybridized by Professor Foëx of MONTPELLIER by crossing Cabernet Sauvignon with *berlandieri*. Despite initial fears to the contrary, 333 EM has sufficient phylloxera tolerance. This rootstock is slightly more lime tolerant than 41 B, and is also drought tolerant.

420 A Millardet et de Grasset is one of the oldest rootstocks obtained in 1887 by Professor Millardet and his assistant the Marquis de Grasset. It is a *berlandieri–riparia* hybrid and is highly regarded for good-quality vineyards, being a lower-vigour rootstock which hastens maturity. It is regarded as 'the *riparia* for chalky soils'. Phylloxera tolerance is high but nematode tolerance is low to moderate.

1103 Paulsen was bred by the director of an American vine nursery in Sicily by crossing *berlandieri* and *rupestris*. It is regarded as a drought-tolerant rootstock with high phylloxera tolerance and moderate nematode resistance. Lime tolerance is intermediate, and vigour moderate to high. It is welcomed by nurserymen as being easy to graft and root.

1613 Couderc is a complex hybrid between Solonis (*riparia–rupestris–candicans*) and Othello (*labrusca–riparia–vinifera*) bred by Georges Couderc in 1881. Phylloxera resistance is low to moderate, but it finds favour because of moderate to high nematode resistance. It is well suited to fertile, sandy, loam soils, and is used mainly in California.

1616 Couderc is a Solonis (*riparia–rupestris–candicans*) cross with *riparia* in 1881 to produce a low-vigour rootstock with high nematode and phylloxera tolerance. It is best suited to more humid soils, and it advances maturity.

3309 Couderc is a *riparia–rupestris* cross made in 1881. George Couderc planted 18 seeds in a row of the nursery where he had added lime; of the five which did not show chlorosis, 3309 C became the most successful. Phylloxera tolerance is high and lime tolerance medium, and it is better suited to humid than drought-prone soils. Rooting and grafting are easy, and the use of this rootstock is widespread. R.E.S.

Galet, P., *Précis de viticulture* (5th edn, Montpellier, 1988).

——and Morton, L. T., *A Practical Ampelography* (Ithaca, NY, and London, 1979).

Hardie, W. J., and Cirami, R. M., 'Grapevine rootstocks', in B. G. Coombe and P. R. Dry (eds.), *Viticulture, i: Resources in Australia* (Adelaide, 1988).

Pongracz, D., *Rootstocks for Grape-Vines* (Cape Town, 1983).

Van Leeuwen, C., and Roby, J.-P., 'Choix du portegreffe', in *Un raisin de qualité: de la vigne à la cuve*, n° Hors Série du *Journal International des Sciences de la Vigne et du Vin* (2001), 61–6.

Winkler, A. J., et al., *General Viticulture* (2nd edn, Berkeley, Calif., 1974).

Roquebrun. See ST-CHINIAN.

Roriz, or **Tinta Roriz,** the official Portuguese names for the Spanish red wine grape variety TEMPRANILLO, used particularly in the Douro valley, where it is the second most planted variety for the production of port. Said to have been named after Quinta de Roriz, where it was first imported into Portugal, it is particularly favoured by growers in the Cima Corgo and Douro Superior subregions where it vies with TOURIGA FRANCA as the most widely planted variety. It is relatively easy to grow in the Douro but has a tendency to over-produce and performs best in those years when yields are inherently low. In the Alentejo, it has been known as Aragónêz.

rosado is Spanish and Portuguese, and **rosato** is Italian, for ROSÉ. See also CLARETE.

Rosana, Spanish name for ROUSSANNE grape.

Rosé de Loire, general, and relatively important, appellation created in 1974 for ROSÉ WINE made from a blend of Loire red grapes (Cabernet Franc, Cabernet Sauvignon, Pineau d'Aunis, Pinot Noir, Gamay, and Grolleau), of which Cabernet constitutes at least 30 per cent. The wine may be produced anywhere within the ANJOU, SAUMUR, and TOURAINE zones and usually lies, in quality terms, somewhere between Rosé d'Anjou and Cabernet d'Anjou, with the distinction that it is always dry.

See also LOIRE.

Rosé des Riceys, rare, still, pink wine made in the commune of Riceys in the Aube *département*, the southern end of the CHAMPAGNE region. This dark, rose-coloured wine is made by careful SAIGNÉE of Pinot Noir grapes, by only three producers. It can be one of France's most serious rosés. Like Champagne's still red wine, Bouzy Rouge (see Coteaux

CHAMPENOIS), part of its appeal may be its name.

Rosenmuskateller, German name for aromatic, pink-berried MOSCATO Rosa Trentini variety particular to Alto Adige, northern Italy.

Rosette, very limited sweet white wine appellation just north of Bergerac in SOUTH WEST FRANCE. It includes some of the PÉCHARMANT zone. Production was down to below 700 hl/ 18,500 gal by 2002.

Rosette is also the name of an old FRENCH HYBRID, also known as Siebel 1000, which once produced pale red wines in New York state.

rosé wine-making, production of wines whose colour falls somewhere in the spectrum between red and white.

Historically, rosé wines have been made by a number of different processes, but today two methods are in general use. The preferred technique is a short MACERATION of the juice with the skins (see SKIN CONTACT) of dark-coloured grapes just after CRUSHING for a period long enough to extract the required amount of colour or ANTHOCYANINS. The juice is then separated from the skins by DRAINING or PRESSING and FERMENTATION proceeds as in WHITE WINE-MAKING. With the red-skinned GRENACHE grape, traditionally much used for rosés partly because of its relative lack of anthocyanins, a maceration of eight to 12 hours is usually sufficient. Highly pigmented grape varieties may need much less contact time, while very lightly coloured grapes may need a day or two's maceration. See also SAIGNÉE.

Some basic rosés are made by blending a small amount of finished red wine into a finished white wine. While a pinkish colour can be achieved by this process, the hue and flavour of such a wine are quite different from those of a wine made by short-term maceration. CHAMPAGNE is one of the few controlled appellations in which the blending method of rosé wine-making is sanctioned—and in practice rosé champagne is more often made by blending than by maceration.

Pink wines may also be made by using CHARCOAL treatments to remove the colour from red wines which are for some reason not saleable as reds.

A VIN GRIS or BLUSH wine is made as above but with no maceration. Both tend to be even paler than most rosés. A.D.W.

rosé wines, suddenly popular wines in any shade of pink, from hardly perceptible to pale red (see COLOUR). For some reason they are rarely known as pink wines, although the English word BLUSH has been adopted for particularly pale rosés. There was also a FASHION in California, from the late 1980s, when wine had to be white to be popular, to label pale pink wines made from dark-skinned grapes White,

as in WHITE ZINFANDEL (which has spawned a host of supposedly White wines made from such darkly coloured grape varieties as Cabernet, Merlot, Grenache, and Barbera).

In France, rosés are particularly common in warmer, southern regions where there is local demand for a dry wine refreshing enough to be drunk on a hot summer's day but which still bears some relation to the red wine so revered by the French. PROVENCE is the region most famous for its rosé, often in a strange skittle-shaped bottle, although, in the greater southern RHÔNE (especially TAVEL), the LANGUEDOC, and ROUSSILLON, rosés are at least as common as white wines. Grenache and Cinsaut are two of the grapes commonly used for rosé in the south of France. The Loire valley also produces a high proportion of rosé wine of extremely varied quality and sweetness levels, particularly around ANJOU, whether lowbrow Rosé d'Anjou or highbrow Cabernet d'Anjou. See also ROSÉ DE LOIRE. VIN GRIS and SAIGNÉE are French terms for particular types of rosé.

Spain also takes pink wines seriously—so seriously that it has at least two names for them, depending on the intensity of the colour. A *rosado* is light pink, while darker pink (light red) wines are labelled *clarete*. Portugal's best-known pink wines are exported, as in MATEUS and LANCERS. Pink wines are not especially popular in Italy, where the term used is usually *rosato* although *chiaretto*, meaning 'claret', is occasionally used for darker rosés. It is only with difficulty that German grapes can be persuaded to yield wines that can genuinely be called red rather than rosé. Official German terms for pink wines include WEISSHERBST and, in WÜRTTEMBERG, SCHILLERWEIN. See also ŒIL DE PERDRIX.

The New World was for long rather bemused by the concept of rosé, although this changed fast in the early 21st century. Chile was innovative. Australia makes some swashbuckling deep pinks and South Africa has a growing market, with several of the wines branded Blanc de Noir (*sic*) to indicate they are produced solely from red grapes.

Roseworthy, town north of Adelaide in the state of SOUTH AUSTRALIA, close to the Barossa Valley, known in the wine world for Australia's first agricultural college, established in 1883. It trained a high proportion of winemakers and viticulturists in Australia and New Zealand and contributed greatly to the technical standing of the Australian wine industry (see AUSTRALIAN INFLUENCE) until 1991 when it was relocated to the Waite campus of the University of Adelaide, where the AUSTRALIAN WINE RESEARCH INSTITUTE and CSIRO were already sited. For more details, see ADELAIDE.

Roșioară. See PAMID.

Rossese, esteemed red grape variety producing distinctively flavoured varietal wines in the north west Italian region of LIGURIA. The variety has a long history in the region and it has its own DOC in the west of the region in Dolceacqua whose wines are admired, though variable.

Rossignola, optional, tart ingredient in VALPOLICELLA.

Rosso Conero, Italian red wine based on MONTEPULCIANO grapes whose full potential is yet to be realized. See MARCHE.

Rosso di signifies a red wine from the Italian zone whose name it precedes, often a declassified version of a long-lived, more serious wine such as BRUNELLO DI MONTALCINO or VINO NOBILE DI MONTEPULCIANO.

Rosso Piceno, Italian red wine based on SANGIOVESE with some MONTEPULCIANO grapes, improving in quality though not yet at the level of the better Sangiovese wines of Toscana or Umbria. See MARCHE.

rot, loose term for the decay, with microbial interference, of any part of the vine. Rot is most commonly used as a synonym for BOTRYTIS BUNCH ROT, which is the most important sort of rot for wine quality. Other fruit rots include BLACK ROT, SOUR ROT, WHITE ROT; rots of other vine parts include ARMILLARIA ROOT ROT and TEXAS ROOT ROT.

rotary drum vacuum (RDV) filter, specialized form of earth FILTRATION designed to cope with very 'dirty' liquids—those which contain a high concentration of solids or particles that would rapidly block other filters. Such liquids arise during the winemaking process when hazy juice or wine is allowed to settle through the action of gravity; the resultant LEES, although still liquid, are frequently very thick and require mechanical sieving to separate the valuable liquid from the solid particles suspended in it.

RDV filtration relies on the constant regeneration of the filter medium, essential if these liquids with a high proportion of solid particles are to be clarified. This is achieved by shaving off a fine layer of the DIATOMACEOUS EARTH (DE) through which the liquid is passed.

The filter comprises a slowly rotating drum (or disk) covered in a fine stainless steel mesh and fitted with an internal vacuum pump, semi-immersed in a trough into which liquid is introduced. The filtration cycle begins when a significant quantity of DE is fed into the trough as a slurry in water; as the water is sucked through the mesh into the drum, the DE forms a 'cake', some centimetres thick, on the outer surface of the drum.

The water is largely removed from the trough and replaced with the turbid juice or wine, which is itself sucked through the earth

by the vacuum and collected in a tank, while the solids are retained on the surface of the DE cake. As the quantity of solids retained quickly blocks the very fine holes in the cake, its surface is regenerated by the removal of the entrapped solids and a small quantity of DE (as little as possible) by a scraper knife, passed once every revolution of the drum or disk. When the entire cake of DE has been removed by the constant shaving off of a small amount, the filter is cleaned and prepared for another batch of juice or wine.

These filters are normally used to clarify the products of settled grape juice or wine, such as lees after crushing, pressing, and settling, and the residue of FININGS such as bentonite. If used carefully, they can recover good-quality wine that is otherwise impossible to separate from such solids and would therefore be either discarded or sent as POMACE for distillation.

Alternative technology such as a modern centrifuge (see FILTRATION) is used in some wineries to the use of DE, which is increasingly considered an undesirable product with which to work, and to dispose of after it has done its task. P.L.

Rotbrenner, vine FUNGAL DISEASE found in most of Europe which can cause severe crop losses. Caused by the fungus *Pseudopezicula tracheiphila*, the disease is encouraged by prolonged rainfall and attacks leaves and young bunches. Satisfactory control is obtained with fungicides applied early in the growing season. R.E.S.

Roter Traminer. See GEWÜRZTRAMINER.

Roter Veltliner, white grape variety formerly widespread in Austria (once planted in California) for the production of table grapes and wine, today grown to a much more limited extent in Lower Austria. Along with Brauner Veltliner, it covers not much more than 200 ha/ 500 acres, or 1 per cent of the area planted with GRÜNER VELTLINER, in the 1990s. In warm years, if yields are restricted, it can make intensely aromatic, concentrated wines with high extract, especially in the Wagram district of Donauland. DNA PROFILING in Austria revealed in 1998 that Roter Veltliner is a parent of ROTGIPFLER, NEUBURGER, and FRÜHROTER VELTLINER. R.H. & J.V.

Rotgipfler, the marginally less noble of the two white wine grape varieties traditionally associated with GUMPOLDSKIRCHEN, the dramatically full-bodied, long-lived spicy white wine of the Thermenregion district of AUSTRIA. (The other is ZIERFANDLER.) There were about 120 ha/300 acres of Rotgipfler in Austria in the mid 2000s; it ripens late, but earlier than Zierfandler, and the wines are particularly high in EXTRACT, ALCOHOL, and BOUQUET. DNA PROFILING in Austria showed in 1998 that Rotgipfler is the progeny of TRAMINER and ROTER VELTLINER.

Rothschilds and wine. The Rothschilds first entered the world of wine in 1853 when Baron Nathaniel (1812–70), grandson of Mayer Amschel and a member of the English branch of the family, bought Brane Mouton and renamed it Ch MOUTON-ROTHSCHILD. This was common practice among more important CHÂTEAU owners. It was a buyer's market in Bordeaux vineyards then devastated by oidium, or POWDERY MILDEW, and the Rothschild purchase was viewed more as a property transaction than as the acquisition of a distinguished vineyard. When the important 1855 CLASSIFICATION placed Ch Mouton-Rothschild top of the second growths, however, the Rothschilds were particularly exercised by what they regarded as its unfairly low placing.

Nathaniel was succeeded by his son Baron James (1844–81) and then Baron Henri (1872–1947), who was more interested in literature than wine, and James's widow was responsible for Mouton until the arrival of Henri's younger son Philippe (1902–88) in 1922.

Baron Philippe de Rothschild was to prove one of the most influential forces in the wine business of Bordeaux and beyond. Not only did he acquire two neighbouring Pauillac FIFTH GROWTH châteaux—Mouton d'Armailhacq (named at various stages Mouton-Baron-Philippe, Mouton-Baronne-Philippe, and, since the late 1980s, d'Armailhac) in 1933 and Clerc Milon in 1970—he established the importance of château BOTTLING, established MOUTON CADET as one of the world's most successful wine BRANDS and an important NÉGOCIANT business in the Médoc, astutely developed the concept (and value) of ARTIST'S LABELS, established the finest collection of wine-related works of art in the world, and in 1979 initiated Opus One, the world's first high profile JOINT VENTURE with Robert MONDAVI of California. In 1988, he was succeeded at Mouton by his daughter Philippine. Under her leadership, Baron Philippe de Rothschild S.A. has diversified into VARIETAL vins de pays from the LANGUEDOC and a joint venture in Chile with Concha y Toro to produce the ambitiously priced Cabernet blend Almaviva.

Meanwhile, Baron James of the French family bought Ch LAFITE in 1868 in the face of local competition. He died a few months later but is said to have visited the property briefly in the spring of that year. His son Edmond (1845–1934) was to sow, and indeed provide, the seeds for the establishment of the ISRAELI wine industry by making a vast donation in 1882. James's great-grandson Élie (1917–) was the family member who eventually took charge of Lafite, subsequently Lafite-Rothschild, until 1975 when his nephew Eric (1940–) became the château's head. In 1962, the fourth growth PAUILLAC Ch Duhart-Milon was acquired. In 1984, the leading SAUTERNES property Ch Rieussec was also purchased, L'Évangile in POMEROL being added in

1990. Since then joint ventures have been established in Los Vascos in CHILE, Ch d'Aussières in Corbières, Quinta do Carmo in Portugal, and Caro with Catena in Argentina. The Lafite Rothschilds were on the point of expanding their California interests but sold Chalone to an acquisitive DIAGEO in 2004.

In 1973 Baron Edmond (1926–97), one of many partners in Lafite but engaged in many other affairs, bought the semi-derelict Ch Clarke of LISTRAC and in 1977–8 built a very large new *cuvier* and *chai*. In 1979, he added Ch Malmaison in the adjoining commune of MOULIS, which was also treated to major renovation, as well as acquiring two more non-classified châteaux in the Médoc. Since 1998, this branch of the Rothschild family have had a JOINT VENTURE with Anton Rupert of South Africa, Rupert & Rothschild.

In 1994, the English financier Lord (Jacob) Rothschild (1936–) opened a wine museum and cellar for the display and sale of Rothschild wines at Waddesdon Manor just north of London. E.P.-R. & J.R.

Littlewood, J., *Milady Vine: The Autobiography of Philippe de Rothschild* (London, 1984).

rotofermenter, or **rotary fermenter**, a horizontal FERMENTATION VESSEL arranged so that the contents can be mixed mechanically either by rotating the vessel, or by rotating an inner shaft fitted with vanes in a stationary vessel. Designed to eliminate the need for PUNCHING DOWN or PUMPING OVER, this equipment speeds the FERMENTATION and MACERATION phases of RED WINE-MAKING. Some European wine producers, notably in Burgundy, have invested in them, as have a number of NEW WORLD winemakers. Like most mechanical systems that promote skin–juice contact, they are expensive and require extensive and robust framing structures to mount and hold the horizontal tank. Rotofermenters are usually controlled by COMPUTERS, with cycles of rotation chosen by the winemaker. Off-setting this convenience is the fact that the fermentation is conducted in a closed system (with CARBON DIOXIDE released by a one-way vent) so AERATION is not easy to include as part of the vinification process. Typically, they allow greater extraction of PHENOLICS and TANNINS and produce more deeply coloured wines than those made in open fermenters. P.J.W.

Roublot, light-berried vine once grown in the Chablis region but abandoned because of its sensitivity to FUNGAL DISEASES.

Rouchalin, sometimes **Rouchelin**, occasional name for CHENIN BLANC in south west France.

Rouchet, Italian red grape variety. See RUCHÈ.

Rougeon, Seibel FRENCH HYBRID red wine variety grown in the north eastern UNITED STATES. Very productive and winter hardy, it produces deep-coloured wines with few hybrid aromas, and sometimes has a meaty note, but needs considerable attention because of it susceptibility to both DOWNY MILDEW and POWDERY MILDREW. D.F.

Roupeiro, Portuguese white grape variety grown particularly in the ALENTEJO producing basic white wine to be drunk as young as possible. DNA PROFILING in Portugal confirmed that it is identical to SÍRIA.

rousing, alternative term for the wine-making operation of STIRRING.

Roussanne, fashionable white Rhône grape which doubtless owes its name to the russet or *roux* colour of its skin. With MARSANNE, with which it is often blended, it is one of only two vine varieties allowed into the white versions of the northern Rhône's red wine appellations HERMITAGE, CROZES-HERMITAGE, and ST-JOSEPH and into the exclusively white but often sparkling ST-PÉRAY. In each of these appellations, Marsanne is far more widely grown because, although the wine produced is not as fine, the vine tends to be hardier and more productive. Roussanne's irregular yields, tendency to POWDERY MILDEW and rot, and poor wind resistance all but eradicated it from the northern Rhône until better clones were selected and even today it is preferred there by a minority of producers such as JABOULET. Nevertheless, French plantings had reached 760 ha/1,900 acres by 2000.

Roussanne's chief attribute is its haunting aroma, something akin to a particularly refreshing herb tea, together with acidity that allows it to age much more gracefully than Marsanne, which, in blends, can lend useful body. It does need to reach full maturity, however, in order to express itself elegantly. In the southern Rhône, Roussanne (but not Marsanne) is one of four grape varieties allowed into white CHÂTEAUNEUF-DU-PAPE, and Ch de Beaucastel has demonstrated that carefully grown Roussanne can respond well to oak ageing. The variety is also grown in Provence (although the more common pink-berried **Roussanne du Var** is a lesser, unrelated variety used for VINS DE PAYS and ordinary table wines) and, increasingly, in the Languedoc and Roussillon, where Roussanne's tendency to ripen late is less problematic than in the northern Rhône and where results can be impressive. Although it is usually classified with Marsanne and Vermentino in appellation regulations, it can make a fine blending partner with the fuller-bodied Chardonnay too. It can suffer in drought conditions, however.

The variety is also beguilingly fine and aromatic at Chignin in SAVOIE, where it is known as Bergeron, but should not be confused with ROUSSETTE. It is grown to a limited extent in Liguria and Toscana, where it is a permitted ingredient in Italy's Montecarlo Bianco, and can also be found in Australia, presumably having been taken there as a partner to the much more successful SHIRAZ. Roussanne is also increasingly popular, both for blending and as a VARIETAL, in California's Central Coast. Acreage has grown from under 20 in 1995 to nearly 200 (80 ha) in 2003 with Renaissance in North Yuba county showing a particular aptitude for it.

Roussette, former name for the ALTESSE grape of SAVOIE now used for a number of wines made in eastern France.

Roussette de Savoie, SAVOIE appellation for some of the region's finest wines, whites made exclusively from ALTESSE. In good vintages, they age well and some producers now ferment and/or age in oak. Four CRUS' names may be suffixed to the appellation: Frangy, Monterminod, Monthoux, and most notably Marestel, a steep south-facing slope in the village of JONGIEUX that yields exceptionally ripe fruit.

Roussette de Seyssel is a SEYSSEL wine made from Altesse. In the nearby Ain *département*, the name of the VDQS **Roussette du Bugey** may be followed by the name of the commune in which the wine was made. W.L.

Roussillon, although first encountered by some outsiders as a suffix to LANGUEDOC, has a quite distinct identity, both cultural and geographical. Its inhabitants are Catalan rather than French or Occitan, with a history rich in Spanish influence, particularly between the 13th and 17th centuries, when it was ruled first from Majorca and then from Aragón. They identify closely with the inhabitants of Spanish CATALUÑA just across the Pyrenees. Quite unlike the flat coastal plains of the Languedoc, Roussillon's TOPOGRAPHY can be guessed at by the fact that today it is effectively the *département* called Pyrénées-Orientales, the eastern section of the Pyrenees, a mountain range so high that much of it remains snow covered throughout the summer. Vines and olives (the latter decimated by the frosts of 1956) are two of the rare agricultural crops that can thrive in the tortured, arid valleys of the Agly, Têt, and Tech—although the lower land is today an important source of soft fruit. The climate is France's sunniest, with an average of 325 days' sunshine a year, frequent winds accentuating the grape-drying process in summer. Wine styles and techniques as well as grape varieties have much in common with neighbouring Spain, as do the relatively low yields. Despite the prevailing temperatures, Roussillon's cellars were some of France's last to install efficient TEMPERATURE CONTROL, and new OAK arrived relatively recently, but the region has been making up for lost time and is now home to some of France's most exciting reds and whites.

Viticulture was probably introduced to the region via the Greek establishment of Marseilles in the 7th century BC and developed by the Romans. It seems highly likely that the MUSCAT vine was the first to be introduced, in an effort to ape the popular sweet wines of the AEGEAN ISLANDS. The RIVESALTES region had certainly earned an important reputation for its Muscat by the 14th century, which probably pre-dated that of the Languedoc's FRONTIGNAN. Sweetness was often concentrated by leaving Muscat grapes to shrivel on the vine, a practice that continued at least until the late 19th century (see DRIED GRAPE WINES). Roussillon became the world's foremost producer of VINS DOUX NATURELS, with BANYULS and to a lesser extent MAURY eventually overtaking Rivesaltes in réclame if not volume (see also GRAND ROUSSILLON).

But this specialization was to be its downfall for much of the 20th century when strong, sweet wines were decidedly unfashionable, and the region's table wines, rather Spanish in terms of their depth of colour and alcohol, were regarded as useful only for blending with the lighter wines of the Languedoc, which has about six times Roussillon's area under vine.

Awarded APPELLATION CONTRÔLÉE status as recently as 1977, **Côtes du Roussillon** has been a name in search of an image outside the region in which it is, with the exception of COLLIOURE, the sole appellation for table wines. **Côtes du Roussillon Les Aspres,** for wines made in the south of the département, gained its own appellation in 2004. Côtes du Roussillon can be white and rosé as well as red, but the **Côtes du Roussillon-Villages** appellation that theoretically designates the region's finest wines is only for red wines made in the northern, hillier third of the region just south of CORBIÈRES and FITOU.

The best reds, as geography suggests, tend to be like a Spanish rendering of Corbières. Côtes du Roussillon reds must be made from at least three grape varieties and, the defining rule, Syrah and/or Mourvèdre must constitute at least 20 per cent. Grenache is the most widely planted variety in Roussillon and its relative Lladoner Pelut is also grown. As has been the Spanish custom, some white Maccabéo can constitute up to 10 per cent of the blend. As in the Languedoc, CARBONIC MACERATION has been much employed to counter Carignan's inherent astringency but more 'traditional' vinification techniques are increasingly employed on the nobler varieties. The reds are robust, rarely subtle, but good value. Within the northern Villages region, the small villages of CARAMANY, LATOUR-DE-FRANCE, Lesquerde, and Tautavel have successfully lobbied to have their names allowed as suffixes to the Côtes du Roussillon-Villages appellation.

Whites, with their relatively low acidity, may be more difficult to make successfully, but they are also more distinctive, their full-bodied fragrance shaped by Grenache Blanc, Maccabéo, and Tourbat (Sardegna's TORBATO and known locally as Malvoisie du Roussillon), which must constitute at least half of any blend. Fragrance comes from the likes of Marsanne, Roussanne, and Vermentino/Rolle, which together must make up at least 20 per cent of any white wine blend. Domaines de Casenove, Cazes, des Chênes, du Mas Crémat, Força-Réal, Gauby, Ch de Jau, Domaines Piquemal, Sarda-Malet, and Singla have all made some excellent wines, although CO-OPERATIVES still dominate.

Muscat and Grenache, the region's dominant vine varieties (other than Carignan) grown for vin doux naturel, are increasingly made into less alcoholic, dry VIN DE PAYS.

A few producers, especially on the coastal plain around Rivesaltes, are trying their luck with such INTERNATIONAL VARIETIES as Chardonnay and Merlot, although it can be difficult to preserve acidity in the first and fruit concentration in the second. These wines are usually labelled as Vin de Pays des Côtes Catalanes in the northern third, Vin de Pays Catalan in the south. A Vin de Pays de la Côte Vermeille was created in the early 21st century for wines made close to the coast around Collioure and Banyuls.

One enclave in the upper Agly valley near the village of MAURY emerged in the early years of this century as an area of real potential for reds not unlike the concentrated, SCHISTOUS essences of PRIORAT across the Pyrenees, and extremely mineral-flavoured whites. Its own vin de pays designation of Coteaux Fenouillèdes was rescinded just when it was most needed and the wines had to be sold as Vin de Pays des Côtes Catalanes, along with wines from a much larger area, from the 2003 vintage. Domaines Gauby, du Soula, Matassa, and du Clot de l'Oum are some of the leading practitioners.

The vine-growers of Roussillon have been some of France's least content with the details of their appellation regulations, which continue to evolve. There can be considerable scepticism about a system devised as far away as Paris and administered from Brussels, especially among those who identify so closely with the inhabitants of Barcelona.

Ponsich, P., 'Histoire de la vigne et du vin en Roussillon', in Éditions Montalba, *Les Vins du Roussillon* (France, 1980).

row spacing, the space between rows of vines in the vineyard. See VINE DENSITY. Since the early 1990s, some NEW WORLD producers have emulated the European practice of using closer row spacing in the hope that this will lead to an improvement in wine quality.

Royalty, also known as **Royalty 1390,** CALIFORNIA hybrid vine variety with red flesh, a TEINTURIER. It was bred by crossing the progenitor of all red-fleshed teinturiers, Alicante Ganzin, with the Jura grape variety TROUSSEAU and was released in 1958 along with the somewhat similar but much more successful RUBIRED. There is little regal about this particular variety, which is difficult to grow, although a few hundred acres persist, almost exclusively in the hot SAN JOAQUIN VALLEY.

RS, common abbreviation for RESIDUAL SUGAR.

Rubin, distinctively BULGARIAN crossing of Nebbiolo and Syrah developed around 1944. It ripens in mid September and has 50 per cent more ANTHOCYANINS than Cabernet Sauvignon, although it appears to have little potential for longevity.　　　　C.G.

Rubired, increasingly popular (in an age when depth of COLOUR is automatically associated with quality) red-fleshed California HYBRID, the result of crossing the progenitor of all red-fleshed TEINTURIERS, Alicante Ganzin, with the port variety TINTO CÃO. It was released, along with the somewhat similar but much less successful ROYALTY, in 1958. Its productivity and depth of colour have made the variety so popular with blenders of wine, California port, and grape juice, that by 2003 there were more than 13,000 acres/5,200 ha in the state, making it California's sixth most popular red grape. It is grown, without any major viticultural problems, mainly in the hot SAN JOAQUIN VALLEY. This useful blending ingredient has also become increasingly popular in Australia.

ruby, style of fortified wine. See PORT.

Ruby Cabernet, red VINIFERA grape variety bred in and for CALIFORNIA in 1949. Dr H. P. Olmo of the University of California at DAVIS (see also EMERALD RIESLING, CARNELIAN) crossed Carignan with Cabernet Sauvignon in an attempt to combine Cabernet characteristics with Carignan productivity and heat tolerance. The slightly rustic Ruby Cabernet enjoyed a heyday in California in the 1960s and is still the state's ninth most planted red wine grape (though is not as popular as the red-fleshed hybrid RUBIRED). Most of its 8,000 acres are in the southern SAN JOAQUIN VALLEY. It is grown by several producers in South Africa, Latin America, and also appeared increasingly on Australian wine labels during that country's red wine shortage of the late 1990s. Plantings in Australia had reached almost 2,000 ha/5,000 acres by 2003, while South Africa had 3,375 ha/5,860 acres in the same year.

Ruchè, Rouchet, or occasionally **Roche,** relatively obscure red grape variety of the

PIEMONTE region in north west Italy enjoying something of a revival with its own varietal DOC around Castagnole Monferrato, occasionally labelled Rouchet. Like NEBBIOLO, the wine is headily scented and its TANNINS imbue it with an almost bitter aftertaste. According to Gleave, it is locally supposed to have been brought from BURGUNDY in the 18th century.

Gleave, D., *The Wines of Italy* (London and New York, 1989).

Rueda, historic Spanish white wine zone named after the unprepossessing town which straddles the main road from Madrid to León in CASTILLA Y LEÓN (see map under SPAIN). In the Middle Ages, vineyards flourished on this bleak Castilian plateau and cellars were hollowed out of the limestone under the town, but after PHYLLOXERA ravaged the zone, Rueda went into rapid decline. The high-yielding PALOMINO grape was used for replanting, a move that in this case was justified since the main local styles were FORTIFIED WINES in the image of SHERRY.

For much of the 20th century, the local VERDEJO grape was Rueda's sleeping beauty. It was awoken in the 1970s, when Bodegas Marqués de Riscal of RIOJA recognized the area's potential for dry white wine and sold a fresh Rueda white alongside its Rioja reds. Rueda was awarded DO status in 1980 and the local Consejo Regulador succeeded in re-launching the native variety of which there were nearly three times as much as of Palomino in the mid 2000s, a radical reversal of the previous situation. Two very different forms of Rueda currently coexist: fortified and unfortified. The fortified wines (Rueda Pálido, with a minimum ALCOHOLIC STRENGTH of 14 per cent developed under a film of FLOR like a coarser FINO sherry, and the stronger Rueda Dorado) are declining, however, and are most often sold in bulk locally and on the northern Spanish coast. In complete contrast, modern Rueda is a light, fruity, dry white wine. It may be made from a blend of Viura (MACABEO) and Verdejo, the latter accounting for at least 50 per cent of the blend, or it may be a SAUVIGNON BLANC varietal. Rueda Superior must contain at least 85 per cent Verdejo and, as more farmers convert their vineyards, there are ever more VARIETAL wines. Sauvignon Blanc was introduced by Marqués de Riscal in the early 1980s. Some fine, elegant wines have resulted, including one from one of the LURTON family of Bordeaux.

TEMPRANILLO produces some typically firm red wine in the zone. In 2002, red wines were admitted in the Rueda DO, although some white wine producers were still battling in court in 2005 to return it to white wine-only status.   R.J.M. & V. de la S.

Peñín, J., *Guía Peñín* (Madrid, annually).

Rufete, early-ripening vine variety capable of making fruity red wines and lightish port in the north of Portugal, where 5,500 ha/ 13,500 acres were planted in 2004, and the west of Spain, where a national total of 686 ha grew in the same year. This variety was previously known as TINTA PINHEIRA.

Ruffiac, Ruffiat. See ARRUFIAC.

rugose wood, a complex of four VIRUS DISEASES which comprises Rupestris stem pitting (RSP), Kober stem grooving (grapevine vitivirus A or GVA), CORKY BARK (grapevine vitivirus B or GVB), and LN33 stem grooving (LNSG). Additionally, grapevine vitiviruses C and D have been been identified but they have not yet been shown to cause disease in grapevines.

Although widespread, this complex of diseases is relatively unknown as all but corky bark are generally symptomless on *Vitis vinifera*. Rugose wood induces graft incompatibility and can kill the vines, especially in the first years after planting. Typical symptoms are pitting or grooving of the wood. All four diseases can be identified by INDEXING. The effect on wine quality of these diseases is still to be evaluated.

Bovey, R., *et al.*, *Virus and Virus-like Diseases of Vines: Colour Atlas of Symptoms* (Lausanne, 1980).

Pearson, R. C., and Goheen, A. C., *Compendium of Grape Diseases* (St Paul, Minn., 1988).

Weber, E., Golino, D., and Rowhani, A., 'Laboratory testing for grapevine diseases', *Practical Winery and Vineyard* (Jan/Feb 2002), 13-27.

Ruiterbosch, wine area in SOUTH AFRICA once known as Mossel Bay.

Ruländer is the more traditional German name for PINOT GRIS, which was propagated in the Rheinpfalz in the early years of the 18th century by wine merchant Johann Seger Ruland. Since the mid 1980s, the name has been reserved for sweeter—and increasingly unfashionable—styles of Pinot Gris, while the increasingly common dry wines are labelled GRAUBURGUNDER. While the vine is prone to GREY ROT, it can also produce some fine BOTRYTIZED sweet wines.

In Austria, where Pinot Gris is typically even earthier and richer than its German counterparts, it is also commonly called Ruländer and is much less common than Pinot Blanc, covering just 1 per cent of the country's vineyard, chiefly in Styria and Burgenland. The variety can produce some highly regarded Austrian whites, sometimes fermented and aged in oak.

The name Ruländer is also used for some of the Pinot Gris that is widely planted in ROMANIA.

Rully, rambling village in Burgundy's CÔTE CHALONNAISE providing approximately equal quantities of red and white wines. The wines are attractive early and rarely age well, being grown on light and sandy soil. Rully is also a good source of sparkling CRÉMANT de Bourgogne. Nineteen vineyards in the village, one-sixth of the total, are designated PREMIERS CRUS, with Grésigny, Rabourcé, and Les Cloux being the most frequently seen.   J.T.C.M.

Rumania. See ROMANIA.

rupestris, species of the *Vitis* genus native to North America much used in developing suitably resistant ROOTSTOCKS and HYBRIDS. For more details, see VITIS.

Russia. Only the most southern parts of the Russian Federation are suitable for viticulture. The principal limiting factors are a short vegetation period, lack of water, and high summer temperatures. After a turbulent period at the end of the 20th century, total vineyard area has stabilized at around 70,000 ha/ 173,000 acres in the mid 2000s but there are official plans to restore this to pre-GORBACHEV levels closer to 150,000 ha by 2010.

History

South Dagestan is Russia's most important ancient viticultural area although WILD VINES growing around the Caspian, Black, and Azov seas were selected and cultivated long ago, and can still be found in the register of varieties permitted within the Russian Federation. There is evidence of viticultural co-operation between those living on the Black and Azov seas and the Ancient Greeks.

In 1880, PHYLLOXERA reached Russia and devastated the country's viticulture.

The first vineyards in the Anapa zone of the Krasnodar region were established in the locality of Pilenkovo and planted to RIESLING and PORTUGIESER varieties. In 1914, the Russian vineyard area averaged 50,000 ha/123,500 acres, but this had halved by 1919. In 1940, vineyards occupied 42,000 ha. The great development of commercial vineyards came at the end of 1950, and Russia had a highly efficient wine production and, especially, processing and bottling system throughout the Soviet era until GORBACHEV's anti-alcoholism campaign began in 1985. Vineyards were abandoned or grubbed up, bottling plants converted to other uses, and then land privatization during the transition to a market economy further shrivelled the Russian wine industry. The Russian Federation's total vineyard area shrank to 72,000 ha by 2000, less than half the area cultivated in the late 1980s, while the total grape harvest shrank to less than a third of its previous level.

Climate and geography

Most commercial vineyards are in the North Caucasus. The climate of most Russian viticultural zones is very CONTINENTAL and winters can be extremely severe, so that up to half of all vines need to be covered with soil in this period for WINTER PROTECTION. The most favourable soil and climate conditions are in the Krasnodar region and Dagestan, with active annual temperature summations of 3,600 to 4,000 °C and, even more importantly, winters warm enough in parts to permit non-protected viticulture.

Krasnodar, the most important Russian wine region is divided into seven agricultural zones, of which the Anapa-and-Taman zone is perhaps most promising for wine production. No winter protection is required for vines here and the active heat summation of 3,400 to 3,600 °C with 193 to 233 frost-free days is sufficient even for quite late ripening varieties. The Black Sea zone is much wetter but winters are not as severe and still, sparkling, and dessert wines are produced here. In most other parts of Krasnodar, vines have to be banked up if they are to survive the harsh winters, although parts of the Central zone on the Azov sea are quite promising for wine production.

Dagestan with its extremely varied climate, some of it semi-desert, is Russia's second most important wine-producing region (and was its principal one in the late 1980s). The flat, southern zone along the Caspian sea between the capital and AZERBAIJAN, with its strong tradition of viticulture, is one of the most propitious parts of the Russian Federation for the restoration of wine production. Grape varieties grown include RKATSITELI, Agadai, White Muscat, Asyl Kara, Red Tersky, SAPERAVI, Jemghug Zala, Premier, Kodryanka, and Moldova.

About 13 per cent of Russian wine is produced in the **Stavropol** region although the active annual temperature summation is only 3,000 to 3,400 °C and the frost-free period usually just 180–90 days. Winter protection is essential. The most common varieties are Levokumski Stable, Sauvignon Blanc, Riesling, Rkatsiteli, and Aligoté.

Even less important as a wine producer is the **Rostov** region with its dry, hot summers, frosty winters and low yields. **Chechnya** also produced considerable quantities of wine, and **Kabardino-Balkariya** continues to do so.

Industry organization
In the late 1970s, Russia had nearly 200,000 ha/ 500,000 acres of vineyard but by 2000 the total vineyard area left after GORBACHEV's anti-alcohol drive and vineyard privatization was just 71,900 ha: 34,600 ha in the Krasnodar region, 20,700 ha in Dagestan, 8,900 ha in the Stavropol region, 5,700 ha in the Rostov region, and 1,100 ha in Kabardino-Balkaria.

Dessert wines are produced in the Don and Kuban valleys, the Stavropol region, Dagestan, and Kabardino-Balkaria.

Sparkling wine is important to Russians with large production centres for SOVIET SPARKLING WINE in the cities.

Viticulture
Vine-TRAINING SYSTEMS changed enormously during the 20th century. Densely planted vineyards (5,000 to 10,000 vines per ha) with single vine supports have given way to TRELLIS SYSTEMS in wider-spaced rows. The many vineyards that need winter protection are either trained with long and medium canes left in one direction and covered with soil in winter by a vine-laying machine, or left to be covered with a high mound of soil. Row and vine spacing is 2.5 to 3.0 m and 1.25 to 2.0 m respectively.

In warmer, non-protected viticultural zones, there may be IRRIGATION in areas with a satisfactory water supply. The trunks of particularly vigorous vines are trained 1.2 m high, their canes being supported vertically, with free-hanging terminal shoots; such vines are planted in rows spaced between 3 and 4 m. Vineyards on non-irrigated lands have medium- and high-TRUNKED forms with row and vine spacing at 2.5 to 3.0 m and 1.25 to 2.0 m respectively.

Vine varieties
The varietal assortment of Russia's vineyards is extremely diverse, with about 100 varieties allowed for commercial cultivation. Depending on the region, 70 to 85 per cent of vineyards are planted to wine grapes, with TABLE GRAPES accounting for 15 to 30 per cent of the total vineyard area. Among wine grapes cultivated in all viticultural regions of Russia, the most common is RKATSITELI, with 45 to 50 per cent. This variety allows various cultural practices and produces a range of different types of wine. Such varieties as ALIGOTÉ, RIESLING, CLAIRETTE, CABERNET SAUVIGNON, TRAMINER, MUSCATS, SILVANER, SAPERAVI, MERLOT, PINOT GRIS, and the indigenous Moldovan variety PLAVAI are also widely planted, as well as the local red Tsimlyansky.

Recently, NEW VARIETIES with improved resistance to FUNGAL DISEASES and FROST have been released by the All-Russia Potapenko Research Institute for Viticulture and Ecology. Most notable among the wine grape varieties are Saperavi Severny and CABERNET SEVERNY. They, and other new varieties such as Stepniak and Fioletovy Ranni, occupy about 10,000 ha/ 25,000 acres on various Russian farms. Com-

mercial cultivation of these new, specially bred varieties has allowed considerable expansion of non-protected viticulture.

In the early 1990s, there was a substantial expansion in the total area planted to new, high-yielding wine grape varieties such as Vydvizhenets, and varieties suitable for both wine and table grapes such as Muscat Derbentski and Zala Gyöngye, as well as to indigenous varieties to be made into wine with CONTROLLED APPELLATIONS of origin such as Sibirkovy, Tsimlyanski Cherny, Plechistic, Narma, and Güliabi Daghestanski.

V.R. & M.R.

Zakharova, E. I., 'The Soviet Federative Republic of Russia' (Russian), in A. I. Timush (ed.), *Encyclopaedia of Viticulture* (Kishinev, 1987).

Russian River Valley, high-quality California wine region and AVA west of Healdsburg along that portion of the river that meanders through the hills of northern Sonoma county toward its mouth. See SONOMA.

Rust, important wine town on the western shore of the Neusiedlersee in the Burgenland region of AUSTRIA historically famous for the production of sweet white AUSBRUCH wines but now also for high-quality reds mainly from Blaufränkisch and Zweigelt and some excellent dry white wines. Rust is also the base of the Austrian Wine Academy, the largest wine education centre in mainland Europe.

Rutherford, important centre of wine production in California's NAPA valley.

Rutherglen, historic wine region in NORTH EAST VICTORIA ZONE, famous for its fortified LIQUEUR MUSCAT and Liqueur Tokay.

Ruwer, small German river, 40 km/25 miles in length, which rises in the Hunsrück mountains and flows into the MOSEL, downstream from Trier. In recent years, some of the vineyards have been replaced by houses, and in the 1960s the area under vine did not expand as it did in the main part of the Mosel-Saar-Ruwer wine region. In steep sites (once in ecclesiastical hands) at Eitelsbach, Maximin Grünhaus, and Kasel, Rieslings from good years are among the best in Germany. They are similar in structure to those of the SAAR, but have a touch of earthiness to add individuality.

See also MOSEL-SAAR-RUWER. I.J.

Ruzica, occasional alternative name for the white DINKA grape.

Saale-Unstrut, small but expanding wine region in eastern GERMANY of terraced and sometimes isolated vineyards, starting to recover from the forlorn condition in which they were left by the former East German regime (see map under GERMANY). The main producers in the 650 ha/1,600 acres under vine are the cellars at Naumburg belonging to the state of Sachsen-Anhalt, and the co-operative cellar at Freyburg. As in nearby SACHSEN, Müller-Thurgau dominates (here with 22 per cent of total vineyard area) and Weissburgunder (here 12 per cent) is increasingly popular. Traditional Silvaner is planted on 9 per cent of the calcareous soils. These are continental Europe's northernmost vineyards, with a CONTINENTAL climate and frequent, dangerous FROSTS. The result is wines that are naturally light in alcohol but relatively rich in extract. It is said that the calcareous soil gives them added BODY, so that they can seem better balanced than many dry wines grown in the slate of the Mosel.   I.J. & D.S.

Saar, river which rises in the Vosges mountains and joins the MOSEL at Konz, near Trier. Downstream from Serrig, Riesling vines grow in slate soil, resulting in steely, firm wines with a powerful aroma and long flavour. In good vintages, they are amongst the most successful in the MOSEL-SAAR-RUWER wine region of GERMANY. Only top estates or, at least, growers with vines in favoured sites can produce good wines in poor vintages. For the rest, their lesser wines can be converted into sparkling wine. Within Germany, Saar Riesling SEKT has a good reputation and a long-established position in the market.

See also RUWER.   I.J.

Saccharomyces. See YEAST.

Sachsen, or **Saxony** in English, the smallest wine region in GERMANY. Formerly in East Germany, it is also known colloquially as the Elbtal, and established the first German viticultural training institute (in Meissen) in 1811–12. A steadily increasing 446 ha/1,100 acres of vineyard follow the course of the river Elbe, from Pillnitz on the southern outskirts of Dresden, to Diesbar-Seusslitz north of Meissen. Sachsen and SAALE-UNSTRUT are the most northerly wine regions in Germany (see map under GERMANY) and have very similar climates. The granite and gneiss-dominated soils are not unlike those of Austria's WACHAU, albeit with less dramatically steep slopes. Yields are low, usually under half the national average. It was in Meissen, known for its porcelain factory, that viticulture in Sachsen was first documented in 1161. It is also the home of the regional co-operative that receives the grapes from 130 ha/320 acres of vineyard, cultivated by 2,500 part-time growers. The region's other main producer, the state wine domaine, is housed in the 18th-century palace

Schloss Wackerbarth at Radebeul. Müller-Thurgau dominates white grape plantings with 21 per cent, but Riesling (16 per cent) and Weissburgunder (13 per cent) are gaining ground, as are red vines with 15 per cent in 2003. Nearly 90 per cent of the wine is bottled dry. Although additional investment is needed to improve quality, the tremendous enthusiasm in the east for home-grown wines and the enthusiasm of so many part-time growers bode well for the preservation of Sachsen's longstanding viticultural tradition.

I.J. & D.S.

sack, name for a white FORTIFIED WINE, imported from Spain or the Canary islands, which was much in vogue in England in the 16th and 17th centuries. Its most famous, fictional, consumer was Sir John Falstaff in Shakespeare's 2 *Henry IV*, *Act IV*, *Scene ii* he delivers his classic speech in its praise. The etymology of sack is disputed. The *Oxford English Dictionary* derives the word from the French word *sec* meaning 'dry', but admits that it cannot produce a convincing explanation for the difference in vowels. Moreover, sack was probably sweet. It was matured in wood for up to two years so it would have been like a cheap OLOROSO. Hence Julian Jeffs proposes another derivation: Spanish *sacar*, to draw out, from which *sacas* became exports of wine. Often the place of production was put before the noun, as in Canary sack (see LA PALMA), Malaga sack, (see Málaga), Sherris (or Sherry) sack. Sherris is JEREZ, hence the modern word SHERRY. From the end of the 17th century, 'sherry' began to replace 'sack' as the generic term, but sack was still used in the 18th century.

Sack was popular in England, even more so when in 1587 Drake raided the Spanish fleet at Cádiz and captured 2,900 PIPES (not BUTTS at this stage) of sherry intended for the Armada and made drinking sack an act of patriotism. Undoubtedly the English colony did not welcome the second raid on Cádiz in 1595; yet sack continued to be exported to England. With the accession of James I in 1603, tension eased and the merchants flourished once more. Sack appears in the works of many of the major English writers of the 17th century, and, however much the Puritans disapproved of the theatre, they did drink sack: when Cromwell paid an official visit to Bristol he was presented with a pipe of sack.   H.M.W.

Jeffs, J., *Sherry* (4th edn, London, 1992).

sacramental wine, saviour of some CALIFORNIA wineries during PROHIBITION. For more details of the sacramental nature of wine, see EUCHARIST.

Sacramento valley, northern part of the vast CENTRAL VALLEY of CALIFORNIA from Lodi northwards, including the vinously important University of California at DAVIS.

Sacy, the white grape variety once widely grown in the YONNE *département*. Its productivity is its chief attribute, its acidity the wine's most noticeable characteristic. This has been used to reasonable effect by the producers of sparkling wines, and the variety, also called Tresallier, is still an ingredient in the white wines of ST-POURÇAIN. See also PINOT.

Sagrantino, lively, sometimes tannic red grape variety grown in UMBRIA in central Italy, particularly in the Montefalco area. **Sagrantino di Montefalco** was elevated to DOCG status in the mid 1990s. Sagrantino has been used as an ingredient in DRIED GRAPE WINES but today shows promise as a carefully vinified dry red, sometimes blended with SANGIOVESE. Outstanding wines from the Arnaldo Caprai winery have created much interest in the variety, but the overall level of viticultural and oenological sophistication in the production zone is not high, as demonstrated by many wines.   D.T.

saignée, French term meaning 'bled' for a wine-making technique which results in a ROSÉ WINE made by running off, or 'bleeding', a certain amount of FREE-RUN juice from just-crushed dark-skinned grapes after a short, prefermentation MACERATION. The aim of this may be primarily to produce a lightly pink wine, or to increase the proportion of PHENOLICS and FLAVOUR COMPOUNDS to juice, thereby effecting a form of CONCENTRATION of the red wine which results from fermentation of the rest of the juice with the skins. The second operation has often been undertaken by ambitious producers of both red bordeaux and red burgundy.

St-Amour, the most northerly of the BEAUJOLAIS crus and an area in which a considerable amount of white Beaujolais Blanc (and ST-VÉRAN) is made. About 320 ha/790 acres of Gamay vines are planted for the production of relatively light but true red Beaujolais. The cru was added several years after most others. One theory is that its name, which indubitably adds to its appeal, comes from a Roman soldier who celebrated a narrow escape from death in Switzerland by converting to Christianity and establishing a mission. He was later canonized as St-Amour. There are other, earlier theories, as one would expect of Beaujolais, perhaps the earthiest of all wine regions.

St-Aubin, village in the Côte de Beaune district of Burgundy's Côte d'Or tucked out of the limelight between Meursault and Puligny-Montrachet, producing two-thirds red wine from Pinot Noir and one-third white from Chardonnay. A high proportion, two-thirds, of the vineyard area is designated PREMIER CRU, notably Les Charmois, La Chatenière, En Remilly, and Les Murgers Dents de Chien, part of a swathe of mostly south west-facing vineyards lying between the borders of Chassagne-Montrachet and Puligny-Montrachet and the hamlet of Gamay, which is included in the St-Aubin appellation. The remaining vineyards have the ideal south and south easterly exposition but are less favourably situated further up the cooler valley.

White St-Aubin has some of the character of Puligny-Montrachet, especially in the warmer vintages; the reds resemble a more supple version of red Chassagne-Montrachet. Hubert Lamy is one of several fine producers based in St-Aubin.

See also CÔTE D'OR, and map under BURGUNDY.   J.T.C.M.

St-Bris was granted full appellation status from the 2001 vintage for its crisp, cool climate Sauvignon, having been a VDQS since 1974. About 100 ha/250 acres of Sauvignon vines in the communes of St-Bris-le-Vineux, Chitry, IRANCY, Quenne, and parts of Vincelottes south of AUXERRE and west of CHABLIS are currently in production. The wine is too obscure to be made with anything other than artisan passion, but it lacks the breed and concentration of great Loire Sauvignon made to the south west. Being technically Burgundian but made from a decidedly non-Burgundian grape, it is a curiosity.

St-Chinian, good-value appellation in the LANGUEDOC in southern France which extends over arid, spectacular, mountainous terrain in the foothills of the Cévennes between the MINERVOIS and FAUGÈRES appellations (see map under LANGUEDOC). Some fresh, dry rosé and increasingly interesting whites are also made. The small town of St-Chinian itself is in the middle of the zone, which extends upwards and northwards as far as Vieussan, including Berlou and its respected CO-OPERATIVE, whose wines are sometimes labelled Berloup. In the mid 2000s, a total of about 2,800 ha/6,900 acres were dedicated to the production of appellation wine within the zone, which can be divided into two very different sections. In the northern zone around Berlou and Roquebrun, which earned their own appellations **St-Chinian Berlou** and **St-Chinian Roquebrun** for red wines in 2005, vines at around 200 m/656 ft altitude grow on arid schists and yield low quantities of extremely sharply etched wines with distinct minerality. In the southern zone closer to St-Chinian itself, the clays and limestone, typically at about 100 m, tend to result in fuller, softer wines. Carignan vines, limited to 40 per cent of any red, are being gradually replaced by Syrah, Grenache, Lladoner Pelut, and Mourvèdre, the four of which must total at least 60 per cent of any blend. Cinsaut may represent no more than 30 per cent. St-Chinian Roquebrun is a blend of Mourvèdre, Grenache, and particularly schist-grown Syrah whereas St-Chinian Berlou must also contain at least 30 per cent Carignan, almost invariably from old vines. Grenache Blanc, with Marsanne, Roussanne and some Vermentino are the main white grapes. Many producers here also grow other varieties with which to make some excellent VIN DE PAYS. Other fine producers include Domaine Borie La Vitarèle, Canet Valette, Cazal-Viel, Ch Maurel Fonsalade, Mas Champart, Ch Moulinier, Domaine Navarra, and Ch Viranel.

St-Christol, the easternmost named TERROIR within the Coteaux du LANGUEDOC appellation in southern France, named after a village on the eastern boundary of the Hérault *département* with Gard. Production of appellation wine is relatively low here, and is chiefly in the hands of the village CO-OPERATIVE although quality is fast improving on estates such as Domaine de la Coste.

St-Drézéry, the smallest named TERROIR within the Coteaux du LANGUEDOC appellation in southern France. Like neighbouring ST-CHRISTOL it is named after a village on the eastern boundary of the Hérault *département* with Gard and such appellation production as there is is chiefly in the hands of the village CO-OPERATIVE although Ch Puech-Haut makes fine reds and whites.

Ste-Croix-du-Mont, most important of the sweet white wine appellations on the right bank of the GARONNE in the BORDEAUX region. At their best, these wines can resemble the wines made across the river in SAUTERNES and BARSAC, being high in alcohol, sugar, and concentration. Prices are considerably lower, however. The topography and soil structure of Ste-Croix-du-Mont are generally more promising than those of its right bank neighbours LOUPIAC and CADILLAC, for some of the vineyards here are on gravel slopes well situated for the development of NOBLE ROT. An increasing number of producers are prepared to take the risks necessary to produce BOTRYTIZED wines, and BARREL FERMENTATION, such as introduced for the prestige cuvées of Chx des Arroucats, La Rame, and du Mont, is becoming increasingly common (see SAUTERNES for details). Some very ordinary, sugary MOELLEUX is also made, however.

Ste-Foy, or **Ste-Foy-Bordeaux**, 350 ha of vineyards in the extreme east of the BORDEAUX region on the border with, and arguably more properly part of, BERGERAC. The appellation is named after its principal town, just 22 km/14 miles west of the town of Bergerac. Its red wines are very similar to red Bergerac and BORDEAUX AC, while its white wines are often sweet and mostly undistinguished.

St-Émilion, important, fast-changing red wine district in Bordeaux producing more wine than any other RIGHT BANK appellation, and home of most of the extravagantly priced

MICROCHÂTEAUX. It takes its name from the prettiest town in the Bordeaux region by far, and one of the few to attract tourists to whom wine is of no interest.

The town's historical importance is undisputed, and obvious to the most casual of visitors. In the 8th century it was a collection of caves hollowed out of the cliff on which a fortified medieval town was to be built. In the Middle Ages its port, Pierrefitte, played an important part in shipping wine down the DORDOGNE river, until it was overtaken by LIBOURNE a few miles downstream. It was on the pilgrim route to Santiago de Compostela, and even today its CONFRÉRIE the **Jurade de St-Émilion** prides itself on maintaining the district's reputation for hospitality. As outlined in BORDEAUX, history, St-Émilion was a wine region long before the Médoc on the left bank of the Gironde, even though for most of the 19th century it was less important commercially. In the early 20th century, the wines of St-Émilion were left to the merchants of Libourne to sell in northern France and northern Europe, while the BORDEAUX TRADE concentrated on selling LEFT BANK wines. The reputation of St-Émilion grew steadily throughout the second half of the 20th century, accelerating towards the end of the century, not least because of international interest in the microchâteaux, or garagistes. As a result, rivalry between the left and right banks intensified, with St-Émilion and the scores of wine shops lining its narrow cobbled streets being the focus of right bank wine activity.

Whereas the Médoc is made up of large, grand estates, most of St-Émilion's 400 or so smallholders are essentially farmers, albeit dedicated to a single crop.

That crop is dominated by the Merlot and Cabernet Franc (here called Bouchet) vine varieties, Merlot accounting for more than 60 per cent of all vine plantings and imbuing the wines with their characteristic almost dried fruit sweetness. A little Cabernet Sauvignon is grown, but it can be relied upon to ripen profitably only in very selected spots in the generally cooler soils and MACROCLIMATE of the right bank, and then only if a suitable CLONE has been planted.

Grape varieties apart, variation is the hallmark of this extensive region. The quality of its wines can vary from light, fruity, serviceable clarets to the finest FIRST GROWTHS capable of ageing for a century or more. The diversity of soils in the district is such that Bordeaux's most diligent geologist, Henri Enjalbert, devoted his *tour de force* to the region.

Although conventionally the St-Émilion district has been divided into two general soil types—the *côtes* or hillsides below the town, and the *graves* or gravelly limestone plateau to the west of it—there are inevitably myriad soil types within the 5,400 ha/13,300 acres of St-Émilion vineyard. More than 3,000 ha lie on the plain between the town and plateau and the river Dordogne. Wines made on this lower land, a mixture of gravel, sand, and alluvial soils, tend to be lighter and less long lived than the wines produced on the plateau or the hillsides, and most, but not all, of them qualify for the most basic appellation, **St-Émilion**.

But the St-Émilion district also boasts a diversity of appellations and, uniquely in France, has a CLASSIFICATION of individual properties which is regularly revised, and depends on tasting. This classification was first drawn up in 1955 and is revised every ten years. Several hundred properties are accorded the misleadingly grand-seeming **St-Émilion Grand Cru** status. In 2004, for example, just 1,850 ha qualified for the simple St-Émilion appellation while more than 3,600 ha qualified as St-Émilion Grand Cru for the 1996 harvest. The 2006 classification, published too late for this edition, was suspended in 2007 but reinstated in 2009.

But the classification's most significant task is to identify which properties rank as **St-Émilion Grand Cru Classé** and which few qualify as **St-Émilion Premier Grand Cru Classé.** See CLASSIFICATION for details of the 1996 classification, which rated 68 properties Grands Crus Classés, of which 13 are Premiers Grands Crus Classés.

Most of the district's most highly ranked properties are either on the steep, clay-limestone hillsides immediately below the town or on a gravelly section of the plateau 5 km/3 miles west of the town and immediately adjacent to the POMEROL appellation. Of St-Émilion's two most highly ranked properties, Chx AUSONE and CHEVAL BLANC, the first is the archetypal *côtes* property, with a tiny, vertiginous vineyard, and cellars hewn out of the hillside, and the second is on particularly gravelly soils with clay and some of the iron-rich deposits characteristic of neighbouring Pomerol. The startling difference in the style of these wines, the second the only great wine to be made predominantly from Cabernet Franc grapes, is a telling demonstration of the variety that St-Émilion can offer.

Of traditionally famous St-Émilion properties, Ch Figeac, which pre-dated and claims to rival Ch Cheval Blanc, is (unusually for the appellation) attached to Cabernet Sauvignon. Since most other St-Émilions lack this tannic ingredient, the district's wines in general mature much faster than their left bank counterparts.

This is particularly true of the new wave of small properties which emerged in the 1990s, some of whose wines have been offered at prices in excess of the famous and established FIRST GROWTHS. See MICROCHÂTEAU.

At the other extreme of value, the St-Émilion CO-OPERATIVE, l'Union des Producteurs de St-Émilion, is one of France's most ambitious, and bottles a quarter of St-Émilion's production. The whole region is characterized by a strong sense of local identity.

The satellite appellations

On the outskirts are the so-called St-Émilion satellites, **Lussac-St-Émilion, Montagne-St-Émilion, Puisseguin-St-Émilion**, and **St-Georges-St-Émilion**, encircling St-Émilion proper to the north and east. On this more rolling countryside north of the Barbanne (see LALANDE-DE-POMEROL), the vine is grown alongside other crops and viticulture now accounts for well over half of the total area, or 4,000 ha. Co-operatives are important here and Montagne- and Lussac-St-Émilion produce significantly more wine than either Puisseguin or, especially, St-Georges, which was for many years sold as Montagne-St-Émilion. The grape varieties planted are similar to those in St-Émilion proper but the standard of wine-making is generally more rudimentary. There are, nevertheless, bargains to be sought out.

Coates, C., *Grands Vins* (London, 1995).

Duiker, H., and Broadbent, M., *The Bordeaux Atlas* (London, 1997).

Echikson, W., *Noble Rot* (New York, 2004).

Enjalbert, H., *Great Bordeaux Wines: St Émilion, Pomerol, Fronsac* (Paris, 1983; English trans., 1985).

Parker, R. M., *Bordeaux* (4th edn, New York, 2003).

Penning-Rowsell, E., *The Wines of Bordeaux* (6th edn, London, 1989).

The vine variety

St-Émilion is also a synonym for the widely planted white grape variety called UGNI BLANC in France and TREBBIANO in Italy. The name is used particularly in Cognac in south west France, where it is widely planted.

St-Estèphe, the northernmost of the four important communal appellations in the Haut-Médoc district of Bordeaux. St-Estèphe is separated from the vineyards of Pauillac's Ch LAFITE only by a stream—indeed Ch Lafite owns some land in the commune of St-Estèphe itself. To the immediate north of St-Estèphe, across a stretch of polder, lies the Bas-MÉDOC, the lower, lesser portion of this most famous region.

The soils of St-Estèphe contain their fair share of GRAVEL, but these layers of gravel are often to be found on a CLAY base. These more poorly drained soils are cooler and can delay ripening, leaving St-Estèphe grapes higher in acidity than their counterparts further south in the Médoc. In Bordeaux's low-rainfall vintages, such as 1990, the water-retaining clays of St-Estèphe have an advantage.

A high proportion of grapes grown on St-Estèphe's stable area of 1,200 ha/2,960 acres of vines have found their way into the vats of the village's co-operative, which often uses the name Marquis de St-Estèphe. The village may boast fewer famous names and CLASSED GROWTHS than MARGAUX, PAUILLAC, and ST-JULIEN, but its wines have a distinctive style that is deep coloured, full of extract, perhaps a little austere in youth, but very long lived. This style was perceptibly softened during the 1980s as higher proportions of Merlot grapes blurred the edges of the Cabernet, and wine-making techniques, particularly CONCENTRATION, have been harnessed to make the wines seem softer and fuller.

The stars of St-Estèphe are its two second growths, Ch Montrose and Cos (formerly Ch Cos d'Estournel), whose fortunes and reputations have alternated throughout the village's relatively recent history as a fine wine producer. Cos (pronounced 'koss') d'Estournel has the Médoc's most eye-catching architecture, in a façade of pure oriental folly beside the main road through the Médoc's wine villages. Its wines are the commune's most ambitious, styled for many decades to come with occasional reliance on concentration techniques. Its sister property Ch Marbuzet was in effect treated as a SECOND WINE until the emergence in the late 1990s of Les Pagodes de Cos. Ch Montrose produces much more traditionally structured, almost Ch LATOUR-like wines.

St-Estèphe's other classed growths are the increasingly dramatic third growth Ch Calon-Ségur, the reliable fourth growth Ch Lafon-Rochet, well sited between Ch Lafite and Cos, and the modest fifth growth Ch Cos-Labory. Some of the village's most conscientiously made wines, however, are such CRUS BOURGEOIS as the exotic Chx Haut-Marbuzet, Meyney, de Pez, and Beauséjour (both owned by ROEDERER), Les-Ormes-de-Pez (the latter run in tandem with Pauillac's Ch Lynch-Bages), and Ch Beau-Site.

For more information, see MÉDOC and map of BORDEAUX.

Coates, C., *Grands Vins* (London, 1995).

Duijker, H., and Broadbent, M., *The Bordeaux Atlas* (London, 1997).

Ginestet, B., *St-Estèphe* (Paris, 1984).

Parker, R., *Bordeaux* (4th edn, New York, 2003).

Penning-Rowsell, E., *The Wines of Bordeaux* (6th edn, London, 1989).

Ste-Victoire, subappellation within Côtes de PROVENCE.

St-Georges d'Orques, named TERROIR within the Coteaux du LANGUEDOC just outside Montpellier where estates such as Ch de Fourques, Domaine de la Prose, and Domaine Henry (whose chief produce is VARIETAL vins de pays) are proving the zone's worth.

St-Georges-St-Émilion, satellite appellation of ST-ÉMILION in Bordeaux.

St-Jean-de-Minervois is the small mountain village in the far north east of the MINERVOIS region that gives its name to the Languedoc's most individual VIN DOUX NATUREL appellation, Muscat de St-Jean-de-Minervois. Like the other Muscats of FRONTIGNAN, LUNEL, and MIREVAL, it is made exclusively from the best Muscat variety, MUSCAT BLANC À PETITS GRAINS, to which alcohol is added half-way through fermentation to produce a wine with at least 15 per cent alcohol and 125 g/l residual sugar. Unlike these other Muscats produced closer to the Mediterranean, however, St-Jean's vineyards are hacked out of the *garrigue* 200 m/660 ft above sea level and the grapes ripen a good three weeks later. The altitude and less reliable weather can affect both quality and yields, which often have difficulty reaching the permitted maximum of 28 hl/ha (1.6 tons/acre), but the resulting wines are more reliably interesting and display more of the variety's delicate orange-flower flavours than is usually the case in Muscats other than those of BEAUMES-DE-VENISE. Domaines de Barroubio and Montahuc are the leading labels.

St-Joseph, ambitiously expanded northern RHÔNE west bank appellation producing mainly red wines from the SYRAH grape but also some full-bodied dry whites from the MARSANNE and, occasionally, ROUSSANNE grapes. The vineyard area increased sixfold during the 1970s and 1980s although a more stringent development plan was put into place in the early 1990s as the better producers realized that the reputation of this relatively new appellation (1956) would hardly be enhanced by the produce of the new vineyards on the plateau. The appellation now extends from CONDRIEU in the north (where there is some overlap) to a small pocket of St-Joseph vineyards between ST-PÉRAY and the town of Valence and totalled 875 ha/2,160 acres in 1996 and nearly 1000 ha by the mid 2000s. The heart of the region, however, is the stretch of old, terraced vineyards around the town of Tournon (including the communes of Vion, Lemps, St-Jean-de-Muzols, Tournon, Mauves, and Glun) just across the wide river Rhône from the hill of HERMITAGE. The wines are lighter and certainly faster maturing than this north northern Rhône archetype, not so much because the soils are very different—on the best sites granite predominates, supplemented by sand and gravel—but because St-Joseph's east-facing vineyards simply lose the sun up to two hours earlier in the crucial ripening season. For this reason, locals view St-Joseph as their answer to BEAUJOLAIS, a fruity wine for drinking in the first three years or so. Those less accustomed to the sheer weight of a good northern Rhône red may prefer to drink them at between two and six years old, depending on the character of the vintage, but Gripa's VIEILLES VIGNES bottling can easily repay a decade's bottle age. Red St-Joseph can be a delightfully transparent expression of Syrah fruit, and is one of the most flattering northern Rhône reds to taste young. The best should be approached in a much less reverential way than a Hermitage or a CÔTE RÔTIE, the rest (which comprise too high a proportion of the total) can be too light and insubstantial to be worth the price premium that St-Joseph can, often inexplicably, command over the other basic northern Rhône appellation CROZES-HERMITAGE. White St-Joseph represents less than 10 per cent of the appellation's total production and the best can provide lovers of white Hermitage with a good-value alternative. Other top producers include Pierre Coursodon, Durand, and Pierre Gaillard.

St-Julien, one of the most homogeneous, reliable, and underrated village appellations in the Haut-Médoc district of Bordeaux. St-Julien may suffer in popular esteem because, unlike PAUILLAC to its immediate north and MARGAUX a few miles to the south, there is no FIRST GROWTH property within its boundaries. Instead, however, it can boast five superb second growths, two excellent third growths, four well-maintained fourth growths, and, from the 1980s at least, an unrivalled consistency in wine-making skill. St-Julien is the commune for wine connoisseurs who seek subtlety, balance, and tradition in their red bordeaux. The wines may lack the vivid, sometimes almost pastiche, concentration of a Pauillac, the austerity of a classic ST-ESTÈPHE, or the immediate charm of a stereotypical (if all too rare) Margaux, but they embody all the virtues of fine, long-lived blends of Cabernet and Merlot grapes, being deep coloured, dry, digestible, appetizing, persistent, intriguing, and rewarding.

The appellation, the smallest of the Médoc's most famous four, has for years encompassed about 900 ha/2,220 acres of vineyard within the communes of St-Julien and Beychevelle to its immediate south. Both gravelly soils and subsoils here are relatively homogeneous, broken only by a narrow strip of river bank on either side of the *jalle* that bisects the zone and flows into the Gironde north of Ch Ducru-Beaucaillou. South of St-Julien is a considerable extent of land classified merely as Haut-Médoc, but to the north the appellation is contiguous with the southern border of Pauillac, and Ch LÉOVILLE-LAS-CASES in the extreme north of St-Julien shares many characteristics with some fine Pauillac wines, notably Ch LATOUR, which is well within sight.

The Léoville estate, as Penning-Rowsell points out, must have been the largest in the entire Médoc in the 18th century, before it was divided into the three second growths known today as Chx Léoville-Las-Cases, Léoville-Poyferré, and Léoville-Barton.

Léoville-Poyferré, which includes the original château building, enjoyed a heyday in terms of its reputation in the 1920s, but also demonstrated something of a return to form in the 1980s. Best value, and perhaps most representative of the appellation, is Léoville-Barton, run from Ch Langoa-Barton, a fine third growth, by Anthony BARTON.

Chx Gruaud-Larose and Ducru-Beaucaillou are the other two St-Julien second growths, and produce two of the Médoc's finest wines in most vintages. Gruaud-Larose is usually the richer of the two, and the property was well run for most of the 20th century by Cordier but was sold to the Merlaut family in 1997. The particularly distinctive Victorian box that is Ch Ducru-Beaucaillou ('beautiful pebble') is, unusually for a Médoc château, the home of its owner, Bruno Borie.

The third growth Ch Lagrange was much improved in the 1980s by investment from the Japanese spirits firm Suntory, while fourth growths Chx St Pierre, Talbot, Branaire-Ducru, and Beychevelle are generally well run.

St-Julien's classed growths account for about three-quarters of the appellation's total production, and even such unclassified properties as Chx Gloria, Hortevie, and Lalande-Borie do not believe in underpricing their admittedly admirable produce.

For more information, see MÉDOC and map of BORDEAUX.

Coates, C., *Grands Vins* (London, 1995).

Duijker, H., and Broadbent, M., *The Bordeaux Atlas* (London, 1997).

Ginestet, B., *St-Julien* (Paris, 1984).

Parker, R., *Bordeaux* (4th edn, New York, 2003).

Penning-Rowsell, E., *The Wines of Bordeaux* (6th edn, London, 1989).

St-Laurent, as well as being one of the few villages of any size in the MÉDOC, is the name of a black grape variety for long thought to be related to PINOT NOIR and today most commonly encountered in lower AUSTRIA and the Austrian wine region Burgenland. It is capable of producing deep-coloured, velvety reds with sufficient concentration—provided yields are limited—to merit ageing in oak and then bottle. The variety was brought to Württemberg in southern Germany from Alsace in the early 19th century. Thanks to the German red wine boom of the 1990s, total German plantings had reached 600 ha/1,500 acres by 2003. If attention is paid to the successes of those few vintners in the Pfalz and the much larger number in Austria who have been carefully cultivating this variety since well before the 1990s, then its reputation is likely to grow.

The Austrians already see considerable potential. Certainly it has had several centuries to adapt itself to conditions in Thermenregion, Lower Austria, and Burgenland, where its viticultural disadvantages, dangerously early budding, tendency to drop its flowers and susceptibility to COULURE and rot, are less problematic than in Alsace, for example. It also ripens well ahead of Pinot Noir and can be cultivated on a much wider range of sites. St-Laurent wine can resemble a powerful Pinot Noir and the variety is undergoing an important renaissance in Austria.

The variety is also cultivated in the CZECH REPUBLIC, where it is once again known as Svatovavřinecké. During the communist regime it was referred to simply as Vavřinecké without reference to the word 'saint'.

DNA PROFILING in Austria established a parent–offspring relationship with Pinot in 2000.

St-Macaire, town in the BORDEAUX region just across the river GARONNE from Langon in the GRAVES district. It lends its name to **Côtes de Bordeaux-St-Macaire**, an almost extinct BORDEAUX AC regional appellation for sweet white wines.

St-Mont, Côtes de, VDQS heading for AC status in the Armagnac region dominated by the dynamic Plaimont CO-OPERATIVE. The zone is effectively a northern extension of the MADIRAN area and much the same grape varieties are planted, although yields are generally higher. TANNAT must constitute at least 60 per cent of some surprisingly juicy reds with increasing proportion of FER Servadou (called Pinenc here), together with the Cabernets. For whites, local varieties ARRUFIAC (Ruffiac), and PETIT COURBU are being encouraged, in some cases rescued from extinction, at the expense of the MANSENGS, thereby differentiating this wine from JURANÇON to the south. Clairette is being phased out. More than 950 ha/2,350 acres of vineyard are dedicated to this wine, about three-quarters of it to red wine production. Quality is increasing with every vintage, as is the price differential between it and the local VIN DE PAYS des Côtes de Gascogne. The Plaimont co-op dominates production and has worked hard on its Le Faite bottlings.

St-Péray, small and shrinking appellation of just 60 ha/150 acres for white SPARKLING WINES that seem something of an anomaly in the northern RHÔNE, famous for the weight and longevity of its wines. Soils and MESOCLIMATE here are admittedly cooler than most of the rest of the Rhône, but the Marsanne and Roussanne or Roussette (Altesse) grapes grown here produce few wines of great finesse, despite the fact that the MÉTHODE TRADITIONELLE is employed to transform them into sparkling wine. A considerable proportion of production is given its first fermentation at the co-operative of Tain l'HERMITAGE before being made sparkling in the St-Péray co-operative cellars. A small quantity of still St-Péray is also made which is not unlike white St-Joseph.

St-Pierre Doré, almost extinct, very productive, light-berried vine once used in ST-POURÇAIN.

St-Pourçain, sometimes called **St-Pourçain-sur-Sioule**, small appellation in the cereal-and OAK-producing ALLIER *département* almost precisely in the centre of France. (Because of this St-Pourçain cannot be found on maps of French wine regions; only on detailed maps of the whole *hexagone*—see map under FRANCE.) It was an important site in Roman times, near RIVER transport and

offering suitable HILLSIDE VINEYARDS. White St-Pourçain was one of the most respected wines in France in the Middle Ages (see LOIRE, history, and MEDIEVAL LITERATURE) but is today more of a cool climate curiosity. From about 650 ha/1,600 acres of vineyard on varied soils of limestone, granite, and gravel, a wide range of wine colours and flavours are made, being typically dry, light in body, and relatively high in acidity.

The traditional vine variety was TRESSALLIER, the local variant of SACY, but modern white wines are increasingly likely to be made from CHARDONNAY or even SAUVIGNON and there is a legal limit (50 per cent in the mid 1990s) on the amount of Tresallier which may be used. GAMAY is the most common grape used for pink and light red St-Pourçain, although some PINOT NOIR is also grown. The increasingly effective CO-OPERATIVE in the town of St-Pourçain-sur-Sioule itself dominates production.

George, R., *French Country Wines* (London, 1990).

St-Romain, exquisitely pretty village perched on top of a cliff in the Côte de Beaune district of Burgundy producing red wines from Pinot Noir and white wines from Chardonnay. There are no PREMIERS CRUS in the appellation, which was granted only in 1967, and applies to just 98 ha/240 acres (44 for red wine and 54 for white).

The vineyards of St-Romain are situated behind those of Auxey-Duresses and at higher altitude, 300 to 400 m/985 to 1,310 ft above sea level, than is usual in the Côte d'Or. In lesser vintages, the grapes do not ripen as well as elsewhere but in warmer years the wines can be excellent value. St-Romain is also home to one of the region's best-known COOPERS, François Frères. Alain Gras makes particularly fine wines here.

See also CÔTE D'OR, and map under BURGUNDY. J.T.C.M.

St-Sardos, wine region on the left bank of the GARONNE near Montauban promoted to VDQS status in 2005.

St-Saturnin, one of the more exciting of the named CRUS within the Coteaux du LANGUEDOC appellation in southern France named after the eponymous village but including parts of St-Guiraud, Jonquières, and Arboras. Just west of MONTPEYROUX, this zone is also in high, rugged country where little other than the vine will grow. The St-Saturnin CO-OPERATIVE is particularly dynamic, as are such individual producers as Mas Jullien, who coax maximum character out of local grape varieties grown here on the south-facing slopes of the Cévennes (although Olivier Jullien's wines are presented as straight Coteaux du Languedoc).

Saintsbury, Professor George (1845–1933). Though a distinguished man of letters in his day, Saintsbury is now principally remembered for *Notes on a Cellar-Book*, a seminal work on wine which was an immediate success and has run to many editions.

He was born on 23 October 1845 in Southampton, where his father was superintendent of the docks. The family moved to London in 1850 and Saintsbury attended King's College School, where he acquired his deep love of literature. Aged 17 he won a Postmastership to Merton College, Oxford, but to his everlasting regret he failed to win a Fellowship. For ten years, from the age of 21, he was a schoolmaster but eventually settled in London with his wife and two sons, becoming a journalist, and for a time was assistant editor of the *Saturday Review*.

The actual cellar book was a simple exercise book in which Saintsbury listed the contents of just two cellars, the first in his London house in West Kensington, the second in Edinburgh, where from 1895 to 1915 he held the Regius Chair of Rhetoric and English Literature at Edinburgh University.

In June 1915 he retired from the Chair in Edinburgh, having some ten years previously developed gout, which prevented him from drinking red wine. He eventually retired to Bath, where he published 13 volumes, including *Notes on a Cellar-Book*, which first appeared in July 1920, as well as innumerable articles and pamphlets.

The SAINTSBURY CLUB was founded in 1931 but, although nominated president, the Professor, due to ill health, never attended a meeting. See also LITERATURE OF WINE.　　J.M.B.

Saintsbury, G., *Notes on a Cellar-Book* (15th edn, London, 1978).

Saintsbury Club, perhaps the most famous of all DINING CLUBS connected with wine, founded in 1931 in honour of Professor George SAINTSBURY. The Club meets twice a year, as nearly as possible on his birthday 23 October and on his name day 23 April St George's Day.

Its beginnings were unremarkable. At a luncheon given by André SIMON, J. L. Squire casually mentioned Saintsbury, old and ill in Bath. Shortly after, in May 1931, a dinner was organized, and it was at this that Maurice Healy (author of *Stay me with Flagons*) suggested that a Saintsbury Club should be founded 'to perpetuate and honour his name'. The first meeting, or dinner, was held at Vintners' Hall (see VINTNERS) on Saintsbury's 86th birthday.

The membership, limited to 50, has always comprised men of letters, wine lovers, both professional and amateurs, with a good sprinkling of DOCTORS and lawyers. The perpetual president George Saintsbury himself never attended a meeting, but his health is toasted by the members at each meeting. André Simon was, unsurprisingly, a leading light and the original cellarer and treasurer. Founder members included Sir John Squire

as 'editor'; Vyvyan Holland, son of Oscar Wilde, as honorary secretary; and such luminaries as H. Warner Allen, Hilaire Belloc, Duff Cooper, Sir Gerald du Maurier, the Marquis of Hartington, Maurice Healy, A. P. Herbert, and Compton Mackenzie. Representing the wine trade were Col. Ian Campbell, John HARVEY, Francis Berry, and William Byass (of GONZALEZ BYASS). The president of Le Club des Cent in Paris is ex officio an honorary member.

Members, upon election, donate fine wine, and the Club cellar, at Vintners' Hall, is of a high order. Once a year a member of the Club is invited to give the Saintsbury 'oration', which is then privately printed for members. Current members include Michael BROADBENT and Hugh JOHNSON.　　J.M.B.

Saints Glaces, the ICE SAINTS of France. Most commonly these are St Mamert on 11 May, St Pancrace on 12 May, and St Servais, sometimes St Gervais, on 13 May, although, as for Germany's EISHEILIGEN, there is also Ste Sophie on the limit of supposedly possible dates for disastrous FROST, 15 May.

St-Véran, appellation created in 1971 for white wines from the Chardonnay grape in southern Burgundy, between Mâconnais and Beaujolais, to include much of the wine that was once sold as Beaujolais Blanc. St-Véran encompasses seven communes: Davayé, Solutré-Pouilly, and Prissé on classic LIMESTONE soil adjacent to POUILLY-FUISSÉ and Chânes, Chasselas, Leynes, and St-Vérand, where the sandy red soil of Beaujolais is mixed with limestone. By the mid 2000s, 645 ha/1,590 acres qualified for this appellation, whose star is arguably Domaine des Deux Roches, although most fine Pouilly-Fuissé producers also make good St-Véran.

The wines frequently have more body and ageing ability than a typical MÂCON-VILLAGES without rivalling the power and persistence of the wines of Pouilly-Fuissé, which forms an enclave within St-Véran.　　J.T.C.M.

salary, wine as. The practice of paying workers in wine is an old one (and certainly older than the payments in salt from which the word 'salary' is derived). In Ancient PERSIA, for example, wine rations were strictly ordered and were often far in excess of any individual's possible personal consumption.

More recently, labourers, and in particular grape-pickers on the bigger BORDEAUX estates, would expect to receive some quantity of wine (rarely of great quality and often lowly PIQUETTE) in addition to wages.

The most notorious, and now outlawed, instance of paying workers with deliberately stupefying quantities of wine was the so-called *dop* system once prevalent in SOUTH AFRICA.

Salice Salento, DOC for robust red wine made mainly from NEGROAMARO grapes in south east Italy. For more details, see PUGLIA.

salinity, the concentration of salt (sodium chloride) in soils or irrigation water. Among agricultural crops, grapevines are relatively sensitive to salt injury. Salt in the rootzone affects grapevines in two ways: firstly, it is harder for the vines to extract water from the soil, and they may suffer from drought. Secondly, salt can be toxic in high levels in the vines' tissues. When vines are irrigated by sprinklers with water containing excessive salt, or grown on excessively saline soils, leaves may be burnt, and in severe cases this leads to defoliation. Similar effects can occasionally be found in coastal vineyards affected by wind-borne salt. MERLOT vines are particularly susceptible. Saline soils are typically found in hot and dry climates where IRRIGATION has been introduced. For example, salinity is seen as a potential problem for the inland irrigated vineyards of Australia, along the Murray–Darling river systems. The problem is also found in southern France, where there are 10,000 ha/24,700 acres or more of vineyards planted on ancient marine deposits. Salinity can be overcome by applying more irrigation water than the vines use, so as to leach the salt. Some vine varieties such as COLOMBARD are tolerant of salt, and there are ROOTSTOCKS such as Dog Ridge and Ramsey which show some salt tolerance. Grape juice and hence wine can contain elevated sodium and chloride levels. These appear unaffected by variety, and to result primarily from sprinkler irrigation (which wets the foliage) with saline water. Wine from vineyards with saline soils may contain elevated levels of salt.　　R.E.S.

salt can affect vines. See SALINITY. Some, but very few, wines may taste slightly salty (see TASTE).

Salvagnin, Vaud name for a light red blend of Pinot Noir with a bit of Gamay in SWITZERLAND. Similar to but less common than the DÔLE of Valais.

Salvagnin (Noir) is a Jura name for PINOT NOIR, disconcertingly similar to the name of one of the Jura's own vine varieties, SAVAGNIN.

Sämling 88, common Austrian synonym for the SCHEUREBE vine variety of which 300 ha/740 acres are planted in the southern Austrian wine regions of Burgenland and Styria. It can make some excellent BOTRYTIZED wines.

Sámos, see GREECE.

sampling, important part of a continuum of wine quality control procedures which begin in the vineyard and may end when a consumer picks a bottle out of a CASE in his or her CELLAR.

A very small proportion of a vineyard's fruit may be sampled to assess its chemical composition to help predict the HARVEST date, as well as to indicate likely quality and, in some cases, eventual wine style. Grape sampling might simply consist of selecting some berries haphazardly from the vineyard and expressing juice into a REFRACTOMETER to measure sugar content (see MUST WEIGHT; see also RIPENESS).

The person taking the sample must be careful to avoid any bias which might affect the sampling result. Either berries or bunches are taken, and a normal sample may weigh 300 g (10.5 oz) to several kilograms. Typically the sample is taken to the winery laboratory and crushed or pressed to obtain juice, which is then analysed for sugar and perhaps also ACIDITY and PH. Some modern laboratories use spectrophotometry or near infrared spectroscopy (NIRS) to analyse the concentration of extractable ANTHOCYANINS. Spectrophotometry can also determine the total PHENOLIC compounds in the grapes. The total extractable anthocyanin value has been shown to correlate well with the potential wine quality. See also PHYSIOLOGICAL RIPENESS.

Many vineyards are harvested without a fruit sample being taken, however, particularly in more primitive traditional regions.

A second sampling is frequently made when a load of grapes is delivered to the winery, particularly if the grapes have been bought by contract, since grape PRICES are often based on sugar levels.

During FERMENTATION samples are taken at least daily to verify the regular conversion of sugars to ALCOHOL. Later, during ÉLEVAGE, regular sampling provides the winemaker with valuable guidance. Finally, shortly before BOTTLING, samples are taken for detailed analysis to ensure that the wine meets all regulations and is free of FAULTS and CONTAMINANTS.

An important part of selling wine EN PRIMEUR is the release of **cask samples,** or *échantillons* in French, samples drawn from the containers in which the wine is still being matured, typically a BARREL, on which wine merchants and wine writers can base their assessments. Such raw wines, often roughly drawn off into small sample bottles, have not undergone STABILIZATION and can suffer OXIDATION and other faults after only a week or two. The best way to judge a young wine still in cask is sampling in the cellar or winery itself, tasting it straight from the barrel, but sampling the contents of a wide range of different barrels. R.E.S., A.D.W., & J.R.

Samsó, Penedès name for the CARIGNAN grape.

Samtrot. See MÜLLERREBE.

San Benito, small CALIFORNIA county inland from MONTEREY county. The one exception to a prevailing mediocrity is a one-vineyard AVA named Mount Harlan (see map under CALIFORNIA) after the limestone-rich slopes on which Calera winery's several celebrated blocks of Pinot Noir grow. The county has other AVAs (Cienega Valley, Lime Kiln Valley, Paicines) from which little is seen. B.C.C.

Sancerre, dramatically situated hilltop town on the left bank of the upper Loire which lends its name to one of the Loire's most famous, and famously variable, wines: racy, pungent, dry white Sauvignon Blanc, which enjoyed enormous commercial success in the 1970s. The town's situation on such a navigable RIVER, and the favourable DRAINAGE and TOPOGRAPHY of the rolling countryside around it, assured Sancerre's long history as a wine producer; the suitability of the site for viticulture was obvious from Roman times. Until the mid 20th century, however, Sancerre produced red wines, and white wines from the Chasselas table grape. Sancerre's dramatically simple, piercing Sauvignon flavours of gooseberries and nettles were initially introduced into the bistros of Paris as a sort of white wine equivalent of Beaujolais, but, by the late 1970s and early 1980s, Sancerre was regarded as the quintessential white wine for restaurants around the world.

The average altitude of the Sancerre hills is between 200 m and 400 m/655–1,310 ft. The Sauvignon has adapted well to many of the varied TERROIRS around Sancerre, where, in 14 different communes, vines are cultivated, particularly on south-facing slopes. There are three distinct areas: the 'white' western vineyards are made up of clay and limestone soils with some Kimmeridgean marne, especially in the cru of Chavignol, that produce quite powerful wines; those between here and the town of Sancerre are high in gravel as well as limestone and produce particularly delicate wines; while those close to Sancerre itself are rich in flint (*silex*) and yield longer-living, particularly perfumed wines. Comparisons with POUILLY-FUMÉ, made just a few miles upstream on the opposite bank, are inevitable, although both are relatively large, heterogeneous appellations, Sancerre even more than Pouilly. The total area given over to the Sancerre appellation, which had declined to about 700 ha/1,730 acres in the 1960s, had reached 2,600 ha by the mid 2000s. Being further from the main road than Pouilly, the growers of Sancerre possibly have to work harder to sell their wines.

A wide range of agricultural activity takes place on this terrain, and in many of the outlying villages the vine plays a subordinate role, but viticulture is particularly important in Bué and in nearby Chavignol, where the meticulous grower Henri Bourgeois is based and which is famous for its goat's cheese.

The climate here is distinctly CONTINENTAL, and the vineyards are easily subject to spring FROSTS, but the river to the east and the forests to the west moderate low temperatures. Vines are generally CORDON or single GUYOT trained.

Sancerre's popularity has brought with it the inevitable increase in the proportion of mediocre wine produced, sometimes over-produced, within the zone. In particularly cool years, even the best producers have to work hard to avoid excessive VIGOUR, resulting in unpleasantly HERBACEOUS aromas and a lack of fruity substance but techniques such as grassing, de-budding, and leaf plucking are starting to result in healthier grapes and more concentrated wines. Most Sancerre is ready for drinking almost as soon as it is bottled, and rarely improves beyond two or three years, although the best certainly keep. There have since been attempts to marry Sancerre fruit with OAK, with varying degrees of success. In years as ripe as 1989, some sweet VENDANGE TARDIVE wine was produced by the likes of Alphonse Mellot and Henri Bourgeois. Other fine producers include Lucien Crochet, Cotat, Vincent Pinard, and Vacheron.

Sancerre also exists in light, often beguiling, red and rosé versions, made from Pinot Noir grapes. These wines enjoy a certain following, mainly in France, but need very high standards of wine-making and good weather to imbue them with a good core of fruit.

See also LOIRE, including map.

Friedrich, J., *A Wine and Food Guide to the Loire* (New York, 1996 and London, 1997).

sand, description of sediment or soil which is made up of relatively large particles (bigger than silt, and much bigger than clay). See SOIL TEXTURE and GEOLOGY for more details of this particular form of soil classification. Sandy soils can be difficult to cultivate because of their poor ability to store water or nutrients, but they are notable in viticulture for providing a good measure of protection from the PHYLLOXERA louse. Vineyards dominated by sand include those of COLARES in Portugal, the Camargue in the south of France, the Great plain of HUNGARY, and Maipo valley in CHILE.

Sandeman, port and sherry house with one of the most famous logos in the wine trade, the black-cloaked Sandeman Don created in 1928. It was founded in London by a Scotsman, George Sandeman, who in 1790 established his shipping business with a £300 loan from his father. He began by shipping sherry and moved swiftly on to port. After being taken over by the North American multinational corporation Seagram in 1980 for £17 million, Sandeman saw an increasing emphasis on quantity rather than quality. In 1990, George Sandeman (representing the seventh generation of the family to make port) moved to OPORTO to manage the company, becoming the first Sandeman to live in Portugal since 1868. In 2001, Sandeman's port and (less important) sherry interests were acquired by SOGRAPE.

Halley, N., *Sandeman: Two Hundred Years of Port and Sherry* (London, 1990).

sandstone, a sedimentary rock composed of SAND-grade particles which are usually QUARTZ. The rock may be unconsolidated or the grains may be held together by another material such as calcium carbonate forming a CALCAREOUS sandstone, or the rock may be hardened by the quartz grains growing into one another. These variations mean that sandstones vary greatly in fertility and drainage. Sandstones occur in the higher alluvial ground of the river Dordogne, just below the *côtes* of ST-ÉMILION, and in similar settings elsewhere.

J.M.H.

Sangiovese, qualitatively variable red grape variety that is Italy's most planted and is particularly common in central Italy. In 1990, almost 10 per cent of all Italian vineyards, or more than 100,000 ha/247,000 acres, were planted with some form of Sangiovese. In its various clonal variations and names (BRUNELLO, Prugnolo Gentile, Morellino, NIELLUCCIO), Sangiovese is the principal vine variety for fine red wine in TOSCANA, the sole grape permitted for BRUNELLO DI MONTALCINO, and the base of the blend for CHIANTI, VINO NOBILE DI MONTEPULCIANO, and the vast majority of SUPERTUSCANS. It is, in addition, the workhorse red grape of all of central Italy, widely planted in UMBRIA (where it gives its best results in the DOCG wines Torgiano and Montefalco), in the MARCHE (where it is the base of Rosso Piceno and an important component of Rosso Conero), and in LAZIO. Sangiovese can be found as far afield as Lombardia and Valpolicella to the north and Campania to the south.

Sangiovese is widely thought to be of ancient origin, as the literal translation of its name ('blood of Jove') suggests, and it has been postulated that it was even known to the ETRUSCANS. Yet in 2004, researchers Vouillamoz and Grando at SAN MICHELE ALL'ADIGE identified the parents of Sangiovese: the Tuscan 'cherry grape' CILIEGIOLO and Calabrese Montenuovo, an obscure variety found in Campania though probably originating from Calabria. Other Italian researchers had established a direct link between Sangiovese and Ciliegiolo in 2002, but the parentage remained incomplete until Calabrese Montenuovo was DNA-typed by chance at San Michele all'Adige and identified as the other parent. As a result, Sangiovese's DNA is probably half Tuscan and half southern Italian. Ciliegiolo was already cited in Toscana in 1590 by Giovanvettorio Soderini under the name Ciriegiulo. In his book, Soderini also mentioned the variety Sangiogheto. This is commonly accepted as the first historical mention of Sangiovese, but there is no evidence that Sangiogheto actually was Sangiovese. Indeed, when Soderini writes about the ways to make a very good wine, he says 'beware of the Sangiogheto, who thinks to make wine from it will make vinegar'. Moreover, Sangiovese was

rare or almost unknown in Toscana prior to 1700, whereas TREBBIANO and MALVASIA were the most widespread grapes. This is consistent with Sangiovese's probably being born some time before 1700 from a spontaneous cross between Ciliegiolo and Calabrese Montenuovo. Calabrese Montenuovo is not a registered variety, and its true identity is still not known, but researchers were prompt to make it clear that it is not NERO D'AVOLA from Sicilia, a variety often called Calabrese. In fact, the name Calabrese is commonly used for several distinct CULTIVARS in Italy, even for Sangiovese.

Cosimo Trinci, in 1738, observed that wines made solely from Sangiovese were somewhat hard and acid, but excellent when blended with other varieties, a judgement echoed by Giovanni Cosimo Villifranchi in 1883. Bettino RICASOLI found a way to tame Sangiovese's asperity—a substantial addition of sweetening and softening CANAIOLO—which became the basis of all modern Chianti and of Vino Nobile di Montepulciano (although Ciliegiolo, MAMMOLO, and COLORINO as well as the white grapes Malvasia and, especially, Trebbiano were subsequently added to the blend). The use of small oak barrels, begun in the 1970s, can be seen as a modern solution to the same problem of excessive asperity.

Conventional ampelographical descriptions of Sangiovese, based on the pioneering work of G. Molon in 1906, divide the variety into two families: the Sangiovese Grosso, to which Brunello, Prugnolo Gentile, and the Sangiovese di Lamole (of Greve in Chianti) belong, and the Sangiovese Piccolo of other zones of Toscana, with the implicit identification of a superior quality in the former. Current thinking is that this classification is too simplistic, that there is a large number of CLONES populating the region's vineyards, and that no specific qualitative judgements can be based on the size of either the berries or the bunches. Significant efforts are at last being made to identify and propagate superior clones; MASS SELECTION in the past sought principally to identify high-yielding clones without any regard for wine quality. The variety adapts well to a wide variety of soils, although the presence of limestone seems to exalt the elegant and forceful aromas that are perhaps the most attractive quality of the grape.

Sangiovese's principal characteristic in the vineyard is its slow and late ripening—harvests traditionally began after 29 September and even today can easily be protracted until or even beyond mid October—which gives rich, alcoholic, and long-lived wine in hot years and creates problems of high ACIDITY and hard TANNINS in cool years. Over-production tends to accentuate the wine's acidity and lighten its colour, which can also OXIDIZE and start to brown at a relatively young age. The grape's rather thin skin creates a certain susceptibility to ROT in cool and damp years,

which is a serious disadvantage in a region where rain in October is a frequent occurrence. Too often Sangiovese has been planted with scant attention to exposure and ALTITUDE in Toscana, where the vine is often cultivated at up to or even beyond 500 m/1,640 ft. A good part of contemporary viticultural research in Toscana—which involves increased VINE DENSITY, lower YIELDS per vine, better clones, more appropriate ROOTSTOCKS, lower vine-TRAINING SYSTEMS, small oak BARRELS, more suitable supplementary varieties for blending, different temperatures and lengths of FERMENTATION—is dedicated to resolving a single problem: how to put more meat on Sangiovese's bones, how to add flesh to its sizeable, but not always sensual, structure.

Throughout modern Toscana, Sangiovese is now often blended with a certain proportion of the Bordeaux grape CABERNET SAUVIGNON, whether for Chianti (in which case the interloper should not exceed 15 per cent of the total) or a highly priced VINO DA TAVOLA. This highly successful blend, in which the intense fruit and colour of Cabernet marries well with the characterful native variety, was first sanctioned by the DOC authorities in CARMIGNANO.

In UMBRIA, the variety dominates most of the region's best red wine, as in the Torgiano of the producer LUNGAROTTI. But in terms of quantity rather than quality, Sangiovese is most important in Romagna (see EMILIA-ROMAGNA), where SANGIOVESE DI ROMAGNA is as common as the LAMBRUSCO vine is in Emilia. Sangiovese di Romagna wine is typically light, red, ubiquitous, and destined, quite properly, for early consumption. The most widely planted Sangiovese vines planted in Romagna appear to have little in common with Toscana's most revered selections, although there has been some careful CLONAL SELECTION in Romagna with promising results, and two of the best clones currently being used to repopulate Tuscan vineyards, R24 and T19, are in fact from Romagna. Some Sangiovese is grown in the south of Italy, where it is usually used for blending with local grapes, and the success of Supertuscans has inevitably led to a certain amount of experimentation with the variety to the north of Toscana too.

D.T. & J.V.

Outside Italy

Like other Italian grape varieties, particularly red ones, Sangiovese was taken west, to both North and South America, by Italian emigrants. In South America it is best known in Argentina, where there are several thousand hectares, mainly in Mendoza province, producing wine that few Tuscan tasters would recognize as Sangiovese.

In California, however, international recognition for the quality of Supertuscans brought a sudden increase in Sangiovese's popularity in the late 1980s and 1990s. In 1991, its acreage was climbing towards 200, or about as much land as CABERNET SAUVIGNON had commanded in

1961. By 2003, acreage had increased to nearly 3,000. There are some significant plantings in the NAPA valley, but other successful plots can be found in SONOMA county, SAN LUIS OBISPO county, SANTA BARBARA county, and the SIERRA FOOTHILLS. Despite some doubts over the quality of Sangiovese cuttings available from California NURSERIES, early results gave hope to Californians. Some had the faintly floral aromas veteran drinkers of Chiantis and Brunellos would recognize as Sangiovese, although the wines were made in a more FRUIT-DRIVEN style. Quality is expected to increase with VINE AGE and identification of CLONAL variations. Robert Pepi, Seghesio, and Atlas Peak, in which the Tuscan firm of ANTINORI had an important stake, were some of the earliest commercial producers; Villa Ragazzi and Noceto were pioneers on a smaller scale. Benessere has successfully joined the varietal fray, while Dalla Valle, Shafer, and Stolpman have shown a talent for blends.

The grape is also grown in Washington state, although it can be difficult to match clone to site, especially given Washington's mono-clonal history.

Bastianich, J., and Lynch, D., *Vino Italiano: The Regional Wines of Italy* (New York, 2002).

Belfrage, N., *From Barolo to Valpolicella: The Wines of Northern Italy* (London, 1999).

—— *From Brunello to Zibibbo: The Wines of Southern Italy* (London, 2001).

Sangiovese di Romagna,

quantitatively important VARIETAL central Italian red made from the most widely cultivated grape variety in ROMAGNA. In the DOC zone, 6,900 ha/17,500 acres were planted in the late 1990s, with an average annual production of 130,000 hl/3.4 million gal. The reputation of the zone has been sullied by the mediocre quality of much of the wine produced, and by the efforts of a number of Tuscan producers to blame the low quality of Tuscan wines between 1965 and 1980 on the infiltration of their vineyards by high-yielding, low-quality Sangiovese di Romagna. Just like the SANGIOVESE of Toscana, the Sangiovese of Romagna exists in many clonal variations, some of which do indeed produce abundant quantities of indifferent wine, but the better clones of Sangiovese di Romagna are by no means inferior to those of Toscana, and the occasional bottles of fine Sangiovese produced in Romagna give tantalizing hints of possibilities yet to be exploited.

The variety is cultivated throughout the region and, in the past, took on a distinctive personality in the various subzones in which it was planted: lighter and fruitier in the eastern and western extremes (near the border with the Marche and close to Bologna); fuller, richer, and more tannic in the central provinces of Ravenna and Forlì. Modern WINE-MAKING techniques and practices have partially flattened and standardized these differences, but there can be few doubts that the best Sangiovese di

Romagna comes from the hills to the south of the ancient Via Emilia, where the terrain rises towards the Apennines. The DOC reflects this widely accepted view of the most suitable terrain, confining the territory of Sangiovese di Romagna to the eastern hills of the province of Bologna and the Apennine zones of the provinces of Ravenna and Forlì. Here the mixture of sandstone and clay in the soil and the high summer temperatures succeed in ripening Sangiovese and could, with more commitment and more professional wine-making, give products of real distinction. A tradition of CASK AGEING has long existed and, in the area extending from Marzeno to Modigliana to the west and Predappio to Meldola and Bertinoro in the east, successful experiments with small oak barrels have given results comparable to a good Tuscan Sangiovese. These superior products remain, for the moment, mere drops in the bucket: permitted yields of 11 tons/ha and the domination of the large CO-OPERATIVES have tended to reduce Sangiovese di Romagna to its lowest common denominator. Highly successful commercial fruit production in Romagna has given the paradoxical result of a high level of professional preparation and the tendency to treat grapes as a mere cash crop whose value can be assessed only by calculating the price per ton and the potential tonnage per hectare. Sixty per cent of Romagna's production is controlled by co-operatives, and another 25 per cent is controlled by large commercial wineries. The virtual elimination of vine-growers from the process of transforming their grapes into wine continues to impede the kind of quality revolution for Sangiovese that transformed Tuscan wines between 1975 and 1990.   D.T.

sangría, a mixture of red wine, lemonade, and, sometimes, spirits and fresh fruit, served with particular gusto in Spain's tourist resorts.

sanitation. See HYGIENE.

San Joaquin valley,

southern half of the vast Central valley in CALIFORNIA, and that part of the state which produces the great bulk of its wine, and its TABLE GRAPES and DRYING GRAPES. It stretches almost 300 miles/480 km from Stockton down to Bakersfield, and approaches 60 miles in width at its widest. Its great expanses of vineyard include more than 100,000 acres/40,000 ha of wine grapes. It is California's Languedoc-Roussillon or Mezzogiorno, but so far only as a bottomless well of cheap, everyday wine. Except for the distinct AVAS of LODI and CLARKSBURG at its very northern end near the confluence of the San Joaquin and Sacramento rivers, it resists any internal dividing lines because its climate and soils are so relentlessly consistent.

Huge as it is, its wineries match. The immense E. & J. GALLO is unquestionably the most important name in it, although

CONSTELLATION's huge Guild winery, Bronco, and the Wine Group (Franzia) are major players too.

Sanlúcar de Barrameda, one of the three Spanish towns in which SHERRY is made and matured. MANZANILLA is a delicate, pale, dry sherry matured in Sanlúcar.

San Luis Obispo, wine-producing county in the CENTRAL COAST AVA of CALIFORNIA midway between Los Angeles and San Francisco. Many of California's coastal counties demonstrate why the American AVA system, its embryonic answer to France's APPELLATION CONTRÔLÉE, tries to avoid political boundaries in the shaping of vineyard districts. San Luis Obispo county does so more vigorously than most. A boiling summer sun beats down on the high, sheltered plain that is the Paso Robles AVA while fogs hang over a narrow, cool coastal shelf holding the Edna Valley AVA near San Luis Obispo city. The two AVAs are fewer than 20 miles/32 km apart, and well within the same county. A third AVA, Arroyo Grande, runs from the coast back up into the mountains, thus capturing examples of both extremes within its boundaries.

Arroyo Grande Valley AVA

A long range of hills sloping towards Pismo Beach at the southern edge of San Luis Obispo county, Arroyo Grande was viticulturally distinguished in the 1980s only by the painstaking decision to plant 350 ha/865 acres of it for Maison Deutz, the California arm of Champagne house Deutz. This has now been sold. The location is one of the coolest in California. Hundred-year-old Zinfandel vines behind lake Lopez do magnificently well for Saucelito Canyon winery, while Pinot Noir does quite well for Talley Vineyards in lower lying portions of the AVA.

Edna Valley AVA

Directly south of the coastal town of San Luis Obispo, Edna Valley won quick fame for its Chardonnays, beginning in the mid 1970s. Edna Valley Vineyards, part of the Chalone group, is the principal winery. Gewürztraminer has also done well, but it is not widely planted. Pinot Noir has been variable. Low hills on three sides give the small valley a soup-tureen shape, allowing it to collect moisture-laden air from the Pacific ocean, making FUNGAL DISEASES a frequent threat despite low rainfall. Cool, even temperatures and fog cover result in a very long growing season, often 50 per cent longer than Burgundy. Alban is a particularly fine producer of Rhône varieties in the southern corner of the AVA.

Paso Robles AVA

An isolated inland plain, where the headwaters of the Salinas river congregate, Paso

Robles earned an early reputation as a place where outlaws could hole up, no questions asked. Locals still cultivate the impression that this is a haven for the disconnected—James Dean ended his briefly rebellious life in a nearby automobile accident in the 1950s. From the 1880s onward, its role as a wine district was to produce the kind of sun-baked, high-alcohol, fiercely tannic Zinfandels that could pull an outlaw into a saloon on the bleak, wintry nights that are almost as common hereabouts as blistering summer days. Since its confirmation as an AVA, newcomers in an expanding roster of local wineries have moved on to embrace Cabernet Sauvignon, Syrah, Sauvignon Blanc, and Chardonnay in vineyards set on a restlessly rolling plain of former alfalfa fields east of Paso Robles town. Wines from these new territories can charm early, but few have shown long staying power. The Zinfandelists have stuck with their traditional haunts in high hills to the west of town, but now even they are joining up as growers of Cabernet and Chardonnay. Meridian, J. Lohr, and Arciero represent the large players; Justin, Wild Horse, Eberle, and Castoro the new artists. Interesting recent entrants include the Perrin family (Ch de Beaucastel) of CHÂTEAUNEUF-DU-PAPE, making Rhône varieties as Tablas Creek in the western sector of the appellation, and SOUTHCORP of Australia, which has planted 400 acres of Syrah and Cabernet Sauvignon in the eastern part near Creston.

York Mountain AVA

A small appellation contiguous with and cooler than the western edge of the huge Paso Robles AVA.

San Marino, tiny republic within Italy between the regions of EMILIA-ROMAGNA and the MARCHE. The quality of wine produced rose dramatically in the 1980s and is mostly 'exported', to tourist resorts on the Adriatic.

San Michele all'Adige, Istituto Agrario di, one of Italy's better-known wine schools and centres of ACADEME. It was founded in 1874 in what was then the Austrian South Tyrol and is now the province of Trento in the far north of the country. Its activities have always spanned both education and research, and now encompass fruit crops other than wine, and dairy farming. Its first director was Edmund Mach, highly regarded in the former Austro-Hungarian empire as an OENOLOGIST. A wide range of viticultural research is undertaken, from the study of indigenous grape varieties to the molecular genetics and genomics of grapes in collaboration with international research institutes, and oenological concerns include the analysis of flavour and PHENOLICS, microbiology, and sensory analysis (see TASTING). The institute hosts the most important ampelographic collection in Italy, with

varieties from Italy and all over the world, as well as producing a range of wines under its own label.

Santa Barbara, southern CALIFORNIA city which gives its name to the southernmost in a string of three heavily planted wine counties on California's CENTRAL COAST (see also MONTEREY and SAN LUIS OBISPO). Its southernmost vines grow hardly more than 100 miles/160 km from downtown Los Angeles. The city of Santa Barbara has one of the dreamiest climates man could hope to find, almost rain free, and so mild that semi-tropical plants grow in lush profusion. And yet Pinot Noir and Chardonnay are prized varieties in the county because many of its vineyards hug the Pacific ocean shore north of cape Concepcion, where nearly eternal sea fogs create conditions cooler and cloudier than either CARNEROS or much of SONOMA county's Russian River. MISSIONARIES brought vines to the region in the 1770s (see CALIFORNIA, history), and a few commercial wineries dotted the landscape during the later 19th century, but it was not until the wine boom of the 1970s that Santa Barbara began to assert any serious claims as a wine-producing area. Its potential seems particularly bright, in no small part because of its proximity to the trend-setting megalopolis of Los Angeles, and indeed the 2005 Academy Award-winning movie *Sideways* set here created an instantaneous American fascination with the district (and Pinot Noir). It has only two AVAs, and they do not encompass all of its recently swollen 20,000 acres/8,000 ha of vineyard, but its reliance on fog as a cooling agent gives it remarkably complex shadings.

Santa Maria Valley AVA

Located on the San Luis Obispo border, this district is climatologically and geographically an extension of the coastal sections of its northern neighbour. A flock of distinctive Pinot Noirs brought this AVA swift identity during the 1980s. It also has proven well adapted to Chardonnay in a short career that began only with the 1970s. The floodplain of the Santa Maria river runs true east–west, and thus is wide open to the prevailing sea fogs of the region. Much more heavily planted than the Santa Ynez Valley to the south, it has only a sparse handful of wineries. Byron, Qupé, and Au Bon Climat were its most prominent wineries at the outset of the 1990s, but more recently KENDALL-JACKSON's purchase of the Tepusquet Vineyard has made them an extremely important player (mainly under the Cambria label). Some small artisan wineries such as Foxen have also enjoyed acclaim, especially among day visitors from Los Angeles. Most of its grapes go to cellars outside the county. Much of the part that stays home goes to wineries in other parts of the county.

Santa Ynez Valley and Santa Rita Hills AVAs

Although far from being the only schizophrenic AVA in California, the Santa Ynez Valley comes close to being the extreme case. It starts as a narrow, fog-beset river course between steep east–west hills that run inland from the Pacific shore at Lompoc as far as the village of Solvang. There the main valley is joined by tributary canyons from the north, which are much warmer because they are sheltered from sea fogs by elevation and higher hills. The lower end seems best suited to Pinot Noir, Chardonnay, and, perhaps, Riesling. WIND is a serious consideration, and the best sites are in the lee of hills, not on top of them. In recognition of its climatological distinction, this lower section (west of the main coastal freeway, Highway 101) is now a sub-AVA of Santa Ynez Valley named Santa Rita Hills. Sanford, Babcock, Melville, and Lafond are prominent producers in this western section. The upper, eastern end appears to do better by Sauvignon Blanc and, mostly in blends, Cabernet Franc, Merlot, and Cabernet Sauvignon. Judgements on these varieties remain tentative, however; early plantings here came only after 1970, and acreage remains small. Firestone Vineyards was the pioneer, followed by Zaca Mesa. More recent entrants to have garnered acclaim include Fess Parker (known to all Americans over 45 for his television roles as Daniel Boone and Davy Crockett) and Andrew Murray. Syrah is a good at demonstrating differences between the two sections of Santa Ynez Valley: in the Santa Rita Hills AVA it gives peppery nuances and leaner body while in the eastern canyons it is fuller, more leathery, and berry-scented.   B.C.C.

Santa Clara Valley, California wine region and AVA south of San Francisco. Its colloquial name, Silicon valley, explains its status in the computer industry. In spite of a long vinous history, factories, shopping malls, and homes began to supplant most of its vineyards in the 1950s. By the 1970s, the transformation was nearly complete and the final chapters were being written for once-important winery names such as Almadén and Paul Masson. Mirassou remains today but its vineyards are now in the Salinas valley in MONTEREY. A few acres of Santa Clara vines persist to the west in the SANTA CRUZ MOUNTAINS and at its southern end in the Hecker Pass district, but luxury homes for computer programmers make all these vineyards more of a toy than a viable agricultural investment. San Ysidro District AVA east of Gilroy is a single grower, owned by a New York winery.   B.C.C.

Santa Cruz Mountains, diverse CALIFORNIA wine region and AVA immediately south of San Francisco. Its vineyards amount to a light dusting of freckles on a long, lopsided, bony body. In a stretch of coast ranges that begins as the ridgepole of the San Francisco peninsula and continues south as far as the city of Santa Cruz, climates and soils would be so diverse as to beggar description even if vineyards were not separated one from another by miles of redwood forest, meadows, and artist colonies populated by cyber-refugees earning a living through the optical fibre. The most useful points to make about it are: it is one of California's cooler growing regions; Pinot Noir has a rich history here, although Riesling and Zinfandel had their day in the last century; Cabernet Sauvignon has won the AVA its greatest fame albeit on the inland slopes of the ridgeline; and a prominent RHÔNE RANGER, Bonny Doon's Randall Grahm, started in the counterculture woods behind UC Santa Cruz. Top wineries include Ridge, David Bruce, Mt Eden, Fogarty, and Storrs. At the southern end of the AVA, overlooking Monterey bay, the hamlet of Corralitos is the geographical centre of activity for many small-scale producers of Pinot Noir which have sprung up since the mid 1990s.

B.C.C.

Santa Maddalena, known as **St Magdelener** by the many German speakers who make and drink it, was historically the most famous wine of ALTO ADIGE in north east Italy. (In an Italian government classification of 1941, it was for political purposes ranked after Barolo and Barbaresco as the country's most significant wine, a rating which would be unlikely to be repeated today.) It takes its name from the hill of Santa Maddalena to the east of the city of Bolzano (Bozen), long considered a particularly suitable site for the cultivation of the SCHIAVA (Vernatsch) grape from which the wine is made. Some 300 ha/760 acres are planted in the DOC zone and produce approximately 24,000 hl/633,600 gal per year. Like other Italian DOCs, Santa Maddalena underwent a significant enlargement of its production zone from the original nucleus (now called Santa Maddalena CLASSICO) of the communes of Santa Maddalena, Retsch, Justina, Leitach, and St Peter. The zone with its well-known name now stretches all the way to Settequerce (Siebeneich) in the Val d'Adige to the west and to Cornedo (Karneid) in the Val d'Isarco to the east. These latter zones undoubtedly give a Schiava of good quality but with less personality than the Schiava of Santa Maddalena; fortunately over 85 per cent of the current production of Santa Maddalena is Santa Maddalena Classico. Historically, most of the wine was sold to the Austrians and the Swiss, who appreciated Santa Maddalena's light style of red wine. As this style has fallen out of fashion, and as the Swiss and Austrians have found themselves drawn to other Italian wines, production of Santa Maddalena had fallen by over 25 per cent by the mid 2000s.

D.T. & D.C.G.

Santa Maria Valley, California wine region and AVA. See SANTA BARBARA.

Santarém, capital of the RIBATEJO in central, southern Portugal, former IPR and now a subregion of DOC Ribatejo.

Santa Rita Hills, promising California wine region and sub-AVA of Santa Ynez Valley. See SANTA BARBARA.

Santa Ynez Valley, California wine region and AVA. See SANTA BARBARA.

Santenay, somewhat forgotten village and spa in the Côte de Beaune district of Burgundy producing red wines from Pinot Noir and occasional whites. The soils in Santenay are a little richer in MARL than most of the Côte d'Or, producing red wines tending to the rustic more than the elegant. They are not counted among Burgundy's finest, although they are capable of ageing well. The vineyards are trained and pruned according to the CORDON DE ROYAT system in place of the usual GUYOT.

Most of the best vineyards, the PREMIERS CRUS La Comme, Clos de Tavannes, and Les Gravières, form an extension from Chassagne-Montrachet. Also reputed are La Maladière, situated behind the main village, and Clos Rousseau on the far border of Santenay, beyond the casino and thermal waters of the higher village. Vincent Girardin is one of the best, and certainly most prolific, Santenay producers.

See also CÔTE D'OR, and map under BURGUNDY.

J.T.C.M.

Santorini, one of the southern Cyclades islands that are part of GREECE, known in classical times as Thíra.

History

The island is a part of the core of an ancient volcano, which erupted *c.*1640–1620 BC (perhaps a century earlier), destroying the Minoan civilizations of Thíra and, it is thought, neighbouring Crete. A large part of Thíra became submerged, and has remained so to this day.

In antiquity, the island was not especially famous for its wine, but this was to change in the Middle Ages. It belonged to the Byzantine empire until the CRUSADERS sacked Constantinople in 1203–4 and Santorini was given to one of the Venetian conquerors, remaining in his family until 1336. It then became part of the duchy of Naxos but VENICE retained a strong influence; 1479–89 was another period of direct Venetian rule. It was Venetian enterprise that made Santorini an important wine producer. The wine it exported was made from a mixture of grapes, chiefly the white ATHIRI and red MANDELARIA, and it was prized for its sweetness and high alcohol which enabled it to withstand the six-month sea voyage, via Venice, to western Europe. Santorini was conquered by the Ottoman Turks in 1579, but the

Turks did not discourage the production of the only cash crop that the island's volcanic soil could sustain.

Loanwords from Italian still in use in Santorini today testify to Venice's importance in its wine-making past. The local dialect word for the vintage is *vendemma* from Italian *vendemmia* and the sweet, 13–15 per cent alcohol wine has been called Visanto, from Italian *vin santo* (but is now officially known as Vinsanto).

See GREECE for details of modern wines.

H.M.W.

Lambert-Gócs, M., *The Wines of Greece* (London, 1990).

Manessis, N., *The Illustrated Greek Wine Guide* (Corfu, 2000).

Saperavi, distinctive Georgian red wine grape variety notable for the COLOUR and ACIDITY it can bring to a blend. As a VARIETAL wine, it is capable, not to say demanding, of long BOTTLE AGEING. The flesh of this dark-skinned grape is deep pink, so that Saperavi has much in common with TEINTURIER grape varieties. It ripens late, is relatively productive, and is quite well adapted to the cold Russian winters, but not so well that the Russian Potapenko viticultural research institute has been discouraged from producing a **Saperavi Severny**, a hybrid of SEVERNY and Saperavi which was released in 1947 and incorporates not just Saperavi's VINIFERA genes, but also those of the cold-hardy VITIS *amurensis*.

Traditional Saperavi is planted throughout almost all of the wine regions of the former Soviet republics. It is an important variety in RUSSIA, UKRAINE, MOLDOVA, GEORGIA, KAZAKHSTAN, UZBEKISTAN, TAJIKISTAN, KYRGYZSTAN, and TURKMENISTAN, although in cooler areas the acidity may be too marked for any purpose other than blending, despite its relatively high sugar levels. It has also been grown in BULGARIA for some time.

See also MAGARACH, the Crimean wine research centre which has crossed Cabernet Sauvignon and Saperavi to produce the promising Magarach Ruby and also devised Magarach Bastardo for FORTIFIED WINES by crossing the Portuguese BASTARDO with Saperavi.

Sardegna, known as **Sardinia** in English (the Italian adjective is **Sardo**), Mediterranean island 200 km/125 miles off the coast of Italy at its nearest point, governed by CARTHAGE before conquest by Ancient ROME, and subsequently by Byzantines, Arabs, and Catalans. (See map under ITALY.) Sardegna became an integral part of Italy only in 1726, when it was ceded to the House of Savoy. Historically, linguistically, and culturally, as well as geographically, the island seems detached from the mainstream of Italian civilization, and it is therefore no surprise that most of its significant grape varieties—VERMENTINO, CANNONAU, Carignano (CARIGNAN), Bovale (thought to be BOBAL)—are of Spanish origin and that, due to limited local demand, and few commercial contacts with the mainland, viticulture dedicated to quality is developing so slowly.

Vines in any case play only a small part in a total agricultural economy in which over 40 per cent of the land is dedicated to the grazing of animals—sheep in particular—for milk and meat. While the total area under vines and the total production of wine underwent a significant increase in the post-war period, aided by lavish subsidies both from Rome and from the regional government, the result has not been a self-sustaining wine industry. As markets for Sardinian wines have contracted and the flow of public funds to CO-OPERATIVE wineries has dwindled to a trickle, the total vineyard surface decreased from a high of 70,000 to 40,000 ha/ 100,000 acres in the early 1990s and the island's total production of wine has dropped from a high of 4.5 million hl to an average of only just over 800,000 hl between 1999 and 2003.

The production of DOC wine meanwhile dropped from close to 90,000 hl in the mid 1980s to below 60,000 hl in 1990 before rising to 167,000 hl/4.3 million gal in 1997. As a percentage of the total production, this is not particularly low for a region in Italy's south (see PUGLIA, for example). The powerfully alcoholic wines of Sardegna have long been prized more for beefing up wines produced in cooler climates to the north than for drinking on their own. Little has been done within the DOCs to match individual vine varieties to proper soils and climates. The production zones of the most popular varieties—Vermentino and Cannonau—have been extended to include the entire surface of the island; and yields have been allowed to rise to 105 hl/ha (6 tons/acre) for the Carignano del Sulcis DOC, 130 hl/ha for the Vermentino di Sardegna DOC, and 140 hl/ha for the Nuragus di Cagliari DOC—extremely high for Italy. The result has been a general flight from DOC 'status', with several—Monica di Cagliari, Giro di Cagliari, Nasco di Cagliari—having become virtually inactive. The Arborea DOC, approved in 1987 in an attempt to launch the well-known vine varieties SANGIOVESE and TREBBIANO in a zone of commercial fruit cultivation, established 135 hl/ha as its official maximum permitted yield, and has not been a commercial success.

The existence of four different types of wine—dry, sweet, a *liquoroso*, or higher-alcohol, dry wine, and a *liquoroso* sweet wine—in many of the DOCs (Malvasia di Cagliari, Monica di Cagliari, Giro di Cagliari, Nasco di Cagliari, Cannonau di Sardegna) seems programmed to create confusion, and it is far from clear that Sardegna's powerfully alcoholic wines need to reach still higher ALCOHOLIC STRENGTHS.

If the overall picture is far from encouraging, small quantities of good wines do exist and suggest that Sardegna's soil and climate have potential. Vernaccia di Oristano, although dwindling in quantities produced,

can be a good approximation of a dry SHERRY with a clean and bitter finish, and the hard to find Malvasia di Bosa justly enjoys a certain reputation as a dessert wine. Refreshing bottles of Vermentino di Gallura, produced in the island's north, do exist, though hardly in sufficient quantity to merit the wine's promotion to DOCG status in 1996, even though it was accompanied by the lowering of yields to 10 tonnes/ha, are unquestionably a positive step for the future. An occasional good bottle of Nuragus di Cagliari only underlines the absurdity of allowing such high yields. Carignano del Sulcis has produced some of the island's best wines in recent years, especially those from the co-operative in Santadi. This producer, Argiolas, and Barrua, a more recent JOINT VENTURE between Santadi and the Incisa family of SASSICAIA, with winemaker Giacomo Tachis.

Cannonau, thought to be a clone of GRENACHE and accounting for 20 per cent of the island's total production, has produced some good wines in the province of Nuoro, particularly in the subzone of Oliena. Attempts to extend its cultivation to the provinces of Cagliari and Sassari have been a fiasco from both quantitative and qualitative points of view, however.   D.T. & D.C.G.

Sárfehér, undistinguished, very productive white grape of Hungary traditionally grown on the sandy Great plain for TABLE GRAPES and sparkling wines.

Sárga Muskotály, or **Sárgamuskotály,** occasional Hungarian name for MUSCAT BLANC À PETITS GRAINS.

Sassella, subzone of VALTELLINA in the far north of Italy.

Sassicaia, trail-blazing central Italian wine made, largely from CABERNET SAUVIGNON, originally by Mario Incisa della Rochetta at the Tenuta San Guido near BOLGHERI and one of the first Italian reds made in the image of fine red bordeaux. The first small commercial quantities were released in the mid 1970s. For more details, see VINO DA TAVOLA. In the late 1990s, Sassicaia was granted its own DOC, the only wine from a single estate in Italy to enjoy this privilege.

Saumur, town in the Loire giving its name to an extensive wine district and several appellations. Saumur is effectively a south western extension of TOURAINE, yet is more of a centre for the wine trade of Anjou–Saumur than is Angers. The grapes grown in these latter two neighbouring regions are very similar, except that Saumur does not have Anjou's range of potentially great sweet white wines.

Saumur's most important wine (and France's most important mousseux) is **Saumur Mousseux,** a well-priced sparkling wine made from Chenin Blanc grapes with increas-

ing amounts of Chardonnay and, usually less successful, Sauvignon Blanc. These grapes can come from an even wider area than that permitted for still Saumur, and the quality of wine-making is high among the larger houses of the town of Saumur, such as Gratien & Meyer, Langlois Chateau, and Bouvet Ladubay, and also at the important CO-OPERATIVE at St-Cyr-en-Bourg, with its extensive underground cellars hewn out of the local TUFFEAU. This CALCAREOUS rock predominates around Saumur, and was much quarried, both locally and abroad (according to Duijker it was used for rebuilding after the Great Fire of London, and also extensively in the Dutch city of Maastricht). This left the Saumurois with readymade wine cellars, perfect not just for mushrooms, one of their most important products, but also for the maturation of their acidic wines which, as in CHAMPAGNE, had a natural tendency to retain some carbon dioxide in spring. Ackerman-Laurance was the first producer of sparkling Saumur, in the early 19th century. The wines have enjoyed considerable commercial success, although an increasing proportion of the base material for Saumur Mousseux is expected to be fashioned into CRÉMANT de Loire, for which the criteria are rather more rigorous: yields of 50 rather than 60 hl/ha and 12 rather than nine months' TIRAGE.

Saumur Blanc can be remarkably difficult to distinguish from Anjou Blanc, being made substantially from Chenin Blanc and being both high in acidity and potentially long lived. Only such conscientious growers as Chx du Hureau, de Targé, Villeneuve, and Domaine des Roches manage to coax much fruit out of them, however, by picking in TRIES and employing OAK for fermentation and maturation, resulting in a graceful, limestone alternative to the firmer dry white ANJOU made on schist. The parallel between still white Saumur and the still white wines of Champagne, Coteaux CHAMPENOIS, is an apt one for the négociant wines meanwhile.

Saumur Rouge is a much more successful wine, made on soils similar to those of CHINON and BOURGUEIL. It may be made from Cabernet Franc, Cabernet Sauvignon, or Pineau d'Aunis grapes, but is usually made almost exclusively from Cabernet Franc and can be a refreshing, relatively light, fruity wine. A little more Saumur Rouge is produced than Saumur Blanc, but the most significant still wine of the region is **Saumur-Champigny,** whose extraordinary expansion in the 1970s and 1980s was originally due to FASHION, and mainly Paris fashion at that, but has been sustained by growers' determination to maximize vineyard potential and reach full ripeness. The Saumur-Champigny zone, prettily named after the village of Champigny, is on a tuffeau plateau that lends itself well to viticulture, as in neighbouring Touraine. Its high LIMESTONE content made the Chenin Blanc vine traditionally grown here prone to CHLOROSIS in the post-PHYLLOX-ERA era, but by the mid 2000s more than 1,330 ha/3,200 acres of vines were producing Saumur-Champigny. It was the dominant St-Cyr-en-Bourg co-operative in particular that encouraged the planting of Cabernet Franc vines and developed the still red wine appel-lation with such success. Much Saumur-Champigny is too light to be worth ageing, although it is usefully, and quintessentially, fruity and flirtatious. Particularly reliable pro-ducers include Filliatreau, Foucault, Ch du Hureau, Domaine des Roches Neuves, and Ch de Villeneuve.

A small amount of light rosé **Cabernet de Saumur** is made, usually considerably drier and less ambitious than Cabernet d'Anjou, while **Coteaux de Saumur** is Saumur's me-dium sweet white, made in very small quan-tities from Chenin Blanc grapes.

See also LOIRE, including map.

Friedrich, J., *A Wine and Food Guide to the Loire* (New York, 1996, and London, 1997).

Saussignac, very small sweet white wine appellation in SOUTH WEST FRANCE. It lies within the BERGERAC district to the west of Monbazillac and produces sweet white wines, from Sémillon, Sauvignon Blanc, and some particularly successful Muscadelle grapes. Since the mid 1990s, the appellation has be-come an enclave of great SWEET WINE-MAKING, led by Clos d'Yvigne and Domaine de Richard. In 2004, appellation laws were strengthened to insist on manual picking and completely nat-ural sweetness, generally due to BOTRYTIS.

Atkinson, P., *The Ripening Sun: One Woman and the Creation of a Vineyard* (London, 2004).

Sauterne, occasionally found on labels of GENERIC sweet white wine. Real SAUTERNES always ends in *s*.

Sauternes. The special distinction of this region embedded within the Graves district south of BORDEAUX is that it is dedicated, in a way unmatched by any other wine region, to the production of unfortified, sweet, white wine. In Germany or California, say, where superlative sweet Rieslings are occasion-ally made, such wines are the exception rather than the rule, and emerge from vines that more usually produce drier or medium sweet wines.

In Sauternes the situation is quite different. The appellation is reserved for wines from five communes that must adhere to regulations stipulating minimum levels of ALCOHOLIC STRENGTH (13 per cent) and a tasting test that requires the wine to taste sweet. Three grape varieties are planted: Sémillon, Sauvignon Blanc, and Muscadelle. Sémillon is the princi-pal grape, because it is especially susceptible to noble rot, and it accounts for about 80 per cent of a typical estate's ENCÉPAGEMENT. Sauvignon often attracts BOTRYTIS earlier than Sémillon, and its naturally high acidity can give the wine a freshness that balances the richer, broader

flavours of Sémillon. Muscadelle's contribu-tion is mostly aromatic, but its viticultural frailty leads many growers to find it more trouble than it is worth.

No one is exactly sure when sweet wine pro-duction became the norm here. The style was well entrenched by the late 18th century, when Thomas JEFFERSON and others were purchas-ing wines from the district's most famous property Ch d'YQUEM that were evidently sweet; and harvesting details from the 1660s suggest, but do not prove, that the wines made then were probably sweet.

Sauternes is the product of a specific MESOCLIMATE. The communes of Sauternes, Barsac, Preignac, Bommes, and Fargues are close to two rivers, the broad GARONNE and its small tributary, the Ciron. When, in au-tumn, the cool spring-fed Ciron waters flow into the warmer tidal Garonne, evening mists envelop the vineyards until late morning the following day, when the sun, if it shines, burns the mist away. This moist atmosphere encourages *Botrytis cinerea*, a fungus that at-tacks the grapes and causes them to shrivel and rot (see BOTRYTIS BUNCH ROT). Mist acti-vates the botrytis spores in the vineyards, and the alternating sunshine completes the process of desiccation.

The onset of botrytis is crucial to the evolu-tion of the grapes. Without it, they may in-deed ripen sufficiently to ensure that a sweet wine can be made, if fermentation ceases be-fore all the sugar has been converted into alcohol, but the result will lack complexity. As outlined in more detail in NOBLE ROT, the overall effect of a benevolent botrytis infec-tion is to increase the concentration of SUGAR IN GRAPES and, to a lesser extent, that of TARTARIC ACID; to stimulate the production of GLYCEROL that contributes to the wine's VISCOSITY; and to alter considerably the AROMA and flavour of the finished wine.

The essential difference between mediocre and great Sauternes hangs on the willingness of estate owners to wait until botrytis arrives. This act of patience is largely responsible for the cost of Sauternes. There are years, such as 1978, 1985, and those of the early 1990s, when botrytis either fails to develop at all or arrives very late in the year. Proprietors must then de-cide whether to delay or to begin the harvest. Delay is a risky strategy: the chances of frost or rain, both of which can wreck the harvest, clearly increase as the autumn months wear on, but by picking too early the estate can end up with insipid sweet white wine while its more scrupulous neighbours are in a pos-ition to market great BOTRYTIZED wine.

This introduces an economic issue unique to this region. Sauternes is exceptionally costly to make. There are a number of vintages each decade in which it is either impossible to make good sweet wine (and some grapes may be sal-vaged to make a dry white that qualifies only as a BORDEAUX AC) or in which, as in 1991, it can

be produced only in minute quantities. Even in excellent VINTAGES, maximum YIELDS are re-stricted to 25 hl/ha (1.4 tons/acre), a quantity infrequently attained. At Yquem, the average yield is a trifling 9 hl/ha, and at most conscien-tious estates the yields probably fluctuate between 12 and 20 hl/ha—although total pro-duction of the appellation, perhaps tellingly, does not vary nearly as much. (In the red wine districts of MÉDOC or ST-ÉMILION, yields of more than 45 hl/ha are routine.)

In addition, the harvest is unusually pro-tracted. Botrytis occasionally swoops over en-tire vineyards, as in 1990 and 2003, but this is rare. More commonly, it performs its un-sightly activities patchily. A typical harvesting pattern might be as follows: an attack of botrytis on Sauvignon grapes allows half of them to be picked in late September; two weeks of drizzle follow, during which picking is suspended; finer weather resumes, grapes affected by undesirable GREY ROT are elimin-ated, and in late October another attack of botrytis allows the Sémillon and remaining Sauvignon grapes to be picked over a three-week period. The necessity for selective har-vesting, or TRIAGE, essential for Sauternes, is expensive, as teams of pickers must be kept available for a very long period. More than any other wine, Sauternes is made in the vine-yard. Once the grapes have been picked, they are difficult to manipulate. Their MUST WEIGHT (sugar content), their PHYSIOLOGICAL RIPENESS, and the degree of botrytis infection will all de-termine quality before the winemaker has got to work. None the less, Sauternes calls for care-ful vinification. Pressing should be as gentle as possible, and some leading estates still use old-fashioned hydraulic or basket PRESSES for this purpose. Fermentation takes place in tanks or, more usually since the mid 1980s, in BARRIQUES, of which a third or more are likely to be new (see BARREL FERMENTATION). Fermen-tation either stops of its own accord when the wine has achieved a balance of about 14 per cent alcohol and a RESIDUAL SUGAR level that is the equivalent of a further 4–7 per cent al-cohol, or it is arrested with the addition of SUL-FUR DIOXIDE. For more details, see BOTRYTIZED wine-making.

In weaker vintages, CHAPTALIZATION may be permitted, although better estates avoid the practice, which merely adds sweetness ra-ther than complexity and is often used to dis-guise lazy harvesting. The wine is usually aged in oak barrels for between 18 and 36 months (see BARREL MATURATION). The necessary invest-ment in these barriques also contributes to the high cost of production. Some estates—Chx d'Yquem, Raymond-Lafon, La Tour Blanche—use up to 100 per cent new oak, while others, such as Chx Climens or Doisy-Daëne, prefer a lesser proportion. It is a question of style ra-ther than quality. Less distinguished lots of wine are usually sold off to NÉGOCIANTS; in 1978, Yquem bottled only 15 per cent of the crop under its own label, and in 1987, many estates marketed no wine at all.

A technological development introduced in 1985 has stirred considerable controversy. CRYOEXTRACTION can help growers to save part of a crop that might formerly have had to be rejected. Grapes are chilled for 20 hours in a cold chamber before pressing, thus eliminating water and the least ripe grapes. Cryoextraction has no effect on chemical components of the grape and its must but it is a rescue operation only, and its major drawback is cost. None the less, in damp vintages such as 1987 it came in useful for estates such as Yquem which had invested in the process.

Although the prevalence of botrytis and overall geographical location are common to all Sauternes, specific MESOCLIMATES and SOIL STRUCTURES affect the styles of the different estates. BARSAC is the most distinctive commune, and is entitled to its own appellation, although it can also be sold as Sauternes. Its proximity to the Ciron and its ALLUVIAL soil give wines that are often lighter and more elegant than its neighbours. The communes of Bommes and Sauternes itself tend to give the fattest wines, although exceptions are numerous. There are also differences in maturation dates: the grapes at Ch Filhot, for instance, often ripen a week later than those of Barsac.

All these factors were taken into account when in 1855 the existing estates were classified. Successful candidates were ranked as either first or second growths, with Yquem rightfully given its own super-status (see CLASSIFICATION). In the 1960s especially, standards slumped. The wines were out of FASHION and there was a string of poor vintages. Only the richest estates could afford to maintain standards. Elsewhere, corners were cut, grapes were picked too early, and barriques were replaced with tanks. For two decades many classified growths produced wines that were mediocre at best, even in fine vintages. Only with the excellent 1983 vintage did matters improve. Prices rose, and wise proprietors invested in long overdue improvements, which bore fruit in the superb 1986, 1988, 1989, and 1990 vintages and, more recently, the 1996, 1997, 2001, and 2003. The official 1855 classification is once again a reasonably reliable guide to quality, although a number of unclassified growths, such as Ch de Fargues (owned by Comte Alexandre de Lur-Saluces who used to manage Yquem), Gilette, and Raymond-Lafon, are often of first growth quality, and price.

After a bad patch, Sauternes is again showing the quality of which it is capable. It combines power, voluptuousness, and elegance, and good bottles can evolve and improve for up to 50 years (longer in the case of Yquem). Given the risks and costs involved in its production, it remains underpriced in relation to the enormous pleasure it brings to those growing numbers of wine lovers who find a fine

Sauternes has an undeniable place on the dinner table. In 2004, a total of more than 1,700 ha/4,200 acres produced Sauternes while almost 540 ha were registered in the Barsac appellation.   S.B. & J.R.

Brook, S., *Sauternes, and Other Sweet Wines of Bordeaux* (London, 1995).

Olney, R., *Yquem* (London, 1986).

Sauvignonasse, surprisingly common white grape, also known as Sauvignon Vert, which is quite distinct from but in some places has been confused with the more famous SAUVIGNON BLANC. In general the wines produced from Sauvignonasse are much less crisp and aromatic than those of Sauvignon Blanc and this vine is much more sensitive to DOWNY MILDEW and ROT. DNA PROFILING at SAN MICHELE ALL'ADIGE confirmed Galet's opinion that Sauvignonasse is identical to TOCAI FRIULANO. Sauvignonasse is also widely planted in CHILE, often called simply Sauvignon, and has been casually mixed, from vineyard to bottle, with SAUVIGNON BLANC. VINE IDENTIFICATION was well under way in the late 1990s so that Chilean varietal statistics in 2005 distinguished between the country's 7,400 ha of Sauvignon Blanc and surprisingly low total of 200 ha of Sauvignon Vert. Galet also maintains that the variety called Sauvignon Vert in California, where a few scattered plantings remain, is in fact the MUSCADELLE of Bordeaux.

Galet, P., *Dictionnaire encyclopédique des cépages* (Paris, 2000).

Sauvignon Blanc is the popular vine variety solely responsible for some of the world's most distinctively aromatic dry white wines: Sancerre, Pouilly-Fumé, and a tidal wave of Sauvignon Blanc and Fumé Blanc from outside France. The direct, obvious, easy-to-appreciate nature of varietal Sauvignon Blanc seems to answer a need in modern wine consumers who are perhaps more interested in immediate fruit than subtlety and ageing ability—which is not to deny that in many great white wines, both dry and sweet, it does also add nerve and zest to its most common blending partner SÉMILLON.

It has always shared a certain aromatic similarity with the great red wine grape Cabernet Sauvignon (something approaching HERBACEOUSNESS) and in 1997 Sauvignon Blanc's standing in the world of wine rose when DNA PROFILING established that, with Cabernet Franc, Sauvignon Blanc was a parent of Cabernet Sauvignon, the result of a spontaneous field crossing, probably in the 18th century, in Bordeaux. The variety has always seemed to have its origins in Bordeaux, where it has been enjoying a revival in popularity. Additional DNA profiling in Austria subsequently suggested that Sauvignon Blanc might be related to CHENIN Blanc and TRAMINER.

Sauvignon Blanc's most recognizable characteristic is its piercing, instantly recognizable

aroma. Descriptions typically include 'grassy, herbaceous, musky, green fruits' (especially gooseberries), 'nettles', and even 'tomcats'. Research into FLAVOUR COMPOUNDS suggests that METHOXYPYRAZINES play an important role in Sauvignon's aroma. Over-productive Sauvignon vines planted on heavy soils can produce wines only vaguely suggestive of this but Sauvignon cautiously cultivated in the central vineyards of the Loire, unmasked by oak, can reach the dry white apogee of Sauvignon fruit with some of the purest, most refreshingly zesty wines in the world. The best Sancerres and Pouilly-Fumés served as a model for early exponents of New World Sauvignon Blanc, although by the 1980s it was the Loire vignerons, and winemakers all round the world, who were more likely to copy their counterparts in New Zealand (which achieved rapid fame with this variety) in experimenting with fermentation and maturation in oak, and picking the grapes at different levels of RIPENESS to add nuance and pungency to the aroma and weight to the palate.

Oak-aged examples usually need an additional year or two to show their best, but almost all dry, unblended Sauvignon is designed to be drunk young, although there are both Loire and Bordeaux examples that can demonstrate durability, if rarely evolution, with up to 15 years in bottle (see POUILLY-FUMÉ and Pavillon Blanc de Ch MARGAUX, for example). As an ingredient in the great sweet white wines of SAUTERNES, on the other hand, Sauvignon plays a minor but important part in one of the world's longest-living wines.

The vine is particularly vigorous, which has caused problems in parts of the Loire and New Zealand. If the vine's vegetation gets out of hand, the grapes fail to reach full maturity and the resulting wine can be aggressively herbaceous, almost intrusively rank. (And underripe Sémillon can exhibit very similar characteristics—just as underripe Cabernet Sauvignon can smell like Cabernet Franc.) A low-vigour ROOTSTOCK and CANOPY MANAGEMENT can help combat this problem.

Sauvignon buds after but flowers before Sémillon, with which it is typically blended in Bordeaux and, increasingly, elsewhere. Until suitable clones such as 297 and 316 were identified, and sprays to combat Sauvignon's susceptibility to POWDERY MILDEW and BLACK ROT were developed, yields were uneconomically irregular. In 1968, for example, Sauvignon was France's 13th most planted white grape variety but within 20 years it had risen to fourth place and by 2000 its French total of well over 20,000 ha/50,000 acres put it behind only Ugni Blanc and Chardonnay in France.

In Bordeaux it was not until the late 1980s that Sauvignon overtook Ugni Blanc, or TREBBIANO, as second most planted white grape variety after Sémillon, which still outnumbers Sauvignon almost two to one in terms of area planted—although the newer clones of Sauvignon are much more productive than the important but rapidly declining Sémillon. The Gironde's Sauvignon is concentrated in the Entre-Deux-Mers, Graves, and the sweet wine-producing districts in and around Sauternes. In each of these areas, it is dominated by and usually blended with Sémillon, particularly in Sauternes, where the typical blend incorporates 80 per cent of the more rot-prone Sémillon together with a little Muscadelle. BORDEAUX BLANC owes much to Entre-Deux-Mers Sauvignon although low yields and, often, expensive oak ageing, as in the best dry white PESSAC-LÉOGNAN, GRAVES, and the handful of expensive Médoc whites (sold as BORDEAUX AC), are prerequisites for a memorable performance from Sauvignon in Bordeaux. It is perhaps no coincidence that the average Loire Sauvignon has more Sauvignon character than the average all-Sauvignon Bordeaux Blanc when the official maximum yield for the first is 10 hl/ha (0.6 tons/acre) lower than the 65 hl/ha allowed in Bordeaux.

As with red wines, the satellite areas of SOUTH WEST FRANCE reflect Bordeaux's spread of vine varieties and Sauvignon is often an easily perceptible ingredient in the dry whites of such areas as BERGERAC, Côtes du MARMANDAIS, and Côtes de DURAS.

It is in the Loire that Sauvignon is encountered in its purest, most unadulterated form. In the often limestone vineyards of SANCERRE, POUILLY-FUMÉ, and their western satellites QUINCY, REUILLY, and MENETOU-SALON, it can demonstrate one of the most eloquent arguments for marrying variety with suitable TERROIR. The variety is often called Blanc Fumé here and has happily replaced most of the lesser varieties once common, notably much of the Chasselas in Pouilly-sur-Loire. Most of these wines are designed to be drunk, well chilled, within two years and are none the worse for that.

From this concentration of vineyards, which might well be considered the Sauvignon capital of the world (however much the inhabitants of Marlborough in NEW ZEALAND's South Island might dispute it), Sauvignon's influence radiates outwards: north east towards Chablis in ST-BRIS, south to ST-POURÇAIN-sur-Sioule, and north and west to Coteaux du GIENNOIS and CHEVERNY, as well as to a substantial quantity of eastern Loire wines, typically labelled TOURAINE. Such Sauvignons tend to be light, racy, and, of course, aromatic. With Chardonnay, it has also been allowed into the vineyards of Anjou, where it is sometimes blended with the indigenous CHENIN BLANC.

Elsewhere in France, Sauvignon Blanc has been an obvious, though not invariably successful, choice for those seeking to make internationally saleable wine. In Languedoc-Roussillon, there were well over 4,000 ha by 2000 even if yields are often too high to extract quite enough varietal character for the VINS DE PAYS made from the vine. Small plantings of Sauvignon can also be found in some of the Provençal appellations.

Across the Alps, Sauvignon's most successful Italian region is the far north east in FRIULI, with some ALTO ADIGE and COLLIO examples exhibiting particularly fine fruit and purity of flavour. Many of the better bottles from the north east are made from the extremely pungent and recognizable R3 clone of the Rauscedo vine nursery. Attempts to transfer Sauvignon to central Italy have been notably less successful. In the 1980s, Italy's plantings of Sauvignon doubled to nearly 3,000 ha/ 7,410 acres but it is overall a relatively minor grape outside the far north east.

The Podravje region across the SLOVENIAN border from here is known as a source of delicate Sauvignon Blanc, with a particularly distinctive version coming from Meranovo in the Maribor district. In Vipava and Brda districts both barrel-aged and unoaked styles are produced. The variety also thrives in Styria in AUSTRIA, stylishly combining fruit with aroma. In Germany, as 'Muskat-Silvaner' it is grown but rarely, and many would argue that young Riesling can provide the same sort of crisp, aromatic white. It is planted to a certain extent further east—even if the wines tend to be progressively heavier and sweeter. Parts of SERBIA, the Fruška Gora district of VOJVODINA, and some of the CZECH REPUBLIC clearly have potential. ROMANIA had 2,600 ha of Sauvignon Blanc in the mid 2000s, and neighbouring MOLDOVA also had sizeable plantings of the variety.

Sauvignon Blanc has probably been the most successful of the INTERNATIONAL VARIETIES for white wine imported into Spain, ahead of Chardonnay, even if total planted area is only 460 ha according to official 2004 figures. It is produced by the most dedicated internationalists such as TORRES, but also in the up-and-coming region of RUEDA. Certainly Portugal and north western Spain have no shortage of indigenous varieties (see MINHO and GALICIA) capable of reproducing vaguely similar wine styles. There is a tendency for Sauvignon Blanc to taste oily when reared in too warm a climate, as it sometimes does in Israel and other Mediterranean vineyards where those with an eye to the export market put it through its paces.

This was clearly perceptible in many of Australia's earlier attempts with the variety, although by the early 1990s, there was even keener appreciation of the need to reserve it for the country's cooler sites (see AUSTRALIA for more on the wines produced) and since the second half of the 1990s sales (and plantings) have soared, reaching 3,400 ha by the mid 2000s. Nonetheless Chardonnay plantings outnumber those of Sauvignon Blanc by more than eight to one in Australia.

In New Zealand, on the other hand, Sauvignon Blanc overtook Chardonnay in 2003 and this relatively minute wine industry can boast twice as much Sauvignon (7,000 ha/ 17,500 acres in 2006) as Australia and considerably more than either the Loire or Bordeaux. This is the variety that introduced New Zealand wine to the world and did it by developing its own pungent style: intensely perfumed, more obviously fruity than the Loire prototype, with just a hint of both gas and sweetness and, occasionally, gooseberries or asparagus. This style of Sauvignon can now be found in Chile, South Africa, the cooler areas of North America, and in virtually all parts of France where Sauvignon is grown.

Chardonnay overtook 'Sauvignon' in Chile only early this century and, although there is now a serious attempt to distinguish SAUVIGNONASSE from true Sauvignon Blanc, there is a preponderance of Sauvignon of both sorts in the Maule region and a dominance of Sauvignon Blanc in Casablanca (see CHILE).

California clones of Sauvignon Blanc have been widely planted in Chile but tend to suffer from excessive VIGOUR. High yields also help depress the keynote aromas of Sauvignon Blanc in other South American wines labelled Sauvignon. Brazil's 'Sauvignon' is usually SEYVAL BLANC, according to GALET.

Thanks to Robert MONDAVI, who renamed it FUMÉ BLANC, Sauvignon Blanc enjoyed enormous success in California in the 1980s, and the late 1990s saw a second great wave of popularity for California Sauvignon Blanc so that plantings had reached over 13,000 acres/ 9,500 ha by 2004. See CALIFORNIA for more on the wines, which are very occasionally sweet and even botrytized, a sort of Semillon-free Sauternes. There has also been an increase, as elsewhere in the New World, in blending in some Semillon to dry white Sauvignon to add weight and fruit to Sauvignon's aroma and acidity. Like California, WASHINGTON state makes both Sauvignon Blanc and Fumé Blanc from its declining acreage (down to 600 acres by 2005) of Sauvignon, a poor third to Chardonnay and Riesling. Of other American states, TEXAS has had particular success with the variety.

But perhaps Sauvignon's real success in the New World, New Zealand excepted, has been in SOUTH AFRICA, where, for want of genuine Chardonnay perhaps (see AUXERROIS), local wine drinkers fell upon the Cape's more successful early Sauvignons as a fashionable internationally recognized wine style. By 1990, there were 3,300 ha of Sauvignon Blanc to South Africa's barely 2,400 ha of Cabernet Sauvignon. By 2002 this had doubled again to 6,500 ha/ 15,970 acres and was still growing. Cape Sauvignon Blanc, particularly from the cooler vineyards of Elgin, Darling, and Cape Agulhas, shows intense capsicum flavours and reasonable ageing potential.

Sauvignon Blanc is often simply called **Sauvignon**, especially on wine labels, but it has mutated into variants with darker-coloured berries, notably **Sauvignon Rose** and **Sauvignon Rouge**, an unrelated version of which is found in the hills of Oriolo dei Fichi in ROMAGNA.

Bowers, J. E., and Meredith, C. P., 'The parentage of a classic wine grape, Cabernet Sauvignon', *Nature Genetics*, 16/1 (1997), 84–7.

Sauvignon Gris, sometimes sold as a VARIETAL, is another name for Sauvignon Rose and has discernibly pink skins. It can produce more substantial wines than many a Sauvignon Blanc, and has an increasing following, notably in Bordeaux and the Loire. See also FIÉ.

Sauvignon de St-Bris. See ST-BRIS.

Sauvignon Vert, synonym for SAUVIGNONASSE.

Savagnin is a fine but curious vine variety with small, round, pale berries. In France, it is as much a viticultural curiosity as the wine it alone produces, VIN JAUNE, is a wine-making oddity. Today, under the name Savagnin, it is cultivated almost exclusively in the JURA in eastern France, and presumably only those producers rewarded by the high prices fetched by vin jaune would persist with a vine that can yield so churlishly.

France's vineyard census of 2000 found a grand total of 412 ha/1,000 acres of this variety cultivated to a limited extent throughout the Jura vineyards because it may be included in any of the region's white wine appellations, although most is reserved for the sherry-like vin jaune. The contents of barrels rejected for vin jaune are used for OXIDATIVE dry white wines. Since the late 1990s, however, a new breed of fresh, unoxidized Savagnin has emerged, and caused a stir amongst traditionalists. The vine is well adapted to the ancient, west-facing MARL slopes of Jura but many believe it is at its finest in the vineyards of CHÂTEAU-CHALON, where it may sometimes be left to ripen as late as November. The resulting distinctively nutty wine is the product of six years' ageing in cask, under a FLOR-like film, and it can continue to evolve for many years in bottle, the special 62 cl *clavelin*.

Called Gringet, it is also the principal ingredient in the still and sparkling wines of AYZE in SAVOIE. It is also grown, at particularly high altitudes, in Valais in SWITZERLAND, where it is called either Païen or Heida.

DNA PROFILING at Milan confirmed Galet's contention that Savagnin is identical to the TRAMINER which was once grown widely in Germany, Alsace, Hungary, and Austria, and that GEWÜRZTRAMINER is the pink-berried MUSQUÉ mutation of Savagnin, Savagnin Rosé. This makes Savagnin a PINOT relative, which would explain why Pinot Noir is sometimes called Savagnin Noir in Jura. Certainly a non-Musqué Savagnin Rosé is still cultivated to a very limited extent in Alsace, where it is sometimes called KLEVNER or Klevener de Heiligenstein. Austrian Traminer is, like

Jura's Savagnin, famous for its aroma and ability to age.

Galet, P., *Dictionnaire encyclopédique des cépages* (Paris, 2000).

Savagnin Noir is a Jura name for PINOT NOIR.

Savatiano, Greece's most common wine grape, widely planted on up to 20,000 ha/ 50,000 acres throughout Attica and central GREECE. This light-berried vine, with its exceptionally good DROUGHT resistance, is the most common ingredient in RETSINA, although RHODITIS and ASSYRTIKO are often added to compensate for Savatiano's naturally low acidity. On particularly suitable sites, Savatiano can produce well-balanced dry white wines.

Savennières, distinctive and much celebrated dry white wine appellation in the Anjou region of the Loire, immediately south west of the town of Angers. Total production of the appellation is less than 30,000 cases in a good vintage but these examples of dry CHENIN BLANC display such an unusual combination of nerve, concentration, and longevity that they have won devotees around the world (although mainly in northern France). Many producers have abandoned the south east-facing SLATE and SANDSTONE slopes on the north bank of the Loire. In its Napoleonic heyday, Savennières was a sweet wine, but today almost all of it is dry, and unusually concentrated because maximum permitted yields are relatively low. The best wines can last for several decades, and can be unappetizingly tart at less than seven years old. Within Savennières are the two subappellations **Savennières-Coulée de Serrant**, a single estate of just 7 ha/17 acres run by the Joly family on BIODYNAMIC lines, and the 33 ha of **Savennières-La Roche-aux-Moines**, in which several different producers struggle to make a living in this frost-prone corner of the Loire valley. Domaine des Baumard makes some of the best Savennières, but this is a wine for intellectuals, not neophytes. More recently, top Coteaux du LAYON producers have bought land here and, by applying better vineyard management and selective picking techniques, are achieving much higher ripeness levels which result in wines with both accessibility and complexity in youth, even if they may not last as long as more traditional Savennières. Examples include Germain's Ch de Varennes, Domaine des Forges, Ch Pierre Bise, and Jo Pithon.

Across the river to the south east are the sweet white wine appellations of Anjou: BONNEZEAUX; Chaume; Coteaux de l'AUBANCE; Coteaux du LAYON; and QUARTS DE CHAUME. See also LOIRE, including map.

Savigny-lès-Beaune, a small town in BURGUNDY near Beaune, as *lès* (Old French for near) implies, with its own appellation for red

wine and a little white. The reds are agreeable, rivalling those of BEAUNE itself, but lack the depth and character of wines from villages such as Pommard or Volnay more prominently sited on the LIMESTONE escarpment.

The village is divided by the river Rhoin. Those vineyards on the southern side, including PREMIERS CRUS Les Peuillets, Les Narbantons, Les Rouvrettes, and Les Marconnets, are on sandy soil and produce wines similar to those of Beaune, although lighter. Those on the other side of the village, towards Pernand-Vergelesses, including Les Lavières and Les Vergelesses, are on stonier soil.

An engraving dating from 1703 at the Château de Savigny describes the wines as nourishing, theological, and disease-defying— 'nourrissants, théologiques et morbifuges'. A little white wine is produced from Chardonnay. Chandon de Briailles is the leading producer based here.

See also CÔTE D'OR, and map under BURGUNDY. J.T.C.M.

Savoie, eastern French alpine region on the border with Switzerland, sometimes Anglicized to **Savoy**, comprising the two *départements* Savoie and Haute-Savoie together with small parts of neighbouring Ain and Isère. This dramatic countryside is so popular with visitors for both winter sports and summer relaxation that only a small amount of the wine ever leaves the region.

Such was the influence of the House of Savoy at one time that Savoie and much of northern Italy were part of the same kingdom. This may help to explain Savoie's particularly distinctive family of apparently indigenous vine varieties. Most Savoie wines are white and are sold under the much-ramified appellation **Vin de Savoie**, although CRÉPY, SEYSSEL, and ROUSSETTE de Savoie have their own appellations. Crépy and Seyssel are specific areas, while Roussette denotes those wines made from ALTESSE, Savoie's finest white grape variety, produced anywhere in the Vin de Savoie zone.

Much of the terrain here is too mountainous for viticulture and the Savoie vineyards tend to be widely dispersed, clustered in the flatter, more sheltered parts of the region. Some vineyards are on the banks of the river RHÔNE as it flows from lake Geneva towards the wine region known as the Rhône valley. Seyssel is here as well as the communes of CHAUTAGNE and JONGIEUX, two of the 17 CRUS which can append their names to the appellation Vin de Savoie.

South of here, close to the town of CHAMBÉRY, famous for its VERMOUTH, is a cluster of CRUS whose names may be more familiar to some wine enthusiasts than the main appellation itself: ABYMES, APREMONT, ARBIN, CHIGNIN, CRUET, and MONTMÉLIAN.

Further north, in Haute Savoie the Chasselas grape predominates in a cluster of vineyards on the southeastern shores of lake Geneva and makes a range of light, almost Swiss wines under the names of the crus MARIGNAN, Marin, RIPAILLE, and the appellation Crépy. Towards Chamonix, the isolated cru of AYZE (which Michelin insists is Ayse) makes still and sparkling wine from the obscure GRINGET variety.

The characteristics of these Vins de Savoie and the environments in which they are produced are sufficiently different to justify their being granted separate appellations. Total vineyard area for the Vin de Savoie appellation increased from about 1,650 ha/4,075 acres in 1990 to around 1,800 ha in 2005. About two-thirds of production is white: crisp, delicate, lightly scented, often chaptalized in the Swiss manner, and essentially alpine. The most widely planted variety is JACQUÈRE, popular with growers because of its productivity. Chardonnay is grown in some parts, and some producers are experimenting with BARREL MATURATION, but the finest varieties are ALTESSE, with its own appellation ROUSSETTE DE SAVOIE, and limited plantings of ROUSSANNE, or Bergeron, responsible for the cru CHIGNIN BERGERON.

Most of Savoie's wines are VARIETAL and, among reds, Gamay and Pinot Noir imported from Beaujolais and Burgundy respectively can be perfectly respectable, if light, examplars. Most inspiring, however, is MONDEUSE, with its deep colour, peppery flavour, and slight bitterness. Mondeuse grown at Arbin has a particular reputation, and such wines go well with the local cheese-dominated cuisine. Leading producers include Dom de St-Christophe, Louis Magnin, and André et Michel Quénard.

A small amount of sparkling wine may be sold as **Mousseux de Savoie** and **Pétillant de Savoie**.

See also the Vins du BUGEY made just over the border in the Ain *département*.   J.R. & W.L.

George, R., *French Country Wines* (London, 1990).
Messiez, M., *Les Vignobles de pays du Mont-Blanc—Savoie, Valais, Val d'Aoste* (Quart, Vallée d'Aoste, 1998).

scale, types of insects which attack grapevines, comprising at least 13 different species. Scale insects feed by sucking sap, and heavy infestations can weaken vine VIGOUR. Some scale insects excrete honeydew, which can spoil any bunches because a black, sooty mould usually grows on the honeydew. If many bunches are affected, this may taint the resultant wine.   R.E.S.

Scandinavia, part of northern Europe which includes Norway, Sweden, Denmark, Finland, and Iceland. Of these countries, only DENMARK has a liberal attitude towards alcoholic drinks and their sale—and also has vineyards. Elsewhere wine has been sold by state MONOPOLIES, which has had the effect of restricting choice. High levels of TAXATION have made the lot of the Scandinavian wine

drinker even harder, although Scandinavian cellars provide famously good, if slow, conditions for wine BOTTLE AGEING. The climate may be unsuitably cold for vine-growing, but can be excellent for STORING WINE.

Scheurebe is the one early 20th-century GERMAN CROSSING that deserves attention from any connoisseur, and the only one named after the prolific vine breeder Dr Georg Scheu, the original director of the viticultural institute at Alzey in Rheinhessen. Sometimes called simply **Scheu**, it was developed with specific, sandy, Rheinhessen soils around Dienheim in mind but has achieved its greatest popularity in the PFALZ. Although recent DNA PROFILING suggests otherwise, Scheurebe is thought to have been a Silvaner × Riesling cross, but it is much more than a riper, more productive replica of Riesling. Provided it reaches full maturity (like such other German crossings as BACCHUS and ORTEGA it is distinctly unappetizing if picked too early), Scheurebe wines have their own exuberant, racy flavours of blackcurrants or even rich grapefruit. It is one of the few varietal parvenus countenanced by quality-conscious German wine producers, not just because it can easily reach high PRÄDIKAT levels of ripeness, but because these are so delicately counterbalanced with the nerve of acidity—perhaps not quite so much as in an equivalent Riesling—but enough to preserve the wine for many years in bottle. Furthermore, for all its inherent aromatic exuberance, Scheurebe also follows the noble cousin Riesling in reflecting soil and mesoclimate, generating for example some striking and site-typical variations not just in the Pfalz, but in Franken, and in rare instances along the Nahe and around Boppart in the Mittelrhein.

Despite its distinct virtues and distinctive flavours, Scheurebe has been in steady decline in Germany over recent decades, slipping to 2,200 ha/5,400 acres by 2003. This may be because it is associated with sweet wine, which is unfashionable in Germany, particularly in the Pfalz and Franken. Such prejudice seems unwarranted. Estates such as Müller-Catoir, Pfeffingen, and Lingenfelder in the Pfalz and Wirsching in Franken have for more than 20 years vinified impressive, full-bodied dry Scheurebe. (Dr Becker even makes a respectable sparkling version in Scheurebe's home base in Dienheim.) Since the mid 1990s, some notable Pfalz estates have reintroduced Scheurebe, in some cases just after having ripped it out. If the quality of the best wines as well as the passionate pronouncements of propagandists such as Rainer Lingenfelder begin to exert influence on German wine politics and FASHION, there might yet be a Scheurebe renaissance.

The variety is also grown in southern Austria, where it is known as SÄMLING 88 and can make fine sweet wines such as those of Alois Kracher.   J.R. & D.S.

Schiava, Italian name for several undistinguished dark-skinned grape varieties known as Vernatsch by the German speakers of Alto Adige, or Südtirol as they would call it; and as TROLLINGER in the German region of Württemberg, where they are widely grown. The name Schiava, meaning 'slave', is thought by some to indicate Slavic origins.

The Schiava group is most planted in TRENTINO-ALTO ADIGE in northern Italy, where several forms were recently characterized as genetically distinct cultivars by DNA PROFILING at Milan. The most common is **Schiava Grossa** (Grossvernatsch), which is extremely productive but is not associated with wines of any real character or concentration. Plantings are in decline as the lighter style of wine produced by Schiava, once highly prized by the Swiss market, has lost favour. DNA PROFILING showed it is a parent of MUSCAT HAMBURG.

Schiava Gentile (Kleinvernatsch) produces better quality, aromatic wines from smaller grapes. The most celebrated, and least productive, clone is Tschaggele. Schiava-based wines in general are definitely less fashionable than a generation ago, when they enjoyed much popularity in Austria and southern Germany and, as vineyards in Trentino-Alto Adige are being replanted, it is frequently being replaced by INTERNATIONAL VARIETIES.

Schiava grapes are found in most of the non-varietal light red wines of Trentino-Alto Adige.

Schilcher, rosé wine found mainly in Western Styria in AUSTRIA that is light, acid, fruity and made from Blauer Wildbacher grapes.

Schillerwein, pink wine speciality from blending red and white wines made in the WÜRTTEMBERG region in Germany. The term is also used in German SWITZERLAND for a similar sort of wine.

Schioppettino, red grape variety native to the FRIULI region of north east Italy. It probably originated in the border area between Prepotto and SLOVENIA, where wine made from Schioppettino is cited in a marriage ceremony in 1282. In spite of official attempts to encourage its replanting, Schioppettino was substantially neglected after the PHYLLOXERA epidemic of the late 19th century in favour of the new imports from France: Merlot, Cabernet Franc, and Cabernet Sauvignon. It seemed destined to disappear until a EUROPEAN UNION decree of 1978 authorized its cultivation in the province of Udine (see also PIGNOLO). The wine is deeply coloured, medium bodied, with an attractively aromatic richness hinting at violets combined with a certain peppery quality reminiscent of the RHÔNE. Although vine plantings and therefore wine production are still limited, and concentrated in the COLLI ORIENTALI, the potential seems notable. Prepotto is considered its elective home, but quite good quality has also come from the Buttrio-Manzano area. D.T.

schist, a large group of coarsely crystalline metamorphic rocks that can be split into thin layers because their micaceous minerals have become aligned. The history of the DOURO valley in northern Portugal demonstrates the role played by schist (see also DELIMITATION). The schists in this terrain split and crumble easily, and are set in the midst of a tumbled, wild country which is otherwise almost entirely GRANITE. Schist is otherwise an uncommon rock type beneath vineyards, but occurs in PRIORAT, CÔTE RÔTIE, and in some parts of northern ALSACE. The French word *schiste* means SLATE as well as schist, and is sometimes used loosely to mean SHALE. J.M.H.

Schloss Johannisberg, German wine estate in the RHEINGAU with a history closely interlinked with that of the entire region. Around 1100, the Benedictine monks of Mainz built a monastery on the site, the first in the Rheingau. In 1130, the hill, monastery, and village were renamed Johannisberg after St John the Baptist. In 1716, the abbey was purchased by Konstantin von Buttlar, the prince-abbot of Fulda. Neglected vineyards were restored and planted, in particular with the Riesling grape, an important and innovative move which eventually led to the variety's being known in some parts of the world (notably modern California) as Johannisberg Riesling. Legend has it that Schloss Johannisberg played an important role in the discovery of BOTRYTIZED wines. Grapes affected by NOBLE ROT were first harvested at Johannisberg unwittingly, leading the administrator to record on 10 April 1776: 'I have never tasted such a wine before.' The discovery gave rise to the AUSLESE, BEERENAUSLESE, and TROCKENBEERENAUSLESE styles. In 1802, Johannisberg became secularized and the property of the prince of Orange. It was won four years later by Napoleon, who presented it to Marshal Kellerman, duke of Valmy, who owned it until 1813. From 1813 to 1815, the property was administered by the allies Russia, Prussia, and Austria; it was then given to the Habsburg Emperor Francis I of Austria at the Vienna Congress. In 1816, the emperor presented it to his State Chancellor Clemens Wenzeslaus, prince of Metternich-Winneburg, a gift which entailed an obligation to pay an annual tithe of the harvest to the Habsburgs or their legal successors. Today Schloss Johannisberg belongs to the Austrian state chancellor's great-grandson, Prince Paul Alfons of Metternich-Winneburg.

In 1811, Peter Arnold Mumm, a successful banker and wine merchant, purchased the entire Schloss Johannisberg vintage for 32,000 florins. He made a healthy profit and decided to invest in the estate. Ever since there has been a close association between the Mumm wine estate and Schloss Johannis-

berg and today they are run in tandem under the same ownership, with the wine of both estates made at von Mumm's cellars and the administration based at Schloss Johannisberg. Of von Mumm's 59 ha/145 acres of vineyards, 83 per cent are planted with Riesling and the remainder with Pinot Noir. Of the seven vineyard sites belonging to Johannisberg, three are almost totally owned by the von Mumm estate, Schwarzenstein, Hansenberg, and Mittelhölle, while they also own a sizeable share of the remaining four: Hölle, Klaus, Goldatzel, and Vogelsang. In addition, the estate owns parts of the Berg Schlossberg, Rottland, and Roseneck vineyards in Rüdesheim; the Klauserweg in Geisenheim; and the Hollenberg, Hinterkirch, and Frankenthal in Assmannshausen. The vineyards of Schloss Johannisberg itself cover an area of 86 acres, and are planted entirely to Riesling but were not ranked among Germany's finest in the late 1980s and early 1990s.

See also GERMAN HISTORY. S.A.

Schönburger, pink-berried 1979 GERMAN CROSSING with Pinot Noir, Chasselas Rosé, and Muscat Hamburg among its antecedents which has been more useful to the wine industry of ENGLAND than to its native Germany, where it is hardly grown. It has good disease resistance, yields reasonably well, and its tendency to lack acidity is a positive advantage as far from the equator as Kent and Somerset. Its wines are white and relatively full bodied.

Schoonmaker, Frank (1905–76), highly influential American wine writer and wine merchant. Born in South Dakota, he first became interested in wine when researching travel books in Europe in the late 1920s. Immediately after the Repeal of PROHIBITION, he wrote a series of wine articles for the *New Yorker* which were published as *The Complete Wine Book* in 1934. Soon afterwards he founded an eponymous wine import company and travelled extensively, becoming noted for his abilities as a judge of young wines, his espousal of DOMAINE BOTTLING in Burgundy, and his expertise in German wines. An early advocate of American wines, he was highly critical of the habitual GENERIC naming of them. In the 1940s, he was hired as consultant to the large California producer Almaden, for whom he created the best-selling VARIETAL Grenache Rosé, having been inspired by the French wine TAVEL. Schoonmaker employed Alexis LICHINE, who was to occupy a very similar, if not more public, post immediately before the Second World War and the two men were to publish the first editions of their respective wine encyclopedias in 1964 and 1967. He published five wine books and numerous shorter works on wine.

Bespaloff, A., *The New Frank Schoonmaker Encyclopedia of Wine* (New York, 1988).

Schwarzriesling, or 'black Riesling', is a German synonym for Pinot MEUNIER. Now

grown on a total of more than 2,500 ha/5,700 acres, it is most common in WÜRTTEMBERG, which has its own minor, low-yielding mutation called Samtrot, literally 'red velvet'.

Sciacarello (sometimes written **Sciaccarello**) is a speciality of the French island of CORSICA. The grape variety is capable of producing deep-flavoured if not necessarily deep-coloured reds and fine rosés that can smell of the island's herby scrubland. The vine has good disease resistance and thrives particularly successfully on the granitic soils in the south west around Ajaccio and Sartène. It buds and ripens late and may well have been imported by the Romans but no one has yet identified its Italian cousin. Only a few hundred hectares remain on the island, and it is now much less important than NIELLUCCIO.

science. For long it was maintained that WINE-MAKING was an art, but the proportion of the world's wine made by individuals with no grasp of the basic principles of OENOLOGY has shrunk rapidly. Meanwhile, the vineyards of the world are increasingly managed by individuals who have been taught at least the rudiments of the science of VITICULTURE. By the late 1980s, it had even become difficult to discuss wine with many of those who grow and make it without being conversant with a wide range of scientific terms and concepts, including a host of measurements such as PH, TA, RS, GA (GALLIC ACID), and IPT (indice des polyphénols totaux). The dramatically improved overall quality of wine since ACADEME took a role in teaching and researching wine-related subjects is eloquent testimony to the beneficial effect of the increasingly scientific approach of all those involved with wine. As in all fields, however, the best scientists are often those who seek to explain rather than dominate, and in OLD WORLD regions whose wines have been admired for centuries, the best results are often obtained by those who combine scientific knowledge with a respect for TRADITION. For specific applications of science, see, for example, DNA PROFILING, GLOBAL POSITIONING SYSTEMS, GLYCOSYL-GLUCOSE, REVERSE OSMOSIS, and MINERALS.

scion, in viticulture, is the piece of the fruiting vine that is grafted on to the quite separate ROOTSTOCK. When grown, such a plant will have the leaves and desired fruit of one VINE VARIETY (Cabernet Sauvignon, for example), but the roots of the other, rootstock, variety (110 Richter, for example). GRAFTING is very widely used in viticulture since rootstocks are needed to combat soil-borne pests or diseases, such as PHYLLOXERA and NEMATODES. B.G.C.

scoring individual wines, and many aspects of their production, is an increasingly popular pursuit with professionals and amateurs alike.

Scoring vineyards

Vineyards may be scored to assess their suitability for producing good-quality wine grapes. The most famous system is that used in the DOURO valley of northern Portugal for PORT production. Vineyards are allocated points, from plus 1,680 for the most promising, to minus 3,340 for the least favoured, taking into account YIELD, SOIL TYPE, MESOCLIMATE, vineyard maintenance, GRAPE COMPOSITION, ENCÉPAGEMENT, and VINE AGE. Highly classified vineyards are entitled to produce as much wine as they are able each year, while the production from lower classifications can be restricted to meet demand. The CHAMPAGNE region of north east France has a similar, if considerably less precise, system whereby whole COMMUNES are given a percentage rating, between 80 and 100.

Vineyards may also be scored for their adherence to organic growing principles as part of their accreditation (see ORGANIC VITICULTURE).

For the growing practice of linking price to grape quality, see PRICE.

A newer system for assessing vineyards for potential wine quality was developed by this writer in New Zealand. This is based on the principles of CANOPY MANAGEMENT, but also allows for assessment of vine VIGOUR. This system, or variants of it, is being used as the basis of assessing both the quality and price of grapes in Australia and New Zealand. R.E.S.

Smart, R. E., and Robinson, M., *Sunlight into Wine: A Handbook for Winegrape Canopy Management* (Adelaide, 1991).

Scoring wines

The increasing tendency of WINE WRITERS to award scores to individual wines is understandable. Wine drinkers are, happily, presented with more choice than ever before. Unhappily, we all seem to have less and less time to make decisions. A score which can be interpreted at a glance is one obvious way of solving those two problems. Some of the various scoring systems are discussed in NUMBERS AND WINE but the prototype is that used by the American writer Robert PARKER, who did much to promote the controversial but highly influential practice of awarding points out of 100 between 50 and 100, modelled on the American high school system. Effectively, wines of interest to readers of his and the many other publications which now use points out of 100 are those which score more than 85. Serious COLLECTORS and INVESTORS tend to concentrate on those which score more than 90, or even 95, so-called TROPHY WINES.

These scores have had an extraordinary effect on the wine market. They enable potential INVESTORS, and even FINE WINE TRADERS, to take a position and affect the market, without necessarily knowing anything whatever about wine. They empower new wine drinkers to make decisions independently of wine traders.

And because, unlike TASTING NOTES, they can be understood universally, they can guide potential wine buyers all over the world, thus opening up the wine market in general and the fine wine market in particular to countries without an established wine culture. Scores undoubtedly played a part in ASIA's dramatic and inflationary entry into the fine wine market in the mid 1990s, for example, just as they have since encouraged interest from new wine buyers not just in established markets but in expanding markets such as South America and Russia.

The implications of extending the market so widely for a commodity as finite as fine wine are obvious, and the effect on prices for the most restricted fine wines of all, the so-called Bordeaux MICROCHÂTEAUX, has in some cases been to lift them even above those of the traditional FIRST GROWTHS. It is reasonable to assume that the price differential between the cheapest and the most expensive wines will widen yet further.

Quite apart from price and demand, however, scoring has affected the wines themselves. Because scores are invariably arrived at as a result of a comparative TASTING, of many different samples of the same sort of wine, it is inevitable that some of the more subtle wines are overlooked and, particularly with red wines, the deeper-coloured, stronger, more concentrated wines are likely to make a more immediate, and often favourable, impression. Of course this varies with the taster(s), but it is undeniable that, overall, wines have become more alcoholic, more concentrated, smoother-textured, and less acid—all as an indirect result of comparative tasting.

There is another, more obviously beneficial, effect of the prevalence of scoring individual wines. New, good, wine producers can make a name for themselves and their wines very

much faster than has ever been the case. A sample judiciously sent to Robert Parker and the *Wine Spectator* can ensure immediate commercial success, and direct communication with potential consumers, within the vast American market, for example. The downside for wine drinkers, of course, is that prices will inevitably rise steeply.

Wine scores, as those who award them try vainly to point out, can never substitute for description. But in the 1990s at least, the market seemed much more interested in numbers than words.

For more detail of the practicalities and weaknesses of wine scoring, see NUMBERS AND WINE.

Scotland, northern British country too cold for vine-growing but with some fine wine merchants and a long tradition of importing wine, notably from Bordeaux.

Kay, B., and Maclean, C., *Knee Deep in Claret* (Edinburgh, 1983).

Scott Henry, a vine-TRAINING SYSTEM whereby the CANOPY is divided vertically and the shoots are separated and trained in two curtains, upwards and downwards (see diagram). The canopy is about 2 m/6.5 ft tall, and the leaves are held in place by foliage wires. The system was developed by an Oregon vine-grower of the same name in the early 1980s when his vines were so vigorous that both yield and quality were reduced. The system was originally developed for CANE PRUNING; a later spur-pruned version has now generally been superseded by the SMART–DYSON system.

The Scott Henry system is suited to moderate-vigour vineyards with row spacing of about 2 m or more. It became widely used in many New World countries in the 1990s because of its suitability for MECHANICAL

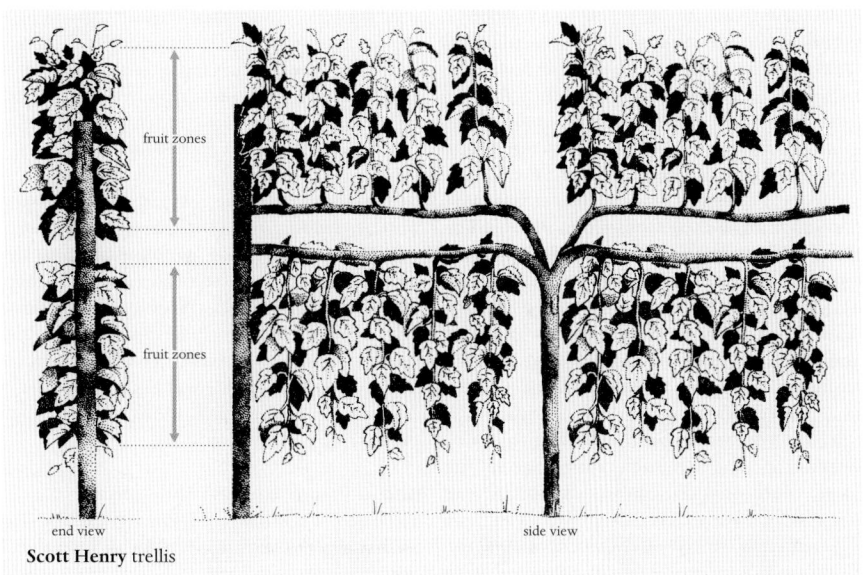

Scott Henry trellis

HARVESTING and potential for improving wine quality.   R.E.S.

Smart, R. E., and Robinson, M., *Sunlight into Wine: A Handbook for Winegrape Canopy Management* (Adelaide, 1991).

screw caps, sometimes known as ROTEs (roll-on, tamper-evident), and often by the brand name Stelvin®, have emerged as the leading competitor to cork in terms of performance if not yet in terms of usage. They are cheaper than top-quality corks, and no capsules are needed, but the cost of new bottling equipment and bottles can deter smaller producers.

Screw caps as an alternative to cork for bottling wine were first used in 1959, when a French company introduced the Stelcap-vin, which had already proved successful for a range of spirits and liqueurs. The rights to manufacture this closure were acquired by Australian Consolidated Industries Ltd (ACI) in 1970 and it was renamed Stelvin® for the Australian market. ACI trials of four closures (three screw caps with different wadding materials and a cork for comparison) on three red and three white wines, first reported in 1976, concluded that screw caps were ideal for sealing wine bottles but only if they had the right wadding material and a satisfactory seal between bottle and cap. An industry push towards screw caps at that time lost momentum, partly through lack of consumer acceptance, and partly because awareness of the shortcomings of cork were not as widespread then as now.

As dissatisfaction with cork gradually increased, there were sporadic attempts to introduce screw caps to the market place. In 2000, winemakers in Australia's Clare Valley, famous for its Rieslings, banded together to take a stand on the issue. The Clare winemakers, many of whose wines are made in a style that shows up any cork-related faults particularly transparently, had to overcome a significant logistical obstacle: at the time, no Australian supplier could offer bottles and caps of the required style and quality. As a result, they had to gather together enough like-minded producers willing to adopt screw caps to generate the threshold order of 250 000 bottles from Pechiney in France. Their effort made the headlines and the momentum increased so that by the 2004 vintage some 200 million wine bottles were sealed with screw caps in Australia. This Clare initiative prompted New Zealand winemakers to form the New Zealand Screw Cap Initiative in 2001. By 2004, an estimated 70 per cent of New Zealand's wines were sealed under screw cap, up from just 1 per cent three years earlier. Whether or not screw caps establish such a presence in the more traditional European wine-producing countries remains to be seen.

Screw caps consist of two components: the aluminium alloy cap, which comes attached to the sleeve, and the liner, which is made of an expanded polyethylene wadding. The liner typically contains a tin foil layer that acts as a barrier to gas exchange, overlain by a PVDC (Saranex®) film that provides an inert surface in contact with the wine. In production, the screw cap is not screwed on but is held down tight over the end of the bottle and a set of rollers moulds the sleeve of the cap over the ridges on the outside of the top portion of the neck. This holds the whole closure firmly in place. The cap itself is joined to the sleeve by a series of small metal bridges, which are broken when the cap is twisted. To obtain a tight seal it is especially important that the lip of the bottle be free of defects.

Although they are often considered as a single closure type, not all screw caps are alike. The most significant difference is in the nature of the liner. In some caps this lacks the tin foil layer; the closure therefore has higher oxygen transfer properties and is less suited to long AGEING of wines.

Trials have shown that screw caps with tin/Saranex® liners provide a more effective barrier to gas exchange than all but the very best corks. Screw caps are inert and can last many years (and have kept white and red wine in good condition for more than 30 years). They also have the advantage of requiring no equipment to remove them. Some industry commentators predict that they will eventually replace corks for almost all wine types. However, controversy remains over whether they are the best closure type for red wines destined for long ageing and for some styles of white wine. While some scientists argue that wine ageing is an anaerobic process most successful in the complete absence of extrinsic oxygen, others suspect that the tiny amounts of oxygen transmitted by the less than perfect seal of corks—or screw caps without a metal foil layer in the lining—is important for red wine ageing. Because the chemistry of wine ageing is incompletely understood, it is likely that only long-term trials with red wines sealed under different closures will settle this debate.   J.A.G. & T.M.S.

Goode, J., *Wine Science* (London, 2005).

Scuppernong, the best known of the vine varieties belonging to the *Vitis rotundifolia* species of the MUSCADINIA genus planted in the south east of the United States and in Mexico. Like other Muscadines, the grapes (in this case bronze-skinned) are very distinctively flavoured. Some well-structured sweet, dark gold wines are made which taste markedly different from the much more widely known product of VINIFERA varieties.

sec is French for DRY while **secco** is Italian and **seco** is Spanish and Portuguese for dry. See SWEETNESS and DOSAGE for official European Union sugar levels.

secateurs, hand-held scissors used for winter PRUNING of vines. Two-handled secateurs are used for cutting larger-diameter and older wood of the vine. Pruning can be faster, more effective, and less tiring with pneumatic or electric secateurs (see MECHANICAL PRUNING).
                                                    R.E.S.

secbutyl-methoxypyrazine (SBMP). See METHOXYPYRAZINES.

sécheresse, French for both DROUGHT and WATER STRESS. When the stress is mild, this is a recognized contributor to wine quality.

secondary fermentation, a fermentation that occurs after the completion of the normal alcoholic FERMENTATION. This may be a FERMENTATION IN BOTTLE, or the evolution of carbon dioxide that accompanies a MALOLACTIC FERMENTATION, or simply a restarting in the winery of an alcoholic fermentation of a wine that still contains fermentable SUGARS. This can happen if, for example, there is a rise in TEMPERATURE or a more powerful YEAST is introduced. The GOVERNO wine-making process associated with TOSCANA in central Italy is another example of deliberate provocation of a secondary fermentation.

second crop, crop that may form after the main one on secondary LATERAL SHOOTS. The amount of lateral shoot growth is correlated with that of the whole shoot; on weak shoots, laterals can barely be seen, while on long, strong shoots and at NODES near the cut ends of trimmed shoots, laterals can grow so strongly as to resemble primary shoots. Second crop bunches are most abundant on strong laterals. In some varieties, a second crop is rare, but on others, such as PINOT NOIR and many MUSCAT varieties, this crop can be large. Usually the existence of a second crop is a negative factor for wine quality since its development runs six to eight weeks behind the main crop and it competes for nutrients, as well as complicating the development and control of VINE PESTS and VINE DISEASES. Worse, it adds a proportion of immature fruit to the HARVEST (especially where MECHANICAL HARVESTERS are used), which usually adversely affects the quality of the resulting wine.   B.G.C.

second growth. See the CLASSIFICATION of Bordeaux.

second wines are wines made from cuves or vines considered not good enough for the principal product, or *grand vin*, made at an estate. The phenomenon was born in BORDEAUX in the 18th century, and was revived in the early 20th century at Ch LAFITE but was hardly developed commercially until the 1980s, when increased competition forced ever more rigorous selection at the ASSEMBLAGE stage. Some of the more famous second wines are Ch LATOUR's Les Forts de Latour and Ch MARGAUX's Pavillon

Rouge. (The branded wine MOUTON CADET began life as the second wine of Ch MOUTON-ROTHSCHILD, which much more recently created Le Petit Mouton as its modern second wine.) Second wines are likely to contain the produce of young vines together with the least satisfactory lots. In particularly unsuccessful VINTAGES, some properties make no *grand vin* at all so that the second wine, or *second vin*, is the only wine produced that year. In general, a second wine from a poor vintage (when a *grand vin* was also bottled) is rarely an exciting drink, but a second wine from a quality-conscious producer in a good vintage can represent good value—so long as it is not consumed alongside the *grand vin*. Some proprietors have even developed labels for their third wines.

sediment, the solid material which settles to the bottom of any wine container, whether it be a bottle or a vat, tank, cask, or barrel. This sediment is a very heterogeneous mixture which at the start of wine-making consists mainly of dead yeast cells (the gross LEES), the insoluble fragments of grape pulp and skin, and the seeds that settle out of new wine. At subsequent stages it consists of TARTRATES and, from red wines, PHENOLIC polymers, as well as any insoluble materials added to assist CLARIFICATION or to facilitate FILTRATION.

Sediments in bottled wines are relatively rare, and usually signal a fine wine that has already spent some years in bottle. So unaccustomed have modern wine consumers become to sediment that many (erroneously) view it as a fault. Many winemakers therefore take great pains to ensure, through clarification, STABILIZATION, and filtration, that the great majority of wines made today, and virtually all of those designed to be drunk within their first few years, will remain free of sediment for at least a few years. Wines designed for long periods of BOTTLE AGEING, on the other hand, frequently deposit crystals of tartrates, white in white wines and dyed red or black in red wines. Red wines, in addition, deposit some PIGMENTED TANNINS that are the result of phenolic polymerization. The heavy deposits in bottles of vintage port are a particularly dramatic example of this phenomenon. Winemakers deliberately leave more tartrates and phenolics in wines designed for long ageing in bottle so that they are able to develop the compounds that constitute BOUQUET. A bottle of wine containing sediment needs special care before SERVING.

Environmentally responsible disposal of sediment from wine production presents a problem: skins, stems, seeds, and pulp residues can be processed for the recovery of small amounts of sugar, tartaric acid, colouring agents (see OENOCYANIN), and grapeseed oil, but in most wine regions the costs of recovery greatly exceed the market value of the recovered substances. The solid sediments are frequently returned to the vineyard and worked into the soil instead. See also WINERY WASTE.

See also the quite different phenomenon of BOTTLE DEPOSIT. A.D.W.

seedling, the young plant that develops when a seed germinates. Grape seeds have tiny embryos which develop rapidly as the seed germinates, growing a freely branching tap-root and a shoot. The growth of seedlings is important in VINE BREEDING, but not otherwise in commercial viticulture, as vines are propagated from cuttings (see VEGETATIVE PROPAGATION). B.G.C.

seeds. For details of grape seeds, see GRAPE.

For details of the historical evidence provided by finds of ancient grape seeds (and other parts of the grape), see PALAEO-ETHNOBOTANY.

Ségalin is a recent INRA crossing of Jurançon Noir × Portugais Bleu which has good colour, structure, and flavour and is authorized in SOUTH WEST FRANCE. (See also CALADOC, CHASAN, PORTAN.)

Ségurs, important family in the history of the BORDEAUX wine region, originally from the village of PAUILLAC. In 1670, Jacques de Ségur, a notary who was a councillor of the legal Parlement of Bordeaux, became the second husband of Jeanne de Gasq, daughter of another Parlement councillor. As a dowry she brought with her the *seigneurie* of LAFITE, to add to others he had including Calon in ST-ESTÈPHE, and an estate of about 1,000 ha/2,470 acres to the north of Pauillac. Their son Alexandre de Ségur was born in 1674. His father died in 1691, but in 1695 he married Marie-Thérèse de Clausel, the heiress of LATOUR, which gave him all the southern part of Pauillac and another very large estate. Their son, the future Marquis Nicolas-Alexandre de Ségur, was born in Bordeaux in 1697, and when his father died in 1716 he took over the very large domaine, which then included the farm of MOUTON before it passed in the 1730s to the Marquis de Branne. The marquis, a vice-president of the Bordeaux Parlement, was said to have been called 'le prince de vignes' by Louis XV. He is reputed to have said, 'I make wine at Lafite and Latour, but my heart is at Calon,' and on the label of Ch Calon Ségur there is today a large heart. When he died in Paris in 1755 he left a substantial fortune. He had four daughters and their descendants owned Ch Latour until it was acquired by HARVEYS of Bristol and, principally, 'the family interest of Lord Cowdray' (the British Pearson group) in 1962. E.P.-R.

Penning-Rowsell, E., *The Wines of Bordeaux* (6th edn, 1989).

Seibel, common name for many of the FRENCH HYBRID vine varieties bred by Albert Seibel of the Ardèche in the late 19th and early 20th centuries, most of them identified by number and many of them given a more colloquially appealing name. Seibel 5455 is more often called PLANTET, for example, while Seibel 4986 is Rayon d'Or and Seibel 9549 is DE CHAUNAC. The variety once known simply as Seibel in France is Seibel 7053, which is known as CHANCELLOR in New York state. Small quantities of various Seibels such as VIGNOLES are planted in some cooler wine regions around the world.

Sekt, word used in German-speaking countries to describe quality SPARKLING WINE as defined by the EUROPEAN UNION. Its etymology is uncertain but is popularly said to be the result of a misunderstanding between the German classical actor Ludwig Devrient and a waiter at Lutter & Wegener's restaurant in Berlin in November 1825. Devrient, a regular customer for CHAMPAGNE, quoting from his Falstaff role, cried 'Give me a cup of SACK, rogue. Is there no virtue extant?' (*I Henry IV*, Act II, Scene iv). He was served with his usual champagne, and a new meaning for the word Sekt had been invented, which, according to the authority on German sparkling wine, Professor Dr Helmut Arntz, had been accepted throughout Germany by 1900.

Of Germany's total annual sparkling wine production of more than 375 million bottles (a figure that steadily increases), 94 per cent can be described as Sekt, of which about 85 per cent is white. Most Sekt is very inexpensive.

About 90 per cent of Sekt made in Germany is based on Italian, French, or other non-German still wine, and most is sold as dry (TROCKEN) or medium dry (HALBTROCKEN). The average Sekt consumer buys a branded wine, and is interested neither in its method of production (98 per cent acquires its sparkle by the tank method; see SPARKLING WINE-MAKING), nor in the origin of the base wine.

Deutscher Sekt, however, is made solely from German base wine, and it is in this small part of the market where there is fine, elegant sparkling wine, mainly BRUT or extra dry.

In the 1980s, there was a marked increase in the number of enterprises (including producers' associations, co-operative cellars, and private estates) making Deutscher Sekt for the wine lover—as opposed to the less demanding traditional sparkling wine market. These new high-quality sparkling wines are sold under the name of a region and vineyard of origin, bearing a vintage and almost always the name of a vine variety. The acidity and finesse of RIESLING in particular make a most stylish sparkling wine, and Sekt from the PINOT family is also very successful. Sparkling wines from a private estate may be made either by a contract Sekt manufacturer or by the estate itself. Where an estate is making its own Sekt, the relatively small volume of liquid involved requires the wine to be BOTTLE FERMENTED.

Austria's Sekt producers, many of which were established during the time of the Austro-Hungarian empire, are based in Vienna and source their grapes from the Weinviertel in Lower Austria. I.J. & D.S.

selection, increasingly important ingredient in maximizing wine quality whereby only the finest grapes or lots of wine are allowed in the final blend. See TRIAGE and ASSEMBLAGE.

Selection, official German wine designation since 2000 for a class of German wines that taste dry (having a maximum 12 g/l RESIDUAL SUGAR if Riesling, otherwise 9 g/l) and are hand-harvested from fruit cropped at no more than 60 hl/ha and no less than 12.2 per cent POTENTIAL ALCOHOL. The area to be picked for Selection must be declared by the vintner no later than 1 May of the growing season. See also GERMAN WINE LAW.

sélection clonale is French for CLONAL SELECTION, while **sélection massale** is French for MASS SELECTION.

Sélection de Grains Nobles, the richest, most sumptuous ripeness category of ALSACE wines.

selfed vine, a plant created by one VINE VARIETY crossed to itself. This is not a very successful breeding strategy, since most varieties carry deleterious recessive genes, and there is consequently a strong inbreeding depression. This is avoided by crossing unrelated vines, which is a feature of successful VINE BREEDING. See also NEW VARIETIES. R.E.S.

semi-carbonic maceration, winemaking process which involves a short CARBONIC MACERATION phase followed by a normal alcoholic FERMENTATION. In such wines, winemakers rely upon an initial period of maceration of the grapes in an anaerobic (oxygen-free) atmosphere, followed by crushing and traditional fermentation of the resultant MUST. The great majority of Beaujolais NOUVEAU and most other PRIMEUR wines are made in this fashion. Such wines have a very distinct aroma reminiscent of bananas or kirsch, arising from the distinctive by-products of the intracellular fermentation occurring within the whole berries and without yeast, during the first phase.

Before the days of mechanical CRUSHER-DESTEMMERS, most red wines would have been made by a very similar process. Under these circumstances, in which whole grape clusters or bunches were placed into fermentation vessels, some juice was liberated from berries broken during handling. Ambient YEASTS then set off spontaneous FERMENTATION of this small amount of juice, thus generating the CARBON DIOXIDE which provided the anaerobic conditions necessary to sustain carbonic maceration of the intact berries distributed throughout the vessel. The extent of the carbonic maceration was therefore affected by the size and shape of the vessel; the deeper the vessel, the greater the proportion of grapes in an anaerobic atmosphere, and the greater proportion that underwent carbonic maceration. A.D.W. & P.L.

Sémillon, often written plain **Semillon** in non-francophone countries, a golden grape variety from south west France, is one of the unsung heroes of white wine production. Blended with its traditional partner SAUVIGNON BLANC, this golden-, sometimes copper-, berried vine variety is the key ingredient in SAUTERNES, arguably the world's longest-living unfortified wine, as it is in most of the great dry whites of Graves (see PESSAC-LÉOGNAN). Unblended, in Australia's HUNTER VALLEY, it is responsible for one of the most idiosyncratic and historic wine types exclusive to the New World. Thanks to its widespread establishment in Bordeaux and much of the southern hemisphere, it has been the world's most planted white grape variety capable of top-quality wine production but is not fashionable and has been declining in importance.

Outside Sauternes, Sémillon seems destined to play a supplementary role. The wines it produces tend to fatness and, although capable of ageing, have little aroma in youth. Sauvignon Blanc, with its internationally recognized name, strong aroma, high acidity, but slight lack of substance, fills in all obvious gaps. But if Sémillon had traditionally been blended with Sauvignon, it attracted another blend-mate in the early 1990s, if for entirely different reasons. Sémillon does not exactly complement Chardonnay so much as provide neutral padding for it and, in a world desperate for Chardonnay, Sémillon found itself the passive ingredient in commercially motivated blends sometimes, even, called SemChard—most notably but not exclusively in Australia. And here, as elsewhere in the New World, Sémillon's weight, and high yield, make it a popular base for commercial blends.

As a vine, Sémillon is easy to cultivate. It is almost as vigorous as Sauvignon Blanc with particularly deep green leaves, but flowers slightly later and is not particularly susceptible to COULURE. Nor is it a victim of disease, apart from rot, which, in favourable conditions, is the blessed NOBLE ROT rather than the destructive GREY ROT. This makes Sémillon a particularly productive vine, which was doubtless a factor in its widespread popularity.

Its greatest concentration is still in Bordeaux, where, although total plantings halved between 1968 (when it was the most planted variety of either hue) and 1988, it was still the most planted white grape variety by far with nearly 9,200 ha/22,700 acres in 2000. On the left bank of the Garonne, in the Graves, Sauternes, and its enclave BARSAC, Sémillon still outnumbers Sauvignon in almost exactly the traditional proportions of four to one, while in the ENTRE-DEUX-MERS, where most Sémillon has been planted, Sauvignon (together with varieties for financially more rewarding red wine production) is fast replacing it.

In the great, long-lived dry whites of Graves and Pessac-Léognan, Sémillon usually predominates and inspires rich, golden, honeyed, viscous wines quite unlike any Sémillons made elsewhere. Low yields, old vines, oak ageing, and Sauvignon all play their part. In Sauternes, Sémillon's great attribute is its proneness to noble rot. This special mould, *Botrytis cinerea*, concentrates sugars and acids and shrinks yields so that the best of the resulting wines such as Ch d'YQUEM may continue to evolve for centuries. Again, oak ageing deepens Sémillon's already relatively deep gold (really ripe grapes may almost look pink). Thus one of Sémillon's disadvantages, a tendency to overcrop, is eliminated. Similar, but usually less exciting, sweet whites, the most ordinary made simply by stopping fermentation or adding sweet grape must, are made in the nearby appellations of CADILLAC, CÉRONS, LOUPIAC, and STE-CROIX-DU-MONT.

In quantitative terms, however, Sémillon's most common expression, other than as basic white for local consumption in CHILE, is as an important ingredient in basic white bordeaux, although it is increasingly used as ballast to the nervier, more aromatic Sauvignon Blanc.

Like Sauvignon Blanc, Sémillon is allowed in many other appellations for dry and sweet whites of SOUTH WEST FRANCE but is perhaps most notable in qualitative terms in MONBAZILLAC. Thanks to its (declining) importance throughout BERGERAC, Sémillon is still the most planted variety in the Dordogne, its 4,000 ha in 2004 still, just, outnumbering Merlot, and is the most planted white-berried variety in the Lot-et-Garonne *département*, although little of it finds its way into APPELLATION CONTRÔLÉE wine. It is technically allowed in most appellations of PROVENCE, but has made little impact on the vineyards of the Midi, where acidity is at a premium.

Sémillon's other great sphere of influence has been South America in general and Chile in particular, where there were still about 1,800 ha/4,400 acres planted in 2004 even though Chilean varietal Semillon is very, very much rarer than Sauvignon.

In North America, Sémillon is generally rather scorned, lacking the image of Sauvignon Blanc, although a significant number of producers use the former to add interest to the latter. Total area planted in California had fallen to about 1,200 acres/490 ha by 2004. A few producers have experimented with producing BOTRYTIZED wines in the image of Sauternes from it and it also adds weight to Sauvignon in white bordeaux MERITAGE blends. Historically LIVERMORE VALLEY has produced the best fruit for dry white VARIETALS, while it can also perform well in parts of NAPA, SONOMA, and Santa Ynez Valley in SANTA BARBARA county. Sémillon also has a relatively significant presence—50 acres (to Sauvignon's 1,000)—in Washington, where it often displays grassy, Sauvignon-like aromas, but is taken seriously by the likes of L'Ecole 41.

It is quite widespread, without being particularly important, throughout eastern Europe, but it is in both SOUTH AFRICA and AUSTRALIA where Sémillon had a particularly glorious past. In 1822, 93 per cent of all South African vineyard was planted with this variety, imported from Bordeaux. So common was it then that it was simply called Wyndruif, or 'wine grape'. It was subsequently called Green Grape, a reference to its abnormally green foliage, but has been declining in importance so that today the Semillion, as it is sometimes called, accounts for hardly 1 per cent of Cape vineyards with just over 1,000 ha in total. The recent growth in Sauvignon Blanc plantings in South Africa has brought an increase in sophisticated white BORDEAUX BLENDS, often oak aged.

While all the Australian pale grape focus was on the growth of Chardonnay (and the decline of Riesling) since the early 1990s, Semillon's plantings stealthily grew from 2,713 ha/6,700 acres in 1990 to 6,200 ha/15,300 acres in 2004. Its role in the Hunter Valley is well known: to produce low alcohol (10.5 to 11 per cent) wines with unmatched cellaring potential. It has also enjoyed success as a wooded style, blended with Sauvignon Blanc, in the Adelaide Hills and Margaret River. But its position in the Barossa Valley, where it is the most widely planted white variety, comes as a surprise. Likewise, its plantings have grown rapidly in the Riverland and Riverina. See AUSTRALIA for more details.

In New Zealand, where its 2006 total plantings of 270 ha make it very minor compared with Sauvignon Blanc, Sémillon often demonstrates the same sort of grassiness as in Washington state. Some interesting sweet wines have been coaxed out of Sémillon in Gisborne and Hawkes Bay.

The variety was also exported to Israel to establish vineyards there at the end of the 19ᵗʰ century.

Brook, S., *Sauvignon Blanc and Sémillon* (London, 1992).

sequence of wines to be served. See ORDER.

Serbia, the largest and most central republic in what was YUGOSLAVIA (see map in that article) and now in a loose federation with MONTENEGRO. Serbia, excluding VOJVODINA, produces around one-third of all ex-Yugoslavian wine, both red and white—about 1.6 million hl from 73,000 ha according to OIV figures for 2002. Between the flattish countryside around Belgrade and Skopje in MACEDONIA is a series of valleys, some with easily worked, fertile,

open slopes and some wilder, steeper, and more wooded. Broadly, the vineyard trail follows the Morava river from the Danube due south towards its source in the mountains of KOSOVO, leaving the border hills of BULGARIA to the east.

Immediately to the south of Belgrade in the Šumadija-Velika Morava region, the rather ordinary white grape variety SMEDEREVKA grows, around the town of Smederevo, from which it takes its name. Here too, and to the south in the Oplenac subregion, a more ambitious range of white grape varieties are now growing. SAUVIGNON BLANC with a potentially excellent intensity of flavour can be produced, but winemaking practices frequently leave much to be desired.

Serbia is at its best producing red wines. Its own PROKUPAC grape, used by itself or blended with more internationally known varieties, grows in all Serbian wine regions. It predominates in the small but ancient district of Zupa in the Zapadna Morava region not far south of Belgrade. The wines are well balanced, pleasantly coloured, and can demonstrate an easy, if sometimes light, fruit quality which can be used to bolster PINOT NOIR and GAMAY. While Pinot Noir wines can have a very true BOUQUET, occasionally more reminiscent of German than French versions, 'Gamay' rarely shows at all true to its Beaujolais archetype, tending rather to produce a coarse, overextracted red if it is not well handled.

Many of the most promising red wine vineyards lie in the region of Juzna Morava from around the towns of Niš, Leskovac, and Vranje towards the Bulgarian border. Healthy CABERNET and MERLOT grapes are being grown here, often in big privately owned vineyards as well as some belonging to bottler/brand owners who correctly identified the region as climatically suitable for these classic Bordeaux red wine varieties in the early 1980s; their investments should be bearing fruit now that the vineyards are mature.

Further east, by the Bulgarian border, Timok is also being developed as a vineyard area with similar potential for classic reds, although without a modern vinification plant, potential cannot be transferred from vineyard to bottle.   A.H.M.

Sercial, Portuguese white grape variety once quite commonly planted on the island of Madeira but subsequently used to denote the lightest, most acid, latest-maturing style of MADEIRA rather than the grape variety from which it was made. Sercial is the last of the white grapes to ripen on the island and retains its characteristically high level of acidity almost wherever it is planted. On the Portuguese mainland it is known as ESGANA CÃO.

Servanin, old, very rare red wine grape of the Isère tributary of the southern Rhône.

service of wine. See SERVING WINE and SOMMELIERS.

serving wine involves a number of fairly obvious steps, but mastering each of them can maximize the pleasure given by any individual wine. See OPENING THE BOTTLE, BREATHING, DECANTING, GLASSES, FOOD AND WINE MATCHING, ORDER, and LEFTOVER WINE for details of these aspects of serving wine.

Perhaps the least obvious requirement of anyone serving wine is that they appear superficially mean, by filling glasses no more than two-thirds, and preferably less than half, full. This allows energetic agitation of the glass if necessary, and enables the all-important AROMA to collect in the upper part of the bowl (see TASTING).

The factor which probably has the single greatest effect on how a wine tastes, however, is temperature, and this is a factor which can be controlled by whoever is serving. Because of the well-known general rule that white (and rosé) wines should be chilled and red wines should be served at something called room temperature, and because many refrigerators are set at relatively low temperatures, in practice many white wines are served too cool and many red wines dangerously warm. See TEMPERATURE for some guidance on specific recommended serving temperatures for certain styles of wine. Few wine drinkers have wine thermometers, however, so a certain amount of experimentation with ways of modifying serving temperatures is advisable.

Cooling wine in a refrigerator is much slower than cooling wine in a container holding water and ice (two hours rather than 30 minutes to cool an average bottle from 22 to 10 °C/50 °F). An ice box would do the job faster but has the serious disadvantage that the bottle will be cooled right down to icebox temperature if left there. This may well freeze the wine and push the cork out. Some main refrigerator cabinets are, furthermore, set at such low temperatures that wines may emerge simply too cool. (Note that a container full of ice cubes but no water is not a very effective cooler as it provides relatively little contact between the bottle and the cooling medium.)

It is a happy coincidence that the ideal cellar temperature, around 15 °C/59 °F, is also ideal for serving a wide range of wines such as complex dry white wines and light-bodied red wines, and is not so low that it takes long to warm tannic red wines to a suitable serving temperature.

In cool climates, wine drinkers may have difficulty in warming bottles of red wine to suitably high temperatures for serving. This is one argument for decanting, into a decanter warmed with hot water. Direct heat should not be applied to a bottle, and even contact with a radiator can heat wine to such a dangerously high temperature that some of the more volatile FLAVOUR COMPOUNDS are lost and the ALCOHOL can dominate so that the wine tastes unbalanced.

One of the most effective ways of warming wine, whether intentionally or not, is to pour it out into glasses in a relatively warm environment or, even faster, to pour the wine into a decanter or glasses which previously held hot water. This effect is accentuated if the glasses are cupped in human hands. For this reason, it is usually wise to serve wines slightly cooler than the ideal temperature at which they are best appreciated. Warming wine in microwave ovens can be effective if the oven is big enough, and if great care is taken not to overheat the wine and to remove the CAPSULE if it is metallic.

Ambient temperature, or even the precise temperature of the taster, can affect how a wine tastes: crisp, light wines taste either delightfully refreshing or disappointingly meagre when the taster is hot or cold respectively. On the other hand, in tropical climates, where both temperature and humidity are high, it can be almost impossible to find suitable conditions in which to serve even the finest red wine as, without air conditioning, drinks heat up so rapidly that a red wine has either to be served well chilled or run the risk of being almost MULLED. Light red wines with marked ACIDITY such as BEAUJOLAIS and reds from cooler climates such as the LOIRE, NEW ZEALAND, TASMANIA, NEW YORK, and CANADA can taste much more appetizing in hot climates than CLASSED GROWTH red bordeaux or fine burgundy.

One final aspect of serving wine, about which the Latin poet HORACE wrote extensively, is matching wine to guest and occasion. Part of what might generally be called CONNOISSEURSHIP, this is a pleasure associated with wine which can be almost as great as drinking it, but is too complex to prescribe or describe here.

See also TASTING for the special conditions of serving wine for this particular purpose, a very different one from actually drinking it.

set, the process by which vine flowers become berries. See FRUIT SET.

setting, stage in plant development after FLOWERING when the flowers either fall off or adhere to the plant and fruits start to grow.

For more information. See FRUIT SET.

settling, the wine-making operation of holding MUST or wine in a vessel so that suspended solids fall to the bottom. The French term *débourbage* is sometimes used for the most common example of settling, to begin the CLARIFICATION of freshly drained and pressed white musts before FERMENTATION. Fermentation is delayed by adding SULFUR DIOXIDE and by cooling before pumping to the settling vessel.

Red wines, whose skins are included in the fermentation vessel, are settled after fermentation and MACERATION when the purpose is to remove not just grape debris but also dead yeast cells, or LEES.

Settling is governed by such factors as the size of the solid particles, the difference in their DENSITY from that of the liquid, and the extent to which the liquid moves within the settling vessel. Because must and cloudy grape juice are so much denser than wine, they are much more difficult to settle. Solids as large and dense as seeds and stem fragments settle rapidly. Finely divided pulp debris and dead yeast cells which are very small settle more slowly and are easily resuspended by currents within the settling vessel. COLLOIDS, which have dimensions of large molecular size, are very slow to settle because their movement is influenced by the smallest liquid movement within the vessel. The settling of colloids can be greatly assisted by the addition of clarifying or FINING agents such as BENTONITE, which adsorbs them and grows them into complexes large enough to settle. Settling of particularly viscous grape juice can also be encouraged by the addition of ENZYMES designed to break chains of PECTINS.

Settling may also be part of processing and finishing in wine-making. Unless time is a critical factor, settling, possibly followed by a light filtration, is preferable to the more expensive options of CENTRIFUGATION or FILTRATION.

A.D.W.

Setúbal, port on the Sado estuary south of Lisbon, the capital of PORTUGAL, is also the name of a Portuguese FORTIFIED WINE with its own DOC region (see map under PORTUGAL). It is made predominantly from Moscatel (MUSCAT) grapes growing on the lower slopes of the Arrábida hills and the plain around the town of Palmela. The region was officially demarcated in 1907 for Moscatel de Setúbal. In the past producers could blend in up to 30 per cent of other white grape varieties, ostensibly to lend acidity. This is no longer permitted under the rules of the DOC which were revised in 1997 and 1999 in line with EUROPEAN UNION regulations that for a wine to be labelled with a variety it must be made with at least 85 per cent of the specified grape. The principal type of Moscatel is the so called Moscatel de Setúbal or Moscatel Graúdo (MUSCAT OF ALEXANDRIA) but a tiny amount of pink skinned Moscatel Roxo is bottled separately as a varietal wine. To begin with, Setúbal is made in much the same way as many other sweet fortified wines, the FERMENTATION being arrested with GRAPE SPIRIT. After vinification, however, pungent Muscat grape skins are left to macerate in the wine for five or six months, which imparts a taste of fresh dessert grapes and gives Setúbal its intense aroma and flavour. Most Setúbal is bottled after spending four or five years in large oak vats, by which time the wine has

an amber-orange colour and a spicy, raisiny character. Small quantities, however, are bottled after 20 years or more in cask, by which time the wine is deep brown and has a rich, grapey intensity. José Maria da FONSECA Successores, by far the largest producer of Setúbal, hold stocks of wine dating back to the mid 19th century, which are occasionally bottled and released for sale.

For details of the unfortified wines made on the Setúbal peninsula, see TERRAS DO SADO.

R.J.M.

Mayson, R., *The Wines and Vineyards of Portugal* (London, 2003).

Severny, Russian vine variety developed at the All-Russia Potapenko Institute from a Malengra seedling with a member of the famously cold-hardy VITIS *amurensis* vine species native to Mongolia.

See also SAPERAVI Severny and CABERNET SEVERNY. There is small-scale experimentation with a Severny variety in CANADA, where winters are as harsh as in Russia.

sexual propagation, reproduction by seed involving the union of male and female sex cells (POLLEN and ovule respectively). The important feature of this type of propagation is that the parent plants are genetically different, so the seedling is in turn genetically different from either parent. Throughout the world of nature, this is how genetic diversity is continued, permitting selection of those progeny best suited to survive. In commercial viticulture, this process has been circumvented by propagating selected, desirable individuals and propagating them vegetatively (see VEGETATIVE PROPAGATION). The varieties RIESLING and CABERNET SAUVIGNON are excellent examples of this process. Originally sexual seedlings, they have been propagated asexually for many centuries with substantially the same genetic constitution. Sexual propagation is used for VINE BREEDING throughout the world to produce NEW VARIETIES. Success depends on selecting suitable parents, and many years of painstaking evaluation.

B.G.C.

Seyssel, small wine appellation within the eastern French region of SAVOIE producing light, dry and off-dry white still and sparkling wines from vineyards concentrated on the steep slopes of the upper Rhône valley about 40 km/25 miles downriver of Geneva. This is one of the few Savoie wines to escape the region itself, notably in the form of sparkling Seyssel from producers Varichon et Clerc (owned by the giant BOISSET group). ALTESSE (still often called Roussette) is the dominant grape variety here, although the local MOLETTE is also grown for sparkling wines, which must contain at least 10 per cent Altesse, whose Savoyard roots are said to be here. The sparkling wines need to have a POTENTIAL ALCOHOL of just 8.5 per cent at harvest and must be BOTTLE

FERMENTED in the region. They are light, refreshing, and the best can develop in bottle, but most are drunk locally.

Seyssuel, village on which the dynamic VIN DE PAYS des Collines Rhodaniennes is based.

Seyval Blanc, useful light-skinned FRENCH HYBRID, the most widely planted SEYVE-VILLARD hybrid, number 5276, the result of crossing two SEIBEL hybrids. It is productive, ripens early and is well suited to relatively cool climates such as that of ENGLAND, where it is the single most planted vine variety. It is also popular in CANADA and, to a lesser extent, in the eastern UNITED STATES, notably in NEW YORK state. Its crisp white wines have no hint of FOXY flavour and can even benefit from BARREL MATURATION but, because the variety has some non-VINIFERA genes, it is outlawed by European Union authorities for QUALITY WINE production. In the UK it is mainly used for blending and is particularly successful for sparkling wine production. As a sparkling wine, it can (somewhat unexpectedly in view of its hybrid origins) be labelled as Quality Sparkling Wine.

Seyve-Villard, series of about 100 FRENCH HYBRIDS developed by hybridizer Bertille Seyve and his partner and father-in-law Victor Villard, much planted in France in the mid 20th century. Perhaps the most famous, however, is SEYVAL BLANC.

Sforzato, Sfursat, Sfurzat, all names for a DRIED GRAPE WINE made in the VALTELLINA zone in the far north of Italy.

SGN. See SÉLECTION DE GRAINS NOBLES.

shade, the absence of sunlight in a vine CANOPY. This is due to leaves blocking out sunlight, as the transmission of light through one leaf is less than 10 per cent of full sunlight. In most vineyards, the blocking leaves are other vine leaves, but occasionally they may be the leaves of weeds or even adjacent trees, as occurs in the VINHO VERDE region of Portugal. For most vineyards in the world, shade is due to vigorous vines being trained to restrictive vine-TRAINING SYSTEMS.

Sunlight levels in the centre of dense canopies with many leaf layers can be as little as 1 per cent of the levels above the canopy. At this very low level of light, PHOTOSYNTHESIS is almost zero, and in time the leaves turn yellow and then fall off. Leaves deep in the canopy also experience filtered sunlight with altered colour composition, in that red light is reduced and far red light relatively enriched. The ratio of red to far red light can act as a signal system for the vine and other plants, and may play a role in the vine's response to shade. Since the vine evolved in forests, it has mechanisms like tendrils for avoiding shade by climbing towards the sunlight.

Shade can reduce both vine YIELD and grape quality. Shade has been shown to reduce bud INITIATION, BUDBREAK, FRUIT SET, and hence berry number, as well as BERRY SIZE. So shade can reduce yield dramatically, and yields may increase up to threefold where shade has been removed by improving the training system and allowing the sunlight in.

Many studies around the world, for a range of vine varieties in a range of climates, have also demonstrated that shade alters grape chemical composition and reduces wine quality. Shade is known to decrease levels of SUGARS, ANTHOCYANINS, PHENOLICS, TARTARIC ACID, monoterpene FLAVOUR COMPOUNDS, and apparent varietal character. Other negative effects of shade on wine quality are increases in MALIC ACID, PH, POTASSIUM, and in the so-called HERBACEOUS characters. Shaded fruit is also more susceptible to BOTRYTIS BUNCH ROT and POWDERY MILDEW. CANOPY MANAGEMENT can reduce shade in the canopy and, in high-vigour vineyards, may improve yield and quality simultaneously.   R.E.S.

Champagnol, F., *Éléments de physiologie de la vigne et de viticulture générale* (St-Gely-du-Fesc, 1984).
Smart, R. E., and Robinson, M., *Sunlight into Wine: A Handbook for Winegrape Canopy Management* (Adelaide, 1991).

shale, a dark, clay-grade sediment which splits easily into very thin layers. It is much more easily crumbled than SLATE. Both as a ROCK and in SOILS, shale behaves as a clay for cultivation.   J.M.H.

shanking, see BUNCHSTEM NECROSIS.

sharpshooters, insects which feed on vine foliage and can carry important vine diseases. See LEAFHOPPERS.

shatter. See FRUIT SET.

Shaulis, Nelson (1913–2000). Born in Pennsylvania, Nelson Shaulis was destined to have a greater impact on world viticultural practice than most of his scientific contemporaries. His eastern US origin was appropriate, as this was the region of his greatest influence. He began his career at the Agricultural Experiment Station, Geneva (see CORNELL), in 1948, and retired as Professor of Viticulture in 1978.

Shaulis can be considered the father of CANOPY MANAGEMENT, although the term was not coined by him. In his early experiments with CONCORD grapevines, he realized that limits to YIELD and RIPENESS were a consequence of SHADE within the grapevine CANOPY. The solution was simple enough in hindsight, but revolutionary for the time. By dividing a dense canopy into two less dense canopies, shade could be reduced, and suddenly yield and ripeness could be dramatically increased. The new TRELLIS design, first published in the mid 1960s, was called the GENEVA DOUBLE CURTAIN.

As an important further extension to this work, Shaulis and colleagues developed the world's first MECHANICAL HARVESTER of grapes and subsequently undertook important primary research on MECHANICAL PRUNING.

The impact of Shaulis's research has been felt in every country of the world, but the NEW WORLD, free of yield limits, has benefited most. Shaulis influenced many younger researchers who made canopy management an accepted practice globally, including Carbonneau from Bordeaux (see LYRE), Intrieri and Cargnello from Italy, Kliewer from California, and Smart from New Zealand.   R.E.S.

Shenandoah Valley is the name of two AVA wine regions. For details of the California region, see SIERRA FOOTHILLS. There is also a Shenandoah Valley in VIRGINIA.

sherry, seriously undervalued but slowly reawakening fortified wine from the region around the city of Jerez de la Frontera in ANDALUCÍA, south west Spain. 'Sherry' was used as a generic term for a wide range of FORTIFIED WINES made from white grapes, but in the mid 1990s the sherry trade successfully campaigned to have the name restricted—at least within the EUROPEAN UNION—to the produce of the Jerez DO. (For details of other once-prominent producers of similar wine styles, see CYPRUS, SOUTH AFRICA, and BRITISH WINE.)

Sherry production was steady in the late 1990s, after a sharp reduction earlier in the decade, averaging about 700,000 hl/18.5 million gal a year. Apart from Spain, the two most important markets for sherry have been the Netherlands and Great Britain.

Sherry is the English corruption of the word Jerez, while Xérès is its French counterpart and is also the French name for sherry. The words Jerez-Xérès-Sherry appear on all bottles of sherry, on paper seals granted by the CONSEJO REGULADOR to guarantee the origin of the wine. Within the Jerez DO, there are three centres for sherry maturation: JEREZ DE LA FRONTERA, SANLÚCAR DE BARRAMEDA, and PUERTO DE SANTA MARÍA, each of which imparts subtle differences to the wines. Throughout this article, the types of wine made naturally in sherry BODEGAS are referred to in lower case italics, as in *oloroso*, while the sherry styles created for commercial use on the label are referred to with a capital letter, as in Oloroso.

Sherry is initially made to conform to two principal types: pale, dry *fino* (or, in Sanlúcar de Barrameda, *manzanilla*), which ages under the influence of the film-forming yeast FLOR, and dark, full, but dry *oloroso*. All sherry styles found on labels (Manzanilla, Fino, Amontillado, Oloroso, Pale Cream, Cream, etc., in generally ascending order of BODY) are derived from these two main types. The only exception is Palo Cortado, which is a naturally resulting intermediate type and style between Amontillado and Oloroso. PEDRO XIMÉNEZ is an intensely sweet wine, usually for blending, made from the grape variety of the same name often grown outside the sherry region.

History

Jerez is one of the oldest wine-producing towns in Spain. It may well have been established by the PHOENICIANS who founded the nearby port of Cádiz in 1110 BC. The Phoenicians were followed by the CARTHAGINIANS, who were in turn succeeded by the ROMANS. Iberian viticulture advanced rapidly under Roman rule and Jerez has been identified as the Roman city of Ceritium. After the Romans were expelled around AD 400, southern Iberia was overrun by successive tribes of Vandals and Visigoths, who were in turn defeated by the Moors after the battle of Guadalete in 711 (see ISLAM). The Moors held sway over Andalucía for seven centuries and their influence is still evident, not least in the architecture of Seville, Cordoba, and Granada. Under Moorish domination, Jerez grew in size and stature. The town was named 'Seris' and this later evolved into Jerez de la Frontera, when it stood on the frontier of the two warring kingdoms during Christian reconquest in the 13th century.

Viticulture, which continued despite Moorish occupation, was revitalized by the Christians, although the region around Jerez continued to be plagued by war until the 15th century. Exports began and, in spite of periodic setbacks, trade with England and France was well established by the 1490s, when it was declared that wines shipped abroad would be free from local tax. In 1492, the Jews were expelled from Spain, their vineyards were confiscated, and foreigners, many of them English, took their place as merchants. Certain basic quality controls were established, including the capacity of the sherry cask or BUTT, which has not changed to this day.

At the end of the 15th century, after Christopher Columbus had discovered America from his base in Andalucía, the sherry town of Sanlúcar de Barrameda became an important port for the new transatlantic trade and in the 16th century large quantities of wine were shipped to the Americas from Jerez. In his book *Sherry,* Julian Jeffs speculates that Vino de Jerez (sherry) was almost certainly the first wine to enter North America.

Relations between England and Spain began to deteriorate in the 16th century and, although trade continued, the colony of English merchants trading from Sanlúcar began to suffer privations. In 1585, after a number of raids by Sir Francis Drake and his fleet, English merchants were arrested and their possessions seized. Exports ceased. Two years later, in an attack on Cádiz, Drake both 'singed the King of Spain's beard' and captured '2,900 pipes' of wine. This plunder helped to establish sherry as a popular drink in Elizabethan England.

After the death of Elizabeth I, trade became easier and 'sacke', or SACK, returned to royal circles. The English colony re-established itself and prospered, often by shipping poor-quality wines.

By the 17th century, 'sherris-sack' was well established in England and was drunk by Samuel Pepys, who in 1662 records that he mixed sherry and MÁLAGA. Pepys visited the English colony in Sanlúcar de Barrameda in 1683. At that time, until the construction of a railway in the mid 19th century, most of the sherry bodegas were located on the coast at Sanlúcar and Puerto de Santa María for easy export.

The sherry industry suffered many setbacks at the beginning of the 18th century, when England and Spain became embroiled in a series of conflicts beginning in 1702 with the War of the Spanish Succession. The METHUEN TREATY (1703) diverted trade to Portugal and a series of restrictive measures imposed by the Gremio or Wine Growers Guild of Jerez sent merchants to Málaga in search of wine. However, the latter half of the century was an era of increasing prosperity stimulated by the arrival of a number of French and British merchants. The firms of Osborne, Duff Gordon, and Garvey date from this period.

The Peninsular Wars (1808–14) devastated Jerez. Andalucía became a battleground, occupied for a time by the French, who pillaged the sherry bodegas and forced a number of families to flee to the relative safety of the Cádiz garrison. With the defeat of the French, merchants set about rebuilding their businesses with spectacular success. Pedro DOMECQ took over the firm of Juan Haurie in 1822 and Manuel María González Angel, founder of GONZÁLEZ BYASS, began trading in 1835. Sherry exports rose steadily from about 8,000 butts in the early years of the century to over 70,000 butts in 1873, a figure not exceeded again until the 1950s. In the 1850s, the sherry industry was greatly helped by the construction of a RAILWAY linking Jerez and Puerto de Santa María, and a number of merchants left their quayside bodegas. Many new producers took advantage of the sherry boom only to be wiped out by PHYLLOXERA and economic depression a few years later.

By the end of the 19th century, the sherry industry was on the brink of collapse. The boom gave rise to numerous spurious 'sherries' from South Africa, Australia, France—and from Germany, where a sherry-style potion was made from potato spirit. A spiral of price-cutting began and sherry was stretched with poor-quality wine imported from other parts of Spain. Demand fell as Victorian society refused sherry, alarmed by scare stories that the wine was detrimental to health. The predations of the phylloxera louse from 1894 helped to stabilize the market and the shippers who survived the depression held large stocks of unsold wine to tide them through the lean years when all the vineyards were replanted.

In 1910, the leading traders united to form the Sherry Shippers Association, which campaigned vigorously to restore the fortunes of the beleaguered industry. After the First World War exports returned to their late 19th century levels. In 1933, a CONSEJO REGULADOR was formed to protect and control the sherry industry and in 1935, a year before the outbreak of the Spanish Civil War, Jerez established its own DO region. The Civil War (1936–9) had little effect on sherry exports, but trade collapsed during the Second World War.

The most dramatic episode in the recent history of sherry began in 1944 when Don Zoilo Ruiz-Mateos y Camacho, mayor of the town of Rota, bought out a small sherry stockholder whose business had suffered badly during the war. In the late 1950s, his son, the now legendary José María Ruiz-Mateos, secured a 99-year contract to supply the important BRAND owners HARVEYS of Bristol with all their sherry requirements. With help from the banks, he began buying up other bodegas and in 1961 established the Rumasa empire. In the 1970s, Ruiz-Mateos acquired substantial wine interests outside Jerez (see RIOJA), as well as in banking, construction, retailing, tourism, chemicals, and textiles. The group is said to have bought three banks in a single day. Although Ruiz-Mateos contributed greatly to the modernization of the Spanish wine industry, Rumasa initiated a price-cutting spiral which continued to blight the long-term interests of sherry well into the 1990s. Ruiz Mateos's empire building came to an abrupt end in 1983 when, fearing imminent collapse, the government nationalized Rumasa, which at that point controlled about a third of the sherry industry. Rumasa's component parts were subsequently returned to the private sector.

Since the mid 1980s, the sherry industry has been facing decline. The total vineyard area has been reduced to 10,350 ha/25,560 acres; less than half what it was at the end of the 1970s. Plots of sunflowers and cereals are now commonplace among the vines. In the early 1990s, with a worldwide market estimated to be around 1.09 million hl/28.7 million gal, stocks were drastically reduced as the sherry industry attempted to bring supply and demand back into balance.

Significantly, one of the main actors as the industry seeks to renovate and relaunch itself in the early 21st century is none other than Ruiz Mateos himself. He has rebuilt a sizeable group based on Garvey, with successive additions including the Spanish interests of Sandeman, and early signs of wine quality are promising. A few new names have appeared on the Jerez landscape, such as Tradición, Rey Fernando de Castilla, Dios Baco, and El Maestro Sierra. They have typically acquired older soleras from bodegas which either disappeared or were taken over by others.

Another leading actor has been the Estévez group, led by the idiosyncratic José Estévez (died 2005), the inventor of a controversial system to remove HISTAMINE from sherries. This group now includes Marqués del Real Tesoro, Tío Mateo, and Valdespino. Also showing signs of dynamism have been the Sanlúcar de Barrameda bodegas, from the giant Barbadillo to smaller ones such as Hidalgo-La Gitana and Pedro Romero.

Amid calls to rejuvenate the concept of sherry, including the promotion of a larger number of vintage-dated wines (a concept adopted by González Byass for some top-end Olorosos, Amontillados, and Palos Cortados), the Consejo Regulador responded in 2000 by creating two new categories of high quality sherry: VOS (Very Old Sherry or *Vinum Optimum Signatum*), for wines with an average age surpassing 20 years, and VORS (Very Old and Rare Sherry or *Vinum Optimum Rare Signatum*), for wines over 30, in four categories: Oloroso, Palo Cortado, Amontillado and Pedro Ximénez. Such methods as carbon dating were introduced to ascertain the age of the wines submitted by bodegas, and demanding blind tastings were instituted to accept or reject samples. This new category has stirred up fresh interest in sherry and qualified wines command high prices. But inevitably this is an elite category of minor presence on the market as most of the brands release just a few hundred bottles of their prized elixirs every year.

See also SPAIN, history, and SACK.

Geography and climate
The climate of the Jerez region is strongly influenced by its proximity to the Atlantic. Sea breezes from the gulf of Cádiz alleviate extremes. The oceanic influence is strongest in the coastal towns of Sanlúcar de Barrameda and Puerto de Santa María, where temperatures in July and August may be 10 °C/18 °F lower than in Jerez, 20 km/12 miles inland. Winters are mild and damp with most of the region's annual average rainfall of 650 mm/25 in falling between late autumn and spring. There is almost no rainfall between June and October. Summer temperatures often reach 30 °C inland, occasionally rising to 40 °C with the *levante*, a piercing, dry, dusty wind from the south east.

The vines are sustained during the dry summer months by the porous, white ALBARIZA soils that are at the heart of the Jerez DO. The demarcated region is roughly triangular in shape and extends from the town of Chiclana de Frontera in the south east to the river Guadalquivir in the north west, tapering inland. However, the best albariza soils cover a stretch of rolling country north of the river Guadalete between Jerez and Sanlúcar de Barrameda. These outcrops of albariza are known collectively as Jerez Superior and the majority of these vineyards are within the municipality

of Jerez de la Frontera, with secondary pockets around Sanlúcar de Barrameda, Puerto de Santa María, Chipiona, and Rota.

The albariza zone is divided into subdistricts. Those with the deepest, but not necessarily the most CALCAREOUS, albariza soils like the famous Balbaina, Macharnudo, Carrascal, and Añina districts produce the most delicate wines for the finest Finos and Manzanillas (see Wine-making below). The most calcareous soils, known as *tajón*, are generally unsatisfactory for viticulture because of potential CHLOROSIS. The finest albarizas include a proportion of sand and clay and tend to vary with depth, with a limestone content of 25 per cent or more on the surface rising to 60 per cent in the rooting zone 80 to 100 cm/39 in below the surface. In between the hills of albariza, barro soils have more clay and produce fuller, coarser wines and slightly higher yields. On the sandy soils known as arenas, yields are twice as great as on the albariza but the quality of the wine is poor. Arena soils were popular with growers at the end of the 19th century as the phylloxera louse found it difficult to survive in sand. However, with the recent rationalization of the sherry industry, viticulture is increasingly concentrated on the albariza soils and over 80 per cent of the region's vineyards are situated in Jerez Superior.

Viticulture and vine varieties
In the 19th century, a variety of different vines were planted around Jerez but, after phylloxera wiped out most of the vineyards in the 1890s, many varieties were never replanted. Only three varieties are now authorized for new vineyards in Jerez: PALOMINO, PEDRO XIMÉNEZ, and MUSCAT OF ALEXANDRIA. Of these, Palomino is the most important and accounts for around 95 per cent of the total vineyard area. There are in fact two types of Palomino: Palomino Basto (also known as the Palomino de Jerez) and Palomino Fino. Palomino Basto has largely been supplanted by Palomino Fino, which provides better YIELDS and is more resistant to disease. Palomino Fino has proved to be a particularly versatile grape and is used for most types of sherry.

Moscatel Gordo Blanco (Muscat of Alexandria) represents about 3 per cent of the Jerez vineyard and is planted principally in the more sandy soils on the coast around Chipiona. It is mainly used for sweetening although some producers make and market their own VARIETAL Moscatel wines.

Pedro Ximénez (known for short as PX) has given ground to Palomino and currently represents less than 100 ha/250 acres of vineyard since Palomino Fino is easier to cultivate. Most sweet wine is now made from Palomino although some smaller producers still maintain small PX SOLERAS which they bottle as a varietal wine. In recent years, special dispensation

has been granted for the, now routine, importation of PX must from MONTILLA-MORILES to compensate for the lack of PX in Jerez.

Since phylloxera swept through Jerez, all vines have been grafted onto American ROOTSTOCKS which are selected according to the soil's LIME content. In the past vines were planted in a hexagonal pattern known as *tresbolillo* but, with increasing MECHANIZATION, vineyards are planted in orderly rows at a maximum VINE DENSITY of 4,100 vines per ha (1,660 per acre). Yields from the Palomino are high, although the maximum permitted yield for the entire DO has been set at 80 hl/ha (4.5 tons/acre).

With the onset of mechanization, modern vineyards are trained on WIRES, although the PRUNING method, called *vara y pulgar*, is unchanged, and similar to the GUYOT system. A *vara* (meaning stick or branch) with seven or eight buds produces the current year's crop. The *pulgar* (meaning thumb) is a short shoot with one bud which will produce the following year's *vara*.

Wine-making
The HARVEST begins when the Palomino has reached a MUST WEIGHT of at least 11 °BAUMÉ, traditionally on 8 September. It lasts for about a month.

Grapes are loaded into plastic crates and transported to large automated wineries, where they are destalked and pressed. Most bodegas use horizontal plate or pneumatic PRESSES to control the extraction rate, which may not legally exceed 72.5 l/19 gal of juice from 100 kg/220 lb of grapes (16 per cent higher than the extraction rate permitted for CHAMPAGNE, for instance). Others, especially the COOPERATIVES, use continuous de-juicers which tend to produce coarser wines with more solids and PHENOLICS. Today acid levels are adjusted with the addition of TARTARIC ACID prior to fermentation, and cold STABILIZATION before bottling is usually essential.

After SETTLING or CENTRIFUGATION, fermentation generally takes place in temperature-controlled, stainless steel tanks, although a few shippers continue to ferment a small proportion of their wine in butt, mainly to impregnate and season new casks of American oak that are to be used for maturation. (New BARRELS are not valued in Jerez.)

The modernization of the sherry industry which began in the 1960s and continued through the 1970s and 1980s has removed much of the mysticism that once surrounded the production of sherry. The modern winemaker can predetermine which of the two initial sherry types—*fino* and *oloroso*—each lot of grapes becomes.

The first selection takes place in the vineyard. Wines for the best *finos* are sourced from older vines growing on the best albariza soils while *olorosos* are made from grapes grown on the heavier clays. Elegance is crucial to *finos*, also made from the best FREE-RUN juice, which has fewer impurities than the slightly coarser and more astringent juices from the press, which are set aside for *olorosos* or inferior *rayas*, particularly coarse *olorosos*. Wine destined for *fino* tends to be fermented at a lower temperature than that made for *oloroso*. Barrel-fermented wine is often too coarse and astringent for the production of *fino*.

The second selection takes place soon after the end of fermentation. Although many shippers producing table wine endeavour to persuade otherwise, Palomino-based wine is fairly flat and characterless with a natural alcohol content of 11 or 12 per cent. Depending on the style of the wine, sherry is fortified with grape spirit to between 15 or 15.5 and 22 per cent. The appearance of FLOR, the veil of yeast that forms on the surface of the wine and distinguishes *fino* from other styles of sherry, is determined by the degree of fortification. Growth is inhibited by an ALCOHOLIC STRENGTH much above 16 per cent. Wines destined to develop into *finos* are therefore fortified to 15 or 15.5 per cent. *Olorosos*, which mature without flor, are fortified to a higher strength of around 18 per cent.

The sherry bodegas are teeming with the flor YEAST strains. This beneficial FILM-FORMING YEAST grows naturally on the surface of the wine, although some houses now choose to cultivate their own flor culture. Butts used for *fino* are only partially filled to around five-sixths of their 600- to 650-l (160–70-gal) capacity because flor, which both protects the wine from OXIDATION and changes its character, feeds off OXYGEN as well as alcohol.

Flor is also extremely sensitive to heat and in the warm summer months it tends to die. In Montilla, for example, flor is reduced to a scum-like film in July and August, while in the cooler Jerez region it grows all the year round. However, there are significant climatic differences within the Jerez region (see Geography above). Flor grows more thickly and evenly in the cooler, more humid coastal towns of Sanlúcar de Barrameda and Puerto de Santa María than it does in the bodegas situated in Jerez de la Frontera itself. This accounts for many of the subtle differences in style between Jerez Fino, Puerto Fino, and Manzanilla outlined below.

Left to its own devices, flor would feed on the nutrients in the wine and die before having a profound influence on the wine's character. However, flor is kept alive in casks of *fino* for six years or more by continually replenishing the butt with younger wine, and replenishing the yeast nutrients. This is the basis of the SOLERA system, a method of fractional blending which, apart from nurturing flor in *fino*, also maintains a consistent style for other sherry styles.

A sherry solera comprises a number of groups of butts, each of which is known as a criadera. Wine is withdrawn from the group containing the oldest wine, which is itself

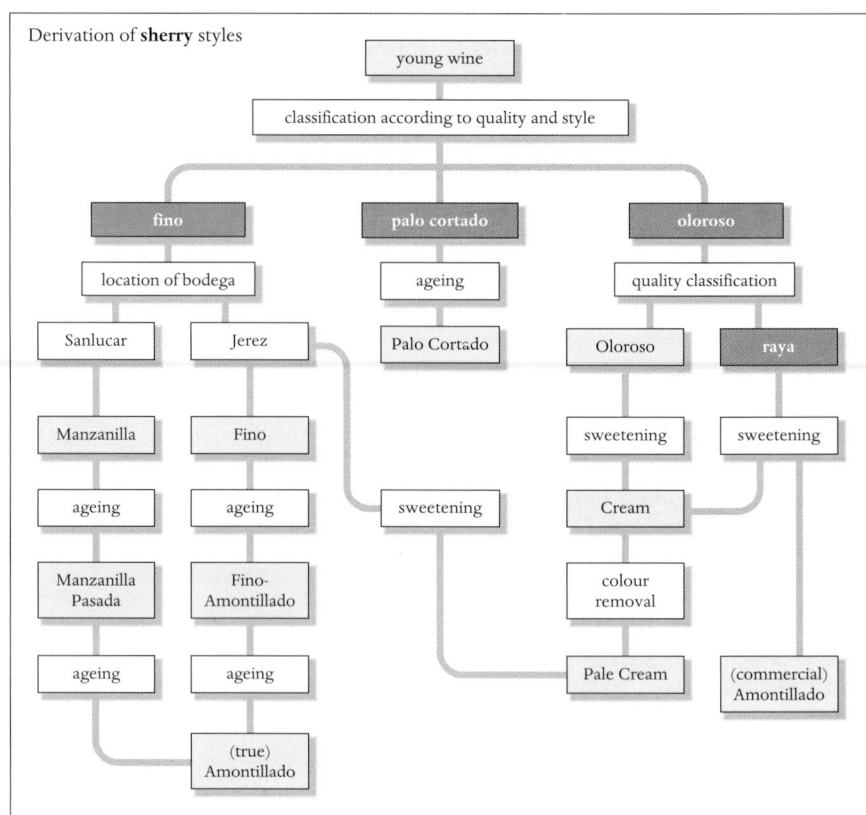

Derivation of **sherry** styles

called the solera. This is replenished from the butts that form the first criadera, which is in turn replenished by wine from the second criadera, a process known as 'running the scales'. Simple soleras are fed by three or four criaderas while more complex systems run to as many as 14. The whole system is fed with new wine from the most recent harvest. Up to 33 per cent of the wine in a solera may be withdrawn in any one year. *Fino* soleras need to be refreshed the most frequently, and by running the scales at regular intervals (usually two or three times a year) flor may be kept alive for eight to ten years.

Styles of sherry

The diagram above shows how commercial styles of sherry are made from the types of wine naturally formed.

Before bottling as Fino or Manzanilla styles of sherry, *finos* are filtered and fortified to a minimum of 15.5 per cent. Some of the more commercial BRANDS are slightly sweetened.

Finos which lose their covering of flor become a sherry type known as *amontillados*, turning amber in colour and changing in character due to greater contact with the air. *Amontillados* evolve naturally if the flor has exhausted its supply of nutrients, or the style may be induced if the flor is killed off by fortification to 16 per cent alcohol or above. A *fino* beginning to take on the characteristic of an *amontillado* may be bottled as a *fino-amontillado* or, in

the case of a wine from Sanlúcar de Barrameda, a Manzanilla Pasada. True Amontillados are completely dry and the finest examples age for many years in their own soleras. Most so-called 'Amontillados' are no more than medium dry sherries blended from inferior quality *rayas* and sweet wines, however (see AMONTILLADO).

Having been fortified to 18 per cent, *olorosos* on the other hand develop without recourse to flor. They age in greater contact with the air, turning dark brown and gaining in concentration with age. The alcoholic content increases with slow EVAPORATION such that the strength of an old *oloroso* may approach 24 per cent. In their natural state, *olorosos* are dry, although old wines may taste full and concentrated. *Rayas* (inferior *olorosos* used in blending) may be aged in the open air. A certain proportion of Oloroso on the market is natural, dry OLOROSO; the majority is sweet wine of various quality levels.

Sweet sherries, most of them styled Cream, are made in a number of different ways. The finest sweet sherries such as Oloroso dulce (sweet oloroso) are produced by blending intensely sweet wines made from sun-dried Pedro Ximénez grapes. However, today Palomino grapes are frequently dried to raisins under plastic tunnels, pressed, and fortified before fermentation to make a MISTELA. This is never as sweet or as powerfully concentrated as PX, but the method is widely used for the production of more commercial sherries. Commercial Cream sherries may be very ordinary blends to which sweetening and colouring wines have been added.

The darkest sherries may be adjusted with ARROPE grape concentrate, or *vino de color*, a dark, sweet syrup that has been prepared by boiling down fresh grape must. Pale Cream sherry, typically a blend of *fino* and sweet wine, is normally adjusted with RECTIFIED CONCENTRATED GRAPE MUST and fresh Palomino must, vacuum CONCENTRATED, and the colour removed with activated CHARCOAL. A few bodegas sweeten their wines with fortified Moscatel but this tends to produce a rather obvious, aromatic, grapey style of sherry.

In the early 2000s, two new designations were introduced, with some success, for particularly old sherries: VOS, Very Old Sherry or *Vinum Optimum Signatum*, for blends at least 20 years old and VORS, *Vinum Optimum Rare Signatum* or Very Rare Old Sherry, for blends at least 30 years old. This provided some incentive for the release, or re-branding, of some bodegas' greatest treasures.

Organization of the trade

Although few boundaries are visible, there are over 6,000 individual vineyards in Jerez farmed by over 5,000 different growers. A few sherry firms have vineyard holdings that amount to 2,000 ha/4,940 acres but the majority of properties are small, averaging little over a hectare. The majority of growers sell their grapes either directly to a shipper or to one of seven CO-OPERATIVES. Some co-ops maintain their own soleras but most sell the wine to one of the sherry bodegas.

Four classes of sherry bodega are recognized by the Consejo Regulador:

Bodegas de Producción: wine-making bodegas which are not permitted to mature wine.

Bodegas de Elaboración: wine-making bodegas which are allowed to hold stocks of wine for a short period of time before selling it on.

Bodegas de Crianza y Almacenado: firms which mature and keep stocks of wine or ALMACENISTAS. These bodegas are required to have a minimum of 1,000 hl/26,400 gal of which 60 per cent must be from Jerez Superior.

Bodegas de Crianza y Expedición: firms which both mature and sell wine for consumption. These bodegas are required by law to maintain a minimum stock of 12,500 hl/330,000 gal of wine of which 60 per cent must be from Jerez Superior. Exporters of sherry must hold a government licence.

See also individual articles on sherry shippers CROFT, DOMECQ, GONZÁLEZ BYASS, HARVEY, and SANDEMAN; and see specific styles of sherry: FINO, MANZANILLA, AMONTILLADO, OLOROSO, CREAM, PALO CORTADO, and PEDRO XIMÉNEZ.

R.J.M. & V. de la S.

Gonzalez Gordon, M., *Sherry: The Noble Wine* (London, 1990).

Jeffs, J., *Sherry* (5th edn, London, 2004).

Peñín, J., *Guía Peñín* (Madrid, annually).

Radford, J., *The New Spain* (2nd edn, London, 2004).

shipping. See TRANSPORT OF WINE.

Shiraz, the Australian name for the SYRAH grape, widely used elsewhere, and therefore a name better known by many consumers than its Rhône original. Because Australian Shiraz has been so successful in European markets, the word Shiraz has been used on wine labels for Syrah grown all over the world, notably SOUTH AFRICA. Shiraz appears on possibly the majority of Australian red wine labels, either in lone varietal splendour or in conjunction with, most often, Cabernet Sauvignon—typically labelled simply Cabernet Shiraz or Shiraz Cabernet, depending on which is the dominant variety. Viticulturally Shiraz is identical with Syrah but the resulting wines taste very different, with Australian versions tasting much sweeter and riper, more suggestive of chocolate than the pepper and spices often associated with Syrah in the Rhône. From the early years of the 19th century onwards, Shiraz (variously called Scyras, Syrah, or Hermitage) was the dominant red variety in Australia. When the linked red wine and export booms began in the second half of the 1980s, plantings in all regions, very cool to very warm, increased in tune. The result has been a range of style from elegant, cool-grown, spicy Rhône styles (increasingly using a dash of Viognier—see CO-FERMENTATION) through half a dozen important and regionally distinctive richer, riper styles, some traditional (Barossa Valley), some new (Heathcote). For more detail, see AUSTRALIA.

The grape variety shares a name, but little else, with the medieval capital of PERSIA, although the (white) wine of Shiraz has been enthusiastically documented.

Shiroka Melnishka. See MELNIK.

Shoalhaven Coast, region on the NEW SOUTH WALES coast south of Sydney capable of producing surprisingly good Semillon. It also relies on Chambourcin.

shoestring root rot, vine disease. See ARMILLARIA ROOT ROT.

shoot, new growth in a plant that develops from a bud and consists of a stem with leaves. Collectively, the shoots and leaves of a vine form its CANOPY. The BUDS of a grapevine burst in spring to begin a new shoot (see BUDBREAK). Shoot growth gradually accelerates to a maximum rate before FLOWERING, then slows to a stop at about VERAISON, although in humid regions shoots can continue to grow after veraison. See also WATER SHOOT, however.

VIGOUR, which effectively means shoot growth rate, varies hugely between and within vines. A vigorous shoot is evident by its long internodes, large leaves, strong lateral shoots,

Shoot system: each spring buds burst and produce shoots as shown, which shoots in turn develop (axillary) buds at each node or leaf position along the shoot. If these buds are retained at winter pruning and burst in spring then a new sequence of shoot growth begins.

and long tip tendrils well before flowering; weak shoots are the opposite. Despite these differences in growth rate and length at full bloom, shoots, whether weak or vigorous, have 17 to 20 visible internodes. Later in summer the stem of the shoot changes from green to brown and thus becomes a CANE (see CANE RIPENING). See also SHOOT TIP.   B.G.C.

shoot positioned, term used to describe vine-TRAINING SYSTEMS in a very general way. Shoot-positioned vines have shoots normally trained upwards and held between pairs of foliage or catch wires. Also the tips of the shoots are normally TRIMMED, because otherwise they can fall down the sides and cause shading. The typical vine-training system of Germany is shoot positioned, as are all VERTICAL TRELLISES. Some important examples of non-shoot-positioned canopies are found in drier climates, such as the GOBELET-trained vines of the Mediterranean, and also the 'drooping' canopies of vigorous vines in California and Australia. See SHOOT POSITIONING.   R.E.S.

shoot positioning, spring and summertime viticultural practice of placing vine SHOOTS in the desired position to assist in TRIMMING, LEAF REMOVAL, and HARVEST operations, and to facilitate the control of VINE DISEASES and VINE PESTS.

The practice is by no means universal but is more common in wet and humid climates with high vineyard VIGOUR and a high risk of FUNGAL DISEASES, particularly in Germany, Alsace, and New Zealand. In the drier climates of southern

France, Spain, Portugal, California, and Australia, the risk of fungal diseases is much lower and shoot positioning is relatively rare.

Typically the shoots are positioned upwards and are held between two pairs of so-called foliage wires, and sometimes the foliage wires themselves are moved to catch the shoots. Generally the operation is carried out manually, but a VINE FOLIAGE LIFTER may also be used. They are then trimmed to resemble a neat hedge. This then facilitates other vineyard operations such as SPRAYING and general cultivation, and enables mechanical operations such as leaf removal. For some training systems, such as GENEVA DOUBLE CURTAIN and SCOTT HENRY, shoots are positioned downwards.

R.E.S.

Smart, R. E., and Robinson, M., *Sunlight into Wine: A Handbook for Winegrape Canopy Management* (Adelaide, 1991).

shoot thinning, vineyard operation normally carried out by hand in the early spring which consists of breaking off unwanted shoots arising from the vine's HEAD or CORDON. Sometimes these shoots have no bunches and are called WATER SHOOTS. The shoot-thinning operation can be done most quickly when the shoots are 20–40 cm/8–15 in long and the bunches are quite visible, which allows discrimination between fruitful and non-fruitful shoots. The aim of shoot thinning is to reduce the density of the CANOPY and to avoid leaf congestion later in the season. This can help improve wine quality (see CANOPY MANAGEMENT) but is common only in regions with plentiful, relatively inexpensive LABOUR. Shoot thinning is the subject of mechanization research, with early prototypes developed by Professor Justin Morris at the University of Arkansas. See also DESUCKERING. R.E.S.

shoot tip, the 1 cm/0.4 in of shoot furthest from the vine's original bud, also known as the shoot apex. This small piece of tissue competes very effectively with the grapes for food produced by the mature leaves, and so a vigorously growing vine may slow fruit RIPENING. These nutrients may be diverted to the grapes by TIPPING the shoots. The balance between shoot growth and fruit growth has important effects on grape RIPENING and wine quality (see BALANCE, LEAF TO FRUIT RATIO, and VINE PHYSIOLOGY). **Shoot tip growth** is being increasingly used to monitor vine growth as a guide to vine management. For example, irrigation should be regulated so that shoot growth stops by the time of VERAISON, and Californian studies have related shoot tip appearance to measurements of vine WATER STRESS. Also, a vine which is in BALANCE and has been pruned appropriately will not have excessive numbers of shoot tips from the main and lateral shoots.

B.G.C. & R.E.S.

Greenspan, M., 'Integrated irrigation of California winegrapes', *Practical Winery and Vineyard* (Mar/Apr, 2005), 21–34.

short, tasting term for a wine whose impact on the PALATE is not persistent; the opposite of LONG.

shot berry. A very small, immature, usually seedless berry resulting from insufficient pollination. A large number of shot berries leads to uneven FRUIT SET. See MILLERANDAGE.

shows, wine. Now a universal phenomenon, wine shows are a particularly important phenomenon in Australia's wine culture, taking place in each AUSTRALIAN state's capital (originally offshoots of general agricultural shows), with some uniquely Australian features.

Each class (established by variety and vintage(s)) is judged by a panel of three judges, one being panel chair, and three associate judges. If one or more of the judges has given gold medal points to a wine, it will automatically be retasted and discussed and the show chair may well be called in.

The more experienced judges officiate at up to ten regional and capital city shows a year, know each other well, and have mutual respect for each other. While the discussion—in best Australian fashion—may be robust, it seldom, if ever, becomes ill-tempered. The most important part of the discussion will continue to turn on style issues.

The trophies and medals awarded to the more successful exhibitors are used extensively in marketing and promotion, and are accepted as reliable indicators of quality by retailers and consumers alike. But the greater long-term benefit has been for the winemaker judges, drawn from the leading wineries and schooled by chairs in the tradition of Len EVANS. J.H.

See also JUDGING and COMPETITIONS.

shut down, vine. Under severe WATER STRESS the ripening process ceases.

Sichel, influential wine family now made up of two very distinct branches. The family originated in Germany and was involved with wine from the early 19th century. The direct descendants of the German founders established the wine and spirits distribution company H. Sichel Söhne at Mainz in Germany in 1857 and it grew to be an important commercial force. Its activities were severely curtailed during the First World War but a successful export business was developed in the 1930s, based increasingly on the branded wine BLUE NUN Liebfraumilch. Walter Sichel re-established a London office for Sichel in 1927 and had to work to overcome prejudice against all things German. In 1935, he became a naturalized British citizen, and the Sichels remaining in Germany were dispersed to Britain, France, and the United States. It was during the 1950s that Blue Nun began to establish itself as one of the world's most successful wines. It was cleverly marketed, in this era of uncertainty about wine and etiquette, as the

wine to be drunk 'right through the meal', whatever was being eaten.

The fact that the quality of Blue Nun was vastly superior to that of the average LIEBFRAUMILCH also presumably played a part in the success of the brand, of which in the mid 1980s about 2 million cases a year were sold in 81 countries. Peter M. F. Sichel directed the firm's fortunes from New York, widening the range of Blue Nun products in partnership with Sichel's American distributors Schieffelin Somerset, a subsidiary of LVMH, until his retirement when the Blue Nun trademark was sold (see BLUE NUN).

The Anglo-French-Scandinavian branch of the Sichel family is descended from a Dane who married a Sichel of Mainz, worked for the firm, and took his wife's name. He was sent to Bordeaux in 1883 to establish a Sichel & Company there. His son married another Dane, and extended the Bordeaux business into château ownership. His grandson Allan Sichel, who married a Swede, was an influential member of the British wine trade in the mid 20th century, introducing Harry WAUGH among others to the delightful, if hazardous, business of buying wine *sur place* in post-war France, and writing *The Penguin Book of Wines*, which was published in 1965.

Allan's son Peter A. Sichel continued his father's tradition of writing an annual report on Bordeaux, the vintage, and the market. He lived for many years in MARGAUX at the family's Ch d'Angludet running the Bordeaux NÉGOCIANT Maison Sichel, developing a number of French wine BRANDS. The Bordeaux Sichels are also substantial shareholders in Ch Palmer. Peter was a president of the Union des Grands Crus from 1988 to 1991, being one of the most articulate voices in defence of TRADITION and subtlety in the wines of Bordeaux. He took over the business of Pierre Coste of Langon in the GRAVES in 1992, and was an early investor in CORBIÈRES in the Languedoc, in Domaine du Trillol. The considerably expanded business is now run by his five sons, who have invested in Ch d'Argadens just across the Garonne from Langon.

Sicilia (known as **Sicily** in English), large, often hot, and viticulturally important island off the toe of ITALY (see map under ITALY) which is in the throes of modernization.

Ancient history

In startling contrast to the present day, Sicilia was famed throughout classical antiquity for its agricultural produce, not least its wines. The settlement of colonies of Greeks around the island in the 8th century BC was an undoubted spur to the development of viticulture. Flourishing vineyards are testified for the 5th century at the later Greek settlement Akragas (Agrigento). Sicilia may have played a key role in the development of viticulture on the Italian peninsula (see ITALY, ancient history). Vines from Morgantina and Tauromenium were transplanted to POMPEII around Vesuvius, the Colli ALBANI, and southern Etruria, where they were well established by the 2nd century BC (Pliny, *Natural History* 14. 25, 35, and 38). The most notable characteristic of Sicilian wines was their sweetness. The most famous were Mamertine, a sweet, light wine from the north east of the island around Messina, and a very similar wine from Tauromenium (Taormina); but there is evidence for wine production right down the east coast. Much of the rest of the island had its own wines. Inland there was the Murgentina vine from Morgantina (Serra Orlando). Inscriptions on AMPHORAE testify to a so-called 'Mesopotamian' wine from the south coast near Gela. Sicilian wines were certainly exported (references to Tauromenian, for example, appear on amphorae), but the scale of the trade is difficult to judge, since the identification of Sicilian amphora types remains a tantalizing problem.   J.J.P.

Wilson, R. J. A., *Sicilia under the Roman Empire* (Warminster, 1990).

Medieval history

Throughout the Middle Ages, Sicilia's main export product was grain. It also produced olives, citrus fruits, and wine, but wheat has the advantage of being far less capital intensive: whereas olive trees, citrus fruit trees, and vines take years to come into full bearing, wheat can be harvested months after it has been sown. Medieval Sicilia owed its wealth to grain, and wine was not its most important commercial product.

Under the Normans, who governed Sicilia from 1130 to 1194, smallholders owned most of the land, and they made their living mainly by growing wheat or, in the mountainous parts of the island, keeping livestock. They grew vines as well, but the wine made in these small vineyards was usually for domestic consumption. In the course of the 14th century, demand for high-quality wine rose, and vineyards spread through Sicilia. Many of these vineyards, which produced wine for well-to-do Sicilians or for export, were owned by members of the feudal aristocracy or the local nobility. The principal wine-making towns were strung along the north eastern and eastern coasts: Cefalù, Patti, Aci, Catania, Augusta, and Syracuse. These not only produced large surpluses of wine, they were also able to ship their wine safely to Messina, from where it was taken to Africa and the Levant. From Patti, wine was carried to Constantinople, and Syracuse traded with nearby MALTA. Messina also imported wines from CALABRIA, which it then shipped to northern Italy; Messina and Palermo also carried Sicilian wines to the towns of northern Italy.

Palermo was Sicilia's largest and most important city. In the early 14th century, it had 100,000 inhabitants, as did NAPLES; in the whole of Europe, only VENICE and Milan, with populations of 200,000, were larger. Because of its size, Palermo and its surrounding countryside could never make enough wine for the city's needs, and so it imported wine from Naples and Calabria, which was cheaper than transporting wine overland from eastern Sicilia. This provoked the wrath of the citizens of Catania. Palermo exported wine as well.

From the late 14th century onwards, more and more vineyards around Palermo, Messina, and Catania came to be owned by members of the upper classes, and so, after 1400, did taverns. In the 15th century, most of the wine continued to be made in areas near ports: Aci, Catania, Messina, Taormina, and, in the west, Trapani. But further inland, Noto and Randazzo were also important. By far the biggest exporter was Messina, but Francavilla, Patti, Trapani, and Palermo handled a lot of the foreign trade in wine, too.

The wines that Sicilia exported were, for the most part, the strong, sweet wines which were capable of surviving the sea voyage, such as VERNACCIA and Muscatello. Other names of wines mentioned in documents are Mantonico (also called Mantonicato), which could be red or white; a white wine named Cuctumini; and finally Mamertino, which shares its name with the classical Mamertinum, which PLINY tells us was grown in Messina (*Natural History* 14. 66).   H.M.W.

Epstein, S. R., *An Island for Itself: Economic Development and Social Change in Medieval Sicilia* (Cambridge, 1992).

Matthew, D., *The Norman Kingdom of Sicily* (Cambridge, 1992).

Modern wines and other vine products

With total vineyard area reduced to just over 125,000 ha/312,500 acres, Sicilia's annual wine production averaged 7 million hl/185 million gal between 1999 and 2003. This decline in production from its old volumes of 10 million hl is attributable to a fall in demand for the sort of blending wines in which Sicilia excels: deep-coloured, high-strength wines that were used to bolster feebler efforts from more northerly climes, not only within Italy.

The island's geography and climate—a hilly and mountainous terrain with poor soil, intense summer heat, and low RAINFALL—make it ideal for the classic Mediterranean agriculture of grain, olive oil, and wine, and Sicilia's viticulture, in fact, enjoys a series of natural advantages which have not yet been fully exploited: HILLSIDE VINEYARDS with excellent exposures, abundant SUNLIGHT, and high TEMPERATURES to ripen the grapes; excellent ELEVATION (it is by no means unusual to find a flourishing vineyard at 500 to 900 m/1,640–2,950 ft above sea level); good diurnal TEMPERATURE VARIABILITY; and a range of native VINE VARIETIES with real personality. The concentration on quantity over quality, systematically encouraged by the regional gov-ernment's subsidies for the transformation of the traditional GOBELET training systems into more productive WIRE-trained or TENDONE systems between 1960 and 1987, has done no small harm to Sicilian viticulture and has led to a chronic cycle of over-production, declining prices, and wines which are impossible to market.

Things started to change in the late 1990s. By the mid 2000s, about 90,000 ha of the island's vineyards were GUYOT trained, while 14,700 ha were still ALBERELLO (bush vines), and 15,650 ha were tendone trained. The fact that over 70 per cent of Sicilia's vines are now wire trained illustrates a move to mechanization, and a readiness to start addressing high production costs. In addition, investment by producers in northern Italy such as Zonin, Girelli, and G.I.V. has shown the promise that exists, and the work of CONSULTANTS such as Alberto Antonini, Riccardo COTARELLA, and Carlo Ferrini has resulted in the production of some impressive wines from Sicilian-owned wineries Baglio Curatolo, Morgante, and Donnafugata respectively.

Despite all this, DOC production is still low, usually no higher than 2 per cent of total wine production as many producers prefer to use the IGT Sicilia denomination, as it allows greater flexibility. Significant producers include NÉGOCIANT Duca di Salaparuta winery, whose Corvo BRAND was for years one of Italy's most prominent, Regaleali, and Planeta, one of Sicilia's huge success stories in recent years. Its owner, Diego Planeta, is also the president of Settesoli, Sicilia's most important CO-OPERATIVE winery, and has done more than most to present the modern face of Sicilian wine to the world.

Most of these producers have drawn on Sicilia's wealth of indigenous grape varieties. CATARRATO is the island's most widely planted grape variety, accounting for about 38 per cent of plantings. Its presence accounts for the large production of GRAPE CONCENTRATE that Sicilia still produces and exports to the rest of Italy (CHAPTALIZATION is not permitted in Italy, but grape concentrate is used for ENRICHMENT by the majority of Italian producers). INZOLIA, which accounts for about 7 per cent of Sicilia's area under vine, has the potential to produce attractive and modern wines, as does GRILLO whose 2,300 ha represent less than 3 per cent of plantings. Chardonnay is the most popular of the imported varieties, with 3,637 ha of vineyard, but even the most expensive bottles suggest that the vine has found it just too hot in Sicilia. On the whole, however, Sicilia's white wines have improved dramatically in recent years, as advances in the cellar have ensured that the flavours captured in the grapes are preserved by the use of protective measures such as REFRIGERATION, rather than dissipated or OXIDIZED, as once was the case.

Of the red varieties, NERO D'AVOLA, accounting for 13 per cent of total vineyard, is the most exciting. Its deep colour and robust tannin structure has long made it a favourite of blenders, but it is now staking a claim as a Sicilian classic VARIETAL. Attention seems destined to turn to PERRICONE and NERELLO MASCALESE to see if by any chance either can rival Nero d'Avola. Syrah, a variety similar in many respects to Nero d'Avola, seems ideally suited to the climate in central Sicilia, and is already producing very exciting wines from some of the 4,400 ha planted. As with Chardonnay, Sicilia just seems too hot for the likes of Merlot and Cabernet Sauvignon.

In the southeast of the island, Cerasuolo di Vittoria, made from a blend of at least 40 per cent of FRAPPATO and no more than 60 per cent of Nero d'Avola (here known as Calabrese), has improved in recent years. In the north east, much attention has been focused on planting vineyards on the higher slopes of Mount Etna in the belief that the volcanic soil and high altitude will combine to produce great wines. Early efforts show promise.

Sicilia once enjoyed a great reputation for SWEET WINES, and attempts to revive the tradition are currently under way, although the once famous Moscato of Siracusa seems irremediably extinct, and Moscato of Noto, despite attempts to revive it, on the verge of becoming so. Moscato of Pantelleria returned to the market with convincing evidence of its inherent quality, and the Malvasia delle Lipari of the late Carlo Hauner which emerged in the 1980s has demonstrated that the reputation of this wine was not entirely mythical either. Today the Barone di Villagrande winery is building on the work done by Hauner.

D.T. & D.C.G.

Bastianich, J., and Lynch, D., *Vino Italiano: The Regional Wines of Italy* (New York, 2002).

Belfrage, N., *From Brunello to Zibibbo: The Wines of Southern Italy* (London, 2001).

Sideritis, Greek light-berried vine variety found to a limited extent near Patra and often blended with RODITIS.

Siegerrebe is a modern German vine crossing grown principally, like certain giant vegetables, by exhibitionists, *Sieger* meaning 'champion'. In Germany it can break, indeed has broken, records for its ripeness levels, but the flabby white wine it produces is so rich and oppressively flavoured that it is usually a chore to drink. It was bred from Gewürztraminer and a red table grape and has been known to reach *double* the Oechsle reading required for a TROCKENBEERENAUSLESE. So powerful is its heady flavour that a fine Riesling is quite overpowered by even 10 per cent of Siegerrebe. Total German plantings had blessedly dwindled by 2003 to a mere 129 ha/318 acres. The variety has also been used to bolster some blends in ENGLAND.

Sierra Foothills, wine region in GOLD RUSH country in CALIFORNIA and an AVA. This is basically the *piemonte* area on the western edge of the Sierra Nevada, the snowy mountains which separate California from the rest of the US (from reality in the minds of many). Thousands flocked here after 1849 and, miners being notoriously thirsty, the region's vineyards go back almost that far. The Sierra Foothills AVA blankets all of the vineyards in El Dorado, Amador, and Calaveras counties, takes in a few others in the flanking Nevada and Mariposa counties, and, in the process, points to most of the abandoned mines still there. California Shenandoah Valley and Fiddletown are AVAs within Amador county; El Dorado AVA and the subappellation Fair Play take in the vineyards in that county. North Yuba AVA is, not surprisingly, in Yuba county.

El Dorado and Fair Play AVAs
Where most of Amador county's vines grow at an altitude of 800 to 1,200 ft/240 to 360 m, El Dorado's start close to 1,500 ft and range up above 3,600 ft/1,160 m. Predictably, conditions are cooler, and the choice of varieties leans toward Cabernet Sauvignon, Merlot, Chardonnay, and Riesling, with some Syrah and other varieties thrown in. Representative, established wineries include Sierra Vista, Boeger, Lava Cap, and Madroña. The subdistrict Fair Play AVA is south of the El Dorado vineyards, which cluster around Placerville (known as Hangtown during the Gold Rush), about halfway to Amador county, but not along the aptly named main road, Highway 49. Thus Fair Play is a mildly isolated destination. But the gaggle of small wineries in Fair Play has a justly deserved reputation for good times and for good value wines. So a steady stream of visitors regularly make the trek.

Fiddletown AVA
Fiddletown adjoins the upper, eastern end of California Shenandoah Valley, in the Sierra Nevada Mountain foothills east of the town of Plymouth. Amid rolling meadows and patchy pine forest, it grows some of the state's oldest plantings of ZINFANDEL in a region now most famous for that grape, and going back to gold rush days.

California Shenandoah Valley AVA
California is tacked onto the front of Shenandoah Valley to distinguish this one from one in Virginia. The California model is a mesa between two rivers east of the town of Plymouth. It became famous for hearty Zinfandels before the turn of the century and, after a long slumber, has regained some of its old momentum since the late 1970s, again with Zinfandel at the heart of the matter. More than a score of wineries share a modest acreage that also includes Sauvignon Blanc, Sangiovese, Syrah, and Petite Sirah. Monteviña initiated the resurgence after Sacramento retailer Darrell Corti encouraged Napa wineries to bottle some of the old-vine Amador Zinfandels. Leon Sobon's Shenandoah Vineyards, Domaine Terra Rouge, and Renwood carry the region's banner commercially, while Young's has become a cult destination selling mainly at the winery.

B.C.C.

Sierras de Málaga, Spanish DO created in the early 21st century as effectively a subappellation of MÁLAGA to encompass those producers of this famous strong, sweet wine whose bodegas lie outside the town itself. It also includes a number of relatively new vineyards producing dry, unfortified wines, some in a subzone known as Serranía de Ronda around the inland town of Ronda, of which Cortijo de las Monjas is probably the best producer.

silica gel and **silica sol**, amorphous forms of silicon dioxide in which there is no crystalline structure, used in wine-making as FINING agents. Silicon and OXYGEN are the two most abundant elements on earth and their compound, silica, is similarly ubiquitous. Both forms of silica are useful because of their ability to adsorb and precipitate undesirable compounds such as PROTEINS which could cause a haze in bottled wines. Silica is used almost interchangeably with BENTONITE but is used rather more often in Europe than the United States, presumably because bentonite, principally an American product, is more expensive. It is also used in conjunction with GELATIN as it moderates the activity of gelatin and reduces the risk of overfining.

A.D.W.

silt, description of particles of intermediate size between clay and sand. See SOIL TEXTURE and GEOLOGY for more details of this particular form of soil classification. Grains of silt dominate LOESS and are often predominant in ALLUVIAL soils. Silt is a major component of many of the soils in California's Napa valley.

Silvaner, Grüner Silvaner, or **Sylvaner,** early-ripening, productive, if frost-sensitive white grape variety grown mainly in Germany and central Europe (see SYLVANER for an account of it in France). Its very name suggests romantic woodland origins, and certainly it has a long history over much of eastern Europe, where it may indeed first have been identified growing wild. DNA PROFILING in Austria established that Silvaner is the progeny of TRAMINER and Österreichisch Weiss, a variety often mistaken for Silvaner. The crossing probably took place in what is now Austria (although hardly any true Silvaner is grown there today) and it certainly came to Germany from the banks of the Danube. A vine known as Silvaner was widely grown throughout the extensive vineyards of medieval Germany. Its arrival from Austria at Castell in FRANKEN in 1659 is well documented and the variety is still the second most planted in Franken where distinctive clay-limestone soils seem to play a defining role in making full-bodied, firm, if aromatically discreet wines. Silvaner enjoyed its greatest popularity in the first half of the 20th century, when it overtook ELBLING to become Germany's most planted vine variety and established a dominant position in Rheinhessen. At 5,800 ha/14,300 acres in 2003, the variety is now a distant third to the even more productive MÜLLER-THURGAU, which rapidly surpassed it in area after the Second World War.

This vigorous vine buds a few days before Germany's quintessential RIESLING, and can suffer spring frost damage. It is not notable for its disease resistance but it is productive. The chief characteristic of the wine produced is its high natural acid, generally lower than Riesling's in fact but emphasized by Silvaner's lack of body and frame. (It is significant that the German name for Sauvignon Blanc, a variety essentially notable for its aroma and high acid, is Muskat-Silvaner.) Provided yields are not too high, it can provide a suitable neutral canvas on which to display more geographically based flavour characteristics (see TERROIR) but Silvaner is not noted for either its longevity or its high must weights.

Most of Germany's finest Silvaners come from Franken, where Riesling is difficult to ripen and Silvaner has remained popular. Occasional and encouraging examples are made elsewhere, however—such as in certain calcareous, sandstone, or porphyry sites in Rheinhessen—where talented growers have achieved transparency of flavour and distinctive finishing character while avoiding the curse of a coarse, thick mid-palate. Silvaner is certainly more than capable of producing versatile, workhorse white wine, and the vintners of Rheinhessen have been at pains since the early 1990s to generate consumer awareness and a better image for this grape, even if it is largely with wines of that unassuming sort. Total plantings in Germany nevertheless continue to decline, even in Rheinhessen.

Blauer Silvaner is a local, dark-berried mutation that is a speciality of Württemberg.

Outside Germany, Silvaner is relatively important, as Sylvánské Zelené, in the CZECH REPUBLIC, is still grown in SLOVENIA as Zeleni Silvanec and around Lake Balaton in HUNGARY, and is prized in RUSSIA for its ability to ripen early. It is also planted in ALTO ADIGE, where it can provide light and piercing wines for youthful consumption.

In Valais in SWITZERLAND, it is called Johannisberg and seems positively luscious in comparison with French Switzerland's ubiquitous CHASSELAS. Sylvaner is the second most planted white grape variety in Valais, where it is often called Rhin, or Gros Rhin (as opposed to Petit Rhin, the local synonym for RIESLING). The variety ripens later than Chasselas and, in villages as warm as Chamoson, Leytron, and Saillon, can result in wines with more body, character, and race.

Despite its useful acidity levels, Silvaner is not widely grown in the New World, although California and Australia still grow it to a strictly limited extent.

Simon, André Louis (1877–1970). Simon

was the charismatic leader of the English wine trade for almost all of the first half of the 20th century, and the grand old man of literate CONNOISSEURSHIP for a further 20 years. In 66 years of authorship, he wrote 104 books. For 33 years he was one of London's leading champagne shippers; for another 33 years active president of the Wine & Food Society. Although he lived in England from the age of 25, he always remained a French citizen. He was both Officier de la Légion d'Honneur and holder of the Order of the British Empire.

Simon was born in St-Germain-des-Prés, between the Brasserie Lipp and the Deux Magots (the street has since been demolished), the second of five sons of a landscape painter who died (of sunstroke, in Egypt) while they were still youths.

From the first his ambition was to be a journalist. At 17 he was sent to Southampton to learn English and met Edith Symons, whose ambition was to live in France. They married in 1902 and remained happy together for 63 years. Simon was a man of judgement, single-mindedness, and devotion all his life.

He was also a man of powerful charm, the very model of his own description of the perfect champagne shipper, who 'must be a good mixer rather than a good salesman; neither a teetotaller nor a boozer, but able to drink champagne every day without letting it become a bore or a craving'.

He became a champagne shipper, the London agent of the leading house of Pommery, through his father's friendship with the Polignac family. It gave him a base in the centre of the City's wine trade, at 24 Mark Lane, for 30 years. From it he not only sold champagne; he soon made his voice heard as journalist, scholar, and teacher.

Within four years of his installation in London he was writing his first book, *The History of the Champagne Trade in England*, in instalments for the *Wine Trade Review*. A. S. Gardiner, its editor, can be credited with forming Simon's English prose style: unmistakably charming, stately, and faintly whimsical at once. He spoke English as he wrote it, with a fondness for imagery, even for little parables—but with an ineradicable French accent that was as much part of his persona as his burly frame and curly hair.

His first *History* was rapidly followed by a remarkable sequel: *The History of the Wine Trade in England from Roman Times to the End of the 17th Century*, in three volumes in 1906, 1907, and 1909—the best and most original of his total of over 100 books. None, let alone a young man working in a language

not his own, had read, thought, and written so deeply on the subject before. It singled him out at once as a natural spokesman for wine, a role he pursued with maximum energy, combining with friends to found (in 1908) the Wine Trade Club, where for six years he organized tastings and gave technical lectures of a kind not seen before; the forerunner by 45 years of the Institute of MASTERS OF WINE. In 1919 he published *Bibliotheca vinaria*, a catalogue of the books he had collected for the Club. It ran to 340 pages.

The First World War ended this busy and congenial life, full of dinners, lectures, book-collecting, and amateur theatricals. Before war was declared Simon was in France as a volunteer, serving the full four years in the French Artillery, where as 'un homme de lettres' he was made regimental postman, before being moved on to liaison with the British in Flanders and on the Somme. It was in Flanders that the irrepressible scribbler wrote his best seller, *Laurie's Elementary Russian Grammar*, printed in huge numbers by the War Office in the pious hope of teaching Tommy, the British soldier, Russian.

In 1919, Simon bought the two homes he was to occupy for the rest of his life: 6 Evelyn Mansions, near Westminster Cathedral (where he attended mass daily), and Little Hedgecourt, a cottage with 28 acres beside a lake at Felbridge in Surrey. Gardening these acres, making a cricket pitch and an open-air theatre, and enlarging the cottage into a rambling country house for his family of five children were interspersed with travels all over Africa and South America to sell Pommery, until suddenly, in 1933, caught in the violent fluctuations of the franc–pound exchange rate when Britain came off the gold standard, he could no longer pay for his champagne stocks and Pommery, without compunction, ended their 33-year association.

Simon began a second life at 55: that of spokesman of wine and food in harmonious association. Already, with friends, he had founded the SAINTSBURY CLUB in memory of the crusty old author of *Notes on a Cellar-Book* (see also SAINTSBURY). With A. J. A. Symons he founded the Wine & Food Society (now INTERNATIONAL WINE & FOOD SOCIETY). Its first (Alsace) lunch at the Café Royal in London in the midst of the Depression (and for 10s. 6d.) caused a sensation. But its assured success came from the ending of PROHIBITION in America. Sponsored by the French government, Simon travelled repeatedly to the US, founding its first Wine & Food Society branch in Boston in December 1934 and its second in San Francisco in January 1935.

Meanwhile, while working briefly for the advertising agency Mather & Crowther, he conceived the idea of *A Concise Encyclopedia of Gastronomy* to be published in instalments. It sold an unprecedented 100,000 copies. Research, writing, and editing (and finding paper to print) the *Encyclopedia* and the Society's *Quarterly* occupied him throughout the Second World War. His daughter Jeanne and her family moved into Little Hedgecourt for the war and thereafter. His son André was a wine merchant. His two other daughters and a son all retired from the world into religious communities.

Simon was a better teacher than a businessman. He was repeatedly helped out of difficulties by adoring friends. Thus the National Magazine Company gave him an office in Grosvenor Gardens in 1941, to be followed by the publisher George Rainbird, still in central London at Marble Arch. In 1962, his friend Harry Yoxall suggested that at 85, daily responsibility for the Society and its magazine was too burdensome and bought the title from him for Condé Nast Publications. But in his 90s, Simon was still exceptional company at dinner and gave little picnics for friends beside his woodland lake.

His final book, *In the Twilight*, written in his last winter, 1969, recast the memoirs he had published as *By Request* in 1957. On what would have been his 100th birthday, 28 February 1977, 400 guests at the Savoy Hotel in London drank to his memory in CLARET he had left for the occasion: Ch LATOUR 1945.   H.J.

Sirah is the name by which some PETITE SIRAH is known in South America. It should not be confused with the true Syrah of the northern Rhône.

Síria, very widely planted white wine grape in Portugal known as Crato Branco in the Algarve (300 ha in the official early 2000s' vine census), Roupeiro in Alentejo (2,300 ha), Códega in the Douro, Alva in the northern Alentejo, and sometimes Coda Pinhel. There were 4,000 ha in Beiras and 7,000 ha in Trás-os-Montes, making a national total of about 12,300 ha/ 30,300 acres. The wine is rarely exciting.

site climate, the climate of a specified site, for instance a vineyard or part of a vineyard. The scale of definition usually falls within that of MESOCLIMATE.

site selection. See VINEYARD SITE SELECTION.

Sizzano, red wine DOC in the Novara hills in the subalpine north of the PIEMONTE region of north west Italy. The proportion of NEBBIOLO grapes in Sizzano is usually lower than in either Gattinara or nearby LESSONA and BRAMATERRA in the Vercelli hills across the river Sesia. Sizzano is also usually plumper and earlier maturing than its northern neighbours in the Novara hills GHEMME and BOCA, although FARA may be lighter still. For more details, see SPANNA, the local name for Nebbiolo.

skin, grape. For details of grape skins, see GRAPE.

skin contact, *macération pelliculaire* in French, wine-making operation with the aim of extracting FLAVOUR COMPOUNDS, FLAVOUR PRECURSORS, and ANTHOCYANINS from grape skins into grape juice or wine. In its widest sense, it is identical to MACERATION, and some form of skin contact is essential to ROSÉ WINE-MAKING, but the term is generally used exclusively for the maceration of white grapes for about four to 24 hours before PRESSING and FERMENTATION with the aim of increasing flavour, BODY, and AGEING potential. Skin contact tends to reduce must acidity and increase pH. It also increases the concentration of AMINO ACIDS, leading to a better rate of fermentation. Vine varieties frequently processed with skin contact are Sémillon, Sauvignon Blanc, Muscat, and Riesling. Grapes must be healthy and fully ripe. Denis DUBOURDIEU and his team have been responsible for its application to white bordeaux since the late 1980s. It is important to arrest skin contact before excessive amounts of bitter PHENOLICS (which may also darken colour) are extracted. In some vintages and in some regions, especially when the skin is rich in tannin due to a hot, dry climate, the technique simply does not work as too much undesirable material is extracted with the minimum amount of additional flavour compounds.

Ribéreau-Gayon, P., Dubourdieu, D., Donèche, B., and Lonvaud, D., *Traité d'Œnologie* I: *Microbiologie du vin: Vinifications* (Paris, 1998), translated by J.M. Branco, as *Handbook of Enology* I: *The Microbiology of Wine and Vinifications* (Chichester, 2000).

slashing, vineyard operation of mowing or cutting a COVER CROP, or cutting vine shoots in summer (see TRIMMING).

slate (*schiste* in French and *Schiefer* in German), a group name for various very finely crystalline, fissile rocks derived from clay, shale, mudstone, and other fine-grained sediments, sometimes with silt, which have been metamorphosed into a moderately hard, dark, slab-like rock. Some of the vineyards in southern Beaujolais are on a brown soil over weathered slates. Just north of here the vineyards of POUILLY-FUISSÉ are also partly over slates. The most celebrated vineyard occurrence of slate is the MOSEL-SAAR-RUWER region of Germany, where Riesling vines grow in slate which holds moisture and heat, and reradiates warmth at night. Several vineyard names end in *-lay* or *-ley*, a reference to the slatiness of the soil. See entries prefixed SOIL.   M.J.E. & J.M.H.

slope, or incline, an important characteristic of any vineyard site that is not completely flat. For more details, see TOPOGRAPHY.

Slovakia. When this eastern part of what was Czechoslovakia voted to split from the Czech Republic in the early 1990s, it failed to privatize its wine industry successfully. With notable exceptions such as the fine Rieslings of Kastiel Béla, a JOINT VENTURE involving renowned Mosel grower Egon Müller, Slovakia consumes all the wine it produces except for that exported to the Czech Republic and some local Polish towns. With total vineyard area having fallen from around 25,000 ha/ 62,000 acres to just 14,000 ha in 2002, producing 315,000 hl according to OIV figures, yields are apparently extremely low. This shortfall may be explained by FROST, lack of funds for vineyard treatments such as SPRAYING, post-privatization lack of vineyard maintenance, and small-scale undeclared private production for barter or home consumption. New wine laws came into force in 1996. The wine regions are located next to the central mountainous plateau, along the western and southern borders, including its far-eastern TOKAJ region, which is an extension of Hungary's, though vineyards are few and far between and prices are much lower (see map on p. 221).

For more details on viticultural and wine-making history, see CZECH REPUBLIC, with which it shares its traditions.

A.H.M. & H.K.B.

Slovenia, small country in Central Europe with a long wine-making history. CELTS and Illyrian tribes were making wine here before the ROMANS. In the Middle Ages, wine production was carried out by MONKS AND MONASTERIES. Slovenia was part of Austro-Hungarian Empire and since 1918 it was part of what was to become YUGOSLAVIA. After the Second World War, production was limited to CO-OPERATIVES, where quantity not quality ruled. However, many excellent and long-lived wines were produced in those times, especially in the Podravje region. Commercially important private sector wine businesses started to emerge in the 1970s. In 1967, PSVVS (Business Association for Viticulture and Wine Production) was founded which introduced a seal of approval for wines of Slovenia. In 1991, Slovenia was the first republic of Yugoslavia to establish its independence. It has established by far the most successful wine industry and now has fully implemented and well-policed wine laws, a thriving private sector incorporating many excellent estates, in addition to the co-operatives. In 2004, Slovenia joined the EUROPEAN UNION.

Slovenia has a total of 24,600 ha/59,300 acres of vines. More than 40,000 winegrowers are registered, resulting in highly fragmented vine-growing and wine-making. Annual production is around 1 million hl, three-quarters of it white. Around 50,000 hl/2.6 million gal (5 per cent of the total) was exported in 2004 (to BOSNIA AND HERZEGOVINA, CROATIA, the UNITED STATES, GERMANY, and ITALY) and about the same quantity imported (from MACEDONIA, FRANCE, ITALY, SPAIN, and CROATIA). Production is focused on quality and premium quality (*vrhunsko*) wines, with only about 30 per cent of basic TABLE WINE quality. TOURISM plays an increasing role in premium wine distribution. Officially consumption in 2004 was around 30 l/8 gal a head per year; unofficially it must be around 50 l/12 gal a head per year.

Slovenia is divided into three wine regions: Podravje in the north east of the country; Primorska in the west , close to Italian border and the Adriatic; and Posavje in the south east. It is further divided to 14 wine districts.

Geographically Slovenia is very diverse with many different MESOCLIMATES with vines growing on either gentle or steep slopes, many of them terraced. The climate is generally CONTINENTAL, with hot summers, and cold and rather dry winters. Annual rainfall averages 800 to 1,400 mm. The climate in Primorska is influenced by the MEDITERRANEAN, especially in Koper district. Spring FROST, summer HAIL, and even DROUGHT is experienced in most wine districts.

Double or single GUYOT is the most common training system. The high-yield PERGOLA training system (*latnik*) and *casarsa* (similar to GDC) were common in Primorska but are being replaced with guyot. As terrain is steep, manual harvesting is the norm.

Wines were traditionally vinified in old wooden casks either from Slovenian or Slavonian oak. Modern practice includes stainless steel and barrel maturation either in Slovenian or French oak of different sizes. MALOLACTIC FERMENTATION for reds and whites is common in Primorska and is more and more practised for reds in Podravje and Posavje. As in all ex-Austro-Hungarian Empire countries, the best wines have tended to be VARIETAL, but blends, red and white, are becoming more common. The majority of wine is produced in large, often well-equipped cooperatives but private producers are increasingly popular and can often command higher prices.

By law all wines must be chemically analysed, tasted, and scored to determine their quality level before going to market. Designations are: *namizno vino* (table wine); *deželno vino PGO* ('country wine' coming from a single region); and *kakovostno vino ZGP* (quality wine) and *vrhunsko vino ZGP* (premium quality wine), both of which come from single district.

Zaščiteno geografsko poreklo (ZGP) is the equivalent of European QWPSR, Quality Wine Produced in Specified Region but many top producers in Slovenia label all their wines merely as *kakovostno*. *Posebno tradicionalno poimenovanje* (PTP) is a designation reserved for traditional wines coming from a delimited origin. To date, Cviček PTP from Dolenjska and Teran PTP from Kras are carry this designation. According to the RESIDUAL SUGAR level all wines in Slovenia are designated either as *suho* (dry), *polsuho* (medium-dry), *polsladko* (medium-sweet), or *sladko* (sweet).

Podravje with 10,500 ha of vines is the largest wine region in Slovenia. It is divided into seven wine districts. Laški Rizling (WELSCHRIESLING) and Šipon (probably FURMINT) are the dominant varieties, usually ending up in bulk wine or inexpensive blends. Renski Rizling (RIESLING), CHARDONNAY, SAUVIGNON BLANC, Sivi Pinot (PINOT GRIS), Beli Pinot (PINOT BLANC), Dišeči Traminec (GEWÜRZTRAMINER), and Modri Pinot (Noir) are mostly used for higher quality VARIETAL wines.

The beautiful Ljutomer-Ormož district famous for the village of Jeruzalem and Šipon, the Maribor district, and Radgona-Kapela district, where Ranina (BOUVIER) and Dišeči Traminec are specialities, produce the best wines in Podravje. Haloze, with the steepest vineyards in the country, is struggling but has potential. Šmarje-Virštanj, Srednje Slovenske Gorice, and Prekmurje are of local importance.

All but 3 per cent of the wines grown in Podravje are whites, although reds, especially Modri Pinot, are increasing. Locals prefer the traditional semi-dry style in whites but modern whites are dry, crisp, and medium bodied with distinctive and expressive varietal aromas.

Other grape varieties planted in this region are: Rumeni Muškat (yellow MUSCAT), Muškat Ottonel (MUSCAT OTTONEL, often spelt Otonel on Slovenian labels), Zeleni Silvanec (SYLVANER), Rizvanec (MÜLLER-THURGAU), KERNER, Portugalka (PORTUGIESER), Kraljevina, Ranfol, Žlahtnina red and white (CHASSELAS), GAMAY, and ZWEIGELT.

Posavje with 5,500 ha of vines is the smallest and least important region in Slovenia, producing slightly more reds than whites. Production is extremely dispersed and bulk wine prevails. Posavje is divided into three wine districts. Bizeljsko-Brežice is known for sparkling wine and the highly acidic local white Rumeni Plavec. Bela Krajina can produce the best Modra Frankinja (BLAUFRÄNKISCH) and Rumeni Muškat in the country. It is home to a traditional red blend called Metliška Črnina. Dolenjska is home to the highly popular Cviček, a light, pale, ruby, highly acidic blend of red and white grapes, usually Žametovka and Kraljevina. Other grapes planted in this region are Sauvignon, Chardonnay, Beli Pinot, Sivi Pinot, Renski Rizling, Traminec, Šipon, Ranina, Neuburger, Modri Pinot, Šentlovrenka (SAINT-LAURENT), Gamay, Zweigelt, and Rdeča Žlahtnina.

Primorska with 8,000 ha has made great progress in quality since early 1990s and is today the most appreciated Slovenian wine region. It produces the majority of Slovenia's best reds, although whites prevail and are generally of better quality and value. International varieties such as Chardonnay, Sauvignon Blanc, Sivi Pinot (Gris), Merlot, Cabernet Sauvignon, and Modri Pinot (Noir) play an important role in the region, however local varieties, especially Rebula, Tokaj, and Refosco, are also popular. Primorska is divided into four districts. Goriška Brda, the continuation of Italy's COLLIO DOC and influenced by its Italian neighbours, boasts many good producers and is currently Slovenia's most esteemed wine district, having begun the move to quality in the late 1980s. Many of best wines are matured white and red blends based on Rebula (RIBOLLA) and MERLOT–CABERNET SAUVIGNON respectively. The Vipava valley is proud of its native Zelen and Pinela; both are light, crisp and grassy. Kras (Carso), a plateau up behind Trieste, is the home of Teran, a distinctive, highly popular and highly acidic dark red made from Refošk (REFOSCO) grapes. Koper on the Slovenian cost and in Istria is the warmest district in the country. Extremely popular Refošk and Malvazija (MALVASIA) prevail. Other grapes grown in Primorska are Rumeni Muškat, Beli Pinot, Laški Rizling, Vitovska Grganja, Klarnica, Glera, Cabernet Franc, Barbera, Syrah, Cipro, and Maločrn.

In 1852, Slovenia's first sparkling wine (*penina*) produced by the TRADITIONAL METHOD was made in Gornja Radgona in the Radgona-Kapela district of Podravje and has continued since, no longer in isolation. Podravje is also where the country's best BOTRYTIZED wines are made, and labelled, Germany according to sugar level: *pozna trgatev* (SPÄTLESE), *izbor* (AUSLESE), *jagodni izbor* (BEERENAUSLESE), *ledeno vino* (EISWEIN), and *suhi jagodni izbor* (TROCKENBEERENAUSLESE). The best sweet wines are made from Šipon, Laški Rizling, and Renski Rizling. Typically they are expensive but some can be of world class quality. In Primorska, some great sweet wines are made in PASSITO style. Other sweet wines are typically made from Rumeni Muškat. Sweet Verduc (VERDUZZZO) and Pikolit (PIKOLIT) are specialities of Brda.

Slovenia makes very good whites, especially from varieties such as Pinot Gris, Sauvignon Blanc, and Chardonnay. Reds have improved considerably since the early 1990s. However, Slovenia will probably find its identity on the international market through Rebula, Laški Rizling, Refošk, Šipon, Zelen, and Pinela; and blends made from these local varieties might well have an impact. R.Go.

Nemanič, Dr J., and Bogataj, Prof. Dr J., *Wines of Slovenia* (Ljubljana, 2004).

Smaragd, the most valuable category of white wines made from the ripest grapes on the best sites of the Wachau in AUSTRIA. Alcohol levels must be more than 12.5 per cent. Smaragd wines can age up to 20 years. The category is named after the green lizard that basks in the sun on the Wachau's hottest steep stone terraces above the river Danube. See also STEINFEDER and FEDERSPIEL.

Smart–Dyson, vine TRAINING SYSTEM developed in the early 1980s in California and

Smart–Dyson vines are always spur pruned

1.15m

2-bud spur

vertically divided canopy

by the late 1990s adopted in new plantings in Argentina, the United States, Australia, Chile, Portugal, and Spain. Towards the end of the 20th century, the use of the trellis increased, especially in California and Spain. Some growers have used it in conjunction with ORGANIC VITICULTURE because the open canopy discourages disease.

The system was devised by Richard Smart of Australia and John Dyson of New York, and initially trialled on Dyson's ranch in Gilroy, California, in 1992 with Merlot vines. It is a vertically divided training system like SCOTT HENRY, but the vine is CORDON trained and there are upwards- and downwards-pointing SPURS giving rise to the two canopies. It is compatible with MECHANICAL PRUNING, unlike the Scott Henry system, and it can be MECHANICALLY HARVESTED as readily.   R.E.S.

Smart, R., 'Introducing the Smart–Dyson trellis', *Practical Winery and Vineyard* (Nov/Dec 1993), 48–9.

Smederevka, white grape variety commonly planted and admired throughout the south of what was YUGOSLAVIA. It takes its name from the town of Smederevo south of Belgrade and is planted extensively in SERBIA and VOJVODINA. As a VARIETAL wine, it is usually dry and relatively high in both alcohol and acidity, but it is often blended with other varieties, notably LAŠKI RIZLING. It is also planted to a much more limited extent in HUNGARY.

smell. The smell of a wine is probably its single most important attribute, and may be called its AROMA, BOUQUET, odour or off-odour if it is positively unattractive, or even FLAVOUR.

The sense of smell is the most acute human tasting instrument (as witness how a blocked nose robs food and drink of any flavour) but since it is so closely related to what we call the sense of taste, it is considered in detail under TASTING.

smudge pot, burner, usually fuelled with oil, lit in frost-prone parts of an orchard or vineyard on still nights when lethal frost seems imminent to create air convection currents which mix relatively warm upper air with the chilled air settled at ground level. They have lost favour because of the numbers of pots required, not to mention fuel, smoke, lost sleep, and the general inconvenience of operating them in the cold darkness of the early morning. Other approaches to frost avoidance are available: see FROST.

J.G. & R.E.S.

snails, vine pests of which at least two types can be of economic significance to wine production: the white Italian snail, *Theba pisana*, and the brown or English snail, *Helix aspersa*. They are mainly a problem in early spring, and can strip vines of young foliage if they are in large numbers, which happens particularly in wet conditions. They will contaminate fruit and wine if they are present at HARVEST time. Clean CULTIVATION is an important preventive measure, and sprays or baits used early can also control snails. Copper-based FUNGICIDES used on vines also affect snails by repelling and killing them. Ducks and geese feed on snails, and their presence in vineyards will keep numbers down.   M.J.E.

Soave, dry white wine from the VENETO region of north east Italy. Like the neighbouring VALPOLICELLA zone, the Soave zone has expanded enormously with the creation of the Soave DOC in 1968. At the time, both regions were enjoying an export boom, so production flowed off the small hilly zone onto the alluvial plain of the Adige river. The CLASSICO zone, first defined and delimited in 1927 and currently comprising about 1,100 ha/ 2,720 acres of mostly HILLSIDE VINEYARDS, is the source of superior Soave. The eastern part of the zone, in the commune of Monteforte d'Alpone, where the vineyards are planted on decomposed volcanic rock, produces steelier wines than those from the western part in the commune of Soave, where the higher per-

centage of limestone in the soil and the warmer afternoon sun gives fuller, more forward wines.

Today, there are also about 4,000 ha of vineyard on the plain, and these are responsible for the bulk of ordinary Soave. The quality-oriented producers from the hills have long struggled with the fact that their wines, no matter how good, will always be associated with these lower priced wines. The introduction of DOCG in 2002 seemed a good time to deal with this issue, but compromise won the day. Instead, the whole issue of Soave was complicated further: DOCG was introduced for Soave Superiore, which can be made only from grapes grown on the hills previously mapped out for the Recioto di Soave DOCG. If in the Classico zone, this wine will be Soave Classico Superiore DOCG; if from outside the Classico zone, but from the hills, it will be Soave Colli Scaligeri Superiore DOCG. But not all wines from the hills will be DOCG; this being dependent on them having a minimum alcohol level of 12 per cent.

On a more positive note, the new law has seen Trebbiano Toscano excluded from the blend for DOCG. This interloper was introduced to the area in the 1960s, when high yields were more important, and it soon displaced the local Trebbiano di Soave (which is, in fact, Verdicchio). The new law allows for a minimum of 70 per cent Garganega and up to 30 per cent of Trebbiano di Soave, Chardonnay, or Pinot Bianco, although Trebbiano Toscano remains a mainstay in the bulk of Soave from the plain. As a result, there are about four bottles of very basic Soave produced for every bottle of Soave Classico.

When yields are controlled, GARGANEGA can give wines of real class. A late-ripening variety, it has a thick skin that helps protect it against the autumn mists rising from the northern part of the Po valley. Producers such as Pieropan, Gini, Pra, and Ca' Rugate are now illustrating the real potential not only of Garganega but also of the Soave zone.

Garganega is also the mainstay of the sweet RECIOTO di Soave, a PASSITO made from raisined Garganega grapes with a long local tradition. DOCG status was granted in 1998 and about 1,800 hl were produced in 2003.

D.T. & D.C.G.

sodium, element that is not a required nutrient for vine growth. Sodium chloride (common SALT) is, however, a major hazard for vine-growers, particularly in hot, irrigated areas where ground waters are saline, or where salty irrigation water is applied to the leaves. Sodium has an unfavourable effect on soil fertility because it reduces water infiltration due to its tendency to disperse clay particles. This can be overcome by addition of CALCIUM to the soil, normally as gypsum. See also SALINITY.   R.E.S.

Sogrape, Portugal's largest wine producer, owned by the Oporto-based Guedes family, whose success is founded on MATEUS Rosé. In the mid 1980s, Sogrape began to diversify, now producing a wide range of wines and owning enterprises throughout Portugal in the Douro, Minho, Dão, Bairrada, and Alentejo, including table wine brands such as Grão Vasco, Duque de Viseu, Gazela, Planalto, Quinta de Azevedo, Quinta dos Carvalhais, Vinha do Monte, and port shippers FERREIRA, SANDEMAN, and Offley. It has also acquired Finca Flichman of ARGENTINA.

soil, the sediment at the surface of the Earth capable of supporting the growth of plants, including vines, is the result of the alteration of the geological layer by climate and vegetation. There is no absolute dividing line between soil and the underlying ROCK, another term used in geology. A typical early 20th-century definition of soil was 'rocks that have been reduced to small fragments and have been more or less changed chemically, together with the remains of plants or animals that live in it or on it'. For most purposes this is still a satisfactory working definition, emphasizing as it does the ORGANIC MATTER content.

For modern soil scientists, this definition is inadequate, however, as it fails to include the stratification into 'horizons' which are present in all soils (in Britain, for example, eight horizons are recognized above the bedrock); it fails to bring out variations in porosity and permeability which affect plant roots; and it fails to take account of very wide variations over the world associated with different CLIMATES and different belts of vegetation.

For vines, the problems of distinctions between soils and rocks are exacerbated by the fact that many vineyards are in areas where the underlying bedrock is not a hard rock but an unconsolidated young sediment, so that the dividing line between soil and bedrock is even less obvious than normal, and by the fact that vines have ROOTS long enough to extend below the soil into the bedrock.

See GEOLOGY, STONES AND ROCKS, SUBSOIL, TERROIR, TOPOGRAPHY, and other entries prefaced by SOIL, below, most importantly, SOIL AND WINE QUALITY. J.M.H.

Van Leeuwen, C., and Chéry, P., 'Quelle méthode pour caractériser et étudier le terroir viticole: analyse de sol, cartographie pédologique ou étude écophysiologique?' in *Un raisin de qualité: de la vigne à la cuve*, n° Hors Série du *Journal International des Sciences de la Vigne et du Vin* (2001), 13–20.

soil acidity. The problem of high soil acidity, or low soil PH, occurs where hydrogen cations (H+) predominate relative to those of the alkaline elements CALCIUM, POTASSIUM, and MAGNESIUM adsorbed to the fine particle surfaces of the CLAY and ORGANIC MATTER. Acidity is found mainly where the alkaline mineral elements have been leached down or out of the soil profile under heavy rainfall over long

ages, and their places in the so-called 'exchange complex' on the soil particles have been taken by hydrogen ions. Problems of soil acidity are to be expected in most viticultural regions with high rainfall, and affect parts of Europe and the east coast of Australia.

Soils of pH below about 6 are described as acid; below 5 as highly acid; and below 4 as extremely acid. The last are clearly unsuitable for most plants, while grapevine root growth is inhibited below pH 5 because aluminium, which is toxic to vine roots, is soluble when pH is less than 5. Soils more acid than that are best avoided for viticulture; if this is not possible, then LIME should be applied. The soil acidity of the MÉDOC in Bordeaux, for example, also promotes COPPER toxicity where there has been a build-up of copper in the topsoil from spraying vines with BORDEAUX MIXTURE.

Acidity also has an effect on the supply of nitrogen to the vine. Organic matter contains 5–10% nitrogen, and 1–2% of the organic matter in the soil is mineralized per year, thus releasing nitrogen. Acidity influences the speed at which organic matter is mineralized so that a soil pH of 5.5–6 can limit excessive nitrogen supply to the vines in soils rich in organic matter (over 1.5%).

Soil acidity should be contrasted with SOIL ALKALINITY, which is more common in arid areas. It does not follow that soil acidity bears any relation to wine ACIDITY.
J.G., R.E.S., & C.V.L.

soil alkalinity. A soil is said to be alkaline when the measured PH (see SOIL ACIDITY) is above about 8.0. Above pH 8.5 usually implies a content of free lime or common salt (sodium chloride) in the soil; while many less alkaline surface soils sit above chalk or limestones, or contain limestone rocks. Saline soils should definitely be avoided for viticulture, but some of the best vineyard soils in cool climates are associated with LIMESTONE or CHALK.

High lime and pH can induce deficiencies of IRON, ZINC, and MANGANESE or BORON in the vines. Lime-induced iron deficiency can cause CHLOROSIS. These deficiencies can usually be controlled by the selection of particularly well-adapted varieties of ROOTSTOCK. Spraying the leaves is another approach.

Soils high in free lime can also create nutritional difficulties through the reduced availability of POTASSIUM. J.G. & C.V.L.

soil amelioration, a viticultural practice for improving soils by the addition of so-called **soil amendments**. These can include FERTILIZERS to overcome mineral nutrient deficiencies (such as superphosphate to add phosphorus); LIME, which will overcome SOIL ACIDITY; and gypsum and ORGANIC MATTER, which will improve SOIL STRUCTURE. These ameliorants are spread on the soil surface, and occasionally turned in by CULTIVATION. Where there is a need for deep placement, as

in liming, then large and powerful bulldozers are used, normally before planting. When the lime and gypsum are finely ground, special applicators allow these normally insoluble products to be added through DRIP IRRIGATION systems. R.E.S.

Coombe, B. G., and Dry, P. R. (eds.), *Viticulture, ii: Practices* (Adelaide, 1992).

soil and wine quality. The SOIL has many attributes that can influence the vine grown in it, and thence the quality of both grapes and wine. Quite how influential these attributes are remains a matter of debate, with a fairly marked divergence between the OLD WORLD and NEW WORLD, if not of opinion, then of interpretation.

Old World versus New World
Old World opinion, especially in France, strongly emphasizes soil effects at a vineyard level, particularly in relation to vine water status. These are fundamental to the concept of TERROIR which underlies the official French APPELLATION CONTRÔLÉE system, although their influence is less significant than that of climate. In Germany, large local differences in climate associated with TOPOGRAPHY are often considered to override soil effects (see MESOCLIMATE and CLIMATE AND WINE QUALITY), although soils are still regarded as an important factor governing wine quality. SOIL COLOUR can be critical at the extreme cool limit of viticulture in determining whether grapes will ripen at all. Fregoni and Berry give examples.

New World opinion has tended to minimize the role of soil, and instead to stress major differences in regional climate, or MACROCLIMATE. Amerine and Winkler's 1944 CLIMATE CLASSIFICATION of California into five temperature regions epitomizes this view.

Much of the divergence in approach can be ascribed to differences in historical, geographical, and commercial background. Traditional European vineyards were small, and the identities of their wines often uniquely established over many generations. It was observed that certain sites consistently produced different and/or better wines than others, apparently regardless of VINE MANAGEMENT and WINE-MAKING practices, and sometimes in the absence of discernible differences in mesoclimate. One general observation, especially marked in Bordeaux, was that the best sites stood out most clearly in poor VINTAGE YEARS. These sites maintained a relative consistency of high quality, whereas others, superficially similar and often very close, suffered greatly diminished quality. The only possible reason seemed to lie in unalterable (and perhaps invisible) properties of the soil.

New World viticulture generally lacks this experience. Individual vineyards are often much larger, and until recently grapes from individual plots have rarely been fermented separately. Moreover, its dominant commercial organizations have tended to employ extensive BLENDING of wines from different soils and regions, so that any individualities are often masked or lost.

Differences in agricultural history have also influenced the choice of soils for planting vines. In Europe, all the fertile land was needed for cereal production or grazing to provide sufficient food for the people. Since vines would grow almost anywhere, they were planted on the poorest soils to optimize land use. In the New World, viticulture emerged in the context of excess food supply and often replaced fruit production, with fertile soils and irrigation the norm. It was not until several decades later that growers became aware that certain limiting conditions, such as cool climate, poor soils, limited water and nitrogen supplies, were necessary for wine quality.

Despite all this, the absolute need for quality (and in some cases, wine individuality) in a now highly competitive world market means that the New World can no longer afford to neglect any avenue to excellence. This has become especially evident with recent advances in SOIL MAPPING as part of VINEYARD DESIGN and in PRECISION VITICULTURE, notably in North America and Australia. This approach enables different plots to be identified by soil type and to be managed and harvested separately, even in extensive vineyard developments. The results obtained support Old World experience, as reported by Smart. It is important to note, nevertheless, that the effect of soil on wine quality is reduced in warmer climates, which is why the influence of terroir is so much more marked in marginal climates such as that of Burgundy.

The Old World meanwhile is busy trying to identify more closely the reasons why some soils can give better wines than others. Pre-eminent in this field has been the work of the Bordeaux researcher Dr Gérard Seguin, which forms a background to the discussion that immediately follows. Other French studies of note are of PREMIER CRU vineyards in Burgundy by Meriaux and Chrétien reported by Berry. In this account we distinguish between chemical and physical soil attributes.

Physical soil attributes

Scientific opinion now almost universally agrees with Seguin's conclusion that soil physical characteristics predominate as the main influence over grape and wine qualities other than CLIMATE; and further, that, among the physical characteristics, the most important are those which govern water supply to the vine. These and their relationship to individual soil types are discussed in some detail under TERROIR. See also SOIL WATER, SOIL TEXTURE, DRAINAGE, and VINE PHYSIOLOGY.

Here we may note briefly that the best wines come from soils that are very well drained, and furnish a steady, but only moderate, water supply to the vines. When combined with ap-propriate restrictive mineral VINE NUTRITION, this ensures that growth is restrained. The leaf area, especially the secondary leaf area on the LATERAL SHOOTS, remains relatively small, and nearly all leaves and bunches are well exposed to SUNLIGHT. Smaller berries are also usually less liable to congestion and compression within the bunch, and are therefore less likely to split or suffer spoilage as a result of FUNGAL DISEASES or BACTERIA. WATER STRESS needs to be just enough to attain these ends, and not enough to reduce photosynthesis too much.

Some other physical properties of soils almost certainly influence wine qualities in subtle ways.

SOIL COLOUR affects soil temperature and that of the air immediately above. Dark-coloured soils absorb and convert nearly all of the light falling on them into heat, and so are warmer than light-coloured soils, and, at night and during daytime cloud cover, radiate more warmth back to the vines and bunches. This can be critical in some cold marginal viticultural climates, allowing fuller RIPENING and thus better wine quality (as in the bituminous soils of the Neckar valley in WÜRTTEMBERG or the Meuse valley of southern BELGIUM for example).

The presence of STONES AND ROCKS in the soil or on its surface influences both water and temperature relations. A high proportion of stones throughout the soil profile is commonly associated with very good profile DRAINAGE, but at the same time reduces water-holding capacity and encourages desirably extensive ROOT GROWTH to assure its water supply. In Bordeaux, where the main risk is excessive water supply to the vines, the most important positive effect on wine quality of stones in the soil is the limitation on water-holding capacity, leading to the level of water stress that promotes red wine quality. Studies at CHÂTEAUNEUF-DU-PAPE have shown the benefits of stone cover in improving temperatures and fruit ripening. A cover, or mulch, of stones or rocks also protects against surface EVAPORATION, leading to a greater consistency of water supply. A mulch also protects against soil erosion, and allows the exploitation of MESOCLIMATES which are probably beneficial for wine quality but might otherwise be too risky. The steep, rubbly slate surfaces of many of the MOSEL-SAAR-RUWER vineyards in Germany are a good example. Stony soils, whether sloping or not, usually have the further advantage for wine quality that they are at most only moderately fertile, as discussed below.

Soils containing a large proportion of rock or stone have the additional advantage that they most readily absorb heat and transmit it to depth, because solid rock is a comparatively good conductor of heat: much better than dry or loose soil. Stony soils are warm mainly because they hold less water. Water has a high specific calorific capacity and needs a lot of energy to warm it. Wet soils are therefore cold soils. Moderately damp soil beneath surface stones is both a reasonable heat conductor and a good heat storer, because of the high heat storage capacity of its water content. It is also protected from evaporative cooling. Such soils are efficient at absorbing and storing warmth, and retransmitting it to the above-ground vine parts during cloud cover and in the evening. See TEMPERATURE VARIABILITY and CLIMATE AND WINE QUALITY.

Whatever the mechanisms, there can be little doubt that stony and rocky soils produce many of the world's great wines; and that, within given areas, the stoniest or rockiest usually produce the best. Typical are the coarse gravels that characterize the most eminent châteaux of the MÉDOC in Bordeaux, the large stones that completely cover some of the best sites of CHÂTEAUNEUF-DU-PAPE in the southern Rhône, the coarsely stony gravels that give wines of outstanding quality in the Marlborough region of NEW ZEALAND's South Island, and more recently in the Gimblett Gravels region of Hawkes Bay in the North Island.

Chemical attributes

The relationship between soil chemistry and wine quality is in the main very poorly understood. In some quarters there is the belief that soil influences wine quality because the vine takes up flavour compounds direct from the soil but this viewpoint is unsubstantiated.

Soil NITROGEN is in part an exception to this lack of knowledge. It is clear from Seguin's work, and that of other European researchers, that the optimum nitrogen supply to the vine is at most only moderate. The optimum supply for red wine production is lower than for white wine because nitrogen deficiency increases berry skin PHENOLICS but also limits the build up of aroma precursors in white grapes (see Peyrot des Gachons et al. and Choné et al.). Vines receiving much nitrogen, unless severely constrained by other factors, have vigorous and leafy growth. This leads readily to excessive SHADE within the canopy, and thence to poor fruit quality (see CANOPY MICROCLIMATE). The effects of nitrogen, water supply, and various other nutritional and environmental factors can to varying degrees reinforce or counteract each other in this regard. The best combination among them is that giving optimum vine BALANCE. A major problem in New World viticulture is excessive nitrogen fertilization, leading to excessive vigour.

A further complication has arisen from recent research showing that low nitrogen contents in the berries can be a cause of difficulties in wine-making, leading to STUCK FERMENTATIONS and the presence of HYDROGEN SULFIDE and its malodorous MERCAPTAN derivatives in the wine. This is especially common with grapes grown in warm, sunny climates. While it is now known that at least much of the problem can be overcome by adding nitrogen-based YEAST nutrients during fermentation, the problem of combining suitable nitrogen nutrition for vine balance with optimum concentrations of natural nitrogen compounds in the berries remains largely unsolved.

POTASSIUM availability is another soil factor with mixed relationships to wine quality. Deficiencies are common in cool and humid climates, where the efficiency of water use for growth and yield (see HUMIDITY and CLIMATE AND WINE QUALITY) means that potassium and some other elements are diluted in the plant. Potassium-deficient vines are more than usually susceptible to DROUGHT and VINE DISEASES, and the fruit lacks sugar (see SUGAR IN GRAPES) as well as COLOUR and flavour.

Conversely, vines in hot, atmospherically arid climates readily accumulate excess potassium in the leaves, stems, and fruit. High potassium levels in grapes can lead to high wine PH, with all its attendant quality defects. It should be stressed, however, that the problem is not necessarily correlated with high soil potassium content, nor even always with atmospheric aridity but it may be the result of too much potassium fertilizer. Excessive leaf shading in a poor canopy microclimate contributes importantly in many cases, and improved CANOPY MANAGEMENT can help greatly in assuring more appropriate fruit potassium levels. However, the effect of potassium on grape quality is far less significant than that of nitrogen.

The rule for other nutrient elements appears to be that adequate supplies are needed equally for vine health and for fruit and wine quality though there is very little evidence concerning the possible role of elements such as magnesium, phosphorus, or iron.

Possible specific quality roles for the trace elements (COPPER, ZINC, MANGANESE, IRON, BORON, and molybdenum) remain obscure but potentially interesting. Their contents in the soil and availability to the plant vary enormously from soil to soil, and, in often disparate ways, with SOIL MANAGEMENT. Fregoni and Champagnol cite some cases where differences in wine quality or character from different soils could conceivably be associated with the amounts or balances of trace elements in the soil, vines, or grapes. At the moment, however, no trace element constituent has been shown to be a decisive factor, either in wine quality or in any particular wine characteristic (although see MINERALS for details of vineyard 'fingerprinting'), and opinions about the effect of trace elements on grape quality are highly speculative and sometimes exaggerated in non-scientific literature.

SOIL ACIDITY and SOIL ALKALINITY are further possible influences; but again, little firm evidence exists at present. Extremes in either direction, sufficient to upset vine nutrition and health seriously, seem unlikely to improve wine quality. On the other hand, vines can tolerate a fairly wide soil pH range without evident harm, while the potential trace element deficiencies that are often encountered at high pH levels can in most cases be readily overcome by spraying leaves or by judicious choice of ROOTSTOCKS. Fregoni cites examples of acclaimed wines coming from the full range of soil pH levels. Robinson gives a comprehensive account of this and other aspects of VINE NUTRITION.

The subject of ORGANIC MATTER in soils for viticulture needs careful evaluation. On the one hand, soils naturally high in organic matter tend to be too fertile, and to supply too much nitrogen and water, for good wine quality (as explained above). Soils naturally low in organic matter have a reduced nitrogen supply (unless fertilizers are added), which is good for red wine-making. On the other hand, many respected TERROIRS that have otherwise favourable characteristics for wine quality are naturally too low in organic matter, or have become so, so that both their physical condition and vine health would benefit from its build-up and maintenance (see ORGANIC VITICULTURE). Very sandy soils need organic matter to give them sufficient capacity to store water and nutrients. All soils, and especially clayey soils, benefit from having some organic matter, to give them friability (see SOIL STRUCTURE), and to encourage the activity of earthworms, which help to keep them well aerated and freely draining. The speed of mineralization in clayey soils is slow because they are less well aerated, so excessive nitrogen supply to the vine is not a major risk.

The natures and geological origins of the ROCKS or sediments from which soils are formed (see GEOLOGY) are further factors sometimes held to influence wine qualities. Soils formed from CHALK and LIMESTONE, for example, are highly valued in some cool climates, although not generally in warm regions such as the south of France (see, for instance, Champagnol). Most researchers consider this to be related to their free DRAINAGE and the ability of the SUBSOIL to store water. Certain grape varieties, particularly Pinot Noir and Chardonnay, are also regarded by some as having a special requirement for chalk or limestone soils to produce their best wines; but again, this seems to be a largely northern French view. Experience elsewhere, especially in the New World, lends it little support. One universally positive role of chalk and limestone (or deliberately adding LIME) is that the resulting high level of calcium absorption to the soil clay particles helps to maintain crumbly texture in the soil, thus encouraging aeration, even at very high clay contents (see SOIL TEXTURE).

On the general role of geology, we can conclude that any influence is mostly indirect, via the shaping of TOPOGRAPHY determined by the underlying GEOLOGY, and through effects which are more properly those of the derived soil rather than of the rock or sediment. There can be some direct effects on water supply, however, where vine roots penetrate into the geological stratum underlying the soil. Chalk in Champagne (see above) and the Médoc gravel beds of Bordeaux (see SOIL WATER) have been cited in this regard.

Other factors

These relations are often obscured in practice, and great variation of soils over even short distances means that generalizations of any kind are dangerous. In some vineyards, especially those on alluvial soils, the soil type may change dramatically over a few metres, despite an apparent uniformity at the surface. For the same reason, SOIL MANAGEMENT procedures are seldom equally appropriate across an entire vineyard, let alone between different vineyards.

A second point is that, despite this, management technologies are increasingly becoming available which obviate many of the effects of this variability. This is especially so in the New World. Among the more important is adoption of DRIP IRRIGATION, which in climates with a dry summer can go far towards giving the vines a controlled optimum water regime that is little influenced by soil type. Similarly, techniques of soil and (especially) leaf or PETIOLE analysis are making possible a more controlled optimum vine nutritional regime, so that differences in nutrient supply by the soil are moderated, or even, potentially, eliminated. Remaining soil characteristics, for instance those influencing the vine's temperature and light microenvironments, then perhaps assume greater prominence as being more difficult to manipulate.

A third point is that most vineyards throughout the world are now grafted to PHYLLOXERA-tolerant ROOTSTOCKS. The various rootstocks differ in their ability to take up mineral elements and water, in their capacity to root to depth, and in their effects on the VIGOUR of the vines grafted onto them. It is therefore possible to compensate for and adapt to particular soils as a means of approaching an optimal combination of vigour, nutrition, and canopy management for vine balance. Any consideration of soils now has to acknowledge the role of rootstocks.

At the same time it is salutary to remember that no single rootstock variety can be identified in France which in any case distinguishes the GRAND CRU vineyards from their less celebrated neighbours; nor have vineyard reputations changed much, whereas rootstock usage has. These facts support the conclusion that the main effects of both soil and rootstock on wine quality are mediated by observable effects on the vine that can be subsequently manipulated by management, and are not due to any direct influence of the soil or rootstock itself.

The growing awareness of soil effects on wine quality in the New World has several repercussions. One is to plant vineyards on the less fertile hillside soils, as is evident in California and Chile, for example. Another is to perform detailed SOIL MAPPING before planting, and as a prerequisite to VINEYARD DESIGN. More recently, ZONAL VITICULTURE concepts arising out of GLOBAL POSITIONING SYSTEM and GEOGRAPHICAL INFORMATION SYSTEM technologies allow differential management, including harvesting of separate zones of a vineyard block to maximize quality. These effects, identified by REMOTE SENSING, are by and large due to soil differences.

Conclusions

There can be no doubt that soil characteristics do influence wine quality. However, in most situations the effects of soil are subsidiary to those of CLIMATE, VINE VARIETY, and VINE MANAGEMENT (see van Leeuwen et al.). Of the influential soil characteristics, the most important are those governing the supply of water to the vine, probably followed by those influencing temperatures in and above the soil. Soil chemistry and vine nutrition, within the bounds of normal vine health and growth, play little role that has yet been discerned, other than the role of nitrogen in vegetative vigour and berry nitrogen content, and in some situations that of excess potassium on the pH of must and wine.

Most typically, the best soils for wine quality are:

- generally shallow, with the exception of gravelly soils, because deep soils tend to be too fertile (see SOIL DEPTH);
- fairly light textured, often with gravel through much of the profile and at the surface; almost any texture, from heavy clay to coarse gravel, though intermediate soil textures such as silt or loam tend to hold a significant amount of water and are therefore less suited to wine quality (see SOIL TEXTURE);
- free draining;
- sufficiently high in organic matter to give soil friability, a healthy worm population, and adequate nutrient-holding capacity, but not, as a rule, particularly high in organic matter;
- overall, relatively infertile, supplying enough mineral elements for healthy vine growth, but only enough nitrogen early in the season to promote moderate vegetative vigour.

J.G., R.E.S., & C.V.L.

Berry, E., 'The importance of soil in fine wine production', Journal of Wine Research, 1 (1990), 179–94.

Champagnol, F., Éléments de physiologie de la vigne et de viticulture générale (St-Gely-du-Fesc, 1984).

Choné, X., Van Leeuwen, C., Chéry, P., and Ribéreau-Gayon, P., 'Terroir influence on water status and nitrogen status of non-irrigated Cabernet Sauvignon (Vitis vinifera): vegetative development, must and wine composition', South African Journal of Enology and Viticulture, 22/1 (2001), 8–15.

Fregoni, M., 'Effects of the soil and water on the quality of the harvest', Proceedings: International Symposium on the Quality of the Vintage (Cape Town, 1977).

Jackson, R., Wine Science: Principles, Practice, Perception (San Diego, 2000).

Peyrot des Gachons, C., Van Leeuwen, C., Tominaga, T., Soyer, J.-P., Gaudillère, J.-P., and Dubourdieu, D., 'The influence of water and nitrogen deficit on fruit ripening and aroma potential of Vitis vinifera L. cv Sauvignon blanc in field conditions', Journal of the Science of Food and Agriculture, 85/1 (2005), 73–85.

Robinson, J. B., 'Grapevine nutrition', in B. G. Coombe and P. R. Dry (eds.), Viticulture, ii: Practices (Adelaide, 1992).

Seguin, G., ' "Terroirs" and pedology of wine growing', Experientia, 42 (1986), 861–72.

Smart, R., 'Terroir unmasked', Wine Business Monthly (June 2004), 34–38.

Tregoat, O., Gaudillère, J.-P., Choné, X., and Van Leeuwen, C., 'Étude du régime hydrique et de la nutrition azotée de la vigne par des indicateurs physiologiques. Influence sur le comportement de la vigne et la maturation du raisin (Vitis vinifera L. cv Merlot, 2000, Bordeaux)', Journal International des Sciences de la Vigne et du Vin, 36/3 (2002), 133–42.

Van Leeuwen, C., Friant, P., Choné, X., Tregoat, O., Koundouras, S., and Dubourdieu, D., 'Influence of climate, soil, and cultivar on terroir', American Journal of Enology and Viticulture, 55/3 (2004), 207–17.

soil colour, a term normally referring to the surface colour of a soil. Viticultural folklore associates red wine with red soils, and white wines with white or grey soils. However, while the balance of circumstantial evidence does seem to support such a relationship, many exceptions exist. Present explanations for the apparent correlation are largely speculative.

Colour can certainly affect soil temperature, and that of the air immediately above it. Fregoni discusses this in some detail. Dark-coloured soils or rocks absorb most of the incoming light energy and convert it to heat. Therefore, whereas they reflect less light than light-coloured soils, they radiate more heat at night and when the sun is shaded. In cool climates this may be especially beneficial to red grapes, which in general need more warmth than white grapes to ripen fully. Other examples of the exploitation of these thermal characteristics include the vineyards of Deidesheim in the PFALZ region of Germany, where black basalt rock is mined and spread on the vineyards to help produce wines of unusual sweetness. Fragmented dark grey SLATE helps Riesling to ripen in the otherwise very cool MOSEL-SAAR-RUWER. 'Bituminous' SCHIST soils are reportedly the only ones on which grapes can be ripened at the extreme northern limit of viticulture in BELGIUM. At the other extreme, the exceedingly reflective white ALBARIZA soils of JEREZ in southern Spain produce the best (white) grapes for sherry in a very hot climate, which would seem counter-intuitive.

The relationships of soil colour to temperature suitability for vine-growing are far from straightforward, however. Many reddish and brown soils are still favoured for viticulture in hot regions such as the Mediterranean wine regions and also in much of Australia and California. Presumably the greater warmth radiated during the evening can still result in a net benefit for the vines and wines, despite possibly adverse effects in the heat of the day: see CLIMATE AND WINE QUALITY.

One point of potential speculation is the role of light reflected back from the soil into the vine CANOPY, and to the grape bunches. Little is known about this, but either or both of the quantity and spectral quality of light could conceivably be significant in various ways. White soils obviously reflect back most light (but radiate least heat). A red soil, on the other hand, may be fairly efficient at absorbing and radiating heat, but still reflect the light wavelengths most useful for PHOTOSYNTHESIS back into the canopy. Recent French experiments have shown an improvement in grape (and apple) colour from using reflective foil on the soil surface. See further discussion under SUNLIGHT.

Soil colour is in any case a useful indicator of some of its other properties. Black shows a high content of ORGANIC MATTER. Red or brown are due to the presence of oxidized IRON compounds, and normally indicate good DRAINAGE. A grey soil surface, or soil layer, shows that most of the original iron compounds have been reduced as a result of bad drainage, and eventually leached downwards, often to be deposited in a heavier-textured SUBSOIL.

The colour of the subsoil is a particularly important indicator of soil suitability for viticulture. Except where it consists largely of decomposing chalk or LIMESTONE, a white, grey, or mottled subsoil shows drainage that is usually too poor for viticulture; or at least, a need for artificial drainage. J.G.

Fregoni, M., 'Effects of the soil and water on the quality of the harvest', in Proceedings, International Symposium on the Quality of the Vintage (Cape Town, 1977).

soil depth, a loose term for the depth to the boundary between the SOIL and its parent ROCK material; or, alternatively, the depth to which plant ROOT GROWTH is possible before reaching some impenetrable barrier. Examples of the latter include the tight and/or poorly drained subsoils of some podzolic soils; cemented ironstone, or 'coffee rock', which forms at the base of some iron-rich soils that have been subject to leaching; or layers with excessively high or low pH, or of salt or some other toxic factor which effectively prevents further root penetration.

Soil fertility is combination of fertility per soil volume unit and the rooting depth, which determines the amount of soil available for each vine. Seguin's work shows that if soil is fertile or moderately fertile per soil volume unit, deep rooting leads to excessive soil fertility (due to the availability of water and nutrients) and thus excessive vigour. As a result, in most cases, shallow rooting is a quality factor, because it reduces vigour and yield. Only in soils with very poor fertility per soil volume unit, such as the gravelly soils of the Médoc, is deep rooting an advantage. These soils have such a low water-holding capacity per soil volume unit that deep rooting is necessary to provide a regular supply of water to the vine. Seguin has also shown that deep rooting in these soils where water drains very rapidly prevents the rapid absorption by the root system of rain shortly before harvest, thus helping to prevent rot.

There is a great deal of evidence that in most other situations, great wines are produced on soils where vine rooting is shallow. For example, most great St-Émilions are produced on the limestone plateau, where vine rooting rarely exceeds 60 cm/23 in and can be as little as 30 cm (as in parts of the vineyard of Ch AUSONE). The roots do not penetrate the rock, although Duteau *et al.* have shown that water can move from the bedrock to the roots by capillarity. On the heavy clay soils in Chx PÉTRUS and CHEVAL BLANC, vine rooting does not exceed 130 cm/50 in because of the clay's physical resistance to root penetration. In the Languedoc, the best wines are produced on shallow soils on the hillsides and simple wines are produced on the plains, where rooting is much deeper.

Shallow soils are therefore of major importance in cool, wet climates, while somewhat deeper soils might be an advantage in very dry climates, especially when irrigation is not allowed or not possible. J.G. & C.V.L.

Duteau, J., 'Contribution des réserves hydriques profondes du calcaire à Astéries compact à l'alimentation en eau de la vigne dans le Bordelais', *Agronomie*, 7/10 (1987), 589–865.

Seguin, G., 'Influence des terroirs viticoles', *Bulletin de l'OIV*, 56 (1983), 3–18.

—'"Terroirs" and pedology of wine growing', *Experientia*, 42 (1986), 861–72.

soil disinfection. See FUMIGATION.

soil erosion, shifting or removal of soil by wind or running water. Wind erosion is fairly uncommon in established vineyards, because the vines themselves constitute an effective WINDBREAK at ground level, although it can be a problem in young vineyards. Driving sand, in particular, can seriously injure young vines, and there can in addition be irreparable loss of the most valuable topsoil. The danger can be minimized by growing COVER CROPS such as rye, which act as windbreaks as well as directly binding the soil. More recently, VINE GUARDS have been used to protect young vines from sand blasting.

Erosion by water, on the other hand, is always a potential problem on the sloping sites that normally afford the best MESO-CLIMATES for wine quality (see HILLSIDE VINEYARDS). Some steeply sloping sites, such as in the MOSEL-SAAR-RUWER region of Germany and the northern RHÔNE, necessitate a constant and laborious replacement of soil from the bottom of the slope to the top.

VINEYARD SITE SELECTION and the selection of suitable soils are important elements in the avoidance of erosion. STONES AND ROCKS of the soil surface can offer protection by breaking the flow of water across the surface, and by shielding the fine soil from direct battering and dispersion by raindrops. Plant cover and MULCHES (including vine prunings) have a similar effect. Permanent cover crops between the rows offer the best protection against erosion but are feasible only in those situations where water and NITROGEN supplies are sufficient for both grass and vines. Too much competition for nitrogen can cause problems, especially with white grapes. In Germany, for example, cover crops have been found to increase the problem of ATYPICAL AGEING. Planting on convex hill slopes helps too, to the extent that there are no external sources of flowing water. Where occasional water flowing onto or across a site cannot be avoided, it can often be made harmless by diversionary banks, directing the flow into drains or permanently grassed waterways which follow the natural flow line.

Avoidance of unnecessary cultivation is essential, together with other measures which maintain the soil's ORGANIC MATTER content and physical crumb structure (see SOIL STRUCTURE and SOIL MANAGEMENT). These enable rain to be absorbed readily where it falls. Row orientation and such cultivation as is unavoidable should ideally be directed just a little off the contour, so that any water flow along furrows will be gentle and harmless, and able to spill out onto permanently grassed natural waterways. Cultivation straight up and down slopes lends itself to general erosion.

The practicalities of vineyard design often limit control over the direction and slopes of cultivation. The best control of erosion is therefore through its avoidance as far as possible, and adoption of the other planning and management measures described above.

J.G.

soil fertility, the physical and chemical characteristics of a soil determining its ability to support vigorous plant growth. A fertile soil is generally understood to be one with a high content of available plant nutrients, moderate to high ORGANIC MATTER content, good SOIL STRUCTURE and DRAINAGE, and most typically a SOIL TEXTURE high in LOAM which can store vast amounts of water. Neither SOIL ACIDITY nor SOIL ALKALINITY will be excessive, so that the nutrient elements will all be in a favourable balance of availability for plant growth.

Highly fertile soils, especially those rich in NITROGEN, are undesirable for wine grapes because they encourage excessive vegetation and a congested CANOPY MICROCLIMATE. This in turn can reduce both YIELD and, especially, the quality of the grapes for wine-making. Although vineyard management cannot greatly improve this state of affairs, vigour may be reduced by planting permanent COVER CROPS,

using low-vigour ROOTSTOCKS, avoiding the use of fertilizers except to correct nutrient deficiencies, and by not irrigating the vines. On the other hand, the notion that only infertile soils can make good wines is undoubtedly mistaken. CANOPY MANAGEMENT techniques can allow vigorous vines on moderately fertile soils to mimic the canopy microclimates of traditional vineyards on less fertile soils, with resultant improvements in quality. Carbonneau and Casteran have elucidated these principles in the Bordeaux environment.

See also SOIL AND WINE QUALITY, CLIMATE AND WINE QUALITY, and BALANCE. J.G. & R.E.S.

Carbonneau, A. P., and Casteran, P., 'Interactions "training system × soil × rootstock" with regard to vine ecophysiology, vigour, yield and red wine quality in the Bordeaux area', *Acta horticulturae*, 206 (1987), 119–40.

soil management, the practices of cultivation, or non-cultivation, of soils in vineyards, including the use of COVER CROPS and MULCHES, and other measures to improve the soil's physical condition or improve SOIL FERTILITY. In the broadest sense this term can also embrace IRRIGATION, the use of HERBICIDES, and the addition of FERTILIZER.

In the past, soil management has consisted primarily of clean cultivation to control WEEDS. The advantages of this approach include the avoidance of herbicides, an improvement in SOIL STRUCTURE (if carried out when the soil is dry), and forcing roots to go down deeper. The disadvantages of this approach are increasingly recognized, however. Modern soil management seeks to conserve and, if necessary, increase the ORGANIC MATTER content; to conserve and improve SOIL STRUCTURE and porosity, and thereby improve aeration and free absorption and DRAINAGE of SOIL WATER and resistance to SOIL EROSION; and to maintain a reserve of nutrients in organic and slowly available inorganic forms to provide a steady and balanced supply of VINE NUTRIENTS matched to the plants' needs. It is also expensive.

Aspects of soil management include growing plant covers and green manure crops, with minimal cultivation for their establishment; using inorganic fertilizers (as needed) mainly to grow these crops, and thence to supply the vines as far as possible from organic sources; summer mulching with the residues of the cover and green manures grown *in situ*, or with imported vegetable materials or manures; and, when essential, the use of environment-friendly herbicides to control cover crops and weeds. This approach forces the roots to go down deep, improves machine access to the vineyard after rain, helps to control vigour, reduces the use of herbicides and is inexpensive. However, it may also lead to too much competition in low fertility soils with regard to NITROGEN, especially in the case of white grapes (see ATYPICAL AGEING).

Measures by which undesirable soil compaction can be reduced include the use of lighter equipment in the vineyard, and avoidance of all traffic when the soil is wet. In large vineyards it is feasible to apply some sprays from the air (see HELICOPTERS). Similarly the future greater use of biological methods for pest control (see ORGANIC VITICULTURE and INTEGRATED PEST MANAGEMENT) should help to reduce the movement of equipment in the vineyard. The use of LIME or gypsum may be indicated for some soils. All these measures serve to improve soil physical conditions for vine ROOT GROWTH, thereby improving vine health, YIELD, and in some instances wine quality.   J.G. & R.E.S.

McCarthy, M. G., Dry, P. R., Hayes, P. F., and Davidson, D. M., 'Soil and management and frost control', in B. G. Coombe and P. R. Dry (eds.), *Viticulture*, ii: *Practices* (Adelaide, 1992).

soil mapping, procedure used before vineyard planting to assist in design decisions about irrigation layout, variety and rootstock location, and choice of TRAINING SYSTEM. Soil mapping is becoming more common in vineyard developments in the New World, and represents acceptance of the Old World notion that local conditions, especially the soil, have important effects on quality. The procedure consists of digging pits, normally on a grid at about 90 m spacing, so that the soil can be sampled and described by a soil specialist. Maps are prepared for use in vineyard design, the most useful of which is that of 'readily available water' or RAW. See TERROIR for a full discussion of the relevant issues, also SOIL, SOIL AND WINE QUALITY, and PRECISION VITICULTURE.   R.E.S.

Smart, R. E., 'Vineyard design to improve wine quality—the Orlando way', *Australian and New Zealand Wine Industry Journal*, 11 (1996), 335–6.

soil nutrients, elements occurring in the soil which are taken up by plant root systems. Soils which are rich in nutrients are often termed fertile, but such soils do not usually produce good-quality wine (see SOIL FERTILITY). The amounts of nutrients that are available to the vine depend on the soil's mineralogy, the amount and nature of ORGANIC MATTER, and also the soil PH. Soils with a long history of COVER CROPS have high levels of surface organic matter and are typically rich in NITROGEN but this is not necessarily available to the vine since the cover crop may compete with the vine for nitrogen. Old vineyard soils on the other hand are often relatively impoverished of organic matter, but may have high levels of COPPER as a result of repeated FUNGICIDE application. Many nutrients including nitrogen and PHOSPHORUS, for example, are less available in acid soils. Others such as IRON and MANGANESE are less available in alkaline soils. Nutrient deficiencies are diagnosed by symptoms on the vines, or by plant and soil tests, and can be remedied by applying FERTILIZERS.   R.E.S.

Robinson, J. B., 'Grapevine nutrition', in B. G. Coombe and P. R. Dry (eds.), *Viticulture*, ii: *Practices* (Adelaide, 1992).

soil preparation, the treatment of SOIL before PLANTING a vineyard, can be an important viticultural operation. Proper attention at this stage can determine the long-term success or otherwise of a VINEYARD.

Having selected the best possible site (see VINEYARD SITE SELECTION, TOPOGRAPHY, and TERROIR) and vineyard layout, and assured suitable DRAINAGE, the potential vine-grower should in most soils undertake deep RIPPING along the paths of the future vine rows. This should be done when the soil is as dry as possible, and aims to break through any pre-existing hard pans and to open up the SUBSOIL to facilitate penetration of the vine roots.

If a vineyard is replanted, particular care must be taken to remove the roots of the old vines since these can harbour VIRUS DISEASES or FUNGAL DISEASES.

If the SOIL ACIDITY is high, with a pH at a depth of 3 cm/1.2 in of less than, say, 5.5, adding LIME will be beneficial. SOIL TESTING should establish the suitable application of lime and other fertilizers.

Finally, WEEDS need to be controlled. In most climates it is usual to grow an autumn–winter green manure crop to add ORGANIC MATTER prior to vine planting in spring.   J.G.

Boehm, E. W., and Coombe, B. G., 'Vineyard establishment', in B. G. Coombe and P. R. Dry (eds.), *Viticulture*, ii: *Practices* (Adelaide, 1992).

soil structure, the physical structure of soils, an important vineyard characteristic, as governed by bonding of the primary particles (as described in SOIL TEXTURE) into larger aggregates. The size and stability of these aggregates help to determine the soil's friability or crumb structure, and hence its porosity for air movement, water DRAINAGE, and ROOT penetration, and its capacity to withstand the effects of CULTIVATION and compression by vineyard machinery and the elements.

Soil structure depends on the following factors:

1. The amount and chemical nature of the clay. To have stable structure, a soil must have at least a moderate CLAY content. Montmorillonite clays swell and shrink with wetting and drying, leading to a desirable 'self-mulching' soil character. At the other extreme, good structure is hard to build up and preserve in kaolinitic soils. Illitic clays (see GEOLOGY) are intermediate.
2. Relative contents of CALCIUM and SODIUM. Calcium helps to build up good soil structure, sodium causes breakdown and dispersion of the aggregates.
3. ORGANIC MATTER content. Humus is necessary for good structure in most soils, especially where the clay is kaolinitic. It is formed from decaying plant roots, leaves, etc. deposited at the surface, and the remains of microflora and microfauna living in the soil. Gummy substances excreted by living roots and soil organisms also play an important part in forming and preserving soil aggregates.
4. Soil disturbance by cultivation. All cultivation can be destructive of soil structure if it is done when the soil is wet, especially when the clay content is low and of unfavourable chemical nature, and the organic matter content is low. However, if done when the soil is dry, it can improve soil structure.

Good SOIL MANAGEMENT aims principally to preserve and strengthen soil structure.   J.G.

soil testing, or analysis by laboratory techniques, seeks to determine the concentrations of nutrient elements in the soil, and to give other information on its physical and chemical state. Soil testing is a useful part of SOIL MAPPING to determine PH (see SOIL ACIDITY, SOIL ALKALINITY) and specific VINE NUTRIENTS. Tissue analysis of the vines themselves usually gives a better guide to any FERTILIZER requirements than soil testing.

Soil tests nevertheless do give useful preliminary information for some nutrients. Carried out before planting, they allow the placement of any necessary nutrients such as PHOSPHORUS, POTASSIUM, CALCIUM, MAGNESIUM, and BORON below the vine rows, at depths where they will remain readily, and more or less permanently, available to the roots (see SOIL PREPARATION). Field inspection to determine SOIL TEXTURE and its natural DRAINAGE to as great a depth as possible is of course an essential preliminary to any vine planting. See also SOIL AND WINE QUALITY, TERROIR, and VINEYARD SITE SELECTION.   J.G. & R.E.S.

soil texture, the overall physical nature of the soil as determined by its proportions of constituent clay, silt, sand, STONES AND ROCKS, and ORGANIC MATTER. The individual constituents are defined below. Soils predominantly of clay are described as heavy textured. Loams are medium-textured soils, normally containing a fairly even balance of clays, silt, and sand, together with a moderately high organic matter content. Sands are light-textured soils, often loose and gritty, with at most a low clay content. Certain mineral elements, most notably CALCIUM, complement textural differences in helping to determine soil friability (see SOIL STRUCTURE).

Clay is the finest of the inorganic soil fractions, with particles conventionally set at less than 0.002 mm in diameter. If mixed in water, most of the particles remain in colloidal suspension for a long time. Because their surface areas are so large relative to their volumes, they have by far the greatest capacity for combining with, adsorbing, and holding plant nutrient elements and water. Fertile soils normally have at least a moderate proportion of clay.

Silt is an intermediate fraction, comprising the particles ranging between 0.002 and 0.05 mm in diameter. Being small enough to be carried in suspension by turbulent rivers, but large enough to settle out fairly quickly, silt particles are prominent in alluvial soils deposited by river floods.

Sand particles are the largest of those generally thought of as truly constituting soil, and range from 0.05 mm up to 2 mm in diameter. Unless mixed with a proportion of clay, sand remains loose under most conditions. In contrast to clay, the surface area of a sand particle is small relative to its volume, so it has little capacity for surface binding and storing of plant nutrients or water.

Organic matter plays an important complementary role, especially on very sandy soils where it is practically the only medium for nutrient and water storage. Organic matter also helps to make clay soils more friable.

Stones and rocks appear to have particular significance for viticulture, through their effects on limiting soil water-holding capacity and, additionally, on TEMPERATURE both within and immediately above the soil. Stony soils are also usually well drained and have a low water-holding capacity, while a surface layer of stones greatly enhances resistance to SOIL EROSION and reduces surface water loss by evaporation.

Commercial viticulture is carried out across a very wide range of soil textures. Clay and clay-loam soils can be suitable provided they contain ample calcium (as in most LIMESTONE- or CHALK-derived soils) and at least some organic matter. The strongest growth of vines, as with most other plants, is usually on loams and silty soils. Whether or not this is desirable depends on various other management and environmental factors, as described for example under SOIL FERTILITY and VIGOUR. Soils in the clay to loam texture range will store in the vicinity of 15 mm/0.6 in of WATER per 10 cm/ 4 in of soil depth, in forms that the vine roots can extract.

Soils consisting mostly of sand can pose problems for viticulture because of their lack of storage capacity for both water and nutrients. Typically they will hold 10 mm or less of root-available water per 10 cm of soil depth. The great depth of some sandy soils can be an offsetting factor, however, as in parts of the Bordeaux region, because vine roots penetrate many metres if the SUBSOIL texture and DRAINAGE permit, and can thus exploit a large enough volume to compensate for the low water-holding capacity per soil volume unit. On some very sandy soils, the problems of water supply are overcome by supplying carefully controlled amounts by drip IRRIGATION. Nutrients can be supplied at the same time, in a process known as FERTIGATION.

An ideal soil for wine quality, depending on CLIMATE and the rate of EVAPORATION, together with the potential for irrigation, will balance texture against root-available depth to give an adequate storage capacity for water and nutrients, and to provide the vine with a steady moderate supply of both for BALANCED growth

and fruiting. No single soil texture has a monopoly of these characteristics. Seguin notes that in the Bordeaux region the soils giving the best water regimes and producing the best wines range from the dominant deep, stony sands of the MÉDOC, because of their low water-holding capacity to heavy (but well-structured) clays in POMEROL, because the water is present but not easily available to the vines. Thus in Bordeaux, extreme textures are generally better than intermediate textures such as silt or loam soils, which can hold significant supplies of water readily available to the vine.

See also GEOLOGY.   J.G. & C.V.L.

Seguin, G., 'Influence des terroirs viticoles' ('Influence of viticultural terroirs'), *Bulletin de l'OIV*, 56 (1983), 3–18.

soil types. For types of SOIL and ROCK, see individual entries on ALBARIZA, ALLUVIUM, CALCAIRE, CHALK, CLAY, GRANITE, GRAVEL, LIMESTONE, LOAM, LOESS, MARL, QUARTZ, RENDZINA, SAND, SANDSTONE, SCHIST, SHALE, SILT, SLATE, TERRA ROSSA, TUFFEAU, and VOLCANIC. See also SOIL AND WINE QUALITY and GEOLOGY, however, for evidence of soil's relatively indirect role in shaping wine and wine quality.

soil water, that water held by the soil, within the potential rooting zone for plants, after any surplus has drained away (if it can). It exists in varying degrees of bondage to the finer soil particles (see SOIL TEXTURE) and ORGANIC MATTER, as well as in open soil pores, which either drain away quickly (in well-drained soils) or remain in a stagnant state under waterlogging. In the last case, a lack of OXYGEN quickly kills most plant roots.

Water supply to the vines is the key factor in grape quality. Vines are Mediterranean plants that need very little water: they can easily grow in climates with only 400 mm/ 15 in of rainfall a year, providing that the soil has at least an average water-holding capacity. Water deficits resulting in a certain level of WATER STRESS are essential to grow good quality grapes, particularly for red wine-making.

Water supply to the vine depends on climatic parameters (RAINFALL, potential EVAPOTRANSPIRATION), soil parameters (water-holding capacity), and plant-related factors (rooting depth, leaf area, crop load). Studies on TERROIR by Seguin, Duteau *et al.*, Morlat, and Koundouras *et al.*, for example, show that terroir that produces high-quality red wine supplies only moderate amounts of water to the vines, thus inducing water deficit stress. The gravelly soils of the Médoc were the first in the world to be seriously studied by Seguin, who used a neutron moisture probe to investigate vine–water relations in these soils as early as 1966. However, the fact that these soils are deep is rather an exception than a general rule, and can be explained only by their high gravel content and their low clay content

(see SOIL DEPTH). These soils can be subject to temporary waterlogging until flowering, but generally the water table is not within reach of the roots during ripening. If it is, wine quality suffers, as explained in van Leeuwen *et al.* (1994).

Regular or permanent waterlogging, even if only of the subsoil or the zone immediately overlying it, is a clear counter-indicator for vines, particularly if it occurs during the vine growing season. The optimum soil water regime is thus usually found where there is an adequate depth of well-drained soil, with at least moderate contents of clay, silt, and organic matter so that water can be supplied steadily from soil reserves over a long period. The less the clay and organic matter content, the deeper the soil needs to be to achieve that end. Note, however, that too much available soil water can be counter-productive in viticulture if it promotes too much vegetative VIGOUR, or helps to prolong vegetative growth into the fruit-ripening period. (See also CLIMATE AND WINE QUALITY, SOIL AND WINE QUALITY.)

Ideally there should be ample available soil water during FLOWERING and FRUIT SET, diminishing so as to create just enough mild WATER STRESS before VERAISON to inhibit further vegetative growth. Opinions vary as to the optimum water supply between veraison and RIPENING, but most agree at least that there should be no severe stress through this period; nor should there be so much water available, especially after preceding stress, as to encourage a sudden uptake into the berries or renewed vegetative growth.

The binding capacity of the soil for the water that remains after free DRAINAGE has its own significance for vine–water relations. Some is so tightly bound to the CLAY and ORGANIC MATTER that roots cannot extract it at all, and some can only be extracted slowly. This explains why heavy clay soils, such as those of Ch PÉTRUS in Pomerol which induce early water deficits, can produce very fine red wines (see van Leeuwen *et al.* (1994)). The small amount of water held in sandy soils, on the other hand, is readily and quickly available, and therefore easily exhausted. However, in sandy soils, vine rooting is often very deep and water-holding capacity can be too high to grow high quality fruit. See van Leeuwen *et al.* (1994, 2004), Duteau *et al.*

Even in Mediterranean climates with very low summer rainfall, the best soils are not those on the plains with a high water-holding capacity but the more shallow, stony soils of the slopes, which have lower water-holding capacity. However, when water-holding capacity is very low (shallow and very stony soils on hard limetone bedrock, as in La Clape, near Narbonne), water stress might be so severe as to reduce wine quality. In such climates, relatively shallow soils, or sandy/stony soils with limited water-holding capacity, combined with supplementary irrigation when needed (and permitted), can have advantages in allowing the best control over water availability to the vines.   J.G., R.E.S., & C.V.L.

Duteau, J., Guilloux, M., and Seguin, G., 'Influence des facteurs naturels sur la maturation du raisin, en 1979, à Pomerol et Saint-Emilion', *Connaissance de la Vigne et du Vin*, 15/3 (1981), 1–27.

Morlat, R., 'Le terroir viticole: contribution à l'étude de sa caractérisation et de son influence sur les vins. Application aux vignobles rouges de la moyenne vallée de la Loire', PhD thesis, Bordeaux University II, 1989.

Seguin, G., '"Terroirs" and pedology of wine growing', *Experientia*, 42 (1986), 861–73.

Van Leeuwen, C., Friant, P., Choné, X., Tregoat, O., Koundouras, S., and Dubourdieu, D., 'Influence of climate, soil, and cultivar on terroir', *American Journal of Enology and Viticulture*, 55/3 (2004), 207–17.

Van Leeuwen, C., and Seguin, G., 'Incidences de l'alimentation en eau de la vigne, appréciée par l'état hydrique du feuillage, sur le développement de l'appareil végétatif et la maturation du raisin (Vitis vinifera variété Cabernet franc, Saint-Emilion, 1990), *Journal International des Sciences de la Vigne et du Vin*, 28/2 (1994), 81–110.

solar, Portuguese term meaning a 'manor house', which (like CHÂTEAU in France) may also be a wine-producing property.

solera, system of fractional blending used most commonly in JEREZ for maintaining the consistency of a style of SHERRY which takes its name from those barrels closest to the *suelo*, or floor, from which the final blend was customarily drawn. The system was created for commercial reasons in the second half of the 19th century. Previously, sherry was vintage-dated just like claret.

The system is designed to smooth out the differences between vintage years and is effectively a more subtle, and very much more labour-intensive, version of the BLENDING of inexpensive table wines between one vintage and another, although the solera system concerns barrel-aged liquids and is made up of several different scales. Depending on market demand, a fraction of wine is removed from the oldest scale of the solera, the so-called solera barrels themselves, and replaced (although the barrels are never filled completely) with wine from the next scale of barrels containing wine of the same type but one year younger, the so-called first criadera. They in turn are replenished from the scale two years younger (the second criadera) and so on, the youngest scale being replenished with new wine. This system is particularly useful for FLOR wines because it refreshes each barrel with younger wine and provides micronutrients to sustain the flor yeast for several years. It takes several years' operation for a solera to reach an equilibrium average age. Many soleras in Jerez were started decades ago and, since no barrel is ever emptied, there is always some of the oldest wine in the final blend. Fewer scales are needed to produce a

consistent AMONTILLADO or OLOROSO sherry than a FINO or MANZANILLA sherry because these fuller, richer wines vary less from year to year.

Even using modern pumps, a solera system is extremely labour-intensive and it is only in regions where LABOUR costs are relatively moderate that a large solera is feasible.

The solera system is also used for blending Brandy de Jerez, and for many other fortified wines such as MÁLAGA, MONTILLA, MADEIRA, LIQUEUR MUSCAT and Liqueur Tokay in Australia, as well as in the production of top-quality VINEGAR. If a product is labelled 'Solera 1880', for example, it should come from a solera established in 1880.

For mathematical calculations of the average age of a solera, and the time required to reach equilibrium average age, see Baker *et al.*

Baker, G. A., Amerine, M. A., and Roessler, E. B., 'Theory and application of fractional blending programs', *Hilgardia*, 21 (1952), 383–409.

soluble solids, also called total soluble solids (TSS) and total dissolved solids (TDS), refers to the collective concentration in unfermented grape juice of all solutes (dissolved molecules and ions). The predominant solutes, accounting for about 90 per cent of the total, in the juice of ripe grapes are the reducing sugars GLUCOSE and FRUCTOSE; others are acids (MALIC and TARTARIC), ions (organic and inorganic), and literally hundreds of inorganic and organic molecules that together contribute to the characteristics that make grapes such an adaptable and useful product. Collective concentrations of TSS range from 5 to over 25 per cent and may be expressed in many ways, most usually either as degrees BRIX, BAUMÉ, or OECHSLE. With all such measurements, TEMPERATURE control or correction is necessary.
                                          B.G.C.

sommelier, widely used French term for a specialist wine waiter or wine steward. The sommelier's job is to ensure that any wine ordered is served correctly and, ideally, to advise on the individual characteristics of every wine on the establishment's wine list and on FOOD AND WINE MATCHING. In some establishments, the sommelier may also be responsible for compiling the list, buying and storing the wine, and restocking whatever passes for a CELLAR. (All too few restaurants today have their own serious collection of wines, although there are notable exceptions such as the Tour d'Argent in Paris, whose cellar is but a few feet from the river Seine, and Taillevent, whose cellar is so important that it has spawned a retail wine business.)

A sommelier should present the wine or wines ordered to the host before they are opened to ensure that there has been no misunderstanding (and so that the host can especially check that the vintage corresponds to expectations). This is a good time for the

host to check that the bottle feels at the right SERVING temperature. The bottle should be opened in view of the host, and, if a wine is to be DECANTED (and that is an option that any decent sommelier should be able to offer), that operation should be performed in public too.

Some sommeliers offer the cork to the host to smell, which is well meaning but is no certain guide to whether or not the wine is FAULTY. Some sublime wines come from under some rather unpleasant-smelling corks, and vice versa.

A surer guide to whether a particular bottle happens to be one of the relatively few to exhibit a FAULT (CORKINESS is the most common) is to examine the small tasting sample usually offered by the sommelier to the host for this very purpose. A glance will confirm that it is not cloudy, dull, or fizzing when it should not. A swift inhalation should confirm that it smells 'clean'. Few people can then resist actually tasting a mouthful, but it is generally unnecessary as the most common faults are apparent to the eye or nose. Besides, tasting a wine should clearly reveal its all-important TEMPERATURE. This is the moment to ask for an ice bucket (for red wines if necessary) or for a bottle to be taken out of an ice bucket.

In many countries there are official associations of sommeliers, often with a series of examinations, qualifications, or at least competitions. The Court of Master Sommeliers (www.courtofmastersommeliers.org) holds exams and awards the initials MS not unlike the Institute of MASTERS OF WINE. French, and other, sommeliers compete in these events all over the world and, such is the average French person's reverence for the wine knowledge of a sommelier, to win the title Meilleur Sommelier du Monde (Best Sommelier in the World) is henceforth to inhabit another world.

Somontano, wine zone in the foothills of the central Pyrenees, in ARAGÓN in north east Spain (see map under SPAIN). Somontano (meaning 'under the mountain') is one of the most impressive of Spain's recently designated DO regions. In stark contrast to much of inland Spain, Somontano looks like winemaking country. The heavy winter rains are supplemented by a network of rivers and streams flowing off the mountains. Even in summer, when temperatures can easily reach 35 °C/95 °F, the fields remain green and productive.

Bodega Pirineos, once the region's COOPERATIVE, together with the ultra-modern, recently created wineries Viñas del Vero (vintage 1986) and Enate (1991), make virtually all Somontano's wine. The red MORISTEL grape (no relation with Monastrell) dominates, closely followed by the newly planted varieties imported into the region such as Tempranillo, Cabernet Sauvignon, Merlot, and even Pinot Noir, which are preferred by the two newcomers. Pirineos has continued to develop Moristel-based wines and is recovering the almost extinct red Parraleta vine, which traditionally gave backbone to blends dominated by Moristel. Garnacha was on the wane, and mainly used for rosés, until Viñas del Vero discovered and relaunched the impressive old vineyards at Secastilla with a very distinctive single-estate Garnacha red. For whites, the traditional Macabeo and almost extinct Alcañón have been joined by Chardonnay and Gewürztraminer. The modern, crisp wines now produced have nothing in common with Somontano's traditional, rustic wines.

R.J.M. & V. de la S.

Sonoma, northern CALIFORNIA town, valley, and one of the state's most important wine counties. **Sonoma county** is one of the larger of northern California's coastal counties, and one of its most historic. **Sonoma valley** is a very small portion of Sonoma county but it rivals and occasionally beats nearby NAPA valley for *réclame*. Vineyards are everywhere in the county, and have been since the last third of the 19th century. Sprawling, geologically and climatically diverse, it is the most resolutely amoebic of all the fine wine regions, having divided and redivided itself into AVAs and sub-AVAs until they run three layers deep in several places, four in a few, and eight in one. Growing conditions are a little more homogeneous than the welter of names suggests, but Sonoma still gives would-be gurus some of their most engaging opportunities to define subtle boundaries by taste and taste alone. The full roster follows.

Alexander Valley AVA

The largest and most fully planted of Sonoma county's many vineyard valleys, Alexander Valley takes in the Russian river watershed upstream of Healdsburg north all the way to the Sonoma–Mendocino county line north of Cloverdale. If the general history is long, with vines dating back to the 1850s, the particular history of noble varieties is—a few rare plantings excepted—as short here as almost everywhere else in California. The valley awakened from a long drowse of mixed black grapes for bulk red only in the late 1960s and early 1970s. Simi winery started the renaissance in 1970, when a new owner breathed life into a moribund cellar. Chateau Souverain picked up the traces in 1973 and then Jordan Vineyards added a stamp of elegance in 1976. Growth has been steady since then. KENDALL-JACKSON's 1996 purchase of the mountain vineyards on Gauer Ranch represented another step forward for Sonoma, while GALLO's acquisition of nearly 1,500 acres/600 ha since 1988 in Alexander Valley alone signalled a new era for both Gallo and Alexander Valley.

Alexander Valley is noteworthy among other Sonoma county appellations for the fleshy voluptuousness of its wines. A wide range of grape varieties is grown at least passably well, which has distracted from the question of what the district does best. Accessibility is much more likely to be a general descriptor than longevity, however. Cabernet Sauvignon has gained a certain currency, with a signature note of chocolate warmth and agreeable MOUTHFEEL. Chardonnays also tend to bold statement and ample girth. These varieties, market driven, dominate plantings. Sauvignon Blanc and Zinfandel succeed often enough to make one wonder if they are not suited best to these particular suns and soils. Most of its substantial plantings are on a broad and nearly flat valley floor very nearly bisected by the river, but some significant ones creep into the east hills. Other wineries that brought Alexander Valley to wide attention in recent years were Geyser Peak, Clos du Bois, and Murphy-Goode. Wineries outside the area whose significant reputations have been based primarily on grapes grown in Alexander Valley include Rodney Strong, Silver Oak, Chateau St Jean, and the red wines of Estancia.

Chalk Hill AVA

In essence a small sub-AVA in the foothills behind the Russian River district, Chalk Hill is at its eastern edge near the town of Windsor. It occupies the western slope of the hills which separate the southern end of Alexander valley from the Santa Rosa plain.

Dry Creek Valley and Rockpile AVAs

For years a sparsely settled tributary of the Russian river drainage, Dry Creek Valley has slowly emerged over the past decade as one of Sonoma county's most intriguing appellations. Among white varieties, Sauvignon Blanc stands head and shoulders above Chardonnay. Among reds, the race is more even between Zinfandel and Cabernet Sauvignon. The sad thing, from the point of view of Zinfandel fanciers, is that nowhere else is that grape nearly so voluptuous, while Cabernet does at least as well and perhaps better in several other zones in California. Still, until the mid 1990s economic considerations favoured Cabernet to a degree that no farmer could ignore, and plantings shifted accordingly. Since 1995, however, (red) Zinfandel has been resurgent and an undersupply has made these highly regarded vineyards tantalizing to second careerist refugees from San Francisco.

The valley heads north and west from Healdsburg, where Dry creek flows into the Russian river. For many years plantings stopped at Warm Springs dam. The reservoir above drowned some good patches of Zinfandel; but now the area north of the lake has been planted and christened Rockpile AVA. It is the source of at least one exceptional, sun-drenched, chewy Zin from Rosenblum. The terrain further west was historically considered too wild to be cultivated, although a few picturesque inroads are now being made.

Italian immigrants planted the early vineyards. Italian names remain commonest among vineyard owners, but they are far from having a monopoly in the modern era. Dry Creek's most prominent wineries in the late 1990s included Ferrari-Carano, Nalle, Preston, Michel Schlumberger, and Rafanelli.

Knights Valley AVA

A small, handsome, upland valley in Sonoma county separates the upper end of the Napa valley from the lower end of the Alexander valley. It was originally developed by Beringer Vineyards, but now has several growers and a prominent winery owned by British businessman Peter Michael. The most impressive grape variety to date has been Cabernet Sauvignon.

Northern Sonoma AVA

This oddity of an AVA encompasses all of Sonoma that drains into the Pacific, which is to say all but Sonoma valley and some of the Petaluma river watershed; it was proposed and is mainly used by E. & J. GALLO, but has proven useful to a few others with scattered vineyards.

Russian River Valley and Fort Ross AVAs

Most of the Russian river's course is through other AVAs in MENDOCINO and Sonoma counties. Only when the river escapes from Alexander valley through a narrow gorge in the mountains at Healdsburg, then flows on, first south, then west, in its journey to the Pacific do the watercourse and the Russian River Valley AVA become one and the same.

Cool, often foggy, the AVA blossomed as a wine-producing region only after 1970 when new winery owners in the area began bottling locally grown grapes under Sonoma county labels. It has taken the district fewer than 20 years to prove itself eminently well adapted to still wines from Chardonnay and Pinot Noir as well as to sparkling wines from the same varieties. In a few HILLSIDE locations such as Martinelli's Jackass Vineyard, Zinfandel does amazingly well. Joe Swan was an early pioneer. Dehlinger, Sonoma-Cutrer, Rochioli, Gary Farrell, and Williams & Selyem are some of the region's best-known wineries. Interest in Pinot Noir exploded in the region during the late 1990s, with vineyard acreage more than tripling from around 4,000 acres then to over 12,000 in 2003.

Fort Ross is a new AVA in the mountains north of the Russian River appellation, and near to the historic Russian encampment from which it takes its name, where sea otters were extensively hunted in the early 1800s. Proximity to the coast led many observers to assume that Pinot Noirs grown in the Fort Ross AVA would be leaner and more acidic than their Russian River cousins, which originally drove the price for these grapes to extremely high levels. But the elevation of most vineyard sites in the Fort Ross AVA puts them continuously above the maritime fog layer so that the grapes bud early and often ripen in late August. Big body and bold fruit have frequently been the signature of the AVA. Hirsch and Flowers are well-known producer-growers.

Sonoma-Green Valley AVA

A sub-AVA of California's Russian River Valley AVA described above, Sonoma-Green Valley lies at the western edge of the larger region, and answers to all the same descriptions. Its best-known estate is Iron Horse.

Sonoma Coast AVA

This AVA stands out as a purely artificial construction. Its sponsors (including Sonoma-Cutrer) drew boundaries to include widely scattered vineyards so they could continue to describe their wines as ESTATE BOTTLED after tightened federal regulations began requiring that both winery and vineyard be within the same AVA to qualify. The AVA covers some otherwise excluded vineyards along Sonoma county's shore, but swings inland to encompass parts of the Russian river and Sonoma valleys, and Carneros.

Sonoma Mountain AVA

A sub-AVA of Sonoma Valley (see below) best known for Cabernet Sauvignon, it occupies the east-facing slopes of the 2,400-ft/730-m mountain from which it draws its name and which separates Sonoma valley from the Petaluma river watershed to the west. The AVA sits above the towns of Glen Ellen and Kenwood. Its most prestigious winery is Laurel Glen.

Sonoma Valley AVA

For history, especially romantic history, no other AVA in California compares with Sonoma Valley. In addition to being the site of the ragtag revolt, which eventually secured Alta California for the US rather than Mexico, it had the last of the Franciscan MISSIONARY vineyards, one of the earliest commercial vineyards north of San Francisco (General Mariano Vallejo appropriated the Franciscan plantings), and, courtesy of public relations master Agoston HARASZTHY, the first great winery name of northern California, Buena Vista. In more modern times, its Hanzell Vineyard started the rush to using French oak BARRELS to age California wines and thereby revolutionized their style, most especially Chardonnay's. The valley parallels the Napa valley to the east, and nearly touches the Russian river valley to the north west. Its southern extremity doubles as the Sonoma portion of CARNEROS. A long, thin comma of a trough in the coast ranges, it warms markedly from south to north because San Francisco bay's influence dwindles mile by mile. Steep mountains on each side make it geologically as well as climatically complex. Some of its memorable wines portray that diversity: Zinfandel, Gewürztraminer, Pinot Noir, Chardonnay, and Cabernet Sauvignon. Sonoma Mountain

(see above) is a sub-AVA. Sebastiani and Gundlach-Bundschu are the old-timers of the valley. Others of note include Kenwood, Benziger, St Francis, and Kunde. Carmenet is in the AVA in the eastern mountains, as is Ravenswood's tasting room; Matanzas Creek is in a spur called Bennett valley to the north; Viansa and Cline are in the Carneros section to the south.

Sopron, wine region in the extreme north west of HUNGARY which is geographically part of the Neusiedlersee wine regions of AUSTRIA. Its climate is much more temperate than that of most of the rest of Hungary, with cooler, wetter summers and milder winters. From the 14th century, when Hungary was recognized as a useful source of fuller, richer wines than those of northern Europe, Sopron was an important centre of the wine trade, dispatching not just its own wines but those of the rest of Hungary to Austria, Poland, and Silesia. Today Sopron produces mainly red wines, more tannic than the Hungarian norm, from grape varieties such as KÉKFRANKOS, Cabernet, and Merlot.

sorbates. See SORBIC ACID.

sorbic acid (2,4-hexadienoic acid), winemaking additive and preservative discovered in 1940 to inhibit the growth of YEAST and other FUNGI. Sorbic acid, or its salt potassium **sorbate**, is used widely in food and drink production to inhibit the growth of yeast and mould, notably on cheese and meat. It is classified as one of the safest food preservatives. Sorbic acid use has permitted the wide range of everyday commercial wines currently available which contain some RESIDUAL SUGAR but whose ALCOHOLIC STRENGTH alone is not sufficient to inhibit yeast metabolism.

There is a drawback, however. While most people detect about 135 mg/l, a small proportion of humans are sufficiently sensitive to sorbic acid to find about 50 mg/l in wines. It has a particular taste and a rancid odour to some palates, even at levels that are hardly high enough to inhibit yeast. The EU limit in finished wines is 200 mg/l.

Sorbic acid inhibits the growth of some BACTERIA but not, unfortunately for winemakers, the large group of LACTIC ACID BACTERIA. SULFUR DIOXIDE must be used together with sorbic acid in sweet wines that are low in alcohol in order to prevent the growth of lactic acid bacteria. Some of these lactics metabolize sorbates to produce compounds such as 2-ethoxyhexa-3,5-diene, which has a perception threshold of around 10 ng/l and smells of crushed geranium leaves—definitely a wine FAULT.   A.D.W.

sorbitol, one of the ALCOHOLS present in trace amounts in grapes and wines, and closely related to GLUCOSE. It has a mildly sweet taste, is very soluble in water and, when present in

high concentrations, confers a sense of BODY on a liquid.

Since sorbitol can be made easily and cheaply from many agricultural raw materials, this property has been harnessed by a few unscrupulous wine bottlers to increase consumer acceptance of thin, acid, ordinary wines. Sorbitol is not harmful to humans but its use is prohibited by most wine regulations.   A.D.W.

sorì is a PIEMONTESE dialect term used for vineyard sites of the highest quality, particularly for those with an exceptional favourable southern exposure. More subtle variations also exist: a 'morning' sorì (*sorì di mattino*) with a south eastern exposure or an 'evening' sorì (*sorì di sera*) with a south western exposure. The term was first used on a wine label by Angelo GAJA for his Sorì San Lorenzo Barbaresco 1967 and was widely imitated in the subsequent quarter-century.   D.T.

sorting of grapes. See TRIAGE.

sotolon, compound (3-hydroxy-4,5-dimethyl-2(5H)-furanone) that is an important component of the spice fenugreek and is found in a wide range of products from BOTRYTIZED wines to roasted tobacco. It is responsible for the hazelnut and particularly spicy 'curry' aromas found notably in VIN JAUNE from Jura but also in TOKAJI and some fortified wines including VIN DOUX NATUREL and PORT, especially those that are RANCIO. It forms partially during the ageing process, particularly if this is oxidative, but in vins jaunes it is known to increase after bottling. Discovered by Japanese scientists in the late 1970s as a flavour compound in raw cane sugar, sotolon has a very low flavour threshold and is formed in carbohydrate-rich media.   W.L. & P.J.W.

Kobayashi, A., 'Sotolon identification, formation and effect on flavor', in American Chemical Society, *Flavor Chemistry Trends and Developments* (Washington, DC, 1989).

sour rot, a breakdown of mature grapes caused by a mixture of fungi, bacteria, and yeast which invades damaged berries. The fruit takes on the smell of vinegar, and juice from rotting berries can spread the infection, as can FRUIT FLY. Common entry points for the mixture of microbes are bird pecks as well as splits in berry skin caused by rain. Some organisms involved are the fungi *Aspergillus*, *Botryosphaeria*, *Cladosporium*, *Monilia*, *Penicillium*, and *Sclerotinia* and the yeast *Saccharomyces*. The rot is encouraged by rain and high humidity, and control relies on avoiding fruit damage as well as encouraging fruit aeration.   R.E.S.

Pearson, R. C., and Goheen, A. C., *Compendium of Grape Diseases* (St Paul, Minn., 1988).

Sousão, known as **Souzão** and **Sousón** in Spain's GALICIA, is a dark-skinned grape variety widely planted in northern Portugal, where the wine is notably high in acidity as well as colour and is therefore increasingly valued in PORT blends. It is an ingredient in QUINTA DO NOVAL Nacional, and in the nearby Minho it is known as Vinhão, its official Portuguese name, and makes particularly tart red VINHO VERDE. Portuguese plantings totalled about 8,800 ha/ 21,700 acres in 2004, when there were 573 ha in Spain. Spelt variously Sousão, Souzao, and all stations in between, it has also been planted by aspirant makers of port-style wines in California and Australia, with a certain degree of success.

South Africa, prolific southern hemisphere wine producer with a lustrous past and now in the midst of a significant renaissance. The famous Muscat-based dessert wines of CONSTANTIA seduced 18th-century Europe at a time when names like LAFITE and Romanée-Conti (see DOMAINE DE LA ROMANÉE-CONTI) were still in the making. The two centuries which followed were, by comparison, a disappointment, with the ordinary being too plentiful and the individual too rare. Only since the late 1980s has the Cape begun to shake off its political notoriety and vinous obscurity.

The Cape (South Africa's vineyards are in the hinterland of the Cape of Good Hope) functioned as a vast distillery for most of the 20th century, draining a partly subsidized annual wine lake and guaranteeing a certain quality of life to a politically powerful farming lobby. The growers' body founded in 1918, the KWV (Co-operative Wine Growers' Association), was until 1998 legally empowered to determine production quotas, fix minimum prices, and predetermine production areas and limits—a system which tended to handicap the private wine producer and favour the bulk grape-grower. Under pressure, the KWV began to relinquish most of these powers in 1992, and set the stage for a much freer, livelier production scene.

By the late 1990s, the requirements of the country's considerable brandy industry were more or less separately met, with plantings of high-yielding varieties increasingly developed expressly for this purpose. This forced growers of poorer vine varieties in lower-yielding regions to reconsider their commercial strategies. No longer assured of economically viable minimum prices for DISTILLATION wines, they were obliged to decide whether to replant with premium varieties or grub up their vineyards and replace them with alternative crops. At the same time, increased demand for superior wines led to new vine-growing ventures in completely new viticultural areas and to the rediscovery of certain regions whose potential had long been overlooked.

Until recently, the Cape's wine industry could be divided between the quantity-producing majority and the quality-conscious minority. However, the export-led boom which followed democratic elections in 1994 transformed an industry in which as recently as 1990 less than 30 per cent of the harvest reached the market as wine. In 2003, over 70 per cent of the grape crop was used to produce wine, with the remainder supplying the domestic brandy industry and the fruit juice sector.

With 1.5 per cent of the world's vineyards, South Africa ranks about 17th in area under vines, but its annual output, at just over 10 million hl/264 million gal, makes it definitively one of the world's top ten wine producers. Most vineyards are irrigated; there are no checks on yields, which rise to about 350 hl/ha (20 tons/acre) along the Orange river, where most of the harvest is destined for distillation and fruit juice concentrate. However, the national average is about 80 hl/ha, indicating that the yield in the better vineyards compares with that in Europe's better vineyards. Total area of vineyard for wine grapes has been growing and was about 110,000 ha/ 270,600 acres by 2003. There are now more than 500 cellars which crush grapes, a number that more than doubled between 1994 and 2004—although this number is but a small proportion of the 4,435 registered grape growers.

The risks and discipline of cooler environments suited to classic, low-yielding varieties have been braved by those who represent the innovative side of the South African wine industry. Together with a few wholesale merchant-producers, such wine-growers began to revolutionize the Cape wine scene in the 1980s, preparing the way for the significant transformation—in both plantings and in quality—which characterized the first post-apartheid decade.

An ever-strengthening export market which is slowly recognizing the nuances possible in the higher-priced brackets has been helped by a buoyant domestic economy.

As in Europe and America, people are drinking less, but better, and the growing black middle class has added significantly to the number of domestic consumers. An important percentage of the Cape's production used to be the staple, low-price, alcoholic beverage of the mainly Coloured population of the Western Cape. Political resistance, and an important swing to BEER which began in the 1980s, resulted in a near 30 per cent drop in per capita consumption between 1970 and 2003, to nearly 8 l per year. Meanwhile, to an increasing extent, wine is the beverage of choice of middle class families in the Cape and in the inland areas around Johannesburg. This shift away from a beer-and-spirit-only consumption pattern has seen the growth of a more sophisticated domestic market. Coupled with a tenfold increase in exports between 1993 and 2003, this means that there is now a powerful incentive to vine-growers to pursue quality rather than quantity.

This scramble for excellence has confirmed the benefits of cooler sites and matching locality to grape varieties. The historic Constantia area has been rediscovered and replanted. Climatic conditions here and in newly pioneered areas such as Elgin, Walker Bay, Elim, and Cape Agulhas (see below) on the eastern seaboard and alongside the cold Benguela current along the west coast, differ dramatically from those in the hot hinterland.

Chenin Blanc, still sometimes known as Steen, remains the farmers' favourite vine variety, making almost any and every style of white wine and comprising just over 17 per cent of all plantings. It is the base of myriad sweetish wines, sometimes locally called Stein, often sold by the 5-l BOX, a frequent fixture at a *braai*, as barbecues are known in South Africa.

In the late 1990s, less than 18 per cent of Cape vineyards produced red grapes. By 2003 this proportion had topped 40 per cent. As a result, the traditional, tough, burly red blends featuring Cabernet Sauvignon, Shiraz, Cinsaut, Tinta Barroca, and the Cape's own crossing PINOTAGE have been dethroned by newer styles. Growth in plantings of the premium red varieties has seen Cabernet Sauvignon move from 4.9 per cent of total plantings in 1996 to 11.7 per cent in 2003. In the same period, Shiraz vineyards increased sevenfold, Merlot trebled and Cabernet Franc more than doubled. Small OAK ageing was introduced in the late 1970s and became widely used for commercial wines in the second half of the 1980s. Now most of the country's smaller cellars, and all of the producing wholesalers, use French oak for both reds and whites. Controlled MALOLACTIC FERMENTATION is widely practised while reduced dependence on flavour-stripping FILTRATION and STABILIZATION processes has also helped improve the quality of the better wines. New CANOPY MANAGEMENT strategies and increasing VINE DENSITIES also played a role.

However, poor grape quality—often due to VIRUS-infected planting material—has hindered even greater progress. LEAFROLL, FANLEAF, and CORKY BARK viruses affect tens of thousands of hectares of vineyards (partly explaining the popularity of hardy, bulk-producing grape varieties such as Cinsaut and Chenin Blanc).

While counterparts elsewhere in the New World streaked ahead, South Africa's progress was slowed by the application of unnecessarily arduous plant importation regulations and the steadfast refusal by members of the industry's own vine improvement body to recognize the extent of the problem. The first virus-free vineyards produced maiden wines only in the late 1980s. Poor handling techniques in disseminating this material as well as virus-infected ROOTSTOCKS have ensured that many of the newer vineyards have already succumbed to virus problems.

A few fundamental natural handicaps exist. Apart from isolated CALCAREOUS outcrops, Cape soils tend to be excessively acid, requiring heavy LIME amendments, tartaric acid

South Africa

Wine-growing regions

0 ——————— 100 km

Upington •
ORANGE RIVER
Douglas •
Orange
0 ——————— 100 km

Johannesburg •
Durban •
Cape Town •

Vredendal •
OLIFANTS RIVER
Citrusdal •
PIKETBERG
Piketberg •
Olifants
SWARTLAND
TULBAGH
Tulbagh •
Malmesbury •
WORCESTER
Touws
Worcester •
Calitzdorp •
Oudtshoorn •
KLEIN
KAROO
Paarl •
Montagu •
PAARL
Robertson •
DURBANVILLE
ROBERTSON
Bonnievale •
Durbanville •
Franschhoek •
RUITERBOSCH
Cape Town •
Stellenbosch •
Swellendam •
CONSTANTIA
STELLENBOSCH
Mossel Bay •
ELGIN
Caledon •
Breede
OVERBERG
Hermanus •
WALKER
BAY
Cape Agulhas •
Indian Ocean

adjustments to musts and wines, and severe TARTRATE removal procedures before bottling (see SOIL ACIDITY).

If great wines are made by their markets, the Cape in the past suffered from another disadvantage. Its core market was distant and small: 3 million middle class consumers in and around Johannesburg, two days' drive to the north east of the Cape. Transporting wine from Cape Town 1,600 km/1,000 miles to Johannesburg costs almost as much as container-shipping it to Europe. However, the TOURISM boom which has boosted the Cape's economy, as well as a vibrant export trade, has made this largely a problem of the past.

History

The father of the South African wine industry was a 33-year-old Dutch surgeon sent to establish a market garden to reduce the risks of scurvy on the long sea passage between Europe and the Indies. Jan van Riebeeck, the Cape's first European settler, was a reluctant pioneer, and no viticulturist. But his brief was to set up a supply station for DUTCH EAST INDIA COMPANY sailors on the spice routes; and the Cape's MEDITERRANEAN CLIMATE suggested vines might well flourish.

Seven years after sailing into Table bay on 6 April 1652, at the head of a ragtag mercenary band, he recorded: 'Today, praise be to God, wine was pressed for the first time from Cape grapes.' The cuttings came from 'somewhere in western France' according to Professor C. Orffer, South Africa's leading academic viticulturalist. Conditions and quality improved when a new governor, Simon van der Stel, established the legendary 750-ha/1,850-acre CONSTANTIA wine estate outside Cape Town in 1685.

Constantia again became the focal point of the wine industry in 1778, when the estate was bought by a talented and ambitious grower, Hendrik Cloete. His Constantia dessert wines soon became the toast of European aristocracy. Cape wine exports flourished under British rule, even if mainly of cheap wines. When in 1861 the Gladstone government removed empire preferential tariffs, French wines had only the Channel to cross to capture the British market and far-flung Cape colony products became uncompetitive.

PHYLLOXERA struck in 1866, adding a 20-year recuperation period to the trade's already unhealthy fortunes. Making up for lost time, growers rebuilt the industry, planting some 80 million high-yielding vines such as Cinsaut by the early 1900s. A manageable flow swelled into a deluge; unsaleable wine was poured, literally, into local rivers.

This fuelled the formation in 1918 of the Cooperative Wine Growers' Association (KWV), which was subsequently legally empowered to limit production and set minimum prices. Relative stability ensued, with the emphasis increasingly on brandy and FORTIFIED wines.

Burman, J., *Wine of Constantia* (Cape Town, 1979).

Leipold, C. L., *Three Hundred Years of Cape Wines* (Cape Town, 1952).

Oppermann, D. J. (ed.), *Spirit of the Vine* (Cape Town, 1968).

Climate and geography

It has been suggested that if South Africa jutted another 200 km/124 miles south into the Atlantic, the cooler climate would slow grape ripening and produce wines of greater elegance. Producers in the south of France may happily boast of their *vins du soleil*, but Cape growers are not keen to emphasize the intense African sunshine when describing their otherwise MEDITERRANEAN CLIMATE. The Benguela current from Antarctica makes the Cape cooler than its LATITUDE may suggest, however, and many new vineyard areas south towards Agulhas as well as on the west coast offer the prospect of a long, slow ripening season.

Warm summers from November to April are moderated by cold, wet, blustery winters, frequently with snowfalls on the higher mountains. Late frosts are rare; so are unseasonally heavy summer rains.

The winelands are widely dispersed throughout the Western and Northern Cape, some 700 km/420 miles from north to south and 500 km across, strung between the Atlantic and Indian oceans.

Climates and soils vary as dramatically as landscapes: mountains rear out of the sea, unfolding into lush valleys, sere drylands, and a series of inland mountain chains. In the Stellenbosch district alone, just outside Cape Town, there are more than 50 soil types. On the hillsides, decomposing granite prevails. Soils tend to be low in PH (4.5), with a predominance of clay (25 per cent and more), but are well drained and moisture retentive. That portion of the harvest reserved mainly for brandy and fruit juice comes from hot, irrigated river valleys such as the Orange, Olifants, and Breede, where vineyards yield prodigiously. Around inland Robertson there are some calcareous lime-rich outcrops akin to the calcareous soil of Burgundy's CÔTE D'OR. But in the cooler coastal areas, such soils must be man-made with substantial LIME additions.

Annual rainfall rises from 250 mm/9.7 in in the near-desert Klein Karoo to 1,500 mm in the lee of the Worcester mountains, about 120 km inland from Cape Town. Growers, particularly in the semi-desert areas who depend on IRRIGATION argue they merely make up the shortfall to reach the 900 mm annual rainfall of a vineyard in the Bordeaux region of France.

Average summer daily temperatures often exceed 23 °C/ 73 °F during the February and March harvest months, and maximum summer temperatures can rise to nearly 40 °C. However, an increasing proportion of new, cooler vineyard sites are making this caricature of the Cape as a hot climate viticultural region as questionable a generalization as the old belief that Cape vintage variations are insignificant.

A unique but mixed blessing is the frequent gale-force summer south easter, the 'Cape Doctor' WIND, that reduces humidity, mildew, and other FUNGAL DISEASES, but also sometimes batters vines.

Most wine regions would, according to the WINKLER scale, be classified Region III sites (as in Oakville, Napa valley), IV (like Sydney and Florence), and some in V (Perth). But a number of areas experience cooler European (or Winkler II) conditions, especially in high-altitude or sea-cooled vineyards. New appellations such as Walker Bay (on arenaceous shale), Constantia (granite and sandstone), Elgin (shale), and Cape Agulhas have stretched horizons and broadened the Cape's climatological repertoire.

Burger, J., and Deist, J., *Viticulture in South Africa* (Cape Town, 1981).

Wine regions

Constantia Fabled name in the annals of Cape wine (see CONSTANTIA), now a demarcated wine ward in Cape Town's southern suburbs, on the slim peninsula pointing into the south Atlantic, cooled by the sea on two sides for relatively slow summer ripening with average daily temperatures of 18–19 °C, and very wet but moderate winters (average annual rainfall over 1,000 mm/39 in). Rich, loamy Table Mountain sandstone and decomposed granite soils nurture vigorous growth and even shy-bearing classic vines require ruthless SUMMER PRUNING and CROP THINNING. Here five vineyards have, since the mid 1980s, once again been producing classic wines from land that once formed part of the historic 750-ha Hendrik Cloete estate, since subdivided.

Stellenbosch Charming university town 45 km east of Cape Town, its Cape Dutch, Cape Georgian, and Victorian buildings shaded by long-established oaks, in the heart of the Cape winelands and traditionally home of the country's finest reds. After Constantia, it is the oldest wine region, established in 1679. The government Oenological and Viticultural Research Institute (OVRI), the STELLENBOSCH University Oenology Department, the Wine & Spirit Board, government experimental vineyards, the biggest wine wholesaler Distell with its 10,000-barrel maturation cellars, are all here, surrounded by valleys of vines and the soaring blue-grey mountains of Stellenbosch, Simonsberg, and Helderberg. The district's five wards—Jonkershoek Valley, Papegaaiberg, Simonsberg-Stellenbosch, Bottelary, and Devon Valley—all yield wines displaying distinctive differences. Vineyards on the Helderberg (which runs from Stellenbosch to False bay at Somerset West) also enjoy a considerable reputation. Soils and climate vary, from sandy alluvial loam along the valley floors and river courses to deep, moisture-retaining decomposed granite on the hillsides. The climate is tempered by the Atlantic sweeping into False bay, a 15-minute drive from the town. Average daily summer temperatures are about 20 °C.

Although best known for Cabernet Sauvignon, Merlot, Shiraz, and Pinotage, Stellenbosch produces a host of wine types including port-style wines and some excellent Chardonnays and Sauvignon Blancs. Stellenbosch returns lower average yields than hotter, more extensively irrigated inland regions. It is the source of only about 14 per cent of the country's total wine production although it boasts the greatest concentration of leading estates, an extensive wine route network, and scores of restaurants. Estates and cellars particularly famous for their wines include Delheim, Hartenberg, Jordan, Kaapzicht, Kanonkop, Meerlust, Morgenhof, Mulderbosch, Neil Ellis, Rustenberg, Rust-en-Vrede, Saxenburg, Simonsig, Stellenzicht, Thelema, Uitkyk, Vergelegen, Vergenoed, Warwick, Waterford, and Zevenwacht.

Paarl Warm home of the KWV and an increasing number of well-known estates. The district reaches north into Tulbagh (a separate area of origin) and Wellington and east toward Franschhoek (meaning 'French corner'), home of the first French Huguenot settlers. The best-known cellars include Backsberg, Bellingham, Boschendal, Cabrière, Fairview, Glen Carlou, Graham Beck, Plaisir de Merle, Rupert & Rothschild Fredericksburg, Veenwouden, and Welgemeend. The biggest producer is Nederburg, with a comprehensive range of 40 labels; it produced the Cape's first BOTRYTIZED wine, labelled Edelkeur, from Chenin Blanc in 1969.

Worcester Extensive, fertile district beyond the Du Toitskloof mountains and within the Breede River Valley region, delivering 20 to 25 per cent of the national crop, mainly bulk varieties for distillation or FORTIFICATION. Generally warm and needing irrigation, the district is still dominated by numerous CO-OPERATIVES.

The region's wine production includes a high percentage of Colombard and Chenin Blanc, although it also accounts for almost half the Cape's Semillon plantings and a third of its Ruby Cabernet. Worcester is the home of many a national champion fortified red and white MUSCADEL and dessert HANEPOOT. The Slanghoek ward has had success with Sauvignon Blanc and botrytized wines.

Robertson Warm, dry district within the Breede River Valley region and home of many estates and co-operatives producing some fine whites, including bold Chardonnays, and an increasingly creditable array of reds, most notably Shiraz. Bonnievale is the best known of the district's wards. Most vineyards fringe the Breede river, which provides irrigation and alluvial soils although calcium-rich outcrops are also found. Most of the international varieties perform well here although Robertson has long enjoyed a reputation for lovely Muscats, including fortified Muscadels, off-dry Colombards, and striking Chardonnays. A few memorable Sauvignon Blancs emerged recently despite the warm harvest conditions. Best-known producers include Bon Courage, De Wetshof, Weltevrede, Van Loveren (all whites), Graham Beck (sparkling wines), Springfield, and Zandvliet (Shiraz). Robertson produces almost 15 per cent of the national harvest. Average daily growing season temperatures are about 22 °C, while rainfall is less than 400 mm annually, making irrigation essential.

Olifants River Chiefly bulk grape-producing region among mountains and along the Atlantic western seaboard, the majority of whose growers supply large co-operatives with wine mainly for distillation but increasingly for export. South Africa's biggest single winery, the progressive Vredendal Co-operative, vinifies more than 40,000 tonnes of grapes annually.

Orange River Hottest, most northerly, and most recently established (in the 1960s) of South Africa's wine regions, producing nearly 12 per cent of the national crop. Bulk wines, huge yields—40 tonnes per ha or 140 hl/ha—are common, thanks to irrigation schemes.

Klein Karoo (**Little Karoo**) Inland, semi-desert ostrich- and sheep-farming region. A few enterprising estates here such as Boplaas and Die Krans are making hearty port-style wines and fortified Muscadels, as well as some dry table wines.

Ruiterbosch Small, new ward with promising cool vineyards. South Africa's most southerly wine region fronting the Indian ocean, almost outside the Mediterranean climate area with its winter rainfall, producing individual white wines made from Sauvignon Blanc and Rhine Riesling. Pinot Noir is also planted.

Walker Bay Southerly, relatively cool maritime vineyards producing among South Africa's most promising wines made from the Burgundy grapes Chardonnay and Pinot Noir, from Hamilton Russell Vineyards and Bouchard-Finlayson.

Elgin Cool, high vineyards in apple orchard country east of Cape Town. A recently designated wine ward whose early vintages of Sauvignon Blanc showed intense individuality. Hopes are also high for Pinot Noir here.

> Hughes, D., and Hands, P., *Complete Book of South African Wine* (Cape Town, 1988).
> Knox, G., *Estate Wines of South Africa* (Cape Town, 1982).
> Platter, J., *John Platter's South African Wine Guide* (Stellenbosch, annually).

Viticulture

The stark contrast between the traditional and the progressive in South African viticulture, often visible on adjoining farms, reflects the disparate objectives of growers. The bulk grape-farmer delivering to one of the less progressive co-operatives strives for quantity; the grower bottling his own crop knows quantity can be the enemy of quality.

The tractor, trellising, wide planting spaces, and chemical pest and weed control became common features by the 1960s, but on some farms vineyard workhorses could still be seen drawing simple tilling implements between traditional, densely planted rows of untrellised BUSH VINES planted only 1.2 m/4 ft apart to a density of 7,000 vines per ha (2,800 per acre), similar to many French vineyards.

In the 1990s quality wine producers have put the horses out to pasture but are swinging back to close planting; more restrained ORGANIC and biological pest controls; careful CLONAL SELECTION; painstaking SOIL PREPARATION that can involve additions of over 20 tons of lime per ha to achieve higher pH, calcium-balanced soils; and PRUNING for lower yields.

Average planting densities are around 3,300 vines per ha (1,300 per acre). Yields in cooler, coastal climates are appreciably lower than the national average: about 49 or 56 hl/ha (2.8 or 3.2 tons/acre) for Cabernet Sauvignon and Chardonnay are considered consistent with quality in Cape conditions. Yields from a still significant number of virus-infected vineyards can drop to below 28 hl/ha (1.6 tons/acre).

Most vineyards (outside Paarl, Stellenbosch, and the coastal areas) are IRRIGATED in summer, with overhead sprays or fixed sprinkler systems supplying individual vines, a typical regime delivering 200 to 700 mm/7.8–27.3 in of extra moisture a year in evenly spaced intervals. Producers who do not water make a marketing feature of wines from DRYLAND vineyards.

The most common trellising system is a simple vertical 'hedge row' developed from a split vine cordon, supported by a wire raised about 750 mm/2.4 ft for ease of pruning. The summer foliage is trained upright in a canopy held by one or more wires above the cordon. Short-SPUR PRUNING is commonly practised (eight to ten spurs, four to five on each cordon, pruned back to two or three buds each).

Most vine diseases and pests found their way from the northern hemisphere long ago. Chemical pesticides are in wide use—the ladybird, a natural predator of the dreaded MEALY BUG, is increasingly rare—though farmers are now encouraged by OVRI to experiment with INTEGRATED PEST MANAGEMENT programmes, emphasizing biological and physical measures and minimizing the use of insecticides. Baboons are also a pest in several areas.

POWDERY MILDEW, locally called 'white rust', is the most serious common disease. DOWNY MILDEW poses a seasonal threat. Both are containable by systemic fungicides. BOTRYTIS is not a serious problem most years, and is welcomed by growers specializing in dessert wines.

Cape vineyards were decimated by PHYLLOXERA from 1866 and virtually all vines are grafted onto resistant American ROOTSTOCKS, the most common being Richter 99 and 101-14.

Virus-infected vines are widespread, shortening the productive lifespans of vineyards. Affected vines succumb to LEAFROLL, CORKY BARK, and FANLEAF, inhibiting PHOTOSYNTHESIS and ripening, diminishing yields but not improving grape quality.

From the mid 1980s, heat-treated, virus-tested plant material was more freely available, along with a greater selection of imported clones of classic varieties. Healthier vineyards are the result, but scientists warn the virus will eventually affect these too, although more slowly. Virus-free Cabernet Sauvignon vineyards planted with Schleip clone 163 ripen in mid February, four to six weeks earlier than diseased vineyards, and at higher sugar levels.

Developing a significant pattern of regional/varietal characteristics is Cape viticulture's current challenge.

> Burger, J., and Deist, J., *Viticulture in South Africa* (Cape Town, 1981).

Wine-making

Although wine-making in South Africa remains in a state of flux and experimentation, today largely following international whims and tendencies, at some point in the 1980s, almost in the twinkling of an eye, the small French BARRIQUE transformed the face and taste of top Cape wines.

But in general, heavy irrigation, high yields, a hot climate, and low pH soils still produce musts that are low in ACIDITY from the majority of commercial vineyards, requiring TARTARIC ACID additions most years.

> Platter, J., *John Platter's South African Wines* (Cape Town, annually).

Vine varieties

In South Africa, a vine variety is known as a cultivar, and South Africa is a cultivar-conscious wine country. Regional wine characteristics are still insufficiently well defined to challenge grape variety as the determining factor for

---

Chile has no shortage of valley floor vineyards that can be worked much more easily than sites as steep as Errazuriz's Dom Maximiano vineyard in Aconcagua but, just as in California, an increasing proportion of vines are now being planted on **hillsides** with their shallow soils and good **drainage**.

quality, style, and even labelling and marketing of a wine.

White varieties constitute by far the majority of Cape vineyards. Chenin Blanc, known sometimes as Steen, has for long been the dominant grape variety in South Africa, and was still planted on nearly 20 per cent of all vineyard in 2004. From the 1980s, Sauvignon Blanc and Chardonnay boomed (although Sauvignon Blanc was widely planted in the 19th century) but together they made up little more than 15 per cent of the country's total vine plantings by 2004. Other major white wine grapes include, in decreasing quantity: Colombar(d), Cape Riesling (see CROUCHEN), Sémillon, (Weisser) Riesling, Gewürztraminer, as well as various Muscats. Muscat of Alexandria, locally known as Hanepoot, doubles as a table grape. White and a mutant red MUSCADEL (Muscat Blanc à Petits Grains) remain important for fortified wines. Chenel and Weldra, both Cape crossings of Chenin Blanc and Ugni Blanc, have not caught on, producing wine so neutral it is suitable only for brandy.

Highest-priced reds are Cabernet Sauvignon and BORDEAUX BLENDS, including Merlot and/ or Cabernet Franc, which proliferated from the early 1980s. Cabernet Sauvignon is South Africa's most planted INTERNATIONAL VARIETY, planted on more than 13 per cent of the nation's vineyard. Syrah (Shiraz in South Africa) is becoming popular, on its own and blended. Pinot Noir has been generally disappointing but new clones are being tried. PINOTAGE, the Cape's own crossing of Pinot Noir and Cinsaut, is becoming increasingly popular and was the single most planted new red vine variety in 1996 (Chardonnay was the white) although it still represented only 6.7 per cent of the nation's vines in 2004.

For most of this century, high-yielding Cinsaut was the most widely planted red, but it has declined in importance and represented only 3 per cent of vineyard in 2004. There are yet smaller plantings of Grenache, Carignan, Zinfandel, Ruby Cabernet, and some port varieties, most commonly TINTA BARROCA, often made into a dry red. PONTAC is another South African speciality, on a minuscule scale. Gamay has made a modest impact in its Beaujolais-style CARBONIC MACERATION mode.

Other varieties planted to a considerable extent but used principally for blending, fortified wines, distillation, or grape concentrate are all white berried. The most important are Sultana and Palomino (known curiously as White French in South Africa). Others include an undistinguished Midi variety called Servin, Servan, or Raisin Blanc; a rot-prone South African speciality known variously as Canaan, Kanaän, or Belies; and Pedro Luis or False Pedro.

Orffer, C. J., *Wine Grape Cultivars in South Africa* (Cape Town, 1979).

Pongracz, D. P., *Practical Viticulture* (Cape Town, 1978).

Wine of Origin and labelling

Wine of Origin (WO) legislation introduced in 1973, and variously updated since then, ended decades of a labelling free-for-all in which confused South African wine nomenclature and unverified vintage and grape variety claims baffled the consumer. The following types of wine production zones are now classified: geographical unit (e.g. Western Cape), region (e.g. Coastal), district (e.g. Stellenbosch), and ward (e.g. Bottelary). While the larger units are broadly geographical and/or political, a ward is based on shared soils, climate, etc. (i.e. aspects of TERROIR). 'Estates' are no longer official places of origin, but registered 'estate wines' must be grown, made, and bottled on a single property. Single vineyards may be indicated as such on labels provided they are registered in accordance with the legal provisions.

A wine may also be 'certified' for vintage provided at least 85 per cent comes from one harvest. For a wine to be labelled as a single VARIETAL, it must contain at least 85 per cent of the variety stated. Varieties in a blend may be indicated only if they are vinified separately.

Participation is voluntary and about 35 per cent of Cape-bottled wine is certified. Non-certified wine is liable to spot-check analysis for health requirements.

Wines may state a single origin but be blends of the products of several regions. The authorities have merged, on paper, various wine-growing areas. Parts of the Coastal Region, stretching for nearly 400 km/240 miles, are far from the sea. Local wags call this the Wine of Mixed Origin system.

South Africa meets requirements on prohibition of additives, and for labelling, which must state the ALCOHOLIC STRENGTH (from 1992) to within half a per cent. TRADITIONAL METHOD Cape sparkling wine is labelled Méthode Cap Classique even locally. FLOR yeast fortified wines matured in a SOLERA system are in decline but not exported as sherry.

Although the WO regulations borrow from France and Germany, there are no rulings on crop YIELDS, fertilizer quantities, or IRRIGATION levels. Chaptalization and all other forms of ENRICHMENT are banned. ACIDIFICATION is permitted.

The definition of 'dry' in relation to South African wines sold on the domestic market has recently been changed: the maximum RESIDUAL SUGAR content is now 5 g/l rather than 4 g/l. (See also SWEETNESS for a comparison with official terminology within the European Union.)

www.sawis.co.za

South African Wine Industry Trust

Wine for certification is submitted to the government-appointed Wine & Spirit Board. The wine must pass an analytical test and is blind tasted by a panel which may reject wines judged faulty or atypical, and often does.

The South African Wine Industry Trust (SAWIT) was established in 1999 when the KWV put up R369 million in an agreement with government to focus on the transformation of the industry through its Section 21 Companies, Busco (Wine Industry Business Support Company), Devco (Wine Industry Development Support Company), and Wieco (Wine Industry Empowerment Company), and a number of Special Purpose Vehicles dedicated to Black Economic Empowerment (BEE). These include export promotion, technology transfer, and Labour Development. SAWIT's guiding principle is that long-term, sustainable development of the South African wine business is only possible through the active participation of South Africa's previously disadvantaged communities in the mainstream economy. To that end, it tries to facilitate entrepreneurial development and large BEE equity transactions for black communities linked to the wine and spirits industry. SAWIT has also driven the development of a BEE Charter for the South African wine industry.

J.P. & M.F.

South African Riesling. See CAPE RIESLING.

South America, the world's second most important wine-producing continent, after Europe, with ARGENTINA being by far the biggest producer, followed by CHILE and BRAZIL. Other, relatively minor, wine producers are, in descending order of importance, URUGUAY, PERU, PARAGUAY, and BOLIVIA, although see also ECUADOR and VENEZUELA. The North American wine producer MEXICO produces much more wine than Uruguay, for example. Spain and, in some parts, Portugal were important influences in the 16th and 17th centuries, although more recently France, Italy, and the United States have helped to shape South America's wine industries. Wine quality has improved extremely rapidly in those countries—Chile, Argentina, and to a lesser extent Uruguay—which have (relatively recently) turned their attention to exporting.

History

The late 15th century European voyages of discovery, notably to the Americas, were followed by migrations of European settlers there, associated with substantial movement of animals and plants between the two continents. Although indigenous varieties of vine grew in Central America (see VITIS), there is no evidence that the Aztecs made wine from them, and it was thus with the arrival of the Spanish conquistadores in the 16th century that vine cultivation and wine-making were first introduced to the region. Mexico was the first part of the continent to witness the introduction of European VINIFERA vines, and as early as 1522 Cortés is recorded as having sent for vine cuttings from Spain. Moreover, by 1524 the planting

The effects of **Pierce's disease** on Cabernet vines in California's Napa valley. Once leaves are affected by this fatal bacterial disease, they shrivel and vine plants are likely to die within one to five years of being infected. It is a particular threat in the southern and western states of the US.

of vines was a condition of *repartimiento* grants, through which the Spaniards were granted land and labour on the foundation of Mexico City. From Mexico, the spread of viticulture followed swiftly on the heels of Spanish conquests.

Vines were planted in Peru soon after Pizarro's defeat of the Incas between 1531 and 1534, and within 20 years Spanish commentators described vineyards producing a substantial quantity of grapes. Some of the earliest Peruvian vines appear to have been introduced from the CANARY ISLANDS, whereas others seem to have been derived from the seeds of dried grapes brought from Spain. From Peru, viticulture and wine-making then spread south to Chile and Argentina, where vines were cultivated as early as the mid 1550s, although there were even earlier experimental plantings on Argentina's coast. See also MONKS AND MONASTERIES.

The traditional explanation for the rapidity of this spread was that the Spanish conquerors required a ready supply of wine for the EUCHARIST, and that monks therefore played a central role in establishing vineyards. There is, however, little evidence to support this view, and most of the early vineyards and attempts to produce wine were on secular estates. Economic factors, such as the cost of importing wine and the difficulties of transporting it overland, meant that the early Spanish conquerors had a very real interest in establishing vineyards if they wished to continue to consume the main alcoholic beverage that they had known in Iberia. In particular, the long sea voyage across the Atlantic, followed by an overland haul across Panama, and then a further voyage down the Pacific coast, meant that most wine reaching Peru and Chile from the Iberian peninsula was likely to have been of poor quality.

By the end of the 16th century, Spanish restrictions on wine production in 'New Spain', designed to protect the metropolitan wine producers and merchants in Iberia, served to limit further secular development of viticulture in Mexico, but they also appear to have provided an incentive to Peruvian producers, who rapidly became the dominant wine suppliers to the region as a whole. Subsequently, in the 17th century, Jesuit MISSIONS along the coastal valleys of Peru became the most important centres of viticulture in the region. P.T.H.U.

Blij, H. de, *Wine Regions of the Southern Hemisphere* (Totowa, NJ, 1985).

Dickenson, J., and Unwin, T., *Viticulture in Colonial Latin America: Essays on Alcohol, the Vine and Wine in Spanish America and Brazil* (Liverpool, 1992).

Hyams, E., *Dionysus: A Social History of the Vine Wine* (London, 1965).

South Australia, the wine state in AUSTRALIA.

At a little under 50 per cent, South Australia's contribution to the annual CRUSH may be falling from its high point of 75 per cent in the 1940s and 1950s, but it still dominates the country's wine output. Vine-growing and wine-making are major contributors to South Australia's gross domestic production, yet they occupy only a small percentage of the state's vast land mass. Vine-growing is concentrated in the south eastern corner, much of it within an hour's drive of the capital Adelaide. The two outposts are the Riverland sprawling along the Murray river (the Lower Murray Zone); and Coonawarra and nearby Padthaway 325 km/200 miles south east of Adelaide, not far from the border with VICTORIA (the Limestone Coast Zone).

The **Barossa Valley**, an hour north of Adelaide, vies with the Hunter Valley as Australia's best-known wine region. To this day, the Germanic influence of its 19th-century Silesian immigrants is everywhere to be seen—in the town names, the Lutheran churches, the stone buildings, and in the names of the leading families.

The once-dominant Riesling has bowed to the inevitable as Chardonnay (and also Semillon) has swept past it, although part of the change has come about as a consequence of Riesling's move to the EDEN VALLEY, Clare Valley, and (less importantly in absolute terms), the ADELAIDE HILLS.

This shift reflects two things: first, the warm climate of the valley floor, more suited to red wine production; second, a fundamental reappraisal of the function of the Barossa valley proper. For decades vine plantings shrank while production soared, not because of increased yields, but because the Barossa Valley wineries process a major part of the grapes grown in the Riverland, Coonawarra, Padthaway, McLaren Vale, and Langhorne Creek.

Most of Australia's largest companies are based here. The presence of PENFOLDS, and the creation of its masterwork Grange, embody the glory of the Barossa Valley: substantial plantings of Shiraz dating as far back as 1860, dry farmed (no IRRIGATION) and BUSH pruned, often yielding as little as 16 hl/ha (1 tonne/acre) of inky, dark purple essence.

While the Barossa Valley has 80 or so wine producers within its precincts, the McLaren Vale region, 45 minutes due south of Adelaide, has 90 and is often called the home of the small winery. These wineries represent a mixture of the old and the new, thus reflecting the dynamics which have operated here no less than in the Barossa Valley.

At the northern end, urban sprawl has swallowed up many once-substantial vineyards, and encircles the few remaining plantings at Reynella. However, with one important qualification, the southern end of the fashionably cool and increasingly important Adelaide Hills to the east, the open plains of McLaren Vale, and the hills of the Fleurieu Peninsula offer abundant suitable land for the new plantings. The qualification is the availability of increasingly scarce WATER, and ever-more stringent controls on the use of surface water (by dams), artesian water (by bores) and river water.

McLaren Vale is a strongly maritime-influenced region, with considerable variation in MESOCLIMATE. Once famous for its supposedly iron-rich red wines exported to England under the Emu and Glenloth labels and prescribed by (surely enlightened) physicians around the turn of the century as tonics, the emphasis in the 1970s and 1980s turned to its melon-and citrus-tinged Chardonnay, pungent gooseberry Sauvignon Blanc, and full-flavoured Semillon. But with the resurgence of the red wine market, attention has once again focused on its generous, gutsy red wines. Here the long-forgotten virtues of its DRYLAND Grenache have been rediscovered; whether used to make a single varietal red wine, or blended with Shiraz, many consider it Australia's best example of Rhône-style red. The high quality of the grapes, and hence the wines, is better understood by the industry than by the public, and (even more with rapidly growing neighbour **Langhorne Creek**) much of the production ends up in regional blended wines, the labels of which may or may not show the composition of that blend. Langhorne Creek is the principal source of Jacob's Creek and these two regions between them account for 20 per cent of the state's output.

The Limestone Coast Zone includes these regions of rapidly growing importance: Mount Benson, Robe, Wrattonbully, Coonawarra, and **Padthaway**. The twins of **Coonawarra** and Padthaway in the far south east of the state are generally recognized as producing Australia's finest Cabernet Sauvignon (Coonawarra) and some of its best Chardonnay, Sauvignon Blanc, and Shiraz. Both are cool regions (Coonawarra is the cooler of the two) with considerable LIMESTONE (TERRA ROSSA in Coonawarra), and an extensive underground water-table. **Mount Benson** is cooler again, with sand and limestone interspersed, and seems destined to produce wines of greater elegance but less weight and structure.

While vines were first planted in Coonawarra in 1890 (by John Riddoch), for all practical purposes both regions date from the early 1960s. This explains why both areas are exclusively planted to premium grape varieties, and why the major wine companies are the dominant landholders (there are six wineries in Padthaway, more than 30 in Coonawarra). After two decades of darkness in the 1980s and 1990s, in which all the focus was on the cost of growing grapes and not on maximizing their quality, there has been a major turnaround in the approach of the major companies. Apparently having spent millions of dollars in legal fees arguing about the boundaries of Coonawarra, they then turned their attention to making the best possible wine, with Cabernet Sauvignon (accounting for almost 60 per cent of the 5,500 ha under vine in 2004) the flagbearer.

Wrattonbully had a face lift in 2004 with the formation of the Tapanappa joint venture between Brian Croser, Jean-Michel Cazes (of Château Lynch Bages in Pauillac) and the parent company of Champagne Bollinger. It purchased the original Koppamurra Vineyard, from which it will produce estate-based wines, setting a formula for future ventures elsewhere.

The **Clare Valley**, just to the north west of the Barossa Valley, but joined with the **Adelaide Hills** in the Mount Lofty Ranges Zone, is one of the unspoilt jewels of South Australia. The narrow, twisting folds of the hills provide an intimacy in total contrast to the flat, featureless plain of Coonawarra. Like the Barossa Valley, it is steeped in history, with splendid stone buildings and wineries. Its strongly continental climate, with warm days but cool to cold nights in summer, produces Australia's finest Riesling, which is a fragrant yet steely wine which ages superbly, taking on the aroma of lightly browned toast with a twist of lime as it ages.

Most of the wineries are small; almost all produce Riesling, Shiraz, and Cabernet Sauvignon, the red wines being intensely coloured, deeply flavoured, and long lived, often with a skein of eucalypt mint running through them. MALBEC also flourishes here as nowhere else, used as a blend component with Cabernet Sauvignon (sometimes with a dash of Shiraz thrown in for good measure).

The Fleurieu Zone, as well as being home to McLaren Vale and Langhorne Creek, takes in the exotic **Kangaroo Island**, plus **Currency Creek**, and **Southern Fleurieu**. All are highly MARITIME, and hence cooler than McLaren Vale. Kangaroo Island is one of the (largely) undiscovered nature paradises of Australia, viticulture as yet of small compass. Southern Fleurieu is also largely unspoilt and of considerable beauty.

Finally, there is the **Riverland**, stretching along the mighty Murray river from Waikerie to Renmark, producing nigh on 55 per cent of South Australia's total crush and over 30 per cent of the nation's. The continuing increase in premium grape plantings, and the decline in lesser or multipurpose varieties, is nowhere more evident than in the fact that Chardonnay, Shiraz, and Cabernet Sauvignon accounted for 57 per cent of total Riverland plantings by 2004, the once-dominant Muscat Gordo Blanco and Sultana for just 9 per cent. J.H.

South Burnett, young, relatively hilly Australian wine region in south east Queensland. It has a subtropical climate, with summer rainfall a real problem; coupled with generally fertile red soils. Ripening tannins can be challenging, but in the right vintages there have been impressive results with Semillon, Chardonnay, Shiraz, and Cabernet Sauvignon. It is also a very pretty region, well worth the two and a half hours' drive from Brisbane.

South Coast, name loosely defining vineyards close to the CALIFORNIA coast from Los Angeles southwards to the Mexican border. TEMECULA has the only substantial vineyards within the region. San Diego county's SAN PASQUAL also falls within it.

South Coast Zone of NEW SOUTH WALES stretches more than 400 km from north of Sydney, Australia, to the Victorian border in the south, but extends inland to take in Sydney itself, the Blue mountains, and the Southern Highlands and Shoalhaven Coast regions.

South Eastern Australia, official 'super zone' which takes in all relevant wine regions in QUEENSLAND, NEW SOUTH WALES, VICTORIA, and SOUTH AUSTRALIA, used for multiregion, inexpensive blended wines constituting a significant proportion of all wine exported from Australia.

Southern Fleurieu, new, strongly maritime wine region in SOUTH AUSTRALIA, the most northerly region in the state. Altitude is the key moderator of climate.

Southern Flinders Ranges, newest and most northerly wine region of SOUTH AUSTRALIA.

Southern Highlands, Australian wine region high on the Great Dividing range south east of Sydney. A somewhat schizophrenic climate, cold in winter and humid in late summer with rainfall then a problem. A popular weekend retreat for wealthy Sydney residents is partial explanation for its rapid development.

South West Australia Zone comprises the Blackwood Valley, Geographe, Great Southern, and Margaret River wine regions, not to be confused with the South East Australia Super Zone.

South West France, recognized region within FRANCE which incorporates all of the wine districts in the south western quarter of the country with the exception of BORDEAUX and COGNAC. This means in effect all of the upriver wines once regarded as serious commercial rivals by the Bordelais (most notably Bergerac, Monbazillac, Côtes de Duras, Cahors, Buzet, Côtes du Frontonnais, and Gaillac travelling away from and roughly clockwise round Bordeaux), together with those made in GASCONY and BASQUE country (Côtes de St-Mont, Madiran, Pacherenc du Vic-Bilh, Jurançon, Béarn, and Irouléguy).

Few generalizations can be made about such an extensive area, except that the climate is heavily influenced by the Atlantic.

The vine was cultivated in most of these districts in the Roman era (see FRANCE and GAUL) but wine-making was developed only under the medieval influence of MONKS AND MONAS-TERIES. During the CRUSADES some of these areas came under direct English protection.

The history of the first group of wines has been heavily influenced, nay hampered, by the commercial muscle of protectionist Bordeaux. The fact that these wines were made up river of but outside Bordeaux in the 'high country', or HAUT PAYS, meant that they were penalized at their exit port, and the HUNDRED YEARS WAR was to have an everlasting effect on their trading history, opening the door for the DUTCH WINE TRADE to take the place of once-powerful ENGLAND. The commercial progress of wines from the second group was long hindered by the difficulty of navigating the Adour river down to the port of Bayonne, and by competition with other crops.

The grape varieties grown in the first group of wine districts is generally very similar to the ENCÉPAGEMENT of Bordeaux, while the southern districts can boast one of the most exciting collections of local vine varieties in Europe, including the likes of ABOURIOU, BAROQUE, DURAS, FER (Servadou), LEN DE L'EL, MANSENG, MAUZAC, NÉGRETTE, ARRUFIAC, TANNAT, JURANÇON Noir, and PETIT COURBU. Many producers ignore the letter of the AC law regarding the proportions in blends of local with INTERNATIONAL VARIETIES in favour of the former. Culturally, Gascony is one of the proudest and greediest regions of France; the region needs wines to drink with *foie gras*, duck, and goose.

For more details, see the individual entries for all the APPELLATION CONTRÔLÉE wines BÉARN, BERGERAC, BUZET, CAHORS, Côtes de DURAS, FRONTON, Côtes du MARMANDAIS, GAILLAC, IROULÉGUY, JURANÇON, MADIRAN, MARCILLAC, MONBAZILLAC, PACHERENC DU VIC-BILH, PÉCHARMANT, ROSETTE, and SAUSSIGNAC. See also the VDQS wines, some of them produced in only very small quantities, Côtes de ST-MONT, Côtes du BRULHOIS, LAVILLEDIEU, ST-SARDOS, TURSAN, Vins d'ENTRAYGUES, and Vins d'ESTAING. See also LIMOUX.

George, R., *French Country Wines* (London, 1990).

soutirage, French term for RACKING, or moving clear wine off its sediment and into a clean container. It can also be used for the wine serving process of DECANTING.

Soviet sparkling wine is a specific term which, in tune with EUROPEAN UNION law, replaced the term Soviet champagne, or *champanskoe*, in the early 1990s. Although bottle-fermented sparkling wines have been made in what has variously been called Russia, the Soviet Union, the CIS and the ex-Soviet republics since the 18th century, consumer demand for sparkling wine was most notably demonstrated at the end of the 19th century, when the imperial court of Tsar Nicholas II regularly imported 800,000 bottles of, usually sweet, CHAMPAGNE. (The late 19th-century Champenois defined champagne sweetened to satisfy the *goût russe* as one with 273 to 330 g/l of RESIDUAL SUGAR, as opposed to the *goût anglais* of 22 to 66 g/l for the English.)

High import taxes led to the development of a domestic industry initially constructed on base wines imported from France in barrel, made sparkling according to champagne production techniques. This led to the development of vigorous sparkling wine industries based on grapes grown in the CRIMEA and around Odessa in UKRAINE, where Henri ROEDERER of Rheims established a Franco-Russian sparkling winery in 1896.

Soviet Union, the Union of Soviet Socialist Republics, which, following the fall of communism, fragmented into its 16 constituent republics. See, in very approximate declining order of wine production (not the same as order by vineyard area), RUSSIA, MOLDOVA, UKRAINE, CRIMEA, GEORGIA, KAZAKHSTAN, AZERBAIJAN, UZBEKISTAN, ARMENIA, KYRGYZSTAN, TAJIKISTAN, and TURKMENISTAN.

spacing of vines. See VINE DENSITY.

Spain, country in the grip of vinous revolution with the most land under vine in the world (1,154,000 ha/2,851,600 acres in 2005, of which 23 per cent was (mainly drip) irrigated) and yet only the world's third most important producer of wine. Thanks to Spain's arid climate, this vast area of vines yields on average only about 30 hl/ha (1.7 tons/acre), reflecting the extreme physical conditions in much of central Spain, where DROUGHT is a persistent problem (see below). Far greater use of DRIP IRRIGATION increased Spain's annual average wine production from 35 million hl/924 million gal in the early 1990s to nearly 45 million hl in the mid 2000s.

Spain occupies most of the Iberian peninsula and is the third largest country in Europe, extending from the Pyrenees that form the frontier with France in the north to the strait of Gibraltar just 15 km/9 miles from Africa to the south. Spain is a diverse country with distinct regional and cultural differences. The principal language spoken throughout Spain is Castilian, although CATALUÑA, GALICIA, and the BASQUE country have their own regional tongues, which are now generally used within those regions in preference to Castilian.

The country's regional diversity is reflected in her wines, which range from light, dry whites in the cool Atlantic region of Galicia to heavy, alcoholic reds in the Levante and the Mediterranean south. ANDALUCÍA in the south west is known for the production of fortified and dessert wines, the most famous of which is SHERRY.

Spain is a significant beneficiary of recent improvements in wine-making TECHNOLOGY. Modern production methods were slow to reach Spain but, when they did, typically in the early 1990s, they did so with a vengeance,

with modernization sweeping one region after the other, including some (but not all) of the less glamorous ones. A programme of investment which began a decade earlier was further helped by Spain's accession to the EUROPEAN UNION in 1986. In 1996, vineyard IRRIGATION was legalized throughout the country, radically changing prospects for the drought-stricken central and south-eastern areas.

History to Columbus

Although the wine-growing PHOENICIANS founded Cádiz *c.*1100 BC on the coast of southern Spain, they did not introduce viticulture to the Iberian peninsula, for the vine had been cultivated in Spain since between 4000 and 3000 BC. Grapes, found in Spain from the close of the Tertiary era onwards, pre-date *Homo sapiens* by millions of years.

Cádiz, gateway to the Atlantic, was an important Phoenician trading post. After the Phoenicians came the Carthaginians, themselves inhabitants of a city—CARTHAGE—founded by Phoenicians. The Carthaginians grew wine in Spain; more importantly, they were a threat to the emerging republic of Ancient ROME.

The 2nd century BC was a time of much unrest under Roman rule in Spain, and no systematic colonization was attempted until Rome finally 'pacified' the whole of the peninsula under Augustus. Political stability furthered trade: as the evidence from AMPHORAE shows, a great deal of wine from Baetica (which approximated to ANDALUCÍA) and Terraconensis (TARRAGONA) was sold in Rome, and Spanish exports far exceeded exports of Italian wine to Aquitaine and south eastern GAUL via Bordeaux. Spanish wine reached the Loire valley, Brittany, Normandy, and England, and it was given to the troops guarding the Roman frontier with Germany. Literary evidence confirms the discoveries of archaeology. Strabo says in his *Geography* (completed AD 9) that, since the fall of Carthage, Baetica has been famous for the beauty of its many vineyards. COLUMELLA, a native of Cádiz in Baetica, sees the wine imports from Baetica and Gaul as symptomatic of the decline of Roman agriculture (I, *Praefatio.* 20).

Most of the Spanish wines, and particularly that of Saguntum, sold in Rome appear to have been PLONK: perfect for getting the porter of one's mistress drunk on, is Ovid's advice (*Ars amatoria* 3. 645–6). Some wines earn praise, however: PLINY says that Terraconensis is good (*Natural History* 14. 71) and so repeatedly does MARTIAL, himself a native of Spain.

Spain was no mere outpost of empire. It was the birthplace of other Roman authors besides Martial and Columella: Seneca, Lucan, and Quintilian. The emperors Hadrian and Marcus Aurelius came from Spanish families. When the Roman empire disintegrated, Spain was invaded by barbarians, first by the Suevi and then by the Visigoths. We do not know what hap-

pened to viticulture and the wine trade: presumably it continued.

The overthrow of the Visigoths by the Moors in 711 did not mean the end of viticulture, for the ISLAMIC conquerors were enlightened rulers, who did not impose their own way of life on their subjects. Better still, many of them liked wine themselves. The Moorish position with regard to wine was ambiguous. Although the Prophet forbade the use of wine, the emirs and caliphs of Spain grew wine; although its sale was illegal, it was subject to excise (see TAXATION). By the time ENGLAND was importing considerable quantities of wine from Spain, the mid 13th century, the Christians had largely succeeded in their reconquest.

Around 1250, wine was regularly shipped from Bilbao to the English ports of Bristol, Southampton, and London. The quality of the wines varied. The best wines were very good indeed: when Edward III fixed maximum prices for wines in 1364, a cask of the best Spanish wine was to cost as much as a cask of the best GASCON, which fetched more than wine from LA ROCHELLE. Spanish wines were popular because being from a hot climate they were high in alcohol and therefore kept better than French or German wines. But some of these wines were just high in alcohol, and that was their only merit. Hence they were often used to ADULTERATE more expensive and weaker wines. Laws forbidding this practice were widely disregarded.

See also SACK, and ARNALDUS DE VILLANOVA and EIXIMENIS, two important medieval commentators on aspects of wine who were Catalan by birth.   H.M.W.

Blazquez, J. M., 'La economía de la Hispania Romana', in A. Montenegro *et al.* (eds.), *Historia de España: España romana* (Madrid, 1982).
Curchin, L. A., *Roman Spain* (London, 1991).
Jeffs, Julian, *Sherry* (4th edn, London, 1992).
Keay, S. J., *Roman Spain* (London, 1988).
Tchernia, André, *Les Vins de l'Italie romaine* (Paris, 1986).

History from Columbus

Spain emerged as a united, Christian country under a single crown in January 1492 following the final defeat of the Moors at Granada. Christopher Columbus discovered the West Indies in October of the same year, opening up a whole NEW WORLD to Spanish trade.

The wine regions around Cádiz and MÁLAGA, both important Spanish ports, were the first to attract the attention of foreign traders, and SHERRY, often called SACK, became a popular drink at the English court. Foreign traders in the sherry town of SANLÚCAR DE BARRAMEDA were granted special privileges by the duke of Medina Sidonia in 1517 and an English church was built to encourage more merchants. But relations between England and Spain began to deteriorate in the 1520s and after Henry VIII's divorce from Catherine of Aragón in 1533

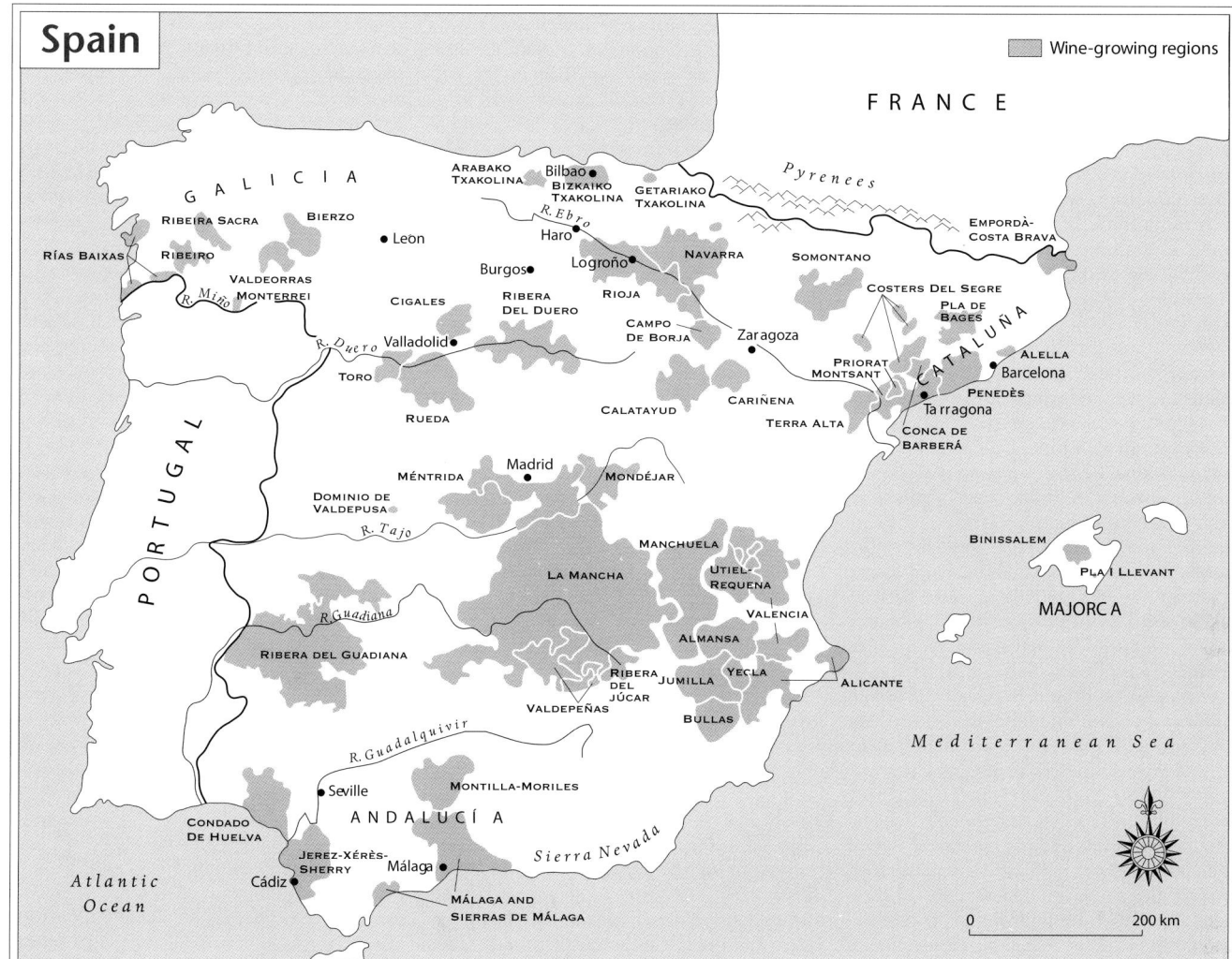

Spain

Wine-growing regions

FRANCE

Pyrenees

GALICIA

ARABAKO TXAKOLINA
Bilbao
BIZKAIKO TXAKOLINA
GETARIAKO TXAKOLINA

RIBEIRA SACRA
BIERZO
León
Haro
NAVARRA
SOMONTANO
EMPORDÀ-COSTA BRAVA

RÍAS BAIXAS
RIBEIRO
Burgos
Logroño
RIOJA

VALDEORRAS
MONTERREI
CIGALES
RIBERA DEL DUERO
COSTERS DEL SEGRE
PLA DE BAGES

R. Miño
CAMPO DE BORJA
Zaragoza
CATALUÑA
ALELLA
Barcelona

PORTUGAL
R. Duero
Valladolid
PRIORAT MONTSANT
PENEDÈS
Tarragona

TORO
CARIÑENA
CONCA DE BARBERÁ

RUEDA
CALATAYUD
TERRA ALTA

MÉNTRIDA
Madrid
MONDÉJAR
BINISSALEM

DOMINIO DE VALDEPUSA
PLA I LLEVANT

R. Tajo
MANCHUELA
MAJORCA

LA MANCHA
UTIEL-REQUENA

R. Guadiana
VALENCIA

RIBERA DEL GUADIANA
ALMANSA

RIBERA DEL JÚCAR
JUMILLA
YECLA
ALICANTE

VALDEPEÑAS
BULLAS

Mediterranean Sea

R. Guadalquivir

Seville
MONTILLA-MORILES

CONDADO DE HUELVA
ANDALUCÍA
Sierra Nevada

JEREZ-XÉRÈS-SHERRY
Málaga

Atlantic Ocean
Cádiz
MÁLAGA AND SIERRAS DE MÁLAGA

0   200 km

brought English merchants into direct conflict with the Spanish. In the latter part of the century, war erupted between the two countries. English settlers fled fearing the Spanish Inquisition and trade between the two nations diminished.

The English defeat of the Armada in 1588 destroyed Spain as a seafaring power and, on the death of Philip II ten years later, the country was left with a crippling debt despite its immense colonial wealth. Trade in wine soon resumed and, after the death of Elizabeth I, sack became a favoured drink in the court of James I. But 17th-century trade was sporadic and trade in Spanish wines was blighted by excessive English import duties. Not surprisingly, the Spanish fostered markets elsewhere in Europe and the New World.

Spanish wine has historically depended on exports to a larger extent than the wines from other traditional producing nations in Europe (and this continues to be the case today). During the 17th and 18th centuries, exports to Spain's American colonies surpassed in volume and value those to Britain and northern Europe. Vines had been planted all

over the Americas since the very first days of Spanish colonization, and wine was made in MEXICO from the early days of the 16th century. But successive monarchs, particularly Philip III, tried to stop the development of a local industry, to protect the flourishing export trade from the mainland. Between 1605 and 1620 he wrote edicts curtailing the spread of American vineyards. These were followed very unevenly—the local administration practically ignored them in Chile, but in Argentina they served to virtually quell all attempts at developing a national wine industry until independence came in the early 19th century. For more details, see SOUTH AMERICA.

See SHERRY for details of 18th- and 19th-century trade in that important SPANISH WINE.

At the same time, Málaga also enjoyed a spectacular increase in popularity, producing an estimated 35,000 BUTTS of wine in 1829, equivalent to 175,000 hl. 'Mountain', as the wine was popularly known in its 19th-century heyday, sat alongside PORT, MADEIRA, and sherry as one of the world's great FORTIFIED wines.

By all accounts there was little wine of exportable quality from the rest of Spain. Even

RIOJA, already Spain's leading table wine at the turn of the 19th century, found few markets other than neighbouring Basque country and South America. The chronicler Richard Ford writing in 1846 notes that Spanish 'wine continues to be made in an unscientific and careless manner'. Cyrus REDDING writing in the 1851 edition of the *History and Description of Modern Wines* observes 'the rude treatment of the grape' in Spain. It seems that outside Jerez and Málaga little had changed since Roman times. In central and southern Spain, wines continued to be made in crude earthenware TINAJAS, while to the north wooden casks were used. Wine was frequently stored in *cueros*, pigskins lined with pitch or resin which tainted the wine. Wine-making progressed slowly in Spain.

From the middle of the 19th century, wholesale change was forced on the Spanish wine industry, first by POWDERY MILDEW, which was found in Cataluña in the 1850s, and then much later by PHYLLOXERA. This devastating aphid was to arrive in Málaga in 1878, where it destroyed the livelihoods of thousands of vine-growers, many of whom left to establish a new life in South America, and Málaga's wine industry never fully recovered. But phylloxera spread relatively late and slowly through Spain, partly because of the long distances between the various Spanish wine regions, and in the 1860s the French, who had also suffered powdery mildew (oidium) for ten years, had crossed the Pyrenees to compensate for the shortfall in French wine. Rioja and NAVARRA, the closest wine regions to BORDEAUX, benefited most from France's misfortune, and the resulting influx of French influence and expertise.

The BARRICA (225-l/59-gal oak cask) which is now used throughout Spain was introduced from Bordeaux and wine-making was refined along the Bordelais lines (although American OAK continued to be preferred thanks to Spain's flourishing transatlantic trade in the late 18th century, to the hardness of American oak—much appreciated in Jerez—and to its relatively low cost). Rioja BODEGAS belonging to Marqués de Murrieta, Marqués de Riscal, López de Heredia, and CVNE date back to this period when up to 500,000 hl of wine a month were shipped across the Pyrenees to France.

Phylloxera took hold in Jerez in 1894 and reached Rioja in 1901, by which time the epidemic had been controlled by grafting European vines on to resistant American ROOTSTOCKS. Vineyards were replanted throughout the country but many traditional, indigenous VINE VARIETIES in such regions as Galicia and Cataluña were rendered virtually extinct. In Cataluña, the post-phylloxera period coincided with the development of the sparkling wine industry which is today one of the largest in the world. Following a visit to the Champagne region, José Raventós introduced the TRADITIONAL METHOD for the production of sparkling wine to the family firm of Codorníu in 1872. The wine, originally christened *champaña*, was a success, and vineyards around the town of San Sadurni de Noya were replanted with the trio of white grapes that now produce over a million hl of CAVA annually.

The first half of the 20th century was a turbulent era for Spain. Political infighting led to the abdication of Alfonso XIII in 1931 and the proclamation of a republic. However, one of the lasting measures introduced by the monarchist dictator General Primo de Rivera was the DO system of controlled appellations administered by a CONSEJO REGULADOR, which was first established in Rioja in 1926. Jerez and Málaga followed suit respectively in 1933 and 1937.

In June 1936, following the election victory of the Popular Front, Spain erupted into civil war. For three years sentiment ran high and Spain tore itself apart, often along regional, separatist lines. Some parts of the country, notably Cataluña and VALENCIA, were affected more than others but throughout country vineyards were neglected and wineries were destroyed. The Nationalist victory in 1939 brought political stability to Spain under General Franco but economic recovery was hampered by the Second World War, which effectively closed European markets to Spanish exports.

In the 1950s, the wine industry began to revive, helped by the nationwide construction of large CO-OPERATIVE wineries which had begun some years earlier. This turned Spain, with its vast area of vineyard, into a natural source for inexpensive bulk wine either sold under proprietary BRAND names, or labelled with spurious GENERIC names such as Spanish Chablis or Spanish Sauternes, subsequently outlawed by European Union authorities.

The post-war history of the Spanish wine industry was for some time marked by the Rumasa saga, outlined under SHERRY. But Rumasa's horizons ran far beyond Jerez and by the late 1970s José María Ruiz-Mateos seemed to control Spain. Ruiz-Mateos contributed greatly to the much-needed modernization of the Spanish wine industry but by the early 1980s there were signs that the empire was in trouble—see SHERRY.

The 1960s sherry boom was followed by the international 'discovery' of Rioja, which had reached the top in the domestic market early this century. In the 1970s and 1980s, the family firm of TORRES wrought a single-handed transformation of the wines of PENEDÈS. The death of General Franco in 1975 and the restoration of the monarchy set the foundations for a modern, multi-party democracy in Spain. Greater economic freedom has led to the growth of an urban middle class which has in turn stimulated a new interest in high-quality wine. Economically deprived rural regions such as La Mancha and Galicia have further benefited from EU finance, which is helping to change the face of the Spanish wine industry. In the 1990s, a fast-paced chain of events brought about more changes than during possibly the previous 90 years. International FLYING WINEMAKERS flocked to Spain; private estates overtook CO-OPERATIVES in most regions; INTERNATIONAL VARIETIES became commonplace in vineyards from La Mancha to Navarra; irrigation and WIRE-trained vineyards sprouted up everywhere; and wine styles changed radically to the fruitier type favoured on international markets.

Spanish wine law

Since joining the EU, Spain has brought her wine law into line with that of other European countries. There is now a four-tier system administered by INDO, acronym for the Madrid-based Instituto Nacional de Denominaciones de Origen. Every autonomous region, however, controls its own appellations, following the lead of Cataluña through INCAVI, the Institut Català de la Vinya i del Vi, and Castilla-La Mancha through IVICAM, the Instituto de la Viña y el Vino de Castilla-La Mancha. Only the appellations encompassing more than one autonomous region (Rioja, Jumilla, and Cava) are controlled by the Ministry of Agriculture through INDO.

VINO DE MESA (VdM) at the bottom of the pyramid includes all the wine made from unclassified vineyards or wine that has been declassified by blending. This is Spain's equivalent of the EU category TABLE WINE, and (as in Italy) it now includes some of the country's most expensive and prestigious wines.

VINO DE LA TIERRA (VdlT) applies to wine from a specific region provided producers conform to certain local norms. This is Spain's counterpart to France's VIN DE PAYS.

VCIG is a proposed denomination just below Denominación de Origen, or DO.

DO regions are the mainstay of the system, each with its own Consejo Regulador which regulates the growing, making, and marketing of wines, ensuring that they comply with specified regional standards. In 2005, there were 64 DO regions covering two-thirds of the total vineyard area of Spain. In the 1990s, INDO introduced a new category:

Denominación de Origen Calificada (DOC, previously known as DOCa), which equates with Italy's DOCG. Rioja was the first region to be awarded DOC status, in 1991, and was followed in 2003 by Priorat, which calls itself DOQ, Denominaciò d'Origen Qualificada in Catalan.

Geography and climate

Around much of Spain, the land rises steeply from the coast reaching a maximum altitude of 3,482 m/11,420 ft at Mulhacén in the Sierra Nevada just 50 km/30 miles from the Mediterranean. Iberia's dominant feature is the vast plateau that takes up much of central Spain. Known as the *meseta*, this undulating table land ranges in altitude from 600 to 1,000 m, tilting slightly towards the west. Four of Iberia's five major rivers (the Duero, Tajo, Guadiana, and Guadalquivir) drain westwards into the Atlantic, with the Ebro flowing south east to the Mediterranean. Other rivers are seasonal, many drying up completely in the summer months.

Great mountain ranges known as *cordilleras* divide Spain into distinct natural regions. The north coast, from Galicia to the Pyrenees, is relatively cool and humid with few extremes. Annual RAINFALL in this part of Spain ranges from 1,000 mm/39 in on the coast to over 2,000 mm on the mountain peaks inland. Galicia, Asturias, and the BASQUE country are intensively cultivated and densely populated.

The Cantabrian cordillera, a westerly spur of the Pyrenees which rises to over 2,600 m in the Picos de Europa, protects the main body of Spain from cool, rain-bearing north westerlies. Rioja in the upper Ebro valley is therefore shielded from the bay of Biscay so that, although annual rainfall reaches around

1,500 mm on the Basque coast, it declines sharply to the east and is just 450 mm at Haro, the wine-making capital of Rioja, only 100 km inland.

The Spanish climate becomes more extreme towards the centre of the central plateau. Winters are long and cold with temperatures falling well below freezing point (the lowest recorded temperature is −22 °C/−7.6 °F in Albacete). Summers here can be blistering hot with daytime temperatures sometimes rising above 40 °C. Little rain falls in the summer months and DROUGHT is a constant problem. Agriculture has adapted to the lack of rainfall, which struggles to reach 300 mm in places. Much of this comes in sudden downpours in spring and autumn which sometimes cause devastating flash floods.

South and east from the central plateau the climate is increasingly influenced by proximity to the Mediterranean. The climate on the narrow coastal littoral is equable with long, warm summers giving way to mild winters. These are Spain's holiday Costas, but there are lush market gardens producing rice and citrus fruit around Valencia, and, on the mountain slopes inland, olives, almonds, and TABLE GRAPES are important crops. The hottest part of Spain is the broad Guadalquivir valley in Andalucía, north of the Sierra Nevada, where summer temperatures rise to 45 °C. The south west corner of Andalucía has a climate of its own, strongly influenced by the gulf of Cádiz and the Atlantic (see SHERRY).

Viticulture

Throughout much of Spain, YIELDS are notably low. In most of central and southern Spain, vines are widely spaced to survive the summer drought with VINE DENSITIES ranging from 900 to 1,600 vines per ha (375–650 per acre) according to the amount of water available (less than one-eighth of the vine density in some MÉDOC or CÔTE D'OR vineyards, for example). Growers have adopted a system of planting known as the *marco real* with 2.5 m between each vine in all directions. In all but the most modern vineyards (which tend to be planted with increasing MECHANIZATION in mind), vines tend to be free standing, BUSH trained, and pruned according to the GOBELET method known as *en vaso* in Spain. Yields from these vineyards, many of which are over 40 years old, are frequently less than 20 hl/ha (1.1 tons/acre). The records for the DO of JUMILLA, for example, show, despite a marked increased during the 1990s, average yields of just 18 hl/ha (one-eighth of customary yields in many an Italian DOC).

However, one considerable advantage that accompanies a dry climate is the lack of FUNGAL DISEASES. POWDERY MILDEW, DOWNY MILDEW, and BOTRYTIS BUNCH ROT are virtually unknown in central Spain.

IRRIGATION was one of the most important new developments of the 1990s. The practice

had begun to spread unofficially—particularly during the DROUGHTS in south-east Spain of 1994 and 1995—and was formally legalized in 1996. Drip irrigation, pioneered on the Marqués de Griñón Valdepusa estate in Toledo province under the supervision of Australian viticulturist Richard Smart, is the favourite of many growers. Subsurface drip irrigation, which minimizes the losses due to EVAPORATION, became increasingly popular in the early 21st century. Irrigation has been followed by considerably increased yields in such areas as Rioja Baja. This, together with a rapid increase in new plantings, triggered concerns about wine quality in the late 1990s.

Viticultural practices vary sharply from one part of Spain to another. In areas such as Rioja and Penedès, where more systematic replanting is taking place, vines are more densely planted (up to 5,000 vines per ha) and are increasingly trained on wires. With irrigation, yields may reach 70 or 80 hl/ha, far above official limits. In Galicia, vines were traditionally trained on pergolas (see TENDONE), both to make maximum use of the limited space in this densely populated part of Spain and to lessen the risk of fungal diseases in this humid climate. Newer vineyards are planted on lower vine-TRAINING SYSTEMS to ease cultivation but have to be regularly sprayed to combat disease. Yields are frequently high, sometimes surpassing 100 hl/ha in RÍAS BAIXAS.

Traditionally, most grapes were harvested by hand and grapes frequently arrived at co-operative wineries already starting to ferment, having been squashed when loaded into large trailers. Quality-conscious bodegas increasingly provide growers with stackable plastic containers to keep the grapes whole during transportation (see HARVEST). Some firms also set out a harvest regime refusing grapes delivered after midday when they have been heated by the sun. Some estates are now harvesting at night. The number of MECHANICAL HARVESTERS is increasing as fast as the acreage of vineyards supported on wires.

Vine varieties

The Spanish claim to have up to 600 different grape varieties, although 80 per cent of the country's vineyards are planted with just over 20 of them. Since the arrival of phylloxera at the end of the 19th century, farmers tended to favour varieties well adapted to local climatic conditions, but irrigation has changed this tendency considerably. The drought-resistant white AIRÉN is planted throughout central Spain, occupying more than one-quarter of the area under vine. Airén traditionally produced base wines for Spain's brandy industry and oxidized, alcoholic white wines for local bars and cafés, but with careful handling and improved vinification (see below) it is capable of producing some simple but refreshing dry wines. Dark-skinned TEMPRANILLO has overtaken GARNACHA to become the second

most widely planted variety with 190,000 ha in 2004, an increase of 68 per cent on the area planted with Tempranillo in 2003. It travels under such aliases as Cencibel, Ull de Llebre, and Tinto Fino in different parts of the country.

BOBAL and Monastrell (the MOURVÈDRE of France) perform Garnacha's role in the Levante, where they each cover around 100,000 ha/ 250,000 acres. Both varieties yield dark, alcoholic reds and the occasional dry rosé.

Other white varieties which are also important in Spain are the sherry grapes PALOMINO (planted in Jerez, RUEDA, and parts of Galicia) and PEDRO XIMÉNEZ (Montilla-Moriles and Málaga). The white MACABEO (also called Viura) is widely planted in Rioja and Cataluña, especially Penedès, where, along with Parellada and Xarel-lo, it is grown for Cava sparkling wine. High-quality white varieties which are gaining ground include ALBARIÑO (Galicia) and VERDEJO (Rueda), while other promising grapes which are making a more limited comeback include the white LOUREIRA, TREIXADURA, and GODELLO (all three in Galicia) and the red GRACIANO (Rioja) and MENCÍA (Galicia and Castilla y León).

INTERNATIONAL VARIETIES are making significant inroads in some parts of Spain. CABERNET SAUVIGNON, SYRAH, MERLOT, SAUVIGNON BLANC, and CHARDONNAY are increasingly important in Cataluña, Somontano, Navarra, Castilla y León and Castilla-La Mancha.

Wine-making

Spanish wine-making has changed radically since the 1960s. Stainless steel, once a rarity, is now commonplace and most bodegas have the means of TEMPERATURE CONTROL for fermentation. These improvements transformed Spanish wines, especially in La Mancha and the Levante, where temperature control is essential to preserve the primary fruit character in both red and white wine. Traditional TINAJAS are rarely used today, while the epoxy-lined concrete tanks still to be found in some co-operative wineries are regaining favour with top producers for red wines, as are oak vats, in a return to traditional fermentation vessels which ensure less temperature variation than stainless steel tanks.

A vogue for crisp, technically perfect, simple young whites was followed in the 1990s by a resurgence of barrel-fermented whites, in effect a revival of a 19th-century tradition that had given way to whites fermented in tank and matured in oak that were generally flat and OXIDIZED.

Spain continues to foster the long-established tradition of ageing red wines in OAK. The use of wooden BARRELS as vessels for fermentation and storage dates back many centuries but in the second half of the 19th century the French introduced the 225-l BARRIQUE (*barrica*) to Rioja, and its use has subsequently spread throughout the country. Unlike the

French, however, most Spanish winemakers use American oak, which is not only considerably cheaper than French oak, it can also impart a stronger flavour to the wine. The Tempranillo grape in particular seems to produce wine that responds to maturation in new oak. However, French oak has made significant inroads since the early 1990s. Spanish oak-aged reds are usually denoted by the words CRIANZA, RESERVA, or GRAN RESERVA, which are enshrined in local legislation. From the 1970s to the 1990s, the wines often showed a pungent, vanilla character but this is being superseded by more FRUIT-DRIVEN aromas and flavours, partly in response to FASHION.

Most Spanish DOs also stipulate minimum BOTTLE AGE and traditionally very few Spanish wines were released before they were were ready to drink. But some growers, led by Alejandro Fernández of RIBERA DEL DUERO and the PRIORAT newcomers, started a new habit of renouncing both crianza and Reserva back labels, selling oak-aged wine as vino JOVEN, often with little bottle age.

For specific wine regions, see ANDALUCÍA, ARAGÓN, BASQUE, CASTILLA-LA MANCHA, CASTILLA Y LEÓN, CATALUÑA, GALICIA, LEVANTE, NAVARRA, and RIOJA.

See also SHERRY.   V. de la S.

Jeffs, J., *The Wines of Spain* (London, 2000).

Peñín, J., *Guía Peñín* (Madrid, annually).

Radford, J., *The New Spain* (2nd edn, London, 2004).

Spanna, local name for the NEBBIOLO grape in eastern PIEMONTE in north west Italy, particularly around Gattinara in the hills of the Vercelli and Novara provinces. This just may be the *uva spinea* mentioned by PLINY, who added that this is the variety *quae sola alitur nebulis*. Nebbiolo, a very late-maturing vine variety, may well be said to 'breathe the fog' of the Piemonte autumn.

Six DOC wines and one DOCG, Gattinara, are made either wholly or in part from Spanna: three in the Vercelli hills (BRAMATERRA, GATTINARA, LESSONA) and four in the province of Novara (BOCA, FARA, GHEMME, and SIZZANO). Only Gattinara and Ghemme, with 100 and 85 ha (250 and 210 acres) respectively and responsible for the longest-lived Spanna wines, have a significant production, and several of the others are virtually of postage stamp size (Boca is 15 ha, Lessona 6.5 ha). In the 19th century, this area had greater plantings, and was more famous for its wines, than the LANGHE. Today, the wines display strong Nebbiolo personality, although only Lessona can be 100 per cent Spanna, the other DOCs requiring blending with the less interesting VESPOLINA and BONARDA Novarese grapes. Spanna wines had an excellent reputation before the Second World War and were quite popular in the major market of nearby Milan, but the postwar period has seen a definite loss of ground to the richer and more professionally made Nebbiolo wines of the Langhe; the combination of excessive CASK AGEING in old casks, and imperfectly executed or non-existent MALOLACTIC FERMENTATIONS have not been helpful to the reputation of these wines. In addition, the grape Spanna became confused with the wine Spanna, which became almost generic and often included more blending wine from the south of Italy than they did Nebbiolo from the hills of Novara and Vercelli. Today, Spanna is DOC in the Colline Novaresi. The extreme fragmentation of vineyard property and a workforce that moved to the textile factories of nearby Biella also accelerated the decline of winemaking in this area, but in the mid 2000s Spanna looked set for a modest revival in its historic area of production.   D.T. & D.C.G.

sparging a wine means stripping it of OXYGEN or CARBON DIOXIDE by purging it with fine bubbles of an INERT GAS, usually NITROGEN. The technique is not widely used because it removes not only oxygen but also significant amounts of volatile FLAVOUR COMPOUNDS. A tank or bottle may also be sparged with an inert gas. Sparging can also refer to the use of CO_2 to increase the concentration of CO_2 in the wine.   A.D.W.

sparkling wine, wine which bubbles when poured into a glass, an important and growing category of wine. The bubbles form because a certain amount of CARBON DIOXIDE has been held under pressure dissolved in the wine until the bottle is unstoppered (see FIZZINESS).

Sparkling wine may vary in as many respects as still wine: it can be any wine COLOUR (it is usually white but pink fizz and sparkling reds such as BURGUNDY (Bourgogne Mousseux) and Australian sparkling Shiraz have enjoyed a certain following); it can be any degree of SWEETNESS (although a high proportion tastes bone dry and may be labelled BRUT, while Italians specialize in medium sweet SPUMANTE); it can vary in ALCOHOLIC STRENGTH (although in practice most dry sparkling wines are about 12 per cent, while the sweeter, lighter Spumante are between 5.5 and 8 per cent); and it can come from anywhere in the world where wine is produced.

According to EUROPEAN UNION regulations, the sweetness level of EU wines must be shown on the label. For official EU definitions, see DOSAGE. Sparkling wines produced outside the EU but sold within the EU do not have to indicate the sweetness level but if it is specified, only the EU-designated terms may be used.

Sparkling wines also vary in fizziness, not just in the actual pressure under which the gas is dissolved in the wine, but also apparently in the character of the foam. Some sparkling wines froth aggressively in the mouth while others bubble subtly. The average size, consistency, and persistence of the bubbles also vary considerably. Study of foam and foaminess, along with research into YEASTS, are two of the few areas which unite the (sparkling) wine industry with the BEER industry.

To the winemaker, however, the most obvious way in which sparkling wines differ is in how the gas came to be trapped in solution in the wine: traditional method, transversage, transfer, Charmat, or carbonation, in declining order of cost, complication, and likely quality of sparkling wine, together with the rarer *méthode ancestrale* and *méthode dioise*. (See SPARKLING WINE-MAKING for details of each method.)

The most famous sparkling wine of all is CHAMPAGNE, the archetypal sparkling wine made in north eastern France, which represents about 8 per cent of global sparkling wine production. A significant proportion of all sparkling wine is made using the same basic method as is used in Champagne (now called the traditional, rather than the champagne, method), much of it from the same grape varieties Pinot Noir, Chardonnay, and, to a lesser extent outside Champagne, Meunier, even though different wine regions often stamp their own style on the resulting sparkling wine. Examples of such wines were made with ever-increasing frequency in the 1980s and early 1990s in CALIFORNIA, AUSTRALIA, and ITALY particularly.

A host of fine, very individual sparkling wines is made using the traditional method but with non-champagne grapes, however. The most prodigious example of this is the popular Spanish CAVA. The LOIRE region of France also produces traditional method sparkling wine in great quantity, notably in SAUMUR. All of France's new CRÉMANTS also use the traditional method. In almost every wine region in the world with aspirations to quality, some traditional method wine has been made. Wines made by this, the most meticulous method, may be described on the label within Europe as *méthode traditionnelle*, *méthode classique*, or *méthode traditionnelle classique*. Other descriptions include bottle fermented (although strictly speaking wines made by the transfer method, described below, may be labelled 'bottle fermented', while only those made by the traditional method can be labelled 'Fermented in *This* Bottle').

Similarly, in almost every wine region in the world, Charmat process sparkling wine is made in considerable quantity, often for specific local BRANDS, especially for SEKT in Germany and a host of wines such as LAMBRUSCO and ASTI in Italy. RUSSIA has been an enthusiastic market for sparkling wines ever since the imperial court imported such vast quantities of champagne (and base wine to make sparkling) at the end of the 19th century. Today SOVIET SPARKLING WINE is still made in enormous quantity in both Russia and UKRAINE. Asti and a number of other low-alcohol, sweet Italian, or Italianate, sparkling wines are made using a variation of the Charmat process.

The transfer method is used for some better-quality branded wines, particularly in Germany and the United States (giving rise to the defiant description on some American sparkling wine labels 'Fermented in *This* Bottle' for products made by the traditional method).

Some characterful sparkling wines are made eschewing DISGORGEMENT and selling the part-fermented, still-sweet wine together with the LEES of its second fermentation in bottle. These include some GAILLAC, LIMOUX, and CLAIRETTE DE DIE made by specific but similar local methods sometimes called *méthode ancestrale*.

See also OPENING THE BOTTLE, LABELLING IN-FORMATION, and DOSAGE.

sparkling wine-making, making

SPARKLING WINES, most obviously involves the accumulation of gas under pressure in what was initially a still 'base wine' or, ideally, blend of base wines. The most common methods of achieving this are discussed below but these are matters of technique rather than substance. Almost all of them depend on initiating a second FERMENTATION, which inevitably produces CARBON DIOXIDE, and most of them incorporate some way of keeping that gas dissolved under pressure in the wine, while separating it from the inconvenient by-product of fermentation, the LEES. What matters most to the quality of a sparkling wine, however, is the quality and character of the blended base wines.

Making and blending the base wine

Wines that are good raw material for the sparkling wine-making process are not usually much fun to drink in their still state. They are typically high in acidity and unobtrusively flavoured. There is a school of thought that the austerity of the still wine of the CHAMPAGNE region, Coteaux CHAMPENOIS, is the most eloquent argument of all in favour of champagne's carbon dioxide content.

It is not just in Champagne, however, that sparkling winemakers argue that BALANCE is the key to assembling a base wine to make sparkling, and that the best sparkling wines are therefore essentially blended wines. Some fine VARIETAL sparkling wines exist (some of the best BLANC DE BLANCS champagnes, for example), but a great sparkling wine never tastes just like the still wine version plus gas; the very nature of sparkling wine-making is to try to make a sum that is greater than the parts (although this may not be achieved, or even attempted, for cheaper wines). Those who aspire to make good sparkling wine are acutely aware that any minor fault in a base wine may be amplified by the sparkling wine-making process.

Accordingly, for better sparkling wines, grapes had invariably been hand picked up

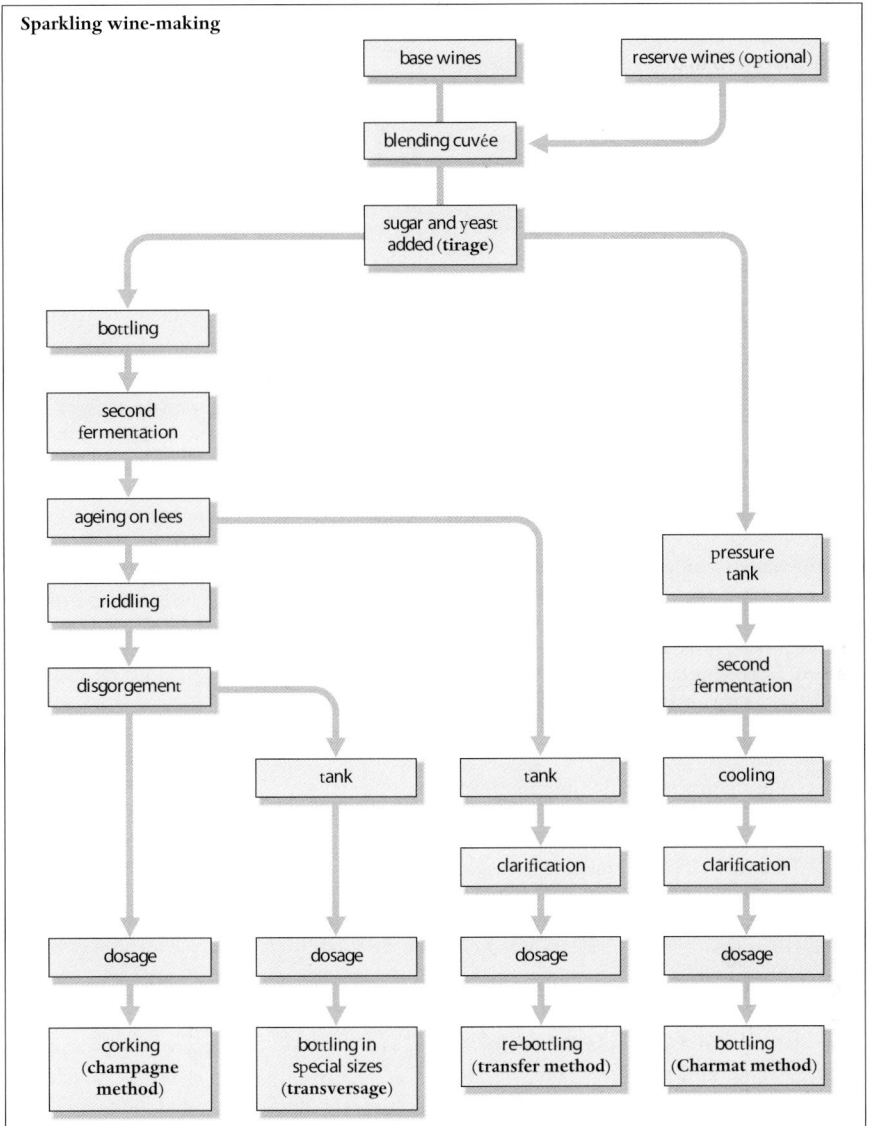

Sparkling wine-making

to the early 1990s since WHOLE BUNCH PRESSING was the norm, and such MECHANICAL HARVESTERS as had been tested by then risked splitting berries and extracting harsh PHENOLICS into the grape juice, which could cause astringent, coarse characteristics which would be magnified by the pressure of bubbles. It is possible that gentler mechanical harvesters will change this, although it is essential to press grapes as soon as possible after picking. Press houses in the vineyards have long been *de rigueur* in Champagne and are increasingly common for other top-quality sparkling wines.

Grapes destined for sparkling wines are usually picked at lower MUST WEIGHTS than the same varieties would be if they were to be sold as a still wine. In very general terms, average YIELDS can be higher for sparkling wines than still wines (see below), partly because there is no imperative to achieve high sugar levels. In California, for example,

HARVEST begins in mid, or sometimes early, August for Pinot Noir and Chardonnay destined for sparkling wines. In Australia, the aim is to pick such varieties just as HERBACEOUS characters have been lost when ripe fruit FLAVOUR COMPOUNDS are beginning to develop (in practice at about 17 to 20 °BRIX in Australia's cooler areas.

PRESSING is an important stage in sparkling wine-making, particularly in Champagne, where black grapes are used, as it is essential that the concentration of phenolics, both ASTRINGENCY and COLOUR, is kept to a minimum. There has been much experimentation with horizontal presses of various types, and modern airbag or tank presses can certainly offer a reliably high standard of HYGIENE, but modern technology has found it difficult to improve upon the traditional vertical presses of Champagne, although they are LABOUR intensive. So-called 'thin layer' presses which minimize pressure, and therefore the extraction of phenolics by pressing a layer of grapes no more than 70 cm/27 in thick, are used increasingly.

The winemaker can then make the usual still white wine choices concerning OXIDATIVE versus PROTECTIVE methods of JUICE HANDLING; juice CLARIFICATION; choice of YEAST strain and FERMENTATION rate; protein STABILIZATION; and MALOLACTIC FERMENTATION (sparkling wines made from wines which have not undergone malolactic fermentation may be simpler and fruitier in youth).

Then comes the crucial blending stage, the true art of making sparkling wine, and one in which experience is as important as SCIENCE. A large champagne house such as MOËT & CHANDON may be able to use several hundred base wines in order to achieve the house style in its basic expression, that year's NON-VINTAGE blend. A small, independent concern, especially outside Champagne, may have access to only a very limited range of base wines—a disadvantage in a poor vintage, although not necessarily in a good one. And a producer of the most basic Charmat process wine may simply blend the cheapest vaguely suitable ingredients available in the market place.

Traditional method (champagne method)

This method, once known as the champagne method and now known variously as traditional method, classic method, *méthode traditionnelle*, and *méthode classique*, is the most meticulous way of making wine sparkle; the raw ingredients vary considerably but the basic techniques do not.

Pressing and yield Pressing is the first operation defined in detail by the traditional method, which understandably differentiates rigorously between the fractions of juice from each press load, for the first juice to emerge from the press is highest in sugar and acidity and lowest in phenolics, including pigments. A maximum extraction rate is usually defined in any regulations concerning sparkling wine production (such as those for France's CRÉMANTS). Those who produce traditional method sparkling wine acknowledge that the first juice to emerge from the press is generally the best, even if there is a certain amount of VINTAGE variation. From 1992, the permitted extraction rate for champagne was reduced so that 160 kg (350 lb) of grapes rather than 150 kg of grapes were required to produce 100 l (26.4 gal) of wine, about the same extraction rate as that used by producers of top-quality sparkling wine anywhere in the world. (This compares with an approximate average extraction rate of 100 l of wine from about 130 kg of grapes for still red wines; see YIELD.)

Base wines After the making of the base wines (described above), which usually takes place over the winter following the harvest, the final blend is made after extensive tasting, assessment, and BENCH BLENDING. There is extreme flexibility in blending a non-dated wine and a high proportion of 'reserve wine' made in previous years may be used. Some champagne houses include up to 45 per cent of reserve wines in their NON-VINTAGE blend. (KRUG indulge in the luxury of using base wines from up to six different vintages being held in reserve.) The ingredients in a vintage-dated sparkling wine are more limited (often by necessity for those new to sparkling wine-making, by law in Champagne). Many of the base wines made from dark-berried grapes, however lightly pressed, may have a light pink tinge at this stage, although the PIGMENTS are precipitated during *tirage*, the crucial next stage during which the blended wine rests on the lees of a second fermentation in bottle. As soon as the new blend has been made in bulk blending tanks, it usually undergoes cold STABILIZATION in order to prevent subsequent formation of TARTRATES in bottle.

Second fermentation This new blend then has a mixture of sugar and yeast added to it before bottling in particularly strong, dark BOTTLES, usually STOPPERED with a CROWN CAP, so that a second fermentation will occur in bottle, creating the all-important fizz. Conventionally, an addition or *tirage* of about 24 g/l of sugar is made. This creates an additional 1.2 to 1.3 per cent ALCOHOLIC STRENGTH and sufficient carbon dioxide to create a pressure inside the bottle of five to six atmospheres after disgorgement (see below), which is roughly the FIZZINESS expected of a sparkling wine, and one which can safely be contained by a wired champagne cork. During this second fermentation, known as *prise de mousse* in French, the bottles are normally stored horizontally at about 12 °C/54 °F until the fermentation has produced the required pressure and bubbles, usually for four to eight weeks.

Special types of YEAST culture which help sparkling winemakers have been developed (and are much used for still wines too). Such yeasts are particularly good at flocculating, and produce a granular deposit that is easy to riddle, or shake, to the neck of the bottle for extraction.

At this stage, RIDDLING agents are increasingly added with the yeast and sugar. Made of some combination of TANNINS, BENTONITES, gelatines, or alginates, they help to produce a uniform skin-like yeast deposit that does not stick to the glass but slips easily down it during the riddling process. The development of smoother glass bottles has also helped.

Ageing on lees Timing of the riddling process after the second fermentation is a key element in quality and style of a traditional method sparkling wine, the second most important factor affecting quality after blending the base wine. The longer a wine rests on the lees of the second fermentation in bottle, the more chance it has of picking up flavour from the dead yeast cells, a process known as yeast AUTOLYSIS.

Most regulations for traditional method sparkling wines specify at least nine months ageing on lees, and the minimum period for non-vintage champagne was increased to 15 months in the early 1990s (vintage champagnes are usually aged for several years). During the bottle ageing process, the yeast cells autolyse, releasing increasingly complex flavour compounds. The chemistry of autolysis is not fully understood, but it seems that autolysis has significant effects only after about 18 months on the lees, and that the most obvious changes occur after five to ten years of lees contact, which inevitably increases production costs considerably. It may be that compulsory periods of lees contact in bottle of only a few months have less effect on quality than has been imagined.

Riddling The riddling process, known as *remuage* (or shaking) in French, is one of the most cumbersome (and most publicized) parts of the traditional method, but it is undertaken for cosmetic rather than oenological reasons: to remove the deposit that would otherwise make the wine cloudy (as it does in the *méthode ancestrale* described below).

Traditionally, bottles were gradually moved from the horizontal to an inverted vertical by hand, by human *remueurs* or riddlers who would shake them and the deposit every time they moved them towards the inverted vertical position in special *pupitres* or riddling racks. This was a slow and extremely labour-intensive way of moving the deposit from the belly of the bottle to its neck. The CAVA industry based in Cataluña developed an automatic alternative in the 1970s, the *girasol* or GYROPALETTE, which has since been widely adopted for traditional method sparkling wine-making the world over. The bottles are stacked, 504 at a time, in large metal crates, and their orientation changed at regular intervals (including night time, unlike the manual method), with accompanying shake, from the horizontal to inverted vertical by remote control. Using riddling agents, well-adapted yeasts, and gyropalettes, bottles may now be riddled in as little as three days, as opposed to the six weeks or more needed for hand *remuage* without riddling agents.

Disgorgement and dosage The final stage in a sometimes short (but inevitably complicated) production process compared, say, with a fine oak-aged red is to remove the deposit now in the neck of an inverted bottle. The conventional way of achieving this is to freeze the bottle neck and deposit by plunging the necks of the inverted bottles into a tray of freezing solution. The bottles are then upended, opened, and the deposit flies out as a solid pellet of ice. Bottles are then topped up with a mixture of wine and sugar syrup, the so-called DOSAGE, stoppered with a proper champagne CORK held on with a wire MUZZLE, and prepared for labelling. Most dry sparkling wine is sweetened so that it contains between 5 and 12 g/l RESIDUAL SUGAR, and the further from the equator the grapes are grown, the more dosage is generally required to counterbalance high natural ACIDITY, although the longer a wine is aged on lees, the less dosage it needs.

Alternative methods Riddling and disgorgement are unwieldy processes which contribute nothing to the innate quality of the sparkling wine. It is not surprising therefore that, in the 1980s, as LABOUR costs spiralled, there was considerable research into alternative methods of expelling the sediment.

One of the most successful has been the development of encapsulated yeast. Yeast can be trapped in a 'bead' made of calcium alginate. Such beads are about a few millimetres in diameter and are able to hold the yeast trapped in their interior while having big enough pores to admit sugar and nutrients into the bead so that a full second fermentation can proceed as normal. The great advantage is that the riddling stage takes seconds as the beads simply drop into the neck of the inverted bottle. The only brake on the adoption of encapsulated yeasts has been the development of reliable machinery which will dispense beads into bottles without shearing them. Although MOËT & CHANDON successfully trialled the use of such beads, the company decided it was more practical and economical to continue to use gyropalettes to move the sediment to the neck of the bottle.

Another possible method is to insert a membrane cartridge into the neck of the bottle. Yeast is dispensed into it and it is then plugged before the bottle is stoppered with the usual crown cap. Like the beads, the cartridge allows ingress of sugar and nutrients for fermentation to take place there, as well as allowing the carbon dioxide gas out. In this case there is no need at all for riddling, and disgorgement simply entails taking off the crown cap and allowing the pressure inside the bottle to expel the cartridge. This alternative could be particularly useful to small wineries for whom the investment in riddling and disgorgement equipment has been prohibitive.

Transversage

Transversage is an occasional twist on the traditional method whereby, immediately after disgorgement, the contents of bottles of sparkling wine made by the traditional method are transferred into a pressure tank to which the dosage is added before the wine is bottled, typically in another (often small) size of bottle, under pressure. This is how many half-bottles, all airline 'splits' or quarter-

bottles, and virtually all BOTTLE SIZES above a jeroboam of champagne are filled.

Transfer method

The transfer method, known as *méthode transfert* in French and Carstens in the United States, also depends on inducing a second fermentation by adding sugar and yeast to a blend of base wines and then bottling the result. It differs from the traditional method, however, in that riddling and disgorgement are dispensed with and, after a period of lees contact, the bottles are chilled, and their contents transferred to a bulk pressure tank where the sediment is removed by clarification, usually FILTRATION. A suitable dosage is then added and the result is once again bottled, using a counter pressure filler, before being corked and wired. The transfer method is likely to be abandoned in the long term because it has all the disadvantages of the traditional method but does not produce all its qualities in the wine.

Continuous method

This process was developed in the USSR for SOVIET SPARKLING WINE and is now used in Germany and Portugal. The method involves a series of usually five reticulated tanks under five atmospheres of pressure, the same FIZZINESS as in most sparkling wines. At one end, base wine together with sugar and yeast (usually rehydrated dried yeast) is pumped in and the second fermentation crucial to virtually all methods of sparkling wine-making begins. This creates CARBON DIOXIDE, which increases the pressure in the tank, but the yeast cannot grow under this pressure and so further yeast has to be added continuously. The second and third tanks are partly filled with some material such as wood shavings, which offer a substantial total surface area on which the dead yeast cells accumulate and a certain amount of AUTOLYSIS, or at least reaction between the dead yeast cells and the wine, takes place. In the fourth and fifth tanks there are no yeast cells and the wine eventually emerges relatively clear, having spent an average of perhaps three or four weeks in the system. See also LANCERS.

Charmat process or tank method

This very common method, also called *cuve close* (French for sealed tank), tank, or bulk method, *granvas* in Spanish, *autoclave* in Italian, was developed by Eugene Charmat in the early years of the 20th century in Bordeaux. Its advantages are that it is very much cheaper, faster, and less labour intensive than the above processes, and is better suited to base wines which lack much capacity for AGEING. A second fermentation is provoked by yeast and sugar added to base wine held in bulk in a pressure tank and, after a rapid fermentation, the fermentation is typically arrested by cooling the wine to $-5\,°C$ when a pressure of about five atmospheres has been reached. The result

is clarified, a dosage is added and the resulting sparkling wine is bottled using a counter pressure filler. This style of sparkling wine is the most likely to taste like still wine with bubbles in it, rather than to have any of the additional attributes which can result from fermentation in bottle.

Carbonation

Also known as the injection, or simply the 'bicycle pump', method, carbonation of wine is achieved in much the same way as carbonation of fizzy, soft drinks: carbon dioxide gas is pumped from cylinders into a tank of wine which is then bottled under pressure, or very occasionally it is pumped into bottles. Fizziness must by law be at least three atmospheres in Europe. The result is a wine which has many, and large, bubbles when the bottle is first opened, but whose mousse rapidly fades. This is the cheapest, least critical, and least durable way of making wine sparkle and is used for perhaps the cheapest 10 per cent of all sparkling wines.

Méthode ancestrale or méthode rurale

This method is rarely used and results in a lightly sparkling, medium sweet wine, often with some deposit, but it most closely parallels how wines were originally made sparkling. It involves bottling young wines before all the RESIDUAL SUGAR has been fermented into alcohol. Fermentation continues in bottle and gives off carbon dioxide. Variants on this theme are still made in Gaillac, where the method is sometimes known as the *méthode gaillacoise*, from the Blanquette grape in LIMOUX, and may still occasionally be found in SAVOIE.

The wine is designed to be sweeter and less fizzy than a traditional method sparkling wine and no dosage is allowed. The wine may in some cases be decanted off the deposit and rebottled under pressure in a form of transfer method.

Méthode dioise

This is an unusual variation on the *méthode ancestrale* above and the transfer method, producing wines similar to ASTI. It is used for the sweet wine CLAIRETTE DE DIE, most of which is made by the local CO-OPERATIVE. The base wines are fermented in stainless steel tanks at very low temperatures over several months. The wine is then filtered, bottled, and fermentation continues in bottle until an alcoholic strength of about 7.5 per cent has been reached. The wine is disgorged six to 12 months after bottling (by inserting a pipe through the crown cap and sucking out the clear wine under pressure) before being filtered again and immediately transferred to new bottles.

Spätburgunder is the chief synonym in GERMANY for PINOT NOIR and the grape variety that experienced the most dramatic rise in popularity in Germany in the 1990s. Such is German enthusiasm for red wine that Germany's total plantings increased from 3,400 ha/8,400 acres in 1980 to 5,500 ha in 1990 and more than 11,000 ha by 2003. There is considerable dispute over the vine's importance in Germany during the Middle Ages but in modern times, until the late 1980s, it was cultivated largely in parts of the RHEINGAU (notably Assmannshausen) where it owes its toehold to the same 13th-century Cistercian MONKS responsible for its rise to fame in the Côte d'Or, and along the steep slate slopes of the AHR. Then the typical Spätburgunder was pale, sweetish (and all too often tinged with rot-related odours). Today it is much deeper coloured, as alcoholic as climate and CHAPTALIZATION regulations will allow, fermented out to dryness, and well structured, thanks to the much lower yields, longer MACERATION, and BARREL MATURATION associated with Germany's most ambitious producers. Few of these wines are exported since demand so much exceeds supply within Germany, and prices are high. Growers in the Ahr (notably Meyer-Näkel), and the Rheingau (above all August Kesseler of Assmannshausen) are building on local growing traditions to achieve an international reputation for German Pinot Noir. But it is now important in other regions: Baden (the leader at 5,600 ha), the Pfalz (whose Pinot area is the fastest-growing in Germany), and Rheinhessen. On occasion, nobly sweet or (since the first recorded instance in 1983 at Koehler-Rupprecht in the Pfalz) Eiswein are also made from Spätburgunder in Germany, as in Austria.

Spätlese, one of the PRÄDIKATS in the QMP quality wine category defined by the GERMAN WINE LAW. Spätlese means literally 'late harvest' and the grapes should have been picked at least a week after a preliminary picking of less ripe grapes. In practice, however, this requirement is quite weak and Spätlese may well—depending on conditions in any given vintage—be picked prior to the bulk of wines that will be labelled as QbA or Kabinett. Specific minimum MUST WEIGHTS are laid down for each combination of vine variety and region. These wines' additional ripeness, and therefore POTENTIAL ALCOHOL, make them excellent candidates for bottling as TROCKEN (dry) wine. The top dry wines from any given estate are most often labelled as Spätlese trocken, even if they exceed the minimum must weight stipulated for Auslese. See also AUSTRIA.   D.S.

Spätrot, synonym for ZIERFANDLER.

special late harvested, term which should according to EU labelling law be applied to wines of more than 15 per cent alcohol made in Australia from 'fresh ripe grapes of which a significant proportion has been desic-cated under natural conditions in a manner favouring the concentration of sugars in the berries'.

specific gravity. See DENSITY.

Spergola, white grape variety from the Emilia region of Italy.

spiced wines. See FLAVOURED WINES and MULLED WINE.

spinning cone column, gas-liquid counter-current device for making DEALCO-HOLIZED WINE or GRAPE CONCENTRATE and for removing SULFUR DIOXIDE from juice, and reducing some wines' ALCOHOLIC STRENGTH, particularly in California. Spinning cone technology is an advance on the processes operating in a one- or two-stage vacuum evaporator. The device consists of a vertical stainless steel column containing two internal and alternating series of inverted cones; one series is fixed and attached to the column wall, the second series is parallel to the first and attached to a central rotating shaft. Liquid flows down the upper surfaces of the stationary cones under gravity, and moves up the upper surfaces of the rotating cones in a thin film due to the centrifugal force from the spinning action. Vapour that is evaporated from the thin film of liquid (under vacuum at low temperature, and with the aid of an inert stripping gas) flows up the column in the spaces between the successive fixed and rotating cones. Through a process of repeated evaporation and condensation on the cones, the volatiles are enriched in the up-flowing vapour stream. The volatiles, after passing through a condenser, are finally captured in liquid form at the top of the column while the stripped liquid is pumped out the bottom of the column. Spinning cone technology offers extremely high separation efficiency, with a low pressure drop across the column and low liquid hold up, hence the juice or wine has a short residence time in the column. Accordingly, alcohol and aroma removal are achieved with much less of the product evaporated than in a traditional evaporator. Also, the aroma fraction is recovered separately from the alcohol and can be back added to the wine to restore the flavour profile at a lower alcohol concentration. One application of the spinning cone column is reducing the alcoholic strength of excessively alcoholic wines by between one and three per 3 per cent without loss of FLAVOUR COMPOUNDS to produce a wine with the flavour intensity afforded by fully ripe fruit but without an unacceptable alcohol content. About 10 per cent of the wine is passed through the spinning cone column and, after having the volatile flavour compounds restored, is then added back to the remainder.

Advocates of the spinning cone column claim it can be used to selectively remove unwanted flavours from a finished wine such as those from HYDROGEN SULFIDE, MERCAPTANS, and even excess HERBACEOUS notes. Because of the cost of equipment, this is mainly a service industry since very few producers can afford to buy a spinning cone themselves. An alternative and equally popular technique for reducing alcohol levels in wines is REVERSE OSMOSIS.

P.J.W.

spitting is an essential practice at professional TASTINGS where several dozen, often more than 100, wines are regularly offered at the same time. Members of the wine TRADE, and WINE WRITERS, rapidly lose any inhibitions about spitting in public. Since there are no taste receptors in the throat, spitting allows the taster to form a full impression of each wine, while minimizing the blunting effects of ALCOHOL. It does not, unfortunately, leave the taster completely unaffected by alcohol. Some ethanol is vaporized and absorbed in the nose and mouth and, no matter how assiduous the taster, it is extremely difficult to prevent any liquid from dribbling down the throat. According to the estimates of this writer, tasting 30 wines can involve ingesting almost a glass of wine.

Whatever tasters spit into is a **spittoon**. These can vary from specially designed giant metal funnels, through wooden CASES filled with sawdust, to ice buckets, jugs, or, particularly convenient at a seated tasting, personal plastic or cardboard beakers. Most professional tasting rooms are equipped with channels, or sinks with running water designed to drain away expectorated wine.

spraying, a vineyard practice of applying AGROCHEMICALS to control pests, diseases, and weeds. Late last century, vineyard sprayers were often drawn by draught animals and operated with manual pumps; nowadays they are usually mounted on tractors or drawn by them, and sometimes mounted on MECHANICAL HARVESTERS in order to spray several rows at once.

The aim of economically and environmentally sound spraying is to achieve maximum coverage of the 'target' (leaves, bunches, or weeds) by applying minimum amounts of the appropriate agrochemical. There should be ideally no chemical lost to the surrounding environment as 'spray drift'. Good coverage depends on having very small droplets, although these are more readily blown off target by wind than large drops. A recent and welcome development is the so-called tunnel sprayer, which prevents spray escaping into the environment. The vine canopy beside the tractor is enclosed by a cover or tunnel, usually made of fibreglass, with the spray jets mounted inside the tunnel. Any spray droplets not caught by the vine are caught by the opposite side of the tunnel and can therefore be retrieved and returned to the spray cart. Such units save a lot of spray material, especially early in the growing season when the 'target' is small.

Vineyards can be sprayed from the air as well as from the ground, using fixed-wing aircraft or HELICOPTERS. Costs can be lower, but coverage is typically not as good as for ground spraying and low wind conditions are required. Aerial spraying can be used when ground conditions are unsuited for tractors, such as following heavy rain.

Relatively few vineyards are now sprayed from containers strapped on workers' backs, although this is still done in Portugal's DOURO valley and on one-man properties. The costs of such spraying operations are of course very high, and generally not sustainable for most commercial vineyards. Agrochemicals in dry powder form are applied by a process known as DUSTING.   R.E.S.

Coombe, B. G., and Dry, P. R. (eds.), *Viticulture*, ii: *Practices* (Adelaide, 1992).

sprinklers are used for IRRIGATION, and in some vineyards to control FROST (the water freezes to form a protective coating of ice round the young vine buds). Sprinkler irrigation has largely been replaced by DRIP IRRIGATION, which uses much less water, and does not leave wet leaves vulnerable to FUNGAL DISEASES and SALINITY damage. It is important to avoid waterlogging, which can readily cause injury to the newly growing roots. It has also been used in hot regions of Australia for vineyard cooling, by operating the system intermittently during the hottest part of the day.

J.G. & R.E.S.

spritzer, common name for a mixture of white wine and fizzy water that is usually drunk as an APERITIF.

spritzig, German term for semi-SPARKLING, applied widely to wines which are not meant to be particularly FIZZY but which have a small but attractive concentration of CARBON DIOXIDE in solution such that there is a slight prickle on the tongue when they are tasted. **Spritz** has become an international tasting term, perhaps for onomatopoeic reasons.

spumante, Italian word for sparkling wine from the verb *spumare*, to foam or froth, which is disappearing from labels. The most important of these is ASTI (once known as Asti Spumante), made from the MOSCATO BIANCO grape cultivated in the provinces of Asti, Cuneo, and Alessandria, of which over 80 million bottles may be made in an average year.

Significant quantities of sparkling wines from CHARDONNAY and PINOT NOIR, the classic grapes of CHAMPAGNE, are also produced in Italy, principally from three areas: the TRENTINO-ALTO ADIGE, the OLTREPÒ PAVESE, and FRANCIACORTA. The Italians, unlike the Champagne houses, also employ PINOT BLANC

and PINOT GRIS in their blends. Some of these wines are produced using the CHARMAT process, but the majority are fermented in bottle like champagne and are labelled 'metodo classico'. The Talento association of producers of TRADITIONAL METHOD sparkling wines eliminated the word spumante from their labels, as have those of FRANCIACORTA whose DOCG applies only to sparkling wine.

A vast number of other types of sparkling wine are made in Italy from a bewildering range of grape varieties, in a dazzling array of colours, ALCOHOLIC STRENGTHS, and RESIDUAL SUGAR levels. Over 30 DOCs allow sparkling wine to be made: Bianco di CUSTOZA, Colli Albani, Colli Euganei, Colli Piacentini, Colli Tortonesi, CORTESE dell'Alto Monferrato, FRASCATI, GAVI, GRECO DI TUFO, Locorotondo, Marino, Roero ARNEIS, TREBBIANO di Romagna, Velletri, and VERDICCHIO dei Castelli di Jesi are some of the more significant white sparklers. Red sparkling wines are permitted within the AGLIANICO, BRACHETTO, Cesanese di Olevano Romano, Elba Rosso, FREISA, and LISON-PRAMAGGIORE (from MERLOT, CABERNET, or REFOSCO) DOCs. In addition to these there are myriad sparkling wines made and sold as a VINO DA TAVOLA: from VERNACCIA di San Gimignano, from Trebbiano grown in ORVIETO and many, many more. One can conclude that Italians simply like CARBON DIOXIDE in their wine and do not, unlike the French perhaps, require that it resembles a single paradigm.

See also FRIZZANTE.   D.T.

spur, a viticultural term for a shortened grapevine cane. A spur is a stub formed by pruning the CANE to between one and four NODES, usually two. Spurs are used to provide the next season's fruiting SHOOTS. Of all PRUNING systems, SPUR PRUNING is the most severe since over 90 per cent of the previous year's cane growth is removed. Spurs are also left on cane-pruned vines to augment replacement canes at next pruning.   B.G.C.

spur pruning, a form of winter vine PRUNING whereby the canes are cut back to two bud SPURS (see diagram). Normally the spurs are spaced along a CORDON top and point upwards (although see SMART–DYSON). There are several advantages to spur pruning, in that it takes less time to prune by hand and the operation can also be mechanized easily using pre-PRUNING MACHINES. Also, setting the spur spacing results in the correct shoot spacing in the canopy, which in turn leads to well-exposed leaves and fruit (see CANOPY MICROCLIMATE). Spur pruning is not particularly well suited to very vigorous vineyards, however, as excessive SHADE can lead to the loss of both yield (due to low bud fruitfulness) and quality. The other main form of vine pruning is CANE PRUNING. See also CORDON TRAINING.

R.E.S.

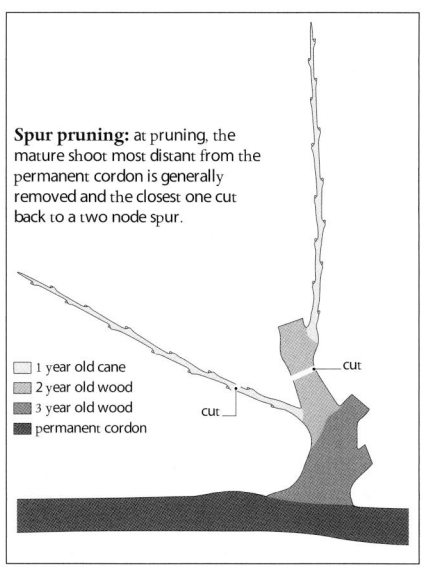

Spur pruning: at pruning, the mature shoot most distant from the permanent cordon is generally removed and the closest one cut back to a two node spur.

☐ 1 year old cane
▨ 2 year old wood
▨ 3 year old wood
■ permanent cordon

Squinzano, DOC for robust red wine made mainly from NEGROAMARO grapes in south east Italy. For more details, see PUGLIA.

Sri Lanka (formerly Ceylon), tropical Indian ocean island nation with two fledgling ventures making wine from established plantings of Cardinal, Black Muscat and a variety called Israel Blue vines originally grown for TABLE GRAPES.   D.G.

stabilization, group of wine-processing operations undertaken to ensure that the wine, once bottled, will not form hazes, clouds, or unwanted deposits; become gassy; or undergo rapid deterioration of flavour after BOTTLING. A quick recovery from BOTTLE SICKNESS and subtle changes in flavour that occur with lengthy AGEING are considered normal in a **stable** wine.

Everyday wines are usually more thoroughly stabilized than fine wines since consumers have come to expect them to be crystal clear. Fine wines are normally less drastically stabilized since those who buy them are expected to understand about TARTRATES and the slow throwing of a SEDIMENT, and also because it is believed that the less stable constituents contribute to the AGEING process. (The fine wine process of BARREL MATURATION has the effect of stabilizing a wine naturally in any case.)

Stabilization includes two sorts of operations: one to counter physical and chemical changes and another to counter microbiological changes.

Physical and chemical stability
Young wines are supersaturated in tartrates; REFRIGERATION and cold FILTRATION will reduce the concentration of tartrates below the level that would subsequently form crystals in the bottle.

Young white wines often contain high concentrations of rapidly browning PHENOLICS which, if left in the wine, will cause undue darkening of the wine after bottling. Selective FINING can remove the offending type of phenolic and ensure longer light colour in young white wines. Young red wines may also contain excessive amounts of TANNINS which taste bitter and astringent unless allowed to POLYMERIZE during extended bottle ageing. Red wines designed to be drunk young can be fined to remove some of these tannins.

Some varieties of white grape such as MUSCAT contain large amounts of heat-unstable PROTEINS which can coagulate and appear as a haze in the bottle unless it is kept at a constant, low temperature. These proteins can be removed by fining with BENTONITE or, less effectively, some other fining agents.

Microbiological stability

Measures to ensure microbiological stability have to counter the growth of either YEAST or BACTERIA. The simplest way to avoid yeast growth which could result in a SECONDARY FERMENTATION, is to ensure that the wine is free of fermentable sugar, and its RESIDUAL SUGAR is negligible. If some residual sugar is necessary to balance, say, high ACIDITY in the wine, then sterile filtration and STERILE BOTTLING are the surest way of guaranteeing stability. Failing the necessary equipment and trained personnel, additions of SULFUR DIOXIDE and SORBIC ACID will sufficiently inhibit most yeast growth, at some marginal depreciation of wine quality.

Stabilization of wine against bacterial attack is not so much of a problem in clean, modern wineries where the level of HYGIENE is high. The most harmful bacteria, those which turn wine into vinegar, ACETOBACTER, can operate only in the presence of OXYGEN and so stability can be assured by protecting the wine from air. Furthermore, sulfur dioxide, which is invariably used by winemakers, helps by suppressing the growth of acetobacter, and that of LACTIC ACID BACTERIA. Lactic acid bacteria can also be inhibited by removing all fermentable sugars and all of the MALIC ACID (by MALOLACTIC FERMENTATION), two substrates for growth of some lactics.

No cellar treatments are needed against micro-organisms harmful to humans since wine's high levels of acidity and alcohol naturally inhibit their growth. A.D.W.

Stags Leap District, California wine region and AVA. See NAPA.

stainless steel is widely used for holding wine, both for AGEING and, especially, for FERMENTATION. For wines made PROTECTIVELY it has the great advantage over wood that it is easy to clean and OXYGEN can be completely excluded from it, by the use of INERT GAS to fill head space if necessary. It has the advantage over concrete, still much used (including at Ch PÉTRUS), that TEMPERATURE CONTROL is even easier, especially with refrigerated jacketing and cooling/warming coils, and any TARTRATES can be hosed out rather than having to be chipped off the concrete walls. For some wines, the exclusion of oxygen can be a disadvantage, however, and there is a risk of REDUCTION.

Nor is there any possibility of the gradual, natural CLARIFICATION and STABILIZATION process that is possible in wooden containers.

stake. The simplest form of vine support is a stake driven into the ground beside the vine. A stake supports an individual vine, whereas POSTS, which are usually thicker than stakes, support several vines from suspended wires. Stakes are a very traditional form of vine support, having been used for centuries. Vines trained to stakes are most common in the OLD WORLD, although the vineyards of California are a significant exception. Since vines are climbing plants, they are unable to support themselves unless specially trained with a short trunk as for GOBELET vines.

Materials used for stakes vary enormously between different wine regions, reflecting local availability. Most common is WOOD, which has been used for centuries, although it is only recently that timber has been treated chemically, preventing softwoods from rotting in the ground. Sometimes stakes are made from round timber, as in much of Europe, or from sawn timber as in California. They can also be made from stone (slaty schist) as in the Douro valley of Portugal, or from cement as in parts of Italy. Stakes made from steel, plastic, or fibreglass have become more common in recent times and can be installed already notched and punched for wires.

See also POST. R.E.S.

stalk. For information about the stalk of an individual grape or berry, see PEDICEL. For information about the stalk of a bunch of grapes, see BUNCHSTEM. See also STEM.

stamen, pollen-bearing part of a flower that consists generally of an ANTHER borne on a filament. A grapevine flower is small and has five erect stamens that become evident after the CALYPTRA or cap has fallen off at FLOWERING. B.G.C.

standard drinks, unit of measurement used by governments to quantify a normal or regular pour of alcoholic drink by the amount of pure ALCOHOL it contains; also known as a unit of alcohol. Once this has been agreed upon, the theory goes, it is easier for authorities to set safe limits for consumption. There are many stumbling blocks, however, including wide variance among countries with regard to how much alcohol a 'standard drink' contains, ranging from 13.6 g in Canada, to 10 g in Australia, to 8 g in the UK. In addition, both standard servings and the average ALCOHOLIC STRENGTH of wine are greater than when the standards were first set (see HEALTH, Sensible drinking). In some countries such as Australia, it is compulsory to state on wine labels the number of standard drinks each bottle contains. B.B.

starch, vine, an insoluble carbohydrate polymer composed of GLUCOSE residues. It is non-osmotic and is the principal storage substance in plants, forming as starch grains. Starch grains occur in the leaf and in cells of storage tissue in stems and roots of the vine. During daylight hours, when SUCROSE levels rise in leaves due to PHOTOSYNTHESIS, starch grains build up. At night they are metabolized to provide the sugar needed for RESPIRATION (this is also their fate in the human gut). Starch, natural storage reserves, are remobilized when buds burst and shoots begin to grow. Unlike many fruits, grape berries do not contain much starch, which is one reason why grapes do not ripen after picking (apart from changes associated with dehydration). Starch is the principal CARBOHYDRATE reserve of vines. B.G.C.

state wine-making has been important, not just in eastern Europe during the communist era when all activity took place under the auspices of the state, but also in TURKEY, Germany, where the state has owned a number of important vineyards and cellars, including KLOSTER EBERBACH, and in North African countries such as ALGERIA, EGYPT, and MOROCCO.

staves are the shaped wooden planks that are cut and formed into BARRELS. See BARREL MAKING for more details.

Shorter lengths designed to impart OAK FLAVOUR to wines stored in used barrels or in tanks may are be called **inner staves** (see BARREL INSERTS and INNER STAVES, respectively).

Steen, name by which CHENIN BLANC used to be known in South Africa, although all of South Africa's premium Chenin Blanc is now sold under that name. It is the Cape's most common white vine variety, present in all wine regions. Steen is also South Africa's most versatile grape, producing an astonishing spectrum of wine styles: dry, sweet, BOTRYTIZED, sparkling, brandy, and sherry types. Confusingly, some wines are still labelled either Chenin Blanc or Steen at the whim of the producer. It is the major and often sole grape in local wines labelled **Stein**, denoting not grape variety but an off-dry to semi-sweet white, once the country's biggest-selling wine category. Vinified at low temperatures, the wine can show lively fruity appeal for a year or two but this attraction tends to fade in dry Cape Steens. J.P. & M.F.

Steiermark, wine region in AUSTRIA known in English as STYRIA.

Steinfeder, light, fragrant, SPRITZIG white wines of the Wachau region in AUSTRIA. The grapes for Steinfeder must have a must reading of 15° to 17 °KMW (73 to 83 °Oechsle) and may not be chaptalized. The maximum alcohol level allowed is 11 per cent. This category's symbol is the *stipa pennata*, a featherweight grass species indigenous to the Wachau's steep vineyard terraces. See also FEDERSPIEL and SMARAGD.

Stellenbosch, important wine district in South Africa, famously beautiful town within it, and the name of the only university in South Africa offering professional degrees in both VITICULTURE and OENOLOGY. Informal teaching in these two subjects started in 1889 but the Department of Viticulture and Oenology was formally opened only in 1917, with Professor A. I. Perold as director. The university has been (for better and for worse, it should be said) an important influence on the Cape wine industry over the decades, and continues to produce many of the Cape's leading wine-makers and wine-researchers. The town is also home to the Nietvoorbij Institute for Viticulture and Oenology; and the Cape Institute for Agricultural Training with its experimental farm is nearby in Elsenburg.

As elsewhere (see the University of BORDEAUX, DAVIS, GEISENHEIM, for example), the PHYLLOXERA crisis was a powerful motivation for viticultural research, and from 1890 until about 1920 most of Stellenbosch's work was concentrated on re-establishing the phylloxera-devastated vineyards of the Cape.

During the 1920s, considerable effort was expended on improving the quality of fruit-bearing vine SCIONS, a range that was naturally restricted by strict QUARANTINE regulations. This involved VINE BREEDING which led to NEW VARIETIES, of which PINOTAGE has been the most widely acclaimed.

Under the guidance of Stellenbosch oenologists, South Africa was one of the first wine-producing countries to apply widespread TEMPERATURE CONTROL to fermentations. Stellenbosch graduates also played a major part in forming South Africa's WINE OF ORIGIN legislation in 1973.

The university's Institute of Wine Biotechnology has an international reputation.

See SOUTH AFRICA for more detail of the Stellenbosch wine region.

Stelvin, see SCREW CAPS.

stem. The terms stem and stalk tend to be used somewhat carelessly by winemakers, if not by viticulturists. For information about the stem of an individual grape or berry, see PEDICEL. For information about the stem of a bunch of grapes, see BUNCHSTEM. For informa-tion about the stem of a vine plant, see SHOOT. See also DESTEMMING.

stemming, paradoxically alternative term for DESTEMMING grapes.

stem pitting, vine virus disease. See RUGOSE WOOD.

stemware, see GLASSES.

sterile bottling, or, more correctly, **aseptic bottling**, is the technique of getting wine into a closed bottle without incorporating any micro-organisms (notably YEAST and harmful BACTERIA). Borrowed from the pharmaceutical packaging industry, this technique does the job of PASTEURIZATION without the use of heat. Aseptic techniques have become the norm for wine bottling because the use of membrane filters (see FILTRATION) has made the task very simple. Many everyday modern wines have small amounts of RESIDUAL SUGAR and therefore require bottling in an aseptic manner, but the degree of care needed depends upon the levels of residual sugar and alcohol. Very light, off-dry wines such as German QbA need high standards of sterility for machinery and packaging materials.

It involves the highest level of HYGIENE but the necessary equipment is also considerably more expensive than that for regular BOTTLING, which is why it is justified primarily for high-volume, relatively low alcohol wines containing some residual sugar which could suffer SECONDARY FERMENTATION if yeast cells are allowed into the bottle, typically LIEBFRAUMILCH and other mass-market German blends.

An aseptic bottling line involves the creation of a germ-free room, modifying the usual equipment so that it may be sterilized easily. The room is kept under a slight positive pressure of sterilized air and entry, through a double door system, is restricted to the few specially trained and clothed personnel required. Micro-organisms are removed from the wine by depth membrane sterile FILTRATION and the corks or other CLOSURES are sterilized by gaseous SULFUR DIOXIDE or other chemical sterilizing agents such as paracetic acid. The bottling and corking machines are usually sterilized by steam, or by chemical sterilants. Frequent sample bottles are removed at random for microbiological analysis, and each bottling run is held in storage until it is certain that no organisms are growing.

A.D.W. & D.B.

Bird, D., *Understanding Wine Technology* (2nd edn, Newark, 2005).

steward, wine. See SOMMELIER.

stickie, Australian term for sweet, usually fortified, wines. Typical examples are the Muscats and Tokays of Rutherglen and Glenrowan in North East VICTORIA.

stigma. See vine FLOWER.

stilbene, see RESVERATROL.

stirring, wine-making term which may be used as a synonym for LEES STIRRING or may refer to the important operation of stirring, usually in much larger containers, when blending disparate components in a blend. This is particularly necessary when grape spirit is added to wine, as during FORTIFICATION, since the spirit, with its lower DENSITY, tends to float on top of the wine. Stirring, or dynamizing, also plays an important role in the production of some BIODYNAMIC preparations.

stomata (plural of **stoma**), minute openings on the surface of leaves bordered by two guard cells which open and close, thus regulating the exchange of gases between the atmosphere and the air chambers inside the leaf, especially of water out and carbon dioxide in (see TRANSPIRATION and PHOTOSYNTHESIS). The stomata of the grapevine occur only on the underside of each leaf blade, and there are also some on berries. B.G.C.

stones and rocks, as visible constituents of the soil or its surface (cf. the underlying ROCK), loom large in the folklore of wine quality. They figure prominently in the older French concepts of TERROIR. Nineteenth century French writers such as Rendu and Petit-Lafitte laid particular emphasis on the proportions of stone or gravel in the soils of the best vineyards. The stonier the soil, they said, the better in general is the wine quality.

Present thinking broadly supports the old ideas. Rocky and stony soils are usually well drained, but at the same time not too fertile. A high proportion of stones also reduces water-holding capacity (see SOIL WATER, which is especially critical to red wine quality in Bordeaux, for example). Both factors are significant in climates and management systems where excessive vine VIGOUR, leading to unsatisfactory CANOPY MICROCLIMATES, is a threat. Forcing the vine to develop a sparse, but extensive, ROOT system also helps to buffer it against sudden changes in nutrition or water supply. Beyond that, a rocky or stony soil is thought to help by efficiently absorbing heat during sunshine and reradiating it during the evening and cloudy periods—thereby perhaps affording the ripening fruit a better temperature regime for flavour RIPENING (see CLIMATE AND WINE QUALITY). Verbrugghe *et al.* document the temperature effects on ripening grapes of the famously large stones of CHÂTEAUNEUF-DU-PAPE in the southern Rhône. Stones and rocks also form an efficient mulch against surface evaporation, and offer protection against SOIL EROSION.

See also SOIL AND WINE QUALITY. J.G.

Petit-Lafitte, A., *La Vigne dans le Bordelais* ('The vine in the Bordeaux region') (Paris, 1868).

Rendu, V., *Ampélographie française* ('Ampelography of France') (Paris, 1857).

Verbrugghe, M., Guyot, G., Hanocq, J. F., and Ripoche, D., 'Influence de différents types de sol de la basse vallée du Rhône sur les températures de surface de raisins et de feuilles de Vitis vinifera' ('Influence of different soil types of the lower Rhône valley on the temperatures of the berry surface and leaves of *Vitis vinifera*'), *Revue française d'œnologie*, 128 (1991), 14–20.

stoppers, wine bottle. See CLOSURES.

storing wine is an important aspect of wine consumption, since wine is relatively sensitive to storage conditions and is one of the very few consumer products that can improve with age (although see AGEING for details of how few, and which, wines this applies to). Until the era of inflation, the wine trade regarded storing and ageing wine as part of their business, but since the 1960s they have steadily relinquished this role. The development of the EN PRIMEUR market and the increase in the number of wine COLLECTORS leaves many more ordinary wine drinkers with the problem of how to store wine over long periods, often a decade or two.

There are two basic choices: to consign the bottles to professional storage and/or to establish some form of domestic cellar. If wine is put in storage, it is vital that a specialist in wine storage is found, since wine is a much more fragile commodity than most things kept in warehouses, and needs specialist treatment and conditions. It is important that the wine storage specialist is in sound financial health itself, it understands the detail of storage conditions needed, and that it provides some facility for marking individual CASES with some identification of their owner. In the case of business failure, this can make the difference between establishing possession and not.

For more details of how to identify and, if necessary, convert part of a home into a suitable place to store wine, see CELLAR.

Storage conditions

Even in Ancient GREECE there was some appreciation of the importance of storage conditions on the evolution and health of wine. The key factors are TEMPERATURE, light, HUMIDITY, and security.

If wine is kept too hot, or exposed to strong sunlight, it rapidly deteriorates. If it is kept too cold, it can freeze, expand, and push out the stopper of whatever container it is held in.

For bottles stored for a few weeks, the primary concern is to keep them from strong direct light (white wines in colourless glass are most at risk) and to ensure that they do not reach temperatures more than about 25 °C/77 °F (although there is some latitude here, depending on the fragility of the wine), at which point the wine may be spoilt and forever afterwards taste cooked.

A fairly wide range of temperatures is suitable for wine storage, although, in general, the lower the storage temperature, the slower the reactions involved in wine maturation and, the theory goes, the more complex the wine eventually. Dramatic temperature swings should be avoided and an average temperature somewhere in the range 10–15 °C (50–9 °F) is considered suitable (see TEMPERATURE for more details).

Some degree of humidity is beneficial, to ensure that the exposed end of the cork does not dry out and allow in oxygen. A level of 75 per cent relative humidity is usually cited, although this, like so many aspects of wine consumption rather than production, suffers from a lack of scientific research. The disadvantage of very damp cellars is that damp labels eventually deteriorate and make identification difficult (and some COLLECTORS, perversely, prefer pristine labels so any resale price is not prejudiced).

Bottles to be stored for more than a few weeks, however, should be stored so that any cork is kept damp and there is no possibility of its drying out and allowing in the enemy, OXYGEN. This usually entails storing the bottles horizontally, ideally in a wine rack so that individual bottles can easily be extracted, or in a BIN full of wines of the same sort. Many wine producers deliberately mark their cases in an effort to keep bottles upside down, and corks damp, during shipment. The increased use of alternative CLOSURES however, particularly SCREW CAPS, suggests that horizontal storage may no longer be necessary but the stopper is much less likely to be damaged than if bottles are stored vertically on top of one another.

The wine itself in an inverted bottle comes to no harm. Research in the late 1990s suggested that an ideal storage position for wine bottles stoppered with a natural cork is at a slight angle from the horizontal so that the cork is kept damp but the air bubble of ULLAGE just touches the cork rather than lying on top of the middle of the bottle. It has also been suggested by some that champagne ages most gracefully when stored in bottles that are kept upright rather than horizontal but this has not been proven.

If a maturing wine is agitated, it may disturb the sediment and therefore the AGEING process (although this is an unproven hypothesis). Some cellars are specifically designed with rubber racks for bottles in order to minimize any likely vibration. The need for a secure storage space is obvious, especially since bottles of alcoholic drink seem to be widely regarded as common currency rather than private property.

It is also important that there are no strong, persistent smells in a long-term wine storage area.

See also BULK STORAGE.

Straccia Cambiale, synonym for the white grape BOMBINO BIANCO.

Strathbogie Ranges, hilly, elevated Australian wine region in central VICTORIA. Elevation, aspect, and soil differences provide a multiplicity of opportunity.

straw wines, sweet wines made from grapes dried on straw. See VIN DE PAILLE, ALSACE, AUSTRIA, CZECH REPUBLIC, VIN SANTO, and DRIED GRAPE WINES.

Stück, German term for a large wooden BARREL, typically one with a capacity of 1,200 l/317 gal used in RHINE regions of GERMANY. (In the MOSEL-SAAR-RUWER region the FUDER is more common.) A **Halbstück** contains 600 l, and was commonly used for transporting wine in the pre-tanker era, while a **Doppelstück** contains 2,400 l.

stuck fermentation, winemaker's nightmare involving an alcoholic FERMENTATION which ceases before completion. Such fermentations are notoriously difficult to restart and the wine is at risk of spoilage from OXIDATION and BACTERIAL DISEASE. Before cooling equipment was commonplace, fermentation TEMPERATURES could reach a dangerously high level, often in excess of 35 °C/95 °F. In extreme cases, with temperatures nearing the range at which YEASTS are killed, over 40 °C, the yeast cells release compounds which inhibit future yeast growth, thereby making it difficult or impossible to restart such fermentations, even after cooling.

Stuck fermentation has many documented causes. The tendency over recent decades to harvest grapes at higher maturity levels has resulted in wines with a higher alcohol content, and unless fermentation conditions are optimal, various stresses culminate in reduced or, in some cases, complete cessation of fermentation activity. One of the most common causes is a deficiency of the essential nutrient NITROGEN. Grapes which come from vineyards deficient in nitrogen have a low ratio of nitrogen to sugar; this is especially the case with Riesling and Chardonnay. This limits the development of yeast cells, and fermentation activity is not sustained after the yeast become starved of nitrogen. This problem is exacerbated in the fermentation of juices prepared from white grape varieties where the winemaker, aiming to produce a wine low in PHENOLICS, with clean, accentuated VARIETAL character, highly clarifies the must (see CLARIFICATION) to produce a juice with very low levels of suspended grape solids. Fermentation at low temperature (below 15 °C/60 °F) with strict protection from air greatly increases the risk of stuck fermentation. In the absence of oxygen, the grape solids, which contain LIPIDS, are essential for strong yeast growth and for sustaining high yeast cell viability during the critical final stage of fermentation.

There are several ways to reduce the risk of stuck fermentation but these can affect the style of wine produced: adding nitrogen to the juice, either in the form of an ammonium salt (most commonly diammonium phosphate) or a proprietary yeast food which contains organic or inorganic nitrogen; adding back must settlings to increase the level of grape solids; using a yeast starter culture of a high-alcohol-tolerant strain that has been propagated with excess air; or adding nitrogen and exposing the fermentation to a small amount of air once the yeast is active. These options are usually effective, especially when several are used in combination. The latter treatment is most simply achieved by stirring or PUMPING OVER. Failure of the yeast inoculum to dominate the wild yeasts that are invariably present in grape must can result in a stuck fermentation if the wild yeasts have a lower tolerance to alcohol. Wild yeasts, which produce 'killer toxin' (zymocidal yeasts), can be especially aggressive by actively eliminating the sensitive wine yeast. Certain LACTIC ACID BACTERIA, which can rapidly grow during the early stages of fermentation when sulfites have not been added to the must prior to fermentation, have been found to inhibit yeast activity. Inhibition of fermentation by wild yeasts and bacteria can be diminished considerably by using a highly active yeast starter culture, choosing a yeast that is resistant to killer toxin (broad spectrum resistant strains are not yet available commercially), and by any method that reduces the number of wild micro-organisms present in the must. Cool harvesting and processing conditions, and FILTRATION, CENTRIFUGATION, or PASTEURIZATION are usually effective.   P.H.

Alexandre, H., and Charpentier, C., 'Biochemical aspects of stuck and sluggish fermentation in grape must', *Journal of Industrial Microbiology and Biotechnology*, 20 (1998), 20–7.

Bisson, L. F., and Butzke, C. E., 'Diagnosis and rectification of stuck and sluggish fermentations', *American Journal of Enology and Viticulture*, 51 (2000), 168–77.

Henschke, P.A., 'Stuck fermentation: causes, prevention and cure', in M. Allen, P. Leske, and G. Baldwin (eds.), *Proceedings of the Australian Society of Viticulture and Oenology: Advances in Juice Clarification and Yeast Inoculation* (Adelaide, 1997), 30–8, 41.

Sturm, the cloudy, part-fermented, very slightly sparkling sweet grape juice that is a local speciality at harvest time in AUSTRIA. It is generally white but red versions are also produced. The German equivalent is Federweisser, in Luxembourg it is known as Fiederweissen, and in Alsace it is known, confusingly, as *vin nouveau*. It tends to be drunk with hearty autumn food such as *Zwiebelkuchen* (onion tart).

Styria, small but fashionable wine area in the far south east of AUSTRIA, most famous for aromatic, lively dry whites.

subjectivity plays an unavoidable part in wine TASTING. Personal preferences inevitably play some role in wine assessment. For more discussion of this, see PHILOSOPHY AND WINE and QUALITY IN WINE.

subsoil, the usually heavier-textured layer of a SOIL which underlies the main zone containing ROOTS and ORGANIC MATTER. It overlies the native ROCK or sediments from which the soil is formed. The contrast in texture between surface soil and subsoil is greatest in ancient soils and in forest (especially pine forest) regions, due to the progressive downward leaching of the heavier minerals and fine CLAY particles. Such subsoils are, however, typically depleted of many of the important nutrient elements, because roots have continuously extracted them from depth and deposited them at the surface in leaf litter and derived organic matter.

A fairly heavy-textured subsoil, provided that it drains freely enough, can have advantages for viticulture because it provides a good store of moisture that is well protected against direct EVAPORATION and exploitation by shallow-rooted WEEDS. The usual relative sparseness of vine roots in the subsoil, together with the strength with which clay particles hold water (see SOIL WATER and SOIL TEXTURE), ensures that the stored water can be used only at a limited rate. Seguin cites the clay soils of POMEROL as an example of this. It helps to provide the vine with the consistent regime of water supply that Seguin believes to be important for wine quality. See also TERROIR and SOIL AND WINE QUALITY.

On the other hand, many heavy subsoils impede DRAINAGE, particularly those formed from acid rock materials. These can be detrimental to viticulture, unless carefully drained and, possibly, LIMED to overcome SOIL ACIDITY and improve the SOIL STRUCTURE.   J.G.

Seguin, G., 'Influence des terroirs viticoles', *Bulletin de l'OIV*, 56 (1983), 3–18.

—— '"Terroirs" and pedology of wine growing', *Experientia*, 42 (1986), 861–72.

subsoiling, vineyard practice normally conducted before PLANTING that is designed to break up SUBSOIL, removing barriers to root growth and improving water infiltration. Subsoiling is synonymous with RIPPING.   R.E.S.

succinic acid, an acid found to a limited extent in both grapes and wine. Present in low concentrations in ripe grapes, it is a contributor to the fresh or tart taste of the fruit, albeit to a much lesser extent than TARTARIC ACID or MALIC ACID. Like these two principal grape acids, pure succinic acid is a white crystalline solid that is very soluble in water and alcoholic water solutions such as wine.

Succinic acid concentrations tend to be much higher in wine than grapes because the acid is a by-product of the complex nitrogen metabolic processes involved in YEAST growth during FERMENTATION. Concentrations are generally higher in red wines than in whites. In some wines, a considerable proportion of the succinic acid reacts with one molecule of ETHANOL to form an ESTER, mono-ethyl succinate, which has a very mild, fruity aroma. Very small amounts of the compounds resulting from the reaction of both acid groups of succinic acid with ethanol are also found but these are non-odoriferous.   A.D.W.

Coulter, A. D., Godden, P. W., and Pretorius, I. S., 'Succinic acid: how is it formed, what is its effect on titratable acidity, and what factors influence its concentration in wine?', *Australian and New Zealand Wine Industry Journal*, 19/6 (Nov/Dec 2004), 16–25.

suckering. See DESUCKERING.

sucrose, cane sugar, the most common of the SUGARS, is ubiquitous in plants because it is the preferred compound for PHLOEM translocation of energy and carbon around the plant. Sucrose consists of a GLUCOSE joined to a FRUCTOSE. Breakdown (HYDROLYSIS) of sucrose is achieved readily by the enzyme INVERTASE, which 'inverts' it to these hexoses.

Invertase in the vine occurs in CELL wall spaces but not in those of the leaf, which is why sucrose is confined in vines mainly to leaves and phloem tubes. Invertase is abundant in grape berries both in the cell walls and in the vacuoles; hence the sugars that accumulate in berries are mainly glucose and fructose.   B.G.C.

Südtirol, or South Tyrol. See ALTO ADIGE.

sugar addition, wine-making practice more usually called CHAPTALIZATION or, in European Union parlance, ENRICHMENT.

sugar concentration in grapes. See MUST WEIGHT.

sugar in grapes, the *raison d'être* of VITICULTURE. The central role of sugar in the utility of grapes for wine, TABLE GRAPES, DRYING GRAPES, and other viticultural products cannot be over-emphasized. SUGARS produce SWEETNESS and ferment to produce ETHANOL, both of which are valued by humans. However, of all sugary plant produce, none yields a commodity as highly valued or widely produced as grape wine.

The free sugar that accumulates in grapes, GLUCOSE and FRUCTOSE, is the result of translocation of SUCROSE photosynthesized in leaves and moved via PHLOEM tubes into grape berries during RIPENING, where it is inverted (hydrolysed) by the enzyme INVERTASE. The astonishing feature of grapes is that this accumulation occurs at the same time as water is accumulating in the berry, yet concentration is also increasing; in other words, sugar is increasing proportionately more than water. Other phloem-provided sucrose moves throughout the vine dispensing energy and the carbon skeletons for all organic molecules throughout the vine. Additionally, sugar is used for carbon storage, as STARCH in wood, and for the formation of GLYCOSIDES in the storage of secondary metabolites in vacuoles of cells (see FLAVOUR PRECURSORS and FLAVOUR COMPOUNDS).

While total sugar content (see MUST WEIGHT) is a key factor in determining optimum RIPENESS of grapes for wine, sugar–acid balance is equally important; hence the use of sugar–acid ratio as a guide to the date of harvest. See also PHYSIOLOGICAL RIPENESS and GRAPE QUALITY ASSESSMENT.   B.G.C.

Winkler, A. J., *et al.*, *General Viticulture* (2nd edn, Berkeley, Calif., 1974).

sugars, simpler members of the large group of natural organic chemical compounds called CARBOHYDRATES. The sugar of common parlance, SUCROSE, comes from either sugar cane or sugar beet plants and is a major international commodity. To scientists, sucrose is a molecule made up of one unit of each of GLUCOSE and FRUCTOSE linked together with the elimination of a molecule of water.

Plants produce sucrose by PHOTOSYNTHESIS, many of them accumulating sucrose within their cells but others, such as the common wine vine *Vitis* VINIFERA, breaking this sucrose down into its two simpler constituent parts, glucose and fructose, which are stored in the berries. AMERICAN VINES store small amounts of sucrose in the fruit along with the two simpler forms. Over the millennia during which people have selected grape vines, they have chosen those capable of photosynthesizing an excess of sugars and storing them in berries. For more detail, see SUGAR IN GRAPES.

Although the amounts of sugars other than glucose and fructose detected in grape must are very small, the process of photosynthesis involves sugars with three, four, five, and seven carbon atoms as well as the six-carbon glucose and fructose. It would be surprising, therefore, if traces of some of these were not identified in grape juice, and in wines some dozen different residual sugars have been reported.

Sucrose, usually in the form of sugar beet concentrate or some form of GRAPE CONCENTRATE, may be added to some grape musts before fermentation in order to increase the ALCOHOLIC STRENGTH of the resultant wine (see CHAPTALIZATION).

The total amount of sugars left in a finished wine is called its RESIDUAL SUGAR.

Some of the sucrose resulting from photosynthesis, stored in the berries as glucose and fructose before grape harvest, is converted into STARCH and stored in the vine's trunk and larger arms and roots during winter DORMANCY until spring temperatures begin the annual cycle of leaf and fruit production once more, and the starch is remobilized to soluble sugars, mainly glucose.

See also MUST WEIGHT.   A.D.W.

sulfide and **disulfide** are the compounds of SULFUR with hydrogen or metallic elements in which the sulfur atom exists in its most reduced state, that is having gained two electrons from the other element or elements in the compound (see REDUCTION).

Sulfides occur naturally during winemaking. As FERMENTATION nears completion, the REDOX POTENTIAL can fall so low that elemental sulfur residues on the grapes from fungicides, and even SULFUR DIOXIDE itself, can be reduced to HYDROGEN SULFIDE. The winemaker can detect this problem easily because hydrogen sulfide has an intense smell of bad eggs. Fortunately, the compound is very volatile and can usually be removed by simple AERATION.

In a wine-making context, any reference to 'sulfide' or 'sulfides' is invariably a criticism and usually means hydrogen sulfide. Sulfides should not be confused with SULFITE, however.

In the 19th and early 20th centuries, copper and bronze were commonly used for winery equipment and small amounts of copper would dissolve in the wine. If traces of hydrogen sulfide were present, copper sulfide, one of the least soluble of all compounds, would be formed. Later, after bottling, the colloidal copper sulfide would form a cloud or haze with some of the wine proteins. This problem has been averted by the widespread use of STAINLESS STEEL.   A.D.W.

sulfite and **bisulfite**, the negatively charged ions liberated when sulfurous acid dissociates, as shown below:

$$H_2SO_3 \rightleftarrows H^+ + HSO_3^-$$
sulfurous acid   hydrogen ion   bisulfite ion

$$HSO_3^- \rightarrow H^+ + SO_3^{--}$$
bisulfite ion   hydrogen ion   sulfite ion

The analytical method usually used for the measurement of sulfite determines all of the various forms which are active in terms of smell, effect on YEAST and BACTERIA, and potential danger to asthmatics (see SULFUR DIOXIDE). The term sulfites, or sulphites, is therefore used on wine labels (as in 'Contains sulfites/sulphites') as an inclusive term for free sulfur dioxide, sulfurous acid (hydrated sulfur dioxide), bisulfite ion, sulfite ion, and some forms of complexed sulfite. See LABELLING INFORMATION.   A.D.W.

sulfur, an element that constitutes about 0.5 per cent of the weight of the Earth's crust and one of the more important elements for mankind. It is extremely important in wine production because of the wide-ranging uses of SULFUR DIOXIDE. A pale yellow, brittle, solid substance at room temperature, it was already known to the speakers of Ancient Sanskrit as *sulvere*. The book of Genesis in the Bible refers to sulfur as brimstone. In its combined form as sulfuric acid, sulfur is used in so

many manufacturing processes that the tonnage consumed by a nation can be taken as an indication of the health of its economy.

History

Sulfur has been used as a cleansing agent and wine preservative since antiquity. Among the various substances, such as pitch and resin, used by the Romans to prepare vessels in which wine was stored and to assist in the preservation of wines, authors such as CATO and PLINY also mention the use of sulfur. It seems probable that the pungent smells given off when ores containing sulfur were burned led to their association with a cleansing action, and experimentation would then have revealed the most efficacious methods of use. In the late 15th century, a German decree specifically refers to the use of sulfur, with wood shavings, powdered sulfur, herbs, and incense being burned in barrels before they were filled. By the 18th century, sulfur wicks were being regularly used to sterilize barrels in the best châteaux of Bordeaux (having been introduced by the DUTCH), and advances in chemistry had also led to the synthesis of derivatives of elemental sulfur, thus enabling inorganic salts containing sulfur to become widely used in wine-making. Sulfur dioxide is today used in the production of virtually all wines, albeit kept to a minimum in high-quality winemaking. In the vineyard, sulfur products are widely used to protect vines against both POWDERY MILDEW and DOWNY MILDEW.   P.T.H.U.

Johnson, H., *The Story of Wine* (London, 1989).

Viticulture

Sulfur is essential for vine nutrition, although sulfur deficiency in vineyards is very rare. Vines usually obtain sufficient quantities from soil supplies, or from FUNGICIDES. Continued application of sulfur to vineyards to control powdery mildew for over a century has led to excess SOIL ACIDITY in France. Carbon bisulfide was injected into vineyard soils in the late 19th century to control PHYLLOXERA, although the practice was replaced by the use of resistant rootstocks. See also SULFIDE.   R.E.S.

Wine-making

Sulfur is most familiar to winemakers as sulfur dioxide (although it can also react with oxygen to form sulfur trioxide, implicated in the problem of acid rain).

Residues of elemental sulfur used in the vineyard can combine with hydrogen in new wine to produce HYDROGEN SULFIDE, the compound responsible for the foul smell of bad eggs. See also MERCAPTANS.

Everyday wines to which high sulfurs additions have been made for particular operations, or for transport, may be **desulfured**.

See also SULFITE.   A.D.W.

sulfur dioxide, or **SO₂**, formed when elemental sulfur is burned in air, is the chemical compound most widely used by the wine-maker, principally as a preservative and a disinfectant. Sulfur dioxide, as fumes from burning sulfur, has been used since antiquity to preserve and disinfect during the production and storage of foods (see SULFUR for more historical detail).

Sulfur dioxide reacts with OXYGEN and so prevents OXIDATION, which has undesirable effects on the colour and flavour of wine. It is often added to freshly picked grapes in the form of metabisulfite. (The compound is therefore widely, often more liberally, used in the preparation of other foods and drinks, particularly fruit juices and dried fruits.) Sulfur dioxide has the further property, of particular value to the winemaker, of inhibiting or killing BACTERIA or wild YEAST, and of encouraging a rapid and clean FERMENTATION. Other less important reasons for using sulfur dioxide in wine-making are that it helps brighten the colour of red wines and encourages the extraction of compounds from the grape skins during MACERATION. Sulfur dioxide's efficacy is influenced by the wine's PH. Less is needed at a lower pH because the pH level determines how much of the free sulfur dioxide (see below) is molecular, the only form in which it is effective as an antimicrobial agent.

At room temperatures and normal atmospheric pressures, the compound exists as a colourless gas with a pungent, choking aroma similar to that of a struck match or burnt coke.

The disadvantage of using sulfur dioxide (which all but a fraction of 1 per cent of winemakers do) is that its aroma can be quite unpleasant even at fairly low concentrations, especially to some particularly sensitive tasters (who are likely to find it most noticeably on sweet Loire wines, sweet bordeaux, and German wines). Tests using both experienced and inexperienced wine tasters have shown that concentrations of 11 mg/l of sulfur dioxide in water are just detectable. In wines, the threshold is much higher, partly because the acid-tasting effect of sulfur dioxide which is so obvious in pure water is overwhelmed by the acids naturally present in wine. The minimum detectable sulfur dioxide concentration for most people is just over 200 mg/l in white wines and 100 mg/l in reds, although palates can vary considerably in their sensitivity.

The threshold at which sulfur dioxide can be detected also varies with wine type, because sulfur dioxide reacts or combines to form 'bound' sulfur dioxide with up to 50 other wine constituents, including notably ACETAL-DEHYDE and PYRUVIC ACID; this interferes with sulfur dioxide perception because only 'free', or uncombined, sulfur dioxide is active in terms of its effect on aroma. More significantly, it is only the free fraction that is effective as an antioxidant and microbicide. However, regulations about maximum permit-

ted sulfur levels tend to concern the total amount of sulfur dioxide present, both free and bound. Good wine-making practice aims to maximize the free to bound ratio of sulfur dioxide; this permits winemakers to add less total sulfur dioxide to achieve the same level of protection for the wine. Free sulfur dioxide can be difficult to measure in red wines.

During the latter half of the 20th century, maximum levels of sulfur dioxide permitted by law were systematically reduced. From permitted levels of up to 500 parts per million (ppm) in 1910, they were well under half this limit for dry wines by the early 1990s. (Sweet wines need higher levels of sulfur dioxide to inhibit possible fermentation of the RESIDUAL SUGAR.) These reductions have been made partly because the smell of sulfur dioxide is undesirable, but they are also a response to lobbyists, especially in the United States, concerned about the effect of high doses of sulfur (more than any single bottle of wine contains) on asthmatics. This latter force has resulted in compulsory LABELLING INFORMATION in various countries. (For more details, see LABELLING INFORMATION, allergen labelling.)

Within the EU, maximum permitted levels of total sulfur dioxide are 160 mg/l in dry red wines, 210 mg/l in dry white, dry rosé, and sweet red wines, and 260 mg/l in sweet white and rosé wines. Certain very sweet wines could contain up to 400 mg/l, however, including all sweet white bordeaux, Jurançon, and a number of sweet white Loire wines, Beerenauslese, Trockenbeerenauslese, and Ausbruch wines. The maximum level permitted in Australia was reduced to 250 mg/l in the 1990s, except for wines with 35 g/l or more residual sugar, for which up to 300 mg/l sulfur dioxide is permitted.

There have been attempts to produce wines without any addition of sulfur dioxide. Such wines are particularly prone to oxidation and the off-flavours generated by wild yeast and bacteria. They need careful handling and possibly even PASTEURIZATION. It would be impossible to produce an entirely sulfur-free wine since a small amount of sulfur dioxide is one of the by-products of the metabolic action of yeast during fermentation when the material being fermented contains sulfate salts. Since sulfate salts are natural components of such fermentable materials as dough and fruit juices, it is normal to encounter small amounts of sulfur dioxide in such fermented products as bread and wine.

A.D.W. & J.A.G.

Goode, J., *Wine Science* (London, 2005).
Robinson, E. M. C., and Godden, P. E., 'Revisiting sulphur dioxide use', *Australian Wine Research Institute Technical Review*, 145 (2003).
Rose, A. H., 'Sulphur dioxide and other preservatives', *Journal of Wine Research*, 4 (1993), 43–7.

sulphate, **sulphide**, **sulphite**, and **sulphur**, the British and non-technical spellings of

SULFATE, SULFIDE, SULFITE, and SULFUR respectively. This volume follows the International Union of Pure and Applied Chemistry (IUPAC) nomenclature recommendations and uses sulfate, sulfide, sulfite, and sulfur throughout since the terms are generally used in a technical context.

Sultana, the most important white grape variety used to produce the pale brown DRYING GRAPES sometimes called SULTANAS and the single most-planted vine variety in the world covering an estimated 344,000 ha/850,000 acres of vineyard, much of it in the Middle East. The fruit of the Sultana vine, called Thompson Seedless in California, is remarkable for its versatility. As well as being dried, it can be vinified into a neutral white wine and, especially after treatment with GIBBERELLIN growth regulators to increase BERRY SIZE, is a much sought-after crisp, green, seedless TABLE GRAPE. In some viticultural regions, such as Australia's RIVERLAND and California's CENTRAL VALLEY, the Sultana harvest can be diverted to whatever happens to be the most profitable end use, including wine in times of wine grape shortage.

It is originally from the eastern Mediterranean, where it may be known as **Sultanine**, **Sultanina**, variants on Kismis in the former Soviet Republics and eastern Europe, and Cekizdecsis in Turkey. It is still much grown and used both for dried fruit and table grapes in countries such as AZERBAIJAN and ARMENIA. This variety, producing thin-skinned, seedless grapes, is too susceptible to a variety of FUNGAL DISEASES to be grown in most of western Europe, but it can be very productive in hot, dry conditions. In widely varying locations, it provides base material for some, usually undistinguished, wines.

sultanas, pale brown DRYING GRAPES made from the SULTANA grape variety, also known as THOMPSON SEEDLESS.

Sumer. In Ancient Sumer (3500–1900 BC), the earliest literate civilization of southern MESOPOTAMIA, wine and BEER were both widely consumed, and are often mentioned as being drunk on the same occasion. 'Wine' almost certainly refers to grape wine in most contexts, although date wine was also prepared by the Sumerians.

At the sacred city of Nippur, just downstream from Babylon, which stood on an important branch of the river Euphrates, the principal quay of the temple was known as the 'Quay of the Vine', although it is not clear if this refers to an original commercial activity or is simply an ornate epithet of the sort beloved of Sumerian poets. In praise poetry addressed to King Shulgi, who was deified in his own lifetime (c.22nd century BC), the king's martial prowess with the double-edged axe is eulogized with the image of him 'spilling his enemies' blood on the mountain-side like the contents of a smashed wine jug'.

DRUNKENNESS seems to have carried no stigma of disapprobation. In a number of Sumerian literary works, the gods get drunk on wine and beer in circumstances which are not merely amusing but are dramatically important.   J.A.B.

Bottéro, J., 'Getränke', *Reallexikon der Assyriologie und vorderasiatischen Archäologie* (the standard reference work) (Berlin, 1928–).

Kinner Wilson, J. V., *The Nimrud Wine Lists* (London, 1972).

summer pruning, optional vineyard operation designed to sacrifice quantity for quality. See PRUNING and CROP THINNING.

Sumoll, Spanish red wine grape grown in CONCA DE BARBERÁ and, increasingly, in TARRAGONA.

sunburn can damage grapes and is a viticultural term used loosely for a range of conditions. Classical sunburn produces a round halo of burnt skin on the side of the berry facing the sun. Such sunburn is due to a combination of bright sunshine, high air temperatures, and low winds, and the so-called 'hot spot' can be up to 12 °C/54 °F above air temperature. Berries which were previously shaded from the sun are most sensitive, as their skins have not been conditioned by exposure to sunlight. Sunburn sensitivity is higher for vineyards suffering WATER STRESS.

The condition in which grapes develop pigmentation in response to the ultraviolet component of sun exposure is also loosely called sunburn. This is particularly obvious with some white varieties, and the skin can develop deep yellow or even brown colours. Whether such exposure is harmful to the berry is arguable, and exposure to sun encourages the production of QUERCETIN (see FLAVONOLS), which is associated with wine quality and bitter flavours. Such berries may be smaller, and exposed fruit has been shown to produce better-quality table wine (see CANOPY MICROCLIMATE).
                                    R.E.S.

Winkler, A. J., *et al.*, *General Viticulture* (2nd edn, Berkeley, Calif., 1974).

Sunbury, historic Australian cool climate wine region in VICTORIA close to Melbourne's northern suburbs, and even closer to its domestic and international air terminal. Craiglee and Goona Warra are two wineries steeped in history, Craiglee a top flight producer of spicy, elegant SHIRAZ.

sunlight, the ultimate energy source of all life, and of wine itself. Through a process known as PHOTOSYNTHESIS, part of its energy is used by plants to combine CARBON DIOXIDE from the air with WATER taken up from the soil, to form SUGAR IN GRAPES. This is the building block for other plant products, as well as being the immediate source of energy for all of a plant's biochemical processes, via its RESPIRATION back to carbon dioxide and water.

In climatology, the traditional measurement of sunlight is as hours of bright sunlight. Such measurements of hours of bright sunshine have limitations when applied to the study of climatology of grapevines. When continuously illuminated, the leaves become saturated with light at only about one-third of average sunlight intensity, at which point other plant processes or environmental factors become more directly limiting to plant growth and RIPENING, the most important in cool climates being TEMPERATURE.

Moreover, sunlight can still support photosynthesis, albeit at diminishing rates, down to quite low intensities. This means that significant amounts of usable sunlight are not registered by these standard bright sunlight measurements. More recently, electronic sensors have been used in climate recording networks which give readings of total energy, rather than of bright sunlight only.

Some implications follow for the CANOPY MICROCLIMATE and CANOPY MANAGEMENT of grapevines. Displaying leaves obliquely to bright sunlight encourages maximum efficiency of photosynthesis. For the same reasons, exposure to sunlight such as in the early morning and late afternoon, and as predominates at high latitudes, can be more photosynthetically effective than that of the leaves directly facing for example the overhead sun. This is especially so for vines with a VERTICAL TRELLIS, and also in hot climates, where midday photosynthesis may be reduced anyway because of excessive temperatures and WATER STRESS. Finally, leaves that are only partly or intermittently illuminated by direct sunlight use what energy they get with an enhanced efficiency.

Another important role of sunlight in viticulture is that of heating the vines and the soil. Grape berries for example may be heated up to 15 °C above air temperature for black berries exposed to bright sunlight in low wind conditions. Leaves are heated less when exposed to sunlight, as they are evaporatively cooled by the process of TRANSPIRATION. Berry temperatures are of considerable importance in affecting the chemical make-up of the grapes. Similarly, leaf temperatures have important effects on photosynthesis and respiration and this also directly affects GRAPE COMPOSITION AND WINE QUALITY. Soil temperature depends on the reflectivity to sunlight of the soil surface; thus dark soils absorb more sunlight and are warmer than white or light coloured soils (see SOIL COLOUR). The total amount of sunlight energy over all of the spectrum is important in heating vines and soils.

The intensity of sunlight is not its only characteristic of importance to grapevines. Another is spectral quality or the proportion of sunlight at different wavelengths. This does not vary greatly from region to region, or under full sunlight versus cloud; but it does vary enormously within the vine CANOPY.

The total spectrum of solar radiation comprises ULTRAVIOLET RADIATIONS, visible light, and infrared (heat) radiations, in order of increasing electromagnetic wavelengths. Visible light is in the wavelength range 400 to 760 nanometres (nm) (1 nm is a millionth of a millimetre). Within that range, in order of increasing wavelength, are the component colours of the visible light spectrum: violet, indigo, blue, green, yellow, orange, and red.

Most of the wavelengths between 400 and 700 nm are absorbed by leaves, and are used to varying degrees for photosynthesis. Those absorbed and used most efficiently are in the blue and (especially) red parts of the spectrum, centred around 440 and 660 nm respectively. It is the partial reflection of the intermediate wavelengths, by the photosynthetically active pigment chlorophyll, that gives plant leaves their characteristic green colour. Thus shade light, as well as being much less intense than full sunlight, is still more impoverished of its photosynthetically useful wavelengths. If overall light intensity is reduced eight- or tenfold, that of red light around 660 nm can be reduced a hundredfold in deep canopy shade.

Also important physiologically are the barely visible 'far red' wavelengths, between 700 and 760 nm. These and the adjacent infrared wavelengths are hardly absorbed at all, being either reflected or transmitted through the leaves. Canopy shade light is therefore relatively rich in them. The ratio of normal red to far red wavelengths (measured as 10-nm-width bands centred around 660 and 730 nm, and known as the R : FR ratio) is between 1.0 and 1.2 in the open, whereas in deep canopy shade it can be 0.1 or less.

It is the R : FR ratio, rather than light intensity as such, that appears to govern many plant reactions to shading within the canopy, probably through the action of a wavelength-sensitive pigment known as phytochrome. A low R : FR ratio, characteristic of deep canopy shade, promotes rapid spindly stem growth (trying to reach the light); sparse leaves and light green colour; sparse lateral branching; and poor bud FRUITFULNESS. Conversely, a high R : FR ratio, as in normal external light, promotes stocky growth, with strong lateral branching; deep green leaf colour; and good bud fruitfulness. Direct exposure of the bunches to such light also promotes the formation of ANTHOCYANIN pigments in the berry skins of red wine grape varieties, and appears to be associated with superior flavour and potential wine quality. The practice of LEAF REMOVAL around the bunches is in part a response to this.

The fact that such wavelength discrimination can still occur at quite low light intensities raises further interesting questions on which, at present, there is little direct information for grapevines. They include the effects of height, orientation, and distance between rows on the quality of the light reaching the lower canopy and bunches; also those of different soil colours, MULCHES, or COVER CROPS on the intensity and spectral quality of light reflected back to the lower canopy and bunches.

Smart reviews general aspects or light-quality effects on grapevine growth and fruit composition. He also deals comprehensively with sunlight relations in the context of vine canopy microclimate, canopy management, and wine quality.

See also VINE PHYSIOLOGY.   J.G. & R.E.S.

Smart, R. E., 'Principles of grapevine canopy micro-climate manipulation with implications for yield and quality', *American Journal of Enology and Viticulture*, 35 (1985), 230–9.

——'Influence of light on composition and quality of grapes', *Acta horticulturae*, 206 (1987), 37–47.

——'Canopy management', in B. G. Coombe and P. R. Dry (eds.), *Viticulture*, ii: *Practices* (Adelaide, 1992).

Supérieur, Supérieure, or Supérieures may be found suffixed to the name of an AP-PELLATION CONTRÔLÉE on French wine labels. The regulations for a Supérieur wine usually demand a slightly higher minimum ALCO-HOLIC STRENGTH (typically by half a per cent). The term is often optional and Quelquechose Supérieure is by no means infallibly superior to plain Quelquechose.

Superiore, Italian term applied to DOC wines which are deemed superior because of their higher minimum ALCOHOLIC STRENGTH, usually by a half or 1 per cent, and a longer period of AGEING before commercial release. Among the more significant wines which fall into this category are the three BARBERA DOCs of PIEMONTE (Alba, Asti, Monferrato), BARDOLINO, CALDARO, GRAVE DEL FRIULI, SOAVE, VALPOLICELLA, and VALTELLINA (where the use of the word Superiore is strictly linked to the sub-denominations of Grumello, Inferno, Sassella, and Valgella and indicates to all intents and purposes the CLASSICO zone of Valtellina). Both Barbera d'Alba Superiore and Barbera d'Asti Superiore must be aged in wood for at least one year, in addition to the requirement of an extra half a per cent of alcohol compared with the regular Barbera bottlings of the two zones.   D.T.

super second, a specialist term in the FINE WINE market for CLASSED GROWTH wines from BORDEAUX to denote the best-performing wines ranked as second growths in the 1855 CLASSIFICATION of the Médoc and Graves. There is no absolute agreement about which properties qualify as super seconds but Chx Pichon-Longueville-Lalande, and more recently Pichon-Longueville (Baron), in PAUILLAC, Cos and Montrose in ST-ESTÈPHE, and LÉOVILLE LAS CASES and Ducru-Beaucaillou in ST-JULIEN have all been nominated at one

time or another. Other strong candidates (although not second growths) include Ch Palmer in MARGAUX, and Ch La MISSION-HAUT-BRION in PESSAC-LÉOGNAN.

super-Spanish. See MÉNTRIDA and VINO DE MESA.

Supertuscan, term sometimes used by English speakers to describe the innovative wines labelled as VINO DA TAVOLA made in the central Italian region of Toscana which emerged in the 1970s. Prototype Supertuscans were TIGNANELLO and SASSICAIA, both initially marketed by ANTINORI. The vino da tavola denomination was replaced by IGT in 1994, but the term Supertuscan remains. For more details, see TOSCANA.

sur lie, French term meaning 'on the lees', customarily applied to white wines whose principal deviation from everyday WHITE WINE-MAKING techniques was some form of LEES CONTACT. The term has been used most commonly for the French dry white MUSCADET to differentiate those wines which remained on their lees after fermentation, usually in tank, in an effort to increase flavour and texture. The practice, and term, has since spread south to the LANGUEDOC and even outside France and has proved a useful way of adding flavour and value to the produce of relatively neutral grapes such as Chenin Blanc in South Africa.

surmaturité, French expression often used by Anglophones for overripeness, a usually undesirable stage in grape maturity whereby grapes start to shrivel and acid levels fall to a dangerously low level, although see the fashion for extended HANG TIME. Some Australians refer to this stage as exhibiting 'dead fruit' flavours.

surplus production has for years been the single greatest problem facing the world's wine industry, aggravated by improved efficiency in the vineyard and falling consumption in most important wine markets. The most palatable effect of this surplus for wine consumers has been its dampening impact on PRICES at the bottom end of the wine market.

Even in the late 1950s, the world produced almost 15 per cent more wine than it consumed, but wine consumption was rising rapidly, and it was assumed that it would catch up. By the late 1970s, average YIELDS began to increase substantially. This was largely the result of increased viticultural proficiency, but also reflected the availability of particularly productive CLONES of established vine varieties, as well as the more widespread use of AGRO-CHEMICALS to combat VINE DISEASES, and FER-TILIZERS. Just at this point, consumption began to decline, especially markedly in the principal wine-producing countries (which had been the

principal wine markets): France, Italy, USSR, Spain, and Argentina.

The exceptionally large European harvests of 1979 and 1980 plunged what is now the European Union into crisis and forced measures which included compulsory DISTILLATION of about a fifth of total production (only of the lowest-quality wine), a VINE PULL SCHEME, and a somewhat fruitless attempt to control yields, which continued to rise by an average of about 0.5 per cent a year. By the late 1980s, the world was producing 19 per cent more than it could consume (see table overleaf), with particularly marked surpluses in France, Italy, and Spain, and a marked surplus of industrial ALCOHOL as a result of compulsory distillation.

The breakup of the Soviet Union, for long a net wine importer, and the introduction of free market economies within the former Soviet Republics meanwhile deprived many eastern European wine producers of their traditional, and none too fastidious market, creating fresh pressure on the world's wine suppliers.

Surpluses on a smaller scale, sometimes simply of the wrong type of wine, have resulted in national vine pull schemes such as those enacted in NEW ZEALAND and ARGENTINA in the late 1980s and early 1990s respectively.

By the early and mid 1990s, there was overproduction in all continents except the Americas, but most especially in Europe and particularly of poor quality TABLE WINE. This did nothing to alleviate severe shortages in the mid to late 1990s of red wines suitable for export in many countries, however, most notably in South Africa and Australia, where there was a shortage of commercially desirable wine grapes of both colours. Substantial plantings of Chardonnay vines in the mid 1990s in Australia and California resulted in a surplus of that grape variety. As the table shows, the overall surplus was generally declining at the beginning of the 21st century but was still uncomfortably high.

For more details of European efforts to curb surplus wine production, see EUROPEAN UNION.

Surrentine wine from vineyards on the slopes of the Sorrento peninsula in southern Italy achieved prominence from the latter half of the reign of Augustus in the first decade of the 1st century AD. It ranked high in Classical ROME, but behind CAECUBAN and FALERNIAN, in PLINY's assessment. It was produced from the vine known as the Aminnea Gemina Minor, which, unusually for one of the classic wines, was trellised rather than grown up trees. The wine itself was a rather thin white wine, which nevertheless could be described as 'strong'. It may well have had a high acidity. There are recommendations to age it for 20 to 25 years. It never won universal approval—'a high class vinegar' was the opinion of both the emperors Tiberius and Caligula, and there are some signs that its MEDICINAL properties were among its most important selling points.   J.J.P.

World totals in million hl of wine				
	Production	Consumption	Surplus	% Surplus
1976–80	326.0	285.7	40.3	12
1981–85	333.6	280.7	52.8	16
1986–90	292.8	237.0	55.8	19
1991–95	261.3	222.7	38.6	15
1991	258.5	232.8	25.7	10
1992	294.7	226.6	68.1	23
1993	254.1	216.3	37.8	15
1994	245.5	215.2	30.3	12
1995	253.6	222.7	30.9	12
1996	272.5	223.2	49.3	18
1997	264.4	223.5	40.9	15
1998	262.1	227.8	34.4	13
1999	281.2	225.1	56.1	20
2000	280.0	226.6	53.4	19
2001	266.6	226.9	39.7	14.9
2002	257.8	228.6	29.2	11.3
2003	266.7	234.7	32.0	12

Note: These figures are based on OIV official statistics.

Pliny the Elder, *Natural History*, trans. by H. Rackham (London, 1945), Book 14.

sur souches, French expression meaning 'on the stumps' or, in the context of a purchase of a future vintage of wine, 'on the vine'. The BORDEAUX TRADE has, at times of particularly buoyant sales, occasionally bought futures in a crop before even it was harvested.

Süss, literally 'sweet' in German. Used on labels in AUSTRIA to designate wines whose RESIDUAL SUGAR is more than 45 g/l.

Süssreserve, German term for SWEET RESERVE, the sweetening agent much used, especially in the 1970s and 1980s, for all but the finest or driest German wines. Its use is declining for two main reasons: GERMANY is making an increasing proportion of dry wines (see TROCKEN and HALBTROCKEN); better producers of off-dry and medium wines prefer to stop the fermentation while there is still some RESIDUAL SUGAR in the wine rather than add unfermented juice.

sustainable viticulture, a form of viticultural practice which aims to avoid any form of environmental degradation while maintaining the economic viability of the vineyard. It is defined by the Sustainable Agriculture Research and Education Program at the University of California at DAVIS as 'the principle that we must meet the needs of the present without compromising the ability of future generations to meet their own needs'.

In reality, the term is applied quite liberally and almost invariably falls short of environmentalist ideals of being completely self-sustaining. The Sustainable Winegrowing New Zealand (SWNZ) initiative, for example, was established in 1995 to provide a 'best practice' environmental model for both vineyard and winery. SWNZ is reliant on voluntary audits and stops short of prohibiting man-made inputs such as PESTICIDES. However, such programmes can, via grower education, significantly reduce the number and strength of chemical SPRAYINGS, which is of both environmental and economic benefit. A related approach is INTEGRATED PEST MANAGEMENT, as are LISA or LEISA, acronyms which stand for Low (External) Input Sustainable Agriculture, terms often used for programmes in North America and Australia.

ORGANIC growers may claim to practise sustainable viticulture but still obtain organic fertilizer or seed for cover crops from an external source, thus burning fossil fuels in transportation. Even in biodynamic wine-growing, in which external inputs are be minimized to create self-sustaining farms, growers are invariably reliant on copper sulfate (as BORDEAUX MIXTURE) and sulfur dust, both of which are finite resources and, in the case of copper, decompose in the soil only with great difficulty.

A mere handful of the world's organic and biodynamic vineyards are farmed without mechanization, notably smallholdings on vertiginous terrain in Switzerland for example.

Some wineries, for example Fetzer in California, are moving towards renewable energy, partly based on recycling carbon dioxide gas produced during alcoholic fermentation. Renewable energy use is becoming more widespread worldwide through legislative pressure and as the price of alternative energy sources such as solar-powered cells fall.

See also LUTTE RAISONNÉE. M.W.

Ingels, C., 'Sustainable agriculture and grape production', *American Journal of Enology and Viticulture*, 43 (1992), 296–8.

Reganold, J., Papendick, R., and Parr, J., 'Sustainable Agriculture', *Scientific American*, 262 (1990), 112-120.

Susumaniello, lively, deep-coloured red wine grape that has crossed the Adriatic to be grown on the heel of Italy.

Svatovavřinecké, Czech name for ST-LAURENT.

Swan District, the hot, traditional, once-dominant wine region of WESTERN AUSTRALIA. **Swan Valley** is now a subregion fighting back from the brink of oblivion, and very dependent on TOURISM.

Swan Hill, Australian wine region on the Murray river, partly in VICTORIA and partly in NEW SOUTH WALES.

sward. See COVER CROP.

sweetness. Wines taste sweet mainly because of the amount of RESIDUAL SUGAR they contain (although the impact of this on the palate is greatly influenced by factors such as the levels of ACIDITY, TANNINS, and CARBON DIOXIDE in the wine as well as by the serving TEMPERATURE). ETHANOL, or alcohol, can also taste sweet, as can GLYCEROL and a high level of PECTINS. A dry wine with a residual sugar of less than 2 g/l that is relatively high in alcohol, such as many a Chardonnay for example, can taste quite sweet. A sweet VOUVRAY, on the other hand, made in a cool region from the naturally acidic grape variety CHENIN BLANC, may contain well over 30 g/l residual sugar, but in youth can taste dry.

A wide variety of different terms in different languages are used to describe sweetness, although they invariably relate strictly to the residual sugar rather than to the taste impression. The table opposite gives the official EU classification of sweetness levels. Producers are not obliged to put this information on the label of a still wine, though it is mandatory for sparkling wines. See DOSAGE for specific terminology.

Some wine drinkers have been conditioned to be suspicious of any sweetness in a wine, perhaps because neophytes generally prefer some residual sugar (which is why so many wine BRANDS contain some) and sweetness is therefore associated with a lack of sophistication. Some of the greatest wines of the world are sweet, however. So long as there is sufficient ACIDITY to balance the sweetness, a sweet wine is by no means cloying. Indeed, a comparative tasting of great young sweet wines is more likely to leave the taster with the impression of excess acidity than excess sugar.

See SWEET WINES and SWEET WINE-MAKING for more details of sweeter wines.

sweet reserve, preserved GRAPE JUICE held for BLENDING purposes, usually to sweeten, or at least soften, wines high in ACIDITY. The unfermented grape SUGARS counterbalance the tart flavours of wines produced from grapes grown in cool regions such as much of GERMANY (where it is such juice is known as *Süssreserve*) or grapes naturally high in acidity such as UGNI BLANC and COLOMBARD.

Historically grape juice was preserved simply by adding offensively high doses of SULFUR

RS g/l	English	French	German	Italian	Spanish
up to 4 (or not exceeding 9 provided that the total acidity expressed as grams of tartaric acid per litre is not more than 2 grams below the RS content)	dry	sec	trocken	secco or asciutto	seco
more than 4 and not exceeding 12 (or not exceeding 18 where the minimum total acidity has been set by the member state)	medium dry	demi-sec	halbtrocken	abboccato	semiseco
more than 12 and not exceeding 45	medium (or medium sweet)	moelleux	lieblich	amabile	semidulce
at least 45	sweet	doux	süss	dolce	dulce

DIOXIDE. Modern REFRIGERATION and near-sterile FILTRATION enable the production of sweet reserve that does not reek of sulfur dioxide. The sweet juice usually undergoes CLARIFICATION and refrigeration so as to precipitate any TARTRATES and can be stored at very low temperatures for up to 12 months.

In many wine regions, sweet reserve is being replaced by GRAPE CONCENTRATE or RECTIFIED GRAPE MUST. Grape concentrate is cheaper to store because it is much richer in sugar, which also prevents the growth of micro-organisms so that it can be stored without recourse to expensive refrigeration. Rectified grape must is preferred simply because it more closely resembles a solution of sugar and water than does preserved juice.   A.D.W.

sweet wine-making, the production of wines with noticeable amounts of RESIDUAL SUGAR which may vary considerably in ALCOHOLIC STRENGTH and production techniques. Local regulations differ considerably but, with a few exceptions, non-grape sugar may be added only (and rarely) for the purposes of CHAPTALIZATION, to increase the final alcoholic strength, and not to add sweetness after fermentation. The most common method of sweetening basic wine is the addition of some form of sweet grape juice, followed by STABILIZATION (for any wine containing sugar is theoretically susceptible to SECONDARY FERMENTATION).

The finest sweet wines are made by concentrating the SUGAR IN GRAPES, however, and the combined effect of the alcohol produced and the residual sugar tends to inhibit further YEAST activity. The three common ways of doing this are by the benevolent NOBLE ROT effect of the botrytis fungus on the vine as it nears maturity in perfect conditions (see BOTRYTIZED WINES); by processing frozen grape clusters (see EISWEIN and CRYOEXTRACTION); or by drying mature grapes either on the vine or after picking (see DRIED GRAPE WINES). Many sweet wines are made by simply leaving the grapes on the vine for as long as possible in order to concentrate the grape sugars. If BOTRYTIS BUNCH ROT fails to materialize, the grapes simply start to raisin or shrivel, a condition known in French as *passerillé*. Such wines, sweet JURANÇON, for example, described as *moelleux* in French, can be extremely rich and satisfying, but are typically less complex

and less long-lived wines than those made from grapes transformed by the action of noble rot.

Some everyday sweet wines are made nowadays, however, simply by fermenting the wine out to dryness and subsequently adding SWEET RESERVE, GRAPE CONCENTRATE or RECTIFIED GRAPE MUST just before a sterilizing membrane FILTRATION and sterile BOTTLING. These wines owe their stability not to their composition but to the fact that all micro-organisms have been filtered out. They are best drunk within a year of bottling and within a day or two of opening the bottle. Most sweet German wines of QBA level, such as LIEBFRAUMILCH, are examples of this type of wine, and the sweetening agent is called SÜSSRESERVE in German.

Another technique, commonly employed for inexpensive sweet white French wines, is to ferment a must relatively high in sugars, between 200 and 250 g/l, until the alcohol level has reached about 11 or 12 per cent, and then add a substantial dose of SULFUR DIOXIDE.

One quite different way of transforming grapes into a liquid that is both sweet and stable is to add spirit to grape juice either before fermentation (see VIN DE LIQUEUR) or during it (see VIN DOUX NATUREL). Such liquids are usually more than 15 per cent alcohol, much stronger than most table wines.

Many FORTIFIED WINES are sweet. See also WHITE WINE-MAKING, RED WINE-MAKING, ROSÉ WINE-MAKING, and, particularly, BOTRYTIZED WINES, DRIED GRAPE WINES, and EISWEIN for details of how these particularly fine sweet wines are made.

sweet wines are widely under-appreciated, especially in view of how difficult some of them are to make. Sweet wines have been popular for various periods since ancient times; indeed most of the most admired wines of classical ROME were sweet and white, many of them DRIED GRAPE WINES made by deliberate raisining to concentrate the sugars. In the Middle Ages the great city states of Italy such as VENICE and GENOA profited from the popularity of wines made so much sweeter than northern European wines by the effects of the MEDITERRANEAN CLIMATE. By the late 17th century. the DUTCH WINE TRADE was energetically profiting from the sweet wines of western France. And subsequently the sweet wines of

CONSTANTIA and TOKAJI in particular were considered the height of FASHION.

For specific modern sweet wines see AUSLESE, BANYULS, BARSAC, BEERENAUSLESE, BONNEZEAUX, BOTRYTIZED WINES, CADILLAC, CÉRONS, CLAIRETTE DE DIE, EISWEIN, JURANÇON, LAYON, LOUPIAC, MAURY, MOELLEUX, MONBAZILLAC, MONTLOUIS, various MOSCATELS, MOSCATO, MUSCAT, PICOLIT, QUARTS DE CHAUME, RASTEAU, RECIOTO, RIVESALTES, SÉLECTION DE GRAINS NOBLES, STE-CROIX-DU-MONT, SAUTERNES, SPECIAL LATE HARVESTED, TROCKENBEERENAUSLESE, VENDANGE TARDIVE, VIN DE PAILLE, VIN SANTO, and VOUVRAY.

See SWEETNESS for details of sweet wine descriptions in various languages and what they entail.

Switzerland, small, alpine country in central Europe beginning to look outwards into the greater world of wine. Annual wine production is steady at more than a million hl/ 26.4 million gal from about 15,000 ha/37,050 acres of often spectacular vineyards. The majority of these are in the western, French-speaking part of the country, Suisse romande. There are also extensive vineyards all over eastern, German-speaking Switzerland (or Ostschweiz), and many vineyards in Ticino, the Italian-speaking south of Switzerland (or Svizzera Italiana). The country is divided into 23 cantons, of which all produce some wine (see map overleaf). For many years, Swiss wine labelling lacked the discipline applied to the north in Germany or the controls imposed to the west in France, but from the early 1990s an APPELLATION CONTRÔLÉE system was applied with increasing rigour, initially in French-speaking Switzerland. Since controls on wine imports were relaxed in the mid 1990s (and disappeared altogether for white wines in 2001), the Swiss wine industry has been forced to seek customers abroad, particularly for the most common style of wine produced in Switzerland: light, white, and relatively neutral. An increasing proportion of Swiss wine is seriously good, however. CHASSELAS is the principal grape variety and, when well vinified, it can express well the country's diversity of soils and climates. Valais has a clutch of interesting indigenous grapes and some increasingly sophisticated red wines are made in all Swiss wine regions, particularly Ticino and Bündner Herrschaft.

Switzerland

History

Grape seeds of the neolithic age, between 3000 and 1800 BC, have been found at St-Blaise in Neuchâtel, and the Romans (see Ancient ROME) certainly cultivated the vine in most modern Swiss wine regions. In the Middle Ages, vine-growing spread under monastic influence, notably that of the Cistercians (see MONKS AND MONASTERIES), who planted the original Dézaley vines in Vaud. As elsewhere, medieval wines were thin, acid, and often helped by the addition of honey and other flavourings. In the 17th century, Swiss vignerons were already feeling the effects of wine imports from hotter climes, notably from further down the RHÔNE valley.

Switzerland was far more seriously affected by the viticultural catastrophes of the late 19th century (DOWNY MILDEW, PHYLLOXERA, POWDERY MILDEW) than most other wine-producing countries. Between 1877 and 1957 the total Swiss vineyard declined by 60 per cent from 33,000 to 12,500 ha, a decrease encouraged by competition from cheaper imported wines, increasing industrialization, and development of the all-important lakesides. In the mid 20th century, CLONAL SELECTION and FERTILIZERS were harnessed with particular enthusiasm in attempts to increase productivity from Switzerland's relatively inconvenient, expensive-to-work vineyards. More recent de-velopments in both vineyard and cellar are concerned with quality.

Climate

Although Switzerland is on a particularly suitable latitude for wine production, between 45 and 47 degrees, a high proportion of the country is simply too high. However, the country's lakes and the föhn, a local wind which warms up sizeable portions of the south of the country, particularly Graubünden in the upper Rhine valley, enable full grape ripening to take place in many valleys and on lake-sides. And in Valais in the south west, the upper Rhône valley, sunshine is so dependable (an average of more than 2,000 hours a year, rising sometimes to more than 2,500 hours) that vineyards can be as high as 750 m/ 2,460 ft and one, at Vispertenminen, is 1,100 m above sea level. Valais is sheltered by the alps and, like south east Switzerland, benefits particularly from the föhn, but it can be dry and IRRIGATION with mountain water is sometimes necessary. The slope of some vineyards is as steep as 90 per cent. Most Swiss wine regions have an annual rainfall of between 500 and 1,800 mm/19.5–70 in a year, the wettest region being Ticino, which suffers violent but short storms and is also the hottest with average July temperatures of more than 21 °C/70 °F. Elsewhere, average July temperatures are be-tween 17.5 and 20 °C, there is good day–night TEMPERATURE VARIABILITY, and winter temperatures in the vineyards rarely fall below danger level for vines. Valais is most at risk.

Viticulture

The slope and, in some regions, rainfall make SOIL EROSION many Swiss vine-growers' prime concern. REMONTAGE and TERRACES are common in Switzerland's steep vineyards, and COVER CROPS are increasingly common. Sophisticated MECHANIZATION is possible only on some of the flatter vineyards on the plain, or on some of the terraces of eastern Switzerland. A wide variety of training methods are used, including CORDON, GOBELET, GUYOT, TENDONE (in Ticino), and the Swiss German speciality *taille à l'onglet* designed to protect the vines against spring FROST danger there. Elaborate monorail systems may be used to transport equipment and, at harvest, grapes.

Many vine-growers sell their grapes direct to NÉGOCIANTS or CO-OPERATIVES but an increasing number make and sell their own wine. YIELDS are nationally restricted, according to Switzerland's somewhat microscopic unit of measurement, to 1.4 kg/sq m for Chasselas grapes and 1.2 kg/sq m for red and superior white grapes, the equivalent of more than 105 hl/ha (6 tons/acre) and 84 hl/ha respectively. Some cantons, such as those of eastern

The distinctive turrets of Château Pichon-Longueville, once known as Château Pichon-Baron, provide a backdrop to these Merlot grapes being picked in the autumn sunshine for this second growth **Pauillac**.

Switzerland and Geneva, Neuchâtel, and Valais, apply their own stricter limits, however, and national average yields are about the same as in France.

The most common viticultural problems are downy mildew, powdery mildew, botrytis bunch rot, soil erosion, and occasional spring frost in the east of the country.

Switzerland's most famous viticultural research stations are at WÄDENSWIL in German-speaking Switzerland and CHANGINS at Nyon in Suisse romande.

Wine-making

The essential stylistic difference between Swiss wine and that of neighbouring Germany and Austria is that ACIDITY is seen as an evil rather than a virtue and MALOLACTIC FERMENTATION is routinely practised. The resulting softness in Swiss wine is emphasized by the additional alcohol provided by CHAPTALIZATION. This prefermentation sugar addition has been almost de rigueur for many Swiss wines, although the practice is unnecessary in much of Valais and the Rhine valley, and is declining elsewhere. Ordinary wines may have their alcohol content increased by up to 3 per cent, although Swiss consumers are increasingly favouring lighter, drier wines.

Swiss PRESSES, made by Bucher and Sutter, are known throughout the wine-making world, and are put to particularly effective work in their native land, where the aim is to extract as much juice as possible from the country's precious grapes with only the gentlest of pressure from an inflatable membrane.

DESTEMMING is the norm and some form of CARBONIC MACERATION is often employed for German-speaking eastern Switzerland's red wines. As elsewhere, BARREL MATURATION has become increasingly popular for Swiss reds in general.

Switzerland has several pink wine specialities: white wines made from Pinot Noir and/or Gamay grapes such as Valais's DÔLE Blanche. Œil de Perdrix, 'partridge eye', is made only from Pinot Noir, originally in Neuchâtel, while Gamay provides rosé. Federweisser or WEISSHERBST is a product of German Switzerland where SCHILLERWEIN is a local rosé.

BLENDING has played an important part in the Swiss wine industry for decades. As Switzerland remains outside the EUROPEAN UNION, Swiss wine merchants are unencumbered by the mass of regulations which protect wines within EU countries and have long depended on imported wines, particularly deeply coloured red ones, to add bulk to many of their less expensive blends. (In the late 1990s, for example, Switzerland was importing about 150 times as much wine, mainly red, as it exported, and two large orders in 2004 were enough to boost total exports to almost double 2003 levels.) Such blending is under the supervision of the Ordonnance sur les Denrées Alimentaires (ODA). The introduction of a full APPELLATION CONTRÔLÉE system within Switzerland is focusing attention on authentic domaine-bottled all-Swiss products but small additions of imported wines were still allowed in the late 1990s.

Vine varieties

Switzerland's most planted variety, covering 45 per cent of the country's vineyard land and responsible for a remarkable 60 per cent of the country's total wine production, is CHASSELAS, or Gutedel as it is known by German speakers. In Valais it is called Fendant, while in Vaud wines are sold under their geographical appellation names rather than by its old local synonym Dorin. The same applies to Geneva, where the traditional local name is Perlan. In Valais, the second most important variety is SYLVANER, whose wines, fuller bodied than Chasselas, are sold as Johannisberg. Gros Rhin is a Valais synonym for Sylvaner. Petit Rhin (RIESLING) is relatively rare and can be reliably ripened only on the schists around Sion in Valais.

The conveniently early-ripening MÜLLER-THURGAU, in Dr Müller's native land known as Riesling–Sylvaner, is the most common white grape variety in German Switzerland, having substantially replaced the historic RÄUSCHLING vine, particularly around Zurich just south of the German border. There are signs of a revival of interest in the more distinctive variety, however. A Müller-Thurgau relative, Findling, has been introduced in Geneva canton.

Other white grape varieties include PINOT GRIS, called Malvoisie in Valais; PINOT BLANC; a little GEWÜRZTRAMINER; CHARDONNAY, which can be elegant in the cantons of Neuchâtel and Geneva, and richer in Vaud and Valais; and ALIGOTÉ, COMPLETER, SAUVIGNON BLANC, KERNER, and SÉMILLON.

PINOT NOIR, called Blauburgunder in German, is Switzerland's most widely planted red grape variety by far (and the most planted vine of any sort in German Switzerland), although the productive GAMAY is more important in Vaud and Geneva, and MERLOT reigns in Ticino to such an extent that it accounts for three-quarters of production. BONDOLA is a local red grape of Ticino, and SYRAH can produce a respectably ripe wine in sheltered parts of Valais such as Leytron and Chamoson.

A number of crossings have been developed as suitable for Switzerland's very particular growing conditions: FREISAMER, Charmont (Chasselas × Chardonnay), Gamaret and Garanoir (both Gamay × REICHENSTEINER), and, a Valais speciality, Diolinoir (Rouge de Diolly × Pinot Noir), of which some nurture great hopes.

But of most interest to students of AMPELOGRAPHY is Valais's rich collection of a dozen ancient indigenous varieties, each with substantial body, ageing potential, and its own whiff of history: the AMIGNE of Vétroz; the elegant PETITE ARVINE of Fully (now planted at MAS de Daumas Gassac in southern France); the powerfully scented HUMAGNE BLANCHE; the almost extinct RÈZE; and, among dark-skinned varieties, the noble CORNALIN DU VALAIS and the powerful HUMAGNE ROUGE. MARSANNE Blanche, also known as Ermitage, Muscat du Valais (MUSCAT BLANC À PETITS GRAINS), and Païen or Heida (SAVAGNIN Blanc) are also grown in Valais, the latter high up at Visperterminen.

The wine regions

The country's emerging appellation contrôlée system is applied by each canton individually.

Valais The 5,200 ha of productive vineyards of this south western canton produce 40 per cent of every Swiss vintage. Concentrated on the south-facing slopes of the sunny upper Rhône valley, the region is known as 'the California of Switzerland'. Many of these beautiful vineyards are terraced, some into so-called *tablars*, horizontal slices of vineyard cut into the mountainside, farmed as a part-time activity by 22,000 smallholders. Typical of what they produce is the ubiquitous FENDANT (made from the Chasselas grapes which cover one third of the *vignoble*), and medium-weight reds labelled either Pinot Noir or DÔLE, a blend in which Pinot Noir must dominate the Gamay element. (Dôle Blanche is made from a blend of Pinot Noir and Gamay grapes vinified as a white wine.)

Some of the most concentrated Sylvaners, sold here as JOHANNISBERG, come from particularly well-favoured sites at Chamoson. Petite Arvine of Fully is accorded the greatest respect, however, for its exotic intensity, while Cornalin du Valais and Humagne Rouge make some of Switzerland's most seriously age-worthy reds. Fine, sweet, late-harvest wines, made from Johannisberg (Sylvaner), Amigne, Ermitage (Marsanne), Malvoisie (Pinot Gris), and Petite Arvine picked in November and December, can easily reach 20 per cent POTENTIAL ALCOHOL. They may be described as FLÉTRI, or withered, a reference to partial raisining on the vine. Wines made from such indigenous varieties as Gwäss, Lafnetscha, Himbertscha, or Rèze are curiosities. VIN DES GLACIERS from the Val d'Anniviers above Sierre is another local rarity with a long tradition. Superior Valais producers include Marie Thérèse Chappaz, Jean-René Germanier, and Didier Joris.

Vaud Switzerland's second most important wine canton is also in French Switzerland, round the northern shore of lake Geneva, or lac Léman (almost everything has at least two names in Switzerland). The canton's six wine regions are La Côte, Lavaux, and Chablais on the north shore of lake Geneva, Les Côtes de l'Orbe on the plain between lakes Geneva and Neuchâtel, Bonvillars on lake Neuchâtel, and Vully on lake Morat. In all, 26 villages have their own appellation, and there are two GRANDS CRUS: Dézaley in the commune of Puidoux and Calamin in the commune of Epesses. Chasselas accounts for 70 per cent of the production from just under 3,900 ha, although, under the influence of the Vaud's varied soils, its character can vary from almost insultingly innocuous to an almost POUILLY-FUMÉ-like steeliness. In La Côte, the aromatic floral notes of the variety itself tend to dominate the wines. In Yvorne, Aigle, Bonvillars, and Calamin the mineral character of individual soils can easily dominate the fruit, while Dézaley and St-Saphorin often manage to demonstrate both fruit and minerals.

A little Chardonnay and Pinot Gris are also grown here. Red wines, especially Gamay, are a speciality of La Côte. Salvagnin, a designation accorded by a special tasting panel, approximates to a Vaud version of Valais' Dôle, although it can be made from Pinot Noir or Gamay or both. Similarly, Terravin is a Chasselas whose quality has a local seal of approval. Many of Switzerland's largest NÉGOCIANTS are based here.

The best producers include Domaine La Colombe, Pierre-Luc Leyvraz, and Bernard Ravet.

Geneva The 1,400 ha of vineyards around the city at the south western end of the lake are much flatter than those of Valais and Vaud and benefit from good sunlight, those next to the lake often escaping spring frost danger. Chasselas dominates, Riesling–Sylvaner is on the wane, while all manner of newcomers, including Chardonnay, Aligoté, Sauvignon, Sémillon, Kerner, Freisamer, Merlot, and even Cabernet Sauvignon, are increasingly popular with growers and consumers alike. Gamay is particularly successful here, whether as a well-structured red, a PRIMEUR, or a rosé. This was the birthplace of Switzerland's burgeoning appellation contrôlée laws. GAMARET and GARANOIR perform well here, and plantings of the former are expected to reach 100 ha by 2007. Reliable producers include Domaine des Balisiers, Charles and Jean-Michel Novelle of Le Grand Clos, Domaine Grand Cour, and Domaine du Paradis.

Neuchâtel Only 600 ha of the ancient CALCAR-EOUS soils, on the well-situated south-facing slopes above lake Neuchâtel, grow vines, but with characterful results. Chasselas as usual predominates, but Pinot Noir is also important, just as it is over the French border in the JURA. The pale pink Pinot Œil de Perdrix is a Neuchâtel invention. This was the first canton to restrict yields.

Eastern cantons In the 17 German-speaking cantons of Switzerland are 2,600 ha of vines, ranging from 0.2 ha in Nidwald to more than 600 ha in the canton of Zürich. Schaffhausen, effectively an outcrop into south BADEN in Germany, has nearly 500 ha of vines. Here in eastern Switzerland nearly 80 per cent of production is red wine, particularly the rot-resistant Mariafeld and 2-45 clones of Blauburgunder (Pinot Noir) and, to a lesser extent, the crossings Gamaret and Garanoir developed locally at the CHANGINS viticultural research station. Räuschling is once again gaining ground in Limmatal and on the shores of the lake south of Zürich, where Blauburgunder is often labelled Clevner. Riesling–Sylvaner (Müller-Thurgau) is the dominant white grape variety of eastern Switzerland, while Completer is a local speciality of Bündner Herrschaft near the border with Austria and Liechtenstein in Graubünden, where a small quantity of sweet Freisamer and serious red wine, mainly Blauburgunder, is also produced. Fromm, Gantenbein, and Schlossgut Bachtobel and some of the most effective producers.

Italian-speaking Switzerland There are just over 1,000 ha of vineyard in the southern canton of Ticino, and barely 30 ha over the border with Graubünden in the Italian-speaking Mesolcina valley. This makes Ticino Switzerland's fourth most important wine canton, and nearly 85 per cent of its production is of the Bordeaux red variety Merlot, imported in the first half of the 20th century. Here, vineyards lower than 450 m are sunny enough to ripen this variety, although higher vineyards may have to concentrate on Pinot Noir. Merlot del Ticino can be relatively light or, from well-sited vineyards and carefully vinified, often using new oak, can be a serious challenge for fine red bordeaux. Pale pink Merlot Bianco has also been popular. Sopraceneri, north of Monte Ceneri, is an important wine region of which the local red grape variety Bondola is a speciality. It tends to be included in the rustic local version of 'house wine' called Nostrano, or 'ours', as opposed to Americano, which may include the HYBRIDS and AMERICAN VINES still representing 7 per cent of total production here. Some of the most interesting producers are Castello Luigi, Castel San Pietro, Daniel Huber, Adriano Kaufmann, Werner Stucky, and Christian Zündel.

Other cantons The German-speaking but central canton of Berne has more than 200 ha of vines, mainly on the north shore of Lake Bienne, although there are some vines on the Thunersee west of Interlaken. On the southern shores of lake Neuchâtel are 100 ha of mainly Chasselas and Pinot Noir in the canton of Fribourg, most of them on the north shore of lake Morat. The Swiss canton of Jura also has a few hectares of vines.

Joris, D., *Connaissance des vins suisses* (Geneva, 1992).
Schweizer Weinführer (Bern, 2004).
Sloan, J. C., *The Surprising Wines of Switzerland* (London, 1995).

Sylvaner is the French name for the eastern European variety known in German as SILVANER (under which name details of all non-French plantings appear). In France, it is practically unknown outside ALSACE, where it was the most planted vine in the lower, flatter, more fertile vineyards of the Bas-Rhin until Riesling overtook it in the 1990s. A total of 1,900 ha/4,700 acres was planted in Alsace in 2000.

Sylvaner may be an old vine and, at one time, an extremely important one in Germany at least, but in Alsace many of the wines are dull, even if quite full bodied with good acidity (unlike many Pinot Blancs). Only specific TERROIRS and old vines manage to imbue Alsace Sylvaner with as exciting a character as the best FRANKEN Silvaners.

Sylvoz, a vine-TRAINING SYSTEM developed by the Italian grower Carlo Sylvoz in which canes of up to, say, ten buds in length are tied to a wire below a high CORDON. The vines can be trained with a high cordon, about 2 m/6.5 ft, or a mid height cordon at about 1 m. Depending on the number of buds retained, the system can be very high yielding. A variation of the Sylvoz is the Casarsa system common in northern Italy, where the canes are not tied below the cordon, but fall downward as a result of their own weight. The Sylvoz system is suited to vines of high vigour where it is necessary to minimize pruning labour.

R.E.S.

Eynard, I., and Dalmasso, G., *Viticoltura moderna: manuale pratico* (Milan, 1990).

Symingtons, dominant family of port wine shippers for four generations whose group of port companies includes W. & J. Graham, Warre, Dow's Port (Silva & Cosens), Quarles Harris, Quinta do Vesuvio, and Smith Woodhouse. They are also joint owners of Quinta de Roriz with their distant cousin João van Zeller. Founder of the family firm was Andrew James Symington, who arrived in Oporto from Glasgow in 1882 at the age of 19. Originally he joined the firm of Warre & Co., rising to become a partner. At the time George Warre was senior partner at Dow's, and in 1912 a swap took place whereby Symington took a share in Dow's while Warre regained a part of the firm that his family had founded. The Symingtons ran production and the vineyards for the two firms while the Warre family ran sales and marketing in London. The Warre family sold their remaining shareholding to the Symingtons in 1961. W. & J. Graham & Co. was purchased from the Graham family in 1970 along with the smaller sister company of Smith Woodhouse. The family owns Quinta do Bomfim near Pinhão, which provides much of the fruit for Dow's (along with Quinta da Senhorada Ribeira, acquired in 1998). It also owns Warre's Quinta da Cavadinha in the Pinhão valley and Graham's Quinta dos Malvedos at Tua. The group was instrumental

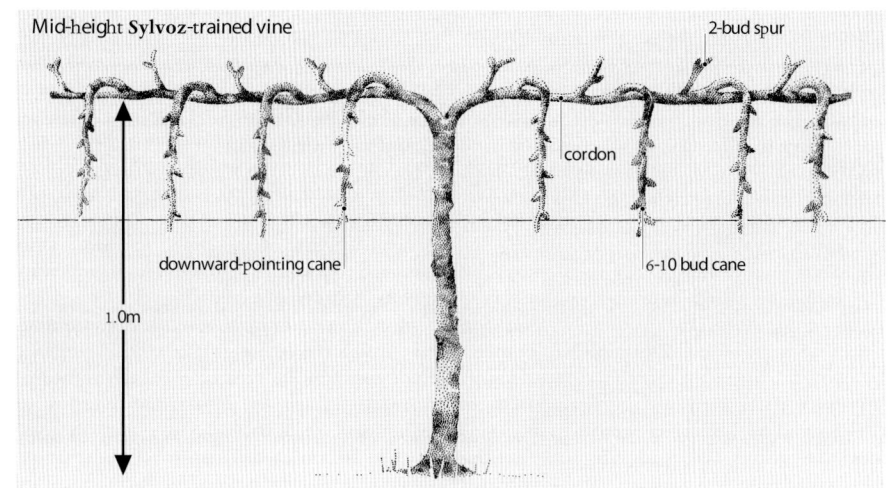

Mid-height **Sylvoz**-trained vine

2-bud spur

cordon

downward-pointing cane

6-10 bud cane

1.0m

in reviving interest in single-quinta ports in the late 1980s (see PORT, styles). In 1989 the Symingtons acquired Quinta do Vesúvio, a 400-ha/990-acre estate widely regarded as one of the finest vineyard sites in the Douro, but in need of some restoration (see FERREIRA). The vineyards have been extended and improved and, from 1992, Quinta do Vesúvio has been marketed as a brand in its own right. The family own substantial additional vineyards whose fruit is sold to their various different port companies. In 1988, the extensive Quinta do Marco plant in VILA NOVA DE GAIA was opened and it bottles more than 1.5 million cases of port annually. In 1996, a new winery, Quinta do Sol near Regua, was opened with an annual wine-making capacity of 6,000 PIPES, or 3.2 million litres, of port. Despite this integration, each company within the group has its own separate stocks and the group maintains a full range of vintage and wood ports for each company.

In 1988, the BLANDY family approached the Symingtons and offered a partnership in their MADEIRA business, hoping to reverse a general decline in sales of madeira. The Symingtons have since acquired a controlling interest in the Madeira Wine Company, an important producer of island-bottled madeira. Madeira brands held by the Blandy and Symington families include Blandy's, COSSART GORDON, Leacock, and Rutherford & Miles. The Symingtons have established their own import companies in Britain and the US.

The Symingtons have eventually become firm believers in DOURO table wines. Their flagship wine Chryseia is made jointly with Bruno Prats, past owner of Ch Cos d'Estournel of ST-ESTÈPHE. Red Douro single estate wines are made at Quinta de Roriz and sold under this name. There is also a standard quality Altano BRAND as well as an Altano Reserve.

S.A. & J.R.

Symphony, white-berried vine crossing of Grenache Gris and Muscat of Alexandria developed in CALIFORNIA at DAVIS by Dr H. P. Olmo. It lives the tenuous existence of all crossings, especially ones that make powerfully aromatic wines, although in the early 1990s it enjoyed a small vogue as an off-dry table wine something like a MALVASIA Bianca, and as a sparkling wine too. The state total had grown to more than 700 acres/280 ha by 2004.

symposium (meaning 'drinking together') was one of the most important social forms in the world of Ancient Greece, and was a considerably less cerebral affair than its 20th century counterpart. From Greece it spread to Etruria and the rest of Italy and flourished until the end of antiquity. Symposia were usually intimate gatherings: the room normally held seven or 11 couches, on each of which two men reclined on their left side, a custom adopted from oriental feasting; respectable women did not take part, and the servants and entertainers were mostly handsome slaves, both male and female. As part of the lifestyle of the leisured class, symposia were lavish affairs: in the richest households, the vessels for the mixing and drinking of wine would have been of gold or silver, although most will have been content with fine painted pottery. Both the shapes and the decoration of Greek pottery bear witness to the strong influence of the symposium.

The drinking of wine at the symposium followed the meal and was distinct from it, although a dessert of nuts, fruit, cakes, and the like often accompanied the wine. The end of the meal proper was marked by the drinking of a small amount of neat wine in honour of the 'Good Daemon' as a 'demonstration of the power of the good god', after which the tables were removed and the guests washed their hands and were offered garlands and perfumes. The wine was then mixed with water in a *krater* (mixing bowl; see CRATER) according to one of the numerous possible ratios (as detailed under Ancient GREECE). From each bowl,

a LIBATION was first offered together with a prayer (the god or gods invoked seem to have varied), and the Paean, a hymn of praise to Apollo, was also sung at the beginning of the proceedings by the whole company. A standard *krater* had a capacity of 14 l/3.7 gal, and various ancient writers indicate that three *kraters* would be emptied at a temperate symposium, so, although the alcoholic strength of the mixture was not high, the amount consumed must have been considerable (42 l for 14 or 22 people, apparently). The ratio for the dilution of the wine was determined by a *symposiarch* or master of ceremonies, chosen from the company, who also regulated the progress of the drinking: he could propose toasts, and order any member of the company to drink more, the aim being to maintain a level of pleasurable but controlled intoxication. However, since the drinking involved an element of competition, and since the proceedings might last all night, the outcome was often outright DRUNKENNESS, as VASE PAINTINGS and literary evidence make clear.

The most basic forms of entertainment arose out of the drinking itself: there were various drinking challenges with forfeits, and the heeltaps of wine were used to play the game of *kottabos*, in which each drinker would shoot the last drops of wine from his cup with a flick of the wrist at the target, which was usually a light bronze disc, balanced on top of a stand or tripod; when hit, it would fall into the basin beneath with a satisfying clatter.

Music and poetry played an important part in the entertainment: most, if not all, of the LYRIC POETRY of archaic Greece is now thought to have had its origins in the symposium, with its preoccupations of warfare and politics, wine and feasting, and love. Some extemporized poetry was no doubt sung at classical symposia, but it was more normal to perform existing poems, which often celebrated the great men and deeds of the past: the collection of Athenian songs of this type (*skolia*) preserved in ATHENAEUS' *Deipnosophistae* (694-96 BC) offers a sample of the traditional songs of one city.

Like the drinking, the singing was both communal and competitive: a branch of myrtle was passed round, and each man as he received it had to sing, sometimes picking up the song from the last singer, although good singers might be called on for a 'party piece'. Singers often accompanied themselves on the lyre, but slave girls were also hired to play the flute to entertain the company, to accompany singers, and to provide music for dancing, and professional dancers, acrobats, and mimes might also perform. Flute players would also be expected to provide sexual services at the end of the evening if required (hence the assumption that any women present at a symposium were not respectable).

Urbane and cultured conversation was also an essential feature; at times this might be structured, and given a competitive aspect, by the posing of riddles or the exchange of witty (and often abusive) comparisons applied to fellow guests. This too might be stimulated by professional help: the career of the parasite who pays for his dinner with his jokes and clowning can be traced back to HOMER. The genre of the literary symposium, a gathering of learned figures conversing on literary or philosophic issues, as in Plato's *Symposium* (whence the modern use of 'symposium'), may give a misleadingly high-minded impression of the average Greek symposium, but such discussion clearly had its place, albeit at a less rarefied level.

Finally, those revellers still awake might go out into the street as a *komos*, a mobile party with wine and music, calling on other symposia or making rowdy attempts to rouse those now asleep.   R.B.

Bibliographical note: O. Murray, 'The Greek Symposium in History', in E. Gabba (ed.), *Tria corda: scritti in onore di Arnaldo Momigliano* (Como, 1983), discusses historical and political aspects; O. Murray (ed.), *Sympotica* (Oxford, 1990) and O. Murray and M. Tecuşan, *In vino veritas* (Rome 1995) chs. 6–10 are collections of essays on particular aspects, with very full bibliographies, while J. Davidson, *Courtesans and Fishcakes* (London 1997), ch. 2, analyses Athenian attitudes to drinking. Athenaeus' *Deipnosophistae* collects many stories of symposia, while XENOPHON's *Symposium* gives the flavour of a classical symposium better than the more famous one of Plato; both are accessible in translation in the Loeb Classical Library.

synthetic closures, also known rather imprecisely as 'plastic corks', have proved popular with both consumers and producers. They satisfy the wine drinker's need to wrestle with a CORKSCREW while alleviating the risk of CORK TAINT but they have the disadvantage of not being biodegradable. It has proven surprisingly difficult to find synthetic materials that replicate the natural properties of cork in order to provide a tight seal while remaining easy enough to extract from the neck of the bottle. The first brands to establish a market presence, most notably Supremecorq and Integra, were based on a one-piece injection-moulded design. These early examples were hard to extract and almost impossible to reinsert. They also allowed too much oxygen transfer, making them suitable only for wines intended for early consumption. The better-performing synthetic closures now available are made by an extrusion process, some with a separate smooth plastic sleeve (Nomacorc and Neocork), some without. There are indications that these improved synthetics may also be suitable for wines intended for ageing. Another concern surrounds the capacity of synthetic closures to 'scalp' flavour by absorbing volatile components from the wine (see FLAVOUR SCALPING). Natural corks also do this but to a lesser extent. Synthetic closures continue to be popular because they are cheaper than all but the poorest quality natural corks and they do not require producers to adopt new bottles and BOTTLING LINES.

J.A.G.

Syrah, one of the noblest and currently most fashionable red wine grapes, if nobility is bestowed by an ability to produce serious red wines capable of ageing majestically for decades and if fashionability is measured by the extent to which new cuttings are currently going into the ground all over the world. So valued was the durability of France's HERMITAGE, arguably Syrah's finest manifestation, that many red bordeaux were in the 18th and 19th centuries *hermitagé* (see ADULTERATION AND FRAUD). And so popular has the variety become today that some estimates reckon it is the world's fifth most planted red wine grape with a total of 137,000 ha/338,000 acres.

Syrah's origins have been the subject of much debate and hypothesis, involving Syracuse in SICILIA, Ancient PERSIA (SHIRAZ being its most common synonym, especially in Australia), the vine family VITIS *allobrogica* recognized as producing fine wine in the Rhône since Roman times (see RHÔNE, history). DNA PROFILING at DAVIS and MONTPELLIER in 1998 however established that Syrah is in fact the progeny of two vines from southeast France, DUREZA and MONDEUSE BLANCHE.

The vine is relatively productive and disease resistant, sensitive to COULURE but conveniently late budding and not too late ripening. Care has to be taken with rootstocks because it is sensitive to CHLOROSIS. Its deep, dark, dense qualities are much reduced once the yield is allowed to rise and it has a tendency to lose aroma and acidity rapidly if left too long on the vine.

Many vignerons in the northern Rhône, Syrah's homeland, distinguish between a small-berried, superior version of Syrah, which they call Petite Syrah (not to be mistaken for the variety known in North and South America as PETITE SIRAH), and the larger-berried Grosse Syrah, which produces wines with a lower concentration of PHENOLICS. AMPELOGRAPHERS reject this distinction, although connoisseurs have reason to be grateful for it. The total ANTHOCYANINS in Syrah can be up to 40 per cent higher than those in the tough, dark Carignan, which makes it, typically, a wine for the long term that responds well to OAK maturation, even new oak when the grapes are really ripe.

The most famous prototype French Syrahs—Hermitage and CÔTE RÔTIE—are distinguished by their longevity or, in the case of newer producers, ambition. Only ST-JOSEPH and that paler shadow CROZES-HERMITAGE can sensibly be broached within their first five years. Syrah that has not reached full maturation can be simply mean and astringent, with more than a whiff of black pepper or burnt rubber. When planted on the fringes of the Rhône such as in the ARDÈCHE, Syrah may avoid this fate only in the ripest vintages.

Until the 1970s, French Syrah plantings were almost exclusively in and around the very limited vineyards of the northern Rhône valley and were dwarfed in area by total Syrah plantings in the vine's other major colony, Australia, where it is known as Shiraz and has been that country's major black grape variety for decades (see below).

Since then, however, Syrah has enjoyed an extraordinary surge in popularity throughout southern France so that total French plantings rose from 2,700 ha/6,670 acres in 1968 to exactly ten times that 20 years later and had reached 50,700 ha by the turn of the century. The increases were noticeable throughout the southern Rhône, particularly in Châteauneuf-du-Pape country, where Syrah has been increasingly valued as endowing Grenache with life expectancy, but have been most spectacular in Languedoc-Roussillon, where Syrah has been most enthusiastically adopted as an officially approved 'improving variety' that has added structure to wines both APPELLATION CONTRÔLÉE and VIN DE PAYS. By 1993, there were 24,000 ha in Languedoc-Roussillon alone (increased to 30,400 by 2000), and Syrah has frequently been responsible for the Midi's most successful varietal wines, usually labelled Vin de Pays d'Oc. Yields very much in excess of the low yields that characterize the arid hill of Hermitage have tended to dilute its northern Rhône characteristics in many cases, producing a much more supple, more obviously fruity, if still savoury, style of Syrah, often characterized by a particularly polished TEXTURE. In the northern Rhône it is rarely blended, except perhaps with a little Viognier (the original CO-FERMENTATION recipe), while in the south it is typically blended with Grenache, Mourvèdre, and perhaps Carignan and/or Cinsaut. In Provence, the very Australian blend of Syrah and Cabernet Sauvignon is relatively common, and Syrah is one of the most successful noble vine imports to Corsica, where there are several hundred hectares in production.

Shiraz, then known as Scyras, was probably taken to Australia, possibly from Montpellier, in 1832 by James BUSBY. It flourished so obviously that it was rapidly adopted by New South Wales and spread therefrom. Today Australian Shiraz can vary from a brown, baked, dilute everyday red to the glorious, almost porty concentration of Australia's most famous wine, Penfolds Grange. For more details, see SHIRAZ.

Another unexpectedly successful site for mature, concentrated Syrah is Valais in Switzerland, particularly around the suntrap village of Chamoson on the upper reaches of the Rhône valley. Here classic northern Rhône techniques are employed, sometimes to great effect. Italy too is increasingly planting Syrah, most successfully so far around Cortona in southern Toscana. The variety was initially introduced from MONTPELLIER, in 1899 in Piemonte. Spain had nearly 3,000 ha planted in 2004 with particular success both in Toledo and Manchuela. In Portugal, it is planted in the Alentejo and also in the Ribatejo and Estremadura, with experimental plantings in the Douro.

To ripen fully, Syrah demands a warm climate, which has imposed some limits on its spread, but it has been particularly successful in California, both in Napa and Sonoma and, particularly, in warmer parts of the Central Coast. Californians were slow to distinguish between true Syrah and PETITE SIRAH and even slower to import suitable plant material so that, despite a modishness achieved thanks to the RHÔNE RANGERS, there were still barely 400 acres of it in the state in 1992 but by 2003 there were 17,000 acres/6,800 ha. For more details, see CALIFORNIA.

Promising results from such vineyards as Red Willow, Cayuse, Boushey, and various Red Mountain vineyards suggest that WASHINGTON state may have considerable potential for fine, bright Syrah wines. In 1999, only a handful of Washington Syrahs were produced. Just six years later, Syrah was being made by some of the state's most respected producers, as well as by some specialist newcomers passionately committed to the grape. Syrah has become markedly fashionable in Washington, with many producers releasing fine examples. Total acreage surpassed 2,400 acres/970 ha in 2005, and threatens to surpass Cabernet Sauvignon and even possibly the venerable Merlot with time.

South Africa's total of this variety, usually called Shiraz except for examples deliberately fashioned in a Rhône rather than New World style, has increased dramatically since the mid 1990s. In 1995, it represented 1 per cent of the total area of vineyard. By 2003, this proportion had risen to 7.7 per cent, or 8,100 ha/ 19,900 acres. While most of these plantings tend to be concentrated around Stellenbosch and Paarl, Shiraz now comprises 18 per cent of the vineyard area of Malmesbury, 11 per cent of Robertson and Olifants River, and 12.6 per cent of Worcester. Wines produced from the new, virus-free clones have begun to enjoy international recognition.

Much of New Zealand is too cool for Syrah but plantings have increased to well over 200 ha in the North Island, chiefly Hawkes Bay.

CHILE has shown considerable potential with its Syrah, of which about 2,500 ha had been planted by the mid 2000s. The wines are rich and dense, and have presumably inspired such imitation as is so far evident on the other side of the Andes, where total Argentine plantings grew from fewer than 1,000 ha in 1990 to 9,500 ha by 2002. It is not far-fetched to suggest that Syrah/Shiraz may soon be as popularly familiar a name as Cabernet.

'La Syrah', supplement to *Le Vigneron des Côtes du Rhône et du Sud-Est* (1992), 341.

Norman, R., *Rhône Renaissance* (London, 1995).

Syria, country in the Middle East with a declining total area of vineyard but still 56,000 ha/138,000 acres in 2002 according to OIV. Vines have been dedicated to the production of TABLE GRAPES and DRYING GRAPES rather than wine since the rise of Islamic fundamen-

talism in the late 1970s (see ISLAM). Average annual Syrian wine production in the late 1970s was 63,000 hl/1.6 million gal but fell to 8,000 hl in the early 1980s and was too small to register on OIV's statistics by the early 21st century.

Syria has a particularly long history of wine production, however (see ORIGINS OF VITICULTURE). See also MESOPOTAMIA.

Szekszárd, wine region in southern HUNGARY with a special LOESS soil as deep as 10 to 15 m in places. The landscape is very varied which allows different MESOCLIMATES to shape the wines. The Szekszárd hill is 100–120 m high on average. The steep slopes are dissected by erosional valleys and ravines with the eastern and southern slopes generally providing the best wines. The KADARKA grape, once the chief component of Bikavér, made Szekszárd's viticulture famous in the 18th and 19th centuries but its attractively scented, relatively soft wine is today made only on a very small scale. Villány may be more famous for reds but Szekszárd vines need a shorter ripening period. Kékfrankos, Merlot, and Cabernet Franc are grown widely in the region. Olaszrizling and Chardonnay are the chief white grapes but the white wines here can lack acidity.   G.R. & G.M.

Szürkebarát, Hungarian name for PINOT GRIS, which is quite widely planted there; but its naturally low acidity can result in slightly flabby wines, particularly on the Great plain. It is most revered within HUNGARY as Badacsonyi Szürkebarát, a rich, heavy, sometimes traduced, wine from the north shore of lake Balaton. It can yield livelier wines from Mátra.

TA. See TOTAL ACIDITY.

table grapes, the common term for those grapes specially grown to be eaten as fresh fruit. Of the grapes grown worldwide, table grapes represent the third most frequent use, following wine and dried grapes. About 16 million tonnes are grown each year. The most important producing countries are China, Iran, Turkey, Italy, India, and Egypt. The fruit is consumed primarily within the producing country because it is relatively low in value and perishable. However, with refrigeration the opportunities for export are increasing and Chile, for example, has developed a substantial export trade in table grapes over the last three decades.

The varieties of grapes for fresh consumption are usually specialized and different from those for wine and drying. They should taste good, have a reasonably consistent BERRY SIZE, bright colour, firm flesh texture, not too many seeds, and skins tough enough to withstand storage and transport. Recently developed seedless varieties are increasingly popular. Some important table grape varieties are Barlinka, Calmeria, CARDINAL, CHASSELAS, Dattier, Emperor, Flame Seedless, Gros Vert, Italia, MUSCAT OF ALEXANDRIA, MUSCAT HAMBURG, Perlette, Ruby Seedless, Ribier, and SULTANA (or Thompson Seedless).

Table grapes are typically grown in warm to hot regions to encourage early maturity and freedom from any ROT brought on by rain. Low night temperatures assist the colour development of some varieties, while both very high and very low day temperatures may inhibit colour development. Many of the table grape regions of the world are inland DESERT areas.

There are some important differences between table grape and wine grape vineyard management. For table grapes, the aim is generally to produce maximum berry size, and so IRRIGATION and FERTILIZERS are used more liberally than for wine grapes. Sloping and overhead trellis systems such as the pergola and TENDONE are common, where the shoots and leaves form a canopy over the fruit, avoiding excessive and direct sun exposure (see SUNBURN).

Because they are worth more than most wine grapes (although see Ch d'YQUEM, MONTRACHET, and DOMAINE DE LA ROMANÉE-CONTI), table grapes typically require more manual vineyard work. This can include SHOOT THINNING, CROP THINNING, and sometimes berry thinning. These practices lead to larger berries which ripen early. GROWTH REGULATORS are also commonly used to thin flowers, but more particularly to increase berry size of seedless varieties such as Sultana. CINCTURING or girdling can also be used to hasten ripening.

Table grapes are harvested earlier than wine grapes as a lower sugar level and higher acidity make them taste more refreshing, in the range of 15 to 18 °BRIX (whereas wine grapes would preferably be harvested for dry wines at about 22 °Brix).

Some table grape varieties can be kept in cool stores for up to 20 weeks, although eight to 12 weeks is more common. Long storage life is promoted by low temperatures such as 21 °C (at which the sugar content stops them freezing), a relative humidity of about 96 per cent, and SULFUR DIOXIDE fumigation for mould control. R.E.S.

Table grapes are used widely by the emerging wine industries of ASIA.

table wine, term used internationally to distinguish wines of average ALCOHOLIC STRENGTH from FORTIFIED WINES, which have been strengthened by the addition of alcohol. In this context, 'table wines' rely solely on FERMENTATION for their ALCOHOLIC STRENGTH, which tends to be between 9 and 15 per cent.

Within the EUROPEAN UNION, however, the term 'table wine' has a specific meaning and is applied to the vast but declining quantity of wine produced within it that does not qualify as superior QUALITY WINE.

Within France, table wine is known as VIN DE TABLE. The distinct and superior category is VIN DE PAYS.

Within Italy, the situation is rather different. Although all of Italy's most basic wine (and there is a great deal of it) is designated vino da tavola, that designation has also been used in its time, confusingly, by a considerable number of the best producers for some of their best wines, notably SUPERTUSCANS (see VINO DA TAVOLA for more details). Italy also has an embryonic counterpart to France's vin de pays, IGT, but by far the largest part of Italian wine is designated vino da tavola.

The reverse is the case in Germany, where less than 5 per cent of total production is deemed to be Deutscher Tafelwein or its superior category LANDWEIN. See below, however.

Spain's table wine—and some new wines made in the image of SUPERTUSCANS outside the official quality wine system—are called VINO DE MESA. Spain also has a small superior category, VINO DE LA TIERRA.

Portugal's table wine is known as VINHO de mesa and its even more nascent superior subcategory is IPR.

Greek table wine is called epitrapezios oinos within Greece and is rarely exported.

Most of Luxembourg's wine qualifies as quality wine, and the rest is called vin de table. See also ENGLAND.

Within the EU, table wines from different countries may be freely blended to produce **European table wine**. This is particularly common in Germany, where it may be called EWG Tafelwein, or simply Tafelwein. Within France, however, a significant proportion of France's considerable imports from Italy and, more recently, Spain, are blended with French vin de table to produce a Vin de Table des Pays Différentes de l'EU.

In the US, the term table wine denotes wine less than 14 per cent alcohol while wines between 14 and 24 per cent alcohol are officially 'dessert wines' whether fortified or not.

Tâche, La, great red GRAND CRU in Burgundy's CÔTE D'OR. For more details, see VOSNE-ROMANÉE and DOMAINE DE LA ROMANÉE-CONTI.

Tacoronte-Acentejo, DO wine region on the west-facing slopes in the north east of the volcanic island of Tenerife in the CANARY ISLANDS. Tacoronte-Acentejo produces red wines made predominantly from the dark-berried LISTÁN Negro and Negramoll grapes. The volcanic soil imparts a peculiar character to these improving wines.   R.J.M. & V. de la S.

taille, French term for PRUNING and also, by extension, for vine-TRAINING SYSTEM. The name is also used in CHAMPAGNE and sometimes elsewhere for the coarser, later juice which flows from the press in the traditional method of SPARKLING WINE-MAKING.

Taiwan, otherwise known as the Republic of China, island off, and independent of, CHINA. The progressive dismantling of the government alcohol MONOPOLY following Taiwan's accession to the World Trade Organization in 2001 now allows private companies to make wine. Among the many new ventures producing a diverse range of FRUIT WINES is a small number combining grapes and other fruits in various wine confections. Domaine Shu-Sheug, established by a grower who previously supplied grapes to the monopoly, produces red wines from Black Queen grapes and an 'ice' wine from Golden Muscat.   D.G.

Tajikistan, mountainous, ex-Soviet, central Asian republic between UZBEKISTAN and China producing only about 60,000 hl of wine from 36,000 ha of vineyards in 2002 according to the OIV. Lowlands, plateaux, foothills, and mountain slopes suitable for viticulture occupy only 7 per cent of Tajikistan's area. The climate of the country is CONTINENTAL. In the lowlands and valleys at 900 m/2,950 ft above sea level, the average January temperature is 2 to −3 °C/27 °F and the average July temperature is 26 to 31 °C, while the annual rainfall is 150 mm to 600 mm/23 in. On the foothills, at an altitude of 1,000 m to 1,500 m, the average January temperature varies from 0 to −5 °C, that of July is 23 to 25 °C, and the annual rainfall is 350 to 850 mm.

Viticulture and wine-making were developed in Tajikistan even before the military campaigns of Alexander the Great in the 4th century BC. Ancient documents testify to the cultivation of numerous VINE VARIETIES in the country, which were made into wine, vinegar, and *bekmes* (CONCENTRATED GRAPE

MUST), as well as being traded as TABLE GRAPES and RAISINS. Viticulture was highly developed in Osrushan in Ura-Tyube, Fergana, and in the Zeravshan river valley.

The adoption of ISLAM in the north prohibited the consumption of wine and changed the country's range of grape varieties. Wine varieties were grubbed up and table and raisin varieties were planted in their place. Central, south, and south eastern parts of the country were also affected by this trend but to a lesser extent. In the 1920s, small private vineyards were amalgamated to form large farms, and the total vineyard area continued to increase in order to meet the needs of commercial wine production. The first state farms specializing in viticulture were established and wineries in the towns of Ura-Tyube, Leninabad, and Pendzhikent were built.

In 1940, the total vineyard area was 8,200 ha/20,250 acres, with the gross yield of grapes being 49,000 tons and the grape wine production accounting for 27,900 hl/736,500 gal. Thereafter, the raw material base of the industry and grape-processing facilities continued to increase.

Tajikistan can be divided into three viticultural zones: the Leninabad region in the north, the Ghissar valley in the centre, and the Vakhsh valley together with the Kuliab regions in the south. Although most vines are trained into fan-shaped TRAINING SYSTEMS with numerous canes on vertical trellises and high-trunked forms, several areas still have vines trained to horizontal trellises. Most vineyards need WINTER PROTECTION, and irrigated vineyards account for 75 per cent of the total.

In the 1990s, 25 grape varieties were in commercial cultivation, with ten wine varieties such as RKATSITELI, SAPERAVI, CABERNET SAUVIGNON, RIESLING, Tagobi, Bayan Shirey, and Muscat Rosé. The 20 wineries of Tajikistan (including four secondary vinification enterprises) in the early 1990s produced more than 50 brands of wine, most of them strong and sweet.   V.R.

Kirillov, I. F., Brodnikovski, M. I., Savchenko, A. D., and Podkolzin, I. V., *Viticulture of Tajikistan* (Russian) (Dushanbe, 1969).

Kiselev, N. A., *Viticultural Regions and Wines of Tajikistan* (Russian) (Moscow, 1967).

Savchenko, A. D., 'The Soviet Socialist Republic of Tajikistan' (Russian), in A. I. Timush (ed.), *Encyclopaedia of Viticulture* (Kishinëv, 1986).

Talia, occasionally written **Thalia**, Portuguese name for the ubiquitous white grape variety known in France as UGNI BLANC and in Italy as TREBBIANO.

Tamarez, Alentejo name for the Portuguese white grape TRINCADEIRA DAS PATRAS.

Tamar River, wine region in TASMANIA.

Tămâioasă, name for MUSCAT grape or wine in ROMANIA. Thus **Tămâioasă Alba** is

Romanian for MUSCAT BLANC À PETITS GRAINS, **Tămâioasă Hamburg** or **Tămâioasă Neagră** is MUSCAT HAMBURG, **Tămâioasă Ottonel** is MUSCAT OTTONEL. **Tămâioasă Românească** is another Romanian synonym for Muscat Blanc à Petits Grains, and there were more than 600 ha planted in Romania in 2005. It is also grown in Bulgaria as **Tamianka**.

Taminga, grape variety bred specifically for AUSTRALIAN conditions (see also TARRANGO) by A. J. Antcliff. Taminga is capable of ripening and producing white wine of fair quality in a wide variety of different sites with an average yield of 90 hl/ha (5 tons/acre).

Tamyanka, Russian name for MUSCAT BLANC À PETITS GRAINS.

tank method, alternative name for a bulk SPARKLING WINE-MAKING process which involves provoking a second fermentation in wine stored in a pressure tank. Other names include Charmat process and *cuve close*.

tanks. See CONTAINERS.

Tannat, distinctive, tough, deep black-berried vine variety most famous as principal ingredient in MADIRAN, where its inherent astringence is mitigated by blending with Cabernet Franc, some Cabernet Sauvignon, and FER, and wood ageing for at least 20 months. If Madiran is Tannat's noblest manifestation, slightly more approachable, if more rustic, wines are made to much the same recipe for Côtes de ST-MONT, as well as for the distinctively hard reds and rosés of IROULÉGUY and the rare reds and pinks labelled TURSAN and BÉARN.

Although it can also be found as a minor ingredient in such wines as Côtes du BRULHOIS, overall plantings in France have been declining so that there were fewer than 3,000 ha/7,400 acres by 1988 and just 2,760 ha in 2000. Although it may owe its French name to its high tannin content, the vine is almost certainly Basque in origin and, like MANSENG, was taken to URUGUAY by Basque settlers in the 19th century, where it is by far the most important vine variety and, rather like MALBEC in ARGENTINA, seems to thrive better in the warmer climate of its new home in South American than SOUTH WEST FRANCE. In Uruguay, where it has been called Harriague after its original promulgator, there are several thousand hectares, and strategies for softening the grapes' tannins include blending with such grapes as Pinot Noir and Merlot as well as all the usual winemaking techniques (see MACERATION in particular). Port and Beaujolais styles have also been made from it. From Uruguay it spread to Argentina, where it is still grown to a very limited extent and we can probably expect to see Tannat in many more wine regions. It had a presence in California by the early 2000s.

tannins, diverse and complex group of chemical compounds that occur in the bark of many trees and in fruits, including the grape. Strictly speaking, a tannin is a compound that is capable of interacting with PROTEINS and precipitating them; this is the basis of the process of tanning animal hides (hence the name tannin) and is also a process that is believed to be responsible for the sensation of ASTRINGENCY. Tannins in wine come predominantly from the grapes and, to a much lesser extent, from the WOOD in which the wine is aged. See also OAK FLAVOURS.

The natural tannins of grapes, or condensed tannins, also called PROANTHOCYANIDINS since they release red anthocyanidin pigments when heated in acidic media, are FLAVONOIDS consisting of oligomers and polymers of CATECHINS. Formation of proanthocyanidins occurs under the control of ENZYMES as part of the metabolism of the grape but they may rearrange to longer or shorter molecules in the acidic wine medium. Other catechin polymers can be formed in wine as a result of enzymatic or chemical oxidation reactions. These polymeric flavonoids that can range from colourless through light yellow to amber, as well as PIGMENTED TANNINS resulting from reactions of anthocyanins with catechins and tannins, may also be regarded as tannins. Wine may also contain hydrolysable tannins, deriving from gallic acid and ellagic acid, extracted from oak cooperage in the course of barrel ageing, from OAK CHIPS, or added as OENOLOGICAL TANNINS.

Tannins play an important role in the AGEING of wine, particularly red wines, where pigmented tannins are crucial to the colour and sensory properties. Handling tannins during RED WINE-MAKING is one of the most critical steps in optimizing the quality and character of a red wine, yet the process is based almost totally on experience and intuition because of our understanding of the principles involved is still rudimentary.

The tannins in grapes are predominantly in the SKINS and SEEDS of each berry and also the STEMS, the amount of tannins in grape pulp being relatively insignificant. Thus, the more skins, seeds, and stems are involved in the wine-making process, the higher the possible resultant level of tannins. Tannin levels in white and rosé wines, which are made largely by excluding or minimizing these grape components, are therefore lower than in reds. Although white wines have similar structures to the pigmented tannins of a red wine, the absence of ANTHOCYANINS condensed into the tannins of white wines accounts for how different they look.

Tannins are most often encountered by the human palate in over-steeped tea, and by wine drinkers in young reds designed for a long life in bottle and in whites made with excessive SKIN CONTACT. They produce the taste sensation of bitterness and the physical tactile 'dry-ing' sensation of astringency. Catechins and small tannins are responsible for bitterness, while larger ones elicit the astringency sensation, presumably by interaction with the proteins on the tongue and insides of the cheek.

Traditional methods for measuring tannins report them as if they were all gallic acid, and such analyses, including the widely used Folin Ciocalteu method, are popular because of their analytical convenience. Alternative methods for measuring the phenolic compounds of grape tannins more directly and as other than gallic acid are time consuming and require considerable analytical expertise. Gallic acid or GA equivalent concentration averages about 300 mg/l in white wines, but 1,800 mg/l in reds. The tannin types and their extraction rates vary considerably with VINE VARIETY and WINE-MAKING methods. Varieties notably high in tannins include CABERNET SAUVIGNON, NEBBIOLO, SYRAH, and TANNAT.

Since the late 1980s, much research into red wine-making has been aimed at minimizing the bitter and astringent impression made by tannins on the palate while enhancing the TEXTURE and ageing properties which they confer on a wine. These studies have involved, among other variations, ever more refinement of MACERATION techniques and deliberately controlled exposure to OXYGEN at various points during the wine-making process (see MICRO-OXYGENATION, for example). It is also widely recognized that the influence of such viticultural factors as grape RIPENESS and grape composition on the properties of tannins is not yet understood. Of the many institutions involved in chemical studies of tannins, the INRA station at MONTPELLIER is notable and scientists there have made considerable advances in determining the structures of grape tannins and understanding the chemical reactions affecting phenolics in the course of wine-making.

Different WOOD TYPES contain different sorts of tannins, but these have most effect on wine when the COOPERAGE is new. The tannins of the various species and varieties of OAK, the most common wood used in wine-making, vary among themselves, and according to how the oak was seasoned (see BARREL MAKING). Oak tannins differ in significant ways from grape tannins, although the consequences of such differences on the stability of wine colour and on the sensory properties (including mouthfeel) of barrel-matured red wines in particular are yet to be scientifically rationalized. For more details, see OAK FLAVOUR. Wine consumers have come to expect a certain amount of wood oak flavour in a wide range of wines, including some relatively immature wines, both red and white, whether the result of genuine BARREL MATURATION or the use of OAK CHIPS. They are therefore often exposed to the effects of tannin on the palate, which can be considerably mitigated by the right choice of accompanying FOOD.

Winemakers can adjust excessively high tannin levels by FINING with casein, gelatin, or albumin, which selectively precipitate large-sized astringent tannins. Formation of soluble complexes with macromolecules such as proteins and POLYSACCHARIDES may also prevent tannins from interacting with salivary proteins and eliciting astringency. Given sufficient time, tannins are removed naturally, however, during wine ageing. The tannins polymerize and form aggregates that eventually precipitate as SEDIMENT so that they no longer have any bitter or astringent effect on the palate. Depending on the wine composition and pH, reactions of tannins can also yield smaller tannins and pigmented tannins, thus resulting in lower astringency.

See also OENOLOGICAL TANNINS, which may be deliberately added in the course of wine-making to increase a wine's tannin level.

A.D.W., P.J.W., & V.C.

Cheynier, V., and Fulcrand, H., 'Analysis of proanthocyanidins and complex polyphenols', in C. Santos-Buelga and G. Williamson (eds.), *Methods in Polyphenol Analysis* (London, 2003), 282.

Tasting tannins

Tannins cannot be smelt or tasted; they cause tactile sensations. A significant development of the 1990s was a keener appreciation of the different sorts of sensory impact of tannins on the palate (see TEXTURE). In Australia, this has led in particular to the development of a MOUTHFEEL wheel rather like the AROMA WHEEL, and American tasters can sometimes seem more preoccupied by a wine's texture than its flavour. Tannins may be variously described as hard, bitter (if accompanied by BITTERNESS), green, ripe (if perceptible but only after the impact of fruit that has reached PHYSIOLOGICAL RIPENESS has been felt on the palate), coarse, grainy, wood (if obviously the effect of CASK AGEING), long chain (an American expression for POLYMERIZED), short chain, and polymerized. This is clearly an area in which considerably more scientific rigour will be applied.

Cheynier, V., Prieur, C., Guyot, S., Rigaud, J., and Moutounet, M., 'The structure of tannins in grapes and wines and their interactions with proteins', in T. Watkins (ed.), *Wine: Nutritional and Therapeutic Benefits* (Washington, DC, 1997).

Noble, A. C., 'Astringency and bitterness of flavonoid phenols', in P. Given and D. Paredes (eds.), *Chemistry of Taste: Mechanisms, Behaviors, and Mimics* (Washington, 2002), 192–201.

Vidal, S., Francis, L., Noble, A., Kwiatkowski, M., Cheynier, V., and Waters, E., 'Taste and mouth-feel properties of different types of tannin-like polyphenolic compounds and anthocyanins in wine', *Analytica Chimica Acta*, 513/1 (2004), 57–65.

Tanzania. German settlers planted vines just south of mount Kilimanjaro in the 1930s and an ambitious vine nursery was established by another German in the 1980s. Today Tanganyika Vineyards produce serviceable

Chenin Blanc and a red from two grape harvests a year.

Platter, J. & E., *Africa Uncorked* (London, 2002).

Tarragona, Mediterranean port in Spanish CATALUÑA which has played an important part in a flourishing wine industry since Roman times (see SPAIN, history, and map). Until the 1960s, wines called Tarragona were predominantly sweet, red, fortified, and drunk as a cheap alternative to PORT. Awarded DO status in 1976, Tarragona continues to ship communion wine all over the Christian world (see EUCHARIST). Over 70 per cent of Tarragona's wine production today is white, however, a large proportion of which is sold to the CAVA houses in PENEDÈS. Many of the best unfortified reds, made in the fashionable style of neighbouring PRIORAT by such producers as Josep Anguera and the Capçanes CO-OPERATIVE, are now part of the separate MONTSANT DO created in 2001.   V. de la S. & J.R.

Tarrango, red wine grape variety developed at Merbein in AUSTRALIA in 1965. The aim of this TOURIGA × SULTANA crossing was to provide a slow-ripening variety suitable for the production of light-bodied wines with low TANNINS and relatively high ACIDITY. As a result, some Australian wines have been fashioned in the image of BEAUJOLAIS but the variety will ripen satisfactorily only in the hot irrigated wine regions of Australia such as the RIVERLAND. Brown Brothers of Milawa have been particularly persistent with this variety, planted on almost 200 ha in Australia in the mid 2000s. Other varieties developed by A. J. Antcliff specifically for Australian conditions included Carina and Merbein Seedless for drying and Tulillah, Goyura, and TAMINGA for white wines.

tartaric acid, the most important of the ACIDS found in grapes and wine. Of all the natural organic acids found in plants, this is one of the rarer. The grape is the only fruit of significance that is a tartrate accumulator, and yet it is of critical importance to the winemaker because of the major part it plays in the taste of the wine. Furthermore, because tartaric acid exists in wine partially as the intact acid and partially as the acid tartrate, or bitartrate ion, it is the principal component of the mixture of acids and salts that constitutes wine's all-important buffer system (see BUFFERING CAPACITY) and maintains the stability of its ACIDITY and COLOUR.

Tartaric acid is of further interest because its potassium acid salt, potassium tartrate or cream of tartar, while being moderately soluble in grape juice, is only partially soluble in alcoholic solutions such as wine. Most winemakers therefore try to ensure that no excess tartrates remain in the wine when it is bottled lest these crystals frighten less sophisticated consumers by their resemblance to glass

shards. See TARTRATES for more on this important by-product of the wine-making process.

Grapes and the resultant wines vary considerably in their concentrations of tartaric acid. Among the thousands of cultivated VINE VARIETIES, some are noted for their high concentrations of tartaric acid, while others are remarkably bland. In general, wine grapes have higher concentrations of acids than table grapes. Among wine grape varieties, however, there is considerable variation in concentrations of the two principal acids: tartaric acid and MALIC ACID. Palomino, the sherry grape, for example, is particularly high in tartaric acid, while the Pinot Noir of Burgundy and Malbec, or Côt, are relatively low in tartaric.

The relative amounts of these two acids that are present in grapes do not necessarily govern the relative amounts in wines, however. Precipitation of potassium acid tartrate, as outlined above, limits total tartaric acid concentration, while malic acid is frequently decomposed by MALOLACTIC FERMENTATION. Wines that have not undergone this secondary fermentation generally have slightly more tartaric acid than malic acid, while those which have undergone this 'softening' process usually have many more times tartaric than malic acid; they are also more stable.

Weather and soil, as well as grape variety, affect the amounts of different acids in the grape and wine. Cooler climates in general favour higher concentrations of acids and lower levels of POTASSIUM in the grape skins. Malic acid is much more effectively decomposed by excessive heat during the grape ripening period than is tartaric acid. Soils deficient in potassium, or potash, may result in grapes of high acid concentration and low PH because low potassium levels allow greater concentrations of acid tartrate ion to stay in solution. Another curious difference is that tartrate levels are very high in grape flowers. Tartaric acid is not respired during ripening, meaning that its amount per berry stays relatively constant during berry RIPENING. More than half of the tartrate in ripe berries can be present as a salt. The proportion of free to salt form varies with variety and the concentration of metal cations in the juice; potassium is by far the most abundant.   A.D.W. & B.G.C.

tartrates, the general term used by winemakers to describe the harmless crystalline deposits that separate from wines during FERMENTATION and AGEING. In English the substances are also called argols, in French *tartres* and in German *Weinsteine* (literally, 'wine stones'). The principal component of this deposit is potassium acid tartrate, the potassium salt of TARTARIC ACID, which has therefore given rise to the name. Small amounts of pulp debris, dead yeast cells, precipitated phenolic materials such as TANNINS and PIGMENTED TANNINS, and traces of other materials

make up the impurities contaminating the potassium acid tartrate (see SEDIMENT).

The LEES, the thick layer of dead yeast and grape skins, seeds, and pulp fragments that sinks to the bottom of the FERMENTATION VESSEL during the later stages of fermentation as deposit, contains lower concentrations of tartrates than do the crystalline deposits that form on the walls of the vessel. Lees are a commercial source of tartrates, but extraction and purification of potassium acid tartrate from lees is much more expensive and time consuming than from the crystalline deposits on walls, the preferred source for commercial tartrates.

The main forms of tartrates used commercially are pure crystalline tartaric acid used as an acidulant in non-alcoholic drinks and foods, cream of tartar (pure potassium acid tartrate) used in baking, and Rochelle salt (potassium sodium tartrate) used mainly in electroplating solutions. The wine industry is the only source of tartrates available to commerce and the crystalline encrustations left inside fermentation vessels are therefore regularly scraped off and purified for eventual commercial use.

Tartrates separate from new wines because potassium acid tartrate is less soluble in solutions of alcohol and water such as wine than it is in plain water, or grape juice. The exact figures for wines vary slightly according to grape variety and region, but experience shows that about a half of the tartrate soluble in grape juice is insoluble in wine. The problem is that the tartrate may remain in a supersaturated state in the complex wine mixture only to crystallize at some unpredictable later time.

Only the most informed consumers appreciate the harmlessness of tartrate crystals in bottle. Although tartrates precipitated in red wines usually take on some red or brown colouring from adsorbed wine pigments and are commonly regarded as mere sediment, in white wines they can look alarmingly like shards of glass to the uninitiated. The modern wine industry has in the main decided that tartrate STABILIZATION is preferable to consumer education.

Tartrate instability was recognized as a problem only in the 19th century when, with greater wine production and standardization of BOTTLE production, bottle-aged wines first became common. Previously wines were not expected to be perfectly clear and many would routinely be strained, but producers of most modern wines, and all inexpensive white wines, believe that their customers expect a brilliantly clear liquid to emerge from the bottle, no matter how long it has been there.

With the efficient degrees of FILTRATION possible today, it is relatively easy to ensure perfect clarity immediately prior to BOTTLING. The problem is to ensure that the wine will remain clear. Historically, wines were stabilized against tartrate precipitation by letting the cellar cool to temperatures near or below freezing during the winter. Low temperatures for three to four months would usually remove so much potassium acid tartrate that further precipitation was unlikely. The modern equivalent is to use REFRIGERATION to chill the wine before bottling to between −5 and −10 °C/24 to 14 °F for two to three weeks. Precipitated tartrate crystals are then filtered from the cold wine before it is warmed back to cellar temperature. Sometimes small amounts of finely divided CHARCOAL or BENTONITE clay are mixed into the wine to be chilled to act as nucleation centres for the supersaturated potassium acid tartrate and therefore induce crystal formation. A more recent and faster technique involves the stirring up of finely ground potassium acid tartrate in the wine, which is then cooled to a low temperature and the cold wine and crystal mixture immediately filtered. This method depends on the rapid crystallization of tartrates from the wine on the millions of fine crystals added that act as nucleation centres. This method saves both time and power. See also ELECTRODIALYSIS.

Metatartaric acid, produced by heating tartaric acid, is used widely in the UK and occasionally in Germany at a maximum level of 100 mg/l. Its use is permitted in Australia and elsewhere but it is not very popular because it is effective only for a matter of months. Metatartaric acid dissolves in wine and inhibits the formation of tartrate crystals. However, it is unstable and reverts to tartaric acid within 3–18 months (depending on temperature), with the risk of yet more tartrate crystals.

Some everyday wines produced in large quantities contain enough calcium to cause precipitation of calcium tartrate during bottle ageing, although this was most common in the era of the concrete tank. When the concrete tanks were new, or had had their protective coating of tartrates removed, wine dissolved enough calcium carbonate from the concrete surface to cause subsequent calcium tartrate instability. Stainless steel tanks, or lined concrete ones, have largely overcome the problem of calcium tartrate instability.

Tartrates are most commonly encountered in bottles of German wine because, coming from a relatively cool region, they have the greatest concentration of tartaric acid. In white wines, colourless, perfectly shaped crystals of potassium acid tartrate are found. In red wines, there are usually sufficient adsorbed TANNINS and PIGMENTED TANNINS to colour the crystals reddish brown and to ensure that they are small and irregular in shape.

A.D.W.

Ribéreau-Gayon, P., Glories, Y., Maujean, A., and Dubourdieu, D., Traité d'Œnologie 2: Chimie du vin: Stabilisation et traitements (Paris, 1998), translated by Aquitrad Traduction as Handbook of Enology 2: The Chemistry of Wine Stabilization and Treatments (Chichester, 2000).

Tasmania, small island state to the cool south of AUSTRALIA, with most of its vineyards clustered round Launceston in the north or Hobart in the south of the island and on the east coast around Bicheno. So far there has been no move to seek registration of any regions, or even zones, notwithstanding the diversity of climate noted below. The creation of two zones, one north and one south, would be a logical first step, the boundary easy to draw. Regions could then follow once they gained the sufficient critical mass of 500 tonnes.

In volume terms, the Tasmanian wine industry is as tiny as its potential is large. It crushed a total of nearly 7,000 tonnes of grapes in 2004 but a revival in the long-depressed state economy (and rising house prices) will underwrite the continued growth of the wine industry. This is reflected by the rash of takeovers discussed below, and the money (and expertise) the new Tasmanian corporate players have injected.

Outside observers not only habitually exaggerate the extent of Tasmania's viticulture, but are oblivious to the diversity of TERROIR and climate in the island's extremely complex geography. There are sites which are both warmer and very much drier than southern Victoria (for example the **Coal River/Richmond** region in the east of Hobart, and, in terms of warmth, the **Tamar River** south of Launceston) and there are sites cooler and wetter (for example **Pipers Brook**, east of Launceston). The one clear pattern is that Pinot Noir finds itself at home in all parts of the state, with the qualified exception of parts of the Tamar River.

Zinfandel was once grown successfully at the Coal River; the colour and extract of the Tamar River red wines is extraordinary, hinting misleadingly at a warm to very warm climate. The island's major producers have hitched their future to such cool-climate varieties as Riesling, Pinot Gris, Chardonnay, and Pinot Noir (the latter two for both table and sparkling wine use). However, the apparent effect of climate change—or at least, some warm vintages—has led to some impressive MERLOT, CABERNET SAUVIGNON, and SHIRAZ coming from the warmer sites of the Tamar River and from the Coal River, where Domaine A struts its stuff.

Tasmania has also seen the merger and acquisition games played on the mainland by the big corporates. In chronological order: the JAC group headed by Joe Chromy buys Heemskerk and Rochecombe (1994); St Matthias is purchased by Moorilla Estate (1995); Pipers Brook buys Rochecombe and Heemskerk from Chromy (1998); Chromy fast-tracks development of Tamar Ridge in wake of sale; Rochecombe and Heemskerk labels disappear (the latter to reappear as part of the large Cellarmaster direct-sale business); Rosevears Estate is founded and takes in Notley Gorge and Iron Pot Bay (1999); Belgian-owned Kreglinger takes control of Pipers Brook (2001); Hardys develops Bay of Fires (2001); Andrew Pirie abruptly leaves Pipers Brook (2003); Gunns Limited buys Tamar Ridge from Chromy and announces major vineyard expansion in new area in Tasmania's north east under the direction of Dr Richard Smart, viticulture editor of the first and second editions of this book (2003); Andrew Hood sells Wellington Wines to principals of organic producer Frogmore Creek, which announces plans for major new winery solely dedicated to organically grown grapes (2003); Andrew Pirie takes long-term lease of Rosevears Estate Winery to make his own Pirie wines and continue contract making of Rosevears, Notley Gorge, and Iron Pot Bay wines (2004). And so on.

Over this period, the future of the Tasmanian wine industry has taken shape. Larger vineyards are being established by well-funded groups; Hardys, Australia's pre-eminent sparkling winemaker (Arras, Sir James, etc.), now sources all of its ultra-premium base wine from Tasmania; Pinot Noir has improved out of all recognition and is being made in larger volumes; and its distinctively elegant Riesling and Chardonnay, with high natural acidity, have an increasingly receptive audience.

The quality of Tasmanian wine has never been in dispute, but will get better and better as VINE AGE increases, and the terroir/variety dating game becomes even more sophisticated.

The Taste of Tasmania is a highly effective part-government-, part-industry-funded ongoing annual promotion of the wine and food of the state, linking into lifestyle TOURISM, and firmly points the direction for the future. J.H.

taste. What we call the sense of taste is to a very great extent the sense of smell. See TASTING for more details. As for our own personal taste in wine, it is overall SUBJECTIVE. There are no rights and wrongs in wine preferences. See also QUALITY IN WINE.

tastevins, or wine tasters, as they are known by collectors of wine antiques, are shallow, often dimpled, saucers used for TASTING by professionals (and occasional self-conscious amateurs). Because they were usually used in a cellar, or on purchasing journeys where robust construction was essential, they were almost invariably made of silver. The earliest English references to tasters date from the 14th century but only a single extant example pre-dates 1600. British tasters mostly copy the BORDEAUX model, being 65–110 mm (2.5–4.5 in) in diameter with sloping sides, a domed base, and lacking a handle. Very few were made after 1800. Extremely rare tasters were made of glass or porcelain, usually Worcester.

Tastevins are far more plentiful in France than elsewhere. Most have a single handle and a slightly domed base. Many are decorated with a different pattern on either side of the handle. Late 19ᵗʰ- and 20ᵗʰ-century examples are often plated. R.N.H.B.

Some BURGUNDY producers still use tastevins in their own cellars, where they can be useful to demonstrate hue and clarity even in a dim light. For actual tasting, GLASSES are more efficacious, even if more fragile and less easily portable. Contemporary manufacture of tastevins is sustained by many CONFRÉRIES, most obviously the Burgundian Chevaliers du Tastevin.

Mazenot, R., *Le Tastevin à travers les siècles* (Grenoble, 1973).

tasting, the act of consciously assessing a wine's quality, character, or identity (see BLIND TASTING). It is certainly not synonymous with, nor necessarily contemporaneous with nor accompanied by, the act of drinking it. The ideal conditions for the act of tasting, and the organization and classification of formal wine tastings, is outlined under TASTINGS. This article is concerned with the activities and mechanisms involved in consciously receiving the sensory impressions a wine can stimulate.

Ancient Greek tasters

The existence of an organized trade in wine in Ancient GREECE must have created a class of specialized MERCHANTS. Both for them and for discerning members of the public, skill in tasting was necessary, and the Greeks had a word for the wine taster and his art: *oinogeustes/-geustikē*. The first attestation of this activity is through the cognate verb meaning 'to taste wine', found as early as the 4ᵗʰ century BC.

References to the professionals are extremely rare; one is found in a document of the 3ʳᵈ century AD from Roman Egypt (*Oxyrhynchus Papyrus* 3517), where it is said, 'The wine taster has declared the Euboean wine to be unsuitable.'

The most enlightening ancient text is by Florentinus, a writer of the early 3ʳᵈ century AD, who gives the following advice (preserved in the *Geoponica* 7. 7).

When and how to taste wine. From Florentinus. Some people taste wines when the wind is in the north, because then the wines remain unchanged and undisturbed. Experienced drinkers prefer to taste when the wind is from the south, because this has the most effect on the wine and reveals its nature. One should not taste when hungry, because the sense of taste is blunted, nor after heavy drinking or a large meal. The person tasting should not do so after consumption of food with a sharp or very salty taste, or anything which affects the sense of taste strongly, but should have eaten as lightly as possible and be free from indigestion.

See MERCHANTS for a continuation of this advice, as applied to the art of selling wine. N.G.W.

How we taste

Most of what is commonly called the sense of taste is in fact the sense of SMELL, whether applied to wine, or any food or drink, since by chewing we transform our food into liquid which gives off smellable vapour. To verify this it is enough to eat or drink something with the nose pinched shut, or to consider the extent to which we 'lose our appetite' when we have a head cold which blocks the nose. The human brain senses what we call flavours and aromas in the olfactory bulb, which, as Buck and Axel so elegantly demonstrated in their Nobel prize-winning work, is reached via a thousand different olfactory receptor cells, each expressing a single odorant receptor gene, these genes representing about 3 per cent of an individual's genetic make-up. Unexpectedly, each olfactory receptor cell is sensitive to a very small group of related aromas. From the olfactory bulb these messages are sent to other parts of the brain and processed, combining them and forming a pattern. Most aromas are made up of many different molecules, each of which activates several of these olfactory receptors, making odorant patterns, so that humans are able to recognize and, particularly, memorize up to 10,000 different aromas. The olfactory bulb is reached mainly by the nostrils, and to a lesser extent by a channel at the back of the mouth called the retronasal passage (which is why most healthy people can still perceive some flavour even if they do not consciously smell what they consume). The human olfactory sense is extremely acute (although not as acute as that of some animals).

Concentrations of some compounds of one part per 10,000 can be sensed, recognized, and remembered by the average person. A single whiff can transport us immediately to something experienced many years before.

The tasting capacity of the mouth is much more limited. In the mouth, our tactile sense can register FIZZINESS, TEMPERATURE, VISCOSITY, EXTRACT, the apparent heat generated on the palate by excessive ALCOHOL, and the sensation induced by TANNINS of drying out the insides of the cheeks.

The tongue also has certain taste receptors we call taste buds, which can sense the four 'primary tastes' of SWEETNESS, ACIDITY, BITTERNESS, and saltiness together with the more recently recognized UMAMI. There is considerable genetic variation in how many taste buds we have, with roughly a quarter of the population considered extremely sensitive 'supertasters'. To supertasters the substance PROP (6-n-propylthiouracil) tastes extremely bitter and taste sensations in general are intensified and exaggerated. To so-called 'non-tasters', PROP is virtually tasteless, while about half of us are 'medium tasters', find PROP mildly bitter, and experience taste sensations without distorting extremes. Although it is a rather simplistic generalization, our taste buds have different sensitivities so that those at the front of the tongue are usually particularly sensitive to sweetness, those on the edges of the tongue are particularly sensitive to acidity, those at the back of the tongue are particularly sensitive to bitterness, and those at the front edges are particularly sensitive to saltiness. With the exception of some wines matured near the sea such as MANZANILLA or some produced from vineyards with a serious SALINITY problem, very few wines taste salty, and in even fewer can umami be detected. Sweetness and acidity, on the other hand, are two of the most important measurements of a wine. During tasting, therefore, the front of the tongue can usually detect the apparent sweetness of a wine (which is not necessarily the same as its RESIDUAL SUGAR). The sides of the tongue react quite markedly in many people to acidity; so markedly that a smell of a particularly acid wine is enough to make the sides of the tongue tingle in anticipation in an experienced taster. Some wines taste quite bitter (bitterness often accompanies, but is not the same as, astringency) and this bitterness is most commonly sensed on the flat rear portion of the tongue.

It is clear that the mouth's tasting ability, apart from being usefully linked to the olfactory bulb by the retronasal passage, is in *measuring* the wine, assessing its dimensions of sweetness, acidity, bitterness, fizziness, viscosity, potency, and ASTRINGENCY. The mouth is capable of making an overall assessment of a wine's TEXTURE, while the nose senses what we call its flavour. Just as what is commonly called the sense of taste is really the sense of smell, so what is commonly called flavour is really AROMA or, in older wines, BOUQUET. (See FLAVOUR, however, for a proposal that the word be used to incorporate all the measurements sensed by the mouth.)

The essential character and most complex distinguishing marks of any wine are in its smell, which is made up of hundreds, probably thousands, of different FLAVOUR COMPOUNDS, present in widely varying permutations and concentrations in different wines.

What is commonly called tasting therefore involves persuading as many of these flavour compounds as possible to reach the olfactory bulb, while ensuring that contact is made between the wine and all of the inside of the mouth for the purposes of assessing a wine's dimensions and texture.

How to taste

The operation of tasting is generally divided into three stages involving sequentially the eye, the nose, and the mouth (although, as outlined above, this is not the same as the simple sequential application of the senses of sight, smell, and taste).

Eye The job of the eye in wine tasting is mainly to assess clarity and colour, as well as to monitor the presence of CARBON DIOXIDE and ALCOHOL (the former indicated by bubbles, the latter possibly by any TEARS of the wine that may form on the inside of the glass when it is rotated).

The clarity of a wine is an indication, hardly surprisingly, of the extent to which CLARIFICATION has been carried out, but also of the wine's condition. Many wine FAULTS result in a haze of some sort. In the late 1990s, anti-FILTRATION sentiment was so strong in California that some highly priced Chardonnays looked positively cloudy. A wine with particles floating in it, however, may simply be an innocent casualty of poor SERVING technique in which a wine has not been properly separated from its entirely harmless sediment. Experienced tasters can sometimes discern quality simply by looking at a wine's luminescent clarity and subtle range of hues.

The colour of a wine, both its intensity and its hue, is one of the potentially most valuable clues to any BLIND TASTER. Intensity of colour is best judged by looking straight through a glass of wine from directly above (preferably against a plain white background). Different grape varieties tend to make deeper or lighter coloured wines (Cabernet Sauvignon, Syrah, and Nebbiolo make particularly deep red wines; Gewürztraminer and Pinot Gris are examples of varieties which make particularly deep white wines, because the grape skins are deep pink). A deep colour also indicates youth, long MACERATION (possibly over-EXTRACTION), and thick-skinned grapes in a red wine; sometimes age, some OXIDATION, BARREL MATURATION, although not if preceded by BARREL FERMENTATION, in white wines.

The actual hue can also provide clues, and can be best assessed by tilting the glass away at an angle so that the different shadings of colour at the rim can be seen, again preferably against a plain white background. A bluish tinge in a red wine indicates youth, while orange/yellow indicates AGE (or OXIDATION). Very pale green in a white wine may indicate Riesling, while a pink tinge suggests that the wine was made from pink-skinned grapes such as Gewürztraminer and Pinot Gris. For more information, see COLOUR.

This stage in tasting for any purpose other than identification is usually very short and, if tasters are SCORING various aspects of a wine, many wines gain maximum points for appearance.

Nose As demonstrated above, this is the single most important stage in wine tasting. The trick is to persuade as many flavour compounds as possible to vaporize and come into contact with the olfactory bulb (although what we smell is in fact an AZEOTROPIC mixture of many, rather than isolated, individual, flavour compounds). It is then necessary, of course, to be in a suitable frame of mind to interpret the messages received by the olfactory bulb, which is why the act of tasting requires concentration.

The simplest way to maximize the evaporation of a wine's volatile elements is by the judicious use of TEMPERATURE and agitation.

Higher temperatures encourage any sort of evaporation so ideal tasting temperatures tend to be slightly higher than ideal SERVING temperatures. It is unwise to taste wines so hot that the alcohol starts to evaporate at such a rate that it dominates the flavour, however, so an ideal tasting temperature for wines, red or white, is somewhere between 15 and 20 °C/59–68 °F. At these relatively elevated temperatures, faults as well as attributes should be perfectly apparent. What is lost is the refreshment factor, but then the point of tasting rather than drinking is analysis rather than pleasure. Sparkling wines tend to be tasted slightly cooler to retain the carbon dioxide.

Many professional tasters first smell, or 'nose' a wine without agitating it to see how powerful its aroma is without this encouragement before deliberately increasing the number of molecules liberated by a wine by agitating the wine and increasing its surface area, preferably rotating it in a bowl-shaped glass with a stem (see GLASSES) so that no wine is lost.

As soon as the wine has been agitated, the aroma collects in the bowl of the partly filled glass above the wine and can be transmitted to the olfactory bulb up the nostrils with one thoughtful inhalation.

The taster monitors first whether the wine smells fresh and clean, or whether any off-odours indicate the presence of a wine FAULT. The next basic measurement might well be of the intensity of the aroma (if it is an attractive smell, then intensity is preferable). And then comes the complex part of the operation which is much more difficult to describe: the sensation and attempt at description of the individual components that make up the aroma, or 'bouquet' as it is called if it has taken on the complexities associated with AGEING. For a discussion of this, see TASTING TERMS.

Quite apart from those components which result from the grapes themselves, the aroma can provide certain overall hints about viticulture and wine-making techniques. LEAF ALDEHYDES suggest that the grapes were less than fully ripe. Oak ageing may be betrayed by a certain amount of OAK FLAVOUR; scents of spices and toast can be the result of the degree of TOAST which the barrels received. Tropical fruit aromas suggest that the fermentation was particularly long and cool. DIACETYL, which can smell like butter and other dairy products, is a particularly obvious sign of MALOLACTIC FERMENTATION. The subject is too complex for more than the most cursory treatment here, but the books cited below provide more detail.

As a wine undergoes gentle AERATION in the glass, it may well begin to give off other compounds with time. World-famous taster Michael BROADBENT, for example, keeps a series of records of how a single glass of wine tastes, marked according to how long after pouring each note was made. Most good wines seem to

get better with time and then to start to deteriorate. In blind tasting, however, a taster's first impressions are usually the most accurate, and insights are rarely provided by constant repetition of the 'nosing' process.

Mouth In terms of aroma, 'flavour' in its narrow sense, the mouth, or palate as it is sometimes called, usually merely confirms the impressions already apparent to the nose when some vapour escapes the mouth and reaches the olfactory bulb via the retronasal passage. Many tasters take in a certain amount of air over their mouthful of wine to encourage this process (and are often mocked for the accompanying noise).

The main function of the mouth in the tasting process is to assess the texture and measure the dimensions rather than the character of a wine by assessing sweetness, acidity, bitterness, viscosity, and tannin level. Monitoring the combination of sweetness, viscosity, and any sensation of 'heat' gives a good indication of the likely alcohol content of any individual wine, ETHANOL tending to leave a burning sensation in the mouth. The insides of the mouth may also register the TEXTURE, analysing the impact of the TANNINS. For this reason, it is a good idea to rinse the mouth thoroughly with wine so that all possible taste receptors may come into contact with it—another reason why wine tasting looks both ridiculous and disgusting to outsiders.

After rinsing a wine around their mouths, and noting the impressions given by the vapour rising up the retronasal passage, most professional tasters then demonstrate their devotion to duty rather than alcohol by SPITTING. There are no taste receptors in the throat. The taster then notes how LONG the impressions given by the wine seem to persist after spitting, or swallowing.

Conclusions Perhaps the most important stage, however, is a fourth stage of analysis, in which all previous impressions are evaluated. This includes most particularly considering whether the measurements taken by the mouth suggest that the wine is in BALANCE, and monitoring the LENGTH of the aftertaste, these last two factors being important indicators of quality. A fine wine should continue to make favourable sensory impressions throughout the entire tasting process.

Experience is necessary to judge balance. A significant, if decreasing, proportion of young red wines designed for long-term evolution, for example, are not by any objective criterion in balance. Their tannins may still be very marked and make the wine an unpleasantly astringent drink, even if they suggest that the wine will keep well. (Making red wines with less obvious tannins so that they can be both aged and drunk in their youth is one of the prime current preoccupations of winemakers.) Similarly, the acidity in a young German wine may be aggressively dominant, but experience shows that it is essential to preserve a top-quality Riesling, for example, for the ten or 20 years' bottle ageing it may deserve. (Some would also argue that a perceptible level of SULFUR DIOXIDE was also acceptable in such a wine.)

Professional tasting usually involves making **tasting notes**, typically under the four headings noted above. It may also involve SCORING by allotting NUMBERS to different elements according to a carefully predetermined scale, especially if wine JUDGING is involved. Tasting notes can be set out in many different ways and experienced tasters tend to devise their own abbreviations and symbols.

Tasting for pleasure, which is what most wine drinkers do every time they open a bottle, requires nothing more complicated than a moment's concentration and an open mind.

Factors affecting taste

We cannot know what other tasters experience for the tasting mechanism is far from public. Furthermore, individuals vary in their sensitivity to different compounds and dimensions of wine. But even as individuals, the way our brain processes information sent from sensory receptors changes all the time so that the same wine will have a different effect on us depending on the state of our palate. The most obvious example of this is how different something tastes before and just after we have had a mouthful of red hot chili. But even something as apparently innocent as a particularly hot drink or salty solution can affect the way we taste. An acid wine will seem less acid if tasted immediately after a very acid one, which is why the ORDER of serving and tasting is crucial, but extremely difficult to get right until every wine has been tasted. See also FOOD AND WINE MATCHING.

Our overall physical well-being affects how we taste. If we are run down, we tend to produce less saliva and, because saliva contains compounds which have a buffering effect on many aspects of taste, both foods and drinks can taste quite different (this is quite apart from the fact that good HEALTH is needed to tackle a succession of alcoholic liquids).

How we taste can be quite markedly affected by our mood, and of course by the physical environment in which we taste (see TASTINGS below). Tasting in a very humid atmosphere is markedly more difficult than when the atmospheric pressure is high, flavour compounds are readily volatilized, and taste impressions seem crystal clear.

Broadbent, M., *Wine Tasting* (9th edn, London, 2003).

Buck, L., and Axel, R., *Cell*, 65 (1991), 175–87.

Duffy, V. B., Miller, I. J., and Bartoshuk, L. M., '6-n-propylthiouracil (PROP) supertasters and women have greater number of fungiform papillae taste buds', *Chemical Senses*, 19 (1994), 465.

Peynaud, É., *The Taste of Wine* (2nd edn, New York, 1996).

Robinson, J., *Jancis Robinson's Wine Tasting Workbook/How to Taste* (London, 2000).

Schuster, M., *Essential Winetasting* (London, 2000).

tasting notes are the usual record of professional or serious wine TASTINGS. They are conventionally divided into notes (and sometimes SCORES or NUMBERS) for what is sensed by the eye, the nose, and the mouth, together with overall conclusions (see TASTING). The thoughtful organizer of a tasting prepares a **tasting sheet** which provides as a minimum a list of complete names of all the wines served, in the relevant ORDER of serving, with sufficient space to write full tasting notes. Sometimes these are carefully divided into sections—Appearance, Aroma/Bouquet, Taste, and Conclusions, for example—but this is an optional extra as tasters vary according to how much they want to write on each aspect. Most experienced tasters develop their own shorthand, and good and bad habits. The number of words in a personal average tasting note can vary between one and 100 or, in the case of a particularly complex wine which evolves in the glass, more. Tasting notes, especially of wines worth AGEING, are all the more valuable if they are dated. Most tasting notes remain of personal use only, but Michael BROADBENT has produced two important books based entirely on his, the majority of Robert PARKER's output is made up of his. Comparison of the two authors provides a reasonable guide to the different styles of British and American tasting notes respectively. The advent of sophisticated INFORMATION TECHNOLOGY has introduced the possibility of entering tasting notes directly into a computer database, and many wine WEBSITES are made up principally of tasting notes, although any nearby liquid poses a threat to a keyboard (which can become unpleasantly sticky during a tasting of sweet wines). This method of record-keeping should, in theory at least, lessen the usual problem of declining legibility of tasting notes towards the end of a tasting.

tastings, events at which wines are tasted. Informal tastings take place every time a bottle of wine is opened by a wine enthusiast. More formal ones take place when wine producers show their wines to potential buyers or commentators. The most common sort of formal tasting is one held for the purposes of wine assessment, typically by wine MERCHANTS keen to sell their wares, sometimes by a generic body keen to promote wines of a particular style or provenance. Formal tastings are also held by wine clubs and societies for less commercial purposes: EDUCATION or simple pleasure perhaps.

A **horizontal tasting** is one in which a number of different wines of the same VINTAGE are compared, while a **vertical tasting** is a comparison of different vintages of the same wine, most commonly the same Bordeaux

CHÂTEAU. George SAINTSBURY is credited with the first recorded use of these expressions.

A BLIND TASTING is one whose purpose is that the taster assesses and possibly identifies unknown wines as closely as possible.

A **comparative tasting** is one in which various different examples of the same sort or style of wine—CLASSED GROWTHS of the same vintage, or wines from the same APPELLATION, or a single VARIETAL, for example—are tasted and compared. Such tastings increasingly form the basis of modern WINE WRITING and should be conducted blind for a true, unprejudiced assessment.

Equipment

The only essential equipment for a wine tasting, apart from the wine, is suitable GLASSES and, if bottles are stoppered with a cork, a CORKSCREW, but it is almost impossible to hold a tasting without a substantial area of flat surface on which to put bottles and glasses safely, usually in the form of a table to which there is good access. Next most useful objects are undoubtedly spittoons (see SPITTING), and something in which to pour away LEFTOVER wine from a tasting sample (bottles plus funnels are customary although spittoons can also be used for this purpose). The thoughtful organizer ensures that there is some plain white surface against which to hold a glassful of wine (see TASTING). This typically involves lining up bottles on a table with a white surface (to see a wine's colour and clarity most easily) or a covering such as a tablecloth or sheet. A truly assiduous host provides tasters with a tasting sheet on which is a full and accurate list of wines to be tasted, in the correct order, with appropriate space for tasting notes. Water for rinsing of glasses and palates and some neutral-tasting food for 'cleaning the palate' can be helpful too. Cheese is usually too strong (see FOOD AND WINE MATCHING); bread or dry, savoury crackers are generally preferred by professionals.

Conditions

Ideal conditions include a strong natural light, ambient temperature between 15 and 18 °C/59–64 °F, and an absence of any extraneous smells. (It is clear therefore that tasting in most cellars, even those of the finest winemakers, is far from ideal.) In practice, a tasting that involves many people inevitably generates its own heat and smell, so it is wise to begin at a lower ambient temperature and not to be too exercised about a whiff of aftershave or polish, which is soon absorbed into the ambient atmosphere.

Organization

One glass per taster usually suffices, and no more than a fifteenth or even twentieth of a bottle is needed to give someone a decent tasting sample. Ensuring that tasters are served rather than serving themselves can limit wine consumption.

A suitable number of different wines to be shown at a single tasting is controversial. Some tasters claim to be able to assess up to 200 wines in a day at JUDGING sessions such as the Australian wine SHOWS, while the most experienced professionals in CHAMPAGNE deliberately limit themselves to fewer than a dozen wines at a time. A novice taster should probably start with no more than four wines while a professional might feel a tasting which offered only 15 was hardly worth the detour.

What is clear is that it is difficult to *enjoy* more than a dozen wines at a time, and that the ORDER in which any selection is served is vital to the impression they give.

tasting terms, the myriad and oft-mocked words used by tasters in an often vain attempt to describe sensory impressions received during TASTING.

The difference between a taster and a social drinker is this need to describe, to attempt the difficult task of applying words to individual, invisible sensations, particularly the aromas sensed by the olfactory bulb.

The sense of smell is an exceptionally private one, for which there is no common public domain which can be codified. The best we can do is describe aromas by other aromas of which they remind us. Hence 'blackcurrant' or CASSIS, frequently for Cabernet Sauvignon; 'strawberry' or 'raspberry' for Pinot Noir; 'vanilla' for OAK. Science is starting to correlate the FLAVOUR COMPOUNDS found in different GRAPE VARIETIES (if not yet different APPELLATIONS) with those found in the objects used as taste descriptors.

There is as yet no official wine-tasting LANGUAGE, although there have been many valiant attempts at establishing one and, particularly as research on flavour compounds and FLAVOUR PRECURSORS continues apace, this is becoming an increasingly attainable goal. The Scottish doctor Alexander HENDERSON was one of the first to attempt it in the English language in *The History of Ancient and Modern Wines* in 1824, CHAPTAL having applied about 60 French terms in his *L'Art de faire le vin* in 1807. These early tasting vocabularies tended to concentrate on the dimensions of a wine rather than its flavour or aroma, and applied words such as 'acidic, sweet, bitter, light'.

Terms used for mouth sensations

The most straightforward of these 'dimensional terms', which describe what is sensed in the mouth (and the even more public and obvious visual impressions), are still in use today and, since for the most part they describe what is measurable, are useful, indisputable, and not affected by SUBJECTIVITY. Inevitably, some jargon has evolved, of which the following are the most obvious examples.

Body—a noun; see BODY.
Big—high in alcohol.

Concentrated—having intense (though possibly) subtle flavours.
Crisp—attractively high in ACIDITY.
Fat—full bodied and viscous.
Flabby—lacking in ACIDITY.
Finish—a noun for aftertaste.
Full—of BODY.
Green—too acid, made of unripe fruit.
Hard—too much TANNIN and too little fruit.
Heavy—too alcoholic; too much EXTRACT.
Hot—too alcoholic.
Legs—see TEARS.
Light—agreeably light in BODY.
Long—impressively persistent aftertaste; see LONG.
Short—opposite of LONG.
Smooth—imprecise term for pleasing TEXTURE.
Soft—low in tannins.
Well balanced—having good BALANCE.

Terms used for aroma

It is in their attempts to find 'character terms' to apply to these more subtle, more private olfactory sensations that wine tasters can seem so foolish.

Some 'idioterms' are just plain fanciful, descriptions obviously applied in sheer desperation at the apparent impossibility of the task. In this category come the 'fading but well-mannered old lady', and who can forget James Thurber's 'naive domestic burgundy but I think you'll be amused by its presumption'? A more recent example is 'sexy', an increasingly common, but delightfully imprecise, tasting term.

Other sorts of terms, 'simile terms', are applied in a serious attempt to recall palpable objects which give rise to similar aromas: the fruits, flowers, vegetable, and mineral descriptors, for example.

Particularly common terms used to describe aroma, or flavour, include:

Buttery—see DIACETYL.
Fruity—intense impact of fruit flavours, sometimes a euphemism for 'slightly sweet.'
Grapey—mixture of intensely aromatic and the aromas associated with MUSCAT grapes.
Oaky—pejorative term for a wine excessively marked by OAK.
Toasty—see TOAST.

There are also 'derivative terms', which must once have been coined by an authority and continue to be widely used even though they are literally inaccurate. So many wine tasters have been taught to describe the powerful and characteristic smell of GEWÜRZTRAMINER as 'spicy', for example (perhaps because *Gewürz* is German for 'spice'), that this is the most common tasting term for the aroma, even though it does not smell like any particular spice at all (much more like lychees, in fact).

It will be of the 'simile terms' that a common tasting vocabulary is finally composed—although there is the obstacle of many different languages and national conventions to be overcome first. Max Leglise, a researcher in Burgundy, has attempted to concoct essences of each of his approved terms so that there is

an objective standard for them. (Unfortunately, synthetic flavourings deteriorate.) Professor Ann C. Noble at DAVIS, clearly frustrated by the looseness with which tasting terms are applied, has done sterling work with her aroma wheel. This corresponds sufficiently closely with the tasting terms suggested by Professor Émile PEYNAUD, Bordeaux's tasting guru, to give us all hope that soon an international tasting language that is no more ambiguous than any other will be available to the world's wine tasters.

Brochet and DUBOURDIEU established in 2001 that each expert taster has his or her own set of tasting terms which typically correspond to a personal set of prototypes, 'ideal' wines, rather than detailed analytical description. In a separate study involving white wines coloured red, they also demonstrated that many tasting terms are colour-specific and that if tasters see red wine, they will assign tasting terms associated with objects of that colour.

See also AROMA WHEEL and LANGUAGE OF WINE.

Broadbent, M., *Wine Tasting* (9th edn, London, 2003).

Brochet, F., and Dubourdieu, D., 'Wine descriptive language supports cognitive specificity of chemical senses', *Brain and Language*, 77 (2001), 187–96.

—— and —— 'The color of odors', *Brain and Language*, 79 (2001), 309–20.

Peynaud, É., *The Taste of Wine* (2nd edn, New York, 1996).

Rankine, B., *Tasting and Enjoying Wine* (Adelaide, 1990).

Taurasi, the best-known high-quality wine of the CAMPANIA region (promoted to DOCG status in 1993) and arguably of the whole of southern Italy, is produced from the AGLIANICO grape in a zone north east of the city of Avellino. The village of Taurasi is a mere 64 km/40 miles from Barile, the centre of the AGLIANICO DEL VULTURE production zone, and, like the most famous wine of BASILICATA, Taurasi demonstrates the heights which Aglianico can reach in the volcanic soil which it prefers. Although by the mid 2000s there were 293 producers and over 421 ha/1050 acres in the Taurasi zone, the firm of Mastroberardino was until the early 1990s the only label on the market. The zone's maximum potential production is 32,400 hl/858,000 gal per year, but seldom exceeds 7,000 hl in a normal vintage. DOCG regulations require three years of ageing, one of which must be in wood, and RISERVA bottlings must be aged for four years. The permitted production zone sprawls over a large and heterogeneous area, with little regard for the fact that Aglianico gives its best results only at a certain altitude, with most of the best wines coming from vineyards at 400 to 500 m above sea level. In the past decade, Taurasi has been given greater prominence by the rise to fame of I Feudi di San Gregorio, whose first vintage was only in 1992. Along with Vesevo, another new producer, they now produce the best wines in the zone. D.T. & D.C.G.

Tautavel, subappellation of Côtes du ROUSSILLON-Villages.

Tavel, right bank appellation for dry rosé in the southern RHÔNE whose historic reputation is still sufficient to justify a sometimes unwarranted price premium over other rosés, although Tavel at its best manages to combine refreshment with interest and concentration of flavour. Tavel was already favoured by Louis XIV in the 18th century, and writers Balzac and Mistral continued to promulgate its superiority. Grapes can reach such levels of RIPENESS here that the appellation enforces a maximum ALCOHOLIC STRENGTH of 13.5 per cent.

The wine is always bone dry, but the Grenache and Cinsaut grapes give the blend a certain apparent sweetness. Chilling is essential, and the wine should be drunk young, as an alternative to red wine in hot weather. Grenache is the dominant grape variety, as throughout the southern Rhône, but may not exceed 60 per cent of the blend.

Such was demand for the wine in the 1950s that the area was considerably extended, by clearing *garrigue*. A steady 900 ha/2,220 acres of sand and clay is shared mainly by members of the Tavel CO-OPERATIVE, although there are some quality-minded estates. Ch d'Acqueria was for long the best-known estate but some of the best wine is made by Domaine de la Mordorée in nearby LIRAC, a more dynamic and often more remarkable appellation.

Tavira, fishing port and DOC in southern Portugal. See ALGARVE

Távora-Varosa, DOC immediately south of the DOURO in central-northern Portugal. Much of the region's production is dry, white base wine for the local sparkling wine industry, not entitled to the denomination.
R.J.M.

tawny, style of FORTIFIED wines usually associated with extended CASK AGEING. See PORT, for example.

taxation. Wine has attracted the attention of the taxman since ancient times. Its production, sale, and distribution have been so closely regulated by the authorities for one simple reason: revenue, whatever their attitude to alcohol. The civilizations of the ancient Middle East (see Ancient EGYPT and MESOPOTAMIA) were the first to recognize this useful attribute. It was carefully regulated in parts of Ancient GREECE, but it was the Romans who, in this as in many other aspects of wine history, helped realize its potential.

In Ancient ROME tax was paid from the moment the grape appeared on the vine (Roman vine-growers paid a vineyard tax calculated on the quality of the land) to when it was consumed. It was paid either in kind or in cash and represented a huge proportion of state income. Some areas in the empire, CALABRIA, then the heel of Italy, for example, paid their entire tax to Rome in wine, which was then sold or distributed free to the urban masses.

Medieval kings found wine taxation fabulously lucrative. During England's occupation of western France, for example, the crown benefited doubly by receiving duties paid on wine exported from BORDEAUX, and then again on the same wine as customs when it entered London. During the early part of the 14th century, when this trade was at its peak, wine duties collected in Bordeaux surpassed the king's total tax revenue in England.

Not surprisingly, taxes on wine have been perceived as a fast, easy way of raising cash and the state has shown no scruples in doubling or tripling them at times of emergency—often to pay for wars such as the HUNDRED YEARS WAR, the English Civil War, and the Napoleonic Wars.

Although they may complain, in certain circumstances wine merchants have been happy to pay tax because it legitimizes their business. Wine merchants within the Islamic empire of the caliphs (usually Jewish or Christians) viewed their payments as a kind of insurance policy; the state would not outlaw their activities, despite the Koranic ban on alcohol, because the income was so useful (see ISLAM).

Wine taxation has uses beyond mere revenue. Different levels can be used to reward or punish trading partners. For example, throughout the 18th century, French wines attracted twice as much DUTY as Portuguese wines (see METHUEN TREATY). Not surprisingly, trade in French wines suffered and port became the staple English wine (see WAR).

Differential taxation has also been used to manipulate consumer tastes for reasons of health or morality. Gladstone's Act of 1860 reduced the duty on light, less alcoholic wines in an attempt to switch the British palate away from the heavy, fortified wines and spirits that earlier taxation had favoured.

Taxation has at times had indirect consequences. During the 18th century, when duties were high and complicated (French wines were subject to 15 separate duties), ADULTERATION AND FRAUD and smuggling increased in England. Grievances against excessive taxation of wines entering Paris have been recognized as one of the sparks that lit the fire of revolution in 1789.

It was inevitable that, as soon as wine was taxed, certain parties should be exempt. Traditionally these have included the crown, the Church, and sections of the nobility; such exemptions go back at least as far as Ancient EGYPT. This privilege has been extended in modern times (so far as customs duties go) to travellers via the system of duty-free allowances.
H.B.

Briggs, A., *Wine for Sale: Victoria Wine and the Liquor Trade 1860–1984* (London, 1985).
Francis, A. D., *The Wine Trade* (London, 1972).
Hyams, E., *Dionysus: A Social History of the Vine* (2nd edn, London, 1987).

Taylor's, important independent PORT shipper known in full as **Taylor, Fladgate & Yeatman** and part of the FLADGATE PARTNERSHIP. The original firm of port shippers was established in 1692 by Job Bearsley, and between then and 1844 there were no fewer than 21 name changes. However, with the arrival of Joseph Taylor in 1816, John Fladgate in 1837, and Morgan Yeatman in 1844, the company assumed its present full name, and Taylor's for short. In 1744, Job Bearsley's son Bartholomew bought Casa dos Alambiques at Salgueiral near Régua, the first known British port shipper's property in the DOURO valley. Salgueiral is still one of the company's vinification centres.

In 1808, a new partner, Joseph Camo, arrived, the first American to be admitted into partnership in a port company and until recently the only non-British shipper ever to be allowed into meetings of the British Association at the FACTORY HOUSE. As an American, Camo remained neutral during the Peninsular Wars, and was important in keeping export routes open in the face of French invaders.

Taylor's best-known property, Quinta da Vargellas high up in the Douro, was acquired in 1893, when it was still suffering from the ravages of PHYLLOXERA. This acquisition marked the start of Taylor's now considerable landowning and farming activities. In 1948, Taylor's bought FONSECA Guimaraens, with its three quintas: Panascal, Cruzeiro, and Santo António. Quinta da Terra Feita, which had been supplying port to Taylor's since at least 1903, was bought in 1974, adding a further 37 ha/91 acres of well-placed vines. In 1990, Terra Feita de Cima was added, followed in 1993 by São Xisto, which was further extended in 1999 to over 41 ha, and in 1998 by Quinta do Junco, adding a further 85 ha.

Taylor's vintage port is consistently one of the most admired and longest lived of the year, and its Quinta de Vargellas single quinta bottling can often be almost as concentrated.

The principal shareholder is now a nephew of Mrs Dick Yeatman, Alistair Robertson, who took over the firm in 1967, since when the firm has been one of the most successful companies in VILA NOVA DE GAIA, doing much to revitalize the selling and marketing of port, notably by popularizing the filtered LBV, or 'late bottled vintage', style. A new generation of the family joined in 1994: Natasha Bridge (née Robertson) with responsibilities for blending and Adrian Bridge as managing director.

Foulkes. C. (ed.), *A Celebration of Taylor's Port* (London, 1992).

Tazzelenghe, 'tongue-stinging' red grape of Italy's Colli Orientali in FRIULI.

TBA, understandably common abbreviation for TROCKENBEERENAUSLESE. And also for **2,4,6-tribromoanisole**; see TRIBROMOANISOLE.

T-budding, a BUDDING method used extensively in woody horticultural plants, including the grapevine, normally for field GRAFTING onto a ROOTSTOCK. The method entails making two T-shaped cuts in the bark of the rootstock, when the bark is slipping, then lifting back the flaps to permit insertion of a shield-shaped piece cut from the scion with a bud on it. After insertion, the bud is wrapped tightly with budding tape to ensure close contact of the tissues and high humidity around the cuts. T-budding can be done when the bark of the stock lifts freely, during two to three months over midsummer. Scion buds may be taken from stored winter cuttings or green current shoots. As with CHIP BUDDING, T-budding may be used for TOP GRAFTING. B.G.C.

TCA, or **2,4,6-trichloranisoletrichloroanisole**, the unpleasant-smelling compound associated with CORKED wine. See TRICHLORO-ANISOLE.

Tchelistcheff, André (1901–94), consultant oenologist and founding father of the modern California wine industry. Tchelistcheff was born in Moscow, the sickly son of a Russian professor of law. After a brush with death in the army, he trained as an engineer-agronomist in Czechoslovakia, then at the age of 36 decided to study VITICULTURE and OENOLOGY in more detail, in Paris. While working on a farm near Versailles, he became a graduate assistant to the director of the department of viticulture at the National Institute of Agronomy as well as taking a course in wine microbiology at the Institut PASTEUR. An obviously talented student, who combined intellectual rigour with a philosophical bent, he worked briefly at MOËT & CHANDON and had already been offered jobs in Chile and China before being introduced to his future employer. Georges de Latour was a Frenchman who had established himself as a highly successful businessman and owner of Beaulieu Vineyard in the Napa valley but was anxious to import a French-trained winemaker for the post-PROHIBITION era.

During his 35-year career at Beaulieu, Tchelistcheff introduced the principles of winery HYGIENE as well as pioneering temperature-controlled FERMENTATION, mastery of MALOLACTIC FERMENTATION, and frost damage prevention techniques such as the orchard heaters and WIND MACHINES which dominate Napa valley to this day. He also made considerable progress in the prevention of various VINE DISEASES and established a reputation as both wine and vineyard CONSULTANT.

From his first years in California, Tchelistcheff established an identity independent of Beaulieu, with his own small laboratory in St Helena advising other Napa and Sonoma wineries and training a younger generation of winemakers such as the young MONDAVI brothers. He was a consultant to Buena Vista winery, for example (see HARASZTHY), from 1948, and in 1967 began a long association with Ch Ste Michelle in WASHINGTON state. He was also one of the first to recognize the viticultural potential of the CARNEROS district of northern California. Although he retired from Beaulieu in 1973, four years after it was sold to the Heublein corporation, he continued to be an active consultant to a host of California wineries as well as to Ornellaia of BOLGHERI in Italy (where his son Dimitri subsequently advised). In 1991, however, he was wooed back to Beaulieu by the multinational corporation which by then owned it.

Tchelistcheff was a charter member of the American Society of Enologists and was made a Chevalier de l'Ordre du Mérite Agricole by the French government in 1954, being promoted to Officier in 1979. Tchelistcheff was unique in the wine world for the geographical breadth and historical depth of his singularly acute views on the contemporary wine scene.

TCP, see TRICHLOROANISOLE.

TDN, the FLAVOUR COMPOUND norisoprenoid hydrocarbon 1,1,6-trimethyl-1,2-dihydronaphthalene found particularly in RIESLING.

tears (to rhyme with 'ears'), tasting term used to describe the behaviour of the surface liquid layer that is observable in a glass of relatively strong wine. The wine wets the inside of a clean glass and climbs up a few millimetres. At the upper edge of the thin layer on the inside wall patches of the film thicken, become more drop-like, and eventually roll back down the inside wall to the liquid surface. These traces of what look like particularly viscous droplets are also sometimes called 'legs', and may give some indication of a wine's ALCOHOLIC STRENGTH. (But note that some of the finest German wines may have only 7 or 8 per cent alcohol but still form very obvious tears.)

James Thomson, a British physicist and engineer, observed and correctly explained in 1855 what he called 'tears of strong wine'. Unfortunately his work was overlooked and the explanation for the action is usually credited to Marangoni who published in 1871.

Four physical relationships are involved in producing tears. The attractive forces between molecules in a liquid are called surface tension forces and are what hold the liquid together. The same type of force also acts between a liquid molecule and the molecules of a solid surface, but is called interfacial tension. If the interfacial tension between a liquid and a glass is a bit greater than the surface tension, then molecules of liquid will adhere to the glass and wet areas higher and higher above the liquid surface. A point is reached at which the weight of the liquid clinging to the wall just balances the force trying to lift more liquid up the wall surface. If the liquid is a pure single substance, action stops at this point and no tears are observed.

Wine is not a single component substance, however, but is mainly a solution of alcohol and water. While the thin film of wine climbs up the inner wall of the glass, another physical action occurs: the alcohol evaporates faster than the water from the film surface. This changes the composition of the film, increasing its concentration of water and thereby increasing its surface tension and index of refraction. This increase in surface tension of an area of film depleted in alcohol causes the film to assume a drop-like form and to grow at the expense of the surrounding film. Eventually the drop becomes so heavy that interfacial tension can no longer hold it to the glass surface. It then runs down the wall, forming a tear or leg. The change of refractive index makes the boundary between the water-rich drop and the alcohol-rich film clearly visible.

Dubious readers can convince themselves of this somewhat complicated explanation of an apparently simple phenomenon by observing the lack of tears in glasses of pure water (or pure alcohol). That evaporation is necessary can be demonstrated by simply covering a glass that previously demonstrated **tearing**. Tearing ceases, and will resume upon removal of the cover.

It is often thought that tears are the result of GLYCEROL but in fact entirely unrelated phenomena are responsible. The small changes in VISCOSITY and index of refraction make the drop contrast with the liquid film on the glass surface. Tears are *not* a measure of viscosity.

Although the tears phenomenon occurs in any multicomponent liquid mixture, it is most obvious in wines above about 12 per cent alcoholic strength because the higher alcohol evaporates faster. A.D.W.

TeCA, or **2,3,4,6-tetrachloroanisole**, see TETRACHLOROANISOLE.

teinturier literally means 'dyer' in French, which is the function for which these vines with their red-fleshed grapes were initially grown, notably in the Midi, to add at least apparent depth to the pale wines of the dominant ARAMON in the early years of the 20th century. The original variety called **Teinturier**, or sometimes Teinturier du Cher, was probably extremely ancient, possibly a selection of WILD VINES, and was first noted around Orléans in the 17th and 18th centuries, where it imbued the pale pink wines of the region with valuable colour.

As long ago as 1824, the Frenchman Louis BOUSCHET decided to try to breed vines with coloured flesh, and the 1828 crossing of

Aramon × Teinturier du Cher resulted in the popular Petit Bouschet. Henri Bouschet, Louis's son, crossed Petit Bouschet with Grenache to produce the very popular ALICANTE BOUSCHET, a deeply coloured *teinturier*, known as Garnacha Tintorera in Spain, *tintorera* being Spanish for *teinturier*. Other red-fleshed varieties bred by the Bouschet family and used for their 'dyeing' properties at one time include Morrastel Bouschet, Carignan Bouschet, and GRAND NOIR DE LA CALMETTE.

Red-fleshed versions of the lightly coloured GAMAY grape have been widely grown, not just in the Loire but outside France. The Gamay *teinturiers* include Gamay Fréaux, Gamay de Bouze, and Gamay de Chaudenay. Gamay Fréaux and Gamay de Chaudenay are said to be mutants of Gamay de Bouze. Colobel (Seibel 8357) is a *teinturier* FRENCH HYBRID which was the only such variety to be authorized in France.

Germany's useful red-fleshed varieties include Carmina, Deckrot, DUNKELFELDER, Kolor, and Sulmer. ROYALTY 1390, Salvador, and the increasingly popular RUBIRED are all California creations, while the important Georgian *teinturier* is SAPERAVI, which is, if not red fleshed, then certainly pink fleshed.

R.E.S. & M.J.E.

Galet, P., *Dictionnaire encyclopédique des cépages* (Paris, 2000).

Robinson, J., *Vines, Grapes and Wines* (London, 1986).

Temecula, CALIFORNIA high DESERT wine region and AVA inland of the coastal mountain range 35 miles north of San Diego. Temecula is the viticultural aspect of a mixed-use residential and industrial development called Rancho California. Beginning in the late 1960s, insurance company developers used vineyards as part of their sales pitch to urban-weary escapees from Los Angeles and San Diego. Rainbow Gap, a narrow opening in the coastal ridge, funnels cool marine air across a 5-mile swathe of sanded desert allowing grapes to be grown in what would otherwise be a deeply inhospitable home for vines. IRRIGATION water is imported by pipeline. As the vineyards began to weave an image of moderate, salubrious weather, housing developments came swiftly to the undulating mesas all the way from Riverside south to San Diego. Within 20 years, grape-growers in the band of cool afternoon breezes at Temecula began to find themselves squeezed between rows of residences. However, enough vines still exist to satisfy about 20 small wineries. One good-sized one, Callaway, is still there, but has moved to sourcing most of its grapes in other areas, reportedly because of PIERCE'S DISEASE infestation. Sauvignon Blanc seems to do well, and occasionally Viognier. Hart and Baily are the most artistically successful among the small pioneering outfits.

Orfila is a singularly successful operation in the nearby San Pasqual Valley AVA, a Pierce's disease hot spot, surrounded on three sides by riverine growth, but the disease seems to be under control here. The valley stretches eastward from Escondido in San Diego county in the South Coast region. B.C.C.

temperate, a broad class of climates, usually taken to include those with an annual average temperature of less than 20 °C/68 °F, but a warmest month average temperature greater than 10 °C/50 °F, the latter being the approximate poleward limit of tree growth.

Just as wine is considered a beverage of temperate people, so the grapevine is a plant of temperate climates. It is specially so when the grapes are to be used for WINE-MAKING, and still more so for table wines. Excessive heat during ripening leads to a loss of the more delicate fruit aromas and flavours from the grapes, and therefore from the wines. Insufficient warmth leads to incomplete RIPENING in which FLAVOUR COMPOUNDS, which become manifest only late in the ripening process, are lacking. (The gross geographical limits for commercial viticulture resulting from temperature constraints are noted under LATITUDE.)

At a more detailed level may be added the further relevant concept of 'equability', or lack of extreme variation about given average temperatures through the vine growing and ripening seasons. This seems a particularly relevant consideration for cool and warm rather than hot climates.

See TEMPERATURE VARIABILITY and CLIMATE AND WINE QUALITY. J.G.

temperature is critically important to VITICULTURE, WINE-MAKING, wine MATURATION, and wine SERVICE, each in very different ways.

Climate, viticulture, and temperature

Temperature is widely considered the most important climatological factor affecting grapevines, although others such as SUNLIGHT, RAINFALL, HUMIDITY, and WIND are also important. Coombe and Gladstones comprehensively review the role of temperature in viticulture.

Vines in cool climates start growing in the spring at about the time when the mean air temperature reaches 10 °C/50 °F. The rate of vine growth and development then increases to a maximum at about 22 to 25 °C (72–7 °F), before falling away at even higher temperatures. Temperature is often discussed in viticulture as mean temperature, that is maximum plus minimum temperatures divided by two. These facts underlie the traditional methods for viticultural CLIMATE CLASSIFICATION, which are based on excesses of monthly average mean temperatures over 10 °C. Such classifications can at best be only approximate, however, if only because mean temperatures seldom truly reflect the real average temper-

atures as they might be measured continuously throughout the 24 hours, and as experienced by the vine (McIntyre *et al.*). Nor do established long-term temperature recording sites, from which most of the available data come, often truly represent existing or potential vineyard sites (see TOPOGRAPHY, MESOCLIMATE, CLIMATE CHANGE).

Prescott proposed that viticultural climates could be characterized just as accurately as by any other existing method, by the average mean temperature of their warmest month. Smart and Dry adapted this for use in Australia as mean January temperature (MJT): an index now quite widely used for approximate comparisons of viticultural climates, although July should be substituted for January in the northern hemisphere. Average mean temperatures for the full growing season can also be a reasonable basis for broad comparisons (see COOL CLIMATE VITICULTURE).

The risk of killing dormant vines in winter is a second basis for defining climatic suitability for viticulture, being the main limiting factor in cool climates with marked CONTINENTALITY. Most fully dormant VINIFERA vines with well-matured canes can withstand air temperatures down to about −15 °C/5 °F. Native AMERICAN VINE SPECIES are in general hardier, and AMERICAN HYBRIDS, their hybrids with European varieties, intermediate. However, there is considerable variation among VINE VARIETIES within each group.

The winter hardiness of RIESLING, for instance, is almost certainly one of the reasons for its historical success in Germany. See also WINTER FREEZE.

The chance of winter killing of vines in Europe increases from south west to north east (see RUSSIA, for example). Extensive commercial viticulture without WINTER PROTECTION reaches its limit where the average mean temperature of the coldest month falls below about −1 °C/30 °F (Prescott).

Air temperature is not the only kind governing vine growth and fruiting, however. Vines and soils are warmed by sunlight, which has major effects on grape berry temperature, leaf temperature, grape composition, and hence wine quality (see VINE PHYSIOLOGY). Some evidence now confirms the old belief that soil temperature is also important. This control appears to be mediated by the root-produced hormone CYTOKININ, although soil temperature can also affect vine temperature, especially at night. The composition of the soil, its colour, drainage, and duration and angle of exposure to the sun are all important factors in this respect. See SOIL COLOUR, STONES AND ROCKS, TOPOGRAPHY, MESOCLIMATE.

Soil and air temperatures at particular stages of vine growth or during ripening can have specific effects. Winter and early spring temperatures govern BUDBREAK in spring. Air TEMPERATURE VARIABILITY largely determines the risk of FROST damage after budbreak.

Temperatures around FLOWERING contribute to differences in FRUIT SET (by influencing COULURE, most notably) and to the FRUITFULNESS of the developing new buds which form shoots and bunches the following year. Both fruit set and bud fruitfulness are favoured by moderately high temperatures. Finally, both average temperature and temperature variability during ripening can have a direct influence on fruit and wine qualities, as discussed under CLIMATE AND WINE QUALITY.   J.G.

Coombe, B. G., 'Influence of temperature on composition and quality of grapes', *Acta horticulturae*, 206 (1987), 23–35.

Gladstones, J., *Viticulture and Environment* (Adelaide, 1992).

McIntyre, G. N., Kliewer, W. M., and Lider, L. A., 'Some limitations of the degree day system as used in viticulture in California', *American Journal of Enology and Viticulture*, 38 (1987), 128–32.

Prescott, J. A., 'The climatology of the vine (*Vitis vinifera*): 3. A comparison of France and Australia on the basis of the warmest month', *Transactions of the Royal Society of South Australia*, 93 (1969), 7–15.

Smart, R. E., and Dry, P. R., 'A climatic classification for Australian viticultural regions', *Australian Grapegrower and Winemaker*, 196 (1980), 8, 10, 16.

Wine-making and temperature

Temperature and TEMPERATURE CONTROL are of critical importance in making good-quality wine (although great wine may have been made fortuitously, long before the theory of temperature control was understood and temperature was deliberately manipulated). Temperature has direct effects on the rates of the biochemical reactions involved in FERMENTATION, and on the slower reactions involved in CLARIFICATION and STABILIZATION of wine. Years of experiment and calculation have demonstrated that most chemical reactions happen about twice as fast if the temperature is raised by 10 °C/18 °F—and it is for this reason that REFRIGERATION slows down the reactions of harmful BACTERIA, as well as the reactions involved in AGEING.

In warm regions, therefore, care should be taken to ensure that grapes arrive at the winery in a cool, and relatively undamaged, condition. The harmful effects of ACETOBACTER and wild YEAST are encouraged by high temperatures. Low temperatures are vital if there is any interval between HARVEST and CRUSHING; the potential quality of white wines in particular can be lost through carelessness at this early phase of wine-making. During DESTEMMING and crushing, when the PHENOLICS in grape juice are in direct contact with oxygen, OXIDATION begins at a rate proportional to the temperature. To slow browning of white grape juice, therefore, care is usually taken to keep temperatures as low as possible (see MUST CHILLING). SULFUR DIOXIDE may also be added. Oxidation of red grape juice is less of a problem because its higher phenolic content, including the red colour compounds, can conceal small amounts of amber or brown, although lower

temperatures during prefermentation processes are in general desirable whatever the colour of the grape skins.

If temperature control is desirable prior to fermentation, it is critical during it. At temperatures below 10 °C/50 °F most yeasts will act prohibitively slowly or not at all, while at temperatures above 45 °C/113 °F they are damaged and finally killed. Secondly, higher fermentation temperatures speed up some reactions so that undesirable flavour compounds become apparent. Thirdly, at higher temperatures, some of the desirable FLAVOUR COMPOUNDS are volatilized in the rapidly evolving stream of carbon dioxide, literally 'boiled off'. The result of this is a wine low in fruit and marked by 'hot' fermentation characteristics. In the extreme case of temperatures nearing the range at which yeasts are killed, the yeast cells secrete compounds which inhibit future yeast growth, thereby making it difficult or impossible to restart this STUCK FERMENTATION even after cooling.

There are yeast strains which grow and ferment very slowly at very low temperatures, only just above freezing. Such strains are particularly useful in cool wine regions such as Switzerland and parts of Germany but fermentation rates are so slow that a single FERMENTATION VESSEL can be used only once after each harvest, which therefore affects the capital cost of production, as it does at the most ambitious wineries elsewhere where there has been investment in fermentation capacity for any year's total production.

White wines are in general fermented at lower temperatures than red, partly in order to conserve the primary grape AROMAS, partly because there is no MACERATION for which heat may be useful in encouraging the extraction of phenolics and other flavour compounds from the grape skins. White wine temperatures between 12 and 17 °C (50–54 °F) are common for fermentation in the New World to yield fruity, well-balanced, light coloured wines quickly enough that the fermentation vessel can be used two or three times in a season (although see also BARREL FERMENTATION). Grape varieties such as Sauvignon Blanc, Riesling, and Muscat tend to be fermented at the lower end of this temperature range, whereas more neutral varieties, with a less complex blend of grape flavours to be conserved, may be fermented at the upper end and rely on the accumulation of secondary fermentation aromas. Old World white wine fermentation temperatures are likely to be 18 to 20 °C (64–68 °F) or cooler. The techniques of barrel fermentation and LEES CONTACT, such as are often applied to Chardonnay grapes, often involve slightly higher fermentation temperatures too, although the small size of the barrel (in comparison with the normal stainless steel tank) helps to control temperature.

Temperature control is also extremely important during red wine-making. The main

concern here is the extraction of sufficient TANNINS, ANTHOCYANINS, and flavour compounds from the grape skins. Temperature is one of the factors governing this extraction, agitation and time being the others. Fermentation temperatures between 25 and 30 °C (generally produce the best flavour and extraction in red wines, provided other conditions (and grape variety, agitation, and time all play a part interlinked to temperature in the maceration process) are optimal. Temperatures higher than this threaten the yeast activity while temperatures below it inhibit extraction.

Temperature continues to be an important factor in wine production long after the fermentation phase. Oxidation and loss of fruitiness in white wines can be discouraged by low temperatures, while the bacterial activity that stimulates MALOLACTIC FERMENTATION can be positively encouraged by storing the newly fermented wine between 25 and 30 °C (77–86 °F) until this secondary fermentation is completed.

Fermentation temperatures govern the types of ESTERS that are formed and accumulate in the wine. Lower temperatures (10 to 15 °C/50–59 °F) favour both the production and retention of the fruity esters, which have lower molecular weights. Among these are nearly all of those possible by reactions between ACETIC, propionic, isobutyric, and isovaleric acids with ETHANOL, propyl, isobutyl, and FUSEL OILS. These are the esters which give tropical fruits their characteristic flavours (ISOAMYL ACETATE, for example, is the flavour material of ripe bananas), which is why cool-fermented wines so often taste of tropical fruits. The aroma compounds of each grape variety are also better retained at these lower temperatures.

Higher fermentation temperatures (20 to 25 °C/68–77 °F) favour heady, heavier esters and, at the same time, destroy more of the VARIETAL character of the grape. Temperatures of 30 °C and higher result in the loss of much of the fruity ester complex through hydrolysis and volatilization and its replacement by substances which smell 'cooked'.   A.D.W.

Storage temperature

In the same way that it affects the reactions involved in wine-making, temperature becomes the governing factor in the much slower reactions in bottle that constitute wine AGEING. Interactions among the thousands of natural organic chemicals in the wine during this important phase of its maturation are directly affected by temperature. Applying the general scientific formula for temperature's effect on chemical reactions, a CELLAR temperature of 30 °C/86 °F should in theory mature a wine twice as fast as storage at 20 °C/68 °F—except that at such a high temperature compounds with a cooked or jammy note are formed and may well dominate the more desirable compounds. A cellar temperature of 10 °C/

50 °F should in theory age wine at half the speed of a 20 °C cellar, which is to say very slowly, although not quite so slowly as a cellar kept at 0 °C/32 °F, which would also result in extremely high deposits of TARTRATES and PHENOLICS. In practice, a reasonable cellar temperature for ageing wines to be drunk within one's own lifetime is somewhere between 10 and 15 °C (50–59 °F). (The cellars of the Swedish state MONOPOLY were so cold that any fine, old wine bought in Sweden would taste markedly different from the same wine aged in the more temperate climate of France, for example.)

Even lower down the temperature scale, wine freezes at a temperature below 0 °C, that is roughly half its ALCOHOLIC STRENGTH, so usually somewhere between −5 and −8 °C (23 and 18 °F). For this reason, in cool climates, care should be taken to insulate wine stored in places such as garden sheds or garages where winter temperatures are not maintained at a level acceptable to humans.

Serving temperature

The temperature at which a wine is served has a profound effect on how it smells and tastes. Different styles of wine deserve to be served at different temperatures to enhance their good points and try to mask any faults. The following are some general observations, with suggested guidelines in italics.

The higher the temperature, the more easily the volatile FLAVOUR COMPOUNDS evaporate from the surface of wine in a glass. So, to maximize the impact of a wine's AROMA or BOUQUET, it is sensible to serve it relatively warm, say between 16 and 18 °C (61–4 °F) (at temperatures over 20 °C/68 °F the ALCOHOL can begin to evaporate so markedly that it unbalances the wine). *Serve complex and mature wines relatively warm.*

Conversely, the lower the temperature, the fewer volatiles will evaporate and, at a serving temperature of about 8 °C/46 °F, all but the most aromatic wines appear to have no smell whatsoever. *The gustatory faults of a low-quality wine can be masked by serving it very cool.*

The higher the temperature, the more sensitive is the PALATE to sweetness, so it makes sense to serve sweet wines which may not have quite enough ACIDITY to counterbalance the sweetness quite cool, say at about 12 °C/54 °F. For the same reason, medium dry wines served with savoury food will probably taste dry if served well chilled. *In general, chill sweet wines.*

The lower the temperature, the more sensitive the palate to TANNINS and BITTERNESS. Peynaud points out that the same red wine will taste 'hot and thin at 22 °C/72 °F, supple and fluid at 18 °C/64 °F, full and astringent at 10 °C/50 °F'. *Tannic or bitter wines such as many Italian red wines and any young red designed for ageing should be served relatively warm.*

The effect of temperature on apparent acidity is more widely disputed by scientists, but it is generally observable that flabby wines can seem more refreshing if they are served cold, say at 10 °C/50 °F. (This may be related to the effect of temperature on sweetness described above.) *To increase the refreshment factor of a wine, serve it cool.*

Temperature also has an observable effect on wines containing CARBON DIOXIDE. The higher the temperature, the more gas is released, which means that fizzy wines can be unpleasantly frothy at about 18 °C/64 °F. *Sparkling and lightly sparkling wines are generally best served well chilled.* Since very few wines with a complex bouquet ever have any perceptible gas, this is no great limitation (those who make Australia's extraordinary sparkling Shiraz claim it is best served at room temperature, but these sparkling wines are not particularly fizzy).

General rules are therefore:

Serve tannic red wines relatively warm, 15–18 °C (59–64 °F).

Serve complex dry white wines relatively warm, 12–16 °C (54–61 °F).

Serve soft, lighter red wines for refreshment at 10–12 °C (50–5 °F).

Cool sweet, sparkling, flabby white and rosé wines, and those with any off-odour, at 6–10 °C (43–50 °F).

Of course wine tends to warm up to match the ambient temperature, so initial serving temperatures at the bottom end of these brackets are no bad thing, especially in warmer environments. For more details of how to cool and warm bottles, see SERVING WINE.

See also TASTING (as opposed to drinking) for its different requirements of wine temperature.

Peynaud, E., *The Taste of Wine* (2nd edn, New York, 1996).

temperature control during WINE-MAKING is crucially important, as outlined in TEMPERATURE. Although it has been widely and systematically practised only since the 1960s and 1970s, its efficacy was appreciated as long ago as Roman times (see DIE). See REFRIGERATION for details of how wine may be cooled at various points in its life. In cool wine regions or particularly cool years, a FERMENTATION VESSEL may need to be heated to encourage alcoholic FERMENTATION, most easily by circulating warm water in equipment also designed to carry cooling cold water or, in smaller cellars, simply by closing doors and installing a heater or two. Some form of heating may also be required to encourage MALOLACTIC FERMENTATION.

temperature variability, a characteristic of climates referring to the short-term variability of temperature between night and day (diurnal temperature variation or thermal amplitude), and from day to day. It is unrelated to annual temperature range, as described under CONTINENTALITY, and clearly distinct in its VITICULTURAL and OENOLOGICAL implications. Temperature variability plays an important role in determining the risks of FROST damage to dormant vines in spring and autumn, and of HEAT STRESS and direct heat damage to the vines and fruit in summer. There is a more speculative suggestion of relevance to cool regions (see CLIMATE AND WINE QUALITY) that it also influences the formation of PIGMENT, AROMA, and FLAVOUR in the vines and ripening berries: these processes being favoured, relative to the mere accumulation of SUGAR IN GRAPES, by a narrow daily temperature range and minimal temperature fluctuations from day to day. However, in warm to hot regions, a greater temperature variability may be an advantage for wine quality as it implies cooling effects at night.   J.G.

Much is made in certain regions (e.g. WACHAU in Austria, the Uco valley in Argentina, much of Chile, and the SANTA CRUZ MOUNTAINS in California) of the beneficial effects of a wide diurnal temperature variation (night temperatures must be lower than 15 °C)—often due to altitude—but it is not clear whether this is simply because the ripening period is thereby extended, allowing grapes to reach PHENOLIC RIPENESS without losing the desired sugar/acid balance, or whether the variation has some more complicated, as yet unidentified, influence of the ripening process and the accumulation of phenolics.

Gladstones, J., *Viticulture and Environment* (Adelaide, 1992).

Tempranillo is Spain's answer to Cabernet Sauvignon, the vine variety that puts the spine into a high proportion of Spain's most respected red wines, and is increasingly planted elsewhere. Its grapes are thick skinned and capable of making deep-coloured, long-lasting wines that are not, unusually for Spain, notably high in alcohol. Often replacing GARNACHA, BOBAL, or MONASTRELL, it has become the most popular red wine grape in Spain and was planted on a total of 183,500 ha/453,000 acres in 2004.

Temprano means early in Spanish and Tempranillo probably earns its name from its propensity to ripen early, certainly up to two weeks before the Garnacha (GRENACHE) with which it is still regularly blended to make RIOJA. This relatively short growing cycle (Tempranillo buds neither early nor late) enables it to thrive in the often harsh climate of Rioja's higher, more Atlantic-influenced zones Rioja Alta and Rioja Alavesa, where it constitutes up to 70 per cent of all vines planted. Tempranillo has traditionally been grown in widely spaced bushes here, but this relatively vigorous, upright vine has responded well to recent efforts to train it with more rigour on WIRES.

Wine made from Tempranillo grown in relatively cool conditions, where its tendency to produce musts slightly low in acidity is a positive advantage, can last well but the variety does not have a particularly strong flavour identity. Some find strawberries, others spice, leather, and tobacco leaves, but yields and wine-making skill are critical in determining its style.

In Rioja, it is traditionally blended with Garnacha, Mazuelo (Carignan), Graciano, and Viura. In Penedès, where it is known as Ull de Llebre, Tempranillo softens the local Monastrell. In Valdepeñas, it is known as Cencibel. The variety is ideally suited to the cool conditions of Ribera del Duero, where, as Tinto Fino, it is by far the principal grape variety, but the seasoning of varieties imported from Bordeaux is an ingredient of some importance in that high plateau's most famous wine VEGA SICILIA. Indeed, throughout Spain, blends of Tempranillo with Cabernet Sauvignon and/or Merlot are becoming prevalent, notably in Navarra and Castilla-La Mancha.

Tempranillo is now grown in practically all red wine regions of Spain. The variety is so well entrenched in northern and central Spain that Spain's total Tempranillo plantings were well over 31,000 ha/76,600 acres in Rioja alone. Its synonyms also include Tinto Madrid, Tinto de la Rioja, Tinta del Pais, Tinto Aragónes, and Tinta de Toro, where its particularly concentrated form has played a major part in the newfound popularity of TORO wines.

Tempranillo is one of the very few Spanish varieties to have been adopted to any real extent in Portugal, where it is known officially as RORIZ and planted on an estimated 13,000 ha/32,000 acres in 2004. It was probably introduced to Portugal from Spain in the mid 19th century and gained ground in the wake of PHYLLOXERA. Under the name Tinta Roriz, it is the second most planted variety in the Douro (after Touriga Franca), where it is valued for port and unfortified Douro wines. However, Tinta Roriz has a tendency to over-produce and only performs well when yields are low. Given its importance in the region, it is no coincidence that declared port vintages tend to be those when Tinta Roriz has done well. As Aragónez, it is widely planted in the Alentejo, where it is sometimes bottled as a varietal but is often blended with the local Trincadeira. It is also gaining ground in the Dão region (where it is known as Tinta Roriz) and in other parts of Portugal.

As Tempranillo or **Tempranilla** and making rather light, possibly over-irrigated reds, it has been important in Argentina's wine industry but lost ground to more marketable varieties in the late 1980s, with plantings having declined to 5,000 ha/12,350 acres by 2002, mainly in Mendoza, although the Spanish-owned O. Fournier makes a particularly interesting example.

There were 1,500 ha/3,700 acres in southern France in 2000, most notably in the Aude and used for blending. Tempranillo is almost certainly the true identity of the unfashionable low-acid variety known in California as Valdepeñas, of which 400 acres/160 ha remained, mainly in the Central valley, in the mid 1990s. Since that time, interest has perked up with another 400 acres finding a home in areas such as the Sierra foothills. Stevenot is a noteworthy California producer here, while Abacela pioneered fine Tempranillo in southern Oregon.

As vine-growers the world over search for new, recognizably high-quality products, Tempranillo is spreading around the world, notably in Australia, where plantings totalled more than 250 ha/620 acres by the mid 2000s.

tendone, the Italian name for the overhead vine-TRAINING SYSTEM widely used in southern Italy. It is also common in South America, where it is used for both TABLE GRAPES and wine grapes, and is called *parral* (Argentina) or *parron* (Chile). English terms used include both arbour and pergola, although the system is little used in English-speaking countries.

The vines are normally trained with trunks about 2 m/6.5 ft high and a system of wooden frames and cross wires supports the foliage and fruit. Arbours are normally high enough from the ground to allow tractors and implements to pass underneath, but not so high as to make hand work difficult. The vines are pruned to either canes or spurs (see PRUNING). Because all of the sunlight is captured, the system can be very productive: 30 to 70 tonnes of grapes per hectare when water supply is plentiful.

Such training systems are limited in use because of the expense of their construction and the high cost of LABOUR required to manage them. Worker productivity is lower because of fatigue, and, where the vines are vigorous, the leaves form a very dense CANOPY on top and so the fruit and lower leaves are heavily shaded (see SHADE). This reduces both yield and quality, and increases the risk of POWDERY MILDEW.

Furthermore, the ventilation under such canopies is very restricted and the build-up of humidity favours BOTRYTIS BUNCH ROT. The arbour system is used for table grapes in many parts of the world, and has the advantage that the fruit hangs freely and makes access easy. Inclined overhead trellis systems which do not completely cover the ground are often used for table grapes, as in South Africa (where it may be called the verandah system), and for wine grapes around the borders of fields in the VINHO VERDE region of Portugal.   R.E.S.

tendril, coiling, clasping organ that enables the stems of plants to climb (see WILD VINES). In many plants, these organs are modifications of stems, leaves, or leaflets, but in the grapevine they are modified INFLORESCENCES, developing at two of every three consecutive NODES. Tendrils are sensitive to touch; when sufficiently elongated, they react to pressure on their surface by coiling around the touched object, be it a wire, a part of the vine, or any other adjacent material. Once coiled, the tendrils become lignified and very tough.   B.G.C.

tent, medieval term for strong red wine from Iberia, mainly Spain (notably deeper in colour that the CLAIRET then still associated with Bordeaux). It is an Anglicized version of the word TINTO, Spanish and Portuguese for red.

tenuta, Italian word for a fairly substantial agricultural holding or estate (larger than, for example, the usual PODERE).

Téoulier, old white grape variety once grown in south east France.

Teran, Terrano, names for a subvariety of the REFOSCO group, used, respectively, in CROATIA and the Kras district of SLOVENIA and the CARSO DOC in the extreme east of Friuli. One of them, Teran Bijeli, was shown to be identical to PROSECCO by DNA PROFILING at Zagreb.

Terlano, or **Terlaner** in German, white wines from around the town of Terlano in ALTO ADIGE.

Termeno Aromatico. See GEWÜRZTRAMINER.

termites, can be pests in older vineyards, where they tunnel into old wood and can weaken it so much that the vine may collapse. Occasionally newly planted cuttings are attacked where growing conditions are poor.   M.J.E.

Teroldego, grape variety which makes deep-coloured, seriously lively, fruity wines named Teroldego Rotaliano because they are made almost exclusively in the Rotaliano plain in TRENTINO, north east Italy, with suitable tannins for relatively early drinking. Wine made from this variety is rather prone to REDUCTION. Teroldego is traditionally trained in PERGOLA, but from 1985 onwards the Foradori winery initiated a qualitative revolution by doing MASS SELECTION and introducing the Guyot VINE TRAINING system in Trentino. Foradori's Granato beame the benchmark for classic and age-worthy Teroldego. The variety was known in the Rotaliano plain as early as the 15th century, and DNA PROFILING at SAN MICHELE ALL'ADIGE recently showed that Teroldego and LAGREIN from Alto Adige have a parent–offspring relationship. See also MARZEMINO.   J.V.

terpenes, distinctive FLAVOUR COMPOUNDS associated with the floral aromas found in wines made from such varieties as Muscat, Gewürztraminer, and Riesling. They are also found in oak, particularly American oak (see OAK FLAVOUR).

terpenoids, an important group of plant chemicals including many essential oils, CAROTENOIDS, plant HORMONES, sterols, and rubber. They contribute much to the unique qualities of the vine. Chemically, they are multiples of branched, five-carbon (isoprene) units yielding a variety of compounds with diverse properties: the C10 monoterpenes make an important contribution to floral aromas (see FLAVOUR COMPOUNDS); the C15 sesquiterpenoids include the hormone ABSCISIC ACID, and the C20 diterpenes include the GIBBERELLIN hormones. Carotenoids, with 40 carbon atoms, contribute to the skin colour of so-called white grapes and are metabolized to nor-isoprenoid flavour compounds that play a large part in non-floral aroma of grapes. See also terpenes in OAK FLAVOUR. B.G.C. & P.J.W.

Terra Alta, Spanish for 'high land', is the highest of the DO wine zones in Spanish CATALUÑA (see map under SPAIN). Its recent development parallels that of TARRAGONA, which adjoins Terra Alta to the east. As in Tarragona, growers are following the lead of PRIORAT, notably recovering and relaunching their formerly despised GARNACHA BLANCA grapes and making some impressive red blends.
R.J.M. & V. de la S.

terraces make work in vineyards planted across sloping land considerably easier, and can also help combat SOIL EROSION. Terraces more or less follow the contours of the land, and so row spacing may be irregular. Terraces are created when the hillside is re-formed into a series of horizontal steps between the rows. The world's most famous vineyard terraces are those of the PORT wine region of the DOURO valley in northern Portugal where there has been considerable experimentation with different designs, although they are common in much of SWITZERLAND, the northern RHÔNE, and elsewhere.

In centuries past, such terraces were laboriously constructed by hand and supported by stone walls. For modern vineyards, the cost of laying stones by hand can be prohibitive, and so most modern terraces are formed by bulldozers. Terraces are expensive to create, and are therefore justified only for expensive wines. There is a modern tendency to avoid planting vineyards on such slopes.

An alternative to creating terraces is to plant vines up and down the hillsides, as in Germany and other parts of northern Europe. This practice avoids the expense of forming terraces but can lead to soil erosion and worker fatigue, and some slopes are too steep for tractors. See also HILLSIDE VINEYARDS. R.E.S.

Terrano, synonym for Teran or REFOSCO.

Terrantez, synonym for the Portuguese white wine grape FOLGASÃO that is practically extinct on the island of MADEIRA but can occasionally be encountered in historic bottles.

terra rossa, red-brown LOAM or CLAY directly over well-drained LIMESTONE found typically in regions with a MEDITERRANEAN CLIMATE. Such soils are found in southern Europe (in Spain's La MANCHA, for example), North Africa, and parts of Australia. The quality of many wines made from Cabernet Sauvignon and Shiraz grapes grown at Coonawarra in SOUTH AUSTRALIA is said to owe much to the terra rossa soils there. M.J.E.

Terras do Sado, VINHO REGIONAL in southern PORTUGAL encompassing the SETÚBAL peninsula between the Tagus and Sado estuaries and a section of the Atlantic coast (see map under PORTUGAL). The warm, maritime climate is particularly well suited to winemaking. In the 19th century, the north-facing slopes around the village of Azeitão were planted with a number of different Moscatel (MUSCAT) grape varieties to make sweet, fortified Setúbal but, since this wine has declined in popularity, other varieties have taken their place.

Although there are many individual growers, production is largely concentrated in the hands of two firms, José Maria da FONSECA Successores in Azeitão and J. P. Vinhos (known for its João Pires brand) based nearby. In the 1980s, two skilled OENOLOGISTS, trained respectively at DAVIS in California and ROSEWORTHY in Australia, helped to modernize wine-making in the region. As a result of experiments that were partly inspired by the NEW WORLD, the Terras do Sado region produces a wide range of different wines including such well-established brands as Periquita and Pasmados, and single estate wines such as Quinta de Camarate, and Quinta da Bacalhôa.

The most important red grapes are the indigenous varieties, especially CASTELÃO (here commonly nicknamed Periquita), which is used for red, rosé, and sparkling wines. MUSCAT OF ALEXANDRIA (called Moscatel de Setúbal locally) is the most significant white variety, together with ARINTO, FERNÃO PIRES, and ESGANA CÃO. Chardonnay, Cabernet Sauvignon, Merlot, and Syrah have also been grown successfully on the limestone Arrabida hills and producers are now experimenting with other indigenous grape varieties from the north of Portugal such as Touriga Franca and Touriga Nacional.

Within the Terras do Sado region is the Palmela DOC formed by the merger of two former IPRs and now a region with two distinct terroirs: the limestone hills of the Serra da Arrabida, and the sandy soils of the plain which extends eastwards from the fortress town of Palmela, which is where the widely planted Castelão grape performs at its best, making distinctive, structured wines that are capable of ageing well in bottle. R.J.M.

Terras Durienses, subregion of VINHO REGIONAL Trás-os-Montes which corresponds to the Douro region. See DOURO and TRÁS-OS-MONTES for more details.

Terras Madeirenses, VINHO REGIONAL for the unfortified wines of the island of MADEIRA. Despite considerable EU investment in a new winery at São Vicente, as well as experimental plantings of Cabernet Sauvignon, Merlot, and Syrah, these wines are all consumed on the island. R.J.M.

Terrasses du Larzac, appellation within the Coteaux du LANGUEDOC in southern France created in 2005 for red wines made from Syrah, Grenache Noir, Mourvèdre with, possibly, some Cinsaut and Carignan, grown in some of the highest vineyards of the Coteaux du Languedoc on the slopes of the Cevennes.

Terret is one of the Languedoc's oldest vine varieties and, like PINOT, has had plenty of time to mutate into different shades of grape, which may even be found on the same plant. Indeed, Galet claims to have seen different-coloured grapes in the same bunch. **Terret Gris** was once by far the most planted white wine variety in the Languedoc, even if it was concentrated in the Hérault *département*, where there were 2,600 ha/6,400 acres of **Terret Blanc** still growing in 2000. Either grape can be made into a relatively full-bodied but naturally crisp varietal white, but as a name Terret lacks the magic of INTERNATIONAL VARIETIES. Although light-berried Terrets are in decline, combined they were planted on about 3,000 ha of French vineyard in 2000. They are allowed into the white wines of Minervois, Corbières, and, to a decreasing extent, Coteaux du Languedoc.

Terret Noir is the dark-berried version, which was grown on nearly 400 ha/1,000 acres in 2000 and is one of the permitted varieties in red CHÂTEAUNEUF-DU-PAPE, to which it can add useful structure and interest. All Terrets bud usefully late and keep their acidity well.

Galet, P., *Dictionnaire encyclopédique des cépages* (Paris, 2000).

terroir, much-discussed term for the total natural environment of any viticultural site. No precise English equivalent exists for this quintessentially French term and concept. Dubos and Laville describe it fully, and how it underlies and defines the French APPELLATION CONTRÔLÉE system. A definition is given in van Leeuwen *et al.* Discussion of terroir is central to philosophical and commercial differences between OLD WORLD and NEW WORLD approaches to wine.

Major components of terroir are SOIL (as the word suggests) and local TOPOGRAPHY, together with their interactions with each other and with MACROCLIMATE to determine MESOCLIMATE and vine MICROCLIMATE. The holistic combination of all these is held to give each site its own unique terroir, which is reflected in its wines more or less consistently from year to year, to some degree regardless of variations in methods of VITICULTURE and WINE-MAKING. Thus every small plot, and in generic terms every larger area, and ultimately region, may have distinctive wine-style characteristics which cannot be precisely replicated elsewhere. The extent to which terroir effects are unique is, however, debatable, and of course commercially important, which makes the subject controversial.

Opinions have differed greatly on the reality and, if real, the importance of terroir in determining wine qualities. Major regional classifications of European vineyards have been largely founded on the concepts of terroir, although these may be based on climate rather than soil. New World viticulturists and researchers, on the other hand, have tended to dismiss it as a product of mysticism and established commercial interest. Dickenson canvasses the issues in detail, and is likewise mostly sceptical. But against these views it might also be justly charged that 'newer' viticulture has notoriously attempted to imitate the products of the great vineyards without regard to terroir, and therefore has a commercial reason for belittling its potential contribution.

It can certainly be argued that modern improvements in vineyard and winery technology, by raising and unifying standards of wine quality, have to some extent obscured differences in both style and quality of wines that in the past were (sometimes wrongly) attributed to terroir in its true sense. But paradoxically, the same improvements can serve to unmask genuine differences due to terroir. By eliminating extraneous odours and tastes derived from faulty wine-making, they allow the fuller expression of intrinsic grape qualities, which can be related to site. The wines of Burgundy are most often cited as evidence of the reality of the terroir effect. Many growers have different plots which they cultivate in the same way. They then vinify the grapes from these plots in a similar way, yet the wines produced differ significantly in quality and style. GUIGAL's single-vineyard bottlings in Côte Rôtie are another example of this approach to terroir.

Laville lists the following factors (components) as determining terroir:

- Climate, as measured by TEMPERATURE and RAINFALL.
- Sunlight energy, or insolation, received per unit of land surface area (see SUNLIGHT).
- Relief (or TOPOGRAPHY, or geomorphology), comprising altitude, slope, and aspect.
- Geology and pedology, determining the soil's basic physical and chemical characteristics (see GEOLOGY).
- Hydrology, or SOIL–WATER relations.

An essential notion of terroir is that all its components are natural, and that they cannot be significantly influenced by management.

The main emphasis in nearly all recent French writings is on the soil, and especially its role and interactions with other elements of the environment in governing water supply to the vine. The most important evidence for this comes from the studies of Dr Gérard Seguin, of the University of BORDEAUX. He found that, while many of the acknowledged best Bordeaux vineyards are on the Quaternary (recently laid down) gravelly sands, by no means all are. Neither geological origin nor SOIL TEXTURE could explain the region's best terroirs, as judged by the wines they produce. The best in fact covered extremely diverse soil textures, ranging from heavy CLAYS, as in Pomerol, through CALCAREOUS brown soils, to sandy LOAMS and SANDS over clay (podzols), to the deep, gravelly sands most typical of the Médoc. An analysis of the soils' chemical properties showed them also to be extremely variable.

Two unifying themes did, however, emerge among the top CRUS. First, none of their soils was very fertile, but then none of the vines showed mineral element deficiencies either (see VINE NUTRITION). Secondly, their soils regulated water supply to the vines in such a way that it was nearly always just moderately sufficient, without extremes in either direction. DRAINAGE was always excellent, so that both water-logging and sudden increases in water supply to the vines were avoided no matter how much the rainfall. In the case of clay soils, this depended on their having fairly high ORGANIC MATTER and/or CALCIUM contents, so that they maintained friability and an open pore structure through which water could move readily (see SOIL STRUCTURE).

At the same time, the capacity to store soil water within a SOIL DEPTH accessible to the vine ROOTS was great enough to ensure supply through prolonged rainfall deficits. This might be achieved either by great soil depth and a deep, sparse root system, in the case of sandy soils with little water storage capacity per unit volume; or a lesser depth in heavier soils, combined with a capacity of the clay and organic matter to hold some of the water tightly enough that it is only slowly available to the roots. The deep, gravelly sands of the MÉDOC exemplified the former situation, the heavy clays of POMEROL, the latter. This explained why the best terroirs maintain their wine quality notably better in poor seasons than the rest, a consistency which has always been one of the most striking features of the Bordeaux CLASSED GROWTHS.

Van Leeuwen et al. found that the effect of soil is secondary to that of climate. However, both the climate and the soil effects are mediated through their influence on water supply to the vine.

Studies of terroir in Burgundy, cited and illustrated by Johnson, and by Halliday and Johnson, have led to similar conclusions. There the best wines are from stony clay loam soils, formed on the middle slopes from MARL (a clay

and soft limestone mixture) mixed with SILT and rubble from outcropping hard LIMESTONE further up. These soils combine good drainage with just the right capacity to store and supply water to the vines.

Extensive studies by Carbonneau and colleagues in the Bordeaux region, and by Smart and colleagues in Australia and New Zealand, have revealed a further common feature of vineyards producing the best wines. All have a high degree of leaf and bunch exposure to direct sunlight, with little complete shading of internal and lower leaves (see further discussion under SUNLIGHT, CANOPY MICROCLIMATE, and CANOPY MANAGEMENT). Variation in this respect is explained by differences in vegetative VIGOUR and vine BALANCE. Best quality is associated with only moderate vigour, which typically results from a somewhat restricted water supply, limited NITROGEN, and (in some cases) appropriate TRAINING SYSTEMS. These studies suggest that soil effects on wine quality are indirect; i.e. soil conditions regulating water and nitrogen supply to the vine affect vine vigour, which in turn affects fruit and leaf exposure to sunlight, which in turn affects wine quality. While exposure to sunlight is amenable to management control on soils that are not too fertile, vine supply of water, in the absence of IRRIGATION, is very largely not. It is therefore a prime contributor, together with local TOPOGRAPHY, to the immutable influence of terroir.

An implication is that GEOLOGY, often cited as a basis of terroir, has in general no more than an indirect role. To varying degrees, parent ROCK materials do contribute to the natures of the soils derived from them; they also shape local topography and therefore MESOCLIMATE. Occasionally the parent materials contribute directly because vine roots can penetrate them, as in the cases of CHALK subsoils and the recent ALLUVIAL deposits of the Médoc. In the broad sense, however, it remains the soil itself, and its water relations, that play the decisive role.

The effect of terroir on wine quality is now quite well understood: it is mainly mediated through vine water supply by the soil and the climate, although mineral supply (and especially nitrogen supply) can also play a role. This effect of terroir can partly be obtained by good canopy and irrigation management in dry climates. However, the effect of terroir on wine style is still poorly understood. The high quality of Chx AUSONE (limestone), CHEVAL BLANC (gravel and clay), and PÉTRUS (heavy clay) can be explained by the water regime. But why do they taste different and why do they each have their own style, despite very similar viticultural and oenological practices? This aspect of terroir is extremely interesting, because top wines are not only very good, but also unique, with their own style.

Another aspect of terroir is that its greatest expression occurs when grape ripening is relatively slow and therefore late in the season. This occurs in cool climates, or in warmer climates when varieties are sufficiently late ripening. In all quality wine regions in Europe, growers have chosen varieties that just achieve ripeness under the local climatic conditions. When grapes ripen in August in the northern hemisphere, or in February in the southern hemisphere, it is very difficult to produce refined wines with sought-after aromatic expression. Terroir can only be understood when soil, climate, and vine are taken into account simultaneously. A poor understanding of terroir in New World countries has in some instances led producers to plant varieties regardless of the local climatic conditions. When early-ripening varieties are planted in warm climates, wines are heavy, lacking freshness and aromatic expression (except for aromas produced by wine-making practices). This is the case with warm climate Chardonnay, for instance. A much better expression is obtained in cool climates (Chardonnay in Chablis, Sauvignon Blanc in New Zealand). Growers in the New World are becoming more aware of this and seeking out cooler regions—Carneros instead of the Napa valley, for example, or high altitude vineyards in Argentina, New Zealand, and Tasmania.

An international concept?

The question remains as to how far the French concept of terroir, with its primary emphasis on soil, is relevant to other regions and viticultural systems. An overriding influence of soil and its water relations can be easily enough understood in the Bordeaux environment, with its relatively flat topography and, as a consequence, few really major differences in mesoclimate. The situation is clearly different in areas such as Germany's MOSEL-SAAR-RUWER region at the cold limit of commercial viticulture. The topographic differences between individual sites decide whether grapes, particularly the high-quality varieties such as RIESLING, will ripen fully at all. Topography and mesoclimate are inescapably major components of terroir (or its German equivalent).

Moreover, it has been argued that mesoclimatic differences may not merely govern the degree of ripeness attained. Some believe that they could also affect more subtle grape and wine qualities of the kinds commonly attributed to terroir; see CLIMATE AND WINE QUALITY and TEMPERATURE VARIABILITY. Soil might similarly influence grape and wine qualities through its effect on MICROCLIMATE; see STONES AND ROCKS, SOIL COLOUR, and SOIL AND WINE QUALITY.

The New World approach to vineyard design is now much more likely to take soil differences into account. New World vineyards were once most likely to have been subdivided according to existing boundaries, shape, topography, or whim. Today it is increasingly common to allow a soil survey and SOIL MAPPING to determine choice of variety, rootstock, even trellis system—a concession to the wisdom of Old World experience.

Any such effects serve, of course, to underline terroir as a real concept, and not something expressed merely through the relationships between vine vigour, balance, and the vine canopy. The distinction is critical because, to the extent that the latter is true, other approaches are often available to achieve the same end. Two stand out in importance.

1. The use of larger or more complex vine-TRAINING SYSTEMS, such as Carbonneau's LYRE trellis, making it possible to maintain good leaf and fruit exposure on larger and more productive vines. This in turn allows the exploitation of moister, and possibly more fertile, soils, giving higher yields without any necessary loss of fruit and wine quality.

2. In regions with dry summers, the use of controlled IRRIGATION, especially that made possible by DRIP IRRIGATION. This allows vegetative vigour to be held at appropriate levels for vine balance, but water to be supplied during ripening as needed. It is an important advance in regions of MEDITERRANEAN CLIMATE, enabling them to duplicate many of the terroir characteristics of the long-established best table wine areas, but with fewer climatic risks.

It seems inconceivable, however, that these developments will ever totally eliminate the regional and local differences in wine qualities that have been traditionally ascribed to terroir. Differences in MACROCLIMATE, MESOCLIMATE, and soil MICROCLIMATE remain, while there are many conceivable avenues by which differences in soil chemistry—for instance, in trace element balances—might have small effects on wine flavours and aromas which are nevertheless detectable by the sense of TASTE. To the extent that terroirs remain unique, and poorly understood, one can therefore hope that they will continue to help mould the infinite variety and individuality of the best wines, giving the special nuances of character that make wine such a fascinating study for winemaker and consumer alike. *Vivent les différences!*

J.G., R.E.S., & C.V.L.

Bohmrich, R., 'Terroir', *Journal of Wine Research*, 7/1 (1996–7), 33–46.

Dickenson, J., 'Viticultural geography: an introduction to the literature in English', *Journal of Wine Research*, 1 (1990), 5–24.

Falcetti, M., 'Terroir ou cépage: de l'opposition des concepts face au défi vitivinicole du XXIème siècle', *Bulletin de l'OIV*, 791–2 (1997), 25–36.

Halliday, J., and Johnson, H., *The Art and Science of Wine* (London, 1992).

Johnson, H., and Robinson, J., *The World Atlas of Wine* (5th edn, London and New York, 2001).

Laville, P., 'Le Terroir, un concept indispensable à l'élaboration et à la protection des appellations d'origine comme à la gestion des vignobles: le cas de la France', *Bulletin de l'OIV*, 709–10 (1990), 217–41.

Riou, C., Morlat, R., and Asselin, C., 'Une approche intégrée des terroirs viticoles. Discussion sur les critères de caractérisation accessibles', *Bulletin de l'OIV*, 68/767–8 (1995), 93–106.

Seguin, G., ' "Terroirs" and pedology of wine growing', *Experientia*, 42 (1986), 861–73.

Smart, R. E., 'Vineyard design to improve wine quality the Orlando way', *Australian and New Zealand Wine Industry Journal*, 11 (1996), 335–6.

Van Leeuwen, C., and Chéry, P., 'Quelle méthode pour caractériser et étudier le terroir viticole: analyse de sol, cartographie pédologique ou étude écophysiologique?', in *Un raisin de qualité: de la vigne à la cuve*, n° Hors Série du *Journal International des Sciences de la Vigne et du Vin* (2001), 13–20.

—— Friant, P., Choné, X., Tregoat, O., Koundouras, S., and Dubourdieu, D., 'Influence of climate, soil, and cultivar on terroir', *American Journal of Enology and Viticulture*, 55/3 (2004), 207–17.

tête de cuvée, term occasionally used for selected top bottlings.

tetrachloroanisole, more properly **2,3,4,6-tetrachloroanisole,** or **TeCA,** is a musty- or dusty-smelling compound that can taint wine if the concentration is above the perception threshold of 10–15 ng/l in red or white wine and about 4 ng/l in sparkling wine. It is caused by the microbial degradation by fungi in the winery of pentachlorophenol (PCP) used in some pesticides, herbicides, and insecticides, including those used in wood treatment. Although such pesticides are no longer permitted for vines, it is thought that they may contaminate the vineyard or winery environment. PCA or 2,3,4,5,6-pentachloroanisole has a much higher perception threshold, at around 5000 ng/l but is nearly always present with TeCA.

Texas, south western state in the UNITED STATES, currently the country's fifth largest wine-producing state after California, New York, Washington, and Oregon with about 3,200 acres/1,300 ha planted mainly with VINIFERA vines. The first vineyard was planted by the Spanish at the Ysleta Mission near what is now El Paso in the early 1660s. The production built to more than 200,000 gal/7,570 hl by 1853. In the 1880s, the famous VITIS taxonomist T. V. MUNSON, from Denison, Texas, shipped native Texas vine species to France and saved the European wine community from devastation by PHYLLOXERA. In the early 20th century, the Texas wine industry was almost eliminated by PROHIBITION. Dr Clint McPherson and Robert Reed of Texas Tech University revived the modern wine industry in 1976 with the creation of Llano Estacado Winery. In 2004, 70 bonded wineries produced 1.9 million gal/71,900 hl of wine from 7,500 tons of grapes and by early 2005 there were 86 wineries.

Wine is grown in all parts of the state and conditions vary greatly. Texas is divided into three main regions. The **North-Central Region** runs across the northern third of the state from the Panhandle border with New Mexico east towards Dallas, but excludes north east Texas. One of the best quality wine regions, the Texas High Plains AVA, and the largest concentration of grape growers are both in the western part of the North-Central Region. To the east around Dallas, Fort Worth, and Grapevine, which has fashioned itself as a major wine destination, the humidity makes it difficult to grow VINIFERA vines though a few hardy souls persevere.

The eastern third of Texas, the **South-Eastern Region** around the cities of Austin, San Antonio, and Houston, suffers from PIERCE'S DISEASE, the biggest problem for the Texas grape-growing industry. In the far north east portion of the South-Eastern Region are warm, humid pine forests suitable for MUSCA-DINE grapes. Pierce's disease-resistant Lenoir (Black Spanish), Cynthiana, and Blanc du Bois varieties are grown in this north east area. In the centre of the South-Eastern Region, how-ever, including the Texas Hill Country AVA, Bell Mountain AVA, and Fredericksburg in the Texas Hill Country AVA, fine VINIFERA wines are produced. In the south of the South-Eastern Region, on the Mexican border, is DESERT and the oldest winery in Texas, Val Verde, which has operated continuously for over a century and is known mainly for sweet, FORTIFIED wines.

The central-western third of the state is the **Trans-Pecos Region** whose high-altitude vineyards amidst arid mesas produce about 40 per cent of the grapes in Texas from its 1,208 acres/489 ha, about the same production as that of the Texas High Plains vineyards.

The University of Texas owns almost 1,000 acres/400 ha of vines in the Trans-Pecos Region near Fort Stockton. The vineyard is leased to, farmed, and the grapes vinified by Mesa Vineyards, a Texas-based company that purchased the property from the French com-pany Cordier in 2005. More than two-thirds of all Texas wine is produced here. Vineyards are otherwise divided among the state's inde-pendent vine-growers and bonded wineries, al-though new plantings are expected to be primarily in the western part of Texas.

Cabernet Sauvignon and Chardonnay lead in total number of acres planted; Chenin Blanc (making particularly successful wines here) and Sauvignon Blanc lead in tonnage. Some growers are having success with grapes more suited to Texas' warm weather such as Syrah, Tempranillo, Sangiovese, Viognier, and Pinot Gris. The primary enemies of Texas vines are Pierce's disease, winter freeze, hail, wind, drought, black rot, cotton root rot, black berry moth, and crown gall. Grapes and wine are routinely imported from California, New Mexico, and France to augment Texas produc-tion.

Texas has seven designated AVAS plus one pending in 2005, listed below in chronological order.

The Mesilla Valley (1985) extends from New Mexico into Texas, but is generally considered a New Mexico AVA.

Bell Mountain (1986), won on behalf of the unique quality and concentration of Cabernet Sauvignon grown in this small area in north east Gillespie county 15 miles north of Fredericksburg.

Fredericksburg (1989), within Texas Hill Country is known for good-quality Cabernet Sauvignon and Chardonnay.

Texas Hill Country (1991), the largest AVA in the US, includes 15,000 square miles but fewer than 800 planted acres of vineyard in the late 1990s. It produces mainly pleasant whites and relatively soft reds.

Escondido Valley (1992), an area of about 50 square miles in Pecos county in the Trans-Pecos Region near Fort Stockton. This small AVA is the home of Ste Mesa Vineyards, the state's biggest winery and grower of 40 per cent of the state's grapes.

Texas High Plains (1993), the state's most con-sistent AVA so far, especially for Cabernet Sauvignon and Chardonnay. A high elevation with fertile red soils, hot days, cool nights, and frigid winters that allow full vine DORMANCY.

This region grows a further 40 per cent of Texas grapes from about 1,200 acres.

Texas Davis Mountains, one-winery AVA granted in 1998 producing very good Cabernet Sauvignon and a small quantity of Sauvignon Blanc.

Texoma (AVA status pending 2005) will in-clude parts of both Texas and Oklahoma.

D.E.T. & R.M.M.

English, S. J., *The Wines of Texas* (4th edn, Austin, Tex., 2002).

Texas root rot, caused by the fungus *Phymatotrichum omnivorum*, which lives in the soil. This vine FUNGAL DISEASE can prevent grape-growing in parts of the south western United States. A circular patch of vines can suddenly die in summer. The disease is avoided by planting disease-free material in non-infested soil. The vigorous ROOTSTOCK Dog Ridge can be planted where the fungus is sus-pected.

R.E.S.

texture, the dimension of tasting that draws together attributes such as smoothness and ASTRINGENCY that produce tactile rather than flavour sensations on the surface of the mouth. These sensations are often referred to collect-ively as MOUTHFEEL, especially in relation to red wines. In practice, the sensory perception of texture, experienced through the sense of touch and arising from the trigeminal nerve, is closely intertwined with the senses of taste and smell. ASTRINGENCY, BODY, VISCOSITY, BIT-TERNESS, and ACIDITY are among the inter-related factors influencing texture. Because of the complexity of the interactions among the many wine constituents that may be in-volved, formal sensory studies relating wine composition to texture are limited. Neverthe-less, a start has been made on this daunting task and evidence to date indicates that wine

TANNINS, PIGMENTED TANNINS, and ETHANOL are all involved with this sensation. Research in 2004 showed that wine POLYSACCHARIDES also probably play an important role in the textural properties of wine. Current work at DAVIS, ADELAIDE, and INRA MONTPELLIER is aimed at discriminating among the ways astringency manifests itself, and relating these to the texture and tannin composition of the wine. Tasting notes sometimes try to describe the texture of a wine by comparing it to a type of material such as silk or velvet, or by likening it to the texture of a foodstuff, e.g. grainy or chewy. A mouthfeel wheel was developed in Adelaide in Australia in answer to Davis's AROMA WHEEL (illustrated under MOUTHFEEL). Its purpose is to establish a vo-cabulary for describing the sensations of tex-ture in red wines.

P.J.W. & J.Ha.

Gawel, R., Oberholster, A., and Francis, I. L., 'A "mouth-feel wheel": terminology for communicat-ing the mouth-feel characteristics of red wine', *Australian Journal of Grape and Wine Research*, 6 (2000), 203–7.

Vidal, S., Francis, L., Williams, P., Kwiatkowski, M., Gawel, R., Cheynier, V., and Waters, E., 'The mouth-feel properties of polysaccharides and anthocyanins in a wine like medium', *Food Chemis-try*, 85 (2004), 519–25.

Thailand, south east Asian country where viticulture began in the 1960s on the low plain around the capital Bangkok and has flour-ished, despite the challenges involved in TROP-ICAL VITICULTURE. Although the early vineyards were developed to produce TABLE GRAPES, the main varieties planted were VINIFERA, includ-ing MALAGA BLANC, MUSCAT HAMBURG, Perlette, CARDINAL, and POKDUM. A total of around 4,000 ha/10,000 acres had been planted by 2001.

In the mid 1980s, grapes from these vine-yards became the raw material for a popular wine cooler (called Spy) produced by the Siam Winery, a venture established by the man who devised the energy drink Red Bull. A more conventional wine-making operation, Château de Loei, based on mainstream wine grape varieties (principally Chenin Blanc and Syrah) began in 1991 in the cooler Phurua Highland district in north east Thailand (at 600–800 m) along the Loei river, close to the border with Laos. The venture was the personal project of the late Dr Chaijudh Karnasuta, a prominent Thai industrialist. A third frontier was forged in the mid 1990s by an offshoot of the giant Boon Rawd Corporation, brewer of Singha beer, with trial plantings of 50 wine grape varieties in the highlands around the Khao Yai National Park north of Bangkok. Chenin Blanc and Syrah also performed well here, forming the backbone of the premium wines released by the founding winery, PB Valley, and by Chateau des Brumes and GranMonte Estate that have followed PB Val-ley. Other varieties for which expectations are high in this region include Cabernet

Sauvignon, Pinot Noir, Tempranillo, Dornfelder, and Zinfandel.

Meanwhile, Siam Winery has strengthened its position as the largest producer of wine in Thailand, with a capacity of more than half a million cases a year. It added the Chatemp label to its line-up in 1999 and the appropriately named Monsoon Valley label in 2003. The early releases are based on the Malaga Blanc and Pokdum growing in the so-called 'floating vineyards' in the Chao Phraya delta. Siam Winery has also established substantial vineyards with more conventional varieties in Khao Yai and at Hua Hin, south west of Bangkok. D.G.

Theophrastus (370–288 BC), philosopher and botanist from Lesbos who discusses viticulture in his 'plant researches'.

thermal amplitude. See TEMPERATURE VARIABILITY.

thermotherapy, a technique to eliminate VIRUS DISEASES from grapevines by growing infected plants at high temperatures (about 38 °C or 100 °F), and then propagating from SHOOT TIPS. These shoot tips can produce plants free of virus diseases, but diseases such as FANLEAF DEGENERATION virus are eliminated much more easily than others—LEAFROLL, for example. Each tip produced must be checked to see whether it is virus-free, and can become registered as a new CLONE. New techniques of TISSUE CULTURE have generally been found more effective at virus elimination. R.E.S.

thermovinification, process sometimes used in RED WINE-MAKING, particularly in cool climates such as those of upper NEW YORK state or after particularly cool growing seasons, whereby heat, about 70 °C/158 °F, is applied to grape clusters or MUST before FERMENTATION to liberate ANTHOCYANINS, or colour, from the skins (see TEMPERATURE effects). The heat treatment is immediately followed by PRESSING to liberate coloured juice, which is then fermented much as in traditional WHITE WINE-MAKING. Thermovinification is particularly valuable in making everyday wines from grape varieties low in anthocyanins, or from better-coloured grape varieties affected by moulds such as BOTRYTIS rot, which destroys colour in dark-skinned grapes. In the latter case, the heat inactivates the colour-destroying enzymes secreted by the mould. The heat also destroys pectoclytic enzymes, making CLARIFICATION more difficult, and oxidases such as LACCASE, reducing the risk of oxidation, especially useful for botrytis-affected grapes. Thermovinification is rarely used in making fine wines, however, which almost invariably rely on extended MACERATION to extract colour and flavour from the grape skins. However, at Ch de Beaucastel in the Rhône, the Perrins have for many years heated the grapes very briefly to 80 °C/176 °F immediately after destemming. The grapes are then cooled to cellar temperature prior to fermentation. This is said to increase the extraction of colour and flavour and avoid the addition of sulfur to the must. See also FLASH DÉTENTE.

A.D.W. & J.Ha.

thiamine. See VITAMINS.

Thiniatiko, red grape occasionally found on the Greek island of Cephalonia making rich wines. It may be related to MAVRODAPHNE.

thinning vines. See CROP THINNING and SHOOT THINNING.

thiols. See MERCAPTANS.

third growth. See the CLASSIFICATION of Bordeaux.

Thompson Seedless is the common CALIFORNIA name for the seedless white grape variety SULTANA. It acquired this name from an early grower of the variety, near Yuba City, one William Thompson. Thompson Seedless is California's most planted grape variety by far. Almost all of California's Thompson Seedless is planted in the hot, dry SAN JOAQUIN VALLEY, with nearly two-thirds in Fresno county, the powerhouse of California raisin production. In 1960, almost 70 per cent of all grapes crushed for white wine were Thompson Seedless, clearly indicating what made up the 49 per cent of 'other grapes' then allowed in wines labelled as VARIETALS. In the 1970s, Thompson Seedless was particularly useful to the California wine industry in helping to bulk out inexpensive white JUG WINE blends at a time when demand far outstripped supply of premium white wine grape varieties. Today, however, it is used mainly either for DRYING GRAPES, as material for DISTILLATION, or for GRAPE CONCENTRATE to sweeten bottled waters or cold tea drinks.

Thouarsais, Vins du, small southern Loire VDQS just west of HAUT-POITOU. In the mid 2000s, only about 20 ha/50 acres were officially producing this particularly light wine, mainly from Chenin Blanc with a little Chardonnay although a little light red is produced too.

thrips, tiny (1–2 mm long), winged insects which readily feed on grapevine flowers and developing bunches, causing scarring and dwarfing of new shoots in early spring. While thrips are sometimes thought to be the cause of poor FRUIT SET, there is little evidence to support this. M.J.E.

Tibouren could almost be said to be *the* Provençal grape variety. It has a long history and the ability to produce such quintessentially Provençal wines as earthy rosés with a genuine scent of the *garrigue* (its wine is not naturally deep in colour). With total 2000 plantings of about 450 ha/1,110 acres, almost all in the Var, Tibouren is cultivated by a number of the more quality- and history-conscious producers of Provence and some of them bottle it as a varietal rosé. It is sensitive to COULURE and therefore yields irregularly. The deeply incised shape of its leaves reminds Galet of some Middle Eastern vine varieties, and certainly it could possibly have been imported by the Greeks via Marseilles, although its original sphere of influence was around St-Tropez, where it is thought by some to have been imported as recently as the end of the 18th century by a naval captain Antiboul, after whom it was named.

Galet, P., *Dictionnaire encyclopédique des cépages* (Paris, 2000).

Tierra de Barros. Spanish wine zone. See EXTREMADURA.

Tierra del Vino de Zamora, promising VCIG in Spain in CASTILLA Y LEÓN.

tight spacing, American colloquial expression for closely planted vineyards, see VINE DENSITY.

Tignanello, seminal central Italian wine first produced by the house of ANTINORI as a single-vineyard Chianti Classico in the 1970 vintage and then as a ground-breaking VINO DA TAVOLA in the 1971 vintage. For more details, see VINO DA TAVOLA and SUPERTUSCANS.

time and wine. See AGEING.

Timorasso, rare Piemontese vine variety making aromatic, durable white wine and grappa.

tinaja, large, earthenware vessel, probably developed from the Roman AMPHORAE, occasionally still used to ferment and store wine in central and southern SPAIN. *Tinajas* are used by some producers in La MANCHA, VALDEPEÑAS, and MONTILLA-MORILES, although modern versions are mostly made from reinforced concrete. They are relatively cheap, but have the disadvantages that they are not very efficient in terms of space, are difficult to clean, and offer relatively poor TEMPERATURE CONTROL.

tinta, the Spanish and Portuguese feminine adjective for red, is therefore the first word of many, unrelated Spanish and Portuguese names and synonyms for dark-skinned vine varieties. For Tinta Roriz, see RORIZ, for example.

Tinta Amarela, productive dark-skinned Portuguese grape variety grown in the DOURO for PORT. It can yield fine, attractively scented wines but suffers the singular disadvantage of being particularly sensitive to ROT. Nonetheless it accounts for around 20 per cent of vines in the Baixo Corgo, the coolest and wettest of the Douro's three subregions. As TRINCADEIRA, its official name, it is a highly regarded variety in the more arid regions of the Alentejo and southern Portugal, where it produces rich, powerful dry reds.

Tinta Barroca, common, relatively thick-skinned port grape variety which is the third most planted in Portugal's DOURO valley, grown on a total of 7,400 ha/20,200 acres of Portuguese vineyard in 2004. It is favoured by growers for yielding large quantities of grapes with exceptionally high levels of sugar and is widely planted on higher or north-facing slopes. However, Barroca is easily damaged by extreme heat and the berries have a tendency to shrivel on the vine. By no means as highly prized as the other leading port grapes, Touriga Franca and Tinta Roriz (Aragónez), Barroca produces reasonably well-structured but slightly jammy, rustic wines which can be useful in a blend. In Portugal, Tinta Barroca is rarely used as a varietal but it has been one of the most popular varieties for fortified port-like wines in South Africa's vineyards, and full-throttle, unfortified VARIETAL Tinta Barroca dry(ish) red (sometimes described as **Tintas das Baroccas** and often misspelt **Tinta Barocca**) is a South African speciality.   J.R. & R.J.M.

Tinta Caiada, Portuguese red grape variety also known as Tinta Lameira in the Douro.

Tinta de Toro, one of many names for TEMPRANILLO.

Tinta Francisca (not to be confused with TOURIGA FRANCA), lesser red grape variety used in the production of port in Portugal's DOURO valley, where it is not regarded as one of the finest varieties. The wine produced can be notably sweet but is not particularly concentrated. Some see similarities with Pinot Noir.

Tinta Miúda, 'small red one', Portuguese red wine grape grown traditionally around LISBON but now found in ESTREMADURA. The vine is low-yielding but can produce seductive and powerful wines. Identical to the GRACIANO of Rioja and MORRASTEL of the Languedoc, it ripens late and is susceptible to rot but is valued by winemakers for the colour and acidity it contributes to a blend.

Tinta Negra Mole, by far the most commonly planted vine variety on the island of MADEIRA. Although its background is unknown, Negra Mole is a VINIFERA variety (unlike many of the vines that replaced the noble varieties SERCIAL, VERDELHO, BUAL, and MALVASIA after the ravages of POWDERY MILDEW and PHYLLOXERA in the 19th century). It yields relatively high quantities of sweet, pale red wine which turns amber with the madeira production process and then yellow-green with age. A variety with the same name, but which may be quite distinct, is grown on the Portuguese mainland in the Algarve and, as Negramoll, on 1,200 ha/3,00 acres in Spain.

Tinta Pinheira, former name for the Portuguese grape variety Rufete.

Tinta Roriz, official Portuguese name for TEMPRANILLO. See also ARAGÓNEZ.

tinto, Spanish and Portuguese for red, so that *vino* (*vinho* in Portuguese) *tinto* is red wine (as opposed to the lighter red CLARETE produced in Spain). This is the origin of name of the red wine once known in England as TENT.

Like TINTA, Tinto is also the first word of many Spanish and Portuguese names and synonyms for black grape varieties. TEMPRANILLO, for example, is known as Tinto Fino in Ribero del Duero.

Tinto Cão, meaning 'red dog', top-quality black grape variety for the production of PORT. Having almost disappeared from the vineyards of the DOURO valley in northern Portugal (despite its long history there), it is being planted with greater enthusiasm since it was identified as one of the five finest port varieties, although it is not one of the deepest coloured. It is also grown in the Dão region and has also been planted experimentally at DAVIS in California, and in Australia were it has been known as Tinta Cao.

Tinto del Pais, synonym for TEMPRANILLO, as is **Tinto Fino** in Ribera del Duero.

tipping, the viticultural practice of cutting off SHOOT TIPS at flowering. Normally about 10 to 20 cm (8 in) of shoot tip are removed. This can help reduce the problem of COULURE, or poor FRUIT SET, for some susceptible varieties.

tirage, French for that part of the SPARKLING WINE-MAKING process during which sugar and yeast are added to the blended base wines in order to provoke a second fermentation, thereby creating CARBON DIOXIDE gas. It is sometimes used to include the entire period during which the sparkling wine matures on the LEES of this second fermentation.

tissue culture, the culturing of excised cells, tissues, and organs using artificial media of salts and nutrients, used especially in GENETIC MODIFICATION. The techniques can be used to develop vines with particularly useful properties much faster than by conventional PROPAGATION. Usually a CALLUS develops first, then roots and buds develop within the callus, leading to a new vine that can flower and set seed. The formation of roots or buds is achieved by subtle changes in the ingredients of the culture solution, especially in the relative amounts of the hormones AUXIN and CYTOKININ. Aseptic conditions are essential. Meristem culture, or the culture of the terminal 1 mm of vine shoot, especially after its fragmentation, has permitted the production of large numbers of plantlets in tubes that

are free of some VIRUSES and CROWN GALL disease. Large numbers of vine plantlets can be 'micro-propagated' by these methods, which can rapidly build up populations of scarce VINE VARIETIES. See diagram opposite.   B.G.C.

titratable acid. See TOTAL ACIDITY.

toast (*chauffe* in French), given to a barrel when forming it over a heat source, is one of the processes in BARREL MAKING that most obviously affect eventual wine flavour. The heat source also inevitably toasts the inside of the barrel to a degree that varies according to the heat of the fire and the length of time the barrel is held over it. This heating process dramatically alters the wood's physical and chemical composition. The toast provides a buffer between the ALCOHOL in wine and the TANNINS in wood. In general, the less a barrel is toasted, the more tannins and other wood characteristics will be leached into the wine by the alcohol. Wine matured in lightly toasted barrels therefore tends to taste 'oaky', 'woody', or even 'vegetal', while wine matured in heavily toasted barrels is more likely to taste 'toasty' or 'spicy'. See also OAK FLAVOUR.

Burgundy barrels are in general more heavily toasted than Bordeaux barriques, perhaps partly because the STAVES are thicker, and partly because a heavy toast is better suited to the flavours of Pinot Noir and Chardonnay grapes than to those of Cabernet Sauvignon, Merlot, Sauvignon Blanc, and Sémillon. The following terms are used, although they are imprecise, and New World winemakers are more likely to employ them than their European counterparts.

Light toast: there is little colour change in the wood, which has probably been toasted over the fire, after the shaping has been completed, for about five minutes at a surface temperature of 120–180 °C (248–356 °F). Wines aged in these barrels are usually quite fruity but can be somewhat tannic.

Medium toast: the wood is browner, probably having been toasted for approximately 10 minutes at 200 °C/392 °F). Wines aged in such barrels are said to have smells of vanilla and coffee. The greater toasting provides a buffer between the alcohol in the wine and the wood tannins. Therefore, wines aged in these barrels will normally be less tannic than those aged in light toast barrels. They are often described as rounder, smoother, and more persistent.

Heavy toast: the wood is very dark, having been toasted for around 15 minutes at 225 °C/ 440 °F. Wines aged in these barrels are usually marked by aromas of roasted coffee beans, toasted bread, ginger, nutmeg, cloves, and smoked meats. The above flavour descriptions apply to wine aged in French oak barrels.

The word 'char' is usually associated with American whiskey barrels, which are made over steam or natural gas but then set on fire. Traditionally American oak wine barrels were

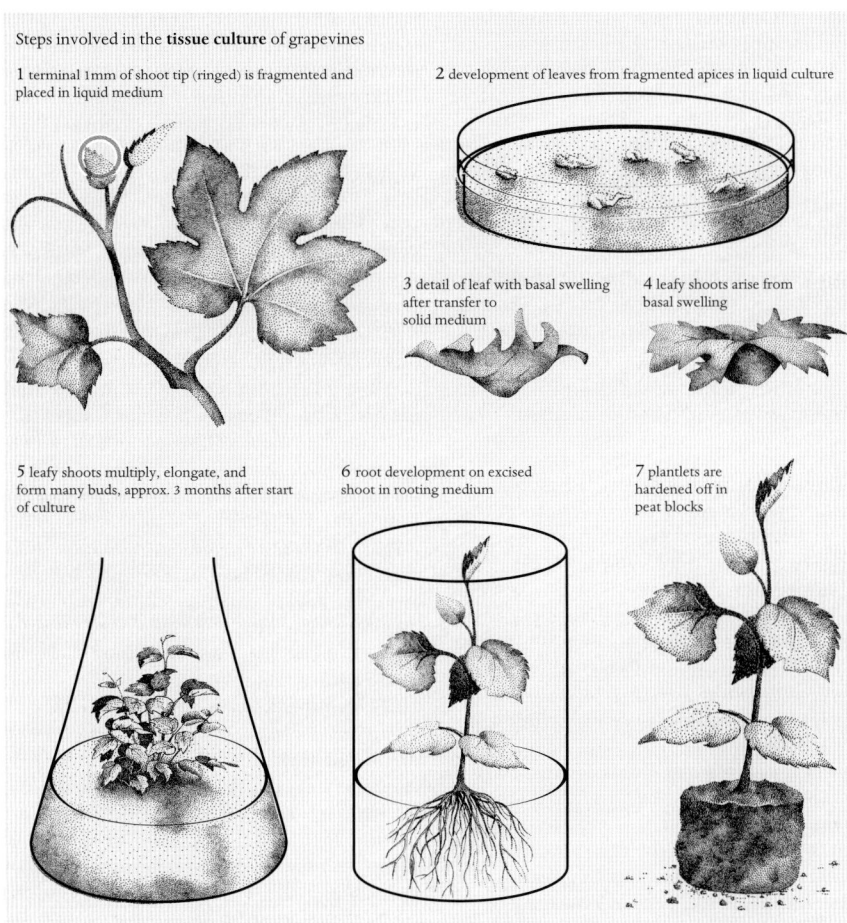

Steps involved in the **tissue culture** of grapevines

1 terminal 1mm of shoot tip (ringed) is fragmented and placed in liquid medium

2 development of leaves from fragmented apices in liquid culture

3 detail of leaf with basal swelling after transfer to solid medium

4 leafy shoots arise from basal swelling

5 leafy shoots multiply, elongate, and form many buds, approx. 3 months after start of culture

6 root development on excised shoot in rooting medium

7 plantlets are hardened off in peat blocks

simply un-charred bourbon barrels but American cooperages now toast to the customer's specifications.   M.K.

Tocai, or **Tocai Friulano**, old Friulan name for SAUVIGNONASSE, the most popular and widely planted white grape variety of the FRIULI region in north east Italy. It has no connection at all with Tokay d'Alsace (an Alsace synonym for the PINOT GRIGIO which grows alongside Tocai in Friuli), and is also completely unrelated to the great TOKAJI wine of Hungary, which is why the Hungarians managed to persuade EU authorities to ban use of the term from 2007.

Even by late 2005, it was decidedly unclear whether the grape would be renamed Sauvignonasse, its synonym Vert (dangerously unItalian but saleable), Friulano, or something completely different.

In Friuli, this productive, late-budding vine variety produces the staple wine of the region's taverns and trattorie. At the time when renaming became necessary, about 1,500 ha/ 3,750 acres were in production in the major DOC zones (COLLI ORIENTALI, COLLIO, GRAVE DEL FRIULI, and ISONZO), accounting for nearly 20 per cent of the total vineyard area of these zones, and over 30 per cent of the total area devoted to white varieties. Buttrio, Manzano,

and Rosazzo in the Colli Orientali, and the areas between Cormons and Brazzano, between Brazzano and Dolegna, and Capriva di Friuli in the Collio DOC are classic subzones. The wine itself is light in colour and body, floral in aroma, and has pronounced almond notes on the palate and on the nose. It is designed to be drunk young.

Some 'Tocai', not identical to Tocai Friulano, is also grown in VENETO.

California grows a few hundred acres of Tocai Friulano, and it is also produced by Millbrook in the Hudson valley, NEW YORK.

Tocai Rosso is also used as an Italian synonym for GRENACHE Noir.

A variety called Tocai Friulano is also cultivated to a limited extent in ARGENTINA.
                                                   D.T. & J.V.
Galet, P., *Dictionnaire encyclopédique des cépages* (Paris, 2000).

Tokaji, great Hungarian sweet white wine from the Tokaj (formerly Tokaj-Hegyalja) region in the far north east of HUNGARY of such renown it is even mentioned in the national anthem. Wines from the village of Tokaj itself may be called **Tokaj**; all others are conventionally known as Tokaji, the 'i' denoting the adjectival form or 'from the region of'. In English-speaking countries, it was long

known as **Tokay.** (See also LIQUEUR TOKAY and PINOT GRIS.)

History

Hungarian researcher Iván Balassa has shown that wines have been made here using **aszú** grapes since the second half of the 16th century. This occurred in connection with the introduction of a third hoeing, which resulted in a later harvest; and also from an intention to emulate MALVASIA wines of the time. However, since the term **aszú** originally referred only to 'dry' or 'shrunken' grapes, we cannot be certain that the BOTRYTIS fungus was also recognized as early as the late 16th century, rather than the traditional attribution to the mid 17th century.

The market for Tokaji wine grew apace in the course of the 16th and 17th centuries, particularly in north east Hungary (now in eastern SLOVAKIA) and POLAND. Its value to the regional and national economy was such that the vineyards of this region were some of the first to have been subject to CLASSIFICATION, in 1700.

By the 18th century, this extraordinary wine had been introduced to the French court (see HUNGARY, history), and was subsequently introduced to the Russian imperial court by the Habsburgs. Only CONSTANTIA from the Cape of Good Hope, and to a lesser extent Moldavian COTNARI, rivalled this wine, generally known outside Hungary as 'the wine of kings and king of wines' during this period of sweet wine worship, with Tokay Essencia or Tokaji Esszencia regarded as an all-purpose restorative.

During most of the 20th century, Tokaji languished. Its recovery from PHYLLOXERA was slow, and was far from complete even at the outset of the Second World War. Further, its reputation suffered with the dissolution of the Austro-Hungarian Empire in 1918 and the disappearance of the vaunted IMPERIAL TOKAY. Under Soviet domination, quantity rather than quality was encouraged, although a surprising number of individual growers and winemakers continued to uphold traditions and some exceptional wines were made.

Wine writer Hugh JOHNSON and other private investors set up the Royal Tokaji Wine Company in 1989 and the early 1990s saw an unusually cosmopolitan range of investors, including AXA Millésimes and another insurance giant from France and VEGA SICILIA from Spain, dedicated to restoring the image of this noble wine, with styles of wine varying quite widely in how they are made. In 1995, a new vineyard classification was created.

Geography

The Tokaj region comprises 5,800 ha/14,500 acres of vineyards and 28 villages, including Tokaj near Hungary's northernmost boundary, which has given its name to the appellation and the region as a whole. (A further 1,400 ha of land with excellent potential could be planted.) The most famous vineyards are in Tarcal, Mád, Tállya, Mezőzombor, Bodrogkeresztúr, Tolcsva, and Tokaj itself. The quality and character of the wine differs according to the situation of individual rows in the vineyard. Two of the original Tokaj villages were ceded to SLOVAKIA after the First World War so that Slovakia is also authorized to use the name Tokaj (Tokajsky Vyber) for sweet wines made in these villages.

Soils in the region are volcanic CLAYS, particularly thin and poor on the steepest slopes, with LOESS and sedimentary clay on the gentler foothills and more SAND around Tokaj. The volcanic origins of the soil and the presence of volcanic debris (known as tuff) result in a high level of trace elements, giving many wines a high degree of minerality.

The warming effect of the Carpathian mountains, which shelter the region from the east, north, and west, results in a MACRO-CLIMATE of humid nights and long, warm autumns, which combination, together with the confluence of the Tisza and Bodrog rivers, favours the development of noble rot most years, resulting in BOTRYTIZED sweet wines.

Grape varieties and viticulture

The principal grape variety grown here on about two-thirds of the vineyard is the fiery FURMINT, blended with the indigenous HÁRSLEVELŰ, and occasionally perfumed by small quantities of the golden mutant of MUSCAT BLANC À PETITS GRAINS, here sometimes called Muscat Lunel, Yellow Muscat, or Sárga Muskotály. ZÉTA (formerly Oremus) is also allowed, and since 2004 the regulations permit the inclusion of the historic Kövérszőlő. Vineyards planted before the mid 20th century were usually of mixed varieties.

Strict PRUNING is needed to limit yields and maximize the likelihood of noble rot. The harvest is generally very late and picking often continues late into November. Close and frequent inspection of vineyards is necessary in order to determine which of the varied sorts of Tokaji can be made from each part.

Types of wine

According to legislation current in 2005, the following wine types are produced in Tokaj.

Dry and semi-dry wines

Fresh or briefly matured wines Typically fermented dry but potentially containing some RESIDUAL SUGAR. With a few exceptions, they are fermented in stainless steel and will last three to five years, depending on the vintage. These wines are made from mostly overripe grapes left in the bunches after the aszú berries (see below) have been picked out.

Matured dry wines Invariably matured in wood, with a small proportion also fermented in wooden casks. Very long cellaring potential. As botrytis is undesirable in these wines, the grapes must come from high-altitude vineyards (about 250 m/820 ft above sea level) cultivated specifically for this purpose. Highly priced examples come from the likes of Szepsy and Árvay.

Szamorodni Ripeness comparable to BEEREN-AUSLESE, but fermented dry and subjected to subtle maturation (under a FILM-FORMING YEAST). Contains botrytized grapes and tastes not unlike VIN JAUNE of the Jura.

Főbor Historic style of wine, identified by Balassa (1991) as the forerunner of Szamorodni. Unlike Szamorodni, contemporary Főbor is not matured in OXIDATIVE conditions; Főbor can be either dry or sweet, depending on the natural proportion of SPÄTLESE-type overripe fruit and shrivelled, possibly botrytized berries.

Sweet wines

Szamorodni Typically made in the sweet style, when the sugar content of the grapes is so high that the must will not ferment fully dry. The residual sugar of sweet Szamorodni is comparable to a 2 or 3 puttonyos Aszú (see below), sometimes more. It needs to be matured for two or three years, and is lightly oxidized in character.

Reductive sweet wines Ready for release 12–16 months after harvest, this new 'satellite' genre emerged since the late 1990s from producers who could not afford the time and capital required to mature Aszú wines. Often marked by mineral character, the wines may contain 50–180 g/l residual sugar and a ratio of botrytized berries comparable to Aszú wines. Some wineries make them in stainless steel, while others such as Árvay, Oremus, and Szepsy use new oak barrels for both fermentation and maturation.

Aszú sweet wines The table below shows minimum residual sugar and EXTRACT required for each style.

Traditionally the concentration of Aszú wines has been measured by the number of hods or *puttonyos* (about 27 l each) of aszú berries included per Gönc, the 136-l barrel named after Gönc, a village in the northern Zemplén mountains that used to be famous for its cooperage. (The word *puttonyos* on Tokaji Aszú labels is not the plural of the noun meaning 'hod'—the traditional measure used for the aszú paste—as some non-Hungarian commentators have erroneously suggested (this would be *puttonyok*), but an adjective formed by a suffix comparable to English *-ed*, as in

'seven-headed monster'. Thus, *3 puttonyos Aszú* means '3-hodded Aszú'.) The aszú berries were traditionally crushed very gently by foot or rubber rollers and then macerated in the so-called base wine. According to current legislation, this base wine must be wine, must, or partly fermented must of the same vintage as the aszú berries. At present the aszú berries are not crushed, and the old measurement is not used, but the number of *puttonyos* still appears on labels.

Essencia The free-run juice of hand-picked pure BOTRYTIZED berries, with over 450 g/l sugar (800 g/l or more is not unheard of). Essencia takes years to achieve a modest alcohol level of 4–5 per cent. It is rarely sold commercially, and is typically used for blending to improve the concentration of Aszú wines. The 1997 wine law set a minimum of five years in cask.

Fordítás Made by refermenting wine or must poured on Tokaji Aszú paste (MARC) left after pressing. Sweet wines, typically with more than 60 g/l sugar.

Máslás Made by refermenting new wine or must poured on Tokaji Aszú lees. Sweet wines, typically with 50–90 g/l sugar.

Wine-making

Formerly the aszú berries were selected after the harvest, with non-botrytized berries used for dry wines. Nowadays aszú berries are selected on the vine, typically three or four times in a good autumn. Selected berries and the base wine are blended, with the macerated berries in contact with the base wine for 24–36 hours. Only then does a modest pressing and a very long fermentation start. (Alcohol may not be added.) Aszú wines today are typically fermented in new Hungarian oak casks of 220, 300, or 500 l. At least two years' ageing in oak and one in bottle is required by law.

In sections of the vineyard where half or more of the berries have turned into shrivelled aszú grapes, the berries are picked individually. In parts where the proportion of aszú berries is less than 50 per cent, such a laborious process is deemed unprofitable and the mixture of grapes is harvested and called Szamorodni, or 'as it comes'. Thus the harvest yields three different basic ingredients: the selected aszú grapes from which Aszú wine is made; the szamorodni mixture from which Szamorodni wine is made (dry or sweet depending on sugar content); and grapes without any aszú content from which either base wine for Tokaji Aszú or VARIETAL wines are made. These varietal wines may be labelled Tokaji Furmint, Tokaji Hárslevelű, or Tokaji Sárga Muskotály and are bottled in regular 75-cl bottles instead of the long-necked 50-cl flask special to Tokaji.

As one might perhaps expect of a combination of proud Hungarians and foreign investors, Tokaji has been a hotbed of vino-political ferment, particularly with respect to

Style	Residual sugar (g/l)	Dry extract (g/l)
3 puttonyos Aszú	60	25
4 puttonyos Aszú	90	30
5 puttonyos Aszú	120	35
6 puttonyos Aszú	150	40
Aszúeszencia	180	45

maturation time and techniques for the botrytis wines. The most highly regarded producers include István Szepsy, Tokaj Hétszőlő, Árvay és Társa, Tokaj Oremus (owned by VEGA SICILIA), Disznókő (owned by AXA), and the Royal Tokaji Wine Company.

G.R., G.M., & M.L.-G.

Alkonyi, L ., *Tokaj* (Budapest, 2000).
——*Tokaj—the Myth of Terroir* (Budapest, 2004).
Balassa, I., *Tokaj-Hegyalja Szőleje és Bora* (Tokaj, 1991). Tokaj-Hegyalja Vineyard and Wine, English summary.
Lambert-Gócs, M., 'Tokaji: forever amber', *Gastronomica* (Summer 2002), 59–63.
Rohály, G., Mészáros, G., and Nagymarosy, A., *Terra Benedicta—Tokaj and Beyond* (Budapest, 2003). *Tokaj-Hegyaljai Album* (1867).

Tokay d'Alsace, or simply **Tokay**, was for long the Alsace name for PINOT GRIS. The variety was probably taken to Hungary in the 14th century, where it was cultivated as Szürkebarát and, it is thought, brought back two centuries later by General Schwendi after his campaign against the Turks, to be planted in Kientzheim as 'Tokay', the name of Hungary's most famous wine even then (although the famously restorative wine TOKAJI depends not on Pinot Gris but on FURMINT vines).

To avoid confusion with the famous Hungarian wine of the same name (although the winemakers of Alsace would probably be horrified if anyone found the distinctive aromas of Hungarian Tokaji in their Pinot Gris), Europe's vinous lawmakers proposed **Tokay Pinot Gris** as an alternative, an intermediate stage towards the eventual elimination of the word Tokay from Alsace required by April 2007.

Galet, P., *Dictionnaire encyclopédique des cépages* (Paris, 2000).

Tomar, former IPR and now a subregion of RIBATEJO in central, southern Portugal.

tonneau, traditional Bordeaux measure of wine volume, once a large wooden cask holding 900 l, or 252 imperial wine gallons, the equivalent of four BARRIQUES. A PARIS tonneau was 800 l, but, because of the prominence of GASCON merchants in London and English merchants in Bordeaux, the Bordeaux measure became the standard. By the end of the 18th century, tonneaux had been replaced by the easier to transport smaller barrique, yet the tonneau, the exact equivalent of 100 CASES of wine, is still the measure in which the Bordeaux wine trade deals.

Such was the importance of wine to medieval trade in general (see BORDEAUX and DUTCH WINE TRADE), that a tonneau, or ton in English, evolved from being the space occupied by a tun of wine, to become the unit of measurement for the carrying capacity of any ship, whatever its load.

Tonnerrois, an up-and-coming wine area near CHABLIS around the town of Tonnerre.

top grafting or **top working**, the viticultural operation of changing the fruiting VINE VARIETY of a mature vineyard by inserting a bud of the selected variety in each vine, but retaining the established root system. An array of approaches is available: CLEFT GRAFTING, NOTCH GRAFTING, CHIP BUDDING, or T-BUDDING, usually applied high on the original trunk just below the HEAD. If the operation is done well, only one season's crop is lost. The main risk is that of systemic disease spread from the original planting, especially VIRUS DISEASES to which different varieties and rootstocks have different tolerances. This operation was initially most common in the NEW WORLD as a response to changes in market demand and FASHION, but is becoming increasingly prevalent in Old World regions.

B.G.C.

topoclimate, a local climate as determined by TOPOGRAPHY, for instance that of a particular hill, valley, or slope. It is commonly subsumed under the broader term MESOCLIMATE.

topography, a term describing the land surface features of any area, which can have considerable implications for local climate and therefore for viticulture. Geiger gives the most comprehensive general account of topographic effects on local climate. Some suggested detailed adjustments to temperature records, to allow for actual topographic features of vineyard sites, are used by Gladstones in his discussion of regional climate. Topographic elements having the most influence on the climate are local ELEVATION or altitude; slope; the relative isolation of hills; aspect; and proximity to water masses such as oceans, lakes, and rivers.

1. Local elevation or altitude Other things being equal, temperature falls by about 0.6 °C/1.1 °F per 100 m/330 ft greater altitude.

2. Slope At night, air is chilled by direct contact with a land surface which is rapidly losing heat by radiation. The chilled air, being denser, flows down slopes to the flat land or valleys below, and is replaced by warmer air from above the land surface. The turbulent surface air over slopes at moderate elevations is therefore usually warmer at night, and in the early morning, than that settled over the adjacent flats and valley floors. This band on a hill slope is known as its 'thermal zone', and especially in cool climates is valued for viticulture because of its enhanced ripening potential and length of frost-free period. The steeper the slope, the more pronounced is its thermal zone. See also HILLSIDE VINEYARDS.

3. Relative isolation of hills Thermal zones are strongest on isolated and projecting hills or mountains, because these have little or no external source of surface-chilled air. Cooled air from their own surfaces that slips away can be replaced only by totally unchilled air from above. The implications of this are discussed under CLIMATE AND WINE QUALITY; see also TERROIR. Examples of viticulturally famous isolated hills include the hill of Corton at ALOXE-CORTON in Burgundy; the Kaiserstuhl in BADEN; and, on a larger scale, the Montagne de Reims in CHAMPAGNE.

4. Aspect Slopes which face the sun through much of the day (southerly aspects in the northern hemisphere, and northerly aspects in the southern hemisphere) are the warmest, and those facing away from the sun are the coolest. The most important consequences are felt at night. The differences in soil heating

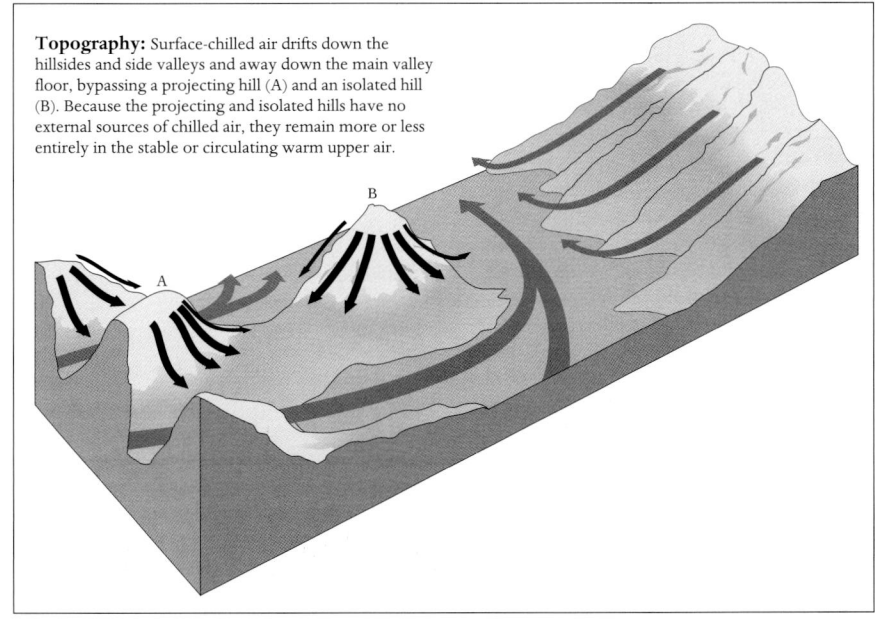

Topography: Surface-chilled air drifts down the hillsides and side valleys and away down the main valley floor, bypassing a projecting hill (A) and an isolated hill (B). Because the projecting and isolated hills have no external sources of chilled air, they remain more or less entirely in the stable or circulating warm upper air.

during times of sun exposure directly govern warming of the vines by reradiation at other times, when temperatures are lower and therefore more limiting. Differences in average soil temperature are themselves directly influential as well, through their effect on the vine roots. Warmth and activity of the roots are important not only for nutrition of the vine, but also for growth and fruiting through export of the growth substance CYTOKININ to the vine tops.

The climatic contrasts among aspects are greatest at high latitudes, and also early and late in the vine-growing season, these being the situations and times when the sun is furthest from the vertical. Similarly, the steeper the slope, the more aspect will affect its climate.

Easterly aspects have the advantage that they are warmed earliest in the day, when soil and air temperatures are lowest, and therefore most limiting to vine growth or ripening. Also, east-facing slopes are typically the most sheltered from cold, stormy winds, which throughout the world come predominantly from the west; while to the extent that they are in the lee of major hill or mountain ranges, they generally enjoy the warmest and sunniest climates of their regions, which is a clear advantage in otherwise cool, wet regions. Notable examples of this are found in the CÔTE D'OR of Burgundy, and in the RHINE valley of Germany and Alsace. The combined result is that slopes facing east to south tend to be favoured for viticulture in the northern hemisphere, and those facing east to north tend to be favoured in the southern hemisphere, especially towards the cool limit of viticulture. West-facing slopes do, however, have some compensation in that they maintain their warmth longer into the night; while in west coastal regions, they can have better exposure to afternoon sea breezes (see below).

5. Proximity to oceans, lakes, and rivers Water absorbs and stores large quantities of heat, with relatively little change in temperature because of the depth to which the heat penetrates, together with the high specific heat of water compared with rocks or dry soil. Its resulting temperature inertia greatly modifies the temperature regimes of adjacent land, largely by the convectional circulation of air. Cool air from over the water is drawn to replace heated air rising over the land in the afternoons, while at night a reverse convection results from chilled air descending from the cold land surface and rising over the now relatively warm water. This daily alternating pattern of air circulation, when not prevailed over by stronger winds, makes the climate adjacent to water significantly more equable than it would otherwise be, in terms of both temperature and humidity. Both factors are important in CLIMATE AND WINE QUALITY. There is also a reduced incidence of spring FROSTS and WINTER FREEZE injury in regions liable to

these. Examples of this LAKE EFFECT are found in NEW YORK state and the vineyards of Ontario in CANADA.

The effects of rivers and lakes are normally confined to their immediate valleys, but maritime influences can extend considerable distances inland from coasts in the form of land and sea breezes. Notable examples of the latter occur in the BORDEAUX region of France; the NAPA valley and SONOMA and other near-coastal regions of California; and the HUNTER VALLEY and SWAN VALLEY of Australia's east and west coasts respectively.   J.G.

Geiger, R., *Das Klima der bodennahen Luftschicht* (4th edn, Brunswick, 1961), trans. as *The Climate near the Ground* (Cambridge, Mass., 1966).

topping, the viticultural practice of cutting shoots to remove the younger growth. Normally *c*.30 cm/12 in of shoot is cut off, which is significantly more than by the operation of TIPPING. See TRIMMING.

topping up, *ouillage* in French, the operation of refilling any sort of wooden container to replace wine lost through EVAPORATION. The container should be kept full or nearly full lest the ubiquitous ACETOBACTER use OXYGEN from the head space to start the process of transforming wine into VINEGAR. The well-run winery will have a strict regime of topping up all wooden containers on a regular basis.

A really good, tight BARREL closed with a sound, new, inert plastic BUNG loses liquid by diffusion through the barrel's staves. The HEAD SPACE created by this liquid loss is filled with water and alcohol vapours, together with traces of CARBON DIOXIDE. Since no oxygen can enter the head space, there is no danger of acetification and topping up is not necessary.

With older barrels, especially those in poor condition, it is nearly impossible to achieve such a tight seal. Air inevitably seeps in around the bung or through poorly fitting joints between staves or heads. A regular topping-up regime is the only insurance against the development of vinegar in such containers.

Winemakers differ in what they view as the ideal topping-up regime for various different wines, but modern practice is to top up at least monthly, using wine of the same provenance and, often, filling the barrel so that some wine is ejected when the BUNG is driven into the bung-hole.

Depending on the amount of evaporation and the spare time available to the winery staff, topping up is done anywhere from twice a week to once every six weeks. In Bordeaux the bung is left at the top of the barrel so as to maximize AERATION of the young wine for the first six months, after which the barrel is rolled to one side so that the bung is in the so-called bung-over position. Thus the bung and bung-hole region are kept moist and aeration is reduced. Many New World

wineries have adopted this practice, even for Burgundian varieties, as it is much less labour intensive than constant topping up.

See also ULLAGE.   A.D.W. & M.K.

Torbato is a white-berried grape variety today most obviously associated with SARDEGNA, where varietal dry whites are produced. Like GRENACHE Noir, known as Cannonau in Sardegna, its origins are disputed, thanks to the past extent of the kingdoms of Majorca and Aragón. Many believe it to be a Spanish variety which was imported many centuries ago. It is particularly successful around Alghero.

It was once quite widely cultivated in ROUSSILLON, where it is known as TOURBAT, or Malvoisie du Roussillon, but was abandoned before new and healthier plant material was imported from Sardegna in the 1980s.

Torgiano, small hillside DOC zone between Perugia and Assisi in the central Italian region of UMBRIA. It has produced small quantities (about 7,500 hl/200,000 gal in a normal year) of what was considered Umbria's finest red wine in the 1960s and 1970s. The production of bottled wine is almost entirely in the hands of the Lungarotti family, whose efforts have demonstrated that the SANGIOVESE vine can yield important results outside TOSCANA. A significant amount of CANAIOLO grapes is used in the blend, but more important yet is the wine-making philosophy which until the 1970s emphasized a relatively brief period of CASK AGEING in large oval casks, and some BARREL MATURATION thereafter, followed by a lengthy period of BOTTLE AGEING—up to ten years for the RISERVA, which was awarded DOCG status in 1990.   D.T. & D.C.G.

torna viagem, literally means 'round trip' in Portuguese and is occasionally found on labels of ancient SETÚBAL which have been subjected to lengthy sea voyages for ageing purposes. This is the equivalent of the *vinho da roda* of MADEIRA.

Toro, revolutionized Spanish red wine zone in CASTILLA Y LEÓN (see map under SPAIN) whose wines were famous within Spain in medieval times. This wild and remote zone spans the Duero valley east of Zamora. It was accorded DO status in 1987. At an ALTITUDE of between 600 and 750 m/2,000–2,800 ft, growing conditions are severe. The dry, stony soils can support cereals or vines. The region's principal grape variety, Tinta de Toro, is a local variant of Rioja's TEMPRANILLO which has adapted to the climatic extremes of this part of Spain. The grapes need careful handling. Left to their own devices, they will easily ripen to a POTENTIAL ALCOHOL level of 16 per cent. Local regulations permit a maximum ALCOHOLIC STRENGTH of 15 per cent but the best wines usually have a strength of around 13.5. A small number of producers have fostered a move away from the heavy, bulk reds of recent times, a move which gained notable momentum when some of the greatest names in Ribera del Duero, Rioja, and even Bordeaux were awakened to the region's potential and launched their own estates, particularly Vega Sicilia's Pintia, Mauro's San Román, Sierra Cantabria's Numanthia-Termes, Michel Rolland's Campo Elíseo, Telmo Rodríguez's Pago La Jara, Jacques Lurton's El Albar, in addition to the home-grown Bienvenida Sitio del Palo, Dos Victorias, and Quinta Quietud. By the mid 2000s, Toro's 5,300 ha/1,300 acres of vineyard supplied well over 30 bodegas.

R.J.M. & V. de la S.

Peñín, J., *Guía Peñín* (Madrid, annually).

Torontel, Chilean name for the aromatic white grape variety TORRONTÉS Riojano, of which there is a steady planting of about 1,000 ha/2,500 acres in Chile, mainly in Maule. It is an ingredient in pisco.

Torres SA, Miguel, Spain's largest family-owned producer of wine and Spanish brandy, based in PENEDÈS in north east Spain.

The present company was founded in 1870 with the fruits of a chance investment by Jaime Torres in a Cuban oil company. A winery was established at Vilafranca del Penedès near Barcelona and its produce was shipped to Cuba in a fleet also belonging to Torres, whose heir was his nephew Juan. Juan expanded the business within Spain and left a thriving family business to his son Miguel in 1932. After confiscation, disruption, and even winery destruction during the Spanish Civil War, Miguel rebuilt the business and as early as the 1950s decided to concentrate on selling wine in bottle rather than in bulk.

Perhaps the most significant development in the history of Torres came in 1959 when Miguel's son Miguel A. Torres went to study in DIJON. This resulted in experimental plantings of vine varieties imported from France and Germany such as Cabernet Sauvignon, Chardonnay, Riesling, Gewürztraminer, and Sauvignon Blanc. Torres also introduced vine TRELLIS SYSTEMS. A modern laboratory was established, temperature-controlled stainless steel fermentation vessels were installed, and red wines were bottled after just 18 months' BARREL MATURATION in cool cellars hewn out of the hillside. All of these techniques, and a host of other innovations, were then quite unknown elsewhere in Spain.

Vindication of Miguel A. Torres's achievements came in 1979, when, in the well-publicized 'wine olympics' organized by the French gastronomic magazine *Gault-Millau*, Torres Gran Coronas Black Label 1970 was voted winner of the top Cabernet class. In 1982/3 he spent a sabbatical year at MONTPELLIER, and has introduced higher VINE DENSITIES, increasingly ORGANIC methods, and MECHANICAL PRUNING. About a third of all

Spanish wine produced by Torres is exported, notably to Sweden, Denmark, and the US.

On the death of his father in 1991, Miguel A. Torres became president of the company with particular responsibilities for winemaking. He has also been one of Spain's most prolific wine writers, and runs the 220-ha estate near Curicó in CHILE which he established in 1978. By the mid 2000s, Torres owned 1,900 ha of vineyard in Penedès, Priorat, and other areas of Cataluña. In 2004, the company invested in Ribera del Duero, Jumilla, and Toro. His sister Marimar is a food writer based in San Francisco and manages a 56-ha vineyard in SONOMA county's Russian River Valley. In 1998, the Spanish company embarked on a JOINT VENTURE in China involving 400 ha of vines. Miguel's son, another Miguel, directs the Jean Leon winery which Torres acquired in 1994 and his daughter Mireia heads the company's technical department.

Torres Vedras, DOC in western Portugal. See ESTREMADURA.

Torrontés, name of several white grape varieties grown in and characteristic of ARGENTINA and of a different but also distinctively flavoured indigenous variety in GALICIA in north west Spain that is particularly common in the white wines of RIBEIRO. Within Spain, the variety is occasionally found around Cordoba. In the Canary Islands the name Torrontés is used for a different grape variety—MADEIRA's Terrantez.

Much more important, however, are the three varieties known as Torrontés in Argentina (**Torrontés Riojano, Torrontés Sanjuanino,** and **Torrontés Mendocino**). Official 2001 figures found 8,100 ha/20,000 acres of Torrontés Riojano, making it Argentina's most-planted white wine grape by far. Although there was considerable emigration from Galicia to Argentina, no definite relationship between Spanish and Argentine Torrontés had been established before DNA PROFILING at DAVIS suggested that Torrontés Riojano and Torrontés Sanjuanino are each the progeny of a crossing between MUSCAT OF ALEXANDRIA and CRIOLLA CHICA (the MISSION of California) and that Torrontés Mendocino is also likely to be a progeny of Muscat of Alexandria, although the other parent has not been identified.

The fragrant Torrontés is often seen as the Argentine white wine variety with the greatest potential although it can be over-alcoholic and is often bitter. Carefully grown and vinified, Torrontés can produce wines that are high in acidity, and intriguingly aromatic in a way reminiscent of but not identical to MUSCAT, although much is also used for blending. The variety seems particularly well adapted to the arid growing conditions of Argentina, particularly the high, sandy vineyards of Cafayate where at ALTITUDES of over 1,600 m/5,250 ft its

high natural acidity and assertive flavour are particularly distinguished.

Torrontés Riojano (known as Torontel in Chile) is the most common and highest quality Argentine subvariety and takes its name from the northern province of La Rioja, where it is by far the most planted single vine variety. **Torrontés Sanjuanino** (known in Chile as MOSCATEL DE AUSTRIA) is more commonly associated with the province of San Juan in Argentina and is rather less widely planted. It is less aromatic, and has bigger berries and more compact clusters. Argentine vineyard statistics also distinguish the relatively rare **Torrontés Mendocino**, sometimes called **Torrontés Mendozino**, which is most common in Río Negro province in the south and lacks Muscat aroma.

Toscana, important central Italian region known in English as TUSCANY (under which term details of its history are to be found).

Geography and vine varieties
Toscana produces just under 3 million hl/79 million gal of wine a year. The Tuscan countryside is famously undulating. A full 68 per cent of the region is officially classified as hilly (a mere 8 per cent of the land is flat) and HILLSIDE VINEYARDS, at ALTITUDES of between 150 and 500 m (500–1,600 ft) supply the vast majority of the better-quality wines. The SANGIOVESE vine, the backbone of the region's production, seems to require the concentration of SUNLIGHT that slopes can provide to ripen well in these latitudes, as well as the less fertile soils on the hills. Growers also value the significant TEMPERATURE VARIABILITY between day and night as an important factor in developing its aromatic qualities.

Sangiovese has been, until recently, virtually synonymous with fine wine in Toscana and, although the variety is widely planted throughout central Italy, the Tuscan climate (harsh in winter) and the calcium-rich MARLS in the best zones have thus far given incomparable results for this variety. From CARMIGNANO, Rufina, and the hills around Vinci in the north through the CHIANTI CLASSICO area to the zones of VINO NOBILE DI MONTEPULCIANO and BRUNELLO DI MONTALCINO, Sangiovese is the recurring theme in Tuscan wine although it has traditionally been blended with such other varieties as Canaiolo, Malvasia, and, in the 20th century, Trebbiano. Since the 1980s, however, attempts have been made to make great wines from Sangiovese alone. The pursuit of quality that began in earnest in the late 1970s in Chianti Classico and Montepulciano focused on Sangiovese, but producers soon discovered that the wave of enthusiasm that followed the introduction of the DOC laws in the late 1960s had resulted in large plantings of unsuitable CLONES on poor ROOTSTOCKS in many unsuitable sites. The past 25 years has seen a series of small steps to redress this situation, and many new vineyards now have far superior clones of Sangiovese, and are producing infinitely better wines as a result.

Tuscan viticulture was dominated historically by large estates owned by wealthy local families, the majority of them of noble origin, and tilled by a workforce of sharecroppers. The demise of this system in the 1950s and 1960s led to a hiatus in investment or even ordinary maintenance, deterioration of the vineyards and cellars, plummeting quality, and eventual sales of the properties to new owners with the requisite capital and energy to carry on the viticultural traditions of the past. Tuscan ownership of Tuscan viticulture is now part of history, but the new wave of vintners from Milan, Rome, and Genoa—joined in the 1980s by a sizeable contingent of foreigners—has shown both a commendable commitment to quality and an equally commendable openness to new and more cosmopolitan ideas. See also ANTINORI, FRESCOBALDI, and RICASOLI, local noble families with considerable wine interests.

White wines

Trebbiano has been for white wine what Sangiovese has been for red wine, the basis of the regional production, and more than a dozen Trebbiano-based DOC wines currently exist in Toscana. The grape has been cultivated principally for its high productivity and its acid-conserving qualities in hot areas, plus its resistance to frost in cool, damp areas, but the wines have little character and have gradually gone out of FASHION in the market place; they seem destined to be used exclusively for VIN SANTO. Scattered patches of VERMENTINO exist along the Tuscan coast up to the border with Liguria, but the variety has yet to establish a clear identification with Toscana as a region. Interest in white wines was strong in the 1980s, however, and pioneering producers in Chianti experimented with white INTERNATIONAL VARIETIES—principally CHARDONNAY and SAUVIGNON—in higher vineyards where Sangiovese ripens poorly. Results have been mixed thus far, with only a handful of Chardonnays of note.

Supertuscans

Far less marginal are the new breed of Tuscan red wines, the so-called Supertuscans, often made with the assistance of French VINE VARIETIES and in an international style. Their development dates from the late 1960s and early 1970s, first as experiments or even for mere *divertissement*, but the startling results obtained in such all-CABERNET wines as Sassicaia and such Sangiovese/Cabernet blends as Tignanello from ANTINORI have established these products as a fundamental category in the overall Tuscan picture. Few estates in Chianti have not joined in the scramble to produce a wine of this prestigious type, and small BARREL MATURATION, now extended to Sangiovese, has yielded a new style of Tuscan wine greatly appreciated by consumers who once disdained Chianti. MERLOT is increasingly planted as an alternative to Cabernet, with impressive results, and in the 1990s significant amounts of SYRAH vines began to bear fruit, with uneven results.

Chianti still towers over these new wines, none the less. With over 900,000 hl/23.7 million gal produced in an abundant year, it is Italy's largest single group of DOCGs (although it should be remembered that Chianti's name has been extended to subzones near Florence, Pisa, Pistoia, Arezzo, and Siena which have nothing to do with the historic zone of Chianti Classico between Florence and Siena).

For more details of specific Tuscan wines, see BOLGHERI, BRUNELLO DI MONTALCINO, CARMIGNANO, CHIANTI, CHIANTI CLASSICO, CHIANTI RUFINA, ELBA, GALESTRO, MONTECARLO, PREDICATO, VERNACCIA, VINO DA TAVOLA, VINO NOBILE DI MONTEPULCIANO, VIN SANTO.

D.T. & D.C.G.

Bastianich, J., and Lynch, D., *Vino Italiano: The Regional Wines of Italy* (New York, 2002).

Belfrage, N., *From Brunello to Zibibbo: The Wines of Southern Italy* (London, 2001).

total acidity, TA, or **titratable acidity**, measure of the total ACIDITY, both FIXED ACIDS and VOLATILE ACIDS, present in grape juice or wine. With ALCOHOLIC STRENGTH and RESIDUAL SUGAR, total acidity is one of the most common wine measurements involved in any wine ANALYSIS.

It is obtained by a laboratory process called titration, in which very small additions of an alkali of known strength are made to a measured quantity of the grape juice or wine until the amount of added alkali just equals the amount of acids in the sample. The value of these total acids can be calculated and expressed as grams of any number of different acids per litre of juice or wine. By tradition, different wine regions have chosen to express total acidity variously as TARTARIC ACID or sulfuric acid, or simply as the amount of acidic hydrogen ions (see PH) per litre.

In France and much of the rest of Europe, for example, it has become nearly standard to measure acids as if they were all sulfuric, even though the amount of this compound in grapes and wine is minuscule. In Germany, on the other hand, rather than choose a particular acid for reporting purposes, the measurement is often in milligrams of hydrogen ion per litre. In the United States, Italy, South Africa, Australia, New Zealand, and the United Kingdom meanwhile, total acidity is reported as if all acids were tartaric (and, as if the situation were not complicated enough already, sometimes titrated to an end point not of pH 7, but of pH 8.2). The total acidity of a young red bordeaux, for example, might be reported as 6.5 g/l of tartaric acid in Australia, 3.9 g/l of sulfuric acid in France, or 87 mg of hydrogen ions per l in Germany, even though the the wine in fact contains a complicated mixture of many different ACIDS.

The total acidity of wines expressed as tartaric acid normally varies between about 4.5 g/l (the minimum permitted within the EUROPEAN UNION although some hot climate wines may be less acid than this) and 8 g/l for wines made from underripe grapes or naturally high-acid grape varieties. The total acidity of ripe grape juice or must should ideally be in the general range of 7 to 10 g/l expressed as tartaric acid, although it may in practice be between 3 and 16 g/l. (Some acid is usually lost during wine-making, as a result of MALOLACTIC FERMENTATION and cold STABILIZATION, so one may need to start with a higher acidity than the final one desired.) However, CARBONIC ACID and a small amount of SUCCINIC ACID are produced during fermentation and in some vintages this might reduce the overall loss of ACIDITY.

A.D.W.

total dry extract, or **TDE**. See EXTRACT.

Toul, Côtes de, in the far north east of France, remains, with the even more northerly French wine region on the MOSELLE, as a reminder of what was once a flourishing Lorraine wine industry. It was subsequently marginalized by industrialization, injudicious replanting after PHYLLOXERA, the First World War, and the delimitation of the nearby CHAMPAGNE region which had once drawn wine from here. Today Gamay is the most planted vine variety in the appellation and is the usual ingredient in the local pale pink speciality VIN GRIS; such Pinot Noir as remains is reserved for Toul's relatively light reds. AUXERROIS is the most successful variety for dry whites.

George, R., *French Country Wines* (London, 1990).

Touraine, the most important Loire region centred on the town of Tours (see map under LOIRE). This is 'the garden of France', and Loire château country *par excellence*, a series of playgrounds for France's pre-revolutionary aristocrats, and now the Parisian weekender's rural paradise. The local TUFFEAU was quarried extensively to build these and more distant châteaux, leaving caves ideal for wine-making and wine maturation.

Touraine's most famous wines are the still red wines from the individual appellations of BOURGUEIL, CHINON, and St-Nicolas-de-Bourgueil and its still and sparkling, dry to sweet whites from VOUVRAY and MONTLOUIS.

Wines called simply Touraine come from a much larger zone, incorporating about 5,300 ha/13,000 acres of vineyard in total extending from SAUMUR in the west as far as the city of Blois in the east, encompassing very varied soils which may include clay, sand, tuffeau, and gravel. Viticulture is concentrated on the steep banks of the Loire and its tributary the Cher east of Tours. Cereals predominate on the cooler soils of the plateaux between river valleys. The climate of the region also shows considerable variation, with that of the most eastern vineyards being distinctly CONTINENTAL and affected by seriously cold winters, while vineyards at the western extreme are tempered by the influence of the Atlantic.

If soil and climate vary considerably throughout Touraine, there is an enormous range of grape varieties too. For all its proximity to Paris and the INAO headquarters, Touraine has presented the APPELLATION CONTRÔLÉE authorities with their most severe test in their avowed aim to remove all VARIETAL names from labels of AC wines. White Touraine, for example, may be made from any combination of Chenin Blanc, Arbois (increasingly rare), Sauvignon Blanc, and Chardonnay grapes, so long as Chardonnay constitutes no more than 20 per cent of the blend.

Touraine Rouge, made in about the same quantity as Touraine Blanc, may be made from an even less specific blend, incorporating any or all of Cabernet Franc, Cabernet Sauvignon, Cot (Malbec), Pinot Noir, Meunier, Pinot Gris, Gamay, Pineau d'Aunis, and Grolleau.

In very general terms, Sauvignon and Gamay tend to be grown in the far east of the region, and are, respectively, the most common white and red varieties used for the Touraine appellation. From a conscientious producer, a Sauvignon de Touraine can provide a less expensive alternative to the Loire's more famous Sauvignons produced in appellations such as SANCERRE and POUILLY-FUMÉ and these less expensive Touraine wines can be particularly successful in riper vintages such as 1996 and 2003. Red Touraine is usually a distinctly leaner variant on the BEAUJOLAIS theme, however, although the relationship has been used to develop a Touraine PRIMEUR, and the adoption of SEMI-CARBONIC MACERATION has improved quality. Some producers tried labelling more substantial blended reds, made from Gamay, Cabernet, and Cot, Touraine Tradition but a new appellation **Touraine Chenonceaux** was being developed in the mid 2000s for blends of Cabernet and Cot. Some white and red Touraine is, confusingly, made in quite a different style, however, most commonly but not necessarily from Chenin Blanc and Cabernet Franc grapes.

Small quantities of **Touraine Mousseux** (about one-tenth as much as Saumur Mousseux, for example, even smaller quantities of **Touraine Pétillant**, and large quantities of **Touraine Primeur** (see PRIMEUR) are made but the region also has three subappellations in areas allowed to add their name to that of Touraine, although they are of declining importance.

From its 220 ha/540 acres of vines on both banks of the Loire close to the famous château of Amboise, **Touraine-Amboise** produces mainly red wines from Gamay, Cabernet Franc, and Cot, the last of which can yield some wines with sufficient stuffing to be worth ageing. The appellation's white wines, dry to medium dry (or even moelleux—notably produced by Amboise's excellent viticultural college Domaine de la Gabillière) depending on the year, are made exclusively from the long-lived Chenin Blanc.

Touraine-Azay-le-Rideau comprises about 90 ha/220 acres of vineyard on both banks of the Indre, south of the Loire between Tours and Chinon on soil that is clearly superior to that of the general Touraine appellation. It produces roughly equal quantities of crisp whites from Chenin Blanc and light rosés mainly from Grolleau, which can be considerably more sprightly than the Rosé d'Anjou with which the variety is more readily associated.

Touraine-Mesland in 2005 comprised about 110 ha of vineyard on a sand and gravel plateau immediately above the right bank of the Loire between Amboise and Blois. Gamay plus some Cabernet Franc and Cot is responsible for durable reds and rosés, and Chenin Blanc, together with some Chardonnay and Sauvignon, for dry whites. Touraine-Mesland's pale pink VIN GRIS enjoys a certain reputation.

Touraine-Noble Joué is a small appellation just south of Tours created in 2001 for pink wines made from Meunier with Pinot Gris and Pinot Noir.

Tourbat is the ROUSSILLON name for Sardegna's white grape variety TORBATO. It is alternatively known as Malvoisie du Roussillon and is one of the many varieties allowed into the several VINS DOUX NATURELS of the region and Côtes du Roussillon whites.

Touriga is used as an Australian synonym for TOURIGA NACIONAL, but the Touriga of California is probably TOURIGA FRANCA.

Touriga Franca (formerly known as **Touriga Francesa**) is the most widely planted grape variety in the DOURO valley, accounting for around one-fifth of all vines. It has no proven conection with France and seems to be a relatively new grape in the Douro, where it flourishes on warmer south-facing slopes for both port and Douro wines. It is classified as one of the best port varieties, although the wine it produces is not as concentrated as that of TOURIGA NACIONAL. Favoured by growers for its consistent yields, it is respected by winemakers for its wines' perfume and persistent fruit. It is also widely planted in TRÁS-OS-MONTES and is slowly being disseminatated to other Portuguese regions such as ESTREMADURA, the RIBATEJO, and TERRAS DO SADO. Portuguese plantings totalled about 14,000 ha/35,000 acres in 2004, four times those of Touriga Nacional.

Touriga Nacional, the most revered vine variety for port and, increasingly, for fine dry reds, and not just in PORTUGAL. It produces small quantities of very small berries in the DOURO valley and the Portuguese DÃO region (where it probably originated) which result in deep-coloured, very tannic, concentrated wines. The vine is vigorous and robust but is prone to poor FRUIT SET and may produce just 300 g/10 oz of fruit per vine, making it very unpopular with growers. This almost led to its extinction in the mid 20th century but considerable work has been done on CLONAL SELECTION of the variety so that newer cuttings are slightly more productive and average sugar levels even higher. Touriga Nacional today represents about 2 per cent of Douro vines but should constitute at least 20 per cent of all red Dão. Touriga Nacional is slowly migrating south into other parts of Portugal, including ESTREMADURA, the RIBATEJO and the ALENTEJO. Portuguese plantings totalled about 3,500 ha/8,750 acres in 2004. The variety is also grown in Australia, although not (yet) the best clones, and in Spain and is expected to make an impact elsewhere.

tourism. Wine-related tourism continues to be increasingly important to both producers and consumers. For many centuries, not even wine merchants travelled, but today many members of the general public deliberately make forays to explore a wine region or regions. This is partly a reflection of the increased interest in both wine and foreign travel generally, but also because most wine regions and many producers' premises are attractive places. VINEYARDS tend to be aesthetically pleasing in any case, and the sort of climate in which wine is generally produced is agreeable at least during the growing season and very possibly for most of the year. Getting to grips with this specialist form of agriculture combines urban dwellers' need to commune with nature with acquiring privileged, and generally admired, specialist knowledge. And then there is the possibility of TASTING, and buying wines direct from the source, which may involve keen prices and/or acquiring rarities. (Cellar-door sales can be particularly attractive to wine drinkers living in countries with high DUTY levels on alcohol.)

Wine tourism is certainly not new to Germany. The RHINE has long welcomed tourists, who are encouraged to travel by steamer and stop at wine villages en route, and the MOSEL valley is surely one of the most photographed in the world. German tourists, on the other hand, have long plundered the Weinstuben of ALSACE and represent an important market for the region's wines.

In France, wine tourism was often accidental. Northern Europeans heading for the sun for decades travelled straight through BURGUNDY and the northern RHÔNE and could hardly fail to notice vineyards and the odd invitation 'Dégustation–Vente' (tasting–sale). (And it is true that a tasting almost invariably leads to a sale.) Wine producers in the LOIRE have long profited from their location in the midst of châteaux country, and within an easy Friday night's drive of Paris.

BORDEAUX was one of the last important French wine regions to realize its potential for wine tourism. The village of ST-EMILION has had scores of wine shops and restaurants for decades but it was not until the late 1980s that the MÉDOC, the most famous cluster of wine properties in the world, had a hotel and more than one restaurant suitable for international visitors. Alexis LICHINE was mocked for being virtually the only CLASSED GROWTH proprietor openly to welcome visitors.

Much of southern Europe is simply too hot, and too far from suitable resorts, to make wine tourism comfortable and feasible, but *agriturismo* has played an extremely important part in the viticultural economy of Italy.

In various NEW WORLD wine regions, tourism has also become an important aspect of business. Prominent examples here include NAPA and SONOMA, now almost part and parcel of the San Francisco tourist experience; SOUTH AFRICAN vineyards within easy reach of Cape Town; NEW ZEALAND, the most southerly wine areas of which are just as breathtakingly beautiful as those of the Cape; HUNTER VALLEY for visitors to and residents of Sydney; upper NEW YORK state; and even the vineyards of ENGLAND, whose owners depend heavily on income from farmgate sales.

Some tour operators and travel agents specialize in wine tourism, and the number of wine regions without their own special wine route or winery trail is decreasing rapidly.

tourne, wine fault caused by BACTERIA which turn the wine brown and cloudy.

tractor, the most common vineyard machine. Tractor dimensions have had a significant impact on vineyard design. In many parts of Europe where tractors replaced horses, tractor designers obliged by creating either narrow, or row-straddling, tractors (known in France as *tracteurs-enjambeurs*). The narrowest vineyard tractors are not much wider than their drivers, about 80 cm/31 in. In the New World, however, vineyards were changed to accommodate the tractors, which included row spacings of 3 to 4 m to allow early tractor models between the rows.

The introduction of tractors and other forms of MECHANIZATION to viticulture has had profound economic and sociological effects. Less LABOUR was required, encouraging the population drift to the cities. However, a few growers concerned about soil compaction or constrained by steeply sloping vineyards have returned to horse-drawn ploughs. R.E.S.

trade, wine. Wine is better known for its sociability than its profitability. What is needed to make a small fortune in the wine business is said to be a large fortune. The wine trade is considerably more amusing, however, than many others. It routinely involves immersion in an often delicious product, travel to some of the more beautiful corners of the world (see TOURISM), and provides widely admired expertise.

One of the attractions of the wine trade is the people. It has for long attracted a wide range of individualists who, if they were not interesting and amusing before they or their visitors have tasted their wares, seem so afterwards. Producers and merchants alike tend to be generous, and to appreciate the fact that it is difficult to sell or buy wine without tasting and sharing it.

Apprenticeship is probably the easiest route into the wine trade, although some form of specialist EDUCATIONAL qualification can help too. The general areas in which full-time employment may be found include vineyard management, wine-making and quality control, sales and marketing, wholesaling, retailing, and, the job with potentially the most power and perks, buying. There is also the overcrowded field of WINE WRITING. See also wine MERCHANTS.

tradition, defined by oenologist Émile PEYNAUD as an experiment that has worked, is an extremely important ingredient in viticulture and wine-making in many Old World regions. A significant proportion of older small-scale producers in regions such as Burgundy and the Rhône, for example, do things in the vineyard and cellar precisely because their fathers did, even if their own children are likely to have been exposed to SCIENCE through some sort of formal training. These graduates of ACADEME may understand the reasons for some of these supposedly traditional methods better than their parents, but they do not necessarily change them.

Some peasant wine-growers, for example, will perform operations such as RACKING or BOTTLING only when the moon is in a certain phase (see BIODYNAMIC VITICULTURE), or when the wind is, or is not, blowing from a certain direction. Superstition plays a very small part in making wine, and these traditions are likely to have evolved for a reason, often one that is eventually explained by science.

traditional method, official EU term for the most painstaking way of making wine sparkle, once known as the champagne method. See SPARKLING WINE-MAKING.

training in a wine context usually means VINE TRAINING. See below.

training systems, methods of VINE TRAINING, which vary considerably around the world. Since the grapevine is a true VINE, and is not self-supporting like a tree, innumerable training systems for vines have been devised over the millennia of cultivation (see OENOTRIA for example). Confusion between the terms training systems, TRELLIS SYSTEMS, and PRUNING is widespread. In fact they are three distinct, if closely related, entities. A trellis is a man-made physical structure, consisting normally of wood and wires. The word training describes the actions of pruning in winter and summer, and SHOOT and CANE placement, so that the vine's TRUNK, ARMS, and CORDONS and BUDS are appropriately located on the trellis system. Those training systems which involve trellises are often named after the trellis.

The viticulturist's choice of training system will be affected by the cost of the system, the availability of any materials required, the availability of the skilled LABOUR required to install and manage it, CLIMATE, TOPOGRAPHY, vine VIGOUR, VINE VARIETY, MECHANIZATION requirements, and, in many instances, knowledge of alternative systems. In many places in the world, especially the OLD WORLD, little thought is given to using any but the region's traditional system. In the New World, much consideration is given to the choice of training system, because of recent research into CANOPY MANAGEMENT which has shown substantial benefits in terms of YIELD, wine quality, and disease reduction by adopting new designs. Training systems may be dictated by requirements for MECHANICAL HARVESTING and MECHANICAL PRUNING.

A basic difference in training systems about which the casual observer may wonder is why some vineyards have trellis systems with wires, and others not. While self-supporting GOBELET vines are common in southern Europe, in many countries such vineyards are considered old-fashioned, and WIRES to suspend foliage are used instead. The control of vine VIGOUR and VINE DISEASES are the principal reasons for adopting more elaborate systems. If vines were planted to the gobelet system in an area of summer rainfall such as northern France, the vines could be very prone to FUNGAL DISEASES because the leaves and fruit would be in a shaded, humid environment. It would also be difficult to gain access to the vineyard, as the shoots would cover the ground. Lifting the foliage up and containing it between wires allows TRIMMING of the ends and LEAF REMOVAL for better fruit exposure. Both tractor access to the vineyard and airflow within it are also improved.

The vine is pruned in winter as a means of training the framework and buds into an appropriate position to be supported by the trellis system.

A vine-training system should aim to maximize yield and quality, and to facilitate cultural operations such as spraying, cultivation, harvesting, and pruning. As the degree of mechanization increases, so does the need for the vineyard to be uniform and orderly. For example, mechanical leaf removal and harvesting are made easier by locating the bunches of grapes in a single zone. Similarly, mechanization of summer and winter pruning is made easier if the vine shoots and canes all point in the same direction, vertically upwards, for example. The vine framework should ideally be at a convenient height for any hand operations, neither too high nor too low. Some would argue that the fruit should be near the ground to absorb reflected heat, although this can involve back-breaking labour at HARVEST and pruning, and is extremely difficult to mechanize.

Until the 1960s, it was extremely rare for any training system other than that traditional in a given region to be considered. In many parts of the world, little has changed, although the recently developed vineyards of some NEW WORLD regions have evaluated the various systems and adopted those best suited to their requirements.

There is an almost infinite variety of vine-training systems; there are few plants whose cultivation can vary as much as between the densely planted (10,000 vines per ha or 4,000 per acre), neatly trimmed vertical hedges of the vineyards of the Médoc and the vineyards of a few hundred vines per hectare trained up trees around agricultural fields in the Vinho Verde region of Portugal.

Vine-training systems can be classified in a number of ways. In France, it is common to classify vines as low-trained (*vignes basses*) or high-trained (*vignes hautes*). For low vines, the trunk is up to 50 cm/20 in high, but usually shorter. Such training systems are more economical, and are suited to lower-vigour vineyards. Grape RIPENING may benefit from the fruit being closer to the ground, but both HARVEST and PRUNING are much less comfortable manual operations, and vines may also be more disease prone. The many examples of low-trained vines in France include the extensive southern areas of GOBELET, the CORDON DE ROYAT vines of Burgundy and Champagne, and the double GUYOT of Bordeaux.

High vines are less common in modern France but were certainly known by Roman authors (see AGRICULTURAL TREATISES). Interest in high vines was more recently rekindled by the 1950 publication of the Austrian LENZ MOSER. He recommended low-density vineyards with wide rows of trunks about 1.25 m/ 4 ft high. Higher training does reduce FROST risk, but requires thicker and more expensive supports, although vineyard work is made easier. 'High-culture' vines can be trained either cordon or Guyot. Vineyards of the New World have typically used high vine-training systems. Overhead trellises such as Italy's TENDONE are special examples of high vines.

There are other possible ways of classifying vine-training systems, however. The cordons may be classed as short, as in the 0.5 m in a closely spaced cordon de Royat, or many metres in length as for the Portuguese cruzeta (see below). An alternative classification takes account of whether the foliage is free, as for example in the gobelet vines of the Midi, or SHOOT POSITIONED or constrained into a plane, such as the vertical systems common in Alsace and Germany in which the foliage is held in place by WIRES and maintained by TRIMMING.

The vine canopies can also be classified by their plane: arbours or tendone-trained vines have horizontal canopies about 2 m above the ground, while the Tatura trellis developed in Australia is inclined at 60 degrees to the ground, and most shoot-positioned canopies are vertical. Some canopies have shoots all growing upwards, as in the lyre trellis, while the GENEVA DOUBLE CURTAIN (GDC) has shoots which grow downwards, and the SCOTT HENRY and SMART–DYSON systems have shoots trained both upwards and downwards. Vines may have a DIVIDED CANOPY in either the horizontal plane such as the GDC or LYRE trellis, or vertically as in the Scott Henry. Training systems can be simple, like the free-standing gobelet vines of the Rioja, or elaborate, like the Ruakura twin two tier (RT2T) developed in New Zealand, which is both horizontally and vertically divided, and requires 20 wires per row to support fruit and foliage.

The following list gives brief details of some of the training systems in use around the world, including traditional and some new ones being used for deliberate CANOPY MANAGEMENT.

Alberate, an old form of vine-training system used in parts of Italy where the vines are trained on or between trees. There are local variations, such as those in Bologna, Toscana, Veneto, and Romagna, with the common feature being that trees are used for support.

Alberello, see GOBELET.

Arbour, see TENDONE.

arched cane, a variation on many different forms of training systems where canes are arched rather than being tied horizontally, see GUYOT. Alternative names include bow trained, *arcure* in French, Capovolto or Guyot *ad archetto* in Italy. This practice is claimed to lead to better BUDBREAK in the centre of the canes, where buds do not normally burst well. It can be considered a variation of Guyot training.

Ballerina, a form of Smart–Dyson developed in King Valley, VICTORIA, Australia. One vertical and two transverse curtains are created from one or two cordons trained to spurs pointing upwards. Many bilateral cordon training systems can easily be converted to Ballerina.

Barra, used for monoculture in Vinho Verde whereby vines are trained in one direction along a single wire at shoulder height.

basket training, often used for free-standing vines where canes are wound one around the other for mutual support. Common for some BUSH VINE systems which are pruned. Typically they are of low vigour.

Bush vines, see BUSH VINES and GOBELET.

Casarsa, or Casarsa Friuli, an Italian training system like the SYLVOZ, except the canes are not tied down after pruning.

Cassone padavano, a horizontally divided Italian system, pruned like the Sylvoz.

Cazenave, an Italian vine-training system which uses a modified form of Guyot pruning where short arms containing spurs and canes (five to six buds) are arranged along a horizontal CORDON. The canes are tied about vertically to a wire above. Because the pruner is able to leave so many buds per vine, this system is suited to fertile soils.

Château Thierry, a form of GUYOT training where the cane is tied in an arch to a stake beside the free-standing vine.

Cordon de Cazenave, an Italian and French system used for fertile soils, with one or more canes left on a CORDON DE ROYAT.

Cordon de Royat, see CORDON DE ROYAT.

cordon trained, American term to distinguish a training system using cordons as opposed to canes. These are typically horizontal and bilateral but in the late 1990s, in California as in Europe, unilateral cordons were in vogue.

cordon vertical, a vertical cordon with alternating spurs to either side. Not used very commonly as growth tends to be mainly from the top buds.

Cruzeta, a system used in the VINHO VERDE area of Portugal where vines are trained to a wide cross arm about 2 m off the ground. More sophisticated than *latada* but less so than *barra*.

Duplex, a system developed in California in the 1960s with flexible cross arms to allow for machine harvesting. While the fruiting wires are horizontally divided by 1 m/3 ft, the foliage was not shoot positioned to create two separate curtains as for the GENEVA DOUBLE CURTAIN. As a consequence, it is not nearly as beneficial in terms of yield, quality, and disease resistance.

Espalier, see ESPALIER.

Éventail (meaning 'fan'), a French system with multiple arms, each giving rise to a spur or short cane. Originally the form used in Chablis, with the arms lying on the ground, this has been modified to the taille de Semur system, where each arm is tied to a lower wire in the one plane.

factory roof system, commonly used for TABLE GRAPES, in South Africa and Israel, for example, where the CANOPY is trained up at an angle to meet in a gable near the row centre. This may also be called a closed, one-arm PERGOLA, and provides excellent access to the fruit for any hand work required.

fan shaped, a training system distantly related to *éventail* that is used in central Europe, particularly Russia, where the vine trunks are spread out in the shape of a fan, which makes it easier to bury vines for WINTER PROTECTION. The Italian version is called *ventagli*.

Flachbogen, the German name for a training system like the Guyot whereby one cane is laid horizontally either side of the head, and shoots trained vertically between foliage wires. The shoots are trimmed at the top. See VERTICAL TRELLIS.

Geneva double curtain (GDC), see GENEVA DOUBLE CURTAIN.

gobelet, see GOBELET.

Guyot, see GUYOT.

Halbbogen, a German training system whereby the vine is pruned to one cane of about 15 buds' length, and is arched in the middle over a wire about 25 cm/10 in above the base and end of the cane. Shoots are trained each year vertically between foliage wires, and are trimmed at the top.

head trained, common American term for a vine trained so that a group of spurs arise in one zone, called the head. Such vines are normally cane pruned, but may also be spur pruned. Here the spurs elongate into arms and the resulting structure is something of a hybrid between a vertical cordon and a gobelet.

Hudson River umbrella, a system used in the eastern US, where canes are arched downwards from a high head.

Isère, a training system much like Ch Thierry, where the cane is trained in a bow to a stake beside the vine.

Latada, traditional 3-m high trellis used in the Vinho Verde region for vines grown around fields of other crops.

Lenz Moser, see LENZ MOSER.

Lincoln canopy, a horizontal canopy developed at LINCOLN University in New Zealand. It is like the arbour, but is at waist height and allows tractor access between rows.

lyre, see LYRE.

MPCT, or minimal pruned cordon trained, which describes the system developed and extensively used in Australia, mainly for bulk wine production. Young vines are trained to a form of CORDON at about 1.5 m height and, apart from wrapping early cane growth on the wire, receive minimal hand work, including pruning. See MINIMAL PRUNING.

Palmette, an Italian training system, with one vine trained to four horizontal canes, one pair above the other.

Parral, see TENDONE.

Parron, see TENDONE.

Pendelbogen, the German name for the arched cane training system described above. There is a 50-cm height difference between the end of the cane and the highest point, which is thought to improve budbreak in the middle of the cane. Most of the shoots are trained vertically upright between foliage wires, and normally require trimming at the top. Pendelbogen means 'pendulum bow', and there are related training forms called not just Halbbogen ('half bow'), but also Rundbogen ('round bow') and Doppelbogen ('double bow'). The name has also been applied to a mid-height Sylvoz system in New Zealand.

Pergola, see PERGOLA.

Perold, form of vertical trellis used in South Africa.

pyramid, an Italian training system where vine shoots are trained over a group of stakes tied together at the top, forming a pyramid.

Ramada, alternative name for *latada* above.

Raggi Bellussi, an Italian overhead training system suspended from above and with two vines planted together and trained in four directions. Pruned like the Sylvoz.

Raggiera or **raggi**, an Italian training system where vines are trained overhead on wires like the spokes of a wheel. Either one vine may be trained up a central stake or tree and divided into cordons, or several vines may be at the one position with each trained along a different radius.

Ruakura twin two-tier (RT2T) trellis, a system developed at the Ruakura Research Centre in New Zealand with the canopy divided into four curtains, two above two. Well suited for high-vigour vineyards, but no mechanical harvester had been developed for it by the 1990s.

Scott Henry, see SCOTT HENRY.

shelf, or *tana*, local name for overhead trellis in Japan.

slanting trellis. The canopy is trained along an inclined support. This trellis can be used for both table- and wine-grape production.

Smart–Dyson trellis, see SMART–DYSON.

Sylvoz, see SYLVOZ.

Tatura trellis. Developed at the Tatura Research Station in Australia and consisting of two inclined canopies at 60 degrees meeting in the middle of the row. Early studies indicated high productivity, but the system has not been used commercially for wine grapes, probably because of mechanization difficulties.

Te Kauwhata two tier (TK2T). Developed at the Te Kauwhata Research Station in New Zealand, this system is vertically divided, with shoots trained vertically upwards. Limited commercial use in California and New Zealand.

Tendone, see TENDONE.

three-wire trellis. Another California trellis system with a pair of fixed foliage wires above the cordon. Shoots are not positioned, and fall across these wires under their own weight.

traverse trellis. European name for the T trellis.

T trellis. Common in Australia, where the vine is trained to two horizontal cordons about 0.5 m apart. It takes its name from the appearance of the vine trunk and cordons. Shoots are not positioned, and so the canopy is not divided. Can be machine pruned and harvested, and is widely used in bulk wine-producing areas.

tunnel, an alternative name for a form of overhead vine training where the vines are planted in two rows and trained overhead.

two-wire vertical trellis. Common terminology in California, where one wire is occupied by the cordon and the second is a fixed foliage wire. Shoots grow up and over this wire and fall under their own weight to form a bell-shaped canopy. When the vines are vigorous, the canopy is very shaded.

U, an alternative name for the LYRE trellis.

umbrella kniffin, a system used in eastern America, where canes from a mid-height head are trained over a top wire and tied below.

V, a vine-training system in the shape of the letter where shoots are trained upwards into two curtains. This form does not work as well as the LYRE or U system, where the cordons are separated at the base.

vase, another name for the GOBELET training system.

vertical cordon, a rare training system as top buds tend to burst first, making it difficult to manage.

vertical trellis, see VERTICAL TRELLIS.

VSP, or vertical shoot positioning, which describes a system used throughout the world where annual shoot growth is trained vertically and held in place by foliage wires. See VERTICAL TRELLIS.

Y, a vine-training system in the shape of the letter and equivalent to the V system except that the trunk of the vine forms the vertical part of the letter.

The above cannot pretend to be a comprehensive list of the multitude of training systems used worldwide, nor of all their local names, and how patterns of usage are changing, especially in the New World, but it does give some indication of the extraordinary variation in vine-training systems. The greatest complexity of training systems in the world is to be found in Italy, while those used in France tend to be determinedly regional.   R.E.S.

Ambrosi, H., and Becker, H. (eds.), *Der deutsche Wein* (Munich, 1978).

Eynard, I., and Dalmasso, G., *Viticoltura moderna: manuale pratico* (Milan, 1990).

Galet, P., *Précis de viticulture* (5th edn, Montpellier, 1988).

Huglin, P., *Biologie et écologie de la vigne* (Lausanne, 1986).

Smart, R. E., and Robinson, M., *Sunlight into Wine: A Handbook for Winegrape Canopy Management* (Adelaide, 1991).

Trajadura, early-ripening white grape variety used to add body and a certain citrus character to Portugal's VINHO VERDE if it is picked sufficiently early. It is known as TREIXADURA across the Spanish border in Galicia. It is often blended with LOUREIRO and sometimes with ALVARINHO.

Traminer, the less aromatic, paler-skinned variant of the pink-skinned white wine grape variety Gewürztraminer. It has been grown, for example, in Moravia in what was Czechoslovakia, where it is also known as Prinç. The name derives from the village of Tramin, or Termeno, in ALTO ADIGE. In countries as different as Germany, Italy, Austria, Romania, many of the former Soviet republics, and Australia, however, Traminer is also used as a synonym for GEWÜRZTRAMINER, under which name many more details can be found.

transfer method, SPARKLING WINE-MAKING process, now less common than it was, involving provoking a second fermentation in bottle and then transferring its contents into a tank, where the wine is separated from the deposit.

translocation, plant physiological process whereby soluble materials such as dissolved salts, organic materials, and growth substances are moved around the vine in the PHLOEM. (The phloem tissue is in the outer part of the trunk or stems, and so can be disrupted by CINCTURING.) Sucrose is the principal form in which CARBOHYDRATES are moved, and the phloem sap also contains amino acids and organic acids, inorganic nutrients, plant hormones, and alkaloids. Examples of translocation are the movement of inorganic nutrients absorbed by roots from the soil to other parts of the vine, for example POTASSIUM going into the fruit, which may prejudice wine quality. Translocation also includes the important movement of SUCROSE formed by PHOTOSYNTHESIS away from the leaves to the fruit which will eventually become ALCOHOL in wine. From the point of view of wine, the translocation of sucrose, MALIC ACID, TARTARIC ACID, elements, and compounds containing NITROGEN during RIPENING are crucial to the chemical composition of grapes, and thus to eventual wine quality.

Movement of foodstuffs is invariably towards points of need, such as growing shoot tips for the early part of the season, flowers, then developing berries, and also towards the permanent vine parts such as trunks and roots for the accumulation of reserves later in the season. HORMONES such as auxins, cytokinins, and gibberellins play an important role in regulating translocation. The vine is capable of translocating products over long distances and so, even though the shoot supporting a bunch may be shaded, the grapes will still ripen depending on materials imported from other parts of the vine.   R.E.S.

Champagnol, F., *Éléments de physiologie de la vigne et de viticulture générale* (St-Gely-de-Fesc, 1984).
Winkler, A. J., *et al.*, *General Viticulture* (2nd edn, Berkeley, Calif., 1974).

transpiration, physiological process whereby water taken up from a vine's roots is evaporated through the leaves, important in preventing the vine from overheating in sunny weather. Water and dissolved elements move in the so-called transpiration stream through the woody part of the vine called the XYLEM. The xylem fluid also contains relatively large amounts of amino acids, especially glutamine, organic acids, especially malic, and small amounts of sugars. Total water loss from

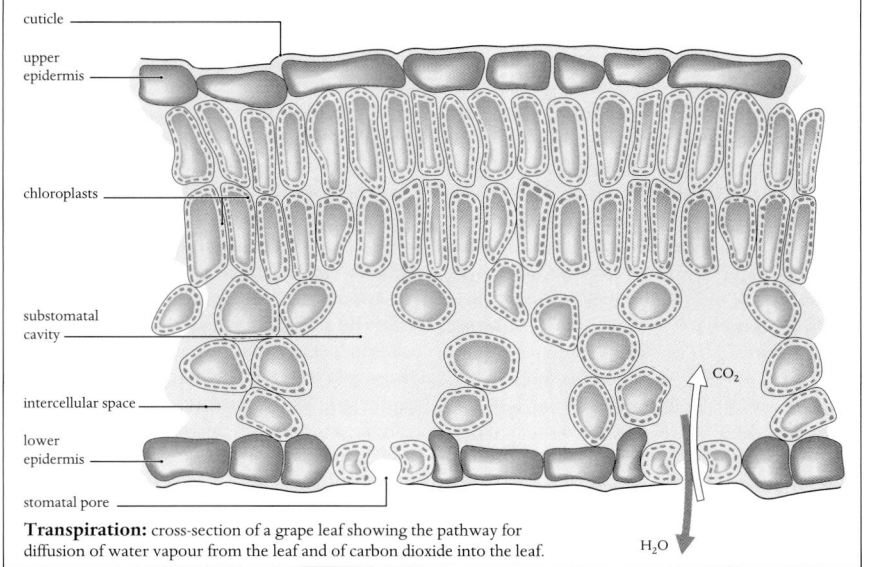

cuticle
upper epidermis
chloroplasts
substomatal cavity
intercellular space
lower epidermis
stomatal pore
CO_2
H_2O

Transpiration: cross-section of a grape leaf showing the pathway for diffusion of water vapour from the leaf and of carbon dioxide into the leaf.

a vineyard is called evapotranspiration, and this includes transpiration from the vines and also any weeds or cover crop present, plus EVAPORATION from the soil surface.

Transpiration is an energy-driven process, with the energy being provided by leaves absorbing SUNLIGHT. Water vapour passes from the leaf to the atmosphere via small pores on the underside called STOMATA. Energy is required to provide the latent heat of evaporation for the phase change from liquid (water) to gas (water vapour), which takes place in the cavity below the stomata. The cell walls of the substomatal cavity are wet from a long column of water extending to the roots. Provided the vine is well supplied with water, leaves facing the sun will be only 2–3 °C (36–7 °F) warmer than the air, while if water supply is limited then this figure can exceed 10 °C (18 °F) and the vine will suffer both HEAT STRESS and WATER STRESS.

Transpiration is controlled by both atmospheric and plant factors. High transpiration rates are due to weather patterns of low humidity, and high sunshine, temperature, and wind speed. Typically, during the day as temperature rises, humidity falls, and so transpiration is fastest in the early afternoon. As soils dry, the risk of water stress increases and so, by partially closing stomata, the vine is able to regulate its water status to some extent. However, as stomata close then PHOTOSYNTHESIS stops, as carbon dioxide entry into the leaf is inhibited.

Rates of transpiration vary with the weather and growth stage of the vineyard. For a vineyard in full leaf in the middle of the season, daily evapotranspiration rates may be as high as 40,000 l/ha for a hot, dry, and sunny climate. For a vineyard planted with 2,000 vines per ha, this rate is equivalent to 20 l (4.4 gal) per vine per day. The amount of water transpired

is very high relative to both the vine's growth overall and the fruit produced. For example, measurements cited by Smart and Coombe show 5,000 g and 80 g of water respectively for each gram of plant dry weight and gram of fruit produced.   R.E.S.

Champagnol, F., *Éléments de physiologie de la vigne et de viticulture générale* (St-Gely-de-Fesc, 1984).
Smart, R. E., and Coombe, B. G., 'Water relations of vines', in T. T. Kozlowski (ed.), *Water Deficits and Plant Growth*, vii (New York, 1983).
Winkler, A. J., *et al.*, *General Viticulture* (2nd edn, Berkeley, Calif., 1974).

transport of wine has changed considerably over the ages but a wide variety of different methods, from tanker to a bottle sent by mail, are still used.

Ancient history
Wine was transported in bulk in antiquity in a variety of ways: in huge wineskins loaded on the backs of two- or four-wheeled carts or in BARRELS on carts, but water-borne transport had a great advantage because of the inefficiency of the harnesses used on animals. For most of the Mediterranean area, wine was carried in large AMPHORAE, which were loaded in the holds of ships. The pottery jars required considerable packing (heather, straw, etc.) to cushion them against breakages. They could be transferred to smaller vessels for transport up inland waterways. A recent discovery has been of wrecks carrying *dolia* (see DOLIUM), as a kind of tanker for the bulk transport of wine. Barrels were widely used in northern Europe (see CELTS) and later in the Mediterranean, although the amphora tradition died out completely only in the medieval period.   J.J.P.

Moulin, M. M., 'Le Transport du raisin ou du vin par la route à l'époque romaine en Gaule et dans les provinces voisines', in R. Chevallier *et al.*, *Archéologie de la vigne et du vin* (Paris, 1990).

Peacock, D. P. S., and Williams, D. F., *Amphorae and the Roman Economy* (London, 1986).

Modern transport

In the Middle Ages, RIVERS played an important role in transporting wine, and only those wine regions with access to good water transport (by sea and/or river) were likely to develop much trade. In the 19th and early 20th centuries, the advent of a RAILWAY system transformed wine regions as dissimilar as the LANGUEDOC, ROUSSILLON, Mendoza in ARGENTINA, RIOJA, and CHIANTI. Today wine is generally transported by road and sea (although, at the height of Beaujolais NOUVEAU's popularity in the early 1980s, planes, parachutes, and vintage cars were just some of the means used to race that particular wine to the consumer).

For centuries, the transport of wine meant BULK TRANSPORT, and the most common container used for transporting wine was the barrel. SHERRY, for example, was still shipped to British bottlers in its special casks, or BUTTS, until well into the 20th century (when the empty butts were used for Scotch whisky maturation). In the latter half of the 20th century, however, container shipment in bulk tankers became the norm, although, as an increasing proportion of wine is bottled not just in its country or region of origin but actually at the winery, the most common container for transport today is probably the BOTTLE. Barrels may be an awkward shape, but bottles are breakable, and pilferage of bottled wine is considerably easier than stealing BULK WINE. Wine transport across national frontiers or state lines can involve the additional problems associated with any product subject to TAXATION.

From the consumer's point of view, the most important aspect of the transport of wine is TEMPERATURE. If wine is exposed to high temperatures, it may well deteriorate considerably, even if it has been subject to effective STABILIZATION. Spikes of temperature can also lead to spoilage due to OXIDATION. Conscientious producers try to avoid shipping wine in high summer, while scrupulous wholesalers insist that insulated containers are used for shipments in hot weather and/or through the TROPICS but this adds to the costs. Stowing the wine below sea level minimizes the temperature variation. Exposure to light can also be a problem: research indicates that exposure to UV light at any point in the distribution chain may convert amino acids into MERCAPTANS, thus damaging wine quality. The risk is reduced by the use of brown rather than clear bottles.

In the late 1990s, the transport of wine, and direct shipment in particular, became even more legally restricted in the UNITED STATES, although a Supreme Court ruling in 2005 suggested some relaxation of controls.

transversage. See SPARKLING WINE-MAKING.

Trás-os-Montes, VINHO REGIONAL in north east Portugal. Meaning 'behind the mountains', Trás-os-Montes is locked in by high mountains on one side and the Spanish frontier on the other (see map under PORTUGAL). The inhabitants of Trás-os-Montes have always prided themselves on their independence but since the 1960s the economy has suffered as local people have been forced to leave this remote agricultural region to find profitable work in the coastal cities or abroad. The mountains which isolate Trás-os-Montes from the rest of Portugal cast a rain shadow over the region which becomes progressively more arid towards Spain. The climatic extremes and shallow granite-based soils make cultivation difficult, although farmers have been helped considerably by funds from the European Union and the World Bank.

Wine is an important commodity in Trás-os-Montes, which includes the northern half of the PORT wine region and, with a total of 69,000 ha/170,000 acres under vine, there are more vineyards here than in any other part of Portugal. However, as yields are low, production is exceeded by that of both ESTREMADURA and the RIBATEJO. The high vineyards here, north of the DOURO valley, also supply wine for MATEUS Rosé and a number of imitative brands. Table (unfortified) wines from the Douro region, not entitled to the Douro DOC because of the grape varieties used, are entitled to their own Vinho Regional: Trás-os-Montes—Terras Durienses. Three Trás-os-Montes regions have their own IPRS: Chaves, Valpaços, and Planalto-Mirandes. R.J.M.

Trbljan, relatively important light-berried vine variety grown particularly on the coast of CROATIA just north of Zadar. Several thousand hectares are planted. The grape is also sometimes called Kuč.

Trebbiano, most common name for the undistinguished Ugni Blanc white grape variety in Italy, where it is by far the most planted white grape variety. The word Trebbiano in a wine name almost invariably signals something light, white, crisp, and uninspiring. This gold-, even amber-berried grape variety is so prolific, and so much planted in both France and Italy, the world's two major wine-producing countries, that it probably produces more wine than any other vine variety in the world—even though Spain's AIRÉN and Garnacha/GRENACHE each cover a larger total vineyard area. Trebbiano in its many forms covers a greater area of vineyard even than SANGIOVESE. It is cited in more DOC regulations than any other single variety (about 80) and may well account for more than a third of Italy's entire DOC white wine production.

In France, where it found its way as a result of the Mediterranean trade that flourished between Italian and French ports during the 14th century, the variety is the country's most important white vine. See under its most common French name UGNI BLANC for details of Trebbiano in France.

Ugni Blanc's most common use, as base wine for brandy, provides a clue to the character of the wine produced by Trebbiano. It is, like most copiously produced wines, low in extract and character, relatively low in alcohol, but usefully high in acidity. This exceptionally vigorous vine buds late, thereby avoiding most spring frost damage, which underscores its high yields, which can easily reach 150 hl/ha (8.5 tons/acre). Its relative immunity to frost has made it quite popular for difficult, cool positions in central Italy and replacing it with more characterful varieties as vineyards are replanted is not always easy. It has good resistance to POWDERY MILDEW and GREY ROT but can succumb to DOWNY MILDEW. Because it ripens relatively late, often as late as October in parts of Italy, there is a natural geographical limit on its cultivation but in areas such as Charentes it is simply picked before it is fully ripe, as indeed it is in southern Italy to maximize acidity.

There are almost as many possible histories of Trebbiano as there are different varieties called Trebbiano in Italy. Trebbiano Toscano (Tuscan) and Trebbiano Giallo (yellow) ripen rather earlier than most other Trebbiano. PLINY mentions a *vinum trebulanum* in CAMPANIA. There is no shortage of possible geographical references, with many towns and villages incorporating words like Trebbiano, and the river Trebbia in EMILIA-ROMAGNA providing another possible source. The Bolognese agronomist PETRUS DE CRESCENTIIS certainly described the vine Trebbiano as early as 1303.

Today Trebbiano is planted all over Italy (with the exception of the cool far north), to the extent that it is likely that the great majority of basic *vino bianco* will contain at least some of the variety, if only to add acidity and volume. Its stronghold, however, is central Italy. **Trebbiano Toscano**, covering just over 42,000 ha/106,680 acres, was Italy's third most planted vine variety in 2000, while there were more than 20,000 ha of **Trebbiano Romagnolo**, nearly 8,700 ha of **Trebbiano d'Abruzzo** or **Trebbiano Abruzzese**, and under 5,000 ha of **Trebbiano Giallo**.

Trebbiano di Soave and **Trebbiano di Lugana** are not related to Trebbiano, despite their name, and are in fact VERDICCHIO.

TREBBIANO DI ROMAGNA dominates white wine production in Emilia-Romagna, made chiefly from Trebbiano Romagnolo or the almost amber-berried Trebbiano della Fiamma. Some idea of Trebbiano's ubiquity is given by listing just some of the wines in which it is an ingredient: VERDICCHIO, ORVIETO, FRASCATI, together with in the north SOAVE (from Trebbiano Toscano, which was planted in place of Trebbiano di Soave in the 1960s and 1970s, when yield was a more important consideration than quality). The variety has after all had many centuries to adapt itself to local conditions. Between Toscana and Rome, in UMBRIA, the variety can be known as Procanico, which some agronomists believe is a superior, smaller-berried Trebbiano. Only the fiercely varietal-conscious north eastern corner of Italy is virtually free of this bland ballast.

Trebbiano's malign influence was most noticeable in central TOSCANA in much of the 20th century, however, where Trebbiano was so well entrenched that CHIANTI and therefore VINO NOBILE DI MONTEPULCIANO laws sanctioned its inclusion in this red wine, thereby diluting its quality as well as its colour and damaging its reputation. Trebbiano is now very much an optional ingredient, however, which is increasingly spurned by the quality-conscious red wine producers of Toscana.

Once Trebbiano fell out of favour with Chianti producers, an attempt was made to transform it into innocuous dry whites such as GALESTRO. Fortunately, the market for these wines has dwindled, and in the 2000s much Trebbiano in Toscana was grubbed up, or used in VIN SANTO.

Perhaps Italy's most exciting Trebbiano, Valentini's Trebbiano d'Abruzzo (see ABRUZZO), is not a Trebbiano at all but is made from BOMBINO BIANCO.

Trebbiano has also managed to infiltrate Portugal's fiercely nationalistic vineyards, as Thalia, and is widely planted in BULGARIA and in parts of GREECE and RUSSIA. As well as being used for MEXICO's important brandy production, Trebbiano is well entrenched in the southern hemisphere, where its high yields and high acidity are valued. There were more than 4,000 ha/9,800 acres of 'Ugni Blanc' in Argentina by the end of the 1980s as well as extensive plantings in Brazil and Uruguay.

South Africa also calls its relatively limited plantings Ugni Blanc but relies more on COLOMBARD for brandy production and cheap, tart blending material, as does California, whose few remaining hundred acres of the vine called 'St-Emilion' there are exclusively in the Central valley, although interesting VARIETAL versions are not entirely unknown. Australia, where Colombard is also more important, has about 800 ha of Trebbiano, planted mainly in the irrigated areas, where it provides a usefully tart ingredient in basic blended whites and is also sometimes used by distillers.

The influence of Trebbiano/Ugni Blanc will surely decline as wine drinkers seek flavour with increasing determination.

Trebbiano di Romagna, abundant VARIETAL central Italian dry white made from a grape variety which differs little either in AMPELOGRAPHY or wine personality from the TREBBIANO of Toscana. The variety is cultivated across a wide swathe of ROMAGNA in the provinces of Bologna, Forlì, and Ravenna, with a total of approximately 4,800 ha/12,000 acres producing about 69,000 hl/1.82 million gal of DOC wine a year. Permitted yields of almost 100 hl/ha (5.7 tons/acre) do little to assist a grape not known for its striking personality, and most Trebbiano di Romagna is, at best, suitable for a picnic.   D.T. & D.C.G.

Treixadura, Galician name for Portugal's scented, delicate white TRAJADURA and treated in much the same way. This is the main grape of Ribeiro and may be blended with Galician Torrontés and Lado. It is also grown in the Rías Baixas region, where it is often blended with Albariño and possibly LOUREIRA. Total Spanish plantings were 660 ha/163 acres in 2004.

trellis systems, support structures for the vine framework required for a given TRAINING SYSTEM. Normally these are man made, although vines are still occasionally trained to trees. The trellis system in its simplest form consists of a STAKE driven beside a vine to which the vine trunk or shoots are tied. Nowadays WIRES are used to support vines and foliage, as posts are installed at intervals along the row.

There are several designs of end assemblies but they are all firmly anchored in the ground so as to support the strain in the wire due to the weight of the crop, the vines, and any wind stresses. At intervals along the row are intermediate posts, which also help carry the vine weight. In a well-constructed trellis system, the wires should be strained so tight that the wire does not sag, and this in turn facilitates MECHANIZATION. Details of some common trellis systems and end assemblies are given by Smart and Robinson. Vineyard POSTS are made from wood, concrete, plastic, steel, stone, or even cane. If made from softwood, vineyard posts must be chemically treated to stop wood-rotting fungi.

The majority of the world's vineyards, however, have very simple trellis systems. For many, the vines are free standing (see GOBELET), or have loose wires running from vine to vine supported by occasional stakes. The major support for the weight of the vine and crop is from the vine trunk.

For more information on the wide range of trellis systems used in various regions, see TRAINING SYSTEMS.   R.E.S.

Freeman, B. M., Tassie, E., and Rebbechi, M. D., 'Training and trellising', in B. G. Coombe and P. R. Dry (eds.), *Viticulture*, ii: *Practices* (Adelaide, 1992).
Smart, R. E., and Robinson, M., *Sunlight into Wine: A Handbook for Winegrape Canopy Management* (Adelaide, 1991).

Trentino, the southern and principally Italian-speaking half of Italy's central alpine region of TRENTINO-ALTO ADIGE. Trento is the regional capital. Viticulture is centred on the valley of the Adige and the hills immediately to the east and west of the river, with an occasional excursion to side valleys such as the Valle dei Laghi and the Val di Cembra. The terrain further east and west into the Dolomites and the Gruppo di Brenta mountains is too rugged and mountainous for viticulture. Although the region is far to Italy's north, and Trento is on the 46th degree of LATITUDE, the climate is not necessarily cool, as heat rapidly builds up at lower altitudes during the summer months (see TOPOGRAPHY). Viticulture is therefore by no means confined to early-ripening vine varieties. Annual average regional production has fallen from over 1 million hl to 700,000 hl/18.5 million gal. More than 70 per cent of the vineyards are registered for DOC wine production, a proportion second only to ALTO ADIGE in Italy.

The DOC structure consists of one large regional DOC, supplemented by the various VARIETAL wines, together with five more or less geographically specific supplementary DOC zones. The Sorni DOC is minuscule. Teroldego Rotaliano suggests that the TEROLDEGO grape seems to have found its ideal soil in the GRAVELLY, pebbly terrain of the Rotaliano plain. The DOC limits of 120 hl/ha (6.8 tons/acre) do not encourage quality, but the Foradori winery has demonstrated Teroldego's potential for serious, concentrated wines. The DOC zone of Caldaro, on both sides of lake Caldaro, is shared with Alto Adige and SCHIAVA is the dominant grape. Valdadige, a long stretch of the Adige river, including a part of Alto Adige and a north western chunk of Veneto, is the DOC for predominantly a red blend of Schiava and LAMBRUSCO and a white blend of various INTERNATIONAL VARIETIES (PINOT BLANC, PINOT GRIS, MÜLLER-THURGAU, CHARDONNAY, and WELSCHRIESLING) as well as for varietals from Pinot Bianco, Pinot Grigio, and Chardonnay. Casteller is a DOC zone on both sides of the border with the province of Verona for a red blend of Schiava, MERLOT, and Lambrusco.

Trentino's most important wines, however (with the exception of the 5 million bottles of Chardonnay-based SPUMANTE produced every year), are unquestionably the 17 VARIETAL wines of the Trentino DOC. Chardonnay is the most important white, followed by Pinot Grigio, Müller-Thurgau, and Pinot Blanc; Cabernet, Merlot, MARZEMINO, LAGREIN, and Pinot Noir are the leading reds. Yields from the predominantly TENDONE vineyards are too generous (from 14 to 15 tonnes per ha for the whites, from 13 to 15 tonnes per ha for the reds) to give wines of superior quality, but Trentino's greatest handicap is the market-driven spirit of wine production, which has planted and vinified according to consumer tastes of the moment without much regard for specific characteristics of soil and MESOCLIMATE. The fact that 117 of the 222 townships of the Trentino are in one or another of the various DOCs is eloquent testimony of this productivist viewpoint. The general improvement in quality of the wines of Alto Adige which marked the decade between 1985 and 1995, and created a new interest in the wines, was much less obvious further south.

Significant historical traditions matching individual varieties and individual subzones do exist none the less: Müller-Thurgau in Faedo and the Val di Cembra; Cabernet in the Vallagarina and between Pressano and Lavis; Lagrein in the Campo Rotaliano and in Rovereto della Luna; NOSIOLA in Lavis, Faedo, and the Valle dei Laghi; Pinot Noir in Civezzano and in the hills to the north of Trento; Chardonnay in vineyards over 400 m/ 1,300 ft in altitude. High-level Chardonnay, Müller-Thurgau, Cabernet and Merlot, and Pinot Noir, frequently treated to BARREL MATURATION, began to emerge from these specific subzones in the 1980s, indicating an important potential for high-quality wines which has yet to be tapped. CO-OPERATIVES market nearly three-quarters of the total production. The region's centre of ACADEME is SAN MICHELE ALL'ADIGE.   D.T. & D.C.G.

Bastianich, J., and Lynch, D., *Vino Italiano: The Regional Wines of Italy* (New York, 2002).

Belfrage, N., *From Barolo to Valpolicella: The Wines of Northern Italy* (London, 1999).

Trentino-Alto Adige, northern Italian region through which flows the Adige river (called Etsch by the region's many German speakers). It is made up of ALTO ADIGE, or the South Tyrol, in the north and TRENTINO in the south (see map under ITALY).

Trepat, indigenous red wine grape of north east Spain, particularly in Conca de Barberá and Costers del Segre. About 1,500 ha/ 3,700 acres are grown, used mainly for light rosés, but it has shown some intriguing potential for fine reds.

Tressallier, spelt **Tressalier** by GALET, is a white grape variety grown in the Allier *département* notably for ST-POURÇAIN that is closely related to the SACY of the Yonne. It is certainly traditional there, but not unanimously acclaimed nowadays.

Galet, P., *Dictionnaire encyclopédique des cépages* (Paris, 2000).

Tressot, very ancient red grape variety of Burgundy, already described in the 14th century along with PINOT NOIR. Tressot is exclusively cultivated in the Yonne (CHABLIS country) where it has now almost disappeared. DNA PROFILING at DAVIS suggested that Tressot is a natural cross between DURAS and PETIT VERDOT. Confusingly, it is also a Burgundian name for the Jura's (unrelated) TROUSSEAU vine.   J.V.

tri, French for a sorting process, notably postal but, in a wine-making context, it means the selection of suitable grapes. This usually takes the form of a TRIAGE on reception of the grapes at the winery or cellar, using a sort-ing table or *table de tri*. However, in the production of BOTRYTIZED wines a *trie* (note the feminine form), or several *tries*, is made in the vineyard whereby the pickers proceed along the rows selecting only those clusters, and occasionally only those berries, that have been successfully attacked by NOBLE ROT.

tri, table de, French for 'sorting table'. See TRIAGE.

triage is the French and common winemaking term for the sorting of grapes according to quality prior to wine-making. Most commonly, freshly picked bunches of grapes are spread on a *table de tri*, a sorting table or slowly moving and sometimes vibrating belt, so that substandard examples can be manually plucked off and thrown away (along with any leaves and stems that have crept in). For most wines, clusters that are unevenly ripe, or underripe, or have suffered DISEASE or VINE PEST damage are rejected. In the production of BOTRYTIZED sweet white wines, however, all but the grapes uniformly infected with NOBLE ROT are rejected. In some wineries, the grape berries are sorted after the bunches have been through the destemmer, and may even be sorted twice, both before and after DESTEMMING. Such sorting is a labour-intensive process that requires training and has so far resisted mechanization. However, an automated sorter which works on the basis of grape density and is used after destemming has recently been developed in France. Ripe grapes sink in the floating tank; unripe grapes remain on the surface. The cost of sorting can be justified only for relatively fine wines but the practice increased considerably in the early 1990s, with the damp vintage of 1992 resulting in particularly widespread adoption in Bordeaux.   A.D.W. & J.Ha.

tribromoanisole, more properly **2,4,6-tribromoanisole,** or **TBA,** is a musty- or dusty-smelling compound which may affect wine produced in a contaminated winery. The cause so far identified is the microbial degradation by fungi in the winery of tribromophenol (TBP) used in wood preservatives or as a flame retardant in paints and plastics. It is therefore only indirectly related to cork, which can act as a 'carrier' of the taint. The perception threshold in red and white wines is approximately 3–4 ng/l, down to 2 ng/l in sparkling wine. Further research is needed to assess the frequency of this FAULT. It has not so far been possible to distinguish TBA from TCA by TASTING.

Tricastin, Coteaux du, extensive and recently expanded appellation on the eastern fringes of the southern RHÔNE for mainly red and rosé wines with a very small amount of white. Although the climate here is definitively MEDITERRANEAN, the higher ALTITUDES and more exposed terrain produce rather lighter wines than those of the Côtes du Rhône which they resemble. The best wine comes from sheltered, south-facing slopes, but acidity levels are usually noticeable beneath the superficial warmth of the southern vine variety perfume. The region was substantially redeveloped by *pieds noirs* returning from North Africa in the late 1960s. Large areas of scrub were cleared and planted with southern Rhône vine varieties. The appellation has benefited from standard-bearers such as Domaines Tour d'Élyssas and de Grangeneuve.

Grenache and Syrah are the principal vine varieties grown, although up to 15 per cent of Carignan, Mourvèdre, or Cinsaut is allowed (to a maximum of 30 per cent between them). Of the permitted white varieties, Grenache Blanc, Clairette, Bourboulenc, Marsanne, Roussanne, and Viognier, may also be included. The basic maximum yield allowed is 52 hl/ha (3 tons/acre).

The wines are similar to those of the much larger Côtes du VENTOUX appellation to the immediate south, which was also promoted to full APPELLATION CONTRÔLÉE status in 1973. A total of more than 2,600 ha/6,400 acres was devoted to Tricastin in the mid 2000s.

trichloroanisole, more properly **2,4,6-trichloroanisole,** or **TCA,** is a potent taint compound associated with musty odours and flavours in a range of food and beverages. It is the unpleasant-smelling compound most commonly considered responsible for CORK TAINT. The formation of TCA begins when chlorine reacts with organic phenols to form chlorophenols such as trichlorophenol (TCP). These in turn react with mould in the presence of moisture to form TCA. The enzyme methylase acts as a catalyst. Such phenols are present in all organic matter and are highly prevalent in the winery: in corks, barrels, wooden pallets and in wood used in the structure of the building such as beams. TCA is extremely potent, with an aroma threshold in wine of 2–5 ng/l in red and white wines, reduced to 1–1.5 ng/l in sparkling wine because the CARBON DIOXIDE volatilizes taint compounds.   J.A.G. & J.Ha.

Trimbach, family-run wine producer based at Ribeauvillé in ALSACE. The company was established in 1626. Its wines are characterized by very fine fruit and high acidity. Even its Sylvaner can stand many years' BOTTLE AGEING. Two of its most famous bottlings are Rieslings: the very fine, rare, and long-lived Clos Ste-Hune (in fact from the Alsace Grand Cru Rosacker) and Cuvée Frédéric Émile, named after the 19th-century Trimbach who expanded the business to become an important merchant house as well as vine-grower.

trimming, the vineyard operation of removing unwanted SHOOT growth which can cause SHADING and hinder SPRAYING. Although it is usually done with a trimming machine mounted on a tractor, it may also be carried out with a hand-held machete or similar device. The operation normally removes the SHOOT TIP and a few leaves below it, or about 30 cm/12 in of growth, thus leaving the shoots trimmed to about 10–20 NODES, or 70–150 cm/ 27–58 in. Trimming is essential in vineyards with high VINE DENSITY to stop shoots from adjacent rows from growing together. Regrowth may be such as to demand up to six trimmings a year, particularly in vineyards well supplied with water (by rainfall or irrigation). If shoots are trimmed too short then there may be insufficient leaf area to ripen the crop properly (see LEAF TO FRUIT RATIO). Resulting wines will be lower in alcohol and of lighter body and colour. Sometimes vineyards are trimmed so neatly on the top and sides that vine rows can look like a recently trimmed hedge, hence the term hedging.

R.E.S.

Trincadeira, sometimes called **Trincadeira Preta,** or black Trincadeira, is a red grape highly valued by winemakers in southern PORTUGAL and grown on a total of 13,000 ha/32,500 acres of Portuguese vineyard. Known in the DOURO as TINTA AMARELA, it is very susceptible to rot and therefore only performs well in the driest of climates. Trincadeira is therefore ideally suited to the ALENTEJO, where it can produce deep-coloured, spicy wines in the right conditions but tends to herbaceousness if not picked at the right time.

R.J.M.

Trincadeira das Pratas, traditional Portuguese white grape grown mainly in Estremadura, the Ribatejo, and Terras do Sado. It can, but does not always, produce delicate, perfumed dry white wines and is known as Tamarez in the Alentejo.

Triomphe (d'Alsace), HYBRID bred by Kuhlmann in Alsace from KNIPPERLÉ and a *riparia-rupestris* AMERICAN VINE. It has good resistance to mildew but the wine produced, however deep coloured, tastes FOXY. The vine is responsible for some English reds.

trocken, German for dry, and an emotive as well as legally defined term when applied to the wines of GERMANY. Wines so-labelled first appeared in the 1970s and in the decade following became the overwhelming preference of German consumers. By the late 1980s, German vintners of all regions were selling largely trocken or HALBTROCKEN wines in their domestic market. The late 1990s marked a gradual return of consumer interest within Germany in sweeter styles of Riesling. Foreigners are slowly being won over by the trocken products of particularly ripe vintages.

The term can be applied in German-speaking countries within the European Union to a still wine with a maximum of 4 g/l RESIDUAL SUGAR, or up to 9 g/l if the TOTAL ACIDITY is less than the residual sugar by no more than 2 g/l (9 g/l residual sugar and total acidity not less than 7 g/l). The proportion of German still wine that is described as trocken varies considerably between regions (with a higher proportion in southern regions) but averages about 28 per cent (from just 16 per cent in the mid 1990s).

Because CARBON DIOXIDE reduces the impression of sweetness, a sparkling wine containing between 17 and 35 g/l residual sugar may be described as trocken. Many of the big-volume sparkling wines produced in Germany (see SEKT) are trocken, while top-quality versions are usually drier and labelled BRUT or extra brut. See also DOSAGE.

See also HALBTROCKEN, FEINHERB, and SWEETNESS.

J.R. & D.S.

Trockenbeerenauslese, sometimes known as **TBA**, the ripest and rarest of the Prädikats in the QMP quality-wine category defined by the GERMAN WINE LAW. *Trockenbeeren* refers to grapes (*Beeren*) shrivelled by NOBLE ROT. Many VINTAGES have yielded no Trockenbeerenauslese wine at all in Germany (it is more frequent in Austria's Neusiedlersee region), but warmer weather and scrupulous standards of selection have dramatically increased the frequency of TBA bottlings by many top German estates since 1988. Even riper grapes and higher MUST WEIGHTS are needed for this ultra-rich, usually deep golden-orange, usually heavily BOTRYTIZED wine than for BEERENAUSLESE. An even higher minimum POTENTIAL ALCOHOL is required than for SAUTERNES, generally produced in a much warmer climate. It is inevitable therefore that these rarities command exceptionally high PRICES, which go some way to compensating the producer for the many passages (see TRI) through the vineyard, the risk of losing all the grapes to GREY ROT or rain, and the difficulty of vinifying such sticky juice.

See also AUSTRIA.

J.R. & D.S.

Trois Glorieuses, annual weekend devoted to wine, and food, in and around Beaune. See HOSPICES DE BEAUNE and MEURSAULT for more details.

Trollinger, or **Blauer Trollinger,** is the most common German name for the distinctly ordinary black grape variety known as SCHIAVA in Italy, VERNATSCH in the Tyrol, and Black Hamburg by many who grow and buy table grapes. It almost certainly originated in what is now the Italian Tyrol (see ALTO ADIGE) and its German name is a corruption of Tirolinger. In Germany, it is associated exclusively with WÜRTTEMBERG, where it has been cultivated since the 14ᵗʰ century (see GERMAN HISTORY). This southern region's 2,600 ha/6,400 acres sufficed as of 2003 to sustain the variety's position as Germany's fourth most planted red wine vine, a rather astonishing statistic when one considers that virtually all of the resultant pale red is drunk by thirsty Württembergers.

Tronçais is a sort of French OAK named after a forest near NEVERS.

trophy wines, small group of wines more expensive than any others and becoming more so under sustained attack from the world's best-heeled COLLECTORS, INVESTORS, and drinkers. A Bordeaux FIRST GROWTH, Ch PÉTRUS or Le PIN from a fine VINTAGE is a trophy wine, as was in the late 1990s virtually every bottle produced by one of the MICROCHÂTEAUX. Most wines from DOMAINE DE LA ROMANÉE-CONTI and Domaine LEROY count, as do the single-vineyard bottlings of GUIGAL, most PRESTIGE CUVÉES from Champagne, TROCKENBEERENAUSLESEN from top German growers and Austrians such as Kracher, VEGA SICILIA, L'Ermita of PRIORAT, Dominio de Pingus, and the most lauded SUPERTUSCANS and GAJA bottlings. New World trophy wines include PENFOLDS Grange and all the CALIFORNIA CULT wines. The key to identifying trophy wines is their international fame (often determined by a particularly high SCORE, notably from the American wine critic Robert PARKER) and, especially, PRICE. Their prices rose markedly in the late 1990s because of the dramatic increase, particularly in ASIA, in the number of potential buyers of these 'limited edition' wines prepared to acquire them at any price.

tropical viticulture. Although the grapevine is regarded by many as a strictly temperate plant, it is now increasingly grown in the tropics, defined approximately as the region bordered by the tropics of Cancer and Capricorn. Countries in which some grapes are cultivated in tropical conditions include AUSTRALIA, Colombia, BOLIVIA, BRAZIL, ECUADOR, INDIA, INDONESIA, KENYA, Laos, MEXICO, MYANMAR, NAMIBIA, Nigeria, the Philippines, SRI LANKA, TANZANIA, THAILAND, VENEZUELA, and VIETNAM.

Within the tropics there are many different climates, modified by differences in ALTITUDE and RAINFALL. Lowland tropical trunk areas can be divided into those regions which are almost continuously wet, those with pronounced wet and dry seasons, and those which are virtually arid. In the lowland wet tropics, grapevines adopt an evergreen growth habit and can be manipulated into cropping more than once per year, mainly by TRIMMING SHOOTS to encourage fruit development rather than leaf growth and by the application of chemicals which induce dormant buds to burst. Other chemicals are used, particularly for TABLE GRAPES, which retard growth and induce flower buds to form (see GROWTH REGULATORS).

In areas with pronounced wet and dry seasons, pruning and removing all vegetation can induce a form of DORMANCY.

In arid tropical areas, IRRIGATION is essential to permit vine growth, not least because soils and therefore root development are very different from Europe's. Here budburst is initiated by pruning and withholding irrigation water. Highland tropical areas with altitudes in excess of 1,000 m/3,280 ft can have climates that are almost temperate with temperatures that are sufficiently low (less than 15 °C/59 °F) to induce normal dormancy and allow grapevines to follow a climate-controlled growth cycle.

The majority of tropical grapes are consumed as TABLE GRAPES. However, increasing amounts are used as DRYING GRAPES, especially in India, or fermented into wine. Grapevines can be very productive in the tropics, giving YIELDS of fresh fruit of 140 to 280 hl/ha, or 8 to 16 tons/acre, more than once a year—so tropical viticulture can yield relatively inexpensive wine, as in the far north of Brazil, for example, although in Thailand producers are increasingly encouraging vines to produce a single higher quality crop every 12 months.

Depending on the climate, tropical grapes can be programmed to reach maturity at times of the year when other fresh fruit is not available, or when international prices are very high. J.V.P., & H.-P.H.

Trousseau is the name of one of the two principal dark grape varieties indigenous to the JURA, and is more robust and deeply coloured than POULSARD although it is in serious decline as Pinot Noir, and Chardonnay, become ever more popular. It buds late and therefore avoids devastation by most spring frosts but is an irregular yielder. As long ago as the mid 19th century, the early French AMPELOGRAPHER Comte A. Odart maintained that Trousseau is the same as Portugal's BASTARDO, and a variety for long called Cabernet Gros and occasionally, erroneously, Touriga in Australia. In both of these countries it is commonly used for sweet, dessert wines and flourishes in very different conditions from its native Jura.

Galet, P., *Dictionnaire encyclopédique des cépages* (Paris, 2000).

trunk, the main stem of a tree, from the ground to the first branches or, in the case of a grapevine, to the CORDONS or HEAD. Newly formed vine trunks are pliable and need support (see VINE TRAINING). The height of the trunk of a grapevine is variable, from 10 cm/4 in (in BUSH VINES) to more than 10 m/30 ft (in vines growing up trees), and is determined by the specifications set for each TRAINING SYSTEM and TRELLIS. The trunk height determines the position of the CANOPY relative to the ground. Vine trunks are woody and form part of the bulk needed for storage

reserves, especially of CARBOHYDRATES and NITROGEN compounds. In climates with freezing winters, multiple trunks are used to facilitate replacement after winter killing, and in extremely cold climates trunks are buried during the winter (see WINTER PROTECTION).

The trunk of any plant (including the OAK tree, used for COOPERAGE and CORKS) contains a sleeve of conducting tissue with the CAMBIUM in its centre, bark (with PHLOEM) on the outside, and wood (with XYLEM) on the inside. Through these tissues, xylem sap moves upward, carrying water, minerals, and compounds from the roots to the leaves, and phloem sap moves multi-directionally carrying sugars and elaborated molecules from the leaves to the rest of the vine. The downward passage of phloem sap in vines can be interrupted by trunk CINCTURING or girdling.

B.G.C.

trunked, a common form of VINE TRAINING where the vine has a trunk of variable height which ends in a HEAD or CORDONS. The term trunked is particularly used in eastern Europe and the former Soviet Republics, where such vines are considered high or low trunked, in contrast with trunkless vines, which are easier to bury for WINTER PROTECTION.

Tsaoussi, white grape speciality of the Greek island of Cephalonia, where it may be blended with the more distinctive ROBOLA.

Tsolikauri, relatively important white wine grape of GEORGIA, although only about a tenth as widely planted there as the popular RKATSITELI.

TTB, teetotal acronym for the Alcohol and Tobacco Tax and Trade Bureau, the US regulatory body responsible for AVA approvals, federal taxation, and label approval. (These are enforced by the Bureau of Alcohol, Tobacco, and Firearms, now known as ATF.)

tufa, a common mistranslation of the French term TUFFEAU.

tuffeau, a common rock type in the central LOIRE. *Tuffeau blanc* is CALCAREOUS but provides much better DRAINAGE than most LIMESTONES. This is the rock used to build many of the châteaux of the Loire and remaining hollows in the rock have been adapted for wine-making and storage. The overlying *tuffeau jaune* is more sandy, and is particularly suitable for the Cabernet Franc vine, underlying some of the best vineyards in CHINON and SAUMUR-CHAMPIGNY.

J.M.H.

Tumbarumba, relatively new high ALTITUDE, cool Australian wine region especially suited to Sauvignon Blanc, Chardonnay, and Pinot Noir, the last two both for table and sparkling wine production. Spring frost is the major threat. See NEW SOUTH WALES.

Tunisia, North African country which was once an important wine producer. Viticulture was probably introduced when the Phoenicians established the city of CARTHAGE on the coast and was certainly developed during the Roman occupation. The Phoenician agronomist Mago recorded contemporary vinegrowing and wine-making practices in his *Treatise of Agronomy*.

French occupation until 1956 led to vineyard development on a vast scale, but independence was followed by a decline in local expertise. Wine production continued but total vineyard area had fallen to about 26,000 ha/64,250 acres by the early 2000s with 15,000 ha dedicated to wine production as opposed to TABLE GRAPES. Italians, Swiss, Germans, and Austrians have all invested in the Tunisian wine industry in the last ten years, bringing with them both wine-making and viticultural expertise.

Annual rainfall is between 250 mm and 500 mm, with the great majority of precipitation in mid autumn. The average annual temperature is 20 °C. The most important varieties include Carignan, Mourvèdre, Cinsaut, Alicante Bouschet, Grenache, Syrah, and Merlot for reds and Muscat of Alexandria, Chardonnay, and Pedro Ximenez for whites. An APPELLATION CONTRÔLÉE system, loosely based on the French one, is in place in an effort to control quality. The vast majority of wine production is centred in and around the Cape Bon region in the north east of the country. The most important wine centres in Tunisia are Khanguet, Grombalia/Tekelsa, Tebourba, and Bizerte for rosé and reds, and Kelibia for dry Muscat.

Annual wine production had fallen to just over 270,000 hl by 2002 according to OIV statistics—60–70 per cent rosé, 25–30 per cent red, and less than 10 per cent white.

With some five million tourists a year and minimal imports of foreign wine, only about 30 per cent of annual production is exported, mainly in bulk to Germany and France. L.D.

Platter, J. & E., *Africa Uncorked* (London, 2002).

Turkey, eastern Mediterranean country that is the world's fourth most important grower of grapes, only a very small proportion of which is made into wine. Turkey's 590,000 ha/1.5 million acres of vineyard (OIV 2004 estimates) makes it the world's fourth most important grower of vines. It is regularly one of the world's biggest producers of TABLE GRAPES and is also an important producer of DRYING GRAPES. Its wine production has been increasing significantly, however, and was put at 330,000 hl by the OIV in 2002.

Modern Turkey includes Mount Ararat (see BIBLE) in ASIA MINOR, part of the region most closely identified with the ORIGINS OF VITICULTURE. Archaeological finds support the theory that wine was produced there at least 6,000 years ago (and see PALAEOETHNOBOTANY for details of even earlier finds). The region is therefore rich in indigenous VINIFERA vine varieties, of which between 600 and 1,200 have been identified but fewer than 60 are grown commercially. Many serve as table grapes as well as wine grapes, which is how they survived many centuries of Ottoman rule and the ban on alcohol consumption under ISLAM. Kemal Atatürk himself, founder of modern Turkey, established the country's first winery for seven centuries in 1925 as part of his westernization programme.

The country's grape-growing regions include considerable climatic variation. The Thrace region, with many vineyards on the sea of Marmara, in the hinterland of Istanbul, is very much part of Europe and shares the warm coastal climate of its neighbours the far south west of BULGARIA and the extreme north east of GREECE. Responsible for 40 per cent of Turkish wine production, the region is home to the country's first 'boutique' winery Sarafin and grows such European grape varieties as Gamay, Cinsault, Sémillon, and Riesling as well as such Turkish varieties as Yapincak and Papazkarasi. European varieties such as Sémillon, Grenache, and Carignan are also grown on the Aegean coast, which accounts for about 20 per cent of Turkey's wine production, also from high-yield, low-altitude vineyards. Cabernet Sauvignon and Merlot are increasingly popular in both these regions.

Anatolia, which produces the remainder of Turkish wine, has the most demanding climate, where vineyards, up to 1,250 m/4,000 ft above sea level, have to withstand very severe winters with temperatures sometimes down to −25 °C/−13 °F. Average summer temperatures are extremely high, however, and average sunshine up to 12 hours a day. Narince grapes produce white wines in Central Anatolia. Eastern Anatolia, where grape varieties Oküzgözü and Boğïazkere are grown for reds, borders IRAN, Iraq, and Syria and has similar climatic conditions. Yields average less than 35 hl/ha (2 tons/acre).

Wine production is dominated by Tekel, once owned by the state but acquired by a group of private companies in 2004, and Kavaklidere of Anatolia and Doluca of Thrace. REFRIGERATION and STAINLESS STEEL tanks were still novelties in the late 1990s but have become routine in the country's more modern wineries.

Wine production is divided fairly equally between increasingly sophisticated whites and relatively alcoholic reds with a few rosés. Buzbağ is the most memorable brand of Tekel, which makes almost a quarter of each year's wine production into brandy and the aniseed-flavoured spirit *raki*. Wine is generally for export and tourists.

Turkmenistan, central Asian republic and former state of the Soviet Union that sprawls between the Caspian sea, UZBEKISTAN, AFGHANISTAN, and IRAN. Its approximately 28,000 ha/69,200 acres of vineyards specialize in TABLE GRAPES and RAISINS but according to OIV figures, 240,000 hl of strong, mainly sweet wine were produced in 2002. The vast Karakumy desert occupies a large part of this hot, dry country.

There are large daily and annual temperature fluctuations. The average January temperature is −4 °C/25 °F; that of July is 28 °C. The annual rainfall is 80 mm/3 in in the north east and 300 mm in the mountains, the largest amount of rainfall being recorded in spring and winter. Evidence of vine-growing in the country dates back to the 3rd century BC. Greek and Roman writers report that grapes were cultivated in Marghian (the Murgab valley) and in Aria (the Tejen valley). The Kopetdag ravines still have a great diversity of WILD VINES that have served as a basis for many indigenous varieties. Different wine vessels depicting grape bunches found during excavations of the village of Baghir near the capital Ashkhabad testify to the fact that Turkmenistan has a long history of wine-making.

For many years the nomadic way of life of Turkmenistan's population did not favour the development of agriculture, viticulture included, which had to wait until the country was annexed to RUSSIA at the end of the 19th century and the Ashkhabad RAILWAY was built. In 1898, the total vineyard area was just 308 ha/760 acres. Thereafter it increased and reached 2,500 ha in 1928, 4,000 ha in 1940, 11,000 ha in 1975, and 27,000 ha in 1990.

Almost all vineyards need IRRIGATION, but only the north part of the Tashauz region needs WINTER PROTECTION. The Karakumy canal provided the chance to increase vineyard areas and their production. In the early 1990s, viticultural farms were changing over to large-scale technological grape cultivation. Trellises were introduced into vineyards previously planted with GOBELET vines.

The vineyards are in the Ashkhabad region (70 per cent of the total grape area), the Mary region (15 per cent), and the Chardzhou region.

Turkmenistan is a unique region suitable for early-, mid-, and late-maturing table and raisin grapes. Provided assorted varieties are planted, grapes can be harvested from the middle of June until October. Only 21 grape varieties were cultivated on a commercial scale in the early 1990s, however, with eight wine varieties such as Terbash, Tara Uzüm Ashkhabadski, RIESLING, SAPERAVI, Kizil Sapak, and Bayan Shirey. V.R.

Tursan, small VDQS in the Landes in SOUTH WEST FRANCE producing wine made from mainly red, mainly TANNAT grapes, mostly from the Geaune CO-OPERATIVE and sold locally. The white version is of more interest and is virtually a one-producer wine, but what a producer: three-star chef Michel Guérard of Eugénie-lès-Bains who sells his oaked version of the local white grape variety BAROQUE under the name Baron de Bachen.

Tuscany, the most important region in central ITALY (see map under ITALY), where it is known as TOSCANA. Today Toscana is at the centre neither of Italy's economic life nor of its political life, but it is the region which formed Italy's language, its literature, and its art, and has thus assumed a central place in the country's culture and self-image. The landscape, immortalized in the work of artists from Giotto to Michelangelo and part of every European's cultural baggage, has remained largely unchanged to this day: a succession of hills and valleys covered with cypresses, umbrella pines, vineyards, and olive groves.

Ancient history

In the ancient world, Toscana, and at certain points of its history a much larger area, was known as Etruria. See ETRUSCANS for the ancient history of Toscana.

Medieval history

If we know more about the wines of medieval Toscana than we do about the wines of other regions of medieval Italy, it is not because they were better or there were more of them: the reason is Toscana's, and particularly Florence's, economic and political importance.

Viticulture flourished despite the frequent, small-scale civil wars. The region produced more or less equal amounts of oil and wine, but by far the largest crop was wheat. Smallholders were rare in this part of Italy, since the land was mostly owned by monasteries, the local aristocracy, and, increasingly, by merchants in the cities. The system of agriculture was often that known as *mezzadria*, whereby the landowner would provide the working capital and the land in return for half (*mezzo*, hence the name) the crop. In 1132, for instance, the Badia (Abbey) di Passignano (whose wine is now made and sold by the merchants ANTINORI) leased some of its land to a wealthy cobbler for half his crop of olive oil and wine.

The regional centre for market sales was the Mercato Vecchio in Florence. The earliest reference to wine retailers in the city dates from 1079, and in 1282 the wine sellers formed a guild, the Arte dei Vinattieri. Giovanni di Piero Antinori joined it in 1385, a member of the noble family that continues to make and sell wine in Toscana today. In order to uphold the profession's reputation, the guild imposed a strict code of practice. The statutes insisted on cleanliness and exact measures; the shop was not to be situated within 100 yd of a church and it was not to serve children under 15. No cooked food could be sold, and shops were not to shelter ruffians, thieves, or prostitutes. The wine trade was vital to the Florentine economy. Tax records show that more than 300,000 hl/7.9 million gal of wine entered the city every year in the 14th century. The Florentine historian Villani, writing in 1338, estimated that weekly consumption of wine was a gallon a head. Given that Florence had approximately 90,000 inhabitants, this meant that well over 90 per cent was sold elsewhere, to the surrounding country or other Tuscan cities, some overseas via the port of Pisa, mainly to Flanders, PARIS, and Marseilles.

By no means all of this wine would have been Tuscan: a lot of it had come from Crete (Candia), Corsica, or NAPLES. Toscana itself produced red wine, which was usually called simply *vino vermiglio*, but occasionally names appear. The reds of MONTEPULCIANO and Cortona were heavy, those of Casentino lighter. In the late 14th century, we find Montalcino referred to as BRUNELLO. The most important of Toscana's white wines were called 'Vernaccia' and 'Trebbiano', probably named after their respective grape varieties VERNACCIA and TREBBIANO, but neither was an exclusively Tuscan wine. Of the two, Vernaccia was the more highly reputed. In its sweet form it was associated primarily with LIGURIA, and particularly with Cinqueterre and Corniglia, although sweet Vernaccia was also made in Toscana. The dry style of Vernaccia, made in San Gimignano (but also elsewhere), which is not found before the 14th century, was not exported overseas, because only the sweet version was capable of surviving the long sea voyage to France, Flanders, or England. Trebbiano, too, could be dry or sweet. The first recorded mention of CHIANTI is in the correspondence of the Tuscan merchant Francesco di Marco Datini in 1398, and it is a *white* wine. Datini was fond of it: in 1404 Amadeo Gherardini of Vignamaggio, which is still a well-known estate, wrote to Datini sending him half a barrel of his personal stock. Another of Datini's favourites was (red) CARMIGNANO.

Datini's letters give us an idea of what a rich merchant bought for his own consumption. He had MALMSEY sent to him from Venice and Genoa, and, more exotically, the equally strong, sweet wine of Tyre from Venice. These foreign wines were luxury items. Another expensive wine from outside Toscana that Datini loved was Greco. It was grown in PUGLIA and so highly prized was it that in the 14th century the commune of San Gimignano abandoned its tradition of giving distinguished visitors a few ounces of saffron and instead made them a present of the precious Greco.

Dante and Boccaccio both mention Vernaccia, a byword for luxury. No Tuscan author wrote exclusively about the wines of the region until Francesco Redi. His *Bacco in Toscana* ('Bacchus in Toscana'), published in 1685, is subtitled *ditirambo*, the Greek dithyramb being a choral lyric in praise of DIONYSUS. Redi's poem, however, has little to do with the classical genre and is no more than an excuse for showing off his learning to fellow members of the Accademia della Crusca: he provides 228 pages of unhelpful and pretentious notes to deluge 980 lines of verse. Neither the poem nor the notes contains anything interesting or new about Tuscan wine and viticulture, and the notes Leigh Hunt wrote to his translation (1825) of *Bacco in Toscana* are a good deal more amusing (although of more use to the historian of language than to the historian of wine). The only wines Redi mentions, and praises, are VERNACCIA, CHIANTI, CARMIGNANO, and, finally, MONTEPULCIANO, which he regards as the king of all wines. H.M.W.

For the detail of today's Tuscan wines and vines, see TOSCANA.

Flower, R., *Chianti: The Land, the People and the Wine* (London, 1979).

Melis, F., 'Produzione e commercio dei vini italiani nei secoli XIII–XVIII', *Annales cisalpines d'histoire sociale*, 1/3 (1972), 107–33.

Txakoli, usually white wine made in Spain's BASQUE country, known as **Chacolí** in Castilian. Like VINHO VERDE it is strongly Atlantic influenced and is usually sold young, very slightly sparkling, and low in alcohol. A century ago over 1,000 ha of vines stretched from Bayonne to Bilbao, but after PHYLLOXERA ravaged the region, few vineyards were replanted. With cool summers, and an annual RAINFALL of 1,500 mm/58 in, this is hardly ideal grape-growing country. The high trained Hondarribi Zuri white grape variety, which accounts for 85 per cent of Txakoli, traditionally produced thin wines, but quality noticeably improved during the 1990s. Hondarribi Beltza makes light reds for local consumption.

Getariako Txakolina is the principal appellation yet is still one of Spain's smallest DO regions and a matter of considerable pride to those few BASQUE farmers who stubbornly refuse to give in to the elements and have even increased their vineyards to reach 84 ha/201 acres on the rocky Biscay coast west of San Sebastian (see map under SPAIN). **Bizkaiko Txakolina** is an even smaller DO region with just 60 ha/144 acres of vineyards scattered in Vizcaya province around the main city of Bilbao. The predominance of FOLLE BLANCHE grapes makes for more acidic and herbaceous wines than in Getariako. **Arabako Txakolina** is the newest DO for Txakoli and comprises just 50 ha of vineyards in the Ayala valley near Vizcaya. Hondarribi Zuri and Hondarribi Beltza are the main grape varieties, while Petit Manseng, Petit Courbu, and Gros Manseng are also permitted. V. de la S.

typicality, the original English word for **typicity,** a wine tasting term adapted from the French *typicité* or Italian *tipicità* for a wine's quality of being typical of its type, geographical provenance, and even its VINTAGE year—a wine characteristic much discussed by professionals. And it is perhaps because typicality is a SUBJECTIVE notion, rather than a physical attribute that can be measured by ANALYSIS, that it is so much discussed. Individual tasters are likely to differ as to what they consider typical of a particular wine description, just as they are likely to differ in their impressions of the wine under consideration.

Typicality need not and may not concern the average wine drinker, who is right to demand merely that the wine tastes good, but it becomes important in wine JUDGING if the wine has been entered into a particular class. It is also important to professional wine buyers, particularly when choosing wines to represent a GENERIC style.

Each wine type demands a different set of characteristics. For example, a deep white wine of modest ACIDITY and relatively high ALCOHOLIC STRENGTH, smelling strongly of ALDEHYDES, would be extremely atypical of Chablis, but would display the typicality of a FINO style of SHERRY. Similarly, a very young red wine smelling strongly of CARBONIC MACERATION would be accorded high marks for typicality if a young BEAUJOLAIS, but none as a young BORDEAUX.

It should be added, however, that, as winemakers increasingly travel between wine regions, absorbing and applying different techniques, some distinctions between what were regarded as wine archetypes are being eroded, and there is more disagreement than ever as to what constitutes typicality. See also REGIONALITY.

typicity, see TYPICALITY.

Tyrian, Australian NEW VARIETY. See CIENNA.

Tyrol. Hardly any wine is made in this western part of Austria, but considerable quantities are made in that part of the Tyrol ceded to Italy after the First World War, now known as the South Tyrol, Südtirol in German, or ALTO ADIGE in Italian.

Uclés, promising new Spanish DO in the Cuenca province of CASTILLA-LA MANCHA.

Ugni Blanc (which is in fact Italy's ubiquitous TREBBIANO) is France's most planted white grape variety by far, outnumbering Chardonnay's area five to two at the turn of the century, and yet is rarely seen on a wine label. Just as AIRÉN, Spain's most planted white variety, supplies that country's voracious brandy stills, so the copious, thin, acid wine of Ugni Blanc washes through the stills of the Cognac and Armagnac regions. Cognac is particularly reliant on Ugni Blanc, often calling it St-Émilion.

But despite EUROPEAN UNION encouragement to pull up poorer-quality vines, and a distinctly sluggish market for brandy, France's total plantings of Ugni Blanc fell only 10,000 ha between the late 1980s and the turn of the century to 90,000 ha/225,000 acres.

Ugni Blanc supplanted the FOLLE BLANCHE that was pre-PHYLLOXERA the main ingredient in French brandy production because of its good resistance to oidium, or POWDERY MILDEW, and grey rot.

It is not, however, a French variety but was imported from Italy, probably during the 14th century when the papal court was established at Avignon. Other Italian varieties were presumably similarly transported but Trebbiano's extraordinarily high yields and high acidity may have helped establish it in southern France, where it is still grown widely today. Often called Clairette Ronde (although not related to CLAIRETTE), it was still by far the most planted white wine grape in the southern Rhône and Provence in 2000 and it is still widely planted in the north west of the Gironde, where, like COLOMBARD, it is allowed in Bordeaux Blanc up to 30 per cent and is sometimes tellingly called Muscadet Aigre, or 'sour Muscadet'.

For more details of this variety, which probably produces more wine than any other, see TREBBIANO (although the variety is usually known throughout South America, where it is widely planted, as Ugni Blanc). Argentina had 2,600 ha and Bulgaria 2,300 ha in the early 2000s.

Uhudler, strange wine speciality of Südburgenland and some parts of Styria in AUSTRIA made from vines that are AMERICAN HYBRIDS such as ISABELLA, Elvira or CONCORD.

Ukraine, independent state of the former Soviet Union and an important wine producer. Odessa and the autonomous CRIMEA regions account for 80 per cent of all Ukrainian vineyards which totalled just over 100,000 ha/247,000 acres producing 2.4 million hl of wine in 2002 according to OIV figures.

History
Grapes were grown in what is now Ukraine as early as the 4th century BC. The south coast of the Ukraine, including Crimea, was a developed centre of grape culture in ancient times. Archaeological evidence has revealed stone fences, remnants of viticultural plots and wineries, and wine AMPHORAE in the Tauric settlement of Uch-Bash near Inkerman (as old as the 10th to 7th centuries BC) and in the ancient town of Mirmecium in the east portion of the Kerch peninsula. The tomb of a SCYTHIAN chief of 500 BC was unearthed arranged with an amphora of Chian wine at its head. In the northern parts of Ukraine, wine production originated in monastic vineyards established there much later, in the 11th to 12th centuries.

Viticulture and wine production waxed and waned in Ukraine since the land suffered numerous raids of nomadic tribes and witnessed long periods of war. The development of capitalism in Ukraine necessitated new profitable branches of agriculture, vine-growing and wine-making included. In 1913, the total vineyard area of Ukraine was 54,000 ha/133,000 acres and the gross yield of grapes was 79,000 tons. The grape and wine industry suffered heavily after the First World War, however, and as a result of PHYLLOXERA. By 1919, the total vineyard area had been reduced to 13,000 ha.

Thereafter the restoration of viticulture took place steadily, and by 1940 the total vineyard area was 103,000 ha. However, the Second World War also caused great damage to the industry. The total vineyard area decreased once more, to 68,000 ha. Vineyards were completely neglected, with the proportion of missing vines reaching 40 to 50 per cent. In the post-war period, state farms specializing in viticulture were established and were subsequently amalgamated into specialized trusts and large companies. Nurseries were also established to meet the need for propagation material.

In 1960, vineyards occupied 400,000 ha, but there has since been a steady and significant decline. Viticulture in the southern parts of Ukraine accounts for up to 20 per cent of agricultural activity however.

Climate and geography
Ukraine is mostly flat and sometimes hilly, with the Ukrainian Carpathian mountains in the south west and the Crimean mountains in the south.

The climate is mild, mostly CONTINENTAL. The difference between summer and winter temperatures increases in the south, when rainfall and humidity drop, the thickness of snow cover decreases, and snow holds for a shorter period of time. The average temperature in January ranges from −8 °C/10 °F in the north east to +2 °C/35 °F on the south coast of the Crimea, while the average temperature in July is 19 °C (66 °F) in the north west to 24° in the south east. The duration of the frost-free period is 230 days in the north and 290 days in

the south. The active temperature summation is 2,900–3,700 °C. The annual rainfall is 350–400 mm (13–15 in) in the south east and 1,200–1,500 mm in the Carpathian mountains.

Commercial viticulture is concentrated in the Crimea (34,600 ha), in the Odessa region (40,000 ha), the Kherson region (7,600 ha), the Nikolayev region (8,400 ha), the Transcarpathian region (4,600 ha), and in the Zaporozh'ye region (500 ha). About 500 state and collective farms grow grapes, and the largest of them are located in the Crimea. State farms in the Ukraine may export to Russia, KAZAKHSTAN, MOLDOVA, and other former Soviet republics.

Viticulture

Average YIELDS in Ukraine have fallen significantly in recent years to about 26.5 hl/ha (2.1 tons/acre).

A typical modern Ukraine vineyard allows large-scale cultivation of widely spaced vines that do not need WINTER PROTECTION (unlike RUSSIA) and which are trained high enough to permit MECHANIZATION of 60 per cent of all vineyards. New varieties with improved resistance to environmental factors are increasingly planted. Since most vineyards are located in drier zones, IRRIGATION has played a major part in doubling yields. The irrigated vineyard area accounts for more than 25,000 ha.

Vine varieties

Vineyards are planted mostly to VINIFERA varieties grafted on phylloxera-resistant ROOTSTOCKS, although some MUSCADINES are also grown, according to the Institute MAGARACH. Ukraine had 65 wine and 45 table vine varieties planted in 1992. The largest areas are planted to wine grapes such as RKATSITELI, ALIGOTÉ, CABERNET SAUVIGNON, SAPERAVI, RIESLING, SAUVIGNON Vert, GEWÜRZTRAMINER, PINOT GRIS, SERCIAL, BASTARDO, Fetiaska (see FETEASCĂ), Bastardo Magarachski, and white Sukhomlinski. Newly bred varieties also being introduced (see RUSSIA) include Golubok, Saperavi Severny, Pervenets Magaracha, Fioletovy Ranni, Podarok Magaracha, Karmraiut, Stepniak, Olimpiiski, Sorok let Oktiabria, and a range of TABLE GRAPES. Areas planted to indigenous grape varieties such as Kefessia, Soldaia, Sary Pandas, Kokus Bely, and Jevat Kara are being restored. Wine grapes account for 80 per cent of the total vineyard area but table grapes are gaining ground.

Sixty viticultural regions have been specified for Ukraine.

Wines produced

The Crimea has the most favourable soil and climatic conditions for viticulture. Wines produced by the MASSANDRA winery are the pride of the republic.

The Crimea also produces high-quality white and red table wines and 'yellow' FORTIFIED wines such as Sercial Magarach, Massandra, and Oreanda as well as sherry- and madeira-style wines.

Microzones in the foothills near Sevastopol produce grapes to be made into dry white VARIETALS: Aligoté Zolotaia Balka, Rkatsiteli Inkermanskoie, Riesling Alcadar, and Riesling Krymski (Crimean Riesling). Dry red wines such as Cabernet Kachinskoie, Cabernet Kolchuginskoie, and Alushta (a blend of mainly Cabernet Sauvignon, Morrastel, and Saperavi) are produced in the western valleys of the Alma, Belbek, and Kacha in the Crimea, and in the vicinity of the town of Alushta.

The southern coastal steppes of Ukraine and the Dnepr right bank area have a moderately continental climate and increasingly warm temperatures towards the end of summer. This favours the production of full-bodied, dry wines such as Perlyna Stepu, Nadneprianskoie, and Oksamit Ukrainy.

Dry white wines such as Beregovskoie, Promeniste, Serednianskoie, and Riesling Xakarpatski are made in the Transcarpathian region.

Industry organization

In 2003, Ukraine produced 1.9 million hl/50 million gal of wine, a steep decline from the 5.8 million hl average of the early 1980s before GORBACHEV's anti-alcohol campaign.

SOVIET SPARKLING WINE production is important in Ukraine and wineries producing 50 million bottles of this popular drink each year are in the capital Kiev and in Artemovsk, Odessa, Sevastopol, Sudak, and Kharkov. In 1882, the Russian winemaker prince Leo Golitsyn established a winery in the village of Novy Svet in the Crimea which marked the beginning of the production of sparkling wines in Russia. Most common grape varieties used for base wines are Pinot Blanc, Aligoté, Riesling, and Fetiaska (**Fetească**).

Viticultural and oenological research in Ukraine is carried out by the most famous centre of wine academe in the ex Soviet Union, the Institute for Vine and Wine MAGARACH, founded in 1828 in Yalta in the Crimea. There is also the Tairov Institute for Viticulture and Oenology in Odessa founded in 1905.

Of all ex Soviet states, Ukraine has made most notable progress towards establishing its own wine law. V.R. & A.L.

ullage, which derives from the French *ouillage*, has had a variety of meanings and uses in the English-speaking wine trade. It can mean the process of EVAPORATION of wine held in wooden containers such as a BARREL. The HEAD SPACE left in the container is also called the ullage, or 'ullage space', and the wine in that state is said to be 'on ullage'. The word ullage is also used for any space in a stoppered wine bottle not occupied by wine (see FILL LEVEL). And ullage is also used as a verb so that a bottle or barrel not entirely full is said to be 'ullaged'.

The ullage space in a barrel is not empty but contains water and alcohol vapours together with some CARBON DIOXIDE previously dissolved in the wine. If the container is not completely gas tight, some air will seep in around poorly fitting joints between staves, the tank head, or the bung. Only relatively new and well-made barrels approach the degree of tightness required to prevent the entry of air, and with it the risk of OXYGEN. When wine is matured in any other form of wooden container it is particularly important that the ullage space is minimized by regular TOPPING UP. A.D.W.

Ull de Llebre, meaning 'hare's eye', is the CATALAN name for TEMPRANILLO.

ultrafiltration, a form of cross-flow FILTRATION which can be used for ALCOHOL REDUCTION and possibly also for TANNIN removal or concentration.

Wollan, D., 'Physico-chemical tuning of wine composition', presentation given at the 12th Australian Wine Industry Conference (Adelaide, 2004).

ultraviolet radiation, radiation of shorter wavelength than so-called visible light, and which is very damaging to all life because of its mutation-inducing properties. PHENOLIC compounds absorb ultraviolet radiation, and levels of QUERCETIN in grape berries are related to ultraviolet exposure. It is argued that ultraviolet exposure increases levels of phenolics and therefore COLOUR in red wines, which can be an advantage of vineyards at high ALTITUDE, and those close to the 'ozone hole' over the Antarctic. This leads to the intriguing possibility that the more southerly regions of the southern hemisphere have a wine quality advantage over northern hemisphere wine regions. R.E.S.

umami, Japanese term derived from two words meaning 'delicious' and 'essence' and used to refer to what some consider to be the fifth primary taste. More a quality than a specific flavour, it is variously described as 'savoury' or 'meaty' and is found in high levels in foods such as soy sauce, Parmesan, fresh tomato juice, tuna and seaweed. Umami levels in other foods are increased by the addition of monosodium glutamate.

Eastern thinking has for many centuries recognized five primary tastes but it was not until 1907 that Professor Ikeda of Tokyo Imperial University identified and isolated the AMINO ACID glutamate, or glutamic acid, as the source of the flavour he named 'umami'. He subsequently developed the seasoning monosodium glutamate so that umami levels in other foods might be increased. Recent research identifying the receptors on the tongue that detect amino acids gives further credibility to the existence of this fifth taste.

The level of amino acids in wine is thought to be affected by the ripeness of the grapes and the process of fermentation. However, it is extremely difficult to isolate the taste of umami in wine because of the way it interacts with the other four primary tastes.

Proponents of umami suggest that its presence brings a 'completeness' to the flavour of a wine but warn that it may increase the bitterness and astringency of some tannic reds.

See also TASTING.

Umbria may be the fourth smallest of ITALY's 20 regions in terms of both physical size and population (see map under ITALY), with its viticulture of only minor significance in the regional economy, but it is undergoing some exciting vinous developments. Umbria's annual production of 1 million hl/26 million gal per year (only 17 per cent of it of DOC quality) is just one-third that of neighbouring Toscana (where DOC wine represents over one-third of the total volume). Despite the geological and climatic similarities between these two central Italian regions, Umbria has so far remained well in the shadow of its Tuscan neighbour. There are some encouraging signs, however.

ORVIETO is still the region's biggest DOC, accounting for 80 per cent of Umbria's total DOC production. Other DOC white wines based on TREBBIANO grapes, simple products at best, are made in the zones of Colli del Trasimeno, Colli Perugini, TORGIANO, Colli Altotiberini, Colli Martani, and Colli Amerini. Trebbiano is often referred to as Procanico in Umbria, although some claim that Procanico is actually a superior CLONE of Trebbiano which gives smaller bunches and a finer wine. So far their efforts to transmute the dross of Trebbiano into the finely spun gold of Procanico have been more theoretical than practical, but work goes on. SANGIOVESE is the region's principal red grape variety, giving pleasant, if not memorable, wines in the Colli Altotiberini, Colli Amerini, Colli Martani, Colli Perugini, and Colli del Trasimeno DOCs; the wines produced near lake Trasimeno are allowed up to 40 per cent of the GAMAY grape in the blend, and to the west of the lake some all-Gamay wines are produced, although they are more an oddity than a serious imitation of BEAUJOLAIS.

Sangiovese has reached its heights in Umbria in the wines produced by LUNGAROTTI in the Torgiano DOCG and, as Rosso di Montefalco, also gives good results in the hillside vineyards of the small Montefalco DOC zone between Assisi and Terni, where it is blended with a small percentage of the local SAGRANTINO. This last variety, which in the past yielded notably rustic wines high in TANNINS, demonstrated in the 1990s that it can respond well to more careful vinification and ageing techniques. There was a considerable improvement in general in Umbrian Sangiovese in the 1980s and 1990s, rewarded with the promotion of Torgiano from DOC to

DOCG. The elevation of Sagrantino di Montefalco to DOCG status, however, is perhaps more of a vote of confidence in the future than an accurate reflection of the prevailing quality level of all producers.

More surprising yet perhaps was the number of high-quality wines to emerge from Umbria in the 1990s, thanks in no small part to the work of Orvieto native Riccardo COTARELLA and to the input from Tuscan investors and OENOLOGISTS. No discernible pattern emerged, either in terms of grape varieties or of precise geographical zones. Sangiovese continued to improve, but many of these new wines were from Merlot, Cabernet Sauvignon, Pinot Noir, and Chardonnay, the last at times blended with GRECHETTO to provide a distinctively Umbrian style of BARREL-FERMENTED white wine (pioneered by ANTINORI at the Castello della Sala and developed by Cotarella, brother of Antinori's head winemaker Renzo Cotarella). In the late 1990s, interest in these new wines was high, both in Italian and international markets, not least because many were priced well below similar products from nearby Toscana.   D.T. & D.C.G.

Bastianich, J., and Lynch, D., *Vino Italiano: The Regional Wines of Italy* (New York, 2002).

Belfrage, N., *From Brunello to Zibibbo: The Wines of Southern Italy* (London, 2001).

United Kingdom. See Great BRITAIN.

United States of America, increasingly important producer of wine and DRYING GRAPES, and a significant consumer of fine wine. The US is the world's fourth biggest producer of wine with forecast output of 515 million gall/19.5 million hl in 2004, having overtaken Argentina in the early 1990s. Only France, Italy, Spain, and Turkey have more vines planted than the United States' 1.1 million acres/445,000 ha, although an estimated third of this total is devoted to raisins and, to a lesser extent, TABLE GRAPES. CALIFORNIA is by far the most important wine-producing state, followed by WASHINGTON, OREGON, and then NEW YORK.

History

European settlement in what is now the US goes back to the late 16th century (see also VÍNLAND), but it was two centuries later that wine was first successfully produced there. The long delay was not for lack of trying. The abundant native AMERICAN VINE SPECIES immediately drew the attention of the first settlers; wine-making was an official aim of the VIRGINIA and Carolina colonies, and it was encouraged and repeatedly tried in all of the American colonies.

The first trials quickly showed that wine acceptable to European palates could not be made from the unameliorated native grape varieties. The next step was to import cuttings of European VINIFERA vines, beginning

in Virginia around 1619. The experiment was frequently repeated over the whole length of the Atlantic seaboard with vines from every great European wine region, but the result was uniform failure. The vines were destroyed by extremes of climate, by native PESTS, and by previously unknown VINE DISEASES. The facts were not clearly understood for more than two centuries, since the trials were isolated and uncoordinated, and no adequate knowledge of plant pathology existed. The cycle of hopeful experiment followed by complete failure went on in profitless repetition (see Thomas JEFFERSON for example).

All Europe took part in the effort. French VIGNERONS were imported along with French vines by the Virginia Company in 1619, and French expertise continued to be sought thereafter: Huguenot exiles were employed in Carolina in 1680, in Virginia in 1700, in Pennsylvania in 1683. Germans attempted wine-growing at Germantown in Pennsylvania; in Florida a colony of Greeks, Italians, Frenchmen, and Spaniards tried vine-growing in 1767. All of these, and innumerable other efforts, were based on VINIFERA varieties and were accordingly doomed to rapid and entire failure (see PHYLLOXERA and FUNGAL DISEASES).

A new direction was taken through the discovery of a chance HYBRID—the combination of a native *Vitis labrusca* and an unknown *vinifera*—called the Alexander grape, in Pennsylvania, not far from where William Penn had planted *vinifera* in 1683. Its hybrid character was unrecognized for many years, but it in fact showed the way in which vine-growing in the eastern United States would be developed. The first successful commercial wine production in the US, based on the Alexander, began in Indiana around 1806. Thereafter, many new AMERICAN HYBRIDS of American vine species either with each other or with a European *vinifera* variety, formed almost invariably by chance, were introduced and contributed to the possibilities of wine-making in the US.

The most important were the CATAWBA, DELAWARE, ISABELLA, and NORTON, all introduced in the first half of the 19th century. With the exception of Norton, most were better adapted to white wine production than to red, and most had more or less of the so-called FOXY aroma. Whatever their defects, they would at least survive under American conditions, and they made wine production possible.

Permanent and extensive wine production was first established around Cincinnati, Ohio, in the 1830s by Nicholas Longworth; when the Cincinnati *vignoble* was devastated by BLACK ROT, the Ohio wine industry moved north to the shores of lake Erie. The other main wine-making centres were around Hermann, MISSOURI, a German colony on the Missouri river (second only to California at the turn of the century), and around the Finger lakes of upstate New York (see NEW YORK for more historical detail of the state's wine industry).

In the south before the Civil War, some wine-making, based both on the native hybrids and on the native MUSCADINE vines of the American south, grew up in the Carolinas and Georgia. Scattered vineyards, all growing American native or hybrid vines, and small wineries could be found throughout the settled regions, and extended to the frontiers of TEXAS and Kansas. The federal government supported vine-growing through plant exploration, the distribution of plants, and experimental work in the analysis of grapes and wines. In the decade before the Civil War, interest in vine-growing burgeoned and many new hybrid varieties were introduced, some of them now the outcome of controlled rather than accidental hybridizing.

The most important single result of this activity was the CONCORD, a vine with good resistance to pests and diseases, well adapted to the extreme growing conditions of the area that then constituted the United States, but whose extremely FOXY grapes were particularly unsuitable for wine (or at least wine as most wine drinkers know it). The ubiquity of the Concord has had a large part in establishing a taste for grape juice rather than for wine among Americans.

Meanwhile, although the fact was quite unknown in the US, *vinifera* grapes were successfully grown and wine made in the Spanish settlements on the Rio Grande in New Mexico and Texas (beginning around 1626) and in the Franciscan missions of California (beginning around 1779). The Mexican War of 1846–7, followed by the GOLD RUSH of 1849, brought the *vinifera*-growing regions of the south west into the US; since then, California has dominated American wine production. At the time of the American conquest, the vine was already grown on a small but commercial scale in Los Angeles. Plantings thereafter spread over the state and production grew rapidly, from a few hundred thousand gallons in 1860 to more than 30 million gal/1.1 million hl by the end of the century.

The first *vinifera* variety grown in New Mexico and California was the MISSION, probably a New World seedling of an unknown European parent; it is at best a mediocre grape for wine. Importations and trials of many superior *vinifera* varieties quickly began, and although the Mission grape long dominated California, plantings of other, better varieties increased steadily. Among the most interesting is the distinctively California ZINFANDEL, which is still widely grown.

The economic growth of the California industry was unstable: a cyclical pattern of boom and bust persisted until 1894 (see CALIFORNIA, history), when the California Wine Association, a union of the largest producers and dealers in the state, was formed. The CWA was not a MONOPOLY, but it controlled so large a share of the wine production of the state that it could stabilize costs and prices, and did so until Prohibition. The CWA distributed its wines throughout the US (where wine drinking continued to be almost wholly confined to the cities) and developed export markets, particularly Great BRITAIN.

Outside California, vine-growing continued to develop slowly, in much the same way. New Jersey, Virginia, and Arkansas were added to the states where viticulture was already established: New York (where the production of sparkling wine had become a speciality), Ohio, and Missouri. By 1919, the last year before national PROHIBITION was enforced, the US produced 55 million gal of wine. During the Prohibition years, from 1920 to 1933, some commercial wine production was allowed, and HOME WINE-MAKING became more popular than ever before or since, resulting in an increase in total vine acreage thanks to demand for GRAPE CONCENTRATE, but the industry was destroyed.

Upon Repeal (from 1934), the US industry had to reconstitute itself. Some of the old firms reappeared; many new firms mushroomed. But it took time to put things right: the market was ignorant, or perverted by the intemperate habits encouraged by Prohibition; the producers were uninstructed or, sometimes, unscrupulous. The country was in the lowest depths of economic depression, and wine was an unfamiliar luxury. High-alcohol sweet wines became the mainstay of the trade, and remained so for the next generation. The federal government failed to re-establish its research programmes for wine, but important OENOLOGICAL and VITICULTURAL research was carried out by the state universities of California at DAVIS and New York. Promotional work was largely in the hands of the Wine Institute of California, founded in 1934.

The Second World War, by cutting off European supplies, brought new prosperity to US industry but brought new instability as well. Large distilling companies bought up established wineries in order to have a product to sell. A seller's market prevailed until, after the war, the artificially stimulated demand collapsed. The distillers departed from the wine trade, which fell into somnolence. Little effort was made to develop new markets; wineries typically sold their wines in bulk to wholesalers for bottling under their own brands; American wines, after the bad old example set in the 19th century, continued to use GENERIC names such as Burgundy, Chablis, Sherry, and Champagne, and most wineries produced an entire 'line' of such types from a severely limited range of grape varieties.

In the east, especially, the decline was marked; in Ohio, for example, the 149 wineries of 1940 had dwindled to 47 in 1960. One valuable new development was the introduction, by Philip WAGNER, of hybrid grape varieties developed in France (see FRENCH HYBRIDS) such as SEYVAL, SEIBEL, and BACO into the eastern vineyards; these gave larger yields and made more attractive and interesting wines than the old American hybrids could produce. Another innovation was the effective introduction of VARIETAL labelling by the American merchant Frank SCHOONMAKER, a practice that was to become standard.

Beginning around 1970, wine production in the US suddenly took on a new energy and a new glamour, a development not entirely explained but doubtless the result of many different, slowly gathering social forces. New wineries, large and small, were started in California where there were 240 wineries in 1970, 770 in 1989, and almost 1,700 in 2004. New vineyards were planted, and wine-growers made unprecedented efforts to find the best matches between grape variety and location. They increasingly concentrated on relatively few grape varieties and wine types instead of producing the old comprehensive 'line' of wines, aspiring to new levels of quality and complexity. Innovation in technology was eagerly sought, at the same time as traditional European methods were introduced and adapted. Large-scale foreign investment from Japanese, British, French, Spanish, Swiss, and German companies was attracted to the American wine industry, notably a number of French CHAMPAGNE firms who invested, some of them briefly, in California sparkling wine production in the 1980s.

The explosion of new activity in the industry was matched by consumer developments: wine classes, internet sales and websites, wine societies, wine publications proliferated to exploit the interest and anxieties of a public long ignorant and indifferent but now eager to learn. Consumption of wine—now dominated by table wine—rose from 267 million gal/ 10 million ha in 1970 to 668 million gal in 2004, about 3 gal (11 l) per adult (18 year-olds are classified adults by America's census-takers but have to wait three years before being allowed to drink legally). As wineries proliferated, they offered a variety of choices such as Americans had never before seen. One firm, GALLO of Modesto, California, succeeded in becoming the largest winery in the world, only to be passed in 2004 through the legerdemain of mergers and acquisitions by CONSTELLATION.

Outside California the boom in wine was, proportionately, even greater. The old regions—New York and Ohio especially—began to sprout new enterprises after a long quiescence. The vineyards were transformed by the introduction not only of hybrids developed in France such as Seyval and Seibel, but by *vinifera* varieties, now, thanks to modern understanding of plant pathology and the availability of PESTICIDES and FUNGICIDES, at last grown successfully in the eastern US after more than three centuries of failure. States such as New Jersey, Pennsylvania, and

Virginia which had once supported viticulture on only a modest scale now saw the growth of a renewed and expanded industry. Texas and New Mexico, sites of very old but very small-scale *vinifera* wine-making, now boasted large viticultural developments. The Yakima valley in WASHINGTON and the Willamette valley in OREGON undertook large plantings of *vinifera* and began to develop a reputation for particular types of wine. Thanks largely to the *labrusca*-based products of Constellation Brands' Canandaigua Wine Company, New York continues to produce more wine than any state other than California. Washington, South Carolina, and Georgia all produce more wine than Oregon. The number of commercial wineries in the entire country in the mid 2000s was more than 3,500.

Many obstacles to the production and sale of wine still exist, however, some of them natural, such as climate, some of them man made, such as the different taxes and restrictions imposed by the different states. The spirit of Prohibition is still vigorous, whether it takes the old form of moral disapproval or the newer forms of disapproval on grounds of diet, HEALTH, and safety. Since 1989, the federal government has required warning labels on all bottles of wine sold in the US. And in the late 1990s further, sometimes severe, restrictions were placed on the shipment of wine between states, making it even more difficult for consumers to buy wine direct from wineries (although see Regulations below).

But, on any view, the US wine industry in the latter half of the 20th century underwent a remarkable development from the ruins left after Prohibition, renewing old activities, spreading into new regions, expanding production, developing new methods in viticulture and wine-making, and reaching new levels of quality. T.P. & J.R.

Adams, L., *The Wines of America* (4th edn, New York, 1990).

Lapsley, J. T., *Bottled Poetry: Napa Winemaking from Prohibition to the Modern Era* (Berkeley, Calif., 1996).

Pinney, T., *A History of Wine in America—From the Beginnings to Prohibition* (Berkeley, Calif., 1989).

—— *A History of Wine in America—From Prohibition to the Present* (Berkeley, Calif., 2005).

Schoonmaker, F., and Marvel, T., *American Wines* (New York, 1941).

Sullivan, C., *Napa Wine: A History from Mission Days to the Present* (San Francisco, 1994).

Regulations

Following repeal of Prohibition in 1933, each of the 48 (now 50) states was allowed to set its own regulations governing the sale and distribution of alcoholic beverages. As a result an arcane, confusing regulatory environment involving in effect 50 separate countries has evolved. The prevailing 'three-tier' system is, however, under increasing economic and legal pressures. The consistent theme throughout the rules is that no enterprise can act as supplier, wholesaler (distributor), and retailer. A chief exception to this rule is California, where wineries can circumvent this structure. In many states, BOUTIQUE (farm) wineries can sell their wines directly to consumers, but most sell them to wholesalers, which then sell to retailers and restaurateurs. After a series of aggressive acquisitions, the number of different wholesalers was literally decimated between 1985 and 2005, each enjoying what is effectively a state-sanctioned monopoly on alcohol sales and profits. An actual state MONOPOLY operates in Pennsylvania and New Hampshire.

A potentially revolutionary 2005 US Supreme Court ruling gave all states a choice: either allow inside-the-state and into-the-state shipping by wineries, or prohibit both; such shipments would enable consumers interested in buying directly to bypass the three-tier system. But that system is not likely to disintegrate, because most producers need wholesalers to display and to distribute their wares across the immense continent. Seeking to protect their privileges, wholesalers have amassed clout in state legislatures nationwide by giving sizeable contributions to officeholders' fund-raising campaigns.

Label approval, AVAS, and federal taxation, are overseen by the TTB. D.F. & H.G.

Modern wine production

Wine is made in each of the 50 states comprising the US. Much of it is humble, created only for the TOURIST traffic that provides the majority of sales for most small wineries. While small wineries on the West Coast have garnered boutique and even cult status, the rest of the US has not yet produced wine of equal quality, at least not according to the wine media. Nonetheless, the number of wineries outside California, Oregon, and Washington trebled to about 1,500 between 1993 and 2005.

Increasingly, non-West Coast wineries are finding nearby urban markets receptive to their wines. Seven per cent of the wine sold in the state of MISSOURI is produced by Missouri wineries, much of it consumed in the cities of St Louis and Kansas City. The wineries of southern Illinois are beginning to enjoy acceptance in Chicago. Even Washington, DC, which has often snubbed the wine brands of neighbouring VIRGINIA, is opening up to its increasingly well-made wines.

The American wine industry comprises an odd collection of monied hobbyists, enthusiastic HOME WINEMAKERS, retired professionals in search of a glamorous lifestyle, and a diminishing number of increasingly powerful international wine and spirits conglomerates (see GLOBALIZATION).

A gradual easing of regulatory constraints has kept pace with these developments, and many states can now boast of official wine trails and state grapes, wine festivals, concerts, and events, even if the majority of states still limit or prohibit altogether the shipping of wines within or across their borders.

Despite these successes, the national retail chains and the behemoth wholesalers are little interested in the pioneering work required to promote wines from little-known US wine regions. The dramatic growth of these wineries has come despite the wineries' inability to ship wines in most states and the lack of support from the powerful retail companies.

Most of the wineries in the lesser-known areas are reliant upon the tourist trade in order to provide consistent revenue. This requires that wines be made expressly for tourists: typically, wines that are soft, mildly flavoured and often slightly sweet. These wineries become the victims of their own success: as their volumes of tourist wine increases, their reputation for the drier wines sought by more sophisticated customers, the restaurant sector in particular, decreases. Few wineries in these regions have a well-established distributor network nearly as effective as their sales at the winery.

Compounding these challenges, many wineries use HYBRID grapes unknown to their potential customers. Most American customers are fairly sure how a Chardonnay or Merlot is likely to taste. But few have even heard of Vignoles, Norton, or Marechal Foch.

The developing wine industries in NEW YORK, VIRGINIA, TEXAS, and in the southwest may increasingly use VINIFERA varieties but much of the rest of the US is dependent upon hybrids or native AMERICAN VINE varieties such as Delaware, Catawba, Niagara, or Norton. Vinifera has consistently struggled in these areas, due to pressures from PHYLLOXERA, PIERCE'S DISEASE, and the numerous other challenges associated with hot, humid summers and/or fiercely cold winters. In many of eastern America's vineyards, winter hardiness is the overriding selection criterion.

Red hybrid grapes such as BACO NOIR, CHANCELLOR, CHAMBOURCIN, CHELOIS, CONCORD, DE CHAUNAC, MARECHAL FOCH, and ROUGEON are increasingly common as new vineyards and wineries spring up in America's viticultural hinterlands. White hybrid plantings are dominated by AURORE, CAYUGA, SEYVAL BLANC, VIGNOLES, and VIDAL BLANC.

Other hybrids are poised for the leap from experimental plantings to commercial vineyards. As with many of the new winery and vineyard projects in the non-traditional areas of America, the success and failure of these grapes is still in flux. Some wineries eschew these hybrids as inappropriate for dry table wines, but many of America's best dessert wines have so far been based on such hybrids as Vidal Blanc and Vignoles. As the significant wine-producing states of Texas, Virginia, and New York are abandoning hybrids (except for dessert wines), it will increasingly be left to other, less important wine-producing states to explain and market these grapes and wines to buyers.

However, regional pride, local media, and plain old curiosity offer small wineries opportunities that are unavailable to large-scale wine areas. In Missouri, approximately 1.5 million people visit its wineries each year; wine TOURISM has proved to be an attraction to wine drinkers and non-wine drinkers alike.

Other US states

While CALIFORNIA, IDAHO, MICHIGAN, MISSOURI, NEW YORK, OREGON, TEXAS, VIRGINIA, and WASHINGTON have their own entries in this book, much of the wine made in every other US state is surprisingly good. Greater understanding of the viticultural and winemaking challenges associated with these areas, and the hybrid and native American varieties upon which they often rely, has given rise to a burgeoning wine industry far from the famous coastal wine regions.

The states of **Hawaii** and **Alaska** can be said to have derived a marketing advantage from their tourist industries. Many other states, **North Dakota** and **Maine** being extreme examples, suffer from the considerable limitation of having such a short growing season that they have no commercial vineyards and therefore have to import grapes, must, or grape concentrate and/or produce FRUIT WINES. But wineries exist in these states in response to perceived interest in local agricultural products, as well as an increasing curiosity about, and acceptance of, wine in American society. (Between 1990 and 2003 the annual amount spent on wine per American adult increased from $12 to $33.) While Maine and the other New England states (excluding New York) support about 200 wineries, most are dependent upon grapes purchased from New York or Pennsylvania. This is a common phenomenon in new US wine regions where many wineries function as brands built upon grapes imported from more famous wine-producing states, particularly California, Washington, and New York.

The creation of new AVAs in New England, as in so many of the new regions, reflects wishful thinking, and marketing more than viticultural reality. Only the minority of these AVAs host legitimate commercial wine production from locally grown grapes and many are so large as to make a mockery of the concept supposedly enshrined in the AVA definition. The Ohio River Valley AVA, for instance, is a delimited region of over 16 million acres/6.5 million ha. Southeastern New England AVA is hardly better defined. At just under 2 million acres/750,000 ha, it sprawls across three states' coasts, but at least it has coastal proximity as its common thread. But with so few successful vineyards to draw on, the two dozen or so wineries in the three states of **Massachusetts**, **Rhode Island**, and **Connecticut** have found it necessary to create such a flexible AVA. Sakonnet, Rhode Island's best known winery, utilizes grapes grown throughout the AVA for its well-made sparkling wines. Among other wineries, Sharpe Hill Vineyard has made some excellent wines from purchased grapes and grapes in the western portion of the state. The Western Connecticut Highlands AVA abuts the New York state border and New York's famously picturesque Hudson valley. The short growing seasons and cool nights throughout the northeastern US necessitate a reliance on white varieties if *vinifera* grapes are grown—and Riesling Gewurztraminer, and Muscat are more successful than the ubiquitous Chardonnay grown in response to the perceived market demands.

The newfound fame and financial rewards reaped by New York's Finger lakes' producers of Riesling and other aromatic wines is being emulated elsewhere in the north east. **New Jersey**'s Warren Hills AVA, the Central Delaware Valley AVA (shared by New Jersey and **Pennsylvania**), and Pennsylvania's Lancaster Valley AVA and the Cumberland Valley AVA, have all produced some well-balanced examples of white *vinifera*-based wine, but have had more success with white and red hybrids. Pennsylvania's more than 90 wineries, including the ubiquitous Chaddsford and the benchmark Clover Hill wineries, are almost wholly dependent upon hybrids. Alba, Tomasello, and Unionville wineries in New Jersey are also best known for their hybrids such as Chambourcin, even if some notable Riesling has been made.

The Lake Erie AVA is shared by New York, Pennsylvania, and Ohio and its 20,000 acres of vineyard produce vast quantities of grapes, less than a quarter of which is converted to wine. Most is CONCORD for jelly and juice.

Although wine production has been sporadically attempted along the eastern seaboard since the founding of the Jamestown colony in the 16th century, it has only recently become a product worthy of national and international trade. Philip Wagner of **Maryland**'s Boordy Vineyard played an important role in the story in the improvement of eastern US wines through its adoption of hybrid vines in the late 20th century. See also VIRGINIA.

North Carolina boasts over 40 wineries as well as one of the area's chief tourist destinations, the Biltmore Estate. This sprawling mansion enjoys more than a million visitors annually, many of whom taste the estate's increasingly well-made wines. Surprisingly, many of the grapes used are from the state of **Georgia**, which has more acres under vine than any southeastern state apart from Virginia. **South Carolina** and Georgia's vineyards hug the Atlantic coast, many perched upon hills close to the sea. Although the mainstay has always been hybrid and the well-known if little-respected MUSCADINE vines, *vinifera* plantings have increased considerably, and Georgia's Blackstock Vineyards, while producing no wine itself, is the source of many estimable *vinifera* wines from this part of America.

Florida's hot and humid weather is ideal for citrus crops but offers only a suffocating hot-house environment for *vinifera* and even hybrid grapevines. Gulf Coast states Alabama, Mississippi, and Louisiana fare little better and generally import grapes.

But there has been progress for the grapevine in the interior states of **Arkansas**, **Illinois**, **Indiana**, and, to a much lesser degree, in **Tennessee**, **Kentucky**, and **West Virginia**. In Arkansas, the Altus and Arkansas Mountain AVAs are beginning to find their feet with new experimental hybrid plantings. In these states, WINTER FREEZE may be only a marginal issue, but the hot, humid summers have so far proved to be discouraging to efforts with *vinifera* vines.

The two largest producing states in this part of America are **Ohio** and MISSOURI. Ohio features prominently in the story of American wine (see above) and today about 750,000 gal/28,000 hl of wine are made here each year, most of it sold to the state's residents. Markko Vineyard, Ferrante Winery, Valley Vineyards, and Chalet Debonné are the old hands among the nearly 80 wineries in Ohio. The small AVAs of Grand River Valley and Loramie Creek are home to some new small wineries producing both *vinifera* and hybrid wines. Although Ohio's grapevine production is more *vinifera* than hybrid, much of the *vinifera* wine has so far been lacklustre. The most reliable wines have been dessert wines created from hybrid grapes but Troutman and Tarula wineries suggest that *vinifera* quality is rising. One of the more unusual American AVAs is the Isle St George AVA encompassing four islands in the middle of lake Erie, a ferry boat ride away from Cleveland,

Indiana, the state to the immediate west of Ohio, hosts a smaller wine industry but one with equal promise and Oliver Winery, Huber Winery, and Turtle Run have all produced reliable wines including Huber's Heritage, a blend of hybrid and *vinifera* grapes. Throughout the Midwest, FUNGAL DISEASES are a constant concern and fuel the continued interest in hybrids.

Until recently, **Illinois** lagged behind but its vineyard acreage his overtaken Indiana's and some exciting hybrid wines are being produced in the southwest of the state not far from Missouri's Augusta AVA. Alto Vineyards and Galena Cellars are notable producers among the state's two dozen wineries and, since climatic conditions are similar to MISSOURI, many of the same hybrids such as Seyval Blanc, Vidal Blanc, and Chambourcin are likely to succeed.

The states to the north are mostly afflicted by the severity of the winters. MICHIGAN may be protected by its Great lakes but **Wisconsin**, **Iowa**, **Minnesota**, **Nebraska**, and the **Dakotas** have very little wine production and as yet relatively few vineyards, but their small successes have been based upon some of the grapes and styles proven in MISSOURI, as well as varieties created by the late Elmer Swenson. An amateur viticulturist for most of nine decades of life, Swenson created dozens of winter-hardy hybrids, and his cuttings continue to see experimentation and commercialization in these High Plains states as well as Canada. So, in addition to the usual hybrids, Plains vineyards are planted with Brianna, Diamond, Fredonia, FRONTENAC, LaCrosse, St Croix, and St Pepin. Notable wineries include Alexis Bailly and WineHaven (Minnesota), Tabor Home (Iowa), Cuthills Vineyards and James Arthur Vineyards (Nebraska), HolyField Winery (Kansas), and Stone Bluff Cellars (Oklahoma). But most are still working to match hybrid varieties and site.

Only Wisconsin's eastern portion and the Lake Wisconsin AVA seem to offer the hope of *vinifera* production. Wisconsin's most prolific wineries, Cedar Creek and Wollersheim, make very good wine but principally use grapes purchased from less viticulturally challenging states.

The Mountain states are relatively unimportant wine producers but **Colorado**'s increasing vineyard area (nearly 1,000 acres) and growing number of wineries (over 50) are beginning to provide wines of quality to its major tourist market as well as Denver, America's tenth largest city. The dry conditions allow healthy *vinifera* production but varieties have yet to produce characterful wines despite a usefully hot growing season. Riesling, Chardonnay, Gewurztraminer, Merlot (the most widely planted), Cabernet, Syrah and, perhaps surprisingly, Lemberger have all produced wines of interest. Wineries such as Bookcliff, Carlson, Garfield, Plum Creek, Spero, S. Rhodes, Stone Cottage, and Terror Creek are all notable.

The rest of the Southwest, including TEXAS, **New Mexico**, and **Arizona**, also have warm, dry growing conditions resulting in short seasons and grapes that often lack flavour and PHENOLIC RIPENESS. But, as with Colorado's best vineyards, ALTITUDE seems to be the solution for both New Mexico and Arizona's best vineyards. Arizona's sole AVA, Sonoita, includes vineyards at 4,000 to 5,000 feet /1,200 to 1,500 m, and the best of the dozen or so wineries in the state use fruit from these lofty vineyards. Syrah and Zinfandel can be almost shockingly good here and Dos Cabezas, Sonoita, and Callaghan have also made impressive white wines. New Mexico has 30 wineries and the best of their vines are grown at more than 4,000 feet. Good reds have been produced by wineries such as Milagro Vineyards but Gruet Vineyards is one of the few US wineries outside the major wine-producing states to have genuinely national distribution. This is no mere stroke of luck but reflects the high quality sparkling wines produced in high altitude vineyards, vineyards which might be as warm as 90 °F/32 °C during the day but

will usually cool to less than 60 °F/15 °C during the night.

See also AVA and specific entries on CALIFORNIA, WASHINGTON, OREGON, IDAHO, TEXAS, VIRGINIA, MICHIGAN, MISSOURI, and NEW YORK.

D.F.

Adams, L., *The Wines of America* (4th edn, New York, 1990).

Cass, B. (ed.), *Oxford Companion to the Wines of North America* (Oxford and New York, 2000).

Gayot, A., *Guide to the Best Wineries of North America* (New York, 1993).

Lukacs, P,. *American Vintage: The Rise of American Wine* (New York, 2000).

Morton, L. T., *Winegrowing in Eastern America* (Ithaca, 1985).

www.wineamerica.org

www.wineinstitute.org

Upper Goulburn, high altitude, cool Australian wine region in VICTORIA with the snowfields of mount Buller on one extremity, Strathbogie ranges on the other.

Uruguay is South America's fourth most important wine-producing country with an area under vines of more than 8,500 ha/21,000 acres of which more than 95 per cent is for wine production. The relatively small 2005 harvest was of 850,000 hl/17 million gallons.

The history of wine-making in the country is comparatively recent, starting as late as 1870, with vineyards planted by immigrants, mainly Basques and Italians. This tradition of 'peasant' smallholdings continues, with the average vineyard size being no more than 5 ha. In all there are over 3,500 growers. Wine was initially produced for local consumption and, with half the population of the country living in the capital Montevideo, four-fifths of the vineyards are in the immediately neighbouring *departmentos*. Domestic wine consumption is high, and rising, currently standing at 32 l/8.45 gal per person per year.

With the formation of Mercosur, announced at the end of the 1980s, the Uruguayans realized that they would have to protect their wine industry from Chilean and Argentine wine, with their lower production costs. In order to achieve this, the Uruguayan National Institute for Vitiviniculture (INAVI) embarked on a three-pronged campaign. Firstly, encouragement was given to growers to plant VINIFERA varieties, rather than the AMERICAN VINES and HYBRIDS that then dominated. Secondly, the Uruguayans were urged to be proud of their own wines, with stress being laid on their purity and 'naturalness'. Finally efforts were made to conquer export markets despite limited promotional resources. BRAZIL, because of a shortage of domestic red wine, is by far the most important export market, accounting for over 60 per cent of the total.

Wines are divided into two classes, VCP (*Vino de calidad preferente*) and VC (*Vino Común*). VCP wines, which account for about

one-tenth of total production, must be made from *vinifera* grapes and be sold in 75cl, or smaller, bottles. VC wine, which is sold widely in demijohns and tetrapacks, is predominantly rosé based on MUSCAT HAMBURG grapes.

For better quality wines the dominant grape variety is TANNAT, introduced to Uruguay by Basque settlers and made with increasing enthusiasm and expertise. It accounts for 36 per cent of all plantings of noble varieties. Other red wine grapes are Merlot (10 per cent), Cabernet Sauvignon (6 per cent), and Cabernet Franc (4 per cent) while white wines tend to be made from Chardonnay (7 per cent) and Sauvignon Blanc (6 per cent).

Most of the vineyards lie on deep clay soils on gently rolling hills to the north of Montevideo, but there are vines in 16 out of the 19 *departmentos*. Of particular interest are recent plantings in the Cerro Chapeu region on the Brazilian border and in El Carmen and Carpinteria in the centre of the country. In all three cases the soils are poorer and there is a bigger diurnal temperature variation (see TEMPERATURE VARIABILITY).

The climate in Uruguay is influenced by the Atlantic, with both rainfall and heat summation being similar to that of Bordeaux. Humidity can be excessive so the LYRE training system is popular. High soil fertility has resulted in excessive yields although the more serious producers are addressing this.

International interest in Uruguayan wines has been shown by a number of JOINT VENTURES with international groups such as Jean-Claude BOISSET of Burgundy (with Pisano), Bernard Magrez of Bordeaux, (with Juanicó), and FREIXENET of Spain (with Carrau). C.C.F.

Bigongiari, B. (ed), *Viñas, Bodegas y Vinos* (Buenos Aires, 2003).

Fielden, C., *The Wines of Argentina, Chile and Latin America* (London, 2003).

Waldin, M., *Wines of South America* (London, 2003).

US. See UNITED STATES of America.

USSR. See SOVIET UNION.

Utiel-Requena, large, workmanlike Spanish wine region producing some sturdy reds, and mostly rosés, in the hills inland from VALENCIA in south east Spain (see map under SPAIN). Utiel-Requena is the coolest of the five wine regions of the LEVANTE and was once famous for its heavy DOBLE PASTA reds. Consequently the region is dominated by the sweet, dark BOBAL grape variety (Bobal Clásico must be made from vines more than 50 years old), although the TEMPRANILLO vine is rapidly gaining in importance, followed by Syrah, Merlot, and Cabernet Sauvignon. Utiel-Requena produces large amounts of GRAPE CONCENTRATE.

V. de la S. & J.R.

Peñín, J., *Guía Peñín* (Madrid, annually).

Uva Abruzzi, occasional name for the red MONTEPULCIANO grape.

Uva di Troia, good-quality southern Italian red grape variety named after a village near Foggia and fast declining in popularity with growers although there are at least a thousand hectares in PUGLIA. It forms the base for the Castel del Monte DOC, although it has yet to each the potential already demonstrated by the likes of PRIMITIVO or NEGROAMARO further south.

Uva Rara, red wine grape variety too widely grown in the OLTREPÒ PAVESE in Lombardia in northern Italy to justify its Italian name, whose literal translation is 'rare grape'. Often called, misleadingly, BONARDA Novarese, it is grown in the Novara hills and used to soften the SPANNA grapes grown here in a range of scented red wines.

Uzbekistan, independent central Asian republic with Tashkent as its capital. It is a major supplier of TABLE GRAPES and wine production has been declining fast but it still produced 336,000 hl/near 9 million gal of wine in 2002 according to OIV figures.

History
The grapes and wines of Uzbekistan have long been famous beyond its own frontiers. Between the 6th and 2nd centuries BC people in the Fergana valley grew wheat, barley, and grapes using artificial irrigation and Fergana grapes were prized in CHINA to the east.

It is thought that some central Asian VINE VARIETIES originated as the wild subspecies VITIS *silvestris* Gmel as a result of long-term selection. Some varieties were brought to Uzbekistan from IRAN between the 6th and 4th centuries BC and other varieties were brought by Greeks and Arabs in the 7th and 8th centuries AD.

Archaeological excavation has revealed grape seeds dating back to the 5th century BC during excavations of Tali Barzu near Samarkand.

Viticulture and wine-making flourished in Uzbekistan until the end of the 7th century, when, as a result of the Arab conquest of central Asia, wine grape varieties gave way to table, raisin, and seedless raisin varieties (see ISLAM).

After central Asia was annexed to RUSSIA in the second half of the 19th century, demand for table grape varieties with good shipping qualities developed rapidly. European wine varieties from MOLDOVA, the Crimea in UKRAINE, and other regions were also imported into Uzbekistan. In 1917, Uzbekistan had 37,000 ha/91,000 acres of vineyards, mainly owned by individual smallholders. The first specialized state farms were established in the 1920s.

Modern viticulture
With about 90,000 ha of vines, the great majority of which are devoted to TABLE GRAPES, Uzbekistan is in the very heart of central Asia, on the same latitude as Italy. The country's relief varies considerably, with the Tian-Shan and the Pamir and Alai spines in the east, and mountains accounting for about 30 per cent of the total area of the country. The climate of Uzbekistan is very CONTINENTAL. The average January temperature is 3 to $-3\,°C/37$–$22\,°F$ and that of July is 26 to $32\,°C/79$–$89\,°F$. Late spring and early autumn FROSTS are commonplace. The active temperature summation is 4,000 to 4,500 °C. The annual rainfall is 100 mm (4 in) in the lowlands to 1,000 mm in the mountains.

Commercial grape culture is centred on the ten zones of Uzbekistan with the most suitable soil and climate conditions. The leading viticultural zones, accounting for about 75 per cent of vines, are the Samarkand, Surkandaria, Namandan, Tashkent, Bukhara, and Kashkadaria regions. About 90 per cent of vines need WINTER PROTECTION. Only vineyards in the mountains, at an altitude of 800–1,500 m (2,600–5,000 ft), where the annual rainfall is at least 450 mm, do not require IRRIGATION.

The country's assortment of vines, all ungrafted, still has features typical of the viticulture of central Asia. Table grape varieties predominate and the grape conveyor system is employed whereby early-, mid-, and late-maturing grapes are harvested continuously for about 120 days. In the 1990s, 36 varieties were officially allowed for commercial viticulture, of which 20 were table and dried fruit varieties. Wine grape varieties included ALEATICO, RIESLING, Kuljinkski, Hungarian Muscat, MUSCAT Rosé, Soiaki, Bayan Shirey, SAPERAVI, RKATSITELI, MORRASTEL, and Khindogny.

Uzbekistan's wine industry was still run substantially by the state in the early 2000s and more dynamic than many other central Asian republics'. Wines tend to be sweet, often strong, and many are sparkling.

The Shreder Research Institute for Horticulture, Viticulture, and Oenology is Uzbekistan's centre of wine ACADEME and sole vine NURSERY.   V.R.

Akhramov, I. K., 'The history of viticulture and enology in the Fergana valley' (Russian), *Vinodelie i vinogradarstvo SSSR*, 7 (1966), 43.

Julia, F., and Beillon, D., *Uzbekistan—Rehabilitation of the Vine and Wine Sector* (Bordeaux, 2001).

Mirzayev, M. M., 'The Soviet Socialist Republic of Uzbekistan' (Russian), in A. I. Timush (ed.), *Encyclopaedia of Viticulture* (Kishinëv, 1986).

Vaccarèse, rare, relatively light red grape variety permitted in CHÂTEAUNEUF-DU-PAPE producing wines similar to CINSAUT.

Vacqueyras, after GIGONDAS, the second one of the Côtes du Rhône villages to be awarded its own appellation, in 1990. Vacqueyras may be red, white, or rosé, although only a minuscule proportion of its dramatically expanded vineyard total of 1,000 ha/2,500 acres is planted with white grape varieties. Most of the wine is like a super-concentrated Côtes du Rhône-Villages, made in the communes of Vacqueyras and Sarrians between Gigondas and BEAUMES-DE-VENISE (see map under RHÔNE). The appellation rules are very similar to those of Gigondas, and thus to those of Châteauneuf-du-Pape, although only half the grapes in a red Vacqueyras have to be Grenache. The rest are usually Syrah, Mourvèdre, and Cinsaut. Vacqueyras tends to be slightly more rustic than good Gigondas, but producers such as Domaines des Amouriers and de la Monardière and Ch des Tours, now operated in conjunction with Ch Rayas of CHÂTEAUNEUF-DU-PAPE, at least back up that rusticity with power and concentration.

vacuole, the central compartment of plant CELLS, separated from cytoplasm by a membrane. In grape berries, vacuoles within flesh cells contain the solution that forms grape juice. B.G.C.

vacuum evaporation. See CONCENTRATION.

Valdadige, or Etschtaler in German, basic appellation of the Adige (Etsch) valley that, unusually, extends across three regions, though is used principally by producers in TRENTINO and also by some in northwestern VENETO. Vineyards in ALTO ADIGE theoretically qualify but the Alto Adige appellation is usually used instead.

Valdeorras, easternmost wine zone in GALICIA in north west Spain (see map under SPAIN). Steeply terraced vineyards are planted predominantly with inappropriate but productive vine varieties such as Garnacha Tintorera (ALICANTE BOUSCHET) and the white PALOMINO. The indigenous white GODELLO, which had all but disappeared from Galicia in the wake of PHYLLOXERA, is being aggressively replanted. This moderately productive variety is susceptible to disease, but Valdeorras is protected from the Atlantic by mountains immediately to the west. If carefully vinified, it can produce an aromatic wine with an ALCOHOLIC STRENGTH of 12 to 13 per cent. In the late 1990s, some of Spain's most acclaimed BARREL-FERMENTED whites were Godello wines from Valdeorras made by the Guitián family, who pioneered this style. The MENCÍA grape, which makes fruity reds, is similarly respected by a new wave of producers in Valdeorras. R.J.M. & V. de la S.

Valdepeñas, wine region in CASTILLA-LA MANCHA in south central Spain producing soft, ripe red wines. The sea of rolling vineyards that is Valdepeñas is really an extension of La MANCHA (see map under SPAIN), but Valdepeñas has developed a reputation for quality over and above its larger neighbour and has consequently earned a separate denomination, or DO. Physical conditions in Valdepeñas are similar to those in La Mancha. The Sierra Morena dividing CASTILE from ANDALUCÍA immediately to the south is a barrier to the moderating influence of the Mediterranean. At an altitude of 700 m/2,300 ft above sea level, Valdepeñas shares the arid, CONTINENTAL conditions that prevail through much of central Spain.

As in La Mancha, the white, DROUGHT-resistant AIRÉN is the dominant grape variety but the red Cencibel, as the TEMPRANILLO of Rioja is known here, has been gaining ground in Valdepeñas' 30,000 ha/75,000 acres of vineyard. Much of the 'red' wine made in the region is a blend of red and white grapes somewhat lacking in colour and BODY. The best red wines, however, are made exclusively from Cencibel, which has the capacity to age well in OAK and increasingly they include Cabernet Sauvignon, Merlot, Syrah, and even Petit Verdot. The best wines have the soft, smooth, vanilla character, although not the price tag nor the complexity, of a well-aged RIOJA.
R.J.M. & V. de la S.

Valdepenas is also the name of a relatively unusual red grape variety grown in California which is thought to be TEMPRANILLO.

Valdiguié, sometimes called Gros Auxerrois, enjoyed its finest hour in the late 19th century when, as a dark-berried grape variety from the Lot, it was valued for its productivity and its resistance to oidium (POWDERY MILDEW). In the early 20th century, it was known as 'the ARAMON of the south west' for its emphasis on quantity at the expense of quality. It has now been all but eradicated from France, where a few hectares remain, mainly in the Tarn *département*.

In 1980, French ampelographer Galet visited the US and identified the variety then sold rather successfully as Napa Gamay as none other than this undistinguished vine from south west France, of which there were then 4,000 acres/1,600 ha planted in California. By the 1990s, it had disappeared from official statistics but occasionally turned up on the label of a fruity VARIETAL wine.

Galet, P., 'La Culture de la vigne aux États-Unis et au Canada', *France viticole* (Sept–Oct 1980 and Jan–Feb 1981).

Valençay, small region on the south bank of the Cher tributary of the Loire in northern France, promoted to AC status in 2004. Only

about 100 ha/250 acres of clay soils with a certain amount of limestone, flint, and silt are planted with a wide range of LOIRE grape varieties. Some of the most successful are Sauvignon Blanc (Valençay is only about 20 miles/30 km from the appellations QUINCY and REUILLY) but crisp wines of all three colours are made for drinking young from Cabernets, Cot (Malbec), Gamay, Pinot Noir, Chardonnay, and Arbois.

Valencia, Spain's biggest port and third largest city, also lends its name to an autonomous region and one of five wine denominations (see DO) in the Levante (see map under SPAIN). The vineyards are well away from the city, inland from the fertile market gardens and paddy fields bordering the Mediterranean. Production of white wine exceeds red. Neutral dry whites are made from the MERSEGUERA grape, although the local Moscatel Romano (MUSCAT OF ALEXANDRIA) produces some good, pungent dessert MISTELAS. MONASTRELL and the dark-fleshed Garnacha Tintorera (ALICANTE BOUSCHET) together produce rather coarse red wines, although the latter can produce some fresh, dry rosé. Five large producers dominate Valencia and the surrounding DOs. For more details, see LEVANTE.   R.J.M.

Valgella, subzone of VALTELLINA in the far north of Italy.

Valle d'Aosta. See AOSTA.

Valle de Güimar, denominated wine region occupying a valley in the dry south eastern part of Tenerife in the Spanish CANARY ISLANDS. A few tiny wineries, technically improved with EUROPEAN UNION subsidies, make surprisingly distinguished wines from the white LISTÁN Blanco grape, but in such small quantities that they are hardly known even on the island.   V. de la S.

Valle de la Orotava, denominated wine region covering the lush northern flanks of the Teide mountain on Tenerife in the Spanish CANARY ISLANDS. Much improved reds, whites, and rosés from the typical Canary Islands grape varieties are rarely seen outside Tenerife.   V. de la S.

Valle Isarco, or Eisacktaler in German, source of pure, dry white wines from ALTO ADIGE.

Valpaços, IPR in north east Portugal. See TRÁS-OS-MONTES.

Valpolicella, red wine from the VENETO region in north east Italy. The Valpolicella, like a number of other historic areas of Italy, saw its production zone greatly enlarged when it achieved DOC status in 1968. The historical

zone, north west of the town of Verona, encompassed the hills extending from Sant'-Ambrogio in the west to the outskirts of Verona in the east. In 1968, it was extended eastward as far as the very boundaries of the SOAVE white wine zone, and south onto the fertile plains on the northern edge of the Po valley. The original Valpolicella zone, whose wines alone may be labelled Valpolicella CLASSICO, now accounts for just over 40 per cent of the total production of about 460,000 hl/12.2 million gal. The subzone of the Valpantena, a valley to the east of Verona that has historically produced wines that are every bit as good as those in the Classico zone, is a legally permitted subdenomination on labels.

The name Valpolicella is derived from a mixture of Latin and Greek, as in 'the valley of many cellars'. CORVINA has historically been regarded as the best grape of Valpolicella, being used to produce a wide range of styles, all from the same hills. The youthful wines resemble a good Beaujolais in that they can be enjoyed chilled and have, at their best, a delicious sour cherry character. The fuller wines come from better sites on the hills, as do the RECIOTO and AMARONE wines made from dried grapes. Traditionally, the sweet Recioto was the great wine; Amarone was regarded as a mistake, a 'Recioto that had run away'. Amarone was produced commercially for the first time in the 1953 vintage, by Bolla and Bertani.

By the late 1960s, when the DOC regulations were drawn up, any pretence of quality wine production seemed to have been abandoned. Lesser grape varieties MOLINARA and RONDINELLA were allowed as part of the blend, and excessive yields were permitted. As a result, quality fell almost as quickly as the prices paid to growers for their grapes. By the late 1980s, many of the vineyards on the hills in the Classico zone were abandoned, as remunerative viticulture became increasingly impossible. Only those growers on the plains, where yields were several times higher than those from the hills, were able to make money. Consequently, the grapes from these prolific vineyards made most Valpolicella, and these were the wines that shaped the image of the wine.

Viticulture on the hills was salvaged by the increase in popularity of Amarone during the 1990s. Production of Amarone increased from 46,500 hl/1.2 million gal in 1990 (up from 19,772 hl in 1972) to 116,752 hl in 2000. As the price paid for grapes for Amarone is usually three times higher than that paid for those used for Valpolicella, this development led to many new plantings on the hills, and many more growers willing and able to invest in their vineyards.

Amarone, along with Recioto, applied for DOCG status in 2005. It is a complicated application, for as in Soave no solution has been

found to the historical travesty of expanding from the hills to the lesser sites on the plains. The compromise solution sees growers on the plains being allowed to select a lower percentage of their grapes for drying than those from the hills. Whether this messy solution works in practice remains to be seen. Since 2000, production of Amarone has risen to 148,000 hl, and now constitutes 25 per cent of the total production of Valpolicella whereas in 1990 it comprised well under 10 per cent. That too many unsuitable sites are being used to produce Amarone risks a decline in the wine's popularity as rapid as its recent rise.

In 2003, the positive step was taken of removing Molinara as an obligatory component in the blend for Valpolicella, and all mention of it has now been excised from the DOCG proposal for Amarone. It produces, at best, light and short-lived wines. Rondinella, which can comprise from 5 to 30 per cent of the blend for Amarone, is superior to Molinara but not as good as Corvina or CORVINONE, which together can comprise between 40 and 80 per cent of the blend. Producers such as Allegrini, Bussola, Ca' La Bionda, Quintarelli, and, more controversially, Dal Forno, have all helped raise the profile of Amarone.

The RIPASSO technique, once employed for boosting the strength, body, and durability of standard Valpolicella, is now becoming more widely used. The increase in production of Amarone has, not surprisingly, been accompanied by an increase in the production of Ripasso wines, a development that has made Valpolicella more appealing to a wider market, for the Ripasso wines are fuller and softer than traditional Valpolicella. The future for both Valpolicella and Amarone is now brighter than it has been at any time since the early 1970s; it is up to the producers to ensure that in the future, unlike the recent past, quality triumphs over quantity.   D.T. & D.C.G.

Belfrage, N., *Barolo to Valpolicella: The Wines of Northern Italy* (London, 1999).

Valréas, one of the Côtes du Rhône villages. See RHÔNE.

Valtellina, the northernmost zone in Italy where the NEBBIOLO grape (here called Chiavennasca) is cultivated, is a narrow valley formed by the river Adda as it flows from east to west before emptying its waters into lake Como. Despite its 46-degree latitude, the valley—protected to the north by the Rhaetian and Lepontine alps—has a relatively privileged climate (not unlike the warmer wine regions across the border in SWITZERLAND) with a high percentage of sunny days during the year. The longer days of the summer supply ample amounts of solar radiation for grape RIPENING, partially compensating for lower median temperatures compared with the classic areas for Nebbiolo in PIEMONTE to the south west. A certain amount of daytime heat is also stored and released during the cooler hours of the evening and night by the very rocky soils of the vineyards. Nonetheless, the wines themselves, while unmistakably Nebbiolo, do tend to have less body and roundness, and more perceptible TANNINS and ACIDITY, than the classic wines of the LANGHE or those made from SPANNA in the Novara-Vercelli hills, and can be sold only at considerably lower prices. Although Nebbiolo seems well adapted to Valtellina, it arrived relatively recently: the detailed works of Francesco Saverio Quadrio in the 17th century make no mention of the grape and the beginning of its cultivation in Valtellina appears to date from the early 19th century.

The production zone is divided into nearly 500 ha/1,250 acres of Valtellina SUPERIORE, elevated to DOCG status in 1998 (including the legally recognized subzones of Grumello, Inferno, Sassella, and Valgella; Paradiso, another name which frequently appears on labels, is not a legally recognized subzone, although its wines can be among the valley's best), and the nearly 600 ha of regular Valtellina. The Superiore zone, the historical nucleus of the valley's viticulture, produces an average of 16,000 hl/413,000 gal per year with a minimum ALCOHOLIC STRENGTH of 12 per cent. The 17,500 hl/462,000 gal yearly production of regular Valtellina is generally a simpler and less age-worthy wine which need reach only 11 per cent alcohol. Production levels from the increasingly mature vineyards have significantly declined in recent years and this, in addition to the difficulties of mechanizing the narrow TERRACES of the vineyards in order to contain costs, may prejudice the future of the valley's viticulture.

Three thousand growers share the 1,176 ha/2,900 acres of DOC vineyards, which has encouraged the commercial domination of the NÉGOCIANT houses, which market 88 per cent of Valtellina's production. Another substantial portion, 10 per cent, is marketed by CO-OPERATIVE wineries, leaving the zone with a virtual absence of the small producers whose work has been so fundamental in improving the quality and image of the famous Langhe wines BAROLO and BARBARESCO. Wine-making is not always scrupulous at these négociant houses and insufficiently mastered MALOLACTIC FERMENTATIONS and long ageing in old casks continue to mark a certain percentage of Valtellina's wines.

Valtellina also produces a wine called Sforzato (also seen with dialect names of Sfursat or Sfurzat) from DRIED GRAPES. Like AMARONE, the wine is dry and must have a minimum of 14.5 per cent of alcohol. But, just as in the Valpolicella, too much emphasis is often given to this type of wine, considered the zone's most prestigious, and too little attention given to the regular Valtellina bottlings. See DRIED GRAPE WINES for more details.

D.T. & D.C.G.

value brands, wine category that emerged in California in the early 2000s as consumer buying of skilfully marketed inexpensive wines became not cheap but clever. The best known representative of this new category was a Franzia product labelled Charles Shaw and priced in some outlets at $1.99, colloquially called 'Two Buck Chuck' by its legion of American fans.

Vandyke Price, Pamela (1923–). The first woman to write seriously about wine in Britain did more than most to popularize wines after the Second World War. Author of about 30 books on food and wine, she is probably most distinguished as a performer, however, having trained initially as an actress.

Vandyke Price, P., *Woman of Taste* (London, 1990).

vanillin, phenolic ALDEHYDE found in grapes and a component of the lignin structure of OAK wood; responsible for the vanilla note in wines. It is especially extracted from barrel wood. If new oak casks are used for wine maturation, this vanillin adds complexity to the flavour (see OAK FLAVOUR).

varietal, descriptive term for a wine named after the dominant grape variety from which it is made. The word is increasingly misused in place of VINE VARIETY. A varietal wine is distinct from a wine named after its own geographical provenance (as the great majority of European wines are), and a GENERIC wine, one named after a supposed style, often haphazardly borrowed from European geography, such as 'Chablis' and 'Burgundy'. Varietal wines are most closely associated with the NEW WORLD, where they constitute the great majority of wines produced. The concept was nurtured by Maynard AMERINE at the University of California at DAVIS in the wake of PROHIBITION as a means of encouraging growers to plant worthy vine varieties. It was advocated with particular enthusiasm by Frank SCHOONMAKER in the 1950s and 1960s, and was embraced during the CALIFORNIA wine boom of the 1970s to distinguish the more ambitious wines, often made from Cabernet Sauvignon and, increasingly, Chardonnay, from the lack-lustre generics of old. Varietal labelling was also adopted, for a similar purpose, in AUSTRALIA, SOUTH AFRICA, NEW ZEALAND, and elsewhere.

Originally, when the United States' acreage of classic vine varieties was relatively limited, a varietal needed only 51 per cent of that variety in the blend to be so labelled. In 1973, this requirement was increased to 75 per cent (although some particularly strongly flavoured NEW YORK state vine varieties were exempted from this increased requirement; see FOXY). Despite the emergence of the MERITAGE category of superior blends, varietal wines continue to be viewed by many as California's premier statement of quality. See also LABELLING INFORMATION.

The French INAO authorities are hostile towards varietal labelling, understanding that they have nothing to gain and much to lose by entering into this commonwealth of nomenclature. Within France, varietal wines (typically VIN DE PAYS) are called *vins de cépage*, and are widely regarded as of lower rank than APPELLATION CONTRÔLÉE wines. INAO stated in the early 1990s that its eventual aim was to eradicate grape varieties from the names and labels of all appellation contrôlée wines, possibly even those of ALSACE and certainly such familiar combinations of grape and geography as Sauvignon de TOURAINE. This has not prevented even quite eminent producers in BURGUNDY from printing 'Pinot Noir' and 'Chardonnay' on their export labels in addition to the geographical name of the appellation.

In their 1990s attempts to reformulate the DOC system and wine-quality categories, the Italian authorities were equally keen to emphasize their uniqueness, place, over grape variety. Such attitudes are understandable and, in the long term, may pay dividends, but there is little doubt that an important factor in the success of many New World wines has been the ease with which consumers can grasp the concept of varietal labelling. In the 1980s, Chardonnay and Cabernet Sauvignon became the most recognizable names in the world of wine.

Most varietal wines are based on a single vine variety but examples made up of a blend of two or even three different varieties have become increasingly common, especially when there is a shortage of certain popular varieties. Common varietal blends are Semillon/Chardonnay (possibly stretched with some Colombard or Chenin Blanc) and Sauvignon/Semillon among white wines and Cabernet/Merlot, Cabernet/Shiraz, Syrah/Merlot, and Grenache/Shiraz/Mourvèdre. It is usual to list the varieties on the label in declining order of importance in the blend.

For more details, see VINE VARIETIES.

variety of vine or grape. See VINE VARIETIES.

Varois, Coteaux, enclave within the Côtes de PROVENCE appellation which takes its name from the Var *département*. The wine achieved AC status in 1993 and by the mid 2000s, 1,900 ha/2,200 acres of vines were producing vast quantities of rosé, while one-third of production was red wine, some of it potentially exciting, and there was a little extremely varied white. The wooded hills around Brignoles are based on LIMESTONE and are so buffered from warming MARITIME influence by the hills of Ste-Baume that vines will not ripen at all reliably at altitudes of more than about 350 m/1,100 ft.

Reds and rosés may incorporate an almost dazzling array of varieties: Grenache, Syrah, Cinsaut, Mourvèdre (which will ripen only in the warmest sites), Cabernet Sauvignon,

Carignan (limited to half of any one parcel of vines), and the ancient Provençal variety Tibouren. This gives the better producers an exciting palette from which to work; some of them produce several different blends which vary in style by virtue of both varietal mix and ÉLEVAGE. For white wines, Grenache Blanc is added to those varieties permitted for Côtes de Provence Blanc (see PROVENCE), although Rolle is increasingly appreciated. Chx La Calisse and Routas and Domaine du Deffends are dependable exporters.

Varro, Marcus Terentius (116–27 BC)

was a prolific Roman writer who wrote on subjects as diverse as grammar, geography, history, law, science, philosophy, and education; the rhetorician Quintilian called him 'the most learned man among the Romans' (*Institutio oratoria* 10. 1. 95). Yet the only one of his works to survive in its entirety is his manual of agriculture, *De re rustica*. Varro started it in his 80th year and addressed it to his wife, who had bought a farm. Varro was a man of letters, and, unlike CATO's treatise, from which he borrows occasionally, his own is a literary exercise, written in a highly wrought style. *De re rustica* is full of antiquarian learning as well as practical advice, and Varro often looks back to the time when the inhabitants of Italy were all hard-working honest farmers and there was none of the decadence that prevails among the city dwellers of his day. The treatise is divided into three books, each of which is a dialogue; most of the material on wine comes in the first book. He defines old wine as at least a year old; some wine goes off before that, but some, like FALERNIAN, becomes the more valuable the longer it is kept. Varro's work was used by later writers such as VIRGIL, PLINY, COLUMELLA, and PALLADIUS. Varro's own chief authority, by his own admission, is Mago of CARTHAGE, about whom nothing is known and of whose work nothing survives. Among the many Greek authors he mentions as his sources are Aristotle, Xenophon, and Theophrastus. H.M.W.

Skydsgaard, J. E., *Varro the Scholar* (Copenhagen, 1968).

vase painting.

Vases in Ancient GREECE from 600 to 300 BC are an important source of information about the SYMPOSIUM, the VINTAGE, and VITICULTURE generally.

vat,

large CONTAINER for STORING wine and/or AGEING or maturation. A vat may also be used as a FERMENTATION VESSEL. In English-speaking countries they may also be known as tanks; in France they are called CUVES.

For many centuries, WOOD was the most common material but in the mid to late 20th century inert materials such as cement, enamel, epoxy resin, and STAINLESS STEEL replaced wood except in particularly traditional or traditionalist areas. At the start of the 21st century, wooden fermentation vats are once again becoming more fashionable though they are very expensive.

For details of wine maturation in wooden vats, see CASK AGEING.

vat size

varies enormously. FERMENTATION VESSELS in large commercial wineries contain, typically, between 50 and 300 hl, although smaller enterprises may use much smaller wooden vats. The ratio of height to width has implications for red wine-making in determining the area of the CAP. Blending tanks may contain several thousand hl: 15,000 hl/ 396,000 gal in the case of Lindemans' Karadoc winery in Australia. Grupo Peñaflor, Argentina's largest wine company, boasts the largest wine vat in the world, with a capacity of about 50,000 hl—large enough to hold a dinner party for several hundred inside, though it is no longer used in wine-making.

Vavřinecke,

former Czech name for the red ST-LAURENT grape. See SVATOVAVŘINECKÉ.

VCIG,

Spanish wine denomination proposed in 2005 for Vinos de Calidad con Indicación Geográfica for wines better than VINO DE LA TIERRA but below DO level. It was used for the first time by the Castilla y León regional government for such regions as Benavente, ARRIBES, LEÓN, Tierra del Vino, and Arlanza.

VDN

is sometimes used as an abbreviation for VIN DOUX NATUREL.

VDP,

or the Verband Deutscher Prädikatsweingüter, the most influential and prestigious German growers' association, incorporating 200 of the finest wine estates in GERMANY. In 1910, just two years after consolidating the top MOSEL-SAAR-RUWER estates into the GROSSER RING, the mayor of Trier persuaded likeminded organizations in the RHEINGAU and PFALZ to band together to form a national association for the purpose of selling its members' wines at AUCTION. Over the years, other regional groups joined the VDP and by the late 1990s its membership included estates in all 13 wine-growing regions. Although its collective holdings account for a mere 3.5 per cent of Germany's total vineyard area, this group produces a remarkable proportion of its finest wines.

In their effort to preserve German wine culture, the national and regional branches of the VDP still maintain their tradition of wine auctions, although auction prices today, prestige notwithstanding, have little bearing on market prices. The VDP's contribution to the image of fine and rare German wines is based on its members' uncompromising dedication to high quality, starting with stringent, self-imposed regulations. These stipulate that members must have holdings in the top vineyard sites; produce lower YIELDS and higher MUST WEIGHTS than required by the GERMAN

WINE LAW; plant at least 80 per cent of their vineyards with varieties traditionally associated with their regions; practise environmentally sound methods; be established as fulltime growers of sound reputation; and submit to regular (at least every five years) VDP compliance inspections. Members' labels and capsules carry the VDP name and logo, an eagle and grape cluster. See also GROSSES GEWÄCHS.

VDQS

stands for **Vin Délimité de Qualité Supérieure**, France's minuscule interim wine quality designation between VIN DE PAYS and APPELLATION CONTRÔLÉE, which accounts for well under 1 per cent of the nation's wine production. The VDQS category (also known as AO-VDQS) is very much a testing ground for smaller wine regions, many of which are eventually promoted to full AC status. Some VDQS date from the early 1950s; none was created between 1984 and 1994, when Côtes de MILLAU was created from Vin de Pays des Gorges et Côtes de Millau. There is a relatively high concentration of VDQS designations on the fringes of the LOIRE, and of SOUTH WEST FRANCE. The VDQS system is overseen by the AC authorities, INAO, and the regulations governing the more recently granted VDQS wines are every bit as strict as AC rules. The VDQS category will be scrapped after the 2010 vintage.

Vega Sicilia,

concentrated and long-lived red wine that is Spain's undisputed equivalent of a FIRST GROWTH, made on a single property now incorporated into the RIBERA DEL DUERO denomination. The wine was being made long before the present DO region took shape in the 1980s. This 1,000-ha/2,500-acre farm either side of the main road east of Valladolid has been making wine in its present form since 1864 when Eloy Lacanda y Chaves planted vines from Bordeaux alongside Tinto Fino, also known as Tinta del País (a local strain of TEMPRANILLO). The current style was defined around 1910, when the winery was leased by Cosme Palacio, a Rioja grower. A succession of different owners has since managed to maintain the quality and reputation of Vega Sicilia as Spain's finest red wine. However, Vega Sicilia fell on lean times at several junctures, and was able to make a substantial leap in quality and, more importantly, in consistency after being bought by the Alvarez family in 1982.

The more than 200 ha/500 acres of vineyard on LIMESTONE soils overlooking the river Duero (DOURO in Portugal) are planted mainly with Tinto Fino but CABERNET SAUVIGNON, MERLOT, and a little MALBEC together make up about 20 per cent of the total production. A tiny quantity of old-vine white ALBILLO remains.

Bodegas Vega Sicilia produces three wines, all red. Valbuena is a five-year old VINTAGE-dated wine aged in American oak. Vega Sicilia Unico, which is restricted to the best VINTAGES and is often released after spending about ten years in a combination of wooden tanks, small, new BARRIQUES, large, old barrels and bottles, attracts the most attention. Vega Sicilia can hardly be described as an exuberant wine and, perhaps because of its high price, the Unico occasionally attracts criticism. It is, however, an extraordinarily compact yet powerful, persistent wine with a restrained yet complex character that is uncommon in most of Spain. The best vintages of Vega Sicilia Unico and the third wine produced here, the rare multi-vintage Reserva Especial, last for decades.

In 1991, Bodegas Vega Sicilia acquired the nearby Liceo winery and created the immediately acclaimed Bodegas Alión, which makes much more modern reds from 100 per cent Tempranillo grapes, aged in new French oak. In 2001, Pintia, Vega Sicilia's bodega in the TORO region, produced its first vintage.

R.J.M. & V. de la S.

Peñín, J., *Vega Sicilia—Journey to the Heart of a Legend* (Madrid, 2002).

vegetarian and vegan wines are increasingly requested by consumers. The main area of concern is the use of animal-based products for FINING and STABILIZING wine. Of the five most common agents, only BENTONITE is suitable for vegans as well as vegetarians; CASEIN and albumin (see EGG WHITES) are acceptable to most vegetarians; ISINGLASS and GELATIN would be unacceptable to most vegetarians and vegans. Although such materials are processing aids rather than additives, it is impossible to guarantee that there is absolutely no residue in the wine and some wine drinkers may object to the actual use of an animal-derived product. Some winemakers and retailers have started to make this information available on the bottle or at the point of sale. See also LABELLING INFORMATION.

vegetative propagation, reproduction of a plant by asexual means. In viticulture, CUTTINGS on which both roots and shoots will grow are used. In those limited locations where PHYLLOXERA and other root pests are not present and ROOTSTOCKS are not used, LAYERING can be used to replace missing vines. Micropropagation (see TISSUE CULTURE) is a modern application in which small amounts of a MOTHER VINE may be propagated in large numbers rapidly. Unlike SEXUAL PROPAGATION, the progeny of vegetative propagation is genetically identical, unless MUTATION intervenes.

B.G.C.

vein banding, vine disease. See FANLEAF DEGENERATION.

Veltliner, Valtlin Zelene, Veltlinske Zelené, Veltini, common eastern European names for the four distinct Austrian grape varieties supposedly originating from VALTELLINA in Lombardia (northern Italy): GRÜNER VELT-LINER, ROTER VELTLINER, FRÜHROTER VELTLINER, and occasionally Brauner Veltliner.

J.V.

vendange, French word for HARVEST. A *vendangeur* is a grape-picker, and a temporary lodging for grape-pickers may be called a *vendangeoir*.

Vendange Tardive, means literally 'late harvest' and in France is restricted to ALSACE, where strict regulations cover its production, even if too many producers are meeting only the bare minima. Although all Alsace Vendange Tardive wines are made from ripe grapes, and without the aid of CHAPTALIZATION, the wines themselves vary considerably in how sweet they are, with some of them tasting rich but almost bone dry. Labels give no clue as to how sweet these wines taste, making FOOD AND WINE MATCHING particularly difficult. SÉLECTION DE GRAINS NOBLES is Alsace's even riper category. See also AUSLESE and BEERENAUSLESE, their counterparts in Germany, and LUXEMBOURG.

vendange verte, see CROP THINNING.

vendemmia, Italian for VINTAGE year or HARVEST. **Vendimia** is Spanish for harvest.

Vendômois, Coteaux du, appellation (since 2001) producing a wide range of wines between the Coteaux du LOIR and the city of Vendôme. The wines are necessarily light and crisp, this far from the equator, but a pale pink VIN GRIS from the PINEAU D'AUNIS grape can be an attractive local speciality. Slightly more solid reds may be made from Pinot Noir, Gamay, or either Cabernet, and Chenin Blanc is the principal grape, nowadays often aided and abetted by Chardonnay, for some particularly tart white wines which represent about one bottle in six.

See also LOIRE, including map.

Veneto, historically and currently very important wine region in north east ITALY (see map under ITALY). It stretches westward to lake Garda and northward to the Alps and the Austrian border from the terra firma behind the lagoons and city of VENICE, an important power in the wine trade of the Middle Ages whose legacy has shaped some wines in Veneto and elsewhere. Since the mid 1990s, Veneto has overtaken Puglia and Sicilia to become Italy's largest wine-producing region with production of more than 9.2 million hl/230 million gal in 2004. As production in the south of Italy has fallen, that in Veneto has increased. A large part of this increase is due to success of Pinot Grigio, though the entrepreneurial spirit of the producers and the CO-OPERATIVES has also played a role.

In theory, a significant proportion of Veneto wine is of good quality, with DOC wine representing well over a quarter of the total. The reality is somewhat different. This proportion has been artificially inflated both by drastic enlargements of the DOC zones (to plains which were cereal-growing areas prior to the Second World War in the case of Valpolicella and Soave) and/or by sanctioning extremely generous YIELDS (in the case of Valpolicella, Soave, Bardolino, and Prosecco). The resulting wines, though nominally of DOC level, are too frequently characterless. Good bottles of Bardolino, Valpolicella, and Soave are not difficult to find, however, and the CORVINA vine variety which forms the basis of Valpolicella, and GARGANEGA, the base of Soave, are capable of making interesting wines if grown in the proper area: the hills on the 45 degrees 30 minutes of LATITUDE which run eastward from lake Garda, to the north of the fertile Adige river plain. Other HILLSIDE zones of real potential are scattered about the region and include the Colli Berici to the south and Breganze to the north of Vicenza, the Colli Euganei to the south west of Padua, the hillside part of the Piave DOC zone. Native varieties such as Tocai, Garganega, and Verduzzo, are cultivated in these zones, as are imports such as Merlot and Cabernet (brought to the area in the wake of the Napoleonic invasion in the early part of the 19th century). The Garganega-based Bianco di Custoza and Gambellara, two country cousins of Soave, the lightly sparkling Prosecco of Conegliano, and the Moscato of the Colli Euganei (no rival to MOSCATO D'ASTI but with the true, grapey character) round out the regional picture, a picture characterized by large quantities of pleasant and easy drinking wines which seem to suffer from a lack of ambition and competitive spirit. Veneto's centre of ACADEME is the experimental viticultural institute at CONEGLIANO.

For details of notable specific wines, see AMARONE, BARDOLINO, BIANCO DI CUSTOZA, BREGANZE, GAMBELLARA, LISON-PRAMAGGIORE, PIAVE, PROSECCO, RABOSO, RECIOTO, SOAVE, and VALPOLICELLA.

D.T. & D.C.G.

Bastianich, J., and Lynch, D., *Vino Italiano: The Regional Wines of Italy* (New York, 2002).

Belfrage, N., *From Barolo to Valpolicella: The Wines of Northern Italy* (London, 1999).

Venezuela is a minor South American wine producer, and consumer, but TROPICAL VITICULTURE has been practised, mainly for TABLE GRAPES, since the arrival of European immigrants at the end of the 19th century—although there is evidence that Jesuit MISSIONARIES first planted vines at Cumana in the 16th century, and vine-growers emigrated here from Baden in the early 19th century; see GERMAN HISTORY. According to OIV statistics, there were only about 1,000 ha/2,500 acres of vines in the early 21st century and a thriving DRIED GRAPE industry. Producers have tended to use GRAPE CONCENTRATE as their raw material for products that range from LAMBRUSCO-like blends to base wines for SANGRÍA. Average temperatures are about 27 °C, vine DORMANCY is impossible, and the two harvests per year are dictated by the rainy seasons. One of the most viticulturally suitable regions is Mérida in Lagunillas, where at altitudes of about 1,100 m/3,600 ft the climate is cooler than elsewhere and annual total rainfall (unevenly spread) is between 300 and 400 mm. Vines are also grown in Barquistimeto and in even drier areas to the north. Most of the vine varieties grown are table grapes, HYBRIDS such as Jacquez and ISABELLA, and a relative of CRIOLLA. A little GRILLO, BARBERA, and MALVASIA are also grown, however.

Venice, north east Italian cultural and, once, commercial centre which was to exert considerable and sometimes lasting influence on the wines of the world. Medieval Venice had no agriculture or viticulture and obtained its wine and grain from LOMBARDIA to the west; Venice's importance was in its trade. In 840 a treaty, known as the Pactum Lotharii, between CHARLEMAGNE's grandson Lothair and the doge of Venice, protected Venice's neutrality and guaranteed its security from the mainland. This treaty made Venice independent from the west and from Byzantium. Thus Venice became the most important of the Italo-Byzantine ports, and its position was strengthened when the Byzantines discovered that Venice's rivals Amalfi, NAPLES, and Gaeta had been collaborating with the Saracens. Initially Venice owed its wealth to its trade, acquiring possession of Crete, Modon, and Coron in the Aegean and being granted exemptions from the TAXATION in Constantinople that was to ruin the Byzantine economy (see GREECE, medieval history). The CRUSADES only strengthened Venice's position at the frontier between northern Europe and the eastern Mediterranean.

With its eastern expansion came the trade in sweet wines, so much more esteemed by northern Europeans than their own thinner FERMENTS. Most of these were from Crete, known then as Candia. Many of them carried the name of the Greek port from which they were shipped, Monemvasia (hence MALVASIA di Candia, and MALMSEY). Some of these wines were sold in Constantinople, others were taken to Venice for redistribution, either overland to Florence (via Ferrara), or by sea to Paris, England, and Flanders. In addition to buying and selling Aegean wines, Venice also dealt in Italian wines, from Trevi, the northern Adriatic, and the MARCHE, and in the even richer wines of Tyre (in modern LEBANON), which was owned by the Venetians for most of the 13th century.

However, in trade with Syria and Palestine, Venice came second to GENOA, and the rivalry extended to the trade with northern Europe: Genoa led the way there, and Venice, which was less well placed, did not start shipping wine to northern Europe until the early 14th century. By that time Genoa had already won the bat-

tle: at the end of the 13th century, Venice had ceased to be the richest and most important port in Italy, but not before having imported the Greek techniques of increasing sugar and alcohol content by deliberately making DRIED GRAPE WINES. Johnson suggests a direct link between such practices, employed on the islands along the Dalmatian coast, and those subsequently, indeed currently, used by some in the VENETO hinterland of Venice to make PASSITO versions of Valpolicella and Soave.

Venice was also to become the centre of GLASS production, and therefore played an important, if indirect, role in the history of wine.

See also ITALY. H.M.W.

Johnson, H., *The Story of Wine* (London, 1989).

Lopez, R. S., 'The trade of mediaeval Europe: the south', in *The Cambridge Economic History of Europe*, 7 vols., ii: *Trade and Industry in the Middle Ages* (Cambridge, 1987).

Melis, F., 'Produzione e commercio dei vini italiani nei secoli XIII–XVIII', *Annales cisalpines d'histoire sociale*, 1/3 (1972), 107–33.

Nicol, D. M., *Byzantium and Venice* (Cambridge, 1988).

Ventoux, Côtes du, large and growing appellation on the south eastern fringes of the southern RHÔNE between the Coteaux du TRICASTIN and the Côtes du LUBERON. The 7,700-ha/19,000-acre appellation, renamed Ventoux in 2008, takes its name from Mont Ventoux, the 2,000-m/6,500-ft high peak which dominates the region. The communes entitled to the appellation are on the western and southern flanks of this land mass, which has a significant cooling effect on the southern Rhône's generally MEDITERRANEAN CLIMATE. Historically this has been an area for producing TABLE GRAPES (along with other tree fruits such as cherries).

The predominantly red and rosé wines are made mainly from a blend of Grenache, Syrah, Cinsaut, and Carignan—very similar to those of Tricastin, except that the maximum permitted proportion of Carignan is 30 per cent in Ventoux, twice as much as in Tricastin. Ventoux is even more dominated by the CO-OPERATIVES than Tricastin, and the wines can taste even lighter than those of Tricastin. Since the 1990s, however, a number of ambitious, distinctly superior producers emerged, notably Domaines de Fondrèche and Le Murmurium and Chx Pesquié and Valcombe. Clairette, Bourboulenc, and Grenache Blanc are the principal varieties for the small quantities of white produced.

Livingstone-Learmonth, J., *The Wines of the Rhône* (3rd edn, London, 1992).

Parker, R., *Wines of the Rhône Valley* (2nd edn, New York, 1997).

veraison, word used by English speakers for that intermediate stage of grape berry development which marks the beginning of RIPENING, when the grapes change from the hard, green state to their softened and col-

oured form. It is derived from the French term *véraison*. At the beginning of veraison, the berries are hard and green, and about half their final size. During veraison, the berries change skin colour and soften, SUGARS and volume increase, and ACIDITY decreases. The colour of the grape before veraison is due to green chlorophyll, and at veraison berry skin changes colour to red-black (see ANTHOCYANINS) or yellow-green (see CAROTENOIDS), depending on the variety.

For any one berry, the inception of veraison is rapid and dramatic. The berries soften and begin to accumulate GLUCOSE and FRUCTOSE, and begin to grow about six days later. However, not all berries on a vine, nor indeed in a bunch, show veraison simultaneously. The first berries to soften are those which are exposed and in warmer MICROCLIMATES (near a stake, post, or wall, for example, and benefiting from nocturnal reradiation from the soil); the last berries to undergo veraison are those in the CANOPY shade and on short shoots. It is difficult therefore to be precise about the single date of veraison; more commonly a date is recorded when, say, 50 per cent of the berries on a vine show veraison. At about the same time as veraison occurs, CANE RIPENING begins.

The onset of veraison (and cane ripening) is controlled by both plant and environmental factors. Exposed grapes on vines which have a high LEAF TO FRUIT RATIO and which are experiencing mild WATER STRESS (and hence no active shoot growth) undergo veraison first. By contrast, veraison is delayed in vines with large crops, with many actively growing shoot tips and shaded fruit. Veraison is observably early in vineyards producing high-quality fruit, with both veraison and cane ripening developing quickly. Environmental factors associated with the early onset of veraison are warm, sunny, and dry weather. R.E.S. & B.G.C.

See also ENGUSTMENT.

Champagnol, F., *Éléments de physiologie de la vigne et de viticulture générale* (St-Gely-du-Fesc, 1984).

Huglin, P., *Biologie et écologie de la vigne* (Paris, 1986).

Vérargues, or **Coteaux de Vérargues**, one of the named CRUS within the Coteaux du LANGUEDOC appellation in southern France. The zone overlaps substantially with that of MUSCAT DE LUNEL east of Montpellier and is immediately south of ST-CHRISTOL.

Verdea, light-berried vine speciality of the Colli Piacentini in north central Italy.

Verdeca, Puglia's most popular light-berried vine producing neutral wine suitable for the VERMOUTH industry and declining in popularity. DNA PROFILING at SAN MICHELE ALL'ADIGE suggests a parent–offspring relationship with the widespread Dalmatian variety PLAVINA crna, interestingly indicating an ancient viticultural bridge across the Adriatic sea. J.V.

Verdejo, characterful grape grown on a total of 6,000 ha/15,000 acres of Spanish vineyard in 2004 with a distinctive blue-green bloom that is the Spanish RUEDA region's pride and joy (and has staved off a challenge for primacy from imported SAUVIGNON BLANC, with which it is often blended). DNA PROFILING at Madrid showed it is a synonym of PLANTA FINA from Valencia in southern Spain, but although the vine looks quite similar to the VERDELHO of Madeira and the Azores, their DNAs are distinct. Wines produced are aromatic, herbaceous (somewhat reminiscent of laurel), but with great substance and extract, capable of ageing well into an almost nutty character.

Verdelho, name once given to several Portuguese white grape varieties, and most closely associated with the island of MADEIRA, where the Verdelho vine became increasingly rare in the post-PHYLLOXERA era but the name was for long used to denote a style of wine somewhere between SERCIAL- and BUAL-levels of richness. The relatively few Verdelho vines on Madeira produce musts with moderate levels of sugar and high acidity. The Verdelho found on Madeira is the same as that found growing in the Azores and this Verdelho, cuttings of which were presumably picked up on one of these Atlantic islands en route to the antipodes, was extremely important in 19th-century Australia. It has had notable success in vibrant, tangy, full-bodied table wines in more recent times, particularly in the Hunter valley of New South Wales, Victoria, and some of the hotter regions of Western Australia. See AUSTRALIA for more details.

A quite distinct variety once called Verdelho, but now officially renamed GOUVEIO, is planted on the Portuguese mainland, particularly in the Alentejo, Dão, and Douro. There is also a rare red Verdelho, **Verdelho Tinto,** grown today in Portugal and sometimes known as **Verdelho Feijão.**

Verdello, white grape variety known both in UMBRIA, where it was once prized for its ACIDITY but is now rapidly losing ground, and SICILIA.

Verdesse, minor white grape of BUGEY in eastern France whose wine can be powerful and highly aromatic.

Verdicchio, one of central Italy's classic white wines, is produced from the Verdicchio grape in two DOC zones of its home territory (since at least the 14th century) of the MARCHE: Verdicchio dei Castelli di Jesi, to the west of Ancona and a mere 30 km/20 miles from the Adriatic sea, and Verdicchio di Matelica, considerably further inland and at higher altitudes, close to the regional border with UMBRIA. The wines share common characteristics, although the Verdicchio di Matelica,

with lower yields (13 tonnes/ha against the 14 tonnes permitted for Verdicchio dei Castelli di Jesi) and better exposed HILLSIDE VINEYARDS, can be a fuller, more characterful wine. Matelica's 300-odd ha (750 acres) are dwarfed, however, by the more than 3,150 ha of the Castelli di Jesi. This latter DOC is divided into a CLASSICO zone, with over 90 per cent of the total vineyard area, and a zone of regular Verdicchio dei Castelli di Jesi with a mere 270 ha. Close to 60 per cent of the production of the Castelli di Jesi DOC is controlled by CO-OPERATIVES, and NÉGOCIANT houses control three-quarters of the remaining 40 per cent; small producers are of marginal significance both in terms of volume and in their impact on the market.

The wine's fame was largely due to the efforts of Fazi-Battaglia, a large négociant firm with extensive vineyard holdings, which pioneered the large-scale marketing of Verdicchio and still controls over 20 per cent of the total production. It was Fazi-Battaglia which introduced the amphora-shaped bottle and scroll-shaped label, initially a positive factor in gaining recognition for the wine but later responsible for the image of kitsch and frivolity with which Verdicchio has been saddled.

Like many central Italian white wines, Verdicchio was once fermented on its skins, giving it a certain fullness and authority albeit often at the expense of any delicacy. The GOVERNO technique, whereby a second fermentation is induced by the addition of the must from dried grapes after the conclusion of the initial fermentation, was also employed to add a contrasting sweetness and an enlivening dash of CARBON DIOXIDE to the wine. These practices have been largely abandoned and Verdicchio is now made in a modern style, without SKIN CONTACT and with temperature-controlled fermentations. It is now a more 'correct', if perhaps less distinctive, wine, although the lemony acidity and the bitter almonds of the aftertaste are still identifiably present in better bottles. A notable improvement in quality in the two DOC zones in the 1990s modified opinions of the grape's potential. As yields decreased, EXTRACT increased and ACIDITY, while remaining high, is balanced by a relatively high PH giving the wines more roundness. As the vines—currently trained quite high with very wide spacing—are planted to more ambitious designs, Verdicchio is expected to become one of central Italy's most interesting wines.

The Verdicchio grape is also present in northern Italy, where it is known as Trebbiano di Soave, the superior variety that adds perfume to the steely Garganega in Soave. Further to the west, it is known as the Trebbiano di Lugana, where it is grown on its own in a warmer zone to give full-bodied wines of real interest.

Perhaps partly because of its high natural acidity, Verdicchio was one of the first Italian SPUMANTES, with a tradition which can be

traced back to the middle of the 19th century, and pleasant bottles of bubbly Verdicchio remain an integral part of the DOC production. Total Verdicchio plantings were nearly 4,000 ha/9,900 acres in the early 1990s.

D.T. & D.C.G.

Verdiso, lively light-skinned grape speciality of Treviso in north east Italy.

Verdoncho, undistinguished La Mancha white grape.

Verdot. See PETIT VERDOT for details of both this and Gros Verdot.

Verduzzo, white grape variety with a long documented history in north east Italy. It is cultivated principally in FRIULI (with the significant exception of the PIAVE DOC in the bordering province of Treviso in Veneto) in six different DOC zones: AQUILEIA, COLLI ORIENTALI, GRAVE, ISONZO, LATISANA, and LISON-PRAMAGGIORE. Only the Grave and the Colli Orientali produce significant quantities—respectively 15,700 hl (424,500 gal) and 5,000 hl (132,000 gal) annually—and the Verduzzo of the Colli Orientali is qualitatively far superior, the grape showing a decided preference for HILLSIDE VINEYARDS. The wine exists both in a dry and a sweet version, although the latter, obtained either by late harvesting or by raisining the grapes (see DRIED GRAPE WINES), can frequently be more medium dry than lusciously sweet. Sweet Verduzzo, although less common than dry Verduzzo, is the more interesting wine, golden in colour and often with a delightful density and honeyed aromas, even if it lacks the complexity of an outstanding dessert wine. Dry Verduzzo is less characterful, and the grapes' TANNINS often impart an odd astringency which is more noticeable when it has been fermented dry.

Ramandolo, to the north of Udine, is considered the classic zone for fine sweet Verduzzo, but the Colli Orientali di Friuli DOC, when first established, permitted the use of the name Ramandolo for any sweet Verduzzo in the production zone, converting, as it were, a place-name into a generic name. This anomaly was recently corrected with the establishment of a separate Ramandolo DOC. Occasional bottles of Verduzzo from the Collio production zone can also be found that are superior to the Verduzzo of the Grave DOC if not as good as the Colli Orientali Verduzzo. They qualify only as a VINO DA TAVOLA, however.

Italy's 1990 vineyard survey found 2,600 ha/6,400 acres of the much less characterful Verduzzo Trevigiano vines and 1,800 ha of Verduzzo Friulano.

D.T.

verjus, or **verjuice,** the tart, apple-flavoured juice of unripe grapes, has many variations and many culinary uses, especially in dressings and sauces. It adds ACIDITY to a dish but unlike vinegar does not clash with wine. Traditional in many countries of the world, it is made from underripe grapes cut during CROP THINNING or from second crop berries that are unripe at harvest. One method is to press the grapes then preserve the partially fermented but highly VOLATILE juice with salt. Alternatively, the grapes may be boiled before pressing to kill the yeast and prevent fermentation but must then be used immediately or frozen. Most commercial producers gently press the grapes, cold settle and filter the juice before packaging, in which case STERILE BOTTLING is essential to prevent the verjus from fermenting.

Vermentino, attractive, aromatic white grape variety widely grown in Sardegna, Liguria, to a limited extent in Corsica, and to an increasing extent in Languedoc and Roussillon, where it is a recently permitted variety in many appellations, including white Côtes du Roussillon. DNA PROFILING showed it is identical to the Ligurian PIGATO and the Piedmont variety FAVORITA. It is also thought by most, but not all, authorities to be identical to the variety long grown in eastern Provence as ROLLE and sometimes called Rollo in north western Italy. In CORSICA it is sometimes called Malvoisie de Corse, and some believe that the variety is related to the MALVASIA family. Vermentino is Corsica's most planted white grape variety and dominates the island's white APPELLATION CONTRÔLÉE wines. In Sardegna, it is picked deliberately early to retain acid levels but still manages to produce lively wines of character, although attempts at a richer, fuller style have also emerged, notably from Capichera in the **Vermentino di Gallura** DOCG, created in 1996. The interest in indigenous white grape varieties has been a boon for those growers along the Tuscan coast who had either the foresight or good fortune to plant Vermentino, for prices in the 2005 vintage were very high, with demand far outstripping supply.

Italy has nearly 4,000 ha/10,000 acres of Vermentino vines while France had more than 2,600 ha in 2000, mainly on Corsica.

vermouth, herb-flavoured FORTIFIED wine available in many different styles and qualities but usually a much more industrial product than wine. The Romans certainly made herb-flavoured wines, and the Greeks before them used a wide range of additives (see Ancient GREECE), often using wormwood or *artemesia absinthum*, which was thought to have curative powers for gastric ills. Such FLAVOURED WINES were strictly of local minority interest until the 16th century when a Piemontese, d'Alessio, began to market a medicinal wine similar to those he had noted in Bavaria flavoured with wormwood, there called *Wermuth*. The medicine, which enjoyed a certain success in French

royal circles, subsequently became known as *vermutwein* and, in Anglicized form, vermouth. The diarist Samuel Pepys noted 'a glass of wormwood wine' without the comment it would have elicited had it been anything other than commonplace in late 17th century London. Modern large-scale vermouth production dates from 18th-century Piemonte, close to the alps which could supply the necessary herbs. Brands such as Cinzano, Martini, and the French NOILLY PRAT threw off any pretence at curative powers during the cocktail age and were particularly popular in the early and mid 20th century.

So many herbs and spices are now used to flavour fortified wines that the definition of vermouth is necessarily elastic. The more classic version is the almost dry, bitter drink with the strong aroma of wormwood and other bitter herbs. The Italian Punt e Mes is one of the better-known examples. But the more popular version by far is sweeter, about 17 per cent alcohol, and more vaguely herbal. Such vermouths are traditionally known as Italian if red and sweet and French if gold and drier, although these styles are made wherever vermouth is produced. France's most delicately alpine vermouth is CHAMBÉRY, while the vermouth most closely linked to fine wine is Lillet of Bordeaux, for long owned by the Borie family of the ST-JULIEN property Ch Ducru-Beaucaillou.

The vermouth industry has never sought fine wine as its base and is a useful outlet for some of the European WINE LAKE, absorbing millions of litres of basic table wine from the south of Italy and France. The alcohol used for FORTIFICATION comes from much the same source. Traditionally vermouths were flavoured by infusion of 'botanicals', herbs, peels, and spices gathered from the wild. Modern vermouth is more likely to be flavoured by the addition of a concentrate designed for consistency to match an imagined ideal blend of botanicals. After sweetening, usually with MISTELLE, and fortification, most modern vermouth is chilled for tartrate STABILIZATION and subjected to PASTEURIZATION and FILTRATION.

Vernaccia, name used for several, unrelated Italian grape varieties, mainly white but sometimes red, from the extreme north of the peninsula (VERNATSCH being merely a Germanic version of Vernaccia) to the fizzy red **Vernaccia di Serrapetrona** of the MARCHE and the **Vernaccia di Oristano**, which is an almost SHERRY-like wine made on the island of SARDEGNA. The most highly regarded form is VERNACCIA DI SAN GIMIGNANO, which has no relationship to the Sardinian **Vernaccia di Cagliari** vine, according to the studies of Professor Liuzzi of Cagliari in the early 1930s.

The name is so common because it comes from the same root as the word 'vernacular', or indigenous. Wines called Vernaccia, or sometimes **vernage**, are often cited in the records of

London wine merchants in the Middle Ages, but the term could have been used for virtually any sort of wine, Latin being the common language then. Vernaccia was a particularly common product of LIGURIA in north west Italy and Toscana. For more details of medieval trade in Vernaccia, see GENOA, ITALY, and TOSCANA.

Vernaccia di San Gimignano, distinctive dry white wine made from the local VERNACCIA vine variety, probably unrelated to any other Vernaccia, cultivated in the sandstone-based soils around the famous towers of San Gimignano in the province of Siena in TOSCANA in central Italy. There are references to Vernaccia in the archives of San Gimignano as early as 1276. The wine was elevated to DOCG status in 1993.

DOC recognition had been awarded in March of 1966, making Vernaccia di San Gimignano the first ever DOC, which saved the wine from what seemed a fatal decline: the Dalmasso Commission of 1932 had described the wine as a curiosity and the wine became even rarer after the Second World War when so much TREBBIANO and MALVASIA were planted in the zone. Since the late 1960s, the wine has enjoyed a measure of success, thanks to its unquestioned superiority over the standard bland Tuscan white blend of Trebbiano and Malvasia.

At its best, the wine has a crisp, refreshing quality and an attractively bitter finish. Despite its renewed popularity and attempts to give it further complexity with small BARREL MATURATION, the wine has attained only modest quality and price levels. In the long run, it may well have a lesser significance in its own place of origin, as leading producers in San Gimignano have begun to achieve striking success with serious red wines based on SANGIOVESE grapes (which have always been grown here), and with more international varieties such as CABERNET SAUVIGNON and CHARDONNAY. D.T.

Vernatsch, German name for the undistinguished light red grape variety SCHIAVA.

Veronelli, Luigi (1926–2004), Italy's most influential food and wine critic since 1956, when he founded the magazine *Il Gastronomo* and began to collaborate with Italy's major daily newspapers, news weeklies, and RAI-TV, the national television network. Born into an affluent Milanese family with a broad European culture, Veronelli was an unabashed Francophile from his first writings and a frank admirer of the French APPELLATION CONTRÔLÉE system, in particular of its designated CRUS, a CLASSIFICATION which he attempted to apply to Italian vineyards and their products in his many books on his country's wines. Polemical in character and a romantic anarchist in his political convictions, Veronelli long championed the cause of the small peasant proprietor and was a particularly bitter opponent of Italy's DOC systems, which he considered rigged in favour of the country's large commercial wineries. His campaigns against the DOC system earned him a period of banishment from Italian television in the 1970s and 1980s. A trip to California in the early 1980s converted him to an enthusiast of the BARRIQUE, then almost unknown in Italy, and his writings were extremely influential in spreading the use of small oak barrels in Italy.

For many years Veronelli represented the only possible means of obtaining commercial recognition and visibility for Italy's small producers and he can be credited with the discovery and identification of many of the country's better producers, a role which won him a group of devoted friends and an equally large group of sworn enemies. If the career was a controversial one, it is safe to say that the current Italian wine scene would be virtually unrecognizable without his work, and the emergence of Italian VITICULTURE and OENOLOGY dedicated to quality would have been considerably slower and more uncertain.

D.T. & J.R.

Belfrage, N., *Life beyond Lambrusco* (London, 1984).

vers de la grappe, insect pest and an important cause of BOTRYTIS BUNCH ROT. The term is generally used to refer to cochylis and eudemis (see MOTHS).

vertical trellis, a vine-TRAINING SYSTEM widely used throughout the world, in which the shoots are trained vertically upwards in summer. The system is commonly called **vertical shoot positioning**, or **VSP**, in the New World. The shoots are held in place by foliage wires which, in turn, are attached to vineyard posts. In many vineyards there are two pairs of foliage wires, and commonly the vines are subjected to TRIMMING at the top and sides to maintain a neat, hedge-like appearance. Both SPUR PRUNING and CANE PRUNING are possible. This trellis system is widely used in Alsace, Germany, eastern Europe, the United States, and New Zealand, with high vines (trunks of about 1 m/3 ft) and relatively low-density plantings. The vineyards of Bordeaux, Burgundy, and Champagne are also vertically shoot positioned, although the vines are planted closer together and the trunks are much shorter.

R.E.S.

verticillium wilt, FUNGAL DISEASE which causes apparently healthy vines to collapse suddenly. The fungus *Verticillium dahliae* lives in the soil, and attacks new vineyards. Young vines are usually affected, and often the vine recovers. There is no control apart from avoiding planting on sites where the fungus exists.

R.E.S.

Vespaiola, white grape variety grown in the VENETO region of north east Italy, said to take its name from the wasps (*vespe*) attracted by the sugar levels of its ripe grapes. Its most famous product is the Torcolato sweet wine of BREGANZE, although in this Vespaiola is blended with Tocai and Garganega, and the DRIED GRAPE WINE-making technique may well be the most important ingredient. As a dry white wine, Vespaiolo is acidic and neutral.

Vespolina, low-yielding red grape variety known almost exclusively in, and therefore probably native to, the area around GATTINARA in the PIEMONTE region of north west Italy. Commonly blended with NEBBIOLO, occasionally in the company of BONARDA Piemontese, it is also grown in the OLTREPÒ PAVESE zone across the border in LOMBARDIA, where it is known as Ughetta. DNA PROFILING showed a parent–offspring relationship with NEBBIOLO.

Anderson, B., *The Wine Atlas of Italy* (London and New York, 1990).

Veuve Clicquot Ponsardin, Champagne house as famous for its eponymous founder, the first great champagne widow (*veuve* in French), as for its wines. Nicole Barbe Ponsardin (1777–1866) married François Clicquot, an owner of Champagne vineyards, in 1798. The wedding took place in a Champagne cellar as churches were not yet reconsecrated following the French Revolution. François Clicquot died in 1805, leaving Mme Clicquot in charge of the company, which she renamed Veuve Clicquot Ponsardin. The widow steered the house carefully through the turbulent years of the First and Second Empires, defying Napoleon's blockades to ship the wine to Russia, and finding an export market in virtually every European court. 'La Grande Dame' is credited with inventing the riddling process called REMUAGE, and adapting a piece of her own furniture into the first riddling table for that purpose. She devised the famous yellow label, still used for the NON-VINTAGE wine. On her death, the company passed to her former chief partner, another shrewd businessman, Édouard Werlé, and the house remained in the hands of the Werlé family until in 1987 it became part of the Moët Hennessy-Louis Vuitton group (see LVMH). The house style is based on Pinot Noir grapes and, in particular, those grown at Bouzy, where the house has large holdings. La Grande Dame is Clicquot's PRESTIGE CUVÉE, named, of course, after the widow. In 1990, the Champagne house purchased a majority stake in the WESTERN AUSTRALIAN winery Cape Mentelle and its New Zealand subsidiary CLOUDY BAY, completing the purchase in 2000.

S.A.

Crestin-Billet, F., *Veuve Clicquot, la grande dame de la Champagne* (Grenoble, 1992).

Vézelay, commune near AUXERRE whose white wines from local Chardonnay grapes

have their own appellation Bourgogne Vézelay, given a fillip by the village's well-known restaurant.

Victoria, third most important wine state in AUSTRALIA. From its nadir in the mid 1950s, when there were fewer than 30 wineries in operation, Victoria has recovered to the point where its viticultural map once again resembles that of the 19th century, populated by almost 600 wine producers, more than any other state.

Hubert de Castella came to Victoria in 1854 from his native Switzerland, and was a leading figure in the golden age of Victorian viticulture up to 1890 (when it produced half the wine made in Australia). He wrote several books, the most famous entitled *John Bull's Vineyard*, a eulogy suggesting Victoria could supply England with all the wine it might ever need. Instead, a combination of PHYLLOXERA, changing land use, changing consumption patterns, the removal of inter-state duties, and the First World War saw the end of the hundreds of vineyards and wineries spread across the very cool southern half of the state.

What is now the North East Victoria Zone, with **Rutherglen** as its epicentre, became the focus of wine-making, producing a range of FORTIFIED and red table wines, the latter almost indistinguishable from some of the former. Foremost among the fortified wines were, and are, the unctuous LIQUEUR MUSCAT and Liqueur Tokay, wines of unique style and extraordinary concentration of flavour deriving in part from the shrivelled grapes and in part from long BARREL MATURATION in tin sheds which unconsciously mimic the *estufas* of MADEIRA. The North East Victoria Zone is currently divided into five regions: Rutherglen, Glenrowan, King Valley, Alpine Valleys, and Beechworth, although there was a move in the mid 2000s to excise parts of the King Valley and create a new region called Whitlands High Plateau.

Rutherglen and **Glenrowan** add massively rich full-bodied dry reds (from mainly Shiraz and Durif), and a range of other, less convincing, table wines, but their very warm summer and autumn days (and cold nights) provide a climate best suited to fortified wines.

Alpine Valleys and **Beechworth** provide a total contrast. Their altitude creates a significantly cooler climate eminently suited to table wines, albeit with a wide spectrum of varieties. **King Valley** is an incubator for varietal wines of every hue and shape: GRACIANO, MARZEMINO, MONDEUSE, PETIT MANSENG, SAGRANTINO, SAPERAVI, and TANNAT.

The Port Phillip Zone has five regions clustered around Melbourne: **Yarra Valley**, **Mornington Peninsula**, **Geelong**, **Sunbury**, and **Macedon Ranges**. Over 250 wineries here enjoy a range of climatic conditions all cooler than those of Bordeaux, variously cooled by

ALTITUDE or MARITIME influences. Pinot Noir and Chardonnay are the dominant varieties, capable of producing wines of world class, with the Yarra Valley, Mornington Peninsula, Geelong and the southern part of Gippsland leading the way.

Shiraz is sometimes seen as a newcomer in Victoria, but Craiglee (at Sunbury) made superb Shiraz evidenced by a cache of 1872 discovered almost 100 years later buried in the then defunct winery. Yeringberg removed its Shiraz in 1981 because it didn't sell as well as its other wines (and has since replanted it), while Yarra Yering has been producing its No. 2 Dry red for 30 years, quietly using a little VIOGNIER. Shiraz–Viognier is the new star, with Geelong, and the Yarra Valley (Yering Station) seen as leaders. With appropriate site selection, and warmer rather than cooler vintages, both Cabernet Sauvignon and Merlot can be superb.

Heathcote is the darling of the Central Victoria Zone, with its ancient (500 million-year-old Cambrian) soils, decompressed igneous greenstone which has become a vivid red-brown with age. The temperate climate and soil combination is producing some of Australia's most striking Shiraz, deeply coloured and velvety rich, albeit with the high alcohol (14° to 15.5°) levels necessary for full sensory ripeness. **Bendigo**, which once included Heathcote, is likewise red wine country, with Cabernet Sauvignon also excellent.

The **Goulburn Valley** is the oldest Victorian region with a continuous history of viticulture thanks to Tahbilk (formerly Chateau Tahbilk), which still makes an icon Shiraz exclusively from vines planted in 1860. Marsanne grows alongside Shiraz, Cabernet Sauvignon, and, of course, the ever-present Chardonnay.

The **Upper Goulburn** (previously Central Victorian High Country) and **Strathbogie Ranges** are paired in much the same way as the Alpine Valleys and Beechworth. Here altitude provides a cooler climatic background, but not cool enough in the Strathbogie Ranges to prevent generous flavours and MOUTHFEEL in the red wines. Riesling, Gewurztraminer, Pinot Gris, Chardonnay, and Viognier are the dominant white varieties.

The **Pyrenees** (quaintly named, for the slopes are gentle and far from dramatic) on the eastern side, abutting the **Grampians** (with Great Western seeking registration as a subregion) continue the red wine dominance, this time in the Western Victoria Zone. The Pyrenees on the eastern side can provide Shiraz and Cabernet Sauvignon every bit as sumptuous as that of Heathcote or Bendigo, but as you move west into the Grampians, the subtly cooler climate yields wines with more elegance and finesse, pepper, spice, and eucalypt mint along with the vibrant red fruit flavours.

The sparsely populated **Henty** is dramatically cooler; indeed on some criteria it is the coolest region on the Australian mainland.

Ultra-fine and intense Riesling, Semillon Sauvignon Blanc and steely, elegant Chardonnays are the mainstays, but micro-quantities of magnificent Pinot Noir to rival Bass Phillip (Gippsland) and Bindi (Macedon Ranges) are made by Tarrington Estate.

North West Victoria Zone takes in the **Murray Darling** and **Swan Hill** regions on the Murray river as it meanders for 500 km/305 miles marking the border between New South Wales and Victoria before moving through South Australia's Riverland. The story is no different: modified hydroponics in desert sand with (so far) unlimited WATER provide sky-high yields of at times surprisingly good quality grapes. The focal point is Lindemans' Karadoc winery, now the eastern states' wine-making, bottling and packaging centre for Southcorp's empire. Lindemans Bin 65 Chardonnay was born here, and notwithstanding the arrival of [yellow tail] (*sic*), remains one of the world's leading brands of Chardonnay.   J.H.

Halliday, J., numerous works including *The Wine Atlas of Australia and New Zealand* (2nd edn, Sydney, 1998) and *Australia Wine Companion* (Sydney, annually).

Vidal, white grape variety and a FRENCH HYBRID more properly known as **Vidal Blanc** or **Vidal 256** and widely grown in CANADA, where it is particularly valued for its winter hardiness. Grown to a limited extent in the eastern UNITED STATES, particularly NEW YORK state, it is a hybrid of Ugni Blanc and one of the Seibel parents of SEYVAL BLANC. The wine produced, like Seyval's, has no obviously FOXY character and can smell attractively of currant bushes or leaves. Its slow, steady ripening and thick skins make it particularly suitable for sweet, late harvest (non-botrytized) wines and ICEWINE, for which it, with RIESLING, is famous in Canada. Vidal-based wines do not have the longevity of fine Rieslings, however.

Vidigueira, subregion of ALENTEJO in southern Portugal. Despite being one of the hottest parts of the country, Vidigueira, with its large CO-OPERATIVE winery, produces mainly white wine.

vieilles vignes is French for 'old vines'. The term is used widely on wine labels in the hope that potential buyers are aware that wine quality is often associated with senior VINE AGE. There are few effective controls on the use of the term, however, and little agreement about exactly how many years it is before a vine can be deemed old. BOLLINGER was one of the first producers to use the term, for the produce of ungrafted vines in one walled vineyard.

Vien de Nus, special red grape variety grown around the town of Nus in Italy's Valle d'AOSTA.

Vienna, capital city of AUSTRIA and, unusually, a wine region and wine area in its own right.

Vietnam, small, south east Asian country with a history of viticulture dating from French colonial times. Recent attempts to revive viticultural traditions and make wine have had mixed results. The most suitable locations for conventional viticulture in this hot and wet country are in the highlands—on the slopes of Ba Vi mountain west of Hanoi, for example, where VINIFERA vines were grown by French colonists about a century ago, or on the upper slopes of the central highlands. Contrarily, however, Vietnam's first commercial grape wine-making venture, the Thien Thai Winery, was established on the steamy southern coastal plain at Phan Rang, in Ninh Thuan province, 350 km/210 miles north east of Ho Chi Minh City (formerly Saigon). The attraction was the existence of established vineyards producing up to 50,000 tonnes of TABLE GRAPES a year from red CARDINAL vines grown on PERGOLAS. The winery, with an initial one million bottle capacity, was a JOINT VENTURE between the British firm Allied Domecq and a local company. The first wines, both still and sparkling, were released in 1995 but the winery was mothballed in 2002. Subsequently, though, two Hanoi-based FRUIT WINE companies, Thang Long and Viet Nang, began drawing on grapes grown in Ninh Thuan to extend their range to include sparkling and still grape wines. Lam Dong Foodstuff Company is another fruit wine producer that has successfully drawn on these grapes to tap into the growing market for grape wines with its Dalat label. Most other domestic wine labels were using imported bulk wine in the mid 2000s.

Under natural conditions, the southern vines bear almost continuously (see TROPICAL VITICULTURE). Systematic PRUNING has been adopted, however, to induce three output peaks ('vintages') in order to facilitate a manageable crushing schedule. INTERNATIONAL VARIETIES have been trialled under Australian technical supervision—on land which was, until 1995, a minefield left over from the Vietnam war. CHAMBOURCIN produces prolifically and copes best with the humidity. In the trials, a number of varieties progressed from CUTTINGS to fruit in a single year.   D.G.

Doyle, S., 'Assessing the potential of viticulture in Vietnam', *Australian Grapegrower and Winemaker*, 394 (Oct 1996).

vigna is Italian for VINEYARD, while a **vignaiolo** is a vine-grower.

vigne is French for a VINE, and sometimes VINEYARD. **Vigneron** is French for a vine-grower, some say derived from *vigne ronde*, implying that a vigneron actually prunes the vines himself whereas a VITICULTEUR merely grows them.

The term *vigneron* is now used widely outside France for a wide range of people engaged in wine production. A **vignoble** is French for a VINEYARD, although the term *vignoble* can be used more broadly as in 'the entire French *vignoble*'.

Vignoles, also known as Ravat 51, FRENCH HYBRID popular in cooler wine regions in the eastern UNITED STATES. It can make fresh, delicate white wine and is particularly well suited to sweet wine production. The low-yielding vine was bred by Ravat from SEIBEL and Pinot Noir.

vigour in a viticultural sense is the vine's vegetative growth, an important aspect of any vine. This may seem of unlikely interest to wine drinkers, but the level of vineyard vigour is a vital factor in wine quality. Low-vigour vines do not always have sufficient leaf area to ripen grapes properly, while high-vigour vines typically produce thin, pale, acidic wines often wrongly thought to result from OVERCROPPING.

Vines of high vigour show a lack of BALANCE between shoot and fruit growth. Vigorous vineyards show rapid shoot growth in the spring, and shoots continue to grow late into the growing season, even past VERAISON, the beginning of fruit ripening. Shoots on vigorous vines have long INTERNODES, thick stems, large leaves, and many LATERAL SHOOTS. Vigorous vineyards are usually, but not necessarily, associated with high YIELDS. The rank, vegetative growth may produce so much SHADE that FRUITFULNESS declines, leading to even more vegetative growth and a loss of varietal character, colour, body, and general wine quality.

Vine vigour is easy to quantify using PRUNING WEIGHTS and other vine measurements as outlined by Smart and Robinson, and so these approaches along with SCORING can be used as a form of quality control. For an alternative approach to the assessment of vine vigour, see NORMALIZED DIFFERENCE VEGETATION INDEX.

The vigour of a vineyard is essentially dependent on two features, the size and health of the root system, and also the pruning level. First, what grows above ground is some sort of mirror of what grows below. A vine with a large and healthy root system will have the reserves of CARBOHYDRATES and balance of HORMONES to support vigorous shoot growth. On the other hand, a vine with a small and/or unhealthy root system, be it due to shallow soil, drought, root pests such as PHYLLOXERA, or diseases such as ARMILLARIA ROOT ROT, will support only low-vigour growth.

Vines should be pruned to bud numbers relative to the amount of early shoot growth they can support. This is the concept of BALANCED PRUNING, and one criterion used is to retain at winter PRUNING about 30 buds per kg of pruning weight. Use of this sort of rule

means that the subsequent shoot growth will be in balance with the vine's carbohydrate reserves, ensuring balance between shoot and fruit growth, and moderate vigour.

High vigour is a common problem of modern vineyards, for many and varied reasons. The vines may be planted in a region with a benign climate on too deep a soil, which is well supplied with water (from rainfall and/or irrigation) and nutrients (from natural fertility or fertilizers or added compost). Such soils are said to have high SOIL POTENTIAL in that they promote excessive vine vigour. Modern control methods can also keep vines free of stress associated with weeds, pests, and diseases. CANOPY MANAGEMENT techniques are used to maintain yield and wine quality in such situations.

An alternative approach is to devigorate the vines. The most common approach is to control the water supply, which is of course easier to do when irrigating in an arid climate than when vineyards are supplied by rainfall alone. Other techniques include nutrient stressing, increasing crop load by leaving more buds at winter PRUNING, or by growing shoots downwards as in the GENEVA DOUBLE CURTAIN training system.   R.E.S.

Smart, R. E., and Robinson, M., *Sunlight into Wine: A Handbook for Winegrape Canopy Management* (Adelaide, 1991).

Winkler, A. J., *et al.*, *General Viticulture* (2nd edn, Berkeley, Calif., 1974).

Vijariego (also known as Bujariego and Vidijariego), white grape variety from the CANARY ISLANDS which produces distinctive dry wines there on vineyards totalling nearly 600 ha/1,500 acres, notably that made by Bodegas Viñátigo.

Vilana, white grape variety that is native to and the most widely grown on the island of Crete (see GREECE). It is responsible for the most delicate examples of spicy dry white Peza made there.

Vila Nova de Gaia, or Gaia New Town, cramped, cobbled suburb on the opposite side of the DOURO estuary from the Portuguese city of OPORTO where PORT is traditionally aged. From the waterfront, long, single-storey buildings called LODGES rise in steps up the hillside. Under the clay-tiled roofs, shippers mature their stocks of port, as well as TASTING, BLENDING, BOTTLING, and selling it. Until 1986, the law required that all port destined for export had to be shipped from within the strictly defined area of the Gaia entrepôt. Port may now be shipped from anywhere within the demarcated Douro region so that export markets are open to small firms, quintas, and co-operatives without premises in Vila Nova de Gaia.   R.J.M.

Villages, common suffix of an APPELLATION CONTRÔLÉE name for a French wine. Generally

speaking, an X-Villages wine must be made from one or several of a selection of communes whose produce is known to be superior to that of the rest of the X zone. See, for example, BEAUJOLAIS, MÂCON, and Côtes du Rhône.

village wine is a term used particularly in Burgundy for a wine which qualifies for an APPELLATION that coincides with the name of the village or commune in which the wine is made. It contrasts with a lesser GENERIC wine, which takes the name of a region, and wines from PREMIER CRU and GRAND CRU vineyards.

Villány-Siklós, wine region in HUNGARY on the terraced southern and eastern slopes of the Villány mountains which protect the vineyards from cold northern influences resulting in a special sub-MEDITERRANEAN mesoclimate. (See map under HUNGARY.) The Villány mountains consist of calcareous rocks deposited in the marine basins of the Mesozoic. Dolomite, marl and limestone are covered direct with sandy loess. This layer is sometimes mixed up with limestone debris, having a higher concentration of calcium. This is the cropland of more acidic wines, while the purely loess soil produces softer wines. Villány is mostly known for its red BORDEAUX BLENDS, sometimes rather heavy and tannic but with good ageing potential. Cabernet Franc grows well here and Cabernet Sauvignon also produces exciting wines. The everyday drinking wine is the softer PORTUGIESER and KÉKFRANKOS is often used in blends. In the last decade, Pinot Noir and Syrah have been planted, producing wines that can be heavy and lacking in elegance. The whites are mostly grown in the Siklós part of the region. As in SZEKSZÁRD, wines are often low in acid, high in alcohol and do not suit long ageing. Olaszrizling, Chardonnay, and Hárslevelű are widely planted. The region is well suited to TOURISM.   G.R. & G.M.

Villard is the common French name for a great French viticultural secret, their most commonly planted HYBRIDS. Most are members of the vast SEYVE VILLARD group.

In France, Villard Blanc is Seyve Villard 12.375 while Villard Noir is Seyve Villard 18.315. Villard Noir was planted all over France, from the northern Rhône to Bordeaux, and was treasured for its resistance to DOWNY MILDEW. Villard Blanc made slightly more palatable wine (though the must can be difficult to process). Both varieties yield prodigiously and for that attribute were so beloved by growers that in 1968 there were 30,000 ha/74,000 acres of Villard Noir and 21,000 ha of Villard Blanc in France (making them fifth and third most planted black and white grape varieties respectively).

To the great credit of the authorities, and thanks to not inconsiderable bribes for grubbing up, within 20 years these respective totals had been shaved to 2,500 ha and 4,600 ha and to 600 ha and 740 ha by the turn of the century, mainly in Tarn and Ardèche.

Other hybrids once widely planted in France are BACO, CHAMBOURCIN, COUDERC, PLANTET, and various other members of the Seibel and Seyve Villard families.

For more information, see FRENCH HYBRIDS.

vin, French for wine and therefore a much-used term (see below). **Vin blanc** is white wine, **vin rosé** is pink, **vin rouge** is red wine, **vin mousseux** is sparkling wine, and so on. For **vin ordinaire**, see VIN DE TABLE. For **vin biologique** (more correctly, **vin issu de raisins biologiques** or **vin issu d'agriculture biologique**), see ORGANIC WINE. For **vin blanc cassis**, see KIR.

viña, viñedo. Spanish word for VINEYARD.

Vincor, CANADA's largest wine company, was the fourth largest in North America, when it was acquired by the American giant CONSTELLATION early in 2006. Vincor owns wineries in British Columbia, Ontario, Quebec, and New Brunswick in Canada; wineries R H Phillips in California, Hogue Cellars in Washington state, Goundrey and Amberley in Western Australia, Kim Crawford in New Zealand, and Western Wines, one of the largest wine importers in the UK and owners of the Kumala brand in South Africa. In addition to wine it sells other 'refreshment products' and wine kits in Canada. The company had its beginnings in 1989 through a management buyout of the wine division of John Labatt, owners of Chateau Gai. In 1992, it merged with Inniskillin, the first winery since PROHIBITION to be granted a licence, in 1974, to make and sell wine in Ontario. A year later the company merged with Brights Wines. Subsequent purchases in the next two years included Okanagan Vineyards in British Columbia and London Winery in Ontario. One of Vincor's premium VQA lines, Jackson-Triggs, opened a showcase winery at Niagara-on-the-Lake in 2001. Vincor's other premium wine brands in Canada include Sumac Ridge, and Hawthorne Mountain in BC. Its JOINT VENTURES in British Columbia are significant: Nk'Mip Cellars, opened in 2003 with the Osoyoos Indian Band, is North America's first aboriginal-owned winery, while Osoyoos Larose winery, opened in 2004 in partnership with Bordeaux's Groupe Taillan, owner of Château Gruaud Larose, represents the first European producer to invest in BC. Le Clos Jordan in Niagara, Ontario, is a joint venture with BOISSET of Burgundy.

Vin Délimité de Qualité Supérieure, France's interim wine quality designation between APPELLATION CONTRÔLÉE and VIN DE PAYS. See VDQS for more details.

vin de liqueur, strong, sweet drink made by adding grape spirit to grape must, so-called MUTAGE. The alcohol is added before the juice begins to ferment so that the resulting liquids have an alcoholic strength of between 16 and 22 per cent but no secondary products of fermentation such as GLYCEROL or SUCCINIC ACID. The term has also been adopted by EUROPEAN UNION authorities (although not by this book) to encompass all FORTIFIED wines.

The principal members of this special category of French specialities, sometimes known as *mistelles*, are the PINEAU DES CHARENTES of Cognac country, its Armagnac counterpart FLOC DE GASCOGNE, and MACVIN DU JURA, made from local MARC added to grape juice and tasting strongly of the former. Most vins de liqueur are pale gold, but soft, fruity rosé versions of both Pineau and Floc can be found in the regions of production. Vin de liqueur differs from VIN DOUX NATUREL in that the alcohol is added earlier and the resulting drinks therefore tend to be, and taste, more spirit dominated. Some Muscat de FRONTIGNAN may also qualify. Many wine regions have their own versions of this easy-to-make strong, sweet aperitif: Champagne has its Ratafia, the Rhône its Rinquinquin, while the Languedoc has Cartagène, although, where there are no regulations governing their production, they are sometimes made further along the scale towards vins doux naturels. Like vins doux naturels, these sweet wines can be enhanced by serving them cool, and the wine in an opened bottle should retain its appeal for well over a week.

vin de paille is French for 'straw wine' (*Strohwein* in German), a small group of necessarily expensive but often quite delicious, long-lived, sweet white wines. These are essentially a subgroup of DRIED GRAPE WINES made from grapes dried on straw mats. Cyrus REDDING's catalogue of wines produced in the early 19th century makes it clear that vins de paille were much more common then and, although he was most enthusiastic about 'Ermitage-paille' (from HERMITAGE vines), he found vins de paille in JURA, ALSACE, and Corrèze. At about the same time some producers in Rust in AUSTRIA were also using the technique.

Today, production of this rarity is virtually confined to particularly ripe vintages and the most conscientious producers of Hermitage, ARBOIS, occasionally L'ÉTOILE, and Côtes du JURA. For much of the 20th century no vin de paille was made in Hermitage, but Gérard Chave revived the practice with healthy, not late-picked, Marsanne grapes in 1974, dried on straw in the attic, and has since been followed by CHAPOUTIER and others.

Average yields are minuscule once the grapes have been raisined, but the results are luscious in the extreme, and are invariably sold in half-bottles.

Today the Jura producers usually dry their SAVAGNIN, POULSARD, or Chardonnay grapes in boxes rather than laying them out on straw. The minimum POTENTIAL ALCOHOL allowed is 18 per cent (as opposed to 14 per cent in Hermitage). The grapes are generally pressed in January, and 100 kg/220 lbs of grapes may yield fewer than 20 l/5 gal of juice. Jura producers must age their vins de paille in cask for at least three years and the wines often have a natural alcoholic strength of at least 14.5 per cent. They are capable of long BOTTLE AGEING.

There is renewed, if limited, experimentation with making vin de paille in Alsace and, unlike BOTRYTIZED wine, this is one wine style with which any curious and dedicated winemaker can experiment. See also LUXEMBOURG.

Livingstone-Learmonth, J., *The Wines of the Northern Rhône* (Berkeley, 2005).

vin de pays, French expression meaning 'country wine' which was adopted for an intermediate category of wines created in FRANCE in 1973, and formalized in 1979, to recognize and encourage the production of wines that are distinctly superior to basic VIN DE TABLE, and which, in theory at least, offer some stamp of regional identity. Hence the creation of more than 140 different vins de pays, all of them carrying some geographical designation mirroring the principles of the APPELLATION CONTRÔLÉE (AC) system. To qualify as a vin de pays, a wine must not be blended across zones, must be produced in limited quantities, must be made of certain specified grape varieties, must reach a certain minimum ALCOHOLIC STRENGTH, and must be submitted to a tasting panel, as well as coming from a specified area. By 1993, more than one-fifth of all wine produced in France was sold as a vin de pays of some sort and the proportion rose to more than 30 per cent by the turn of the century.

In many regions, the vine-grower has a clear choice between making an appellation wine and producing a vin de pays, either because yields are too high to qualify for an AC, or because he or she grows grape varieties permitted by the local vin de pays regulations but prohibited by those of the local AC (as is often the case with new or imported INTERNATIONAL VARIETIES). In general, vins de pays may be produced from grapes which yield up to 90 hl/ha (5 tons/acre) while 50 hl/ha or so is a more likely maximum YIELD permitted by appellation regulations.

There are three levels of vin de pays:

There are five at the regional level: Vin de Pays d'Oc from the LANGUEDOC and ROUSSILLON; Vin de Pays du Jardin de la France from the LOIRE; Vin de Pays du Comté Tolosan, most of SOUTH WEST FRANCE; Vin de Pays des Comtés Rhodaniens, incorporating ARDÈCHE, BEAUJOLAIS, JURA, SAVOIE, and the northern RHÔNE; and Vin de Pays Portes de la Mediterranée from the south east of France and Corsica.

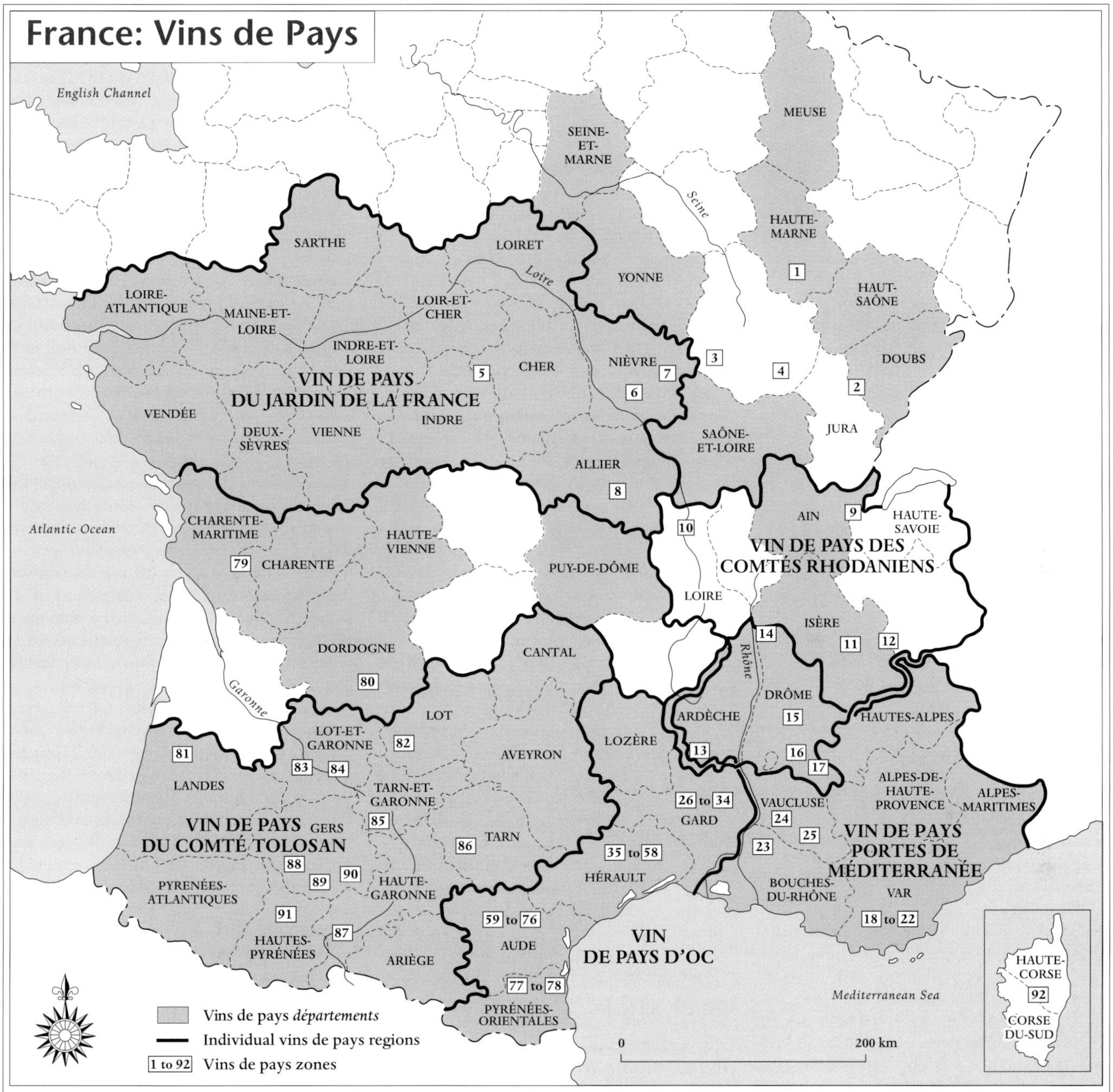

France: Vins de Pays

English Channel

Atlantic Ocean

Mediterranean Sea

vin de pays

737

VIN DE PAYS DU JARDIN DE LA FRANCE

VIN DE PAYS DES COMTÉS RHODANIENS

VIN DE PAYS DU COMTÉ TOLOSAN

VIN DE PAYS PORTES DE MÉDITERRANÉE

VIN DE PAYS D'OC

Départements and regions labelled: SARTHE, LOIRE-ATLANTIQUE, MAINE-ET-LOIRE, LOIR-ET-CHER, LOIRET, YONNE, SEINE-ET-MARNE, MEUSE, HAUTE-MARNE, HAUT-SAÔNE, DOUBS, INDRE-ET-LOIRE, CHER, NIÈVRE, SAÔNE-ET-LOIRE, JURA, VENDÉE, DEUX-SÈVRES, VIENNE, INDRE, ALLIER, AIN, HAUTE-SAVOIE, CHARENTE-MARITIME, CHARENTE, HAUTE-VIENNE, PUY-DE-DÔME, LOIRE, ISÈRE, DORDOGNE, CANTAL, ARDÈCHE, DRÔME, HAUTES-ALPES, LOT-ET-GARONNE, LOT, AVEYRON, LOZÈRE, GARD, VAUCLUSE, ALPES-DE-HAUTE-PROVENCE, ALPES-MARITIMES, LANDES, TARN-ET-GARONNE, GERS, TARN, BOUCHES-DU-RHÔNE, VAR, HÉRAULT, PYRÉNÉES-ATLANTIQUES, HAUTE-GARONNE, AUDE, HAUTES-PYRÉNÉES, ARIÈGE, PYRÉNÉES-ORIENTALES, HAUTE-CORSE, CORSE-DU-SUD

Rivers: Seine, Loire, Garonne, Rhône

Legend

- Vins de pays *départements*
- Individual vins de pays regions
- 1 to 92 Vins de pays zones

0 — 200 km

1 Vin de pays des Coteaux de Coiffy
2 Vin de pays de Franche-Comté
3 Vin de pays des Coteaux de l'Auxois
4 Vin de pays de Sainte Marie La Blanche
5 Vin de pays des Coteaux du Cher et de l'Arnon
6 Vin de pays des Coteaux Charitois
7 Vin de pays des Coteaux de Tannay
8 Vin de pays du Bourbonnais
9 Vin de pays d'Allobrogie
10 Vin de pays d'Urfé
11 Vin de pays des Balmes Dauphinoises
12 Vin de pays des Coteaux du Grésivaudan
13 Vin de pays des Coteaux de l'Ardèche
14 Vin de pays des Collines Rhodaniennes
15 Vin de pays des Coteaux des Baronnies
16 Vin de pays du Comté de Grignan
17 Vin de pays des Coteaux de Montélimar
18 Vin de pays des Coteaux du Verdon
19 Vin de pays de Mont-Caume
20 Vin de pays des Maures
21 Vin de pays du pays d'Argens
22 Vin de pays de la Sainte Baume
23 Vin de pays de la Petite Crau

24 Vin de pays d'Aigues
25 Vin de pays de la Principauté d'Orange
26 Vin de pays des Sables du Golfe du Lion
27 Vin de pays du Duché d'Uzès
28 Vin de pays des Cévennes
29 Vin de pays de la Vistrenque
30 Vin de pays des Côtes du Vidourle
31 Vin de pays de la Vaunage
32 Vin de pays des Coteaux de Cèze
33 Vin de pays des Coteaux du Pont du Gard
34 Vin de pays des Coteaux Flaviens
35 Vin de pays du Val de Montferrand
36 Vin de pays du Mont Baudile
37 Vin de pays des Côtes du Ceressou
38 Vin de pays des Monts de la Grage
39 Vin de pays des Coteaux d'Enserune
40 Vin de pays des Coteaux du Libron
41 Vin de pays des Coteaux de Murviel
42 Vin de pays des Coteaux de Laurens
43 Vin de pays des Côtes de Thongue
44 Vin de pays de la Bénovie
45 Vin de pays de Cassan
46 Vin de pays de la Haute Vallée de l'Orb

47 Vin de pays de Saint-Guiihem-le-Désert
48 Vin de pays des Coteaux de Bessilles
49 Vin de pays des Côtes du Brian
50 Vin de pays de Cessenon
51 Vin de pays des Coteaux du Salagou
52 Vin de pays de la Vicomté d'Aumelas
53 Vin de pays des Collines de la Moure
54 Vin de pays de Caux
55 Vin de pays des Coteaux de Fontcaude
56 Vin de pays de Bessan
57 Vin de pays de Bérange
58 Vin de pays des Côtes de Thau
59 Vin de pays des Coteaux de Peyriac
60 Vin de pays de la Haute Vallée de l'Aude
61 Vin de pays des Coteaux de Narbonne
62 Vin de pays des Côtes de Prouilhe
63 Vin de pays de la Cité de Carcassonne
64 Vin de pays de Cucugnan
65 Vin de pays du Val de Dagne
66 Vin de pays des Coteaux du Littoral Audois
67 Vin de pays des Côtes de Pérignan
68 Vin de pays des Coteaux de la Cabrerisse
69 Vin de pays des Hauts de Badens

70 Vin de pays du Torgan
71 Vin de pays des Côtes de Lastours
72 Vin de pays du Val de Cesse
73 Vin de pays de la Vallée du Paradis
74 Vin de pays des Coteaux de Miramont
75 Vin de pays d'Hauterive
76 Vin de pays Catalan
77 Vin de pays des Côtes Catalanes
78 Vin de pays de la Côte Vermeille
79 Vin de pays Charentais
80 Vin de pays du Périgord
81 Vin de pays des Terroirs Landais
82 Vin de pays des Coteaux de Glanes
83 Vin de pays de Thézac-Perricard
84 Vin de pays de l'Agenais
85 Vin de pays des Coteaux et Terrasses de Montauban
86 Vin de pays de Côtes du Tarn
87 Vin de pays de Saint-Sardos
88 Vin de pays des Côtes de Montestruc
89 Vin de pays des Côtes du Condomois
90 Vin de pays des Côtes de Gascogne
91 Vin de pays de Bigorre
92 Vin de pays de l'Ile de Beauté

About 50 are departmental, named after one of France's *départements*, or counties, such as Vin de Pays de l'Hérault, Vin de Pays de Loire-Atlantique, Vin de Pays de Tarn-et-Garonne, or Vin de Pays de l'Ardèche (these are, respectively, specific *départements* within each of the regions above). See also BORDEAUX AC for 2005 proposals to introduce a Vin de Pays in the Gironde *département*.

Even more are locally specific. These may be named after some historical or geographical phenomenon such as Vin de Pays des Coteaux de Murviel, Vin de Pays des Marche de Bretagne, Vin de Pays des Coteaux du Quercy, or Vin de Pays des Collines Rhodaniennes (each a local denomination within the four departmental vins de pays specified above, the last a name used for some serious reds and whites made outside the official appellations of the northern Rhône).

Some of these locally specific vins de pays names are virtually unused, some of the smaller ones have been developed as commercially useful exclusivities by individual merchants, and many of them are unknown outside their district of origin. Their names in many cases bear no relation to current geography—although historical nomenclature has clearly been a useful source for local officials charged with finding names which would present no confusion with the name of any existing AC or VDQS wine. (The French authorities have been keen to make a very clear distinction between vins de pays and wines which are accorded the full sanction of AC status.) Some of the local names are simply too difficult for export markets, often unsure of the exact spelling of even vin de pays, to grasp. Vin de Pays des Coteaux du Grésivaudan, for example, is rarely asked for by name outside Savoie, while the name of the south western Vin de Pays des Coteaux et Terrasses de Montauban seems unnecessarily pedantic.

Other exercises in nomenclature have represented strokes of genius. The image of Corsica is transformed in the name Vin de Pays de l'Île de Beauté, just as the Loire sounds even prettier as the Jardin de la France, while Roussillon's vins de pays quite rightly emphasize the region's ethnic origins in Vin de Pays des Côtes Catalanes.

A small amount of red, and some white, vin de pays PRIMEUR is produced each year, and may be released on the third Thursday of October (thereby beating Beaujolais NOUVEAU by a full month).

The vins de pays which have enjoyed enormous success outside France are those labelled as VARIETALS, a concept viewed with such distaste by INAO, which oversees AC labelling, that vins de pays present the modern consumer with virtually the only means of acquiring a wine that is both French and labelled with a familiar grape variety such as Chardonnay, Sauvignon Blanc, Merlot, or Cabernet Sauvignon (or, increasingly, with a less familiar variety such as Marsanne, Terret, or Viognier). Some non-French customers could be much more attracted by a Chardonnay, Vin de Pays d'Oc, than, for example, a full AC counterpart carrying a less familiar name such as St-Romain or a Bugey, for example. Reverence for the words 'appellation contrôlée' is a French phenomenon. Vins de pays have been particularly successful in Germany and Great Britain.

The most important single vin de pays is Vin de Pays d'Oc, which is France's prime source of varietal wine. About 85 per cent of all vins de pays come from Languedoc-Roussillon, Provence, or the southern Rhône. A further 6 per cent come from the Loire. Vin de pays has also provided a useful way of selling the surplus produce of vines grown in regions specializing in brandy production. Crisp, dry white Vin de Pays des Côtes de Gascogne has been the commercial saviour of vignerons in Armagnac country since the early 1980s, while the Cognac counterpart is Vin de Pays Charentais.

In every ten bottles of vin de pays, about seven are red, two are rosé, and one is white. In general they are sold at lower prices than most AC wines, often quite rightly as many of these wines can be thin on flavour. Some producers, however, have become increasingly ambitious in their wine-making techniques and a number of vins de pays may be offered, and sold, at relatively robust prices. The pioneer was MAS de Daumas Gassac, an internationally famous wine which is sold merely as a departmental Vin de Pays de l'Hérault, but there are now scores, if not hundreds of equally ambitious producers of vins de pays, especially in Languedoc-Roussillon, making some of the best-value wines in the world.

vin de presse. French for PRESS WINE.

Vin de Savoie. See SAVOIE.

Vin des Glaciers, also known as **Vin du Glacier,** 'glacier wine' is a local speciality in the Val d'Anniviers near Sierre in Valais in SWITZERLAND. The white wine, traditionally made of the now obscure Rèze vine, comes from communally cultivated vines and is stored at high altitudes in casks refilled just once a year on a SOLERA system. The resultant product is deliberately MADERIZED and valued for its rarity.

vin de table, the French form of TABLE WINE and France's most basic level of wine, which, having been a copious embarrassment, is now dwindling to a relative trickle. By 1997 this, the lowliest of French wine categories, accounted for just 15 per cent of the nation's output (excluding wine destined for brandy stills), well under half the amount that qualified as VIN DE PAYS, originally conceived as a sort of superior subcategory of vin de table, and the amount produced continues to diminish as lower quality vineyards are ripped out. Vin de table may not be vintage dated. Occasionally wines from superior producers and vineyards are bottled as vin de table when they transgress some local regulation or because they are deemed atypical in either taste or production method.

Vin de table is, typically, light red wine made in areas of the LANGUEDOC and ROUSSILLON not delimited as APPELLATION CONTRÔLÉE territory. There are no limits on YIELDS in table wine production and typical grape varieties are likely to contain large amounts of high-yielding CARIGNAN, France's second most planted grape variety according to the vineyard census of 2000. Some white vin de table is also made, and some vin de table is produced in virtually every part of France where vines are grown.

France's vin de table has been light and thin ever since the plains of the Languedoc were planted at the end of the 19th century. Red vin de table has traditionally needed BLENDING with darker, more alcoholic wine which was originally imported from ALGERIA and subsequently from southern Italy, Sicily, and Spain.

There is still a serious SURPLUS of vin de table, however, and a significant proportion of it has been subject to compulsory DISTILLATION as part of the EUROPEAN UNION's efforts to remedy this. The area of vineyard dedicated to vin de table production has also contracted markedly as the vin de pays designation has been developed, and as poorer-quality vineyard sites have been targeted by VINE PULL SCHEMES.

Much of it is sold locally, in bulk, for blending, with other table wines or to producers of VERMOUTHS or other FORTIFIED wines and wine-based products.

vin doux naturel translates directly from French as a wine that is naturally sweet but is a term used to describe a French wine speciality that might well be considered *un*naturally sweet. Nature's sweetest wines contain so much grape sugar that the yeasts eventually give up the fermentation process of converting sugar into alcohol, leaving a residue of natural sugars in a stable wine of normal alcoholic strength (see SWEET WINE-MAKING). Vins doux naturels, on the other hand, are made by MUTAGE, by artificially arresting the conversion of grape sugar to alcohol by adding spirit before fermentation is complete, thereby incapacitating yeasts with alcohol and making a particularly strong, sweet half-wine in which grape flavours dominate wine flavours. They are normally made of the grape varieties MUSCAT and GRENACHE, and should have an alcoholic strength of between 15 and 18 per cent and a POTENTIAL ALCOHOL of at least 21.5 per cent.

The Greeks, happily ignorant of DISTILLATION, already knew how to make a sweet wine by adding concentrated must. Almost as soon as the techniques of distillation were introduced into western Europe, it was discovered that distilled wine, or alcoholic spirit, had the power to stop fermentation, thereby reliably retaining the sweetness so prized by our forebears. The Catalan alchemist ARNALDUS DE VILLANOVA (Arnaud de Villeneuve) of Montpellier University's then flourishing medical school perfected the process and in 1299 was granted a patent from the king of Majorca, then ruler of ROUSSILLON, which was to become the world's centre of vin doux naturel production.

This is essentially how PORT as we know it, created nearly 400 years later, is made strong and sweet, and the technique is also used in the production of MADEIRA and MÁLAGA. In each case, spirit is added when the fermenting MUST has reached about 6 per cent alcohol, except that whereas the added spirit constitutes between 5 and 10 per cent of the final volume of a vin doux naturel, typically resulting in an alcoholic strength of just over 15 per cent, the added spirit usually represents 20 per cent of the final volume of port, whose alcoholic strength is closer to 20 per cent. The spirit added to vins doux naturels is considerably stronger than that added to port, however: about 95 per cent alcohol as opposed to the traditional 77 per cent used in port FORTIFICATION. Nowadays, however, the spirit may well come from exactly the same source, one of France's larger distilleries designed to reduce Europe's wine surplus (see WINE LAKE). Thus a vin doux naturel contains less alcohol, and less added water, than port.

A young vin doux naturel therefore, like port, tastes relatively simply of grapes, sugar, and alcohol (although, since some fermentation has usually taken place, it may contain a more interesting array of fermentation products than a VIN DE LIQUEUR). Naturally aromatic MUSCAT BLANC À PETITS GRAINS grapes are therefore particularly well suited to the production of vins doux naturels designed to be drunk young (and, usually, chilled to offset the sugar and alcohol). The best known of these golden sweet liquids that are made exclusively from this, the finest MUSCAT vine variety, was historically Muscat de FRONTIGNAN. The Languedoc has three other appellation contrôlée vins doux naturels, however: Muscats de LUNEL, MIREVAL, and, an exception far from the coast, ST-JEAN-DE-MINERVOIS, whose vineyards are even higher than most of those for the red, pink, and dry white wines of MINERVOIS. In the 1970s, the similar, often even finer, Muscat made in the Côtes du Rhône village of BEAUMES-DE-VENISE enjoyed renown on an international scale.

Muscat de Beaumes-de-Venise is probably easier for non-natives to appreciate than the southern Rhône's other vin doux naturel appellation of RASTEAU, whose Grenache-based heady red and tawny sweet wines, some of them deliberately made RANCIO, have more in common with the increasingly famous vins doux naturels of Roussillon. The best of these, like the best ports, owe their complex flavours necessarily to ageing, whether in cask, BONBONNE, or, occasionally, bottle. The greatest name is BANYULS, which has benefited from some impeccable winemakers and, most important in this context, wine-éleveurs (see ÉLEVAGE). MAURY is a smaller appellation in the mountains with enormous and, occasionally, realized potential, while the extensive coastal RIVESALTES and Muscat de Rivesaltes appellations are much more varied and sometimes traduced. Grand Roussillon is a largely theoretical vin doux naturel appellation designed as a lesser Rivesaltes.

Non-vintage-dated vins doux naturels are common, particularly among the Languedoc Muscats into which a little of the previous year's output may be blended so as to smooth out vintage differences. It is common in Roussillon, however, to find indications of age and vintage dates, although most vins doux naturels are ready to drink as soon as they are sold. Many, particularly the Muscats, benefit from being served young and chilled, but the alcohol preserves the freshness of wine in an opened bottle for at least a week.

George, R., *The Wines of the South of France* (London, 2001).

Vin du Bugey. See BUGEY.

vine, the plant, often known as the grapevine, whose fruit is transformed into WINE.

A vine in its broadest sense is any plant with a weak stem which supports itself by climbing on neighbouring plants, walls, or other supports. Of this group of plants the grapevine is the most famous, and the most commercially important. (In this work the word vine is used to mean the grapevine.) There are various forms of climbing vines which rely on different mechanisms for attachment. The so-called ramblers rest on each other's plants and some, as for roses, have spines to help adhesion. The grapevine is one of the so-called tendril climbers with TENDRILS on the stem; the garden pea has leaf tendrils.

Because the vine is unable to support itself, it is generally grown on TRELLIS SYSTEMS. Some TRAINING SYSTEMS still use trees for support, as for the *alberate* of Italy. However, most vineyards of the world are trained to some combination of wood posts and wire. Vines can be trained so that they are free standing but this requires special pruning and training to keep the trunk short, otherwise the vine will fall over. The GOBELET of the Mediterranean region is the most widespread of the free-standing forms.

Most of the world's wine is made from the VINIFERA species of the VITIS genus (see BOTANICAL CLASSIFICATION for a more detailed explanation of where the vine fits into the world of plants).

Grapevines are the world's most important fruit crop, with about 7.7 million ha/19 million acres of vineyards producing almost 60 million tonnes of fruit in the late 1990s. Grapes are used for wine-making in all of its forms, for brandy, for consumption as TABLE GRAPES and DRYING GRAPES, for fresh GRAPE JUICE, for GRAPE CONCENTRATE, RECTIFIED GRAPE MUST, and for limited industrial products. However, wine production is the major use and accounts for 80 per cent of all vineyard output.

The grapevine is grown on all continents except Antarctica, but most of the world's vineyards are in Europe. Three countries, Italy, Spain, and France, each have almost 1 million ha/2.5 million acres of vineyards, and Italy and France each produce almost one-quarter of the world's wine. *Vitis vinifera* cannot tolerate extreme winter cold. Requiring warm summers for fruit maturation, the vine is grown approximately between the 10 and 20 °C isotherm in both hemispheres, or about between latitudes 30 degrees north and 50 degrees north, and 30 degrees south and 40 degrees south (see map of WORLD PRODUCTION). Principally in order to minimize the damage associated with FUNGAL DISEASES, the grapevine has traditionally been grown in MEDITERRANEAN CLIMATES with warm, dry summers and mild, wet winters. The ready availability of AGROCHEMICALS, and to a lesser extent diseasetolerant varieties, has allowed this range to be extended, especially since the Second World War. Winter DORMANCY is essential for vine longevity, and the hot and humid climates nearer the equator are not conducive to either grape production or wine quality (although see TROPICAL VITICULTURE).

Most of the world's vineyards are planted with traditional VINE VARIETIES, which have been perpetuated for centuries by vegetative propagation. Different CLONES of these varieties may also be distinguished.

Many viticultural practices are very traditional, especially in Europe, where in many cases they are prescribed by law. Cultural operations and the reasoning behind them are introduced under VITICULTURE, VINE PHYSIOLOGY, VINE DISEASES, and VINE PESTS. The effects of climate and soils are also discussed in, respectively, CLIMATE AND WINE QUALITY and SOIL AND WINE QUALITY.

See VINE MORPHOLOGY for discussion of the parts of the vine, and VINE PHYSIOLOGY for details of how the vine functions. See also VINE GROWTH CYCLE and, for a historical perspective, ORIGINS OF VITICULTURE.   R.E.S.

Mullins, M. G., Bouquet, A., and Williams, L., *Biology of the Grapevine* (Cambridge, 1992).

Winkler, A. J., *et al.*, *General Viticulture* (2nd edn, Berkeley, Calif., 1974).

vine age, easily observable by the width of the vine's trunk, is widely considered a factor affecting wine quality, with widespread consensus that, in general, older vines make better wine. Indeed this idea is enshrined in APPELLATION CONTRÔLÉE legislation which, in many cases, specifically excludes the produce of vines less than three or sometimes more years old. The limited amount of wine from young vines destined to produce AC wine is typically sold as VIN DE TABLE. Some French producers deliberately exclude wine from vines under a certain age from their top bottlings, and put it into SECOND WINES. The concept that older vines make better wine is much used in marketing wine in the Old World (see VIEILLES VIGNES) and has more recently been adopted in the New World, notably by some California and Barossa Valley producers. Conversely, some winemakers observe that young vineyards produce their highest-quality wine in the first year or two of production, perhaps at least partly because yields are relatively low at this point. For example, in the world-famous blind tasting in Paris in 1976 which first pitted California Cabernets and Chardonnays against top-quality red bordeaux and white burgundies, Stag's Leap Wine Cellars S.L.V. Cabernet Sauvignon 1973 came out on top, scoring more highly than Ch MOUTON-ROTHSCHILD 1970 and Ch HAUT-BRION 1970, even though this was the first vintage and the vines were only three years old. Both of these apparently opposed viewpoints may be correct, as will be discussed below.

Conventional VINE TRAINING takes two to three years to form the vine framework, and if any bunches are formed they are traditionally discarded before they ripen. Once a vine produces one to three or so normal crops and is about three to six years of age, it usually fills its allotted growing space above ground, and so the YIELD and annual shoot growth normally stabilize, and will change only with a major alteration to management or growing conditions. Vineyards which are protected from stresses, pests, and diseases, and from too much or too little water and mineral nutrients, can be long living. An outstanding example is the famous vine at Hampton Court Palace near London, which is still producing large crops of grapes (under glass) despite being planted in 1769. Vineyards free from stresses are, however, rare.

The vigour and yield of many commercial vineyards begin to decline after 20 years, and by 50 years many vineyards are yielding at such a low level as to be normally considered uneconomic.

Below ground, however, the picture can be different. Champagnol defines three stages of ROOT GROWTH. During the first stage the root system colonizes available space, and this takes until the seventh to tenth year, taking longer in poor soils and with low VINE DENSITY. In the so-called adult stage there is little change in the volume of soil exploited, but

the final, senescent stage sees a reduction in root activity. This can be through the accumulation of cultivation wounds, or from the effects of drought, or from soil compaction by machinery, or lack of oxygen at depth. Root pests and diseases may also weaken the root system, and continued application of some fertilizers and spray materials can worsen SOIL ACIDITY and so reduce root health.

The parts of the vine above ground do seem to weaken with age, and senescence is more obvious. Despite perceptions to the contrary, winter PRUNING weakens the vine. Pruning wounds also allow the invasion of wood-rotting fungi, and continued summer TRIMMING is devigorating. In addition to this there are the continued effects of cultivation which can prune roots, and the exhaustion of the soil's mineral reserves.

The normal course of events, then, is for vines to show reduced VIGOUR as they age, and this is particularly evident for vines planted on sites with low SOIL potential. The conventional explanation for improved quality with vine age is because of reduction in yield, and indeed for many celebrated vineyards the two go hand in hand. However, since older vines are lower in vigour, exposure of the leaves and fruit to sunlight is better, which may offer an indirect explanation for the effect of vine age on wine quality.

The canopy MICROCLIMATE can also explain the apparent paradox that some vineyards seem to produce their best quality when young, often with the first crop in the third year. Such vines have FRUITFUL buds and so in the first fruiting year there is excellent vine BALANCE of leaves and fruit, and very good exposure of both to sunlight. Commonly the vine is more vigorous in subsequent years, the shoots grow longer and quality is reduced because of increasing SHADE. So such vineyards can produce premium quality for the first few crops and then quality may decline until the vine is old and vigour is low again.

R.E.S. & J.Ha.

Champagnol, F., *Éléments de physiologie de la vigne et de viticulture générale* (St-Gely-du-Fesc, 1984).

Smart, R. E., and Robinson, M., *Sunlight into Wine: A Handbook for Winegrape Canopy Management* (Adelaide, 1991).

vine breeding, the crossing of one vine variety or species with another to produce a new variety. Grapevines are highly heterozygous outcrossers and do not breed true from seed, which is the reason for their universal vegetative PROPAGATION. If both parent varieties belong to the same species (in practice, usually the European VINIFERA) of the VITIS genus, then the result is commonly called a CROSS or crossing, while the results of crossing varieties from more than one species (typically, a *vinifera* variety and a member of an AMERICAN VINE SPECIES) are commonly called HYBRIDS.

These NEW VARIETIES are traditionally created by dusting POLLEN from the male parent on to the receptive stigma of the female parent (see vine FLOWER), and then germinating the seed from the berry which subsequently grows (although see GENETIC MODIFICATION for more recent techniques). There is a very low probability that any one seedling will be a useful variety, and extensive testing, probably over more than ten years, for viticultural and wine-making suitability is required before any new variety is released.

The convention is to express the female parent first, thus EMERALD RIESLING is a Muscadelle × Riesling cross, while BACO 22A is a Folle Blanche × Noah hybrid (Noah itself being an AMERICAN HYBRID).

Vine breeding was particularly important in the early 20th century, notably in France, Germany, and Romania, as a European response to the spread of the PHYLLOXERA pest (see HYBRIDS and FRENCH HYBRIDS). Breeding of new varieties which combined high yields with high MUST WEIGHTS, and subsequently those which combined high wine quality with good resistance to pests and diseases, has been an important activity in such German centres as GEILWEILERHOF and GEISENHEIM.

The prospects for the breeding of new varieties are outlined by Einset and Pratt and Allewedt and Possingham. They emphasize the availability of germplasm among *Vitis* species which contains resistance to the major pests, diseases, and environmental stresses of *vinifera*. *V amurensis* and *V riparia*, for example, contain genes for winter hardiness, and *V vinifera* and *V berlandieri* for lime soil tolerance (see CHLOROSIS). Among various *Vitis* species can be found genetic resistance to the fungal diseases DOWNY MILDEW, POWDERY MILDEW, BOTRYTIS BUNCH ROT; the bacterial diseases of CROWN GALL and PIERCE'S DISEASE; and the soil pests of PHYLLOXERA and NEMATODES. A desire to minimize the use of AGROCHEMICALS has encouraged breeding DISEASE-RESISTANT VARIETIES to combine these natural resistances, notably in Germany and the United States.

Because of increasing emphasis on a few familiar VINE VARIETIES, and also the lingering suspicion of hybrids caused by the poor wine performance of the early French hybrids, some consumers view the results of breeding programmes with suspicion. Yet such programmes can offer the opportunity of an improved range of flavours and styles produced from vineyards which do not require any other means of pest and disease protection.

See also NEW VARIETIES. R.E.S.

Alleweldt, G., and Possingham, J. V., 'Progress in grape breeding', *Theoretical and Applied Genetics*, 75 (1988), 669–73.

—— Spiegel-Roy, P., and Reisch, B., 'Grapes (*Vitis*)', in J. N. Moore and J. R. Ballington (eds.), *Genetic Resources of Temperate Fruit and Nut Crops: Acta horticulturae*, 290 (1990), 289–327.

Einset, J., and Pratt, C., 'Grapes', in J. Janick and J. N. Moore (eds.), *Advances in Fruit Breeding* (West Lafayette, 1975).

Huglin, P., *Biologie et écologie de la vigne* (Paris, 1986).

vine density is a measure of how closely spaced vines are in the vineyard, both within the row and between rows. The choice of vine spacing is one of the most fundamental decisions in PLANTING a vineyard, and between, even within, the world's wine regions there is enormous variation in spacing. The traditional vineyards of France's Bordeaux, Burgundy, and Champagne regions have about 10,000 plants per ha (4,050 per acre) (and sometimes more), with vines spaced typically 1 m apart both within and between the rows. In many NEW WORLD vineyards, on the other hand, a spacing of 2.5 m/8 ft between vines along the row and 3.7 m/12 ft between rows, or 1,080 vines per ha, is quite common. Probably the most widely spaced vineyards of the world are those of the Vinho Verde region in Portugal, La Mancha in Spain, and some parts of Chile, Japan, and Italy (see TENDONE), with spacings as wide as 4 m by 4 m, or just 625 vines per ha.

It is widely held that high vine densities lead to improved wine quality. It is true that many of the world's most famous vineyards, especially in the Old World, have very narrow spacings, and so high densities, but it is difficult to argue that this is a prerequisite for quality production. Narrow spacings are indeed appropriate to vineyards of moderate VIGOUR, often a reflection of TERROIR effects and soil (see SOIL AND WINE QUALITY). Some New World vignerons have been encouraged to plant high-density vineyards on fertile vineyard soils in expectation of matching the quality of famous Old World vineyards. The theory is that such dense planting will cause root competition and substantial devigoration, but this has infrequently, if ever, been demonstrated, and the result is often a vineyard of high vigour which is very difficult to manage. The quality of fruit is affected by excessive SHADE, and this potentially also reduces quantity. The belief that 'tight spacing' encourages wine quality was widely promulgated in the 1980s and 1990s in California. Despite many commercial experiments, it remains to be demonstrated that wine quality is automatically increased, while the costs of establishing and running such a high-density vineyard certainly are. Research and commercial experience in Europe indicate that close row and vine spacings are suited only to vineyards of low SOIL FERTILITY, or more correctly of low soil potential. In high-vigour situations, some New World vine-growers have responded by removing one vine in two down the row, and sometimes two in three. This has been found to restore vine BALANCE, and yield and quality have subsequently improved.

High-density vineyards are the traditional form of viticulture in many parts of the world, as spacing need only be sufficient to allow the workers unhindered access. Some vineyards are not even planted in rows but were haphazardly arranged, like a field of wheat. Before PHYLLOXERA invaded Europe, unhealthy plants could be replaced by LAYERING a cane from an adjacent vine. These considerations, and the fact that vines then were generally less vigorous, encouraged high-density vineyards and densities were as high as 40,000 plants per ha, or just a quarter of a square metre per plant. Once GRAFTING to ROOTSTOCKS developed as a response to phylloxera, however, then the additional cost of each plant encouraged lower vine densities. The introduction of first animals and then TRACTORS led to the planting of vineyards in rows with a further reduction in vine density. The final factor leading to wider spacing between vines has been the need to provide sufficient space for modern, more vigorous vines. This follows from effective control of vine pests and diseases and weeds using AGROCHEMICALS, as well as the use of plants both VIRUS free and subject to CLONAL SELECTION.

OLD WORLD vineyards are generally planted more densely than those of the New World. Many New World vineyards were planted after the introduction of tractors, necessitating row spacings of about 3 m/10 ft or more. By contrast, most European vine-growers have chosen to persist with narrow rows and to develop either narrow tractors, or over-row tractors, known in France as *tracteurs enjambeurs*.

Vineyard density is a major consideration affecting the vineyard's yield, quality, cost of establishment and maintenance, and therefore profitability. Planting costs are proportional to the number of plants used; costs for TRELLIS SYSTEMS and DRIP IRRIGATION are higher with narrower row spacings. The time taken to plough and spray is also greater when rows are closer together.

Under most circumstances, the YIELD of densely planted vineyards is higher, especially in the first years of the vineyard's life and with vines planted on low soil potential. R.E.S.

Champagnol, F., *Éléments de physiologie de la vigne et de viticulture générale* (St-Gely-du-Fesc, 1984).

Galet, P., *Précis de viticulture* (5th edn, Montpellier, 1988).

vine diseases. Diseases caused by microbes can limit the distribution of vines and affect both yield and quality. See BACTERIAL DISEASES, FUNGAL DISEASES, VIRUS DISEASES, PHYTOPLASMA diseases, and the names of individual diseases. See also CLIMATE EFFECTS ON VINE DISEASES.

vine extraction. See RIPPING OUT for how it is done and VINE AGE and VINE PULL SCHEMES for some reasons why.

vine foliage lifter, machine which lifts vine foliage in the growing season. Once the foliage is vertical it can be secured by WIRES and is then well placed for TRIMMING to maintain a constant CANOPY outline. This is a particular aid to CANOPY MANAGEMENT. See also SHOOT POSITIONING.

vinegar, sour liquid condiment that depends etymologically, and often materially, on wine. The French word for it, composed of *vin* (wine) and *aigre* (sour), is a direct descendant of its Latin equivalent. Not just wine but any solution containing a low concentration (less than 15 per cent) of ETHANOL will turn to vinegar if exposed to OXYGEN. The ethanol is oxidized first into an ALDEHYDE and then to ACETIC ACID by the oxygen in the atmosphere. Winemakers over the centuries have learned to shelter wine from the action of atmospheric oxygen, and nowadays will do all they can to prevent their wines turning to vinegar, and 'vinegary' is a tasting term of great disapprobation (while 'winey' is quite a compliment when applied to a vinegar). Once the VOLATILE ACIDS in a wine have reached a certain point, however, it can have a potable future only as wine vinegar.

The OXIDATION of any dilute aqueous alcohol solution is greatly hastened by the action of a group of bacteria known as ACETOBACTER from the environment. These bacteria also hasten the reaction of some of the alcohol with some of the newly produced acetic acid to form the ESTER known as ETHYL ACETATE. This compound has a fruity flavour which, when added to the tart taste of acetic acid, gives the complex character to a good wine vinegar.

The everyday vinegar of the market place varies geographically. In southern Europe wine vinegar is the norm, for example, while in northern Europe malt, cider, and distilled vinegars predominate, and in the Far East rice vinegar is most usual.

Today a wide range of vinegars are produced, many flavoured with herbs and fruits, some, such as Italian balsamic vinegar, given BARREL MATURATION according to rules as strict as those governing APPELLATION CONTRÔLÉE wine production. The most powerful vinegars are so strong in ethyl acetate that their flavour can overpower that of a subtle wine. In foods served with subtle wines, wine itself can be used as a condiment, contributing the same sort of ACIDITY as a vinegar would have done. See also VERJUS.

A domestic vinegar SOLERA is one solution for wine LEFTOVERS. A.D.W.

vinegar fly. See FRUIT FLY.

vine growth cycle, the annual march of the vine's development, which begins at budbreak in the spring, and concludes at leaf fall in the autumn. There are distinct developmental stages along the way (see PHENOLOGY), the principal ones being BUDBREAK, FLOWERING, FRUIT SET, VERAISON, HARVEST,

	Winter			Spring			Summer			Autumn		

Vine growth cycle: patterns of root, shoot, and berry growth for the grapevine, for northern and southern hemispheres.

| South | Jun | Jul | Aug | Sep | Oct | Nov | Dec | Jan | Feb | Mar | Apr | May |
| North | Dec | Jan | Feb | Mar | Apr | May | Jun | Jul | Aug | Sep | Oct | Nov |

❶ first flush　　❹ cane maturation　　❻ flowering　　❽ veraison
❷ second flush　　❺ fruit bud initiation commences　　❼ fruit set　　❾ harvest
❸ budbreak　　　　 for following year's crop

when the grapes are mature, and LEAF FALL. The pace of development between these phenological stages varies greatly with vine variety. Very early varieties, such as MADELEINE ANGEVINE, go through the stages up to ripeness in a short time, and can therefore ripen in regions with a short growing season and relatively cool temperatures. In late varieties, such as MOURVÈDRE, CARIGNAN, and CLAIRETTE, all stages are prolonged and much more heat and time are needed to bring them to maturity. The length of the growth cycle also depends on climate, especially temperature. In hot regions, the period from budbreak to harvest may be as short as 130 days for early varieties, but in cooler regions this period can be over 200 days.

The vine often begins to grow later in the spring than most other deciduous plants, when the average air temperature is normally about 10 °C/50 °F in cool climates. The first sign of impending growth is vines BLEEDING as the soil warms, then the buds swell, and eventually the first tinges of green are seen in the vineyards as the shoot tips burst from the buds. The young shoots grow very slowly at first, producing small leaves on each side of the shoot. This early shoot growth depends on the reserves of CARBOHYDRATES stored in the vine, but soon the leaves are old enough for PHOTOSYNTHESIS and produce the carbohydrates which become the tissue of further shoot growth.

After about four weeks in warm climates, the principal period of growth begins, and shoots grow much more rapidly. Shoots may grow more than 3 cm/1 in a day, and

the observant can notice changes in shoot length from day to day. Shoot growth slackens at flowering or bloom, 40 to 80 days after budbreak depending on TEMPERATURE, but can continue to the end of the season under conditions of mild temperatures and overgenerous supplies of water and nitrogen. More commonly, WATER STRESS reduces shoot growth between flowering and veraison (or the beginning of grape RIPENING), and it may cease altogether later in the season. The shoot tips are sometimes trimmed, but will often grow again from lateral buds.

Small flower clusters are apparent on the young shoots as buttons, and in the few weeks before flowering they enlarge and the individual flowers are obvious. Flowering takes place when the average daily temperatures are about 15 to 20 °C (59–68 °F), and is followed by the so-called fruit set process.

The next significant stage is that of veraison, when grapes change colour and begin to ripen. This takes place about 40 to 50 days after fruit set. Between set and veraison, the berries grow to about half their final size, but remain green and hard. They contain low concentrations of SUGARS, but are high in organic ACIDS. Veraison is an easily observable stage when the berries change colour to either red-black or yellow-green, depending on the variety. The berries also soften, and they begin rapidly to build up sugar (see ENGUSTMENT). During this stage, the vines also rapidly accumulate carbohydrate reserves in the roots, trunk, and arms.

The most appropriate date of harvest depends on the desired stage of RIPENESS for

WINE-MAKING. It is earliest for sparkling wines, intermediate for table wines, and delayed for dessert and fortified wines. Harvest date may also be influenced by weather conditions. Fruit ripening normally proceeds quickly in hot areas, with rapid increases in sugars and PH and a decline in ACIDITY, especially MALIC ACID. In cooler regions the rate of ripening is slower, and the fruit typically has lower sugars and higher acidity. Rainfall near harvest can cause problems due to berry splitting, BOTRYTIS, and other bunch rotting fungi (see ROT). After rain, there is normally a rush to harvest grapes while they are still sound.

Leaf fall marks the end of the season, and of all the developmental stages it is the least precisely marked. Some leaves may fall off during the growing season, especially if the vine comes under stress, for example by drought, disease, or shade. A significant proportion of the leaves may also be removed by MECHANICAL HARVESTING. With continued warm and sunny weather following harvest, the leaves remain healthy and are photosynthetically active in replacing carbohydrate reserves in the vine trunk and roots. Once these levels are built up, the vines often lose their green chlorophyll colour and turn yellow. The first frost of the season causes leaf fall, and the vines are then in a dormant state. After PRUNING in winter, the vines are ready for the growth cycle to begin again.

See also VINEYARD ANNUAL CYCLE.　　R.E.S.

Champagnol, F., *Éléments de physiologie de la vigne et de viticulture générale* (St-Gely-du-Fesc, 1984).
Coombe, B. G., 'Grape phenology', in B. G. Coombe and P. R. Dry (eds.), *Viticulture*, i: *Resources* (Adelaide, 1988).
Winkler, A. J., *et al.*, *General Viticulture* (2nd edn, Berkeley, Calif., 1974).

vine guards, plastic tubes which became popular internationally in the 1980s and 1990s to protect young vines. As well as protecting vines from WIND, they also protect from HERBICIDES and vineyard PESTS, especially rabbits, and reduce vine-training costs, although in warmer wine regions they can create just too hot a MICROCLIMATE around the young plant. The guards are normally in place for one year, sometimes two. Wine tourists now witness coloured vine guards as the most obvious feature of new plantings.　　R.E.S.

vine identification. See AMPELOGRAPHY and DNA PROFILING for details of these two very different methods of identifying different VINE VARIETIES.

vine improvement, a group of practices designed to improve vine planting material for the benefit of vineyard YIELD and the quality of the fruit and wine produced. This is currently focused on eliminating harmful VIRUS DISEASES and also on genetic improvement. Some virus diseases such as LEAFROLL cause delayed RIPENING and can therefore have dramatic effects on wine quality. CLONAL SELECTION is a technique which, by selecting high-performance vines, can achieve both ends. Other techniques of virus elimination include THERMOTHERAPY and TISSUE CULTURE. Genetic improvement can also be achieved through beneficial MUTATION and selection, by GENETIC MODIFICATION, and by VINE BREEDING.

Although virus diseases had affected European vines since the end of the 19th century, it took some time for preventive action to be taken on a national scale. The first attempt at controlling the quality of planting material in France was made in 1944, when the Section de Contrôle des Bois et Plantes de Vigne (now part of ONIVIT) was formed, charged with avoiding the spread of virus diseases, and also with ensuring that all rootstocks used had sufficient resistance to phylloxera. Previously, nurserymen had been free to propagate whichever vines they chose, with sometimes disastrous effects for their clients.

In Germany there has been a high regard for the health of buds and rootstock for grafting, and rigorous clonal selection programmes and registration of CLONES has ensured high-quality planting material. Similar schemes operate in other European countries.

In non-European countries there has also been an awareness of the importance of quality control of propagation material. After the Second World War, the California wine industry created a model system for improving the quality of planting material. Research at the University of California at DAVIS had demonstrated the importance of virus diseases, and had shown how they might be detected. A so-called 'clean rootstock program' was developed which aimed to distribute only virus-free cuttings to nurseries, using thermotherapy and INDEXING in particular to produce virus-free plants. This has subsequently become known as FOUNDATION PLANT SERVICES (FPS), and has distributed high-health vines all around the world. In Australia and New Zealand, government officials worked with industry personnel to create at regional or state level a Vine Improvement Organization which became self-funding by the sales of improved planting material. R.E.S.

McCarthy, M. G., 'Grape planting material', in B. G. Coombe and P. R. Dry (eds.), *Viticulture*, i: *Resources* (Adelaide, 1988).

vine management, a term embracing all management practices in the vineyard, including especially SOIL PREPARATION and DRAINAGE; PRUNING and CANOPY MANAGEMENT; use of FERTILIZERS, MULCHES, and COVER CROPS; CULTIVATION and WEED CONTROL; use of FUNGICIDES and PESTICIDES; IRRIGATION; vine TRIMMING and LEAF REMOVAL; CROP THINNING to control YIELD; and HARVEST methods.

vine morphology is the study of the form and structure of the vine plant, as distinct from vine physiology, which is the study of its function. See ANTHER, ARM, BEARER, BERRY, BRUSH, BUD, BUNCH, BUNCHSTEM, CAMBIUM, CALYPTRA, CANE, CELL, CORDON, FLOWERS, GRAPE, HEAD, INFLORESCENCE, INTERNODE, LATERAL SHOOT, LEAF, NODE, OVARY, PEDICEL, PERICARP, PETIOLE, PHLOEM, POLLEN, PULP, ROOT, SEEDS, SHOOT, SPUR, STAMEN, STEM, STOMATA, TENDRIL, TRUNK, VINE, WATER SHOOT, and XYLEM. B.G.C.

vine nutrition, the supply of inorganic nutrients (sometimes called mineral nutrients or nutrient elements) to the vine. Vines, like other plants, require three major nutrients, NITROGEN, PHOSPHORUS, and POTASSIUM, and the minor or trace elements MAGNESIUM, MANGANESE, IRON, ZINC, COPPER, and BORON.

Among horticultural plants, the vine is regarded as having low nutrition requirements. For example, a common recommendation for apple orchards is to apply an annual fertilizer dressing of 80 to 300 kg/ha (70–270 lb/acre) of nitrogen (N), 50 to 250 kg/ha of phosphorus (P), and 50 to 800 kg/ha of potassium (K). A similar suggestion for vineyards would be 0 to 100 kg/ha N, 0 to 50 kg/ha P, and 0 to 120 kg/ha K. These low requirements reflect the low levels of nutrients that are removed from the vineyard each year by the grape HARVEST.

Measurements have been made in many countries of the amounts of elements contained in the grapes picked, and also in the leaf litter and winter prunings. These values vary with region, variety, and yield, but are about 50 kg/ha of N, 15 kg/ha of P, and 45 kg/ha of K. A general recommendation therefore would be to apply this amount of FERTILIZER if there was any doubt that the vineyard soil would be able to supply it. In general, SOIL TESTING before PLANTING can indicate any likely deficiencies. In mature vineyards, the standard procedure is to test either the leaves or the leaf stalks (PETIOLES) for their nutrient content, and apply fertilizers only as the need is indicated. For many

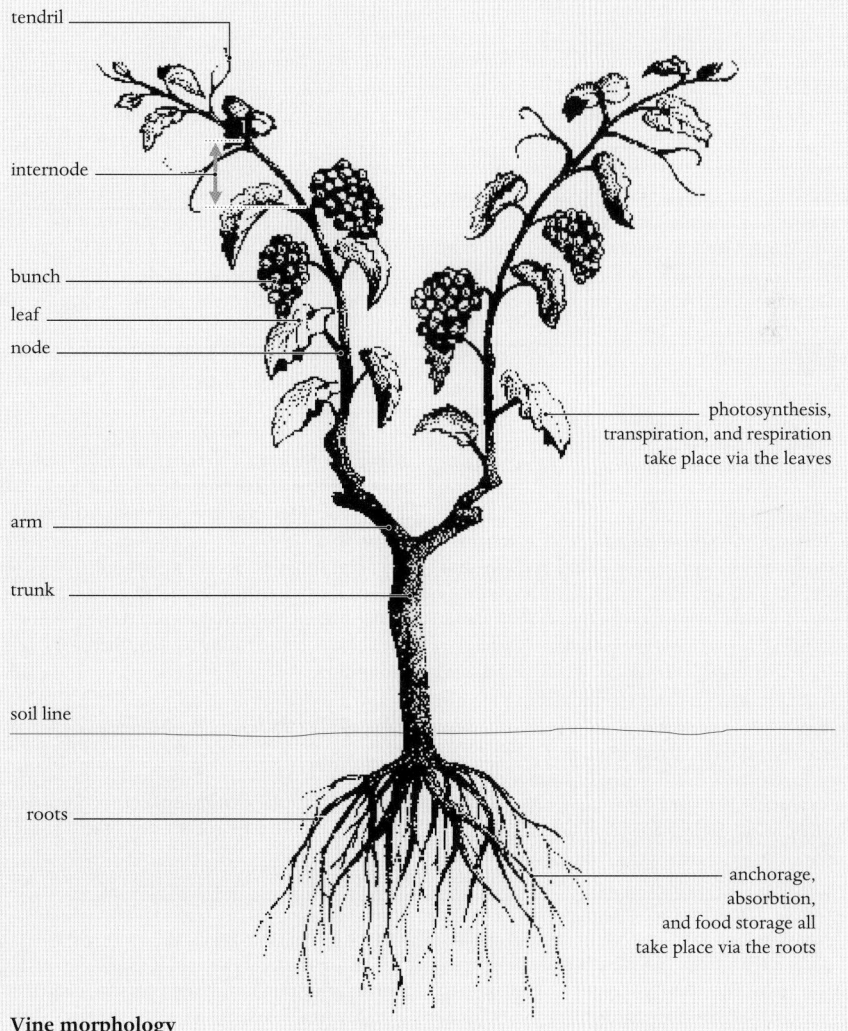

tendril

internode

bunch

leaf

node

photosynthesis, transpiration, and respiration take place via the leaves

arm

trunk

soil line

roots

anchorage, absorbtion, and food storage all take place via the roots

Vine morphology

crops, an annual addition of fertilizer will do little harm if it is not needed. For vines, however, such an addition is likely to be unnecessary and even wasteful since their needs are so low, and there is always the danger of over-fertilization, especially with nitrogen, which can directly and indirectly reduce wine quality. Similarly, high levels of potassium in soils can reduce wine quality because of increased wine PH.

Continued use of the same parcel of land for viticulture over extended periods of time reduces the levels of nutrients. Studies of old vineyard soils in Bordeaux have shown that fertility can be restored by heavy applications of ORGANIC MATTER, LIME, phosphorus, and potassium. Organic matter such as mulches and animal manures can be used to fertilize vineyards, but they are typically lower in nutrient content and more expensive. They often, however, improve soil structure by their organic matter content. Such forms of fertilizer are favoured for ORGANIC VITICULTURE.

Despite the common opinion to the contrary, there seems to be little connection between nutrition of the vine and wine character or quality other than through influences on vine VIGOUR. The lay perception is that soil directly affects wine quality through giving wines a special chemical signature which relates to their quality. Recent studies in Canada and elsewhere have shown that the vineyard origin may be determined by analysis of a wine's trace elements, but there is no necessary relationship to wine quality. See MINERALS for more explanation, and also SOIL AND WINE QUALITY and TERROIR.   R.E.S.

Danzer, K., De la Calle Garcia, D., Thiel, G., and Reichenbacher, M., 'Classification of wine samples according to origin and grape varieties on the basis of inorganic and organic trace analyses', *American Laboratory* (Oct 1999), 26–34.
Winkler, A. J., *et al.*, *General Viticulture* (2nd edn, Berkeley, Calif., 1974).

vine pests can make viticulture uneconomic and can have drastic effects on wine quality unless controlled. They include animals, insects, and nematodes (while VINE DISEASES include the microbes bacteria, fungi, phytoplasma, viroids, and virus).

The principal commercial wine grape VITIS VINIFERA is indigenous to Eurasia, whilst the majority of severe vine pests and diseases come principally from east and south east North America. Their accidental introduction to Europe from the 1850s onwards had dramatic consequences for local viticulture. The fungal disease POWDERY MILDEW was bad enough but fortunately a control was soon at hand. The insect pest PHYLLOXERA was not so easy to control, and for a period following its introduction in 1863 the entire French wine industry was threatened. Fortunately it was solved by grafting *vinifera* vines on to ROOTSTOCKS derived from AMERICAN VINE SPECIES which have natural resistance to phylloxera. This practice is now used worldwide.

In general, vine pests are easier to control than diseases, although the AGROCHEMICALS used to control insects (PESTICIDES) are among the most potent used in viticulture. The modern tendency is to depend less on pesticides and to develop strategies such as INTEGRATED PEST MANAGEMENT. Phylloxera is a threat to only a small proportion of the world's vineyards as over 85 per cent are grafted to rootstocks considered resistant. However, the insect pest MARGARODES is at present confined to only a few vineyard regions of the southern hemisphere, and at present there is only limited chemical control.

Vine pests can have dramatic effects on wine quality. One end of the spectrum is the pest causing the vine severe stress, as for example with root damage due to NEMATODES or phylloxera. Indeed this effect is frequently transient as it is a prelude to death and/or vine removal (see RIPPING OUT).

The following are some examples of how some pests can affect vines and reduce wine quality. Leaf area removal by beetles, deer, kangaroos, LOCUSTS, MOTHS, rabbits, and SNAILS can jeopardize PHOTOSYNTHESIS and grape RIPENING. Leaves can also be damaged and photosynthesis reduced by LEAFHOPPERS and MITES. Vine growth and yield are reduced by attacks on roots from gophers, phylloxera, margarodes, nematodes, and squirrels, and by destruction of the trunk and arms by BORERS and TERMITES. Damage to the grapes themselves by insects and birds can lead to BUNCH ROTS, which can be spread by fruit fly. Some pests can taint grapes, as for example the honeydew of MEALY BUGS and SCALE. Last but not least is the very important role of pests in carrying (vectoring) diseases. The dreaded and lethal bacterial PIERCE'S DISEASE is spread by leafhoppers, as is the phytoplasma disease FLAVESCENCE DORÉE. Important VIRUS DISEASES which can substantially reduce wine quality and yield are spread by nematodes and mealy bug.

For more detail see major entries under ANIMALS, BEETLES, BIRDS, FRUIT FLY, INSECT PESTS, MITES, NEMATODES, PHYLLOXERA; other entries are to be found under the pests' common name.   R.E.S.

vine physiological status, term often used to describe the condition of the vine. How the vine is responding to its environment is a most important consideration for the production of premium wine quality, especially during the fruit RIPENING period, but also during the preceding year.   R.E.S.

vine physiology, the science of the function of the VINE, including the growth and development of the vine shoot and root systems, its fruiting, and the major physiological processes such as PHOTOSYNTHESIS, TRANSLOCATION, and TRANSPIRATION. Physiology is also concerned with controls on plant growth and development, including both environmental and internal control by HORMONES. Both VINE NUTRITION and degree of WATER STRESS are affected by the vineyard soil, and TEMPERATURE and SUNLIGHT are the most important climate influences.

The vine's physiology can be manipulated by vineyard management techniques to alter growth, yield, and quality. For example, decisions on TRAINING SYSTEMS and PRUNING levels will alter the light incident on leaves, thus affecting photosynthesis and sugar supply to the grapes during RIPENING. The term VINE PHYSIOLOGICAL STATUS is often used to describe the condition of the vine, as for example the degree of water stress it is experiencing. Manipulating such conditions is the aim of the vineyard manager intent on maximizing wine quality.   R.E.S.

Champagnol, F., *Éléments de physiologie de la vigne et de viticulture générale* (St-Gely-du-Fesc, 1984).
Mullins, M. G., Bouquet, A., and Williams, L., *Biology of the Vine* (Cambridge, 1992).
Winkler, A. J., *et al.*, *General Viticulture* (2nd edn, Berkeley, Calif., 1974).

vine products, the range of products produced from the vine. The GRAPEVINE is the world's most important fruit crop, and WINE and its brandy distillates are by far the most important of its products. Other products include DRYING GRAPES, TABLE GRAPES, GRAPE JUICE, GRAPE CONCENTRATE, VINEGAR, VERJUS, grapeseed oil, and RECTIFIED GRAPE MUST. There are other minor products: grapevine cuttings (*sarments* in French) can be used for propagation or for barbecue firewood (although the latter is indeed a minor use); and vine leaves are used in Middle Eastern and Greek cuisine and for wrapping certain cheeses.   R.E.S.

vine pull schemes, schemes whereby growers receive some sort of incentive to pull out vines, a process known as *arrachage* in French. The most comprehensive of these schemes to combat various wine SURPLUSES is that embarked upon by the EUROPEAN UNION in 1988, which in the first eight years encouraged growers, mainly in southern France and southern Italy, to pull out a total of 500,000 ha/1,235,5400 acres, more than the entire vineyard area in the world's fourth biggest grower of vines, the United States. This reduced the EU surplus by an estimated 25 million hl. Many ageing vine-growers in these areas have come to expect this vine pull payment as they come to the end of their working life, regarding it as a retirement bonus. In few areas, however, have satisfactory alternative agricultural uses for the land been found. In 1998, the European Commission proposed retaining its grubbing up scheme for a further transitional period as part of a major reform of the wine sector. The plan

Still unpruned vines producing **Blanc de Morgex** at La Salle, Valle d'Aosta, on the Italian side of the alps, already dusted with early winter snow. It can be difficult to achieve high alcohol levels at this sort of **altitude** but the wines have an attractive delicacy.

put before European Union farm ministers proposed targeting member states and regions that were systematically over-producing wines for which there was little or no demand. With the reform of the EU Common Market Organization for Wine in 1999, a shift in policy created new planting rights for 51,000 ha/ 126,021 acres. Since the enlargement of the EU in 2004, the vineyard area has increased by 105,000 ha, so that the current area under vine is around 3.2 million ha.

An even more comprehensive vine pull scheme than the European Union's was enacted within a single country, the Soviet Union, as part of GORBACHEV's attempts to curb alcohol consumption. Between 1985 and 1990, the total area under vine in the old USSR fell from more than 1.3 million ha to 880,000 ha/2.2 million acres.

Other national vine pull schemes may be directed at particular types of vine in an effort to reduce production of certain wine types—usually in recent history wine of the most basic sort. Such schemes were applied in both ARGENTINA and NEW ZEALAND in the late 1980s, for example.

For details of the mechanics of pulling out vines, see RIPPING OUT.

vine removal. See RIPPING OUT.

vine spacing. See VINE DENSITY.

vine training, the process of establishing a vine framework in the required shape. Training includes tying down and trimming growing shoots in summer, followed by suitable winter PRUNING. Normally vines are trained to a supporting structure which may be as simple as a stake in the ground, or may be a more complex trellis system made from wire and wood, metal, or concrete posts. Training is normally complete within the first two or three years of a vine's life and well established before grape production begins. It will, however, take longer where vines are planted at wide distances apart and with complex trellis systems such as the TENDONE. Training normally consists of forming the TRUNK, the CORDONS or HEAD, and any arms required.

See under TRAINING SYSTEMS for more details of individual forms, and see also TRELLIS SYSTEMS for more details of their supports.

R.E.S.

vine-training systems. See TRAINING SYSTEMS.

vine varieties, distinct types of vine within one species of the vine genus VITIS (see also BOTANICAL CLASSIFICATION). Different vine varieties produce different varieties of grape, so that the terms vine variety and grape variety are used almost interchangeably. Each variety of vine, or grape, may produce distinct and identifiable styles and flavours of wine. Vine variety is *cépage* in French, *cepa*

in Spanish, *Rebsorte* in German, and *vitigno* in Italian. Professional botanists favour the term grapevine CULTIVARS.

All of the vine varieties we know today initially originated from WILD VINES. Domestication was made possible by propagating the best vines (see ORIGINS OF VITICULTURE) either by CUTTINGS or LAYERING (see PROPAGATION), thus producing genetically identical new plants. Afterwards, new vine varieties could originate from natural crossings between the vine varieties that had been selected, or between vine varieties and wild vines, or by selecting other wild vines. DNA PROFILING recently revealed several pedigrees of traditional and widespread modern vine varieties.

Most important vine varieties used to produce wine are of the European vine species *Vitis* VINIFERA. A number of varieties of AMERICAN VINE SPECIES and their AMERICAN HYBRIDS have also been used to make wine, however, although many suffer a bad reputation because of the resultant wines' FOXY character (the dark-skinned NORTON is a notable exception). American species are also used as ROOTSTOCKS. Wine has also been made from a range of Asian vine varieties and from the FRENCH HYBRIDS.

It is clear that specific vine varieties were recognized in Ancient GREECE and ROME, since some are already described in CLASSICAL TEXTS such as those of Pliny and Columella (see ANCIENT VINE VARIETIES). The extent to which the vine varieties of Europe originate from wild vines or were introduced is not known. Also, with the fall of the Roman empire, cultivated vineyards were abandoned, and such varieties as were deliberately cultivated presumably interbred with local wild vines and native *Vitis vinifera*. The result of this intermixing over time is that many European regions have developed their own local varieties.

There are approximately 10,000 known varieties of *vinifera*. Ampelographers Pierre Viala and Victor Vermorel listed about 5,000 different varieties in their great seven-volume AMPELOGRAPHY published between 1901 and 1910 (see MONTPELLIER). Many of these were synonyms, and modern French authorities list fewer than 220 varieties of commercial significance in modern France. Italy and Portugal have a particularly rich heritage of vine varieties, however, and Galicia in north west Spain is reputed to boast as many as 1,000 indigenous vine varieties. VINE IDENTIFICATION and the study of individual varieties' characteristics and aptitudes is as yet an underdeveloped field of activity.

Vine varieties are often named for the colour of their berries, with many French varieties, for example, coming in *noir* (black), *rouge* (red), *violet*, *rose* (pink), *gris* (grey-pink), *jaune* (yellow), *vert* (green), and *blanc* (white) hues. Not least because this is what usually appears on wine labels, this book uses the

convention of adopting a capital letter for each word in a vine variety's name, even though 'Pinot noir' may be botanically more correct than 'Pinot Noir'. Examples of mutants are Pinot Blanc and Pinot Gris, while Sauvignon Vert is a quite different variety from Sauvignon Blanc. See individual variety names for more details.

Varieties were classified and grouped into families by Levadoux, but DNA PROFILING is now shedding light on the true origin for many varieties. Varieties can be broadly grouped into three major botanical categories called PROLES, which are related to their geographical origins, and to some extent their end use. Varieties can also be classified in more detail by their country or region of origin, although as some varieties are becoming more international (see INTERNATIONAL VARIETIES) this distinction is becoming unclear.

Varieties may also be differentiated by their morphological features (see VINE MORPHOLOGY), of which a range is used to distinguish varieties and species in a scientific activity known as ampelography, recently supplemented by DNA profiling. Another classification is by end-product use, and so vine varieties may be described as being for wine, TABLE GRAPES, DRYING GRAPES, GRAPE JUICE, or for ROOTSTOCKS (although some varieties, such as SULTANA, are in practice used for several of these). Among wine vine varieties, some varieties are particularly well suited to different styles of wine: sparkling, fortified, sweet, or dry still wine, for example. Within each group there are noble varieties and those suitable only for lower-value products.

Most widely planted varieties

Of all vine varieties, remarkably few have achieved an international reputation, and most of these are French. Obvious examples of these INTERNATIONAL VARIETIES include Cabernet Sauvignon, Pinot Noir, Syrah/Shiraz, Merlot, Chardonnay, Sauvignon Blanc, and Riesling. As an increasing proportion of all wine is labelled VARIETALLY, there is increasing correlation between these most famous varieties and those which cover the greatest total area of vineyard land. Nevertheless most estimates agree that more of the earth's surface is devoted to Sultana/Thompson Seedless and AIRÉN (planted to Spain's relatively low VINE DENSITY) than it is to any well-known wine grape.

The table overleaf lists what appear to be the 20 most planted wine grape varieties in the world, although calculations were hampered by the fact that some of the statistics are described as 'estimates'.

Choice of variety

Vine-growers are rarely free to choose which vine variety to plant in a given vineyard. They may have acquired a planted vineyard in full production and cannot afford the

Drying Moscato grapes on rush mats in Piemonte. The ancient technique of deliberately concentrating the sugar in grapes after they have been picked to make **dried grape wines** is far more common in Italy than anywhere else.

Grape (synonyms in brackets)	Area in ha/acres 1998 (estimated)	Area in ha/acres 2004 (estimated)	Principal countries
Airén W	423,100/1,045,000	306,000/756,300	Spain
Cabernet Sauvignon R	146,200/361,000	262,000/648,300	France, Chile, USA, Bulgaria, Australia
Merlot R	162,200/400,600	260,0000/642,100	France, Italy
Garnacha R (Grenache, Cannonau)	317,500/784,500	209,800/518,500	Spain, France
Tempranillo R (Cencibel, Ull de Llebre, Tinta Roriz)	101,600/250,900	202,100/499,500	Spain, Portugal
Chardonnay W	99,000/244,400	179,300/443,100	USA, France, Australia, Italy
Syrah R (Shiraz)	Not in top 20	142,600/352,300	France, Australia, Argentina, South Africa
Ugni Blanc W (Trebbiano)	203,400/502,400	136,100/336,300	France, Italy
Rkatseteli W	128,600/317,700	127,500/315,100	Georgia, Russia, Ukraine, Bulgaria
Carignan R (Mazuelo, Carignane)	244,330/603,500	111,100/274,600	France
Bobal R	106,200/262,300	89,000/219,800	Spain
Pinot Noir R (Spätburgunder)	Not in top 20	86,500/213,700	France, Moldova, Germany, USA
Sauvignon Blanc W	60,700/150,000*	79,300/196,000	France, Moldova, Ukraine
Sangiovese R (Nielluccio)	98,900/244,300	77,000/190,300	Italy, Corsica
Monastrell R (Mourvèdre, Mataro R)	117,800/291,000	74,500/184,100	Spain, France
Cabernet Franc	Not in top 20	54,500/134,600	France, Argentina, USA, Canada
Catarratto W (Bianco Comune and Bianco Lucido 18,650)	75,400/186,200	50,900/125,850	Italy
Welschriesling W (Laški/Olasz Rizling, Graševina, Riesling Italico)	76,300/188,400	50,300/124,300	Ex-Yugoslavia, Hungary, Romania
Macabeo W (Maccabeu)	Not in top 20	49,700/122,800	Spain, France
White Riesling	Not in top 20	48,700/120,400	Germany, China, Ukraine, Australia
Muscat of Alexandria W (Moscatel de Málaga, Gordo, Hanepoot)	66,900/165,300	48,500/119,800	Spain, Chile, Algeria, Argentina
Aligoté W	71,800/177,400	45,000/111,300	Russia, Ukraine, Moldova, Bulgaria
Cinsaut R (Cinsault)	86,200/212,900	44,400/109,600	France, South Africa
Chenin Blanc W (Steen)	53,900/133,100	39,200/96,800	South Africa, USA, France

* approximate figure based on the unproven assumption that most of Chile's Sauvignon is not Sauvignon Blanc but all of that growing in eastern Europe is.

crop loss involved in changing variety either by RIPPING OUT established vines or by FIELD GRAFTING a new variety onto the trunk and root system of the old one. Different varieties need different conditions of soil and climate. Cabernet Sauvignon simply will not ripen regularly in cool regions, for example.

In France, and much of the EUROPEAN UNION, the varieties permitted may be regulated. Some of these restrictions can be traced back to the Middle Ages (see PINOT NOIR), but formalization took place from 1935 with the APPELLATION CONTRÔLÉE (AC) laws which authorize only specified varieties for each appellation, distinguishing between principal and secondary varieties (see appendix 1 for full details). Similarly, some varieties were completely banned (although it required more than 30 years for this law to have its effect). For the production of more basic VIN DE TABLE, l'Institut des Vins de Consommation Courante (IVCC, the precursor of ONIVIT) decreed in 1953 for each viticultural region three classifications of varieties: recommended, authorized, and tolerated until eventual removal. These laws have subsequently been overtaken by EU laws with the similar intent of allowing only specified varieties. For discussion of these restrictions, see VINE VARIETIES, EFFECT ON WINE.

In the New World, the choice of vine variety or varieties is often in practice determined by the style of wine that is eventually desired, many of them involving just one vine variety (typically sold as a VARIETAL wine). Examples of mono-varietal AC wines within France are Muscat de Frontignan, Muscadet, and Sancerre. Blends of two varieties often include those which are complementary, such as the productive and full-bodied Marsanne mixed with the lighter, rarer Roussanne for the white Hermitage, or the lightly coloured Aramon deepened by Alicante-Bouschet. Celebrated blends of three varieties include Sémillon, Sauvignon Blanc, and Muscadelle in Sauternes, and Pinot Noir, Chardonnay, and Meunier in champagne. Even more complex blends of varieties are common in red bordeaux and in Châteauneuf-du-Pape, both styles which are emulated in the New World. The mix of vine varieties that go into a single wine is called an *assemblage* in French and *uvaggio* in Italian and the mix of vine varieties that are planted on a single property, appellation or region, is called *encépagement* in French and does not exist in other languages.

Varieties themselves are often subdivided into various CLONES. While particular clones of many varieties have been selected through performance evaluation by CLONAL SELECTION, in many cases they cannot be separated by appearance.

See also NEW VARIETIES.   R.E.S., J.V., & J.R.

Galet, P., *Dictionnaire encyclopédique des Cépages* (Paris, 2000).

— *Précis de viticulture* (5th edn, Montpellier, 1988).

Mullins, M. G., Bouquet, A., and Williams, L., *Biology of the Grapevine* (Cambridge, 1992).

Olmo, H., 'The origin and domestication of the vinifera grape', in P. E. McGovern, S. J. Fleming and S. H. Katz (eds.), *The Origins and Ancient History of Wine* (Amsterdam, 1995).

Van Leeuwen, C., 'Choix du cépage en fonction du terroir dans le Bordelais', in *Un raisin de qualité: de la vigne à la cuve*, n° Hors Série du *Journal International des Sciences de la Vigne et du Vin* (2001), 97–102.

vine varieties, effect on wine. Of all the factors such as SOIL, CLIMATE, VITICULTURE, and detailed WINE-MAKING techniques which have an effect on wine quality, vine variety is probably the easiest to detect in a BLIND TASTING. The colour of the grapes' skin determines what COLOUR of wine can be produced: red wine can be produced only from dark-skinned grapes. Only grape varieties which ripen readily and/or are prone to NOBLE ROT are likely to produce good SWEET WINES, while only those with high levels of natural acidity are likely to produce good brandy or SPARKLING WINES. But, even more important in identification, individual grape varieties tend to produce wines with identifiably different flavours. Indeed, in very general terms, it is a mark of quality in a vine variety that it is capable of producing wines with distinguished flavours, even if those flavours are heavily influenced by weather and TERROIR and vineyard practice. Lesser vine varieties tend to produce wines that are neutral and undistinguished, however promising the vineyard site.

When more than one vine variety is used to produce a single wine, it is important that the wines produced by those varieties are complementary. Cabernet Sauvignon tends to blend well with wines that have more obvious fruit such as Merlot or warm-climate Syrah/Shiraz, for example, while the weight of Sémillon is a good foil for the aroma and acidity of Sauvignon Blanc. Other French examples copied elsewhere include Grenache with Syrah and, possibly, Mourvèdre and Cabernet Sauvignon with Syrah.

Wine quality is maximized if the vine variety or vine varieties are well suited to the site, in terms of climate, soil structure, ROOTSTOCK, VINE DENSITY, TRAINING SYSTEM, PRUNING regime, and other viticultural methods. Although to an increasing extent varieties are selected for new vineyards on the basis of climatic similarity with a classic wine region (see HOMOCLIME), matching vine variety to site is considered in its infancy in most of the NEW WORLD (even if certain combinations such as Coonawarra for Cabernet Sauvignon vines, or Central Coast and Oregon for Pinot Noir, established themselves earlier than most). In parts of the Old World, on the other hand, the matching of vine variety to site, or even whole regions, is so entrenched (see VINE VARIETIES above) that some would argue it amounts to restriction. The varieties Cabernet Sauvignon and Merlot undoubtedly perform extremely well in Bordeaux, but it is perhaps an unnecessary constraint to forbid Bordeaux vine-growers from planting, say, the Syrah grape of Hermitage.

Varieties vary in the range of environments they can tolerate. Chardonnay and to a slightly lesser extent Syrah, for example, are extremely versatile. Chardonnay can produce good wine in climates which vary from the coolness of Chablis to the hot interior valleys of California. Varieties such as Pinot Noir and Nebbiolo, on the other hand, appear to be extremely fastidious. See also CLIMATE AND WINE QUALITY.

The French APPELLATION CONTRÔLÉE system, which officially disapproves of citing vine varieties on the label, even as interpretation of a geographical appellation, is predicated on the belief that for every appellation there is an ideal vine variety or ENCÉPAGEMENT, or that the character of the appellation is stronger than that of any vine variety. While this is an attractive proposition (and it is certainly true that, for example, the appellation of a red bordeaux or a white Alsace wine is often more strongly identifiable than any single vine variety), it seems questionable for most wine regions, even within France. Regulations in other EUROPEAN UNION wine-producing countries tend to emulate those of France.

R.E.S. & J.R.

Galet, P., *Précis de viticulture* (5th edn, Montpellier, 1988).

Moran, W., 'The wine appellation: environmental description or economic device', *Auckland Cool Climate Symposium* (1988), 356–60.

Pouget, R., 'L'Encépagement des vignobles français d'appellation d'origine contrôlée: historique et possibilités d'évolution', *Bulletin de l'OIV*, 685–6 (1988), 183–95.

vineyard, name given to the field where grapevines are grown.

The contrast in connotations between the very words vineyard and field illustrates something of the special nature of vines as a crop. This may be partly connected with the symbolism of and pleasures associated with wine, but is also a function of the aesthetic appeal of vineyards in all seasons, whether the increasingly luxuriant green canopy of spring and summer, the flame-coloured leaves of autumn, or the rows of poignant black stumps in winter. The beauty of vineyards and vines plays an important part in wine TOURISM; it is difficult to imagine substantial numbers of people making a pilgrimage to a region famous for any other agricultural crop.

In most parts of the world, the vineyard is a well-defined entity, generally well demarcated by the borders of the straight rows. *Vignoble* is a common French term for a vineyard at all quality levels. In Bordeaux, and elsewhere, CRU may be used synonymously with a top-quality vineyard, while in Burgundy the terms CLIMAT or, in the case of a walled vineyard, CLOS are more common. In Italy the terms cru, VIGNA, SORÌ, and RONCO are all used. Recognition of single vineyards is less developed in Spain although innovator Miguel TORRES uses the term *pago*.

In an agricultural sense, vineyards are typically monocultures with vines the only plants growing, apart from COVER CROPS and WEEDS. Less frequently, however, vineyards are grown intermingled with other crops, the so-called *coltura promiscua* that was once the norm in much of central Italy. In the VINHO VERDE region of northern Portugal, vines are typically grown as borders around other fields which may contain field crops or orchards. Originally trained to wires attached to bordering trees, the vines of Vinho Verde are nowadays more commonly trained on wooden or metal supports, although they still surround fields in which other crops are grown.

Any one vineyard may be made up of smaller units, parcels, or fields, which may contain different vine varieties, clones, rootstocks, or vines of different ages. Sometimes fields are separated, as for example by headlands, hedges, or drainage ditches, and otherwise may be contiguous one with another.

Even relatively small vineyards are rarely homogeneous in terms of SOIL, TOPOGRAPHY, and MESOCLIMATE. Soils in particular may vary considerably within one single vineyard (see VOUGEOT or MONTRACHET, for example). Sometimes, when the soil, topography, and climate are uniform over an area much larger than a single vineyard, as in COONAWARRA in South Australia (although the soils are much, much more varied than the climate or topography), then the region as a whole may earn a reputation for good quality rather than certain vineyards within it.

Vineyards vary in size, depending on many factors. Owing to fragmentation of vineyards by inheritance, some vineyard owners in BURGUNDY may lay claim to only a few rows often indistinguishable to outsiders from the adjacent vines. At the other end of the scale in the New World, there are often large corporate vineyards. One of the world's largest vineyards is the 2,800-ha/6,920-acre San Bernabe ranch in the Salinas valley of MONTEREY in California.

Some vineyards are particularly famous for their wine because of their particular combination of VINE VARIETY, CLONE, ROOTSTOCK, and climate conditions, which can be distinguished at the various levels of MACROCLIMATE, MESOCLIMATE, and MICROCLIMATE. Of particular importance are the soil conditions, which, together with mesoclimate, constitute what the French (and others) call TERROIR. See under each of these entries for a discussion of their relative contribution. For example, a feature of the famous Bordeaux PREMIERS CRUS is that as well as producing great wine in good years they are also able to do well in acknowledged low-quality years. This is a function not just of appropriate vineyard management, but also of the terroir which allows the vine to ripen the fruit adequately when other, less exalted vineyards cannot.

See also HILLSIDE VINEYARDS, PLANTING, VINEYARD ANNUAL CYCLE, VINEYARD SITE SELECTION.

R.E.S. & J.R.

vineyard annual cycle. The march of the seasons through the year dictates the work to be done in vineyards (see VINE GROWTH CYCLE). Spring is the time of budbreak, and early ploughing and spraying must be done. Early spring is also the common time for PLANTING vineyards. As the temperatures rise, the vine shoots grow more rapidly, and FLOWERING takes place in early summer. This can be a busy period as often fungicide SPRAYS are to be applied, and the first SHOOT POSITIONING is carried out. Soon after FRUIT SET is the time for the second shoot positioning, and often the first TRIMMING. In those vineyards of the world where IRRIGATION is practised, the first applications of water are often made around this time, and may continue up to the time of harvest. About this period the nurseryman is doing BENCH GRAFT-ING, and it is also the time for FIELD BUDDING AND GRAFTING. As the summer progresses, many vine-growers are involved with further spraying of AGROCHEMICALS and often continued cultivation. Depending on the vine variety and region, the HARVEST may be in early, mid, or late summer, and sometimes in the autumn. Whenever it occurs, it is one of the busiest periods in the vineyard, often involving SAMPLING to test grape ripeness before the harvest itself. Depending on the spread of varieties, the harvest may be brief or protracted, but few other jobs are attended to in the vineyard at this time. The period immediately following harvest is busy in the wineries but not so in the vineyards, and vineyard workers and viticulturists often take their annual leave then. This is also the common time for soil RIPPING and maintenance of machinery and TRELLIS SYSTEMS. Once the leaves fall, the serious business of PRUNING begins, and depending on the scale of operations this may continue right up until budbreak. This is also the time when CUTTINGS are taken for PROPAGATION. R.E.S.

vineyard design, important component of vineyard planning before vineyard planting (except in traditional Old World areas where spacings, variety, and rootstock may well be prescribed). In a new vineyard, normally the first step is a topographic survey, followed by a soil survey and SOIL MAPPING, today in some instances using GLOBAL POSITIONING SYSTEM technology. Based on this important information, block layout and irrigation design proceeds, and finally on a block by block basis decisions are made about variety, clone, rootstock, row and vine spacing, and training system. In this way, the vineyard will optimize use of local resources, and in a way emphasize the TERROIR. R.E.S.

vineyard site selection is the single most important aspect of grape production in the NEW WORLD, even if it is not always appreciated as such. On the relatively rare occasions when a vineyard site may be selected in the Old World, it is of course just as crucial. (Most Old World vineyards have been in existence for centuries, and when a new vineyard is created, or re-created, another important consideration may be whether or not it qualifies for a certain APPELLATION.)

Vineyard site selection embraces more than just choosing the vineyard location, as the decision will affect the vineyard's YIELD, quality of the wine produced, and therefore the vineyard's long-term profitability. The site's regional climate, or MACROCLIMATE, for example, determines by virtue of temperature and sunshine hours which VINE VARIETIES should be grown, and the resulting likely wine style and quality. For example, lower temperatures produce more delicately flavoured wines, and

hot climates produce wines relatively high in alcohol. Such effects are discussed under CLIMATE AND WINE QUALITY. Vineyards are often planted at higher ELEVATIONS to take advantage of lower temperatures. The site selection process might include evaluating climatic data from distinguished wine regions in an attempt to locate similar climates, or HOMOCLIMES, as has been done with considerable success in Australia. With its enormous range of LATITUDE and ALTITUDE, Chile has a greater opportunity than most countries to match climates.

Modern science is creating new methods of vineyard site selection, especially based on Geographical Information Systems (GIS) and digitized databases. Researchers at VIRGINIA TECH in the US, for example, have identified sites with the greatest potential by overlaying maps of the same area according to different selection criteria such as elevation and land use, slope and aspect, and winter freeze risk. Such approaches provide a useful alternative to the trial and error more usually employed.

Similarly, rainfall and humidity affect the likelihood of many VINE DISEASES, especially important fungal diseases such as POWDERY MILDEW, DOWNY MILDEW, and BOTRYTIS BUNCH ROT. The likelihood of these diseases can be estimated by reference to climate records. In addition, the threat of NEMATODES may be evaluated by knowledge of indigenous types, or of the previous crops grown on the site. It may even be possible to avoid the introduction of PHYLLOXERA and other pests and diseases by creating a local QUARANTINE. If phylloxera and nematodes are considered a likely problem, the appropriate ROOTSTOCKS can be used.

The site climate, or MESOCLIMATE, affects, for example, the extent to which cold air drains away, and the likelihood of spring and autumn FROST. A site's proximity to bodies of water such as lakes (see LAKE EFFECT) can be important in providing protection from injury due to particularly low temperatures, as in NEW YORK state and SWITZERLAND. These attributes depend on local TOPOGRAPHY.

The balance between rainfall and evaporation indicates the likelihood of DROUGHT, and for some regions at least whether IRRIGATION is desirable, and the amount of water required. In many parts of the world availability of high-quality water for irrigation is an essential factor in site selection. This may involve locating vineyards near streams or rivers, or with access to underground (artesian) water, or opportunities to build dams.

SOIL conditions present at the site will determine vineyard VIGOUR, with deep, fertile soils, for example, leading to vigorous growth and the possibility of high yields, but the concomitant need to manage problems this creates (see CANOPY MANAGEMENT). Premium-quality vineyards are typically found on soils with low water-holding capacity, and low SOIL FERTILITY. Site selection normally involves a process of SOIL MAPPING and physical and

chemical analysis of soil samples. This allows potential problems such as poor DRAINAGE or SOIL ACIDITY to be treated appropriately before the vineyard is planted. Knowledge of soil depth indicates likely vine vigour.

Vegetation growing at the site, and the productivity and quality of other agricultural crops grown in the region, can be used as an indicator of the vineyard performance. The types of trees present give guidance as to the soil properties, and their size for their age indicates soil fertility and water supply.

Not all important features of potential vineyard sites are natural ones. Frontage to busy roads is essential if retail sales are expected from the vineyard site. Good communications with markets and proximity to a supply of LABOUR can also be significant. The performance and reputation of other vineyards in the area can also be commercially important. R.E.S.

vineyard weather stations contain a number of electronic instruments to measure the climate within a vineyard. Normally they comprise sensors for sunshine, air and soil temperatures, wind speed and direction, humidity, rainfall, leaf wetness, and occasionally evaporation. Data are stored in a data logger which may be downloaded to a portable computer, or remotely interrogated by a computer over a wireless or cable telephone connection. Such weather stations are used primarily for disease prediction, especially for fungal diseases such as DOWNY MILDEW and POWDERY MILDEW, and also for predicting vine PHENOLOGY. R.E.S.

vin gris is not, happily, a grey wine but a pink wine that is usually decidedly paler than most ROSÉ, made exactly as a white wine from dark-skinned grapes, and therefore without any MACERATION. No rules govern the term *vin gris*, but a wine labelled **gris de gris** must be made from lightly tinted grape varieties described as *gris* such as CINSAUT or GRENACHE GRIS.

In France, where it is a speciality of the Côtes de TOUL and certain parts of the Loire, *vin gris* is usually made from pressing, but not macerating, dark-skinned grapes, often Gamay, which rarely ripen sufficiently to produce a deeply coloured red. It is also made in the Midi, notably beside the saltpans of the Camargue by Listel, where care is needed to tint rather than dye the resultant wine. The term is also occasionally encountered in the New World—although BLUSH wines are extremely similar to, if almost invariably sweeter than, *gris* wines. See also SCHILLERWEIN and other German light pinks.

The style is particularly popular in Morocco, which produces gris with an orangey-pink hue, mainly from traditional varieties such as Cinsaut and Grenache, but also from Cabernet Sauvignon. Moroccan Gris de Boulaouane is one of the best-selling wines in French supermarkets.

Vinhão, official Portuguese name of the dark-skinned grape SOUSÃO.

vinho, Portuguese for wine, and **vinho de mesa** is Portugal's basic TABLE WINE. A **vinho maduro** is one that has been matured, for at least a year. A **vinho verde,** on the other hand, is a 'green' or young wine, designed to be drunk early.

vinho regional, third tier of designated wine regions in Portugal roughly equivalent in status to the French VIN DE PAYS (see also DOC and IPR). These large regions covering entire provinces—MINHO, TRÁS-OS-MONTES (with the subregion of Terras Durienses for wines from the Douro), BEIRAS, Ribatejano for RIBATEJO, ESTREMADURA, Alentejano for ALENTEJO, Terras do Sado, ALGARVE, and Terras Madeirenses for MADEIRA—permit greater flexibility in terms of permitted grape varieties and ageing requirements. The vinho regional designation is therefore popular with innovative winemakers wishing to bottle relatively young wines or blend Portuguese and foreign grape varieties. In the centre and south of the country (Estremadura, the Ribatejo, Terras do Sado, and the Alentejo), producers are largely ignoring the DOCs and IPRs in favour of vinho regional. R.J.M.

Vinho Verde, DOC in north west PORTUGAL producing light, acidic, often slightly sparkling, and highly distinctive wine whose name means 'green wine', a reference to the youthful state in which it is customarily sold. It is produced in verdant countryside inland from the coast north and east of the city of OPORTO which is known as the Costa Verde or Green Coast (see map under PORTUGAL). The Vinho Verde DOC region extends from Vale da Cambra south of the river DOURO to the river Minho that forms the frontier with Spain over 130 km/80 miles to the north. Rain-bearing westerly winds from the Atlantic support intensive cultivation and the countryside north of Oporto is one of the most densely populated parts of rural Iberia. It is impossible to assess just how much land is occupied by vineyard in the Minho. At the start of the 21st century, official figures recorded over 100,000 vineyards taking up just over 59,000 ha/145,000 acres. For every hundred farmers in the region, 90 count themselves as vine growers and in spite of the rampant industrialization of the region around Oporto, over a quarter of the workforce is still engaged in some form of agriculture. Ninety per cent of holdings are less than 5 ha in extent and the majority are little bigger than a suburban back garden. In order to make the best use of this cramped environment, vines have traditionally been grown high above the ground on pergolas (see TENDONE), stout granite posts up to 4 m/13 ft high leaving space for other crops underneath. Apart from making the best use of the limited available space, high-trained vines help to reduce the risk of GREY ROT, which is endemic during the warm, damp, growing season where average annual rainfall varies from 1,200 mm on the coast to well over 2,000 mm on the mountains inland. These practical advantages, however, are increasingly outweighed by such problems as the impossibility of MECHANIZATION. Many of the larger producers are therefore replanting vineyards on lower TRAINING SYSTEMS.

The Vinho Verde DOC officially divides into six subregions, distinguished by climatic differences and the white grape varieties grown there. The area around the town of Monção on the Spanish border produces one of the best but least typical Vinhos Verdes from the ALVARINHO grape. Alcohol levels of up to 13 per cent set these wines apart, and, thanks to a combination of consumer demand and low yields, they are relatively expensive. Further south along the river Lima and in the increasingly urbanized countryside around the towns of Braga, Barcelos, and Guimarães, the dominant grape varieties are LOUREIRO, TRAJADURA (both known, with slightly different spellings of their names, in GALICIA in Spain), and Pedernã (see ARINTO). These high-yielding vines produce wines that are light and acidic with an alcoholic strength typically between 8 and 10 per cent. Inland towards the river Douro around the town of Baião, AVESSO is the most important variety, producing a slightly fuller style of wine in a warmer, drier climate. With the exception of Alvarinho wines from Monção, under the local legislation Vinhos Verdes may not exceed 11.5 per cent alcohol and wines more alcoholic than this fall into the vinho regional designation of MINHO.

Vinho Verde originated as a rough and ready local wine made on a domestic scale. Following fermentation in open stone LAGARES, the wine would be run off into cask where the secondary MALOLACTIC FERMENTATION produced carbon dioxide. This was retained in the wine, giving it a slight sparkle. Until the 1980s, well over half of all Vinho Verde produced, however, was a fizzy, acidic, light, dry red with only about 10 per cent alcohol made from grapes such as Azal, Vinhão, and Espadeiro. Foreign palates struggle with these deep-coloured, rasping reds and, although it is still prized locally, little red Vinho Verde leaves the north of Portugal. Production of red is declining markedly.

With the drive to make wine for export in the 1950s and 1960s, white Vinho Verde came to be made on a much larger scale.

Most vine-growers now deliver at least a portion of their crop either to the local co-operative or to one of the larger private wineries. Following mechanical pressing and fermentation in vat, the malolactic fermentation is suppressed and CARBON DIOXIDE is injected before bottling to give the wine its characteristic pétillance. Since the 1980s, a number of single estates or QUINTAS have also emerged, some making high-quality VARIETAL wines from grapes such as Alvarinho, Loureiro, and Avesso. Although Vinho Verde is traditionally bone dry, most commercial BRANDS are sweetened to appeal to overseas markets. Few bottles carry a VINTAGE, but both red and white Vinho Verde should be drunk within a year of the harvest while the wine retains its characteristic fruit and freshness. R.J.M.

Mayson, R., *The Wines and Vineyards of Portugal* (London, 2003).

vinifera, the European species of VITIS that is the vine most used for wine production, to which all the most familiar VINE VARIETIES belong. *Vinifera* is not a classical Latin word, but one made up by Linnaeus (see BOTANICAL CLASSIFICATION) to denote 'wine-grape bearing'.

The species is thought to originate in Transcaucasia (see ORIGINS OF VITICULTURE), and has been spread through the Mediterranean and Europe by the Phoenicians and Greeks and later by the Romans. *Vinifera* was spread through the New World, initially by Cortés in SOUTH AMERICA, and subsequently into western North America. The Dutch took *vinifera* grapevines to the Cape of Good Hope in 1616 (see SOUTH AFRICA), and the English to Australia, then New Zealand, beginning in 1788.

Vinifera is one of about 60 species of the *Vitis* genus, the majority of which originate in the Americas or Asia. *Vinifera* grapes are used principally for wine-making, table grapes, and drying grapes. See VINE for more details. There are some 5,000 to 10,000 *vinifera* VINE VARIETIES, grouped into three PROLES.

Vitis vinifera is distinguished from other *Vitis* species by a range of general botanical features, including vigorous shoots mostly free of hair, prominent NODES and BUDS, regularly intermittent TENDRILS, leaves generally orbicular, more or less deeply lobed, PETIOLAR sinus often in a U or lyre shape, and conspicuous dentation (so-called teeth) around the edge of the leaf. *Vinifera* flowers are typically hermaphroditic (both male and female), and there are differences in seeds too (see GRAPE). Because *vinifera* vines are selected for their fruit characters, the seeds typically represent a small proportion of the berry weight, 10 per cent compared with 80 per cent for *Vitis berlandieri*.

Further details about *vinifera* can be found under the following entries, which describe more fully aspects of the commercial culture of this species, emphasizing its use in wine-making. Especially important are the effects of CLIMATE and SOIL. See also VINE VARIETIES, VINE GROWTH CYCLE, VINE BREEDING, VINE DISEASES, VINE MORPHOLOGY, VINE PESTS, VINE PHYSIOLOGY, VINE PRODUCTS, VINE TRAINING, and VITICULTURE. R.E.S.

Jackson, R., *Wine Science: Principles, Practice, Perception* (San Diego, 2000).

vinification, the practical art of transforming grapes into wine. In its widest sense, it is synonymous with WINE-MAKING, but strictly encompasses only those processes which take place in the winery up to the point at which the ÉLEVAGE of the new wine begins. See also OENOLOGY.

vin jaune, meaning literally 'yellow wine' in French, extraordinary style of wine made in France, mainly in the JURA region, using a technique similar to that used for making SHERRY but without FORTIFICATION.

In the Jura, where the most famous *vin jaune* appellation is CHÂTEAU-CHALON, the wine must be made from the curious local white grape variety the SAVAGNIN or Naturé, grown ideally on MARL. The grapes are picked well ripened, often not until late October, ideally at 13 to 15 per cent POTENTIAL ALCOHOL, and fermented as normal. The wine is then put into old 228-l/60-gal casks not quite filled so that there is a good surface of wine on which the local benevolent FILM-FORMING YEAST, called here the *voile* or veil, can develop. It is similar to the FLOR which is responsible for FINO sherries but can develop at a lower alcoholic strength and, because temperatures are generally lower, is not as thick. The *voile* also has to survive the harsher temperatures of a Jura winter, and takes two or three years to develop fully. After full development it will wane in cooler weather. OXIDATION is an important element in making *vin jaune*. The wine is left in cask, untouched other than to allow regular sampling to check the amount of ETHANAL formed (a crucial compound for the taste of *vin jaune*) and for a dangerous rise in VOLATILE ACIDS. It may not be bottled for a full six years and three months after the harvest, although not all of this time must be spent in cask. Considerable research is being undertaken to analyse precisely, and possibly replicate, the *voile*. (George observes that Chardonnay wine will develop *vin jaune* flavour under cultured yeasts designed to replicate the *voile* after about four years, but that it loses this nuttiness rapidly, unlike Savagnin.)

The finest *vin jaune* from the best vintages will last for 50 or more years in its distinctive 62-cl *clavelin* bottle (the amount of wine left after keeping a litre in a cask for six years, supposedly). Research in the 1990s showed that the compound SOTOLON develops in bottle, providing the distinct spicy or light 'curry' flavours in *vin jaune*. The wine should be served at cellar temperature or warmer and the bottle should be opened well in advance. The wine may be drunk with all sorts of savoury dishes, particularly of course chicken cooked in the wine itself, a classic dish, and the local Comté cheese. W.L.

A similar wine, called *vin de voile*, is made by at least one producer in GAILLAC.
George, R., *French Country Wines* (London, 1990).

Vínland. Driven westward by overpopulation in the second half of the 9th century, the Scandinavians colonized Iceland, then Greenland, and finally, a century later, as some sources tell us, Vínland, 'Wine Land', which must have been on the east coast of America.

Two sagas, Grenlinga Saga, the 'Saga of the Greenlanders', composed in the late 12th century, and Eirik's Saga, dated mid 13th century, give accounts of the discovery of Vínland, where wild vines, wheat, grassland and game are found.

Scholars do not agree on the precise location of Vínland. The sagas do not give clues, and, although archaeologists have found what appear to be traces of Norse settlements on the east coast of America, the evidence is not conclusive. Besides, the climate was warmer around AD 1000 than now (hence the colonization of Greenland; see CLIMATE CHANGE) so that vines could survive further north.

Even though the stories told in the sagas differ in some respects, they are not fantasy. An earlier and unrelated source supports the existence of Vínland. Around 1075 Adam of Bremen wrote a history of the archbishopric of Bremen and Hamburg, which until 1104 included the Scandinavian countries. Adam travelled to the royal court of Denmark, where King Svein Ulfsson, nephew of King Canute, tells him that Vínland has wild vines, which make excellent wine, and also wild wheat. So were the first winemakers in America Norse colonists? But if they were, the wine must have been made not from the European *Vitis* VINIFERA, but from native AMERICAN VINE SPECIES, almost certainly VITIS *labrusca*, which grows wild on the eastern coast of the United States. H.M.W.

Jones, G., *The Norse Atlantic Saga Being the Norse Voyages of Discovery and Settlement to Iceland, Greenland, America* (Oxford, 1964).

Magnusson, M., and Pálsson, H., *The Vínland Sagas* (Harmondsworth, 1965).

vin muté, wine that has undergone MUTAGE.

vin nouveau. See STURM.

vino, Italian for wine and, colloquially and unfairly, English for basic quaffing wine, or PLONK.

vino da meditazione, unofficial but useful Italian category of wines too complex (and often too alcoholic and/or sweet) to drink with food. Such wines, many of them extra strong and/or sweet because they are DRIED GRAPE WINES, should be sipped meditatively after a meal.

Although they do not employ the same terminology, and produce wines much lighter in alcohol, some Germans effectively treat fine wine as a *vino da meditazione* to be drunk once the table has been cleared of food and, often, beer.

vino da tavola, Italian for TABLE WINE, the official EUROPEAN UNION category denoting the lowest of the vinous low, but one that played a key role in the transformation of Italian wines in the late 20th century. Historically the great majority of each Italian wine harvest qualified as basic vino da tavola, although vino da tavola was also worn as a badge of honour by many producers who stepped outside the DOC laws of the time and came to designate some of the finest, and most expensive, wines Italy produced.

These new **vini da tavola** were born in 1974 with the appearance of TIGNANELLO and SASSICAIA, both marketed by the Florentine house of ANTINORI. Although the wines were produced in entirely different geographical zones (CHIANTI CLASSICO and BOLGHERI respectively) and from entirely different grape varieties (a predominance of Sangiovese and Cabernet Sauvignon respectively), they shared four significant characteristics that were to mark the evolution of this category of wines. They both represented an attempt to give more body, intensity, and longevity to Tuscan red wines, which had become lean and attenuated. Unlike the prevailing Tuscan red wine norm, these blends excluded white grapes. Non-traditional, non-Italian varieties were used in both blends (the 1975 Tignanello substituted Cabernet Sauvignon for the native CANAIOLO). And, in a move that was to delight French COOPERS, small oak barrels, principally of French origin, were used for the BARREL MATURATION of both wines. This latter innovation was a radical break with the local practice of using large casks of Yugoslav oak, and marked a movement towards a more international style. The move was not welcomed by all in the domestic market and forced Antinori to seek a wider international public for the wines; it also forced them to seek more flavour intensity and concentration in the wines to avoid an overwhelming oakiness.

The vini da tavola were born out of frustration with the DOC laws that came into practice in the late 1960s. These laws enshrined the practices of low quality and high quantity that prevailed in Italy in the post-war years, so any producer who tried to pursue a quality route found his way blocked by absurd laws. In Chianti, for instance, Antinori were compelled by DOC laws to add at least 10 per cent white grapes to their blend. In their effort to produce a superior red wine, they had to ignore this stipulation. Rather than do battle, they stepped outside the legal framework at the urging of Italian wine journalist Luigi VERONELLI, a vehement opponent of the mediocrity of the DOC laws.

The blend of the 1975 Tignanello (80 per cent Sangiovese, 20 per cent Cabernet Sauvignon—

the first vintage had included 3 per cent Malvasia) rapidly became canonical and was to prove extremely influential over the following 15 years. Cabernet Sauvignon has remained principally a blending grape in Toscana due both to a certain unfamiliarity with the variety on the part of growers and to the costs of transforming entire vineyards. A certain number of Cabernet Sauvignon-based wines began to appear, particularly after the middle of the 1980s. The native Sangiovese grape was hardly neglected, however, and a substantial number of BARRIQUE-aged, 100 per cent Sangiovese wines began to appear in the 1980s, the pioneering effort being Montevertine's Le Pergole Torte in 1977.

Experiments with earlier maturing varieties SYRAH and, with notable success, MERLOT became increasingly common in the late 1980s, both for blending with Sangiovese and for VARIETAL wines. The first PINOT NOIRS appeared at the same time, principally from vineyards at over 450 m/1,480 ft in altitude, where Sangiovese has traditionally had difficulties in ripening, although the suitability of this Burgundian variety to the Tuscan climate has yet to be demonstrated. Some non-traditional white varieties were also planted, notably CHARDONNAY and SAUVIGNON BLANC, and various OAK treatments essayed.

Sassicaia was a pioneering wine, not only in its use of Cabernet but also in its revaluation of a zone never known for producing fine or even commercial wine. When first offered commercially, Sassicaia had to be sold as a vino da tavola, not because, as with Tignanello, it eschewed the legal constraints of the area, but because there was no DOC for BOLGHERI reds at the time. Its example has been followed by other peripheral areas of Toscana. At the time, these could not qualify as DOC wines, just as non-traditional varietal wines in an area such as Chianti Classico cannot be given DOC status.

In 1992, the Italian government finally bowed to EU pressure and introduced the Goria law, named after the then Minister of Agriculture. This led to the introduction of IGT with the 1994 vintage, which resulted in the phasing out of such vini da tavola

If these high-priced 'outlaws' were initially confined to Toscana, the mid 1980s saw a significant expansion of the phenomenon. Ambitious producers saddled with poorly conceived DOCs and/or a poor image for the wines of their zone were quick to profit by the example of Toscana. Superior Sangiovese from Romagna and superior versions of INTERNATIONAL VARIETIES from Friuli and the Trentino, frequently barrique aged, followed suit. This latter category of wines was a true reversal of formal values: the fruity and refreshing (if somewhat simple) Cabernet, Chardonnay, Sauvignon, and Pinot Noir of these two regions continued to be released as DOC wines while newer, more ambitious,

more substantial versions of the same varieties, frequently from the same houses, were released as vini da tavola at substantially higher prices. Some of these wines returned to the DOC fold in the 1990s, partly as a result of the greater prestige and credibility now accorded to the wines of their zones and regions, but many important wines were still deliberately sold as vini da tavola in the mid 2000s.

Piemonte, with a more consolidated viticultural tradition and with a certain number of prestigious DOCG wines, was slower to accept the idea that the term vino da tavola could be a viable alternative, but Barbera, the region's most widely planted variety, existed in a bewildering variety of styles. It was therefore almost inevitable that the first important small barrel-aged Barberas in Piemonte were vini da tavola and, as the number of these wines increased, many producers—not only in Asti or the Monferrato, but also in the LANGHE—began to release their basic Barbera as a DOC wine and their superior Barbera as a vino da tavola. As a region with a significant amount of experimentation with newly introduced international varieties, Piemonte eventually followed the Tuscan example. Younger producers' experiments with Nebbiolo/Barbera blends, or even more baroque blends such as Barbera/Cabernet Sauvignon, combinations obviously neither imagined nor covered by existing DOCs, had no alternative to vino da tavola status until the creation of an overall regional DOC in 1995. They are now being marketed as either Langhe Rosso or Monferrato Rosso.

Italian wine thus does not follow the example of French or German viticultural classification, whose finest and most expensive products are almost inevitably the appellation wines and whose respective VIN DE TABLE and TAFELWEIN enjoy a generally low status. Italy has, in reality, two structures: the first is the classic pyramid of DOC, a direct copy of the French AC laws; the second a more modern structure called IGT that accommodates innovation and diversity to an extent that confounds many an envious French producer who feels manacled by AC laws.

Today vino da tavola is found only on wines that do not qualify for a DOC or an IGT, so will increasingly revert to being the lowest rung on the quality ladder, as in France and Germany.

See also SUPERTUSCAN.   D.T. & D.C.G.

vino de la tierra, increasingly important category of wines from specially designated zones in SPAIN which have not qualified for DO status—the equivalent of the French VIN DE PAYS.

vino de mesa, Spanish term for TABLE WINE, the most basic category for wine coming from vineyards that do not qualify for either VINO DE LA TIERRA or DO status.

vino de pago, Spanish term for high-quality, single-estate wines, which in some regions have already been granted their own appellations, be it as VINO DE LA TIERRA (Vino de la Tierra Terrerazo in the Valencia region, for example) or DO (Denominación de Origen), such as Finca Elez and Dominio de Valdepusa in Castilla-La Mancha. See also PAGO.

Vino Nobile di Montepulciano, potentially majestic and certainly noble red wine made exclusively in the township of Montepulciano 120 km/75 miles south east of Florence in the hills of TOSCANA in central Italy. It was one of the first four DOCGs conferred in 1980. Following a change to the DOCG regulations in 1999, the wine can now be made solely from Sangiovese, and must be at least 70 per cent Sangiovese, here called Prugnolo Gentile. Traditionally, producers would have blended in Canaiolo, Mammolo, Trebbiano, and even Gamay, but since the mid 1980s Sangiovese has come to the fore as the principal variety of Montepulciano.

The soil of the zone has a higher percentage of sand than the production zones of Chianti Classico or Brunello; the slopes, which face mainly east to south east, are planted at altitudes of 250 m to 600 m/2,000 ft, although the best wines undoubtedly come from the lower vineyards.

Vino Nobile has an illustrious history, having been lauded as a 'perfect wine' by the cellarmaster of Pope Paul III in 1549, by Francesco Redi in his 'Bacchus in Toscana' of 1685 (he called it 'the king of wines'), and by G. F. Neri in the late 18th century, who gave it the title 'noble'. The area planted rose rapidly after the introduction of the DOC in 1966. Between 1970 and 1989, the total vineyard rose from less than 150 ha/370 acres to 760 ha; production rose from 8,000 hl/211,000 gal to 30,700 hl; and the number of producers bottling their own wine increased from seven or eight to 40. By the mid 2000s there were 820 ha of vineyard in the zone owned by 167 producers who account for an annual production of just under 34,000 hl.

The wine itself is rather fuller in body and more alcoholic than Chianti, reflecting its warmer production zone. It has so far not shown the aromatic finesse and elegance of the best Chianti or Brunello, possibly because of the lack of limestone in the soil, or because of Montepulciano's warmer evenings and nights. In recent years, producers such as Avignonesi and Poliziano have shown the potential that the zone undoubtedly has with Riserva wines such as Grandi Annate and Vigna Asinone, both of which contain some Cabernet. New oak has replaced large old casks in many cellars, and while an excess of oak is evident in some wines, this is balanced by a decrease in the number of oxidized or musty wines that spent far too long in old casks. Legally, the wine must be aged for two years (from January 1 following the vintage) in order to qualify as a Vino Nobile; for Riserva, this period is extended by a year. Despite these improvements, the wines have not been able to gain the prestige or fetch the prices of the better Chianti Classico Riservas and are undoubtedly the poor relation of BRUNELLO DI MONTALCINO.

In an attempt to mirror the success of Rosso di Montalcino, a DOC for Rosso di Montepulciano was created in 1989 for earlier-maturing wines but the total production is less than 5 per cent of that of its big brother. D.T. & D.C.G.

Vino Santo. See VIN SANTO.

Vin Santo, 'holy wine', TOSCANA's classic amber-coloured dessert wine, is produced throughout this central Italian region. It is made traditionally from the local white grapes TREBBIANO and MALVASIA (although the red SANGIOVESE is also used to produce a wine called Occhio di Pernice, or eye of the partridge) which have been dried on straw mats under the rafters, in the hottest and best-ventilated part of the peasant home (see DRIED GRAPE WINES). The grapes were normally crushed between the end of November and the end of March, depending on the desired RESIDUAL SUGAR level in the wine (the longer the drying process, the greater the evaporation and the sweeter the must), and then aged in small barrels holding between 50 l and 300 l/79 gal. These barrels, often bought second hand from the south of Italy, were frequently made of chestnut, but the 1980s saw a decisive turn towards OAK. The barrels themselves are sealed and never topped up, resulting inevitably in ULLAGE and OXIDATION which gives the wine its characteristic amber colour. Some producers believe in using a *madre,* or starter culture, comprised of yeast cells from previous batches of Vin Santo in order to help the fermentation and to add complexity to the blend. Others, in true Tuscan fashion, view the *madre* as a throwback to the time when all Vin Santo was marred by faults and refuse to countenance its use.

The wine comes in a bewildering range of styles from the ultra-sweet to a bone-dry version which more closely resembles a dry FINO sherry than a dessert wine. The habit of keeping the barrels under the roof in a space called the *vinsantaia* encouraged refermentation each year when warm weather arrived and tended to exhaust the unfermented sugars that had remained in the wine. Today, most producers keep their Vin Santo in a cellar with a more constant temperature so as to retain a degree of freshness in the finished wines.

Until recently, most Vin Santo was sold as a VINO DA TAVOLA, simply because the authorities had struggled to codify the bewildering array of styles contained within the many localized traditions. Large DOCs such as Val d'Arbia

and Colli dell'Etruria Centrale, formulated in the mid 1990s, have been superseded by DOCs for specific areas; most of the major wine-producing zones in Toscana now have their own DOC for Vin Santo. Trebbiano and Malvasia are the mainstay of many of these DOCs, as a number of producers argue that the production technique is far more important in determining the style of the eventual wine than the grape varieties used. However, the fact that Occhio di Pernice is a DOC in many zones, where the use of red grapes is permitted, illustrates that even in the production of Vin Santo, varietal quality is a key factor.

The quality of the wine itself varies wildly, not only as a result of variation in grape composition, RESIDUAL SUGAR, and wine-making competence, but because the land is divided between so many smallholders, all of whom seem to feel obliged to produce Vin Santo as an obeisance to the tradition of offering this wine to guests as a gesture of esteem. Although some delicious Vin Santo is made, there is also a considerable proportion with serious wine FAULTS, particularly an excess of VOLATILITY, usually a direct consequence of lengthy BARREL MATURATION. DOC rules insist the wine is matured for at least three years, and the better producers rarely release their Vin Santo before five years. Cask maturation, without RACKING, lasts from four to more than ten years for the most traditionally made wines.

Producers who manage to produce traditional yet fault-free Vin Santo include Avignonesi, Capezzana, Fontodi, Isole e Olena, Poliziano, San Giusto a Rentennano, and Selvapiana. Any bottle called **Vin Santo Liquoroso** will have been made by adding grape spirit to sweet must, and will have been produced in four months rather than four years, something that will be reflected in the price.

Trentino also produces its own version of Vin Santo called **Vino Santo**, made from the NOSIOLOA grape and a decisively sweet DRIED GRAPE WINE. These wines are quite different from Tuscan Vin Santo since they are aged in barrels subject to regular TOPPING UP, although they too are decidedly artisanal and very variable in quality. D.T. & D.C.G.

Vinsanto is the official term for the sweet wines of SANTORINI.

Tachis, G., *Il libro del Vin Santo* (Florence, 1988).

Vins de Moselle. See MOSELLE.

Vinsobres, one of the better Côtes du Rhône villages, awarded its own red wine appellation in 2005. The wine must include a minimum of 50 per cent Grenache and at least 25 per cent of either Syrah or Mourvèdre, with Carignan and Cinsault also permitted. Superior producers include Domaines Chaume-Arnaud, du Coriancon, and du Moulin.

vintage can either mean the physical process of grape-picking and wine-making, for which see HARVEST, or it can mean the year or growing season which produced a particular wine, for which see VINTAGE YEAR. A vintage wine is one made from the produce of a single year.

vintage assessment is important enough to have an immediate effect on PRICE but is also notoriously difficult because quality and character can vary so much between producers and properties. A vintage is often assessed at the most difficult stage in its life, its infancy, for reasons of commerce and curiosity. Wine MERCHANTS and WINE WRITERS habitually taste wines from the most recent vintage in a wine region important for INVESTMENT when they are just a few months old and are still in cask. Quite apart from the fact that the wines are at this stage still being made (see ÉLEVAGE), samples may give a misleading impression because they have been specially chosen and groomed to show particularly well at this early stage, or too long has elapsed since they were drawn from cask (OXIDATION is a common problem), or, if they are tasted directly from cask, because they are undergoing a distorting treatment such as FINING. Furthermore, this sort of vintage assessment may be before the ASSEMBLAGE process and provides only a snapshot of embryonic wine from a small proportion of the total number of barrels produced.

This sort of comparative tasting can usually give some indication as to which are the most and least successful wines of a given vintage, but it can be difficult to stand back from the individual samples, accurately remember exactly how the same wines from previous vintages tasted at the same stage, and make any reliable assessment of the likely characteristics and potential of the young vintage as a whole. Vintages of which the collective assessment at this young stage was subsequently agreed to have been too enthusiastic include 1975 in Bordeaux and 1983 and 1996 in Burgundy, but other examples abound. (Wine merchants have proved themselves much less likely to err on the side of caution.)

The assessment of a mature vintage is a much less hazardous process that is usually undertaken in the form of a horizontal TASTING, although of course SUBJECTIVITY plays its part as it does in all tasting.

Broadbent, M., *Great Vintage Wine Book II* (London, 1991).

—— *Wine Vintages* (London, 1998).

vintage charts are both useful and notoriously fallible, partly because young VINTAGE ASSESSMENT is so fraught with difficulty. Most vintage charts take the form of a grid mapping ratings for each combination of wine region and year. The least sophisticated vintage charts content themselves with a NUMBER for each major wine region: Bordeaux

2003 '8' (out of 10), for instance. More sophisticated charts (such as that regularly updated in Robert PARKER's newsletter) divide Bordeaux into its main districts, and add a letter indicating maturity: Margaux 2003 '91T' (91 out of 100, T for Still Tannic), for instance. The fact that this same vintage chart suggests that Pomerol 2003 is '84E' (E for Early maturing) already demonstrates how difficult it is to generalize about a district in which there may be hundreds of different producers, each with a different wine-making policy and style of wine.

The most useful vintage charts are the most detailed, but also those that are regularly updated on the basis of continuous and relevant tasting. The INTERNATIONAL WINE & FOOD SOCIETY was one of the first to issue a vintage chart, in 1935. The Society has since then issued an annual vintage chart, updated by a committee expressly charged with this task.

vintage port, in France often called *le vintage*. See PORT.

vintage year, the year in which a wine was produced and the characteristics of that year. Most, but not all, of its characteristics result from particular WEATHER conditions experienced. In the southern hemisphere, a **vintage-dated** wine invariably carries the year in which the grapes were picked, even though much of the VINE GROWTH CYCLE was actually in the previous year. In the northern hemisphere, vintage-dated wines carry the year in which both the vine growth occurred and the grapes were picked (with the exception of those rare examples of EISWEIN picked in early January, which are dated with the year whose vine growth produced the wine). The expression 'vintage year' is also sometimes used of a year producing particularly high-quality wines.

In a literal sense, all young wine is vintage wine, being from a single year. Only at the BLENDING stage may wine of a recent year, or vintage, be mixed with older wines into an undated blend. Most everyday wines—such as the TABLE WINE category designated by the EUROPEAN UNION, the JUG WINES of the US, and CASK WINE in Australia—are not vintage dated. Some top-quality CHAMPAGNE and most SHERRY is NON-VINTAGE too. In most circumstances, however, a non-vintage wine is inferior to a vintage-dated one.

The vintage year printed on a wine label can help the consumer decide when to open a particular bottle, being particularly relevant to wine meant for AGEING (others, the great majority of wines, should simply be drunk as young as possible). Since the capacity of a wine to improve with age is one obvious test of its quality, a vintage's status is only fully established in retrospect (whatever those charged with selling it may say; see VINTAGE ASSESSMENT).

The concept of vintage year has a long history. OPIMIAN wine, made in the consular year of Lucius Opimius, 121 BC, was celebrated for decades afterwards as a particularly fine vintage. The celebrated RHINE Steinwein of AD 1540, last drunk in 1961, was made in a freak year so hot and dry that the Rhine dried up, and people could walk across its bed.

Vintage years did not become a normal commercial consideration until the end of the 17th century, when BOTTLES and CORKS replaced BARRELS for long-term wine storage. Vintages became particularly important towards the end of the 18th century, when the modern bottle shape evolved, allowing bottles to be stored on their sides. The better red wines of Bordeaux came to be 'laid down' for many years, and it was then that what is now regarded as the traditional Bordeaux style of WINE-MAKING for prolonged BOTTLE AGEING became established.

Penning-Rowsell gives details of some of the more famous Bordeaux vintages. The celebrated 1784 clarets, sought out and imported by America's wine-loving President Thomas JEFFERSON, were from one of the many fine vintages spanning the late 18th century and first years of the 19th century, culminating in the reputedly outstanding 'comet' year of 1811. Other runs of predominantly good Bordeaux vintages followed in the 1840s and again in the 1860s and the first half of the 1870s: a period long remembered as the crowning glory of the PRE-PHYLLOXERA era. The limited climatic records available suggest that these were predominantly warm periods.

Vintage years in contemporary Bordeaux, and throughout central and western Europe, tend still to be those of ample sunshine (especially in spring, and again in late July and August), and average or higher TEMPERATURES leading to a normal or early HARVEST date. Bad vintage years have almost invariably been cool and/or wet, with below-average sunshine.

In hot and reliably sunny viticultural climates, on the other hand, the best years for table wines are usually average or cooler than average. This generalization does not apply to sweet FORTIFIED WINES, which need more or less unlimited warmth and sunshine. Nor does it necessarily apply to all table wines, or all hot areas. For instance wet, cloudy, and relatively cool summers in the very warm Hunter valley of NEW SOUTH WALES are usually inferior for red table wines, although they may still produce good-quality white table wines.

The reactions of vines and grapes to seasonal conditions or weather events can also differ widely according to SOIL type within an area. As demonstrated by the extensive studies of Seguin in Bordeaux, vines on well-drained, deep soils may be little affected by variations in RAINFALL, whereas those on shallow and poorly drained soils will alternate between drought stress and waterlogging under the same rainfall. For this reason the best vineyards, with favourable TERROIR, are the least subject to vintage variation and can maintain consistently high quality.

In addition, VINE VARIETIES can react quite differently to the weather conditions depending on their individual timings of BUDBREAK, FLOWERING, and RIPENESS, and the relative sensitivities of their berries to rain, diseases, or damaging heat. PINOT NOIR, like most other early-maturing red grape varieties, is very sensitive to heat or direct exposure of the berries to SUNLIGHT, readily suffering *coups de soleil*, or SUNBURN. ZINFANDEL, with its tightly packed bunches, is notoriously sensitive to any rain towards harvest time. The least rain and water uptake causes berry splitting and subsequent total BUNCH ROT. This is probably the main reason its extensive use is confined to California and Puglia, where the ripening season is free of rain. CHENIN BLANC is similarly susceptible, at least in climates such as those of California and South Africa, where the preceding weather is mostly hot and dry. By contrast the CABERNET SAUVIGNON of Bordeaux is relatively tolerant of both heat and rain, and is therefore generally less affected by vintage differences, so long as the weather has been warm enough to ripen it.

A final point is that critical weather events, particularly heavy rainfall and HAIL, are not necessarily uniform within a given district and year. Even if they were, management decisions can lead to quite different results—depending, for instance, on the extent to which SPRAYING has been practised, or whether grapes are picked before, during, or after rains at harvest time.

Nor is weather the only possible external influence on the characteristics of a particular vintage year. Market conditions may dictate how or whether certain viticultural practices such as PRUNING and CROP THINNING are carried out so as to influence crop quality or yield. Social history may also dictate some characteristics of a vintage year, as in some of the vintages ripened in European vineyards during the Second World War. There have also been instances of CONTAMINANTS from a new pesticide which have affected particular vintages of certain wines, sometimes on a less than localized scale, as in the use of Orthene in Germany in 1983.

For all these reasons, vintages are seldom uniformly good, medium, or bad, even within a small area (see VINTAGE ASSESSMENT). A generally recognized 'vintage' year can have its failures, often for reasons totally beyond the competence of vignerons and winemakers. Equally, 'poor' vintages can usually still produce good wines from particular locations and grape varieties.

See AUCTIONS and INVESTMENT. See also LABELLING INFORMATION.   J.G. & R.E.S.

Penning-Rowsell, E., *The Wines of Bordeaux* (6th edn, London, 1989).

Seguin, G., ' "Terroirs" and pedology of wine grow-ing', *Experientia*, 42 (1986), 861–72.

vintner, late Middle English word for wine MERCHANT which superseded **vinter**. Mainly because of England's links with BORDEAUX, vintners were some of the most important people in the City of London in the 14th and early 15th centuries (four mayors of London were vintners in Edward II's reign). The **Vintners' Company** evolved from the 'Mistery of Vintners', a group of London and Gascon merchants who enjoyed a practical monopoly on London's important wine trade with Gascony from at least 1364. It was formally incorporated in 1437, and was recognized by Henry VIII as one of the '12 great' livery companies. It is still based at **Vintners' Hall** by the Thames in London, in a section of the City known as Vintry ward, where for centuries wine would be unloaded for sale throughout southern England. Any member of the Vintners' Company is a freeman of the City of London and is still allowed to sell wine without applying for a licence. Today UK wine trade EDUCATION, regulation, and control are under its auspices, as is the Institute of MASTERS OF WINE.

The word has also come to be used for a wine producer as well as a wine merchant, particularly in North America.

Simon, A., *History of the Wine Trade in England*, ii (London, 1964).

vin viné is a traditional term for a wine made strong and sweet by the addition of alcohol to grape must at some point before fermentation is complete. A VIN DOUX NATUREL and a VIN DE LIQUEUR are both therefore *vins vinés*. See also MUTAGE.

Viognier became one of the world's most fashionable white grape varieties in the early 1990s, mainly because its most famous wine CONDRIEU is distinctive, associated with the modish RHÔNE, and has until recently been relatively scarce. By the mid 2000s, it had become a common blending partner with various red grapes, especially SYRAH, for CO-FERMENTATION. CHÂTEAU GRILLET is the only other all-Viognier French appellation. Through DNA PROFILING in 2004, researchers Vouillamoz at DAVIS and Schneider at Torino suggested a parent–offspring relationship with FREISA from Piedmont, a likely progeny of NEBBIOLO, thus Viognier was claimed Nebbiolo's cousin—something of a surprise.

The vines need a relatively warm climate and can withstand drought well but are prone to POWDERY MILDEW. The grapes are a deep yellow and the resulting wine is high in colour, alcohol, and a very particular perfume redolent of apricots, peaches, and blossom. Condrieu is one of the few highly priced white wines that should probably be drunk young, while this perfume is at its most heady and before the wine's slightly low acidity fades.

The vine was at one time a common crop on the farmland south of Lyons and has been grown on the infertile terraces of the northern Rhône for centuries but its extremely low productivity, often due to poor FRUIT SET, saw it decline to an official total of just 14 ha/35 acres in the French agricultural census of 1968—mostly in the three northern Rhône appellations in which it is allowed, Condrieu, CHÂTEAU GRILLET, and, to an even lesser extent, CÔTE RÔTIE, in which it may be included as a perfuming and stabilizing agent up to 20 per cent of the Syrah-dominated total.

French nurserymen saw an increase in demand for Viognier cuttings from the mid 1980s, however (when the red wines of the Rhône enjoyed a renaissance of popularity), and by 1988 were selling half a million a year. By 1997, more than 100 ha/250 acres of Viognier qualified for the Condrieu appellation and by the turn of the century, Viognier plantings throughout the LANGUEDOC had reached 1,540 ha (from 139 ha in 1993). Considerable further plantings in the northern Rhône, many of them outside appellation boundaries, took the total French area of Viognier up to 2,360 ha in 2000 and it has doubtless continued to increase since then. The great majority of French Viognier is sold as a VIN DE PAYS.

Here and elsewhere the variety has shown itself a willing and able blending partner, not just with other Rhône varieties such as ROUSSANNE, MARSANNE, GRENACHE BLANC, and ROLLE, but also, usefully, with Chardonnay. This latter blend has had some success in Italy, although that country's total plantings of Viognier are extremely modest. Graf Hardegg makes some fine varietal Viognier in Austria.

In California, too, the variety has been much in demand with the state total increasing from 25 acres/10 ha in 1988 to over 2,000 acres/800 ha, particularly in the Central Coast, by 2003. Many examples are notably high in alcohol when ripened under the reliable California sun, but Viognier has to be fully ripe before it reveals its trademark heady aromas. So seductive is it that there has been considerable experimentation with it all over North America, notably in VIRGINIA and CANADA. Both Argentina and Chile, where there are almost 200 ha, have made some convincing examples of this popular variety which is also planted in Brazil and, with particular success, in Uruguay. Australian producers, led by Yalumba, have welcomed it enthusiastically, using it both as a varietal white wine and as a 5–10 per cent blend with Shiraz. Perhaps slowed by its QUARANTINE requirements, South Africa has lagged behind in this particular race.

Today the consumer can choose from a range of recognizably perfumed, if slightly light, southern French varietal Viogniers, some of them produced from vines FIELD GRAFTED over to Viognier from less fashionable varieties. The California way with Viognier is a notably alcoholic one, but when it works these monsters can be magnificent.

Viosinho, low-yielding white variety producing some good white wines, especially at higher altitudes, in the DOURO, nothern Portugal. Traditionally a constituent of white PORT, Viosinho is now also used to make unfortified wines.

Viré-Clessé, white wine appellation created from the 1998 vintage for the communes of Viré, Clessé, Laizé, and Montbellet in the Mâconnais which extended to 219 ha/540 acres by the mid 2000s. It is controversial in that the rules expressly forbid wines with RESIDUAL SUGAR, thus excluding those of the most famous local producer, Jean Thévenet. The names of superior vineyards La Montagne, La Bussière, En Collonge, and Quintaine are sometimes appended.

Virgil (Publius Vergilius Maro) (70–19 BC), Latin poet and good, if unoriginal, source of information on viticulture in Ancient ROME. Like HORACE, Virgil benefited from the patronage of the Emperor Augustus, and much of his poetry was written in praise of Roman and Italian virtues. The rural virtues are expounded in the *Georgics*, a didactic poem about agriculture, published in 37 BC. The second of the four books is devoted mainly to vine-growing. Although it is of little use as a practical manual, it does give a lively and colourful picture of the life and problems of the vine-grower. Like HESIOD, Virgil's purpose was moral, and his main concern is to describe the farmer's virtues of austerity, integrity, and hard work, which made Rome great. Although Virgil is from a literary point of view a more interesting writer than his chief source VARRO, he is not an independent authority, and it is to his predecessors CATO and Varro, and to the later COLUMELLA and PLINY, that we must turn for first-hand information about Roman viticulture.　　　　　　　　H.M.W. & H.H.A.

Griffin, J., *Latin Literature and Roman Life* (London, 1985).

Johnston, P. A., *Virgil's Agricultural Golden Age: A Study of the Georgics* (Leiden, 1980).

Virginia, mid Atlantic state in the eastern UNITED STATES in which wine production has increased substantially since 1980. Grapes have been planted there since the early settlers came to Jamestown in 1607, making the first wine in the New World from indigenous grapes. It is to Thomas JEFFERSON, however, that credit is given for importing fine French wines to his estate at Monticello (now an AVA in central Virginia), and for attempting, unsuccessfully, to grow and vinify VINIFERA varieties. *Vinifera* grapes now outnumber HYBRIDS and native grapes by almost 4 : 1. Chardonnay and the red Bordeaux varieties do exceptionally well, and interesting wines are also made from Norton, Touriga Nacional, Tannat, Petit Verdot, Viognier and Petit Manseng. The growing season is warm and humid so growers have to guard against FUNGAL DISEASES by careful selection of site and variety, CANOPY MANAGEMENT, and SPRAYING regimes. The total number of wineries increased from 6 in 1979 to more than 90 by 2005. Five other AVAs are Virginia's Eastern Shore, influenced by the Chesapeake bay; Northern Neck George Washington Birthplace in northern Virginia close to the ready market of Washington, DC; Shenandoah Valley (not to be confused with the California AVA) bounded by the Allegheny mountains to the west, the Blue Ridge mountains to the east, the James river to the south, and the Potomac river to the north; North Fork of Roanoke; and Rocky Knob in southwest Virginia.

H.L., B.W.Z., & T.K.W.

www.virginiawines.org

Virginia Tech in Blacksburg, VIRGINIA, is home to the Enology–Grape Chemistry Group, part of the Department of Food Science and Technology. The Group was established by B.W. Zoecklein in 1986 for graduate teaching and research, with the aim of helping the wine industry to lower production costs and improve wine quality. Research is mainly in the areas of analytical chemistry, increasing grape aroma/flavour potential, and aroma/FLAVOUR PRECURSORS. The Group provides web-based technical information at www.vtwines.info.

Virginia Tech's viticulture research and extension programmes are conducted through the Agricultural Research and Extension Center at Winchester, in the northern Shenandoah valley, under the direction of Tony K. Wolf. Grape research has focused on aspects of cold stress physiology, vine and vineyard management to optimize crop yield and quality, cultivar and clone evaluations, and pest management. Technical information is disseminated through meetings, web-based resources (http://arecs.vaes.vt.edu/arec.cfm?pid=vitis), and *Viticulture Notes*, a bi-monthly newsletter started in 1986.

B.W.Z. & T.K.W.

viroids, particles smaller than VIRUSES which are thought capable of producing virus-like disease effects in the grapevine. Viroids can be found in nominally virus-free vines following THERMOTHERAPY, and are known to cause significant diseases for other crops. They are transmitted by vegetative PROPAGATION as for viruses, but viroid-free grapevines can be produced by TISSUE CULTURE. No viroids have so far been identified with commercially important grapevine diseases. The viroid Yellow Speckle is widespread in Australia but is not known to harm the vines.

R.E.S.

Mullins, M. G., Bouquet, A., and Williams, L., *Biology of the Grapevine* (Cambridge, 1992).

virus diseases, group of VINE DISEASES caused by very small and simple organisms, consisting of ribonucleic acid wrapped in a protein sheath. Some virus diseases can seriously affect grapevine yield and wine quality, and since they are mainly spread by PROPAGATION in CUTTINGS, there has been an emphasis on VINE IMPROVEMENT and CLONAL SELECTION to prevent their spread. Virus diseases began to affect European vines from about 1890, when ROOTSTOCKS were used in France to control PHYLLOXERA. GRAFTING doubles the risk of virus spread and, unlike many fruiting varieties, rootstocks do not always show virus symptoms.

Virus diseases are mostly spread by taking cuttings from infected plants, although some are spread by NEMATODES and insects. They are mostly detected by inoculating sensitive plants (see INDEXING), and more recently by serological techniques based on immunological reactions (see ELISA) and ribonucleic acid analysis. Often viruses do not kill the vine but each year they reduce both growth and yield. For example, rootstocks infected with leafroll virus show no symptoms but the virus can greatly reduce wine quality as it delays fruit ripening. It is probably the most important vine virus disease in many parts of the world. Considerable viticultural effort has been expended in vine improvement and in developing virus-free vines.

Common virus diseases are CORKY BARK, FANLEAF DEGENERATION, LEAFROLL VIRUS, RUGOSE WOOD, NEPOVIRUSES. See also BACTERIAL DISEASES, FUNGAL DISEASES, PHYTOPLASMA diseases.

R.E.S.

Bovey, R., *et al.*, *Virus and Virus-Like Diseases of Vines: Colour Atlas of Symptoms* (Lausanne, 1980).

Pearson, R. C., and Goheen, A. C., *Compendium of Grape Diseases* (St Paul, Minn., 1988).

Weber, E., Golino, D., and Rowhani, A., 'Laboratory testing for grapevine diseases', *Practical Winery and Vineyard* (Jan/Feb 2002), 13-27.

Visan, one of the Côtes du Rhône villages. See RHÔNE.

viscosity, the quality of being **viscous**, the extent to which a solution resists flow or movement. Honey is more viscous than sugar syrup, for example, which is considerably more viscous than water. Viscosity, which approximates to what wine tasters call BODY, can be sensed by the human palate in the form of resistance as the solution is rinsed around the mouth.

A very sweet wine is more viscous than a dry one, even if they have the same ALCOHOLIC STRENGTH. Alcohol itself is more viscous than water, and higher-strength wines are therefore more viscous than lower-strength wines. An increase of 1 per cent in alcoholic strength increases viscosity relative to water by about 0.04 units, while an increase of 10 g/l in RESIDUAL SUGAR increases viscosity by about 0.03 units. The most viscous wines of all therefore are those that are both sweet and strong. The dissolved solids in wine, the wine's EXTRACT, also add marginally to its viscosity, so the less a wine has been subjected to FILTRATION and FINING, the more viscous it is.

It has been thought that the viscosity and the (quite unrelated) GLYCEROL content of a wine were the main factors in the formation of 'tears' on the inside of a wine glass. While they may be minor factors, the explanation is very different. See TEARS.

A.D.W.

Vitaceae, the family in the plant kingdom which includes the genus VITIS containing the grapevine. There are 12 genera altogether with about 700 species, which are spread through tropical and temperate zones around the world. The plants in the family are characteristically climbers with leaves opposite tendrils. See also BOTANICAL CLASSIFICATION.

R.E.S.

Vital, white grape grown in Estremadura in western Portugal which is known as MALVASIA Corada in the Douro.

vitamins, a group of organic compounds that are essential dietary components, deficiencies causing a variety of well-known disorders in humans. The levels of vitamins in grapes increase during ripening but the final values are relatively low compared with those of many other fruits. The most abundant is ASCORBIC ACID (vitamin C), the levels of which vary considerably—from 15 to 150 mg/l, which is only 10 per cent of that in oranges (although ascorbic acid is often added during winemaking). Average values for the concentrations of other vitamins are about 1 to 10 parts per million (ppm) for niacin, pyridoxine, and pantothenic acid; 0.1 to 1 ppm for thiamine and riboflavin; and 0.001 to 0.01 ppm for biotin and folic acid. These levels in grapes are too low to be considered as a serious dietary source and are further reduced in wine by the use of SULFUR DIOXIDE and YEAST growth (although AUTOLYSIS can add others). Wine also contains low concentrations of vitamin B_{12} (cobalamine).

The 'bioflavonoids', or vitamin P, a complex that includes D-catechin and many other flavonoids, occur in grape juice in large amounts, especially in dark-skinned berries. P is held to be a blood-capillary fragility factor and may play a part in warding off heart disease, although its credentials as a vitamin are contentious (see HEALTH).

B.G.C. & A.D.W.

viticulteur, French term for a vine-grower.

viticulture, the science and practice of grape culture. Viticulture is practised consciously by VITICULTURISTS, often instinctively by grape-growers or vine-growers. Practices vary enormously around the world; some of these differences are highlighted under NEW WORLD.

Grapes can be grown, over a wide range of LATITUDES, in climates ranging from very hot (southern California, central Australia) to very cool (England, Luxembourg). Viticulture is practised in very wet climates (parts of New Zealand) to very dry ones (Copiopo in Chile, Central valley in California). The TOPOGRAPHY can be very steep, as in the Mosel valley of Germany or the Douro of Portugal, or very flat plains, as in many regions of Australia and Argentina. VINE DENSITY can vary enormously: from vineyards planted with large numbers of very small vines, as is common in Champagne and Bordeaux (10,000 vines per ha (4,050 per acre)), to few, large vines as in the Vinho Verde vineyards of Portugal (600 vines per ha). Some vineyards may be tended entirely by manual LABOUR, while others are MECHANIZED. Vineyards may rely on IRRIGATION for their survival where they are grown in deserts, while in others, such as France, irrigation is forbidden.

The following entries follow the sequence of vineyard development from initial planning through to picking: VINEYARD SITE SELECTION; choice of ROOTSTOCK, VINE VARIETY, and CLONE; SOIL TESTING and SOIL PREPARATION; choice of VINE DENSITY and TRELLIS SYSTEM; vine PLANTING, VINE TRAINING, and PRUNING; control of VINE PESTS, VINE DISEASES, and WEEDS; fruit SAMPLING and HARVEST. See also VINEYARD ANNUAL CYCLE.

Effects on wine quality

For still wines, it is arguable that the VITICULTURIST can have a greater impact on wine quality than the WINEMAKER since so many of the factors affecting quality are viticultural. The belief that 'wine is made in the vineyard not the cellar' became increasingly widespread during the 1990s.

Quite apart from the decisions involved in vineyard site selection, there are obvious ways in which viticulture can influence wine quality—selection of vine variety, rootstock, clone—and some where the effects are more difficult to identify.

Usually premium-quality wines come from vineyards planted to soils with good DRAINAGE and of low SOIL FERTILITY. However, inappropriate vineyard management can destroy the potential for wine quality. For example, over-enthusiastic applications of nitrogen FERTILIZERS will result in excess vineyard VIGOUR which may delay RIPENING and encourage FUNGAL DISEASES. The SPRAYING regime adopted by the vine-grower can determine whether the grapes are affected by BUNCH ROT or not.

The choice of vine-TRAINING SYSTEM and associated trellis system can have fundamental effects on wine quality. Limits on YIELD are also imposed by appellation laws in some regions. Where vines are pruned lightly to many buds and carry too low a LEAF TO FRUIT RATIO then the fruit will not ripen properly and wine quality will be reduced.

Vineyards may require judicious IRRIGATION to prevent excessive WATER STRESS (although

the practice is banned in many European regions), but excessive irrigation (like excessive rainfall) can cause delayed ripening and a loss of wine quality.

Vineyards should be subject to grape sampling programmes so that harvest takes place when the fruit is at optimum maturity.

See also VINE DISEASES, VINE PESTS, VINE PHYSIOLOGY, and VINE VARIETIES.   R.E.S.

Coombe, B. G., and Dry, P. R., *Viticulture*, i: *Resources* (Adelaide, 1988).
—— *Viticulture*, ii: *Practices* (Adelaide, 1992).
Galet, P., *Précis de viticulture* (5th edn, Montpellier, 1988).
Winkler, A. J., *et al.*, *General Viticulture* (2nd edn, Berkeley, Calif., 1974).

viticulturist, someone who practises VITICULTURE. In many countries the grape-grower is termed simply 'grower' rather than 'viticulturist', which word is more often used for professional persons who typically have some formal tertiary training in viticulture. Grape-growers or vine-growers may also be termed wine-growers.   R.E.S.

Vitis, the genus of the plant kingdom which includes the VINE (see BOTANICAL CLASSIFICATION). *Vitis* is one of 14 genera according to Galet in the family Vitaceae and contains in turn about 60 species. Most of the *Vitis* species can be found in the east and south east of North America, or in Asia, mainly in the temperate zones of the northern hemisphere, with a few in the tropics. The most important species for wine production is the single European species (strictly, Eurasian) *Vitis vinifera*, often written *V vinifera*, described in detail in VINIFERA.

As shown on the right, there are many different AMERICAN VINE SPECIES. They became the subject of attention by early European settlers as *V vinifera* failed to cope with indigenous diseases in the early colonies on the east coast. However, they proved generally unsatisfactory for wine because of their strongly flavoured berries (see FOXY). These native American species have since been crossed with *V vinifera* to form new varieties (see AMERICAN HYBRIDS), and among themselves to produce the ROOTSTOCKS used in modern viticulture.

Asian species are little studied, and their exact number is still uncertain. One of them, however, *V amurensis*, is the world's most northerly vine species, and has been used to introduce cold hardiness into VINE BREEDING programmes (see AMURENSIS). Varieties of *V amurensis* and *V cognetiae* are grown in JAPAN.

Note: The systematic botanical classification of species within the *Vitis* genus has been a subject of confusion for more than a century. Hedrick documents this early confusion, especially that concerning *V vulpina*, which has often been wrongly confused with *V riparia*, the great taxonomist Linnaeus being the origin of the confusion. GALET clarified the taxonomy in 1967, but there is still some doubt

about the taxonomy of Asian species. The French taxonomist Planchon proposed that *Vitis* species be divided into two so-called sections. The first, *Vitis* (but originally called *Euvitis*), contains the great majority of species including the 'European' wine grape species *vinifera*, and the second MUSCADINIA contains only three species indigenous to the Americas. These two sections differ in chromosome number and many morphological features. The species of the section *Vitis* have proven to be closely enough related to interbreed easily when this has been attempted, but crossings between members of the two sections typically produces sterile hybrids. More recently it has been proposed that *Muscadinia* be considered a separate genus, which is adopted in some modern textbooks such as Mullins *et al.* but not others such as Galet and Antcliff. This volume follows Galet.

The following partial listing, of the most important species, is based on Mullins *et al.*, which in turn is from Galet's thesis. Only the more important species are listed. Other listings may be found in Winkler *et al.* and Galet.

Section Vitis	
European and Middle Eastern species	
Vitis vinifera	Europe, Middle East
American species	
Vitis aestivalis	North America (east)
Vitis berlandieri	North America (east)
Vitis californica	North America (west)
Vitis candicans	North America (east)
Vitis caribaea	North America (east)
Vitis champini[a]	North America (east)
Vitis cinerea	North America (east)
Vitis vulpina (*Vitis cordifolia*)	North America (east)
Vitis doaniana[b]	North America (east)
Vitis girdiana	North America (west)
Vitis labrusca[c]	North America (east)
Vitis lincecumii	North America (east)
Vitis longii[d]	North America (east)
Vitis monticola	North America (east)
Vitis riparia	North America (east)
Vitis rufomentosa	North America (east)
Vitis rupestris	North America (east)
Asian species	
Vitis amurensis	Asia
Vitis coignetiae	Asia
Vitis thunbergii	Asia
Section Muscadinia	
Vitis munsoniana	North America (east)
Vitis rotundifolia	North America (east)

[a] *Vitis champini* (sometimes spelt *champinii*) was originally described by the French ampelographer Planchon as a separate species, but it is now generally regarded as a group of natural *rupestris–candicans* hybrids.
[b] *Vitis doaniana*, a probable natural hybrid with *V candicans*.
[c] *Vitis labruscana* is sometimes used to describe varieties dominated by *V labrusca* but with some *V vinifera* genes too such as Concord.
[d] *Vitis longii* is sometimes given the name *V solonis* from a misreading on a bundle of cuttings sent to Europe. Some regard it as a natural hybrid between *V candicans* and other species, as for *V champini* and *V doaniana*.

For *Vitis sylvestris* see WILD VINES. See also VINE, VINIFERA, AMERICAN VINE SPECIES, VINE VARIETIES, PROLES, CLONE, HYBRIDS, CROSS. R.E.S.

Antcliff, A. J., 'Taxonomy: the grapevine as a member of the plant kingdom', in B. G. Coombe and P. R. Dry (eds.), *Viticulture, i: Resources* (Adelaide, 1988).

Galet, P., *Précis de viticulture* (5th edn, Montpellier, 1988).

Hedrick, U., *The Grapes of New York.* (Albany, NY, 1908).

Mullins, M. G., Bouquet, A., and Williams, L., *Biology of the Grapevine* (Cambridge, 1992).

Winkler, A. J., *et al.*, *General Viticulture* (2nd edn, Berkeley, Calif., 1974).

Vitis vinifera, the species of vine from which most of the world's wine is made. The relationship of *vinifera* to other species of the Vitis genus is described above under VITIS, and details about the species and wine grapes in general are given under VINIFERA. There are many thousands of *vinifera* VINE VARIETIES, which in turn are classified into three PROLES. The relationship of *Vitis vinifera* to other members of the plant kingdom is discussed under BOTANICAL CLASSIFICATION. The commercial culture of *Vitis vinifera* is introduced with the entry VITICULTURE.

Viura is a common Spanish synonym for MACABEO and is therefore what Riojanos call their dominant white grape variety.

Vivarais, Côtes du, wine region promoted to AC status in 1999 on the right bank of the RHÔNE immediately opposite Coteaux du TRICASTIN in the wild and beguiling Ardèche. Widely dispersed vineyards on mainly LIMESTONE soils in a much cooler and wetter climate than the rest of the southern Rhône total 650 ha/1,600 acres and produce mainly light reds and rosés from Grenache and Syrah grapes. A small amount of white is made from Clairette, Grenache Blanc, and Marsanne. Production is dominated by CO-OPERATIVES, whose more profitable business may be producing varietal VINS DE PAYS de l'Ardèche from non-appellation varieties.

Vizetelly, Henry (1820–94), prolific English wine writer whose detailed accounts of the history of port and champagne are particularly celebrated. Vizetelly came from a family of printers, and so it is particularly appropriate that today his influence is perhaps most marked in the continued, and increasingly imprecise, reproduction of the engravings which distinguished his many and various books about wine. He was introduced to wine in 1869 when he was sent to Paris to report on the French vintage for the *Pall Mall Gazette*, narrowly escaping execution during the Franco-Prussian War the next year. He spent much of the 1870s visiting the vineyards of France and Germany and in 1877 visited Portugal, Madeira, and the Canary islands. Whereas JULLIEN and REDDING provided global wine surveys for the specialist reader, Vizetelly managed both to delve more deeply into specific wine regions, and to produce books which appealed to a wider market. When based in France he was one of the first acknowledged wine 'experts' who was invited to serve as a judge of wines at the Vienna and Paris Exhibitions. On his eventual return to England, he became a publisher and as Zola's English publisher, he was imprisoned and financially ruined.

Gabler, J. M., *Wine into Words: A History and Bibliography of Wine Books in the English Language* (Baltimore, 1985).

vocabulary, tasting. See LANGUAGE OF WINE and TASTING TERMS.

Vojvodina, autonomous region within SERBIA in the far north east of what was YUGOSLAVIA (see map with that article). The best of the vineyards enhance the lovely rolling countryside of Fruška Gora district north of Belgrade and south of the Hungarian border. They adjoin the vineyards of CROATIA to the west and sweep south beyond the town of Novi Sad nearly to Belgrade itself. Viticulturally they are an extension of the inland Croatian region with much the same mix of white grape varieties for the most part. There are also some good red wines made from CABERNET SAUVIGNON and MERLOT. The SMEDEREVKA vine, called after the town of Smederevo south of Belgrade, makes large amounts of very ordinary white wine usually drunk with mineral water as a SPRITZER. The Smederevka TRAMINER crossing called Neoplanta has a very perfumed aroma and oily texture not unlike a concentrated Pinot Gris. Some of the wines from this area are potentially the best-balanced whites in what was Yugoslavia.

Close to the Hungarian border lies a region which owes its roots much more to HUNGARY than to Yugoslavia. The sandy plains extend over the frontier; many of the people speak Hungarian more naturally than Serbian: and even the grapes reflect the Hungarian viticultural tradition. Laški Rizling (WELSCHRIESLING) still predominates but red wine grapes include KADARKA and Frankovka (BLAUFRÄNKISCH) while EZERJÓ and Kövedinka (the DINKA of Hungary) are among white wine grapes. Even MUSCAT OTTONEL tends to be more prevalent here and in Hungary than in the rest of Yugoslavia.

The sandy plain continues round into ROMANIA and a further, rather unexciting part of the Vojvodina vineyard sits on the northern bank of the Danube just where it crosses the Romanian border. More Smederevka and more Laški Rizling grow here. BANAT RIZLING grows here and in Romania and is reputed to have a better, more solid style than Laški Rizling. A.H.M.

volatile. All wines are volatile in that they contain volatile FLAVOUR COMPOUNDS and some level of VOLATILE ACIDS, but volatile is used as a pejorative tasting term for a wine in which the level of ACETIC ACID has risen unacceptably high.

volatile acidity of a wine is its total concentration of **volatile acids**, those naturally occurring organic ACIDS of wines that are separable by DISTILLATION. Wine's most common volatile acid by far is ACETIC ACID (more than 96 per cent), which is why it is used as the routine measure of volatile acidity (VA). A few other acids such as formic, propionic, SUCCINIC, and LACTIC, normally present in trace amounts in wines, are also volatile. The EU limit for VA is 1.2 g/l for red wine and 1.08 g/l for white and rosé, though the perception threshold is around 0.8 g/l, depending on wine style.

Acetic acid, in small amounts, is a by-product of the normal action of YEAST in grape juice. However, the major source is the action of a group of BACTERIA known as ACETOBACTER which require OXYGEN for their growth and survival, and cause a reaction between the alcohol of the wine and the oxygen to produce acetic acid. Very low concentrations of acetic acid, below 0.2 g/l, do not affect the taste adversely. Increasing concentrations change the taste of the wine, however, from added complexity and fruitiness to a frankly vinegary flavour at levels much above 1.5 g/l. Most everyday wines are very low in acetic acid but some red wines may be excessively acetic. A few fine wines, usually mature reds in bottle, are rich enough in BODY, TANNINS, and ALCOHOL to bear concentrations of acetic acid that do not impair flavour but are sometimes said to LIFT it.

It is not the acetic acid itself that causes changes in the aroma but the ESTER known as ETHYL ACETATE, the reaction product of acetic acid and ETHANOL.

Exposure of wines to air in the presence of acetobacter starts the process of VINEGAR production, although if exposure to air is limited the wine will probably not be spoiled.

It was the research work of Louis PASTEUR, trying to find a reason for the spoilage of so much burgundy shipped to England, that resulted in the discovery of acetobacter. It also resulted in the discovery that yeast is responsible for the conversion of grape sugars to wine. A.D.W.

volatility, property of having excessive VOLATILE ACIDS.

volcanic, describes rocks which are the product of volcanic eruptions. These are variable in composition and therefore form a wide range of soils. Volcanic rocks seldom underlie major vineyard regions but there are several famous exceptions. In the Kaiserstuhl-Tuniberg region of BADEN in Germany, vines are grown in clays derived from volcanic rocks, while the PFALZ to the north is underlain by basalt. South Nahe has a feldspar-porphyry subsoil. The TOKAJI of Hungary is produced from grapes grown on volcanic rocks, mainly andesite.

The Finger lakes region of NEW YORK STATE has stony but rich soil derived from volcanic rocks, where the vine roots can penetrate far below the winter frost level, and where SOIL WATER is available to the vines in dry summers. See SANTORINI and entries prefixed SOIL.

J.M.H.

Volidza, fine Greek red wine grape from the same area as MAVROUD.

Volnay, attractive small village in the Côte de Beaune district of Burgundy's Côte d'Or producing elegant red wines from Pinot Noir. The wines of Volnay were celebrated under the *ancien régime* for their delicacy: Claude Arnoux describes them as partridge-eye pink in colour, and the finest of all the wines of the Côte de Beaune, although they had to be drunk very young. Since then they have alternated in fame with those of neighbouring Pommard depending on whether FASHION dictated wines of breeding or of power.

More than half Volnay's vineyards are of PREMIER CRU status, stretching in a broad swathe from Pommard to Meursault, continuing into the latter village. Because Meursault is renowned for its white wines, its single really fine red wine vineyard of Les Santenots is sold as **Volnay Santenots**, which has its own appellation. The best part of this vineyard is Les Santenots-du-Milieu, although it is not as typical of Volnay as Le Cailleret, which it abuts, or Champans. These two vineyards express the astonishing, velvety finesse of Volnay. Clos des Chênes, just above Le Cailleret, is also very fine but a little lighter as the soil is even thinner.

Excellent vineyards close to the village include Taillepieds, the Clos de la Bousse d'Or, MONOPOLE of Domaine de la Pousse d'Or, which also owns an excellent enclave within Le Cailleret known as the Clos des 60 Ouvrées, and the Clos des Ducs of the Marquis d'Angerville, whose father pioneered DOMAINE BOTTLING in the 1930s. Volnay's finest producers include Michel Lafarge, Pousse d'Or, de Montille, d'Angerville, and most of the best producers in MEURSAULT who also have vineyards in Volnay.

See also CÔTE D'OR, and map under BURGUNDY.

J.T.C.M.

Arnoux, C., *Dissertation sur la situation de Bourgogne* (Dijon, 1728).

VORS and VOS, classifications for age-dated SHERRY.

Vosges OAK comes from the mountains to the immediate west of ALSACE.

Vöslau, wine centre in lower AUSTRIA in what is now the Thermenregion district.

Vosne-Romanée, village in the Côte de Nuits district of Burgundy's CÔTE D'OR producing arguably the finest red wines made anywhere from Pinot Noir grapes (see

map under BURGUNDY). As well as excellent wines at VILLAGE and PREMIER CRU level, there are six GRAND CRU vineyards, three of which share the name Romanée, the suffix to which Vosne was hyphenated in 1866.

The grands crus are Romanée-Conti, La Romanée, La Tâche, Richebourg, Romanée-St-Vivant, and La Grande Rue. Between them they produce, with Musigny and Chambertin, the greatest wines of the Côte de Nuits. They have more finesse than any other but to this is allied as much power and stuffing as their nearest rivals.

A vineyard formerly known as Le Cloux was rechristened La Romanée in 1651, presumably on account of Roman remains being discovered nearby. In 1760, the property was bought by the Prince de Conti, subsequently becoming known as Romanée-Conti. Just above this sublime vineyard, whose wines can be the most expensive in the world, is La Romanée. Romanée-Conti has brown, CALCAREOUS soil about 60 cm/23 in deep with 45 to 49 per cent CLAY and liable to serious erosion in the upper, steeper part. La Romanée also has a notably steep slope with less clay and more RENDZINA in the make-up of the soil. The former is the monopoly of the DOMAINE DE LA ROMANÉE-CONTI (DRC), the latter of the Liger-Belair family. About 300 cases are made each year from the tiny 0.84 ha/2 acres of La Romanée, double that is produced from the 1.80 ha of Romanée-Conti.

Another monopoly of the Domaine de la Romanée-Conti, and regarded as nearly as fine as the vineyard from which it takes its name, is La Tâche, whose 6 ha (including the vineyard of Les Gaudichots, which used to be separate but is regarded as being of the same quality) produce a wine which is explosively seductive even when young, whereas Romanée-Conti takes longer to show its astonishing completeness. La Tâche seems to thrive even in lesser years, being judged the only wine worthy of bottling by the Domaine de la Romanée-Conti in 1950 and 1951.

The next most sought-after Vosne-Romanée wine is Richebourg, whose 8 ha are shared between ten growers, notably Domaine de la Romanée-Conti, Domaine LEROY, branches of the Gros family, and Domaine Méo-Camuzet. As the name suggests, this is one of the most voluptuous wines of Burgundy and can equal La Tâche in some years.

Romanée-St-Vivant, taking its name from the monastery of St-Vivant founded at Vergy c.900 and subsequent owner of the vineyard, can also make very fine wine but it is usually lighter and less powerful than its neighbours, being further down the slope and having deeper soil. There are half a dozen owners, of which the largest is Domaine de la Romanée-Conti (5.3 ha out of 9.43). Domaine Leroy and Louis LATOUR's Domaine de Corton Grancey are the next largest owners.

Between La Tâche to the south and La

Romanée-Conti to the north lie the 1.4 ha of La Grande Rue, originally classified as PREMIER CRU but promoted, as its location suggests is only right, to grand cru. The vineyard is a monopoly of Domaine Lamarche, whose wines have not so far stood comparison with those of their illustrious neighbours.

Amongst the best of Vosne-Romanée's premier cru vineyards are Clos des Réas, Les Malconsorts, and Les Chaumes on the Nuits-St-Georges side, Cros Parantoux made famous by Henry Jayer, above the grands crus, and Les Beaumonts and Les Suchots abutting Flagey-Échézeaux. Part of Les Beaumonts is actually in the latter commune, although it is sold as Vosne-Romanée, as is the village wine of Flagey.

While the renown of the Domaine de la Romanée-Conti dominates Vosne-Romanée, it should not overshadow other significant influences: Henri Jayer, for his unparalleled wine-making skills; René Engel for his patriarchal influence and local historical research and publications; Lalou Bize-LEROY, who has bought and transformed the former Domaine Nöellat. Other particularly fine domaines are those owned by the various members of the Gros family, Domaine Jean Grivot, and Sylvain Cathiard.

J.T.C.M.

Olney, R., *Romanée-Conti* (Paris, 1991).

Rigaux, J., *Ode aux grands vins de Bourgogne* (Précy-sous-Thil, 1997).

Vougeot, small village in the Côte de Nuits district of Burgundy producing red wines from the Pinot Noir grape. The name is derived from the diminutive of Vouge, a small stream flowing through the village. There are only 4.8 ha/11.8 acres of vineyards producing VILLAGE WINE and 11.7 ha designated PREMIER CRU; the village's fame rests squarely with the 50.6 ha GRAND CRU, Clos de Vougeot.

The fame of Clos de Vougeot is historical since it was the flagship vineyard of the Cistercians, who planted and enclosed what is significantly the largest grand cru vineyard of the Côte d'Or. Geologically, this is not a homogeneous site: the top, abutting Musigny and Grands Échézeaux, has a light chalky and gravelly soil on oolitic limestone which drains beautifully and gives the wines of greatest distinction; the middle section is on softer limestone with clay and some gravel, with moderate drainage on a very gentle slope. The bottom section, almost flat, stretching down to the main RN74 road, consists of poorly drained alluvial clay.

When the wines could be blended by the MONKS to produce a complete wine from differing constituent parts, Clos de Vougeot doubtless deserved its reputation. Now that the vineyard is fragmented between 80 or more owners, far too many of the wines are below standard through the inadequacies of some of the raw material and many of the production techniques of the less conscientious producers.

Classic Clos de Vougeot is likely to be dense and ungiving when young, robust rather than elegant. However, after a decade it opens out into one of the most complete wines of the Côte d'Or with deep, rich flavours reminiscent of truffles and undergrowth.

Of the premier cru vineyards, Le Clos Blanc, the monopoly of Domaine de la Vougeraie in succession to Héritiers Guyot, has produced white wine since first planted by the monks in 1110. The other premier crus are les Cras, les Petits Vougeots, and Clos de la Perrière, monopoly of Domaine Bertagna.

Reliable producers of Clos de Vougeot include Méo-Camuzet, Anne Gros, and René Engel.

See also CLOS DE VOUGEOT, CÔTE D'OR, and map under BURGUNDY. J.T.C.M.

Vouvray, the most important individual white wine appellation in the TOURAINE district of the Loire. The wines of Vouvray vary enormously in quality, thereby offering a true representation of the grape variety from which Vouvray is exclusively made. Vouvray is CHENIN BLANC and, to a certain extent, Chenin Blanc is Vouvray (although ARBOIS grapes are theoretically allowed into Vouvray too). No other wine made only from this long-lived middle Loire grape, often called Pineau de la Loire, is made in such quantity, from more than 2,000 ha/5,000 acres of vineyard. (The proportion of sparkling wine produced increased during the 1990s.) Only COTEAUX DU LAYON can begin to rival Vouvray for the total area of Chenin Blanc planted.

Vouvray itself is a particularly pretty small town on the northern bank of the Loire just east of Tours, whose wines owe much to the MONKS AND MONASTERIES who refined local viticulture from the Middle Ages. It was not until the creation of the Vouvray appellation in 1936 that Vouvray established an identity of its own; before then most of it was shipped out for blending by the energetic DUTCH WINE TRADE, and much of the wine sold as Vouvray came from anywhere in Touraine.

Houses, and wine cellars, have habitually been created out of the TUFFEAU on this right bank of the wide river, with vines planted in the clay and gravel topsoil over the tuffeau on the plateau above, dissected by small rivers and streams so that many vineyards have an ideal sheltered southerly aspect. The locals claim that this is where the Atlantic climate meets the CONTINENTAL climate.

Making top-quality Vouvray MOELLEUX is as hazardous as making any top-quality sweet white wine which owes its sweetness to NOBLE ROT or extreme RIPENESS. The vine-grower is entirely at the mercy of the weather, and the harvest in Vouvray is one of France's last, usually lasting until well into November, often involving a number of TRIES through the vineyard. An increasing number of producers have mastered the art of making top-quality dry Vouvray in less ripe vintages however.

Wine-making here is distinguished by the need to bottle pure fruit and its naturally high acidity as early and as unadorned as possible. Thus, this is one of the few wine regions of the world of little commercial interest to the COOPERAGE business. Neutral fermentation vessels such as large old oak casks or stainless steel tanks are used, MALOLACTIC FERMENTATION is generally avoided, and the AGEING process is expected to occur, extremely slowly, in bottle.

The style of wine made by the best producers such as Huet, Champalou, Domaine des Aubuisières, Clos Naudin, and Domaine de la Taille aux Loups is determined completely by the weather. In the least generous VINTAGES, only dry and possibly sparkling wines are made. The best years yield very sweet, golden nectars that are naturally MOELLEUX, or even LIQUOREUX, but are so high in acidity that most are almost unpleasant to drink in their middle age between about three years old and two to three decades. Some of the finest Vouvrays can still taste lively, and richly fruity, at nearly a century. A relatively high proportion of demi-sec (medium dry) is also produced in many years, and it too has demanded a considerable amount of BOTTLE AGEING before the acidity has muted and the wine can be served as a fine accompaniment to many savoury, richly sauced dishes. Better vineyard management, however, is resulting Vouvrays of all sweetness levels that are more broachable in youth.

Commercial Vouvray also exists, on the other hand, as simply a medium sweet, reasonably acid, white wine that has little capacity for development.

Vouvray Mousseux can often offer more interest than other Loire sparkling wines, to those who appreciate the honeyed aromas of Chenin Blanc, at least. The wines have weight and flavour, and are suitable for drinking with as well as before meals.

See also LOIRE, including map.

VQA, Vintners Quality Alliance, was initially formed as a voluntary organization to identify wines made entirely from grapes grown in CANADA, as opposed to merely blended or bottled there. Today, Ontario's legally enforceable and British Columbia's still voluntary VQA APPELLATION systems are considered the most significant wine-related accomplishment of the 1980s. VQA Canada existed briefly in the late 1990s but is now part of the Canadian Vintners Association, which promotes and regulates Canadian wine nationally and internationally. For more detail, see CANADA.

VQPRD, abbreviation for the EUROPEAN UNION term **Vin de Qualité Produit dans une Région Déterminée**, meaning QUALITY WINE. Although it is essentially a French expression, the initials are sometimes seen on labels of superior bottlings from any European country. In France, the classification includes both APPELLATION CONTRÔLÉE and VDQS wines.

Vranac, red grape variety that is a speciality of MONTENEGRO and MACEDONIA (see map of former YUGOSLAVIA). The wines produced are deeply coloured and can be rich in EXTRACT, responding unusually well to oak AGEING. There is an element of refreshing bitterness on the finish of these wines that suggests some relationship to an Italian variety just across the Adriatic. Indeed, DNA PROFILING at Zagreb in 2001 suggested a parent–offspring relationship with PRIMITIVO, better known in California as ZINFANDEL. Vranac is one of the few indigenous grape variety names to appear on the label of wines exported from what was Yugoslavia.

VSP, vertical shoot positioning. See TRAINING SYSTEMS.

VT. See VENDANGE TARDIVE.

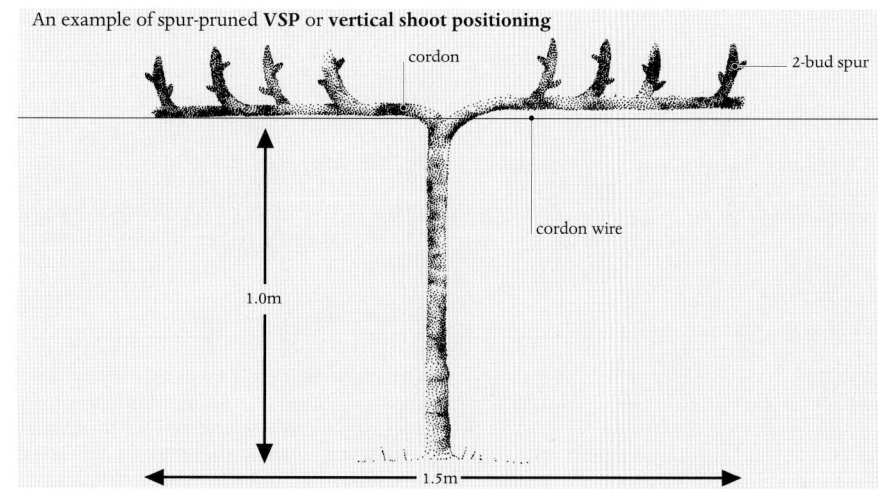

An example of spur-pruned **VSP** or **vertical shoot positioning**

cordon

2-bud spur

cordon wire

1.0m

1.5m

W

Wädenswil, town on lake Zurich and site of a research station in German-speaking SWITZERLAND concerned with fruit growing, horticulture, and viticulture. It was founded in 1890 in response to the viticultural catastrophes of FUNGAL DISEASES and PHYLLOXERA. SUSTAINABLE VITICULTURE, in which pests and diseases are controlled by biological or biotechnological methods, has developed in this environment.

Today Wädenswil is concerned with research, development, testing, control, and extension services in viticulture and wine microbiology. The station has developed a number of YEAST STRAINS for the repair of STUCK FERMENTATIONS and some grapevine CLONES, notably of PINOT NOIR, which have been planted as far away as Oregon, California, New Zealand, and South Africa. A number of plant protection methods have been developed, such as the introduction of predators and pheromones for trapping and confusing INSECTS.

Wädenswil and the research station at CHANGINS in western Switzerland combined under the administration of Agroscope (ACW) in early 2006.

Wagga, abbreviation for the School of Wine and Food Sciences, Wagga Wagga, now part of CHARLES STURT UNIVERSITY.

Wagner, Philip (1904–96), Baltimore newspaper editor, VITICULTURIST, WINEMAKER, and author of books on vines and wine. Beginning as a HOME WINEMAKER during PROHIBITION, Wagner published *American Wines and How to Make Them* (1933). Interested in improving the basis of eastern American winemaking, Wagner began to import and test FRENCH HYBRID vines in 1939 and to distribute them from the nursery and vineyard he founded, Boordy Vineyard, in Maryland. His *A Wine-Grower's Guide* (1945) was the first work to publicize French hybrids in the US; in the same year he opened a winery at Boordy Vineyard and produced the first French hybrid wine on record in the US. Wagner's success with his wines, his activity in supplying French hybrids from his nursery, and the persuasiveness of his writing in favour of a better selection of VINE VARIETIES entitle him to be regarded as the man who changed the course of wine-making in the eastern US. The clarity, grace, and authority of his books gave him an influence far beyond the sphere of Boordy Vineyard.   T.P.

waiter, wine. See SOMMELIER.

Wales. Several small vineyards in sheltered corners of southern Wales produce either Welsh Vineyards QUALITY WINE, Welsh Regional Wine, or United Kingdom TABLE WINE. For more details, see ENGLAND.

Walker Bay, cool climate wine district in SOUTH AFRICA.

Wälschriesling. See WELSCHRIESLING.

war, effects on wine. Wine is a way of life literally rooted in the soil. It is also capital and labour intensive and reliant on a complex distribution network, which make it highly vulnerable during time of war.

The most visible effect of war is the destruction of vineyards. Just as it was customary for warring ancient Greeks to cut down or burn the vines of their enemies, so the barbarian invaders of Roman Europe signalled victory in the same way.

Planting on newly captured territory likewise symbolized success. When the Christians drove the Moors from medieval SPAIN, they planted vines behind them, as did the Crusaders who briefly held parts of the Holy Land. It is difficult to imagine a clearer expression of a battle won and determination to stay than the planting of such a long-term crop as vines.

Certain regions have suffered ruin disproportionately because of their strategic geographical position. The location of the CHAMPAGNE region at the crossroads of northern Europe has ensured the destruction of its vineyards dozens of times, most famously when they were bisected by the trenches of the First World War.

The short-term effects of war have sometimes had permanent consequences. The Thirty Years War (1618–48) which ravaged 17th-century Europe was so destructive that many northern German vineyard areas were never replanted (see GERMAN HISTORY). Recovery was hampered by the sheer scale of the devastation, by lack of manpower through depopulation, and by destruction of capital equipment.

Plundering of existing wine stocks is another common feature of European war, with Champagne, once again, an obvious example. When Russian soldiers occupied the region in 1814 they were not slow to help themselves. In this case the Champagne houses did at least have the subsequent consolation that the Russians became their wines' most loyal peacetime consumers until 1917. In general, however, terrible hardship was the result of forced requisitioning and outright plunder. Civil conflicts, such as the French Wars of Religion in the 16th century, were at least as destructive.

The sale and distribution of wine is a complex operation which is inevitably dislocated by war. TRANSPORT becomes hazardous. During the HUNDRED YEARS WAR (1337–1453) ships carrying wine between Bordeaux and England were attacked so often that convoys were arranged for safety.

Wars also frequently led to a ban on trade with the enemy. When Britain and France were at war in the early 18th century, French wine imports into Britain were prohibited. Smuggling was one answer to the problem, switching to wine produced by the ally Portugal was another. Thus war altered trading and consumption patterns, and PORT became the staple wine of Georgian England.

Wars do not bring uniform misfortune. The demand for wine to provision troops in some cases provided a stimulus to wine regions not directly involved in the fighting. The Roman army needed huge supplies to send it into battle. Records show that, when Edward I embarked on his Scottish campaign in 1300, he first bought in vast quantities of wine from Bordeaux.

It is also probable that the influx of American forces into Second World War Europe and its aftermath was an important factor in building the wine market in the UNITED STATES.

Historically the effects of war on wine, as on so many other commercial activities, have been mixed and in some cases one grower's suffering made another's fortune.   H.B.

Bonal, F., *Le Livre d'or de Champagne* (Lausanne, 1984).

Francis, A. D., *The Wine Trade* (London, 1972).

Johnson, H., *The Story of Wine* (London and New York, 1989).

Warre, important port shipper. See SYMINGTONS.

Washington, dynamic fruit-growing state in the PACIFIC NORTHWEST of the United States which, with little fuss or fanfare, crept into second position behind California as an American VINIFERA wine producer. Producing just 5 per cent of the national wine total, Washington state's 32,500 acres/13,160 ha of vines (an increase of 100 per cent in five years) made it a very distant second behind California's 500,000 or so in the early 21st century, however.

History
In the 1930s, the Washington wine industry was based on the native American grape variety CONCORD, which grows well in the Yakima valley (see below). It is still abundantly planted there but is almost exclusively limited to the making of juice, jellies, and other non-wine confections. In 1969, when California's wine boom was well under way, there were just two wineries in Washington, each of them based on a single, small vineyard. By 2005 there were 345, the number increasing by about 40 every year.

Geography and climate
Washington is the USA's leading apple and hop state, both crops being good viticultural markers, but there is a sharp difference between the climates of western and viticulturally much more important eastern Washington.

Western Washington is mild and damp the year round because of the proximity of the Pacific ocean and the inland sea called the Puget sound, overlooked by Seattle. Population, limited space, and marginal growing conditions combine to limit plantings in western Washington to less than 1 per cent of the state's total. The **Puget Sound** appellation covers the islands and land adjoining the waters of the Puget sound, into the Cascade foothills.

Eastern Washington, a vast area of rolling farmland screened from marine air by the towering barrier of the Cascade mountains (which extend south into OREGON and help shape the viticultural landscape there), has hot, desert-dry summers and cold to arctic winters. This rigorous weather east of the Cascades has failed to halt the march of the vine, however. Vineyard locations here are limited by the reach of IRRIGATION water and by air drainage. The first is vital in summer, the last just as vital in winter, where temperatures can plummet to $-15\,°F/-26\,°C$ and stay there for a fortnight or more. Most vine plantings are on south- and south west-facing slopes for winter rather than summer warmth. Such freeze-susceptible varieties as Merlot are limited to such slopes, although even these locations failed to save some Merlot vines from the big WINTER FREEZE of February 1996 and that of 2003 which affected the exposed **Walla Walla AVA** in particular. The severity of Washington winters increased growers' enthusiasm for the two Cabernets, made them wish Riesling were easier to sell, and revived the Russian technique of fan training which had been used for some early plantings against winter cold (see vine-TRAINING SYSTEMS). Virtually all the vineyards in eastern Washington fall within the 11 million-acre/ 4.4 million-ha embrace of the Columbia Valley AVA. Inside it, in turn, are the important Yakima Valley appellation, which encompasses about 40 per cent of the state's vineyards, the Walla Walla Valley AVA, the newer **Red Mountain AVA** (neither red nor a mountain), **Wahluke Slope AVA** and the new **Columbia Gorge AVA**, which straddles both Oregon and Washington. Soils tend to be sandy loam, a generally inhospitable environment for PHYLLOXERA, so most vines in Washington are planted ungrafted, which helps recovery from winter freeze, widely spaced and trained in bilateral CORDONS. With no exposed graft unions, these vines are better preserved in the cold winters. About 80 per cent of grapes are MECHANICALLY HARVESTED. Clonal diversity has been limited, but by the early 21st century, more diverse plant material was beginning to become available. Washington also claims two hours more sunlight each day during the growing season than California, due to its more northerly, yet still sunny, position. Cool nights help maintain a fresh acidity in the grapes despite the heat of the days.

Vine varieties and wine styles
Virtually all wines are *vinifera*, VARIETAL, and are generally distinguished from those of California by bright fruit and relatively crisp acidity. Although the state is arguably best known for its Merlot, the second most planted grape variety, white grapes have predominated. Fast declining acreage hides the fact, but Riesling remains a variety that the state grows particularly well, for both drier wines and sweeter late harvest ones, some of the latter being BOTRYTIZED. With the exception of the Eroica JOINT VENTURE (see below), SEMILLON can deliver more exciting wines than Riesling, however, and with greater consistency. One after another of these wines has demonstrated the kind of structure and balance that promise well for longevity. The best performances of Riesling and Semillon notwithstanding, Chardonnay dominated vineyard and cellar alike in Washington throughout the 1990s, although total plantings have hardly risen from their late 1990s total of 4,500 acres since red varieties have been favoured for new plantings. While typical Chardonnays range from merely good to quite good, the variety's fortunes were sustained more by consumer demand than inherent superiority. Virtually all wineries use BARREL FERMENTATION, MALOLACTIC FERMENTATION, and LEES CONTACT to broaden and deepen a modest varietal flavour. Other white varieties with good track records from more limited plantings are SAUVIGNON BLANC and CHENIN BLANC. GEWÜRZTRAMINER, generally workaday in quality, has been steadily declining. MÜLLER-THURGAU has shown occasional brightness in a scattering of vineyards in the Puget sound basin, the isolated patch of vines west of the Cascade mountains.

Reds blossomed later than whites in Washington but Merlot enjoyed great popularity in the 1990s and Cabernet Sauvignon and Syrah are current favourites for those currently planting, projected to overtake Merlot in 2007. By nature, Washington reds lean towards ripe flavours and noticeable alcohol levels. The prevailing style has called for ample tannins and hearty oak flavours. The net effect has been wines dramatic in youth but without great staying power in many cases. BORDEAUX BLENDS, with or without CABERNET FRANC, the state's fourth most planted red grape with a static 600 acres, are increasingly common and show promise. SYRAH clearly has a serious long-term future in Washington, and plantings totalled 2,400 acres by 2005. Among other red grape varieties, Washington has an American monopoly on the obscure but usefully low acid variety LEMBERGER, which several wineries produce as a quite rewarding fresh, fruit-rich wine meant to be drunk in its youth. One or two producers have even essayed large-scale, oak-aged wines with it, as in AUSTRIA. There has been some not-entirely-unsuccessful experimentation with SANGIOVESE, NEBBIOLO, and even BARBERA.

The producers

The dominant force in Washington wine is Chateau Ste Michelle Wine Estates (once called Stimson Lane Company), a subsidiary of American Tobacco Company, and the owner of a range of labels which includes Chateau Ste Michelle, Domaine Ste Michelle, Columbia Crest, Snoqualmie, and Northstar, with important high-quality joint ventures with Ernst Loosen of Germany (for Eroica Riesling) and Piero ANTINORI of Italy (for Col Solare). The company collectively controls more than one-third of all vineyard land in Washington, and produces a wide range of wines, including a number of superior single-vineyard bottlings. Some of the most sought-after wines are made in Walla Walla by Leonetti and in Puget Sound (from fruit grown in some of Columbia Valley's top vineyards) by Quilceda Creek and Andrew Will. Other important labels by volume and reputation include the Seattle-based Columbia Winery, which produces fine wines from Red Willow vineyards, Yakima Valley-based Hogue Cellars, and Woodward Canyon in Walla Walla. While Washington produces a few steeply priced bottlings, it has long prided itself on trying to offer good value further down the scale.   L.S.H.

Cass, B. (ed.), *The Oxford Companion to the Wines of North America* (Oxford and New York, 2000).

Gregutt, P., and Prather, J., *Northwest Wines: A Pocket Guide to the Wines of Washington, Oregon, and Idaho* (Seattle, 2004).

Hall, L. S., *Wines of the Pacific Northwest* (London, 2001).

Parker, T., *Discovering Washington Wines* (Seattle, 2002).

Perdue, A., *The Northwest Wine Guide: A Buyer's Handbook* (Seattle, 2003).

www.WinesNorthwest.com

water is the most important constituent of wine (see WINE COMPOSITION) and is as essential to those who produce it as to those who consume it but access to reliable supplies of good-quality water, particularly for IRRIGATION, is likely to become a pressing problem for an increasing number of wine producers—not least because of CLIMATE CHANGE and problems associated with SALINITY.

SOIL WATER, the product of RAINFALL and/or irrigation, is a prerequisite for vine growth and survival. PHOTOSYNTHESIS, without which grapes would never ripen, depends on water being available (which is why RIPENING stops if WATER STRESS is too severe). Water in the form of well-timed rain can also be useful in dusting off grapes immediately prior to HARVEST.

Water is also vital in the winery: HYGIENE's best friend is the hosepipe, and many systems of TEMPERATURE CONTROL depend on copious supplies of water. In a small and decreasing number of wine regions, wine may be diluted to reduce ACIDITY. In warmer regions, however, the operation known euphemistically as HUMIDIFICATION is sometimes undertaken for ALCOHOL REDUCTION.

And then there is water as a drink. For centuries wine was always diluted with water, indeed drinking undiluted wine was the mark of a barbarian in Ancient GREECE and Ancient ROME. Wine was a safer drink than most available water until the 17th century in major cities, and much later than that elsewhere. In the late 1960s, this writer was offered unlimited wine as part of her board when working in a smart Italian hotel, but had to pay for bottled water, the only reliable drinking water.

The modern wine drinker rarely chooses to dilute his or her wine (other than to make the occasional SPRITZER) but for HEALTH reasons he or she is well advised to drink at least as much water alongside every glass of wine. Despite its incontrovertible appeal, wine is a poor quencher of thirst.

water addition. See HUMIDIFICATION .

water berry, an alternative name, current in California, for BUNCHSTEM NECROSIS, the physiological disorder of grape berry stems, drying and shrivelling grapes as they approach RIPENESS.

water shoot, a shoot that arises from the wood of the vine, not from buds left at pruning. In fact they mostly arise from BASAL BUDS embedded in the wood and are generally not FRUITFUL. Suckers are a type of water shoot which arise at the base of the TRUNK at or below soil level.   B.G.C.

water stress is the physiological state of plants, including vines, suffering from a shortage of water. Water stress during the later stages of the viticultural growing season is common, since a considerable proportion of the world's vines are grown in MEDITERRANEAN CLIMATES, where rain falls principally in the winter months. It is commonly held that some water stress is desirable for optimum wine quality, especially for red wines, but there is little agreement about exactly how much. There is, however, almost universal agreement that water stress should be sufficient before VERAISON to stop SHOOT TIPS actively growing. Otherwise they attract assimilates, the products of photosynthesis, away from the ripening fruit, to the detriment of wine quality.

Water deficit, or mild water stress, is essential for growing good-quality dark-skinned grapes. It not only reduces shoot growth but also limits berry size and increases the PHENOLICS in the skins. However, these beneficial effects require low yields. When yields are high, water stress quickly leads to poor ripening due to insufficient photosynthesis. This explains why great wines may be produced in very dry climatic conditions in south-ern France or Spain, for example, but only when yields are kept to 30 hl/ha or less. Peyrot des Gachons *et al.* have shown that water stress is not generally favourable for the quality of white wines, which tend to be less aromatic.

IRRIGATION can be used to overcome water stress, although it is outlawed in some European countries. Water stress results in restriction of growth and loss of yield. Unirrigated DRYLAND vineyards in hot climates may yield only 2 to 5 tonnes/ha, for instance. PARTIAL ROOTZONE DRYING is an irrigation method which aims to stimulate the vines' perception of water stress while minimizing any drop in YIELD. Another irrigation strategy designed to induce water stress is REGULATED DEFICIT IRRIGATION. However, this technique is more likely to reduce yield and can induce excessive water stress in hot weather.

Water stress depends on two components: the water content in the root zone of the vine, and the evaporative power of the atmosphere. The latter depends on factors affecting the rate of EVAPORATION, which is high on sunny, hot, windy days with low humidity. On days with extremely high evaporation, even well-watered vines can show temporary wilting. On the other hand, vines growing in dry soils but in overcast, cool, and humid climates do not show as much water stress. The combination of climate and soil which results in maximum vine stress is high evaporation and low soil water content; minimum stress results from low evaporation and wet soils.

Water stress is measured by vine physiologists as water potential in the plant, but is more easily understood in terms of the effect on the vine. One of the first signs of impending water stress is the drooping, or wilting, of tendrils near the shoot tip, followed by wilting of the young, then the mature, leaves. With severe stress, the leaves exhibit CHLOROSIS, then NECROSIS, and eventually can fall off. Berries start to shrivel. As water stress develops in the vine, the plant responds by endeavouring to reduce water loss. At the end of the 20th century, water stress was usually assessed by measuring SOIL WATER, and irrigation decisions were based on this information. The direct measurement of water stress as experienced by the vine (through so-called 'physiological indicators') has been made possible by the commercial availability in the first decade of the 21st century of equipment such as dendrometers, which measure trunk swelling and shrinking, and PRESSURE BOMBS, which measure leaf water potential. However, both techniques indicate the minute-by-minute fluctuations in water stress which occur during the day.

A well-watered vine opens the pores called STOMATA on the underside of the leaf in response to the first light of dawn, and they remain open all day, allowing the free exchange of water vapour (the air humidity) and CARBON DIOXIDE between the leaf interior and the atmosphere. Water stress causes the vine leaf partially to close stomata during the day, and the hormone ABSCISIC ACID regulates this response. Initially, this may be in the middle of the day, but subsequently, as the stress worsens, they are shut for most of the day. While this action is sufficient to reduce further water loss, PHOTOSYNTHESIS is reduced because of the lack of carbon dioxide.

Water stress also affects a range of other vine functions. It can substitute for winter cold in promoting dormancy in TROPICAL VITICULTURE. During the growing season, drought causes shoot growth to slow and then stop as the leaf tip loses activity. Leaves are smaller and paler in colour, and the growth of LATERAL SHOOTS is also inhibited. Severe stress early in the season can reduce FRUIT SET, and later stress reduces BERRY SIZE.

According to Champagnol, the effect of water stress on wine quality is not straightforward. There is no doubt that severe water stress interrupts grape RIPENING and reduces wine quality (especially when yields are high), as for example may be observed in Algeria. It is not clear whether water stress leads to higher SUGARS and better wine in dry viticultural areas such as the LANGUEDOC and ROUSSILLON in southern France. In humid maritime climates, such as that of BORDEAUX, however, there has been ample demonstration that mild water stress during ripening is favourable to wine quality. For example, the Bordeaux growing seasons of 1996, 1995, 1990, 1989, and 2000, all superior VINTAGES, were all relatively dry. Van Leeuwen *et al.* show that all the driest vintages were good and all the wettest vintages were relatively poor. R.E.S. & C.V.L.

Champagnol, F., *Éléments de physiologie de la vigne et de viticulture générale* (St-Gely-du-Fesc, 1984).

Gaudillère, J.-P., Van Leeuwen, C., and Ollat, N., 'Carbon isotope composition of sugars in grapevine, an integrated indicator of vineyard water status', *Journal of Experimental Botany*, 53/369 (2002), 757–63.

Peyrot des Gachons, C., Van Leeuwen, C., Tominaga, T., Soyer, J.-P., Gaudillère, J.-P., and Dubourdieu, D., 'The influence of water and nitrogen deficit on fruit ripening and aroma potential of *Vitis vinifera* L. cv Sauvignon blanc in field conditions', *Journal of the Science of Food and Agriculture*, 85/1 (2005), 73–85.

Tregoat, O., Gaudillère, J.-P., Choné, X., and Van Leeuwen, C., 'Étude du régime hydrique et de la nutrition azotée de la vigne par des indicateurs physiologiques. Influence sur le comportement de la vigne et la maturation du raisin (*Vitis vinifera* L. cv Merlot, 2000, Bordeaux)', *Journal International des Sciences de la Vigne et du Vin*, 36/3 (2002), 133–42.

Van Leeuwen, C., Tregoat, O., Choné, X., Jaeck, M.-E., Rabusseau, S. and Gaudillère J.-P., 'Le suivi du régime hydrique de la vigne et son incidence sur la maturation du raisin', *Bulletin de l'OIV*, 76/867–8 (2003), 367–79.

Waugh, Harry (1904–2001), English wine merchant famous for his longevity, courtesy, and open mind. He did not enter the wine trade until he was 30, joining as a clerk in a long-established City of London business associated with the fashionable West End company of Block, Grey & Block, where he went to work and first displayed his ability in selecting and selling fine wines. At that time, few British wine merchants visited the sources of their wines, but relied on agents or their principals, who paid regular visits to Britain. In this way, Waugh met such well-known Bordeaux merchants as Christian CRUSE, Jean Calvet, and Ronald BARTON. He also spent an annual holiday in the leading French wine areas with the late Allan SICHEL, wine importer and part-owner of Ch Palmer (see MARGAUX).

During the Second World War, Waugh served in the Welsh Guards, and then at the beginning of 1946 joined the London office of HARVEYS of Bristol. With wine in very short supply after six years of war, there was great demand for red bordeaux, the favoured table wine among regular wine drinkers. Waugh took a further holiday in Bordeaux, where he was introduced by Édouard Cruse to the wines of POMEROL, then almost unknown in Britain. In 1950, he acquired and imported in cask the distinguished 1949 vintage of the then obscure Ch PÉTRUS; as by coincidence did that other Bristol wine merchant Ronald AVERY. He also visited for Harveys other French wine regions, including Beaujolais, then imported as a somewhat anonymous quaffing blend. He bought individual CRU Beaujolais and was invited to form a London chapter of the still flourishing Compagnons de Beaujolais CONFRÉRIE.

After the devastating FROSTS of February 1956, Waugh, by then a director of Harveys, went with a colleague to Bordeaux and, through broker Jean-Paul Gardère, bought large quantities of the fine 1955 vintage, thereby bypassing the BORDEAUX TRADE, for which he was long remembered. He was a regular visitor for his firm to Oxford and Cambridge colleges, and in 1953 instituted an annual Oxbridge undergraduate wine-tasting competition, sponsored until 1990 by Harveys (and subsequently by POL ROGER champagne). During this period, Harveys trained some of the leading lights of the British wine trade, including Michael BROADBENT.

In 1962 the families who owned Ch LATOUR decided to sell, and offered this famous Bordeaux first growth to Harveys. Although Waugh and his chairman were in favour, the majority of the board was against, so that Pearson, publishers of the *Financial Times*, acquired a 51 per cent stake, while Harveys were allotted only 25 per cent. Waugh became one of two Harvey representatives on the board, on which he remained during two changes of ownership. He introduced as joint managers Jean-Paul Gardère and his friend Henri Martin, proprietor of Ch Gloria (see ST-JULIEN). In 1966 when Harveys was bought by Showerings, producers of Babycham, a popular perry, Waugh, then 62, retired. (Seven years later his first children, twins, were born.)

Then began Waugh's close association with wine amateurs in the United States. For many years he made regular lecture tours, and achieved a reputation in the US unequalled by any other British wine professional. Several volumes of *Harry Waugh's Wine Diary* were published as a record of his punishing itineraries. He did much to publicize Ch Latour, as well as other Bordeaux châteaux's wines. He also introduced California wines to British (and east coast American) wine connoisseurs in the early 1970s when they were little known. For his services to French wines, he received the French Mérite Agricole in 1984 and in 1988 he was made a Chevalier de l'Ordre du Mérite National. In 1989, he was made an honorary member of the Institute of MASTERS OF WINE. He will always be remembered for his reply to someone who asked whether he had ever mistaken claret for burgundy: 'not since lunch.' E.P.-R.

Waugh, H., *Harry Waugh's Wine Diaries* vols. i–ix (vols. i–v were individually entitled) (London, 1966–81).

weather, probably the single most exasperatingly unpredictable variable in the viticultural equation, as in most other farming activities. For details of overall weather patterns, see CLIMATE, MACROCLIMATE, and CLIMATE CLASSIFICATION. For accounts of specific climatological phenomena with implications for wine production, see DEW, DROUGHT, FLOODING, FROST, HAIL, RAINFALL, SUNLIGHT, TEMPERATURE, and WIND. The weather in a specific growing season is the most important influence on the characteristics of a particular VINTAGE YEAR.

websites, increasingly important way of selling and communicating about wine. See INFORMATION TECHNOLOGY.

weed control, a range of viticultural practices to avoid WEEDS competing with vines—particularly young vines—for water and nutrients. The practices vary from region to region and with VINE AGE, with the common options being CULTIVATION (ploughing) or HERBICIDES.

Mechanical control of weeds involves cultivating down the row alley using discs or tines. Cultivation directly under the row is more difficult, as the weeding device needs to avoid the trunks. A number of appropriate cultivators have been developed, with the swing back action achieved manually in early models but now controlled automatically by touch sensing the trunk. Even so, such cultivation disturbs the ground under the vine row where the majority of roots are, and many machines can cause some vine damage. Hand hoeing of weeds is still found in some vineyards, although often this is restricted to the control of particularly difficult weeds in young vineyards. The alternative is to use herbicides, and spraying an undervine strip is common.

Mowing between the rows is common in summer rainfall areas, or where there is plentiful irrigation, otherwise the weeds growing there cause excessive WATER STRESS and sometimes NITROGEN deficiency, leading to incomplete fermentations. Other methods of weed control include mulching, using cereal straw, for example, placed as a mat under the rows. This has the added advantage of increasing organic matter, earthworm populations, and water infiltration. Weeds may also be controlled by planting the vines through a strip of plastic. R.E.S.

weeder, implement used in vineyards for removing WEEDS, typically from the vine row. These machines, usually mounted on a tractor, have fallen from favour owing to the death of some vines, and the introduction of some diseases because of vine injury. In many parts of the world, the use of undervine weeders has been replaced by HERBICIDES. R.E.S.

weeds. A weed is defined as a plant out of place, and many vine-growers regard a weedy vineyard as a sign of poor management. The presence of plants other than vines in the vineyard is a feature of ORGANIC VITICULTURE, on the other hand. Some vineyards are excessively ploughed to keep them free of weeds, to the detriment of SOIL STRUCTURE. More recently there has been a tendency to achieve the same result using HERBICIDES, perhaps in combination with CULTIVATION.

There is no doubt that weed growth inhibits the growth of vines, especially in young vines. When the vine root system is small and shallow, weeds compete for water and nutrients, especially NITROGEN, but with older vines the competition can be less as the vine root system is larger and deeper. Some plant species seem to have a further effect in inhibiting others, a phenomenon known as allelopathy. In very weedy vineyards, the weeds may also compete with the vines for light.

Weeds can cause inconvenience and discomfort to vineyard workers and can also harbour vine PESTS and DISEASES, although they can also shelter predators of insect vine pests. Weeds play an important part in the spread of the disease FLAVESCENCE DORÉE. In some vineyards, other plants may be deliberately encouraged to grow between the rows as a COVER CROP.

Weeds which occur in vineyards obviously vary from region to region, and are representative of the local flora. Those present depend on prior land use, soil preparation, seed reserves in the soil, and the extent to which seeds arrive in the vineyard, by wind or on implements, for example. Weeds which are difficult to control and can be found in many vineyards worldwide include field bindweed (*Convolvulus arvensis*), Johnson grass (*Holcus*

halepensis), and Bermuda or couch grass (*Cynadon dactylon*). R.E.S.

Flaherty, D. L., *et al.* (eds.), *Grape Pest Management* (Oakland, Calif., 1992).

weevils. See BEETLES.

weighing of grapes is an important operation at any centre where grapes are received from a number of different growers who are paid by weight. This applies to most wine CO-OPERATIVES and many individual wineries, even if the more progressive take other factors such as grape quality and health into account before determining PRICE. Weighing is normally done with large platform scales on which the lorry is weighed full and empty.

The amount of additives needed during the adjustment operations of ENRICHMENT, ACID-IFICATION, and DEACIDIFICATION, as well as the BLENDING process, can be calculated more precisely on the basis of weight than volume. The weight of wine is calculated from the measured volume and the DENSITY. Blends calculated on a volume basis do not account for the contractions that occur when solutions of differing ALCOHOLIC STRENGTH are mixed. A.D.W.

Wein (pronounced 'vine') means 'wine' in GERMAN. It is therefore the first syllable of a host of important German wine names such as **Weinbau** (vine-growing), **Weinbrand** (basic brandy), and **Weingut** (wine estate) as distinct from a **Weinkellerei**, which buys in grapes, must, or wine but probably owns vineyards only if it describes itself as the all-purpose **Weingut-Weinkellerei**. A **Weinprobe** is a wine tasting, **Weinsäure** is TARTARIC ACID, some of which may eventually be precipitated as crystal TARTRATES, or **Weinsteine**.

Weinviertel, wine area in AUSTRIA and the country's first DAC designaton.

weisser, meaning 'white', is a common prefix in German for pale-skinned grape varieties, e.g. **Weissburgunder** or **Weisser Burgunder** is PINOT BLANC.

Weisser Riesling, common synonym for the great white RIESLING grape variety of Germany.

Weissherbst, special sort of pink wine made from a single grape variety in the AHR, RHEINGAU, RHEINHESSEN, PFALZ, WÜRTTEMBERG, and BADEN wine regions of GERMANY. It may be either a QBA or QMP wine and in Baden Weissherbst made from Spätburgunder (PINOT NOIR) has enjoyed local popularity. See also SCHILLERWEIN. The term is also used in German SWITZERLAND for very much the same style of wine.

Welschriesling, or **Wälschriesling**, white grape variety which, as Germans are keen to point out, is completely unrelated to the great RIESLING grape of Germany. Indeed it

rankles with many Germans that the noble word is even allowed as a suffix in the name of this inferior variety; they would prefer that the word Rizling were used, as in **Welsch Rizling** or **Welschrizling**, which it is in many of its many synonyms.

Welschriesling may be the variety's most common name in AUSTRIA, but Welschrizling is obediently used in BULGARIA, its most common name in HUNGARY is OLASZ RIZLING, in SLOVENIA and VOJVODINA it is LAŠKI RIZLING, and in the CZECH REPUBLIC and SLOVAKIA it is the very similar Rizling Vlassky. Only in CROATIA does it acquire a name of any distinction, Graševina. The Italians call it RIESLING ITALICO (as opposed to Riesling Renano, which is the Riesling of Germany) and variants of this are used all over Eastern Europe. In ROMANIA, where there were 7,300 ha of the variety in the mid 2000s, the grape is usually just marketed as Riesling, as there was no German Riesling in the country up to 2004, although most of the 'Riesling' planted in the ex Soviet republic is true Riesling. The variety is one of the few common white wine grapes in ALBANIA, as it is in what was for long its close political ally CHINA.

The origins of this old variety are obscure. Although French origins have been posited, this seems unlikely as it is quite unknown in France (and Germany), it thrives best in dry climates and warmer soils, and has a tendency to produce excessively acid wines in cool climates.

Welsch simply means 'foreign' in Germanic languages, which provides few clues. But since Vlaska is the Slav name for Wallachia in Romania, and since the variety is particularly successful in that country, it is easy to develop a theory that it originated there, and that Laški is a corruption of Vlassy, or Wallachian.

Although Welschriesling has little in common with Riesling, it too is a late-ripening vine whose grapes keep their acidity well and produce light-bodied, relatively aromatic wines. Welschriesling can easily be persuaded to yield even more productively than Riesling, however, and indeed this and its useful acidity probably explain why it is so widely planted throughout eastern Europe and, partly, why so much of the wine it produces is undistinguished (although low technological standards in many wineries in what was YUGOSLAVIA, for example, have also played a part).

As a wine, Welschriesling reaches its apogee in AUSTRIA, specifically in some particularly finely balanced, rich late harvest wines made on the shores of the Neusiedlersee in Burgenland, where nearly half of Austria's total 4,300 ha/10,600 acres of the variety is planted. In particularly favoured vintages, the NOBLE ROT forms to ripen grapes up to TROCKENBEERENAUSLESE level, while retaining the acidity that is Welschriesling's hallmark. Welschriesling may not have the aromatic character of Germany's Riesling, but since aroma plays only a small part in the appreciation of really sweet wines, this leaves Welschriesling at less of a disadvantage than Riesling addicts might imagine, although Austrian TBAS, sometimes a blend of Chardonnay with Welschriesling, rarely have the longevity of their German counterparts. The bulk of Austria's Welschriesling, however, goes into light dryish wines for early drinking, notably in Weinviertel, Burgenland, and Styria. It is also used for production of Austrian SEKT.

Western Australia, or **WA**. AUSTRALIA'S biggest state has the country's most isolated wine regions in its south west corner.

Nowhere have the winds of change blown harder since 1970 than in Western Australia. In that year, more than 90 per cent of the state's wine was made from grapes grown in the then Swan Valley (now a subregion of the **Swan District** in the Greater Perth Zone); by 1980 the figure was 59 per cent; by 2003 it was less than 11 per cent and still falling notwithstanding the larger geographic compass which takes in the Peel and Perth Hills regions as well. The other side of the coin has been the emergence of the Margaret River and Great Southern regions spanning the far south western corner of the state.

In a manner reminiscent of the Barossa Valley in South Australia, the Swan Valley, with the dubious distinction of being the hottest region in Australia, with harvest typically beginning in January, remains the production centre of much of Western Australia's wine, largely through a single company, Houghton (part of HARDYS). As well as producing Houghton White Burgundy (or HWB, as it is called in Europe) from Verdelho, Chenin Blanc, and Chardonnay grown in the Swan Valley and at Gingin (just to the north), Houghton has large vineyards at Frankland in the Great Southern, and is a major purchaser of grapes throughout that region and the Margaret River. Houghton's ultra-premium Jack Mann and Gladstones red wines from these regions are among Australia's very best full-bodied wines based on Cabernet Sauvignon and Shiraz.

The **Margaret River** has grown both in size and reputation since the mid 1990s. It is now regularly grouped with Coonawarra and the Yarra Valley as the best-known of the newer regions, joining the Barossa and Hunter Valleys representing the traditional regions. Its all-year-round tourist-friendly climate, physical beauty and diverse attractions from surf to woodworks neatly combine with undoubted quality of its wine. While, 240 km/146 miles to the south of Perth, it is still at a latitude of 34 degrees south, and therefore completely reliant upon the cooling influence of the Indian ocean to provide its TEMPERATE climate. Here Cabernet Sauvignon (often blended with Merlot) produces a wine which consistently combines elegance with strength, redcurrant fruit with a seasoning of gravelly

GOÛT *de terroir*. Pungently grassy and intense Semillon and Sauvignon Blanc also perform with distinction, likewise more often than not blended with each other (and sometimes with Chenin Blanc as a third partner). Chardonnay is the other grape of importance, making wine which is invariably complex and often long lived. Leeuwin Estate is regarded by many as Australia's best; Giaconda is the other main contender for the title.

Riesling has never succeeded in the Margaret River, but comes emphatically into its own in the far-flung, colder, and usually more CONTINENTAL subregions of the Great Southern region of **Porongurup**, **Mount Barker**, and **Frankland River**. Here it produces crisp, tightly structured wines which evolve slowly but with grace, mirroring the slow development of the equally taut yet fragrant Cabernet Sauvignon. This is a huge and diverse region. Chardonnay and Shiraz also do well, balancing cool climate elegance and intensity of flavour. The coastal subregions of **Albany** and **Denmark** are far more suited to Sauvignon Blanc, Chardonnay, and (intermittently) Pinot Noir.

The other regions within the South West Australia Zone are of lesser importance in terms of production, and will remain so. The adjacent areas of **Pemberton** (north east) and **Manjimup** (south west) fall within the geographic area generically known as the Warren valley, taken from the Warren river which flows through both. They have remained at loggerheads over their respective boundaries and names, although the majority of vignerons in each favour the Pemberton/Manjimup distinction. These somewhat schizophrenic attitudes are also reflected in the varietal wines of the regions. The distinctly cool, moderately high rainfall, and varied soils (some very fertile) caused the Pemberton pioneers to see their region as a Burgundy equivalent. In fact Merlot and Shiraz have performed as well, if not better than, Pinot Noir while Verdelho challenges Chardonnay. That challenge intensifies in Manjimup, but will likely remain undecided for another decade or so.

The **Blackwood Valley** lies immediately to the north of Manjimup, taking its name from the Blackwood river. The first plantings were only in 1978, and there are just as many questions about the future direction here as there are in Manjimup and Pemberton.

The last region in the South West Australia Zone is **Geographe**, altogether more important and with a clearer focus, albeit with varied climate as one moves inland from the coast. The coastal town of Bunbury is the centre (on the north/south axis), while Capel Vale is the dominant winery. The most important of four rivers are the Collie and Fergusson, creating valleys as they flow to the coast, and a cross-hatch with the Darling range running north–south. Varied terroir is the order of the day, but Chardonnay, Verdelho, and Sauvi-

gnon Blanc lead the white wines and Shiraz, Cabernet Sauvignon, and Merlot the reds, all with flavour and attitude.   J.H.

Halliday, J., numerous works including *The Wine Atlas of Australia*, and *Australia Wine Companion* (Sydney, annually).

western grapeleaf skeletonizer, a vine pest and native insect of Mexico and the states of Arizona, New Mexico, and Texas, first found in California in 1941 in San Diego county. The young larvae feed on the soft leaf tissue, leaving a skeleton framework. Chemical control is effective, but timing is critical. Left unchecked this insect will completely defoliate a vine, seriously affecting RIPENING.   M.J.E.

Western Victoria Zone comprises Grampians, Henty, and Pyrenees regions in Australia.

whip graft, the form used in GRAFTING which simply involves an angled slice across the SCION stem and a similarly angled cut of the stock, with the two cuts then matched and the graft tied tightly with grafting tape. **Whip-and-tongue** is the same except that another cut is made to raise 'tongues' of stem tissue that dovetail with each other and improve the strength of the graft.   B.G.C.

white has a special meaning when applied both to grapes and wine. Any light-skinned grape may be called a white grape, even though the grape skin is not white but anything from pale green through gold to pink. In a similar fashion, white wines are not white, but vary in colour from almost colourless to deep gold. See COLOUR.

White French, inappropriate South African name for the PALOMINO grape, an adaptation of Fransdruif.

White Riesling, common synonym for the great white RIESLING grape variety of Germany.

white rot, FUNGAL DISEASE affecting vines that occurs in those parts of Europe most prone to hailstorms, also known as hail disease. Crop losses can be as high as 80 per cent. The fruit is attacked after a hailstorm and, because the berry skin is lifted from the flesh, the berries appear white, hence the name. High summer rainfall, high humidity, and high temperatures also favour the disease. The fungus responsible is *Coniella diplodiella*, which is controlled by a range of chemical sprays.   R.E.S.

white wine-making, the production of wines with almost imperceptible to golden COLOUR. If the juice is separated from the grape skins gently and soon enough (as in the production of CHAMPAGNE), white wines can be made from black-skinned grapes, but the great majority of white wines are made from grapes with yellow or green skins. White wines can be made from grapes of all hues, so long as there is no SKIN CONTACT or MACERATION with dark-skinned grapes. The only exception to this is the red-fleshed TEINTURIERS. White wines are distinguished from their red counterparts by their absence of ANTHOCYANINS and PIGMENTED TANNINS. As with any WINE-MAKING operation, the production of white wines usually entails CRUSHING and DESTEMMING the grape clusters or bunches on arrival at the winery, although occasionally white grapes may be crushed beforehand at a field pressing station (and see also WHOLE BUNCH PRESSING). After crushing and destemming, the sweet POMACE requires draining and PRESSING to separate the liquid from the solids. The timing of the separation of juice from solids constitutes the major difference between red and white wine-making: before FERMENTATION for whites and afterwards for reds.

Prolonged contact between juice and grape skins (see SKIN CONTACT and MACERATION) encourages the transfer of soluble materials, including PHENOLICS, FLAVOUR COMPOUNDS, and FLAVOUR PRECURSORS, from the skins to the juice. The extracted phenolics, which are essential to a red wine, providing both colour and TANNIN, are generally undesirable in a white wine, for they lead to excessive astringent and bitter tastes and, at higher levels, a coarseness making the wine undrinkable. The skin phenolics also lead to the development of amber to brown colours deemed inappropriate for white wines. The challenge for the white winemaker is therefore to find the balance, through appropriate juice handling techniques, between appropriate transfer of the flavour compounds and minimal phenolic extraction. Because of their light colour and delicate flavours, white wines show the unappetizing effects of OXIDATION much faster than red wines and so white wine-making is in general a more delicate operation than RED WINE-MAKING. Small amounts of ACETALDE-HYDE are produced by the reaction of oxygen with alcohol, and this compound can easily spoil the AROMA of a fresh, fruity young wine. There are two possible solutions to this inconvenience. Exposure to oxygen may be minimized or completely avoided throughout wine-making right up to and including bottling by techniques known collectively as PROTECTIVE. Alternatively, a policy of unprotected handling is adopted whereby the MUST is deliberately, and sometimes in the case of everyday wines violently, aerated so that its susceptible phenolics oxidize, these brown compounds being removed by absorption into the dead yeast cells or LEES after fermentation. This technique is sometimes referred to as hyperoxidation. Most of the acetaldehyde produced by this sort of oxidation is reduced to alcohol during the subsequent fermentation. The disadvantage of this prefermentation oxidation is that it removes some of the compounds that would have contributed to BODY and AROMA as well as a bit of colour.

White wines are usually fermented and processed cooler than normal room TEMPERATURE, although the disadvantages of this are the cost of any REFRIGERATION used and the pressure on available FERMENTATION VESSELS since cool fermentations take longer. Only a small, but much-vaunted, proportion of white wine comes into contact with WOOD but BARREL FERMENTATION followed by BARREL MATURATION is an increasingly common phenomenon, particularly for wines made from the CHARDONNAY grape. Among these barrel-fermented white wines, LEES STIRRING is also popular, as is MALOLACTIC FERMENTATION.

A.D.W. & P.J.W.

white wines, made with much less SKIN CONTACT than red wines. This does not necessarily mean, however, that they are inherently less interesting, or shorter lived (see AGEING). They vary enormously in colour from virtually colourless to deep gold and even, in extreme age, deep tawny (the same colour as some very old red wines). They are made in virtually all wine regions, although in hot regions ACIDIFICATION and some form of REFRIGERATION are usually needed to produce white wines suitable for modern tastes.

French for white is *blanc*, Italian is *bianco*, Spanish is *blanco*, Portuguese is *branco*, German is *weiss*, while in most eastern European languages, including Russian, the word for white is some variant of *byeli*.

White Zinfandel, undeterred by the fact that it is neither white nor crucially Zinfandel, was California's great commercial success story of the 1980s. Although he was not the first to vinify California's ubiquitous ZINFANDEL grapes as a white, and therefore BLUSH, wine, Bob Trinchero of Sutter Home launched 'White' Zinfandel down the

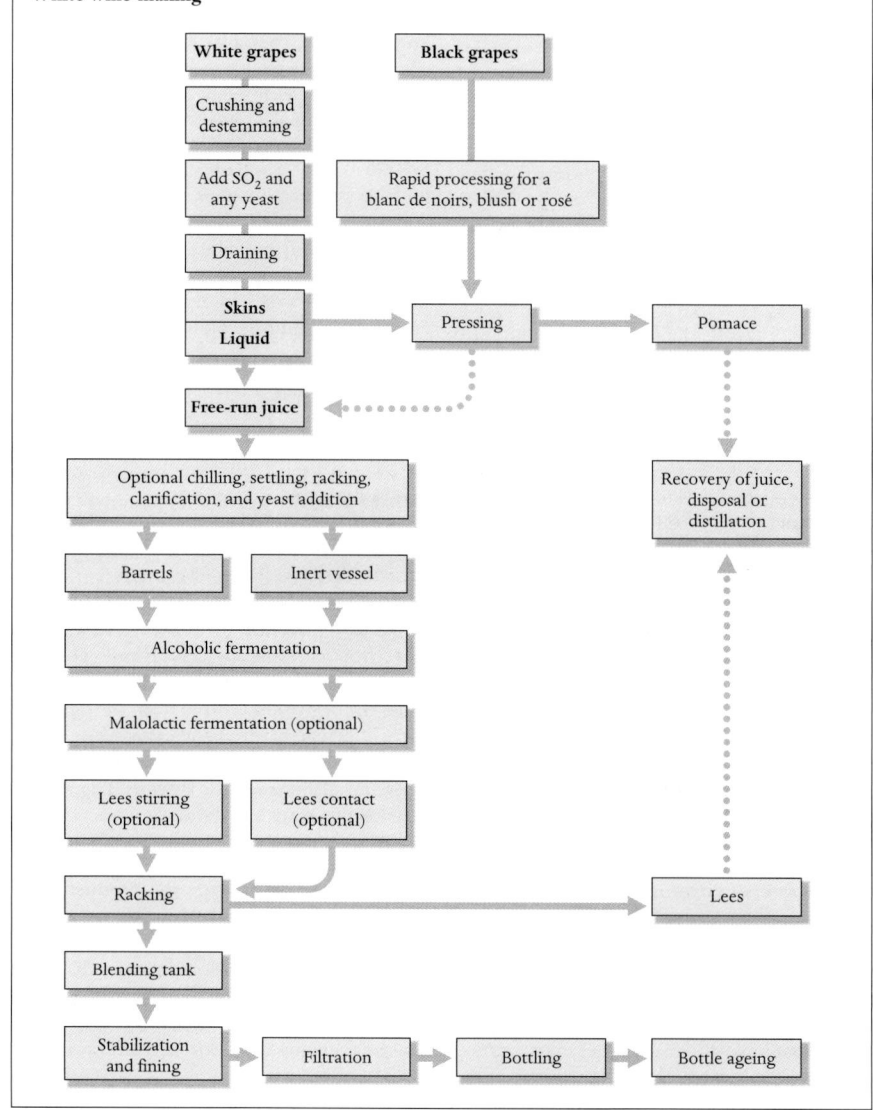

White wine-making

White grapes → Crushing and destemming → Add SO₂ and any yeast → Draining → Skins / Liquid → Free-run juice → Optional chilling, settling, racking, clarification, and yeast addition → Barrels / Inert vessel → Alcoholic fermentation → Malolactic fermentation (optional) → Lees stirring (optional) / Lees contact (optional) → Racking → Blending tank → Stabilization and fining → Filtration → Bottling → Bottle ageing

Black grapes → Rapid processing for a blanc de noirs, blush or rosé → Pressing → Pomace → Recovery of juice, disposal or distillation

Lees

commercial slipway in 1972 and was to see his own sales rocket from 25,000 cases in 1980 to 1.5 million cases six years later. The wine evolved as a way of making California's vast acreage of Zinfandel acceptable to the predominantly white wine-drinking American public. So successful was it that it stimulated an outbreak of new plantings of the variety expressly to keep pace with demand for this decidedly ersatz version. The wine is usually pale pink, decidedly sweet, often enlivened with a touch of gas, and scented with more than a dash of other, more obviously aromatic, grape varieties such as Muscat or Riesling. So successful was the wine that it begat styles such as **White Grenache**, designed to glamorize vineyard Cinderellas.

whole bunch fermentation, ultra-traditional method of red wine FERMENTATION in which grape berries are not subjected to DESTEMMING. The possible disadvantages are that, unless the fruit and STEMS are very ripe and MUST is handled very gently, the stems may impart harsh TANNINS to the wine. The technique also involves a greater total capacity of FERMENTATION VESSELS, which are often open topped to allow PUNCHING DOWN of the CAP (although PUMPING OVER is also practised). The advantages are that the stems can ease the drainage of the juice through the cap, and encourage healthy oxygenation by increasing the cap's interface with the atmosphere during MACERATION. This practice is most common in BURGUNDY.

whole bunch pressing, special WHITE WINE-MAKING technique whereby the grapes are not subjected to DESTEMMING and bunches of ripe grapes are pressed whole, with the stems used as conduits for what can often be particularly viscous juice. This works best for very ripe grapes and would not be suitable if a period of SKIN CONTACT precedes PRESSING since excess TANNINS could be leached into the wine from the STEMS. This technique is almost universal in the production of top-quality SPARKLING WINES and most other white wines from dark-skinned grapes and in the direct pressing of BOTRYTIS-affected clusters of super-ripe grapes as in SAUTERNES. It is also increasingly popular with some quality-conscious producers of white wines in some wine regions since the juice that results tends to be low in PHENOLICS and high in quality.

whole grape fermentation. Alternative name for CARBONIC MACERATION.

Wien. VIENNA as its natives know it.

WIETA, or Wine and Agricultural Ethical Trade Association, organization dedicated to improving social and employment conditions in the wine industry of SOUTH AFRICA. Members include grape-growers, wine producers, trades unions, retailers, agents, importers, and exporters of South African wine. Its code of conduct includes a prohibition on child and enforced labour and obliges members to provide a safe and healthy working environment with freedom of association, the right to collective bargaining, a living wage, reasonable working hours, regular employment, security of tenure, and protection against unfair discrimination. Members are subject to regular audits, and, when compliant, are accredited by WIETA. M.F.

Wildbacher, or **Blauer Wildbacher**, dark-skinned grape variety that is a speciality of western STYRIA in AUSTRIA, where almost all of the 460 ha/1,100 acres grown are located. The variety has been increasingly popular with growers and almost all of it is made into the local pink speciality, Schilcher wine, enlivened by Wildbacher's high acidity and distinctive perfume. DNA PROFILING in Austria suggested a parent–offspring relationship with GOUAIS BLANC.

wild vines, plants of the genus VITIS growing in their natural state without any cultivation by humans. Such vines are lianas and are often found climbing trees but may also grow as shrubs. They are widespread in the Americas, especially in the east and south east, in Asia, and up until the mid 1800s in Europe. Generally the vines are indigenous, but sometimes they are feral, that is, they are derived from plants once cultivated rather than from indigenous plants. Examples of feral vines are the wild vines of the Pays BASQUE and, according to Mullins, the AMERICAN VINE SPECIES *Vitis riparia* and *Vitis rupestris* along the Rhône and Garonne rivers after importation as ROOTSTOCKS. Wild vines are typically spread by birds eating the berries and passing the seeds. Where wild vines of different species grow together, it is common for natural HYBRIDS to develop, as for example in the east of America (see AMERICAN HYBRIDS). Such hybrids can also develop from natural pollen interchange with cultivated grapes.

Perhaps the most famous of all wild vines are those described in the legend about the discovery of VÍNLAND. The early settlers and explorers in the Americas and the Caribbean found profuse growth of wild vines in the woods. Such vines had tolerance to the harsh winter climate and indigenous pests such as PHYLLOXERA, and FUNGAL DISEASES such as DOWNY MILDEW and POWDERY MILDEW, and to PIERCE'S DISEASE, and so could grow without check, while the *Vitis* VINIFERA vines imported from Europe perished in cultivation.

Wild vines of the wine-producing *vinifera* species were more widespread in Europe and western Asia, although they have disappeared from large areas of Europe since the introduction of the American pests and diseases noted above. Sometimes such wild vines are called *Vitis vinifera silvestris*, while cultivated vines are called *Vitis vinifera sativa*, although there are very few differences between the two forms. When they are both grown under the same conditions, they appear similar; indeed, there is more variation among different VINE VARIETIES of cultivated *vinifera* than there is among different types of wild *vinifera*. One fundamental difference, however, is that the wild vines are dioecious, that is that there are both male and female plants. The cultivated vine on the other hand has mostly perfect or hermaphrodite flowers (containing functional male and female parts), which results in better FRUIT SET, and would have been the basis of selection from the wild by humans.

Wild vines are important to modern viticulture as they are the source of many of the present-day varieties. With the collapse of the Roman empire and the abandonment of vineyard cultivation, some ancient varieties became feral and interbred with native wild vines. So those of the modern varieties selected from the wild from that period onwards may have contained germplasm from both wild *Vitis vinifera* and Roman or Gallo-Roman varieties. See also JAPAN. R.E.S.

Jackson, R., *Wine Science: Principles, Practice, Perception* (San Diego, 2000).

Mullins, M. G., Bouquet, A., and Williams, L., *Biology of the Grapevine* (Cambridge, 1992).

Pinney, T., *A History of Wine in America: From the Beginnings to Prohibition* (Berkeley, Calif., 1989).

wind, or strong air movement, is a problem on many coastal and otherwise exposed viticultural sites. Major valleys can also be windy, because they can act as funnels, and have their own distinctive systems of wind force and directions. The mistral of the southern Rhône is one of the more notorious examples of this. The detrimental effects of wind on vines are described under WIND STRESS; installing WINDBREAKS can provide a solution.

Hot, dry winds in summer are a particular hazard of viticultural regions bordering deserts. Some Australian vineyards are periodically affected. The sirocco of North Africa can similarly afflict the vineyards of southern Europe, occasionally reaching France. The hot, very dry, strong *zonda* winds of Argentina can cause major problems for vineyards.

The effects of wind are by no means all detrimental, however. The normally regular afternoon sea breezes of coastal regions with otherwise summer-dry climates, such as those of Portugal, California, and much of southern Australia, have a useful moderating effect on viticultural climate, and are thought to contribute significantly to the quality of their wines (see CLIMATE AND WINE QUALITY). In all environments some air movement is needed to prevent excessive build-up of humidity within the vineyard, and to encourage drying of wet foliage and bunches, thereby reducing the risk of FUNGAL DISEASES. Night winds (or WIND MACHINES) largely prevent radiation

FROSTS, while during sunlight hours the moderate movement of leaves encourages a more uniform spread of intermittent sunlight exposure among them, thus promoting a more efficient use of SUNLIGHT. Some degree of windiness is also often an unavoidable concomitant of the TOPOGRAPHIES that are viticulturally the best in other respects.

In summary, winds cannot be entirely avoided; nor are they wholly undesirable. The selection of sheltered sites, where possible, is important in windy regions. Beyond that, the answers to wind problems lie mainly in suitable vineyard strategies of TRELLISING and where necessary in the use of WINDBREAKS.

J.G.

windbreak, a barrier of vegetation or other materials to break the force of WINDS and avoid WIND STRESS. The benefits of windbreaks go beyond reducing physical vine damage. A combination of reduced wind force and (in dry atmospheres) the maintenance of higher HUMIDITIES among the vines reduces closure of the leaf pores (STOMATA), and therefore enhances potential PHOTOSYNTHESIS. Quite substantial yield increases are commonly recorded in the lee of effective windbreaks, amply exceeding any losses that might be incurred through reduced vine area.

The best natural windbreaks are fast-growing trees or tall shrubs whose roots do not extend too far laterally. Tall winter COVER CROPS such as cereal rye, planted between the vine rows, can also afford useful protection to young vineyards in early spring. VINE GUARDS can also protect young vines from wind.

J.G. & R.E.S.

wind machine, a strong fan for stirring up and mixing cold, dense air settled on the land surface with warmer air from above, thereby preventing FROSTS on still spring nights when there is no WIND to do the job. Such machines, introducing an aeronautical look to vineyards, have been used in slight depressions on valley floors that are prone to radiation frosts, such as in the NAPA valley of California. HELICOPTERS can be used to the same effect.

J.G.

wind stress, can reduce vine YIELD and RIPENING in some exposed vineyards. Severe gusts of wind can have dramatic effects on vineyards, breaking shoots and removing leaves. However, even lower velocity wind can also cause vine problems which are apparent only to the trained eye. Wind cools plants by removing the warming effects of the sun's rays, as well as other more substantial effects on physiology. For some plants, including vines, wind can have a major effect on growth. Shoot length, leaf area, and fruit growth can all be substantially reduced. The problem is particularly acute for young vines, as in older vineyards the CANOPY can usually offer some degree of self-protection.

Some vines respond negatively to movement, probably a response involving plant HORMONES. A major effect of wind is that of closing STOMATA. Freeman and colleagues of the University of California showed that wind speeds of 3 m/10 ft per second in the Salinas valley caused stomata to close partially, which has the effect of reducing both PHOTOSYNTHESIS and TRANSPIRATION. Vines ripening in windy places will show reduced ripening and higher PH.

Simon studied the effects of WINDBREAKS on vines in the San Rafael region of Argentina. Malbec vines adjacent to the 10-m/33-ft tall poplar windbreak showed earlier FLOWERING, FRUIT SET, and VERAISON and longer shoots with more grapes near the windbreak. The windbreak was also effective against occasional very strong winds in reducing mechanical damage.

R.E.S.

Freeman, B. M., Kliewer, W. M., and Stern, P., 'Influence of windbreaks and climatic region on diurnal fluctuation of leaf water potential, stomatal conductance, and leaf temperature of grapevines', *American Journal of Enology and Viticulture*, 33 (1982), 233–6.

Simon, J. C., 'Étude des influences agronomiques des brise-vents dans les périmètres irrigués du Centre-Ouest de l'Argentine. I: Effets des brise-vents sur la croissance et le développement d'une culture type: la vigne', *Annales agronomie*, 28 (1977), 75–93.

wine, alcoholic drink made by fermenting the juice of fruits or berries (see FRUIT WINES). By extension, this most general definition can also include products of the FERMENTATION of sugar solutions flavoured with flowers or herbs, but it normally excludes those of hydrolysed barley starches involved in brewing, and the products of the fermentation of sugar-containing liquids destined for DISTILLATION. There are also certain drinks, such as MEAD, cider, and perry, which depend on sugar fermentations for their alcohol content but for historical reasons merit their own names.

The narrower definition, relevant to this book and accepted throughout Europe, is that wine is 'the alcoholic beverage obtained from the fermentation of the juice of freshly gathered grapes, the fermentation taking place in the district of origin according to local tradition and practice'. This is to distinguish 'proper' wine from alcoholic drinks made from imported grape concentrate, which are known in Europe as MADE WINE. These include BRITISH WINE and a significant proportion of the liquid produced by HOME WINE-MAKING. New World definitions of wine are very similar except that the last phrase is omitted and wine may be made from a mixture of grapes grown many hundreds of miles apart.

Etymology

The modern English *wine* comes from Old English *wīn*, pronounced like modern 'wean':

that indeed was how Chaucer pronounced his *wyn*, but Shakespeare's pronunciation was closer to our own. The Old English form was in turn descended from the Latin *vīnum*, or as the Romans wrote it vinvm, by way of a loan-word represented in all Germanic languages (e.g. German *Wein*, Icelandic *vín*); a similar loan into Celtic has yielded Welsh *gwin* and Irish *f ion*. The explanation is that the Germans and CELTS, whose native beverage was BEER, learnt to drink wine from the Romans; with it came the Latin word, borrowed while Latin *v* was still pronounced [w]. From Germanic territory drink and name passed in turn to the Slavs (e.g. Russian *vinó*) and Balts (Lithuanian *vỹnas*, Latvian *vīns*).

Within Latin itself, from *vīnum* comes the noun *vīnea* 'vineyard'; this word, reinterpreted of a single vine (classically *vītis*, whence 'viticulture'), yielded French *vigne*, which was naturally brought over to England by the Normans. However, once the native English began to learn their masters' language, they adjusted it to suit their own speech habits; since English then as now lacked the palatal sound of French *gn*, it was simplified to *n*, so that *vigne* became *vine*. This was adopted into English and subjected to the normal sound-changes of the late medieval and early modern period: the final *-e* ceased to be pronounced and the long *i* became a diphthong. The French word was also substituted in the term for the place where vines were grown, originally *wīngeard*, now 'vineyard', with the vowel shortened as often in compounds (e.g. 'shepherd' vs. 'sheep').

Whereas *vitis* can be related to an Indo-European verb-root meaning to 'wind' or 'twine', as in English *withy*, the ultimate origins of *vinum* and *vinea* are less clear: similar words are found in many Mediterranean languages, even those belonging to different language-families, but few interrelations can be established. For instance, although Latin *ī* often comes from *ei*, since the change did not take place till the late 2nd century BC it cannot have occurred in *vinum*, for which forms with *vin*- are found in the kindred languages of ancient Italy. This rules out a direct link with the term current in Ancient GREECE, according to dialect *woinos* (Ϝοῖνος) or *oînos* (οἶνος), as in OENOLOGY, akin to the **woiniyo-* (* denotes a reconstructed form) underlying Armenian *gini* and sometimes associated with Sanskrit *veṇi* or *veṇī* 'braid'. The form *wiyana* and *wayana* are quoted from the ancient Anatolian languages (see ASIA MINOR) Hittite and Luvian: outside Indo-European, a Semitic noun **wayn*, 'grape, vine, wine', which yields Hebrew *yayin* and Ethiopic *wäyn* besides an Arabic *wayn* 'black grape' found in an ancient lexicon, has sometimes been considered the source of the Greek word and sometimes a derivative. Even Georgian *γvino* (see GEORGIA) has been proposed: no theory is convincing, except after a few glasses.

L.H.-S.

The **fermentation vessels** for red wines at Rustenberg, one of South Africa's most respected producers, are stainless steel tanks which have been deliberately suspended so as to allow the **press** to be gravity-fed and to move freely about the cellar.

Editorial note:

See WINE COMPOSITION, WINE-MAKING, WINE TYPES and the other entries which immediately follow. The word 'wine' appears in only these titles. Otherwise, for wine press see PRESS, for wine and religion see RELIGION AND WINE, for wine trade see TRADE, etc. For details of specific wines, see under their names or their provenance.

Wine & Spirit Education Trust, the leading provider of wine EDUCATION, based in London, offering courses and qualifications for both wine trade and consumer at several different levels in about 30 countries and seven languages. A WSET Diploma is the usual prerequisite for studying to become a MASTER OF WINE.

wine composition differs quite considerably from GRAPE COMPOSITION, partly because parts of the grape are discarded during WINE-MAKING, and partly because the processes involved effect a complicated series of transformations. Alcoholic FERMENTATION, for example, transforms sugars into alcohol, while MALOLACTIC FERMENTATION reduces the level of malic acid in favour of lactic acid. The precise composition of a wine varies with WINE TYPE, HARVEST conditions and date, VINTAGE characteristics, and the age of the wine (see AGEING for details of how wine composition may change with age). Nevertheless, the table gives some guidance as to the likely range of concentrations of the essential constituents of the approximately 1,000 so far identified.

Navarre, C., *L'Oenologie* (Paris, 1988).

wine grape, a term used to describe grapes used for wine-making, as opposed to TABLE GRAPES for eating and DRYING GRAPES for use by the dried fruit industry. For discussion about the plant which bears wine grapes, see VINE, and for more detail of the fruit itself, see GRAPE.

wine lake, term coined for Europe's wine SURPLUS. With the introduction of compulsory DISTILLATION in 1982, it was rapidly transformed into an ALCOHOL lake. Of a typical annual wine surplus of just under 40 m hl/1,000 m gal, only about 15 m hl is likely to find a use as distilled alcohol. For more details, see EUROPEAN UNION.

winemaker, one who makes WINE. In its broadest sense, the term includes those who engage in HOME WINE-MAKING as a hobby, although in a professional sense a winemaker is someone employed (sometimes by themselves) to produce wine. An increasing proportion of such people recognize that wine production includes every aspect of vineyard management, and there are wine producers all over the world whose production is so small that they personally conduct, or at least oversee, every stage from planting to marketing (usually

Wine Composition		
Component	**Proportions per l**	**Comments**
Dissolved gases		
CARBON DIOXIDE	0–50 cc	
SULPHUR DIOXIDE		
Total	80–200 g	More in some sweet wines
Free	10–50 mg	More in some unstable wines
Volatile substances		
WATER	700–900 g	
ETHANOL (alcohol)	8.5–15% by vol	More in fortified, less in low-alcohol wines
HIGHER ALCOHOLS	0.15–0.5 g	
ACETALDEHYDE	0.005–0.5 g	Higher amounts in sherry and similar wines
ESTERS	0.1–0.3 g	
ACETIC ACID	0.35–0.6 g	
Fixed substances		
RESIDUAL SUGAR	0.8–180 g	According to type of wine; more in sweet and botrytized wines
GLYCEROL	5–12 g	
PHENOLICS	0.2–0.5 g; 1.5–4.0 g	Lower range for white wines, higher range for reds
gums and PECTINS	1–3 g	Depends on fungal levels in grapes
Organic acids		
TARTARIC ACID	5–10 g	Depending on grape origin
MALIC ACID	0–4 g	According to climate and extent of malolactic fermentation
LACTIC ACID	0–1 g	
SUCCINIC ACID	1–3 g	
CITRIC ACID	0–1 g	Found in wines where additions have been made
Mineral salts		
Sulphates	0.1–0.4 g	Expressed as potassium salts
Chlorides	0.25–0.85 g	
Phosphates		
Mineral elements		
POTASSIUM	0.7–1.5 g	
CALCIUM	0.06–0.9 g	
COPPER	0.001–0.003 g	
IRON	0.002–0.02 g	

Based on Navarre, C., *L'Oenologie* (Paris, 1988)

with markedly different degrees of success in each area). A wine production unit of any size, however, will employ both a VITICULTURIST, or vineyard manager, and a winemaker whose active responsibilities begin with receiving grapes from the vineyard and continue with their SAMPLING, CRUSHING, PRESSING, FERMENTATION, ÉLEVAGE, BOTTLING, and storage—all those operations outlined in WINE-MAKING. Larger wine producers may even employ a team of winemakers, each with different responsibilities.

Curiously, there is no obvious synonym for the word winemaker in any of the major European languages, perhaps because historically wine was thought to make itself. The most common candidates have very different literal translations into English: *maître de chai* in Bordeaux; *Kellermeister* in Germany; *enologo* in Italy; *œnologue* in some French wineries. While most (though not all) modern winemakers have studied OENOLOGY, and will certainly consider themselves oenologists, the term OENOLOGIST is more usually applied to an outside CONSULTANT rather than to a full-time employee in Europe. The most temporary winemakers of all are the breed known colloquially as FLYING WINEMAKERS.

Like the chef, the winemaker enjoyed a brief period of near cult status during the early 1980s, when for a time certain men (and a few women) were treated as though capable of fashioning superior wine out of almost any quality of grapes, a FASHION that was most notable in the New World but by no means confined to it. VITICULTURISTS lobbied against this view, however, to become the wine gurus of the 1990s. Today there are ever closer links between those responsible for vineyard and cellar and in an increasing number of cases they are the same person.

Most successful winemakers understand that making fine wine depends not only on a respectful understanding of the complicated biochemistry involved but also, perhaps more importantly, on an appreciation of the greatest potential within each lot of grapes and then the skill and patience to reveal that potential in the finished wine.

Clarke, O., *New Classic Wines* (London, 1991).
Norman, R., *The Great Domaines of Burgundy* (2nd edn, London, 1996).

wine-making, the practical art of producing WINE. In its most general sense, it

Antoine Arena's vineyards in Patrimonio, northern Corsica, are, like an increasing proportion of the world's vines, home to **organic viticulture**. It is considerably easier to manage without fungicides in a climate as dry as Corsica's than in damper/more humid wine regions.

encompasses all operations in both vineyard and cellar but for the purposes of this article, wine-making excludes vine-growing, or VITICULTURE.

Wine-making, while a sophisticated practical art for several millennia, became an applied SCIENCE only towards the end of the 19th century after Louis PASTEUR's discovery of the existence and activities of BACTERIA and YEAST. Since then, knowledge of the detailed chemical and biochemical reactions involved in their metabolic processes has steadily increased, as has the sophistication of the containers and equipment used in the professional cellar.

Wine-making in brief is a series of simple operations, the first of which is CRUSHING or smashing the fruit to liberate the SUGAR in the juice for FERMENTATION, which is the second step and occurs naturally when YEAST cells come into contact with sugar solutions. The new wine must then be subjected to various treatments to ensure CLARIFICATION and STABILIZATION and various other cellar operations which are collectively called élevage before the final step, BOTTLING.

Details in this sequence of operations vary considerably with WINE TYPE and its origin. General (as opposed to local) differences of technique dictated by different sorts of wine are outlined in WHITE WINE-MAKING, RED WINE-MAKING, ROSÉ WINE-MAKING, SWEET WINE-MAKING, SPARKLING WINE-MAKING, and under the names of various FORTIFIED WINES. One of the most obvious is the stage at which the juice is separated from the skins by PRESSING (before fermentation for white wines, after fermentation for red wines).

Before fermentation, some AMELIORATION of the grape juice may be needed. Since more than half the sugar in grape juice is converted to end products other than ALCOHOL (mostly CARBON DIOXIDE), a sugar concentration of about 20 per cent by weight is needed in the crushed grapes (see MUST WEIGHT) to produce a sound wine of around 11 per cent (see ALCOHOLIC STRENGTH for the practical range of alcohol levels in wine). In many cooler wine regions, fermentable sugars may be added to the basic fruit juice to increase the eventual alcoholic strength (see CHAPTALIZATION). In warmer regions, on the other hand, ACIDIFICATION may be permitted at some point during wine-making. Some SULFUR DIOXIDE is almost invariably added at this stage as a disinfectant.

The application of yeast is another crucial step in wine-making. Yeasts are single-celled plants which utilize sugar in building new yeast cells. In the presence of unlimited oxygen, nearly all the sugar would be converted into cells, carbon dioxide, and water, but if the yeast's access to oxygen is restricted, as in a large container, after an initial multiplication phase, the yeast switches to a second metabolic process of which the end products are mainly ETHANOL, potable alcohol, and carbon dioxide. The alcohol produced dissolves additional substances such as plant ACIDS, TANNINS, colouring and flavouring materials from the grape pulp—and skins in the case of red wines. In a very real sense, wine is a by-product of the yeasts' metabolic activity operating under less than optimum conditions. Fortunately, yeasts make a number of other attractive flavour compounds during this second, less efficient metabolic process. Heat is another product generated by the yeasts' metabolism, and REFRIGERATION may well be needed in order to control TEMPERATURE below the level at which yeasts are fatally damaged.

The new wine is usually separated from its LEES once fermentation is complete (except in the case of some white wines deliberately matured with LEES CONTACT). The normal technique is to let all the debris settle on the bottom of the container for a few days before RACKING, drawing off the wine from the top. This wine, opaque with its load of suspended yeast cells and fine debris, is further clarified, usually by FILTRATION or CENTRIFUGATION. This clarification process is often encouraged by adding a FINING agent which attracts suspended particles towards it and then helps them fall to the bottom of the container.

A second, softening fermentation, MALOLACTIC FERMENTATION, may take place in wines high in MALIC ACID, naturally or encouraged, during or after the primary alcoholic fermentation.

Other optional steps include MACERATION of skins and pulp or wine, which may take place before, during, and/or after fermentation, assisted in the case of red wines by REMONTAGE. Alternative methods of vinification include CARBONIC MACERATION and THERMOVINIFICATION.

It is important to minimize the new wine's exposure to OXYGEN, whatever its colour. In older wineries this was accomplished by keeping the wine in wooden containers and TOPPING UP at frequent intervals to replace losses by evaporation. Modern inert containers such as stainless steel tanks, once filled, lose no wine by evaporation. They have the additional advantage that, when there is insufficient wine to fill a tank completely, the empty HEAD SPACE can be filled with nitrogen or carbon dioxide, thus eliminating the problem of exposure of the wine to oxygen.

A common step immediately after red wine fermentation is to rack the wine off the skins into wooden BARRELS as this aids both clarification and the MATURATION process. For the highest-quality red wines, some time in new OAK barrels is common, the shape and size of barrel, duration of stay, and proportion of total production put into new oak varying according to wine type, vintage, and the producer's aspirations. New wine is capable of dissolving considerable flavour and tannins from a new barrel during the first year. Other red wines, or these wines after a year in new oak, may be aged in used oak or larger wooden casks, or red wines may proceed directly to inert storage tanks and omit a wood-ageing stage altogether. See ÉLEVAGE for more detail of the operations required during this post-fermentation stage.

Only a small proportion of white wines are aged in wood, STAINLESS STEEL being the preferred material for both fermentation and storage. An increasing proportion of top-quality white wines (especially those made from the Chardonnay grape), however, are fermented in small oak barrels (see BARREL FERMENTATION). They may then be allowed to rest on the lees from which certain flavour characteristics may be encouraged to develop by LEES STIRRING, or bâtonnage. Most white wine is clarified, stabilized, and bottled early to avoid exposure to oxygen and minimize any risk of OXIDATION.

The great majority of wines, whatever their colour, are bottled before the next vintage (so that storage capacity for only one year's production is needed). Wood-matured table wines will normally be bottled within two years of the vintage, however, while many fortified and some other wines treated to exceptionally long wood maturation (such as some Italian, Spanish, and Portuguese reds) may be matured in cask for much longer than this. (See ÉLEVAGE for a more detailed account of cellar work during this period.)

Before the wine can be bottled, it may be necessary to make a selection from different lots, and to assemble these ingredients into a final blend, although the BLENDING may well have been carried out at a much earlier point in the wine's evolution. (See also ASSEMBLAGE.)

The final step in the wine-making process before bottling is to subject the wine to ANALYSIS in order to check that it is stable and meets legal requirements.

Ideally wines should be given several months' BOTTLE AGEING before dispatch to ensure stability and to allow the wine to recover from the shock of bottling and, more specifically, possible BOTTLE SICKNESS.   A.D.W.

Amerine, M., and Singleton, V., Wine: An Introduction (2nd edn, Berkeley, Calif., 1965).

Halliday, J., and Johnson, H., The Art and Science of Wine (London, 1992).

Rankine, B., Making Good Wine: A Manual of Wine-making Practice for Australia and New Zealand (Melbourne, 1989).

Wine of Origin. Area of origin designation scheme in SOUTH AFRICA.

wine press. See PRESS for details of the equipment used during PRESSING. For the interface between wine and the press, see WINE WRITERS.

winery, modern, essentially NEW WORLD term for the premises on which wine is made;

its first recorded use was in the United States in 1882. It may mean either the entire enterprise, or it may mean specifically the building or buildings used for wine-making. The nearest French equivalent is CAVE. WINERY DESIGN is a specialist art currently being most obviously perfected in northern CALIFORNIA, where, neatly, the FASHION is for caves: wine-making facilities burrowed into hillsides, the cost of maintaining suitable temperatures and humidity in such subterranean tunnels being minimal.

winery design is a specialist branch of building design. Although WINE-MAKING can take place almost anywhere, modern wineries are much more than mere processing facilities. Nowadays wineries should be efficient in energy and resource consumption, suit the individual styles of wine and wine-making and, of equal importance, support the BRAND image, often through architectural appearance, public display of wine-making processes, specialized hospitality and cellar door facilities, and other amenities designed to engage the TOURIST and customer.

To ensure functionality and efficient workflow, a winery layout is based on a thorough understanding of the logistics of the specific wine-making practices and processes from grape receipt through production, bottling, storage, and shipping. Other issues include the need for offices, laboratory, and tasting bench, as well as equipment sizes and types, and finish materials. The impacts of site conditions, environmental concerns, health and safety matters, and maintenance are also considered. Finally architectural requirements in terms of style and functionality of the winery and associated facilities, including cellar door sales, amenities, access, and infrastructure are incorporated.

Building a winery to make an architectural statement is not new; the 19th century CHÂTEAUX of Bordeaux, like the imposing Ch MARGAUX or the whimsical Ch Cos d'Estournel in STE-ESTÈPHE, or Andrea Palladio's 16th-century Villa di Maser in the VENETO make that clear. There are also 21st-century icons created by the world's greatest architects. Ysios by Santiago Calatrava and Marques de Riscal by Frank Gehry are two examples, both in RIOJA, from the Old World; Clos Pegase of NAPA VALLEY by Michael Graves, Craggy Range in NEW ZEALAND by John Blair, and Graham Beck Coastal Cellar in SOUTH AFRICA by Johan Wessels are three from the New World.

Other wineries find beauty in their simplicity and clarity. Many top producers aim for quick, cool, and gentle processing, which means gravity flow instead of PUMPS wherever possible. If the site permits, as many as seven different levels can be achieved, where grapes are received at the highest level and shipping takes place from the lowest. If the winery can be part buried into a hillside, it aids natural

TEMPERATURE and HUMIDITY control in, for example, barrel cellars.

A well-planned winery development can account for resource conservation, management of waste and noise pollution, and ease of maintenance. If located in a vineyard, a winery offers the potential of a high level of sustainability: e.g. the reuse of WINERY WASTE and by-products, such as IRRIGATION using treated waste water, composting of solid waste and uptake of carbon dioxide by the vines. Carefully chosen materials, such as stainless steel, quarry-tile, and epoxy coatings, are attractive but hygienic and easy to clean. Today innovation permeates all stages of winery design and operation.

P.K.C.S.

Dethler J. (ed.), *Châteaux Bordeaux* (London, 1989).
Richards, P., *Wineries with Style* (London, 2004).

winery waste comprises the liquid and solid waste that results from the process of turning fruit into wine. Globally the wine industry has been working to establish sustainable systems to deal with both these waste streams so as to maintain the beautiful rural environments in which wine is often made.

Water is a by-product of the HYGIENE or sanitation required to make wine, for example washing tanks, fermenters, and barrels. Roughly 1.5 volumes (litres/gallons) of water is used in the production of 1 volume of wine, though the exact amount depends on wine-making processes, winery equipment, and winery practices. Over a year, about 70 per cent of the total volume of waste water generated is during the VINTAGE period, so sustainable waste-water systems need to be designed to handle these loads at this time.

Liquid winery waste tends to have a high oxygen requirement or BOD (organic acids, sugars, alcohol, etc.), low levels of nitrogen and phosphorus relative to carbon, and high solids content; it is generally acidic (low PH) due to organic acids, moderately saline (from sodium-based cleaning chemicals); and there may be imbalances in sodium, calcium, and magnesium.

This kind of waste water stored for a period of time releases malodours, turns black, and degrades any land/vegetation that it continually comes into contact with. There are winery waste-water treatment systems all over the world that are now able to turn this liquid waste stream into a reusable resource via solids removal, pH adjustment, aeration, and final polishing. Treated water can be better quality than local water supplies and is often then reused to irrigate golf courses, vineyards, winery gardens, or used back in the winery.

What are collectively known as cleaner production procedures can help minimize water use in the wine-making process and thereby reduce treatment costs and reliance on potable water. These procedures include waste stream segregation, for example keeping stormwater out of the waste system, diverting

heavily polluted waste water (from a still house or ION EXCHANGE) away from less polluted; improved operating practices, for example screening solids from the waste system, sweeping floors rather than hosing them down with water; personnel practices, including management initiatives, employee training and incentives; procedural measures, including documentation, material handling and storage, material tracking, and scheduling and inventory control.

Winery solid wastes include stalks, MARC, LEES (tartrates, grape solids, and dead yeast cells), spent DIATOMACEOUS EARTH used in FILTRATION, and sludge, which is a by-product of waste-water treatment.

Stalks and marc are produced only during the vintage period. Approximately 1 unit of marc is generated for every 10 units of grapes processed. Marc can be distilled to recover alcohol, colour extract, and tannin extract. Lees can also be collected and sent to the still for alcohol recovery. Stalks can be used to improve the organic levels of soils if they are thinly spread and worked into the soil. Many garden COMPOSTS use grape stalks as an ingredient.

Spent diatomaceous earth can be processed by third parties to produce TARTARIC ACID, which may be used as a wine additive in various parts of the world. Spent earth also has agronomic benefits and can be worked into most soils types to improve the soil structure.

Landscape suppliers also like to re-use winery sludge once it has dried out as an ingredient in compost.

When the correct resources, management initiatives, and support are allocated to ensuring winery waste is treated in a environmentally sustainable manner, wineries will continue to exist in harmony with their surroundings. S.J.G.

Wine Society, seminal British member-owned wine club-cum-wine merchant. The International Exhibition Co-operative Wine Society (IECWS), generally known as the Wine Society, was founded in 1874 by an architect, an eye surgeon, and a prominent Customs and Excise official following a food and wine exhibition in London's Albert Hall that year. The objects and rules included a membership holding of one share only, no dividends to be paid on these until extinction on the member's death, and the introduction of unfamiliar wines as well as those in general use—all to be bought 'for ready money only' at the lowest possible price. The Society remained small for many years, and attained its 5,000[th] member only in 1922, but grew substantially between the two World Wars. The number of shares now exceeds 250,000.

Prospective members are sponsored by existing members and elected by the Committee. A dividend of 5 per cent is credited annually to each member shareholder, but is paid out only on the member's death, although, with the agreement of the Committee, many shares are inherited. Edmund PENNING-ROWSELL was the Society's longest-serving chairman, from 1964 until 1987.

The Society's cellars were under the London Palladium theatre and London Bridge railway station (where the London AUCTIONEERS subsequently stored their wine) until the Society moved out of London to purpose-built and regularly extended premises in Stevenage in 1965. In the mid 2000s, the Wine Society was one of the two biggest independent retail wine merchants in Britain (the other being its mail order direct rival Laithwaites) with a turnover exceeding £54 million. The policy of cash-with-order is retained. The Society is distinguished by its far-sighted, even-handed management, the efficiency of its bureaucracy, and the quality of wine STORAGE offered to members.

Australia has a similar, but independent, operation.

wine tasters. The animate sort are humans, often of widely varying abilities, experiences, preferences, and prejudices, engaged in the pursuit of wine TASTING. The inanimate sort are shallow, usually silver, saucers for tasting young wines, known in French, and often in English, as TASTEVINS.

wine types may be classified in several ways, the most usual being by alcohol level. Those whose ALCOHOLIC STRENGTH is entirely due to FERMENTATION, and usually in the range of 9 to 15 per cent, are what we tend to call simply 'wine' or sometimes 'table wine' (although TABLE WINE has a specific meaning within the EUROPEAN UNION). Such wines may be further classified by COLOUR into RED WINES, WHITE WINES, and ROSÉ WINES. Or they may be classified according to their concentration of dissolved carbon dioxide as SPARKLING WINES, still wines, and a host of terms in between such as PERLANT and FRIZZANTE. Wines may also be classified according to SWEETNESS.

Wines with higher concentrations of alcohol, between 15 and just over 20 per cent, are called FORTIFIED WINES in this book since (with the exception of some DRIED GRAPE WINES) they owe some of their alcoholic strength to the process of FORTIFICATION, or the addition of spirit. PORT and SHERRY are the best known of these wines, officially called *vins de liqueur* in EU terminology. This higher-strength category also includes sweet alcoholic drinks made by adding grape spirit to fermenting grape juice at various points, for details of which see VIN DOUX NATUREL and VIN DE LIQUEUR as well as MISTELLE.

Wines which have been deliberately manipulated so that their alcohol levels are particularly low, say below 5.5 per cent, are sometimes called LOW-ALCOHOL wines. (Some regular wines, such as MOSCATO D'ASTI and lighter SAAR wines, may have a natural alcoholic strength of between 5 and 9 per cent.)

Wine types may also be loosely, and somewhat subjectively, classified according to when they are drunk into APERITIF wines (sometimes called 'appetizer wines'), 'food wines' or 'dinner wines', and SWEET WINES. See also VINO DA MEDITAZIONE.

Although geographical classifications are of wines not wine types, once-popular GENERIC wines represent an attempt at a geographical classification of wine types.

wine writers, imprecise term to include all those who communicate through the various media on the subject of wine. Some of them style themselves wine critics (notably the consumerist Robert PARKER) while such literary stylists as Hugh JOHNSON and Gerald Asher are undoubtedly wine writers. One sort of commentator hardly ever writes at all but occupies regular slots on radio or television, often reaching a much wider audience than any author could hope to. And myriad wine WEBSITES have provided some wine writers with an international reputation far quicker than is usually possible with the printed word.

Such has been the increase in wine writing opportunities that by the early 1980s, for probably the first time ever, it was possible, with luck and hard work, to make a living as a wine writer with no other source of income. But it would be unreasonable to expect an activity as pleasurable as wine writing to be lavishly rewarded financially and many wine writers also rely on income from dangerously closely related activities such as trading in wine or undertaking specific commissions for wine companies. Britain had a long tradition of wine merchants who write, who sometimes became wine writers who used to trade. Kermit Lynch is an American example of this phenomenon, Michael Fridjhon a South African one while John Platter and James Halliday are wine producers turned wine writers in South Africa and Australia respectively.

Wine writers in continental Europe such as France's Michel Bettane and Thierry Desseauve, Spain's Jose Peñín, and Italy's phalanx of specialists, tend to concentrate on the wines of their own countries.

Britain may have the greatest concentration of full-time wine writers in the world, perhaps partly because it is a centre of wine book publishing—and possibly because the British wine market is so diverse that British consumers need more advice than most. It certainly has the highest proportion of women among the country's wine writers, whereas in the United States and most European countries, wine writing is still dominated by men although this is slowly changing.

But changes in wine writing have wrought changes in wine writers. Given the preponderance of buyer's guides, TASTING NOTES and SCORING in place of writing, it would be quite possible nowadays to be a highly successful wine writer without ever visiting a vineyard

or cellar. A sound palate and a good database (see INFORMATION TECHNOLOGY) would in theory be quite sufficient, if a poor substitute for the excitement of exploring the world of wine.

See also WINE WRITING.

wine writing, a parasitical activity undertaken by WINE WRITERS enabled by vine-growing and wine-making but more usually associated with wine TASTING, and even wine drinking, than with either of the former. For an analysis of wine books through the ages, see LITERATURE OF WINE and for a discussion of words used to describe wine, see LANGUAGE OF WINE.

Wine writing can now be found not just between hard covers in specialist books but on WEBSITES, in specialist magazines and newsletters, in academic journals, and in general interest magazines and newspapers of even the most populist sort. It is now quite usual for an upmarket and not unusual for a mass-market newspaper to have a regular wine column.

Newsletters are a mainly American phenomenon with Robert PARKER's *Wine Advocate* being the most influential but given some serious competition by the likes of Stephen Tanzer's *International Wine Cellar* (strong on wine-making detail) and Orley Ashenfelder's *Liquid Assets* (of particular interest to INVESTORS). Both of the first two are also published in French.

Virtually all countries of any interest to wine exporters have at least one specialist wine consumer magazine (and major wine-producing and wine-trading countries tend to have specialist trade publications too). The world's best-selling wine magazine is the glossy, New York-based *Wine Spectator*. Its distant American consumer rival is the *Wine Enthusiast* but there are several lively wine trade publications including *Wine Business*. Britain fields the quite widely exported *Decanter* and *Wine & Spirit* (formerly *Wine International*), joined in 2003 by *The World of Fine Wine*. Europe's three major wine-producing countries can offer much less consumer wine coverage than might be imagined: France, for example, has exactly the same number of specialist wine magazines as Singapore. Most of the thousands of food-related titles around the world also have some wine coverage.

In the world of books, food outweighs wine very substantially; indeed many bookstores locate such wine titles as they do stock in an obscure corner of their cookery section. New wine titles continue to appear, perhaps sometimes the result of publishers' famous fondness for the fruits of the vine, but only a handful of authors can generate the sort of sales the increasingly agglomerated book trade now seeks worldwide.

Buyer's guides, typically annual, proliferate; more and more of the words written about wine resemble shopping lists rather than literature. Today's reader seems to want easily understood advice, and often SCORES, more than anything else. Wine writing really has almost become wine tasting.

Winkler, Albert Julius (1894–1989), scientist at the University of California at DAVIS whose name (and that of Maynard AMERINE) is commonly associated with a particular method of CLIMATE CLASSIFICATION involving heat summation whereby California was divided into five viticultural regions, Regions I (the coolest) to V (the warmest). He edited *General Viticulture*, published in 1962 and revised in 1974, which was for long considered the most comprehensive book on viticulture in the English language.

winter freeze, a climatic stress which can be lethal to parts or all of the vine. In areas of high latitude and high altitude the risk of very cold winter weather is substantial, particularly in CONTINENTAL climates away from the moderating effects of oceans (although even in MARITIME climates winter freeze can kill thousands of vines in exceptionally cold winters such as that of 1956 in St-Émilion and Pomerol). Such continental climates typically show colder temperatures, but also greater TEMPERATURE VARIABILITY.

Cold-hardy varieties, such as the American vine CONCORD, can be grown in the midwestern United States in sites with annual minimum temperatures of −29 °C/−20 °F occurring once in three years. European VINIFERA varieties sensitive to cold require relatively warmer sites, however, where annual minimum temperatures of −20 °C/−4 °F) are recorded no more than once in a decade. CROWN GALL disease commonly develops on vines injured by winter freeze.

An essential first step towards avoiding winter freeze injury is wise VINEYARD SITE SELECTION. Sites which export cold air, such as those offering AIR DRAINAGE on free-standing hills, can avoid winter injury by being up to 5 °C/9 °F warmer than sites which import cold air, such as those on valley floors. Vineyard sites within a few kilometres of large bodies of water (such as the Médoc, which suffered far less from the great winter freeze of 1956 than the inland vineyards of St-Émilion and Pomerol, for example) are also preferred because of the moderating effects on temperature (and see LAKE EFFECT in North America).

Selecting varieties with noted winter hardiness is also important. Varieties such as Chardonnay and Riesling are more winter hardy than Pinot Noir, Chasselas, and Cabernet Sauvignon. In turn, *Vitis vinifera* is less hardy than some interspecific HYBRIDS such as SEYVAL, which in turn are less winter hardy than such American varieties as DELAWARE and CONCORD. Choice of ROOTSTOCKS which avoid stress is also critical for vine survival.

The vine's reserves of CARBOHYDRATES act like a biological antifreeze. The aim of vine management to avoid winter stress is to achieve maximum carbohydrate reserves at the end of the growing season. This entails choice of suitable TRAINING SYSTEM, appropriately severe PRUNING level, and THINNING so as to restrict YIELD, which, when excessive, can act to reduce levels of vine carbohydrates.

An alternative strategy to avoid winter kill is to bury the vines in autumn (see WINTER PROTECTION below).   R.E.S.

> Howell, S. A., 'Cultural manipulation of vine cold hardiness', in R. E. Smart *et al.* (eds.), *Proceedings of the Second International Symposium for Cool Climate Viticulture and Oenology: 11–15 January 1988, Auckland, New Zealand* (Auckland, 1988).

winter protection, cumbersome viticultural technique aimed at protecting vines in cold, CONTINENTAL climates against the effects of WINTER FREEZE. Vines are buried in autumn to benefit from the fact that winter temperatures below the soil surface are never more than a few °C below freezing point, whereas the air temperature can be more than 20 °C/36 °F colder. Burying vines is, however, labour-intensive and expensive. This was traditionally practised in central Europe and North America, but is uncommon now because of the cost. Only in the vineyards of RUSSIA, parts of the UKRAINE, some of the central Asian republics, and CHINA is it still considered an acceptable price to pay for viticulture, although some severe winters in upper NEW YORK state in the early 21st century have engendered some reconsideration. The procedure has been modified so that just those few canes to be used for fruiting the following year are buried. Vines are also trained so that they have several trunks, so that those killed in winter can easily be replaced. See fan-shaped TRAINING SYSTEMS.
>   R.E.S. & J.R.

Winzer, which is the German equivalent of the French vigneron, is a common prefix in Germany for a CO-OPERATIVE wine cellar, as in **Winzergenossenschaft, Winzerverein,** and **Winzervereinigung.**

wire, used to form vine TRELLIS SYSTEMS, along with POSTS. Wine consumers might never credit something as mundane as wire in vineyards with their enjoyment, yet it is difficult to conceive of how wine could be so widely produced without it. The widespread use of wire has revolutionized trellising of vines, since it is now possible to train vines to forms which maximize their production and MECHANIZATION. High-tensile wire can support very heavy loads without breaking. Normally, thicker wire is used to support the weight of grapes in a trellis, and thinner wires to support foliage. See TRELLIS SYSTEMS and TRAINING SYSTEMS.   R.E.S.

WO. See WINE OF ORIGIN.

wood has been the most popular material for wine CONTAINERS both for transport and storage for centuries and even today trees are almost as important to some wines as vines. Merchants in Ancient ARMENIA shipped wine down the Tigris in palm-wood casks seven centuries BC, according to HERODOTUS. Wooden BARRELS eventually succeeded AMPHORAE as containers for both shipping and storage in the 3rd century AD.

It was not until the mid 20th century, however, that wood was irrevocably replaced by the bottle and tanker for TRANSPORT and widely replaced by inert materials such as cement and STAINLESS STEEL for STORAGE and FERMENTATION.

For fine wines, wood is still valued as the prime material for maturing (see BARREL MATURATION and CASK AGEING) and for fermenting certain types of white wine and for some handmade red wines (see BARREL FERMENTATION) as well as for some larger fermentation vats.

The chemistry of wine's maturation in wood is still not fully understood but experience shows that wood (unlike amphorae and sealed tanks made of inert materials) inevitably exposes the wine to a certain amount of OXYGEN, and actively aids CLARIFICATION and STABILIZATION of the wine matured in it—quite apart from the wide range of flavours and characteristics which may be added and transformed as a result of exposure to that particular wood, either directly as OAK FLAVOUR or indirectly as WOOD INFLUENCE.

See also WOOD TYPES.

Wood also plays a part in viticulture, not just because the vine's own wood is important (see CANE and TRUNK), but also because wood is a common material for POSTS and STAKES in the vineyard.

For more detail of wood structure, see CAMBIUM and XYLEM.

> Guimberteau, G. (ed.), *Le Bois et la qualité des vins et eaux-de-vie* (Martillac, 1992).

wood alcohol. Alternative name for harmful METHANOL.

wood influence. If a wine is fermented or matured in a wooden container, many different aspects of that container may shape its character and flavour, quite apart from those compounds that may be directly extracted from the oak wood and absorbed into the wine as wood flavour (see OAK FLAVOUR). The most obvious advantage of holding a wine in wood (see BARREL MATURATION and CASK AGEING) rather than an inert material is that wood encourages natural CLARIFICATION and STABILIZATION. The precise influence of a wooden container on any wine held in it is a function of the way that wine was made as well as of the following aspects.

World Distribution Of Vineyards*

(*including those producing table and drying grapes)

See Appendix 2 for details of vineyard area and wine production

EUROPE

Isotherm
10 °C

NORTH
AMERICA

Atlantic Ocean

20 °C

Atlantic Ocean

Equator

AFRICA

SOUTH
AMERICA

20 °C

10 °C

Wine-growing regions

Wood type

Barrels and tanks have been made from a variety of different woods although OAK is generally preferred. The exact choice of wood, or even oak, type can have a powerful effect on flavour and structure. See WOOD TYPES for more.

Manufacturing techniques

Several aspects of BARREL MAKING can have a marked impact on wine flavour. One particularly controversial issue is whether barrels made from hand-split staves are perceptibly superior to their counterparts made from sawn oakstaves; carefully controlled research in this area is rare.

The method of drying the wood can also affect wine character. Wines, particularly wines naturally low in tannins themselves, can taste aggressively tannic after being matured in barrels made from kiln-dried, as opposed to air-dried, wood. It has been assumed that air drying extracts some hydrolysable wood TANNINS (known as ellagitannins) in a process illustrated by the black deposit left on the ground but Australian research by Sefton (see below) suggests that seasoning may be a much more complex process than was previously thought, with seasoning affecting not the actual level of tannins, but their sensory effect.

In an Australian study, lots of the same wood were dried in Australia and in France. The Australian lot, dried under hot and dry conditions, was analysed and compared with the lot aged in France under cool and moist conditions. As the rate of chemical reactions increases dramatically with temperature rise, differences were to be expected. The concentration of certain lactones (see OAK FLAVOUR) was much higher in wood dried in Australia.

The degree to which the staves are heated while being bent, or barrel TOAST, has an obvious and profound effect on flavour. The more slowly this is done the better it is for both flavour and structure of a wine matured in that barrel. A deep medium toast produces the most desirable character for most woods, but there is variation in effect depending on geographic origin of the wood and wine style. Toasting also reduces the concentration of ellagitannins, which may contribute to MOUTHFUL and colour stability.

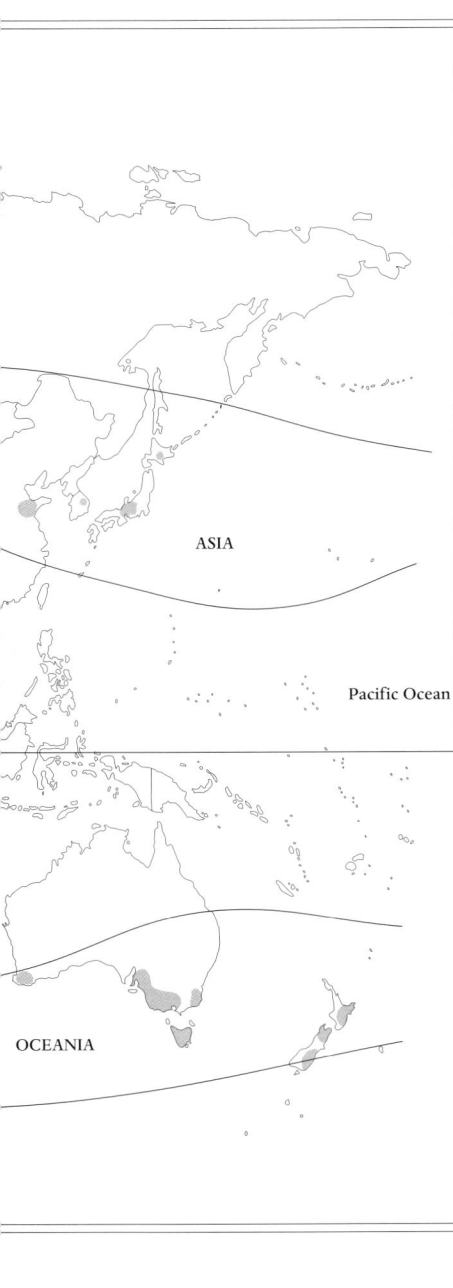

FERMENTATION, as do some Burgundy and Rhône producers. Many of Italy's and some of Germany's and Alsace's most revered wines are the product of CASK AGEING in large, old wooden casks. Proponents of such wooden vats note that some of the greatest wines in the world are made in them and suggest that ageing in large wooden tanks provides a gentle oxygenation of the wine and, hence, a desirable form of pre-bottling maturation. There are some signs of a renaissance in the use of large wooden fermentation vats, though the cost may be prohibitive to many producers.

Age of container

Barrels may be valued simply because they are containers made from a material that clarifies and stabilizes the wine naturally, offers the wine some mild but useful oxygenation, or also because they can actually add OAK FLAVOUR to the wine. The newer the barrel, the more wood flavour it is capable of imparting and in most wine regions new barrels command a premium, with one-year-old barrels selling for approximately 70 per cent, two-year-old barrels selling for less than 50 per cent, and five-year-old barrels selling for just 10 per cent of the cost of a new barrel.

New barrels may be the most expensive but they are not necessarily valued most highly by all winemakers. Their strongly oaky flavour can overwhelm subtle wines and some winemakers, especially in Burgundy, deliberately minimize this effect by using only a small proportion of new barrels or by 'breaking in' new barrels on lesser wines. Within a given type and style of wine, the richest wines will absorb the most oak with positive effects.

New barrels are used systematically for good vintages of classed growth red bordeaux and therefore for a high proportion of better quality wines, especially fine reds and Chardonnays, made by ambitious and well-funded winemakers in newer wine regions. They are used with more moderation elsewhere.

Older barrels are important for wines where the winemaker seeks slow oxygenation of the wine but no perceptible oak flavour, such as in making PORT, SHERRY, and, in many cases, RIOJA.

Some producers, most famously such as Dominique Laurent, new wave NÉGOCIANT in Nuits-St-Georges, boast of using '200 per cent new oak', meaning that wines are first put into one new barrel and then into another. Very few wines can withstand such an onslaught.

Time

Time remains the winemaker's greatest tool. A wine's character is also influenced by how long it remains in wood, which, in the case of new oak, can vary from about two months for relatively light white wines to two years or even three in the case of a top-quality SAUTERNES. More traditionally minded producers in Spain, Italy, and Portugal may keep wines in

old wooden cooperage for even longer. Some BRUNELLO DI MONTALCINO is given four years' CASK AGEING and VEGA SICILIA, for example, has sometimes been matured for ten years in barrel.

Vintage

The character of individual VINTAGE YEARS also affects how they react to wood and therefore the influence of any wood on a wine's flavour. Wines, especially red wines, vary so much from vintage to vintage that it is impossible to specify the perfect barrel for a given wine. For this reason, many winemakers order a range of different WOOD TYPES and with variation of TOAST in anticipation of each harvest. With white wines, which contain far fewer FLAVOUR COMPOUNDS than reds, the choices can be more specific.

Wine-making techniques

Up to this point our concerns have been with direct flavour effects from the wood, but equally important are the indirect or secondary flavour effects that are more the result of the wooden tank's or barrel's environment. For more details, see CASK AGEING and BARREL MATURATION respectively. White wines fermented in barrel may be changed enormously in character. For more details, see BARREL FERMENTATION.

Storage conditions

Exact temperature and humidity, even draughts, can affect the character of a wine held in a wooden container. For more details see BARREL MAINTENANCE. L.B. & M.K.

Naudin, R., *L'Élevage des vins de Bourgogne en fûts neufs* (Beaune, 1989).

Sefton, M. A., 'How does oak barrel maturation contribute to wine flavor?', *Australian and New Zealand Wine Industry Journal* (Feb 1991).

—— *et al.*, 'Influence of seasoning on the sensory characteristics and composition of oak extracts', in *International Oak Symposium* (San Francisco, 1993).

Singleton, V. L., 'Some aspects of the wooden container as a factor in wine maturation', in American Chemical Society, *Chemistry of Winemaking* (Washington, DC, 1974).

Spillman, P. J., Sefton, M. A., Gawel, R., 'The effect of oak wood source and location of seasoning on the chemical composition of oak matured wines', *Australian Journal of Grape and Wine Research*, 10 (2004), 216–26.

wood types. Over the years, many different kinds of wood have been used to make small BARRELS and larger VATS and casks. Acacia, cypress, chestnut, ash, redwood, pine, eucalyptus, and poplar are just a few of the woods that have been used.

Chestnut has long been popular for large oval casks in the Rhône, Beaujolais, and in parts of Italy and Portugal, but as this wood offers strong TANNINS and is also relatively porous, chestnut barrels and tanks are often

Size of container

The larger the container, the lower the ratio of surface area to volume will be. Barrels holding less than 190 l/50 gal can overwhelm wine with OAK FLAVOURS. Containers holding more than 570 l/150 gal will provide little wood oak flavour, particularly after their first use. (See BARREL TYPES for detail of barrel sizes most commonly used.)

The use of large wooden VATS or tanks for wine has largely fallen out of favour since the advent of STAINLESS STEEL and other inert materials, because the latter are much easier to clean than wood and because TEMPERATURE is harder to control in large-volume wooden containers. A few top Bordeaux properties (Chx MARGAUX and MOUTON-ROTHSCHILD, for example) still use large oak vats for red wine coated with paraffin or silicone to neutralize the wood. Wines made in unlined new chestnut barrels can be so tannic as to be undrinkable.

In other countries, pine and eucalyptus have been used for casks, but these woods produce wines with flavours that strike many consumers as odd unless the wood is very well seasoned (see BARREL MAKING) or coated on the inside. Acacia is used successfully, notably in Austria. In Chile, the local evergreen beech, or *rauli*, wood was once common. Redwood was used for large upright tanks in America for many years, although very few have been built since the early 1970s. Redwood is rarely made into barrels because the wood is difficult to bend and the flavours are aggressive. Since the advent of neutral STAINLESS STEEL and enamel-lined tanks, wooden COOPERAGE must offer something extra to the wine to be worth the premium.

By far the most popular wood type in use in wine-making today is OAK, which has none of the disadvantages outlined above and whose particular aspects of WOOD INFLUENCE and OAK FLAVOUR have come to be appreciated by both winemakers and wine drinkers. M.K.

Worcester, warm inland wine district within the Breede River Valley region in SOUTH AFRICA.

world production of wine is concentrated in two bands of generally TEMPERATE to MEDITERRANEAN CLIMATE in each hemisphere, as shown on the map on p. 774. (Parts of the Far East are being developed for viticulture, despite high rainfall in some of these areas, but most of these industries are too young to feature in the OIV statistics on which these figures are based.)

Total production of wine is affected by each year's weather (particularly by FROST or poor FRUIT SET within Europe, as in 1991 and 1994 for example), by the effects of VINE PULL SCHEMES, offset by those of new plantings. The underlying trend is downwards, largely because of determined efforts by the EUROPEAN UNION

to reduce its wine SURPLUS, mirrored by a similar initiative in Argentina, another major producing country. But the 1996 harvest total, for example, was boosted by favourable weather conditions in most of Europe, new plantings in Australia, and a dramatic increase in production in Spain (56 per cent more than in 1995).

See also PRODUCTION, CONSUMPTION, and SURPLUS of wine.

Wrattonbully, substantial wine region just north of Coonwarra in SOUTH AUSTRALIA with a strongly LIMESTONE-based soil. In 2003, a JOINT VENTURE between Brian Croser of Petaluma in the Adelaide Hills, Jean-Michel Cazes of Chateau Lynch Bages in Pauillac, and BOLLINGER purchased the oldest vineyard (1973) in the region and renamed it Tapanappa, giving the area a significant boost.

Württemberg, relatively large and growing wine region in southern GERMANY with 11,460 ha/28,300 acres of vineyard which loosely follow the river Neckar and its tributaries (see map under GERMANY). The main part of the region lies between Stuttgart (including several of the city's suburbs) and Heilbronn with the vineyards to the north mingling with those of BADEN. Steep and expensive-to-maintain terraced slopes look down on the Neckar. Besides being valued for the quality of their wine, these TERRACES add interest to the landscape and attract tourists. Where the gradient is greater than 30 per cent, IRRIGATION is allowed; by assisting PHOTOSYNTHESIS, this can increase the POTENTIAL ALCOHOL content of the grape must by over 1 per cent. The regional climate varies from south to north, but is at its most CONTINENTAL along the Kocher, Jagst, and Tauber, three tributaries at the north eastern edge of the region, where winters can be severe.

Less than one-fifth of the region's vineyards is planted in RIESLING, with that produced at Flein, a few kilometres south of Heilbronn, enjoying much local esteem. Other white wine varieties, notably KERNER, SILVANER, and MÜLLER-THURGAU, account for about 12 per

cent of the area under vine and, like Riesling, are on the wane in favour of red wine varieties, which have become increasingly important since the early 1990s. TROLLINGER is planted on 22 per cent of the region's vineyard, followed by the 17 per cent devoted to Müllerrebe (MEUNIER), known locally as Schwarzriesling. A further third is accounted for by other red wine varieties including LEMBERGER (Blaufränkisch) and Spätburgunder, although the latter is less important here than in neighbouring BADEN.

Judged by international standards, much of the red wine produced here is pale, light, and soft, but that is how the locals like it. Nevertheless, a small number of young turks, or rather young Schwabians, are deliberately making more robust reds, often with well over 13 per cent alcohol. Per capita wine consumption here, 35 l a year, is the highest in Germany, and considerable quantities of red wine are imported to satisfy local demand, which explains why so few of these wines are seen outside the region.

Of the 15,443 registered vine-growers, 82 per cent own less than 1 ha/2.47 acres, so CO-OPERATIVE cellars are necessary. They handle over 75 per cent of the grape harvest. The central cellar at Möglingen processes the entire crop of 36 local co-operatives, while an additional 32 local co-operatives produce and market their own wines. There is a small number of ancient and highly regarded state- and privately-owned estates, of which 13 are members of the prestigious VDP association. The best of their wines are serious and comparable in quality with those from good winemakers in Baden. I.J. & D.S.

Würzer is a Gewürztraminer × Müller-Thurgau CROSSING made at the German viticultural station of Alzey in 1932 and only planted in any significant quantity in the 1980s, peaking in 1995 at 121 ha/300 acres, mainly in Rheinhessen. It is overpoweringly heady, yields well, but a little goes a very long way indeed.

Xante, synonym for the grape variety CURRANT.

Xarel-lo, white grape variety planted on a total of 8,750 ha/21,600 acres of Spanish vineyard in 2004, producing powerful still and sparkling wines in its native CATALUÑA. It is particularly important in ALELLA, where it is known as Pansa Blanca. It is most commonly found in PENEDÈS, however, where, with Parellada and Macabeo, it makes up most CAVA blends. The vine is very vigorous and productive and buds early so is prone to spring frost damage. It needs careful pruning and the wine it produces can be very strongly flavoured. It is the smell of Xarel-lo that often distinguishes so many Cavas from other TRADITIONAL METHOD sparkling wines.

Xenophon, writer in Ancient GREECE in the late 5th century BC famous for his *Anabasis*. In the *Economics*, a dialogue between a farmer, Ischomachos, and the famous philosopher Socrates, the planting and care of vines is discussed: vines should be planted in well-dug earth, at an angle, and the earth should be trodden down around the vine.   H.H.A.

Xérès, French name for both JEREZ and SHERRY.

Xinomavro, black grape variety grown all over northern GREECE as far south as the foothills of mount Olympus, where Rapsani is produced. Its name means 'acid black' and the wines can indeed seem harsh in youth but they age well, as mature examples of Naoussa can demonstrate. One of the few Greek vine varieties which may not reach full ripeness in some years, it is blended with a small proportion of the local Negoska to produce Goumenissa and is also used as a base for sparkling wine on the exceptionally cool, high vineyards of Amyndeo. The wines tend to be relatively soft but to have good acid, attractive bite, and age well.

xylem, the principal water-conducting tissue in vascular plants. In woody stem tissues, the secondary xylem forms the wood. The CAMBIUM differentiates xylem tissue on its inside. A single ring of xylem is produced each year with the first-formed vessels (in spring) being larger than those of late wood. This is how the annual rings which help to assess the age of a plant are formed (see OAK). In the grapevine, the vessels are large and porous so that its wood is very water conductive, a feature of vines generally. In autumn, however, vessels may become blocked by structures which plug the tubes, called tyloses, formed by the 'ballooning' of adjacent cell material into the vessel through pits in the walls; some vessels remain functional for up to seven years, but most become blocked by tyloses in their second or third year. The secondary xylem of QUERCUS forms the wood from which oak barrels are made. (See also PHLOEM.)   B.G.C.

Xynisteri, the most common white grape variety grown on CYPRUS. It is preferred to the dark-skinned MAVRO for the rich fortified wine COMMANDARIA, the island's most distinctive wine.

Yarra Valley, historic Australian wine region that is cool in both senses just north east of Melbourne, VICTORIA; internationally recognized Chardonnay and Pinot Noir. Ever-changing vistas from hillsides of valley floor make it a must-visit region, for wine TOURISTS. Melbourne is but one hour away.

Ycoden-Daute-Isora, complicated name from the Guanche pre-Hispanic times, for the most ancient, but recently denominated, wine region in the Spanish CANARY ISLANDS. It is centred on the town of Icod de los Vinos, where wine has been made since the Spanish conquest in the 15th century. It now produces the best dry whites in the islands, from LISTÁN Blanco and, increasingly, from the much more distinctive Vijariego and Marmajuelo grapes. The region has 2,000 ha/4,800 acres under vines. In the 1990s, coastal vineyards were consistently uprooted and replaced by inland vineyards at much higher ALTITUDES on the verdant volcanic slopes.

V. de la S.

yeast, microscopic, single-celled fungi, having round to oval cells which reproduce by forming buds, are vital to the alcoholic FERMENTATION process, which, starved of oxygen, transforms grape juice to wine. SUGARS are used as an energy source by yeast, with ETHANOL and CARBON DIOXIDE as major by-products of the reactions.

The word yeast (which may be singular or plural unless it encompasses yeasts from more than one species) is an old one whose meaning has changed significantly with the flowering of microbiological science. It originally derived from an ancient word meaning 'to boil', 'to seethe', or 'to be troubled'. In 16th-century English, it referred to the froth on the top of a brewing tank and to the semi-solid material that could be collected both from that froth and from the bottom of the tank. From the mid 17th century, the meaning of the word yeast changed to that of a single-celled plant, a *thallophyte* and one of the lowest members of the vegetable kingdom along with algae, lichens, and fungi.

In common with other fungi, yeasts are differentiated from plant cells by absence of chloroplasts, which contain the plant cell's chlorophyll. The modern fermentative yeasts have evolved from an ancestral yeast by a process of genome duplication, rearrangements and deletions, estimated to have occurred over the past 100 million years.

Nomenclature

The nomenclature of various yeasts is far from straightforward and is in the process of being revised. Taxonomists—scientists who classify and name plants and animals—have traditionally had difficulty with the various micro-organisms because early microscopes revealed little detail, and because the appearance of an organism depended on the conditions of its growth, isolation, and preparation for observation. The result has been that names have changed over time as laboratory equipment improved and as new techniques were perfected. In particular, the development of methods to study the genetic information contained in chromosomal DNA has provided more reliable ways to characterize and classify yeasts. Indeed, a *Saccharomyces cerevisiae* yeast was the first higher organism to have its whole genome sequenced by 1996. Genome analysis has revealed that some yeasts which were thought to be closely related were in fact only distantly related, and vice versa. Furthermore, some characteristics of yeasts that were used to differentiate species, such as the pattern of sugars that can be fermented, were found to represent natural variation within that species, and consequently did not represent different species. For this reason, many yeast names in common usage several decades ago are no longer accepted.

Saccharomyces cerevisiae is the name now most frequently used for the yeast involved in making wine and beer and in leavening bread. *Saccharomyces*, the genus, means 'sugar fungus', and *cerevisiae* derives from the same root as 'cereals'. Older literature frequently called this yeast *Saccharomyces ellipsoideus* because the cells associated with fruit juices appeared more elliptical than circular. Within this yeast species are several hundred different strains or selections, each with real or fancied minor differences. Some strain differences relate to fermentation vigour, lack of off-flavour formation, and enhancement of wine varietal character, such as fruity notes in Sauvignon Blanc. Another species within the same genus, *Saccharomyces uvarum*, is often used in the distilling and brewing industries. This species and other closely related species, *Saccharomyces bayanus* and *Saccharomyces paradoxus*, and their hybrids made by breeding with *Saccharomyces cerevisiae*, are showing potential for increasing the diversity of wine aromas and flavours. Several of the wild yeast species (see below), *Candida stellata*, *Kluyveromyces thermotolerans*, and *Torulaspora delbrueckii*, are now being used experimentally in combination with *Saccharomyces cerevisiae* to introduce new and diverse flavour profiles in wine.

Cultured versus ambient yeast

Ecology studies have shown that intact grape berries harbour a number of other yeast genera in significant populations and frequently participate in the wine-making process. Spread around wineries and vineyards by insects, particularly FRUIT FLIES, and possibly air currents, these are collectively known as **wild yeast,** among which the most common genera are *Klöckera/Hanseniaspora*, *Metschnikowia*, and *Candida*, with *Pichia*, *Hansenula*, *Zygosaccharomyces*, and *Torulaspora* usually representing a low proportion. Contrary to popular belief,

Saccharomyces species are rarely isolated from grape berries unless they are damaged by, for example, disease, birds, insects, or hail. More sensitive to SULFUR DIOXIDE, and intolerant of an ALCOHOLIC STRENGTH much above 5 per cent, these wild yeasts are generally active during the early stages of 'spontaneous fermentations', those occurring when insufficient or no sulfur dioxide is added to the grape juice or must. Fortunately, there are usually enough *Saccharomyces cerevisiae* cells present on the surfaces of harvesting, transportation, and winery processing equipment which enter the grape juice or must, so that these latter yeast continue the fermentation above the unstable alcoholic strength of 5 per cent, depleting the supply of sugar and producing a stable wine. Again, contrary to popular belief, inoculation with *Saccharomyces* yeast does not suppress wild yeasts which are naturally present in juices and musts during the early stages of fermentation. Therefore, wine is commonly the result of a mixed microflora, although the impact of wild yeasts on the wine is usually restricted by the inoculated yeast. Many traditional Old World wineries which use wild yeast consistently, return POMACE and LEES to vineyard soils to encourage the establishment of wild yeast populations. These populations are believed to stabilize with a particular mixture of yeasts suitable for wine fermentation, so that **ambient yeast** may be a more appropriate term. Such mixtures of yeast genera and species, often called **'indigenous yeast'** or **'natural yeast'**, have in the past been much more commonly used than cultured yeast in the traditional wine regions of Europe. The concept of 'château' or resident/indigenous populations of ambient yeast which promote the particular character of an estate wine is controversial among wine scientists.

Increasing numbers of Old World producers, the majority of New World winemakers, and certainly all of those worried about minimizing risk, use **cultured yeast**, however, sometimes called **pure culture**, **selected natural yeast**, or **inoculated yeast**. The advantage of cultured yeasts, of which only one strain is usually added, is that it has been specially selected (from ambient yeasts) so that its behaviour is predictable and the fermentation will proceed smoothly and, of most importance, to completion without the risk of a STUCK FERMENTATION or formation of off-odours. Individual winemakers often favour certain strains of cultured yeast for practical WINE-MAKING reasons. Depending on the strain of yeast, the differences in the wines produced, particularly as the wine ages, may often be too small to be detected by the average consumer. Strains have been selected and exploited by oenologists and winemakers for characteristics such as fermentation vigour, high alcohol and sulfur dioxide tolerance, ability to referment wine to make sparkling wine, freedom from acetic and sulfidic off-flavours, film

or FLOR formation needed for SHERRY production, enhancement of wine varietal character, low foaming, yeasticidal properties, improved red wine colour, better tolerance to nutrient deficiencies, and lower potential to form sulfur dioxide.

The advantage of a well-adapted population of ambient or natural yeast is that there are many different strains and, because of their different abilities and aptitudes, they may be capable of producing a wine with a wider range of flavours and characteristics, a phenomenon that some winemakers believe is even more marked when, as is increasingly the case, LEES CONTACT is encouraged. Such a view had not been confirmed by science in the early 2000s, however, partly because of the difficulty of working with mixed culture fermentations and the difficulties of identifying the yeasts involved.

Cultured yeast characteristics

Yeast are cultured in large sterile tanks with vigorous aeration under conditions which encourage biomass but discourage alcohol formation. They are then filtered, washed, dried, and packed in sterile containers, often under vacuum, for transfer to the winery (or brewery or bakery). Over one hundred different strains are now produced worldwide as active dried wine yeast preparations. Active dried yeast is quickly and simply reactivated with warm water or diluted grape juice at 40 °C/104 °F for 15 minutes. Some wineries culture their favoured yeast in grape juice with or without vigorous aeration and add about 2–4 per cent by volume to the juice or must to initiate fermentation. Following use in wine-making, the yeast and grape debris are freed of as much wine as possible and usually discarded. A minor proportion may be processed to recover alcohol, TARTRATES, and occasionally grapeseed oil.

Among the many genera of yeasts, there are astounding variations in terms of the production and tolerance of alcohol, aroma and flavour, rate of fermentation, temperature tolerance, flocculation characteristics, sulfur dioxide tolerance, REDUCING potential, and micro-nutrient requirements. Although some wild yeasts cannot tolerate alcohol concentrations above 5 per cent, a tolerance of up to 15 or 16 per cent is the norm for yeasts used in the production of dry wine. Some yeast can tolerate concentrations of more than 20 per cent during the special conditions of Sake fermentation. Yeast with a high alcohol production and tolerance may be chosen for FORTIFIED WINES or dry red wine made from over-ripe grapes with very high sugar levels in some New World wine regions; yeast which flocculate particularly well, such as that called Épernay, may be used for SPARKLING WINE-MAKING; yeast which form a film of flor are used to make sherry; while a yeast with good tolerance of sulfur dioxide may be useful in

certain examples of SWEET WINE-MAKING. Some cultured yeast strains are known internationally while others may be used merely locally.   A.D.W. & P.H.

How yeast works

Yeast, like most living organisms, need a good supply of carbon and NITROGEN, a source of SULFUR, PHOSPHORUS, and OXYGEN, various MINERALS and trace elements, and several VITAMINS for growth and reproduction. The usual carbon sources are the six-carbon sugars, GLUCOSE and FRUCTOSE. Wine yeast can also use SUCROSE, which may be added to the juice of underripe grapes (CHAPTALIZATION) and is used in SPARKLING WINE-MAKING to induce the secondary fermentation. Amino acids and ammonium compounds most often supply the nitrogen, and most fruit juices, including grape juice, provide the other components necessary for growth. Nutrients, based on nitrogen or vitamins, may be specially added as growth factors to encourage yeast activity at the beginning of fermentation, especially in the case of underripe grapes, rot, or grapes from low fertility vineyards. Oxygen is an especially important nutrient, which is supplied in large quantity during production of the yeast starter culture. Trace amounts of oxygen may also be supplied during the early or middle stage of fermentation to improve yeast survival and fermentation activity later in fermentation (see STUCK FERMENTATION).

All cells require energy to exist, to grow, and to reproduce. Yeast can release a small amount of the energy stored in glucose and fructose of grape juice by a series of complex biochemical reactions known as GLYCOLYSIS. This nearly universal process among living organisms is so complex and involves so many steps that it has taken scientists years of research to understand it. Using internal ENZYMES, the yeast cell, through a series of reactions, splits the six-carbon sugar molecule into two molecules of three-carbon PYRUVATE. The final two steps, known collectively as fermentation, convert pyruvate to ETHYL ALCOHOL and carbon dioxide. In this fermentative decomposition of pyruvate, the first step is removal of the terminal carbon dioxide from the pyruvate, leaving the two-carbon fragment ACETALDEHYDE. Acetaldehyde is then converted to alcohol, and the carbon dioxide escapes from the fermentation vessel. A small amount of acetaldehyde is also converted to ACETIC ACID, which is required for biosynthesis of lipids, needed to make cell membranes; some acetic acid escapes from the cell and contributes to wine VOLATILE ACIDITY.

When all of the sugar is fermented to alcohol and carbon dioxide, and a small amount of oxygen is present, yeast can reconvert some of the ethyl alcohol back to acetaldehyde. Further oxidative decomposition occurs, by a complex series of reactions, to carbon dioxide and water. This process, which takes place in the mitochondria within the cell and which releases most of the energy originally stored in sugar, is known as RESPIRATION. The exposure of wine to oxygen is, however, rigorously prevented except in some circumstances, such as in the making of FLOR wines such as FINO sherry. Normally wine is protected from air during fermentation by the blanket of carbon dioxide produced.

During fermentation of grape juice, yeast produce small amounts of other compounds from sugar glycolysis, and the metabolism of amino acids and other nutrients. Some of these compounds are volatile and contribute fermentation-derived characteristics to a wine's AROMA. The most important compounds are esters, aldehydes and ketones, fatty acids, higher alcohols, and volatile sulfur compounds (HYDROGEN SULFIDE and MERCAPTANS). Recent research has shown that some of these volatile compounds play a much greater role in the distinctive aroma profile of certain grape varieties than previously believed. Furthermore, advances in the understanding of how yeast control the formation of these aroma compounds is leading to the development of new yeast strains which can alter the emphasis of various aroma notes in wine. GLYCEROL, ACETIC ACID, and succinic acid, which contribute to the taste of wine, are the most important non-volatile compounds produced by yeast.

Research by Swiegers et al. has also shown that yeast can modify some grape-derived compounds which contribute to wine aroma and flavour. Certain hydrolytic enzymes, glycosidases, are released by the cell which can hydrolyse various FLAVOUR PRECURSORS, notably sugar conjugates of MONOTERPENES, norisoprenoids, aliphatics, PHENOLS, and benzene derivatives. Monoterpenes are important to the aroma of wines made from floral grape varieties such as MUSCAT, RIESLING, and TRAMINER. See FLAVOUR COMPOUNDS.

Another class of grape-derived flavour precursors are the cysteine-linked compounds, which, when hydrolysed by enzymes present in some strains of yeast, generate volatile THIOLS with fruity aromas. These compounds, which contribute box tree, passionfruit, grapefruit, guava, and gooseberry aromas, are important in Sauvignon Blanc wines, and have also been identified in wines made from Colombard, Riesling, Sémillon, Merlot, and Cabernet Sauvignon.

Some yeasts also have the ability to degrade phenolic acids to volatile vinyl phenols (e.g. 4-vinylphenol and 4-vinylgaiacol), which contribute a phenolic off-flavour. In red wine, 4-vinylphenol can react with anthocyanins to form stable pigments. BRETTANOMYCES yeasts are able to convert these unstable vinylphenols to the stable ethylphenols (e.g. 4-ethylphenol and 4-ethylgaiacol), responsible for phenolic, medicinal, and barnyard aromas in wine. Yeast also produce carbonyl compounds,

which, under some circumstances, can enhance red wine colour. For example, acetaldehyde and pyruvic acid can react with anthocyanins to form more stable pigmented pyroanthocyanins that can contribute to the stable colour of aged red wines.

After the yeast have converted all of the sugar, they slowly die, flocculate, and fall to the bottom of the vessel, forming a sediment known as gross LEES. In bottle-fermented sparkling wines, the interaction between this sediment and the wine in the bottle is an important element in sparkling wine-making (see AUTOLYSIS). P.H.

Boulton, R. B., Singleton, V. L., Bisson, L. F., and Kunkee, R. E., *Principles and Practices of Winemaking* (Gaithersburg, 1998).

Jackson, R., *Wine Science: Principles, Practice, Perception* (San Diego, 2000).

Swiegers, J. H., Bartowsky, E. J., Henschke, P. A., and Pretorius, I. S., 'Yeast and bacterial modulation of wine aroma and flavour', *Australian Journal of Grape and Wine Research*, 11 (2005), 139–73.

Yecla, denominated wine zone in the LEVANTE, south east Spain, producing mainly rather coarse red wines. Sandwiched between JUMILLA, ALICANTE, and ALMANSA (see map under SPAIN), Yecla is dominated by La Purísima, the single largest CO-OPERATIVE in Spain. The red MONASTRELL represents 85 per cent of all grapes grown in the region. The private Bodegas Castaño is pioneering more ambitious wines by adding Cabernet Sauvignon, Tempranillo, and Merlot to Monastrell. R.J.M. & V. de la S.

yellow mosaic, vine disease. See FANLEAF DEGENERATION.

yellows. See GRAPEVINE YELLOWS.

Yellow Tail, Australian wine BRAND whose early 21st century growth in the US, from a standing start, set records in the history of branding and gave birth to the infamous 'critters' (small animals on labels) wine category. The Casella family had just 16 ha/40 acres of vines in RIVERINA and supplied BULK WINE until John Casella with an aggressive, export-orientated manager planned an assault on the embryonic US market for Australian wines in the late 1990s. A first attempt failed but new branding involving a yellow kangaroo image and the irritating but eye-catching logo [yellow tail] (*sic*), together with particularly fruity, not to say sweet, wines and a bold profit-sharing scheme with the US importer of DUBŒUF paid off. Annual US sales rose from 200,000 cases in the launch year of 2001 to 7.5 million in 2004.

yema bud, alternative name for CHIP BUDDING.

yield, an important statistic in wine production, which measures how much a vineyard produces. It has been a subject of intense

interest from at least the time of classical ROME.

Factors affecting yield

Vineyard yield depends on many factors, which will be briefly described here. For a more complete discussion, see the individual factors listed.

Yield may be measured as either a weight of grapes or a volume of wine (see below), and is usually considered per unit area of vineyard, since this is what matters in farming economics. Those who believe that increasing VINE DENSITY is associated with improved wine quality argue that yield per vine is a more important consideration. Disciples of CANOPY MANAGEMENT, on the other hand, argue that the amount of sunlit leaf area per unit of land is more important than yield per vine.

Yield per vine depends on the number of bunches per vine, and the average bunch weight. The number of bunches per vine depends on the winter PRUNING policy, the BUDBREAK, and the number of bunches per shoot, or FRUITFULNESS. Bunch weight depends on the number of FLOWERS per bunch, and the success of FRUIT SET in forming berries, then on the weight of individual berries.

Yield per vine depends on VINE AGE (very old vines often produce very little), the way the vines have been managed, and on the WEATHER over at least the last two years, together with other factors such as VINE PESTS and VINE DISEASES.

After pruning, the weather is one of the most important factors affecting vineyard yield. Cold winters, for example, promote a high degree of budbreak, but FROSTS in spring can kill young shoots and bunches. Warm, sunny weather promotes FLOWERING and POLLINATION, but cold, wet, and windy weather can cause poor FRUIT SET. Some varieties are more prone than others to poor set. Drought conditions can also reduce fruit set, but the more common DROUGHT effect is to reduce berry size, often to less than half that of vines well supplied with water. Rain will generally increase yield as it causes berries to swell, but too much rain near harvest causes BOTRYTIS BUNCH ROT and potentially a considerable, possibly total, loss in yield.

Strangely enough, the weather the preceding season can also have an effect on yield. It has been shown that warm, sunny weather during flowering encourages bunch INITIATION in the buds that are forming for next growing season. So this weather pattern can prepare the vine for a high potential yield the following year.

How yield is measured

Conventional units of yield are the weight of fresh grapes per unit land area, such as tonnes/ha, or tons/acre. (One ton/acre is about 2.5 tonnes/ha.) This is the standard measurement in most NEW WORLD wine regions.

Although many Italians and Swiss measure yield in weight of grapes, in most European countries production is measured in volumes of wine per unit area, normally expressed as hectolitres per hectare, or hl/ha. In many cases, this measurement is an extremely important one, often limited to a maximum (depending on the VINTAGE) specified by local regulation (see APPELLATION CONTRÔLÉE, DOC, etc. and the note below).

The two measurements interrelate, although the volume of wine produced by a given weight of grapes can vary considerably according to vine variety, individual vintage conditions, winery equipment, wine-making policy, and, most importantly, wine type. To make 100 l (1 hl) of red wine, which is fermented in the presence of grape skins that can be pressed rather harder than white grape skins, about 130 kg (0.13 tonnes) of grapes are needed. To make 100 l of white wine, about 150 kg are needed (more like 160 kg for top-quality SPARKLING WINE-MAKING). Assuming an average of 140 kg of grapes per 100 l of wine, one tonne/ha is about 7 hl/ha, while one ton/acre is about 17.5 hl/ha (typically slightly less for whites and slightly more for reds).

Surprisingly, despite its importance in measuring yield, there is no uniform approach in determining the area of a vineyard. Excluding the essential and normally cultivated areas along the ends (called headlands) and at the sides, which are indubitably part of the productive unit, effectively reduces the size of many vineyards by 10 per cent or so, and the figure may be higher for small vineyards.

Wherever grapes are bought and sold in any quantity, there is normally a government-inspected WEIGHING scale.

Yields and wine quality

A necessary connection between low yields and high-quality wine has been assumed at least since Roman times when 'Bacchus amat colles' encapsulated the prevailing belief that low-yielding HILLSIDE VINEYARDS produced the best wine. Wine law in many European countries is predicated on the same belief and the much-imitated APPELLATION CONTRÔLÉE laws of France specify maximum permitted yields for each appellation (even if an additional allowance is often permitted; see below and PLC).

There is little doubt that heavily cropped vines with a low LEAF TO FRUIT RATIO ripen more slowly, so that in cooler climates the fruit may not reach full RIPENESS and wine quality suffers. It is less widely understood, however, that undercropping can also adversely affect wine quality. A high leaf to fruit ratio will certainly ripen grapes, but the shaded CANOPY MICROCLIMATE will produce grapes high in POTASSIUM and PH and low in PHENOLICS and flavour.

It should also be noted that, within a given wine region (Bordeaux is a notable example), there is no correlation between size of the crop and quality of the wine. Some of the finest red bordeaux VINTAGE YEARS of the 1980s, for example, were also those in which yields were relatively high; while the lowest crop levels of the decade were recorded in lesser vintages such as 1984 and 1980.

There are countless commercial examples of high vineyard yields associated with low quality, however. Very high yields are common to vineyards of high vigour, which in turn is typically due to planting on very fertile (or heavily fertilized) soil, well supplied with water. High-yielding vineyards are also often in hot climates, where the climate reduces the potential for wine quality anyway. Such vineyards are commonly planted with varieties selected for quantity rather than quality.

Very low yields may be the deliberate result of careful pruning, SHOOT THINNING, or even CROP THINNING, but they may also be associated with excessive vine stress. This can be due, for example, to weeds, pests, or disease, or to very shallow soils and WATER STRESS (as in much of Spain, for example), and a vine that is too severely stressed will not function properly and will not produce premium wine.

The yield which a vineyard can ripen properly will depend on the VINE VARIETY, the region, vine management practices (particularly pruning and vine-TRAINING SYSTEMS), and climate as well as weather. For example, a yield of 8 tonnes/ha, or 56 hl/ha, might be considered excessive in a very cool climate, but a yield five times this figure might be easily ripened to a similar or higher sugar level in a warmer climate. Some varieties seem more prone than others to crop level effects on wine quality, and in general red wine varieties are more affected than white. PINOT NOIR is an outstanding example, as the obvious inverse relationship between yield and quality in red burgundy demonstrates. MERLOT is another example.

Some specific examples

Vineyard yields vary enormously around the world and, in some regions with less dependable climates, from year to year. Among the highest reported yields are about 100 tonnes/ha for TABLE GRAPES grown on complex trellises in Israel (if their juice were made into wine, this would convert into about 1,750 hl/ha!). The Argentine vine-breeder Angel Gargiulo was in the 1970s and 1980s encouraged to breed new wine grape varieties specifically designed for the Argentine environment which can yield up to 500 hl/ha (but were commercially planted only to a very limited extent). Commercial, well-managed vineyards in irrigated DESERT regions in California, Australia, and Argentina can routinely produce 15 tons/acre (260 hl/ha). At the other end of the spectrum, pests, disease, drought, or bunch rot can all reduce yields to less than 1 tonne/ha, or 7 hl/ha. See Ch d'YQUEM as well as Domaine LEROY and CHAPOUTIER for some examples of particularly low yields, encouraged for the sake of wine quality.

Some attempt at calculating national average yields may be made using OIV statistics, although these are more reliable for some countries than for others. According to those published in 1996, and discounting those vineyards dedicated to table or drying grapes, the United States has one of the highest national average yields, at 100 hl/ha (5.7 tons/acre). See EUROPEAN UNION for a discussion of yields in Europe.

Certain wine types, most red wines, for example, are more sensitive to yield. Vineyards dedicated to sparkling wines, or base wines for brandy, are in general allowed to yield rather more than those dedicated to still wine production.

From a financial point of view, high yields are attractive to vine-growers, who have traditionally been paid on the simple basis of weight (although quality factors such as MUST WEIGHT are increasingly taken into account; see PRICE of grapes). Vine-growers whose aim is to produce good-quality wine may, however, deliberately restrict yields by such measures as pruning, crop thinning, and shoot thinning. One of the most important economic issues facing modern viticulture is whether high-vigour and high-yielding vineyards can produce high-quality wine using vineyard management techniques such as CANOPY MANAGEMENT.

The fact that yields are officially limited by regulation in the two most important wine-producing countries of France and Italy has undoubtedly encouraged worldwide respect for low yields, and perhaps some inertia in researching ways of increasing both quality and quantity. It should be noted, however, that the official maxima cited in wine regulations are now almost routinely increased in France by a device called the *plafond limite de classement*, or PLC, which allows a certain increase (often 20 per cent) on the base yield according to the conditions of the year. Average yields for the top appellations of the MÉDOC in 1989, 1990, and 1996, for example, were between 55 and 60 hl/ha when the theoretical maximum yield is 45 hl/ha.

See also PRUNING. R.E.S. & J.R.

Coombe, B. G., and Dry, P. R., *Viticulture, i: Resources* (Adelaide, 1988).

Gargiulo, A. A., 'Quality and quantity: are they compatible?', *Journal of Wine Research*, 2/3 (1991), 161–81.

Ross, J., 'Balancing yield and quality, parts I–IV', *Practical Winery and Vineyard* (Mar/Apr 1999, May/June 1999, Nov/Dec 1999, May/June 2000).

yield monitors, sensors fitted to mechanical grape harvesters which assess and record the amount of fruit being harvested in real time. When used in conjunction with a differential GLOBAL POSITIONING SYSTEM, they allow maps of yield to be produced. Such maps are a key to the implementation of PRECISION VITI-CULTURE and ZONAL VITICULTURE.   R.G.V.B.

York Mountain, California wine region and AVA. See SAN LUIS OBISPO.

Yquem, Château d', the greatest wine of SAUTERNES and, according to the famous 1855 CLASSIFICATION, of the entire BORDEAUX region. It is sweet, golden, and apparently almost immortal.

The origin of the name is obscure, although the Germanic *aig-helm* (meaning 'to have a helmet') is claimed. Probably the first vineyard-owning family were the Sauvages, who, from being tenants, bought the estate in 1711. It was acquired by the Lur Saluces family in 1785, when the last Sauvage d'Yquem married Comte Louis-Amadée de Lur Saluces. By then the wine was very well known, for in 1787 Thomas JEFFERSON wrote to 'M. d'Yquem', asking to buy some, stating, 'I know that yours is one of the best growths of Sauterne [*sic*]'. It is not known when Yquem was first made with BOTRYTIZED grapes, those affected by NOBLE ROT, but this painstaking technique probably originated early in the 19th century, although very sweet bottles dating from the latter part of the 18th century have been found. In the second half of the 19th century, Yquem had a world-wide reputation, not least in tsarist RUSSIA. From before the First World War until 1968, the estate was run by the Marquis Bernard de Lur Saluces who was succeeded in 2004 by Comte Alexandre, who also owns Ch de Fargues in Sauternes (although in 1999 LVMH acquired majority ownership after a bitter family struggle). Pierre LURTON, also manager of CH CHEVAL BLANC, was subsequently installed by LVMH.

The château, dating back to the 15th century and the Renaissance, stands on the crest of a small hill, with small towers at each corner and a large inner courtyard. The vineyard on all sides extends to 99 ha/245 acres in production out of a total of 125 ha. The vines planted are 80 per cent SÉMILLON and 20 per cent of the usually more productive SAUVIGNON BLANC. Production averages 8,000 cases, a fraction of the typical output of a top red wine property in the MÉDOC. The secret of Yquem's renown is its susceptibility to noble rot, and its ability to run risks and sacrifice quantity for painstakingly upheld quality. An average of five passages, or TRIES, are made through the vineyard each year so that only the BOTRYTIS-affected grapes are picked. The maximum yield is 9 hl/ha (0.5 tons/acre), compared with the normal 25 in Sauternes. The juice is pressed three times, and then treated to three years' BARREL MATURATION in new oak casks. The cost of the whole operation makes Yquem a very expensive wine. CRYOEXTRACTION, or freeze concentration, was controversially used on the 1987 vintage and, experimentally, in the early 1990s.

Since 1959 a dry white wine, Y, or Ygrec, has been produced but intermittently. Notably alcoholic, it has more than a hint of a Sauternes. In 2005, Pierre Lurton was experimenting with a fresher style of dry white bordeaux from grapes rejected for the Sauternes.

E.P.-R. & J.R.

Olney, R., *Yquem* (Paris, 1985; London, 1986).

Yugoslavia, eastern European union of peoples that existed for barely 60 years before breaking up amid bloodshed, privation, and extreme ethnic tension at the beginning of the post-communist era in the early 1990s.

Viticulture in this war-torn collection of tribes and states is as rich and varied in potential as the people themselves. That potential was just beginning to be realized as civil war intervened. For ease of reference, the name Yugoslavia is still used here, although no political implication is intended. Although Yugoslavia is now sometimes used to refer to the Serbian rump excluding Slovenia, Croatia, Bosnia and Herzegovina, and Macedonia, wine-making techniques and styles described below still apply to much of ex-Yugoslavia except SLOVENIA, which owes a far more direct debt to Italy and Austria. Slovenia does, however, share its viticultural practices with the other countries of the group.

Yugoslavia ran from north west to south east parallel to, and on a latitude with, ITALY. The area of major white wine production runs inland along the north east border from eastern Slovenia through eastern CROATIA and into the northern half of SERBIA. Most of it is on hilly land, higher and steeper in the north and more gentle around the river Danube and its tributaries north and east of Belgrade.

The best of the reds come from the south eastern third of what was Yugoslavia along the coasts of MONTENEGRO and KOSOVO and inland in MACEDONIA and eastern Serbia.

Considerable quantities of wine of both colours is produced along the rest of the coast and islands, the vast majority of which is consumed locally. In addition, Yugoslavia has substantial brandy and VERMOUTH industries.

Considering the geographical proximity and similarity to Italy, Yugoslavian wines are remarkably dissimilar to those produced across the Adriatic sea, mainly because of the differences in vine variety mix and viticultural practices between the two countries, Italy having a higher proportion of high yield, low density plains land plantations. PHYLLOXERA came relatively late to Yugoslavia, affecting the vineyards between 1890 and 1920. As in other countries, many vineyards were pulled out and remained permanently out of production, some were replanted with local grape varieties, but many (far more than in Italy) were converted to the better French, German, and Austrian varieties which were already well known and appreciated in other parts of eastern Europe.

Wine-making practices also frequently differ from Italy's. White wine-making especially is often less industrial, using riper grapes which show more EXTRACTION, and sometimes more AROMA. According to market demand and available resources, reds may be made light, sweet, with a very short time spent on skins for the German market or strong and heavily coloured for the local and more eastern markets. INTERNATIONAL VARIETIES such as Cabernet Sauvignon tend to be more classically handled. Both white and red grapes can show very true, fully ripened varietal characteristics.

Exports, once higher than a million hl a year, fell sharply in the late 1980s and early 1990s. Latterly, dealers from further east in Europe and Russia have taken an interest in Serbia especially. Macedonia has also rebuilt an export trade to both Germany and Slovenia. Relatively little remains of the once enormous trade in light, sweetish red wines shipped to Germany from Kosovo and medium dry Laški Rizling shipped to the UK from Slovenia.

Under the communist regime, Yugoslavia's cost of living was controlled, and there was full employment, but production standards were as low as the market would bear.

Unlike the more hardline communist countries, however, Yugoslavia allowed considerable private land ownership. Even in 1990, 180,000 ha/444,600 acres, more than 70 per cent, of Yugoslavian vineyard was recorded as being in private hands.

Yugoslavia is now split into political components which correspond reasonably well to the boundaries of wine regions previously defined by state law. For more details, therefore, see (roughly from north to south) SLOVENIA, CROATIA, VOJVODINA, SERBIA, KOSOVO, MONTENEGRO, BOSNIA AND HERZEGOVINA, and MACEDONIA.

Viticulture and climate

In most of the vineyards, with the exception of some of the coastal regions, the vines are trained along trellised rows. Although labour has been plentiful and cheap, vineyards are designed wherever possible to permit the passage of tractors for cultivation and treatment purposes. Pruning and harvesting remain almost entirely manual.

Training systems vary from double GUYOT through to LENZ MOSER and VINE DENSITY follows suit. Distances between rows are usually fairly wide except on the more traditionally planted hillsides, where vines may even be trained up their own individual STAKE.

Under state control, little attention was paid to the quality of cultivation or ideal picking date. As a result, YIELDS were typically well under 50 hl/ha (2.8 tons/acre), less than half those of Germany, for example. Healthy red grapes are often picked before they have reached full MATURITY and may then be subjected to trucking for very long distances to reach the winery to which they are contracted.

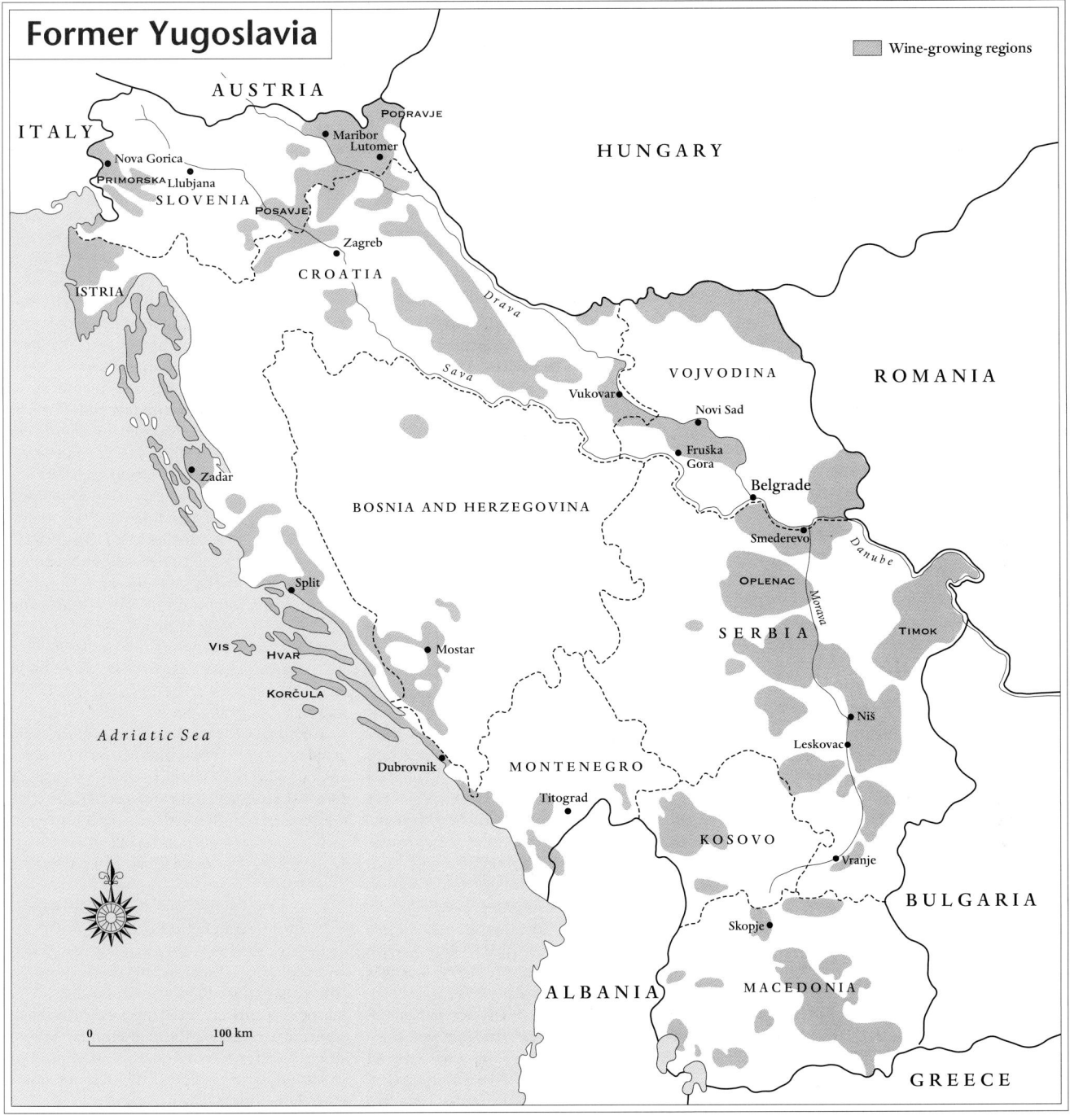

Former Yugoslavia

Wine-growing regions

AUSTRIA

ITALY

PODRAVJE

Nova Gorica

• Maribor
Lutomer

PRIMORSKA Llubjana

SLOVENIA

POSAVJE

HUNGARY

• Zagreb

CROATIA

ISTRIA

Drava

Sava

VOJVODINA

ROMANIA

Vukovar

Novi Sad

• Fruška
Gora

• Zadar

Belgrade

BOSNIA AND HERZEGOVINA

Smederevo

Danube

OPLENAC

• Split

Morava

SERBIA

TIMOK

VIS

HVAR

KORČULA

Adriatic Sea

• Niš

Leskovac

Dubrovnik

MONTENEGRO

• Titograd

KOSOVO

• Vranje

BULGARIA

Skopje

N

ALBANIA

MACEDONIA

0   100 km

GREECE

Wine regions in inland Slovenia and Macedonia are relatively high ALTITUDE, thereby allowing a longer ripening season than latitude may suggest. There is adequate rainfall and most of the countryside, with the exception of Macedonia, is pleasantly green and fertile throughout the growing season, despite the fact that many of the districts have a CONTINENTAL rather than MEDITERRANEAN climate and enjoy a high number of completely dry days. Winters can be very cold, especially inland.

Wine-making

Such progress as Yugoslavia has made in vinification has been led by demand from export customers. The curious hybrid of communism and capitalism by which the wine enterprises have been run developed heavy bureaucratic burdens and a lack of entrepreneurial spirit. There was some investment in the 1980s, but even in the late 1990s, many of the co-operatives (such as one in the heart of Fruška Gora white wine country in Vojvodina) still had massive concrete cellars, three and four

storeys of tanks high, with no means of TEMPERATURE CONTROL. Often machinery which badly needed painting or replacing to avoid metal CONTAMINATION in the wines could not be attended to in time for the harvest. Scant attention was paid to storage TEMPERATURE, which particularly affected the huge surplus of reds so often offered on the world market as part of reciprocal deals by would-be importers. Wines sweetened both for the home market and for export more often than not had such BOUQUET as they possessed flattened by the use of very dull GRAPE CONCENTRATE. All the more regrettable in view of these grapes' potential.

Major exporters included Navip in Serbia, who nursemaided a joint project with the Japanese in a well-equipped winery near Belgrade. They were aware of this potential but in the late 1990s were unwilling to realize it because of the severe price constraints imposed by competition from other, poorer ex-eastern bloc countries.

Since 2000, when land restitution was more or less completed all over central and eastern Europe, many of the old state wineries have been bought out, sometimes by their original management, but more and more often by people who have acquired wealth in other fields. Sometimes with help from international funding, vineyards are being restored and wineries re-equipped. Slovenia and Croatia are among the first to benefit from this new wave of investment. Results available on the international market are as yet patchy but should become much more evident in the next few years. The west may not see as much as expected of this progress since the new wave investors tend to look to their home market and eastwards for their outlets, in part because the west still expects to pay below market prices for anything, whatever its quality, that comes from these countries.

A.H.M.

Zala Gyöngye, Muscat-like TABLE GRAPE crossing of an EGER grape and Pearl of Csaba that is quite widely planted in Hungary, where some undistinguished wine is also made from it. It is also grown in Italy, Croatia, Romania, and Israel for table grapes and is usually called by a local translation of the expression 'Queen of the Vineyards'.

Zalema, Spanish white grape variety grown on 5,100 ha/12,600 acres of vineyard in 2004, particularly in the southern CONDADO DE HUELVA zone, where its musts and wine can oxidize easily. It is being replaced by higher-quality varieties such as PALOMINO.

Zefir, early-ripening 1983 Hungarian CROSS-ING of Leányka and Hárslevelű producing soft, spicy wine.

Zenit, 1951 Hungarian crossing of Bouvier and Ezerjó which ripens usefully early to produce crisp, fruity but not particularly aromatic white wines.

Zentralkellerei, a vast central co-operative wine cellar peculiar to GERMANY, where there are three, including the vast Badische Winzerkeller at Breisach in BADEN. These *Zentralkellereien* draw in wine from smaller CO-OPERATIVES, or *Winzergenossenschaften*. Other *Zentralkellereien* are at Kitzingen in FRANKEN and Möglingen in WÜRTTEMBERG.

Zéta, Hungarian vine crossing of FURMINT and BOUVIER, formerly known as Orémus, which, with Furmint, Hárslevelű, and Sárga Muskotály, is permitted in TOKAJI.

Zibibbo, Sicilian name for the MUSCAT OF ALEXANDRIA white grape variety, sometimes made into wine, notably Moscato di PANTELLE-RIA, although more usually sold as TABLE GRAPES. It is very much less common in Italy than Moscato Bianco (MUSCAT BLANC À PETITS GRAINS).

Zierfandler, the more noble of the two white wine grape varieties traditionally associated with GUMPOLDSKIRCHEN, the dramatically full-bodied, long-lived spicy white wine of the Thermenregion district of AUSTRIA. (The other is ROTGIPFLER.) At the end of the 1980s, there were about 100 ha/250 acres of Zierfandler. It ripens very late, as its synonym Spätrot suggests, but keeps its acidity better than Rotgipfler. Unblended, Zierfandler has sufficient nerve to make late harvest wines with the ability to evolve over years in bottle, but many Zierfandler grapes are blended, and sometimes vinified, with Rotgipfler. The variety, as Cirfandli, is also known in Hungary. DNA PROFILING in Austria suggested a parent–offspring relationship with ROTER VELTLINER.

Zilavka, relatively successful white grape variety planted in Herzegovina (see BOSNIA AND HERZEGOVINA). This distinctive variety manages to combine high alcohol with high acidity and a certain nuttiness of flavour. The Zilavka made around the inland town of Mostar is particularly prized. It is not, however, necessarily made exclusively from Zilavka grapes. Zilavka is also increasingly planted in MACEDONIA.

Zimbabwe, southern African country with small-scale commercial wine industry. Launched in the 1950s, and nurtured in the sanctions period of the 1960s and 1970s, the industry showed a noticeable improvement in wine quality from the late 1980s. In this TROPICAL climate, temperature is moderated by ALTITUDE in some of the better vineyard areas. On the same latitude as much of Bolivia and southern Brazil, Zimbabwe is subject to summer rain from November to April with February being the wettest month. Vines are sprayed with a calcium-based GROWTH REGULA-TOR to induce even budding during the warm, damp early summer. SPRAYING is a frequent necessity against the BOTRYTIS BUNCH ROT that is an annual hazard and the crop can suffer from both dilution and HAIL. Winemakers frequently resort to ACIDIFICATION and sometimes ENRICHMENT (Zimbabwe has no official labelling or wine control regulations). There is no shortage of SUNLIGHT, however, with average daily sunshine of eight hours. Prevailing winds are from the east, blowing off the warm coast of MADAGASCAR. Mean annual temperatures of just under 19 °C/66 °F and an average of 27.5 days of FROST between June and August serve to keep the growers on their toes.

The most promising vineyards are 40 km/ 25 miles east of the capital Harare at Marandera. Chenin Blanc, Colombard, and CAPE RIESLING vines produce passable dry and off-dry whites, with South African PINOTAGE, Merlot, Shiraz, and Cabernet Sauvignon making reds. The Cairns Group (which produces the Mukuyu label) and African Distillers own the biggest wineries, drawing from widely scattered vineyards at Bulawayo and Mutare but each has lost significant farms in President Mugabe's appropriation of white-owned land, including Fighill, which used to produce 25 per cent of African Distillers' wine including their top Chardonnay. Zimbabwe uses South African, German, Australian, and New Zealand wine-making expertise and its wines improved enormously in the late 1990s, thanks to input from FLYING WINEMAKERS.

J.P. & M.Fr.

zinc, essential element for healthy vine growth. A deficiency of zinc affects the plant's ability to synthesize the hormones AUXINS, which in turn results in a failure of the shoots to grow normally. The principal symptoms are CHLOROSIS between the veins of young and old leaves, their small size, and a widened leaf

sinus where the PETIOLE attaches. FRUIT SET can also be poor. Zinc deficiency commonly occurs in vineyards on sandy soils, and is treated by daubing pruning wounds with pastes containing zinc, or spraying leaves in summer.   R.E.S.

Zinfandel is an exotic black grape variety of CROATIAN origin cultivated predominantly in California that has tended to mirror the giddily changing fashions of the American wine business.

For much of the 20th century, the viticultural 'pioneer' Agoston HARASZTHY was credited with introducing this important variety to California from his native Hungary, but a more worthy Zinfandel hero is the California historian Charles L. Sullivan, who unearthed the truth, or at least part of it, about Zinfandel's route to California. It was he who pointed out that there was no mention of Zinfandel in Haraszthy's copious promotional literature in the early 1860s, and that, long before Haraszthy arrived in California in 1849, the variety was well known on the American East Coast.

The vine was imported, possibly unnamed, to the US from the Austrian imperial nursery in Vienna by George Gibbs of Long Island, probably in 1829. He took it to Boston and by the early 1830s it had acquired such names as 'Zenfendel' and 'Zinfindal' among New England growers, many of whom added it to the range of VINIFERA vines they grew under glass as a TABLE GRAPE.

Many of those who participated in the California GOLD RUSH of 1849 turned to agriculture, often dependent on shipments of plant material from the East Coast. 'Zinfindal' was included in a particularly important load which arrived in 1852 and by 1859 the variety was grown in both Napa and Sonoma. In 1862, the secretary of the Sonoma Horticultural Society gave some wine made from these grapes to a French winemaker working in California who reported that it tasted like 'a good French claret'.

These early California growers discovered that the vine was identical to one known in New England as 'Black St Peters', although it is not known how or when Black St Peters arrived there.

Because Zinfandel has no French connection, it had escaped the detailed scrutiny of the world's ampelographic centre in MONTPELLIER and its European origins rested on local hypothesis rather than internationally accredited fact until the application of DNA PROFILING to vines in the early 1990s. Only then was it irrefutably demonstrated what had been suspected, that Zinfandel is one and the same as the PRIMITIVO of southern Italy (which may have been imported from the United States). (The relationship had already been sufficiently acknowledged by the Italians in the 1980s that some were exporting their Primitivo

labelled, in direct appeal to the American market, Zinfandel.) Subsequent DNA profiling at DAVIS established that the variety PLAVAC MALI of Croatia is in fact the progeny of a cross between Zinfandel and Dobričić, an obscure and ancient Croatian variety found on the island of Šolta near Split. This suggested a probable Dalmatian origin for Zinfandel, and Croatian researchers Pejic and Maletic collaborating with Carole Meredith at Davis intensively searched the coastal vineyards for Zinfandel until in 2001 they discovered an ancient and almost extinct variety on the island of Kaštela near Split called Crljenak Kaštelanski (literally 'red grape of Kaštela') that strongly resembled Zinfandel. DNA profiling established that it was Zinfandel, thus supporting a primary Croatian origin for California's Zinfandel.

Zinfandel took firm hold on the California wine business in the 1880s, when its ability to produce in quantity was prized above all else. Many was the miner, and other beneficiary of California's gold rush, whose customary drink was Zinfandel. By the turn of the century, Zinfandel was regarded as California's own claret and occupied some of the choicest North coast vineyard. During Prohibition, it was the choice of many a HOME WINEMAKER but since then its viticultural popularity has become its undoing.

In 20th-century California, Zinfandel has occupied much the same place as SHIRAZ (Syrah) in Australia and suffered the same lack of respect simply because it is the most planted black grape variety, often planted in unsuitably hot sites and expected to yield more than is good for it. Zinfandel may not be quite such a potentially noble grape variety as Syrah but it is certainly capable of producing fine wine if yields are restricted and the weather cool enough to allow a reasonably long growing season.

Zinfandel's viticultural disadvantages are uneven ripening and thin-skinned berries in compact clusters. Bunches often ripen unevenly with harsh, green berries on the same cluster as those that have reached full maturity, and that once grapes reach full ripeness, in direct contrast to its great California rival Cabernet Sauvignon for example, they will soon turn to raisins if not picked quite rapidly. Zinfandel performs best in warm but not hot conditions and prefers well-drained HILLSIDES since it is subject to BUNCH ROT if caught by autumn rains.

Although Zinfandel has been required to transform itself into virtually every style and colour of wine that exists, it is best suited to dry, sturdy, unsubtle, but vigorous reds with an optimum lifespan of four to eight years. Such wines are rarely blends, although Ridge Vineyards are exponents of FIELD BLENDS which include PETITE SIRAH. Since the early 1990s, however, other premium producers have commanded prices which justify more

expensive handling of this ascendant variety, including several picking passes (TRIES) through the vineyard and more luxurious OAK treatments. See CALIFORNIA for more details of Zinfandel the wine, both red and white. Dry Creek valley in SONOMA has demonstrated a particular aptitude for this underestimated variety.

Thanks to the enormous popularity of WHITE ZINFANDEL, Zinfandel plantings, which had been declining, increased by up to 3,000 acres/1,215 ha a year during the late 1980s, mostly in the Central valley, so that they totalled 34,000 acres in 1992, just ahead of California's total acreage of Cabernet Sauvignon at the time. The resurgence of Zinfandel continued in the late 1990s as red Zinfandel began to enjoy mildly cult-like status (with many examples commanding prices over $30), driving total plantings to 50,000 acres/20,000 ha in 2003, only slightly less than Merlot and two-thirds as much as California's most important black variety Cabernet Sauvignon.

Zinfandel is also grown to a much more limited extent in warmer sites in other western states in the US, and some South African growers have also taken advantage of their climate's suitability for Zinfandel. Australia is another obvious location for this unusual variety and Cape Mentelle in Western Australia has been particularly successful with it. There is even an experimental, if discreet, plot in HERMITAGE in the northern Rhône.

Galet, P., 'La Culture de la vigne aux États-Unis et au Canada', *France viticole* (Sept–Oct 1980).

Sullivan, C. L., 'A viticultural mystery solved', *California History*, 57 (Summer 1978), 115–29.

zonal viticulture, form of PRECISION VITICULTURE in which vineyards are divided into zones of characteristic performance in terms of YIELD and/or grape composition. These are then managed as separate units with respect to particular inputs and/or selective harvesting. Typically, zones are identified either on the basis of visual inspection of yield maps, imagery acquired by REMOTE SENSING, and/or maps of other vineyard attributes, simple classification of such data, or through the use of statistically based clustering algorithms. Such an approach particularly facilitates the implementation of precision viticulture where winemakers are equipped for large, as opposed to small, crushes. For example, a block of Cabernet Sauvignon might be mechanically harvested into either of two bins, depending on location within the block, in order to maximize the production of a high-value varietal wine by allocating fruit from areas producing lower-value material to a lower value blended wine. Under conventional uniform management, only the latter would have been produced from the block.

By 2005 this approach had been adopted in several locations in Australia, Chile and the US.   R.G.V.B.

Bramley, R. G. V., and Hamilton, R. P., 'Hitting the zone—Making viticulture more precise', in R. J. Blair, P. J. Williams, and P. B. Hoj (eds.), *Proceedings of the 12th Australian Wine Industry Technical Conference* (Adelaide, 2004).

Bramley, R. G. V., Proffitt, A. P. B., Hinze, C. J., Pearse, B., and Hamilton, R. P., 'Generating benefits from Precision Viticulture through selective harvesting', in J. Stafford (ed.), *Proceedings of the 5th European Conference on Precision Agriculture* (Uppsala, 2005).

Zweigelt or **Blauer Zweigelt** (formerly Rotburger) is Austria's most popular dark-berried grape variety even though this crossing was bred only relatively recently, by a Dr Zweigelt at the KLOSTERNEUBURG research station in 1922. It is a BLAUFRÄNKISCH × ST-LAURENT crossing that at its best combines some of the bite of the first with the elegance of the second, although it is sometimes encouraged to produce too much dilute wine. It is popular with growers because it ripens earlier than Blaufränkisch but buds rather later than St-Laurent, thereby tending to yield generously. It is widely grown throughout all Austrian wine regions and can increasingly make a serious, age-worthy wine, even though most examples are best drunk young. So successful has it been in Austria that the variety has also been planted on an experimental basis in Germany and England. The export fortunes of the variety may, oddly enough, be hampered by its originator's uncompromisingly Germanic surname. If only he had been called Dr Pinot Noir. It is grown in JAPAN.

zymase, group of ENZYMES which encourage the conversion of GLUCOSE and FRUCTOSE into ETHYL ALCOHOL during fermentation.

Appendices

Appendix 1 Complete list of controlled appellations and their permitted grape varieties

It is still impossible to tell from the labels of most geographically named wines which grapes were used to make them. The following is a unique guide to the varieties officially allowed into the world's *controlled* wine appellations (therefore by no means all known wine names), listed by local name alphabetically by country, grouped where appropriate into alphabetically listed regions within that country, and listed alphabetically by appellation name within that region. Italics denote minor grapes. R, W, P, and S denote red, white, pink, and sparkling wines respectively.

VARIETAL APPELLATIONS are not included in this list because they are so numerous and because the region of origin and the grape variety are, in most cases, clearly stated on the label.

AUSTRIA

Weinviertel (W) Grüner Veltliner

CROATIA

Hvar (W) Trbljan
Pelješac, Postup, Dingač, Prošek, Faros, Potomje (R) Plavac Mali

CYPRUS

Commandaria (R) Mavro, Xynisteri

FRANCE

For more detail on subappellations such as Grés de Montpellier or Saint-Christol (within Coteaux du Languedoc), see www.inao.gouv.fr or www.vitis.org.

Alsace and North East
Crémant d'Alsace (S) Riesling, Pinot Blanc, Pinot Noir, Pinot Gris, Auxerrois, Chardonnay
Vin d'Alsace Edelzwicker (W) Gewürztraminer, Riesling, Pinot Gris, Muscat Blanc à Petits Grains, Muscat Ottonel, Pinot Blanc, Pinot Noir, Sylvaner, Chasselas
Other Alsace wines are varietally labelled.
Côtes de Toul (R) Pinot Noir (P) Gamay, Pinot Noir, *Pinot Meunier, Aubin, Auxerrois* (W) Aubin, Auxerrois
Moselle, VDQS Auxerrois, Gewürztraminer, Pinot Meunier, Müller-Thurgau, Pinot Noir, Pinot Blanc, Pinot Gris, Riesling, *Gamay*

Bordeaux
Blaye (R) Cabernet Sauvignon, Merlot, Malbec, Prolongeau (Bouchalès), Béquignol, Petit Verdot (W) Ugni Blanc, *Colombard, Pineau de la Loire (Chenin Blanc), Sémillon, Sauvignon Blanc, Muscadelle*
Bordeaux, Bordeaux Clairet, Bordeaux Rosé, Bordeaux Supérieur, Premières Côtes de Bordeaux (R, P) Cabernet Sauvignon, Cabernet Franc, Carmenère, Malbec, Petit Verdot
Bordeaux Sec (W) Sémillon, Sauvignon Blanc, Muscadelle, *Merlot Blanc, Colombard, Mauzac, Ondenc, Ugni Blanc*

Bordeaux Côtes de Francs (R) Cabernet Sauvignon, Merlot, Malbec (W) Sémillon, Sauvignon Blanc, Muscadelle

Bordeaux Haut-Benauge (W) Sémillon, Sauvignon Blanc, Muscadelle

Bourg, Côtes de Bourg, Bourgeais (R) Cabernet Sauvignon, Cabernet Franc, Merlot, Malbec (W) Sauvignon Blanc, Sémillon, Muscadelle, Merlot Blanc, Colombard

Côtes de Blaye (W) Sémillon, Sauvignon Blanc, Muscadelle, *Merlot Blanc, Folle Blanche, Colombard, Pineau de la Loire (Chenin Blanc)*

Côtes de Castillon (R) Cabernet Sauvignon, Cabernet Franc, Merlot, Malbec (Côt)

Crémant de Bordeaux (W, S) Sémillon, Sauvignon Blanc, Muscadelle, *Ugni Blanc, Colombard* (P, S) Cabernet Sauvignon, Cabernet Franc, Merlot, *Carmenère, Malbec, Petit Verdot*

Entre-Deux-Mers, Entre-Deux-Mers Haut-Benauge (W) Sémillon, Sauvignon Blanc, Muscadelle, *Merlot Blanc, Colombard, Mauzac, Ugni Blanc*

Fronsac, Canon Fronsac, Côtes Canon Fronsac (R) Cabernet Sauvignon, Cabernet Franc (Bouchet), Merlot, Malbec (Pressac)

Graves, Graves Supérieures (R) Cabernet Sauvignon, Cabernet Franc, Merlot, Malbec, Petit Verdot (W) Sémillon, Sauvignon Blanc, Muscadelle

Graves de Vayres (R) Cabernet Sauvignon, Cabernet Franc, Merlot, Malbec, Petit Verdot (W) Sémillon, Sauvignon Blanc, Muscadelle, *Merlot Blanc*

Haut-Médoc, Listrac-Médoc, Margaux, Médoc, Moulis, Pauillac, Pessac-Léognan, St-Estèphe, St-Julien (R) Cabernet Sauvignon, Cabernet Franc, Merlot, Carmenère, Malbec (Côt), Petit Verdot

Pomerol, Lalande-de-Pomerol, Néac, Lussac-St-Émilion, Montagne-St-Émilion, Parsac-St-Émilion, Puisseguin-St-Émilion, St-Georges-St-Émilion (R) Cabernet Sauvignon, Cabernet Franc (Bouchet), Merlot, Malbec (Pressac)

Premières Côtes de Blaye (R) Cabernet Sauvignon, Cabernet Franc, Merlot, Côt (W) Sémillon, Sauvignon Blanc, Muscadelle, *Merlot Blanc, Colombard, Ugni Blanc*

St-Émilion (R) Merlot, Cabernet Sauvignon, Cabernet Franc, Carmenère, Malbec (Côt)

Ste-Foy-Bordeaux (R) Cabernet Sauvignon, Cabernet Franc, Malbec, Petit Verdot (W) Sémillon, Sauvignon Blanc, Muscadelle, *Merlot Blanc, Colombard, Mauzac, Ugni Blanc*

Sauternes, Barsac, Ste-Croix-du-Mont, Loupiac, Cadillac, Cérons, Premières Côtes de Bordeaux, Pessac-Léognan, Côtes de Bordeaux, St-Macaire (W) Sémillon, Sauvignon Blanc, Muscadelle

Burgundy
Regional Appellations

Bourgogne Grand Ordinaire (R) Pinot Noir, Gamay, *César, Tressot* (P) *Pinot Gris, Pinot Blanc, Chardonnay* (W) Chardonnay, Aligoté, Pinot Blanc, Melon de Bourgogne, *Sacy*

Bourgogne Passe-tout-grains (R, P) Gamay, *Pinot Noir, Pinot Blanc, Pinot Gris, Chardonnay*

Bourgogne Mousseux (S) Chardonnay, Pinot Blanc, Pinot Noir, Pinot Beurot, Pinot Liébault, *César, Tressot*

Bourgogne, Bourgogne Clairet, Bourgogne Rosé, Bourgogne Hautes Côtes de Beaune, Bourgogne Rosé Hautes Côtes de Beaune, Bourgogne Clairet Hautes Côtes de Beaune, Bourgogne Hautes Côtes de Nuits, Bourgogne Rosé Hautes Côtes de Nuits, Bourgogne Clairet Hautes Côtes de Nuits, Bourgogne Côte Chalonnaise, Bourgogne Rosé Côte Chalonnaise, Bourgogne Clairet Côte Chalonnaise (R, P) Pinot Noir, Pinot Liébault, Pinot Beurot, *César, Tressot, Pinot Blanc, Pinot Gris, Chardonnay* (W) Chardonnay, *Pinot Blanc*

Bourgogne Aligoté, Bourgogne Aligoté Bouzeron (W) Aligoté, *Chardonnay*

Crémant de Bourgogne (S) Pinot Noir, Chardonnay, Pinot Gris, Pinot Blanc, *Gamay, Aligoté, Melon de Bourgogne, Sacy*

Beaujolais
Beaujolais, Beaujolais Supérieur, Beaujolais-Villages (R, P) Gamay, *Pinot Noir, Pinot Gris, Chardonnay, Aligoté, Melon de Bourgogne* (W) Chardonnay, *Aligoté*

Brouilly, Chénas, Chiroubles, Fleurie, Juliénas, Morgon, Moulin-à-Vent, St Amour (R) Gamay, *Chardonnay, Aligoté, Melon de Bourgogne*

Côte de Brouilly (R) Gamay, *Pinot Noir, Pinot Gris, Pinot Blanc, Chardonnay*

Régnié (R) Gamay

Chablis Region
Irancy (R) Pinot Noir, *Pinot Gris, César*

Petit Chablis, Chablis, Chablis Premier Cru, Chablis Grand Cru (W) Chardonnay

St-Bris (W) Sauvignon Blanc, Sauvignon Gris

Bourgogne-Vézelay (W) Chardonnay, Pinot Blanc

Côte Chalonnaise
Note: The communes indicated with an asterisk contain premier cru vineyards.

Givry (R) Pinot Noir, Pinot Beurot, Pinot Liébault, *Chardonnay* (W) Chardonnay, Pinot Blanc

Mercurey*, Rully* (R) Pinot Noir, Pinot Beurot, Pinot Liébault, *Chardonnay* (W) Chardonnay

Montagny* (W) Chardonnay

Côte d'Or
Côte de Beaune, Côte de Beaune-Villages, Beaune*, Nuits-St-Georges* (R) Pinot Noir, Pinot Liébault, *Chardonnay, Pinot Blanc, Pinot Gris* (W) Chardonnay, Pinot Blanc

Aloxe-Corton*, Maranges* (R) Pinot Noir, Pinot Beurot, Pinot Liébault, *Chardonnay, Pinot Blanc, Pinot Gris* (W) Chardonnay

Auxey-Duresses*, Blagny, Chassagne-Montrachet*, Chorey-lès-Beaune, Côte-de-Nuits-Villages, Fixin*, Ladoix, Marsannay, Meursault*, Monthélie, Morey St-Denis*, Pernand-Vergelesses*, Puligny-Montrachet*, St-Aubin*, St-Romain, Santenay*, Savigny-lès-Beaune*, Vougeot* (R) Pinot Noir, Pinot Beurot, Pinot Liébault, *Pinot Blanc, Pinot Gris, Chardonnay* (W) Chardonnay, Pinot Blanc

Chambolle-Musigny*, Gevrey-Chambertin*, Marsannay Rosé, Pommard*, Volnay*, Volnay Santenots*, Vosne-Romanée* (R) Pinot Noir, Pinot Liébault, Pinot Beurot, *Chardonnay, Pinot Blanc, Pinot Gris*

Côte d'Or—Grands Crus
Bonnes-Mares, Chambertin, Chambertin-Clos-de-Bèze, Chapelle-Chambertin, Charmes-Chambertin, Griotte-Chambertin, Latricières-Chambertin, Mazis-Chambertin, Mazoyères-Chambertin, Ruchottes-Chambertin, Clos des Lambrays, Clos de la Roche, Clos St-Denis, Clos de Tart, Clos de Vougeot, Echézeaux, Grands Echézeaux, Richebourg, Romanée-Conti, Romanée-St-Vivant, La Romanée, La Tâche (R) Pinot Noir, Pinot Liébault, Pinot Beurot, *Pinot Blanc, Pinot Gris, Chardonnay*

La Grande Rue (R) Pinot Noir, *Pinot Blanc, Pinot Gris, Chardonnay*

Musigny, Corton (R) Pinot Noir, Pinot Liébault, Pinot Beurot, *Pinot Blanc, Pinot Gris, Chardonnay* (W) Chardonnay

Corton-Charlemagne, Montrachet, Bâtard-Montrachet, Bienvenues-Bâtard-Montrachet, Chevalier-Montrachet, Criots-Bâtard-Montrachet (W) Chardonnay

Charlemagne (W) Chardonnay, *Aligoté*

Mâconnais

Mâcon, Mâcon-Villages, or Mâcon followed by a commune name (e.g. Mâcon Chardonnay, Mâcon Viré, Mâcon Lugny) (W) Chardonnay

Mâcon or Mâcon followed by a commune name (e.g. Mâcon Chardonnay, Mâcon Viré, Mâcon Lugny) (R, P) Gamay

Pouilly-Fuissé, Pouilly-Vinzelles, Pouilly-Loché, St-Véran (W) Chardonnay

Champagne

Champagne, Coteaux Champenois (S) Pinot Noir, Pinot Meunier, Chardonnay

Rosé de Riceys (P) Pinot Noir

Corsica See Provence and Corsica.

Jura

Arbois, Arbois Mousseux, Arbois Pupillin (R) Poulsard Noir, Trousseau, Pinot Noir (W) Savagnin Blanc, Chardonnay, *Pinot Blanc* (S) Poulsard Noir, Trousseau, Pinot Noir, Savagnin Blanc, Chardonnay, *Pinot Blanc*

Note: Pinot Noir and Pinot Blanc are not permitted for the production of *Vin de Paille*; other grapes are as above. Arbois Rosé may be made from a blend of black and white grapes.

Arbois Vin Jaune (W) Savagnin Blanc

Château-Chalon Vin Jaune (W) Savagnin Blanc

Côtes du Jura (R) Poulsard Noir, Trousseau, Pinot Noir (W) Savagnin Blanc, Chardonnay

Côtes du Jura Mousseux (S) grapes as above

Côtes du Jura Vin Jaune (W) Savagnin Blanc

Crémant du Jura (S) Poulsard, Pinot Noir, Chardonnay, *Trousseau, Pinot Gris, Savagnin*

Côtes du Jura Rosé is made from a blend of black and white grapes.

L'Étoile, L' Étoile Mousseux (W) Chardonnay, Poulsard, Savagnin Blanc

L'Étoile Vin Jaune (W) Savagnin Blanc

Languedoc-Roussillon

Cabardès (R, P) Grenache, Syrah, Cinsaut, Cabernet Sauvignon, Merlot, Cabernet Franc, *Côt, Fer, Carignan, Aubun Noir*

Clairette de Bellegarde, Clairette du Languedoc (W) Clairette

Collioure (R) Grenache, Mourvèdre, Syrah, *Carignan, Cinsaut* (P) Grenache, Mourvèdre, Syrah, *Carignan, Cinsaut, Grenache Gris* (W) Grenache Blanc, Grenache Gris, *Malvoisie, Macabeu, Marsanne, Roussanne, Vermentino*

Corbières (R, P) Carignan, Grenache, Cinsaut, Lladoner Pelut, Mourvèdre, Piquepoul Noir, Terret Noir, Syrah, Maccabeu (W) Bourboulenc, Clairette Blanche, Grenache Blanc, Maccabeu, Muscat Blanc à Petits Grains, Piquepoul Blanc, Terret Blanc, Marsanne, Roussanne, Vermentino (Rolle)

Corbières-Boutenac (R) Carignan, Grenache, Syrah, Mourvèdre

Costières de Nîmes (R, P) Carignan, Grenache, Mourvèdre, Syrah, Cinsaut (W) Clairette Blanc, Grenache Blanc, Bourboulenc Blanc, Ugni Blanc, Roussanne, Vermentino, Macabeu, Marsanne, *Viognier*

Coteaux du Languedoc (R) Carignan, Cinsaut, Grenache, Lladoner Pelut, Mourvèdre, *Counoise Noir (Aubun), Grenache Rosé, Terret Noir, Picpoul Noir* (P) Carignan, Cinsaut, Grenache, Lladoner Pelut, Mourvèdre, *Counoise Noir (Aubun), Grenache Rosé, Terret Noir, Picpoul Noir, Bourboulenc, Carignan Blanc, Clairette, Maccabéo, Picpoul, Terret, Ugni Blanc* (W) Grenache Blanc, Clairette, Bourboulenc, Piquepoul Blanc, Marsanne, Roussanne, Vermentino, *Macabeu, Terret Blanc, Carignan Blanc, Ugni Blanc, Viognier*

Côtes de la Malepère, VDQS (R) Merlot, Côt, Cabernet Franc, *Cinsaut, Cabernet Sauvignon, Grenache, Lladoner Pelut* (P)

Cinsaut, Grenache, Cabernet Franc, *Merlot, Côt, Cabernet Sauvignon, Syrah*

Côtes de Millau, VDQS (R) Gamay, Syrah, *Cabernet Sauvignon, Fer Servadou, Duras* (P) Gamay, *Syrah, Cabernet Sauvignon, Fer Servadou, Duras* (W) Chenin Blanc, Mauzac

Côtes du Roussillon (R, P) Carignan, Cinsaut, Grenache, Lladoner Pelut Noir, Syrah, Mourvèdre, Macabeu Blanc (W) Grenache Blanc, Macabeu Blanc, Tourbat Blanc (Malvoisie du Roussillon), Marsanne, Roussanne, Vermentino

Côtes du Roussillon-Villages (R) Carignan, Grenache, Lladoner Pelut Noir, Syrah, Mourvèdre, Maccabéo

Faugères (R, P) Carignan, Cinsaut, Grenache, Mourvèdre, Syrah, Lladoner Pelut (W) Grenache Blanc, Marsanne, Roussanne, Vermentino, *Clairette, Bourboulenc, Macabeu, Carignan Blanc*

Fitou (R) Carignan, Grenache, Mourvèdre, Syrah, *Lladoner Pelut, Cinsaut*

Minervois (R, P) Grenache, Syrah, Mourvèdre, Lladoner Pelut, Carignan, Cinsaut, Picpoul Noir, Terret Noir, Aspiran Noir (W) Grenache Blanc, Bourboulenc Blanc (Malvoisie), Maccabeu, Marsanne, Roussanne, Vermentino (Rolle), *Picpoul Blanc, Clairette, Terret Blanc, Muscat Blanc à Petits Grains*

Minervois-La-Livinière (R) Grenache, Syrah, Mourvèdre, *Lladoner Pelut, Carignan, Cinsaut, Picpoul Noir, Terret Noir, Aspiran Noir*

St-Chinian (R, P) Carignan, Cinsaut, Grenache, Lladoner Pelut, Mourvèdre, Syrah

Loire and Central France

Anjou, Rosé d'Anjou, Saumur, Saumur Champigny (R) Cabernet Franc, Cabernet Sauvignon, Pineau d'Aunis (P) Cabernet Franc, Cabernet Sauvignon, Pineau d'Aunis, Gamay, Côt, Groslot (W) Chenin Blanc, *Chardonnay, Sauvignon Blanc*

Anjou Coteaux de la Loire (W) Chenin Blanc

Anjou Mousseux (W, S) Chenin Blanc, *Cabernet Sauvignon, Cabernet Franc, Côt, Gamay, Groslot, Pineau d'Aunis* (P, S) Cabernet Sauvignon, Cabernet Franc, Côt, Gamay, Groslot, Pineau d'Aunis

Anjou-Villages, Anjou-Villages-Brissac (R) Cabernet Sauvignon, Cabernet Franc

Bourgueil, St-Nicolas-de-Bourgueil (R) Cabernet Franc (Breton), *Cabernet Sauvignon*

Bonnezeaux (W) Chenin Blanc

Cabernet d'Anjou, Cabernet de Saumur (P) Cabernet Sauvignon, Cabernet Franc

Châteaumeillant (R, W, P) Gamay, Pinot Gris, Pinot Noir

Cheverny (R) Gamay, Pinot Noir, *Cabernet Franc, Cabernet Sauvignon, Côt* (P) Gamay, Pinot Noir, *Cabernet Franc, Cabernet Sauvignon, Côt, Pineau d'Aunis* (W) Sauvignon Blanc, *Chardonnay, Arbois (Menu Pineau), Chenin Blanc*

Chinon (W) Chenin Blanc (Pineau de la Loire) (R, P) Cabernet Franc (Breton), *Cabernet Sauvignon*

Coteaux d'Ancenis (W) Chenin Blanc, Pinot Gris (Malvoisie) (R, P) Cabernet Sauvignon, Cabernet Franc, Gamay, *Gamay de Chaudenay, Gamay de Bouze*

Coteaux de l'Aubance (W) Chenin Blanc (Pineau de la Loire)

Coteaux du Layon, Coteaux du Layon Chaume (W) Chenin Blanc (Pineau de la Loire)

Coteaux du Loir (W) Chenin Blanc (Pineau de la Loire) (R) Pineau d'Aunis, Cabernet Franc, Cabernet Sauvignon, Gamay, Côt (P) Pineau d'Aunis, Cabernet Franc, Cabernet Sauvignon, Gamay, Côt, Groslot

Coteaux de Saumur (W) Chenin Blanc (Pineau de la Loire)

Coteaux du Vendomois (W) Chenin Blanc, *Chardonnay* (R) Pineau d'Aunis, *Gamay, Pinot Noir, Cabernet Franc, Cabernet Sauvignon* (P) Pineau d'Aunis, *Gamay*

Côtes d'Auvergne (R, P) Gamay, Pinot Noir (W) Chardonnay

Côtes de Gien, Coteaux du Giennois (R, P) Gamay, Pinot Noir (W) Sauvignon Blanc

Cour-Cheverny (W) Romorantin Blanc

Crémant de Loire (W, P, S) Chenin Blanc, Cabernet Franc, Cabernet Sauvignon, Pineau d'Aunis, Pinot Noir, Chardonnay, Menu Pineau, *Grolleau Noir, Grolleau Gris*

Fiefs Vendéens (R, P) Gamay, Pinot Noir, *Cabernet Franc, Cabernet Sauvignon, Négrette, Gamay Chaudenay* (W) Chenin Blanc, *Sauvignon Blanc, Chardonnay*

Gros Plant du Pays Nantais (W) Gros Plant (Folle Blanche)

Haut-Poitou, VDQS (W) Sauvignon Blanc, Chardonnay, Chenin Blanc, Pinot Blanc (R, P) Pinot Noir, Gamay, Merlot, Côt, Cabernet Franc, Cabernet Sauvignon, *Gamay de Chaudenay, Grolleau*

Jasnières (W) Chenin Blanc (Pineau de la Loire)

Menetou-Salon (W) Sauvignon Blanc (R, P) Pinot Noir

Montlouis (W) Chenin Blanc (Pineau de la Loire)

Muscadet, Musacadet-Côtes de Grandlieu, Muscadet-Coteaux de la Loire, Muscadet-Sèvre et Maine (W) Melon

Orléans, VDQS (R) Pinot Meunier, *Pinot Noir* (W) Auvernat Blanc (Chardonnay), *Pinot Gris* (P) Pinot Meunier, *Pinot Noir, Pinot Gris*

Pouilly-Fumé, Blanc Fumé de Pouilly (W) Blanc Fumé (Sauvignon Blanc)

Pouilly-sur-Loire (W) Chasselas, Blanc Fumé (Sauvignon Blanc)

Quarts de Chaume (W) Chenin Blanc (Pineau de la Loire)

Quincy (W) Sauvignon Blanc

Reuilly (W) Sauvignon Blanc (R, P) Pinot Noir, Pinot Gris

Rosé de Loire (P) Cabernet Franc, Cabernet Sauvignon, Pineau d'Aunis, Pinot Noir, Gamay, Grolleau

St-Pourçain (R) Gamay, Pinot Noir, *Gamay Teinturiers* (W) Tressallier, St-Pierre-Doré, Aligoté, Chardonnay, Sauvignon Blanc

Sancerre (W) Sauvignon Blanc (R, P) Pinot Noir

Saumur Mousseux (W, S) Chenin Blanc, Chardonnay, Sauvignon Blanc, Cabernet Franc, Cabernet Sauvignon, Côt, Gamay, Grolleau, Pineau d'Aunis, Pinot Noir (P, S) Cabernet Franc, Cabernet Sauvignon, Côt, Gamay, Grolleau, Pineau d'Aunis, Pinot Noir

Savennières (W) Chenin Blanc (Pineau de la Loire)

Touraine, Touraine Azay-le-Rideau, Touraine Amboise, Touraine Mesland (W) Chenin Blanc (Pineau de la Loire), Arbois (Menu Pineau), Sauvignon Blanc, *Chardonnay* (R) Cabernet Franc (Breton), Cabernet Sauvignon, Côt, Pinot Noir, Pinot Meunier, Pinot Gris, Gamay Noir à Jus Blanc, Pineau d'Aunis (P) Cabernet Franc (Breton), Cabernet Sauvignon, Côt, Pinot Noir, Pinot Meunier, Pinot Gris, Gamay Noir à Jus Blanc, Pineau d'Aunis, Grolleau, *Gamay de Chaudenay, Gamay de Bouze, Gamay à Jus Coloré*

Touraine Mousseux (W, S) Chenin Blanc (Pineau de la Loire), Arbois (Menu Pineau), *Chardonnay, Cabernet Franc (Breton), Cabernet Sauvignon, Pinot Noir, Pinot Meunier, Pinot Gris, Pineau d'Aunis, Côt, Grolleau* (R, S) Cabernet Franc (Breton) (P, S) Breton, Côt, Noble, Gamay, Grolleau

Touraine Noble Joué (P) Pinot Meunier, Pinot Gris, Pinot Noir

Valençay (R, P) Cabernet Franc, Cabernet Sauvignon, Côt, Gamay, Pinot Noir, *Gascon, Pineau d'Aunis, Gamay de Chaudenay, Grolleau* (W) Arbois, Chardonnay, Sauvignon Blanc, *Chenin Blanc, Romorantin*

Vouvray (W) Gros Pinot (Pineau de la Loire, Chenin Blanc), Petit Pinot (Menu Pinot)

Vins du Thouarsais, VDQS (W) Chenin Blanc, *Chardonnay* (R, P) Cabernet Franc, Cabernet Sauvignon, Gamay

Note: Gamay means Gamay Noir à Jus Blanc unless otherwise stated.

Loire fringes

Côte Roannaise (R, P) Gamay

Côtes du Forez (R, P) Gamay

Provence and Corsica

Ajaccio (P) Barbarossa, Nielluccio, Sciacarello, Vermentino Blanc, *Carignan, Cinsaut, Grenache* (W) Ugni Blanc, Vermentino Blanc

Bandol (R) Mourvèdre, Grenache, Cinsaut, *Syrah, Carignan* (P) Mourvèdre, Grenache, Cinsaut, *Syrah, Carignan, Bourboulenc, Clairette, Ugni Blanc* (W) Bourboulenc, Clairette, Ugni Blanc, *Sauvignon Blanc, Marsanne, Sémillon, Vermentino*

Bellet, Vin de Bellet (R) Braquet, Folle Noir (Fuella), Cinsaut, *Grenache, Rolle, Roussanne, Spagnol (Mayorquin), Clairette, Bourboulenc, Chardonnay, Pignerol, Muscat Blanc à Petits Grains* (P) Braquet, Folle Noir (Fuella), Cinsaut, *Grenache, Roussanne, Rolle, Spagnol (Mayorquin), Clairette, Bourboulenc, Pignerol* (W) Rolle, Roussanne, Spagnol (Mayorquin), *Clairette, Bourboulenc, Chardonnay, Pignerol, Muscat Blanc à Petit Grains*

Cassis (R, P) Grenache, Carignan, Mourvèdre, Cinsaut, Barberoux, *Terret, Aramon* (W) Ugni Blanc, Sauvignon Blanc, Doucillon (Bourboulenc), Clairette, Marsanne, Pascal Blanc

Coteaux d'Aix-en-Provence, Les Baux-de-Provence (R, P) Cabernet Sauvignon, Carignan, Cinsaut, Counoise, Grenache, Mourvèdre, Syrah (W) Bourboulenc, Clairette, Grenache Blanc, Sauvignon Blanc, Sémillon, Ugni Blanc, Vermentino Blanc

Coteaux de Pierrevert (R, P) Grenache, Syrah, *Carignan, Cinsaut, Mourvèdre* (W) Grenache Blanc, Vermentino, Ugni Blanc, Clairette, Roussanne, *Marsanne, Picpoul*

Coteaux Varois (R) Grenache, Syrah, Mourvèdre, *Carignan, Cinsaut, Cabernet Sauvignon* (P) Grenache, Cinsaut, *Syrah, Mourvèdre, Carignan, Tibouren* (W) Clairette, Grenache Blanc, Rolle, Sémillon, Ugni Blanc

Muscat du Cap Corse (W) Muscat Blanc à Petits Grains

Palette (R, P) Mourvèdre, Grenache, Cinsaut (Plant d'Arles), *Téoulier (Manosquin), Durif, Muscat Noir de Provence, Muscat de Marseille/d'Aubagne, Muscat de Hamburg, Carignan, Syrah, Castets, Brun Fourca, Terret Gris, Petit-Brun, Tibouren, Cabernet Sauvignon* (W) Clairette à Gros Grains/Clairette à Petits Grains/Clairette de Trans/Clairette Picardan/Clairette Rosé, *Ugni Blanc, Ugni Rosé, Grenache Blanc, Muscat de Frontignan, Pascal, Terret-Bourret, Piquepoul, Aragnan, Colombard, Tokay*

Patrimonio (R, P) Nielluccio, *Grenache, Sciacarello, Vermentino Blanc* (W) Vermentino Blanc, *Ugni Blanc*

Côtes de Provence (R, P) Carignan, Cinsaut, Grenache, Mourvèdre, Tibouren, *Barberoux, Cabernet Sauvignon, Calitor (Pécoui Touar), Clairette, Roussanne du Var, Sémillon, Ugni Blanc, Vermentino Blanc (Rolle)* (W) Clairette, Sémillon, Ugni Blanc, Vermentino Blanc (Rolle)

Vin de Corse (R, P) Nielluccio, Sciacarello, Grenache, *Cinsaut, Mourvèdre, Barbarossa, Syrah, Carignan, Vermentino (Malvoisie de Corse)* (W) Vermentino (Malvoisie de Corse), *Ugni Blanc (Rossola)*

Rhône

Beaumes de Venise (R) Grenache, Syrah (plus a total of up to 20% of the other varieties permitted for Côtes du Rhône)

Châteauneuf-du-Pape (R) Grenache Noir, Cinsaut, Syrah, Mourvèdre, *Picpoul, Terret Noir, Counoise, Muscardin, Picardan, Vaccarèse, Clairette, Roussanne, Bourboulenc* (W) Grenache Blanc, Bourboulenc, Roussanne, *Clairette, Picpoul*

Châtillon-en-Diois (R, P) Gamay, *Syrah, Pinot Noir* (W) Aligoté, Chardonnay

Clairette de Die (S) Muscat Blanc à Petits Grains, *Clairette Blanche*

Condrieu, Château Grillet (W) Viognier

Cornas (R) Syrah

Coteaux de Die (W) Clairette Blanche

Coteaux de Pierrevert, VDQS (R, P) Carignan, Cinsaut, Grenache Noir, Mourvèdre, (Petit) Syrah, *Œillade, Terret Noir* (W) Clairette Blanche, Marsanne, Picpoul Blanc, Roussanne, Ugni Blanc

Côte Rôtie (R) Syrah, *Viognier*

Coteaux du Tricastin (R, P) Grenache Noir, Cinsaut, Mourvèdre, Syrah, Picpoul, *Carignan, Grenache Blanc, Picpoul Blanc, Clairette Blanche, Bourboulenc, Ugni Blanc, Marsanne, Roussanne, Viognier* (W) Grenache Blanc, Picpoul Blanc, Clairette Blanche, Bourboulenc, Ugni Blanc, Marsanne, Roussanne, Viognier

Côtes du Luberon (R, P) Grenache Noir, Syrah, Mourvèdre, Cinsaut, Carignan, *Counoise Noir, Picpoul Noir, Gamay, Pinot Noir* (W) Grenache Blanc, Clairette Blanche, Bourboulenc, Ugni Blanc, Rolle, *Roussanne, Marsanne*

Côtes du Rhône (R, P) Grenache Noir, Syrah, Mourvèdre, *Cinsaut, Terret Noir, Carignan, Counoise, Muscardin, Vaccarèse, Camarèse, Picpoul Noir, Grenache Gris, Clairette Rose* (both red and rosé may include a small percentage of the white grapes allowed in the appellation, see below) (W) Grenache Blanc, Clairette, Marsanne, Roussanne, Bourboulenc, Viognier, *Picpoul, Ugni Blanc*

Côtes du Rhône-Villages (R, P) Grenache Noir, Syrah, Mourvèdre (plus a total of up to 20% of the other varieties permitted for Côtes du Rhône) (W) Grenache Blanc, Clairette, Marsanne, Roussanne, Bourboulenc, Viognier (plus a total of up to 20% of the other varieties permitted for Côtes du Rhône)

Côtes du Ventoux (R, P) Grenache Noir, Syrah, Cinsaut, Mourvèdre, Carignan, *Picpoul Noir, Counoise, Clairette, Bourboulenc, Grenache Blanc, Roussanne* (W) Clairette, Bourboulenc, Grenache Blanc, *Roussanne*

Côtes du Vivarais (R) Grenache Noir, Syrah, *Cinsaut, Carignan* (P) Grenache Noir, Cinsaut, *Syrah* (W) Clairette Blanche, Grenache Blanc, Marsanne

Crémant de Die (S) Clairette, *Muscat Blanc à Petits Grains, Aligoté*

Gigondas (R) Grenache Noir, *Syrah, Mourvèdre* (with the exclusion of Carignan, all the other grapes that go into Côtes du Rhône are also allowed) (P) Grenache Noir (plus a total of up to 20% of the other varieties permitted for Côtes du Rhône)

Haut-Comtat, VDQS (R, P) Grenache, *Carignan, Cinsaut, Mourvèdre, Syrah*

Hermitage, Crozes-Hermitage, St-Joseph (R) Syrah, *Marsanne, Roussanne* (W) Marsanne, Roussanne

Lirac (R, P) Grenache Noir, Cinsaut, Mourvèdre, Syrah, *Carignan* (W) Clairette Blanc, Grenache Blanc, Bourboulenc, *Ugni Blanc, Picpoul, Marsanne, Roussanne, Viognier*

St-Péray (W) Roussanne (Roussette), Marsanne (S) Roussanne (Roussette), Marsanne

Tavel (P) Grenache Noir, Cinsaut, Clairette Blanche, Clairette Rose, Picpoul, Calitor, Bourboulenc, Mourvèdre, Syrah, Carignan

Vacqueyras (R) Grenache Noir, Syrah, Mourvèdre (P) Grenache Noir, *Mourvèdre, Cinsaut* (with the exclusion of Carignan, all the other grapes that go into Côtes du Rhône are also allowed) (W) Grenache Blanc, Clairette Blanc, Bourboulenc, *Marsanne Blanc, Roussanne Blanc, Viognier*

Vinsobres (R) Grenache, Syrah, Mourvèdre, *Carignan, Cinsaut*

Rhône fringes

Coteaux du Lyonnais (R, P) Gamay (W) Chardonnay, Aligoté

Savoie and Bugey

Crépy (W) Chasselas

Vin de Bugey, Bugey followed by a commune name (R, P) Gamay, Pinot Noir, Mondeuse (W) Chardonnay, Aligoté, Altesse, Jacquère, Pinot Gris, Mondeuse Blanche

Bugey Mousseux, Bugey Pétillant (S) Chardonnay, Jacquère, Molette, Aligoté, Altesse, Mondeuse Blanche, Pinot Gris, Gamay, Pinot Noir, Mondeuse, Poulsard

Roussette de Bugey, Roussette de Bugey followed by a commune name (W) Altesse, *Chardonnay* (100% Altesse from 2009)

Bugey-Cerdon (P) Gamay, Poulsard

Note: Varietal labelling is used for all the Bugey appellations where a wine is exclusively from one variety.

Roussette de Savoie, Roussette de Savoie followed by a cru name (W) Roussette

Seyssel, Seyssel Mousseux (W) Roussette (S) Molette, Chasselas, Roussette

Vin de Savoie (P, R) Gamay, Mondeuse, Pinot Noir, *Persan, Cabernet Sauvignon, Cabernet Franc, Persan, Étraire de la Dui, Servanin, Joubertin* (W) Aligoté, Altesse, Jacquère, Chardonnay, Chasselas, Gringet, *Velteliner Rouge, Mondeuse Blanche, Roussette d'Ayze, Verdesse*
Note: Persan, Étraire de la Dui, Servanin, Joubertin, and Verdesse are permitted only in the *département* of Isère. Gringet, Roussette d'Ayze, and Chasselas are permitted only in the *département* of Haute-Savoie.

Vin de Savoie followed by a cru name grape varieties as above except:

Arbin (R) Mondeuse

Ayze (W, S) Gringet, *Altesse, Roussette d'Ayze*

Chignin-Bergeron, Bergeron (W) Roussanne

Marignan, Marin, Ripaille (W) Chasselas

Vin de Savoie Pétillant, Vin de Savoie Mousseux (W) grapes as for white Vin de Savoie plus Gamay, Pinot Noir, Mondeuse, and Molette in Haute-Savoie

South West France

Béarn (R, P) Tannat, Cabernet Franc (Bouchy), Cabernet Sauvignon, Fer (Pinenc), Manseng Noir, Courbu Noir (W) Petit Manseng, Gros Manseng, Courbu, Lauzet, Camaralet, Raffiat, Sauvignon Blanc

Bergerac, Bergerac Sec (W) Sémillon, Sauvignon Blanc, Muscadelle, Ondenc, Chenin Blanc, *Ugni Blanc*

Bergerac, Côtes de Bergerac (R, P) Cabernet Sauvignon, Cabernet Franc, Merlot, *Malbec (Côt), Fer Servadou, Merille (Périgord)*

Blanquette de Limoux Mousseux, Crémant de Limoux (W, S) Mauzac, Chardonnay, Chenin Blanc

Blanquette Méthode Ancestrale Mousseux (W, S) Mauzac

Buzet (R, P) Merlot, Cabernet Sauvignon, Cabernet Franc, Malbec (Côt) (W) Sémillon, Sauvignon Blanc, Muscadelle

Cahors (R) Malbec (Côt), Merlot, Tannat

Côtes du Brulhois, VDQS (R, P) Cabernet Sauvignon, Cabernet Franc, Merlot, Fer, Côt, Tannat

Côtes de Duras (W) Sauvignon Blanc, Sémillon, Muscadelle, Mauzac, Rouchelin (Chenin Blanc), Ondenc, *Ugni Blanc* (R, P) Cabernet Sauvignon, Cabernet Franc, Merlot, Malbec (Côt)

Côtes du Marmandais (R, P) Cabernet Franc, Cabernet Sauvignon, Merlot, *Abouriou, Malbec (Côt), Fer, Gamay, Syrah* (W) Sauvignon Blanc, *Muscadelle, Ugni Blanc, Sémillon*

Côtes de Montravel, Haut-Montravel (W) Sémillon, Sauvignon Blanc, Muscadelle

Côtes de St-Mont, VDQS (R, P) Tannat, *Cabernet Sauvignon, Cabernet Franc, Merlot, Fer* (W) Arrufiac, Clairette, Courbu, *Gros Manseng, Petit Manseng*

Fronton (R, P) Négrette, *Côt, Mérille, Fer, Syrah, Cabernet Franc, Cabernet Sauvignon, Gamay, Cinsaut, Mauzac*

Gaillac (R, P) Duras, Fer Servadou, Gamay, Syrah, *Cabernet Sauvignon, Cabernet Franc, Merlot* (W) Len de L'el, Mauzac Rosé, Muscadelle, Ondenc, Sauvignon Blanc, Sémillon

Gaillac Premières Côtes (W) Len de L'el, Mauzac, Mauzac Rosé, Muscadelle, Ondenc, Sauvignon Blanc, Sémillon

Gaillac Mousseux (doux) (W) Len de L'el, Mauzac, Mauzac Rosé, Muscadelle, Ondenc, Sauvignon Blanc, Sémillon (P) Duras, Fer Servadou, Gamay, Syrah, *Cabernet Sauvignon, Cabernet Franc, Merlot*

Irouléguy (R, P) Cabernet Sauvignon, Cabernet Franc, Tannat (W) Courbu, Manseng

Jurançon, Jurançon Sec (W) Petit Manseng, Gros Manseng, *Courbu, Camaralet, Lauzet*

Lavilledieu, VDQS (R) Négrette, Mauzac, Bordelais, Morterille (Cinsaut), Chalosse (Béquignol), *Syrah, Gamay, Jurançon Noir, Picpoul, Milgranet, Fer* (W) Mauzac, Sauvignon Blanc, Sémillon, Muscadelle, Blanquette, Ondenc, Chalosse Blanche (Claverie)

Limoux (W) Chardonnay

Madiran (R) Tannat, *Cabernet Sauvignon, Cabernet Franc/Bouchy, Fer (Pinenc)*

Marcillac (R, P) Fer Servadou, *Cabernet Sauvignon, Cabernet Franc, Merlot*

Monbazillac, Rosette (W) Sémillon, Sauvignon Blanc, Muscadelle

Montravel (W) Sémillon, Sauvignon Blanc, Muscadelle, Ondenc, Chenin Blanc, *Ugni Blanc*

Pacherenc du Vic Bilh (W) Arrufiac, Courbu, Gros Manseng, Petit Manseng, *Sauvignon Blanc, Sémillon*

Pécharmant (R) Cabernet Sauvignon, Cabernet Franc, Merlot, Malbec (Côt)

Saussignac (W) Sémillon, Sauvignon Blanc, Muscadelle, Chenin Blanc

Tursan, VDQS (R) Tannat, *Cabernet Sauvignon, Fer Servadou (Pinenc)* (P) Tannat, Cabernet Franc, *Cabernet Sauvignon, Fer Servadou* (W) Baroque, *Sauvignon Blanc, Petit Manseng, Gros Manseng, Cruchinet (Chenin Blanc)*

Vins d'Entraygues et du Fel, VDQS (R, P) Cabernet Franc, Cabernet Sauvignon, Fer, Gamay Noir à Jus Blanc, Jurançon Noir, Mouyssaguès, Négrette, Pinot Noir (W) Chenin Blanc, Mauzac

Vins d'Estaing, VDQS (R, P) Fer Servadou, Gamay Noir à Jus Blanc, Jurançon Noir, Abouriou, Merlot, Cabernet Franc, Cabernet Sauvignon, Mouyssaguès, Négrette, Pinot Noir, Duras, Castets (W) Chenin Blanc, Roussellou (St-Pierre Doré), Mauzac

GREECE

Amyndeo (R) Xynomavro

Ankhíalos (W) Roditis, *Savatiano*

Archanes (R) Kotsifali, Mandelaria

Daphnes (R) Liatiko

Goumenissa (R) Xynomavro, *Negoska*

Limnos (W) Muscat of Alexandria

Mantinia (W) Moscophilero

Côtes de Meliton (R) Limnio, Cabernet Sauvignon, Cabernet Franc (W) Athiri, Roditis, Assyrtiko, *Sauvignon Blanc, Ugni Blanc*

Náoussa (R) Xynomavro

Neméa (R) Aghiorghitiko

Paros (R) Monemvassia (Malvaria), *Mandelaria*

Pátras (W) Roditis

Peza (R) Kotsifali, Mandelaria (W) Vilana

Rapsani (R) Xynomavro, Krassato, Stavroto

Rhodes (R) Mandelaria (W) Athiri

Sámos (W) Muscat Blanc à Petits Grains

Santorini, Santorini Vissanto (W) Assyrtiko, *Athiri, Aidini*

Siteaia (R) Liatiko

Zitsa (W) Debina

HUNGARY

Egri Bikavér (Bulls Blood of Eger) (R) Kékfrankos, Kadarka, Blauburger, Portugieser, Zweigelt, Kékmedoc, Cabernet Sauvignon, Merlot, Cabernet Franc, Pinot Noir

Tokaji (W) Furmint, Hárslevelű, Muscat Blanc à Petits Grains (Sárga Muskotály), Zéta, Kövérszőlő

Tokaji Muskotály Aszú (Muscat Aszú) (W) Muscat Blanc à Petits Grains (Sárga Muskotály)

ITALY

Abruzzo
All DOC and DOCG wines are varietal.

Basilicata
Terre dell'Alta Val d'Agri (R) Merlot, Cabernet Sauvignon, other local red varieties (P) Merlot, Cabernet Sauvignon, Malvasia di Basilicata, other local varieties

Other DOCs are varietal.

Calabria
Bivongi (R, P) Gaglioppo, Greco Nero, Nocera, Nero d'Avola, Castiglione (W) Greco Bianco, Guardavalle, Montonico Bianca, Malvasia Bianca, Ansonica

Cirò (P, R) Gaglioppo, *Trebbiano Toscano, Greco Bianco* (W) Greco Bianco, *Trebbiano Toscano*

Donnici (P, R) Gaglioppo (Montonico Nero), *Greco Nero, Malvasia Bianco, Pecorello, Greco Bianco* (W) Montonico Bianco, Greco Bianco, Malvasia Blanca, Pecorello

Lamezia (W) Greco Bianco, Trebbiano, Malvasia (P, R) Nerello Mascalese, Nerello Cappuccio, Gaglioppo, Magliocco, Greco Nero, Marsigliana

Melissa (W) Greco Bianco, Trebbiano Toscano, Malvasia Bianca (R) Gaglioppo, Greco Nero, Greco Bianco, Trebbiano Toscano, Malvasia

Pollino (R) Gaglioppo, Greco Nero, Malvasia Bianca, Montonico Bianco, Guarnaccia Bianca

Sant'Anna di Isola Capo Rizzuto (R, P) Gaglioppo, Nerello Mascalese, Nerello Cappuccio, Malvasia Nera, *Nocera*

San Vito di Luzzi (W) Malvasia Bianca, Greco Bianco, Trebbiano Toscano (R, P) Gaglioppo, *Malvasia, Greco Nero, Sangiovese*

Savuto (R, P) Gaglioppo, Greco Nero, Nerello Cappuccio, Magliocco Canino, *Sangiovese, Malvasia Bianca, Pecorino*

Scavigna (W) Trebbiano Toscano, Chardonnay, Greco Bianco, *Malvasia* (P, R) Gaglioppo, Nerello Cappuccio, Aglianico

Verbicaro (R, P) Gaglioppo (Guarnaccia Nera), Greco Nero, Malvasia Bianca, Guarnaccia Bianca, Greco Bianco (W) Greco Bianco, Malvasia Bianca, Guarnaccia Bianca

Campania
Aversa (W, S) Asprinio

Campi Flegrei (W) Falanghina, Biancolella, Coda di Volpe (R) Piedirosso, Aglianico, Sciascinoso

Capri (W) Falanghina, Greco, *Biancolella* (R) Piedirosso

Castel San Lorenzo (R, P) Barbera, Sangiovese (W) Trebbiano Toscano, Malvasia Bianca

Cilento (R) Aglianico, Piedirosso, Primitivo, Barbera (P) Sangiovese, Aglianico, Primitivo, Piedirosso (W) Fiano, Trebbiano Toscano, Greco Bianco, Malvasia Bianca

Costa d'Amalfi (R, P) Piedirosso, Sciascinoso, Aglianico (W) Falanghina, Biancolella

Falerno del Massico (W) Falanghina (R) Aglianico, Piedirosso, *Primitivo, Barbera*

Gallucio (W) Falanghina (R, P) Aglianico

Guardia Sanframondi/Guardiolo (W) Malvasia di Candia, Falanghina (R, P) Sangiovese (S) Falanghina

Ischia (W) Forastera Bianco, Biancolella (R) Guarnaccia, Piedirosso (Per'e Palumno)

Penisola Sorrentina (W) Falanghina, Biancolella, Greco (R) Piedirosso, Sciascinoso, Aglianico

Sannio (R, P) Sangiovese (W) Trebbiano Toscano

Sant'Agata dei Goti (R, P) Aglianico, Piedirosso (W) Falanghina, Greco

Solopaca (W) Trebbiano Toscano, Falanghina, Malvasia Toscana, Malvasia di Candia, Coda di Volpe (R, P) Sangiovese, Aglianico, Piedirosso, Sciascinoso (S) Falanghina

Taburno (W) Trebbiano Toscano, Falanghina (R) Sangiovese, Aglianico (S) Coda di Volpe, Falanghina

Taurasi, DOCG (R) Aglianico

Vesuvio (W) Coda di Volpe (Caprettone or Crapettone), Verdeca, Falanghina, Greco (R, P) Piedirosso (Palombina), Sciascinoso (Oliveila), *Aglianico*

Emilia-Romagna

Bosco Eliceo (W) Trebbiano Romagnolo, Sauvignon Blanc, Malvasia di Candia

Bosco Eliceo Sauvignon (W) Sauvignon Blanc, *Trebbiano Romagnolo*

Cagnina di Romagna (R) Refosco (Terrano)

Colli Bolognesi (W) Albana, Trebbiano Romagnolo

Colli della Romagna Centrale (W) Chardonnay, Bombino, Sauvignon Blanc, Trebbiano, Pinot Bianco (R) Cabernet Sauvignon, Sangiovese, Barbera, Merlot, Montepulciano

Colli di Faenza (W) Chardonnay, Pignoletto, Pinot Bianco, Sauvignon Blanc, Trebbiano Romagnolo (R) Cabernet Sauvignon, Ancellotta, Ciliegiolo, Merlot, Sangiovese

Colli di Parma (R) Barbera, Bonarda Piemontese, Croatina (S) Chardonnay, Pinot Nero, Pinot Bianco

Colli di Rimini (W) Trebbiano Romagnolo, Biancame, Mostosa (R) Sangiovese, Cabernet Sauvignon, Merlot, Barbera, Montepulciano, Ciliegiolo, Terrano, Ancellotta

Colli di Scandiano e Canossa (W) Sauvignon Blanc, Malvasia di Candia, Trebbiano Romagnolo, Pinot Bianco, Pinot Grigio

Colli d'Imola (W) one or more non-aromatic local white varieties (R) one or more non-aromatic local red varieties

Colli Piacentini Gutturnio (R) Barbera, Croatina (Bonarda)

Colli Piacentini Monterosso Val d'Arda (W) Malvasia di Candida Aromatica, Moscato Bianco, Trebbiano Romagnolo, Ortrugo, *Beverdino, Sauvignon Blanc*

Colli Piacentini Trebbianino Val Trebbia (W) Ortrugo, Malvasia di Candida Aromatica, Moscato Bianco, Trebbiano Romagnolo, Sauvignon Blanc

Colli Piacentini Valnure (W) Malvasia di Candida, Trebbiano Romagnolo, Ortrugo

Lambrusco di Sorbara (R, P) Lambrusco di Sorbara, Lambrusco Salamino

Lambrusco Grasparossa di Castelvetro (R, P) Lambrusco Grasparossa, *Fortana (Uva d'Oro)*

Pagadebit di Romagna (W) Bombino Bianco

Friuli-Venezia Giulia

Carso (R) Terrano, *Piccola Nera, Pinot Noir*

Collio Goriziano/Collio (W) one or more local white varieties (R) one or more local red varieties

Colli Orientali del Friuli (W) one or more local white varieties (R, P) one or more local red varieties

Friuli Annia (W) one or more local white varieties (R, P) one or more local red varieties

Friuli Aquileia (P) Merlot (R) one or more local red varieties

Grave Friuli (W) one or more non-aromatic local white varieties (R, P) one or more non-aromatic local red varieties

Friuli Isonzo (W) one or more non-aromatic local white varieties (R, P) one or more non-aromatic local red varieties

Friuli Isonzo Vendemmia Tardiva (W) Tocai Friulano, Sauvignon Blanc, Verduzzo Friulano, Pinot Bianco, Chardonnay

Friuli Latisana (P) Merlot, Cabernet Franc, Cabernet Sauvignon, Refosco Nostrano, Refosco dal Peduncolo Rosso (W, S) Chardonnay, Pinot Bianco, Pinot Nero

Ramandolo, DOCG (W) Verduzzo Friulano

Lazio

Atina (R) Cabernet Sauvignon, Syrah, Merlot, Cabernet Franc

Bianco Capena (W) Trebbiano, Malvasia di Candia, Trebbiano, *Bellone, Bombino*

Castelli Romani (R) Cesanese, Merlot, Montepulciano, Nero Buono, Sangiovese (R) one or more local red varieties (W) Malvasia, Trebbiano

Cerveteri (W) Trebbiano, Malvasia, *Verdicchio, Tocai, Bellone, Bombino* (R) Sangiovese, Montepulciano, Cesanese, Canaiolo Nero, Carignano, Barbera

Circeo (W) Trebbiano Toscano, Malvasia di Candia, other local white varieties (R, P) Merlot, other local red varieties

Colli Albani (W, S) Malvasia, Trebbiano

Colli della Sabina (W) Trebbiano Toscano, Malvasia, other local white varieties (R, P) Sangiovese, Montepulciano, other local red varieties

Colli Etruschi Viterbesi (W) Trebbiano Toscano (Procanico), Malvasia, other local white varieties (R, P) Sangiovese, Montepulciano, other local red varieties

Colli Lanuvini (W) Malvasia, Trebbiano

Cori (W) Malvasia, Trebbiano, Bellone (R) Montepulciano, Nero Buono di Cori, Cesanese

Est! Est!! Est!!! di Montefiascone (W, S) Malvasia, Trebbiano

Frascati (W, S) Malvasia, Trebbiano, *Greco*

Genazzano (W) Malvasia, Bellone, Bombino, Trebbiano, Pinot Bianco (R) Sangiovese, Cesanese

Marino (W, S) Malvasia, Trebbiano

Montecompatri Colonna (W) Malvasia, Trebbiano, *Bellone, Bonvino*

Nettuno (W) Bellone, Cacchione, Trebbiano Toscano (R) Merlot, Sangiovese (P) Sangiovese, Trebbiano Toscano

Tarquinia (W) Trebbiano, Malvasia (R, P) Sangiovese, Montepulciano, Cesanese Comune

Velletri (W) Malvasia, Trebbiano, *Bellone, Bombino* (R) Sangiovese, Montepulciano, Cesanese, *Bombino Nero, Merlot, Ciliegiolo*

Vignanello (W) Malvasia, Trebbiano (R, P) Sangiovese, Ciliegiolo

Zagarolo (W) Malvasia, Trebbiano, *Bellone, Bonvino*

Liguria

Cinque Terre, Cinq Terre Sciacchetrà (W) Bosco, Albarola, Vermentino

Colli di Luni (R) Sangiovese, Canaiolo, Pollera Nera, Ciliegiolo Nero (W) Vermentino, Trebbiano Toscano

Colline di Levanto (W) Vermentino, Albarola, Bosco, other local white varieties (R) Sangiovese, Ciliegiolo, other local red varieties

Golfo del Tigullio (W) Vermentino, Bianchetta Genovese, other local non-aromatic white varieties (R, P) Ciliegiolo, Dolcetto, other local non-aromatic red varieties

Val Polcevera (W, S) Vermentino, Bianchetta Genovese, Albarola, Pigato, Rollo, Bosco (R, P) Dolcetto, Sangiovese, Ciliegiolo, Barbera

Lombardia

Botticino (R) Barbera, Schiava Gentile, Marzemino, *Sangiovese*

Capriano del Colle (R) Sangiovese, Marzemino, Barbera, *Merlot, Incrocio Terzi No. 1*

Cellatica (R) Schiava Gentile, Barbera, Marzemino, *Incrocio Terzi No. 1*

Garda (W) Riesling, Riesling Italico (R, P) Groppello, Marzemino, Sangiovese, Barbera (S) Garganega, Chardonnay

Garda Colli Mantovani (R) Cabernet, Merlot, Rondinella, *Negrara, Sangiovese, Rossanella (Molinara)* (R) Merlot, Rondinella, Cabernet, Sangiovese, Molinara, Negrara Trentina (W) Garganega, Trebbiano, Chardonnay, Sauvignon, Riesling Renano, Riesling Italico

Franciacorta, DOCG (WS) Chardonnay, Pinot Bianco, Pinot Nero (PS) Pinot Nero, Chardonnay, Pinot Bianco

Lambrusco Mantovano (R) Lambrusco Viadanese, Lambrusco Maestri, Lambrusco Marani, Lambrusco Salamino, *Ancellotta, Fortana, Uva d'Oro*

Lugana (W) Trebbiano di Lugana

Oltrepò Pavese (R, P) Barbera, Croatina, Uva Rara, Ughetta (Vespolina), Pinot Nero (S) Pinot Nero, Chardonnay, Pinot Grigio, Pinot Bianco

Riviera del Garda Bresciano (W) Riesling Italico, Riesling Renano (R, P) Groppello Gentile, Mocasina, S. Stefano, Sangiovese, Barbera, Marzemino (P) Groppello

San Colombano al Lambro (R) Croatina, Barbera, Uva Rara (W) Chardonnay, Pinot Nero

San Martino della Battaglia (W) Tocai Friulano

Sforzato di Valtellina, DOCG (R) Nebbiolo (Chiavennasca)

Terre di Franciacorta (R) Cabernet Sauvignon, Cabernet Franc, Barbera, Nebbiolo, Merlot (W) Pinot Bianco, Chardonnay (S) Pinot Bianco, Chardonnay, Pinot Nero

Valcalepio (R) Merlot, Cabernet Sauvignon (W) Pinot Bianco, Chardonnay, Pinot Grigio

Valtellina Rosso (R) Chiavennasca, *Pinot Nero, Merlot, Rossola, Pignola Valtellinese*

Valtellina Superiore, DOCG (R) Nebbiolo (Chiavennasca)

Marche

Colli Maceratesi (W, S) Maceratino, Trebbiano Toscano, Verdicchio, Malvasia Toscana, Chardonnay, Sauvignon, Incrocio Bruni 54, Pecorino, Grechetto (R) Sangiovese, Cabernet Franc, Cabernet Sauvignon, Ciliegiolo, Lacrima, Merlot, Montepulciano, Vernaccia Nera

Colli Pesaresi (R, P) Sangiovese (W) Trebbiano, Verdicchio, Biancame, Pinot Grigio, Pinot Nero, Riesling Italico, Chardonnay, Sauvignon, Pinot Bianco

Conero, DOCG (R) Montepulciano, Sangiovese

Esino (R) Montepulciano, Sangiovese (W) Verdicchio, other local white varieties

Falerio dei Colli Ascolani, Falerio (W) Trebbiano, Passerina, Pecorino, Verdicchio, Malvasia Toscana

Focara Rosso (R) Sangiovese, Pinot Nero, Cabernet Sauvignon, Cabernet Franc, Merlot

Lacrima di Morro d'Alba (R) Lacrima, Montepulciano, Verdicchio

Offida (R) Montepulciano, Cabernet Sauvignon

Roncaglia Bianco (W) Trebbiano, Pinot Nero

Rosso Conero (R) Montepulciano, *Sangiovese*

Rosso Piceno (R) Montepulciano, Sangiovese

Serrapetrona, DOCG (R) Vernaccia Nera

Terreni di San Severino (R) Vernaccia Nera, other local red varieties

Molise

Biferno (R, P) Montepulciano, Trebbiano, Aglianico (W) Trebbiano Toscano, Bombino Bianco, Malvasia

Pentro di Isernia, Pentro (W) Trebbiano Bianco, Bombino Bianco (R, P) Montepulciano, Sangiovese, other local red varieties

Piemonte

Albugnano (R) Nebbiolo, Freisa, Barbera, Bonarda

Alta Langa (R) Pinot Nero, Chardonnay

Acqui, Brachetto d'Acqui, DOCG (R, S) Brachetto

Asti, DOCG (W, S) Moscato

Barbaresco, DOCG (R) Nebbiolo Michet, Nebbiolo Lampia, Nebbiolo Rosé

Barbera d'Asti, Barbera del Monferrato (R) Barbera, *Freisa, Grignolino, Dolcetto*

Barolo, DOCG (R) Nebbiolo Michet, Nebbiolo Lampia, Nebbiolo Rosé

Boca (R) Nebbiolo (Spanna), Vespolina, Bonarda Novarese

Bramaterra (R) Nebbiolo (Spanna), Croatina, Vespolina, Bonarda

Canavese (R, P) Nebbiolo, Barbera, Bonarda, Freisa, Neretto (W) Erbaluce

Carema (R) Nebbiolo

Cisterna d'Asti (R, S) Croatina

Colli Tortonesi (R) one or more local non-aromatic red varieties (W) one or more local non-aromatic white varieties

Collina Torinese (R) Barbera, Freisa

Colline Novaresi (R) Nebbiolo, Uva Rara, Vespolina, Croatina (W) Erbaluce

Colline Saluzzesi (R) Pelaverga, Nebbiolo, Barbera

Coste della Sesia (R, P) Nebbiolo, Bonarda, Vespolina, Croatina, Barbera (W) Erbaluce

Fara (R) Nebbiolo (Spanna), *Vespolina, Bonarda Novarese (Uva Rara)*

Gabiano (R) Barbera, Freisa, Grignolino

Gattinara, DOCG (R) Nebbiolo (Spanna), *Bonarda di Gattinara, Vespolina*

Gavi, Cortese di Gavi, DOCG (W) Cortese

Ghemme, DOCG (R) Nebbiolo (Spanna), *Vespolina, Bonarda Novarese (Uva Rara)*

Lessona (R) Nebbiolo (Spanna), *Vespolina, Bonarda*

Loazzolo (W) Moscato

Monferrato Ciaret/Chiaretto (R) Barbera, Bonarda, Cabernet Franc, Cabernet Sauvignon, Dolcetto, Freisa, Grignolino, Pinot Nero, Nebbiolo

Piemonte Spumante (S) Chardonnay, Pinot Bianco, Pinot Grigio, Pinot Nero

Pinerolese (R, P) Nebbiolo (Spanna), Vespolina, Bonarda Novarese (Uva Rara)

Roero, DOCG (R) Nebbiolo, *Arneis* (W) Arneis

Rubino di Cantavenna (R) Barbera, *Grignolino, Freisa*

Ruchè di Castagnole Monferrato (R) Ruchè, *Barbera, Brachetto*

Sizzano (R) Nebbiolo, *Vespolina, Bonarda Novarese (Uva Rara)*

Valsusa (R) Avanà, Barbera, Dolcetto, Neretta Cuneese

Puglia

Alezio (R, P) Negroamaro, *Malvasia Nera, Sangiovese, Montepulciano*

Brindisi (R, P) Negroamaro, *Susumaniello, Malvasia Nera, Sangiovese, Montepulciano*

Cacc'e Mmitte di Lucera (R) Montepulciano, Uva di Troia, Sangiovese, Malvasia Nera, Trebbiano Toscano, Bombino Bianco, Malvasia del Chianti

Castel del Monte (W) Pampanuto (Pampanino), Chardonnay, Bombino Bianco (R) Uva di Troia, Sangiovese, Aglianico, Montepulciano, Pinot Nero (P) Bombino Nero, Aglianico, Uva di Troia, Montepulciano, Pinot Nero

Copertino (R, P) Negroamaro, *Malvasia Nera di Brindisi, Malvasia Nera di Lecce, Sangiovese, Montepulciano*

Galatina (R, P) Negroamaro (W) Chardonnay

Gioia del Colle (R, P) Primitivo, Montepulciano, Sangiovese, Negroamaro, Malvasia Nera (W) Trebbiano Toscano

Gravina (W) Malvasia del Chianti, Greco di Tufo, Bianco d'Alessano, *Bombino Bianco, Trebbiano Toscano, Verdeca*

Leverano (P, R) Negroamaro, Malvasia Nera di Lecce, Sangiovese, Montepulciano (W) Malvasia Bianca, *Bombino Bianco, Trebbiano Toscano*

Lizzano (P, R) Negroamaro, Bombino Nero, Pinot Nero, Sangiovese, Montepulciano, *Malvasia Nera di Lecce, Malvasia Nera* (W) Trebbiano Toscano, Chardonnay, Pinot Bianco, *Malvasia Lunga Bianca (Malvasia), Sauvignon Blanc, Bianco d'Alessano*

Locorotondo (W) Verdeca, Bianco d'Alessano, *Fiano, Bombino, Malvasia Toscana*

Martina, Martina Franca (W, S) Verdeca, Bianco d'Alessano, *Fiano, Bombino, Malvasia Toscano*

Matino (P) Negroamaro, *Malvasia Nera, Sangiovese*

Nardò (P, R) Negroamaro, *Malvasia Nera di Brindisi, Malvasia Nera di Lecce, Montepulciano*

Orta Nova (P, R) Sangiovese, *Uva di Troia, Montepulciano, Lambrusco Maestri, Trebbiano Toscano*

Ostuni (W) Impigno, Francavilla, *Bianco d'Alessano, Verdeca*

Rosso Barletta (R) Uva di Troia, Montepulciano, Sangiovese, *Malbec*

Rosso Canosa (R) Uva di Troia, *Montepulciano, Sangiovese*

Rosso di Cerignola (R) Uva di Troia, Negroamaro, *Sangiovese, Barbera, Montepulciano, Malbec, Trebbiano Toscano*

Salice Salentino (P, R) Negroamaro, *Malvasia Nera di Lecce, Malvasia Nera di Brindisi* (W) Chardonnnay

San Severo (W) Bombino Bianco, Trebbiano Toscano, Malvasia del Chianti, Verdeca (P, R) Montepulciano, Sangiovese

Squinzano (P, R) Negroamaro, Malvasia Nera di Brindisi, Malvasia Nera di Lecce, Sangiovese

Sardegna

Alghero (R, P) one or more local non-aromatic red varieties (W) one or more local non-aromatic white varieties

Campidano di Terralba, Terralba (R) Bovale Sardo, Bovale di Spagna, *Pascal di Cagliari, Greco (Greco Nieddu), Monica*

Mandrolisai (P, R) Bovale Sardo, Cannonau, Monica

Sicilia

Alcamo (W) Catarratto Bianco Comune, Catarratto Bianco Lucido, *Damaschino, Grecanico, Trebbiano Toscano* (R) Calabrese, Nero d'Avola, Sangiovese, Frappato, Perricone, Cabernet Sauvignon, Merlot, Syrah (P) Nerello Mascalese, Calabrese, Nero d'Avola, Sangiovese, Frappato, Perricone, Cabernet Sauvignon, Merlot, Syrah

Cerasuolo di Vittoria (R) Frappato, Calabrese, *Grosso Nero, Nerello Mascalese*

Contea di Sclafani (W) Catarratto, Insolia, Grecanico (R) Nero d'Avola, Perricone (P) Nerello Mascalese

Contessa Entellina (W) Ansonica, *Catarratto Bianco Lucido, Grecanico Dorato, Chardonnay, Sauvignon Blanc, Müller Thurgau, Pinot Bianco, Grillo* (R, P) Calabrese, Syrah

Delia Nivolelli (W) Grecanico, Inzolia, Grillo (R) Nero d'Avola, Pignatello, Perricone, Merlot, Cabernet Sauvignon, Syrah, Sangiovese (S) Grecanico, Chardonnay, Inzolia, Damaschino, Grillo

Eloro (P, R) Nero d'Avola, Frappato, Pignatello

Erice (W) Catarratto (R) Calabrese, Nero d'Avola

Etna (W) Carricante, Catarratto Bianco Comune, Catarratto Bianco Lucido, *Trebbiano, Minnella Bianca* (P, R) Nerello Mascalese, Nerello Mantellato (Nerello Cappuccio)

Faro (R) Nerello Mascalese, Nerello Cappuccio, *Calabrese, Gaglioppo, Sangiovese, Nocera*

Mamertino di Milazzo (W) Grillo, Ansonica, Inzolia, Catarratto (R) Calabrese, Nero d'Avola, Nocera

Marsala (Oro, Ambra) Grillo, Catarratto, Ansonica, Damaschino (Rubino) Perricone, Calabrese, Nerello Mascalese

Menfi (W) Inzolia, Chardonnay, Catarratto Bianco Lucido, Grecanico (R) Nero d'Avola, Sangiovese, Merlot, Cabernet Sauvignon, Syrah

Monreale (W) Catarratto, Ansonica, Inzolia (R) Calabrese, Nero d'Avola, Perricone

Riesi (W) Ansonica, Chardonnay (R) Calabrese, Cabernet Sauvignon (P) Calabrese, Nerello Mascalese, Cabernet Sauvignon

Sambuca di Sicilia (W) Ansonica (R, P) Nero d'Avola

Santa Margherita di Belice (W) Ansonica, Grecanico, Catarratto Bianco Lucido (R) Nero d'Avola, Sangiovese, Cabernet Sauvignon

Toscana

Bianco della Valdinievole (W) Trebbiano Toscano, Malvasia del Chianti, Canaiolo Bianco, Vermentino

Bianco dell'Empolese (W) Trebbiano Toscano

Bianco di Pitigliano (W) Trebbiano Toscano, Greco, Malvasia Toscana, Verdello, Grechetto, *Chardonnay, Sauvignon Blanc, Pinot Bianco, Riesling Italico*

Bianco Pisano di San Torpe (W) Trebbiano

Bianco Vergine Valdichiana (W) Trebbiano

Bolgheri (W) Trebbiano, Vermentino, Sauvignon Blanc (R, P) Cabernet Sauvignon, Merlot, Sangiovese

Candia dei Colli Apuani (W) Vermentino, Albarola

Carmignano (R) Sangiovese, Canaiolo Nero, Cabernet Franc, Cabernet Sauvignon, Trebbiano Toscano, Canaiolo Bianco, Malvasia del Chianti

Carmignano, Barco Reale di Carmignano (R) Sangiovese, Canaiolo Nero, *Cabernet Franc, Cabernet Sauvignon, Trebbiano Toscano, Canaiolo Bianco, Malvasia*

Chianti (R) Sangiovese, Canaiolo Nero, Trebbiano, Malvasia del Chianti

Colli dell'Etruria Centrale (R) Sangiovese, *Canaiolo Nero, Trebbiano, Malvasia, Cabernet Franc, Cabernet Sauvignon, Merlot* (W) Trebbiano Toscano, *Malvasia del Chianti, Pinot Bianco, Pinot Grigio, Chardonnay, Sauvignon Blanc*

Colline Lucchese (R) Sangiovese, Canaiolo, Ciliegiolo, Colorino, Trebbiano, Vermentino (W) Trebbiano Toscano, Greco, Grechetto, Vermentino Bianco, Malvasia

Elba (W) Trebbiano (Procanico) (R) Sangiovese (Sangioveto)

Montecarlo (W) Trebbiano, Sémillon, Pinot Grigio, Pinot Bianco, Vermentino, Sauvignon Blanc, Roussanne (R) Sangiovese, Canaiolo Nero, Ciliegiolo, Colorino, Malvasia Nera, Syrah, Cabernet Franc, Cabernet Sauvignon, Merlot

Monteregio di Massa Marittima (R) Sangiovese (W) Trebbiano, Vermentino, Malvasia, Ansonica

Montescudaio (W) Trebbiano, Vermentino, Malvasia (R) Sangiovese, Trebbiano Toscano, Malvasia

Parrina (R, P) Sangiovese (W) Trebbiano, Ansonica, Chardonnay

Pomino (R) Sangiovese, Canaiolo, Cabernet Sauvignon, Cabernet Franc, Merlot (W) Pinot Bianco, Chardonnay, Trebbiano

Rosso di Montalcino (R) Sangiovese

Rosso di Montepulciano (R) Sangiovese, Canaiolo Nero

Sassicaia (R) Cabernet Sauvignon

Val d'Arbia (W) Trebbiano, Malvasia, Chardonnay

Val di Cornia (W) Trebbiano, Vermentino, *Malvasia, Ansonica, Biancame, Clairette, Pinot Bianco, Pinot Grigio* (R) Sangiovese, *Canaiolo, Ciliegiolo, Cabernet Sauvignon, Merlot*

Vino Nobile di Montepulciano (R) Sangiovese, Canaiolo Nero

Vino Santo Occhio di Pernice (P) Sangiovese, Merlot

Trentino-Alto Adige

Caldaro/Lago di Caldaro (R) Schiava, Pinot Nero, Lagrein

Casteller (R) Schiava, Merlot, Lambrusco, Lagrein, Teroldego

Klausner Leitacher (R) Schiava, *Portoghese, Lagrein*

Sorni (R) Schiava, Teroldego, Lagrein (W) Nosiola, Müller-Thurgau, Sylvaner, Pinot Bianco

Trentino (W) Chardonnay, Pinot Bianco, *Sauvignon Blanc, Müller-Thurgau, Manzoni Bianco* (R) Cabernet Franc, Cabernet Sauvignon, Merlot (Vin Santo) Nosiola

Trento (WS, PS) Chardonnay, Pinot Bianco, Pinot Nero, Pinot Meunier

Valdadige (W) Trebbiano Toscano, Nosiola, Sauvignon, Garganega, Pinot Bianco, Pinot Grigio, Riesling Italico, Chardonnay, Müller-Thurgau (R, P) Lambrusco a Foglia Frastagliata (Enantio), Schiava, Merlot, Pinot Nero, Lagrein, Teroldego, Cabernet Franc, Cabernet Sauvignon

Umbria

Assisi (W) Trebbiano, Grechetto (R, P) Sangiovese, Merlot

Colli Altotiberini (W) Trebbiano Toscano, Malvasia del Chianti (R) Sangiovese, Merlot, Trebbiano Toscano, Malvasia del Chianti Nero

Colli Amerini (W) Trebbiano Toscano, Grechetto, Verdello, Garganega, Malvasia Toscano (R) Sangiovese, Montepulciano, Ciliegiolo, Canaiolo, Merlot, Barbera

Colli del Trasimeno (R) Sangiovese, Ciliegiolo, Gamay, Merlot, Cabernet (W) Trebbiano Toscana, Grechetto, Chardonnay, Pinot Bianco, Pinot Grigio

Colli Perugini (R, P) Sangiovese, *Montepulciano, Ciliegiolo, Barbera, Merlot* (W) Trebbiano Toscano, *Verdicchio, Grechetto, Garganega,*

Malvasia del Chianti (S) Grechetto, Chardonnay, Pinot Bianco, Pinot Nero, Pinot Grigio

Lago di Corbara (R) Cabernet Sauvignon, Merlot, Pinot Nero, Sangiovese, *Aleatico, Barbera, Cabernet Franc, Canaiolo, Cesanese, Ciliegiolo, Colorino, Dolcetto, Montepulciano*

Montefalco (W) Grechetto, Trebbiano Toscano (R) Sangiovese, Sagrantino

Orvieto (W) Trebbiano Toscano (Procanico), Verdello, Grechetto, Canaiolo Bianco (Drupeggio), Malvasia Toscana

Rosso Orvietano (R) Aleatico, Cabernet Franc, Cabernet Sauvignon, Canaiolo, Ciliegiolo, Merlot, Montepulciano, Pinot Nero, Sangiovese, *Barbera, Cesanese Comune, Colorino, Dolcetto*

Torgiano (W) Trebbiano Toscano, Grechetto (R) Sangiovese, Canaiolo, *Trebbiano Toscano, Ciliegiolo, Montepulciano* (S) Chardonnay, Pinot Nero

Torgiano Riserva, DOCG (R) Sangiovese, Canaiolo, *Trebbiano Toscano, Ciliegiolo, Montepulciano*

Valle d'Aosta

Arnad-Montjovet (R) Nebbiolo, *Dolcetto, Vien de Nus, Pinot Nero, Neyret, Freisa*

Chambave (R) Petit Rouge, *Dolcetto, Gamay, Pinot Nero* (W) Moscato

Donnaz (R) Nebbiolo (Picutener), Freisa, Neyret

Enfer d'Arvier (R) Petit Rouge, Vien de Nus, Neyret, Dolcetto, Pinot Nero, Gamay

Nus (R) Vien de Nus, Petit Rouge, Pinot Nero (W) Malvoisie

Torrette (R) Petit Rouge, *Gamay, Pinot Nero, Fumin, Vien de Nus, Dolcetto, Mayolet, Premetta*

Valle d'Aosta (W) Müller-Thurgau, Pinot Grigio, Petite Arvine, Chardonnay, Blanc de Morgex (R) Petit Rouge, Chambave, Dolcetto, Gamay, Pinot Nero, *Premetta*, Fumin

Veneto

Arcole (R) Merlot (W, S) Garganega

Bagnoli di Sopra/Bagnoli (R) Cabernet Franc, Cabernet Sauvignon, Carmenère, Raboso Piave, Raboso Veronese, Merlot (P) Raboso Piave, Raboso Veronese, Merlot (W) Chardonnay, Sauvignon, Tocai Friulano, Raboso Piave, Raboso Veronese (WS, PS) Raboso Piave, Raboso Veronese, Chardonnay

Bardolino (R) Corvina, Rondinella, Molinara, Negrara, *Rossignola, Barbera, Sangiovese, Garganega*

Bardolini Superiore, DOCG (R) Corvina Veronese, Rondinella, Molinara, Rossignola, Barbera, Sangiovese, Marzemino, Merlot, Cabernet Sauvignon

Bianco di Custoza (W) Trebbiano Toscano, Garganega, Tocai Friulano, Cortese, Malvasia, Pinot Bianco, Chardonnay, Riesling Italico

Breganze (W) Tocai Friulano, *Pinot Bianco, Pinot Grigio, Riesling Italico, Sauvignon Blanc, Vespaiolo* (R) Merlot, *Groppello Gentile, Cabernet Franc, Cabernet Sauvignon, Pinot Nero, Freisa*

Colli Berici Spumante (S) Garganega, *Pinot Bianco, Pinot Grigio, Chardonnay, Sauvignon Blanc*

Colli di Conegliano (W) Incrocio Manzoni 6.0.13., Pinot Bianco, Chardonnay, *Sauvignon Blanc, Riesling Renano* (R) Cabernet Franc, Cabernet Sauvignon, Marzemino, Merlot, *Incrocio Manzoni 2.15*

Colli Euganei (W) Garganega, Prosecco (Serprina), Tocai, Friulano, Sauvignon Blanc, *Pinella, Pinot Bianco, Riesling Italico, Chardonnay* (R) Merlot, Cabernet Franc, Cabernet Sauvignon, Barbera, Raboso Veronese

Corti Benedettine del Padovana (W) Tocai Friulano, Pinot Bianco, Pinot Grigio, Chardonnay, Sauvignon (R) Merlot, Raboso Piave, Veronese

Gambellara (W) Garganega

Garda (W) Riesling, Riesling Italico (R, P) Groppello, Marzemino, Sangiovese, Barbera (S) Garganega, Chardonnay

Lison-Pramaggiore (R) Merlot (W) Tocai Friulano

Merlara (R) Merlot (W) Tocai Friulano

Montello e Colli Asolani (R) Merlot, Cabernet Franc, Cabernet Sauvignon

Monti Lessini/Lessini (R) Merlot Pinot Nero, Corvina, Cabernet Franc, Cabernet Sauvignon, Carmenère (W) Chardonnay, Pinot Bianco, Pinot Nero, Pinot Grigio, Sauvignon (S) Chardonnay, Pinot Bianco, Pinot Nero

Recioto di Soave, DOCG (W) Garganega, Pinot Bianco, Chardonnay, Trebbiano di Soave

Riviera del Brenta (W) Tocai Friulano, Pinot Bianco, Pinot Grigio, Chardonnay (R) Merlot, Cabernet Franc, Cabernet Sauvignon, Carmenère, Raboso Piave, Raboso Veronese, Refosco dal Peduncolo Rosso (S) Chardonnay, Tocai Friulano, Pinot Bianco, Pinot Grigio

Soave, Soave Superiore, DOCG (W) Garganega, Pinot Bianco, Chardonnay, Trebbiano

Valpolicella (R) Corvina Veronese, Rondinella, Molinara, *Rossignola, Barbera, Negrara Trentina, Sangiovese*

Vicenza (R, P) Merlot (W) Garganega

PORTUGAL

Alenquer (R) Castelão, Aragonez, Touriga Nacional, Trincadeira, Tinta Miúda (W) Vital, Arinto, Fernão Pires, Rabo de Ovelha, Seara Nova

Alentejo (including the subregions of Portalegre, Borba, Redondo, Evora, Reguengos, Moura, Granja-Amareleja and Vidigueira) (R) Aragonez, Trincadeira, Castelão, Moreto, Alfrocheiro (W) Antão Vaz, Arinto, Fernão Pires, Perrum, Roupeiro

Arruda (R) Castelão, Aragonez, Trincadeira, Tinta Miúda (W) Arinto, Vital, Fernão Pires, Rabo de Ovelha, Seara Nova

Bairrada (R) Baga, Castelão, Alfrocheiro, Bastardo, Jaen, Touriga Nacional, Rufete (W) Maria Gomes, Bical, Rabo de Ovelha, Cerceal Branco

Beira Interior (R) Baga, Jaen, Marufo, Rufete, Bastardo, Tinta Roriz, Touriga Nacional (W) Siria, Malvasia Fina, Malvasia Rei, Tamarez, Arinto, Bical, Fonte Cal, Rabo de Ovelha

Biscoitos (IPR) (W) Arinto, Terrantez, Verdelho

Bucelas (W) Arinto, Esgana Cão

Carcavelos (R) Castelão, Preto Martinho (W) Galego Dourado, Ratinho Arinto,

Chaves (IPR) (R) Tinta Amarela, Bastardo, Tinta Carvalha (W) Síria, Fernão Pires, Gouveio, Malvasia Fina

Colares (R) Ramisco (W) Arinto, Jampal, Malvasia

Dão (R) Alfrocheiro, Bastardo, Jaen, Rufete , Tinto Cão, Tinta Roriz, Touriga Nacional (W) Bical, Encruzado, Barcelo, Cerceal, Malvasia Fina, Verdelho

Douro (R) Touriga Nacional, Touriga Franca, Tinta Roriz, Tinta Barroca, Tinto Cão, Tinta Amarela, Mourisco, Bastardo (W) Gouveio, Viosinho, Rabigato, Malvasia Fina, Donzelinho

Encostas d'Aire (IPR) (R) Castelão Baga, Trincadeira (W) Fernão Pires, Arinto, Tamarez, Vital

Graciosa (IPR) (W) Arinto, Fernão Pires, Terrantez, Verdelho

Lafões (IPR) (R) Amaral, Jaen (W) Arinto, Cerceal

Lagoa (R) Negra Mole, Monvedro, Castelão (W) Sária

Lagos (R) Negra Mole, Castelão (W) Malvasia Fina

Madeira (R) Tinta Negra Mole, Bastardo, Malvasia Roxa, Verdelho Tinto (W) Sercial, Verdelho, Boal, Malvasia, Terrantez

Óbidos (R) Castelão, Alicante Bouschet, Caladoc, Aragonez (W) Vital, Arinto, Fernão Pires, Rabo de Ovelha, Seara Nova

Palmela (R) Castelão (W) Fernão Pires, Arinto, Rabo de Ovelha, Moscatel Galego Branco, Tamarez

Pico (IPR) (W) Arinto, Terrantez, Verdelho

Planalto Mirandês (IPR) (R) Marufo, Touriga Nacional, Touriga Francesa, Tinta Amarela, Mourisco Bastardo (W) Gouveio, Malvasia Fina, Rabigato, Viosinho

Portimão DOC (R) Negra Mole, Castelão (W) Crato Branco

Port (R) Touriga Franca, Touriga Nacional, Bastardo, Mourisco, Tinto Cão, Tinta Roriz, Tinta Amarela, Tinta Barroca (W) Gouveio, Malvasia Fina, Rabigato, Viosinho, Donzelinho, Síria (Códega).

Ribatejo (including subregions of Almeirim, Cartaxo, Chamusca, Coruche, Santarém, and Tomar) (R) Baga, Castelão, Trincadeira, Preto Martinho (W) Arinto, Fernão Pires, Rabo de Ovelha, Tália, Trincadeira das Pratas, Vital

Setúbal (W) Moscatel Graúdo (R) Moscatel Galego Roxo

Tavira (R) Negra Mole, Castelão (W) Crato Branco

Távora-Varosa (R) Alvarelhão, Bastardo, Castelão, Rufete, Tinta Roriz, Touriga Nacional, Touriga Franca, Tinta Barroca, Mourisco, Vinhão, Pinot Noir (W) Bical, Fernão Pires, Síria, Malvasia Fina, Malvasia Rei, Gouveio, Viosinho, Chardonnay

Torres Vedras (R) Castelão, Tinta Miúda, Aragonez, Touriga Nacional (W) Vital, Rabo de Ovelha, Arinto, Fernão Pires, Seara Nova

Valpaços (IPR) (R) Touriga Nacional, Touriga Franca, Tinta Roriz, Tinta Amarela, Tinta Carvalha, Mourisco, Cornifesto, Bastardo (W) Síria , Fernão Pires, Gouveio, Malvasia Fina, Rabigato

Vinho Verde (R) Vinhão , Espadeiro, Amaral, Borraçal, Brancelho, Pedral (W) Loureiro, Trajadura, Padernã, Azal, Avessò, Alvarinho

ROMANIA

Cotnari (W) Grasă, Tămâioasă, Francusa, Fetească Albă

SPAIN

Note: Single-estate DOs such as Dominio de Valdepusa or Pago Guijoso are not listed below.

Abona (W) Bastardo, Forastera, Listán Blanco, Pedro Ximénez, *Verdello, Gual, Bermejuela, Moscatel* (R) Bastardo, Malvasía Rosada, Tintilla, Vijariego, *Negramoll, Moscatel Negro*

Alella (W) Pansá Blanca (Xarel-lo), Garnacha Blanca, Macabeo, *Chardonnay, Pansá Rosado, Chenin Blanc* (R) Ull de Llebre (Tempranillo), Garnacha Tinta, Garnacha Peluda

Alicante (R) Monastrell, Garnacha Tinta, Bobal (W) Merseguera, Moscatel Romano, Verdil

Almansa (R) Monastrell, Cencibel, Garnacha Tintorera (W) Merseguera

Ampurdán-Costa Brava (R) Garnacha Tinta, Cariñena, Cabernet Sauvignon, Merlot, Tempranillo, Garnacha, Syrah (W) Macabeo, Garnacha Blanca, Chenin Blanc, Riesling, Muscat, Gewürztraminer, Macabeo, Chardonnay, Parellada, Xarel-lo

Arabako Txakolina/Chacoli de Álava (W) Hondarrabi Zuri (R) Hondarrabi Beltza

Bierzo (R) Mencía, Garnacha Tintorera (W) Godello, Doña Blanca, Malvasía, Palomino

Binissalem (R) Manto Negro, Callet, Tempranillo, Monastrell (W) Moll, Parellada, Macabeo

Bizkaiko Txakolina/Chacoli de Vizcaya (W) Hondarrabi Zuri, Folle Blanche (Gros Plant) (R) Hondarrabi Beltza

Bullas (R) Monastrell, Tempranillo (W) Macabeo, Airén

Calatayud (R) Garnacha Tinta, Tempranillo, Cariñena, Juan Ibáñez, Monastrell (W) Viura, Garnacha Blanca, Moscatel Romano, Malvasía

Campo de Borja (R) Garnacha, Tempranillo (W) Macabeo

Cariñena (R) Garnacha, Tempranillo, Cariñena, Juan Ibáñez, Monastrell, Cabernet Sauvignon (W) Viura, Garnacha Blanca, Parellada, Moscatel Romano

Cava (S) Xarel-lo, Parellada, Macabeo, Chardonnay, *Pinot Noir*

Cigales (R) Tempranillo, Garnacha (W) Verdejo, Viura, Palomino, Albillo

Note: All white grapes may be used for rosé wines.

Conca de Barbera (W) Macabeo, Parellada (R) Trepat, Garnacha, Ull de Llebre (Tempranillo), Cabernet Sauvignon

Condado de Huelva (W) Zalema, Palomino, Garrido Fino, Moscatel

Costers del Segre (W) Chardonnay, *Macabeo, Parellada, Xarel-lo, Garnacha Blanca* (R) Tempranillo, Cabernet Sauvignon, Merlot, *Monastrell, Trepat, Mazuelo (Cariñena), Garnacha Tinta*

El Hierro (W) Vijariego Blanco, Bremajuelo, Baboso Blanco, Gual, *Malvasía, Verdello, Pedro Ximénez, Listán Blanco* (R) Listán Negro, Verijadiego Negro, Baboso Negro, *Negramoll*

Getariako Txakoli/Chacoli de Guetaria (W) Hondarrabi Zuri (R) Hondarrabi Beltza

Gran Canaria (W) Listán Blanco, *Gual, Pedro Ximénez, Marmajuelo, Breval, Vijariego, Albillo, Moscatel* (R) Listán Negro, *Negramoll, Tintilla*

Jumilla (R) Monastrell, Garnacha Tintorera, Cencibel (W) Merseguera, Airén, Pedro Ximénez

Lanzarote (W) Burrablanca, Breval, Diego, Listán Blanco, Malvasía, Moscatel, Pedro Ximénez (R) Listán Negro, Negramoll

Málaga (W) Pedro Ximénez, Moscatel de Alejandría, Moscatel Morisco, *Lairén, Doradilla, Colombard* (R) Romé, Cabernet Sauvignon, Merlot, Syrah, Tempranillo, *Garnacha, Cabernet Franc, Pinot Noir, Petit Verdot*

Sierras de Málaga (W) Pedro Ximénez, Moscatel, Chardonnay, Macabeo, Sauvignon Blanc (R) Romé, Cabernet Sauvignon, Merlot, Syrah, Tempranillo, *Garnacha, Cabernet Franc, Pinot Noir, Petit Verdot*

Manchuela (W) Albillo, Chardonnay, Macabeo, Sauvignon Blanc, Verdejo (R) Bobal, Cabernet Sauvignon, Tempranillo, Garnacha, Merlot, Monastrell, Moravia Dulce, Syrah

Monte Lentiscal (R) Listán Negro, *Negramoll, Tintilla, Malvasía Rosada* (W) Listán Blanco, *Malvasía, Gual, Pedro Ximénez, Albillo, Moscatel*

La Mancha (R) Cencibel, *Garnacha, Moravia* (W) Airén, *Pardillo, Verdoncho, Macabeo*

Méntrida (R) Garnacha, Tinto Madrid, Cencibel

Mondéjar (W) Macabeo, Malvar, Torrontés (R) Cabernet Sauvignon, Tempranillo

Monterrei (W) Verdello, Doña Blanca, Palomino, Godello, Treixadura (R) Mencía, *Tinto Fino (Tempranillo)*

Montilla-Moriles (W) Pedro Ximénez, Lairén (Airén), *Baladi, Torrontés, Moscatel*

Montsant (W) Chardonay, Garnacha Blanca, Macabeo, Moscatel, Pansal, Parellada, Trobat (R) Cabernet, Mazuela, Garnacha, Garnacha Peluda, Merlot, Monastrell, Picapoll, Syrah, Tempranillo

Navarra (R) Tempranillo, Garnacha Tinta, Cabernet Sauvignon, Merlot, *Mazuelo, Graciano* (W) Viura, *Moscatel de Grano Menudo (Muscat de Frontignan), Malvasía Riojana, Chardonnay, Garnacha Blanca*

La Palma (W) Albillo, Bastardo Blanco, Bermejuela, Bujariego, Burrablanca, Forastera Blanca, Bual, Listán Blanco, Malvasía, Moscatel, Pedro Ximénez, Sabro, Torrontés, Verdello (R) Almuñeco (Listán Negro), Bastardo Negro, Malvasía Rosada, Moscatel Negro, Negramoll, Tintilla

Penedès (R) Tempranillo, Garnacha Tinta, Cabernet Franc, Merlot, Pinot Noir, Cabernet Sauvignon, Monastrell, Cariñena, Samsó (W) Parellada, Xarel-lo, Macabeo, Subirat Parent, Gewürztraminer, Muscat d'Alsace, Chardonnay, Sauvignon, *Chenin Blanc, Riesling*

Pla i Llevant (W) Prensal Blanc, Moscatel, Macabeo, Parellada, Chardonnay (R) Callet, Fogoneu, Tempranillo, Manto Negro, Monastrell, Cabernet Sauvignon, Merlot, Syrah

Pla de Bages (W) Macabeo, Parellada, Picapoll, Chardonnay, Gerwürztraminer (R) Garnacha, Tempranillo, Merlot, Cabernet Sauvignon, Cabernet Franc, Syrah

Priorato (R) Garnacha Tinta, *Garnacha Peluda, Cariñena, Cabernet Sauvignon* (W) Garnacha Blanca, *Macabeo, Pedro Ximénez, Chenin Blanc*

Rias Baixas (W) Albariño, Treixadura, Loureira Blanca, Caiño Blanco, *Torrontés, Godello* (R) Caiño Tinto, Espadeiro, Loureira Tinta, Sousón, *Mencía, Brancellao*

Ribeira Sacra (W) Albariño, Loureira, Godello, Doña Blanca, Torrontés, *Palomino* (R) Mencía, Brancellao, Sousón, Merenzao

Ribeiro (W) Treixadura, Loureira, Albariño, *Jerez (Palomino), Torrontés, Godello, Macabeo, Albillo* (R) Caiño, Garnacha (Alicante), Ferrón, Sousón, Mencía, Tempranillo, Brancellao

Ribera del Duero (R) Tinto Fino/del País (Tempranillo), *Garnacha Tinta (Tinto Aragonés), Cabernet Sauvignon, Merlot, Malbec, Albillo*

Ribera del Guadiana (W) Alarije, Borba, Cayetana Blanca, Pardina, Viura, Chardonnay, Chelva (Montúa), Eva (Beba de los Santos), Malvar, Parellada, Pedro Ximénez, Verdejo, Cigüente, Moscatel de Alejandria, Moscatel de Gran Menudo, Perruno, Sauvignon Blanc (R) Garnacha Tinta, Tempranillo, Bobal, Cabernet Sauvignon, Graciano, Mazuela, Merlot, Monastrell, Syrah, Garnacha Tintorera, Jaén Tinto, Pinot Noir

Ribera del Júcar (R) Cabernet Sauvignon, Cencibel, Merlot, Syrah, Bobal

Rioja (R) Tempranillo, Garnacha, *Graciano, Mazuelo, and Cabernet Sauvignon (experimental)* (W) Viura, *Malvasía Riojana, Garnacha Blanca, Verdejo, Sauvignon Blanc, Chardonnay*

Rueda (W) Verdejo, Viura, *Sauvignon Blanc, Palomino Fino*

Somontano (R) Moristel, Tempranillo, Cabernet Sauvignon, Merlot (W) Viura, Alcañón, Chardonnay, Pinot Noir, Chenin Blanc, Gewürztraminer

Tacoronte-Acentejo (R) Listán Negro, Negramoll (W) Malvasía, Moscatel Blanco, Listán (Palomino)

Tarragona (R) Garnacha Tinta, Cariñena, Ull de Llebre (Tempranillo), *Cabernet Sauvignon, Merlot* (W) Macabeo, Xarel-lo, Parellada, Garnacha Blanca, *Chardonnay, Muscat*

Terra Alta (W) Garnacha Blanca, Macabeo, *Chardonnay, Colombard* (R) Cariñena, Garnacha Tinta, Garnacha Peluda, *Pinot Noir, Pinot Meunier, Cabernet Sauvignon, Merlot*

Toro (R) Tinto de Toro (Tempranillo), *Garnacha Tinta, Cabernet Sauvignon* (W) Malvasía, Verdejo Blanco

Uclés (R) Cencibel (Tempranillo), Cabernet Sauvignon, Merlot, Syrah, Garnacha Tinta

Utiel-Requena (R) Tempranillo, Bobal, Garnacha Tinta, *Cabernet Sauvignon* (W) Macabeo, Merseguera, *Planta Nova, Chardonnay*

Valdeorras (R) Mencía, Garnacha, Gran Negro, Maria Ordoña (Merenzao) (W) Godello, Palomino, Valenciana (Doña Blanca), Lado

Valdepeñas (R) Cencibel (W) Airén

Valencia (W) Merseguera, Malvasía Riojana, Planta Fina, Pedro Ximénez, Moscatel Romano, Macabeo, Tortosí (Bobal Blanco) (R) Monastrell, Garnacha Tintorera, Garnacha Tinta, Tempranillo, Forcayat

Valle de Güimar (W) Listán Blanco, Malvasía, Moscatel, *Verdello, Vijariego, Gual* (R) Listán Negro, Negramoll, Castellana, *Ruby Cabernet, Shiraz, Merlot, Cabernet Sauvignon*

Valle de la Orotava (W) Gual, Malvasía, Verdello, Vijariego, Bastardo Blanco, Forastera Blanca, Torrontés, Listán Blanco, Marmajuelo, Moscatel, Pedro Ximénez (R) Listán Negro, Malvasía Rosada, Negramoll, Bastardo Negro, Moscatel Negra, Tintilla, Vijariego Negro

Vinos de Madrid (R) Tinto Fino, Garnacha (W) Malvar, Airén, Albillo

Ycoden-Daute-Isora (W) Bastardo Blanco, Bermejuela, Forastera Blanca, Bual, Listán Blanco, Malvasía, Moscatel, Pedro Ximénez, Sabró, Torrontés, Verdello, Vijariego (R) Bastardo Negro, Listán Negro, Malvasía Rosada, Moscatel Negra, Negramoll, Tintilla, Vijariego Negro

Yecla (R) Monastrell, Garnacha, Cabernet Sauvignon, Tempranillo (W) Merseguera, Verdil

SWITZERLAND

Dôle (R) Pinot Noir, *Gamay*

Goron (Valais), Salvagnin (Vaud) (R) Pinot Noir, Gamay

L'Œil-de-Perdrix de Neuchâtel (P) Pinot Noir

Appendix 2A Total vineyard area by country

	'000s hectares	'000s acres		'000s hectares	'000s acres
EUROPE			Korea	27	67
Spain	1,207	2,982	Yemen	25	62
France	887	2,192	Japan	21	52
Italy	868	2,145	Cyprus	17	42
Portugal	249	615	Lebanon	15	37
Romania	239	591	Pakistan	13	32
Moldova	148	366	Israel	7	17
Greece	130	321	Jordan	4	10
Uzbekistan	103	255	Thailand	4	10
Germany	102	252	Other countries	27	67
Bulgaria	99	245			
Ukraine	99	245	Total	1,693	4,183
Hungary	88	217			
Serbia/Montenegro	71	175	**AMERICAS**		
Russia	70	173	United States	415	1,025
Georgia	64	158	Argentina	211	521
Croatia	61	151	Chile	185	457
Austria	48	119	Brazil	72	178
Tajikistan	30	74	Mexico	42	104
Turkmenistan	30	74	Canada	11	27
Macedonia	29	72	Peru	11	27
Slovenia	17	42	Uruguay	10	25
Czech Republic	16	40	Bolivia	3	7
Switzerland	15	37	Venezuela	1	2
Armenia	13	32	Other countries	4	10
Slovakia	13	32			
Kazakhstan	10	25	Total	963	2,380
Azerbaijan	8	20			
Albania	7	17	**AFRICA**		
Kyrgyzstan	7	17	South Africa	132	326
Bosnia and Herzegovina	4	10	Algeria	94	232
Luxembourg	1	2	Egypt	70	173
Malta	1	2	Morocco	50	124
UK	1	2	Tunisia	24	59
			Libya	9	22
Total	4,734	11,698	Tanzania	3	7
			Madagascar	2	5
			Other countries	4	10
ASIA					
Turkey	570	1,409	Total	388	959
China	453	1,119			
Iran	300	741	**OCEANIA**		
India	65	161	Australia	157	388
Afghanistan	50	124	New Zealand	19	47
Iraq	50	124			
Syria	46	114	Total	177	437
			World total	7,955	19,657

These 2003 OIV figures include vineyards dedicated to table grapes and drying grapes.
OIV statistics are given in hectares, so the equivalent figures in acres are approximate.
All figures are rounded. For accuracy, totals are taken separately from the OIV figures, and therefore may not equal the sum of the component numbers.

Appendix 2B Wine production by country

	1986–90		1991–5		1996–2000		2003	
	'000s hectolitres	'000s US gals	'000s hectolitres	'000s US glas	'000s hectolitres	'000s US glas	'000s hectolitres	'000s US gals
France	65,344	1,726,388	54,325	1,435,267	56,271	1,486,523	46,360	1,224,701
Italy	60,226	1,591,171	61,225	1,617,565	54,386	1,436,726	44,086	1,164,629
Spain	33,656	889,192	26,750	706,735	34,162	902,464	42,802	1,130,709
United States	17,121	452,337	16,790	443,592	20,386	538,541	20,770	548,685
Argentina	18,836	497,647	15,587	411,809	13,456	356,262	13,225	349,368
China	2,734	72,232	3,480	91,942	9,581	253,103	*11,600	306,440
Australia	4,463	117,912	4,810	127,080	7,380	195,958	10,194	269,297
South Africa	8,572	226,472	9,529	251,756	7,837	207,032	8,853	233,871
Germany	10,915	288,374	10,939	289,008	9,989	263,881	8,191	216,383
Portugal	8,455	223,381	7,153	188,982	6,828	180,376	7,340	193,902
Chile	4,103	108,401	3,326	87,873	5,066	133,830	6,682	176,519
Romania	7,502	198,203	5,508	145,521	6,173	163,073	5,555	146,748
Russia	n.a.	n.a.	3,110	82,166	2,512	66,360	4,530	119,670
Hungary	4,062	107,318	3,822	100,977	4,126	108,997	3,880	102,499
Greece	4,337	114,584	3,668	96,909	3,832	101,231	3,799	100,359
Moldova	n.a.	n.a.	4,358	115,138	2,151	56,823	3,215	84,931
Brazil	2,918	77,094	3,095	81,770	2,920	77,138	2,620	69,213
Austria	2,854	75,403	2,484	65,627	2,351	62,107	2,526	66,730
Ukraine	n.a.	n.a.	1,793	47,371	1,290	34,078	2,380	62,873
Bulgaria	3,261	86,156	1,885	49,802	2,811	74,258	2,314	61,129
Croatia	n.a.	n.a.	1,869	49,379	2,096	55,370	1,768	46,706
Serbia/Montenegro	n.a.	n.a.	2,615	69,088	2,686	70,957	1,734	45,807
Mexico	1,183	31,255	2,234	59,022	1,340	35,399	1,096	28,953
Switzerland	1,280	33,818	1,202	31,757	1,222	32,282	967	25,545
Japan	542	14,320	552	14,584	1,014	26,787	938	24,779
Macedonia	n.a.	n.a.	1,004	26,526	1,057	27,923	930	24,568
Uruguay	795	21,004	846	22,351	999	26,391	837	22,111
Georgia	n.a.	n.a.	1,056	27,900	1,503	39,705	800	21,134
Slovenia	n.a.	n.a.	822	21,717	476	12,574	671	17,726
Algeria	687	18,151	536	14,161	391	10,329	*580	15,322
New Zealand	464	12,259	443	11,704	568	15,005	550	14,529
Slovakia	n.a.	n.a.	763	20,158	482	12,733	540	14,265
Czech Republic	n.a.	n.a.	506	13,369	514	13,578	510	13,473
Uzbekistan	n.a.	n.a.	1,343	35,482	564	14,899	458	12,099
Cyprus	667	17,622	590	15,588	586	15,480	385	10,171

	1986–90		1991–5		1996–2000		2003	
	'000s hectolitres	'000s US gals	'000s hectolitres	'000s US glas	'000s hectolitres	'000s US glas	'000s hectolitres	'000s US gals
Canada	386	10,198	319	8,428	403	10,646	359	9,484
Morocco	431	11,387	335	8,851	350	9,246	343	9,061
Kazakhstan	n.a.	n.a.	379	10,013	179	4,279	328	8,665
Tunisia	299	7,900	349	9,221	365	9,642	246	6,499
Turkmenistan	n.a.	n.a.	15	396	317	8,374	240	6,340
Turkey	290	7,662	257	6,790	307	8,110	225	5,944
Lebanon	82	2,166	229	6,050	188	4,966	150	3,963
Peru	98	2,589	93	2,457	121	3,196	133	3,513
Luxembourg	165	4,359	173	4,571	136	3,593	123	3,249
Albania	239	6,314	117	3,091	153	4,042	92	2,430
Madagascar	77	2,034	87	2,299	89	2,351	89	2,351
Bosnia and Herzegovina	n.a.	n.a.	101	2,668	46	1,215	76	2,008
Belorussia	n.a.	n.a.	505	13,342	149	3,936	75	1,981
Malta	20	528	28	740	35	925	70	1,849
Tajikistan	n.a.	n.a.	325	8,587	74	1,955	62	1,638
Paraguay	75	1,982	76	2,008	74	1,955	60	1,585
Israel	156	4,122	122	3,223	85	2,245	57	1,506
Azerbaijan	n.a.	n.a.	1,030	27,213	129	3,408	49	1,294
Egypt	20	528	24	634	27	713	42	1,110
Kyrgyzstan	n.a.	n.a.	54	1,427	21	555	36	951
Lithuania	n.a.	n.a.	35	925	40	1,057	36	951
Armenia	n.a.	n.a.	258	6,816	50	1,321	27	713
Bolivia	19	502	20	528	20	528	20	528
Estonia	n.a.	n.a.	15	396	26	687	20	528
England & Wales	11	291	18	476	14	370	15	396
Belgium	2	53	1	26	1	26	2	53
World total	267,568	7,069,148	265,067	7,003,071	272,577	7,200,722	266,728	7,046,208

These figures are based on official OIV statistics.

All figures are rounded. For accuracy, totals are taken separately from the OIV figures, and therefore may not equal the sum of the component numbers.

* OIV estimate.

Appendix 2C Per capita wine consumption by country

	1991		1996		2003	
	litres	US gals	litres	US gals	litres	US gals
Luxembourg	60.30	15.93	50.40	13.32	55.80	14.74
France	67.00	17.70	60.00	15.85	55.40	14.64
Portugal	62.00	16.38	58.46	15.45	52.60	13.90
Italy	60.28	15.93	59.37	15.69	51.10	13.50
Slovenia	40.00	10.57	40.00	10.57	44.40	11.73
Switzerland	47.20	12.47	41.17	10.88	41.40	10.94
Spain	39.77	10.51	37.71	9.96	33.60	8.88
Argentina	55.01	14.53	41.47	10.96	32.10	8.48
Denmark	23.60	6.24	26.80	7.08	31.80	8.40
Hungary	30.00	7.93	30.00	7.93	31.60	8.35
Austria	33.70	8.90	32.00	8.45	29.40	7.77
Germany	26.10	6.90	22.90	6.05	24.40	6.45
Romania	19.30	5.10	31.50	8.32	22.60	5.97
Greece	32.40	8.56	30.93	8.17	22.30	5.89
Netherlands	16.50	4.36	13.30	3.51	22.10	5.84
Uruguay	25.40	6.71	*30.30	*8.01	22.10	5.84
Australia	17.70	4.68	18.10	4.78	21.30	5.63
Cyprus	13.20	3.49	13.10	3.46	20.60	5.44
UK	10.29	2.72	12.50	3.30	17.90	4.73
New Zealand	12.10	3.20	9.90	2.62	17.00	4.49
Sweden	12.78	3.38	12.60	3.33	16.90	4.46
Chile	29.50	7.79	15.80	4.17	16.10	4.25
Ireland	4.50	1.19	7.00	1.85	14.70	3.88
Norway	6.90	1.82	7.58	2.00	12.40	3.28
Czech Republic	*11.80	*3.12	11.80	3.12	11.50	3.04
Slovakia	*11.80	*3.12	13.10	3.46	11.00	2.91
Canada	8.28	2.19	7.08	1.87	10.90	2.88
Finland	4.49	1.19	5.19	1.37	8.70	2.30
Serbia/Montenegro	22.10	5.84	19.90	5.26	8.60	2.27
USA	7.12	1.88	7.70	2.03	8.10	2.14
South Africa	9.06	2.39	9.30	2.46	7.70	2.03
Tunisia	2.20	0.58	3.09	0.82	2.20	0.58
Japan	0.91	0.24	1.39	0.37	2.00	0.53
Peru	0.47	0.12	0.61	0.16	1.90	0.50
Brazil	1.83	0.48	1.58	0.42	1.70	0.45
Morocco	0.99	0.26	1.40	0.37	1.10	0.29
Israel	3.50	0.92	4.20	1.11	0.90	0.24
Turkey	0.47	0.12	*0.40	*0.11	0.20	0.05
Mexico	0.22	0.06	0.28	0.07	0.10	0.03

These figures are based on official OIV statistics.

* OIV estimate.

Complete list of entries by subject

Picture acknowledgements

Colour plates
All full-page colour images in this book have been supplied by Cephas Picture Library, specialists in wine-related photography.

All pictures are facing the page quoted:

CEPHAS/ Mick Rock   72
CEPHAS/ Mick Rock   73
CEPHAS/ Andy Christodolo   96
CEPHAS/ Mick Rock   97
CEPHAS/ Ian Shaw   168
CEPHAS/ R & K Muschenetz   169
CEPHAS/ Mick Rock   192
CEPHAS/ Nigel Blythe   193
CEPHAS/ Andy Christodolo   264
CEPHAS/ Nigel Blythe   265
CEPHAS/ Dario Fusaro   288
CEPHAS/ Andy Christodolo   289
CEPHAS/ Kevin Judd   360
CEPHAS/ Mick Rock   361
CEPHAS/ Nigel Blythe   384
CEPHAS/ Diana Mewes   385

CEPHAS/ Kevin Judd   456
CEPHAS/ R & K Muschenetz   457
CEPHAS/ Ian Shaw   480
CEPHAS/ Kevin Argue   481
CEPHAS/ Mick Rock   552
CEPHAS/ Kevin Judd   553
CEPHAS/ Dario Fusaro   576
CEPHAS/ Andy Christodolo   577
CEPHAS/ Andy Christodolo   648
CEPHAS/ Bruce Fleming   649
CEPHAS/ Mick Rock   672
CEPHAS/ Mick Rock   673
CEPHAS/ Andy Christodolo   744
CEPHAS/ Dario Fusaro   745
CEPHAS/ Alain Proust   768
CEPHAS/ Mick Rock   769

Line diagrams on the pages indicated are drawn by Russell Birkett with reference to the following sources:
American Journal of Enology & Viticulture, Vol. 38, No 2, 1987. Copyright © Dr Ann C. Noble and *American Journal of Enology & Viticulture* 36, 322
B. G. Coombe and P. R. Dry (eds), *Viticulture, Volume 1: Resources in Australia, volume 2: Practices* 134, 170, 178, 475, 661, 699
G. Dalmasso, *Vinocoltura Moderna* 258
R. Huglin, *Biologic et écologic de la vigne* 20
J. Long, *Vignes et Vignobles* 336, 519, 627
R. Mayson, *Portugal's Wines & Wine Makers* 55
M. G. Mullins et al, *Biology of the Grapevine* 709
J. Renfrew, *Palaeoethnobotany* 504
R. Smart and M. Robinson, *Sunlight into Wine* 60, 413, 617, 742
R. J. Weaver, *Grape Growing* 320, 591, 743
Winkler et al, *General Viticulture* 521